EDITOR

NATHAN BRACKETT

DEPUTY EDITOR

CHRISTIAN HOARD

CONTRIBUTING EDITORS

Jenny Eliscu, Nina Pearlman

RESEARCH EDITORS

Brian Gilmore

Jane Lerner

Emily Lemanczyk

Will Levith

Steve Marzolf

Amelia McDonell-Parry

Nicholas Messing

Dara Pettinelli

Jessica Robertson

Patrick Ryan

Janice Schiffman

Jason Stutts

EDITORIAL STAFF

Lauren Gitlin

CONSULTING EDITORS

Anthony DeCurtis, Joe Levy, Holly George-Warren

THIRD EDITION EDITORS

James Henke, Anthony DeCurtis, Holly George-Warren

{ T H E   N E W }

ALBUM
GUIDE

COMPLETELY REVISED
AND UPDATED
FOURTH EDITION

A FIRESIDE BOOK

PUBLISHED BY SIMON & SCHUSTER

New York   London   Toronto   Sydney

FIRESIDE
Rockefeller Center
1230 Avenue of the Americas
New York, NY 10020

First Fireside Edition 2004

For information regarding special discounts for bulk purchases,
please contact Simon & Schuster Special Sales at 1-800-456-6798
or business@simonandschuster.com

Designed by Joy O'Meara

Manufactured in the United States of America

10 9 8 7 6 5 4 3 2 1

Library of Congress Cataloging-in-Publication Data is available.

ISBN 0-7432-0169-8

Introduction
by Nathan Brackett

Welcome to *The New ROLLING STONE Album Guide,* your handbook to every record that matters. This fourth edition covers more than 10,000 albums from the most important artists of rock, punk, hip-hop, techno, soul, dance, blues, jazz, country, gospel, disco, reggae, and Top 40 pop, and is the product of three years of work by more than 70 writers and editors.

It's been a long 12 years since our last *Album Guide,* which was edited by Anthony DeCurtis, Holly George-Warren, and James Henke. More than 350,000 albums have been released. The record business has gone from big profits to experiencing the worst recession since the early '80s. And, more important for a book about albums, there are innumerable more ways for people to learn about music: not just from magazines anymore, but from fan websites; listening kiosks at record stores; music websites such as AllMusic.com and RollingStone.com; online music services such as iTunes Music Store; and, notoriously, file-sharing software such as LimeWire and Kazaa.

So how do you make an album guide that fits into a book bag? Selectively. For the most part, we've tried to limit the artists in this book to the people we think we'll still be listening to when the fifth or sixth edition of the *Guide* comes out, or to the artists who—even if they're not well known anymore—have made a lasting, undeniable contribution to pop music. Everyone in this book has moved the cultural needle in one direction or the other; you won't find many one-hit wonders, unless they were just too fascinating to ignore.

This is not a book for pop music historians, nor is it an encyclopedia (for that, see *The ROLLING STONE Encyclopedia of Rock & Roll,* also published by Fireside/Simon & Schuster). This is a book to be used and enjoyed. Because this is a consumer guide, we've limited ourselves to covering domestically released albums that are currently in print. Our main criterion was that albums needed to be easily available from major online stores such as Amazon.com and Barnes andnoble.com. (One caveat: In special cases, we've included out-of-print or import albums if they are essential to understanding an artist.) In the case of nonrock artists with enormous discographies, such as Miles Davis and Pete Seeger, we've included a selective list to serve as a starting point for the interested beginner.

This book stands upon the foundation of the 1992 *Album Guide,* which was written entirely by just four writers: J.D. Considine, David McGee, Paul Evans, and Mark Coleman. Three of those writers—Considine, Evans, and McGee—have returned to update many of their old entries. Some entries have been cut (so long, Lobo; farewell to the Vogues); hundreds have been added, to the point that approximately 70 percent of this *Album Guide* is entirely new.

In the introduction to the first RS *Record Guide,* published in 1979, editor Dave Marsh noted that "writing about performers as diverse as Roscoe Holcomb, Elvis Presley and the Sex Pistols ought to be confusing," but went on to marvel that "as we progressed, the whole of popular music began to seem a seamless web."

As we started this project, that notion seemed quaint—pop is often described as a fragmented place today, where strange cliques form and multiply. As we got further into it, though, Marsh's original idea didn't seem so odd. Part of the joy of a book like this is the strange juxtapositions: Papa Roach appears on the same page as Charlie Parker; techno pioneer Juan Atkins follows Chet Atkins. But you also get the sense that in 25 years, these distinctions will seem less funny, just as the idea (as any Uncle Tupelo fan can attest) of the Sex Pistols and Roscoe Holcomb in one place doesn't seem so radical today.

Above all—despite the intimidating pages of gray text and official-looking listings—this book is meant to be fun, and to make you want to hear this music. Good hunting!

Ratings

★★★★★
Classic: Essential listening if you're even mildly curious about the artist or genre under discussion. Not only are these albums worthy of your disposable income, they stand a good chance of enriching your life.

★★★★
Excellent: Four-star albums generally represent outstanding performances by immortal artists or peak performances by mere mortals. If you're a fan of the artist or type of music in question, it's hard to go wrong with any of these albums.

★★★
Average to Good: Albums in the three-star range will primarily be of interest to fans of the artist being discussed. Like a B+ movie, these albums are often pleasurable but not necessarily memorable.

★★
Fair to Poor: Albums in the two-star category either fall below the artist's established standard or are failures in and of themselves.

★
Disastrous: Albums in the range of one star or less are wastes of vital resources. Only masochists and completists need apply.

Contributors

EDITORS

Nathan Brackett (N.B.) is a senior editor at ROLLING STONE, where he has edited the record reviews section since 1997.

Christian Hoard (C.H.) is a regular contributor to ROLLING STONE and *The Village Voice*.

WRITERS

Richard Abowitz (R.A.) is contributing editor to *Las Vegas Weekly, Las Vegas Life, Showbiz Weekly,* and *Vegas Magazine*.

Steve Appleford (S.A.) is a regular contributor to ROLLING STONE and the *Los Angeles Times*.

Arion Berger (A.B.) is entertainment editor of *Express* and a freelance writer. She lives in northern Virginia.

Pat Blashill (P.B.) has written for ROLLING STONE, *Details,* and *Wired,* and is the author of *Notes from the Underground: A Secret History of Alternative Rock* (Fireside, 1996).

Jon Caramanica (J.C.) is a regular contributor to ROLLING STONE and has written for *The New York Times, Spin, Vibe, The Village Voice, XXL,* and *Vice*.

Nick Catucci (N.C.) writes about music and books for *The Village Voice*.

Neva Chonin (N.CH.) is a pop-music critic for the *San Francisco Chronicle*.

Mark Coleman (M.C.), a contributor to the previous edition of *The ROLLING STONE Album Guide,* is the author of *Playback: From the Victrola to MP3: 100 Years of Music, Machines and Money* (Da Capo, 2004).

J.D. Considine (J.D.C.), a contributor to the previous edition of *The ROLLING STONE Album Guide,* has written for ROLLING STONE, *Entertainment Weekly, Blender, Guitar World, Bass Guitar, Revolver, The New York Times,* and the *Globe & Mail*.

Bill Crandall (B.C.) is the music editor of RollingStone.com.

Charles R. Cross (C.R.C.) is the author of four books, including 2001's *Heavier Than Heaven: The Biography of Kurt Cobain* and *Roomful of Mirrors,* a biography of Jimi Hendrix.

Andrew Dansby (A.D.) is the entertainment editor at the *Houston Chronicle*. A former news editor for RollingStone.com, he contributes to ROLLING STONE, *XXL, Blender, Harp,* and *Texas Music*.

Matt Diehl (M.D.) is a contributing music editor at *Interview* and managing editor of Flavorpill.net in Los Angeles. He has two books—one on contemporary punk rock, another on no-fall snowboarding—due in 2005.

Ben Edmonds (B.E.) is the U.S. editor of *Mojo* and the author of *What's Going On?: Marvin Gaye and the Last Days of the Motown Sound* (Canongate, 2001).

Jenny Eliscu (J.E.) is an associate editor at ROLLING STONE, where she has worked since 1999.

Paul Evans (P.E.), a contributor to the previous edition of *The ROLLING STONE Album Guide,* has written for *Book Magazine, The Washington Post,* and the *Los Angeles Times.* He teaches English and history in Charlottesville, VA.

Kris Ex (K.X.) has written for ROLLING STONE, *XXL, Vibe,* and *The Source.* He is a former music editor of *The Source,* and is writing a book with 50 Cent, to be published by MTV Books.

Gaylord Fields (G.F.) is an assistant editor at ROLLING STONE, and his work has also appeared in *Spin* and *Time Out New York.* He is also a DJ on the free-form radio station WFMU, in Jersey City, NJ.

Jason Fine (J.F.) is an assistant managing editor at ROLLING STONE.

Sasha Frere-Jones (S.F.J.) is pop music critic for *The New Yorker.*

David Fricke (D.F.) is a senior editor at ROLLING STONE.

Andy Gensler (A.G.) is a music writer and co-founder of the Mishpucha music collective and Legalize Dancing NYC.

Joe Gross (J.G.) is the pop-music critic for the *Austin American-Statesman.* He has contributed to ROLLING STONE, *Spin, The Village Voice,* and others.

Ernest Hardy (E.H.) has contributed to ROLLING STONE, *Vibe,* the *Los Angeles Times,* and many other publications.

Keith Harris (K.H.) is the editor in chief of Red Flag Media Publications in Philadelphia. He has written for ROLLING STONE, *Slate, The Village Voice,* and others.

Geoff Himes (G.H.) has written for ROLLING STONE, *The Washington Post, New Country,* and many other publications.

Steve Hochman (S.H.) covers pop music for the *Los Angeles Times* and is the music critic for the radio news magazine *The California Report,* produced by KQED-FM in San Francisco.

Tom Hull (T.H.) writes about philosophy and music on his websites TerminalZone.net, NotesOnEverydayLife.com, and TomHull.com, as well as for *The Village Voice* and *Seattle Weekly.*

James Hunter (J.H.) writes about music and books for ROLLING STONE, *The Village Voice, The New York Observer,* and *L.A. Weekly.*

Mark Kemp (M.K.) is the entertainment editor for *The Charlotte Observer.* A former music editor of ROLLING STONE, he is the author of *Dixie Lullaby: A Story of Music, Race, and New Beginnings in a New South.*

Rob Kemp (R.K.) has written for ROLLING STONE, *Time Out New York,* and *The New York Observer.* He also plays bass in a punk-rock karaoke band in New York, NY.

Greg Kot (G.K.) is pop-music critic for the *Chicago Tribune* and author of *Wilco: Learning How to Die* (Broadway, 2004).

Ernesto Lechner (E.L.) is a frequent contributor to ROLLING STONE, the *Los Angeles Times,* and other publications. His book on the history of Latin rock will be published in 2005 by the Chicago Review Press.

Joe Levy (J.L.) is a deputy managing editor at ROLLING STONE, where he has worked since 1997.

David Malley (D.MA.) is an assistant editor at ROLLING STONE.

Michaelangelo Matos (M.M.) is the music editor of *Seattle Weekly* and the author of *Sign O' the Times* (Continuum, 2004). He is also a frequent contributor to ROLLING STONE, *Spin,* and *The Village Voice.*

Kembrew McLeod (K.M.) is a professor of communication studies at the University of Iowa, and is the author of *Freedom of Expression: Overzealous Copyright Bozos and Other Enemies of Creativity* (Doubleday, 2005).

David McGee (D.M.) is the author of *Go, Cat, Go!: The Life and Times of Carl Perkins, the King of Rockabilly.* He has contributed to all four editions of *The ROLLING STONE Album Guide,* and has written for ROLLING STONE, *BMI Music World,* and *Pro Sound News.*

Milo Miles (M.MI.) is a commentator for NPR's *Fresh Air* and a longtime contributor to ROLLING STONE, *The New York Times, The Village Voice,* and the *Boston Phoenix.*

Tom Moon (T.M.) writes about music for *The Philadelphia Inquirer*, ROLLING STONE, and *GQ*, and is an on-air contributor to NPR's *All Things Considered*.

Tom Nawrocki (T.N.) is an assistant managing editor at ROLLING STONE.

Chris Nelson (C.N.) is a frequent contributor to *The New York Times*, *Mojo*, and ROLLING STONE.

Elena Oumano (E.O.) is a fulltime communications professor at the City University of New York, and has written about music for *The New York Times*, the *Los Angeles Times*, *Spin*, and *The Village Voice*.

Jon Pareles (J.P.) is chief pop-music critic for *The New York Times*.

Nina Pearlman (N.P.) is managing editor at *Revolver* magazine.

Parke Puterbaugh (P.P.) is a longtime contributor to ROLLING STONE, where he was also a senior editor. He has also written for *USA Today*, *Stereo Review*, and many other publications.

Mac Randall (M.R.) has written for *The New York Times*, the *Daily News*, *Observer*, ROLLING STONE, *Musician*, *Vanity Fair*, and *Mojo*. He is the author of *Exit Music: The Radiohead Story* (Delta, 2000).

Peter Relic (P.R.) has written for ROLLING STONE, *Mojo*, *Vibe*, and *Grand Royal* magazine.

Ann Powers (A.P.) is a senior curator at the Experience Music Project in Seattle, WA, and the author of *Weird Like Us: My Bohemian America*.

Tricia Romano (T.R.) is a dance music and nightlife columnist for *The Village Voice* and has written for *Spin*, ROLLING STONE, *Seattle Weekly*, and *Salon*.

Chris Ryan (C.R.) is a frequent contributor to *Spin* and *The Village Voice*.

Kelefa Sanneh (K.S.) is a pop-music critic for *The New York Times*.

Roni Sarig (R.M.S.) has contributed to ROLLING STONE, *Vibe*, *Spin*, *XXL*, *Salon*, and *Maxim*, and is the author of *The Secret History of Rock: The Most Influential Bands You've Never Heard*.

Bud Scoppa (B.SC.) is a former managing editor of *Hits* magazine, and has written for ROLLING STONE and many other publications.

Scott Seward (S.S.) writes for *The Village Voice*.

Rob Sheffield (R.S.) is a contributing editor to ROLLING STONE.

Dev Sherlock (D.S.) is a former editor at *Musician*, who has written for ROLLING STONE, *Musician*, *Time Out New York*, *N.M.E.*, and *Billboard*.

Laura Sinagra (L.S.) writes about music and film for ROLLING STONE, *The Village Voice*, and *Spin*.

Ben Sisario (B.S.) writes about music and books for *The New York Times*, ROLLING STONE, *Blender*, and other publications.

Richard Skanse (R.SK.) is the editor of *Texas Music* magazine. He contributed to *The ROLLING STONE Encyclopedia of Rock & Roll* and has written for ROLLING STONE, *Tracks*, *Blender*, and the *Austin American-Statesman*.

Franklin Soults (F.S.) is former music editor of the *Cleveland Free Times* and has written for ROLLING STONE, the *Boston Phoenix*, and the *Chicago Reader*.

Carla Spartos (C.S.) is a former senior editor at *The Village Voice* and a freelance music and nightlife writer.

Allison Stewart (A.S.) is a contributing editor to *No Depression* and has written for *The Washington Post*, *Chicago Tribune*, ROLLING STONE, and *The Village Voice*.

David Swanson (D.S.) is an assistant editor at ROLLING STONE.

Greg Tate (G.T.) is a staff writer at the *The Village Voice*, the author and editor of many books on music and culture, and guitarist with the jazz band Burnt Sugar.

Barry Walters (B.W.) is a senior music critic at ROLLING STONE.

Douglas Wolk (D.W.) writes about music for *The Village Voice*, ROLLING STONE, *The Nation*, and *Slate*, and runs the record label Dark Beloved Cloud.

David Wykoff (D.WY.) is an entertainment attorney in Nashville, TN, and former contributor to ROLLING STONE.

Charles M. Young (C.M.Y.) writes for ROLLING STONE, *Men's Journal,* and many other publications. He is also a former editor of ROLLING STONE and *Musician* magazines.

Warren Zanes (W.Z.) is vice president of education at the Rock and Roll Hall of Fame Museum in Cleveland. His album *Memory Girls* was released in 2003 on Dualtone Records.

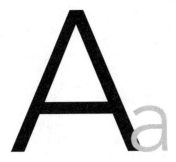

Aaliyah

★★½ Age Ain't Nothing but a Number (Jive, 1994)
★★★½ One in a Million (Jive, 1996)
★★★★ Aaliyah (Virgin, 2001)
★★★★ I Care 4 U (Blackground, 2002)

Appropriately for a nice Midwestern girl, the late Aaliyah Haughton occupied the sensible middle ground of R&B divas. When it came to sexual availability, she was between En Vogue maliciously taunting "You're never gonna get it" and Tweet blankly cooing "Oops, there goes my shirt." You *might* get it, Aaliyah's wary delivery suggested, if the time and place were right, but her clothes weren't about to magically vanish. Her best singles, "Are You That Somebody" and "Try Again," outline the rules a smart but passionate nonvirgin must set to protect herself in an age of sexual free-for-all.

Though her debut was overshadowed by the revelation that her producer, R. Kelly, had married the 15-year-old Chicago-raised starlet, Aaliyah's artistic personality occasionally pokes its nose above Kelly's bland settings. But it wasn't until Timbaland's stuttering beats *challenged* Aaliyah rather than cushioned her (as Kelly had) that her full personality revealed itself. If more critics had attuned their ears to the smooth, just-ever-so offbeat *One in a Million,* Missy Elliott's *Supa Dupa Fly* might have not seemed like such a shock.

The best was yet to come. The *Doctor Dolittle* soundtrack's "Are You That Somebody?," which placed Aaliyah up against the most idiosyncratic twitch of Timbaland's career, remains one of '90s' R&B's most astounding moments. And Aaliyah's third release was self-titled for a reason. On the ballads, she floats assuredly without drifting off into slow-jam tedium, while her commonsense avoidance of melodrama contrasts nicely with Timbaland's Latin tinges.

By her death at the age of 22 in a private-plane crash, Aaliyah had grown from studio puppet to a powerful R&B archetype—a more self-aware Ronnie Spector for a time that requires more self-awareness of its young adults. Sure, Timbaland sculpted her sound throughout, but Aaliyah imprinted herself upon those beats—as a catalyst, she's equaled only by Missy Elliott herself.

The six new tracks on *I Care 4 U*—a partial best-of for an artist who deserves a full career overview—add to the impression that Aaliyah's career was just beginning to blossom creatively. And that legacy lives on: According to the U.S. Social Security Administration annual report, Aaliyah was one of the 100 most popular names for newborn girls in 2001. —K.H.

ABBA

★★★ Ring Ring (1973; Universal, 2001)
★★★ Waterloo (1974; Universal, 2001)
★★★★ ABBA (1975; Universal, 2001)
★★★★ Arrival (1977; Universal, 2001)
★★★★ The Album (1978; Universal, 2001)
★★★ Voulez-Vous (1979; Universal, 2001)
★★★★ Super Trouper (1980; Universal, 2001)
★★★★ The Visitors (1981; Universal, 2001)
★★★ ABBA Live (PolyGram, 1986)
★★★★½ The Millennium Collection (Universal, 2000)
★★★★ The Definitive Collection (Universal, 2001)

Perhaps the first band to force rock elitists to take fluff pop seriously, ABBA made deliriously optimistic, naive, danceable, slightly off-kilter Europop that has enjoyed three heydays: its original one, during the '70s; one during the '80s and '90s, sparked by open-minded fans of the craft; and one that began in 1999, with the success of *Mamma Mia!,* a musical based loosely on ABBA songs. At this point, fans can find virtually every blip and chord the Swedish quartet ever recorded, thanks to Universal's frantic mass release, in 2001, of the band's early albums, remastered and tricked up with bonus tracks. Although the original version of *Waterloo*, the band's second record, is still on the stands, as is 1977's *Arrival*, Universal's rereleases are the ones to seek out.

There's some stylistic variation among ABBA's releases—some are disco, some are Euro-by-way-of-cabaret, some are "serious"—but, thanks to the never-less-than-sterling songwriting gifts of Benny Andersson and Björn Ulvaeus and the clean, pert female vocals of Anni-Frid Lyngstad and Agnetha Faltskog, there's very little variation in the recordings' quality. Some of the rereleases fool around with chronology, but their featured bonuses are plums: *Arrival* sticks in "Fernando" as well as the cheery travelogue "Happy Hawaii"; *ABBA* contains a medley of folk songs recorded for a charity album as well as the B side "Crazy World"; *Waterloo* introduces a Swedish version of the title song and includes a remix of "Ring Ring," which can of course be found, unremixed, on *Ring Ring* the album—early, less bouncy ABBA with the men singing lead. *The Album* offers an early version of "Thank You for the Music"; *Super Trouper* includes an outtake ("Put On Your White Sombrero") and a previously 7-inch-only B side "Elaine." *Voulez-Vous* features no fewer than three bonus tracks: "Summer Night City," "Gimme! Gimme! Gimme! (A Man After Midnight)," and the B side "Lovelight." If none of the above sounds interesting to you, but you still want to own "Dancing Queen" and "Waterloo," buy the airtight *Millennium Collection*.   —A.B.

ABC

★★★★	The Lexicon of Love (Mercury, 1982)
★★★	Beauty Stab (Mercury, 1983)
★★	How to Be a Zillionaire! (Mercury, 1985)
★★	Alphabet City (Mercury, 1987)
★★	Up (Mercury, 1989)
★★★★	Absolutely: The Best of ABC (Mercury, 1990)
★★	Abracadabra (Mercury, 1991)
★★	Skyscraping (Deconstruction, 1997)
★★★★	The Millennium Collection (Mercury, 2000)

ABC's classic debut, *The Lexicon of Love*, holds up as one of the catchiest, funniest, and smartest records to emerge from the '80s' British haircut-pop brigade. Martin Fry had a silver tongue to go with his platinum wedge of hair, and the group dressed up in opera capes and black tie to play suave Roxy Music–style synth funk. Fry unzipped his cocktail croon for witty songs about sex, money, and pop fantasy, playing the cosmopolitan cad with a heart full of secrets he'll keep until he finds a place to sell them. "The Look of Love" and "Poison Arrow" were huge hits, but "Date

Stamp," "Valentine's Day," and "Many Happy Returns" are every bit as tasty, as Fry shops for romance in a material world: "I get sales talk from sales assistants/When all I want to do, girl, is lower your resistance/Everything is temporary, written on that sand/Looking for the girl who meets supply with demand." Bravo. The group also made a hysterically funny feature film to go with the album, the little-seen, Julien Temple–directed *Mantrap*.

For *Beauty Stab*, they made two surprising decisions: they decided to get all serious and they decided to use loud guitars, because, as people tended to believe in 1983, guitars meant sincerity. *Beauty Stab* produced one great single, "That Was Then, but This Is Now"—rarely have the political implications of fruit-based pastry been explored more succinctly than in the line "Can't complain, mustn't grumble/Help yourself to another piece of apple crumble." But after *Beauty Stab* flopped, ABC returned to synth pop for the fabulously poignant 1985 hit "Be Near Me," on *How to Be a Zillionaire! Alphabet City* had the hit "When Smokey Sings," but the barbed irony was gone, and by now ABC could have been Wang Chung or Glass Tiger or Johnny Hates Jazz or any number of bland Brit smoothies. The group dissipated into occasional comeback attempts. *The Lexicon of Love* is a better album than any of ABC's greatest hits collections *(Absolutely, Millennium Collection)*, but you really do need a copy of "Be Near Me" somewhere in your life.   —R.S.

Paula Abdul

★★★	Forever Your Girl (Virgin, 1988)
★	Shut Up & Dance (Virgin, 1989)
★	Spellbound (Captive/Virgin, 1991)
★	Head Over Heels (Captive/Virgin, 1995)
★★★	The Greatest Hits (Virgin, 2000)

The "Forever Your Girl" kid was a disco star in the Hot Radio heyday of Milli Vanilli, Young MC, and Soul II Soul, with a pliant grin and a short skirt that helped America forgive her for having a voice like a pair of windshield wipers. A former choreographer, cheerleader, and Laker Girl, Paula squealed four straight #1 hits: "Straight Up" (she's caught in a hit and run), "Forever Your Girl" (but she loves you anyway), "Opposites Attract" (a rap duet with a cartoon cat), and "Cold Hearted" (snake-hating propaganda with a Bob Fosse–knockoff video and lyrics worthy of vintage Goffin-King). *Forever Your Girl* went platinum seven times over, probably because as a pop bunny in a hip-hop world, Paula was so darn eager to please everybody—she was white on the front cover of her album and black on the back cover. She was very pretty, and if you ever had fantasies of having sex with a chipmunk, you probably bought three copies. She also did a remix album, *Shut Up And Dance,* no doubt because someone asked her very nicely.

Spellbound was Paula's bid to prove that she was (1) a real singer, with (2) something to say, and failed beyond miserably at both efforts. The ballad "Rush Rush" has one of the most laughable vocals ever to reach #1, with Paula squeaking baby talk ("Lover come to me/I wanna see you 'gree with me"? What the hell does that even mean?) over piano and strings. The New Order–like "Promise of a New Day" was a much better song, with a strange video that stretched out Paula's body vertically to make her look skinnier. She finally exhausted the world's last remaining reserves of patience with the career-killing "Vibeology," repeatedly chirping, "I'm in a funky way!" Paula briefly married Emilio Estevez, basically retired, gritted her teeth through the contractual obligation *Head Over Heels,* and finally found her greatest success in 2002 as a cohost of TV's *American Idol.* "Cold Hearted" still sounds pretty good; "Rush Rush" has to be heard to be believed.   —R.S.

AC/DC

★★	High Voltage (1976; Epic, 2003)
★★½	Let There Be Rock (1977; Epic, 2003)
★★½	Powerage (1978; Epic, 2003)
★★★	If You Want Blood, You've Got It (1978; Epic, 2003)
★★★★½	Highway to Hell (1979; Epic, 2003)
★★★★★	Back in Black (1980; Epic, 2003)
★★★	Dirty Deeds Done Dirt Cheap (1981; Epic, 2003)
★★★½	For Those About to Rock, We Salute You (1981; Epic, 2003)
★★½	Flick of the Switch (1983; Epic, 2003)
★★½	'74 Jailbreak (1984; Epic, 2003)
★★½	Fly on the Wall (1985; Epic, 2003)
★★★★	Who Made Who (1986; Epic, 2003)
★★½	Blow Up Your Video (1988; Epic, 2003)
★★★	The Razor's Edge (1990; Epic, 2003)
★★½	AC/DC Live (1992; Epic, 2003)
★★★½	Ballbreaker (EastWest, 1995)
★★½	Stiff Upper Lip (EastWest, 2000)

AC/DC rose to fame during the second half of the '70s, but this veteran Australian quintet forged the archetype for '80s metal with its turn-of-the-decade release *Back in Black.* Perhaps AC/DC's most crucial innovation is the way their lyrics make plain the boys' locker-room conception of sexuality that had previously bubbled just under the surface of most heavy-duty rock. Shamelessly sexist panderers or refreshingly frank entertainers? AC/DC fits both descriptions, but none of it would matter if guitarist Angus Young wasn't such a gargantuan riffmonger equipped with a Godzilla-like rhythm section to boot. Learn to laugh with or at lead singer Brian Johnson's shrieking depictions of those hormonal surges, and AC/DC's thundering musical charge will sweep you up like a riptide.

Original lead singer Bon Scott pioneered the raunchy, high-pitched style that Johnson later perfected; he died shortly after AC/DC's belated American breakthrough, *Highway to Hell.* Produced by pop-metal maven Robert "Mutt" Lange, that album sharpens the band's impact by refining some of its rougher edges. "You Shook Me All Night Long," from *Back in Black,* the Lange-produced platinum followup, epitomizes AC/DC's streamlined attack: a ringing, near-melodic chorus is welded to a granite-shattering beat. "Rock and Roll Ain't Noise Pollution" insists the climactic final cut, but overall *Back in Black* proves that noise pollution, when properly deployed, can qualify as great rock & roll.

Predictably, AC/DC hasn't changed a whit since then. Angus Young still stalks the stage in a schoolboy's uniform, tossing off riffs and abbreviated solos while his brother Malcolm strokes a propulsive rhythm guitar and Brian Johnson shakes the roof. *For Those About to Rock* almost measures up to the heft of *Back in Black,* but successive albums quickly become rote. AC/DC's macho posturing is unspeakably dull when it is not supported by killer hooks. (*Dirty Deeds Done Dirt Cheap* compiles the best of Bon Scott–era AC/DC; the title cut is a trashy, irresistible revenge fantasy.) A quickie soundtrack album, *Who Made Who* nevertheless works as an effective introduction to the group: Previous triumphs ("You Shook Me All Night Long") contrast with reclaimed later efforts ("Sink the Pink," from *Fly on the Wall*) and a completely out-of-character '70s blooze number called "Ride On." Of course, AC/DC returns to business as usual with *Blow Up Your Video,* where even the hottest riffs ("Heatseeker") don't seem to detonate with the same gratifying crunch. But after girding its loins for a few years, AC/DC confidently stalked back into the metal arena with *The Razor's Edge*—loud and proud. "Money Talks" makes the prospect of AC/DC's eventual greatest hits collection seem all the more enticing to non-metalheads.

The rest of the '90s was a victory lap for the band, rereleasing much of its back catalogue and touring behind albums that were just a shadow of their powerful predecessors. A serviceable 1992 live album, *AC/DC Live,* culled from the tour following *The Razor's Edge,* acted as a reminder of their onstage fury. After a three-year break the band returned to the studio for the Rick Rubin–helmed *Ballbreaker.* Perhaps using Rubin, whose work with bands such as the Red Hot Chili Peppers had made him the de facto hard-rock producer of the day, was a stab at relevance. Motivations aside, *Ballbreaker* has a spark that the band had been missing on most of its late-era work, with tracks such as "Hard as a Rock" sitting comfortably next to any other behemoth in its arsenal. The band returned in 2000 with *Stiff Upper Lip,* a somewhat tired collection, lacking the energy of *Ballbreaker* and smelling suspiciously like an excuse to rake in more arena ticket money. Guess what? None of the tens of thousands of fans who packed those concert halls cared one whit. AC/DC were inducted into the Rock and Roll Hall of Fame in 2003.   —M.C./C.R.

Johnny Ace

★★★★   The Johnny Ace Memorial Album (1973; MCA, 1990)

Born John Alexander in Memphis, Johnny Ace was the piano player in a band dubbed the Beale Streeters, which in the late '40s could often be found backing B.B. King and Bobby Bland. But Ace, blessed with a smooth, sturdy baritone voice, had no intention of remaining a faceless backing musician. Signed to the Duke label, he proceeded to cut several R&B hits that showed him comfortable delivering a blues ballad ("So Lonely" and "Never Let Me Go" being two of the most affecting performances of their day) as well as uptempo material ("Don't You Know" and "How Can You Be So Mean" being the only representatives of that style on this album). He didn't have great range, and sometimes he wobbled slightly off key, but Ace did have presence and personality to burn. Among the 12 cuts here is the immortal "Pledging My Love," the velvety R&B ballad that hit the Top 20 and might have made Ace a crossover star if it hadn't made him a legend first. When it was released in 1955, Ace was dead, having expired on Christmas Eve of 1954 after losing a game of Russian roulette backstage before a show that evening at Houston's City Auditorium.

Despite all the archaeology the CD era has inspired, *Memorial Album* is the same package Duke owner Don Robey issued following Ace's death—no bonus tracks or alternative takes (maybe none exist?), and hyperbolic liner notes lacking any references to backing musicians or recording dates. It's only a hunch, but those familiar with some of the early Sun blues sessions will want to check out the scorching, distorted guitar solo on "How Can You Be So Mean," which bears the stylistic trademarks of Ace's friend B.B. King.   —D.M.

Aceyalone

★★★★   All Balls Don't Bounce (1995; Project Blowed, 2004)

★★★½   A Book of Human Language (Project Blowed/Nu Gruv, 1998)

★★★★   Accepted Eclectic (Ground Control/Nu Gruv, 2001)

★★½   Love and Hate (Project Blowed, 2003)

A founding member of Los Angeles rap troupe Freestyle Fellowship, Aceyalone is one of the most underrated MCs currently working. His first solo album, 1995's *All Balls Don't Bounce,* is an arty, loping, good-natured disc whose slice-of-life feel (with a giant side order of disses, including one capped by a dead-on Beavis and Butt-head impersonation) falls halfway between De La Soul's *3 Feet High and Rising* and Atmosphere's *Lucy Ford.* Best of all is the wry "Annallillia," the story of Acey's continued attempts to court a difficult woman with an unusual name ("I bet you think I'm silly, huh, Annallillia?"). Unfortunately, in a hip-hop scene saturated with Wu-Tang rip-offs and Cali gangsta, *All Balls'* boho aura helped the record go precisely nowhere. (The disc was reissued in 2004, after having been out of print for the better part of a decade, with a good bonus disc of remixes and contemporary cuts that add a darker undertone to the original album's often flighty groove.)

Three years later, *A Book of Human Language* reintroduced Aceyalone as even more high-concept, with each track meant to represent a chapter in a book on, you guessed it, language itself. Heady stuff, and occasionally overwhelming, but the jazz-tinged music keeps it light on its feet. The more song-oriented *Accepted Eclectic* was Aceyalone's strongest album to date, from its playful title track (whose twittering cartoon effects recalled early Soul Coughing, of all things) to the brilliant "Rappers, Rappers, Rappers," which celebrates everything from "Ugly rappers/ Pretty rappers, big city rappers, country rappers" to "two-for-fiddy," Hello Kitty, and Frank Nitti rappers. (Even gum wrappers receive a shout-out.) Unfortunately, the newer *Love and Hate* finds Acey sounding unsure where to go next.   —M.M.

Ace of Base

★★★½   The Sign (Arista, 1993)

★★½   The Bridge (Arista, 1995)

★★½   Cruel Summer (Arista, 1998)

★★★½   Greatest Hits (Arista, 2000)

★★★   Platinum and Gold Collection (Arista, 2003)

Look, it's not as if Ace of Base *chose* to come from Sweden. So keep those pathetically easy, inaccurately dismissive ABBA comparisons to yourself. These particular northerners were jaded club rats, not bubblegum Scandi-naifs. Jonas "Joker" Berggren and Ulf "Buddha" Ekberg's seemingly benign Eurodisco thump was actually full of moody undertones; their plastic textures were pristine rather than antiseptic; and their synthetic skank was surprisingly club-wise. And they wrote "The Sign," the wisest, catchiest, most triumphant kiss-off since "I Will Survive."

On the debut disc, an Ennio Morricone–style keyboard whistle marks the welfare-state cautionary tale "All That She Wants." (Dig the "Bhangra Version," though.) "Don't Turn Around" is a logical impossibility—a funky Diane Warren song!—made reality. And if the group wasn't above feigning airheadedness (one lyric has siblings Jenny and Linn Berggren cooing "Kiss me baby, I'm attractive"), you could always spy the smirk underneath.

Though now out-of-print *Lucky Love* was an adequate followup, the palpable desperation audible in Ace of Base's "Cruel Summer" cover was commercial, not sexual. *Greatest Hits* will net you some fine house mixes and Motown fabrications. —K.H.

Adam and the Ants

★★★½ Dirk Wears White Sox (Epic, 1979)
★★★½ Prince Charming (Epic, 1981)
★★★ Friend or Foe (Epic, 1982)
★★ Strip (Epic, 1983)
★★ Vive le Rock (Epic, 1985)
★ Manners and Physique (MCA, 1990)
★★★★ Antics in the Forbidden Zone (Epic, 1990)
★★½ The Peel Sessions (Dutch East India, 1991)
★★★½ B-Side Babies (Epic, 1994)
★ Wonderful (Capitol, 1995)
★★★★ Antbox (Epic, 2000)

Sexual perversion, pirate costumes, visible black lingerie for men, tribal drumming, loud surf guitars, brain-dead lyrics, high-pitched shrieks barely hinting at the moral depravity lurking under the surface—Adam Ant brought an awful lot to the table. He was one of the great New Romantic pop stars, a dandy highwayman swashing his buckle for some of the '80s' most outrageous hits. Adam began as a London artrock leather boy on *Dirk Wears White Sox,* but even though he was still working out his shtick, he was already a sexy phony with a puffy-shirt complex and stiletto cheekbones. (He was also a former teen flame of actress Amanda Donohoe—oh, the humanity.) The music was twisted postpunk kicks, with the incredible "Cleopatra" leading the way for sick thrills like "Car Trouble," "Digital Tenderness," and "Zerox." Hard as it is to believe, some people took Adam incredibly seri-

ously, and they—okay, *we*—have been scarred by the experience ever since.

Adam Ant took a huge leap on *Kings of the Wild Frontier,* where he became a U.K. sensation with his new formula of "Antmusic for Sexpeople." Now here was a poseur among poseurs: Adam dressed up in 18th-century pirate finery, all frills and sleeves and pseudo-Apache warpaint, with the rest of his Ants looking mean in the same costume, ready to go keelhaul some landlubbers. The music was a shameless pop hustle, full of big Burundi-inspired rhythms and stolen guitar hooks, all amped up to headache levels and topped with debauched howls as the Ants fleeced their fans of their money at musket-point. The songs pay homage to art-terrorist inspirations such as Blackbeard, Geronimo, Link Wray, *Planet of the Apes,* and Joe Orton, in slobbering come-ons such as "Dog Eat Dog," "Los Rancheros," "Feed Me to the Lions," or the immortal "Physical (You're So)." "Jolly Roger" was the theme song, with all the Ants chanting in unison, "It's your money that we want!/And your money we shall have!"

Prince Charming was exactly the same album, except with a blue cover. The Ants scored their finest hit with "Stand and Deliver," a rollicking guitar anthem that used stagecoach robbing as a perfect metaphor for rock stardom, advertising a lifestyle in which you dress up to make trouble and ride away under cover of night. Unfortunately, the amazing B side "Beat My Guest" missed the album, finally appearing years later on *Antics in the Forbidden Zone.* Other classics here include "Ant Rap," "Mile High Club," "S.E.X.," and "Picasso Visita el Planeta de los Simios." The title song offered the ultimate New Romantic motto: "Ridicule is nothing to be scared of." On *Friend or Foe,* "Adam and the Ants" officially became "Adam Ant," which made no difference to anyone except people who'd loaned money to the other Ants. The scurvy was obviously reaching Adam's brain by this point, but that just made him sound funnier in the likes of "Try This for Sighs," "Crackpot History and the Right to Lie," and his biggest U.S. hit, "Goody Two Shoes." He also did a cover of the Doors' "Hello I Love You"—it takes a lot of pretension to make Jim Morrison sound sincere, but Adam was maybe the one rock star capable of pulling it off.

Strip was the album where Adam walked the plank. Two of the tracks were produced by Phil Collins, the worst possible sign, although there were still great tunes such as "Puss in Boots" ("Pussycat pussycat, where have you been?/I've been to London and now I'm queen") and the minuet-core title tease. But *Strip* went straight to Davy Jones' locker, and so did his attempted teddy-boy comeback *Vive le Rock,* although in retrospect it had a few Antworthy moments (was Adam the first nondisco pop star to employ the song title "Miss Thing"?). *Manners and Physique* was conformist mainstream pop, and *Wonderful* may as well have been Michael Bolton. By now Adam was concentrating on his acting career *(Slam Dance, Blue Steel),* but his musical cred level remained high thanks to high-profile acolytes such as Elastica, who covered "Cleopatra," and Nine Inch Nails, who covered "Physical (You're So)." *Antics in the Forbidden Zone* was a near-flawless best-of, although loyal Antpeople still cling to the rarities of *B-Side Babies* and the brilliantly titled three-disc *Antbox.* Never one to go quietly, Adam Ant was arrested in a bizarre 2002 incident in which he supposedly whipped out a gun in a London pub. It turned out to be a toy. By George, he's still got it.   —R.S.

Bryan Adams

★★	You Want It, You Got It	(A&M, 1981)
★★★	Cuts Like a Knife	(A&M, 1983)
★★★½	Reckless	(A&M, 1984)
★★	Into the Fire	(A&M, 1987)
★★★	Waking Up the Neighbours	(A&M, 1991)
★★★	So Far So Good	(A&M, 1993)
★★★	Live! Live! Live!	(A&M, 1995)
★★	18 'til I Die	(A&M, 1996)
★★	MTV Unplugged	(A&M, 1997)
★½	On a Day Like Today	(A&M, 1998)
★★★	Greatest Hits	(A&M, 1999)
★★½	Best of Me	(A&M, 2001)

As a singer, Adams can't quite master Rod Stewart's tender gruffness. As a writer, he falls more than a few notches short of Bob Seger's small-town mythologizing. But in the early '80s Adams tried valiantly to match these strengths—and on his singles, at least, came close to delivering an easier, radio-perfect version. Beginning as a songwriter for Bachman-Turner Overdrive, Kiss, and Bob Welch, the harmlessly leather-jacketed Canadian embodied the rock-as-career-choice approach of his moment; he was crafty, modest, competent, likable. "Cuts Like a Knife" (1983) and "Summer of '69" (1985) were perfect as bright, chunky singles. "(Everything I Do) I Do It for You," off *Waking Up the Neighbours,* sold in stratospheric amounts, but it was Adams at his slickest, not his best. There's more of Adams' sappy, big-screen balladry on *Best of Me. So Far So Good* stresses the rockin' hits.   —P.E.

Faye Adams

★★★	The Herald Recordings	(Collectables, 1990)

Among the virtues that led Atlantic Records to sign Joe Morris' Blues Cavalcade in the early '50s was its lead singer, Faye Adams, whose big, aching voice bore an uncanny resemblance to Dinah Washington's. When the Cavalcade broke up before it had even cut a side for Atlantic, Adams signed with the small Herald label and emerged as a distinctive voice in postwar R&B. She could belt the blues with anyone, and her voice had an exciting trill in it that could make devastating work of a ballad such as "Anytime, Anyplace, Anywhere" or, even better, her signature song, "Shake a Hand" (written by Joe Morris), a slow, churning vow of devotion featuring Adams' gutsy reading backed by a personable small combo with a tinkling blues piano prominent in the mix and a monolithic horn section blowing chunky, foreboding chords in the distance. Adams' recordings were marked both by a rawness that lent them the feel of live tracks and by strong, often inventive instrumental work—"Takin' You Back" swings along at a heady pace and then hits a stop-time phrase to make room for a couple of energetic burps from a tenor sax; and several of her dramatic ballads are lent richer atmosphere by robust, Jimmy McGriff–like organ lines.

Her first Herald single, 1953's "Shake a Hand," topped the R&B chart and crossed over to become a #22 pop record; she followed that with another R&B chart-topper, the stomping, sax-powered "I'll Be True," and in 1954 topped the R&B chart for the third and final time with "Hurts Me to My Heart." Adams moved to the Imperial label in 1957, and subsequently recorded for several other independents—including Savoy and Prestige—without much success. She retired in 1963, leaving *The Herald Recordings* as her admirable legacy. This collection supplants the label's earlier *Golden Classics* LP, and includes all three of the artist's #1 R&B hits, plus 11 other choice tracks that offer ample evidence of her versatility and persuasive vocalizing.   —D.M.

Ryan Adams

★★★★½	Heartbreaker	(Bloodshot, 2000)
★★★	Gold	(Lost Highway, 2001)
★★★	Demolition	(Lost Highway, 2002)
★★★½	Rock N Roll	(Lost Highway, 2003)
★★★½	Love Is Hell	(Lost Highway, 2004)

Ever since the demise of his '90s alt-country band Whiskeytown, Ryan Adams has shown himself to be a skilled and fearsomely prolific tunesmith with a voice that's as suited to caustic punk as it is to mopey folk. If you can make it past Adams' self-conscious streak—some of his songs practically scream "I am a Major American Artist, and you will recognize my brilliance!"—there's plenty to enjoy on these discs.

Recorded with fellow lovers of twang Gillian Welch

and David Rawlings, *Heartbreaker* is the closest Adams has come to classic tear-in-my-beer country. His tender duet with Emmylou Harris on "Oh My Sweet Carolina" is a career highlight. The sprawling followup, *Gold,* is Adams' first outright attempt to don the genius mantle, via a loving pastiche of various '70s singer-songwriters. Though admirably ambitious, the album is bottom-heavy, with most of its standout tracks ("Enemy Fire," "Touch, Feel and Lose," "Goodnight, Hollywood Blvd.") clustered near the end.

Adams allegedly recorded four albums' worth of material within months of *Gold's* release. *Demolition* grabs 13 songs from that pile. Good songs, too, but despite gritty rockers like "Gimme a Sign" and heart-in-throat ballads like "Cry on Demand," the end result doesn't hang together. On *Rock N Roll* and *Love Is Hell,* Adams makes some serious chameleon moves. The former transparently references every hard-rockin' band from the Stooges to the Strokes, while the latter, originally released in 2003 as two EPs, aims for a moody mix of the Smiths, Radiohead, and Jeff Buckley. Excellent songs abound, and yet it's hard to locate a distinct personality at work here. Adams' high level of talent is obvious; here's hoping that in the future he'll offer more than a tour through his record collection. —M.R.

King Sunny Ade

★★★★½	Juju Music (Mango, 1982)
★★★★	Synchro System (Mango, 1983)
★★★	Live Live Juju (Rykodisc, 1988)
★★★½	E Dide (Get Up) (Mesa, 1995)
★★★★	Odu (Atlantic/Mesa, 1998)
★★★	Let Them Say & Edide, Classics, Vol. 1 (Masterdisc, 2001)
★★★½	Ekilo Fomo Ode & The Way Forward: Classics, Vol. 2 (Masterdisc, 2001)
★★★	The Good Shepherd & The Child: Classics, Vol. 3 (Masterdisc, 2001)
★★★½	Mo Ti Mo & Destiny: Classics, Vol. 4 (Masterdisc, 2001)
★★★	Surprise & Conscience: Classics, Vol. 5 (Masterdisc, 2001)
★★★	Merciful God & Baba More Pe O, Classics, Vol. 6 (Masterdisc, 2001)
★★★★½	King of Juju—The Best of (Wrasse, 2002)
★★★★½	The Best of the Classic Years (Shanachie, 2003)

A superstar in his native Nigeria since the late '60s, juju bandleader King Sunny Ade was introduced to audiences in Europe and the U.S. in 1982 as "the next Bob Marley"—a sales pitch aimed more at stoking the engines of hype than accurately describing Ade's music. Granted, juju (as Ade plays it) is a catchy and exotic sound, but far more foreign to Western ears than reggae ever was. Instead of being centered around the vocal line, juju accords equal or greater importance to its guitars and drums, with episodic melodic development instead of regular verse-chorus structures.

Moreover, the fact that Ade sang only in Yoruba meant that his lyrics were largely unintelligible to non-Nigerians. Even so, Ade's Western recordings are surprisingly accessible. Well-versed in musical technology even before signing with Mango, Ade's African Beats had no difficulty absorbing the synths and drum machines added by producer Martin Meissonnier to *Juju Music* and *Synchro System.* After beefed-up electronics and even a Stevie Wonder cameo on the now-deleted *Aura* did little to improve sales, Ade was dropped from the label, and he disbanded the African Beats.

In 1986 he returned to recording with a new group, whose sound is somewhat more techno-intense and percussive. *Live Live Juju* gives a reasonable approximation of that group in concert, though no live recording has been able to capture the diverse interactions of the African Beats in full flight. After another pause of several years, Ade began releasing calmer, more autumnal sets (as befit a performer now in his 50s) that show he'd kept up with technology. *Odu* has the warmest sound and the most cleanly organized layers of rhythm, voice, keyboards, and guitar of any Ade album. The Masterdisc series presents Ade's own selections from his back catalogue and is hugely recommended to fans: *Ekilo Fomo Ode & The Way Forward* has the most lambent guitar workouts, *Mo Ti Mo & Destiny* the prettiest tunes.

Ade has never been as well represented in the era of digital music as he is now. The *King of Juju* import presents highlights from all three Island LPs and a selection of his more aggressive and electronic sides of the same vintage. *The Best of the Classic Years* is what it says: Ade's modern juju before it went international—an engrossing dream of interlocked beats, pealing guitars, and sweet voices. Although he failed to conquer America, Ade refused to fade away. In a huge affirmation for veteran Ade fans, his sterling retrospectives and confident new releases show he's both determined to stay and strong enough to last. —J.D.C./M.MI.

Aerosmith

★★★★	Aerosmith (Columbia, 1973)
★★★	Get Your Wings (Columbia, 1974)
★★★★½	Toys in the Attic (1975; Columbia, 1993)
★★★★½	Rocks (Columbia, 1976)
★★	Draw the Line (Columbia, 1977)

★ Live Bootleg (Columbia, 1978)
★ A Night in the Ruts (Columbia, 1979)
★★★★★ Aerosmith's Greatest Hits (Columbia, 1980)
★ Rock in a Hard Place (Columbia, 1982)
★★ Classics Live (Columbia, 1984)
★★ Done With Mirrors (Geffen, 1985)
★★ Classics Live II (Columbia, 1987)
★★ Permanent Vacation (Geffen, 1987)
★★ Gems (Columbia, 1988)
★★★★ Pump (Geffen, 1989)
★★★ Pandora's Box (Columbia, 1991)
★★★ Get a Grip (Geffen Universal, 1993)
★★★ Big Ones (Geffen, 1994)
★★ Box of Fire (Columbia, 1994)
★★ Nine Lives (Columbia, 1997)
★★ A Little South of Sanity (Geffen, 1998)
★★★ Just Push Play (Columbia, 2001)
★★★ Young Lust: The Aerosmith Anthology (Geffen, 2001)
★★★★½ O, Yeah! Ultimate Aerosmith Hits (Columbia, 2002)
★★★½ Honkin' on Bobo (Columbia, 2004)

In the days when drugs and alcohol were required substances on the road to rock & roll nirvana, Aerosmith blazed the path of excess, American-style. Though the Boston quintet's glam-rock swagger paved the way for Guns n' Roses, Mötley Crüe, and countless others, the originals greased their lip-smacking arena-rock dramatics with hip-shake rhythms out of an earlier era steeped in R&B and blues. Their affinity for the groove provided a logical bridge for the first rock-rap crossover, Run-D.M.C.'s inner-city reincarnation of Aerosmith's "Walk This Way."

Aerosmith establishes the formula that would carry the so-called Toxic Twins—singer Steven Tyler and guitarist Joe Perry—through three decades in which they'd swing wildly between hits and hokum, shotgun-blues raunch and purple balladry. Perry brought riffs by way of the Rolling Stones and the Yardbirds, and Tyler the bawdiness, while second guitarist Brad Whitford, bassist Tom Hamilton, and drummer Joey Kramer applied the lubrication, a rhythm section that never forgot that it don't mean a thing if it ain't got that below-the-belly-button swing. "Dream On" is the debut's signature piece, a "Stairway to Heaven"–style ballad that suggested these hard-rock bad boys had arena aspirations from the get-go.

That goal became reality after the twin triumphs of *Toys in the Attic* and *Rocks,* hard-rock landmarks that bring the melody without stinting on the toughness. But the band's excesses soon swallowed them up, as evidenced by a bankrupt series of studio albums from *Draw the Line* through *Done With Mirrors.* Things got so bad during this period that Perry and later Whitford briefly quit.

Ignited by the Run-D.M.C. collaboration, the reunited and newly cleaned-up Aerosmith began marshalling a comeback. An audacious single, "Dude (Looks Like a Lady)," perked up the otherwise thin *Permanent Vacation,* but *Pump* made their return to hard-rock glory official: the first wall-to-wall classic since *Rocks.* It revealed a previously well-concealed social consciousness on "Janie's Got a Gun" and still managed to snarl through the slick production. Its success ushered in a new era of studio puffery, with ballads and gimmicks competing for space with the rockers on *Get a Grip.* As a live act, the new Aerosmith came across like multimillionaire craftsmen; their hook-filled but disconcertingly sanitized bombast is documented on the live disc *A Little South of Sanity.*

Nine Lives sees the band resorting to repeating itself and others, with "Hole in My Soul" revising "Dream On," while Led Zeppelin's "Kashmir" is the template for "Taste of India." *Just Push Play* continues to press the same buttons that recharged the band's career: power ballads so overblown they might make Mariah Carey blush, the occasional contemporary production touch (turntable scratching, drum loops), plus the time-tested arsenal of dirty guitar licks and lip-smacking, jive-rapping sexual innuendo. There's something sleazy and craven about the whole affair—no surprise from a band that shared a stage with Britney Spears and 'N Sync during the 2001 Super Bowl. The blues covers that dominate *Honkin' on Bobo* allow Aerosmith to play it looser and raunchier, and this time there're no gratuitous pop concessions to muck up the low-rent thrills.

Among a truckload of hits compilations and retrospectives, the priciest is *Box of Fire,* which repackages the 12 albums from the band's first Columbia Records era with a marginal five-song bonus disc. The best is *O, Yeah! Ultimate Aerosmith Hits,* which combines the classic '70s material with the best of its "Janie's Got a Gun"–era hits for Geffen. —G.K.

Aesop Rock

★★★ Float (Mush, 2000)
★★★★ Labor Days (Def Jux, 2001)
★★★★ Daylight (EP) (Def Jux, 2002)
★★★ Bazooka Tooth (Definitive Jux, 2003)

White New York City rapper Aesop Rock rhymes as if he's trying to recite his internal monologue, smothering exotic beats in bizarre observations and confessional narratives seemingly woven from the utterances of someone talking in their sleep. On *Float,* the breakthrough that—along with Cannibal Ox's *The Cold*

Vein—ushered in the postmillennial "undie" (short for "underground") hip-hop movement, Aesop even provided liner notes explaining the ambitious, oblique, and sometimes simple ideas that inspired each song. About "6B Panorama" he writes, "Home. Studying my surroundings from the inside looking out. Taking notice of the overlooked elements of one day." These elements include pigeons, vagabonds, princesses, junkies, "batty" senior citizens, jaywalkers, and men "slapping dominoes down"—the details of a "city, a village, a neighborhood, a ghost town."

And he goes on. And on, and on, over the croak of '70s funk synth and a stripped-down, skipping beat he produced. Blockhead, Omega, and, most famously, Slug (the voice behind fellow undie stalwarts Atmosphere) also create Aesop's music, which is usually elegant but sometimes hook-deficient. The funny, meditative, and startlingly original *Labor Days,* however, brims with crooked details that snag one's attention, like the bursts of woolly synth on "Labor," the flutelike lead and melodic bassline on "Daylight," the Asian ambience of "Flashflood." Aesop's dorky and subtly ironic voice courses through every track like a snake digesting a recent meal, as he ponders the metaphysics of working nine to five, relates the life and times of a wannabe artist named "Lucy," and makes obscure references (to mythology, for instance) that even the careful listener will never parse. More than dense, Aesop Rock's food-for-thought rhymes are delectably rich. And every so often he delivers a zinger, like this one from "Daylight": "Life's not a bitch/life's a beautiful woman/you only call her a bitch 'cause she wouldn't let you get that pussy."

"If cameras are guns, one of y'all is gonna shoot me to death," Aesop intones at the start of "Easy," overestimating the amount of press his last two discs earned him. *Bazooka Tooth* suffers from his premature effort to stay underground: the beats are crafted for close listening, not casual enjoyment, and the rhyme flows are overly dense and therefore seem less impassioned.   —N.C.

Afghan Whigs

★	Big Top Halloween (Ultrasuede, 1988)	
★★½	Up in It (Sub Pop, 1990)	
★★★½	Congregation (Sub Pop, 1992)	
★★★½	Uptown Avondale (EP) (Sub Pop, 1992)	
★★★★½	Gentlemen (Elektra, 1993)	
★★★½	What Jail Is Like (EP) (Elektra, 1994)	
★★★½	Black Love (Elektra, 1996)	
★★★	1965 (Columbia, 1998)	

Too alt-identified (or complicated) for the mainstream, too straightforward (or cock-rockish) for many indie lifers, the Afghan Whigs never found the mass audience to which their cinematic, oddly addictive soul-rock infernos aspired. Much of the admiration they did inspire centered on frontman Greg Dulli, an inspirationally pudgy, manic-depressive cad who would have creeped out Don Giovanni. Dulli's a Catholic boy blessed with a filmmaker's sense of story, a robust, overly industrious voice that can't quite stay on key, sexual hang-ups for days, and the seeming conviction he may, in fact, be black. Dulli could introduce a song "Ladies/Let me tell you about myself/I've got a dick for a brain/And my brain is gonna sell my ass to you" and let his corrosive charisma and charred voice do the rest.

After a fetal 1988 debut called *Big Top Halloween* they've longed to forget, *Up in It* showed some signs of ambition beyond the Sub Pop Singles Club, but thudding production hides the band's latent smarts in sludge. The quantum leap that is *Congregation* shows they ditched grunge for soul because they were no damn good at the former and ladies dig the latter. Dulli's sex-god persona is coming into focus. Convinced submission ("I'm Her Slave"), predation ("Tonight"), and absolution ("This Is My Confession") are all necessary to balance out the guilt and pleasure, and he macks like an expert at all of them. The hidden track, "Miles Iz Dead," brings a terrific faux-funk riff to life and sums up Dulli's seduction strategy thus: "Don't forget the alcohol."

The placeholding *Uptown Avondale* dives into soul covers such as Freda Payne's "Band of Gold" and the Supremes' "Come See About Me." It'd be nice if Dulli stayed on key the whole time, but the band's hearts and hips are in the right place.

But *Gentlemen* they will take to their grave. A brilliant, knowing record sleeve hides one of '90s rock's messiest psychodramas. Reportedly written after a particularly nasty breakup, the *Gentlemen* song cycle portrays the artist as a grandmaster headfucker, the kind of guy you would keep your slightly obsessive sister away from at all costs even as she is, once again, climbing into his car. Dulli chronicles the melodramatic chess of maximum codependence with vengeful loathing, self- and otherwise, while the band—guitarist Rick McCollum in particular—pounds out complex, almost proggy R&B. From the howling single "Debonair" and the subtle, savage fuck-off "Be Sweet" to the plaintive "What Jail Is Like" and the astoundingly bitter "When We Two Parted," *Gentlemen* dissects the sort of emotional train wreck few bands have ever documented as unflinchingly. *Gentlemen* is toxic and cunning, hopelessly arrogant and just plain hopeless. (*What Jail Is Like* is more soul covers and killer live tracks, demonstrating that almost any live bootleg from here forward is worth a spin.)

"Tonight I say goodbye/To everyone that loves me," opens *Black Love*, a smoother, more flagrantly soulful, and somehow even darker album. Where *Gentlemen* at least felt like the catharsis of vibrant autobiography, *Black Love*'s noir-novel vibe balls up in the pit of your stomach and eats right through. The album's overtly cinematic feel works like a distancing effect until you realize just how fucked up Dulli sounds. The opening "Crime Scene Part One" is thunderously dramatic, but the funk on "Going to Town" and the "Honky's Ladder" jive feels more shticky than sticky.

Created after an increasingly ill Dulli received treatment he clearly really, *really* needed for clinical depression, *1965* is the headfucker on Zoloft. Instead of hating himself and the world, Dulli, who's never sung better, sounds like he's actually enjoying sex because sex is fun and not just a power trip he can't escape. He shouts out Nas on "Omerta," and "John the Baptist" and "Somethin' Hot" shake what his mama gave him, while "Neglekted" is just plain dirty. At the time, *1965*'s groove thang felt like a mild letdown from the previous trilogy's relentlessness, but in hindsight it's clear Dulli wasn't as used to joy as pain, and probably had as much to say about the former as the latter. Having been almost famous for a little too long, the Afghan Whigs called it a day in February 2001.   —J.G.

A.F.I.

★★	Answer That & Stay Fashionable (1995; Wingnut, 2000)
★½	Very Proud of Ya (NIT, 1996)
★★½	Shut Your Mouth & Open Your Eyes (NIT, 1997)
★½	Fire Inside (Adeline, 1998)
★★★	Black Sails in the Sunset (NIT, 1999)
★★★	The Art of Drowning (Nitro, 2000)
★★★★	Sing the Sorrow (DreamWorks, 2003)

By the time of the release of their major label debut, *Sing the Sorrow*, A.F.I. had transformed themselves from lightning-fast hardcore-punk torchbearers to scary goth-metal freakazoids on a mission to gather up an army of alienated youth. It's clear from the opening minutes of that album—where the music lurches to a sludgy crawl more than a couple times—that A.F.I. are on to something new, weaving electronic drums, synths, punk rhythms, anthemic choruses, creepy-crawly lead vocals, and metal riffage into a dark, near-perfect album for even darker times. The A.F.I. of *Sing the Sorrow* come off as the Damned for the new metal generation, whereas the A.F.I. of their debut, *Answer That & Stay Fashionable*, could have been just about any hardcore-obsessed garage

band from the 1980s or 1990s. The transition from a generic Southern California punk band to something more substantive and original began with 1999's *Black Sails in the Sunset*, in which they started slowing things down and finding their own voice. Earlier releases like the four-song EP *Fire Inside* (not a cover of the Bob Seger song, but a reference to the band's name, which stands for "A Fire Inside") seem to end almost as soon as they begin, which is even true of blitzkrieg full-length albums like *Answer That & Stay Fashionable* and *Very Proud of Ya*.   —K.M.

Christina Aguilera

★★	Christina Aguilera (RCA, 1999)
★★½	Stripped (RCA, 2002)

Of the teen divas who revived bubblegum in the late '90s, Christina Aguilera had the distinction of being the one who could "really sing"—meaning she did better impressions of Whitney Houston and Mariah Carey than anybody else. Groomed for showbiz from the time her teeth first sparkled, she appeared on *Star Search* at age eight (she sang "The Greatest Love of All," and lost) and, like Britney Spears and the boys of 'N Sync, was a cast member on Disney's *The New Mickey Mouse Club.* By the time she recorded her debut album at eighteen, she was a fully formed hitmaker. *Christina Aguilera* has two alluring anthems of pop femininity, "Genie in a Bottle" and "What a Girl Wants" (both by coed songwriting teams), but the remainder is generic Top 40 pop that sounds like she had not quite outgrown the sexless Disney mindset. In that she lost market share to Spears, who straight from the start exuded a vampishness that appealed to teenagers and pedophiles alike.

Fans of Aguilera had to wait three years for the sluttification of their American idol: *Stripped,* decorated with images of the singer in varying states of piercings and undress, claims to be an honest self-portrait, "no hype, no gloss, no pretense," despite a superabundance of hype, gloss, and pretense. The hip-hop–influenced songs, mostly written or cowritten by Aguilera—with some much needed help from Linda Perry ("Beautiful") and Alicia Keys ("Impossible")—finally bring her in step with the times, but she's more chameleon-like than ever, claiming an uncompromising, defiant individuality in songs that have little.   —B.S.

Air

★★★★½	Moon Safari (Astralwerks, 1998)
★★★½	Premiers Symptomes (Source/Astralwerks, 1999)
★★★½	The Virgin Suicides: OST (Source/Astralwerks, 2000)

L'amour, c'est bleu, and nobody captures the sound of posh melancholy quite like the sad-eyed gentlemen who call themselves Air. The French duo of Nicolas Godin and Jean Benoit Dunckel specialize in moody space pop, combining the digital flash of outré dance music with the tropes of '60s French easy-listening schlock: bongos, castanets, vintage electric piano, and shag-carpet organ straight from the soundtracks of movies such as *Un Homme et Une Femme.* You can practically hear Anouk Aimee pouring them some Riunite on ice in the background. But the sound is too lavishly sentimental to be just a joke, and Air makes for resonant late-night listening, when you can hear the sadness under all the glitz.

Air's debut, *Moon Safari,* takes off with the sleazy cocktail grooves of "La Femme d'Argent," "Sexy Boy," and "Kelly Watch the Stars." Guest vocalist Beth Hirsch coos a few *très tragique* café ballads, "New Star in the Sky" recalls David Bowie in his Jacques Brel mode, and "Ce Matin Là" gets you weeping along with a tuba solo. It's just a shame *Moon Safari* isn't available on reel-to-reel. *Premiers Symptomes* is a fab collection of early singles. The duo did the superb soundtrack for Sofia Coppola's film *The Virgin Suicides,* with '70s-style keyboard nostalgia such as "Afternoon Sister," "Bathroom Girl," and "Dirty Trip." To avoid typecasting, Air changed their sound completely for the drastic departure *10,000 Hz Legend.* In theory, this is an admirable idea, but theories suck and so does *10,000 Hz Legend,* as well as its companion remix album, *Everybody Hertz.* The sound is harsh, dry, disjointed, and completely humorless, with the exception of an ode to fellatio starring Cibo Matto's Miho Hatori, "Wonder Milky Bitch." *Talkie Walkie* was a significant return to form, with the cheerfully whistled chorus of "Alpha Beta Gaga," the happiest melody they've ever written.   —R.S.

Arthur Alexander

A gentle singer with a penchant for the pathos of love, Arthur Alexander was one of the pioneers of country soul, and arguably its finest interpreter. Born in Alabama, Alexander grew up on country music; as a teenager in the late '50s he wrote songs that used his forlorn, gospel-influenced vocal delivery to lift the clichéd commonplaces of country (cheating hearts, etc.) into the realm of high art.

The first song Alexander recorded, 1962's "You Better Move On," was his biggest hit, and was later covered by the Rolling Stones. Subsequent singles didn't fare nearly as well, but by then Alexander was established as a writer, and his earnest songs became hits for others: The Beatles recorded "Anna" and "Soldier of Love," while Esther Phillips and Percy Sledge both had success with "Set Me Free." Elvis Presley had his last monster hit with "Burning Love," a song Alexander introduced but didn't write.

Alexander's own versions, gathered on the well-curated starting point *The Ultimate,* remain marvels of poised, brilliantly understated phrasing—the plaintive "Anna (Go to Him)" and the more anguished "Whole Lot of Trouble" show why other singers, including Otis Redding, considered Alexander one of the masters. Coming out of his first retirement in 1972, Alexander released *Arthur Alexander* (reissued, with several additional tracks, as *Rainbow Road*). The album, recorded in Memphis, has a tighter, more assertive rhythm attack, and songs saturated with slow-burning emotional torment and disconsolate heartache.

Embittered, Alexander left the business in 1981, and was driving a bus for a Cleveland social-services agency when he was rediscovered in the early '90s. *Lonely Just Like Me,* which reunited him with Dan Penn and others from his past, combines sharply rendered updates of Alexander's old songs interspersed with surprisingly emotional new material, including the plaintive "If It's Really Got to Be This Way." The album won near universal praise, but this return was also bittersweet: Alexander died of heart failure in June 1993, just before he was to embark on a summer tour.   —T.M.

Alice Cooper

★★   Trash (Epic, 1989)
★★   Hey Stoopid (Epic, 1991)
★★½   The Last Temptation (Sony, 1994)
★★   Muscle of Love (1973; WEA Int., 1995)
★★   Classicks (Epic, 1995)
★   A Nice Nightmare (Excelsior, 1998)
★★★★ The Life and Crimes of Alice Cooper (Rhino, 1999)
★★★   Brutal Planet (Spitfire, 2000)
★★★★ The Best of Alice Cooper (Rhino, 2001)
★   Alice Cooper Live (Delta, 2001)
★★★   Dragontown (Spitfire, 2001)
★★★   Billion Dollar Babies Deluxe Edition (Rhino, 2001)
★★   The Essentials (Rhino, 2002)
★★★   The Eyes of Alice Cooper (Eagle, 2003)
★★★   Poison (Music Media, 2003)

Rock lost the ability to shock so long ago that Alice Cooper's original impact is hard to fathom now. A true early-'70s antihero, Alice bridged the old generation gap and defined a new one: Concerned older siblings and parents alike couldn't fathom what young teenagers saw in the scrawny cross-dressing geek and the simplistic blare his band passed off as music. These days, the only shocking thing about the records is just how perfect the early ones still sound. *Love It to Death* and *Killer* flesh out Alice's theatrical fantasy trip with sublime, straight-ahead rock & roll: punchy guitar riffs, roadworthy rhythms, defiant melodies, and, yes, memorable lyrics.

It was certainly a shock when "I'm Eighteen" became a hit single in early 1971, as you couldn't have found a band with less hit potential than Alice Cooper. The L.A. (via Phoenix) quintet—and Alice Cooper was the name of the group, not just of its singer, minister's son Vincent Furnier—had recorded two forgettable albums of painfully arty psychedelia for Frank Zappa, and were known only for the speed with which they repelled paying customers. (The dreadful *Alice Cooper Live* dates from the 1969 Toronto Rock & Roll Revival; you'll walk out on the CD, too.) But relocating to Detroit, they found specific inspiration sharing stages with the MC5 (streamlined rock), Stooges (the danger of Iggy), and Parliament/Funkadelic (theatrical outrage). Encouraged by rabid Motor City audiences, Alice Cooper simultaneously became tighter and even more outrageous. Caked with makeup, wrapped in a live boa constrictor, Alice's late-night horror-show act dramatized his fans' barely spoken fears. Producer Bob Ezrin was the final piece of the newly revved-up band's puzzle, and the exemplary hard rock of *Love It to Death* and *Killer* (both 1971) helped transform unlikeliest-to-succeed

Alice into one of '70s rock's first great arena attractions.

The group possessed genuine songwriting talent (particularly guitarist Michael Bruce), so even their most theatrical pieces had enough musical underpinning to hold up on record, and a knack for concocting catchily subversive singles. The title track of *School's Out* was the biggest and best, a liberating gust of pure adolescent rebellion. Unfortunately, the corny *West Side Story* quotes on "Gutter Cats vs. the Jets" pointed toward Alice's imminent future—pure show biz. *Billion Dollar Babies* still carries some kick, especially the 2001 *Deluxe Edition* featuring a 1973 concert disc. But "shock" numbers such as "I Love the Dead" were becoming predictable, and the group's fixation on its own success did not portend well. The wages of fame, and the internal frictions inevitable when group and singer answer to the same name, took their toll, and the sagging *Muscle of Love* was an unfitting end for what had been an exhilarating four-year run. Singer and band parted company, but *Greatest Hits* collects all their hard-rock battle cries from those decadent days of yore—"I'm Eighteen," "Under My Wheels," "School's Out," "No More Mr. Nice Guy"—in one irresistible, timeless album.

The now-solo Alice Cooper held his ground by hiring the Detroit guitar tag team of Steve Hunter and Dick Wagner for *Nightmare*. "Only Women Bleed" came out of left field to become a pop hit in 1975, and he would return to ballads ("I Never Cry," "You and Me," "How You Gonna See Me Now") for chart sustenance throughout the decade. He'd need them. Golfing with George Burns, goofing on *Hollywood Squares*, Alice started making wan, lazy albums that sadly reflected his shifting priorities. 1977's live *The Alice Cooper Show* featured the able Hunter-Wagner band pummeling the early classics—nostalgia, already. Throughout the rest of the '70s and much of the '80s Alice was adrift, trying on styles from new wave to pop metal in a series of albums now mercifully disappeared. The 1989 comeback *Trash,* produced to mainstream specifications by songsmith Desmond Child, rewarded a defanged Alice Cooper with his first platinum in fifteen years. *Hey Stoopid* has a bit more bite, the cautionary title tune containing welcome flashes of the old reprobate's wit and wisdom: "Hey, bro, take it slow, you ain't livin' in a video."

Classicks, A Nice Nightmare, and *Super Hits* are all collections of this early-'90s material, and unessential. *The Best of Alice Cooper* is more utilitarian: the bulk of 1974's *Greatest* plus the lighter cream of the solo years. At four CDs *The Life and Crimes of Alice Cooper* box set may be too long by a disc, but it's hard to listen to its ups and downs without acquiring newfound respect for the old pro's counterpunching abilities. And he's not done yet. *Brutal Planet* (2000) and *Dragontown* (2001) are purported to be the completion of a trilogy begun in 1994 with *The Last Temptation,* but their main attraction is simply that they rock harder than anything he's done in two decades, and provide Vince Furnier with an excuse to take the stage one more time and become Alice Cooper, the beloved heavy metal entertainer.

Alice dialed down the metal for *Eyes.* Its more mainstream rock recalls the classic Cooper group, appropriate for an album whose central track is "Detroit City" and features MC5 guitar slinger Wayne Kramer. *Poison* is a double-disc compilation of later Alice, with live versions of some of the earlier, bigger hits thrown in. Vigorous and entertaining but not terribly essential. —M.C./B.E.

Alice in Chains

★★★	Face Lift (Columbia, 1990)
★★★	Sap (EP) (Columbia, 1991)
★★★★½	Dirt (Columbia, 1992)
★★★½	Jar of Flies (EP) (Columbia, 1993)
★★★	Alice in Chains (Columbia, 1995)
★★★	MTV Unplugged (Columbia, 1996)
★★	Nothing Safe: Best of the Box (Columbia, 1999)
★★½	Music Bank (Columbia, 1999)
★★★	Live (Columbia, 2000)
★★★	Greatest Hits (Columbia, 2001)
★★★	Essential Alice in Chains (Sony Legacy, 2004)

Heavy metal was every bit as crucial an ingredient as punk in the mix of influences that became Seattle grunge. Though often underrated next to more celebrated grunge progenitors such as Nirvana, Mudhoney, and Soundgarden, Alice in Chains' slow-grind roar may be even more influential; later bands such as Godsmack (named after an Alice song), System of a Down, and Creed would be unimaginable without them.

That said, the quartet's output was relatively small and its accomplishments undercut by singer Layne Staley's long-running battle with heroin, which prematurely broke up the band and eventually took his life in 2002. That tragic history is presaged by "We Die Young," the first song on the band's debut album. Death, drugs, and the struggle to transcend both would be the band's enduring themes, and Alice created a signature sound that fit the dire imagery. It's heard to devastating effect on "Man in the Box," the defining moment on *Face Lift:* guitarist Jerry Cantrell's black-angel chords distended by a relentless wah-wah pedal, with Staley moaning in harmony.

Staley's hell-awaits wail, augmented by monks-of-doom harmonies, is as eerie as mainstream metal gets in the '90s, Seattle's version of Black Sabbath's '70s encounters with Beelzebub. Essential to the atmosphere is Cantrell's guitar playing, a slow-motion death spiral that places a premium on space and density. The rhythm section specializes in slow burn; uptempo moods, like humor, are virtually nonexistent in the Alice lexicon. *Dirt* is a contender for bleakest multiplatinum album in rock history. It contains Alice's best-known song, the unusually melodic "Would?," which also appears on the soundtrack to Cameron Crowe's movie *Singles.* But the album's dark heart lies in the remorseless "Sickman," "Godsmack," "Hate to Feel," and "Junkhead," in which Staley distills his self-destructive attitude with a chilling offhandedness: "What's my drug of choice? Well, what have you got?" Cantrell's "Rooster," about a war veteran, paints a different, equally riveting portrait of against-the-odds survival.

Jar of Flies may have been designed as a stopgap between major albums but the seven-song EP sounds like Alice's answer to *Led Zeppelin III*—an inspired change of pace. Staley's voice floats over acoustic guitars, harmonica, and strings, and the melodies are among the band's most durable. But with the singer's health deteriorating, Alice begins repeating itself on its final studio album, *Alice in Chains.* Its legacy is kept alive by a steady stream of vault-clearing retrospectives, none of which matches the impact of the original studio creations. —G.K.

Tha Alkaholiks

★★★★	21 & Over (Loud/RCA, 1993)
★★★½	Coast II Coast (Loud/RCA, 1995)
★★★½	Likwidation (Loud/RCA, 1997)

Tha Liks

★★½	X.O. Experience (Loud/Columbia, 2001)

Music critics and the masses alike largely ignored this '90s West Coast rap trio, but not since '50s lounge comedy has anyone gotten so much mileage out of playing drunk. Dean Martin and others milked the bottle because it offered some kind of hysterical release to repressed white suburbanites. On their wonderful 1993 debut, *21 & Over,* Tha Alkaholiks aimed tighter (so to speak), offering simple, hedonistic release to upstanding "alternative rap" fans, while also providing smart, comic relief from the hardcore gangsta scene that thrived in the crew's home base, L.A.

It wouldn't have worked without the trio's intoxicating chemistry. Cali native J-Ro (James Robinson) was a charismatic card: He sounded like L.L. Cool J's younger brother as he burped his way through "Only When I'm Drunk," staying on the beat even as he staved off the heaves. Two friends transplanted from Ohio provided counterpoint, Tash (Rico Smith) with tighter, grimier raps and E-Swift (Eric Brooks) with an infectious blend of jazzy instrumentation and brittle sound effects (his occasional raps held their own, too).

On *Coast II Coast*, E-Swift's mixes came to the fore, tinged with a new darkness and harder funk to underpin the 'Liks' tacit acknowledgement that maturation was unavoidable. But if they hinted at breaking out of their haze (the reality check "21 and Under"), occasionally the stupor just turned stupid (the misogynistic "Hit and Run"). *Likwidation* was even more uneven, featuring throwaway skits and guest raps but also many of the crew's finest creations, from the extended dis of "Captain Hook" to the Stevie Wonder bliss of "All Night."

After threatening breakup, the group shortened their name and came back with *X.O. Experience*, a disc that goes all the way hard by hooking up with the Neptunes and other edgy, electrified youngsters. Teetering is one thing, losing all sense of balance another. —F.S.

Allman Brothers Band

★★★★	The Allman Brothers Band (Capricorn/PolyGram, 1969)
★★★★	Idlewild South (Capricorn/PolyGram, 1970)
★★★★★	At Fillmore East (Capricorn/PolyGram, 1971)
★★★★	Eat a Peach (Capricorn/PolyGram, 1972)
★★★★★	Beginnings (Capricorn/PolyGram, 1973)
★★★★	Brothers and Sisters (Capricorn/PolyGram, 1973)
★★★	Win, Lose or Draw (Capricorn/PolyGram, 1975)
★★★½	The Road Goes On Forever (1975; Universal, 2001)
★★½	Wipe the Windows, Check the Oil, Dollar Gas (Capricorn/PolyGram, 1976)
★★★	Enlightened Rogues (Capricorn/PolyGram, 1979)
★★★★★	Dreams (PolyGram, 1990)
★★★½	Live at Ludlow Garage (PolyGram, 1990)
★★★	Seven Turns (Epic, 1990)
★★★½	Shades of Two Worlds (Epic, 1991)
★★★★	A Decade of Hits 1969–1979 (PolyGram, 1991)
★★★½	An Evening with the Allman Brothers Band (Sony, 1992)
★★★★	The Fillmore Concerts (PolyGram, 1992)
★★★½	Where It All Begins (Sony, 1994)
★★	Hell & High Water: The Best of the Arista Years (Arista, 1994)
★★★½	An Evening with the Allman Brothers Band: 2nd Set (Sony, 1995)
★★★½	Mycology: An Anthology (Sony, 1998)
★★½	Peakin' at the Beacon (Sony, 2000)
★★★	The Millennium Collection (PolyGram, 2000)
★★★	Hittin' the Note (Peach/Sanctuary, 2003)

Duane Allman

★★★★	An Anthology (Capricorn/PolyGram, 1972)
★★★★	Anthology, Vol. 2 (Capricorn/PolyGram, 1974)

Gregg Allman

★★★	Laid Back (Capricorn/PolyGram, 1974)
★★★	The Gregg Allman Tour (Polydor, 1974)
★★★½	Playin' Up a Storm (Capricorn/PolyGram, 1977)
★★★	I'm No Angel (Epic, 1987)
★★★	Just Before the Bullets Fly (Epic, 1988)
★★★	Searching for Simplicity (Sony, 1997)
★★★	One More Try: An Anthology (Capricorn, 1997)
★★★	No Stranger to the Dark: The Best of Gregg Allman (Epic/Legacy, 2002)
★★★	The Millennium Collection (Universal, 2002)

Don't be fooled by the two lead guitars, the two drummers, the legendary concerts that only kicked into gear around the two-hour mark: Boogie-'til-you-puke overkill really isn't a part of the Allman Brothers' recorded legacy. Guitarist Duane and singer-organist Gregg Allman knocked around Los Angeles in the late '60s, polishing their chops in third-billed psychedelic ballroom bands such as the Hour Glass and Allman Joys. Moving back to Macon, GA, in 1968, the Allmans put together a powerhouse outfit of similarly inclined players: second guitarist Dickey Betts, bassist Berry Oakley, drummers Butch Trucks and Jai Johanny Johanson. At the same time, Duane Allman began doing session work at the Muscle Shoals studio in Alabama—where this skinny white hippie quickly earned a reputation as a stinging, soulful accompanist. Duane and Gregg both exhibited a natural feel for black music that the much-hyped British "blues masters" of the period couldn't begin to match. Growing up in the South, they absorbed gutbucket R&B and sanctified gospel along with the more common influences of soul and freedom jazz, and came up with an unprecedented sound: a searching, polyrhythmic extension of rock. Duane and Dickey Betts shied away from distortion and overamplified special effects; instead, they stroked clean, precise lines out of their Gibsons. On a good night, they seemed to nudge and push each other toward new heights, supported by a massive, rock-solid wall of rhythms. And Gregg's capacity as a blues belter—already startling when he was in his early 20s—grows deeper and more resonant with time.

The "Don't Want You No More"/"It's Not My Cross to Bear" medley kicks off the debut in definitive style. After a fluid jazzy intro ("Don't Want You") the band explodes into a slow blues ("Not My Cross") where Duane's guitar and Gregg's voice join in a beautifully anguished duet—wailing from the very depths of their souls. The bittersweet, organ-drenched "Dreams" showcases the band's easy-rolling melodic punch, while "Whipping Post" draws up a sturdy blueprint for the cathartic concert extrapolations that would become the Brothers' signature.

Idlewild South is way too skimpy timewise, but the musical development is stunning. The Bible-thumping "Revival" points up a crucial country music influence and the haunting, melancholy "Midnight Rider" fully asserts Gregg's identity as a singer. Once again, "In Memory of Elizabeth Reed" presents the blueprint of a concert warhorse, capturing the Allmans at their most adventurous. This is what jazz-rock fusion groups of the mid-'70s should have aspired toward.

Some would say *At Fillmore East* is the peak achievement of the band. Certainly, it communicates all the excitement and drama of the group's concert explorations. The blues standards sound grittier and more rockin' than anything on the first two albums, and after "Whipping Post" builds to its shuddering peak, that long spacey fade-out provides sheer post-orgasmic bliss. Nevertheless, *Beginnings* (the debut album and *Idlewild* packaged together) gets the nod over *Fillmore* since it takes account of the band's considerable pop-song potential as well as its instrumental prowess. But rock jamming just doesn't get any better than *Fillmore East*—except, perhaps, on 1992's expanded, double-CD version, *The Fillmore Concerts*.

Just a few months after *At Fillmore East* was recorded, Duane Allman died in a motorcycle accident. He was 24. The stopgap *Eat a Peach* extracts even more magic from the historic Fillmore stand. Perhaps the live "Mountain Jam" (almost three quarters of an hour long) loses something in the translation to disc, but the snarling cover of Sonny Boy Williamson's "One Way Out" and devastatingly pretty studio tracks such as "Blue Sky" add quite a bit to the legend.

Bassist Berry Oakley was killed in similar circumstances in 1972, just a little more than a year to the day after Duane's accident. Miraculously, the remaining group bounced back strong with *Brothers and Sisters*, wisely adding a pianist, Chuck Leavell (rather than trying to replace Duane with another guitarist), and emphasizing Dickey Betts' country-tinged picking and singing. The Brothers' refurbished, slightly twangier sound soon became the flagship model of a new genre—"Southern rock." The instrumental "Jessica" isn't quite up to the standard of "Elizabeth Reed," but the liquid guitar leads on the hit single "Ramblin' Man" introduced the pop mainstream to a tangy, intoxicating regional delight.

Hard touring (and the resultant hard living) took an inevitable toll on the band, though. *Win, Lose or Draw,* a lackluster live album *(Wipe the Windows, Check the Oil, Dollar Gas),* and a passable best-of *(The Road Goes On Forever)* show further signs of strain. *Enlightened Rogues,* from 1979, has its moments, though the presence of guest star Bonnie Bramlett on the best cut ("Crazy Love") doesn't bode well for this proudly self-contained band. The band reached its low point with a pair of rudderless albums on Arista *(Reach for the Sky* and *Brothers of the Road,* both mercifully out of print) and seemed to break up for good in the early '80s.

Inevitably, the Brothers reconvened during the nostalgic summer of 1989, but the group's live shows (featuring the added muscle of new guitarist Warren Haynes) quickly laid to rest any accusations of reputation pimping. Gregg's voice emerges with a fresh, whiskey-ruined authority on the respectable *Seven Turns* (1990), and somehow the 1991 followup, *Shades of Two Worlds,* actually expands on that renewed promise. The timeless, soaring improvisations of "Desert Blues" and "Sort of Bird" firmly reassert the band's unique, enduring brand of blues power, while Gregg fills his sobriety songs with the shaky conviction of lived experience: He's been to the "End of the Line" and back. Betts, meanwhile, contributes one of the best songs of his Allman Brothers career with *Where It All Begins'* "Back Where It All Begins." Never mind the soaring beauty of his country-jazz guitar soloing that pads out the song's nine-minute-plus running length; the real hook is in his warm and heartfelt delivery of the song's catchy chorus, which Dave Matthews would kill for. But *Where It All Begins* would mark Betts' swan song with the group (apart from 2000's *Peakin' at the Beacon,* the weakest of the band's three live releases of the decade). He was booted from the group in early 2000, and his characteristic country rock soul is missed on 2003's *Hittin' the Note.* That said, the album finds Gregg and the remaining players hitting the note more often than not, even if they never quite hit on anything new. The twin guitars of Haynes (back in the group after sitting out the second half of the '90s) and new kid Derek Trucks pack plenty of punch—both in the extended jams and the opening "Firing Line," a particularly potent, straight-up blues rocker—and Gregg's brutally trenchant "Old Before My Time" is one of the most effectively world-weary life-on-the-road songs in a long, long time.

With four discs covering not only the band's greatest hits but also solo cuts and a sampling of Gregg and Duane's earlier work in Hour Glass and the Allman Joys, the 1991 box set *Dreams* is the definitive Allman Brothers Band anthology. After that, the 2001 expanded double-disc version of *The Road Goes On Forever* improves on the original with 13 extra tracks, though the tighter *A Decade of Hits* is just as (if not more) potent. *Mycology* makes a convincing case for the reunited band's '90s output, but *Hell & High Water*, which picks through the wreckage of the two best-forgotten Arista albums, is for completists only.

For Duane Allman enthusiasts, both volumes of *An Anthology* collect sterling examples of the late guitarist's session work—including tracks with the Hour Glass, Wilson Pickett, and Eric Clapton—and are highly recommended to guitar students and Southern-soul buffs alike. His famous solo on Aretha Franklin's "The Weight," on *Volume One,* is worth the price of admission alone. The same volume also features Derek and the Dominos' "Layla," but it's hard to imagine anyone shilling out for either of these collections who doesn't already own that album. Brother Gregg, meanwhile, has had more time to work on his solo résumé. Never a prolific songwriter, he recast some of his Allman Brothers tunes as moody blues pop on his 1974 solo debut, *Laid Back,* and scored a surprise hit. *The Gregg Allman Tour*—which features a 24-piece orchestra—is lush but not without soul. The harder-hitting *Playin' Up a Storm,* from 1977, actually eclipsed most of the Allmans' work of the same period. A decade later, Gregg made a few tentative steps back in the right direction with *I'm No Angel* (1987), followed by *Just Before the Bullets Fly* (1988); the title track of the former presents a battle-scarred veteran with a surprising amount of fire left in his bones. The workmanlike *Searching for Simplicity* (1997), however, failed to turn up anything new. *No Stranger to the Dark* sums up the three latter albums, while the skimpier *Millennium Collection* focuses on the first three. *One More Try* devotes an exhausting two discs to solo Gregg—overkill, to say the least, though the abundance of previously unreleased and alternate tracks (including versions of many Allman Brothers Band tunes) doubtless lends the collection collector appeal. —M.C./R.SK.

America

★★ America (Warner Bros., 1972)
★★ Homecoming (Warner Bros., 1973)
★ Hat Trick (Warner Bros., 1973)
★★ Holiday (Warner Bros., 1974)
★★ Hearts (Warner Bros., 1975)
★★★ History: Greatest Hits (Warner Bros., 1975)
★★ Hideaway (Warner Bros., 1976)
★½ America Live (Warner Bros., 1977)
★ Harbor (Warner Bros., 1977)
★ Silent Letter (One Way, 1979)
★ Alibi (One Way, 1980)
★ A View from the Ground (One Way, 1982)
★ Your Move (One Way, 1983)
★ Perspective (One Way, 1984)
★ Encore: More Greatest Hits (Rhino, 1991)
★ Ventura Highway & Other Favorites (Columbia, 1992)
★ Hourglass (American, 1994)
★ King Biscuit Flour Hour (King Biscuit, 1996)
★ Human Nature (Oxygen, 1998)
★ Highway: 30 Years of America (Rhino, 2000)
★★½ The Complete Greatest Hits (Rhino, 2001)
★★½ Definitive America (WEA, 2001)

America was to '70s folk rock what the Archies were to Beatlesque pop. The trio camouflaged its songs with earnest, three-part harmonies (à la Crosby, Stills & Nash) and earthy, pseudo-cosmic lyrics, but its music was little more than bubblegum for adolescent hippies.

Dewey Bunnell, Dan Peek, and Gerry Beckley cantered out of the gate in 1972 with a #1 hit ("A Horse with No Name") that duplicated the laid-back yawn of Neil Young. But the song was weighed down by clunky, banal lyrics ("In the desert, you can remember your name/ 'Cause there ain't no one for to give you no pain") and a repetitive melody.

Though they tried, America never achieved the emotional scope or instrumental inventiveness of Young and his sometime vocal partners CSN. America's early-'70s hits all were variations on the same themes: mawkish love songs ("I Need You"), clumsy impressionism ("Horse," "Ventura Highway"), childhood fairy-tale metaphors ("Tin Man"), and corny affirmations ("Lonely People"). By the middle '70s, the group had enlisted former Beatles producer George Martin to brighten their acoustic sound with lush pop arrangements, but the songs remained the same.

In 1979 America switched labels and forged ahead with a new Adult Contemporary sound. The music and lyrics were as tepid as ever, with the group replacing the faux folk-pop of its past with overproduced, Eagles-lite rockers. The new America fit well into early-'80s MOR playlists, and the group scored two more hits ("You Can Do Magic" and "The Border") before fading into the murk of MTV-friendly synthesizer pop.

For those who have a desire to revisit their '70s

childhood memories, *History: Greatest Hits* offers all the America anyone needs. The interchangeable *Complete Greatest Hits* and *Definitive* add songs from the group's post-1975 albums. The boxed set *Highway* is mind-numbing overkill. —M.K.

American Hi-Fi

★★ American Hi-Fi (Island, 2001)
★½ Live from Tokyo (Island, 2002)
★★ The Art of Losing (Def Jam, 2003)

Maybe it's because he felt oppressed by females as drummer for Veruca Salt, but when Stacy Jones (who also drummed for another '90s alt mainstay, Letters to Cleo) formed American Hi-Fi with guitarist Jaime Arentzen, bassist Drew Parsons, and skinsman Brian Nolan, he used the forum to smear the human race's better half. While his overdetermined pop punk and hypersensitivity set Jones apart from losers such as Limp Bizkit's Fred Durst, even his tunefulness sounded turgid. "Flavor of the Weak," the Cheap Trick–meets–Green Day hit off their self-titled debut, poisons Billie Joe Armstrong's snotty delivery with barely concealed disgust. Jones' crush, it turns out, dares to date a dude who likes "Nintendo" and getting "stoned." What happens when he gets the girl? He blames her for the loss of something unnamed but apparently very important: "You fucked it out of me," he half wails, half sneers at a lover in "My Only Enemy." *The Art of Losing*, released after a pointless live disc, matches *American Hi-Fi*, cut of bitter fluff for cut of bitter fluff. "Run away from me," he snarls in "Beautiful Disaster." Happily. —N.C.

Tori Amos

★★★★½ Little Earthquakes (Atlantic, 1992)
★★★★ Crucify (EP) (Atlantic, 1992)
★★★★ Under the Pink (Atlantic, 1994)
★★½ Boys for Pele (Atlantic, 1996)
★★★½ From the Choirgirl Hotel (Atlantic, 1998)
★★★ To Venus and Back (Atlantic, 1999)
★★ Strange Little Girls (Atlantic, 2001)
★★★½ Scarlet's Walk (Epic, 2002)
★★★★ Tales of a Librarian: A Tori Amos Collection (Atlantic, 2003)

Tori Amos seemed to come out of nowhere in 1992. Though she'd materialized briefly four years before, fronting a best-forgotten hairspray band that also included future Guns n' Roses drummer Matt Sorum, her solo debut, *Little Earthquakes*, was one of that year's most improbable success stories. At the time, rock was mostly a boys' club, and a girl who played piano was out of the question. *Little Earthquakes*

trumpeted a sea change, heralding the return of the singer/songwriter and helping to pave the way for Lilith Fair–types from Paula Cole to Ani DiFranco. Its songs are like confidences, full of intimate personal detail, sexual candor ("so you can make me cum/that doesn't make you Jesus"), and playfully surreal language that somehow makes emotional sense. The a capella "Me and a Gun" unflinchingly faces her own rape experience; like the love child of Kate Bush and Kurt Cobain, this is an arty singer/songwriter with a jagged alternative edge. This alt-worthiness was reinforced when her piano-and-voice version of "Smells Like Teen Spirit" (from the *Crucify* EP, which also includes Tori treatments of the Stones and Led Zep) garnered significant alternative airplay. Still, word of Amos spread like an exotic rumor until *Little Earthquakes* was suddenly platinum.

Under the Pink is nearly as good. It beats the sophomore jinx by taking more chances—breaking away from personal pain in "God" ("Do you need a woman to look after you?") and "Cornflake Girl," even as her lyrics dive deeper into abstraction. Her popularity had become so great that *Boys for Pele* entered the charts at #2, but this difficult album resists meeting comprehension even halfway. The pain displayed on "Hey Jupiter" is clear and convincing, but elsewhere the melodies can be as elusive as the words, an insular personal language that only the most committed fan will be motivated to decipher. The move to a band format on *From the Choirgirl Hotel* provides the focus that had been lacking on the previous album, and pushes her singing to carry as much meaning as the words. *To Venus and Back* is an ambitious, and only intermittently successful, double-CD set. The studio disc consists of new songs cut with a minimum of preproduction. The spontaneity suits the elementary lilt of "Concertina," but on more demanding constructs such as "Bliss" ("maybe we're bliss/of another kind") she and the band simply sound underrehearsed. The second disc, recorded live on her 1998 tour, passes over her signature songs in favor of B sides, obscurities, and neglected album tracks.

The mission of *Strange Little Girls* is gender reversal—Tori takes on a collection of songs ostensibly written from a male viewpoint and turns the tables. The only track that truly fulfills this premise is her hushed reading of Eminem's "'97 Bonnie and Clyde," which unmasks the full horror of his tale of dumping a murdered girlfriend's body. Tom Waits' "Time" and Depeche Mode's "Enjoy the Silence" at least play to her strengths, which cannot be said of her reconstructions of Neil Young, the Beatles, and Slayer. There's also a concept to *Scarlet's Walk*, its suite of songs chronicling a cross-country journey in the aftermath of 9/11. The booklet's color-coded roadmap isn't necessary; these songs *feel* like a triptych. Quietly intense, it is her most carefully crafted and inviting album since *Little Earthquakes,* the caressing melodies and relatively straightforward narratives of "A Sorta Fairytale" and "Crazy" acknowledging our overriding need for connection. *Scarlet's Walk* is an unexpectedly accessible gift from Tori Amos, an artist blessed with a substantial audience willing to follow wherever she may lead. No compilation could possibly please her famously fussy and proprietary audience, but *Tales of a Librarian* does a reasonable job of cherry-picking her catalogue, remixing many tracks and reworking some.   —B.E.

Trey Anastasio

★★½	One Man's Trash (1998; Phish Dry Goods, 2002)
★★★	Trey Anastasio (Elektra, 2002)
★★★½	Plasma (Elektra, 2003)
★★★	Seis de Mayo (Elektra, 2004)

Phish guitarist Trey Anastasio's solo albums tend to explore areas that he avoids with his usual henchmen—which, considering his old band's eclecticism, is saying something. Officially, Anastasio's solo career began with the total-improv freakouts of 1996's *Surrender to the Air* (now out of print) and continued with two interesting but nonessential collections of demos and home-studio experiments, only one of which, *One Man's Trash,* remains in print. But for most intents and purposes, *Trey Anastasio* is the real beginning of our story, showcasing his singing, songwriting, and guitar-playing talents; songs with deceptively tight arrangements that often gambol into jazz-rock fusion territory (see Nicholas Payton's hot licks on "Last Tube").

Plasma captures Anastasio live with a 10-piece band, ditching some of his studio albums' complexity and replacing it with lengthy but rewarding jams. Much of the material on the all-instrumental *Seis de Mayo* was originally performed by Phish, but the tunes are rearranged for a variety of ensembles, including (on the closing "Guyute") a full orchestra. Ambitious but far from pompous, it's both an intriguing detour and, now that Phish is history, an indication of a possible future main route.   —M.R.

Laurie Anderson

★★★	Big Science (Warner Bros., 1982)
★★★★	Mister Heartbreak (Warner Bros., 1984)
★★★	United States Live (Warner Bros., 1984)
★★★	Home of the Brave (Warner Bros., 1986)
★★★★	Strange Angels (Warner Bros., 1989)
★★★½	Bright Red (Warner Bros., 1994)
★★★	The Ugly One With the Jewels and Other Stories (Warner Bros., 1995)
★★★★	Talk Normal: The Laurie Anderson Anthology (Rhino, 2000)
★★★★½	Life on a String (Nonesuch, 2001)
★★★★	Live at Town Hall, New York City, September 19–20, 2001 (Nonesuch, 2002)

Performance artists are entertainers as much as they are artists—sometimes even more so—and as such, the skills Laurie Anderson most relies upon tend to be comic, not musical: timing, for instance; inflection; a sense of character that allows her to slip effortlessly out of her normal deadpan and into a believable secondary voice; and, of course, the ability to distill an idea in the fewest and most effective words possible. That's not to slight her music. Although Anderson isn't much of a singer (or, at least, wasn't until *Strange Angels*), she does know how to delegate, and fleshes out her compositions with meticulously produced—if melodically minimal—arrangements. In other words, her albums are competent and listenable, and the work they showcase can be wonderfully illuminating. In the end, however, what you're left with is closer to theater than to music, and frankly, theater isn't as suited to the home stereo as it is to the stage.

Even so, what got Anderson's career going was, ironically enough, a hit single: "O Superman." Granted, it was a hit only in the U.K., and owed its success mostly to the way its hypnotic strangeness transformed the mundane (an answering machine message) into the surreal. But it did understand the form and function of a single, and it fits in perfectly well with the rest of *Big Science.* Here, Anderson's speech is the central focus, and her musical support—keyboards, percussion, and occasional saxophone or bagpipe—is skeletal and hypnotic, relying mostly on repetition and teasingly attenuated phrases. All of its selections came from Anderson's massive theater piece *United States,* which is offered in its entirely on *United States Live,* a four-and-a-half-hour marathon that heaps pronouncements, gags, epigrams, and shaggy-dog stories into an amiable, enigmatic statement on America's inscrutability. Despite its epic sprawl, the set moves along nicely—although it's doubtful many listeners will want to plough through it more than twice.

Anderson's albums aren't always so ambitiously conceptual, and as such generally make for somewhat easier listening. *Mister Heartbreak* has the shiny patina of pop, thanks to Bill Laswell's eclectic, atmospheric production on "Sharkey's Day" and "Sharkey's Night," not to mention the Peter Gabriel collaboration

"Excellent Birds" (which can also be found, under a slightly different title, on his album *So*). The soundtrack *Home of the Brave* remakes the Sharkey songs and features some attractive guitar work by Adrian Belew, although the Nile Rodgers–produced "Language Is a Virus" is more clever than successful.

Strange Angels finds Anderson moving toward a more musical approach, singing more than talking and relying on meatier, more melodic arrangements. While that doesn't completely transform these words-and-music constructions into songs, the cheerful melodies and flowing, Caribbean cadences make it a remarkably engaging and approachable album. With *Bright Red*, however, she returns to material that is more word-focused and atmospheric (although with Brian Eno as producer, the atmospheres are exquisite). Still, even that is more "pop" in approach than *The Ugly One With the Jewels*, a collection of pieces drawn from her book *Stories From the Nerve Bible*. It's witty, captivating, and slyly musical, but more the musical equivalent of an illuminated manuscript than a pop album. (*Talk Normal* neatly and intelligently summarizes Anderson's recorded output to this point.)

With *Life on a String*, Anderson returns to the sort of song-form material she explored in *Strange Angels*. It's a remarkable piece of work—lush, evocative, provocative, and unexpectedly catchy. While still not pop in the conventional sense, it uses the pop vocabulary with a knowing deftness, pulling the listener in even as she undermines her audience's expectations. *Live at Town Hall* takes material from that album, as well as assorted Anderson "oldies," and refracts them through the lens of the 9/11 terrorist attacks on New York and Washington, D.C. (which occurred mere days before these performances). As always, her timing is excellent.   —J.D.C.

Angry Samoans

    ★★½   Live at Rhino Records (Triple X, 1990)
    ★★★★   The Unboxed Set (Triple X, 1995)
    ★★½   The 90's Suck & So Do You (Triple X, 1999)

Though not featured in the film *The Decline of Western Civilization*, the Angry Samoans were as much a part of the early L.A. hardcore scene as more celebrated bands such as X, Fear, Black Flag, the Germs, and the Circle Jerks. Formed in 1978 by two rock critics, "Metal" Mike Saunders and Gregg Turner, the Samoans were as offensive as they were tuneful. Only East Coast counterparts the Meatmen came close to rivaling the homophobia, misogyny, and generally retarded sexuality on early Angry Samoans cuts such as "Homo-Sexual," "They Saved Hitler's Cock," and "Steak Knife."

Fueled by garage-rock riffs baked in pop charm, the Samoans' music was more advanced than the dumb metal of the Meatmen or almost any other hardcore band. As a result, the band quickly alienated itself from the dogmatic scene that birthed it, and later releases focused more on the band's love of bubblegum pop. The *Unboxed Set* includes on a single disc almost everything the band recorded during its glory years. *Live at Rhino* captures an early incarnation of the band doing a sloppy set of originals and covers. Though the original band split in 1988, Saunders, with a largely new lineup, revived the Samoans name for *The 90's Suck & So Do You*, which offers less than 15 minutes of inconsequential tracks.   —R.A.

The Animals

    ★★★★½   The Best of the Animals (1966; Abkco, 1988)
    ★★   House of the Rising Sun (1970; Brentwood, 2002)
    ★★★½   Before We Were So Rudely Interrupted (1977; Repertoire, 2002)
    ★★★   Ark (1983; Castle, 1997)
    ★★★½   The Best of Eric Burdon and the Animals (Polydor, 1991)
    ★★   In the Beginning (Sundazed, 1993)
    ★★★   The Best of Eric Burdon and the Animals (PolyGram Special Markets, 1997)
    ★★★★½   Animalisms (Repertoire, 2000)
    ★★   Taken Alive (Fuel, 2002)

Monstrously talented, the Animals were second only to the Rolling Stones as British purveyors of R&B in the '60s. But internal divisiveness dogged them from the start, and while popular during their short peak, they never mustered the survivalist smarts of the Stones, and their songwriting fell consistently short of Jagger and Richards'. England never produced a finer singer, however, than Eric Burdon at his best. Hailing, as did his bandmates, from Newcastle-on-Tyne, Burdon was the archetypal working-class hero, a short, boozing scrapper gifted improbably with an amazing voice. Blues and R&B perfectly suited his skills and sensibility; the U.K. equivalent of Mitch Ryder, he sang black music with almost eerie assurance. Searching for a singer, the Alan Price Combo (Price: keyboards; Hilton Valentine: guitar; Chas Chandler: bass; John Steel: drums) enlisted Burdon, guaranteeing themselves success, but also tension—Price would soon prove no match for the charismatic Burdon. So frantic were the group's early stage shows that they renamed themselves the Animals, and in their reworking of the blues standard off Dylan's first album, "House of the Rising Sun," they gained a #1 hit with only their second single. The band then scored with a brilliant cover of Nina Simone's "Don't Let Me Be Misunderstood" and with Mann-Weill's "We Gotta Get Out of This Place," both featured on the Abkco *Best of. Animalization,* however, remains their most fully realized album—effects-heavy and menacing, the guitar work on Goffin-King's "Don't Bring Me Down" is Valentine at his toughest; "Gin House Blues" is Burdon singing with frightening authority; "Inside—Looking Out" builds to a ferocious climax (this 1966 masterpiece is repackaged along with "Animalism," another gem from that year, on Repertoire's *Animalisms*). Although Price left in 1965, the substitution of classically trained Dave Rowberry ensured that organ and piano would contribute heavily to the group's distinction—and the playing of the other Animals was always first-rate. But Burdon was the ace. Remarkable phrasing and unwavering focus characterized all of his work with the band; *The Best of the Animals* covers most of the essential stuff, from the anthemic "It's My Life" to their snappy last single, "See See Rider"—but the compilation isn't really extensive enough to do them justice. And it's a good idea to supplement it with the live *In the Beginning,* great in-concert fare from 1963.

In September 1966, the original Animals fell apart. Burdon was becoming enraptured with nascent psychedelia and gobbling acid; so LSD-addled had Valentine become that he began believing he was Jesus; and the rest of the group was simply exhausted. A new band, Eric Burdon and the Animals, was the result: Taking along only drummer Barry Jenkins (replacing Steel, who had left in 1966), Burdon moved to California and left R&B behind. Polydor collected the trippy stuff on *The Best of Eric Burdon and the Animals* (don't confuse it with the lesser album of the same name on PolyGram Special Markets). The original Animals got back together in 1977 on *Before We Were So Rudely Interrupted.* A better reunion album than most, its highlight is Burdon's tortured version of "Many Rivers to Cross." Another comeback bid, *Ark,* from 1983, was less successful. —P.E.

Anthrax

★★	Fistful of Metal (1984; Megaforce, 1995)
★★★	Armed & Dangerous (1984; Megaforce, 1995)
★★★½	Spreading the Disease (Island, 1985)
★★★	Among the Living (Island, 1987)
★★★½	I'm the Man (Island, 1987)
★★★	State of Euphoria (1988; Island, 1990)
★★★½	Persistence of Time (Island, 1990)
★★★½	Attack of the Killer B's (Island, 1991)
★★★	Sound of White Noise (Elektra, 1993)
★★★	Anthrax Live: The Island Years (Island, 1994)
★★★	Stomp 442 (Elektra, 1995)
★★★★	Return of the Killer A's: The Best of Anthrax (Beyond, 1999)
★★★½	Madhouse: The Very Best of Anthrax (Island, 2001)

Up until *I'm the Man,* Anthrax seemed a perfectly typical thrash act. *Fistful of Metal* (recorded with original lead singer Neil Turbin) finds them starting out playing fairly straightforward hard rock, while the version of "God Save the Queen" on *Armed & Dangerous* (featuring subsequent vocalist Joe Belladonna) points up its debt to punk. *Spreading the Disease* shows off its chops (check the "Theme from *Masterpiece Theatre*" quote in "Gung-Ho"), while *Among the Living* emphasizes its ferocity ("Caught in a Mosh," "Efilnikufesin") and *State of Euphoria* its uncompromising point of view ("Make Me Laugh," "Schism").

I'm the Man, however, not only features a rap tune—"I'm the Man"—that beats the Beastie Boys at their own game, but also balances it with a Black Sabbath cover. In other words, not only was the group down with rap, but it refused to recognize a difference between rap and thrash—a powerful gesture in the pre–rap rock era.

But there's the rub. Even though Anthrax's subsequent hip-hop hit, a duet version of "Bring the Noise" with Public Enemy (included on *Attack of the Killer B's, Return of the Killer A's,* and *Madhouse*) is clearly a landmark performance, Anthrax was largely played out by the early '90s. The band hit its peak with *Persistence of Time,* which adds an epic sweep to "Blood" and "H8 Red," expands its social commentary with "All in the Family" (about inbred prejudice), and even has a Joe Jackson cover ("Got the Time"). *Attack of the Killer B's* maintains that plateau, thanks to "Bring the Noise" as well as a nasty country-style attack on record labeling ("Startin' Up a Posse"). But despite its clever title, *Sound of White Noise* opens no new ground for the band, while *Stomp 442* (the title of which refers to the displacement of a classic Oldsmobile engine) delivers more punch than it does memorable material.

Of the two best-ofs, *Madhouse* takes a straightforward anthology approach, while *Killer A's* offers several remixes and includes illuminating commentary in the liner notes. —J.D.C.

Antipop Consortium

★★½	Tragic Epilogue (75 Ark, 2000)
★★★½	Arrhythmia (Warp, 2002)
★★	Antipop Consortium vs. Matthew Shipp (Thirsty Ear, 2003)

Vets of New York's underground hip-hop and poetry scenes, High Priest, Beans, and M. Sayyid formed

Antipop Consortium circa 1997 with ambitions of bringing the unbridled creative freedom of the avant-garde—jazz, poetry, who knows—to rap. Though they never exactly broke free from the chains of the form, they went about as far with experimental hip-hop as anybody did in the '90s, or is ever likely to do, with stuttering, uncomfortable beats and torrents of free-associative lyrics that are always just a few quick syllables away from total incomprehensibility.

Tragic Epilogue is a thorough but joyless manifesto of the Antipop philosophy, with deliberately amateurish electronic programming, simple yet uncomfortably off-kilter beats, and abstract, rambling lyrics seemingly straight out of the poetry slam. The pseudoscientific jargon and pretense of futurism gives them a unique way to boast and taunt, but after a while it becomes apparent that they're simply self-satisfied nerds. "The world is flat, ha ha, you fell off/Hoping that the laws of gravity will bring you back to Earth/If not, okay, your words fall lighter than air/So throw it away and disappear to a black hole, son" is a typically shrugworthy line: while impressive in its dense poetics, it's meaningless.

They mended things considerably with *Arrhythmia,* which manages to be funky and catchy—uh-oh, sounds like pop—without compromising the essential weirdness of their vision. Every line is a nonsequitur, and some of it is even quite funny. "Mega" ends with grandiose operatic cadences, and the rhythm track of "Ping Pong" is built, as though on a dare, around the sound of balls bouncing between the speakers, a trick used by the Beastie Boys in *Paul's Boutique* but not as cleverly folded into the rhythm as here, a testament to the skills of their producer, Earl Blaize.

The group broke up in mid-2002 but early the next year issued—without Sayyid—a collaboration with Matthew Shipp, one of the most adventuresome jazz pianists to emerge in the '90s. Shipp finds some fascinating points of contact with the slippery Antipop grooves, but for the most part the project is unproductive. Not exactly a tragic epilogue, but an unfortunate one nonetheless. —B.S.

Aphex Twin

★★★★ Analogue Bubblebath (EP) (1991; TVT, 1994)
★★★ Analogue Bubblebath II (EP) (Rabbit City, 1991)
★★★★ Selected Ambient Works 85–92 (1992; PIAS, 2002)
★★★★ Analogue Bubblebath III (EP) (Rephlex, 1993)
★★★ Caustic Window (Rephlex, 1993)
★★★ Selected Ambient Works, Vol. 2 (Warp/Sire, 1994)
★★★ Classics (1995; PIAS 2002)
★★★½ I Care Because You Do (Warp/Sire, 1995)

★★★★ Richard D. James Album (Warp/Sire, 1996)
★★★ 51/13 Aphex Singles Collection (WEA Australia, 1996)
★★★★ Come to Daddy (EP) (Warp/Sire, 1997)
★★★★★ Windowlicker (EP) (Warp/Sire, 1999)
★★★★ Drukqs (Warp/Sire, 2001)
★★★ 26 Mixes for Cash (Warp, 2003)

Polygon Window

★★★ Surfing on Sine Waves (1993; Warp, 2002)

No one looms larger in '90s electronic music than Cornwall's own Richard D. James, a.k.a. Aphex Twin, a young man who started his career rewiring his keyboards to make acid-house tracks and ended up a quasi-religious figure to followers of electronica. James' output is influential and frustrating in equal parts, following the arc of a gifted child's primary school report card. James often starts with a brilliant idea, plays it out halfway and then drops it, bored. Scattered through his catalogue are ideas other groups took up later with more success. His reputation in the press as an eccentric and eternal adolescent is somewhat borne out by tendencies in his work: the obsession with childhood ("milk," "child," and "boy" show up in titles); samples of children's voices; and a sonic palette that recalls nursery mobiles and toys. The young-man aesthetic is also manifest in his detailed, complex compositions and flashes of bathroom humor. This bedroom auteur actually sounds like he's in his bedroom, giggling and farting to his infamy. But that doesn't mean he isn't a genius—just that the act of making records often seems to be secondary to the act of simply being Richard James. (If anyone ever cried out for a well-curated best-of, it's Dr. Aphex.)

The title track of his 1991 debut EP, *Analogue Bubblebath,* was a juicy redrawing of ambient techno aesthetics, with hints of the mania to come in the track "AFX2." Soon, James released the effective but less innovative acid-house track "Digeridoo," started his own label, Rephlex, and got signed to Belgian label R&S. (Most of this period of work is compiled on *Classics.*) This is the last time James sounds like he's part of a movement other than his own—"Flaphead" is an anonymous acid-house track and "Polynomial-C," though effective, could have been any number of people working in the ambient techno field in 1991. The germs of what's to come are here—the distorted drums of "Phloam" prefigure later tracks such as "Ventolin" (and much of Autechre's *Anvil Vapre* EP), and "Quinophec" presages the soft, pastoral sounds that Aphex uses for much of 1994 and 1995 (and out of which Boards of Canada have made an entire career). "Isopropanol" marks the debut of the children's voices and hectic programming that would become his dominant tactic in the late '90s.

Prolific and fond of games, James released new albums almost instantly under different names. *Caustic Window* is James still working within the confines of the dance community. Both "Joyrex" tracks take acid house's 4/4 foundation and twist it into knots without losing the beat. The remainder is, confusingly, not that different from other James records of the time, with the exception of the distorted beats on "Astroblaster" and "AFX 114." A title such as "On the Romance Tip" suggests that Aphex is having a laugh, except that it also sounds like many of his "serious" tracks. Not for the last time, it is hard to tell which bits are piss-takes and which are the "real" tracks. *Selected Ambient Works 85–92* shows Aphex mostly tossing the jokes and doing some of his best work, floating between dub and techno but never settling. Tracks like "Tha" and "Ageispolis" opened up ambient syntax, hinting at work from later practitioners such as Pole and the Basic Channel family in Berlin. James' virtuosity is clearest, paradoxically, when he isn't being particularly virtuosic and lets his innate sense of hierarchy and pace drive his sounds.

Signing to Warp, the Motown of '90s electronic music, Aphex showed up first as Polygon Window with the *Surfing on Sine Waves* album. It's an archetypal James affair, beginning brilliantly with "Polygon Window" and "Audax Powder," one of his best tracks, then wandering through dodgy interrogations of beatmaking ("Quoth") and sappy soundtracks ("Is It Really Me?"). The last vestiges of acid house and off-the-rack ambient are gone, though, and the Aphex everyone knows begins to emerge.

Then, to keep everyone off balance, comes *Selected Ambient Works, Vol. 2,* an almost beatless two-disc series of untitled compositions. Some thought it was a joke, others threw themselves at James' feet. Roughly in the ambient genre as Eno first imagined it, *Selected* simply drifts with lots of minor-key themes and digital reverb. Occasionally beautiful, it does sound sometimes as if James hooked up a loop, put it through a reverb device, and went out to lunch. (Not that there's anything wrong with that.) Another puzzler. *I Care Because You Do* is actually of a piece with *Selected,* adding an increasingly active drum foundation (inspired, in part, by the increasing presence of drum and bass in the UK). String sounds begin to creep in on tracks such as "Icct Hedral," and his overall sound becomes denser and stranger. "Ventolin" is the ghost of "Phloam" beefed up brilliantly. (Often missed is James' own annotations of his track listings, indicating that some of the tracks date back as far as 1990. The best are the newest, from 1994.) The artwork is

another James joke: Tagged as a "faceless" techno artist, James strikes back with the album cover, an oil painting of himself, smiling. The sincerity of the title itself is in doubt, but James' liking of his own face isn't. It will show up again, many times.

The Richard D. James Album is a rollicking combination of hyperkinetic drum-and-bass patterns, silky strings, and crosstalking oddities. "Girl/Boy" was something of a hit in the U.K., and the vaguely obscene lyrics of "Milkman" got James even more press as an enfant terrible. By this point, Trent Reznor and Philip Glass were both calling to work with James, and it was obvious that his brio and skill could read to people far removed from dance music and bedroom electronics. (James' collaboration with Glass, as well as some other singles, are available on the solid *51/13* compilation.)

Two of James' best works are the EPs that followed *RDJ, Come to Daddy* and *Windowlicker.* Both were driven to market by controversial videos directed by Chris Cunningham, each making extensive use of a latex mask of James' face. (We won't spoil the effect, but it is quite likely that one or both videos will offend you.) In smaller doses, James' work improves. "Come to Daddy" is NIN gone nerdy but too comic to be really scary, while the delicate "Flim" and the athletic "Bucephalus Bouncing Ball" are two of James' most important tracks. "Windowlicker" is possibly the Aphex apex, a deft, inviting, and weird blend of all his interests. Start here.

Drukqs is a two-disc set dedicated to testing how far James can push his aesthetics, from total programming nightmares ("Omgyjyaswitch 7") to murky death dub ("Gwely Mernans"). To these extremes, James adds a series of very short piano and harpsichord pieces apparently inspired by Satie. They break up the action well; the second disc of *Drukqs* is his best-sequenced chunk of work. Weirdly dismissed by many, *Drukqs* is often spectacular.

There was an oft-repeated, possibly apocryphal story about James and his ubiquitous remixing services in the '90s. A messenger from an unnamed label showed up to retrieve a promised Aphex Twin remix. Delinquent but unfazed, James allegedly handed them a DAT off the shelf and took the cash. Nobody knew better. The title *26 Mixes for Cash* doesn't exactly dispel rumors of cynicism such as this, nor does some of the work. For every amazing piece such as his remix of Wagon Christ's "Spotlight" or the remix of 808 State's "FlowComa," (simply listed as "Remix by AFX") there are five others that just go through the motions. As with all AFX product, the high points are great (the "Windowlicker acid edit" is unusually organic and funky), so it's up to you to decide if you really need your cash or the mixes. Ultimately, Aphex is essentially '90s—the perfect music for working at a desk and watching the money roll in: unfailingly intelligent, occasionally astonishing, but often lighter than the air that surrounds it. Bubbletronica. —S.F.J.

Aphrodite

★★★½ Takeover Bid: Round One (Razor & Tie, 1998)
★★★★ Aphrodite (V2, 1999)

Few dance producers reign over their subgenre as unquestionably as Gavin King dominates jump-up. Fusing reggae-style intensity with funk beats as hard as they are hyper, the results are similar to dancehall, but without those muppet-voiced Jamaican dudes threatening to off batty boys. Aphrodite's self-titled American debut is a compilation of older tracks that still sound fresh. The shifting bass lines offer melodies before King drops the proceedings into freefall. Snippets of melodic ornamentation—electronic seagulls, soul saxophones, unmoored organ vamps—surface then plunge away beneath the breakbeat surf. And the awesome "B.M. Funkster" is jump-up's defining moment, sampling a loping horn riff from James Brown protégé Marva Whitney's "Unwind Yourself" for maximum funk impact.

As with most dance music producers, King has scattered more singles, mixes, and remixes about than any album guide can take into account. For starters, though, *Takeover Bid* is an ace mix disc. King has also masterminded numerous remixes—of Nine Inch Nails, among others. His self-released import tracks are worth hunting for, as are tracks released under the names Alladin and Amazon II—pseudonyms are yet another way the dance underground tries to elude you. This time, at least, it's worth the quest. —K.H.

Fiona Apple

★★★ Tidal (Epic, 1996)
★★★½ When the Pawn Hits the Conflicts He Thinks Like a King What He Knows Throws the Blows When He Goes to the Fight and He'll Win the Whole Thing 'Fore He Enters the Ring There's No Body to Batter When Your Mind Is Your Might So When You Go Solo, You Hold Your Own Hand and Remember That Depth Is the Greatest of Heights and if You Know Where You Stand, Then You Know Where to Land and if You Fall It Won't Matter, 'Cuz You'll Know That You're Right (Epic, 1999)

Fiona Apple, the waiflike singer/songwriter with a whale of a voice, was only 19 when her debut album came out in 1996. By then the New York native had already been writing songs for seven years and playing piano for eleven. Seductively miserable, *Tidal* was packed with jazzy torch songs and twitchy electronic flourishes. It was remarkably mature stuff, on par with the music Alanis Morissette and Tori Amos were releasing at the time, and two cuts—"Shadowboxer" and "Criminal"—became hit singles. Apple was open about the fact that she had been raped years earlier, although in songs like "Sullen Girl" ("But he washed me ashore and he took my pearl—and left an empty shell of me"), her agony was better communicated by her throaty, soulful voice than by her often sophomoric lyrics. Her bratty rant at the 1997 MTV Music Awards ("This world is bullshit!") proved again that this precocious Maya Angelou fan wasn't very economical with or smart about her choice of words. Then came her second album, with a 90-word title that does not adequately represent how much Apple had improved since *Tidal:* As her own turn of phrase in "A Mistake" suggested, she had "acquired quite a taste for a well-made mistake," trading two-dollar words for more subtle phrasings. On "Fast As You Can," and "Get Gone," she toys with lopsided rhythms and her voice turns more defiant and pissed-off, more self-aware and playful than on *Tidal.* Though it is more musically complex and melodically advanced, *Pawn* keeps the focus on Apple's sultry voice and moody piano playing, which consistently make up for any of her dysfunctional self-indulgence. —J.E.

The Apples in Stereo

★★★½ Fun Trick Noisemaker (spinART/Elephant 6, 1995)
★★★½ Science Faire (spinART/Elephant 6, 1996)
★★★★ Tone Soul Evolution (spinART/Elephant 6, 1997)
★★½ Her Wallpaper Reverie (spinART/Elephant 6, 1999)
★★★ The Discovery of a World Inside the Moone (spinART/Elephant 6, 2000)
★★★ Let's Go! (EP) (spinART, 2001)
★★★½ Velocity of Sound (spinART, 2002)

Led by Robert Schneider, a writer/producer who can practically make two tin cans and a comb sound like *Revolver,* the Apples in Stereo are the core of the Elephant 6 Recording Company, a loosely affiliated set of bands in love with the psychedelic hues of '60s pop (others include Neutral Milk Hotel and Olivia Tremor Control). *Fun Trick Noisemaker* is Elephant 6's statement of purpose, bursting with inventiveness and energy, and graced with gleefully lysergic arrangements and Beach Boys–inspired harmonies. *Science Faire* collects a few earlier, rawer singles, recorded at home on a four-track tape machine—if you heard them on an AM radio, though, you'd never know the difference.

With *Tone Soul Evolution,* the Apples got to play in a big studio for the first time, and you can hear their delight with their new toys—they layer on track after track of horns and piano and doot-doot-doot backing vocals like they're determined to use all 24. Schneider's songs aim for the simple elegance of the classic pop he adores, and usually get there; "Seems So" and "Shine a Light" are almost impossibly catchy, and he scatters them with sweetly bent guitar solos that conjure up vintage George Harrison. The subsequent *Her Wallpaper Reverie*—seven songs, plus eight little instrumental doodles—gets lost in suspicious fumes in much the same way as its lesser psychedelic ancestors, although it does include the stately *Magical Mystery Tour* homage "Strawberryfire."

The Discovery of a World Inside the Moone raises the stakes again—the production compresses half an hour's worth of classic-rock-radio harmonies, hip-swinging beats, and guitar crunch into every three minutes. After the opening slam dunks of "Go" and "The Rainbow," though, the tunes aren't as memorable as the lush, varied recording implies they are. *Let's Go!* is a nifty quickie for kids, featuring two versions of "Signal in the Sky," the irresistible rocker they recorded for TV's *The Powerpuff Girls,* plus a sloppy-but-fun live cover of the Beach Boys' very Apples-esque "Heroes & Villains."

The Apples ditched the fancy production and streamlined their boogie on *Velocity of Sound.* Schneider's new model seems to be *Nuggets*-style caffeine-buzz garage psychedelia, drummer Hilarie Sidney's two tunes match his hook-for-hook, and the band's got its fuzz pedals cranked all the way up. Average track time: 2:38. —D.W.

Archers of Loaf

★★★½ Icky Mettle (Alias, 1993)
★★★★ Vee Vee (Alias, 1995)
★★★½ The Speed of Cattle (Alias, 1996)
★★★½ All the Nations Airports (Alias/Elektra, 1996)
★★★ White Trash Heroes (Alias, 1998)
★★★ Seconds Before the Accident (Alias, 2000)

Every college town in America shelters a gaggle of underemployed noisemakers throttling haphazardly tuned guitars in the hope some unkempt sense will waft out of the din. But these unfortunately named North Carolina smart guys were distinguished by the precision of their barrage. Here was a band so in control of its crosscut dissonance and go-go-*stop* rhythms

that even its obligatory grab bag of B sides and leftovers, *The Speed of Cattle,* stands as a solid, listenable whole.

Icky Mettle is a sparring match between the two cannily dissonant guitars of two cannily dissonant Erics, Bachmann and Johnson. Darting upward, dipping downward, shouldering each other for space in the mix, these serrated lines jut, slash, sear, and occasionally fit their teeth into each other's groove. To be heard over this clash, Bachmann must bark the verbal piecemeal of his lyrics ("All I ever wanted was to be your spine!", "There's something wrong with my toast!") so vehemently that they cohere into rousing shout-along catchphrases in spite of themselves.

With the roiling swell of *Vee Vee,* the Archers sculpted a lively testament to heroic failure. Not only does a mob forcibly drown the "frontman/For the world's worst rock and roll band," but before we get to the rousing finale, "Underachievers March and Fight Song," Bachmann is already hoping that "the worst is yet to come!" Prophetic? Maybe, but only because the band peaked so early. By the time Alias scored major-label distribution, the Archers were *so* over the sort of postpunk anthemry that might have gotten them noticed: Rife with prickly images of terrorism and consumer fraud, *All the Nations Airports* was arid, arty, and angular.

By *White Trash Heroes,* Bachmann's voice was largely blown. (*Accident,* recorded around this time, showcases a great live band hobbled by this vocal setback). This regrouping album, sometimes soft and mournful, adorned with elegiac overtones and brooding synthesizers, offers a ruminative coda to an otherwise screechy career. Going out not with a bang but a whimper never sounded so poignant. —K.H.

Arrested Development

★★★★ 3 Years, 5 Months & 2 Days in the Life of . . . (Chrysalis, 1992)
★★★ Unplugged (Chrysalis, 1993)
★★½ Zingalamaduni (Chrysalis, 1994)
★★★ Extended Revolution (Stateside, 2003)

Speech

★★ Spiritual People (Vagabond, 2002)

Inspired by the political awareness of Public Enemy and the spiritual missives of the Native Tongues tribe, Atlanta-based collective Arrested Development came out of nowhere in 1992 with what was then a novel sound: consciousness-raising hip-hop that was funky, easygoing, and instantly accessible.

Their debut, *3 Years, 5 Months & 2 Days In the Life of . . .* —a reference to the amount of time it took the group to secure a recording contract—is pure audio delight from start to finish, a triumph of smartly turned rhythm tracks and the mellow verbal dexterity of rapper Speech, who, on the imploring "Give a Man a Fish," advises listeners, "Malt liquor got you licked, it's your powerful master" and "Raise your fist but also raise your children." One of the rare documents that's equally successful as a political statement and as pop art, *3 Years* covers a daunting range of topics and musical styles, rehabilitating Sly Stone ("People Everyday" is a canny update of "Everyday People") and advocating for old-fashioned morality ("Fishin' 4 Religion"), humanizing homelessness ("Mr. Wendal"), and envisioning a utopia ("Tennessee"). The album sold over 4 million copies and won several Grammys, but perhaps more important, it became the model for much of the so-called enlightened rap that would become an alternative to the gangsta-thug material that ruled much of the '90s.

Alas, the group never again reached the heights of *3 Years.* The quickie followup *Unplugged* is predictably erratic—though Arrested Development toured, they were never revered for their live show. The official studio followup, 1994's *Zingalamaduni,* is loaded with rhetoric, and more than a little strident: Despite several idyllic melodies, tunes such as "Ache'n for Acres" and "In the Sunshine" sound pedantic and forced. Speech made one forgettable solo record, and in 2003 he participated in an Arrested Development remix project, *Extended Revolution,* which boasts several intense reworkings from electronica pioneer Paul Oakenfold.   —T.M.

Ashanti

  ★★   Ashanti (Murder Inc., 2002)
  ★½   Chapter II (Murder Inc., 2003)

Ashanti was better than her first album indicated. Onstage she was a natural, sultry and light, at ease and with real power in her young voice. Only under the guidance of Murder Inc. kingpin Irv Gotti could a hot diva whispering "Baby, baby, baby, baby!" sound so damn boring. Ashanti's self-titled debut followed her appearances in star-making duets with Ja Rule ("Always on Time") and Fat Joe ("What's Luv"). The sound was strictly radio-ready R&B circa 2002, up-to-date and anonymous, and no threat creatively to contemporaries Alicia Keys and India.Arie. She curses undependable men on "Foolish" in a girlish vamp submerged in gloss, but taps a small vein of funk for "It's Over." Ashanti sounds most genuine on "Dreams," a delicate ballad that edges toward Stevie Wonder's sentimental side. But it's not enough to turn soul clichés into something real.

Chapter II is even lighter, without a single new trick

but with plenty of boasting and dumb chatter between songs. "Then Ya Gone" is a torrid and potent funk duet with rapper Chink Santana, while "The Story of 2" is a distant echo of ancient girl-group soul. Too much of the rest is empty of feeling, turning this Murder Inc. princess into just another lovesick diva tumbling back down the charts.   —S.A.

Asian Dub Foundation

  ★★★½   Facts and Fictions (1995; Beggars, 2002)
  ★★★½   Rafi's Revenge (London, 1998)
  ★★   Conscious Party (Virgin France, 1998)
  ★★★½   Community Music (Virgin France, 2000)
  ★★★   Frontline 1993–97: Rareities and Remixes (2001; Beggars, 2002)
  ★★½   Enemy of the Enemy (EMI, 2003)

Though it has not enjoyed quite the exposure or recognition of fellow tablas-'n'-breakbeats Londoners Talvin Singh and Cornershop, this collective—formed in 1993 at a music-technology workshop run by bassist Dr. Das (Aniruddha Das), with civil rights worker and DJ Pandit G (John Pandit) and a young Bengali rapper named Master D (Deeder Zaman)—has set a high standard for its uncompromising politics and clever mingling of very old and very new musical traditions. With postcolonial fury and a sample box, the group has made some of the most righteously and intelligently angry pop music to come out of England since the Clash, eagerly taking up the flame of anti-imperialist, multicultural rock in a new decade and a tense new world order.

Fact and Fictions finds ADF's sound—frenetic reggae meets drum-and-bass beats—fully formed. "We ain't ethnic, exotic, or eclectic/The only 'E' we use is electric," Master D barks in "Jericho," a song boldly introduced as speaking "for the consciousness of the nation."

The heat builds on *Rafi's Revenge,* with yet more controversial topics and a sound that pushes the bubbling tabla drums, slippery guitar patterns, and frenzied rhythms to explosive heights. "Naxalite," one of the most impassioned political songs since U2's "Sunday Bloody Sunday," cries, "We must never give up/Until the land is ours . . . / 'Til we have taken the power."

A mediocre live disc *(Conscious Party)* held the place while ADF recorded its most carefully articulated and varied album, *Community Music.* Toning down the inflammatory stuff, the group makes more cogent and nuanced social criticisms than ever before. "Real Great Britain" castigates the "shoegazer nation" that won't look its problems in the face, while "Collective Mode" and "Memory War" call for unity and truth in the face of propaganda.

Master D left the group at the end of 2000, and following a collection of remixes and miscellany, the group released *Enemy of the Enemy*, with a series of guest MCs taking D's place. None of them match his wild, lispy charm, and underwhelming guest spots by Sinéad O'Connor and Radiohead guitarist Ed O'Brien don't help either.   —B.S.

The Association

★★½	The Association's Greatest Hits (Warner Bros., 1968)
★	The Association's Golden Heebie Jeebies (Edsel, 1987)
★★	Just the Right Sound: The Association Anthology (Rhino, 2002)

White-bread, saccharine, fake flower-power shmaltz. Atop elevator-music instrumentation, the Association crooned. While hits such as "Windy" and "Along Comes Mary" convey the daffy zing of toothpaste ads, and "Cherish" tingles as a makeout classic, the band bombed on anything more ambitious, such as, for example, the antiwar dirge "Requiem for the Masses" or the Pepsi Generation anthem "Enter the Young." With more than 50 cuts, the Rhino collection induces sugar shock.   —P.E.

Ass Ponys

★★★★	Some Stupid with a Flare Gun (Checkered Past, 2000)
★★★½	Lohio (Checkered Past, 2001)

"Standing on the highway, pants around my knees/I'd write her name out on the road but I can't piss 'Denise.' " That classic couplet is now largely lost to history. The Ass Ponys' *Electric Rock Music*, the album that gave us that boozy confession, is, like the rest of the Ponys' '90s output, shamefully out of print. In fact, by the time these Cincinnati oddballs resurfaced in 2000, they were little more than a historical footnote, a band fondly remembered by a handful of critics and college-radio jocks. The Ponys' loose, rootsy jangle coexisted with a dark undertow of dissonance, a split personality that neatly matched Chuck Cleaver's deft sketching of mid-American weirdos.

Fine as they were, though, most of those early records lacked the rocket-launch freewheeling of guitarist Bill Alletzhauser, whose presence on *Flare Gun* inspires the rhythm section to a crunch rarely even approximated in the band's heyday. Perhaps fearful of being pegged as a novelty artist, Cleaver shies away from outright comedy here, but his vignettes of loners with overactive imaginations retain a quiet emotional pull without straining toward melodrama.

Lohio was more varied yet, with drum flurries of almost Who-like intensity mixed in among looser, countrified shuffles. Still, if you ever run across a cutout or used copy of *Electric Rock Music*, snatch it up. Until then, feel free to write disgruntled letters to whoever supervises A&M's back catalogue. Oh, and maybe ask 'em what happened to the Feelies' *Time for a Witness* while you're at it.   —K.H.

Chet Atkins

★★★★	Chet Atkins in Hollywood (RCA, 1959)
★★	Plays Back Home Hymns (RCA, 1962)
★★★	The Guitar Genius (RCA Camden, 1963)
★★½	Chet Atkins Picks on the Beatles (RCA, 1966)
★★½	Relaxin' With Chet (RCA Camden, 1969)
★★½	Reflections (RCA, 1980)
★★★	Stay Tuned (Columbia, 1985)
★★★	Street Dreams (Columbia, 1986)
★★★½	Sails (Columbia, 1987)
★★★½	Chet Atkins, C. G. P. (CBS, 1988)
★★★★½	Galloping Guitar: The Early Years (Bear Family, 1993)
★★★	Read My Licks (Columbia, 1994)
★★★	My Favorite Guitars/It's a Guitar World (One Way, 1995)
★★★	The Most Popular Guitar/Down Home Guitar (One Way, 1995)
★★★	Caribbean Guitar/Travelin' Guitar (One Way, 1995)
★★★½	The Essential Chet Atkins (RCA, 1996)
★★★	Almost Alone (Columbia, 1996)
★★★	Me and My Guitar/The First Nashville Guitar (One Way, 1997)
★★	Pickin' the Hits (Sony Music, 1997)
★★★½	The Day Finger Pickers Took Over the World (Sony, 1997)
★★★	Super Hits (RCA, 1998)
★★★	Mister Guitar/Chet Atkins in Three Dimensions (One Way, 1998)
★★★	Picks on the Hits/Superpickers (One Way, 1998)
★★★½	Me and Chet/Me and Jerry (One Way, 1998)
★★★	Finger Style Guitar/Stringin' Along With Chet Atkins (One Way, 1998)
★★★	Hum and Strum Along With Chet Atkins/The Other Chet Atkins (One Way, 1998)
★★★½	Chester and Lester/Guitar Monsters (One Way, 1998)
★★★★	Chet Atkins (Camden, 1999)
★★★	Chet Atkins/Doug Stone (Platinum Disc, 2000)
★★★★	Guitar Legend: The RCA Years (Buddha, 2000)

★★★ Guitar Country/More of That Guitar Country
(Collectables, 2001)
★★★ A Master and His Music (RCA, 2001)
★★★★ RCA Country Legends (Buddha, 2001)
★★★★ Chet Picks on the Grammys (Columbia, 2002)
★★★ Tribute to Bluegrass (BMG Special Products, 2002)

with Mark Knopfler
★★★★ Neck and Neck (Columbia, 1990)

Like Nashville's other ace instrumentalists (Floyd Cramer, Boots Randolph, Charlie McCoy), guitarist Chet Atkins spent a long time releasing albums that showcased remarkable skill—in contention with syrupy string arrangements, baby-talk back-up vocalizing, and mediocre material. That said, his technical dexterity and trademark twangy fluidity were such that a goodly amount of that mass of material (he began recording in the late '50s) rewards exploring. *In Hollywood* is a good place to start—such smooth fare as "Let It Be Me" and "Greensleeves" shows off the virtuosity that earned Atkins the name of "Mr. Guitar." *Picks on the Grammys* continues in the same vein: hits from 1967 to 1996 ably covered by the master. For an exhaustive serving of classic early Atkins, guitar fanatics will drool over *Galloping Guitar*, a massive box set. One Way has also done an excellent job of assembling twofers of vintage Chet; *Hum and Strum Along With Chet Atkins/The Other Chet Atkins* is a nice novelty featuring Latin tunes. *Almost Alone* is great six-string work, almost unaccompanied. Both *The Essential* and *Guitar Legend* are fine compact overviews of Atkins at his solo best, but some of his more exciting works are collaborations. *Chester and Lester* pairs him with Les Paul, and a sweet fire gets going between the two old stalwarts.

Mainly turning out hokum during the '70s, Atkins revived in the next decade. Helped out by bassist David Hungate and keyboardist Darryl Dybka, he released a series of albums that, for all their jazz-lite glossiness, surrounded him with very accomplished players. A guitar conclave, *Stay Tuned* joins him with Earl Klugh, Steve Lukather, George Benson, and Dire Straits mainman Mark Knopfler, and, while the tunes are formulaic, the playing is impressive. A followup, *Sails,* is easy listening raised to an artform. *Neck and Neck* is irresistible—with Atkins and Knopfler as equal partners, this labor of love ranges in style from Stephane Grappelli to Don Gibson. Its strength, however, lies in its country numbers—on a few of which Atkins actually sings (quite creditably). *The Day Finger Pickers Took Over the World* is Atkins acoustically dazzling, trading riffs with Aussie composer/guitarist Tommy Emmanuel.   —P.E.

Juan Atkins
★★★★ Wax Trax! Mastermix, Vol. 1 (TVT/Wax Trax!, 1998)
★★★ Legends, Vol. 1 (OM, 2001)
Model 500
★★★★ Classics (R&S, Austria, 1995)

It is impossible to overstate Juan Atkins' importance in the history of dance music. As a member of Cybotron (alongside Rick Davis) in the early '80s, Atkins essentially wrote the blueprint for Detroit techno, and as a DJ and producer he has continued to map the genre's terrain. His most important work post-Cybotron came under the moniker Model 500, whose singles, including the great "No UFO's," "Off to Battle," and "Night Drive (Time, Space, Transmat)," are collected on *Classics.* "No UFO's" keynotes Atkins' *Wax Trax! Mastermix Vol. 1,* a slamming DJ set that also serves as a smart history lesson, ranging from early techno (Rhythim Is Rhythim's "Nude Photo") to obscure disco (Martin Circus' "Disco Circus") to ghetto-tech (DJ Assault's "Sex on the Beach") to European minimalism (Maurizio's "7"). 2001's *Legends, Vol. 1* is less historically minded and more overtly interested in moving asses, and while a few tracks stand out (Isoleé's "Beau Mot Plage"), most don't.   —M.M.

Atmosphere
★★★½ Overcast! (Rhymesayers Entertainment, 1997)
★★★★½ Lucy Ford: The Atmosphere EPs (Rhymesayers Entertainment, 2001)
★★★★ God Loves Ugly (Fat Beats/Rhymesayers Entertainment, 2002)
★★★★ Seven's Travels (Rhymesayers/Epitaph, 2003)

Minneapolis underground hip-hoppers Atmosphere began in the mid-'90s, when Slug (né Sean Daley), rhyme partner Spawn, and producer Ant (born Anthony Davis) began releasing homemade cassettes; by 1997, they'd become one of the most popular live acts in the Twin Cities, a position solidified by the self-released *Overcast!,* which introduced Slug as a skillful braggart with a penchant for offering to take your girl home.

Cassettes such as the excellent, out-of-print *Se7en,* as well as a rigorous touring schedule and vigorous networking (Slug often played shows with punk, rock, and R&B acts as well as fellow hip-hoppers), earned Atmosphere a sizable cult following. But it was 2001's *Lucy Ford* that made Slug a hot commodity. Playing like a cross between De La Soul's 3 *Feet High & Rising* and Modest Mouse's *The Lonesome Crowded West, Lucy Ford* is both a day-in-the-life-of-a-slacker classic and a great break-up album. There's almost no boasting, plenty of self-examination, and Ant's loops and beats match Slug's goofy, warm, worried persona at every step; "Guns and Cigarettes" is one of the most drunk-sounding hip-hop tunes ever recorded.

God Loves Ugly, the followup, pulled a 180-degree switch, with a heavy concentration on bully-boy boasting ("The Bass and the Movement," "Flesh") and vitriol ("Fuck You Lucy"). But "Modern Man's Hustle" may be his best single to date, finding a middle ground between Slug's introverted and extroverted sides. A year later, Rhymesayers, Atmosphere's label, signed to punk indie Epitaph for distribution and released the excellent *Seven's Travels*—recorded at the same time as *Ugly* but with a markedly different sensibility (jaunty maturity rather than growing pains). The semihit video for "Trying to Find a Balance," as well as their appearing twice on the Warped Tour, helped make Slug indie rap's icon du jour and threatened to turn him into a bona fide star.   —M.M.

At the Drive-In

★★½	Alfaro Vive, Carajo! (EP) (Headquarter, 1995)
★★½	Acrobatic Tenement (Flipside, 1996)
★★★	El Gran Orgo (EP) (One Foot, 1997)
★★★½	In/Casino/Out (Fearless, 1998)
★★★★	Vaya (EP) (Fearless, 1999)
★★★½	At the Drive-In/Sunshine [Split] (Big Wheel, 2000)
★★★★	Relationship of Command (Virgin, 2000)

Sparta

★★★	Austere (DreamWorks, 2002)
★★★★	Wiretap Scars (DreamWorks, 2002)

Mars Volta

★★★	European Tour Sampler (Southern, 2002)
★★★½	Tremulant (EP) (Gold Standard, 2000)
★★★★	De-Loused in the Comatorium (Gold Standard/Universal, 2003)

At the Drive-In reinvigorated American postpunk, combining emo's unabashed passion with a politically edged fury reminiscent of the MC5. The El Paso, TX, fivesome—singer Cedric Bixler, guitarist Omar Rodriguez, guitarist Jim Ward, bassist Paul Hinojos, and drummer Tony Hajjar—established their formula early on, combining the rough-edged emo of underground favorites Jawbreaker with Rage Against the Machine's bombastic punk-metal attack. *El Gran Orgo*'s six tuneful tracks sound more focused than previous album *Acrobatic Tenement*'s sprawl of tricky rhythms and noisome textures: On "Picket Fence Cartel," Bixler spits a barely discernible barrage of bitter words over stop-start guitars and stomping-yet-precise drums and bass, before breaking into what was to become his trademark yowl in the strangely catchy chorus.

With emo's aggressive longing distilled into Bixler's convulsion of a voice, the band ditched its vestigial pop-punk niceties on *In/Casino/Out* and played harder and faster than ever before. Explosive and frequently pretty, the disc would sound spastic were it not so carefully orchestrated. The bass growls like a Rottweiler, the guitars twine like two strands of razor wire, and the cascading drums leap out of the mix. (Bixler's lyrics, on the other hand, become completely confused. On "Pickpocket," he blathers that "In the humble stench of nativity/hummed the smell of television snow" as if it actually meant something.)

The seven-song EP *Vaya* actually scales back the simulated chaos and dials in some exquisite, restrained tension. The lissome groove on "300 MHz" puts Rage Against the Machine's quiet parts to shame, and includes a bridge with Bixler's vocals being played backward (either that or he's truly spouting gibberish), while "Heliotrope" gallops into slinky, frenetic funk that repeatedly seizes and recovers, then drops down to Bixler's hoarse whisper and explodes. "198d" even proves the band's ability as balladeers.

Their major label debut, *Relationship of Command,* ratchets the levels back up to 11. In comparison to *Vaya, Command* sounds a little icy. But this is owed mostly to Ross Robinson's all-edges production; ATDI play as deftly as ever, unleashing a fireworks display of competing yet complementary sound bursts. The sinisterly schizo "One Armed Scissor" enthralled indie-oriented hard-rock fans who had yet to hear from the Strokes or the White Stripes, but personal differences broke At the Drive-In apart before they could make a mark on MTV.

Bixler and Rodriguez (the ones, famously, with MC5-inspired afros) went on to form Mars Volta, but it was Sparta—Paul Hinojos and Tony Hajjar, with Jim Ward on guitar and vocals—who capitalized on ATDI's momentum, essentially by re-creating their sound. Sparta obviously intended the startlingly good *Wiretap Scars* for an audience wider than At the Drive-In's. Ward can't help but sing more conventionally than Bixler, although he flits quite comfortably between vulnerable coo and outraged shout. Big guitars and beats abound, but so do melodies, and the pretty parts stretch out, interrupted only by explosive choruses.

Mars Volta's three-song EP *Tremulant* also smoothes out At the Drive-In's spiky textures, but with a psychedelic sheen and smidgens of ambient electronica. The almost absurdly ambitious *De-Loused in the Comatorium*—a well-received concept album about the drug-related death of a friend—moves like tropical weather, squalling in tremendous bursts, then settling into hushed interludes that sound like breezes playing on loose debris. Bixler fully releases his helium-fed voice, playing on every crash and whisper, ultimately breaking through the cast of rage that defined At the Drive-In. Sparta scored a hit with "Cut Your Ribbon"; one hopes Mars Volta will someday vault onto radio. If At the Drive-In did it, anything's possible. —N.C.

Audioslave

★★★ Audioslave (Sony, 2002)

The combination of Rage Against the Machine and Chris Cornell looks on paper like something that could be achieved only in a game of fantasy rock baseball, or a really excellent impromptu jam session. This supergroup of noise came together after singer Zack de la Rocha's departure left Rage without a frontman; Cornell's Soundgarden had already split, so the pairing was set. Their debut album is a sonic assault that bears more similarity to Cornell's former team, albeit with actual ballads such as "I Am the Highway," the prettiest of the bunch. "Light My Way" lands at the other end of the spectrum, a full-on pan of boiling water in the face that proves guitarist Tom Morello listened to his fair share of Nugent albums while studying at Harvard. Cornell's lyrics can seem a bit New-Agey when set to Morello's guitar histrionics, but when the group sets to rocking, there is much firepower present. Still, as with most supergroups, or corporate mergers, past résumés hang heavy over these songs. —C.R.C.

Autechre

★★½	Incunabula (Wax Trax!, 1994)
★★½	Amber (TVT, 1994)
★★★★	Tri Repetae ++ (1995; Wax Trax!, 1999)
★★★	Chiastic Slide (Warp, 1997)
★★★	LP5 (Warp, 1998)
★★★	EP7 (Nothing, 1999)
★★★	Confield (Warp, 2001)
★★★	Draft 7.30 (Warp, 2003)

Blip, buzz, zap: Sean Booth and Rob Brown, the two knob-twiddlers behind Autechre, were among the leaders of the electronica renaissance of the mid-'90s, blending the cool minimalism of '70s pioneers such as Kraftwerk and Brian Eno with stark avant-garde noise, plus a touch of the block-rocking intensity of '80s hip-hop and electro-funk. As with Aphex Twin, Mouse on Mars, and other innovators, their treatment of electronic dance music is at once a cerebral deconstruction that demands close listening on headphones (and far away from a dance floor) and a challenge to other experimental music makers to produce work

that can elicit a physical, sexual response. No wonder it's called intelligent dance music.

The group began slowly, with smart if unexciting ambient watercolors on Incunabula and Amber that give no indication of the innovations to follow. On Tri Repetae ++, Booth and Brown hit a stride that carried them through nearly a decade of intensely challenging music. Pushing the limits of danceability, the album squeezes faster, tighter, and more bizarre rhythms out of an arsenal of tones ranging from the squiggly and percussive to the breezily melodic. The soundscapes, made of complex patterns that alter and intersect in ever changing ways, retain an excitable pulse while veering dangerously out of orbit and into a noisy outer realm where there is no disco ball and no bar.

So how do you top a visionary work that challenges the very nature of dance music? Unfortunately, you don't. After Tri Repetae, Autechre albums have a mind-numbing sameness despite their minute-by-minute ingenuity. Like, say, Chicago, they basically made the same album—and the same EP, and the same remix—many, many times. Chiastic Slide is a dull sequel, but LP5 kicks in with faster and more jarring rhythms. Confield and Draft 7.30 continue in familiar patterns of crunching, robotic rhythms and clean, spacey melodies that swarm in and out of focus. Mindlessly repetitive, yes, but in the best sense possible. —B.S.

The Auteurs

★★★★	New Wave (Caroline, 1993)
★★★	Now I'm a Cowboy (Vernon Yard, 1994)
★★★	After Murder Park (Hut, 1996)

Baader Meinhof

★★★½	Baader Meinhof (Caroline, 1997)

Black Box Recorder

★★★★	England Made Me (Jetset, 1999)
★★★★½	The Facts of Life (Jetset, 2001)
★★★	The Worst of Black Box Recorder (Jetset, 2001)
★★★★	Passionoia (One Little Indian, 2003)

Luke Haines was too sardonic and overeducated to rouse the masses at Wembley Stadium, so he deployed power chords as a framework for his unrequited, self-referential show biz obsessions. On the band's debut, "Don't Trust the Stars" and "Starstruck" pun off the connections between astrological coincidences and showbiz success, while "American Guitars" mocked rock-god aspirations as well as the British Haines' own aesthetic incompatibility with such aspirations.

New Wave offered a survey of that low-rent district where the privileged bohemian poor rub shoulders with the criminal underground, a world of lack more than want, grasping and pathetic and lively. Haines conflates cynicism and charm so freely that his targets rarely matter: When he discredits thrift-shop chic with a casual "Lenny Bruce never walked in a dead man's shoes," the elliptical angle of his assault is the hook. By the time of *After Murder Park* Haines was hinting at dangers and calamities that he couldn't quite pin down with lyrics or music. So, naturally, he orchestrated a likeably tense little one-off concept album about German terrorists Baader Meinhof.

Having learned a bit of electronics from that detour, Haines formed Black Box Recorder with Jesus and Mary Chain drummer John Moore and pert, pouty, posh Sarah Nixey on vocals. Right as rain and just as damp, *The Facts of Life* watches synth patterns trickle past spare drumbeats in a languid contest to see which can seem the most innocuous. Call it drip-hop—aural drizzle as an indicator of romantic malaise. But just because Nixey coos with the calm tenderness of a latent sociopath doesn't mean she wants to hurt you. *Passionoia* is a bit more wan musically, but two Nixey set pieces play off her prim sexpot persona smashingly. On the title cut, she's a frosty, disciplinary headmistress; on "Andrew Ridgley," she eulogizes the go-go '80s from the perspective of a poor little rich girl.   —K.H.

The Avalanches

★★★★   Since I Left You (Modular/Sire, 2001)

Anyone with a sampler can create a new song out of bits and pieces of existing music, but it takes real panache to balance the familiar and obscure. *Since I Left You,* the first album from Australian quintet the Avalanches, strikes that balance perfectly. Composed of hundreds of samples, the disc's playful, airy grooves are ecstatic with the endless possibilities of sound, evoking the Beastie Boys' *Paul's Boutique* refracted through the rave-kissed bliss of Primal Scream's "Loaded." What sticks, though, is the disc's surprisingly resonant emotional core, which explores the thrill and dread of leaving a stifling relationship and entering the wider world—in this case, the night world of club culture—in order to find yourself.   —M.M.

Roy Ayers

★★★	Daddy Bug and Friends (Atlantic, 1967–69)
★★★	Ubiquity (Polydor, 1971)
★★★½	He's Coming (Polydor, 1972)
★★★★	Live at the Montreux Jazz Festival (Verve, 1972)
★★★	Coffy (Polydor, 1973)
★★★½	Virgo Red (Polydor, 1973)
★★★	Mystic Voyage (Polydor, 1975)
★★★	Vibrations (Polydor, 1976)
★★	You Might Be Surprised (Columbia, 1985)
★★★★	Evolution: The Polydor Anthology (Chronicles/Polydor, 1995)
★★	Live at Ronnie Scott's (Silverline, 2001)
★★★★	Virgin Ubiquity: Unreleased Recordings, 1976–1981 (Rapster/BBE, 2004)

Like many music makers of the '60s and '70s, vibraphonist Roy Ayers, known for his crisp instrumental funk, has enjoyed an echoing multigenerational success: Not only are the records he made then considered classics in their own right, but via sampling, they've provided the foundation for countless hip-hop and acid jazz productions from DJ Jazzy Jeff, 2Pac, Outlawz, and others.

A native of San Francisco, Ayers discovered the vibraphone at age 17, and by his early twenties was recording with West Coast jazzers Jack Wilson and the Gerald Wilson Orchestra. He joined flutist Herbie Mann's group in 1966, and under Mann's direction recorded his first solo efforts, which featured tenor man Joe Henderson and are collected on *Daddy Bug and Friends.* Forming the Roy Ayers Ubiquity in 1970 with Billy Cobham and other jazz-rock heavyweights, Ayers began his most consequential recording period: Hits included "We Live in Brooklyn, Baby" from 1971's *He's Coming* and "Coffy Is the Color" from the 1973 soundtrack to *Coffy,* while several other records, including the 1972 *Live in Montreux,* show that Ayers and his ensemble were rare among the jazz-rock "fusion" outfits of the day because they were capable of sliding between heavy-backbeat music and crisp traditional swing without compromising in either direction. Though many individual titles are out of print, the essentials of the Ayers canon are collected on the two-disc *Evolution: The Polydor Anthology,* which showcases the leader's wry, agile solo play.

By the 1980s, Ayers' own records grew listless and overproduced, devoid of the sparky interplay that once defined his groups. He continued, however, to record, collaborating with Afro-pop star Fela Anikulapo Kuti and guesting on Guru's pathfinding jazz–hip-hop experiment *Jazzmatazz* in 1993. Ayers continues to record; his most recent efforts, including several live albums recorded at London's Ronnie Scott's, don't significantly expand his legacy.

Ayers finally opened his vaults in 2004, and the result is *Virgin Ubiquity,* a set of previously unreleased studio sides made during one of the vibraphonist's most prolific periods. Three vocalists take turns doing leads, but the highlights are the instrumentals—an alternative version of "Mystic Voyage" and the funky "Green and Gold," which captures Ayers' chattering exchange with Bobby Lyle on electric piano.　—T.M.

AZ

★★★	Doe or Die (EMI, 1995)
★★½	Pieces of a Man (Virgin, 1998)
★★½	S.O.S.A. (Virgin, 2000)
★★	9 Lives (Motown, 2001)
★★★½	Aziatic (Motown, 2002)

AZ's career is, in some ways, a testament to the staggering influence that his fellow Queensbridge rapper Nas had over the hip-hop world in the early '90s. After appearing on Nas' excellent debut, *Illmatic*, AZ found himself on the tip of many a rap fan's tongue, as people wondered when the passionate MC from Nas' "Life's a Bitch" would drop his own album. Those questions were answered with 1995's *Doe or Die*, a literate, sensitive look at street life that sits comfortably, as a companion, next to Nas' masterpiece. After appearing on the Nas-led (and rather ill-conceived) "supergroup" the Firm, AZ made his followup, the disappointing *Pieces of a Man*. Like Nas, AZ began relying on shinier production (handled mostly by the Trackmasterz) and smoothed out his sound to appeal to an R&B audience.

S.O.S.A. is a slight return to the raw style that brought him prominence, but it still suffers from AZ's concessions to the mainstream sounds of Puff Daddy and Bad Boy. *9 Lives* sadly found AZ sinking into obscurity with little to no contributions from any top-notch producers or MCs. AZ couldn't carry the weight all by himself and the album suffers from a generic feel. Happily, *Aziatic* is a return to form. Coming out in the shadow of Jay-Z's *The Blueprint*, *Aziatic* has a similar, soul-drenched sound, using the production of veterans such as DR Period (M.O.P.) to highlight his exceptional lyrical talents.　—C.R.

Babes in Toyland

- ★★★ Spanking Machine (Twin/Tone, 1990)
- ★★ To Mother (EP) (Twin/Tone, 1991)
- ★★★★ Fontanelle (Reprise, 1992)
- ★★ Nemesisters (Reprise, 1995)
- ★★ Further Adventures of Babes in Toyland (Fuel 2000, 2001)

Hailing from Minneapolis, Babes in Toyland came out of the same hardcore scene that a few years earlier had produced the Replacements and Hüsker Dü. But Babes in Toyland proved to be a more traditional punk band than either of those predecessors. Kat Bjelland, dressed in a tattered wedding dress, came on like Miss Havisham on the war path. Led by Kat's sloppy guitar and screams from the gut, Babes on *Spanking Machine* and *To Mother* (a followup EP) helped inspire the nascent riot grrrl movement perhaps even more than former Babes member Courtney Love's far more successful Hole. Still, it was a surprise when Babes was signed to a major label. But unlike, say, the major-label debut of the Replacements or Hüsker Dü, *Fontanelle*—produced by Sonic Youth's Lee Ranaldo—finds Babes using the big recording budget to create the trio's most uncompromising effort. Ranaldo does a fantastic job capturing the dissonance in Bjelland's guitar as well as the band's hard-driving rhythm section. On tracks such as "Bruise Violet" and "Handsome and Gretal," Bjelland purrs sweet nothings one minute and howls like a banshee the next. Though angry enough to scare anyone with a dick, Bjelland is never dogmatic on *Fontanelle*. Instead, she is all feminist rage sans feminism; in short, *Fontanelle* is great punk rock played by an all-chick band. Sadly, by *Nemesisters* the band members had become expert enough players to evolve into just an average metal band. Babes split up in 1997; *Further Adventures* offers a gathering of the influential group's live recordings, rarities, and outtakes. —R.A.

Baby

see HOT BOYS

Babyface

- ★★ Lovers (1986; Solar/Epic, 1989)
- ★★★ Tender Lover (Solar, 1989)
- ★★★ A Closer Look (Solar, 1991)
- ★★★ For the Cool in You (Epic, 1993)
- ★★★½ The Day (Epic, 1996)
- ★★ MTV Unplugged, NYC 1997 (Epic, 1997)
- ★★★ Christmas With Babyface (Epic, 1998)
- ★★★★ A Collection of His Greatest Hits (Epic, 2000)
- ★★★½ Love Songs (Epic, 2001)
- ★ Face2Face (Arista, 2001)
- ★★ The Spirit of Christmas (Sony Special Products, 2002)

For a time in the '90s, Kenneth "Babyface" Edmonds was half of the hottest hit-making team in pop, along with his songwriting and production partner, Antonio "L.A." Reid. His Midas touch generated massive hits for Whitney Houston, Boyz II Men, Paula Abdul, and even Eric Clapton. But where Reid used that momentum to climb the corporate ladder (eventually becoming head of Arista Records), Babyface followed his art and ended up a spent force—but not before having a number of smoothly unobtrusive R&B hits.

Lovers, recorded after L.A. and Babyface had left their band the Deele is competent but predictable, with the singer lavishing his light tenor on slow, soulful ballads like the Stylistics' "You Make Me Feel Brand New." Unsurprisingly, *Tender Lover* also includes a few powerhouse ballads, the best of which (such as "Whip Appeal") capture the insinuating cadences of a lover's pillow talk. *A Closer Look* provides highlights from both albums, as well as two live tracks and duets Babyface recorded for albums by Karyn White and Pebbles.

For the Cool in You further refined that formula,

increasing the potency of the uptempo tunes while scoring a major hit with the warmly sentimental "When Can I See You Again," and then Babyface peaked with *The Day,* an all-star, hit-encrusted effort that more or less epitomized the R&B pop aesthetic of the mid-'90s. But after the nakedness of *MTV Unplugged* exposed his weaknesses as a singer, his career stalled and his creativity crashed. *Christmas With Babyface* is low key and agreeably traditional, and would have made a nice, quiet exit. (*A Collection of His Greatest Hits* would make nice time capsule fodder.) But Babyface, convinced he could somehow seem hip, came back with *Face2Face,* a painful grab for street cred on which the only thing more painful than the maudlin "Still in Love With U" is hearing Snoop Dogg work his persona on "Baby's Mama." —J.D.C.

Burt Bacharach

★★½	Reach Out (A&M, 1967)
★★★	Butch Cassidy and the Sundance Kid (A&M, 1969)
★★★	Make It Easy on Yourself (A&M, 1969)
★★★	Burt Bacharach (A&M, 1971)
★★½	Burt Bacharach's Greatest Hits (A&M, 1974)
★★★	Woman (A&M, 1979)
★★½	Classics, Vol. 23 (A&M, 1987)
★★★	Plays the Burt Bacharach Hits (MCA, 1997)
★★★★	The Look of Love (Rhino, 1998)
★★★★	One Amazing Night (NK2, 1998)
★★★½	The Millennium Collection (Interscope, 1999)
★★★★	The Very Best of Burt Bacharach (Rhino, 2001)
★★★★	What the World Needs Now: Burt Bacharach Classics (A&M, 2003)

with Elvis Costello

★★★½	Painted from Memory (Mercury, 1998)

Classically trained and phenomenally industrious, Burt Bacharach began writing hits in the '50s for performers as various as Perry Como, Marty Robbins, and Gene Pitney, after having honed his arranging skills as conductor for Marlene Dietrich. With lyricist Hal David, he went on to deliver an astonishing series of '60s pop singles for Dionne Warwick. Combining Tin Pan Alley craft, Gershwinesque jazz flourishes, and daring offbeat rhythms, his songs became Muzak staples—a sad but inevitable fate.

On his own, he made albums that featured lush, symphonic versions of his work for other artists. He sometimes sang (very poorly); more often, he assembled dreadful choirs who crooned like jingle hacks. If you can get beyond this, his arrangements still pack punch and surprise. Overfond of whimsical instrumentation (harpsichords, bossa-nova guitars), he still

comes off as a distinctive musical intelligence—he does "light" with more class than almost any other AOR composer. *Woman,* a semiclassical epic, is his most ambitious work, but nonobsessives will be much more interested in his greatest-hits sets, which contain such ubiquitous singles as "Alfie," "I Say a Little Prayer for You," "Promises, Promises," and "What the World Needs Now Is Love." In the late '90s, Bacharach appeared alongside Elvis Costello in *Austin Powers: The Spy Who Shagged Me* as a living embodiment of slightly kitsched-up elegance, and a new generation of indie rockers took Bacharach's soft, orchestrally rich pop in arty (and sometimes ironic) new directions. Bacharach and Costello also teamed up for 1998's *Painted From Memory,* which showed that Bacharach's gift for melody remained undiminished; Costello added a layer of hip credibility. Bacharach's new trendiness also spurred some terrific best-ofs, the best being Rhino's *The Look of Love,* and the all-star tribute album *One Amazing Night.* The latter underscores Bacharach's wide appeal—check out Wynonna's killer version of "Anyone Who Had a Heart" and a nifty take on "Raindrops Keep Falling on My Head" courtesy of Ben Folds Five. —P.E.

Bachman-Turner Overdrive

★★	Bachman-Turner Overdrive (Mercury, 1973)
★★★	Bachman-Turner Overdrive II (Mercury, 1974)
★★★	Not Fragile (Mercury, 1974)
★★	Four Wheel Drive (Mercury, 1975)
★★	Head On (Mercury, 1975)
★★★	Best of Bachman-Turner Overdrive (So Far) (Mercury, 1976)
★★	Freeways (Mercury, 1977)
★	Street Action (Mercury, 1978)
★	Rock 'n' Roll Nights (Mercury, 1978)
★★★½	Best of B.T.O. (Remastered Hits) (Mercury, 1998)

Bachman-Turner Overdrive launched a million bad jokes about spare tires and hefty metal, but this beefy Canadian band's shimmering power hooks still motor past all tasteful objections. Toughening his old group's pop sensibilities with a big guitar sound, ex–Guess Who member Randy Bachman hit the ground running in his '70s vehicle. "Let It Ride," "Roll on Down the Highway," and "You Ain't Seen Nothing Yet" all sound like they rolled off the same assembly line—on purpose. B.T.O. maintained a fairly high standard of quality across its initial releases, pumping out tuneful filler alongside the aforementioned hits. However, the optimistically titled *Best of Bachman-Turner Overdrive (So Far)*—reissued in 1998 with the parenthetical *(Remastered Hits)*—is all the B.T.O. general listeners need to hear. Tossing in the FM standard "Gimme Your Money Please" (about a mugging) and the ambitious "Lookin' Out for #1," this one qualifies as essential if your car still has a tape deck. On the post–*Four Wheel Drive* titles, B.T.O. sputters and eventually stalls, and the plethora of collections and live CDs that keep coming out on a variety of labels can't jump-start this rusty old engine.   —M.C./M.K.

Backstreet Boys

★★½   Backstreet Boys (Jive, 1996)
★★★½   Millennium (Jive, 1999)
★★   Black & Blue (Jive, 2000)
★★★   The Hits: Chapter One (Jive, 2001)

Five young men from the time-honored teen-pop proving grounds of church choirs and regional theater, the Backstreet Boys were, in their heyday—before they were unseated by 'N Sync—the biggest teen sensation since the Monkees, at the crest of the late-'90s pubescent-pop tidal wave.

Under the aegis of Orlando impresario Lou Pearlman, the Backstreet Boys signed to Jive Records in 1994, releasing their self-titled 1996 debut to great success in Europe and Canada before issuing it stateside the next year. Packed with soon-to-become unavoidable hits—"Quit Playin' Games (With My Heart)," "Everybody (Backstreet's Back)," "As Long As You Love Me"—*Backstreet Boys* served as the blueprint for boy bands to come, mixing soulful, sexually inoffensive ballads with harmony-heavy R&B and mildly edgy dance tracks. It eventually sold 13 million copies, though the Boys' popularity wouldn't actually peak until the release of *Millennium* (which would sell more than 1 million copies in its first week) two years later. While *Millennium* wasn't as shamelessly hook-filled as *BSB,* it did offer up the Boys' best-ever track, "I Want It That Way," a near-perfect slice of puppy-dog soul.

Released the next year, *Black & Blue* followed roughly the same formula as its predecessors, with decidedly lesser results. With the exception of the irresistibly cheesy "Shape of My Heart" and the just-plain-bad cheating-boyfriend apologia "Call," most of the tracks here are unexceptional.

Dogged by bad reviews, heart ailments, substance abuse, and encroaching facial hair, the Boys have had a relatively rough time of things since their 1999 heyday, but their 2001 best-of collection, *The Hits: Chapter One,* brings to mind happier times. Every smash is here, and every modest success as well, from "All I Have to Give" to "Drowning," a new single with little of the kick of the group's best work. Unlike most retrospectives, *The Hits* doesn't exactly chart the band's musical evolution—there hasn't been one to speak

of—but it does offer an impressive tribute to their hit-making power.   —A.S.

Bad Brains

★★★★★ Bad Brains (1982; ROIR, 1996)
★★★★   Rock for Light (1983; Caroline, 1991)
★★★★★ I Against I (1986; SST, 1990)
★★★   Live (1988; SST, 1990)
★★★   Quickness (Caroline, 1989)
★★★★   Youth Are Getting Restless: Live in Amsterdam (Caroline, 1990)
★   Rise (Epic, 1993)
★★   God of Love (Maverick, 1995)
★★★★★ Black Dots (Caroline, 1996)
★★★½   Omega Sessions (EP) (Victory, 1997)
★★★½   Banned in DC: Bad Brains Greatest Riffs (Caroline, 2003)

Bad Brains would have been as important as fluoridated water if their only contribution to pop music had been their 1980 debut 45 "Pay to Cum," an impossible freight train of sound and speed-singing that split American hardcore into Before and After. But they did much more, including simply being black, which made their white-hot punk a quintessentially American triumph. The skinny Rastas in the Lacoste shirts fled, banned, from D.C. to New York in 1979, fronted by Joseph "HR" Hudson. Combining the moves and vocals of James Brown and Johnny Rotten with some Nadia Comaneci acrobatics, HR was hilarious, scary, unscripted, and beautiful. To watch HR start a show by doing a backflip off the drum riser and land on the downbeat was as close to God as many of us will come. And his band was black and they played all this dub. What *were* they doing?

Just being New York's greatest hardcore band, blowing every mind they touched. Dimwits have called their 1982 debut ROIR cassette "badly recorded," which is like saying the guitar on "You Really Got Me" sounds funny. *Bad Brains* is one long thought, starting with the dangerously torqued and catchy "Sailin' On" and continuing through an articulation of punk as political liberation and reggae as spiritual salvation that has yet to be fully unpacked. Their music was the word as act, almost unbearable live, barely containable on tape. Some analogies: late-period John Coltrane, a broken water main emptying into your house, an amplified rockslide. The debut's only flaw is that "Pay to Cum" is included only in a live version. The priceless original appears on *Banned in DC: Bad Brains Greatest Riffs,* a solid best-of that goes too heavy on the live versions to be a definitive introduction.

Rock for Light was their slightly more visible 1983 debut on Caroline, produced by Ric Ocasek with an infuriating lack of low end. It's still unapologetic and brilliant, if just for adding older set numbers such as "How Low Can a Punk Get?" and "We Will Not." Like Monk or Hendrix, there is no limit to how many times you can hear them play their best songs.

After some heavy touring, the band began to suffer from some of HR's less helpful tendencies, such as ending up in jail. But they made another landmark album in 1986, *I Against I*, a fusion of punk and metal that put moshing on the map and gave stadium sports an anthem: "Re-Ignition." The reggae element was reduced and the live show honed to a terrifying point. The hooks on "Let Me Help" and "She's Calling You" sounded almost like Love, and the multipartite structure of the title track revealed that, yes, these guys really *had* been a jazz fusion band called Mind Power before they heard the Dead Boys in 1977. But that's OK.

That was it for making history. *The Youth Are Getting Restless* is the live album to own; the others attempt to cash in on the studio records. *Quickness*, recorded in large with Cro-Mags drummer Mackie recording in place of HR's brother, Earl Hudson, has the essential Brains track "Soul Craft" and a few stormers but is marred by HR's increasingly homophobic and bonkers worldview. Sans HR, the band signed to Epic in 1993 and made the miserable *Rise* with replacement singer Israel Joseph. (Imagine ABBA with different singers. Sensible?) HR rejoined for the Maverick reunion *God of Love* but got into new trouble, and the band ended up with neither a label nor their band name, which lawyers at Maverick held on to for sentimental reasons. The band reformed for the umpteenth time as Soul Brains and still tours under that name. The band is great, but HR stands still on stage and imitates Haile Selassie's Mona Lisa smile. The major addition to their discography was *Black Dots*, the 1996 Caroline release of the four-track basement demos made in 1979 with D.C. engineer Don Zientara. (HR recorded his vocals on the lawn.) Stripped of any studio enhancements, the band is even more terrifying, and this might be the record to start with for novices. There is nothing else like them in American music.   —S.F.J.

Bad Company

★★★½   Bad Company (Swan Song, 1974)
★★★   Straight Shooter (Swan Song, 1975)
★★½   Run With the Pack (Swan Song, 1976)
★★½   Burnin' Sky (Swan Song, 1977)
★★★   Desolation Angels (Swan Song, 1979)
★★½   Rough Diamonds (Swan Song, 1982)
★★   Fame and Fortune (Atlantic, 1986)
★★   Dangerous Age (Atlantic, 1988)
★★★★   10 From 6 (Atlantic, 1988)

★★   Holy Water (Atco, 1990)
★★   Here Comes Trouble (Atco, 1992)
★   The Best of Bad Company Live . . . What You Hear Is What You Get (Atlantic, 1993)
★★   Company of Strangers (East West, 1995)
★★   Stories Told & Untold (East West, 1996)
★★★½   The "Original" Bad Company Anthology (Elektra, 1999)
★★   In Concert: Merchants of Cool (Sanctuary, 2002)

This mid-'70s supergroup picks up precisely where lead singer Paul Rodgers old band left off. Bad Company coarsens and distorts Free's economical blooze attack just enough to put it across to a howling, smoke-filled arena. Compared to his shrieking competition (from Ian Gillan in Deep Purple to Sammy Hagar in Montrose and later Van Halen), Rodgers is a remarkably soulful hard-rock frontman. And former Mott the Hoople guitarist Mick Ralphs proves an able foil; his stuttering riffs and clipped solos boldly copy Free guitarist Paul Kossoff's signature sound, while ex–Free drummer Simon Kirke provides thundering foursquare rhythms.

Bad Company came as a breath of fresh air amid arena rocks' increasing stench, but this particular breeze quickly turned into a gust of hot air. Rodgers and Company never could get beyond the "Baby I'm a Bad Man" stance of Bad Company. The no-bullshit minimalism and rhythmic thrust of the debut becomes a rut by the third album. The post-Rodgers releases—beginning with *Fame and Fortune*—find Ralphs and Kirke keeping company with a couple of unfortunate Rodgers clones, Brian Howe and later Robert Hart. The albums aren't bad enough to be abominations, or shameless enough to be successes.

That said, there's not a bum riff or bogus groan to be found on *10 From 6*, a collection that mixes the full bore earthquakes ("Can't Get Enough") and half-acoustic lust ballads ("Shooting Star") alongside musings on the road ("Movin' On") and the music ("Rock & Roll Fantasy")—it's essential to any survey of '70s rock. While *The "Original" Bad Company Anthology* is overkill, it's a not-bad selection from the band's first five albums plus a handful of B sides and four new Rodgers-fronted tunes. Of the two live discs, only *Merchants of Cool* is worth hearing, as it brings Rodgers back for some fairly spirited takes on the chestnuts.   —M.C./M.K.

Badly Drawn Boy

★★½   How Did I Get Here? (Toys Factory [Japan], 1999)
★★★★   The Hour of Bewilderbeast (XL, 2000)

★★★ About a Boy (Artist Direct, 2002)
★★★½ Have You Fed the Fish? (Artist Direct, 2002)
★★★½ One Plus One Is One (Astralwerks, 2004)

England's Damon Gough, who performs as Badly Drawn Boy, is a big Bruce Springsteen fan. Seems strange at first, because he's one of a young cluster of wounded-romantic singer/songwriters, not an arena rocker. His songs feel intimate even when they are dense with strings and horn charts, and he's convincingly sensual either in a whisper or a shout. But the Springsteen connection is clear during Badly Drawn Boy concerts, both in his determined outreach to fans and in their sense of knowing him like a friend. He gathers you in. The most frequent comparison is to Elliott Smith, another essentially acoustic fabulist of the heart's troubles who was fond of sinuous, insistent melodies. But where Smith often presented soiled boys and girls who found love to be broken, for Badly Drawn Boy, love is forever part of "All Possibilities." Clever at taking the temperature of a relationship and ardent but able to take hard knocks, he can be sweetly caring, as in "I Need a Sign" and "Pissing in the Wind," without coming off like a quivering sap or a fraud. Also like Springsteen, Badly Drawn Boy's mature work is meticulously crafted.

So, combining early EPs with a few scattered tracks, *How Did I Get Here?* is a product purely for dedicated fans, since the songs, if not exactly badly drawn, are at least incomplete sketches. All of Badly Drawn Boy's abilities snap into place for *The Hour of Bewilderbeast*. It's less experimental instrumentals, more song form and conversational, and presents one of the most beguiling and fully formed sensibilities to pop out of nowhere since Beck's *Mellow Gold*. If "Magic in the Air" evokes your favorite summer night of shifting passions, Badly Drawn Boy has breached your defenses for good.

Comely, affecting, light on its feet, reflective, and witty, *About a Boy* matches its movie as well as any soundtrack this side of *Magnolia*, and it plays as well on its own. Worth adopting. Even more encouraging, *Have You Fed the Fish?* indicates that success won't spoil Badly Drawn Boy. He cherishes his young family and his hugely expanded audience without being either smug or abashed by either. The album delivers rich, multi-instrument arrangements that sound like he invented them rolling out of bed, plaintive laments that could not be more unplugged, and thoughts about angels and rewinding to move forward that he makes sound like pearls. Meet a sensitive soul for our time.

Judging only from the recorded evidence on *One Plus One Is One*, Gough still wasn't getting out of his bedroom enough, but the sense of personal warmth triumphing over everyday melancholia is one of the album's biggest charms. On songs such as "Life Turned Upside Down," "Logic of a Friend," and the tear-jerking "Year of the Rat," Gough writes to the sound of his own conversational murmuring and fills in the blank spots with rumbling timpani, keyboards, and a children's choir.   —M.MI.

The Bad Plus

★★★★ These Are the Vistas (Columbia, 2003)
★★★★ Give (Sony, 2004)

Look solely at the instrumentation of the Bad Plus—acoustic piano, upright bass, drums, no vocals—and you'd think they were a jazz trio. While that assumption's not wrong, it doesn't do them justice. These quirky Midwesterners have jazz chops and jazz panache, but they apply those traits with the muscle of a rock band. Oh yeah, they play rock songs, too: Nirvana's "Smells Like Teen Spirit" and Blondie's "Heart of Glass" on *These Are the Vistas*, the Pixies' "Veluria" and Black Sabbath's "Iron Man" on *Give*. A neat gimmick, and well executed—especially the triumphant crescendoes of the Sabbath cover—but in the end, it's just a gimmick; the real rewards here are to be found in the band's own compositions. The droll singsonginess of "Keep the Bugs off Your Glass and the Bears off Your Ass" (*Vistas*) and the off-center lyricism of "Frog and Toad" (*Give*) demonstrate yet again that truly cool music sneers at the concept of category.   —M.R.

Bad Religion

★★★ How Could Hell Be Any Worse? (Epitaph, 1982)
★ Into the Unknown (Epitaph, 1983)
★★★ Suffer (Epitaph, 1988)
★★★ No Control (Epitaph, 1989)
★★★★ Against the Grain (Epitaph, 1990)
★★★ 80–85 (Epitaph, 1990)
★★★ Generator (Epitaph, 1992)
★★★ Recipe for Hate (Epitaph/Atlantic, 1992–93)
★★★★ Stranger Than Fiction (Dragnet/Sony, 1994)
★★★ All Ages (Epitaph, 1995)
★★ The Gray Race (Atlantic, 1996)
★★★ Tested (Epic, 1997)
★★ No Substance (Atlantic, 1998)
★★ The New America (Atlantic, 2000)
★★★ The Process of Belief (Epitaph, 2002)
★★★ The Empire Strikes First (Epitaph, 2004)

In the late '70s, Southern California's cookie-cutter suburbs were a breeding ground for Ramones mania among bored, leather-jacketed misfits, and their response was to create hardcore: a faster, harder, less melodic version of CBGB-era punk. Bad Religion brought braininess to the mix, and its multisyllabic lyrics—ranging from latchkey-kid autobiography to cautionary political commentary—resonated on a level that set the quintet apart from its smashmouth peers.

Lacking a record label, the band simply started its own, and Bad Religion and the Epitaph imprint became something of a West Coast counterpart to Washington, D.C.'s Dischord, run by Minor Threat bandmates Ian MacKaye (later in Fugazi) and Jeff Nelson. Epitaph became a hothouse for the '90s pop-punk explosion, nurturing the Offspring, Rancid, NOFX, and Pennywise, among others—bands who in many cases eclipsed Bad Religion in commercial impact, but all of whom owe their sound and their careers to the pioneering hardcore band's '80s output.

The place all of those pop-punk disciples started is compiled on *80–85*, which repackages Bad Religion's debut album and other early recordings. It's the quintessential L.A. hardcore primer, an unrefined but exciting mix of compressed musical fury (two-minute or shorter screeds) and angry-nerd lyrics by singer and future biology Ph.D. Greg Graffin, then only in his teens. But the band struggled for years to take the next step. *Into the Unknown*—conspicuously excluded from *80–85*—remains the black sheep of the back catalogue, a head-scratching 180-degree turn toward '70s keyboard pop that essentially broke up the band for a few years.

On *Suffer,* the reunited Bad Religion distills its essence to 15 blast-furnace songs in under 30 minutes; the melodies build to anthemic choruses and then crash abruptly. *No Control* refines the formula and *Against the Grain* perfects it, beefing up the multipart harmonies and achieving a howling clarity. It's the band's mid-career peak, a manifesto on the price of modernization that presages the premillennial hand-wringing heard in countless rock albums a decade later.

Subsequent releases struggle to live up to that standard, and on *Recipe for Hate* the band invited a bevy of admirers (Eddie Vedder among them) to vary the increasingly predictable arrangements. The great leap forward finally arrived with Andy Wallace, hired as the band's first outside producer, who brought a blue-flame clarity to *Stranger than Fiction.* Suddenly the band's songs lunged at the listener with a previously unheard fist-meets-face ferocity, drummer Bobby Schayer proved he could do more than deliver a punk polka beat, and the compact melodies soared, particularly the title song and a sharp remake of "21st Century (Digital Boy)" (originally heard on *Suffer*). Both of the latter tunes were written by guitarist Brett Gure-

witz, and his departure from the band after the release of *Stranger than Fiction* coincided with its demise as a creative force. Graffin's pseudophilosophical lyrics sounded clumsy without Gurewitz's melodies to offset them, and the shared songwriting of *No Substance* and celebrity producers on *The Gray Race* (Ric Ocasek) and *The New America* (Todd Rundgren) did little to pull the band out its rut. Gurewitz's return for *The Process of Belief* and *The Empire Strikes First* restored the balance, and though they broke no ground, the discs were easily the band's strongest releases in a decade. —G.K.

Erykah Badu

★★★   Baduizm (Universal, 1997)
★★★   Live (Universal, 1997)
★★★½   Mama's Gun (Motown, 2000)
★★★   World Wide Underground (Motown, 2003)

She has a sweet-and-sour voice, she preaches self-respect and social idealism, and she's got a love for the cool grooves, minor keys, and impressionistic surprises of jazz. Erykah Badu incorporated all of these strengths into *Baduizm,* a mellow, tasteful album of intelligent R&B, garnering comparisons to Billie Holiday upon its release. Badu cowrote all the record's tracks except for a cover of Atlantic Starr's "4 Leaf Clover," and on songs such as "Appletree," "Afro," and "Certainly" she evinces an impressive sense of loungey sass. It's an ambitious album despite the wobbles in quality—at her best, Badu is just the jaundiced, tenderhearted but realistic jazzy torch singer that the '90s, with its spate of plasticky R&B dolls, needed.

Badu kept the momentum from her debut at a boil with the release of *Live,* a document of how much of a crowd favorite she'd become. A masterful performer in full control of her audience and her material, Badu covers familiar territory—tracks from *Baduizm*—and includes a couple of surprises as well. She does a cocktail-lounge version of the disco hit "Boogie Nights" and unleashes the magnificent "Tyrone," a can't-take-it-anymore lament of monumental proportions.

Mama's Gun looks back toward '70s soul and angular jazz; it's less elliptical and less thickly textured than *Baduizm.* This cool breeze of an album brings hip-hop boasting into the lounge with the mellow "Cleva" and incorporates tricky stop-start jazz instrumentation into an updated girlfight on "Booty." The album spawned a hit with "Bag Lady," but the song is a naive number, offering spiritual aphorisms (such as "Pack light") and lousy advice ("I betcha love can make it better") to the titular down-and-outer. *World Wide Underground* gets too caught up in its gentle hip-hop groove, never going anywhere, except on a few tracks—most notably the vibrant "Danger." —A.B./N.B.

Joan Baez

★★★★   Joan Baez (1960; Vanguard, 1987)
★★★★   Joan Baez 2 (1961; Vanguard, 1987)
★★★★   In Concert/Part One (1963; Vanguard, 1988)
★★★½   In Concert/Part Two (Vanguard, 1963)
★★★★   Joan Baez 5 (Vanguard, 1964)
★★★★   Farewell Angelina (Vanguard, 1965)
★★★   Noel (1966; Vanguard, 1987)
★★★   Portrait (Vanguard, 1966)
★★½   Joan (Vanguard, 1967)
★★★½   Baptism (Vanguard, 1968)
★★★   Any Day Now (Songs of Bob Dylan) (1968; Vanguard, 1987)
★★½   David's Album (Vanguard, 1969)
★★½   One Day at a Time (Vanguard, 1970)
★★★★   The First Ten Years (1970; Vanguard, 1987)
★★★   Blessed Are (Vanguard, 1971)
★★½   Carry It On (Vanguard, 1972)
★★   Come From the Shadows (A&M, 1972)
★★   Where Are You Now, My Son? (Vanguard, 1973)
★★★   Hits, Greatest and Others (Vanguard, 1973)
★★★★   Ballad Book (1974; Vanguard, 1987)
★★★   Gracias a la Vida (Here's to Life) (A&M, 1974)
★★★½   Diamonds and Rust (A&M, 1975)
★★   Live in Japan (Vanguard, 1975)
★★★   Lovesong Album (1976; Vanguard, 1987)
★★★   From Every Stage (A&M, 1976)
★★   Gulf Winds (A&M, 1976)
★★★   Blowing Away (Portrait, 1977)
★★★   Best of Joan Baez (A&M, 1977)
★★½   Honest Lullaby (Portrait, 1979)
★★★½   Country Music Album (1979; Vanguard, 1987)
★★★★   The Night They Drove Old Dixie Down (1979; Vanguard, 1985)
★★½   Very Early Joan Baez (1982; Vanguard, 1987)
★★★   The Contemporary Ballad Book (Vanguard, 1987)
★★★½   Recently (Gold Castle, 1987)
★★★½   Diamonds and Rust in the Bullring (Gold Castle, 1989)
★★★   Play Me Backwards (Virgin, 1992)
★★★   Rare, Live and Classic (Vanguard, 1993)
★★★   Ring Them Bells (Guardian, 1995)
★★★½   Live at Newport (Vanguard, 1996)
★★★½   Greatest Hits (A&M, 1996)
★★★½   Gone from Danger (Guardian, 1997)
★★★   Vanguard Sessions: Baez Sings Dylan (Vanguard, 1998)
★★★½   Live in Europe '83: Children of the Eighties (BMG, 1999)
★★★½   The Millennium Collection (A&M, 1999)
★★★★   Joan Baez, Vol. 2 (Vanguard, 2001)

Joan Baez's musical and political significance are so intertwined that it's hard to assess her impact solely on aesthetic grounds. A leading participant in the '60s cultural revolution, she lent intelligent credibility to radical ideas; and not only did her perfectly enunciated versions of Bob Dylan and Tim Hardin songs win highbrow listeners over to the new music, but her chaste—if sometimes overbearing—seriousness made the message of that music appear all the more critical and "legitimate." In the '70s, long after many of her peers had given up on the notion of music as message, Baez persevered. By the time of the U.S.A. for Africa revival of social consciousness a decade later, she had become a figure largely ignored, dismissed as unhip. The subsequent triumph of intelligent, strong female folk singers, however, testifies, no matter how indirectly, to Baez's spiritual influence— Tracy Chapman and Sarah McLachlan are as certainly her psychic daughters as they are Joni Mitchell's.

Gathered together on a dizzying array of repackagings, Baez's early work is traditional folk ("Man of Constant Sorrow," "Streets of Laredo," "Silver Dagger") of the most pristine variety. Baez's high, resonant, vibrato delivery is sometimes more musically satisfying than interpretively acute; her acoustic guitar playing can be equally hyperprecise, and, too often, the songs sound like a folklorist's reverent guide to the form rather than a singer comfortably emoting. But *Very Early* and *In Concert* are strong collections of Scots/Irish traditionals; and *Ballad Book, Lovesong Album,* and *Country Music Album* remain admirable.

Joan Baez 5 found the singer branching out, delivering an impressive Villa-Lobos classical piece with light-operatic grace and crusading for contemporary songwriters by covering Richard Farina's "Birmingham Sunday," Phil Ochs' "There but for Fortune," and Bob Dylan's "It Ain't Me Babe." Paired romantically with Dylan during the early '60s as the "King and Queen of Folk," she concentrated throughout the decade on reverent readings of his songs. Championing his genius proves to be one of her most endearing gestures—but as her Dylan collection, *Any Day Now,* attests, it's exactly by handling his lyrics as Holy Writ that Baez betrays her signal weakness. As a singer she triumphs when rendering dignified pathos; the ambivalence of Dylan eludes her. *Baptism* is mid-period Baez at her most ambitious. Having nearly exhausted standard folk music, she tries out sung and spoken readings of Welsh ballads, spirituals, and poems by Garcia Lorca, Yevtushenko, Whitman, and e. e. cummings. With orchestral arrangements by Peter Schickele (P.D.Q. Bach), the record has its gorgeous moments, but it's an effortful listen; like a PBS special, it's too apparently "good for you."

In the early '70s, Baez turned out artful covers of Kristofferson and Beatles songs, hit a high point with her version of the Band's "The Night They Drove Old Dixie Down," and on *Hits, Greatest and Others* shows herself to be a creative, if not very revealing, interpreter of high-end pop. She begins, too, to write more of her own material—and *Gulf Winds, Come From the Shadows,* and *Diamonds and Rust* are certainly smarter than most singer/songwriter albums of the time. But her best work *(From Every Stage)* remains her less obviously personal—"Swing Low, Sweet Chariot" and "Joe Hill" are strong and effortless, betraying none of the fretful quality that sometimes weakens her autobiographical songs.

Generating no interest from record companies, Baez was absent from the scene in the early '80s. When she finally returned, however, her work had gained in assurance. *Recently* and *Speaking of Dreams* are graceful sets; working with the Gipsy Kings, Paul Simon, and a host of studio aces, her delivery more casual than in her heyday, she sings about old loves and current causes—and she sounds not only wise but comfortable. *Play Me Backwards* won a deserved Grammy for Best Contemporary Folk Recording; *Gone from Danger* emphasized her contemporary appeal, as she convincingly covered songs by younger writers (Indigo Girls, Mary Chapin Carpenter). In fact, her career and stature were significantly revived in the '90s, as a new audience came to appreciate not only the clarity of her voice but also the courage of her convictions.   —P.E.

LaVern Baker

★★★★	LaVern Baker Sings Bessie Smith (1958; Atlantic, 1988)
★★★★★	Precious Memories/LaVern Baker Sings Bessie Smith (1959, 1958; Collectables, 2000)
★★★★★	Soul on Fire: The Best of LaVern Baker (Atlantic, 1991)
★★★	Live in Hollywood '91 (Rhino, 1991)
★★½	Woke Up This Mornin' (DRG, 1992)
★★★★½	LaVern/LaVern Baker (Collectables, 1998)
★★★½	See See Rider/Blues Ballads (Collectables, 1998)
★★★★★	The Legend at Her Best (Collectables, 2000)

If anyone came to her profession with an unassailable pedigree, it was LaVern Baker. Born Delores Williams in Chicago in 1929, the niece of Memphis Minnie,

Baker started her recording career in 1950 with the Eddie Penigar Band. Those sides were unissued, but a year later she appeared on three Okeh singles as Bea Baker, then billed herself as Little Miss Sharecropper and recorded for National, RCA/Victor, and Columbia. In 1952, using the name LaVern Baker, she joined Todd Rhodes and His Orchestra and recorded for King; she then signed to Atlantic the following year. There, she delivered the sultry slice of urgent R&B "Soul on Fire," a cataclysmic performance that found Baker employing a stunning array of vocal tools ranging from a deep, longing blues growl to tearful glottal stops to wanton upper-register shouts. It was a portent of things to come. In early '55 she had her first hit, "Tweedlee Dee," which had a near-three-month run on the pop chart, peaking at #14; between 1956 and 1963 she placed six more singles in the Top 50, with 1956's "Jim Dandy" rising to the Top 20 and 1958's wrenching "I Cried a Tear" peaking at #6 in its five-month chart run.

As her Aunt Minnie had done more than 20 years earlier, Baker stepped into a man's world, making a lasting impression on fans and on female vocalists who came after her. Hers was a voice that would not be denied, whether she was belting out an uptempo pop hit or probing the nuances of Doc Pomus' poignant blues ballad "My Happiness Forever," which demands the singer put across equal measures of resilience and vulnerability from one phrase to another. And on those occasions when she got hold of a song that took her back to her Baptist church roots, as she did on Leiber and Stoller's "Saved," she could testify with the best, using her big, booming voice to proclaim the Lord's goodness and mercy for all to hear. She was never better than on her 1959 gospel album, *Precious Memories,* on which she sounds like a cross between Mahalia Jackson and Sister Rosetta Tharpe. Her measured, mesmerizing version of Thomas A. Dorsey's standard "Precious Lord" is alone worth the price of admission, but housewreckers such as the propulsive "Didn't It Rain" and the ebullient gospel-soul of "Everytime I Feel the Spirit" will get the blood boiling and the spirit soaring.

The Atlantic years are succinctly documented on *Soul on Fire.* The other essential document from this time is the one that best reveals the depth and breadth of Baker's artistry: *LaVern Baker Sings Bessie Smith* links the former most dramatically to the latter's legacy, not merely by its title but by the intelligence and personality of Baker's interpretations. Here she is by turns bawdy ("Baby Doll"), strong and independent ("I Ain't Gonna Play No Second Fiddle," "Young Woman's Blues"), vulnerable ("Empty Bed Blues," "After You've Gone"), and bowed but proud ("Nobody Knows You When You're Down and Out"). Among a stellar supporting cast of players, Buck Clayton on trumpet and Vic Dickenson on trombone stand out with solo turns that buttress Baker's tour de force with eloquent instrumental commentaries. In asserting her heritage, Baker tells anyone who will listen that this music defines her. She sings Bessie Smith in grand style—but the control, phrasing, and attitude are all LaVern Baker, whose best-known work barely suggests her great gift as an artist.

These critical years in Baker's career have been fleshed out recently by the Collectables label, which has reissued six of her Atlantic albums on single-disc twofers and has combined four of those titles on the double CD *The Legend at Her Best.* The best of the lot is the gospel album *Precious Memories* packaged on the same disc with *LaVern Baker Sings Bessie Smith*— rarely have God and Mammon been evoked so profoundly as they are here, but the line between the two is almost indistinguishable when Baker digs into a song. Another twofer combines Baker's first two albums, *LaVern* and *LaVern Baker,* and here is an object lesson in how Atlantic transformed one of its greatest singers into an artist who made her commercial bones singing frothy novelty songs. On *LaVern,* she's a gut-bucket R&B singer, growling and shouting her way through Chuck Willis' "Of Course I Do" and one of her own songs, "Lots and Lots of Love," putting a bluesy spin on the pop classic "Harbor Lights," and turning "Everybody's Somebody's Fool" into an anguished torch song with pop affectations. On *LaVern Baker* she's lightened up her husky tone just a bit, dropped the blues singer's bent notes and sultry growls and supplanted them with a perky, wailing style better suited to overtly commercial (and lightweight, albeit irresistibly bouncy) material such as "Jim Dandy," "Tra La La," and "Tweedlee Dee." Not that she abandoned her essence—a hymnlike treatment of "That Lucky Old Sun" takes her right back to the church, whereas Doc Pomus' "My Happiness Forever" is strictly after-hours R&B testifying. The blues belter and balladeer reigns on the twofer featuring *See See Rider* and *Blues Ballads.* The latter is the gut wrencher of the two, featuring some first-rate songs from Doc Pomus and Mort Shuman ("You're Teasing Me"), Neil Sedaka and Howie Greenfield ("I Waited Too Long"), Leiber and Stoller ("Whippersnapper"), along with W.C. Handy's "St. Louis Blues" and a Baker original, "So High, So Low." There's no going wrong with any of these Collectables twofers—the song selection, the arrangements, and especially Baker's sense of the song as expressed in her interpretive choices are all impeccable and frequently stunning. In the absence of a box set, the double CD *The*

Legend at Her Best is a satisfying choice in that it offers all the tracks from *LaVern/LaVern Baker* and *Precious Memories/LaVern Baker Sings Bessie Smith*—a really broad perspective on the range Baker exhibited in these years on the four strongest albums of her Atlantic tenure.

When the hits stopped coming in the '60s, Baker continued touring and recording before dropping out of sight by decade's end. When found almost 20 years later, she was happily engaged as the entertainment director of a U.S. military NCO club in the Philippines, where she had been raising a family and performing for GIs. In 1988 she returned to the States to participate in Atlantic's 40th-birthday celebration at Madison Square Garden—where she brought the house down. Gradually she made her way back, performing selected concert dates, cutting "Slow Rollin' Mama" for the 1988 *Dick Tracy* soundtrack, then following her friend and former Atlantic artist Ruth Brown in the starring role in Broadway's *Black and Blue.* In early 1991 she was elected to the Rock and Roll Hall of Fame, and followed that honor with her return to recording. *Live in Hollywood '91* is the resulting document of her early comeback, being a performance recorded at Hollywood's Cinegrill club in the Roosevelt Hotel. The years have been kind to her voice; here, it sounds even more powerful than it does on some of the Atlantic sides, and age has lent it an earthy huskiness that deepens the feeling she brings to bluesier material such as "Tomorrow Night," a song identified with Lonnie Johnson. Biggest surprise: the venerable "Tennessee Waltz" done up in a strutting tempo, with Baker tossing off the verses as if she were engaged in idle chitchat; then she swoops and glides through the chorus, her voice suddenly exposing the hurt and longing she feels below the surface—a remarkable performance.

Six months after her Cinegrill performance, Baker ended her 20-year exile on record by cutting a studio album, *Woke Up This Mornin',* in New York with a host of top-flight musicians, among them guitarist Cornell Dupree, bassist Chuck Rainey, drummer Bernard Purdie, and powerhouse Ronald Cuber, who manhandles the baritone sax in delivering one sterling solo after another. Technically out of print now, this album remains available on some retail Internet sites, and is well worth seeking out. True to her versatile nature, Baker assays a wide range of material here. Blues and R&B dominate the proceedings, with the torchy reading of "Body and Soul" standing out, although she one-ups herself on "Trouble in Mind," going low for some deep blues as Dupree and Cuber support her with well-crafted, emotion-packed solos. Elsewhere, she makes a good, lusty run at the Bee Gees' "To Love

Somebody," imbuing the song with a bold eroticism uncommon to most interpretations; does Otis Redding proud with a fiery take on "Can't Turn You Loose"; then closes out the proceedings with another reading of "Tennessee Waltz," again done uptempo, but with Baker's performance even more nuanced than that heard on her live album. There are a few missteps here—the treatments of Eddie Floyd's "Knock on Wood" and William Bell's "You Don't Miss Your Water" are a bit too stolid in their arrangements, and Baker sounds unduly restrained as a result.

Recipient of a Pioneer Achievement Award from the Rhythm and Blues Foundation in 1989, Baker performed in her later years despite advancing physical disabilities. A diabetic, she eventually lost both of her legs to the disease, and also suffered a series of strokes in the '90s. Undeterred, though, she continued performing from a wheelchair until her disease caught up with her for good on March 10, 1997, stilling one of the most authoritative voices of the last half century. —D.M.

Afrika Bambaataa

★★ United DJ's of America: Electro-Funk Breakdown (Moonshine/DMC, 1999)
★★★ Looking for the Perfect Beat 1980–1985 (Tommy Boy, 2001)
★★★ Afrika Bambaataa Presents Eastside (Obsessive, U.K., 2003)

Afrika Bambaataa is one of hip-hop's seminal figures, both as DJ (his nickname was "Master of Records") and as record maker. *Looking for the Perfect Beat* covers his early work as handily as you could want—all that's missing is some liner notes. It kicks off with 1980's "Zulu Nation Throw Down," in which Bam's then-crew, the Cosmic Force, chants party rhymes over live funk (including a drummer who paradiddles just this side of disastrous) to the breaka-breaka-dawn with the infectious brio of the Furious 5 or the Funky 4 + 1. 1981's "Jazzy Sensation" beefs up the sound and smooths out the rhymes, but it's "Planet Rock," from 1982, that changed the world. Combining a pair of Kraftwerk tunes ("Numbers" and "Trans-Europe Express") over an earth-quaking groove and fuzzy call-and-response vocals from the Soul Sonic Force, the record codified both electro and Latin freestyle and remains a classic that can rock any party, any crowd, anytime. Its formula pointed the way to Bambaataa's future, including two more hits in the same vein (1983's "Looking for the Perfect Beat" and 1984's "Renegades of Funk") and the more humdrum fare that takes up *Perfect Beat*'s second half. Similarly, Bam's DJ mix *United DJs of America* is electro-heavy

but lacks inspiration, though a couple of tracks (Uberzone's "Freaks," Bam's "2 Kool 4 Skool") almost make up for it. —M.M.

Bananarama

★★½ Deep Sea Skiving (London, 1983)
★★★ Bananarama (London, 1984)
★★½ True Confessions (London, 1986)
★★★ Wow! (Polydor, 1987)
★★★★ Greatest Hits Collection (Polydor, 1988)
★★ Pop Life (London, 1991)
★★★½ The Essentials (Rhino, 2002)

It would not be too great an exaggeration to suggest that Bananarama was the original Spice Girls—except that in this case, the emphasis would be on sugar and everything nice. Starting off with more enthusiasm than talent, the trio—Sarah Dallin, Keren Woodward, and Siobhan Fahey—found stardom despite its musical limitations.

As in the old days, most of the credit for their success belonged with Bananarama's producers, the suitably anonymous teams of Swain-Jolley and Stock-Aitken-Waterman. *Deep Sea Skiving*, an agreeable hodgepodge that flaunted Bananarama's amateurishness while nonetheless delivering a few decent singles, is most memorable for the mock-exotic "Aie a Mwana" and the chipper, Swain-Jolley–produced "Shy Boy." Not wishing to mess with a winning formula, Swain-Jolley were retained to produce all of *Bananarama* and most of *True Confessions*, although with somewhat diminishing returns; their embrace of unison vocal lines pulls a certain poignancy from the B-girls' voices (as "Cruel Summer," from *Bananarama*, demonstrates), but diminishes their overall pop appeal.

Enter S-A-W, a neo-disco production team that in 1986 was just entering its ascendancy. Not only did S-A-W hand the trio its biggest U.S. hit with an impossibly upbeat remake of the Shocking Blue hit "Venus," but it gave the group backing tracks so irrepressibly tuneful that Bananarama's vocal strengths (or lack thereof) were essentially beside the point. As such, *Wow!* is a perfect pop bonbon, from hook-heavy dance tunes such as "I Heard a Rumour" and "I Can't Help It" to relatively low-key confections such as "Nathan Jones." No wonder *The Greatest Hits Collection*—track for track, the group's best album—relies so heavily upon this period.

Success, however, is a cruel mistress, turning the head of even the most marginally talented. Siobhan Fahey, after marrying Dave Stewart of Eurythmics, left just before *Hits*, and Jacquie O'Sullivan was brought in as B-girl number three, a change more noticeable in the album art than in the sound of the music. The effect of the absence of Stock-Aitken-Waterman on *Pop Life,* however, was much more pronounced. Despite the efforts of ex–Killing Joke bassist Youth to add some edge to the girls' sound, their meringuelike voices seem largely unaffected by his efforts, and consequently *Pop Life* suffers.

O'Sullivan bailed, whereupon Dallin and Woodward recorded several albums—*Please Yourself, Violet,* and *Exotica*—as a duo. Mercifully, the first two have been deleted, while the third never saw U.S. release. —J.D.C.

The Band

★★★★★	Music From Big Pink (Capitol, 1968)	
★★★★★	The Band (Capitol, 1969)	
★★★★	Stage Fright (Capitol, 1970)	
★★½	Cahoots (Capitol, 1971)	
★★★★	Rock of Ages (Capitol, 1972)	
★★★	Moondog Matinee (Capitol, 1973)	
★★★½	Northern Lights—Southern Cross (Capitol, 1975)	
★★★★	The Best of the Band (Capitol, 1976)	
★★½	Islands (Capitol, 1977)	
★★★★	The Last Waltz (Warner Bros., 1978)	
★★★	Jericho (WEA/Rhino, 1993)	
★★★	High on the Hog (WEA/Rhino, 1996)	
★★★½	Jubilation (WEA/Rhino, 1998)	
★★★	The Best of the Band, Vol. 2 (WEA/Rhino, 1999)	
★★★★½	Greatest Hits (Capitol, 2000)	

The Band didn't have a bona fide star, but the first two albums from the mostly Canadian outfit are essential influences for almost every country-rock band that followed, from Little Feat to Lucinda Williams to Uncle Tupelo. While honing their chops in Canada as backup players for the Arkansas-born rockabilly singer Ronnie Hawkins, the Band developed a strong sense of their roles as musicians and singers. They also heard a lot of tall tales about the American South that would inspire their later music. When the group left Hawkins to eventually back Bob Dylan during his mid-'60s transformation from acoustic folkie to rock poet, guitarist Robbie Robertson and keyboardist Richard Manuel absorbed Dylan's literary approach to songwriting. In 1967, the Band moved into a country house (dubbed "Big Pink") in upstate New York, where they came up with the songs for their extraordinary first album.

Music From Big Pink introduces a group with a clarity of vision that had never before been heard in rock & roll. While the Beatles were downing LSD and writing about tangerine dreams and marmalade skies,

Big Pink was remarkably simple and direct, right down to the tiniest details. In the opening track, "Tears of Rage," the sensitivity and grace of the singing and nuances of each instrumental brushstroke underscore the desperate plea of a father saddened by his daughter's hotheadedness: "We carried you in our arms on Independence Day/And now you'd throw us all aside and put us all away."

From Robertson's stinging Stratocaster leads to Levon Helm's raunchy drumming, Rick Danko's down-home bass lines, Manuel's gospel/R&B piano playing, and Garth Hudson's majestic, churchlike organ textures, it seemed at times as if the Band was trying to work up a soundtrack for Democracy itself. But it was Robertson's remarkable ability to match the songs with the right voices—Helm's Southern twang, Danko's mournful croon, or Manuel's haunting tenor—that elevated the Band from a great musical ensemble to artful storytellers. *Big Pink* is basically a collection of short stories about ordinary Americans—as powerfully and gracefully painted onto a musical canvas as Twain's characters were written into books. The album's most famous track, "The Weight," encapsulated the mood of the album and of the times, offering a simple tale of human vulnerability in a time of great upheaval.

Robertson and company expanded on their reputation as American storytellers on *The Band.* Kicking off with the sweeping "Across the Great Divide," the group's second album combines uptempo songs (the rural dance tune "Rag Mama Rag" and working-class allegory "Up on Cripple Creek") with more delicate personal meditations (the ethereal solitude of "Whispering Pines" and bitter betrayal of "Unfaithful Servant"). This time, Arkansas native Helm's influence on Robertson's songwriting is evident, and his voice is more prominent on the album. His Southern drawl gives credibility to "The Night They Drove Old Dixie Down," a populist anthem written from the bitter perspective of a proud but powerless Civil War soldier.

With the success of the Band's first two albums came the by-products of fame: substance abuse, exhaustion, grandiosity, and greed. As a result, *Stage Fright* found the Band slipping. Robertson's songwriting took a more personal turn as he dealt with the psychological toll on his group. The highlights—"The Shape I'm In," "Daniel and the Sacred Harp," and "Stage Fright"—reveal a growing sense of anxiety and cynicism. While the playing—especially Hudson's evocative organ and accordion parts—remains first rate, the sharply detailed character sketches of the first two albums are in shorter supply.

Cahoots is a near-total wash. The carnivalesque atmosphere of the music and cinematic sweep of the lyrics never completely gel. Only the lead-off track, "Life Is a Carnival," "4% Pantomime" (with a guest spot by Van Morrison), and Helm's gorgeous interpretation of Dylan's "When I Paint My Masterpiece" deliver anything approaching the quality of the Band's previous work. The dubious distinction of *Cahoots* is that it contains Robertson's first truly awful song, "The Moon Struck One." Perhaps the most portentous song is the prophetic plea "Where Do We Go From Here?"

The Band never completely recovered from the lost innocence of *Stage Fright* and *Cahoots*. While *Rock of Ages* is an excellent double-disc document of the group's early-'70s live performances, *Moondog Matinee* finds the Band retreating to the safety of its collective childhood with a set of interesting if unremarkable cover versions of '50s and '60s R&B songs. On *Northern Lights—Southern Cross* Robertson reclaims his reputation as one of rock's great songwriters ("Ophelia," "Acadian Driftwood," and "It Makes No Difference"), although the synthesizer flourishes date the overall sound. *Islands* is a barely listenable collection of outtakes the Band released to fulfull its contractual obligations to Capitol Records.

When the Band decided to call it quits (at least, for a while), they staged a farewell concert in San Francisco featuring an all-star cast of their musician friends (including Neil Young, Joni Mitchell, Van Morrison, Eric Clapton, the Staple Singers, Muddy Waters, Dr. John, and Emmylou Harris) and mentors (Ronnie Hawkins and Bob Dylan). *The Last Waltz*, the Martin Scorsese film that chronicled the concert, is one of the best rock movies of all time, and the concert album of the same name (recently expanded into a four-CD box set) is an excellent companion piece.

In 1983, the Band (without Robertson) regrouped and began touring small clubs again, but they didn't record a new album for another decade. *Jericho* was dedicated to Manuel, who had committed suicide while on the road with the Band in the mid-'80s. It was a surprising return to form for the Band, even without Robertson, its primary songwriter and guiding light. Gone are the sweeping storylines and stinging guitars, but the Band's signature blend of vocals, instrumentation, and American musical styles remains intact. *Jericho* lacks the edge of the Band at its prime, but the interpretations of Bruce Springsteen ("Atlantic City"), Bob Dylan ("Blind Willie McTell") and Muddy Waters ("Stuff You Gotta Watch") and the moving tribute to Manuel ("Too Soon Gone") make this album a fascinating milestone in the group's development. *High on the Hog* basically repeats *Jericho*'s formula, with less

successful results. *Jubilation* finds the reunited Band growing, its mix of acoustic instruments and roughened voices revealing a new, dignified maturity. By 1999, however, the death of Danko and the loss of Helm's voice to throat cancer treatments effectively put an end to the Band.

Greatest Hits is a misnomer—"Up on Cripple Creek" was the Band's only Top 30 single—but it's a solid chronological anthology of the group's best songs, and offers more music than the earlier collection, *The Best of the Band*. *The Best of the Band, Vol. 2* is a decent overview of the reunited Band's work. All of the original albums have been remastered and reissued with previously unreleased outtakes and detailed liner notes, and are well worth seeking out.   —M.K.

The Bangles

★★★   All Over the Place (Columbia, 1984)
★★½   Different Light (Columbia, 1985)
★★½   Everything (Columbia, 1988)
★★★   Greatest Hits (Columbia, 1990)
★★½   Doll Revolution (Koch, 2003)

Mining the early Beatles for rock & roll catchiness and the Mamas and the Papas for vocal harmonies, this self-conscious L.A. girl group began with '60s revivalism of an earnest, unexamined sort and ended up with lush, radio-perfect pop. Extremely capable practitioners of hitcraft, the band played tightly and chose their songs well—and achieved gigantically the dubious triumph of sound over significance. With "Going Down to Liverpool" and "Hero Takes a Fall," *All Over the Place* presented a quartet of British Invasion fans well versed in the chiming guitars and brisk melodies of a competent second-string act of that era (the Bangles were hardly fake Kinks, for example; more like fake Searchers).

Different Light reaped hits aplenty, in Prince's "Manic Monday," the funky novelty "Walk Like an Egyptian," and Jules Shear's lovely "If She Knew What She Wants." Rhythm guitarist Susanna Hoffs mastered a singing style that combined pep, coy sweetness, and an occasional plaintive resonance; bassist Michael Steele's "Following" featured tough-talk vocalizing that nicely leavened the band's tendency toward a cloying, somewhat arch delivery.

On *Everything*, Hoffs' "In Your Room" caught definitively the Bangles' gift for pastiche—its strings recalled the Stones' "2,000 Light Years from Home," its organ riffs echoed the Detroit Wheels, its guitar was crunchy like sanitized punk. "Eternal Flame" was a widescreen, fairly bathetic ballad, its orchestral sweep connoting a new, unwelcome "seriousness." Predictably, *Greatest Hits* is the best Bangles—no real thematic consciousness enlivened their individual albums, and on the compilation there's the nice addition of two sharp singles, Paul Simon's "Hazy Shade of Winter" and the Grass Roots' "Where Were You When I Needed You?" Far more authentic an enterprise than, say, the Monkees, the Bangles put out smart, clean, calculated pop music. After a number of ill-fated solo projects, the group came together in 2000 for the inevitable reunion. But even nostalgia has its limits. —P.E./E.L.

Buju Banton

★★★	Stamina Daddy (VP Records, 1992)	
★★★	Mr. Mention (Penthouse, 1993)	
★★★½	Voice of Jamaica (Penthouse/Mercury Records, 1993)	
★★★★½	'Til Shiloh (Penthouse/Loose Cannon, 1995)	
★★★★	Buju Banton: The Early Years (Penthouse/VP Records, 1996)	
★★★½	Inna Heights (Penthouse/VP Records/Island Records/PolyGram, 1997)	
★★★½	Unchained Spirit (Penthouse Productions/Epitaph, 1999)	
★★★	Buju Banton and Posse: Rudeboys Inna Ghetto (IMC Music, 1999)	
★★★	Friends for Life (Penthouse/Epitaph/VP Records, 2003)	

When he was 17, he penned and voiced "Boom Bye Bye"; two years later, thanks to that track, which advocates shooting gay men in the head, Buju Banton was the international poster boy for homophobia. No excuses, but "batty bwoy" lyrics are de rigueur for Jamaican MCs, yet today's Buju is the sole reggae artist to publicly acknowledge one's right to love whom one chooses.

Despite his grave juvenile error, Buju is the worthiest successor to the mantle of Bob Marley. "He's our sun," says the respected DJ (reggae rapper/producer) Tony Rebel. "Every other reggae artist revolves around him." Cleaving to Bob's implicit rule that yuh haffe sing rough for the sufferah and following the Gong's generous example of lyrical inclusiveness, Buju's coarse, resinous vocals are more compelling than just about anyone else's tones.

The 15th child of an inner-city Kingston family, Buju descends from Jamaica's Maroons—fugitive slaves who tormented the British for nearly 100 years, until the colonial government was forced to sign a treaty that guaranteed Maroons perpetual freedom and self-government. Chubby baby cheeks earned Mark Myrie his first name—*buju* is the Maroon term for "breadfruit"—but soon after Buju passed through the gates of the fabled Penthouse Studio, he con-

quered Jamaica's dancehalls as a gangly, rail-thin, gravel-voiced teen, a.k.a. Mr. Mention.

That sobriquet became the title of his debut set, a collection of fifteen sizzling boomshots. Dropping his tightly coiled, percussive bass flow over relentless digital beats, Buju slugs rhymes fast, hard, and deep, like Ali at his prime. Even if non-Jamaicans sometimes can't penetrate his thick patois flow, like all reggae greats Buju draws listeners into his world. Tracks such as "Batty Rider," a bouncing hymn to scantily clad dancehall "models," evoke dancehall's escape from tropical ghetto pressures via blissful self-regard and sinewy hip grinds. Yet even then, Buju revealed a razor-keen social conscience in "How the World a Run," an incisive dissection of 20th-century postcolonialism.

In 1993, soon after NYC-based indie Loose Cannon released Buju's aptly titled *Voice of Jamaica,* "Boom Bye Bye" surfaced in a reggae compilation and Buju's crossover plans tanked. Two years later, though, he stunned the international reggae axis by regenerating roots-style reggae with *'Til Shiloh.* Alternating his signature DJ bluster with a new Marley-esque yet quintessentially Buju singing style, *Shiloh* is powered by a shatteringly honest emotionalism and a soul guidance unmarred by the usual pieties.

Buju sings in "Prelude," "Though you may think my faith is in vain/'Til Shiloh we will chant Rastafari's name," then chuckles and muses, "All my days/seems they have been wasted, eh?" Buju had been down to the river and reborn as a Rasta man, but he hadn't wasted a day. Whether wringing every drop of emotion from the soaring title track or treading more familiar good-body-gal turf in the rough-riding "Champion," Buju proves that a reggae artist can praise Jah and Janet equally. With that release, dancehall and roots styles became simply opposite ends of reggae's wide-ranging territory. Followup albums *Inna Heights* (nearly as sublime as *Shiloh*), *Unchained Spirit,* and *Friends for Life* offer the same compelling blend of reggae's rowdy and rapturous. —E.O.

Barenaked Ladies

★★★	Gordon (Reprise, 1992)	
★★★	Maybe You Should Drive (Reprise, 1994)	
★★	Born on a Pirate Ship (Reprise, 1996)	
★★★½	Rock Spectacle (Reprise, 1996)	
★★★½	Stunt (Reprise, 1998)	
★★½	Maroon (Reprise, 2000)	
★★★½	Disc One: All Their Greatest Hits (1991–2001) (Reprise, 2001)	
★★	Everything to Everyone (Reprise, 2003)	

From the Coasters to Biz Markie, comedy has occupied an important place in rock history. But from

"Purple People Eater" to Jimmy Fallon, it's occupied a dubious (often downright irritating) space as well. Repetition is the key to pop brilliance—a song has to sound better each time you hear it. But repetition makes jokes stale—when's the last time you laughed at a bumper sticker? Musicians seem to realize this. Maybe that's why no one wants to be a gag band. Or maybe it's just that pranksters get laid less often than brooding types.

So, for all their shortcomings, you've got to give the Ladies credit for not going all serious on us. These amiable Canadians are actually more endearing the weaker their jokes are. You root for the songwriting team of Ed Robertson and Steven Page, who are considered a national treasure among their countrymen. Both the intensity of their cult and the limitations of its size were surely earned—they deserved as much notice and not much more. Tracks such as "Be My Yoko Ono" are so benign they never threaten to split your sides. But if you're warmed by the chuckle, most any of these discs will make you smile and tap your feet.

For the rest of us, there's the best-of. In the late '90s, when pop mutations thrived amid a confused marketplace, the absurdist "rap" "One Week" was the big breakthrough. Even better is "It's All Been Done," a wise (not to mention catchy) perspective on continuing to make new stuff this late in the history of stuff. No, they won't be giants, but the gawky "If I Had $1,000,000" uncovers the elusive secret at the heart of the Ladies' popularity—how to overindulge in modesty without resorting to a self-effacing cringe. —K.H.

MC Paul Barman

★★★★   It's Very Stimulating (Wordsound, 2000)
★★★   Paulellujah! (Coup d'État, 2002)

Paul Barman—Brown graduate, sometime illustrator and puppet-maker, short, bespectacled Jew—found a perfect partner in legendary hip-hop producer Prince Paul, himself a comedian of some repute. Despite appearances, it was an inspired pairing. The producer's bemused, jovial beats on *It's Very Stimulating* proved to be a dream fit for Barman's not-quite-on-the-beat flow and nasal pitch. As an MC, Barman had nothing but surprises: a predilection for polysyllabic rhymes, esoteric lyrical references, and an aww-shucks folksiness that's only available to genre outsiders. His debut name-checked Chuck Close, Wallace Shawn, and Krzysztof Kieslowski, and also boasted that "my dandy voice makes the most anti-choice granny's panties moist." Elsewhere, he argued against test-based school curricula and fantasized about making it in the Metropolitan Museum of Art.

Paulellujah!, his first full-length album, stretched the shtick to its extreme. "I make def tunes," he says on "Excuse Me," "take from MF Doom and Jeff Koons." Barman uses a host of producers here, and the lack of sonic consistency holds him back, although some of his most transcendent storytelling comes on the two-part "Anarchist Bookstore," a rambling tale about the late-afternoon goings-on of a leftist gaggle. At his worst, Barman is clunky and awkward, but at his best, his songs are like tone poems with a purpose, exploring the multitudinous permutations of good ol' syllables, and the various meanings such an experiment might evoke. —J.C.

Syd Barrett

★★★   The Madcap Laughs (1970; EMI, 1990)
★★★   Barrett (Capitol/EMI, 1970/1990)
★★★   The Peel Sessions (Dutch East India/Strange Fruit, 1987)
★★   Opel (Capitol/EMI, 1989; Alliance, 1996)
★★   Crazy Diamond (Harvest/EMI, 1993)
★★★½   The Best of Syd Barrett: Wouldn't You Miss Me? (Harvest/Capitol/EMI, 2001)

With Brian Wilson, Roky Erickson, Kurt Cobain, and a handful of others, Syd Barrett is among rock's most egregiously troubled geniuses, a drug casualty whose primary legacy is his crucial role in founding Pink Floyd and steering the band through its initial batch of singles and a monumental debut album, *The Piper at the Gates of Dawn*. On that album, Barrett pioneered space rock with his singing, songwriting, and guitar playing only to lose his grip on the band, and reality, as LSD slowly did him in. His subsequent solo recordings—done with the empathetic production assistance of friends such as manager Peter Jenner and David Gilmour, the guitarist who replaced him in the Floyd—provide mere glimpses of what might have been.

At their best, *The Madcap Laughs* and *Barrett* can be entrancing. Against muted backdrops that suggest a warmer, more bucolic answer to the Floyd's epic psychedelia, Barrett strums a guitar and gently sing-speaks lyrics that combine nursery-rhyme innocence with nightmare visions. His idiosyncrasies meld with haunting melodies on "Octopus," "Terrapin," and "Baby Lemonade," but the albums contain too many fragments, wanderings, and false starts to qualify as more than cult items—it's like listening to a meltdown in slow motion, with the listener as voyeur. The problem is exacerbated on *Opel*, which collects leftovers such as "Word Song," in which the singer sounds like he's trying to identify the strange pictures floating through his ravaged mind. *Crazy Diamond* collects all three albums, plus even more depressing bonus tracks, to create a picture of madness that verges on the exploitive.

The Best of Syd Barrett, on the other hand, plays like a celebration of eccentricity. Bereft of the filler that marred Barrett's studio releases, it's a coherent statement of outsider art, fleshed out with two previously unreleased songs. These include the solo acoustic "Bob Dylan Blues," a witty and charmingly low-key take on a singer that Barrett, in a better world, might've one day rivaled. —G.K.

Basement Jaxx

★★★★	Atlantic Jaxx Recordings: A Compilation (1998; Astralwerks, 2001)
★★★★	Remedy (Astralwerks, 1999)
★★★★½	Rooty (Astralwerks, 2001)
★★★★½	Kish Kash (Astralwerks, 2003)

House music tends to mythologize itself as an urban wonderland where anything can happen, but few artists make music that lives up to that fantasy the way Basement Jaxx's does. South Londoners Simon Ratcliffe and Felix Buxton, who began recording tracks together in the mid-'90s, reimagine Prince's Paisley Park as a bustling, shape-shifting grooveathon taking in dub, psychedelia, Vocoder chants, soca horns, Latin-jazz vibes, football-hooligan yell-alongs, and tuff-girl vocals, all set to a luscious, irresistible 4/4 beat.

You can hear Ratcliffe and Buxton's vision taking shape on the dozen early sides collected on *Atlantic Jaxx Recordings: A Compilation.* "Samba Magic" and "Belo Horizonti" (the latter credited to the Heartists) explore Latin music with an assurance shocking in a pair of pasty Englishmen, while the thuggish stomp of "Set Yo Body Free" and the euphoric synth stabs of "Fly Life" are definitive mid-'90s club anthems. It's *Remedy,* though, where the duo goes nova. From the Spanish guitar strum that hooks the synth-string disco of "Rendez-Vu" to the carnival-bound horn blasts of "Bingo Bango" to "Same Old Show" 's playful retooling of the Selecter's "On My Radio," the album displays more variety than most house DJs demonstrate in a six-hour set. The disc's masterpiece was "Red Alert," the best "1999" rewrite ever, complete with a bass hook every bit as irresistible as Prince's synth riff.

Improbably, *Rooty* was even better. Some club rats cried sellout because the Jaxx made the tunes short and structured them like actual songs instead of stretches of beat punctuated by occasional stuff on top. Everybody else danced their asses off. The irresistible "Romeo" plays follow-the-bouncing-hook, while "Get Me Off" and "S.F.M. (Sexy Feline Machine)" make electro bleeps signify like hot-'n'-heavy

breathing. And "Where's Your Head At" turns a Gary Numan sample until it both jacks your body and bangs your head at once, escaping house's often narrow parameters by refusing to put on the same old show. *Kish Kash,* released in 2003, is more kaleidoscopic-leaning pop, with 'N Sync's JC Chasez buttering up the swarming rock-dance "Plug It In," Siouxsie Sioux making the punk-disco title cut stick like porcupine quills, and Meshell Ndegéocello paying explicit homage to Prince on the nasty "Right Here's the Spot." Unknowns like Emily (the piping "Hot and Cold") and Totlyn Jackson ("Supersonic") hold their own, as Buxton and Ratcliffe prove themselves to be the best production team in the world this side of the Neptunes. —M.M.

The Beach Boys

★★★/★★★	Surfin' Safari/Surfin' USA (1962/1963; Capitol, 2001)
★★★★/★★★	Surfer Girl/Shut Down, Vol. 2 (1963/1964; Capitol, 2001)
★★★/★★	Little Deuce Coupe/All Summer Long (1963/1964; Capitol, 2001)
★★	Beach Boys Christmas Album (1964; Capitol, 2001)
★★★/★★★	The Beach Boys Concert/Live in London (1964/1970; Capitol, 2001)
★★★★/★★	Today!/Summer Days (and Summer Nights!!) (1965; Capitol, 2001)
★★★/★★	Party/Stack-o-Tracks (1965/1968; Capitol, 2001)
★★★★★	Pet Sounds (Capitol, 1966)
★★★/★★★★	Smiley Smile/Wild Honey (1967; Capitol, 2001)
★★★★/★★★★	Friends/20/20 (1968/1969; Capitol, 2001)
★★★★★/★★★	Sunflower/Surf's Up (1970/1971; Capitol, 2000)
★★/★★	Carl and the Passions—So Tough/Holland (1972/1973; Capitol, 2000)
★★★	The Beach Boys in Concert (Capitol, 1973)
★★/★★★★	15 Big Ones/Love You (1976/1977; Capitol, 2000)
★/★	M.I.U./L.A. (Light Album) (1978/1979; Capitol, 2000)
★/★	Keepin' the Summer Alive/The Beach Boys (1980/1985; Capitol, 2000)
★★★★	Good Vibrations Box (Capitol, 1993)
★★★★★	Pet Sounds Box (Capitol, 1997)
★★★	Greatest Hits, Vol. 1, 2, 3 (Capitol, 1999)
★★	Endless Harmony (Capitol, 2000)

No pop musician has expressed the thrill and pain of being a teenager better than the Beach Boys' Brian Wilson. Early hits such as "Surfin' U.S.A.," "Little Deuce Coupe," "Fun, Fun, Fun," and "I Get Around" provided a road map to '60s suburban California kicks, and put dreams of riding the waves at Doheney, Del Mar, Tressles, and Laguna in the minds of kids who'd never even seen the Pacific Ocean. Of course, not all the songs were about waves and cars—from the start many were about Brian Wilson's own loneliness, vulnerability, and deep psychic pain. The delicately melancholy "In My Room" and the yearning ballad "Surfer Girl," both from 1963, hinted at a heavy undertow pulling below the group's frothy surface.

Wilson formed the Beach Boys in 1961 when he was 20, with his two younger brothers, Carl and Dennis, their cousin Mike Love, and neighbor Alan Jardine (who was replaced on two early albums by another childhood friend, David Marks). The group's first recording, the crude doo-wop anthem "Surfin," became a regional radio hit and drew the attention of Capitol Records. The next single, "Surfin' Safari," released on Capitol in 1962, hit #14 on the pop charts and was followed by "Surfin' USA," which mapped out Wilson's vision: to combine Chuck Berry's rock & roll guitar with the intricate vocal harmonies of the Four Freshman. Listening to the Beach Boys' early material is a thrill—you can hear Wilson's confidence and abilities grow with each new song, as he crafts increasingly daring instrumental arrangements, drives the group's sunny vocal harmonies into unexpected, often magical places, and develops ingenious ways of using the studio to make his music come to life. "Don't Worry, Baby" and "The Warmth of the Sun," from 1963's *Shut Down, Vol. 2*, are among the most lush and wonderful songs the Beach Boys ever recorded. "I Get Around," with its handclap rhythm, surf guitar riff, and Wilson's wild falsetto, is a career high point. Even the mediocre *Beach Boys Christmas Album* is memorable for Wilson's use of studio orchestration—something that would come to mark his brilliant mid-'60s productions.

By 1964, the Beach Boys rivaled the Beatles as the world's preeminent pop group—and it was a rivalry Wilson took extremely seriously. Touring took its toll on the Beach Boys' leader, though, and at the end of a 1964 European trip Wilson suffered a nervous breakdown and decided to quit the road. While the rest of the group toured (with Glen Campbell initially replac-

ing Wilson on stage, later Bruce Johnston), Brian stayed home to work on new songs. This marked a turning point—allowing Brian unlimited time to perfect his arrangements and develop his studio craft. For *Today!*, he wrote most of the lyrics, cut the backing tracks, and planned the vocal arrangements. By the time the group came home, all they had to do was lay down their vocals. The Beach Boys had essentially become Brian's band. And Brian wasn't writing novelty surf songs anymore.

The results crystallize on side two of *Today*. The music is orchestral, idiosyncratic, and revealing—a direct line into Wilson's troubled romantic soul. "Kiss Me, Baby" and "Please Let Me Wonder," in particular, are as complex and personal as any pop music ever made. While *Pet Sounds*, from two years later, remains Wilson's masterpiece, the second side of *Today* is where that album really starts.

Following *Today*, the Beach Boys rushed out *Summer Days (and Summer Nights!)*, notable mainly for the stellar single "California Girls," then Brian went back to the studio to finish *Pet Sounds*. Inspired by the Beatles' *Rubber Soul*, *Pet Sounds* was Wilson's attempt to make an entire coherent, emotionally honest record—a song cycle of loneliness, hope, and the search for love. It was also his most elaborate production, for which Wilson created complex, unorthodox instrumental landscapes to give his songs a breathtaking majesty. "God Only Knows," one of the great love songs of all time, and "Caroline, No," Brian's heartbreaking meditation on lost innocence, may be the most remarkable tracks, but from start to finish *Pet Sounds* is mind-blowingly transcendent even 29 years after it was made.

Ironically, *Pet Sounds* didn't sell well—the next album, *Party*, a mostly acoustic "live" album recorded with friends (including Jan and Dean) in the studio, sold much better on the strength of its #2 single, "Barbara Ann." Also notable are three Beatles covers and a version of Dylan's "The Times They Are a-Changin'."

Brian soon returned to the studio with the idea of making an album even more complex than *Pet Sounds*—one he intended to change pop music forever. Collaborating with lyricist Van Dyke Parks, Wilson started on *Smile*, which featured intricate vocal sections, songs divided into suitelike parts, and generally the most far-out experiments he'd attempted. The other Beach Boys didn't support Brian's extravagant efforts, and Wilson, already wrestling with his own mental instability and the emotional fallout from experiments with pot and LSD, buckled under the pressure. The album was abandoned. Rerecorded versions of various songs appear scattered over '70s albums, but it wasn't until 2004 that Wilson went back into the studio to complete the project he intended to be his masterpiece (see Brian Wilson entry).

One hint at what Wilson was initially attempting with *Smile*, however, is "Good Vibrations," which he had started during the *Pet Sounds* period and released as a single in 1966. Recorded in three studios over six months, it is one of the most densely woven songs ever recorded—a "pocket symphony," Wilson called it, in which he layered vocal track upon vocal track, and employed instruments including tubas, marimbas, and a theremin, to create three and a half of the most riveting minutes in pop music. Released as a single in October 1966, "Good Vibrations" stayed in the Top 40 for 12 weeks.

The next Beach Boys album, *Stack-o-Tracks,* is essentially a Beach Boys karaoke record containing just instrumental backing tracks that "you can play along to"—fascinating for Beach Boys obsessives, perhaps, but unnecessary for anyone else. The group attempted to salvage the *Smile* fiasco with the inconsistent *Smiley Smile,* for which they pieced together rerecorded portions of *Smile*'s epic "Heroes and Villains," "Vegetables," and the lovely "Wonderful." (It also contained the "Good Vibrations" single.) Released in September 1967, at the height of the summer of love, LSD, and political turmoil over the Vietnam War, the album was like a strange throwback—it highlighted how out of touch these suburban California surfers had become with the psychedelic times. The album bombed, and the Beach Boys' commercial career never quite recovered.

But while the group wouldn't have another #1 song until "Kokomo" in 1988, the Beach Boys continued to make some fascinating, mostly overlooked music into the '70s. One of the great thrills of discovering the Beach Boys, in fact, is to dig through these later albums for hidden gems. *Wild Honey, Friends, Sunflower, Surf's Up,* and *Love You* are all fantastic albums in their own way, and great songs can also be found buried on the often-dismissed *Carl and the Passions, 15 Big Ones,* and *Holland.*

Wilson floated in and out of the group during this time, no longer intent on being the producer or dominant songwriter, but just an occasional contributor. Brothers Carl and Dennis stepped up to fill Brian's shoes—Carl proved himself a talented producer and the group's most exciting lead singer, with a warm R&B-styled sound; Dennis also produced tracks, and demonstrated a gift for writing songs with gentle, introspective melodies. Unlike the grand productions of Wilson's mid-'60s records, these albums are sparse, simple, free of studio flourishes—not as ambitious, for sure, but easygoing and warm.

Friends, from 1968, typifies the period. If you can get past sappy wannabe-hippie tracks such as "Wake the World" and "Transcendental Meditation," the album is gorgeous, with standout moments including "Meant for You," one of Mike Love's finest vocals, and Brian's "Busy Doin' Nothin'," a samba shuffle in which Wilson details his homebound life—the lyrics even include a to-do list for the day and an invitation to come visit him (complete with directions to his house). *Wild Honey* is a rougher album of California soul, on which Carl contributes his finest vocals on the excellent "Darlin' " and "I Was Made to Love Her," a tribute to Stevie Wonder. *20/20,* similarly, features excellent vocals by Carl on songs such as "I Can Hear Music" and "Time to Get Alone," as well as Dennis's sweet "Be with Me" and another of Brian's stay-at-home gems, "I Went to Sleep."

The next album, *Sunflower,* is the epitome of '70s California cool. Songs such as "This Whole World," "Add Some Music to Your Day," "Forever," and "Cool, Cool Water" are filled with crisp melodies, delicate harmonies, and a mood of hope and sunshine. While it's often written that the Beach Boys never recovered once Brian abdicated leadership, *Sunflower* is a testament to what they could still do as a group. *Surf's Up* is darker, with a four-minute title track (including the lines "surf's up/there's gonna be a tidal wave") that's like the hangover to all the group's early surf-song highs. The album also features the excellent "Long Promised Road," "Feel Flows," and Brian's heartbreaking " 'Til I Die." *Carl and the Passions—So Tough* is weaker, with a few standout cuts such as "You Need a Mess of Help to Stand Alone" and "Marcella." *Holland* is a mess of an album recorded mainly in Holland without Brian, but features a pair of his excellent songs, "Sail on Sailor" and "Funky Pretty" (both sung by drummer Ricky Fataar.) *15 Big Ones,* featuring mostly covers, was an attempt to capitalize on Brian's return to the band (which didn't last), but the next year's *Love You* is one of Wilson's most overlooked works, essentially a Brian solo album, with gentle piano melodies in songs that show a man who's been damaged but not destroyed. (It also features some hilarious and bizarre tunes, such as "Johnny Carson," an adoring ode to the late-night television host.)

The album didn't get much attention, and the Beach Boys went on without Brian, releasing a string of inconsequential albums including 1978's *MIU,* produced by auxiliary Beach Boy Bruce Johnston, 1979's *L.A. (Light Album),* and the abysmal *Keepin' the Summer Alive.* In 1988, the Beach Boys topped the charts with "Kokomo," from the *Cocktail* movie soundtrack, but the next and last album, 1992's *Sum-*

mer in Paradise, produced by Mike Love, is perhaps the group's worst.

Unfortunately, the great Beach Boys two-record compilation *Endless Summer* from 1974—an album that helped put them back on the map after their '60s, slide—is out of print. But after a long period of mismanagement, the group's catalogue is back in stores with well-done two-for-one releases of all the original albums (with superb liner notes), and a new series of greatest-hits packages. Though it's a behemoth collection (five discs in all), even casual fans will find plenty to love on *Good Vibrations,* which includes key parts of all the group's albums, plus an excellent selection of alternative takes, a capella tracks, and demos, as well as the only officially released portion of the *Smile* sessions. It also includes a bonus disc of unreleased material including great tracking sessions, demos, and rarities. Also wonderful is the *Pet Sounds Box* set, a painstakingly compiled five-disc collection (with a 125-page explanatory booklet) that includes the first ever stereo mix of *Pet Sounds* (Brian recorded in mono, because he was deaf in one ear), as well as bonus tracks, in-progress studio sessions, vocal-only tracks, and alternative takes.

Beach Boys Greatest Hits, Vols. 1–3 is a basic introduction that breaks down the group's major songs chronologically. *Endless Harmony* is a mixed bag of unreleased tracks, including stereo mixes of "Kiss Me, Baby," a great live version of "Do It Again," and another mix of Brian's devastating " 'Til I Die." *Hawthorne, CA: Birthplace of a Musical Legacy* is two discs of leftovers, alternate versions, studio clowning, and other arcana—nothing essential but lots of fun. The only other current collection is *Sounds of Summer: The Very Best of the Beach Boys,* which gathers all their hits, from "Surfin' Safari" to "Kokomo." Perhaps modeled after *The Beatles 1,* a massive success, *Sounds of Summer* is not nearly as impressive—unlike the Beatles, the Beach Boys' best stuff often wasn't the hits, but the secret treasures.   —J.F.

Beanie Sigel

★★★   The Truth (Roc-A-Fella, 1999)
★★★   The Reason (Roc-A-Fella, 2001)

Earning the nickname Broad Street Bully for a punishing, brutal rhyme style and unforgiving portraits of Philadelphia crime life, Beanie Sigel has acted as Roc-A-Fella's muscle. Coming up under Jay-Z's benevolent wings, Sigel debuted in 1999 with *The Truth,* featuring the searing title track (produced by a then-unknown Kanye West) and other grim entries, such as the prison tale "What Ya Life Like." The monochromatic delivery, with it's simplistic yet effective word-

play, and the limited variety of content takes a toll. For his sophomore effort, Beanie lightened up a bit, engaging the club-track template on songs like "Beanie" and remaking an EPMD classic with Roc cohort Memphis Bleek, "So What You Saying." Sigel played to his strengths with songs like the West-produced "Nothing Like It" and the emotional "Mom Praying," with Scarface. Sadly, Sigel proved just how real he kept it when he found himself in a heap of legal trouble that stemmed from various 2002 and 2003 incidents in. His career seems to be indefinitely derailed.   —C.R.

Beastie Boys

★★★★★   Licensed to Ill (Def Jam/Columbia, 1986)
★★★★★   Paul's Boutique (Capitol, 1989)
★★★½   Check Your Head (Grand Royal/Capitol, 1992)
★★   The In Sound From Way Out! (Grand Royal/Capitol, 1992)
★★★★   Ill Communication (Grand Royal/Capitol, 1994)
★★★½   Some Old Bullshit (Grand Royal/Capitol, 1994)
★★★★½   Hello Nasty (Grand Royal/Capitol, 1998)
★★★★   Sounds of Science (Grand Royal/Capitol, 1999)
★★★★   To the 5 Boroughs (Capitol, 2004)

The Beastie Boys—Adam "Ad Rock" Horovitz, Adam "MCA" Yauch, and Michael "Mike D" Diamond—have spent their entire career trying to live down their first record and live up to their second. That they have managed to do either, let alone both, is one of the not-particularly-minor miracles of reinvention that rock & roll has long thrived on.

There is little overstating the importance of the Beasties' debut, *Licensed to Ill.* It arrived out of nowhere, following some negligible hardcore punk singles, one hilarious prank phone call on wax ("Cookie Puss"), and two singles on the then-upstart Def Jam label. (Not for nothing did the Beasties collect this early material under the name *Some Old Bullshit,* aka *S.O.B.,* which can be summed up thusly: enjoyable, yes; essential, no). From the Led Zeppelin sample that opened the album to the *Green Acres* sample that closed it, *Licensed to Ill* was bombastic and hilarious, driven equally by Saturday-morning cartoons, punk attitude, Jamaican bass, '70s rock strutting and '80s street swagger. It was also a phenomenon: It was the first credible hip-hop album from a white group, and it became the fastest-selling debut in Columbia Records history, something that never would have been possible if the record company had not convinced the Beasties to drop their original title, *Don't Be a Faggot.*

Make no mistake: Although the Beasties matured

quickly and continually, at this point, they were adolescents with microphones and the chance to tell the world to suck their dicks, which is exactly what they did. *Licensed to Ill* is filled with enough references to guns, drugs, and empty sex (including the pornographic deployment of a Wiffle-ball bat in "Paul Revere") to qualify as a gangsta-rap cornerstone. The Beasties would later try to explain away their *Licensed* personas as a joke—"the most illingest B-boy" as a parody of rock-star excess—and though it's doubtless more complicated than this, it's also clear from the pirates-on-the-prowl boasts of the first cut, "Rhymin' & Stealin'," that there's a lot of playground playacting at work.

Producer Rick Rubin had already rolled out skeletal hip-hop rhythms with L.L. Cool J's *Radio* (1985) and had topped the charts in 1986 with a blend of rock guitars and rap on Run-D.M.C.'s "Walk This Way." For *Licensed to Ill*, the producer upped the ante on both styles—the beats clanked harder and rumbled deeper, the guitars aped the skunk rock of Alice Cooper and Motörhead. "Fight for Your Right" became the pop-metal anthem the Beasties would forever try to live down (going so far as to apologize for it on the liner notes of their 1999 retrospective, *The Sounds of Science*). But the music of "The New Style" and "Hold It Now, Hit It" was radical and inventive, full of electro-rhythms and cavernous bass punctuated by guitar slams and breakbeats. For their part, the Beasties brought a sensibility born of cathode-ray-tube overexposure and liberal-arts majors—MCA name-checks *Barney Miller*'s Abe Vigoda and Picasso. But they also brought with them a dream cultivated by coming of age in downtown Manhattan clubs in the early '80s, with punk ebbing and rap ascendant: a vision of black and white music and audiences not just side by side but thoroughly inseparable. Ad Rock's nasal sneer was an instant hip-hop classic (you can hear its effect on Cypress Hill's B-Real, to say nothing of Eminem); MCA's growl got the party started right; and Mike D, well, Mike D tried hard to keep up and did.

Licensed to Ill sold 9 million copies, and after the Beasties fell into a royalty dispute with Def Jam, they decamped from Manhattan for Los Angeles, where they rented a house in the Hollywood Hills and began work on their second masterpiece. *Licensed to Ill* was the Beasties as the Three Stooges, full of comic aggression; *Paul's Boutique* was the Beasties as the Marx Brothers, full of comic surrealism. With producers the Dust Brothers, the Beasties introduced a dense, and densely funky, music woven of endless samples. It was, as they named the suite that ended the album, "B-boy Bouillabaisse," and the references flew faster

and wilder than ever: David Bowie, Bob Marley, Clint Eastwood, Pink Floyd, the Funky Four Plus One, the Beatles, Fred Flintstone, J.D. Salinger, Jimi Hendrix, the Brady Bunch, Joni Mitchell, Galileo, Run-D.M.C., Ricky Powell, and on and on until the break of dawn. Moving to the West Coast, the Beasties pioneered psychedelic hip-hop, which was mind-expanding in text and texture. It would take seven years until the world would catch up with the expansive grooves and mindset of *Paul's Boutique,* at which point the Dust Brothers would be helping to make Beck a star. Meanwhile, the Beasties were still rhyming about girls, drugs, guns, and watching television, though now with a growing social conscience: They wear condoms, offer compassion to the homeless bum of "Johnny Ryall," and preach that "racism is a schism on the serious tip" to the knuckleheads in "Looking Down the Barrel of a Gun."

When *Paul's Boutique* stiffed commercially, the Beasties regrouped at their G-Son studios, in L.A., built themselves a skate ramp, and began to re-create themselves as a total cultural experience. *Check Your Head* arrived with the Beasties' own magazine and label, both named Grand Royal, and a Beastie-approved wardrobe, which was sold at Mike D's X-Large stores in New York and L.A. The album took its name from *Flex Your Head,* a 1982 compilation of Washington, D.C., hardcore on the Dischord label, marking a return to the Beasties' hardcore-trio roots. This is where they went back to the basics, returning to their instruments, so they could try to play the beats they once sampled and bash their way through sloppy rock songs like "Gratitude." Conceptually, it was a breakthrough; but of all their records, *Check Your Head* has aged the worst. The freestyling on "Pass the Mic" (where Mike D rhymes "commercial" with "commercial" and offers the novel advice to "be true to yourself") sounds stiff, and when they try to replicate '70s lounge-funk on the organ-driven "Lighten Up," it's downright embarrassing. (Their not-rare-enough rare grooves are collected on *The In Sound From Way Out!,* and you are advised to spend your money on any random Grant Green or Meters record.) Despite standouts like "So Whatcha Want," the indie-rockrap-band concept didn't really gel until *Ill Communication* was released.

For one thing, the Beasties—with help from Mario Caldalto—had gotten better at producing themselves. *Ill Communication* was more layered and tricked-out, not as spare and homemade as *Check Your Head.* Now the beats sounded like they had been cooked up in a laboratory, not knocked together in a garage; the album unfolded with strange, dubbed-up sonic detours into flute interludes and fuzzed-out rock and organ jams that offered the surprises of a good DJ set. (And the instrumentals centered on keyboardist Money Mark, who could actually play.) Mike D got his yoga on in "Root Down"; in "Sabotage," Ad Rock struck back at media snoopers who'd crashed a friend's wedding; and MCA was the spiritual seeker who'd discovered Buddhism while snowboarding. He was the group's moral center, laying down the law in "Sure Shot" ("The disrespect to women has got to be through"), laying out his mission in "Do It" ("Slowly but surely I seek to find my mind"), laying out hip-hop genealogy in "Alright Hear This" ("I give respect to what's been borrowed and lent/I know this music comes down from African descent"), and bringing back the old dream of black and white audiences together, also on "Sure Shot" ("Send my rhymes out to all nations/Like Ma Bell, I've got the ill communications"). In the year Kurt Cobain checked out, 1994, the Beasties became indie-rock leaders, headlining that year's Lollapalooza alongside the Smashing Pumpkins.

In the four years that followed *Ill Communication,* the Beasties moved back to New York and produced a nearly perfect synthesis of their early and later work. *Hello Nasty* combined the anarchic wiseass humor of *Licensed to Ill* with the musical reach of *Paul's Boutique,* and yes, they played the instruments (or some of them). The return to New York brought back an old-school vibe: "Super Disco Breakin' " the lead cut, and references to mid-'80s hip-hop abound, from long-gone dances like the wop to *Krush Groove* and a sample of the Beasties' own "The New Style." But in truth, the old school the Beasties reconnected with wasn't old-school hip-hop; it was New York bohemia. They had long since stopped being a hip-hop group and were by now an indie-rock group that rapped. This was the first Beasties album to include singing—five songs, no less (six if you include dub-master Lee Perry's preaching on the estimable "Dr. Lee, PhD"). MCA gets existential on the bossa nova "I Don't Know," and Ad Rock takes on the objectification of women on "Song for the Man," which sounds like '60s French pop. He also contributes "And Me," which sets a thrumming melody to a drum-and-bass beat that spirals into the strangest sounds ever to appear on a Beasties album. Ad Rock—who had indulged his jones to keep on making records with the hardcore band DFL and beat merchants BS 2000—provides much of *Hello Nasty's* drive and probably more than few twisted beats. He closes the album with "Instant Death," an attempt to come to terms with the loss of his mother.

To the 5 Boroughs arrived after a six-year layoff, during which time MCA and Mike D had started families. And much more had changed: The Twin Towers, depicted on the album's cover, had been leveled. The country was at war. It was an election year. The sound of *To the 5 Boroughs* is stripped-down and straightforward—no instrumental interludes or singing, just hip-hop beats and straight-up rapping. But that sound has nothing to do with the hip-hop of their contemporaries—the disc is driven by breakbeats and scratches, as if the Beasties were trying to rock a Bronx roller rink in 1979. There is so much scratching, in fact, that the album serves as a de facto tribute not just to the spirit of New York but also to fallen comrade Jam Master Jay, from Run-D.M.C., who'd been shot dead two years earlier. There is also much editorializing from the Beasties—much of it necessary some of it pretty funny. The message was simple: more gun control, no war, and if the five boroughs can work together, so can the rest of us. "We need a little shift on over to the left," advises MCA on the dancehall jam "Time to Build," before Mike D, always the Beasties' business genius, starts rapping about the national debt. On such a high-minded album, the MC boasts come off stranger than ever. (What rapper had stepped up to the Beasties in the last 15 years?) But after six albums in a 20-year career, it all came down to the old dream, rekindled on "An Open Letter to NYC," which sampled CBGB punks the Dead Boys as well as Queens punks 50 Cent and Nas. The dream: black and white music and audiences, together forever. The chorus: "Brooklyn, Bronx, Queens, and Staten/From the Battery to the top of Manhattan/Asian, Middle Eastern, and Latin/Black, white, New York—you make it happen."   —J.L.

The Beatles

★★★★★   Please Please Me (1963; Capitol 1987)
★★★★½   With the Beatles (1963; Capitol 1987)
★★★★★   A Hard Day's Night (1964; Capitol 1987)
★★★★½   Beatles for Sale (1964; Capitol 1987)
★★★★★   Help! (1965; Capitol 1987)
★★★★★   Rubber Soul (1965; Capitol 1987)
★★★★★   Revolver (1966; Capitol 1987)
★★★★★   Sgt. Pepper's Lonely Hearts Club Band (1967; Capitol 1987)
★★★½   Magical Mystery Tour (1967; Capitol 1990)
★★★★★   The Beatles (1968; Capitol 1989)
★★½   Yellow Submarine (1969; Capitol 1990)
★★★★★   Abbey Road (1969; Capitol 1987)
★★★   Let It Be (1970; Capitol 1990)
★★★★★   The Beatles 1962–1966 (1973; Capitol 1993)
★★★★½   The Beatles 1967–1970 (1973; Capitol 1993)
★★★★   Live at the Hollywood Bowl (Capitol, 1977)
★★   Live at the Star Club in Hamburg, Germany (Bellaphon, 1977)

★★★★★ Past Masters, Vol. One (Capitol, 1988)
★★★★½ Past Masters, Vol. Two (Capitol, 1988)
★★★★ Live at the BBC (Capitol, 1994)
★★★ Anthology 1 (Capitol, 1995)
★★★ Anthology 2 (Capitol, 1996)
★★★ Anthology 3 (Capitol, 1996)
★★★★ The Yellow Submarine Songtrack (Capitol, 1999)
★★★★★ The Beatles 1 (Capitol, 2000)
★★★ Let It Be . . . Naked (Capitol, 2003)

John had the vision, Paul had the heart, George had the spirit, and Ringo had two fried eggs on toast, please. Together, they were the Beatles, four working-class Liverpool boys who came out of nowhere to conquer the world with the greatest songs ever heard. In case you're from Mars, John Lennon (the Smart One) and Paul McCartney (the Cute One) wrote the tunes. George Harrison (the Quiet One) played lead guitar. Ringo Starr (the Drummer) played drums. They all sang. They invented the idea of the self-contained rock band, writing their own hits and playing their own instruments. They invented the idea that the world's biggest pop group could grow up into arty, innovative musicians. For that matter, they invented the idea that there was any such thing as the world's biggest pop group. They also invented drugs, beards, bed-ins, India, concept albums, round glasses, the Queen, breaking up, and vegetarians.

The Beatles left behind more great music than anybody can process in a lifetime. Sheer abundance is part of their story: Life with the Beatles means vaguely disliking a chestnut like "Nowhere Man" or "Blackbird" for years until it sneaks up and gets into your blood for good. Just check out "I Want to Hold Your Hand," which explodes out of the speakers with the most passionate singing, drumming, lyrics, guitars, and girl-crazy howls ever—it's no insult to the Beatles to say they never topped this song because nobody else has either, although the lads came pretty close themselves with "You're Going to Lose That Girl." It's the most joyous three minutes in the history of human noise.

The Beatles were already bar-band veterans when they released their 1962 debut single, "Love Me Do," toughened by speed-fueled all-nighters in the sleazy clubs of Hamburg. They banged out *Please Please Me* in one marathon 10-hour session with producer George Martin on February 11, 1963. It's a blueprint of everything the Beatles would ever do, mixing up doo-wop, country, R&B, girl groups, Chuck Berry, Buddy Holly, Little Richard, and Tin Pan Alley into their own exuberant sound. John and Paul sang the openhearted originals "Ask Me Why," "There's a Place," and "I Saw Her Standing There." Ringo

shouted, "All right, George!" in his gender-flipped cover of the Shirelles' ultrafemme "Boys." All four Beatles sang and played with total emotional urgency, holding nothing back, knowing their first shot at getting out of Liverpool could have been their last. You can hear John completely blow out his voice in the last track, "Twist and Shout."

On *With the Beatles,* the mop-tops stepped out with a bunch of great Motown tributes: "Please Mister Postman," "You Really Got a Hold on Me," and the window-rattler "Money (That's What I Want)." They also shone with the originals "It Won't Be Long" and "All My Loving," George's "Don't Bother Me," and the Ringo showcase, "I Wanna Be Your Man." Unfortunately, there's also some real crapola here, such as "Little Child" and "Devil in Her Heart." The old show tune "Till There Was You" would rank as the Beatles' all-time ghastliest moment—if not for the horrifying "Hold Me Tight" ("It's you!/You, you, you!") which happens to be an original.

The full-length originals didn't come out in America until 1987. Today, the out-of-print U.S. versions don't even have nostalgia value, except maybe *Meet the Beatles.* The U.S. *Rubber Soul* adds acoustic tunes from *Help!* for an interesting album more conceptually unified than the U.K. original—although shorter, and not as good.

A Hard Day's Night, the soundtrack from the Beatles' superb debut film ("Don't touch Ringo's drums—they loom large in his legend"), was also the first album comprised entirely of Lennon-McCartney originals. Although they were now the four most famous people in the world, the toppermost of the poppermost, bigger than Elvis, bigger than Jesus, they were still holding nothing back emotionally or musically: Just listen to "If I Fell" or "You Can't Do That."

The strain of Beatlemania shows in *Beatles for Sale,* as the lads unload some of the ickiest covers from their bar-band days. But they keep growing with "What You're Doing" and "I'm a Loser." The harmonies of "Baby's in Black," the hair-raising "I still loooove her" climax of "I Don't Want to Spoil the Party," the eager hand claps in "Eight Days a Week"—it all makes "Mr. Moonlight" easy to forgive.

Help! was a big step forward, exploring doubt, loneliness, alienation, adult sexual longing, acoustic guitars, electric piano, bongos, castanets, and the finest George songs known to man. The Cute One suddenly proved he was also the Smart One, the Smart One proved he could sound cuter than the Cute One, the Quiet One got Smart as well as Cute, and "Act Naturally" proved how much they all loved Ringo. *Help!* was utterly ruined in its U.S. version, which cut half the songs and added worthless orchestral soundtrack filler, so it's always been underrated. But *Help!* is the first chapter in the astounding creative takeoff the Beatles were just beginning: the soulful bereavement of "Ticket to Ride," the impossibly erotic gentleness of "Tell Me What You See," the desperate falsetto and electric punch of "You're Going to Lose That Girl."

On *Rubber Soul*, the Beatles grew up with an album of bittersweet romance, singing adult love ballads that feel worldly but not jaded. "Drive My Car" was a brash pop-life satire featuring Ringo's hottest drumming, while "Girl" upped the folk-rock ante on Bob Dylan. "Norwegian Wood" wove sitar and acoustic guitar together as John cryptically sang about an affair so his wife wouldn't guess what the song was about. (The rest of us can get confused as well—does he light up a joint at the end or burn the girl's house down?) John and Paul both took off as singers: "Nowhere Man" might be slight as social commentary but it's heartbreaking as music, while "I'm Looking Through You" and "Wait" bare the vulnerable emotion in Paul's vocals. "In My Life" was one of the last Lennon-McCartney songs that the pair actually wrote together, and it could well be a loving farewell to each other before the friendship turned sour.

For *Revolver*, the Fabs tuned in to Dylan, the Stones, the Beach Boys, the Byrds, and decided to top them all. They also decided to make Ringo sing the one about the yellow submarine. On top of the world, at the peak of their powers, competing with one another because nobody else could touch them, the Beatles breezed through acid rock ("She Said She Said"), chamber music ("For No One"), raga ("Love You To"), R&B ("Got to Get You Into My Life"), and everything in between with superhuman confidence. It contains their prettiest music ("Here, There, and Everywhere"), their bitchiest ("And Your Bird Can Sing"), their friendliest ("I Want to Tell You"), and their scariest (the screaming-seagull acid-nightmare "Tomorrow Never Knows"). John's songs are the best, but Paul gets in the funniest line: "If I am true I'll never leave,/and if I do I know the way there."

Revolver got butchered particularly badly in its U.S. release, which only gave John three songs, the same number as George. Incredibly, Americans didn't get to hear the uncut *Revolver* until the CD came out in 1987. Ever since *Revolver* has steadily climbed in public estimation. These days, *Revolver* has earned its reputation as the best album the Beatles ever made, which means the best album by anybody.

Sgt. Pepper's Lonely Hearts Club Band, the psychedelic soundtrack of the Summer of Love, was the first Beatles album released in its original uncut version in America, where fans hadn't even heard the full *Re-*

volver yet. So it was a revelation of how far artists could go in a recording studio with only four tracks, plenty of imagination, and a drug or two. It's a masterwork of sonics, not songwriting—the words and melodies are a lot more rickety than on the previous three albums. But with Paul overdubbing every instrument under the sun and George Martin fixing the holes, *Sgt. Pepper* still sparkles, especially the jangly "Getting Better," the half-past-dead "A Day in the Life," and Ringo's greatest hit, "With a Little Help from My Friends."

Sgt. Pepper marked a turning point: No longer playing live, increasingly dimmed by drugs, the Beatles were drifting apart. They collaborated less and worked solo, isolating John's caustic rock edge, Paul's light pop whimsy, and George's sere spiritualism. *Magical Mystery Tour* was a lot goopier than *Sgt. Pepper*, though lifted by the cheerful "All You Need Is Love" and the ghostly "Strawberry Fields Forever." Her Majesty the Queen had the best comment: "The Beatles are turning awfully funny, aren't they?" By now, the Beatles didn't need to push—they could have hit #1 with a tape of themselves blowing their noses, which would have been catchier than "Hello Goodbye" or "Lady Madonna." *Yellow Submarine* was a flat soundtrack rather than a real album, but here's a question: Why is George's "It's All Too Much" not heralded as one of the top five all-time psychedelic freakouts in rock history?

The Beatles wrote most of the White Album on acoustic guitars while on retreat in Rishikesh, India, a place where they had no drug connections, which probably explains why they came up with their sturdiest tunes since *Revolver*. As John recalled, "We sat in the mountains eating lousy vegetarian food and writing all these songs." Even Ringo: a big hand, please, for the man who wrote "Don't Pass Me By." The double-disc White Album, officially entitled *The Beatles*, has loads of self-indulgent filler—even the justly maligned "Revolution #9" is more fun than "Honey Pie" or "Yer Blues." Before CDs, most people just made a 45-minute tape of highlights for actual listening; now you can program "Sexy Sadie" and "Long, Long, Long" without having to lift the needle to skip over "Helter Skelter." But nobody would pick the same highlights, which is part of the fun, and besides, if the Beatles had edited it down to one disc, "Rocky Raccoon" would have been the first to go, which would have been tragic. "Martha My Dear," "Blackbird," "Dear Prudence," "Julia," "Cry, Baby, Cry," "Savoy Truffle," and "Happiness Is a Warm Gun" are all among the Beatles' finest songs, even if nobody will ever understand how they talked George Martin into permitting that godawful bass feedback at the end of the otherwise perfect "Julia."

As a strange footnote, the White Album acquired permanent notoriety during Charles Manson's 1969 trial, when an L.A. district attorney floated the theory that the album had inspired an alleged hippie murder cult. Silly stuff, but the accusation stuck, even though there's never been any evidence behind it; as Charlie himself admitted, he was more of a Bing Crosby man. Oh, well—"Helter Skelter" still sucks anyway.

Despite its solo vocals, the White Album was the last Beatles album to evoke the old team spirit. *Let It Be,* the ill-fated documentary soundtrack, wasn't even released until 1970. The singing, playing, and writing are weak, despite the White Album–style gems "Dig A Pony" and "Two of Us." "The Long and Winding Road" is actually a not-terrible tune under Phil Spector's orchestral dreck (just listen to Aretha Franklin sing it on *Young, Gifted, and Black*). Fortunately, the band decided not to go out like that, and reconvened to make the farewell *Abbey Road.* Slick, polished to the point of easy listening, *Abbey Road* devotes side two to a Paul-dominated "pop symphony," as George's "Here Comes the Sun" gives way to a medley of inspired tunelets such as "Golden Slumbers," "Sun King," and "The End." The spottier side one has John's "I Want You (She's So Heavy)," his de facto sequel to "I Want to Hold Your Hand," and Ringo's kiddie fave "Octopus's Garden," which makes "Yellow Submarine" sound like "The Wreck of the Edmund Fitzgerald." Good night, everybody. Everybody, everywhere. Good night.

Beatles reissues are a story in themselves. Over the years, Capitol has cranked out Beatles anthologies from every conceivable angle—*Love Songs, Reel Music, Rock & Roll Music, Rarities,* and so on. Hardly any of them have been rip-offs, however; Elvis Presley should be so lucky as to have his legacy preserved with this much care. *The Beatles 1962–1966* and *1967–1970,* the "Red" and "Blue" albums, became the canonical sets in the '70s, and they still sound great, although they're overpriced, each spreading a single CD's worth of great music over two discs—and nobody has ever explained what the hell "Old Brown Shoe" is doing on the Blue Album. *Hollywood Bowl* is a loving tribute to the screaming girl fans who drown out the band in these 1964–65 shows; those girls were heroes on the rock & roll frontier, and they deserve to be the lead instrument on a Beatles album of their own. *Live at the Star Club* is a dull live set from the tail end of the group's early Hamburg days, right about the time the Beatles were making it at home and going through the motions in Hamburg. *Past Masters* collects their singles on two CDs, including essential nonalbum cuts such as "She Loves You," "Hey Jude," "Yes It Is," and "Rain." The 1977 *Love Songs* had a nice cover.

The long-bootlegged *Live at the BBC* has excellent radio performances of the lads chattering, nattering, cracking one another up, dedicating songs to their aunties out there in radio land, and playing many otherwise unrecorded covers, as well as the great original "I'll Be On My Way." The all-outtakes *Anthology* sets are too much of a good thing, good for only a couple of listens apiece, although *Anthology 3* has "Junk," a sweet acoustic White Album ballad Paul revived on his solo debut. The three surviving Beatles reunited in 1995 to touch up the John outtake "Free as a Bird," which in retrospect wasn't a bad song at all, although the very idea was dead grotty. The song peaked at #2 in the U.K. and therefore missed inclusion on *1,* the budget-priced collection of #1 hits that shocked the music business by selling zillions of copies, even though everybody on earth already has all the songs. In fact, the Beatles were the top-selling act of 2001. "Free as a Bird," no doubt, will appear on the inevitable sequel *2,* which will also have "Please Please Me" and "Strawberry Fields Forever"; also brace yourself for the Beatles' *H,* so everybody can buy new copies of "Help!," "Hello Goodbye," "Hey Bulldog," and "Her Majesty." The Paul-supervised *Let It Be . . . Naked* remix isn't worth the trouble.

The Four Historic Ed Sullivan Shows Featuring the Beatles came out on DVD in 2003 with no fanfare and a clumsy title, but it's essential. You get 20 1964–1965 Beatles performances, including three versions of "I Want to Hold Your Hand," but the real revelation is how badly the rest of the show sucked. Mitzi Gaynor singing show tunes? Mr. Acker Bilk doing a clarinet solo called "Acker's Lacquer"? Magic from the Great Fantasio, acrobats, card tricks, and a host who resembles a suburban funeral director with a mouthful of Vicodin? So *this* is what people did for fun before the Beatles came along? No wonder America freaked out. —R.S.

Beatnuts

- ★★★ Intoxicated Demons (Relativity, 1993)
- ★★½ Street Level (Relativity, 1994)
- ★★★ Stone Crazy (Relativity, 1997)
- ★★★ A Musical Massacre (Relativity, 1999)
- ★★½ Take It or Squeeze It (Loud, 2000)
- ★★ Originators (Landspeed, 2002)
- ★★ Milk Me (Penalty, 2004)

For over a decade Psycho Les and JuJu of the Beatnuts have been pumping out gritty New York street rap with remarkable consistency and uneven quality. As producers, these two Queens natives, along with DJ Premier, are the architects of a brand of hardcore East Coast hip-hop known by its heavy drums and sparse loops. As MCs, Psycho and JuJu stick to the basics: gunplay and bedroom antics. The subject matter and music may not vary significantly from album to album, but for what they do, the Beatnuts are some of the best. *Intoxicated Demons* is as good a place as any to start, as it features their anthem, "Reign of the Tec," a tribute to vengeance as exhilarating as any early-'90s rap track.

Street Level sits comfortably with the typical rough-neck rap of the day (think Mobb Deep and Notorious B.I.G., minus the highs). *Stone Crazy* was something of a breakthrough for the duo, giving them a bona fide hit with "Off the Books" (a track that also served as an introduction of sorts to Big Punisher). *A Musical Massacre* is more of the same, with an "Off the Books" sequel of sorts in "Watch Out Now."

By 2000's *Take It or Squeeze It* the formula was starting to get tired. While the production continued to reveal nuances in the 'Nuts' minimal palette, the lyrics were beginning to run thin on ideas. After finding themselves in label limbo with the folding of Loud Records, the Beatnuts returned to the underground with *Originators*. The album sadly rested on the laurels of their past achievements, offering little new in the way of musical or lyrical ideas.   —C.R.

Beats International

★★★½   Let Them Eat Bingo (Elektra/Asylum, 1990)
★★½   Excursion on the Version (London/PolyGram, 1992)

The grandfather of mash-up/bootleg culture is Beats International's debut album, and especially its dance hit "Dub Be Good to Me"—an ingenious combination of the S.O.S. Band's "Just Be Good to Me" and the bass line from the Clash's "The Guns of Brixton." The group's mastermind was Norman Cook, who'd just spent a few years as the Housemartins' bassist and hadn't yet become Fatboy Slim. Beats International was a transitional band for him, as he started to play with making new grooves out of fragments of other people's recordings, but also wrote some splendid original songs. "For Spacious Lies" is a mournfully perky assessment of the distance between political principles and practice: "Freedom's just a song by Wham!, but we pretend." (The following year's *Excursion on the Version*, now out of print, is more dub-obsessed and less clever.)   —D.W.

The Beautiful South

★★★★   Welcome to the Beautiful South (Elektra, 1989)
★★★   Choke (Elektra, 1990)
★★★½   0898 (Elektra, 1992)
★★★★½   Carry On Up the Charts (Mercury, 1995)

★★★★   Blue Is the Colour (Ark 21, 1996)
★★★   Quench (Mercury, 1999)
★★★½   Painting It Red (Ark 21, 2000)

The dissolution of British pop socialists the Housemartins at the end of the '80s was one of the most productive breakups in rock history. Bassist Norman Cook transmogrified into Fatboy Slim. But by targeting sentimental suburbans rather than club rats, Paul Heaton achieved a stranger, more nuanced triumph. As the Beautiful South, Heaton and guitarist David Rotheray fashioned soft facsimiles of housewife balladry, but their lyrics worked deftly cynical twists on romantic truisms. The results are simultaneously sweet and painful—like a razor blade hidden in a chocolate bar.

Welcome to the Beautiful South kicks off with an acid critique of a callous songwriter's transformation of his love life into chart-topping gold. It closes by taunting a fickle pop audience: "Twenty years from now, will you come to my cremation?" Future albums found the band concentrating less on the crudities of showbiz, more on expressing Heaton's empathy for his plodding, unloved listeners. That empathy prevents *Beautiful South* from degenerating into a sardonic, wiseass scam. After all, in the U.K., Heaton's gently wafting bitterness actually registered as pop—these songs did indeed carry on up the charts, as their best-of declares. Proof that pop fans are smarter than either elitist highbrow snobs or cynical label execs happen to believe.

Blue Is the Colour brings Heaton's empathy to the fore, offering crafted pop for people desperately seeking an alternative to middle-class stasis, folks who've "lost the difference between bored and lonely." Auxiliary vocalist Jacqueline Abbot makes her intentions immediately clear, offering a two-way way out of domesticity's confines on the disc's opening track, "Don't Marry Her": "Fuck me." "Liar's Bar" beelines for the standard British escape, the pub, while it imagines a Disney apocalypse: "The world won't end in darkness/It'll end in family fun." Sometimes wistful, sometimes resigned, the Beautiful South's resistance to such a bland decline in subsequent albums amounts to the kind of small-scale heroism they celebrate in their songs.   —K.H.

Beck

★★★★★   Mellow Gold (Bong Load/DGC, 1994)
★★★½   Stereopathetic Soulmanure (Flipside, 1994)
★★½   One Foot in the Grave (K, 1994)
★★★★★   Odelay (DGC, 1996)
★★★   Mutations (DGC, 1998)
★★★½   Midnight Vultures (DGC, 1999)
★★★★½   Sea Change (DGC, 2002)

Beck is the king of the Hanna-Barbera blues singers, a rock & roll dumpster diver trying to make folk music dangerous again by looting American culture for toys, whether they're acoustic guitars or drum machines or two turntables and a microphone. He's a joker, a smoker, a midnight Bram Stoker, an L.A. boho who mixes up Gertrude Stein and Grandmaster Flash with last night's *Welcome Back, Kotter* rerun. Although he's a folkie at heart, acoustic minimalism cannot contain his more-is-more sensibility. Beck always sounds most himself when he piles on the star wars and other galactic funk.

Beck first blew up with the epochal 1994 hit "Loser," in which he skated to glory on a hot-wired Duane Allman guitar lick and a cheap beatbox. Like the rest of *Mellow Gold,* "Loser" sounded brilliantly disposable at the time, which was part of the fun. But the musical imagination and emotional resonance of *Mellow Gold* hold up long after the surprise wears off. It's a nonstop gas, collecting the best of his homemade recordings: the scruffy valentine "Nitemare Hippy Girl," the psychedelic death trip "Steal My Body Home," the hip-hop goof "Beercan," the scam-artist tearjerker "Pay No Mind (Snoozer)." *Mellow Gold* was nothing short of miraculous: Bob Dylan's *Bringing It All Back Home* as choreographed by Sid and Marty Kroft.

Having fluked into a major-label hit, Beck defied all commercial logic by releasing two more albums that same year, both on indie punk labels. He earned some cred with the acoustic folk blues of *One Foot in the Grave,* which was sincere but dull: too much Sigmund, not enough Sea Monsters. *Stereopathetic Soulmanure* collected random home-taping junk from 1988 to 1994, from the cathartic punk of "Tasergun" and "Pink Noise (Rock Me Amadeus)" to the gorgeous Deadhead country of "Modesto." Even at this formative stage, Beck proved himself the kind of folkie who can ride boxcars with Depression-era hoboes in "Waitin' for a Train" and then give props to "Ozzy." He sings with giddy abandon whether he's indulging in elaborate Guthrie-esque tropes ("Plastic donut can of Spam/There's no kindness in this land") or just letting it all hang out ("So what/I lost my job at the Hut/My ass got cut").

But Beck really got crazy with the Cheez Whiz on *Odelay,* the smash hit that proved he could do it all. As the title suggests, it's his ode to L.A., mixing up his folk and rap and punk and hippie passions into cosmopolitan American slop, with help from his producers the Dust Brothers. Beck shimmies in and out of his musical guises, strumming acoustic guitar in "Ramshackle," rocking the Catskills hip-hop-style in "Where It's At," blaming it on the bossa nova in

"Readymade," or murmuring his most beautiful ballad ever in "Jack-ass." It's a vision of an America of wide-open cultural frontiers—in "Where It's At," when Beck announces, "There's a destination a little up the road," he's imagining a future of sonic and sexual freedom that never arrived, never really even came close, although at the time it seemed so near we could reach out and touch it. *Odelay* could have come off as a bloodless art project, but Beck gets lost in the jigsaw jazz and the get-fresh flow until his playful energy makes everyone else sound tame. Put it together, it's a strange invitation.

Odelay was the last time Beck tried so many tricks on one album; his subsequent records basically explore one side of his music at a time. *Mutations* slowed it down for an album of depressive ballads about locking yourself indoors and waiting to die, produced (too loudly) by Nigel Godrich of Radiohead fame. While *Mutations* was sensitively fashioned, it was also incredibly boring, hitting duller-than-dog-breath lows by the third verse of practically every song, so the outright comedy record *Midnite Vultures* came as a relief. Fans of his serious side were appalled by gimmicky funk throwaways such as "Get Real Paid," "Hollywood Freaks," and "Mixed Bizness." ("She's mixing business with leather"—how the hell did Beck beat Prince to that one?) But for anyone who doesn't believe melancholy is inherently deeper than fun, *Midnite Vultures* is a hoot, especially the climactic slow jam "Debra," where he picks up a lucky lady in his Hyundai to take her for a real good meal.

Sea Change was a return to acoustic shoegazing, with gorgeous, downbeat reflections on a broken relationship, brooding in the style of Nick Drake and Serge Gainsbourg. But this time Beck came up with the first-rate melodies he left out of *Mutations,* and the emotion of the music was no joke at all. All over *Sea Change* he sounded like the same open-eared, warily ironic busker who recorded *Mellow Gold*—except eight years after "Loser," he sounded like he knew how it feels to actually lose something worth keeping. How long can he keep this up? Well, Beck has always been eager to flaunt how fallible he is. But that destination is still a little up the road, a little farther than it used to be, and Beck is one musician who's in the journey for the long haul.   —R.S.

Jeff Beck

★★★½ Truth (Epic, 1968)
★★½ Beck-Ola (Epic, 1969)
★★★ Rough and Ready (Epic, 1971)
★★ Jeff Beck Group (Epic, 1972)
★★ Beck, Bogert & Appice (Epic, 1973)
★★★★ Blow by Blow (Epic, 1975)

Between his virtuosic command of the fretboard and his daredevil feel for feedback and distortion, Beck's playing is rarely less than astonishing. But he lacks the vision and determination necessary to convert that instrumental intensity into any viable group chemistry, a weakness that has kept his solo career from amounting to much more than a few dazzling moments scattered through a lot of disappointing music.

Perhaps the closest he's ever come to fronting a band that could balance and enhance his strengths as a soloist was with the group he formed after leaving the Yardbirds. Because both singer Rod Stewart and bassist/guitarist Ron Wood had enough presence and confidence to hold their own ground alongside Beck, the music they made together was often as cohesive as it was exciting. *Truth,* despite a tendency to confuse showboating with ambition, is an excellent example of the heights Beck and his bandmates could achieve; had they continued in this vein, in time they could have eclipsed even the mighty Led Zeppelin. Unfortunately, it was not to be; although *Beck-Ola* features a couple of amusingly energized Elvis covers ("Jailhouse Rock" and "All Shook Up"), the group's attempts to add a heavier edge to its sound only succeed in making the music more lugubrious.

After losing Stewart and Wood to the Faces, Beck's next group opted for a funkier approach, built around jazz-oriented keyboardist Max Middleton and David Clayton-Thomas imitator Bob Tench. It wasn't an ideal match. *Rough and Ready* stumbles whenever faced with a ballad but otherwise offers a passable gloss on the sort of vaguely improvisatory white soul Traffic made popular. But *Jeff Beck Group* pushes the band's mannerisms to the point of self-parody. Beck then tried the power-trio approach, but the results, as embodied by *Beck, Bogert & Appice,* aren't much better, offering all the self-indulgence of Cream but none of the focus or pop appeal. (A concert recording from this period, *Beck, Bogert & Appice Live,* is even more embarrassing, but was released only in Japan.)

By rights, Beck's next attempt at reinvention—this time as a fusion jazz star—ought to have been just as disastrous as the previous three, but thanks to producer George Martin, the all-instrumental *Blow by Blow* emerges as one of the most listenable and consistent albums of the guitarist's career. An eloquent player with absolutely nothing to say, Beck isn't much of a jazzman, but Martin works around the guitarist's limitations, elegantly framing the solos with sympathetic rhythm arrangements and lush string orchestrations.

With *Wired,* Beck leaps into the deep end, abandoning all his *Blow by Blow* playmates except Middleton to work with Mahavishnu Orchestra alumni Jan Hammer and Narada Michael Walden. Beck plays gamely, but it's really Hammer's album, since his synth solos are what ultimately galvanize the group. *Jeff Beck With the Jan Hammer Group Live* would seem a natural outgrowth from this collaboration, but the actual results are a mess, with Beck getting by on feedback and flash while Hammer's group tries to hold the music together. *There and Back* returns Beck to the studio with a more sympathetic set of collaborators (Hammer, drummer Simon Phillips, keyboardist Tony Hymas), but still goes nowhere.

Astonishingly, Beck's next album, *Flash,* was a pop outing with Wet Willie alumnus Jimmy Hall singing on most tracks. Thanks to producers Nile Rodgers and Arthur Baker, it's consistent and accessible, but threw sparks only when the guitarist reunited with Rod Stewart for a version of "People Get Ready." Bored, Beck went back to fusion and the empty acrobatics of *Jeff Beck's Guitar Shop,* but that didn't last. His next album, *Crazy Legs,* was a tribute to Gene Vincent & the Bluecaps guitarist Cliff Gallup that found Beck playing in classic rockabilly style with the Big Town Playboys, while the soundtrack album *Frankie's House* found him working in a enough different styles (R&B, New Age, semimetal) to show off his versatility, but without enough focus for the music to make much of an impression.

Although not quite a career summation, the box set *Beckology* includes highlights from the above, as well as Beck's first recordings (with the Tridents), a good sampling of his Yardbirds material, and a smattering of arcana. By rights, it should have been a solid career summation, but in the late '90s Beck discovered techno and found himself creatively refreshed. Partly live and partly studio-concocted, *Who Else!* had its moments, but never quite gelled. *You Had It Coming* offered a more cohesive approach, particularly in its interplay with guitarist Jennifer Batten (the first real fretboard sparring partner Beck has had since the Yardbirds) and in its approach to such roots material as the blues standard "Rollin' and Tumblin'." *Jeff* more fully embraced the studio-based aesthetic, pairing Beck with only a producer (mostly Andy Wright and Apollo 440) and one or two musicians for most tracks. But because his guitar reacts purely to the tracks, it's as if all filters have evaporated; not only does he recapture the improvisational abandon of *Wired,* he actually takes the music a step forward. Who says the keyboard is mightier than the fretboard? —J.D.C.

Walter Becker

  ★★½   Mose the Fireman (Rabbit Ears, 1993)
  ★★★   11 Tracks of Whack (Giant, 1994)

When Steely Dan took a hiatus from 1981 through 1994, their work ethic went to hell. Donald Fagen and Walter Becker (who for all intents and purposes were the group) yielded a grand total of three solo albums over those 14 years. Sure, they produced some albums for other folks (Becker oversaw discs for Rickie Lee Jones, Michael Franks, China Crisis, John Beasley, Jeremy Steig, etc.), but one of the most prolific songwriting teams of the '70s released just 26 songs during that period.

Nonetheless, those solo albums revealed who contributed what to the Steely Dan partnership. Fagen's *The Nightfly* proved that he had the voice, the melodies, and the romanticism. Becker's *11 Tracks of Whack* showed that he was the iconoclast, the one who gave the acerbic edge to the lyrics and the unpredictable shiftiness to the chord changes. Becker's thin, nasal, cramped voice is a real barrier to appreciating these songs, but if you can get past that handicap, the songs are quite good, unsettling portraits of a "Junkie Girl," "This Moody Bastard," and other self-destructive characters on society's margins. It was the first Fagen-Becker coproduction since 1980, and the tracks glistened. Oh, but that voice.

Becker is also credited as the cocreator of the children's album *Mose the Fireman.* Becker and John Beasley composed the ragtime and Dixieland music and led the quartet that played it behind Michael Keaton's narration about a mythical New York fireman. The music is then repeated without the narration. You will also see albums credited to Becker and Fagen; these are the duo's early songwriting demos before they finally landed their Steely Dan deal. Fewer than 30 songs are involved; some of them were later redone by Steely Dan, but most were not. The better-than-forgettable, less-than-compelling leftovers have been assembled into countless compilations too numerous and transitory to list. For completists only. —G.H.

The Bee Gees

  ★★½   Bee Gees 1st (1967; Polydor, 1988)
  ★½   Horizontal (1968; Polydor, 1988)
  ★½   Idea (1968; Polydor, 1989)
  ★★★   Odessa (1969; Polydor, 1987)
  ★★★   Best of Bee Gees (1969; Polydor, 1987)
  ★½   Cucumber Castle (1970; Polydor, 1989)
  ★★½   Trafalgar (1971; Polydor, 1989)
  ★½   2 Years On (1971; Polydor, 1989)
  ★½   To Whom It May Concern (Atco, 1972)
  ★★   Best of the Bee Gees, Vol. 2 (1973; Polydor, 1987)
  ★½   Life in a Tin Can (RSO, 1973)
  ★½   Mr. Natural (RSO, 1974)
  ★★★½   Main Course (1975; Polydor, 1988)
  ★★★   Children of the World (1976; Polydor, 1989)
  ★★★½   Bee Gees Gold, Vol. 1 (RSO, 1976)
  ★★★   Here at Last . . . Live (1977; Polydor, 1990)
  ★★★½   Greatest Hits (RSO, 1979)
  ★★★   Spirits Having Flown (1979; Polydor, 1989)
  ★★★½   Bee Gees Greatest (1979; Polydor, 1988)
  ★★½   Living Eyes (RSO, 1981)
  ★★   E.S.P. (Warner Bros., 1987)
  ★★   One (Warner Bros., 1989)
  ★★★½   Tales from the Brothers Gibb: A History in Song, 1967–1990 (Polydor, 1990)
  ★★   High Civilization (Warner Bros., 1991)
  ★★   Size Isn't Everything (Polydor, 1993)
  ★★   Still Waters (Polydor, 1997)
  ★★★   One Night Only (Polydor, 1998)
  ★★   Tomorrow the World (Magnum, 1999)
  ★★★½   This Is Where I Came In (Universal, 2001)
  ★★★★   Their Greatest Hits: The Record (Polydor, 2001)

Nothing if not professional, the Aussie Brothers Gibb—leader Barry and twin followers Maurice and Robin—enjoyed two mega-careers playing two sorts of music: lush, Beatles-like pop and high-gloss disco. Milking the pop sensibility that prizes gesture over authenticity, they made remarkable '60s jukebox love songs, their trademark warbling conveying genuine passion about as accurately as Hollywood kisses capture the mess and tangle of real love. The trick, however, to "Holiday," "Words," "I Started a Joke," and "To Love Somebody" was that the Bee Gees understood their teenage make-out audience. So what if the lyrics didn't make sense? Who cared, when everything was so digestible?

After *Odessa,* the *Sgt. Pepper's* copy that all '60s headliners felt driven to attempt (the Bee Gees' wasn't bad; faulting it for pretentiousness makes absolutely no sense), the Bee Gees faded, resurfacing occasionally with such ace radio balladry as "How

Can You Mend a Broken Heart?" Then, with the out-of-nowhere timing of melodrama, they returned in the '70s with brilliant, plastic R&B. Pumped by finger-popping bass and swishing high-hat cymbals, *Main Course, Spirits Having Flown,* and, most spectacularly, their contributions to *Saturday Night Fever* didn't create disco but mainstreamed it with stunning craft. They had gigantic hits, of course. A third bid at stardom seemed to risk the ire of even the most indulgent of gods. The '80s Bee Gees appeared tentative and flailing.

Still, they persevered. Driven by the irresistible single "You Win Again," 1987's *E.S.P.* was a huge international hit (stateside listeners remained unconvinced). *One* fared even better. *High Civilization, Size Isn't Everything,* and *Still Waters* found them in a holding pattern, although the brothers' 1997 induction into the Rock and Roll Hall of Fame sparked a revival of interest. They ended the '90s with a fairly urgent live album, *One Night Only,* and entered the new century with one of their strongest albums in years, *This Is Where I Came In.* Mixing the AOR-funk of their latter years with melodic pop that echoed their early glory days, it wasn't exactly their Third Coming, but by that point most newcomers were interested in the Bee Gees' slew of hits, which has been collected most completely on *Their Greatest Hits: The Record* and *Tales from the Brothers Gibb,* a four-disc collection that's a little heavy on filler material. The Bee Gees continued to tour occasionally until January 2003, when Maurice Gibb died of cardiac arrest while receiving treatment for an intestinal blockage. Following his death, Robin and Barry declared that the Bee Gees were finished.   —P.E.

Bell Biv DeVoe

    ★   Hootie Mack (MCA, 1993)
  ★★★   Best of Bell Biv DeVoe (MCA, 2000)
   ★★   BBD (MCA, 2001)

After the teen outfit New Edition lost Bobby Brown to solo success and a life in the tabloid headlines, the three remaining singers regrouped as Bell Biv DeVoe—for Ricky Bell, Michael Bivins, and Ronnie DeVoe—and forged on. On their debut album, *Poison,* now out of print, the boys leave behind New Edition's syrupy odes to sodas and hand-holding, and their meltingly harmonious vocals prove just as suited to such adult fare as scheming lovers ("Poison"). The followup, *Hootie Mack,* inexplicably still available, sounds like the rush release it was. Eight years later, the group gave it another go with *BBD,* awkwardly and blatantly trying to adjust to the times with a potty-mouthed mix of hot kink, bling, and bling. The best

that can be said about *The Best of* is that it gives fans access to songs from the first album; the worst is that it vividly demonstrates how completely these young men squandered their talents.   —A.B.

Belle and Sebastian

 ★★★★   Tigermilk (1996; Matador, 1999)
★★★★★   If You're Feeling Sinister (The Enclave, 1996)
 ★★★★   The Boy With the Arab Strap (Matador, 1998)
 ★★★★   Lazy Line Painter Jane (Matador, 2000)
 ★★★½   Fold Your Hands Child, You Walk Like a Peasant (Matador, 2000)
   ★★   Storytelling (Matador, 2002)
 ★★★★   Dear Catastrophe Waitress (Rough Trade, 2003)

When Belle and Sebastian (named after a children's television series) made their debut album, *Tigermilk,* they were barely even a band. Singer/guitarist/keyboardist Stuart Murdoch assembled a sextet to record his tender, introverted compositions; the record was originally released (on vinyl only) in early 1996 as a Glasgow vocational school's class project. It would surely have passed immediately into obscurity, except that the songs are astonishingly great—sly, literate, interlocking stories of disaffected youth, set to unstoppable melodies. ("I gave myself to God," Murdoch murmurs in "The State I Am In." "There was a pregnant pause before he said OK.") The arrangements jangle, shuffle, and don't get in the way of the tunes; they're occasionally graced with elegant trumpet lines, in homage to Murdoch's beloved Love.

With *If You're Feeling Sinister* Murdoch gets everything exactly right. This time, the songs are even more audacious, lyrically and sonically: the blasting harmonica that powers "Me and the Major," the self-referential games of "Judy and the Dream of Horses," the orgasmic orchestral crests of "The Stars of Track and Field." Murdoch's characters' sexual confusion and personal failings are unsparingly cast, but drawn with consummate compassion and wit, and he's come up with another set of impossibly hooky melodies. A perfect album.

The three 1997 EPs collected as *Lazy Line Painter Jane* gave the band a chance to experiment a bit, with mostly spectacular results. Guest singer Monica Queen bursts into the title track halfway through and transforms it into a Dusty Springfield–via–Velvet Underground barnstormer; the Murdoch-sung "A Century of Fakers" and an odd little spoken piece by guitarist Stuart David, "A Century of Elvis," are radically different takes on a single backing track; "Dog on Wheels" is Murdoch's most overt Love homage yet. (The band has continued to release nonalbum singles ever since; the best are "Legal Man," a goofy fake-1971 dance number, and the slow-simmering "This Is Just a Modern Rock Song.")

The Boy With the Arab Strap finds Murdoch delegating some of the songwriting to his bandmates. That's not an intrinsically bad idea—Isobel Campbell's fey "Is It Wicked Not to Care?" is charming, and anticipates the records she made under the name the Gentle Waves—but he's a great songwriter, and the others are merely pretty good. Murdoch himself is singing as gently as ever, but his lyrics are seething with oddly embittered rage. Musically, though, the band's on top form. "Sleep the Clock Around" builds on a pulse by degrees until it lets loose with a triumphal trumpet-and-bagpipe coda, and the title track is a rollicking update of vintage glam rock.

Even more of a group effort, the still darker *Fold Your Hands Child, You Walk Like a Peasant* has a couple of Murdoch's most finely wrought songs ever, especially "The Model" and its Proustianly complex melody. It's also got B&S's first actively embarrassing moment (the leaden Lee Hazlewood pastiche "Beyond the Sunrise"), another Campbell-sung winner ("Waiting for the Moon to Rise"), and a handful of barbed references to the Bowlie Weekender music festival the band headlined in 1999, including "The Chalet Lines," which Murdoch sings from the perspective of a woman raped at it.

Storytelling—music written for Todd Solondz's movie of the same name, and barely used in it—is a filler-y comedown, with grandiose instrumentals and half a dozen songs that could mostly pass for a subtle Belle and Sebastian parody. Only the garage-rocking, 75-second "Scooby Driver" is a sign of hope that they're not trapped by their own songwriting habits. Although Campbell left the band shortly after *Storytelling* was released, Belle and Sebastian soon began crafting *Dear Catastrophe Waitress*. Pop maximalist Trevor Horn (who had worked with the likes of Seal and Rod Stewart) was an unlikely choice to produce the album, but he worked out beautifully. *Dear Catastrophe Waitress* has a lush, detailed sound and shows Murdoch in a playful mood, imagining that his boss seduces him on "Step Into My Office, Baby" and alluding to Thin Lizzy with "I'm a Cuckoo." (He has also offered his most overtly Christian lyrics to date.) It ends with a fabulous rocker, "Stay Loose," proof that the band has left its stylistic cul-de-sac behind.   —D.W.

Belly

  ★★★½ Star (Sire/Reprise, 1993)
  ★★★ Baby (Silvertooth, 1993)
  ★★★ King (Sire/Reprise, 1995)
  ★★★★ Sweet Ride: The Best of Belly (Rhino, 2002)

Tanya Donelly

  ★★ Lovesongs for Underdogs (Warner Bros., 1997)
  ★ Beautysleep (4AD, 2002)

Distorto-melodic Throwing Muses featured slasher-burner Kristin Hersh doing the most throwing and stepsister Tanya Donelly doing the bulk of the musing. By 1992, Donelly had skipped out for a one-album Pixies-ish twist with Kim Deal's Breeders, then alighted again to make it big with her own Belly (with ex-Muse Fred Abong on bass, plus drummer and guitarist brothers Chris and Tom Gorman). The band's strong first EP, *Slow Dust*, hit #1 on the U.K. indie charts, and 1993's full-length *Star* debuted just as stateside aggro-grunge gloom gave way to alt's broader palette. Confident pop fables, such as the jaunty, puppeteering "Gepetto," Gypsy nightmare "Slow Dog," and radio-glistening "Feed the Tree" give witchy weirditude serious (if shoegazey) melodic muscle. The even more songful 1995 followup *King* (produced by rock icon maker Glyn Johns) is another ebullient charmer, its showpiece tune "Now They'll Sleep." But *King*'s commercial nonstart ended up breaking up the band, and the quiet self-analysis of Donelly's 1997 solo debut, *Lovesongs for Underdogs*, is more a postcard from an old friend than a blazoned manifesto, and on 2002's *Beautysleep*, songs such as the ultrasound-heartbeating "Life Is But a Dream" and the Stevie Nicks–ish "Night You Saved My Life" reveal our onetime dervish in the creative thrall of motherhood. In "Night," she sings, "Now I sit with my baby at my breast/I was never this good at my best," bringing her spiritual quest to the domestic sphere.   —L.S.

Pat Benatar

  ★★★ In the Heat of the Night (Chrysalis, 1979)
  ★★★ Crimes of Passion (Chrysalis, 1980)
  ★★ Precious Time (Chrysalis, 1981)
  ★★ Get Nervous (Chrysalis, 1982)
  ★★ Live From Earth (Chrysalis, 1983)
  ★★ Tropico (Chrysalis, 1984)
  ★★ Seven the Hard Way (Chrysalis, 1985)
  ★★ Wide Awake in Dreamland (Chrysalis, 1988)
  ★★★ Best Shots (Chrysalis, 1989)
  ★ True Love (Chrysalis, 1991)
  ★ Gravity's Rainbow (Chrysalis, 1993)
  ★ Innamorata (CMC, 1997)
  ★★ 8-15-80 (CMC, 1998)
  ★★½ Synchronistic Wanderings (Chrysalis, 1999)

Just as there are a lot of songwriters who have no business singing, there are a lot of singers who would really be better off not writing. Pat Benatar, for instance. As a singer, her ability was obvious from the first, for not only did *In the Heat of the Night* do more with John Mellencamp's "I Need a Lover" than he ever did, but its emphasis on metallic, Suzi Quatro–style rockers such as "Heartbreaker" and the title tune gave her a saleable image and a sound. *Crimes of Passion* follows much the same pattern, thanks to such tough-but-tuneful offerings as "Treat Me Right" and "Hit Me with Your Best Shot" (although the latter got her into hot water with anti–sexual abuse activists). But Benatar wanted more than cover-song success; she wanted to prove her mettle as a writer, and actually does so with "Hell Is for Children" (from *Crimes*), an anti–child abuse song written by Benatar and bandmates Neil Geraldo and Roger Capps.

"Hell" was a fluke, unfortunately, and *Precious Time* proved it, with original songs that are either silly or clichéd, and sometimes both. *Get Nervous* continues the decline, while *Live From Earth* (eight concert recaps of earlier hits, plus two studio tracks) perks up only when it gets to "Love Is a Battlefield"—a song Benatar and band didn't write.

Tropico moves away from arena rock and toward a more intricately arranged sound, but only Lowen & Navarro's "We Belong" does anything with the approach. Tellingly, *Seven the Hard Way* is loaded with outside material, and Benatar soars through the likes of "Sex as a Weapon" and "Invincible" (though her version of "7 Rooms of Gloom" is enough to make one wonder if she'd ever heard Motown before).

About the only thing on *Wide Awake in Dreamland* that's worth hearing is "All Fired Up," and it—along with most of Benatar's hits—can be found on *Best Shots* (which is, song for song, a better deal than the career-encapsulating *Synchronistic Wanderings*, which, at three CDs, is about two discs longer than casual fandom would warrant). As for *True Love*, Benatar's painfully earnest bout with the blues, it seems to be the product of a misunderstanding; traditionally, one must suffer to earn the right to sing the blues, not just listen to it. Since then, she has retreated to the nostalgia circuit and its CD corollary, CMC Records. —J.D.C.

Ben Folds Five

★★★★ Ben Folds Five (Passenger/Caroline, 1995)
★★★ Whatever and Ever Amen (550, 1997)
★★½ Naked Baby Photos (Caroline, 1998)
★★★½ The Unauthorized Biography of Reinhold Messner (550, 1999)

Ben Folds

★★★★ Rockin' the Suburbs (Epic, 2001)
★★ Ben Folds Live (Epic, 2002)

★★ Speed Graphic (EP) (Sony, 2003)
★★★ Sunny 16 (EP) (Sony, 2003)

The Bens

★★★½ The Bens (EP) (Sony, 2003)

When North Carolina trio Ben Folds Five arrived with its self-titled debut in 1995, a still grunge-heavy modern-rock climate made the guitarless group seem almost a novelty. But actually, Folds' aggressive piano playing falls in line with ivory-pounding rockers from Jerry Lee Lewis through Elton John, and the group's keyboard-based pop quirks draw from Todd Rundgren and Joe Jackson, among others. At the very least, then, *Ben Folds Five* marked the arrival of a formidable new addition to the tradition. In particular, songs such as "Uncle Walter" and "Boxing" display Folds' knack for character sketches, something relatively rare among his alt-rock peers. Meanwhile, "Underground"—with its faux-dramatic opening, multiple vocal parts, and skewering of the so-called alternative scene—typifies Folds' sharp humor as well as the threesome's ability to mount surprisingly complex arrangements with limited resources.

A more sardonic, even bitter, voice emerges on the group's major-label debut, *Whatever and Ever Amen*, which screams "break-up album" all over—particularly on the revenge-fantasy opener, "One Angry Dwarf and 200 Solemn Faces," and the self-explanatory "Song for the Dumped." Its most notable exception, "Brick," features a rather contrite, sullen narrator recounting, without political agenda, a trip to the abortion clinic. It's beautifully executed, and even became an unlikely hit for the group. Elsewhere, though, *Whatever*'s dark obsessions snuff out a lot of the topical humor that made the group's debut a delight, even as the musical approach remains largely unchanged.

Naked Baby Photos is the group's former indie label attempting to benefit from "Brick" 's success—a somewhat premature odds-and-ends compilation of the formative years: outtakes, original versions, studio goofs, and early live recordings. *The Unauthorized Biography of Reinhold Messner*, the trio's third and final studio album, marked a significant change in direction. Though not as heady or literal as its title suggests, it has the feel of a concept album—an extended treatise on a man coming to terms with his shortcomings, demons, regrets, and mortality—complete with string and horn orchestrations, plus other divergences from the trio's familiar piano-bass-drums aggregation. Mostly, it's as serious as it sounds and the writing is often good enough to do its subjects justice. But tracks such as "Army" and "Your Redneck Past" leave room for Folds' dark humor as well, making *Reinhold*

Messner the group's most sophisticated, accomplished record, if not the most easy to enjoy.

Rockin' the Suburbs is Folds' proper solo debut, (there is a very odd set of instrumental and spoken-word tracks that he released under the name Fear of Pop, which you can safely ignore). With its bright production ("Annie Waits") and character-driven romps ("Zak and Sara," "The Ascent of Stan"), *Suburbs* marks a partial return to the writing style that made *Ben Folds Five* so successful. New additions to the sonic vocabulary include drum-machine hand claps, synthesizers, multitracked vocals, even guitars—both acoustic ("Still Fighting It") and full-on electric (the hilarious title track, also a single). Integrating elements of all the things Folds does best—biting irony, bittersweet tales, expertly crafted sketches—the pianist seems to have reached a new level of comfort and consistency on this engaging record.

Ben Folds Live features concert recordings from Folds' 2002 solo piano tour. However, since most of his songs are dominated by piano anyway, hearing them without additional accompaniment doesn't offer much of a new twist. A cover of Elton John's "Tiny Dancer" and a pair of songs that don't appear on other albums hardly make *Live* a must-hear, either, though an included DVD featuring eight live video clips might entice fans. Instead of a proper followup to his solo debut, Folds released two EPs in rapid succession, which were available for sale online only. *Sunny 16* and *Speed Graphic* feature five tracks, including one cover song each (the Cure's "In Between Days" on the first; Divine Comedy's "Songs of Love" on the second). While limited-edition EPs would seem the perfect place to experiment, the eight originals are mostly just standard Folds fare, and not particularly his best work. *Sunny 16* is the more notable of the two, with humorously topical songs like "There's Always Someone Cooler Than You" and "Rock Star."

The Bens, released the same year, showcases the tantalizing union of Folds with indie-rock singer/songwriters Ben Lee and Ben Kweller. While the prospect of three Bens in one band might have been too good a novelty to pass up, in fact, the four-song collection scores on each track—from the CSN-style harmonies of "Just Pretend" to the new-wavey romp of "Xfire." Like the best EPs, this one leaves you wanting more. —R.M.S.

Tony Bennett

★★★½   The Beat of My Heart (1957; Columbia, 1997)

★★★★   Tony Bennett with Count Basie [original title: Basie Swings, Bennett Sings (with Count Basie)] (1959; Roulette, 2000)

★★★★   I Left My Heart in San Francisco (1962; Columbia, 1988)

★★★★   I Wanna Be Around (1963; Columbia, 1995)

★★★★   Who Can I Turn To (1964; Columbia, 1995)

★★★★   If I Ruled the World: Songs for the Jet Set (1965; Columbia, 1997)

★★★   The Movie Song Album (1966; Columbia, 1988)

★★★★   Snowfall: The Tony Bennett Christmas Album (Columbia, 1968)

★★★   Something (1970; Columbia, 1995)

★★★★   Tony Bennett's All-time Greatest Hits (1972; Columbia, 1997)

★★★★   The Tony Bennett/Bill Evans Album (1975; Fantasy, 1990)

★★★★   Together Again: Tony Bennett & Bill Evans (1976; Rhino, 1999)

★★★★   16 Most Requested Songs (1986; Columbia, 1991)

★★★★   The Art of Excellence (Columbia, 1986)

★★★★   Bennett/Berlin (1987; Sony, 1990)

★★★★★   Tony Bennett Jazz (Columbia, 1987)

★★★★   Astoria: Portrait of an Artist (Columbia, 1990)

★★★★★   Forty Years: The Artistry of Tony Bennett (Columbia/Legacy, 1991)

★★★★★   Perfectly Frank (Columbia, 1992)

★★★★   Steppin' Out (Columbia, 1993)

★★★★   The Essence of Tony Bennett (Columbia/Legacy, 1993)

★★★½   MTV Unplugged (Columbia, 1994)

★★★★   Here's to the Ladies (Columbia, 1995)

★★★★   Tony Bennett on Holiday (Columbia, 1997)

★★★★   3 Pak (I Left My Heart in San Francisco, The Art of Excellence, Astoria) (Sony, 1997)

★★★★   Sings His All-time Hall of Fame Hits (Columbia, 1997)

★★★★   Tony Bennett's All-time Greatest Hits (Columbia, 1997)

★★★½   Tony Bennett at Carnegie Hall, June 9, 1962—The Complete Concert (Columbia, 1997)

★★★½   The Playground (RPM/Columbia, 1998)

★★★   Bennett Sings Ellington/Hot and Cool (RPM/Columbia, 1999)

★★★★   Sings Rodgers & Hart Songs (Rhino, 1999)

★★★½   The Ultimate Tony Bennett (RPM/Columbia Legacy, 2000)

★★★   Playin' With My Friends: Bennett Sings the Blues (Sony, 2001)

with Bill Evans

★★★½   Together Again (1977; Rhino, 1999)

with k.d. lang

★★★½   A Wonderful World (Sony, 2002)

That Tony Bennett is as popular, if not more so, in the 21st century as he has been at any other time in his 50-plus years in show business is more than testimony to the power of persistence or to the MTV generation appreciating his individual sense of style as a mark of unassailable cool. When he sings, Bennett, by the very personal nature of his lyric readings, creates new worlds and reveals the heart's deepest desires. He has never lost sight of the wisdom proffered by two early mentors, Frank Sinatra and Count Basie, to wit, insist on singing the best songs (Sinatra) and "economy of line, keep it simple, keep it swingin' " (Basie).

Exhibit A in defense of the above observations is the four-CD box set *Forty Years: The Artistry of Tony Bennett,* released in 1991. Its 87 songs, from Bennett's first single, 1950's overblown "Boulevard of Broken Dreams," to 1989's "When Do the Bells Ring for Me," show songwriter credits from the pantheon: notably Jule Styne, Richard Rodgers, Johnny Mercer, Cole Porter, Kurt Weill, Harold Arlen–Ira Gershwin, Cy Coleman–Carolyn Leigh, Carl Sigman, Gordon Jenkins, Jerome Kern, Oscar Hammerstein, Johnny Mandel, Betty Comden–Adolph Green, Jimmy Van Heusen, and Hank Williams (whose "Cold, Cold Heart" Bennett and producer Mitch Miller transformed with strings and a pop arrangement into a single that had a six-week run atop the pop chart in 1951, the first country-to-pop mutation embraced by the masses). He worked well with a number of producers ("some terrible, some terribly artistic," he writes in his liner notes) whose styles varied, including Mitch Miller, Ernie Altschuler, Helen Keane, Teo Macero, and his own son, Danny Bennett, and found a comfort zone where he could deliver honest performances. And it never hurts to have the kind of backing Bennett was blessed with during these years, particularly that of his longtime (since 1956) piano accompanist/ musical director Ralph Sharon, the Count Basie Orchestra, Bill Evans, Jo Jones, Jimmy Rowles, Joe La Barbera—a mile-long list of the finest musicians of the day. And this litany hasn't yet accounted for the superb arrangers on these sessions, such as Robert Farnon, Torrie Zito, George Siravo, Marion Evans, et al.

The box set documents the breadth and depth of Bennett's art in all its remarkable variety. His first producer, Mitch Miller, knew nothing of subtlety, favoring instead a big, bright sound, full of rising strings, orchestral crescendos, and big-voiced backup singing. Still, Bennett had a productive run with Miller, as disc one of this set shows. Elsewhere, though, the textures become richer as new producers and arrangers pass through and Bennett becomes a singer, as opposed to the belter he often had to be under Miller's aegis. In

this light, disc four is a revelation, as it showcases Bennett in more austere settings, digging deep into his lyrics and delivering again and again with deeply felt but introspective probings of the human condition, particularly with regard to feelings of love and the passing of time. The apex of this 22-song disc—and the entire box set, some might argue—is three songs cut in 1975 with the evocative minimalist pianist Bill Evans providing the sole instrumental support. On his solo forays Evans steps out, but gingerly, with atmospheric, discursive variations on the theme, then backs off when Bennett returns, supporting the vocalist's moody deliberations with solemn right-hand fills.

The box set becomes the jumping-off point for all of Bennett's work in the years leading up to his 1990s "rediscovery." For one, the artist himself is now engaged in a reconsideration and repackaging of his catalogue, with titles reissued as the Tony Bennett Master Series. These are perfect products of their times: 1963's *I Wanna Be Around,* comprised of the entire original *I Wanna Be Around* album and seven tracks from another 1963 LP, *This Is All I Ask,* captures the mood of American pop in its final, florid orchestral stage before the British Invasion and rock & roll in general took control of the radio and of the American cultural mainstream; 1964's *Who Can I Turn To,* released at the height of Beatlemania, reads like a troubled internal monologue conducted in the aftermath of a love affair gone south, with the material reflecting the appropriate contrasting moods, from desolation ("Who Can I Turn To") to tearful reflection ("There's a Lull in My Life") to the determination to move on ("The Best Thing to Be Is a Person," a blues ballad that closes the album as an optimistic philosophical bookend to the opening title track); 1965's lush, mesmerizing *If I Ruled the World: Songs for the Jet Set* could have been the soundtrack for a Claude LeLouche–directed romance. When it swings, it does so subtly, not bombastically; when it goes into a dreamy mode, Bennett sings with the lightest, most affecting of touches, as the Ralph Sharon Trio provides delicate accompaniment, the Will Bronson Chorus harmonizes sotto voce, Al Cohn occasionally steps in with a sensuous tenor sax solo, and the strings hum softly and evocatively in the background. The material is made to order for romance: "Fly Me to the Moon"; the Latin-tinged breakup song "How Insensitive," written in part by Antonio Carlos Jobim; Sammy Cahn and Jimmy Van Heusen's poignant monologue of a man determined to turn his life around, "All My Tomorrows"; a horn-rich, swinging interpretation of Richard Rodgers' "Two By Two"; and a previously unissued take on a classic Richard Rodgers–Lorenz Hart discourse on the condition known as being in love, "Falling in Love With Love," with which Bennett has such a good time that he chuckles to himself at the end of the second verse. On 1970's *Something*, Bennett finds his emotional touchstones in contemporary material such as the George Harrison–penned title track; Lennon-McCartney's "The Long and Winding Road"; a swinging version of Fred Neil's "Everybody's Talkin' "; and a deliberate, almost conversational reading of the Bacharach-David gem "Make It Easy On Yourself" to which Bennett imparts a mature acceptance of the inevitable while also suggesting the bombastic emotion found in the Walker Brothers' 1965 hit version and the poignancy of Dionne Warwick's 1970 hit.

Astoria, an autobiographical song cycle, is a special entry in the Bennett catalogue owing to the songs being carefully chosen to reflect the ideas and moods of the singer's formative years in New York, where he was born Anthony Dominick Benedetto in 1926 to immigrant Italian parents. *Astoria* provides perspective on a life, *Tony Bennett Jazz* on a career. As the box set indicates, Bennett has blurred the lines between jazz and pop singing by working effectively in both styles. On *Jazz* he assays an assortment of sides cut between 1954 and 1967, adding grist to the argument that he ranks with the best jazz singers of any generation; along the same lines, his two after-hours summits with Bill Evans, *The Tony Bennett/Bill Evans Album* and *Together Again,* are treasures barely hinted at even by the exceptional cuts on the box set. Other recommended forays into more pronounced jazz encounters should start with *Tony Bennett Sings Rodgers & Hart Songs,* which features Bennett accompanied with great sensitivity by the Ruby Braff–George Barnes Quartet on a 20-song overview of two Rodgers and Hart albums Bennett cut for his own Improv label in 1976 and 1977; even by Bennett standards these represent a daunting standard of interpretive singing and imaginative accompaniment. Check out the astonishing, near-whisper vocal Bennett employs throughout most of "Lover," and the mind-bending evocation of a lonely man for whom the turning of the earth does not bring renewal in an autumnal reading of "Spring Is Here." In a celebratory spirit, Bennett leaves the blues behind on the scintillating *Basie Swings, Bennett Sings* with Count Basie and His Orchestra.

Bennett/Berlin teams the master interpreter with a set of Irving Berlin tunes less obvious than one might imagine, despite the inclusion of "White Christmas." Focusing on several melancholy entries in the Berlin canon, Bennett in effect delivers a concept album quite moving in its depictions of shattered love. A 1986 album, *The Art of Excellence,* finds a low-key, dispassionate Bennett ruminating over aspects of love

in a performance enlivened by a humorous, topical call-and-response duet with Ray Charles on "Everybody Has the Blues."

Given that he had 32 Top 40 singles between 1951 and 1965, with all but two rising into the Top 30, the purely commercial aspect of Bennett's art demands some sort of representation. And so it is that three "greatest hits"–type compilations exist. *Tony Bennett's All-time Greatest Hits* and *16 Most Requested Songs* assemble the most successful singles in their respective packages, while *The Essence of Tony Bennett* aspires to an elevated plateau. On the latter, timeless moments such as "Because of You," "Solitaire," and "I Left My Heart in San Francisco" are present and accounted for, but so are less obvious but equally scintillating entries.

From the first quiet notes and heartfelt lyrics of "Time After Time," the opening track on *Perfectly Frank,* it's apparent something special is going on. And something is: this is Tony Bennett paying homage to Frank Sinatra, the man who, on national television in 1974, called Bennett his favorite singer and subsequently extolled his virtues many times over. Sensitively backed by the Ralph Sharon Trio, these intimate readings are direct and passionate, the ambience is strictly late-night, small club, and the theme is romance. Warming up to the challenge of the album's concept, Bennett tackles trademarked Sinatra fare such as "Nancy" and "One for My Baby" as well as less prominent selections in the Chairman of the Board's repertoire, gives it all a respectful, swinging spin, and for a moment owns each of the 24 tracks. No mere masterful tribute, *Perfectly Frank* is a vivid demonstration of a peerless interpreter at the top of his game. His first studio effort after the *Forty Years* box returned him to the public eye in a major way, *Perfectly Frank* was the launching of an artistic renaissance for Bennett that has continued unabated into the new millennium.

In the wake of his tribute to the singer's singer, Bennett tipped his hat to the stylist's stylist in a collection of Fred Astaire chestnuts. Best known through his film roles as the epitome of upper-crust elegance and a dancer nonpareil, Astaire's unique way with a song marked him as a formidable stylist, very nearly the equal of the giants of his generation. His range would not wow anyone, and his singing voice was soothing but not especially rich in colors. Yet he understood and knew how to sell the sophisticated lyrics he sang, be they celebrations of high life (Irving Berlin's "Steppin' Out with My Baby") or high romance (George and Ira Gershwin's "He Loves And She Loves").

American popular song gets no better than *Steppin' Out,* with 18 tracks written by Irving Berlin, the

Gershwins, Arthur Schwartz–Howard Dietz, Cole Porter, and A.J. Lerner. Again backed by the Ralph Sharon Trio, Bennett finds new points of personal reference in the Astaire canon as he explores the worldly wise texts of Cole Porter's "I Concentrate on You" and the Gershwins' "Nice Work If You Can Get It," the latter being an especially nice bit of work as the mood and tempos change from the jaunty, cocky opening bars into a solemnly described account of love's end.

Continuing to pay tribute to those who had influenced him, Bennett surfaced again in 1995 with *Here's to the Ladies,* 18 songs otherwise associated with some of the top female vocalists of the past half-century—the likes of Billie Holiday, Peggy Lee, Rosemary Clooney, Sarah Vaughan, Margaret Whiting, Ella Fitzgerald, Dinah Washington, and others—expertly executed by the Ralph Sharon Trio supplemented by a big band. With Sharon on piano and backed by an unobtrusive orchestra, Bennett focused his attention solely on Billie Holiday in the 1997 release *Tony Bennett on Holiday.* Ambience counts for much here, and Bennett, who coproduced with his son Danny, keeps things resolutely quiet, his vocals floating free with feathery tenderness across the medium-cool soundscape. An electronic duet between Bennett and Billie Holiday on "God Bless the Child" (the only track produced by Phil Ramone, he being the architect of Frank Sinatra's *Duets* albums) sounds as pasted together as it really is. Even though this is the only opportunity we have to hear these two remarkable vocalists in the same place at the same time, the concept worked better in theory than it does in practice. It doesn't undermine the album, but it wasn't necessary. In keeping with the theme nature of his latter-day albums, *The Playground* is an odd but ultimately captivating entry in that, although its songs are taken from the classic American-pop songbook, it's an album expressly aimed at children.

2001's *Playin' With My Friends: Bennett Sings the Blues* teams the vocalist nonpareil with a cross-generational mix of guest artists, with contemporaries such as B.B. King (on a rousing treatment of "Let the Good Times Roll") and Ray Charles (an engaging take on "Evenin' ") and young upstarts Diana Krall and Sheryl Crow (who does not acquit herself well with a dolorous treatment of "Good Morning Heartache") bridged by Stevie Wonder, Billy Joel, and Bonnie Raitt. It's a likable album, but hardly ranks with Bennett's transcendent work.

MTV Unplugged documents Bennett's transformation into alternative rock icon with his appearance on the in-concert show that gives this album its name. Here Bennett and the Sharon Trio work out on a compelling set of classics, including "Old Devil Moon," "Fly Me to the Moon," "Body and Soul," as well as the signature songs (which also qualify as classics) "Rags to Riches" and "I Left My Heart in San Francisco." Elvis Costello and k.d. lang make guest appearances, the latter harmonizing nicely with Bennett on a medium-cool version of "Moonglow" and taking her own well-considered solo turns; the less said about Costello's affected performance the better. Now we know he can't sing pop, either. Lang teamed up with Bennett in 2002 for an album of duets, *A Wonderful World,* heavy on some tried-and-true standards that the duo has a splendid time turning inside out in delicate fashion, especially "A Kiss to Build a Dream On" and the album-closing "If We Never Meet Again."

Oh, yes. In addition to the advice given him by Sinatra and Basie, there is one other tenet to which Bennett has held firm over the years, one borne out by the half-century-plus of artistry documented here. The words, his own, are as elegant as his singing: "I believe in music being truthful and beautiful, and that has become the premise for what I am doing." Well said; well sung. —D.M.

Chuck Berry

★★★★	Chuck Berry Is on Top (1959; Chess/MCA, 1987)	
★★★★	Rockin' at the Hops (1960; Chess/MCA, 1987)	
★★★★	New Juke Box Hits (Chess, 1961)	
★★★★½	From St. Louis to Liverpool (Chess, 1964)	
★	Chuck Berry's Golden Hits (Mercury, 1967)	
★★	The London Sessions (Chess, 1972)	
★★★	Rockit (Atco, 1979)	
★★★★★	The Great Twenty-eight (1982; Chess/MCA, 1984)	
★★★★	Rock 'n' Roll Rarities (Chess/MCA, 1986)	
★★★★★	The Chess Box (Chess/MCA, 1988)	
★★★★	Missing Berries: Rarities, Vol. 3 (Chess/MCA, 1990)	
★★★	His Best Vol. 1 (Chess, 1997)	
★★★	His Best Vol. 2 (Chess, 1997)	
★★	The Millennium Collection (MCA/Universal, 1999)	
★★★★★	The Anthology (MCA/Universal, 2000)	
★★★½	Blues (Chess, 2003)	

with Bo Diddley

★★	Two Great Guitars: Bo Diddley & Chuck Berry/The Super Super Blues Band: Howlin' Wolf, Muddy Waters, Bo Diddley (1964; BGO, 2002)

By now it's easy to see that rock & roll was an inevitable outgrowth of all the seemingly disparate musics emerging in the post–World War II years, rather than something that fell out of the sky full-blown on the day Elvis Presley walked into the Memphis Recording Service. All the early rock & roll giants occupied distinctive niches defined by their musical approach. Chuck Berry was the first important writer, performer, and instrumentalist in the rock & roll style, a man whose immediately identifiable playing and powers of observation and eloquence have remained touchstones for succeeding generations of artists, one of the standards by which great rock is measured. Had he been only a profound influence on Bob Dylan, the Beatles, and the Rolling Stones he would merit distinction; but Berry's signature shows up frequently in current performers from punks to singer/songwriters.

At a time when critics discounted rock & roll as adolescent caterwauling, Berry was not only defining a subculture, he was providing running commentary on a country in the midst of change, more mobile, more affluent, more restless, free for the moment from the specter of war but bitterly divided internally over racial issues. Aiming his messages unequivocally at the younger generation, Berry made poetry of the seemingly mundane complexities of adolescent life. His was folk music for teens, with references to a world with its own language, symbols, and customs.

But as much as he was a chronicler of young American culture, so was Berry given to deeper ruminations. "Too Much Monkey Business" is a vivid depiction of the drudgery and ennui of the working life. If you get past the clever images spicing "Brown-Eyed Handsome Man" the story becomes one of black men overcoming the strictures of segregation. A touching memory of love lost and love renewed is rendered in mellow, bluesy fashion in "Time Was." The force and sincerity behind "I've Changed" will move anyone familiar with Berry's checkered history with the law. At a time when American families are breaking up in record numbers, the story of a divorced father's desperate search for his daughter in "Memphis" takes on new relevance. He also wrote the greatest songs *about* rock & roll in "Sweet Little Sixteen," "Around and Around," "Rock and Roll Music," and "Roll Over, Beethoven."

Those seeking classic Berry all in one place now can take three steps up: the flawlessly programmed *The Great Twenty-Eight* (easy to find used), the more in-depth and fully rounded *The Anthology,* or the hefty *Chess Box.* The *Box* also offers the pleasure of side trips into Berry's lesser-known work, much of it in a blues vein and some of it instrumental. The *His Best* and *20th Century Masters* anthologies are simply lesser versions of the same package. When he arrived at Chess in 1955, Berry was familiar with a number

of styles. In his longtime pianist Johnnie Johnson he had an accompanist equally at home in blues, boogie-woogie, R&B, and rock & roll, and at Chess he worked with the sterling players populating the label's studio: Willie Dixon, Fred Below, Jimmy Rogers; even Bo Diddley and his maraca man Jerome Green sit in on a few cuts. Completists, then, are advised to grab the *Rock 'n' Roll Rarities* collection and seek out *Missing Berries, Volume 3,* now missing itself and a much sought-after sampling of blues-oriented material.

Also noteworthy are the out-of-print former LPs *Chuck Berry Is on Top, Rockin' at the Hops,* and *New Juke Box Hits.* These show how Berry was wedging in what might be called alternative material amid his rock & roll—check out Berry's steel guitar on the instrumental "Blues for Hawaiians" from *Chuck Berry Is on Top,* the deeply felt covers of Jay McShann's "Confessin' the Blues" and Charles Brown's timeless "Driftin' Blues" on *Rockin' at the Hops,* and a stirring treatment of B.B. King's "Sweet Sixteen" on *New Juke Box Hits.* The most important deleted original LP, however, is *St. Louis to Liverpool.* The title is a reminder that in 1964, when this album was released, it was clear that the Beatles, the Rolling Stones, and lesser British rockers were deeply indebted to the man. In addition to classic tracks—"Little Marie," "Promised Lan'," "You Never Can Tell," and "No Particular Place to Go"—the album includes one of the best cover versions of the Charles Brown classic "Merry Christmas, Baby," a tough rendition of Guitar Slim's "Things I Used to Do," and a searing instrumental, "Liverpool Drive"; then Berry calms down with a mellow, after-hours blues, "Night Beat." Another easily found cutout, *The London Chuck Berry Sessions* (1972), is notable for producing Berry's only #1 single, "My Ding-a-Ling," a dreadful fluke novelty now mercifully forgotten.

Berry left Chess to record for Mercury between 1966 and 1969, producing nothing of note. *Chuck Berry's Golden Hits* consists of reworkings of some of the great Chess sides, plus one new track, the unremarkable "Club Nitty Gritty." Accept no substitutes for the originals. In particular, the many latter-day live recordings with various pickup bands are to be shunned. Apart from the Chess material, the other Berry album of note is *Rockit,* originally released on Atco in 1979. No gem this, but an exemplary return to good rockin' form. Guitar aficionados may find something of interest in the teaming of Berry and Bo Diddley on two of the four extended instrumental tracks on *Two Great Guitars,* but for these two masters, the workouts are fairly routine (currently reissued as a twofer with the equally forgettable *Super Super Blues Band*). An excellent item for the confirmed Berry fan,

Blues includes Nat "King" Cole–style blues pop and jump blues in addition to modified Delta blues twangers. The disc is wonderful for comparing Berry to Chess blues masters and for hearing how he concocted rock from the roots.   —D.M./M.MI.

The Beta Band

★★★★	The Three E.P.'s (Astralwerks, 1998)
★★	The Beta Band (Astralwerks, 1999)
★★½	Hot Shots II (Astralwerks, 2001)
★★★★	Heroes to Zeros (Astralwerks, 2004)

For a while there, it looked as if Scotland's Beta Band was destined to be one of those outfits that never match their earliest work. To be fair, though, following *The Three E.P.'s* would have been tough for just about anyone. Originally released as three separate discs—*Champion Versions, The Patty Patty Sound,* and *Los Amigos del Beta Bandidos*—the album dazzles with its kaleidoscopic inventiveness, as the Betas gobble up every conceivable pop style, from prissy folk to sweaty funk, and convert them into long, multisegmented song suites, full of seemingly offhand melodies and goofy humor. The quartet's digestive process isn't always reliable, but the cumulative effect is impressive.

On *The Beta Band* and, to a lesser degree, *Hot Shots II,* the Betas come close to losing their way. The humor has gone from goofy to nearly incomprehensible, and the interesting musical snatches are undone by countless irritating digressions. When the arrangements get sparse (as on *Hot Shots II*'s "Gone"), things tend to work, but that just doesn't happen often enough.

Heroes to Zeros is a very different kettle of kippers. As the opening track, "Assessment" (which tips its hat rather broadly to U2's "I Will Follow"), suggests—and the rest of the album conclusively demonstrates—the Betas have figured out how to streamline their sound without killing their creativity. Songs like "Space Beatle" and "Liquid Bird" reach Wilsonian (Brian Wilsonian, that is) heights of complexity but never come ungrounded. Four albums into its career, the Beta Band has finally beaten the sophomore slump.   —M.R.

Bettie Serveert

★★★½	Palomine (Matador, 1992)
★★½	Lamprey (Matador, 1995)
★★★½	Dust Bunnies (Matador, 1997)
★★★½	Private Suit (Hidden Agenda, 2000)
★★★★	Log 22 (Palomine, 2004)

When it was first released, *Palomine* was hailed as college rock's *London Calling.* And yet: Repeated listening reveals that, despite standouts such as the title track's bittersweet vow of friends forever or the persona-defining "Tom Boy," these Dutch pals of ours were better at sustaining a vague mood than concretely bringing their desires, their fears, and their tunes into focus. *Lamprey* proved itself merely a pleasant, vacant wash. But while no one was listening, Bettie Serveert got better. *Dust Bunnies* finds the band wondering if it should be sadder that it isn't famous, why it doesn't like its friends more than it does, and if disillusionment is anything more than an immense cosmic gag. (Their answer: a resounding "Hmm, dunno.") This is the testament of a band whose limited success denied it the luxury of outright failure—like it or not, it was just going to keep on rocking, or droning, or jangling, or whatever it was it did—and that writes and plays funnier and freer as a result.

For *Private Suit,* the band submitted to the iron hand of P.J. Harvey associate John Parish, who shoehorned them into a snug girl-singer-plus-backupband template. With Visser limited to reeling off quick hooks, this arranged chamber pop seems claustrophobic after the rangy expanse of *Dust Bunnies.* But the girl singer sounds more womanly and self-possessed than ever. "Took a Tylenol and an hour's drive," she begins the album, "and somehow found a reason why I'm still alive."

On *Log 22,* produced by Visser, the band loosened up considerably, kicking into full-on Velvets-as-jamband mode. "Wide-Eyed Fools" indicated that these boho ramblers had no intention of assuming a quiet, normal life anytime soon.   —K.H.

Beyoncé
see DESTINY'S CHILD

The B-52's

★★★½	The B-52's (Warner Bros., 1979)
★★★★★	Wild Planet (Warner Bros., 1980)
★★★★	Party Mix (Warner Bros., 1981)
★★	Mesopotamia (Warner Bros., 1982)
★★★	Party Mix/Mesopotamia (1981–82; Warner Bros., 1991)
★★	Whammy! (Warner Bros., 1983)
★★	Bouncing off the Satellites (Warner Bros., 1986)
★★★	Cosmic Thing (Warner Bros., 1989)
★★	Good Stuff (Warner Bros., 1992)
★★★★	Time Capsule: Songs for a Future Generation (Warner Bros., 1998)
★★★	Nude on the Moon: The B-52's Anthology (Rhino, 2002)

A party band in the truest sense of the term, the B-52's were one of the first pop acts to pick up on the ironic attitude of the postpunk underground. Taking its cue from acts such as Blondie and the Sic Fucks, *The B-52's* is obsessed with the detritus of hip, embracing such trash icons as lava lamps and beehive hairdos (the latter having in fact inspired the band's name). Yet for all its playful sarcasm, the album manages to avoid the usual pitfalls of camp, never daring to act as if the band was somehow superior to its material.

Even so, that would likely wear thin in a hurry were it not for the band's other strength: its music. Applying the amateurism of New York punk to the abandon of beach music (the soulful Carolina kind, not the twangy California stuff), the band came up with a sound unlike anything else on the scene. It wasn't Ricky Wilson's idiosyncratic guitar lines or the simple stomp of Keith Strickland's drumming that did it, so much as the way their jerry-rigged groove reinforced the campy quality of Fred Schneider's declamations and Cindy Wilson and Kate Pierson's B-girl harmonies. This was the chemistry that made "Rock Lobster" so oddly arresting, and that spirit carries over to the rest of the album, from the sci-fi silliness of "Planet Claire" to the fevered insistence of "Dance This Mess Around."

Wild Planet improves on the formula by fleshing out the musical mannerisms with actual songs, offering everything from the dark, enigmatic groove of "Private Idaho" to the near pathos of Cindy Wilson's "Give Me Back My Man." That triumph was short-lived, however. After *Party Mix*, a collection of club-oriented remixes of the most danceable songs from *The B-52's* and *Wild Planet*, *Mesopotamia* found the band out of its element as it tried to swap its fun-loving frivolity for the arch art rock of bands such as Talking Heads (whose David Byrne produced the album). Never had the group's music sounded so boring or pretentious. (Both EPs have since been combined on a single CD.)

Whammy! is an attempt to return to the silliness of the first albums, but is unable to overcome either its self-conscious songs (which range from the mock-utopian "Song for a Future Generation" to the pseudo-Southern culture of "Butterbean") or the stiffness of its drum machine–driven rhythm tracks.

With the death of Ricky Wilson in 1985, the B-52's were thrown even further into disarray, having not only to augment the band's lineup with session players but also to virtually reinvent its sound. No wonder *Bouncing off the Satellites* flops miserably; solid as the singing is—note how neatly Cindy Wilson and Kate Pierson harmonize on "Summer of Love"—it sounds hollow and contrived. So the band went back to its roots and hit the jackpot. Commercially, *Cosmic Thing* was far and away the band's most successful ef-

fort, producing two Top 5 singles and spending nearly a year in the *Billboard* Top 40. Artistically, though, it's less heartening. Despite their no-nonsense melodicism, most of the songs here reprise the band's early sound without any edge or ambiguity. Thus "Love Shack," instead of sending up beach music dance parties, becomes a straight-up tribute—an act of imitation, not transcendence. And while the considerably slicker production doesn't stop the band from generating a simulacrum of its original groove on the likes of "Channel Z" and "Deadbeat Club," the B-52's tumble into self-caricature.

Cindy Wilson left the group once *Cosmic Thing* had run its course, and thus bears no responsibility for the hash that is *Good Stuff.* Clearly, the group had run out of gas, artistically and commercially. *Songs for a Future Generation* compiles all the B-52's classic tracks, but dilutes the effect somewhat by padding the disc with such second-rate fare as "Hallucinating Pluto." *Nude on the Moon* is an even longer version of the same exercise, and is useful mainly as a cure for nostalgia. —J.D.C.

B.G.

★★	Chopper City (Cash Money, 1997)
★★	It's All on U, Vol. 1 (Cash Money, 1997)
★★½	It's All on U, Vol. 2 (Cash Money, 1997)
★★★½	Chopper City in the Ghetto (Universal, 1999)
★★	True Story (Universal, 1999)
★★★	Checkmate (Universal, 2000)
★★	Livin' Legend (Koch, 2003)

The young prince of Cash Money, B.G., a.k.a. Baby Gangsta, was plucked out of the notorious Uptown ghetto of New Orleans by Cash Money founders Baby and Slim Williams when he was just eleven years old. Rather than play up the prodigy's youthful innocence, the Williams brothers capitalized on the somewhat disturbing thrill of hearing a hardly pubescent boy spitting grime-filled rhymes laced with violence and sex talk. Over in-house producer Mannie Fresh's sparkling electro beats, he quickly established himself as a regional superstar on the Southern rap scene. As was their way, Cash Money, recognizing a star when they saw one, released album after album from B.G., paying little heed to established artist-release schedules. In 1997 alone, B.G. put out three albums, the best of which, *It's All on U, Vol. 2,* helped Cash Money link up with Universal Music in a lucrative distribution deal. He also, along with labelmate Juvenile, was made one of the cornerstones of Cash Money's supergroup, Hot Boyz.

Chopper City in the Ghetto, from 1999 was a phenomenal success, placing Cash Money on the national map, making B.G. a household name, and adding the word *bling* to the cultural vocabulary. With its smash hit, "Bling Bling," and its anthemic roll call, "Cash Money Is an Army," it stands as B.G.'s best work. 1999 also saw the rerelease of B.G.'s first album, recorded at the tender, and one would think innocent, age of 11. Its pleasures are largely cheap thrills. *Checkmate* would be B.G.'s final record with Cash Money, as he departed unamicably from the empire soon afterward. His followup, released three years later, would go mostly unnoticed, suffering from the absence of Mannie Fresh and his Cash Money cohorts. —C.R.

Big Audio Dynamite

> ★★★ This Is Big Audio Dynamite (Columbia, 1985)
> ★★★★ No. 10, Upping St. (Columbia, 1986)
> ★★★★ Tighten Up, Vol. 88 (Columbia, 1988)
> ★★★ Megatop Phoenix (Columbia, 1989)
> ★★★ The Globe (Columbia, 1991)
> ★★★ Higher Power (Columbia, 1994)
> ★★½ F-Punk (Radioactive, 1995)
> ★★★★ Planet B.A.D.: Greatest Hits (Columbia, 1995)
> ★★★ Superhits (Columbia, 1999)

After the Clash, guitarist Mick Jones—whose pop sense provided that band with some of its biggest hits—decided to abandon punk entirely and embrace a more modern sound, one that reconciled guitar-based rock with the electrobeats and sonic manipulation of hip-hop. Dubbed Big Audio Dynamite (because it was B.A.D., geddit?), his new group's initial experiments were more gimmicky than illuminating, but by *No. 10, Upping St.* its use of samples was no longer simply a matter of sonic special effects, with "C'mon Every Beatbox" using its electronics to create a common ground between hip-hop, rock, and reggae. *Tighten Up, Vol. 88* expanded the music's base even further to include ska, rockabilly, and even country music. Yet even as B.A.D. was laying the groundwork for later work by Jesus Jones, the Farm, and EMF, the group's refusal to embrace dance music outright, combined with Jones' predilection for predictable, singsong melodies, kept it from topping its early success—leaving *The Globe* and *Higher Power* mired in mediocrity. *F-Punk* tried to relight the fire by cranking the guitars, but to little avail. —J.D.C.

Big Black

> ★★★ Lungs (EP) (1982; Touch and Go, 1992)
> ★★★ Bulldozer (EP) (1983; Touch and Go, 1992)
> ★★★★ Racer X (EP) (1984; Touch and Go, 1992)
> ★★★★½ Atomizer (1985; Touch and Go, 1992)
> ★★★½ Headache (EP) (1986; Touch and Go, 1992)

> ★★★★ The Hammer Party (1986; Touch and Go, 1992)
> ★★★★ Songs About Fucking (Touch and Go, 1987)
> ★★★★½ The Rich Man's Eight Track Tape (1987; Touch and Go, 1992)
> ★★★½ PigPile (Touch and Go, 1992)

Rapeman

> ★★★ Budd (EP) (Touch and Go, 1988)
> ★★★★ Two Nuns and a Pack Mule (Touch and Go, 1989)

It's like watching an optical illusion in which white dots on a black background switch places across the page. In the wildly influential Big Black, punk polymath and indie philosopher-king Steve Albini's flesh-shredding riffs and freight-train drum machine sought to destroy everything in his band's path with disciplined, scabrous noise and caustic yellow journalism.

Big Black's debut EP, *Lungs*, is a mere skeleton of future triumphs: thin, angular guitars, a relentless drum machine named Roland, humorless screeds. The followup EP, *Bulldozer*, the first with brilliant guitarist Santiago Durango, is thicker and more fully realized ("Cables," about the slaughterhouse as theme park, became a fan fave). The *Racer X* EP is the first fully conscious Big Black record, with the band's savage aesthetic in its final form: British postpunk set alight by American hostility. (All three EPs benefit from their compilation on *The Hammer Party*.)

Atomizer is a full-bore revelation, a key document of 1980s underground culture and one of the most influential albums of the age. Durango and bassist Dave Riley aid Albini in setting these odes to tabloid America on "liquify"; guitars have simply never sounded so annihilating. Topics include child abuse, racial self-loathing, sex-plus-arson (the catchy, haunting "Kerosene"), and a live reprise of "Cables." And contrary to popular belief, there's a (misinterpretable) half-assed morality at play; Big Black doesn't make the horror, it just reports it, soaked in wit and loathing. You get it? Fine. You don't? Fuck you. (*The Rich Man's Eight Track Tape* combines *Atomizer*—minus the useless near-instrumental "Strange Things"—a single covering Wire's "Heartbeat," and the inferior-by-comparison followup EP *Headache*.)

The smart bombs on *Songs About Fucking* feel still more focused but less inspired, the songwriting less diverse. Their lyrical focus hasn't budged, and the sound is starting to calcify into shtick. Big Black still stuns, but it no longer surprises, and it's no wonder Durango split for law school and the band called it quits—at the height of its indie fame—on the eve of *Fucking*'s release. (The *Fucking* CD appends one single.) A fun-but-not-revelatory live album and video appeared in 1993.

Albini soon formed Rapeman with bassist David Wm. Sims and human drummer Ray Washam, both late of Texas noise maniacs Scratch Acid. They didn't last very long, hampered by a protest-worthy name, but *Two Nuns and a Pack Mule* is a scorcher, an underrated slice of funny, brutal skreepunk that slams vegetarians, covers ZZ Top, and shouts out Sonic Youth. (The *Nuns* CD is appended with the band's fetal debut EP *Budd*, notable only for the brilliant title track.) —J.G.

Big Brother and the Holding Company

★★	Big Brother and the Holding Company (1967; Columbia, 1971)
★★★½	Cheap Thrills (Columbia, 1968)
★★	Big Brother and the Holding Company Live (Rhino, 1985)
★★½	Live at Winterland '68 (Columbia/Legacy, 1998)
★★	Do What You Love (Cheap Thrills, 1999)

Complete with R. Crumb cover art, endless, warped guitar solos, and clunky, hippie homages to "da blooze," *Cheap Thrills*, Big Brother and the Holding Company's second album, sums up acid rock in all its messy, pseudo-psychedelic glory. Even the group's name was an underground pun—"holding" being doper's slang for possessing drugs. What makes the record more than a period piece is, of course, its singer, Janis Joplin. While her more focused work came later, Joplin already thrills like a force of nature: "Piece of My Heart" and Big Mama Thornton's "Ball and Chain" unleash a vocalist whose urgency finds no equal in mainstream rock. From her ripest beginnings, Joplin comes on as an archetypal desperado, her passion ripped from the same inner source as that of the timeless bluesmasters Ma Rainey, Howlin' Wolf, and the like. *Live at Winterland '68,* for better and worse, is even more unleashed. —P.E.

Big Daddy Kane

★★★★	Long Live the Kane (Cold Chillin', 1988)
★★★★	It's a Big Daddy Thing (Cold Chillin', 1989)
★★★½	Taste of Chocolate (Cold Chillin', 1990)
★½	Prince of Darkness (Cold Chillin', 1991)
★★★	Looks Like a Job For . . . (Cold Chillin', 1993)
★★½	Daddy's Home (MCA, 1994)
★★½	Veteranz Day (Blackheart, 1998)
★★★★	The Very Best of Big Daddy Kane (Rhino, 2001)

Tall, dark, and handsome, Big Daddy Kane was all that and then some: the undisputed champion playboy

MC of the Western world at a time when fast rap was the freshest sound around. Kane was born Antonio Hardy on September 10, 1968—his stage name was an acronym for "King Asiatic Nobody's Equal." Before his personal charisma and skills on the mike came to the fore, Kane was a ghostwriter, penning raps for Biz Markie ("Pickin' Boogers," "The Vapors") and Roxanne Shante ("Have a Nice Day"). The goofy, hefty Biz was the flipside of Kane's cock-diesel loverman look: The pair joined legendary Queens producer Marley Marl's Juice Crew and signed to Marley's Cold Chillin' label. Kane waxed his debut single, "Raw," ("chillin'/killin' like a villain/the meaning of RAW is Ready And Willin' ") for Cold Chillin' in 1987, and that set the stage for his great late-'80s albums. An appearance alongside Vanilla Ice in Madonna's salacious *Sex* book in 1992 gave rise to vicious rumors that didn't help the popular perception that Kane had taken his smooth lothario persona too far. Kane has defended his R&B-flavored material, pointing out that early hip-hop hits such as "Rapper's Delight" were essentially rhymes laid over R&B tracks like "Good Times." Then there's the fact that by the late '90s, sung R&B hooks became de rigueur in both underground and mainstream hip-hop. So either Kane was unfairly penalized for being a trendsetter, or he deserved his lambasting for setting a wack precedent; either way, his R&B-flavored hits such as "Smooth Operator" cannot hold a candle to his energetic fast rap classics "Raw," "Ain't No Half-Steppin' " and "Set It Off" (all of these tracks are on *The Very Best of*). *Taste Of Chocolate* (1990) featured intriguing collaborations with the likes of Barry White (the pair, who met while contributing to Quincy Jones' *Back on the Block* album, delivered the ballad "All Of Me"), Malcolm X's daughter, Gamilah Shabazz (for the duet "Who Am I"), and rhyming comedian Dolemite (on the hilarious dis-fest "Big Daddy Vs. Dolemite"). Kane also gave a young Jay-Z a leg up, featuring him along with Ol' Dirty Bastard on "Show & Prove" from *Daddy's Home*. Also worth seeking out is the DJ Premier–produced "Platinum Plus," featuring Kane on Big L's 2000 album *The Big Picture*. —P.R.

Big L

★★	Lifestylez ov da Poor and Dangerous (Sony, 1995)
★★★	The Big Picture (Rawkus, 2000)

Born Lamont Coleman, and a member of Fat Joe's DITC (Diggin' in the Crates) crew, Big L's first album, 1995's *Lifestylez ov da Poor and Dangerous*, garnered little notice, but by the late '90s he'd become one of the most well-respected underground hip-hop

MCs in New York, thanks in large part to the 1998 single "Ebonics." Unfortunately, Coleman was murdered in Harlem on February 15, 1999, a couple of months shy of his 25th birthday. *The Big Picture* is an uneven collection of music he was working on before his shooting; tracks such as "Ebonics," "Holdin' It Down," and "Flamboyant" portray Big L as a rapper full of potential that his early death squandered, one of the sadder what-if stories of recent hip-hop.   —M.M.

Big Pun

★★★½	Captial Punishment (Loud-RCA, 1998)
★★★★	Yeeeah Baby (Loud-Columbia, 2000)
★★★½	Endangered Species (Loud-Columbia, 2001)

Despite his untimely passing and limited discography, Bronx rapper Big Pun (born Christopher Rios) is widely acknowledged to be one of the most gifted MCs ever to breathe life into a microphone. His main claim to pop success was his debut's radio-friendly "Still Not a Player," but there's much on *Capital Punishment* worthy of praise. The music is filled with ominous bass loops, sharp drum stabs, and soul-filled R&B. When Pun teams up with other MCs—the Roots' Black Thought on "Super Lyrical;" mentor Fat Joe on "Twinz" (a remake of Dr. Dre and Snoop Doggy Dogg's "Deep Cover"), Wyclef on "Caribbean Connection,"; Noreaga on "You Came Up,"; Mobb Deep's Prodigy; and Wu-Tang's Rebel INS (Inspectah Deck) on "Tres Leches"—he shines with intricately laced, breathless strings of words. On his own he's just as deadly, as he proves on "The Dream Shatterer" and "Beware" where he boasts, "Y'all niggas can't do shit to me/Physically, lyrically, hypothetically, realistically/I'm the epitome of catching wreck."

Rios died of a heart attack in 2000. Released two months after his death, *Yeeeah Baby* is musically adventurous, blending sublime R&B ("It's So Hard"), operatic stylings ("Off With His Head"), raunchy ballads ("My Dick"), and Latin tunes ("100%"). His legendary humor is on display through self-deprecating skits and numbers like "Laughing at You" and "Nigga Shit." He's still as ferocious an MC as ever, letting off beautifully scripted barrages of rhyme on "We Don't Care" and "Leather Face."

The posthumous *Endangered Species* features former highlights, unreleased numbers, and past cameos. The inclusion of star-studded posse cuts such as "John Blaze," "Wishful Thinking," and "Banned from TV," next to remixes of Brandy's "Top of the World" and Ricky Martin's "Livin' la Vida Loca," showcases the full range of Pun's verbal dexterity and makes this a worthy sendoff for a star that shone bright but briefly.   —K.X.

Big Star

★★★★	#1 Record (Ardent, 1972)
★★★★★	Radio City (Ardent, 1974)
★★★★★	Third/Sister Lovers (1978; Rykodisc, 1992)
★★★★★	#1 Record/Radio City (Line/Fantasy, 1992)
★★½	Big Star Live (Rykodisc, 1992)
★★★½	I Am the Cosmos (Rykodisc, 1992)
★★	Columbia: Live at Missouri University 4/25/93 (Zoo, 1993)
★★	Nobody Can Dance (Norton, 1999)

Big Star toiled in obscurity in the '70s, making off-kilter garage pop that hardly anybody noticed at the time. The Memphis popsters were too light and tuneful to connect with the hard-rock crowd, too weird for mainstream attention. But their music kept steadily blowing young minds and influencing other musicians, and by the time the American indie underground came into its own in the '80s, they were rightfully acclaimed as forefathers. Poignant, plaintive, brainy, Big Star devised a cool rock & roll swagger that was quintessentially Southern; the music was arty and bohemian, yet had nothing at all to do with New York or L.A., and it has made these men cult heroes to generations of restless small-town kids. All three Big Star albums have taken their places as classics.

Lead singer Alex Chilton was already a jaded music-biz castaway by the time the band started. After singing the Box Tops' hit "The Letter" as a teenager, he'd sunk back into obscurity. With Big Star, his voice got higher and lighter, meshing with the jagged guitar chime of *#1 Record*. Along with drummer Jody Stephens and fellow singer/songwriter Chris Bell, Chilton had a bent style of Beatles songcraft, with guitar ravers such as "Feel" and "In the Street" alongside one of the all-time great love songs, the acoustic "Thirteen." *Radio City* is even sharper and smarter, with Chilton's boyish, angelic, occasionally zonked-out vocals on top of slashing guitar and barbed harmonies. "September Gurls," "Life Is White," and "Mod Lang" became underground classics, rewriting the *Rubber Soul* songbook with a bittersweet Memphis edge, and while Bell was almost entirely absent from the album, bassist Andy Hummell contributed the killer "Way Out West." The Fantasy and Line reissues both put *Radio City* and *#1 Record* on the same CD, which makes both albums sound even better.

Radio City didn't sell, and Big Star's followup took years to get released. Originally issued in 1978 as *Third*, more commonly known by its original title, *Sister Lovers*, it's a truly amazing album of catatonic grandeur, full of long, slow, rambling melodies that sink to the depths of despair ("You're sitting down to dress/And you're a mess," goes one typical lyric). Chilton's songs are stark and brilliant, with piano, strings, heavy studio reverb, eccentric soul flourishes, and a cover of Lou Reed's "Femme Fatale." It's often been reissued with varying track listings and running order—the longest version is Rykodisc's 1992 version—but however you find it, the music is stately ("Stroke It Noel," "Nightime"), sometimes joyous ("Thank You Friends," "O Dana"), and always gorgeous ("Blue Moon"). A late-night masterpiece.

Alex Chilton eventually reemerged with a solo career in the '80s, looking a little surprised to find himself still kicking around. As Big Star started getting posthumous respect, archival reissues popped up: *Big Star Live* is a 1974 concert featuring a nasty version of Loudon Wainwright's "Motel Blues"; *Nobody Can Dance* is more raw and punkish. In 1993 Chilton and Stephens reunited for a one-off show (backed up by the Posies) recorded as *Columbia: Live at Missouri University*. Chris Bell was killed in a 1978 car crash after recording a solo album that never got released in his lifetime. *I Am the Cosmos* finally appeared in 1992, with the adolescent yearning of "You and Your Sister" and the acoustic desolation of "I Am the Cosmos." —R.S.

Big Tymers
see HOT BOYS

Bikini Kill

★★★★	The C.D. Version of the First Two Records (Kill Rock Stars, 1992)	
★★★★	Pussy Whipped (Kill Rock Stars, 1994)	
★★	Reject All American (Kill Rock Stars, 1996)	
★★★	Singles (Kill Rock Stars, 1998)	

Julie Ruin

★★ Julie Ruin (Kill Rock Stars, 1998)

Le Tigre

★★★★ Le Tigre (Mr. Lady Records, 1999)
★★★ From the Desk of Mr. Lady (EP) (Mr. Lady Records, 2001)
★★★ Feminist Sweepstakes (Mr. Lady Records, 2001)

Feeding subtlety, recording quality, and centuries of female subservience into the meat grinder of punk, the pioneering *Bikini Girl* fanzine—devoted to "Revolution Girl Style Now"—spawned an even more potent and far-reaching monster: the Olympia, WA, quartet Bikini Kill. Led by editor/rabble-rouser/singer Kathleen Hanna, the band's shows consciously set out to create a new, female-centric agenda for rock and nurtured the inner feminist in rockers from Sleater-Kinney to Nirvana's Kurt Cobain, whose "Smells Like Teen Spirit" was inspired by a slogan Hanna spray-painted graffiti-style on his wall.

The band's early recordings are rougher than burlap on baby skin, and the politics is very earnest and sometimes preachy, Hannah's intensity breathtaking in bad-girl manifestos such as "Double Dare Ya," "Suck My Left One," and "Rebel Girl," cowritten with Joan Jett. The sound captured on *The C.D. Version of the First Two Records* is caustic, daring, and shamelessly didactic, a two-by-four to the chops of patriarchy. *Pussy Whipped* compresses a dozen more songs into 24 minutes and climaxes midway with Hanna screaming like she's being knifed on "Tell Me So" and riding a lascivious guitar riff on "Sugar," then a few songs later exits on the uncharacteristically tender "For Tammy Rae." It would prove to be the band's last essential recording; *Reject All American* quickly loses steam and *Singles* is a slight epitaph, marking the third appearance on CD of "Rebel Girl."

Hannah sketches out a transition strategy on *Julie Ruin*, in which she sings, writes, and plays most of the instruments herself. It introduces a more rhythmic and melodic approach, but is no less blunt in its politics or low-fi in its sonics, with a cheap drum machine and cheesy sampler making this the femme-punk equivalent of a Throbbing Gristle B-sides album. "I Wanna Know What Love Is" answers NWA's "Fuck tha Police," while "Crochet" disembowels another favorite target: the media.

With Le Tigre, Hannah asks, "Who took the bomp from the bompalompalomp?" The electro-rock trio answers its own musical question on *Le Tigre*, which makes Hannah's hot rock only seem more palatable with its Shin-Dig!-worthy beats and Shangri-La's-like vocal give-and-take. The self-titled album flat-out swings while namechecking feminist icons in "Hot Topic," and mulls the genius-feminist divide on "What's Yr Take on Cassavetes."

Feminist Sweepstakes keeps the party rolling: The "LT Tour Theme" celebrates "rollerskate jams" with diabolical laughs and an Iron Maiden–worthy guitar solo, and "Dyke March 2001" is a sci-fi protest anthem. But the stakes are very much the same as they were on Bikini Kill's first album, with stories of dead-end jobs and marginalized lives—snapshots from a world in which gender and sexual orientation too often dictate the difference between economic success and failure, social acceptance and ostracism. All of which makes Le Tigre one of the most subversive dance bands in rock history. —G.K.

Biz Markie

★★★ I Need a Haircut (Cold Chillin', 1991)
★★★★ All Samples Cleared (Cold Chillin', 1993)

Considering it came out in 1988, the same year as Public Enemy's sonically dense *It Takes a Nation of Millions to Hold Us Back*, Biz Markie's debut, *Goin' Off*, is either the last of the old-school rap records or the first release of the old-school revival. With tracks built around a basic drum-machine pattern and DJ cuts and scratches, the sound is decidedly schoolyard lo-fi. Unconcerned with depicting street life or expressing black consciousness, Biz Markie's raps—some written for him by Big Daddy Kane, or with producer Marley Marl—are designed purely to be party entertainment, vocal candy to accompany the dance beat. Novelties delivered in Biz's distinctive nasal slur, including the gross-out "Pickin' Boogers," the crowd rocker "Biz Dance Pt. 1," and the human beatbox display of "Make the Music with Your Mouth Biz" introduce Biz as hip-hop's clown prince.

Reissued together with *Goin' Off* in a two-CD set, Biz Markie's second release, 1989's *The Biz Never Sleeps*, continues in this jokey, party-time vein with tracks such as "The Dragon," an ode to body odor, and "Mudd Foot," his dance tribute to a "Fat Albert" character. But this time, Biz is at the helm, and with writing and production help from his cousin and DJ, Cutmaster Cool V, he cooks up an album that's still relatively spare, but far more musically sophisticated than the debut. In particular, tracks such as "Check It Out," "Biz in Harmony," and "Just a Friend"—the latter Biz's biggest pop hit, later revived by teen crooner Mario—offer original musical accompaniment, back-up harmonies, and melodies that manage to be catchy even when delivered with Biz's mock-earnest off-key singing.

I Need a Haircut further refines Biz's now-trademark blend of slobbering rap comedy, interpolations of familiar songs, and tracks built on classic R&B riffs. "Road Block" is typical, casting Biz as an everyman loser in love as he sings (butchers) the melody of "American Woman." In the same vein, "Alone Again" centers or the chorus of Gilbert O'Sullivan's 1972 hit, "Alone Again (Naturally)." Biz's song, featured on original copies of *Haircut* but absent from the current version, became the focus of a copyright-infringement battle between O'Sullivan and Biz that changed hip-hop, setting a new precedent for sample clearances. *Haircut's* most memorable track, however, is "T.S.R. (Toilet Stool Rap)," which is at once a gross-out novelty similar to *Goin' Off*'s "Pickin' Boogers" as well as a clever slice of life about that place of quiet repose where so many creative ideas are born.

All Samples Cleared is both a good-natured reference to Biz's "Alone Again" ordeal and also a statement of fact in the newfound hip-hop landscape: Kool and the Gang, Lee Dorsey, James Brown, Cannonball Adderley, Rufus Thomas, and other more obscure names all get credited (and, presumably, paid) for use of their music in constructing these songs. It also happens to be Biz's most accomplished and engagingly melodic record. "I'm the Biz Markie" opens with a fast-flowing vocal performance and track reminiscent of Brand Nubian. Elsewhere, Biz offers his most topical material: an honest admission of his looks ("I'm a Ugly Nigga [So What]"); a rundown of his colorful relations ("Family Tree"); cautionary tales of folk wisdom ("Bad By Myself"); madcap adventures in sexual pursuits ("Young Girl Bluez," "Hooker Got a Boyfriend"), and, for good measure, another Biz-created dance step ("The Gator [Dance]").

By 2003, there was no reason to expect Biz would ever release another album. So when *Weekend Warrior* arrived, it not only seemed to come out of nowhere, it also surprised fans by being every bit as good as any of the records he had made during his prime. With solid production and star cameos from P. Diddy, Elephant Man, and others, *Warrior* offers pleasant surprises all the way through. Still defiantly old-school, Biz's hilariously tossed-off rhymes and random gabbing are pure entertainment, reanimating the party spirit of hip-hop's earliest rapping DJs.

Two Biz best-ofs—both contain his most familiar material and almost identical track listings—are also available. *The Best of Cold Chillin'* offers seventeen tracks, including the post-*Samples* single "Studda Step" and a couple other nonalbum cuts. *Greatest Hits* features fourteen songs, among them Biz's 2001 comeback single, "Turn tha Party Out." —R.M.S.

Björk

Somehow, over the course of a decade, Björk Gudmundsdóttir has transformed herself from the singer of a decent Icelandic alt-rock band into the world's most successful avant-garde musician—the person who turns everyone else's difficult-listening experiments into pop praxis. *Debut,* her coming-out party after the breakup of the Sugarcubes, was produced by Soul II Soul's Nellee Hooper, with songs that serve the gasping, note-stretching eccentricities of her voice. It scored three dance hits in "Human Behaviour," "Violently Happy," and "Big Time Sensuality," and although not all of her stylistic about-faces succeed, the horny daydream "Venus as a Boy" is cute as a button.

Hooper returned for *Post,* this time joined by more top-rank producers, including Tricky and 808 State's Graham Massey. It's very much like the good parts of *Debut,* but with more assured melodies for Björk's voice to circle like Christmas lights, especially "Isobel," a light-headed ode to self-adoration. Comedy relief comes from "It's Oh So Quiet," an unlikely big-band cover of Betty Hutton's 1948 novelty song "Blow a Fuse" that became an even less likely hit. *Telegram* is remixes and rerecordings of most of *Post* (done with the likes of the Brodsky Quartet and Pan Sonic's Mika Vainio) that actually shed new light on the songs. There's also a cool little collaboration with percussionist Evelyn Glennie and a new mix of "I Miss You."

Homogenic announces itself from the get-go as unlike any other pop record in sight, and then transforms its peculiarity into sheer majesty. A swooning string section meets noise splatters as beats (courtesy of Mark Bell and Howie B.), and Björk's glorious vocal acrobatics coax them all into bed together. She's also blossoming as a songwriter, especially on "Jóga," a gesture of devotion to a friend, and the radiant "All Is Full of Love."

The brief soundtrack for Björk's starring role in the film bummer *Dancer in the Dark, Selmasongs* includes duets with Catherine Deneuve and Radiohead's Thom Yorke. It's a terrific exercise in constructing lush movie-musical songs around the rhythms of heavy industry, and her voice is in top form; it just feels a bit skimpy.

Vespertine, on the other hand, is a banquet in the hall of Björk's personal erotics. The lyrics (mostly by the diva herself, with filmmaker Harmony Korine and the late poet e.e. cummings pitching in) obliquely concern life-changingly great sex, and she lingers ecstatically over every syllable. It's not the stuff of radio hits, but the music is spectacular, gently transplanting cutting-edge digital art music into lush, euphonious pop, with contributions from experimental electronic duo Matmos, avant-garde harpist Zeena Parkins, and, on a trio of songs, a custom-made music box. And her voice is still a marvel: Her subsequent world tour in-

cluded a few shows in venues small enough that she could sing *without a microphone.*

The lineup of *Greatest Hits* was determined by a survey on Björk's Web site. The set combines alternate mixes and a negligible new song, "It's in Our Hands," with an otherwise solid if unilluminating survey of her career peaks. *Family Tree* is an extravagance for serious fans: one disc of Björk's own picks from her previous records, plus five three-inch mini-CDs surveying her pre-*Debut* recordings and alternate arrangements of a few familiar songs that feature the Brodsky Quartet. Nice but unessential. The same goes for *Livebox,* a five-disc set that documents live versions of her four proper studio albums (and throws in a DVD of five more tracks). She rearranges her songs cleverly and her singing is as wonderful as ever, but there's nothing revelatory here.   —D.W.

Frank Black

★★★★   Frank Black (4AD/Elektra, 1993)
★★★½   Teenager of the Year (4AD/Elektra, 1994)

Frank Black and the Catholics

★★   Frank Black and the Catholics (spinART, 1998)
★★½   Pistolero (spinART, 1999)
★★★   Dog in the Sand (What Are Records?, 2000)
★★★   Black Letter Days (spinART, 2002)
★★★½   Devil's Workshop (spinART, 2002)
★★★   Show Me Your Tears (spinART, 2003)

Between 1986 and 1993, Charles Thompson IV, a.k.a. Black Francis, headed one of America's greatest alt-rock bands, the Pixies. In the music he's made since then, under the new handle Frank Black (get it?), you can still hear the stylistic features that distinguished his first group: wildly lurching melodies and chord progressions; sudden shifts of meter, tempo, and dynamics; guitar parts that run the gamut from surf sparkle to hardcore chug; and vocals that alternately coo and howl words covering every shade of peculiar. But as the Black catalogue stretches into the present, those features fade into the background. Clearly, Thompson has mellowed over time, becoming more sensible, more direct, and less interesting.

Coproduced by fellow oddball Eric Drew Feldman (Captain Beefheart, Pere Ubu), Black's self-titled debut remains his best album. Songs such as "Places Named After Numbers" and the near-epic "Parry the Wind High, Low" achieve a menacing kind of catchiness, while "I Heard Ramona Sing" features a typically left-field lyric: "I hope if someone retires/They pull another Menudo." A good chunk of *Teenager of the Year*'s whopping 22 tracks sound underdeveloped, but there's enough top-shelf material ("Headache," "Pie in the Sky") to make it worthwhile.

From here the pickings get thinner. Black's next album, *The Cult of Ray* (now out of print), is a punk-metal disaster. His first disc with new band the Catholics goes for a live garage-rock vibe; the energy's great but the songs aren't memorable. *Pistolero* is a slight improvement, interspersing a few sterling tunes ("I Switched You," "So Hard to Make Things Out") among the filler.

On *Dog in the Sand* and its followers, Black regains some of his former juice, adding extra musicians, including Feldman, to the Catholics' basic rock quartet setup and exploring country, folk, and blues influences. They're all decent records—*Devil's Workshop* is the standout—and yet they still miss that lunatic spark of old. —M.R.

Blackalicious

★★★½   A2G (EP) (Quannum Projects, 1999)
★★★★   Nia (Quannum Projects, 2000)
★★★½   Blazing Arrow (MCA, 2002)

Xavier Mosley (Chief Xcel) and Tim Parker (Gift of Gab) got together as Blackalicious back in 1991. They came out of the Sacramento/Davis underground rap scene, which released records as Solesides and Quannum Projects. Over the nine years until they released their first full-length album, they cut a handful of singles and two EPs and contributed some of the best things on comps such as *Solesides Best Bumps* and *Quannum Connection*. But while their basic shtick wasn't unusual for alt-rap—Gab's torrent of gangsta-free words flooding Xcel's utility beats and turntableism—they showed quite a knack for memorable hooks such as, in the seven-cut *A2G*, the alphabet sequence of "A to G," the p-funky chorus in "Rock the Spot," or the "by any means necessary" refrain to "Making Progress."

By the time they assembled *Nia* (Swahili for "purpose") they had 45 songs to choose from; the biggest problem with the nineteen that they chose (including three repeats from *A2G*) is that hooks and messages pile up so fast that it's hard to keep them straight. But "Ego Trip by Nikki Giovanni" (whose protagonist created the pyramids and the Nile, sent an ice age to Europe and burned out the Sahara, gave oil to the Arab world, and can fly) stands on its own, not least because Erinn Anova handles the vocal. Then there's the speech at the end of "Cliff Hanger," the "Blackalicious, we keep it fat, delicious" chorus on "Smithsonian Institute of Rhyme," the "un-huh"s that stomp home "Reanimation," the subliminal "drifting"s on the lullaby "Sleep."

Given that the market for underground rap is a good hundred times that for, say, underground jazz,

major labels beckoned, and for better and worse, *Blazing Arrow* was the result. The deal gives them access to samples from the likes of Harry Nilsson, on "Blazing Arrow," and De La Soul, on "Paragraph President," and the guest stars queue up, although they still hang with old friends such as DJ Shadow and Cut Chemist. But in the end it's still much the same record: fast beats and scratches, lots of words, a few less hooks, but the refrain on "Sky Is Falling" (lifted from one of those B-boys—Beethoven, I think) is awesome. Two lines sum them up nicely: "passion, the drive to press, to strive for best," but especially, "aural pleasure, y'all." —T.H.

Black Box Records
see AUTEURS

The Black Crowes

★★★½   Shake Your Money Maker (American, 1990)
★★★★   The Southern Harmony and Musical Companion (American, 1992)
★★★★   Amorica (American, 1994)
★★½   Three Snakes and One Charm (American, 1996)
★★★½   By Your Side (American, 1999)
★★★★   Greatest Hits 1990–1999: A Tribute to a Work in Progress (American, 2000)
★★★   Live at the Greek (with Jimmy Page) (TVT, 2000)
★★   Lions (V2, 2001)
★★★   Live (V2, 2002)

The Black Crowes seemed little more than blues-rock throwbacks when they swaggered onto MTV in 1990, with a low-budget, live-in-concert video for their Stonesy debut single, "Jealous Again." Soon after, the band dropped a hard-rocking, blue-eyed remake of Otis Redding's funky "Hard to Handle," and music critics cried sacrilege. But what the critics didn't know, the little girls understood: The Black Crowes—along with Guns n' Roses and Lenny Kravitz—put the roll back into rock at a time when hip alternative bands were downplaying the music's sexuality. Guitarist Rich Robinson's raunchy riffs sliced into the funky grooves of the Georgia band's rhythm section like a serrated knife into peach pie, laying a foundation of sweet, soulful boogie for the spastic, Jagger-esque moves and throaty moans of frontman Chris Robinson.

The Crowes hit the ground running on their first two CDs. They don't just ape classic rock on these albums, they actualize the quality of the Rolling Stones' prime years (*Sticky Fingers* and *Exile on Main Street*), thereby reclaiming the Southern American roots of late-'60s and early-'70s British blues rock. Even without the two aforementioned hits, *Shake Your Money Maker* displays a rare maturity for a debut album. In 1990, "She Talks to Angels" was one of the most achingly sublime ballads about drug addiction to appear on a rock record in years—and more empathetic than the Stones' "Sister Morphine." The raw riffage and whiplash boogie of "Thick 'n Thin" pays tribute to the Crowes' regional forebears Lynyrd Skynyrd. With its sharper, beefier attack, *The Southern Harmony and Musical Companion* is even better. The highlights— "Remedy," "Thorn in My Pride," "Hotel Illness," and a gospelish remake of Bob Marley's "Time Will Tell"—find the Crowes effortlessly gliding over all the rock & roll bases: dirty-ass guitar licks, decadent lyrics, soulful vocals, and acoustic-blues pensiveness.

On *Amorica,* the Black Crowes really come into their own as a contemporary hard-rock boogie band. Here, they downplay the Stones influences and focus on their strengths: Chris Robinson's increasingly potent vocals and ever-darkening lyrics; Rich Robinson and Marc Ford's furious guitar interplay; drummer Steve Gorman's Zeppelinesque workouts with bassist Johnny Colt; and Eddie Harsch's churchy piano parts. Percussionist Eric Bobo (of Beastie Boys fame) lends a hypnotic, Latin-tinged seasoning to the music, while the haunting pedal-steel guitar of American Music Club's Bruce Kaphan underscores the album's overall sense of dread. In the wah-wah-fueled funk of "A Conspiracy," sad country soul of "Wiser Time," and resigned country blues of "Descending," the group locks into a sound that owes debts to no one in particular—except the Black Crowes themselves.

Three Snakes continues in the more eclectic vein of *Amorica,* but the album lacks the strong material of its predecessor. While the Robinson brothers are in top form, their solid musicianship can't rescue this album from the awkward, grunge-inspired pop of "Nebakanezer," the psychedelic pretentiousness of "How Much for Your Wings?" or the silly, Sly Stone–via–Lenny Kravitz funk of "(Only) Halfway to Everywhere." On the much better *By Your Side,* the Crowes return to what they do best: lean, mean Southern boogie. At times, they dip back into their stylistic catalogue a bit too literally, once again invoking the Stones ("Kickin' My Heart Around") and Faces ("By Your Side").

In 2000, the Black Crowes toured with former Led Zeppelin guitarist Jimmy Page; the resulting *Live at the Greek* finds Page and the Crowes whipping out brawny performances of such Yardbirds and Zeppelin classics as "Shapes of Things" and "Whole Lotta Love." Page's influence can be heard all over the Crowes' next studio album, *Lions,* as the band continues its back-to-basics approach on a new label. But all the lumbering stomp and Zeppelinesque bombast in the world can't prop up the album's weak, unmemorable songs.

With the various Crowes itching to fly the coop, the band capped its career (at least temporarily) with the double-disc *Black Crowes Live.* It's a fitting farewell; the Crowes always soared highest onstage, and here they kick out the hippie jams ("Cosmic Friend"), swagger like Ronnie Van Zant ("Wiser Time"), and reach for the heavens with stoned abandon ("She Talks to Angels"). *Greatest Hits 1990–1999* is a solid selection of the Crowes' best American Recordings. —M.K.

Black Dice

★★★½ Black Dice (Troubleman, 2001)
★★★★½ Cold Hands (Troubleman, 2001)
★★★½ Beaches and Canyons (DFA, 2002)
★★★½ Creature Comforts (DFA, 2004)

If the Strokes revived vintage CBGB rock and the Yeah Yeah Yeahs embodied Brooklyn's hipster cool, Black Dice represented the cutting edge of New York City's postmillennial punk. The foursome started out in the Providence, RI, noise scene, which was established by Rhode Island School of Design students and centered on the legendary underground venue Fort Thunder. Unlike Providence's other leading band, Lightning Bolt—a bass-and-drums duo who recycle riff-happy heavy metal into amphetamine-kicked skronk—Black Dice set about tearing apart the rigid structures of '90s hardcore.

When Black Dice's lead screamer, effects-board maestro, and youngest member, Eric Copeland, elected to attend New York University, his guitarist brother, Bjorn, bassist Aaron Warren, and drummer Hisham Bharoocha decided to move with him to Brooklyn. Their first, self-titled release after the move, on respected New Jersey hardcore label Troubleman, sounds like a building collapsing: Screeching and buzzing guitar and bass crash into convulsing beats, while Eric's wordless cries approximate both outrage and anguish. Stripped of recognizable repetition and language itself, the songs don't even have names.

Originally known for assaulting audiences at their shows—both physically, by jumping into the crowd swinging, and sonically, by cranking their amps to almost literally unbearable levels—Black Dice slowly began focusing on musical performance, attentively twiddling knobs and pushing buttons in order to orchestrate layers of on-the-spot loops and yet more obscurely wrought noise. *Cold Hands* jumps from splintered screamo to almost pastoral, yet still creepy, passages: The hushed title track's jagged motif could be the slow winding of a music box, its pretty melody reversed and twisted, or ghostly echoes in a deserted boatyard.

Beaches and Canyons, released by much-hyped upstart Manhattan label DFA, fully revealed Black Dice's long-simmering fetish for Japanese noiseniks the Boredoms, whose experimental thrash punk gave way over time to an expansive, spiky psychedelia. (Back-to-nature Brooklyn-by-way-of-Baltimore aggregate Animal Collective also influenced *Beaches and Canyons.*) Black Dice drummer Bharoocha, who spent part of his childhood in Japan, creates tribal polyrhythms instead of breaking beats; Eric literally coos, whoops, and screeches like a monkey; and everyone tries their hand at gee-whiz effects tools, including the "Korg Kaos Pad, Flip 2 Power VT-X Tremelo, Electro Harmonix Poly Chorus, and DOD Gonkulator." (We're not making these up, although they might have.) However Black Dice made it, the combination of whipping feedback, frenetic rhythms, and tidal washes encapsulates the concrete jungle's controlled chaos unlike the sound of any other New York City band.

The hushed, amorphous *Creature Comforts* was made, painstakingly, to be heard on headphones: The highly processed guitars, hand drums, and God knows what else subtly suggest surf, dub, and shoe gazer but also Ed Wood sound effects, jungle racket, and conversation. —N.C.

Black Eyed Peas

★★★	Behind the Front (Interscope, 1998)
★★★½	Bridging the Gap (Interscope, 2001)
★★½	Elephunk (Interscope, 2003)

L.A.-based hip-hop trio Black Eyed Peas started out as the unofficial West Coast franchise of the East Coast's iconic Native Tongues collective, desperate to show the world that not all West Coast rap devotees were about was blingin', bangin', and bitches: Former break dancers garbed in boho gear, comprised of various races and stressing positivity, the trio was a pointed antidote to the gangsta and ghetto fabulousness of the day. Their 1998 debut, *Behind the Front* produced the irresistible club hit, "Joints and Jams," but the group hadn't found their voice yet and the album sinks under the weight of its slick production. Their followup, *Bridging the Gap,* is a more organic-feeling representation of their considerable skills and vision: Tracks such as "On My Own" and "Weekend" display uncluttered and muscular production, deft samples, and smart rhymes.

The group wanted to crack the big time, though, and they did with *Elephunk,* breaking out some mar-

quee names—Justin Timberlake, Papa Roach, Brazilian samba legend Sergio Mendes—as well as adding a female member, Fergie, to their crew. The would-be *What's Goin' On*–era Marvin Gaye track "Where Is the Love" became an Up With People anthem, and the Parliament-inflected "Let's Get Retarded" achieved their booty-shaking goals (and became a theme song for the NBA). The production is meticulously detailed, but the crew's clichéd observations, preachy lyrics, and MTV-ready posturing make *Elephunk* their least inspiring album. —E.H.

Black Flag

★★★	Jealous Again (EP) (SST, 1980)
★★★★½	Damaged (SST, 1981)
★★★	Everything Went Black (SST, 1982)
★★★★	The First Four Years (SST, 1983)
★★★	My War (SST, 1983)
★★	Family Man (SST, 1984)
★★★	Slip It In (SST, 1984)
★★	Live '84 (SST, 1984)
★★	Loose Nut (SST, 1985)
★★★	The Process of Weeding Out (EP) (SST, 1985)
★★★	In My Head (SST, 1985)
★★★	Who's Got the 10"? (SST, 1986)
★★★★★	Wasted . . . Again (SST, 1987)

Lords of the Huntington Beach surf-punk scene and pioneers of the California hardcore aesthetic, Black Flag was an enormously influential band in its day, and it made a handful of indisputably great recordings—as well as an unconscionable number of mediocrities. Granted, a good bit of that had to do with the rapid rate at which the band churned out new albums (six titles in one two-year stretch), but far more damaging was its fondness for poetry readings and dissonant, self-indulgent instrumental recordings. Henry Rollins, the singer/poetry reader who fronted the band from *Damaged* on, was clearly the star, and he made a career as a bandleader/actor/writer and alt-celebrity after Black Flag broke up. But the band's real strength was guitarist Greg Ginn, whose slash-and-burn rhythm work and short, searing solos recall the classic cacophony of Johnny Thunders.

Perhaps the best place to start is *Damaged,* a stunning display of suburban disaffection. Black Flag's writing is cuttingly sharp here, and the band makes some telling points in such consumer-culture parodies as "Gimmie Gimmie Gimmie" and "TV Party." Beyond that, the band's discography becomes a minefield of missteps, spotty albums, and ramshackle reissues. *The First Four Years,* which recaps the band's early singles and EPs, is worth owning; the career-spanning best-of *Wasted . . . Again* is essential listening, but *Everything Went Black,* a collection of early studio sessions and outtakes, is pretty much for collectors only. *My War, Slip It In, Loose Nut,* and *In My Head* each have their moments, but only *Slip It In* manages enough of them to justify a full album. *Live '84* is rambling and chaotic, but *Who's Got the 10"?* cuts through its occasional self-indulgence with brutally intense playing. And though almost every solo on *The Process of Weeding Out* goes on too long, at least it spares us the poetic recitations that make *Family Man* so hard to bear.   —J.D.C.

Black Grape
see HAPPY MONDAYS

Black Rebel Motorcycle Club
★★★★   B.R.M.C. (Virgin, 2000)
★★★   Take Them On, On Your Own (Virgin, 2003)

A tried-and-true rule of rock & roll: It's okay for an American band to sound British if at least one member hails from the U.K. In the case of Los Angeles trio Black Rebel Motorcycle Club, it's their drummer, Nick Jago, whose presence helps justify the band's hefty debt to '80s Brit-rockers such as the Jesus and Mary Chain and Love and Rockets. The band's debut album—named, like the group itself, for Marlon Brando's biker gang in *The Wild Ones*—adds a heavy bass groove to the swirly, psychedelic sound of the U.K. groups that inspired them. Dark, dizzying, and heavy with distortion, *B.R.M.C.* is the best '80s Brit-rock album since, well, the '80s. "Whatever Happened to My Rock & Roll" is a spacey, blues-rock romp, and "Rifles" coasts on drugged-out vocals and shimmering guitars.

Take Them On, On Your Own has fewer hooks, but at least BRMC is starting to sound like their own band. "Stop" declares its presence with a wet, sexy bass line—the song's melodic anchor for Peter Hayes' droning guitar. Other numbers ("Six Barrel Shotgun") rev hard and fast, exactly like Detroit garage rock would sound to three California Anglophiles. On "Ha Ha High Babe," they indulge their psychedelic tendencies with an impenetrable tangle of noise that loops and loops and loops all the way out to space while Hayes pants, "You're ha ha high baby/You can't keep it on the ground." Original, it's not. But it still sounds awfully good while it's happening.   —J.E.

Black Sabbath
★★★★★   Black Sabbath (Warner Bros., 1970)
★★★★★   Paranoid (Warner Bros., 1971)
★★★★   Master of Reality (Warner Bros., 1971)
★★★   Volume 4 (Warner Bros., 1972)
★★★★   Sabbath Bloody Sabbath (Warner Bros., 1973)
★★★★   Sabotage (Warner Bros., 1975)
★★   Technical Ecstasy (Warner Bros., 1976)
★★★★   We Sold Our Soul For Rock 'N' Roll (Warner Bros., 1976)
★★★   Never Say Die (Warner Bros., 1978)
★★★★   Heaven & Hell (Warner Bros., 1980)
★★★   Mob Rules (Warner Bros., 1981)
★★★   Born Again (Warner Bros., 1983)
★★   Seventh Star (Warner Bros., 1986)
★★   The Eternal Idol (Warner Bros., 1987)
★★   Headless Cross (I.R.S., 1989)
★   TYR (I.R.S., 1990)
★★   Dehumanizer (Warner Bros., 1992)
★★   Cross Purposes (IRS, 1994)
★   Forbidden (Capitol, 1995)
★★★★   Best of Black Sabbath (Castle, 2000)
★★★★   Symptom of the Universe: The Original Black Sabbath 1970–1978 (Rhino/Warner Bros., 2002)
★★★★★   Black Box: The Complete Original Black Sabbath 1970–1978 (Rhino, 2004)

Black Sabbath the album, the song, and the band have been studied by metalheads with all the fervor accorded the Dead Sea Scrolls. "Black Sabbath" the song starts off the not-feeling-so-fab four's 1970 debut, and from the moment that its first fearsome notes were unleashed on an unsuspecting public it has remained one of the unshakeable cornerstones of heavy metal. While Led Zeppelin, Deep Purple, and even earlier gods of noize such as Blue Cheer and Jimi Hendrix are also responsible for the storied future of hard rock and metal, this Birmingham, England, quartet stands apart from its peers on a high mountain peak of doom, cannabis, and the monster riffs that—along with evil T-shirts, volume, and shaggy hair—have fueled a million basement dreams of dark glory. They took the blues out of blues-rock and replaced it with Wagner, creating epic battle rhythms filled with a tension and release that any adolescent boy would know about firsthand. Thanks to Roger Bain's production, *Black Sabbath* sounds really big and really unhealthy. It's an album that eats hippies for breakfast; also, it has even been statistically determined that if a brain cell were the size of a grain of sand, the amount lost while listening to this record upon its first year of release could easily fill the Grand Canyon.

What people forget about Black Sabbath—and it's understandable given their demonic imagery and All Hallow's Eve vibe—was that it was one of the most God-driven, puritanical, wet-blanket rock bands in history. Its "mankind is evil and must repent for its wicked ways" thesis would influence almost all the future bards of the metallic arts. On their second and supremely heavy album *Paranoid,* there are laments on the destruction of war and the hypocrisy of politicians ("Electric Funeral" and "War Pigs"), the perils of technology ("Iron Man"), the perils of drug abuse ("Hand of Doom"), and the perils of mythical creatures and their choice of footwear ("Fairies Wear Boots"). On "Hand of Doom," Geezer Butler's subatomic bass, Ozzy Osbourne's tortured bullfrog yelp, Bill Ward's smack-you-in-the-face drums, and Tony Iommi's fuzz guitar lead mesh seamlessly into something so unholy and beautiful that it would take lesser bands years of back-to-the-drawing-board grunt work to achieve such badassed symmetry.

Hot on the heels of *Paranoid* came *Masters of Reality,* an even darker album, if that's possible. The moralizing reaches new heights and the world is given the generous gift of "Sweet Leaf" and "Children of the Grave." *Vol. 4* is one of those difficult "cocaine" albums that bands were fond of making back then. Sabbath was rich, bored, huge in America, and it was the '70s—you do the math. Sluggish and muddy, it nonetheless has its moments and remains a hard-to-beat monument to bloat and excess. Plus, it features a heartfelt ballad from Ozzy called "Changes" that just might be the scariest song the band ever committed to tape.

Sabbath Bloody Sabbath, from 1973, is yet another drugs album, but there is inspiration here that suggests the band found another supplier. Not even Yes's Rick Wakeman can kill the schizophrenic weirdness of a track like "Sabbra Cadabra." Ambitious and tortured, the group creates the first conceptless concept album. "Killing Yourself to Live" is a keeper, as is the now-classic title track. *Sabotage* continues the theme of themeless epic suites with twisted stoner-prog anthems that rock as hard as the early days, but also hyperextend themselves in unexpected ways. It might be the most underrated of their albums, and was certainly the original band's last stab at greatness together. Songs such as "Hole in the Sky," "Symptom of the Universe," and "The Writ" are weird, wild, and massive.

Technical Ecstasy is the '70s-era Sabbath album least likely to be found in a hard-rock fan's collection. It's not horrible, but you wonder if anyone in the band remembers making it. Is it an ill-fated attempt to snag some of the boogie-rock money that Ted Nugent was rolling around in? Or had they just run out of steam? Tony Iommi's guitar is the only thing left alive. The same might be said of *Never Say Die,* the last album Ozzy appeared on before taking a hike and finding solo fame. The songs are better, though, especially the title tune, and it sounds like someone poked Bill Ward with a stick because the drum work is great throughout. Not a blaze of glory for the original foursome but better than people might remember.

There are several good-to-great Sabbath compilations out there, most of which are heavy on Ozzy-era material. Shy, retiring types and scaredy cats looking for an easy way into Black Sabbath's diabolical cosmology can't go wrong with the 1976 best-of *We Sold Our Soul for Rock 'n' Roll,* which is all a weekend blasphemer could ever need. For a more complete overview of Sabbath's glory days, check out *Black Box,* which collects the first four albums and tacks on a load of bonus material. (*Symptom of the Universe* is the abridged version.)

Buyer beware: Of the post-Ozzy albums—and a good many of them should have been sold under the name the Tony Iommi Experience—there are three essential purchases. *Heaven & Hell* and *Mob Rules,* featuring the elfin dragon-slayer Ronnie James Dio on vocals, are both excellent. *Born Again,* recorded with ex–Deep Purple yelper Ian Gillan, is likewise a monstrous beast and one of the best Sabbath albums that hardly anyone has heard. Anything after that is recommended only to diehard freaks who can't go a day without hearing yet another spitfire lick from their master's Gibson, fans of train wrecks who want to hear *The Eternal Idol* (one of Iommi's attempts to cross over into the world of '80s pop metal), and Otto the bus driver.   —S.S.

Black Sheep

★★★★   A Wolf in Sheep's Clothing (Mercury, 1991)

Like its cohorts in the pioneering Native Tongues clique—De La Soul, A Tribe Called Quest, and the Jungle Brothers—New York hip-hop duo Black Sheep approached its music with humor, wit, and creativity. Its 1991 debut, *A Wolf in Sheep's Clothing,* is all youthful energy and cocky strut, with Dres and Mista Lawnge goofing on sell-out rappers, dodging homely honeys, and mocking envious haters. The pair specialized in call-and-response hooks, the most memorable of which, "You can get with this/Or you can get with that," popped out of speakers on the classic "The Choice Is Yours." Mostly though, Black Sheep were girl crazy, and *A Wolf in Sheep's Clothing* is rife with bedroom boasts, horny come-ons, ménage à trois fantasies, and meditations on fly females. Thanks to the duo's comical approach, the subject matter stays fun and light, and offbeat production touches such as the flute sample flitting through "Hoes We Knows" and the rhythmic dog barks that punctuate "Similak Child" make the album consistently engaging.   —K.M.

Blackstreet

★★½   Blackstreet (Interscope, 1994)
★★★½   Another Level (Interscope, 1996)
★★½   Finally (Interscope, 1999)
★★   Level II (DreamWorks, 2003)
★★★★   No Diggity: The Very Best of Blackstreet (Interscope, 2003)

The brainchild of producer Teddy Riley (Bobby Brown, Michael Jackson, etc.), Blackstreet was the sound of Riley getting back into the groove of performing, which he hadn't done since his former group Guy broke up. After single-handedly defining the New Jack Swing sound that swept R&B in the early '90s, Riley stretched out musically on his group's four studio albums, the best of which is *Another Level,* which features the brain-melting, ass-moving single "No Diggity." The song stood out because of its minimalist production, dark vibe, and a guest rap by Dr. Dre that made it absolutely impossible to ignore (it was surpassed as the single of 1996 only by another Dr. Dre–related song, Tupac's "California Love"). Neither *Finally* or *Level II* contain a single like "No Diggity," in either quality or pop impact, though these albums still continued Blackstreet's visibility on the R&B scene. Like many groups in the same vein, their best-of compilation stands as their most consistent album; *No Diggity: The Very Best of Blackstreet* is an awe-inspiring example of bump and grinding single after single. A party favorite.   —K.M.

Black Uhuru

★★★   Love Crisis (Third World, 1977)
★★★★   Showcase (Heartbeat, 1979)
★★★★   Sinsemilla (Mango, 1980)
★★★   Black Sounds of Freedom (Shanachie, 1981)
★★★★½   Red (Mango, 1981)
★★★★   Guess Who's Coming to Dinner (Heartbeat, 1981)
★★★   Tear It Up—Live (Mango, 1982)
★★★   Chill Out (Mango, 1982)
★★★★   The Dub Factor (Mango, 1983)
★★★   Anthem (Mango, 1984)
★★★★   Reggae Greats (Mango, 1984)
★★★★   Brutal (RAS, 1986)
★★★★   Brutal Dub (RAS, 1986)
★★★   Positive (RAS, 1987)
★★★★   The Positive Dub (RAS, 1988)
★★½   Now (Mesa, 1990)
★★½   Now Dub (Mesa, 1990)
★★½   Iron Storm (Mesa, 1991)
★★½   Iron Storm Dub (Mesa, 1992)
★★½   Mystical Truth (Rhino, 1993)
★★½   Mystical Truth Dub (Mesa, 1993)
★★★★★   Liberation: The Island Anthology (Island, 1993)
★★   Strongg (Rhino, 1994)
★★   Strongg Dub (Mesa, 1994)
★★★   Ras Portraits (RAS, 1997)
★★★½   Ultimate Collection (Hip-O, 2000)
★★   Dynasty (RAS, 2001)
★★★   The Millennium Collection (Universal, 2002)

In retrospect, it's tempting to describe Black Uhuru as the Fugees of '80s reggae. Not necessarily because both trios had the same gender breakdown, but because at its peak Black Uhuru was blessed with a similar understanding of how to make Caribbean culture accessible to mainstream America. Black Uhuru never sold as well as the Fugees; only two of their albums (*Chill Out* and *Now*) ever cracked the Billboard Hot 200 album chart. But with the release of *Red,* Black Uhuru was recognized as the most important roots reggae act to have emerged since Bob Marley's Wailers first splashed down in the U.S. Like its predecessors, *Red* made ample use of lead singer Michael Rose, whose elaborately ornamented phrasing at times has more in common with cantorial singing than with typical reggae vocal style; likewise, the album's rhythm work—by producers Sly Dunbar and Robbie Shakespeare and their cohorts—is flawless and enticing. But the writing is what really makes this album sizzle, from the spiritual wisdom of "Youth of Eglington" and "Carbine" to the sensual pleasures of "Sponji Reggae" and "Puff She Puff."

Black Uhuru's output up to this point was solid, if a bit hard to track. Its debut, *Love Crisis* (which was later remixed and reissued as *Black Sounds of Freedom*) has many of the same vocal and instrumental strengths as *Red,* but suffers from overly conventional material; *Showcase,* a collection of singles that was later repackaged as *Guess Who's Coming to Dinner,* is much stronger, thanks to stirringly militant numbers such as "Abortion" and "Guess Who's Coming to Dinner." *Sinsemilla* consolidates these strengths, and makes somewhat better use of Puma Jones (who joined during the period covered by *Showcase*).

Regrettably, the group's live album, *Tear It Up,* doesn't, but that poor showing may simply reflect the changes Black Uhuru was going through as the group developed a more cosmopolitan attitude and approach. *Chill Out* is far more urban (and far less doctrinaire) than its predecessors, but even that album seems cautious and conservative when compared to the techno-intense sound of *Anthem.* Taken simply on the strength of its groove, *Anthem* is certainly one of the group's most insinuating efforts, but apart from tunes such as "Party Next Door" and a version of

Miami Steve Van Zandt's "Solidarity," the songwriting is less than convincing.

Rose left the group at this point, and was replaced on *Brutal* by Junior Reid. His performance isn't terribly distinctive, but the songs and production more than make up the difference, particularly on the Arthur Baker–remixed "Great Train Robbery." Reid takes more of a leading role with *Positive* (Jones' last album with the group), although here the dub version almost outclasses the original. But he, too, left the group soon after, leaving founding member Duckie Simpson to recruit Don Carlos and Garth Dennis (both of whom had sung in Black Uhuru's very first lineup) for the polished but increasingly pedestrian *Now, Iron Storm, Mystical Truth,* and *Strongg* (all followed by obligatory dub versions). Of the various best-ofs, *Liberation* gives the best overview of the band at its peak, while *The Ultimate Collection* has the highest hits-per-dollar ratio. —J.D.C.

Rubén Blades

★★★	De Panamá a Nueva York: Con la Orquesta de Pete Rodríguez (Alegre, 1970)
★★★★	Metiendo Mano! (Fania, 1977)
★★★★½	Siembra (Fania, 1978)
★★★½	Maestra Vida: Primera Parte (Fania, 1980)
★★★★½	Canciones del Solar de los Aburridos (Fania, 1981)
★★½	The Last Fight (Fania, 1982)
★★★	El Que la Hace la Paga (Fania, 1982)
★★★★½	Buscando América (Elektra, 1984)
★★★	Mucho Mejor (Fania, 1984)
★★★★	Escenas (Elektra, 1985)
★★	Crossover Dreams (Elektra, 1986)
★★★★	Doble Filo (Fania, 1986)
★★★★	Agua de Luna (Elektra, 1987)
★★	Nothing but the Truth (Elektra, 1988)
★★★★	Antecedente (Elektra, 1988)
★★	Ruben Blades with Strings (Fania, 1988)
★★★★	Live! (Elektra, 1989)
★★★★	Caminando (Elektra, 1991)
★★★	Amor y Control (Sony Discos, 1992)
★★★	Tras la Tormenta (Sony International, 1995)
★★★½	La Rosa de los Vientos (Sony, 1996)
★★★	Tiempos (Sony, 1999)
★★★★	Mundo (Sony, 2002)

Presidential candidate in his native Panama, Hollywood actor, and legendary *salsero:* Rubén Blades is Latin music's great renaissance man. And yet his loftiest achievement has probably been his protean transformation of Afro-Caribbean music into a sociopolitically conscious genre that reflects the never-ending carnival of Latin American reality with humor and poignancy.

Blades the salsa master was also a product of a specific time and place—New York in the '70s, where the Fania record label spearheaded the salsa revolution by revamping the old Cuban rhythms with a gritty, modern-day influence and subtle echoes of American R&B. Blades was one of the shiniest stars in the Fania constellation, which also included Celia Cruz, Eddie Palmieri, Johnny Pacheco, Héctor Lavoé, and visionary trombonist/producer Willie Colón.

It was Colón who took Blades under his wing, collaborating with him on the smoldering, thickly textured *Metiendo Mano!* A year later, *Siembra* would become the best-selling album in salsa history (an honor it held for a few decades) thanks to Blades' anthemic "Pedro Navaja," a seven-minute dance epic fueled by biting social commentary, deliciously dark humor, and an impossibly sticky chorus.

Wanting to distance himself from traditional Afro-Caribbean terrain and bring his music closer to a new, savvier pop hybrid, Blades dropped his customary big band in favor of a jazzier sextet (Seis del Solar), signed with Elektra in 1984, and released the masterful *Buscando América*. The music had lost none of its swing, but the lyrics were deeply reflective and melancholy. By then, it was quite clear that Blades was one of Latin America's all-time essential songwriters.

Instead of recycling the *Buscando América* formula, Blades used his Elektra tenure as an opportunity to continue experimenting. The inevitable lapses in judgment included an English-language album that failed to ignite much interest from the mainstream.

After reuniting with Colón for a lackluster 1995 session that found both performers recording their alleged duets in separate studios, Blades took an even bolder step away from the tropical sounds that had made him famous. Limiting the salsa repertoire to his fiery, nostalgia-tinged concert appearances, he released a series of albums that embraced all kinds of Latin folklore while searching tirelessly for a mature pan-global statement that at times bordered dangerously close to world lite. But he finally got it right with *Mundo,* his most eclectic effort to date and a soulful statement of purpose for a man who really believes that the heart of an honest musician knows no cultural boundaries. —E.L.

Blake Babies

★★★	God Bless the Blake Babies (Zoë/Rounder, 2001)

During their original 1986–91 run, Boston's Blake Babies were darlings of college radio for embodying things eternally fresh: amateurish talent, love/hate passions, youthful voices. When the band—which parted ways as singer/bassist Juliana Hatfield staged a successful solo career—reformed a decade later, they wisely refrained from trying to go home again. *God Bless* is a refined, adult set. It even feels like a family disc: Hatfield, guitarist John Strohm, and drummer Freda Love Smith all sing lead, and longtime collaborator Evan Dando of the Lemonheads turns up as well. Occasionally the professionalism they acquired on sabbatical polishes any ardor off the work, and "What Did I Do" reverts to dorm-room angst. But in songs like "Picture Perfect" and "When I See His Face," the Blake Babies sound like a band that knows how to settle down in style.   —C.N.

Bobby "Blue" Bland

★★★	The Best of Bobby Bland (1972; MCA, 1987)
★★★★★	Two Steps from the Blues (1973; MCA, 1991)
★★★	Dreamer (1974; MCA, 1991)
★★★	Members Only (1985; Malaco, 1995)
★★★	After All (1986; Malaco, 1995)
★★★	Blues You Can Use (Malaco, 1987)
★★★	First Class Blues (1987; Malaco, 1990)
★★★★	Midnight Run (Malaco, 1989)
★★★	Portrait of the Blues (Malaco, 1991)
★★★★★	I Pity the Fool: The Duke Recordings, Vol. #1 (MCA, 1992)
★★★	Years of Tears (Malaco, 1993)
★★★★★	Turn On Your Love Light: The Duke Recordings, Vol. 2 (MCA, 1994)
★★★	Sad Street (Malaco, 1995)
★★★★★	That Did It!: The Duke Recordings, Vol. 3 (MCA, 1996)
★★★★	Greatest Hits, Vol. 1 (MCA, 1998)
★★★½	Memphis Monday Morning (Malaco, 1998)
★★★	Greatest Hits, Vol. 2: The ABC-Dunhill/MCA Recordings (MCA, 1998)
★★★	Live on Beale Street (Malaco, 1998)
★★★	Blues & Ballads (MCA, 1999)
★★★	The Millennium Collection (MCA, 2000)
★★★★	The Anthology (MCA, 2001)
★★★	Blues at Midnight (Malaco, 2003)

with B.B. King

★★★★	B.B. King & Bobby Bland: Together for the First Time Live (1974; MCA, 1990)
★★	B.B. King & Bobby Bland: Together Again . . . Live (1976; MCA, 1990)

Less celebrated than his contemporary B.B. King (for whom he served briefly as valet and chauffeur) and lacking King's major-label support, Bobby "Blue" Bland nonetheless has a lot more than staying power going for him. Although nearly 50 years have passed since his early, scuffling days working joints on

Memphis's Beale Street with King, Roscoe Gordon, and Johnny Ace, he has quietly become one of the best-selling and most frequently charted R&B artists of all time, well ahead of some of his celebrated peers.

Born in 1930 near Memphis, the young Robert Calvin Bland received his first lessons in direct, heartfelt singing while a member of various church groups in town; in the late '40s he took to Beale Street and began honing a singular vocal approach out of the gospel, blues, and early R&B that had become his artistic touchstones. Bland didn't, and doesn't, have a big, powerful voice. Rather, his was the quiet storm of postwar blues—forceful and determined in a macho kind of way on the uptempo numbers, but with an underlying tenderness that could put the hurt in a ballad to a degree approached in his peer group only by B.B. King. Although his artistic growth was far from complete when he cut his first sides at Sam Phillips' Memphis Recording Service in 1951, he sounds every bit the assured vocalist, recording in his hometown backed by musician friends from Roscoe Gordon's band; a year later he was signed to the Houston-based Duke label, teamed with players unfamiliar to him (Johnny Board and His Orchestra), and lost nary a step—in fact, Board brought a big, ambitious sound to Bland's sessions by way of a prominent horn section and an organist and vibraphonist whose embellishments brought a jazz feel to the arrangements, prompting even more richly textured performances from Bland. Such was the genesis of a signature style that embraced not only florid, emotionally charged blues (and borderline pop) ballads but also hard-driving blues and jump blues orchestrations, extending a tradition pioneered in the '30s by Big Joe Turner and the boogie-woogie cats from Kansas City.

An exemplary reissue program has restored order to Bland's Duke recordings, thanks primarily to the three essential well-annotated two-CD collections, *I Pity the Fool: The Duke Recordings, Volume One, Turn on Your Love Light: The Duke Recordings, Volume Two,* and *That Did It! The Duke Recordings, Volume Three.* The ultimate aim of this program is to bring the entirety of Bland's 20-year Duke recording history to the market in chronological order, including alternate takes, rarities, and previously unissued sides. Lower-budget Duke retrospectives include the single CDs *The Best of Bobby Bland* (which includes "Farther Up the Road" and two other certified Bland classics in "I Pity the Fool"—his second #1 single, from 1960—and "Turn On Your Love Light"); *Greatest Hits, Vol. 1,* with its 16 essential tracks (although the omission of "Little Boy Blue" is puzzling); and the 12-cut

20th Century Masters—The Millennium Collection: The Best of Bobby "Blue" Bland set ("I Pity the Fool," "Turn On Your Love Light," the scabrous "Poverty," and the exquisite, monumental "Lead Me On" from Two Steps from the Blues are the highlights of this truncated overview).

Among the non–greatest hits albums, the one absolute must-have is Two Steps from the Blues, one of the most powerful R&B albums ever recorded. From the raw-boned confessional blues of the opening title song to the final, touching "I've Been Wrong So Long," Bland constructs a concept album devoted to intimate reflections on love and longing so personal and atmospheric that it comes off as R&B's answer to Sinatra's brilliant forays into thematic unity, Only the Lonely and In the Wee Small Hours. Check out the aching plea "Lead Me On" for a heartbreaking sample of this artist's deeply felt balladeering style—this one's strictly Mount Olympus in grandeur.

Aging as gracefully as his friend B.B. King, Bland, after some fallow years on ABC in the mid- to late-'70s (the highs and lows of which are encapsulated on the two live albums with King, and on the 16-track Greatest Hits, Vol. 2: The ABC-Dunhill/MCA Recordings, which includes a couple of interesting forays into country with "Today I Started Loving Her Again" and "I Hate You"), found a home on Malaco and has stayed the course with gospel-soul stylings and exemplary song selection in a traditional R&B vein. A good starting point for this era is First Class Blues, something of a greatest-hits package comprising several tracks from Bland's first two Malaco albums, After All and Members Only, as well as fresh interpretations of "Two Steps from the Blues" and another Bland evergreen from the Duke years, "St. James Infirmary." On a fervent interpretation of "In the Ghetto," Bland, all soul on ice, gives a slow, deliberate reading that has the effect of making vivid the desperation of inner-city life. This latter stage of Bland's career finds him affecting an odd strangled wail he calls "the squall." It's a truly weird effect on disc, but in concert it still elicits squeals of delights from the women in the audience. The Members Only album is one premier showcase for "the squall," but in no way does it undercut the powerful but nuanced sadness he brings to the wistful title song, which remains one of his towering performances in the recording studio. The inspired Midnight Run, Portrait of the Blues, 1998's Memphis Monday Morning, and especially 1993's Years of Tears show the mature vocalist in splendid form, working his turf, moving hearts, and sounding as involved in his material as he was at the outset of his career. Remarkable—then and now. —D.M.

Mary J. Blige

★★★★ What's the 411? (Uptown/MCA, 1992)
★★★½ My Life (Uptown/MCA, 1994)
★★½ Share My World (MCA, 1997)
★★★½ Mary (MCA, 1999)
★★★★ No More Drama (MCA, 2001)
★★★ Love and Live (Geffen, 2003)

Mary J. Blige's authoritative, sometimes bellicose voice and no-bull delivery made her one of the important new voices of the '90s. A bridge between the R&B world and the hip-hop nation, she pioneered the movement that would later become neo-soul, generating gripping songs that were also massive radio hits. Blige has the distinction of being the first to fully seize the narrative possibilities of rap: Her tough-girl persona and streetwise lyrics give even the sweet songs of her 1992 debut What's the 411? a gritty undertone and a realism missing from much of the devotional love songs ruling the charts at that time.

Growing up in a housing project in Yonkers, Blige listened to everything from "Planet Rock" to Anita Baker; she was initially discovered by Uptown's Andre Harrell, then came under the wing of Sean "Puffy" Combs, who coproduced What's the 411?, situating her voice in capricious, playful settings just edgy enough to rate time on hip-hop mix shows.

Blige's vocal skills shine more completely on the followup, 1994's My Life, which finds Combs guiding her into more conventional R&B-ballad territory. Blige sings of hard times, men who hurt her, and struggles she's known, sometimes veering precariously close to overly emotional hand-wringing. The most compelling material, however, is the more sensual songs, among them the hit "Mary Jane (All Night Long)" and the brisk "You Bring Me Joy."

The success of her first two projects enabled Blige to call the shots on her next one, and she moved even further toward the R&B mainstream by hiring Jimmy Jam and Terry Lewis, Babyface, and others to produce. Share My World, which entered at #1 on the Billboard charts, displays Blige's hit-song savvy but fewer memorable performances. 1999's Mary more fully realizes Blige's vision for Share My World. Its songs include a beautiful duet with Lauryn Hill, "All That I Can Say," and two smart appropriations: "Deep Inside" interpolates Elton John's "Bennie and the Jets," while "Time" borrows portions of Stevie Wonder's "Pastime Paradise" and Al Green's "I'm Glad You're Mine."

By the time Blige returned with No More Drama in 2001, her neo-soul approach had helped artists such as Macy Gray become stars. Sensing the potential for burnout, Blige makes the music more assertive (Dr. Dre produces the percolating dance-floor anthem "Family Affair") and the lyrics more uplifting and compassionate. Several songs, including the title track, pursue the theme of reconciliation, and there's even an ode to the emotional trials of "PMS." As in the past, Blige gathers an enormous amount of talent to help her—from rappers Eve, Missy Elliott, and Ja Rule to Combs, now P. Diddy, who does a remix of the title track—and, on this set, the intense singer makes sure that everyone shines.

Blige's reunion with P. Diddy, *Love and Life,* doesn't quite hark back to the pair's enduring *What's the 411?,* but is a feast of contrasts: Some of the tracks catch Blige celebrating the joy of romance, and others, particularly tracks with Method Man and 50 Cent providing rap cameos, offer craftily produced chronicles of sex and its aftermath.   —T.M.

Blind Faith

★★★★   Blind Faith (Polydor, 1969)
★★★   Blind Faith Deluxe Edition (Polydor, 2001)

When Eric Clapton and Ginger Baker (from the recently dissolved Cream), Steve Winwood (on hiatus from Traffic), and Rick Grech (from Family, which was a big deal in Britain, at least) got together in 1969 as Blind Faith, they had created something new to rock & roll: the supergroup. But like almost every supergroup since, Blind Faith was never quite the sum of its parts. Although its one album had some incredible moments—the ethereal "Presence of the Lord" and "Can't Find My Way Home"—too much of the album was given over to directionless jamming.

The quartet held together for barely a year, breaking up after its first tour. Nonetheless, the band left enough in the way of unreleased material to allow Polydor to issue a *Deluxe Edition* of *Blind Faith,* on which the original album is augmented by an hour and a half of studio leftovers (including an entire CD of unfocused, uninspired instrumental jams). If ever a product proved that less is more, this deluxe edition is it.   —J.D.C.

Blind Lemon Jefferson

★★★★   Blind Lemon Jefferson (1974; Milestone, 1992)
★★★★½   King of the Country Blues (Yazoo, 1988)
★★★   Penitentiary Blues (Collectables, 1989)
★★★★   Moanin' All Over (Tradition, 1996)
★★★★★   The Best of Blind Lemon Jefferson (Yazoo, 2000)
★★★½   Blue on Blues (Varèse Sarabande, 2002)

Among the influential guitarists of the 1920s only Lonnie Johnson claims a stature comparable to that of

Blind Lemon Jefferson. Blind at birth, Jefferson began performing in his early teens, playing in the streets, at parties, wherever he could find an audience. As the years progressed, his repertoire expanded to include not only blues but also field hollers, work songs, ballads, prison songs, hymns—all expressed in the idiosyncratic style he had developed. His guitar style is marked by unpredictable riffs and irregular rhythms that are free of any easily pinpointed influence. As a writer Jefferson was given to the dark, brooding tales, but he leavened chilling narratives such as " 'Lectric Chair Blues" and "Prison Cell Blues" with the light of salvation proffered in gospel numbers ("He Arose from the Dead," "I Want to Be Like Jesus in My Heart") and a randy sense of humor ("Match Box Blues"). Recording steadily during the last four years of his life, Jefferson left a body of work that made a significant impact on succeeding generations of blues artists—Lightnin' Hopkins, T-Bone Walker, and B.B. King are among the giants who acknowledged Jefferson's impact on their own styles—and signature songs such as "See That My Grave Is Kept Clean," "Black Snake Moan," and "Easy Rider Blues" that were recognized as genre classics. In addition he became a footnote in early rock & roll history when his "Match Box Blues" served as the foundation for Carl Perkins' 1957 rewrite, "Match Box," which was later covered by the Beatles.

The Yazoo and Milestone albums are highly recommended, as all three offer a broad overview of Jefferson's best-known work with a minimum of song duplications and uniformly solid annotation. By contrast, the skimpy nine-track *Penitentiary Blues* duplicates a few of the songs on the Milestone set, and its generic annotation fails to provide any information about the album itself. Aficionados, however, will find the two versions of "Black Snake Moan" interesting, as well as the starkly rendered title song. The newest Jefferson title, *Blue on Blues* from Varèse Sarabande, divides a dozen cuts between Jefferson and Charlie Patton, with Jefferson's representative tracks including "See That My Grave Is Kept Clean," "Black Snake Moan," and "Penitentiary Blues." While the domestic releases do an exemplary job in telling Jefferson's story, completists will want to check out Document's four-volume *Complete Recorded Works* collection.   —D.M.

Blind Melon

★★   Blind Melon (Capitol, 1992)
★   Soup (Capitol, 1995)
★   Nico (Capitol, 1996)

Blind Melon's lone hit, the acoustic ditty "No Rain," gave off sweet hippie love vibes for the summer of

1993, with forlorn vocals and a moving video starring the Bee Girl, an awkward adolescent girl in a bee costume and glasses who roamed the grassy wastelands of youth in search of other hive folk to buzz and bumble with. When she finally found her apiary soulmates at the end of the video, "No Rain" was an instant tearjerker and an MTV classic. But not even the support of the insect community could get Blind Melon a second hit. Not so much hippies trying to pass for grunge as metalheads trying to pass for hippies, the Melon men didn't have their hearts in faking it. For their followup, *Soup,* they evidently just stitched some contorted practice-tape highlights together and hoped nobody would care. Nobody did. The lead singer, Shannon Hoon, died of drugs soon afterward; *Nico* collects posthumous scraps. Oh, Bee Girl, wherever you are: We remember. —R.S.

Blink-182

★★½ Buddha (1994; Kung Fu, 1998)
★★½ Cheshire Cat (1995; Cargo/Uni, 1998)
★★★ Dude Ranch (Grilled Cheese, 1997)
★★★★ Enema of the State (MCA, 1999)
★★★★ Take Off Your Pants and Jacket (MCA, 2001)
★★★★ Blink-182 (Geffen, 2003)

If Green Day's bratty emotion defined pop-punk in the mid-'90s, Blink-182's alternately gushy and goofy radio hits updated it for the new millennium. On their first two albums, *Buddha* and *Cheshire Cat,* the San Diego–area trio slapped together lilting melodies and racing beats in an attempt to connect emo, hardcore's sullen "emotional" branch, and skate punk, a sort of pop hardcore. In 1997, the year Green Day discovered acoustic balladry and harmonica on *Nimrod,* Blink-182 finally focused their sound with *Dude Ranch.* Guitarist Tom DeLonge plays the straight man, singing sturdily and deadpan, while the squeakier-voiced bassist Mark Hoppus bleats urgently about romance gone wrong. Drummer Scott Raynor (who was replaced by Travis Barker in 1998), sticks to double time, but his songwriter bandmates hang their old weepie-and-wedgie routine on shiny new hooks. And while later pop-punk bands such as the Promise Ring will implausibly deny their emo tendencies, the scrupulously unpretentious Blink actually name one of their bitter anthems after the frequently derided genre. (Don't ask where they got the inspiration for "Dick Lips.")

Were it not for three classic singles, Blink-182's major-label debut, *Enema of the State,* would've sounded like just another visit to the *Dude Ranch.* "Adam's Song" took its controversial place in rock history alongside Ozzy Osbourne's "Suicide Solu-

tion" when a teen killed himself in his bedroom while the track played on repeat. DeLonge announces the song's plain opening lines, "I never thought/I'd die alone," just as chiming guitar gives way to a handful of pent-up chords. The chorus, a sluice of pounding, harmony-laced redemption, transforms the melancholy into triumph: "The tour is over, I've survived/I can't wait till I get home/to pass the time in my room alone." The point, of course, is that teens trapped in their rooms *aren't* alone.

And then there's hiding in your room with someone else. "All the Small Things" is Blink's most subtle song about sex—the title does not refer to the band's penises. (Don't ask where they got the inspiration for "Dysentery Gary.") In its schoolyard-chant verse and na-na-na chorus, Hoppus sweetly tilts at his "little windmill," a love interest who comes to his shows, gives him roses, and thinks about spending the night. An adolescent fear of sex animates *Enema of the State*'s best cut, the blithely jubilant "What's My Age Again?" "We started making out/and she took off my pants," DeLonge narrates obliviously, "but then I turned on the TV." How better to close the '90s than by posing and then answering the question "What the hell is ADD?" in under two and a half minutes?

Essentially a concept album about being a teenager, *Take Off Your Pants and Jacket* nimbly touches on disenchantment with adult life, socializing online, meeting girls at rock shows, first dates, Christmas Eve with only two presents wrapped, mother jokes, grandparents shitting their pants, ejaculating into socks, discovering punk rock, puking from a "sip" of alcohol, breakups, parents getting divorced, wanting to leave home, and coming home anyway. If none of this album's singles stand out quite as much as those from *Enema of the State,* it's because of *Jacket*'s unprecedented cohesion: Almost every song interweaves gently plaintive moments with bolts of frantic energy. Kids discovering punk rock could do much worse than starting here. *Blink-182* showed that Mark, Tom, and Travis channeled their adolescent angst by deepening their sound. Mixing in expert electronic touches and drawing on the stormy tumult and openhearted expressiveness of underground emo punk, full-bodied barn burners such as "Feeling This" and "Asthenia" are both deep-feeling and catchy as all get-out. And just to prove that they'd really grown up, they even named a tune after the Stockholm Syndrome, a psychological condition wherein hostages identify with their captors. —N.C.

Blondie

★★★★ Blondie (1976; Private Stock/Chrysalis, 1977)
★★★ Plastic Letters (Chrysalis, 1977)

★★★★½ Parallel Lines (Chrysalis, 1978)
★★★½ Eat to the Beat (Chrysalis, 1979)
★★★ Autoamerican (Chrysalis, 1980)
★★★★½ Best of Blondie (Chrysalis, 1981)
★★ The Hunter (Chrysalis, 1982)
★★★ No Exit (Beyond, 1999)
★★★★½ Greatest Hits (Capitol, 2002)
★★ The Curse of Blondie (Sanctuary, 2004)

"Blondie Is a Group!" announced the ads for this New York combo's first album, somewhat defensively. For once, the hype was correct, though lead singer and focal point Deborah Harry certainly had the ability to steal a spotlight—and hold on to it. One of the earliest punk bands, Blondie was pretty much a second-string act at CBGB until its debut album came out in late 1976. Harry, guitarist Chris Stein (also Harry's longtime boyfriend), and cohorts flaunt an enthusiasm for pop effluvia that's absolutely contagious. Surf music, girl groups, Motown, bubblegum, glitter rock, even a touch of heavy metal—everything gets boiled down into sweet little concoctions that release surprisingly complex, lasting pleasures. Eventually, Stein and Harry's devotion to the Bowie/Eno/Roxy Music school of art rock overwhelmed their pure pop impulses, but for a while, Blondie's stylistic experiments yielded impressive results. While Debbie Harry was hardly a punk antistar like Patti Smith, her sex symbolism exuded street smarts and a knowing sense of humor. Clearly, this woman was nobody's bimbo.

Blondie revels in the trashiest strains of '60s pop, adding a dry Manhattan twist to "X Offender" and "Rip Her to Shreds." *Plastic Letters,* the followup, sounds rushed and hollow, though the catchy singles "Denis" and "(I'm Always Touched by Your) Presence, Dear" both tap into Harry's emotional reserves. *Parallel Lines,* recorded with an expanded lineup, represents a huge leap in musicianship and overall conception. From the dynamite rock & roll opener "Hanging on the Telephone" to the rock-disco crossover "Heart of Glass," Blondie keeps the hooks—and ideas—coming fast. *Eat to the Beat* strives for the same natural balance, and comes surprisingly close.

You have to admire Blondie's artistic gumption. However, by the time of *Autoamerican,* the band's eclecticism begins to diffuse. "Rapture" and "The Tide Is High" were satisfying singles, but Blondie's grasp of hip-hop and reggae (respectively) wasn't nearly as strong as its hold on good ol' rock & roll. The end came in the early '80s during Chris Stein's prolonged illness with a rare disease (he's since recovered): Blondie's last tour and album *(The Hunter)* were distracted, painful affairs.

Although it was nice to have the band back for *No Exit,* the album is clearly the work of a group that has experienced some loss of muscle. Only "Maria" signals a return to the deep, dangerous pop well of Blondie's youth; otherwise, the record fails to recapture the gorgeous possibilities the group was previously able to make out of the pop buffet. The band's old eclecticism returns on *The Curse of Blondie*— there's a rap-rock attempt, as well as some jazz— mostly to ill effect.

All of Blondie's '70s and '80s recordings have been released with uninteresting live, and often fuzzy, tracks tacked on. What they show is that, up through *Eat to the Beat,* at least, Blondie came up with one revelation after another, tapping '60s pop with such ferocious verve and goodwill that even the weirdest moments, such as the sonic experimentation of *Eat,* remain rivetingly listenable.   —M.C./A.B.

Bloodhound Gang

★★½ Use Your Fingers (Columbia, 1995)
★★★ One Fierce Beer Coaster (Geffen, 1996)
★★ Hooray for Boobies (Interscope, 2000)

By turns offensive and just plain dorky, the Bloodhound Gang will not likely ever get much credit for being one of the earliest groups of suburban white guys to integrate rap into their rock and pop music. After an independent debut EP, *Dingleberry Haze,* brought attention to the band's blend of early Beastie Boys brattiness, Ween's sick-in-the-head stoner humor, and a musical vocabulary defined by watching too much MTV in the '80s, the group arrived nationally with *Use Your Fingers.* While passing mild misogyny off as playful fun and attempting other assaults on political correctness ("You're Pretty When I'm Drunk," "She Ain't Got No Legs"), Bloodhound Gang rampages through the detritus of low-pop culture, referencing Kajagoogoo and *Sanford & Son.* While doing its best to act dumb, the music is deceptively eclectic, ranging from early rap-rock fusion to human beatbox a cappella. Ultimately, though, how much you can take of this record depends mostly on your tolerance for the group's middle-school humor.

One Fierce Beer Coaster offers more of the same, but in smaller, more easy-to-swallow doses: There's the postmodern kitchen-sink pop references, the eager-to-offend lyrics ("I Wish I Was Queer So I Could Get Chicks," "Kiss Me Where It Smells Funny"), and the mix of rap rock with moments that indicate a wider musical palette. And "Fire Water Burn," which combines old-school hip-hop with Cake-like monotone and a Pixies quote, is accessible enough to have earned the group its first notable airplay.

After a four-year absence, the Bloodhound Gang returned with *Hooray for Boobies,* the group's most musically varied release and also its most hateful, complete with purportedly playful takes on prison torture ("I Hope You Die"), rape ("A Lap Dance Is So Much Better When the Stripper Is Crying"), and angry sex ("Yummy Down on This") that, regardless of intent, don't sound like much fun (or very funny) at all. The exception is the record's minor hit, "The Bad Touch," a catchy pop song set to a synth-pop/house beat that indicates the group's ability to temper its sophomoric attitude into something worth hearing.   —R.M.S.

Blood, Sweat and Tears

★★★★	Child Is Father to the Man (Columbia/Legacy, 1968)
★★½	Blood, Sweat and Tears (Columbia/Legacy, 1969)
★★½	Blood, Sweat and Tears 3 (1970; Columbia, 1986)
★★	Blood, Sweat and Tears 4 (1971; Legacy, 1999)
★★★	Greatest Hits (Columbia, 1972)
★★	Nuclear Blues (LAX, 1980)
★★	Found Treasures (Columbia, 1990)
★★★	Live (Rhino, 1994)
★★★	What Goes Up: The Best of Blood, Sweat and Tears (Columbia, 1995)
★★★	Super Hits (Columbia, 1998)

Frighteningly pretentious, BS&T were fired by the same questionable impulse to fuse rock and jazz that compromised Miles Davis and nearly killed off Jeff Beck. Convinced that rock & roll just wasn't bright enough, these high-culture bullyboys figured that what was missing was brass. Horns, of course, had been a brilliant mainstay for Little Richard and James Brown, but what BS&T had in mind was fat big band—Woody Herman, Glenn Miller, et al. Soon staging a saxophone shootout with contemporary rivals Chicago, BS&T delivered hits that indeed featured breathtaking arrangements and playing—but their virtuosity was wholly misbegotten.

Dylan sideman and ex–Blues Project member Al Kooper founded BS&T, but held on only long enough for their first, and best, record. Featuring such classy writers as Harry Nilsson and Randy Newman, *Child Is Father to the Man* showed a band not yet gripped by terminal condescension; it's an elegant, ambitious record. Then came David Clayton-Thomas. Bearish, amiable, and deeply desirous of the chintz mantle earned by being "a great entertainer," C-T was a scenery chewer of a singer, radiating bogus black soul

and arrogant "chops." Bellowing "And When I Die," "Spinning Wheel," and "You've Made Me So Very Happy," he made their second album hit-heavy and hollow—and primed them for a career of unintended Vegas-aspiring. BS&T is best represented by an album of its live work—the band really gets to stretch out and, even if the material is still inflated, there are passages of crack playing as expert as, say, the Johnny Carson–era *Tonight Show* orchestra.   —P.E.

Kurtis Blow

★★★	Kurtis Blow (Mercury, 1980)
★★	Deuce (Mercury, 1981)
★★	Tough (Mercury, 1982)
★★★	Party Time? (Mercury, 1983)
★★	Ego Trip (Mercury, 1984)
★★★	America (Mercury, 1985)
★★	Kingdom Blow (Mercury, 1986)
★★	Back by Popular Demand (Mercury, 1988)
★★★½	The Best of Kurtis Blow (Mercury, 1994)

Kurtis Blow was the first rapper to cut albums for a major label, a breakthrough that would have been more impressive had Blow actually been an album artist. But he was essentially a singles act, meaning that while his original albums have their moments— "The Breaks" on *Kurtis Blow,* say, or "Basketball" from *America*—moments are usually all they offer. The exception is *Party Time?* (which, at five songs, is actually more like an EP than an album), where Blow's temporary alliance with the Washington, D.C., band EU produces the first meaningful rap/go-go fusion, a genuine footnote in hip-hop history. By the mid-'90s, Blow had so completely disappeared from the scene that Chris Rock, playing a millionaire rapper in the comedy *CB4,* joked that he was going to go out and "find Kurtis Blow!" Far easier to find is *The Best of Kurtis Blow,* which offers all the classic singles, as well as a few less-than-classic tracks.   —J.D.C.

Blue Öyster Cult

★★★★	Blue Öyster Cult (Columbia, 1972)
★★★★½	Tyranny and Mutation (Columbia, 1973)
★★★★½	Secret Treaties (Columbia, 1974)
★½	On Your Feet or On Your Knees (Columbia, 1974)
★★★★	Agents of Fortune (Columbia, 1976)
★★	Spectres (Columbia, 1977)
★★	Some Enchanted Evening (Columbia, 1978)
★★	Mirrors (Columbia, 1979)
★½	Cultosaurus Erectus (Columbia, 1980)
★★★	Fire of Unknown Origin (Columbia, 1981)
★	Extraterrestrial Live (Columbia, 1982)
★	The Revolution by Night (Columbia, 1983)

★ Club Ninja (Columbia, 1986)
★★ Imaginos (Columbia, 1988)
★★★ Career of Evil (Columbia, 1990)
★ Cult Classics (Herald, 1994)
★★★½ Workshop of the Telescopes (Columbia, 1995)
★½ Heaven Forbid (CMC, 1998)
★★★½ Super Hits (Columbia, 1998)
★★★½ Don't Fear the Reaper: The Best of (Columbia, 2000)

"This Ain't the Summer of Love," Blue Öyster Cult sneered in 1976, and they meant it, man. BÖC were a metal band who sent up hippie spiritualism with their own readymade mythology: the funniest name and lyrics in metal history, plus a cryptic logo that got spray-painted in every parking lot in America. These Long Island dudes looked like a bunch of stereo salesmen, but they wanted you to know they were really, really evil. And they sound surprisingly fresh today because their sensibility was pure punk. Buck Dharma, Allen Lanier, Eric Bloom, and producer Sandy Pearlman invented a guitar sound that purged all the emotion away, crisp and clean and scientific, speeding up rock licks with an unsentimental technocratic wit. Demanding "Cult" status while refusing to pay their Summer of Love dues, BÖC have become pariahs on classic-rock radio, but there are plenty of tasties in their oeuvre for those who dare to dig.

Blue Öyster Cult introduces the band with thought-provoking titles such as "I'm on the Lamb But I Ain't No Sheep" and "She's as Beautiful as a Foot." "And Then Came the Last Days of May" is a tale of hippie dope dealers killing each other, as the wide-open spaces of the psychedelic frontier implode into banally murderous capitalism. *Tyranny and Mutation* revs both the velocity and the irony for a four-song opening suite as perfectly paced as Wire's *Pink Flag.* With "The Red and the Black" (later covered by the Minutemen), "7 Screaming Dizbusters" (and you know how those dizbusters can scream), and "Hot Rails to Hell" (Lucifer rides the subway!), it's one molten hook after another. *Secret Treaties* turns up the volume with stun-guitar riffs and ridiculously demonic lyrics. "Dominance and Submission" has zip to do with sex—it's about listening to the radio. Lanier's then girlfriend Patti Smith cowrote the even funnier "Career of Evil," with its unforgettable threat, "I'll spend your ransom money/But still I'll keep your sheep."

After a limp live album and Lanier's appearance on Smith's *Horses,* the Cult regrouped for *Agents of Fortune.* "Don't Fear the Reaper" is their masterpiece, guitars whispering in your ear about sex and death and Romeo and Juliet, limpid Beach Boys voices floating with a truly chilling blandness, a libretto about "40,000 men and women" making no sense whatsoever: It all made a perfect radio creepshow for the summer of *The Omen. Agents* also offers some anomalously pretty love ballads ("I love you like sin/But I won't be your pigeon"?) and a vocal cameo from Patti herself. But punks like Patti soon cornered the market on sarcastic hard rock, and BÖC got left behind.

They settled into a grind of live rehashes and studio flops, refusing to release a proper best-of (*Cult Classics* looks like one, but it's a pathetic set of 1994 re-recordings; *Career of Evil* and *Workshop of the Telescopes* suffer from too many live versions and post-*Agents* filler; *Super Hits* and *Don't Fear the Reaper* are superior). Too cold and cerebral for the '80s metal revival, BÖC never adapted to punk despite bequeathing guitar sounds to everyone from Tom Verlaine and R.E.M. to Pavement and Stereolab. *Mirrors* is notable for "In Thee," a moving Lanier ballad about breaking up with Smith. *Fire of Unknown Origin,* a frequent item in dollar bins, is definitely worth a buck for "Burnin' for You," a spooky, sexy anthem cowritten by rock critic Richard Meltzer that became a fluke 1981 hit. As for the rest—well, nobody ever said it was easy making a career of evil. —R.S.

Blues Traveler

★★★ Blues Traveler (A&M, 1990)
★★★ Travelers and Thieves (A&M, 1991)
★★★ Save His Soul (A&M, 1993)
★★ Four (A&M, 1994)
★★ Live from the Fall (A&M, 1996)
★★ Straight on Till Morning (A&M, 1997)
★★★ Bridge (A&M, 2001)
★★ Travelogue: Blues Traveler Classics (A&M, 2002)
★★★ Truth Be Told (Sanctuary, 2003)

Linchpins of the late '80s jam-band scene that also disgorged Phish, the Spin Doctors, and Widespread Panic, Blues Traveler borrowed the strategy of the Grateful Dead and built a steady following by emphasizing chops over image and relentless touring over studio-crafted radio hits. The New York quartet is best known as catalysts for H.O.R.D.E., one of the most successful festival tours to emerge in the wake of Lollapalooza.

Though Blues Traveler's albums boast few truly memorable melodies, they're uniformly competent blues-based rock, distinguished by John Popper's acrobatic harmonica runs and gruff vocals, Chan Kinchla's agile guitar playing, Bobby Sheehan's aggressively melodic bass playing, and the spacious drumming of Brendan Hill. When Popper sings about "mulling it over" on the debut album, he summarizes the band's ethos: The quartet loves to chew over a simple melody and explore all the flavors before exhausting it. Popper himself is not short of ambition, sometimes to his detriment—he's a wordy lyricist and an effusive soloist who has trouble reining himself in. *Blues Traveler* provides a blueprint for all the band's studio releases: exotic but danceable grooves in sometimes unconventional time signatures, and guitar fills and baroque harp flourishes that start out as mere decoration but build into more open-ended jams as the album progresses and the songs widen.

The formula, reprised on *Travelers and Thieves* and *Save His Soul,* finally broke through to a mainstream audience on Blues Traveler's slightest album, *Four.* The radio hit "Run-Around" captured the band at its most amiable, Popper's ebullient solo back-flipping like a frisky pup. "Hook" is in a similar vein, but "Look Around" and "The Mountains Win Again" show the band brooding in the slow-build atmosphere, the soloists biding their time until they can open up and wail.

Showboating prevails on the double-CD *Live from the Fall,* a noodlefest that will appeal to fans of fancy harp and guitar solos, but no one else. *Straight on Till Morning* presents Blues Traveler at its bluesiest on "Make My Way" and "Carolina Blues," and virtuosity serves the song on the hard-charging "Great Big World." Still, Popper's cringe-inducing lyrics and embarrassing stabs at scat singing make this a typically mixed bag for nonbelievers. Sheehan's death prompted a retooling of the lineup for *Bridge,* though some of the old excesses remain—there's even a drum solo. When the band truly focuses on interplay, *Bridge* burns brightest. Keyboardist Ben Wilson is a welcome addition, his clavinet whipping up the funk with Popper on "You Lost Me There" and turning up the flame underneath "You're Burning Me." The effusive Popper is still prone to overreach as a lyricist ("When you're living, you're just a series of atmospheres"), but Sheehan's death brought out a disarming directness in the singer's songwriting on "Pretty Angry," a beautifully paced slow-burn elegy embroidered by Wilson's piano. The keyboardist also infuses *Truth Be Told* with inventive technique, and the disc finds the band in top form, with compact solos folded into tautly arranged songs.   —G.K.

Blur

★★½   Leisure (Food/SBK, 1991)
★★★½   Modern Life Is Rubbish (Food/SBK, 1993)
★★★★½   Parklife (Food/SBK, 1994)
★★★★½   The Great Escape (Food/Parlophone/Virgin, 1995)
★★½   Blur (Virgin, 1997)
★★★   13 (Food/Parlophone/Virgin, 1999)
★★★★½   Blur: The Best of (Food/Parlophone/Virgin, 2000)
★★★   Think Tank (Virgin, 2003)

In their youth, this British quartet of art-school pretty-boy popsters was caught between two of the U.K.'s dominant early-'90s styles: the noisy quasi-psychedelia of shoegazers such as My Bloody Valentine and Ride and the groovy quasi-funk of "Madchester" bands such as the Stone Roses and Happy Mondays. While *Leisure* has some engaging moments—"She's So High," "Bang," "Repetition"—its indecisiveness sinks it.

By the time *Modern Life Is Rubbish* was released, Blur had undergone a remarkable transformation. Spurred by disgust at the wave of American grunge washing over England, principal singer/songwriter Damon Albarn was now writing detailed third-person character studies such as "For Tomorrow" and "Chemical World" and decking them out with complex musical arrangements that recalled such defiantly British acts as XTC, the Buzzcocks, Madness, and the godfathers of them all, the Kinks. Though not a perfect collection, *Modern Life* had a colossal influence on the Britpop movement of the '90s.

On Blur's next two albums, Albarn's storytelling and hook-crafting savvy reached its pinnacle. *Parklife* dissected the mating habits of young Brits on their Mediterranean holidays to a Duran Duran–style disco beat ("Girls and Boys") and made a music-hall knees-up out of the daily routines of the chronically unemployed (the title track). *The Great Escape*'s "Country House" sneered at the idle rich, while "Ernold Same" empathized with the plight of the commuter class. And with "This Is a Low" *(Parklife)* and "The Universal" *(The Great Escape),* Blur proved it had the majestic-anthem angle covered too.

Having established a winning sound (and engaged in a pointless media-fueled rivalry with Oasis), Blur promptly transformed itself again. Irony, clever craftsmanship, and devotion to all things English were jettisoned, as the band turned to American indie rock for inspiration. The resulting self-titled album can politely be called transitional. "Song 2," a primeval riff-o-rama punctuated by Albarn's fevered "whoo-hoo"-ing, was the band's first U.S. hit (up to this point, they were major stars just about everywhere *except* America), but the rest is uneven and often unconvincing. The followup, *13,* lacks focus and runs on too long; even so, it's more rewarding than its predecessor. "Battle" and "Caramel" are mesmerizing space rock, and on "Tender" and "No Distance Left to

Run," Blur dares to be both vulnerable and bluesy. Despite its exclusion of some crucial *Modern Life*–era cuts, *The Best of* makes a strong case for Blur as the preeminent British singles band of the last decade. *Think Tank,* the group's first album without founding guitarist Graham Coxon, carries the stylistic expansiveness of *13* even further, but otherwise ace tracks like "Out of Time" are undone by atypically shallow lyrics, which leads one to wonder whether Albarn's heart is still in writing pop songs.   —M.R.

Boards of Canada

★★★★ Music Has the Right to Children
(Warp/Matador, 1998)
★★★ In a Beautiful Place Out in the Country (EP)
(Warp, 2000)
★★ Geogaddi (Warp, 2002)

The Scottish duo of Michael Sandison and Marcus Eoin, Boards of Canada took the often-impenetrable formula known as IDM (intelligent dance music) popularized by Autechre in the mid-'90s, and softened the form's rough edges by adding austere atmospheres that were often as chilly as they were beautiful. Their debut album, *Music Has the Right to Children,* coupled eerie, foreboding walls of sound with a heavy, thudding hip-hop beat while whimsical harmonies play off of dark, processed vocals. The otherworldly, off-kilter rhythms of "Telephasic Workshop" are brought back to earth with the simplest trick: a catchy tune.

BOC followed up *Music* with a five-song (EP), *In a Beautiful Place Out in the Country,* discarding the strong backbeats of their debut in favor of the willowy, soft textures prominently featured on the title track. Their long-awaited second full-length, *Geogaddi,* disappointed, however. The shock of the new no longer applied, so the contrast of evil undertones and electronic lullabies simply wasn't as compelling. Still, a few tracks—with their offbeat explorations of sound—demonstrate why BOC remain influential and important contributors to experimental techno.   —T.R.

Body Count

★★★ Body Count (Sire/Warner Bros., 1992)
★★ Born Dead (Virgin, 1994)
★ Violent Demise: The Last Days (Virgin, 1997)

Body Count began as a thrash-metal side project for West Coast gangsta rapper Ice-T, but briefly eclipsed his hip-hop albums in notoriety for the song "Cop Killer." The song was initially released on Body Count's self-titled debut, then deleted when the

rapper's label, Warner Brothers, caved in to public pressure from, among others, President George Herbert Walker Bush, who took the song far too literally. "Cop Killer" was deleted from subsequent versions of the album, replaced by a First Amendment rant by former Dead Kennedys singer Jello Biafra.

It was much ado over one of the weaker songs on what is otherwise an album of darkly satiric and politically pointed commentary, sexist rants, and ghetto storytelling by Ice-T—who was then at the height of his powers after two extraordinary hip-hop albums, *The Iceberg/Freedom of Speech . . . Just Watch What You Say* and *O.G. Original Gangster.* Body Count is a middle-tier thrash band at best, but Ice-T is an entertaining front man, trafficking in outrage, whether imagining a tryst with a white supremacist's daughter in "KKK Bitch" or dissecting integration tensions in "There Goes the Neighborhood."

The novelty of a celebrity rapper mixing politics and speed metal wore off by the time of *Born Dead* and the stillborn *Violent Demise.* Lesser material focusing on locker-room juvenilia is partially to blame, and so is the band's relative lack of thunder when compared to nastier crews such as Slayer and Pantera.   —G.K.

Michael Bolton

★★ Michael Bolton (Columbia, 1983)
★★½ The Hunger (Columbia, 1987)
★★ Soul Provider (Columbia, 1989)
★★ The Early Years (RCA, 1991)
★ Time, Love & Tenderness (Columbia, 1991)
★ Timeless (The Classics) (Columbia, 1992)
★½ The One Thing (Columbia, 1993)
★★ The Greatest Hits 1985–1995 (Columbia, 1995)
★½ This Is the Time—The Christmas Album (Columbia, 1996)
★★ All That Matters (Columbia, 1997)
★★★ My Secret Passion: The Arias (Sony Classical, 1998)
★ Timeless (The Classics), Vol. 2 (Columbia, 1999)
★★ Love Songs (Columbia, 2001)
★½ Only a Woman Like You (Columbia, 2002)

Easily one of the most reviled figures in mainstream pop, Michael Bolton has a powerful, expressive, remarkably versatile voice—and an almost perverse sense of how to apply it. While he owed his initial popularity to he-man power ballads that made him a late-'80s heartthrob, his subsequent decision to remake various R&B chestnuts made him a figure of derision and disdain in some circles.

Bolton began life as Michael Bolotin, and sang in several nondescript Connecticut hard rock bands before being signed to Columbia in 1982. (The cover-heavy *The Early Years* offers all anyone need hear from that period.) *Michael Bolton* is better balanced and more pop-savvy, but falters when he attempts an over-burdened rendition of the Supremes' "Back in My Arms Again."

Finally having learned to relax, *The Hunger* finds him turning to Otis Redding's "(Sittin' on) The Dock of the Bay," which gets an earnest, respectful reading so faithful to the original you'd think Bolton had begun doing impressions. Chuffed by that single's success, he takes greater liberties with *Soul Provider,* overemoting his way through such classics as "Georgia on My Mind" (as expected, Bolton goes through "Georgia" like Sherman). By *Time, Love & Tenderness,* his approach to the likes of "When a Man Loves a Woman" seems almost a parody of soul singing.

A pity, really, because when left to his own material, Bolton's singing is quite bearable. "Walk Away" and "That's What Love Is All About" (from *The Hunger*) may look like pro forma rock ballads, but Bolton understands how to play the inner dynamics to add drama to their heartbreak sentiment. While that may easily lead to schmaltz, performances such as "How Am I Supposed to Live Without You" or "How Can We Be Lovers" (both from *Soul Provider*) suggest that Bolton could be capable of greatness.

But it was not to be. He continued to ransack the classics through cover versions, offering a pair of albums shamelessly dubbed *Timeless: The Classics* (and if you think what he does to R&B is cruel, wait 'til you hear his cheerily bombastic take on "Like a Rolling Stone" from *Timeless, Vol. 2*), but otherwise seemed stylistically adrift. *The One Thing* compiles most of the worst clichés of '80s MOR rock, while *All That Matters* (despite some nicely subtle singing on "Safe Place from the Storm") is muddled and unconvincing. By contrast, *My Secret Passion,* his foray into operatic arias, is surprisingly good—not quite Metropolitan Opera caliber, but tasteful and quite competent. But what his public preferred was the soppy emotionalism of the material collected in *Love Songs,* and so *Only a Woman Like You* delivered the sad spectacle of Bolton trying to seem relevant through wan attempts to catch some of Marc Anthony's buzz through soppy, Latin-inflected love songs. Sad, very sad.   —J.D.C.

Gary U.S. Bonds

★★★   On the Line (1982; BMG/Razor & Tie, 1991)
★★★★ The Very Best of Gary U.S. Bonds: Original Legrand Masters (Varèse Sarabande, 1998)
★★★   Back in 20 (M.C., 2004)

Some of the liveliest feel-good, party-down singles of the early '60s pre-Beatles period came out of a Norfolk, VA, recording studio owned by Bronx, NY–raised producer/Legrand Records label chief Frank Guida, whose principal client was a local club singer named Gary Alexander. Guida had cowritten a rousing rocker of a tune called "New Orleans," intending to give it to another vocalist, Leroy "Bunchy" Toombs. Preferring to cut his own original material instead, Toombs passed on the song, so Guida turned to Alexander.

On first listen, Guida found Alexander's performance a bit thin, not because of any deficiency in the singer—who had energy and expressiveness to burn—but rather in the somewhat limited technology of the day. So Guida had Alexander double his vocal, and "New Orleans" was done. On a billboard down the street from the studio was an advertisement exhorting Americans to "Buy U.S. Bonds!" The enterprising Guida recognized it immediately as Gary Alexander's new stage name, and the late summer of 1960 saw the release of Legrand single 1003 by Gary U.S. Bonds. With the studio band, the Church Street Five (propelled by Emmett Shields' double-bass-drum beat), rocking furiously behind him, Bonds set the rowdy atmosphere by shouting the opening lines, "I said-a hey, hey, hey, hey, yeah!" and was answered with equal enthusiasm by the band as saxophonist Earl Swanson began wailing. The assault didn't let up, and almost three minutes later the party wound down, leaving listeners everywhere breathless but eager for more. By the fall "New Orleans" was peaking at #6 on the pop chart. A rock & roll juggernaut had been launched that would roll on for only two years but leave an indelible mark on a generation of rockers and producers then coming of age at the dawn of the British Invasion. Bonds' third single, "Quarter to Three," not only topped the chart, but its sizzling, dense sound established Guida as one of the most innovative and influential producers of his time. "Quarter to Three" was a tribute in song to the intoxicating effects of the music of "Daddy G'" (he being the Church Street Five's other saxophonist, Gene Barge) on the all-night revelers saluted in the lyrics. In addition to the usual hyperkinetic Bonds vocal, Guida enlisted 14 children to whoop it up in the studio, and they came through, sounding for all the world like the most debauched human beings on the planet at that moment. To this Guida added five more overdubs of party ambience. The end result proved irresistible. Succeeding singles were variations on this formula, and a number of them worked in grand fashion: "School Is Out," the raucous followup to "Quarter to Three," went to #5, a sequel, "School Is In" (clearly a less interesting topic), topped out at #28, but Bonds closed out 1961 with a return to the Top 10 with "Dear Lady Twist." This exhilarating ride continued into 1962, beginning with another dance-oriented number, "Twist, Twist Señora," which spiced its hand-clapping and ensemble shouting with a pop-calypso flavor, all of which met with approval to the tune of a #9 pop hit.

Bonds barely broke a sweat in making his final appearance in the Top 30 as a Legrand artist. For the Richard Lester–directed film *It's Trad, Dad*, the legendary songwriting team of Doc Pomus and Mort Shuman penned the jovial but slightly wistful doo-wop-influenced "Seven Day Weekend" (which finds the singer lamenting that his life can't be one long party); in about 10 minutes' time, Bonds was filmed lip-synching the song in a New York studio, collected his money, and went home. Peaking at #28, "Seven Day Weekend" marked the end of Bonds' hit-making tenure with Guida, despite several good singles cut over the next four years.

Varèse Sarabande's 16-track *The Very Best of Gary U.S. Bonds: The Original Legrand Masters* tells the story of the exemplary work Bonds and Guida did for each other (the latter remains woefully underacknowledged for his sculpting of a distinctive sound signature in the studio). All the abovementioned hits are here, as well as nonhit sides that demonstrate the admirable consistency of the artist's and the producer's efforts over the years. Consistency is not the same as diversity or the mark of an artist taking chances; rather, Bonds and Guida had an infectious formula and they worked it for all it was worth. No shame in that: the music stands.

Bruce Springsteen was one of those budding rockers who became infatuated with Bonds' music in the early '60s, and he later made "Quarter to Three" a staple of his live shows. In 1981 the Boss returned the favor by coproducing, with his E Street Band guitarist Steve Van Zandt, two albums for Bonds, *Dedication* (1981) and *On the Line* (1982). Now out of print, *Dedication* featured the Springsteen-penned "This Little Girl," very much in a Guida vein sonically, with some E Street edge, which propelled Bonds back onto the chart, peaking at #11. *On the Line* made its mark via the single "Out of Work," which peaked at #21, Bonds' final appearance in the Top 50. With four Springsteen songs and appearances by most of the E Streeters in support roles, *On the Line* has the feel and energy of the long encores the Boss used to do in which he put his stamp on '60s rock and soul tunes that had influenced him. Completists are advised to check the online services for twofer import releases (via the Ace label) of Bonds' Legrand albums.   —D.M.

Bone Thugs-n-Harmony

★★★★ Creepin On Ah Come Up (EP) (Ruthless, 1994)
★★★★ E. 1999 Eternal (Ruthless, 1995)
★★★½ The Art of War (Ruthless, 1996)
★★★½ BTNHResurrection (Ruthless/Epic, 2000)
★★★½ Thug World Order (Ruthless/Epic, 2002)
★★★★ The Collection: Volume One (Ruthless/Epic, 1998)
★★★★ The Collection: Volume Two (Ruthless/Epic, 2000)

Mo Thugs Family

★★★ Mo Thugs Family, Family Scriptures (Relativity, 1997)
★★★½ Mo Thugs Family, Chapter II: Family Reunion (Relativity, 1998)
★½ Mo Thugs Family, III: The Mothership (Koch, 2000)

Bizzy Bone

★★★ Heaven'z Movie (Ruthless, 1998)
★★ The Gift (AMC, 2001)

Krayzie Bone

★★★½ Thug Mentality 1999 (Ruthless, 1999)
★★ Thug on Da Line (Ruthless, 1999)
★★ L-Burna AKA Layzie Bone, Thug by Nature (Ruthless, 2001)

Bone Thugs-n-Harmony—the resilient group comprised Cleveland, OH, natives Anthony "Krayzie Bone" Henderson, Charles "Wish Bone" Scruggs, Steve "Layzie Bone" Howse, and (from nearby Columbus) Byron "Bizzy Bone" McCane—redrew the hip-hop map. When Bone burst onto the scene, commercially successful hip-hop came almost exclusively from New York and California. A telephone audition with Eazy-E of L.A.'s most notorious group, N.W.A, provided Bone with its break. Eazy-E sent Bone bus tickets to Los Angeles, where the group signed to Ruthless Records. Bone's unique sound—light-speed, snappily syncopated raps combined with round-toned, sweet soul harmonies—was already in evidence on its eight-song debut proper, *Creepin On Ah Come Up*. Their grimy East Cleveland street origins and Eazy-E's gangsta tutelage informed the EP's breakout hits "Thuggish Ruggish Bone" and "For tha Love of $."

In March 1995, while Bone was recording its full-length debut, *E. 1999 Eternal*, Eazy-E died of AIDS. His passing deepened Bone's sense of purpose. The group's tribute to its mentor, "Crossroad," got a radio-ready remix rebirth as "Tha Crossroads" and became its biggest hit, tieing the Beatles' 32-year-old record for the fastest-rising *Billboard* single. Clad all in white, the group performed the song on that year's

Grammy Awards, and took home the trophy for Best Rap Performance.

Followup double album *The Art of War* spawned hit singles "Look into My Eyes" and "If I Could Teach the World" but was plagued by an excess of rote material. (This problem can be attributed at least in part to Bone's prolific output, making both *Collection* CDs welcome distillations of their weighty catalogue.) *The Art of War* did, however, contain the Cameo-sampling nugget "Blaze It," suggesting that even though Cypress Hill are hip-hop's most famous herb advocates, Bone's blissful, plentiful pot paeans take you higher.

Though there is something to recommend on all of Bone's solo albums, the group recognizes its superior unified strength. Later albums *BTNHResurrection* and *Thug World Order* even suggest that their soul-stirring singing is well suited to the mellowness of age.

Now that there are rap superstars from every corner of the country, it's easy to overlook Bone's early role in expanding hip-hop's geographic boundaries. That it also broadened the genre's artistic parameters is to the group's lasting credit. When its staccato rhyming cadence is purposely copied—as Biggie Smalls did on his rousing Bone collabo "Notorious Thugs"—it makes the group's unique identity clear. Having recorded with everyone from 2Pac to Mariah Carey, Bone Thugs-n-Harmony remains one of popular music's most intriguing and enduring propositions. —P.R.

Bon Jovi

    ★★   Bon Jovi (Mercury, 1984)
    ★½   7800° Fahrenheit (Mercury, 1985)
  ★★★½ Slippery When Wet (Mercury, 1986)
    ★★   New Jersey (Mercury, 1988)
    ★★½ Keep the Faith (Mercury, 1992)
  ★★★★ Cross Road: 14 Classic Grooves (Mercury, 1994)
    ★★½ These Days (Mercury, 1995)
    ★★   Crush (Island, 2000)
   ★★★ One Wild Night: Live 1985–2001 (Uptown/Universal, 2001)
    ★★   Bounce (Island, 2002)
  ★★★½ This Left Feels Right (Island, 2003)

Jon Bon Jovi

    ★★   Blaze of Glory (Mercury, 1990)
   ★★★ Destination Anywhere (Mercury, 1997)

Emerging in the wake of the '80s pop-metal boom, Bon Jovi's early recordings fused the crass popcraft of Journey and Starship with the average-Joe populism of Bruce Springsteen for a sound that aspired to rock & roll grandeur without achieving it. *Bon Jovi* and *7800° Fahrenheit* understand the basic formula, but offer little in the way of memorable material, sticking close to pop conventions like heartbreak lyrics and strident, minor-key choruses (although *Bon Jovi* does at least hint at things to come with "Shot Through the Heart"). The band is nearly redeemed by *Slippery When Wet*, an album which in its better moments— "Livin' on a Prayer," say, or "Wanted Dead or Alive"— actually delivers enough melodic razzle-dazzle to make the band's shameless posturing almost forgivable. Unfortunately, the band's massive sales encouraged the lads to show how little success had changed them, which they did through the bombastic Springsteenisms of *New Jersey*.

Bon Jovi the band went on hiatus, during which time frontman Jon Bon Jovi released the solo album-cum-soundtrack *Blaze of Glory* (written for the film *Young Guns II*), which updates "Wanted Dead or Alive" but otherwise makes the Wild West sound suspiciously like East Jersey. After regrouping, the band quickly returned to form with the cheerfully clichéd *Keep the Faith*, which at least balanced the bombast with the corny but heartfelt ballad "Bed of Roses." *Cross Road*, a relentlessly tuneful best-of, has charms enough to be a guilty pleasure for all but the most cynical, and even adds to the canon with "Always." (A second best-of, *This Left Feels Right*, dilutes the catalogue's charm with later and lesser hits.)

From there, the band continued on as if the '90s never happened, cranking out variations on the old formula and somehow continuing to fill arenas (stadiums in its home state). It hardly matters that *These Days* sounds like it should have been called *Those Days* (though it's hard not to admire the shamelessness of "Lie to Me"). *Destination Anywhere*, Jon Bon Jovi's second solo project, sounds more like a collection of demos than a fully-realized album, but it did give the singer the opportunity to flex his melodrama muscles on "August 7, 4:15." *Crush* is summed up in the chorus to "Two Story Town," which complains of "the same old sights, the same old sounds," but *Bounce* finds the band briefly revitalized by the tragedy of 9/11. Not that the blunt, jingoistic "Undivided" deserves comparison to the similar-but-superior "The Rising," but it wouldn't be Bon Jovi if the band didn't continue to aspire to Springsteen. —J.D.C.

The Bonzo Dog Band

    ★★   Gorilla (Liberty, 1967)
   ★★★ History of the Bonzos (BGO, 1987)
   ★★★ Cornology (EMI, 1998)
    ★★   Anthology (Voiceprint, 1999)
    ★★   Vol. 1: The Intros (EMI, 2000)
    ★★   Vol. 2: The Outros (EMI, 2000)
    ★★   Vol. 3: Dog Ends (BMI, 2000)

Before Monty Python, there was Bonzo. A remarkably inventive gang of wits, this late-'60s London quintet did twisted vaudeville, delivering custard-pie funny bits with an acid-era sense of the absurd. Lord Buckley and Lenny Bruce were among their influences; the satirical pieces of the Mothers of Invention provided an American parallel (although the Bonzos were far more cheery). Keeping close watch on the zeitgeist, the Bonzos sent up mod mania on "Cool Britannia" and hippie preoccupations on "Kama Sutra" and "Can Blue Men Sing the Whites?"; Paul McCartney produced their 1968 hit, "I'm the Urban Spaceman." As is true of most comedy acts, the Dog Band's routines were uneven, but its box set, *Cornology,* proves how often it did score. Plus, the boys could really play their saxes, guitars, and assorted devices. *Anthology* assembles the band's rarities; the EMI volumes repackage early work and are mainly for fanatics.   —P.E.

Boogie Down Productions

★★★★★ Criminal Minded (B-Boy, 1987)
★★★★½ By All Means Necessary (Jive, 1988)
★★★★ Ghetto Music: The Blueprint of Hip Hop (Jive, 1989)
★★★★ Edutainment (Jive, 1990)
★★★ Live Hardcore Worldwide (Jive, 1991)
★★★ Sex and Violence (Jive, 1992)
★★★★ Best of B-Boy Records (Landspeed, 2001)

KRS-One

★★★ Return of the Boom Bap (Jive, 1993)
★★★★ KRS-One (Jive, 1995)
★★★★ I Got Next (Jive, 1997)
★★★★ A Retrospective (Jive, 2000)
★★★ The Sneak Attack (Koch, 2001)
★★½ Spiritual Minded (Koch, 2002)
★★★★ The Mix Tape (Koch, 2002)
★★★ Kristyles (Koch, 2003)
★★★ Keep Right (Grit, 2004)

Laurence Krisna Parker (born August 20, 1965) was living in a Bronx homeless shelter in 1985 when he met social worker Scott Sterling (a.k.a. Scott LaRock). The pair formed the hardcore rap group Boogie Down Productions, releasing only their debut album *Criminal Minded* (an unadulterated classic and the template for all subsequent gangsta rap) before LaRock was fatally shot at a party in the Bronx. KRS-One soldiered on as BDP, his personal acronym (Knowledge Reigns Supreme Over Nearly Everyone) blossoming on *By All Means Necessary* as he declared "Some people say I am a rap missionary/some people say I am a walking dictionary/some people say I am truly legendary/but what I am is simply a black revolutionary." While many early BDP story-raps were

street-level parables, KRS did not fall prey to gangsta caricatures; in the liner notes to *Edutainment* he castigated "gangster pop star pimps" for "acting the way the government wants black people to act." Earning his nickname the Teacher, KRS-One produced info-packed lectures in rap form on topics including U.S. government complicity in the drug trade ("Illegal Business" on *By Any Means*), African-American history ("You Must Learn" from *Ghetto Music*), and vegetarianism ("Beef" from *Edutainment*), delivered in a commanding voice often inflected with Jamaican patois. His songs featured sonic calling cards and iconic choruses such as the whooping alert of "Sound of da Police" and the titular chant of "Black Cop" (both on *Return of the Boom Bap*) that became ingrained in the consciousness of multiple generations of hip-hop devotees. In 1993, KRS shelved the BDP moniker in favor of his own name, although in tone and quality his overall oeuvre remained relatively seamless. Despite dipping popularity in the face of fickle fashion, and even considering his gospel (!) effort *Spiritual Minded,* KRS-One has never made the concessions that would result in a wack album. In the summer of 2004, he embarked on an intimate U.S. club tour, performing a furious nonstop sequence of his greatest hits (there are many) to a distilled, fervent fan base, laying a very strong claim to being the greatest MC of all time. "Kool Moe Dee has a new book out where he claims Melle Mel was the greatest ever," said KRS-One at these shows, "and I took Melle Mel out, so . . ." So think about it: KRS-One lyrically destroyed rappers from MC Shan (on "The Bridge Is Over," off 1987's *Criminal Minded*) to Nelly (check "Ova Here" on 2002's *The Mix Tape*), and looks set to continue recording strong material past his 40th birthday. He has a point.   —P.R.

Booker T. and the MG'S

★★½ Green Onions (Stax, 1962)
★★ Soul Dressing (Atlantic, 1965)
★★★ And Now, Booker T. and the MG's (Atlantic, 1966)
★★★★ The Best of Booker T. and the MG's (1968; Rhino, 1989)
★★★½ Hip Hug-Her (1968; Rhino, 1992)
★★★ Soul Limbo (1968; Stax, 1991)
★★★ Uptight (1968; Stax, 1991)
★★★ The Booker T. Set (1969; Stax, 1987)
★★★ McLemore Avenue (Stax, 1971)
★★★½ The Very Best of Booker T. and the MG's (Rhino, 1994)
★★ That's the Way It Should Be (Sony, 1994)
★★★½ Time Is Tight (Box) (Stax, 1998)

Backing up Otis Redding and a host of Stax all-stars, Booker T. and the MG's were among the prime movers behind the Memphis Sound. Adamant in their insistence that less is more, each of the quartet's players was a lean and efficient virtuoso. One of the inventors of funk guitar, Steve Cropper played trebly, swift riffs; his lead lines were telegraphic and never flashy. An unorthodox player, Donald "Duck" Dunn seldom relied on the blues patterns of most R&B players—his bass, instead, provided essential punctuation. Drummer Al Jackson's spare drumming was soul music's counterpart to that of Rolling Stone Charlie Watts. Only Booker T. Jones himself, a teenage wunderkind when he started out at Stax, was a more expansive talent: The eloquence of his organ lent the band's records an insinuating grace.

The MG's masterworks are '60s instrumentals such as "Green Onions," "Hip Hug-Her," "Groovin'," and "Soul Limbo." All of the Stax records have worthwhile cuts; and each of the best-of compilations—especially the *Time Is Tight* box—has timeless, elegant funk. *That's the Way It Should Be,* a reunion effort, still shows them in strong form on both originals and covers ranging from U2's "I Still Haven't Found What I'm Looking For" to Dylan's "Gotta Serve Somebody." —P.E.

Boredoms

One of the most adventurous bands on the planet, Osaka, Japan's Boredoms are rarely easy to take, but—especially on their later records—they're also sublime and monumentally powerful. Led by the indefatigable Eye Yamatsuka (later Yamantaka Eye, or simply EYE), they smash every preconception of what rock music is supposed to be like into splinters, and then build a palace out of them.

Boredoms' first album, *Osorezan to Stooges Kyo* ("The Stooges Craze and Osorezan"), was subsequently compiled with the earlier *Anal by Anal* EP *as Onanie Bomb Vs. the Sex Pistols.* It's a total mess—they've clearly decided that they want to destroy everything predictable about music, but haven't a clue what to replace it with. There's a lot of vehement shrieking in a made-up language, riffs that self-destruct after a few seconds, and incoherent clattery mayhem. *Soul Discharge* is a real improvement. It's still hilariously berserk, but the epileptic rhythms are purposeful more than accidental, and they're actually sort of engaging with pop, albeit from somewhere outside our solar system—check out the B-52's disembowelment "52 Boredom" and the punk-metal freakout "Sun, Gun, Run."

With *Pop Tatari,* Boredoms had a decent recording budget for the first time, and used it to make their most agitated and discombobulated record yet. It starts with 30 seconds of a piercing sine wave (called "Noise Ramones"), and thereafter whirls into an hour-long schizophrenic frenzy—*Eye*'s voice sounds like an entire zoo fighting to the death. *Wow2* is Boredoms live in the studio and attempting to pass for a heavy rock band, which is sort of like Frankenstein's monster attempting to pass for a professional wrestler.

Around this time, Boredoms made their first real splash in America, opening the Lollapalooza tours of 1994 and 1995 with their legendary live show, as much acrobatic theater of the absurd as rock performance. Beneath the howling anarchy of tracks such as the Bore anthem "Shock City," though, *Chocolate Synthesizer* is a genuine work of compositional art, featuring melodic motifs that recur through the album, battered into every conceivable shape, as well as the band's newfound willingness to stay in their fabulously twisted grooves.

Having pushed chaos to the limit, they started to get serious about building a set of tools for their music with a series of EPs and albums called *Super Roots*—experimental records, which by this band's standards is saying something. The first *Super Roots* EP is an attempt to record something quiet (or, as Eye put it, "ambient hardcore"); they were still constitutionally incapable of not bashing things and squealing, but it's fun to hear them try to restrain themselves, and "Budokan Tape Try (500 Tapes High)" even sort of paraphrases Grace Jones' version of "Demolition Man." *Super Roots 2* is an ultra-limited single that includes lots of silence; *Super Roots 3* is the entire band hammering at a one-chord riff for half an hour; there is no *Super Roots 4,* since 4 signifies in Japanese roughly what 13 does in English; *Super Roots 5* is an hour-long noise cloud; *6* is a series of scraggly but intense exercises in rhythm and timbre.

And then they proved what all that research had been for. *Super ae* is a pounding, astounding psychedelic masterwork, the raw power of Boredoms' early records harnessed and directed into sustained riff-laden sun worship. Its centerpiece, "Super Going," rises and breaks and rises again with tidal majesty; elsewhere, its drones and chants blow up to monomaniacal electric force and fall again to heart-stopping acoustic splendor. It's beautiful, which they'd never been before, and it sounds like a new kind of hymn.

Two more *Super Roots* discs followed *Super ae: 7* is a very long, delightful band-plus-electronics jam on the riff from the Mekons' "Where Were You?" and *8* is just a single, a frenetic jungle-influenced cover of an old Japanese cartoon theme. *Vision Creation Newsun* is the real sequel to *Super ae*, and at times even more intense—there are shades of drum and bass in its pattering rhythms—although it recycles a few of the same themes and structures. *Suncidal Cendencies* is an album-length "EP" with two variations on one of *Vision*'s tracks, plus a 24-minute, five-percussionist workout credited to "Uoredoms."

The *Rebore* discs are extended megamixes of the Boredoms catalogue (leaning most heavily on *Super ae* and *Vision*); vols. *1, 2,* and *3* are respectively remixed by U.N.K.L.E., Ken Ishii, and DJ Krush, and don't alter the source material much beyond throwing in the occasional breakbeat. Eye himself takes over for *Vol. 0,* and unsurprisingly does odder things. The members of Boredoms are also staggeringly prolific outside the band, with more than 50 recorded side projects—the records Eye has made with turntablist Otomo Yoshihide as MC Hellshit & DJ Carhouse are particularly insane, and he's collaborated memorably with Sonic Youth and with John Zorn's Naked City project. Eye's cover artwork for the *Shock City Shockers* compilation of Bore pals was subsequently appropriated as the back cover of Beck's *Midnite Vultures*. —D.W.

Boston

★★★½	Boston	(Epic, 1976)
★★½	Don't Look Back	(Epic, 1978)
★½	Third Stage	(MCA, 1987)
★★★	Greatest Hits	(Epic, 1997)
★★	Rock and Roll Band	(Sony Music, 1998)

After painstakingly experimenting in his basement studio for years, Boston guitarist and MIT-trained engineer Tom Scholz channeled his frustrations into a song called "More Than a Feeling." This 1976 pop

Top 10 ushers in the long, cold winter of arena rock; Boston's soaring combination of high-tech metal guitar punch and smooth pop vocal hooks quickly became the cornerstone of Album Oriented Radio. But as slick as it sounds, "More Than a Feeling" also strikes an uncommonly resonant emotional note.

In retrospect, it's a classic one-shot-to-glory tale. Only problem is, Boston went on to make two far less distinctive and even more popular albums. *Boston* itself sports two satisfying, if similar, followups ("Peace of Mind" and "Hitch a Ride"), alongside a couple of cleaned-up boogie crowd-pleasers ("Smokin' " and "Rock & Roll Band"). The title track of *Don't Look Back* would hold its own on the debut, but Boston's formulaic virtuosity dulls rather quickly. Perhaps Scholz realized this: He retired for eight years after the second album. When the long-delayed *Third Stage* finally saw the light of day, the Boston concept seemed a little musty. That didn't stop "Amanda" from climbing to the top of the charts, of course. *Greatest Hits* charts the band's descent from genre builders to also-rans. —P.E.

Bottle Rockets

★★★	The Bottle Rockets	(East Side Digital, 1993)
★★★★	The Brooklyn Side	(1994; Atlantic, 1995)
★★★★	24 Hours a Day	(Atlantic, 1997)
★★	Leftovers EP	(Doolittle/New West, 1998)
★★★	Brand New Year	(Doolittle/New West, 1999)
★★★	Songs of Sahm	(Bloodshot, 2002)
★★	Blue Sky	(Sanctuary, 2003)

The Bottle Rockets, from rural Missouri, are the thinking person's hillbilly bar band. At their best, they bridge the worlds of the hicks and the hippies, blues junkies and potheads, Motörhead and Hank Williams. The songs of singer-guitarist Brian Henneman are odes to blue-collar rednecks, trailer-park denizens, and divorcees who solve their problems by downing shots, flinging fists, driving fast, or going down slow. His humor is cut by poignancy, an affection for his motley down-on-their-luck characters that is vividly descriptive but rarely judgmental.

The Bottle Rockets finds Henneman coming off his gig as a guitar roadie for Uncle Tupelo to write songs in a similar vein: countrified rock that blends electric guitars and banjo, and sparse production that frames stories of death ("Kerosene"), Southern bravado ("Wave That Flag"), and lust ("Trailer Mama").

The Brooklyn Side has a similar arc with sharper production, opening with an acoustic country ballad and then adding carefully calibrated doses of bombast until Henneman is ranting like a drunk in boxer shorts on the oddly moving "Sunday Sports." There are hints of Neil Young, Sun Records rockabilly, and Chuck Berry rock & roll in an album that packs a Saturday-night kick even as it acknowledges the Sunday-morning hangover.

24 Hours a Day is more concise, the specifics in songs such as the darkly comic "Indianapolis" and the rueful title track honed with literary precision, while the band perfects its mix of barbed-wire guitars and stringed instruments.

There's truth in advertising on *Leftovers:* Outtakes such as "Coffee Monkey" come off as amusing B sides. *Brand New Year* boasts the slickest sound yet on a Rockets album, at odds with the typically homespun subject matter. *Songs of Sahm* gets the band back on track with a collection of genre-defiant songs written by kindred spirit Doug Sahm, the late cosmic cowboy from San Antonio. The Rockets' affinity for Sahm's brand of blues, acid rock, honky tonk, and Tejano balladry stamps them as worthy heirs to his maverick Americana legacy.

Blue Sky is the most subdued Bottle Rockets yet, as the bar-band brashness of old is replaced with a more reflective tone. Henneman's songs are as oddly touching and humorous as ever, but musically, he's gone soft. —G.K.

David Bowie

★★	David Bowie (Deram, 1967)
★★★	Space Oddity (1969; Virgin, 1999)
★★★½	The Man Who Sold the World (Mercury, 1970)
★★★★★	Hunky Dory (1971; Virgin, 1999)
★★★★★	The Rise and Fall of Ziggy Stardust and the Spiders From Mars (1972; Virgin 1999)
★★★★★	Aladdin Sane (1973; Virgin, 1999)
★★	Images 1966–1967 (London, 1973)
★★	Pin Ups (1973; Virgin, 1999)
★★	David Live (1974; Virgin, 1999)
★★½	Diamond Dogs (1974; Virgin, 1999)
★★★	Young Americans (1974; Virgin, 1999)
★★★★★	Station to Station (1976; Virgin, 1999)
★★★★★	Changesonebowie (1976; Virgin, 1999)
★★★★★	Low (1977; Virgin, 1999)
★★★★½	Heroes (1977; Virgin, 1999)
★★★½	Stage (1978; Virgin, 1999)
★★★★★	Lodger (1979; Virgin, 1999)
★★★★½	Scary Monsters (1980; Virgin, 1999)
★★★★½	Changestwobowie (RCA, 1981)
★★★½	Let's Dance (Virgin, 1983)
★	Tonight (Virgin, 1984)
★	Never Let Me Down (Virgin, 1987)
★★★★	Sound and Vision (1989; Virgin, 2003)
★★★★★	Changesbowie (1990; Virgin, 1999)
★	Black Tie White Noise (Virgin, 1993)

★★★★★	The Singles 1969–1993 (Rykodisc, 1993)
★	Outside (Virgin, 1995)
★	The Buddha Of Suburbia (Virgin, 1995)
★★½	Earthling (Virgin, 1997)
★★★★	Essential David Bowie: Best of 1969–1974 (Virgin, 1997)
★★★★	Essential David Bowie: Best of 1974–1979 (Virgin, 1997)
★★	Hours (Virgin, 1999)
★★★★	Bowie at the Beeb: Best of the BBC Radio Sessions 1968–1972 (Virgin, 2000)
★★★	Heathen (Columbia, 2002)
★★★	Reality (Columbia, 2003)

Is David Bowie's "Young Americans" the greatest song ever? It could be. Over grand, lurching piano glam, Bowie testifies like a deranged soul crooner about the new breed of young Americans coming to save the world. They're the pretty things who drive their mamas and papas insane, the chosen people sent by the gods of rock to bring action and adventure and romance and sex sex sex back to a dead-end society. Bowie was only 27 at the time, but he sounds much older, a slinky vagabond rooting for the hot tramps and glitter kids of the future. He sounds old and English, almost like a vampire, but he's saved by the young Americans. All night he wants the young Americans: he wants to do us, he wants to be us, he wants what we want. For the five minutes of the song, all anyone could ever want is to be or do a young American. David Bowie's whole world, and everything great about rock & roll, is in this tune.

Rock & roll had pretensions long before it had a David Bowie, but Bowie invented whole new levels of theatrical posing, stylistic diddling, and sexual provocation, doing for pretensions what Jimi Hendrix did for electric guitars. The erstwhile David Jones had begun in the late '60s wasting his ambitions on costumes that didn't quite fit: mod, folk music, mime. He was clunky as a mod (the results have been recycled as *David Bowie, Love You Till Tuesday, Images, Early On*), and wispy as a folkie *(Space Oddity)*, but he began to rock on *The Man Who Sold the World,* more bluesily than he ever would again, teaming up with guitarist Mick Ronson and producer Tony Visconti for heavy visions such as "Width of a Circle."

And then one day David visited New York, where a friend turned him on to the Velvet Underground's "Sweet Jane." The result: *Hunky Dory,* Bowie's first classic, an album of Nico-style cafe ballads about queen bitches falling in love with pretty things. On *Hunky Dory,* the David in Miss Jones finally got loose, reveling in pansexual lust, visionary gossip, glam flamboyance, and you're-soaking-in-it decadence. Brilliant tunes, too—Barbra Streisand covered the best song here ("Life on Mars?"), while Dinosaur Jr covered the second best ("Quicksand"), and that pretty much sums up the bizarro impact of *Hunky Dory*. The bubbleglam rocker "Queen Bitch" pays tribute to Lou Reed while giving David a chance to look swishy in his bipperty-bopperty hat.

Hunky Dory made Bowie the star he has remained ever since. But *Ziggy Stardust* remains the most famous of all glam records, turning up Ronson's boogie guitar for a concept album about an androgynous rock star from outer space. Bowie took it all too far, and he couldn't even play guitar, but he works his fey vibrato in "Suffragette City," "Starman," and "Moonage Daydream," while "Five Years" is one of the all-time great album openers, with doomy drums and a chanting choir to announce the end of the world and the dawn of the new Bowie era. The Rykodisc reissue adds the key rarities "Velvet Goldmine" and "Sweet Head," which has the credo "Before there was rock, you only had God."

Aladdin Sane cranks up the hard, slick, sensationalistic energy of *Ziggy*, minus the draggy bits, for a sequel that sounds even better than the original, driven by the guitar swagger of "Watch That Man" and the swoony postapocalyptic love song "Drive-In Saturday." *Pin Ups* was a set of '60s Swinging London covers with Twiggy on the cover; the one great moment is the Yardbirds' "Shapes of Things," where Bowie becomes an unlikely ecologist, whimpering "Please don't destroy the lands/Don't make them desert sands" even though he doesn't sound biodegradable. *Diamond Dogs* announced the end of the world (again?) with a certain boy-who-cried-wolf quality, despite "Rebel Rebel" and the title song, which celebrates "the year of the scavenger, the season of the bitch." Bowie boasts he has never listened to *David Live*, and good for him; the *Ziggy* film soundtrack is a waste. The real live document of the Ziggy period is the little-screened BBC documentary *Cracked Actor*, which has to be seen to be believed, especially when Bowie sings the title tune while jamming his tongue into a human skull like a glam Hamlet.

Bowie switched gears for the surprisingly warm R&B homage *Young Americans*, which he described as "plastic soul." Cut in Philadelphia with background vocals from a young Luther Vandross, it's short on tunes aside from the title song. But it was the warm-up for *Station to Station*, the album where Bowie dyed his hair blond, proclaimed himself the Thin White Duke, and made the most intense music of his life. "TVC15," "Golden Years," and "Stay" combine heavy guitar grooves and shiny vinyl funk beats, plus nutzoid lyrics

("Light is so vague when it brings someone new/This time tomorrow I'll know what to do"). It all explodes in the heart-pounding 10-minute onslaught of the title song, inspired by the Catholic devotion of the Stations of the Cross and apparently quite generous helpings of drugs. *Station to Station* is a space-rock masterpiece, even if Bowie admits he can barely remember making it.

Low, released the week Bowie turned thirty, marked a new beginning. After burying himself in white powder in Los Angeles, he fled to Berlin for some personal detox and began his famous "Berlin trilogy." Side one of *Low* consists of seven synth-pop fragments; side two consists of four brooding electronic instrumentals. Bowie sings about spiritual death and rebirth, from the electric blue loneliness of "Sound and Vision" to the doomed erotic obsession of "Always Crashing in the Same Car." Thanks to producer Tony Visconti, keyboardist Brian Eno, and the fuzzed-out guitars of Ricky Gardner and Carlos Alomar, it's the music of an overstimulated mind in an exhausted body, as rock's prettiest sex vampire sashays through some serious emotional wreckage.

Heroes expands the formula with guitarist Robert Fripp, a thicker, fuller sound, a more prominent role for Eno, and the killer title hymn. The finale of the Berlin trilogy, *Lodger* is that rarest of rock & roll artifacts: an underrated Bowie album. Not even the artiste himself has ever made grand claims for this one, but it rocks as hard as *Station to Station* or *Aladdin Sane*, with razor-sharp musical corners and new layers of wit and generosity in the songwriting, especially "Boys Keep Swinging," "D.J.," and "Fantastic Voyage." *Lodger* guitar hero Adrian Belew also appears on *Stage*, a surprisingly decent live album that perversely turns Side Two of *Low* into arena fodder.

Scary Monsters turns up the Fripp guitar for a sleek, chilly-chic set, not as bold as *Lodger* but excellent nonetheless, especially the terrifying "Space Oddity" update "Ashes to Ashes" and the anthemic "Young Americans" update "Teenage Wildlife," which proved beyond any doubt that when Bowie decided not to sing, he could out-not-sing any nonsinger in rock & roll. By now, Bowie's pop clout was bigger than ever, as entire genres sprouted from phases of his past, including goth, punk, techno pop, and the New Romantic poseurs. Bowie cashed in with *Let's Dance*, a slight but pleasant pop record with a few big MTV hits, including the touching rocker "Modern Love."

At the time, Bowie fans debated whether *Let's Dance* was a stylistic triumph, a pop sellout, or just a table-setter for future glories. But it's safe to say nobody suspected it would go down as Bowie's last stand. Still only 36, the most iconic and influential active artist in rock, Bowie seemed to lose his touch overnight, wheezing unpleasantly through the rest of the decade. *Tonight* was an expensive quickie padded with lame covers, while *Never Let Me Down* made things even worse with originals. But the noose he chose to hang himself with was guitar sidekick Reeves Gabrels, who ruined everything left to ruin in Bowie's music. Gabrels collaborated with Bowie in the misbegotten Tin Machine project, producing three albums of dreary art-metal wankeroo. *Black Tie White Noise* had a witty cover of Morrissey's "I Know It's Gonna Happen Someday," the sound of Bowie imitating one of the all-time great Bowie imitators. *The Buddha of Suburbia* was soundtrack filler. *Outside* was a poor reunion with Eno, who presumably had bills to pay.

There were signs of life on Mars in *Earthling* and *Hours,* which offered strong songs ("Looking for Satellites," "Seven," "Thursday's Child") damn near ruined by Gabrels' cheesy guitar glop. *Heathen* and *Reality* were redeemed by Gabrels' exit and a lighter songwriting touch as well as funny covers of Neil Young, the Pixies, and the Legendary Stardust Cowboy. The last few albums prove that Bowie's creative powers are alive and well—as always, he just needs collaborators who can get him pushing.

Bowie's hits collections are as much fun as his proper albums, because his genius for the grand statement and the big splash meant that he didn't skimp when it came to dreaming up hit singles. The 1976 *Changesonebowie* is the original crash course for the ravers. The 1990 *Changesbowie* combines *Changesonebowie* and *Changestwobowie* for a one-disc whammy, although there are too many shortened single edits and it's hard to forgive that "Fame '90" remix. The double-disc *Singles* runs too far into the '80s and '90s; *Sound and Vision* is a mostly redundant three-disc box; *Bowie at the Beeb* collects early BBC live material, including Lou Reed and Chuck Berry covers. The two separately available *Essential* volumes are both eccentric, but present worthy rarities such as Bowie's original version of "All the Young Dudes." Hot tramps in search of a handy introduction should use *Changesbowie* as a map and then start playing around. Despite his image as an alien Major Tom figure, what endures most in Bowie's music is the lust for life you can hear in "Young Americans," "Fantastic Voyage," "Teenage Wildlife," "Five Years," and so many more. His music will always sound great as long as the world still has kooks, cracked actors, glitter babes, and young folk going through that difficult phase. Mother Nature clearly didn't intend David Bowie to become a singer, but his whole career proves that sometimes it's nice to fool Mother Nature, because she's a kook like us. —R.S.

Bow Wow Wow

★★★	Your Cassette Pet (EMI Harvest, 1980)	
★★★	See Jungle! See Jungle! Go Join Your Gang Yeah! City All Over! Go Ape Crazy (RCA, 1981)	
★★	The Last of the Mohicans (EP) (RCA, 1982)	
★★	I Want Candy (RCA, 1982)	
★★★½	Original Recordings (Capitol, 1982)	
★	When the Going Gets Tough the Tough Get Going (RCA, 1983)	
★★	Girl Bites Dog (EMI, 1993)	
★★★½	Best of Bow Wow Wow (RCA, 1996)	
★★	Live in Japan (Receiver imp., 1997)	
★★	Wild in the U.S.A. (Cleopatra, 1998)	

Bow Wow Wow was Malcolm McLaren's first big project after the Sex Pistols imploded, and the erstwhile media manipulator made sure his new band bounded onto the scene with a whole gaggle of gimmicks. The first was Annabella Lwin, a 14-year-old Burmese immigrant McLaren found working in a laundry and decided to remake into a postpunk goddess. Then there was what used to be Adam's Ants, the trio of Matthew Ashman (guitar), Leroy Gorman (bass), and Dave Barbarossa (drums), whom McLaren introduced to African music—specifically, the sound of Burundi tribal drumming—then induced to dump Adam and follow him.

But it was the product that ultimately pulled the package together. Bow Wow Wow's cassette-only first single, a home-taping anthem called "C-30, C-60, C-90 Go!," had little going for it musically—a basic Burundi-beat groove topped with a chant-along vocal—but made quite a stink when it hit the charts smack in the middle of the British Phonograph Industry's "Home Taping Is Killing Music" campaign. No surprise, then, that the group's cassette-only first and now out-of-print album, *Your Cassette Pet,* was almost pure provocation, filled with such nudge-wink nasties as "Uomo Sex al Apache" (say it real fast) and "Sexy Eiffel Towers" (a tribute to the famous Gallic phallic symbol). But between the Bow Wow boys' vigorous rhythm work and Annabella's charmingly hammy vocals, even the likes of "Louis Quatorze"—in which Annabella breathily recounts her ravishings by the beastly Louis—seems more silly than scandalous.

Much the same can be said for the impossibly titled *See Jungle! See Jungle! [etc.]* which introduced the group to this country. But American pop radio proved less than enamored of McLaren's recastings of Rousseau ("Go Wild in the Country") and McLuhan (["I'm a] T.V. Savage"), so RCA turned the Bows over to a proven hitmaker: Kenny Laguna, who converted the band's Burundi beat into a jazzy Bo Diddley groove and gave it a near-hit with a remake of the

Strangeloves' "I Want Candy." The out-of-print *Last of the Mohicans* includes the single and three others, but since all four tracks also appear on *I Want Candy,* the only real reason to seek it out is its cover photo, which finds an unclothed Annabella posed with the rest of the band in McLaren's last art-school joke: a re-creation of Manet's *Déjeuner.*

I Want Candy did well enough to encourage Capitol to issue *12 Original Recordings,* an LP edition of *Your Cassette Pet* and the band's first British singles. But *Candy's* lack of material—half its tracks are remakes of earlier recordings—and spiritless performances marked the beginning of the end for the band. By the time the McLaren-less group got around to cutting the slick, empty *When the Going Gets Tough,* smart listeners knew to keep going.   —J.D.C.

Box Tops

★★★	The Letter/Neon Rainbow (1967; Sundazed, 2000)
★★★	Cry Like a Baby (1968; Sundazed, 2000)
★★★	Nonstop (1968; Sundazed, 2000)
★★	Dimensions (1969; Sundazed, 2000)
★★★½	The Ultimate Box Tops (Warner, 1987)
★★★	Tear Off! (Last Call, 1998)
★★★★	Best of the Box Tops: Soul Deep (Arista, 1996)

Revered by indie rockers for his highly personal brand of power pop in Big Star and the eccentricity of his solo albums, Alex Chilton achieved his greatest commercial success as the 16-year-old lead singer of the Box Tops. The Memphis quintet was cobbled together by veteran Memphis producer Dan Penn to record a single, "The Letter," a huge hit that blended a sophisticated string arrangement with a jaunty, calliope-like keyboard riff and the sound of an airplane taking off. But it was the gravelly, remarkably mature wail of the teenage Chilton that separated "The Letter" from other Summer of Love radio fodder. The subsequent debut album is steeped in Memphis soul, with touches of country and blues, an approach that would remain intact on subsequent releases.

The Penn-written title track of *Cry Like a Baby* produced another major hit, and Chilton began contributing to the songwriting (the negligible "Nonstop") while cementing his status as a transfixing blue-eyed soul stylist on "I Met Her in Church." With Penn giving way to Chips Moman as resident studio guru, *Dimensions* took a more eccentric turn, with a lascivious novelty ("Sweet Cream Ladies, Forward March"), a leering Chilton blues ballad ("I Must Be the Devil"), and an ill-advised guitar jam (a nine-minute "Rock Me Baby"). *Tear Off* found a reunited Box Tops ripping it up persuasively on a batch of vin-

tage blues, soul, and rockabilly tunes that inspired their sound three decades earlier. Of the hits compilations, *Best of the Box Tops* provides the most expansive introduction to Chilton's formative years.   —G.K.

Boyz II Men

★★★	Cooleyhighharmony (Motown, 1991)
★★★★	II (Motown, 1994)
★★★	Evolution (Motown, 1997)
★★	Nathan Michael Shawn Wanya (Universal, 2000)
★★★	Legacy: The Greatest Hits Collection (Universal, 2001)
★★	Full Circle (Arista, 2002)
★★★	The Millennium Collection (Motown, 2003)
★★★	The Christmas Collection (Motown, 2003)

You don't become the most commercially successful R&B act of all time—resetting the record for most weeks at #1 on the *Billboard* singles chart a jaw-dropping three times—by bragging about the size of your dick. Tailoring their advances to the most timid sexual prey, these four nice Philadelphia boyz carefully cushioned a come-on such as "I'll make love to you" with a polite "When you want me to." Their hands-off sensuality made the existence of white idols such as the Backstreet Boys and 'N Sync all but inevitable, while their ladies-first approach offered a triumphant twist on the old adage "Nice guys finish last."

As protégés of Bell Biv Devoe's Michael Bivins, BIIM initially assayed New Jack Swing on their most atypically thumping hit, "Motownphilly." The remainder of *Cooleyhighharmony* was recklessly unafraid of schmaltz, a counterbalance to the breakbeat swagger of the New Jack era. Though the quartet was ever peering back over its shoulder at doo-wop, its nostalgia sounded contemporary, because rather than attempting to re-create the past, it made it sound, sadly, forever lost.

It's no coincidence that the group named its first album after a flick and that its whopper hit "End of the Road" sprang from the *Boomerang* soundtrack—BIIM's sentimentality always emitted overtones of Hollywood. So while *Legacy* is amazing track by track, it's a disorienting overall listen, like watching the last five minutes of a dozen different romantic comedies spliced together. *II* is more coherent and no less popwise—the uptempos benefit from the nuances of Dallas Austin and Jimmy Jam and Terry Lewis, the ballads ("I'll Make Love to You," "Water Runs Dry") are Babyface at his most romantic.

The rest of the group's output is an increasingly wimpier whimper. Once, the Boyz' harmonies seemed like a collective counterbalance to hip-hop's aggrandizement of the individual. And so the collective anonymity of *Full Circle*'s weak balladry is sadder than any of the group's heartbreak songs. —K.H.

Billy Bragg

★★★★	Talking With the Taxman About Poetry (Elektra, 1986)
★★★★	Back to Basics (Elektra, 1987)
★★★	Help Save the Youth of America (Elektra, 1988)
★★★½	Workers Playtime (Elektra, 1988)
★★★½	The Internationale (Elektra, 1990)
★★★½	Don't Try This at Home (Elektra, 1991)
★★★	William Bloke (Elektra, 1996)
★★★½	Reaching to the Converted (Rhino, 1999)
★★★½	England, Half English (Elektra, 2002)
★★★★½	Must I Paint You a Picture (Rhino, 2003)

Billy Bragg is a folksinger, less because of his musical roots (which in fact owe more to the Clash than to the Child ballads) than his principal interest: that is, average folk like you and me. Bragg's overriding sense of humanity puts the heart into his love songs, the sparkle into his social sketches, and keeps even his most stridently ideological material from turning into socialist harangues.

These qualities can be found in their rawest form on *Back to Basics*, a 21-song album compiling the whole of Bragg's first three U.K. releases *(Life's a Riot With Spy vs. Spy, Brewing Up With Billy Bragg,* and *Between the Wars)*. Recorded for the most part with little more than Bragg's electric guitar behind his rough-hewn vocals, the best of these songs—"The Milkman of Human Kindness," "A New England," "Love Gets Dangerous," "Which Side Are You On"— are tuneful and affecting despite their stripped-down simplicity. Nor does *Talking With the Taxman About Poetry* add much in the way of accompaniment, but that hardly keeps him from pulling a sense of drama from "Levi Stubbs' Tears" or lending "Ideology" the sort of power-chord majesty associated with bands like the Who.

Bragg begins to move toward a full-band sound with *Workers Playtime*, an album that bears the subtitle "Capitalism Is Killing Music." (And if you think Bragg doesn't see the joke in having such a legend on a major label release, you seriously underestimate his sense of humor.) As usual, the love songs are well-drawn and emotionally involving, but this time around the political tunes—particularly the countryish "Rotting on Remand" and the triumphant "Waiting for the Great Leap Forwards"—have the edge melodically. That's also the case with *The Internationale*, although Bragg can't take credit, since most of these songs are well-known anthems. *Don't Try This at Home* is easily the most accessible of Bragg's albums, with love songs ("Moving the Goalposts," "You Woke Up My Neighbourhood," and, especially, "Sexuality") that are winning and witty, and issue songs ("God's Footballer," "North Sea Bubble") that suck the listener in with melody before springing their message.

Sadly, the dour *William Bloke* doesn't match that sense of fun (or even the wit of its title). *Reaching to the Converted,* a miscellany of tracks that never made it onto U.S. albums, is hardly essential, but it does include some gems, including the wry, wistful "Scholarship Is the Enemy of Romance" and a lovely cover of the McGarrigle sisters' "Heart Like a Wheel." Bragg fully returns to form with *England, Half English,* which matches typically impish, insightful reflections on politics (on both the interpersonal and national levels) with some of the best-realized band arrangements of Bragg's career (the reggae-inflected title tune is especially nice). *Must I Paint You a Picture* summarizes his career to date, compiling enough first-rate songs to leave any listener wondering why this guy isn't more famous. —J.D.C.

The Brand New Heavies

★★★½	The Brand New Heavies (Delicious Vinyl, 1991)
★★	Heavy Rhyme Experience, Vol. 1 (Delicious Vinyl, 1992)
★★★★	Brother Sister (Delicious Vinyl, 1994)
★★★	Original Flava (Hollywood, 1995)
★★½	Shelter (Delicious Vinyl, 1997)
★★★★	Trunk Funk Classics: 1991–2000 (Rhino, 2000)

Years in the making, *The Brand New Heavies* sounds today almost as good as it did in the early '90s, the heyday of the so-called acid jazz movement, and the beginning of a return of sorts to natural sounds and the kind of sexy syncopation that only a live drum kit can generate. The group's powerful instrumental alchemy (the Heavies' main lineup had been jamming together in the West London suburb of Ealing since 1985) was bolstered by the regal vocals of Atlanta, Georgia, native N'Dea Davenport. Although her involvement with the group remained sporadic throughout the years, Davenport quickly became the Heavies' most memorable persona.

With its overblown gallery of guest rappers, the much-anticipated followup *Heavy Rhyme Experience, Vol. 1* was an ambitious, cluttered affair—the kind of conceptual record that sounds better on paper than in real life. Two years later, the Heavies emerged from the studio with *Brother Sister,* their ultimate funk manifesto and a bona fide commercial success. One listen to the jubilant "Back to Love" was proof enough that

Davenport and company had grown up listening to the right records. Granted, there was nothing new and innovative about their festive R&B revival. So tight and life affirming was the Heavies' groove, however, that it was virtually impossible to stop dancing and question the validity of it all.

That sobering moment came in 1997 with *Shelter.* Slicker than its predecessors and with a new vocalist to boot (Siedah Garrett) it went platinum in the U.K. with a fun, still-energetic sound that was slowly beginning to feel formulaic. Not much has been heard since then from the Heavies, except for the release of a compilation that included (surprise, surprise) a newly recorded cut with the ever-excellent Davenport. —E.L.

Brand Nubian

★★★★ One for All (Elektra, 1990)
★★★ In God We Trust (Elektra, 1993)
★★★ Everything Is Everything (Elektra, 1994)
★★★ Foundation (Elektra, 1998)
★★★★ Best Of (Rhino, 2001)
★★½ Fire In The Hole (Babygrande, 2004)

Sadat X

★★★ Wild Cowboys (Loud/RCA, 1996)
★★ No Better Way (Light, 1996)
★★ The State of New York vs. Derek Murphy (Relativity, 2000)

Grand Puba

★★★ Reel to Reel (Elektra, 1992)
★★ 2000 (Elektra, 1995)
★★ Understand This (Koch/Rising Son, 2001)

When Brand Nubian stepped onto the scene at the dawn of the 1990s, it seemed as if funky, mindful, barrier-breaking hip-hop albums were coming out every day. De La Soul and A Tribe Called Quest were at the height of their powers, and nearly forgotten groups such as KMD and the Goats were dropping gems. Brand Nubian, a quartet from New Rochelle, New York, made crucial contributions to this era of hip-hop richness. Maxwell "Grand Puba" Dixon, Lorenzo "Lord Jamar" Dechelaus, Derrick "Sadat X" Murphy, and DJ Alamo wore wooden necklaces and colorful, batik-printed shirts on the cover of the classic debut *One for All,* and from the start they had a sobering lyrical style equally effective whether promoting African-American consciousness ("Concerto in X Minor") or telling hoes to chill (the Edie Brickell–sampling "Slow Down"). Sporting two MCs with classic voices (the lithe-tongued Grand Puba and the sinewy, nasal Sadat X), the group's sound was instantly recognizable. But Puba went solo after *One for All,* taking DJ Alamo with him. Lord Jamar and Sadat X brought DJ Sincere

aboard and continued under the Brand Nubian banner for *In God We Trust* where they furthered their commitment to the Nation of Islam on "Meaning of the 5%" and the chanting "Allah and Justice." That album blew up on the strength of the Diamond-produced single "Punks Jump Up to Get Beat Down," whose gay-bashing lyrics raised eyebrows and objections. *Everything is Everything* didn't have any hits, but it was just as effective. Brand Nubian's original lineup reunited in 1998 for *Foundation.* While by no means a perfect album (it has a number of light, corny tracks—particularly the instantly dated single "Let's Dance" with Busta Rhymes), it includes fine production from Gangstarr's DJ Premier on "The Return" and incisively addresses social topics such as questionable police procedure ("Probable Cause") and maligned black women ("Sincerely") on some of the group's best work. While Brand Nubian's *Best Of* wisely includes essential solo cuts such as Grand Puba's "360 Degrees," anyone interested in latter-day Nubian cream should pick up the compilation *Soundbombing II* (Rawkus, 1999), which includes Grand Puba and Sadat X joining Sir Menelik on "7XL" and the superb Sadat X/Common collabo "1-9-9-9." Sadat X also appears on "Come On," the best cut on the Notorious BIG's posthumous *Born Again,* and the awesome title track from 2002's *Art of War,* an album by Berlin-based DJ Desue available only in Germany. Grand Puba, Lord Jamar, and Sadat X reunited for *Fire in the Hole.* —P.R.

Brandy

★★½ Brandy (Atlantic, 1994)
★★★½ Never Say Never (Atlantic, 1998)
★★★½ Full Moon (Atlantic, 2002)
★★★½ Afrodisiac (Atlantic, 2004)

Listening back over Brandy Norwood's R&B career, it's tempting to say she developed as a singer. And perhaps her pipes did strengthen over the years—she definitely grew into her persona. But it's more to the point to say that stardom entitled her to better songs and more inventive producers. There's a greater contrast between the lackluster "I Wanna Be Down" and the wonderful "Almost Doesn't Count" than there is between her vocal delivery on either song. And while *Full Moon* was her "adult" album as advertised, her vocals hadn't matured so much as her tracks had grown up—the crushing off-kilter beat of "What About Us" is certainly not kiddie stuff.

Which isn't to deny Brandy's vocal presence. On paper, "Sittin' up in My Room" (from the epochal *Waiting To Exhale* soundtrack) is just another ode to unrequited puppy love. But Brandy's voice, forlorn yet with a ghost of a chirp lingering, retains a sense of perspective—you can hear that she knows she won't be lonely forever. And on paper, her duet with Monica, "The Boy Is Mine," couldn't have been more of a vocal mismatch. Brandy's girly breathiness up against Monica's baby-diva suavity—it was like Ronnie Spector versus Aretha (albeit on a much, much smaller scale). But Brandy more than held her own, and the result was a definitive clash between distinct female pop archetypes.

Only a greatest hits will properly highlight Brandy's contributions to the past decade's R&B. But her work with top-line producers like Rodney Jerkins and Dallas Austin ensures that there are few lulls in between the hits on her albums. And she accomplished no small feat, starring in a half-decent sitcom while putting her name on some classic pop singles. Can Alyssa Milano claim the same? Patty Duke? John Stamos?   —K.H.

Bratmobile

> ★★★½   Pottymouth (Kill Rock Stars, 1993)
> ★★★   Peel Sessions (BBC, 1993)
> ★★★★   The Real Janelle (Kill Rock Stars, 1994)
> ★★★½   Ladies, Women, and Girls (Lookout, 2000)
> ★★★   Girls Get Busy (Lookout, 2002)

These pioneering riot grrrls have been one of indie rock's most consistently kicky bands over the past decade or so, committed to toughing it out in a world grown increasingly hostile to both unruly women and low-budget rock bands. But for all their political smarts, their records are more fun than a barrel of monkeys. The main reason is guitarist Erin Smith, who whips out the surfy, rock-lobster trash riffs that make the music go bang. Molly Neuman hits the drums, while wiseacre Allison Wolfe takes care of business on the mike, even when she's just chanting "Girl germs, girl germs/Can't hide out—they're everywhere."

Bratmobile first revved up in the early '90s with stray singles and compilation tracks, including "Girl Germs" (on the 1991 Kill Rock Stars compilation), "Cool Schmool" (a 1991 split single with Sleater-Kinney bassist Corin Tucker's original band, Heavens to Betsy), and the great 1992 7-inch "Kiss and Ride"/"Queenie." Its long-awaited debut, Pottymouth, appeared in 1993, remaking some of these songs and adding others, including "Panik," "Bitch Theme," and a gender-pretzeled cover of Joan Jett's "Cherry Bomb." The Real Janelle is their most dynamic, fullest-sounding album, with the sad ballad "And I Live in a Town Where the Boys Amputate Their Hearts."

Bratmobile broke up for a while, with Neuman joining the Frumpies and the Peechees while Wolfe and Smith formed Cold Cold Hearts. Though these bands were decent, it was happy news when the festive ladies reunited for Ladies, Women, and Girls and Girls Get Busy. The Brat spirit was fully intact in rave-ups like "I'm in the Band," "Gimmie Brains," and "Cheap Trick Record." The band's live shows were better than ever, too—proof positive that the punk rockers who can tackle adulthood tend to be the ones who learn to dance.   —R.S.

Toni Braxton

> ★★★   Toni Braxton (LaFace, 1993)
> ★★★★   Secrets (LaFace, 1996)
> ★★   The Heat (LaFace, 2000)
> ★★   Snowflakes (Arista, 2001)
> ★★★½   More Than a Woman (Arista, 2002)
> ★★★★   Ultimate Toni Braxton (Arista, 2003)

Kenny "Babyface" Edmonds likes to make women suffer. That's what pop songwriters do, for the most part, and Edmonds has employed some of the most talented women in the field to consciously explore the full continuum of romantic pain. But Toni Braxton was the sort of multiplatinum masochist a songsmith stumbles across once in a career. Her taut huskiness was palpably physical, as if her sadness was literally constricting her throat: She sings "I shall never breathe again" as if in need of mouth-to-mouth. As for the remainder of the material, one title said it all: "Another Sad Love Song."

If her debut hinted that Braxton's romantic despair was a narrow patch of turf to mow, best sampled a single at a time, Secrets allowed Braxton to move through a wider range of emotions than anyone had reason to previously suspect. Though both songs are thematically similar, the aural striptease of "You're Makin' Me High" couldn't be farther from the girlish flirtatiousness of "I Love Me Some Him." And "Un-Break My Heart" is Braxton at her most monolithically abject—maintaining a pained, almost heroic dignity as she prostrates herself before her tormentor.

Success was not kind to Braxton's musical persona—stars don't need to play the victim, after all. And The Heat allows Braxton to breathe heavily over the gently strummed Spanish guitars beloved by Babyface as well as most directors of soft-core porn. The catty "He Wasn't Man Enough" steams things up. The rest is just hot air. By contrast, Snowflakes, a quickie Christmas moneymaker, is as chilly as its title, with Braxton's refined stylings toppling over into sanctimony.

But Braxton was at her toughest on More Than a Woman—in fact, no other woman in R&B was coming up with kiss-offs like "Hit the Freeway" and "Let Me Show You the Way (Out)." Ultimate renders most of her studio albums redundant, and the steady increase in sass as her career progresses is fun to track. —K.H.

The Breeders

★★★★	Pod (4AD/Elektra, 1990)	
★★★	Safari EP (4AD/Elektra, 1992)	
★★★★½	Last Splash (4AD/Elektra, 1993)	
★★	Title TK (4AD/Elektra, 2002)	

The Breeders started as a Boston supergroup, featuring the Pixies' bassist Kim Deal (writing most of the songs and playing guitar) along with guitarist Tanya Donelly from Throwing Muses, violinist Carrie Bradley of local heroes Ed's Redeeming Qualities, and a couple of out-of-towners: Slint's drummer Britt Walford (who called himself "Shannon Doughton" and later, ahem, "Mike Hunt") and British bassist Josephine Wiggs (from the Perfect Disaster). Originally planned as a one-off project, *Pod* was striking enough to spawn a career. It's hazy and creepily erotic, showcasing Deal's thin purr and bizarre, skeletal songs—you're never sure if they're going to make it to the next phrase—as well as a sinuous cover of the Beatles' "Happiness Is a Warm Gun." Aside from the racing "Hellbound," it's as elliptical as rock gets, and it was just what college radio had been waiting for.

With *Safari*, Kim Deal added her identical twin sister Kelley on lead guitar (never mind that Kelley, legendarily, could barely play) and vocals. More or less a concept EP about Kim's breakup with her husband, it featured more-fleshed-out original songs and a spunky take on the Who's "So Sad About Us."

Donelly and Walford left, and new drummer Jim MacPherson arrived, before the Breeders hit it out of the park with the summery alternative-rock landmark *Last Splash*. With its scraping, rhythmic hooks and headlong three-chord chorus, "Cannonball" was an MTV hit, and the rest of the album developed Kim's loopy melodies and oblique words into an unpredictable guitar-rock tornado. "Divine Hammer" is a chiming tribute to her favorite part of men's bodies; "Drivin' on 9" resurrects an old Ed's Redeeming Qualities favorite as tender country. Kelley even sings lead on a spiteful little rocker, "I Just Wanna Get Along." The band had never sounded more assured or more ebullient.

And then there was silence. The Breeders of *Last Splash* toured the world, but only managed to eke out one more single; Kelley was busted for heroin; Kim and some Ohio pals, as the Amps, made a ramshackle album, *Pacer* (forgettable aside from its title track, another of Deal's perfect garage-rock readymades). Finally, after nine years, the Deals and new hired hands delivered the mostly dreadful *Title TK*—journalistic

slang for "we'll fill it in later." It's an attempt to return to the protean, stripped-down aesthetic of *Pod*, but the songs (one recycled from *Pacer*) just seem unfinished and aimless, and the stark arrangements and recording do them no favors. —D.W.

Bright Eyes

★★	A Collection of Songs Written and Recorded 1995–1997 (Saddle Creek, 1997)	
★★★½	Letting Off the Happiness (Saddle Creek, 1998)	
★★★½	Every Day and Every Night (EP) (Saddle Creek, 2000)	
★★★½	Fever and Mirrors (Saddle Creek, 2000)	
★★★	Oh Holy Fools [split with Son, Ambulance] (Saddle Creek, 2001)	
★★★★½	There Is No Beginning to the Story (EP) (Saddle Creek, 2002)	
★★★★½	Lifted or the Story Is in the Soil, Keep Your Ear to the Ground (Saddle Creek, 2002)	
★★	A Christmas Album (Saddle Creek, 2002)	

Desaparecidos

★★★½	Read Music/Speak Spanish (Saddle Creek, 2002)	

There are exceptions—the compilation of his teenage experiments, a split EP with an obnoxious-voiced friend, and an ill-advised Christmas disc that at least benefits a charity—but the remarkable consistency of Bright Eyes' output cannot be denied. In fact, it suggests a myth the collective-fronting singer/songwriter himself, Conor Oberst, would probably jump at having granted: that his voice, once discovered, channeled a perpetually precocious talent. Young—he turned 22 the year *Lifted or the Story Is in the Soil, Keep Your Ear to the Ground* ended up on many critics' year-end lists—hair-in-those-bright-eyes sexy, and as romantically, existentially sad as he is romantically, existentially opposed to straight-laced society and its discontents, Oberst piles on the drama and then self-consciously peels it back, enthralled with what makes things sad and beautiful at the same time.

Oberst's older brother Justin started Saddle Creek records in 1993 to put out tapes Conor recorded. Less than 10 years later, the label headed up an acclaimed Omaha, NE, scene including Conor's buddies in Cursive and the Faint. *Letting Off the Happiness* was the label's breakthrough, even if the rest of the country didn't know it yet. Always in confessional mode, Oberst strums an acoustic guitar along with his own sweetly warbling voice only some of the time, as on the seemingly caffeine-fueled "June on the West Coast." Often he's joined by friends on drums, bass, pedal steel guitar, keyboards, organ, samplers, and finger cymbals. Recorded in houses around town—haphazardly, judging by the liner notes—the disc sounds loose but not shambolic, casually buoying Oberst's notebook poetry and cathartic melodies, which he whispers or shouts in jagged chunks.

The tender *Every Day and Every Night* EP turns the normal travails of teenhood—boredom, love lost—into meditations on the joys and disappointments of making art. On paper, this sounds like a snoozefest, but Oberst races through the philosophy books he's probably only partly read to get at the stinging, soaring questions that remain after the last page has been turned. *Fever and Mirrors*—the title refers to Oberst's search for rapture in sickness and obsessive self-reflexivity—opens with a young boy haltingly reading aloud a book he clearly doesn't understand. The album's pretty, almost poppy second-to-last track, "An Attempt to Tip the Scales," ends with a too-long, tacked-on radio interview in which Oberst describes his deep depression in excruciating detail. It is only here, in mocking his self-indulgence, that Oberst slips—who wants to hear about it, except in a tune?

As a sojourn from defining art, love, and life itself, Oberst turned his focus to late capitalism and economic injustice with Desaparecidos. His crimped holler perfectly suits the raucous, new wave–inflected indie rock, but it was on the next Bright Eyes full-length, *Lifted or the Story Is in the Soil, Keep Your Ear to the Ground,* that Oberst (and a small army of musicians playing accordion, mandolin, cello, etc.) finally quit squinting in the spotlight he'd been occupying all along. Take "You Will. You? Will. You? Will. You? Will." Oberst, his voice and guitar echoing in what sounds like a large room—a change from earlier recordings, where the only air seems to come from his breath—confirms a lover's accusations: "You say that I treat you like a book on a shelf/I don't take you out that often 'cause I know that I've completed you/and that's why you are here/that's the reason you stay here/how awful that must feel." The song's climax, a woozy hoedown in which Oberst drags the title's ambivalent thicket of grammar up and down the musical scale, encapsulates and animates as never before this young dude's struggle to step outside of himself without simply tumbling into someone else's embrace or ideas. And while he's as prone to drama as ever, Oberst asserts that people aren't just characters in books—or songs. —N.C.

Garth Brooks

★★★   Garth Brooks (Capitol, 1989)
★★★★   No Fences (Capitol, 1990)
★★★★   Ropin' the Wind (Capitol, 1991)
★★★½   The Chase (Capitol, 1992)
★   Beyond the Season (Capitol, 1992)
★★★½   In Pieces (Capitol, 1993)
★★★★½ The Hits (Capitol, 1994)
★★   Fresh Horses (Capitol, 1995)
★★   Sevens (Capitol, 1997)
★★   Double Live (Capitol, 1998)
★   Garth Brooks & the Magic of Christmas (Capitol, 1999)
★   Garth Brooks in . . . the Life of Chris Gaines (Capitol, 1999)
★★★   Scarecrow (Capitol, 2001)

If ever there was a more over-the-top country-music entertainer than Garth Brooks, then he or she has not yet been discovered. His performances combine arena-rock spectacle with aw-shucks sentimentality, and his record sales are astronomical. Brooks personifies the kind of slick country music that took Nashville from its Southern working-class roots smack into the politically moderate values of Clinton-era middle-class America. The singer's mix of country with '70s-style singer/songwriter music, album-oriented rock, and middle-of-the-road pop came just as the Baby Boom generation was looking beyond contemporary pop and classic rock for a new sound to grow old with. But Brooks' music also resonates with younger heartland fans who fall outside the postpunk and urban demographics. The singer's impact on popular music cannot be overestimated; his influence runs that deep.

Brooks' first album is a collection of music typical of the New Traditionalist sound of '80s country. The album did well—yielding four hits, including two chart-toppers—but its overall sound is unremarkable. It was on *No Fences* that Brooks began genre-hopping his way to superstardom. The album has all the ingredients that would come to define him—sensitive ballads, power ballads, honky-tonk barnburners, and pretty pop. Opening with "The Thunder Rolls," a dead ringer for the heartland arena sound of Bob Seger, the album builds up to Brooks' smash hit "Friends in Low Places"—pure honky-tonk with a seductive pop hook. He fleshes out *No Fences* with heart-tugging singer/songwriter fare ("Victim of the Game") and Tin Pan Alley–style Western swing ("Mr. Blue"). *No Fences* wound up selling more than 10 million copies, and forever changed the way country music was made.

Ropin' the Wind was even bigger and better. Kicking off with a gutbucket Southern rocker ("Against the Grain") that outdoes Charlie Daniels at his own game, Brooks brings an edge to the music that he'd not previously shown, combining all the elements that made *No Fences* such a gargantuan hit to even greater effect.

Ropin' the Wind has your sentimental love ballads ("What She's Doing Now") and your cheatin' songs ("Papa Loved Mama"), but it also includes a Billy Joel cover ("Shameless") that confirms what was becoming increasingly clear: Garth Brooks is the Billy Joel of the South—a pop star for weekend warriors. It may be slick, and it may be little more than ear candy, but there's nary a bad cut on this record.

Garth got ambitious on *The Chase,* and his sales suffered. Still, the gospel choir on "We Shall Be Free," covers of songs by Little Feat ("Dixie Chicken") and Patsy Cline ("Walking After Midnight"), and Brooks' more confessional writing make for an album of greater depth than anyone imagined. After *The Chase*'s disappointing sales, country's pudgy poster boy returned to straight crackle 'n' pop country on *In Pieces,* another solid collection of puffed-up anthems, emotional overkill, and cinematic C&W for the upwardly mobile.

By the middle '90s, Brooks' formula was getting stale. How many times can a cowboy beat his dead horse before the beast starts stinking? On *Fresh Horses,* Brooks turns in a bad Aerosmith cover one moment, a bad Dylan cover the next, and fills the spaces with tired honky-tonk and increasingly tedious pop schlock. To quote his own damn self, he's "so New York and then L.A. and every town along the way." *Sevens* is worse. Here, Brooks becomes a bona fide parody of himself (which is to say he's become a parody of a parody). On *In the Life of Chris Gaines,* he attempts to remedy the problem by adopting an alt-rock alter ego. The album comes with a fictional biography describing Garth-as-Gaines as a legendary Aussie rocker—complete with facial hair and a wig—but the music was neither legendary nor rock. Gaines was the most monumentally disastrous marketing idea that mainstream pop had seen in years, and the album tanked. Brooks never recovered from the embarrassment of the Gaines fiasco, and *Scarecrow* found him returning to the country, rock, and pop blend that only Garth Brooks can pull off.

The Hits is a fine set of Brooks' best songs. *Beyond the Season* and *Magic of Christmas* are his huge-selling holiday collections that, depending on your tolerance for schmaltzy Christmas songs, are dispensable. *Double Live* is one of those "you had to be there" performance sets wherein the singer brings absolutely nothing new to the original versions of his songs. —M.K.

Big Bill Broonzy

★★★★ Feelin' Low Down (GNP Crescendo, 1973)
★★★★ Big Bill Broonzy and Washboard Sam (1986; Chess/MCA, 1991)
★★★★ Big Bill Broonzy Sings Folk Songs (Smithsonian Folkways, 1989)
★★★★½ Good Time Tonight (Columbia, 1990)
★★★★★ The Young Big Bill Broonzy 1928–1935 (Yazoo, 1991)
★★★★★ Do That Guitar Rag 1928–1935 (Yazoo, 1991)
★★★★½ The 1955 London Sessions (Collectables, 1994)
★★★½ Baby, Please Don't Go (Drive Archive, 1994)
★★★★ The Complete Bluebird (1934–1935) (RCA Bluebird, 1995)
★★★★ Black, Brown & White (Drive Archive, 1995)
★★★½ Treat Me Right (Tradition, 1996)
★★★½ Warm, Witty & Wise (Columbia/Legacy, 1998)
★★★ Absolutely the Best (Varèse Sarabande, 2000)
★★★★ Trouble in Mind (Smithsonian/Folkways, 2000)

An important transitional link between acoustic country blues and electrified urban blues, Big Bill Broonzy, born in Mississippi and raised in Arkansas, helped shape the force that became Chicago blues after moving to the Windy City in 1920 upon completing a tour of duty in the army. A fiddle player at that time, he switched to guitar and began playing the instrument as if born to it, and was often seen in the company of local stars such as Blind Lemon Jefferson and Sleepy John Estes. Even among this crowd, his style was distinctive: basic, fundamental guitar accompaniment highlighted by stark, single-string solos and forceful chording and a smooth but plaintive cry of a singing voice (which moved easily from a world-weary moan to a mellow, sanguine tone) suited to deliver self-penned songs focused on the travails of big city life, social inequities, and hard times with women. More than any guitarist of his time, he made effective use of silence as a dramatic component of his music, sometimes employing only a few strong, angular retorts to punctuate key lyric sections, but at the same time he was an unqualified master of many styles, from ragtime and blues fingerpicking to a flatpicking style that echoed with country influences. And he was prolific: At his death in 1958, over 300 songs had been copyrighted with his name as composer.

Broonzy's early years are well documented on the Yazoo, Columbia, and Legacy collections. The Yazoo discs focus primarily on solo acoustic or duet recordings from 1928 to 1935, whereas Columbia's *Good Time Tonight* and *Warm, Witty & Wise* single-disc sets offer both solo acoustic and combo recordings spanning the years 1930 to 1940. A notably delicious treat recommending *Do That Guitar Rag* is the inclusion of four bawdy numbers featuring scintillating musical dialogues between Broonzy on guitar and Georgia Tom Dorsey on piano (obviously before he saw the light and began writing the songs that defined modern gospel music), supporting Jane Lucas' sassy vocalizing.

An engaging live performance is captured on Evidence's *Black, Brown & White*, with seven tracks recorded in concert in Antwerp, Belgium, in 1952, and six others recorded in 1955 at a friend's house in Brussels. Playing acoustic, or with pianist Blind John Davis, Broonzy samples virtually every type of song in his repertoire. Topical songs are represented by the brutal title track ("If you's white/you's all right/ if you's brown/stick around/but if you's black/oh, brother, get back, get back, get back"), with its light, lilting rhythm quite at odds with the lyric's frontal assaults on racism ("I helped build the country/and I fought for it too/Now I bet you can see/what a black man have to do").

That Broonzy never left his social conscience behind is indicated on the opening track of Collectables' first-rate *The 1955 London Sessions*, "When Do I Get to Be Called a Man," an explicit litany of the sacrifices a man had made for his country and what his country had withheld in return—dignity, for one; respect, for another. Apart from the solo acoustic sides, Broonzy is teamed here with a septet on some bluesy, boozy performances with a decidedly New Orleans feel about them, notably "Southbound Train," with trumpeter Leslie Hutchinson blowing piercing, muted fills. Drive Archive's *Baby, Please Don't Go* suffers only from a lack of adequate liner information, but what's there indicates these 10 tracks were recorded between 1952 and 1955. The key track: the dramatic interpretation of "Backwater Blues (I Got Up One Mornin' Blues)"—not only one of the most haunting tracks Broonzy ever recorded, but ranks with Bessie Smith's version in terms of the profound sense of loss the singer communicates. Similarly, but with far better annotation, the Smithsonian Folkways entry, *Big Bill Broonzy Sings Folk Songs*, collects some recordings Broonzy made for the label near the end of his life as well as several live tracks, some featuring Pete Seeger on harmony vocals and banjo, all of which underscore the remarkable breadth and depth of Broonzy's repertoire. From the same label comes a second excellent over-view, *Trouble in Mind*, containing 24 tracks (including several alternate takes) from the artist's 1956–57 sessions. Seeger is here too, pitching in on banjo and vocals on a stirring live version of "This Train (Bound for Glory)," but Broonzy's solo with acoustic guitar carries the day.

GNP Crescendo's *Feelin' Low Down* is a set of acoustic sides, raw and potent, but lacking any dates or session information. Apart from that oversight, its 14 cuts feature vintage Broonzy in many moods on songs ranging from his own moving originals (including "Big Bill Blues" and "Lonesome Road Blues") to stirring covers, such as the heavyweight treatment he gives the traditional folk number "John Henry." Before he died of throat cancer in 1958, Broonzy had helped ignite a folk and blues revival in this country that brought attention to many of his contemporaries who might otherwise have died in obscurity. Today he is far less known among the general public than, say, Robert Johnson, but his most penetrating and personal songs remind us of the important issues of his time that remain relevant to our own. —D.M.

Charles Brown

★★★½   Boss of the Blues (1964; Mainstream/Legacy, 1993)
★★★★   One More for the Road (1986; Alligator, 1989)
★★★★   All My Life (Bullseye Blues/Rounder, 1990)
★★★★★   Driftin' Blues: The Best of Charles Brown (1992; Collectables, 1995)
★★★★   Someone to Love (Bullseye Blues/Rounder, 1992)
★★★★   Blues and Other Love Songs (1992; 32 Jazz, 2000)
★★★★   Just a Lucky So and So (Bullseye Blues/Rounder, 1994)
★★★★   Blues n' Brown (Jewel, 1995)
★★★½   Cool Christmas Blues (Rounder, 1994)
★★★½   These Blues (Verve, 1995)
★★★½   Honey Dripper (Verve, 1996)
★★★½   So Goes Love (Verve, 1998)
★★★   In a Grand Style (Bullseye Blues, 1999)
★★★½   A Life in the Blues (Rounder, 2004)
★★★★   Alone at the Piano (Savoy Jazz, 2004)

Late night, lights down low, bottle of wine at hand, someone to dream with, and Charles Brown, blues elegance personified—now there's a scenario suitable for any true romantic. Blues and R&B have had any number of outstanding boudoir balladeers, but Charles Brown, who died on January 21, 1999, always brought a special warmth and engaging personality to his efforts, and thus carved out for himself an exalted place among his peers and, for a few years in the late '40s and early '50s, the general public as well.

Born in Texas City, TX, Brown's burgeoning interest in music led him to Los Angeles after he graduated from Prairie View College. He formed an association with Ed Williams and Johnny Moore in a group they called the Three Blazers. Of their three wonderful voices, none stood out more than Brown's in its laconic grace and soothing timbre (comparable to Nat "King" Cole's "smoky gray" quality), attributes made more effective by the singer's unerring sense of pro-

priety with regard to a lyrical phrase—gingerly knead-
ing key words, or stretching them over a few beats, to
draw out an underlying feeling—and frugal use of ornamentation (deep bass dips, or a conversational or
recitative style) for greatest emotional impact. The
Three Blazers hit it big out of the box in 1945 with
"Driftin' Blues," a song Brown had written in high
school, which remained on the R&B chart for nearly
six months, until Brown went solo. On his own, he
wrote and recorded numerous upper-level R&B chart
singles—nine in 1949 alone—including two #1s in
1949's "Trouble Blues" and 1951's "Black Night." All
the while this was happening, a Christmas song he
wrote and recorded with the Three Blazers in 1947,
the melancholy "Merry Christmas, Baby," was becoming a seasonal classic, charting every year in the
first three years after its release. While "Driftin' Blues"
is regarded as his signature song, "Merry Christmas,
Baby" has lived on in numerous cover versions, by far
the most powerful being Elvis Presley's tour de force
of blues vocalizing on his *Elvis Sings the Wonderful
World of Christmas* LP. Collectables' *Driftin' Blues:
The Best of Charles Brown* is the must-have CD charting these fruitful years.

Brown's chart run ended in 1952, and he became
so low-profile he seemed to have dropped off the Earth
for a couple of decades. Brown in fact stayed
on the road, and every so often found a small label
here or there that was happy to have him for a moment. *Blues n' Brown*, released in 1995, is a ten-song
collection of low-down blues—most of them cowritten by Brown—recorded at the Modern/Kent studios
in Los Angeles in 1971, with producer Maxwell Davis.

Praise be to Bullseye Blues, which performed a
great service in giving Jimmy McCracklin and Charles
Brown a home, to the benefit of both artists. Brown's
first Bullseye effort, *All My Life*, is another smooth, assured outing showing off the artist's interpretive powers. Throughout these sessions his vocals reflect a
stronger sense of love as an impermanent state in
being more resonant, more nuanced, more ambivalent
than on any of his other recordings.

Possibly as a response to the harder edge of *All My
Life, Someone to Love* is soft, mellow, back-to-the-
boudoir fare, beginning with the Brown–Bonnie Raitt
duet on the title track, which finds the two singers engaged in the vocal equivalent of long, meaningful
looks into each other's eyes, and discreet, under-the-
table hand-holding. The same year he recorded *Someone to Love*, Brown slipped into a San Francisco
studio for three days and came back with *Blues and
Other Love Songs* (originally released on Muse in
1992, it has been reissued by 32 Jazz), produced by
the formidable tenor saxophonist Houston Person,

who lent his distinctive touch to five of the songs, including a barn-burning workout on his version of
"One Mint Julep."

Brown's 1994 Bullseye release, *Just a Lucky So and
So*, is a more ornate affair in that Brown is backed not
only by a small combo, but also by the Crescent City
Horns (the album was recorded in New Orleans) and
the New Orleans Strings. The pleasing result is a combination of the best of the Mainstream style with
the small-combo midnight blues of *Someone to Love*.

In the late '90s Brown and his regular working
combo—a tight, tasty quartet that included Clifford
Solomon on tenor sax, Danny Caron on guitar (and
providing some savvy business guidance to Brown's
career), Ruth Davies on bass, and Gaylord Birch (who
passed away after the sessions for the 1996 release,
Honey Dripper) on drums—cut three fine albums for
Verve that turned out to be Brown's final, stirring testimony on disc. Although his voice was now a matured,
slightly weathered instrument, his phrasing and
preternatural cool remained things of wonder, his
piano playing retained its characteristic ebullience
and sensitivity, and the band played tight, economical
support behind him. Some of the most memorable moments in this album trifecta come when Brown goes
minimalist, as on the solo piano and vocal on a moody
version of Duke Ellington's "I Got It Bad (and That
Ain't Good)" and a grand, stately reimagining of
"Amazing Grace," both from *These Blues;* or the angular, New Orleans–style solo piano ruminations underpinning his solo performance of Thomas A. Dorsey's
gospel monument "Precious Lord" on *Honey Dripper*
(which also features, in addition to the Joe Liggins title
tune, two new Brown songs: the slow-grinding blues of
"News All Over Town" and a lively jump blues quite at
odds with the subject matter, "I Cried Last Night," enlivened by robust tenor sax solos courtesy of Clifford
Solomon and some fleet-fingered runs by guitarist
Danny Caron); or, on *So Goes Love*, a gospel-
influenced rendition of "Stormy Monday," with
Brown's smooth crooning supported only by his steady
rolling piano lines and Solomon's restrained tenor sax
punctuations, and an album-closing solo piano-vocal
downcast blues ballad, "Blue Because of You." Those
were the last notes of Brown's career on record, and
when all was said and done he had produced a body of
work over the course of 53 years that was remarkable
for its consistency and its soulful expressiveness. Gone
he may be, but Charles Brown's music lives on, timeless and majestic to the highest degree.   —D.M.

James Brown

★★★   Please Please Please (King, 1959)
★★½   Try Me (King, 1959)

★★★★ Think (King, 1960)
★★½ The Amazing James Brown (King, 1961)
★★★★ James Brown Presents His Band (King, 1961)
★★★½ Excitement Mr. Dynamite (King, 1962)
★★½ James Brown and His Famous Flames Tour the U.S.A. (King, 1962)
★★★★★ Live at the Apollo (1963; Polydor, 2004)
★★★ Prisoner of Love (King, 1963)
★★★★ Pure Dynamite! (King, 1964)
★★½ Showtime (Smash, 1964)
★★½ Grits and Soul (Smash, 1964)
★★★★ Papa's Got a Brand New Bag (King, 1965)
★★½ James Brown Plays James Brown Today and Yesterday (Smash, 1966)
★★★★ I Got You (I Feel Good) (King, 1966)
★★★ Mighty Instrumentals (King, 1966)
★★★ James Brown Plays New Breed (The Boo-Ga-Loo) (Smash, 1966)
★★★½ It's a Man's, Man's, Man's World (King, 1966)
★★ Christmas Songs (King, 1966)
★★★ Handful of Soul (Smash, 1966)
★★ The James Brown Show (Smash, 1967)
★★★★ James Brown Sings Raw Soul (King, 1967)
★★★ James Brown Plays the Real Thing (Smash, 1967)
★★★ Live at the Garden (King, 1967)
★★★★ Cold Sweat (King, 1967)
★★½ James Brown Presents His Show of Tomorrow (King, 1968)
★★★ I Can't Stand Myself (When You Touch Me) (King, 1968)
★★★ I Got the Feelin' (King, 1968)
★★★ James Brown Plays Nothing but Soul (King, 1968)
★★★★★ Live at the Apollo, Vol. II (1968; Universal, 2001)
★★★½ Thinking About Little Willie John/A Few Nice Things (King, 1968)
★★ A Soulful Christmas (King, 1968)
★★★★ Say It Loud, I'm Black and I'm Proud (King, 1969)
★★ Gettin' Down to It (King, 1969)
★★★ The Popcorn (King, 1969)
★★★ It's a Mother (King, 1969)
★★½ Ain't It Funky (King, 1970)
★★½ Soul on Top (King, 1970)
★★★★½ It's a New Day—Let a Man Come In (King, 1970)
★★★★½ Sex Machine (King, 1970)
★★½ Hey, America (King, 1970)
★★★ Super Bad (King, 1971)
★★ Sho Is Funky Down Here (King, 1971)
★★★½ Hot Pants (Polydor, 1971)

★★★½ Revolution of the Mind (Live at the Apollo, Vol. III) (Polydor, 1971)
★★★★½ There It Is (Polydor, 1972)
★★★½ Get On the Good Foot (Polydor, 1972)
★★ Black Caesar (Polydor, 1973)
★★ Slaughter's Big Rip-Off (Polydor, 1973)
★★★ The Payback (Polydor, 1974)
★★★★ Hell (Polydor, 1974)
★★½ Reality (Polydor, 1975)
★★ Sex Machine Today (Polydor, 1975)
★★ Everybody's Doin' the Hustle & Dead on the Double Bump (Polydor, 1975)
★★★ Hot (Polydor, 1976)
★★★ Get Up Offa That Thing (Polydor, 1976)
★★ Bodyheat (Polydor, 1976)
★★½ Mutha's Nature (Polydor, 1977)
★★★★★ Solid Gold (Polydor UK, 1977)
★★½ Jam 1980's (Polydor, 1978)
★★★ Take a Look at Those Cakes (Polydor, 1979)
★★★ The Original Disco Man (Polydor, 1979)
★★★ People (Polydor, 1980)
★★★ Hot on the One (Polydor, 1980)
★★★★ Soul Syndrome (1980; Rhino, 1991)
★★★ Nonstop! (Polydor, 1981)
★★½ The Greatest Hits Live in Concert (1981; Sugar Hill, 1991)
★★★½ Bring It On! (Churchill/Augusta, 1983)
★★★★½ The Federal Years, Part One (Solid Smoke, 1984)
★★★★ The Federal Years, Part Two (Solid Smoke, 1984)
★★★★½ Ain't That a Groove (Polydor, 1984)
★★★★★ Doing It to Death (Polydor, 1984)
★★★½ Gravity (Scotti Bros., 1986)
★★★ The CD of JB (Sex Machine and Other Soul Classics) (Polydor, 1985)
★★★★½ James Brown's Funky People (Polydor, 1986)
★★★★★ In the Jungle Groove (Polydor, 1986)
★★★★ The CD of JB II (Cold Sweat and Other Soul Classics) (Polydor, 1987)
★★★½ I'm Real (Scotti Bros., 1988)
★★★★ James Brown's Funky People (Part 2) (Polydor, 1988)
★★★★ Motherlode (Polydor, 1988)
★★★★½ Roots of a Revolution (Polydor, 1989)
★★★★ Messing With the Blues (Polydor, 1990)
★★★★★ Star Time (Polydor, 1991)
★★★★ Love Over-Due (Scotti Bros., 1991)
★★★★★ 20 All-Time Greatest Hits! (Polydor, 1991)
★★★½ The Greatest Hits of the Fourth Decade (Scotti Bros., 1992)
★★ Universal James (Scotti Brothers, 1992)
★★★★ Soul Pride: The Instrumentals, 1960–1969 (Polydor, 1993)

★★★ James Brown's Funky Christmas (Polydor, 1995)

★★ Live at the Apollo, 1995 (Scotti Brothers, 1995)

★★★½ 70s Funk Classics (Universal, 1995)

★★★ Get on the Good Foot (Polydor, 1995)

★★★★★ JB40: 40th Anniversary Collection (Polydor, 1996)

★★★★ Foundations of Funk: A Brand New Bag, 1964–1969 (Polydor Chronicles, 1996)

★★★★★ Funk Power, 1970: A Brand New Thang (Polydor Chronicles, 1996)

★★★★ Make It Funky: The Big Payback, 1971–1975 (Polydor Chronicles, 1996)

★★★★ Dead on the Heavy Funk: 1975–1983 (Polydor, 1998)

★★★★ Say It Live and Loud: Dallas, 1968 (Polydor, 1998)

★★ I'm Back (Private I, 1998)

★★½ James Brown's Original Funky Divas (Polydor, 1998)

★★★ Living in America (Scotti Brothers, 1999)

★★★½ The Millennium Collection (Polydor, 1999)

★★★ Godfather of Soul (Polydor, 2000)

★★★★ Ballads (Polydor, 2000)

★★★★ Live at the Apollo, Vol. II, Deluxe Edition (Polydor, 2001)

★★★½ The Millennium Collection: Vol. 2 (Polydor, 2002)

★★½ The Next Step (Fome, 2002)

James Brown may never have captured the zeitgeist as Elvis Presley or the Beatles did, nor can he be said to have dominated the charts like Stevie Wonder or the Rolling Stones, but by any real measure of musical greatness—endurance, originality, versatility, breadth of influence—he rivals or even betters them all. Brown has been astonishingly productive over the first four decades of his recording career, churning out more than 100 albums (give or take a few anthologies) as a singer, bandleader, or instrumentalist; many are great, and nearly all are worth hearing. And even though none of the 44 singles he put into the Billboard Top 40 ever made it to #1—indeed, only two cracked the Top 5—in retrospect, that reflects worse on the pop audience than it does on his music.

Indeed, Brown has long boasted that his best ideas were years ahead of their time, and history has borne him out. Hip-hop borrowed freely from his catalogue, as rappers such as Rob Base, Kool Moe Dee, and Eric B. & Rakim all powered singles with beats Brown produced as much as 20 years earlier. Nor were they the only ones, for by the early '90s the churning fatback pattern immortalized in Brown's "Funky

Drummer" (1969) was a staple among club-savvy alternative rock acts. Even Michael Jackson's celebrated moonwalk was little more than an update of a Brown move called the camel walk.

Dealing with a body of work so wide-ranging and important is not easy, particularly for those starting from scratch. Certainly, there are greatest-hits albums available, of which 20 All-Time Greatest Hits is the best buy (JB40: James Brown's 40th Anniversary Collection is more expensive, but makes for a nicely compact history). Those interested in specific eras of his career may prefer the close focus of such sets as Funk Power, 1970: A Brand New Thang or Dead on the Heavy Funk: 1975–1983. But the single best introduction to Brown's work is Star Time, a wonderfully annotated, admirably representative four-disc box set that follows Brown's career from "Please Please Please," his 1956 debut, to "Unity," a 1984 collaboration with hip-hop godfather Afrika Bambaataa. In addition to including all the intervening hits, it restores some singles to their full-length versions, offers a fair amount of non-LP material, and includes several illuminating rarities, among them the previously unreleased original version of "Papa's Got a Brand New Bag." Five stars are barely enough.

As for the rest of his work, well, let's just start at the beginning. Roots of a Revolution, focusing on the 1956–62 period, with two songs each from 1963 and 1964, gives a strong sense of Brown's early evolution, but because the set purposely excludes Brown's best-known titles from that period, it should be seen as a "second step" album for fledgling fans.

Then there are the original albums. Of these, Think is by far the best, in part because it has the highest hit quotient ("Think," "I'll Go Crazy," "Good Good Lovin'") but mostly because it offers Brown's most distinctive work to that point, particularly in its chugging title tune. Please Please Please, despite including Brown's first single (the raw, gospel-inflected title track) and his first R&B chart-topper (the more traditional R&B tune "Try Me"), is mostly given over to derivative material such as "Chonnie-on-Chon" and "Let's Make It." Try Me—which was reissued in 1964 as The Unbeatable James Brown—repeats "Try Me" but otherwise leans more toward the blues, thanks to such songs as "I Want You So Bad" and "Messing with the Blues," while The Amazing James Brown shows off the increasing proficiency of his band through gritty titles such as "Dancin' Little Thing" and "Come Over Here."

With Presents His Band, Brown moves into the instrumental realm and delivers his epochal remake of Jimmy Forrest's "Night Train" (a huge hit in the U.K.), but Excitement Mr. Dynamite—which has also been available as *Shout and Shimmy*—returns Brown and company to the hard-hitting vocal approach of *Think*, even to the point of repeating "Good Good Lovin'."

At that point in his career, Brown was still better-known for his live show than for his recordings, a fact that explains the somewhat misleading title to the studio album *James Brown and His Famous Flames Tour the U.S.A.* Incredibly, King Records president Syd Nathan felt there was no market for a real James Brown live album, so the singer went ahead and recorded *Live at the Apollo* at his own expense; it turned out to be the album that finally put him on the map—and no wonder. It doesn't just present the hits, but also shows off the incredible precision of Brown's band as well as the uncanny bond he had with his audience. *Pure Dynamite!*, an even more energetic set recorded before a raucously appreciative crowd at Baltimore's Royal Theatre, followed a year later, and Brown would release eight more live albums after that, including three more recorded at the Apollo: *Live at the Apollo, Vol. II*, with its itchy, intense rendition of "There Was a Time"; and *Revolution of the Mind: Live at the Apollo, Vol. III.* (*Live at the Apollo 1995* is by that point a needless exercise in nostalgia for both star and venue.) Because Brown toured with an entire revue, *The James Brown Show* puts its emphasis on the other players in the show, including his band; likewise, *James Brown Presents His Show of Tomorrow* features only two tracks by Brown, with the rest given over to members of the revue. Brown also put out a couple of "faked" live albums—studio recordings with audience noise dubbed in later. Perhaps the most notorious of these was *Showtime* (fortunately, its best tunes appear without embellishment on *Messing with the Blues*), but *Super Bad* repeats the ruse, as does the first half of the double-album *Sex Machine*, although the loping, hypnotic groove generated by his band on "Give It Up or Turnit a Loose" makes such fakery almost forgivable.

Brown later admitted that his model for *Live at the Apollo* was Ray Charles' concert album *In Person*. That wasn't his only nod to Brother Ray; *Prisoner of Love*, with its string sweetening and choral cushioning, is self-consciously in the vein of Charles' ABC recordings—although Brown remains far too raw a singer to seem much at home in these MOR arrangements. No matter; the direction Brown takes with *Papa's Got a Brand New Bag* would soon leave Charles in the dust, at least from an R&B perspective. This, in effect, is the birth of funk, as Brown's songs grow lean and repetitious, with fewer and fewer chord changes and a greater emphasis on rhythmic tension. Granted, nothing else on the album

takes that idea quite as far as its two-part title tune, but that was more than enough. The revolution truly had begun.

Brown suggests in his autobiography that the revolution had actually begun with *Out of Sight*, an album he recorded for Smash shortly before *Brand New Bag*, but a legal battle among Brown, King Records, and Smash resulted in a court order withdrawing the album shortly after its release (the single "Out of Sight" can be found on *Star Time*). Part of the loss when *Out of Sight* was put out of the picture was a track entitled "I Got You (I Feel Good)," but Brown, typically, turned the situation to his advantage and recut the song with a harder groove; both versions of the song can be found on *Star Time*, but the funkier and more familiar of the two is the centerpiece of *I Got You (I Feel Good)*. Brown didn't cut down on his balladry during this period, however. *It's a Man's, Man's, Man's World* certainly has its share of funk, including the two-part "Ain't That a Groove," but there's room enough for the slow ones, including the title track and a tearfully intense number called "The Bells." Likewise, *James Brown Sings Raw Soul* alternates rhythmically intense tunes such as "Money Won't Change You" and "Let Yourself Go" with soppy ballads along the lines of "Tell Me That You Love Me." Even the unstoppable groove of "Cold Sweat"— which, with its driving, monolithic bass pulse and exquisite Maceo Parker sax break, was a milestone almost as important as "Papa's Got a Brand New Bag"—is flanked on *Cold Sweat* by MOR numbers such as "Mona Lisa" and "Nature Boy" as well as a smattering of rock & roll oldies.

Of course, some of that was simply a reflection of Brown's determined eclecticism. Like Ray Charles, Brown refused to see himself as a one-dimensional musician and regularly fleshed out his albums with material that ranged far afield from the sound of his singles. Sometimes, he did whole albums of these songs, such as *Thinking About Little Willie John* and *A Few Nice Things*, a tribute to the influential R&B stylist that boasts a touching cover of John's "Talk to Me!" He also flirted with jazz, trying his hand at lounge singing with the Dee Felice Trio on *Gettin' Down to It* and recording *Soul on Top* with the Louis Bellson big band.

But Brown's most consistent sideline was playing organ, piano, and vibraphone. Although by no means a master technician, his solos are remarkably fluid, and at their best compare well with the work of such jazz-funk players as Les McCann and Ramsey Lewis. In all, Brown released 11 all-instrumental albums between 1961 and 1971; some, such as *James Brown Plays the New Breed*, *James Brown Plays the Real*

Thing, or *James Brown Plays James Brown Today and Yesterday* feature his funky, Jimmy McGriff–style organ solos; others, such as *Mighty Instrumentals, The Popcorn,* and *Ain't It Funky* put the emphasis on his band. Most have been written off as inconsequential, but the music is often quite good, particularly on rhythmically centered tunes such as "Peewee's Groove in 'D,'" from *Real Thing,* or "Soul Pride," from *Popcorn.* Finding the original albums may be a bit of a trick, but fortunately *Soul Power: The Instrumentals, 1960–1969* includes all the highlights and then some. Nor should we forget the albums he produced for his backing band, the JBs, and their various spin-offs, a sampling of which is spread between *James Brown's Funky People* and *James Brown's Funky People (Part 2).*

With *Say It Loud, I'm Black and I'm Proud* Brown states what had long been implicit in his music; the black power sentiment of the title tune generated a certain amount of controversy at the time, but the album isn't all politics, as the loping "Licking Stick—Licking Stick" makes clear. Brown's band was getting funkier with each passing month; even his outtakes are astonishing, as evidenced by the selection on *Motherlode. It's a New Day So Let a Man Come In* is especially strong, thanks to "Give It Up or Turnit a Loose," a mesmerizing workout with interlocking guitar and bass patterns, as well as such lesser greats as "It's a New Day" and "Let a Man Come in and Do the Popcorn." But many of Brown's hottest singles from this period—"Funky Drummer," for instance—didn't make it to album until Brown began to be anthologized in the '80s and '90s. Some of these tracks turn up in remixes on *In the Jungle Groove,* a DJ-oriented release that augments "Funky Drummer" with a three-minute "Bonus Beat Reprise," while *Star Time* offers a choice selection of complete versions of key tracks such as "Mother Popcorn." But if what you want to hear is what Brown heard during this period, your best bet is *Funk Power 1970: A Brand New Thang,* which not only offers a clear picture of the Brown band with bassist Bootsy Collins but also presents a number of hits in their original, unedited form.

Brown took the notion of funk quite literally with *Hot Pants,* and gets down even further with *There It Is* (including "I'm a Greedy Man" and the marvelously kinetic "Talkin' Loud & Sayin' Nothing," as well as the message song "King Heroin"). After the double album *Get on the Good Foot,* Brown released several soundtracks, of which only *The Payback* is worthwhile; from there, he went straight to *Hell,* a somewhat mixed double album that includes the Nixon-inspired "Funky President (People It's Bad)." By this point, Brown was losing his edge, and as he

tried to cope with the disco era, his albums grew increasingly spotty. Some, such as the remake-oriented *Sex Machine Today* or the uncharacteristically mellow *Everybody's Doin' the Hustle & Dead on the Double Bump,* are conceptual failures, while others—*Bodyheat, Mutha's Nature, Jam 1980's,* or *People*—are uninspired. Still, he had his moments: *Hot,* on which Brown copied David Bowie's "Fame" for "Hot (I Need to Be Loved, Loved, Loved)"; *Get Up Offa That Thing,* with its insistent title tune; and "For Goodness Sakes, Look at Those Cakes," on *Take a Look at Those Cakes.* With *The Original Disco Man,* he even came to terms with disco itself, and proved on *Soul Syndrome* that he could imitate the Miami sound as well as anyone.

By the early '80s, Brown was in limbo, with no label and a waning audience. Recorded at Studio 54, *The Greatest Hits Live in Concert* isn't even as good as the live-in-Japan *Hot on the One,* recorded a year earlier. He tried going independent, releasing the pleasantly retro *Bring It On!* through the tiny Churchill/Augusta label; it's a good album heard by almost no one. He even went Hollywood for a time, appearing in and contributing to the soundtracks of *The Blues Brothers* and *Dr. Detroit;* the latter has the more interesting musical performance. But it wasn't until he cut "Living in America" for the soundtrack to *Rocky IV* that Brown was able to reestablish himself. Ironically, part of the reason "Living in America" works is that it plays off the cliché James Brown–isms that had come back into vogue, resulting in Brown imitating himself (as he is through the rest of *Gravity*). *I'm Real* takes the opposite approach, with Brown complaining about rappers ripping him off, over rhythm tracks largely built around sampled James Brown records. *Soul Session Live* is the soundtrack from a Cinemax special that offers more stars (Aretha Franklin, Joe Cocker, Wilson Pickett) than memorable music, but *Love Over-Due,* recorded after Brown's release from prison on drug charges, is a return to form that boasts a sharp new band and a classic sense of material. From there, Brown went mostly into repackaging—even in the movies, with Jackie Chan (!) impersonating him in *The Tuxedo.* He did record with his touring band, but despite some fine playing *The Next Step* clearly leads nowhere. —J.D.C.

Jackson Browne

★★★★	Jackson Browne (Asylum, 1972)
★★★★	For Everyman (Asylum, 1973)
★★★★★	Late for the Sky (Asylum, 1974)
★★★½	The Pretender (Asylum, 1976)
★★★★★	Running on Empty (Asylum, 1978)
★★	Hold Out (Asylum, 1980)

Cowritten by Jackson Browne and the Eagles' Glenn Frey, "Take It Easy" pinpoints the attitudinal and musical changes taking place at the start of the '70s: "Don't even try to understand/Just find a place to make your stand/And take it easy." While the Eagles pursued the more hedonistic implications of that agenda, "trying to understand" is what Jackson Browne has always been about. Though he has focused on events in the world around him since the mid-'80s, Browne refined and perfected the role of the dark, sensitive singer/songwriter in the 1970s. He took the autobiographical charge of Joni Mitchell's early transmissions and raised the voltage. His philosophical slant endeared Browne to a generation of smart teenagers who'd read a bit and were asking Big Questions. Along with Mitchell, Jackson Browne served as a combination of bard, sex symbol, and intellectual mentor. Though both these L.A. troubadours also commanded sizable audiences among adults, their formative influence on subsequent singers and songwriters—not to mention other people—can't be overstated.

Browne's debut lays the groundwork for future heart-and-soul excavations. "Doctor My Eyes," an early hit single, communicates the subdued, subtle power of his half-spoken melodies, while "Rock Me on the Water" and "Song for Adam" foreshadow the free-ranging contemplation to come. *For Everyman* strikes a balance between the cool introspection of "I Thought I Was a Child" and "Sing My Song to Me" and the warm humor of "Ready or Not" and "Redneck Friend." David Lindley's loping slide guitar and arsenal of stringed instruments buoys Jackson's occasional slides into melancholy. "These Days," an FM-radio hit for Gregg Allman, stands as one of Browne's most intricately detailed emotional scenarios.

Late for the Sky strengthens and solidifies Browne's approach; it's the quintessential Browne album. The metaphorical complexity of "Fountain of Sorrow" and the clear-eyed poignancy of "For a Dancer" would be a tough act to follow; unsurprisingly, "The Fuse" and "Sleep's Dark & Silent Gate" (both from *The Pretender*) aren't quite as eloquent.

They are effective, though; Browne's once-hesitant singing improves with each album. But even when his songwriting is sharp, the mellowing trend in his music dulls the impact. Browne eerily predicts the rise of the yuppie on *The Pretender*'s title track, only to have his point undercut by a creeping string section.

Just when it seemed that mellow inevitably turned to mush, Browne made good on all the singer/songwriters' claims to confessional integrity. At a time when the overdub-enhanced live double album was a rock commonplace, Browne released a real concert document. *Running on Empty* collects new material, previously unrecorded cover versions, motel jams, loose ends, rough edges, mistakes, and unexpected moments of triumph. The album exudes intimacy, revealing the empathetic, flexible bond between Browne and his audience.

Hold Out returned to the popification program begun on *The Pretender,* though even the catchiest ruminations (the title track and "Hold On Hold Out") don't sink in over time like Browne's thoughtful hooks of old. *Lawyers in Love* marked the singer/songwriter's transition from the personal to the political. The title track is a cutting slice of social observation, but the remainder of the album is muddled. For the first time, Browne seems unsure of himself. Interestingly, both Browne and Mitchell started writing topical songs in the mid-'80s. Browne has stuck with it. The subsequent albums convey his passion and commitment, though the well-intentioned broadsides and liberation anthems never quite connect with the musical setting: tasteful, state-of-the-art L.A. studiocraft. Little Steven Van Zandt's "I Am a Patriot," from *World in Motion,* is the only truly memorable song on Browne's trilogy of protest albums.

Fortunately, Browne left the politics behind on *I'm Alive,* returning to his forte: the personal joy and agony of day-to-day human interaction. Here, he deals with the various stages of a failed relationship, from the thrill of attraction (the reggae-tinged "Everywhere I Go") to post-honeymoon-period worry (the gentle "Too Many Angels") and, ultimately, the grief of breaking up (the piano-based "Two of Me, Two of You"). Browne continued his renewed introspection on *Looking East,* to slightly lesser success. Looser, warmer, and more live sounding than Browne's other recent work, *The Naked Ride Home* takes on domestic mysteries (on the title track) and political realities ("Casino Nation"), and is passionately crafted and sung.

Despite its subtitle, *The Next Voice You Hear* is not the best of Jackson Browne. Though it contains some of his most well-known album tracks ("These Days," "Fountain of Sorrow") and biggest hits ("Doctor My Eyes," "Lawyers in Love"), so much great material is missing—and too many weak songs appear on the collection—that it doesn't adequately represent his oeuvre. For a true overview, pick up the 32-song *Very Best of,* compiled by Browne himself. —M.C./M.K.

Bubba Sparxxx

★★★ Dark Days, Bright Nights (Beat Club/Interscope, 2001)
★★★★ Deliverance (Beat Club/Interscope, 2003)

Bubba Sparxxx (born Warren Anderson Mathis, in tiny Lagrange, GA) is the Ronnie Van Zant of rap. Like the scrappy late singer of Lynyrd Skynyrd, Mathis brings his background as a white, working-class Southern man into a popular new arena—in his case, hip-hop. Some critics initially dismissed Mathis' rural, country-tinged rap, just as some had scorned Skynyrd's gritty mix of blues, country, and '70s hard rock. Some people even summoned the tired old demeaning "redneck" term. But it's not lack of smarts that mars Bubba's first album; it's lack of a coherent vision and consistent delivery. He's not the most elegant rapper, but his topics—and the dazzling production of Timbaland (Jay-Z, Missy Elliott)—make up for his sometimes clunky rhymes. Bubba's concerns are as valid as Van Zant's, and when he lashes out at old prejudices about the poor, white South or conveys the fears of threatened factory workers, he joins a long line of proud, Southern-rock provocateurs. *Dark Days* delivered a hit with "Ugly" (#15 pop; #6 rap), but some pundits wrote off the Bubba/Timbaland partnership as a lesser clone of the Eminem/Dr. Dre dream team. It was a superficial comparison, but Bubba's hayseed video for "Ugly" also only reinforced the white-trash stereotypes his songs rose above.

Deliverance was a big step forward. The rapping is more assertive, the album more coherent. Bubba acknowledges the country and blues roots of his hip-hop without resorting to the disingenuous overstatement of Kid Rock. In "Nowhere," Bubba offers an allegory about coming from a rural backwater over a spooky mix of house-music vocals and hip-hop ambience. "She Tried" is the tale of a guilt-ridden cheater told over ancient Appalachian fiddles and contemporary beats. Timbaland incorporates Irish whistle, acoustic guitars, banjo, and pedal steel, but the instruments don't come off as mere novelty. On *Deliverance,* Bubba writes from his experiences growing up in the dirty South of the 1990s, but he also proves that he is, first and foremost, a legitimate rapper. —M.K.

Buck 65

★★★ Language Arts (1997; WEA, 2002)
★★★½ Vertex (1999; WEA, 2002)
★★★★ Man Overboard (2001; WEA, 2002)
★★★½ Synesthesia (2001; WEA, 2002)
★★★½ Weirdo Magnet (WEA, 2002)
★★★★ Square (WEA, 2002)
★★★★ Talkin' Honky Blues (V2, 2004)

Buck 65 (Richard Terfry) is a DJ/rapper from Nova Scotia who's not just underground, but off the beaten path. Or, as he puts it: "Street credibility: zero. Dirt road credibility: up the yin yang." But he became a legend in Halifax for his elemental beats, deft scratches, obscure dubs, and plainspoken but brainy rap, and he impressed Warner Music Canada enough to not just sign him but release his six-album back catalogue. Five are installments in the *Language Arts* series. The other, *Weirdo Magnet,* collects older tapes going back to 1988. While his music is often inventive, it mostly serves to set up his words: He tells amazing stories, waxes philosophical, obsesses over his craft, and on occasion exposes himself with radical honesty—although I'd bet against his having been in the Sex Pistols, and the only incontrovertible detail of his centaur tale is that he for sure has a complex mind. And while he can easily conjure up his former childhood, he can also project profound maturity and age; in short, he gives you much to think about. For example, on *Weirdo Magnet* he has a piece where he spouts unclichéd, unironic platitudes such as "the most expensive indulgence is hate/the most dangerous man is the liar."

The first *Language Arts* album is the most underground, with lots of scratches and a long pastiche at the end. *Vertex* is best known for "Centaur," about the trials of someone "built like a horse from the waist down," but he also goes shopping for records and announces, "the older I get, the more life starts to make sense, and the less I care." *Man Overboard* is richer melodically and more diverse, assuming many voices, but none more immediate than his own as he mourns his late mother, whom he never managed to take to Graceland, but whose pride motivated his music. *Synesthesia* (expanded in the 2002 reissue, and now listed as part five of *Language Arts*) is a darker, grumpier album, where he disavows the f-word and frowns on groupies and regrets that "you can't chop wood with an axe made of words," but it's also his densest, most rhythmic work. In *Square,* he returns more to storytelling: a heavy-handed man, "born with his heart on the outside," afraid to touch his loved ones; a stigmatized girl from his hometown; but it also features paeans to science and food, and admits that "sometimes dumb crimes blow my mind." *Talkin' Honky Blues* is even better, introducing a band replete with pedal steel for a richer sound that still serves primarily to set up the words of an older, more worn persona, "a road hog with an old dog," who boasts, "I run with the bulls and swim with the pool sharks." So he came from nowhere, but he's been around. He gets compared to DJ Shadow and Laurie Anderson, but he's so original you never know what's coming next. A major talent, but in his own words, "it's possible that I can be huge, but I doubt it."   —T.H.

Lindsey Buckingham

★★★★   Law & Order (1981; Warner Bros., 1987)
★★★½   Go Insane (1984; Warner Bros., 1991)
★★★★   Out of the Cradle (Reprise, 1992)

The fact that Fleetwood Mac's 2003 offering *Say You Will* began life as a Lindsey Buckingham solo album is something of a shame. Mac albums may sell like Big Macs, but Buckingham's solo ventures are rare, weirdly wonderful birds. While Fleetwood Mac's *Tusk* more than hinted at the guitarist's closet experimental tendencies, *Law & Order* is the first true glimpse of Buckingham unleashed, and the result is a meticulously crafted beautiful mess. The hit "Trouble" was irresistible bait; with a firm rhythmic assist from Mick Fleetwood on drums, Buckingham wraps an artfully strummed melody line around a seductive, breathless reverie. It's like listening to a long, sweet sigh. After that, *Law & Order* is an unruly, one-man-band grab-bag of McCartney-esque pop ("Shadow of the West"), doo-wop ("September Song"), and wickedly gleeful, oddball cheek ("That's How We Do It in L.A."). Remarkably, it never feels overly indulgent, as Buckingham matches every quirk with an equally inventive hook. The moodier *Go Insane* could use a little more of its predecessor's sense of organic fun, if only to counter that distinctly '80s synth-and-drum-machine chill and the slump that sets in after the strong opening triptych of "I Want You," "Go Insane," and "Slow Dancing." *Out of the Cradle*, by contrast, is Buckingham at his most sublime, almost to a fault. Buffed to a flawless, sparkling sheen, it's essentially an album of transcendent pop lullabies ("Don't Look Down," "You Do or You Don't") for the middle-aged, with a few snarling, paranoid nightmares ("Wrong") thrown in for good measure. How catchy is it? Suffice to say, had Mick Fleetwood and Co. snatched this baby from Buckingham's cradle, the '90s might have sounded a lot more like the late '70s.   —M.C./R.S.K.

Jeff Buckley

★★★★   Live at Sin-é (Columbia, 1993)
★★★★★   Grace (Columbia, 1994)
★★½   Sketches for My Sweetheart, the Drunk (Columbia, 1998)
★★★   Mystery White Boy (Columbia, 2000)
★★★★   The Grace EPs (Columbia, 2003)
★★   Songs to No One: 1991–1992 (Knitting Factory Works, 2002)
★★★★   The Complete Live at Sin-é (Columbia, 2003)

Jeff Buckley's voice had supernatural shapeshifting powers—he could sing like angels in rapture one minute and moan with the anguished deprivation of '60s soulmen the next, or lash out like an ornery cornered cat. The son of iconoclastic folkie Tim Buckley, the singer, songwriter, and guitarist became a rock figure to watch on the basis of just a scruffy EP (*Live at Sin-é*) and then one full studio album, 1994's transcendent *Grace*. After struggling with various versions of the followup, which he'd tentatively titled *My Sweetheart, the Drunk*, Buckley finally began recording in Memphis during the spring of 1997, only to drown in the Mississippi River in late May. He was 30.

Buckley didn't rush into the record business. Setting up shop first in Los Angeles and then New York, he kicked around in several bands and collaborated with all kinds of musicians—among them Captain Beefheart guitarist Gary Lucas, with whom he formed Gods and Monsters and cowrote "Mojo Pin" and "Grace," both represented in demo form on the mostly dreary set of experiments entitled *Songs to No One*. His early New York tenure, captured on the acoustic-guitar-based *Live at Sin-é* EP and a new expanded two-disc set, reveals an introspective bent and a penchant for fitful vocal improvisations that show the influence of qawwali master Nusrat Fateh Ali Khan, Van Morrison, and, of course, his father.

Buckley's maturation as a vocalist was nearly complete by the time he recorded *Grace*, which features a full band and finds him fully inhabiting songs that glance toward Led Zeppelinish mysticism (the slow-building "So Real," the grandiose and gorgeous "Mojo Pin") or the hushed intimacy of the post-Dylan troubadours (a cover of Leonard Cohen's "Hallelujah"). The gorgeously recorded album, which made many critics' 10-best lists, led to nearly a year of constant touring with an increasingly hard-rocking band; the erratic *Mystery White Boy* captures the outfit at its most coherent. The *Grace EPs* collect material Buckley recorded during the sessions for *Grace;* two of them, *Peyote Radio Theater* and *So Real*, were intended as promo-only items, and each of the others contains at least one track from *Grace*. Gems include extended live versions of "Mojo Pin," Leonard Cohen's "Hallelujah," and Van Morrison's "The Way Young Lovers Do," all revealing different facets of Buckley's gift for rapturous vocal improvisation.

Buckley wrote lots of songs after *Grace*, obviously

in pursuit of a slightly different sound. He convinced Television's Tom Verlaine to produce him, and the two demoed coy, inventively experimental versions of the songs—the best of them begin the odd, inevitably erratic two-disc *Sketches for My Sweetheart, the Drunk,* which gathers material from several different sessions and eras. Verlaine abandoned the project well before its completion; Buckley was in the midst of rerecording the material he'd concocted with Verlaine, as well as newly written songs, when he died.   —T.M.

Tim Buckley

★★★	Tim Buckley (Elektra, 1967)	
★★★★	Goodbye and Hello (Elektra, 1967)	
★★★★	Happy/Sad (Elektra, 1969)	
★★★	Lorca (Elektra, 1970)	
★★★★	Blue Afternoon (1970; Enigma/Retro, 1989)	
★★★★	Starsailor (1971; Enigma/Retro, 1989)	
★★★	Greetings from L.A. (1972; Enigma/Retro, 1989)	
★	Sefronia (1974; Enigma/Retro, 1989)	
★	Look at the Fool (1974; Enigma/Retro, 1989)	
★★★	Dream Letter (Live in London, 1968) (Enigma/Retro, 1990)	
★★★	Live at the Troubadour, 1969 (Rhino, 1994)	
★★★	Honeyman (Manifesto, 1995)	
★★★½	Morning Glory: The Tim Buckley Anthology (Rhino, 2001)	

Dreamily handsome, possessed of a genuine, if eccentric, poetic gift, capable of singing a veritable choir of voices, and brandishing an archetypal romantic sensibility, Tim Buckley was a sort of late-'60s folkie Coleridge—overwhelmed by the gods with too many gifts. His work was as ambitious as that of any of his contemporaries: It was also a commercial disaster. His fatal overdose in 1975, however metaphorically apt, was a tragedy—and for a long time even the Buckley myth was an obscure one, as most of his records had gone out of print.

With such curious instrumentation as bottleneck guitar, harmonium, kalimba, and the vibes that would become a Buckley trademark, *Goodbye and Hello* drew critical raves for its meandering beauty, willful vision, and strange grace. Somewhat psychically akin to Van Morrison's *Astral Weeks* and Leonard Cohen's earliest work, this was orphic, amorphously lovely stuff. With titles such as "Phantasmagoria in Two" and "I Never Asked to Be Your Mountain," the record's lyrics recalled Wallace Stevens, and Buckley's voice seemed almost a little mad in its dramatic versatility (he sounds alternately like a child, a crone, and a straightforwardly expert folk singer). With his tone poems extending to 10 and 12 minutes on *Happy/Sad,*

the songs soared past any verse-chorus-verse structure; this was abstract expressionism of a rare bravery. So were Buckley's next three albums, with the jazzy *Starsailor* being that cluster's standout. Perhaps frustrated with his cult status, Buckley then veered wildly—*Greetings from L.A.* was rock, of a sort, and *Look at the Fool* was desperate (his voice sounds like a croaking Al Green, and the record funks around to no purpose). In his glory hour, however, Buckley was a solid live performer who flourished in concert, and both *Dream Letter* and *Honeyman* are outstanding. The mid-'90s witnessed a welcome revival of interest in the singer, largely due to the arrival of his son, Jeff, yet another brilliant talent, who also, sadly, died young.   —P.E.

Buffalo Springfield

★★★½	Buffalo Springfield (Atco, 1966)	
★★★★★	Buffalo Springfield Again (Atco, 1967)	
★★★	Last Time Around (Atco, 1968)	
★★★	Retrospective (Atco, 1969)	
★★★★½	Box Set (Rhino, 2001)	

Creative tension between Stephen Stills, the highly proficient craftsman, and Neil Young, the erratic, extreme genius, produced, in Buffalo Springfield, one of America's best '60s bands. Simultaneously more of a mainstream musical pro and more of an unexamined hippie than the idiosyncratic Young, Stills sang declamatory vocals and played tremolo guitar on "For What It's Worth," a 1967 Top 10 hit decrying the Sunset Strip riots in which flower children faced off the police. Young's standout from the debut was the characteristically ambitious "Nowadays Clancy Can't Even Sing" with its surreal poetry and keening vocals.

Potentially nearly an American Beatles, the supergroup employed orchestral arrangements, four-part vocals, Wild West mythmaking, unrivaled instrumental prowess—and a fertile internal explosiveness along the lines of the Who's. Stills' finest hour came with the band; "Bluebird" and "Rock & Roll Woman" find him a stronger singer and more versatile guitarist than he's ever been since. And in Buffalo Springfield, Young tried out not only such bravura cinematic fare as "Broken Arrow," but premiered the artful naiveté of "I Am a Child," its resonant simplicity paving the way for his solo hits.

The other members were hardly slouches. Rhythm guitarist Richie Furay's "Kind Woman" served as a blueprint for the refined country rock he'd later make with Poco. Bassist Jim Messina would join Furay in Poco, and then pair with Kenny Loggins in one of the '70s' biggest soft-rock acts. The band's twin peaks, of course, would fitfully collaborate again in Crosby,

Stills, Nash & Young—an inflated Springfield that, for all its musical achievement and countercultural significance, lacked the buoyancy of its prototype.

Only two years after its dazzling start, the Springfield was just a memory. But a memory that lingers: Rock & roll this expert and melodic would prove hard to find in the years to come. The group's legacy was aptly served by the 2001 release of the plainly named *Box Set*. The 88-song/four-disc compilation includes 36 unreleased tracks, the highlight being bare-bones acoustic demos of several of the Springfield's greatest moments. —P.E./G.F.

Jimmy Buffett

★★★½   A White Sport Coat and a Pink Crustacean (MCA, 1973)
★★★½   Living and Dying in 3/4 Time (MCA, 1974)
★★★★   A1A (MCA, 1974)
★★★   Havana Daydreamin' (MCA, 1976)
★★★½   Changes in Latitudes, Changes in Attitudes (MCA, 1977)
★★★   You Had to Be There (MCA, 1978)
★★★½   Son of a Son of a Sailor (MCA, 1978)
★★★   Volcano (MCA, 1979)
★★★   Coconut Telegraph (MCA, 1981)
★★   Somewhere Over China (MCA, 1981)
★★★   One Particular Harbor (MCA, 1983)
★★½   Last Mango in Paris (MCA, 1985)
★★★★   Songs You Know by Heart (MCA, 1985)
★★★   Floridays (MCA, 1986)
★★★   Hot Water (MCA, 1988)
★★½   Off to See the Lizard (MCA, 1989)
★★★   Feeding Frenzy (MCA, 1990)
★★★★   Boats, Beaches, Bars & Ballads (MCA/Margaritaville, 1992)
★★   Before the Beach (MCA/Margaritaville, 1993)
★★½   Fruitcakes (MCA/Margaritaville, 1994)
★★½   Barometer Soup (MCA/Margaritaville, 1995)
★★½   Banana Wind (MCA/Margaritaville, 1996)
★★★½   Don't Stop the Carnival (Island/Margaritaville, 1998)
★★★   Christmas Island (MCA, 1999)
★★★½   Buffett Live: Tuesdays, Thursdays, Saturdays (Mailboat, 1999)
★★½   Far Side of the World (Mailboat, 2002)
★★   Live in Las Vegas (Mailboat, 2002)
★★½   Live in Cincinnati (Mailboat, 2003)
★★   Live in Auburn, WA (Mailboat, 2003)
★★   Live in Mansfield (Mailboat, 2003)
★★★½   Meet Me in Margaritaville (Universal, 2003)
★★★½   License to Chill (RCA, 2004)

Jimmy Buffett put his adopted hometown of Key West on the map with a deep catalogue of albums that found him adding a Caribbean lilt to his country- and folk-based songs. His subject matter—neatly summed up in the definitive box set *Boats, Beaches, Bars & Ballads*—illuminated a subtropical state of mind that found favor with fans of margaritas and sunsets. No matter that much of Buffett's audience works from nine to five in their daily lives; his songs offer companionable escapist fantasies, while his legendary live performances served as mobile Floridian beach parties. Buffett's fans—the colorfully attired "Parrotheads"—have become as much a part of the cultural landscape as the man himself.

Buffett got his start in Nashville, recording a pair of overlooked and now long out-of-print albums—collected on the 1993 album *Before the Beach*—before making a southerly change in latitude. A former journalist and history major, Buffett unassumingly puts his literate background to good use. His story-songs resonate with sharp observations; his travelogues include a strong sense of time and place; his shaggy-dog tales stay on the leash. And most important, he applies his wry sense of humor to his brand of counterculture hedonism, even as he celebrates it.

He found his voice as a transplanted Floridian in the early '70s with *A White Sport Coat and a Pink Crustacean* and *Living and Dying in 3/4 Time*. The beautiful "Come Monday," from the latter album, established him on the pop charts, and that plainspoken ache and quiet melody still cut deep. Both albums mix chunky little bits of honky-tonk and Western swing into Buffett's defiantly left-of-center sensibility.

Then followed a string of albums on which Buffett created his very own beachgoing post-hippie subculture. If you closed your eyes, you could practically hear the palm trees swaying on *A1A*, his highwater mark as a recording artist. *A1A* (named after Florida's coastal highway) introduces the seafaring theme on cuts like "Trying to Reason With Hurricane Season," "A Pirate Looks at Forty" and "Nautical Wheelers." Buffett captures the lazy serenity of a steamy late summer day on "Life Is Just a Tire Swing."

Changes in Latitudes, Changes in Attitudes made him a superstar, thanks largely to "Margaritaville"—the first Top 10 hit of Buffett's career and something of a national anthem for the figurative Conch Republic (i.e., those who live in Key West or wish they did). The sound is breezy, Caribbean-scented soft rock, but the self-recriminating edge is pure country: "Some people say there's a woman to blame/but I know it's my own damn fault." After that flash of insight, Jimmy Buffett began retreating to his own personal "Margaritaville"—lost in a pleasant, unchallenging haze where he began to sound a bit routine. His last essential albums were 1979's *Volcano* and 1981's *Coconut Tele-*

graph. With *Somewhere Over China,* Buffett sounded for the first time like he was treading water.

Much of the rest of Buffett's '80s output is music that only a Parrothead could love. There were a few high points, such as the fan favorite *Floridays* and *Hot Water,* on which he attempted to stretch himself as a songwriter. Along the way came a nice single-disc compilation, wryly titled *Songs You Know by Heart: Jimmy Buffett's Greatest Hit(s);* a near-definitive twofer, *Meet Me in Margaritaville: The Ultimate Collection;* and the smartly compiled box set *Boats, Beaches, Bars & Ballads.*

Of course, there also have been plenty of live albums: *You Had to Be There* (1978), *Feeding Frenzy* (1990), *Buffett Live: Tuesdays, Thursdays, Saturdays* (1999). In 2003, on his own Mailboat label, he released four intact concerts, raw and uncut, for Parrothead degustation. But Jimmy Buffett is not the Grateful Dead. Even longtime fans questioned the sound quality and the point. Let's just say that you had to be there.

Buffett did great business on the road in the '90s and beyond, but as a songwriter he seemed to have lost a compelling voice. *Fruitcakes, Barometer Soup,* and *Banana Wind* are solid and craftsmanlike, but still a few mangos shy of a load. At least when he did get around to cutting the inevitable Christmas album *Christmas Island,* he managed to throw in some left-field twists, such as Chuck Berry's "Run Rudolph Run" and John Lennon's "Happy Xmas (War Is Over)." And his 1998 collaboration with Herman Wouk, which resulted in the musical *Don't Stop the Music,* showed an admirable sense of adventure. Coming from the man who put Key West on the map, *Don't Stop the Carnival* displays surprising candor in unveiling the conflicts and tensions that underlie the superficial enchantments of life on a tropical island.

By the time of 2002's *Far Side of the World,* he was back to preaching to the choir and largely making his mark as a staple of summer shed tours. And then Jimmy found his mojo again: In 2004 Buffet cut his first overtly country album and was rewarded with his first #1 album. Given that the contemporary C&W crowd freely embraced the Eagles and Fleetwood Mac, it's no surprise that a reflective singer/songwriter with a party-hearty streak like Buffett should find favor as an icon, too. *License to Chill* is a case of a mature artist getting his second wind. To his credit, Buffett made the move on his own terms, adapting country music to his folky, Floridian style rather than the other way around. Steel drums, slide guitar, marimba, and endless references to the good life on or near the water comfortably bob alongside fiddle, steel guitar, and his duettists' twangy voices. The result is a

union of sensibilities best described by the title of a Buffett original: "Conky Tonkin'," a droll slice of life about a pair of rootless party mavens "headin' down U.S. 1" to (where else?) Key West.   —P.P./M.C.

Built to Spill

★★★½	There's Nothing Wrong with Love (Up, 1994)
★★	Built to Spill Caustic Resin EP (Up, 1995)
★★½	The Normal Years (K, 1996)
★★★½	Perfect From Now On (Warner Bros., 1997)
★★★★	Keep It Like a Secret (Warner Bros., 1999)
★★★½	Live (Warner Bros., 2000)
★★★½	Ancient Melodies of the Future (Warner Bros., 2001)

Doug Martsch

| ★★★★ | Now You Know (Warner Bros., 2002) |

The American indie rock scene of the 1990s didn't produce many guitar heroes, but Doug Martsch, leader of the Boise, ID–based collective Built to Spill, definitely qualifies. Following the trail first blazed by Neil Young and Dinosaur Jr's J Mascis, Martsch (the only person to play on every Built to Spill record) is equally comfortable with intricate textural overdubs and unhinged fuzz-o-rama soloing. He also sings in a Neil Young–ish whine and writes clever, cutting songs. In short, he's a talent more people ought to know about.

Built to Spill's opening gambit, *Ultimate Alternative Wavers,* is out of print but worth hunting down for the noisy catharsis of "Revolution" and "Nowhere Nothin' Fuckup." More restrained and more focused, *There's Nothing Wrong with Love* shines brightest in the quiet moments; the wayward backing vocals and slide guitar on "Cleo" lend extra charm to the lyrics, sung from the perspective of Martsch's then-newborn son. A rambling EP cut with the help of another Boise band, Caustic Resin, is for fans only, as is *The Normal Years,* a collection of early singles and outtakes.

Thanks to a major-label production budget, *Perfect From Now On* is Built to Spill's tightest-sounding album yet, though the songs are still discursive: "Stop the Show," for instance, starts with an ominous, vaguely flamenco three-minute intro, morphs into loud, snotty rock, turns right on a jangle-and-chime hook, then left for a gut-busting lead. *Keep It Like a Secret* is punchier and poppier, boasting delightful hide-and-seek tunes such as "Center of the Universe" and "Time Trap." It's probably the best initial buy for new listeners. *Live* is a raw and energetic concert record that boasts plenty of Martsch's guitar-o-rama wailing and a 20-minute-plus version of Young's "Cortez the Killer."

Ancient Melodies sticks to the *Secret* formula, with

hardly less impressive results. Martsch's excellent first solo album, *Now You Know,* emphasizes his acoustic slide playing, but leaves just enough room for a trademark wah-wah freakout on "Impossible." —M.R.

LTJ Bukem

★★★	Mixmag Live! Continuous DJ Mix (1995; Moonshine, 1996)
★★★★	LTJ Bukem Presents Logical Progression, Level 1 (1996; Sire, 2001)
★★★	Progression Sessions Featuring MC Conrad (Good Looking, 1999)
★★★	Journey Inwards (Good Looking/Kinetic, 2000)
★★★★	Producer 01 (Good Looking, 2001)
★★	Producer 05: Rarities (Good Looking, 2002)

Twelve-inch single releases are dance music's real medium, not albums, so it should not be surprising that LTJ Bukem (a.k.a. Danny Williamson) has released only one "real" album of new material thus far in his career. However, his influence on the genre of drum-and-bass music—as an artist, label head, producer, remixer, and DJ—is immeasurable.

Drum and bass, initially termed "jungle," exploded in the clubs of London in the early '90s and Bukem was one of its earliest proponents. By taking the form's skittering breakbeats and melding them with a blend of funk grooves and spacey synths, he was creating a more atmospheric and soulful style than his peers, who opted to explore the music's darker edges with colder, more metallic digital soundscapes.

As head of his own label group, the Good Looking Organization, Bukem has released countless compilations of his roster's material (ranging from the more straight-ahead drum and bass of his Good Looking and Looking Good labels to the more ambient-funk-driven *Earth* and more soulful *Cookin'* series), but none more important than *Logical Progression, Level 1,* a landmark drum-and-bass album showcasing tracks of his own and a host of other like-minded artists and future drum-and-bass superstars, including Peshay, PFM, and ILS. A fantastic introduction to the genre, not only did it signal a fresh, more musical direction for drum and bass at the time, but it continues to serve as a blueprint for many of today's drum-and-bass artists. This ranks alongside Goldie's debut, *Timeless,* as perhaps one of the two most important drum-and-bass releases of the decade.

Increasingly, Bukem was finding space within this inventive and futuristic new style of electronic music to incorporate the music of his teenage idols, '70s jazz-funk fusioners such as Herbie Hancock and Beastie Boy faves Lonnie Liston Smith and Roy Ayers.

This was most in evidence on his double-CD solo album. *Journey Inwards* was just that: thoughtful compositions with Rhodes keyboards, nature sounds, female vocals, drifting synths, and wah-wah guitar all giving life to the stiffer programmed beats while paying homage to his influences. It made for a much more organic, instrumental, and downtempo collection than his previous output.

The *Mixmag Live* DJ set is an early statement of intent from Bukem but, as it was not widely released at the time, serves more as a historical document now than anything. The *Progression Sessions* series showcases GLO artists in a more exciting live-mix setting with Bukem on the turntables and sidekick MC Conrad freestyling (more singing than rapping) over the top. The MC is a common feature in live drum-and-bass club sets but, unless you're looking to re-create a Sunday night out in Brixton (and despite Conrad's prowess), it does tend to distract from an otherwise superb tune selection.

The other two all-Bukem albums, *Producer 01* and *Producer 05,* collect his numerous single releases and are both very good, but the first stands out on account of such early classics as "Music" and the once-hard-to-find "Demon's Theme." Fans may also want to seek out the Bukem-compiled *Points in Time* and *Looking Back* series. —D.S.

Solomon Burke

★★★★	If You Need Me/Rock 'N' Soul (1963, 1964; Collectables, 1998)
★★★	Lord, We Need a Miracle (1979; Savoy, 1990)
★★★	Take Me, Shake Me (1983; Savoy, 2001)
★★★★	Soul Alive (Rounder/PGD, 1989)
★★★	Into My Life You Came (Savoy, 1990)
★★★	This Is His (Savoy, 1990)
★★★	The Best of Solomon Burke (Curb, 1991)
★★★★	Home in Your Heart: The Best of Solomon Burke (Rhino/Atlantic, 1992)
★★★½	Home Land (Manifesto, 1993)
★★★½	Soul of the Blues (1993; Black Top, 1998)
★★★	A Change Is Gonna Come (Rounder/PGD, 1994)
★★★½	Live at the House of Blues (Black Top, 1994)
★★½	Definition of Soul (Pointblank, 1997)
★★★★	The Very Best of Solomon Burke (Rhino, 1998)
★★★	Not by Water, but Fire This Time (CGP, 1999)
★★★	Proud Mary: The Bell Sessions (Sundazed, 2000)
★★★	The King of Blues 'N' Soul (Fuel, 2001)
★★★★	Don't Give Up On Me (Fat Possum, 2002)
★★★★	Got to Get You Off My Mind and Other Hits (Rhino, 2003)

When Solomon Burke won a Grammy Award for his 2002 album *Don't Give Up On Me,* it was an honor both well deserved and long awaited. Even during his peak commercial years during a seven-year stint with Atlantic Records in the '60s, Burke was hardly a top-drawer soul star, although his fans were legion and devoted. But it seemed like someone was always bigger, always stealing the headlines, whether it was his friend Sam Cooke (whose death was the inspiration for Burke's easy-rolling 1965 hit, "Got to Get You Off My Mind") or more flamboyant contemporaries such as Otis Redding and Wilson Pickett. But Burke kept his nose to the soul and gospel grindstone, staying close to the music he felt in his heart, cutting a bunch of exemplary records, some of which earned rave reviews but were no longer suitable stylistically for the mainstream of contemporary black music.

But *Don't Give Up On Me* couldn't be ignored as a statement, even if its commercial potential seemed limited. In his younger days Burke could sound startlingly like Nat "King" Cole or Brook Benton, master crooners both; nowadays, the sexagenarian artist emotes in a gruff, husky tone, occasionally rising into sandpapery shouts when he really gets into testifying from the soul music pulpit. The weight of the years in his voice, and the intensity of his identification with a song's story line, bring an immediacy and urgency to every performance on *Don't Give Up On Me.* Producer Joe Henry did right by the aging Burke, ditching full-bodied Southern soul arrangements for an austere approach, backing the artist with a small combo of guitar, bass, piano/keyboards, and drums/percussion, supplemented by the rich, churchy organ of Rudy Copeland, who handles those same duties in Burke's own church. The assembled musicians do work themselves into a churning, edgy froth once in a while—most effectively on a lowdown, bluesy treatment of Bob Dylan's bitter "Stepchild"—but the dominant mode is deep introspection framed by subdued support. The stark landscape suits Burke to a tee, and he digs into some gems supplied by Van Morrison ("Fast Train," "Only a Dream"), Nick Lowe ("The Other Side of the Coin"), Brian Wilson and Andy Paley ("Soul Searchin'," the most overt foray into R&B in Wilson's history), and Tom Waits and Kathleen Brennan, whose expressions of streetwise pragmatism in the rich gospel tones of "Diamond in Your Mind" is not only the highlight of the album but one of the stellar interpretive moments of Burke's entire career—a truly towering performance of breathtaking feeling.

But to those who had been following the Philadelphia-born Burke's career lo these many years, *Don't Give Up On Me* was an unsurprising show of strength: He's been doing this sort of thing pretty much since he stepped into a recording studio in 1955 to cut "Christmas Presents from Heaven" for the Apollo label. At that point he was already a boy wonder on the gospel circuit, not as a vocalist but as a real live preacher who was actually billed as the "Wonder Boy Preacher," and could be heard delivering his sermons on radio as well. He dressed in regal garb—a king's crown and rhinestone-studded cape—worked himself and his flock into a lather, then wowed 'em with a rousing gospel number to bring it all home.

Signing with Atlantic in the early '60s, he was teamed variously with producers Jerry Wexler and, most successfully, Bert Berns. Over the course of seven years, Burke ranged across his entire musical vocabulary, cutting classic Southern soul with full-throttle rhythm and horn sections and shouting female gospel singers in the background, as well as gospel, pop, and especially country—his first crossover hit was a beautiful, crooning version of the country song "Just Out of Reach (Of My Two Open Arms)," which peaked at #24 in 1961. Possessed of a keen social conscience, Burke also cooked up what he thought would be an empowering project for the black community in the wake of segregation's end, in the form of a super summit called the Soul Clan. This musical group was to have been composed of soul stars Burke, Wilson Pickett, Otis Redding, Don Covay, and Joe Tex, and its aim was to take profits from a planned album and reinvest them in black neighborhoods, building good housing and rehabilitating local businesses so that blacks wouldn't abandon their own communities for the better-appointed white-dominated business districts and neighborhoods. Alas, the group's demand for a $1-million advance was dismissed out of hand by Atlantic, Redding was killed in an airplane crash, and Pickett bowed out. Arthur Conley and Ben E. King joined up, but the sole fruit of this labor was a single, "Soul Meeting," and then Soul Clan receded into history.

The glorious years on Atlantic are well documented, although much remains out of print. Still, the essential recordings, singles and album tracks alike, are pretty much all available, but not in one place. A great starting point is Rhino's double-CD, 40-track collection, *Home in Your Heart: The Best of Solomon Burke,* which contains the five pop hits (apart from those already mentioned, these include "If You Need Me," "Goodbye Baby [Baby Goodbye]," and "Tonight's the Night"), a moving country-soul take on Mel Tillis' "Detroit City," and a frightful, devastating account of the wages of bad love, "The Price" (the legend behind this one being that Burke improvised the lyrics onstage shortly after being served with divorce papers). At 16 tracks, another Rhino entry, *The Very*

Best of Solomon Burke, suffers by comparison, but all of the hits are here as well as the Soul Clan single, "Soul Meeting," which is not on *Home in Your Heart.* For a look at what Burke was really up to, check out the Collectables twofer combining 1963's *If You Need Me* and 1964's *Rock 'N' Soul* albums. The former's title song was a #37 pop single and the latter leads off with 1964's #33 pop hit, "Goodbye Baby (Baby Goodbye)," but go deeper into the disc, and there's Burke's blistering, self-penned self-condemnation, "Stupidity"; two fine country numbers, "I Really Don't Want to Know" done as a saloon song and a heartbreaking interpretation of the Jim Reeves hit "He'll Have to Go"; a sensitive reading of the Lloyd Price–penned, Little Richard–recorded "Send Me Some Loving"; and even a lively stab at Woody Guthrie's "Hard Ain't It Hard."

Since leaving Atlantic in the late '60s, Burke has bounced from label to label, with mixed results leaning toward the positive. For a while he returned to the gospel fold, with his tenure on Savoy producing the best work in that vein. The Savoy albums are by turns fire and brimstone and soothing and meditative, with the message always coming through loud and clear no matter the approach. Burke's two Rounder albums brought him back to the secular world. *Soul Alive* is a live album that catches him in one of his most expansive moods, ranging across a typically broad spectrum of material. *A Change Is Gonna Come,* a studio album, is a spotty attempt at updating Burke's sound. When it works, it's mesmerizing—his take on "A Change Is Gonna Come" is given added resonance by the overwhelming sadness in Burke's delivery, a sadness no doubt composed of equal parts mourning over the loss of his friend Sam Cooke and despair over the title sentiments ever applying in a profound way to the black community. *Proud Mary: The Bell Sessions* documents Burke's 1969–70 stint on the Bell label, notable mainly for a fiery cover take of John Fogerty's "Proud Mary," which was a soul chart hit. At this point Burke was making a more aggressive move to incorporate some rock glide in his stride (viz, "Proud Mary" and a bonus track featuring a fairly fierce cover of Bob Dylan's "The Mighty Quinn"), but otherwise he clings to his soul and gospel sensibility with the likes of Otis Redding's "These Arms of Mine" and Marvin Gaye's "I'll Be Doggone," and tips his hat to country with a powerful "She Thinks I Still Care." The one misstep in recent years is 1996's *The Definition of Soul.* This is a heavily produced, ham-handed attempt at social commentary a la latter-day Bo Diddley that is no more successful than Diddley's and almost as embarrassing. You don't have to get too far into the proselytizing album opener, "Why Can't We Come Together," before it's apparent that Burke is out of his

element. Saving grace: the teaming with Little Richard on "Everybody's Got a Game," because the famous Mr. Penniman makes everything better whenever and wherever he shows up. None of this foretold the coming of *Don't Give Up On Me,* though, which ought to be a template for more great work to come as Burke ages most gracefully. —D.M.

T Bone Burnett

★★★	Truth Decay (Takoma, 1980)
★★★½	Trap Door (Warner Bros., 1982)
★★	Proof Through the Night (Warner Bros., 1983)
★★★	T Bone Burnett (Dot, 1986)
★★★★	The Talking Animals (Columbia, 1988)
★★★	The Criminal Under My Own Hat (Columbia, 1992)

A terrific songwriter but a terrible sermonizer, T Bone Burnett—back in the days before he devoted himself to producing such rootsy soundtrack albums as *O Brother, Where Are Thou?* and *Cold Mountain*—made albums that offer an intriguing, sometimes maddening mixture of roots-oriented rock and high-minded rant. His first album, *Truth Decay,* is a solidly melodic, rockabilly-based outing that gets a little ham-fisted with its message (as in his the-devil-is-an-adman number, "Madison Avenue") but keeps the music light and lithe. Amazingly, *Trap Door* uses the same band but offers a completely different sound, which at its best—"Hold On Tight," say, or "I Wish You Could Have Seen Her Dance"—has all the chiming effervescence of a latter-day Byrds album. The production values are even higher on *Proof Through the Night,* which brings in a passel of high-profile guest musicians (Ry Cooder, Mick Ronson, Richard Thompson, Pete Townshend), but the high-gloss sound doesn't much help the material, which ultimately collapses under the weight of its bitterly pedantic lyrics.

Burnett throws a curve ball with *T Bone Burnett,* a conventional country album that's wonderfully well-sung but a tad too low-key. *The Talking Animals,* on the other hand, not only finds him returning to rock & roll but also regaining the ground lost with *Proof Through the Night* through wickedly funny songs such as "Image," a tango in four languages, or the dementedly Pirandellian "The Strange Case of Frank Cash and the Morning Paper." But *The Criminal Under My Own Hat* found his writing again falling prey to cleverness and studio gloss, which may explain his subsequent focus on production work. —J.D.C.

R.L. Burnside

★★★★	Mississippi Delta Blues (Arhoolie, 1967)
★★★★½	Raw Electric (Inside Sounds, 1979–80)

★★★★	Mississippi Hill Country Blues (Fat Possum, 1984)
★★★½	Bad Luck City (Fat Possum, 1991)
★★★★	Too Bad Jim (Fat Possum, 1994)
★★★★	A Ass Pocket of Whiskey (Fat Possum, 1996)
★★★½	Come On In (Fat Possum, 1998)
★★★★½	Wish I Was in Heaven Sitting Down (Fat Possum, 2000)
★★★½	Well Well Well (Fat Possum, 2001)
★★★★	Burnside on Burnside (Fat Possum, 2001)

After a 30-year career spent in near obscurity in small-time northern Mississippi juke joints, R.L. Burnside was "discovered" by Fat Possum Records in the late 1980s, for which he's recorded a series of traditional blues sides as well as rowdy, remarkably experimental works that are credited with inspiring all kinds of punk blues, from the Jon Spencer Blues Explosion to the White Stripes.

A farm laborer, Burnside learned the blues from his neighbor Mississippi Fred McDowell, and was first recorded in 1967 *(Mississippi Delta Blues)*. That record led to a string of festival appearances and the development of his first bona fide band, which included members of his large family on guitar. Burnside's growly intensity was first heard by rock audiences in 1991, when Fat Possum released *Bad Luck City*. The subsequent *Too Bad Jim*, recorded at the club of another important rural-blues belter, Junior Kimbrough, is even more intense—its droning modal harmonies providing the perfect backdrop for Burnside's hectoring, woeful-but-not-pitiful incantations.

Breakthrough comes with *A Ass Pocket of Whiskey*, recorded with the Jon Spencer Blues Explosion, and the subsequent blues-meets-loops odyssey *Come On In*, experiments that prove it's possible to expand even the most raw, primal blues. Along the way, Burnside has made several hauntingly spare acoustic records, including the uniformly good live document *Burnside on Burnside*. Since attaining a national profile, several reissues of work he did in the '80s have surfaced—among them *Mississippi Hill Country Blues*, recorded in 1984, and the incredibly energetic *Raw Electric*.   —T.M.

Bush

★★★½	Sixteen Stone (Trauma/Interscope, 1994)
★★★½	Razorblade Suitcase (Trauma/Interscope, 1996)
★★	Deconstructed (Trauma/Interscope, 1997)
★★½	The Science of Things (Trauma/Interscope, 1999)
★★	Golden State (Atlantic, 2001)

Bush was the grunge heartthrob of 1995, an unlikely blend of punk guitars, perfect cheekbones, and the shakiest American accents to cross the Atlantic since Tim Roth in *Reservoir Dogs*. Nobody gave a toss for these Londoners at home, but millions of Americans inhaled the teen-spirit aroma emanating from lead singer Gavin Rossdale, a grunge sexpot with eyelashes you could hang Christmas tree ornaments on. Gavin had a bruised, boyish ache in his voice that made him sound gorgeously tormented, while his band plowed efficiently through the loud-quiet-loud Seattle songbook. Hipsters complained that Bush was just a mishmash of Nirvana and Pearl Jam, but if we had had any idea how much uglier rock radio was about to get, we all would have appreciated Bush for the excellent singles band it was, especially "Glycerine," "Mouth," and "Machinehead." "Swallowed," from the Steve Albini production *Razorblade Suitcase*, remains one of the '90s' great forgotten hits, an anguished power ballad wherein Gavin yowls, "I'm here with everyone/And you're not." The hits stopped coming, but Rossdale remained in the public eye as one of the few male rock stars of his time to trade on sex rather than violence, while also serving as elbow candy for No Doubt's Gwen Stefani.   —R.S.

Kate Bush

★★★	The Kick Inside (EMI America, 1978)
★★	Lionheart (EMI America, 1978)
★★★	Never for Ever (EMI America, 1980)
★★★	The Dreaming (EMI America, 1982)
★★★	Kate Bush (EP) (EMI America, 1983)
★★★★	Hounds of Love (EMI America, 1985)
★★★★	The Whole Story (EMI America, 1986)
★★★★	The Sensual World (Columbia, 1989)
★★★	The Red Shoes (Columbia, 1993)
★★★★	This Woman's Work Anthology 1978–1990 (EMI import, 1998)

Eccentric and idiosyncratic, Kate Bush's work is an odd offshoot of English art rock, capturing much of its spirit while avoiding the worst of its instrumental indulgences. Despite an occasional flash of pop accessibility, her early efforts are easily dismissed. *The Kick Inside*, with its effusive arrangements and parade of dead lovers, seems almost a parody of rock romanticism; *Lionheart* was a rush job, and sounds it; *Never for Ever*, though stylistically adventurous, is undercut by uneven arrangements. Eventually, Bush discovered digital synthesis, and with it constructed a universe better suited to her songs. Unlike her early albums, the sound of *The Dreaming* and *Hounds of Love* is as focused as it is fantastic, lending credibility to her witches, sorcerers, and demon lovers. After *The*

Whole Story, a greatest hits collection, Bush jettisoned such juvenalia altogether; though her music maintained its sense of aural adventure, she addressed herself assiduously (if less affectingly) to more mature (and markedly feminine) material in *The Sensual World* and *The Red Shoes. This Woman's Work,* an import-only box set, surveys her pre-*Sensual World* output with the completist ardor of a devoted fan; objective, it is not. —J.D.C.

Busta Rhymes

★★★½	The Coming (Elektra, 1996)	
★★★½	When Disaster Strikes (Elektra, 1997)	
★★★½	Extinction Level Event (The Final World Front) (Elektra, 1998)	
★★★	Anarchy (Elektra, 2000)	
★★★★	Total Devastation: The Best of Busta Rhymes (Rhino, 2001)	
★★★½	Genesis (J, 2001)	
★★★½	It Ain't Safe No More (J, 2002)	

Woo-hah! Busta Rhymes is hip-hop's Godzilla, a fire-breathing giant whose marketable cuddly side has kept him perpetually serialized in apocalyptic-themed blockbuster albums; no matter their overblown conceits, they always deliver a few of the spine-tingling moments that had attracted you in the first place. Rhymes was still a teenager when he moved from his Flatbush, Brooklyn, birthplace to Long Island, where he formed the group Leaders of the New School with high school chums Dinco D, Charlie Brown, and Cut Monitor Milo. The group delivered two albums: the exuberant *A Future Without a Past...* (Elektra, 1991), which featured Busta's pillowy ode "Feminine Fatt," and *T.I.M.E.* (Elektra, 1993), the darker, semi-sci-fi brainfreaker. Public Enemy's Chuck D was the one who gave Busta Rhymes the handle, and Busta's energetic rhyming and wacky chuckle were obviously inspired by Flavor Flav. When Busta stole the show with his dragon impersonation on A Tribe Called Quest's "Scenario" in 1993, solo stardom was a given.

With his Cheshire cat perma-grin and medusa head of dreads, Busta's manic microphone antics have proved impressively durable. Each of his albums spawned at least one hit single (though often more), from "Who-hah!! Got You All in Check" off *The Coming,* straight through to the ridiculous, lascivious "Make It Clap," from *It Ain't Safe No More.* His singles, which function like memorable action sequences from Hollywood blockbusters, burst with sonic special effects layered over classic grids of funky drums and tight bass loops. And then there's Busta, a sex-craved comedian nearly hyperventilating as he finds yet another catchy way of saying not much at all ("Hit you

with no delayin' so what you sayin', yo? Silly with my nine milly, what the dilly yo?" from the 1997's "Put Your Hands Where My Eyes Could See"). An absolute master of the club-bangin' anthem (often to an absurd degree; the P. Diddy party jam "Pass the Courvoisier" took things to a new level of decadent product placement), Busta has stayed in microwave rotation on TV and radio for nearly a decade. As he once rapped, "Gotta listen to how radio be playin' us/30 times a day make you delirious." The Flipmode majordomo's presence was definitively captured in Hype Williams' clip for the Janet Jackson duet "What's It Gonna Be?" None of Busta's albums are essential, and while Rhino's 18-cut best-of is superior (it includes two Leaders of the New School tracks), his recent releases have rendered it out-of-date. —P.R.

Butthole Surfers

★★★	Butthole Surfers Live/PCPEP (Latino Bugger Veil, 1983)	
★★★★	Psychic . . . Powerless . . . Another Man's Sac (Latino Bugger Veil, 1985)	
★★★★	Rembrandt Pussyhorse (Latino Bugger Veil, 1986)	
★★★★	Locust Abortion Technician (Latino Bugger Veil, 1987)	
★★★★	Hairway to Steven (Latino Bugger Veil, 1988)	
★★★	Double Live (Latino Bugger Veil, 1989)	
★★	Pioughed (Capitol, 1991)	
★★★	Independent Worm Saloon (Capitol, 1993)	
★★★	The Hole Truth . . . and Nothing Butt! (Trance Syndicate, 1995)	
★★★★	Electriclarryland (Capitol, 1996)	
★★★★	Weird Revolution (Hollywood, 2001)	
★★	Humpty Dumpty LSD (Latino Bugger Veil, 2002)	

Gibby Haynes

★★★	Gibby Haynes and His Problem (Surfdog, 2004)	

Actors often complain that comedy is hard and doesn't get much credit when it's time to pass out the awards. One can make the same case regarding the Butthole Surfers, a band beloved and much deciphered by those who got the joke (and got beyond the joke) while those who didn't went no further than the name. Beyond the joke, the Buttholes were always crazy in frightening, fractured ways reminiscent of folk art by some wacked-out peasant trying to warn his neighbors about the looming catastrophe of . . . what?

Beyond the psychosis, there was a unique amalgam of alienation from and affection for American culture. They pursued sensuous guitar tones and new noises with an acid-fueled fervor as their lyrics erased the coordinates of whatever cosmos you thought you were inhabiting. People who fit nowhere else in the world found a home at their unique live shows.

Many musicians have been Buttholes over the years. The center of the band has always been vocalist Gibby Haynes and guitarist Paul Leary, who became friends at Trinity University in San Antonio in the late '70s; King Coffey has laid down the tribal drumbeat under their psychedelic explorations almost from the beginning. Touring relentlessly on the punk circuit from their home base in Austin during the '80s, they plowed all their money back into the band, buying obsolete and bizarre electronics to record some of the most original music in rock history.

Their first and second EPs on Alternative Tentacles are now combined on *Butthole Surfers Live/PCPEP,* released on their own label, Latino Bugger Veil. Sometimes called *A Brown Reason to Live,* the first EP is still fall-on-the-floor funny, though slightly dated in its pop-culture references. The vision is there, the sound not quite in place yet. The second EP is sort of a joke as a live reprise of their first EP (it being a tad early for a greatest-hits collection), but it is interesting to hear Leary's Dionysian guitar come into its own in a club setting.

Their first full-length, *Psychic . . . Powerless . . . Another Man's Sac* (originally released on Touch and Go), is about as good as psychedelia gets this side of Hendrix. Haynes figures out what to do with his not-naturally-great voice by running it through a bullhorn and various effects boxes that add new dimensions of mystery to his surreal lyrics, while the band careens from chaos to grooved riff-bashing with occasional moments of crystalline beauty. If you're not hooked by "Cherub," a study in atmospheric feedback and psychotic ranting, you're probably just not going to get the Buttholes.

Rembrandt Pussyhorse (the CD also includes their EP *Cream Corn from the Socket of Davis*) has hilarious covers of "American Woman" (dig the supercompressed drums) and the theme from *Perry Mason,* two versions of their angst epic "Creep in the Cellar," and the tribute to demented old bluesmen "Movin' to Florida." *Locust Abortion Technician* opens with "Sweat Loaf," more and less a cover of Black Sabbath's "Sweet Leaf" that was always a frenzied high point of their live show and proceeds as a tour through all levels of metaphysical discombobulation. *Hairway to Steven* never spelled out the song titles, but you can sorta figure them out from the drawings and lyrics, and Gibby gets real intense about seeing an X-ray of a girl passing gas and reaches a peak with his wordplay in the mini-opera "Johnny Smoke."

The sound quality on *Double Live* is subpar, but the album does approximate the BHS concert experi-ence. Leary's uniquely fluid guitar bashing and Haynes' hypersonic satire on popular culture (check out his obscene take on Jim Morrison at the beginning of "Sweat Loaf") will make your knees go weak if you heed the advice on the back cover, "VERY LOUD IT PLAY." As one of the biggest underground acts in the country, the Buttholes decided to go the overground, corporate route in the '90s, signing with Capitol in hopes of wider distribution. The results were varied. *Pioughed* has some good moments but doesn't quite reach the extremes of inspiration and surprise of its predecessors (best joke: "No, I'm Iron Man"). Produced by Led Zeppelin bassist John Paul Jones, *Independent Worm Saloon* is as close as the Buttholes ever came to producing a punk album. "Who Was in My Room Last Night?" was a high-velocity minor hit with a good video, but "Goofy's Concern" had the better chord progressions and made a rare political statement in the midst of a lot of nihilism ("I don't give a fuck about the CIA").

Electriclarryland contains the Buttholes' sole major radio hit, "Pepper," as close to a perfect song as they'd ever write: great hooks in verse and chorus, wonderfully eerie production (by Paul Leary), and Haynes doing a shell-shocked monotone rap about all his demolished and/or dead friends. After recording an aborted album, *After the Astronaut,* for Capitol, the Buttholes rerecorded much of it for Hollywood as a new album, *Weird Revolution.* The title track, a Malcolm X parody, calls for solidarity among the weird to resist the injustice of the straight man. "The Shame of Life," written with Kid Rock, is a dirge rap that sorta celebrates and sorta mourns the rock lifestyle. Funniest cut: "Shit Like That," a rant about your life falling apart. Big hit that somehow didn't get recorded right: "Intelligent Guy." Overall it was their best album since the '80s, but it didn't quite connect with the public as the band toured after 9/11.

The Hole Truth . . . and Nothing Butt! has live odds and ends; *Humpty Dumpty LSD* offers demos and recording-studio odds and ends. Both will make fans happy but aren't the place to begin if any of the above intrigues you.   —C.M.Y.

The Buzzcocks

★★★★ Spiral Scratch (EP) (New Hormones, 1977)
★★★★ Another Music in a Different Kitchen (UA, 1978)
★★★★ Love Bites (UA, 1978)
★★★★ A Different Kind of Tension (UA, 1979)
★★★★★ Singles Going Steady (IRS, 1979)
★★★ Lest We Forget (ROIR, 1988)
★★★ The Peel Sessions Album (Strange Fruit/Dutch East India Trading, 1991)

★★★★ Time's Up (UK Receiver, 1991)
★★★★½ Operators Manual: Buzzcocks Best (IRS, 1991)
★★★ Entertaining Friends: Live at the
Hammersmith Odeon March 1979
(IRS, 1992)
★★★½ Trade Test Transmissions (Caroline, 1993)
★★★ All Set (IRS, 1996)
★★ Modern (Go-Kart, 1999)
★★★★ Buzzcocks (Merge, 2003)

In Britpunk's class of '77, the Buzzcocks were the horny, goofy, slightly baffled guys sitting in the back of the room, unsure whether to hide their boners, show them to the person sitting next to them, play with them, or what. So they wrote razor-sharp pop songs about all the feelings (some complicated, some not) that brought said boners about, played 'em fast and rough (the songs, not the boners, but the brilliant "Orgasm Addict" is about both) and became punk's ultimate three-minute heroes, inventing and perfecting a catchy/fast dynamic that would inspire garage bands for decades.

Howard Devoto and Pete Shelley brought the Sex Pistols to Manchester in 1976, forming their own band with drummer John Maher and bassist Steve Diggle around the same time. This lineup lasted all of one EP, the iconic *Spiral Scratch,* one of the very first DIY, self-released punk singles. It's a hot and wired four-song blurt, but you can already hear brainiac Devoto's mind wandering. He soon split to form the also excellent but far artier Magazine. (*Time's Up* is a collection of Devoto-era sessions that finally saw legit release in 1991.) Guitarist Shelley started to sing, Diggle moved to guitar, some guy named Garth played bass and suddenly the Buzzcocks were a world-historical pop force. If you can buy only one Buzzcocks album, make it *Singles Going Steady,* an anthology of post-*Spiral* 45s. It's packed with twitching, tuneful song after twitching, tuneful song about human relationships in all their frantic glory; "Orgasm Addict," "What Do I Get," "Ever Fallen in Love (With Someone You Shouldn't Have)," and "Noise Annoys" (which became the name and anthem of roughly 8 trillion college radio shows) are only the most famous cuts. The 16 cuts offer the sound of a band knowing that punk was about articulating desires directly and playing them like it was all they could do to keep from, well, exploding.

Other albums aren't nearly as well-known as *Singles,* but they're nearly as good. *Another Music in a Different Kitchen* rants and raves about being "lost without a clue." On "Sixteen," Shelley can't decide if he remembers that age with fondness or irony even when he's making out with someone that age, and

"Fiction Romance" wobbles between hope and despair. At the heart of it all is, of course, desire. "I need sex/I need love/I need drink/I need drugs/I need food/I need cash/I need you to love me back," sings Shelley in "I Need." Well, yes, that about sums it up. *Love Bites* is the not-as-great followup. Clearly a guy who spends a lot of time in his own head, maybe Shelley likes "The Real World" and maybe he doesn't. "Ever Fallen in Love" is the clear highlight, but the rest bops along nicely.

A Different Kind of Tension closes out the first part of their career with a slightly heavier sound, more complex songwriting, and Shelley's ever more bummed visions of the world. "You Say You Don't Love Me" and the anthemic "I Believe" ("there is no love in this world any more") pretty much speak for themselves. Nowhere near done, the band broke up over a label conflict in 1981. *Lest We Forget* is a powerful live album with typically dicey ROIR sound; *Entertaining Friends* also has some howl to it. The astounding *Product* box set is long out of print, but contains pretty much every studio track they ever made until 1981. Surely, this slice of heaven can be found on eBay. If you can't find it, *Operator's Manual* is a tidy best-of, not quite as concise as *Singles Going Steady,* but with more album tracks.

Shelley and Diggle got back together in 1989 and released *Trade Test Transmissions.* Picking up exactly where they had left off, the songs address masturbation ("Palm of My Hand"), sorrow ("Who'll Help Me Forget?"), and love of all sorts. Time and production values have made the guitars bigger, but the tunes still career across the room and hurl you their heart. *All Set* is more of the same, but *Modern* slips badly. This is Buzzcocks as plastic new wave, with electronic beeps and synth drums sprinkled around the guitar power. There are still great hooks (witness "Thunder of Hearts"), but *Modern* might as well have been named *1983.* In 2003, iconic American indie rock label Merge Records—whose flagship band, Superchunk, clearly committed every Buzzcocks song to memory—released *Buzzcocks.* Astoundingly, it's the finest album of their postreunion career. Twenty-five years after throwing their first spitball at an object of desire, Shelley and Diggle retain their wit, their obsession, the heart, their riffs, and their roar, every boner a perfect hook.   —J.G.

The Byrds

★★★★★ Mr. Tambourine Man (Columbia, 1965)
★★★★½ Turn! Turn! Turn! (Columbia, 1965)
★★★★½ Fifth Dimension (Columbia, 1967)
★★★½ Younger Than Yesterday (Columbia, 1967)
★★★★½ The Byrds Greatest Hits (Columbia, 1968)

★★★★★	The Notorious Byrd Brothers (Columbia, 1968)
★★★★★	Sweetheart of the Rodeo (Columbia, 1968)
★★★	Dr. Byrds & Mr. Hyde (Columbia, 1969)
★★★½	The Ballad of Easy Rider (Columbia, 1969)
★★	Live at the Fillmore West February 1969 (Columbia, 1970)
★★	Untitled (Columbia, 1970)
★★	Byrdmaniax (Columbia, 1971)
★★	Farther Along (Columbia, 1972)
★★	The Byrds (Asylum, 1973)
★★★★	Preflyte (Columbia, 1973)
★★★★	In the Beginning (Rhino, 1988)
★★★½	Never Before (Murray Hill, 1989)
★★★★	The Byrds [Box Set] (Columbia/Legacy, 1990)
★★★★★	Greatest Hits (Columbia/Legacy, 1999)
★★★★	The Complete Flyte (Sundazed, 2000)

The Byrds were one of the great '60s bands, evolving from sure-footed pop craftsmen to astral travelers with their own innovative style of guitar glimmer. Roger McGuinn was a folkie who'd gotten turned on to rock & roll when he saw the Beatles in *A Hard Day's Night,* and his chiming 12-string Rickenbacker sound became a permanent part of rock's musical language from the opening notes of "Mr. Tambourine Man." The Byrds' first big hits were covers, so they've been consistently underrated as a songwriting band, but Gene Clark, who mostly just stood around and banged a tambourine onstage, wrote some of the best tunes of the '60s. McGuinn, Clark, the pre-Stills, pre-Nash folkie David Crosby, bluegrass-bred bassist Chris Hillman, and pouty-lipped drummer Michael Clarke were the very definition of folk-rock exuberance, five mod California boys high on guitar power.

Mr. Tambourine Man is one of rock's greatest debut albums, with the frail, kindly, and basically anonymous voices weaving together in folkish harmonies to float in the sound, submerging the lyrics in a rush of pure electric energy. The attention getters were the Bob Dylan covers (particularly the title hit and an ace "Spanish Harlem Incident"), but actually, the most vital songs on the album are the Gene Clark originals such as "Here Without You," "I Knew I'd Want You," and "I'll Feel a Whole Lot Better." Like all the early Byrds albums, *Mr. Tambourine Man* benefits from the superb Columbia/Legacy reissue series, which presents definitive versions of each album with outtakes and singles; the prize on *Mr. Tambourine Man* is "She Has a Way."

Turn! Turn! Turn! was a hasty followup, but the band had plenty of material on hand, going back to the well for more Clark songs: the almost Lou Reed–like ramble "Set You Free This Time," the dev-

astated drone "If You're Gone," the morosely up-tempo "The World Turns All Around Her." As a sign of things to come, the band also did the country standard "Satisfied Mind," and, for some reason, "O Susanna." The Legacy reissue adds the essential B side "She Don't Care About Time."

Fifth Dimension is the Byrds' most underrated album. Clark was gone by this point, but the band made up for the holes in the songwriting by turning up the guitars. It's an album of bold, expansive machine-head psychedelia, mixing ancient Celtic folk standards ("Wild Mountain Thyme," "John Riley") with the space-age electric charge of "I See You" and "2-4-2 Fox Trot (The Lear Jet Song)." The groundbreaking hit "Eight Miles High" is the band's highest of highs, blending Coltrane-influenced 12-string squiggles with eerie harmonies for a truly hypnotic sound. And the lyrics are about airplane travel. Right! There's filler (a weak "Hey Joe," the inept R&B instrumental "Captain Soul"), but David Crosby contributes the catchily mush-headed "What's Happening?!?!" *Younger Than Yesterday* is a smoother version, with Chris Hillman bringing a straightforward country influence to "Time Between" and "Have You Seen Her Face." Unfortunately, the songs trail off halfway through, with Crosby's "Mind Gardens" a real monstrosity.

The Notorious Byrd Brothers was Roger McGuinn's attempt to make his own *Pet Sounds* or *Sgt. Pepper;* he missed, but with producer Gary Usher, he came up with a unique and powerful elegy for '60s idealism, overlooked at the time yet recognized as a classic now. It's ethereal, mournful, beautiful, hardly ever rocking, with a touching sadness in spaced-out melodies such as "Natural Harmony" and "Dolphin's Smile." "Goin' Back" is a great old Goffin-King ballad, originally a hit for Dusty Springfield, here remodeled into a farewell to the Summer of Love; "Draft Morning" is a Vietnam song that ends with McGuinn playing "Taps" on guitar. It's a very comforting album to put on when you're hungover.

For *Sweetheart of the Rodeo,* the Byrds became a totally different band, exploring the new frontier of country rock. New member Gram Parsons was the catalyst, as the band cut back on the electricity to embrace a rootsy sound of fiddle, banjo, and pedal steel twang, doing reverent covers of Merle Haggard and Louvin Brothers songs. *Sweetheart* peaks with a great version of Dylan's scary "Nothing Was Delivered," as well as the Parsons ballads "Hickory Wind" and "One Hundred Years from Now." Unfortunately, much of Parsons' singing was erased because of legal conflicts; the 1997 reissue restores the complete Parsons vocals for a definitive edition of one of '60s rock's most influential albums.

Sweetheart was the last of the Byrds classics. Parsons and Hillman left to form the Flying Burrito Brothers, who brought the country moves of *Sweetheart* to fruition with the 1969 masterpiece *The Gilded Palace of Sin*. Meanwhile, McGuinn assembled a new band and started making de facto solo records under the Byrds name. *Dr. Byrds* has "Drug Store Truck Driving Man," a showcase for guitar picker Clarence White. *Easy Rider*, the best of the later Byrds albums, has the oddly funky long-hair Jesus-freak anthem "Jesus Is Just All Right" and a beautiful reading of Woody Guthrie's "Deportee." The last gasps: the largely live double album *Untitled*, the studio-slick *Byrdmaniax*, the tired *Farther Along*, the failed reunion *Byrds*. *Preflyte* was a collection of pre–*Mr. Tambourine Man* acoustic sessions, with top-notch originals such as "Boston" and "The Airport Song." *In the Beginning* has largely different versions of this material; the complete collection, a must for fans, is Sundazed's *The Complete Flyte*. *Never Before* and the box set *Byrds* introduced many rarities, most now best heard on the reissued original albums. *Greatest Hits* downplays the band's weirdness, with too many Dylan covers, but still makes an excellent introduction, especially the expanded 1999 edition with the key album tracks "Have You Seen Her Face" and "Set You Free This Time." —R.S.

Cabaret Voltaire

Part of the problem with pioneering electronic acts is that the music they produce is often more influential than it is listenable. Take Cabaret Voltaire as an example. This duo was among the first rock acts to tie electronic dissonance to trancelike rhythms, and also to lead the way in the use of "found sound"—that is, taped snippets of TV preachers or police announcements that would later be incorporated as ironic commentary into the group's recordings. In fact, most of what has since been done to death by avant-garde dance-music groups like Revolting Cocks or Front 242 was done first by Cabaret Voltaire.

So why are so many of Cabaret Voltaire's albums so excruciatingly dull? Part of the problem is that the Cabs were frequently more interested in musical method than compositional content, meaning that the "how" of their music frequently outweighed the "why." Thus, most of the group's early output, from the primitive singles and live tracks collected on *The Living Legends . . .* to the densely layered textures of *3 Crépuscule Tracks*, is gratingly monotonous; *Three Mantras* is interesting for its Eastern influences and *Voice of America* has a few intriguing soundbites, but that's about as far as it goes. Things begin to change, though, with *Red Mecca*, on which the interplay between the synths and the percussion lends an exotic flavor to the music on "A Touch of Evil" and its ilk. There are also some interesting touches on *2 x 45*, particularly the sparring saxophones on "Protection" and the subtle Middle Eastern groove behind "Get Out of My Face." Still, it isn't until *Micro-Phonies* that Cabaret Voltaire is able to convert its interest in static structures into anything resembling conventional dance music. Although the melodic interest remains fairly limited, there's a surprising amount of pop appeal in the way Stephen Mallinder's vocals play off Richard H. Kirk's churning electronics on "Do Right" and the slow-churning "Spies in the Wires." Both *Drinking Gasoline* and *The Covenant, the Sword and the Arm of the Lord* further the advances made by *Micro-Phonies*, but it isn't until the hard, mechanical pulse of *Code* that Cabaret Voltaire finds the ideal balance between accessibility and menace; between the hard-edged funk of "Sex, Money, Freaks" and the clanking pulse powering "Here to Go," this is perhaps the duo's most exhilarating work. Strangely, from there the Cabs coast into predictability with the house-influenced *Groovy, Laidback and Nasty,* which sounds almost pop-friendly on tunes like the buoyant "Keep On (I Got This Feeling)." But *Body and Soul* returns the group to the brittle minimalism of yore, while the nastier moments of *Colours* manage to turn the beat-driven colorism of acid house into the musical equivalent of a bad trip.   —J.D.C.

The Cadillacs

★★★   The Cadillacs Meet the Orioles (Collectables, 1991)

★★★½   For Collectors Only (Collectables, 1992)

The Cadillacs were a golden-age-of-doo-wop group who made a far greater impact than might be presumed from the group's lone national hit, "Speedo," a rocking ode to the title character—spirited lead singer Earl "Speedo" Carroll—and his skill with the ladies. Of all the vocalists who wore Cadillacs accoutrement through the years (and there were some good ones, notably Earl Wade, who had been with the Crystals and Opals; and Jim Bailey, who fronted an Earl Carroll–less configuration of the group and sang a sweet lead on the exuberant "My Girlfriend," a doo-wop standard), Carroll's personable singing always defined the group. As a balladeer Carroll stood out in a doo-wop field rife with formidable romantic crooners such as the Harptones' Willie Winfield, the Flamingos' Nate Nelson, the Moonglows' Harvey Fuqua, and the Orioles' Sonny Til; in fact, Carroll is front and center on one of doo-wop's legendary ballads, the ethereal "Gloria," the prototype of all New York–style slow grinders. Fueled by Carroll's distinctive vocal presence, the Cadillacs cut several fine love songs— "Zoom," "You Are," the lush "Tell Me Today," the eerie "Wishing Well," among others—that ceded nothing to any other group in the way of heart and soul, as the lead singer demonstrated his impeccable sense of nuance and control, caressing the high notes just so at the right moment, coming back soft and tender in other passages. But as group harmony gave way to new musical trends in the late '50s–early '60s, so did the Cadillacs finally call it a day.

Collectables' three-CD *For Collectors Only* anthology tells the Cadillacs' story pretty much in its entirety, from the group's first recordings for the Josie label ("Wishing Well," "I Wonder Why") to Carroll's final masterpiece, 1960's "Tell Me Today," with of course the original versions of "Speedo," "Gloria," and the landmarks mentioned above, as well as a bopping rendition of "Rudolph the Red-Nosed Reindeer" for all the Yuletide music buffs. As with too many Collectables releases, though, the liner notes offer a thumbnail group history but give short shrift to dates, and no shrift at all to session information of any kind. The closest thing to a hits compilation still in print is another Collectables title, *The Cadillacs Meet the Orioles*, which features six Cadillacs sides ("Gloria" and "Speedo" among them, of course) and six Orioles sides (including "Crying In the Chapel").   —D.M.

Café Tacuba

★★★   Café Tacuba (WEA, 1992)

★★★★   Re (WEA, 1994)

★★★   Avalancha de Exitos (WEA, 1996)

★★★★   Reves/Yosoy (Warner Bros., 1999)

★★★★   Tiempo Transcurrido: The Best of Café Tacvba (WEA, 2001)

★★★   Vale Callampa (MCA, 2002)

★★★★½   Cuatro Caminos (MCA, 2003)

This Mexico City quartet isn't just one of the more daring and creative bands of the rock en español movement, it is one of the more daring and creative bands to come out of any country during the alternative-rock boom of the 1990s. Café Tacuba's idiosyncratic collision of modern pop styles (from rock to hip-hop and electronica) with Latin folk traditions (including mariachi, *ranchera, tejano, banda,* and samba) is unlike anything in rock's rich, colorful history. Despite Café Tacuba's eclecticism and innovative use of instrumental textures, this music doesn't come off as schizophrenic. The group's distinctive sound is funneled through the grainy vocals of dynamic frontman Rubén Albarrán, who sings with a bratty punk sneer at one moment and a gentle coo the next.

After forming in the late 1980s, Café Tacuba released its self-titled debut on WEA Latina. On that album, the band did what many Mexican rock acts of the time were doing: mixed elements of British and U.S. rock, new wave, ska, funk, and hip-hop with Latin styles and lyrics sung in Spanish. But Café Tacuba's interpretations of Anglo pop didn't sound as dated and copycatted as the music of fellow Mexican rockers such as Maná or Caifanes. *Re* was an ambitious leap forward for Café Tacuba. The band continued experimenting with musical textures inspired by rock pioneers such as the Beatles, PiL, the Pixies, and even Ministry. The sensational *Re* set the tone for the band's eclectic stretches on subsequent albums. *Avalancha de Exitos* is a transitional collection that pays cockeyed tribute to an array of Latin artists with inventive interpretations of some unlikely hits. Café Tacuba puts cello and a sizzling techno foundation to the Mexican rock band Botellita de Jerez's "Alármala de Tos," a bright violin to Dominican merengue superstar Juan Luis Guerra's "Ojalá Que Llueva Café," and a loopy indie-rock feel to "Cómo Te Extraño Mi Amor" by Mexican pop crooner Leo Dan.

As inventive as Café Tacuba had already proved to

be, no one could have predicted the ambitious sound of the double-disc *Reves/Yosoy*, a gorgeous fusion of styles that includes one disc of song-based pop and rock and another of instrumental music. Collaborating with New York contemporary-classical ensemble the Kronos Quartet, the *Reves* disc flows from minimalist soundscapes that conjure the film scores of Ennio Morricone to clattering electronica and musique concrète.

When Café Tacuba switched from WEA to MCA, the band not only got better North American distribution but also delivered its most focused album to date. That's not to say *Cuatro Caminos* isn't equally as eclectic as anything the band had done before. Working with producers Dave Fridmann (Flaming Lips) and Andrew Weiss (Ween), as well as longtime cohorts Gustavo Santaolalla and Anibal Kerpel, *Caminos* careens from the brutish postrock swagger of "Eo" and "Recuerdo Prestado" to the hypnotic melodicism of "Eres" and the Beatles/Zeppelin–style Middle Eastern touches in "Hoy Es." An absolute beauty.

The four-song *Vale Callampa* is an odd but delightful tribute to the Chilean band Los Tres and includes the Brian Wilson–inspired harmonies of "Olor a Gas." *Tiempo Transcurrido: The Best of Café Tacuba* is the band's contract-ending compilation for WEA, collecting the Latin American hits from its first four albums; it's an excellent place to begin a journey into the music of this outstanding band. —M.K.

Cake

★★★½	Motorcade of Generosity	(Volcano, 1994)
★★★½	Fashion Nugget	(Volcano, 1996)
★★½	Prolonging the Magic	(Volcano, 1998)
★★	Comfort Eagle	(Columbia, 2001)

Whenever the music industry is at a loss for trends, novelty artists prosper. And so, the mid-'90s were predictably ripe with one-off jokes—still smarting from the emotional hangover of grunge, radio listeners wouldn't look a gag gift in the mouth. But despite Cake's quirky surface—singer John McCrea's deadpan delivery and Vince Di Fiore's oddball mariachi trumpet initially sounded like a put-on—the members of Cake weren't the one-dimensional wise guys their humorous singles suggested. As the surface of their songs became familiar, the humor faded to reveal a sense of pathos so strong, it was a wonder it remained concealed for so long.

That humorous sheen enabled Cake to discuss matters Modern Rock often ignored. *Motorcade*'s "Rock 'n' Roll Lifestyle," for instance, mocked trust-fund scenester rebels, surreptitiously examining class relations right there on the radio for all to hear. The

album's lyrics also twisted clichés, as with "You think she's an open book/But you don't know which page to turn to." *Fashion Nugget* is better still, distinguished by a broad taste in covers: In addition to a moving cover of "I Will Survive," Cake also exhumes Willie Nelson's "Sad Songs and Waltzes" and anticipates the Cuban-music revival with the Havana dance-band standard "Perhaps, Perhaps, Perhaps."

The title of *Prolonging* was a good joke but a bad lie. The magic was gone, leaving competence in its wake. Offering fewer quirks, the newer songs seem emotionally overripe or intellectually strained. Yet Cake proved honorable even in its decline. The band could have dragged on forever as a novelty act. After all, Weird Al Yankovic hasn't told a half-decent joke since before Lil' Bow Wow was born, and it may take total nuclear annihilation, or at least an act of Congress, to stop him. —K.H.

J.J. Cale

★★★★	Naturally	(Mercury, 1971; PolyGram, 1990)
★★★★	Really	(Shelter, 1972; PolyGram, 1990)
★★★	Okie	(Mercury, 1974; PolyGram, 1990)
★★★	Troubadour	(Shelter, 1976; PolyGram, 1990)
★★★★½	5	(Shelter, 1979; PolyGram, 1990)
★★★	Grasshopper	(Mercury, 1982; PolyGram, 1990)
★★★	Special Edition	(Mercury, 1984; PolyGram, 1990)
★★★★	Travel Log	(Silvertone, 1990)
★★★	Number 10	(Silvertone, 1992)
★★★	Closer to You	(Virgin, 1994)
★★★	Guitar Man	(Virgin, 1996)
★★★★	Anyway the Wind Blows: The Anthology	(Mercury, 1997)
★★★★	The Very Best of J.J. Cale	(1998, Mercury)
★★★	Live	(Narada, 2001)
★★★	In Session	(Classic, 2003)
★★★★	To Tulsa and Back	(Sanctuary, 2004)

In addition to Eric Clapton's slightly stodgy hit versions of "After Midnight" and "Cocaine," J.J. Cale has been covered by everyone from Lynyrd Skynyrd and Bobby "Blue" Bland to Spiritualized, a disparate array of acts encompassing British blues, Southern boogie, sweet soul, and space rock, reflecting the inherent adaptability of Cale's great songs. And although his star shines brightest as a songwriter, Cale's own studio work was often superior to the more popular cover versions of his songs. His mellow declaration "Call Me the Breeze" (covered by Skynyrd and Johnny Cash) is perhaps best described as a shuffle in loose shoes, exemplifying a narcotized, countrified state of being that sounds utterly effortless, Cale's trademark. Born

Jean-Jacques Cale (no relation to Velvet Underground's John Cale) on December 5, 1938, in Oklahoma City, J.J. soon moved to Tulsa, where he began playing in clubs in the 1950s with his own band, Johnny Cale & the Valentines.

Cale's early career included a three-year mid-'60s residence in Los Angeles, which included a brief stint playing with Delaney and Bonnie and a membership in California psychedelic band the Leathercoated Minds, whose album, *A Trip Down the Sunset Strip,* appeared in 1967. Cale returned to Tulsa in 1967. Clapton got hold of a Cale demo and turned "After Midnight" into a smash hit in 1970. With that boost, Cale made his debut, *Naturally* (an album whose cover depicts a grinning, top-hat-toting raccoon), inaugurating a career-spanning string of fine, stylistically similar albums. An especially good set of Tulsa-fied roots rock, 1979's 5 features the overdue-for-a-vacation groover "Let's Go to Tahiti" and "Mona," a gorgeous tune with great work from bassist Carl Radle (who also played on Clapton's *Layla* sessions). On songs like 1983's "Losers" (about the "exclusive club that we're in"), Cale's lyrics had something of the wry bonhomie of Warren Zevon.

In a somewhat peculiar turn in 1990, Cale landed with British label Silvertone, then home to Manchester's baggy champs the Stone Roses, and released *Travel Log,* a gem with lock-tight grooves courtesy of bassist Tim Drummond and drummer Jim Keltner. Cale underwent a subsequent unexpected renaissance when Widespread Panic began playing his songs, and if bemused by the jam band's noodlesome onanism, he appreciated the new fans.

To Tulsa And Back, from 2004, was Cale's first set of new songs in eight years. It was originally conceived as a collaboration with his original producer Audie Ashworth, but when Ashworth passed away, Cale made an album that retained the intended flavor: typically languid, typically excellent.   —P.R.

John Cale

- ★★★½   Vintage Violence (1970; Columbia/Legacy, 2001)
- ★★★★½   Paris 1919 (Reprise, 1973)
- ★★★★½   The Island Years (1974–77; Island/Chronicles, 1996)
- ★★★½   Artificial Intelligence (Beggars Banquet, 1985)
- ★★★½   Seducing Down the Door (1970–90; Rhino, 1994)
- ★★★   Fragments of a Rainy Season (Hannibal, 1992)
- ★★★½   Eat/Kiss: Music for the Films of Andy Warhol (Hannibal, 1997)
- ★★   Day of Niagara (Table of the Elements, 2000)

- ★★★   Sun Blindness Music (Table of the Elements, 2000)
- ★★★   Dream Interpretation (Table of the Elements, 2002)
- ★★★½   Stainless Gamelan (Table of the Elements, 2002)
- ★★★   Hobo Sapiens (EMI, 2004)

John Cale/Brian Eno
- ★★★★   Wrong Way Up (Warner Bros., 1990)

John Cale/Lou Reed
- ★★★½   Songs for Drella (Sire, 1990)

With his classical training, devotion to the '60s avant-garde, and arty slumming in the Velvet Underground behind him, John Cale could put on imposing airs for an early-'70s fringe rocker. He soon made his mark as a producer, working with Nico, the Stooges, Patti Smith, and the Modern Lovers. He collaborated with minimalist Terry Riley. He recorded his own hip neo-classical music as *The Academy in Peril* and knocked off two albums of enigmatic songs, *Vintage Violence* and the often beautiful *Paris 1919.* He played everything from bass to harpsichord to viola and had a rare knack for building songs that seemed equally balanced around piano and guitar.

In 1974, he returned to England and hooked up with Brian Eno, performing a terroristic rendition of "Heartbreak Hotel" on the Island Records showcase *June 1, 1974.* He stuck with Eno and Island for three albums, which are his main claim to being a godfather of punk rock: the paranoid "Fear Is a Man's Best Friend," the extended guitar antics of "Gun," the nasty revelry of "Dirtyass Rock 'n' Roll," the fury of "Guts," and the unbridled hysteria of "Leaving It Up to You"—the last shocking enough for Island first to suppress the song, then to feature it on the *Guts* compilation. Those songs were last seen on *The Island Years,* a comprehensive two-CD set, but the period also fills up a quarter of Rhino's two-CD *Seducing Down the Door.*

Cale's '80s work wanders around a bit. The second CD of *Seducing* covers Cale's work up to 1990; out-of-print albums offer mostly slivers of past ideas, such as the exotic chant of "Chinese Envoy" and the live butchering of "Waiting for the Man." *Artificial Intelligence* is perhaps the best of the '80s albums, another set of oblique songs with arresting rhythm figures, like "Dying on the Vine" and "Satellite Walk."

And in the '90s, Cale wanders even more, working on soundtracks, dance music, tributes, collaborations (including a brief Velvet Underground reunion), and all sorts of odds and ends. The duet albums with Brian Eno *(Wrong Way Up)* and Lou Reed *(Songs for Drella)* are perhaps more reflective of Cale's partners but rank among his better work. In *Fragments of a Rainy Season*, Cale reprises his songbook, performing solo, most impressively on piano. *Eat/Kiss* is quasi–film music that Cale wrote for revivals of two Warhol films; the set is characteristically eclectic and includes one of Cale's spoken pieces performed in the tradition of "The Gift."

Cale's most interesting recordings are his least recent: a set of mid-'60s experiments that are mostly beatless, minimalist avant-garde noise. For instance, *Day of Niagara,* with La Monte Young, was built around an amplified viola drone that anticipated the Velvet Underground's sound, if none of the music; in retrospect, the album seems like an even less funky preview of Lou Reed's famous *Metal Machine Music.* The *Inside the Dream Syndicate* discs have far greater musical variety; *Stainless Gamelan* is rather enjoyable, starting with a 10-minute piece of percussive Cembalet, then devoting almost 30 minutes to a surrealist soundscape allegedly concerned with Mozart and Joseph Conrad, and spending eight minutes on a cha-cha with a soprano sax improvisation that sounds like something you might imagine Evan Parker and Han Bennink were doing when they were teenagers. In the end, Cale's attraction to the avant-garde was the same as his attraction to punk—he's made a career of subversion, and all that classical training has served him well.   —T.H.

Cameo

★★★	Cardiac Arrest (1977; Mercury, 1994)
★★½	Ugly Ego (1978; Universal, 2003)
★★½	We All Know Who We Are (1978; Mercury, 1998)
★★★	Cameosis (1980; Mercury, 1993)
★★★	Knights of the Sound Table (1981; Mercury, 1993)
★★★	She's Strange (1984; PolyGram, 1990)
★★★½	Single Life (1985; PolyGram, 1990)
★★★★½	Word Up! (1986; PolyGram, 1990)
★★★	Machismo (1988; PolyGram, 1990)
★★★	Real Men . . . Wear Black (Polydor, 1990)
★★★	Emotional Violence (Reprise, 1992)
★★★★	The Best of Cameo (Mercury, 1993)
★★★	The Best of Cameo, Vol. 2 (Mercury, 1996)
★★	Nasty (Intersound, 1996)
★★	Best of Cameo (PSM, 1997)
★★★	Ballads Collection (Mercury, 1998)
★★★	Greatest Hits (Mercury, 1998)
★★★½	12" Collection and More (Mercury, 1999)
★★	Sexy Sweet Thing (Universal/Private Eye, 2000)
★★½	The Millennium Collection (Mercury, 2001)
★★★★	Cameo Anthology (Mercury, 2002)

Cameo has been funking around since the mid-'70s, somehow stumbling into the sort of career in which hits anthologies have begun to outnumber studio albums. Starting out as 10-piece-plus, P-Funk-styled R&B band and ending up, many albums later, as a three-piece, techno-intense brain trust, Cameo parallels the evolution of R&B from show-oriented bands to studio-based recording projects.

Many of the band's early titles are out of print, and it's just as well: Only a hard-core funk fiend would find much interesting in the derivative grooves fueling *Secret Omen* (1979) or *Alligator Woman* (1982).

She's Strange is another story entirely. Although most of the album is given over to run-of-the-mill funk tunes, "Talkin' Out the Side of Your Neck" is brash, brassy, and angrily politicized (anti-Reagan), while "She's Strange" augments its groove with dreamy, atmospheric synths and vocals that walk the line between rap and soul. With its title tune, *Single Life* expands impressively on the synth-and-rhythm combination "She's Strange" introduced, building the verse around a tension-building six-note bass riff and grounding the chorus with a whistling synth hook swiped from Ennio Morricone's *The Good, the Bad and the Ugly.* From there, it's just a simple step to *Word Up!* and "Word Up!," which uses a strikingly similar rhythmic strategy—another bass-driven verse, the same Morricone lift—but ups the impact by tying it to a stronger melodic idea. More important, *Word Up!* doesn't come off as an album's worth of B sides surrounding one good single; between the rap-flavored "She's Mine" and the jazzy "Back and Forth," the album is irresistible from beginning to end.

That's hardly the case with *Machismo*, which seems too concerned with production technique to deliver much in the way of melodic interest. *Real Men . . . Wear Black* and *Emotional Violence* may find the band getting back to basics, but there isn't enough melodic interest to make its beefed-up grooves worth celebrating. After that, any album not involving a reissue isn't worth the bother.

So, on to the various hits compilations. Details matter; *The Best of Cameo* is worth owning, *Best of Cameo* is not. With two discs affording genuine career breadth, *Cameo Anthology* is by far the best value for money. The discs, seemingly predicated on the assumption that any given fan really wants only two of the band's hits, shuffle which two you're likely to get.   —J.D.C.

Camper Van Beethoven

★★★	Telephone Free Landslide Victory (1985; spinART, 2004)
★★★★	II & III (1986; spinART, 2004)
★★★½	Camper Van Beethoven (1986; spinART, 2004)

★★★ Vampire Can Mating Oven (EP) (Pitch a Tent/Rough Trade, 1987)
★★★★½ Our Beloved Revolutionary Sweetheart (Virgin, 1988)
★★★★ Key Lime Pie (Virgin, 1989)
★★★ Camper Vantiquities (IRS, 1993)
★★★★ Camper Van Beethoven Are Dead: Long Live Camper Van Beethoven (Pitch a Tent, 2000)
★★★½ Cigarettes & Carrot Juice (spinART, 2002)
★★½ Tusk (Pitch-a-Tent, 2002)

Fond of unexpected juxtapositions, arcane musical styles, and lyrical non sequiturs, Camper Van Beethoven stands as proof that a band can get away with almost anything provided it has a sense of humor and a way with melody. Admittedly, the Campers' initial success had more to do with the former than the latter, thanks to the wacky "Take the Skinheads Bowling," from *Telephone Free Landslide Victory*. But what kept the group from succumbing to the sort of novelty-act status accorded the Dead Milkmen or Mojo Nixon was its ability to surround its punch lines with artful, intriguing numbers like "Vladivostock" and "Balalaika Gap."

The group's second album, *II & III*, sharpened the music's focus by tightly integrating the various influences, leading to a sound one song aptly describes as "ZZ Top Goes to Egypt." Again, there's plenty of wit in the writing, as in the suburban satire of "(Don't You Go to) Goleta," but the Campers' obvious affection for country and folk idioms kept things from getting too glib. That didn't help much with *Camper Van Beethoven*, however, a more audacious outing that added multi-instrumentalist Eugene Chadbourne to the lineup and augmented relatively conventional tunes like "The History of Utah" with experimental efforts like "Stairway to Heavan (sic)." That combination, unfortunately, isn't quite as interesting as it sounds. (Camper Van Beethoven, or members thereof, collaborated with Chadbourne on two albums for Fundamental records, *Camper Van Chadbourne* and the live *Eugene Van Beethoven's 69th Sin Funny*. Both alternate between arty deconstructions of country music and seemingly directionless free improvisation.)

After an EP's worth of odds and ends (*Vampire Can Mating Oven*, which was later reissued with additional tracks as *Camper Vantiquities*), CVB moved to the majors, signing with Virgin. The box set *Cigarettes and Carrot Juice* compiles all its recordings to this point. The band's introduction to the mainstream was *Our Beloved Revolutionary Sweetheart*, easily its best effort. Because the songs make the most of the band's melodic instincts while somehow finding room for its stylistic quirks, *Sweetheart* is an ideal showcase for

the Campers' quirky charms. *Key Lime Pie* falls short of that mark, but not by much; although the album's mood is much darker, there's still plenty of sparkle to the likes of "When I Win the Lottery" and "All Her Favorite Fruit." Sadly, the band broke up soon after; singer David Lowery pursued a career with Cracker, while guitarist Greg Lisher, bassist Victor Krummenacher, and drummer Chris Pedersen continued with their side project, the Monks of Doom.

In 1999, Lowery and the others reunited to assemble *Camper Van Beethoven Are Dead: Long Live Camper Van Beethoven*, a heavy reworking of old and unreleased material that, while not quite amounting to new music, amounted to more than just a dip in the vaults. They also released *Tusk*, a cover of the Fleetwood Mac album the group recorded "as a joke" between sessions for *Revolutionary Sweetheart* and *Key Lime Pie*. Sadly, they forgot to dub in the laugh track. —J.D.C.

Cam'ron

★★ Confessions of Fire (Epic, 1998)
★★ S.D.E. (Epic, 2000)
★★★ Come Home With Me (Roc-a-Fella, 2002)
★★ Diplomatic Immunity (Roc-a-Fella, 2003)

Cam'ron has recently found the platinum-level success he's long coveted, but he's no overnight sensation. The Harlem native started rapping with neighborhood cronies Mase (who would later find fame with P. Diddy and the Bad Boy family) and Big L (the legendary late MC of the Diggin' in the Crates Crew). After a brief association with Bad Boy, Cam dropped his first album in 1998, *Confessions of Fire*. His debut and its followup, 2000's *S.D.E.* (which stands for sports, drugs, and entertainment and gives you an idea of Cam's priorities), contain several rap radio hits, such as "Horse & Carriage" and "What Means the World to You," as well as some workmanlike uptown crime rap, but his popularity remained regional, a New York radio celebrity.

After a two-year break due to label disputes, Cam'ron found himself under the patronage of fellow Harlem rap entrepreneur Dame Dash and his Roc-A-Fella records imprint. *Come Home With Me* featured the hits "Oh Boy" and "Hey Ma." Cam's flow evolved into a brutally simple conversational style, eschewing lyricism for easily understood boasts and threats. While he may not be the most thought-provoking MC in the world, Cam's style has a charm all its own due mostly to his unapologetically controversial sense of humor. The production on *Come Home With Me* is exceptional, with beats provided by Roc-A-Fella in-house beatmakers Just Blaze and Kanye West. That disc was quickly followed by the solid if overlong *Diplomatic Immunity*, a group album by Cam'ron and his uptown crew, the Diplomats. —C.R.

Can

★★★★	Monster Movie (UA, 1969)
★★★½	Soundtracks (UA, 1970)
★★★★★	Tago Mago (UA, 1971)
★★★★	Ege Bamyasi (UA, 1972)
★★★½	Future Days (UA, 1973)
★★★	Soon Over Babaluma (UA, 1974)
★★★	Landed (Virgin, 1975)
★★★	Unlimited Edition (Caroline, 1976)
★★	Flow Motion (Virgin, 1976)
★★	Saw Delight (Virgin, 1977)
★	Out of Reach (Peters International, 1978)
★★★★½	Cannibalism (UA, 1978)
★★★½	Can (Laser, 1979)
★★★★	Delay 1968 (Spoon, 1981)
★½	Rite Time (Mercury, 1989)
★★★½	Cannibalism 2 (Spoon, 1992)
★★★½	The Can-Anthology 25 Years (Spoon, 1994)
★★	Cannibalism 3 (Spoon, 1994)
★★★	Sacrilege (Mute, 1997)
★★½	Can Box (Spoon/Mute, 1999)

When Can (then known as the Can) debuted with *Monster Movie*, they seemed like a particularly strange psychedelic band: four hard-jamming Germans (with backgrounds in avant-garde classical music and jazz), fronted by a sandpaper-voiced black American, Malcolm Mooney. Nobody knew yet that they'd become the godfathers of the German experimental rock movement. Can didn't write songs in the usual sense; instead, they'd improvise for hours on end, rooted by drummer Jaki Liebezeit's crisp, inventive patterns, and then bassist Holger Czukay would edit the results down to their good parts. Michael Karoli's wailing, atonal guitar parts are wilder than almost any other psych band dared at the time, but their specialty is hitting a groove and staying there, as on the 20-minute lust letter, "Yoo Doo Right."

Delay 1968, recorded around the same time, is so good it's hard to believe it stayed in the, er, can for another 13 years. It's Can's most raucous and insistent record, with Karoli riffing harder than he ever would again, and Mooney's hoarse, off-key cries suiting its avant-garage vibe. (Radiohead has been known to cover "Thief" in concert.)

Mooney left in 1970, partway through a series of movie-music sessions, and was promptly replaced by Damo Suzuki, an itinerant freak from Japan who integrated his voice into the band's improvisations more than Mooney had. Most of *Soundtracks* sounds like the transitional album it is—gentle psych in the vein of some of the things Pink Floyd was doing around the same time—but the band shines on the extended one-chord freakout "Mother Sky," and Mooney gets in a quiet, jazzy one, "She Brings the Rain."

Tago Mago is Can's masterpiece, a double album with seven long, trippy pieces that were years ahead of their time. The vicious, stealthy crack of "Mushroom" became a standard at post-punk-era clubs; "Aumgn," an echo-crazed bad-trip showcase for Karoli and keyboardist Irmin Schmidt, sounded right at home in ambient chill-out rooms two decades later. And "Halleluhwah" is almost 20 minutes of a rib-crushing Liebezeit beat, with Suzuki and the rest of the band percolating along at full strength. A terser, somewhat calmer variation on the sound and style of *Tago Mago*, *Ege Bamyasi* (named after a can of okra) consolidated Can's fan following with the singalong "Spoon," which became a hit in Germany. Elsewhere, the amorphous experimental piece "Soup" shows off Czukay's chops as an editor, and Suzuki delivers terrifying pronouncements that probably made sense to him ("You are losing your vitamin C!"). *Future Days* sets its sights a little lower. Suzuki mostly sticks to the background, aside from a peculiar attempt at a pop song ("Moonshake"); the rest of the album is three long, dreamy pieces that suggest Can had been listening to electric-era Miles Davis (and are the closest they ever got to their "krautrock" scenemates Neu! and Kraftwerk).

Suzuki departed before *Soon Over Babaluma*, and Can found itself without a singer for the first time—from then on, Karoli handled most of their relatively rare vocals. The album is mellow and almost timid in places; Karoli had started playing violin as well as guitar, and Liebezeit mostly holds himself back to tippy-tapping beats. The one great exception is "Chain Reaction," whose swift, slamming pulse anticipates techno records of 20 years later. *Landed* starts strongly with the proto–new wave "Full Moon on the Highway," maybe the most conventional pop song Can ever recorded (it's still pretty weird), and gradually loosens up until "Unfinished" disintegrates into blurs of industrial noise.

Unlimited Edition—an expanded version of a limited-edition record from a couple of years earlier—compiles weird little sketches and outtakes from 1968 to 1975, including a handful of vocals by Suzuki and Mooney (the latter's "Connection" is a brief, punchy rocker), and the first five installments in the band's intermittent "Ethnological Forgery Series." Its centerpiece is the sprawling "Cutaway," an 18-minute cross-section of instrumental doodles that never quite gets off the ground.

Flow Motion spawned an actual hit single in the U.K., "I Want More," a stab at disco graced with a fabulous Karoli tremolo riff. Otherwise, though, the album is something of a mess: It sounds as if they wanted both to make a slick, commercial record (partly inspired by reggae) and to sabotage the attempt with woozy atonality. Czukay stopped playing bass after *Flow Motion,* and drifted out of the band (although he continued to edit their records); he was replaced by bassist Rosko Gee and percussionist Reebop Kwaku Baah from Traffic. *Saw Delight* has a few more curious disco experiments, including a long instrumental jam called "Animal Waves" on which Czukay plays a shortwave receiver, but you can smell the desperation for crossover success, and it doesn't suit them.

The leaden, meandering *Out of Reach* is dismissed by the band as a ghastly mistake, and they're right. Remarkably, they pulled it together one last time for the second half of *Can* (sometimes known as *Inner Space*), featuring the tense, jagged postdisco groove "Aspectacle" and a hilarious cover of Jacques Offenbach's kick-line classic "Can Can." Johnny Rotten, a huge fan, wanted to become their singer, but by that point they'd decided to quit while they were ahead.

In 1986, the original lineup of Can—including Malcolm Mooney—reunited for the sessions that became *Rite Time,* but they don't seem to have been too excited about them; the album didn't appear for almost three years. It's identifiably Can, and not embarrassing, but the old magic is absent, and Mooney bellows away without much relevance to what the band is playing. Skippable. Since then, the members of Can have continued to make occasional appearances on each other's records, and Karoli and Liebezeit toured in Damo Suzuki's band in the late '90s. Michael Karoli died of cancer in 2001.

The first *Cannibalism* compiles tracks from Can's first six albums (including three of *Monster Movie's* four songs), lovingly sequenced and reedited by Czukay—it's not exactly a greatest-hits, but it gives a good sense of what they were up to. *Cannibalism 2* carries the story up through *Delay,* with Czukay abridging nearly every piece he includes and throwing in a few previously unreleased scraps. The third disc in the series actually isn't by Can: It's a collection from the four core members' post-Can solo records, and (aside from Czukay's perverse take on the East German national anthem, "Der Osten Ist Rot") mostly reveals how lost they were without each other to curb their excesses.

Sacrilege, 1997's remix collection, is mostly an excuse for Can's disciples—Sonic Youth, Brian Eno, the Orb, Carl Craig, and others—to show respect for their forefathers. They have some fun with the source material, but they don't exactly improve on it. *Can Box,* released to commemorate the band's 30th anniversary, contains a book, a video, and two CDs; the latter are decent but slightly dull live recordings from 1972, 1975, and 1977.   —D.W.

Candy Butchers

★★★½ Play With Your Head (RPM/Sony, 2002)
★★★½ Hang On Mike (RPM, 2004)

If the voice of Candy Butchers leader Mike Viola sounds familiar, that's probably because you've seen the 1996 Tom Hanks flick *That Thing You Do!,* for which Viola cowrote and sang the title song. His own music isn't quite as shamelessly retro as that of the movie's fictional group the Wonders, but at times it's not far off, matching the sunny melodicism of Squeeze and Marshall Crenshaw with the sour lyrical attitude of early Elvis Costello and Graham Parker. *Play With Your Head* covers the power-pop angle splendidly, with occasional cute asides like the sitar riff on "My Monkey Made a Man Out of Me." The sound has gotten sparser and the lyrics seem more personal on *Hang On Mike,* but otherwise, it's more of the same, and nothing's wrong with that. Two earlier, out-of-print Candy Butchers releases, *Live at La Bonbonniere* (1996) and *Falling into Place* (1999), are worth the hunt if you like what's here.   —M.R.

Canibus

★★★½ Can-I-Bus (Universal, 1998)
★★★ 2000 B.C. (Before Canibus) (Universal, 2000)
★★ C True Hollywood Stories (Archives, 2001)
★★ Mic Club: The Curriculum (Babygrande, 2002)
★★½ Rip the Jacker (Babygrande, 2003)

Hip-hop is a fickle biz, and battle rappers make enemies at a faster clip than most. Still, few MCs have seemed so determined to arouse bad will as Canibus. From L.L. Cool J, whom he savaged in his career-making single, "Second Round K.O.," to Wyclef Jean, whose eccentric production on *Can-I-Bus* he quickly disowned, Canibus lashed out against every collaborator who'd given him a leg up. His ferocious skill actually hampered his career—his bad attitude is emphasized by a clipped, snide delivery that makes every jibe sound personal. At least his albums will never be bogged down with the redundant guest spots that spoil so many hip-hop albums.

Following Canibus' series of explosive underground singles, hip-hop tastemakers declared his 1998 debut the most eagerly anticipated hip-hop album of the year, and tossed that disc aside, upon its release, as one of hip-hop's greatest disappointments. This was undeserved: The mix of Wyclef's glossy production and Bus' loony sci-fi-inflected paranoia is an odd one—it makes the Fugee's pop moves sound weirdly avant-garde and the MC's complex rhymes sound simpler than they are. But from the rock guitar track to the Roxanne Shante sample, *Can-I-Bus* was as wide-ranging as any hip-hop album to emerge from the late '90s.

Keeping an ear to the streets, Canibus lashed out against Wyclef's production on *B.C.*, a less ambitious and fairly decent followup. But by the time of *True Hollywood Stories*, Bus' wit seemed embittered. When he rescues Eminem's fan Stan from his car crash and invites the kid on tour, his assault on the more successful rapper seems as desperate a plea for attention as Stan's plunge off the bridge. As does his jibe at Jay-Z, "The only difference between me and you is a budget." The frothing, antiterrorist "Draft Me" turned out not to be an empty boast: Canibus ended up enlisting in the Marines, but as *Mic Club* and *Rip the Jacker* attest, that didn't make for better music.   —K.H.

Canned Heat

★★★½	Living the Blues (1968; Akarma, 2001)
★★★★	Future Blues (1970; Repertoire, 2002)
★★★½	Live at the Topanga Corral (1971; Repertoire, 2002)
★★	Historical Figures and Ancient Heads (1972; Beat Goes On, 2002)
★★★½	The Best of Canned Heat (1972; EMI, 1995)
★★	New Age (1973; Beat Goes On, 2001)
★★	Human Conditions (1978; Aim, 2002)
★★	Internal Combustion (River Road, 1994)
★★★★	Uncanned! The Best of Canned Heat (Capitol, 1994)
★★★	King Biscuit Flower Hour (King Biscuit, 1996)
★★	Gamblin' Woman (Mausoleum, 1996)
★★★½	On the Road Again (Aim, 1997)
★★★	Canned Heat Blues Band (1996; A&M, 1998)
★★	Boogie 2000 (Ruf, 1999)
★★★½	Live at the Kaleidoscope 1969 (Varèse, 2000)
★★★	Canned Heat 1967–1976: The Boogie House Tapes (Ruf, 2000)
★★★★	The Very Best of Canned Heat (EMI, 2001)
★★★★	Far Out (Akarma, 2001)
★★	Big Road Blues (Prestige Elite, 2002)
★★★	Live Concert '70 (Beat Goes On, 2002)
★★½	Don't Forget to Boogie: Vintage Heat (Varèse, 2002)
★★★★½	Canned Heat Cookbook: Their Greatest Hits (Fuel 2000, 2002)
★★	Live in Oz (Mystic, 2002)
★★½	Friends in the Can (Varèse, 2003)

with John Lee Hooker

★★★★½	Hooker 'n Heat (1970; Capitol, 1991)
★★½	Hooker 'n Heat Live (1987; Rhino, 1990)
★★★★	The Best of Hooker 'n Heat (Capitol, 1996)

Canned Heat was the brainchild of Bob "The Bear" Hite, Al "Blind Owl" Wilson, and Henry "Sunflower" Vestine, a trio of Los Angeles record collectors and blues fanatics who came together in 1966 to put their passion into practice. These serious young men fancied themselves purists—after all, Vestine had been among the first '60s blues-heads to rediscover Skip James, and Wilson had played guitar with Son House. But like most white blues bands of the era, their value was not in how close they came to the traditional sources, it was in their unconscious mutation of those traditions. The demo collection *Don't Forget to Boogie* is the group at its most restrained, probably because it was recorded by Johnny Otis not long after they formed in 1966. Signed by Liberty following their appearance at the 1967 Monterey Pop Festival, Canned Heat was positioned to be something like a West Coast equivalent of the Butterfield Blues Band—zealous white blues missionaries.

Three-hundred-pound frontman Hite was the lead singer, but it was two of Al Wilson's occasional vocal turns that provided the band with an unexpected breakthrough. Wilson, whose brilliant slide and harp playing were the soul of Canned Heat, set his shaky falsetto against Vestine's mildly psychedelic guitar drone for a reworking of "On the Road Again," a Memphis Jug Band tune from the '20s. It became a left-field hit in the summer of 1968, followed months later by the even bigger hit "Going Up the Country," with a flute line so resolutely cheerful that Madison Avenue continues to license it decades later. It graced the third Canned Heat album, the double *Living the Blues*, a fan favorite because of the 20-minute jam "Parthenogenesis" and all 40:51 minutes of the immortal "Refried Boogie," both now unlistenable to all but the most committed Heat-heads. The entire *Future Blues* album takes less time than "Refried Boogie," but it may be the band's best. Harvey Mandel replaces Vestine on lead guitar, and Bob Hite finally gets his own hit with their version of Wilbert Harrison's "Let's Work Together." Wilson died shortly thereafter, but not before taking part in Canned Heat's 1970 sessions with boogie master John Lee Hooker. *Hooker 'n Heat* is credited to the band but belongs to John Lee; the version of "Burnin' Hell," with only Wilson's harp for accompaniment, is a career highlight. When the full crew joins in for extended workouts on "Peavine" and (of course) "Boogie Chillen No. 2," their unfettered hippie spirit allows them to follow wherever Hooker's famously eccentric time-keeping leads. With *Hooker 'n Heat*, the archivists made some blues history of their own. Highlights from this double CD are available as *The Best of Hooker 'n Heat*. The live volume, unfortunately, is from a night when their gears never quite meshed.

Canned Heat lost a lot of flair with Wilson's passing, but not its sense of mission. *Historical Figures* (with a Little Richard cameo), *New Age*, and *Human Conditions* were workmanlike efforts that did their best to ignore the deepening '70s. Not even Bob Hite's death in 1981 could derail this boogie train; the band has continued under the leadership of drummer Fito de la Parra, often with Vestine (until his death in 1997) and bassist Larry Taylor. But when people remember Canned Heat, it will be the original incarnation found on the hits packages *Best of, Cookbook, On the Road Again,* and the more expansive *Very Best of.* The two-CD *Uncanned!* has the right size canvas to offer a definitive portrait, but its failure to include either "Fried Hockey Boogie" or "Refried Boogie" is not likely to be forgiven by the hard-core. *Far Out* is a double that collects alternate takes and rarities; another double compilation, *The Boogie House Tapes,* is often of bootleg quality but is a completist's wet dream. *Live at the Kaleidoscope 1969* (a.k.a. *Live at the Topanga Corral*) is the recommended live document—Henry Vestine stakes his claim as one of the era's most underrated guitarists with his manic solo bursts on "Bullfrog Blues," while Alan Wilson actually breathes life into the Elmore James warhorse "Dust My Broom," a minor blues miracle. Despite contributions from Roy Rogers, Taj Mahal, and John Lee Hooker, *Friends* doesn't ignite.   —B.E.

Cannibal Ox

> ★★★★   The Cold Vein (Definitive Jux, 2001)

Vast Aire

> ★★   Look Ma . . . No Hands (Chocolate Industries, 2004)

Manhattan hip-hop duo Cannibal Ox made a startling debut in 2001 with their album, *The Cold Vein.* On it, the uptown crew accomplished the mighty task of creating a whole new way to view inner-city life. Produced entirely by Definitive Jux chief El-P, MCs Vast Aire and Vordul crafted a startling world that resembled an impoverished Harlem as imagined by sci-fi writer Philip K. Dick. Over jagged beats laden with thick keyboards, Vast and Vordul kick clear-eyed rhymes of hope ("Atom"), despair ("Iron Galaxy"), and fond nostalgia ("A B-Boy's Alpha"). *The Cold Vein* is a testament to the independent creative spirit that fueled the best of underground hip-hop.

Sadly, Can Ox has yet to make a followup. In 2004, Vast Aire released a rather underwhelming solo debut. Despite the presence of top-notch producers such as Madlib and RJD2, the MC seems to have abandoned the mixture of sensitivity and toughness that made him so special.   —C.R.

Capone-n-Noreaga

> ★★★★   The War Report (Penalty, 1997)
> ★★★   The Reunion (Tommy Boy, 2000)

Noreaga

> ★★★   N.O.R.E. (Penalty, 1998)
> ★★   Melvyn Flynt—Da Hustler (Penalty, 1999)
> ★★   God's Favorite (Universal, 2002)

The career arc of Queens-based rappers Capone and Noreaga mirrors the transformation of New York City mainstream rap from gritty representation of crime-riddled streets to glossy fantasies of the good life. The duo immediately distinguished itself with Capone's nasal delivery and clear-eyed vision of street life, coupled with Noreaga's often hilarious and nonsensical rhymes ("I run laps around the English Channel," is one of his choice lines). Their 1997 debut, *The War Report,* proved an instant sensation with songs like "L.A., L.A.," in which the two threw themselves into the fray of the East Coast/West Coast rap battles that were raging at the time.

The group faced adversity early on, when Capone was sent to jail before *The War Report* was released. With his partner in rhyme turning to crime, Noreaga released his first solo album, 1998's *N.O.R.E.* Noreaga's union with then up-and-coming producers the Neptunes was a kind of rap alchemy, collaborating on anthems like "Superthug"—and many more in the future. *N.O.R.E.* made Noreaga a viable solo act, but his followup, *Melvyn Flynt—Da Hustler,* is an unfocused let down, offering little humor and no exhilarating club track, perhaps due to the passing of Noreaga's father. In 2000, Noreaga reunited with Capone for the forgettable *The Reunion,* which lacks the chemistry of their debut. Noreaga, rechristened N.O.R.E., released *God's Favorite* in 2002, reteaming with the Neptunes for two stellar cuts, "Nothin' " and "Grimey," though the album was plagued by too many guest appearances from some of N.O.R.E.'s less talented cohorts.   —C.R.

The Cardigans

> ★★★½   Emmerdale (1994; Minty Fresh, 1999)
> ★★★★   Life (Minty Fresh, 1995)
> ★★★½   First Band on the Moon (Mercury, 1996)
> ★★   Gran Turismo (Mercury, 1998)
> ★★   Long Before Daylight (Koch, 2004)

From a distance, the Cardigans fit all the adjectives usually heaped upon Swedish pop groups: Bubbly. Perky. Winsome. Cute. But this lounge-pop five-some's world isn't all sweetness and light. Front-woman Nina Persson's breathy, girlish voice may seem carefree, but the words she sings often carry a uniquely Scandinavian gloom, shadowing the corners of an otherwise sunny vista.

Graced with delectable retro production by Tore Johansson and packed with clever arrangements featuring such nonrock instruments as bassoon and vibraphone, *Emmerdale* hits its peak on a gloriously bizarre disco reinterpretation of Black Sabbath's "Sabbath Bloody Sabbath." Lyrics like "Symptoms are so deep/Something here's so wrong/Nothing is complete/Nowhere to belong" ("Sick & Tired") are worthy of grunge's sulkiest angst merchants but somehow never break the prevailing chipper mood.

Even more musically upbeat, *Life* improves on *Emmerdale* by showing off the tightness of the Cardigans' playing. More than just catchy tunes, "Hey! Get Out of My Way," "Fine," and the Motown-influenced "Tomorrow" are great grooves too. Twee? Sure. But "light" pop has rarely sounded this excited, or exciting. Consumer note: The U.S. versions of *Life* and *Emmerdale* share six tracks, including "Sabbath Bloody Sabbath."

First Band on the Moon contains the Cardigans' biggest hit, "Lovefool," which, typically, disguises the desperate plea of a jilted lover as a lively neo-Blondie dance number. Elsewhere, the music takes on a harder edge. The macho riffs on "Been It" and "Losers" betray the group's fondness for metal without diminishing the delicacy of the melodies. And there's another goofy Sabbath cover—"Iron Man" this time.

Up to this point, the dark patches in the Cardigans' songs could be written off as fashionable ennui. But on *Gran Turismo,* the going gets well and truly somber. Replacing the vivacious beat-combo sound of old with icy layers of electronics, it's the least fun record in the band's catalogue, and that's not a good thing.

Regrouping after a lengthy hiatus for *Long Gone Before Daylight,* the Cardigans seemed to have completely forgotten what had once made them so special. The synthscapes are gone and the impeccable group playing is back, but the lugubrious, down-tempo songs just don't hold up. With a couple of lyrical tweaks, the opening cut, "Communication," could fit comfortably on a Faith Hill album—and that's *really* not a good thing.   —M.R.

Mariah Carey

★★★   Mariah Carey (Columbia, 1990)
★★★   Emotions (Columbia, 1991)
★★   Music Box (Columbia, 1993)
★★★   Daydream (Columbia, 1995)
★★★★   Butterfly (Columbia, 1997)
★★   Rainbow (Columbia, 1999)
★   Glitter (Virgin, 2001)
★★   Charmbracelet (MonarC/Island, 2002)
★★★   The Remixes (2003, Columbia)

She wasn't exactly a child star, but Mariah Carey has grown up in public, reaching the charts first as a 20-year-old Whitney Houston copycat with a somewhat fictional "five-octave" vocal range, and emerging in the next century as almost-salty thirty-something hip-hop-loving pop diva who's been divorced, dropped from her label, rehabbed, and slagged off by both Eminem and *Us Weekly*—but now seems more human than she did at the start of her career. In the interim, she's become one of the top-selling pop stars of all time, and influenced a generation of female pop-R&B singers with her fluttering vocal trills.

Carey debuted with an album of uplifting dance pop and R&B ballads, each song's composition cocredited to Carey and each providing an opportunity to unleash her wide vocal range. Carey's strong, soulful voice served the sinewy R&B of "Vision of Love," her first #1 single, and the dance ballad "Someday." Carey had a number of essential and winning qualities—the novelty of her vocal top end, the tensile strength of her singing on the soulful verses, and the ability to convey a genuine joy behind the mike when she's let loose to romp through something as felicitous as "Emotions." Carey's followup to her top-selling debut finds the singer relaxing into her form, less self-conscious about her vocal tricks and hooked up with a sassier studio crowd, notably the postdisco super-producers David Cole and Robert Clivilles.

Carey softens her approach on *Music Box,* putting a damper on the just-for-fun disco of her previous records, and mainstreaming her lite soul into "uplifting" beauty-pageant ballad territory. "Hero" soared on wings of Carey's golden tone to the #1 chart slot and became an instant standard of weddings, funerals, auditions, and Miss Harvest Queen competitions. While there's nothing wrong with Carey singing relatively straight for 10 songs, there is a sore lack of power here: baleful soaring ballads, pop optimism along the lines of smiling through the tears and believing in yourself (or him, or Him), and hardly a decent tune in the lot. Clivilles and Cole roar back for the electro-synth dance number "Now That I Know," but neither Babyface nor frequent collaborator Walter Afanasieff can pull Carey out of this soft-rock slump.

Carey edges toward the harder end of the musical spectrum in baby steps on *Daydream.* She enlists Tina

Weymouth and Chris Frantz of the Tom Tom Club and the British producer Adrian Belew to rewrite Tom Tom Club's "Genius of Love" as her own love song "Fantasy," unleashing again the whiplike high register that made her famous. "Fantasy" is the kind of collaborative effort that retains its party atmosphere on record, as backup singers, snippets of the original tune, and a twiddling synth line weave in and out of Carey's vocals. Afanasieff returns to cowrite his strongest tunes yet, the sweet, bouncy "Underneath the Stars" and "One Sweet Day," a yearning R&B ballad on which Carey shares vocal duties with Boyz II Men. Aside from an ill-advised cover of Journey's "Open Arms," *Daydream* adheres to the classic radio-friendly diva format, alternating between frisky dance tunes and overscaled ballads.

Names like Puffy, Krayzie and Wish Bone, Missy Elliot, Timbaland, Q-Tip, and David Morales show up in the liner notes of Mariah Carey's *Butterfly*, and more interestingly, the sounds that made those names recognizable are all over the record as well. Carey doffs her trademark slit-sided miniskirts for denim hot pants and takes her considerable vocal range to the streets. And it works. The pulsing mid-tempo "Honey," cowritten by Puffy, doesn't sound much different from previous Carey singles except for asides from Mase and the Lox. Songs like "Butterfly," "Close My Eyes," and "Breakdown" speak indirectly of Carey's pending extraction from the tentacles of her powerful husband, then–Sony president Tommy Mottola.

But *Rainbow* is an uneasy exercise in hip-hop bombast, pumping up the jams to operatic lengths and complexity and declaring the singer's independence in a handful of braying ballads in which Mariah serenades "the light in me." Worse, she reprises the "Genius of Love" underpinnings for the lead-off single, "Heartbreaker," featuring Jay-Z, and this piece of desperate unoriginality is the best song on the album. Carey is credible as neither a diva nor a homegirl; her bloated "Can't Take That Away (Mariah's Theme)" is both self-indulgent and self-aggrandizing, and the spiteful "Did I Do That?," a nervy excoriation of her celebrity marriage, blames Mottola for making a fool of her. The harder-edged numbers paint the singer as a sassy, strong-spirited flirt, the slower ones as a wide-eyed little girl with big dreams. *Rainbow* left Carey at a crossroads, and the album's sales did not yield the expected pot of gold.

With the possible semi-exception of "Loverboy," there's nothing to recommend the infamous *Glitter* except its novelty status as the product of a dramatic public meltdown. Carey's career crashed and burned in a spectacularly center-stage fashion as she struggled to define herself post-Mottola and post-Columbia (she signed to Virgin and was notoriously bought out from her contract thanks to *Glitter*). Her voice is only getting stronger, and if *Rainbow* was Mariah's vocal peak, *Glitter* isn't quite a comedown—it's the songs and the production, the horrible sequencing and general lack of conviction among the players, that tarnished this bit of miscalculated tinsel.

Carey bounded back post-*Glitter* with a recording that isn't markedly unlike *Glitter* itself, which isn't to say it's bad. Questions of quality as regards her body of work become moot over time, because it's timing that creates the crests and dips in her success arc—if the hip-hop-inspired *Rainbow* wasn't substantially worse than *Butterfly*, which outsold it by miles, neither is *Charmbracelet* a substantial drop in quality or change in sensibility from her previous collections of lushly produced, trembling-lipped ballads of vulnerable romance. But *Charmbracelet* did its job—reestablishing the perception that she had reclaimed her career and her sanity.   —A.B.

Wendy (Walter) Carlos

★★★½	Switched-On Bach (1968; East Side Digital, 2001)	
★★★	Sonic Seasonings (1972; East Side Digital, 1998)	
★★★	A Clockwork Orange (1972; East Side Digital, 1998)	
★★	Tron (1982; East Side Digital, 2002)	
★★★	Digital Moonscapes (1984; East Side Digital, 2000)	
★★★	Beauty in the Beast (1986; East Side Digital, 2000)	
★★★	Switched-On Brandenburgs (1987; East Side Digital)	
★★	Switched-On Bach 2000 (Telarc, 1995)	
★★	Tales of Heaven and Hell (East Side Digital, 1998)	
★★★½	Switched-On Boxed Set (East Side Digital, 1999)	
★★★	Well-Tempered Synthesizer (East Side Digital, 2001)	
★★★	Switched-On Bach II (East Side Digital, 2001)	

Walter Carlos caused a stir in the late '60s with *Switched-On Bach*, a kind of Johann's "greatest hits" played exclusively on synth. Classical purists balked, but the record was trailblazing—no longer could the Moog machine be relegated to the role of a special effect; it could deliver "Jesu, Joy of Man's Desiring" as music, not as a series of squawks. Choosing Bach was smart; while the dynamics and tone of the music certainly lost something in translation into blips and bleeps, the mathematical precision of the composer's style lent itself to the fastidiousness of the electronic approach. And Carlos is a dazzling technician—he demonstrated the capabilities of the new instrument in ways that proved influential for years to come. After his '60s heyday, Walter, through means of a sex-change operation, became Wendy—and experimented with original music. Much less satisfying than that of such avant-gardists as Terry Riley, her work flashed more technique than imagination. *Beauty in the Beast* and *Digital Moonscapes* might now be filed under New Age—a genre Carlos largely pioneered—and they're pleasant. *Tales of Heaven and Hell* is basically a gothic joke. The *Brandenburgs*, obviously, are Bach, and they remain intriguing. *Well-Tempered Synthesizer* takes on Monteverdi and Haydn along with other high classical greats, and it's nearly as good as the Bach sets. —P.E.

The Carpenters

★★	Offering/Ticket to Ride (A&M, 1969/1970)
★★½	Close to You (A&M, 1970)
★★★★	Carpenters (A&M, 1971)
★★★★	A Song for You (A&M, 1972)
★★	Now and Then (A&M, 1973)
★★★	The Singles: 1969–73 (A&M, 1973)
★★½	Horizon (A&M, 1975)
★★½	A Kind of Hush (A&M, 1976)
★★	Passage (A&M, 1977)
★★	Christmas Portrait (A&M, 1978)
★½	Made in America (A&M, 1981)
★	Voice of the Heart (A&M, 1983)
★	Lovelines (A&M, 1989)
★★½	From the Top (A&M, 1991)
★★★	Love Songs (A&M, 1998)

Hating the Carpenters was pretty much mandatory up until the '90s, when '70s nostalgia and the resurgence of lounge music made it okay for discerning listeners to enjoy the duo's crystalline productions and undeniable ear for bittersweet pop. In 1994, the *If I Were a Carpenter* tribute album found artists as diverse as Sonic Youth, the Cranberries, and Sheryl Crow covering the siblings' greatest hits without a hint of irony. Sure enough, there was much to love in the Carpenters' first few efforts. Songwriter/producer Richard Carpenter's clean-cut arrangements and good-humored ditties were beautifully complemented by his sister Karen's voice. Sweet and pure, the latter was able to express infinite amounts of longing, even while working the catchiest, most superficial of choruses.

The Bacharach/David medley on 1971's *Carpenters* is arguably the group's most impressive

moment—light and breezy, slightly jazzy, the work of two young idealists who are still in love with life and its endless possibilities. A year later, "Road Ode," a meditation on the emptiness of show biz marked by a profoundly melancholy piano line and soaring vocal harmonies, brings *A Song for You* to a dramatic, almost painful finale.

The Carpenters' subsequent releases were less arty and subtle, but the bubbly hits kept coming at a rapid pace up until *Passage*. After that, the group was unable to adapt itself to the changing sounds of the late '70s. The music lost its old-fashioned loveliness, and Karen died of anorexia in 1983.

Selecting all the wrong tracks and seriously botching their sequencing, the Carpenters' four-disc set *From the Top* misrepresents the duo's legacy and is recommended only to obsessive-compulsive completists. Contrary to popular belief, the Carpenters were not necessarily a singles band. The many compilations available out there are mostly scattered collections of too-familiar tunes. The duo's early, semiconceptual records deliver a much more poignant picture of the hidden depth that lay beneath the smiley faces and saccharine hooks. —E.L.

James Carr

★★★½	The Complete James Carr, Volume One (Goldwax, 2000)
★★½	24 Karat Soul (Soultrax, 2001)
★★★★	The Complete Goldwax Singles (Kent, 2001)

James Carr's best-known single, "The Dark End of the Street," written by Dan Penn and Chips Moman, was covered by Linda Ronstadt, Aretha Franklin, and the Flying Burrito Brothers, among others. Carr's version, released in 1967, peaked at #10 on the R&B charts and stalled at #77 on the pop charts. Which is to say, Carr's influence has been more keenly felt among the players and the cognoscenti than among the record-buying public (remember them?). To be sure, James Carr never found the audience that Otis Redding and Percy Sledge did. But as a soul singer, Carr delivered some of the finest gospel-inflected music of his era. On that haunting song "The Dark End of the Street," Carr rendered his material sublime, making the song a kind of companion piece to the folk standard "Long Black Veil."

It is a measure of James Carr's undeserved obscurity that various U.S.-released compilations have gone out of print. Most recently, Razor & Tie's fine 1995 collection, *The Essential James Carr,* has been cut from their catalogue. Yes, the revived Goldwax label issued *The Complete James Carr, Volumes One and Two;* but these remain intermittently available and not as consistent as Razor & Tie's release. The 2001 Soultrax project, *24 Karat Soul,* thick with unflattering rerecordings of '60s material, is finally the U.S. release that, even if inadvertently, leads the listener to an important point: perhaps it's time to consider imports.

The U.K.'s reliable Kent Soul imprint offers very fine Carr albums. Most notably, *The Complete Goldwax Singles* brings together 28 sides from between 1964 and 1970, including the aforementioned classic and a number of other exceptional examples of what has come to be called "deep soul." Harlan Howard's "Life Turned Her That Way" is a natural for Carr, rightly suggesting that the singer is in his element with material like "The Dark End of the Street" that deals with fate's bitter theater. Indeed, lighter lyrics don't work as well with Carr's church-born singing style. Even on "A Man Needs a Woman," which features a beautifully urgent vocal performance, the credibility of the song almost collapses when Carr hits the unfortunate line, "Just like a hamburger needs a bun." By contrast, the unlikely Barry and Robin Gibb song "To Love Somebody" lands right in Carr territory, likewise the classic "Pouring Water on a Drowning Man." Do yourself a favor: pay the extra shipping and hear one of the unsung heroes of deep soul. —W.Z.

The Cars

★★★★½   The Cars (Elektra, 1978)
★★★★½   Candy-O (Elektra, 1979)
★★   Panorama (Elektra, 1980)
★★★½   Shake It Up (Elektra, 1981)
★★★   Heartbeat City (Elektra, 1984)
★★★½   Greatest Hits (Elektra, 1985)
★   Door to Door (Elektra, 1987)
★★★★   Just What I Needed: The Cars Anthology (Rhino, 1995)
★★★★   The Cars: Deluxe Edition (Rhino, 1999)

The Cars were never exactly rock stars, and they were never exactly anybody's favorite band. But everybody always liked them, and their cold, shiny guitar hooks are still in rock-radio rotation years after their 1987 breakup. The band were older pros who'd been kicking around Boston a while before hopping onto the new-wave thing, and their approach was sleek and ironic from the get-go, starting with their name—it wasn't their style to call themselves the Corvettes or the Trans Ams or anything else that might suggest they really cared about cars.

"Good Times Roll" kicks off *The Cars* and sets the tone for their whole career, an expertly engineered guitar/synth machine that tweaks clichés with self-conscious irony. Wobbly-voiced robot boy Ric Ocasek keeps threatening to "brush your rock & roll hair,"

and you'd best believe, when it comes to rock & roll hair, Ric *knows* what he's talking about. "Just What I Needed" complains about sexually insatiable girls who come around and waste all your time-time, while "My Best Friend's Girl" pines for a fickle teen seductress with nuclear boots, drip-dry gloves, and suede-blue eyes. Some deluded souls dismiss *Candy-O* as a synthed-up sophomore slump, but they are wrong, wrong, wrong. Every song was a massive hit in Boston, and many made it outside Route 128 as well; in "Dangerous Type," "Lust For Kicks," and "It's All I Can Do," Ric Ocasek and Ben Orr sing mournful high-tech tales of a teen romantic frustration that couldn't possibly be more theoretical. (Would a girl who was the "Dangerous Type" ever go out with one of the Cars?) The best song, "Double Life," explains the Cars' sexual philosophy: "When you idle at the stoplight/better get the signal right."

Panorama was Ocasek's art record, and not a very good one at all. *Shake It Up* went back for direct pop pleasure and got it right in the first three songs: "Shake It Up," "Since You're Gone," and "I'm Not the One." *Heartbeat City,* produced by future Shania svengali Mutt Lange, has more anonymous hits and a mushier sound; it's basically a Def Leppard album without the guitars. After the flop *Door to Door,* the Cars quietly pulled into that big garage in the sky. It should have been a snap to compile an undeniable best-of, but *Greatest Hits* bungles the job by picking the blandest items and muddling them up in nonchronological order. The two-disc *Just What I Needed* piles on more demos and rarities than even a hard-core fan could sit through, but it still somehow manages to leave out essential hits like "All Mixed Up," "Lust For Kicks," and "Bye Bye Love." The deluxe edition of *The Cars* packages the debut with a bonus disc of alternate versions. Ben Orr died of pancreatic cancer in 2000. —R.S.

Derrick Carter

★★★★   Mixmag Presents . . . The Cosmic Disco (DMC, 1997)
★★★★   About Now (611, 2001)
★★★½   Squaredancing in a Roundhouse (Classic, 2002)
★★★½   Choice: A Collection of Classics (Azuli, U.K., 2003)
★★★   Nearest Hits and Greatest Misses (Classic, 2003)

Luke Solomon & Derrick L. Carter

★★★   Thanks for Coming By . . . (Classic, 2001)

Derrick Carter is probably the most popular house DJ in Chicago as well as the United States. He began his career when he was nine, playing at family reunions, and began making his own records in the late '80s. His recording career stalled, however, until the mid-'90s, when he began releasing 12-inches on Organico, quickly becoming a draw on the Midwestern rave circuit. *Mixmag Presents . . . The Cosmic Disco,* his first major mix CD, is a cult classic among house fans for its shrewd showcasing of Chicago talent like DJ Sneak ("You Can't Hide From Your Bud"), Gene Farris ("Visions of the Future"), Green Velvet ("Answering Machine," "Land of the Lost"), and Carter himself, whose remix of Cajmere's "Only 4 U" closed out the set. Around the same time, Carter and British house DJ and Freaks member Luke Solomon started the Classic Recording Company. *Thanks for Coming By . . . ,* a label showcase, features a CD-length mix from each; Carter's mix is the more engrossing of the two, and Isolée's classic "Beau Mot Plage" is the highlight. Months later, Carter issued *About Now . . . ,* a sterling manifesto whose first half outdid *The Cosmic Disco* in its fierce joy. Even jazzy touches (the horns on Eddie & the Eggs' "Me & My Watermelon," the luxe keyboard riff of Kojak's "You Can't Stop It") feel less supper-club smooth than late-night jam-session nasty. Late 2002 saw the issue of Carter's playful, accomplished *Squaredancing in a Roundhouse,* his second full album (1995's *Pagan Offering* is out of print). Carter's volume of the *Choice* compilation series, in which various DJs select personal favorites, is an intriguing mix of rarities (the Staple Singers' "Slippery People") and house classics like Mr. Fingers' "Mysteries of Love (Dub Mix)," while the misleadingly titled *Nearest Hits and Greatest Misses* is another DJ set that brings together strange but surprisingly compatible bedfellows like postrockers Tortoise and ecstatic housemongers Roy Davis Jr. and Peven Everett.   —M.M.

James Carter

★★★★ JC on the Set (DIW, 1994)
★★★★ Jurassic Classics (DIW, 1995)
★★★★★ The Real Quietstorm (Atlantic, 1995)
★★★★★ Conversin' With the Elders (Atlantic, 1996)
★★★★ In Carterian Fashion (Atlantic, 1998)
★★★★ Layin' in the Cut (Atlantic, 2000)
★★★★★ Chasin' the Gypsy (Atlantic, 2000)
★★★½ Gardenias for Lady Day (Columbia, 2003)
★★★★ Live at Baker's Keyboard Lounge (Warner Bros., 2004)

It's too late for anyone to return jazz to the golden age of Charlie Parker and John Coltrane, but if anyone could have in the last decade, it would have been James Carter. Taken as a group, it's now clear that the

one and only purpose of jazz saxophonist James Carter's first three albums is to impress the hell out of the listener. He plays sax in four weight divisions, plus bass clarinet and bass flute. He's mastered just about every sound those horns can produce, from honks through squeals, and particularly enjoys those pops and clicks on the valves that make for self-accompanied percussion. He shows off his circular breathing. The only thing he doesn't do is human beat-box.

Carter also shows off his mastery of the history and lore of the saxophone, not only using Ellington and Monk standards as launchpads, but digging up Sun Ra, and resurrecting Don Byas and little-known Texas tenor John Hardee. The DIW albums careen between tradition and avant-garde, but Carter's real breakthrough comes in *The Real Quietstorm,* where he concentrates on ballads and lets the luscious melodies outshine the performance.

Having established himself as the most imposing young saxophonist since Sonny Rollins, Carter next moved to consolidate his reputation by *Conversin' With the Elders.* Of course, when you're as young as Carter, elders can be as modern as Hamiett Bluiett and Lester Bowie, or as ancient as Buddy Tate and Sweets Edison, and the juxtaposition, which lets Carter reprise "Moten Swing" (from the Robert Altman movie *Kansas City*), play reggae with Bowie, and do dueling baritones with Bluiett, is one of Carter's most broadly enjoyable albums.

Carter's major-label efforts are all concept albums. *In Carterian Fashion* is meant to be a tenor-organ showcase, but it defies all expectations: Carter has no desire to settle into a soul-jazz groove, so his pairing with three organists starts as jousts and quickly turns into a rout: his most out recording, but not an especially successful concept.

The next two albums represent Carter's first work with guitarists. *Layin' in the Cut* features two electric guitarists and funk bassist Jamaaladeen Tacuma working out of a groove perhaps a bit too reminiscent of Ornette Coleman's group Prime Time. Meanwhile, *Chasin' the Gypsy* uses two acoustic guitarists to reconsider Django Reinhardt's swing, with cousin Regina Carter playing Stephane Grappelli on violin, resounding evidence that everything old can be new again. Plus, it lets Carter show off his new bass saxophone.

After an unseemly hiatus, Carter switched to Columbia, and Warners flushed out a live album that Atlantic had been sitting on since 2001. *Gardenias for Lady Day* was overstrategized: Ostensibly a Billie Holiday tribute, half of the songs had nothing to do with her, the two vocals were hammed up by an Ella wanna-be, "Strange Fruit" was reconceived as a noise break, and much of the rest was buried in maudlin strings. On the other hand, the rhythm section was perfectly tuned for Carter's postmodern '40s jones, and Carter was incandescent. *Live* is another oddball, with a panoply of guest saxophonists who can hardly get a note in edgewise—Franz Jackson even resorts to a blues shout. Carter is bursting with talent and ideas; it's a shame that he doesn't get more opportunities to work out.   —T.H.

The Carter Family

★★★★★ The Carter Family: Country Music Hall of Fame Series (MCA, 1991)
★★★½ On Border Radio, Vol. 1 (Arhoolie, 1995)
★★★½ On Border Radio, Vol. 2 (Arhoolie, 1997)
★★★ Country by the Carter Family (Vanguard, 1997)
★★★★ Best of the Best of the Original Carter Family (King Special, 1998)
★★★★★ On Border Radio, Vol. 3 (Arhoolie, 1999)
★★★★ Can the Circle Be Unbroken: Country Music's First Family (Sony Legacy, 2000)

The year 2027 will mark the 100th anniversary of the release of the first Carter Family recordings, and if history has taught us anything, it's that we'll still be talking about the enormous reach and influence the Carters' music continues to exert on roots musicians of all stripes. There will be a list of latter-day Carter Family acolytes joining the likes of Woody Guthrie, Bob Dylan, Doc Watson, Freakwater, The Be Good Tanyas, Dolly Varden, and others.

Here's where the history of modern country music begins, its ground zero being Bristol, TN, in 1927, when Victor A&R scout Ralph Peer came to town looking for new talent (and not least of all an effort to get a piece of what he hoped would be some lucrative publishing). As documented on the Country Music Foundation's essential *The Bristol Sessions* CD, Peer perhaps found more than he had bargained for, because a trove of outstanding artists committed their songs to vinyl, including the Stonemans (who had already been recorded), Blind Alfred Reed, and the feisty Kentucky preacher Alfred G. Karnes. But two artists leaped out of the Bristol sessions to change the course of music history: Mississippi's consumptive Singing Brakeman, Jimmie Rodgers, and Maces Springs, VA's Carter Family. In addition to his classic songs, Rodgers' forays into Hawaiian music and black blues expanded country's musical palette by a quantum leap. The dour, proper A.P. Carter, his wife, Sara, and her cousin Maybelle Addington (who had married A.P.'s younger brother Ezra and become a Carter herself) advanced a repertoire A.P. had gleaned from the hills and hollows of the region, hundreds of songs of British/Irish/Scottish/Appalachian origin that he retooled, refining the songs' ancient texts into plainspoken country poetry that reflected the traditions, trials, and mores of the rural South. A.P. was the model song-catcher; he had great affection for the haunting tales he heard in his own small part of the world and would tap any source for ideas, be it family, friends, or passing strangers. Where the original songs leave off and Carter's rewrites begin is now a moot point: The body of work has become, sui generis, Carter Family songs for all time, and many of them have entered into the lingua franca of American popular song: "Wildwood Flower," "Wabash Cannonball," "Worried Man Blues," "Will the Circle Be Unbroken," "Single Girl, Married Girl," "Little Log Cabin by the Sea," "The Storms Are on the Ocean," "Keep On the Sunny Side," "Little Darlin' Pal of Mine"—the list goes on and on. Their popularity aside, the early Carter Family recordings take on the aspect of monuments, both in the commitment and expressiveness of the performances and in terms of the repertoire's deep influence on succeeding generations of country, folk, and bluegrass musicians.

Prior to the Bristol sessions, country records were largely instrumental, string-band affairs. But by 1927, advances in microphone technology allowed the subtle harmonic blends of mountain singers such as the Carters to be distinguishable on record for the first time, and the keening alto of an untutored but instinctively gifted vocalist such as Sara Carter was heard with a clarity impossible to achieve in earlier years. As opposed to their progeny—A.P. and Sara's daughter Jeanette; Maybelle's daughters June, Helen, and Anita—the original Carter Family's voices were hardly great instruments from a technical standpoint, but the stark beauty of their blend, with baritone A.P. holding down the bottom as Sara and Maybelle carried the message, engendered a riveting immediacy. The very plainness of their singing became a thing of inestimable beauty, simply on the strength of the emotional punch their voices packed, sans embroidery. The X factor in their performances was the added rhythmic thrust provided by Maybelle's then-forward-looking guitar technique, which found her picking the melody lines on the bass strings as she strummed the rhythm on the treble strings. Her style, immediately emulated by other pickers, became one of the most influential ever.

The Carters recorded prolifically during the Victor years, from 1928 through 1935, when the bulk of their celebrated songbook was committed to disc. The Depression wreaked havoc on their concert appearances, limiting them to low-paying gigs in schoolhouses and such in Virginia, until the group parted ways for economic reasons, with A.P. moving to Detroit to seek work, and Maybelle and her husband following suit to Washington, D.C. Sara and A.P. separated in 1932, but the trio continued to gather for recording sessions, moving in 1935 from Victor to the American Record Company (ARC), then a year later signing with the Decca label. This coincided with their landing a handsome contract with radio station XERF, which beamed their broadcasts nationwide, thanks to a huge antenna built across the border in Mexico, and thus invulnerable to U.S. government regulations. The Decca years proved commercially and economically fruitful. A.P. and Sara split for good in 1939, but the band continued to perform and record together, returning to the ARC and Columbia labels briefly in the early '40s, then re-signing with Victor in 1941. These later recordings have their moments, but Sara sounds increasingly distracted in the post-Decca years, and finally plain bored.

The original Carter Family odyssey—from Maces Springs, in the shadow of Clinch Mountain, to national acclaim—ended in 1943, when Sara retired and moved to California with her new husband, who happened to be A.P.'s cousin, Coy Bayes. Maybelle continued, however, and incorporated her daughters into her road show; for his part, A.P. settled in Maces Springs and ran a country store, which today houses the Carter Family museum. In 1952, A.P. re-formed the Carter Family with Sara and their daughter Jeanette, who filled in for Maybelle; the group disbanded four years later. A.P. passed away in 1960; in 1966, Maybelle and Sara reunited and cut a memorable album (now out of print) for Columbia and played numerous folk festivals around the country. Sara then bowed out again, but Maybelle and her girls carried on, eventually providing haunting backing harmonies for Johnny Cash. Maybelle died in 1978, Sara a year later.

Domestically, the Carters' catalogue is once again in disarray, now that the eight-volume series from Rounder *(The Complete Victor Recordings)* is out of print. For the important Victor recordings, the best available option is King Special's budget-priced *Best of the Best of the Original Carter Family,* although at 10 songs, it's a skimpy overview of a lengthy, towering tenure. At least the 10 are prime-time numbers, including "Keep On the Sunny Side," "Wabash Cannonball," "Worried Man Blues," "Wildwood Flower," and "I'm Thinking Tonight of My Blue Eyes." The Carters' commercially and critically productive two years with Decca are summarized on MCA's splendid 16-track *Country Music Hall of Fame Series* entry.

They cut 60 sides for Decca, so these 16 tracks do include a number of the finest songs in the catalogue. "In the Shadow of Clinch Mountain" is one of the sweetest evocations of the homeland ever set to music; the sprightly "My Dixie Darling" is as heartfelt as playful love sentiments come; and the eerie death ballad "Answer to Weeping Willow" contains some of the most vivid, haunting imagery in any Carter Family song. *Clinch Mountain Treasures: The Complete October 1940 ARC Recordings* documents their return to recording after A.P. and Maybelle's 28-month day-job hiatus. If this isn't the Carters' most inspired work, it nonetheless has its strengths. "Give Him One More as He Goes" shows off a seldom employed sense of humor about the human condition; "Meeting in the Air," "Look Away From the Cross," and "There'll Be No Distinction There" are powerful, unadorned gospel performances; and A.P.'s finest hour among his rare solo appearances is on his own mesmerizing love ballad, "I Found You Among the Roses," a genuinely affecting and deeply felt performance from the most unexpected source. Arhoolie's three-volume *On Border Radio* series captures the Family's entertaining shows from station XET in Monterrey, Mexico. And it is a family in the broadest sense: In addition to A.P., Sara, and Maybelle, Jeanette appears, as do Maybelle's daughters, in their earliest professional appearances. There are plenty of deep, moving moments here—A.P.'s tender reading of "My Virginia Rose" on *Vol. 3;* the original Carters' stirring rendition of "On the Sea of Galilee" on *Vol. 1;* Sara and Maybelle's delightful guitar duet on "Shortning Bread," June and Helen's playful rendition of "Polly Wolly Doodle All Day," and Jeanette's heart-tugging "I Never Will Marry," all on *Vol. 2.*

Like *On Border Radio, Country by the Carter Family* emphasizes the family aspect in its blending of 1940 recordings by A.P., Sara, and Maybelle with contemporary recordings made by the Carter Sisters and Mother Maybelle and contributions by Johnny and Rosanne Cash as well. Johnny's narration of the sentimental "A Song to Mama," with the Carter women singing background vocals, is one of the unalloyed highlights here, along with the Carter Sisters' haunting reading of Gordon Lightfoot's classic "For Lovin' Me." This is not the most essential of Carter discs, but its charms make it a winner all the way.

To get to the heart of Carter Family music, it's necessary to visit the import section. There, the fan will find a splendid two-volume, multi-CD collection from the British label JSP, *The Carter Family: 1927–1934* and *The Carter Family, Vol. 2: 1935–1941,* which contains virtually everything the trio recorded during the years in question; each volume boasts five CDs—the first volume weighs in with 126 songs, the second with 130 songs. Hard-core completists should consider Bear Family's 12-CD *In the Shadow of Clinch Mountain*. This rich box set contains nearly every recording the Carters made for their various labels, from Victor to Bluebird. Disc 12 is an interview with Mother Maybelle and Sara, conducted in 1963 by Pete Seeger's brother Mike and Carter Family historian Ed Khan. A dozen pricey discs may seem like a lot to get through, but the peculiar charm of Carter Family recordings, their music, and the stories they tell touch a fundamental part of almost anyone who crosses their path. —D.M.

Neko Case

★★★ The Virginian (Bloodshot, 1997)
★★★★ Furnace Room Lullaby (Bloodshot, 2000)
★★★★ Blacklisted (Bloodshot, 2000)

The Corn Sisters

★★★ The Other Women (Mint, 2000)

A teenage punk-rocker turned alt-country chanteuse, Neko Case was born in Alexandria, VA, and raised mainly in Tacoma, WA. She spent the mid-'90s attending art college in Vancouver, B.C., where she met Carolyn Mark, with whom Case would form the duo the Corn Sisters, whose *The Other Women* is a loose album consisting mostly of covers, and the future members of power poppers New Pornographers (see separate entry). On her own, though, Case is the most arresting female alt-country singer since the Mekons' Sally Timms. *The Virginian*, her debut, is heavy on covers, mostly country (Ernest Tubb, Loretta Lynn) but with a nod toward rock-hipster tastes with its version of Scott Walker's "Duchess." *Furnace Room Lullaby* is even more assured, and features the great "Thrice All American," a tribute to Tacoma ("I wanna tell you about my hometown/It's a dusty old jewel in the south Puget Sound") that's become a theme song of sorts for Case. *Blacklisted* turned down the twang and cranked up the noir, bringing to mind a more down-home k.d. lang or an updated, David Lynch-ian Patsy Cline, particularly on the two cover tunes, Ketty Lester's "Look for Me (I'll Be Around)," and Aretha Franklin's "Running Out of Fools." Just as impressive are Case's own songs, particularly the haunting "Deep Red Bells," written about the Puget Sound's infamous Green River Killer. —M.M.

Johnny Cash

★★★★ Johnny Cash With His Hot and Blue Guitar (1957; Varèse Sarabande, 2002)
★★★★ Johnny Cash Sings the Songs That Made Him Famous (1958; Varèse Sarabande, 2003)

★★★★ The Fabulous Johnny Cash (1959; Legacy, 2002)
★★★ Hymns by Johnny Cash (1959; Sony, 2002)
★★★½ Songs of Our Soil (1959; Legacy, 2002)
★★★★ Greatest! (1960; Varèse Sarabande, 2003)
★★★ Johnny Cash Sings Hank Williams and Other Favorite Tunes (1960; Varèse Sarabande, 2003)
★★★ Ride This Train (1960; Legacy, 2002)
★★½ Now, There Was a Song! (1960; Legacy, 1994)
★★★ Blood, Sweat and Tears (1963; Legacy, 1994)
★★★ Ring of Fire: The Best of Johnny Cash (1963; Legacy, 1995)
★★ Bitter Tears: Ballads of the American Indian (1964; Legacy, 1994)
★★★½ Orange Blossom Special (1965; Legacy, 2002)
★★★ Ballads of the True West (1965; Legacy, 2002)
★★★ Carryin' On With Johnny Cash and June Carter (1967; Legacy, 2002)
★★★★★ At Folsom Prison (1968; Legacy, 1999)
★★★ At San Quentin (1969; Legacy, 2002)
★★★ America (1972; Legacy, 2002)
★★½ Ragged Old Flag (1974; Legacy, 2002)
★★★ Silver (1979; Legacy, 2002)
★★★ Johnny Cash Is Coming to Town (1987; Universal, 2003)
★★★★ Johnny Cash: Columbia Records 1958–1986 (Columbia, 1987)
★★★★ Classic Cash/Hall of Fame Series (Mercury, 1988)
★★★★ Water From the Wells of Home (Mercury, 1988; Universal, 2003)
★★★★ The Sun Years (Rhino, 1990)
★★½ Boom Chicka Boom (1990; Universal, 2003)
★★★ The Mystery of Life (Mercury, 1991; Universal, 2003)
★★★★ The Gospel Collection (Legacy, 1992)
★★★★ Come Along and Ride This Train (Bear Family, 1994)
★★★★★ The Man in Black 1959–62 (Bear Family, 1994)
★★★★★ American Recordings (American, 1994)
★★★★★ The Man in Black 1963–69 (Bear Family, 1995)
★★★★ Unchained (American, 1996)
★★★½ The Man I Am (Vanguard, 1999)
★★★★ 16 Biggest Hits (Legacy, 1999)
★★★★★ The Complete Sun Singles (Varèse Sarabande, 1999)
★★★★ Love, God, Murder (Legacy, 2000)
★★★★ American III: Solitary Man (American, 2000)
★★★½ Return to the Promised Land (Renaissance, 2000)
★★★½ The Road Less Traveled: Sun Recordings (Varèse Sarabande, 2001)
★★★★★ Essential Sun Singles (Varèse Sarabande, 2002)

★★★ The Millennium Collection (Universal, 2002)
★★★ 16 Biggest Hits, Vol. 2 (Legacy, 2002)
★★★★ The Essential Johnny Cash (1955–1983) (Columbia/Legacy, 1992; Legacy, 2002)
★★★★ At Madison Square Garden (Legacy, 2002)
★★★½ American IV: The Man Comes Around (American, 2002)
★★★ Live Recordings From the "Louisiana Hayride" (Scena, 2003)
★★★★ Unearthed (Lost Highway, 2003)

with Jerry Lee Lewis and Carl Perkins

★★★★ The Survivors: Johnny Cash, Jerry Lee Lewis, Carl Perkins (Columbia, 1982)

with Willie Nelson

★★★★ VH1 Storytellers (American, 1998)

When Johnny Cash died in 2003, he left behind a vast legacy of recorded music spanning half a century. Cash was a mythical figure who embodied much of what was good, bad, and sometimes contradictory about America. In his early days on Sun Records, he walked the line between rockabilly and country, demonstrating a common touch that appealed to both audiences. He was a born-again Christian whose gospel albums thundered with indignation over humankind's sinful ways. He was also a recidivist drug addict whose bad habits led to periods of ill health and rehabilitation. He espoused political stances and created an indelible persona. On 1971's *Man in Black,* which found him at peak popularity, he declared his intention to protest poverty, prejudice, and society's ills by cloaking himself in black until things changed. His seeming contradictions only underscored his complexity, and he continued to wear black until his death, at age 71.

To be sure, Cash's prolific discography—numbering over a hundred albums, not counting compilations, repackages, box sets, and greatest hits—includes its share of mediocrities. There are even some outright duds and follies. (*Mean as Hell!* and *Everybody Loves a Nut,* from the '60s, and *The Junkie and the Juicehead Minus Me* and *Look at Them Beans,* from the '70s, leap to mind.) Still, Cash moved fearlessly forward and kept at his calling with a righteous sense of mission. Much of the time, remarkable things happened when Cash hit the studio or stage. He cut one of the better (and more popular) albums of his career in 2002, with *American IV: The Man Comes Around.* Such things just don't happen to popular musicians at age 70. The secret: Johnny Cash stayed hungry and remained true to himself.

Signed to Sun Records in 1955, Cash was the most countrified artist in the label's original rockabilly class. The Cash sound was set with "I Walk the Line";

Marshall Grant slapped away at his bass and Luther Perkins picked simple riffs and lead lines on his guitar's lower strings while Cash strummed insistent rhythm. Their minimalist sound endures to this day as a template for rockabilly at its most stripped. Cash's deep baritone, which only deepened with age, was powerful and expressive. Its raggedness and oftentimes wobbly nature worked in Cash's favor, making him seem not so different from the average guy. He also happened to sing great songs, many of which he wrote himself. Invariably, the topics were love, murder, prison, and trains, and his flair for striking imagery and the cutting phrase elevated his material to the level of poetry. Some of his best Sun sides came from Jack Clement, the label's house producer and talent scout, and he gave Clement's songs—"Ballad of a Teenage Queen," "Guess Things Happen That Way"—definitive interpretations.

Considering the magnitude of his Sun recordings, it's sometimes difficult to believe he was with the label only two years before splitting for Columbia in 1958. Rhino's *The Sun Years* and Varèse Sarabande's *Essential Sun Singles* provide great single-disc overviews (with 18 and 25 tracks, respectively). For a deluxe overview, Varèse Sarabande's 40-track double-disc *The Complete Sun Singles* is the item to own. These discs demonstrate the evolution of Cash's sound from the spare trio arrangements of the early sides to the use of background choruses and additional instruments (piano, drums, fiddle, pedal steel) on the later ones. Varèse Sarabande has also reissued, with bonus tracks, the albums that came out on Sun from 1958 to 1960: *Johnny Cash With His Hot and Blue Guitar, Johnny Cash Sings the Songs That Made Him Famous, Greatest!,* and *Johnny Cash Sings Hank Williams. The Road Less Traveled: Sun Recordings* collects demos, alternate takes, and nonoverdubbed originals from the Sun years.

Throughout the '60s, Cash came on like the title of Sun's 1970 compilation, *The Rough-Cut King of Country Music.* His move to Columbia in 1959 inaugurated the populist-folksinger period of his career, aspects of which would largely define his musical persona from that decade forward. He kicked off his lengthy tenure at the label with *The Fabulous Johnny Cash,* which covered a lot of stylistic ground and yielded a few hits ("Don't Take Your Guns to Town," "Frankie's Man, Johnny"), plus the classic loner's lament, "I Still Miss Someone." It's been claimed that Cash left Sun because Sam Phillips wouldn't let him record gospel, and he did just that at Columbia with *Hymns,* which perhaps paved the way for fellow Sun exile Elvis Presley's run of gospel albums. *Ring of Fire* reprises Sun-era material, but it also finds Cash coming on tough and embattled on June Carter's title cut, which featured an inventive use of horns and a weary-as-sin vocal performance by Cash. In 2003, "Ring of Fire" ranked fourth on Country Music Television's elite list of the 100 Greatest Songs of Country Music.

The ever-ambitious Cash became a determined storyteller and chronicler of the American experience, exploring themes that ranged from trains and travelogues *(Ride This Train)* to Native Americans *(Bitter Tears: Ballads of the American Indian)* and rugged tales of frontier life *(Ballads of the True West,* a double album). He invested considerable research and effort in these concept albums, stamping himself as a champion of old ways and, in the process, a kind of American conscience.

Blood, Sweat and Tears introduced the Harlan Howard classic "Busted" and has more of a country-blues slant than other albums from this period. *Orange Blossom Special* is notable for Cash's interpretations of three Bob Dylan songs ("It Ain't Me Babe," "Don't Think Twice," "Mama, You Been on My Mind"). It was inevitable that Dylan and Cash—two of the greatest, gruffest outlaw voices—would become friendly. They duetted (rather awkwardly, it must be admitted) on "Girl From the North Country," televised on Cash's prime-time variety show in May 1969, and the symbolism of their union helped bridge musical generations.

Cash peaked in the '60s with a pair of concerts delivered behind prison walls. *At Folsom Prison* found him accompanied by wife-to-be June Carter and the Tennessee Three in a raucous, powerhouse performance at the notorious California penal institution. Many of the songs are about murder, prison, and life on the lam. The final moments of a convict on death row are chillingly detailed in "25 Minutes to Go." The Cash-Carter duet on "Jackson" is sassy and sexy, while the mighty "Folsom Prison Blues" roars disapproval of prisons and class disparity. Cash's other prison album, *At San Quentin,* was an even wilder ride, which took the incarcerated audience from near-riotous frenzy ("San Quentin") to gospel serenity ("Peace in the Valley"). Cash's rambunctious reading of Shel Silverstein's "A Boy Named Sue" became his biggest single, reaching #2 in 1969, and "Wanted Man," written by Bob Dylan, paid sly, salty tribute to the outlaw spirit. In their latest CD incarnations, *At Folsom Prison* and *At San Quentin* have been expanded by three and nine tracks, respectively, and both are essential documentaries of an outsider artist and audience bonding as never before or since.

Cash greeted the '70s with *Hello, I'm Johnny Cash* (1970), which found him writing and finding good songs by other writers. It has more of a country-folk

feel than many of his records, thanks to the inclusion of Tim Hardin's "If I Were a Carpenter," Kris Kristofferson's "To Beat the Devil," and Cash's own folk-flavored "Southwind." Like much of his '70s output, *Hello, I'm Johnny Cash* remains out of print but is deserving of reissue. Returning to gospel, *Johnny Cash Sings Precious Memories* (1975) offered stately readings of well-known country hymns. *Five Feet High and Rising* (1974) is another notable album from this period, and *Johnny Cash and His Woman* (1973), a series of duets with June Carter Cash, has its pleasures, too. Although a lot of his '70s titles have gone missing, a couple of patriotic-themed albums, *America* and *Ragged Old Flag,* got a new lease on life in 2002.

Cash also hit his stride on *Strawberry Cake* (1975), a live album recorded in London. June Carter Cash and sister Helen performed a medley of Carter Family songs, and their high, keening mountain harmonies are simply exquisite. *The Last Gunfighter Ballad* (1977) is a somewhat half-baked concept album saved by the Carter Family's harmonizing on such extraordinary tracks as "Far Side Banks of Jordan" and "That Silver Haired Daddy of Mine." *The Rambler* (1977), another concept album, interspersed dialogue with songs about travel, and it worked to spectacular effect. All the songs were written by Cash, and some—"Hit the Road and Go," "Lady," "If It Wasn't for the Wabash River," "My Cowboy's Last Ride"—are among his best.

On *Gone Girl* (1978), he took stock of his life, and the wistful mood was immensely moving. His ragged cover of the Rolling Stones' "No Expectations" tells quite a story—to wit, Cash's own. "It Comes and Goes" paints a picture of a man bored with his station in life but lacking motivation to change it. The final track, a moving cover of Rodney Crowell's "A Song for the Life," finds Cash giving muted thanks for having learned to "listen to a sound like the sun going down." *Silver* (1979) continued in the vein of *Gone Girl:* strong tunes that reveal Cash's inner feelings and promote no cause save that of unburdening his soul. Produced by Brian Ahern (known for his work with Emmylou Harris), it is another standout from this resurgent period.

In the '80s, Cash reconciled with his past. It began with the Jack Clement–produced *Rockabilly Blues* (1980), which wasn't rockabilly per se, but hard country with rockabilly overtones. Nice cover choices included Nick Lowe's "Without Love," with Lowe and Dave Edmunds playing along, and Steve Goodman and John Prine's wise and witty "The Twentieth Century Is Almost Over." The Cash-penned title song recounted life on the road circa 1955. *The Survivors* (1983) captured a performance in Stuttgart, Germany, where erstwhile labelmates Carl Perkins and Jerry Lee Lewis showed up. If it wasn't exactly the Million Dollar Quartet (as Cash, Perkins, Lewis, and Elvis Presley were briefly dubbed back in the old days), it was good, nostalgic fun from three fourths of the crew many years later.

The Adventures of Johnny Cash (1982) and *Rainbow* (1986) teamed Cash with producers Clement and Chips Moman, respectively. The former disc's highlights include songs by John Prine ("Paradise"), Billy Joe Shaver ("Georgia on a Fast Train"), and Merle Haggard ("Good Old American Guest"). *Rainbow* is enlivened by a moving rendition of Creedence Clearwater Revival's "Have You Ever Seen the Rain," and a tender treatment of "Love Me Like You Used To."

Cash moved to Mercury in 1986, ending an association with Columbia that had lasted a quarter century. While at Mercury, he was produced almost exclusively by Jack Clement, and the partnership yielded some strong results. The must-have album from the Mercury years is *Water From the Wells of Home,* a towering effort that is tender, romantic, nostalgic, tough, and moving, with traditional instrumentation and crisp arrangements. A sleeper among them is the 1986 gospel album, *Believe in Him,* on which majestic country hymns are mostly given spare, acoustic arrangements, creating the intimate effect of a bunch of pickers bringing guitars, mandolins, and banjos over to Cash's place for a good old-fashioned round of praise. Two more albums from the Mercury years, *Johnny Cash Is Coming to Town* and *Boom Chicka Boom,* were paired on a 2003 reissue. Caveat emptor: *Classic Cash* (from Mercury's *Hall of Fame* series) consists of rerecordings of his early work at Sun and Columbia, and therefore has offended purists, though some of his vocal retakes are strong enough to merit an objective listen. You may also wish to avoid the skimpy *Millennium Edition* collection.

In the final chapter of a glorious career, Cash moved to Rick Rubin's American Recordings in the mid-'90s. Between 1994 and 2002, Cash released a quartet of studio albums for American that served as a kind of serial coda. Raw and unvarnished, often featuring just voice and guitar, these four titles—*American Recordings; Unchained; American III: Solitary Man; American IV: The Man Comes Around*—reestablished Cash as a formidable persona and a spiritual godfather to the grunge generation. *American Recordings* is indispensable; it's a stark, rough-hewn folk chiaroscuro whose simplicity is its strength. Subsequent volumes have been strong, too, and even though Cash's voice was frail and faltering on 2002's *American IV: The Man Comes Around,* the artist's truthful essence shone through. Of all improbable things, his

rendition of Nine Inch Nails' "Hurt," and the artistic, unsparing, Grammy-nominated video that was made for it, helped to raise his profile one more time, even as his body was faltering at the end of his life.

In the midst of this stellar string of recordings came the soundtrack of a 1998 summit meeting between Willie Nelson and Johnny Cash for the *VH1 Storytellers* series. With no prior planning, these two country-music greats sat down with their guitars and played whatever came to mind, bantering easily and swapping stories.

There are numerous Cash retrospectives from which the casual or even devoted fan can choose. The 20-song retrospective *Johnny Cash: Columbia Records 1958–1986* hardly does justice to so much work over so long a time (though it does include Cash's spectral version of Bruce Springsteen's "Highway Patrolman"). However, *The Essential Johnny Cash (1955–1983),* the first box set devoted to Cash, squarely hit the mark. In 2002, the release of the double-disc *Essential Johnny Cash* (not to be confused with the earlier three-disc box set of the same title) coincided with Cash's 70th birthday. It offers a satisfying overview, and the CD booklet is filled with glowing testimonials from fellow artists. For those desiring more music and a thematic overview, the three-CD box set *Love, God, Murder* was organized disc-by-disc around the major themes that motivated and conflicted this grassroots folk legend. The three CDs were also released individually under their one-word titles. *At Madison Square Garden*—a previously unreleased concert from 1969, a year that found Cash at the height of his power and popularity—is a welcome addition.

In the mid-'90s, the German Bear Family label issued a series of box sets for hard-core fans. *Come Along and Ride This Train* (which focuses on Cash's American-history songs), *The Man in Black 1959–62,* and *The Man in Black 1963–69* fill four, five, and six discs, respectively. Completists will have a field day, but the average fan will fare well with Legacy's more affordable bounty.

Several collections of Cash's sacred music remain in print. *The Gospel Collection,* a 24-track disc from Legacy, compiles some of his most compelling early gospel recordings for Columbia. Another archival collection, *Just as I Am,* appeared on Vanguard in 1999. A year later, the Cash-financed *Return to the Promised Land*—the uncut soundtrack from a long-form 1994 video of the same name—appeared on the Renaissance label. It features unsyrupy gospel from Johnny Cash and June Carter Cash and heartfelt between-song testimonials.

Incidentally, the new millennium has seen the release of several fine Cash tribute albums from his legion of musical disciples. *Dressed in Black—A Tribute to Johnny Cash* (Dualtone, 2002) is raw, high-spirited fun, and the truest to Cash's early sound. *Kindred Spirits: A Tribute to the Music of Johnny Cash* (Sony, 2002) features bigger names, such as Bruce Springsteen, Bob Dylan, and daughter Rosanne Cash. *Johnny's Blues* (Northern Blues, 2003) finds such artists as Corey Harris and Maria Muldaur covering Cash with a bluesy slant.

In 2003, the year of his death, a pair of releases served to bookend Johnny Cash's remarkable career. *Live Recordings from the "Louisiana Hayride"* collects spunky performances from radio broadcasts dating back to 1955; though the fidelity is unsurprisingly rough in spots, Cash and company were in fine form. The five-disc set *Unearthed* culls buried treasure from the other end of his career: his final decade at American Recordings. The material on four of the discs (including one of spirituals) is of previously unreleased material, while the fifth, in this context, is a perhaps superfluous best-of from his tenure at American. *Unearthed* proves, as if further proof were needed, that Johnny Cash was a bottomless well of Americana.   —P.P.

June Carter Cash

★★★   Press On (Dualtone, 1992; Dualtone, 2003)
★★★½   Wildwood Flower (Dualtone, 2003)

with Johnny Cash

★★★   Carryin' On With Johnny Cash and June Carter (Columbia, 1967)

If there is a royalty of American music, June Carter Cash spent her life in the high court, witness to its riches. She was the daughter of Maybelle Carter, niece to A. P. Carter and Sara Carter (these three the legendary Carter Family), mother of Carlene Carter and stepmother to Rosanne Cash, and lest we forget, wife of Johnny Cash.

She was also a formidable singer and songwriter in her own right, although June Carter Cash's music is not as readily available on CD as is the vast output of certain among her family members. But thanks to Dualtone Records, we do have some fine material by which to remember the singer and songwriter, who died in 2003.

Press On is a Grammy-nominated collection originally released in 1992. The recording finds June Carter Cash involved in something like a musical inventory, a reverential but hardly somber look backward at the music that was her native world. She draws from the Carter Family catalogue as easily as she moves ahead to the years in which country music saw certain among its bright lights returning to "traditional" sounds, Marty Stuart and Ricky Skaggs included. Highlights include a duet with Johnny on "The Far Side of the Banks of Jordan" and a moving version of "Ring of Fire," which she cowrote.

Wildwood Flower (2003) proves to be a worthy continuation of *Press On*'s musical memory project, done in the light of husband Johnny's remarkable—and not altogether foreseeable—emergence as an MTV emblem of hipness. Produced by son John Carter Cash, this recording, like *Press On*, features Norman Blake on acoustic guitar. The bulk of the material comes from the Carter Family catalogue. "Keep on the Sunny Side" kicks off the CD, but the more meditative, darker material such as "Storms Are on the Ocean" proves the most stirring. Her voice is frail at times and the performances sometimes loose, but June Carter Cash's *Wildwood Flower* reminds the listener of a time when music was something people played for one another, not simply a package shipped from an Internet warehouse.

For those who are hooked by these recordings, it's worth checking out *Carryin' On With Johnny Cash and June Carter*. Mostly from 1967, the *Carryin' On* material is marked by a very real willingness to get silly. Through these songs, such as "Long Legged Guitar-Pickin' Man" (on which June unleashes some Wanda Jackson-like growls) and "Jackson," the humor that was an important part of country music's "hillbilly" origins emerges again—and it's a breath of fresh air, even if this recording is a bit thin when put beside the best work of these two artists.   —W.Z.

Rosanne Cash

★★★½   King's Record Shop (1987; Columbia, 1990)
★★★½   Hits, 1979–1989 (Columbia, 1989)
★★★★   Interiors (Columbia, 1990)
★★★★   The Wheel (Columbia, 1993)
★★★½   Retrospective (Columbia, 1995)
★★★½   Super Hits (Columbia, 1998)

Rosanne Cash's original songs are journeys of self-discovery; sometimes, as she revealed on *Interiors*, other people get in the way of that pursuit, and the resulting pain cuts deep. Since the outset of her career, Cash (the first-born daughter of Johnny Cash and his first wife, Vivian Liberto) has evinced a skeptical view of relationships, which often wind up not in the happily-ever-after realm but in moral, philosophical, and physical disintegration. Marriage (first to Rodney Crowell, then to John Leventhal, both of whom entered her professional life as producers) and motherhood seem to have only deepened her conviction that anything put together will fall apart. If all this sounds deadly serious, it is. Nevertheless, until *Interiors*, she always found a way to leaven her dark internal monologues with a dash of humor. In her two post-*Interiors* studio albums, the now out-of-print *10 Song Demo* (which is not a demo recording and contains 11 songs) and *The Wheel*, she has not shrunk from aiming a pointed barb at others— "I throw your roses in the fire/To make the flames a little higher/I watch your roses turn to dust/I know no man I can trust" is her reaction to someone sending her flowers in "Roses in the Fire," from *The Wheel*—but the focus has become ever sharper on self-analysis, and she's never easy on herself. Even in a song as melodically beautiful and atmospherically seductive as *The Wheel*'s "Sleeping in Paris," she can't help but admit, "No one sees behind the mask/No one knows I'm sinking fast," as she awaits the expected salvation of lying beside her lover when he arrives in the City of Light.

Although her first four albums are technically out of print, three anthologies hit many of the high points of those and later years. *Hits 1979–1989* contains most of the obvious chart entries, starting with 1979's captivating single "No Memories Hangin' Round," and concluding with 1988's "Black and White." Some of the choice tracks include a country take on Lennon and McCartney's "I Don't Want to Spoil the Party" (a nonalbum track); "Tennessee Flat Top Box," featuring a terrific guitar solo courtesy of Randy Scruggs; one of Cash's finest heartbreakers, "Blue Moon with Heartache," from *Seven Year Ache;* and a powerful, haunting country ballad penned by Crowell for *Right or Wrong*, "No Memories Hangin' Around," with Cash duetting with Bobby Bare, Ricky Skaggs getting all the ache possible out of his fiddle solos, and James Burton adding an astringent, affecting guitar solo. Bare's reading of the Crowell lyric "I ain't fakin' feelin' far away" alone is worth the price of this disc, as is the beautiful blending of his and Cash's voices, one grizzled and weary, the other young and tender. *Super Hits* is a bit short at 10 tracks, but there's no arguing with the song selections: "Seven Year Ache," "Blue Moon with Heartache," "The Way We Make a Broken Heart," "Tennessee Flat Top Box," "I Don't Want to Spoil the Party," and others—all first-rate performances and productions.

Retrospective comes highly recommended, even though it focuses heavily on latter-day albums, especially her masterpieces, *Interiors* and *The Wheel*, with nothing from the worthy but out-of-print *Right or Wrong* or *Seven Year Ache* ("to delve back further, you'll just have to buy those old albums," Cash advises in her liner notes). —D.M.

Cat Power

★★★ Dear Sir (Plain, 1995)
★★★ Myra Lee (Smells Like Records, 1996)
★★★★ What Would the Community Think (Matador, 1996)
★★★★½ Moon Pix (Matador, 1998)
★★★★ The Covers Record (Matador, 2000)
★★★★ You Are Free (Matador, 2003)

Cat Power is the Georgia-born indie-rock songwriter Chan Marshall, famed for her coldblooded, intimate voice; her shaky guitar; and her propensity for onstage meltdowns. Cat Power first gained notoriety in 1996 for "Not What You Want," the closing track of her second album, *Myra Lee*. For nearly six minutes, Marshall strums her guitar and wails the title phrase over and over, wistfully at first, and then desperately; by the end, she's moaning and screaming and banging her head against the wall. It's nails-on-chalkboard for nonfans, a sublime moment of hag-rock transcendence for true devotees, and Cat Power's entire career in a nutshell.

What Would the Community Think is leaner and tougher, powered by the rhythm section of Two Dollar Guitar guitarist, Tim Foljahn and Sonic Youth drummer Steve Shelley. Marshall intones a memorable cover of Smog's "Bathysphere," and rocks out in the vaguely creepy, definitely cathartic "Nude as the News," yelping "I still have a flame gun for the cute ones" with her own cryptic sort of menace. *Moon Pix* is even stronger, a long, bleak night of cold sweat scored for guitar, and it still holds up as one of the '90s great singer/songwriter triumphs. While musicians from the Dirty Three play atmospheric folk-punk background, Marshall sings raggedy, sorrowful ballads like "Metal Heart" and "Say," stretching her vowels out into forlorn moans. It's a quiet album, but the songs get more powerful the closer you listen, as Marshall testifies to her unbearable longing for an unbearable love.

You Are Free was even more expansive musically than *Moon Pix*, ranging further afield in terms of songwriting (with a few gaffes) but with a renewed sense of emotional urgency, bringing in flourishes of gospel and even disco uplift in great songs like "Free," "Speak for Me," and "Good Woman." In between, Marshall had her most eccentric success with *The Covers Record*, paying tribute to her personal hit parade with versions of songs by Lou Reed, Moby Grape, Smog, Michael Hurley, and Baptiste/Koury's "Sea Of Love." Best of all, Marshall strips down the Stones' "Satisfaction," ditching the chorus and wailing over just acoustic guitar. "Baby baby baby, come back," she pleads. "Can't you see I'm on a losing streak?" She waits a week. He doesn't come back. She still can't get no satisfaction. Scary shit, and a typical Cat Power bone chiller. —R.S.

Nick Cave and the Bad Seeds

★★★½　From Her to Eternity (Mute, 1984)
★★★★　The First Born Is Dead (Mute, 1985)
★★★　Kicking Against the Pricks (Mute, 1986)
★★★½　Your Funeral . . . My Trial (Mute, 1986)
★★★★　Tender Prey (Mute, 1988)
★★★½　The Good Son (Mute, 1990)
★★★★　Henry's Dream (Mute, 1992)
★★★★　Live Seeds (Mute, 1993)
★★★★　Let Love In (Mute, 1994)
★★★　Murder Ballads (Reprise, 1996)
★★★★　The Boatman's Call (Reprise, 1997)
★★★★　The Best of Nick Cave and the Bad Seeds
　　　　(Mute, 1998)
★★★½　No More Shall We Part (Warner Bros., 2001)
★★★　Nocturama (Anti, 2003)

Birthday Party

★★★　Hee-Haw (1979–80; Buddha, 2000)
★★★　Prayers on Fire (1981; Buddha, 2000)
★★★　Junkyard (1983; Buddha, 2000)
★★★★　Mutiny/The Bad Seed (1983; Buddha, 2000)
★★★½　Hits (4AD, 1992)
★★★　Live, 1981–1982 (4AD, 1999)
★★★　John Peel Sessions (Fuel 2000, 2001)

Nick Cave wasn't the first punk with literary ambitions, nor was he the first rock singer to be fascinated and inspired by suffering, religion, or the gothic lore of the American South. But few have explored these themes with Cave's passion and determination, or lasted as long. Scholarly and tasteful, yet unafraid to plunge into genuinely disturbing territory, Cave's songs of dark romance and soulful pain are articulations of a worldview that champions any source of deep, honest emotion, be it love or hate.

Cave and his first group, the Birthday Party, moved from Australia to London in 1980 and took the post-punk scene there by storm. With frantic, explosive songs that seemed to barely hold together as they were played, and Cave's maniacal ravings ("Release the bats! Release the bats!/Pump them up and explode the things") delivered in a Mephistophelean baritone, the group—guitarist Roland S. Howard, drummer Mick Harvey, bassist Tracey Pew, and a rotating cast—set a post-Stooges standard for chaos in rock.

The band's sloppiness drained some of the music's force (the live set attests to this), but at its best, as in the late sessions collected on *Mutiny/The Bad Seed,* they summon fearsome demons. The Birthday Party was built to collapse, and in its wake Cave formed a new band, the Bad Seeds, with Birthday Party alumni (Harvey and *éminence grise* Anita Lane) and others of like minds (bassist Barry Adamson, guitarist and noisemonger Blixa Bargeld from Einstürzende Neu-

bauten). From the first notes of *From Her to Eternity* Cave's new vision is clear: a group with the power and control to channel the morbid grandeur of his lyrics. A cover of Leonard Cohen's "Avalanche" and the title track are slow exorcisms, with brooding, bluesy mantras building into erotic floods; only the silly cover of Elvis' "In the Ghetto" breaks the spell.

With *The First Born Is Dead,* Cave confronted head-on the specter of the blues that had hovered over his work from the beginning. The album's eight songs are a baptism in the blues as a demonic force, an almost unbearably intense experience that moves from the mythic birth of Elvis Presley ("Tupelo") to a trip on the bluntly metaphoric "Train Long-Suffering" ("In the name of pain and suffering/There comes a train/ . . . Woo-woo! Woo-woo!") to a grisly death of strangled guitar ("Six Strings That Drew Blood"). Reinterpreting the blues for the merciless climate of the '80s, it is one of Cave's most unflinchingly powerful statements.

Kicking Against the Pricks is a missable collection of covers that merely codifies obvious influences (Johnny Cash, Velvet Underground), but *Your Funeral . . . My Trial* and *Tender Prey* break bold new ground. Barely three years since his howling days with the Birthday Party, Cave ably slides into the guise of an unsmiling crooner; with a few tricks borrowed from U2 and Tom Waits, the Bad Seeds supply subtle and atmospheric instrumentation. After *Your Funeral's* haunted dreamscape, *Tender Prey* is a cold-eyed, all-too-real trip through hell on earth, beginning with an agonizing first-person narrative of death by electrocution in "The Mercy Seat" ("I think my head is smoking/And in a way I'm hoping/To be done with all these looks of disbelief"). "Up Jumped the Devil" and "Deanna," a love letter to a bad girl as only Cave can deliver it, are his first strong pop singles.

In 1989 Cave moved to Brazil and found new inspiration in the concept of *saudade,* a mixture of longing, sadness, and deep sensuality. *The Good Son* opens with a reverie sung partially in Portuguese, "Foi Na Cruz" ("It Was on the Cross"), and reintroduces Nick Cave as a compassionate, Christlike absorber of mournful emotions ("The Good Son," "Sorrow's Child," "The Weeping Song"). *Henry's Dream* takes those emotions and runs with them in quasi-conceptual narrative form. Henry (along with a series of other Cave-like characters) is man adrift in a cruel world, who struggles to express his woe ("Brother, My Cup Is Empty") but is always stymied ("Suspicion and dark murmurs surround me/Everywhere I go they confound me"). There isn't much of a literal plot, but the emotional narrative is painfully clear, and the songs—some of Cave's best, like "Papa

Won't Leave You, Henry" and "Straight to You"—are played with a masterly eloquence by the Bad Seeds, now sounding like true vets.

Let Love In is Cave and the Bad Seeds at a peak moment of songwriting and instrumental skill, every nuance played with total confidence and control (captured beautifully on *Live Seeds*). "Red Right Hand," written by the group as a whole, is a gothic masterpiece with a creeping rhythm and a creaking organ line, one of the band's most instantly catchy tunes. Cave is truly loving his sinister Elvis act throughout, but sings with a faith and earnestness in "Lay Me Low" and "Let Love In." *Murder Ballads* is a set of gimmicky duets sung with P.J. Harvey, Kylie Minogue, and Shane MacGowan; Cave's solo songs ("Stagger Lee," "O'Malley's Bar") show what he can do without such celebrity distractions.

Cave's '90s masterpiece is *The Boatman's Call,* a solemn and steady collection of introspective piano ballads. "Into My Arms," sung with just piano and bass, contemplates divine versus earthly love, as Cave says, "I don't believe in an interventionist God," and then hedges: "But if I did, I would kneel down and ask Him/Not to intervene when it came to you." In "People Ain't No Good," he struggles unconvincingly to hold on to his misanthropy. This is mature, confessional songwriting, vividly interpreted for the postgoth age. *No More Shall We Part* treads similar but more maudlin ground; the highlight is a deliciously vicious jab at paranoid fundamentalism, "God Is in the House." *Nocturama* is more of the same, and though it's beautiful stuff, like *No More* it lacks the bare emotional force of its predecessors. (Though you might forget that listening to the 15-minute ode to passion and obsession, "Babe, I'm on Fire.")   —B.S.

Cee-Lo
see GOODIE MOB

Kasey Chambers

★★★½   The Captain (EMI, 2000)
★★★½   Barricades & Brickwalls (EMI, 2002)

Australian Kasey Chambers is proof that you don't have to be an American hillbilly riding a losing streak to convincingly sing country music. Growing up, Chambers heard her mom and dad (and older brother Nash, now her producer) sing folk tunes nightly around a campfire—the family lived a nomadic existence on Australia's Nullarbor plains. Returning to civilization when Kasey was nine years old, the Chambers family launched a career as the Dead Ringer Band, and their brand of New Australian country caught on, leading to a string of seven successful albums.

Kasey Chambers began her solo career in 1998, after her parents separated. She recorded her solo debut, *The Captain,* in a frenzied, two-month live-recording binge on remote Norfolk Island, but word of her blunt, unsparingly direct songs soon spread to Nashville. Among her early fans were Buddy and Julie Miller, who contributed backing vocals to four of the album's songs.

The Captain, released in 1999 in Australia and 2000 elsewhere, established Chambers as a talent to watch: It won best country album at Australia's version of the Grammy Awards, and, as an opening act on several tours, the body-pierced Chambers earned the respect of some of the feistiest women in American country, among them Emmylou Harris and Lucinda Williams, who guests on *Barricades & Brickwalls'* trenchant "On a Bad Day."

Where *The Captain* brilliantly negotiates a balance between country and rock, *Barricades & Brickwalls* is more of a roots-music thoroughbred: Buoyant, fiddle-driven reels alternate with sour drinking songs, and rock guitars turn up as an occasional spice, not the primary ingredient. This keeps the focus on Chambers, whose laconic, down-to-earth singing style makes everything she sings sound like wisdom learned the hard way, lessons that could apply equally in the Tennessee hills and the Aussie outback.   —T.M.

Gene Chandler

★★★½   20 Greatest Hits (Collectables, 1994)
★★★   Live at the Regal (Collectables, 1994)
★★½   Rainbow '80: A Golden Classics Edition (Collectables, 1994)
★★½   Just Be True (Collectables, 1996)
★★★½   The Duke of Earl—The Best Of Gene Chandler (Collectables, 2000)

Gene Chandler's 1962 single "Duke of Earl" is a magnificent record, a blend of doo-wop background choruses and pop-soul lead vocals that was writ large in rock & roll history by the conviction of Chandler's performance: He digs into the lyric as if he believes every word of the tale about a man become royalty by dint of his romantic illusions. He promises to take his paramour—identified as the "Duchess of Earl"—on a walk through "my Dukedom, and a paradise we will share," all under the protection of the invincible Duke ("nothing can stop me now/because I'm the Duke of Earl"). Then he swoops into a keening falsetto wail and really gets his swerve on. This was a soul man whose macho bluster never subsumed his sensitive side. On "The Duke of Earl" the pose worked brilliantly, giving Chandler a chart-topping hit, and a career-defining one at that.

Chandler was never again to impact the culture so dramatically, but he carved out a solid career over the course of nearly three decades of recordings. The critical Vee Jay and Constellation recordings of the '60s can be found on two first-rate collections, *The Duke of Earl—The Best of Gene Chandler* and *20 Greatest Hits,* whereas 1980's *Rainbow '80—A Golden Classics Edition* is a 17-track overview of Chandler's late-career Chi-Sound years in the '70s.   —D.M.

Tracy Chapman

★★★★½ Tracy Chapman (Elektra, 1988)
★★★★ Crossroads (Elektra, 1989)
★★★ Matters of the Heart (Elektra, 1992)
★★★½ New Beginning (Elektra, 1995)
★★★½ Telling Stories (Elektra, 2000)
★★ Let It Rain (Elektra, 2002)

One of those rare talents who seem to have sprung full-grown, Chapman found instant success with her 1988 debut. For a while, singers like Suzanne Vega and Rickie Lee Jones had been making the world safe for sharp, no-nonsense women singers, and the climate was right for Chapman's arrival. Still, no one was prepared for the depth and breadth of the album—for its dignity, seasoned musicality, or thematic reach.

"Fast Car" was the first marvel, a folk song real enough to acknowledge the existence of convenience stores and a woman's thirst for speed. And it sounded great, too: Drum heavy and tough, its efficiency allowed Chapman's voice to glide and slur. Then there was "Talkin' 'Bout a Revolution," its '60s spirit revamped by a Reagan-era urgency (and by the fact that Chapman was no countercultural vet, but a young black woman). "For My Lover" showed that she could also handle the intimate revolution: A hip defense of loving however you want to love, it alluded to both a Virginia jail and psychoanalysis, encapsulating Chapman's neat blending of archetypal folk references and the talk of today.

Chapman's followup, *Crossroads,* was also fine. Again, she offered folk's perennial philosophy—working-class solidarity, a yearning for independence and release—alongside newer ways of thinking: woman power, African-American pride, and self-help stubbornness. With violin played by ex-Dylan accompanist Scarlet Rivera, "This Time" revealed the writer's new capacity for elegance; Neil Young, reprising the childlike piano of "Helpless," added grace to "All That You Have Is Your Soul." And throughout the record, Chapman's knowing vocals sounded wise beyond her years. *Matters of the Heart,* an introspective album, didn't break any new ground; none of its at-

mospheric songs really stood out. *New Beginning* was subtler and richer, and its Grammy-winning single, "Give Me One Reason," spurred a Chapman revival. *Telling Stories* was strong and steady—clear-eyed, poetic folk/funk of the kind that first got Chapman noticed. On *Let It Rain* Chapman seems a little stuck, both stylistically and emotionally: there are no revelations here. But stay tuned.   —P.E.

Charlatans U.K.

★★ Some Friendly (1990; Beggars Banquet, 1998)
★★★ Between 10th and 11th (Beggars Banquet, 1992)
★★★ Up to Our Hips (Beggars Banquet, 1994)
★★★½ The Charlatans U.K. (Beggars Banquet, 1995)
★★★★ Tellin' Stories (Beggars Banquet, 1997)
★★★★ Melting Pot (Beggars Banquet, 1998)
★★★ Us and Us Only (MCA, 1999)
★★ Wonderland (MCA, 2001)
★★★ Songs From the Other Side (Beggars Banquet, 2002)

The Charlatans had the misfortune to hail from Manchester, England, during roughly the same period as groups like the Stone Roses and the Happy Mondays, and have spent the better part of their career living down the association. The fact that their 1990 debut, *Some Friendly,* was a derivative ode to dippy, Hammond-happy psych-pop didn't help. On their darker second effort, the Charlatans (who would soon add the "U.K." to their American releases to avoid confusion—and litigation—with the '60s Bay Area psychedelic group of the same name) first demonstrated their growing fascination for classic rock of the Doors/ *Exile on Main Street* variety. Though there's nothing much memorable here (except for the fine, if workmanlike, "Tremelo Song") and not a hook in sight, it was nevertheless a strong step forward from their debut.

In 1994 *Up to Our Hips,* a comparatively uncomplicated pop record mostly notable for containing the great semi-hit "Can't Get Out of Bed," ushered in an era of intra-band turmoil that would play out over the next few records and included lineup changes, the embezzlement conviction of the band's accountant, and the armed robbery conviction of keyboard player Rob Collins, who would later be killed by a drunk driver. The albums from this period—1995's *The Charlatans U.K.* and 1997's *Tellin' Stories*—are the group's finest, charting their progression from Mancunian faux-pop hedonists to England's most assured purveyors of soulful Brit-rock. Tracks like "North Country Boy" and "Here Comes a Soul Saver" suggest a growing fondness for country-folk and blues-rock that, all previous evidence to the contrary, oddly suits them, and the psychedelic flourishes are no longer laid on with a trowel.

The greatest hits/odds and sods compilation *Melting Pot* followed, offering all of the band's hits and a track remixed by the Chemical Brothers, with whom the Charlatans often collaborated. *Us and Us Only* served mostly as a showcase for the group's growing Bob Dylan fascination, with the usual pop and psychedelia sprinkled throughout. Released September 11, 2001, and quickly forgotten (stateside, at least) *Wonderland* mixes electronica, pop, rock, and disco grooves in a not entirely satisfying way. Though singer Tim Burgess adopts a passable falsetto on tracks like "I Just Can't Get Over Losing You," and the record-opening "You're So Pretty—We're So Pretty" is atypically witty, this is the group's most disjointed effort since their debut. Though not as essential as *Melting Pot*, 2002's *Songs From the Other Side* collates seven years' worth of Beggars Banquet B sides, and includes several remixes and instrumentals.   —A.S.

Ray Charles

★★★½   The Great Ray Charles (1956; Atlantic, 1987)
★★★★   Ray Charles (Atlantic, 1957)
★★★★½   The Genius of Ray Charles (Atlantic, 1959)
★★½   The Genius Hits the Road (ABC, 1960)
★★★   The Genius After Hours (1961; Atlantic, 1985)
★★★★   The Genius Sings the Blues (1961; Atlantic Import, 2003)
★★★★   The Greatest! (Atlantic, 1961)
★★★   Dedicated to You (ABC, 1961)
★★★★½   Genius + Soul = Jazz/My Kind of Jazz (1961; Rhino, 1997)
★★★★   Ray Charles and Betty Carter (1961; DCC, 1988)
★★★★★   Modern Sounds in Country and Western Music (1962; Rhino, 1988)
★★★½   Berlin, 1962 (Pablo, 1996)
★★★★★   Modern Sounds in Country and Western Music, Vol. 2 (ABC, 1963)
★★★½   Ingredients in a Recipe for Soul/Have a Smile With Me (1963, 1964; Rhino, 1997)
★★★½   Sweet and Sour Tears (1964; Rhino, 1997)
★★★★   Live in Concert (ABC, 1965)
★★★   Together Again (ABC, 1965)
★★★½   Crying Time (ABC, 1966)
★★★   Ray's Moods (ABC, 1966)
★★★   A Portrait of Ray (ABC, 1968)
★★★½   The Best of Ray Charles (1956–58) (Atlantic, 1970)
★★★   Volcanic Action of My Soul (ABC, 1971)
★★★★★   25th Anniversary in Show Business Salute to Ray Charles (ABC, 1971)

★★½   Through the Eyes of Love (ABC, 1972)
★★★   Jazz Number II (Tangerine, 1972)
★★★★   Renaissance (Crossover, 1975)
★★★   True to Life (Atlantic, 1977)
★★½   The Early Years (1978; King, 1996)
★★½   Love & Peace (Atlantic, 1978)
★★★   Ain't It So (Atlantic, 1979)
★★★   Brother Ray Is at It Again (Atlantic, 1980)
★★★★   A Life in Music (1956–59) (Atlantic, 1982)
★★★   Wish You Were Here Tonight (Columbia, 1983)
★★   Do I Ever Cross Your Mind (Columbia, 1984)
★★½   Friendship (Columbia, 1984)
★★   The Spirit of Christmas (1985; Rhino, 1997)
★★   From the Pages of My Mind (Columbia, 1986)
★★★★   Ray Charles Live (1958–59) (Atlantic, 1987)
★★★★★   Greatest Country & Western Hits (1962–65) (DCC, 1988)
★★★★   Greatest Hits, Vol. 1 (1960–67) (Rhino, 1988)
★★★★   Greatest Hits, Vol. 2 (1960–72) (Rhino, 1988)
★★½   Just Between Us (Columbia, 1988)
★★★★★   Anthology (Rhino, 1989)
★★   Seven Spanish Angels and Other Hits (Columbia, 1989)
★½   Would You Believe? (Warner Bros., 1990)
★½   My World (Warner Bros., 1993)
★★★★★   The Birth of Soul (1952–59) (Atlantic, 1991)
★★★★½   Genius & Soul: The 50th Anniversary Collection (Rhino, 1997)
★★★   Standards (Rhino, 1998)
★★★★½   The Definitive Ray Charles (Rhino, 2001)
★★★   Ray Charles Sings for America (Rhino, 2002)

with Milt Jackson
★★★   Soul Brothers (Atlantic, 1958)
★★½   Soul Meeting (Atlantic, 1962)
★★★   Soul Brothers/Soul Meeting (1957–58) (Atlantic, 1989)

with Cleo Laine
★★★★★   Porgy & Bess (1976; RCA, 1989)

One of popular music's most protean talents, Ray Charles tried almost every imaginable style in his 40-odd years as a recording artist, building a body of work that includes not only classic R&B and rock numbers, but also forays into country, jazz, and even middle-of-the-road pop. His heartfelt eclecticism has resulted in some astonishing music, but it has also led to enough misguided and mediocre work to make even the most sympathetic listener wish that the singer's judgment was as sterling as his talent.

Charles made his first recordings in 1947 and 1948 and began releasing singles on the Downbeat label (which eventually became Swingtime) in 1949. These sides have been assembled in low-cost packages of varying content and quality; to that extent, *The Early Years* is typical, offering minimal fidelity and little or no recording information, though habitués of bargain bins and used-record stores will surely find others. Musically, the value of these collections is marginal, as Charles' earliest singles owe much to the sound of Charles Brown or Nat "King" Cole. But the singer's maturity is immediately apparent, even if his future greatness is not.

As such, the Ray Charles story begins, for all intents and purposes, in 1952, when his contract with Swingtime was purchased by Atlantic Records. Atlantic was where Charles' sound finally came into focus, and where he recorded his first, and in many ways his most influential, R&B hits, although it took a few years for him to build up to that point. Those interested in a chronological view of his progress should proceed directly to the triple-album *The Birth of Soul,* which finds the young singer/pianist starting with more or less conventional blues ("The Sun's Gonna Shine Again") and jump tunes ("Mess Around," "Jumpin' in the Morning") before hitting on the formula that would beget "I Got a Woman," "Hallelujah I Love Her So," and other breakthrough singles. What makes these singles so affecting is the way they fuse jump-blues rhythm work to a gospel-inflected vocal, an approach that electrified pop fans (but scandalized churchgoers, who felt its marriage of secular and spiritual was nothing short of sacrilege). "I Got a Woman," "Mess Around," and "Hallelujah I Love Her So" are all on *Ray Charles,* though lesser tunes like "Funny but I Still Love You" and "Losing Hand" are just as interesting, if only for Mickey Baker's growling guitar work. *Yes Indeed!!* adds Charles' first Top 40 hit, "Swanee River Rock (Talkin' 'Bout That River)," as well as the similarly soulful "Leave My Woman Alone" and "Lonely Avenue," while *What'd I Say* delivers the singer's first Top 10 pop hit, the supercharged call-and-response number "What'd I Say," as well as the churchy "Tell All the World About You" and a surprisingly swinging version of the Scottish folk song "My Bonnie." "I Believe to My Soul" and "Hard Times" are the highlights of *The Genius Sings the Blues,* but the album flanks those performances with lesser numbers from Charles' earliest sessions for the label. (*The Birth of Soul* includes everything on these four albums, which have been deleted but are widely available on import.) *Live* augments the 1958 recording *Ray Charles at Newport* with six selections recorded a year later (and originally released on *Ray Charles in Person*) and is a stunning testament to the power of Charles' live band, particularly Margie Hendrix of the Raeletts.

Even though his commercial success was strictly with R&B tunes, Atlantic considered Charles a jazz musician as well as a pop star; indeed, his Atlantic discography contains almost as much instrumental work as vocal. Unfortunately, his Atlantic jazz sessions have been packaged and repackaged so many times over the years that it takes some work to sort it all out. Even the easy, one-stop double-disc sampler of such sides, *Blues + Jazz,* is now out of print. Several titles have been reissued by Rhino as twofers, often joining a weaker set with a stronger one.

Whether it's worth sifting through these titles is, of course, another issue entirely. Charles isn't a bad jazz pianist, but he isn't an especially inspiring one, either, being more adept at rhythm work and accompaniment than strict improvisation. Then again, these aren't terribly demanding jazz dates, tending more toward the sort of soul-jazz groovesmanship of Ramsey Lewis or Ahmad Jamal, with only the Milt Jackson collaborations pushing the playing beyond the pedestrian. Some of that can be chalked up to the fact that *Soul Brothers* and *Soul Meeting* find Charles collaborating with a better class of musician (Oscar Pettiford, Connie Kay, Kenny Burrell), but both recordings feature Charles on alto saxophone, an instrument that brings out much of the same soulful passion that informs his singing.

Perhaps the most important of his albums for Atlantic is *The Genius of Ray Charles*—not because it's full of hits (it isn't) or contains his best work for the label (it doesn't), but because it introduces the musical approach he would follow for much of the '70s. Although *The Genius of Ray Charles* puts him in front of a big band, the sound he pursues is nothing like that of the swing-era bands, or even the jazzy, large-ensemble sound that singers like Frank Sinatra and Dean Martin went for; instead, what Charles comes up with is a curious hybrid of the brassy R&B of his pop-oriented recordings and the showy schmaltz favored by the era's middle-of-the-road acts. Hence, Charles bounces from the powerhouse blues of "Let the Good Times Roll" or "Two Years of Torture" to overblown, gimmicky renditions of fare like "Alexander's Ragtime Band," although at times, he's able to incorporate elements of both ("Come Rain or Come Shine"). (Be aware, however, that the album is abysmally recorded, with frequent overmodulation muddying its brasher moments.)

By the dawn of the '60s, Charles had jumped to ABC Records, negotiating a deal that gave him, among other things, full ownership of the master tapes of the recordings he made for the label. Ironically, Charles' control of these recordings is part of the reason most of his albums from this era have been out of print for years, despite the fact that this period produced his biggest hits, including such singles as "Hit the Road Jack" and "Unchain My Heart." Granted, most of Charles' Top 40 hits from this period have been collected on the two Dunhill CDs, *His Greatest Hits, Vol. 1* and *Vol. 2,* but considering Charles first began to think in terms of albums instead of singles and planned his recordings with that in mind during this phase, serious listeners have little choice but to seek out the used-record market.

Still, it helps to shop carefully, for in the early '60s, Charles had an unfortunate fondness for conceptually organized albums, an approach that often led to trouble. His first album, for instance, was a collection of place-name songs called *The Genius Hits the Road,* which on the one hand boasts "Georgia on My Mind," perhaps his greatest ballad performance ever, and on the other drags in such dreck as "Moon Over Miami" and an appallingly gimmicky "Deep in the Heart of Texas." *Dedicated to You* focuses on songs featuring women's names in their titles; *Sweet and Sour Tears* offers songs about crying; *Have a Smile With Me* goes for allegedly funny songs like "Two Ton Tessie" and "The Man With the Weird Beard"; and so on. Most seem a trifle forced, but when Charles gets hold of a theme that grabs him—say, "Let's Go Get Stoned"—the results are amazing.

Nowhere is that more the case than on *Modern Sounds in Country and Western Music,* an album of country songs performed Ray Charles–style. This wasn't unknown territory for a singer who had grown up listening to country music and had even played piano in a hillbilly band, but what makes the album work is his ability to transform these songs. Consider, for instance, the way he turns Floyd Tillman's twangy "It Makes No Difference Now" into a jaunty, horn-driven blues or adds a jazzy edge to Hank Williams' "Hey, Good Lookin'." But it was his sturdily straightforward reading of the Don Gibson hit "I Can't Stop Loving You" that struck a strong chord with the pop audience. Even more stunning is his soulful take on "You Are My Sunshine," from *Modern Sounds in Country and Western Music, Vol. 2* (and added as a bonus track to Rhino's CD version of *Modern Sounds in Country and Western Music*), which treats it as a groove tune, with solid rhythm work and scintillating interplay with the Raeletts. But then, Charles' second *Modern Sounds* album is generally superior to the first because of its smoother balladry (his version of Williams' "Your Cheatin' Heart") and because the blues tunes rock harder (his smouldering rendition of Gibson's "Don't Tell Me Your Troubles").

As he had done at Atlantic, Charles continued to make jazz albums for ABC. *Genius + Soul = Jazz* is by far the best of the lot, since its big-band-and-organ arrangements retain much of the sound of his pop albums. But the low-key and swinging *Ray Charles and Betty Carter* also shines, particularly when the two genially spar through "Baby, It's Cold Outside." There are also a few jazzy moments on *Live in Concert,* much as there were on his Newport album for Atlantic. But his self-indulgent '70s jazz albums are easily ignored, apart from the funkier moments of *My Kind of Jazz* ("Booty Butt").

By the mid-'60s, much of Charles' output was solidly middle-of-the-road, with a heavy emphasis on string-laden ballads. That's not to say he had abandoned the soul side of his sound, just that it grew ever more compartmentalized. And by the mid-'70s, Charles was better known for what he'd done than for what he was doing. That didn't stop him from making good records, of course—the *Porgy & Bess* he recorded with Cleo Laine is easily one of the best pop performances those songs have seen, at times surpassing even the legendary Louis Armstrong/Ella Fitzgerald version—but the good ones were becoming increasingly rare. He returned to Atlantic in 1977 and released four albums, none of which particularly demand hearing, though they have their moments: his "Oh, What a Beautiful Morning," from *True to Life,* for instance; the quasi-disco "You 20th Century Fox," from *Love & Peace,* is a genuine hoot; the way he rephrases the Dobie Gray hit "Drift Away" on *Ain't It So.*

There was worse to come, however. Charles jumped to Columbia in 1983, where he proceeded to turn himself into a country singer. It wasn't a complete transformation, of course; *Just Between Us* is mostly blues and features a rollicking "Save the Bones for Henry Jones," recorded with Lou Rawls and Milt Jackson, while *The Spirit of Christmas* reverts to the MOR/R&B formula that served him so well in the '60s. When Charles did sing country for Columbia, though, he sang it straight, without any of the R&B overtones that marked his first C&W experiments. And frankly, the music gains nothing from his fidelity. If anything, the reverse is true, as most of these albums are indistinguishable from the Music Row hackwork Charles' producer, Billy Sherrill, churned out for his other clients. Granted, the singer does occasionally rise above the production-line predictability of his material, as when he breathes life into "3/4 Time" on *Wish You Were Here Tonight,* or joins Merle Haggard in savoring the loneliness of a "Little Hotel Room" on *Friendship.* Still, saying these albums aren't entirely bad hardly counts as a recommendation. The indefatigable Charles followed his first, ragged Warner Bros. release, *Would You Believe?,* with a Pepsi commercial that proved more popular than any of his contemporary recordings. And the clever, enjoyable repackaging of *Sings for America* confirms that Charles has repertoire for all circumstances and sensibilities. Part of his genius is that he can never be counted out for good.

Given the breadth of Charles' output, it might seem that the best introduction would be a well-balanced best-of album. *A 25th Anniversary in Show Business Salute* is perhaps the best singles package ever assembled, inasmuch as its 35-song selection draws from his Atlantic and ABC recordings; the trouble is, the set has been long out of print. Nowadays, *Definitive Ray Charles* makes a very decent substitute. The five-CD *Genius & Soul: The 50th Anniversary Collection* attempts to be the definitive update of the *25th Anniversary* set, though the quality wobbles on the later discs. Still, it remains the Charles box for those who want a big one. *Standards* concentrates on Charles' pop-soul proclivities, as do the well-organized *Greatest Hits* volumes on Rhino, which add welcome energetic cuts. Rhino's *Anthology* is an excellent collection that includes the ABC hits and other recordings of interest. Perhaps the most satisfying way to celebrate the ongoing legend of Ray Charles is through a pair of vivid performance DVDs: *In Concert* (Image, 2001) and *Live at Montreux Jazz Festival* (Geneon, 2002). Before his death in June 2004 at the age of 73, Charles finished an album of duets, released as this book goes to press. —J.D.C./M.M.

Cheap Trick

★★★★	Cheap Trick (Epic, 1977)	
★★★★	In Color (Epic, 1977)	
★★★★	Heaven Tonight (Epic, 1978)	
★★★★	Live at Budokan (Sony, 1979)	
★★★	Dream Police (Epic, 1979)	
★★	All Shook Up (Epic, 1980)	
★★	One on One (Epic, 1982)	
★★★	Next Position Please (Epic, 1983)	
★★	Standing on The Edge (Epic, 1985)	
★★	The Doctor (Epic, 1986)	
★★★	Lap of Luxury (Epic, 1988)	
★	Busted (Epic, 1990)	
★★★	Woke Up With a Monster (Warner, 1994)	
★★★	Cheap Trick (Red Ant, 1997)	
★★½	Special One (Big 3, 2003)	
★★★★	The Essential Cheap Trick (Epic/Legacy, 2004)	

From bar band could-be's to arena rocking superstars, from bargain bin has-beens to objects of hipster rediscovery, Cheap Trick has always been, well, Cheap Trick. Playing Beatlesque melodies with the might of Kiss or Nugent, they're humorous, hook-filled, bracingly loud, and subtly sensitive. Coming out of the Midwest bar-band scene in the mid-'70s, the band de-

buted with *Cheap Trick,* a sharp collection of power pop with an almost metallic edge. Songs like "He's A Whore" displayed all the band's weapons: Rick Nielsen's savage yet melodic guitars, Bun E. Carlos' seemingly multilimbed fills, Tom Petersson's driving bass, and Robin Zander's archetypal rock & roll voice (capable of an earthy, raw tone as well as sugar-sweet cooing). The band went on a three-album run to start their career, with *In Color* and *Heaven Tonight* following up the debut. These albums contain more anthems ("Surrender" being the absolute zenith of their art) than you can pump a fist at. The seminal *Live at Budokan* is a testament to both their tremendous power as a live act and the near maniacal devotion of their Japanese fans. Riding high off the success of one of the great live records of all time, the band made *Dream Police,* which drops a bit in consistency and sadly ups the sheen to the production end of things (though the title track remains a classic).

The band continued to pursue ill-fitting production when they teamed with Beatles producer George Martin on *All Shook Up.* Power-pop Svengali Todd Rundgren helped the band adjust to new-wave sonics on the underrated *Next Position Please,* which contains the gorgeous "I Can't Take It."

The group saw both their commercial rewards and their aesthetic standards take a dip for much of the '80s until 1988's *Lap of Luxury,* which features two of that year's most ubiquitous hits: "The Flame" and the Elvis Presley cover "Don't Be Cruel." When Cheap Trick finally got paid it was almost too late; they were thought of as senior members of the hair-metal movement, and one-hit wonders at that.

The band had a quiet first half of the '90s with two forgettable albums, but their second self-titled release was a return to form, shedding much of the glossy production that had hampered so many of their records. *Special One* was a case of forgettable self-parody, but with the reissue of several of their early albums, Cheap Trick nonetheless earned the respect they deserved. —M.C./C.R.

Chemical Brothers

★★★	Exit Planet Dust (Astralwerks, 1995)	
★★★★	Dig Your Own Hole (Astralwerks, 1997)	
★★★	Surrender (Astralwerks, 1999)	
★★½	Come With Us (Astralwerks, 2002)	
★★★½	Singles 93–03 (Astralwerks, 2003)	

Manchester, U.K., duo Tom Rowlands and Ed Simons put the arena-rock bombast in Britain's rave scene by blending power-chord guitars with old-school house, hip-hop breakbeats, and soul dusties. Little wonder that the Chemical Brothers translate to mainstream American audiences far better than some of their more adventurous and esoteric U.K. peers.

Exit Planet Dust sets the template for what became known as Big Beat, an offshoot of techno that turns the four-four kick drums of house into a battalion of virtual John Bonhams, augmented by screeching sirens and shape-shifting sound effects that doubled as a soundtrack for ecstasy trips. Tim Burgess (Charlatans U.K.) and a then-unknown Beth Orton add cameo vocals, but the album never quite matches the peaks of the duo's live sets.

Dig Your Own Hole refines the formula and becomes a defining record for the new rave generation: a mix of cameo vocalists, walloping drum loops, and disco psychedelia that crushes barriers between genres. "Block Rockin' Beats" sets the tone, driving Nine Inch Nail–sized beats through a Schooly D hip-hop sample, while "Setting Sun" channels the Beatles' "Tomorrow Never Knows" through Oasis' Noel Gallagher, whose melodic instincts balance the Chems' AC/DC-like penchant for turning everything up past eleven.

The electro-beat high starts to wear off on *Surrender,* which plays like a series of homages to the duo's influences: Kraftwerk on "Music: Response," *Revolver*-era Beatles on "Let Forever Be" (with Gallagher again on vocals), and New Order on "Out of Control" (with New Order's Bernard Summer on vocals). *Come With Us* is a return to a more "underground" sound; that is to say, it owes more to house than rock. But only the tripped-out, nearly beatless atmospherics of "Hoops" qualify as innovative.

Singles 93–03 nicely summarizes the Brothers' decade-long run while reflecting their decline; the latter-day tracks seem gimmicky and uninspired compared to the early rave classics. —G.K.

Clifton Chenier

★★★★ Louisiana Blues and Zydeco (1965; Arhoolie, 1990)
★★★★ Bon Ton Roulet (1966–73; Arhoolie, 1990)
★★★★ Black Snake Blues (1967; Arhoolie, 1997)
★★★ Sings the Blues (1969; Arhoolie, 1988)
★★★★ Bayou Blues (Specialty, 1971)
★★★★ Out West (1971; Arhoolie, 1991)
★★★★½ Bogalusa Boogie (1975; Arhoolie, 1990)
★★★★ Live at Montreux (1975; Arhoolie, 1991)
★★★ Boogie in Black and White (Jin, 1976)
★★★★ Boogie 'N' Zydeco (Maison de Soul, 1977)
★★★ Red Hot Louisiana Band (Arhoolie, 1978)
★★★ New Orleans (GNP Crescendo, 1978)
★★★ King of Zydeco (Home Cooking, 1980)
★★★★ Classic Clifton (Arhoolie, 1980)
★★★ King of Zydeco (Arhoolie, 1981)

★★★★★ I'm Here (Alligator, 1982)
★★★ Country Boy Now Grammy Award Winner 1984! (Maison de Soul, 1984)
★★★ Live at the San Francisco Blues Festival (Arhoolie, 1986)
★★★★ 60 Minutes with the King of Zydeco (Arhoolie, 1988)
★★★ Clifton Chenier & Rockin' Dupsie (Flyright, 1989)
★★★ Live at St. Mark's (Arhoolie, 1990)
★★★★★ Zydeco Dynamite: The Clifton Chenier Anthology (Rhino, 1993)

Clifton Chenier wasn't just the King of Zydeco—he pretty much invented zydeco as we know it. Although he came up playing the same Creole party music as his father and grandfather, the young accordionist began to incorporate blues elements into his sound in the mid-'50s, and in so doing redefined zydeco. Although Chenier made his first recordings for the tiny Elko label in 1954, his earliest work in print at this writing are his 1955 sessions for Specialty, collected on *Bayou Blues:* tracks like "I'm On My Way" and "Eh, Petite Fille" are typical of his blues-fueled style. His only other recordings from this period to have made the transition to digital can be found on the first eight tracks of *Clifton Chenier & Rockin' Dopsie,* but as much as these sessions capture the sweaty enthusiasm of his playing, their heavily distorted sound makes them of interest only to dedicated fans.

Chenier's recordings thereafter simply refined the style he'd developed in the '50s. *Bon Ton Roulet* shows how well he could rock it, while the solidly traditional two-steps and waltzes included on *Louisiana Blues & Zydeco* are proof that Chenier was by no means just a rocker. Still, perhaps the best of Chenier's albums is *Bogalusa Boogie,* a near-flawless recording that vividly captures the accordion-and-washboard interplay between Clifton and his brother Cleveland as well as the solidly soulful groove of their Red Hot Louisiana Band.

A diabetic, Chenier's health began to fail in 1979, but that hardly slowed his recording schedule; if anything, it increased. Unfortunately, of the albums recorded between 1979 and his death in 1987, only *I'm Here* manages any consistent degree of quality; the rest, though generally superior to most of his competition, lack the sparkle of his earlier output. —J.D.C.

Cher

★★ Gypsies, Tramps & Thieves (MCA, 1971)
★★★ Cher (Geffen, 1982)
★★ Half Breed (MCA Special Products, 1992)
★★½ It's a Man's World (Reprise, 1996)

★★ Believe (Warner Bros., 1998)
★ Bittersweet: The Love Songs Collection (MCA, 1999)
★★½ The Millennium Collection—The Best of Cher (MCA, 2000)
★★★ Song for the Lonely (Warner Bros., 2001)
★★★½ The Very Best of Cher (Rhino, 2003)

Everybody knows Cher. In the '60s, she was the taller half of Sonny & Cher, singing "I Got You, Babe," "The Beat Goes On," and other showbiz-hippie hits with her shaggy husband, Sonny Bono. As early as 1965, she'd commenced what has become her unthinkably long string of solo hits, first scoring heavily when "Bang Bang (My Baby Shot Me Down)" went to #2 on the 1966 pop charts.

Between then and now, much has gone on in the life of Cher: TV shows, the break-up of her marriage to Bono, an acting career that yielded a Best Actress Oscar in 1987 for *Moonstruck,* several husbands and boyfriends; the death of Sonny; controversy concerning her relationship with her outspoken lesbian daughter, Chastity; beauty products sold on cable TV; face-lifts; megashopping—everything reported on in the media with the care, consistency, and detail usually reserved for the ongoing chronicling of popes. Cher never goes away. When she wrote her autobiography a few years back, she implied, in her unfailingly straightforward yet kindhearted way, that it was easy being a rock-identified female icon like Chrissie Hynde or Debbie Harry—but that, as a proud child of Hollywood, it was rather more of a feat to do it in feathers.

As a singer, she's always been a great celebrity, but that's not to say Cher hasn't had her grand moments in recorded sound. She has definitely had a way of making people want to hear her, over the course of decades and in several styles, at least in three-and-a-half-minute shots. Her sense of rhythm is nothing special, and her enunciation is often notably poor, but what Cher has is a rich, deep throb in her voice, usually at the lower end of her upper range, that she keeps returning to, keeps lavishing sound upon, keeps climbing upward into; at times, she sings more like someone trying to do an impersonation of a classy guitar soloist. This bent makes *Bittersweet,* a collection of standards, unlistenable, especially given Bono's goofy arrangements and his earless production of Cher's singing, which is horrible here. But her weird power makes throttle-heavy baroque '80s rock numbers such as "I Found Someone" or "We All Sleep Alone" (from *Cher*) seriously kick.

Gypsies, Tramps & Thieves and *Half Breed* are the original-release albums named for the enormous-selling hits, from 1971 and 1973 respectively, of their titles, and both pure stirring junk; spotty as collections, these albums indicate that Cher has usually worked best as a singles artist. The *20th Century Masters* anthology goes a way toward collecting her various hits from different record companies—a nice, long, musically chewy mix of "Take Me Home," Cher's 1979 disco debut; "The Way of Love," a signature ballad the size of Arizona. The job, however, didn't really get done until recently, when Rhino released *The Very Best of Cher.* It entered the pop album charts at #7.

The first track on that collection was "Believe," Cher's 1998 electronicized pop stroke that turned out to be her biggest record ever, a piece of music beloved by everyone from grocery store moms to Damon Albarn of Blur, who pronounced it brilliant. In 1995, she'd tried a proper adult pop album of the sexy and considered sort that Tina Turner, say, excels at. *It's a Man's World,* it was called, and Cher sang well enough, particularly on songs as important and well chosen as Paul Brady's "Paradise Is Here" and "The Sun Ain't Gonna Shine Anymore," the Walker Brothers' old '60s 45-rpm aria. Expensive, intelligently produced and conceived, the album was still only a little better than okay.

What Cher needed was a big fat hit—she just couldn't compete with Tracey Thorn—even if the producer did wildly alter her voice electronically. "Believe" was that tune. In her 50s, Cher had done an iconistic variation on her own iconhood. After September 11, 2001, she released "Song for the Lonely," a no-holds-barred dance-music prayer believably concerned about heroes, tragedy, people with recently broken hearts, and hope. Cher's transformation into the world's all-purpose kindhearted rock-identified female icon seemed complete. It was the triumph of feathers. —J.H.

Neneh Cherry

★★★★ Raw Like Sushi (Virgin, 1989)
★★★ Homebrew (Virgin, 1992)

A former punk singer and the daughter of jazz cornet player Don Cherry, Neneh Cherry won accolades for her unclassifiable debut from hip-hop, pop, R&B, and dance partisans alike. *Raw Like Sushi* focuses her ferocious energy on an honest treatment of social ills—specifically their effect on women—and witty takes on boy-girl culture. The music is refreshingly diverse, transforming the inoffensive R&B-inspired British dance music of the time into a delivery system for hard beats, rhymes, and rock instrumentation. The album's hit, "Buffalo Stance" (a cover of an obscure new-wave

B side), turned Cherry into a feminist star both hip-hoppers and popsters could love.

Sidelined for three years, Cherry finally followed up her acclaimed debut with *Homebrew,* a measured study of the same subjects covered on *Raw Like Sushi. Homebrew* goes further with the rock sound, particularly on the fierce "Money Love" and "Trout," the latter a duet with R.E.M.'s Michael Stipe. The rest is pride and optimism, up-from-the-ghetto stories and better-do-right demands, connected by the complex web of syncopated beats and arcing trip-hop lines of sound that give the record a mellow, loungey feel. Cherry's social idealism remains impeccable, but her earnestness is a bit of a letdown for those inspired by the sassy, keen-eyed commentator she so cleverly played on *Raw.* —A.B.

Vic Chesnutt

★★★	Little (1990; New West, 2004)
★★★½	West of Rome (1991; New West, 2004)
★★★½	Drunk (1993; New West, 2004)
★★★	Is the Actor Happy? (1995; New West, 2004)
★★★★	About to Choke (Capitol, 1996)
★★★★	The Salesman and Bernadette (Capricorn, 1998)
★★★	Left to His Own Devices (spinART, 2001)
★★	Silver Lake (New West, 2003)

Brute

★★	Nine High a Pallet (1995; Velocette, 2002)
★★	Co-Balt (Widespread, 2002)

Vic Chesnutt and Mr. and Mrs. Keneipp

★★★	Merriment (Backburner, 2000)

"I'm not an optimist/I'm not a realist/I might be a subrealist," sings Vic Chesnutt on *About to Choke*'s "Myrtle," a darkly comic, self-effacing riddle in a career filled with dark comedy, self-deprecation, and poetic riddles. Chesnutt, who was confined to a wheelchair after a car crash at age 18, has been one of the most prolific and enigmatic songwriters of his generation, writing in a simple style that nonetheless communicates immediate sensitivity and pain. His best songs capture, in the same breath, hope and disappointment, escape and self-destruction, love and pity—stories without a plot so much as a "subrealist" attention to detail.

Chesnutt was discovered in Athens, GA, by Michael Stipe, who produced his first two albums with a light hand. *Little*'s instrumentation is, for the most part, just Chesnutt and his guitar, which lends stark power to the album's most dramatic points. Chesnutt the poet appears fully formed here. "Gepetto" pictures Pinocchio's lonely creator left behind after his creation outgrows him, while closer to home, he tells of the anxiety of catching an opossum and a kitten in a rabbit trap and the relief when "we all three escaped safely." *West of Rome* expands the sound with a band but doesn't touch Chesnutt's outlook.

On *Drunk* and *Is the Actor Happy?*, Chesnutt delves deep into his psyche with portraits of a man bent on slow self-annihilation. "Sleeping Man" contemplates inactivity, while elsewhere on *Drunk,* he pictures cowardice of a more painful sort: "When I ran off and left her/She wasn't holding a baby/She was holding a bottle/And a big grudge against me." Chesnutt never says whether it's a bottle of formula or beer, but he makes his disappointment with himself quite clear. The reissues of the first four albums add more than 30 bonus tracks and telling essays by Stipe, Ian MacKaye of Fugazi, and other admirers.

Although Chesnutt's strong poetic voice is a constant—as is his thin, wavering little wail of a singing voice—his albums are a zigzag of varying instrumentation. *About to Choke* and *The Salesman and Bernadette* offer his most solid backing, as well as his most disciplined songwriting. "Degenerate" encapsulates *Choke*'s death-feeds-life theme with a prayer on the beauty and tragedy of ruin and transformation. "I am a rough ball of twine," he says. "But now I am frazzled and aloof/Degenerate, disintegrate the tight knots." The character sketches on *Bernadette* are easier to take, and the breezy accompaniment by the alt-country ensemble Lambchop is a delight. Chesnutt's wry humor, always present but usually smothered, gets a chance to shine: "She said her father looked like Woodrow Wilson. I saw him once and thought he looked a little bit like Truman. I know for a fact he has an Eisenhower ashtray." *Left to His Own Devices* was recorded by Chesnutt solo, and even though it features some outstanding songs, such as "Deadline," a chilling nursery rhyme about pressure, its unevenness can be irritating. The two albums he made under the name Brute, with the bland jam band Widespread Panic backing him, are anything but uneven—but also anything but memorable. That cannot be said, however, for *Merriment,* an unpolished yet utterly charming collaboration with Kelly and Nikki Keneipp, a couple in the Chesnutt circle who have also worked with Jack Logan. They wrote all the music, which is played clunkily but with heart. "Bless the idiot/That makes us split a gut" is one of the many brilliantly tossed-off lines that makes one wonder if there's any limit to Chesnutt's creativity.

Silver Lake, recorded in a Los Angeles mansion with a large, expert band, is warm, commodious, and a bit too slick. Many of the songs are not up to his usual standard, though that's slightly forgivable once you get to "In My Way, Yes," a rare glimpse of joy: "I never thought/I'd ever have a life like this/I never dreamed/I'd be alive." —B.S.

Chic

★★★	Chic (Atlantic, 1978)
★★★★	C'est Chic (Atlantic, 1978)
★★★★	Risqué (Atlantic, 1979)
★★★★½	Dance Dance Dance: The Best of Chic (Atlantic, 1991)
★★	Chic-ism (Warner Bros., 1992)
★★★	The Best of Chic, Vol. 2 (Rhino, 1992)
★★½	Live at the Budokan (Sumthing Else Music Works, 1999)
★★★★	The Very Best of Chic (Rhino, 2000)

Formed by New York session men Nile Rodgers and Bernard Edwards, Chic presided over the end of the disco era with a string of hits that celebrated the decadent high life with razor-sharp funk arrangements and classic pop hooks. Eschewing drippy orchestration and big-band anonymity, their style was slightly out of step with the times, or perhaps ahead of them: Chic's 1979 megahit "Good Times" formed the basis of both the Sugarhill Gang's joyously inventive "Rapper's Delight," a seminal hip-hop hit, and Queen's bloodless introduction to the materialistic rat race of the '80s, "Another One Bites the Dust."

With slick costumes, runway poses, and sophomoric French catchphrases ("Le freak/C'est chic"), the early albums exude a faux sophistication that is completely at odds with the band's tight grooves and all-American cheer-along vocals. Guitarist Rodgers and bassist Edwards reached to James Brown for the funk licks, but applied them to simple, hummable tunes, leaving plenty of negative space for you to get out there and dance. When it works, it's pop magic of the highest order: "Le Freak," "Good Times," "Dance, Dance, Dance (Yowsah, Yowsah, Yowsah)," and "I Want Your Love" are some of the most irresistible dance songs of all time. And when it fails, it's only disco. (Four later albums that dabbled in electro-funk thankfully are out of print.) *Dance Dance Dance* has all the essentials, and *The Best of Chic, Vol. 2,* making no pretense about delivering any more hits, mines the occasionally dazzling album cuts ("Hangin'," "Stage Fright"). The later Rhino set is skimpy and omits some essentials ("Chic Cheer," "Savoir Faire").

Rodgers and Edwards, who became two of the most sought-after producers in the business, reunited in 1992 for *Chic-ism,* a mostly dry run that only gets going on the last track, "M.M.F.T.C.F. (Make My Funk the Chic Funk)." Edwards died of pneumonia in 1996, at age 43, shortly after the Tokyo concert that resulted in *Live at Budokan.* —B.S.

Chicago

★★★	Chicago Transit Authority (Columbia, 1969)
★★½	Chicago II (Columbia, 1970)
★★½	Chicago III (Columbia, 1971)
★	Chicago IV: Live at Carnegie Hall (Columbia, 1971)
★★	Chicago V (Columbia, 1972)
★★½	Chicago VI (Columbia, 1973)
★★	Chicago VII (Columbia, 1974)
★★	Chicago VIII (Columbia, 1975)
★★★½	Chicago IX: Chicago's Greatest Hits (Columbia, 1975)
★★½	Chicago X (Columbia, 1976)
★★★	Chicago XI (Columbia, 1977)
★★½	Hot Streets (Columbia, 1978)
★	Chicago 13 (Columbia, 1979)
★½	Chicago XIV (Columbia, 1980)
★★★	Greatest Hits Volume II (Columbia, 1981)
★	Chicago 16 (Warner Bros., 1982)
★★★½	Hard to Say I'm Sorry (Columbia, 1983)
★	Chicago 17 (Warner Bros., 1984)
★	Chicago 18 (Warner Bros., 1986)
★	Chicago 19 (Reprise, 1988)
★½	Chicago's Greatest Hits 1982–89 (Warner Bros., 1989)
★	Chicago Twenty 1 (Warner Bros., 1991)
★★½	Group Portrait (Columbia/Legacy, 1991)
★	Night and Day (Giant, 1995)
★★	The Heart of Chicago 1967–1997 (Reprise, 1997)
★★	The Heart of Chicago 1967–1998, Vol. 2 (Reprise, 1998)
★½	Chicago 25: The Christmas Album (Chicago, 1998)
★★★	Best of Chicago (Rhino, 2002)

Doing for Roman numerals what Kiss did for lipstick, Chicago was the quintessential hippie-dad band of the '70s. These furry-headed guys employed a lot of horn players and dabbled in jazz-fusion schlock, but they were never as slimy as Blood, Sweat and Tears. Their forte was harmlessly groovy soft-rock hits like "Make Me Smile," "Does Anybody Really Know What Time It Is?," and everyone's favorite, "Saturday in the Park." They saved the indulgent flute-and-bongo solos for their album tracks, and rocked out in "25 or 6 to 4." They didn't have a star frontman: just a logo, goopy ballads, a little R&B grit now and then, smooth '70s lingo ("Can you dig it? Yes, I can!"), whimsical shots like "Harry Truman," and a name that disguised how totally L.A. they were. It was a version of hippiedom for people who had to get up in the morning, although the quadruple-vinyl monstrosity *Live at Carnegie Hall* proved that Chicago could also sell to the burnout crowd. Robert Lamm sang the best hits, but Peter Cetera sang their best ever, 1977's enigmatic and slightly scary "Baby, What a Big Surprise."

Chicago actually gave its twelfth album a title, *Hot Streets,* clearly the act of desperate men in the throes of a crisis. "Alive Again" was a perky hit, but the verbal-album-title gambit was soon abandoned, and it was a transitional period for the band after guitarist Terry Kath accidentally killed himself playing with a handgun. By the next big hit, "Hard to Say I'm Sorry" in 1982, Chicago was barely recognizable: horns and Roman numerals gone, synthesizers and Arabic numerals here to stay, Peter Cetera's whine up top. The Chicago of the '80s was an easy-listening franchise that really could have used a stoned clarinet solo or two to liven things up. In the '90s, as the radio hits disappeared, the band continued to have success as a live oldies act. *Night and Day* was a big-band tribute; *25,* a Christmas album. The best '70s hits are on 1975's *Chicago IX,* with the let's-paint-the-logo-on-the-wall cover. Most of the same songs appear on the *Group Portrait* box, the 2002 Rhino *Best of Chicago* (although in some inferior edits), and the 1983 *If You Leave Me Now,* which confusingly came out between *Chicago 16* and *Chicago 17.* Predictions that Chicago could kick Boston's ass have yet to be tested empirically. —R.S.

Alex Chilton

★★★★	Like Flies on Sherbert (Peabody, 1979)	
★★★★	Bach's Bottom (Razor & Tie, 1981)	
★★	Live in London (Aura, 1982)	
★★★½	Document (Aura, 1985)	
★★★	Alex Chilton's Lost Decade (Fan Club, 1985)	
★★★½	Feudalist Tarts (Big Time, 1985)	
★★★½	No Sex (Big Time, 1986)	
★★★½	High Priest (Big Time, 1987)	
★★★★	Black List (New Rose, 1990)	
★★★★	Stuff (New Rose, 1991)	
★★★★	19 Years: A Collection (Rhino, 1991)	
★★★	Clichés (Ardent, 1994)	
★★★★	High Priest/Black List (Razor & Tie, 1994)	
★★½	A Man Called Destruction (Ardent, 1995)	
★★½	1970 (Ardent, 1996)	

Alex Chilton is your basic professional cult legend. Barely ever inspired to work, famously surly, musically brilliant, commercially nonexistent, he's bounced around the edge of the music business for over thirty years, the picture of dapper wastedness. The first phase of his strange career was in the mid-'60s, when as a 16-year-old Memphis boy, Chilton sang the manfully gruff lead vocals on the Box Tops' huge hit "The Letter." By the time he returned with his own group,

Big Star, he had a completely different voice, high and sweet. But when Big Star collapsed, Chilton began the third and most durable phase of his career: the charismatic, self-destructive Southern grifter scamming his way to musical glory.

Chilton's discography is a complete mess. In the late '70s, he spent his famous "lost decade" coughing up material for scattered indie and import quickies. His first proper solo album, *Like Flies on Sherbert,* is a generously lubricated assault on any notion of production values, with pop gems like "My Rival" and "Hey! Little Child" falling apart at every chord change. The covers range from a ragged "I've Had It" (Ceroni/Bonura) to KC and the Sunshine Band (a damn fine "Boogie Shoes"). The only real musical parallels are the Lindsey Buckingham basement tapes included on Fleetwood Mac's *Tusk,* and the early Pavement singles that came out years later. *Like Flies on Sherbert* sank like a stone, which only added to Chilton's growing legend. *Live in London* was even messier. Eventually, his recordings appeared on cult collections such as *Lost Decade* and the well-titled *Dusted in Memphis.* The 1994 edition of *Bach's Bottom* is the best place to hear these songs, especially his eternal cry of physical love, "Take Me Home and Make Me Like It." "Free Again" is off-the-cuff country, "Bangkok" is off-the-cuff rockabilly, and the incoherent acoustic ramble "Walking Dead" is so far off the cuff it's rolling across the floor.

Chilton dropped out for a while, working as a dishwasher in New Orleans, but in the mid-'80s, with young bands like R.E.M. and the Replacements tooting his horn, he made one last stab at a steady career. He came back as a New Orleans soul hipster, with a funny voice and a half-assed rhythm section. Specializing in EPs, presumably because they're easier than real albums, he did great covers of R&B obscurities (Eve Darby's "Take It Off," Willie Tee's "Thank You John") beside occasional originals ("Lost My Job," "Thing For You"). *High Priest,* an actual full-length album, has a hilarious version of "Volare." *Black List* was his best retro EP, with Furry Lewis's "I Will Turn Your Money Green" and the nasty original "Jailbait" ("Every time I turn my back/Jailbait's driving my Cadillac"). Since then Chilton has mined the same vein with diminishing returns (*A Man Called Destruction, Set*), although he does a nice "My Baby Just Cares for Me" on *Clichés. Stuff* is the closest thing to a coherent introduction, which isn't to say it's terribly coherent. *19 Years* is easier to find than *Stuff* but not as good; the 1985 summary *Document* is premature; the early solo recordings released as *1970* are even more chaotic than *Bach's Bottom.* Currently touring the oldies circuit with the reunited Box Tops, Chilton may never sing "Take Me Home and Make Me Like It" again in his life, but a fan can dream.   —R.S.

Chocolate Genius

★★★★   Black Music (V2, 1998)
★★★★   Godmusic (V2, 2001)

Marc Anthony Thompson, a.k.a. Chocolate Genius, relishes the fact that he's an African-American artist making music that recalls white indie rockers like Paul Westerberg and Mark Eitzel, and he named his debut *Black Music* just to underline that point. Still, the album title has less to do with the color of Chocolate Genius' skin than with the content of his compositions, which are about as morose as you can get: "Half a Man," "Don't Look Down," "A Cheap Excuse," "Hangover Five," "Hangover Nine," "Stupid Again." As rendered by Thompson in a husky near-whisper, this is gripping stuff, turning despair into ghostly beauty. The album's centerpiece, "My Mom," about a parent's slow fade into the depths of Alzheimer's disease, is a guaranteed tearjerker.

Godmusic is marginally more positive. A few of its early songs mine modern R&B grooves, in marked contrast to its very "white"-sounding (despite the moniker) predecessor. But the cocktail turns out to be subtly spiked; sure, Thompson sounds a lot like Al Green on "For One More Look at You," but would the good reverend ever lend his voice to lines such as "Born by fire and bred with weasels/Flex up accordingly, my child"? By the record's midpoint, the Genius has moved on to spacier, almost psychedelic terrain, and the results—"Bossman Piss (In My Lemonade)," "To Serve You," "Infidel Blues"—are simply sublime.

Back in the 1980s, before he was Chocolate Genius, Thompson recorded two albums of Prince-style soul-pop for Warner Bros. under his own name. Both *Marc Anthony Thompson* (1984) and *Watts and Paris* (1989) are out of print but well worth hunting down.   —M.R.

Chuck D

★★★   Autobiography of Mistachuck (Mercury, 1996)

The sole solo album by the great, booming voice of Public Enemy isn't so much an autobiography as a catalogue of what pisses him off, although for this dissenter-for-life, that may indeed constitute his story. Over bare, soulful backing tracks that avoid an overload of samples or Flavor Flav, the former Carlton Ridenhour—that's "the commissioner" to you, kid—takes aim at hip-hop's violent infighting and coldhearted materialism, exploitive media, drugs, and those "modern-day Stepin Fetchits" ignorant of the

heritage of black radicalism. One track is a simple list: "No Land Cruisers, no drug users/ . . . No Negroes with egos/No mo' shows callin' women bitches and hos." Easy targets, maybe, but what is he going to talk about, finding renewable energy sources?   —B.S.

Chumbawamba

★★★   Tubthumper (Republic/Universal, 1997)
★★★½   Uneasy Listening (EMI [UK], 1999)
★★★★   WYSIWYG (Republic/Universal, 2000)
★½   Readymades (Republic/Universal, 2002)

The first that most of the world heard of Chumbawamba was its 1997 worldwide hit, "Tubthumping," an inescapable party classic about drinking and singing. By that point, though, they'd already been a band for almost 15 years—an anarchist punk collective from Leeds, England, with a handful of traditional close-harmony folk tunes mixed into its repertoire and a sweet tooth for the pop charts. The band's first six albums are usefully condensed into the import collection *Uneasy Listening*. It's got Chumbawamba's angriest songs, and some of its funniest and most tuneful: broadside slams on homophobia, the British poll tax, nouveau riche architecture, and everything else that's not specifically anarchist. Best line: "Nothing ever burns down by itself/Every fire needs a little bit of help."

Once that I-get-knocked-down-but-I-get-up-again chorus connected, though, the group had all the help it needed. Considered as the populist agitprop it was meant to be, *Tubthumper* is an abject failure: It's perfectly possible to listen to it without getting a hint of its politics beyond polite up-with-people-ism, and releasing it on a major label made Chumbawamba come off as a multinational corporation's declawed pet anarchist. As a party record, though, it's swell, with thickly layered hooks and harmonies everywhere, and enormous choruses popping up every minute or so.

WYSIWYG solves the problem by making its politics a lot more blatant, and the band seems a lot more enthusiastic laying into planned communities, Microsoft, and, ultimately, itself ("Dumbing Down"). Its 22 songs and splinters flow like a single suite, produced with the allusive high-density gloss of a TV commercial and sung with tongue nailed into cheek—the deadpan irony of "Celebration, Florida" hits harder than a full-volume rant possibly could. The shenanigans pause only for a lovely near–a cappella take on the Bee Gees' "New York Mining Disaster 1941." *Readymades*, on the other hand, is a vacant, hookless dud: folk-song samples and bland singing pasted onto prefab dance grooves. Skippable.   —D.W.

Cibo Matto

★★★★   Viva! La Woman (Warner Bros., 1996)
★★★½   Super Relax (Warner Bros., 1997)
★★   Stereo Type A (Warner Bros., 1999)

Butter 08

★★★   Butter 08 (Grand Royal, 1996)

Cibo Matto were bright lights in the anything-goes days of the mid-'90s, two crazy-sexy-cool Japanese women hooking up in the East Village to dance this mess around with thrift-shop funk, punk-rock fashion, third-hand hip-hop beats, and lyrics about sex and food. (Their name is garbled Italian for "food madness.") Yuka Honda and Miho Hatori released their excellent indie debut single "Birthday Cake" in 1995, chanting "Extra sugar! Extra salt! Extra oil and MSG!" The flip side was a very strange cover of Soundgarden's "Black Hole Sun," slowed down to a dirge and sung in French. After that aperitif, *Viva! La Woman* was the full-course feast: "Know Your Chicken," "White Pepper Ice Cream," "Artichoke," "Beef Jerky," and for dessert, a disturbingly erotic version of "The Candy Man." The Cibos mixed up hip-hop, dub, lounge, and Japanese pop, while dropping multilingual science into their Beasties-style raps: "Spare the rod and spoil the chick/Before you go and shit a brick."

Viva! La Woman brought Cibo Matto surprisingly broad success—*Time* magazine even named it one of the 10 best hip-hop albums of all time, presumably on a day when there were a lot of paint fumes drifting through the office. But *Stereo Type A* was a bland flop, despite the single "Sci-Fi Wasabi." Hatori has sung with many other artists, including the Beastie Boys ("Start!"), Air ("Wonder Milky Bitch"), and the Gorillaz ("19–2000"). The *Super Relax* EP is worth finding for goofball versions of the Stones' *Satanic Majesties* oddity "Sing This All Together" and the bossa-nova standard "Aguas de Marco," a duet between Hatori and Russell Simins of the Jon Spencer Blues Explosion. Hatori and Honda also joined Simins in the East Village supergroup Butter 08. The group's sole album, 1996's *Butter 08,* holds up surprisingly well as one of the great indie-rock flukes of the '90s, summing up its time and place in the high-spirited grooves "Butter of 69," "Mono Lisa," and "Butterfucker." —R.S.

Circle Jerks

★★★   Group Sex (Frontier, 1980)
★★½   Wild in the Streets (Faulty Products, 1982)
★★½   Golden Shower of Hits (LAX, 1983)
★½   Wönderful (Combat Core, 1985)
★★   VI (Relativity, 1987)
★★★½   Gig (Relativity, 1992)
★★★   Oddities Abnormalities and Curiosities (Mercury, 1995)

Circle Jerks' cartoon punk logo tells you everything you need to know: a blond punk, close-cropped hair, ripped jeans, spike armbands, big boots, chain around the waist, in mid-mosh. First and foremost and possibly only, this is dumb, funny music for running into one other. If Beavis and Butt-Head listened to hardcore instead of metal (and were, like, ten years older), they would both be slavish Jerks fans.

Former Black Flag singer Keith Morris recruited former Redd Kross guitarist Greg Hetson to form the joyously, fearlessly, speedily obnoxious Jerks around 1980. *Group Sex* is an iconic SoCal skate-punk album: 16 whole minutes of real fast, kinda tuneless, kinda tasteless, self-explanatory hardcore whomp, complete with titles like "I Want Some Skank" and "World Up My Ass." *Group Sex* was witty and rude where other bands from the time period come off as self-obsessed and cranky.

Wild in the Streets is not as wasted as the debut, but that cover of "Put a Little Love in Your Heart" is pretty genius. *Golden Shower of Hits* sports one of the all-time great album covers and a couple of classics, "Coup d'État" (also heard on the fabulous soundtrack to *Repo Man*), "When the Shit Hits the Fan," and the fairly stupid "Jerks on 45," which Jerks-izes such hits as "Along Comes Mary," "Close to You," and "Love Will Keep Us Together."

Wönderful isn't, it's just the sound of a silly hardcore band trying to figure out where all the punks went. *VI* is more focused, confident, and powerful, but it's still miles less interesting than most of the noise rock that Morris' peers were making. The band went on an extended hiatus soon after, with members moving on to other projects (Hetson joined punk-lifers Bad Religion, for example). *Gig* chronicles a solid reunion show, with rip-snorting energy, and Morris' obnoxious charisma adds some juice to even the later, *Wönderful* and *IV* songs.

The Jerks ended up on a major label for *Oddities, Abnormalities and Curiosities,* and the result is a perfectly respectable hard-rock album that neither betrays old glories nor breaks significant new ground, a record that in no way diminishes the timeless advice they gave us: "We all have to duck/when the shit hits the fan." —J.G.

Eric Clapton

★★★½   Eric Clapton (RSO, 1970)
★★★   Eric Clapton's Rainbow Concert (Polydor, 1973)

★★★★★	461 Ocean Boulevard (RSO, 1974)	
★★★	There's One in Every Crowd (RSO, 1975)	
★★★	E.C. Was Here (RSO, 1975)	
★★★	No Reason to Cry (RSO, 1976)	
★★★★★	Slowhand (RSO, 1977)	
★★★½	Backless (RSO, 1978)	
★★★½	Just One Night (RSO, 1980)	
★★★	Another Ticket (RSO, 1980)	
★★★★	Timepieces (RSO, 1982)	
★★★½	Timepieces, Vol. II: Live in the Seventies (RSO, 1983)	
★★★★	Money and Cigarettes (Duck/Warner Bros., 1983)	
★★★½	Behind the Sun (Duck/Warner Bros., 1985)	
★★★	August (Duck/Warner Bros., 1986)	
★★★★★	Crossroads (Polydor, 1988)	
★★★	Homeboy (Virgin, 1989)	
★★★★	Journeyman (Duck/Warner Bros., 1989)	
★★★	24 Nights (Reprise, 1991)	
★★★½	Rush (Reprise, 1992)	
★★★★	Unplugged (Duck/Warner Bros., 1992)	
★★★½	From the Cradle (Reprise, 1994)	
★★★	The Cream of Clapton (Polydor, 1995)	
★★½	Crossroads 2—Live in the Seventies (Polydor, 1996)	
★★½	Pilgrim (Duck/Reprise, 1998)	
★★★	Reptile (Reprise, 2001)	
★★★	One More Car, One More Rider (Warner Bros., 2003)	
★★★★	Martin Scorsese Presents the Blues: Eric Clapton (Polydor, 2003)	
★★★	Me and Mr. Johnson (Warner Bros., 2004)	
★★★½	The Millennium Collection (Universal, 2004)	

with Simon Climie (As T.D.F.)

★½	Retail Therapy (Warner Bros., 1997)	

with B.B. King

★★½	Riding with the King (Duck/Reprise, 2000)	

Eric Clapton may have earned his reputation with his guitar, but he owes his solo career to his voice. It's his singing that has carried his best work, from the frenetic gospel groove of "After Midnight" to the pained melancholy of "Tears in Heaven." In fact, his least interesting recordings tend to be those that most emphasize his solos—an irony, perhaps, but also a testament to the fact that Clapton is at the end of the day more than just another guitar hero.

Eric Clapton, the album that launched his solo career, was recorded with musicians he'd met while a part of Delaney & Bonnie & Friends (he was a featured player on the duo's 1970 release, *On Tour*) and boasts similar blues-and-gospel overtones. Although his lithe, understated vocals make the most of "Blues Power" and a cover of J.J. Cale's "After Midnight,"

Clapton seems somewhat overwhelmed by the size of the band here; perhaps that's why he grabbed the rhythm section—Bobby Whitlock, Carl Radle, and Jim Gordon—and ran off to form Derek & the Dominos. But that band fell apart in 1971, and Clapton, beset by depression and a heroin problem, wasn't heard from until 1973, when Pete Townshend organized the star-studded (but generally forgettable) *Eric Clapton's Rainbow Concert*.

Joining forces with producer Tom Dowd, Clapton went to Florida to record *461 Ocean Boulevard*, the album that first showed his pop-star potential. Although the material isn't obviously commercial, being given mainly to blues (Robert Johnson's "Steady Rollin' Man"), oldies (Johnny Otis' "Willie and the Hand Jive"), and reggae ("I Shot the Sheriff," by the then unknown Bob Marley), Clapton's affectless delivery is almost irresistible, cutting to the heart of the blues while avoiding the sort of guttural mannerisms most pop listeners found off-putting. The album was a massive success, but its standard wasn't easily maintained. *There's One in Every Crowd*, for instance, virtually duplicates its predecessor's approach, but with considerably less success, commercial or artistic. Mostly, the difference was the writing, as no amount of reggae groove is going to make Clapton's "Don't Blame Me" as memorable a song as "I Shot the Sheriff."

After a passable live album, *E.C. Was Here*, Clapton returned to the studio in search of a new direction. *No Reason to Cry* wasn't quite it; despite a duet with Bob Dylan ("Sign Language") and a backing band that includes Ron Wood, Robbie Robertson, and Georgie Fame, the only track that really works is the amiable, calypso-tinged "Hello Old Friend." So Clapton ditched the all-star tack, and took a low-key approach to *Slowhand*.

Bingo—the best album of his career. Working with his own band and once again relying more on the songs than the groove, Clapton seems utterly at home here, from the wistful balladry of "Wonderful Tonight" to the stoned shuffle of "Cocaine" (yet another Cale composition) to the jauntily lustful "Lay Down Sally." And though there's plenty of blowing room—check the slide work on his version of Arthur Crudup's "Mean Old Frisco"—it's the strength of the material that gives the solos a worthwhile starting point.

Backless tries hard to re-create that balance but falls short in spite of a few lovely songs ("Tell Me That You Love Me" in particular) and some inspired rhythm work (especially on the Marcy Levy feature, "Roll It"). As had by then become customary, it was time for another live album, but *Just One Night* improves on the usual, thanks to a crack new band that keeps Clapton on his toes through the extended versions of "Double Trouble" and "Cocaine." Unfortunately, that dynamic didn't quite translate to the studio, and apart from the quietly dramatic title tune, *Another Ticket* is a disappointment.

Clapton changed labels soon after, a switch that prompted a predictable round of best-ofs. Apart from a non-LP version of "Knockin' On Heaven's Door," *Timepieces* boasts few surprises (though some fans may object to its preference for the live version of "Cocaine"), but *Timepieces, Vol. II: Live in the Seventies* is easily ignored. *The Cream of Clapton* justifies a third dip into this repertoire by padding his solo hits with singles by Cream, Blind Faith, and Derek & the Dominos, yet inexplicably manages to overlook "Lay Down Sally."

Meanwhile, Clapton's new deal was already producing impressive changes. Although *Money and Cigarettes* stumbled commercially, it's hardly a disappointment musically, thanks to a comfortable collection of songs and a backing band that includes slide virtuoso Ry Cooder and Stax session man Duck Dunn. Charming and unassuming, it's classic Clapton. *Behind the Sun*, on the other hand, is perhaps the guitarist's most daring effort, a (mostly) Phil Collins–produced project that finds him gamely trying everything from guitar synthesizer (on "Never Make You Cry") to what can best be described as 12-bar art rock (on "Same Old Blues"). Unfortunately, not everyone appreciated such risk-taking, and Warner Bros. honchos Ted Templeman and Lenny Waronker later added three tracks—including the tepid but radio-friendly "Forever Man"—to increase the album's commercial appeal. Perhaps that's why *August*, also produced by Collins, backs off a bit from its predecessor's innovations and does nothing more radical than adding a layer of synths to its version of Robert Cray's "Bad Influence." (It does, however, include "Tearing Us Apart," a raucous, sexually charged duet with Tina Turner that ranks among Clapton's finest vocal performances.)

Any such failings, however, were completely forgotten with *Crossroads*, a career-spanning, 73-song retrospective that included all of Clapton's most memorable recordings, from his days with the Yardbirds to the *August* sessions. It's an absolutely stunning collection, and goes a long way toward demonstrating that Clapton is, indeed, the greatest of all rock-guitar heroes. Unfortunately, *Crossroads 2: Live in the Seventies* is a shabby followup that isn't even entirely live (four selections are unreleased studio leftovers). Although most of the previously unreleased recordings have their moments, as in a Santana-ish run through "Eyesight to the Blind/Why Does Love Got to Be So Sad," the set's relative lack of scope and consistency makes it of interest only to completists.

Journeyman, the studio album following *Crossroads,* seems by the very nature of its title to shrug off intimations of greatness, and as such turns out to be a remarkably relaxed and satisfying album. After that minor success, however, Clapton's output becomes maddeningly diffuse, with the guitarist moving in several different directions artistically without making great progress in any of them. The concert recording *24 Nights* was an early symptom, with Clapton offering blues-themed sets, standard pop/rock fare, and even a set of tunes performed with an orchestra conducted by composer/arranger Michael Kamen.

Kamen (who later collaborated with Metallica on their album *S&M*) was no stranger to Clapton, having previously worked with the guitarist on the soundtracks for *Homeboy* and *Lethal Weapon II.* Clapton seemed to enjoy his work in Hollywood, and did the writing himself for his next soundtrack, *Rush.* But the dramatic instrumentals weren't what people noticed; instead, it was a dolorous ditty dubbed "Tears in Heaven" that drew all the notice. Reportedly inspired by the death of his infant son, Connor, the song was already a minor hit when Clapton recut it—along with an assortment of blues and classic rock chestnuts—for an episode of MTV's *Unplugged.* Released as an album, the Grammy-winning *Unplugged* reinvented Clapton yet again, and proved one of the biggest hits, commercially or artistically, of his later career.

Typically, Clapton responded to this burst of popularity by retreating into the blues. *From the Cradle* finds him diligently rerooting himself in the material that was his earliest inspiration, underplaying the solos and stressing the vocal element in the songs. As such, the best moments—whether in his swinging remake of Freddie King's "I'm Tore Down" or his impassioned run through the upbeat "Motherless Child"—stress the songs above all.

Clapton laid low for a few years after that, offering only a lame attempt at techno under the pseudonym T.D.F. (which may have meant "to die for" but should be taken as "to definitely forget"). Embarrassing as it was, the album marked the beginning of a long collaboration with former Climie Fisher keyboardist Simon Climie. *Pilgrim,* which Climie coproduced with Clapton, made some interesting inroads into smooth soul with "My Father's Eyes," no doubt in hopes of capitalizing on the success of the Babyface-produced "Change the World," which appeared on the soundtrack to the flick *Phenomenon,* starring John Travolta. But apart from the beautifully sad "Circus" and boogie-fueled "She's Gone," *Pilgrim* is a turkey.

Failure though it was, it sold well enough for Clapton and Climie to repeat the formula, with minor variations, on *Reptile,* a pleasant but inconsequential effort typified by the light soul of "I Ain't Gonna Stand for It" and the smooth jazz aspirations of the title tune. The rock-gospel harmonies of the Impressions are a particular annoyance. The polished but not especially passionate *One More Car, One More Rider* offers a live run through much of this material; it's also available (and somewhat more entertaining) on DVD, or as a CD/DVD combo.

On the whole, though, Clapton's fans were more interested in seeing him as a grizzled—if genteel—bluesman, hence the unexpected success of *Riding With the King,* a collaboration with B.B. King that involves more coasting than actual riding. The oily cover of Sam & Dave's "Hold On, I'm Coming" is particularly embarrassing. Still, that hasn't deterred Clapton, whose next venture into the blues was *Me and Mr. Johnson,* a tribute to Robert Johnson that somehow completely sidesteps the unearthly dread that once made these blues so compelling to young Brit rockers. Instead, the arrangements emphasize the songs' boogie bounce, to such an extent that even "Hellhound on My Trail" seems oddly upbeat. If that seems a betrayal of Clapton's youthful blues purism—a perspective neatly framed by the early recordings, with collaborators ranging from John Mayall to Duane Allman, compiled on *Martin Scorsese Presents the Blues*—it's worth remembering that the blues have been very, very good to Eric Clapton. Who can blame him for feeling good about that?   —J.D.C.

Petula Clark

★★★	The Other Man's Grass Is Always Greener (Warner Bros., 1968)	
★★★	Memphis (Warner Bros., 1970; Sequel, 1996)	
★★	Today (1971; Sequel, 1997)	
★★★	Live at the Copacabana (Sequel, 1994)	
★★★	International Collection (Bear Family, 1999)	
★★★	Downtown: The Greatest Hits of Petula Clark (Buddha, 1999)	
★★★½	Anthology: Downtown to Sunset Boulevard (Uptown/Universal, 2000)	
★★★	A Sign of the Times (Castle, 2001)	
★★	Jumble Sale: Rarities and Obscurities (Sequel, 2002)	

In a flourish of threatened, institutional antihipness, the Grammy Awards committee voted Pet Clark's "Downtown" Best Rock and Roll Recording of 1965. The ditty's nice bounce, of course, had nothing to do with Elvis or Little Richard—but Clark's Brit appeal, coinciding with the Beatles' advent, together with the relative assertiveness of the song's drum track, must

have tricked fogies into thinking that this wasn't merely MOR given a mild Phil Spector–ish production. Actually, Petula's cool, clipped delivery proved that while she was no Dionne Warwick, her orchestral fare wasn't retread Doris Day either. A showbiz pro from age 11, Clark was canny enough to read the signs of the times, and her choice of material carefully avoided the ultrasunniness of pre-'60s pop. "The Other Man's Grass Is Always Greener," "Don't Sleep in the Subway," and "I Know a Place," all included on the Buddha *Greatest Hits* and the more comprehensive *Anthology,* gave her fairly spirited successes nearly into the '70s—and they remain enjoyable. For Clark maniacs, *International Collection* is a treat: 108 lush pop tunes, in German, French, Italian. *A Sign of the Times* is Pet on tour circa 2001, still in very fine voice.   —P.E.

The Clash

★★★★★	The Clash (Epic U.K., 1977)	
★★★★	Give 'Em Enough Rope (Epic, 1978)	
★★★★★	The Clash (Epic, 1979)	
★★★★★	London Calling (Epic, 1979)	
★★★★	Black Market Clash (Epic, 1980)	
★★★★	Sandinista! (Epic, 1980)	
★★★½	Combat Rock (Epic, 1982)	
★★	Cut the Crap (Epic, 1985)	
★★½	The Story of the Clash (Epic, 1988)	
★★★★½	1977 Revisited (Relativity, 1990)	
★★★½	Clash on Broadway (1991; Sony, 2003)	
★★★★	Super Black Market Clash (Epic, 1993)	
★★★½	Live: From Here to Eternity (Sony, 1999)	
★★★★	The Singles (Legacy, 2000)	
★★★★½	The Essential Clash (Epic, 2003)	

The Clash were the romantics of the London 1977 punk explosion. They were the ones who took the noise to heart, who pushed hardest to see how far the new freedoms could go. They were also the ones who wrote the best songs, burning with political rage and mean guitars. Joe Strummer ranted in his guttersnipe slobber, while guitarist Mick Jones shaped the noise into high-speed anthems. They sounded friendly and scary at the same time, mixing up the punk anger of "Complete Control," the street aggression of "London's Burning," the urban loneliness of "Up in Heaven (Not Only Here)," and the jolly laughs of "Safe European Home." They were inspired by Nicaragua's Sandinista revolutionaries, but they weren't above a little art-for-art's-sake—after all, Sandino himself was a Wordsworth man, and the Clash made dramatic music out of their garageland politics.

The raw, messy U.K. debut is still the toughest

punk album ever, so full of fury and passion and humor it sounds like it's going to burst into flames every time Mick lights up the coda to "Remote Control," every time Joe rasps, "I hate all the brightness/I hate all the cops" at the end of "Hate and War." The Clash sounds like young men wrestling with monsters, but not turning into monsters themselves—maybe even finding their humanity. But the record company deemed *The Clash* too rude for U.S. release and shelved it for two years. The belated, reshuffled American version deleted four great songs but added three not-bad ones, one great one ("White Man in Hammersmith Palais"), and maybe the greatest punk anthem ever, "Complete Control." The 35-minute U.K. version and the 43-minute U.S. version are both now separately available; apparently it's too much goddamn trouble for Sony to put all 19 songs on one 52-minute CD, so you'll have to do it yourself. While you're at it, add "Groovy Times" and "Gates of the West," two amazing songs from the bonus seven-inch that originally came with the U.S. version, for an incomparable 60-minute Clash buzz.

Give 'Em Enough Rope has cleaned-up sound and too much easy military shtick, despite killers such as "Safe European Home" and "Guns on the Roof." Like Martin Scorsese's *Raging Bull*, the double-vinyl *London Calling* dropped just in time to welcome the new decade, and wound up topping many critics' best-of-the-'80s lists. Also like *Raging Bull*—a film Scorsese directed while constantly playing *The Clash* at top volume for inspiration—it's an expansive portrait of doomed wiseguys, working-class anger, and American mythology, aiming for a grandiose death-or-glory scale. The Clash dabbles in reggae, ska, rockabilly, even New Orleans R&B, stretching out for classics like "London Calling," "Spanish Bombs," and the huge hit "Train in Vain (Stand by Me)."

Some fans liked *Sandinista!* even better: It's a big triple-vinyl mess, deliberately provocative and offensive from its title on down to the kiddie-chorus version of "Career Opportunities." The Clash's dub, hip-hop, and art-funk experiments get pretty dodgy, but even the many spliffed-out failures are fun to hear once, and that still leaves 14 or 15 great songs. The geopolitical stuff—"The Call Up," "Washington Bullets," "Charlie Don't Surf"—is dense, lyrical, informative, dreamlike, unlike any other protest-rock before or since. "Up in Heaven (Not Only Here)" is a shout-out from the London slums that produced punk to the New York projects that were producing hip-hop. "Hitsville U.K." has a nifty xylophone solo. *Combat Rock*, even artier than *Sandinista!* yet cleverly packaged as a pop move, had some excellent tunes ("Rock the Casbah," "Ghetto Defendant"), but the cover

looked stupid and the band was audibly falling apart. Strummer kicked out Jones and replaced him with two handsome nobodies for the career-killing *Cut the Crap* (alternate title: *Contra!*), which offered only the bitter "This Is England" and the proto–Andrew W.K. synth-metal chant "We Are the Clash." Six people bought it, five actually played it all the way through, and everyone else was content to applaud the Clash for resisting reunion gigs after that.

Like the Doors, ABBA, and any other band that checks out, leaving a hungry corporation to feed, the Clash has been repackaged way past any point of dignity. The best compilations are *1977 Revisited, Super Black Market Clash,* and the first disc of the pricey gyp *Clash on Broadway,* which all collect the essential early singles that aren't on *The Clash*—don't get stuck without "Gates of the West," "Groovy Times," "Armagideon Time," or "Bankrobber." *The Singles* is a straightforward collection that hits a few bumps ("Know Your Rights," ugh) but gets the highs and lows of their music right; from the rebel swagger of "White Riot" and "Complete Control" to the arty exuberance of "This Is Radio Clash" and "Rock the Casbah," *The Singles* makes the Clash's whole career sound like a risk worth taking. Joe Strummer died suddenly of a heart attack in December 2002. The music world mourned for both the man and the old-fashioned idea that a rock star could ever try so hard to understand the world around him. His epitaph was from one of his greatest songs, "The Call Up": "There is a rose I want to live for/Although, God knows, I may not have met her/There is a dance an' I should be with her/There is a town—unlike any other." R.I.P. —R.S.

Jimmy Cliff

★★★½	Wonderful World, Beautiful People (A&M, 1970)
★★★	Struggling Man (Mango, 1973)
★★★	In Concert: The Best of Jimmy Cliff (Reprise, 1976)
★★	Special (Columbia, 1982)
★★½	The Power and the Glory (Columbia, 1984)
★★	Cliff Hanger (Columbia, 1985)
★★	Hanging Fire (Columbia, 1988)
★★★½	Ultimate Collection (Universal, 1999)
★★★	We Are All One: The Best of Jimmy Cliff (Columbia/Legacy, 2002)
★★★½	Anthology (Hip-O, 2003)
★★★½	20th Century Masters (Universal, 2004)

Jimmy Cliff's two best performances—both groundbreaking reggae classics—are included on the soundtrack of *The Harder They Come* (see ANTHOLOGIES). Twice. Apart from "You Can Get It If You Really Want

It" and "The Harder They Come," the rest of Cliff's career has been devoted to a frustrated, one-sided affair with the American pop-soul mainstream. *Wonderful World, Beautiful People* contains his only other true contender—"Vietnam," a searingly melodic and rhythmically bold interpretation of the reluctant draftee blues. But the title track of this 1970 album exhibits the shallow sentimentality that sinks his subsequent efforts. At least "Wonderful World, Beautiful People" is catchy enough to get your attention for three minutes; Jimmy Cliff's later albums don't even get that far. Avoid the slick remakes of earlier material on *In Concert: The Best of Jimmy Cliff,* and stick with *The Harder They Come.* —M.C.

Patsy Cline

Time has been Patsy Cline's greatest ally. Not that she had that much of it in her brief life, which ended in a plane crash near Camden, TN, on March 5, 1963, when she was 30. At her death, she'd had a handful of hit singles, three of them crossing over from country to reach the pop chart's Top 20, but she wasn't yet a commercial or artistic force in either genre. But the hits endured, growing in stature as the years progressed; and as other recordings became available posthumously, Cline became everything her career had portended before tragedy struck—her albums started selling and haven't stopped yet. The secret of Cline's undiminished appeal is not dissimilar to Elvis Presley's: Hers are great songs, performed with conviction and passion, telling simple stories people understand about love and longing and all the varieties of experience embraced by those two conditions.

Cline's first work, recorded in the late '50s, was with the Pasadena, CA–based 4 Star Music Sales. Critics have not always been kind to the 4 Star material, but in fact those five years produced some good work—not the monumental efforts that were to come, of course, but some good, solid traditional country; even the stillborn experiments in a pop direction have an adventurous quality that makes for interesting listening. The 1958 "I Can See an Angel" has a loping, country beat and supple pop background vocals from the Anita Kerr Singers supporting Cline's bright vocal. The upbeat shuffle "I Don't Wanta," recorded in 1956, features a whooping, unidentified female background chorus and guitar licks lifted from Scotty Moore's solos on Elvis' "Mystery Train." The standout from these years is "Walkin' After Midnight" and its B side, the evocative "Poor Man's Roses (Or a Rich Man's Gold)" (from the pens of pop songwriters Bob Hilliard and Milton Delugg), a #12 pop single in 1957. The allure of "Walkin'" is in its foreboding atmosphere—although there's a full combo behind her, Bob Moore's steady, loping bass line and Don Helms' swirling pedal steel lines dominate the soundscape, falling in beautifully behind Cline's bluesy, bone-weary vocal.

The 4 Star recordings take up most of the first two discs of MCA's gold-standard, absolutely essential box set, *The Patsy Cline Collection,* which contains all of her studio recordings from June 1, 1953, through February 7, 1963, and one stunning live cut recorded at the Ryman Auditorium (home of the Grand Ole Opry), the spiritual "Just a Closer Walk with Thee." Unlike the other collections of 4 Star recordings, those in the MCA box are sequenced chronologically, so it's possible to hear Cline gaining confidence as a vocalist, phrasing with more assurance and attitude as the years pass, adding nuance to her readings, shading lyrics, adding blues phrasings, and generally letting her feelings flow freely as her self-consciousness in the studio fades away.

Laserlight's *Great American Legends: The Patsy Cline Collection* collects the 4 Star material on three discs, but it's a typically skimpy Laserlight package: no liner info whatsoever. Still, it's 39 cuts of Cline in her formative years at a price point below the MCA box. Varèse Sarabande's *25 All Time Greatest Recordings: The 4 Star Sessions 1955–1960* is really 26 takes with the inclusion of an alternate take of "I Don't Wanta," but the disc is misleadingly titled anyway, since these are hardly all-time greatest recordings. The most essential supplement to the MCA box in rounding out the 4 Star years is Razor & Tie's excellent live album, *The Birth of a Star.* Assembled here are 17 performances from Cline's regular appearances on Arthur Godfrey's taste-making national TV show in 1957–58. Again, the material is not the classic Cline of 1960–63, but it's generally top-notch anyway, as are all of Cline's performances.

Come late 1960, Cline's 4 Star contract was winding down. Cline's producer Owen Bradley brought in a song for her first post–4 Star session cowritten by two fellows who would go on to carve out a substantial name for themselves in country music: Harlan Howard and Hank Cochran. Their song, "I Fall to Pieces," was a measured, dramatic, blues-tinged ballad recounting the singer's soul-shattering inability to get on with life in the wake of a failed romance. Cline sang as if she were barely able to maintain emotional ballast, her voice rising and falling, at times sounding so wounded she seemed near tears. Few country records, even great ones Patsy made after this, were so perfectly realized in every component as "I Fall to Pieces."

For the next three years Cline didn't do anything much different from what she had been doing at 4 Star—that is, assaying a wide range of tunes in and out of the country genre—but the quality of her material improved markedly, her performances matured, and Bradley's production intuition remained infallible. Along with Chet Atkins, Bradley had pioneered a new era in country music—the Nashville Sound—and successfully broadened country's appeal much as Roy Acuff had done upon his debut at the Grand Ole Opry in 1938. The classic songs—"Sweet Dreams," "Back in Baby's Arms," "Crazy," "Strange," "Heartaches," "You're Stronger Than Me," "Leavin' On Your Mind," "Faded Love," "Always," "Crazy Arms," and "Why Can't He Be You"—plus a host of nonsingle album tracks that sound like hits today, were written by people like Willie Nelson, Hank Cochran, Harlan Howard, Bob Wills, Carl Perkins, Don Gibson, Hank Williams, Cole Porter, Bill Monroe, Irving Berlin, Mel Tillis, Wayne Walker/Webb Pierce, and Floyd Tillman, among the most prominent.

The last eight of 27 cuts on Disc 2 of the MCA box, all 28 cuts on Disc 3, and all 22 cuts on Disc 4 chronicle the legacy Patsy Cline left. It doesn't get any better than that, but it does get more concise and cheaper for those desiring mostly the prime cuts.

A sure winner is the original 1967 release, *Patsy Cline's Greatest Hits,* containing a dozen certified classics—"Walkin' After Midnight," "Sweet Dreams," "I Fall to Pieces," "Back in Baby's Arms," and "Crazy"—the choice stuff. On the other hand, *20th Century Masters: Classic Patsy Cline* is an odd collection of nonhits such as "Half as Much," "Have You Ever Been Lonely (Have You Ever Been Blue)," and others that hardly substitute for the most famous tracks; ditto for Curb's *Best of Patsy Cline,* a shoddy package inside and out.

Note also three live albums, one being a volume of songs recorded at the Grand Ole Opry between 1956 and 1962 that shows Cline every bit as compelling a performer as she was a singer. *Live Volume Two* is actually a series of studio cuts with canned applause recorded in 1956 and transcribed for broadcast on shows sponsored by the Armed Forces. In some ways the most vital of the live albums—because it shows Cline giving a terrific performance under tough conditions—is MCA's *Live at the Cimarron Ballroom.* This 1961 performance at the Tulsa, OK, venue where Bob Wills and the Texas Playboys held forth every Saturday night for years marked Cline's return to the stage following a near-fatal car accident. She jokes about her condition between songs, but gets down to business when it's time to sing. The set list is interesting in that it includes hard country fare that a Tulsa audience would have eaten up at that time—"Lovesick Blues," "San Antonio Rose," "Walkin' After Midnight," "I Fall to Pieces," "Foolin' Around"—and some curveballs on the order of "Shake, Rattle & Roll," "Stupid Cupid" (the 1958 Connie Francis chart smash that Patsy performed at an army show that same year, preserved as a radio transcription on Disc 2 of *The Patsy Cline Collection*), and "When My Dreamboat Comes Home," which had been a Top 20 hit for Fats Domino in 1956. Given that she was still banged up from the car wreck, Cline's performance is remarkable for its energy and enthusiasm, as well as for the quality of the music she offered.

The one absolute must-to-avoid in the Cline catalogue is Island's abysmal and infuriating *Duets,* on which some industry types decided to wipe off Owen Bradley's arrangements, dub "contemporary" arrangements in behind Cline's original vocals, and then further dub in duet voices with Patsy's. Other than "Walkin' After Midnight," the song selection is lesser fare from the 4 Star years, but the newly recorded "duet" partners don't do justice to the project. Glen Campbell on "Too Many Secrets" is unlistenable, which might be said for everyone else involved as well. —D.M.

Clinic

★★★	Internal Wrangler (Domino, 2000)
★★★★	Walking With Thee (Domino, 2002)
★★★	3 EPs (Domino, 2002)
★★	Winchester Cathedral (Domino, 2002)

Donning surgical masks in concert, Clinic takes a back-to-the-lab approach to postpunk. On its first album, *Internal Wrangler,* the Liverpudlian group mixes and mismatches the styles of krautrock, the Fall, U.S.-servicemen-turned-bizarro-beat-group the Monks, reggae dub, and Pere Ubu into tracks made out of ambling rhythms that are both shambling and hypnotic. The song "Internal Wrangler" is Roky Erickson's 13th Floor Elevators reinterpreted by a surf band, and "DJ Shangri-La" is a hilarious 58-second parody of every self-important mixmaster from Rza to Shadow. Clinic has more than a little in common with Scotland's Beta Band. They both will steal whatever is lying around and reconfigure it for optimum aesthetic pleasure no matter how little sense is made, or whether words come out wrong or are made up on the fly. The group's core setup of garage organ, muddy bass, overmiked drum beats, weedy free-associative singing, melodica, and sloppy postpunk guitar leaves plenty of room for experimentation. This is great news for lovers of adventurous stereo trickery. For the straight and narrow fan of alt rock, Clinic will probably be met with raised eyebrows and the universal gesture for the smoking of intoxicating substances.

To say that the followup, *Walking With Thee,* is a more polished album than *Internal Wrangler* is to say that it sounds like it took the musicians longer than half an hour to record it and that they spent more than a dollar on the process. The basic elements are the same, but there is an opening up and airiness to the tracks that give them a less unfinished feeling. There is a wholeness and consummation of intent. With a band like Clinic you wouldn't want anything too slick, or it would lose that element of risk that makes the best songs sound so vital. Nonetheless, it's telling that the first line on the opening track, "Harmony," is "I believe in harmony." All the instrumentation on *Walking With Thee* fits together naturally. This results in a quieter record with fewer sudden shifts or disorienting tonal juxtapositions. In the end, sound and technique end up taking a backseat anyway, because the songs are so damn good, a string of memorable melodies and vocal tics. Less bombastic or self-consciously weighty than a Radiohead, Clinic uses rock to push against warmth and groove to create beautiful noises that are not only fun but fun to think about. A collection of earlier EPs is recommended to fans who want their Clinic uncut, unhinged, and decidedly unclean.

Winchester Cathedral strikes a bit closer to the debut's Radiohead-on-benzedrine feel, but much of the time it sounds like the band members are just playing around with their noisemakers and not having much fun. Although "The Magician" and the guitar-driven "WDYYB" get by on typically high-strung grooves, atmospheric slow-burners such as "Home" and "Falstaff" sacrifice oddball charm for dull moodiness. Ade Blackburn's half-intelligible slur renders the songs more annoying than memorable, and *Winchester Cathedral* proves Clinic has finally succumbed to that which *Internal Wrangler* fended off so well: art rock. —S.S.

Clipse

★★★★	Lord Willin' (Star Trak/Arista, 2002)

Clipse—Virginia Beach siblings Malice and Pusha-T—began rhyming in the mid-'90s, back when they were high school friends with Pharrell Williams and Chad Hugo. After a 1998 album, *Exclusive Audio Footage,* went unreleased, their future seemed uncertain—until Williams and Hugo, a.k.a. superproducers the Neptunes, came to the rescue. *Lord Willin'* is unrepentant playa-rap, a guided tour of a day in the life of a coke dealer. Though the duo's matter-of-fact delivery is hardly original—Mobb Deep is an obvious influence—they offer so much gripping detail and action-packed forward motion it doesn't matter. And the Neptunes' beats never miss, from the ravey, tuned-static synth hook of "When the Last Time" to the grunting James Brown sax of "Young Boy" to the shockingly austere drum-theory-as-groove of "Grindin'." It's the most consistent, and best, album they've ever produced. —M.M.

The Clovers

★★★★½	Down in the Alley (Atlantic, 1991)
★★★★	The Very Best of the Clovers (Rhino, 1998)
★★★★	The Clovers/Dance Party (Collectables, 1998)

The first rock & roll vocal group, the Clovers racked up 21 Top 100 singles, including "Ting-A-Ling," "Don't You Know I Love You," and "From the Bottom of My Heart." Formed in 1946 as a pop-influenced, Ink Spots–style trio, the group was led by Harold "Hal" Lucas, who was joined in the venture by a couple of his friends from Washington, D.C.'s Armstrong High School, tenor Thomas Woods and bass singer Billy Shelton. Next into the fold was John "Buddy"

Bailey, a gifted lead vocalist whose soaring, plaintive tenor became a signature for the Clovers. Renamed the Four Clovers, the quartet in 1949 replaced Woods with second tenor Matthew McQuarter, and Shelton was replaced by Harold Winley. The Four Clovers officially became the Clovers with the addition of guitarist Bill Harris, also in 1949. Atlantic's *Down in the Alley* and Rhino's *The Very Best of the Clovers* are both first-rate overviews of the Clovers' important contributions to the style of R&B that evolved into soul music in the '60s. At 21 tracks, the Atlantic disc has more to offer than Rhino's 16, but both titles cover the ultimate, essential recordings. For added perspective, Collectables' single-disc *The Clovers/Dance Party* offers two complete early albums. Of these, *The Clovers* is by far the more interesting, with "Lovey Dovey," "Ting-A-Ling," "Blue Velvet," and "Devil or Angel" among its featured tracks, making it something of an essential primer on postwar R&B. —D.M.

The Coasters

★★★½ The Ultimate Coasters (Warner Bros., 1990)
★★★★★ 50 Coastin' Classics: The Coasters Anthology (Rhino/Atlantic, 1993)
★★★★ The Very Best of the Coasters (Rhino, 1994)

The story of the Coasters is the story of two songwriter/producers, two groups, and two labels. It's also the story of brilliant record making in low-tech times and a body of work with depth, humor, feeling, and some sly social commentary.

As a concept, the Coasters were born in the fertile imaginations and driving ambition of Jerry Leiber and Mike Stoller, two white, East Coast, R&B fanatics (Leiber a native of Baltimore, Stoller of New York City) who had migrated to the West Coast and become friends, often double-dating with their black girlfriends. Stoller was a talented piano player, familiar not only with current styles in black popular music, but also conversant with jazz harmonic structure and well versed in contemporary classical music. No musician he, Leiber had aspirations as a writer for the legitimate theater but carried around a notebook in which he penned original blues lyrics, its contents betraying his playwright's sensibility—he didn't write songs, he wrote minidramas, minicomedies, and created characters.

The pair took their mutual interest in R&B to the next level and began working out songs of their own. Their first bite came in 1951, when they sold "That's What the Good Book Says" to the Robins, who were recording for the Modern label. Over the next couple of years, their songs were recorded by Ray Charles, Big Mama Thornton (the original "Hound Dog"), Little Willie Littlefield ("K.C. Loving," later retitled "Kansas City"), and Charles Brown, among the most prominent. In 1953, they paired with music-business veteran Lester Sill and founded their own label, Spark Records, and made the Robins one of their first signings.

The third Spark release was the Robins' first single, "Riot in Cell Block #9," and it was a gem. The Robins boasted a terrific lead tenor singer in Carl Gardner, and Bobby Nunn, a bass singer who could be as emotive as the Ravens' Jimmie Ricks, also had a comedic flair that set him apart from the competition. Nevertheless, neither of these resources suited Leiber and Stoller's ideal for the lead vocal, so they brought in another R&B singer, Richard Berry (now best remembered as the man who wrote "Louie Louie"), to add the proper degree of menace to their tale of a prison uprising told by an inmate serving time for "armed robb-er-y." Berry's unrepentant performance—he sounds like one of those scary psychos who dispassionately recount dismemberments on A&E's *Justice Files*—was buttressed by the sound of sirens wailing; tommy guns firing; a tough, bluesy arrangement punctuated by stop-time figures lifted from Muddy Waters; and wailing, protesting, down-and-dirty blues saxophone riffing by Gil Bernal. And in a quintessentially Leiber literary touch, the riot ends with the prisoners back in their cells after being teargassed, as Berry closes out the tale with an ominous aside, "but every now and then . . ." and the song fades out over the course of nearly 30 seconds of stop-time riffs and gutty sax solos.

With "Riot in Cell Block #9," a mold had been cast. Not only did the Robins sound different, thanks to Stoller basing their harmonies on a jazz approach, but as a lyricist, Leiber was laying down some sly social commentary. "Riot" didn't fool anyone in radio, where it was deemed too controversial, as was the followup single, "Framed." In this story, Bobby Nunn tells of "walking down the street, minding my own affairs" when he is picked up by the cops, put in a lineup, and framed for a liquor store robbery by a stool pigeon. From the cops to the DA and the judge, every authority figure is corrupt to the bone; when the song fades out with Nunn repeating "I was framed" until he is no longer audible, the implication is clear that this character will not quietly accede to the injustice he's experienced any more than the prisoners in cell block #9 had been rendered impotent by tear gas. This was heady stuff for 1953, but it was in the air. In 1950, Percy Mayfield had applied the velvet hammer to racial prejudice in his beautiful chart-topping hit, "Please Send Me Someone to Love," and here was Leiber daring to say the American system was flawed, that everyone was not equal in the eyes of the law. The Robins' singles weren't hits, and Spark, like small labels then and now, had distribution problems that made their releases difficult to find even in the "race music" market. Still, these recordings were part of the first, small intimations of great social change on the horizon in postwar America.

Come 1955, and another sort of change was spurred by Spark's release of the Robins' "Smokey Joe's Café." This Leiber lyric, concerning a knife fight over a woman in the establishment named in the title, was bolstered musically by a captivating, twangy guitar solo by jazz stalwart Barney Kessel and a smoldering, slightly stuttering sax solo from Gil Bernal, which prefigured the King Curtis sound signature of later recordings. "Smokey Joe's Café" made the national R&B charts—a first for a Spark release—and caught the attention of the Ertegun brothers and Jerry Wexler at Atlantic Records in New York. They made an offer Leiber and Stoller couldn't refuse: sell Spark to Atlantic and come to New York to make records for Atlantic as independent producers (a first in the music industry, since labels had always had in-house artists and repertoire personnel to scout and sign artists, shape their material, and then produce it in the studio). The deal split the Robins, with Billy Richards, Roy Richards, and Ty Tyrell opting to sign with their manager's new label, and Gardner and Nunn joining Leiber and Stoller in New York, where they were teamed with Leon Hughes and Billy Guy and dubbed the Coasters, in honor of their West Coast origins. Atco, an Atlantic subsidiary, re-released "Smokey Joe's Café" and sold 100,000 copies of the single, a respectable number in those days.

The Coasters got off to a good start at Atco with 1956's "Down in Mexico," a slice-of-life set in a Mexican honky-tonk, driven in part by the Latin percussion provided by conga player Chico Guerrero. In 1957, though, they crossed over from R&B to pop with smashing results, and for two solid years could do no wrong, racking up six consecutive Top 10 hits and topping the pop chart in 1958 with "Yakety Yak," a resonant, rocking bit of anti-authoritarian teen humor that featured the debut of King Curtis and his stuttering sax solos as regular features of the group's soundscape and of late-'50s rock & roll. The 1959 followup to "Yakety Yak," "Charlie Brown," an unabashed celebration of the school misfit, topped out at #2 for three weeks and was followed into the Top 10 later in the year by the minidrama of bad versus good "Along Came Jones" (featuring a hilarious, overwrought comic turn by Carl Gardner as the melodramatic narrator), and then by "Poison Ivy," a Latinized warning about a woman who is nothing but trouble,

intentionally subverted by Nunn and Gardner's lusty lead vocals, which do everything but announce, "For a good time, call. . . ."

The Coasters were Top 40 staples through 1961 as they continued to cut rich, sub-three-minute playlets provided by Leiber and Stoller. "Run Red Run," from 1960, tells the story of a monkey who gets educated, realizes how he's been exploited, and in Leiber's words, "becomes a revolutionary." The exotic 1961 single, "Little Egypt," the group's final appearance in the Top 40, uses a carny sideshow come-on, King Curtis' smoldering, stuttering sax, and Stoller himself adding a "chipmunk" voice on the fade-out to conjure a seductive portrait of an exotic dancer. "Soul Pad," a non-charter from 1967, describes an offbeat cast of characters populating "a room with a feeling," its funky ambience heightened by some pungent piano and Hammond-organ interjections by one of New Orleans' greatest piano players, James Booker.

All of these career highlights and more are contained on the essential Rhino double-CD set, *50 Coastin' Classics*. Among the more obscure tracks are the original version of "D.W. Washburn," which was a hit not for the Coasters but, in a 1968 cover version, for the Monkees, and a 1959 New Orleans–style rocker, "That Is Rock & Roll," featuring Jerry Leiber adding a gravel-voiced lead vocal in the style of Clarence "Frogman" Henry. An accompanying booklet reprints critic Robert Palmer's liner notes from a 1982 double-vinyl Coasters retrospective, *Young Blood,* and includes song-by-song annotation by Leiber and Stoller, plus complete sessionography and release dates. The photos of the group with L&S in the studio are priceless.

Lower-priced, single-disc retrospectives from Rhino and Warner Bros. touch all the commercial high points for those interested in only the essential documents and minimal annotation. Beware of a disc on the Prime Cuts label titled *The Coasters—Greatest Hits*. The group featured is not the original Coasters, but rather a 1996 incarnation rerecording the originals' best-known songs.   —D.M.

Eddie Cochran

    ★★★   Greatest Hits (Curb, 1990)
   ★★★★   Somethin' Else: The Fine Lookin' Hits of
             Eddie Cochran (Razor & Tie, 1998)

Acknowledged as one of the most gifted of the early rock & roll artists, Eddie Cochran died in a car accident in 1960, leaving unsettled his standing in relation to other first-generation rockers. Between 1957 and 1959, he had only three Top 40 hits, the biggest being the classic "Summertime Blues," which peaked at #8 in 1958. While Buddy Holly and Ritchie Valens had established strong individual identities by the time of their deaths, leaving open to speculation only the question of how their careers might have evolved, Cochran died only having released some spirited sides but without establishing a point of view distinctively his own. On balance, the tracks on the 1998 near-definitive anthology *Somethin' Else* simply don't measure up to the best work of Cochran's peers. True, "Summertime Blues" and "Twenty Flight Rock" remain among the very best singles of the '50s, and have proven to be inspirational touchstones for succeeding generations of unreconstructed rockers who find in Cochran the essence of early rock & roll's rebel spirit. But many of Cochran's recordings sound more like blueprints made by an artist searching for his voice. While he's barely on the radar in his home country, the fact that his death took place during a U.K. tour with Gene Vincent brought Cochran legendary status there, and his slim body of work is more fully represented on Brit collections. —D.M./B.SC.

Cocteau Twins

★★★	Garlands (1982; Capitol, 1991)
★★	Lullabies (EP) (1982; Capitol, 1991)
★★★	Head Over Heels (1983; Capitol, 1991)
★★½	Peppermint Pig (EP) (1983; Capitol, 1991)
★★★½	Sunburst and Snowblind (EP) (1983; Capitol, 1991)
★★★½	Pearly-Dewdrops' Drops (EP) (1984; Capitol, 1991)
★★★½	Treasure (1984; Capitol, 1991)
★★★★	The Pink Opaque (1985; Capitol, 1991)
★★★	Aikea-Guinea (1985; Capitol, 1991)
★★★	Tiny Dynamite (EP) (1985; Capitol, 1991)
★★★	Echoes in a Shallow Bay (EP) (1985; Capitol, 1991)
★★★½	Victorialand (1986; Capitol, 1991)
★★★½	Love's Easy Tears (1986; Capitol, 1991)
★★★½	The Moon & the Melodies (1986; Capitol, 1991)
★★★½	Blue Bell Knoll (4AD/Capitol, 1988)
★★★½	Iceblink Luck (EP) (4AD/Capitol, 1990)
★★★★	Heaven or Las Vegas (4AD/Capitol, 1990)
★★★★	Cocteau Twins (4AD/Capitol, 1991)
★★★½	Four Calendar Café (Capitol, 1993)
★★★	Otherness (Capitol, 1995)
★★★½	Twinlights (EP) (Capitol, 1995)
★★★½	Milk & Kisses (Capitol, 1996)
★★★½	BBC Sessions (Ryko, 1999)

Punk's embrace of inspired amateurism has been responsible for many musical surprises, but none so delightful as the Cocteau Twins. This Scots combo—

Robin Guthrie, Elizabeth Fraser, and, eventually, Simon Raymonde—doesn't write songs so much as shape sounds into some semblance of a verse-chorus construction, after which Fraser appends her other-worldly melodies and inscrutable lyrics. It's not the most musicianly way of doing things, and the band's early efforts, *Garlands* and the EP *Lullabies,* flail more than they fly. But when the Cocteaus hit their mark, as they do on *Garlands'* "Wax and Wane," the result is deliriously tuneful, like a snippet from some fairy melody or a song heard in a dream.

That's the sort of magic the Cocteaus worked best; trouble is, it took them—that is, Fraser and Guthrie—a while to get good at it. Apart from the strident "Musette and Drums" and the rattletrap "When Mama Was Moth," *Head Over Heels* is too noisily primitive to cast much of a spell, while *Peppermint Pig* presents an unseemly brusqueness. Then, almost unexpectedly, comes the luscious, shimmering beauty of *Sunburst and Snowblind,* which includes a much-improved "Sugar Hiccup" (a coarser cousin can be found *on Head Over Heels*) and the gorgeous, moody "From the Flagstones." Raymonde joins up in time for *Pearly-Dewdrops' Drops,* which introduces the tasty title song. *Treasure* continues the Twins' ascent into aural bliss, thanks to such infectious concoctions as "Lorelei" or the hauntingly sibilant "Aloysius." Highlights from those records, along with the otherwise-unavailable "Millimillenary," may be found on the compilation *The Pink Opaque.*

With *Aikea-Guinea,* the degree of craft that went into the group's soundscapes began to increase while the melodic content declined. That doesn't exactly work against *Aikea-Guinea, Tiny Dynamite,* or *Echoes in a Shallow Bay,* as each eloquently conveys its own individual sense of atmosphere, but it does diminish the band's pop appeal. *Victorialand,* recorded without Raymonde, goes even further in its pursuit of the ineffable, as the aptly titled "Lazy Calm" and "Fluffy Tufts" make clear. Yet the duo could still summon its melodic gifts if so moved, as demonstrated by the slippery refrain to "Whales Tails," as well as the classic lines of "Love's Easy Tears" and the quirky choruses of "Orange Appled," both from the *Love's Easy Tears* EP. Even *The Moon & the Melodies,* a collaboration with minimalist composer Harold Budd, manages to deliver tuneful gems like "Sea, Swallow Me" and the slow, deliberate "She Will Destroy You."

Blue Bell Knoll inaugurated the group's association with Capitol Records in the U.S., and though the album can hardly be considered "commercial," it does boast an added sense of sparkle, from the giddy arabesques of Fraser's vocal on "Carolyn's Fingers" to the implied funk of "A Kissed Out Red Floatboat."

Iceblink Luck enhances that sense of groove to near dance-single strength, offering a prelude of sorts to *Heaven or Las Vegas*, wherein the Cocteaus ground their soft-focus soundscapes with low-key, bass-driven rhythm tracks, a strategy that nicely enhances the music's appeal. *Four Calendar Café* continues in the same vein, although particularly with impassioned singing from Fraser and a more lustrous sense of studio polish. *Otherness*, released two years later, is a bit of a red herring, as the looped abstractions of "Feet Like Fins" seem to suggest a retreat into arty opacity. That was hardly the case, though, as the semi-acoustic *Twinlights* EP finds the Cocteaus sounding more conventional than ever, especially on "Half-Gifts," which owes more than a little to Leonard Cohen's "Suzanne." As such, *Milk & Kisses* makes an appropriate farewell, neatly balancing the textural detail of the group's early work with a sophisticated and accessible sense of melody.

Although the Cocteaus were able to approximate their studio sound onstage, the fact that it's only an approximation makes *BBC Sessions* an album for hard-core fans only. The boxed set *Cocteau Twins* is a collection of the group's EPs (at least, up until 1990, anyway), plus a bonus disc containing several non-LP and previously unreleased tracks.   —J.D.C.

David Allan Coe

★★★★ The Mysterious Rhinestone Cowboy/Once Upon a Rhyme (1974/1976; Bear Family, 1994)

★★★ Longhaired Redneck/Rides Again (1976/1977; Bear Family, 1994)

★★★ Tattoo/Family Album (1977/1978; Bear Family, 1995)

★★ Human Emotions/Spectrum VII (1978/1979; Bear Family, 1995)

★★½ Compass Point/I've Got Something to Say (CBS 1979/1980; Bear Family, 1995)

★★½ Invictus Means Unconquered/Tennessee Whiskey (1981; Bear Family, 1995)

★★★ Castles in the Sand/Once Upon a Rhyme (Columbia 1983/1975; Collectables, 1999)

★★★½ For the Record: The First 10 Years (Columbia, 1984)

★★★ 17 Greatest Hits (Sony, 1985)

★★½ Super Hits (Sony, 1993)

★★½ Super Hits, Vol. 2 (Sony, 1996)

★★★ Live: If That Ain't Country . . . (Lucky Dog/Columbia, 1997)

★★½ The Ghost of Hank Williams (King, 1997)

★★½ 20 Road Music Hits (TeeVee, 1997)

★ Johnny Cash Is a Friend of Mine (King, 1998)

★★★½ Recommended for Airplay (Lucky Dog/Columbia, 1999)

★★★ 16 Biggest Hits (Sony, 1999)

★★ Long Haired Country Boy (King, 2000)

★★★★ Songwriter of the Tear (Cleveland International, 2001)

★★½ The Original Outlaw of Country Music (King, 2001)

★★ 20 All-Time Greatest Hits (TeeVee, 2002)

★½ Sings Merle Haggard (King, 2002)

★½ At His Best (King, 2002)

★★ Live at the Iron Horse Saloon (CoePop, 2002)

★★★ Live at Billy Bob's Texas (Image Entertainment, 2003)

A legend in his own mind, country artist David Allan Coe is a shameless self-promoter whose propensity for name-dropping is as much a trademark as his tattoos and long-haired redneck rebel image. And almost in spite of it all, he also happens to be a genuinely gifted songwriter, albeit a frustratingly inconsistent one.

The Ohio-born Coe emerged on the Nashville scene in the early '70s, calling himself the Mysterious Rhinestone Cowboy and boasting he had served nearly two decades in prison, including a stint on death row for murder. As it turned out, he had served time—primarily in various juvenile reformatories—but the murder rap turned out to be a product of Coe's imagination. Undaunted by this revelation, Coe maintained a rough and rugged public persona and promptly aligned himself with the outlaw movement, scoring an early hit as a songwriter with Tanya Tucker's cover of his "Would You Lay With Me (In a Field of Stone)." The song's success helped land him a Columbia deal (following his long-out-of-print 1969 Plantation debut, *Penitentiary Blues*, and the followup, *Requiem for a Harlequin*), and both *The Mysterious Rhinestone Cowboy* and *Once Upon a Rhyme* (which features his own version of the Tucker hit) were highly enjoyable showcases for Coe's rich, Merle Haggard–like voice, strong originals, and great taste in covers; Steve Goodman's "You Never Even Called Me by My Name," from *Once Upon a Rhyme*, would become Coe's signature anthem. Both albums—now compiled as part of Germany's Bear Family Records' reissue series of Coe twofers—stand as exemplary examples of mid-'70s country at its best. After that, his recordings have been considerably less consistent, reeling from the rock-solid, bare-knuckled, blue-collar bravura of "If That Ain't Country" (from *Rides Again*) and "Take This Job and Shove It" (*Tattoo*) to the obnoxious, full-blown self-mythologizing of "Willie, Waylon and Me" (*Rides Again*) and the title track of *Longhaired Redneck*, in which the only name he drops heavier than Johnny Cash's and Merle Haggard's is his own. The redneck shtick hit its nadir with a pair of late-'70s/early-'80s independent "X-rated" albums Coe peddled through a biker magazine; songs like "Little Suzie Shallow Throat" and "Nigger Fucker" earned him a rep as a sexist racist which still dogs him, though he has since denounced the records (both out of print). The superslick Billy Sherrill–produced albums of the same period—*Human Emotions, Invictus Means Unconquered,* and *Castles in the Sand*—were another matter entirely. Although Coe turned out an above-average song here and there, this is more *Urban Cowboy* fare than outlaw, as safe as milk even when Coe likens himself to Bob Dylan ("Castles in the Sand"). Grab the *Rhinestone Cowboy/Once Upon a Rhyme* disc if you can find it, or stick with the solid *For the Record: The First 10 Years* anthology.

By the beginning of the '90s, Coe was bankrupt and eking out a living by constant touring. A brief return to the majors (Sony's Lucky Dog) yielded 1997's *Live: If That Ain't Country . . . ,* a satisfyingly rowdy affair bolstered by lead-guitar work from Allman Brothers/Gov't Mule axeman Warren Haynes, and *Recommended for Airplay,* an exceptional studio album showcasing some of Coe's best originals since the early '70s—and a sense of humor, to boot. The refreshing "Song for the Year 2000," with its "it takes all kinds of people to make the world go round" hook, seemed a sincere and heartfelt (but not sappy) apology for some of his more offensive slurs in the past, while "A Harley Someday" poked gentle fun at a wanna-be "weekend warrior" biker before concluding, "We all started out just like that."

The even stronger *Songwriter of the Tear* skips the humor and goes right for the heart, with devastating results. In the span of 11 mostly terrific new originals, Coe proves that a world-class songwriter still lurks deep underneath all the layers of buffoonish self-parody. Unfortunately, he's still a risky gamble. The two most recent live albums—both featuring a handful of clunkers cowritten with Coe fan (natch) Kid Rock—are warts-and-all affairs, though *Live at Billy Bob's* sounds a lot better and features another outstanding new original in "Heaven Only Knows." The TeeVee and King compilations are uniformly awful, featuring either inferior new recordings of his best-known songs or pointless "tributes" to his heroes—er, close, personal friends—like Haggard and Cash.   —D.M./R.SK.

Leonard Cohen

★★★★★	Songs of Leonard Cohen (Columbia, 1968)
★★★½	Songs From a Room (Columbia, 1969)
★★★★★	Songs of Love and Hate (Columbia, 1971)
★★	Live Songs (Columbia, 1973)
★★★★½	New Skin for the Old Ceremony (Columbia, 1974)
★★★★★	Best of Leonard Cohen (Columbia, 1975)
★	Death of a Ladies' Man (Columbia, 1977)
★★★	Recent Songs (Columbia, 1979)
★★★½	Various Positions (PVC, 1985)
★★★★	I'm Your Man (Columbia, 1988)
★★★★	The Future (Columbia, 1992)
★★★	Cohen Live (Columbia, 1994)
★★★½	Best of, Vol. 2 (Columbia, 1997)
★★★★	Field Commander Cohen: Tour of 1979 (Columbia, 2001)
★★★★	Ten New Songs (Columbia, 2001)
★★★★	The Essential (Columbia, 2002)

Leonard Cohen is the Jewish Bryan Ferry. In the excellent liner notes of his 1975 *The Best of Leonard Cohen,* he explains the suave cover photo: "I rarely ever look this good, or bad, depending on your politics." That sums the man up. Running for the money and the flesh, especially the flesh, Cohen was the literary rogue who strummed his acoustic guitar and croaked of love and its torments. He emerged from Montreal in the 1960s, an acclaimed poet and novelist well into his thirties before he even made his first album. Yet for all his poetic angst and folkie sorrow, Cohen could never hide the fact that he was getting more rock-star booty than any Canadian before or since. Whispering in his glamorously tattered voice, he still makes his songs sound like sinful confidences shared over bottles of bloody-red wine.

He already had his style down on *Songs of Leonard Cohen.* No one has ever accused him of being a real guitarist, but for some reason, you can always tell it's him playing. In "Suzanne," "Master Song," and the peerless "So Long, Marianne," he sounds bemused by his own romantic travails, inventing what critic Robert Christgau called "his tuneless, grave, infinitely self-mocking vocal presence." His songs are strictly verse-chorus-verse, with hardly any bridges or fancy bits. Robert Altman used three of the tunes in the soundtrack to *McCabe & Mrs. Miller,* adding to Cohen's legend.

Songs From a Room is thin and sparse, weighed down by "Bird on a Wire," which became a schlock standard. But *Songs of Love and Hate* is the gangsta shit—even the one with the children's choir is so intense you can't turn it off. Cohen sings about jealous rivals ("Famous Blue Raincoat"), demon lovers ("Avalanche"), cold and lonesome virgin warrior goddesses ("Joan of Arc"), and God knows what else ("Let's Sing Another Song, Boys"), bursting with wit and imagination. *New Skin for the Old Ceremony* is almost as great, featuring the boho romance "Chelsea

Hotel No. 2." Note: Oral sex on unmade hotel beds is almost always a bad idea, since those bedspreads are laundered usually about once every five years, but songs about it are still cool.

Since then, Cohen has recorded sporadically—he apparently has the novel idea that before you make an album, you should wait until you have an album's worth of good songs. The only total waste is the Phil Spector collaboration *Death of a Ladies' Man. Recent Songs* has "Came So Far for Beauty." (Next line: "And I left so much behind.") *Various Positions* has "Hallelujah," which unexpectedly became Cohen's signature song after Jeff Buckley revived it in the 1990s. *I'm Your Man* perversely adds cheesy Eurodisco synths and disco-girl vocals to some of his bleakest tunes: "Everybody Knows," "First We Take Manhattan," "Tower of Song." *The Future* has a hilarious eight-minute send-up of Irving Berlin's "Always," plus political/spiritual statements along the lines of "Anthem" ("There is a crack in everything/That's how the light gets in").

By now, Cohen was bigger than ever, inspiring doom disciples such as Kurt Cobain, Trent Reznor, and Nick Cave. He spent most of the 1990s on a mountaintop Zen Buddhist retreat, while Cobain was down in Seattle singing, "Give me a Leonard Cohen afterworld/So I can sigh eternally." *Ten New Songs* offered "Alexandra's Leaving," "In My Secret Life," and "You Have Loved Enough," the epitaph Cohen has been writing for himself throughout his career. Of his three live albums, the good one is *Field Commander Cohen.* Cohen's record company has released three best-of anthologies, but bizarrely, none of them include "Joan of Arc." —R.S.

Coldplay

★★★½ Parachutes (Nettwerk, 2000)
★★★★½ A Rush of Blood to the Head (Capitol, 2002)

At first, Coldplay was burdened—along with Travis, Doves, Muse, and a few other young bands busting out of post–*OK Computer* Britain—by various media types with the dreaded designation "the new Radiohead." You can hear why: The widescreen melancholy of their first two albums wears the influence of Thom Yorke and company like a comfortable old overcoat, without shame or apology. But the influence of Jeff Buckley and U2 is nearly as strong, and singer Chris Martin's empathetic, often falsetto vocals are all his own.

Gangly, awkward, and charming as only hypersensitive teenagers can be, the Coldplay of *Parachutes* obviously had some growing-up issues to deal with. Both the songs and the playing here can sound tentative at times. But that just makes the great bits all the more magical, and there are plenty of those: the ambient guitar textures of "Don't Panic," the swooning chorus of "Shiver," and the U2-style singalong special "Yellow," to name but three.

A Rush of Blood to the Head delivers on the promise of *Parachutes* and then some. Tracks like "Politik," "God Put a Smile Upon Your Face," and "Warning Sign" are exhilarating epics that ache with beauty. And yet even as the music's ambition balloons, there's still something pleasantly unassuming at its heart. Coldplay knows it's good but doesn't want to get bigheaded about it—a refreshing attitude that may well make it one of the new millennium's prime contenders. —M.R.

Lloyd Cole & the Commotions

★★★★ Rattlesnakes (Capitol, 1984)
★★★ Easy Pieces (Capitol, 1985)
★★★★ Mainstream (Capitol, 1987)

Lloyd Cole

★★★★ 1984–1989 (Capitol, 1989)
★★★½ Lloyd Cole (Capitol, 1990)
★ Bad Vibes (Ryko, 1993)
★★★ Love Story (Ryko, 1995)
★★★★ Collection (PolyGram, 1998)
★★★ The Negatives (March Records, 2001)
★★★ Etc. (XIII Bis, 2001)
★★ Plastic Wood (XIII Bis, 2001)
★★★ Music in a Foreign Language (One Little Indian Records, 2004)

Formed at the University of Glasgow, Lloyd Cole & the Commotions made their debut in 1984 with the single "Perfect Skin," a U.K. hit and an American college radio fave that arrived amid a wave of smart guitar-pop bands (Aztec Camera, Prefab Sprout, the Smiths). But it is just one of numerous highlights on their charming debut, *Rattlesnakes*. Painfully romantic and teeming with lovelorn bohemian characters, literate references (Simone de Beauvoir, Leonard Cohen), and guitarist Neil Clarke's exquisite playing, it remains a high-water mark in Cole's yeoman's career. The followup, *Easy Pieces*, suffers slightly from rushed second-album syndrome and synth-heavy '80s production but remains a fan favorite due to such classics as "Why I Love Country Music" and "Lost Weekend." Cleanly produced and oft-overlooked, Cole's third and final Commotions album, the cynically titled *Mainstream*, is also his most well-rounded. After critical comparisons to Morrissey, Lou Reed, and Dylan, Cole finally finds his own voice on tracks such as the cheeky, upbeat "Sean Penn Blues" and gorgeous, melancholic "These Days."

Something of a love letter to his new hometown, New York City, *Lloyd Cole* was fueled by his late-night lifestyle and a band that included former Voidoids/Lou Reed players Fred Maher (drums) and Robert Quine (guitar). The songs rock harder than Cole ever had before—or has since. It has aged well and finds balance in its gentler moments, such as the quietly resigned "To the Church," wherein he begs, "Driver, can't you drive me a little more slowly . . . can't you find me some George Jones on your radio?"

Dropped by his label as part of a massive house-cleaning and left to his own devices and home studio, Cole resurfaced with the limp, glam rock–dabbling *Bad Vibes*. A new deal with U.S. indie label Ryko (which finally gave *Bad Vibes* a U.S. release) resulted in a mid-'90s comeback of sorts with the effervescent *Love Story*, a pleasant return to the Cole style of old (including guitar contributions from former Commotion Neil Clarke). *The Negatives* announced another rebirth of sorts with Cole this time hooking up with a younger group of NYC musicians (including Jill Sobule and ex-Dambuilder Dave Derby) and delivering another set of solid and upbeat, if familiar, songs. A pair of low-key "catch-up" releases followed: *Etc.* is a surprisingly good collection of outtakes/demos/extras (including a Dylan cover) from the late-'90s that any fan will love, while *Plastic Wood* is a less engaging foray into ambient instrumentals. Either of the best-of collections are decent starting points, but newcomers would also do well to just head straight for the classic *Rattlesnakes*. —D.S.

Ornette Coleman

★★★	Something Else!!! (Contemporary, 1958)
★★★	Tomorrow Is the Question! (Contemporary, 1959)
★★★★★	The Shape of Jazz to Come (Atlantic, 1959)
★★★★	Change of the Century (Atlantic, 1960)
★★★★½	This Is Our Music (Atlantic, 1961)
★★★★½	Free Jazz (Atlantic, 1961)
★★★★	Ornette! (Atlantic, 1962)
★★★★½	Ornette on Tenor (Atlantic, 1962)
★★½	Town Hall, 1962 (ESP, 1965)
★★★½	At the "Golden Circle" Stockholm, Vol. 1 (Blue Note, 1966)
★★★½	At the "Golden Circle" Stockholm, Vol. 2 (Blue Note, 1966)
★★★½	The Empty Foxhole (Blue Note, 1967)
★★★	New York Is Now! (Blue Note, 1968)
★★★	Love Call (Blue Note, 1968)
★★★½	The Art of the Improvisers (Atlantic, 1970)
★★★★	Science Fiction a.k.a. The Complete Science Fiction Sessions (Columbia, 1971/2000)
★★★½	Skies of America (Columbia, 1972)

★½	Dancing in Your Head (A&M, 1977)
★★½	Body Meta (Harmolodic/Verve, 1978)
★★★½	In All Languages (Harmolodic/Verve, 1987)
★★	Virgin Beauty (Columbia, 1988)
★★★★★	Beauty Is a Rare Thing (Rhino/Atlantic, 1993)
★★	Tone Dialing (Harmolodic/Verve, 1995)
★★½	Sound Museum: Hidden Man (Harmolodic/Verve, 1996)
★★½	Sound Museum: Three Women (Harmolodic/Verve, 1996)

Ornette Coleman & Charlie Haden

★★½	Soapsuds, Soapsuds (Harmolodic/Verve, 1979)

Ornette Coleman & Joachim Kühn

★★★	Colors (Harmolodic/Verve, 1997)

Most jazz greats sweep you along with them. Ornette Coleman sits himself down, defiantly, in your path, and demands you reckon with him. In almost 45 years' worth of recording, his music has ranged from challenging to difficult to teeth-gnashingly impossible. But his great albums have changed the path of jazz, and even the worst are noble failures, rarely less than intriguing. His concept of "harmolodics" is central to his work, and nearly impossible to grasp, although the gist of it seems to be freeing improvisation from the exclusive command of chord changes, and giving melody, harmony, rhythm, and mood equal importance.

From the first notes of his debut, *Something Else!!!*, blared out on a plastic alto saxophone and longtime partner Don Cherry's trumpet, it's clear that Coleman has a genuinely original voice. His tone is a rough, dry blues honk, and his compositions are freakishly structured tunes with chords that never go where you expect them to. The presence of pianist Walter Norris normalizes things a little—"The Blessing" could pass for ordinary jazz of the time—but Coleman's clearly straining at the bar lines. *Tomorrow Is the Question!* yokes Coleman and Cherry to the aggressively straightforward rhythm section of bassists Red Mitchell and Percy Heath and drummer Shelly Manne. The themes are even wilder 16th-note barrages, and Coleman and Cherry revel in the chance to play literally fast and loose with them.

Later in 1959, Coleman signed to Atlantic Records, who let him record with his actual quartet: Cherry (on cornet), bassist Charlie Haden, and drummer Billy Higgins. The result, *The Shape of Jazz to Come*, lives up to its title—more than 40 years later, jazz musicians still sound ahead of the curve when they follow its example. Perfectly attuned to each other's quirks, the quartet stretches and compresses notes, phrases, and whole structures, systematically splintering every rule of theme-and-variations jazz. And if Coleman has a single "greatest hit," it's the album's opener, "Lonely Woman," a slow, luscious theme that proceeds at its own uneven pace while Higgins plays like it's an uptempo number.

Cherry switched to pocket trumpet for *Change of the Century,* but the album's pretty much an extension of *Shape,* even if the band doesn't sound quite as desperate to prove itself. Haden gets to stretch out on "The Face of the Bass," and the title track's theme unfolds itself like a string of high explosives. Ed Blackwell takes over on drums for *This Is Our Music,* on which the quartet plays around a little with typical jazz forms in much the same way that a leopard plays with its prey. "Blues Connotation" is a jaunty blues track that promptly goes off somewhere else entirely; "Embraceable You" is an elegant but edgy reading of the Gershwin standard that hints at Coleman's days as an R&B honker.

Free Jazz was a leap into the unknown, years ahead of its time. The "double quartet"—Coleman's regular group, plus Higgins, Eric Dolphy (on bass clarinet), bassist Scott LaFaro, and trumpeter Freddie Hubbard—plays a frenetic little head, holds a few long notes, and then throws away the map and puts the pedal to the floor for 37 minutes. It could be cacophony, and it's not—this is a lively discussion, not an argument, and the eight musicians track each other's improvisations closely. How many albums get a genre named after them, anyway?

Recorded a month later, with LaFaro taking over for Haden in the new edition of the quartet, the four long tracks of *Ornette!* are casual but masterful. Coleman and Haden get to take long, spiraling solos, reeling out what Robert Palmer rightly calls "a series of dependent clauses": Every phrase is an improvisation on the one before it. Yet another bassist, Jimmy Garrison, appears on *Ornette on Tenor,* which is just that, though switching horns doesn't appreciably alter Coleman's barbed rasp. By this point, the group had their pattern down: gnarled high-speed head, open-ended solos for a while, repeat head, end. Nonetheless, the mock "false start" and unaccompanied Coleman free-association that open "Cross Breeding" still sound crisp and shocking.

The Art of the Improvisers is a series of outtakes from the 1959–61 period; nothing especially revelatory, but this is a fine band at the top of its form. Every track from the Atlantic period (including six previously unreleased compositions) is anthologized in chronological order on the six stunning discs of *Beauty Is a Rare Thing,* one of the finest and richest jazz box sets ever released.

Coleman has dabbled in fully scored music for decades, and the live *Town Hall 1962* is the first sign of that—one of its four pieces is a not-so-hot composition for string quartet. The other three, with a trio including bassist David Izenson and drummer Charles Moffet, are distinctively Ornettish, but he doesn't seem to have adjusted to playing without Cherry yet: There are a lot of open spaces where the two horn players used to harmonize. The same trio sounds much stronger on the Swedish gigs documented on the two *Golden Circle* albums. Coleman's left the stylistic double-dares of his Atlantic period behind him—in part because the jazz world, originally violently divided over his work, has started to catch up with him—and he's concentrating on swinging. His improvisations are still knotty and free-flailing: *Vol. 2*'s "Snowflakes and Sunshine" finds him alternating between violin and trumpet, neither of which is exactly his specialty. Still, compositions like "Dee Dee" (on *Vol. 1*) are as close to hummable as he's gotten since "Lonely Woman."

A strange one even by Coleman's standards, *The Empty Foxhole* is a trio date with Haden and a new drummer—very new. The leader's son, Ornette Denardo Coleman, was 10 years old and still very clearly learning how to play drums. His dodgy sense of rhythm, though, was a welcome challenge to Coleman and Haden: You can hear them having fun working around it on "Good Old Days" and the waltzlike title track. The amateur spirit only really gets out of hand on "Sound Gravitation," on which Dad attempts to play violin again. (Daaaad!)

Coleman's last two Blue Note albums, *New York Is Now!* and *Love Call,* were recorded simultaneously, with John Coltrane's old rhythm section of bassist Jimmy Garrison and drummer Elvin Jones (Coleman had played at Coltrane's memorial service), as well as tenor saxophonist Dewey Redman. They're transitional records, and they sound like it: They've got a peculiar lineup, with Coleman pretending he's a multi-instrumentalist again, and he's not making any particular breakthroughs.

Many of Coleman's albums from the late '60s and early '70s, like the ferocious *Crisis,* have been out of print for ages. *Friends and Neighbors* from 1971 is particularly worth digging up, though, for its bizarre title track: a near-funky groove, recorded live at his New York storefront Artists House, with Ornette torturing a fiddle and everyone in the neighborhood chipping in on vocals.

Coleman's next move was both backward and forward. *Science Fiction,* originally released in 1971, reunited him with Cherry, Haden, Higgins, Redman, and Blackwell, and pieces like "Civilization Day" are stylistic throwbacks to the Atlantic years, if more precise sounding. But then he goes way out on a limb: Two songs have vocals by Indian pop singer Asha Puthli, and the title track's big-band noisefest features overdubbed baby noises and David Henderson reading a poem one word at a time. Weird and fabulous. The 2000 CD reissue augments it with the outtakes that became 1982's *Broken Shadows,* including the cyclonic "Happy House," Webster Armstrong singing a dissonant jump blues, and "School Work," the earliest recording of a singsong melody Coleman's listeners would come to know well.

Skies of America was originally intended as a concerto for jazz quartet and the London Symphony Orchestra; for various reasons, it turned into a sprawling orchestral work with Coleman playing saxophone in places. His harmonic sense is splendid, lush, and tartly dissonant, although the arrangements actually sound better here when he's not playing than when he is. "The Good Life," incidentally, is just "School Work" in orchestral drag.

Possibly Coleman's most irritating album, *Dancing in Your Head* gives us 26 exasperating minutes of "Theme from a Symphony"—which is, yes, "School Work" 's nagging eight-note hook again. This time, it's accompanied by two electric atonal guitars, bass, and drums, playing the kind of funk you can't actually dance to. The album's filled out by a brief, misfiring collaboration with the Master Musicians of Joujouka. The next year's *Body Meta* keeps the electric band and the wonky funk vibe, but does a bit better by them, even though everyone occasionally seems to be playing entirely different songs. The distorted free-for-all "Home Grown" even anticipates New York's no-wave sound. And just as dissonant, arty funk was taking off, what did Ornette release? Why, *Soapsuds, Soapsuds,* of course—an album of relaxed acoustic duos with Charlie Haden, opening with a cover of the theme from *Mary Hartman, Mary Hartman.*

The electric band of *Dancing in Your Head* and *Body Meta* became the seven-piece Prime Time, who released several now-out-of-print albums before *In All Languages* paired 13 performances by them with 10 by the reconvened Cherry/Haden/Higgins quartet (eight of them the same songs). Advantage: oldsters, in almost all cases—they're tighter and terser than ever. And "Peace Warriors" is a fabulous two-and-a-half-minute honk-bam-boom.

Following a fine collaboration with Pat Metheny, *Song X,* Coleman returned to the studio with Prime Time. *Virgin Beauty* features Jerry Garcia on three tracks, although it's not terribly Grateful Dead–ish. Its hints of Afro-pop ("Happy Hour") hold up better than its ersatz Prince beats ("Singing in the Shower"), but

the production and showoffish slap 'n' pop bass date it badly. *Tone Dialing,* the final Prime Time record to date, is even more confused (hint: a rapper on an Ornette album is just not a good idea). It attempts to apply harmolodic principles and Ornettian eclecticism to contemporary R&B, but ends up meandering listlessly.

The two *Sound Museum* albums, *Hidden Man* and *Three Women,* are simply alternate takes on a nearly identical set of songs, including a couple of old favorites like "Home Grown" and "Mob Job." The sympathetic acoustic quartet includes Denardo Coleman, Charlie Moffett's son Charnett, and pianist Geri Allen. It's fairly lively, if not nearly as fiery as classic Ornette, but the harmolodic lack of hierarchy seems more like an excuse to sell the same record twice to the same people. (It doesn't help that Coleman's liner notes make no sense at all.) *Colors,* an assured, ungimmicky live duo with German pianist Joachim Kühn, presents Coleman with more of a challenge—he even lets Kühn outplay him a couple of times, as on the hyper-dense "Three Ways to One." —D.W.

Collective Soul

★★½   Hints, Allegations, and Things Left Unsaid (Atlantic, 1994)
★★★   Collective Soul (Atlantic, 1995)
★★★   Disciplined Breakdown (Atlantic, 1997)
★★½   Dosage (Atlantic, 1999)
★★   Blender (Atlantic, 2000)
★★★½   7even Year Itch: Greatest Hits, 1994–2001 (Atlantic, 2001)

The typical Collective Soul song has a one-word title, runs between three and five minutes, prosecutes a catchy '70s-style melody over warm, burbling '90s-style guitars, frets about the human condition, and dominates rock radio for months at a time. These mellow Georgia boys have never been anywhere near fashionable, but they have enjoyed a longer and more fruitful run than most of their flashier grunge-era peers, despite one of the sorriest names any worthy band has ever saddled itself with. Ed Roland, a Southern preacher's kid who was forbidden to listen to rock & roll growing up, is the singer, songwriter, guitarist, and producer whose spiritual concerns and studio perfectionism define the band, and each of Collective Soul's albums has its share of smartly crafted hits. The best are on *Collective Soul,* which features the rumbling ballad "December" (you remember, it's the one that goes, "Turn your head now, baby, just spit me out"), and *Disciplined Breakdown,* which has the gorgeous "Listen." "December" sounds a bit like Nirvana, "Listen" sounds a lot like Three Dog Night, and those parameters pretty much sum up the band's sound. Both of these high points appear alongside "Gel," "Heavy," "Run," and other hits on Collective Soul's stellar best-of collection, which is recommended despite the extremely regrettable title *7even Year Itch.* —R.S.

Bootsy Collins

★★★	Stretchin' Out in Bootsy's Rubber Band (Warner Bros., 1976)	
★★★	Ahh . . . The Name Is Bootsy, Baby! (Warner Bros., 1977)	
★★★½	Bootsy? Player of the Year (Warner Bros., 1978)	
★★½	Ultra Wave (Warner Bros., 1980)	
★★½	What's Bootsy Doin'? (Columbia, 1988)	
★★★★	Back in the Day: The Best of Bootsy (Warner Bros., 1994)	
★★★	Blasters of the Universe (Rykodisc, 1994)	
★★★	Keepin' Dah Funk Alive 4-1995 (Rykodisc, 1995)	
★★½	Fresh Outta 'P' University (Private I/WEA, 1998)	
★★★½	Glory B, da' Funk's on Me!: The Bootsy Collins Anthology (Rhino, 2001)	
★★	Play With Bootsy: A Tribute to the Funk (EastWest/WEA Germany, 2002)	
★★	Play With Bootsy (2002; Thump, 2004)	

Zillatron

★★	Lord of the Harvest (Rykodisc, 1993)	

Bootsy's Rubber Band was the most entertaining and longest-running spin-off of George Clinton's eternal P-Funk circus, and that's because Bootsy is a true star, the clown prince of comic, psychedelic, good-times funk—if he weren't such a genius of the bass, you'd think he was Jimmie Walker in a sequined costume, star-shaped mirrored shades included. His career is like a Horatio Alger story based in Chocolate City: Plucked from teenage obscurity in 1969 to play with James Brown, the former William Collins of Cincinnati brought a slap-happy zest to JB's sound, then hooked up with Clinton and was reborn in his image, with a little help from LSD.

The groove flows free on a string of six albums for Warner Bros. from 1976 to 1982 (of which four remain in print), with Bootsy ably leading a top-notch band of mostly P-Funk vets, including his brother Catfish Collins on guitar, Bernie Worrell on keyboards, and a horn section including Fred Wesley and Maceo Parker. Though Clinton produced the albums and cowrote most of the material, Bootsy emerges as a character all his own. At first he's "Casper" ("not the friendly ghost/but the holy ghost"), the benevolent black spirit that was his alter ego in P-Funk. But before

long his personae grow so numerous—like Bootzilla, the funkiest wind-up toy on the market, "equipped with stereophonic funk-producin', disco-inducin', twin-magnetic rump receptors"—that he's simply Bootsy, an indefinable.

The flash and goofiness can obscure Bootsy's formidable chops, as well as the quality of the songwriting. Clinton let some gems get away, like *Stretchin' Out*'s impossibly sweet "I'd Rather Be With You" and the second album's "The Pinocchio Theory" ("don't fake the funk or your nose will grow"). The melodies are smooth and rich, and Bootsy's bass admirably unobtrusive; unlike some P-Funk discs from this period, the sound is focused and uncluttered, more akin to carefree disco than Clinton's utopian head trip.

The '80s were a transitional time for Collins. As disco died, he sought to modernize his groove with *Ultra Wave* and, after a hiatus of several years, the hip-hop-influenced *What's Bootsy Doin'?*, which was one of the first of many collaborations with bassist and avant-ish producer Bill Laswell. One of them, Zillatron (others are Praxis and Axiom Funk), has Bootsy assuming the monstrous guise of Fuzzface and muttering nonsense through a distorted microphone. Not quite as amusing as his Bootzilla adventures, although it does take Clinton's "space funk" concept to a new level of some sort.

As the '90s dawned, Bootsy was happily trading in nostalgia. After his appearance on Deee-Lite's 1990 party anthem "Groove Is in the Heart" put him back in the public eye, he established a New Rubber Band (with Catfish, Worrell, and some other holdovers) and hit the studio. *Blasters of the Universe,* a double that needn't be a double, finds him back in his grand '70s game with disco ballads and spunky crowd-rousers. The live *Keepin' Dah Funk Alive* (another double) is his standard set: 75 percent oldies from the *Stretchin' Out* era, 20 percent P-Funk faves ("One Nation Under a Groove," "Night of the Thumpasorus Peoples"), and maybe something recorded past 1979, if he's feeling frisky. Bootsy's later albums are quickies involving a lot of wide-eyed guest stars (Snoop Dogg, Fat Boy Slim, Fat Joe), but they keep him on the road, where he belongs.

Despite impressive packaging (including a Bootsy pop-up centerfold) on the *Glory B* two-disc set, the leaner and more selective *Back in the Day* is the Bootsy anthology of choice. The blistering live take on "Psychoticbumpschool" is worth the sticker price alone. —B.S.

Phil Collins

★★★	Face Value (Atlantic, 1981)	
★★½	Hello, I Must Be Going (Atlantic, 1982)	

★★★½ No Jacket Required (Atlantic, 1985)
★★½ 12"ers (Atlantic, 1988)
★★½ Buster (soundtrack) (Atlantic, 1988)
★★½ . . . But Seriously (Atlantic, 1989)
★★★½ Serious Hits . . . Live! (Atlantic, 1990)
★★★ Both Sides (Atlantic, 1993)
★★ Dance into the Light (Atlantic, 1996)
★★★★ . . . Hits (Atlantic, 1998)
★★★ A Hot Night in Paris (Atlantic, 1999)
★★½ Tarzan: Original Soundtrack (Disney, 1999)

For a time, Phil Collins was nearly inescapable on the radio, and enormously popular with the listening public—something that made him an obvious target for critics. Despite his *lumpen*-pop appeal, however, Collins is an incisive songwriter and resourceful musician. Of all his albums, *Face Value* sounds most like his work with Genesis. "I Missed Again" and "If Leaving Me Is Easy" carry the same mournfulness of *Duke*, while "In the Air Tonight" condenses *Wind and Wuthering*'s musical dramatics to a five-minute mini-epic. With *Hello, I Must Be Going*, Collins begins to find his own voice, flirting with soul (although soul didn't always flirt back, as his remake of "You Can't Hurry Love" demonstrates) and sharpening his skills at ballad-writing (which finally paid off in 1984, with "Take a Look at Me Now," from the *Against All Odds* film soundtrack). Collins pulled it all together with the aggressively likeable *No Jacket Required*, which had solid rockers, great ballads, and a pleasantly silly rewrite of Prince's "1999" ("Sussudio").

Unfortunately, the peripatetic Collins was unable to sustain that momentum. *12"ers* was an unconvincing collection of dance remixes, the *Buster* soundtrack squandered "Two Hearts" (cowritten with Motown auteur Lamont Dozier) on what was otherwise an oldies album, and . . . *But Seriously* put more emphasis on its message than its music. *Serious Hits Live!*, however, is a delightful surprise, a live album that actually improves on its material.

With the home-recorded *Both Sides*, Collins turns serious and socially conscious, a move that should have been commercial suicide but instead revealed hidden depths (as well as a tendency to preach). Perhaps in compensation, the worldbeat-flavored *Dance Into the Light* is almost willfully frivolous, sounding at times as if Collins were trying to channel Lionel Richie. *A Hot Night in Paris* goes for something completely different, as Collins drives a jazz big band through arrangements of Genesis oldies and his own tunes. A Buddy Rich album this isn't. Likewise, *Tarzan* isn't exactly a Phil Collins album, as his characteristically jaunty originals share space with Mark Mancina's more conventionally Disney-fied film music.

Still, it does include Collins' long-awaited duet with 'N Sync on "Trashin' the Camp." —J.D.C.

John Coltrane

★★★★½ Giant Steps (Atlantic, 1960)
★★★½ Coltrane Jazz (Atlantic, 1961)
★★★★½ My Favorite Things (Atlantic, 1961)
★★★ Bags & Trane (Atlantic, 1961)
★★★★ Africa/Brass a.k.a. The Complete Africa/Brass Sessions (Impulse!, 1961)
★★★★★ Live at the Village Vanguard a.k.a. Live at the Village Vanguard—The Master Takes (Impulse!, 1962)
★★★ Olé Coltrane (Atlantic, 1962)
★★★★ Coltrane (Impulse!, 1962)
★★★½ Coltrane Plays the Blues (Atlantic, 1962)
★★★★ Ballads (Impulse!, 1963)
★★★ Duke Ellington & John Coltrane (Impulse!, 1963)
★★★★ John Coltrane and Johnny Hartman (Impulse!, 1963)
★★★★ Impressions (Impulse!, 1963)
★★★½ Live at Birdland (Impulse!, 1964)
★★★ Coltrane's Sound (Atlantic, 1964)
★★★ Crescent (Impulse!, 1964)
★★★★★ A Love Supreme (Impulse!, 1965)
★★★★½ The John Coltrane Quartet Plays (Impulse!, 1965)
★★★★★ Ascension (Impulse!, 1965)
★★★½ Kulu Se Mama (Impulse!, 1966)
★★★★ Meditations (Impulse!, 1966)
★★★ The Avant-Garde (Atlantic, 1966)
★★★★½ Live at the Village Vanguard Again! (Impulse!, 1966)
★★★ Expression (Impulse!, 1967)
★★★★½ Live in Seattle (Impulse!, 1970; full version in 1994)
★★★½ Transition (Impulse!, 1970)
★★★★ Sun Ship (Impulse!, 1971)
★★★½ Live in Japan (Impulse!, 1973; full version in 1991)
★★★½ Interstellar Space (Impulse!, 1974)
★★★½ First Meditations (Impulse!, 1977)
★★★ Dear Old Stockholm (Impulse!, 1978)
★★★★ A John Coltrane Retrospective: The Impulse! Years (Impulse!, 1992)
★★★★½ The Major Works of John Coltrane (Impulse!, 1992)
★★★★ Newport '63 (Impulse!, 1993)
★★½ The Last Giant: The John Coltrane Anthology (Rhino/Atlantic, 1993)
★★★★ The Heavyweight Champion: The Complete Atlantic Recordings (Rhino/Atlantic, 1995)
★★★★ Stellar Regions (Impulse!, 1995)

For most of the '50s, John Coltrane was merely a first-rate jazz saxophonist. (He recorded a mountain of albums during that time, which aren't included in the discography above.) On or about March 2, 1959, he abruptly became God, and that's where we pick up the story. Between Coltrane's first session for Miles Davis' *Kind of Blue* (taped that day) and his death from liver cancer at the age of 40 on July 17, 1967, he recorded a massive, brilliant, perpetually evolving, and staggeringly influential body of work.

If you're just starting to listen to Coltrane, the sheer mass of stuff out there can be paralyzing (our discography omits most of the zillion or so compilations and best-ofs currently in print). It's useful to bear a few things in mind, though. First of all, parts of Coltrane's early-'60s records now seem like fairly normal jazz, but if anything he did is a cliché, it's because everyone after Trane has copped his ideas. At the time, in fact, his playing seemed shockingly radical, and he was called "the most avant-garde of the avant-garde." Second, as far out as Coltrane could get, he loved tunes. There's the pure melodic sense of the American popular song tradition hiding in the core of almost all of his work, and if you get lost in any period of it, you can always orient yourself by the simple waltzes he played right up to the end—especially, believe it or not, "My Favorite Things." Yes, the "raindrops on roses" one.

Giant Steps, the first album Coltrane released on Atlantic, was where he declared that everyone had to sit up and pay attention to him. It includes three stone classics: the light-speed title track (which burns through chords so fast that pianist Tommy Flanagan famously can't keep up in his solo—Coltrane swoops in and rescues him), "Mr. P.C.," and an exquisite slow tribute to Trane's then wife, "Naima." (*Bags and Trane,* a collaboration with vibraphonist Milt Jackson, was actually recorded four months earlier; it's one of those solid but unexceptional jazz discs Trane piled up in the '50s.) As occasionally happens in his discography, Coltrane followed up a radical album with an attempt to prove he wasn't so radical as all that; *Coltrane Jazz* is nicely played, but disappointingly straight-ahead, aside from some freaky blowing on "Harmonique."

The Avant-Garde, credited to Coltrane and trumpeter Don Cherry, is a fascinating diversion, recorded in 1960 but not released for another six years. Three of its five tracks are Ornette Coleman tunes, and a fourth is by Coleman's associate Cherry; the rhythm section is Coleman's, too. Normally a tenor saxophonist, Coltrane tries out soprano sax for the first time. He's not entirely at home in the harmolodic maze, but you can hear him trying to open himself up to its possibilities.

The next time he recorded, he played the soprano again, and scored a hit with the title track of *My Favorite Things:* a brilliant 13-minute-plus reimagining of the singalong from *The Sound of Music* as a waltz-time framework for modal improvisation. His racing scales and trills are neatly accompanied by the block chords of pianist McCoy Tyner and the simpatico swing of drummer Elvin Jones; both became part of his group for almost the rest of his life. The three standards that make up the rest of the album are pretty nifty, too, including a tweaked variation on George Gershwin's "Summertime." The same three days' worth of sessions that produced *My Favorite Things* also yielded two more albums, *Coltrane Plays the Blues* (what it sounds like) and *Coltrane's Sound* (smoother originals and another couple of standards)—the former, particularly, has some entertaining twists on basic blues structures.

In early 1961, multi-instrumentalist Eric Dolphy—sort of the Brian Jones of jazz—joined Coltrane's group and became his creative foil, and in May and June they recorded two albums with expanded lineups. *Olé Coltrane* is loose and casual—the two spur each other on over the two-chord Latinate vamp of "Olé," featuring a seven-piece band, and bat around a simple blues and a calm Tyner original. *Africa/Brass,* on the other hand, sounds like a Major Project; built around Dolphy's big-band arrangements, it features "Africa," a hulking, dramatic piece featuring African-inspired rhythms and bass drones. It's also got the first of Coltrane's many versions of "Greensleeves," another modal waltz on which he plays soprano. (He was contractually unable to rerecord "My Favorite Things" for a few years after he left Atlantic, but he treats "Greensleeves" basically the same way.) The currently available version is *The Complete Africa/Brass Sessions,* which pads the album out to two discs with five alternate versions and outtakes.

For all he could do in the studio, though, Coltrane's real wizardry happened onstage, where he could solo as long and intensely as he pleased, and the tapes of his performances at a New York club from early November 1961 were his next big breakthrough. *Live at the Village Vanguard,* in its original incarnation, is three long, astonishing tracks—most notably "Chasin' the Trane," 15 minutes of Coltrane blazing away without a theme at all. A couple of infamous reviews subsequently accused Coltrane and Dolphy of "musical nonsense . . . being peddled in the name of jazz" and called "Chasin' the Trane" "one big air-leak." More nonsense and air-leaks, please: Two more stormers from the Vanguard tapes, "Impressions" (a variant of Miles Davis' "So What") and the drone-based "India" supplement the original three on the current CD version (*The Master Takes*); they also make up the bulk of *Impressions,* along with two brief studio tracks (including the exquisite ballad "After the Rain"). *The Complete 1961 Village Vanguard Recordings* is the motherlode: 22 tracks on four discs, some even more daring than the familiar versions, like a take on "India" with Trane's usual crew supplemented by an extra bassist, Dolphy on bass clarinet, Garvin Bushell playing oboe, and oud player Ahmed Abdul-Malik! It's a splendid opportunity to hear how Coltrane's music could evolve over the space of a few days.

Dolphy left the group in the spring of 1962, and the "classic quartet" was solidified: Coltrane, Tyner, Jones, and bassist Jimmy Garrison. Their first studio project, *Coltrane,* is slightly tamer than the Vanguard tapes. It's basically an attempt to show off all the saxophonist's specialties: long, discursive solos ("Out of This World"), polite balladeering ("Soul Eyes"), the "My Favorite Things"/"Greensleeves" routine ("The Inchworm"), bluesy modal struts ("Tunji"), and formal experiments ("Miles' Mode," based on a 12-tone row—a trick from European classical music). The "deluxe edition" appends a disc of unsurprising outtakes and alternates.

By this point, Coltrane had a reputation as a radical bomb-thrower, so his next three albums were essentially an image-rehabilitation program. *Ballads* is jukebox-length renditions of eight tunes from his slow-dancing days, all done up for a night in at the bachelor pad—only a few, like "You Don't Know What Love Is," even hint at his "sheets of sound." (The "deluxe edition" is recommended to those who crave five consecutive alternate takes of "Greensleeves," followed by seven of "It's Easy to Remember.") *Duke Ellington & John Coltrane* is effectively an endorsement from jazz's Old Guard: Duke contributes most of the songs, Trane plays gracefully but conservatively (he stretches out just a little on "Angelica"), and nobody feels threatened. An anomaly in the Coltrane catalogue, *John Coltrane and Johnny Hartman* finds the classic quartet backing up a smooth torch singer on half a dozen more ballad standards. It's one of Coltrane's least innovative records, but impeccably dignified and elegant.

All this time, though, the group was honing its less restrained art on stage, night after night. They toured Europe several times between 1961 and 1963; those performances have been widely bootlegged, and seven discs' worth of them are collected on *Live Trane: The European Tours* (parts of which had previously appeared as *The Paris Concert, Bye Bye Blackbird, The European Tour,* and *Afro Blue Impressions*). The sound quality's a little murky, but the band is gliding on air, finding new perspectives on its central repertoire over and over. (The set includes no fewer than six versions of "My Favorite Things," totaling over two hours.) Note, though, that Coltrane discographers believe that the box's recording information is seriously flawed—three tracks even appear to be from New York!

Elvin Jones was incarcerated for a while in mid-1963, and the somewhat splashier Roy Haynes filled in for him on drums. *Newport '63* is the altered quartet's three-song plumage-display from that July's Newport Jazz Festival (including a radiant, trilling "My Favorite Things"), plus another piece from the 1961 Vanguard tapes. Coltrane celebrated Jones' return with *Live at Birdland.* Only the first three tracks were actually recorded at the New York club in question, and as virtuosic as they are (particularly Trane's unaccompanied coda for "I Want to Talk About You"), they're basically a status report. The real gem of the set is a devastating, elegiac studio track, "Alabama," which became a classic of the civil rights movement. (The album's initial pressing included a long false start by accident; eventually, everyone decided they liked it that way.)

Crescent shows off Coltrane's rhythm section: "Lonnie's Lament" and "The Drum Thing," respectively, let Garrison and Jones stretch out. The title track swoops elegantly, though the album as a whole drags a bit. *A Love Supreme,* on the other hand, is a hands-down masterpiece of ensemble musicianship: a four-part suite in which the quartet moves as with a single mind. Intended as a piece of sacred music, it's one of the most eloquent prayers of the 20th century. "Acknowledgement," a masterful exegesis of a four-note call to God, appears on virtually every Coltrane anthology, and with good reason.

Recorded in February and May of 1965, *The John Coltrane Quartet Plays* was the last gesture Coltrane made toward the pop audience; from there on out, they'd have to come to him. Its covers of "Chim

Chim Cheree" (another soprano waltz) and Nat "King" Cole's "Nature Boy" are bases from which the quartet locks together and heads for terra incognita, and the two originals are dense, bold, and painterly. The posthumously released *Transition* and *Living Space*, both recorded over the following month, are beautifully played (the experimentally overdubbed extra saxophone part on the latter's title track is a bracing, original idea), but suffer from underdeveloped material—*Transition*'s "Suite" can't quite let go of its more conventional jazz passages, and three of *Living Space*'s five tracks never got real titles.

At the end of June, Coltrane took his next giant step. *Ascension*, recorded with an 11-piece mob including the up-and-coming tenor saxophonists Archie Shepp and Pharoah Sanders, bypasses the elegant modal techniques Coltrane had mastered for a howlingly intense 40-minute free-improv monsoon. (The originally released version was immediately supplanted by an alternate take; the CD includes both.) Over 35 years later, it still blows the roof off.

The classic quartet's days were numbered by then, but they still recorded two more albums' worth of material on August 28 and September 2. *Sun Ship*, an album-length exploration of rhythm with rudimentary, raw thematic material, plays with opened-up time. Jones' drumming is the hardest he ever recorded with Coltrane; sometimes there's a regular tempo, usually there's not, and the group surges forward eloquently, alternating tenderness and force. The session issued as *First Meditations* is a suite on the model of *A Love Supreme*, but much more abrasive in places—you can hear Coltrane trying to push the rest of the group toward the shriekadelic extremes of *Ascension* in "Consequences," and they're clearly more used to the smoother waters of "Love" and the cheerful bop of "Joy."

Pharoah Sanders, whose specialty in those days was screeching, growling extended sax techniques, joined the group as a second saxophonist, and the two-disc *Live in Seattle* documents the expanded group (also featuring bassist/bass clarinetist Donald Rafael Garrett) at the end of September. The ruckus-raising of "Cosmos" and "Evolution," and the way "Out of This World" veers away from its theme and into the wilderness, are what you might expect; the free-sailing but respectful and relaxed 21-minute rendition of "Body and Soul" is more of a surprise.

By the middle of October, it'd been almost a month since Coltrane's last radical move, so the sextet hooked up with singer Juno Lewis and percussionist Frank Butler for the 18-minute title track of *Kulu Se Mama* (which was filled out with two long quartet pieces from June). Heavily influenced by African music, especially in its multiple percussion parts, it often seems more Lewis' show than Coltrane's, and anticipates some of the Afro-pop of the following decade—except when Sanders starts pulling bubbling demons out of the dark corners of his tenor sax.

November's breakthrough was *Meditations*, in which the quartet (plus Sanders and drummer Rashied Ali) revisits its suite from a few months before in much freer, more chaotically energetic style. The highlight, though, is the all-new opener, "The Father and the Son and the Holy Ghost," on which Coltrane and Sanders blow so hard they practically splatter the rest of the group against the walls. It's not pretty, and not much like *A Love Supreme*, but it's undeniably powerful.

Elvin Jones and McCoy Tyner both left Coltrane's group after *Meditations;* Garrison and Sanders stayed on, Ali joined full-time, and Alice Coltrane (John's wife) took over on piano. The new group's sessions from early 1966 are currently unavailable, so the earliest music we have from them is May's extraordinary *Live at the Village Vanguard Again!* Even in the middle of the free-music vortex, Trane never gave up his love of tunes, and the album consists of extended cruises through, above and around two of his favorites: "Naima" and "My Favorite Things." Sanders slashes the melody of "Naima" to ribbons and then tears the ribbons into confetti, Alice imitates Tyner's style as well as she can, and John keeps gravitating back toward the themes as if they were the North Star.

Live in Japan, a four-disc set from two July dates, is even more expansive—this time "My Favorite Things" goes on for almost an hour, though the first quarter is a bass solo. Coltrane and Sanders had been given alto saxophones on the tour, and they gave their new instruments a workout. The group was thinking on a grand scale by this point, and it can be exhausting to wait out their leisurely free ruminations, but if you've got the patience for it, there's some gorgeous, challenging music here.

Expression, recorded in February and March of 1967, was the last album personally approved by Coltrane. It's a bit scattered: "Ogunde" is built around a stately fanfare, and "Offering" and "Expression" work up some free-improv steam, but "To Be," featuring Coltrane on flute (!) and Sanders on piccolo (!!), churns on far too long. On the other hand, *Stellar Regions*, recorded at the first of those sessions but unreleased for 28 years, is a gem, jagged as a rock-lined shore but as lyrical as anything in Coltrane's catalogue. The new quartet (without Sanders) runs the tiniest of thematic ideas (like the fragmentary head of "Transonic") through the improvisational mill, and they emerge sparkling and razor-sharp. A week later, Coltrane and percussionist Ali recorded *Interstellar Space* as a duo. They match each other's frantic energy—"Leo," which had been in the quartet's repertoire for the better part of a year, emerges at hardcore speed and intensity. Trane has picked up some of Sanders' blatantly abrasive tone on the tenor, but he's still thinking—and playing—at a million notes per minute.

A private tape of one of Coltrane's final performances, from April 23, 1967, surfaced recently as *The Olatunji Concert,* and it sounds like the statement the other 1967 recordings were heading toward. The recording is rough and bristly, but thankfully, so is the performance: The new quartet (plus Sanders and an extra percussionist or two) lunges into half-hour-long savagings of "Ogunde" and, what else, "My Favorite Things," and it's a marvel that the Olatunji Center's walls were still standing when it was all over. By ten minutes into the show, the group has become a screaming white-noise machine. The rest is silence: Three months later, Coltrane was dead.

The Heavyweight Champion collects every extant bit of music Coltrane recorded for Atlantic on seven discs, including one that's all alternate takes and false starts (nine of "Giant Steps" alone)—and he's one of those artists where every scrap counts. *The Classic Quartet: Complete Impulse! Studio Recordings* is an eight-disc monster that could singlehandedly justify Western civilization: all of *Coltrane, Ballads, Crescent, A Love Supreme, Quartet Plays, Sun Ship, First Meditations, Transition,* and *Living Space,* plus odds and ends and a disc of "works in progress." *The Major Works of John Coltrane* is fantastic but misleadingly titled; it might better be called *The Major Works of John Coltrane That Used an Expanded Ensemble During a 15-Week Period in the Middle of 1965.* It's got both versions of "Ascension," as well as "Kulu Se Mama," "Selflessness" (from the "Kulu" session), and a shrieking half-hour-long blowout called "Om," recorded the day after *Live in Seattle,* that's possibly the most difficult track of Coltrane's original albums—but still influential in the noise world.

Dear Old Stockholm compiles five studio tracks on which Roy Haynes substitutes for Elvin Jones in the classic quartet; all good stuff, but as a set it has no real reason to exist. The unbalanced two-disc anthology *The Last Giant* spends rather a lot of time on Coltrane's formative years (as early as 1946!), lingers over the Atlantic era, throws in a live 1961 "My Favorite Things," and then vaults straight over the Impulse! period to 90 seconds from 1967. *A John Coltrane Retrospective: The Impulse! Years* is three discs' worth of Trane's more accessible and tuneful

stuff from the '60s, mostly in studio renditions (with a few *Village Vanguard* treats). Impulse!'s *Very Best of* likewise plays up his smoother side; its bait is an otherwise unavailable studio version of "Impressions." —D.W.

Combustible Edison

★★ I, Swinger (Sub Pop, 1994)
★★ Schizophonic! (Sub Pop, 1996)
★★½ The Impossible World (Sub Pop, 1998)

After the dissolution of their rock band Christmas, Liz Cox and Michael Cudahy renamed themselves Miss Lily Banquette and the Millionaire, formed Combustible Edison, and hurled themselves into cocktail-lounge retro hell. Fun for a single or two, the band rarely transcended kitsch; it could do a perfectly good impression of '50s exotica, but it had nothing new to add to it. "Our host is a real scene-maker," Miss Lily croons on *I, Swinger*'s "The Millionaire's Holiday"—she may have been serious about it, but that's still no reason not to cringe. Only creditable covers of "Cry Me a River" and Kurt Weill's "Surabaya Johnny" are entirely unembarrassing.

In 1995, Combustible Edison provided most of the soundtrack to Quentin Tarantino's *Four Rooms*—the remainder being by easy-listening O.G. Esquivel, who outclasses them by a million tiki-decorated bar lengths. *Schizophonic!* is more of the same: entirely fluent in its idiom, entirely uninspired, and unnecessary in a world where Martin Denny records can be found at garage sales. Their farewell, *The Impossible World,* breaks the mold a bit with postproduction touches by electronic voyeur Scanner that bring their space-age bachelor-pad doodles into the post–space age. Cox gets to sing the genuinely strange "Tickled to Death," and her scat-vocalizing elsewhere is graceful. —D.W.

Commodores

★★★ Machine Gun (Motown, 1974)
★★★ Commodores (Motown, 1977)
★★★½ Commondores Live! (Motown, 1977)
★★★ In the Pocket (Motown, 1981)
★★★ Nightshift (Motown, 1985)
★★★★ The Ultimate Collection (Motown, 1997)
★★★½ The Millennuim Collection (Motown, 1999)
★★★★ Anthology (Motown, 2001)

Formed at the Tuskegee Institute in Alabama, this versatile septet signed to Motown in the early '70s—just as the funk movement began to gather steam. The Commodores brought a graceful Southern lilt to its plunking bass lines and sharp horn punctuations. Balancing that party-hearty attack with lead singer Lionel Richie's penchant for soft-soul balladry, the Commodores rode out the '70s on a hot crossover streak. *Commodores* (1977) and out of print albums such as *Caught in the Act* (1975), *Movin' On* (1975), *Hot on the Tracks* (1976), and *Natural High* (1978) all feature seductive après-disco moods along with the overheated dance-floor attitudes. *The Ultimate Collection* sums up the group's heyday quite well; it begins with the flawless thumper "Brick House" and ends with the borderline-unctious "Three Times a Lady." In between those extremes come equally funky throwdowns and considerably less cloying love songs. Just compare the Commodores' sweet, soothing "Easy" to one of Lionel Richie's solo bubble baths—if you dare. *In the Pocket* includes Lionel Richie's last one-two punch with the Commodores: the soaring "Lady (You Bring Me Up)" and the schlocky "Oh No." The out-of-print *Nightshift* is the best Commodores album with replacement singer J. D. Nicholas, mostly due to its hit title track: "Night Shift" is a subtly synthesized, beautifully understated tribute to the late Marvin Gaye and Jackie Wilson.   —M.C.

Common

★★½	Can I Borrow a Dollar? (Relativity, 1992)
★★★★	Resurrection (Ruthless, 1994)
★★★½	One Day It'll All Make Sense (Relativity, 1997)
★★★★	Like Water for Chocolate (MCA, 2000)
★★★½	Electric Circus (MCA, 2002)

Originally based in Chicago, back when he went by Common Sense and before a ska band of that name sued him, this quirky hip-hop artist showed quite a bit of promise on his first two albums. But only after relocating to Brooklyn, NY, would he begin his most artistically fertile period. *Can I Borrow a Dollar?* saw the South Side–born rapper emerge as a post–Native Tongues anti-gangsta rapper, and on his breakthrough second album, *Resurrection,* his profile rose nationally. *Resurrection* sports a trio of killer tracks: the title song, "Book of Life," and "I Used to Love H.E.R.," another in a long line of clever allegories that documented hip-hop's creative decline (like Jeru the Damaja's "One Day," released around the same time). While a few hip-hop faithful grumbled sellout after the release of *One Day It'll All Make Sense,* it wasn't the sort of artistic treason that some saw in Nas' *It Was Written.* Both albums, incidentally, contain singles featuring Lauryn Hill. Common's collaboration with Hill, "Retrospect for Life," subtly interpolates Stevie Wonder's achingly melancholy "Never Dreamed You'd Leave in Summer" into a sad story about the abortion of a couple's child.

Like Water for Chocolate marked yet another shift in direction, as he teams here with kindred spirits the Roots. Featuring excellent guest turns on the mike—like Goodie Mob's Cee-lo and the Roots' Black Thought, as well as a moderately successful single with Macy Gray—the album was much more of a musical affair. *Electric Circus,* in 2002, took the black-rock fusion even further, and was alternately hailed as either a work of genius or dull and boring. Giving Common the benefit of the doubt, it falls more on the genius side, though it does suffer from meandering arrangements and grooves that sometimes spin their wheels. On the other hand, part of what makes the album so remarkable is the hypnotic noodling that steered hip-hop into new directions.   —K.M.

Company Flow

★★★½	Funcrusher Plus (Rawkus, 1997)
★★★	Little Johnny From the Hospitul: Breaks and Instrumentuls, Vol. 1 (Rawkus, 1999)

El-P

★★	Fantastic Damage (Definitive Jux, 2002)
★★★½	Fantastic Damage Plus: Remixes & Instrumentals (Definitive Jux, 2002)

Company Flow became heroes to hundreds of alternative rap fans when they released their *Funcrusher* album at the tail end of the '90s. The grimy lo-fi production, simple beats, and unobtrusive samples thrilled underground hip-hop-heads, as did the front and center rhyming skills of verbose white boys El-Producto and Big Jus, who battled furiously to out-mystify their audience. The lack of hooks, choruses, or a musical motif that would somehow separate one track from another made the words of these chaotic, integrity-obsessed, science-fiction-spouting, mainstream-rap-hating MCs paramount. Underneath their surreal stream of words they seemed to value above all else the days of old when rap was a simpler world of battles, b-boys, DJs, and lyrical prowess. The one thing missing from their equation was that old-school rap was also a helluva lot of fun to listen to.

More interesting, and more fun to listen to, is the all-instrumental *Little Johnny From the Hospitul.* Reminiscent of DJ Shadow in its overcast stoner ambience, it's also a beat junkie's delight. In the hands of El-P and Co Flow DJ Mr. Len, sound effects, vocal snippets, and low-riding bass become the stuff of dreams, nightmares, art, and the soundtrack to a late-night ride down pitch-black streets.

After the members of Company Flow went their separate ways, El-P started a label, Definitive Jux, giving a home to like-minded souls who believed that going back to the future was the best way to wrest rap from the hands of pedestrian gangstas and bling-bling wanna-bes. *Fantastic Damage* goes a long way toward cementing El's reputation as a masterful creator of noisy, industrial, clanging, and decidedly radio-unfriendly sonic landscapes. El-P's bullying tone matches the sounds, but unless you're a conspiracy theorist or a Philip K. Dick fan, his mile-a-minute verbal deluges get old real fast. For enthusiasts of mostly excellent metallic buzzing noises and fractured sound collages, El-P was kind enough to release an instrumental version of his album as well. —S.S.

Ry Cooder

★★½	Ry Cooder (Reprise, 1970)	
★★★	Into the Purple Valley (Reprise, 1972)	
★★★½	Boomer's Story (Reprise, 1972)	
★★★	Paradise and Lunch (Reprise, 1974)	
★★★★	Chicken Skin Music (Reprise, 1976)	
★★½	Jazz (Warner Bros., 1978)	
★★½	Bop Till You Drop (Warner Bros., 1979)	
★★	Borderline (Warner Bros., 1980)	
★★★	The Long Riders (Warner Bros., 1980)	
★★★½	The Border (Backstreet, 1981)	
★★	The Slide Area (Warner Bros., 1982)	
★★★½	Alamo Bay (Slash, 1985)	
★★	Blue City (Warner Bros., 1986)	
★★	Crossroads (Warner Bros., 1986)	
★★½	Get Rhythm (Warner Bros., 1987)	
★★★½	Johnny Handsome (Warner Bros., 1989)	
★★★	Paris, Texas (Warner Bros., 1989)	
★★★	A Meeting by the River (Waterlilly, 1993)	
★★★½	Mambo Sinuendo (Nonesuch, 2003)	

To say that Ry Cooder is an extremely gifted musician is not only an understatement, but misleading as well. Certainly, Cooder has achieved an extraordinary level of technical proficiency in his playing, but what truly makes his music exceptional is the degree of stylistic expertise he has attained. Simply put, Ry Cooder can play damn near anything, from slide guitar to mandolin to banjo, saz, or tiple, or any style, be it gospel, folk, blues, calypso, Tex-Mex, or Hawaiian slack-key guitar. But if Cooder's ability is unquestionable, his taste is not. Despite credentials that include studio work with Taj Mahal, the Rolling Stones, Captain Beefheart, and Eric Clapton, Cooder's own work ranges in quality from the intriguingly experimental to the utterly embarrassing.

Why this is the case isn't entirely clear, but it must have to do with the guitarist's willingness to try anything. That seems to be the undoing of his debut, *Ry Cooder*. Although the album has its moments, including Randy Newman's acrid "Old Kentucky Home" and a delightfully unadorned mandolin version of Sleepy John Estes' "Goin' to Brownsville," it also ends up lumbered with the overwrought arrangements of "One Meatball" and Leadbelly's "Pig Meat." Fortunately, Cooder scales back for *Into the Purple Valley*, and the music improves immensely. Cooder still can't help tinkering with the arrangements, but this time around, the unexpected touches—for instance, the celesta in "Denomination Blues"—work in his favor. But the best moments, like the traditional "Billy the Kid" or his slide guitar rendition of Woody Guthrie's "Vigilante Man," are generally straightforward, presenting each song with minimal ornamentation.

Both *Boomer's Story* and *Paradise and Lunch* proceed in a similar vein, with minor variations and occasional cameos. Cooder brings in Sleepy John Estes for a version of "President Kennedy" on *Boomer's Story*, although that album's highlight is probably Cooder's slide guitar treatment of "Dark End of the Street." For *Paradise and Lunch*, Earl "Fatha" Hines is on hand to add stride piano flourishes to "Ditty Wah Ditty." But *Chicken Skin Music* takes this guest-star strategy to new levels by bringing in two exceptional and distinctive players: Tex-Mex accordion legend Flaco Jimenez and Hawaiian slack-key guitar whiz Gabby Pahinui. It's marvelous enough when the music is geared to their specialties, but when Cooder changes the context—by using Jimenez for a rendition of Ben E. King's "Stand By Me," say—the results are stunning. Sadly, *Jazz* (1978) doesn't quite meet *Chicken Skin Music*'s standard. Even though it includes tunes by Jelly Roll Morton and Bix Beiderbecke, *Jazz* isn't a jazz album. Nor does Cooder intend it to be, since he's far more interested in showing parallels between Morton's *habañiera* and the Bahamanian guitar style of Joseph Spence. And it makes for a fascinating lesson, if a tad too pedantic to be truly entertaining.

With *Bop Till You Drop*, Cooder makes a serious wrong turn, applying his rootsy eclecticism to material culled from rock and R&B. It's not a particularly novel approach for him—*Purple Valley*, for instance, included a version of the Drifters' "Money Honey"—but it brings out the worst in his music. *Bop*, at least, is able to balance its excesses with refreshingly rootsy instrumentals like "I Think It's Going to Work Out Fine"; *Borderline*, on the other hand, goes completely off the deep end. "Down in the Boondocks," "634-5789" and "Crazy 'Bout an Automobile (Every Woman I Know)" are songs that barely needed to be remade, much less reinvented as false nostalgia. Cooder downplays that tendency on *The Slide Area*, offering a blues shuffle treatment of "Blue Suede Shoes" but otherwise sticking with more modern material like the Little Feat–ish "I'm Drinking Again" or "UFO Has Landed in the Ghetto." But *Get Rhythm* finds him fiddling with the oldies again, slogging through an overblown boogie makeover of "All Shook Up" and a version of Johnny Cash's "Get Rhythm" done as imitation doo-wop.

Uneven as those albums are, Cooder was still making great music during this period—he just happened to be doing it for movie studios instead of record companies. Cooder was no stranger to soundtrack work, having contributed to both *Performance* and *Candy* before cutting his first solo album, but it wasn't until he provided some Southwestern atmosphere for Walter Hill's *The Long Riders* that his soundtrack career truly got into gear. Ironically, Cooder actually wound up making better rock records for movies than he did for himself; compare *The Border* to *The Slide Area* or *Get Rhythm,* and it's obvious that the focused demands of film-scoring bring out the best in his playing. *Alamo Bay* is impressively protean, with selections ranging from the sweetly harmonized "Quatro Vicios" (featuring David Hidalgo and Cesar Rosas from Los Lobos) to the punkish "Gooks on Mainstreet," while *Paris, Texas* is eloquently atmospheric, conveying a palpable sense of the town's barren landscape. Neither *Blue City,* which tends to predictable rock & roll, nor *Crossroads,* which is too heavy on overstuffed blues, are terribly impressive, but *Johnny Handsome* gets everything right, from the ominous quiet of the "Main Theme" to the jaunty good mood of "Clip Joint Rhumba." *A Meeting By the River* is a fruitful collaboration with Indian multiinstrumentalist V. M. Bhatt. Much of Cooder's work in the late '90s was dominated by one of his most commercially successful projects, *Buena Vista Social Club* (see ANTHOLOGIES). *Mambo Sinuendo* is another old-time Cuban music project in the same vein with Buena Vista alumnus Manuel Galbán. —J.D.C.

Sam Cooke

- ★★★★ The Best of Sam Cooke (1962; RCA, 1990)
- ★★★★ The 2 Sides of Sam Cooke (1970; Specialty, 1990)
- ★★★★ Live at the Harlem Square Club, 1963 (1985; RCA, 1990)
- ★★★ Forever (Specialty, 1986)
- ★★★★★ Sam Cooke With the Soul Stirrers (Specialty, 1991)
- ★★★★ Night Beat (1963; RCA, 2001)
- ★★★ Earliest Recordings (Specialty, 1992)
- ★★★★★ Jesus Gave Me Water (Specialty, 1992)
- ★★★★★ The Last Mile of the Way (Specialty, 1994)
- ★★★ The Rhythm and the Blues (RCA, 1995)
- ★★★★ Greatest Hits (1998, RCA)
- ★★★ Sam Cooke at the Copa (ABKCO, 1999)
- ★★★★★ The Man Who Invented Soul (RCA, 2000)

- ★★★★½ Sam Cooke's SAR Records Story 1959–1965 (ABKCO, 2002)
- ★★★★ Keep Movin' On (ABKCO, 2002)
- ★★★★ The Complete Specialty Recordings of Sam Cooke (Specialty, 2002)

One of the towering figures in postwar American popular music, Sam Cooke emerged from the gospel world already a full-blown star, young, handsome, graceful as a ballet dancer, and blessed with a degree of onstage charisma and sensuality that had previously been confined to secular heartthrobs. As with Elvis Presley, his image and the sex appeal threatened to obscure the powerful artistry underneath it all, but ultimately the music triumphed. In Cooke's case, his move to the pop field laid the foundation for modern soul music, not only in his forward-looking blend of gospel, pop and R&B, but also in his songwriting, which revealed a burgeoning social conscience informed by gospel's shouts of struggle, peace, and freedom. For Cooke, the political was personal, as he embraced the ideal of economic and political self-determination with the same fervor with which he infused his gospel performances. To that end, he set himself apart in a white-dominated industry by taking control of his career both as an artist and as a businessman. Thanks to the skills of the accountant who became his manager, Allen Klein, Cooke gained creative control of his music, past and present, and moved aggressively to shape a future that would enable him to fully realize his artistic vision. He formed his own label (SAR/Derby), music publishing firm (Kags Music), and management company, and set out to be as much a factor behind the scenes as he was in the spotlight. "My future lies more in creating music and records than in being a live performer," he told *Billboard* magazine in 1964. That same year he also told the British publication *Melody Maker,* "Real gospel music has got to make a comeback," a prediction he did his best to make come true at SAR, where he made gospel, mostly through the Soul Stirrers, the cornerstone of the label.

As a pioneering black businessman in the music industry, Cooke's achievements remain significant, but in the decades since his death in 1964, when he was shot to death in a Los Angeles motel by a woman who claimed he had attacked her, it is the music that remains the brightest beacon for ensuing generations. In the gospel world he became the star attraction of the genre's most popular and influential group, the Soul Stirrers, whose venerable lead singer, R.H. Harris, took the 19-year-old Cooke under his wing and helped him develop an individual style. Cooke took it from there: Once he was in front of audiences, the word got out and soon hordes of adoring teenage girls were flocking to the Soul Stirrers' shows, worshipping the young Adonis more than the word he was espousing. His work in the gospel realm is well documented and still resonant: *Sam Cooke With the Soul Stirrers, Jesus Gave Me Water, The Last Mile of the Way, The 2 Sides of Sam Cooke,* his *Earliest Recordings,* and *The Complete Specialty Recordings of Sam Cooke* chart this exhilarating journey in Cooke's story, from a 1951 recording of Thomas A. Dorsey's "Peace in the Valley" to his entry into the secular realm in 1956 via "Lovable," on which he was billed as Dale Cooke so as to avoid offending his gospel constituency. Some observers feel Cooke was never better than he was in his gospel days, and the performances on these discs give their argument a potent charge. A Cooke original, "Touch the Hem of His Garment," is two minutes of vivid narrative and restrained emotional perfection, but the readings of "Jesus Gave Me Water," the old Baptist hymn "Were You There," and James Cleveland's "One More River" are close behind.

Upon being released from his Specialty contract, Cooke signed with the Keen label, founded by the enterprising talent scout, producer, and would-be mogul Bob Keane, who was soon to discover and produce Dick Dale and Ritchie Valens. Cooke's first Keen single, the lilting love ballad "You Send Me," was leased from Specialty and had a three-week run atop the pop charts in 1957. That success began an eight-year run of hits that included 28 Top 40 pop singles and 30 Top 40 R&B entries.

At Keen from 1957 through mid-1960, Cooke recorded material that was light and upbeat and in a pop vein, barely revealing the artist's deep involvement with gospel and R&B. When he signed with RCA in 1960, and subsequently gained control of his work, Cooke went back to the source, to gospel and blues, for inspiration and added depth. Many of the songs from this period are built on the life experiences he understood as a black man in a segregated world in upheaval, and spoke nearly as directly to his black audience as had his music with the Soul Stirrers. There was always room for a bright, soaring love song such as "Cupid" or a double-edged dance tune on the order of "Having a Party," but Cooke also covered harder blues such as the Howlin' Wolf–Willie Dixon cowrite "Little Red Rooster" and sophisticated classic pop on the order of the Gershwins' "But Not for Me" and the Sammy Cahn–Jimmy Van Heusen classic "All the Way." His first significant record in a harder vein was 1962's "Bring It On Home to Me," a soulful plea enlivened by an urgent gospel call-and-response section featuring Cooke sparring with his backup vocalist, Lou Rawls, as if they were back in church working up the congregation to full lather. By most standards his shining hour on RCA came with the posthumous release "A Change is Gonna Come" (1965), a #31 pop single that has taken on a life far greater than any chart position could reveal. Attuned to the temper of the times—after a president had been assassinated, after Bull Connor had sicced his dogs and trained his hoses on black protesters in Birmingham, after George Wallace had intoned "segregation now, segregation tomorrow, segregation forever" in his gubernatorial inaugural address, after Governor Wallace had stood in the doorway at the University of Alabama to block the admission of black students—"A Change is Gonna Come" was a somber, determined message, in keeping with the Movement's early embrace of Gandhian pacifism, that communicated the certainty of a new day dawning even as Cooke's world-weary vocal accepted the truth of a long, hard journey ahead.

The mainstream Cooke is easily accessible. For those who prefer the chart hits with a minimum of side trips, the enduring title remains 1962's *The Best of Sam Cooke,* which features 11 familiar tunes— "Cupid," "You Send Me," "Only Sixteen," "Having a Party," "Bring It On Home to Me"—and only one, a version and alternate take of the Gershwins' "Summertime," that failed to chart. *Greatest Hits* includes not only the hits on *The Best of* but adds, in its 21 tracks, lesser-known Top 20 items such as his versions of "Little Red Rooster" and "Frankie and Johnny." The deepest and most meaningful look at the man's secular career comes via the four-CD box set, *The Man Who Invented Soul,* which omits only the gospel tracks and songs cut during the final year of his career. These latter are owned by Allen Klein's ABCKO label, and are being reissued separately. One entire disc is given over to Cooke's Keen recordings, thus constituting the most thorough overview of those years on disc. The remaining discs offer a vivid look at the RCA years, including, on Disc Four, the entire, extraordinary *Night Beat* album from 1963, and another gritty live performance from 1963 issued in 1985 as *Live At the Harlem Square Club.* Needless to say, this is as essential a box set as any around, even without the formidable gospel recordings.

A focused, exciting look at Cooke's artistic growth is provided on the single-CD overview from ABKCO, *Keep Movin' On,* which centers on the studio recordings from 1963–64 and quite simply showcases some of the finest, most gripping singing Cooke ever committed to tape. The songs range from his own ebullient hit "Good News" to "A Change Is Gonna Come," with stops at a beautiful, haunting take on an Appalachian ballad, "The Riddle Song," a lovely "Tennessee Waltz," the exquisitely observed "When a Boy Falls in Love," and several other Cooke originals from this period. Best of all, Peter Guralnick, currently at work on a biography of Cooke, provides detailed annotation that places this period and the music it yielded in the proper context of Cooke's development. *Night Beat* belongs in any proper Cooke collection, as it is the sole album-length treatise featuring Cooke backed only by a small combo, which has the agreeable effect of heightening the impact of that glorious voice by keeping it way out front and center, unadorned and mesmerizing in its natural beauty. Apart from the spirited renditions of "Little Red Rooster" and "Shake, Rattle and Roll," the repertoire here is moody blues, some, such as "Mean Old World" and "You Gotta Move," being Cooke originals; others, such as the traditional "Nobody Knows the Trouble I've Seen" and "I Lost Everything," are of a piece with the introspective nature of the originals, lending the entire affair the feel of listening in on an intimate interior dialogue being conducted by one of the great artists of the 20th century. *The Rhythm and the Blues*, from 1995, is something of a companion volume to *Night Beat* in its focus on bluesier material performed in pared-down arrangements; *Night Beat* is far superior, but Cooke's readings of "Cry Me a River" and Rodgers and Hart's poignant "Little Girl Blue," as well as Duke Ellington's bittersweet "Don't Get Around Much Anymore," are worth the price of admission. Two live albums offer contrasting views of Cooke. *Live at the Harlem Square Club* finds Cooke working the largely black audience in gritty, get-down fashion with a backing band that includes the red-hot sax work of King Curtis to bump up the intensity a couple of notches. The songs are all familiar—"Chain Gang," "Twistin' the Night Away," "Having a Party," "Bring It On Home to Me," "Cupid"—but the down-home feel of the set gives the listener an idea of the energy to which the young gospel audiences must have responded with such gusto back in the early '50s. By contrast, the slick, big-band performance captured at the Copa in New York City on July 8, 1964, and issued as *Sam Cooke at the Copa* is genial and even a bit cheesy in a jivey, Vegas kind of way, but nonetheless spirited in its own right. It's the canapés to the *Harlem Square Club*'s collard greens. Cooke doesn't drive the band as hard as he does in the *Harlem Square* performance, nor they him, but he still digs in for a nice take on "Nobody Knows You When You're Down and Out," and the love ballads, especially "When I Fall in Love," are warm and tender in a way only Sam Cooke could be warm and tender. Finally, to get an idea of where Cooke was heading, check out the two-disc box set *Sam Cooke's SAR Records Story 1959–1965*, which features Cooke's productions of Soul Stirrers tracks featuring lead singers Paul Foster and Jimmy

Outler, and four cuts (two produced by Cooke) of R.H. Harris' post–Soul Stirrers group the Gospel Paraders, as well as Cooke-produced gospel tracks by the Womack Brothers (featuring Bobby Womack). On the secular side, featured SAR artists include Cooke (a demo of "You Send Me" is here, as well as other studio tracks), Mel Carter, post–Soul Stirrers Johnnie Taylor, Billy Preston, the Womack Brothers recording as The Valentinos, and others. As with *Keep Movin' On*, this box includes detailed annotation by Peter Guralnick, again an authoritative, informed guide through this critical chapter in an important career. —D.M.

Coolio

★★★½ It Takes a Thief (Tommy Boy, 1994)
★★★★ Gangsta's Paradise (Tommy Boy, 1995)
★★★½ My Soul (Tommy Boy, 1997)
★★★½ Fantastic Voyage: The Greatest Hits (Tommy Boy, 2001)

In the mid-'90s, several actions were undeniably not cool in hip-hop: lifting obvious R&B samples for your hit singles; regular participation in MTV sporting events; calling yourself Coolio. Artis Leon Ivey Jr. committed all these sins, and had not only his biggest hit but his hairstyle parodied by Weird Al as punishment. And yet without Coolio's trailblazing efforts, Puffy might have never had the gumption to rip off Diana Ross, a reputed MC like Method Man would have never showed up on *Rock n Jock* to drop an easy pop fly, and Beavis would have had one less weird mantra to obsess over when he OD'd on sugar.

But though you made Coolio's acquaintance on the radio or MTV, don't go reaching for that greatest hits just yet, even if it is the only Coolio disc where you can find his fun contribution to the Nickelodeon network, "Aw Here It Goes (Theme From Kenan & Kel)." The original albums carefully place those party jams in a sometimes desperate urban context, most effectively on *Gangsta's Paradise*. Once the mood is set by the high gothic tone of the title track, LV's harrowed vocal straining for release as Coolio's slow burn sinks deeper into paranoia, the primarily upbeat remainder of the album sounds less like R&B frivolity and more like a collection of momentary escapes from despair. Coolio's sales slumped with *My Soul*, but his music remained consistent—"C U When U Get There" is one of the few hip-hop elegies to rise above maudlin self-pity.

Coolio's visual legacy shouldn't be ignored, either—and I'm not just talking about the hair. The videos for "Fantastic Voyage" and "1,2,3,4 (Sumpin' New)" document the downside of California dreamin' from a pedestrian's perspective. From Brian Wilson to Dr. Dre, after all, that West Coast fantasy has always rested on the mobility that comes from a sharp ride. But no matter how he got there, Coolio's parties always seemed worth the effort—way more fun that those Snoop Dogg snoozers where everyone gets comatose on cheap weed and lounges around playing Gameboy while bored strippers give them head. —K.H.

Chris Cornell

★★½ Euphoria Morning (A&M, 1999)

The crooner lurking inside Chris Cornell through countless screamfests with Seattle grunge-metal pioneers Soundgarden finally comes out to play on the singer's solo debut. *Euphoria Morning* preempts comparisons to his former band by turning down the volume and upping the variety, with straight blues, acoustic folk, and Beatles-like psychedelic pop. In contrast to Soundgarden, Cornell's voice is way up front in the mix, and he swoops, swoons, and sweats through these ballads with enough conviction to make explicit his debt to the late Jeff Buckley. But it's an influence that he never quite transcends. —G.K.

Cornershop

★★★ Hold On It Hurts (Merge, 1994)
★★★½ Woman's Gotta Have It (Luaka Bop, 1995)
★★★★ When I Was Born for the Seventh Time (Luaka Bop, 1997)
★★★½ Handcream for a Generation (Luaka Bop/Virgin 2002)

One of the few '90s acts embraced by both rock critics and antirock club kids, Cornershop embodies all the possibility and spectacular excess of the global cut-and-paste culture. Although the British five-piece first established itself with conventional alt-rock songs, it has gone on to incorporate all kinds of noise into ambitious collage-style productions: The sweet Punjabi singing of leader Tjinder Singh's heritage, the scattershot crunch of sample-based beats, the idyllic sitar of Anthony Saffery, and the blistering funk of James Brown.

The initial Cornershop efforts, *Hold On It Hurts* and several out-of-print EPs, showcase a band with a taste for energetic pop and strident antiracist rhetoric. By the second full-length disc, the taut rock structures were overrun by sounds from the world bazaar: *Woman's Gotta Have It* is primarily an Indian pop record with wry English lyrics and an inclusive musical sensibility reflective of the burgeoning Asian Underground movement among British musicians and DJs of Indian ancestry.

The band's breakthrough came in 1997 with the hit "Brimful of Asha," a worshipful tribute to Bollywood singer Asha Bhosle that heralded the uniformly tremendous *When I Was Born*. A showcase for the beatific talk-singing of Singh, that single and other more assertively funky bits (including "When the Light Appears Boy," a collaboration with poet Allen Ginsberg) established Cornershop alongside Beck and others as purveyors of a new kind of hybrid pop, one that treated ethnicity as something to be messed with, explored, and exploited, not treated with kid gloves.

It took years for Cornershop to put together a formal followup—there were several EPs and a lo-fi side project called Clinton, which debuted the chant "People Power in the Disco Hour"—and when *Handcream for a Generation* finally arrived, in 2002, some considered it a faint echo of *When I Was Born*. Talkier and less rhythmic, it lacked an accessible single but instead offered several sprawling experiments, including the gospely "Staging the Plaguing of the Raised Platform," bolstered by a children's choir, and the sample-heavy philosophical treatises "Motion the 11" and "Lessons Learned From Rocky I to Rocky III." —K.M.

The Corrs

★★ Forgiven, Not Forgotten (Atlantic, 1995)
★★½ Talk on Corners [Special Edition] (Atlantic, 1999)
★★★ Unplugged (Atlantic, 1999)
★★★½ In Blue (Atlantic, 2000)
★★★½ VH1 Presents the Corrs: Live in Dublin (Atlantic, 2002)
★★★ Borrowed Heaven (Atlantic, 2004)

With their sparkling, sisterly harmonies and knack for breathless pop, the sibling act the Corrs come off somewhat like Ireland's belated answer to ABBA—or, given their respectable instrumental chops and photogenic looks, a Gaelic Dixie Chicks (albeit with a dude, brother Jim, on guitar). Unfortunately, while there seems to be much potential here, too often the music slips into forgettable adult contemporary mush—making the occasional lovely instrumental (showcasing Sharon Corr's fiddle, lead vocalist Andrea's tin whistle, and drummer Caroline's bodhran) or indelibly catchy pop jewel (like *In Blue*'s hit "Breathless") almost frustrating. *Forgiven, Not Forgotten* is immaculately sung, forgettable fluff, like Wilson Phillips without the hooks. Said hooks start to come out of hiding on *Talk on Corners*—released stateside as a remix-heavy "Special Edition"—which dispenses with the instrumental interludes almost entirely in favor of unadulterated high-gloss pop. It's still fluff, but giddy trifles like "So Young" are not without some charm.

But be forewarned—the Corrs' otherwise harmless cover of Fleetwood Mac's "Dreams" is presented here as a numbing dance mix.

In Blue, buoyed by the near-flawless "Breathless" and two other sugar bombs produced by hit maestro Robert John "Mutt" Lange in the same dare-you-to-resist-this style of Shania Twain (one is actually called "Irresistible"), is far and away the Corrs' most consistent studio effort. The two live albums, however, are the better value. *Unplugged* isn't quite the lively Irish reel showcase one might expect (there are only two instrumentals), but the sisters' crystal-clear harmonies soar over the stripped-down arrangements, and the closing cover of R.E.M.'s "Everybody Hurts" is a nice touch. Inspired—if not quite definitive—covers also light up *Live in Dublin*. Pretty but featherweight versions of Neil Young's "Only Love Can Break Your Heart," Jimi Hendrix's "Little Wing," and the Stones' "Ruby Tuesday" all float away without much impact (despite help from guest Ron Wood), but U2's Bono—in typical spotlight-hogging form—lends genuine soul and weight to the proceedings by singing with Andrea on alt-country brat Ryan Adams' gorgeous "When the Stars Go Blue" and the old Lee Hazlewood/Nancy Sinatra hit "Summer Wine."

Bono pops up again (as a songwriter) on the studio set *Borrowed Heaven* via "Time Enough for Tears," a ballad cowritten with Gavin Friday and Maurice Seezer, though it's the Corrs' own slowly percolating "Hideaway" that really evokes shades of prime U2. Too much of the rest of the album seems to be trying a little too hard, though. There's no denying the catchiness of songs such as the single "Summer Sunshine," but the insistent hooks seem to pander and force their way into the head rather than charm with the polished-but-endearing finesse that carried "Breathless." *Borrowed Heaven*'s most memorable and engaging melodies are all packed into the closing "Silver Strand," the album's sole instrumental—proof that the Corrs are at their best when it sounds like a hit single is the last thing on their minds. —R.SK.

Elvis Costello

★★★★★ My Aim Is True (Columbia, 1977; Rhino, 2002)
★★★★★ This Year's Model (Columbia, 1978; Rhino, 2001)
★★★★ Armed Forces (Columbia, 1979)
★★★★½ Get Happy (Columbia, 1980)
★★★½ Taking Liberties (Columbia, 1980)
★★★★★ Trust (Columbia, 1981)
★★ Almost Blue (Columbia, 1981)
★★★½ Imperial Bedroom (Columbia, 1982; Rhino, 2002)

★★★ Punch the Clock (Columbia, 1983)
★★ Goodbye Cruel World (Columbia, 1984)
★★★ The Best of Elvis Costello and the Attractions (Columbia, 1985)
★★★★★ King of America (Columbia, 1986)
★★★★½ Blood & Chocolate (Columbia, 1986)
★★★★ Out of Our Idiot (Demon U.K., 1987)
★★ Spike (Warner Bros., 1989; Rhino, 2002)
★★★ Girls Girls Girls (Columbia, 1989)
★★ Mighty Like a Rose (Warner Bros., 1990)
★★ The Juliet Letters (Warner Bros., 1993)
★★★★ 2 1/2 Years (Rykodisc, 1993)
★★½ Brutal Youth (Warner Bros., 1994; Rhino, 2002)
★★★½ The Very Best of Elvis Costello (Rykodisc, 1994)
★★★ Kojak Variety (Warner Bros., 1995)
★★½ All This Useless Beauty (Warner Bros., 1996; Rhino, 2001)
★★★ Extreme Honey: The Very Best of the Warner Bros. Years (Warner Bros., 1997)
★★★★ Painted From Memory (Mercury, 1998)
★★★★ When I Was Cruel (Mercury, 2002)
★★ North (Deutsche Grammophon, 2003)

"Don't put your heart on your sleeve/When your remarks are off the cuff," Elvis Costello once warned, and like the great rock & roll romantic he is, he's spent a whole career betraying his own good sense. Costello emerged from the London punk explosion of 1977 as the resident singer-songwriter, using his smart mouth to turn sexual and political troubles into musical outrage. Elvis has gone through many changes since then, often coasting on mere craft, or the memory of it. But his key to greatness has always been his passion—his "Let It Bleed" means more than his "Lush Life." A wit, a blackguard, a moralist, a poet, a bitch, a Celtic folk ranter, a grinning pop tunesmith, a radio sweetheart with a sullen punk stare, he's a true original whether he's rocking on out or just trying to look Italian to the musical Valium.

Costello made a big splash right off with *My Aim Is True*, an attack on pop romance in all its guises, with the kind of venom that could only come from a true believer in spite of himself. With backup from a fluffy California bar band, Costello sneers about sex ("Watching the Detectives"), politics ("Less Than Zero"), and religion (the bad-Catholic-boy classic "Waiting for the End of the World")—although the one he'll be stuck singing for the rest of his life is the reluctant love ballad, "Alison." Elvis really found his voice when he got the Attractions together, souping up the music into the Stones/*Nuggets* garage-band racket of every teenage rock geek's dreams, with Steve

Nieve's nagging headache of an organ standing in for the brutal guitar Costello couldn't play. *This Year's Model* is the peak of the angry young Elvis, channeling the rage into the furious hooks of "Lip Service," "Lipstick Vogue," and "No Action."

Armed Forces soon followed—too soon, probably, since it suffers from a heavy case of road fatigue. The shrill, cluttered keyboards, almost all treble, suit the paranoia of the politically charged lyrics ("She's my self-touch typewriter/And I'm the great dictator"). *Get Happy* loosens up for a tour de force of 20 tracks imitating Booker T and the MG's at Ramones velocity, although "Opportunity" and "Riot Act" showed what a supple ballad singer Elvis had become. *Trust* has always been underrated because there's no real angle— just 14 brilliantly barbed pop tunes about men paying the wages of masculinity and suffering for their sins, with Pete Thomas's punchiest drumming and Steve Nieve's glossiest piano. In great songs such as "Watch Your Step," "New Lace Sleeves," and "You'll Never Be a Man," Elvis finally comes clean about his woman problems, with enough wit to suggest a way out: "Shot With His Own Gun," indeed. Not as epochal as *This Year's Model* or *King of America*, *Trust* still marks Elvis's summit as a singer, songwriter, and miserable-Irish-bastard pin-up boy.

Costello spent the next few years stretching out stylistically, starting with the well-chosen, miserably sung country covers of *Almost Blue*. The Cole Porter homage *Imperial Bedroom* buries a few excellent songs ("Beyond Belief," "Man Out of Time") under too many layers of vocal overdubs, strings, horns, harpsichords, guitar solos, and *Sgt. Pepper* studio gimmicks. *Punch the Clock* and *Goodbye Cruel World* imitate Top 40 radio, actually more of a stretch for Elvis than country or Cole Porter, with rare successes like the anti-Thatcher protest "Shipbuilding" and the fabulous real-world hit "Every Day I Write the Book."

By the mid-'80s, Costello was sounding a bit redundant: His thunder had been stolen by look-alike Steve Albini, who took the smoldering geek rage of *This Year's Model* to new sonic heights with Big Black. But Elvis roared back in 1986 with two of his best albums, both clearly influenced by his work producing the Pogues. *King of America* is where Costello harkens to his folkie roots, busting out the acoustic guitar, hooking up with T Bone Burnett and an unlikely passel of grizzled session dudes for a masterpiece. *King of America* gets off to a mighty slow start, but once you hit "Indoor Fireworks" at track six, settle in for one gem after another (okay, not "The Big Light" or "Eisenhower Blues"), from hoarse political rants like "Little Palaces" and "Sleep of the Just" to soulful love ballads like "Jack of All Parades." The Attractions

returned for *Blood & Chocolate,* completing the one-two punch with one of Elvis's loudest, funniest records. Although the songs have the rugged acoustic strum of *King of America,* the Attractions' ham-fisted garage rock animates the Celt-folk passion of "Tokyo Storm Warning," "Poor Napoleon," and "Crimes of Paris." Best line: "She hit him with that paperweight Eiffel Tower."

Since then, Elvis has kept busy, but with only occasional moments of interest on his new records. *Spike* features more all-star help (from Paul McCartney to the Dirty Dozen Brass Band), but except for the righteously Thatcher-bashing "Tramp the Dirt Down," it's pretty words and no action; *Mighty Like a Rose* is less of the same. *The Juliet Letters* is—get this—a classical song cycle about Romeo and Juliet, with none of the literary merit of "Mystery Dance." *Brutal Youth* is a lightweight Attractions reunion; *All This Useless Beauty* offers muted balladry like the poignant "I Want to Vanish." But the covers collection *Kojak Variety,* with sharp versions of Mose Allison's "Everybody's Crying Mercy" and Randy Newman's "I've Been Wrong Before," was shaping up to be Elvis's best '90s album until his Burt Bacharach collaboration, *Painted From Memory.* What could have been a camp joke becomes a magnificently bittersweet career summary for both gentlemen—the heartbreaking "Toledo" is, if anything, too good for Dionne Warwick to sing. *When I Was Cruel,* a belated and gratuitous return to guitar rock, finds Elvis thriving again on his commitment to tricky hooks, funny lyrics, and the head-scratching career moves that will keep his fans on their toes for the rest of his days.

Costello's greatest-hits albums don't flow very well, since he puts his heart and soul into his discrete concept albums. *Girls Girls Girls* is a bulky and eccentric set annotated by the maestro himself, who's always worth reading (the opening of his liner notes to the 1994 reissue of *Goodbye Cruel World* is "Congratulations! You have just purchased our worst album!"). *Taking Liberties* and *Out of Our Idiot* collect some of the stray B sides and outtakes Costello was leaving in his wake; most of these songs appear as bonus tracks on the various CD reissues of the Costello catalogue. Ones to keep an eye out for: "Black Sails in the Sunset," "Hoover Factory," "Talking in the Dark," and his ragged cover of Sam Cooke's "Get Yourself Another Fool." In the late '90s, Elvis began a strange new career appearing as himself in movies, such as *Spice World, 200 Cigarettes,* and *Austin Powers: The Spy Who Shagged Me,* in which he appears with Burt Bacharach to sing "I'll Never Fall in Love Again." It's the funniest thing in the movie. *North* is a return to jazz ballads, with

Costello sounding a little stiff and dusty, but any guy who can write songs such as "Episode in Blonde," "Alibi," and "When I was Cruel" while pushing 50 is in no danger of burning out. —R.S.

Counting Crows

★★★½ August and Everything After (DGC, 1993)
★★ Recovering the Satellites (DGC, 1996)
★★ Across a Wire—Live in New York City (DGC, 1998)
★★★ This Desert Life (DGC, 1999)
★★★ Hard Candy (Geffen, 2002)
★★ Films About Ghosts: The Best of . . . (Geffen, 2003)

August and Everything After instantly established erstwhile coffeehouse folkie Adam Duritz and his San Francisco–based band as the latest heirs to the Van Morrison/Bob Dylan/Bruce Springsteen songwriting tradition; Duritz even subbed for Morrison when the Irish soul troubadour failed to show for his Rock and Roll Hall of Fame induction. The ambitions are spelled out in the breakthrough single "Mr. Jones," which mimics Morrison's "sha-la-la" and namechecks Dylan. The Crows bridge the worlds of rock, folk, and soul with an emphasis on living-room intimacy, thanks to T Bone Burnett's transparent production. The tunes are direct, melodic, uncluttered. The same can't be said for Duritz, whose wordy introspection is marred by a voice that whines as much as it wails.

These flaws are exacerbated on *Recovering the Satellites*, a more ambitious album with stabs at string orchestration and Memphis soul. The color gray, phones that don't ring, "the smell of hospitals in winter"—Duritz sounds as self-obsessed as Morrissey, without the humor. He sings about the malaise of being a rock star in a voice that wanders the octaves in perpetual discomfort, even as the band compensates with its hardest rocker yet, "Angels of Silences," and the buoyant Eagles-like twang of "Daylight Fading."

The self-indulgence becomes insufferable on *Across a Wire*, a premature live double CD. "Angels of Silences" is reconfigured as an inspired jug-band blues, but Duritz sounds even mopier than usual. How ironic that while many of his songs struggle with life as a pop icon, the album prominently displays the MTV and VH1 logos and contains laudatory liner notes written by a VH1 executive.

Duritz snaps out of it on the best portions of *This Desert Life*, which comes out bustling with his gotta-get-out-of-town answer to "Born to Run" ("Hangin' Around") and follows it with "Mrs. Potter's Lullaby,"

which just keeps on rollicking through verse after verse with barely a pause, the guitars knifing through for air. Duritz loosens up just enough to join the rest of the Crows in the joy of the moment, rather than marching them down to the whipping post. For the self-proclaimed "king of the rain," the sky is beginning to clear ("I'm doing alright these days," he declares on "I Wish I Was a Girl") and the melancholy tunes mostly soar instead of wallow.

Though not particularly more optimistic than previous efforts, *Hard Candy* gives listeners a lot more to sing along with, even, as on "Black and Blue," when the singer imagines writing a suicide note. Rather than framing the singer's pain as on previous albums, the Crows' music counterbalances it. The abundant melodies are more instantly apparent, buffed into concise packages that take the Crows outside of their roots-rock cradle and into a more overtly pop realm, where sonic continuity matters less than the unique character of each song: dreamy piano balladry on "Butterfly in Reverse," new-wave keyboards for "New Frontier," Drifters-meet-Springsteen orchestrations on "Miami," the Mamas and Papas vocal vibe that pervades "Why Should You Come When I Call?" It's the most consistently tuneful of all the Crows albums, and it makes Duritz's moping almost tolerable.

Films About Ghosts is a skimpy career overview fleshed out with two tossed-off new tracks, one of which is a Grateful Dead cover. —G.K.

Don Covay

★★★★ Mercy!/See-Saw (Atlantic, 1964, 1966, Koch, 2000)
★★★ Adlib (Cannonball, 2000)

Don Covay and the Lemon Jefferson Blues Band

★★★½ House of Blue Lights (Atlantic, 1969; Sepia Tone, 2002)

At a time when soul veterans with less-than-high profiles, like Solomon Burke, are getting some respectful dues, Don Covay may be the most neglected old master out there. Born in 1938, the son of a Southern Baptist minister, Covay grew up in Washington, D.C., where he became a protégé of Little Richard. By the early 1960s, he was writing the songs and recording the singles for Atlantic that established him as among the most clever inheritors of the Sam Cooke style. His tunes included hit classics like Aretha Franklin's "Chain of Fools" and little-known should-be classics like Little Richard's "I Don't Know What You've Got (But It's Got Me)." As a songwriter Covay has a knack for dramatizing very plain, down-home situations and attaching an indelible phrase, as in his tale of motel infidelity "I Was Checkin' Out (She Was Checkin' In)." Although out of print, his exceptional career overview *Mercy Mercy: The Definitive Don Covay,* particularly valuable for including singles before and after his Atlantic years, can still be found used. A worthy substitute is the combination release of his first two Atlantic LPs, *Mercy!/See-Saw.* Covay had as much blues bark as church shout in his vocals, which made him a prime inspiration for Mick Jagger and Peter Wolf of the J. Geils Band, among others. *House of Blue Lights,* his third Atlantic, is a rough-and-ready response to the heavy-blues fashions of the late '60s and now sounds only a bit more earthbound than his celebrated earlier sides. Covay was not the most consistent stage act, and he spent long stretches away from music.

Though few noticed, *Adlib* was a sharp, well-paced comeback album boosted by help from Wilson Pickett, Huey Lewis, and Lee Konitz. Recovering from a stroke, Covay reined in his voice a bit, but whether he was anguished or exultant, he remains what the geezers call a solid sender.   —M.MI.

Cowboy Junkies

★★★	Whites Off Earth Now (1986; RCA, 1990)
★★★★	The Trinity Sessions (RCA, 1988)
★★	The Caution Horses (RCA, 1990)
★★	Black-Eyed Man (RCA, 1992)
★★★	Pale Sun, Crescent Moon (RCA, 1993)
★★	200 More Miles: Live Performances 1985–1994 (RCA, 1995)
★★★	Lay It Down (Geffen, 1996)
★★	Studio: Selected Studio Recordings 1986–1995 (RCA, 1996)
★★	Miles From Our Home (Geffen, 1998)
★★	Rarities, B-Sides and Slow, Sad Waltzes (Valley, 1999)
★★★	Open (Latent/Zoe, 2001)
★★	Best of Cowboy Junkies (RCA, 2001)
★★	The Radio One Sessions (Strange Fruit, 2002)
★★	One Soul Now (Zoe, 2004)

The Toronto quartet Cowboy Junkies have made a career out of its soft-focus sound, initially emphasizing the drowsily pretty vocals of Margo Timmins, with brother Michael Timmins' droning guitar leads gradually assuming a bigger role. They've maximized that rather limited approach by evincing exquisite taste, particularly on the covers-heavy early albums, and by playing off the tension between Margo's lullaby voice and the frequently dire imagery of Michael's lyrics. The maelstrom-beneath-the-calm subtext was broached on the debut album, *Whites Off Earth Now,* notably on a Robert Johnson blues, in which Margo

Timmins vows, "I'm gonna beat my man/Until I get satisfied."

Armed with a single microphone, the Cowboy Junkies took 14 hours to record the followup: *The Trinity Sessions.* The songs were recorded in a church, and the band takes the notion of "hushed atmosphere" to a glorious and mesmerizing extreme on what remains its signature album. *The Trinity Sessions* is so seamless it makes the songs of Hank Williams, Patsy Cline, and the Velvet Underground sound like long-lost companions.

The deceptively tough female persona that first glimmered on *Whites Off Earth Now* is coaxed to the surface by Michael Timmins' ambitious songwriting on *The Caution Horses* and *Black-Eyed Man,* but the drowsy arrangements sound somehow less compelling with fuller production. The band's streak of ace covers ends on *Caution Horses* with a lukewarm version of Neil Young's "Powderfinger."

Young-like guitar feedback plays a more prominent role on *Pale Sun, Crescent Moon,* signaled by an unlikely cover of Dinosaur Jr's "Post." *Lay It Down* slips back into old habits, the most stripped-down recording since *Trinity,* with a greater sense of groove, thanks to Alan Anton's rubbery bass lines. The band concentrates on honing its strengths, exploring absence (of a lover, or of feeling itself) with uncommon empathy and insight—and it gives the album the feeling of a small but noble achievement.

Desperation sets in on *Miles From Home,* with producer John Leckie (Radiohead, Verve) on board to beef up the sound. He does, but what distinctiveness the Junkies once had is lost in an avalanche of post–Lilith Fair orchestration and backing vocals. *Open* marks a more palatable progression; Michael Timmins' Southern-gothic tales of death and betrayal have never sounded creepier, and his acid-washed guitar provides a suitably menacing counterpoint to his sister's ghost-walking vocals. *One Soul Now* picks up on these sonic cues, but the songs aren't distinctive enough to exploit them.   —G.K.

Carl Cox

★★★½	F.A.C.T. Vol. 2 (Moonshine, 1997)
★★★★	The Sound of Ultimate B.A.S.E. (Moonshine, 1998)
★★	Phuture 2000 (Moonshine, 1999)
★★★½	Mixed Live (Moonshine, 2000)
★★	Global (ffrr/Strictly Rhythm, 2002)
★★★★	Mixed Live, 2nd Session (Moonshine, 2002)

Carl Cox's funky techno and hard-hitting house is as big and gregarious as he is, which may explain why his muscular music has earned him legions of fans worldwide. The British jock has been repeatedly crowned "World's Best DJ" in a career that's spanned decades: He put the bang in Brixton's acid-house explosion and has incited jump-up fervor at many a "Summer of Love" massive. It was at a 1988 Sunrise rave outside London that Cox hooked up a third turntable *and* his signature sound, earning him the moniker "3 Deck Wizard" and an album deal with Paul Oakenfold's Perfecto label. But while Cox's music crossed into the mainstream—his 1992 "Does It Feel Good to You" broke the Top 40—he spent the rest of the decade mining a more underground sound geared at jacking sweaty dance floors.

The 1995 *F.A.C.T.* ("Future Alliance of Communication and Technology") mix sold a stunning quarter million copies, and its followup, 1997's *F.A.C.T. 2,* alerted Americans to how tremendous in scope Cox's techno triptych could be. Obliterating popular tracks by dance dons Fatboy Slim, Cajmere, and Underworld, *F.A.C.T. 2* churns funk, house, tribal, breaks, and beyond into an unyielding techno tirade. The turntable trickery continues on *The Sound of Ultimate B.A.S.E.* Drawing upon his U.K. club night of the same name, it's an ass-shaking assault of dark, mutant house, and the clever changeups on tracks like Freq.'s "Xirtam 2" cut furiously before pummeling the listener with aggressive beats and basslines. Soon after, Cox released his second artist album, *Phuture 2000,* a ho-hum hodgepodge of Latin flava, patois rap, and jungle fury that spawned a couple of forgettable hits. Recorded live at Chicago's Crobar club, you can't help but wish you were hearing *Mixed Live*'s top-of-the-hour techno and progressive house on a thumping Phazon sound system. *2nd Session* fares better on home stereos: Recorded in Detroit on the Area2 tour, a frisky Cox digs heavily from his own Intec label, but the results are surprisingly eclectic and, in typical Cox fashion, unrelenting. It's a far superior sound for him: Coming from big, bad Cox, the mediocre house of *Global*—released the same year—sounds plain wimpy.   —C.S.

Cracker

★★★	Cracker (Virgin, 1992)
★★	Kerosene Hat (Virgin, 1993)
★★	The Golden Age (Virgin, 1996)
★★	Gentleman's Blues (Virgin, 1998)
★★★	Garage D'Or (Virgin, 2000)
★★	Forever (Back Porch, 2002)
★★	Hello Cleveland! Live from the Metro (Cooking Vinyl, 2002)
★★★★	Countrysides (Artist Direct, 2003)

If only David Lowery really had been as giddy about selling out as he seemed, Cracker might have been

the big slobbery raspberry in the face of alt-rock sanctimony he pretended it was. Cracker's rootsy backbeat thrust swaggered with a populist immediacy supposedly more democratic than the collegiate whimsy of Lowery's old band, much-lauded eclectic absurdists Camper Van Beethoven. Lowery declared, "I don't know what the world needs now/But I'm sure as hell that it starts with me" on his first single ("Teen Angst") with the commitment of a long-overlooked talent finally commandeering the spotlight.

But belated success didn't dilute the sourness of a dude who has felt unjustly ignored for the better part of a decade. Rockers have sneered their way to genius many a time, but *Kerosene Hat* drowns in the world-weary whininess Lowery diagnosed as indie rock's terminal condition back on Camper Van's "Life Is Grand." Bitch slaps like "Get Off This" sound more strident than the indie purists it chided for securing Perkins Loans, piercing their nipples, and knowing all the words to "Where the Hell Is Bill?" Lowery sounds as clueless as Mark Knopfler dissing pop stars with earrings back in 1985. The curdled resentment of *The Golden Age*'s "I Hate My Generation" stunk so rankly of old-fartism that if you didn't check Lowery's birth certificate, you might suspect that the contemporaries Lowery was lashing out at were pushing 60.

Recently, Lowery has made peace with his past, reuniting the Campers, even resuscitating his old indie label Pitch-A-Tent. But neither the Spice Girls, Puffy Combs, nor Bobby Brown could get away with calling a record *Forever,* and though he'll outlast them all, neither can David Lowery. *Countrysides* includes songs from writers as varied as Merle Haggard, Terry Allen, and Bruce Springsteen. Lowery unexpectedly recovers his sense of humor here—he kicks off Hank Williams Jr.'s "Family Tradition" with an absurd "Alternative country singers have always been a real close family." Collecting 16 of Cracker's wisest cracks, *Garage D'Or* is probably your best bet, if just for the fondly sardonic "Eurotrash Girl."   —K.H.

The Cramps

★★★½	Gravest Hits (IRS, 1979)
★★★½	Songs the Lord Taught Us (Illegal, 1980)
★★½	Psychedelic Jungle (IRS, 1981)
★★½	Smell of Female (Enigma, 1983)
★★★★	Bad Music for Bad People (IRS, 1984)
★★★	A Date with Elvis (1986; Enigma, 1990)
★★½	Stay Sick! (Enigma, 1990)
★★★½	Look Mom No Head! (Restless, 1991)
★★	Flamejob (Medicine, 1994)
★★	Big Beat from Badsville (Epitaph, 1997)
★★★★	Greatest Hits (BMG Special Products, 1998)

Holing up at the corner of rockabilly raunch and sick psychedelia, the Cramps gleefully embody all of early rock's sleaziest impulses. Their first release, *Gravest Hits,* (which has since been released on CD with *Psychedelic Jungle*) contrasts the itchy anxiety of "Human Fly" against an earnest cover of the Trashmen classic "Surfin' Bird." A similar dichotomy can be found on *Songs the Lord Taught Us,* where Lux Interior's Gene Vincent–meets–Fred Schneider delivery generates maximum friction against the brittle edges of the band's punkabilly instrumental attack. (*Bad Music for Bad People* combines the best of *Songs the Lord Taught Us* with highlights from *Gravest Hits* and *Psychedelic Jungle*). Sadly, neither the low-key *Psychedelic Jungle* nor the live *Smell of Female* is able to match that edgy chemistry, but the unrepentant sexism of *A Date With Elvis* almost makes up the difference; after all, where else are you likely to hear songs as tastelessly titled as "The Hot Pearl Snatch" or "Can Your Pussy Do the Dog?" *Stay Sick!* adds a few kinks to the Cramps' lyrics (e.g., "Journey to the Center of a Girl"), but musically, the group seems to have shot its wad, as the album's only original move is the rheumy cover of "Muleskinner Blues." But *Look Mom No Head!* not only picks up the tempo on most tunes, but brings in Iggy Pop for the thoroughly demented "Miniskirt Blues," then one-ups it with the single-entendre rocker "Bend Over, I'll Drive." If only *Flamejob* and *Big Beat From Badsville* could match their bad impulses with a similar sense of style. —J.D.C.

Cranberries

★★★★	Everybody Else Is Doing It, So Why Can't We? (Island, 1993)
★★★½	No Need to Argue (Island, 1994)
★½	To the Faithful Departed (Island, 1996)
★★★½	Bury the Hatchet (Island, 1998)
★★★	Wake Up and Smell the Coffee (Universal, 2001)
★★★½	Stars: The Best of 1992–2002 (Universal, 2002)

The Cranberries sugary debut could have been merely another wispy bit of dream pop, as effervescent and forgettable as a Sundays album. But rather than aiming for ethereal lightness, singer Dolores O'Riordan was one of the first singers to rework Sinead O'Connor's swoop for her own purposes; unlike pretty-poo thrushes such as Sarah McLachlan, however, O'Riordan also inherited O'Connor's self-determination and even a bit of her righteousness.

For its desired effect, *Everybody Else* required a glossy coat, and Stephen Street, who'd produced the Smiths and the Psychedelic Furs back when, supplied

it. This is music that delights in its own sound— "Linger" isn't so much a broken heart's lament as a celebration of how it feels to sing that particular word over and over. *No Need to Argue* was just as luxurious, but with a harsher undertone. The antiwar fury of "Zombie" was a shocker—it was almost as if Karen Carpenter had released a single skewering Henry Kissinger. Sharp and deeply felt, this foray into the political was also the beginning of the end for O'Riordan's development as a lyricist.

The titles on *To the Faithful Departed* say it all: "I Just Shot John Lennon," "Bosnia," "War Child." "Free to Decide" was a proud statement of autonomy, but the rest of the album was practically an argument against allowing such unchecked freedom for clumsy songwriters such as Dolores. Someone must have talked some sense into somebody before they went back into the studio: *Bury the Hatchet* was a giant leap backward, and not a moment too soon. *Wake Up and Smell the Coffee* is even more modest and gentle in its melodicism. The age of tuneful modern rock has passed, and adult contemporary is the smart way to go. After all, everybody else is doing it. —K.H.

Cream

★★★	Fresh Cream (Polydor, 1966)
★★★★	Disraeli Gears (Polydor, 1967)
★★★★	Wheels of Fire (Polydor, 1968)
★★★	Goodbye (Polydor, 1969)
★★	Live, Vol. 1 (Polydor, 1970)
★★	Live, Vol. 2 (Polydor, 1972)
★★★★★	Strange Brew: The Very Best of Cream (Polydor, 1983)
★★★★	Those Were the Days (Polydor/Chronicles, 1997)
★★★★	The Millennium Collection (Uni/Polydor, 2000)

Cream was rock's first power trio, its first significant psychedelic blues band, and the first to make a fetish of instrumental virtuosity. Its success catapulted Eric Clapton, Jack Bruce, and Ginger Baker to superstardom, and inspired several generations of hard-rock heroes, from Grand Funk to Van Halen. Even 20 years after the trio called it quits, Cream remains a staple of AOR radio. Yet for all that, it's easy to overestimate the value of the Cream's recorded output. Sure, the group cut some astonishing singles—"Badge," "Sunshine of Your Love," "White Room"—but it also made some incredibly misdirected and embarrassing live albums. It was almost as if Cream existed with two distinct identities, one a pithy singles act, and the other a self-indulgent jam band.

Although neither side completely emerges on *Fresh*

Cream, it's easy enough to see the shape of things to come. "I Feel Free" and "I'm So Glad" were slick and tuneful, handily showing off the group's ability to pull pop from the blues, while "Toad" and "Rollin' and Tumblin' " bore witness to the trio's propensity for showboating. Things on the pop side tightened up considerably when producer Felix Pappalardi came aboard; not only did he dress up *Disraeli Gears* with odd instruments and exotic sounds, but he kept the band's instrumental interplay in check, so that even a song as seemingly heavy as "Sunshine of Your Love" came across as singles fodder.

Wheels of Fire brought further refinements in Pappalardi's pop eclecticism. It added such exotic sounds as cello, marimba, and tonette, expanded his studio role from producer to player, and offered the first recorded example of Cream's concert approach; from the focused fury of "White Room" to the rambling, 16-minute version of "Toad," it remains the most representative slice of the Cream legacy. Sadly, things went downhill soon after, and *Goodbye,* recorded in the band's death throes, balances some of the band's most exquisite studio work ("Badge" in particular) with so-so concert recordings; it barely seems a complete album. *Strange Brew* is essentially a singles compilation and holds up well to repeated listening, but the two volumes of *Live Cream* are muddled leftovers released solely to cash in on the band's enduring popularity. *Those Were the Days* is a box set that compiles all of Cream's output, both live and in the studio, in a single package.   —J.D.C.

Creed

★★½	My Own Prison (Wind-Up, 1997)
★★★	Human Clay (Wind-Up, 1999)
★★½	Weathered (Wind-Up, 2001)

At their best, Creed resembled a ham-handed version of early Pearl Jam: the same vague, portentous lyricism and Zeppelin-style riffage married to melodic Top 40 hooks. But Creed replaced the '80s punk sensibilities of its Seattle grunge influences with an extra dollop of *Spinal Tap*–worthy bombast. The Florida-based band's debut, *My Own Prison,* unapologetically embraced '70s-style stadium rock, moving between thundering metallic tracks and sweeping ballads, yielding four hit singles ("Torn," "One," "What's This Life For," and the title track) that pretty much served as album highlights as well.

Prison, which the band originally released themselves before signing with the then-obscure label Wind-Up, turned Creed into superstars, and the group's subsequent discs followed roughly the same template. The 10-times-platinum *Human Clay,* while

covering little new sonic ground, was a satisfying hunk of post-grunge cheese; the immediacy of monster hits like "With Arms Wide Open" was hard to deny. Lead singer Scott Stapp's Eddie Vedder–like mannerisms—the great, emotive growl, the hair-tossing solemnity—seemed to grow in direct proportion to the band's success; by the time they released their third major label disc in 2001, Creed's utter lack of either humor or self-awareness had become its most distinctive trait. *Weathered* boasted several decent songs ("One Last Breath," "Stand Here With Me"), one great guilty pleasure ("My Sacrifice"), and more filler than either the band's fans or even its many critics had come to expect. The band called it a day in the summer of 2004.   —A.S.

Creedence Clearwater Revival

★★★½	Creedence Clearwater Revival (Fantasy, 1968)
★★★★	Bayou Country (Fantasy, 1969)
★★★★★	Green River (Fantasy, 1969)
★★★★★	Willy and the Poor Boys (Fantasy, 1969)
★★★★★	Cosmo's Factory (Fantasy, 1970)
★★★★½	Pendulum (Fantasy, 1970)
★★★	Mardi Gras (Fantasy, 1972)
★★★★	Creedence Gold (Fantasy, 1973)
★★	Live in Europe (Fantasy, 1973)
★★★	More Creedence Gold (Fantasy, 1973)
★★★★★	Chronicle (Fantasy, 1976)
★★★	Creedence 1969 (Fantasy, 1978)
★★★	Creedence 1970 (Fantasy, 1978)
★★½	The Concert (Fantasy, 1980)
★★★	Creedence Country (Fantasy, 1981)
★★★★½	Chronicle, Vol. 2 (Fantasy, 1986)
★★★	At the Movies (Fantasy, 1998)

They say when you get lost in the woods, you should walk downhill until you find the river, and then follow it to town. But for Creedence Clearwater Revival, America was never that simple, and its songs endure as a map of the country's traps, terrors, treasures, and pleasures. CCR was a classic hippie guitar band, soaking in the Northern California air, but it stood apart from the San Francisco psychedelic bands, partly because of its blue-collar earthiness, and partly because its drummer didn't suck. John Fogerty's spit-and-growl voice was the purple mountain majesty above the fruited plain of phenomenal rhythm section Doug Clifford and Stu Cook, California's answer to Wyman and Watts. The guys rambled their tamble while Fogerty ran down the road, chased by a tombstone shadow under a bad moon rising.

The first two albums show that Creedence could jam and get loose with any of the ballroom acid rockers, but with a much tougher sound honed during its years playing swamp blues, country, and rockabilly as an East Bay bar band—they had been playing together, for the sheer love of it, ever since they met in junior high school. Even at its rootsiest, the music was full of mystery and menace: The apocalyptic guitar riff of "Walk on the Water" was scary enough to inspire the Clash's "London Calling." But Creedence truly arrived with *Green River*, from the pastoral beauty of "Green River" to the sexy nightmare of "Sinister Purpose." John Fogerty sings about a river, pure and unpolluted, with the power to "let me remember things I don't know." But his green river is alive with the noise of all the drowned souls it carries—the ghost cries of flatcar riders and cross-tie walkers, pharaohs and Israelites, husbands and gamblers. Absurdly underrated as a lead guitarist—just listen to his terrifying one-note solo in "Tombstone Shadow"—Fogerty sings his hairy ass off, whether his struggles are personal ("Lodi") or political ("Wrote a Song for Everyone").

Willy and the Poor Boys is Fogerty's songwriting peak, with the sharp working-class anger of "Fortunate Son," "Don't Look Now," and "It Came Out of the Sky" (one of rock's first attacks on "Ronnie the Popular"). *Cosmo's Factory* shows off in two fantastic jams, the seven-minute "Ramble Tamble" and the 11-minute "I Heard It Through the Grapevine." Fogerty waxes world-weary in "Lookin' Out My Back Door" and "Long as I Can See the Light," while breathing fire in the demented raveup "Travelin' Band." *Pendulum* is spottier but peaks high with a couple of pensive farewells to the '60s, "It's Just a Thought" and "Have You Ever Seen the Rain?" At this point, Creedence had just released four all-time classic albums in 16 months; arguments over which one's the best will be going on for as long as those big wheels keep on turnin', but my quarter's down on *Green River.* Or maybe *Cosmo's Factory.* Hmmm . . . side two of *Willy?*

The band was falling apart by *Mardi Gras:* Rhythm guitarist Tom Fogerty, John's older brother, had quit, while Clifford and Cook started taking equal shares of the songwriting, although the best they could do was Clifford's "Need Someone to Hold." CCR split bitterly, and it's been depressing to watch the grudge fester over the years—in the late '90s, Fogerty even sued to keep Clifford and Cook from touring as Creedence Clearwater Revisited. All four band members kept recording, but without the old Creedence magic—the closest any of them came was "Rock and Roll Girls," from John Fogerty's only solo hit, 1985's *Centerfield.* The label kept putting out redundant compilations and weak live albums; the 20-song *Chronicle* is a superb place to start, the greatest hits of a band populist enough to put its greatness into its hits. Unlike so many of its peers, CCR was staunchly committed to

the public pleasures of rock & roll, making music anyone could love at first listen, which is why its songs have been sung by everyone from Richard Hell to Pavement, from Bonnie Tyler to the Minutemen, from the halls of Tina Turner to the shores of Bon Jovi. In short, for a couple of years there, Creedence was as great as any rock & roll band could ever be.   —R.S.

Marshall Crenshaw

★★★★	Marshall Crenshaw (1982; Warner Archives/Rhino, 2000)
★★	Field Day (Warner Bros., 1983)
★★★	Downtown (Warner Bros., 1985)
★★	Mary Jean and 9 Others (Warner Bros., 1987)
★★	Good Evening (Warner Bros., 1989)
★★★	Life's Too Short (Paradox/MCA, 1991)
★★	Marshall Crenshaw Live . . . My Truck Is My Home (Razor & Tie, 1994)
★★★	Miracle of Science (Razor & Tie, 1996)
★★	The 9 Volt Years: Battery Powered Home Demos & Curios (1979–198?) (Razor & Tie, 1998)
★★	No. 447 (Razor & Tie, 1999)
★★★★	The Best of Marshall Crenshaw: This Is Easy (Warner Archives/Rhino, 2000)
★★	I've Suffered for My Art . . . Now It's Your Turn (King Biscuit Flower Hour, 2001)
★★★	What's in the Bag? (Razor & Tie, 2003)

Power-pop fanatics—the children of Big Star and Cheap Trick's *In Color*—still genuflect in the direction of *Marshall Crenshaw*, an album whose only crime was to come out at about the same time as synth pop was usurping the place of guitar-based songwriting on the charts. The melodies and arrangements are so clean, plain-spoken, and punchy that it's possible to take their make-it-look-easy brilliance for granted. Most of the songs were recorded by a boisterous trio, though the hard-rocking "Cynical Girl" is a Crenshaw one-man-band tour de force.

That Crenshaw has never quite equaled his debut isn't so much a slight on him as an indication of just how completely he realized his ambitions, fusing hillbilly twang, Motown's tambourine-inflected groove, and brisk Beatles-by-way-of–Everly Brothers melodies. His recordings all inevitably are distinguished by his concisely inventive guitar playing, boyish tenor vocals, and songs addressing love's post-adolescent gray areas. Their charm lies as much in what he steadfastly leaves out: cleverness, earnestness, sanctimony.

That said, he has tried to shake up his formula by trying a variety of production approaches. *Field Day* remains his most divisive recording for that reason;

Steve Lillywhite swamps Crenshaw's fresh-faced tunes in echo and bombast. *Downtown* is something of a baroque roots-pop album, with session pros giving Crenshaw's short, sharp tunes a walloping directness. But his late-'80 struggles to widen his audience included the covers-dominated *Good Evening,* on which he resorts to covering schlock-mistress Diane Warren. *Life's Too Short* marks an attempt to revisit the smart, sparse turf of the first album, but with an arena-rock sense of proportion: Ed Stasium's slamming production, and Crenshaw fronting an all-star power-trio that includes Kenny Aronoff on drums and Fernando Saunders on bass.

In the '90s, his recording pace slowed, and even his studio albums are padded with filler: *#447* includes no less than three instrumentals. But, as usual, his choice of covers is astute, in particular Grant Hart's "Twenty-Five Forty-One," from *Miracle of Science.* Midlife reckoning and melancholy songs dominate *What's in the Bag?,* even as Crenshaw's pop sensibilities remain acute and his guitar work continues to astonish. Never an artist burdened by conceptual designs, Crenshaw and the enduring charms of his three-minute she-done-me-wrong jingle-jangles are better heard on the career-spanning compilation *This Is Easy.* —G.K.

Crosby, Stills and Nash

★★★★	Crosby, Stills and Nash (Atlantic, 1969)
★★★	CSN (Atlantic, 1977)
★★★	Replay (Atlantic, 1980)
★★	Daylight Again (Atlantic, 1982)
★	Live It Up (Atlantic, 1990)
★★★	CSN (Atlantic, 1991)
★★	After the Storm (Atlantic, 1994)

While dominated instrumentally by Stephen Stills, founder of the pioneering folk rockers Buffalo Springfield, CSN's impressive debut album reflected three distinct sensibilities. Enraptured at the time with Judy Collins, Stills led with "Suite: Judy Blue Eyes"; the seven-minute mini-epic conveyed his easy mastery of a number of styles (folk ballad, light rock, Latin-inflected rhythm), highlighted his sharp guitar work, and introduced the soaring ensemble harmonies that would become the group's trademark. Nash's slight but charming "Marrakesh Express" extended from the fluid pop he'd perfected with the Hollies. Ex-Byrd David Crosby turned in the loosely structured ballad "Guinevere"—all drifty atmosphere and wide-eyed poetry, it exemplified his hippie mysticism. Of as much sociological as musical interest, the album exactly captured the spirit of the last high moment of the American '60s. Exhausted by Vietnam, embarked upon mind expansion and lifestyle rebellion, the CSN

generation found in the band both spokesmen and representatives; the singers' slightly weary utopianism, their bucolic fantasies, and their songs about love and its losses reflected the inward turning of an aging youth culture, the movement away from public struggle to self-examination.

By the time of *CSN,* the moment that lent intensity and credibility to the trio's songs had passed, and its music had become nice, bland, and comfortable. Perhaps unsurprisingly, Nash's simple popcraft produced the most dependable of *CSN*'s mild pleasures. *Daylight Again* was no great shakes, either, even if Crosby's voice sounded stronger than his years of highly publicized hard living might suggest. "Might As Well Have a Good Time" underscored the album's air of drastically lowered expectations—and the song wasn't even an original. *Live It Up* was an embarrassment; overreliant on outside writers for inspiration, the group sounded tired and confused, and a techno-happy production, full of synthesizer rhythm tracks, didn't help. *After the Storm,* one more attempt to rekindle the fire, was also disappointing. *Replay* is a compilation of material from the debut and the singers' solo projects. With 25 of its 77 selections being alternate takes or previously unreleased rarities, the *CSN* box set not only documents the group's history thoroughly, but it unearths quite a few pleasant surprises. —P.E.

Crosby, Stills, Nash and Young

★★★★	Déjà Vu (Atlantic, 1970)
★★½	4 Way Street (Atlantic, 1971)
★★★	So Far (Atlantic, 1974)
★★★	American Dream (Atlantic, 1988)
★★	Looking Forward (Reprise, 1999)

Enlisting the aid of Stephen Stills' Buffalo Springfield collaborator (and rival), Neil Young, proved a risky move on the part of Crosby, Stills and Nash—Young's urgency and depth would make any CSN record that featured him gain immensely in power; his absences from their other albums, however, would equally resound. Contributing "Helpless," one of his loveliest and leanest ballads, as well as the gorgeous three-song suite "Country Girl" to *Déjà Vu,* Young also added jagged guitar work that counterbalanced Stills' more technical grace—and his keening, wise-child vocals lent haunting dimension to the trio's harmonies. Though Young's songs were the strongest, the other band members rose to his challenge.

It is the juxtaposition of CSN&Y's individual styles, in fact, that makes *Déjà Vu,* released in 1970, an even more accurate time capsule than *Crosby, Stills & Nash*—the tension of the band's fitful union reflects the restlessness that pervaded the end of the '60s, and each member's songs capture a facet of the countercultural experience. With Crosby's melodramatic "Almost Cut My Hair," the communal rebellion of the protest era is reduced to an individual, symbolic gesture; Nash's "Teach Your Children" and "Our House" express the urge toward domesticity on the part of former rebels; Stills' strong, electric reworking of Joni Mitchell's "Woodstock" takes on, in retrospect, the air of a last hurrah. The Stills-Young collaboration "Everybody I Love You" is so sweeping as to now sound a bit desperate, and Crosby's reincarnation saga "Déjà Vu" hints at the New Age e-z mysticism that would eventually preoccupy many survivors of the CSN generation.

Unsurprisingly, CSN&Y soon came apart—Young's forward-looking vision being antithetical to the air of comfort that inflated *CSN*. The live *4 Way Street* distinctly lacked team spirit; and a best-of set, *So Far*, seemed perfunctory. *American Dream* was still stronger than any Crosby, Stills and Nash record—even if Young's four songs were hardly standouts, the trio sounded more vital with Neil on board. The record's most touching number, however, was Crosby's "Compass," an apologia for his years of substance abuse. On that graceful note of redemption, this edgy brotherhood temporarily retired. They resurfaced with 1999's *Looking Forward*, a pleasant-enough disc that, however, signaled no real advance. —P.E.

Sheryl Crow

★★★	Tuesday Night Music Club (A&M, 1993)
★★★★	Sheryl Crow (A&M, 1996)
★★½	The Globe Sessions (A&M, 1998)
★★	Sheryl Crow and Friends Live From Central Park (A&M, 1999)
★★★★	C'mon, C'mon (Interscope, 2002)
★★★★½	The Very Best of Sheryl Crow (A&M, 2003)

On first hearing, Sheryl Crow's songs sound charmingly loose and off-the-cuff. But take a closer listen and you'll realize that countless hours went into creating this incredible simulation of rootsiness. Not just a talented songwriter and an excellent '70s-style rock & roll singer—sort of a cross between the younger Stevie Nicks and the older Bonnie Raitt—Crow's also a master of production craft. The only problem is that sometimes her perfectionist impulses get in the way of the emotions she's trying to express.

After several years spent as a songwriter and backup vocalist, Crow commenced her solo career with *Tuesday Night Music Club*. The airheaded "All I Wanna Do" scored big on the charts, but the real jewels here are more serious numbers like "Strong Enough" and "No One Said It Would Be Easy." Enjoyable as the album is, it's obviously a committee project. Eight different songwriters besides Crow contribute, making it hard to decipher the personality behind the music.

Crow's second release is a different story. Producing herself and cutting down on the collaborators, she comes up with a record that's classy and full of character. "Everyday Is a Winding Road" and "A Change Would Do You Good" are irresistible pop, while "If It Makes You Happy" (with its almost inevitable followup line "Then why the hell are you so sad?") is the quintessential Sheryl Crow song, capturing the hurt and world-weariness underneath the studio veneer.

The Globe Sessions gets off to a splendid start with the alluring "My Favorite Mistake," but except for the lovely Celtic-flavored folk of "Riverwide," few of the other originals measure up, and even the cover of Bob Dylan's "Mississippi" is surprisingly shallow. The star-studded live album that followed is no great shakes and, unless you've been dying to hear Crow duet with Eric Clapton on "White Room," easily skippable. *C'mon, C'mon* is a welcome return to form, though, offering sassy rock ("Steve McQueen"), buoyant bubblegum ("Soak Up the Sun"), and heart-on-sleeve balladry ("Weather Channel") with equal flair. —M.R.

Rodney Crowell

★★★★	Ain't Living Long Like This (Warner Bros., 1978)
★★★★	Diamonds & Dirt (Columbia, 1988)
★★★	Keys to the Highway (Columbia, 1989)
★★★★	The Rodney Crowell Collection (Warner Bros., 1989)
★★★	Life Is Messy (Columbia, 1992)
★★★★	Greatest Hits (Columbia, 1993)
★★★	Let the Picture Paint Itself (MCA, 1994)
★★★	Jewel of the South (MCA, 1995)
★★	Super Hits (Columbia, 1995)
★★★★	The Houston Kid (Sugar Hill, 2001)
★★★★	Small Worlds: The Rodney Crowell Collection (Raven, 2002)

Taking his cues from the rock & roll primitivism of such late-'70s British power-popsters as Nick Lowe and Dave Edmunds, Rodney Crowell became an important link between the hippie-era country rock of Gram Parsons and the post-punk Americana of Lucinda Williams and Ryan Adams; Crowell even did time in Emmylou Harris' Hot Band. His style of singing and songwriting owes more to the playfulness of Buddy Holly and the sublime beauty of Roy Orbison than to the chaos and crackle of Jerry Lee Lewis or Johnny Cash. As a songwriter, Crowell's written a handful of classic country-pop tunes ("Till I Gain Control Again," "Leaving Louisiana in the Broad Daylight"), and delivered hits for artists as varied as the Oak Ridge Boys and Bob Seger.

In the decade following his excellent debut—a country-rock hybrid that updates the late Parsons' so-called Cosmic American Music—Crowell floundered, putting out a couple of now-deleted albums for Warner Bros. and one for Columbia. But on *Diamonds & Dirt,* he developed the sound he's cultivated since then: that of a cosmopolitan neorockabilly singer/songwriter whose heart-tugging ballads and uptempo dance tunes set the standard for Nashville's New Traditionalist movement. Crowell's songs aren't based so much on old-school cliché and wordplay as on real-life pathos served up with a hip sense of humor—kind of like Parsons'. And country fans ate it up; *Diamonds* produced five #1 hits, bringing Cosmic American Music squarely into the Nashville mainstream.

On *Keys to the Highway,* Crowell's songwriting became more confessional. "Things I Wish I'd Said," inspired by the death of his father, and the folky "Many a Long and Lonesome Highway" are among his strongest songs. But the album was a commercial disappointment, and Nashville turned its fickle back on Crowell. His follow-up, *Life Is Messy,* is lyrically bleak, with music that brings much more of a rock edge to the songs. Crowell was coming out of a divorce from Johnny Cash's singer/songwriter daughter Rosanne, and his feelings bleed through nearly every track. When Crowell switched record labels for *Let the Picture Paint Itself* and *Jewel of the South,* he ventured further into pop-rock singer/songwriter territory, but his writing had lost much of its sting.

After a six-year sabbatical, Crowell returned in 2001 with the best album of his career. *The Houston Kid,* released on the independent country-folk label Sugar Hill, is straight-up autobiography. Plaintive, laid-back, and utterly honest, this raw, cinematic song cycle tells Crowell's story through snapshots, extended scenes, confessions, and anecdotes. It's a songwriter's masterpiece, and at its center is a rewriting of his former father-in-law's classic "I Walk the Line," with a spoken story about the impact it made on Crowell the first time he heard the song.

The Rodney Crowell Collection is a solid overview of his Warner Bros. years, and *Greatest Hits* compiles his best Columbia material. *Super Hits* overlaps with *Greatest Hits,* but leaves off important songs. —M.K.

The Crystal Method

  ★★★ Vegas (Outpost, 1997)
  ★★ Tweekend (Outpost/Geffen, 2001)
  ★★ Community Service (Ultra Records, 2002)
★★★½ Legion of Boom (V2, 2004)

The Crystal Method are a pair of basement beat scientists rocking out in suburban Los Angeles, techno kings as comfortable on the dance floor as on rock radio, and just as wildly uneven. At their best, partners Ken Jordan and Scott Kirkland match power and hooks in dance tracks that throb with raw inspiration and intense sexual energy. Its early reputation built on the strength of furious 12-inch singles ("Now Is the Time"), the Crystal Method finally stepped beyond the rave scene with *Vegas;* "Busy Child" was a medium hit that momentarily busted open the '90s mainstream in league with Prodigy and the Chemical Brothers. Aggressive beats, found voices, and desperate hooks collide and tumble at a brutal pace. If only it all rocked this hard. "High Roller" is like a metal drum solo that won't end, and "Comin' Back" hasn't progressed much beyond the most disposable '70s Eurodisco. The revolution won't survive on filler alone.

What followed had just as much padding, minus the hard-hitting club rockers. The groove on *Tweekend* is hopelessly adrift, resorting to the same big-time rock excesses that techno was supposed to replace—tracks of endless noodling and simplistic beats. The Method hadn't learned the lessons every metal band must eventually grasp: A riff is not a song, and a hot beat is not nearly enough. *Community Service* is an inessential gathering of cluttered remixes that take too long to ignite (Orbital, P.O.D., Rage Against the Machine) or go nowhere at all. *Legion of Boom* is a sudden return to relevance. The beat still reigns supreme, but the Method is finally bored with simple repetition, incorporating live vocals and guitars (Limp Bizkit's Wes Borland) without surrendering the techno flag. There is no career-defining "Busy Child," but *Boom* is easily the duo's most consistent collection, all slash, burn, and bounce, and an energetic commitment to the concept of electronics as rock & roll. —S.A.

The Cult

  ★★ Dreamtime (Beggars Banquet, 1984)
  ★★½ Love (Sire, 1985)
★★★½ Electric (Sire, 1987)
★★★½ Sonic Temple (Sire, 1989)
  ★★★ Ceremony (Sire/Reprise/Beggars Banquet, 1991)
★★★½ The Cult (Sire/Reprise/Beggars Banquet, 1994)

★★★★ High Octane Cult (Reprise/Beggars Banquet, 1996)

★★★★ Pure Cult: The Singles 1984–1995 (Beggars Banquet, 2000)

★★★ Rare Cult (Beggars Banquet, 2000)

★★★½ The Best of Rare Cult (Beggars Banquet, 2000)

★★★ Beyond Good and Evil (Lava/Atlantic, 2001)

★★ Rare Cult: The Demo Sessions (Beggars Banquet, 2002)

Ian Astbury

★★★ Spirit\Light\Speed (Beggars Banquet, 1999)

Although one imagines principals Ian Astbury (vocals) and Billy Duffy (guitar) bristling at the thought, at the end of the day, the Cult boils down to a really great singles band. The virtually identical *High Octane Cult* and *Pure Cult* collections make a solid case for this, distilling an often lugubrious catalogue down to one airtight disc of dark but undeniably danceable and fist-pump-worthy hard rock, from the early goth anthems "Spiritwalker" and "Rain" (from *Dreamtime* and *Love,* respectively) to the arena-rock bombast of "Lil' Devil" and "Sweet Soul Sister" (*Electric* and *Sonic Temple*) and 1992's terrific techno experiment, "The Witch" (from the movie *Cool World*). The actual albums are more hit than miss, but the hits pack a wallop. (*The Best of Rare Cult,* a single-disc sampler of the exhaustive, for-diehards-only box set *Rare Cult,* is also better than most of the studio albums.)

Essentially a heavy-metal band for folks who think they're above such things, the Cult built its sound from equal parts postpunk guitar aggression and neo-hippy mysticism, a combination that quite naturally results in some of the silliest, most pompous music rock has seen since the heyday of the Doors. Typically, it was some time before the band got even that good, as *Dreamtime* never quite gets up a head of steam, while the frenzied, unfocused playing on *Love* squanders the melodic potential of its best songs ("She Sells Sanctuary" and the overlong "Brother Wolf, Sister Moon").

With producer Rick Rubin on hand to tighten and toughen the group's sound, *Electric* manages to kick ass even when its lyrics make no sense, as on the relentless "Love Removal Machine." (Note to the band: There's a difference between "trippy" and "stupid.") But when it found a formula, the Cult wasted no time in hammering it into the ground. *Sonic Temple,* the band's bestseller, may attempt an epic sweep on some songs—most notably the hit "Firewalker" and the power ballad "Edie (Ciao Baby)"—while *Ceremony* tries a sort of hard-rock transcendentalism, but neither disc adds enough variation to the music to necessitate further distinction. The underrated *The Cult*

jacked up the band's sound with a liberal dose of the techno-rock approach that distinguished "The Witch" and produced "Coming Down," the band's last great single. Following an extended hiatus that found Duffy collaborating with the Alarm's Mike Peters in the band Colorsound and Astbury fronting the short-lived Holy Barbarians and releasing a better-than-average electrorock solo album (*Spirit\Light\Speed*), the Cult reconvened for its heaviest record, 2001's relentlessly rocking but charmless *Beyond Good and Evil.* Better that, though, than Astbury's inevitable-in-hindsight portrayal of the Lizard King alongside Robby Krieger and Ray Manzarek in the nostalgia outfit the Doors of the 21st Century. —J.D.C./R.SK.

Culture Club

★★★ Kissing to Be Clever (Virgin, 1982)

★★★ Colour By Numbers (Virgin, 1983)

★★ Waking Up With the House on Fire (Virgin, 1984)

★ From Luxury to Heartache (Virgin, 1986)

★★★★ At Worst . . . The Best of Boy George and Culture Club (Virgin, 1993)

★★½ 12" Collection Plus (Caroline, 1997)

★★★ VH1 Storytellers/Greatest Moments (Virgin, 1998)

Should anyone ever doubt the amount of charisma Boy George once exuded, the fact that Culture Club was able to generate such extraordinary popularity on the basis of such utterly ordinary music ought to be proof enough. Listening to them now, it seems incredible that these albums produced six Top 10 singles (eight in Britain); one can only wonder what sort of national delusion would have resulted in such success.

Yet it wasn't delusion, really, it was charm, pure and simple. Just listen to George's tremulous tenor imploring, "Do You Really Want to Hurt Me" on *Kissing to Be Clever;* how could anyone resist a voice so guileless? Never mind that the rest of the album is chockablock with bleached funk and bland reggae, offering only the denatured carnival rhythms of "I'll Tumble 4 Ya" as inducement (or that "Time [Clock of the Heart]," which Epic eventually appended to the album during its original run, has since been deleted by Virgin); sheer force of personality was what carried the day back then. And the same goes for *Colour By Numbers;* outré as the metaphor in "Miss Me Blind" might have been, outright silly as the chorus to "Karma Chameleon" truly was, the point remains that Boy George made us believe, if only for a moment.

So what happened? Well, sad to say, the Boy turned serious. *Waking Up With the House on Fire* opens with the overwrought "message" of "Dangerous Man," and goes straight downhill from there, through the insufferable sanctimony of "The War Song" to the sheer inanity of "Crime Time" and "Mistake No. 3." Worse, the closest to catchy any of the above gets is "The War Song," which is overstuffed to the point of making "Hair" sound like a Dylan tune. By *From Luxury to Heartache,* the slide into irrelevance was so complete that the album's only real virtue was Boy George's voice—an obvious case of too little, too late. Nonetheless, Boy and the lads reunited in 1998 for the inevitable wallow in nostalgia, the apex of which was the band's appearance on VH1's *Storytellers* (conveniently available in album form for those who forgot to set the VCR). —J.D.C.

The Cure

★★★½	Three Imaginary Boys (Fiction, 1979)
★★★½	Boys Don't Cry (Elektra, 1980)
★★★½	Seventeen Seconds (Elektra, 1980)
★★★	Faith (Elektra, 1981)
★★★	Pornography (Elektra, 1982)
★★★★	The Walk (Sire, 1983)
★★★★	Japanese Whispers (Sire, 1983)
★★½	The Top (Sire, 1984)
★★	Concert: The Cure Live (Fiction, 1984)
★★★★	The Head on the Door (Elektra, 1985)
★★★★★	Staring at the Sea: The Singles (Elektra, 1986)
★★★★	Kiss Me, Kiss Me, Kiss Me (Elektra, 1987)
★★★★★	Disintegration (Elektra, 1989)
★	Mixed Up (Elektra, 1990)
★★★½	Wish (Elektra, 1992)
★★	Paris (Elektra, 1993)
★★	Show (Elektra, 1993)
★★	Wild Mood Swings (Elektra, 1996)
★★★★	Galore (Elektra, 1997)
★★★	Bloodflowers (Elektra, 2000)
★★★★	Greatest Hits (Elektra, 2001)
★★★★½	The Cure (Geffen, 2004)

The Cure's Robert Smith is one of the most significant sex symbols rock has ever produced, all wet and disheveled in the throes of an angst that only makes him so wonderfully, wonderfully pretty. He was the cool older sister you never had, with his big sticky hair, his pear-shaped body, his eyelashes for hours, his voice shaking like milk as he sings his tales of adolescent torpor and dolor. All swirled up in lipstick and rouge, wearing more face than his face could even hold, he smeared his cosmetics with a conspicuously unmothered flair that made him look like he'd eaten his way through the Clinique counter. He's the biggest lesbian rock star ever, even if he's technically a straight guy. He bridged the gap between goth and new wave, be-

tween gloom and glamour, becoming a figure of fascination for millions of depressive '80s kids. Maybe you've never been in love with Robert Smith, and maybe you've never even made out with anybody who's in love with Robert Smith, but you've definitely made out with someone who's made out with someone who's in love with Robert Smith, and that means he's under your skin whether you like it or not.

The Cure began as an arty postpunk trio, doing skewed guitar tunes about reading Camus ("Killing an Arab") and not crying ("Boys Don't Cry"). But Robert Smith was just warming up for the deluge of proto-goth gloom rock that he would unleash over the next few years. *Seventeen Seconds, Faith,* and *Pornography* hold up smashingly well, offering motionless slabs of lavishly textured angst, often decorated with gorgeous synths, as Smith sobbed and sniffled his tormented poetry. But it was the 1982 single "Let's Go to Bed" that introduced the Robert Smith we know and love today. The miserable sob was still there, but now it was playing around with witty lyrics that accurately summed up at least 20 percent of any real-life romantic relationship ("The two of us together again/It's just the same, a stupid game") and a bouncy, hum-along synth-pop melody that made the situation sound more funny than hopeless.

The Cure had hit upon a perfect musical formula, shaping all its depressive moods into actual songs, and the band started to attract increasingly worshipful legions of fans in black nail polish and eyeliner. Smith also joined Siouxsie and the Banshees as a guitarist, doing double duty for two great big-hair bands, which increased his cool quotient immeasurably. His melodies got richer with *The Walk, Japanese Whispers,* and *The Head on the Door,* his king-of-the-mopey-Brits smackdown, as he proved he could outdo New Order ("In Between Days") and Depeche Mode ("Close to Me") at their own games. Best of all was the single "The Love Cats," a brazen piano ditty that revealed that making out could be kind of fun. "Should we have each other for dinner?/Should we have each other with cream?"—mee-*yow!*

Standing On A Beach put the Cure on a roll, and *Kiss Me, Kiss Me, Kiss Me* had the Cure's best-known, best loved, and just plain best song ever, "Just Like Heaven." Smith sings about spinning on that dizzy edge with a dream muse, and then waking up the next morning feeling alone—no, make that alone, *alone*—above the raging sea, one alone little dude indeed.

Disintegration is the Cure's high point for most fans, especially male ones born in the late '70s; according to the kids on *South Park,* it's the greatest album ever made. Although it's dark and depressive, it spawned the hit "Love Song." *Wish* is lighter and frothier, a valentine to the band's younger girl fans, with bubblegoth love ditties like "High," "Friday I'm in Love," and "A Letter for Elise," which nicked the melody from Bon Jovi's "Never Say Goodbye." Smith had a long dry spell in the '90s; he even stopped wearing makeup around the time of *Wild Mood Swings* and *Bloodflowers.* But *The Cure* had the band's most passionate music since *Disintegration,* hitting an all-time peak in the twisted romantic devotion of "Before Three": "Whispering dreams, so fucked and high/It's hard to hold this night inside."

Galore collects the best of the late '80s/early '90s Cure, plus a load of late filler. *Greatest Hits* has seven songs from *Standing On a Beach*—the seven best, for that matter—plus "Just Like Heaven," so it's a bargain. But who wants a Cure album with a title like *Greatest Hits? Join The Dots* is a cult collection of rarities; *Galore* is a feeble remix album; *Show* and *Paris* are weak live albums. These days, Robert Smith is coasting on a wave of good will from a new generation of fans who weren't even born for "Boys Don't Cry," inspiring high-profile bands such as Interpol, Franz Ferdinand, Mogwai, and the Rapture. He remains one of rock's most beloved figures—a love cat with nine lives.   —R.S.

Cypress Hill

★★★★½   Cypress Hill (Ruffhouse/Columbia, 1991)
★★★   Black Sunday (Ruffhouse/Columbia, 1993)
★★   Cypress Hill III: Temples of Boom (Ruffhouse/Columbia, 1995)
★   IV (Ruffhouse/Columbia, 1998)
★   Skull and Bones (Columbia, 2000)
★★   Till Death Do Us Part (Columbia, 2004)

Cypress Hill's formula has been imitated so much, it's easy to forget how shocking it originally sounded: crazy Latino voices, Spanglish gangsta threats, blunted '70s funk beats that made you laugh out loud. B-Real and Sen Dog come on as a hip-hop Cheech and Chong, praising the sweet leaf with a devotion rarely seen beyond the parking lot at a Phish show. While the rappers twist their "Latin Lingo" into *vato* rhymes about blunts, guns, and 40 oz., DJ Muggs pumps bongloads of bass into paranoid sound collages like "Hand on the Pump," and when you turn it up loud, the beat goes boo-ya. The combination of whiny singsong flow and low-riding bass made the album hugely influential, most notably on Dr. Dre, but nobody quite duplicated that perfect balance of humor and horror—not even Cypress Hill themselves. The followup, *Black Sunday,* was jokier, with the hit "Insane in the Brain" and the definitive "I Wanna Get High." Subsequent releases reflect poorly on the relationship between cannabis intake and creative inspiration.   —R.S.

Da Brat

   ★★½   Funkdafied (Chaos, 1994)
   ★★½   Anuthatantrum (Sony/So So Def, 1996)
   ★★★   Unrestricted (Sony/So So Def, 2000)
   ★★½   Limelite, Luv & Niteclubz (Arista, 2003)

The first female MC to go platinum, Da Brat (a.k.a. Shawntae Harris) became the protégé of Jermaine Dupri after being discovered by *Yo! MTV Raps* in the early '90s. Her debut, the snappy, energetic *Funkdafied,* was a smash thanks largely to its title single. Though Da Brat was initially positioned as a female Snoop Dogg (her unapologetic love of herb didn't hurt), by the time her sophomore effort was released in 1996, she had honed her rapidfire delivery to such an extent that comparisons to the terminally mellow Snoop no longer applied.

    Anuthatantrum made it painfully evident that Da Brat, who relied heavily on uninspired samples and reheated get-the-party-started grooves, didn't have much to say beyond the usual recitation of her likes (weed, stretch limos, the occasional reggae groove, weed) and dislikes (haters).

    By the time Brat released *Unrestricted* in 2000, she was facing assault charges, a sagging film career (which would, unfortunately, later include a costarring role in *Glitter*), and worse, the emergence of flashier and more shameless female rappers like Lil' Kim. While Ja Rule, Kelly Price, and Mystikal make pro forma appearances, Da Brat doesn't need the help: *Unrestricted* is her best album to date. Tracks like "What' Chu Like" and "Runnin' Out of Time" are stunners, showcasing her newfound appreciation for NC-17 wordplay and R&B respectively, while the title of the club anthem "Fuck You" pretty much says it all.

    Limelite, Luv & Niteclubz, from 2003, followed mostly the same formula as its predecessor, with slightly diminished returns. Showcasing a mixture of R&B and club beats, but this time with an eye toward *TRL* (indeed, the almost freakishly catchy "In Love wit Chu" became one of Brat's most successful singles), *Limelite* featured guest turns from Mariah Carey and Anthony Hamilton and included frequent references to church that were, you have to figure, probably metaphorical.   —A.S.

Daft Punk

   ★★★   Homework (Virgin, 1997)
  ★★★½   Discovery (Virgin, 2001)
   ★½   Alive 1997 (Virgin, 2001)

The French duo Daft Punk's essential, career-defining insight is that the problem with disco the first time around was not that it was stupid but that it was not stupid enough. After an abortive career in rock as Darlin', Thomas Bangalter and Guy-Manuel de Homem Christo renamed themselves after a review and recorded *Homework,* the 4/4 whomp of house music slowed down to bumping speed, then ducttaped to squelchy acid noise and strutting synthesizer themes straight out of the Giorgio Moroder songbook. Its audacity is a hoot, and the robot two-step of "Around the World" (and its video) became a club perennial.

    Daft Punk took its time recording the followup; meanwhile, Bangalter and some friends, as Stardust, made a glorious and much-compiled straight-up disco single "Music Sounds Better With You." *Discovery* follows the same path, throwing in vocoders and vintage analog synths: Who needs a song if you have a hook? The dance hit "One More Time" leads the march of the boogying cyborgs, and the more they dumb the album down, the funkier it gets. Housecleaning music all night long!

    Alive 1997 is an extended rehash of four *Homework* tracks with a bit of crowd noise. It's great if you have a billion-watt sound system and a mountain of drugs at home, but it's not too useful otherwise.   —D.W.

The Dandy Warhols

★★★ Dandys Rule OK? (1995; Dandy Warhols Music, 2000)

★★★ . . . The Dandy Warhols Come Down (Capitol, 1997)

★★★★ Thirteen Tales From Urban Bohemia (Capitol, 2000)

★★★½ Welcome to the Monkey House (Capitol, 2003)

Their wacky name made people think the Dandy Warhols were a hipster novelty act when they first appeared in the mid-'90s—an impression reinforced by titles like "Lou Weed," from their 1995 indie debut album, and "Not If You Were the Last Junkie on Earth," their first single for Capitol, two years later. It soon became apparent that the Portland, OR–based quartet wasn't a joke, though leadman Courtney Taylor (or Taylor-Taylor, as he later renamed himself) purveys a distinctive brand of irony-laced humor, which is part of the Dandys' recipe. First album *Dandys Rule OK?* establishes a tone of subterranean artiness that draws in equal measure from the dry-ice cool of the Velvet Underground and the droning space-rock of the Byrds—along with a touch of the Cars in their use of loopy analog-synth lines (provided by producer Tony Lash), but it's the style, not the material, that leaves the deeper impression. While much of the subsequent *Come Down* seems obscured under a layer of psychedelic haze, the momentum and wit of "Last Junkie" and "Cool as Kim Deal" burst through the murk, setting the stage for the band's strongest album, 2000's *Thirteen Tales From Urban Bohemia*. Here, the spaghetti Western soundscapes of "Godless" and "Mohammed" and the rock-symphonic "Nietzsche" combine to form a mesmerizing 16-minute opening suite, clearing the air for the signature tracks "Get Off," "Cool Scene," and—best of all—"Bohemian Like You," which combines a particularly wry sociocultural vignette with what may be the most muscular Stones guitar riff of the last 20 years. If *Bohemia* is a total delight, *Welcome to the Monkey House* is at best an intermittent one. The premise is pure Taylor-Taylor: He brought in Duran Duran synthesist Nick Rhodes to play on and produce the album, which re-creates the robotic feel of '80s synth pop in such a way that it's unclear whether the move is a send-up or an homage. Most of the tracks seem stuck between the two extremes, the exceptions being the killer single "We Used to Be Friends" and "You Were the Last High," which comes across with the world-weary romanticism of Roxy Music circa *Country Life*. The Dandy Warhols are a heady band, to be sure, but it remains to be seen whether they turn out to be an important one. —B.SC.

Craig David

★★★ Born to Do It (Wildstar, 2000; Atlantic, 2001)

★★★ Slicker Than Your Average (Wildstar/Atlantic, 2002)

The British dance genre two-step (a.k.a. U.K. garage) rose out of the clubs and blew up across the British Isles at the end of the '90s, combining elements of pop, R&B, and dance music over a quickened, jagged breakbeat. Craig David was among the scene's first personalities and certainly its first bona fide superstar—while still in his teens, no less. Two-step producers the Artful Dodger featured David's vocals on two of their biggest hits, "Re-Rewind" ("The crowd say Bo! Selectah!") and "Woman Trouble." A solo career followed and his slick debut, *Born to Do It*, featured two of the year's best singles, "Fill Me In" and "7 Days." Both tracks featured David's playfully smooth vocal flow and dealt playfully with the single life. The young, sexy star also struck a chord with America's R&B audience, ultimately selling over 7 million copies. Followup *Slicker Than Your Average* found David both trying to defend his street cred while also making a more obvious stab at mainstream pop/R&B. As on his debut, among the best tracks are the production/writing collaborations with the Artful Dodger's Mark Hill. Less interesting is the album's one duet, featuring (gulp) Sting. —D.S.

Dick Dale & His Del-Tones

★★★ Greatest Hits (1975; GNP Crescendo, 1992)

★★★★½ King of the Surf Guitar: The Best of Dick Dale & His Del-Tones (Rhino, 1989)

★★★½ Tribal Thunder (Hightone, 1993)

★★★ Territory (Hightone, 1994)

★★★ Calling Up Spirits (Beggars Banquet, 1996)

★★★★ Better Shred Than Dead: The Dick Dale Anthology (Rhino, 1997)

★★★½ Spacial Disorientation (Sin-Drome, 2002)

Dick Dale is the one true king of surf guitar, the ne plus ultra, the sine qua non, alpha and omega, everyone else pack up and go home. The least of his accomplishments is documented in his appearances in '60s beach movies in which the renegade picker sports a hoop earring—placing him about a decade ahead of the cultural curve with regard to male fashion accessorizing. With the release of his first single in 1961, "Let's Go Trippin'," he created an entire genre, surf music, as well as one of the most unique and influential guitar styles in rock & roll history. Among Dale's notable acolytes was Jimi Hendrix, who, as a guitarist in Little Richard's band, caught one of Dale's shows in the early '60s and, according to reports, spent a great deal of time afterward questioning Dale about his sound and style. In "Third Stone From the Sun," on *Are You Experienced?*, Hendrix signs off one poetic interlude with the words, "You'll never hear surf music again." That quote has been widely interpreted by critics as Hendrix's way of kissing off a moribund genre, but in fact it was an homage to Dale, whom everyone at the time (except Dale, apparently) thought was in the terminal stage of rectal cancer.

Dale's achievements are measured in far more than hot licks, though. Hendrix is acknowledged as having given birth to the guitar-effects industry, but Dale's sonic innovations of the early '60s set the stage for everything to come. Working closely with Leo Fender, founder of the Fender Electric Instrument Company, Dale, insisting he needed a "louder, thicker sound" for the crowds he was playing to in spacious ballrooms, pushed the development of an amplifier that would break all known sonic barriers. After Dale had tested and blown up dozens of prototypes, Fender made the first 85-watt output transformer ever used in an amp, and dubbed it the "Dick Dale Transformer." All that was needed, then, was a speaker that wouldn't disintegrate under the assault. Fender and Dale struck up an alliance with J.B. Lansing (of JBL speakers), who, after some initial skepticism, took Dale's specs and developed a 15-inch speaker that was the marquee component of the legendary Showman amplifier. Impressed but still pushing the envelope, Dale had another 15-inch speaker built into the cabinet, and thus was born the Dual Showman, one of the most popular amplifiers in history. When Dale unapologetically refers to himself as "the king of loud," it's hard to argue with his assessment. He was also one of the pioneer end users of the legendary Fender Reverb Unit, which he used initially on his vocals; later he plugged his Strat into it, producing a steamroller effect on audiences.

A multi-instrumentalist and first-rate surfer, Dale was in the vanguard of a sport beginning to attract a new, younger generation of fanatic hodads and gremmies, as well as civilian hangers-on who emulated the real athletes' fashions, language, and carefree attitude toward everything but surfing. The music Dale played and the culture he was immersed in were separate but equal entities until the late '50s, when he and his father reopened the grand Rendezvous Ballroom in Balboa, CA, formerly a big-band palace, and began drawing thousands of teenagers there and to similar venues he played in other areas of Southern California. In 1961, Del-Tone released the instrumental single "Let's Go Trippin' " (the title was slang for "going to see someone"), and it not only made *Billboard*'s Top 100 singles chart, it stayed there for nine weeks. Its dominant

features were a chorus shouting, "Let's go trippin'!" at the start, Dale's trebly, glissando-rich guitar lines spitting out the melody, and a wailing saxophone solo from one of the Del-Tones, Dale's backing band. In November 1962, Del-Tone released an album, *Surfer's Choice*, recorded live in the studio, that cemented Dale's image and sound. "He's the choice of surfers all over Southern California and all over the world because he's one of them. He plays their kind of music and surfs right along side of them," say the uncredited liner notes; the cover and two photos on the back of the album depict Dale riding a wave with the same panache he brings to his musicianship. Then the music speaks: It's a relentless, unforgiving assault, full of exuberant war whoops; ferocious drumming; razor-edged, double-picked guitar, heavy on treble; piano interludes that have a honky-tonk feel; and ballsy sax retorts to Dale's guitar juggernaut. *Surfer's Choice* contains Dale's most famous song, but in a version quite different from the one that found new life as the vibrant opening track of Quentin Tarantino's 1994 film *Pulp Fiction*. "Misirlou Twist" features violins screaming in response to Dale's breakneck picking, surging orchestral sections that add a Wagnerian grandeur, and a chorus of horns blaring in the background. The "Misirlou" of *Pulp Fiction* fame was released as a single in May 1962 and became a #1 single in Los Angeles in early 1963. In "Let's Go Trippin' " and *Surfer's Choice*, surf music found its genesis; in "Misirlou," its instrumental masterpiece.

Dale's second album, *King of the Surf Guitar* (not to be confused with the Rhino overview listed in the above discography), includes a swinging take of Leiber and Stoller's "Kansas City" and a rough-and-ready workout on Ray Charles' "What I Say." For the folkies, Dale delivered a tender reading of "Sloop John B" on *Surfer's Choice*; his country roots began showing on *King of the Surf Guitar*—"You Are My Sunshine" and "Riders in the Sky" are on the same album that featured one of his fiercest vocals, on Hoyt Axton's "Greenback Dollar," another folk standard, and a brisk rendition of "Hava Nagila," a "Misirlou"-like exploration of Middle Eastern melody.

Dale's audience was a niche group—he never sold albums or singles in numbers even remotely comparable to the Beach Boys and Jan and Dean. In 1965, after five albums and diminishing commercial appeal in the wake of the British Invasion, Dale walked away from the music business. A year later, he was diagnosed with rectal cancer and given only a few months to live. Surviving against all odds, he set out on a program of personal growth—embracing issues such as environmentalism and endangered species while also nourishing his own burgeoning spirituality—and eventually began performing again, in 1970, with a new group of Del-Tones backing him. In 1975, he rerecorded some of his early classics for GNP Crescendo, on an album released as *Greatest Hits.* Having lost nary a step during his self-imposed retirement, Dale's playing was rich and expressive as ever. However, he was more than 10 years past the original recordings of many of the songs, and had retooled several of them with radically new arrangements. The "Misirlou" here, for example, bears little resemblance to the original single or album-track cuts from 1961, and Dale's singing is a bit more restrained than it had been; "Sloop John B." sounds fairly tepid in comparison to the *Surfer's Choice* version.

Two excellent compilations of the classic Dale performances from the '60s are available on Rhino. *King of the Surf Guitar: The Best of Dick Dale & His Del-Tones* from 1989 offers 16 tracks covering the 1961– 1964 era; throws in a rare promotional-only 12-inch track from 1986, "One Double One Oh!"; and closes with a spectacular version of "Pipeline," the Chantays' surf classic, that Dale recorded with the late Stevie Ray Vaughan in 1987 for the *Back to the Beach* soundtrack. Otherwise, the fare is strictly vintage, from *Surfer's Choice* and *King of the Surf Guitar,* primarily: "Let's Go Trippin'," "Misirlou," "Surf Beat," "King of the Surf Guitar" (with background vocals by the Blossoms, whose membership included Darlene Love), "Hava Nagila," "The Wedge," "Mr. Eliminator"—the lingua franca of surf music, in short.

In 1997, Rhino released a more ambitious Dick Dale overview via *Better Shred Than Dead: The Dick Dale Anthology.* Featuring 39 cuts on two discs plus a detailed booklet recounting Dale's life and career and valuable session info, the set includes, from the early years, the Del-Fi demo that became his first Del-Tone single, "Ooh-Whee Marie," and two other rare early Del-Tone singles; and from the later years, several choice cuts from Dale's '90s studio albums for High Tone and Beggars Banquet, along with some cuts from the now-deleted 1983 live album, *The Tiger's Loose,* and an album-closing treat by way of "In-Liner (Surf Beat '97)," a song Dale wrote and recorded for the CD-ROM game *Rocket Jockey.*

A year before *Pulp Fiction* revived his career, Dale made some noise on his own with a formidable return to the recording studio for *Tribal Thunder;* his work for the past decade has been remarkably consistent. As Dale himself would say: Pray for surf!   —D.M.

Evan Dando

   ★★   Live at the Brattle Theatre/Griffith Sunset (Modular, 2001)
  ★★★   Baby I'm Bored (Bar None, 2003)

A grievous, grievous angel is he. When the Lemonheads' final record, *Car Button Cloth,* converged with alt-rock's 1996 nosedive, our erstwhile Lemonhead was well on his way to becoming a legendary crackhead. Fans of his sweet, deceptively simple (some say just simple, or even saccharine) melodies worried about him the same way fans of Elliott Smith's doomed love poems rightly doubted their hopeless troubadour's ability to say when. For much of the latter half of the decade, Dando was nowhere to be found. When he showed up on a New York stage with Giant Sand and Vic Chesnutt in 2000, many in the audience gasped. That night, Dando treated the crowd to a rusty but still sexy baritone, moving tentatively through some tunes from his upcoming record, whose title would mock the glamour of fame, the mystery of his absence, and the Dionysian promise of drugs: *Baby I'm Bored.*

His first official release, though, was a live-show recording, 2001's *Live at the Brattle Theatre/Griffith Sunset,* which contained a few Lemonheads favorites, some works-in-progress, and covers like Victoria Williams' "Frying Pan" and the Louvin Brothers' "My Baby's Gone." On *Bored,* released in 2003, the songs—lushly midwifed by producer Bryce Goggin— can be quite lovely, though anyone who was expecting the alt-pop of yore probably had his own boredom issues to contend with here. The disc drifts into Elliott Smith solipsism on fragments like "Why Do You Do This to Yourself?" But the twisty narcissism of songs with titles like "The Same Thing You've Thought Hard About Is the Same Part I Can Live Without" prove that Dando's own brand of wicked deprecation is still in effect. The collaborations with Ben Lee, "Hard Drive" and "All My Life," have a kind of mundane grace that nods to both the serenity and teetering frustration of life off the pipe.   —L.S.

D'Angelo

  ★★★★   Brown Sugar (EMI, 1995)
  ★★★★   Voodoo (Virgin, 2000)

D'Angelo seemed like the perfect R&B loverman for a generation raised on rap music. The Virginian had the voice of a Sam Cooke or a Donny Hathaway, yet delivered his songs with considerable swagger. A classicist, in other words, cloaked in the guise of a hip-hop roughneck. "Brown Sugar," for example, passed itself off as a love ode, even though it was actually serenading weed, an old hip-hop trick. For most of his debut album, D'Angelo sticks to genuine love songs, a genre in which he's stunningly fluent. "Lady," "Cruisin'," and the imaginatively titled "Me and Those Dreamin' Eyes of Mine" are masterpieces, eyes-shut pleas for a romance that good, and oh, so bad.

D'Angelo's second album, *Voodoo,* isn't a collection of songs so much as one elongated mood piece. It's a fitting result, considering that the album was the product of more than a year of late-night sessions at New York's legendary Electric Lady Studios, during which D'Angelo collaborated with a who's who of '90s soul music: drummer Ahmir "?uestlove" Thompson, bassist Pino Palladino, songwriter/guitarist Raphael Saadiq, producer James Poyser (other guests include Roy Hargrove, Charlie Hunter, and Q-Tip). Apart from "Left & Right," which features guest verses from Method Man and Redman, *Voodoo* is seamless. From the DJ Premier–produced "Devil's Pie" and the fiery, nasty "Chicken Grease" (where D comes off like a minimalist Prince) to the deliciously understated "Untitled (How Does It Feel)," D'Angelo achieves through nuance what some singers with decades of experience and training never achieve: a throbbing, vital presence that demands attention, even as it shuns it. —J.C.

Olu Dara

  ★★★½ In the World: From Natchez to New York
           (Atlantic, 1999)
  ★★★ Neighborhoods (Atlantic, 2001)

For more than 20 years, the trumpet player and singer Olu Dara was a fixture on the New York cutting-edge jazz scene: Recording only sporadically under his own name, he contributed to important works by Henry Threadgill and David Murray. Dara's bell-ringing tone and intense melodic sense separated him from all others in the frenetic world of free jazz.

And then in 1999, the Natchez, MS, native recorded a different kind of album with the band he'd quietly led for years, the Okra Orchestra: *In the World* celebrates all kinds of African-American music, from chanting Delta blues to tony cocktail-lounge swing. It was musically vital and extraordinarily sensual—in one much-heard refrain, Dara proclaims, "Your lips, your lips are juicy"—and helped Dara to establish a broader audience, one that wanted to hear him sing more than play trumpet. The followup, *Neighborhoods,* mined similar territory, but despite several spirited performances (notably the title track and the Latin-flavored "Massamba"), it proved to be less uniformly engaging. —T.M.

Terence Trent D'Arby

  ★★★½ Introducing the Hardline According to
           Terence Trent D'Arby (Columbia, 1987)
  ★★★½ Neither Fish Nor Flesh (Columbia, 1989)
  ★★★★ Symphony or Damn (Columbia, 1993)
  ★★½ Vibrator (Work, 1995)
  ★★★ Wild Card (Compendio, 2001)

It's tough to recall just how famous Terence Trent D'Arby was supposed to be. He was the great post-everything soul hope, a black American living in England with a Napoleonic sense of pop destiny, Eurotrash pretensions, and really amazing plaited braids. Packaged as a shiny new Prince at a time when one didn't seem nearly enough, this dude was slated to be more popular than Jesus. You might have noticed this didn't really come to pass, although the guy is no less (but no more) brilliant now than he was then.

Columbia probably suspected something was up with his first album title, *Introducing the Hardline According to Terence Trent D'Arby.* A pastiche of Europop slickness, soulman croon, and mild funk, *Introducing* is just dripping with look-ladies-no-hands ambition. In fact, the ambition is all you hear in spots; his Sam Cookeish voice is spotless, but most of songs ("If You Let Me Stay," "Rain") bounce right past. Ballsy enough to include a five-minute a cappella tune called "As Yet Unnamed," an excellent Smokey Robinson cover ("Who's Lovin' You"), and two terrific singles. "Wishing Well," with its sex-shuffle rhythm and whistling hook, is a keeper, but the man's finest hour is "Sign Your Name," a slow burner that smolders like Sade and that got hands under blouses at middle school dances the nation over.

Unimpressed with market validation and looking to make an even grander statement, D'Arby turned his ambitions up to deafening levels and released the semibaffling *Neither Fish Nor Flesh* two years later. An overtly experimental, cranky mishmash that makes the Beatles' White Album look precision-tooled, *Neither Fish* can't concentrate D'Arby's obvious talents on a single musical idea for more than one tune. Song by song, the uneven collection has aged fairly well, considering the drubbing it took at the time. But as an album, *Fish* meanders, moving from unfortunate Staxish soul ("I'll Be Alright") to a sharply realized schoolboy R&B tune about AIDS ("Billy Don't Fall") to rockabilly riffs and "To Know Someone Deeply Is to Know Someone Softly," a frictionless slice of bedroom soul R. Kelly has clearly listened to about a million times. Some critics found his scope visionary if diffuse, and his voice still aces, but most of *Hardline*'s fan base were flummoxed by the thing and moved on with their lives.

D'Arby took some time off to figure out where it all went horribly wrong and returned with *Symphony or Damn.* Neither a techno-fish nor entirely flesh, less ditzy yet still diverse, *Symphony* hangs together quite well, finding voice and focus for his neon messiah complexes. "Penelope Please" holds on to 17 as long as he can, "Turn the Page" uses the Funky Drummer break in the service of blissful Britpop, and he even scored a minor hit with the glammy is-he-talking-about-a-blowjob-or-what? rocker "She Kissed Me." And yet, the masses stayed away in droves.

1995's *Vibrator* is dedicated to Muhammad Ali and "all the underappreciated giants still in our midst like for example Todd Rundgren, Bobby Womack, and Kate Bush," rendering reviews pretty much moot. It's more of *Symphony*'s chromium soul rock—the guy's pretty much found a sound he likes—but for the first time a D'Arby album sounds samey and indistinct; *Vibrator* swings the pendulum of eclecticism too far back. *Symphony* if you do or damned if you don't, I guess.

Unless someone figures out how to get people to shell out for his often limitless talents—or he starts producing albums for other, hipper people, preferably young women—all that's left for TTD is a *Behind the Music* and a box set. And one final thought: Lauryn Hill, pay very close attention to how this man's career has played out. Consider yourself warned.   —J.G.

Bobby Darin

★★★½	Bobby Darin (1958; Atlantic, 1994)
★★★½	That's All (1959; Atlantic, 1994)
★★★½	This Is Darin (1960; Atlantic, 1994)
★★★★	The 25th Day of December (1960; Atlantic, 1997)
★★★	Darin at the Copa (1961; Atlantic, 1994)
★★★	The Bobby Darin Story (1961; Atlantic, 1990)
★★★½	Earthy/Golden Folk Hits (1963; Exemplar, 2002)
★★★½	You're the Reason I'm Living/18 Yellow Roses (1963; Exemplar, 2002)
★★★½	From Hello Dolly to Goodbye Charlie/Venice Blue (1964, 1965; Exemplar, 2002)
★★★	Greatest Hits (Curb, 1985)
★★★★	The Ultimate Bobby Darin (Warner Bros., 1988)
★★★★	Capitol Collectors Series (Capitol, 1989)
★★★½	Splish Splash: The Best of Bobby Darin, Vol. I (Atco, 1991)
★★★½	Mack the Knife: The Best of Bobby Darin, Vol. 2 (Atco, 1991)
★★★★★	As Long as I'm Singing: The Bobby Darin Collection (Rhino, 1995)
★★★½	Great Gentlemen of Song: Spotlight on Bobby Darin (Capitol, 1995)
★★★½	A&E Biography: Bobby Darin—A Musical Anthology (Capitol, 1998)
★★★★	Wild Cool & Swingin' (Capitol, 1999)
★★★½	If I Were a Carpenter: The Very Best of Bobby Darin 1966–1969 (Varèse Sarabande, 1999)
★★★	Swingin' the Standards (Varèse Sarabande, 1999)
★★★★	The Hit Singles Collection (Rhino, 2002)

with Johnny Mercer

★★★	Two of a Kind: Bobby Darin & Johnny Mercer (1961; Atco, 1990)

On its surface, Bobby Darin's is one of the strangest, saddest stories in popular music. Restless and driven, the man born Walden Robert Cassotto in the Bronx hit the upper reaches of the pop charts in 1958 with the novelty ditty "Splish Splash" and stayed on the charts steadily through 1967. His only #1 came in 1959, and stayed at the top for nine weeks straight, with a swinging interpretation of Brecht-Weill's "Mack the Knife" that exuded Rat Pack ring-a-ding-ding brio. That hit provided his entrée into adult pop and the Vegas circuit, where he became one of the town's most popular draws through the remainder of the ensuing decade. When Ray Charles fused country and R&B on his 1963 LP, *Modern Sounds in Country & Western Music,* Darin followed suit with a #3 single in the same vein, "You're the Reason I'm Living," and his own experiment with various fusions involving country music. But that same year, he positioned himself in the vanguard of the folk-rock movement, assembling a band that included future Byrds founder Roger McGuinn on guitar.

Given the temper of the times—with the civil rights movement hitting its apex, a growing awareness among the general public of a debacle brewing in Southeast Asia, and more musical artists dissenting in song—Darin, who was seen in some critical quarters as an opportunist with regard to his stylistic flip-flopping, was genuinely moved by the day's rampant suffering, intolerance, and violence (an early supporter of Rev. Dr. Martin Luther King Jr., he participated in the 1965 march from Selma to Montgomery, AL; and he stood a seven-hour vigil at the grave of the assassinated Robert F. Kennedy). In response, he turned inward musically, his repertoire blossoming with spirituals, protest songs, and literate, sensitive songs about love and relationships. Bob Dylan's "Blowin' in the Wind" and "I'll Be Your Baby Tonight" were in the mix, as well as Oscar Brown Jr.'s "Work Song," several stirring Tim Hardin songs (one of which, 1966's "If I Were a Carpenter," was Darin's last Top 10 hit), John Sebastian's "Lovin' You" and "Darling Be Home Soon," and not least of all, a clutch of his own well-crafted folk-pop originals, including, in 1969, one of the most effective and subtle topical songs of the era, "Simple Song of Freedom."

On record, Darin was tremendously effective, no matter what style he was into at the time. But in public, his frequent image changes made him seem not so much authentic as desperate for attention. As the protest movement heated up in the '60s, he ditched his suits, ties, and clean-cut mien for long hair, facial hair, blue jeans, paisley shirts, and beads. He wasn't old—he was only 30 in 1966—but in his new guise, he gave off the desperate air of an aging hipster willing to endure any humiliation for one more crack at the charts. Eventually he returned to his original incarnation as a classic pop singer, donned the stylish suits once more, signed with Motown, and in 1973, landed his own short-lived TV variety series. Afflicted with a rheumatic heart since childhood, Darin died in 1973, during open-heart surgery. Posthumously, friends have said that if Darin's career drive sometimes veered into desperation, then it was because his heart condition had made him more aware of his own mortality and the need to make the most of what he was sure would be a short life. Indeed, Bobby Darin was only 37 years old at the time of his passing.

A Musical Anthology, the companion disc to the A&E network's biography of Darin, features a good sampling of the artist in his many guises, the highlights being live versions of "18 Yellow Roses" and "If I Were a Carpenter," a bit of soul strutting in "(Your Love Keeps Lifting Me) Higher and Higher," and some classic pop forays into "The Good Life" and "Call Me Irresponsible." *Swingin' the Standards* announces its content and approach in its title, but the actual songs are something else again: a stunning reading of the Tom Jones–Harvey Schmidt evergreen from the off-Broadway play *The Fantasticks,* "Try to Remember"; Leslie Bricusse's "Talk to the Animals"; Sammy Cahn and Jimmy Van Heusen's "Everybody Has the Right to Be Wrong," and others of this caliber. The material is from the Atlantic years.

And not least of all—in fact, most definitively—is the superb four-disc box set from Rhino, *As Long as I'm Singing: The Bobby Darin Collection,* which is divided into one disc from "The Rock & Roll Years," two volumes of "The Pop Years," and a fourth focused on "The Folk & Country Years." It's an exhilarating look at the entirety of Darin's career, with all his label associations (save Motown) represented, demo and live versions of "Simple Song of Freedom," and a live version of Dylan's "I'll Be Your Baby Tonight," along with the usual impeccable and thorough annotation common to Rhino boxes. Seven years after the box set's release, Rhino issued the 20-track *Hit Singles Collection,* which, along with Warner Bros.' *The Ultimate Bobby Darin,* comprises two concise overviews of Darin's hit recordings for Atlantic. In the end, it says a lot about Darin's artistry to observe that a listener could cherry-pick from his current discography and not find a mediocre album. Darin always brimmed with confidence, but if he were still with us, even he might be surprised at how good he was through all those years and styles. —D.M.

The Darkness

★★★½ Permission to Land (Atlantic, 2003)

The Darkness burst out of Norfolk, England, in 2003 with a party-hearty anthem called "I Believe in a Thing Called Love," a slightly retro barn burner full of huge-ass guitars and Justin Hawkins' Tiny Tim–worthy falsetto shrieks. Like many turn-of-the-century hard-rock revivalists, this British quartet is immersed in the one-two punch of AC/DC and early Queen, but *Permission to Land* is no irony-damaged novelty. Songs such as "Get Your Hands Off My Woman" and "Givin' Up" display industrial-strength riffs, vigorous hammer-on guitar solos, and a rhythm section that swings like a wrecking ball. —R.K.

Dashboard Confessional

★★★★ The Swiss Army Romance (Drive Thru/Fiddler, 2000)

★★★★ The Places You Have Come to Fear the Most (Vagrant, 2001)

★★★ MTV Unplugged 2.0 (Vagrant, 2002)

★★★ A Mark, a Mission, a Brand, a Scar (Vagrant, 2003)

Dashboard Confessional is a band, but it's easy to use the name to cover the cult of personality of just one man: singer/songwriter Chris Carrabba. Taking cues from the more confessional and personal vein of '90s indie punk, known somewhat derisively as "emo," Carrabba turned the idea into a one-man cottage industry of sad-boy folk-punk numbers. His debut, *The Swiss Army Romance,* is an intimate, almost claustrophobically tight album. The odd background vocal disrupts Carrabba's reverie, but it's almost exclusively his therapy session. Clearly, Carrabba's never met a woman he didn't alienate, or whom he wasn't alienated by, or both. "You're dying to look cute in your blue jeans," he gripes on the title track, "but you're plastic just like everyone/You're just like everyone." And so it goes. Carrabba sings with a piercingly clear whine, infecting all his ramblings with an accent of desperation, whether it's getting overwhelmed by the detritus of love lost ("Living in Your Letters") or driving home, stewing in his own pain ("The Sharp Hint of New Tears").

With the addition of Sunny Day Real Estate bassist Dan Bonebrake to the lineup, Dashboard Confessional sounded more powerful on its second album, *The Places You Have Come to Fear the Most.* And thanks to the breakout single "Screaming Infidelities" (reworked from the debut), people outside the band's dedicated, Internet-centric emo fan base were able to channel Carrabba. What they found was even more fatal femmes—women who lie, cheat, and run away without explaining why. On "The Good Fight," "The Best Deceptions," and "Saints and Sailors," Carrabba bleeds anguish, creating some of the most plainspoken and effective music for catharsis in recent memory.

Dashboard Confessional's music is nothing short of fanatical in nature, so it's not surprising that the band has fostered an unusually fervent fan base of disaffected teens. Those acolytes came out in full force for Dashboard Confessional's taping of MTV's *Unplugged,* creating easily the most interactive session the program has ever seen. On the recording, a wailing Carrabba encourages the audience members to shout their pain along with him, and on many of the songs, they chant along so loudly that Carrabba steps away from the mike. Their hurt matters just as much as his.

The adoration of scores of lovelorn teens didn't guarantee major-label success for Carrabba, though. *A Mark, a Mission, a Brand, a Scar,* the first fruit of a strategic alliance between his label Vagrant and Interscope, traded his earlier albums' intimacy for radioready soundscapes. "Hands Down," which scored big on an earlier EP, sounds drowned in feedback here, as does much of the album. The quiet tunefulness that had been Carrabba's stock-in-trade was mostly gone, and while songs like "Carry This Picture" and "Ghost of a Good Thing" sport his trademark wordy-yeteffective melodies, they're not enough to keep the album afloat. —J.C.

Miles Davis

★★★½ Timeless (1945; Savoy, 2002)
★★★ Bopping the Blues (1946; Black Lion, 1987)
★★★★★ Birth of the Cool (1949–50; Capitol, 2001)
★★★½ Miles Davis and Horns (1951; Prestige, 1989)
★★★★ Dig (1951; Prestige, 1991)
★★★ Our Delight (1952; Prestige, 1992)
★★★★ Miles Davis, Vol. 1 (1952–54; Blue Note, 1988)
★★★★½ Miles Davis, Vol. 2 (1953; Blue Note, 1990)
★★★★½ Collector's Items (1953, 1956; Prestige, 1987)
★★★★ Blue Haze (1953–54; Prestige, 1988)
★★★ At Last! (1953; Contemporary, 1985)
★★★★ Bags Groove (1954; Prestige, 1987)
★★★★ Walkin' (1954; Prestige, 1987)
★★★★ Quintet/Sextet (1955; Prestige, 1990)
★★★½ Blue Moods (1955; Debut, 1990)
★★★½ Musings of Miles (1955; Prestige, 1997)
★★★★ The New Miles Davis Quintet (1955; Prestige, 1982)
★★★★★ Cookin' With the Miles Davis Quintet (1956; Prestige, 1993)
★★★★★ Relaxin' With Miles (1956; Prestige, 1994)

★★★★★ Workin' With the Miles Davis Quintet (1956; Prestige, 1987)
★★★★½ Steamin' With the Miles Davis Quintet (1956; Prestige, 1994)
★★★★ L'Ascenseur pour L'Échafaud (1957; Philips, 1989)
★★★★ Compact Jazz (1951; 1957–58; Philips, 1989)
★★★★★ 'Round About Midnight (1955; Columbia/Legacy, 2001)
★★★★½ Miles Ahead (1957; Columbia/Legacy, 1997)
★★★½ Jazz Showcase (1958; Prestige, 1994)
★★★★ Milestones (1958; Columbia/Legacy, 2001)
★★★ At Newport 1958 (Columbia/Legacy, 2001)
★★★★★ Porgy and Bess (1958; Columbia/Legacy, 1997)
★★★★ '58 Sessions (1958; Columbia/Legacy, 1991)
★★★★½ Jazz at the Plaza (1958; Columbia/Legacy, 2001)
★★★★★ Kind of Blue (1959; Columbia/Legacy, 1997)
★★★½ Live in Stockholm (with Sonny Stitt) (1960; Secret, 1989)
★★★★★ Sketches of Spain (1960; Columbia/Legacy, 1997)
★★★★ Someday My Prince Will Come (1961; Columbia/Legacy, 1999)
★★★★ In Person: Friday Night at the Blackhawk (1961; Columbia/Legacy, 1988)
★★★★ In Person: Saturday Night at the Blackhawk (1961; Columbia/Legacy, 1989)
★★★★½ Miles Davis at Carnegie Hall: The Complete Concert (1961; Columbia/Legacy, 1998)
★★½ Quiet Nights (1963; Columbia/Legacy, 1997)
★★★★ Seven Steps to Heaven (1963; Columbia/Legacy, 1992)
★★★★ Miles Davis in Europe (Columbia/Legacy, 1963)
★★★★ The Complete Concert, 1964: My Funny Valentine and "Four" and More (1964; Columbia/Legacy 1992)
★★★★ Miles In Tokyo (1964; Sony Japan, 1996)
★★★★ Miles In Berlin (1964; Sony Japan, 1996)
★★★★ Heard 'Round the World (1964; Columbia/Legacy, 1983)
★★★★½ ESP (1965; Columbia/Legacy, 1991)
★★★½ Cookin' at the Plugged Nickel (1965; Columbia/Legacy, 1987)
★★★★★ The Complete Live at the Plugged Nickel (1965; Columbia/Legacy, 1995)
★★★★ Highlights From the Plugged Nickel (1965; Columbia/Legacy, 1996)
★★★★ Miles Smiles (1966; Columbia/Legacy, 1992)
★★★½ Sorcerer (1967; Columbia/Legacy, 1993)
★★★★★ Nefertiti (1967; Columbia/Legacy, 1990)

★★★½ Water Babies (1967–68; Columbia/Legacy, 2002)

★★★½ Miles in the Sky (1968; Columbia/Legacy, 1993)

★★★★½ Filles de Kilimanjaro (1968; Columbia/Legacy, 2002)

★★★★★ In a Silent Way (1969; Columbia/Legacy, 2002)

★★★★½ Greatest Hits (1955–63; Columbia/Legacy, 1969)

★★★★★ Bitches Brew (1969; Columbia/Legacy, 1999)

★★★★ 1969 Miles: Festiva de Juan Pins (1969; Sony Japan, 1993)

★★★★★ A Tribute to Jack Johnson (1970; Columbia/Legacy, 1992)

★★★ At Fillmore: Live at the Fillmore East (1970; Columbia Legacy, 1997)

★★★ Black Beauty: Live at the Fillmore West (1970; Columbia Legacy, 1997)

★★★★½ Live/Evil (1970; Columbia/Legacy, 1997)

★★★½ On the Corner (1972; Columbia/Legacy, 2000)

★★★½ In Concert: Live at Philharmonic Hall (1973; Columbia/Legacy, 1997)

★★★ Big Fun (1974; Columbia/Legacy, 2000)

★★★★ Get Up With It (1974; Columbia/Legacy, 2000)

★★★½ Dark Magus (1974; Columbia/Legacy, 1997)

★★★★★ Pangaea (1975; Columbia/Legacy, 1990)

★★★★½ Agharta (1975; Columbia/Legacy, 1991)

★★★★ Circle in the Round (1955–70; Columbia/Legacy, 1979)

★★★★ Directions (1960–70; Columbia/Legacy, 1981)

★★★½ The Man With the Horn (Columbia/Legacy, 1981)

★★★★ Miles! Miles! Miles! Live in Japan 1981 (1981; Sony Japan, 1993)

★★★★ We Want Miles (Columbia/Legacy, 1982)

★★★½ Star People (Columbia/Legacy, 1983)

★★★★ Decoy (Columbia/Legacy, 1984)

★★★★½ Aura (1984; Columbia/Legacy, 1989)

★★★ You're Under Arrest (Columbia/Legacy, 1985)

★★★★½ The Columbia Years 1955–85 (1988; Columbia/Legacy, 2001)

★★★½ Miles Davis and the Modern Jazz Giants (1951–56; Prestige, 1986)

★★★★ Tutu (Warner Bros., 1986)

★★★★½ Siesta (Warner Bros., 1987)

★★★★★ Chronicle: The Complete Prestige Recordings (1951–56; Prestige, 1987)

★★★★ Ballads (Columbia/Legacy, 1988)

★★★ Amandla (Warner Bros., 1989)

★★½ Dingo (with Michel Legrand) (Warner Bros., 1991)

★★★★★ Miles Davis and the Jazz Giants (Prestige, 1991)

★★ Doo-Bop (Warner Bros., 1992)

★★★½ The Best of the Capitol and Blue Note Years (Blue Note, 1992)

★★★★★ Live at Montreux (Warner Bros., 1993)

★★★★ Live Around the World (1988–90; Warner Bros., 1996)

★★★★ Ballads & Blues (1952–58; Blue Note, 1996)

★★★★ Miles Davis & Gil Evans: The Complete Columbia Studio Recordings (1957–62; Columbia/Legacy, 1996)

★★★★½ The Best of Miles Davis & Gil Evans (Columbia/Legacy, 1996)

★★★★ This Is Jazz #8: Acoustic (Columbia/Legacy, 1996)

★★★ Bluing (1951–56; Prestige, 1996)

★★★ This Is Jazz #22: Miles Davis Plays Ballads (Columbia/Legacy, 1997)

★★½ This Is Jazz #38: Electric (Columbia/Legacy, 1998)

★★★★★ The Miles Davis Quintet, 1965–68: The Complete Columbia Studio Recordings (Columbia/Legacy, 1998)

★★★★ The Best of the Miles Davis Quintet (Columbia/Legacy, 1998)

★★★½ Jazz Profile (Blue Note, 1998)

★★★★★ The Complete Bitches Brew Sessions (Columbia/Legacy, 1999)

★★★ Panthalassa: The Remixes (Columbia/Legacy, 1999)

★★★½ Love Songs (Columbia/Legacy, 1999)

★★★★★ Miles Davis & John Coltrane: The Complete Columbia Recordings, 1955–1961 (Columbia/Legacy, 2000)

★★★ Blue Miles (Columbia/Legacy, 2000)

★★★★½ Ken Burns's Jazz (Sony, 2000)

★★★★½ Live at the Fillmore East (March 7, 1970) (Columbia/Legacy, 2001)

★★★½ The Best of Miles Davis & John Coltrane (Columbia/Legacy, 2001)

★★½ The Complete Vocalist Sessions (1947–1957; Definitive, 2001) Import

★★★★★ The Essential Miles Davis (Columbia/Legacy, 2001)

★★★½ Super Hits (Columbia/Legacy, 2001)

★★★ The Complete In a Silent Way Sessions (Columbia/Legacy, 2001)

★★★ Blue Moods (Columbia/Legacy, 2002)

★★★★★ The Best of Miles Davis (Columbia/Legacy, 2002)

★★★★ The Complete Miles Davis at Montreux: 1973–91 (Columbia/Legacy, 2002)

★★★   Love Songs 2 (Columbia/Legacy, 2003)
★★★★   In Person Friday and Saturday Nights at the Blackhawk, Complete (Columbia/Legacy, 2003)
★★★★½   The Complete Jack Johnson Sessions (Columbia/Legacy, 2003)
★★★½   Birdland 1951 (Blue Note, 2004)

Inarguably one of the two or three most important jazz musicians who ever lived, Miles Davis started out at the top and managed to stay there for the rest of his 46-year career. As a soloist, his ideas were startlingly original and his tone utterly unmistakable; as a leader, he often recognized talent well before anyone else, and knew how to get the most out of almost any sideman.

But it was as a stylist that Davis had his greatest impact. Most jazzmen are lucky if they can be linked to even a single formal breakthrough; Davis can be credited with several. After the teenage trumpeter graduated from Charlie Parker's groundbreaking quintet, he turned bebop's frenetic virtuosity on its head with an acerbic series of small-group recordings introducing what came to be known as "cool" jazz. A few years later, he and his quintet had swapped cool's languid lyricism for a tougher, more intense sound, and were acknowledged leaders in the hard-bop movement. Next came his embrace of modality, which shifted his improvisational emphasis from the chord-based approach of bebop to a scale-based strategy similar to that of Indian classical music. And then, after being among the first to incorporate electric instruments in a jazz rhythm section, he abandoned the music's traditional dependence on swing and began working with rock- and funk-based rhythms, thus setting the groundwork for such fusion bands as Weather Report, Return to Forever, and the Mahavishnu Orchestra.

Like Louis Armstrong and Charlie Parker, his importance was as much social as it was musical. The son of a St. Louis dentist, Davis was born into the African-American professional class, and brought a sense of purpose and intellectual rigor to jazz that made it easy for listeners and critics to see the music as being just as "serious" as the symphony. At the same time, Davis never shied away from the coarser, "street" aspects of African-American culture, and would happily show off his newest Italian suit with a practiced pimp strut. This duality—for instance, being as obsessed with Stockhausen as he was with Sly & the Family Stone—made Davis both an inspiration and an enigma to generations of musicians.

Like most jazzmen, Davis began his career as a sideman. He had played in Billy Eckstine's big band and Charlie Parker's quintet before making his recording debut in 1945 with saxophonist Herbie Fields, a session that would likely have been forgotten had Davis not become so famous later (it may be found on the import collection *The Complete Vocalist Sessions*). The first sides issued under Davis' own name are to be found on *Timeless*. Cut with Parker and a rhythm section featuring John Lewis and Max Roach, its basic form is straight bebop, but the young trumpeter's voice can already be heard in its adventurous writing and measured phrasing. It's far preferable to *Bopping the Blues*, a sideman date finding Davis blowing blues obbligatos behind singers Earl Coleman and Ann Baker.

Still, the sessions that made Davis' reputation as a leader are the ones collected under the title *Birth of the Cool*. Using either an octet or nonet, Davis and arranger Gil Evans generated a sound that conveys the coloristic range of a big band while maintaining a chamber music sense of dynamics. Moreover, because the playing manages to employ all the harmonic sophistication of bebop while trading instrumental flash for a more leisurely, contemplative approach to soloing, it produced jazz that was far closer to the depth and consideration of art music than anything that had gone before. Although the recordings hardly marked a commercial breakthrough on Davis' part, their influence was incalculable, as groups ranging from the Modern Jazz Quartet to the Gerry Mulligan/Chet Baker quartet to Stan Kenton and his Orchestra all learned from them.

Ironically, the Davis nonet existed only for the *Cool* project, which, like most of his early-'50s output, was the product of one-off recording sessions. The same is true of the boppish Blue Note dates compiled as *Volume One* and *Volume Two*, and the deliciously unconventional *Blue Haze*, recorded with Charles Mingus. Even Davis' recordings for Prestige, the label that was more or less his home in the early '50s, were varied and episodic. That had its advantages, though. Given the tension between Davis and Thelonious Monk evident on the sessions they cut together (included, variously, on *Bags Groove*, *Miles Davis and the Jazz Giants*, and various anthologies over the years), it would be difficult to imagine them coexisting in a working band, but the fire in these recordings will make most listeners glad the two got together at least once. The all-inclusive *Chronicle* is perhaps the best way to tackle Davis' days with Prestige, since it includes all his sessions as a leader as well as four tunes recorded under Lee Konitz's name, and spares listeners the occasional redundancies that occur when buying the albums individually.

Those interested only in the highlights, however, should seek out *Dig*, recorded with the redoubtable Sonny Rollins on tenor, and then skip ahead to 1955, when Davis introduces saxophonist John Coltrane into his hard-bop quintet. Although Coltrane's contributions are relatively low-key on *The New Miles Davis Quintet,* his aggressive, questing solos offer a dynamic contrast to the acerbic economy of the trumpeter's own playing. Add the wry elegance of the rhythm section (Red Garland, Paul Chambers, and the incomparable Philly Joe Jones), and these albums—*Cookin', Relaxin', Workin',* and *Steamin'*—constitute the best of his work for that label.

This version of the quintet followed Davis when he moved to Columbia Records and can be heard on the lovely *'Round About Midnight.* But the album that truly introduces Davis' Columbia period is *Miles Ahead,* which featured a large ensemble under the direction of Davis' old *Birth of the Cool* collaborator Gil Evans. Theirs was an uncommonly sympathetic pairing, for Evans' coloristic approach to arranging brought out the best in Davis' dark, warm tone (particularly when the trumpeter switched to flugelhorn), while Evans' inventive voicings seemed to inspire Davis to ever more brilliant improvisations. Together, they produced material for a half-dozen albums, and, apart from the halfhearted bossa nova of *Quiet Nights,* it's uniformly excellent. *Porgy and Bess,* a setting of selections from the Gershwin opera, was particularly popular in its time, but their masterwork is undoubtedly *Sketches of Spain,* a work of unparalleled grace and lyricism. (A concert rendition of its "Concierto de Aranjuez" appears on *Miles Davis at Carnegie Hall.*) *Miles Davis/Gil Evans: The Complete Columbia Studio Recordings* augments the original albums with exquisite outtakes, plus enough rehearsal material to underscore just how exacting a bandleader Evans could be.

Davis continued his small group work, of course, adding alto saxophonist Cannonball Adderley on *Milestones* and *At Newport 1958,* and replacing Kelly and Jones with, respectively, pianist Bill Evans and drummer James Cobb for the *'58 Sessions.* (Davis also appears as a sideman on Adderley's *Somethin' Else* at this time.) Splendid as these albums are, though, they seem minor when compared to *Kind of Blue,* perhaps the greatest jazz album of its era. To begin with, Davis conceived the session as an act of revolution, moving away from the chord-based improvisation that had served him (and almost everyone else in jazz) since the birth of bebop. In its place, he introduces the concept of modal improvisation, in which the soloist works from a predetermined set of scales (a method not unrelated to the raga system of Indian classical music). But it isn't the theoretical breakthrough that makes this worth hearing—it's the charged spontaneity and elegant lyricism of the performances that

makes the album so continually rewarding. Even after a thousand replays, *Kind of Blue* remains startlingly vital.

Coltrane would spend the rest of his life refining the concepts introduced on that album, but he'd do it without Davis' help; the swinging and incisive *Someday My Prince Will Come* was his last album with the trumpeter, as Hank Mobley was added on tenor at that point (and he is the only saxophonist on the two *In Person* albums). *Miles Davis & John Coltrane: The Complete Columbia Recordings 1955–1961* is a deserved monument to what is generally considered Davis' "first" great quintet.

His second great quintet was on the horizon, but took some time to assemble. With *Seven Steps to Heaven* Davis replaced Mobley with the fleet-fingered George Coleman on tenor, and also brought in a new rhythm section, with Ron Carter on bass and either Victor Feldman and Frank Butler or Herbie Hancock and Tony Williams on piano and drums. It was the latter pair who stuck. Although much younger than Davis' previous cohorts (Hancock was 23, Carter 25, and Williams just 18), these three played with astonishing energy and insight, and the sheer physicality of their live work—as evinced by *Miles in Europe* and *The Complete Concert 1964: My Funny Valentine and "Four" & More*—is breathtaking.

Coleman's input was less consistently dazzling, although his best work recalls the fire of Coltrane. Saxophonist Sam Rivers added an interesting twist to *Miles in Tokyo,* but it wasn't until Art Blakey alumnus Wayne Shorter joined, on *Miles in Berlin,* that Davis found a saxophonist whose harmonic imagination matched his own. *Live at the Plugged Nickel* shows how Shorter fits into the format established with Coleman, though *The Complete Live at the Plugged Nickel*—which spreads two full nights of music over seven CDs— offers an excellent picture of how he and the others were more than happy to push those boundaries. From there, the music grows ever more daring, from the angularity of *E.S.P.* through the moody eloquence of *Nefertiti,* until it seems to tug at the very seams of mainstream jazz.

For some listeners, and indeed many musicians, this was as good as it got, and the fire and style delineated by these albums—and offered in chronological order in *The Miles Davis Quintet, 1965–68: The Complete Columbia Studio Recordings* box—has since been imitated by many others, from early Wynton Marsalis to Hancock's own *V.S.O.P.* recordings (with Shorter, Carter, Williams, and various trumpeters).

By the end of the '60s, however, Davis was eager to move on, and in particular to explore the possibilities posed by electric instruments and funk rhythms. *Miles in the Sky, Filles de Kilimanjaro,* and *Water Babies* mark the first steps, as electric guitar (courtesy of George Benson on *In the Sky*) and electric piano (played both by Hancock and the young Chick Corea) are added to the lineup, while the trancelike rhythmic patterns explored on *Nefertiti* are elongated. Davis wasn't the only one in the quintet itching to go electric: Williams (who was known as the band's resident Beatles fan) was also toying with rock instrumentation in his own band, Lifetime, while Hancock toyed with rock ideas in the music he contributed to the soundtrack for Michelangelo Antonioni's epochal meditation on swinging London, *Blow-Up.*

But Davis, as ever, was searching for something different. For *In a Silent Way,* he borrowed the young English guitarist John McLaughlin from Williams' Lifetime, and had the Austrian keyboardist Joe Zawinul (who had come to notice through Cannonball Adderley's combo) on electric organ. He replaced Carter with another Englishman, Dave Holland, and had both Hancock and Corea on electric piano. It was a big band, but the music wasn't especially loud, as its rambling, riff-based approach to composition was as prone to pastoral grace as to funky grooves. Moreover, as *The Complete In a Silent Way Sessions* make plain, Davis had also begun to take a more pop/rock approach to the recording studio. Where once his albums were more or less unvarnished documents of how his current group sounded, the sessions for *In a Silent Way* found him recording what were essentially experiments in sound, which his producer—composer Teo Macero—would then splice into album tracks. By pop standards, this was a totally reasonable way to make records, but it seemed near heretical by jazz standards.

In that sense, the contemporary listener has an enormous advantage over those who bought Davis' albums in the early '70s. They had only the finished albums to deal with, and at times, what Davis delivered—abrupt shifts in texture, odd electronic effects, an almost episodic sense of melody—seemed nearly impossible to apprehend by the normal rules of jazz. Tellingly, although the various "complete sessions" sets make it possible to hear the music as it was originally recorded, the full-length versions of pieces are seldom as compelling as the versions that were edited and spliced into existence by Macero.

In any case, there was no turning back for either Davis or his audience after *Bitches Brew.* Where *In a Silent Way* merely flirts with funk, *Bitches Brew* openly courts its rhythmic insistence. Naturally, the jazz community was in an uproar over the album, with some of the more conservative fans condemning Davis for having "abandoned" jazz. Yet even though *Bitches*

Brew was a commercial breakthrough for the trumpeter (it peaked at #35 on the *Billboard* album chart), it is by no means a pop record. Despite the funk grooves, Davis' compositions remained melodically oblique and harmonically challenging. (The import-only *1969 Miles: Festiva de Juan Pins,* recorded a month before the *Bitches Brew* sessions, is markedly more conservative.)

With *Bitches Brew,* Davis' career splits into two paths. On the one hand, there are his studio recordings, which involved a wide variety of musicians and which ranged from kaleidoscopic epics to texturally intriguing miniatures. On the other hand, there was his live band, which involved a relatively stable cadre of players and specialized in marathon performances of varying abstraction. As such, his studio albums of the early '70s—*A Tribute to Jack Johnson, Live/Evil, On the Corner, Big Fun, Get Up With It*—seem wildly experimental, portraying Davis as a musical chameleon. *Jack Johnson,* powered by drummer Billy Cobham and featuring an unusually aggressive McLaughlin, draws from R&B and hard rock, while *Live/Evil* presents the psychedelic side of Davis' band (just compare Keith Jarrett's gospel-schooled piano on "What I Say" to Bruce Hornsby's work with the Grateful Dead). *On the Corner* was abstract funk, like a 23rd-century Sly & the Family Stone, while *Get Up With It* found him viewing Africa and the Caribbean through the lens of electronic music. Only *Big Fun*—compiled from *Bitches Brew* leftovers and twice the length on CD that it was on LP—defies easy categorization, although its dark, moody tracks boast a strong undercurrent of Indian classical rhythms in addition to the expected swathes of rock and funk.

Live, Davis' bands were less inclined to groove and more apt to burn, which made their recordings considerably less commercial than his studio output. Indeed, half (*Black Beauty, Dark Magus,* and *Pangaea*) weren't even released domestically until well into the CD era, consigning hard-core fans to expensive Japanese imports. The three Fillmore albums were all recorded in 1970, and draw largely from the *Bitches Brew* songbook. *Live at the Fillmore East (March 7, 1970),* with Shorter on saxophone, is considered a sort of "missing link," as it represents the last connection between Davis' last hard-bop quintet and his subsequent electric bands. *Black Beauty,* recorded the following month on the opposite coast, finds Steve Grossman in the sax chair, and takes a much more aggressive approach, with the distortion on Corea's electric piano cranked to the max (although there is a touchingly gentle dip into "I Fall in Love Too Easily" midway through the first disc). Back in New York two months later, *At Fillmore* adds Jarrett to the proceedings and trades its predecessors' lyricism for a frenzied, clangorous approach.

Two years later, when *In Concert* was recorded at Philharmonic Hall in New York, Davis had a whole new band and an entirely different approach, drawing heavily from the worldbeat fusion of *Get Up With It.* Although occasionally fascinating, the busily churning rhythms often seem oddly static, as if the band were laboriously treading water. *Dark Magus,* recorded in 1974 with mostly the same rhythm section but with three guitars instead of one, not only makes more sense of the band's roiling rhythms but manages to balance the eagerness to improvise with a willingness to rock. *Pangaea* and *Agharta,* culled from a single show the following year in Osaka, Japan, pares the guitarists down to two: the post-Hendrixian Pete Cosey and the slyly soulful Reggie Lucas. The music—alternately audacious, poetic, hypnotic, and abrasive—has held up better than much of his '70s concert recordings.

They were also his last recordings of the decade, thanks to medical problems that sent him on a downward spiral of ill health and chemical dependence. His return to music-making, in 1981, seemed to play more on his celebrity than his musical imagination. With only drummer Al Foster held over from his last combo, Davis' '80s bands eschewed the rhythmic exoticism of his '70s work, opting instead for a more straightforward fusion approach. That seemed frankly dull on his overarranged and underadventurous studio comeback, *The Man With the Horn.* Onstage, however, the playing was more lively and inventive, as can be heard on either the import-only *Miles! Miles! Miles! Live in Japan* or the domestic release *We Want Miles.* But apart from *Aura*—an adventurous and pointedly non-pop-oriented big-band suite conceived by Danish jazzman Palle Mikkelborg—his final studio recordings for Columbia lacked the insight and daring that marked his prior efforts, although *You're Under Arrest,* which found him covering tunes recorded by Michael Jackson and Cyndi Lauper, came reasonably close to balancing his need for pop relevance with his jazz inclinations.

Davis left Columbia for Warner Bros. in 1985, and his first album for the label was *Tutu,* a one-on-one pairing with producer/multi-instrumentalist Marcus Miller (who, in addition to having played bass in Davis' comeback band, coproduced a number of Luther Vandross' albums). Although its automated hermeticism rubbed jazz purists the wrong way, *Tutu* holds up well, both compositionally and improvisationally. It was followed by the more assured soundtrack album *Siesta,* which marvelously updates the Iberian groove of *Sketches of Spain.* The vaguely

African *Amandla* returns to full-band format for the studio, but apart from Foster and saxophonist Kenny Garrett, relies mostly on session players and as such tends toward conservatism. Davis made one last stab at pop with *Doo-Bop,* a much-reviled but ultimately worthy attempt at fusing hip-hop and jazz. Had Davis teamed with MCs less hackneyed than J.R. and Easy Mo Bee, the album could have been a classic.

Dingo, Davis' other Warners soundtrack, released shortly after his death in 1991, is also intriguing, in part because it includes his first attempts at traditional, bop-derived jazz in 23 years, but its significance is diminished by the fact that half of what we hear is actually the work of trumpeter Chuck Findley. Still, it neatly set the stage for his final album, *Live at Montreux,* in which he and a Quincy Jones–led ensemble revisited the glory of his Gil Evans collaborations. He died three months later.

Perhaps the greatest failing of Davis' Warner Bros. years was that its emphasis on work created for the studio left no sense of what his touring band sounded like. The posthumous *Live Around the World* showed that what Davis did onstage during this period was far more daring than his pop-striving studio work, but the best evidence that Davis' final years have been woefully underrated comes with *The Complete Miles Davis at Montreux, 1973–1991.* Although its 20 CDs make a heavy demand on any listener, the consistent daring of his later bands—and the occasionally stunning contributions of such otherwise overlooked sidemen as keyboardist Kei Akagi and drummer Ricky Wellman—suggests that the trumpeter's final years were wrongly written off by most jazz critics.

Since his death, Davis' work has been anthologized in every manner imaginable, from straightforward best-ofs to specially themed compilations. There are also a number of box sets, organized by label or by project. Nearly all have something to recommend them; the issue is, how much?

Of the best-ofs, only *Ken Burns Jazz* attempts to cover the whole range of Davis' career; it's not a bad representation of his acoustic work, but it reduces his output after 1970 to a single track. *Jazz Profile* draws nicely from *Birth of the Cool* and Davis' earliest sessions as a leader, while *Miles Davis and the Jazz Giants* offers the best sampling of his recordings for Prestige. But the bulk of his career—some 30 years—was spent with Columbia, and summing that up in a single disc seems near impossible. *The Best of Miles Davis* is as close as you'll get, a brisk run through the classics that covers most of the essentials; even so, you're better off spending a little extra and getting the double-disc *Essential Miles Davis,* which conveys a better sense of the scope of his output. As for the theme-oriented collections, *Love Songs* is actually quite sweet, *Bluing* is an attempt at showing his approach to the blues, while *Blue Moods* offers more mood than blues, acting more as high-class background music than an introduction to jazz classics. *Panthalassa: The Remix Collection* is as disappointing as it is ambitious, while *This Is Jazz #38: Electric* woefully misrepresents that aspect of his catalogue by opting for short pieces instead of the more typical long workouts.

With the box sets, it's worth remembering that more is sometimes less. *Chronicle: The Complete Prestige Recordings* is a wonderful resource but a less enjoyable listening experience than the original albums. But that's the problem with many of the Davis box sets. If you're interested in the history—the process of the music-making—and patient enough to sit through the alternate takes and rehearsal snippets, then such sets as *Chronicle* or *Miles Davis & Gil Evans: The Complete Columbia Studio Recordings* or *The Complete Live at the Plugged Nickel* are worth the investment of time and money. If not, then stick with the original albums.

The Columbia Years would seem an obvious analogue to *Chronicle,* but hardly attempts to match the latter's completism; instead, this four-CD set culls most of the obvious highlights but shortchanges both Davis' electric period and his Evans albums. *Miles Davis & John Coltrane: The Complete Columbia Recordings* is, surprisingly, a less confusing way of absorbing the later recordings of that first great quintet than a march through the original albums would be; likewise, *The Miles Davis Quintet, 1956–68: The Complete Columbia Recordings* is a very handy way of dealing with the second quintet—and, oddly, makes the group's dissolution seem a natural outgrowth of its experimentation. But neither is as illuminating as *The Complete In a Silent Way Sessions,* which actually starts at *Filles de Kilimanjaro,* and makes Davis' transition from acoustic to electric music seem almost obvious, while *The Complete Bitches Brew Sessions* feeds the ongoing hunger for unheard Davis, as well as providing a better sense of how Macero's editing process worked. A grateful nation gives its thanks.   —J.D.C.

The Spencer Davis Group

★★½ Funky (Date, 1968; One Way, 1997)
★★★ The Best of the Spencer Davis Group (EMI America, 1996)
★★½ I'm a Man (1967; Sundazed, 2001)

Two triumphant singles, "Gimme Some Lovin'" (1966) and "I'm a Man" (1967), featuring Steve Winwood's earliest (and some of his best) singing, made this Birmingham quartet one of Britain's classiest

and toughest R&B outfits. A trad-blues fan, Davis had the luck to discover the 16-year-old Winwood, and the smart modesty basically to hand over the band to the precocious soulster. Winwood obviously came through—had the rest of this band been even half so tough, the Spencer Davis Group would've rivaled the Animals. *I'm a Man* collects material from the group's second English album of bluesy rock. Davis went on to found other incarnations of his group: *Funky* is a strong representative of the music after Winwood left. The band's early original albums are out of print or hard to find, but EMI's greatest-hits album is a good summation of the high points.   —P.E.

Kimya Dawson
see THE MOLDY PEACHES

Dead Boys

★★★★ Young Loud and Snotty (Sire, 1977)
★★ We Have Come for Your Children (Sire, 1978)
★★ Night of the Living Dead Boys (Bomp!, 1981)
★★★ Younger Louder & Snottier (1989; Bomp!, 1997)
★★ All This & More (Bomp!, 1998)
★ Liver Than You'll Ever Be (Pilot, 2002)

Compared to the piranha bite of vintage Sex Pistols or the Ramones' goony joie de vivre, the Dead Boys sound like borderline-competent heavy metal. But on *Young Loud and Snotty*—led by Stiv Bators' self-destructive, hate-filled, sexist explosions—the band makes up for lack of chops with plenty of nasty, vicious attitude. The Dead Boys' only other studio effort, *We Have Come for Your Children,* offers more of the same though with less effect. The shtick had worn thin. Before they became Dead Boys, Cheetah Chrome (guitar) and Johnny Blitz (drums) were in the groundbreaking Cleveland proto-punk band Rocket From the Tombs, along with Pere Ubu founders Peter Laughner and David Thomas. In fact, many of the best cuts on both Dead Boys albums are Rocket holdovers: *Young Loud and Snotty*'s rousing antianthem "Sonic Reducer" (notably sampled by the Beastie Boys on their 2004 track "Open Letter to NYC") is cowritten by Thomas, while *We Have Come for Your Children*'s morose and compelling "Ain't It Fun" is the late Peter Laughner's unsparing elegy for himself (cowritten with Chrome). So much loutish behavior and public indecency has been committed in the name of punk, but few went further than the Dead Boys. Live, Stiv Bators took Iggy Pop's daredevil stage antics three cocky steps forward into utter anarchy. Not surprisingly, the various live albums—all of which sound to varying degrees like muddy fan bootlegs—capture more chaos than music. For anybody who witnessed Bators' simulation of hanging himself while broken glass rained down onstage, his snarling tagline on the Stooges soundalike "All This and More" (on *Snotty*) was no joke: "I'll die for you if you want me to." Bators did, in fact, meet his maker after being hit by a bus in Paris in 1990.   —R.A.

Dead Kennedys

★★★★	Fresh Fruit for Rotting Vegetables (IRS, 1980)
★★★★	In God We Trust, Inc. (Alternative Tentacles, 1981)
★★★	Plastic Surgery Disasters (Alternative Tentacles, 1982)
★★★	Frankenchrist (Alternative Tentacles, 1985)
★★★	Bedtime for Democracy (Alternative Tentacles, 1986)
★★★★	Give Me Convenience or Give Me Death (Alternative Tentacles, 1987)

The Dead Kennedys' confrontational politics and total scorn for the status quo led many to consider this pioneering California hardcore band the only American punk act on par with the Sex Pistols. Most of the Kennedys' impact derived from the inspired vitriol of Jello Biafra's lyrics, not the music behind him. Indeed, where the Sex Pistols' semi-metal roar seems threatening even when Johnny Rotten isn't singing, the DKs' frenetic rave-ups usually substitute speed for power, noise for intensity.

The most lasting material on *Fresh Fruit for Rotting Vegetables* is its most conventional—post-Ramones rockers like "Kill the Poor" or "California Über Alles"—although there is a certain nasty glee to be found in the likes of "Let's Lynch the Landlord." There's even more righteous rage (or is it rage against righteousness?) on *In God We Trust, Inc.*, but even the ferociously catchy "Nazi Punks Fuck Off" sacrifices some of its musical power to the lyrics' occasionally awkward cadences. Much the same can be said of *Plastic Surgery Disasters, Frankenchrist,* and *Bedtime for Democracy,* where the group's increasingly didactic material seems to exist more as political commentary than as rock & roll. In that respect, it's almost ironic that the group's undoing wasn't its often scabrous assault on the establishment, but an obscenity suit prompted by a poster (of H.R. Giger's "Landscape #XX") included in *Frankenchrist.* Although the band eventually won that battle, it lost the war, disbanding not long after *Bedtime for Democracy;* its final release, *Give Me Convenience or Give Me Death,* is a compilation album collecting many of its most listenable songs.

The band itself had an ugly denouement: In the late '90s, the group became embroiled in litigation, with Biafra and other members of the band suing one another over management and royalty issues.   —J.D.C.

Dead Prez

★★★★	Let's Get Free (Loud, 2000)
★★★½	Turn Off the Radio: The Mixtape Vol. 1 (Holla Black/Full Clip, 2002)
★★★	Turn Off the Radio: The Mixtape Vol. 2: Get Free or Die Tryin' (Landspeed, 2003)
★★½	RBG: Revolutionary But Gangsta (Columbia, 2004)

In an era when hip-hop had all but forgotten its political obligations, Brooklyn's Dead Prez stepped up to the challenge. Rappers M-1 and stic.man were Afrocentric activists nonpareil, and their debut, *Let's Get Free,* was one of the finest examples of agit-rap since Public Enemy's *It Takes a Nation of Millions.* "They Schools" was a vicious skewering of the American educational system; "Be Healthy" advocated the benefits of a holistically inclined lifestyle; "I'm a African" contended just that. And not only were Dead Prez excellent rappers, but their choice of beats was open-minded—as on the mildly conspiratorial, yet truly crunk "Hip-Hop"—opting for bottom-heavy bass that hinted at the time the two spent living in the South.

The next two albums, the independently released *Turn Off the Radio* mixtape series, found the insurgent MCs rapping over urban-radio-standard instrumentals—Aaliyah's "We Need a Resolution" ("We Need A Revolution"), Black Rob's "Whoa" ("Like War"). They kept up the firebrand lyrics, too, rapping "The only free ride I get is the one with a siren" on "Tallahassee Days" and pressuring the pols on "Know Your Enemy": "You want to stop terrorists?/Start with the U.S. imperialists/Ain't no track record like America's." By the time their Sony debut, *RBG,* was released, their agit-rap momentum had dimmed somewhat. The album is strangely dour, filled with stories about crime in the name of struggle, the need to politically organize, and the corruptive influence of media. But unlike *Let's Get Free,* the new songs stagnate, and without the bounce, the didactic messages are hard to swallow.   —J.C.

Death Cab for Cutie

★★★	Something About Airplanes (Barsuk, 1999)
★★★	We Have the Facts and We're Voting Yes (Barsuk, 2000)
★★★★	Forbidden Love E.P. (Barsuk, 2000)
★★★★½	The Photo Album (Barsuk, 2002)
★★	Stability EP (Barsuk, 2002)

★★★ You Can Play These Songs With Chords
(Barsuk, 2002)
★★★½ Transatlanticism (Barsuk, 2003)

No one made prettier postmillennial indie rock than Bellingham, WA, foursome Death Cab for Cutie. Smarter and more sensitive than almost any of his studiously introspective peers, singer/songwriter/guitarist Benjamin Gibbard formed the band—with bassist Nicholas Harmer, guitarist-organist Christopher Walla, and, eventually, crack drummer Michael Schorr—after the tape of his solo cassette EP, *You Can Play These Songs With Chords,* suggested there was a market for charming little photocopies of Built to Spill's quieter, reverb-warped tunes. (Barsuk's 2002 reissue bundles these with later, equally charming alternate takes and rarities.)

On *Something About Airplanes,* DCFC took a baby step toward what would become its defining sound, smoothing over Built to Spill's jittery bombast with Gibbard's salve of a voice (previously a squeak) and slow builds. The five rerecorded cuts from *You Can Play These Songs With Chords,* subtly streamlined, showcase the band's new emphasis on delicacy over dissonance. The critical breakthrough *We Have the Facts and We're Voting Yes* applied the same principle, plus a smattering of psychedelia, to a new batch of songs with better melodies. But the best of that album's tracks, "Company Calls Epilogue" and "405," are fully realized as simple strummers on *The Forbidden Love E.P.,* which came out later that year.

While sometimes nostalgic, as its brilliant name suggests, *The Photo Album* showcases Gibbard's most scathing, not to mention most beautiful, songs to date. The urgent yet dreamy "Why You'd Want to Live Here" joins rock's long tradition of ripping into L.A.—"You can't swim in a town this shallow/You will most assuredly drown tomorrow"—and barrels into a break that's smoggy with fuzz and shot through with sunbursts of chiming guitar. In "Styrofoam Plates," gorgeously gentle but for its broken, unrelenting beat, Gibbard addresses his "bastard" father as he spreads the man's ashes, the weariness in his voice giving way to anger: "You're a disgrace to the concept of family/The priest won't divulge that fact in his homily/And I'll stand up and scream if the mourning remain quiet/You can deck out a lie in a suit but I won't buy it." And how does he end the song? "La la la la la-la/la la la la la-la."

Transatlanticism is whipped cream to *The Photo Album*'s curdled milk, smooth but rarely stunning. Gibbard plants a land mine in the gently rippling guitar reverb of "Tiny Vessels," recounting, for once, a one-sided romance in which "she was beautiful/but

didn't mean a thing to me." Tracks like this and "Title and Registration" show the band at its best, pushing lovely melodies with borderline-restive rhythms. But elsewhere, particularly the almost eight-minute-long title track, the band's slack with melancholy—perhaps a little too full of themselves. —N.C.

Deee-Lite

★★★★ World Clique (Elektra, 1990)
★★★ Infinity Within (Elektra, 1992)
★★ Dew Drops in the Garden (Elektra, 1994)
★★★½ Sampledelic Relics and Dancefloor Oddities (Elektra, 1996)
★★★★ The Very Best of Deee-Lite (Rhino, 2001)

Too far ahead of their time to have been accorded the respect they deserved, Deee-Lite not only presaged the crotch-level charm of post-house dance pop, but co-opted enough of the '60s peace-and-love aesthetic to fool mainstream media into thinking their music was wholesome and innocent.

Instead, Deee-Lite's deceptively frothy dance pop, with its deep grooves and strong sense of soul, eased the way for electronica's brief stand as the Next Big Thing. Of course, because Deee-Lite's music emphasizes song structure as much as rhythm tracks, the group was never pigeonholed, and as such had more pop appeal than most dance acts.

Even so, whatever inroads "Groove Is in the Heart"—the big hit from *World Clique*—might have made, Deee-Lite's moment in the spotlight was relatively short. *Infinity Within* did an admirable job of expanding on the post-hippie optimism of the debut, but *Dew Drops in the Garden*—recorded after the departure of DJ Towa Tei—seems more dippy than hippie.

Sampledelic Relics is a nice collection for hard-core fans, but is ignorable otherwise. *The Very Best* is an apt single-disc summation of the group's efforts, but those interested in further examination would do well to acquire DJ Towa Tei's *Sound Museum.* —J.D.C.

Deep Dish

★★★½ Junk Science (Deconstruction/Arista, 1998)

Since the early '90s, Washington, D.C.'s progressive house emissaries Deep Dish have blown ecstasy-besotted minds from Moscow to Ibiza and along the way remixed the likes of Madonna and the Rolling Stones.

Deep Dish released their first mix CD, 1995's *Penetrate Deeper,* on Tribal America. But it was the duo's massive mix of De'lacy's "Hideaway" the same year that jammed open the remix floodgates as Michael

Jackson, Tina Turner, and even Beth Orton lined up for the pair's beat-mining skills. In 1998 they dropped the masterful and eclectic *Junk Science,* a joint that cuts its house with jazz, techno, funk, and assorted ambient chasers. "The Future of the Future (Stay Gold)" became an instant dance-floor classic with Everything But the Girl's Tracey Thorn's golden voice soaring high above techno beats and watery synth lines. They released five rather indistinguishable mix CDS between 1999 and 2003 under banners like Global Underground, Yoshiesque, and Renaissance that don't come close to *Junk*'s originality. —A.G.

Def Leppard

★★★½	On Through the Night (Mercury, 1980)
★★★	High 'n' Dry (Mercury, 1981)
★★★★½	Pyromania (Mercury, 1983)
★★★★★	Hysteria (Mercury, 1987)
★★★★	Adrenalize (Mercury, 1992)
★★½	Retro Active (Mercury, 1993)
★★★★★	Vault—Greatest Hits, 1985–1990 (Mercury, 1995)
★★½	Slang (Mercury, 1996)
★★★	Euphoria (Mercury, 1999)
★★½	X (Mercury, 2002)

It may be hard to believe, but Def Leppard came up in the same late '70s scene that produced Iron Maiden and Motörhead, the so-called new wave of British metal. At that time, no one could have imagined that the scene's reborn ferocity would lead to a sound as carefully crafted or pop-friendly as Def Leppard's. Neither would anyone have predicted that the plucky teens who recorded *On Through the Night* would end up as the era's most popular metal band or that the group would overcome unimaginable tragedy on its way to the top.

On Through the Night, after all, was a fairly modest start for the band, offering tuneful if formulaic songs played with more competence than fury. *High 'n' Dry* stuck with that approach, though as "Bringin' On the Heartache" demonstrates, the writing grew more intricate and involved.

The rules changed for good with *Pyromania.* Not only is the band's traditional heavy-rock instrumentation—twin guitars, bass, drums—augmented by digital keyboards and state-of-the-art special effects, but that sound-shaping technology often becomes part of the song. Consequently, the backward snare and carefully contoured backing vocals don't just add depth and texture to "Photograph," they actually change the way the music flows and the melody develops. And that's as true of "Rock of Ages," "Foolin'," and most of the other songs on the album.

Hysteria is even more techno-intense, yet the obviously painstaking production never gets in the way of the music. If anything, from the processed vocals in "Animal" to the multiple layers of echo that sheathe the groove in "Pour Some Sugar on Me," the overload of aural detail enhances the album's melodic allure, underscoring the material's pop appeal without dulling its metallic edge.

During the making of *Hysteria,* drummer Rick Allen lost an arm in an auto accident, but he continued to record and perform with the band. While the band was working on the followup, *Adrenalize,* guitarist Steve Clark died from drug and alcohol abuse. Despite the double tragedy, neither the band's sound nor its lyrical concerns changed; singles such as "Let's Get Rocked" furthered the band's carefree, good-time reputation.

After releasing a best-of *(Vault)* and a rarities collection *(Retro Active),* Def Leppard updated its sound, outfitting *Slang* with industrial vocals on "Truth" and shimmering U2-style guitar on "Where Does Love Go When It Dies." Although it was interesting, the album flopped, and the Leps reverted to formula, filling *Euphoria* with power ballads ("It's Only Love") and fist-pumping rockers (the Gary Glitter–ish "Back in Your Face"). Nothing endures forever, so by its 10th album, *X,* Def Leppard seemed creatively tapped out, able to offer only deftly arranged echoes of its once glorious past. —J.D.C.

The Deftones

★★	Adrenaline (Maverick, 1995)
★★	Around the Fur (Maverick, 1997)
★★★½	White Pony (Maverick, 2000)
★★★	Deftones (Maverick, 2003)

The multiracial, multicultural, multimusical Deftones have the strange distinction of being perhaps the least critically maligned band associated with new metal. Maybe that's because their breakthrough, *White Pony,* showed signs that they were as familiar with the Cure's *Disintegration* and things that girls might like as with downtuned bass, chunk style riffs, and screaming about their various aches and pains. Or maybe it's because the songs are built around singer Cheno Moreno's voice in ways other "heavy music" acts are not. Whatever it is, Deftones' *Adrenaline* is one thud after another, but even on the monochromatic debut, you can tell there's a depth of focus lurking just out of reach. Moreno has a charisma lacking in other new metal frontmen; you get the sense he would have beer with you without trying to talk to you about serial killers.

Around the Fur focuses their sound into overt aggression. This is pure rock fury, the sound of guys who are smarter than you give them credit for, trying to prove to themselves that they're as tough (and horny) as everyone thinks. Songs like "Be Quiet And Drive (Far Away)" wants to fuck the pain away, but there's never any satiation, never any true release.

But the smarts eventually won out, with impressive results. *White Pony* strikes a remarkable balance between the raw and the cooked, between beat science and rock dynamics, between metal overkill and quieter moments, between mecha and orga. The pure bulldozer metal on "Elite" gives way to atmospheric, percussive near-balladry on "RX Queen." "Teenager" is as close to warm as new metal gets, while "Korea" shows just how well bassist Chi Cheng and guitarist Stephen Carpenter lock up when called upon to throw down. Through it all, DJ Frank Delgado never lets the beats pull focus away from the songs, providing color without the "hey, we have a DJ!" antics that plague their peers. Perhaps most impressively, Moreno gets off on lyrical nuance and his voice actually signifies passion, instead of the atonal warble that most new metal thinks means they mean it, man. A great leap forward and one of the few new metal albums that wholly justifies the genre.

After three years, *Deftones* sounds born-again hard even while incorporating *White Pony*'s generic expansiveness. Moreno tears his voice to shreds on songs like "Hexagram," while Carpenter's riffs have gotten more compact and focused, and Delgado's scratching has become more musical. "Lucky You" floats into the sunset, while the epic shimmer of "Minerva" is their loveliest moment. Apparently, the Deftones hear things in new metal that most bands wouldn't dare acknowledge. —J.G.

Desmond Dekker

  ★★★½ Desmond Dekker and the Aces (Trojan, 1985)
  ★★★ King of Ska (Trojan, 1991)
  ★★★ Music Like Dirt (Trojan, 1992)
  ★★★★ Rockin' Steady: The Best of Desmond Dekker (Rhino, 1992)
  ★★★ King of Kings (Trojan, 1995)
  ★★★ Moving Out (Trojan, 1996)
  ★★★ Intensified (Lagoon, 1997)
  ★★★½ First Time for a Long Time: Rarities (Trojan, 1997)
  ★★★ Writing on the Wall (Trojan, 1998)
  ★★★ Halfway to Paradise (Trojan, 2000)
  ★★★½ Israelites: Anthology 1963–1999 (Trojan, 2001)

In 1969, straight out of Kingston, Jamaica, Desmond Dekker scored a Top 10 hit with the reggae single "Is-

raelites," paving the way for stronger talents like Bob Marley. Although in the U.S. Dekker remained a one-hit wonder, his influence in Britain was more substantial. Championing the outlaw ethic ("Rude Boy Train"), Dekker's early work was low-tech and punchy; but even with slicker fare, like his cover of Jimmy Cliff's "You Can Get It if You Really Want," his sly vocal style cuts through. The Rhino set is the fabulous '60s stuff (check out "007 [Shanty Town]") and *Desmond Dekker and the Aces* is also vintage excellence, especially the brilliance of the Aces, D.D.'s backup vocalists. The later work is heartening, if not quite so strong. *King of Kings* pairs Desmond with the Specials, the next generation of ska heroes and perhaps Dekker's greatest fans. —P.E.

Delaney & Bonnie

  ★★★★½ On Tour With Eric Clapton (Atco, 1970, 1989)
  ★★★★ The Best of Delaney & Bonnie (Rhino, 1990)

In their toughest, 1969 incarnation—an 11-piece revue—Delaney & Bonnie made Southern soul-rock with scorching expertise. Honing her R&B chops as history's only white Ikette, powerhouse vocalist Bonnie Bramlett and husband Delaney, an ace picker and country-tinged singer, had the talent and charisma to attract breathtaking sidemen: Leon Russell, Bobby Keys, Carl Radle, Rita Coolidge, Jim Keltner—and, at various times, Eric Clapton and Duane Allman. As one of the best bands in rock & roll, they make *On Tour* a triumph: Clapton tears up Steve Cropper's "Things Get Better," D&B exult the funk on "I Don't Want to Discuss It." The acoustic "Motel Shot" is another kind of wonder: traditionals like "Going Down the Road Feeling Bad" and "Will the Circle Be Unbroken" played with a casual, loving freedom. The Rhino collection starts off with *Accept No Substitute*, which formulated D&B's synthesis of Stax/Volt, gospel, and hard country and then gives us the career highlights of a duo who created genuinely credible big-band rock. Their sound remains exciting and groundbreaking: The musicians they introduced are also featured on Clapton's first solo album and Joe Cocker's *Mad Dogs and Englishmen*. —P.E.

De La Soul

  ★★★★★ 3 Feet High and Rising (1989; Tommy Boy, 2001)
  ★★★★½ De La Soul Is Dead (Tommy Boy, 1991)
  ★★★★½ Buhloone Mindstate (Tommy Boy, 1993)
  ★★★★ Stakes Is High (Tommy Boy, 1996)
  ★★★½ Art Official Intelligence: Mosaic Thump (Tommy Boy, 2000)

When you're a group of minds way out of time, you invent your own era. That's just what Long Island, NY, teenagers De La Soul did for their 1989 debut, *3 Feet High and Rising*. In their hip-hop, there were no drug dealers; no gangsters; no hoodlums. Just Posdnuos, Mase, and Trugoy, a triumvirate of psychedelically dressed boho would-bes—and their equally eccentric producer, Prince Paul—with more ideas than they could ever hope to confine to a simple audio record. They certainly did try on *3 Feet*, a cluttered classic crammed wall-to-wall with bizarro concepts that set De La apart from almost all of their contemporaries. Songs touched on the social issues of the day ("Say No Go," "Ghetto Thang"), teenage lust ("Jenifa Taught Me," "Buddy") and an assertive individuality ("Me Myself & I"). In every case, the production was boisterous, teeming with whimsical samples from a range of genres, and demonstrating facility with everything from television commercial jingles to the club music pastiche. Just as fascinating were the skits, in which a collection of increasingly preposterous characters competed in mock game shows. Not only did these brief, absurd interludes help give *3 Feet* a narrative arc, they also helped establish De La as quirky artists with heart, willing to poke fun at themselves.

The exuberance, sadly, was short-lived. Most artists are loath to become pigeonholed, but accept that path as a means to an end. Not De La, though. *3 Feet* was so widely accepted, and so broadly caricatured in the popular sphere, that on their followup, they abandoned its ethic almost completely. Whereas they'd coined their movement the D.A.I.S.Y. Age on *3 Feet,* the cover of *De La Soul Is Dead* featured an overturned pot of daisies. The group was still outré by hip-hop standards, but the whimsy was all but gone. The single "Ring Ring Ring (Ha Ha Hey)" was a classic music industry lament, and the best songs were deeply pessimistic: "Millie Pulled a Pistol on Santa," a story about sexual abuse, remains one of the genre's most moving tracks, followed closely by "My Brother's a Basehead," allegedly based on Posdnuos' true-life experiences. Relatively speaking, *Dead* was a commercial flop, and the group's third album, *Buhloone Mindstate,* didn't do much better, even though it reclaimed some of *3 Feet's* vitality on tracks like "Breakadawn" and the classic "Ego Trippin' (Part Two)."

Given their creative track record, it would have been easy to think that De La just wasn't much interested in commercial success. With that in mind, the group's fourth album, *Stakes Is High,* was a brilliant gambit, the crew's answer record to hip-hop's increasing commercialization. From a group that had made three brilliant concept records, it was stunningly straightforward, almost a conscious attempt to retrofit the group as part and parcel of the genre they'd been trying to inject with life for several years. On songs like "The Bizness," "Itzsoweezee (Hot)," and "Supa Emcees," their production was more straightforward than it ever had previously been. The same could be said of the title track, although a listen to the lyrics revealed a skepticism as thorough as that evinced on *De La Soul Is Dead.*

In 2000, the group released the first in what was to be a triptych of albums, the *Art Official Intelligence* series, which they hoped would gain them a wider audience, deliberately aiming for the mainstream with a retinue of well-known guests—Xzibit, Busta Rhymes, Redman, Slick Rick. As usual, the songs were musically accomplished, but they lacked the passion of the group's early work. Due to label difficulties, the third part of the series wasn't released, although the first two installments proved that De La's best moments were behind them. After years of cult status—it would take *3 Feet* over a decade to go platinum—they'd eased into the role of hip-hop's cranky uncles: respected by everyone, but just a step or three out of sync with the times.   —J.C.

The Delfonics

The Delfonics were the agents by which producer Thom Bell crafted a new subgenre of soul. Blending lush, pop-influenced orchestrations with a group harmony approach (complete with soaring, romantic tenor leads) updated from the '50s doo-wop aesthetic, Bell and the Delfonics were the pioneers who blazed the trail in the late '60s for the Philly Soul explosion of the '70s.

Formed in Philadelphia, the Delfonics were high-school buddies who came together as the Orphonics in the early '60s, led by Washington, D.C.–born vocalist-songwriter William "Poogie" Hart. The original lineup included lead vocalist Hart, his brother Wilbert singing baritone, Ricky Johnson singing bass, and second tenor Richard Daniels. In 1965, Daniels and Johnson left, and the Harts added tenor man Randy Cain and moved on as a trio.

In 1968 Bell and the Delfonics cut William Hart's "La La Means I Love You" (the title sentiment was inspired by a phrase Hart heard his young son utter one night), a song that combined Bell's symphonic soul arrangement, the trio's close-knit harmonizing, and Hart's smooth, seductive lead vocal. "Ready or Not Here I Come (Can't Hide from Love)" put the trio back on the charts in 1969, in advance of its defining, and monster, hit, 1970's "Didn't I (Blow Your Mind This Time)," a Top 10 pop single that was even bigger than its chart position, or its Grammy Award for Best R&B Performance of 1970, indicated. It was most certainly the first pop hit to put the phrase "blow your mind" into a romantic context, free of even the most remote drug connotations, and Hart's gently pleading, soft-as-satin reading of the lyric "I gave my heart and soul to you, girl/Now didn't I do it, baby, didn't I do it, baby."

The group's eponymous fourth album, led by "Didn't I (Blow Your Mind This Time)," yielded no less than five hit singles (out of only 10 cuts), and stands as the definitive statement of the Delfonics–Thom Bell collaboration. For one, the trio was at its absolute vocal peak in these sessions, love men to the hilt on the ballads, and testosterone-fueled go-getters on frantic uptempo fare such as "Funny Feeling," a soul workout spiced with psychedelic flourishes. Even nonsingle tracks that may have been intended as filler reveal the trio's pride in craftsmanship and ability to wring all the emotion out of a lyric—witness the breathtaking flight of William Hart's falsetto on "Delfonics' Theme (How Could You)," a rather drab title masking a potent performance.

Long after the Delfonics disbanded, William Hart resurfaced in 1990, along with Major Harris and another vocalist, Frank Washington, and returned to the studio to cut the album *Forever New* for the Volt label. Harris, and especially Hart, were in good form vocally, but the album sounds dated. Producer Fred Pittman, who also cowrote a number of the songs, seemed ready to relegate the reconstituted Delfonics to the Vegas lounge circuit with his and Preston Glass's stillborn, simplistic arrangements and melodramatic lyrics better suited for a Hallmark greeting card than for vocalists of Hart's and Harris' stature.

One could do worse than to buy *The Delfonics* and leave it at that. But then, the Buddha/BMG re-issues of the group's other two Bell-produced early albums, *The Sound of Sexy Soul* and its debut, *La La Means I Love You*, merit close inspection as well. The latter contains Top 40 hits ("I'm Sorry," "Break Your Promise") and a couple of interesting covers of Hal David/Burt Bacharach songs ("Alfie" and "The Look of Love") that seem to be Bell's way of tipping his hat to one of his primary influences. Like the other Buddha/BMG reissues, new liner notes bring the listener up to speed on the course of the Delfonics' career and the music at issue, and complete discography info is published as well.

The Sound of Sexy Soul, the group's second album (the third was a greatest-hits album), contains a few more crossover hits in "Somebody Loves You" and "Ready or Not Here I Come," and some inspired cover choices among its dozen tracks. Marvin Gaye's "Ain't That Peculiar" is done close to the Motown style of Gaye's original single, oddly enough, whereas "Scarborough Fair" finds Bell and the trio dabbling in psychedelia, albeit less effectively than they would on *The Delfonics'* "Funny Feeling." Finally, for those who prefer their Delfonics straight, no ephemera, Arista's aptly titled *La-La Means I Love You: The Definitive Collection* is the winning ticket. All the hits are here, supplemented by the cream of the album tracks, including "Delfonics' Theme (How Could You)." —D.M.

The Dells

★★★★	There Is (1968; Chess/MCA, 1989)
★★★½	The Dells vs. the Dramatics (1974; Chess/MCA, 1997)
★★★½	Music From the Motion Picture: The Five Heartbeats (Virgin, 1991)
★★★	Passionate Breezes: The Best of the Dells 1975–1991 (Mercury, 1995)
★★★½	Oh What a Night: The Great Ballads (MCA, 1998)
★★★★	Anthology (Hip-O, 1999)
★★★½	The Millennium Collection (MCA, 2000)
★★★½	Ultimate Collection (Hip-O, 2004)

In 1956, this Chicago harmony quintet scored with the elegant, sexy "Oh, What a Night." The Dells' followup hit came twelve years later; "Stay in My Corner" is a standard-issue lover's plea lifted by its dynamic vocal arrangement and Marvin Junior's warm baritone. When the group reemerged on Chess later in the '60s, after knocking around on several independents, its bold new sound left that classic street-corner casualness far behind. A full quotient of strings and horns contrast and emphasize the play of voices. When everything falls into place, as it does on the heaven-bound "There Is," the Dells' harmonies rumble and flash like an approaching storm. *There Is* duplicates the original Cadet LP. The leaner sound of early '70s soul nuggets like "Give Your Baby a Standing Ovation" and "Bring Back the Love of Yesterday" offsets the remade earlier hits: The Dells explain doowop to people too young to remember the real thing.

For a pickup match, *The Dells Vs. the Dramatics* never lapses into hot-dog tricks. Sensitive arrangements carry the day: "Love Is Missing From Our Lives" is clearly a duet between two harmony groups, not two lead singers. Dramatics main man Ron Banks erupts with gruff, joyous Stax soul on "Choosing Up On You," but the Dells' Marvin Junior invests "Strung Out Over You" with tragic, helpless beauty. This battle royal comes out a draw—everyone's a winner. The Dells' more recent—and far less necessary—efforts on Mercury and Private have fallen out of print. But once again, this veteran group rebounded: "A Heart Is a House for Love," taken from the *Five Heartbeats* soundtrack, sounds comfortable and assured on the 1991 R&B charts. The best available compilation, *Anthology,* collects all the essential Cadet sides as well as their fine later singles onto two discs.   —M.C./G.F.

The Dell Vikings

★★★★ For Collectors Only (Collectables, 1992)
★★★★ 1956 Audition Tapes (Collectables, 1993)
★★★½ Golden Classics (Collectables, 1993)

One of the first interracial groups in rock & roll history, the Dell Vikings assembled in 1955 when all five of its original members were stationed at the same air force base in Pittsburgh. Signed to the local Fee Bee label, the group notched 15 charting hits, the most enduring being two Top 10 hits from 1957, "Come Go With Me" and "Whispering Bells," both featuring complex vocal parts, driving rhythms, imaginative production, and the plaintive, soaring lead vocals of tenor Kripp Johnson. When the group tried to jump to the greener pastures of a major-label affiliation with Mercury (which had been scoring big with the Platters), Johnson, who was of legal age when the group signed with Fee Bee, couldn't get out of his contract; his mates, on the other hand, had all been underage and were free to go. Johnson then formed a new Dell Vikings, which included Chuck Jackson, who would find greater success as a solo artist in the early '60s with "I Don't Want to Cry" and "Any Day Now," two of the decade's finest pop-soul singles. A court ruling allowed Mercury's group to use the Dell Vikings name, so Johnson changed his group's name to the Versitiles. Not that it mattered in either case: Neither Mercury's Dell Vikings nor Johnson's Versitiles had a hit, and by 1960, both were history.

The original Dell Vikings left behind some wonderful recordings—wonderful then and remarkable still for their exuberance, energy, and sheer musicality. For a total immersion in all things Dell Viking, try Collectables' two-disc overview, *For Collectors Only,* which includes not only the two indelible hits, but outtakes, a couple of alternate takes, the audition tape of "Come Go With Me," and an a cappella rendition of the delightful group-harmony bopper, "Cry Baby." The less ambitious *Golden Classics* also includes the two essential hits, and a number of lesser-known gems such as a heartrending version of "Over the Rainbow."

The most curious Dell Vikings entry is *1956 Audition Tapes,* which may or may not be a true audition tape (there's no credible evidence in either direction). On the other hand, even demos are expected to show some professional polish, and this one does: The voices are rich and personable, the arrangements note-perfect but not lacking vitality or youthful zeal; there's nary a false note or ragged edge anywhere, and the harmonies are intricate and layered, worked out to their final form. A disc jockey who identifies himself as Barry Kay of WJAS in Pittsburgh introduces the tape and crops up between songs with brief commentary on the next tune's origins; at the end of the disc he advises, "This is just an audition tape; we used only drums and electric guitar. Now it's up to you."

Well, drums and electric guitar do show up, but the instruments are often mixed so low that the vocalists sound as if they're performing a cappella. What these performances do show, indisputably, is a group rooted in a close, sweet harmony sound far less percussive than the approach that made their Fee Bee recordings irresistible. Although *1956 Audition Tapes* isn't the Holy Grail of doo-wop, it is a fascinating document of some formative experiments in adapting the doo-wop ethos to a pop sensibility.   —D.M.

Del tha Funkee Homosapien

★★★★ I Wish My Brother George Was Here (Elektra, 1991)
★★★★ No Need for Alarm (Elektra, 1994)
★★★½ Both Sides of the Brain (Red Urban, 2000)
★★★ Deltron 3030 (75 Ark, 2000)
★★★½ The Best of Del tha Funkee Homosapien: The Elektra Years (Rhino, 2004)

With his lip ring, sweat-crusted baseball cap, and taste for mushrooms and video-game marathons, Del tha Funkee Homosapien was a prime couch-potato candidate. And while Del's indulgences contributed to his sketchy rep as a live performer and probably factored into his extended '90s hiatus, the rapper born Teren

Delvon Jones is a funny, socially conscious iconoclast who nearly single-handedly presented an alternative to the gangsta rap that ruled the West Coast when he emerged. Del even had some gangsta connections. His cousin Ice Cube (Del appeared for about three seconds in "Turn Off the Radio" on *AmeriKKKa's Most Wanted*) helped produce Del's debut album, *I Wish My Brother George Was Here,* which rolled along on fat Funkadelic samples. No other P-Funkcentric rapper embodied George Clinton's mix of social consciousness and scatological hilarity quite like Del. With a voice seemingly suffering from slight sinusitis, Del laid down nonsensical character-sketch classics such as his classic single, "Mistadobalina" ("The way you're on my dick must really hurt your knees"), "Dr. Bombay," slacker send-off "Sleepin' on My Couch," and Donald Byrd–sampling "Ya Lil' Crumbsnatchers," making a truly timeless debut that was playful and serious. (As he said on "Ahonetwo, Ahonetwo": "It pays to steal a groovy sample from the archives/ Use my mental staff to eliminate apartheid").

The underrated followup *No Need for Alarm,* with tracks like "Wack MC's" and "Booboo Heads," came ready to battle; it lacked the debut's crossover appeal, which was cool with Del but not so agreeable with his record company. Dropped by Elektra, Del indulged in a five-year "lost weekend" (sightings placed him working as a stock boy at a record store in Berkeley), commiserating with his fellow Hieroglyphics crew members Casual and Souls of Mischief, who'd undergone their own major-label horror stories.

In 1998, Del surfaced on the cassette-only *Future Development,* released in-house on Hiero Imperium. The new millennium saw Del reemerge big-time with the bugged-out self-produced *Both Sides of the Brain* (guests include El-P and Casual) and with Dan the Automator and Kid Koala in the group Deltron 3030. And in 2001, Del had the biggest hit of his career with Gorillaz, a project headed by Britpop stalwart Damon Albarn, of Blur, whose creeping dubby single "Clint Eastwood" featuring Del was a #1 hit in the U.K. While Del's *Best* mines only his Elektra era, it excavates "Undisputed Champs," on which Del and Q-Tip trade great verses, giving fans cause to exalt, in the words of Bob Dobalina, "Glory Hallastoopid!"   —P.R.

Iris DeMent

★★★½ Infamous Angel (Philo, 1992; Warner Bros., 1993)
★★★★ My Life (Warner Bros., 1994)
★★★ The Way I Should (Warner Bros., 1996)

The youngest of 14 children born to an Arkansas farm family, Iris DeMent makes music that reflects those humble origins, bridging the gap between old-timey mountain soul and the lyricism of contemporary singer/songwriter folk rock. Her first two albums are luminous, bare-bones affairs, with a drummerless string band framing DeMent's songs, which celebrate the commonplace with uncommon eloquence. On *Infamous Angel,* she avoids the drinkin' and romancin' songs of country clichés to celebrate faith, love, rural simplicity, and singin' along to the country radio. But this yearning for clarity is muddled by doubt: "Let the Mystery Be" brings an agnostic's skepticism to DeMent's Pentacostal upbringing, and in "Our Town" she assumes the perspective of a much older woman forced to move on because of economic hard times. DeMent's voice—a heartbreakingly pure soprano—embodies that sense of lost innocence.

Even though its stripped-down acoustic arrangements are nearly identical to the debut's, *My Life* digs even deeper into the metaphysical with songwriting that is more consistently strong. DeMent's originals ring with timeless longing, even when stacked alongside a couple of beauties drawn from Maybelle Carter, an obvious inspiration, and Lefty Frizzell.

The Way I Should casts off the pristine, highly introspective tone—and the prerock string-band sound that accompanied it—for a more world-wise approach, but the results are mixed. The musical accompaniment is more varied and punchier, thanks in part to the first-time appearance of a drummer on a DeMent record. The more aggressive sound is matched by a new sense of freedom in DeMent's singing, whether she's bringing a hymnlike ardor to "There's a Wall in Washington" or trading bluesy yowls with Delbert McClinton on "Trouble." But the socially conscious themes of "Quality Time" and "Wasteland of the Free" come off more as complaints, and introduce an unseemly element of finger-pointing into DeMent's lexicon.   —G.K.

Sandy Denny

★★½ Fotheringay (Island, 1970)
★★★ The North Star Grassman and the Ravens (1971; Hannibal, 1991)
★★★★ Sandy (A&M, 1972)
★★★ Like an Old Fashioned Waltz (1973; Hannibal, 1991)
★★★ Rendezvous (1977; Hannibal, 1991)
★★★★ The Best of Sandy Denny (Hannibal, 1987)
★★★ Sandy Denny and the Strawbs (Hannibal, 1991)
★★★ Gold Dust: Live at the Royalty Theater (PolyGram, 1998)
★★★★ No More Sad Refrains (A&M, 2000)
★★½ Listen, Listen (PolyGram, 2000)

★★★ The Original Sandy Denny (Trojan, 2001)
★★ The Millennium Collection (Universal, 2002)

One of the finest singers England has ever produced, Sandy Denny was a linchpin of the original Fairport Convention. Delivering, alongside Richard Thompson and Ian Matthews, a radical mixture of Dylan covers and Renaissance music, she helped make Fairport leaders of Britain's '60s Olde Musik revival. Her earliest recordings, issued now as *The Original Sandy Denny,* are straight-folk workouts with mostly just voice and guitar digging into a revealing selection of cover tunes ("Pretty Polly," "Last Thing on My Mind"). Some may prefer its simple purity to Denny's next batch of work, from when she was briefly a member of a sort of lesser Fairport, the Strawbs.

Hannibal's *Sandy Denny and the Strawbs,* a 1991 reissue of their unreleased 1967 tapes, captures exactly her early promise—on assured folk numbers by Dave Cousins, she sings with unerring precision, her bell-like delivery coming across as a very natural gift. *No More Sad Refrains* includes selections from her Fairport work—and while the individual albums represented (*Unhalfbricking, Liege and Lief*) remain essential—the compilation's choices do her justice.

After Fairport, she formed Fotheringay, whose style continued along the lines of lutes 'n' flutes. *The North Star Grassman and the Ravens* is her final triumph of the style, making way for the fine modern folk of *Sandy* and *Like an Old Fashioned Waltz* (the latter features a deft remake of Cahn-Chaplin's "Until the Real Thing Comes Along," suggesting a never-developed jazz direction). Casting her as pop singer didn't quite work on *Rendezvous*—the album is dogged by a busy "Candle in the Wind" and a merely capable "Silver Threads and Golden Needles." Although a classy single-disc distillation is available as an import, Denny's glorious three-CD retrospective, *Who Knows Where the Time Goes?,* is now out of print, which leaves the double-CD *No More Sad Refrains* to present her work with the Fairport and Fotheringay as well as solo recordings (including some demos and rarities). The PolyGram import *Listen, Listen* gets its survey onto one disc, but the pure-solo-career selection doesn't do Denny justice. Avoid the cheap but shamefully brief *Millennium Collection.*

In a tragic accident, Denny died in 1978 after falling down a flight of stairs. *Gold Dust: Live at the Royalty Theater* draws on her last concert, when she was fighting a cold and with wobbly sound quality. With some parts now rerecorded and the tapes cleaned up, it's a treasure for committed fans, because so little live Denny is available. Today's neo-folkies owe her a debt, and all those enthralled by Eva

Cassidy should pounce posthaste onto *No More Sad Refrains.* —P.E./M.M.

Depeche Mode

★★★★ Speak and Spell (Sire, 1981)
★★★ A Broken Frame (Sire, 1982)
★★ Construction Time Again (Sire, 1983)
★★ People Are People (Sire, 1984)
★★★ Some Great Reward (Sire, 1984)
★★★★½ Catching Up With Depeche Mode (Sire, 1985)
★★★★½ Black Celebration (Sire, 1986)
★★★★½ Music for the Masses (Sire, 1987)
★★★½ 101 (Sire, 1989)
★★★★½ Violator (Sire, 1990)
★★★½ Songs of Faith and Devotion (Sire, 1993)
★★ Songs of Faith and Devotion . . . Live (Sire, 1993)
★★ Ultra (Reprise, 1997)
★★★★★ The Singles '81–'85 (Sire, 1998)
★★★★★ The Singles '86–'98 (Sire, 1998)
★★ Exciter (Reprise, 2001)

Ask average people about Depeche Mode, and they might give you responses such as "synthesizers," "gloom," "doom," "depressed," and "my soul is a sea of sin." But the most common reply will be, "Jesus, are they still around?" The answer is yes, and always will be. Depeche Mode has outlived its logical career span by more than 20 years now, still bringing the 1980s-style heat for their devoted cult. Black leather? Stylish hair? White jeans? Synth beats? All there.

Original mastermind Vince Clarke departed after just one album, *Speak and Spell,* which included the immortal hits "Dreaming of Me," "New Life," and "Just Can't Get Enough." Clarke went on to found Yaz and Erasure, remaining one of pop's top songwriters. But against all odds, Depeche Mode rolled on with Martin Gore composing and David Gahan singing. "See You," their first hit without Vince Clarke, was a masterpiece of Bowie-style new-wave erotics, longing for an invisible lover to heal the pain of getting ignored by physical heartbreakers. The hits kept coming, dividing roughly into songs about decadent sex rituals ("Work Hard," "More Than a Party") and songs about needing a good cry ("Somebody," "Blasphemous Rumors").

The Depechies scored a big U.S. crossover hit in the summer of 1985 with "People Are People," despite the fact that other Brit synth boys were going down like lambs to the slaughter. The band still wasn't getting any respect, but it packed arenas with black-clad Catholic schoolgirls who could sing all the words to "Master and Servant." It was time for an artistic statement: the trilogy of *Black Celebration,*

Music for the Masses, and *Violator.* Even Mode-phobes have to admit how brilliant these albums are. *Black Celebration* answers "A Question of Lust" with the New Romantic power ballad "Stripped," on which Dave Gahan seethes over and over, "Let me see you stripped down to the bone." *Music for the Masses* amps up the kinky/morbid fun for "I Want You Now," "Little 15," and "Pleasure Little Treasure," which apparently inspired the hook of Sonic Youth's "Teen Age Riot." The songs are mostly about heavy-breathing, trouser-swapping car adventures—and judging from the king-size whomp of "Never Let Me Down Again" and "Behind the Wheel," Dave was getting some serious mileage. *Violator* was an even bigger hit, featuring the rock-guitar shuffle "Personal Jesus." It was crazy to leave "Sea of Sin" and "Happiest Girl" off the album (both are stuck on the essential *World in My Eyes* 12-inch), but at least there's the closeted paranoia of "Policy of Truth." It's a lot, it's a lot, it's a lot like life.

The band had to retreat after Gahan almost drugged himself to death. But Depeche Mode's still-devoted cult embraces the recent records, including solo albums Gahan and Gore released in 2003. Of all the group's compilations, the sentimental fave is still the first, the 1985 *Catching Up With Depeche Mode,* but you can't go wrong with either *Singles '81–'85* or *Singles '86–'98.* Unfortunately, neither includes "But Not Tonight," the closing theme from the classic '80s Valley Girl flick *Modern Girls,* which you can still catch on late-night basic cable. The best recent Depeche is the Freelance Hellraiser's 2002 bootleg mash-up of "Just Can't Get Enough" and D-12's "Purple Pills"; Eminem sounds right at home over that perky synth beat, rapping, "Oh shit, now I started a mosh pit!" Depeche Mode's legendary *101* concert film finally came out on DVD in 2004, complete with extra performance footage and brand-new interviews with the group. Personal to Martin Gore: Love the new teeth!   —R.S.

Derek and the Dominos

★★★★★ Layla and Other Assorted Love Songs (Uni/A&M, 1970)
★★★★ In Concert (RSO, 1973)
★★★★ The Layla Sessions (Uni/Mercury, 1990)
★★★★ Live at the Fillmore (Uni/Mercury, 1994)

An astonishing evocation of unrequited love, "Layla" is almost as celebrated for its real-life circumstances as for its emotionally involving sound. Written for the most part by Eric Clapton and inspired by the classical Persian love poem "Layla," the song sprung from a love triangle between Clapton, his best friend (George Harrison), and the best friend's wife (Patti Boyd).

Heavy stuff, to be sure; indeed, Clapton later admitted that "being Derek was a cover for the fact that I was trying to steal someone else's wife." Of course, everyone knew Derek was Eric, just as they knew that the Dominos were the rhythm section Clapton had picked up through his association with Delaney & Bonnie. But it was just as obvious that the pain and longing expressed in the single was real, and that the genuine show of emotion put an edge on Clapton's vocals and fire in his guitar playing, helping his churning rhythm work throw sparks against the tart counterpoint of Duane Allman's slide. But it's Jim Gordon's stately, pastoral piano figure that has the final word, adding an air of hope and transcendence that seems almost to answer the pleas of the opening verses. Rarely do tragic love songs provide such a sense of redemption.

That isn't the only place such anguish comes across on *Layla and Other Assorted Love Songs*—"Have You Ever Loved a Woman" and "Why Does Love Got to Be So Sad" spring to mind—but the album isn't just an exploration of love denied. Instead, what *Layla* is ultimately about is the transformation of the blues, a process Clapton and his band mates manage through a variety of means. "Bell Bottom Blues," for instance, distills the pop-blues approach of Blind Faith and Cream into a memorable chorus and exquisite metaphor; "Tell the Truth" brings the white-soul groove Clapton mastered with Delaney & Bonnie to its fruition; while the exquisitely arranged "Little Wing" pulls a pathos (that even Hendrix missed) from the song.

As with any masterpiece, it wasn't easy to achieve such clarity of vision, and anyone wishing to hear just how much mediocre music had to be thrown away in making the album need only listen to the almost two and a quarter hours of outtakes and jam sessions included in *The Layla Sessions.* Although this 20th-anniversary-issue box set will doubtless be of interest to guitar fiends (thanks to more than an hour's worth of Clapton/Allman jams) and Clapton collectors, the sheer volume of material seems almost to lessen the original album's achievement. Great albums, it seems, are like sausage—you really *don't* want to know how they're made.

Live at the Fillmore expands on *In Concert,* and at least it has the advantage of a slightly different set list (one that includes Blind Faith's "Presence of the Lord" and three songs from Clapton's first solo album), but that isn't quite enough to overcome the interminable solos and often rambling playing.   —J.D.C.

Descendents

★★★ Fat (SST, 1981)
★★★★ Milo Goes to College (SST, 1982)

★★★	Bonus Fat (SST, 1985)
★★★★	I Don't Want to Grow Up (SST, 1985)
★★	Enjoy (SST, 1986)
★★★	All (SST, 1987)
★★½	Liveage (SST, 1987)
★★★★	Two Things at Once (SST, 1988)
★★	Hallraker: Live! (SST, 1989)
★★★★	Somery (SST, 1991)
★★	Everything Sucks (Epitaph, 1996)
★★★	Cool to Be You (Fat Wreck, 2004)

As they say in *Spinal Tap*, it's such a fine line between stupid and clever. Los Angeles punk band Descendents knew exactly where that line was, and was always happy to cross it. At its best, the group was uniquely able to be silly and smart at the same time, turning childish rants about food, fucking, parents, and girls into tales of adolescent ennui. In a scene where you could only be cool if you were an outcast, vocalist Milo Auckerman easily occupied the role Angus Young fills in AC/DC; both band member and band mascot, whose persona is a pissed-off geek with a perpetual hard-on. Most of the band's album covers include a Bart Simpson–looking doodle that caricatures Auckerman, a cartoonishness well-suited to the band's extremes.

With their 1981 debut EP, *Fat*, Descendents established their ongoing MO—hyperspeed punk songs with lyrics like, "I like food, food is good." The original version of that record did not include the group's first single, "Ride the Wild" b/w "It's a Hectic World," recorded before Auckerman joined the group. Although those two cuts appear on *Bonus Fat*, they can't be considered much of a bonus. *Milo Goes to College* is all straight-ahead punk—15 songs in less than a half hour, each full of metally riffs and lightning-speed plucking by bassist Tony Lombardo, who was always the band's secret weapon. Much like the Who, Descendents often used the bass for melodies and the guitar to bash out a steady rhythm. *Parents* shows a British punk influence, with Auckerman spitting the complaint: "They don't even know I'm a boy/They treat me like a toy, but little do they know that one day I'll explode." Both *Fat* and *Milo Goes to College* were later repackaged as *Two Things at Once*, an essential introduction to the group.

After Milo really did go to college, Descendents regrouped in 1985, and the resultant album, *I Don't Want to Grow Up*, featured the most singable tunes the band had ever written. "Good Good Things," "In Love This Way," and "Can't Go Back" were positively sunny by Descendents standards; the Beach Boys–gone-punk vibe was an obvious precursor to Weezer. The real advance was their ability to give strong melodies to thrash songs: "My World" and "Silly Girl" border on heavy metal but leave out the goofy excess and include way more self-pity.

Enjoy is weak overall, due in part to Lombardo's departure, though mostly because of the scatological humor on the title track. ("Sniff my ass while I pass gas," goes but one pearl.) The album is rescued by a cover of the Beach Boys' "Wendy" and the band's own "Sour Grapes," on which Auckerman gets rejected by a snooty new-wave girl. *All* is often underrated because of the strange pseudo-arty instrumental tracks on its second half; nonetheless, the album features three of the band's best songs, "Cameage," "Coolidge," and "Clean Sheets." The subjects are perennial, but Auckerman's sophistication as a lyricist has grown. "Coolidge" is about accepting one's uncoolness, and "Clean Sheets" talks of being forced to sleep on the floor after a lover's infidelity sullies the sheets.

Given its superior selection of songs, *Liveage* is the better of the band's two concert recordings; but Descendents weren't the kind of band to switch things up in concert, and these albums are for completists only. By contrast, the 1991 anthology, *Somery*, is the only Descendents record to qualify as must-have. It's got virtually all of the winning songs, from the goofy hardcore tunes like "Kids," "Weinerschnitzel," and "My Dad Sucks" to the more commercial-sounding rockers like "Hope," "Silly Girl," and "Sour Grapes."

For some unforgivable reason, the band reformed in 1996 with *All* bassist Karl Alvarez and guitarist Stephen Egerton. Their new album, *Everything Sucks*, lived up to its name. *Cool to Be You* (2004), on the other hand, finds the band sticking their toes into more adult themes (divorce, dead parents, complaints that "punk rock won't pay my bills"), amid some formidable hooks. —J.E.

Jackie DeShannon

★★★	The Very Best of Jackie DeShannon (Collectables, 1996)
★★	You Know Me (Jag/Varèse Sarabande, 2000)
★★★½	Best of Jackie DeShannon, 1958–1980; Come and Get Me (Raven, 2000)
★★★	Classic Masters (Capitol, 2002)

Jackie DeShannon scored massive hits in 1965 and 1969 with Burt Bacharach and Hal David's "What the World Needs Now Is Love" and her own "Put a Little Love in Your Heart"—but despite possessing a terrific, sexy-hoarse singing style, and releasing a number of instrumentally impressive albums (which have all fallen out of print), she has remained a behind-the-scenes wonder, best known for her songwriting.

DeShannon was born in Kentucky but moved to L.A. when she was 16, and began churning out hits for Brenda Lee and collaborating with Randy Newman and Phil Spector cohort Jack Nitzsche. Her early singles were orchestral-rock gems such as "When You Walk in the Room," which was a hit for the Searchers. For a while she turned out note-perfect Supremes homages ("Love Is Leading Me," "Are You Ready for This") before going the singer/songwriter route in the late '60s. In the early '70s she produced top-notch country rock, and in 1975 cowrote "Bette Davis Eyes," the song that made Kim Carnes a star. De-Shannon's solo albums aren't easy to find; *You Know Me* is fine later work. The Raven collection is nice: nearly 30 cuts of prime popcraft; the Capitol best-of only scratches the surface. —P.E.

Destiny's Child

★★★ Destiny's Child (Columbia, 1998)
★★★★ The Writing's on the Wall (Columbia, 1999)
★★★½ Survivor (Columbia, 2001)
★★ 8 Days of Christmas (Columbia, 2001)

Beyoncé

★★★★ Dangerously in Love (Sony, 2003)

Trying to keep track of who's in Destiny's Child is almost as hard as trying to get "Say My Name" out of your head. The Houston R&B gals aren't just a pop group, they're a soap opera, each hit single another chapter in their ongoing saga of lineup changes, lawsuits, sex, shopping, gossip, and all-around fabulousness. The star is Beyoncé Knowles. Her father is the manager, and her mother is the stylist. With her oft-nervous-looking band mates, Michelle (formerly Tenetria) Williams and Kelly (formerly Kelendria) Rowland, she rules the radio with fluid R&B harmonies, skitter-skatter beats, and more floss than the American Dental Association. Their message to the world is a simple one: Bounce, baby, bounce! Shake, baby, shake! Twist, baby, twist! Oh, and stay in school!

Destiny's Child first appeared as a quartet with the 1998 hit "No, No, No," which wiggled seductively while begging the question, Since there are four ladies in the group, shouldn't that be "No, No, No, No"? Or is one still making up her mind? The first hit from *The Writing's on the Wall*, "Bills, Bills, Bills," took the same three-out-of-four-divas approach as "No, No, No," for a lackluster rip of TLC's "No Scrubs." But "Say My Name" (seething paranoia!) and "Jumpin', Jumpin' " (way, *way* down with O.P.P.!) were catchy enough to turn any no-no-no scrub into yeah-yeah-yeah paying customer. By the time of their *Charlie's Angels* theme, "Independent Women," the D-Child ladies were down to three, with some lovely part-

ing gifts for the other contestants (thanks for the memories, Farrah; keep in touch, LaTavia; don't ever change, Toya). They were also on a major roll, saluting the kind of "Independent Women" who require an army of hair stylists, nail techs, and publicists just to clear their throats.

"Survivor" should have been called "Survivor, Survivor, Survivor." The ladies kissed off their former band mates with the immortal words, "I'm not gonna dis you on the Internet/'Cause my mama taught me better than that." But mama didn't teach them a thing about jelly, so it was time for "Bootylicious," an absolutely filthy sugar-walls anthem set to a Stevie Nicks guitar sample. All that remained to establish Destiny's Child as an American institution was (1) a pathetic performance at George W. Bush's inauguration, and (2) a Christmas album, both of which were accomplished in 2001. Overall, *The Writing's on the Wall* is a little catchier than *Survivor*, and remains the one to get until the inevitable greatest-hits album, which will be a doozy. Recommended title: *Beyoncé, Beyoncé, Beyoncé!*

Beyoncé finally made her solo debut in the summer of 2003, *Dangerously in Love*, and although she didn't have any other songs as great as "Crazy in Love," she didn't need any. "Crazy in Love" made Beyoncé the most important person in the world for a few months, a position she will no doubt continue to hold intermittently for the rest of her life. —R.S.

Devo

★★★★ Q: Are We Not Men? A: We Are Devo (Warner Bros., 1978)
★★★ Duty Now for the Future (Warner Bros., 1979)
★★★½ Freedom of Choice (Warner Bros., 1980)
★ Devo Live EP (Warner Bros., 1981)
★★★ New Traditionalists (Warner Bros., 1981)
★★ Oh No! It's Devo (Warner Bros., 1982)
★ Shout (Warner Bros., 1984)
★ E-Z Listening Disc (Rykodisc, 1987)
★★ Total Devo (Enigma, 1988)
★★ Now It Can Be Told (Enigma, 1989)
★ Smooth Noodle Maps (Enigma/Capitol, 1990)
★★ Hardcore Devo, Vol. 1: 1974–1977 (Rykodisc, 1990)
★★★★ Greatest Hits (Warner Bros., 1990)
★★½ Greatest Misses (Warner Bros., 1990)
★★★ Devo Live (The Mongoloid Years) (Rykodisc, 1992)
★★ Adventures of the Smart Patrol (Warner Bros./Sire/Discovery, 1996)
★★★★ Greatest Hits (BMG Special, 1998)
★★★½ Pioneers Who Got Scalped (Warner Bros., 2000)

Devo was a highly elaborate and pretty good joke. Embarking on a furious, mystic mission to redeem rock of its signature "excesses"—passion, rhythm, tunefulness, and aspirations to meaning—these '80s postmodernists dubbed themselves "suburban robots here to entertain corporate life forms." The product of a sensibility spun from William Burroughs, Andy Warhol, Kraftwerk, and drive-in sci-fi, Devo's vigorous embrace of technology paid off in hilarious, deadpan videos, daffy futuristic uniforms, and a neat mythology: With its mascot/idol the Kewpie-freak Booji Boy, the Devo shtick celebrated "de-evolutionized" blankness, as the corporation replaces love and family, and the microchip fills in for the soul.

Like most radical gestures, Devo was best in its first flexing. *Q: Are We Not Men? A: We Are Devo* was a brilliant hoot, with the fearsome five clinically deconstructing the Stones' "Satisfaction" and, in "Mongoloid" and "Jocko Homo," penning anthems to hail the victory of aliens over animals. The group's snappiest single was *Freedom of Choice*'s "Whip It"; its danceability seemed almost to subvert the tight-hipped Devo ideology, or to suggest that even androids sometimes like to funk it up. "Through Being Cool," off *New Traditionalists*, is swift; it celebrates sheer wimpery. The album also boasts one of the band's patented, debunking covers: Lee Dorsey's "Working in the Coalmine," done with an assembly-line sense of swing. The rest of Devo is the same gestalt, funny but monochromatic. Devo's overall cultural significance remains significant, however—they unleashed computer-nerd chic.   —P.E.

Neil Diamond

- ★★ Velvet Gloves and Spit (MCA, 1968)
- ★★ Brother Love's Traveling Salvation Show (MCA, 1968)
- ★★ Touching You, Touching Me (MCA, 1969)
- ★★ Tap Root Manuscript (MCA, 1970)
- ★★½ Stones (MCA, 1971)
- ★★ Moods (MCA, 1972)
- ★★★★ Hot August Night (MCA, 1972)
- ★★ Rainbow (MCA, 1973)
- ★ Jonathan Livingston Seagull (Columbia, 1973)
- ★★★★ 12 Greatest Hits (MCA, 1974)
- ★ Serenade (Columbia, 1974)
- ★ Beautiful Noise (Columbia, 1976)
- ★★★ Love at the Greek (Columbia, 1977)
- ★★ I'm Glad You're Here With Me Tonight (Columbia, 1977)
- ★★ You Don't Bring Me Flowers (Columbia, 1978)
- ★ September Morn (Columbia, 1979)
- ★★½ The Jazz Singer (Columbia, 1980)
- ★ Heartlight (Columbia, 1982)
- ★★★★ 12 Greatest Hits, Vol. 2 (Columbia, 1982)
- ★★★★ Classics: The Early Years (Columbia, 1983)
- ★ Primitive (Columbia, 1984)
- ★ Headed for the Future (Columbia, 1986)
- ★★ Hot August Night 2 (Columbia, 1987)
- ★ The Best Years of Our Lives (Columbia, 1988)
- ★ Lovescape (Columbia, 1991)
- ★★★ The Greatest Hits (1966–1992) (Columbia, 1992)
- ★★★★ Glory Road: 1968–1972 (MCA, 1992)
- ★ Up on the Roof (Columbia, 1993)
- ★ Live in America (Columbia, 1995)
- ★ Tennessee Moon (Columbia, 1996)
- ★★★★ In My Lifetime (Columbia, 1996)
- ★★ The Movie Album (Columbia, 1998)
- ★★★½ 20th Century Masters—The Millennium Collection (Columbia, 1999)
- ★★★★ Collection (Columbia, 1999)
- ★★★★ Ultimate Collection (Columbia, 1999)
- ★★★½ Stages: Performances 1970–2002 (Columbia, 2003)

The Jewish Elvis achieved his greatest artistic transcendence on the cover of his live album *Hot August Night*. Look at him: Neil Diamond, at one with the music. His head bows in reverence and his hair forms a halo above his silver-studded blue-denim jumpsuit, as yet another classic Neil tune explodes from his lungs. The soft-rock balladeer has earned his reputation as a master of crowd-pleasing showmanship. He is Brother Love, he is love at the Greek, he is love on the rocks. He is the sun, he is the moon, he is the words, and we are his tune. Reaching out. Touching me. Touching you. And no matter what he does, Neil Diamond exudes that raw sexual magnetism that never fails to keep Rosie cracklin', Holly holy, and Caroline sweet.

Diamond began in the '60s as a New York singer/songwriter; he was already on the charts himself by the time the Monkees had a #1 hit with his "I'm a Believer." His early Bang records output was a lean, mean run of catchy folk-rock hits like "Cherry Cherry," "Girl, You'll Be a Woman Soon," and "Red, Red Wine." He had a weird side from the beginning, manifested by lesser-known tunes such as "Two Bit Manchild" and "Crunchy Granola Suite." By the late '60s, he had recorded standards like "Sweet Caroline" and the genuinely demented "Brother Love's Traveling Salvation Show." He got more serious in the '70s, beginning with the over-the-top talking-chair soliloquy "I Am . . . I Said." His double-live *Hot August Night* is the triumph of Neilness; musically, it's a bit lax compared to the studio work, but it's festive, and the audio experience is considerably enhanced by the excellent back-cover notes ("ELECTRIC . . . his audience falls like plums at his feet!").

The hits rolled on: the ominous, mysterious "If You Know What I Mean," a sex-and-death torch song worthy of Nick Cave; "Desiree," where Neil confesses, "I became a man at the hands of a girl almost twice my age"; "Forever in Blue Jeans," with the line "Honey's sweet/But it ain't nothin' next to baby's treat" defining a new Neil lyrical sublime. By all accounts one of the true gentlemen in the music biz, Diamond keeps on keeping on. It would be ideal to have a succinct two-CD summary of his early hits, but none exists yet; the deceptively titled *Greatest Hits (1966–1992)* includes 13 inferior live remakes. If you're willing to shell out box-set money, the three-disc *In My Lifetime* at least keeps it strictly business with the real versions of the right songs; good to bear in mind for when your mom is having a bad day. Otherwise, 1983's *Classics: The Early Years* has the great Bang material; the 1999 *Collection* takes you from 1968 to 1972, with *Glory Road* a more expansive two-CD version; 1982's *12 Greatest Hits, Vol. 2* tells the rest of the story. His film work includes *The Last Waltz* (why he was there has never been explained), *The Jazz Singer* (featuring the hit "America"), and *Saving Silverman.* —R.S.

The Dictators

★★★★ Go Girl Crazy! (1975; Norton, 2003)
★★★ Manifest Destiny (East West, 1977)
★★★ Bloodbrothers (1978; Dictators Multimedia, 1998)
★★★ New York, New York (1981; ROIR, 1998)
★★★½ D.F.F.D. (Dictators Multimedia, 2001)

These hard-partying wrestling fans from the Bronx—singer "Handsome" Dick Manitoba, bassist-singer Andy Shernoff, and guitarist Scott "Top 10" Kempner, principally—never quite fit in with the NYC punk scene they helped create. Like the New York Dolls pumped with testosterone and laughing gas, the Dictators swaggered through three albums of sloppy, catchy-as-fuck novelty tunes, then disappeared, only to release one of their best discs 20 years later. *Go Girl Crazy!* set the template with its ironic, offensive, but never nihilistic lampoon of white urban culture. There are two types of songs: beach-life fantasies lifted straight from the '60s—"(I Live for) Cars and Girls," with its sunny drive and faux–Beach Boys harmonizing, and crass surf shouter "California Sun"—and rousing, square-baiting goofs like "Master Race Rock" and "Back to Africa." There's also a deadpan—and actually very pretty—cover of "I Got You Babe." The best thing about *Manifest Destiny* is the scorching cover of the Stooges' "Search and Destroy." On *Bloodbrothers,* "Handsome" Dick Manitoba maintains his brilliantly ragged bluster. But the album suffers from the ponderous influence of late '70s metal, and the jokes, while mostly warm and good-humored, aren't always silly enough to sustain themselves. For *D.F.F.D.,* their postmillennial comeback, the Dictators wisely ditched the over-the-top gags in favor of airtight blasts of early punk attitude buoyed by shout-along melodies and hilariously acid put-downs. The only hint of nostalgia is on "Who Will Save Rock and Roll?"; for the band's no-nonsense worldview, skip to the canonworthy "I Am Right!" and "Pussy and Money." Hint: The latter's "What's it all about?" is a rhetorical question. You'd have to ask them why they reunited when there's so little money to be made. —N.C.

Bo Diddley

★★★★ Bo Diddley/Go Bo Diddley (1958, 1959; Chess, 1987)
★ Live (1975; Triple X, 1994)
★★½ The Mighty Bo Diddley (1985; Triple X, 1994)
★★★★ The Super Super Blues Band (1986; MCA Special Products, 2002)
★★★★ Superblues: Bo Diddley, Muddy Waters and Little Walter (Chess, 1986)
★★★★ The Chess Box (Chess, 1990)
★★ This Should Not Be (Triple X, 1992)
★★½ Promises (Triple X, 1994)
★★ A Man Amongst Men (Code Blue/Atlantic, 1996)
★★½ Mona (Drive, 1996)
★★★★ His Best (Chess, 1997)
★★★½ The Millennium Collection: The Best of Bo Diddley (MCA, 2000)

In the beginning, Bo Diddley took a simple shave-and-a-haircut-six-bits rhythm and covered it with layer upon layer of rhythmic variation, courtesy of Jerome Green's maracas and his own tremolo-heavy guitar, on which he played two different rhythms simultaneously. Having created form, he added complexity in myriad harmonic and textural conceits. Then he brought his world to life in song by blending gospel and blues, and spicing these bedrock ingredients with quotes from black street-corner culture ("Say Man" being an early example of Diddley's use of "the dozens," ritualized insults, boasts, and dares). Bringing it all home in a deep, confident baritone vocal strut, the fellow born Ellas McDaniel in McComb, MS, became the absolute ruler of his dominion, an artist whose sound remains a touchstone for rock & roll guitarists and percussionists, and whose standing as "500 percent more man," as he asserted in one of his memorable lyric flights, remains unassailed four decades after "Say Man" became his sole Top 40 hit.

The logical place to begin assessing Diddley's work is *The Chess Box,* two CDs containing 45 tracks recorded between 1955 and 1968, including all the best-known songs—"Who Do You Love," "I'm a Man/Bo Diddley," "Mona," "Say Man," an extended version of "Signifying Blues"—as well as a host of alternate takes, B sides, and previously unreleased tracks. In the set's accompanying booklet, critic Robert Palmer offers a rigorous, authoritative dissection of Diddley's music, demanding the artist's oeuvre be reconsidered in serious musicological terms.

The Chess Box may be the alpha and omega of Diddley's output, but anyone inspired by Palmer's essay to look for further justification of Diddley's genius will find ample rewards in the catalogue (despite the white-hot *Bo Diddley Is a Gunslinger* having been deleted). Near the top of the A-list is *The Super Super Blues Band,* teaming Diddley with Muddy Waters and Howlin' Wolf on a fabulous set of raw, electric blues, with all three participants toasting each other at every turn. For sheer drive, few albums approach the jiving, juking, incendiary summit meeting heard on *Superblues.* Diddley, Muddy Waters, and Little Walter Jacobs play like men on a mission, talking trash and spurring each other on to more resonant performances. The version of Diddley's "Who Do You Love" included here is the model for the raging, near-meltdown performance of the tune that Diddley delivered on the *La Bamba* soundtrack. Jacobs blows low and mean behind Diddley and Waters on "I'm a Man," as the two guitarists spar instrumentally and verbally. Diddley's first two album releases, *Bo Diddley* and *Go Bo Diddley,* are now available in a twofer CD and represent in 24 tracks prime early Diddley; this is a good alternative to the more expensive box set for anyone on a limited budget or with only a casual interest in Diddley's work, as it contains a number of the best-known sides as well as scintillating items such as "Diddy Wah Diddy" and "Before You Accuse Me." By far the best single-disc summation of Diddley's Chess years is the 20-song *His Best,* a 1997 release that speaks the Diddley lingua franca from its first essential cut—"Bo Diddley," of course—to the final heated notes of the last cut, "Ooh Baby." A more concise but less satisfying overview of the most familiar material is provided on the 12-song *The Millennium Collection: The Best of Bo Diddley,* which includes "Bo Diddley," "I'm a Man," "Say Man," "Mona," and "Can't Judge a Book by Its Cover" among its marquee songs. Drive's *Mona* long player is even skimpier, but the 10 tracks are choice, among them the title cut, another Jerome Green showcase in "Bring It to Jerome," and a couple of tenderhearted Diddley paeans in "I'm Sorry" and "Tonight Is Ours."

In the early '90s, Diddley found a home on Triple X Records, with fair to middling results. At the desultory end of the scale, *Bo Diddley Live,* originally released in 1975, is five tracks of pointless jamming over steadily percolating P-Funk-influenced rhythms. At no point does Diddley distinguish himself on guitar in this mess, and one can only imagine how dreary a night it must have been for the audience as the noodling went on ad nauseam, rarely broken up by flashes of the headliner's lyrical wit or hilarious self-aggrandizement. This album comprises five songs, the shortest running slightly under 10 minutes, the longest a shade over 12 minutes. Later Diddley released *Mighty Bo Diddley,* a stronger effort in that it features some good new original songs and a few instrumental sparks from Diddley himself. Lascivious as ever, Diddley busts a move on the now-aging Mona's sister, in "Mona, Where's Your Sister," and gets in the face of an imagined competitor in "I Don't Know Where I've Been," an uptempo 12-bar blues effort that would have been right at home in Muddy Waters' repertoire. Before taking off on a stinging solo turn, Diddley warns, "I'm gonna make my guitar fit yo' head like a baseball cap!" One of the real treats on any Diddley album comes here, near the end, in a slow, deep, eight-bar blues, "Evil Woman," featuring a shouting, exasperated lead vocal—all B.B. King in style—and a series of tight, crying guitar solos, tart and angular with nary a superfluous note, that demonstrate the depth of feeling sometimes lost in the guitarist's customary flash. Caveat emptor: At this point, Diddley began displaying a social conscience in his lyrics, and these efforts, while well-meaning, are uniformly embarrassing. "Ain't It Good to Be Free" would like to have been Diddley's take on Merle Haggard's "Fightin' Side of Me," but it has nothing of the latter's wit or sense of purpose; "Gotta Be a Change" and "I Don't Want Your Welfare" ("If you wanna give me something/Give me a job," Diddley declares in the chorus) might have been compelling in third-person anecdotal form rather than first-person invective.

Over swirls of anthemlike electronic chords, Diddley's first words on the 1992 release, *This Should Not Be,* sound prescient post-9/11: "People of America/Our great nation is under attack/In this country/This should not be." He goes on to catalogue the social ills he sees around him—singling out hunger and homelessness—and extends the message of "this should not be" to every nation in the world. Prescience suddenly evolves into stridency, hardly whetting the appetite for what's ahead. Yet his other ventures into topicality are more measured and thus more convincing. "U Don't Look So Good" addresses a friend whose irresponsible behavior lands him behind bars; "Mind Yo Business" rails against invasions of privacy by casting the villains in the roles of nosy neighbors; hip-hop and gospel meet in "My Jesus Ain't Prejudice," Diddley's spoken-sung testimony of faith in a God whose love transcends racial boundaries and opposing philosophies. Elsewhere, Diddley gets down with some gutbucket rock & roll on "The Best," a vintage bit of manly bluster proclaiming his superior cocksmanship; makes a stylish foray into contemporary R&B love balladry in "Let Me Join Your World"; and gets with some Prince-inspired grooving on "U Ugly" (Prince seems to have influenced Bo's spelling of late, too). However effective these performances, though, Diddley the guitarist is buried beneath the electronic grooves, almost to the point of being inaudible. And what is a Bo Diddley album without Bo Diddley's guitar?

The title of his 1994 album, *Promises,* keyed to the song of the same name about a woman's duplicity, is more directly related to the overall theme of the rewards life holds for those who keep their heads on straight and stay straight at the same time. The title cut kicks off the set in sizzling fashion, with Tuck Tucker's soaring lap-steel lines adding some country funk to the foot-stomping Diddley beat. Diddley the writer delivers one of his strongest melodies ever and Diddley the singer accommodates it with a powerful, rocking vocal as the band wails behind him.

While retooling his signature rhythm for the electronic age in the swaggering (some might add "obnoxious") "I'm Gonna Get Your Girlfriend," Diddley addresses the younger generation in blunt terms on two songs inveighing against the lure of the street ("Kids Don't Do It" and "Hear What I'm Sayin' "), then closes the album with a troubling nightmare scenario suggested by the national colloquies on date rape (the cases of William Kennedy Smith and Mike Tyson spring to mind when Diddley plays out an imagined courtroom diatribe). In "She Wasn't Raped," Diddley the defendant declares to the jury, "That girl wasn't raped/She gave it up," and proceeds to plead his case over a wash of thumping electronic drums and angry, foreboding synthesizer retorts. Once again, the guitar is conspicuous by its absence. None of this amounts to much, though "She Wasn't Raped" has a certain brutal power in the righteous passion fueling Diddley's monologue. It's hard to fault the man for being engaged by the issues, but on this one he doesn't get it. Considering his own sexual posturing over the

years, the "she gave it up" line in "She Wasn't Raped" is chilling in its insensitivity. She was asking for it, she wanted it—all those repugnant, disingenuous formulations meant to excuse irresponsible, sometimes criminal behavior. Such simplistic thinking is what caused the problem in the first place, Bo.　—D.M.

Dido

  ★★★½　No Angel (Arista, 1999)
   ★★★　Life for Rent (Arista, 2003)

It is no coincidence that *No Angel* sounds surprisingly mature for a debut album. Before becoming an "overnight" global diva, the London-born Florian de Bounevialle Cloud Armstrong had already honed her musical skills with her brother Rollo's band Faithless. But it was *No Angel* that struck a universal chord with lovers of sophisticated, catchy dream-pop songs with trip-hop undertones (think Portishead-lite with a dash of Beth Orton charm and a hint of Sinéad O'Connor mysticism). Even Eminem liked "Thank You" enough to sample its first verse on his subsequent megahit "Stan." Dido's mellow approach and pretty melodies are a bit too laid-back to qualify as groundbreaking. But it would be cynical to altogether dismiss the *chanteuse*'s sincere intentions and gorgeous voice. In 2003, Dido avoided the sophomore slump with *Life for Rent,* a polished followup that reflected on her breakup with her fiancé while delivering dark pop gems such as the atmospheric "See the Sun."　—E.L.

Ani DiFranco

   ★★★½　Ani DiFranco (Righteous Babe, 1990)
   ★★★½　Not So Soft (Righteous Babe, 1991)
   ★★★★　Imperfectly (Righteous Babe, 1992)
   ★★★★　Puddle Dive (Righteous Babe, 1993)
   ★★★½　Like I Said: Songs 1990–91 (Righteous Babe, 1993)
   ★★★½　Out of Range (Righteous Babe, 1994)
   ★★★★　Not a Pretty Girl (Righteous Babe, 1995)
   ★★★★　Dilate (Righteous Babe, 1996)
   ★★★　More Joy, Less Shame EP (Righteous Babe, 1996)
 ★★★★½　Living in Clip (Righteous Babe, 1997)
   ★★★★　Little Plastic Castle (Righteous Babe, 1998)
   ★★★½　Up Up Up Up Up Up (Righteous Babe, 1999)
   ★★★½　To the Teeth (Righteous Babe, 1999)
   ★★★½　Swing Set EP (Righteous Babe, 2000)
   ★★★　Revelling/Reckoning (Righteous Babe, 2001)
   ★★★★　So Much Shouting, So Much Laughter (Righteous Babe, 2002)
   ★★★　Evolve (Righteous Babe, 2003)
   ★★½　Educated Guess (Righteous Babe, 2004)

Ani DiFranco/Utah Phillips

★★★★   The Past Didn't Go Anywhere (Righteous Babe, 1996)
★★★½   Fellow Workers (Righteous Babe, 1999)

Ani DiFranco learned early to live by her wits. As a teenager, she worked her way around Buffalo, NY, folk clubs and relocated to NYC before she turned 20. Two things made her become a folksinger: It was cheap (all the overhead she needed was an acoustic guitar), and it didn't get in the way of her saying her piece. And she had a lot to say—when she cut her first homemade tape, something to sell at the clubs she played, her guitar wasn't much more than a prop that she assaulted between breaths, but her words were fully formed, deeply personal, and rigorously political, and there were a lot of them. But she wasn't a folkie, and despite her looks, she wasn't a punk, either—she was a complete, irreducible original.

Her first two albums were just girl with a guitar, and possibly the most arresting piece on them was "Not So Soft," where she laid the guitar down and just spoke her poem. But she already had all the mouth she would ever need, and she exuded enough presence to make you hang on her every word. A few years later, on *Like I Said,* she returned to those early songs, fleshing them out with newfound musical skills, but the improvement is minor. However, on *Imperfectly,* she starts working with other musicians, most notably drummer Andy Stochansky. This adds powder to the explosive "What If No One's Watching." But DiFranco's own musicianship had also made a great leap forward, as on "If It Isn't Her," with just Ani playing quirky guitar and singing, "I have been playing/Too many of them boy-girl games/She says honey you are safe here/This is a girl-girl thing."

The albums that followed—*Puddle Dive, Out of Range, Not a Pretty Girl, Dilate*—are full of sharply observed lyrics and increasingly innovative music; it's a remarkable series of albums. Meanwhile, DiFranco's intense fan base grew large enough to put her self-released albums on the charts, leading to the inevitable two-CD *Living in Clip,* an extraordinary career summation selected from various concerts with her trio (Stochansky on drums, Sara Lee on bass). The set works both as a greatest-hits and as a performance showcase—DiFranco's guitar, especially on "Out of Range," has the same urgency and definition that she's long demonstrated with her voice.

The next series of albums might be considered her progressive period: While the lyrics continue to reflect her political concerns, they are less clearly anchored in her personal life (or perhaps her personal life as a record-company exec just isn't interesting enough), but her expanding musical skills often make for compelling listening. *Little Plastic Castle* starts out with horns and a Latin beat, and winds up with the meditative "Pulse," with Jon Hassell on trumpet. *Up Up Up Up Up Up* is looser and jazzier, while *To the Teeth* meanders into rap ("Swing") and ska-punk ("Freakshow") and hard to say what else. The sprawling two-CD *Revelling/Reckoning* is less successful, its lyrics hiding behind the music instead of jumping out. The second live double, *So Much Shouting, So Much Laughter,* is a lot more fun, partly because it recycles a familiar songbook under the guise of documenting her new band with all the snazzy horns. But the set also restores some bite to her political songs, especially "Self-Evident," though even there she seems to have outgrown her early, intense fusion of the personal and the political, relegating her political impulses to the more conventional realm of protest songs. Another long protest-song poem, "Serpentine," adds topical relevancy to *Evolve,* but for once, the fancy music gets the best of the muted messages.

On the other hand, her all-solo move, *Educated Guess,* contorts her elegant wordplay over a sharply stinging acoustic guitar, then tortures both with birdlike vocal overdubs. The only pleasure here is when she just recites, or just plays.

The two Utah Phillips albums comprise a fascinating side project. *The Past Didn't Go Anywhere* starts with Phillips saying, "What I do is I collect stories," but then you notice that he's been sampled and looped—folk music as mix tape. The music is decidedly unfolkie synth drums and New Age guitar, which Phillips talks and lectures and hectors over. Fascinating stories, too, especially the ones about deserting from the Korean War and finding pacifism as a 12-step program. And he's observant enough to quote an old geezer on his wife's New Age bookstore: "No matter how New Age you get, old age's gonna kick your ass." *Fellow Workers* dispenses with the trip-hop for tales of Mother Jones and Joe Hill and some old-fashioned labor struggle sing-alongs. Which just serves to remind us that one of DiFranco's most important innovations has been to build her own record label—a rare case of a worker who owns the means of production.   —T.H.

Digable Planets

★★★½   Reachin' (A New Refutation in Time and Space) (Pendulum, 1993)
★★★★   Blowout Comb (Pendulum, 1994)

In the early 1990s, while Suge Knight's Death Row records dominated hip-hop with artists like Dr. Dre and Tupac, Digable Planets chose the same high road

that De La Soul and A Tribe Called Quest had already taken—they all but ignored gangsta culture. MCs Doodlebug, Butterfly, and the sweet-voiced Ladybug combined a positive vibe with jazz samples to create ultra-laid-back joints that provoked head bobbing rather than drive-bys. Their debut, *Reachin'*, invaded college boom boxes and birthed the Top 20 hit and Grammy winner "Rebirth of Slick (Cool Like Dat)." While *Reachin'* preached self-belief, it also waxed political with cuts like the pro-choice narrative "La Femme Fétal" and avoided substance altogether on the nonsensical "Appointment at the Fat Clinic." Some of the tracks on *Reachin'* follow Tribe's blueprint to the letter, but by the time they released their second record, *Blowout Comb,* the Digables had clearly found their own sound. *Blowout* plays like a treatise for good living, an ethic that includes real live instruments and seven-minute epics such as the Afrocentric "Black Ego." "The Art of Easing" picks up where "Rebirth of Slick" left off, and "Borough Check," which features Gang Starr's Guru and a Roy Ayers sample, is a territorial pissing that you can dance to. Although it contained no obvious single, *Blowout* still cracked the Top 40. The group wasn't as lucky, though, and the Digables disbanded in 1995 due to creative differences.
—D.MA.

Digital Underground

★★★★	Sex Packets (Tommy Boy, 1990)
★★★★	Sons of the P (Tommy Boy, 1991)
★★★★	The Body-Hat Syndrome (Tommy Boy, 1993)
★★★½	Future Rhythm (Tommy Boy, 1996)
★★★½	Who Got the Gravy? (Tommy Boy, 1998)
★★★★	No Nose Job: The Legend of Digital Underground (Tommy Boy, 2001)
★★★★	Playwatchalike: The Best of Digital Underground (Rhino, 2003)

George Clinton is second only to James Brown as the originator of hip-hop's musical language—the beats with which California seized the airwaves from New York in the early '90s would be unthinkable without Parliament Funkadelic's blueprint. But unlike their g-funk peers, who replaced P-Funk's wacked-out sexiness with smug misogyny, Oakland's Digital Underground remained true to Clinton's original sensibility, celebrating sex as something squishy, giggly, and mutually pleasurable, and using comedy, with Shock-G, a.k.a. Humpty Hump, as lascivious ringleader.

The terrifically goofy "The Humpty Dance," emerging at the height of *Yo! MTV Raps,* defined the group's image, but the pansexual free-for-all "Doowhatchalike" was their true statement of purpose. The first two albums are solid, but their third was the most

accomplished. The Humpty Hump showcase "Return of the Crazy One" is one of the all-time fabulous raps; the rest of the disc is hooked to a fittingly Parliamentary concept: The world is full of so many evil ideas, you need a condom for your brain. Too bad it was released at a moment when their giddiness was too pop and too weird for a hip-hop world defined by the monochromatic retreads of Dre and his cronies.

When the history of hip-hop is written, these inventive goofballs may be remembered as novelty footnotes whose biggest gift to the music was first bringing Tupac Shakur into the studio. That would be a crime. For all its sexual boasting, rap has produced only a few MCs—L.L. Cool J, Notorious B.I.G.—who sound like they'd actually be any fun in bed; Humpty is freakier than any of them. Like Uncle Jam before them, their commitment to the groove was enough to keep even their minor efforts from going soft. Ice Cube, Snoop, and, yes, Tupac—none of Cali's most honored MCs can say the same.   —K.H.

Dinosaur Jr

★★	Dinosaur (Homestead, 1985)
★★	You're Living All Over Me (SST, 1987)
★★	Bug (SST, 1988)
★★★½	Green Mind (Blanco y Negro/Sire, 1991)
★★★	Where You Been (Blanco y Negro/Sire, 1993)
★★½	Without a Sound (Blanco y Negro/Sire, 1994)
★★★	Hand It Over (Blanco y Negro/Sire, 1997)
★★½	The BBC Sessions (Varèse, 2000)
★★★	Ear-Bleeding Country: The Best of Dinosaur Jr (Rhino, 2001)

After getting it together on three explosive but uneven indie records (*Bug* is the best) and five years of touring, Massachusetts' Dinosaur Jr released a bang-up masterpiece in 1991: *Green Mind.* For guitar maniacs only, this crunching, thunderous happy stuff recalls Neil Young at his Crazy Horse rawest; at other times, the ghost of Hendrix grins. Mainly, however, it's to the early Replacements that Dinosaur owes a heavy nod. Mastermind vocalist/axeman J Mascis writes raveups recalling the amphetamine melodies of the Mats; his voice doesn't sound dissimilar to Paul Westerberg's, and even the persona behind his songs is reminiscent of Westerberg, with its bad-boy-with-a-big-heart charm. Giddily entertaining, Dinosaur can even redeem a title like "Puke + Cry," and "How'd You Pin That One on Me" is the glorious noise every garage band dreams of making. Mascis gradually began to turn down the volume after *Green Mind;* his songwriting, however, remained powerful. The Rhino collection is comprehensive and makes a convincing argument for the band's significance.   —P.E.

Dio

★★	Holy Diver (Warner Bros., 1983)
★½	Last in Line (Warner Bros., 1984)
★	Sacred Heart (Warner Bros., 1985)
★½	Dream Evil (Warner Bros., 1987)
★★	Lock Up the Wolves (Warner Bros., 1990)
★	Strange Highways (Reprise, 1994)
★★	Diamonds—The Best of Dio (Reprise, 1994)
★	Angry Machines (Mayhem, 1996)
★	Inferno: Last in Live (Mayhem, 1998)
★½	Magica (Spitfire, 2000)
★★	The Very Beast of Dio (Rhino, 2000)
★	Killing the Dragon (Spitfire, 2002)
★★★	Stand Up and Shout: The Dio Anthology (Rhino, 2003)

A real traditionalist, Ronnie James Dio makes heavy-metal albums the old-fashioned way, with plenty of sludgelike guitar, dime-store satanism, and the sort of vocal vibrato usually found in aging Salvation Army workers. Granted, none of that offers enough to distinguish *Holy Diver, Last in Line,* or *Sacred Heart* from one another (though *Heart* was recorded live, and therefore has a somewhat flatter sound), but if foolish consistency is your favorite heavy-metal hobgoblin, the albums should be right up your alley.

Astonishingly, *Dream Evil*—recorded after guitarist Vivian Campbell had left to join Whitesnake—alters the formula, as "Sunset Superman" possesses an almost-catchy melody. But that would soon pass, and *Lock Up the Wolves* merely reinvents the old sound with (apart from Dio himself) an entirely new cast of players. Apparently having learned his lesson, Dio and crew continue to flog the same old formula—slow-grinding riffs and howling vocals with occasional spurts of mock-orchestral synths—for another half-dozen albums. Guess you *can't* teach an old devil new tricks. —J.D.C.

Dion

★★★	Presenting Dion and the Belmonts (1960; Collectables, 1983)
★★★	Runaround Sue (1961; The Right Stuff, 1993)
★★★	Reunion: Dion & the Belmonts (1973; Rhino, 1989)
★★★	Yo Frankie! (BMG/Arista, 1989)
★★★½	Bronx Blues: The Columbia Recordings (Columbia, 1990)
★★½	Rock n' Roll Christmas (1993; The Right Stuff, 1999)
★★★½	The Road I'm On: A Retrospective (Columbia/Legacy, 1997)
★★★	Déjà Nu (Collectables, 1999)
★★★★★	King of the New York Streets (The Right Stuff, 2000)
★★	Super Hits (Columbia/Legacy, 2000)
★★½	The Wanderer: Then and Now (Collectables, 2001)
★★★	The Complete Dion & the Belmonts (Collector's Choice, 2001)
★★★	The Wanderer: His Greatest Hits on Laurie Records (Collectables, 2003)
★★★½	Drip Drop: His Greatest Hits on Columbia Records (Collectables, 2003)
★★★★	Greatest Hits (Capitol, 2003)

Dion DiMucci was one of the greatest singers of the late-'50s, early-'60s rock period before the Beatles arrived in the U.S. Born July 18, 1939, in the Bronx borough of New York City, Dion came on the scene at the tail end of the doo-wop era, in 1958, bringing with him a solid musical foundation that found him conversant not only with pop music and R&B, but with country and blues as well. By suggesting (in his wonderfully nuanced phrasing as well as in the words he sang) vulnerability and a tender, even sentimental heart quite at odds with the confident swagger definitively associated with this former member of the Fordham Baldies street gang, Dion challenged his listeners in ways few of his less daring contemporaries could.

Dion's recording career began in 1957 with two singles for the Mohawk label. For the second single, he recruited for support his Bronx buddies Angelo D'Aleo, whose tenor voice was nearly as beautiful and expressive an instrument as Dion's; second tenor Fred Milano; and bass singer/drummer par excellence Carlo Mastrangello. Dion dubbed the group the Belmonts, in honor of Belmont Avenue, in the guys' Italian neighborhood in the Bronx.

Considering how the very mention of their name causes doo-wop aficionados' hearts to flutter, Dion and the Belmonts had only a brief fling together on record—brief but memorable, to the tune of seven Top 40 hits between 1958 and 1960—before Dion went solo. Their second single, "I Wonder Why," launched them onto the charts, peaking at #22, and introduced not a trademark sound but a striking one: Mastrangello kicks it off with a forceful rat-a-tat-tat attack of nonsense syllables before the other three voices come in, one after another, until they're all in harmony and singing the intro setup for Dion's soaring, plaintive entrance: "I-I wonder why/I love you like I do . . ."; it's one of the all-time great singles in rock & roll history. Two followup singles, "No One Knows" and a downbeat ballad, "Don't Pity Me," hit #19 and #40 in 1958 and early 1959, respectively, setting the stage for the group's breakthrough hit, "Teenager in Love," from the pens of the formidable songwriting team of Doc Pomus and Mort Shuman. "Teenager in Love" peaked at #3 and was followed in short order by another #3 single, a version of Rodgers and Hart's pop standard "Where or When," done in the close harmony style of early '50s pop vocal groups such as the Ames Brothers and the Four Aces. At the moment "Where or When" reached its chart apex, Dion was in a hospital trying to kick his drug habit. Two more charting singles followed in 1960—"When You Wish Upon a Star" and "In the Still of the Night"—but by that time, the group had already performed its final shows together. Dion and the Belmonts' brief, incandescent history is documented best on Collectables' reissue of the 1959 Laurie album, *Presenting Dion and the Belmonts*. Disc one of the *King of the New York Streets* box set, titled "The Wanderer," contains six Dion and the Belmonts tracks, among them four of the seven charted singles ("I Wonder Why," "Don't Pity Me," "A Teenager in Love," and "Where or When"). The group reunited in 1972 to play a reunion show for 20,000 fans at New York's Madison Square Garden, and it turned out to be a great night, as preserved on Rhino's *Reunion: Live at Madison Square Garden 1972* CD.

As a solo artist on Laurie, Dion hit the Top 20 right off the bat with 1960's "Lonely Teenager." What happened next created a rock & roll legend. On his first 1961 single, "Runaround Sue," Dion unleashed the persona that had only been hinted at in his work with the Belmonts, and it was credible enough to ensconce the 45 at #1 for two weeks. It was followed immediately by "The Wanderer," a #2 single whose title— and a swaggering, bravura lyrical interpretation that bestowed an autobiographical feel on the song's account of inveterate, heartless womanizing (the guys in the old neighborhood must have loved it)—gave Dion a nickname he still answers to professionally. Over the next three years, he cut a succession of singles that reinforced his image as a tender-tough street kid. "Coming from that Italian macho background, with the gangs and everything," he comments in the updated liner notes on the reissue of his first solo album, 1961's *Runaround Sue*, "you couldn't express loneliness or compassion, any kind of empathy, directly. But when you sang about those things, guys would say, 'That's great!' . . . That was an okay way of saying 'I'm lonely and I'm frightened.'" *Runaround Sue* also documents Dion's nascent forays into well-crafted '60s teen pop, though the results are mixed. A weird version of Bobby Darin's "Dream Lover" finds Dion adding "mmm" and "yeah" to the end of several lyric lines and working to an arrangement of no particular

distinction, save that common to a smarmy lounge singer. An album-closing take on Goffin and King's "Take Good Care of My Baby," which had been a #1 single for Bobby Vee only three months before Dion's album was released, features a nice, low-key reading appropriate to the singer's plea for reconciliation, but neither the vocal performance nor the arrangement would make anyone forget why the Snuff Garrett– produced Vee single topped the chart. Nevertheless, *Runaround Sue* is a portrait of Dion at a particular moment in his career and in rock history, and as such, it provides an interesting perspective on the options he felt were open to him at that juncture.

Options appear to be the point of Dion's move to Columbia in 1962. In the same way labelmate Johnny Cash was leaping stylistic boundaries in search of material and selflessly championing other songwriters' work even while developing his own writer's voice, so did Dion use the Columbia years to delve deeper into the roots music that had first influenced him back in the Bronx, gradually supplanting the odes to teen misery with more mature musings on the state of the heart and the world. His first Columbia hit single was both familiar and new: "Ruby Baby," which lodged three weeks at #2 in early 1963, was a tough, grinding Leiber-Stoller blues for the Drifters, but Dion's uptempo treatment featured de rigueur background hand claps and a solid backbeat supporting a loose, swinging vocal. At the same time this evolution was under way, Dion remained true to the street, cutting some fine pop/doo-wop singles, including "Can't We Be Sweethearts" (one of his best) and "This Little Girl," the latter peaking at #21. As 1963 wound down, he landed on the charts twice more with remarkable performances. The best of the two, "Donna the Prima Donna," is a big, deep production keyed by insistent hand claps, woodblock percussion, rich background voices alternately singing the titular girl's name and settling into smooth "ooohhhs" as Dion wails the verses.

Peaking at #6, "Drip Drop" was Dion's last chart appearance until 1968, when he returned to Laurie. But he never stopped recording, and for the next three years, he made some of the best music of his career, even though the general public heard little of it. In 1965, he cut a scorching version of an obscure Bob Dylan song, "Baby, I'm in the Mood for You," with a full rock & roll band; that same year, he also delivered a fierce rendition of Willie Dixon's "Spoonful" in an arrangement that echoes the murky, sinister ambience of Bo Diddley's records. No doubt his worsening drug problem and his diminishing commercial fortunes played into his mind-set. His anxiety and insecurity produced some beautiful moments, though, such as 1964's "The Road I'm On (Gloria)" and 1965's "Time in My Heart for You." The Columbia years are now well represented on two releases: The first was 1990's *Bronx Blues: The Columbia Recordings,* a collection of 20 tracks including the chart hits and eight songs that do not appear on the other Columbia overview, 1997's two-disc *The Road I'm On: A Retrospective.* Among the essentials on *Bronx Blues* is a little-heard Pomus-Shuman gem, "Troubled Mind," a terse, shuffling blues with gospel overtones a la "Nobody Knows the Trouble I've Seen," and the recording of Dylan's "Baby, I'm in the Mood for You." A less satisfying Columbia package is the ill-conceived *Super Hits,* a skimpy 10-song long player with no discernible conceptual glue.

In 1966, Columbia dropped Dion and he wound up briefly on ABC, where he reunited with the Belmonts for a few engaging rock & roll sides, one of which, "My Girl the Month of May" (the final track on disc one of the *King of the New York Streets* box) is a monstrous recording with a Brit-pop feel. Finally, though, he dropped out of sight to overcome his drug addiction, and when he returned sober and focused to Laurie Records in 1968, he was fully engaged in folk, blues, and folk rock. His first release, "Abraham, Martin and John," written by Dick Holler (nom de plume for country songwriter Dick Feller), caught the zeitgeist and rejuvenated his career. A somber, orchestral, folk-based tribute to three slain leaders came on like a soothing balm to a nation rocked by violence and internal strife centered on the civil rights movement and the undeclared war in Vietnam. As illustrated on *Dion,* his now-out-of-print album for Laurie.

On signing with Warner Bros. in 1969, Dion went full-tilt into folk rock on five intimate, introspective albums, all now out of print, though representative tracks from that period comprise the bulk of disc two of *King of the New York Streets.* Despite beautiful, affecting songs such as "Sanctuary," the Warners period produced no commercial hits; to make matters worse, a dream project with Phil Spector was deemed such a dud that the label declined to release it domestically, though it was available in England.

Moving to Lifesong in 1979, Dion remained on the upswing aesthetically, if not commercially, with *Return of the Wanderer.* A single, "I Used to Be a Brooklyn Dodger," is one of his most poignant vocals, finding him looking back in fondness and with regret at his youth and what he has lost over time. Rejected by the secular market, Dion turned to gospel and recorded several first-rate albums for the Word label, all extolling his newfound faith in God. One of those, *I Put Away My Idols,* won a Dove Award and earned a Grammy nomination in 1983.

But the journey was far from over; in fact, it continues to the present day. Dion returned to the secular field following the publication of his autobiography in the late '80s; and in 1989, he teamed up with producer Dave Edmunds for the inspired *Yo Frankie* on Arista. Edmunds keeps Dion front and center, while surrounding him with a guitar-heavy wall of sound and lush backup vocals. Although the album trades some on the artist's nostalgia value with "King of the New York Streets," "Written on the Subway Wall," and "Little Star," the blending of new and vintage themes inspired impassioned performances, serving notice that work remained unfinished here.

Nineteen ninety-three saw the release of a delightful Christmas album, *Rock n' Roll Christmas. Déjà Nu,* released in 2000, combines two songs Dion wrote for the film *The Wanderer* with more recent recordings in tribute to, as he writes in his liner notes, "Cars, Girls, Love." It gets a bit deeper than that, thanks to two moving covers of Bruce Springsteen songs: "Book of Dreams," done reverently, with a doo-wop-style close harmony chorus in the background; and "If I Should Fall Behind," which closes the album on an a cappella note, with the Wanderers providing a classic, bopping backdrop, complete with burbling bass and wailing falsetto, as Dion sings the vows of devotion with stirring sensitivity. However retro its sensibilities (even the Springsteen songs, evocative and eloquent though they be, are of a piece with a romantic's idealistic view of the world), *Déjà Nu* is a solid effort that shows 61-year-old Dion DiMucci forever young and in command, in voice and in spirit. —D.M.

Celine Dion

- ★ Unison (550 Music/Epic, 1990)
- ★ Celine Dion (550 Music/Epic, 1992)
- ★ Colour of My Love (550 Music/Epic, 1993)
- ★ Dion Chante Plamandon (550 Music/Epic, 1994)
- ★ Power of Love (550 Music/Epic, 1995)
- ★ French Album (550 Music/Epic, 1995)
- ★½ Falling Into You (550 Music/Epic, 1996)
- ★½ Let's Talk About Love (550 Music/Epic, 1997)
- ★ These Are Special Times (550 Music/Epic, 1998)
- ★★ All the Way . . . A Decade of Song (550 Music, 1999)
- ★ The Collector's Series, Vol. 1: (550 Music, 2000)
- ★½ A New Day Has Come (550 Music/Epic, 2002)

Rockers like to imagine that this Quebeçoise thrush embodies all that is Not Rock—mushy soundtrack ballads, windswept weepers for your girlfriend's mom, cloying Hallmark poesy. We should be so lucky—unfortunately, rock makes plenty of space for those qualities. In fact, Dion is harder than most chart-topping gangstas, and her sentimentality is bombastic and defiant rather than demure and retiring. "My Heart Will Go On" wasn't a doormat's plaint, after all; it was a threat of incommutability as ferocious as any crap metal band's profession of dominance.

Though she always used her voice as a club with which to bonk listeners, her earliest hits—"Beauty and the Beast" with Peabo Bryson, "If You Asked Me To"—were as harmless as they were dreadful. Unless you'd accidentally preprogrammed a Lite FM station onto your car stereo or spent too much time in the grocery store, you could safely avoid repeated exposure. Until 1996, that is, when an anonymous "house" rhythm was grafted onto "It's All Coming Back to Me Now" (written by Jim Steinman, the Meatloaf accomplice), granting Dion entrée into the cheesier clubs and pop stations. But her ambitions were both grander and more crass than that, and were well served by the confluence of interests that brought her into contact with both Diane Warren and James Cameron.

In a way, Dion's attention-getting appearance on VH1's *Divas* was sadly appropriate—she stands at the end of the chain of drastic devolution that goes Aretha-Whitney-Mariah. Far from being an aberration, Dion actually stands as a symbol of a certain kind of pop sensibility—bigger is better, too much is never enough, and the riper the emotion the more true.   —K.H.

Dire Straits

★★★½	Dire Straits (Warner Bros., 1978)
★★★½	Communiqué (Warner Bros., 1979)
★★★	Making Movies (Warner Bros., 1980)
★★★★	Love Over Gold (Warner Bros., 1982)
★★★	Twisting by the Pool EP (Warner Bros., 1983)
★★★★½	Brothers in Arms (Warner Bros., 1985)
★★★	Alchemy (Warner Bros., 1984)
★★★★	Money for Nothing (Warner Bros., 1988)
★★★★	On Every Street (Warner Bros., 1991)
★★	On the Night (Warner Bros., 1993)
★★★	Live at the BBC (Warner Bros., 1995)
★★★★	Sultans of Swing—The Very Best of Dire Straits (Warner Bros., 1998)

Dire Straits was originally a band, a four-piece whose singer and lead guitarist, Mark Knopfler, happened to do the bulk of the writing. Over time, however, the group slowly became less a unit than Knopfler plus backing players. On one level, this had a certain Darwinian inevitability to it; being both a winningly acerbic tunesmith and virtuoso guitarist, it was only natural that Knopfler would come to the fore.

But it's a mistake to assume that Dire Straits was little more than the Mark Knopfler show because, as their recordings make plain, this was clearly a case of the parts exceeding the whole. Regardless of what Knopfler's songwriting and fancy picking brought to the party, the feel of the performances made the music click. In other words, Dire Straits was nothing if not a groove band.

That's not the same thing as calling it a soul or funk band, of course; the group's sense of rhythm has more in common with the swampy, low-key blues of J.J. Cale and later Eric Clapton. That much was made clear with the quartet's first success, an insinuating bit of bar-band mythmaking called "Sultans of Swing." Even though Knopfler's lyrics paint a vivid picture of an overlooked and underappreciated pub combo, what ultimately reels the listener in is the laid-back insistence of the band's rhythm work, a quality abundant throughout *Dire Straits,* from the Dylanesque flavor of "Wild West End" to the galloping groove of "Down to the Waterline." (*Live at the BBC,* recorded in 1978, illustrates that groovesmanship was also very much a part of their live show.)

Communiqué continues in that fashion for the most part, but expands the scope of Knopfler's storytelling through the moody, elegiac "Once Upon a Time in the West." With the departure of rhythm guitarist David Knopfler (Mark's brother), the band's size is scaled down, but the music on the aptly titled *Making Movies* moves in the opposite direction, toward sprawling story songs like the sweet, Springsteenian "Romeo and Juliet," although, as "Skateaway" indicates, the band's pursuit of musical drama sometimes comes at the expense of the melody. Fortunately, the band regains its focus for *Love Over Gold,* on which the Straits—now a quintet—easily sustain the mood and melodic structure of the 14-minute megawork "Telegraph Road." Even better, they're able to augment such epics with material as sharply funny as the wry character number "Industrial Disease" or the lighthearted title tune from *Twisting by the Pool.*

Alchemy, an ambling, long-winded live album, focuses almost exclusively on the band's larger works, offering some flashes of instrumental brilliance but little insight into the material, something that makes the radio-friendly brevity of *Brothers in Arms* all the more surprising. It may be easy to find parallels to the album's biggest hits in the band's early output—for instance, the way "Walk of Life" seems to cross "Sultans of Swing" with "Twisting by the Pool," or how "Money for Nothing" taps the same satiric vein as "Industrial Disease"—but the reality is that *Brothers* is the exception to Dire Straits' sound.

Perhaps that's why Knopfler and company waited

so long to deliver that album's followup, *On Every Street.* (*Money for Nothing,* like *Sultans of Swing: The Very Best of,* is simply a hits collection.) Although the album has its lighter moments, such as the dead-Presley "Calling Elvis" or the consumerist sarcasm of "Heavy Fuel," the bulk of its songs find Dire Straits doing what it does best, stretching dry, reflective words and tunes over moody, effortlessly maintained grooves. But that was it; after releasing *On the Night,* a live album culled from the *On Every Street* tour, Dire Straits quietly disbanded as Knopfler pursued the solo career most fans thought he was already leading. —J.D.C.

Dirty Dozen Brass Band

★★★	My Feet Can't Fail Me Now (George Wein Collection, 1984)
★★★	Live: Mardi Gras in Montreux (Rounder, 1986)
★★★½	Voodoo (Columbia, 1989)
★★★★	The New Orleans Album (Columbia, 1990)
★★★★	Open Up: Whatcha Gonna Do for the Rest of Your Life? (Columbia, 1992)
★★★	Jelly (Columbia, 1993)
★★★½	This Is Jazz #30 (Columbia, 1997)
★★★	Buck Jump (Mammoth, 1999)
★★★★½	Medicated Magic (Rope a Dope, 2002)

In classic New Orleans tradition, the Dirty Dozen Brass Band started out as an all-acoustic ensemble in which everyone but the drummers played wind instruments. Things have changed over the years—the group's recordings include guitarists and keyboard players—but the group's marching-music roots remain so strong that almost everything it records uses a sousaphone instead of a string bass.

The term "classic New Orleans tradition" makes sense only if you accept the notion that progress is a natural part of the city's heritage. Hence, applying the "roots" label to both George Clinton and Ferdinand "Jellyroll" Morton is patently obvious to the band, even if it isn't always clear to the listener. *My Feet Can't Fail Me Now* finds the group starting off with a fondness for jazz that its subsequent output doesn't support; *Mardi Gras in Montreux* covers similar territory but with more humor and greater energy (not to mention a killer revision of *The Flintstones* theme). *Voodoo,* though, is much more ambitious, augmenting the group's usual groove with cameos by Dizzy Gillespie, Dr. John, and Branford Marsalis. And even though *The New Orleans Album* continues that vein with an Elvis Costello feature, its emphasis on such guests as Dave Bartholomew and Eddie Bo makes it closer in spirit to the insider cool of the Big Easy's annual Jazz

and Heritage Festival than the calculated glitz of Mardi Gras.

Whatcha Gonna Do for the Rest of Your Life? needs no outside help to stretch the limits of the band's sound—the Dirties do it themselves, through the sassy funk of "Use Your Brains" and the eloquent lament of "The Lost Souls (of Southern Louisiana)." Sadly, *Jelly*—a well-meaning but overtly studious tribute to Mr. Morton—puts the group in a far more serious mood than necessary.

On *Buck Jump,* the Dirties try hard to balance their jazz ambitions with their street-funk roots and succeed more than half the time. But *Medicated Magic,* with its feel-good emphasis on Creole R&B classics, ultimately proves the combo's mettle. With guest stars ranging from Dr. John and Norah Jones to DJ Logic, its groove-conscious renditions of "Cissy Strut," "Junko Partner," and "Walk on Gilded Splinters" elevates the Dirty Dozen to the status of Crescent City Classics.   —J.D.C.

Dirty Vegas

★★½	Dirty Vegas (Capitol, 2002)

Dirty Vegas Sound System

★★½	A Night at the Tables (Ultra, 2003)

In a sense, South London suburbanites Paul Harris, Steve Smith, and Ben Harris got the usual order of things backward. As Dirty Vegas, the trio achieved notoriety when its first single, "Days Go By," had already been included in a television ad (for Mitsubishi's Eclipse), rather than waiting until it had become a club hit, or at least included on an album, first. Unfortunately, *Dirty Vegas* has little beyond that song (quite seductive even minus the visual appeal of a popping-and-locking girl) to recommend it, though the hit does pretty much indicate what the rest of the disc's contents sound like. Not quite so with *A Night at the Tables,* a mix CD that the trio rushed out a few months after their first album, which is more likable than you might expect from such a pushy group of tracks. Sure, the synth glides are bombastic, but occasionally—as on Underworld's "2 Months Off" or a mix of Frankie Knuckles featuring Nicki Richards' "Keep On Moving (King Unique Re-Edit)"—they generate an appealingly rocklike push.   —M.M.

Dismemberment Plan

★★★	! (DeSoto, 1995)
★★★	Dismemberment Plan Is Terrified (DeSoto, 1997)
★★★★	Emergency & I (DeSoto, 1999)
★★★	The Dismemberment Plan/Juno (DeSoto, 2001)

★★★★   Change (DeSoto, 2001)
★★★★   A People's History of the Dismemberment Plan (DeSoto, 2003)

By the time the Dismemberment Plan broke up in early 2003, the Washington, D.C., foursome had become among the most influential bands in underground emo. But, while they deserved every bit of the credit they got, singer-guitarist Travis Morrison, drummer Joe Easley, bassist Eric Axelson, and guitarist Jason Caddell (all but Easley also played keyboard) did not represent their subgenre so much as twist it into a pretzel, crossing punk, funk, new wave, and smarty-pants pop.

! could not have been better titled. Morrison rants, screams, and even sings prettily over a mish-mash of sounds that draws from D.C. punk's long history: Minor Threat's jittery hardcore, Rites of Spring's fractured emo, Jawbox's majestic melancholy, and Fugazi's own dub-influenced hodge-podge. Easley, one of indie rock's best drummers and the Dismemberment Plan's purest talent, hadn't even joined the band yet. Morrison's oddball sense of humor even cut through all the racket; an otherwise dark number features the chorus (also its title), "Onward, Fat Girl."

In a reversal as sudden as the band's time-signature changes, *The Dismemberment Plan Is Terrified* ditched in-your-face punk in favor of brainy anything-goes indie. Morrison squeaks most of "That's When the Party Started" in a playful falsetto, as if he's just huffed helium, and guitar and keyboard intertwine in a woozy, screeching breakdown. In one of the best emo songs ever, "The Ice of Boston," Morrison delivers a deadpan spoken-word narrative over a cool lounge-rock groove, and breaks into an anthemic but still lovely chorus. Relating a shitty New Year's Eve, he describes "two million drunk Bostonians/ singing 'Auld Lang Syne' out of tune," stripping and pouring champagne on his head as his mother calls on the phone, and confronting a former lover: "So I guess the party line is I followed you up here/Well, I don't know about that/Mainly because knowing about that would involve knowing some pathetic, ridiculous, and absolutely true things about myself/that I'd rather not admit to right now." More than just another indie rocker fixated on romantic dysfunction—and there are plenty of them—Morrison was admitting absolutely true things about himself, and unearthing as much joy as disappointment.

In 1998, the Plan released an EP, *The Ice of Boston,* on Interscope, but were soon dropped from the label. (The disc is no longer in print.) Their distinguished return to the indie world, *Emergency and I,* includes a frantic meditation on what would happen if the sun simply went out, named for how long it takes sunlight to reach the earth: "8½ Minutes." That space of time, when feelings would be not only bared but driven to extremes, dramatizes what the album is all about. "Memory Machine," an ironic fantasy about someday being able to erase "longing" ("Poetry, Aldous Huxley—yeah, yeah, yeah, it'll be a relief"), sounds like a mechanical failure, with Easley's spectacularly stuttering beat, almost random bursts of bass, and alarm bells of guitar and keyboard, but the song also captures the chaos of emotion. The frenetic, inventive rockers and borderline-creepy ballads here begin to make sense of that chaos.

The exceedingly tender and exquisitely tense *Change,* on the other hand, hums like a car cruising down a lonesome highway. Even at the end of "Superpowers," where one pounding guitar chord gives way to astringent, off-key notes, the inexorable pull of the desire—to return to the past for a better future, for anything other than the here and now—cannot be shaken. In the live staple "Time Bomb," Morrison quavers, "I lay forgotten at the bottom of your heart/I'm fine, ticking away the years, until I blow your world apart." Having exploded the conventions of emo and indie rock itself, the Dismemberment Plan left behind a catalogue of music that will surely continue to change the inner worlds of young romantics. —N.C.

Disturbed

★★   Sickness (Giant, 2000)
★★½   Believe (Warner Bros., 2002)

Drawing equally on thudding new-metal riffology and the gothic industrial disco of their hometown of Chicago, Disturbed was part of the first wave of post-Korn new-metal bands. On *Sickness,* singer Dave Draiman—he of the spiky hair, chin stud, and surprisingly solid voice for a new-metal vocalist—bellows and rants about pain he's felt (whisper-to-scream rage on "Stupify") and radio hits he loved as a youth (Tears for Fears' "Shout" gets an appropriately thudding cover). The "Don't hit me, Mommy" crap at the end of the oddly danceable "Down With the Sickness" could be sick-joke funny if you let it, but much of *Sickness* feels like hollow formula.

That didn't stop it from selling 2 million copies, and making the followup, *Believe,* one of 2002's more hotly anticipated new-metal albums, on which they turn up the industrial brattle and gothic melodrama. Draiman makes a deal with God on the clattering "Prayer," but you can practically hear the walls bleed on "Rise" and "Intoxication." And they can't seem to avoid the inadvertently hilarious. The album closer

"Darkness" finds Draiman getting his croon on, singing for the laughter and singing for the tears, because with any luck, maybe tomorrow the Good Lord will take him away. —J.G.

The Divine Comedy

- ★★★ A Short Album About Love (Setanta, 1997)
- ★★★ Fin de Siècle (Setanta, 1998)
- ★★★★ A Secret History: The Best of the Divine Comedy (Tristar, 1999)
- ★★★ Regeneration (Nettwerk, 2001)
- ★★★★ Absent Friends (Nettwerk, 2004)

Neil Hannon, the Northern Irish singer, songwriter, and multi-instrumentalist who bills himself on record as the Divine Comedy, is the kind of musical personality they just don't breed in America. Equal parts Scott Walker, Burt Bacharach, Michael Nyman, and Noël Coward, Hannon pokes fun at all aspects of modern life and culture in his lushly, sometimes kitschily arranged pop ditties. His lyrics rarely fail to display erudition with a nod and a wink, but it's his dramatic baritone and knack for writing unshakable tunes that make the Divine Comedy more than just a chucklesome novelty act.

Recorded live with a full orchestra, *A Short Album About Love* isn't consistently brilliant, but "In Pursuit of Happiness," "Everybody Knows (Except You)," and the gorgeous "Timewatching" are top-notch examples of Hannon's craft. *Fin de Siècle* charms with "National Express," "Commuter Love," and "Eric the Gardener," then overindulges in smarmy grandiosity. *Regeneration* finds Hannon working with Radiohead producer Nigel Godrich and adopting a more restrained tone. The laugh quotient is down, unfortunately, but the melodies are as sweet as ever. On *Absent Friends,* Hannon reconnects with his wit and his love of lushness (the orchestra's back); he also allows himself a new, plainspoken emotionalism that, at its deepest ("Leaving Today," "Charmed Life"), is surprisingly touching.

A Secret History does a decent job of compiling Hannon's '90s work, though several tracks lack for the context of their original albums. "Your Daddy's Car," "The Summerhouse," and "Becoming More Like Alfie" are standouts. Still, the best introduction to the Divine Comedy can be found only in the import racks, via three British Setanta releases: *Liberation* (1993), *Promenade* (1994), and *Casanova* (1996). Each of these discs is a witty chamber-pop tour de force, worthy of at least four stars. —M.R.

Dixie Chicks

- ★★★½ Wide Open Spaces (Monument, 1998)
- ★★★½ Fly (Monument, 1999)
- ★★★★ Home (Sony, 2002)
- ★★★½ Worldwide Live (Sony, 2004)

All through 2000, country radio was flooded with "Goodbye Earl," a song about how a battered wife and her high school pal decide to off the abusive husband with a bowl of "special" black-eyed peas. Some stations ran public-service announcements following the Dixie Chicks' "Goodbye Earl" about how to properly report spousal abuse. Sure, they were increasing community awareness, but it almost seemed as if they also feared a rash of Chick-related poisonings. And who could blame them for worrying? Not only did the women make the operation sound rational, but the giddy menace with which Natalie Maines inflected "Earl had to *die*" was infectious.

Sisters Martie Maguire (fiddle) and Emily Robison (banjo) had three dull traditional records to their name before enlisting Maines' nasally pinched sass. Things changed quickly. The title track of *Wide Open Spaces* follows a young girl who leaves home because she needs "room to make big mistakes." On "Let 'Er Rip," Maines growls at a lover to dump her now rather than take all night to break it to her gently. And a closing romp through Bonnie Raitt's "Give It Up or Let Me Go" showcases Maguire's and Robison's chops in a taut band context.

Fly finds the trio flexing its autonomy that much more brashly. "Ready to Run," which makes fear of commitment an equal-opportunity affliction, is a genuine stroke of idiosyncratic freedom. In this context, the pathetic "Cowboy Take Me Away" is an unforgivable sentimental evasion. Still, even if the Chicks never fully wriggled out of the corset Nashville laced them into, they at least got a good start on loosening a few of the stays. *Home* was in many ways a feint toward authenticity, invoking the ladies' acoustic and bluegrass roots, so timely in the era of *O Brother, Where Art Thou?* But in song after song, from the defiant "Long Time Gone" to the heartbreaking "Travelin' Soldier" (the latter a hit even after Natalie foolishly exercised her right to free speech and criticized President George W. Bush), the album title referred sharply to that place you can never go back to. The live album is as redundant as most, of course, but full of verve regardless, and a decent introduction for civil libertarians, Toby Keith–haters, and other latecomers to the Chicks' camp. —K.H.

Willie Dixon

- ★★★★ Willie's Blues (1959; Bluesville/Prestige, 1990)
- ★★★★ I Am the Blues (1970; Columbia Legacy, 1993)
- ★★★ The Original Wang Dang Doodle (MCA/Chess, 1995)

★★★★★   The Chess Box (Chess/MCA, 1988)
★★★½   Poet of the Blues (Sony, 1998)
★★★½   Mr. Dixon's Workshop (Fuel, 2001)
★★★★   In Paris: Baby Please Come Home/Memphis Slim (Original Blues Classics, 1996)

Without ever establishing a style as distinctive as those of the artists with whom he worked, Willie Dixon became one of the architects of urban blues on the strength of his skills as a songwriter, bandleader, musician, arranger, producer, and diplomat. In these roles, Dixon reigned supreme at Chess Records in the 1950s and early 1960s, when he worked in one capacity or another with every significant artist on a label blessed with an abundance of them. Even a cursory listing of his many songwriting credits indicates the breathtaking scope of his contributions to American music and to the language of the blues: "My Babe," "You Shook Me," "Back Door Man," "Little Red Rooster," "Spoonful," "Wang Dang Doodle," "I Can't Quit You Baby," "I'm Your Hoochie Coochie Man," "You Can't Judge a Book By Its Cover," "The Seventh Son," "I Just Want to Make Love to You." Muddy Waters, Howlin' Wolf, Little Walter, Bo Diddley, Lowell Fulson, and Jimmy Witherspoon are only the most prominent of the musicians in Dixon's debt. They and others are heard on the two-CD *The Chess Box* collection, which is an essential blues overview. It's impossible to listen to the 36 tracks and then understate Dixon's stature—even the abused term *giant* seems insufficient considering the magnitude of the man's achievements. Other examples of Dixon's early postwar blues work can be found on *Mr. Dixon's Workshop.* This disc is less focused on Dixon's classics than on rare and obscure sides that showcase some terrific performances and outstanding artists. Jessie Fortune's "Too Many Cooks" features a young Buddy Guy on guitar, along with Big Walter Horton on harp; Guy turns up again on "Sit and Cry the Blues," a solo recording from 1958. "My Babe" is here, not in its classic Little Walter version but in a furious rockabilly reading by Jerry Lee Lewis's cousin Mickey Gilley, years before he found success as a mainstream country artist.

Oddly, Dixon's solo work was the least of his accomplishments. As a musician and producer, he was beyond reproach. Vocally, his was a genial, even moving, voice on occasion, but he never sounded as completely immersed in or defined by his material as did, for example, Muddy Waters or Howlin' Wolf. The zone these and other artists inhabited, in which passion, pain, and technique came together in one explosive package, is one Dixon visited in other capacities, but not on his own releases.

That said, it should be added that Dixon's recordings have some stirring moments. The earliest of these, Columbia's *Big Three Trio,* finds Dixon near the outset of his career, joined by Leonard Caston and Ollie Crawford in a trio purveying blues-tinged popular music in the style of the Mills Brothers. Among the interesting tracks is the Dixon-Caston-penned "If the Sea Was Whiskey," the first verse of which has shown up in countless songs, most notably "Rollin' and Tumblin'." *Poet of the Blues* takes a then-and-now look at Dixon's career in 16 tracks, nine featuring the Big Three Trio (actually a quartet, with Charles Sanders on drums) from the late '40s through the early '50s and seven of Dixon's monuments ("Back Door Man," "I Can't Quit You Baby," "Spoonful") recorded in 1970 in Chicago and issued on the *I Am the Blues* long player. His band, the Chicago Blues All-Stars, included Sunnyland Slim on piano, Johnny Shines on guitar, and Clifton James on drums.

Bluesville/Prestige has reissued Dixon's first album as a bandleader, *Willie's Blues,* recorded in 1959 and featuring the redoubtable Memphis Slim on piano. Imbued with a dark, after-hours ambience, the album is by far Dixon's strongest solo recording. His stuttering vocal on "Nervous" is one of his most effective on record; one of the better tracks is the loping "Youth to You," a thinly disguised reworking of "I Just Want to Make Love to You." Dixon's fruitful if short-lived association with Memphis Slim is further documented on the fabulous live disc *Baby Please Come Home,* recorded in Paris in 1962 with Phillipe Combelle joining the duo on drums and adding vocal support on the rousing set-closer, "All By Myself."

I Am the Blues features Dixon's own interpretations of nine of his best-known songs, and for this reason alone it becomes a good companion volume to the Chess box and the other extensive MCA overview, *The Original Wang Dang Doodle,* with tracks cut between 1954 and 1990. "The blues is about life," he once said. "If it ain't about life, it ain't the blues." When death brought an end to his remarkable career, in 1992, Willie Dixon had walked it like he talked it, staying true to his own maxim right up to the end of his days. —D.M.

Dizzee Rascal

★★★★   Boy in da Corner (Matador, 2004)

When 19-year-old Londoner Dizzee Rascal debuted in 2004 with the excellently unorthodox *Boy in da Corner,* he seemed like a gangsta from another planet, with a high, wound-up, desperate voice that sometimes sounds like Eazy-E, Shabba Ranks, and Gary Numan, all stuck inside the same body. *Boy in da Cor-*

ner presents a phantasmagoric vision of the future of hip-hop and techno, as Dizzee stays clear of assembly-line beats and backs his Cockney-accented flow and streetwise lyrics with jungle and techno drones. The signature tracks are "I Luv U" and "Wot U On": Dizzee used a PlayStation 2 to make some of the martial beats in the former, and the slutbot vocals, 2D melodies, and hardcore techno pound of "Wot" sound like the inside of a bloody video game. Just as N.W.A once captured the realities of the hood, Dizzee evokes 21st-century street life—the real, the virtual, and the violent.   —P.B.

DJ Jazzy Jeff and the Fresh Prince

★★★	Rock the House (Jive, 1988)
★★★½	He's the DJ, I'm the Rapper (Jive, 1988)
★★	And in This Corner (Jive, 1989)
★★★	Homebase (Jive, 1991)
★	Code Red (Jive, 1993)
★★★½	Greatest Hits (Jive, 1998)

Before Will Smith got jiggy in blockbuster films like *Men in Black,* he called himself the Fresh Prince and seemingly spent a good portion of the '80s picking up girls at the local food court with homeboy Jeff Townes (a.k.a. DJ Jazzy Jeff). Sporting a high-top fade and acid-wash jeans, Smith wove comic coming-of-age tales to Townes' considerable scratch skills. Their corny highjinks translated into sitcommy skits and MTV hits that foreshadowed Smith's successful acting career and nabbed him a hit TV show, *The Fresh Prince of Bel Air,* predicated on his nonthreatening street style. Instead of boasting about ho's and libidos, Smith's raps showcase a self-deprecating humor—he's scared of Freddy Krueger; he's laughed at in school for rocking Zips, not Adidas.

The Philadelphia duo's debut, *Rock the House,* featured the sophomoric hit "Girls Ain't Nothing But Trouble," in which boy-next-door Smith is preyed on by sirens to an *I Dream of Jeannie* sample. Their best work, though, is on the 17-track followup, *He's the DJ, I'm the Rapper,* since it spotlights both Smith's likable lyrics ("Parents Just Don't Understand," "Nightmare on My Street") and Townes' mixing mettle ("As We Go," "Pump Up the Bass"). Smith's schlock wears thin on *And in This Corner* and his Chuck D impression on *Code Red* is plain embarrassing. *Homebase,* on the other hand, is buoyed by Townes' disco-electro-funk beats, and contains 1991's breezy beach anthem "Summertime." That hit was remixed and rereleased on 1998's *Greatest Hits,* a laid-back list sometimes overshadowed by megastar Will Smith's solo efforts ("Men in Black," "Just Cruisin' ").   —C.S.

DJ Quik

★★★★	Quik Is the Name (1991; Arista, 1998)
★★★	Way 2 Fonky (1992; Arista, 1998)
★★★	Safe + Sound (1995; Arista, 1998)
★★	Rhythm-Al-Ism (Arista, 1998)
★★★	Balance & Options (Arista, 2000)
★★★	Under tha Influence (Ark 21, 2002)

As a teenager in the '80s in the Los Angeles suburb of Compton, David Blake was a member of the notorious Treetop Piru Bloods street gang. When Blake took a construction job, a coworker introduced him to the delights of that famous hip-hop accessory, the SP-1200 sampler. Blake became DJ Quik and at age 20 he saw his debut album go platinum on the strength of the hit single "Tonite." N.W.A had put Compton on the map, and the hardworking Quik took full advantage of the national attention. His G-funk–heavy, danceable, melodic music worked in clubs and on radio, and like Dr. Dre, Quik was a triple threat who could write, produce, and bust rhymes. Quik has always had notable hair, whether the fully-activated Jheri curl of his early days or his more recent shoulder-length relaxed locks. He's also known for his longstanding beef with MC Eiht (of Compton's Most Wanted); Quik once goofed Eiht all the way to the spelling bee as "having no G in him." None of this would matter if Quik wasn't a durable innovator. *Balance & Options* (2000) led off with the chugging chant "Change da Game," a track featuring sizzling synthesizers and a talented Quik-discovered MC named Mausberg (who was shot and killed in Compton in July 2000 at age 21). "Roger's Groove" was a talkbox tribute to the late great Roger Troutman of Zapp. The album also included "U Ain't Fresh!" (featuring EPMD's Erick Sermon), in which Quik mocked an unnamed producer as an ecstasy-popping homosexual. The track was assumed to be about Dr. Dre, but the hatchet was buried in time for Dre to produce "Put It on Me" on 2002's *Under tha Influence* (the track also appeared on the *Training Day* soundtrack). While he has never stopped wearing Blood colors, Quik has moved beyond celebrations of the gang-banging lifestyle. Partying remains his favorite subject in his crudely humorous sex rhymes, which is why it's noteworthy that intellectual and highly lyrical East Coast MCs such as Talib Kweli and Pharoahe Monch guest on *Under tha Influence.* Since 2000, Quik has also produced tracks on albums by Xzibit and Dre protégé Truth Hurts.   —P.R.

DJ Shadow

★★★★★	Endtroducing (Mo' Wax/FFRR, 1996)
★★★★	Preemptive Strike (Mo' Wax/FFRR, 1998)
★★★★	The Private Press (MCA, 2002)

DJ Shadow is one mad scientist who obviously doesn't get out of the lab much. Shadow, otherwise known as Northern California beatmaster and vinyl fetishist Josh Davis, became one of the leading lights of DJ culture with a string of head-spinning singles in the '90s, weaving more obscure rare-groove samples than any lawyer could trace into an expansive new style of headphone funk. He defined the tripping, hopping Mo' Wax sound, so that by the time he got around to releasing his debut album *Endtroducing*, in 1996, it already sounded not just familiar but inevitable. *Endtroducing* mixed countless samples and special effects into a hypnotic pastiche, especially in the cinematic crawl of tracks like "Midnight in a Perfect World" and "Building Steam With a Grain of Salt." All slow-motion tension and release, Shadow's grooves evoked a late night in the heart of the city, with your body poised right on the edge of utter fatigue.

DJ Shadow kept a low profile over the next few years. In 1998 he masterminded the U.N.K.L.E. project *Psyence Fiction*, a botched attempt at an all-star supergroup. *Preemptive Strike* was a collection of early work, including the excellent spaghetti Western soundtrack "High Noon." He also made some of his wildest, most entertaining music with Cut Chemist, especially 2001's *Product Placement*, which kicked off with a sample from Oscar the Grouch's "I Love Trash." *The Private Press* was his first proper solo album since *Endtroducing*, mixing beats, sound effects, machine hums, and found voices into mock-symphonic patterns of robot noise. As on *Endtroducing*, the best tracks take their time to let the momentum build: "Fixed Income," "Meets His Maker," "You Can't Go Home Again." And since Radiohead freely admit how much they've been influenced by DJ Shadow, it's only right that "Giving Up the Ghost" should sound like primo Radiohead, with nerve-rattling guitar and a lonesome violin howling away. —R.S.

DMX

- ★★★★ It's Dark and Hell Is Hot (Ruff Ryders/Def Jam, 1998)
- ★★★½ Flesh of My Flesh, Blood of My Blood (Ruff Ryders/Def Jam, 1998)
- ★★★½ . . . And Then There Was X (Ruff Ryders/Def Jam, 1999)
- ★★½ The Great Depression (Ruff Ryders/Def Jam, 2001)
- ★★★ The Grand Champ (Ruff Ryders/Def Jam, 2003)

Former stick-up kid DMX emerged from Yonkers, NY, to become a multiplatinum hip-hop phenom who rhymed about blood and grime at a time when the status quo was champagne and diamonds. Using Jekyll-and-Hyde rhyme flows, a manic-depressive persona, and, when words won't do, barks, snarls, and yelps, the Dark Man X laid out his formula on his first LP. *It's Dark and Hell Is Hot* features odes to crew ("Ruff Ryders' Anthem"), deals with the devil ("Damien"), conversations with God ("The Convo"), detailed scripts from the underworld ("ATF," "Crime Story"), and good old-fashioned shit talking ("Fuckin' wit' D," "Get At Me Dog"). The production—by Swizz Beatz, Dame Grease, and Irv Gotti—is brooding and ominous, with gothic underpinnings. Built around shards, chunks, and crashes of smoking, aggressive noise, the album sounds like a burned-down cathedral in a post-apocalyptic ghetto.

DMX's next two albums were released in rapid succession. *Flesh of My Flesh, Blood of My Blood* came out the same year as his debut, making X the first artist to debut at the top of the *Billboard* charts twice in the same calendar year. Despite his prodigious success with *Flesh* and . . . *And Then There Was X*, DMX continued to spit his pavement poetry with the same desperation that made him a blue-collar hero. While the production is a bit more polished—most notably on . . . *And Then There Was X*'s Dru Hill team-up "What These B*****s Want"—nothing ever comes off rehearsed, fabricated, or disingenuous.

Perhaps because he released three albums in two years, DMX didn't take stock of his celebrity until his fourth album, *The Great Depression*. There he taunts his competition: "15 million, nah-nah-nee-nah-nah," and he assumes the role of guardian of the hip-hop game, deriding the music's rampant materialism and excess. He also forays into rock ("Bloodline Anthem") and party music ("Trina Moe") and, of course, he prays, raps with God, deals with the devil, writes a letter to his dead grandmother, and barks every now and then. *The Grand Champ* is more of the same, but tracks such as "Where the Hood At" show that DMX can still deliver exhilarating fight music. —K.X.

The D.O.C.

- ★★★★ No One Can Do It Better (Ruthless, 1989)
- ★★ Helter Skelter (Giant, 1995)
- ★★★ Deuce (Red Urban, 2003)

A native of the West Dallas projects, the D.O.C. (real name Tracy "Tray" Curry) came up as a member of the Dallas rap group Fila Fresh Crew. In 1988 the group's minor hit "I Hate to Go to Work" appeared on *The Posse—Chapter 2*, a compilation on the small but influential Los Angeles–based Macola label that also included early tracks by Ice T and Digital Underground. The D.O.C. came to the attention of a young Dr. Dre, who invited him to come to Compton. Thus, the D.O.C. became involved—writing lyrics primarily—for infamous early Ruthless Records albums like N.W.A's *Straight Outta Compton*. (Ice Cube allegedly referred to the D.O.C. as N.W.A's "unsung hero.") Dre then produced *No One Can Do It Better*, the D.O.C.'s excellent debut album. With an assertive, astringent voice not unlike DMC from Run-D.M.C. and Big Daddy Kane, the D.O.C. devoted himself to lyrical boasting, not gangsta tales. The album included some of Dre's best productions to date (except for the tinny heavy-metal track, "Beautiful But Deadly"). In retrospect, although the D.O.C.'s flow is old school, his facility at relentlessly fast rapping on "Portrait of a Masterpiece" remains impressive. Prospects looked good for the D.O.C. when in November 1989 his larynx was crushed in a car accident. Five years would pass before he recuperated enough to record again, and his comeback album *Helter Skelter*—dominated by resurrection imagery—began with a skit reenacting the accident. Lead track "Return of da Livin' Dead" recycled the beat from his first album's big hit "It's Funky Enough" and was the best beat on the album (with Dre absent, production was handled unexceptionally by the D.O.C. and Erotic D). With his voice reduced to an ineffective rasp, the D.O.C. virtually disappeared for the rest of the '90s. Apparently the D.O.C. maintained ties with his old buddies, however, as his protégé Six Two appeared on "Xxplosive" on Dre's *Chronic 2001*. Having returned to his original stomping ground of Dallas, the D.O.C. formed his own record label and released his third album, *Deuce*, the highlight of which is "Tha Shit," a posse cut featuring Ice Cube, MC Ren, and Snoop. —P.R.

Dr. Dre

★★★★★ The Chronic (Death Row, 1992)
★★ Dr. Dre Presents . . . The Aftermath (Aftermath/Interscope, 1996)
★ First Round Knock Out (Triple X, 1996)
★ Back N Tha Day (Blue Dolphin, 1996)
★★★★ 2001 (Interscope, 1999)
★★★★ Chronicle: Best of the Works (Death Row, 2002)

With its late-'80s Cali-thug breakthrough albums, N.W.A basically told East Coast hip-hop to take its jazz-rap and shove it. And its preachy politics, too. After the group disbanded, producer Dr. Dre founded Death Row records and took that flipoff to the next level. His 1992 solo smash *The Chronic* features system-busting Funkadelic beats designed to rumble your woofer while the matter-of-fact violence of the lyrics blows your smoke-filled mind. On top of it all, Dre's trademark

snaky keyboard twists give tunes like "Nothin' But a G Thing" an ominous melodic elegance. Dre's secret weapon, of course, was the young Snoop Doggy Dog, who graces several tracks with his behind-the-beat drawl. The duo brilliantly played off their home region's escalating gang tensions, mythologizing their alliance with Godfatherlike gravity—"Compton and Long Beach together now you know you're in trouble." The album's release dovetailed with the palpable rage surrounding L.A.'s Rodney King riots, becoming in retrospect a de facto soundtrack of unrest. Dre and Snoop inspired many imitators but no real duplicators of their patented ability to give pure voice to the numb genius of a cannabis high amid solutionless chaos.

Dre produced Snoop's *Doggystyle* in 1993 and, among other projects, worked up tracks for Mary J. Blige and put the dig in Blackstreet's "No Diggity." Dre also worked with Death Row's recent acquisition Tupac, supposedly heralding a new dynastic era with the chummy "California Love," but soon ditched the label and its mounting legal problems to form Aftermath, releasing the uneven guest-artist compilation *Dr. Dre Presents . . . The Aftermath*. The only hit from that record was the good-riddance-to-bad-rubbish kiss-off "Been There Done That." Dre's next big move was discovering his next Snoop in white rapper Eminem. The two fell easily into fruitful collaborative mode. Again Dre played the cool, collected voice of wisdom to a burgeoning young talent. But where Snoop was a burnout savant, Eminem was a speed-freak hothead poet. Dre introduced the character of Slim Shady to the world on the comer's debut single "My Name Is." And in case anyone forgot about Dre's own rhyme skills (quite easy to do), his protégé stepped up the props on "Forgot About Dre," the single off his mentor's 1999 album, the confusingly titled *2001*, which also includes monster gangsta-pop trades such as "The Next Episide" and "Still D.R.E." There has yet to be compiled a best-of that harnesses the full force of Dre's career highlights, but 2002's *Chronicle: Best of the Works* at least favors the Snoop years over lesser hits from his pre-N.W.A work. —L.S.

Dr. John

★★★ Gris-Gris (1968; Collectors' Choice, 2000)
★★ Babylon (1968; Wounded Bird, 2002)
★★ Remedies (1969; Wounded Bird, 2002)
★★ Sun, Moon, Herbs (1971; Wounded Bird, 2002)
★★★★ Dr. John's Gumbo (Atco, 1972)
★★★½ In the Right Place (Atco, 1973)
★★★½ Desitively Bonnaroo (1974; Label M, 2001)
★★½ Hollywood Be Thy Name (1975; One Way, 1997)

★★   Tango Palace (Horizon, 1978)
★★★   City Lights (Horizon, 1979)
★★★★   Dr. John Plays Mac Rebennack (Clean Cuts, 1981)
★★★★   The Brightest Smile in Town (Clean Cuts, 1983)
★★★★   The Ultimate Dr. John (Warner Special Products, 1987)
★★½   In a Sentimental Mood (Warner Bros., 1990)
★★½   Bluesiana Triangle (Windham Hill, 1990)
★★   Bluesiana 2 (Windham Hill, 1991)
★½   On a Mardi Gras Day (Great Southern, 1991)
★★½   Going Back to New Orleans (Warner Bros., 1992)
★★★★½   Mos' Scocious: The Dr. John Anthology (Rhino, 1993)
★★   Television (GRP, 1994)
★★   Afterglow (GRP, 1995)
★★★   The Very Best of Dr. John (Rhino, 1995)
★★½   Anutha Zone (Pointblank/Virgin, 1998)
★★★   Duke Elegant (Blue Note, 2000)
★★★½   Creole Moon (Blue Note, 2001)
★★★★   The Essentials (Elektra, 2002)
★★★★   Dr. John Plays Mac Rebennack: The Legendary Sessions, Vol. 1 (Clean Cuts, 2002)
★★★   N'Awlinz: Dis, Dat or D'Udda (Blue Note, 2004)

Mac Rebennack began his musical career in the '50s as a teenage guitarist and pianist on the New Orleans R&B scene, eventually following Earl Palmer, Harold Battiste, and other N.O. session players to Los Angeles in the mid-'60s. And the musical persona Rebennack assumed for much of his solo career—that of Dr. John Creaux, the Night Tripper—was a product of the collision between Louisiana creole funk and West Coast hippie mysticism. Take, for instance, the way *Gris-Gris* parlays the imagery of voodoo magic (the historical Dr. John Creaux was proclaimed the King of Voodoo in 19th-century New Orleans) into the hallucinatory groove of "I Walk on Gilded Splinters," ending up with a sound that draws equally on bayou funk and psychedelic rock.

That fusion didn't always take, of course. *Babylon* quickly dissolves into hippie foolishness, and while *Remedies* has its moments—for instance, the joyful "Mardi Gras Day"—moments just aren't enough. Dr. John didn't really hit his stride until he returned to roots with *Gumbo*, which offers funky updates of such classic New Orleans R&B numbers as "Iko Iko," "Junko Partner," Professor Longhair's classic "Tipitina," and a medley of Huey Smith hits. From there, it's an easy jump to the second-line funk of *In the Right Place*, which was recorded with the Meters

and produced by Allan Toussaint; it contains Dr. John's only Top 10 single, "Right Place Wrong Time." There's more of the same on *Desitively Bonnaroo*, thanks to the irresistible rhythms of "(Everybody Wanna Get Rich) Rite Away" and "Quitters Never Win." *The Ultimate Dr. John* compiles highlights from *Gris-Gris, Gumbo, Remedies,* and *Desitively Bonnaroo,* but not necessarily the tunes every fan would have chosen; *Mos' Scocious* is a far more complete and representative anthology.

But the voodoo shtick was just that—a gimmick—and eventually Dr. John decided to try a bit of straight-up rock & roll with *Hollywood Be Thy Name*, a mostly live album that offers mildly spiced renditions of "The Way You Do the Things You Do" and "Yesterday" along with a few Dr. John originals; it's second-rate rock despite his first-rate band. With *City Lights*, he makes a bid for light-jazz respectability, but not even the sympathetic backing of New York studio aces Steve Gadd, Will Lee, and Richard Tee can completely overcome the pedestrian nature of the material; perhaps that's why *Tango Palace* resorts to the jivey insincerity of "Disco-Therapy" and "Fonky Side."

Yet just when it seemed Dr. John was finally played out, he brought his skills back into focus with *Dr. John Plays Mac Rebennack*, a solo piano session that brings him back home to the New Orleans piano stylings he cut his teeth on; essential listening, if only for the rollicking "Memories of Professor Longhair." *The Brightest Smile in Town* broadens the music's scope some with such standards as "Come Rain or Come Shine," but that turned out to be a dangerous precedent, as *In a Sentimental Mood* turned that interest in standards into syrupy pop, despite a coy "Makin' Whoopee" cut with Rickie Lee Jones.

From there it's mostly ping-pong, as Dr. John bounces among light jazz (the *Bluesiana* discs), Mardi Gras revivalism (the touristy *Going Back to New Orleans* and the slightly better *N'Awlinz: Dis, Dat or D'Udda*), empty pop (*Television* and *Afterglow*), and tepid jazz (the well-meant but generally useless *Duke Elegant*). Of his recent albums, *Creole Moon* puts enough spunk into its iteration of N.O. funk to make the tired familiarity of the material forgivable. —J.D.C.

Dr. Octagon
see KOOL KEITH

Fats Domino
★★★★½   Rock and Rollin'/This Is Fats (1956, 1957; Collectables, 1998)
★★★★½   Rock and Rollin' With Fats Domino/Million Sellers by Fats (1956, 1962; Collectables, 1998)

Conservative of dress, mild of manner, and unfailingly polite, New Orleans native Antoine "Fats" Domino carried himself with a dignity that made it virtually impossible for critics of early rock & roll to lump him in with the rogues' gallery that included the salacious Presley, the perverted Berry, the crazy Jerry Lee, and the androgynous Little Richard. No, Fats didn't have much in the way of flamboyance going for him; rather, he pushed the music, period. In one of the most fertile producer-artist relationships in history, Fats' recordings were shaped by bandleader, songwriter, arranger, musician, and producer Dave Bartholomew, a genius and visionary whose labs were the J&M and Cosimo recording studios, where he melded the sounds and styles of the Crescent City's multicultural musical heritage into a singular and furiously propulsive branch of rock & roll, every bit as distinctive and exciting as that of Memphis (Sun Records) or Chicago (Chess Records). "I didn't invent the New Orleans sound," Bartholomew once noted. "I just took it off the streets." Between 1950 and 1963, Domino's Imperial recordings (most written by Domino-Bartholomew) sold 63 million copies, and 23 of them went gold, which rivaled Presley's numbers to that time. And one of those singles that didn't go gold, his 1950 debut, "The Fat Man" (a #2 R&B single), is among the contenders for the first rock & roll record. When Domino signed with ABC-Paramount in 1963, he had fashioned not merely an imposing body of work, but a dynasty. It couldn't have happened to a nicer guy.

Domino's influences were many and varied, encompassing all the important names in New Orleans music in the '40s and the R&B stars of his youth. Professor Longhair and Champion Jack Dupree are the touchstones of his piano style; powerful vocalists such as Big Joe Turner, Roy Brown, and Amos Milburn pointed the way vocally with their clever phrasing and forceful personalities. But above these stood Louis Jordan, whose music rocked mightily before the term "rocked" was even in vogue and who further brought to the table a pronounced joie de vivre, which turned out to be true of Fats as well.

Having been dominant on the R&B charts since the release of "The Fat Man," Domino cracked the pop charts in 1952 with "Goin' Home" and didn't leave until 1963. His first pop Top 10 single came in 1955 with "Ain't That a Shame" (which became a #1 pop hit in a sedate Pat Boone cover version); two years later "Blue Monday" topped the R&B chart, and peaked at #5 in pop, and thereafter Fats was a mainstay in the Top 10 and Top 20 through 1962. Oddly, for having sold so many records, he never had a #1 pop hit; "Blueberry Hill," at #2 in 1957, was as close as he got. Which means nothing at all, because Fats has plenty of other numbers he can roll out, but more than that he has history on his side: His music endures, long after a lot of other #1 records have been forgotten. "Blueberry Hill," "Ain't That a Shame," "I'm Walkin'," "Walking to New Orleans," "Whole Lotta Lovin'," "Blue Monday," "I'm Gonna Be a Wheel Someday," "Valley of Tears," "Wait and See," "Sick and Tired"—as Little Richard would say, "Shut up!"

Capitol's four-CD box set, *Walking to New Orleans,* a repackaging of EMI's late-1991 four-CD box set, *They Call Me the Fat Man,* tells the whole glorious Imperial story in one outstanding package. Domino is reported to have cut some 260 sides for the label, and 100 of those are in the box set. Only one track, "Darktown Strutters' Ball" from 1958, is previously unreleased; only three tracks are alternate versions. The set also comes with an entertaining and informative biography by veteran New Orleans music historian Jeff Hannusch that is further buttressed by complete discographical and session details (although the lack of personnel credits on the sessions is an unfortunate oversight). Finally, a great American artist, whose most important work had fallen largely out of print save for a couple of hits collections, was given his just due. As a low-cost alternative to the box set, *The Fat Man: 25 Classic Performances* distills four CDs' worth of material to one vital disc of Imperial monuments, with abridged but essential annotation; a further distillation of essential hits comes from the same label via the 20-track *Fats Domino Jukebox.* The Imperial years have been further rounded out by four wonderful twofer discs from Collectables, comprising eight Imperial albums, plus two bonus tracks per disc, for a total of 104 cuts, not all of which are on the EMI box set. This is the Domino-Bartholomew team in its prime: The four CDs contain a wealth of their song collaborations that were either single B sides or album cuts only, making each disc essential for appraising the evolution of the team's artistry. Amazing, overpowering, life-affirming music, this. Curb's *All-Time Greatest Hits* disc distills Domino's catalogue even further, down to a dozen choice tracks. Although the liner copy notes erroneously that Domino was discovered playing in Dave Bartholomew's band, the disc is otherwise a solid, albeit abridged, document of the glory years.

After leaving Imperial, Fats recorded into the early '70s for ABC, Mercury, and Reprise, without commercial success but not for lack of quality music. Little of this period remains in print, but one interesting artifact from 1968, the Richard Perry–produced *Fats Is Back,* has been returned to print on the Bullseye Blues label. Perry became one of the most successful producers of the '70s and '80s on the strength of his work with Barbra Streisand, Leo Sayer, Ringo Starr, Carly Simon, Art Garfunkel, the Pointer Sisters, and others, but the Fats project came at the start of his estimable career, following his first production, Captain Beefheart's *Safe as Milk.* Perry would become famous for his big, state-of-the-art productions later, but he wisely kept it close to the bone with Fats, and like Bartholomew before him let the artist lay his personality on a set of solid songs, including a vibrant reading of Barbara George's "I Know" and two powerhouse covers of Lennon-McCartney songs, "Lady Madonna" and a smokin' rendition of "Lovely Rita." The nicest touch is at the end, with the wistful, bluesy "One More Song for You," sung with sincerity and grace by an artist who was always ready to play another song for the fans who had made an international star of the youngest of nine children born in 1928 to a poor family in New Orleans' Ninth Ward. The performance resonates with the weight of his history.

Tomato/Rhino's two-disc *Antoine "Fats" Domino* collection is credited as a live recording, although no audience is heard on the discs. Recorded in 1979 in Galveston and Houston, TX, with a band that featured a number of Domino's stalwart hands from the Imperial years—Herb Hardesty leading the orchestra and wailing on tenor sax; Fred Kemp on tenor sax; Lee Allen on tenor sax—Fats is in a genial mood on 34 mostly familiar tracks heavy on hits (how many artists

can release 34 tracks and have them be described accurately as "heavy on hits"?) and the band is simply outstanding, blowing wild and hard on the uptempo numbers and deeply melancholy on introspective songs such as the instrumental version of "Misty" included here. Fats, of huskier voice but with his sly phrasing intact, still brings the passion and presence of his younger years to each number. A better live album choice would be Atlantic's *Live at Montreux,* recorded in 1973 in Montreux, Switzerland, at the Golden Rose Television Festival. The 14 songs Fats pumps out with his band are mostly familiar Domino monuments, and he barely takes a breath between songs. But he's in great voice, high spirits, and is playing his tail end off on piano—it's the best live capture of Domino's exceptional keyboard artistry. After a rousing version of "When the Saints Go Marching In," Domino closes out the set by adding a little New Orleans gumbo to spice up an instrumental version of the old pop standard "Sentimental Journey," sending the crowd home happy.

Fats' latest studio effort came in 1993 with his self-produced yuletide gem, *Christmas Gumbo* (originally released as *Christmas Is a Special Day*). This one finds Fats in a reflective mood for the most part, which makes the long player more suitable for late-night chilling out in a room illuminated only by Christmas-tree lights. That said, the album opens on a bopping note, with "I Told Santa Claus"—an appeal for a woman to be left under his Christmas tree—and Fats takes "Jingle Bells" and "Frosty the Snowman" at a brisk pace, but he closes out the album with "White Christmas," "Please Come Home for Christmas," and a somber "Amazing Grace," to wind things up on thoughtful note. The electronic keyboards don't do a lot for Fats' sound, but his New Orleans twist on the seasonal standards makes for a warm, engaging outing nonetheless, one that could only have come from a man as big-hearted as Fats Domino.   —D.M.

The Donnas

★★   The Donnas (1996; Lookout, 1998)
★★   American Teenage Rock 'n' Roll Machine (Lookout, 1998)
★★★   Get Skintight (Lookout, 1999)
★★★   The Donnas Turn 21 (Lookout, 2001)
★★★   Spend the Night (Atlantic, 2002)

Like obvious inspirations the Ramones and AC/DC, the Donnas couldn't care less about reinventing themselves with every album. They're four sugar-and-spite femme fatales cruising for boy toys in their lemon-scented rides and pretending they're mini-mart punk's answer to Kiss, circa *Destroyer,* over and over again. At their best, the Donnas offer a guileless take on adolescent alienation; they traffic in kicks, not catharsis, fun rather than rage, and they absolutely, positively, do not do ballads.

Together in various incarnations since grade school in Palo Alto, CA, the four Donnas initially performed songs written for them by producer Darin Raffaelli, who played Kim Fowley to the girls' underage Runaways. On the debut, they sing juvenile-delinquent anthems such as "Everybody's Smoking Cheeba" and "I Wanna Be a Unabomber" at blitzkrieg-bop tempos. *American Teenage Rock 'n' Roll Machine* gives the quartet a twist of glam-rock, but it's with *Get Skintight* that the quartet finds its voice: the suburbia-in-excelsis worldview of a John Hughes flick transplanted to a post–Green Day world. The production by Steve and Jeff McDonald of California kitsch-pop maestros Redd Kross slows down the tempos just a notch and fattens the melodies into arena-rock bad-girl sing-alongs. *The Donnas Turn 21* is *Skintight* Part 2; it reshuffles the same five chords, lives to "party like Cheech and Chong," and substitutes a faithful cover of Judas Priest's "Living After Midnight" for the previous album's take on Mötley Crüe's "Too Fast for Love." On *Spend the Night*, the sound and themes haven't changed, but the skills of the musicians have improved markedly, particularly Donna R.'s Ace Frehley-inspired guitar work. —G.K.

Donovan

★★★½	Catch the Wind (1965; DCC, 1988)
★★★	Fairy Tale (1965: Silverline, 2002)
★★½	Sunshine Superman (1966; Epic, 1990)
★★½	Mellow Yellow (Epic, 1967)
★★★½	A Gift From a Flower to a Garden (Epic, 1968)
★★★	Donovan in Concert (Epic, 1968)
★★★½	Hurdy Gurdy Man (1968; Epic, 1986)
★★★	Barabajagal (1969; Epic, 1987)
★★★★★	Donovan's Greatest Hits (Epic, 1969)
★★½	Open Road (Epic, 1970)
★★	Cosmic Wheels (Epic, 1973)
★★½	Essence to Essence (Epic, 1974)
★★★	7 Tease (Epic, 1974)
★★½	Slow Down World (Epic, 1976)
★★★★	Troubadour: The Definitive Collection, 1964–1976 (Epic/Legacy, 1991)
★★★	Sutras (American, 1996)
★★★★	The Essential Donovan (Sony Legacy, 2004)

Epitomizing flower power, Donovan's trippy musings are redeemed from '60s nostalgia not only by his belief that there's nothing funny about peace, love, and understanding, but also by the sheer pop charm of his songs. Coming on as Bob Dylan's breathlessly

sincere Scots twin, Donovan was a quintessential folkie—acoustic guitar, harmonica, story songs, benign rebellion, and, making him distinctive, a Celtic romanticism. Dewy with hope, confident and ambitious, the title track of *Catch the Wind* and "Ramblin' Boy" radiated mythic, wide-eyed yearning.

As Dylan had, Donovan then went electric. But if Bob's rock was tough and bluesy, Donovan's was pop, spun from the sassy tunefulness of his mod peers. And it was psychedelic. Indeed, "Sunshine Superman" bounced along as a wry, ultrahip manifesto, its winking delivery hinting at all manner of illicit pleasures. "Mellow Yellow" (supposedly about the arcane high of smoking banana peels) outright broadcast the theme of blow-your-mind wisdom.

With its cover shot of the maharishi and swooning ditties like "Wear Your Love Like Heaven," *A Gift From a Flower to a Garden* delivered the Donovan persona to the max—a troubadour Saint Francis who filed his lyrics with exotic poetry that promoted a bliss straight out of William Blake's *Songs of Innocence*. After a string of late-'60s hits, produced fancifully by Mickie Most, celebrating a private wonderland—"Jennifer Juniper," "Hurdy Gurdy Man," and "Barabajagal" (with Jeff Beck)—Donovan's moment had passed. Such later work as *Open Road* and *Cosmic Wheels* showed occasional strength, but compared to the golden-hour singles, the music was less remarkable.

Troubadour collects all his best work; the strong liner notes help put it in context. In 1996, the singer teamed up with Rick Rubin in an attempt to present a lean, essential Donovan (somewhat in the way Rubin had presented the older Johnny Cash). The resulting *Sutras* was fine, accomplished folk with Buddhist shadings, but it didn't catch fire. —P.E.

Doobie Brothers

★★	The Doobie Brothers (Warner Bros., 1971)
★★★	Toulouse Street (Warner Bros., 1972)
★★★	The Captain and Me (Warner Bros., 1973)
★★½	What Were Once Vices Are Now Habits (Warner Bros., 1974)
★★	Stampede (Warner Bros., 1975)
★★★	Takin' It to the Streets (Warner Bros., 1976)
★★★★	The Best of the Doobie Brothers (Warner Bros., 1976)
★★½	Livin' on the Fault Line (Warner Bros., 1977)
★★★	Minute by Minute (Warner Bros., 1978)
★★	One Step Closer (Warner Bros., 1978)
★★★★	Best of the Doobies, Vol. 2 (Warner Bros., 1981)
★★	Farewell Tour (Warner Bros., 1983)
★½	Cycles (1989; One Way, 2002)
★	Brotherhood (1991; One Way, 2002)

★★	Rockin' Down the Highway: The Wildlife Concert (Sony/Legacy, 1996)
★★½	The Best of the Doobie Brothers Live (Sony/Legacy, 1999)
★★★★	Long Train Runnin' 1970–2000 (Rhino, 1999)
★	Sibling Rivalry (Pyramid, 2000)
★★★★	Greatest Hits (Rhino, 2001)
★★½	Doobies' Choice (Rhino, 2002)

The quintessential biker-meets-hippie California band, Doobie Brothers yielded a succession of soft-rock hits in the mid-'70s that have come to symbolize the complacent but irresistible charms of the era. Moving from mellow boogie to slick blue-eyed soul, this long-running group actually improved along the way. The Doobies began as a bar band in Northern California, earning a following among the Hell's Angels for their Sunday-afternoon jam sessions. The group's debut floated away to oblivion, but the Doobies honed a couple of sharp hooks on *Toulouse Street,* and bagged a winner. The formula was set—toe-tapping power chords ("China Grove"), a strum-along buzz ("Listen to the Music"), high group harmonies, and choruses repetitive enough to drill their just-groovin'-on-it platitudes into listeners' skulls—and would serve them well for much of the decade. Laid-back to the point of appearing blank, the Doobies come on like a slightly heavier Eagles—or a slimmed-down Bachman-Turner Overdrive. *The Captain and Me* belies the extent of the group's vision: "Rockin' Down the Highway" and "Long Train Runnin' " are virtual clones of the previously mentioned songs, though that didn't stop them from becoming just as popular.

By the fourth album, lead guitarist and chief composer Tom Johnston starts to seem tapped out. Rhythm guitarist Patrick Simmons supplies the ersatz country-rock hit "Black Water," but the rest of *Vices* barely stays afloat. *Stampede* is led by Jeff "Skunk" Baxter, a studio guitarist for Steely Dan: Centered around a sluggish Motown cover ("Take Me in Your Arms"), the thundering charge never quite gains sufficient momentum. Exit Baxter, enter singer Michael McDonald, another Steely Dan alumnus. His luxurious tone and grain of soulfulness turned the Doobie Brothers' beat around. The 1976 hit "Takin' It to the Streets" steers clear of the funky gutter, reaching instead for a loftier veneer: MOR&B. "Takin' It to the Streets" also revolves around McDonald's vocals, electric piano, and a mildly syncopated beat—the guitars and mellow country-rock gait are conspicuously absent. The Doobies quickly became Michael McDonald's franchise. Johnston left in 1978, and the

Brothers went on to release one of their best. *Minute by Minute*'s title cut and the hit single "What a Fool Believes" flaunt McDonald's suave vocal mastery quite effectively, though this elegant penthouse heart-break is certainly a far cry from the group's origins.

The inevitable reunion (sans McDonald) came in 1989 with *Cycles,* and, God, it's awful. Save for "The Doctor," a vapid sing-along ("Music is the doctor/ Makes you feel like you want to") that became a Top 10 hit, the Brothers seem unable to recapture any of their old magic for simply putting words and music together in an appealing way. Ditto for *Brotherhood,* minus the hit. McDonald joined in for a series of concerts in 1996 benefitting the Wildlife Conservation Society. The resulting live double album, *Rockin' Down the Highway,* is slick to the point of anonymity, and a long haul even for diehard fans; *The Best of the Doobie Brothers Live* trims it down to one palatable disc. When last heard from, on *Sibling Rivalry,* the Doobies were still struggling vainly to put their formula to work again, with hideous consequences. (How's this for hypocrisy: a band named after pot singing "Down on every corner/We got children sellin' dope/Who's gonna send a message/And try to give 'em hope.") McDonald wisely stayed far away.

The Doobies were essentially a singles band; taste more than the hits and you're courting heartburn. *Long Train Runnin',* a four-disc, 79-track box set, is the definitive, if burdensome, anthology. The various stocking-stuffer collections are preferable, but of them, only the Rhino set fully bridges the Johnston and McDonald eras. Avoid *Doobies' Choice,* cuts supposedly chosen by the band: It makes weird choices and pushes the new stuff hard.   —M.C./B.S.

The Doors

★★★★	The Doors (1967; Elektra, 1990)
★★★½	Strange Days (1967; Elektra, 1990)
★★★½	Waiting for the Sun (1968; Elektra, 1990)
★★★	The Soft Parade (1969; Elektra, 1990)
★★★★★	Morrison Hotel (1970; Elektra, 1990)
★★½	Absolutely Live (1970; Elektra, 1990)
★★★½	Thirteen (1970; Elektra, 1990)
★★★★	L.A. Woman (1971; Elektra, 1990)
★★½	American Prayer (1978; Elektra, 1990)
★★★★	Greatest Hits (1980; Elektra, 1990)
★★	Alive, She Cried (1983; Elektra, 1990)
★★★½	In Concert (Elektra, 1991)
★★★½	The Doors/An Oliver Stone Film (Elektra, 1991)
★★★★	The Doors Box Set (Elektra, 1997)
★★★★★	The Very Best of the Doors (Rhino, 2001)
★★★★	Bright Midnight: Live in America (Bright Midnight, 2002)

★★★½   Live in Hollywood, Aquarius (WEA, 2002)
★★★★★   Legacy: The Absolute Best (Rhino, 2003)

Three great American '60s bands rendered versions of the California myth. For the Beach Boys, it was sun, surf, and teenage blondes. The Grateful Dead embodied hippie utopianism, the acid love-in, and the endless, mystic jam. The Doors' California was a construct of the darker psyche; it was L.A. crash pads and needle fever, Hollywood bungalows and film-noir threat. At its far limits were the surrounding hills—rich with the threat and promise of Indian burial grounds and natural mysteries—and the ocean, surging deep into oblivion and release. The Doors were originals—Robbie Krieger, a competent guitarist who sounded best when he kept things either elegant or bluesy; the steady John Densmore on drums; and Ray Manzarek, an organist and electric piano player whose semiclassical turns added a touch of the baroque.

The Doors ultimately, however, were Jim Morrison. He was dangerous, raw, beautiful, half-erect in his skintight leather pants, and fatefully self-destructive. By the end of his life, he was tragic and pathetic. It was no wonder that he cited the French Symbolists—especially Rimbaud and Baudelaire—as inspiration. At their best, his suggestive lyrics were clipped and cinematic, either bursts of street talk or snatches at myth. Calling himself an "erotic politician," Morrison was preoccupied with urge, rebellion, and release—if some of his work now sounds melodramatic or forced, his intensity remains compelling, and his acknowledgment of night, pain, and loneliness comes off as riveting and real.

Although the abbreviated, 45 version hit harder, "Light My Fire" neatly introduced the Doors' effect: vocals alternately commanding and stoned, swirling organ and the message that sex could mean deliverance. "Break on Through," however, is the debut album's better song and the essential Doors statement. "The End" attempted an epic—the song served notice that this band was going deep. With the exception of the hard blues "Love Me Two Times" and the rock tango "Moonlight Drive," Strange Days didn't have the power of The Doors; it sounded instead like twilit, ominous carnival music. "People Are Strange," "Strange Days," and "I Can't See Your Face in My Mind" obsessively examined disconnection and the sense of drifting; "Horse Latitudes" was an early example of sheer atmosphere.

Waiting for the Sun featured "Hello, I Love You," a jagged Kinks ripoff in which Morrison comes on like a rapist; "Five to One" was revolutionary sloganeering. The rest of the record was considerably subtler: Krieger's flamenco guitar on "Spanish Caravan" is stirring, "Summer's Almost Gone" is remarkably tender, and the chanted "My Wild Love," with its affecting, cracked-voice vocal, works well at re-creating an air of primitive folk power.

The Door's shakiest album, The Soft Parade, was cluttered with horns and strings. While not at all music for the band's hard-rock followers, Krieger's "Touch Me" and "Tell All the People" are intriguing; they're pop songs, basically, but sifted through the Doors' sensibilities, they take on a surreal quality. "Wild Child" is Morrison parodying himself, and the long concept title song doesn't work.

A return to form, Morrison Hotel was their most cohesive record; aside from the throwaway grunter "Maggie McGill," every song was masterful—and the band swings tougher and easier than they ever had before. Morrison's voice is almost shot, but its strain lends grit to the rockers ("Roadhouse Blues," "You Make Me Real") and poignancy to the ballads ("Blue Sunday," "Indian Summer"). The lyrics are some of Morrison's finest; "Queen of the Highway," in particular, neatly fuses contemporary reference and myth.

"Riders on the Storm," "Love Her Madly," "L'America," and the title track were the standouts of the final album, L.A. Woman. Inventive playing characterizes every song, but so does a heavy air of psychic exhaustion. Morrison's voice is a ghost of its former glory—doom, heartbreak, and frustration sound in his every note. Difficult and sad, the record has some of the power of Neil Young's Tonight's the Night: It's a straining for catharsis.

The Doors are a bit overrepresented by compilations and live albums, but most casual fans will be well served by Greatest Hits, which covers most of the bases. Fanatics will want to find the four-CD box set that came out in 1997; almost every cut had been previously unreleased. The three surviving band members fill one CD with their personal favorites—we can only imagine which songs Jim would have selected.

But the very best collection of Doors material is 2003's Legacy, a two-CD set that expands the basic greatest-hits format. It features 34 of the Doors' best album tracks in chronological order. Hard-core fans will bemoan the omission of "Love Street," but the span of this collection is wide enough to capture the band in various modifications, yet narrow enough to make most tracks familiar even to casual fans. The previously unreleased "Celebration of the Lizard" renders this an essential set for collectors.

There are a number of anomalous Doors releases, including An American Prayer, which belongs in the books-on-tape category. It features Morrison reading his poetry over atmospherics from the band; it's intriguing but suitable mainly for Morrison fanatics.

Bright Midnight is the band's odds-and-sods release, material that was left off the box set. The sound quality is fantastic: One can hear the powerhouse live show that was the Doors at their prime. Also noteworthy is *Live in Hollywood,* which culls 16 songs from two shows at the Aquarius Theatre in July 1969, more evidence that Morrison was a remarkable performer.

The band reunited in 2002, with Ian Astbury (the Cult) filling in for Morrison. Original drummer John Densmore chose not to reenlist and in 2003 he sued, seeking restrictions on the use of the name "the Doors." —P.E./C.R.C.

Doves

★★★½	Lost Souls (Astralwerks, 2000)
★★★	The Last Broadcast (Capitol, 2002)

Rising from the ashes of completely forgettable dance outfit Sub Sub, Manchester's Doves surprised some people by combining goth-tinged melodrama, pop smarts, and dance-floor energy and sonics. *Lost Souls* evokes Fatboy Slim–style big beats and Beatlesque harmonies on a track like "Here It Comes"; on others, a dollop of '60s psych, some '80s techno, or even the Pink Floyd–inspired headphone rock of the '70s. "Sea Song" sounds suspiciously like *Hurting*-era Tears for Fears, but for the most part, Doves do a good job of masking specific influences to create a general mood of Brit sad-boy loneliness. It's striking how at odds Jimi Goodwin's mundane and homely vocals are with the pyrotechnics erupting around him. And Goodwin's deadpan, some would say dreary, melancholic crooning isn't for everyone. You may not necessarily buy a word of what he's selling, but in the end, it doesn't matter because Doves are so adept at erecting vast FM radio towers of approximated warmth and passion. Real confessions can make you squirm, but *Lost Souls* only touches on what it means to be human, without ever reminding you that life is seldom so pretty or grandly realized.

Their followup, *The Last Broadcast,* is stylistically quite similar to their debut, and just as expansive and ambitious. Lyrically, it's even vaguer than its already kind of emotionally vague predecessor, as if this time around, all attention was put into the aural fireworks. Doves have an amazing ability to write a lilting, harmonious pop song, such as "Words," augmented by the right amount of discordant guitars that rub against the rest of the instruments until the whole construction starts to tilt. Flourishes on *The Last Broadcast* include the Brazilian carnival drums that end "There Goes the Fear," but the disc's highlight is "N.Y.," featuring stately horns, Link Wray–style slash guitars, and Pink Floyd pathos culminating in an ex-hilarating blast of electro-punk noise that trails off slowly into a watercolor English sunset. They pile on the sound via traditional instruments and electronics, along with Goodwin's warbling and sudden changes in mood and tempo, but in the space of a four-minute song, the technique becomes unwieldy. It's hard to fault the band, though, for having too many ideas or for trying so hard to turn a verse/chorus/verse pop confection into something that is twisted and ingeniously crafted. —S.S.

Doug E. Fresh

★★★★	Oh, My God! (Reality, 1987)
★★★	The World's Greatest Entertainer (Reality, 1988)
★★½	Play (Gee Street, 1995)
★★★★	Greatest Hits, Vol. 1 (Bust It, 1996)

Unquestionably one of the greatest beat-boxers of all time, Doug E. Fresh capably created an extraordinary palette of rhythmic and musical noises with his mouth, often in a nimble, giddy mode instantly distinguishable from the booming, raspy tones of the Fat Boys' Human Beat Box (may he rest in peace). Born Doug E. Davis on September 17, 1966, in Barbados, Fresh moved to New York and made his 1983 recording debut on the 12" single "Pass the Budda" with Spoonie Gee on the Spotlight label. Spoonie was the nephew of legendary Harlem record-store and label owner Bobby Robinson, who had issued hits like Bobby Marchan's 1960 R&B #1 "Something on My Mind," a protorap classic. He also released "Just Having Fun" by Douge [sic] Fresh with DJ's Chill Will and Barry Bee on his Enjoy label in 1984, a hard-rocking electro jam that showcased Fresh's stunning beat-box talent.

Fresh's 1985 single "The Show/La Di Da Di," on the Reality label, made him one of hip-hop's biggest stars and launched the career of Slick Rick (then known as MC Ricky D). "The Show" was exactly what its title suggested, both a showcase for Fresh's Get Fresh Crew and a narrative tale leading up to Fresh rocking a live show; most hip-hop fans at the time memorized it verbatim. In fact, Fresh's vitality was due to his ability to rock a crowd (a skill that has unfortunately lost currency as hip-hop has aged), and his debut album, *Oh, My God!,* translated his stage-tested routines superbly to the studio. Although Fresh's popularity had faded by the '90s, he received a memorable name-check on A Tribe Called Quest's track "What?" when Q-Tip wondered, "What is hip-hop if it doesn't have violence? Chill for a minute, Doug E. Fresh said silence." His 1995 comeback album *Play* was an entertaining reinvigoration of old-school styles. Fresh maintains a profile on the hip-hop scene, hosting old-school events in New York's Central Park and elsewhere. In 2002, Fresh authored *Think Again,* the first book in Scholastic's Rap & Read series of children's books, which came with a CD single of Fresh rapping the story over a Prince Paul beat. —P.R.

Mike Doughty
see SOUL COUGHING

Nick Drake

★★★★★	Five Leaves Left (1969; Island, 2003)
★★★★	Bryter Layter (1970; Island, 2003)
★★★★★	Pink Moon (1972; Island, 2003)
★★★½	Time of No Reply (Hannibal, 1986)
★★★★	Fruit Tree (Hannibal, 1986)
★★★★	Way to Blue: An Introduction to Nick Drake (1994; Hannibal, 2003)
★★★	Made to Love Magic (Island, 2004)

Nick Drake climbed to the top of the hot-dead-English-guy charts in the late '80s, when the boxed set *Fruit Tree* first exposed America to this gentle, mystical singer-songwriter. Dead of an accidental prescription drug overdose in 1974, Drake recorded barely two hours' worth of music in his entire career, but he had a warm, intimate voice and acoustic guitar to flesh out his frail love-and-death ballads, and decades after the fact, practically everyone who hears *Pink Moon* still flips for its lunar beauty. Taller than Marc Bolan, foxier than Brian Jones, just plain deader than Syd Barrett, Nick Drake would enjoy a cult following even if he hadn't been a genius, and yet as a cursory listen to "Cello Song" or "Place To Be" should convince anyone, a genius is what he was.

Five Leaves Left (a rolling-paper reference) has long, gorgeous folkie ruminations like "Time Has Told Me," "Saturday Sun," and "The Thoughts Of Mary Jane," with piano and strings to expand on Drake's guitar. *Bryter Layter* has flatter songs and fluffier production, despite the highlights "Fly," "Northern Sky," and the much-maligned "Poor Boy." But *Pink Moon* is perfect: 28 minutes, just Drake murmuring over acoustic guitar and occasional piano, stripped-down songs, most over in two minutes or so, all of them unforgettable. The title song offers a chilly prayer about death, while cryptic fragments like "Ride," "Road," and "Know" have an eerie sensuality to go with that melancholic late-night ambience. Greener than the hills but darker than the deepest sea, modulating from a whisper to a slightly louder whisper, *Pink Moon* is Orpheus wooing Eurydice with a guitar, and "Place To Be" remains one of the most seductive love songs ever written.

Although totally unheard at the time, Drake's songs have kept circulating via soundtracks, commercials, mix tapes, and indie/college radio, not to mention by inheritors like Elliott Smith, Cat Power, and Belle and Sebastian. *Time of No Reply*'s outtakes are for cultists; the compilation *Way To Blue* decently selected; the complete-works box *Fruit Tree* overly pricey (two CDs' worth of music spread over four CDs) but something you won't get tired of any time soon. The rarities collection *Made to Love Magic* unearthed a previously unheard song, "Tow the Line." It also has a few alternate versions, including a solo acoustic "River Man" and heinous orchestral remixes. The 48-minute documentary *A Skin Too Few* is worthwhile, though, unfortunately, no performance footage exists. Much more famous, beloved, and influential today than during his lifetime, Nick Drake continues to reach listeners' hearts, finally finding his own "Place to Be." —R.S.

The Drifters

★★★★★	All-Time Greatest Hits and More 1959–1965 (Atlantic, 1988)
★★★★	The Very Best of the Drifters (Rhino, 1993)
★★★★★	Rockin' & Driftin': The Drifters Box (Rhino, 1996)
★★★★	The Legendary Group at Their Best (Collectables, 2000)
★★★★	Clyde McPhatter & The Drifters/Rockin' & Driftin' (Collectables, 1998)
★★★★	Up on the Roof/Under the Boardwalk (Collectables, 1998)
★★★★	Save the Last Dance for Me/The Good Life With the Drifters (Collectables, 2000)

As Billy Vera points out in his excellent liner notes to the essential box set, *Rockin' & Driftin': The Drifters Box,* the only sensible way to approach this story is to think of the group as a franchise, a trademark name with an ever-shifting lineup rather than a single stable entity that produced stellar music from 1953 into the late '60s. In fact, Atlantic's legendary house engineer Tom Dowd recalls working with "30 to 35 different Drifters over the years. Nobody could pinpoint who sang on what." If the Drifters had become wealthy men for their endeavors, they could be called "the best team that money could buy." That none of them ended up with fat wallets is another infuriating, oft-told tale of music-business chicanery by unscrupulous management in a day when artists were regularly taken to the cleaners financially. Instead, they were simply the best team, in all their incarnations, and their legacy is monumental.

Start with an unbelievable roster of great lead singers, beginning in 1953 with group founder Clyde McPhatter, who passed the torch to Johnny Moore, who passed it to Benny Nelson (better known as Ben E. King), who passed it to Rudy Lewis, who passed it to Charlie Thomas, who passed it back to Johnny Moore and then took it back again. Then reflect on the other group members who would occasionally step out for a memorable lead vocal, such as Gerhardt "Gay" Thrasher, whose stunning performance on 1955's "Your Promise to Be Mine" is an R&B classic, and Bobby Hendricks, whose swaggering take on 1958's mid-level chart entry "Drip Drop" was the blueprint for Dion's #6 pop hit in 1963. They were the vocal equivalent of every banjo hitter on a championship baseball team who suddenly starts knocking the cover off the ball in the World Series. And that's not even counting longtime group member Bill Pinkney, who had a few choice moments of his own in the lead role, including a colead with McPhatter on the group's plaintive rendition of Irving Berlin's "White Christmas," a #2 R&B hit in 1954. These vocalists emerged from long shadows and cast substantial ones of their own: McPhatter links the soulful, falsetto moans of gospel great Claude Jeter to the signature styles developed by Smokey Robinson and Al Green; Ben E. King's muscular, masculine vocalizing is the bridge from the frenetic brio of the Sensational Nightingales' Julius Cheeks to the macho posturing of Wilson Pickett.

From there, consider the masters behind the scenes. The Drifters' first producers at Atlantic Records were a team comprising label founders Ahmet Ertegun and Jerry Wexler, with Ertegun's brother Nesuhi sometimes sitting behind the board on his own; all were aided further by Dowd, whose degree of peer respect in the recording industry surpasses that of almost any other engineer who has ever set foot in a studio. In 1958, Ertegun and Wexler handed the production reins to Jerry Leiber and Mike Stoller, whose personal "lab," the Coasters, already had placed three consecutive singles in the Top 10, including one chart-topper in 1958's "Yakety Yak." When Leiber and Stoller moved on in 1963 to devote their time to starting the Red Bird label, Bert Berns, who'd been coming up with solid chart hits at a time when the New York studio scene was stagnating, signed up for the Drifters' final chart run. Not the least but perhaps the least-known of this cast was arranger/conductor Stan Applebaum, who was responsible for the emotionally charged string arrangements on the great '60s hits (strings being a first on a rock & roll record when Applebaum introduced them on the luminous "There Goes My Baby," the 1959 #1 R&B [#2 pop] hit that introduced Ben E. King as lead singer, along with an entire new supporting cast of Drifters). Session musicians included formidable instrumental-

ists such as Big Al Sears on saxophone, drummer Panama Francis, and guitarist Mickey Baker—players who had deep roots in jazz and small-combo R&B.

Then there were the songwriters. Apart from a few questionable copyrights credited to a man Wexler recalls as "a greasy accountant" and partner of the band's despised manager, along with some other one-shots (not that these were undistinguished folk: Atlantic's house arranger Jesse Stone, an accomplished songwriter, penned the group's first hit, the classic "Money Honey"), the lineup responsible for writing the Drifters' timeless hits includes McPhatter himself ("Honey Love," a #1 R&B hit in 1954), Leiber and Stoller, Doc Pomus and Mort Shuman, Gerry Goffin and Carole King, Barry Mann and Cynthia Weil, Burt Bacharach and Hal David—the cream of the crop of the Brill Building school.

Born and raised in Durham, NC, where he sang in the Mount Calvary Baptist Church choir, McPhatter was 12 when his family moved to Harlem. While in high school he joined the Mount Lebanon Singers, whose membership included author James Baldwin's brothers David and Wilmer. In 1950, McPhatter and his Mount Lebanon cohort Charlie White auditioned for and were hired by Billy Ward for a new R&B group he was assembling. Signed to the Federal label, Billy Ward & His Dominoes, with McPhatter singing lead, became a popular R&B attraction. But after two years, McPhatter was getting restless, and Ward, impatient with his singer's increasing individuality, fired him.

McPhatter was holed up in a Harlem tenement when Atlantic founder Ahmet Ertegun tracked him down and convinced him to sign with his fledgling label. Before his first session, McPhatter assembled a backing group with some of his Mount Lebanon mates, including David Baldwin. A quintet dubbed Clyde McPhatter & the Drifters cut its first session in June 1953, but the session went so poorly that only one track, "Lucille," was ever released, and only as a B side a year later. In early August, McPhatter went back to the studio with a new Drifters lineup: Bill Pinkney, Andrew "Bubba" Thrasher, Gerhart "Gay" Thrasher, and Willie Ferbie. From that session came "Money Honey," which hit #1 shortly after release in August 1953, and the Drifters' saga was officially under way. The group hit #1 once more, with "Honey Love," before McPhatter was drafted into the Army in 1954.

The Drifters continued without him, with Johnny Moore joining as lead singer for 1955's chart-topping "Adorable" and 1956's #10 R&B hit "Ruby Baby" (another Drifters song later done to near perfection by Dion). McPhatter returned from his Army hitch in 1956 and went solo, topping the R&B chart out of the box with "Treasure of Love," again in 1957 with

"Long Lonely Nights," and in 1958 with "A Lover's Question," which also crossed over to #6 pop. In 1956, he also landed at #4 R&B with the towering love ballad, "Without Love (There Is Nothing)." His #7 pop hit from 1962, Billy Swan's "Lover Please," was his last chart appearance before alcoholism destroyed his career and eventually cost him his life. He died of a heart attack in Teaneck, NJ, in 1972.

The Drifters had begun to drift artistically after "Long Lonely Nights." With Bobby Hendricks singing lead, 1958's "Drip Drop" failed even to chart R&B, but it had a weak #58 showing pop. Internal strife between the group members and their manager, George Treadwell, boiled over, and Treadwell fired the entire group. He replaced them with a Harlem vocal group that had been performing as the Crowns. Its personnel included lead singer Benny (Ben E. King) Nelson, Charlie Thomas, James Clark, Dock Green, and Elsbeary Hobbs.

With Leiber and Stoller now producing and Stan Applebaum arranging and conducting, the reconstituted Drifters, with King singing lead, made their debut in 1959 with "There Goes My Baby." Thus began a run of 16 Top 40 singles that lasted five years, into 1964. From that 1959 starting point through 1963, when they moved on to Red Bird, Leiber and Stoller framed great songs from Pomus-Shuman and others with Applebaum's lush orchestrations and arrangements that incorporated a pronounced South American *bailon* rhythm—stylistic flourishes previously unheard in American pop. It was also the template for the soul-pop fusion on which the Motown dynasty was built.

Come 1960, and King exited for a solo career—which would yield two indisputably great singles: his self-penned 1960 Top 10 poetic masterpiece, "Spanish Harlem," and 1961's haunting plea, "Stand By Me," written by King in collaboration with Leiber and Stoller (it peaked at #4 pop and topped the R&B chart)—shortly after the group topped the pop chart with one of the most monumental of all Pomus-Shuman songs, "Save the Last Dance for Me." Enter then, by way of the Clara Ward Singers, Rudy Lewis. Three more years of hits followed, including two Top 10 entries, Goffin-King's "Up on the Roof" in 1962 and Weil, Mann, Leiber, and Stoller's evocative "On Broadway," in 1963. In a history studded with so many highlights, one of the most memorable moments came in 1964, when Lewis died of a heroin overdose on the day of a recording session. Johnny Moore, who had been with the group from 1955 to 1957, following McPhatter's departure, had rejoined in 1963. He stepped up to take the lead on the Bert Berns–produced "Under the Boardwalk," and in the midst of mind-numbing grief, Moore delivered one of the most nuanced and poignant performances in rock & roll history.

Under Berns' guidance, the Drifters cut some good singles in the mid-'60s—Mann and Weil's "Saturday Night at the Movies" (#18 pop, 1964); "I've Got Sand in My Shoes" (#33 pop, 1964); Jeff Barry and Ellie Greenwich's "I'll Take You Where the Music's Playing" (#51 pop, 1965)—but the run was over. Another configuration of the group recorded in England in the early '70s and made the Top 10 several times in 1974 and 1975, but America never heard those songs.

There's only one place to go to get the unexpurgated Drifters story, and that's the Rhino box mentioned above, *Rockin' & Driftin': The Drifters Box.* This three-CD collection includes all the important Drifters sides—not only hits, but B sides that illustrate the group's stylistic evolution as new singers entered the picture—from the beginning to the quiet end in England, as well as McPhatter's and King's solo hits, 79 cuts in all. Supplementing those are Vera's above-mentioned liner notes, literate and accessible, which not only keep the record straight with regard to the exhausting personnel changes but also provide vital insight into the sessions that produced this amazing body of work. As a record collector and historian, Vera drew on his knowledge of the band as well as his personal friendship with many of the key players to offer a fascinating inside look at history in the making. Additional perspective on the group is provided by a brief excerpt from Wexler's autobiography, *Rhythm and the Blues: A Life in American Music* (Alfred A. Knopf, 1993), and via an overview of group harmony's development in the essay "Drifting Into Doo-Wop" by Peter Grendysa. Toss in a well-annotated track listing and a full page of small-print lists of every Drifters iteration along with photographs of each and . . . whew! This is the real deal, a box set with a wealth of vital information and a mother lode of timeless tracks.

Less ambitious (and cheaper) single- and double-disc collections offer viable alternatives to the box set. Foremost among these is Atlantic's double-CD *All-Time Greatest Hits and More,* which hits all the high points of the various Drifters generations and has sharp annotation as well. Ditto for Collectables' double-CD *The Legendary Group at Their Best,* another broad overview of the hits and more but lacking the Atlantic collection's informative liner notes. Rhino's single-disc package, *The Very Best of the Drifters,* supplants Atlantic's out-of-print *The Drifters' Golden Hits,* adding four tracks but still boiling down the history to five years, beginning in 1959 with "There Goes My Baby" and ending with 1964's "Saturday Night at the Movies." It ignores about six years of stellar recordings that came before 1959, so caveat emptor. Completists cannot do without the twofers released by Collectables—three individual discs containing two complete Drifters albums. *Clyde McPhatter & The Drifters/Rockin' & Driftin'* are the group's earliest efforts, and the ones most deeply rooted in R&B: *Clyde McPhatter & The Drifters* features, obviously, Clyde McPhatter on lead vocals (and also includes some of his solo hits); *Rockin' & Driftin'* (not to be confused with the box set) features Johnny Moore on lead. The nonsingle album tracks paint an impressive portrait of a group that brought the same high standard to every song it sang—*filler* is hardly an apt term to describe these cuts when the performances are consistently engaging and emotionally compelling. That's why the Drifters were the Drifters.   —D.M.

Drive-By Truckers

★★★★   Gangstabilly (Soul Dump, 1998)
★★★½   Pizza Deliverance (Soul Dump, 1999)
★★½   Alabama Ass Whuppin' (Second Heaven, 1999)
★★★★   Southern Rock Opera (Soul Dump, 2001)
★★★★   Decoration Day (New West, 2003)
★★★½   The Dirty South (New West, 2004)

Though blessed with literary talent, punk values, and a Muscle Shoals pedigree, the Drive-By Truckers are also unreconstructed rednecks, embodying "the duality of the Southern thing" long before they sang about it on *Southern Rock Opera.* And like true Dixie rebels, their fierce loyalty to their cause has often courted tragedy before glory. On *Gangstabilly,* leader Patterson Hood thanks friends and family for persevering through "the 12 years or so leading up to it." But the band's righteous DIY ethic guaranteed that mostly just friends and family would hear this tour-de-force debut, a taut collection worthy of the Bottle Rockets, Ass Ponys, or Waco Brothers.

Thanks to slightly better distribution and clearer production, *Pizza Deliverance* finally garnered the Truckers some wider attention. If the disc suffers from traditional second-album padding, swaggering rockers like "Nine Bullets" and sweeping ballads like "Bulldozers and Dirt" are as sharp as *Gangstabilly's* best. The rowdy-to-sloppy *Alabama Ass Whuppin'* proves padding has nothing to do with the band's live sound. Still, despite Hood's wonderful stories, few numbers improve on the studio versions. Instead, the guitar-heavy attack (and brief cover of "Gimme Three Steps") just clears the way for the Truckers' masterpiece. The title *Southern Rock Opera* is partly a joke, but the complexity of this two-disc set rivals the Who's *Quadrophenia,* comprising historical, cultural, and autobiographical story lines that eventually cohere in a deeply affecting portrayal of Lynyrd Skynyrd's final flight. And, more than *Quadrophenia,* the project is strengthened by the tension between the band's lofty ambitions and their commitment to an earthbound sound. It finally won the Truckers the attention of bigger labels, but the excellent new *Decoration Day* shows how their rebel pride has matured, not mellowed. The cut entitled "Do It Yourself" is actually about suicide, which they now scorn with the fury of street survivors. Slow, somber, and perfectly titled, *The Dirty South* is another tuneful evocation of the dark side of Southern life. Over alternately jangly and sludgy guitars, Hood, Mike Cooley, and young gun Jason Isbell lament Reagan-era poverty ("Puttin' People on the Moon"), reminisce about their moonshine-swilling daddies ("Where the Devil Don't Stay"), and memorialize a legendary workin' man ("The Day John Henry Died"). Older fans will miss the Truckers' Skynyrdesque raveups, but the gritty self-pity and gin-u-wine gravitas of these tragic vignettes still make for the best new-school Southern rock you can buy.   —F.S.

Dru Hill

★★★   Dru Hill (Island, 1996)
★★★   Enter the Dru (Island, 1998)
★★★★   Dru World Order (2002, Def Soul)

With its first release, this Baltimore quartet turned New Jack Swing inside out. Instead of R&B vocal harmonies with hip-hop flavor, Dru Hill fronted like a hip-hop outfit before revealing its crushed-velvet soul. The group negotiated its persona through mere sound, balancing the rich and the real for surefire chick-bait. Keith Sweat's production is plush on the cheap, and the singers' homeboy-next-door vocals are always sincere, never intimidatingly professional. The single "Tell Me" went Top 5 and proved that chicks, indeed, digged on the Dru. *Enter the Dru* continued the streak (still without explaining the band's attachment to martial-arts/mythical-animal imagery), with enough chart oomph to allow Dru member Sisqo to begin releasing solo projects. After the success of Sisqo's summer novelty "The Thong Song," and the relative disappointment of his album sales, Dru Hill regrouped stronger than ever for *Dru World Order,* folding Sisqo back in and adding sad-eyed Skola, a singer with an expansive gospel vibe. Tamir "Nokio" Ruffin (the "N-Tity") does the production honors, piling on the strings, decelerating the syncopation to a slow tease, and piling the men's voices atop one another like the towering platter of bedroom-cakes they are. If there's a cuter contemporary seduction number than "I Should Be . . . ," Boyz II Men sure didn't record one. —A.B.

D12

★★★   Devil's Night (Shady/Aftermath, 2001)
★★★   D12 World (Shady/Aftermath, 2004)

Imagine an Eminem album without the guided tours of his fucked-up head, the razor-sharp characterizations, or the handful of sensitive moments. Then take away half of his rhymes and substitute some fair-to-above-average MCs, and you have a D12 record. If the *Slim Shady* and *Marshall Mathers* albums were slapstick trips into one man's psychosis and alienation—like the Marx Brothers starring in *Taxi Driver*—then D12's approach is a lot simpler: It's *Friday the 13th*, or maybe a Farrelly brothers version of *Henry: Portrait of a Serial Killer*. On *Devil's Night*, Eminem and his five buddies are stuck in a peer-pressure spiral of trying to outdo each other, with D12 irregulars Kon Artis, Proof, Kuniva, Swifty, and the supremely disturbed Bizarre dropping shock raps that range from silly ("I let my dogs out on the Baha Men") to annoyingly over-the-top ("Smacked this whore for talking crap/So what if she's handicapped?"). Despite all this, *Devil's Night* has more than its share of decent moments, thanks mostly to Eminem. Tracks such as "Shit Can Happen" jump to life when he takes the mike. A few songs pick up where he had left off on *The Marshall Mathers LP*: "Ain't Nuttin' but Music" is a sequel to "The Real Slim Shady," down to Dr. Dre's bouncy synth line and the Britney Spears jokes. Almost every track has a tight concept, a chorus that sticks, and a groove that carries a melody. Songs like the creeping "Pistol Pistol," the woozy "Purple Pills," and the bumping "Blow My Buzz" are just more musical than your average rap song, but don't call attention to the fact.

Much of *D12 World* simply repeats the debut's blend of rote horror-core rhymes, "offensive" humor, and dumb skits. But compared with *Devil's Night*, *D12 World* boasts less shock for the sake of shock, better rhymes, and tales of violence that seem, if not realistic, at least less ridiculous. Cuts like the opening "Git Up" and the Dre-produced "American Psycho II" get by on hooky beats and nimble flows, as D12's members boast of their skills, take target practice, and mostly eschew lame jokes. *D12 World* is still undoubtedly Eminem's show, but the album's best moments find all six MCs dropping rhymes that play off one another—like a group of hoodlums working together to steal your hubcaps. On the bright stoopid single "My Band," everyone contributes solidly comic verses, poking fun at one another while pretending not to understand why the media is so interested in their leader; on the title cut, which is buoyed by an excellent Kanye West beat and a Cypress Hill–sung chorus, everyone speed-rhymes his way through a laundry list of the best stuff in the "world": bitches, hot lead, and liquor, in particular. It's still shock rap, and all too perfunctory at times, but if D12's goal is to establish an identity that anyone over 16 can take seriously, it's getting closer. —N.B./C.H.

Duran Duran

★★★★   Duran Duran (1981; Capitol, 2003)
★★★★½   Rio (1982; Capitol, 2001)
★★★½   Seven and the Ragged Tiger (1983; Capitol, 2003)
★★   Arena (1984; Capitol, 2004)
★★★   Notorious (Capitol, 1986)
★★   Big Thing (Capitol, 1988)
★★★★   Decade (Capitol, 1989)
★★   Liberty (Capitol, 1990)
★★½   Duran Duran (Capitol, 1993)
★★   Thank You (Capitol, 1995)
★★   Medazzaland (Capitol, 1997)
★★★★   Greatest (Capitol, 1998)
★★   Pop Trash (Hollywood, 2000)

Duran Duran represents a turning point in the sexual history of new wave: Girls pulled their hair and screamed, while boys complained that they were fascist pop puppets taking up valuable airtime that rightfully belonged to Black Flag. But the girls were right, as they always are. The Fab Five combined New Romantic synths, disco bass lines, flash guitar, wedge haircuts, and a host of art-glam pretensions into some of the '80s' juiciest pop trash.

Duran Duran's first three albums are butter: Simon Le Bon sings of love and fashion, his mouth alive with juices like wine, while Nick Rhodes presses brightly colored keyboard buttons and all three Taylors boogie down. The debut has the insanely catchy "Planet Earth," the lecherous "Girls on Film," and the nuclear-war-pondering "Is There Something I Should Know?" *Seven* has "Union of the Snake" and "New Moon on Monday." But *Rio* is definitely the one to get—even filler like "Hold Back the Rain" has lipstick cherry all over the lens. The title tune evokes a mysterious femme fatale with a fetish for dancing on the sand, and when she shines she really shows you all she can (huh?). "Save a Prayer" is a drippily suggestive slow jam raising the hermeneutic conceit "Some people call it a one-night stand/But we can call it . . . paradise." "Hungry Like the Wolf" is lycanthropic disco madness, complete with orgasmic moans from some lucky she-wolf or another, culminating as

Simon gets all Romulus on your Remus by the moonlight tide. A classic.

Although their imminent demise has been predicted many times, the Durannies have hung around long enough to age into the despot dowagers of the new-wave empire. Indeed, even a devoted fan has to be puzzled by their staying power. After the live *Arena*, and a lull with the side projects Arcadia and the Power Station, they returned as a trio (minus Roger and Andy) on the Nile Rodgers–produced *Notorious*—and yes, that's 16-year-old Christy Turlington posing seductively on the back cover. The later albums are spottier, but the hits kept coming every couple of years or so, and *Greatest* rounds them up (with a little too much '90s stuff). The earlier best-of *Decade* has an ugly cover and no "New Moon on Monday." *Thank You* was a popular, though not very good, 1995 album of covers, including a version of Grandmaster Flash's "White Lines" that became a fluke urban-radio hit. By *Medazzaland* and *Pop Trash*, John Taylor had dropped out of the group, surely just a temporary glitch. Not until the last Duran Duran fan passes from the earth shall its name go unhonored. And Duran Duran fans shall never, never pass from the earth, not as long as there is sand somewhere upon which Rio can dance. —R.S.

Ian Dury & the Blockheads

★★★½   Sex & Drugs & Rock & Roll: The Best Of (Rhino, 1992)

The late Cockney-accented singer Dury (and his trusty collaborator, keyboardist Chaz Jankel) wittily bridged the gap between the British skinny-tie crowd and the American disco mob (with a touch of vaudeville thrown in) during his 1977–80 heyday. Most of his records' energy came from the tension between Dury's awkward, blustery delivery and the Blockheads' slicked-up grooves, and they milked it for all the charm it was worth. *Sex & Drugs & Rock & Roll*, basically an expanded version of their better-sequenced *Juke Box Dury* compilation, includes all of their dance crossover hits: the deadpan-anthemic title song, "Reasons to Be Cheerful, Part 3," and the funky *and* goofy "Hit Me With Your Rhythm Stick." —D.W.

Dust Brothers

★★★★   Fight Club Soundtrack (Restless, 1999)

They have produced but one twitching, energized album under their own name, but cutting-edge production team the Dust Brothers (John King and Mike Simpson) are responsible for a couple of the most important sampledelic albums of the '80s (Beastie

Boys' *Paul's Boutique*) and '90s (Beck's *Odelay*) and even produced one of each decades' most indelible pop songs (Tone-Lōc's "Wild Thing," Hansons' "Mmmbop"). The soundtrack to *Fight Club*—also known as "The Dust Brothers's Long-Awaited Debut Album"—blends whip-crack drum and bass, electro thud and razor wire rock guitar into a kinetic stew that mirrors the film's strung-out anxiety.   —J.G.

Bob Dylan

★★★★	Bob Dylan (Columbia, 1962)
★★★★★	The Freewheelin' Bob Dylan (Columbia, 1963)
★★★★	The Times They Are a-Changin' (Columbia, 1964)
★★★★½	Another Side of Bob Dylan (Columbia, 1964)
★★★★★	Bringing It All Back Home (Columbia, 1965)
★★★★★	Highway 61 Revisited (Columbia, 1965)
★★★★★	Blonde on Blonde (Columbia, 1966)
★★★★	Bob Dylan's Greatest Hits (Columbia, 1967)
★★★★★	John Wesley Harding (Columbia, 1967)
★★★★	Nashville Skyline (Columbia, 1969)
★	Self Portrait (Columbia, 1970)
★★★★	New Morning (Columbia, 1970)
★★★★★	Bob Dylan's Greatest Hits, Vol. 2 (Columbia, 1971)
★★	Pat Garrett & Billy the Kid (Columbia, 1973)
★	Dylan (Columbia, 1973)
★★★	Planet Waves (Asylum, 1974)
★★★½	Before the Flood (Asylum, 1974)
★★★★★	The Basement Tapes (Columbia, 1975)
★★★★★	Blood on the Tracks (Columbia, 1975)
★★★★½	Desire (Columbia, 1976)
★★	Hard Rain (Columbia, 1976)
★★	Street Legal (Columbia, 1978)
★	Bob Dylan at Budokan (Columbia, 1978)
★★★	Slow Train Coming (Columbia, 1979)
★	Saved (Columbia, 1980)
★★	Shot of Love (Columbia, 1981)
★★★★	Infidels (Columbia, 1983)
★★★	Real Live (Columbia, 1984)
★★	Empire Burlesque (Columbia, 1985)
★★★★★	Biograph (Columbia, 1985)
★	Knocked Out Loaded (Columbia, 1986)
★★	Down in the Groove (Columbia, 1988)
★	Dylan & the Dead (Columbia, 1989)
★★	Oh Mercy (Columbia, 1989)
★	Under the Red Sky (Columbia, 1990)
★★★★★	The Bootleg Series, Vols. 1–3 (Rare and Unreleased) 1961–1991 (Columbia, 1991)
★★★½	Good as I Been to You (Columbia, 1992)
★★★★	World Gone Wrong (Columbia, 1993)
★★★½	Dylan's Greatest Hits, Vol. 3 (Columbia, 1994)
★★½	MTV Unplugged (Columbia, 1995)
★★★★★	Time Out of Mind (Columbia, 1997)

★★★★★ Live 1966 (Columbia, 1998)
★★★★ The Essential Bob Dylan (Columbia, 2000)
★★★★★ Love and Theft (Columbia, 2001)
★★★½ Live 1975 (Columbia, 2002)
★★★★ Live 1964 (Columbia, 2004)

Look on his works, ye mighty, and despair. After 40 years on the job, Bob Dylan still makes all other song-writers sound like scared kittens, and in terms of sheer volume, he's built the largest body of work worth listening to in rock & roll. He's the American song-and-dance man, the sleight-of-hand man, mixing up folk roots, beat poetry, Chuck Berry, Baudelaire, Texas medicine, railroad gin, and his own psychedelic mutations of the blues, singing it all in that intense Book-of-Deuteronomy howl of his. By now, Dylan's failures are as mythic as his successes, but even though he has journeyed through the Valley of Suckdom (and has even rested there for years at a time) he also remains rock's longest-running font of vitality, a mystery tramp with his boot heels wandering all over the map of American music. His career is one rock archetype after another: the arrogant young protest singer in the Huck Finn cap; the mod Chelsea-booted hipster of the mid-'60s, singing the third verse of "I Want You" with all the deadly hip-twitching swing of Chuck Berry's guitar; the grizzled old con man of Love and Theft, croaking biblical blues and Tin Pan Alley valentines out of the side of his mouth while keeping one eye on the exit.

After growing up in rural Minnesota, a teen rock-ability guitarist who idolized Elvis and James Dean, the young Robert Zimmerman discovered Woody Guthrie and ran off to New York to become Bob Dylan. His debut album showed his raw talent and brash singing, with covers like "Baby, Let Me Follow You Down" and "You're No Good" reflecting his apprenticeship in the Bleecker Street folk scene. But he pulled ahead of everybody else on Freewheelin', a virtuosic burst of original songs that combined bitter political protest ("Masters of War"), poetic dread ("A Hard Rain's a-Gonna Fall"), introspection ("Bob Dylan's Dream"), romance ("Girl From the North Country"), and a viciously witty fare-thee-well ("Don't Think Twice, It's All Right").

Still armed with just his acoustic guitar, harmonica, and ragged voice, Dylan became the king of the freewheelin' folk rogues, even as his punk rage and blues rhythms suggested the rock moves to come. The Times They Are a-Changin' had straighter protest songs—some great ("The Lonesome Death of Hattie Carroll"), some simpy (the title track)—that were overshadowed by two out-of-place but excellent breakup songs, "One Too Many Mornings"

and "Boots of Spanish Leather." Another Side show-cased his tormented love/hate ballads, suggesting that Dylan was starting to outgrow acoustic simplicity. It also suggested that Dylan—swooning in the erotic intoxication of "Spanish Harlem Incident" and then begging for a serious bitch-slap in "It Ain't Me Babe"—was maybe not the guy you'd want to set up with your sister.

After getting his mind blown by the Beatles over the radio, Dylan finally bid a restless farewell to folk or-thodoxy, plugging in his guitar for a controversial electric performance at the Newport Folk Festival that scandalized old fans. "The only place where it's hap-pening is on the radio and records," he told an inter-viewer. "That's where the people hang out." Dylan mixed up the medicine to invent a whole new breed of rock & roll on Bringing It All Back Home. On the electric first side, Dylan sneered his absurdist, word-drunk rambles over lean, jittery garage rock, brim-ming over with wild humor, while side two had four brain-frazzling acoustic ballads that made The Times They Are a-Changin' sound like kid stuff. "Mr. Tambourine Man" is surely the friendliest of all drug songs, maybe because it's not so much a drug song as a music song; "She Belongs to Me" and "Love Minus Zero/No Limit" are devotional love songs; "Bob Dylan's 115th Dream" takes a riotously funny cruise through American history and ends the way Dylan once claimed all his songs secretly ended: "Good luck."

Highway 61 Revisited perfected the sound that Dylan dubbed "thin wild mercury music," with a jagged guitar groove, swirling organ, fluid piano, and Dylan's madcap snarl up top, all doomy menace and hallucinatory wit, packing a career's worth of rock & roll innovation into each of the nine songs. He got on the radio with the loud, mean anthem "Like a Rolling Stone," a #2 hit in 1965. But every song here is a classic: the adrenaline-crazed "Tombstone Blues," the raucous "From a Buick 6," the spiteful "Ballad of a Thin Man," the epic "Desolation Row." For all the po-etic complexity, the best line is one of the simplest: "I've been up all night, leaning on the windowsill."

Rolling faster than anyone could follow, Dylan moved on to the double-vinyl Blonde on Blonde. Dylan freaks still love to argue over whether Bringing It, Highway 61, or Blonde is the absolute pinnacle of Zimmerdom; unlike Highway 61, Blonde has weak spots, especially the god-awful opening hit "Rainy Day Women #12 & 35," but it's his greatest album anyway, a surreal fever dream of a record, racing through his sharpest, slickest, scariest, and most se-ductive songs at breakneck speed. Recorded in Nashville with session cats who sound juiced by the chance to cut loose, *Blonde* has "I Want You," "Visions of Johanna," "Stuck Inside of Mobile With the Memphis Blues Again," and ends with the bleary 11-minute love ballad "Sad Eyed Lady of the Lowlands," cut in one long take a few minutes after Dylan finished writing it. *Blonde on Blonde,* released just 15 months after *Bringing It All Back Home,* climaxed the amphetamine rush of Dylan's mid-'60s glory. Wired, fried, the ghost of electricity howling in the bones of his face, Dylan was caught up in the most intense burst of creativity any rock & roller has ever had.

You can see the pace taking its toll in the Dylan documentaries *Don't Look Back,* where he's a fidgety coquette sucking in his cheeks for the camera, and *Something Is Happening,* where he's the vanishing American hidden behind steely shades in the limo with John Lennon. But you can hear Dylan at peak fury on *Live 1966,* the famous Manchester, England concert of May 17, 1966, bootlegged for decades but not officially released until 1998. Dylan foams at the mouth in "Baby, Let Me Follow You Down" and "Tell Me, Momma," as the Band flails ferociously behind him; at the finale, an outraged folkie yells "Judas!," goading Dylan into a positively evil "Like a Rolling Stone." At this point, Dylan was recording gems faster than he could keep track of them, and it took years before essential cuts like "If You Gotta Go, Go Now," "Can You Please Crawl Out Your Window?," "I'll Keep It With Mine," or "She's Your Lover Now" got properly released.

But the frenetic pace came to a halt in July 1966: The official (and possibly fictional) excuse was a motorcycle crash. Dylan retreated to Woodstock, NY, to detox, recover, and plan his next move. While there, he gathered with his friends in the Band to cut the legendary "Basement Tapes," home recordings of a new style of stoner folk music. Songs like "You Ain't Going Nowhere" and "Million Dollar Bash" were loose, offhand, and deeply strange, funny on the surface but mysterious below; after years of bootlegging, the official *Basement Tapes* finally appeared in 1975. Much of the finest Basement Tapes work—"I'm Not There (I'm Gone)," "I Am a Teenage Prayer," "Get Your Rocks Off," "Sign of the Cross"—still has yet to be released; see Greil Marcus' book *The Old, Weird America* for the full story. For his next public move, however, Dylan shocked everyone with the stark simplicity of *John Wesley Harding;* in the era of flower power, he suddenly went all Jewish-cowboy prophet on everybody's ass. It's one of his best albums, 12 ancient-sounding country-rock tunes, mostly just drums, bass, and acoustic guitar spinning fabulist yarns that could be hilarious ("Drifter's Escape"), terrifying ("I Dreamed I Saw St. Augustine"), or both ("The Ballad of Frankie

Lee and Judas Priest"), and finally brightening up for "I'll Be Your Baby Tonight."

Dylan dipped deeper into country for *Nashville Skyline;* he even temporarily quit smoking to sweeten his voice. It has a seductively light touch, especially in "I Threw It All Away" and "Tonight I'll Be Staying Here With You." It also has a great cover photo: Dylan tipping his hat before he sets a spell to sing you some right purty songs. But *Self Portrait* was a disaster that nobody has really ever explained: a double album of deliberately bad throwaways, most of them grumpy covers. Dylan took a while to fully recover—his voice grew phlegmy and his songwriting absentminded; his clothes were dirty, but his hands were too clean. *New Morning* was a lighter, stronger *Nashville Skyline;* his *Pat Garrett* soundtrack had the hit "Knockin' on Heaven's Door"; *Planet Waves* was a modest reunion with the Band. *Dylan* was a set of *Self Portrait* outtakes, released against his will and notable for a hilariously bad "Can't Help Falling in Love." *Greatest Hits, Vol. 2* is an ideal introduction—much more fun than the lightweight 1967 *Greatest Hits*—with superbly chosen album tracks and rarities, especially the soulful new acoustic versions of "I Shall Be Released," "You Ain't Going Nowhere," and "Down in the Flood."

It took marriage troubles to shake Dylan up, and he found his rugged new adult voice in the acoustic heartbreak of *Blood on the Tracks.* It was such a stunning comeback that for years afterward, anything half decent he ever did would get praised as "his best work since *Blood on the Tracks.*" Dylan found himself "Tangled Up in Blue," brooding over lost love with bitterness ("Idiot Wind"), generosity ("If You See Her, Say Hello"), and cheer ("You're Gonna Make Me Lonesome When You Go")—a jack of hearts getting kicked around by the simple twists of fate. "Lily, Rosemary, and the Jack of Hearts," the longest but least-loved song on the album, is nonetheless a great one, a sly shaggy-dog story about how love screws you over even when you don't get your hopes up—so you may as well get your hopes up.

Back in the ring, Dylan knocked off *Desire* in one night, with first-take arrangements full of floppy drums, lazy violin, plenty of tequila, and Emmylou Harris' harmonies. He mourned his broken marriage in "Isis," "One More Cup of Coffee," and "Sara," where he recalled "staying up for days in the Chelsea Hotel writing 'Sad Eyed Lady of the Lowlands' for you." But he also had 20 pounds of headlines stapled to his chest, rambling about current events in "Hurricane" and "Joey." According to Dylan legend, *Desire* was the first album he ever wrote with the aid of a rhyming dictionary, and boy can you tell, especially in the ridiculous gangster epic "Joey," which boasts quite possibly the dodgiest lines of Dylan's whole career: "One day they blew him down/At a clam bar in New York/He could see them coming through the door/As he lifted up his fork."

Having thus reconstituted the shattered fragments of American poetry, Dylan moved on to religion. He started out on Genesis, but soon hit the harder stuff, with a fundamentalist conversion that remains one of the oddest episodes of his career. *Street Legal* was the turning point, a turgid set of pulp-mystic dirges with occult lyrics; it's a musical failure, but it has its own fanatical following, a cult within the Dylan cult. By *Slow Train Coming*, Dylan was a Bible-thumping, born-again Christian who was hearing from the Almighty on a regular basis. You'd think God would have been in a pretty cheerful mood—after all, not only was He omnipotent, He got to hang with Dylan. But no: Apparently, all He did was complain, and so for the next few years, Dylan dutifully passed on the Lord's harangues against heathens, pornographers, and harlots. Not sweethearts, though—sweethearts were okay. *Slow Train* benefited from Mark Knopfler's guitar and "I Believe in You"; *Saved* had the underrated "Solid Rock"; *Shot of Love* had the overrated "Every Grain of Sand."

Dylan briefly returned to form with 1983's *Infidels*, an altogether more worldly batch of songs ("Jokerman," "Sweetheart Like You") lifted high by the Sly & Robbie rhythm section and guitarist/producer Knopfler. It's Dylan's best work of the lost years between *Desire* and *Time Out of Mind*, exploring the human side of his spiritual concerns, even if the jingoistic "Neighborhood Bully" suggested that the album could have been called *Intifada*. The finale "Don't Fall Apart on Me Tonight" added a strange autobiographical detail when Dylan confessed, "I wish I'd been a doctor." A scary thought to be sure, but back home in Minnesota, his mother was presumably pleased.

Like everything else, Dylan sucked in the '80s. He locked into a game of chicken with Neil Young, battling to see who could release more bad albums before the decade was out. (Dylan won, eight to seven.) For years Dylan fumbled around like a complete unknown, lost in *Miami Vice* threads and synth drums, trying to conform to a pop scene that had nothing to do with him. On *Empire Burlesque*, he sounded lucky just to be employed, though "Tight Connection to My Heart" went into the all-time canon of great Dylan songs on lousy Dylan albums. *Knocked Out Loaded*, the absolute bottom of the Dylan barrel, has the *Carol Burnett Show*–style production number "Brownsville Girl," with one classic Dylan line: "I didn't know whether to duck or run, so I ran." *Down in the Groove* has a sing-along goof, "Ugliest Girl in the World," though it's not as funny as the genius self-parody

of "Tweeter and the Monkey Man," buried that same year on the Traveling Wilburys' *Volume One*. *Oh Mercy* and *Under the Red Sky* were studio-slick mush, while *Dylan and the Dead* made one Deadhead friend lament, "I never thought I'd see the day when Jerry Garcia would have to bail someone out vocally."

His best performance of the '80s was hidden on side two of the mostly terrible, completely ignored 1984 concert album *Real Live:* a new version of "Tangled Up in Blue," with just Dylan and his guitar, playing around with the chord changes and improvising new words, using the crowd as an instrument to rewrite one of his classics as a whole new song. Hardly anyone paid attention, not even Dylan himself, but he would eventually revisit this playful spirit in the '90s to make some of his finest music. He hit the road for his Never Ending Tour, and recorded a couple of overlooked oddities, *Good as I Been to You* and *World Gone Wrong*, which comprise solo acoustic renditions of old blues and folk songs. It was now official: Dylan had finally blown out his voice. But that turned out to be good news, because after those last creaky floorboards gave way, the man had to come up with a whole new songwriting style for the voice he was left with, the sinister rusted-muffler growl he introduced on *Time Out of Mind*. Dylan's biggest success in years, *Time Out of Mind* shocked the world because it didn't even echo past glories—it was a ghostly, beautiful new sound, yet another side of Bob Dylan. If he'd trained for *Nashville Skyline* by quitting cigarettes, *Time Out of Mind* sounded as though he'd been sucking exhaust pipes, which perfectly suited the bleak, world-weary wit of "Not Dark Yet," "Standing in the Doorway," and the 17-minute finale, "Highlands."

He hit even harder with *Love and Theft*, a full-blown tour of the American songbook in all its burlesque splendor, veering into country blues, ragtime, vaudeville, cocktail-lounge corn, the minstrel show, and the kind of rockabilly he used to bash out with his high school band. *Love and Theft* is a musical autobiography that also sounds like a casual, almost accidental history of the country. The old man faces the apocalypse in "High Water (For Charley Patton)," finds twisted romance in "Moonlight" and "Bye and Bye," even cracks a knock-knock joke in the borscht-belt blues "Po' Boy." ("Freddy or not, here I come"— oy, gevalt!) Relaxed, magisterial, utterly confident in every musical idiom he touches, Dylan sings in a voice that sounds even older than he is.

Dylan's reissues are a tangled mess already, and we ain't seen nothing yet. *Biograph* was the 1985 box set, spiking the hits with choice rarities from 1963's "Lay Down Your Weary Tune" to 1981's "Groom's Still Waiting at the Altar." The prize is the *Blood on the*

Tracks outtake "Up to Me," with the line, "She's everything I need and love, but I can't be swayed by that." *Biograph* is a sprawl, and you can argue all day about the selections (that's part of the fun), but it's still an excellent way to turn on a new fan, or to become one. The three-disc *Bootleg Series* collects unreleased treasures like "She's Your Lover Now," "Let Me Die in My Footsteps," "Call Letter Blues," and "Blind Willie McTell," as well as the unheralded baseball classic "Catfish." It has hardly any Basement Tapes material, though, undoubtedly because that's getting saved for the inevitable *Basement Box.* The 1995 *Greatest Hits, Vol.* 3 reaches all the way back to the early '70s, which is just crazy. The two-CD, 30-song *Essential* is a handy sampler, despite some dubious picks ("Rainy Day Women," that means you). *Live 1966* is the best live album by far. The 1974 *Before the Flood* is crude, rough fun with the Band; *Live 1975* has windbag Rolling Thunder performances; *Hard Rain* and *Unplugged* are naps; and the Vegas-style revue *Bob Dylan at Budokan* is immaculately frightful. *Live 1964* is the famous October '64 solo acoustic show at Carnegie Hall, long bootlegged as *Halloween Masque,* and prized as his definitive pre-electric live set. "Don't let that scare ya. It's just Halloween," Dylan tells the crowd as he fiddles with the intro to "If You Gotta Go, Go Now." "I have my Bob Dylan mask on." But wherever you start exploring, Dylan's body of work is one to luxuriate in; this is what salvation must be like after a while.   —R.S.

The Eagles

★★★½ Eagles (Elektra/Asylum, 1972)
★★★ Desperado (Elektra/Asylum, 1973)
★★★ On the Border (Elektra/Asylum, 1974)
★★★½ One of These Nights (Elektra/Asylum, 1975)
★★★★★ Eagles: Their Greatest Hits, 1971–1975 (Elektra/Asylum, 1976)
★★★ Hotel California (Elektra/Asylum, 1976)
★★★ The Long Run (Elektra/Asylum, 1979)
★★★★ Eagles Greatest Hits, Vol. 2 (Elektra/Asylum, 1982)
★★ Hell Freezes Over (Geffen, 1994)
★★★ Eagles 1972–1999: Selected Works (Elektra/Asylum, 2000)
★★★★ The Very Best of the Eagles (Warner Bros., 2003)

One of the best-selling bands of all time, the Eagles were an anomaly in the L.A. country-folk-rock scene that they came out of: They didn't expand the great country and folk hybrids of the '60s proffered by Buffalo Springfield, the Flying Burrito Brothers, and Gram Parsons so much as provide a template for the Nashville pop of the '90s, as epitomized by Garth Brooks, Travis Tritt, and Brooks & Dunn (fittingly, several major country stars repaid the debt on the 1993 tribute album *Common Thread: The Songs of the Eagles*).

Eagles is anchored by one of the band's signature songs, "Take It Easy," cowritten with Jackson Browne. It defines their sound: breezy tunes outfitted with golden harmonies about rambling and womanizing in the posthippie hangover days of '70s California. It put the Eagles—particularly cocaptains Don Henley and Glenn Frey—at the center of the burgeoning California rock and singer/songwriter movements. It was also blessed with some virtuoso instrumentalists; Burrito Brothers alumnus Bernie Leadon brings a bluegrass feel to portions of the debut.

The Eagles strain to turn *Desperado* into a concept album, and begin exploring the darkness that would imbue much of their later work, but they present their Old West outlaw conceits as a series of dirges. *On the Border* rocks harder, bolstered by the addition of a new producer (Bill Szymczyk) and a guitarist (Don Felder) whose fills and solos are like miniature songs in themselves. *One of These Nights* is the band's most musically adventurous outing yet, flirting with disco on the title song, a waltz on "Take It to the Limit," and bluegrass psychedelia on Leadon's "Journey of the Sorcerer."

Hotel California is widely regarded as the band's masterpiece, and as a snapshot of '70s decadence and jadedness it'll do nicely: It's resplendent pop music about a spiritually bankrupt age. But the album is mighty thin after the twin peaks of the reggae-tinged title song—easily the band's finest moment—and "Life in the Fast Lane," which boasts a tougher sound and a greater sense of humor than ever before, thanks to the addition of former James Gang guitar slinger Joe Walsh.

Walsh's presence also gives *The Long Run* a rougher edge, while bassist Timothy B. Schmit's "I Can't Tell You Why" just may be the mellowest gold in the Eagles' canon. But the album also marks the beginning of the end. The Eagles scold their critics ("we'll find out in the long run"), even as the title song recycles the melody from Otis Clay's R&B cult classic "Tryin' to Live My Life Without You." A quintessential singles band, the Eagles are best represented by their hits collections; *Their Greatest Hits 1971–1975* focuses on the country-tinged early years, *Vol. 2* nails the more varied and adventurous approach of the late '70s, and the two-disc *The Very Best of the Eagles* provides the most comprehensive career overview. *Hell Freezes Over* includes 11 songs from an *MTV Unplugged* performance, which paved the way for the band's $100-a-seat comeback tour and four new, unremarkable studio recordings. *Selected Works: 1972–1999* repackages older material, devoting one of its four discs to the band's Millennium Concert, which proves they're still experts at stiffly re-creating their studio recordings onstage. —G.K.

Steve Earle

★★★½ Guitar Town (MCA, 1986)
★★★½ Exit 0 (MCA, 1987)
★★★★½ Copperhead Road (Uni/MCA, 1988)
★★★½ The Hard Way (MCA, 1991)
★★★ Shut Up and Die Like an Aviator (MCA, 1991)
★★★ Essential Steve Earle (MCA, 1993)
★★★★ Train a Comin' (Winter Harvest, 1995)
★★★★ I Feel Alright (E-Squared/Warner Bros., 1996)
★★★½ Ain't Ever Satisfied: The Steve Earle Collection (Hip-O/MCA, 1996)
★★★★ El Corazón (E-Squared/Warner Bros., 1997)
★★★½ Transcendental Blues (E-Squared/Artemis, 2000)
★★★ Sidetracks (E-Squared/Artemis, 2002)
★★★★ Jerusalem (E-Squared/Artemis, 2002)
★★★★ Just an American Boy (Artemis, 2003)
★★★★ The Revolution Starts . . . Now (Artemis, 2004)

with Townes Van Zandt and Guy Clark

★★★ Together at the Bluebird Café (American Originals, 2001)

with the Del McCoury Band

★★★★ The Mountain (E-Squared, 1999)

In the sin-and-redemption sweepstakes, few life stories in rock compare to Steve Earle's, and few musical artists can match the depth and power of the body of work he has produced during his journey. Beginning with 1995's acoustic "comeback" album, *Train a Comin',* Earle has been predictable only in the high quality of his work; otherwise, each album has found him challenging himself and his listeners, either with an unexpected concept (teaming with the redoubtable Del McCoury Band on *The Mountain,* a one-album experiment in bluegrass that caught the roots boom on its upward arc) or a bold dive into genre-bending (*Transcendental Blues,* with its pronounced echoes of pre–*Sgt. Pepper's* Beatles production flourishes in the midst of largely traditional country formulations). His early albums are dotted with stories of working-class folks struggling to make a place for themselves in a society of haves and have-nots. Since then he's only sharpened his polemics: His longtime opposition to the death penalty has moved him to write a devastating chronicle of a killer's final hours ("Billy Austin," on *The Hard Way*).

Earle's debut album, *Guitar Town,* was his breakthough. The album-opening title track is rich with a furiously strummed acoustic guitar, electric guitars twanging Duane Eddy–style, a steady humming B3 organ, and a propulsive rhythm section fueling Earle's swaggering recollection of the music's siren song in his life. The beautiful rockabilly breakup song "Think It Over" offsets a rather bitter lyric with a gorgeous melody in a song that could have come out of Buddy Holly's catalogue. "My Old Friend the Blues" starts as a gentle, acoustic-driven paean to the comforting powers of the blues and gradually opens up into a languorous honky-tonk ballad. "Good Ol' Boy (Gettin' Tough)" is a template for numerous Earle narratives to come: bristling Southern rock with an acoustic guitar way up in the mix, and a story about an embattled outsider frustrated in his efforts to get his fair share of the American Dream.

Exit 0 picked up right where *Guitar Town* left off, with "Nowhere Road," a story of a desolate Oklahoma road that serves as a metaphor for policies designed to keep the disenfranchised in their place while seeming to hold out the prospect of opportunity ahead. But it's only a prelude to the masterwork of Earle's MCA years, *Copperhead Road.* Released in 1988, it was the most powerful example of the rock-influenced spectrum of the New Traditionalist movement, which was then cresting commercially in the wake of the mainstream breakthroughs of Dwight Yoakam, the Judds, Randy Travis, and Rodney Crowell, among others. The title song leading off the album details an anti-authoritarian legacy handed down to succeeding generations by his bootlegger granddad, for whom violence is one revenue agent's visit away from erupting. For the remainder of the album's first half, the narrator—a Vietnam vet damaged physically and spiritually by his experience in Southeast Asia—lives a hard-luck life that leads him into chicanery ("Snake Oil"), gunplay (the searing "Devil's Right Hand"), isolation, and paranoia ("Back to the Wall"). Finally, disillusionment with the future sets in on the epic "Johnny Come Lately." In a bit more than four minutes, Earle offers a powerful summation of the personal price a generation paid for serving its country during an unpopular, undeclared war.

Small wonder that Earle couldn't top *Copperhead Road* with its followup, *The Hard Way.* It's not as consistently inspired as its predecessor, but in a few spots it's every bit as potent. The surging, dense atmospherics of "The Other Kind" are an ideal complement to the lyrics' story of an unreformed outsider whose life is on the road, and Earle's snarling delivery makes it apparent how much he identifies with his self-penned sentiments. The centerpiece of the album is the above-mentioned "Billy Austin," a somber, riveting acoustic ballad about a Native American, 29 years old, on Death Row for killing a gas station attendant in a botched robbery attempt.

A live album, *Shut Up and Die Like an Aviator,* marked the end of Earle's MCA tenure. In 1993, the label released its official Steve Earle overview, *The Essential Steve Earle,* a 13-track collection that includes "Guitar Town," "The Devil's Right Hand," "Good Ol' Boy (Gettin' Tough)," "Copperhead Road," and "Nowhere Road," as well as two non-album cuts, the truckin' classic "Six Days on the Road" and "Continental Trailways Blues" (both from the movie *Planes, Trains & Automobiles*). A better option is Hip-O's double-CD, 28-track *Ain't Ever Satisfied: The Steve Earle Collection,* which includes six songs from *Copperhead Road* and "The Other Kind" from *The Hard Way.*

Following a two-year sabbatical during which he underwent treatment for his drug addiction, Earle, thin and gaunt, began popping up in Nashville clubs, playing solo acoustic shows. In 1995 he released *Train a Comin'* on the Winter Harvest label. In an all-acoustic affair, Earle is accompanied by two unassailable masters of stringed instruments, Norman Blake and Peter Rowan, plus the formidable acoustic bass player Roy Huskey (now deceased), and on harmony vocals, Emmylou Harris. Earle's next album, *I Feel Alright,* is both a spit-in-the-eye retort to those who wrote him off and a return to his rock-hard style of days gone by, with harmonicas, twangy guitars, and a powerhouse rhythm section present and accounted for. *El Corazón* features a full-blown, regulation bluegrass number, "I Still Carry You Around," teaming Earle with one of bluegrass music's finest groups, the Del McCoury Band. Thus was the stage set for 1999's collaboration, *The Mountain,* a masterful bluegrass album that featured stirring tracks such as "Harlan Man" and "The Mountain."

Bluegrass is a distant memory on *Transcendental Blues,* which opens with the sound of synthesizer drones and tabla riffs on the title song and features other Beatles touches such as backward orchestral riffing on "The Boy Who Never Cried" and serpentine guitar licks and a stop-time effect right out of *Revolver*'s "Tomorrow Never Knows." A between-albums stopgap, *Sidetracks* is billed as "a collection of unreleased or underexposed songs."

Owing to the controversy sparked by "John Walker's Blues"—a song written from the perspective of "American Taliban" John Walker Lindh—the whole of *Jerusalem* was never fairly addressed. It arrived not with a statement supportive of terrorists—as some conservative critics claimed—but rather with a sensi-

ble explanation of Lindh's unsettling odyssey and a pervasive sense of history in four other powerful songs addressing the events of September 11 and their aftermath.   —D.M.

Earth, Wind & Fire

★★½	Earth, Wind & Fire (Warner Bros., 1970)
★★½	The Need of Love (Warner Bros., 1972)
★★½	Last Days and Time (Columbia, 1972)
★★★	Head to the Sky (Columbia, 1973)
★★★★	Open Our Eyes (Columbia, 1974)
★★★★	That's the Way of the World (Columbia, 1975)
★★★½	Gratitude (Columbia, 1975)
★★★½	Spirit (Columbia, 1976)
★★★	All 'n All (Columbia, 1977)
★★★★★	The Best of Earth, Wind & Fire, Vol. 1 (ARC/Columbia, 1978)
★★★	I Am (ARC/Columbia, 1979)
★★½	Faces (ARC/Columbia, 1980)
★★★	Raise! (ARC/Columbia, 1981)
★★★	Powerlight (Columbia, 1983)
★★½	Electric Universe (Columbia, 1983)
★★★	Touch the World (Columbia, 1987)
★★★★	The Best of Earth, Wind & Fire, Vol. II (Columbia, 1988)
★★½	Heritage (Columbia, 1990)
★★★½	The Eternal Dance (Columbia/Legacy, 1993)
★★★	In the Name of Love (Pyramid/Rhino, 1997)
★★	The Promise (Kalimba, 2003)
★★★	That's the Way of the World: Alive in '75 (Columbia/Legacy, 2002)

It wasn't until Earth, Wind & Fire's fourth album, second label, and umpteenth personnel change that Maurice White and company began their metamorphosis into the quintessential African-American hit band of the '70s. They did it by following the advice of the album's erstwhile title track, "Keep Your Head to the Sky." For the next decade, the group's insistent optimism and spirituality helped EWF rival the accomplishments of its greatest detractor, George Clinton, leader of the Parliament-Funkadelic empire. EWF's black-music synthesis spanned pop, soul, jazz, funk, gospel, African music, and rock (and it glanced off salsa). But no matter the style, nearly every hit got the same treatment, padded and polished with smooth vocal harmonies and horn charts and elevated with exuberantly positive lyrics and Philip Bailey's stratospheric lead vocals. Avoiding the twisted pleasures of deep funk and gritty soul, this enhanced high was a natural correlative to disco, thus winning over a huge multiracial audience. But it also may explain why, after the triumph of gritty hip-hop in the 1980s and '90s, even the group's greatest collection—the 1978 *Best of*—has proven less influential, and sounds more dated, than Clinton's funked-up P-Funk sound.

White had been a session drummer at the Chess studios in Chicago during the '60s before he forged a pack of young local players into the new group in 1969. The Warner Bros. albums lean toward the softer end of jazz-rock fusion, peppered by the occasional R&B-flavored horn chart; the initial Columbia albums are caught in the same muddle, although White had assembled a new band.

Gradually, singer Philip Bailey emerges as the point man for White's cosmic vision and commercial ambition. But although the trademark soaring vocals, catchy platitudes, and buttery melodies start to peek out from under the spacey jams and Africa-spiced percussion on *Head to the Sky*, it was still scant preparation for *Open Our Eyes*. Newly focused songwriting and the ensemble's responsive playing result in uplifting dance strokes ("Mighty Mighty"), convincing soul testimony ("Devotion"), sweet mid-tempo melancholy ("Feelin' Blue"), and an intriguing whiff of the Third World ("Kalimba Story").

That's the Way of the World boils that down to a potent, nourishing pop formula. "Shining Star" and the title track launched EWF's run on the pop charts, while the slow-simmering "Reasons" (Bailey's definitive ballad), the funky "Yearnin', Learnin,'" and "Africano" add balance and depth to a landmark album. *Gratitude* devotes three vinyl sides to EWF live, and the band lives up to its onstage rep. *Spirit* keeps it up, pretty much, though the tone of party anthems such as "Saturday Nite" is noticeably light. So is the beat. Slowly but surely, superefficient disco rhythms and automatic-pilot song material weakened EWF's impact, so despite some encouraging peaks—especially the tough-minded regrouping *Touch the World*, featuring the clear-eyed hit "System of Survival"—the only necessary album from the group's second decade is *Best of Earth, Wind & Fire Vol. II*. It was followed by the group's last Columbia outing, *Heritage*, dragged down by an unnecessary reliance on hammy guest appearances by currently hot rappers.

A career capping three-CD box set, *The Eternal Dance* offers a lovingly annotated and sequenced collection of greatest hits and smoothly integrated obscurities that still doesn't quite merit its extravagant length. If the middle disc rivals the high of either *Best of* volume, the group's confused early jams and synth-logged '80s fare drag the other two. Surprisingly, EWF came back again in 1997 with a fatter, funkier bottom on *In the Name of Love*, convincingly updating their trademark sound throughout the album's first half, though the second slips away on generic light jams. Unfortunately, generic light jams provide most of the highlights on the group's fourth-decade offering, *The Promise*, which returns to the basics so doggedly, the crew sounds like a bland contemporary gospel group heavily indebted to Earth, Wind & Fire. —M.C./F.S.

The Easybeats

- ★★★ Live—Studio and Stage (Raven, 1995)
- ★★★ Gonna Have a Good Time (Retroactive, 1999)

"Friday on My Mind" was a terrific 1967 hit. The Aussies behind its cheerful thunder were the Easybeats' main men, Harry Vanda and George Young (brother of AC/DC's Angus and Malcolm). Never a great stateside success, and defunct by 1970, the Easybeats, on the strength of a crack rhythm section and consistently sharp songs, wear better than much British Invasion pop. Their late-'60s work sounds like the big-ballad Bee Gees. Which isn't bad. Even there, however, an intriguing oddness peeks through. The Raven disc offers tough, punchy rarities; the generous Retroactive collection is for completists. —P.E.

Eazy-E

- ★★★ Eazy-Duz-It (Ruthless, 1988)
- ★★★½ It's On (Dr. Dre) 187um Killa (EP) (Ruthless, 1993)
- ★★★ Str8 Off tha Streetz of Muthaphukkin Compton (Relativity, 1995)
- ★★★ Eternal E (Ruthless, 1995)

The rapper born Eric Wright was negligibly taller than Gary Coleman, sported a Jheri curl greasier than cheap pizza, and rapped about being a hardcore gangsta in a laughable pipsqueak monotone—yet as Eazy-E, the N.W.A member became a bona fide hip-hop icon. Eazy got by more on charisma and pottymouthed humor than by actual rapping talent or creative inspiration, which made for some spotty solo albums. *Easy-Duz-It*, recorded with Dr. Dre, is a quickie N.W.A spinoff, but Dre keeps the quality level up, most notably on the thundering remix of "Boyz in the Hood." Money disputes and mistrust of Eazy's Ruthless Records' partner Jerry Heller led to N.W.A's dissolution and a falling-out among its members; Dre subsequently sniped incessantly at Eazy on *The Chronic*, and the beef inspired the best music of Eazy's career, the *It's On* EP. *Str8 Off tha Streetz of Muthaphukkin Compton* came out shortly after Eazy died of AIDS in March of 1995; its monochrome thuggish lyrics posed a bizarre contrast to the poignant reality of Eazy's death. His legacy is the gangsta rapper archetype, as well as the artists he discovered: both Bone Thugs-N-Harmony and the D.O.C. owe him their careers. —P.R.

Echo and the Bunnymen

★★★½ Crocodiles (1980; Sire/Rhino, 2003)
★★ Heaven Up Here (1981; Sire/Rhino, 2003)
★★★½ Porcupine (1983; Sire/Rhino, 2003)
★★★½ Ocean Rain (1984; Sire/Rhino, 2003)
★★★★ Songs to Learn and Sing (Sire, 1985)
★★½ Echo and the Bunnymen (1987; Sire/Rhino, 2003)
★ Reverberation (Sire, 1990)
★★½ Evergreen (London, 1997)
★★ What Are You Going to Do With Your Life? (London, 1999)
★★★★ Crystal Days: 1979–1999 (Rhino, 2001)
★★ Flowers (SpinArt, 2002)
★★½ Live in Liverpool (SpinArt, 2002)

"Am I singing the blues?" intones Bunnymen singer Ian McCulloch on "Rescue." Well, no, but his band soundtracked a million blue moods. For most of the late '80s, before Sonic Youth and Nirvana exploded indie rock into the mainstream, the Bunnymen served as one of the unofficial bands of large-coiffed, limey-identified high school literary magazine editors. The Bunnymen catered to folks who thought themselves too tough (or too hetero) for, say, the Human League but secretly swooned at Mac's flawless lips and bedroom eyes. The Bunnymen's tasteful neopsychedelia gained fans from Courtney Love to Pavement.

Folks blanch at the arrogance of Oasis' Beatles worship, but at least the Gallaghers kept it on their island. On Crocodiles, the Bunnymen swagger like they're the rightful heirs to the Velvets and the Doors, but the results betray their startling lack of familiarity with pale blue eyes or L.A. women. Give 'em this: The debut embodies that strain of Morrison's apocalypse-now pretension that just refuses to die. Weak production doesn't help, but the songs are mighty tasty. Guitarist Will Sergeant knows his way around a swirling hook, and his chord eddies on "Simple Stuff" and "Villiers Terrace" sold as many trenchcoats as the Cure or Joy Division. Heaven Up Here has a stronger sound, but the gothy, plodding arrangements smother the indistinct songs.

Though disliked by many hard-core fans, Porcupine is the Bunnymen's strongest songwriting effort. "The Back of Love" and "The Cutter" are bold, catchy strokes, proving they could sell a dumb rock ditty when they found one. Unfortunately, it was the atmospheric stuff they loved, and Ocean Rain took those popcorn hooks and poured on the production butter. At its best, the album showed that they had finally learned how to arrange their pomposity to serve a great hook, so when McCulloch sings "Fate/Up against your will" on the "The Killing Moon," the song

lets him sell it. This was the Bunnymen at the peak of their foppish power. Depending on whether you were a black-clad ponce or said ponce stole your squeeze, the shimmering single "Bring On the Dancing Horses" was either the '80s' most romantic fluff-pop moment or one of the most overwrought. An A-sides collection, Songs to Learn and Sing, soon followed, which collects this underrated singles band's finest moments to date.

Echo and the Bunnymen was too little too late. Its stripped-down, slicked-up pop was indistinguishable from the era's other dancey British rock albums. ("Bedbugs and Ballyhoo" might as well have shown up on the Cure's Kiss Me Kiss Me Kiss Me.) But, with "Lips Like Sugar" as its single, this was the album that broke 'em stateside.

Rightly sensing that the Bunnys' dark days were done, McCulloch split in August of 1988. The other guys elected to soldier on with the name, and the 1989 death of drummer Peter DeFreitas simply delayed the inevitable: a Bunnymen album without Ian. Reverberation would have been a perfectly respectable followup to a remarkable career had they simply used another band name. Suffice it to say, the riffs were a little more psych, but nobody cared about an Echo record with someone named Noel Burke singing.

After his solo career stiffed, McCulloch and the remaining Bunnys patched it up when it became clear they (and their landlords) needed one another. On Evergreen, McCulloch's voice is incapable of the soaring that made him famous, though it seems Sergeant can write these sorts of psych-pop riffs until the end of time. What Are You Going to Do With Your Life? from 1999 sounds exactly like a McCulloch solo album; no wonder founding member and bassist Les Pattinson split in the middle of recording the thing.

Crystal Days: 1979–1999 is a flattering four-disc overview. The first three have album tracks, singles, rare material, and demos. Disc four is mostly live covers, including the inevitable stabs at VU tunes, a "Soul Kitchen" that X wouldn't dignify with a glance, a touching run at Television's "Friction," and the funniest and least soulful version of "In the Midnight Hour" ever recorded. A lovely career retrospective, except the career refuses to be over. The year 2001 saw the release of Flowers, which felt more like a fans-only Bunnymen album, and 2002 produced a powerful live record, Live in Liverpool. —J.G.

Duane Eddy

★★½ Have "Twangy" Guitar Will Travel (1958; Jamie/Guyden, 1999)
★★ Twangin' the Golden Hits/Twang a Country Song (1965; One Way, 1998)

★★★ Twang Thang: The Duane Eddy Anthology
(Rhino, 1993)

Twang is the word most closely associated with guitar legend Duane Eddy, and certainly that sound best summarizes his personality on record. But Eddy wasn't all lower-register melodies, liberal tremolo, and omnipresent whammy bar. His instrumentals were the original music-minus-one exercises—only the vocalist was missing. This emphasis on song construction separated Eddy from inspired '50s primitives such as Link Wray and set a standard for the rock instrumental that flowered in the '60s when the Ventures came on the scene, and later with the advent of surf music. As well as his overpowering lyricism—evident from his first hit single, "Rebel Rouser," from 1958—Eddy was supported by outstanding musicians. The sax especially was a key element of Eddy's sound, and on songs such as "Ramrod" and the "Peter Gunn Theme," Eddy's twanging was clearly subservient to the impassioned honking that gave both songs a rugged edge.

Eddy was consistently in the Top 40 between 1958 and 1963, making it as high as #4 in 1960 with the lush theme for the film *Because They're Young*, a vehicle designed to make Eddy a movie star. It bombed, but he kept on twanging. His best recordings were on the Jamie label, with his debut, *Have "Twangy" Guitar Will Travel*, the standout LP release. As the years went on, Eddy rerecorded his most celebrated tunes in various settings. The most restrained and thoughtful were on RCA, with the twofer *Twangin' the Golden Hits/Twang a Country Song*, a useful supplement to his straight-rocker sides, with apt material. The only career-spanning collection with original recordings currently available is the sumptuous and enjoyable double disc *Twang Thang*, which shows how Eddy could handle pop and country, but maybe not electronic dance beats. —D.M./M.MI.

Dave Edmunds

★★★ Rockpile (1972; Repertoire, 2001)
★★★ Subtle as a Flying Mallet (1975; One Way, 1998)
★★★½ Get It (Swan Song, 1977)
★★★½ Tracks on Wax 4 (Swan Song, 1978)
★★★★ Repeat When Necessary (Swan Song, 1979)
★★★½ Seconds of Pleasure (Columbia, 1980)
★★★★ The Best of Dave Edmunds (Swan Song, 1981)
★★★ I Hear You Rockin' (Columbia, 1987)
★★★½ The Dave Edmunds Anthology (1968–90) (Rhino, 1993)
★★★½ A Pile of Rock: Live (Castle, 2001)

★★ Rockpile (1972; Repertoire, 2002)
★★★★½ From Small Things: The Best of Dave Edmunds (Columbia/Legacy, 2004)

Dave Edmunds was one of the first people to look for the future of rock & roll in its past. As the '70s started to look like the decade of singer/songwriters, Edmunds wasn't much more than a guy who loved Chuck Berry and George Jones and played a guitar that owed more to Ike Turner than to Eric Clapton. Edmunds' only claim to fame back then was that he had taken a couple of pieces of classical music, Khatchaturian's "Sabre Dance" and Bizet's "Farandole," and turned them into high-speed guitar romps. But as the '70s unfolded, Edmunds caught two breaks. The first was that he cut a guitar-heavy cover of the Smiley Lewis hit "I Hear You Knocking" that turned into a freak Top 10 single. The second was that he matured as a studio wiz, emerging as the producer of choice for English pub-rock bands Brinsley Schwarz and Ducks Deluxe—bands that played his kind of newfangled old-time rock & roll and gave him the collaborator he needed to relaunch his solo career. Although Edmunds could sing, play guitar, and produce a dense, slightly metallic rockabilly sound, Nick Lowe gave him new songs to go with the oldies that Edmunds expertly picked.

The Edmunds-Lowe collaboration starts with *Get It* and extends through their jointly led band, Rockpile. These are basically high-powered nouveau rockabilly albums: fast, hard, with a taste of country. *Get It* and *Tracks on Wax* are about half originals/half covers, with Edmunds' own songs more firmly in a country vein ("Worn Out Suits, Brand New Pockets," "A. 1. on the Jukebox"), while Lowe's songs tended to be hard rockers ("I Knew the Bride," "Heart of the City").

Repeat When Necessary differed in two respects: The album was played by a real band, Rockpile, and none of the songs was written by the band. But the songs were exceptionally strong ("Girls Talk," "Queen of Hearts"), and it turned out to be Edmunds' best album.

Meanwhile, Rockpile recorded their own album, *Seconds of Pleasure*. For their brief moment together, Rockpile had the reputation of being the best live band in the world, but the album didn't quite live up to the band's reputation, probably because the new songs didn't quite live up to the repertoire that Edmunds and Lowe had accumulated. The original LP came with a bonus EP of Everly Brothers covers, which has been appended to the CD, giving it a rather odd denouement. After an acrimonious split with Lowe, Edmunds continued to record albums in a similar vein, each weaker and less focused than the last. *The Best of*

Dave Edmunds is a solid survey of the period, with only two songs post-*Repeat*.

The two-CD Rhino *Anthology* covers the major arc of Edmunds' career, with about half of its cuts from the prime period with Lowe. Edmunds' earliest work hasn't worn well: *Anthology* includes six cuts from his first band, Love Sculpture, including the instrumentals and a sludgy version of "Summertime." The first solo album, *Rockpile*, has reverb-heavy oldies, including a couple of Chuck Berry tunes and Fats Domino's "Blue Monday." *Subtle as a Flying Mallet* was a one-man-band studio exercise, where Edmunds' falsetto does all the voices on "Da Doo Ron Ron": good practice, and more Chuck Berry tunes. *Anthology* does pick up some good songs from Edmunds' later records—the bluegrassy "Warmed Over Kisses (Leftover Love)," the ballad "One More Night," and the Carlene Carter duet "Baby Ride Easy"—but it runs out of ideas way before it ends. More to the point is Edmunds' *A Pile of Rock: Live,* which reprises his songbook in flat-out mode. *From Small Things* is even more determined to represent Edmunds at his most feverish, which, when all is said and done, definitely is the point.   —T.H.

Eels

★★★	Beautiful Freak (DreamWorks, 1996)
★★★½	Electro-Shock Blues (DreamWorks, 1998)
★★★	Daisies of the Galaxy (DreamWorks, 2000)
★★★	Souljacker (DreamWorks, 2001)
★★★½	Shootenanny (DreamWorks, 2003)

After a couple of song-rich, keyboard-dominated albums released under the Man Called E moniker, Mark Everett morphed into the trio Eels with *Beautiful Freak*. At its best, the debut gives a trip-hop twist to the California singer/songwriter tradition; at its worst, it suggests one more bummed-out wise guy's take on Beck's collage-style rock.

With a sense of humor that skews toward cynicism that's alleviated occasionally by bouts of sincerity, Everett is not the likeliest subject to make a transcendent album about death. But he nearly pulls it off on *Electro-Shock Blues*. The music is somber but not sedate, with bursts of saxophone, off-kilter orchestration, and outright noise evoking the turbulence beneath the deadpan vocals. The singer battles not only depression but also his penchant for irony, and his struggle to move beyond them makes for a fascinating if sometimes morbidly downcast listen.

On *Daisies of the Galaxy,* Eels replace the sprawling sound experiments of the first two albums with a more direct folk-rock approach. "Me, I'm feeling pretty good, as of now," Everett sings, which passes

for euphoria in the Eels' world, and the music's easygoing charm affirms him. *Souljacker* plunges back into the darkness, this time with fuzz-coated guitars and a rudimentary blues-punk attack. It's a suitable backdrop for Everett's favorite subjects—loneliness, alienation, and despair, this time told through the perspective of assorted freaks and misfits such as the "Dog Faced Boy" and the troubled high school student in "Soul Jacker Pt. 1."

The scrappy guitars and just-rolled-out-of-bed vocals return on *Shootenanny*. Surprisingly warm childhood memories ("Saturday Morning") collide with the "Agony" of adulthood, while irony gives way to more resilient traits, summed up by a lyric that might've been unthinkable a decade earlier: "Somebody loves you, and you're gonna make it through."   —G.K.

E-40

★★★½	Federal (Sick Wid It/Jive, 1994)
★★★★	The Mailman (Sick Wid It/Jive, 1994)
★★★½	In A Major Way (Sick Wid It/Jive, 1995)
★★½	Tha Hall of Game (Sick Wid It/Jive, 1996)
★★★½	The Element of Surprise (Sick Wid It/Jive, 1998)
★★★½	Charlie Hustle: The Blueprint of a Self-Made Millionaire (Sick Wid It/Jive, 1999)
★★★	Loyalty & Betrayal (Sick Wid It/Jive, 2000)
★★★★	Grit & Grind (Sick Wid It/Jive, 2002)

One of hip-hop's most prolific voices, E-40 has worked in relative obscurity for much of his career. A resident of Vallejo, CA, 40 is best known in the Bay Area. And like his fellow Bay man Too Short, 40 launched his career without the benefit of a major label, hawking tapes one by one on the streets of his hometown. 40's first two albums, *Federal* and *The Mailman,* were minimalist affairs doused in bass-heavy funk, some of the earliest street rap to emerge from the Bay. But despite his comfort with the dark side, 40 set himself apart as a humorist, as on Mailman's "Captain Save a Hoe," a lighthearted Lothario-as-superhero romp.

40 is one of hip-hop's most unique voices: perpetually bemused and nasal; rapping at a fascinatingly quick clip; consistently inventing new lingo and watching as the mainstream catches on years later. 40 steadily churned out an album a year through the late '90s, and they're impressively consistent. Over increasingly esoteric postfunk, 40 toasted inebriation, recounted days on the sinister streets, and generally kept up good humor. From the game-spitting "Sprinkle Me" (from *Major Way*), to the jubilant "Big Ballin' With My Homies" (from *Charlie Hustle*), to the soultastic tale of penitence "Hope I Don't Go Back"

(from *Element*), to the universal hip-hop anthems "The Slap" and "Rep Yo City" (from *Grit & Grind*), 40 has steadily proved himself to be a hip-hop original. And over the years, dozens of hip-hop's finest—including Tupac, Fat Joe, Busta Rhymes, Juvenile, and Fabolous—have guested on 40's albums, a testament to his widespread influence.   —J.C.

8Ball & MJG

★★★★	Comin' Out Hard (Suave, 1993)
★★★½	On the Outside Lookin' In (Suave, 1994)
★★★★	On Top of the World (Suave, 1995)
★★★	Lyrics of a Pimp (TAM/OTS, 1999)
★★★½	In Our Lifetime, Vol. 1 (SuaveHouse/Universal, 1999)
★★★	Memphis Underworld (TAM/OTS, 1999)
★★★★	Space Age 4 Eva (JCOR, 2000)
★★½	Living Legends (Bad Boy, 2004)

8Ball

★★★	Lost (SuaveHouse/Universal, 1998)
★★★	Almost Famous (JCOR, 2001)
★★½	Lay It Down (Draper Inc., 2002)

MJG

★★★½	No More Glory (SuaveHouse/Universal, 1997)

When Southern rap was far from fashionable, 8Ball & MJG—from the unlikely locale of Orange Mound, TN—gave the burgeoning subgenre brash bravado and a strong identity that would influence the stars who would make the genre enormously popular a decade later. *Comin' Out Hard*, their debut, was a minimal affair: electro-influenced, the beats were stark, and the lyrics—street bravado with a wry Southern perspective—were just as unadorned. Songs like "Armed Robbery" (which interpolates the *Mission Impossible* theme) and "The First Episode" are classics of the genre, just as potent as anything by the Geto Boys (who were at that time the most highly regarded rap group in the South).

The pair stuck to their tried-and-true themes of pimping and drug hustling on their next two albums, which included such influential songs as "Break-A-Bitch College," "Crumbz 2 Brixxx" and "Space Age Pimpin'." (The pair also released solo albums. 8Ball's debut *Lost* was, like the man himself, notable for its heft: it was a whopping triple CD.) *Space Age 4 Eva* (2000) proved the duo had aged well, despite being relegated to hip-hop's margins. On songs like "Buck Bounce" and "Pimp Hard," they showcased nimble lyricism over cutting-edge production. After a few years of label difficulties, the duo signed to P. Diddy's Bad Boy Records for 2004's *Living Legends*, a not-quite-up-to-snuff statement of their importance to the game, though next-generation stars like Ludacris and T.I. appeared to pay their respects.   —J.C.

Elastica

★★★★½	Elastica (DGC, 1995)
★★	6 Track EP (Deceptive [UK], 1999)
★★★	The Menace (Atlantic, 2000)
★★½	The Radio One Sessions (Koch, 2003)

Elastica would've been the finest punk-pop album of 1979, had it not been recorded 16 years later. In fact, songwriters Justine Frischmann and Donna Matthews raided their favorite records of that era for attitude, speed, energy, and, very often, riffs—the hit single "Connection" is basically Wire's "Three Girl Rhumba" with new words, and other songs borrow ideas from Blondie, New Order, and the Stranglers. But there's not a wasted second on the album. Sexy, vicious, and hilarious at the same time (especially the debut single "Stutter," a roaring swipe at a lover who can't get it up), it rocks like a banshee.

It was a mighty hard act to follow, and Elastica basically couldn't. Almost five years later, they coughed up the half-assed *6 Track EP*: a live track, some demos, and a couple of collaborations with the Fall's Mark E. Smith. Most of its songs turned up on *The Menace*, a patchwork assemblage that includes four tracks by the now-departed Matthews, a rewrite of another Wire song, and a cover of Trio's "Da Da Da." Even so, it holds together surprisingly well: The party of *Elastica* turned into a cotton-mouthed hangover, trying to rouse itself with some hair of the dog.

The 21-track, live-in-the-studio *Radio One Sessions*, recorded between 1993 and '99, lacks the fire of Elastica's proper albums, but adds seven songs to their catalogue, including some crisp early rockers and the Christmastime Fall parody, "I Wanna Be a King of Orient Aah."   —D.W.

Electric Light Orchestra

★★★	No Answer (Jet/Epic, 1972)
★★	ELO II (Jet/Epic, 1973)
★★★	On the Third Day (Jet/Epic, 1973)
★★★½	Eldorado (Jet/Epic, 1974)
★★★	Face the Music (Jet/Epic, 1975)
★★★	Olé ELO (Jet/Epic, 1976)
★★★	A New World Record (Jet/Epic, 1976)
★★★	Out of the Blue (Jet/Epic, 1977)
★★½	Discovery (Jet/Epic, 1979)
★★★★	Greatest Hits (Jet/Epic, 1979)
★★½	Time (1981; Epic, 2001)
★★	Secret Messages (1983; Epic, 2001)
★★	Balance of Power (CBS Associated, 1986)
★★½	Afterglow (Epic, 1990)

★ Part Two (Scotti Bros., 1991)
★ Moment of Truth (Edel, 1994)
★★★ Flashback (Epic, 2000)
★★★ Zoom (Epic, 2001)
★★★½ The Essential Electric Light Orchestra (Epic, 2003)

An unabashed late-period Beatlemaniac, Jeff Lynne turned his *Sgt. Pepper's* fixation into a workable pop formula for the '70s. The aspiring guitarist-singer-composer-producer founded Electric Light Orchestra with Birmingham homeboy Roy Wood, who'd led the Move during the late '60s. When Lynne joined the Move in 1970, the seeds for ELO were germinated. Their debut, *No Answer,* strives for an unlikely fusion of rock & roll and classical music; unsurprisingly, only the haunting "10538 Overture" really takes hold. That single sounds more like the Move's dense rock studiocraft than ELO's subsequent hits; Wood soon left ELO to pursue his own eccentric orchestral muse. Though it was a commercial success, *ELO II* didn't bode well for Lynne's artistic future; with its snatches of Beethoven and ham-handed Chuck Berry–isms, "Roll Over Beethoven" quickly became an FM radio irritant—like hearing a one-line joke over and over. Lynne continued to hone his approach, and with *On the Third Day* his knack for hummable tunes and subtle hooks is revealed. Oh, there's still a Grieg-inspired tune to deal with, but the vaguely funky and overtly catchy "Showdown" indicates that Lynne was still keeping an ear trained on the competition. *Eldorado* sustains the glossy Beatles hommage of "Can't Get It Out of My Head" over the course of an entire album—ELO's most consistent and cohesive. Nevertheless, for all the band's ambitions, the evidence insists that ELO is at heart one hell of a singles band. Hits off *Face the Music* ("Strange Magic,") and *New World Record* ("Telephone Line," "Livin' Thing") mark Lynne's creative and commercial apex. *Olé ELO* is an acceptable though incomplete compilation, while the superlative *Greatest Hits* delivers the goods.

Out of the Blue shows Lynne's expansiveness clouding ELO's vision once again; its two discs map incredible peaks ("Turn to Stone") and bottomless valleys (the sidelong "Concerto for a Rainy Day"). After that, the ELO spark fades to an occasional flicker: "Hold on Tight" (from *Time*) and "Rock 'n' Roll Is King" (from *Secret Messages*) foreshadow the sleek roots-rock groove Lynne later perfected with the Traveling Wilburys, Roy Orbison's final sessions, and his own 1989 solo album. Led by veteran Move-ELO drummer Bev Bevan, the short-lived, early '90s ELO "comeback" was a robotic simulation of the original group's sound; not even campy, just depressing.

Lynne's own 2001 ELO revival was a solo record in everything but name, but at least it delivered the goods the few remaining fans were still pining for: The Beatles-like harmonies and classical tendencies were as peppy as ever, with contributions by George Harrison and Ringo Starr. The indisputable glow of ELO's best shots is dimmed somewhat by the clumsily structured *Afterglow.* Yet another three-disc box set, *Flashback* corrects the omissions of its predecessor thanks to Lynne's judicious examination of the band's quirky, uneven, but always melodious output. The single-disc comp *The Essential Electric Light Orchestra* should please all but the hardcore fans. —M.C./E.L.

Eleventh Dream Day

★½ Prairie School Freakout (Amoeba, 1988)
★★ Beet (Atlantic, 1989)
★★ Lived to Tell (Atlantic, 1991)
★★ El Moodio (Atlantic, 1993)
★★½ Ursa Major (City Slang/Atavistic, 1994)
★★★ Eighth (Thrill Jockey, 1997)
★★★ Stalled Parade (Thrill Jockey, 2000)

Indie rockers rightly flaunted their distaste for the failings of the mainstream during the '80s and '90s, but their ranks produced plenty of mediocrity too. These Chicago scenesters are a case in point, with little to distinguish them besides the trends of the times that have bookended their career thus far. A heavy Sonic Youth influence lingers over the jangly and repetitive (and amateurish) first few albums, also recalling X in the howling double vocals of founders Rick Rizzo (guitar) and Janet Beveridge Bean (drums). But hard as they try, the group has neither Sonic Youth's transcendent power nor X's frenzied emotional depth. The guitars strum endlessly because they don't know what else to do, the drums beat out a wobbly shuffle, and the songs go nowhere. How they ended up on a major for *Beet* through the impossibly dreary *El Moodio* is anybody's guess.

Back in indieland, the group's next three were produced by John McEntire, the Brian Eno of '90s Chicago. He remade the band in the image of his group Tortoise by peeling away the wallpaper of open-chord guitars and building focused, articulate arrangements with a minimum of sounds. From the very first notes of *Ursa Major*'s instrumental opening, "History of Brokeback," a new Eleventh Dream Day emerges, with a strong, unhurried rhythm section and clear melodic patterns on guitar. The sound is under control and even interesting. But once the singing begins, they revert back to their old tricks and all advancements disappear. *Eighth* and its successor find the group falling more in line with late-'90s Chicago postrock, which is an improvement over their sloppy beginnings but only leaves them somewhere near the middle of a more up-to-date horse race.   —B.S.

Missy Elliott

★★★★★   Supa Dupa Fly (Elektra, 1997)
★★★   Da Real World (Elektra, 1999)
★★★★   Miss E . . . So Addictive (Elektra, 2001)
★★★★½   Under Construction (Elektra, 2002)
★★★★½   This Is Not a Test! (Elektra, 2003)

Missy "Misdemeanor" Elliott rolled out of Virginia Beach in 1997, with the coolest name, hair, sneakers, album cover, and sound in pop music. *Supa Dupa Fly* made her an instant star, along with producer Timbaland, her partner in crimes against sonic conformity. Ever since then, Missy has ruled everything around music. She sings, she raps, and she drops the bomb of the year, every damn year. Who else keeps us all glued to our radios to hear pop music updated one giant step at a time, in the style of Prince and Madonna in the '80s or the Beatles and Motown in the '60s?

Elliott introduced her recipe on *Supa Dupa Fly.* Her albums always have unbelievably sexy beats and vocals, Virginia swamp-funk hip-hop production from Timbaland, plenty of filler, a couple of terrible R&B slow jams, and Elliott talking wild shit between songs. "Supa Dupa Fly (The Rain)," "Izzy Izzy Aah," and "Sock It 2 Me" were stoned-to-the-bone psychedelic soul, the kind that techno and trip-hop composers had always promised but never delivered so intensely. The avant-garde sound of *Supa Dupa Fly* made Elliott and Timbaland the hottest writer/producer team around, scoring hits such as Nicole's 1998 "Make It Hot" (a Missy single in all but billing, and one of her best) and Aaliyah's "Are You That Somebody?"

Da Real World was the one time Elliott got caught short of material. But *Miss E . . . So Addictive* had the smash "Get Ur Freak On," which sounded like Timbaland playing tabla on your frontal lobes while Missy yells "Holla!" until everybody who doesn't want to party drags that dead ass home. She got unexpectedly personal with *Under Construction,* reaching out to old-school '80s hip-hop in a spirit of playful nostalgia. Missy responds to grief and terror, including the death of her friend Aaliyah, by taking a fantastic voyage through the past in her double-Dutch bus, rocking it from the Dre Day to the Suge Knight. "Work It" was her most bizarre, futuristic, and undeniable hit yet, although fans also loved the slow jam with the chorus, "Pussy don't fail me now."

This Is Not A Test! is almost as great, with Elliott trying everything from gospel to electro to a romantic ballad for her vibrator ("Toyz"). In "Pass That

Dutch," she and Tim set off car alarms, whistles, hand claps, kettledrums, heavy breathing, and party people chanting "Hootie-hoo!" It's an all-nighter at the sweatiest club in town, compressed into three and a half minutes. Elliott's made the single of the year at least three times—four if you count "Make It Hot"—and yet she still sounds as hungry and driven as ever. She refuses to repeat past successes, pushing on to newer and weirder realms while everyone else is catching up to what she was doing years ago. And after all these years, Missy and Timbaland still save their best stuff for each other. Holla!   —R.S.

Eminem

★★★★   The Slim Shady LP (Interscope, 1999)
★★★★★   The Marshall Mathers LP (Interscope, 2000)
★★★★   The Eminem Show (Interscope, 2002)

There's a 71-second stretch near the end of "Stan," a track on Eminem's second album, that is impossible to ignore. Stan, a deranged fan played by Eminem himself, sends a final message to his hero before barreling over a cliff: "Dear Mr. I'm-Too-Good-to-Call-or-Write-My-Fans," he begins, working up a psychotic rant that strings together threats against his doomed girlfriend, a sarcastic quotation of an early Eminem line, and the rather unsettling declaration that he and Em "should have been together." The message ends as Stan goes over the edge, committing a murder-suicide inspired by the fictional killing of Eminem's wife in " '97 Bonnie & Clyde." Backed by a creepy sample from the British songstress Dido, it showcases just about everything great about Eminem: a penchant for arresting detail; a remarkable ability to switch between conversational flow, left-field role-playing, or rage-fueled torrents at a moment's notice; and bouts of surprising self-awareness.

From the moment "My Name Is" hit the airwaves, in spring 1999, Eminem galvanized a white suburban audience that had been waiting quietly for a white rapper who had the skills, tenacity, and shamelessness to be a new kind of rock star. Born in Kansas City to an absent dad and an unstable mom, he moved to a racially integrated part of Detroit, lived in a trailer, and proved himself not particularly good at anything except rhyming. His early recordings (some of which are collected on the now out-of-print *Infinite* album), show a distinctly less badass Em trying to find his voice and sounding a lot like the rapper Nas. After he invented his Slim Shady persona, however, a demo tape found its way to Dr. Dre, who was duly blown away by the immensely talented white kid.

The pair soon put together *The Slim Shady LP,* which found Em turning out a series of amazingly deft shock raps that ranged from comic to downright psychotic, often in the same verse: "Well since age 12, I've felt like I'm someone else/'Cause I hung my original self from the top bunk with a belt/Got pissed off and ripped Pamela Lee's tits off/And smacked her so hard I knocked her clothes backwards like Kris Kross." The album's hooky, low-affect G-funk—courtesy of Dre and a handful of lesser-known producers—gives Em plenty of room to maneuver, and he flat out demands your attention on "My Fault" and "'97 Bonnie and Clyde," horror-core tales in which Em watches one female companion OD on 'shrooms and dumps his wife's body in a lake, respectively. From class clown and workaday outcast to race trickster and a "guilty conscience" reminding his producer of his N.W.A past, *The Slim Shady LP* demonstrated that Shady was both an unavoidable pop creation and a rhymer talented enough for hip-hop heads to take seriously.

Besides establishing Eminem as a Major Talent, *The Slim Shady LP* confirmed that his greatest subject was himself—even if he did make up at least half the shit he said. *The Marshall Mathers LP* delved much deeper into personal pain, and the result was a minor masterpiece that merged iller-than-ill flows with a brilliant sense of the macabre. "The Real Slim Shady" is the obligatory insult-filled single, complete with disses of Christina Aguilera and Will Smith and shout-outs to his growing legion of angry teenage followers. The shock raps were still there ("I'm sorry, Puff/But I don't give a fuck if this chick was my own mother/I'd still fuck her with no rubber," he says of J. Lo on "I'm Back"), but on "Stan," "Marshall Mathers," and the awesomely angry "The Way I Am," Em revved up his already supercharged flow with real-life angst, decrying his celebrity, claiming he was misunderstood, and calling out his momma, who had already filed suit for defamation. "Kim" was another wife-killing fantasy filled will truly disturbing hate-spew; the record's misogyny, casual violence, and homophobia earned the ire of various watchdog groups, many of which had never listened to an Eminem record. Although the controversy has faded, the album's sound is still as unmistakable now as it was during the summer of 2000, when you couldn't run to the mailbox without hearing an album track pouring from someone's boom box or car stereo. The production is darker and more full-bodied on this LP, and while he's always been consistent, Em had never sounded so confident or inspired, employing six different voices in one song alone, constantly switching up his rhythms, and flinging disses with a quotability quotient unmatched in hip-hop history.

After a surreal "Stan" duet with Elton John at the 2001 Grammys, an arrest for brandishing a concealed weapon, and a so-so posse album with his homeboys in D12, Em and Dre reconvened for *The Eminem Show.* Except for another diss-filled lead single, "Without Me," Em completely abandoned the Slim Shady persona and made a concept album about how much it sucks to be a highly controversial rap star. The production's arena-rock bombast and Em's hyperserious lyrics threaten to sink the album, but on "White America," "Till I Collapse," and "Sing for the Moment" (which samples Aerosmith's "Dream On"), Em gets the most out of his anger-addled rant raps. "Cleanin' Out My Closet," a surprisingly tender track on which Em decides to run away from his mom, is as close to soft as anything he's ever done. The album's only truly bizarre moment is "My Dad's Gone Crazy," which begins with his daughter, Hailey, walking in on Daddy as he snorts a couple lines of coke, then uses a loop of Hailey's toddlerspeak for the song's chorus. Much of the album rocked plenty hard, but there were more duds than on any other Eminem record, particularly "Drips," "When the Music Stops," and the annoying sex fantasy "Superman." Less than six months after *The Eminem Show* was released, Eminem proved himself to be a surprisingly agile dramatic actor in the bio-pic *8 Mile* and won an Oscar for the amazing soundtrack cut "Lose Yourself." To date, he has not been arrested again.   —C.H.

English Beat

★★★★★   I Just Can't Stop It (London/Sire, 1980)
★★★   Wha'ppen? (London/Sire, 1981)
★★★★   Special Beat Service (London/Sire, 1982)
★★★★★   Beat This—The Best of the English Beat (Sire, 2001)

To call the English Beat a ska band would be like calling the Beatles a Merseybeat act—accurate as far as it goes, though hardly going far enough. One of the few bands in the 2-Tone movement to extend its integrationist approach to matters of musical style, the Beat (as the band was known in Britain) drew equally from Motown, '60s rock, music hall, and punk to develop a sound that was rich and allusive but always put the songs first.

All of which makes *I Just Can't Stop It* compelling from first to last. It isn't just the ease with which the band recasts "Tears of a Clown" as insinuatingly supple ska or fills its remake of "Can't Get Used to Losing You" with sweet regret; what pushes the album over the top is its authority and ingenuity. Despite the lyric's sarcastic wit, the true power of "Mirror in the Bathroom" is its snaky, obsessive groove, a sound that says more about narcissism than words ever could.

But that sort of aural authority is typical of the album, filling in the bluster behind "Hands Off . . . She's Mine" and adding a sense of withering contempt to the anti-Thatcher "Stand Down Margaret."

After such a strong start, *Wha'ppen?* is a good question; although the band's musical skills are still strong, the songs are disappointingly forgettable. But *Special Beat Service* returns the group to form, escalating the Caribbean influence on the retro-skank of ska to dubwise reggae, as "Pato and Roger a Go Talk" (with Pato Banton) illustrates, and adding instrumental luster to pop gems such as "I Confess." But the writing cinches it for the group—from the catchy, clever "Jeannette" to the irrepressible "Save It for Later," the Beat's music is never less than irresistible. *Beat This* succeeds previous best-ofs with a near-perfect sampling of the band's hits, plus suitably laudatory liner notes.   —J.D.C.

Brian Eno

★★★★	Here Come the Warm Jets (1973; Astralwerks, 2004)
★★★★	Taking Tiger Mountain (by Strategy) (1974; Astralwerks, 2004)
★★★★★	Another Green World (1975; Astralwerks, 2004)
★★★	Discreet Music (1975; Astralwerks, 2004)
★★★★★	Before and After Science (1977; Astralwerks, 2004)
★★★	Music for Films (Editions EG, 1978)
★★★★	Ambient 1: Music for Airports (Editions EG, 1978)
★★★	Ambient 4: On Land (Editions EG, 1982)
★★★	Apollo Atmospheres and Soundtracks (Editions EG, 1983)
★★★	Music for Films 2 (Editions EG, 1983)
★★★	Thursday Afternoon (Editions EG, 1985)
★★★★	More Blank Than Frank (Editions EG, 1986)
★★★★★	Desert Island Selection (1986; Astralwerks, 2000)
★★★	Music for Films 3 (Warner Bros., 1988)
★★★★	Nerve Net (Warner Bros. 1992)
★★★	Ali Click (Warner Bros., 1992)
★★★½	The Shutov Assembly (Opal, 1992)
★★★	Neroli (Gyroscope/Caroline, 1993)
★★★★	Eno Box I: Instrumentals (Virgin, 1994)
★★★★★	Eno Box II: Vocals (Virgin, 1994)
★★½	Begegnungen (Gyroscope, 1996)
★★	Begegnungen II (Gyroscope, 1994)
★★★	The Drop (Thirsty Ear, 1997)
★★★	Lightness (Opal, 1997)
★★★	Kite Stories (Opal, 1999)
★★★	Music for Civic Recovery Centre (Opal, 2000)
★★★	I Dormienti (Opal, 2000)

★★★	Compact Forest Proposal (Opal, 2001)
★★★★	January 07003: Bell Studies for the Clock of Long Now (Opal, 2003)
★★★½	Curiosities, Vol. 1 (Opal, 2003)

Brian Eno/David Byrne

★★★½	My Life in the Bush of Ghosts (Sire, 1981)

Brian Eno/John Cale

★★★½	Wrong Way Up (Opal/Warner Bros., 1990)

Brian Eno/Jah Wobble

★★★★	Spinner (Gyroscope, 1995)

Brian Eno/J. Peter Schwalm

★★★★★	Music for Onmyoji (JVC Japan, 2000)
★★★★½	Drawn From Life (Astralwerks, 2001)

A brilliant conceptualist, a founding member of Roxy Music, and a self-described "nonmusician," the appallingly prolific Brian Eno is probably best known as a producer—he was behind the boards for some of the best albums made by David Bowie, Talking Heads, Devo, and U2—and for having coined the phrase "ambient music." A pity, that; Eno has also made wonderful music of his own, recording entrancing tunes with ingenious countermelodies that should have been hits, but weren't.

Pop content is just one component in the Eno catalogue and melody doesn't seem to interest him half as much as sound itself. Consequently, trawling through the Eno catalogue can be as frustrating as it is rewarding, especially as his later albums tend more toward music that seems airy, empty, and maddeningly diffuse.

In that sense, perhaps the best way to approach the Eno oeuvre is by forgetting chronology and diving in with the box sets. *I: Instrumentals* is a delightful omnibus of sound sketches, studio experiments, and sonic art. Some of it is from collaborations with Bowie, avant-pop trumpeter Jon Hassell, minimalist composer Harold Budd, King Crimson guitarist Robert Fripp, or the German electro group Cluster; some is from solo work using his own keyboards or session musicians. Invariably, Eno finds a certain idiosyncratic element in the sounds produced, and tickles them out. When his teasing tends toward atmospheric stasis, the results are generally dubbed "ambient"— sort of like New Age gets an MFA. But not everything there falls into that category; some tracks, such as "Energy Fools the Magician" or "Chemin de Fer," are as catchy and well-crafted as any pop single.

The second box, *II: Vocals*, has far more of that, and relies heavily on Eno's early albums. Applying what he learned about pop subversion from his tenure in Roxy Music to the revisionist aesthetic of new-wave rock, songs such as "Baby's On Fire," "King's Lead Hat," and "Here Come the Warm Jets" boast all the hook-driven appeal of hit singles, yet without the heard-it-before predictability of conventional pop. Eno rarely took the conventional give-the-singer-the-melody approach, however, and on a number of tracks, the vocal—which may be song, or speech, or some "found" bit of a movie or radio broadcast—is just part of the overall sound, often almost incidental to the instrumental parts.

For fans of his vocal music, the key Eno albums are *Here Come the Warm Jets, Taking Tiger Mountain (by Strategy),* and *Before and After Science.* It may be easy to hear both an anticipation of punk and an echo of Roxy Music in the arch clangor of *Here Come the Warm Jets,* but what shines brightest is the offhand accessibility of the songs. It hardly matters whether he's playing with style (as with the doo-wop undercurrent to "Cindy Tells Me") or fooling with form (the portmanteau construction of "Dead Finks Don't Talk"); the melodies linger on. Listening to it now, the album seems almost a blueprint for the pop experiments Bowie (with Eno producing) would conduct with *Low.*

Taking Tiger Mountain (by Strategy) is just as pop-friendly and eclectic, but shies away from the abrasive textures of its predecessor, swapping distortion and dissonance for blurred edges and open-ended harmonies. Not that the album is entirely without teeth, as there's an itchy aggression to the breathless "Third Uncle" and an ominous urgency to the latter half of "The True Wheel." But Eno keeps such snarls on a tight leash; far more typical is the dry wit of "Back in Judy's Jungle."

But it's *Before and After Science* that stands as the greatest of Eno's "pop" albums. A nearly perfect album, it frames Eno's melodic instincts in every imaginable way, from the chilly funk of "No One Receiving" to the irrepressible vigor of "King's Lead Hat" (an anagram for Talking Heads), to the dreamy cadences of "Here He Comes."

After sitting out the '80s, Eno returned to the pop form in 1990 with the brittle, uneven *Wrong Way Up.* Recorded with John Cale, it's a good attempt at recapturing the old magic, but frankly Cale's intense artiness undercuts Eno's instincts. *My Squelchy Life* was originally intended as the followup, but after making advance copies available to the press, Eno withdrew the album (which is now available only on bootleg). Instead, the unexpectedly funky *Nerve Net* became his next pop effort, and it mostly fizzles. Perhaps sensing the tenor of the times, Eno puts more effort into making good grooves than in writing memorable melodies, and while the resulting tracks are full of good energy and interesting sounds, they lack the hooky good nature of *Before and After Science.*

Then again, after Eno's having spent most of the previous decade releasing album after album on which texture was king, what were we to expect? Although some critics have derided his instrumental albums as being a sort of high-concept mood music, it wasn't mood he was interested in; it was atmosphere. On these discs, he took an almost functional approach to music, manipulating its sonic power in the same way a painter or interior designer might manipulate the power of light, color, and form.

Eno began moving in that direction with *Another Green World.* Here, he uses the studio itself as an instrument, molding directed improvisation, electronic effects, and old-fashioned songcraft into perfectly balanced aural ecosystems such as "Sky Saw" or "St. Elmo's Fire." Initially, he referred to these quiet soundscapes as "discreet" music, and on *Discreet Music* (a wry deconstruction of Pachelbel's Canon in D) demonstrates his basic tools: minimal melodies, subtle textures, and variable repetition. Around this time, he had also been collaborating with the German synth duo Cluster on a pair of moody, coloristic electronic albums, selections from which may be found on the *Begegnungen* and *Begegnungen II* compilations. But it was *Music for Airports* that finally codified these experiments into an aesthetic, and even provided a label for the sound: ambient music.

As much as Eno understands about psycho-acoustics and the relationship between what is heard and what is merely sensed, the largely functional (and mostly tuneless) nature of the music limits the listening pleasure of subsequent ambient releases, such as *On Land, Apollo,* and *Thursday Afternoon.* (Eno also produced albums by other artists for his ambient series: both Harold Budd's rich, moody *Plateaux of Mirror* and Laraaji's shimmering *Day of Radiance* are slightly more energetic and engaging than Eno's own efforts.)

There were, of course, releases that didn't carry the ambient tag but seemed part of the same musical subspecies. The three volumes of *Music for Film* work very much on the same principle as the ambient albums, and feature some of the same collaborators. Likewise, there's an extreme emphasis on atmosphere in the spacey *Shutov Assembly,* the contemplative *Neroli,* and the delicately textured *Drop.*

Meanwhile, Eno continued to collaborate with others. *My Life in the Bush of Ghosts,* which takes its title from Amos Tutuola's novel, was recorded with Talking Headman David Byrne, and offers some insight into the cut-and-paste approach to groove the two applied while making Talking Heads' *Remain in Light.* Its "found art" approach to vocals (however scrupulously footnoted) is an acquired taste, but in hindsight it sounds like a true forerunner of hip-hop sampling. *Spinner,* recorded with former Public Image Ltd. bassist Jah Wobble, boasts gently insistent grooves and strongly Middle Eastern flavors, elements Eno had flirted with on the earlier *Ali Click.* More recently, Eno has been working with the German DJ Jan Peter Schwalm. Their first collaboration, the Japanese-only *Music for Onmyoji* (literally, "Music for the Fortune-teller"), is a double album combining one disc of conventional, deftly crafted synthscapes with a disc of manipulated and collaged recordings based on *gagaku,* the ancient traditional music of the Japanese Imperial Court. *Drawn From Life* is rather less exotic, relying on Western instrumentation and household sounds to generate a rich, surprisingly evocative sonic tapestry celebrating the rhythm of day-to-day life (hence the title).

There's a third stream to Eno's catalogue that isn't represented by a box, and that's his "installations." These are sound sculptures created for specific environments; usually instrumental, they are not compositions in the traditional sense, with a beginning, middle, and end, but are open-ended constructions designed to go on indefinitely without looping or intentionally repeating the material. (Opal is Eno's own label, and these discs are available online from *www.enoshop.co.uk.*) Some, such as *Kite Stories* or *Compact Forest Proposal,* for instance, come from environmental pieces in which multiple CD players, loaded with multiple discs, provide layers of music from varied locations. Obviously, the CD experience can only approximate the installation. Others, such as *Lightness* and *I Dormienti,* are more conventional ambient pieces. Perhaps the most interesting is *January 07003: Bell Studies for the Clock of Long Now,* which treats, toys with, and manipulates the sound of bells, a wonderfully transformative piece that provides new insight into everyday chiming.

More Blank Than Frank and *Desert Island Selection* are best-of albums emphasizing material from *Warm Jets* through *Science.* Of the two, the CD version *(Desert Island)* is preferable, since it offers a slightly more balanced overview. Finally, *Curiosities, Vol. 1* is essentially a collection of leftovers, tracks deemed by Eno too interesting to discard, but too singular to be included elsewhere. Completists only.   —J.D.C.

En Vogue

★★★	Born to Sing (Atlantic, 1990)
★★★	Remix to Sing (Atlantic, 1991)
★★★★	Funky Divas (Atlantic, 1992)
★★★½	Runaway Love (Atlantic, 1993)
★★½	EV3 (Elektra, 1997)
★★★½	Best of En Vogue (Elektra, 1999)
★★	Masterpiece Theater (Elektra, 2000)
★★★★	Very Best of En Vogue (Rhino, 2001)

Arriving during an era in which the girl-group mantle had been inherited by the thin-voiced likes of Exposé and the Cover Girls, En Vogue's full-throated sound immediately set them apart, making them seem the gold standard for R&B pop. Never mind that the quartet was every bit a producer's toy—the group, comprised of former session and background singers, was assembled by Timex Social Club masterminds Denzil Foster and Thomas McElroy—the mere fact they could sing was enough to ensure they'd be revered as soul revivers.

Even so, what carried *Born to Sing* wasn't the vocalizing so much as Foster and McElroy's slick New Jack grooves. It wasn't until *Funky Divas* that the foursome got songs to match the power of their voices (not to mention the persuasion of the beats). Thanks to such singles as "My Lovin' (You're Never Gonna Get It)" and "Free Your Mind," En Vogue was very much in style—and the group's glamour-puss videos only added sizzle to the package.

Following through on such success, however, turned out to be beyond their abilities. The remix-heavy *Runaway Love* recycled *Divas* much in the same way that *Remix to Sing* redid the first album (although "Whatta Man," with Salt-n-Pepa, almost makes the redundancy worthwhile), and by the time En Vogue returned with a full album, the four were reduced to a trio. But it wasn't the lack of a fourth so much as the absence of strong material that left *EV3* wanting; not even contributions from Babyface and Dianne Warren could rekindle the spark of *Divas.* Three years later, the three tried again with *Masterpiece Theater,* but judging from the sound, the title appears to have been meant ironically.   —J.D.C.

Enya

★★★	Enya (Atlantic, 1988)
★★★½	Watermark (Geffen, 1988)
★★½	Shepherd Moons (DGC, 1991)
★★★	The Memory of Trees (Reprise, 1995)
★★★½	Paint the Sky With Stars: The Best of Enya (Reprise, 1997)
★★★	A Day Without Rain (Reprise, 2000)

Throughout the '90s, all things Celtic enjoyed a vogue (James Horner's pipe-laden *Titanic* soundtrack, for one). That vogue began with Enya. Her first U.S. release, *Enya,* is postmodern Gaelic music, strong and lovely, consisting of pleasures that perhaps initially seemed too arcane for all but Yeats fanatics or the most catholic followers of world music. All the more suprising, then, is the fact that this ex-Clannad member and keyboard whiz has become a platinum success. *Watermark*—more accessible than her debut—is the remarkable record that established her. Some of the songs are sung in Irish (and one in Latin), but the pristine strength of Enya Ní Bhraonáin's voice—and the cinematic sweep of her songs' arrangements—translates into an aural landscape of spare ecstasy that carries you away. "Storms in Africa," "Evening Falls," and "Orinoco Flow (Sail Away)" achieve nearly mythic resonance—and her startling fusion of passion and severity make Enya a true original. *Shepherd Moons,* however, is a bit of a comedown, but its inward-looking, lunar intensity continued to win Enya enough adherents that she was soon on her way to releasing a greatest-hits collection. Both *The Memory of Trees* and *A Day Without Rain* are embellishments of *Watermark*—and they're sonically gorgeous.   —P.E.

EPMD

★★★★★	Strictly Business (Priority, 1988)
★★★★	Unfinished Business (Priority, 1989)
★★★★	Business as Usual (Def Jam, 1990)
★★★½	Business Never Personal (Def Jam, 1992)
★★½	Back in Business (Def Jam, 1997)
★★	Out of Business (Def Jam, 1999)
★★★★	Greatest Hits (Def Jam, 1999)

De La Soul and Public Enemy got all the press at the time, but EPMD influenced the shape of '90s hip-hop as much as any late-'80s artist except for N.W.A and Kool G. Rap. They were regular guys who made the hottest tracks: No elaborate concepts here, just one or two funk samples looped to death, and some imperturbably cool, deadpan rhymes on top, courtesy of Long Island guys Parrish Smith and Erick Sermon.

Strictly Business relies on deep funk, usually taken from the catalogue of the J.B.s or George Clinton. On classics like "You Got's to Chill," and "You're a Customer," Sermon's mushy-gravy delivery and Smith's smoother, tightly wound flow trade barbs and brags; the choruses, such as they are, are usually Erick or Parrish speaking the title of the song. It's an incredibly simple formula, but like Rakim's *Paid in Full,* it's a landmark of hip-hop cool—an album that can both wash over you and make you dance.

Unfinished Business is more professional. Still strictly breaks and beats, their sophomore album isn't much of a departure, but it does find them settling into their lyrical personas, Smith the straight-faced heavy and Sermon the comic relief. "The Big Payback" chugs along at such a furious tempo that you forget that James Brown did the music. "So Watcha Sayin' "

is an uptempo masterpiece. *Business as Usual* is the bridge to new-school hip-hop. The music becomes more dense, more layered, incorporating more than just a break and a loop. Smith and Sermon are at the top of their game, dissing fake girls ("Gold Digger") and any rappers who would challenge their supremacy ("I'm Mad," "Rampage").

Business Never Personal has its supporters, and its hot tracks ("Crossover"), but more than anything, it marks the point where Smith and Sermon's partnership started to sour creatively. After a falling-out over money that caused a five-year break between the two, Smith and Sermon reunited for 1997's forgettable *Back in Business*. While the album is far from embarrassing, it's nowhere near the standard of their peak work. Perhaps they knew it, trying to capture some of the old magic on "You Got's to Chill 2."

EPMD took a victory lap in 1999, releasing the swan song *Out of Business* and a best-of compilation. *Out of Business* has its moments, especially a passing-of-the-torch track with Method Man and Redman ("Symphony 2000") but is ultimately unworthy of comparison with their earlier classics.   —C.R./N.B.

Eric B. & Rakim

★★★★★	Paid in Full (4th & Broadway/Island, 1987; 1996)
★★★★½	Follow the Leader (UNI, 1988)
★★★★	Let the Rhythm Hit 'Em (MCA, 1990)
★★★★	Don't Sweat the Technique (MCA, 1992)
★★★★★	Paid in Full: The Platinum Edition (PolyGram, 1998)
★★★★	The Millennium Collection (Universal, 2001)

Eric B. & Rakim's debut 1986 single, "Eric B. Is President," b/w "My Melody (Zakia)," was one of the two or three biggest moments in hip-hop, and the revolution it began continued with their debut album. *Paid in Full* was the first hip-hop album to foreground sampled drumbeats as the primary rhythm bed instead of using them as drop-ins, stabs, and accents. More important, Rakim was the first MC to cross the bar line and let his rhymes scan in idiosyncratic, rhythmic clumps, just like Thelonious Monk had done years before. But that's not why he's the greatest MC of all time. The dark, scratchy-smooth voice is one reason; the ability to compress dignity, humor, and drama into a few words is another: "I need money/I used to be a stick-up kid/so I think of all the devious things I did/I used to roll up/this is a hold up/ain't nothing funny/stop smiling/be still/don't nothing move but the money." Most of all, he swung so hard that a new word entered the hip-hop vernacular when he arrived: flow. If any one MC embodies flow, it's Rakim.

Paid in Full is one of hip-hop's perfect records, from the thumbnail hood ethos of the title track to the dance-floor monster "I Know You Got Soul," which single-handedly resuscitated James Brown in 4:44. Tough guys were thick on the ground, but Islamic philosopher-poets with cowboy equilibrium were something new. *Follow the Leader,* maybe hip-hop's best sophomore album, speeds up their bare bones on the galloping galactic funk of the title track, the epitome of New York sangfroid, "Microphone Fiend," and the perfectly named "Lyrics of Fury." *Let the Rhythm Hit 'Em* opened up the duo's sound, as Rakim attempted a loverman routine in "Mahogany," while mostly sticking with their newly uptempo default position on the title track and "No Omega." (Few groups in pop get faster as they get older, but Eric and Ra did.) The final album before the group split, *Don't Sweat the Technique,* is usually rated lower, but for no apparent reason. "Pass the Hand Grenade," "Know the Ledge," "Casualties of War," and the title track are classics in the fast rap style that they actually spent more time doing than in their first LP mode. *Paid in Full: The Platinum Edition* is more than just marketing hokum: The remixes disc contains Coldcut's version of "Paid in Full," the most influential remix ever, as well as an early version of "Massive Attack," "The Wild Bunch," remixing "Move the Crowd" and Derek B remixing "Paid in Full" with a quote from John Mellencamp's Jack and Diane. Who said mash-ups were new?   —S.F.J.

Roky Erickson

★★★½   The Evil One (1981; Pink Dust, 1987)
★★★½   I Think of Demons (Edsel UK, 1987)
★★★   Don't Slander Me (Pink Dust, 1986)
★   Gremlins Have Pictures (Demon, 1986)
★★★★   You're Gonna Miss Me: The Best of Roky Erickson (Restless, 1991)

As with Syd Barrett, Roky Erickson's reputation has as much to do with his acid-casualty notoriety as with the flashes of brilliance that run through his music. As a member of the 13th Floor Elevators, Erickson is widely credited with having invented psychedelic rock—indeed, the quintet's 1966 debut, *The Psychedelic Sounds of the 13th Floor Elevators,* predates both *Grateful Dead* and Pink Floyd's *The Piper at the Gates of Dawn.* But Erickson's interest in mind expansion inevitably took its toll. He was arrested for marijuana possession in 1968; pleading insanity, he spent almost four years ensconced at the Hospital for the Criminally Insane in Rusk, Texas.

Erickson resumed his musical career in the late '70s, cutting a couple of singles before forming the

Aliens, with whom he recorded an album's worth of demented material in 1980. Originally released as *Roky Erickson and the Aliens* on CBS UK in 1980, expanded versions of the album have since been released under the titles *The Evil One* and *I Think of Demons.* Unlike the showbiz satanism heavy-metal bands dabble in, this is truly disturbing material, as Erickson delivers the likes of "Don't Shake Me Lucifer," "Night of the Vampire," and "Two Headed Dog" with the creepy conviction of one whose demons are a little too real.

Sadly, the novelty of such dementia dissipates rather quickly. Apart from the paranoid title tune, *Don't Slander Me* doesn't seem quite so fascinating, returning Erickson to the blues-based grooves that were the Elevators' meat and potatoes. *Gremlins Have Pictures,* recorded in haphazard sessions with various lineups, is merely a document of Erickson's musical deterioration. *You're Gonna Miss Me: The Best of Roky Erickson* draws from all of the above as well as a smattering of concert recordings, and offers the most representative overview of his solo career.   —J.D.C.

Alejandro Escovedo

★★★★½   Gravity (Watermelon, 1992; Texas Music Group, 2002)
★★★★   Thirteen Years (Watermelon, 1994; Texas Music Group, 2002)
★★★   With These Hands (Rykodisc, 1996)
★★★½   More Miles Than Money: Live 1994–1996 (Bloodshot, 1998)
★★★½   Bourbonitis Blues (Bloodshot, 1999)
★★★★½   A Man Under the Influence (Bloodshot, 2001)
★★½   By the Hand of the Father (Texas Music Group, 2002)

with Buick MacKane

★★★   The Pawnshop Years (Rykodisc, 1997)

By the time he released his debut solo album, Alejandro Escovedo had already spent more than a decade playing punk (with the Nuns); cow punk (Rank & File); and full-tilt, triple-guitar rock & roll (True Believers). But the San Antonio–born artist really came into his own with *Gravity* and its equally stunning followup, *Thirteen Years.* Both albums—smartly produced by guitarist Stephen Bruton—were born out of tragedy, as Escovedo struggled to come to grips with the suicide of his first wife. From the chilling opening couplet of "Paradise" ("Did you get your invitation/ There's gonna be a public hanging") to the sadder-than-Tom-Waits-at-closing-time "Broken Bottle" and the ghostly "She Doesn't Live Here Anymore," *Gravity* plays out like one long, cathartic sigh of grief, even when it rocks out with Faces-worthy abandon ("One More Time"). The air of melancholy lingers through most of the more richly orchestrated *Thirteen Years,* but the Tex-Mex-flavored swell of violins, cello, and harp in "Ballad of the Sun and the Moon" hints at a break in the clouds. Across both albums, Escovedo's triple-threat strength as a writer, singer, and arranger is in full display, his songs alternately evoking shades of the moody romanticism of Nick Drake, the experimentalism of the Velvet Underground, and the unruly, street-poet glam of Mott the Hoople's Ian Hunter. (Both *Gravity* and *Thirteen Years* have been reissued with bonus discs featuring instrumental and live tracks; his cover of Hunter's "I Wish I Was Your Mother" is a highlight on both.)

Escovedo's output for the rest of the '90s fell short of that staggering opening salvo of bitter-sweet pathos, though the uneven *With These Hands* and *The Pawnshop Years* (featuring his endearingly sloppy garage band Buick MacKane) are not without their charms, particularly the former's Willie Nelson duet, "Nickel and a Spoon." The live *More Miles Than Money* makes for a fine introductory set, complemented with wicked viola- and cello-driven covers of the Rolling Stones' "Sway" and the Stooges' "I Wanna Be Your Dog." Smart covers (Hunter's "Irene Wilde," Lou Reed's "Pale Blue Eyes") also carry the weight on *Bourbonitis Blues,* a half-live/half-studio affair. But with *A Man Under the Influence,* Escovedo delivered his most satisfying and fully realized batch of originals since his debut. Among the highlights: "Castanets," his best—and rowdiest—rocker to date; "Velvet Guitar," which channeled *Ziggy Stardust*–era David Bowie; and the darkly atmospheric "Wave," which towers above everything else in his canon. A more restrained version of "Wave" is reprised on *By the Hand of the Father,* a soundtrack to a play about the plight of Mexican immigrants inspired in part by Escovedo's music. It's a moving but imperfect concept album—all the spoken narrative discourages repeated listening. Escovedo's songs get their message across just fine without such extrapolations.   —R.S.K.

Melissa Etheridge

★★	Melissa Etheridge (1988; Island, 2003)
★★	Brave and Crazy (Island, 1989)
★★	Never Enough (Island, 1992)
★★★½	Yes I Am (Island, 1993)
★★★½	Your Little Secret (Island, 1995)
★★★	Breakdown (Island, 1999)
★★½	Skin (Island, 2001)
★★½	Lucky (Island, 2004)

Melissa Etheridge has, over the course of eight albums, transformed herself from an issues-oriented feminist folkie to a love-song-slinging blues rocker.

On the heavily acoustic *Melissa Etheridge,* her songs are less about lust than loss, running the gamut from *Why don't you want me?* to *You used to want me, why don't you want me now?* (A deluxe 2003 reissue augments the original album with such fans-only fare as demos and live recordings.) With the overly ambitious *Brave and Crazy,* she leavens the spurned-lover stuff with attempts at poetry, resulting in such cringe-worthy choruses as "Shame, shame but I love your name/And the way you make the buffalo roam." Ouch. *Never Enough* toughens her sound slightly, but it's not until *Yes I Am* that Etheridge finds her formula. With the bluesy grind of "Come to My Window," Etheridge found not only a hard-rock approach suited to her big, bluesy voice, but also a subject—sexual desire—to which everyone could relate.

Your Little Secret expands on that breakthrough, bringing an almost Springsteenian majesty to some of the songs. Even better, she truly understands the allure of illicit desire, and through the likes of "Such an Unusual Kiss" and "I Want to Come Over" makes it very easy to see the good side of bad love. *Breakdown* tends to prefer heartbreak melodrama to lubricious longing, which isn't as much fun but is nearly as entertaining. "Angels Would Fall" may try to be the pop equivalent of *The Thorn Birds* as Etheridge's protagonist longs to lead a devout lover off the prayerful path, but it serves up its soapy saga with enough musical oomph to make the lyrical excesses forgivable.

The rough and rambunctious *Skin* is less ambitious and much more uneven, but when it works—as on the rousing "I Want to Be in Love"—it shows that Etheridge has lost none of her bite. A pity, then, that *Lucky* keeps coming up boxcars. While there's plenty of desire on display in the lyrics, the music itself seems neither hungry nor horny, while "Tuesday Morning," dedicated to gay 9/11 victim Mark Bingham, seems slightly gratuitous in comparison with songs such as Neil Young's "Let's Roll."   —J.D.C.

Eurythmics

★★★	In the Garden (RCA U.K., 1981)
★★★★	Sweet Dreams (Are Made of This) (RCA, 1983)
★★★★	Touch (RCA, 1983)
★★	1984 (RCA, 1984)
★★★★	Be Yourself Tonight (RCA, 1985)
★★★	Revenge (RCA, 1986)
★★	Savage (RCA, 1987)
★★	We Too Are One (Arista, 1989)
★★★★	Greatest Hits (Arista, 1991)
★★	Live 1983–1989 (Arista, 1993)
★★½	Peace (Arista, 1999)

On one level, Eurythmics was a perfect musical marriage, balancing the full-throated passion of singer Annie Lennox with the studio-savvy popcraft of guitarist/keyboardist/producer Dave Stewart. But at the same time, what worked best about the duo's musical chemistry wasn't necessarily in line with what the two most wanted to do, meaning that their best albums were inevitably based on compromise.

That certainly is the case with *Sweet Dreams (Are Made of This)*, the group's first American album. Although its predecessor, the import-only *In the Garden*, used its electronics mainly as a means of fleshing out standard-issue new wave arrangements, *Sweet Dreams* built a significant portion of its sound around synthesizers. While that added poignancy to "Love Is a Stranger" and the title tune, Lennox truly cuts loose on the duo's cover of the Sam & Dave hit "Wrap It Up." *Touch* not only reprises *Sweet Dreams'* synths-plus-voice formula, but one-ups it with "Here Comes the Rain Again." Unfortunately, *1984*, the soundtrack for Michael Radford's film of the George Orwell novel, uses its musical technology almost too well, lending an oppressive chill to the music.

With *Be Yourself Tonight*, Eurythmics expand from duo to full band, and while that shift doesn't entirely displace the group's electronics—"There Must Be an Angel (Playing with My Heart)," for instance, still relies heavily on synths for its instrumental flavor—it does shift the emphasis. "It's Alright (Baby's Coming Back)," "Would I Lie to You?," and the Aretha Franklin duet "Sisters Are Doin' It for Themselves" take a soulful tack that makes the most of Lennox's delivery. Lennox aside, though, Eurythmics' credibility as R&B stylists is fairly limited, and cracks begin to show in their façade as early as *Revenge*, on which the bluesy bluster of "Missionary Man" sounds dishearteningly hollow. Chastened, Eurythmics return to a techno-intense sound for *Savage*, but by this point the group's sound is too mannered to have much impact; at best, songs like "I Need a Man" and "Beethoven (I Love to Listen To)" come across as little more than academic exercises. Still, that's better than *We Too Are One*, which is unable to eke even the slightest melodic interest from the band's empty professionalism.

Lennox announced she was going on sabbatical shortly after *We Too* was released, and returned as a solo artist in 1992; Stewart, by that point, had two solo projects under his belt. The duo reunited for the lush-but-insubstantial *Peace* in 1999.   —J.D.C.

Faith Evans

   ★★★   Faith (Bad Boy, 1995)
   ★★★   Keep the Faith (Bad Boy, 1998)
★★★½   Faithfully (Bad Boy, 2001)

Known best in hip-hop circles as the Notorious B.I.G.'s widow, Faith Evans matured as an artist only after the murder of her (in)famous husband, from whom she was separated at the time. In fact, she likely made her most lasting impression as a prominently featured vocalist on "I'll Be Missing You," Puff Daddy's tribute to his late friend and business partner. Released in 1995, *Faith* was a decent example of '90s R&B—thoroughly produced and somewhat formulaic—but it only hinted at the depth of her artistry. It wasn't until the release of *Keep the Faith* that Evans began to show the kind of promise that separated her from an army of other R&B vixens (Brandy, Deborah Cox, Kelly Price, Monica, etc.). *Faithfully*, her 2001 release, was by far her best album, with its lush backing arrangements and smooth (but not slick) grooves that recall the '70s soul of Philadelphia International artists such as Harold Melvin and the Blue Notes, the O'Jays, and Billy Paul.   —K.M.

Eve

   ★★★   Let There Be Eve . . . Ruff Ryder's First Lady
            (Interscope, 1999)
  ★★½   Scorpion (Interscope, 2001)
   ★★   Eve-olution (Interscope, 2002)

Philadelphia native Eve Jihan Jeffers is a competent if unexceptional MC whose commercial success has largely been spun from her streetwise brand of flapper glamour. Lacking the outrageousness of Lil' Kim or the lyrical roughness of Lady of Rage, Eve is an easy-to-digest artist as au courant as the musically thin Swizz Beats–produced tracks she often rhymes over. Even after listening to an entire Eve album, it's tough to recall any particularly clever couplets or memorable turns of phrase, and the self-described "pitbull in a skirt" remains best known for her exotic hairstyles and the pawprint tattoos on her chest. Yet due to some well-plotted collaborations, Eve can lay claim to appearing on a couple of truly great tracks.

Eve first drew major attention for the Dr. Dre–produced cut "Eve of Destruction" on the soundtrack for the film *Bulworth*, but it was her appearance on "You Got Me," the classic single from the Roots' 1999 album *Things Fall Apart*, that boosted anticipation for her debut album. *Let There Be Eve* was indeed an enjoyable release, but it displayed a self-aggrandizing lyrical preoccupation with dissing haters that Eve has yet to grow beyond.

Her sophomore effort, *Scorpion*, included "Blow Ya Mind," a Dr. Dre–produced duet with No Doubt's Gwen Stefani that deservedly won a Best Rap/Sung Collaboration Grammy. But what distinguished

"Blow Ya Mind" was Dre's fatback beat (one of his post–*Chronic 2001* best) and Stefani's slinky, catgirl chorus—not Eve's rapping. *Scorpion* was otherwise disappointing, reaching a nadir on the Damien Marley duet "No, No, No," a karaoke-type retread of Dawn Penn's ubiquitous dancehall reggae hit.

Eve's third album featured "Gangsta Lovin'," a duet with Alicia Keys, but while the single went into microwave rotation on MTV, it failed to duplicate the thrill of "Blow Ya Mind." *Eve-olution*—ostensibly a document of spiritual and artistic growth—did not deliver the goods. On "What," she summed up her strength (head-turning looks) and weakness (mundane rapping) with the couplet "Tired of my voice/ Plug your ears/Outrageous by choice/Love the stares." In late 2002, Eve made the transition to the big screen with a small role in the Vin Diesel vehicle *XXX* and a larger part in the Ice Cube flick *Barbershop.* —P.R.

Eve 6

★★½ Eve 6 (RCA, 1998)
★★ Horrorscope (RCA, 2000)
★★½ It's All in Your Head (RCA, 2003)

Eve 6 frontman Max Collins is a curious pop-rock specimen, a songwriter who's just bright enough to write lyrics betraying the extreme limitations of his callow insight. If that betrayal were conscious, he'd be one to watch. But Collins would seem to have psychological conflicts that no mere mass audience can cure. And audiences have a way of wisely easing out of such overly dependent relationships.

Eve 6 spawned the radio staple "Inside Out," a bit of strained catchiness distinguished by a line about depositing his "tender/Heart in a blender"—pop culture's grossest use of that particular appliance since Rerun made a baloney shake on *What's Happening?* But once you notice that Collins' plea to "tie me to the bedpost" makes consensual S&M sound as much fun as having your teeth cleaned, you wonder if the boy's getting out often enough.

In fact, Collins spends the better part of *Eve 6* convincing himself that his sexual impulses are dirty and shameful. And that is *no* turn-on. A cannier (or just less uptight) vocalist might have delivered "May I help you put aside your moral fiber?" in a gentle enough way to turn "Jesus Nitelite" into a funny seduction scenario, but Collins clobbers it with melodramatic self-loathing. *Horrorscope* relaxes a bit, musically and vocally, but neither Collins' take on relationships ("Amphetamines") nor on stardom ("Sunset Strip Bitch") is very enlightening. With *It's All in Your Head,* the band tries for more sophisticated lyrical themes (classism, lost children) and doesn't quite pull it off.   —K.H.

Everclear

★★★★ Sparkle and Fade (Capitol, 1995)
★★½ World of Noise (Capitol, 1995)
★★★½ So Much for the Afterglow (Capitol, 1997)
★★★★ Scenes From an American Movie: Learning How to Smile (Capitol, 2000)
★★★ Songs From an American Movie, Vol. 2: Good Time for a Bad Attitude (Capitol, 2000)
★★ Slow Motion Daydream (Capitol, 2003)

Everclear was initially touted as yet another instamatic Nirvana rip-off when they first arrived, but in fact they honorably represented grunge's tauter, punkier fringe. And in a sense, scene veteran Art Alexakis is the anti–Kurt Cobain. His gift is to make the base, crass motives that alternative rock used to look down upon seem desperate, even heroic, a slob's way of exerting his tiny bit of control over a cruel world. Class consciousness permeates "I Will Buy You a New Life," about the transformative power of new money, and "Rock Star," about a guy (possibly Alexakis himself) who wants to get laid and "a girlfriend who does not drink beer."

The tangled *World of Noise* was too aptly titled, but *Sparkle and Fade* was everything a radio-ready rock record should be: explosive, soul-searching, belligerent. When his proudly flaunted "black girlfriend" on "Heart Spark Dollar Sign" declares "You're possessed by a power bigger than the pain," you want to kick him in the shins. But the awesome "Santa Monica" encapsulates Alexakis' cynically escapist worldview—walking hand in hand away from bland normalcy, "we can watch the world die." The perfectly titled *So Much for the Afterglow* is a worthy successor.

With grunge gone, the two volumes of *Scenes From an American Movie* ply Art's sentimental side, intending to establish him as power-ballad troubadour of nuclear-family fission. But having a pop sensibility isn't the same as possessing pop gifts, and Alexakis employs the same tunes over and over. But the first volume contains nice reminiscences, both personal and cultural, as well as decorative but unobtrusive strings and horns, and the repetition of similar melodies has a cumulatively heart-tugging effect. Volume two thrashes about with less focus, often adequately if not fully convincingly. But the refrain of "Babytalk" ("She's got him by the balls") won't reassure anyone who hoped maturity might temper Art's woman issues. A guy can only rehash his troubled youth so often, however, and so Alexakis surveyed the present on *Slow Motion Daydream.* The best he could come up with was the tepid social commentary of "Volvo Driving Soccer Mom." This is the way alt-rock ends—not with a bang but a whimper.   —K.H.

Everlast

★½	Forever Everlasting (Rhyme Syndicate-Warner Bros., 1990)
★★★	Whitey Ford Sings the Blues (Tommy Boy, 1998)
★★★½	Eat at Whitey's (Tommy Boy, 2000)
★★★	White Trash Beautiful (Island Def Jam, 2004)

Everlast is hip-hop's least likely auteur: a teen discovery of original gangsta Ice-T, who rose from a sullen white boy aping rap clichés to become a brooding artist fluent in hip-hop, folk, rock, and meaningful social commentary. Born Erick Schrody, Everlast first hit the charts with the furious shamrocks-and-beer trio House of Pain, but found his true voice retooled as a solo artist, with a stirring hybrid of turntables and acoustic guitars he called "hick hop," equal parts thug and cracker.

Nothing like that was evident on Everlast's disposable 1990 debut, *Forever Everlasting,* a thin collection of unremarkable beats and raps, stripped down and generic. He works up some empty dance-floor beats for "What is This?" and goes urban romantic (a la LL Cool J) for "On the Edge," and the effect is soft and unconvincing, leaving no impression at all. But Everlast was no Marky Mark either, and soon transformed himself into a burly, tattooed frontman overflowing with attitude and Irish testosterone in House of Pain (1992's double-platinum "Jump Around"). It bounced and rocked, but suggested none of the layers of feeling to come. Everlast was an artist in transition.

Everlast's true self emerged on *Whitey Ford Sings the Blues.* Hip-hop was now just one of many ingredients in his sound, and he was as likely to pick up an acoustic guitar as bust a hard-core rap groove. Mixing guitars and beats was no gimmick but a genuine statement of self, landing him close to Beck's musical territory. Everlast opens with some playful nursery rhyme funk (echoing the Tom Tom Club) that announces, "The white boy is back, and you know he never smoked crack." Jokes aside, he included lots of hardheaded raps circa 1998, all toughness and bluster, rapping on getting laid and paid ("Dolla-dolla-dolla-dolla-bill, y'all!"). More important was the debut of Everlast as postmodern bluesman: he redefined himself as a world-weary troubadour for a new age with "What It's Like." "Ends" rode a similar talking blues groove, colliding guitar with scratches into a new genre, where the real folk blues meet hip-hop, delivering social commentary as potent as Stevie Wonder's "Living for the City."

Eat at Whitey's dug even deeper into roots, cranking up the funk, even turning Slick Rick's "Children's Story" into fresh Delta hoodoo with some human beatbox from the Roots' Rahzel. "Black Jesus" is an ominous, full-boil rocker, with Everlast's white rasp sounding straight outta Lynyrd Skynyrd. The presence of guests Carlos Santana and B-Real suggests the kind of range at his disposal, as does the sticky funk with Cee-Lo on "We're All Gonna Die." This time, however, inspiration didn't translate into radio. But not even disappointing sales for *Eat at Whitey's* shook Everlast's musical muse. Four years later, *White Trash Beautiful* turned his wounded growl further inward; he's still tough but not so limited by machismo that he can't feel loss or longing. The result is often closer to Hank Williams than beat street, as a shell-shocked Everlast rhymes about a woman he used to know, even resorting to pedal-steel guitar on the dreamy "This Kind of Lonely." He rocks harder on the boastful "Soul Music," but the tracks on lost love are devastating. Hard, soft, and soulful, *White Trash Beautiful* isn't the sound of commercial calculation. It's basic instinct.   —S.A.

Everly Brothers

★★★★	Songs Our Daddy Taught Us (1958; Rhino, 1988)
★★★★	The Fabulous Style of the Everly Brothers (1960; Rhino, 1988)
★★★★	The Golden Hits of the Everly Brothers (1962; Warner Bros., 1988)
★★	The Very Best of the Everly Brothers (1964; Warner Bros., 1988)
★★★★	Roots (1968; Warner Bros., 1995)
★★★½	Stories We Could Tell (1972; One Way, 1997)
★★★	Pass the Chicken & Listen (1973; One Way, 1997)
★★★★	The Reunion Concert (1984; Mercury, 1989)
★★★★★	Cadence Classics (Their 20 Greatest Hits) (Rhino, 1985)
★★★★	All They Had to Do Was Dream (Rhino, 1988)
★★★	All Time Greatest Hits (Curb, 1990)
★★★	Best of the Everly Brothers: Rare Solo Classics (Curb, 1991)
★★★★½	Walk Right Back: The Everly Brothers on Warner Bros., 1960–1969 (Warner Archive, 1993)
★★★	Wake Up Little Susie (Laserlight, 1994)
★★★★★	Heartaches & Harmonies (Rhino, 1994)
★★★½	All-time Original Hits (Rhino, 1999)
★★★½	Devoted to You: Love Songs (Varèse Sarabande, 2000)

Raised in Kentucky by parents who were successful folk and country musicians, Don and Phil Everly occupied a special niche in early rock & roll as a direct link to Appalachian folk music, traditional country, and bluegrass. Their keening harmonies were distinctive and deeply moving and most often put to devastating use in some of the most exquisite tales ever written on the timeless themes of teenage misery and true love. The Everlys set a standard for harmony singing that still resonates with contemporary country artists, but their most profound impact was on '60s rock and folk artists such as the Beatles, the Hollies, and Simon and Garfunkel; Don and Phil heard themselves being channeled by the likes of Peter and Gordon and of Chad and Jeremy.

Their first professional experience apart from the family show came in 1955 when the teenage brothers were hired as songwriters by Roy Acuff's music publishing company in Nashville. One of Don's songs, "Thou Shalt Not Steal," became a hit for Kitty Wells, but the brothers' own recording attempts fell flat. Their fortunes changed in 1957 when Cadence Records president Archie Bleyer brought them "Bye Bye Love," written by Felice and Boudleaux Bryant. Thirty acts had already passed on the song, but Bleyer (who had originally declined to sign the Everlys yet had given them an introduction to executives at Columbia Records) saw the duo as Cadence's entrée into the rock & roll market. With Don and Phil's insistent harmonies soaring high over an acoustic guitar–driven beat, "Bye Bye Love" jetted to #2 on the pop chart and was followed in short order by the first of three #1 singles, "Wake Up Little Susie" (again from the Bryant-Bryant pen). Largely on the strength of the Bryants' well-crafted, literate, and often wry commentaries on the teen psyche, the Everly Brothers charted 11 singles in the Top 30 from 1957 through 1959, with the beautiful "All I Have to Do Is Dream" and the whimsical rocker "Bird Dog" also topping the chart. In allowing room for the playful ("Poor Jenny," "Problems") and the poignant ("Devoted to You," "Take a Message to Mary"), the Bryants' songs painted a broad emotional canvas depicting in verse the most extreme emotions roiling the brothers' core audience.

Don and Phil, though, were developing as songwriters, and before long the hits had their credits below the title. In 1959 Don checked in with " 'Til I Kissed You," a Top 10 single, and Phil followed suit a year later with "When Will I Be Loved." In 1960, the brothers began a productive, near decadelong association with Warner Bros. that was marked by a reflective turn in their material. Don's "So Sad (To Watch Good Love Go Bad)" and the Howard Greenfield–Carole King tearjerker "Crying in the Rain" were indicative of the Everlys' journey into love's darker recesses, and with that journey came deeper, more cutting lyrics in their self-penned songs and their cover choices.

Since all travel ultimately leads back home, Don and Phil responded to the intimate, personal songs of a new generation with their own rustic take on *Rubber Soul*: 1968's *Roots*, a moving look back at the sources of their own music and something of a companion volume to a daring album they had released 10 years earlier called *Songs Our Daddy Taught Us*. The latter's song selection includes an Irish ballad, a cowboy song, a folk song, and traditional country songs; although Elvis dipped into roots music for an album cut here and there, not even he had he nerve to do an album as rootsy as *Songs Our Daddy Taught Us*. A year after *Roots* celebrated family values, the family split apart when Phil stalked offstage in mid-concert, leaving Don to announce the group's breakup to a stunned audience.

Years of personal animosity and unsuccessful solo albums followed, until the brothers buried the hatchet and reunited at London's Royal Albert Hall in 1983. Captured on record *(The Reunion Concert)* and filmed for HBO, the concert was a complete triumph; their mature voices had lost none of their power to stir souls and move hearts, and the songs benefited from the subtext brought by middle-aged men who had been around the block a couple of times and knew the difference between puppy love and the real, deep, and giving thing. The reunion concert was followed by a brief tenure at the Mercury label, which was kicked off in grand fashion with the album *EB84* and the jubilant "On the Wings of a Nightingale," penned and produced by Paul McCartney. In songs such as "The Story of Me," "You Make It Seem So Easy," and the tender "Asleep," the brothers work out their reconciliation in forceful detail, and in the process, deliver one of the strongest studio albums in their career. The followup, *Some Hearts,* also in a self-revelatory vein, includes Don's too-true take on love's fleeting nature, "Any Single Solitary Heart." And that was that.

Through the '90s, the Everlys continued to perform live, reportedly arriving and leaving the venues separately and never speaking to each other before or after the show. Their voices have been conspicuously silent during the rise of the New Traditionalist and alt-country movements, given that many of their recordings in the '50s and '60s foreshadowed both trends.

The Cadence years are best represented by Rhino's *Cadence Classics (Their 20 Greatest Hits)* and two Varèse Sarabande titles, *The Complete Cadence Recordings: 1957–1960* and *The Essential Cadence Singles*. Completists will enjoy *All They Had to Do Was Dream*, a collection of outtakes from the Cadence sessions that includes between-songs patter. As for the Warner Bros. years, the place to start is the 50-track, thoroughly annotated retrospective *Walk Right Back: The Everly Brothers on Warner Bros., 1960–1969*, which contains not only the hits but also a sampling of album tracks that demonstrates the brothers' long musical reach and absolute command of country, blues, and rock & roll, from the old-time (Jimmie Rodgers' "T for Texas") to hard-edged Bakersfield honky-tonk (Merle Haggard's "Sing Me Back Home"). *Walk Right Back* incorporates a number of tracks from the *Roots* album. The must-avoid is Warner Bros.' *The Very Best of the Everly Brothers:* It features rerecordings of the Cadence hits, which are fine, but stick with the originals.

The One Way label offers a couple of interesting artifacts from the Everlys' early-'70s tenure at RCA. One, 1972's *Stories We Could Tell,* includes songs by John Sebastian (the title track), Rod Stewart ("Mandolin Wind"), Jesse Winchester's lovely "Brand New Tennessee Waltz," Kris Kristofferson's "Breakdown," and two of the finest songs to carry the Everly copyright, "Green River" (energized by Ry Cooder's stinging bottleneck and Buddy Emmons' pedal steel) and Don Everly's revealing "I'm Tired of Singing My Songs in Las Vegas." *Pass the Chicken & Listen,* filmed by their first producer, Chet Atkins, was the brothers' final album before they split up. It's a more overt mainstream country effort, and while not entirely successful, it does offer a powerful version of John Prine's cautionary tale about the devastation of strip-mining in Kentucky, "Paradise." Post-breakup, the brothers are represented by Curb's *Best of the Everly Brothers: Rare Solo Classics,* but alas, there are not many classics to be found. Since all of their other solo work is out of print, this disc at least fills what would otherwise be a void in their story, but it's for completists only.

Of the multilabel retrospectives, Rhino's 16-track *All-time Original Hits* is a superb anthology of blockbusters, whereas Varèse Sarabande's *Love Songs* ranks especially high in the swoon category. The big picture is definitively captured in Rhino's four-CD, 103-song box set, *Heartaches & Harmonies*, which has the exhaustive annotation and sessionography fanatics demand (including Don and Phil's own song-by-song commentary), illuminating the singular path the Everlys trod. Quite simply, *Heartaches & Har-*

monies is one of the best box sets ever, and it doesn't hurt that the music it contains will always reach out across time to touch hearts and stir souls.   —D.M.

Everything but the Girl

★★★½ Everything but the Girl (1984; Sire, 1995)
★★★★ Love Not Money (1985; Sire, 1995)
★★★ Baby, the Stars Shine Bright (1986; Sire, 1995)
★★★ Idlewild (1988; Sire, 1990)
★★ The Language of Life (Atlantic, 1990)
★★★½ Worldwide (Atlantic, 1991)
★★★ Acoustic (Atlantic, 1992)
★★★½ Amplified Heart (Atlantic, 1994)
★★★★ Walking Wounded (Atlantic, 1996)
★★★ Temperamental (Atlantic, 1999)
★★★★ Like the Deserts Miss the Rain (Atlantic, 2003)

Over the course of their two-decades-long career, U.K. duo Everything but the Girl has evolved from stylized, loungey pop to dance-driven futurist pop. By the time of EBTG's self-titled American debut, Tracey Thorn and Ben Watt had already begun moving away from the cafe pop that had aligned their U.K. debut, *Eden* (which came out earlier the same year), with mannered faux-jazz Brits such as the Style Council. *Everything but the Girl* retreads six of *Eden*'s 12 tracks, and those songs—including "Each and Every One," with its bossa-nova beat and muted trumpet, and "Frost and Fire," with its bongos and organ stabs—define the record's blue, lovelorn mood. But the six tracks not drawn from *Eden*, presumably newer material, lean more toward the literate Northern soul/Brit-pop of contemporaries such as the Smiths and Lloyd Cole, all full of guitar jangle and strum, and less concerned with romance than with issues of feminism and racism. Its followup, *Love Not Money*, continues in this direction, with intricate, melodic guitar lines and punchy beats ("Any Town," "Ballad of the Times") taking precedence over the jazz noir ("This Love [Not for Sale]") and Phil Spector beats ("Heaven Help Me").

Baby, the Stars Shine Bright, with its lush string and choir orchestrations, is a wrong turn that nevertheless offers some worthwhile sights. Arrangements for "Come On Home," "Careless," and "Come Hell or High Water," in particular, are so billowy and grand, they revisit a lost era of easy listening that's quaint and evocative in a way that the group's later excursions toward Muzak would not be. *Idlewild* marks the duo's transition into an unfortunate—though probably inevitable—middle period. As if *Baby* never happened, the album alternates *Love Not Money*'s soulful British pop ("Those Early Days," "The Night I Heard Caruso Sing") with the overly slick R&B lite ("Love Is Here

Where I Live," "Tears All Over Town") that would populate subsequent records.

The Language of Life serves as EBTG's career low point, not only because its smooth-jazz veneer strips away the group's more classic jazz and soul touches, but also because it's quite often a downer. Along with other odes to discontentment and failure, "Me and Bobby D" takes Dylan and Kerouac to task for being male-chauvinist weaklings. Is nothing sacred?

Worldwide is almost as slick, but the lite jazz gives way to a far more digestible soul/pop sound, as well as a brighter mood. Tracks like "Understanding," with its backing track closely resembling Marvin Gaye's "Sexual Healing," or "You Lift Me Up," a slow jam with gospel shadings, bring EBTG about as close as they'd get to commercial R&B. With its title less a reference to internationalism than to the actual act of traveling, *Worldwide* stands as Watt and Thorn's testament to being a band on the road.

No doubt, anyone who believed the twosome's pursuit of studio polish needed tempering welcomed *Acoustic*, EBTG's 180-degree turnaround. The mix of well-chosen covers (Elvis Costello's "Alison," Tom Waits' "Downtown Train") with originals ("Me and Bobby D," "Driving") featured stripped-down and imaginatively reconfigured arrangements—quite a novelty in the years before *MTV Unplugged. Acoustic* also served to revive the duo's faith in acoustic instruments. Not that they were prepared to abandon studio gloss entirely—the followup, *Amplified Heart*, in fact, pushes the group further toward dance and commercial pop than it had ever gone to that point, earning a Top 10 hit with the house-influenced "Missing." But by incorporating organic elements, EBTG's music regains a sense of weight and balance.

With the group emboldened by the success of "Missing" and by Thorn's appearance on trip-hop pioneers Massive Attack's "Protection" single, *Walking Wounded* sees EBTG fully embracing modern electronica. Pairing the cool-blue croon of early records with intricately cut beats—the skittering drum and bass of "Before Today," the house throb of "Wrong," the scratching of "Flipside"—the duo found a wonderful new niche for itself at the forefront of pop currents. A late-career highpoint. With somewhat less success, *Temperamental* continues the path of *Walking Wounded*, exploring various beats and textures while pairing them with soul/pop melodies.

After releasing three anthologies available only on import, the group finally put out a domestic best-of set. Anyone looking to the 20-track *Like the Deserts Miss the Rain* for a definitive hits collection, however, will be disappointed. Instead, Watt and Thorn culled together their personal favorites, mixing most of their best-known material with an appealing selection of album tracks, side projects, rarities, and remixes. —R.M.S.

Cesaria Evora

★★★½ Cesaria (Nonesuch, 1995)
★★★★ Cabo Verde (Nonesuch, 1997)
★★★ Miss Perfumado (Nonesuch, 1998)
★★★ Mar Azul (Nonesuch, 1999)
★★★★½ Café Atlantico (Lusafrica/RCA, 2002)
★★★ Sao Vicente (Windham Hill, 2001)
★★★★ The Very Best of Cesaria Evora (RCA, 2002)

There was plenty for rock & rollers to distrust about the overwhelming reception with which the world music audience greeted Cape Verde's premier chanteuse in the mid-'90s. At her most lively, Evora's version of morna disrupts the mournful strum of fado, the notoriously melancholy Portuguese peasant music, with hearty West African rhythms. But at her most genteel, she's a standard Western fantasy of native grace—an exemplar of the long-suffering "folk" given to dignified pining for the rural good old days. Evora's work, though, is marked by a reluctance to settle easily into that stereotype.

If the barefoot diva's self-titled debut was a vocal showcase, the plaints on *Cabo Verde* are stirred up by swifter arrangements and whirling, almost klezmerlike clarinets. On "Coragem Irmon" ("Take Courage, Brother") the guitars seem to surf forward, powered by the clustered soundwaves generated by saxophone colossus James Carter. Evora tempers her resignation with something approaching indignance on "Mar E Morada de Sodade" ("The sea is the home of nostalgia"): "It separates us from distant lands," Evora sings of the sea. The distant lands of Africa, that is, from which the people of Cape Verde did not leave willingly.

On *Mar Azul*, Evora was laying back, and the result was as dignified as it was dull. *Miss Perfumado* one of the discs that made her a star in France, suffers similarly—its one undeniably classic track, "Sodade," is heard to better effect on the compilation *Adventures in Afropea 3: Telling Stories to the Sea,* which compiles the songs of Portuguese-speaking musicians of African descent from various countries. *Café Atlantico* may be Evora's most joyful album, as well as her most wide-ranging stylistically, assaying rhythms from Cuba and Brazil. But while *Sao Vicente* maintains much in that spirit, Evora's move to the New Age label Windham Hill is worrisome. —K.H.

Fabolous

★★★½ Ghetto Fabolous (Elektra, 2001)
★★½ Street Dreams (Elektra, 2003)

Breezy, monumentally conceited, and blessed with an agile flow and mind for wordplay, Fabolous came closer than anyone to duplicating Jay-Z's singular personality at a time when the latter ruled hip-hop radio. But Fab never struck a workable balance between populism and egotism, a task perfected by his model, who uses one to reinforce the other. Only the off-message Eminem and, later, 50 Cent could truly share center stage with Jay—confident though he may have been, Fabolous could never escape Jay-Z's shadow.

Still, *Ghetto Fabolous* went platinum, and rightfully so: Almost every song combines the sparkling beats of a top producer—Timbaland, the Neptunes, Rockwilder, Just Blaze—with whale-hunting hooks and Fab's lube-smooth rhymes. If the phrase "holla back" ever ends up in the dictionary, we will probably have the album's pager-sampling first single, "Young'n," to thank. Ditto the locution of "Keepin' It Gangsta," which, rather than intimating violence, suggests that maintaining the gangsta lifestyle merely involves drinking expensive champagne and dancing the night away.

Even boring people can be fun at parties. Fabolous, like any other pompous jerk, loses himself in the moment. Plus, changing Biggie's famous line from "I see some ladies tonight that should be havin' my baby" to "I see some ladies tonight that should be drinkin' my babies"—swallowing, that is—makes a fine joke, if not a pickup line. Unfortunately, on *Street Dreams,* Fab's big head gets squeezed into a narrow R&B format that he's simply not sexy enough to inhabit. Too tastefully produced not to score airtime, the first single and typical track "Can't Let You Go" slinks sleepily and finds Fab asserting that "the barrel of [his] gun's big enough to spit out a rocket—oh!" That's a lame attempt at keepin' it gangsta. —N.C.

John Fahey

★★★★ Death Chants, Breakdowns and Military Waltzes (Takoma, 1963)
★★★½ Blind Joe Death (1964; Takoma, 1996)
★★★½ Dance of Death and Other Plantation Favorites (Takoma, 1964)
★★★½ The Transfiguration of Blind Joe Death (1965; Takoma, 1997)
★★★ The Great San Bernardino Birthday Party, Vol. 4 (1966; Takoma, 2000)
★★★½ Death Chants, Breakdowns and Military Waltzes (Rerecording/reissue of 1963 version) (1967; Takoma, 1999)
★★★½ John Fahey Guitar (Takoma, 1967)
★★★½ Blind Joe Death (Vanguard, 1967)
★★★½ Days Have Gone By, Vol. 6 (1967, Takoma, 2001)
★★★½ Voice of the Turtle (1968; Takoma, 1996)
★★★ The Yellow Princess (Vanguard, 1969)
★★★ The New Possibility (Xmas Album) (Takoma, 1969)
★★★½ America (1971; Takoma, 1998)
★★★ Fare Forward Voyagers (Takoma, 1973)
★★★ Essential John Fahey (Vanguard, 1974)
★★★ John Fahey/Leo Kottke/Peter Lang (Takoma, 1974)
★★★½ Old Fashioned Love (1975; Takoma, 2003)
★★★ Christmas With John Fahey (Takoma, 1975)
★★★★ Best of John Fahey (1959–1977) (Takoma, 1977)
★★★½ Live in Tasmania (Takoma, 1981)
★★★½ Christmas Guitar, Vol. 1 (Varrick, 1982)
★★★½ Popular Songs of Christmas and New Year's (Varrick, 1983)
★★★½ Let Go (Varrick, 1985)
★★★½ Rain Forests, Oceans and Other Themes (Varrick, 1985)
★★½ I Remember Blind Joe Death (Varrick, 1987)
★★★½ God, Time and Causality (Shanachie, 1990)

★★★★½ The Return of the Repressed: The Anthology (Rhino, 1994)
★★ City of Refuge (PolyGram, 1997)
★★★★ Of Rivers and Religion (Collector's Choice, 2001)
★★★ After the Ball (Collector's Choice, 2001)
★★½ Red Cross (Revenant, 2003)
★★★★ Best of John Fahey, Vol. 2: 1964–1983 (Takoma, 2004)

John Fahey preferred album titles like *Death Chants, Breakdowns and Military Waltzes,* and *Blind Joe Death,* suggesting either a dark private humor or plain morbid fixation, but this Maryland guitarist's forte is music of an exhilarating, almost rapturous beauty. Uplifting or soothing, tinged with melancholy, his sets of country blues, Scotch-Irish folk, or classically derived melodies showcase often dazzling acoustic-guitar work. Generally unaccompanied and without overdubs, he crafts complex tapestries of sound; his virtuosity is less a matter of speed or jazzy convolution than tone, and Fahey's guitar resounds like no other. Big, bell-like, immediate, helped out by very clear production, his tone comes through like a signature. Confusingly, he rerecorded a number of LPs because he thought his technique had improved, and one of his finest releases, *Of Rivers and Religion,* features a whole band with horn charts. A very consistent artist—the assured delivery of "Old Southern Medley" off *The Transfiguration of Blind Joe Death,* from 1973, isn't dissimilar to his rousing take on Eric Clapton's "Layla" (from *Let Go*)—Fahey kept to a very high standard through much of his 40-year career. Gorgeous mood music that can provoke trance and reverie, his albums might appeal to New Age listeners—but his music is denser and smarter than that genre. He survived for years as a perennial Christmas-music favorite. Fahey's stubborn, outsider nature and his '60s experimental works led to his rediscovery as an indie hero; his final albums, however, are feeble echoes of the more clever curios on *Voice of the Turtle* and *The Great San Bernardino Birthday Party.* Newcomers will do well with *Return of the Repressed* or the best-of anthologies; *Vol. 2,* selected by guitarist Henry Kaiser, is particularly well programmed. Fahey's stoic combination of deep sadness and unshakeable resolve to transcend will keep his work forever in fashion. —M.MI.

Fairport Convention

★★★★★ Fairport Convention (1968; Polydor, 1990)
★★★½ Liege and Lief (Island, 1969)
★★★½ Gladys' Leap (Varrick, 1986)
★★½ Expletive Delighted! (Varrick, 1987)

★★½ Jewel in the Crown (Green Linnet, 1995)
★★½ Who Knows Where the Time Goes? (Woodworm, 1997)
★★★ The Cropredy Box (Woodworm, 1998)
★★★ Fiddlestix: The Best of Fairport Convention, 1970–1984 (Raven, 1998)
★★★★½ Meet on the Ledge—The Classic Years (1967–1975) (A&M, 1999)
★★½ Wishfulness Waltz (Mooncrest, 2000)
★★★ Encore Encore: Farewell Tour (Relix, 2000)
★★½ Close to the Wind (Sanctuary/Trojan, 2001)
★★½ The Wood and the Wire (Compass, 2001)
★★★ XXXV (Compass, 2002)
★★★ Then and Now: The Best of Fairport Convention (Metro, 2002)
★★★½ The Anthology: Some of Our Yesterdays (Sanctuary, 2002)

A remarkable debut, *Fairport Convention* (1968) introduced a British folk-rock band whose instrumental prowess and eclectic repertoire qualified them as a nascent supergroup. Dizzying personnel shifts and haphazard commercial success, however, would dog the band throughout its long career, ultimately making Fairport more a style and a vision than a cohesive aggregation. Whatever the lineup, Fairport's players managed a union of Scotch-Irish folk, rock & roll rhythm, and cunning, elliptical lyrics. *Unhalfbricking* (now out of print) featured a legendary cast: angel-voiced Sandy Denny and guitarist Richard Thompson were a pair of singers as potent as the Jefferson Airplane's Grace Slick and Marty Balin; Dave Swarbrick's violin grounded the band in the Celtic tradition; and drummer Dave Mattacks kept things swinging. Whether soaring through the 11 minutes of "A Sailor's Life" or rendering Dylan's "If You Gotta Go, Go Now," the musicians came off as daunting, witty virtuosos. *Liege and Lief* completed Fairport's first chapter, establishing the group at the forefront of late-'60s experimental British bands. *Meet on the Ledge,* the band's best compendium, is especially good at covering the first, great albums.

By the early '70s, both Thompson and Denny had departed; what was left of Fairport forayed even further into traditional music, which seemed limiting. Subsequent recordings were mainly Swarbrick's shows, and the band suffered from the lack of an outstanding vocalist. *Live Convention* (out of print) briefly brought back Sandy Denny, and the album was one of the band's last true highlights. Denny died in 1978, which was about the time the band's original vision had begun to fade.

Fairport kept on going, however. All the '80s-and-after albums, mainly featuring Martin Allcock on vocals, are worth a listen, but they only echo the long-past glory of the group's first three records. *Expletive Delighted!* (1987) is a fair example of the group's later work; it's an interesting fusion of jazzy licks and Celtic reels. *The Copredy Box* is a fine, three-disc live set that captures the excitement of the massive European folk festival that Fairport has hosted for years. *XXXV* commemorates the 35th anniversary of Fairport Convention, by then a ghost, however charming, of its former self. —P.E.

Marianne Faithfull

★★	Marianne Faithfull's Greatest Hits (1969; Abkco, 1988)
★★½	Faithless (1977; Immediate, 1989)
★★★★	Broken English (Island, 1979)
★★★	Dangerous Acquaintances (Island, 1981)
★★★	A Child's Adventure (Island, 1983)
★★★	Strange Weather (Island, 1987)
★★★	Blazing Away (Island, 1990)
★★★★	Faithfull: A Collection of Her Best Recordings (Island, 1994)
★★★	20th Century Blues (RCA Victor, 1997)
★★★	The Seven Deadly Sins (RCA Victor, 1998)
★★★★	A Perfect Stranger: The Island Anthology (Island, 1998)
★★★	Vagabond Ways (Instinct, 2000)

As Mick Jagger's late-'60s squeeze, Marianne Faithfull played the archetypal Brit-rock-star girlfriend: pale, blond, regal, hip. And this daughter of an Austrian noble could sing—notably, at 18, Jagger-Richard's lovely "As Tears Go By." A few other hits followed, but by 1966, she was finished as a soft-voiced popster. *Greatest Hits* chronicles this period; *Faithless* is a reissue of her '70s pop—her voice is strong, the material is not.

By the dawn of the '80s, experience—in the stark form of heartbreak, drug busts, press notoriety, and suicide attempts—had made Marianne Faithfull an artist. As a demimonde chanteuse, Faithfull is indisputably the real thing: wised-up, courageous, bullshit-free. *Broken English,* with a song about cocksucking and a dramatic reading of Lennon's "Working Class Hero," was her startling adult entrance, unleashing a Gauloises-rich voice and a fierce intelligence. *Dangerous Acquaintances* insinuated its power more softly; its Steve Winwood collaboration, "For Beauty's Sake," took a wary look at obsession. *A Child's Adventure* found her in stronger but still uningratiating voice; while a fine record, especially for the wounded strength of "Falling From Grace," it just missed the cracked accomplishment of her mature debut. With *Strange Weather,* Faithfull darkly covered work by Dylan, Lead Belly, and Jerome Kern. And in *Blazing Away,* she commemorates her life lessons; a sharp live album, it serves as a loose best-of. Of the two official best-ofs, *Faithfull* is the tighter and stronger.

Faithfull kept things interesting in the '90s. *A Secret Life* teamed her with composer Angelo Badalamenti, best known for his film scores for David Lynch's eccentric flicks. The collaboration is a kind of moodiness fest, dark on dark, blue on blue. The live *20th Century Blues* is Marianne doing Kurt Weill to a stark piano and acoustic-bass accompaniment—haunting stuff, as are the album's other songs, by Harry Nilsson and Noël Coward. The Vienna Radio Symphony backs her up on another live rendering of Weill gems, *The Seven Deadly Sins;* again, the effect is unsettling, smart, hypnotic. With *Vagabond Ways,* Faithfull returns to original material, cowriting with Daniel Lanois, among others; the voice has retained its haggard beauty. —P.E.

The Fall

★★★★	Live at the Witch Trials (1979; Cog Sinister, 2002)
★★★★	Dragnet (1979; Get Back, 2002)
★★★★	Totale's Turns (It's Now or Never) (1980; Sanctuary, 2002)
★★★★	Grotesque (After the Gramme) (1980; Sanctuary, 2002)
★★★½	Slates (EP) (Rough Trade, 1981)
★★★★	Early Years 1977–1979 (1981; Cog Sinister, 2002)
★★★★	Hex Enduction Hour (1982; Cog Sinister, 1999)
★★★	Room to Live (1982; Cog Sinister, 2002)
★★★	A Part of America Therein, 1981 (Cottage, 1982)
★★★★	Perverted by Language (1983; Sanctuary, 2003)
★★★½	Fall in a Hole (Flying Nun [NZ], 1983)
★★★★	The Wonderful and Frightening World of the Fall (1984; Beggars Banquet, 1997)
★★★½	Hip Priest and Kamerads (1985; Beggars Banquet, 1995)
★★★★	This Nation's Saving Grace (1985; Beggars Banquet, 1997)
★★★	Bend Sinister (1986; Beggars Banquet, 1997)
★★★	Domesday Pay-Off (Big Time, 1987)
★★★★	Palace of Swords Reversed (Cog Sinister/Rough Trade, 1987)
★★★	The Frenz Experiment (1988; Beggars Banquet, 1997)
★★★½	I Am Kurious Oranj (1988; Beggars Banquet, 1997)
★★★	Seminal Live (1988; Beggars Banquet, 1997)
★★★½	Extricate (1989; Beggars Banquet, 1997)

★★★★ 458489 A Sides (1990; Beggars Banquet, 1994)

★★★½ 458489 B Sides (1990; Atlantic, 1995)

★★½ Shift-Work (Cog Sinister/Fontana, 1991)

★★ Code: Selfish (Cog Sinister/Fontana, 1992)

★★★½ The Infotainment Scan (Matador/Atlantic, 1993)

★★★½ Middle Class Revolt (Matador, 1994)

★★★★ Cerebral Caustic (Permanent, 1995)

★★½ The Twenty-seven Points (Permanent, 1995)

★★★ The Legendary Chaos Tape (Rough Trade, 1995)

★ Sinister Waltz (1996; Sanctuary/Trojan, 2001)

★ Fiend With a Violin (1996; Sanctuary/Trojan, 2001)

★ Oswald Defence Lawyer (Receiver, 1996)

★★★ Light User Syndrome (Jet, 1996)

★ The Fall in the City . . . (Artful, 1997)

★ Archive Series—The Fall (Rialto, 1997)

★ The Less You Look, the More You Find (Receiver, 1997)

★ 15 Ways to Leave Your Man (Receiver, 1997)

★★★½ Levitate (Artful, 1997)

★ Oxymoron (Receiver, 1997)

★ Cheetham Hill (Receiver, 1997)

★★★ Live to Air in Melbourne '82 (Cog Sinister, 1998)

★★ Live Various Years (Cog Sinister, 1998)

★★½ Nottingham '92 (Cog Sinister, 1999)

★★★½ The Peel Sessions (Strange Fruit, 1999)

★★★½ The Marshall Suite (Artful, 1999)

★★ A Past Gone Mad: The Best of 1990–2000 (Artful, 2000)

★★★ Live 1977 (Cog Sinister, 2000)

★★★½ Psykick Dance Hall (Eagle, 2000)

★★½ Live in Cambridge 1988 (Cog Sinister, 2000)

★★★ Live in Reykjavik 1983 (Cog Sinister, 2000)

★ Backdrop (Cog Sinister, 2000)

★★ A World Bewitched—Best of 1990–2000 (Artful, 2001)

★★½ Are You Are Missing Winner (Cog Sinister, 2001)

★½ Live in Zagreb (Cog Sinister, 2001)

★★ 2G+2 (Action, 2002)

★★★★½ Totally Wired—The Rough Trade Anthology (Castle, 2002)

★★★ Listening In: Lost Singles Tracks 1990–92 (Cog Sinister, 2002)

★★★½ Early Singles (Cog Sinister, 2002)

★★★½ The Unutterable (Mister E, 2003)

★★★½ It's the New Thing!: The Step Forward Years (Castle, 2003)

★★★½ Words of Expectation: BBC Sessions (Castle, 2003)

★★★ The Real New Fall LP (Narnack, 2003)

★★★★ 50,000 Fall Fans Can't Be Wrong (Beggars Banquet, 2004)

Mark E. Smith is a ranter, but rarely a crowd-pleaser; he's also a *Twilight Zone* fanatic, a William Blake obsessive, and something of a thug, not to mention, just maybe, Britpunk's poet laureate and philosopher king. He's also the sole constant member of the Fall, one of the most indestructible musical ideas to emerge from British punk.

Using half-sung, half-snarled, sometimes hysterically funny, endlessly quotable lyrics that tear apart class, art, politics, lit, other bands, themselves, and more, Smith spot-welded his harangues to a rough-and-tumble groove that choogled like rockabilly, droned like Euro art rock, and squalled like the gnarliest punk. (It also shone like dance rock and beeped like techno, but that was later.) As long as Smith is alive, the Fall will never vary all that much from this singular, highly rhythmic racket, but they sure as hell don't sound like anyone else, and generations of indie rockers have stolen from Smith as if his name were Chuck Berry.

Add all of this genius to an obscenely huge discography and you have the makings of a serious-ass cult act. Devout Fall fans argue about their favorite albums like rabbis hashing out the Talmud. Most regular humans don't need more than a few of these albums, but everyone needs at least one; any of the '80s singles collections are excellent places to start.

Live at the Witch Trials features fetal but nifty workouts of an aesthetic that was discovered quickly and subsequently refined endlessly. As "Crap Rap" puts it, "We're the crap that talks back." Look for this as a theme throughout Smith's career, people. An excellent debut, but not too far from punkodoxy.

Dragnet is the first record with brilliant guitarist Craig Scanlon, who put up with Smith longer than anyone else. The Fall has never sounded stranger than on this dank, appallingly recorded, and fascinating album. (Not to mention self-aware: "I don't sing/I just shout.") *Totale's Turns* is the first of roughly 1 billion live albums, all of which have moments of high rant and rough, tuneless lows.

Grotesque is the first truly great Fall album, the sound of pieces coming together: the trebly guitar, the weird groove (the amazing "New Face in Hell," which clearly changed Pavement's life), and That Voice spitting, yelling, and jabbering his bent, sinister vision, sneering at the middle-class liberals on "English Scheme" and shouting out his hometown ("The N.W.R.A."). Fantastic.

Early Years 1977–1979, Early Singles, and *It's the*

New Thing!: The Step Forward Years all cover much the same territory, and many of these songs show up as bonus tracks on early '00s pressings of albums from the same era. The "definitive rants" on the *Slates* EP, the endlessly powerful *Hex Enduction Hour,* and the slightly less great *Room to Live* finish out the Fall's first era on a spectacular high. On *Slates'* six spotless tunelets, Smith's dissections get sharper still (the self-defining "Prole Art Threat," "An Older Lover") as the music's palette opens up (outta-nowhere acoustic guitar on "Fit and Working Again"). *Slates* can be found on CD with the solid live album *A Part of America Therein.*

Hex . . . adds a second drummer and higher-fidelity production, turning the smart bombs into a fucking freight train. "The Classical," "Fortress/Deer Park," and the anticritic "Hip Priest" all shine, and Smith has never sounded so . . . large, like an indestructible Saxon magus, totally in control of his singular vision. The weaker followup, *Room to Live,* sports fabulously irritated lyrics aimed squarely at bourgeois Britain ("Hard Life in Country" and the title track) undercut by thinner, less compelling music and an uninterested-sounding Smith. *Fall in a Hole* is the excellent live album from this period. (*Hip Priest* compiles tracks from this same period, as does the totally excellent *Totally Wired* and the rare three-CD box *Psykick Dance Hall.*)

Perverted by Language ushers in a new epoch for the Fall; it's the first album to feature the guitar and songwriting of Smith's now-ex-wife Brix, a Yank with a keen melodic sense and, by all accounts, the patience of a saint. It's yet another keeper, complete with a great "football" tune ("Kicker Conspiracy"), weird pounders ("Smile," "Eat Yrself Fitter"), and the oddly moving "Garden."

The Wonderful and Frightening World of the Fall moves the group into the worlds of dance rock, pop riffs, and mass British fame. The singles from this period ("Oh! Brother," "C.R.E.E.P.") are both fabulously slick and endlessly cool. *This Nation's Saving Grace* wanders even further into the mainstream ("What You Need," the shimmering "L.A."), with by now typically excellent results, and also contains the seriously odd "I Am Damo Suzuki," a shout-out to the Can singer of the same name. *Palace of Swords Reversed* compiles (mostly) great singles from 1980 to 1983.

Then the shine began to fade. *Bend Sinister* is the cranky flip side of *This Nation's Saving Grace's* smooth power. *The Frenz Experiment* is more of the duller same, complete with a hit cover of the Kinks' "Victoria." *I Am Kurious Oranj* is the smart soundtrack to a ballet (check out his cover of Blake's "Jerusalem"). The spotless singles collection *458489 A Sides* is a hit-after-hit cheater tape to the Brix era, which ended when she split in 1989. Producers Craig Leon, Adrian Sherwood, and Coldcut give *Extricate* a glossy sound. Guitarist Martin Bramah, not heard since *Live at the Witch Trials,* rejoins as Smith takes shots at Brix on the fabulously nasty "Sing! Harpy," covers the garage primitives the Monks' "I Hate You" as "Black Monk Theme Part One," and generally wallows in his own dank, not-quite-as-tuneful bitterness. *Shift-Work* and *Code: Selfish* enlist keyboards to ill-fitting effect (though the *Listening In* singles collection makes the best of the weak music).

In 1993, the Fall found themselves on Matador Records, sharing a label with Pavement, who may very well still owe them royalties for egregious gimmick infringement. *The Infotainment Scam* does some light genre-surfing (disco on "Lost in Music," T. Rex on "glam racket," 1983-era Fall on "The League of Bald Headed Men") while retaining That Fall Thing.

Having largely invented the stuff, the Fall do American indie rock quite well on *Middle Class Revolt.* "Behind the Counter" smokes, "15 Ways" is classic Fall pop, and the rest hangs together tunefully and oddly professionally. They were off Matador by *Cerebral Caustic,* which is too bad, as it's a furious return to noisy, reckless rant form. Brix is back, and it seems to have inspired and infuriated both her and Smith. "Don't Call Me Darling" is pure rage, "Bonkers in Phoenix" is epic. (The year 1996 also marked the debut of the dreaded compilations of demos, outtakes, and live material on Receiver Records. Don't bother with any of them unless you are a helpless addict and have purchased almost everything else on this list.)

Cerebral was also the last album with Craig Scanlon, and the post-Craig years have had their ups and downs. *The Light User Syndrome* still has Brix aboard, which adds some zip to the tunes, but something truly fundamental feels missing. *Levitate* mixes drum and bass into the Fall thing for a solid outing, then a few more key musicians left. Could this be the end?

Please: 1999's *The Marshall Suite* and 2000's excellent *The Unutterable* roar the band back to life, the former a three-part suite, the latter an absolute bulldozer of electronic thunder able to stand with any of the group's '90s work. The Fall are back, baby.

Or maybe not. The dull *Are You Are Missing Winner?* of 2001 and the is-it-brilliant-or-awful? mishmash *2G+2* from 2002 did not bode well for the future. (The Fall does keep endlessly recycling the past, however. All of the 2002 comps are good, and the BBC sessions collection just crackles.) But as long as Smith has breath in his ranting little Mancunian body, the Fall will be there, churning out albums as well as bile. The 2003 Fall album *The Real New Fall LP* finally saw the light of day in the States in 2004, and it's another good one, full of loud chugging rock overseen by Smith in all of his mumbling, nasty glory. The double-disc retrospective *50,000 Fall Fans* reaches all the way back to the band's first single, "Repetition," and goes up to "Green Eyed Loco-Man," a gnarly rocker from *The Real New*. Track selections range from good to great ("Victoria" is an amazing cover, though it doesn't belong here); this primer on 25 years of prime bile is the ideal place to start for anyone who wants an overview of the Fall's career. —J.G.

Fastball

★★½	Make Your Momma Proud (Hollywood, 1996)
★★★	All the Pain Money Can Buy (Hollywood, 1998)
★★★	The Harsh Light of Day (Hollywood, 2000)
★★★	Keep Your Wig On (Rykodisc, 2004)

This Austin, TX, trio—complete with two equally talented songwriters in guitarist Miles Zuniga and bassist Tony Scalzo—entered into the pop consciousness in 1998 on the strength of "The Way," one of the great pop-rock radio moments of the era. Scalzo gives the anonymous couple who walk off into "eternal summer slacking" a quietly heroic dignity and grace, turning an everyday romance into epic adventure, "where they won't make it home/But they really don't care." A moving tale flawlessly and efficiently told.

After gaining some notoriety around central Texas, Fastball found the center line down the middle of the cross street where zippy punk-pop trips over nerdy pop-rock, where the guys from Orange County skate to the first Weezer album. Songs on the 1996 debut, such as "Human Torch" and "Are You Ready for the Fallout?" are effortlessly catchy, well crafted, and fairly forgettable.

All the Pain Money Can Buy contained "The Way" and the ballad "Out of My Heads." The rest are slightly rootsier versions of the power-pop on the debut. On *The Harsh Light of Day,* Scalzo's voice is sounding more Elvis Costello–ish by the note, and his songs, like "Love Is Expensive and Free," come complete with horn and string arrangements they can finally afford. Scalzo and Zuniga trade off solid melodies like old pros, but there's still no sign of those folks from "The Way." You get the distinct impression those wandering lovers took the money and ran "without ever knowing the way." *Keep Your Wig On* is a solid, adult reunion album. Scalzo and Zuniga found themselves writing together for the first time ("The Way" and "Out of My Head" were Scalzo's tunes). The results combined the straight-ahead popcraft of

the 1998 glory days with the off-the-cuff rock feel of their earliest albums, the sound of bandmates finally figuring out that they need one another and accepting adulthood. Unlike the folks in the "The Way," looks like Fastball will get old and gray. —J.G.

The Fat Boys

★★★★	The Fat Boys (Sutra, 1984)
★★★½	The Fat Boys Are Back (Sutra, 1985)
★★	Big & Beautiful (Sutra, 1986)
★★★½	Crushin' (Sutra, 1987)
★★★	Coming Back Hard Again (Tin Pan Apple, 1988)
★★★★	All Meat No Filler: The Best of the Fat Boys (Rhino, 1997)

An era-defining mid-'80s hip-hop group, the Fat Boys have been consigned somewhat to history's crumb bin as corny comedy rappers. This assessment is deserved, at least based on their highest-profile moments: 1987's Three Stooges–style hospital high jinks movie *Disorderlies,* and the cheesy hits "Wipeout," a 1987 team-up with the Beach Boys (sadly without a fat Brian Wilson), and "The Twist (Yo' Twist)," a 1988 pairing with the appropriately rotund Chubby Checker. But there are nuggets of greatness studding the Fat Boys' recording career—their first two albums are hard-hitting humorous classics, expertly produced by the great Kurtis Blow—and they set the proverbial buffet table for Biz Markie and Heavy D and the Boyz' subsequent hip-hop feasts. Brooklyn buddies Damon "Prince Markie Dee" Morales, Damon "Kool Rock-Ski" Wimbley, and Darren "the Human Beat Box" Robinson (a.k.a. Buffy, a.k.a. the Ox That Rocks) won a Radio City Music Hall talent show in 1983 and promptly changed their name to the Fat Boys. Wearing matching satin jackets, Kazal glasses with sequin frames, and brightly colored T-shirts sporting iron-on letters spelling FAT BOYS, the group had an approachable, lovable look. Their self-titled debut featured rugged vocals and spare, slamming beats that put them in a league with Run-D.M.C., with Robinson's instantly recognizable hyperventilating beat-box style driving "Human Beat Box." Sophomore album *The Fat Boys Are Back* ("and you know they can never be wack!") was even better. On the title track, Prince Markie Dee set things off: "I'm starving, I'm in the mood/plain and simple I need food/eat some beans and pretty soon/everybody in the place will leave the room!" "Don't Be Stupid" warned of the dangers of vices such as gambling, and "Hard Core Reggae" married an *irie* bass line with shout-outs to fat reggae stars such as Jacob Miller. They would go on to have the aforementioned Top 40 hits, only to splinter in the early '90s when Prince Markie Dee went solo. Sadly, the Human Beat Box died in December 1995 of a heart attack.   —P.R.

Fat Joe

★★½	Represent (Relativity, 1993)
★★★	Jealous Ones Envy (Relativity, 1995)
★★½	Don Cartagena (Atlantic, 1998)
★★★	Jealous Ones Still Envy (Atlantic, 2001)
★★	Loyalty (Atlantic, 2002)

Bronx's Fat Joe, a.k.a. Joey Crack, spent the earlier part of his career outshined by the more senior members of his Diggin' in the Crates crew. With members such as Showbiz & A.G., Lord Finesse, and Diamond D., the crew promoted an occasionally tired, true school version of hip-hop: beats, rhymes, and life dug from the gutter and the classic soul/R&B record bins. Fat Joe's early albums certainly follow this model. This is fair-to-middling '90s New York hip-hop, with a few exceptions: *Represent* put Fat Joe on the map with its minor hit, "Flow Joe," while *Jealous Ones Envy* contains the minor classic street anthem "Shit Is Real."

It wasn't until 2002's *Jealous Ones Still Envy* that Joe was able to escape the shadow of DITC or, even more significantly, that of his late partner in rhyme, Big Pun. Powered by two of that year's biggest singles, "We Thuggin' " (featuring R. Kelly) and the infectious "What's Luv?" (on which he takes a backseat to the Murder Inc. duo of Ashanti and Ja Rule), *J.O.S.E.* made Joe a household name outside the Bronx. The album's decided step up in production values allowed Fat Joe to swing smoothly between the club-oriented singles and more raw cuts like "Fight Club." Unfortunately, perhaps tempted to capitalize on his new success, Fat Joe rushed out *J.O.S.E.*'s followup, *Loyalty*. The single "Crush Tonight" tried to recapture the R&B crossover success of "What's Luv?," but it, and the album, didn't fare as well commercially.   —C.R.

The Feelies

★★★★	Crazy Rhythms (1980; A&M, 1990)
★★★★	The Good Earth (Twin Tone, 1986)
★★★★	Only Life (Coyote, 1988)
★★★★	Time for a Witness (A&M, 1991)

Among the formal breakthroughs accomplished by the Velvet Underground was something called the drone strum. As perfected by Lou Reed, this strum didn't syncopate to emphasize the backbeat the way rock rhythm guitar usually did—in fact, it barely syncopated at all, tending more toward chopped, evenly accented eighth notes dropped squarely on the beat. And it was this nervous *chink-chink-chink-chink-*

chink-chink-chink-chink that gave the anxious edge to the likes of "I'm Waiting for the Man" and "White Light/White Heat."

That same strum is at the heart of the Feelies' sound on *Crazy Rhythms*. Yet as much as it defines the band's groove, it doesn't limit the band's rhythmic vocabulary; indeed, songs like the briskly tuneful "Fa-Cé-La" or the slow-building "The Boy With Perpetual Nervousness" augment the basic pulse with a second line of overdubbed percussion. Moreover, this strictly disciplined approach to rhythm makes even the slightest variation, such as the lengthy breakdown on the title tune, stand out in bold relief.

Six years later, the Feelies—this time sporting a new bassist and drummer as well as a full-time percussionist—returned for round two, *The Good Earth*. This time around the band's groove is more conventional (note the standard folk-rock strum of the acoustic guitars on "On the Roof") but still heavily indebted to Reed and the Velvets. If anything, the group has added a few Velvetisms to its repertoire—in particular, the "Heroin"-style acceleration and explosion of "Slipping (Into Something)." *Only Life* can't quite match that growth (though it does include a cover of Reed's "What Goes On"), though it doesn't backslide, either. But *Time for a Witness* pushes beyond mere imitation as the band refines its sound into something that's at once evocative of the band's influences and yet stylistically distinct, especially on the plangent, bluesy "What She Said" or the dark, moody "Find a Way."   —J.D.C.

Bryan Ferry

★★★★★	These Foolish Things (1973; Virgin, 2000)
★★	Another Time, Another Place (1973; Virgin, 2000)
★★★	Let's Stick Together (1976; Virgin, 2000)
★★★	In Your Mind (1977; Virgin, 2000)
★★★½	The Bride Stripped Bare (1978; Virgin, 2000)
★★★½	Boys and Girls (1985; Virgin, 2000)
★★	Bête Noire (1987; Virgin, 2000)
★★★	Taxi (Reprise, 1993)
★★	Mamouna (Virgin, 1994)
★★★½	As Time Goes By (Virgin, 1999)

Bryan Ferry began his solo career while Roxy Music was still in full flower, and at times he has come close to the glam-rock thrill of Roxy on his own. His first solo album was a conceptual and musical tour de force. *These Foolish Things* is a blasphemous collection of oldies covers, mixing up respectable rock classics such as Dylan's "A Hard Rain's a-Gonna Fall" and the Stones' "Sympathy for the Devil" with the evanescent kicks of Lesley Gore's "It's My Party" and the Paris Sisters' "I Love How You Love Me." Sometimes, it's intensely soulful, as in "River of Salt," and always it's hilarious, especially when Ferry leeringly delivers the solemn poetics of "Hard Rain" with a disco-style beat and a cheesy background chorus.

These Foolish Things was such a shocker that Ferry's basically been trying to top it ever since. *Another Time, Another Place* had a moment or two ("The In Crowd," "Wonderful World"); *Let's Stick Together* has some nice stripped-down Roxy Music remakes, including a smoky "Casanova"; *In Your Mind* is a low-key batch of originals. *The Bride Stripped Bare* was a real puzzle, slicking over some potentially great songs with a hack L.A. studio band (Waddy Wachtel on a Bryan Ferry record?). There's the glorious seven-minute "When She Walks in the Room" and a great version of the Irish folk song "Carrickfergus," but Ferry's "Take Me to the River" has about one eighth of the Big Muddy juice of Al Green's original, and it had the misfortune to come out the same year as Talking Heads' version.

Boys and Girls, his first solo album after Roxy Music broke up, was his disco-friendly bid for solo stardom, and while it's too fluffy, it does have one of his greatest songs ever, the hypnotic slow-dance "Slave to Love." *Bête Noire* and *Mamouna* are tuneless sequels, the latter a reunion with Roxy comrades Brian Eno and Phil Manzanera, neither one particularly listenable. His best recent work has returned to the oldies-cover gambit. *Taxi* is a consistently inspired set that ranges from "Amazing Grace" to "All Tomorrow's Parties." Even better, *As Time Goes By* is a straight-up standards album, torching up old-fashioned songs like "Falling in Love Again," "Where or When," and "September Song" with simpatico backup musicians who swing more than they rock. As Bryan Ferry always understands, the fundamental things apply, as time goes by. —R.S.

50 Cent

★★★½   Guess Who's Back? (Full Cup, 2002)
★★★★   Get Rich or Die Tryin' (Shady/Aftermath, 2003)

Dropping gory yet imperturbably cool rhymes, commanding attention with a media presence that matched Eminem's, and turning the bulletproof vest into a hot fashion accessory, 50 Cent established himself as the most lovable hip-hop villain in years with the release of *Get Rich or Die Tryin'* in early 2003. After securing a $1 million deal with Eminem's Shady/Aftermath label and scoring a hit with "Wanksta," a cut on the soundtrack to his new boss's film debut, *8 Mile,* even casual pop fans were aware of the most arresting part of 50's biography—namely that this former hustler, crack dealer, and inmate had taken more bullets than most platinum-selling rappers have hits.

Born Curtis Jackson in Queens, NY, 50 had already built a solid rep by the time he was shot in 2000. He recorded a full album for Columbia Records (the unreleased but heavily bootlegged *Power of the Dollar*) that presaged the mix of spacious, synth-heavy funk and menacing rhymes 50 and his producers would nearly perfect on *Get Rich or Die Tryin'.* After recovering from his brush with death, 50 (armed with a heavily slurred flow, courtesy of a bullet hole in his cheek) released a cavalcade of underground mix-tapes, most of which featured recycled beats and dis-heavy freestyle rhymes. The mixes made a strong case that 50 was the underground's best MC, and they eventually made their way to Eminem, who touted 50 as "the illest motherfucker in the world." As a bidding war broke out, 50 released *Guess Who's Back?,* the only commercially available collection of his pre–*Get Rich* work. *Guess Who's Back?* finds a middle ground between the off-the-cuff rhymes of 50's underground mixes and the more polished assault of his proper studio recordings. Half the material comes from *Power of the Dollar,* including ghetto-life bangers such as "Life's on the Line" and "As the World Turns." "That's What's Up" features 50 and his fellow G Unit soldiers (who would release a platinum record of their own later in 2003) trading quick-tongued verses over the beat to Wu-Tang's "Y'all Been Warned"; "Too Hot" and "Who U Rep With" showcase above-average cameos from Nas. As a smart distillation of the kind of anything-goes mixes sold on Canal Street in downtown NYC, *Guess Who's Back?* is plenty solid.

By the time 50 recorded *Get Rich,* his main producers Em and Dr. Dre knew they had a potential monster on their hands, and the album succeeded in exploiting both gangsta rap's brawniness and its unflappable cool, not to mention its clichés. Dre, Eminem, and a handful of lesser-known producers were at the top of their game on *Get Rich,* concocting alternately club-ready and spaced-out tracks from dark synth grooves, buzzy keyboards, and a persistently funky bounce. "Wanksta," one of Jam Master Jay's last productions, and the Dre-produced "In Da Club" tore up the pop charts, and it's easy to see why: Each sports a spare yet irresistible synth hook augmented by a tongue-twisting refrain; both sound anthemic even though they don't shout their messages. Elsewhere, the hooks are equally slick and powerful—the half-sung, half-shouted chants of "Life's on the Line," the slick steel drum on "P.I.M.P." Wandering stoned through this engaging sonic landscape, pulling off rounds like he's just cooking breakfast, drawling and balling, 50 complements the production with a steady, laid-back flow whose basic tenor is summed up in "Like My Style": "I'm a New Yorker, but I sound Southern." When Eminem pops up with two excellent cameos, on "Patiently Waiting" and "Don't Push Me," you kind of wish 50 could be as brassy and definitive. But his real strength lies in making thugism sound effortless, and much of the time he glides along so easily, you wonder if he's just freestyling.   —C.H.

Filter

★★   Short Bus (Reprise, 1996)
★★   Title of Record (Reprise, 1999)
★★   The Amalgamut (Reprise, 2002)

Former Nine Inch Nails collaborator Richard Patrick joined forces with programmer Brian Liesegang in Filter and made an immediate impact with "Hey Man, Nice Shot," the breakout single from the debut album, *Short Bus*. Widely—and, according to Filter, incorrectly—interpreted as a darkly sardonic tribute to Kurt Cobain, the song was as significant for its sonics as for its disturbing imagery. It finds a middle ground between grunge's world-weary sense of melody and industrial rock's icy steel-pulse rhythms. But *Short Bus* otherwise fails to take its Nails-Nirvana hybrid beyond formula.

With Liesegang departed, Patrick jettisons the mutter-then-scream approach on *Title of Record*, choosing instead to expose the vulnerability behind the jackboot-and-trench-coat pose. Folk guitar underpins a postindustrial ballad, "Take a Picture," and Eastern percussion puts an intoxicating spin on "Miss Blue." Patrick can croon, but his sensitivity, such as it is, is oppressively downcast, and too many of the songs rehash the Jekyll-and-Hyde dynamics that became alternative rock's creative downfall. *The Amalgamut*, with Filter reconfigured as a four-piece rock band, is Patrick's uninspired bid to keep up with the Ozzfest new-metal audience.   —G.K.

Fischerspooner

★★★½   #1 (Capitol, 2003)

The flamboyant performance troupe Fischerspooner personified the polysexual fashion-oriented electroclash dance fad that grew out of the Williamsburg, Brooklyn, club scene. Formed by Art Institute of Chicago grads Casey Spooner and Warren Fischer, Fischerspooner put on elaborate choreographed stage shows that stripped pop music's sexy varnish to a noxious fume—they get busted lip-synching and have diva-style breakdowns onstage. After fierce bidding

wars for all things electro, the U.K.-based Ministry of Sound signed them for a reported $2 million, an unheard-of sum for a techno band. The buzz grew loudest in May 2002, when Fischerspooner staged six shows (at a reported cost of $300,000) at New York's Deitch Projects, a fashionable SoHo art gallery packed with celebrities and journalists. Not bad for a couple of art pranksters who supposedly had their first gig at a Starbucks and shopped for their sound at an East Village record store. After significant delays, Capitol finally released *#1* in February 2003, and the new-wave anthem "Emerge" became its first single. Yet, despite Fischerspooner seemingly drowning in its own hype, *#1*'s updated electro manages to stay fresh—a trans-Euro dance express out of New York City's gritty punk-rock renaissance.   —C.S.

Fishbone

★★★   Fishbone (Sony, 1985)
★★★   In Your Face (Columbia, 1986)
★★★★   Truth and Soul (Epic, 1988)
★★★½   The Reality of My Surroundings (Sony, 1991)
★★   Give a Monkey a Brain and He'll Swear He's the Center of the Universe (Columbia, 1993)
★★★   Chim Chim's Badass Revenge (Rowdy, 1996)
★★★   The Psychotic Friends Nuttwerx (Hollywood, 2000)
★★★   Live at the Temple Bar and More (Nuttsactor 5, 2002)
★★★★   The Essential Fishbone (Columbia/Legacy, 2003)

Fishbone was formed from a disparate, all-black odd-ball crew at a South Central Los Angeles junior high in 1979. Playing an orgasmic urban gumbo of punk, funk, and ska, the six-man band became a favorite of the L.A. postpunk scene; eventually, the group would become a notoriously powerful live act, opening for the Beastie Boys on their *Licensed to Ill* tour and co-headlining club tours with the Red Hot Chili Peppers. Fishbone's albums have some great moments, but they neither capture the excitement of the band's shows nor hold much commercial appeal; the band still plays to sold-out crowds, but it remains one of the shoulda-beens of '80s alternative rock.

Although Fishbone's 1985 self-titled debut forecasted good things with its essential, butt-wiggling "Party at Ground Zero," it suffered from reed-thin production. The band aimed higher with *In Your Face*, struggling to combine P-Funk, the Specials, and Black Flag, but didn't quite have the songs to pull it off. It all finally clicked on *Truth and Soul*, which was released in 1988; still in their early twenties but already tour veterans, the members of Fishbone were writing combustible anthems. Catchy tracks like "Bonin' in the Boneyard" sound like the musical wheels might fall off if the band dared to stop and breathe. Many songs contained social and political commentary: "Ma and Pa" decries the destructive behavior of divorcing parents, as leader Angelo Moore sings, "There's lots of moneys/for all the attorneys," who are the only winners in divorce. The band's Bone in the USA tour consolidated its strengths as a live act; simply put, there was no better conscious party to be found than a Fishbone show.

Followup *The Reality of My Surroundings* is even sharper productionwise, but its tunes aren't as memorable; the hard-charging *Give a Monkey a Brain and He'll Swear He's the Center of the Universe* is their most rocking disc. Sadly, before that record was released, guitarist Kendall Jones left the band after he apparently suffered a nervous breakdown. On the eve of Lollapalooza '93, the band was decimated, and it never truly recovered. Despite the additional departures of original/long-standing members drummer Philip "Fish" Fisher and keyboardist/trombonist Chris Dowd, Fishbone remains a potent live band; in its prime, it was a wholly unique beast. —P.R.

The "5" Royales

★★★★ Dedicated to You (1957; King, 1994)
★★★½ The "5" Royales Sing for You (1959; King, 1994)
★★½ The "5" Royales (1960; King, 1994)
★★★★½ Monkey Hips and Rice: The "5" Royales Anthology (Rhino, 1994)
★★★½ The Apollo Sessions (Collectables, 1995)
★★★ Take Me With You Baby (Cleopatra, 2000)

One of the crucial prerock R&B groups of the '50s, the "5" Royales (actually a sextet, thus the quotation marks) were formed in 1947, in Winston-Salem, NC, around lead vocalist Johnny Tanner, guitarist/songwriter Lowman Pauling, and, later, second lead Eugene Tanner (Johnny's brother). The Royales, originally known as the Royal Sons Quintet, a gospel group, began recording for the Apollo label in the early '50s; these sides (including several Royal Sons tracks) can be heard on Collectables' *The Apollo Sessions*. Pauling was already writing great, bluesy material like "Baby Don't Do It" and the risqué "Laundromat Blues" ("My baby's got the best machine, the best washing machine in town"). After switching to Cincinnati-based King Records in 1954, the group—one of the hardest-touring acts of the era—had fewer hits but made even better music. They also began releasing albums, the first and best of which was 1957's *Dedicated to You,* which led off with "Think," the

group's final Top 10 hit (#9 R&B), and is considered one of the finest '50s R&B albums. (*The "5" Royales Sing for You* and *The "5" Royales* followed, with diminishing returns.)

The group broke up in 1962 and was largely forgotten afterward, though their material wasn't. "Think" was revamped twice by James Brown, in 1960 and 1973, while both the Shirelles and the Mamas and the Papas had enormous hits with "Dedicated to the One I Love" in 1961 and 1967, respectively. In 1994, Rhino brought forth *Monkey Hips and Rice,* a brilliantly chosen two-CD anthology covering everything from the Royal Sons' early sides to a 1962 rerecording of the early single "Help Me Somebody." Unfortunately, the Rhino compilation is currently out of print, but it's worth the search. *Take Me With You Baby,* another collection, rounds up later material that isn't included on *Monkey Hips and Rice.* —M.M.

The Five Satins

★★★ The Five Satins Sing Their Greatest Hit (1982; Collectables, 1993)

In 1956, Fred Parris wrote a song for his doo-wop group, the Five Satins, titled "In the Still of the Nite" (sometimes listed as "[I'll Remember] In the Still of the Night"). Setting up in the basement of a New Haven church with a two-track tape machine, the Satins (only four sang on the record) made the most out of the crude conditions—the track's sludgy, dense sound threatened to engulf the singers, but the primitive nature of the recording actually added an exotic allure. (Reports that a truck can be heard in the background as it tools past the church are false, but the story makes for good myth.) Singing in a clear, heartfelt tenor, Parris proclaimed his love over a turgid rhythm as his fellow Satins voiced eerie, brooding "shoo-do-shoo-be-do" background chants that heightened both the romantic fiction of love in the shadows and a certain undercurrent of dread over what the morning would bring. Released initially on New Haven's local Standord label, "In the Still of the Nite" became the classic rock & roll story of a B side that gained more attention than the planned A side (in this case, "The Jones Girl"), and it inspired the New York–based Herald/Ember label to purchase the master and reissue it in the late spring of 1956. Today, "In the Still of the Nite" is a doo-wop classic, a song that has permanent rotation on the playlists of oldies stations and still earns Parris and his current group of Satins immediate standing ovations at oldies shows.

A year after "In the Still of the Nite," the Satins hit the Top 30 again with a far less ambiguous love song, "To the Aisle," which featured Bill Baker on lead vocal in place of Parris, who was in the army. Parris finished his tour of duty and returned to the group, but the hits ceased. *The Five Satins Sing Their Greatest Hits* proves, however, that the fellows were a formidable contingent, whether Baker or Parris was singing lead, even if their singles failed to muster much commercial enthusiasm. Of special note are "Shadows," with Baker delivering a masterful performance bursting with powerful feeling and conviction, and a sensitive interpretation of Bing Crosby's 1944 charttopper "I'll Be Seeing You." —D.M.

Flaming Lips

★★ The Flaming Lips (Restless, 1985)
★★ Hear It Is (1986; Restless, 1994)
★★★ Oh My Gawd!!! . . . The Flaming Lips (Restless, 1987)
★★★ Telepathic Surgery (1989; Restless, 1993)
★★★½ In a Priest Driven Ambulance (With Silver Sunshine Stares) (Restless, 1990)
★★★½ Hit to Death in the Future Head (Warner Bros., 1991)
★★★★½ Transmissions From the Satellite Heart (Warner Bros., 1993)
★★★★ Clouds Taste Metallic (Warner Bros., 1995)
★★★ Zaireeka (Warner Bros., 1997)
★★★ A Collection of Songs Representing an Enthusiasm for Recording . . . By Amateurs: 1984–1990 (Restless, 1998)
★★★★★ The Soft Bulletin (Warner Bros., 1999)
★★★ Finally the Punk Rockers Are Taking Acid 1983–1988 (Restless, 2002)
★★★ The Day They Shot a Hole in the Jesus Egg— The Priest Driven Ambulance Album, Demos, and Outtakes (Restless, 2002)
★★★★ Yoshimi Battles the Pink Robots (Warner Bros., 2002)

Rock has produced few stranger or more daring bands in the last 20 years than Oklahoma City's Flaming Lips, who embrace everything from merry prankster psychedelia to orchestral pop. At the outset, the Lips tried to bridge the seemingly insurmountable gap between Butthole Surfers–style dementia and bubblegum pop, with mixed results. Their early albums are jumbles of ideas, the weirdness genuine, the songs expansive and sometimes giddily incoherent. They're as much a response to hardcore punk's inflexible pithiness as to mainstream rock's polish.

With *In a Priest Driven Ambulance*, a coherent vision starts to peek through the chaos. It comes courtesy of an irony-free cover of the standard "(What a) Wonderful World," sung with wobbly conviction by Wayne Coyne. For all its disorienting ugliness and alienating strangeness, the world really is a wonderful place, the Lips insist—an unfashionable stance that the band would continue to explore with increasingly plangent results.

The addition of guitar-effects maestro Ronald Jones and monster drummer Stephen Drozd gave Coyne the musical muscle to carry out his ambitions, and on *Transmissions from the Satellite Heart,* the Lips fashioned their first masterpiece: the Buttholes-bubblegum fusion fully realized in sing-along noise anthems such as "Turn It On" and "Be My Head," and the strangely poignant "Pilot Can at the Queer of God." Despite the fluke hit "She Don't Use Jelly," the album transcends novelty. Its multilayered production rewards headphone scrutiny and inspires headbanging, thanks to Drozd's John Bonham–like beats.

Clouds Taste Metallic is a similarly obtuse but fascinating attempt at making a pop album, while *Zaireeka* represents the Lips at their most indulgent. It's impractical—a box set of four CDs designed to be played simultaneously—and inspiring in its loony ambition. At its best, *Zaireeka* allows listeners to feel as through they're not just hearing the music but standing inside it.

The Soft Bulletin marks a turning point. Instead of clouding Coyne's vulnerability in weirdness, the ornate orchestrations heighten it. The album uses offbeat subject matter—the dizziness caused by a head wound, a poisonous spider bite, two scientists competing to find the cure to a disease—as a doorway to universal subjects such as failure, perseverance, and mortality. Coyne's lyrics display a newfound directness that is disarming, while the retooled lineup bypasses rock in favor of sumptuously arranged, ultramelodic grandeur.

On the surface, *Yoshimi Battles the Pink Robots* is a return to the artfully conceived strangeness of the band's earlier work. Its cover image is a cartoon that depicts a tiny heroine facing off against a forbidding giant: a Power Puff girl versus Black Sabbath's "Iron Man," a not inaccurate simplification of the band's sound. There's a greater emphasis on computerized drumbeats and loops, with sometimes clumsy results. But there's no denying the emotional punch of the songs. Once again, Coyne strips away his emotional armor on "Do You Realize?," an anthem to transcending tragedy that suggests a cross between acoustic John Lennon and a Disney movie soundtrack. —G.K.

The Flamingos

★★★ Flamingo Serenade (1959; Collectables, 1991)
★★★ Flamingo Favorites (1960; Collectables, 1992)

★★★   Requestfully Yours (1960; Collectables, 1991)
★★★   The Sound of the Flamingos (1962; Collectables, 1991)
★★★★   Best of the Flamingos (Rhino, 1990)
★★★½   For Collectors Only (Collectables, 1992)
★★★   The Fabulous Flamingos (Collectables, 1992)
★★★★   The Moonglows and the Flamingos: Their First Recordings (UGGH Records, 2000)

The sweet science of doo-wop group harmony numbers in its pantheon few greater practitioners than the Chicago-based Flamingos, who formed in 1952 and had a viable career (at least as performers) into the early '70s. Formed by two sets of cousins—Zeke and Jake Carey (born in Bluefield and Pulaski, VA, respectively) and Paul Wilson and Johnny Carter (both Chicago natives)—who considered themselves black Jews, the group changed lineups and labels a few times during the '50s. The Flamingos' most notable work was with the formidable lead singer Sollie McElroy for the Chance label: The wondrous "Golden Teardrops" never charted, but it has since been kept alive on oldies stations as an early, great example of doo-wop. A sampling of their work from this period, as well as their work for Chess/Checker, can be heard on Rhino's *Doo Wop Box*.

In 1959, now fronted by lead singer Nate Nelson, the group signed with End Records. This was to be the Flamingos' most productive and most successful period. A sumptuous version of the ultraromantic ballad "I Only Have Eyes for You" rose to #11 on the pop chart in 1959, and was followed in mid-1960 by the Sam Cooke–penned "Nobody Loves Me Like You," which peaked at #30. That would be the group's last charting single, even though it recorded voluminously at End before returning briefly to Checker in 1964, releasing four albums between 1960 and 1962, all of which have been reissued by Collectables. The albums document the group's broadening musical palette, which changed along with the times. Minimalist arrangements give way to lush orchestrations with strings, woodwinds, and horns; the love ballads are balanced by exotic fare on the order of "Besame Mucho" and "Mio Amore," Broadway show tunes, and golden-age pop.

Although the group continued to record into the late '60s, the End years were in fact the end of the Flamingos as a productive, creative entity. As an alternative to the individual albums on Collectables, the double-CD *For Collectors Only* is a 42-track summation of this period, featuring "I Only Have Eyes for You" and a stunning, unspeakably beautiful reading of "I'll Be Home" previously unissued on any other album. There's a lot of buried treasure on the End al-

bums, though, and to ignore them is to underestimate a great group that always kept the faith vocally, whether singing alone, with only a few instruments playing discreetly in the background, or with a full orchestra in unrestrained flight. The group's impeccable harmonies and haunting falsetto flourishes, along with Nate Nelson's genius for lyric interpretation, created doo-wop that had the ability to move the human heart in profound ways.   —D.M.

Flamin' Groovies

★★½   Supersnazz (1969; Sundazed, 2000)
★★★   Flamingo (1970; Buddha, 1999)
★★★★   Teenage Head (1971; Buddha, 1999)
★★★½   Shake Some Action (Sire, 1976)
★★★   Now (Sire, 1978)
★★★   Jumpin' in the Night (Sire, 1979)
★★★★   Groovies' Greatest Grooves (Sire, 1989)
★★   Rock Juice (National, 1992)
★★½   A Collection of Rare Demos & Live Recordings (1992; Marilyn, 1994)
★★★   California Born and Bred (Norton, 1995)
★★½   Supersneakers (Sundazed, 1996)
★★★   In Person!!!! (Norton, 1997)
★★½   Absolutely the Best (1999; Fuel, 2000)
★★   Backtracks (Ranch Life, 2000)
★★★   Slow Death (Norton, 2002)

Some of the greatest riffs of the '60s garage-rock revolution were written in the '70s by San Francisco's Flamin' Groovies—a disconnection that severely curtailed their popularity in their own time but only augmented their legend as the garage scene swelled into an obsessively historicized revival in the '80s and '90s. Their rediscovery led to literally dozens of reissues and bootlegs of live concerts, demos, and other unreleased recordings, of which only a fraction remain widely available. The Groovies' influence is tough to trace since the band's sound is deliberately derivative, but their stripped-down worship of the fundamentals of rock during a decade of excess certainly turned some ears at the dawn of punk, particularly after they moved to England and hooked up with pub rocker extraordinaire Dave Edmunds.

The Groovies formed in 1965 but did not record a disc until 1968's mini-album *Sneakers,* collected with some contemporaneous live tracks on *Supersneakers.* All the basic Groovies elements were loosely in place: the chugging Chuck Berry riffs, the Beatles melodies, the dreamy Byrds chords, the Jaggeresque snarl. But it wasn't until their first proper album, *Supersnazz,* that the young group perfected its distinctive boogie—a heavy mid-tempo swagger leavened by clean, melodic guitar lines and a friendly beat—or its exact relationship to the oldies. *Supersnazz* does that, honoring "The Girl Can't Help It" and "Rockin' Pneumonia and the Boogie Woogie Flu" by not robbing the originals of their beautiful sleaze.

Flamingo and *Teenage Head* tighten the groove but do not budge an inch when it comes to the band's anti-nostalgic vision—they saw themselves as keeping a tradition *alive*, not dancing with a corpse. There's nothing the band recorded during this period that isn't lean, mean, and pulsing with the passion of all the great rockers they sought to emulate; *Teenage Head* itself is a fierce garage-rock masterpiece that in spots ("Yesterday's Numbers," "High Flyin' Baby") handily competes with the best of the Stones of the same period. The Groovies' raw power is especially clear on some of the posthumous collections of demos and rehearsal tracks lovingly collected by Norton and other labels. *California Born and Bred* has some blazing run-throughs of the Who, Little Richard, and Chuck Berry covers, clearly unintended for public consumption, yet in all their raggedness, they now seem vital to the Groovies' story. *In Person!!!!* has a killer Fillmore West show from 1971, *Slow Death* demos, and TV appearances.

By 1972 the band was having much greater success in Europe than the States, so leader Cyril Jordan moved the group to England. (The other songwriting force, Roy Loney, was edged out and replaced by Chris Wilson.) *Shake Some Action* and *Now,* produced by Dave Edmunds, have a lighter sound, closer to the Byrds and *Revolver*-era Beatles than to *Beggars Banquet*. They even cover a couple early Beatles songs, "Misery" and "There's a Place." These albums are slightly more consistent than the earlier records and add smart new textures of guitar and vocal harmonies, but they lack the lust and rhythmic heft of the San Francisco years. (Both, along with the slightly lesser *Jumpin' in the Night,* sadly are out of print, though once again it speaks to the oddity of their legend that it's easier to get many bootlegs than their original albums.)

The band's legend grew during the '80s, and by 1992 a disc of new material emerged under the Groovies' name. But on close inspection, *Rock Juice* credits only two musicians, Jordan and original bassist George Alexander, a slight relief given the weak material.

Despite a vast posthumous discography of demos, B sides, etc., the Groovies have only a handful of true anthologies. The best is *Groovies' Greatest Grooves,* a 24-track retrospective that gets almost everything, including the best of the band's many non-LP singles ("Slow Death," "Tallahassee Lassie"), though it's heavy on the Edmunds years and omits some essentials from the *Teenage Head* era. —B.S.

The Flatlanders

★★★★½ More a Legend Than a Band (1972; Rounder, 1992)
★★★½ Now Again (New West, 2002)
★★★ Wheels of Fortune (New West, 2004)
★★★ Live at the Kite: June 8, 1972 (New West, 2004)

More a Legend Than a Band, recorded in Nashville in 1971, was a masterpiece of the "high and lonesome" Texas country style created by an outlaw C&W supergroup—Joe Ely, Jimmie Dale Gilmore, and Butch Hancock—a musical family of great depth and resolute individuality. The album's acoustic approach (guitars, Dobro, mandolin, fiddle, and string bass) and the loping rhythms of this short-lived septet, which was based in Lubbock, TX, mix lead singer Gilmore's expressive voice and Steve Wesson's quavering musical saw for a plaintive sound that is beautifully evocative of prairie vistas. The songs, chiefly written by Gilmore and Hancock, revolve around the escape from and return to the unrelenting uniformity of the West Texas landscape and small-town life. Gilmore's writing has a spiritual quality (evidenced in "Tonight I'm Gonna Go Downtown," an enthralling glimpse of existential rootlessness) wholly reinforced by his eye for telling, unpretentious images ("Have you ever seen Dallas from a DC-9 at night?/Well, Dallas is a jewel, oh yeah, Dallas is a beautiful sight").

In the years after *More a Legend Than a Band* was recorded, Ely, Gilmore, and Hancock developed into independent-minded artists and arresting performers: Ely as a dyed-in-the-wool roots rocker and versatile singer; Gilmore as a honky-tonk troubadour in the best Lone Star tradition; and Hancock as a Dylanesque folkie and movingly poetic songwriter. They reconvened exactly 30 years after cutting their masterpiece to record the solid, workmanlike *Now Again;* although it holds together just fine, it doesn't resonate. Fans, however, were delighted to have more Flatlanders music at long last, even if tempered by its, well, ordinariness. *Wheels of Fortune,* the individually written second effort by the reunited principals, was just a little bit more ordinary. Sometimes what becomes a legend most is to remain a legend. —D.WY./B.SC.

Fleetwood Mac

★★★★ Fleetwood Mac (Blue Horizon/Epic, 1968)
★★★★ English Rose (Epic/Columbia, 1969)
★★★★½ The Pious Bird of Good Omen (Blue Horizon/CBS, 1969)
★★★ Fleetwood Mac in Chicago (1969; Sire/Warner, 1975)

There are essentially three Fleetwood Macs: the first, a British blues-rock band in the vein of the Yardbirds; the second, a dreamy, laid-back California-style pop outfit; and the third—well, that's the '70s hit-making, dysfunctional, made-for-TV, hippie family unit we've all come to know and love from reruns of *Behind the Music.*

Fleetwood Mac's earliest studio albums are difficult to find, but they comprise such an essential part of the band's catalogue that you can't just pretend they never existed. Inspired by fellow British blues revivalist John Mayall, Fleetwood Mac began life as a straight-ahead blues band, named after its rhythm section: drummer Mick Fleetwood and bassist John McVie. The group's calling card, however, was the twin-guitar attack of Peter Green and Jeremy Spencer, who wielded a sure, sensitive hand with their oft-abused source material. *Fleetwood Mac* and *English Rose* revolve around Green's economical lead lines and Spencer's Elmore James–style slide work; Carlos Santana plucked the guitar solo nearly intact for his own enduring version of Mac's "Black Magic Woman," from *English Rose. Fleetwood Mac in Chicago* (which wasn't released domestically until the mid-'70s) finds the group recording in the Windy City with its American blues heroes, including Willie Dixon and Buddy Guy.

Then Play On is Fleetwood Mac's transition from blues purists to a band that blends elements of psychedelia and British folk rock into a cool, blues-based stew. Adding a third guitarist, Danny Kirwan, and emphasizing Mick Fleetwood's adventurous rhythmic sense alongside Green's virtuosity, the group conjures a sparse, propulsive sound that's more reminiscent of the American West than Chicago or the Mississippi Delta. On the epic "Oh Well," an itchy electric-acoustic shuffle turns into a stately semiclassical fade with echoes of Ennio Morricone's spaghetti-western soundtrack music. More compact cuts like "Coming Your Way" and "Before the Beginning" pack the tangled guitar lines into clear melodic structures, while "Rattlesnake Shake" proves those guitar strings can still sputter and burn when required. The gentle harmonies of Kirwan's "Although the Sun Is Shining" showcase British progressive folk rock at its most spare and beautiful, as well as hints of Fleetwood Mac's future, more pop-oriented sound.

After *Then Play On,* Green split for a religious cult and a brief solo career (*End of the Game*) followed by early retirement. With Kirwan and Spencer in control, *Kiln House* is a low-key charmer, radically different from what folks expected from the blues-based Mac. Balancing spare folk and country songs with earnest nods to early rock & roll, the album is at once eclectic and cohesive. The gently rocking tributes to Buddy Holly (all three of 'em!) point out the difference between loose and sloppy, while the orgasmic guitar workouts (all three of 'em!) build to lazy, quivering peaks. Spencer left shortly after the album came out, and Fleetwood Mac was down to one guitarist. The addition of Christine McVie (née Perfect) on keyboards and vocals turned out to be an important choice. Spencer's replacement, Bob Welch, was another matter; he never quite gelled with the rest of the group, despite his years of trying.

Flashes of Fleetwood Mac's latter-day pop can be found throughout the band's next set of transitional albums: the smooth talk of Kirwan's title track to *Bare Trees;* Christine's disarming "Show Me a Smile" (*Future Games*); her breezily melodic "Remember Me" (*Penguin*) and "Just Crazy Love" (*Mystery to Me*); and her stately ballad "Come a Little Bit Closer" (*Heroes Are Hard to Find*). Taken individually, however, these fair-to-middling albums are too scattershot to hold much interest. When Kirwan left the group after *Bare Trees* came out, Fleetwood Mac floundered for several years—split between the heavy-handed pseudomysticism of Welch and the gentle, mainstream pop-rock balladry of Christine McVie. The group nearly splintered for good at one point; when Welch left in 1975, the McVies and Fleetwood were back at square one.

Stevie Nicks and Lindsey Buckingham were a young, Southern California folk-rock duo with one unremarkable album (*Buckingham Nicks*) under their belts when they joined Fleetwood Mac. Nicks' sultry voice and Buckingham's songwriting knack focused the group's fledgling pop ambitions. On Fleetwood Mac's self-titled album of 1975, Nicks and Buckingham not only fit in, but they stimulated the core trio, turning the group into a hit-making machine at the point when Fleetwood Mac was about to become a has-been. Christine McVie responded to the Buckingham-Nicks material with a brace of catchy songs, while John McVie and Mick Fleetwood lent their blues-rock punch to the smoothed-out mix. The result is easy-listening pop with a kick, and it was just what mainstream music fans were looking for in the mid-'70s. By the following year *Fleetwood Mac* was at #1, easily outdistancing all the band's previous efforts.

The album kicks off with Buckingham's infectious "Monday Morning" and then builds to new levels of pop-music pleasure with each subsequent track. "Rhiannon" establishes Nicks' seductive, sirenlike presence, while "Say You Love Me" unfurls Christine McVie's wry melodic edge. Unlike many blockbusters, the surrounding songs nearly equal the hits. In addition to the bouncy opener, Buckingham struts his tuneful stuff on the heavy centerpiece "World Turning" and soulful closer "I'm So Afraid." What's more, the slow tracks never impinge on the album's overall pace.

Rumours is even better. Using the same formula that propelled *Fleetwood Mac,* the band upped the quality of the songs. Not only did the album go to #1, it stayed there for 31 weeks! Fleetwood Mac's cast of voices cuts even deeper when you consider that the two couples in the group were breaking up as the album went down. Buckingham's "Go Your Own Way" and Nicks' "Dreams" spell out two clear takes on a romantic dilemma. *Rumours* can be heard as a conversation among a loose circle of estranged lovers, culminating with "The Chain" (written by the entire group).

After striking such a perfect balance between self-expression and commercial appeal, Fleetwood Mac succumbed to studio artiness. The double-disc *Tusk* reveals Buckingham's secret fixation: to become Brian Wilson with a touch of Brian Eno thrown in. "Sara" maintains the band's pop profile, but the bulk of *Tusk* sounds cold and fussy next to the emotional heat of *Rumours.* On *Mirage,* Fleetwood Mac returns to simple pleasures, but the band seems to have lost its spirit. Reconvening five years later on *Tango in the Night,* the group carries on as if it were still 1982—or 1977. The hits "Big Love" and (especially) Christine McVie's "Little Lies" surge with all the relaxed soft-rock grace of yore but none of the quiet fire, hinting at a premature nostalgia. Buckingham quit the band prior to the 1987 tour; in retrospect, that last straw seems to have broken this venerable band's back.

Buckingham's L.A. cowboy replacements (Rick Vito and Billy Burnette) add little to the washed-out *Behind the Mask.* When Nicks left shortly after that album's release, Fleetwood Mac entered yet another phase, though short-lived. In spite of the capable vocals of new female singer Bekka Bramlett (Delaney & Bonnie's daughter) and guitar work of Traffic alum Dave Mason, *Time* proved to be a full-on bore. Fleetwood Mac's '70s-era lineup reunited for *The Dance,* but it seemed more of a business decision than an aesthetic one. In an *MTV Unplugged* setting, the band unavoidably devotes most of the album to repeats of its peak-era hits ("Dreams," "Rhiannon," "Go Your Own Way"), but they bring absolutely nothing fresh to the proceedings. The best cuts are new ones by Buckingham ("Bleed to Love Her" and "My Little Demon"), but they get buried in the nostalgia fest. For a band that practically became a brand-name franchise in the late '70s, Fleetwood Mac set a standard of quality that's proven tough to maintain—or equal.

Not surprisingly, for an outfit as schizophrenic as Fleetwood Mac, none of its collections adequately captures the band. *The Pious Bird* is an excellent overview of the group's early Peter Green period, and the 1988 *Greatest Hits* package is a decent collection of the Buckingham-Nicks era. *25 Years: The Chain* is frustrating; if ever there was a band for which a chronological overview is appropriate, it's Fleetwood Mac, whose evolution from blues to pop came slowly but dramatically. For whatever reasons, the compilers chose to mix and mingle the eras on this four-disc set, and it suffers as a result.   —M.C./M.K.

A Flock of Seagulls

★★★ A Flock of Seagulls (Jive, 1982)
★★★ The Best of a Flock of Seagulls (Jive, 1987)
★★★ Platinum & Gold Collection (Jive/BMG Heritage, 2003)
★ I Ran: The Best of (Cleopatra, 2004)

In its prime, Liverpool's A Flock of Seagulls was essentially a two-gimmick band, the first being its blend of minor-key melodies and low-tech electronics, the second being singer Mike Score's hair, an astonishingly ambitious bit of pompadour that spilled over his forehead like a breaking wave. Score's look, along with the arty urgency of the Bill Nelson–produced "Telecommunication," lent *A Flock of Seagulls* a certain cutting-edge sheen at the time, but the old-fashioned hooks of "I Ran" earned the group an audience. Four subsequent albums have gone out of print; no great loss, since the Gulls ran out of compelling ideas pretty fast. The cream of their later catalogue, including the minor hits "Wishing (If I Had a Photograph of You)" and "The More You Live, the More You Love," can be found on *The Best of a Flock of Seagulls.* Swap a handful of that album's lesser-known tunes for a few even more lesser-known ones and you've got *Platinum & Gold Collection*. *I Ran*, misleadingly called a best-of, is actually a bunch of tacky rerecordings perpetrated by Score at the dawn of the 21st century. Steer well clear. —J.D.C./M.R.

The Flying Burrito Brothers

★★★★★ The Gilded Palace of Sin (1969; Edsel, 1994)
★★★½ Burrito Deluxe (1970; Edsel, 1994)
★★★ The Flying Burrito Brothers (1971; A&M/Mobile Fidelity Sound Lab, 1991)
★★★ Last of the Red Hot Burritos (1972; Rebound, 1995)
★★★½ Close Up the Honky-Tonks (A&M, 1974)
★★★★ Farther Along: The Best of the Flying Burrito Brothers (A&M, 1988)
★★★★★ Hot Burritos! The Flying Burrito Brothers Anthology: 1969–1972 (A&M, 2000)
★★★ The Millennium Collection: The Best of the Flying Burrito Brothers (A&M, 2001)
★★★★ Sin City: The Very Best of the Flying Burrito Brothers (Universal, 2002)

After a very brief stint with the Byrds that resulted in the country-flavored *Sweetheart of the Rodeo*, Gram Parsons took his vision of "cosmic American music" and joined forces with fellow ex-Byrd Chris Hillman and Texas bassist Chris Ethridge to form the pioneering country-rock band the Flying Burrito Brothers. Their first and most satisfying effort, *The Gilded Palace of Sin*—unfortunately out of print in the U.S.—strives for a deep understanding of the honky-tonk tradition, digging beneath the good-timin' Saturday-night veneer of hard-core country to get at the music's emotional depths. The sound is a true fusion: volatile, shaky at times, but always stimulating. The band enlisted pedal-steel guitarist "Sneaky" Pete Kleinow, who blended the instrument's syrupy cry with fuzzy rock guitar riffs. The songs mix traditional country themes with contemporary specifics. At times, it's pleasantly effective; at other times, it's enticingly weird. The psychedelic riff at the end of "Hippie Boy" creeps along like a longhair walking past a church parking lot on Sunday morning, while "My Uncle" is a twangy draft dodger's road anthem. Parsons' breaking tenor voice isn't a powerful instrument, but his matter-of-fact tone and affectless delivery speak of the personal commitment that's so central to country singing. Covering the Southern soul classics "Dark End of the Street" and "Do Right Woman" in high honky-tonk fashion, Parsons and the Burritos unearth some deeply buried roots. The emotional high points, however, lie within the originals "Hot Burrito #1" and "Hot Burrito #2."

Burrito Deluxe—also out of print—jacks up the rock quotient and includes the addition of future Eagle Bernie Leadon. The results are far less intriguing, though the cover of the Stones' "Wild Horses" may well be definitive, and the songs "Cody, Cody" and "God's Own Singer" rank among the Burritos' finest. The best tracks from *Deluxe* are included on the *Farther Along* set; so is most of the debut, though "Hippie Boy" and "My Uncle" are inexplicably absent. The anthology *Close Up the Honky-Tonks* does include those songs, along with other cuts from the first two albums as well as outtakes.

After Parsons split from the Burritos in 1970, guitarist Rick Roberts joined up with Hillman. *The Flying Burrito Brothers* hints at the encroaching blandness that would later dog both Roberts and Hillman. However, *Last of the Red Hot Burritos* is a fiery farewell from this edition of the group. Bolstered by bluegrass fiddler Byron Berline on several cuts, the Hillman-led Burritos charge through a live set of mostly Parsons-era material with a verve that's missing from their other work.

Before the release of the live album, the Burritos split up briefly but then reunited after Parsons' death, in 1973. The band has since toured and recorded with a revolving-door lineup that often includes no original members whatever. The Burritos haven't put out anything memorable since their early-'70s heyday, although several worthwhile Parsons-era collections have appeared. Most notable among them is the comprehensive double-disc *Hot Burritos! The Flying Burrito Brothers Anthology: 1969–1972*, which compiles the first two albums in their entirety plus lots of extra stuff. The rest, while good, merely recycle songs on the better compilations. —M.C./M.K.

John Fogerty

★★½ Blue Ridge Rangers (1973; Fantasy, 1991)
★★★½ John Fogerty (Asylum, 1975)
★★★ Centerfield (Warner Bros., 1985)
★★½ Eye of the Zombie (Warner Bros., 1986)
★★★½ Blue Moon Swamp (Warner Bros., 1997)
★★★½ Premonition (Warner Bros., 1998)

John Fogerty's solo albums decisively prove that Creedence Clearwater Revival was a phenomenal band. While his own raw guitar and rawer vocals clearly dominated America's best straight rock outfit of the early '70s, the ramshackle grace of CCR's rhythm section provided crucial, spontaneous verve. Urgency, in fact, was Creedence's hallmark. The band responded to its fitful times with songs crammed with messages and metaphors of tumult and apocalypse: Vietnam, America's own civil war, and the crashing end of the utopian '60s provoked remarkable songwriting from Fogerty and great, ragged playing from the group.

While crafty and sometimes entertaining, Fogerty's early solo records lack the spontaneity inherent in inspired collaboration, and his once edgy lyrics are blunted. No longer confronted with high-profile upheaval, he doesn't have much to say about America's more insidious, ongoing crisis; here, he trades mainly in nostalgia or writes good-time stuff. A well-meaning attempt to pay tribute to Hank Williams, Jimmie Rodgers, Merle Haggard, and trad country music, *Blue Ridge Rangers* is actually Fogerty alone in the studio, playing everything. Such hermeticism, of course, is the antithesis of the familial spirit of classic country, and while Fogerty's musicianship is impressive, it's a cold virtuosity. Even more unfortunate are his vocals. With Creedence, Fogerty expertly mimicked blues belters (Screamin' Jay Hawkins), but steered wisely clear of its subtler interpreters (Muddy Waters, Robert Johnson). On *Blue Ridge,* he's deaf to the complex grace of country singing, hitting all the notes but missing the nuance.

On *John Fogerty*'s "Rockin' All Over the World" and "Almost Saturday Night," he returns, thankfully, to rock & roll. A solid set, though a little too heavy on (pro forma) oldies, the album is Creedence-lite. Hailed at the time as a return to form, *Centerfield* (1985) hasn't held up. "The Old Man Down the Road" is functional swamp rock, "Rock and Roll Girls" is charming but slight, and attempts at his former, seemingly effortless significance fall flat: Neither the title track's baseball-player/journeyman-rocker metaphor nor the baby-boom elegy "I Saw It on TV" lead anywhere. The music, at times, tries to extend beyond Fogerty's trad-rock limits, bespeaking commendable ambition, but the syn-drum break on "Vanz Kant Danz" is the kind of thing a Spandau Ballet roadie could have handled with more panache. The lovely "Sail Away," from *Eye of the Zombie,* features Fogerty's best singing in years; the rest of the record, however—all studio gloss and labored funking—simply marks the high point of his professionalism. And for this soulful artist, *professionalism* should be a dirty word.

In 1997, after a decade's hiatus, he astonishingly returned to strength. *Blue Moon Swamp,* edgily produced and driven by the powerhouse single "Southern Streamline," was vintage Fogerty: primal rock & roll sung in a voice deepened by experience. Somewhat in the fashion of the grizzled Neil Young, Fogerty was hailed as an elder statesman of jagged guitar power and roots-rock credibility and saw his album rewarded with a Grammy for Best Rock Album. The following year, he released the strong live *Premonition,* a tour de force featuring new work and CCR classics.   —P.E.

Folk Implosion

★★★½	Take a Look Inside the Folk Implosion (Communion, 1994)
★★★	Kids: Original Motion Picture Soundtrack (PolyGram, 1995)
★★★	Dare to Be Surprised (Communion, 1997)
★★★½	One Part Lullaby (Interscope, 1999)
★★	The New Folk Implosion (Imusic, 2003)

The Folk Implosion started as a Sebadoh side project, teaming Lou Barlow with indie glam-folkie balladeer John Davis. *Take a Look Inside the Folk Implosion* was a lightweight goof, rocking through 14 catchy songs in 22 minutes, with ramshackle highlights such as "Slap Me" and "Shake a Little Heaven." The story took a strange turn when the Folk Implosion did most of the soundtrack for the cheesy 1995 movie *Kids* and found itself with an accidental Top 40 hit after Modern Rock radio started playing "Natural One." It wasn't the best song on the soundtrack—that honor goes to Slint's "Good Morning, Captain"—but it was adventurous studio pop, meandering around a moody bass line and a Left Banke sample. The success of "Natural One" seemed to break new ground for the band, but the Folk Implosion had no interest in following it up, and *Dare to Be Surprised* was back-to-basics indie rock. *One Part Lullaby* was a surprisingly songful return, especially since it appeared just a few months after a lousy Sebadoh album. But the Folk Implosion had picked the worst imaginable time to go major label, and hardly anyone was listening. Davis' solo work on the Shrimper label is swoonier and moonier than the Folk Implosion: Check out 1994's *Pure Night* first, and then investigate 1995's *Leave Home* and 1997's *Blue Mountains.* In 2003 Barlow delivered *The New Folk Implosion,* recorded without Davis; the result was a bush-league, slightly crisper version of Sebadoh.   —R.S.

Foo Fighters

★★★★	Foo Fighters (Roswell/Capitol, 1995)
★★★★	The Colour and the Shape (Roswell/Capitol, 1997)
★★½	There Is Nothing Left to Lose (RCA, 1999)
★★★½	One by One (Roswell/RCA, 2002)

Who'd have thought it? Turns out Nirvana had *two* great songwriters. A year after Kurt Cobain's suicide, Dave Grohl rebounded with Foo Fighters' self-titled debut, on which he wrote and played practically everything himself. Unsurprisingly, he favors the explosive riff-rockers that let him show off his specialty, the apotheosis of punk-rock drumming. The surprises are a couple of tender pop tunes (including the hit "Big

Me") and the confident melodies behind the torrential momentum of songs like "This Is a Call" and "I'll Stick Around."

By the time they recorded *The Colour and the Shape,* Foo Fighters had become a real band, including fellow Nirvana alumnus Pat Smear on second guitar and Sunny Day Real Estate's Nate Mendel; thanks to drummer turbulence, Grohl ended up playing most of the drums himself again. Nobody complained: On tracks like the loud-louder-loudest love song "Everlong," his drumming provides plenty of hooks on its own. *Colour* is the classic-rock album Grohl had waiting to come out of him, with as much Queen as Pixies in its bloodline. The band piledrives everything with maximum force—"Hey, Johnny Park!" is essentially a mid-'70s ballad with a barrel of rocket fuel under its ass.

There Is Nothing Left to Lose, featuring the full band, is a bit of a disappointment. Its lead-off single, "Learn to Fly," became a hit, but the production and songwriting seem somehow tamed. The album has way too much filler and suggests that Grohl & Co. were trying so hard to sound like everything else on Modern Rock radio that they sanded off all the splintery edges that made them exciting in the first place.

One by One is much more like it, a partial return to the attitude and force of *The Colour and the Shape,* with longtime live drummer Taylor Hawkins coming into his own. There are a handful of references to Grohl's get-in-the-van origins (allusions to Hüsker Dü on "Times Like These," cover artwork by Black Flag affiliate Raymond Pettibon), but the album's most exciting moments are variations on Grohl's favorite formulas: "Tired of You," where he braces for a Nirvana-style explosion that never arrives, and the radio hit "Low," whose instruments skip across the mix like stones on a white-water river. —D.W.

Foreigner

★★★½ Foreigner (Atlantic, 1977)
★★★½ Double Vision (Atlantic, 1978)
★★★ Head Games (Atlantic, 1979)
★★★½ 4 (Atlantic, 1981)
★★★★ Records (Atlantic, 1982)
★★★½ Agent Provocateur (Atlantic, 1984)
★★★ Inside Information (Atlantic, 1987)
★★½ Unusual Heat (Atlantic, 1991)
★★★½ The Very Best . . . and Beyond (Atlantic, 1992)
★★ Classic Hits Live (Atlantic, 1993)
★★½ Mr. Moonlight (Rhythm Safari, 1995)
★★★ Jukebox Heroes: The Foreigner Anthology (Rhino/Atlantic Remasters, 2000)

Even though Boston, Heart, and Styx, among others, deserve credit for inventing '70s arena rock, no band parlayed the stadium sound with such dependable know-how as Foreigner. The key to the band's success has been main man Mick Jones. A battle-scarred, hit-savvy veteran who played with the artful organ-rock outfit Spooky Tooth before founding platinum-selling Foreigner, Jones is not only a master of the hook but also a guitarist of unerring efficiency. In Foreigner's early days, former King Crimson multi-instrumentalist Ian McDonald added a touch of class, but Jones' passion for a streamlined sound meant that the band was soon reduced to a smarter, trimmer rhythm-section core.

And, of course, there's ace vocalist Lou Gramm. Not quite a stylist on the order of Bad Company's Paul Rodgers, Gramm is still one of the finest singers in all of pop metal. Gramm's gift lay in roughening up Jones' shimmering grooves; Gramm brought an R&B, almost bluesy style to bear on the band's rockers, and in time, he became the Pavarotti of the power ballad.

Foreigner's catalogue of car-stereo hits is nearly unrivaled: "Feels Like the First Time," "Cold as Ice" *(Foreigner);* "Hotblooded" *(Double Vision);* "Dirty White Boy" *(Head Games);* "Waiting for a Girl Like You" *(4).* The canny Jones kept the sound fresh by working with different producers on each album and supplying the perfect surprising flourish (Junior Walker's sax coda on "Urgent," for example) for each hit. The band's high point came with *Agent Provocateur*'s "I Want to Know What Love Is"— backed by a gospel choir, Gramm belted away with commendable anguish. *Inside Information* also displayed his growth as a vocalist, and the record's synth-work saw Foreigner keeping pace with the times. By the time of *Unusual Heat,* however, Jones had asked Gramm to depart. New singer Johnny Edwards was ultracompetent, but he hadn't yet developed a distinctive style. *Heat* marked a return to Foreigner's reliable, full-out rocking standard. A complete comeback in terms of original vision didn't take place until 1995's *Mr. Moonlight,* for which Gramm was coaxed back into the fold. It was solid rock, but Foreigner's moment had long passed. *Records* is the group's tightest greatest-hits collection. Every bar band in the world has burned out several copies. —P.E.

Fountains of Wayne

★★★½ Fountains of Wayne (Tag/Atlantic, 1996)
★★★ Utopia Parkway (Tag/Atlantic, 1999)
★★★★ Welcome Interstate Managers (Virgin/ S Curve, 2003)

If Nirvana was the voice of the youthful, emergent Generation X of the early '90s, then New York's Fountains of Wayne are the voice of the same generation a few years on, in the midst of an extended adolescence. Adam Schlesinger and Chris Collingwood, the group's songwriting team, were in their late 20s when they released their self-titled debut, and on that record they write knowingly of characters navigating the gray area between adolescence and adulthood. The band wraps these vignettes in Beatles-influenced melodies that are endearingly sweet and catchy.

Fountains of Wayne ditch the Beatles homage for *Utopia Parkway,* infusing the album with more of a rock sensibility. The lyrics are less insightful this time, but the sweetness remains, particularly on "Troubled Times," a gentle reminiscence of a botched love. *Welcome Interstate Managers* is the band's best album to date—the lyrics are attention-grabbingly smart and the songs are so catchy it's maddening. The Beatles influence has returned, but this time it's diversified with nods to the Byrds, the Cars, and even Simon and Garfunkel. The songs still deal with the same Gen X–angsty topics as before, but now they show a bit of personal growth: "I'm gonna get my shit together" go the (albeit slightly tongue-in-cheek) lyrics to "Bright Future in Sales." It seems the band may be close to embracing adulthood after all.   —N.P.

The Four Seasons

★★★★★	Anthology (Rhino, 1988)
★½	The 20 Greatest Hits: Live (Curb, 1990)
★★★	Christmas Album (Rhino, 1991)
★★★★	Greatest Hits, Vol. 1 (Rhino, 1991)
★★★	Greatest Hits, Vol. 2 (Rhino, 1991)
★★★	Greatest Hits (Curb, 1991)
★½	Oh, What a Night (Curb, 1995)
★★★	Let's Hang On & 11 Others, Vol. 6 (Curb, 1995)
★★★	New Gold Hits, Vol. 7 (Curb, 1995)
★½	Who Loves You, Vol. 8 (Curb, 1995)
★★★½	Dawn (Go Away) and 11 Other Great Songs (Curb, 1995)
★★★	Big Girls Don't Cry and 12 Others (Curb, 1995)
★★★	Sherry (Curb, 1995)
★★★½	Rag Doll (Curb, 1995)
★★★½	Gold Vault of Hits (Curb, 1997)
★★★	Second Gold Vault of Hits (Curb, 1997)
★★★★★	In Season: The Frankie Valli & the 4 Seasons Anthology (Rhino, 2001)
★★★	Off Seasons: Criminally Neglected Sides (Rhino, 2001)

Doo-wop music didn't make it out of the '50s as a commercial force, but New Jersey's the Four Seasons, the genre's Caucasian branch, flourished in a form updated for the go-go '60s. Relying on tight doo-wop group harmony, an utterly distinctive lead tenor (Frankie Valli), and songs of love and loss—with added ballast for the new era provided by exquisite, visionary production that blended the best of Phil Spector–era rock & roll and Motown pop-soul sensibilities—the quartet topped the charts out of the box with "Sherry" in 1962 and maintained a steady presence in the Top 30 before its run petered out in 1968 with a perfectly serviceable remake of the Shirelles' hit "Will You Love Me Tomorrow." By then, the group had sold some 80 million records worldwide. Against all odds, a retooled Seasons lineup—still featuring the same utterly distinctive lead tenor—returned in 1975 and cut two more chart-topping hits before the singer took his songs and went solo for good.

There's a raft of splendid choices available for the hardcore Four Seasons fan as well as for the tourist who wants the prime cuts and nothing more. Among single-disc compilations, Rhino's 26-song *Anthology* assembles most of the '60s and '70s hits, including Valli's solo smash "Can't Take My Eyes Off You," and makes fanciful side trips, such as the 1965 version of Dylan's "Don't Think Twice" recorded by the Seasons in chipmunk voices under the *nom du disque* the Wonder Who. Rhino also offers two solid 15-song *Greatest Hits* collections, with *Vol. 1* completely devoted to the '60s classics, whereas *Vol. 2* includes the Seasons' '70s hits and Valli's solo material.

Curb has issued a trove of Four Seasons material in recent years, including long-out-of-print studio albums and the wonderful *Gold Vault of Hits* collections originally issued in the '60s by Phillips. The studio albums are a mixed bag but do contain some interesting off-road excursions beyond the hit tracks. Of special note is the 1964 album *Rag Doll,* with four blockbuster singles: the title song, "Ronnie," "Save It for Me," and the group's Top 10 cover of Cole Porter's "I've Got You Under My Skin." From the first note to the last, *Rag Doll* is a tour de force of exemplary pop singing. Another first-rate studio album is 1964's *Dawn (Go Away) and 11 Other Great Songs.* Here Valli and the guys return to their doo-wop roots on terrific versions of the Crests' "16 Candles," the Penguins' "Earth Angel," and the Willows' "Church Bells May Ring." There's also a solid interpretation of Sam Cooke's "You Send Me" along with, of course, the towering "Dawn."

Two offbeat titles are worth noting. Rhino's *Off Seasons: Criminally Neglected Sides* offers 20 cuts that purport to be overlooked Four Seasons gems. One of these, "Cry Myself to Sleep," is one of the best tear-jerking ballads the group ever recorded. Rhino also offers the group's only yuletide release, 1964's

The 4 Seasons Greetings, which had been out of print for 20 years when it was finally reissued in 1991. Produced by Bob Crewe, with orchestral arrangements by Sid Bass and Charles Calello and vocal arrangements by Nick Massi, *Greetings* is appropriate seasonal fare. By turns reverent and joyous, it comprises mostly familiar songs and carols—"I Saw Mommy Kissing Santa Claus," "What Child Is This," "The Little Drummer Boy," "Jingle Bells," a warm take on "White Christmas," and one new song penned by Crewe and Bass, "Christmas Tears," a bit bluesy but hardly dreary. Valli keeps the falsetto in check here, which was the right call for this material.

Ultimately, the collection to own is Rhino's 2001 double-CD *In Season: The Frankie Valli & the 4 Seasons Anthology,* which leaves no important '60s track unrepresented and also offers all the solo Valli and '70s Seasons tracks anyone really needs, plus detailed liner and session notes to boot. There's no going wrong with this one, especially the first disc, which contains the bulk of the overpowering '60s hits.   —D.M.

The Four Tops

★★★½	Four Tops (1965; Motown, 1989)
★★★	On Top (Tamla, 1966)
★★★	Live! (1967; Motown, 1991)
★★★½	Reach Out (1967; Motown, 1991)
★★★★	Greatest Hits (1967; Tamla, 1990)
★★½	Still Waters Run Deep (1970; Motown, 1982)
★★½	Changing Times (1970; Motown, 1990)
★★½	Back Where I Belong (Motown, 1983)
★★★	Ain't No Woman Like the One I Got (1987; MCA, 1994)
★★	When She Was My Girl (PolyGram, 1992)
★★★★	Until You Love Someone: More of the Best (Rhino, 1993)
★★★	Keepers of the Castle/Their Best 1972–1978 (MCA, 1997)
★★★★	Best of: The Ultimate Collection (Motown, 1997)
★★★★	Four Tops: The Millennium Collection (Motown, 1999)
★★★	Motown Lost and Found: Breaking Through '63–'64 (Motown, 1999)

As George Jones is to country and Roy Orbison is to early rock & roll, so is Levi Stubbs to '60s soul—its baroque expressionist. The other three Tops (Lawrence Payton, Renaldo Benson, Abdul Fakir) were fine, strong singers, but the fire of the most dramatic of all Motown groups was Stubbs, a vocalist to whom David Johansen and Billy Bragg have offered lyrical tributes. His style is simply synonymous with *yearning.*

The writer-producers Holland-Dozier-Holland found the perfect vehicle for their symphonic aspirations in the Tops—nothing outside of Phil Spector's epic work for the Righteous Brothers and Ike and Tina Turner rivals the sweep of "Baby I Need Your Loving," "It's the Same Old Song," "I Can't Help Myself," or especially "Reach Out I'll Be There" and "Standing in the Shadows of Love." On the last two numbers, both released in 1966, the Tops and Motown came of age via cinematic orchestral arrangements, lyrics of an utmost poetic immediacy, and the straining of Stubbs' voice toward a pitch of just-short-of-transcendent frustration, elements that heighten the spine-tingling intensity of the music. Gothic soul, of a sort.

Because they so perfectly embodied the spirit of Motown's heyday, the Four Tops conformed to poetic justice by becoming has-beens (if decent sellers) in the years that followed. Neither disco nor funk suited these operatic soulsters, and their departure from Motown, while adding two gems to their catalogue ("Keeper of the Castle," "Ain't No Woman Like the One I've Got"), didn't help greatly to revive their flame. Stick with the classics, best represented on *The Ultimate Collection* and the Rhino set.   —P.E.

Foxy Brown

★★★	Ill Na Na (Def Jam, 1996)
★★	Chyna Doll (Def Jam, 1999)
★★★	Broken Silence (Def Jam, 2001)

Half a decade after Queen Latifah first made a stand for hip-hop feminism, the dominant strategy for female empowerment in the rap game was simply to play the nasty card: If they're gonna call you a bitch and a ho, then be the nastiest damn bitch and the skankiest damn ho you can be. Questionable logic, to be sure—though Madonna rode a similar if less explicit whore/queen routine to global fame and lots of feminist hurrahs—but it spawned some of the '90s' boldest and most talented female rap stars. The former Inga Marchand of Brooklyn, who rechristened herself after a Pam Grier flick, was the biggest, and perhaps the nastiest. On *Ill Na Na* she makes bitch-positive declarations of sexuality ("If he don't do the right thing like Spike Lee/Bye-bye wifey, make him lose his Nikes/Hit the road") and boasts about the wild life; her relationship with men is both dependent—she announces "holy matrimony" with her crew, the Firm—and combatively, pornographically flirty. It's equality of the sexes at the lowest order. Then come the morning-after albums, which find her pushing the same material much harder (*Chyna Doll*'s "Dog & a Fox," a duet with DMX, is perhaps the crassest sex-therapy session ever: "Ya bitches suck a dick/Y'all niggaz eat a clit/Yeah, you think you fuckin' slick/Y'all niggaz ain't shit") and, whenever she isn't grabbing her crotch or cussing out sucka lady MCs, moaning with depression and regret: on *Broken Silence*'s "Fallin' " and "The Letter," she contemplates death, perhaps suicide. A hard-knock life indeed. —B.S.

Peter Frampton

★★	Wind of Change (1972; A&M, 2000)	
★	Frampton's Camel (1973; A&M, 2000)	
★	Something's Happening (1974; A&M, 2000)	
★	Frampton (1975; A&M, 2000)	
★★★½	Frampton Comes Alive! (1976; A&M, 2001)	
★	I'm in You (1977; A&M, 2000)	
★½	Where I Should Be (A&M, 1979)	
★	Breaking All the Rules (A&M, 1981)	
★	The Art of Control (A&M, 1982)	
★	Premonition (Atlantic, 1986)	
★	When All the Pieces Fit (Atlantic, 1989)	
★★★½	Classics, Vol. 12 (A&M, 1989)	
★★½	Shine On: A Collection (A&M, 1992)	
★	Peter Frampton (Sony Legacy, 1994)	
★★	Frampton Comes Alive II (IRS, 1995)	
★★★½	Greatest Hits (A&M, 1996)	
★★	The Very Best of Peter Frampton (A&M, 1998)	
★	Live in Detroit (CMC, 2000)	
★★½	Anthology: The History of Peter Frampton (A&M, 2000)	

Peter Frampton was one of those quintessential '70s success stories—a fast burn, a hazy comedown, and lots of embarrassing stains afterward. A journeyman English guitarist formerly of the Herd and Humble Pie, with several dull studio albums behind him and no fans to speak of, Peter suddenly scored one of the decade's biggest hits with *Frampton Comes Alive!* He had a simple formula: frizzy blond ringlets, shirts that probably didn't even have buttons, mellow romantic ballads, long guitar solos, even longer electric-piano solos, a strange guitar/voicebox contraption that could say "that's all roit!!" (which we all found inexplicably exciting at the time), and an audience full of kids in dialogue with all the machines in the strangely inspiring techno-utopian epic "Do You Feel Like We Do?" There must have been a killer light show or something, too, judging from the crowd squeals that popped up during the otherwise none-too-rocking boogie jams. "Baby I Love Your Way" was a superbly goopy acoustic ballad, "Show Me the Way" a slightly tougher sequel, and Frampton sold millions of records.

I'm in You was rushed out before the Framp had a chance to catch his breath. The title song was a nice goosebump-raising piano ballad, but side two had perhaps the flimsiest music ever passed off by a major-label rock superstar, gasping to the finish line with a pair of desperately time-killing Motown-cover jams. Cameron Crowe's liner notes proclaimed *I'm in You* "bloody great," but it was actually pretty darn bad, and it stopped the golden boy cold. Frampton later appeared, looking roughed up, in the Bee Gees' film version of *Sgt. Pepper*. To his credit, he never stopped making music, though, and finally got around to *Frampton Comes Alive II* in 1995. Beware of *Anthology* and *The Very Best of*, which present the hits in their inferior original studio versions; *Greatest Hits* and *Classics, Vol. 12* do better just by adding the song "I'm in You" to the highlights of *Frampton Comes Alive!* "Do You Feel Like We Do?" got used brilliantly in the 1993 Richard Linklater movie *Dazed and Confused* as an endless 8-track loop humming in the background, which in the summer of 1976 is exactly what it was. —R.S.

Aretha Franklin

★★½	Aretha (Columbia, 1961)	
★★★	The Electrifying Aretha Franklin (Columbia, 1962)	
★★½	The Tender, the Moving, the Swinging Aretha Franklin (Columbia, 1962)	
★★★	Laughing on the Outside (Columbia, 1963)	
★★½	Running Out of Fools (Columbia, 1964)	
★★★½	Unforgettable (Columbia, 1964)	
★★★★	Songs of Faith (Checker, 1964)	
★★½	Yeah! Aretha Franklin in Person (Columbia, 1965)	
★★★	Soul Sister (Columbia, 1966)	
★★★	Greatest Hits (Columbia, 1967)	
★★★★★	I Never Loved a Man (the Way I Love You) (1967; Atlantic, 1995)	
★★★	Aretha Arrives (1967; Rhino, 1993)	
★★★★★	Lady Soul (1968; Atlantic, 1995)	
★★★½	Aretha Now (1968; Rhino, 1993)	
★★★	Aretha in Paris (1968; Rhino, 1995)	
★★★½	Soul '69 (1969; Rhino, 1993)	
★★★★	Aretha's Gold (Atlantic, 1969)	
★★★½	This Girl's in Love With You (1970; Rhino, 1993)	
★★★½	Spirit in the Dark (1970; Rhino, 1993)	
★★★½	Greatest Hits (Atlantic, 1971)	
★★★	Live at Fillmore West (Atlantic, 1971)	
★★★½	Young, Gifted and Black (Atlantic, 1972)	
★★★★★	Amazing Grace (Atlantic, 1972)	
★★★	The Great Aretha Franklin: The First 12 Sides (Columbia, 1972)	
★★★½	All-time Greatest Hits (Columbia, 1972)	
★★½	Hey Now Hey (The Other Side of the Sky) (1973; Rhino, 1995)	

★★★   Best of Aretha Franklin (Atlantic, 1973)
★★★   Let Me in Your Life (1974; Rhino, 1995)
★★★   With Everything I Feel in Me (Atlantic, 1974)
★   You (Atlantic, 1975)
★★   Sparkle (Atlantic, 1976)
★★★   Ten Years of Gold (Atlantic, 1976)
★★   Sweet Passion (Atlantic, 1977)
★★   Almighty Fire (Atlantic, 1978)
★★   La Diva (Atlantic, 1979)
★★★   Aretha Sings the Blues (Columbia, 1980)
★★   Aretha (Arista, 1980)
★★★   Love All the Hurt Away (Arista, 1981)
★★★   Jump to It (Arista, 1982)
★★½   Sweet Bitter Love (Columbia, 1982)
★★★½   Get It Right (Arista, 1983)
★★★½   Aretha's Jazz (Atlantic, 1984)
★★★½   Who's Zoomin' Who (Arista, 1985)
★★★★★   30 Greatest Hits (Atlantic, 1985)
★★½   Aretha (Arista, 1986)
★★★   After Hours (Columbia, 1987)
★★★★   One Lord, One Faith, One Baptism (Arista, 1987)
★★★   Through the Storm (Arista, 1989)
★★★   What You Get Is What You Sweat (Arista, 1991)
★★★★★   Queen of Soul—The Atlantic Recordings (Rhino, 1992)
★★★★★   Queen of Soul—The Very Best of Aretha Franklin (Rhino, 1994)
★★★½   A Rose Is Still a Rose (Arista, 1998)
★★★★★   Amazing Grace—The Complete Recordings (1972; Rhino, 1999)
★★   So Damn Happy (Arista, 2003)

A supple mezzo-soprano of astonishing range, Aretha Franklin's voice is a force of nature. What makes her one of the great singers in the history of popular music, however, is the knowing command with which she deploys that force. So artful is her approach to her instrument that she might've chosen any genre within which to triumph. The daughter of Rev. C.L. Franklin, a preacher whose many albums of sermons had earned him the name "the Million-Dollar Voice," Aretha could've inherited Mahalia Jackson's crown as the queen of gospel. Equally, she might've followed after Billie Holiday, conquering the blues, or Sarah Vaughan, mastering jazz. In fact, all of these strains find rich expression in Franklin's work—but her signal passion made her "Lady Soul."

Discovered by John Hammond, the unerring Columbia talent scout who'd also mentored Bob Dylan, Franklin was first forced into the mold of a pop singer, covering such easy fare as "Over the Rainbow." Her work for that label—now best represented on *The Great Aretha Franklin: The First 12 Sides* and a trio of '80s reissues—in no way approaches her coming glory, even if her brilliant piano playing and innate vocal power can't quite be buried by glossy arrangements. Pairing up, in 1966, with Atlantic Records vice president Jerry Wexler and the famed Muscle Shoals, AL, studio players, Franklin found her true voice: Against a backdrop of surging rhythm and punching horns, she turned loose her gospel piano and began singing with such graceful abandon that she became recognized very soon as one of the handful of inventors of hard-core soul. Motown was making R&B with a symphonic sweep and sweet melodicism; Aretha's music—boosted greatly by production assists from Wexler, Tom Dowd, and Arif Mardin—would be consistently tougher, rawer, and, arguably, much deeper.

I Never Loved a Man debuted the new Aretha—and it was a staggering introduction. Her version of Otis Redding's "Respect" knocked cold even his amazing original; and with the title track, "Do Right Woman—Do Right Man," "Dr. Feelgood," and "Save Me," this was music of absolute, fluid assurance. The record may stand as the greatest single soul album of all time.

"Baby, I Love You" enlivened the capable *Aretha Arrives*, but *Lady Soul* was another masterpiece, producing the hits "(You Make Me Feel Like) A Natural Woman," "(Sweet Sweet Baby) Since You've Been Gone," and, most significant, "Chain of Fools." With Aretha singing with infectious swagger and its background vocals recalling the Staple Singers, the song encapsulated the Franklin soul style—while as catchy as any early rock & roll number, it resounded with a much wiser force.

On *Aretha Now,* the singer showed that she could transform pop songs into soul numbers; infusing Burt Bacharach's "I Say a Little Prayer" with swing, she added edge to the delicate melody. And *Soul '69* proved her to be a jazz singer of rare intelligence and dimension. With its great takes on Sam Cooke's "Bring It on Home to Me" and Big Maybelle Smith's "Ramblin' " and its tight brass section featuring King Curtis, *Soul '69*'s highlights can now be found on *Aretha's Jazz.* That compilation also presents the better work from Franklin's later orchestral jazz set with Quincy Jones, *Hey Now Hey (The Other Side of the Sky).*

The early '70s marked the end of Aretha's titanic period. *Greatest Hits* featured "Spanish Harlem," a gospel "Bridge Over Troubled Water," and Ashford and Simpson's "You're All I Need to Get By"; *Young, Gifted and Black* presented the spare, urgent "Rock Steady" and the lovely "Day Dreamin' "; *Live at Fillmore West* found Aretha collaborating with Ray Charles. All of these records are confident and immediate; none, however, matches the majesty of her contemporaneous two-album gospel magnum opus, *Amazing Grace.* Featuring James Cleveland and the Southern California Community Choir, *Grace* is Franklin transcendent, returning to the source of her own—and soul music's—earliest inspiration.

In 1981, Aretha came back from a series of bland, sometimes discofied albums in which she often sounded bored or exhausted, with *Love All the Hurt Away*—a funky pop near-triumph. While it wasn't music of the caliber of the best Atlantic sides, the record showed off her newly energized singing—and its success paved the way for her commercial reemergence with *Who's Zoomin' Who.* In many ways a rock record—there's a duet with Annie Lennox of Eurythmics, a Carlos Santana guitar solo, and sax work by Clarence Clemons—*Zoomin'* may be lyrically slight, but it kicks plenty. With help from the Mighty Clouds of Joy, Jesse Jackson, and Mavis Staples, *One Lord, One Faith, One Baptism* reasserted Aretha's gospel prowess—predictably, it was the best record she'd made in over a decade.

Sadly, Aretha would remain quiet for most of the '90s. *A Rose Is Still a Rose* in 1998 found her collaborating with a coterie of celebrated hip-hop artists. Sure enough, the odd Narada Michael Walden–produced ballad was still there. This time, however, the syrupy pop material competed with more transcendental sessions produced by the likes of Lauryn Hill (the luscious title track) and Puff Daddy ("Never Leave You Again"). Five years later, *So Damn Happy* drowned her royal vocalizing in a tepid sea of lackluster hooks and uninspired arrangements.

While incapable of turning in a vocal performance that doesn't catch fire, Aretha has truly shone only in company with sympathetic producers (Wexler/Dowd/Mardin)—and she's sometimes been overwhelmed by less congenial ones (Van McCoy, Luther Vandross). Occasionally willfull, reticent, or inscrutable, she has the tortured personality of a very private soul, and her career has sometimes suffered from lack of direction. She remains, however, the spirit of soul—a singer of genius. Nearly all of her 1967–72 releases are essential R&B records; the excellent *Queen of Soul,* a four-CD box set, presents Aretha Franklin at her finest. For those with little money to spend, *The Very Best of Aretha Franklin* distills the set's essential moments into one devastating disc of pure R&B gold. —P.E./E.L.

Freestyle Fellowship

★★★★ To Whom It May Concern (Beats & Rhymes, 1991)
★★★½ Inner City Griots (4th and Broadway, 1993)
★★½ Temptations (Ground Control, 2001)
★★★★ Version 2.0 (Beats & Rhymes, 2001)
★★★ Shockadoom (Beats & Rhymes, 2002)

The L.A.-based Freestyle Fellowship is made up of MCs Aceyalone, Mikah Nine, Self-Jupiter, and P.E.A.C.E., a crew of uncompromising hip-hop purists. On its very-limited-edition debut, *To Whom It May Concern,* the group's evangelical rhyming approach is breathtaking (especially for those who got to see the MCs perform at the time). After the release of its second album, the group hadn't quite found a balance between its native environment, the stage, and the studio setting. Whereas *To Whom* was raw, *Inner City Griots* was much more of a traditional hip-hop album (save for the verbal ballistics, the albums could have been made by two different groups). Whatever their faults, these releases delivered on a lot of promise, so the faithful waited—and waited—with bated breath for the next one. Finally, after eight years of various solo albums and mix-tape appearances, 2001 brought *Temptations,* on which the group embraced the ideology of "No Hooks, No Chorus" (also the name of one of the album's tracks). Because the MCs highlight their mic skills here rather than craft compelling beats, they undermine the fellowship's legacy, at least on wax. Ironically, they released an instrumental version of *Temptations,* which is like Billy Bob Thornton listing his country-rock CDs but omitting his movies from his résumé. The chronology of the fellowship's career and catalogue is kind of confusing. For instance, *Shockadoom* was recorded in 1998, so technically it's the followup to *Inner City Griots,* but the disc wasn't released until 2002. And 2001's *Version 2.0* is essentially a reissue of the debut album, of which fewer than 1,000 copies were originally pressed. In 1991, the Freestyle Fellowship was on top of its game, but after 10 years, it became clear that the MCs left out the *fun* in their hip-hop fundamentalism. —K.M.

Freeway

★★★★ Philadelphia Freeway (Roc-A-Fella/Def Jam, 2003)

Philadelphia's Freeway has one of hip-hop's truly distinctive voices, a nasal, raspy wheeze that sounds like a perpetual gasp for air. Originally featured on "Roc the Mic" as part of Beanie Sigel's crew State Property, it quickly became clear that Freeway could stand on his own. He spins grimy yarns about the hustling life on his debut, which are all the more impressive compared to Roc-A-Fella's typically glossier output. Complemented by the best work of the label's two in-house producers, Just Blaze ("What We Do") and Kanye West ("Turn Out the Lights"), Freeway proves that even the most hardened truths can set you free.   —J.C.

Glenn Frey

★★	No Fun Aloud (Asylum, 1982)
★★	The Allnighter (MCA, 1984)
★½	Soul Searchin' (MCA, 1988)
★★★	Strange Weather (MCA, 1992)
★★½	Live (MCA, 1993)
★★★	Solo Collection (MCA, 1995)
★★★	The Millennium Collection: The Best of Glenn Frey (MCA, 2000)

After the Eagles split up (for the first time), guitarist-singer Glenn Frey cut a predictably slick solo debut in his old band's party-boy mode; *No Fun Aloud* is like a Joe Walsh album with (slightly) better singing. Not songs, though; apparently that was Don Henley's department. *The Allnighter* glistens with synthesized oomph, but the sugar coating doesn't sit well on Frey's mannered white R&B loverman act. "Smuggler's Blues," the set piece for the followup, was utilized in an episode of the television show *Miami Vice* (Frey had a small role), jump-starting *The Allnighter* on the charts. "Smuggler's Blues," the catchiest tune on the album by far, was a lot more interesting to watch—like a dramatized video clip—than it is to listen to, however. By *Soul Searchin'*, Frey sounded like he wasn't even trying anymore; his pump-your-body TV gym commercials at the time displayed more sweat and effort. With *Strange Weather*, Frey seemed determined to make a statement. "Love in the 21st Century" was a catchy but disposable rocker in the vein of his *Beverly Hills Cop* soundtrack hit "The Heat Is On," but both "I've Got Mine" and "He Took Advantage (Blues for Ronald Reagan)" found him stumbling around in the same rich-rock-star-as-self-righteous-angry-liberal footsteps as Henley; suffice it to say, neither song came within spitting distance of the dignified grace of Henley's *The End of the Innocence*. Frey fares much better with the album-closing "Part of Me, Part of You"—a feel-good, top-down anthem in the spirit of his easy-rolling Eagles hits "Take It Easy" and "Peaceful Easy Feeling." Of course, that song was first featured in the film *Thelma & Louise*, conclusive proof that as a solo artist, Frey's forte is hooky soundtrack fodder and lousy albums. As such, he's best represented by either of his two best-of collections, both of which offer "Part of Me," "The Heat Is On," "Smuggler's Blues," and his other *Miami Vice* hit, "You Belong to the City." The lackluster *Live* features most of the same hits, along with a handful of reheated Ea-

gles tunes; fans who waited a year got the real deal when Frey rejoined the Eagles for *Hell Freezes Over* in 1994.   —M.C./R.SK.

Lefty Frizzell

★★	American Originals (Columbia, 1990)
★★★★	The Best of Lefty Frizzell (Rhino, 1991)
★★★★½	That's the Way Love Goes: The Final Recordings of Lefty Frizzell (Varèse Sarabande, 1996)
★★★★★	Look What Thoughts Will Do (Sony/Columbia, 1997)
★★★	Songs of Jimmie Rodgers (Koch, 1999)
★★	Country Music Hall of Fame 1982 (King, 1999)

Simply one of the great vocal stylists in country-music history, Texas-born William Orville "Lefty" Frizzell came out of the Southwest honky-tonk circuit to land a recording contract with Columbia Records in 1950, when he was 22 years old; he would become one of the biggest stars in country music only a year later. When his Columbia run ended in 1970, he left with 17 Top 10 hits and six #1 singles on his résumé, plus a host of devoted disciples including Merle Haggard (whose song "The Way It Was in '51" memorialized the total dominance Frizzell and his buddy Hank Williams exerted over country music in one vibrant year) and Willie Nelson, who saw fit to honor one of his major influences with an entire album in 1977, *To Lefty From Willie*. Frizzell was only 47 when he died from a cerebral hemorrhage in 1975, but his legacy lives on in succeeding generations of vocalists such as Clint Black, the late Keith Whitley, and especially Randy Travis, each of whom forged an individual style out of what he had learned from Frizzell's emotionally rich and revealing phrasing.

Frizzell's records, while offering a fair share of heartbreak and despair, are remarkably life-affirming, considering his struggles with alcoholism during his short life. This is especially true of the early smash hits, which build on a traditional country foundation while being streamlined in a way well-suited to the quickening pace of post–World War II America. Lay a personable, gimmick-free tenor voice on top of that, and you've got something that speaks directly to listeners looking for stories relevant to their own lives. The simple affirmations of unconditional and enduring love for parents in 1951's poignant "Mom and Dad Waltz" skirt sentimentality not only in the lyrics but also in the dirgelike fiddle lines and moaning pedal-steel fills, ultimately saying what many feel in their hearts. Similarly, the buoyant expressions of romantic love fueling Frizzell's debut hit, "I Love You a Thousand Ways" (one of his landmark recordings; it's now an acknowledged country classic) effectively encapsulate a starry-eyed view of a significant other, even though the song was written from a jail cell in which the 18-year-old Frizzell was serving a sentence for statutory rape; by the same token, the melancholy strains of "Always Late (With Your Kisses)" describe the kick inside when something's amiss in a relationship, especially in the futility with which Frizzell invests his lyric, "Why oh why do you want to do me this way?" On balance, Frizzell had a way with a love song that brooks few comparisons in all of country-music history—the tenderness he brings to his singing and his uncanny modulations in tone and phrasing to suit the mood of the moment are blueprints in the art of technically adroit, openhearted vocalizing.

The essential overview of Frizzell's Columbia years is the two-CD *Look What Thoughts Will Do.* His music speaks volumes, and there's plenty of it here— 34 songs, from the breakout 1950 double-sided chart-topper, "I Love You a Thousand Ways" and the honky-tonk classic "If You've Got the Money I've Got the Time" to his final #1 single, 1964's brooding, haunting treatment of the folk-styled masterpiece, "Saginaw, Michigan." Of special note is the tasty, low-key country blues from 1952, "Lost Love Blues," previously unissued in the U.S., and two masterful homages to Jimmie Rodgers, "Travellin' Blues" and "My Rough and Rowdy Ways." To his credit, Frizzell approached Rodgers' songs in his own way and found where they lived in his stylistic range rather than attempting to replicate Rodgers' vocal approach and arrangements. Columbia eventually released an entire album of Frizzell's Rodgers covers, *Songs of Jimmie Rodgers,* which has now been reissued on CD by Koch. It's neither classic nor indispensable, but it's an enjoyable album that deepens the impression of an artist who has a sure sense of himself.

Elsewhere, Rhino's *Best of* is an exemplary summary of the Columbia years, albeit less thorough than *Look What Thoughts Will Do.* Columbia's *American Originals* and King's *Country Music Hall of Fame* entries fall woefully short of the mark of the Columbia/ Legacy and Rhino sets.

Finally returned to print after years in the cutout wilderness are Frizzell's ABC recordings from 1972 to 1974, many of them originally issued in the albums *The Legendary Lefty Frizzell* and *The Classic Style of Lefty Frizzell,* in 1973 and 1975, respectively. Given his self-destructive personal habits, it's fair to say *That's the Way Love Goes: The Final Recordings of Lefty Frizzell* features an older if not necessarily wiser artist. —D.M.

John Frusciante

★★★★ Niandra Lades and Usually Just a T-Shirt (American, 1994)

★½ Smile From the Streets You Hold (Birdman, 1997)

★★ To Record Only Water for Ten Days (Warner Bros, 2001)

★★½ Shadows Collide With People (Warner Bros., 2004)

Possibly the most fucked-up record ever issued by a major label, ex–Red Hot Chili Peppers guitarist John Frusciante's home-recorded solo debut is not for the squeamish. Unspeakably sloppy but often genuinely moving, it's full of tortured beauty: the sound of a man scraping away at his own mind's breaking point, letting both his id and his imagination run loose. Hence, for instance, a lyrical, Hendrix-inspired tune called "Your Pussy's Glued to a Building on Fire." Appreciating *Niandra*'s splattered resplendence also requires a certain tolerance for Frusciante's singing voice— think Robert Plant with splinters under his toenails.

The followup, *Smile From the Streets You Hold,* has a couple of moments of scary sublimity, especially "A Fall Thru the Ground" (as well as several collaborations with Frusciante's late friend, actor River Phoenix), but it's mostly agonizing to listen to—haphazardly dumped onto tape at the nadir of Frusciante's heroin addiction, it sounds like he's singing through convulsions and shattered teeth.

Subsequently, he cleaned up, rejoined the Chili Peppers, and made *To Record Only Water for Ten Days,* whose almost normal verses, choruses, and drum machines make it sound like a set of almost bland sketches for RHCP ballads. *Shadows Collide with People* is a bit looser and weirder, featuring a couple of lovely, noisy instrumentals. Frusciante's lyrics seem to wander away every few words ("Sending a dummy to my God/Driving to eat a Carvel cake/Somewhere you know isn't where you think"), and he wins no prize for musical focus, either, but he does sound like he's having fun for a change. —D.W.

Fuel

★★★ Sunburn (Sony/550, 1998)

★★½ Something Like Human (Sony/550, 2000)

★★ Natural Selection (Sony, 2003)

Part of a vanishing herd of post–Pearl Jam grunge-pop contenders, Fuel came straight out of Pennsylvania in 1998 with "Shimmer," a canny mix of strings and hard-rock hooks that was one of the year's guiltiest pleasures and the best thing on their major-label full-length debut, *Sunburn.* Fuel boasted a charismatic lead singer (the somber, improbably named Brett Scallions) and enough decent tracks ("Jesus or a Gun," "Bittersweet") to ensure a better future for itself than, say, Seven Mary 3. With the same reliance on depressive, love-gone-wrong ballads and melodic metal-lite ("Last Time" and "Hemorrhage [In My Hands]"), the band's second effort, *Something Like Human*, was more of a lateral move than an artistic step forward; *Natural Selection* stayed that uninspired course. —A.S.

Fugazi

★★★★ 13 Songs (Dischord, 1989)
★★★½ Repeater + 3 Songs (Dischord, 1990)
★★★½ Steady Diet of Nothing (Dischord, 1991)
★★★★ In on the Kill Taker (Dischord, 1993)
★★★★ Red Medicine (Dischord, 1995)
★★★½ End Hits (Dischord, 1998)
★★½ Instrument Soundtrack (Dischord, 1999)
★★★★½ The Argument (Dischord, 2001)

Fugazi has been such a righteous force in underground rock for so long—charging reasonable prices for concert tickets, scrupulously avoiding any taint from the corporate-level music biz—that it's easy to forget they're an actual *band*. At least until you put their records on, or see one of their legendary live shows. But singer/guitarists Guy Picciotto (whose earlier band Rites of Spring pretty much invented emo) and Ian MacKaye (whose earlier band Minor Threat was the formal pinnacle of hardcore) and the mighty rhythm section of Brendan Canty and Joe Lally are a staggeringly powerful combination. They've been challenging themselves and their audience constantly for 15 years, giving some of the hemisphere's hardest punk rock an increasingly arty, thoughtful spin.

Compiling two early EPs, *13 Songs* leads off with Fugazi's best-known song, the white-hot dub-punk anthem "Waiting Room," and keeps going with one feral rocker after another. Picciotto's "Margin Walker" articulates the specific rage of wanting to destroy the culture that excludes you, but the real knockout here is "Suggestion," an explosive attack on everyday sexism, sung by MacKaye from a woman's POV. *Repeater* is a development and refinement of the same basic approach, this time as a refutation of mass culture: "We owe you nothing/You are not what you own," MacKaye bellows on "Merchandise," and Picciotto's "Blueprint" finds him screaming "I'm not playing with you!" over and over. There's a bit of filler (two instrumentals and a remake of "Provisional" from *13 Songs*), and more energy than craft at work, but you can't accuse them of being undercommitted.

With *Steady Diet of Nothing*, they slow down and dig in, making the music both tougher and more complicated. Lally's bass parts are three parts Joy Division to one part dub; you can hear the band's years of playing together turning into tricky, spacious instrumental patterns, as on "Stacks." MacKaye addresses the Gulf War in "Nice New Outfit" ("There's blood in your mouth, but not in mine"), and there are rumors of war elsewhere in the lyrics, but they're mostly the sort of raw impressionism that the late-'90s emo generation subsequently picked up on.

Illness is everywhere on *In on the Kill Taker*, literally or metaphorically—it shows up all over the lyrics, and there are sick, nasty guitar noises starting or ending most of the songs, like the blistering feedback coda of "23 Beats Off." The band actually quiets down and builds tension a few times, but it's usually to give them somewhere to lunge from. Picciotto's words get weirder and are open to interpretation—"crush my calm, you Cassavetes"—but he declaims them like he's taking his revenge. There's also a fabulous MacKaye punk-rock quickie, "Great Cop" (as in "You'd make a . . ."). *Red Medicine* continues along the same path into even denser, darker territory and suggests that Fugazi is feeding on lots of stuff that's very different from its own music. "Fell, Destroyed" even borrows a hook from Tenor Saw's dancehall reggae hit "Ring the Alarm," and "Version" is an ambitious, if not exactly successful, noise-dub experiment. The MacKaye knockout this time is "Bed for the Scraping," with its battle cry of "I don't want to be defeated"—in his mouth, it comes out as "idawannabeedafeeda."

The disjunction between the anthems and the arty moments of *End Hits* is schizzier still: MacKaye's "Five Corporations" savages music-biz hegemony with laconic precision, and Picciotto sings "Guilford Fall" like his head's exploding, but then there are pieces like the hushed bass gurgle "Pink Frosty" that are unrecognizable as the Fugazi of 10 years earlier. (That's a good thing, but the combination makes for difficult listening.) The recording is curious, too, switching between the audio equivalent of long shots and close-ups. A soundtrack to a documentary about Fugazi's first decade, *Instrument* includes oddities, instrumental doodles, and a half-dozen demos, mostly of *End Hits* songs. It's mostly ragged and unformed, but for confirmed Fugaziphiles, it's a solidly interesting peek into the band's creative process.

The four core members of Fugazi (plus live percussionist Jerry Busher, playing with the group for the first time on record) are clearly pulling in different directions on *The Argument*, and the result, miraculously, is their best album—somehow, they seem to have discovered that pleasure has radical possibilities too (backing vocals! cello! tunes, even!). Picciotto's "Full Disclosure" is as headlong a punk charge as they've ever made, but they've also figured out how to make their points by implication and understatement, musically as well as lyrically. The songs shift their textures restlessly as the band flexes its collaborative instincts, playing as if with a single pair of hands. —D.W.

Fugees

★★★	Blunted on Reality (Ruffhouse/Columbia, 1994)
★★★★½	The Score (Ruffhouse/Columbia, 1996)
★	Greatest Hits (Sony, 2003)

The Fugees arrived quietly with *Blunted on Reality;* they were a trio led by two Haitian-American cousins with a sound grounded in conscious rap that also acknowledged the group's Caribbean heritage, blending elements of traditional and dancehall reggae with hip-hop—seemingly an alternative-rap oddity with few commercial prospects. But the group's musicianship brought another layer to the music, and *Blunted*'s best tracks—the acoustic-guitar-driven "Vocab" and "Some Seek Stardom," a showcase for versatile rapper/singer Lauryn Hill—dazzle with compositional flair. Ultimately, *Blunted* catches the group still finding itself, and some awkward rapping by cousins Wyclef Jean and Pras makes the record more about promise than actualization.

That is not the case with its followup, *The Score,* which very consciously sidesteps the group's weaknesses and accentuates its strengths. Mainly, that means Hill has moved front and center, delivering the album's most memorable rhymes and inviting hooks. The production is also notably stronger and more mature than on the debut, enabling the Fugees to emerge as not only the major pop crossover of the day but—with Hill's relatively faithful vocal on a cover of Roberta Flack's "Killing Me Softly"—the rap group even soccer moms could love. At its best, *The Score* suggests ways in which hip-hop can expand musically (and demographically) without becoming tepid or inane. Perhaps a victim of its own achievements, *The Score* has not been followed up, as Jean (the group's musical force) and Hill have jockeyed the notoriety they earned into successful solo careers. Considering that the Fugees made only two albums, *Greatest Hits* is merely an attempt by Sony to squeeze the last drops of juice from the Fugees' career—once it became apparent no third studio record would ever materialize. Seven of the 10 tracks are from *The Score,* and just two come from *Blunted* (a Lauryn Hill solo track rounds out the album). Thoroughly inessential. —R.M.S.

Funkadelic

★★★½	Funkadelic (Westbound, 1970)
★★★	Free Your Mind and Your Ass Will Follow (Westbound, 1970)
★★★★	Maggot Brain (Westbound, 1971)
★★★	America Eats Its Young (Westbound, 1972)
★★★½	Cosmic Slop (Westbound, 1973)
★★★½	Standing on the Verge of Getting It On (Westbound, 1974)
★★★★	Let's Take It to the Stage (Westbound, 1975)
★★★★	Funkadelic's Greatest Hits (Westbound, 1975)
★★★	Tales of Kidd Funkadelic (Westbound, 1976)
★★★	Hardcore Jollies (1976; Priority, 2002)
★★★★★	The Best of the Funkadelic Early Years (Westbound, 1977)
★★★★	One Nation Under a Groove (1978; Priority, 2002)
★★★★	Uncle Jam Wants You (Warner Bros., 1979)
★★	Connections and Disconnections (LAX, 1981)
★★★½	The Electric Spanking of War Babies (1981; Priority, 2002)
★★★★	Music for Your Mother: Funkadelic 45s (Westbound/Ace, 1992)
★★★★	Live: Meadowbrook, Rochester, Michigan, 12th September 1971 (Westbound/Ace, 1996)

James Brown will always be the Father of Funk, but George Clinton is the Son and Holy Ghost with some pagans thrown in. Clinton's work with Funkadelic and Parliament is still a sample lode for hip-hop (there would be no Dr. Dre without Clinton), and his catholic vision of a rock and funk marriage is sui generis. It didn't all work—Clinton's synthesist tendencies and taste for open-ended improvisations resulted in some pretty confused records—but he started more conversations than anyone in funk.

The band's genealogy is near Biblical, tied up with lawsuits and label hopping, but in short: Detroit songwriter George Clinton had a doo-wop vocal group in the '60s called the Parliaments, who became Parliament and recorded a very Funkadelic-like album, the excellent *Osmium,* and then changed their name for legal reasons. At any point, Parliament and Funkadelic have many of the same members, but the reductive breakdown is Funkadelic = rock, Parliament = disco. The first three Funkadelic records—*Funkadelic, Free Your Mind and Your Ass Will Follow,* and *Maggot Brain*—are heavily weighted in favor of Eddie Hazel's post-Hendrix guitar wailing and a druggy worldview. When it works, it's like the Stooges with swing, a mildly terrifying urban funeral procession that can't decide whether to cry or do the Popcorn. There isn't a Black Sabbath song heavier than "Super Stupid" *(Maggot*

Brain), and songs like "Good Old Music" *(Funkadelic)* and "Hit It and Quit It" *(Maggot Brain)* make one nostalgic for a time when funk didn't necessarily drag gentility along for the ride. These songs are *fierce.* On the other hand, Clinton's spoken word and echo-chamber decoration are mostly entertaining because they suggest a day gone by. They will not go on your mix tape. And Eddie Hazel, for all his emoting, is a one-trick pony: Some of the solos are torrid blues narratives, and some are just really long. When Funkadelic gets above nine minutes, it's usually not a good sign. (The excellent *Live: Meadowbrook* disc proves, though, that this band was a force of nature when they got going on stage.) The themes that will make Clinton Clinton are all here: Sex is the point but also kind of scary; money's a game where the house always wins; and funk will somehow resolve the contradiction between the two, if only by making you forget it.

America Eats Its Young isn't the strongest Funkadelic album, but it introduces key elements that will lead Clinton to Parliament: keyboardist Bernie Worrell; a light, playful sense of humor that favors catchphrases and leavens some of Clinton's ickier scatology; and a massive talent for harmony vocal arranging. The political anger is upped on *America,* but it's the party tunes that will survive ("You Hit the Nail on the Head," "A Joyful Process," "Loose Booty"). You could say much the same of *Cosmic Slop* and *Standing on the Verge of Getting It On,* with qualifications. The title track of *Cosmic Slop* is a painful incantation ("I hear my mother call . . .") answered by a very Temptations vocal and Eddie Hazel's crying. (Think of him more as a black cantor than as the next Hendrix.) "Nappy Dugout" is classic Clinton sex talk, in a good way. *Standing* revives a stomper from *Osmium* called "Red Hot Mama," and then moves into larger, dance-friendly jams (the title track). *Let's Take It to the Stage* (not a live album) was a summing-up of everything Funkadelic had done to date, and is still their most playable record. Clinton's sexual politics aren't at their best ("No Head, No Backstage Pass" says it all) but the band is in high gear, from the old-style rock funk of "Good to Your Earhole" and "Stuffs and Things" to the proto-Parliament party tracks like the title track and "Get Off Your Ass and Jam." Everybody is about to take backseat to the synth squiggles of Bernie Worrell and the dusted ad-libs of the young bassist with the funny glasses—Bootsy Collins—but this album captures what made the band so good.

(*Music for Your Mother* and *Best of the Funkadelic Early Years* both have most of what you need from the pre-Parliament era, the former tending toward unnecessary completeness and the latter leaving out a few

key tunes. But be thankful that *Music* is all single-length edits, which helps.)

Hardcore Jollies attempts to balance the new horizontal, de-rocked groove with some echoes of guitar fire (courtesy of Michael Hampton, the new Eddie Hazel) but it's just pleasant, neither cathartic nor bumpalicious. As Clinton shifts labels from Westbound to Warner Bros., *Tales of Kidd Funkadelic* fulfills a contract with outtakes from the Westbound years (including the excellent "I'm Never Gonna Tell It" and concert favorite "Take Your Dead Ass Home!") without actually achieving albumness. For the next two years, Parliament commands Clinton's attention and Funkadelic is on hiatus.

The 1978 return, *One Nation Under a Groove,* is basically Funkadelic as Parliament, with the crucial help of singer Junie Morrison, formerly of the Ohio Players. The title track is sheer pleasure, a nimble blend of vocal ad-libs, bursts of harmony singing, and a bed of guitar and percussion that reads as Clinton's most explicitly African track to date. It's good enough to buoy up the rest, which is average. The overly polite "Who Says a Funk Band Can't Play Rock?" suggests that a funk band can't, though their early records had already put the question to bed for eternity. "Into You" is a breed of sex ballad that Bootsy would do better on his solo records, but "Cholly" is a durable chunk of funk. Add a lot of talk about shit, literally, and a superfluous live cover of "Maggot Brain," and you still need the title track to live a proper life.

Uncle Jam Wants You is the best Funkadelic-as-disco album, just because of the first two songs. "Freak of the Week" is like slowed-down Chic, a classy chick singing and working around that polyrhythmic, squishy center that *One Nation* relied on. And then there's "(Not Just) Knee Deep," now famous as the basis for De La Soul's "Me, Myself and I," but still its very own gimme on the dance floor. Everyone sings, everything bends in the heat, and at 15 minutes, it's about 20 minutes too short. It's still a great template for communal joy. The title track and "Foot Soldiers" beat the military concept to death, and "Holly Wants to Go to California" is like Clinton trying to imitate Elton John without having heard him. "Field Maneuvers" is Clinton copying Lynyrd Skynyrd, sorta, with much better results. The first 20 minutes of music, though—goddamn.

Connections and Disconnections bears the Funkadelic name, inaccurately, but it's just Fuzzy Haskins and friends in a feud with Clinton, trying to cash in. Avoid. *The Electric Spanking of War Babies,* the final Funkadelic album, is loose and fluid but lacks any of the killer hooks and chants that pull their open-ended funk into focus. "Funk Get Stronger" features Sly Stone doing a surprisingly good job, though Clinton and Stone's real keeper is the stellar P-Funk All Stars album, *Urban Dancefloor Guerrillas. Spanking* is a listenable record, but never hits those epiphanic Clinton heights. —S.F.J.

Nelly Furtado

★★★½   Whoa, Nelly! (DreamWorks, 2000)
★★½   Folklore (DreamWorks, 2003)

A first-generation Canadian whose restless ears never stray too far from her Portuguese roots, Nelly Furtado scored a coup for intelligent female popsters with the release of her debut in 2000. *Whoa, Nelly!* is a wild-ass pop go-go, filled with songs that pursue adventure yet could still make the hit parades. Like high-impact hip-hop but melodically durable and sensuously international, the album jumps on Portuguese and Brazilian styles not as exotic refinements but as cool ways to express yourself in everyday tunes. "Turn off the Light" is a reggae-directed rock-blues tune done with towering confidence.

After three years—during which time she sold 2 million CDs, won a Grammy, and had a baby—Furtado reappeared with *Folklore,* a slick multiculti hodgepodge that sounded like *Whoa, Nelly!* redux, only without a single as good as "I'm Like a Bird." The 24-year-old kicks things off by proclaiming, "I am not a one-trick pony," but fails to back up that claim on the 11 songs that follow. Aside from the mechanized drum loops and assorted world-beat flourishes, she mostly sounds like a funkier Michelle Branch. —J.H./J.E.

Peter Gabriel

★★★	Peter Gabriel (1977; Real World/Geffen, 2002)
★★★	Peter Gabriel (1978; Real World/Geffen, 2002)
★★★★	Peter Gabriel (1980; Real World/Geffen, 2002)
★★★★	Security (1982; Real World/Geffen, 2002)
★★★	Plays Live (1983; Real World/Geffen, 2002)
★★★½	Music from the Film "Birdy" (1985; Real World/Geffen, 2002)
★★★★★	So (1986; Real World/Geffen, 2002)
★★★½	Passion: Music for "The Last Temptation of Christ" (1989; Real World/Geffen, 2002)
★★★★½	Shaking the Tree: Sixteen Golden Greats (1990; Real World/Geffen, 2002)
★★★½	Us (1992; Real World/Geffen, 2002)
★★★	Secret World Live (Real World/Geffen, 1994)
★★★★	Long Walk Home: Music from "Rabbit-Proof Fence" (Real World/Geffen, 2002)
★★★	Up (Real World/Geffen, 2002)
★★★½	Hit (Geffen, 2003)

Over the course of his career, British rocker Peter Gabriel has metamorphosed from theatrical prog-rock cult artist to canny, multimedia pop star to worldly rock sage. It's been a dramatic change: Fans of sly, pop/funk singles like "Big Time" might actually find it hard to accept that their hero was also responsible for the baroque silliness that is "Moribund the Burgermeister."

Gabriel's first three solo albums—each entitled *Peter Gabriel,* although the remastered versions are helpfully numbered *1, 2,* and *3*—were experiments in reinvention. The first *Peter Gabriel* (the cover of which finds our hero half-hidden behind a wet windshield) arrived three years after his last studio recording with Genesis, 1974's arty, ambitious *The Lamb Lies Down on Broadway.* Between the flabby dramatics of "Moribund the Burgermeister" and the forced whimsy of "Excuse Me," it was clear that Gabriel without Genesis wasn't all that different from Gabriel with. Yet the folky economy of "Solsbury Hill" and the understated majesty of "Here Comes the Flood" clearly pushed toward something else—not mainstream pop, exactly, but something close.

The second *Peter Gabriel* (with the fingernails cover) moves closer to that new sound. Produced by King Crimson's Robert Fripp—himself a prog-rock star hoping to remake himself to fit a postpunk world—the album finds Gabriel trying to square his past with the (then) present. "D.I.Y.," his paean to self-produced punk, seems especially prescient in the post-Napster world, while the spare, abstract "Exposure" reveals an unexpected edge. Still, neither the Who-style pomp of "On the Air" nor the ham-fisted pathos of "Home Sweet Home" suggests that Gabriel was surrendering his old turf easily.

It's the third *Peter Gabriel* album (with the melting-face cover) that finally puts him on the proper path. Rather than being written on piano and having the ideas translated to band arrangements, the songs on this album were written using digital synthesis and drum loops. Suddenly, there's a new urgency to Gabriel's voice as he rides the rhythms of "Intruder" and "No Self Control," while the blissfully transcendent "Biko" and "Games Without Frontiers" hint at a pop future very different from the guitar-based world Gabriel came up in.

Security expands on those possibilities by adding world-music elements to the mix. Gabriel had already made moves toward African music in "Biko," which opened with a brief mbube chorale, but that bit of color is nowhere near as dramatic as the burst of percussion that the Ekome Dance Company provides in "The Rhythm of the Heat." It isn't simply exoticism that makes the song (or the similarly flavored "San Jacinto" and "The Family and the Fishing Net") so intriguing; it's the way Gabriel incorporates these rhythmic ideas into his melodic concepts, resulting in a kind of magic that's as applicable to the boisterously tuneful "Shock the Monkey" as the moody, mysterious "I Have the Touch."

Gabriel's internationalist musical strategy didn't translate particularly well to live performance, at least not by the evidence of *Plays Live* (although *P.O.V.,* a 1990 concert video shot with a different band and repertoire, isn't quite so flat). But it does make excellent soundtrack source material. In fact, several selections on the all-instrumental *Music From the Film "Birdy"* are reworkings of tunes from *Security* and the third *Peter Gabriel,* transforming familiar melodies into emotionally evocative mood pieces.

With *So,* Gabriel finally figures out how to play these new tools as pop. Amazingly, he does so without compromising the ambition or adventurousness of his previous efforts. Although the hits "Sledgehammer" and "Big Time" are pointedly funk-driven (and serve up a fair amount of sarcasm with their big-beat arrangements), the rest of the album shows how much Gabriel had gleaned from his world-music side project, the W.O.M.A.D. (World of Music, Arts, and Dance) Festival. There are allusions to Zimbabwean Shona mbira themes in Tony Levin's bassline for "Don't Give Up," and Senegalese mbalax singing (courtesy of Youssou N'Dour) spikes the final choruses to "In Your Eyes." Exotic touches, to be sure, but delivered in a context conventional enough to make them palatable to any pop fan.

Gabriel's second soundtrack album, *Passion* (composed for Martin Scorsese's *The Last Temptation of Christ*), is similarly world-music savvy, though it draws more from the Middle East than Africa. Unlike *Birdy,* it feels more like a genuine film score, covering a range of styles (from Gabrielesque prog rock to quasi-symphonic tone poems), and suggests that there are depths to Gabriel that his pop work barely hints at.

Shaking the Tree, by contrast, makes no such moves in that direction, offering only a representation of his big hits augmented by a fresh collaboration with Youssou N'Dour (the title tune) and a new version of "Here Comes the Flood." *Us,* which followed, did its best to pick up where *So* left off, mixing sophisticated funk-pop ("Steam," "Kiss That Frog") with issue-oriented art rock. In this case, however, the issues were more personal, focusing more on psychosexual drama than on social issues, which lent the whole project the fruity air of postanalytic revelation instead of pop-culture inspiration. None of that was audible in *Secret World Live,* however, which made the pop content seem more like the white funk it wanted to be, while rendering the artier fare all the more indigestible.

That, sadly, seems to have been the high-water

mark for Gabriel. Eight years passed before he finally released a new album, and that turned out to be another *Birdy*-like soundtrack, *Long Walk Home* (from the film *Rabbit-Proof Fence*). Taken on its own, it not only complements the film's vision of the Western Australian outback, but reduces many of the major themes from his subsequent "commercial" release, *Up,* to a far more potent essence. *Up,* on the other hand, manages to make several of Gabriel's stylistic habits—grandiloquent prog, slyly mannered funk—seem less like strengths than tics, and (worse) with the tabloid TV-bashing "Barrie Williams Show" turns his gift for satire into an embarrassing and slow-arriving statement of the obvious. We deserve better—and so does he.

After *Up,* Gabriel seems to have tried to make up for his slack productivity in the '90s by releasing numerous new albums. Sadly, he's done so without producing much in the way of new music. The misleadingly titled *Hit* offers only one new song ("Burn You Up, Burn You Down") while recapping much of *Up* and rounding the disc out with middling rarities plus a sprinkling of actual hits. It's hardly an improvement on *Shaking the Tree.* Simultaneously, he has been releasing concert recordings online through the "Encore Series" (www.themusic.com). There were 21 released from his 2003 tour, and several dozen more planned for his 2004 outing. It beats writing new songs, apparently. —J.D.C.

Serge Gainsbourg

  ★★★★ Comic Strip (Phillips/Mercury, 1996)
  ★★½ Couleur Café (Phillips/Mercury, 1996)
  ★★ Du Jazz dans le Ravin (Phillips/Mercury, 1996)
  ★★★★ Aux Armes et Caetera (Sunnyside, 2004)

The great French pop provocateur Serge Gainsbourg's thirty-year-plus career—or at least the early part of it—has been boiled down to three themed compilations for American listeners. *Comic Strip* is the essential introduction to his deliriously inventive late-'60s hits: lush, witty, campy, and throbbing with the kind of irresistible erotic charisma that only truly ugly people can pull off. "Je T'Aime . . . Moi Non Plus" ("I Love You . . . Me Neither"), his heavy-breathing duet with Jane Birkin, has become audio shorthand for Euro-sleaze. It's amazing how timeless a lot of this stuff sounds: "Requiem Pour un Con," released in 1968, could pass for mid-'90s trip-hop.

The other two comps are for confirmed Gainsbourg fiends only. *Du Jazz dans le Ravin* surveys decent but not particularly inspired jazz-influenced material from the late '50s and early '60s. *Couleur*

Café collects his experiments with African and Latin rhythms, including most of 1964's *Gainsbourg Percussions* album (notably the delightful "Pauvre Lola"). Gainsbourg's deeply improbable 1979 album, *Aux Armes et Caetera,* found him in Jamaica, rasping through reggae versions of "La Marseillaise" (the title track), the early jazz standard "You Rascal You" ("Vielle Canaille"), and a bunch of his own songs, with a band that included Sly Dunbar and Robbie Shakespeare. Even more improbably, it's terrific, and the 2004 reissue (which appends a disc of dubs and newly recorded DJ versions) is doubly entertaining.

Note: Most Gainsbourg is much more fun if you know enough French to understand his legendary and largely untranslatable wordplay.   —D.W.

Galaxie 500

★★★	Today (Rough Trade/Rykodisc, 1988)	
★★★★½	On Fire (Rough Trade/Rykodisc, 1989)	
★★★½	This Is Our Music (Rough Trade/Rykodisc, 1990)	
★★★★	Galaxie 500 (Rykodisc, 1996)	
★★★	Copenhagen (Rykodisc, 1997)	
★★★★	The Portable Galaxie 500 (Rykodisc, 1998)	

Galaxie 500's dusted Boston dream-pop was one of the most influential sounds to emerge from the '80s rock underground. The band took off from reference points such as the usual third albums (Velvets, Big Star) and early New Order for a sound that was seductively drowsy and intimate: Dean Wareham's quavery voice and sparse guitar, Naomi Yang's reverberating bass, and Damon Krukowski's decidedly unrocking drums. Their excellent summer-of-'88 debut single "Tugboat"/"King of Spain" was a foretaste of *Today,* which featured "Temperature's Rising" and a cover of Jonathan Richman's "Don't Let Our Youth Go to Waste." But the Galaxie 500 sound really came together in the chamomile psychedelia of *On Fire,* their best album by far. The band hit a songwriting roll with moody ballads such as "Blue Thunder," "Tell Me," and "Strange." Yang sang haunting vocals on "Another Day," while "Leave the Planet" actually kinda rocked in that if-only-I-could-get-off-the-couch sort of way. The sound was lighter than air but melodically rich enough to float around your head, making *On Fire* an album that holds up—definitely one to break out every April.

This Is Our Music wasn't as strong as *On Fire,* with thinner melodies and an awful title, but it has worn well. Despite the excellence of songs such as "Fourth of July" and "Summertime," you can hear the trio competing for attention: There's only so long you can simmer before you either come to a boil or cool

off. The band split acrimoniously, with boiler Wareham departing for Luna and the other two recording simmery albums as Damon & Naomi and Magic Hour. They also began a useful publishing venture, Exact Change Press, reprinting modernist classics such as Gertrude Stein's *Everybody's Autobiography. Copenhagen* documents a late-1990 gig, with some tasty guitar bits. As Galaxie 500's posthumous cult kept growing, Rykodisc reissued the original albums as well as a well-packaged complete-works box. It has an entire disc of uncollected material, including the B-side cover of New Order's "Ceremony," always a live favorite. The previously unreleased "The Other Side," an acoustic groover sung by Yang, stands as one of the most beautiful songs Galaxie 500 ever recorded.   —R.S.

Gang of Four

★★★★★	Entertainment! (1979; EMI, 2001)	
★★★	Gang of Four (EP) (Warner Bros., 1980)	
★★★	Solid Gold (Warner Bros., 1981)	
★★★★	Another Day, Another Dollar (Warner Bros., 1981)	
★★★	Songs of the Free (Warner Bros., 1982)	
★★	Hard (Warner Bros., 1983)	
★★★★	A Brief History of the Twentieth Century (Warner Bros., 1990)	
★★	Mall (Mercury, 1991)	
★★★½	Shrinkwrapped (Castle, 1995)	
★★★★★	100 Flowers Bloom (Rhino, 1998)	
★★★	Solid Gold/Another Day, Another Dollar (EMI, 2004)	

Oh, the burden of a university education! Gang of Four sprang up around England's Leeds University about the same time as the Mekons, the Au Pairs, and Delta 5, exhibiting a marked fondness for brittle, simplistic funk riffs; jagged, post-Hendrixian guitar noise; and a blunt, Marxist lyrical dialectic. But what kept the Gang of Four from slipping—at least at first—into the sort of postgraduate tedium such a formula suggests was a flair for propulsive, approachable pop and an understanding that the band's ideology should never supersede its musical values.

Entertainment! draws most of its energy from Andy Gill's slash-and-burn rhythm guitar, which uses feedback-singed shards of sound to cauterize the beat until the music is as abrasive as any punk without sacrificing rhythmic agility. Much as Talking Heads' David Byrne turned a white fan's gawky approximations of R&B into an alt-rock touchstone, so Gill's guitar—particularly as contrasted with the slick, disco-schooled pulse of bassist Dave Allen and drummer Hugo Burnham—opened new ground between punk and funk, thus making the whole early-'80s new-wave dance boom possible.

Earlier versions of this approach can be found on the *Gang of Four* EP, but *Solid Gold* downplays Gill in favor of Jon King's bland, hectoring vocals, making it a disappointment despite the rhythm section's valiant efforts. *Another Day, Another Dollar* pumps up the rhythm section even further while restoring Gill to his primacy; as a result, "To Hell with Poverty" stands as the group's finest moment. Unfortunately, bassist Dave Allen—the disco cover band vet who grounded the Gang's groove—left soon thereafter. Although *Songs of the Free* and *Hard* had their moments (such as "I Love a Man in a Uniform" from *Songs*), they were few and far between, as the Gang's efforts to spruce up its sound with slick production merely highlighted King's vocal inadequacies, particularly when framed against soulful backing vocals.

By the '90s, the Gang of Four became, effectively, a Gang of Two, as Gill and King soldiered on with a variety of rhythm sections and backing vocalists to diminishing audience response. This didn't soften the duo's politics; if anything, the songs on *Mall* and *Shrink-wrapped* were more pointedly dialectical than ever. *Mall* was undercut by the duo's inability to adapt to new rhythmic technology, but the guitar-centered *Shrink-wrapped* found something of the original fire returned to the group's sound. Since then, the group has disbanded, and King has left the music business entirely.

A Brief History is a choppy but well-chosen best-of drawn from the first five albums. It has since been superseded by the broader, more inclusive, and better-programmed *100 Flowers Bloom*, which condenses the whole of the band's career into a compelling and quite listenable package. —J.D.C.

Gang Starr

★★★	No More Mr. Nice Guy (Wild Pitch, 1989)
★★★★½	Step in the Arena (Chrysalis, 1991)
★★★★★	Daily Operation (Alliance, 1992)
★★★★½	Hard to Earn (Noo Trybe, 1994)
★★★½	Moment of Truth (Virgin, 1998)
★★★★½	Full Clip: A Decade of Gang Starr (Virgin, 1999)
★★★½	The Ownerz (Virgin, 2003)

Guru

★★★	Jazzmatazz, Vol. 1 (Chrysalis, 1993)
★★	Jazzmatazz, Vol. 2: The New Reality (Chrysalis, 1995)
★★	Streetsoul (Virgin, 2000)

Production maestro DJ Premier and wordsmith Guru have defied convention since Gang Starr's first album, *No More Mr. Nice Guy*, establishing the gold standard for high-quality hip-hop and career longevity. First, there's Premier, probably the most consistent and highly revered producer in hip-hop, making beats for Notorious B.I.G. and Jay-Z and virtually everyone in between. His production résumé includes hundreds of songs—some hits, some not. Guru made a big splash with his solo debut, the pioneering 1993 jazz-rap album *Jazzmatazz, Vol. 1*. The album is notable for introducing America to MC Solaar, the tongue-twisting African-French MC, though a newcomer can skip Guru's solo albums and go straight to the Gang Starr catalogue. Though the group's first release—which contained one of the first DJ cuts on a full-length hip-hop album—was not at all a shabby record, *No More Mr. Nice Guy* pales in comparison to their later releases, but that's only because those records that followed shone so brightly.

Released in 1991, *Step in the Arena* sounded far ahead of its time, both slick and raw, with an unassuming touch of jazz that avoided the clichés of groups such as Digable Planets. Guru stood out as an important MC because of his easy flow and wordy rappinghood, though his only weakness is that 15 years of rhyming experience didn't change or complicate his somewhat simple, monotone delivery. In the sonic context of later albums such as *The Ownerz*, which highlights how far Premier has come as a producer, Guru's rhyme style sounds somewhat antiquated, though that's part of its unpretentious charm. Provided with a bed of beats delivered by DJ Premier, Guru could rhyme from *Popular Mechanics* magazine and still sound hot.

Daily Operation delivered darker, denser atmospherics while still never losing touch with the funk; in the era of gangsta rap, this New York crew rewrote the hip-hop playbook. Premier proved that less is more on the stripped-down opening track, "The Place Where We Dwell," while the rest of the album continued in the inventive vein of its predecessor, though with more claustrophobic production. On *Hard to Earn*, it seemed they could do little wrong, though after this album Gang Starr began a slow slide from relevance, but not a dramatic or devastating one.

For any other group, *Moment of Truth* and *The Ownerz* would be career highs, but for Gang Starr they just didn't live up to their jaw-dropping 1991–94 run of albums. The group's best-of collection, *Full Clip: A Decade of Gang Starr*, is a great introduction, but they really deserve a much closer inspection than this collection of singles and near-misses serves up. —K.M.

The Gap Band

★★	The Gap Band (Mercury, 1977)
★★½	The Gap Band II (Mercury, 1979)

★★★ The Gap Band III (Mercury, 1980)
★★★★ Gap Band IV (Total Experience, 1982)
★★★ The Gap Band V—Jammin' (Total Experience, 1983)
★★★★ Gap Gold: Best of the Gap Band (Mercury, 1985)
★★ Gap Band VI (Total Experience, 1985)
★½ Gap Band VII (Total Experience, 1986)
★½ Gap Band VIII (Total Experience, 1986)
★★★ The 12″ Collection (Mercury, 1986)
★½ Straight From the Heart (Total Experience, 1987)
★★ Round Trip (Capitol, 1989)
★★★ Best of the Gap Band (Mercury, 1994)
★★ Testimony (Rhino, 1994)
★★ Ain't Nothin' but a Party (Rhino, 1995)
★½ Y2K: Funkin' Till 2000 Comz (Big Trax/Mercury, 1999)
★★★★ The Ultimate Collection (Hip-O, 2001)
★★ Love at Your Fingertips (Ark 21, 2001)
★★ Original Artist Hit List (Intersound, 2003)
★★½ Gap Band '80s: The Best of the Gap Band (Varèse, 2003)

So what if the Gap Band's best ideas are generally just P-Funk rip-offs? Originality has always played second fiddle to groove in dance music, and that goes double for this crew. Consisting of brothers Ronnie, Charles, and Robert Wilson, the Gap Band had a handful of solid (if slightly goofy) funk hits spread across its first three albums, including "I Don't Believe You Want to Get Up and Dance (Oops!)" from *The Gap Band II* and "Burn Rubber on Me (Why You Wanna Hurt Me)" from *The Gap Band III*, which also includes the Isley Brothers–style ballad "Yearning for Your Love." But it was *Gap Band IV* that made the group's reputation, stretching as it does from the rhythmic insistence of "Early in the Morning" and "You Dropped a Bomb on Me" to slow and soulful songs such as "Stay With Me" (a thinly veiled rewrite of the Orleans hit "Dance With Me") and "Outstanding."

It's downhill from there, though. *The Gap Band V* does at least deliver a serviceable groove with "Party Train," but *Gap Band VI* begins to fall back on stuff such as "Beep a Freak," which seems derivative even by this band's secondhand standards. *Gap Gold* is the first of many best-ofs, each of which tries hard to make the same old songs seem worth buying again (*Ultimate Collection* offers the best value for money). The rest merely chronicle the Gapsters' slow march to irrelevance. —J.D.C.

Garbage

★★★ Garbage (Almo Sounds, 1995)
★★★★ Version 2.0 (Almo Sounds, 1998)
★★★★ Beautiful Garbage (Interscope, 2001)

A Scottish "supervixen" fronting a band of considerably older Wisconsin rock veterans, Shirley Manson was the ideal embodiment of pop-star-as-one-night-stand on *Garbage*'s debut: sleek, wicked, asking nothing but a reciprocation of her icy lust. Teasing "You can always pull out if you like it too much," Manson offered all the ego boost of attracting your own private stalker without the messy reality of late-night phone calls and restraining orders. Like Manson's lip-licked poses, the cold trickery of the electroid guitar hooks masterminded by *Nevermind* producer Butch Vig flaunted their tawdry disposability. Who could resist? The band hit big with Manson's difficult-woman anthem "Only Happy When It Rains" and the dismissive "Stupid Girl." With *Version 2.0*, Vig increased the density of the debut's dance-rock beats with chilly slabs of electronic sleaze, hitting again with "Push It."

Beautiful Garbage found Manson vamping less and sulking more, and still remaining coldly clinical with her interpretive approach; even the girl-group facsimile "Can't Cry These Tears" is an homage more to Blondie than to the Shirelles. By now many young rockers were starting to copy Blondie themselves, though, and Garbage's version of new wave—from a band that could remember the real thing—seemed a little dated. —K.H.

Jerry Garcia

★★★★½ Garcia (Grateful Dead, 1972)
★★ Garcia (Compliments of Garcia) (Grateful Dead, 1974)
★★ Merl Saunders, Jerry Garcia, John Kahn, Bill Vitt: Live at Keystone (Fantasy, 1973)
★★½ Reflections (Round, 1976)
★★½ Run for the Roses (Arista, 1982)
★★★ Almost Acoustic (Grateful Dead, 1988)
★★★½ Jerry Garcia Band (Arista, 1991)
★★★ Don't Let Go (Arista, 2001)
★★★½ Shining Star (Arista, 2001)
★★★½ All Good Things: Jerry Garcia Studio Sessions (Rhino, 2004)

with David Grisman

★★½ Jerry Garcia/David Grisman (Acoustic Disc, 1991)
★★½ Not for Kids Only (Acoustic Disc, 1993)
★★½ Shady Grove (Acoustic Disc, 1996)
★★★ So What (Acoustic Disc, 1998)
★★★ Been All Around This World (Acoustic Disc, 2004)

with David Grisman and Tony Rice

★★★ The Pizza Tapes (Acoustic Disc, 2000)

Sounding very like the mellower Grateful Dead, Jerry Garcia's solo work is pleasant and unremarkable. In combination with Dead lyricist Robert Hunter, he turned out well-crafted fare—his vocals capable, his guitar, as always, understated and stunning. His first two efforts are the Deadest, very akin to that band's *American Beauty*. *Garcia* is the essential album, boasting songs such as "Sugaree" and "To Lay Me Down," which went on to become Dead staples. On the Dead's label, the live *Almost Acoustic* is delightful; a folk quintet tackles such Dead classics as "Casey Jones" and "Ripple." The aggregation Deadheads dubbed "the Jerry band" debuted with *Jerry Garcia Band,* a live double album featuring Garcia's expert dueling with organist Melvin Seals. *Don't Let Go* features JGB, again in concert, at their strongest and supplest. *Shining Star* collects the best of the outfit—and their range of covers is startling, from Dylan to Irving Berlin to the Stones.

Jerry Garcia/David Grisman initiated a remarkably productive alliance between Garcia and legendary mandolinist Grisman. *Shady Grove* offers the finest of their trad blues and ballads, *So What* finds them turning jazzward, and *The Pizza Tapes*, with second guitarist Tony Rice, presents a very relaxed and charming Garcia. —P.E./N.B.

Art Garfunkel

★★★ Angel Clare (Columbia, 1973)
★★★ Breakaway (Columbia, 1975)
★★★★ Watermark (Columbia, 1977)
★★ Fate for Breakfast (Columbia, 1979)
★★ Scissors Cut (Columbia, 1981)
★ Lefty (Columbia, 1988)
★★★ Garfunkel (Columbia, 1990)
★★ Across America (Hybrid/EMI, 1997)
★★ Songs from a Parent to a Child (Sony Wonder, 1997)
★★★ Everything Waits to Be Noticed (EMI/Manhattan, 2002)

On his own, Art Garfunkel exhibits many of the same strengths that marked his work with Paul Simon—an angelic tenor voice, a fine sense of understatement and subtlety, and a genius for harmony vocals. Unfortunately, that's not enough to support a solo career, and without a strong creative voice to play off, Garfunkel's albums end up seeming as empty as they are pretty. *Angel Clare* is all too typical. When given good material, such as Randy Newman's "Old Man" or Van Morrison's "I Shall Sing," Garfunkel is in his ele-

ment, but when the material slips, as on "Mary Was an Only Child," so does the value of his performance. *Breakaway* keeps that from being a problem, thanks to a soaring rendition of Stevie Wonder's "I Believe (When I Fall in Love It Will Be Forever)" and the aching "99 Miles From L.A." There's even a Simon and Garfunkel reunion on "My Little Town."

Watermark is the high point of Garfunkel's solo career. Built around a Jimmy Webb song cycle, its evocation of longing and loss makes it a perfect vehicle for Garfunkel's voice (even though the cover of Sam Cooke's "[What a] Wonderful World," cut with Paul Simon and James Taylor, was the only hit).

Beyond that, Garfunkel's recordings are pretty much fans-only affairs. *Fate for Breakfast* is a slick and unsuccessful attempt at mainstreaming Garfunkel's sound; *Scissors Cut* is too dull to leave a mark; *Lefty* strikes out; and *Garfunkel* proves only that a greatest-hits package is not necessarily the same thing as a best-of album. No surprise, then, that the singer went on hiatus, returning in 1997 for *Across America,* an oldies-dependent live album that reminds us why the duo was billed as Simon and Garfunkel and not the other way around (though the duet with Taylor on "Cryin' in the Rain" is unexpectedly poignant), and *Songs from a Parent to a Child,* a must-hear for those wondering how well Garfunkel harmonizes with his young son. Still, it may be premature to write him off, as *Everything Wants to Be Noticed* convincingly evokes the wistful charm of his early albums as it explores the difficulties of late-life romance. A bit more of this, and Garfunkel may yet earn a reputation that doesn't depend on an ampersand. —J.D.C.

Marvin Gaye

★★★ A Tribute to the Great Nat "King" Cole (Tamla, 1965)
★★★★★ What's Going On (Tamla, 1971)
★★½ Trouble Man (Tamla, 1972)
★★★★★ Let's Get It On (Tamla, 1973)
★★½ Live (1974; Motown, 1998)
★★½ I Want You (Tamla, 1976)
★★★ Live at the London Palladium (1977; Motown, 1998)
★★★½ Here, My Dear (Tamla, 1978)
★★★ Midnight Love (Columbia, 1982)
★★★ Every Great Motown Hit of Marvin Gaye (Motown, 1983)
★★½ Dream of a Lifetime (Columbia, 1985)
★★★ Romantically Yours (Columbia, 1985)
★★★½ 18 Greatest Hits (Motown, 1988)
★★★ Seek & You Shall Find: More of the Best (1963–1981) (Rhino, 1993)

★★	Motown Legends: I'll Be Doggone (Motown, 1995)	
★★★★½	The Master 1961–1984 (Motown, 1995)	
★★★	Midnight Love & the Sexual Healing Sessions (Columbia/Legacy, 1998)	
★★★	The Millennium Collection: Best of Marvin Gaye, Vol. 1 (Universal, 1999)	
★★★½	Lost and Found: Love Starved Heart (Motown, 1999)	
★★★	The Millennium Collection: Best of Marvin Gaye, Vol. 2 (Universal, 2000)	
★★★★	The Millennium Collection: Best of Marvin Gaye & Tammi Terrell (Universal, 2000)	
★★	The Final Concert (The Right Stuff, 2000)	
★★★★½	What's Going On [Deluxe Edition] (Universal, 2001)	
★★★★½	Let's Get It On [Deluxe Edition] (Universal, 2001)	
★★★★	The Very Best of Marvin Gaye (Universal, 2001)	
★	Super Hits (Sony, 2001)	
★★★★	The Complete Duets [with Tammi Terrell] (Universal, 2001)	
★★★½	Love Songs: Bedroom Ballads (Motown, 2002)	
★★	Love Songs (Sony/Legacy, 2003)	
★★★★	Love Songs—Greatest Duets (Motown, 2003)	

From R&B star and soul-music giant to pop icon, the stature of Marvin Gaye has risen steadily over the years. Others had greater vocal range; there were certainly better performers (Marvin never did fully vanquish his stage discomfort); and for one who is regarded as a creative visionary, his genius often needed to be kick-started by collaborators. Yet few artists in any genre can approach Marvin Gaye's breadth of accomplishment. Following the failure of an album of standards aimed at establishing him as a black Sinatra, Gaye submitted to the conventional Motown hit-making machinery. (He would never lose his desire to become a "serious" singer, as evidenced by his affectionate 1965 tribute to Nat "King" Cole.) His first couple of successes, "Stubborn Kind of Fellow" and "Hitch Hike," were not at all how he saw himself, but they got him in the door and on the charts.

Most of Gaye's early albums are out of print, but the string of hits he recorded between 1962 and '69 with the label's bottomless pool of writers and producers—including Smokey Robinson ("Ain't That Peculiar"), Holland-Dozier-Holland ("You're a Wonderful One"), and Norman Whitfield ("I Heard It Through the Grapevine")—made him Motown's premier male singer and have been the basis of countless compilation

packages. What impresses is not only the endless excellence of Motown's production line, but the ease with which Gaye's voice accommodated the very different demands of each piece, from the gospel exhortations of "Can I Get a Witness" to the breezy swing of "How Sweet It Is (To Be Loved by You)." He maintained a parallel and almost equally successful career as a singer of romantic duets with labelmates such as Mary Wells ("What's the Matter With You Baby"), Kim Weston ("It Takes Two"), and his most significant other, Tammi Terrell ("Ain't No Mountain High Enough"). *Greatest Duets* collects the highlights of all his associations (except, curiously, "Ain't No Mountain"), including a session with gospel singer Ona Page. *The Complete Duets* gives you everything recorded by Gaye and Terrell, arguably the most romantic singing partnership in pop history. (After Terrell's death, Marvin vowed he'd never sing with another partner. Judging by his tepid 1976 album with Diana Ross, it was a vow he should have kept.)

Having worked all these wonders, Marvin Gaye then did something no other Motown artist had ever dared. With *What's Going On* (1971), he committed a revolution. Although it spawned three hits—the anti-war title song, the ecological plea "Mercy Mercy Me," and "Inner City Blues"—this was Motown's first true *album*. Its blend of unembarrassed spirituality and unflinching social realism, as well as relentless percussion set against lush orchestration, was unlike anything that came before it in both form and content. For Gaye, it was a self-produced declaration of independence. (The 2001 *Deluxe Edition* adds an earlier and substantially different mix and a rare live performance of the album from 1972.) After a detour to score the film *Trouble Man*, he followed his masterpiece with the almost equally magnificent *Let's Get It On* in 1973. From the title-track opener to the closing "Just to Keep You Satisfied," it is as unashamedly sexual as its predecessor is spiritual. (Its *Deluxe Edition* bonus disc illuminates Marvin's many false starts with multiple collaborators before he settled on the final framework.)

I Want You boasts the seductive title song and "After the Dance" but is otherwise slight, a disappointment after the twin peaks of *What's Going On* and *Let's Get It On*. *Live* is from a 1974 concert that was his first in two years, and it shows, though the sparks that fly on "Distant Lover" are eternal. *Live at the London Palladium* catches a better show and contains the 12 studio minutes of "Got to Give It Up," proof positive that disco and genuine soul could coexist in a single slab of wax. *Here, My Dear* (1978) was not a successful album saleswise, but it may be his most fascinating. Forced to give up the royalties to his ex-wife in their divorce settlement, Gaye's album brutally chronicles the breakdown of the marriage—no hits, but plenty of bruises. After a European exile and a divorce from Motown, he reappeared in 1982 with *Midnight Love* on Columbia. Its slinky single "Sexual Healing" intertwines his two major themes—sex and salvation—and is as seductive as anything in Marvin's overstuffed little black book of song. That said, the rest is smooth and superficially pleasing but leaves little lasting impression. What was a welcome comeback would prove to be his final album.

Since the tragic shooting death of Marvin Gaye in 1984, collections, compilations, and unissued material have rained down on an apparently insatiable marketplace. Steer clear of the countless packages of bootleg-quality live material drawn from his erratic 1983 comeback tour, issued under titles like *Greatest Hits Live, Performance,* and *In Concert.* Even the best of these, *The Final Concert,* offers only marginally improved sound on a performance that is charitably characterized as adequate. *Super Hits* is not the wonderful 1970 Motown collection, now deleted, but a budget set of *Midnight Love* material. There are no less than three packages trading under the title *Love Songs:* 1) the aforementioned *Greatest Duets;* 2) a Sony comp that again reshuffles the *Midnight Love* material; and 3) *Love Songs: Bedroom Ballads,* assembled by biographer David Ritz to combine the singer's most amorous slow songs with the handful of standards arranged for Gaye by Bobby Scott (previously available as *Vulnerable*). In the same vein as the Ritz collection—imagine an update of Jackie Gleason's '50s albums of makeout music—is *Romantically Yours,* which was compiled by Marvin's mentor and sometime producer Harvey Fuqua.

Love Starved Heart is a true rarity: an album of vault material that doesn't waste your time; Gaye rivals Bob Dylan in the quantity of quality material left on the shelf. *Every Great Motown Hit of Marvin Gaye* ain't all that, but its 17 songs make it an acceptable sampler; ditto *18 Greatest Hits,* but *I'll Be Doggone* is just a Motown mishmash. The two best-of volumes in the *Millennium Collection* series, split between the '60s and '70s, contain only 11 songs each. Pick of the litter is the two-CD *Very Best of Marvin Gaye,* though it is not quite up to the double *Anthology* it replaced in the catalogue. The 1995 four-CD set *The Master* is excellent, as well as being a marked improvement over a botched box attempt earlier in that decade. But in the eight years since its release, so much worthy music has been unearthed that a rethink may be in order. Every time they measure Marvin Gaye for a monument, he's grown a few more inches.   —B.E.

Gloria Gaynor

★★   I Am What I Am (Hot, 1996)
★★   The Best of Gloria Gaynor (PGD Special, 1997)
★★★ I Will Survive: The Anthology (Polydor, 1998)
★★   The Fabulous Voice of Gloria Gaynor (BCI, 1998)
★★   Best of Gloria Gaynor (Cleopatra, 1999)

Although Gloria Gaynor sang R&B during the early to mid-'70s, once she lent her magnificent voice to the late-'70s disco hit "I Will Survive," she became known for little else. Most of her still-available records are compilations—all of them essentially various record labels' attempts to keep "I Will Survive" in circulation—and on them, Gaynor always sings well. But she never sings as pertinently as she did on the song that became an anthem of freedom and self-empowerment for millions of dance-obsessed listeners.   —A.B.

J. Geils Band

★★★½ The J. Geils Band (Atlantic, 1970)
★★★   The Morning After (Atlantic, 1971)
★★★★ Live: Full House (Atlantic, 1972)
★★★½ Bloodshot (Atlantic, 1973)
★★   Ladies Invited (Atlantic, 1974)
★★★★ Nightmares . . . and Other Tales From the Vinyl Jungle (Atlantic, 1974)
★★   Hotline (Atlantic, 1975)
★★★   Blow Your Face Out (Atlantic, 1976)
★★★★ Monkey Island (Atlantic, 1977)
★★★★ Sanctuary (EMI-America, 1978)
★★★★½ Best of the J. Geils Band (Atlantic, 1979)
★★★★ Best of the J. Geils Band Two (Atlantic, 1980)
★★★½ Love Stinks (EMI-America, 1980)
★★★★ Freeze Frame (EMI-America, 1981)
★★   Showtime! (EMI-America, 1983)
★   You're Getting Even While I'm Getting Odd (EMI-America, 1984)
★★★½ Flashback (EMI-America, 1988)
★★★★ Houseparty: The J. Geils Band Anthology (Rhino, 1992)

"Take out your false teeth, mama . . . I wanna SUCK on your GUMS." With these gentle words, the J. Geils Band's frontman, Peter Wolf, seared himself onto rock history, and his henchmen took their place as the finest Jewish blues-rockers ever to do the Boston Monkey. The J. Geils Band had a lean, mean approach to old-school R&B, blasting through John Lee Hooker and Otis Rush classics in a completely nonacademic way, making everything sound tough and crass and ironic. Wolf, the self-proclaimed "Woofa Goofa with the Green Teeth," made David Lee Roth seem like the shy type; Magic Dick played the harmonica; in album-cover photos, the entire band dissolved into one giant Jewish Afro with shades; and naming the band after the nonsinging guitarist (who could barely play) was *so* rock & roll. The Geils gang didn't do much songwriting at first, covering obscure blues and soul treasures instead, though the 1973 hit "Give It to Me" was a freaky seven-minute move into early reggae. But *Full House* (source of the aforementioned "false teeth" patter) proved that J. Geils could rip it up live, from "First I Look at the Purse" to the pounding finale, "Looking for a Love." The Magic Dick showcase "Whammer Jammer" became the "Smoke on the Water" of the harmonica.

Nightmares was the best of the early J. Geils studio albums, with the house party "Stoop Down #39," the stoopid-fresh "Detroit Breakdown" (for some reason, Boston bands are always obsessed with Detroit), and the breakup ballad "Must of Got Lost." The double-live *Blow Your Face Out* had a classic live version of the latter, beginning with a long preacherly rap from Wolf ("this is a song about L-O-V-E and if you abuse it, you're gonna lose it, and if you lose it, you ain't gonna be able to choose it," etc.), and whomping renditions of "Love-Itis" and "Where Did Our Love Go?" But J. Geils was starting to mature, calling itself just "Geils" on the cover of *Monkey Island* as Wolf recited a nine-minute poem about alienation in the title track. *Sanctuary* was even tougher, with the touching "I Don't Hang Around Much Any More," the Italian-girl-worshipping "Teresa," the manic "Jus' Can't Stop Me," and the confusing but kind-of-intense title anthem.

Sanctuary was so damn good, it seemed that J. Geils would never be able to match it, but to everyone's surprise, the band bought a synthesizer and promptly became 10 times bigger than ever. Not with a pop sellout, either: "Love Stinks," with a three-chord riff that later showed up as "Smells Like Teen Spirit." The album added the rollicking "Till the Walls Come Tumbling Down," the failed Eurodisco experiment "Come Back," and the Firesign Theatre rip "No Anchovies, Please." *Freeze Frame* updated the band's rock attack with arty synth-funk beats, resulting in a couple of huge singles ("Freeze Frame," "Centerfold") and a hit album that bridged traditional rock, new wave, punk, disco, and slick pop. The best was the finale "Piss on the Wall," where Wolf pondered the nature of reality: "Some people say the world ain't what it is/All I know is I just got to take a whizz."

Unfortunately, after years of white-knuckling it to the top, the band responded to mainstream success by kicking out Peter Wolf. Keyboardist Seth Justman took over the vocals for *You're Getting Even While I'm Getting Odd,* one of the most disastrous followups in music-biz history, a career ender for everyone involved. (Chili Peppers fans take note: It did include a song called "Californicating.") Wolf went on to solo success, but J. Geils fans still wept for what might have been. *Showtime!* was the band's third and weakest live album. *Flashback* is a flimsy best-of from the band's three big EMI albums; the two-disc *Houseparty* is a much better compilation of both early and late J. Geils. But the best places to start are the Atlantic collections *Best of,* with the bowling pins on the cover, and *Best of Two,* which has classic album tracks such as "Stoop Down #39" and "The Lady Makes Demands." —R.S.

Generation X

★★★½ Perfect Hits 1975–1981 (Chrysalis, 1991)

Thanks to the '80s pop-rock career of singer Billy Idol, nobody ever believes that Generation X were present-at-the-creation London punks. But there they were, along with the Pistols, the Damned, and all the rest. They weren't founding fathers by any stretch, with their fat hooks and a willingness to cover Lennon's "Gimme Some Truth" on their excellent (no, really) pop-punk debut. Punk bands may worship fellow pop-punk visionaries such as the Buzzcocks, and even Stiff Little Fingers get a nod or two. But when was the last time you heard a punk band cover Generation X?

These days, their stock is so low their proper albums are available only as imports. Then again, *Perfect Hits* is all you ever need, including iPod-worthy singles such as "Wild Youth," "Your Generation," and "Ready, Steady, Go," a version of "Dancing With Myself," Idol's brilliant ode to whacking off, and the genuinely groundbreaking "Wild Dub," maybe the very first time a punk band turned punk into reggae, a stunt that would happen *a lot* on both sides of the pond over the next thirty years. —J.G.

Genesis

★★★ From Genesis to Revelation (1969; DCC, 1990)
★★★ Trespass (1970; MCA, 1980)
★★ Nursery Cryme (Atlantic, 1971)
★★★ Foxtrot (Atlantic, 1972)
★★★ Genesis Live (Atlantic, 1973)
★★ Selling England by the Pound (Atlantic, 1973)
★★★★ The Lamb Lies Down on Broadway (Atlantic, 1974)
★★★★ A Trick of the Tail (Atlantic, 1976)
★★★ Wind and Wuthering (Atlantic, 1976)

★★★ Seconds Out (Atlantic, 1977)
★★★★ . . . And Then There Were Three (Atlantic, 1978)
★★★★ Duke (Atlantic, 1980)
★★★★ ABACAB (Atlantic, 1981)
★★★ Three Sides Live (Atlantic, 1982)
★★★★ Genesis (Atlantic, 1983)
★★★★ Invisible Touch (Atlantic, 1986)
★★★★ We Can't Dance (Atlantic, 1991)
★★★ Live/The Way We Walk, Vol. 1: The Shorts (Atlantic, 1992)
★★½ Live/The Way We Walk, Vol. 2: The Longs (Atlantic, 1993)
★★½ Calling All Stations (Atlantic, 1997)
★★★ Genesis Archives, Vol. 1: 1967–1975 (Atlantic, 1998)
★★ Genesis Archives, Vol. 2: 1976–92 (Atlantic, 2000)

Like Rodney Dangerfield, Genesis has had a hard time getting respect. In the early '70s, when the group specialized in ambitious, theatrical story-songs, it attracted an avid cult following but was largely ignored by the rock press and public at large. Later in the decade, lead singer Peter Gabriel was finally recognized as a major talent—but only after he'd left the band, who were at this point being derided as middlebrow throwbacks still in thrall to the pomposities of art rock. Even in the early '80s, when Genesis did finally shed its art-rock inclinations and move toward pop, becoming international stars in the process, the press was unimpressed, dismissing the group as easy-listening lightweights. By the '90s, even the solo success of members Phil Collins and Mike Rutherford was being held against the group, by then one of the best-known rock acts in the world.

All of which, to be honest, has been grossly unfair to the group. Granted, Genesis has made its share of mediocre albums—perhaps even more than its share, considering how long the band has been around. But bad albums? None to speak of.

In fact, the worst that can be said of the group's early albums is that they sound dated, almost quaint. From Genesis to Revelation seems laughably "mod" at points—for instance, the jazzy, bongo-spiked intro to "The Serpent"—but that hardly takes away from the genuinely tuneful quality of the songs. Genesis was hardly a band when this was recorded, however, and it isn't until Trespass that we get any real sense of what this band has to offer. Unfortunately, it's something of a mixed bag. At their best, the lyrics are grippingly mythic, but too often Gabriel's wordplay loses its way in a forest of puns and self-conscious allusions; likewise the music, although often potently melodic and

making nice of use of Tony Banks' semiorchestral approach to keyboards, is frequently sidetracked by too-busy arrangements and needlessly ornate embellishments.

That was pretty much the pattern for the band's early albums, though. Nursery Cryme, for instance, offers Grimm play with Mother Goose tales in the 10-minute "Musical Box," while Foxtrot concludes with the marathon "Supper's Ready," an ambitious, inscrutable 23-minute suite built around such titles as "Apocalypse in 9/8 (co-starring the delicious talents of Gabble Ratchet)." Stilted as this stuff sometimes sounded in the studio, it did have an edge in concert; indeed, the performances on Genesis Live are enough to make even the most skeptical listener reconsider the value of "The Return of the Giant Hogweed." But "edge" wasn't really what this band was looking for, and so Selling England by the Pound continues Genesis' journey into the conceptual, flanking blissfully melodic material such as "I Know What I Like (in Your Wardrobe)" with the self-consciously clever "Dancing with the Moonlit Knight" and its ilk. No wonder, then, that the group's masterpiece move—an intensely abstruse double album entitled The Lamb Lies Down on Broadway—is both brilliant and overblown, with moments of genuine majesty and long stretches of pointless obscurantism.

Gabriel left at this point, and Genesis auditioned hundreds of singers before finally deciding on Collins, who had been drumming with the group since Trespass (and who, in fact, had already sung lead on "More Fool Me," from Selling England). It was a canny choice, for Collins, though obviously possessing a voice of his own, sounded enough like Gabriel to ensure a smooth transition for the band. Even so, it isn't Collins' voice that makes A Trick of the Tail a turning point for the band—it's the writing. Instead of showcasing the band's cleverness, this album puts the emphasis on the music, unveiling an unexpected gift for close-harmony singing in "Entangled." Wind and Wuthering expands the band's musical palette still further; typical is the droll clockwork effect that crops up during an instrumental segment of "One for the Vine." More telling, though, is the ballad "Your Own Special Way," a gorgeously lilting love song that seems a harbinger of the band's pop-friendly future.

Indeed, after Seconds Out—a concert double album apparently intended to prove that Collins and company could handle the band's back catalogue—the band made a genuine pop breakthrough with . . . And Then There Were Three. With guitarist Steve Hackett gone, Genesis' studio lineup is reduced to just Collins, Banks, and Rutherford, and while that doesn't noticeably affect the band's instrumental mix, it does hone the playing so that there's less empty flash and wasted energy. At this point, the songs are the focus, and while that doesn't prevent the band from showing off any (note the odd-metered rhythms of "Down and Out"), it does add power to character songs such as "Say It's Alright Joe" and gave the band its first U.S. pop success, through the winsome, up-beat "Follow You, Follow Me." *Duke* and *ABACAB* further enhance the group's pop reputation—the former through "Misunderstanding," a simple, poignant broken-heart song that brings Collins to the fore as a writer, and the latter through "No Reply at All," a surprisingly complex composition that leaves the band plenty of playing room yet maintains strong melodic content. Unfortunately, these pop-oriented efforts are followed by *Three Sides Live*, a double album that's mostly live and totally tedious.

It hardly mattered, though, for by this point the band's superstar status had been established beyond the shadow of a doubt, and both *Genesis* and *Invisible Touch* merely seemed to confirm its popularity. And not without reason, either, as both are sublimely melodic, producing hits as effortless and idiosyncratic as "That's All" (from *Genesis*) and "Tonight, Tonight, Tonight" (from *Invisible Touch*). But *We Can't Dance*, despite its strong pop inclinations, finds the band trying to reclaim some of its old turf, a move that works surprisingly well, thanks to tuneful-but-extended numbers such as "Driving the Last Spike" and "Fading Lights."

Collins left Genesis after the *We Can't Dance* tour, and Genesis stalled for time by releasing two live albums—one of "short" pop hits, the other of "long" art-rock chestnuts—before finally deciding to move on without him. Scots singer Ray Wilson, formerly of the little-known prog-rock band Stiltskin, was drafted by Banks and Rutherford to take Collins' place. Had he come in after *Foxtrot*, Wilson would have made for a smooth transition, but given the pop expectations engendered by Collins' tenure, his succession was deemed a failure, and Genesis slipped quietly into oblivion. Not that interest in the band evaporated, and *Genesis Archives, Vol. 1* offered an olive branch to older fans by bringing back both Peter Gabriel and Steve Hackett to recut tracks from rare live recordings. *Vol. 2* also relied mainly on live recordings, but without the advantage of reworked performances, it held only marginal interest.   —J.D.C.

Geto Boys/Scarface

★★ Makin' Trouble (Rap-A-Lot, 1988)
★★★½ Grip It! On That Other Level (Rap-A-Lot, 1990)
★★★½ The Geto Boys (Def American, 1990)
★★★★ We Can't Be Stopped (Rap-A-Lot, 1991)
★★★★ Uncut Dope: Greatest Hits (Rap-A-Lot, 1992)
★★★ Til Death Do Us Part (Rap-A-Lot, 1993)
★★★ The Resurrection (Rap-A-Lot, 1996)
★★ Da Good Da Bad & Da Ugly (Rap-A-Lot, 1998)
★★★½ Greatest Hits (Rap-A-Lot, 2002)

Scarface

★★★★ Mr. Scarface Is Back (Rap-A-Lot, 1991)
★★★ The World Is Yours (Rap-A-Lot, 1993)
★★★★½ The Diary (Rap-A-Lot, 1994)
★★★ Untouchable (Rap-A-Lot, 1997)
★★★ My Homies (Rap-A-Lot, 1998)
★★½ Last of a Dying Breed (Rap-A-Lot, 2000)
★★★★ The Fix (Def Jam, 2002)
★★★★ Greatest Hits (Rap-A-Lot, 2002)
★★★ Balls & My Word (Rap-A-Lot, 2003)

Willie D

★★½ Controversy (Rap-A-Lot, 1989)
★★½ I'm Goin' Out Like a Soldier (Rap-A-Lot, 1992)
★★★ Play Witcha Mama (Wrap/Ichiban, 1994)
★★★ Loved by Few, Hated by Many (Rap-A-Lot, 2000)

Bushwick Bill

★★★ Little Big Man (Rap-A-Lot, 1992)
★★★ Phantom of the Rapra (Rap-A-Lot, 1995)
★★½ No Surrender . . . No Retreat (Wrap/Ichiban, 1998)
★★ Universal Small Souljah (Nu Wave, 2001)

When Rick Rubin happened upon them in 1990, Houston's Geto Boys were poised to fill a void the mainstream didn't know it had yet: shock rappers. At the time, a couple of artists had raised hackles in the world outside of hip-hop, but the Geto Boys' seeming lack of a taboo zone marked them as troublemakers before they could even get much momentum. The Rubin-produced *Geto Boys*—a slight reworking of their *Grip It! On That Other Level* album—was packed with absurd, sometimes galling tracks ("Mind of a Lunatic," "Trigga Happy Nigga"). So shocking was the music at the time that Rubin was forced to seek alternate distribution for the project.

The controversy had a perhaps unexpected effect on the Boys: On their next album, *We Can't Be Stopped*, they became unlikely first-amendment crusaders. The title track decried the perceived hypocrisy that led to the group's virtual banning, and "Fuck a War" showed they had political ambition beyond their own personal interests. The cover of *Can't Be Stopped*—a snapshot of Bushwick Bill in the hospital after his girlfriend shot out one of his eyes—attracted as much attention as the content, a collection of morbid, gruesome street tales, including "Mind Playing

Tricks on Me," one of the classics of the genre that showed the seamy underbelly of street life rather than celebrating its spoils. This was their free speech—potent, but potentially costly. After *Stopped,* the group never again released a top-flight album (though *The Resurrection* was a strong effort).

It wasn't more than three years into his career as a Geto Boy before Scarface, né Brad Jordan, decided he needed to branch out. Face was already the ringer in the crew—Willie D was a loose cannon, and Bushwick Bill's physical novelty often outshone his rapping. In the same year that *We Can't Be Stopped* was released, Face dropped his solo debut, *Mr. Scarface Is Back,* and managed to outdo the work he had done with the rest of the group. "Murder By Reason Of Insanity" was vividly unhinged, and on "Good Girl Gone Bad" and the stellar "A Minute to Pray and a Second to Die," Face honed his greatest talent: serving up unglamorous, economical storytelling packed with sympathy and heart. The humanity continued on his third solo album, aptly titled *The Diary.* "I Seen a Man Die" is up there with Face's most psychologically illuminating work, and Ice Cube showed up to pay his respects to his Southern counterpart on "Hand of the Dead Body."

For two solo albums, Face floundered, but with 2002's *The Fix,* Scarface once again proved himself to be a rap music pioneer. This time out, though, the demographic ground he broke wasn't geographic, but age based. For the first time in rap music, the aging gangster became an acceptable character archetype. While scores of younger rappers viewed their careers as a means to financial and personal ends, Face put his history of clear-eyed social criticism to work, delivering an album both tangibly wistful ("Guess Who's Back" featuring Jay-Z and Beanie Sigel) and impossibly world-weary ("Someday," "Heaven"). Unlike other rappers who retire in clunky fashion, Face has been the first to find a way to age gracefully, growing wiser with experience and turning it into great art.

Both Bushwick Bill and Willie D have had solo careers, though neither one has produced particularly distinguished output. Willie D also made a name for himself as a boxer in the late '90s. —J.C.

Get Up Kids

★★ Four Minute Mile (Doghouse, 1997)
★★★★ Something to Write Home About (Vagrant, 1999)
★★½ Red Letter Day/Woodson (Doghouse, 2001)
★★½ Eudora (Vagrant, 2001)
★★★ On a Wire (Vagrant, 2002)
★★★½ Guilt Show (Vagrant, 2004)

With their bouncy name and their middle America hometown (Kansas City, MO), the Get Up Kids embody the clean-cut, nerdy side of the emo subculture. But the Get Up Kids actually only made one true emo bill. On 1999's *Something to Write Home About,* the quintet balanced its earnest romanticism between lurching punk and yearning pop, representing the genre as gracefully as the Promise Ring, Saves the Day, or any other late-'90s emo icon, while also reaching out for something bigger.

Until then, the Kids' talents had been of interest mostly to those who shared their adenoidal awkwardness. Listen closely to 1997's *Four Minute Mile* and you'll hear evidence of a budding talent for memorable melodies and riffs, especially on "Don't Hate Me," which not only features an instantly catchy chorus but also encapsulates how passive-aggressive sensitive young men can be ("Oh Amy don't hate me/For running away from you"). But that evidence is buried among lots of weedy, off-key laments wailed over fast and familiar punk rock. *Eudora* collects all the vinyl singles and compilation cuts of those early years, and although it's less coherent than *Four Minute Mile,* the disc's eclectic covers—from New Order to the Replacements to Mötley Crüe—add a welcome jolt of unpredictability. The *Red Letter Day/Woodson* set offers two EPs separated by three long years of growth, and although 1999's *Red Letter Day* demonstrates a huge leap in songwriting ability from the earlier *Woodson,* it's still hampered by amateurish production. The Get Up Kids found the right sound only by moving to Vagrant for *Something to Write Home About,* and the album's critical and commercial success in turn transformed the struggling label into an indie-rock powerhouse. After grueling tours with arena acts such as Weezer, however, the band retreated in 2002 with *On a Wire,* an album that leaves behind emo's earnest pleading for the comforts of straight pop-rock. Tracks such as "Overdue" and "Walking on a Wire" are gorgeous, but they don't make up for the loss of the group's youthful, punky punch. With 2004's *Guilt Show,* however, the Kids proved themselves all grown up and ready to look beyond their own navels, especially on tracks such as the anti-imperialist plea "Holy Roman" and the twinkling portrait of a dull life, "Martyr Me." Despite a few missteps, their newly confident pop rock is something to write home about again. —F.S.

Ghostface Killah

★★★★ Ironman (1996; Epic/Razor Sharp, 2001)
★★★★ Supreme Clientele (Epic/Razor Sharp, 2000)
★★★★½ Bulletproof Wallets (Epic, 2001)
★★★½ Shaolin's Finest (Epic, 2003)
★★★★ Pretty Toney (Epic, 2004)

The Wu-Tang Clan's best MC, Ghostface Killah developed a narrative style that's deeper, denser, and wittier than any of his groupmates'—and just about any gangsta rapper's, for that matter. Ghostface had it from the start of his solo career: *Ironman* combined the RZA's most soulful production to date with torrents of imagery and eddies of observation, a stream of consciousness funneled through back alleys, gun barrels, and big dicks. (Ghost's guest-spots on Raekwon's classic 1995 debut, *Only Built 4 Cuban Linx*, promised as much.) On "260," which slides in with wagging horn figures and soul-man sighs, Ghostface turns a mundane botched robbery into a grand tragedy.

Sparkling and brassy, *Supreme Clientele* showcases a slightly more self-conscious storyteller swinging from skyscraper-size hooks. After each gymnastic verse in album-opener "Nutmeg," Ghostface lets the dramatic disco-stringed chorus run, taunting not just lesser MCs but every listener in awe of his verbal backflips and rolls: "Yeah! See what I mean, you motherfuckin' crybabies? Get in line, punk." *Bulletproof Wallets* (officially featuring Raekwon) was somewhat derided as a commercial move, and sure enough, every song lunges for the ear. The mostly no-name producers cut can't-go-wrong samples into supple, hard-driving loops and polish it all to a gleam. The tinkly, insistent cowbell in "Flowers" cuts through string-section swoops while Ghostface and Method Man soft-shoe along with it. "Never Be the Same Again," featuring a mournful Carl Thomas, is the most sentimental of Ghostface's "cry" songs, yet this long goodbye to a cheating lover flits so realistically from regret and anger to bewilderment that the trickling sap is fully justified.

Choppy, blaring, and shape-shifting, *Pretty Toney* makes peculiarly effective use of its vintage R&B lifts. A couple of the best cuts are brief experiments billed as skits: "Last Night" sketches an evening that starts with deviant sex and ends with an unanswered call; a phone rings incessantly over a dusty throwback break. In "Keisha's House," Ghost recalls a wet summer night in which he drinks on the stoop, takes a shit in his friend's bathroom, and gets horny looking at every woman except the one he's with; the sampled song could be a boom box playing in the background. In the end, he goes home with his girlfriend. —N.C.

Jimmie Dale Gilmore

★★★ Fair & Square (Hightone, 1988)
★★★ Jimmie Dale Gilmore (Hightone, 1989)
★★★★½ After Awhile (Elektra/Nonesuch, 1991)
★★★★ Spinning Around the Sun (Elektra, 1993)
★★★★ Braver New World (Elektra, 1996)
★★★½ One Endless Night (Rounder, 2000)

There are those who call Jimmie Dale Gilmore's voice an acquired—or impossible to acquire—taste. But don't trust them. Out of all the artists to spring out of the unlikely town of Lubbock, Texas—a heady list including Buddy Holly, Waylon Jennings, Delbert McClinton, and Gilmore's fellow Flatlanders bandmates Joe Ely and Butch Hancock—Gilmore's high, wispy vibrato is the voice that best captures the lonesome wail of the West Texas wind, the peal of a pedal-steel guitar ringing through an old honky-tonk, and the ghost of Hank Williams shooting across the desert sky from a border radio tower. Matched with the right song, it can be an instrument of otherworldly beauty . . . or at the very least, straightforward hillbilly bliss. The traditional country stylings of *Fair & Square* and *Jimmie Dale Gilmore* both fall into the latter category, as Gilmore plays it safe by sticking to the tried-and-true, keep-'em-dancing Lefty Frizzell playbook. The song choices are hit and miss; his shuffling take on Ely's bittersweet "Honky-Tonk Masquerade" *(Fair & Square)* borders on hokum, but his own "Dallas" *(Jimmie Dale Gilmore)* is definitive, and his spin through Hancock's comic "Red Chevrolet" is a hoot. Both albums, however, fail to distinguish Gilmore as an artist with a unique vision.

After Awhile—and pretty much everything in its wake—changed that. While still undeniably drawing from classic country influences, *After Awhile* finds Gilmore liberated from the strictures of a dancehall stage, free to serve song over form in the spirit of a folk artist rather than an entertainer. It's also the first of his albums to showcase his strength as a writer as well as a singer—Gilmore wrote every song but one, among them "Tonight I Think I'm Gonna Go Downtown," "Treat Me Like a Saturday Night," and "Chase the Wind," vaulting him into the ranks of some of the Lone Star state's finest troubadours. *Spinning Around the Sun* is less intimate but no less beautiful, featuring another handful of sterling Gilmore originals, a pair of ace Hancock tunes, and, courtesy of songwriter A. B. Strehli Jr.'s exquisite "Santa Fe Thief" and its opening line, "Oh the townhouse warbler lives far apart in a song," the finest marriage of song and voice of Gilmore's career. The T-Bone Burnett–produced *Braver New World*, meanwhile, lives up to its title, with Gilmore singing over rivers of shivery electric guitar on atmospheric beauties like "Borderland" and rocking out on "Headed for a Fall" (among his best originals) and "Outside the Lines," which sounds something like Roy Orbison fronting Doug Sahm's Tex-Mex Sir Douglas Quintet. Like Gilmore's voice itself, the results are weird and wonderful. *One Endless Night* could stand a few more risks. Despite an exemplary cover of John Hiatt's "Your Love Is My Rest" and some left-field picks (the Grateful Dead's "Ripple" and, in the spirit of Willie Nelson's *Stardust*, "Mack the Knife"), the return to more folksy, familiar territory distinguishes it as Gilmore's safest album in a decade—and by extension, his weakest. That said, it's still head and shoulders over just about anything you'll hear on mainstream country radio. —R.SK.

Gin Blossoms

★★	Dusted (1989; Bakman, 2002)	
★★★	Up and Crumbling (EP) (A&M, 1991)	
★★★½	New Miserable Experience (A&M, 1992)	
★★★	Congratulations . . . I'm Sorry (A&M, 1996)	
★★★½	Outside Looking In: The Best of the Gin Blossoms (A&M, 1999)	
★★★	The Millennium Collection (A&M, 2003)	

In 1987, R.E.M. was rising to superstardom; most rock fans would admit to owning a dB's album; the Replacements had made some of the decade's finest ache; somewhere Alex Chilton was doing something; and even Cheap Trick had a hit single. No wonder the Gin Blossoms got together. Their rootsy, indeterminate power pop, primarily harnessed to the songwriting vision of guitarist Doug Hopkins, would take a few years to gel, but by 1993 they had created one of the best-selling rock records of the year. *Dusted,* from 1989, was a self-released crack at tunes that would (mostly) show up later, and the tough, melodic, five-song *Up and Crumbling* EP pointed toward big things.

Recorded at Ardent Studios in Memphis (where power pop lives!), *New Miserable Experience* took a few months to gather steam, but by the middle of '93 five of the album's seven songs had taken up residence and built houses on various Modern Rock and album-rock radio charts: It was damn hard to hide from tough, tender heartbreakers such as "Hey Jealousy," "Until I Fall Away," "Found Out About You," and "Alison Road."

Hopkins' sharp, melodic songwriting gelled nicely with singer Robin Wilson's bar-band, just-folk vocals. No wonder it went all kinds of platinum. *New Miserable Experience* was Pottery Barn rock, but it was about as good as Pottery Barn rock got. (The album was reissued as a deluxe double CD, with tracks from *Dusted, Up and Crumbling,* outtakes, "Idiot Summer" from *Wayne's World 2,* a cover of Big Star's "Back of a Car," and live material.)

But even before the hits began piling up, the Blossoms sacked Hopkins, having grown frustrated with his drinking. Hopkins committed suicide on December 5, 1993. The band then scored its first post-Hopkins hit with the sweet, folkish "'Til I Hear It From You," which can be found on both hits collections. (Buy both of those, or even one; casual fans don't need anything else.) But the band's bland, Hopkinsless followup, *Congratulations . . . I'm Sorry,* reminded everyone just how important the late guitarist was to the band's punchy sound. The Blossoms broke up soon after, but quietly re-formed in 2003. —J.G.

Ginuwine

★★	Ginuwine . . . the Bachelor (550 Music/Epic, 1996)	
★★★	100% Ginuwine (550 Music/Epic, 1999)	
★★★	The Life (Epic, 2001)	
★★★	The Senior (Epic, 2003)	

Fans knew where they stood in relation to neo-love-man Ginuwine, who introduced himself as "The Bachelor" and just wanted to get close to you. *Ginuwine . . . the Bachelor* went much further musically than it did lyrically, introducing the skittering, complex, superfunk beats of producer Timbaland into the world of smooth soul. *100%* was more of the same, but slightly more refined; even the soul stuff itself had its edges rubbed smooth by chill, trip-hop-style production. The sex-you-up-innuendo-free "Pony" made him a star, and by 2001's *The Life,* Ginuwine had perfected the song's format and expanded it into an album's worth of attitude while sacrificing its beat, to the detriment of this romantically schizo recording. He's the good boyfriend, the domineering bully, the kinky hottie, and the earnest suitor, all at too slow a pace and without anyone remotely as talented as Timbaland at the helm. *The Senior* is buoyed by the R. Kelly party bomb "Hell Yeah." But without his support staff, Ginuwine is revealed as not saying anything more interesting than his similarly shirtless rivals. —A.B.

Girls Against Boys

★★	Venus Luxure No. 1 Baby (Touch and Go, 1993)	
★★★	Cruise Yourself (Touch and Go, 1994)	
★★★	House of GVSB (Touch and Go, 1996)	
★	Freak*on*ica (DGC, 1998)	
★★★	You Can't Fight What You Can't See (Jade Tree, 2002)	

The unfocused Washington, D.C., post-hardcore scene spawned this thrash-rock band with lounge sensibilities, and despite the band's move to New York (where it found a bassist), *Venus Luxure* is a fuzzy piece of bottom-heavy pretense: Call it pop bombast. Scott McCloud's ragged voice burbles up through the sludgy mix like a pond creature surfacing to sneer at idle boaters, and the quartet's prog-rock tendencies—the attenuated length of songs, the lyrics' suggestion of some obscure macro worldview—obviate any headbanging fun inherent in the music's beat-pounding drive. Still, GvsB sounded nothing like early-'90s radio rock, and its thorny confrontationalism, if not exactly pleasurable, seemed at least refreshingly perverse. Tapping its taste for lounge with menacing directness made for a crisper if no more well-adjusted GvsB on *Cruise Yourself.* McCloud remains unfriendly, but the album has a sense of humor not indicated by the group's previous work, with wiry guitars, tricky song structures, and cutely self-conscious cynicism in the lyrics. The slow pace of the songs is much more infectious when stripped of their obfuscating sonic density. *Cruise Yourself* is mean, slow lounge-metal, melodic as any vocal standard and performed in clean, crushing march time, like a swankily tricked-out Panzer rolling through streets where martinis run like blood. For a band that found a million ways not to be tiresome on one recording, *House of GVSB* is an impressive achievement, if not a great leap forward. Ted Nicely's production allows each instrument to force its agenda, especially the bass, always GvsB's secret weapon, which gets funky even while eschewing non-rock elasticity. The songs are built intelligently, bristling with overlap and alluring switches in pace, and McCloud's barbed-wire vocals are more controlled and complex. It looked like the group had nowhere to go but up, but it fulfilled the indie cliché of accepting a major-label contract and releasing a weak distillation of its former sound. Even weirder, the Geffen Company release *Freak*on*ica* adds, or rather teases out, chunky industrial impulses that had been overridden by GvsB's talent for swinging a song. The band then left Geffen and landed on tiny emo label Jade Tree, sounding none the worse for wear on the revved-up *You Can't Fight What You Can't See.*   —A.B.

G. Love and Special Sauce

★★★★ G. Love and Special Sauce (Okeh/Epic, 1994)
★★★ Coast to Coast Motel (Okeh/Epic, 1995)
★★½ Yeah, It's That Easy (Okeh/Epic, 1997)
★★½ Philadelphonic (Okeh/550 Music, 1999)
★★★ Electric Mile (Okeh/Epic, 2001)
★★★½ The Best of G. Love and Special Sauce (Okeh/Epic, 2002)

Guitarist and singer Garrett Dutton, a.k.a. G. Love, grew up listening to hip-hop and classic rock, learned the blues from street musicians in his hometown of Philadelphia, and, like the Roots and others, got his start busking on South Street. His music is a coarse melding of several worlds: groaning slide guitar careening over kicky rap or strutting New Orleans march beats, with vocals that combine Beastie Boys–brattiness with a bluesman's sense of emotional investment.

The eponymous *G. Love and Special Sauce* remains the best representation of the group's gumbo: Songs like "Cold Beverage" and "Garbage Man," which have been subsequently used in ad campaigns, exude a buoyant recklessness, while other pieces, notably "This Ain't Living," suggest that Dutton is a crafty student of hip-hop narrative. While not an instant success, the album established the trio's reputation for feverish live performances, a rep it has sustained through less-than-magical studio output.

Coast to Coast Motel finds Dutton broadening his message to include reggae-tinged uplift anthems; despite clear evidence of musical growth, particularly in Dutton's unconventional guitar playing, only several tracks have the immediacy of the debut. *Yeah, It's That Easy* and *Philadelphonic* are only intermittently interesting, but the group's 2001 effort, *Electric Mile,* marks a return to the scruffy refrains and easygoing grooves of the band's debut.   —T.M.

The Go-Betweens

★★ Send Me a Lullaby (1982; Beggars Banquet, 1996)
★★★ Before Hollywood (1982; Beggars Banquet, 1996)
★★★½ Spring Hill Fair (1984; Beggars Banquet, 1996)
★★★ Liberty Belle and the Black Diamond Express (Big Time, 1986)
★★★½ Tallulah (Big Time, 1987)
★★★½ 16 Lovers Lane (Beggars Banquet/Capitol, 1988)
★★★★ Bellavista Terrace: Best of the Go-Betweens (Beggars Banquet, 1999)
★★½ 78 'til 79: The Lost Album (Jetset, 1999)
★★★½ The Friends of Rachel Worth (Jetset, 2000)
★★½ Bright Yellow Bright Orange (Jetset, 2003)

Grant McLennan and Robert Forster have been the core dyad of the Go-Betweens since they formed in Australia in 1977, a partnership strong enough that they picked up again after a pause of a decade or so without breaking stride. They're about as much a songwriting "team" as Lennon and McCartney—after the early days, each one has generally written the songs he sings—and as different: McLennan is the tender intellectual committed to tunecraft, Forster the bitter intellectual who distrusts the easy pleasures of melody.

78 'til 79: The Lost Album, issued 20 years after it was recorded, is mostly crude rehearsal tapes of some spunky but unformed songs. It's mostly worth it for their joyful early singles, "Lee Remick" and "People Say," and for "The Sound of Rain," recorded for a never-released single. Another few years would go by before their first actual album (in the meantime, their long-standing drummer Lindy Morrison joined). Forster has suggested not buying 1982's *Send Me a Lullaby* "without at least owning three others" from the Go-Bs' discography, and he's right—it's dry and graceless. You can hear the intelligence behind it, and the will to do something different, but the songs aren't much fun.

In mid-1982, the band relocated to London and loosened up a bit. Forster's still attached to tune-deprived art-pop on *Before Hollywood,* but McLennan comes into his own, especially with the exquisite single "Cattle and Cane," still remembered as a classic in Australia. The album is also where they developed the classic Go-Betweens sound: a light touch on acoustic guitars, slightly eccentric rhythms, and near-conversational singing. *Spring Hill Fair* of 1984 (on which they expanded to a quartet with bassist Robert Vickers) was the Go-Betweens' first encounter with high-gloss production, and the booming drums don't sit well with the likes of McLennan's prosy "River of Money." The songwriting is improving by leaps, though, and Forster gets off some great lines: "Man O'Sand to Girl O'Sea" begins "Feel so sure of our love/I'll write a song about us breaking up."

Forster inexplicably tries to reinvent himself as a highbrow sex symbol on the brittle *Liberty Belle and the Black Diamond Express,* and McLennan just gets weird—"The Wrong Road" is a nearly surreal power ballad. It only really clicks on the singles "Head Full of Steam" and "Spring Rain." *Tallulah* expanded the band's lineup once again, with the addition of violinist/oboist Amanda Brown. Laugh if you like, but the oboe part *makes* McLennan's "Bye Bye Pride." It's their most genteel record, populated by postcards from Algiers, gray-haired sisters who "sleep in the back of a feminist bookstore," and rumors of adultery.

16 Lovers Lane was the band's final attempt to go commercial, and sounds like it, in a good way—they played up the acoustic prettiness, and McLennan, in particular, rises to the challenge with some of his most seductive melodies. "Streets of Your Town" was their simplest song since "Lee Remick" and became a college-radio hit.

Bellavista Terrace, the band's third stab at a greatest-hits, gets it right. It skips some of their better songs and nonalbum singles, but it flows smoothly and coherently as an album in its own right—a smarter, more literate bridge between new wave and alternative rock than what actually got on the radio.

A 1999 acoustic tour by McLennan and Forster went so well that they decided to make a new Go-Betweens album (without Morrison), and they were open-minded enough to draw on the generation of indie rock that they'd influenced: On *The Friends of Rachel Worth,* their backing band includes both members of Quasi and guest appearances by Sleater-Kinney. They were never especially invested in being young in the first place, so age hasn't hurt them a bit; the album is inconsistent but intermittently delightful, peaking with Forster's bemused, hard-riffing memoir "German Farmhouse." In mid-2002, the British label Circus released expanded two-CD versions of the Go-Betweens' first three studio records, and Forster and McLennan announced plans for another new album. That album, *Bright Yellow Bright Orange,* is somewhat less eventful than its predecessor; the Go-Betweens have settled comfortably into a routine of mid-tempo jangle, and they're hardly stretching the way they did in the *Liberty Belle* days. Forster, in particular, seems to be repeating himself—he's written "In Her Diary" before and better. Still, McLennan has some lovely songs here, especially "Poison in the Wall."   —D.W.

Godsmack

★★★   Godsmack (Republic, 1998)
★★½   Awake (Republic, 2000)
★★   Faceless (Republic, 2003)
★★½   The Other Side (Republic, 2004)

Godsmack emerged out of Boston's metal scene in the late '90s to become yet another down-tuned, chunky multiplatinum new-metal act that rode that genre's bull market as well as or better than anyone else. The band—Wiccan vocalist Sully Erna, guitarist Tony Rambola, bassist Robbie Merrill, and drummer Tommy Stewart—debuted in 1997 with *All Wound Up,* which was rereleased and mildly resequenced in '98 as *Godsmack.*

The tough, mopey *Godsmack,* reportedly recorded for less than two grand, eventually went all kinds of platinum. The hearty riff that powers the mildly anthemic "Whatever" is new metal in a nutshell: a thick hook driven into the ground with Erna's basso rumble imparting a loathing directed both outward and inward. "Someone in London" is almost vibrant, but the most intriguing moment is "Voodoo," which changes up the formula with a rolling, vaguely tribal percussion, a subtler riff, and a hefty-yet-catchy chorus. A solid if fairly uninteresting debut.

Awake declines to build on or really in any way modify Godsmack's initial success—why fuck with a platinum formula?—so it's merely *Godsmack* with a bigger budget and a larger, if occasionally slightly slower, sound. "Vampires" wander around, "Greed" eats the soul, and Erna (with his awe-inspiring sideburns) is still self-obsessed and cranky, as Godsmack continues to work over the sound of no new ideas. Bummer.

Faceless is one brave-ass album title for a band that keeps falling further into metallic anonymity. The blocky riffs continue to jackhammer away here and swing a bit there, but they still flat-out refuse to make a lasting impression. The band picks up acoustic guitars for *The Other Side*, a seven-song set of old and new tunes that trades whomp for feeling. The highlight is "Touché," which gets its blues on. If Godsmack doesn't want to fall clear into the abyss, the band would do well to take this moment to expand its still limited palette. —J.G.

The Go-Go's

★★★★	Beauty and the Beat (IRS, 1981)
★½	Vacation (IRS, 1982)
★★★	Talk Show (IRS, 1984)
★★★★	Greatest (IRS, 1990)
★★★	Return to the Valley of the Go-Go's (IRS, 1994)
★★★★	Go-Go's Collection (Uni/A&M, 2000)
★★½	God Bless the Go-Go's (Beyond, 2001)

The Go-Go's may have sprung from the same L.A. underground that produced X, Fear, and the Germs, but you wouldn't know it from the group's recordings, which are tuneful, perky, and eminently accessible. Like Blondie, the Go-Go's were punk in the pop sense, owing more to beach music, girl groups, and leather-jacket attitude than to the amped-up snarl of the Stooges and Sex Pistols. *Beauty and the Beat* played up the band's Blondie roots admirably, from Gina Schock's surf-rock drumming behind "We Got the Beat" to the itchy innocence of Belinda Carlisle's vocal on "Lust to Love." Unexpectedly, the album was a hit, which may be why things suddenly got slicker with *Vacation*, which was overproduced and, apart from the title track and "Beatnik Beach," easily forgettable. *Talk Show* brought things back into focus, but by then the band was splintering. Carlisle went solo, as did Jane Wiedlin; the others played in various new bands; eventually, they reunited, but were hardly as productive as before. They cut a version of the Capitols' "Cool Jerk" for *Greatest*, and three forgettable

tracks for the compilation *Return to the Valley of the Go-Go's*. Collection was released in conjunction with their episode of VH1's *Behind the Music*, which apparently bought the band enough time to write a full album's worth of new material, which appears on *God Bless the Go-Go's*. Older and wiser, they re-create the sound they had 20 years earlier while somehow capturing little of its original magic. —J.D.C.

Goldie

★★★	Timeless (FFRR/London, 1995)
★½	Saturnz Return (FFRR/London, 1998)
★★	Ring of Saturn (FFRR/London, 1999)
★★★½	INCredible Sound of Drum 'n' Bass Mixed by Goldie (Sony, 2000)
★★	Goldie.co.uk (Moonshine, 2001)

Anointed "the face of jungle" thanks to his penchant for self- and scene-aggrandizing public proclamations, London graffiti artist, actor, producer, and DJ Goldie began making music under the name Rufige Kru. Early tracks like "Terminator" helped usher jungle and drum and bass from their ravey beginnings as break beat hardcore, and his 1994 singles "Angel" and "Inner City Life" evinced a sonic sophistication then little heard from other junglists. *Timeless*, Goldie's first album, was a double CD that displayed both his best tendencies (the steely breaks of "This Is a Bad") and his worst (the mist-trailing guitars of the godawful "Sea of Tears") in equal measure. Still, the album opened up a lot of ears to the new sound. Three years later, though, *Saturnz Return* helped close many of the same ears, thanks to a turgid, hour-long "opera" titled "Mother" and a second disc of largely undistinguishable drum and bass tunes, as well as lousy cameos from Oasis' Noel Gallagher and KRS-One. *Ring of Saturn* featured seven remixes from *Saturnz Return*, all of which improved on their models, which isn't saying much. Goldie has since concentrated on acting in movies rather than making albums, though he's issued a couple of DJ-mix CDs. *Goldie.co.uk* is a humdrum set that mostly shows how far drum and bass has fallen creatively from its mid-'90s peak, but his volume of *INCredible Sound of Drum 'n' Bass* is a smart history lesson that includes several classic cuts from his Metalheadz label. —M.M.

Gomez

★★★	Bring It On (Virgin, 1998)
★★★	Liquid Skin (Virgin, 1999)
★★	Abandoned Shopping Trolley Hotline (Virgin, 2000)
★★★	In Our Gun (Virgin, 2002)
★★★	Split the Difference (Virgin, 2004)

Gomez strives to do something that was once a proud rite for British bands but hasn't been done in decades: play the blues.

Bring It On shows the band is up for it; graceful and spacious, with calm, unhurried riffs and growling but still intimate vocals by Ben Ottewell, Tom Gray, and Ian Ball, the album is a novel take on the blues, accommodating the soaring bigness of Led Zeppelin and Pink Floyd—via Pearl Jam and Spiritualized, perhaps—with a cutting minimalism learned from indie rock. There's also a refreshing sense of quiet humility, a feeling otherwise absent from much boisterous '90s Britpop. *Liquid Skin* has a greater emphasis on acoustic instruments, resulting in a more sit-down vibe. There's a series of gorgeous pastorals ("Revolutionary Kind," "We Haven't Turned Around"), and though things tend to drag a bit, the sprawl never gets too far out of control, something that could never be said for, say, Derek and the Dominoes. Too bad about the lyrics, though ("Beautiful bitch, I could consider this a simple glitch/You're just a hopeless stitch in time").

After an inessential odds 'n' sods compilation sporting not one but two songs called "Shitbag," a reinvigorated Gomez burst out of the gate with *In Our Gun.* "Shot Shot" is easily the band's most excited track, with funky horns and an uncharacteristically quick tempo. Electronica makes a somewhat unwelcome appearance, with lots of distracting zips and zaps and touches of dub, but when the lads stick to the smooth, restful blues they do so well, everything works fine. *Split the Difference* finds the band back in classic form, channeling gloomy, spacey blues, with some novel instrumentation and a coldly deconstructed Junior Kimbrough tune, "Meet Me in the City."   —B.S.

Rubén González

★★★★½   Introducing . . . Rubén González (Nonesuch, 1997)
★★★★   Chanchullo (Nonesuch, 2000)

Ever wonder what *Buena Vista Social Club* would have sounded like without that damn slide guitar? Pianist Rubén González's first American solo album, cut at the age of 77, retains much of the band Ry Cooder assembled, but trims away the vocals and Yanqui frippery to reveal the band's rhythmic backbone. Bassist Orlando "Cachaito" Lopez strings together the timbales, congas, and other percussion into a lean, swaggering line of polyrhythms. And the leader, who helped Arsenio Rodriguez create modern Cuban music in the '40s, parades stately, semiclassical melodies that he then undercuts with giddily frenetic runs before clanging into some bent clusters of harmonics.

Since González's U.S. output was limited to a single Afro-Cuban All Stars spot, his performing was largely unknown to American audiences prior to *Buena Vista.* Yet *Introducing . . .* was an even more remarkable document than one would expect, introducing not just González but Cuban music in its entirety, plumbing the gamut of Cuban styles from *cha cha cha* to *danzón,* from *guaracha* to *bolero.* Even to Yanquis for whom those styles are just delightfully evocative syllables, the artistry is apparent. González had been in retirement through most of the '90s, claiming arthritis; if it ever existed, that affliction was nonetheless belied by the fluidity of these piano lines. As with most followups, *Chanchullo* offered fewer surprises. But though you've heard González's mix of staccato majesty and fleet upper-register runs, you haven't heard them on *these* songs. And you haven't heard González integrate his piano flourishes so fully into such a collaborative group effort. González has recorded imports awaiting U.S. marketing, and he has appeared on still more group sessions—Nonesuch's release of the 1979 all-star jam *Los Heroes,* credited to Estrellas de Areito, is where González fans should immediately proceed. And González's eighth decade may produce yet more music. What has come before may indeed be only an introduction.   —K.H.

Good Charlotte

★½   Good Charlotte (Epic, 2000)
★★½   Young and the Hopeless (Epic, 2002)

Daddy, where did pop-punk come from? According to the rock & roll bible, original 1977 punks the Buzzcocks begat SoCal punk rockers the Descendents, who begat All, who begat Screeching Weasel, who begat Green Day, who begat the Offspring, who begat . . . you get the point. By the late 1990s we got Blink 182 and Sum 41, and on the sixth day, God created Good Charlotte. More accurately, Epic Records created Good Charlotte, who skipped the indie-label game and went straight to the majors. This gives the group negative 50 punk-rock points, which would be a problem if Good Charlotte—who are led by twin brothers Joel (lead vocals) and Benji (guitar) Madden—cared about such things. Perhaps they knew that a punk group with a guitarist named Benji is an oxymoron, so they decided not to even bother playing the credibility game. The group's breakthrough was the MTV favorite "Lifestyles of the Rich and Famous," which was followed by another major hit, "The Anthem," which has to be the most cynical song written in the postalternative era. The song's chorus sounds like it was created by a random punk song generator: "Do you really want to be like them?/ Do you really wanna be another trend?/Do you wanna be part of that crowd?" Joel Madden continues singing, "This is the anthem/throw all your hands up," as though he knows how clichéd this dumb (but catchy) song is. In all, *Young and the Hopeless* is a tuneful but unsatisfying pop album, though it's far better than their mediocre self-titled debut, which contains what has to be one of the all-time worst hidden bonus tracks, the sincerely titled "Thank You Mom," wherein Madden sings, "You showed me how to love God . . . and I thank you." Thankfully, God rested on the seventh day, so we hopefully won't have to endure more groups like this. —K.M.

Goodie Mob

- ★★★★   Soul Food (LaFace/Arista, 1995)
- ★★★½   Still Standing (LaFace/Arista, 1998)
- ★★★   World Party (LaFace/Arista, 1999)
- ★★★★   Dirty South Classics (Arista, 2003)
- ★★★   One Monkey Don't Stop No Show (Koch, 2004)

Big Gipp

- ★★★   Mutant Mindframe (Koch, 2003)

Cee-Lo

- ★★★½   Cee-Lo Green and His Perfect Imperfections (Arista, 2002)
- ★★★★   Cee-Lo Green . . . Is the Soul Machine (Arista, 2004)

After introducing itself a year earlier on the debut album by OutKast, this Atlanta quartet made a splash of its own with *Soul Food.* True to its name, the record offered a deeper, heartier hip-hop sustenance in the form of soulful singing, particularly through the contributions of raspy-voiced standout Cee-Lo and the earthy chanting and poetry of the entire group. Where OutKast added smarts and musical substance to Southern hip-hop, Goodie Mob went a step further with a more developed political conscience, confronting issues such as low-income housing ("Cell Therapy") and prison overcrowding ("Live at the O.M.N.I."). But even at its most outspoken, the group masks its sentiments in a street-warrior stance that keeps the group connected to its grassroots. And with "Dirty South," Goodie Mob found a name for the Dixie-fried rap that would come to dominate the hip-hop charts in the years ahead.

Still Standing follows largely in the same direction, with slightly diminishing returns. Cee-Lo's versatile voice continues to dominate, and many of the album's finest moments are his, though Big Gipp teams with OutKast for *Still Standing*'s biggest hit, "Black Ice." On the whole, though, the record offers fewer memorable cuts, and a generally darker vibe, than its predecessor.

Hoping to brighten its sound and show the world a side of the group other than its ghetto militance, Goodie Mob embraced an internationalist vision of millennial celebration for its third release. *World Party*'s stab at pop crossover took fans by surprise, particularly its choice of samples (Lionel Ritchie?) and outside producers (including TLC producer Dallas Austin). Tracks such as "Chain Swang" and "Get Rich to This" are easily Goodie Mob's most accessible, reinvigorating the group and injecting a sense of fun into what had begun to get bogged down in self-importance. But just as often as this new approach worked, it also tended to feel awkward—not good for a group whose strength was its rootedness in the red clay of its Georgia home. *World Party* was not quite as freewheeling as it wanted to be, and a little too lightweight for the group's taste.

With the original Goodie Mob lineup fracturing after *World Party,* the best-of compilation *Dirty South Classics* presented a fine summation of the quartet's output over three albums. Most of the group's standouts appear here, providing an adequate taste of Goodie Mob's strengths and significance in the scope of Southern hip-hop. Fans looking for previously unreleased extras will be disappointed, however.

After five years away, Goodie Mob returned to the studio—this time without its de facto frontman, Cee-Lo—and came up with the pointedly titled *One Monkey Don't Stop No Show.* Said monkey might not stop the show, but the absence of his dynamic delivery and melodic sense is certainly noticeable. Without Cee-Lo, though, Goodie Mob still manages to squeeze out a decent record. *Monkey* updates the group's sound by adding in a Southern "crunk" feel that takes advantage of the gruff voices of remaining members T-Mo, Khujo, and Gipp.

With his debut solo outing, *Cee-Lo Green and His Perfect Imperfections,* Cee-Lo manages to strike the balance his group missed on *World Party.* The music is eccentric and eclectic but most of all accessible, with an emphasis on Cee-Lo's warm singing and songwriting over his sharp, rapid-fire rhyming. And while it's not afraid to show its slightly naughty side on the funky "Bad Mutha" and "Closet Freak," *Perfect Imperfections* remains committed to relaying messages—social themes of monogamous love and staking out individuality, if not necessarily political ones. More than anything, the record reveals Cee-Lo's strong pop instincts, whether reaching back to doo-wop ("Awful Thing"), embracing regional flavors ("Country Love"), or going straight piano-man on the powerful closer, "Young Man."

Cee-Lo's second outing, *Cee-Lo Green . . . Is the Soul Machine,* continues along the lines of its predecessor, showcasing his rapping, singing, and compositional talents. This time, however, Cee-Lo makes a more concerted stab at a current pop sensibility, enlisting superstar producers the Neptunes, Timbaland, and Jazze Pha to slicken the sound. The effect makes *Soul Machine* a less sprawling, ambitious affair than *Perfect Imperfections,* but altogether a stronger, more consistent effort.

During Goodie Mob's extended absence, Big Gipp also recorded a solo album, *Mutant Mindframe.* Featuring notable guest spots from OutKast's Andre 3000 and others, it's an uneven affair with some great moments and a refreshing musical variety.   —R.M.S.

Goo Goo Dolls

★★	Jed (Metal Blade, 1989)
★★★	Hold Me Up (Metal Blade, 1991)
★★★	Superstar Car Wash (Metal Blade, 1993)
★★½	A Boy Named Goo (Metal Blade, 1995)
★★½	Dizzy Up the Girl (Warner Bros., 1998)
★★★½	Ego, Opinion, Art & Commerce (Warner Bros., 2001)
★★	Gutterflower (Warner Bros., 2002)

Hugely influenced by Paul Westerberg of '80s postpunkers the Replacements, Goo Goo Dolls singer Johnny Rzeznick transports the aching vocals of Westerberg from the rock dive to the prom, elevating mundane postpunk sentiments to the rarefied atmosphere where the power ballad soars. The Dolls started out as a Buffalo bar band with a punky spark of desperation they didn't so much douse as ease out of. Fans who complained that Replacements comparisons were facile were half right—by the time of *Hold Me Up* they sounded more like Soul Asylum, crafting credibly strained and restrained hard rock with a punk pedigree. *A Boy Named Goo* established them as altrock's answer to Journey and Foreigner—a competent "hard-rock" band whose hits happened to be soft, not-particularly-rockin' ballads. Not-half-bad ballads either—1995 was a wiser age than 1982, and among the "soulful" oversinging of the many Eddie Vedders–thrice-removed crowding the airwaves, Rzeznick was credible, subtle, self-deprecating.

But *Gutterflower* was the glossy work of a band taking fewer chances than ever—Matchbox 20 without the subtext. Ultimately, the Dolls suffer from an inability to push their innate sentimentality beyond the banality of yearbook quotes. "What you feel is what you are/And what you are is beautiful," Rzeznick sang on "Slide." Diane Warren couldn't have said it any better. But Paul Westerberg could

have said it better. But if, as so many deluded fans once predicted, the Replacements had become the world's biggest rock band, could he have said it any more honorably?   —K.H.

Gorillaz

★★½	Gorillaz (2001, Virgin)
★★★½	G-Sides (2002, Virgin)

Not the first band in history to evoke the response "So, what exactly is this, again?" Gorillaz doesn't make confusing music; it just has a confusing pedigree and, technically, doesn't exactly exist. A cyber-conglomerate usually attributed to Blur's Damon Albarn, this hip-hop-rock concept includes musicians like Chris Frantz and Tina Weymouth of Talking Heads and Tom Tom Club, Cibo Matto's Miho Hatori, Afro-Cuban musician Ibrahim Ferrer, Dan "the Automator" Nakamura and his Deltron 3030 posse— Del tha Funkee Homosapien and Kid Koala—as well as comics artist Jamie Hewlett, who conceptualized Gorillaz as an animated troupe of manga-style slacker zombies. What all this means for the music is not as fascinating as how all this looks on TV, where the cryptic, zoned-out horror show "Clint Eastwood" enjoyed a juicy run in short-format video throughout 2001. *Gorillaz'* anime conception evokes a rich and unpredictable landscape, whereas the music recalls Butthole Surferesque "weirdness." The diverse strains of expertise among the musicians makes for a surprisingly smooth blend—parallel-universe neo-soul on "New Genius" (featuring a sample from Odetta), electronica played underwater with falsetto vocals on "Man Research," a comment on punk in the punk style on "Punk," whose existence seems to posit that one's six-year-old can make punk. *Gorillaz* is full of expertly assembled songs-as-references-to-song-styles that range from loungey ("Double Bass") to funky ("19-2000") to salsa-y ("Latin Simone"), all of which is soothing, impressive, and deliberately annoying.

Not B sides, *G-Sides* compiles four alternative versions of three Gorillaz songs from the group's one and only full-length recording, plus five previously unheard songs. Fittingly, the thinky music-makers aren't in the business of demonstrating increasing maturity with each release, but this slim album shimmers the way Cibo Matto can, with sugar and vinegar, march and sway. From the Asian hip-hop/spy-movie groove of "The Sounder" to the spooky hand-claps animating the fuzz on "Ghost Train," *G-Sides* comes closer to the spirit of Jamie Hewlett's cartoonish conception of Gorillaz than the album of the same name.   —A.B.

Gorky's Zygotic Mynci

★★★ Tatay (Ankst, 1994)
★★★ Patio (Ankst, 1994)
★★★ Bwyd Time (Ankst, 1995)
★★★★ Introducing Gorky's Zygotic Mynci (PolyGram, 1996)
★★★ Barafundle (Fontana, 1997)
★★★ Gorky 5 (Fontana, 1998)
★★★ Spanish Dance Troupe (Beggars Banquet, 1999)
★★★ The Blue Trees (Beggars Banquet, 2001)
★★★★ How I Long to Feel That Summer in My Heart (Beggars Banquet, 2001)
★★★★ The Singles Collection (Castle, 2003)

Gorky's Zygotic Mynci (with a hard *c*) is a name that has almost certainly come between this exuberant Welsh band and pop world penetration. Translating loosely as "Gorky's Embryonic Monkey," it's like the Breeders—just a joke on making art in an age of mechanical reproduction.

Though playing together since the late '80s, they didn't release a record in the U.S. until 1996's *Introducing,* a crackerjack collection culled from singles and EPs previously released on local label Ankst. Though hailed as part of a Welsh invasion storming U.S. shores along with the likes of Catatonia and Super Furry Animals, in reality they were never part of a "Welsh scene" and felt more affinity with atmosphericists such as Low than ironic indie hipsters or alt-radio readymades.

GZM's style has morphed as members have come into their own as songwriters. The early records are Beefhearted and chaotic—sung almost exclusively in Welsh, and sporting titles such as "Merched Ya Neod Gwalt Eu Gilydd." After 1999's angularly peppy *Spanish Dance Troupe,* containing the glam Blur-ry single "Poodle Rockin," founder and lead guitarist John Lawrence left GZM. The pop-pastoral vision of guitarist Euros Childs, whose sugar-mountain voice and Christine McVie melodicism now prevail, moved the band further into the realm of the deceptively simple. *The Blue Trees,* an acoustic treat of 2000, is a pleasing set of piano-and-guitar ballads recorded with deliberative spareness. Playing 25 different instruments among them, the six main members can suggest the vista of Welsh cliffs, the blissful arrival of long-delayed spring, and the sad beauty of an industrial valley—sound portraits as vivid as Grandaddy's Southwestern sweep or Low's frozen lakes. *How I Long to Feel That Summer in My Heart,* from 2001, is a lush and lovingly multitracked translation of alone time. The second most prominent songwriter, acoustic guitarist Richard James, has a breathy, Elliott Smith attraction that provides a nice respite from Childs' more intense angel's plea. And Childs' sister Megan has a Mo Tucker tremble that fits her gamboling contribution "Can Megan" perfectly. With lyrics as basic as the weather, melodies move along with forgivable familiarity. —L.S.

Gov't Mule

★★★½ Gov't Mule (Relativity, 1995)
★★★½ Dose (Capricorn, 1998)
★★★ Live . . . With a Little Help From Our Friends (Capricorn, 1999)
★★★½ Life Before Insanity (PolyGram, 2000)
★★★ The Deep End, Vol. 1 (ATO, 2001)
★★★ The Deep End, Vol. 2 (ATO, 2002)
★★★½ The Deepest End: Live in Concert (ATO, 2003)

Beginning in the mid-'90s as a side project for new-model Allman Brothers Warren Haynes and Allen Woody, Gov't Mule quickly became a full-time band in its own right. Tough, bluesy, and not afraid of an epic jam, the Mule, led by Haynes' righteous vocals and guitar heroics, has successfully brought the classic power-trio sound of bands such as Cream and the Jimi Hendrix Experience into the 21st century.

On floor-stomping songs such as "Mother Earth" *(Gov't Mule),* "Blind Man in the Dark" *(Dose),* and "Bad Little Doggie" *(Life Before Insanity),* Haynes and his pals step into a secret time tunnel leading directly to the Fillmore East circa 1970. Disorienting at first, it's lots of fun once you're used to it. Memorable tunes can be tough to locate, but the temperature of the performances is so high it hardly matters. The "friends" at the New Year's Eve '98 show documented on the live album include P-Funk keyboardist Bernie Worrell, who enlivens "Soulshine" and "Mule" with his daredevil Hammond organ work.

Allen Woody's sudden death in 2000 left Gov't Mule with a void in the bass region. Bring on the Deep End project, which pairs Haynes and drummer Matt Abts with a different bassist on each track, from Larry Graham and the Who's John Entwistle on *Vol. 1* to the Dead's Phil Lesh and Metallica's Jason Newsted on *Vol. 2.* The four-alarm playing on display here proves that everyone's up to the challenge, though the music does, understandably, lack consistency. *The Deepest End* takes all this to its logical culmination: nearly six hours of music (on two CDs and one DVD), recorded at Jazzfest 2003 in New Orleans, featuring 12 bassists and a small army of other guests. Good stuff, but perhaps it's time to move on to another idea now. —M.R.

Grandaddy

★★★½ Under the Western Freeway (Will, 1997)
★★★★ The Sophtware Slump (V2, 2000)
★★½ Concrete Dunes (Lakeshore, 2002)
★★★★ Sumday (V2, 2003)

His falsetto as forlorn as Neil Young's, Jason Lytle emanates the wry pessimism of a guy who only skulks reluctantly into town when he needs new guitar strings. *Under the Western Freeway*—the second album from these Modesto, California, indie rockers—is a hidden fortress of hot-wired Casios and antique drum machines, with an uneven acoustic strum at its foundation and dissonant guitar fragments looped around like chicken wire. The regrets yelped in lyrics like "Everything Beautiful Is Far Away" are both callow and moving, as if the feeble protests spray-painted on the Northern California overpasses of I-5 had been composed by the world's smartest teenage burnout.

The Sophtware Slump could be America's answer— its halting, quizzical answer—to the sculpted crystalline grandeur and nail-biting technophobia of *OK Computer*. Make-do Yanks that they are, the Grandaddy boys employ a shimmering synthetic surface to nearly conceal a rickety acoustic infrastructure, in contrast to the Brits' chilly precision. Creeping amid a "Broken Household Appliance National Forest," stranded on the moon and gazing earthward, eulogizing a paranoid android named Jed who drank himself to death, Lytle recognizes that the future has already come and gone here, leaving him to root among its detritus.

As a reward for the many plaudits *Sophtware Slump* earned, the band saw some sketchy early material released by an old label. Some of the tunes are just fine, but the sonic support system that allows Grandaddy to thrive isn't yet in place. There's a lesson for arty pessimists in there: Fear the future all you like, it's the past that always turns to bite you in the ass. *Sumday* was more modest in its lethargic, weary optimism. Lytle's structures were more conventional, resulting in what sounds like a homemade, slacker ELO. —K.H.

Grand Funk Railroad

★★★★ On Time (1969; Capitol, 2002)
★★★★ Grand Funk (1970; Capitol, 2002)
★★★ Closer to Home (1970; Capitol, 2002)
★★★ Live Album (1970; Capitol, 2002)
★★★★ E Pluribus Funk (1971; Capitol, 2002)
★★★ Survival (1971; Capitol, 2002)
★★ Phoenix (1972; Capitol, 2002)
★★★ We're an American Band (1973; Capitol, 2002)

★★ Shinin' On (1974; Capitol, 2002)
★★ All the Girls in the World Beware!! (1974; Capitol, 2003)
★★ Masters of Rock (1975; Capitol, 2003)
★★★½ Caught in the Act (live) (1975; Capitol, 2003)
★★ Born to Die (1976; Capitol, 2003)
★★★ Thirty Years of Funk: 1969–1999 (Capitol, 1999)
★★ Live: The 1971 Tour (Capitol, 2002)
★★★½ Trunk of Funk (Capitol, 2003)

Not for nothing are they Homer Simpson's favorite band: Dumb but with delusions of grandeur, critically reviled but worshiped by '70s stoners, Grand Funk Railroad's vulgarity translated for many into charming exuberance. The Flint, MI, natives—singer/ guitarist Mark Farner, bassist Mel Schacher, and drummer/singer Don Brewer—began mixing up hard rock and boogie in 1969. By '71 they released their best album, the disco-informed hard pop classic *E Pluribus Funk*. From the explosive groove-anthem "People, Let's Stop the War" to the eight-and-a-half-minute stairway-to-hell monster ballad "Loneliness," Farner wails like a cross between Axl Rose and Lynyrd Skynyrd's Ronnie Van Zant, Schacher sprints through fuzz-toned walking basslines, and Brewer guarantees the "funk" promised in the disc's title.

Survival, released later that year, grooves with an unhurried but still spry assurance, each instrument sticking to its respective sweet spot. Until, that is, "Gimme Shelter." Perfectly capable of emulating Marvin Gaye and Stevie Wonder on the disc's original songs, Grand Funk smothers the Stones' R&B beat in coarse, driving guitar—thereby anticipating the imminent dominance of hard rock and heavy metal over rock & roll. The remixed and previously rejected tracks included here, like the bonus cuts on the other reissues, were kept in the vault this long for good reason, so unless you've been aching to hear the "guitar intro, harmonica solo, several extra bridges and verses, and double-time section" of "All You've Got Is Money," hang on to the vinyl if you've got it.

Even without the extended version of its instrumental intro, 1972's *Phoenix* would sound ponderous. Stalwart producer Terry Knight, who quit before the disc was recorded, is sorely missed. The album lacks the rhythmic finesse and walloping drive of GFR's early releases. Rather than trading off between his signature crude riffs and juicy funk chords, Farner attempts to play guitar with a subtlety he just doesn't have, while his flatly cheerful voice lingers over deep thoughts like "been gettin' loaded/too much these days."

Luckily, Don Brewer was still looking for a party.

The first Grand Funk song he wrote himself, *We're an American Band*'s rousing title song, was the band's first #1 hit, a career-defining document of the group's hedonistic touring lifestyle. Politically incorrect by today's standards, the comparably inspired "Black Licorice" concerns a specific type of female fan, one with "slender legs" and "hot, black skin." Farner shrieks the refrain like a man who has rediscovered his favorite vices, and the guys (including recent addition Craig Frost) swing harder than a drunk in a brawl. But the band never recovered from the ensuing hangover. They produced a few more *Phoenix* photocopies, like the mopey, self-fulfilling prophecy *Born to Die;* their embarrassing cover of "The Loco-Motion," from *Shinin' On,* was their second chart topper. Mel Schacher and Don Brewer went on tour as Grand Funk Railroad in 2004, but Mark Farner had long since devoted himself to a successful career in contemporary Christian rock. —N.C.

Grandmaster Flash and the Furious Five

★★★★★ Message from Beat Street: The Best of Grandmaster Flash, Melle Mel, and the Furious Five (Rhino, 1994)
★★★ Greatest Mixes (1997; Castle, 2002)
★★½ The Showdown: Sugarhill Gang Vs. Grandmaster Flash and the Furious Five (Rhino, 1999)
★★★★½ Adventures on the Wheels of Steel (Sequel, 2000)
★★★★ The Message (Castle, 2002)
★★½ The Message: Greatest Hits (BMG/Camden, 2002)

Grandmaster Flash

★★★ Grandmaster Flash Presents Salsoul Jam 2000 (Salsoul, 1997)
★★★★ The Official Adventures of Grandmaster Flash (Strut, 2002)
★★★½ Essential Mix: Classic Edition (Rhino, 2002)

Grandmaster Flash helped invent both an art form, the hip-hop sound, and a type of artist, the turntablist DJ. When the 16-year-old Flash (Joseph Saddler) got into Bronx street parties in 1973, he discovered he had no skills as a break dancer, but he did have a passion for music and tinkering with electronic equipment in his bedroom. Adored, party-throwing DJs such as Kool Herc, Pete DJ Jones, and Grandmaster Flowers inspired Flash to combine the sharpest parts of their acts into something better and stronger. During 1974–75, Flash perfected a way to intercut and extend break beats on the beat, so that dancers could just keep rolling on with the funky bits he selected. He could also assemble pieces of records into complete new

workouts, something everybody takes for granted today. This was so innovative back then that it called for a new style of MC, or rapper, to put it across to an audience. The Furious Five, who were up to the challenge, consisted of exhorter Cowboy (Keith Wiggins), wordslinger Kid Creole (Nathaniel Glover), and Kid's more politically minded brother Melle Mel (Melvin Glover), who brought in Scorpio (Eddie Morris) and love-man Raheim (Guy Williams). The Five began to finish one another's lines and toss around raps rhythmically in time to Flash's turntable work. Together they became the mightiest originators in hip-hop history.

Message from Beat Street contains key underground singles, such as "Freedom"; numbers that made Flash and the Five favorites of the new-wave rock set, such as "It's Nasty (Genius of Love)"; and Melle Mel's most ferocious, relentless performance ever, on "The Message," the gunshot that signaled the rise of gangsta rap. Also very desirable is the British import of *The Message,* the only LP issued while the original group was intact. The clincher is "The Adventures of Grandmaster Flash on the Wheels of Steel," the only prime-period example of Flash's ability to set and shatter moods, with his turntables and faders running through a collage of at least 10 records that sound like hundreds. Those who want to spend more and get a full picture of the group should go for *Adventures on the Wheels of Steel,* with choice rarities. *Greatest Mixes* unfortunately entrusts the sound of Flash and the Five to outsiders, while *The Showdown* and *The Message: Greatest Hits* needlessly pair Flash and the Five with the much more trivial Sugarhill Gang.

When a new generation of DJs such as the Invisible Scratch Piklz revived the art of turntablism a few years ago, Flash finally began to get his due as a pioneer scientist of sound. *Presents Salsoul Jam 2000,* however, shows that Latin disco isn't his finest mode of operation. Much more on target, *Essential Mix: Classic Edition* is a super-solid assembly of cuts that never quite goes delirious. Though a standout, *The Official Adventures of Grandmaster Flash* is rather skimpy, padded by brief interview segments and four vintage jams such as Babe Ruth's "The Mexican," which provide old-skool ambience or something. The CD becomes nearly essential, however, because it contains four restless, scratchedelic, funk-filled "turntable mixes" by Flash that are the first and so far only released followups to "Wheels of Steel." Plus, Frank Broughton and Bill Brewster's liner notes provide a definitive history of Flash's techniques and career. Looking back on his achievements, Flash puts it best: "First is forever." —M.MI.

Grateful Dead

★★ Grateful Dead (1967; Warner Bros., 2003)
★★ Anthem of the Sun (1968; Warner Bros., 2003)
★★★ Aoxomoxoa (1969; Warner Bros., 2003)
★★★★ Live Dead (1970; Warner Bros., 2003)
★★★★★ Workingman's Dead (1970; Warner Bros., 2003)
★★★★★ American Beauty (1970; Warner Bros., 2003)
★★★ The Grateful Dead (1971; Warner Bros., 2003)
★★★ Europe '72 (1972; Warner Bros., 2003)
★★★ History of the Grateful Dead, Vol. 1—Bear's Choice (1973; Warner Bros., 2003)
★★★ Wake of the Flood (Grateful Dead, 1973)
★★★★ Best of the Grateful Dead—Skeletons From the Closet (Warner Bros., 1974)
★★★ The Grateful Dead From the Mars Hotel (Grateful Dead, 1974)
★★★ Blues for Allah (Grateful Dead, 1975)
★★ Steal Your Face (Grateful Dead, 1976)
★★★★ Terrapin Station (Arista, 1977)
★★★★ What a Long Strange Trip It's Been (Warner Bros., 1977)
★★ Shakedown Street (Arista, 1978)
★ The Grateful Dead Go to Heaven (Arista, 1980)
★★ Dead Reckoning (1981; Arista, 1990)
★★ Dead Set (Arista, 1981)
★★★ In the Dark (Arista, 1987)
★ Built to Last (Arista, 1989)
★ Dylan and the Dead (Columbia, 1989)
★★★ Without a Net (Arista, 1990)
★★ One From the Vault (Grateful Dead, 1991)
★★ Dick's Picks, Vol. 1 (Grateful Dead, 1991)
★★★★ Two From the Vault (Grateful Dead, 1992)
★★ Infrared Roses (Grateful Dead, 1994)
★★ Dick's Picks, Vol. 2 (Grateful Dead, 1995)
★★★ Dick's Pick's, Vol. 3 (Grateful Dead, 1995)
★★★ Hundred Year Hall (Grateful Dead, 1995)
★★★★ Grayfolded (Plunderphonics, 1995)
★★★★★ Dick's Picks, Vol. 4 (Grateful Dead, 1996)
★★★ Dick's Picks, Vol. 5 (Grateful Dead, 1996)
★★★ The Arista Years (Arista, 1996)
★★★ Dozin' at the Knick (Grateful Dead, 1996)
★★★ Fallout From the Phil Zone (Arista, 1997)
★★★★ Live at Fillmore East 2-11-69 (Grateful Dead, 1997)
★★★ Dick's Picks, Vol. 6 (Grateful Dead, 1997)
★★★★ Dick's Picks, Vol. 7 (Grateful Dead, 1997)
★★★★★ Dick's Picks, Vol. 8 (Grateful Dead, 1997)
★★ Dick's Picks, Vol. 9 (Grateful Dead, 1997)
★★★ Dick's Picks, Vol. 10 (Grateful Dead, 1998)
★★★ Dick's Picks, Vol. 11 (Grateful Dead, 1998)
★★★ Dick's Picks, Vol. 12 (Grateful Dead, 1998)
★★★ Dick's Picks, Vol. 13 (Grateful Dead, 1998)
★★ Dick's Picks, Vol. 14 (Grateful Dead, 1999)
★★★★ Dick's Picks, Vol. 15 (Grateful Dead, 1999)
★★★★ So Many Roads: Live (1965–1995) (Arista, 1999)
★★★★ Dick's Picks, Vol. 16 (Grateful Dead, 2000)
★★ Dick's Picks, Vol. 17 (Grateful Dead, 2000)
★★★★ Dick's Picks, Vol. 18 (Grateful Dead, 2000)
★★★★ Dick's Picks, Vol. 19 (Grateful Dead, 2000)
★★★★ Ladies and Gentlemen . . . The Grateful Dead: Fillmore East, New York, April 1971 (Arista, 2000)
★★ Dick's Picks, Vol. 20 (Grateful Dead, 2001)
★★★ Dick's Picks, Vol. 21 (Grateful Dead, 2001)
★★★ Dick's Picks, Vol. 22 (Grateful Dead, 2001)
★★★★ Dick's Picks, Vol. 23 (Grateful Dead, 2001)
★★ Nightfall of Diamonds (Arista, 2001)
★★★★ The Golden Road (1965–1973) (Rhino/Warner Bros., 2001)
★★ Go to Nassau (Arista, 2002)
★★★ Steppin' Out With the Grateful Dead: England '72 (Arista, 2002)
★★★★ Postcards of the Hanging: Grateful Dead Perform the Songs of Bob Dylan (Arista, 2002)
★★★ Dick's Picks, Vol. 24 (Grateful Dead, 2002)
★★★★ Dick's Picks, Vol. 25 (Grateful Dead, 2002)
★★★★ Dick's Picks, Vol. 26 (Grateful Dead, 2002)
★★★ View From the Vault II (Grateful Dead, 2002)
★★ View From the Vault III (Grateful Dead, 2002)
★★★★ Birth of the Dead (Warner Bros., 2003)
★★★ Dick's Picks, Vol. 27 (Grateful Dead, 2003)

The Grateful Dead became such a larger-than-life social phenomenon that it would be easy to overlook their music, or simply to dismiss it as self-indulgent noodling for stoned hippies. But the Dead's music occupies a unique niche; their open-ended approach to songs and sound was unprecedented in rock. Their emphasis on live performance and their self-sufficiency—in effect the band became a self-contained music industry—fathered the jam-band movement that flourished in the '90s with Phish, the Dave Matthews Band, Blues Traveler, and countless others. All forged lucrative careers built on the Dead's lead: Music mattered more than image, tours counted for more than slickly crafted studio albums, and concerts were improvised in the moment, assuring that no two would ever be alike.

The Dead began as the house band for the acid tests in mid-'60s San Francisco, making the transition from a jug band to garage-blues rockers documented on the *Birth of the Dead* album, and eventually to something far more difficult to categorize.

This was a band whose legacy was forged on the

stage rather than the studio, in large measure because the Dead used their songs as starting points for improvisation rather than as ideals to be duplicated. They treated America's indigenous music—blues, bluegrass, country, jazz, folk, and early rock & roll—as one long, living tradition that demanded to be transmuted and expanded nightly. They covered the songs of their contemporaries, especially Bob Dylan, but also those of Charley Patton, Marty Robbins, Buddy Holly, Woody Guthrie, the Dixie Cups, and Bobby "Blue" Bland. Bassist Phil Lesh was an accomplished avant-garde composer, guitarist Jerry Garcia recorded with everyone from David Grisman to Ornette Coleman, drummer Mickey Hart was one of the first musicians to introduce world music and rhythms to the rock lexicon, and virtuosos such as Branford Marsalis and Bruce Hornsby sat in with the band. To avoid repeating themselves, they risked looking foolish or inept, and sometimes did.

Garcia applied the dexterity of his bluegrass-banjo background to the electric guitar, and he developed one of the signature styles of the last half century, an unhurried approach to the instrument that stood in sharp contrast to rock's faster-is-better orthodoxy. In addition, his songwriting collaborations with lyricist Robert Hunter provided the foundation for the Dead's career: "Dark Star," "Uncle John's Band," "Ripple," "Bertha," "Casey Jones," "China Cat Sunflower," "U.S. Blues," the epic "Terrapin Station," and their sole Top 10 hit, "Touch of Grey." Garcia's interplay with Lesh and guitarist Bob Weir was supported by two percussionists in Hart and Bill Kreutzmann who favored busy polyrhythms over more conventional rock beats, while a succession of keyboardists brought disparate strengths to the band's many eras: the blues raunch of Ron "Pigpen" McKernan, Keith Godchaux's jazzier voicings, Brent Mydland's versatility with synthesizers.

The early albums, particularly *Anthem of the Sun,* are ambitious but awkward, as the Dead experiments with everything from finger cymbals to crotales and extended song suites. *Live Dead* is where the band finds its voice, particularly on a 24-minute "Dark Star" that is closer in feel to Miles Davis' jazz-fusion than rock. The song is the acid test, if you will, of Dead-dom, both the defining work in the canon and the most demanding. It was among the first Hunter lyrics written for the band and is the centerpiece of countless concert recordings to surface over the next 30 years with its open-ended, modal-jazz structure.

Workingman's Dead, in part inspired by the rustic soul of the Band, ranks as the Dead's studio masterpiece, followed closely by *American Beauty.* The focus is on the songs, rather than the jams, and these would provide the focal point of an era, spanning 1969–74, when the Dead played some of the most remarkable concerts in American history, virtually every one available in some incarnation thanks to the band's dedicated tapers. The band's last major statement as a studio band would be *Terrapin Station,* the epic title track ranking with the finest of the Hunter-Garcia collaborations.

The late '70s and '80s saw the Dead struggling to remain relevant amid unfriendly commercial trends, hitting its nadir in disco experiments such as *Shakedown Street,* but improbably scoring a major hit with the wryly touching "Touch of Grey" from *In the Dark.* That said, the polished pleasantness of most of the Dead's latter-day studio recordings is depressing coming from these erstwhile pranksters. The Dead often found themselves going through the motions in concert as well, providing a soundtrack for a party they no longer had any desire to join.

Garcia's death in 1995 effectively ended the band, but not the flood of recordings. Particularly remarkable is the ongoing *Dick's Picks* series, named after the late Dead tape archivist Dick Latvala, which cherry-picks some of the band's finest concert recordings. Best of the bunch is *Volume 4,* which culls highlights from two masterly 1970 performances at the Fillmore East in New York. Here the full range of the band's arsenal is represented: the luminous "Dark Star," a raging "Not Fade Away," the sheer nastiness of McKernan on his showpiece, "Turn on Your Love Light."

A few months later, the Dead nearly topped that performance; their Harpur College concert in Binghamton, NY *(Vol. 8),* should give pause to anyone who buys into the Dead's reputation as mellow. Fresh off recording *Workingman's Dead,* the band opens in acoustic mode, which brings a more melodic concision to the arrangements and a bite to the voices that carries over to the electric set. Garcia and Lesh slug it out on a majestic "The Other One," while "Viola Lee Blues" and "Morning Dew" build to howling climaxes. The group even wages war on Martha and the Vandellas' ebullient "Dancing in the Street," transforming it into a freakish, funky, antiwar meltdown.

Among Dead arcana, *Grayfolded* stands apart: a two-CD deconstruction of "Dark Star." Sound engineer John Oswald, who coined the term "Plunderphonics" to describe how he manipulates and layers or "folds" recorded music, compresses 25 years of "Dark Star" performances into two epic tapestries, including an "ambient dance" mix that recontexualizes the Dead as precursors of the Orb or Aphex Twin.

The uninitiated looking for an entry point to this bewildering catalogue should seek out *What a Long,*

Strange Trip It's Been, a good one-volume retrospective, or *So Many Roads,* a box set that gives a solid overview of the Dead's many incarnations as a touring band. —G.K.

Gravediggaz

   ★★★   Six Feet Deep (V2, 1994)
  ★★★½ The Pick, the Sickle & the Shovel (Gee Street/ V2, 1997)
    ★★   Nightmare in A-Minor (Empire, 2002)
     ★   6 Feet Under (Cleopatra, 2004)

This blood-and-gore-obsessed side project of Prince Paul and the Wu-Tang Clan's RZA was the prime suspect in the "horrorcore" subgenre that emerged just as gangsta rap was losing its shock value. In lesser hands it would have been a dull novelty indeed, but these gifted and adventurous producers make it work the way great horror movies work: You may come for the violence, but you stay for the characters.

Six Feet Deep is basically a rap *Tales From the Crypt,* with a cast of ghouls (Gatekeeper, Grym Reaper, Rzarector, Undertaker—Frukwan, Poetic, RZA, and Paul, respectively) making corny graveyard/ghetto boasts ("I've been examined ever since I was semen/ They took a sonogram and seen the image of a demon") and reveling in the macabre. The MCs are all in top form, but the production is oddly understated, considering that the album came just a year after RZA's epochal work of ultraviolent sci-fi rap, *Enter the Wu-Tang (36 Chambers).*

Things turn puzzlingly serious on the second album. Suddenly the concept of gravedigging carries immense metaphoric significance to the crew, leading to claims about resurrecting the "mentally dead" with vague mystic teachings. "Hidden Emotions" and "Deadliest Biz" probe fascinating territory about the hyper-masculine world of hip-hop itself. There's still plenty of room for gore, though here it tends to be discussed in the context of "the black-on-black crime saga."

RZA and Paul left after *The Pick,* and the group got a taste of real-life death when Poetic succumbed to colon cancer in July 2001. *Nightmare in A-Minor,* recorded by Poetic and Frukwon as a last testament, is a slow-witted shadow of its predecessors, as is *6 Feet Under,* a pointless postmortem made by Frukwon with one Arnold Hamilton. Death be not proud. —B.S.

David Gray

  ★★★½ A Century Ends (Caroline, 1993)
   ★★★   Flesh (1994; Caroline, 2001)
   ★★½ Sell Sell Sell (1996; Nettwerk, 2000)

   ★★★★   White Ladder (1999; ATO/RCA, 2000)
  ★★★½ Lost Songs 95–98 (ATO/RCA, 2001)
   ★★½ The EPs 92–94 (Caroline, 2001)
   ★★★   A New Day at Midnight (RCA, 2002)

English-born, Welsh-bred performer David Gray sings his earnest songs of love and spirituality in a passion-soaked voice that, powerful as it is, sometimes seems barely enough to withstand his intensity. The ghosts of Bob Dylan and, especially, Van Morrison float close to Gray's fiery folk rock—intimidating ghosts, to be sure, but more often than not he proves himself worthy of them.

Though it's occasionally hampered by melodic sameness and Gray's tendency to overemote, *A Century Ends* is an assured debut nonetheless. "Shine," "Debauchery," and "Birds Without Wings" merge modern and traditional British folk styles with Morrisonesque fervor. *Flesh* is tougher and almost as good; the anthemic "New Horizons" is a standout. Leaning more on loud rock arrangements and sounding less distinctive as a result, *Sell Sell Sell* is a slight misstep, but the album's quieter moments—"Hold On to Nothing," "Smile," "Gutters Full of Rain"—are captivating.

White Ladder, Gray's commercial breakthrough, is also his finest collection to date, harnessing his muse to a tasteful array of sampled and programmed beats. "Please Forgive Me," "Babylon," and the title cut have a warm, human depth that contrasts brilliantly with their high-tech surface. *Lost Songs* isn't as strong as its predecessor, but it's by no means a throwaway. The stately restraint of "Hold On" and "Falling Down the Mountainside" proves once again that Gray is at his best when at his most intimate.

On *A New Day at Midnight,* Gray benefits by calming down. The impact of certain songs ("Last Boat to America," "The Other Side") is enhanced without the heavy breathing, but as a whole, the album edges toward snooziness. When he lets out a lusty whoop on the propulsive "Caroline," it's a relief.

In the wake of Gray's platinum success with *White Ladder,* his former label released a compilation of British EPs from his early acoustic-troubadour years; its best songs were already available on his first two albums. —M.R.

Macy Gray

  ★★★★   On How Life Is (Epic, 1999)
 ★★★½ The Id (Epic, 2001)
 ★★★½ The Trouble With Being Myself (Epic, 2003)

Has there been a voice in recent pop history with more character than Macy Gray's? Okay, put it another way: Has there been a more bizarre voice in recent pop history than Macy Gray's? Raspy and raw, Gray's pipes bear more of a resemblance to Donald Duck's than Aretha Franklin's. Still, linked up (as she usually is) with some sharp melodies and simmering funk grooves, Gray sure sounds soulful. Add in her knack for writing heartfelt, sometimes giddy lyrics and her eye-popping visual style, and you've got one distinctive artist; whether she ends up an unlikely superstar or just a cool cult figure remains to be seen.

On How Life Is didn't gain commercial momentum for nearly a year after its release, but one listen is enough to explain its eventual multiplatinum sales. Though the big hit, "I Try," is a catchy and affecting wounded-love ballad, the album's bedrock is the deliciously slinky "Do Something," which quietly condemns a stoner's retreat from the world. Elsewhere, the spirits of Prince, Sly Stone, and Stevie Wonder lurk in the bouncing beats of "Why Didn't You Call Me" and "Sex-O-Matic Venus Freak."

That word *freak* (used to lovingly describe both oneself and others) shows up all over *The Id* as Gray continues to develop her uninhibited persona; "Gimme All Your Lovin' or I Will Kill You" is a fairly representative title. The retro-soul vibe here is, if anything, even more buoyant than it was on her debut, and "Don't Come Around" is a worthy successor to "I Try." Unfortunately, the album loses direction toward the end. "When I See You," the first track on *The Trouble With Being Myself,* sounds like a lost nugget from Kool & the Gang's archives. The remainder suggests that Gray's stuck in a creative holding pattern. But it's a fun holding pattern.   —M.R.

Adam Green
see THE MOLDY PEACHES

Al Green

★★½	Green Is Blues (1970; Capitol, 2003)
★★★★	Al Green Gets Next to You (1970; Capitol, 2003)
★★★★	Let's Stay Together (1972; Motown, 1983)
★★★★	I'm Still in Love With You (1972; Motown, 1982)
★★★★★	Call Me (1973; Capitol, 2004)
★★★★	Livin' for You (1973; Motown, 1983)
★★★★	Al Green Explores Your Mind (1974; Capitol, 2004)
★★★★★	Greatest Hits, Vol. 1 (1975; Motown, 1982)
★★★½	Al Green Is Love (1975; Capitol, 2004)
★★★½	Full of Fire (1976; Capitol, 2004)
★★★	Have a Good Time (Hi, 1976)
★★★★½	The Belle Album (1977; Motown, 1983)
★★★★½	Greatest Hits, Vol. 2 (1977; Motown, 1983)
★★★★	Truth 'n' Time (1978; Motown, 1983)
★★★★	The Lord Will Make a Way (Myrrh, 1980)
★★★★	Tokyo . . . Live! (1981; Hi, 2000)
★★★★	Higher Plane (Myrrh, 1981)
★★★	Precious Lord (Myrrh, 1982)
★★★★	I'll Rise Again (Myrrh, 1983)
★★★	Al Green Sings the Gospel (Motown, 1983)
★★★½	He Is the Light (A&M, 1985)
★★★	Trust in God (Myrrh, 1986)
★★★½	Soul Survivor (A&M, 1987)
★★★★½	Love Ritual: Rare & Previously Unreleased 1968–76 (MCA, 1989)
★★★½	I Get Joy (A&M, 1989)
★★★★	One in a Million (Word/Epic, 1991)
★★★★	The Supreme Al Green: The Greatest Hits (Hi, 1992)
★★★½	Unchained Melody (Collectables, 1993)
★★★	Your Heart's in Good Hands (MCA, 1995)
★★★	Here I Am (EMI-Capitol, 1995)
★★★½	Unchained Melody (EMI-Capitol, 1995)
★★★½	Back to Back Hits (EMI-Capitol, 1995)
★★★½	Glory to His Name (EMI-Capitol, 1995)
★★★½	Rock of Ages (AMW, 1997)
★★½	Anthology Live (Capitol, 1997)
★★★½	Take Me to the River: Greatest Hits, Vol. 2 (Hi, 1997)
★★★★	Hi Masters (Hi, 1998)
★★★	More Greatest Hits (Capitol, 1998)
★★★	True Love: A Collection (Empire Music, 2000)
★★★	Listen to the Rarities (Hi, 2000)
★★★★	The Hi Singles: A's and B's (Hi, 2000)
★★★½	Greatest Gospel Hits (The Right Stuff, 2000)
★★★	Take Me to the River (Capitol, 2000)
★★★★	Testify: The Best of the A&M Years (A&M, 2001)
★★★★★	The Very Best of Al Green (Music Club, 2001)
★★★	The Love Songs Collection (Capitol, 2003)
★★★½	I Can't Stop (Capitol/Blue Note, 2003)

It is a testament to the fact that the world needs a secular Al Green as much as Green himself needs God that Green's early love-and-hard-times soul recordings remain in print and still essential. And it's a testament to the power of the singer's conviction and his unerring vocal instincts that 1995's gospel recording *Your Heart's in Good Hands* signifies no drop-off in quality even if Green deliberately limits his potential audience.

Al Green's blazing streak of hit singles sweetened the sound of Memphis soul just enough to suit the changing times; he reasserted the music's gospel base without losing that identifying grit. Even though he returned to the church halfway through the decade, Green is the preeminent soul man of the '70s, hands down. And given the proper motivation, he can still move mountains. He'd already been performing gospel in public for several years when his secular debut, "Back Up Train" by Al Green and the Soul Mates, reached the R&B Top 10 during the soul-saturated year of 1967. Moving from Grand Rapids down to Memphis a couple of years later, Green hooked up with producer and bandleader Willie Mitchell—the creative main man at Hi Records, Stax/Volt's crosstown rival. *Green Is Blues* made for a rather tentative (if mostly uptempo) debut. But *Al Green Gets Next to You*, released later that same year, accomplishes its stated goal. Here, Green finds the intimate tone that will become his calling card, and Willie Mitchell finally defines a Hi house sound—slower and sweatier than the bristling Booker T.–Bar-Kays groove, but fully capable of the same supercharged emotional impact. Together, they reshape the Temptations' chesty Motown classic "I Can't Get Next to You" into something fresh—no small feat.

"Tired of Being Alone" and "Let's Stay Together" brought Al Green to the pop charts in 1971, introducing his lush, electrifying romanticism to an apparently ballad-starved general public. Sliding from a gravy-thick lower register to an ethereal, heart-stopping falsetto, Al Green makes his seductive pleading hard to resist throughout *Let's Stay Together.* Hi's house band hits its stride right alongside the label's new star: Former MG's drummer Al Jackson Jr. pumps up a subtle pulse, while guitarist "Teenie" Hodges plucks uncommon, jazz-flavored chord progressions against Mitchell's bittersweet horn and string arrangements.

I'm Still in Love With You refines that approach on the title cut and "Look What You Done for Me," while indicating Green's wide-ranging tastes with cover versions of Roy Orbison's "Oh, Pretty Woman" and Kris Kristofferson's "For the Good Times." If those interpretations are a bit forced, Green breathes natural fire into the Memphis-Nashville connection on his next album, *Call Me.* His readings of "I'm So Lonesome I Could Cry" (Hank Williams) and "Funny How Time Slips Away" (Willie Nelson) merge the country heart-tugging of the originals with some R&B sinew-flexing—magnificent. *Call Me* captures Green at a dizzying peak; the hit title track sums up his preceding achievements, while "Jesus Is Waiting" suggests his future destination.

In retrospect, you can hear Al Green inching closer and closer to the Lord on each subsequent record: "Sweet Sixteen" and "My God Is Real" stand out on the spacey, string-laden *Livin' for You*, while "Take Me to the River" is the testifying centerpiece of the funkier, more direct *Al Green Explores Your Mind.* The

flawless *Greatest Hits* concludes his superstar run, but he's far from finished.

After releasing two increasingly sketchy albums in 1976, Al Green stopped working with Willie Mitchell—and radically changed his tune. Around this time, Green's singles quit crossing over to the pop charts. *The Belle Album* explains just what he'd been going through: a difficult, often painful reassessment of his faith and its relation to his art. Picking up an acoustic guitar, Green began to write and sing about his transformation, about his belief and his nagging doubts. "It's you that I want," he tells his lover on the title track, "but it's Him that I need." Perhaps because of Green's up-front uncertainty, *The Belle Album*'s gently funky heat can melt the coldest, most atheistic resolve. *Truth 'n' Time* plugs this best-of-both-worlds approach back into Green's traditional mix of originals and cover versions; "Say a Little Prayer" and, yes, "To Sir With Love" lend themselves to the task quite well. Al Green's next move comes as no surprise, then: In 1980 he began recording straight-up gospel for the Myrrh label. The import-only live album captures a good-sized chunk—but not all—of Green's seductive stage presence and thrill-a-minute virtuosity, while the outtakes and rarities on *Love Ritual* soar above his official mid-'70s releases (especially the wild, African-influenced mix of the title track).

Expectations of a return to secular music sabotaged these albums for many Al Green devotees at the time of their release. In retrospect, the very best ones (*The Lord Will Make a Way, Higher Plane,* and *I'll Rise Again*) weave a delicious spell all their own; they're not as robust as '70s Green, but just as musically complex and soul-satisfying. Though he's shifted his lyric focus to pure spread-the-word proselytizing, Al Green (now a reverend and preacher with his own church in Memphis) has never really lost his knack for crafting dramatic, catchy pop songs—or his ability to make the most unlikely cover versions sound utterly natural. Take *Higher Plane* as an example; "Amazing Grace" is as good as you'd hope, but nobody else on earth could pull off "The Battle Hymn of the Republic" quite the way Green does. *Precious Lord* is a little too soft, and not all the lightweight pop covers on *Trust in God* get over—he is human, after all.

The long-awaited reunion with Willie Mitchell (*He Is the Light*) sounds bracingly familiar, and yet a curiously uninspired batch of songs (save for the Clark Sisters' "You Brought the Sunshine") makes it something less than a magic moment. To his credit, Green didn't linger at this nostalgic crossroads; *Soul Survivor* and especially *I Get Joy* tastefully integrate some contemporary rhythms and synth textures into his ongoing testimony. *One in a Million* is a frustrating, brutally truncated summary of Al Green's Myrrh period; still, those 38 minutes (including "Amazing Grace") should be enough to convince any skeptic. With Al Green, hearing is believing.

Green's work continued to be diffused among various labels and repackagers long after he bowed out of recording secular soul. Hi kept the hits coming with *The Supreme Al Green,* which belied its claim of featuring the greatest hits by omitting the magnificent "Here I Am (Come and Take Me)." The label did a better job following up *The Supreme* with the companion volume *Take Me to the River* five years later. Hi's cleverest repackaging of its Green catalogue comprised a trio of collector's essentials: *Hi Masters; A's and B's,* a collection of singles and their original 7-inch B-sides; and the aptly titled *Listen to the Rarities* (cuts mysteriously deemed unworthy of release but surely able to stand beside Green's most noteworthy hits).

The Right Stuff waited 23 years to release a second volume of its 1975 *Greatest Hits* with the incohesive *More Greatest Hits,* a poorly paced hodgepodge of hits major and minor. Its *Greatest Gospel Hits,* however, is a welcome introduction to Green's inspirational soul for fans of the secular stuff. In 1995, the budget label Cema Special Markets managed to squeeze Green's sterling work onto a series of well-chosen collections—*Here I Am, Unchained Melody, Back to Back Hits,* and the accessible gospel-driven *Glory to His Name.* Capitol's *Anthology Live* is deceptively slick-looking and massive; it's crammed with fillerlike lengthy interviews and uninteresting live tracks, dragging down any momentum generated by the hits, which are available on less expensive volumes. *Take Me to the River,* this one Capitol's, is equally patchwork, including most but not all of the Hi biggies and some very inferior tracks. Empire dipped into the Green well once, on *True Love,* for a random mess of old love songs and gospel tracks, creating a no-doubt-odd aural disjunction for anyone hearing "God Is Standing By" next to "Ride, Sally, Ride." AMW's tidy *Rock of Ages* compiles 10 gospel standards, while Capitol brings together everything in the Green oeuvre that fits the title profile for *The Love Songs Collection,* thereby omitting his essential, ambivalent secular work. Green completists will surely own every track, somewhere, to be found on the two most important later releases, but both A&M's *Testify* and Music Club's solid, completist *The Very Best* efficiently cover the magnificent panorama of the man's career. Green reunited with Mitchell for another go-round in 2003 for *I Can't Stop.* Mitchell's production still has much of its '70s-soul snap; Green's voice has lost maybe a half step, which still puts him in the top 1 percent of singers. —M.C./A.B.

Green Day

★★½	1,039/Smoothed Out Slappy Hour (Lookout, 1991)
★★★	Kerplunk (Lookout, 1992)
★★★★★	Dookie (Reprise, 1994)
★★★★	Insomniac (Reprise, 1995)
★★★★	Nimrod (Reprise, 1997)
★★★★	Singles Box (WEA, 1999)
★★★★	Warning: (Reprise, 2000)
★★★	Take 2 (WEA, 2000)
★★★	Tune in Tokyo [live] (Reprise, 2001)
★★★★★	International Superhits! (Warner Bros., 2001)
★★★	Shenanigans (Reprise, 2002)

Just weeks before Kurt Cobain killed himself in April 1994, Green Day released its blockbuster major-label debut, *Dookie,* transforming the ennui that ruled the day into a racket that affirmed life, not death. The three East Bay stoners—snotty-not-snooty singer/guitarist Billie Joe Armstrong, fleet-fingered bassist Mike Dirnt, and flailing-armed drummer Tre Cool—played peppy pop-punk uncomplicated by heavy metal or deep thoughts, and lodged it on radio where, at press time, it still remains.

"I declare I don't care no more/I'm growing up and out and growing bored," announced Billie Joe in *Dookie*'s opening lines, his snarl keening in a way that suggested—and would always suggest—brattiness, boyish innocence, adult anxiety, and (rarely noted) guileless flirtation. The rest of the album, like the rest of Green Day's career, would be spent wringing exuberance out of aimlessness, finding the sweet spot in life's sour moments. The band's indie albums showed glints of brilliance—*Kerplunk*'s chugging ballad "Christy Road," for one—but any cut here could light up a room. "She" whips around like a severed power line; "Burnout" explodes like a flare; the tightly coiled "Basket Case" drives like a corkscrew; "When I Come Around" slinks with a naked soulfulness; and, last but not least, "Longview" gleefully reinvents grunge's quiet-loud melodrama.

According to the numbers—about 2 million to *Dookie*'s 8 million sold—*Insomniac* absolutely qualified as a sophomore slump. And indeed, if up until then Green Day had been fueled by speed and weed, it seems that posthigh paranoia had set in. "I'm blowing off steam with/methamphetamine," Armstrong sings in "Geek Stink Breath," his voice edged with desperation and a weird, almost fatalistic excitement, his guitar tone tighter and blacker than ever before. It sounds as if he's got more bottled up than he can blow off. The album's best song and biggest hit, "Brain Stew," sometimes played on radio along with the tacked-on tantrum "Jaded," marked a formal wrinkle in the band's Ramones- and Buzzcocks-derived hum; slivers of silence block off bursts of lead-heavy sound, while Armstrong, "past the point of delirium," stretches his vocal cords over the changes. Gloomy but crackling with energy, *Insomniac* resembles—even rivals—Nirvana's bleak response to sudden fame, *In Utero*. But, squinting in the spotlight or not, Armstrong wasn't about to disappear underground.

Nimrod, for all its familiar complaints—one minute in and Armstrong's declaring "I'm so happy I could die"—glows with the relief of someone who's avoided a brush with death. The band, as tight as they were on the extraordinarily wound-up *Insomniac*, nail the syncopated bounce of "Hitchin' a Ride" like a bleached-blond John Henry, set a rock land-speed record on "Nice Guys Finish Last," convincingly spice "Walking Alone" with harmonica, and blast through the near-ballads "Redundant" and "Worry Rock." And then, marking another formal wrinkle, Armstrong steps out for the effortlessly gorgeous, acoustic, all-the-way-there ballad "Good Riddance (Time of Your Life)."

Life goes on: In a spurt remarkably free of growing pains, Green Day welcomes the new millennium with *Warning:*. Adding strings and one solo's worth of ersatz sax to the acoustic guitar and harmonica ushered in on *Nimrod,* the threesome fully focus on the textures that have always differentiated their sturdy grooves and simple melodies. Armstrong's voice, now as throaty as it's always been whiny, leads a dozen speedy, neatly packaged reinterpretations of pop-rock history, from the Beatles to Creedence Clearwater Revival to the Ramones themselves. Grunge had long ago bit Green Day's dust. —N.C.

Green Velvet

★★★★	Green Velvet (F-111/Warner Bros., 2000)
★★★½	Whatever (Relief, 2001)

Cajmere

★★★	TechnoFunk (311, 2000)

Curtis A. Jones is generally credited with helping revive Chicago's house-music scene in the mid-'90s with his record labels Cajual and Relief and with his production of club hits like "Brighter Days," which he recorded under the name Cajmere. It is under the Green Velvet moniker, however, that Jones has been most successful, indulging his taste for droll, over-the-top satires of the nightlife his music helps soundtrack, as well as stiff, punishing, near-industrial beats. *Green Velvet,* his U.S. debut, is essentially a greatest-hits package of his '90s singles, but it works like a concept album, from "Flash," a gleefully decadent guided tour

of a nightclub, to the creepy first-person narrative "The Stalker," to "Answering Machine," a hilarious litany of bad-luck missives from creditors, neighbors, and ex-girlfriends. *Whatever* is less inspired, but features the great "La La Land," a snide put-down of ecstasy culture ("Who's gonna give me a ride to the after-show?" *"Me!"*), and "GAT (The Great American Tragedy)," whose psychoses ("They say it's just a phase/This is *not a fuckin' phase*") feel more lived-in than usual. Between those albums, Jones switched monikers to Cajmere and released *Techno-Funk,* a smart if sometimes claustrophobic minimal techno DJ set. —M.M.

The Guess Who

★★★	Canned Wheat (1969; Buddha/BMG, 2000)
★★★	American Woman (1970; Buddha/BMG, 2000)
★★½	Share the Land (1970; Buddha/BMG, 2000)
★★★	Best of the Guess Who (1971; RCA, 1990)
★★★	Live at the Paramount (1972; Buddha/BMG, 2000)
★★★★	The Greatest of the Guess Who (1977; RCA, 1990)
★★	American Woman, These Eyes & Other Hits (1985; RCA, 1990)
★★★★	Track Record: The Guess Who Collection (1988; RCA, 1991)
★★	These Eyes (1992; BMG, 1997)
★★★★	The Ultimate Collection (RCA, 1997)
★	The Spirit Lives On: Greatest Hits Live (J-Bird, 1998)
★★★★½	Greatest Hits (RCA, 1999)
★★	Running Back Through Canada (RCA, 2001)
★★½	Shakin' All Over! (Sundazed, 2001)
★★	The Platinum & Gold Collection (RCA, 2003)
★★½	Extended Versions (BMG, 2004)

Rock superstars at home in Canada, the Guess Who had to be content with merely being hitmakers in America. Formed by singer Chad Allan and guitarist Randy Bachman in Winnipeg, the group scored a 1965 hit with its cover of Johnny Kidd's "Shakin' All Over." The early sides collected on the Sundazed anthology show a band of no special distinction (outside of having the good sense to record an early song by fellow countryman Neil Young) that fairly screams "one-hit wonder." Then Allan left, keyboard player Burton Cummings moved out front, Bachman found his writing chops with Cummings, and the band found producer Jack Richardson. The Guess Who was reborn in 1969 with "These Eyes," a gorgeous ballad that was more pop than rock, but did the job of putting the band back in the spotlight.

Any thought that the band was a two-hit wonder was dispelled by its second album that year, *Canned Wheat,* containing the hits "Laughing" and "Undun," and an early version of "No Time." Powered by Bachman's hooky and often fuzz-toned licks and Cummings' robust voice, these records brought rock & roll honor to the pop charts. The pinnacle was "American Woman," with hard-rock rhythms so infectious that this anti-U.S. rant became an American #1. The album of the same name includes the reworked "No Time" and the "No Sugar Tonight/New Mother Nature" medley. Bachman left after this (to found Bachman-Turner Overdrive, another band adept at making Top 40 hard rock) and was replaced by two guitarists who would later give way to Domenic Troiano. "Hand Me Down World" rocks almost as spitefully as "American Woman," but "Share the Land," though a bigger hit, is a rather clumsily attempted anthem that marks the beginning of the band's decline. They recorded four more albums before disbanding in 1974, the crisply delivered *Live at the Paramount* being the only one still available.

The band's final hit, the novelty dreck of "Clap for the Wolfman" with deejay Wolfman Jack, was an unfortunate coda to an impressive run. As earnest and workmanlike as their album filler was, it does the Guess Who no disservice to say they were about the hits. Ignore the skimpy collections *These Eyes* and *American Woman, These Eyes & Other Hits.* On the other hand, the triple-CD *Ultimate Collection* box is too much for all but the most seriously committed devotee; even the double *Track Record* may overstate the case. The 18 tracks on *Greatest Hits* are all you really need. Add to the ignore category: *The Spirit Lives On* from a "reunion" that often featured bassist Jim Kale as the only original member, and *Running Back Through Canada,* an obligatory live album from the band's legitimate reunion tour of 2000. *Platinum & Gold* is a spotty, incomplete compilation. Waste no time with the deceptive *Extended Versions,* which is nothing more than 10 of the tracks from *Live at the Paramount* reshuffled and repackaged. —B.E.

Guided by Voices

★★★ Propeller (Scat, 1993)
★★★ Vampire on Titus (Scat, 1993)
★★ The Grand Hour EP (Scat, 1994)
★★★★ Bee Thousand (Scat, 1994)
★★★½ I Am a Scientist EP (Scat, 1994)
★★★ Box (Scat, 1995)
★★★½ Alien Lanes (Matador, 1995)
★★★★ Under the Bushes Under the Stars (Matador, 1996)
★½ Sunfish Holy Breakfast EP (Matador, 1996)
★★★★ Mag Earwhig! (Matador, 1997)
★★½ Do the Collapse (TVT, 1999)
★★ Suitcase: Failed Experiments and Trashed Aircraft (Luna, 2000)
★★★ Isolation Drills (TVT, 2001)
★★★ Universal Truths and Cycles (Matador, 2002)
★★★½ Hardcore UFOs: Revelations, Epiphanies and Fast Food in the Western Hemisphere (Matador, 2003)
★★★★ The Best of Guided by Voices: Human Amusements at Hourly Rates (Matador, 2003)
★★★ Earthquake Glue (Matador, 2003)

Rock & roll life stories don't come much more heartwarming than Robert Pollard's. Just over a decade ago, he was a schoolteacher in Dayton, OH, with a fun little hobby: writing peculiar pop songs and recording them on crappy 4-track machines, helped out by a loose assemblage of pals that he called Guided by Voices. Ten years on, Guided by Voices are an internationally admired band, and Pollard's regarded as one of modern rock's most inspired tunesmiths. Now in his forties, he doesn't need to teach anymore; instead, he gets to live out all his Robert Plant and Roger Daltrey fantasies on concert stages across the country. Lucky bastard.

At its best, Guided by Voices' music is a winning combination of power pop, indie rock, punk-metal, and stream-of-consciousness psychedelia buoyed by Pollard's lilting melodies and Daltreyesque vocals. Identifying GBV's best work can be a chore, however. Their early albums (the ones recorded on those crappy 4-tracks) helped turn the term "lo-fi" into a '90s buzzword, but that doesn't make it any easier to hear the jewels scattered beneath the sonic sludge. And because Pollard is a prolific writer who doesn't tend to edit or develop his ideas much, most GBV discs are maddeningly inconsistent, packed with dozens of tracks—many of which are more fragments than songs—that run the gamut from transcendent to unlistenable.

Newcomers curious to sample Pollard's wares should start with the Matador best-of, an enticing introduction to the oeuvre. If you get hooked, pick up *Bee Thousand, Under the Bushes Under the Stars,* or *Mag Earwhig!,* all of which boast a highly favorable manna-to-dross ratio. Any of the remaining Matador and Scat albums will reward further investigation. GBV's two-album tenure on TVT was disappointing, but *Isolation Drills* sounds far less compromised by marketplace considerations than the Ric Ocasek–

produced *Do the Collapse.* Although the five-CD *Box,* which brings together GBV's earliest music (1987–90); the four-CD *Suitcase,* an outtakes (!) collection; and the five-CD/one-DVD *Hardcore UFOs,* a career-spanning potpourri, are obviously meant for the converted, there's good stuff to be found there as well. Still, the only perfect Guided by Voices album is the one you compile yourself.   —M.R.

Guns n' Roses

★★	Live! Like a Suicide (Uzi Suicide, 1986)
★★★★★	Appetite for Destruction (Geffen, 1987)
★★★	G N' R Lies (Geffen, 1988)
★★★★★	Use Your Illusion I (Geffen, 1991)
★★★★	Use Your Illusion II (Geffen, 1991)
★★★	The Spaghetti Incident (Geffen, 1993)
★★	Live Era: '87–'93 (Geffen, 1999)
★★★★	Greatest Hits (Geffen, 2004)

Sometimes an album seems like an announcement from the Big Rock Dude in the Sky: its very grooves declare, *This is what must be heard now. Appetite for Destruction* was that kind of inevitable hit. Released at the height of the '80s, *Appetite* expressed the captive energies of young America in a voice—the unbounded scream of W. Axl Rose—that was both horrifying and irresistible. Hard rock seemed so dumb until Guns n' Roses attacked it with smarts, snot, and vitriol, cutting through a decade of hairspray with one nasty punch.

This band of journeymen punks and metalheads had gathered in L.A. to fulfill the get-laid-get-rich dream, and had individually tried glam, indie, and whatever came in between without much success. Together, they found the mix that made hard rock a different beast. What Guns n' Roses did, apparently without much forethought, was embrace contradictions: speed and musicianship, flash and dirt. That's why *Appetite* sounded new—it wasn't any one old thing.

The hard-core rhythm section of Duff McKagan and Steven Adler lit napalm under the butts of riff duelists Slash and Izzy Stradlin, while Rose pinpointed where a punk snarl becomes a metal yell. First track "Welcome to the Jungle" is a Hollywood novel on meth, and what follows never takes a breather: the smack boogie of "Mr. Brownstone," the poisoned anthem "Paradise City," Rose's twisted love-hate song to a hooker, "Rocket Queen." That last song, like the massive power ballad "Sweet Child o' Mine," captured the paradox that made Rose the Golem of rock & roll: The era's most sensitive songwriter was a girlfriend-slapping bigot on a tear. And the band was as mixed-up as Axl's mind, unifying lyricism (via Slash)

and scruffiness (Stradlin), romanticism (Rose) and raw power (the rhythm section).

G n' R's personality crisis became tabloid fodder as Rose's control-freak ways clashed with his bandmates' bad habits, nearly destroying the band out of the gate. The double EP *G N' R Lies* made things worse by matching up the group's most tenderoni ballad, "Patience," with the jokey murder ballad "I Used to Love Her" and "One in a Million," in which Rose trashed gays and immigrants over Slash and Stradlin's sloppy guitar sparring. (*Lies* also contains four pleasantly raw live tracks from a 1986 indie release, *Live! Like a Suicide.*) "Million" is unforgivable mostly because it's stupid; usually Rose says the worst with more forethought.

Forethought definitely fed what came next. *Use Your Illusion I* and *Use Your Illusion II* offered a stunned public nearly three hours of serious exploration and wild fucking around. Interband tensions had destroyed group authorship, and Rose's heroics (as well as drugs, which contributed to Steven Adler's replacement by Matt Sorum) strained his bandmates' good-rockin' chemistry. Critics chided Rose for Queen-like minioperas "November Rain" (from *I*) and "Don't Cry" (on both discs), but those songs have endured, while Stradlin jaunts like "Dust n' Bones" now seem efficient but conservative. Throughout *I* and *II*, it's Rose who takes all the interesting turns. But he still needs his band, especially the adventurous stylings of Slash, to properly negotiate them.

I is the more propulsive record, with Stradlin songs, the Wings/Bond cover "Live and Let Die," and vintage G n' R bullshit like "Back Off Bitch" tempering the grandiosity of the centerpiece "November Rain." The psycho fantasy trip "Coma" appeals more to *Appetite* lovers because it's creepy and it rocks. But the lush "Rain" redefines the band—with Dizzy Reed's expressive keyboards giving both Rose and Slash permission to spew emotion, and that hard-rock bottom still bouncing, this song showed how a ballad could be as bloody as a high-speed assault.

II starts in a similarly expansive space and gets even spacier. "Civil War" is a shattered landscape painting; the cover "Knockin' on Heaven's Door" turns Dylan's West into spaghetti. Nastiness and levity (like McKagan's Johnny Thunders paean "So Fine") counter the weirdness of "Breakdown" and "My World" and the extravagance of the riveting, nine-minute "Estranged." Two songs here, however, show that G n' R can still focus to great effect—the cutting "You Could Be Mine" and the plainly inspirational "Yesterdays."

Though endlessly intriguing, the *Use Your Illusion* albums signaled big trouble for Guns n' Roses. Their lack of cohesiveness represented the state of the band. Stradlin, the cowriter who could best focus Axl's excesses, left in 1991. An enjoyable album of punk, glam, and soul covers, *The Spaghetti Incident* suggested that G n' R might be headed back to its spiritual base of shredding rock. But Rose had something different in mind. His growing interest in industrial music and electronica split him from his bandmates, whose ambitions lay more in the Stones direction. Without officially disbanding, the band began its long retreat.

Live Era: '87–'93 attempted to keep interest alive as late as 1999, but the scattered recordings didn't do justice to any of their studio versions. Slash formed his own mildly successful band, Slash's Snakepit; other members pursued other gigs. Rose became the anti-hero of his own internal rock opera, retreating into the studio, hiring and firing scores of collaborators, and occasionally trotting out a strangely shaped new song. Designed to sell to casual fans looking for something to pop in the players in their Range Rovers, *Greatest Hits* offers the crucial hits and a couple of fun cover tunes. A disastrous Axl-led 2002 tour, canceled halfway through, coincided with his former mates' announcement that they were re-forming without him. Pride may have never dealt so cruel a blow to a rock genius. But for the most Shakespearean of late-20th century stars, the outcome was appropriate. —A.P.

Arlo Guthrie

- ★★★½ Alice's Restaurant (Reprise, 1967)
- ★★★ Running Down the Road (1969; Koch, 1997)
- ★★★ Washington County (1970; Koch, 1997)
- ★★★ Hobo's Lullaby (1972; Koch, 1997)
- ★★★ Last of the Brooklyn Cowboys (1973; Koch, 1997)
- ★★★★ Amigo (Reprise, 1976)
- ★★★ The Best of Arlo Guthrie (Warner Bros., 1977)
- ★★★ Mystic Journey (Koch, 1996)
- ★★ Alice's Restaurant 30th Anniversary Edition (Koch, 1997)
- ★★★★ Outlasting the Blues/Power of Love (Koch, 2002)

with Pete Seeger
- ★★★½ Precious Friend (Reprise, 1982)

As sons of titanic fathers go, Arlo has acquitted himself pretty well. The 20 minutes of "Alice's Restaurant"—the draft protest that thrust him to fame at the 1967 Newport Folk Festival—don't hold up to repeated listening, but Guthrie's comfortable, slightly wiggy persona remains welcome. Contending not only with the potent ghost of Woody (whose simple, prophetic songs form America's definitive folk music) but with Woody's disciple Bob Dylan, Arlo has

opted generally for easier music. As resolutely anti-authoritarian as his forebears, he champions personal and political rebellions, but he's nostalgic in ways they never were, and his humor has little of their bite.

As a vocalist, however, his sunniness lends his delivery charm. "Coming Into Los Angeles," a doper's gleeful apologia, was a big hit at Woodstock and the best thing off *Running Down the Road; Hobo's Lullaby* featured Arlo's other mass exposure, in a cover of Steve Goodman's sweet "City of New Orleans." *Last of the Brooklyn Cowboys* is an ambitious crazy-quilt of all kinds of American music, from country to Latino; *Amigo* was stronger, and perhaps Arlo's best. *Mystic Journey,* coproduced by Arlo's son Abe, finds Guthrie still vital after a 20-year absence from the mainstream.

Best of Arlo Guthrie isn't very intelligently compiled. A much better example of Guthrie at his finest remains 1979's *Outlasting the Blues,* popular music at its most honest. A rigorous self-examination, spurred on by Guthrie's conversion to Catholicism, it meditates deeply on love, faith, and death, and it's paired, on the 2002 release, with the more polished but still profound *Power of Love. Precious Friend* locates Guthrie squarely within the folk tradition; it's a tasty collaboration with Pete Seeger, a genre presence nearly as august as Guthrie's dad. —P.E.

Woody Guthrie

- ★★★ Nursery Days (Smithsonian/Folkways, 1962)
- ★★★★ Woody Guthrie Sings Folk Songs (1962; Smithsonian/Folkways, 1990)
- ★★★★ Dust Bowl Ballads (1964; Buddah, 2000)
- ★★★★ The Early Years (Columbia/Legacy, 1964)
- ★★★★ Struggle (1976; Smithsonian/Folkways, 1976)
- ★★★★ Columbia River Collection (Rounder, 1987)
- ★★★★ Library of Congress Recordings (Rounder, 1988)
- ★★★½ The Greatest Songs of Woody Guthrie (Vanguard, 1988)
- ★★★★ Songs to Grow on for Mother and Child (Smithsonian/Folkways, 1991)
- ★★★★ Ballads of Sacco and Vanzetti (Smithsonian/Folkways, 1996)
- ★★★★ Early Masters (Rykodisc/Tradition, 1996)
- ★★★★★ This Land is Your Land: The Asch Recordings, Vol. 1 (Smithsonian/Folkways, 1997)
- ★★★★★ Muleskinner Blues: The Asch Recordings, Vol. 2 (Smithsonian/Folkways, 1997)
- ★★★★★ Hard Travelin': The Asch Recordings, Vol. 3 (Smithsonian/Folkways, 1998)
- ★★★★★ Buffalo Skinners: The Asch Recordings, Vol. 4 (Smithsonian/Folkways, 1999)
- ★★★★★ The Asch Recordings, Vol. 1–4 (Smithsonian/Folkways, 1999)

Weathered, lean, and kindly, Woody Guthrie's face is the face of American folk music. Born in 1912, this astonishingly prolific composer is to the gritty, acoustic story-song what Louis Armstrong is to jazz and Little Richard and Elvis are to rock & roll—the clearest, deepest source. Writing, according to his friend Pete Seeger, a thousand songs in the years between 1936 and 1954, he recorded with absolute fidelity, wit, and grace the struggles and celebrations of the working class. An Okie leftist (his guitar bore the legend "This machine kills fascists"), he was an activist whose politics were the furthest thing from theoretical—he'd suffered the wrongs he strove so passionately to correct. Outlaws from Jesus Christ to Pretty Boy Floyd, from debtors and prisoners to hobos, formed the misfit pantheon from which he took inspiration—and his hard but ecstatic life was an act of protest and of prayer, of anger and of healing.

Influenced by Jimmie Rodgers and the Carter Family, Guthrie also absorbed the strains of cowboy music, country blues, and the music-hall pop of his day; from that tangled yarn he wove his own bardic, simple music, with each song featuring only a few chords, but containing entire condensed volumes of wisdom. His voice was flat, clear, somewhat trebly, and unerringly direct: He sang like a casually chatting prophet. So profound was his effect on not only American music, but on the American character, that it's not just Dylan, Springsteen, and every single folk musician who owes him a debt, but writers like Kerouac and the rest of the Beats, as well as naturalist filmmakers, vernacular poets, and populist politicians. Alongside Walt Whitman, Guthrie remains a national poet laureate.

While all of his records are worth owning, the best place to start is with any of the Asch recordings, or, better yet, the entire four volume set: Its jewels, "This Land Is Your Land," "So Long, It's Been Good to Known Yuh," "Deportee," "Hard Travelin'," and so many more, form the basis of American folk. *Library of Congress Recordings* is an epic three-record set featuring a good handful of Guthrie's dust-bowl ballads and laconically witty spoken intros to the songs. *Folk Songs* pairs him with his friends Leadbelly, Cisco Houston, Sonny Terry, and Bess Lomax Hawes; *Struggle* concentrates on the political work. *Columbia River Collection* is an excellent round of songs from 1941 that had been lost for 40 years; *The Early Years* is a good one-CD intro. Also essential for full appreciation of the man is his 1943 autobiography, *Bound for Glory.*   —P.E.

Guy

★★★   Guy (MCA, 1988)
★★½   The Future (MCA, 1990)
★★★   Guy III (MCA, 2000)

With Guy, production's the thing. The songs and the singing are ultrapro on these albums, but it's the sound—a percolating hip-hop feast of slamming percussion and floating keyboard textures—that grabs the listener. This makes sense, as one third of the trio Guy is producer Teddy Riley, virtually the creator of New Jack Swing. New Jack, of course, added new musicality and sonic surprise to all manner of rap—and Guy was a proving ground for the form. Michael Jackson hired Riley to produce *Dangerous* (1991) and to take the Gloved One to hipper ground.

Ten years after, *Guy III* proved that the trio hadn't lost its luster—it still sounded soulfully slick.   —P.E.

Buddy Guy

★★★½   I Left My Blues in San Francisco (1967; MCA, 1990)
★★★★   A Man and the Blues (Vanguard, 1968)
★★★   This Is Buddy Guy (Vanguard, 1968)
★★★★   I Was Walkin' Through the Woods (1970; MCA, 1989)
★★★   Buddy and the Juniors (1970; Beat Goes On, 1998)
★★★½   Hold That Plane (1972; Vanguard, 1990)
★★★½   Stone Crazy! (Alligator, 1981)
★★★½   Damn Right, I've Got the Blues (Silvertone, 1991)
★★★★   The Very Best of Buddy Guy (Rhino, 1992)
★★★½   The Complete Chess Studio Recordings (MCA, 1992)
★★★½   My Time After Awhile (Vanguard, 1992)
★★★   Feels Like Rain (Silvertone, 1993)
★★★   Southern Blues 1957–63 (Paula, 1994)
★★★   Slippin' In (Silvertone, 1994)
★★★   Live: The Real Deal (Silvertone, 1996)
★★★★   Buddy's Blues (Chess 50th Anniversary Collection) (MCA, 1997)
★★★   Blues Master (Vanguard, 1997)
★★★½   As Good as It Gets (Vanguard, 1998)
★★½   Buddy's Blues: The Best of the JSP Sessions (JSP, 1998)
★★★   Heavy Love (Silvertone, 1998)
★★★½   Buddy's Baddest: The Best of Buddy Guy (Silvertone, 1999)
★★★★   The Complete Vanguard Recordings (Vanguard, 2000)
★★★   The Complete JSP Recordings: 1979–1982 (JSP, 2000)
★★★★   Sweet Tea (Silvertone, 2001)
★★★   The Millennium Collection (MCA, 2001)
★★★★   Blues Singer (Silvertone, 2003)

with Junior Wells

★★★★ Buddy Guy & Junior Wells Play the Blues (1972; Rhino, 1992)

★★★½ Drinkin' TNT and Smokin' Dynamite (Blind Pig, 1982)

★★★ Alone and Acoustic (Hightone, 1991)

★★★ Last Time Around: Live at Legends (Silvertone, 1998)

Slash-and-burn guitar solos are the specialty of this Louisiana-born Chicago blues mainstay, whose string-sizzling sides for Chess in the '60s (and session work at the label for artists including Muddy Waters and Howlin' Wolf) made a particularly strong impression on Jimi Hendrix and Eric Clapton. *The Complete Chess Studio Recordings* is an exhaustive collection of his early singles, but MCA's single disc *Buddy's Blues* makes a stronger impact by skipping the filler and diving right into his best-known hailstones and firestorms, like *My Time After Awhile* and *Stone Crazy! A Man and the Blues,* his Vanguard debut and first proper album (previous Chess titles had been singles compilations), is similarly drenched in Stratocaster-ignited fire; highlights include a soulful crack at "Money (That's What I Want)," the playful "Mary Had a Little Lamb," and "Just Playing My Axe," an extension of Keith Richard's signature "Satisfaction" riff. Both *Hold That Plane* and the live *This Is Buddy Guy* are fun if not quite as consistent, though they supplement *A Man and the Blues* handily on the three-disc *Complete Vanguard Recordings.* Touring with harmonica player Junior Wells in the '70s, Guy added R&B licks and chunks of rock to his trick bag. *Buddy Guy & Junior Wells Play the Blues* features indebted guests along the lines of Eric Clapton, while *Drinkin' TNT and Smokin' Dynamite* catches the duo's act at the 1974 Montreux Jazz Festival. *Last Time Around,* recorded in 1993 but not released until '98 (after Wells' death), is a document of their last performance together, at Guy's own Legends nightclub in Chicago. Guy recorded less and less frequently during the '70s and '80s, though his intermittent outings during that era found his stun-power relatively undiminished—witness the righteously wailin' *Stone Crazy!* from 1981. Rhino's *The Very Best of Buddy Guy* is an exemplary overview of the guitarist's career through that point, including a pair of singles he cut for the Cobra label before the Chess years.

Beginning with the Grammy-winning 1991 Silvertone set *Damn Right, I've Got the Blues,* however, Guy's comeback began in earnest. Even with its requisite superstar walk-ons (Clapton and Jeff Beck this time), *Damn Right* is a thoroughly satisfying dose of pure Buddy Guy fretwork. *Feels Like Rain* was a decent followup, though this time the guests start to weigh things down. It's not so much that vocalists Paul Rodgers and Travis Tritt stink up the joint, but their presence is unnecessary; while justifiably best known for his guitar playing, Guy is no slouch as a singer—as comfortable here belting out his own rocker "She's a Superstar" as he is easing into Marvin Gaye's "Trouble Man." Fortunately, *Slippin' In* is Guy's show from start to finish, with a crack band including Chuck Berry pianist Johnnie Johnson and Stevie Ray Vaughan's Double Trouble rhythm section, Chris Layton and Tommy Shannon. Nevertheless, by *Live: The Real Deal,* a strong but predictable set featuring G. E. Smith and the Saturday Night Live Band, Guy's Silvertone run seemed fresh out of ideas—until *Heavy Love* and its followup, *Sweet Tea.* The refreshingly modern, if uneven, *Heavy Love* was nothing if not eclectic, offering everything from jump blues to soul to funk to psychedelic hard rock to a ZZ Top cover ("I Need You Tonight"). But *Sweet Tea* was something completely different, returning Guy to his Southern roots for an inspired—and frequently chilling—collection of swampy hill-country blues numbers cherry-picked from the Fat Possum songbook. Spooky fare like Junior Kimbrough's "Done Got Old" and James "T-Model" Ford's juke-joint shakin' (as opposed to big-city nightclub rockin') "Look What All You Got" aren't Guy's normal stock in trade, but he wears it all convincingly well. The acoustic *Blues Singer,* from 2003, is an even more back-to-basics affair, with many of the songs featuring just Guy, his guitar, and those devastating "Hard Time Killing Floor," "Lonesome Home Blues." —M.C./R.SK.

GZA/Genius

★★ Words From the Genius (Cold Chillin', 1991)

★★★★ Liquid Swords (MCA, 1995)

★★ Beneath the Surface (MCA, 1999)

★★★★ Legend of the Liquid Sword (MCA, 2002)

It's no wonder why Wu-Tang Clan believed they needed to follow up *Enter the Wu-Tang (36 Chambers)* with the double-disc album *Wu-Tang Forever.* In the four years that separated the collective's brilliant debut and its overlong sophomore effort, Wu-Tang's Ghostface Killah, Raekwon, and GZA each expanded the parameters of gangsta rap. Ghostface glammed it up with soul on *Ironman.* Raekwon anticipated the bling era with *Only Built 4 Cuban Linx*'s traditional gangster—not gangsta—tales. And on *Liquid Swords,* Genius (born Gary Grice—it's no wonder he changed his name) went goth, painting the Clan's street grime black.

Before all that, Genius made one very middling album for the Cold Chillin' label. Listening to *Words From the Genius* makes it clear that RZA deserves half the credit for Genius' post–*Enter the Wu-Tang* success. But GZA's syrupy flow—which 50 Cent might evoke if he were to master Rakim's tongue acrobatics—coats *Liquid Swords'* minimal beats with seamless mininarratives that stick to the brain like a tar baby. The Genius emerged from a group known for its creepy sonics and samples, but this album's opener, presumably lifted from a cheesy kung fu movie, chills like no other throwaway intro in hip-hop: Over bottom-scraping strings and a woman's tortured cries, a young boy recalls his father, a "decapitator" for the Shogun (possessed of a brain "infected by devils"), who narrowly escaped assassination by ninjas. On the track that follows, "Liquid Swords," Genius claims to "represent from midnight to high noon" over a trancelike combination of violin cuts, bass wash, and a ghostly beat.

If *Beneath the Surface* came from a deep, dark place, every grain of dirt was washed off it. Principal producer Mathematics brightens the corners, and the nonmusical interludes are either laughably overserious or unfunny jokes. Even the album's highlight and one hit, "Breaker Breaker," stretches itself thin straddling GZA's foreboding, minimalist aesthetic and radio's maximalist party vibe. These were dark times for the Wu-Tang empire, challenged as it was by Jay-Z, Eminem, et al.

With *Legend of the Liquid Sword,* Genius chose to reassert his myth rather than sit on his laurels. The intro features children, not unlike the one who opens *Liquid Swords,* telling the story of Wu-Tang's origins trading rhymes on the "floatin' forum" we call the Staten Island Ferry. GZA spits with renewed vigor over stomping beats and shooting synths, similar to Ghostface's, that evoke marching followers and horns announcing the entrance of royalty. On "Fame," he puns on the names of dozens of celebrities ("water dripped out of Farrah's Fawcett into a glass/she was super fly/Curtis Mayfield her ass/Chris Tucker to a show/Ted Turner to a 'ho"), demonstrating—without boasting—his dominion over all.   —N.C.

Sammy Hagar

★★½ Standing Hampton (Geffen, 1981)
★★ Three Lock Box (Geffen, 1982)
★★ VOA (Geffen, 1984)

After making his name as the voice behind Montrose, Sammy Hagar launched his own band in 1976 and spent most of the next decade churning out unmemorable assemblages of raucous, glandular hard rock. At this writing, all but three of his 10 solo albums are out of print, and the world is none the worse for it. Nor is Hagar (who has since replaced David Lee Roth in Van Halen), inasmuch as the remaining albums are the least embarrassing remnants of his solo career.

Although *Standing Hampton* has the veneer of hard rock—loud guitars, loud drums, loud everything else—the writing is surprisingly pop-friendly, and it includes two of Hagar's finest: "There's Only One Way to Rock" and the tuneful, touching "I'll Fall In Love Again." *Three Lock Box* pursues that approach into full-blown pop rock, and ends up sounding like bad-imitation Journey, but *VOA*—which includes the got-a-fast-car anthem "I Can't Drive 55"—returns him to the chest-thumping sound of yore, with predictably tedious results. —J.D.C.

Merle Haggard

★★★ Strangers (1965; Capitol, 2001)
★★★★ I'm a Lonesome Fugitive (1967; Capitol, 2001)
★★★★ Branded Man (1967; Capitol, 2001)
★★★★ Sing Me Back Home (1968; Capitol, 2001)
★★★ Mama Tried (Capitol, 1968)
★★★ Okie From Muskogee (Capitol, 1970)
★★★★ The Best of the Best of Merle Haggard (Capitol, 1972)
★★★★ Merle Haggard's Christmas Present (Something Old, Something New) (Capitol, 1973)
★★★★ A Working Man Can't Get Nowhere Today (Capitol, 1977)
★★★★ Serving 190 Proof (MCA, 1979)
★★★ The Way I Am (MCA, 1980)
★★★★ Rainbow Stew/Live at Anaheim Stadium (MCA, 1981)
★★★ Big City (1981; Epic/Legacy, 1999)
★★★ Merle Haggard's Greatest Hits (MCA, 1982)
★★★ Goin' Home for Christmas (1982; Epic, 2003)
★★★ Going Where the Lonely Go (Epic, 1982)
★★★ The Epic Collection (Recorded Live) (Epic, 1983)
★★★ It's All in the Game (Epic, 1984)
★★★★ His Epic Hits—The First 11 (To Be Continued . . .) (Epic, 1984)
★★★★ His Greatest and His Best (MCA, 1985)
★★★ His Best (MCA, 1985)
★★ Amber Waves of Grain (Epic, 1985)
★★★ Kern River (Epic, 1985)
★★★ Out Among the Stars (Epic, 1986)
★★ A Friend in California (Epic, 1986)
★★★ Chill Factor (Epic, 1987)
★★★★ 5:01 Blues (Epic, 1989)
★★★ More of the Best (Rhino, 1990)
★★★ 1994 (Curb, 1994)
★★★★★ The Lonesome Fugitive: The Merle Haggard Collection (Razor & Tie, 1995)
★★★ 1996 (Curb, 1996)
★★★★ If I Could Only Fly (Epitaph, 2000)
★★★ The Millennium Collection (MCA, 2000)
★★★★ Roots, Vol. 1 (Epitaph, 2001)
★★★★★ 40 #1 Hits (Capitol, 2004)

with Willie Nelson

★★★ Poncho and Lefty (1983; Sony, 2003)
★★★ Seashores of Old Mexico (Epic, 1987)

with George Jones

★★★ A Taste of Yesterday's Wine (Epic, 1982)

Merle Haggard is both a guardian of the country-music tradition and one of that tradition's most important artists. It's tempting but dangerous to dismiss most of the Hag's recent work as inferior to the great Capitol albums from the '60s or some of the interesting titles he released on MCA and Epic in the '70s and early '80s. He's not as consistently brilliant as he was in his younger days, but on sporadic occasions, he's as good as anyone out there. Both *5:01 Blues,* another entry addressing the drudgery of the working life, and *Kern River* have moments of grandeur, and Hag's world-weary delivery brings a cutting edge. Moreover, time has tempered a self-righteous streak in Hag's makeup. Considered as a whole, the body of work Haggard has created is stunning in its stylistic range, historical resonance, and flinty observations on the forces that bring people together and then tear them apart.

Haggard's affinity for the working class is bred in the bone. His family fled from the Oklahoma dust bowl in the early '30s and settled in Bakersfield, CA, where he was born in 1937. Haggard's life came unhinged at age nine when his father died. From that point through his teens, he became familiar with the insides of reform schools and jails, where he was often confined on charges of breaking and entering, petty theft, and other minor offenses. In 1957, he hit rock bottom when he was sentenced to a maximum of 15 years in San Quentin on a robbery charge. Upon his release in 1960, he headed for the Bakersfield club scene, where he found work as a sideman in various local bands. He began recording in 1963 for the small Tally label, and his second single, "Sing a Sad Song," written by Wynn Stewart, who was heading a band for which Haggard was playing, hit the Top 20 on the country chart. After a Top 10 single in 1965, "(My Friends Are Gonna Be) Strangers," Capitol bought out the Tally label, and with it Haggard's contract.

Every aspect of Haggard's earliest work indicates his debt to the plainspoken eloquence of Jimmie Rodgers and the plaintive but solid vocal style of Lefty Frizzell. He has also named Bing Crosby as an influence, and indeed, some of his bluesier phrasings recall Der Bingle's subtle touch. Also, the spirit of Bob Wills hovered over Haggard's eclectic approach. Fittingly, Haggard assembled a band, the Strangers, that could move easily between folk, country, and Western swing; its members included lead guitarists James Burton and Roy Nichols, rhythm guitarist Glen Campbell, Glen D. Hardin on piano, and the estimable Ralph Mooney on pedal steel.

After establishing himself with some standard drinking and cheating songs, Haggard dug into deeper material, beginning in 1966, when he recorded Liz and Casey Anderson's "I'm a Lonesome Fugitive." He also made public his own sordid past and began mining it, immediately penning one of his most poignant songs, "Sing Me Back Home," reportedly written for a friend on San Quentin's death row. These two songs brought an implicit political dimension to Haggard's work that would become more pronounced in the following years, when songs such as "Okie From Muskogee" (written, Haggard insists, as a goof) and "The Fightin' Side of Me" (a conscious blast aimed at Vietnam War protesters) were embraced first as anthems by Nixon-era right-wingers, and shortly thereafter as inspired satires by a younger generation at odds with the president's agenda. This seemed to amuse Haggard, who had taken note of the changing times during a visit to Sunset Strip in the late '60s, where he saw "hippies running down the street with Bibles under their arms and pencils up their asses."

However much of a hero he became to the right wing, Haggard rarely let politics intrude so blatantly on his music again. His best songs from the Capitol years were autobiographical gems on the order of "Mama Tried" and "Hungry Eyes," deeply felt and often tragic adult love songs ("The Emptiest Arms in the World," "Someday We'll Look Back," "It's Not Love [But It's Not Bad]"), and observations on the struggles of the working class. The sadly out-of-print *A Working Man Can't Get Nowhere Today* (1977) is the most sustained statement of policy from this period, and it's also as tough a set of country blues as was released in the '70s. (There is, however, no excusing the racist sentiments of "I'm a White Boy.") *The Best of the Best of Merle Haggard* represents the highlights of the Capitol years, but boiling down Haggard's work to "hits" ignores much of what is essential about the man. All of the above-mentioned albums are worth the price of admission, as are a tribute to Hank Williams and Lefty Frizzell, *The Way It Was in '51; High on a Hilltop;* and the laconic *30th Album,* which finds Hag dipping into blues, Western swing, and traditional country in spare settings.

The MCA and Epic years represent periods of retrenchment, consolidation, and, of late, renewal. Boozing and broken hearts are the dominant themes, save for a recent return to social commentary. If you sift through these selections, a few treasures emerge. By far his best from these years is *Serving 190 Proof,* cut in the midst of a midlife crisis. Hag's contradictory feelings about his life and career produce some mesmerizing, though unsettling, moments; enigmatic and moving, it's a first-rate effort. Apart from this album and the excellent, out-of-print *Ramblin' Fever,* the MCA years are aptly summarized on *The Millennium Collection. Rainbow Stew/Live* captures the star and his band at their peak.

As his music took on a darker shade of the blues,

Haggard remained introspective on his Epic albums. *Going Where the Lonely Go* (1983) is one of the best of this ilk, though its followup, *That's the Way Love Goes*, finds him at his contradictory best on "What Am I Gonna Do (With the Rest of My Life)" and the album's closer, "I Think I'll Stay." Three duet albums, *A Taste of Yesterday's Wine*, with George Jones, and *Poncho and Lefty* and *Seashores of Old Mexico*, both with Willie Nelson, team Haggard with vocalists who can challenge him; the results, though spotty, are always interesting.

There are dozens of Haggard compilations in circulation; the two-CD sets *Lonesome Fugitive* and *40 #1 Hits* are excellent overviews of his career and excellent places to start. Perhaps finding inspiration in the late career renaissance of Johnny Cash, Haggard has made two of his best albums in decades for the punk label Epitaph: the spare, unforced *If I Could Only Fly* and soulful *Roots*. Haggard's singing remains remarkable in his command of phrasing and inflection. He sounds like he knows a little bit more than he's letting on; his great art is in suggesting you better beware of what's coming and strap yourself in for the bumpy ride. With Hag, it's take it day to day, make your stand, and hope the sun comes up tomorrow. —D.M.

Bill Haley & His Comets

★★★½   Bill Haley and His Comets—From the Original Master Tapes (MCA, 1985)
★★   Greatest Hits (MCA, 1991)
★★★½   The Millennium Collection (MCA, 1999)
★   Golden Classics/Lucky 13 (Golden Lane, 2000)

Bill Haley laid much of the groundwork for a cultural and musical rebellion in the early 1950s, but by the end of the decade had been unceremoniously dumped by the genre and the audience he had helped create. Haley died in 1981 a lonely, alcoholic, and mostly forgotten figure, but the wonderful music he made with his band, the Comets, survives and will not be denied.

As early as 1951 he was forging a new style out of country & western, R&B, swing, and blues that eventually featured among its sound signatures a slapback stand-up bass that later became a defining feature of rockabilly music. Also, before Carl Perkins, before Chuck Berry, before Scotty Moore, there was Danny Cedrone, the Comets' extraordinary guitar player, whose intricate, advanced solo on Haley's breakthrough hit, "Rock Around the Clock" (almost the same solo he had crafted for Haley's 1952 single "Rock the Joint"), could be the first great rock & roll guitar break in history, nearly impossible to reproduce

by even the most gifted of players, and a clarion call to an entire generation of budding pickers in postwar America. When Cedrone died of a heart attack in 1954, Haley found another guitar stalwart in Frank Beecher, who came in with solid jazz credentials, having been influenced foremost by Charlie Christian, and boasting a résumé that included stints with jazz bands led by Buddy Greco and Benny Goodman. His approach was less flamboyant than Cedrone's but more melodic and, in his rhythmic sense, more inventive than his predecessor's. A band having even one instrumentalist of Cedrone's or Beecher's caliber would consider itself fortunate; having one replace the other is a luxury few have been allowed. The rest of the Comets were no slouches either, and in wild man Rudy Pompilli, in particular, the band laid claim to having one of the founding fathers of rock & roll saxophone. The final, crucial element that put Haley over was the A&R chief and producer who signed him to Decca, Milt Gabler, a visionary himself who understood that something new was in the air musically, knew how to get the most out of the rudimentary recording gear of the time, and used a good studio, the Pythian Temple in New York City, to maximum effect. Up to the point when he started working with Haley, Gabler had been one of the top jazz producers around, having worked with everyone from Louis Armstrong and Ella Fitzgerald to Louis Jordan, whose jump-blues recordings laid the structural foundation for rock & roll. (He had also founded the first independent label, Commodore, whose roster included some of the jazz world's most respected instrumentalists in addition to one of its preeminent vocalists, Billie Holiday.)

Born William John Clifton Haley on July 6, 1925, in the Detroit suburb of Highland Park, Bill Haley began his professional career as a country & western artist, known in his younger years as the "Rambling Yodeler." His recording career began in 1948, when he and his band, the Four Aces of Western Swing, cut three singles for the Cowboy label. From that time into early 1952, Haley recorded for five other labels; in 1949 the band's name was changed to the Saddlemen, then changed again in 1952, after signing with the Essex label, to Bill Haley and His Comets. Haley's first hint of things to come occurred in 1951, when he cut a cover version of Jackie Brenston's "Rocket 88" for the Holiday label. His single was unsuccessful, but Haley saw enough reaction to it to know there was a large, young, and hungry audience eager for something new. For Essex in 1952, Haley and the Comets cut an uptempo side called "Rock the Joint," which sold 75,000 copies; the next year Haley came up with an original song, "Crazy Man Crazy," that spoke the new lingo and made the charts to boot.

Come 1954, Haley changed labels again, this time signing with Gabler to record for Decca, with "(We're Gonna) Rock Around the Clock" being the group's initial release. A modest success, "Rock Around the Clock" set the stage for Haley's explosion into the mainstream with his next single, a sanitized cover version of Joe Turner's "Shake, Rattle and Roll," which made the Top 10 in the U.S. and in Britain, and sold a million copies. In 1955 "(We're Gonna) Rock Around the Clock" was rereleased and soared to #1; a rebel image also accrued to the rather square, avuncular band leader—who had long since discarded his western wear in favor of loud, plaid sport coats and a spit curl that looped down onto his forehead—as a result of the song being used as the theme for the film *The Blackboard Jungle,* a vivid depiction of urban juvenile delinquency in which rock & roll is inextricably linked to the aberrant behavior of adolescents. In 1955 and 1956 Haley cut 11 Top 40 singles and was the best-known rock & roll artist in the world—riots greeted his 1957 shows in Britain. But his run was doomed with the ascension of Elvis Presley in 1956, followed by a host of other young, handsome, musically dynamic artists who could match the fire of Haley's recordings with their own and had the advantage in being energetic, often rambunctious performers. The tepid "Skinny Minny" in 1958 marked Haley's final Top 40 appearance. He remained active on the concert circuit—especially overseas, where his popularity never waned—and continued recording, without success, for Decca into 1964. For the remainder of the decade, and periodically throughout the '70s, Haley always found a home musically, recording for a number of labels (one of them being Orfeón, based in Mexico, which eventually released three albums' worth of Haley's recordings); in 1971 he made a last stab at returning to the country market from whence he sprang with *Rock Around the Country,* recorded for the Sonet label in Nashville with some of the original Comets, supplemented by several of Music City's A-team session players, and produced by the respected blues scholar Sam Charters. Two other Charters-produced albums for Sonet were also released, the last coming in 1979. "Rock Around the Clock" was introduced to a new generation of fans via the TV show *Happy Days,* but there was no longer a market for Haley's music, and Haley himself struggled to keep the flame burning after Rudy Pompilli lost his bout with cancer in 1976. A three-year hiatus from the music business ensued, then a half-hearted, ill-conceived comeback fizzled, and Haley went into seclusion until his death.

Any of the MCA titles in Haley's catalogue are recommended best bets for most of the prime stuff—or at least all of the hits. Unfortunately, Haley's pre-

Decca recordings, particularly the Essex sides that would best show the progression of the artist's music from staid C&W to the big beat of prototypical rock & roll, tend to pop up only on short-lived budget labels. Caveat emptor when it comes to Golden Lane's *Golden Classics/Lucky 13,* as its selections are rerecordings of the classic Haley canon. Also, some online retail sites offer Haley's Orfeón recordings in a double-CD package titled *30 Exitos,* but these would be of interest only to completists, despite some spirited performances.   —D.M.

Daryl Hall & John Oates

★★	Whole Oates (Atlantic, 1972)
★★★	Abandoned Luncheonette (Atlantic, 1972)
★★½	Along the Red Ledge (Atlantic, 1972)
★★	War Babies (Atlantic, 1974)
★★	Daryl Hall & John Oates (Atlantic, 1975)
★★★	Bigger Than Both of Us (Atlantic, 1976)
★★★	Beauty on a Back Street (Atlantic, 1977)
★★	No Goodbyes (RCA, 1977)
★	Livetime (RCA, 1978)
★★	X-Static (Atlantic, 1979)
★★½	Voices (RCA, 1980)
★★★★	Private Eyes (RCA, 1981)
★★★½	H₂O (RCA, 1982)
★★★★	Rock & Soul Pt. 1: Greatest Hits (RCA, 1983)
★★★	Big Bam Boom (RCA, 1984)
★	Live at the Apollo (RCA, 1985)
★★	Ooh Yeah! (Arista, 1988)
★★½	Change of Season (RCA, 1990)
★★	The Atlantic Collection (RCA, 1980)
★★	Marigold Sky (RCA, 1997)
★★	Master Hits: Hall and Oates (Arista, 1999)
★★★★	The Very Best of Daryl Hall & John Oates (RCA, 2001)
★★★	VH1 Behind The Music: The Daryl Hall and John Oates Collection (BMG Heritage, 2002)
★★	Do It for Love (Imaye, 2003)
★★★★	The Ultimate Daryl Hall & John Oates (BMG Heritage, 2004)

Hall & Oates, the most commercially successful boy-boy duo of the rock & roll era, began in Philadelphia as a pair of soulful folkies, or perhaps folkful soulies. Daryl Hall was the tall, blond lead vocalist, John Oates the mustachioed Gabe Kaplan look-alike, and together they pursued the mellow R&B sound of the Stylistics or the Chi-Lites, although they were initially lumped together with '70s soft-rock duos such as Seals & Crofts, England Dan & John Ford Coley, and the Captain & Tennille. Their early hits were love-bead ballads such as "She's Gone" (one of their few actual harmony duets) and "Sara Smile" (better than Starship's "Sara," not as good as Dylan's, about even with Fleetwood Mac's). Hall & Oates became stars in 1977 with the excellent "Rich Girl," which set a new standard for AM radio profanity by (1) hitting #1 and (2) repeating the word *bitch* three times. Mystery surrounded them: Were Daryl and John lovers? Was "Rich Girl" secretly about Bryan Ferry? What did Oates do, exactly? But they couldn't follow it up, and soon descended back into the soft-rock minor leagues.

Voices was the album that turned Hall & Oates into a hit machine. It wasn't any more solid than *Along the Red Ledge* or *X-Static,* with an awful cover of "You've Lost That Lovin' Feeling." But it did have "Kiss on My List," a slick, bouncy #1 synth-pop smooch that taught Hall & Oates the way to make rock girls, disco girls, and new-wave girls scream together. Wasting no time, they banged out *Private Eyes* and *H₂O,* easily their most consistently hooky albums, and scored hit after hit: "Did It in a Minute," "You Make My Dreams," "Private Eyes," "I Can't Go for That (No Can Do)," and "Head Above Water," the catchiest song on *Private Eyes* although it was never a single. They still had a weakness for boring ballads ("One on One"), but redeemed themselves with sick thrills such as "Maneater," which warned about "a she-cat tamed by the purr of a Jag-u-ar." *Big Bam Boom* found the boys slipping a bit, with echoey production to hide the slackened songcraft, but "Out of Touch" did provide a serial-monogamy credo for the '80s: "Smoking guns, hot to the touch/We'd cool down if we didn't use them so much."

Hall & Oates went on hiatus for a few years, returning with *Ooh Yeah!* in the summer of 1988. But they quickly found that relying on the old man's money was a lot easier than relying on the young girls' money, because their entire fan base had moved on to Bobby Brown and Keith Sweat. "Everything Your Heart Desires" was their last big hit; after that, they settled for a low-key presence, occasionally recording minor hits such as the pleasant "Promise Ain't Enough." Oates' solo career peaked with the title of his 2002 album, *Funk Sui;* Hall's peaked with his 1993 hit "I'm in a Philly Mood," although he'd been in a Philly mood for the entirety of his career, and therefore perhaps should have called the song "I've Got a Philly Obsessive-Compulsive Disorder." By now, we all know that Daryl and John were not actually lovers; however, that leaves the question of what Oates did as mysterious as ever. —R.S.

Hammer

★★★½	Let's Get It Started (Alliance, 1988)
★★★	Please Hammer, Don't Hurt 'Em (Capitol, 1990)
★★	Too Legit to Quit (Capitol, 1991)
★★	The Funky Headhunter (Giant, 1994)
★★	Inside Out (Giant, 1995)
★★★½	Greatest Hits (Capitol, 1996)

The ultimate *Behind the Music* subject: Because his success owes more to hard work and showmanship than to originality, Hammer (who called himself MC Hammer on his first two albums) was frequently reviled as a sellout and a fake in the hip-hop community. The fact is, he didn't do anything musically that Puff Daddy hasn't: His music beds not only borrow from obvious sources—Queen's "Another One Bites the Dust" for "Let's Get Started," Rick James' "Superfreak" for "U Can't Touch This," James Brown's "Superbad" for "Here Comes the Hammer"—but often act as straight-up covers, like *Please Hammer*'s embarrassing remake of the Chi-Lites' "Have You Seen Her." Like Puffy, Hammer understands the value of a strong beat (particularly on *Let's Get It Started*) and knows how to wring every ounce of energy from a dance groove. The relentless criticism took its toll, as *Too Legit to Quit* finds the rapper avoiding sample-based grooves and hedging his bets by moving toward a more explicit R&B sound, an approach that works passably on "This Is the Way We Roll" and the album's title tune, but fizzles elsewhere. On the gangsta'd-out *Funky Headhunter,* Hammer tries to play catch-up with Snoop and Dre, to bad effect; *Inside Out* finds him totally at sea. *Greatest Hits* shows that he might have been better off persevering with his original shameless good-timey sound. —J.D.C./N.B.

Butch Hancock

★★★	West Texas Waltzes & Dust-Blown Tractor Tunes (1978; Rainlight, 2000)
★★★	The Wind's Dominion (1979; Rainlight, 2000)
★★★	Diamond Hill (1980; Rainlight, 2000)
★★★★	Firewater . . . Seeks Its Own Level (1981; Rainlight, 2000)
★★★	Own & Own (Sugar Hill, 1991)
★★★	Own the Way Over Here (1993; Rainlight, 2003)
★★★★	Eats Away the Night (Sugar Hill, 1994)
★★★	You Coulda Walked Around the World (Rainlight, 2000)

Butch Hancock and Marce LaCouture

★★	Yella Rose (1985; Rainlight, 2000)

Butch Hancock and Jimmie Dale Gilmore

★★★★	Two Roads (Caroline, 1992)

In Texas, where the song is king, Butch Hancock is both poet and jester, bringing a wry literary sensibility rooted in traditional folk and country. With Joe

Ely and Jimmie Dale Gilmore, he's one of the founding members of the Flatlanders—alternative-country godfathers who bonded in the late '60s over wide-ranging interests in Eastern philosophy, Beat literature, and *Mad* magazine as much as the music of Bob Dylan, Hank Williams, and the Beatles. They recorded one highly influential album, later issued as *More a Legend Than a Band,* before scattering for solo careers.

Hancock, who grew up on a farm outside Lubbock, was the Flatlanders' primary songwriter, and his solo debut, *West Texas Waltzes & Dust-Blown Tractor Tunes,* is focused more on songs than sonics. His craggy singing, acoustic guitar strumming, harmonica tooting, and foot stomping are raw as a West Texas wind, and the songs update the Americana tradition of Harry Smith's *Anthology of American Folk Music,* Woody Guthrie, early Dylan, and Hank Williams Sr.

The Wind's Dominion and *Diamond Hill* flesh out but don't overpower the songs with band arrangements orchestrated by pedal-steel virtuoso Lloyd Maines. *Firewater . . . Seeks Its Own Level* is even better, with Hancock fronting a small combo in a club setting that suits his offhanded gifts. *Own & Own, Own the Way Over Here,* and *Eats Away the Night* rely on older songs, some of which (the political commentary "Talkin' About That Panama Canal") sound dated. But the sharper production values on *Eats Away* lead to definitive versions of Hancock classics such as "Boxcars" and "If You Were a Bluebird."

You Coulda Walked Around the World brings Hancock full circle, back to the sparse country-folk of his debut. The back-cover image depicts Hancock pondering life alongside sculptures of Socrates and Stan Laurel, and it's a fitting snapshot of his music. Between those two sensibilities, the songwriter stakes his claim as a true Texas original.   —G.K.

Herbie Hancock

★★★★½   Takin' Off (1962; Blue Note,1996)
★★★   Inventions and Dimensions (1963; Blue Note,1990)
★★★★   My Point of View (1963; Blue Note,1999)
★★★★   Empyrean Isles (1964; Blue Note,1999)
★★★★½   Maiden Voyage (1965; Blue Note,1999)
★★★★   Blow-Up (soundtrack) (1966; TCM/Rhino, 1996)
★★★½   Speak Like a Child (1968; Blue Note,1990)
★★★½   The Prisoner (1969; Blue 2000)
★★★½   Fat Albert Rotunda (1969; Warner Bros., 2001)
★★★★   Mwandishi (1971; Warner Bros., 2001)
★★★★½   Crossings (1972; Warner Bros., 2001)
★★★★★   Sextant (1973; Columbia/Legacy, 1998)

★★★½   Headhunters (1974; Columbia/Legacy, 1997)
★★★   Thrust (1974; Columbia/Legacy, 1998)
★★★   Death Wish (soundtrack) (1974; One Way, 2000)
★★★½   Flood (1975; Sony Japan, 1997)
★★★★   Man-Child (1975; Columbia/Legacy, 1988)
★★★   Secrets (1976; Columbia/Legacy, 1988)
★★★★   V.S.O.P. (Columbia, 1977)
★★★½   V.S.O.P.—The Quintet (1977; Columbia/Legacy, 1988)
★★½   Feets, Don't Fail Me Now (Columbia, 1979)
★★   Monster (Columbia, 1980)
★★½   Mr. Hands (1980; Columbia, 1998)
★★★   Magic Windows (1981; Columbia, 1997)
★★★½   Quartet (1981; Columbia/Legacy, 1985)
★½   Lite Me Up (Columbia, 1982)
★★★★   Future Shock (1984; Columbia/Legacy, 2000)
★★★★½   Sound System (1984; Columbia/Legacy, 2000)
★★★½   Round Midnight (soundtrack) (Columbia, 1986)
★★★★   Perfect Machine (Columbia, 1988)
★★★   The Best of Herbie Hancock (Columbia/Legacy, 1988)
★★★★★   Best of Herbie Hancock: The Blue Note Years (Blue Note, 1988)
★★★½   A Jazz Collection (Columbia, 1991)
★★★★   The Herbie Hancock Trio (1991; Sony Japan, 1996)
★★★½   The Herbie Hancock Quartet Live (Jazz Door, 1994)
★★★½   A Tribute to Miles Davis (Qwest, 1994)
★★★   Trio Live in New York (Jazz Door, 1994)
★★★★   The Complete Warner Bros. Recordings (Warner Archives, 1994)
★★★★   Dis Is da Drum (Mercury, 1995)
★★★★½   The New Standard (Verve, 1996)
★★★★★   1+1 (Verve, 1997)
★★★★   The Complete Blue Note Sixties Sessions (Blue Note, 1998)
★★★   This Is Jazz #35 (Columbia/Legacy, 1998)
★★★★   The Best of Herbie Hancock—The Hits! (Columbia/Legacy, 2000)
★★★★½   Ken Burns Jazz (Columbia/Legacy, 2000)
★★★★   Future 2 Future (Transparent, 2001)
★★★★   The Herbie Hancock Box (Columbia/Legacy, 2002)

Herbie Hancock/Foday Musa Suso
★★★★   Village Life (Columbia, 1985)
★★★½   Jazz Africa (1987; Verve, 1990)

Herbie Hancock/Chick Corea
★★★½   An Evening With Herbie Hancock and Chick Corea In Concert (1978; Columbia/Legacy, 1998)
★★★★   Corea/Hancock (1978; Polydor, 1992)

Jazz was once popular music, but as far as the jazz community of today is concerned, the less said about that, the better. For many fans and critics, jazz that is dissonant, demanding, and rhythmically complex is to be cheered, while jazz that is funky and direct is to be scorned. As such, the jazz community remains baffled and bemused by Herbie Hancock, a gifted composer and keyboardist who successfully plays both sides of the street.

Most jazz fans think of him as having started as the pianist in Miles Davis' classic mid- to late-'60s quintet, where his playing bridged the gap between the cool intellectuality of Bill Evans and the edgy abstractions of McCoy Tyner. But actually, Hancock's first big splash was in the pop end of jazz, having composed the Mongo Santamaria hit "Watermelon Man" (which went to #10 in 1963). His own take on the tune, recorded that same year and included on *Takin' Off*, is more hard bop than Latin pop, and uses its supple groove to fuel the improvisatory musings of Freddie Hubbard and Dexter Gordon. Hancock radically reinvented the tune 11 years later with his first dip into electro-funk, *Headhunters*. But there "Watermelon Man" played second fiddle to "Chameleon," the only single to put him within spitting distance of *Billboard*'s Top 40 (it peaked at 42).

But let's get back to the '60s. Where his debut found him playing the sort of funky jazz Horace Silver was known for (though even Silver rarely got so soulful), *My Point of View* finds Hancock moving toward a more abstracted, Davis-oriented sound—although "Blind Man, Blind Man," featuring guitarist Grant Green, does seem to proceed from that "Watermelon Man" groove. His subsequent sessions for Blue Note reflect a steady move away from pop-jazz. That doesn't mean they aren't tuneful; the dreamy title track from *Maiden Voyage*, for instance, quickly became a jazz standard. But *Inventions and Dimensions* (which was briefly available under the title *Succotash*) proffers loosely structured experiments with Latin rhythms; *Empyrean Isles* and *Maiden Voyage* are Davis-influenced small-group sessions with Freddie Hubbard on trumpet; *Speak Like a Child* and *The Prisoner* use slightly larger ensembles to extend the coloristic possibilities of his music. The casually curious may want to settle for Blue Note's *The Best of Herbie Hancock*, which highlights the best of these recordings, while completists should seek *The Complete Blue Note Sixties Sessions*, which includes everything from Hancock's solo albums as well as some notable sessions he cut as a sideman.

Fat Albert Rotunda was Hancock's first album after leaving Blue Note in 1969, but it's more of an aside than an indication of where he was headed. Consisting of material he wrote and recorded for Bill Cosby's *Fat Albert* cartoon series, its funky, R&B-oriented material is actually more of a piece with Hancock's *Blow-Up* score (best known for "Bring Down the Birds," which Deee-Lite sampled for "Groove Is in the Heart") than with his regular jazz output. "Li'l Brother," in fact, seems a continuation of an earlier attempt at instrumental R&B called "Don't Go There" (included on the *Complete Blue Note* set).

Mwandishi, Hancock's first proper album for Warner Bros., was a radical move away from the sound of his Blue Note recordings, recalling the rock-influenced sound of Davis' *Bitches Brew* sessions but augmenting it with the Gil Evans–ish horn voicings heard on *The Prisoner*. *Mwandishi* is dark and dreamy, with its rolling rhythms and swirling electronics, while the sonic tapestry of *Crossings* conveys an almost otherworldly sense of atmosphere, particularly on the haunting, synth-colored "Quasar." But *Sextant* is the standout, thanks to its richly detailed sound and intricate interplay.

Hancock changed direction again with *Headhunters*, dumping two horn players and devoting more energy to synths than to electric piano. But it was the pop credibility he earned through the success of "Chameleon" that truly altered the course of his career. The music on *Headhunters* isn't R&B per se, but Hancock was getting there, and his output became funkier and funkier. *Thrust* plays down the more abstract elements that rounded out *Headhunters*, emphasizing the music's pulse, while *Man-Child* added R&B guitarists to the mix, bringing depth to the groove without compromising the improvised content. (These are the albums emphasized in Columbia's *The Best of Herbie Hancock*.)

Yet despite his pop success (*Headhunters*, *Thrust*, and *Man-Child* all cracked the Top 40 of the *Billboard* album chart), Hancock hadn't given up on jazz. The import-only live album *Flood* shows how easily Hancock's mid-'70s band could move from straight jazz to groove-heavy funk without compromising its sound or identity. *Secrets* went for a similar balance in the studio, and even included an imaginative update of "Cantaloupe Island." *V.S.O.P.*, a 1976 concert recording, presents three sides of Hancock—his then-current funk band, the reunited *Mwandishi* group, and an acoustic quintet featuring his old Davis bandmates Wayne Shorter, Ron Carter, and Tony Williams (Hubbard did the honors on trumpet). Of the three, it was the acoustic group that thrilled jazz fans most, and so they were reconvened for an album of their own: *V.S.O.P.—The Quintet*. Although it has much the same sound as the Davis quintet's classic recordings, it lacks the fire and daring of the Davis albums. (Far more persuasive is the import-only *Herbie Hancock Trio,* which finds Hancock, Carter, and Williams pushing limits with abandon.)

Neoconservatism has always sold well with jazz fans, however, and so Hancock regularly released Davis-schooled live albums with all-acoustic bands. *Quartet* features a young and brash Wynton Marsalis; *A Tribute to Miles Davis* uses shameless Davis-clone Wallace Roney. Fortunately, not all of Hancock's "traditional" recordings mine that vein or are as predictable. *1+1,* an album of duets with Shorter, is quiet, touching, and wonderfully lyrical—a staggering performance by both. *The New Standard,* meanwhile, inverts the pop formula by offering straight-ahead jazz treatments of such tunes as Peter Gabriel's "Mercy Street" and Nirvana's "All Apologies."

By that point in the '90s, it seemed as if Hancock had put his funk days behind him. Although his '70s electronic albums after *Man-Child—Secrets; Feets, Don't Fail Me Now; Monster; Lite Me Up;* and *Magic Windows*—aspired to mainstream R&B, Hancock lacked both the aesthetic insight and commercial touch of Quincy Jones. In a word, the albums stank. Mercifully, hip-hop and high technology saved the day.

With *Future Shock,* Hancock uses drum machines, digital synths, and DJ Grandmixer D.ST to conjure the sound of the urban jungle, an approach that turned "Rockit" into a club hit (and earned Hancock airtime on MTV). *Sound System* adds a world-beat flavor to the mix, thanks to Hancock's use of Gambian griot Foday Musa Suso (with whom he later recorded the wonderfully exotic *Village Life* and a somewhat more predictable live album, *Jazz Africa*), while *Perfect Machine* recruits P-Funk bassist Bootsy Collins and Ohio Player LeRoy "Sugarfoot" Bonner. The ambitious *Dis Is da Drum* found Hancock once again flirting with R&B, but the music was too cerebral to successfully engage the booty. Maybe that's why *Future 2 Future,* despite its use of vocals and flirtation with drum and bass rhythms, chose to offload its overt "pop" content in separately sold remixes; overall, the album has more in common with *Sextant* than *Headhunters.*

In addition to his solo career, Hancock has also been doing soundtrack work since 1966, when he scored Michelangelo Antonioni's *Blow-Up.* Although his contributions can be heard in films ranging from *Death Wish* to *House Party 2,* he's probably best known for the elegiac *Round Midnight,* a score as jazz-soaked and moody as the film itself.   —J.D.C.

Handsome Boy Modeling School
see PRINCE PAUL

Hanson

★★★★	Middle of Nowhere (Mercury, 1997)
★★★	Snowed In (Mercury, 1997)
★★½	3 Car Garage: The Indie Recordings '95–'96 (Mercury, 1998)
★★	Live From Albertane: Hanson Tour (Mercury, 1998)
★★★	This Time Around (Island, 2000)
★★★	Underneath (3CG, 2004)

The Hanson brothers came along in the summer of 1997 with "MMMBop," a song bursting with guitars and harmonies and shockingly unstupid lyrics about the meaning of life. Isaac (16, guitar, the Shy One), Taylor (14, keyboards, the Hot One), and Zac (11, drums, the Bonaduce) only took an mmmbop to melt every barrette in America, as the home-schooled Tulsa boys roller-boogied through a video that looked like a *Dynamite* cover shoot circa 1974, a kiddie utopia of after-school California sunshine. They've never topped the super-sugar-crisp rush of "MMMBop," but songs like that only roll around once in any band's career—the Jackson Five never topped "I Want You Back," either. And Hanson has already made more good records than the Bay City Rollers, Bo Donaldson and the Heywoods, Tony DeFranco and the DeFranco Family, and Kristy and Jimmy McNichol *combined!*

With a little help from its producers, the Dust Brothers, Hanson plays its own instruments and writes its own songs on *Middle of Nowhere,* as Liz Phair look-alike Taylor hits high notes that could make a grown woman blush. "Where's the Love" made teen girls scream "Right here, baby!" at the Taylor posters on their walls, while "Weird" and "Yearbook" were pure adolescent ache. But the Hanson boys were too young to fall in love, and we were all too young to know. One thing Hanson was definitely too young to understand was quality control, because it flooded the market with a Christmas album ("Everybody Knows the Claus"!), a live album ("Money [That's What I Want]"!), and early demos (boys, boys—enough already). By *Underneath,* they already sounded old-fashioned; in the wake of "MMMBop," the radio had clogged up with teen-pop disco, while Hanson was evolving into a bang-up rock & roll band. But "MMM-Bop" still sums up the punch of a perfect pop song—it comes out of nowhere to rock your socks off, and then in an mmmbop, it's gone.   —R.S.

Happy Mondays

★★★½	Pills 'n' Thrills and Bellyaches (Elektra, 1990)
★★	Live (Elektra, 1991)
★★	Yes, Please (Elektra, 1992)
★★★	Double Easy: The U.S. Singles (Elektra, 1993)

Black Grape

★★★★ It's Great When You're Straight . . . Yeah
(MCA, 1995)

Anyone who heard the single "24-Hour Party People" when it came out in 1987 would have been hard-pressed to predict the eventual success and cultural import of its authors, the Happy Mondays. A mess of nonsensical lyrics ("24-hour party people, plastic face can't smile the white's out") that were slurred by the band's buffoonish singer, Shaun Ryder, over a stupidly repetitive synth melody, the song didn't sound like the work of a band that would kick-start the biggest English rock scene into the '90s. And yet kickstart a scene they did. With their heady combination of acid house, Northern soul, and '60s psychedelia, they provided the soundtrack for British kids' ecstasy-fueled nights out, and for a time turned Manchester into "Madchester," the epicenter of British music.

Pills 'n' Thrills and Bellyaches is the best of the band's oeuvre, the sound of Madchester at its peak. (The Mondays' first two studio releases, *Squirrel and G-Man Twenty Four Hour Party People Plastic Face Carnt Smile [White Out]* and *Bummed*, are no longer in print in the States.) The band's extended psychedelic jams transport rather than bore, and Ryder, who has finally learned to sing, displays a unique twisted genius on such lyrical gems as "I'm here to harass you/I want your pills and grass, you/You don't look first class, you/Let me look up your ass, you," from "Holiday," the band's ode to customs officials. The record also contains the Mondays' best song ever, the exuberantly trippy "Step On." A rather muffled version of that song, along with much of *Pills 'n' Thrills*, gets reprised on *Live*, a stopgap album that was recorded at Leeds' United Football Ground—quite possibly from beneath the bleachers, if its muddied tone is any indication.

For the Mondays' next—and last—studio release, *Yes, Please*, the group repaired to Barbados, purportedly so the drug-addled members could get clean. But although the island was free of heroin, Ryder's primary addiction, it happened to be rich in crack, and *Yes, Please* sounds as if the Mondays were high on the stuff the entire time they were recording. The music drags, Ryder's lyrics make no sense, and choruses are repeated at least 10 times per song. The old Madchester magic does return on the songs "Sunshine & Love" and "Angel," but since they appear on *Double Easy*, a 16-track best-of, *Yes, Please* is entirely passable.

When the Mondays disintegrated in 1993, it seemed impossible that Ryder could create anything quite so brilliant again. Yet two years later, he returned with Black Grape, a group that not only was as good as the Mondays but was actually better. The ironically titled *It's Great When You're Straight . . . Yeah* is a nonstop romp that takes the Mondays' dance sensibility and focuses it with straight-ahead Brit-pop melodies, funk, and rap, the latter courtesy of Ryder's new partner in rhyme, the rapper Kermit. Ryder's lyrics approach whole new heights of genius here; soaking his lines in pop culture and (sac)religious references, he comes up with such doozies as "Jesus was a black man/No, Jesus was Batman/No, no, no, no, that was Bruce Wayne," from "Kelly's Heroes." Sadly, the momentum could not be maintained: After releasing a subpar followup, *Stupid, Stupid, Stupid* (now out of print), Black Grape split up.   —N.P.

Ben Harper

★★★ Welcome to the Cruel World (Virgin, 1994)
★★ Fight for Your Mind (Virgin, 1995)
★★ The Will to Live (Virgin, 1997)
★★★½ Diamonds on the Inside (Virgin, 2003)

Ben Harper and the Innocent Criminals

★★★ Burn to Shine (Virgin, 1999)
★★★ Live From Mars (Virgin, 2001)

This California native's four principal weapons are a smooth, airy voice; enviable facility on an unusual instrument (the Weissenborn lap steel guitar); a deep love for American roots music; and a righteous moral compass. By combining these features, he's come up with a socially and spiritually conscious soul/folk hybrid that's often a little lightweight, but never less than pleasant.

Predominantly acoustic, *Welcome to the Cruel World* is the closest Harper's come to making a straight folk record. Though the songs deal with big issues, most notably racism, Harper's too loose to get angry, and the prevailing vibe is one of quiet dignity, broken only by the jaunty, zydeco-infused "Mama's Got a Girlfriend Now." *Fight for Your Mind* dabbles with funk grooves, but except for the extended feedback freakout on "God Fearing Man," it's pretty mellow stuff. Titles like "Oppression," "People Lead," and "Power of the Gospel" show where Harper's head is at; they also display a tiresome penchant for soapbox sloganeering.

With its deft production touches—a backward track here, a cool vocal filter there—*The Will to Live* is a more engaging listen, but by now Harper's laid-back approach is becoming a liability. Even when the band's raging behind him, his voice barely rises above a hushed coo. Finally, on *Burn to Shine*, Harper allows himself to cut loose as a singer, fulfilling the promise he'd always shown. It doesn't hurt that the songs are among his best, from the Curtis Mayfield stylings of "The Woman in You" to the New Orleans brass-band whimsy of "Suzie Blue" and the raunchy, Stones-like title track. Harper's winning streak continued with *Diamonds on the Inside,* which found him further refining and expanding his sound; highlights include the self-explanatory "Bring the Funk" and the a cappella gem "Picture of Jesus," guest-starring Ladysmith Black Mambazo. The guy still preaches too much, but his grooves are so tight that it seems silly to complain.

Two lengthy in-concert discs may be more Ben Harper than a non-fan needs. Still, *Live from Mars* is valuable for demonstrating just how incendiary a performer Harper can be. The covers of Marvin Gaye's "Sexual Healing" and Led Zep's "Whole Lotta Love" are great fun, too.   —M.R.

Slim Harpo

★★★½   Raining in My Heart (1961; Hip-O, 1998)
★★★★½   The Best of Slim Harpo (Hip-O, 1997)
★★★★½   The Excello Singles Anthology (Hip-O, 2003)

James Isaac Moore, professionally known as Slim Harpo, was so naturally gifted a musician that he was credible whether he was singing gutbucket urban blues, R&B, or country blues. Even a partial list of artists and bands that have covered Harpo's songs indicates the broad sweep of his influence, starting with the Rolling Stones (who even paraphrased Harpo's song "Got Love if You Want It" for the title of their first live album, *Got Live if You Want It*) and continuing on through the Kinks, Van Morrison and Them, Dave Edmunds (in Love Sculpture), the Jeff Beck–era Yardbirds, Alex Chilton, and the Moody Blues, who took their band name from a Harpo track. His oft-covered song "I'm a King Bee" has become part of the lingua franca of blues rock; "Rainin' in My Heart" has found favor with blues and country singers through the years.

Harpo's first single, 1957's "I'm a King Bee," features lascivious double-entendre lyrics ("I'm young and able/to buzz all night long"); a laconic vocal that would become Harpo's signature; a solid, stomping rhythm courtesy of drummer Clarence "Jockey" Etienne; some tasty, lowdown harmonica work by Harpo; and Clinton "Fats" Perrodin's ostinato top-string bass lick simulating a bee's buzzing sound. The flip side, "I've Got Love if You Want It," is a variation on the Bo Diddley rhythm, right down to the Jerome Green–style maracas supplying some extra rhumba juice to the upbeat affair. Harpo's second single, "Wonderin' and Worryin' " b/w "Strange Love," was the first evidence on record of Jimmy Reed's influence on Harpo's style, both in the heavy groove and in the propulsive harmonica work.

These worthy efforts were finding little success on the sales front (although in Britain an entire generation of young rockers was eating up Harpo's work). That changed in 1961, when Harpo and Miller came up with "Rainin' in My Heart," a measured shuffle with a decidedly country feel, a haunting, minor-key harmonica intro and fills, a midsong narration not uncommon to country singles of the day, and a weary vocal that conjures a portrait of a man entrenched in deep regret over his mistreatment of the good woman who left him.

Rather than capitalizing on their good fortune with more recordings, though, Harpo and his producer, J. D. Miller, began feuding over his contract; at one point Harpo bolted for the Imperial label in New Orleans, but the sessions went unissued after Miller threatened a lawsuit. Harpo then returned to Miller's studio in Crowley, but three years and a moment had passed by the time Excello issued a feisty instrumental, "Buzzin'," which featured Harpo's gutsy, Little Walter–style harmonica lines bouncing off Al Foreman's angular single- and multistring guitar solos redolent with quotes from jazz, blues, and pop styles in rapid succession. Despite the flop of "Buzzin'," Harpo persisted, and in 1965 he and Miller came up with another chart winner. "Scratch My Back" is about as perfect an example of swamp music as anyone has ever put on record, its identifying features being a murky ambience, an irresistible, slinky, mid-tempo groove, some engaging chicken-pickin' guitar work by either James Johnson or Rudolph Richard, some odd woodblock licks that surface in the song's last few bars, and a low-key, spoken vocal by Harpo so benign in its delivery you could almost overlook its salacious message—as a vocalist, Slim Harpo was nothing if not subversive, really one of a kind in that department. One of the final sessions Harpo cut with Miller produced one of their best efforts, the relentless "Shake Your Hips," a John Lee Hooker–style boogie number that cooked mightily but didn't do much for Harpo's commercial fortunes (it resurfaced in 1972 as "Hipshaker" on the Stones' *Exile on Main Street* album). In 1970 Harpo was contracted to tour Europe and had plans to record in London with some of the British musicians who numbered him among their influences. Neither event happened. A couple of weeks after an early January recording session in Baton Rouge, the 46-year-old Harpo, still a young man in seemingly good health, suffered a massive heart attack and died on January 31.

Hip-O's *The Best of Slim Harpo* provides the best overview extant of the artist's enduring legacy. All of the above-mentioned recordings are included on this 16-song overview, along with other interesting, nonhit studio sides, including a slow-boiling talking blues, "Blues Hangover," and a slow, R&B-flavored instrumental, "Snoopin' Around," which features saxophonist Willie "Tomcat" Parker. Almost half of the songs on *The Best of* can be found on the reissue of Harpo's first Excello album, *Slim Harpo Sings Rainin' in My Heart,* which also includes other interesting fare such as "Moody Blues" and quintessential swamp rock prototypes in "Buzz Me Babe" and "Don't Start Crying Now." An excellent package is further augmented by three bonus tracks, two of which—"My Little Queen Bee (Got a Brand New King)" and "Late Last Night"—are unavailable on *The Best of. The Excello Singles Anthology* includes much of the above and is another fine overview. There's a lot more Slim Harpo material where this came from, but these three albums serve his memory well. —D.M.

Corey Harris

★★★	Between Midnight and Day (Alligator, 1995)
★★★★	Fish Ain't Bitin' (Alligator, 1997)
★★★★½	Greens From the Garden (Alligator, 1999)
★★★★	Downhome Sophisticate (Rounder, 2002)
★★★	Mississippi to Mali (Rounder, 2003)

Corey Harris and Henry Butler
★★★   Vu-Du Menz (Alligator, 2000)

Roughly around the time that OutKast and Goodie Mob rose from the South to represent country manners, several fleet-fingered musicologists were similarly rehabilitating the reputation of acoustic blues. The tradition of Son House and Charley Patton had long been maligned as shabby and backward by young black bluesmen who favored the flashy urbanity of the music's Chicago descendants. Along with Keb' Mo' and Alvin Youngblood Hart, however, Corey Harris was among the young African-Americans who steeped themselves in the styles and ethos of Delta music in the mid-'90s. He soon became the most strikingly original blues writer and performer since Robert Cray.

Of these three, Harris internalized the Delta ethos most startlingly. On *Between Midnight and Day,* Harris performs solo, brawnily adapting blues structures to his own idiosyncratic sense of rhythm—no mean feat for an anthropology major from Denver. On *Fish Ain't Bitin',* a three-piece brass section (two trombones and a tuba) and simple percussion occasionally augment Harris' National steel for an off-kilter New Orleans feel. Meanwhile, his own compositions, which name-check Mumia Abu-Jamal and insist on the persistence of lynching, put the time-honored plaints of poverty and racism in contemporary perspective.

Harris was the most stylistically omnivorous of his Delta-influenced fellows, which meant that he'd never settle into one style forever. He goes electric on *Greens From the Garden,* which roams from reggae to Cajun even as it consolidates Harris' ability to integrate blues licks and lyrics alike into a modern idiom. ("Seen the devil last night, walk like a natural man," he observes on "Basehead," "Had a pipe in his mouth, a rock in his hand.") The roots retrenchment of *Vu-Du Menz,* a duet album with pianist Henry Butler, apparently exorcised his old-timey jones, since Harris was further out than ever when he returned to his electric guitar. *Downhome Sophisticate* rambles from Neville Brothers cover to roadhouse boogie to Central African soukous, too busy accumulating styles to attempt anything as neat as fusion. Murky, sardonic, playful, and restless, this may just be a bluesman's answer to *Stankonia.* —K.H.

Emmylou Harris

★★★	Pieces of the Sky (1975; Rhino, 2004)
★★★	Elite Hotel (1975; Rhino, 2004)
★★★★	Luxury Liner (1977; Rhino, 2004)
★★★½	Quarter Moon in a Ten Cent Town (1978; Rhino, 2004)
★★★½	Profile: The Best of Emmylou Harris (Warner Bros., 1978)
★★★½	Blue Kentucky Girl (1979; Rhino, 2004)
★★★★	Roses in the Snow (1980; Rhino, 2002)
★★	Evangeline (Warner Bros., 1981)
★★½	Cimarron (1981; Eminent, 2000)
★★★	Last Date (1982; Eminent, 2000)
★★★½	White Shoes (Warner Bros., 1983)
★★★½	Profile II: The Best of Emmylou Harris (Warner Bros., 1984)
★★★	The Ballad of Sally Rose (Warner Bros., 1985)
★★★	Thirteen (Warner Bros., 1986)
★★★½	Angel Band (Warner Bros., 1987)
★★★½	Trio (Warner Bros., 1987)
★★★	Bluebird (Reprise, 1988)
★★★★	Duets (Reprise, 1990)
★★	Brand New Dance (Reprise, 1990)
★★★★	At the Ryman (Reprise, 1992)
★★★★	Cowgirl's Prayer (Elektra/Asylum, 1993)
★★★½	Songs of the West (Warner Western, 1994)
★★★★★	Wrecking Ball (Elektra, 1995)
★★★★	Portraits (Reprise Archives, 1996)
★★★½	Spyboy (Eminent, 1998)
★★½	The Christmas Album: Light of the Stable (Warner Bros., 1999)
★★★★	Red Dirt Girl (Elektra, 2000)
★★★★	Anthology: The Warner/Reprise Years (Rhino, 2001)
★★★★	Stumble Into Grace (Nonesuch, 2003)

Emmylou Harris is the patron saint of what's come to be known as alternative country. Her sad soprano harmonies on Gram Parsons' two early-'70s solo albums (*GP* and *Grievous Angel*) introduced a young interpretive singer who would help to alter the look and sound of Nashville. Stepping out on her own, Harris forged a soft country-rock style that appeals to fans of both genres. Her enduring influence on music is wide ranging, spanning from New Traditionalist country singers like Dwight Yoakam to such postpunk country rockers as Ryan Adams and Kasey Chambers. Harris' immaculate tone and gentle phrasing may not sit well with purists (of rock or country), but it's hard to argue with her creative spirit, her taste in material—or her execution.

Harris' albums are inconsistent up until *Luxury Liner,* on which her signature crystalline voice really takes shape. Her interpretations of the Louvin Brothers ("When I Stop Dreaming"), Townes Van Zandt ("Poncho and Lefty"), and even Chuck Berry ("[You Never Can Tell] C'est La Vie") are strikingly original. The newfound confidence she brings to the album can be attributed, in part, to the strong backing band, which includes such future country-rock luminaries as Ricky Skaggs, Rodney Crowell, and Brit picker Albert Lee.

On *Quarter Moon,* Harris breaks her dependence on the music of her mentor; for the first time she doesn't cover one of Gram Parsons' songs. Instead, she focuses on living songwriters like Crowell, and the result is an album that feels alive (especially her reading of Dolly Parton's protofeminist missive "To Daddy"). Sparked by the bluegrass accompaniment of Skaggs, Harris made a convincing roots move on *Blue Kentucky Girl* and *Roses in the Snow,* the latter of which flows with grace and respect for the old-time, Anglo-Celtic origins of her sound.

Harris stumbled in the early 1980s, having lost some of her audience to punk and new wave. Her albums suffered. Save for a heartfelt rendering of James Taylor's compassionate "Millworker," *Evangeline* stalled at the gates; *Cimarron* wasn't much better. To her credit, Harris kept "Movin' On" when the New Traditionalist movement—which she'd prefigured by a decade—began churning out cookie-cutter cowboys. Turning to pop with the same measured grace she brought to folk and bluegrass, she fills *White Shoes* with some boggling cover selections (Donna Summer's "On the Radio"?) and boldly flirts with autobiography on her *Red Headed Stranger*–like concept album *The Ballad of Sally Rose.*

On her lucky *Thirteen,* Harris returns to her roots again, but with less success than she had on *Roses in the Snow. Angel Band* is a solid but low-key set of old-time gospel songs, and *Trio* finds the singer joining forces with her sometime collaborators Parton and Linda Ronstadt for a light but enjoyable set of harmony-based songs. Harris closed out the '80s with *Bluebird,* a set of folk and country rock from left-field songwriters such as Kate and Anna McGarrigle, Tom Rush, and Texas troubadour Butch Hancock. The highlight, however, is her simple, aching interpretation of Johnny Cash's "I Still Miss Someone." Harris' last album for Warner Bros. *(Brand New Dance)* was an uninspired misfire, complete with a bad Bruce Springsteen cover.

When she switched from Warner Bros. to Elektra, in 1993, Harris got a renewed blast of creative energy. The mix of lightness and depth on *Cowgirl's Prayer* goes to the heart of her talents as an interpretive singer. And the song selection is sterling, from the Leonard Cohen–penned title track to Harris' down-and-dirty version of Lucinda Williams' "Crescent City." Nothing, however, prefigured the grace and brilliance of *Wrecking Ball,* on which Emmylou Harris shoves at the boundaries of both country and pop. Enlisting producer Daniel Lanois (Bob Dylan, U2) to give her sound the atmospheric feel of artists normally associated with the experimental-rock label 4AD (Cocteau Twins, Breeders), Harris reinterprets the music of a variety of songwriters, from Neil Young (the title track) and Jimi Hendrix ("May This Be Love") to Kate McGarrigle ("Going Back to Harlan"), Lucinda Williams ("Sweet Old World"), and Gillian Welch ("Orphan Girl"). *Wrecking Ball* polarized the critics, but no one can deny the gauzy sizzle of Harris' voice, her gorgeous, emotional phrasing, or the haunting nature of these interpretations. If for no other reason (and there are many reasons), the sheer ambitiousness of *Wrecking Ball* makes it Harris' masterpiece—a full two decades into her solo career.

Having taken the road less traveled with *Wrecking Ball,* Harris wrote and recorded *Red Dirt Girl* with the same atmospheric feel as its predecessor, but this time she sang her own songs. It was only the second time Harris had recorded an album of all-original material (*The Ballad of Sally Rose* being the first), and the strength of the material raises the question "Why?" From the gospelish "Pearl" to the heartbreaking title track and the tough talk of "I Don't Wanna Talk About It," *Red Dirt Girl* reveals the natural songwriter that's been lurking inside Harris all along. *Stumble Into Grace* continues in the vein of *Red Dirt Girl,* with Harris writing most of the songs and producer Malcolm Burn staying with the spare and gauzy sound begun on *Wrecking Ball.* While the atmospherics are no longer so refreshingly new, *Stumble* is as strong as its two predecessors. The sound now fits Harris like the white dress she wears on the cover, and the collaborations—with Kate and Anna McGarrigle on "Little Bird" and Lucious Jackson's Jill Cunniff on the biting social commentary of "Time in Babylon"—are just right. Harris teams with her old friend Linda Ronstadt on "Strong Hand," a powerful ode to American music matriarch June Carter Cash.

The two *Profile* albums are solid best-of collections, but their brevity makes them less than satisfying. *Duets* is a definitive selection of what some folks feel is Harris' true calling: harmony vocals. *Songs of the West* gathers her cowboy laments. *Anthology* is a solid place to start for a summary of Harris' purest years on Warner Bros. Records. But nothing fully represents Harris' pre-Elektra years as well as the three-CD *Portraits,* a strong selection of songs that includes a handful of her early duets with Gram Parsons. The live *Last Date* is a bit schizophrenic, but she makes up for it on *At the Ryman,* a wide-ranging assortment of covers performed at the original home of the Grand Ole Opry, with the all-acoustic Nashville Ramblers. *Spyboy* is a post-Lanois live set that lends Harris' newfound atmospheric feel to some of her old chestnuts. —M.C./M.K.

Deborah Harry

- ★★ Rockbird (Geffen, 1986)
- ★★ Once More Into the Bleach (Chrysalis, 1988)
- ★★½ Collection (Disky, 2000)

The former Blondie singer's fake-tough-girl act on her solo records proves that Deborah Harry needs her ex-Blondie songwriting partner, Chris Stein, like a fish needs gills. Her only semidecent solo effort, 1989's *Def, Dumb & Blonde,* wandered out of print, but its one hit, the crisp, driving "I Want That Man," can be found on the otherwise pointless *Collection.* —A.B.

PJ Harvey

- ★★★½ Dry (Indigo, 1992)
- ★★★★½ Rid of Me (Indigo, 1993)
- ★★★½ 4-Track Demos (Island, 1993)
- ★★★★½ To Bring You My Love (Island, 1995)
- ★★★½ Is This Desire? (Island, 1998)
- ★★★★★ Stories From the City, Stories From the Sea (Island, 2000)
- ★★★½ Uh Huh Her (Island, 2004)

When Polly Jean Harvey burst out of a tiny English farm town and into the hearts of adoring cultists in 1992, the world may not have been ready for her. A guitar-toting succubus with a remarkably elastic voice, Harvey found common ground in the blues and opera and made sexpot melodrama and metaphysical yearning sound kind of fun. If you look for sunniness in your pop music, she may actually frighten you. Her music is doggedly dark and her lyrics never stray too far from something a sexually liberated Emily Dickinson might have turned out— but give Harvey a chance, and she'll get under your skin something fierce. Also, she's made three world-class albums: *Rid of Me; To Bring You My Love;* and *Stories From the City, Stories From the Sea.*

Dry announced Harvey in all her stark, hard-rocking glory. As Harvey wailed like a modern-day Howlin' Wolf and cranked out sloppy guitar noise, her power trio (collectively known as PJ Harvey) ripped through blues-inspired songs that match the anything the hair-flailing grunge boys could deliver. On the superb single "Sheela-na-gig," Harvey even supplies an honest-to-goodness hook of sorts, rhyming "Gonna wash that man right outta my hair" with "Gonna take my hips to a man who cares," but standouts such as "Dress" and "O Stella" get by on Harvey's rough-hewn and undeniable presence.

Rid of Me burns with the same raw, DIY intensity, but by then, PJ Harvey, abetted nicely by producer Steve Albini, was pushing herself to extremes. On "50 Ft. Queenie" (possibly about a cock that grows longer throughout the song), Harvey declares herself "the king of the world"; on the title track, Harvey whispers, "You're not rid of me" over and over again, before the band erupts into a torrent of noise and Harvey tells a lover that he'll eventually wish he had never met her. For heroic good measure, Harvey also provides a perfectly rocking version of "Highway 61 Revisited." Harvey's original sketches for most of the *Rid of Me* material are presented on *4-Track Demos,* augmented by several unreleased songs (including the excellent "Reeling," on which she urges Robert De Niro to sit on her face). The disc isn't revelatory, but it's nice to be able to clearly discern the over-the-top emoting that was ambushed in *Rid of Me*'s guitar onslaught.

With U2 producer Flood (along with Harvey and percussionist John Parish) behind the boards, *To Bring You My Love* was inspired by the blues only figuratively, in its slow ache and in her dancing with the devil. No longer so sex-obsessed (or driven to make sex-fueled music), Harvey tones down her guitar attack and draws on keyboards and eerie electroatmospherics for a set of songs that are slow, beautiful, and preternaturally dark. Over the title track's slow, spare riff, Harvey calls out to Jesus himself, and from there she keeps up the metaphysical oompah, most notably on the creepy, cabaret-influenced "Down by the Water," the psychotically pounding "Meet ze Monsta," and "C'mon Billy," on which she begs a lover to come home with her and meet their kid.

Harvey resolved not to fuck with her formula too much on *Is This Desire?* Like its predecessor, *Desire* is atmospheric, haunting, and vaguely evil, but it's also more cerebral and beholden to Eurogloom textures; Harvey layers keyboards, acoustic guitars, and electrobeats with subdued precision. The gothic third-person narratives—featuring characters named Leah, Angelene, and Elise, among others—don't quite radiate the immediate presence of Harvey's best stuff, but the desperate, truly disconcerting "Joy" and the whispered, creepy "The Wind" rank high in her catalogue.

After a two-year hiatus, Harvey returned with her finest album, *Stories From the City, Stories From the Sea,* pulling a truly shocking about-face: She sounds downright happy, or at least well-sexed. Recalling the loud-and-fast guitar tumult of her first two albums augmented by a mature elegance and a lingering fondness for texture, "Big Exit," "Kamikaze," and "The Whores Hustle and the Hustlers Whore" are expansive and strangely rousing. She drops some deliciously dark and slow moments (especially "Beautiful Feeling" and the Thom Yorke–assisted "This Mess We're In"), but she also gets drunk and wanders happily around New York City. And on the bombastic and awesomely raunchy "This Is Love," arguably her best song ever, she says a big fuck-you to psychosis and sadness as guitars crunch and garments hit the floor: "I can't believe life's so complex/When I just wanna sit here and watch you undress." For anyone wondering what the big deal is about PJ Harvey, this is the place to start.

Uh Huh Her once again found Harvey in entrancing blues-poet mode, conjuring disturbed, historically significant females such as Clytemnestra, Emily Dickinson, and . . . Polly Jean Harvey. Raw, riff-heavy numbers such as "Who the Fuck?" and "The Letter" revisit her punkish early days, while "It's You" and the delicately atmospheric "You Come Through" recall the slow-burning metaphysical turn she took with *To Bring You My Love.* As usual, the songs don't exactly greet you with open arms; instead, they ask you to meet her and her elastic, evocative goth-croon halfway while she wanders badlands of dissatisfaction and desire, comparing a lover's words to poison ("The Life and Death of Mr. Badmouth"), dreaming of good times ("You Come Through"), and brandishing a knife to thwart off marriage (the magnificently creepy "Pocket Knife").   —C.H.

Juliana Hatfield

★★½   Bed (Zoë/Rounder, 1998)
★★½   Beautiful Creature (Zoë/Rounder, 2000)

★★★   Juliana's Pony: Total System Failure (Zoë/Rounder, 2000)
★★★   Gold Stars 1992–2002: The Juliana Hatfield Collection (Zoë/Rounder, 2002)
★★★   In Exile Deo (Zoë/Rounder, 2004)

Blake Babies singer/bassist and occasional Lemonheads member Juliana Hatfield has often seemed like the James Taylor of '90s alt rock: a decent enough writer and performer, but one who consistently lacks the fuel to turn sparks into fire. But while singer/songwriters of the 1970s aimed to go down easy, Hatfield's girlish voice combined with sex-and-drugs lyrics are often harder to swallow. From song to song, the mix can add up to either intriguing juxtaposition or tired coquetry. The obit on the Blake Babies was barely finished when Hatfield began working on her solo debut. Because her early albums—*Hey Babe* (1992), *Become What You Are* (1993), and *Only Everything* (1995)—have fallen out of print, snatches from that work are most readily available on the first half of *Gold Stars 1992–2002.* That's where you'll find mainstream near-misses such as "Spin the Bottle" and the engagingly adolescent "My Sister." Unreleased cuts and covers (the Police, Neil Young) cap the disc—treats for fans, but inessential.

Bed swaps Blake Babies jangle for a tighter rock sound, which is a rare progressive step on an album devoted to people making bad choices or harboring ugly self-opinions. Hatfield, who once penned a track called "Nirvana," lets the rock references fly, with not-so-subtle nods to Tom Petty and Stevie Nicks as well as John Mellencamp.

In 2000, she issued two albums simultaneously. The quieter *Beautiful Creatures,* originally intended as a slate of demos, unveils a distinctly adult point of view. Despite its title, "Cool Rock Boy" is invective more personal than professional; "Choose Drugs" is a heartbreaking junkie tale ("I say it's me or drugs/You choose drugs"). Finally, the characters in Hatfield's songs are taking control, which comes across better still on the noisy, assertive *Juliana's Pony: Total System Failure* (though the title suggests she just can't leave the little-girl imagery behind). The previously wallowing Hatfield spews vitriol like buckshot (toward bad corporations, bad drivers, bad parents, bad dressers, and the bad music industry), and goes nearly an entire record without dishing pity, even for herself.

After an indie-rock excursion in the band Some Girls (*Feel It* [Koch, 2003]) with Blake Babies drummer Freda Love and bassist Heidi Gluck, Hatfield returned with *In Exile Deo,* a gratifying album on which she mingles laid-back grooves and wistful sounds with doses of familiar jangle and aggressive rock. While dark themes still lurk, Hatfield finally sings like she's ready to claim responsibility for living. "I've been sleeping through my life," she says. "Now I'm waking up and I want to stand in the sunshine." —C.N.

Donny Hathaway

★★★★½ Everything Is Everything (Rhino/Atlantic, 1970)
★★★★   Donny Hathaway (Rhino/Atlantic, 1971)
★★★½   Extension of a Man (Rhino/Atlantic, 1973)
★★★★   A Donny Hathaway Collection (Atlantic, 1990)
★★★½   These Songs For You, Live! (Atlantic, 2004)

Voices such as Donny Hathaway's come along maybe once a decade. Before his brief but influential career was cut short by suicide in 1979, Hathaway proved himself a maestro of protest soul who effused equal amounts of political anger and romantic tenderness. With that being so, it's a curious fact that despite his vocal gifts and his acknowledged influence on today's crop of neosoul singers, his back catalogue is very poorly served, especially in the compilation category. But a few of his early LPs are still in print, such as his debut, the spiritual and political *Everything Is Everything,* a stirring introduction to Hathaway's many vocal and songwriting influences (gospel, jazz, classical) and where he strove to take them. *Donny Hathaway* consists mainly of his redefining interpretations of the current Top 40, like his shiver-inducing versions of the Leon Russell/Carpenters tune "A Song for You" and the Hollies' "He Ain't Heavy, He's My Brother." *Extension of a Man* is his ambitious, "heavy" album, featuring the epochal "Someday We'll All Be Free" and the LP's grandiose orchestral opener, "I Love the Lord, He Heard My Cry (Parts 1 & 2)."

The 15 songs on *A Donny Hathaway Collection* include the work he's best known for by the casual music fan: namely his synergistic duets with Roberta Flack, such as "Where Is the Love" and "The Closer I Get to You." Only the omission of the more creatively challenging songs of Hathaway's early years prevents it from being definitive. *These Songs for You, Live!* culled from several early '70s concerts, displays the passion and charm that have inspired artists from Alicia Keys to the Neptunes, and attest to his knack for finding a great band. But what emerges most is Hathaway's irrepressible charisma and talent. The casual seduction of "You've Got a Friend" turns into a joyous sing-along; and in his hands, even "Yesterday" becomes a blues lament nonpareil. —G.F./J.C.

Ronnie Hawkins

★★★½   The Best of Ronnie Hawkins and the Hawks (Rhino, 1990)
★★★   Ronnie Hawkins/Folk Ballads of Ronnie Hawkins (Collectables, 1999)
★★   Mr. Dynamo/Sings the Songs of Hank Williams (Collectables, 1999)

Born (January 10, 1935) and raised in Arkansas, unrepentantly rockabilly Ronnie Hawkins may go down in history as a footnote for his band, the Hawks, having once included the musicians who became as legendary as the Band. (Some no doubt will recall him as the cousin of Dale Hawkins, whose 1957 Top 30 single, "Susie-Q," has been overshadowed by Creedence Clearwater Revival's cover version.) He had but one chart hit in the States—1959's indelible, incendiary "Mary Lou," one of the great one-hit smashes—but carved out a substantial niche for himself in Canada, where he has lived since 1958. It's a shame that had it not been for "Mary Lou" and the Band connection he might have been forgotten, because the recent reissue of four of his late '50s–early '60s studio albums makes it clear that Canada picked up on something the U.S. had overlooked.

Hawkins didn't have a great vocal instrument in terms of range, but his voice was loaded with personality and feeling. Plus he had a sure sense of phrasing and nuance, and knew how to twist a lyric just so to express futility, anger, exasperation, heartbreak, or tender-hearted yearning. Throw in some good original songs—most of which he cowrote with others, including Hawks (and the Band) drummer Levon Helm—along with some flawless, spirited band support, and attention must be paid.

Rhino's *Best of* is the best place to start, because it offers a thorough overview of Hawkins through the years, concluding with a 1970 cut, "Down in the Alley," that shows the artist in a peak performance. In "Mary Lou" he can lay legitimate claim to being among the artists who carried the rockabilly banner into the '60s even as its leading practitioners from the '50s, hoping to remain commercially viable, were moving on to mainstream rock & roll or country. All of the '50s sides here showcase to good effect in other contexts the trademark Hawkins growl heard most effectively on "Mary Lou." The hot stuff on this disc has stood the test of time: the driving rewrite of Chuck Berry's "Thirty Days," retitled as "Forty Days"; the moody "One of These Days"; a taste of the honky-tonk in "Odessa." Any one or all of these songs could have been as big as or bigger than "Mary Lou," but none even made it to the Top 40. So goes the luck of the draw in show bidness. —D.M.

Richie Hawtin

   ★★★★   Decks, EFX & 909 (Novamute, 1999)
   ★★★★½   DE9: Closer to the Edit (Novamute, 2001)

Richie Hawtin and Sven Väth

   ★★★   The Sound of the Third Season (Mute, 2002)

Plastikman

   ★★★   Sheet One (Novamute, 1993)
   ★★★   Musik (Plus 8, 1994)
   ★★★   Mixmag Live!, Vol. 20: Plastikman (Mixmag, 1995)
   ★★½   Consumed (Novamute, 1998)
   ★½   Artifakts [bc] (Novamute, 1998)
   ★★   Closer (Mute, 2003)

Born in England and raised in Windsor, Ontario, just over the border from Detroit, Richie Hawtin is one of techno's most celebrated DJs and producers. On its own, his music tends to be forbiddingly austere; he's best heard in the mix, where his tracks and others like them—usually deliberately unfinished—can be stacked and interlocked like Lego pieces. As a DJ, Hawtin connects them like a gamelan orchestra conductor, lining up single rhythms into an undulating whole, and it tends to be livelier and more physical than most of the music-as-music he makes, either under his own name or as Plastikman or F.U.S.E.

This isn't to say there isn't a certain . . . well, *charm* is overstating it, but Hawtin's early work has an impressive intensity. Starting Plus 8 Records in 1990 with friend and fellow Windsor DJ John Acquaviva, Hawtin helped push techno into faster, harder terrain, and his early work, which explores the nuances of the jabbering "acid" sound of the Roland TB-303 bass synth, ranks among the most influential music of the early '90s. Often, though, the music is too nuanced for its own good. The three various-artists *Plus 8 Classics* compilations offer both Hawtin's crucial work from the period and that of other artists such as Acquaviva, LFO, and Kenny Larkin. This means relief, something not afforded by later Plastikman albums *Consumed* and especially *Artifakts [bc]*, which take minimalism so far it becomes near-immobile.

Hawtin's DJ work is something else. *Mixmag Live! Vol. 20* covers much of the acidic (in both the 303 and bitter-metallic-aftertaste senses) style that marks his early work, but it's with 1999's *Decks, EFX & 909* that Hawtin began stretching out, layering 35 records atop one another, adding texture and space via a Roland TR-909 drum machine and a handful of the titular effects and processors, making for the most impressively physical music he'd made since the early '90s. *DE9: Closer to the Edit* breaks it down even further by expanding the number of sound sources (there are some 100 tracks utilized here) but limiting the amount

of surface texture. The results resembled a continuously flowing composition like Steve Reich's *Music for 18 Musicians,* with the beat and bass lines mutating continuously as tiny melodic fragments sprout up every so often, surprisingly approachable and gratifyingly beautiful. *The Sound of the Third Season,* a gauzy mix by Hawtin and German trance jock Sven Väth, was a pleasant stopgap. Hawtin returned as Plastikman with 2003's *Closer,* even adding some vocals to his usual mix, but the music was more claustrophobic and less inviting than ever. —M.M.

Isaac Hayes

   ★★★★   Presenting Isaac Hayes (1967; Stax, 1995)
   ★★★★   Hot Buttered Soul (1969; Stax, 1995)
   ★★½   The Isaac Hayes Movement (1970; Stax, 1990)
   ★★½   To Be Continued (1970; Stax, 1991)
   ★★★   Black Moses (1971; Stax, 1990)
   ★★½   Shaft (1971; Stax, 2004)
   ★★½   Joy (1973; Stax, 1991)
   ★★½   Live at the Sahara Tahoe (1973; Stax, 1990)
   ★★   Chocolate Chip (1975; Stax, 1998)
   ★★   Groove-a-Thon (1976; Stax, 2002)
   ★★★½   Best of Isaac Hayes, Volume 1 (1986; Stax, 1989)
   ★★★   Best of Isaac Hayes, Volume 2 (1986; Stax, 1989)
   ★★½   Love Attack (1988; Columbia, 1990)
   ★★★★   Greatest Hit Singles (Stax, 1991)
   ★★★½   Double Feature: Truck Turner/Tough Guys (Stax, 1993)
   ★★   Wonderful (Stax, 1994)
   ★★★½   Branded (Pointblank, 1995)
   ★★½   Raw and Refined (Pointblank, 1995)
   ★★★★   Greatest Hits (Fantasy, 1995)
   ★★★½   The Best of Isaac Hayes: The Polydor Years (Polydor, 1996)
   ★★★★   Ultimate Collection (Hip-O, 2000)
   ★★   Instrumentals (Stax/Ace, 2003)
   ★★★★   Isaac Hayes at Wattstax (Stax, 2003)
   ★★★★   Greatest Love Songs (Hip-O, 2004)
   ★★   For the Sake of Love/Don't Let Go (Raven, 2004)

Shades, dashiki, gleaming bald pate: Isaac Hayes cut an imposing figure during his early '70s heyday. The hulking auteur behind the ultra funky "Theme From *Shaft*" was actually a Barry White prototype, given to steamy bedroom raps and lush orchestrations. Or maybe he wasn't: The remainder of the *Shaft* soundtrack is rather mundane action-movie music, spiced by the occasional burst of streetwise syncopation or vocal color. A far cry from Curtis Mayfield's *Superfly,* to say the least. However, Hayes shouldn't be written off as a period oddity. His rambling soundtracks (two of which, *Truck Turner* and *Tough Guys,* are available on a single CD) and full-blown cover versions had a big effect on soul music in general, broadening and softening the instrumental palette. Hayes paved the way for disco; whether he deserves credit or blame is a matter of taste.

Hayes and David Porter made up one of the most successful songwriting and production teams at Stax/Volt. When they started to drift apart in the late '60s, Hayes began to record under his own name. *Presenting Isaac Hayes,* his 1967 debut, is a loose and bluesy after-hours jam session. *Hot Buttered Soul,* the 1969 followup, must have seemed like the eccentric vanity project of a brilliant behind-the-scenes man—until it reached the pop Top 10, anyway.

Elongated and embellished to the point of sonic overkill, "Walk On By" and "By the Time I Get to Phoenix" saunter through full-blown rearrangements. The former song entered the Top 40 as an edited single, although the full-length version of the latter (*Soul*'s entire second side on vinyl) establishes the Hayes game plan. Using the basic melody as theme and springboard, Hayes ruminates on the vagaries of romance in a spoken intro that takes up nearly half the song. His words aren't cued to the rhythm like a modern rapper's, but the contrast between the smoothly spoken and haltingly sung sections adds a delicate tension. *Hot Buttered Soul* is a landmark album.

Spread across two hour-long CDs, *The Best of Isaac Hayes* conveys the maddening expansiveness of his Stax records. *Volume 1* holds "Theme From *Shaft*" and "Walk On By," along with all 19 minutes of the rote "Do Your Thing." *Volume 2* includes a delicious silk-and-molasses crawl through "Never Can Say Goodbye" and the full version of "By the Time I Get to Phoenix." A collection of single edits—a distillation album—would be less authentic, but more approachable. Several of Hayes' biggest hits are included on a dynamite series of Stax samplers: *Original Big Hits Volumes 1–4.*

Though he occasionally dented the charts in the mid- to late '70s, Hayes sounds like he's playing catch-up on his disco period entries. (Most of his work from this period, including *Disco Connection, New Horizon,* and *Don't Let Go,* is unavailable on CD.) Even the bubbly track "Don't Let Go," from 1980, has nowhere near the commanding presence of earlier Hayes concoctions. And "Ike's Rap," from the otherwise forgettable *Love Attack,* lays claim to hip-hop over a soupy, unsympathetic beat. Perhaps modern technology makes Hayes and his bodacious sense of scale seem anachronistic, but then again, *Shaft*'s stuttering wah-wah rhythm has launched many a rap jam.

Hayes has continued to release albums regularly in recent years, but his only consequential recent work was 1995's *Branded,* cut for the boutique blues label Pointblank. He was introduced to the contemporary audience via the '90s animated series *South Park;* his deathless "Chocolate Salty Balls" is on the *South Park*–related *Chef Aid* as well as the soundtrack to the feature film *South Park: Bigger, Longer, Uncut.* More recently, he appeared in the remake of *Shaft* (2000) and on Alicia Keys' best-selling album *Songs in A Minor.* —M.C./B.SC.

Heart

★★★ Dreamboat Annie (1976; Capitol, 1990)
★★★ Little Queen (1977; Epic/Legacy, 1994)
★★ Magazine (1978; Capitol, 1990)
★★½ Dog and Butterfly (1978; Epic/Legacy, 2004)
★★★ Bebe Le' Strange (1980; Epic/Legacy, 2004)
★★★ Greatest Hits—Live (Epic, 1980)
★★½ Private Audition (Epic, 1982)
★★½ Passionworks (Epic, 1983)
★★½ Heart (Capitol, 1985)
★★½ Bad Animals (Capitol, 1987)
★★ Brigade (Capitol, 1990)
★★½ Rock the House "Live" (Capitol, 1991)
★★★★ The Road Home (Capitol/EMI, 1995)
★★★★ Greatest Hits (Epic/Legacy, 1998)
★★★★ Greatest Hits: 1985–1995 (Capitol, 2000)
★★★ Jupiter's Darling (Sovereign, 2004)

Along with debut albums from Foreigner and Boston, Heart's *Dreamboat Annie* ushered in the era of arena rock and Album Oriented Radio. The album sees the band's sister team of Nancy and Ann Wilson shrewdly pulling off a Led Zep role reversal. Lead singer Ann can shift from pop-thrush blandness to piercing shrieks with the stroke of a power chord, as she does on "Crazy on You" and "Magic Man." *Little Queen* ups the heavy quotient on hits like "Barracuda" with satisfying results, but murky folk-rock filler like "Dream of the Archer" cuts away at the record's overall power. The clunky *Dog and Butterfly* merely proves that some aspects of Led Zeppelin's legacy are better left alone. *Magazine* was a rush-job release of demo tapes, perpetrated when Heart skipped from the Canadian label Mushroom over to Epic.

Bebe Le' Strange shows strong signs of development: On "Even It Up," for example, Ann's vocals are bolstered by a snappy horn chart and firm beat. *Greatest Hits—Live* kicks off well, pulling together the obvious high points—and promptly falls apart, concluding with a turgid cover of Zeppelin's "Rock & Roll." *Pri-*

vate Audition is a failed attempt at regaining *Bebe*'s relatively adventurous spirit. *Passionworks* introduces the Wilsons' latter-day approach on cuts like "Allies" and "How Can I Refuse"—supercharged bathos encased in a glossy production.

Another label change, from Epic to Capitol, jump-started Heart's career a second time. *Heart* and *Bad Animals* are the repositories for half a dozen interchangeable power-ballad smashes, any one of which could break your heart or turn your stomach. Oddly enough, *Rock the House "Live"* is not the second-time-around summation fans might have expected. It's a realistic tour documentary, at best: a hodgepodge of minor album cuts and several resounding nonhits from the middling *Brigade*. Yet another live album, *The Road Home,* which collects the band's early hits, strips down the bombastic, arena-rock Heart of the '80s and reveals its sweet folkie soul. —M.C./A.B.

Heavenly

★★½   Heavenly Vs. Satan (1991; K, 2001)
★★★   Le Jardin de Heavenly (K, 1992)
★★★★   P.U.N.K. Girl (EP) (K, 1995)
★★★   The Decline and Fall of Heavenly (K, 1994)
★★★½   Operation Heavenly (K, 1996)

Oxford, England's Heavenly became avatars of the bouncy and saccharine indie-rock style known variously as "shambling," "twee pop," and "cuddlecore," and became an important influence on British and American indie rock, most notably Belle & Sebastian. Though the quartet had already recorded as Tallulah Gosh in the late '80s, lead singer Amelia Fletcher still sounded like a prep-school freshman on Heavenly's eight-song debut, *Heavenly vs. Satan,* breathily crooning with passive, pitch-challenged yearning about teen topics such as a "Cool Guitar Boy" ("There's heaven in his eyes!"). A twee-pop touchstone, the 1991 album was rereleased a decade later with six additional tracks, but although the tunes are strong throughout and several lyrics suggest dark recesses beneath Heavenly's sunny sound, the songcraft is ultimately overwhelmed by the gangly tumble of knock-kneed beats and off-key vocals. A year later, Heavenly was ready to channel its talents more smoothly on *Le Jardin de Heavenly.* Newcomer Cathy Rogers helps—she adds light keyboard fills and solid vocal harmonies behind the perennially tone-challenged Fletcher—as do memorable experiments such as "C Is the Heavenly Option," a duet with K Records' gravelly honcho, Calvin Johnson.

Still, the improvements were hardly preparation for the jolt of *P.U.N.K. Girl,* a musically diverse, themati-

cally unified EP that plants Heavenly's feet on the ground with newly assertive lyrics—at least one of the five songs is about date rape—and newfound tinges of musical menace beneath the retro pop cutesiness. The group eased up on that menace on its following release, but this short album still earns its title, *The Decline and Fall of Heavenly.* "I'm not the same girl that you once knew," sings Fletcher on "Modestic," one of several numbers in which she finds her man falling short of her dreams. For that matter, Heavenly isn't the same band, exploring its '60s pop-rock influences more explicitly than ever before, with horn charts here, girl group melodies there, even a "Tequila"-tinged instrumental ("Sacramento"). *Operation Heavenly* dares even more with a harder rock sound, and Fletcher finally sings tough enough to qualify as a p.u.n.k. girl herself, upsetting romantic conventions with an easy sneer on almost every song. Sadly, the suicide of Amanda's brother and the group's drummer, Matt Fletcher, ended Heavenly only weeks after *Operation Heavenly*'s release, though the surviving members later regrouped as Marine Research. —F.S.

Richard Hell

★★★★½   Blank Generation (Sire, 1977)
★★★   Destiny Street (Razor & Tie, 1982)
★★★½   Time (Matador, 2002)

Kentucky-born Richard Hell deserves credit (or blame) for originating much of the punk imagery and style associated with the London scene. Musically, though, the Voidoids resemble Captain Beefheart's Magic Band much more than the Sex Pistols. And Hell has never managed to capitalize on his early notoriety.

The sullen, punked-out *Blank Generation* stings like a casual insult. "Love Comes in Spurts"—if you're lucky. Behind the sliced T-shirts and ear-scorching amplification, however, lurks an underrated band: The Voidoids focus Richard Hell's boundless alienation into bold, innovative rock & roll. Lead guitarist Robert Quine (who would later gain recognition for his work with Lou Reed) spikes the angry rush of sound with quick runs and sudden explosions; Quine milks each tender electric nerve of his Fender for all it's worth. Hell's no more a poet than he is a bass player, but his snarl-to-a-croak vocal range sounds downright affecting here, not affected. His indictments of society (and himself) are propelled by his band's headlong attack: There's not a wasted growl or gust of feedback on *Blank Generation.*

But during the long layoff between *Blank Generation* and *Destiny Street,* Hell's creative momentum froze; the latter album sounds testy, a little hedging—

not exactly what you'd expect from the author of scathing rave-ups like "Betrayal Takes Two" and "New Pleasures." Though he made a brief return in the supergroup Dim Stars, after *Destiny Street*, Hell mostly abandoned music to focus on acting and writing. Quine committed suicide in spring 2004, months after the death of his wife, Alice.

Time brings together all the odds and ends—many of which were first included on *R.I.P.*—into a two-disc set that includes Voidoids-era outtakes, lo-fi live recordings, an odd 1984 New Orleans session, and some crude, compelling demos from Hell's howling tenure with Johnny Thunders and the Heartbreakers. —R.A.

Helmet

★★★	Strap It On (Amphetamine Reptile, 1990)
★★★½	Meantime (Interscope, 1992)
★★★½	Betty (Interscope, 1994)
★★★	Born Annoying (Interscope, 1995)
★★★	Aftertaste (Interscope, 1997)
★★★½	Unsung: The Best of Helmet 1991–1997 (Interscope, 2004)

Quintessential noise-rockers from lower Manhattan, Helmet is a rhythm juggernaut. Guitars, bass, and drums play interconnecting lines and shift tempos with machinelike precision. The quartet's tight, taut sound bridges the gap between thrash metal and the art-damaged vocabulary of New York City guitar innovators such as Glenn Branca and the Band of Susans, both of whom employed Helmet founding member Page Hamilton. The music's cold relentlessness is broken by Hamilton's hellish wails and terse, punishing guitar solos. Yet it's the band's tightly wound compositions and canny use of silence that distinguish the debut, *Strap It On*, from typical headbanging fare.

Once relying solely on dynamics to carry the music, the band introduced melody and actual singing to its repertoire on its 1991 single "Unsung," which is reprised on *Meantime*. *Betty* expands the musical choices considerably, touching on Wes Montgomery ("Beautiful Love") and primordial blues ("Sam Hell"). By *Aftertaste*, the formula has been perfected: Hamilton stretches guitar lines like high-tension wires across a grid of cross-rhythms, and when the wire snaps, it's cathartic. But too often the band's workmanlike rock sounds like work, and Hamilton's get-a-grip, commonsense lyrics take no risks. *Unsung* culls the stronger tracks from the quartet's hit-and-miss albums, and it builds a persuasive case for Helmet as songwriters as well as sonic ball-crushers. —G.K.

Jimi Hendrix

★★★★★	Are You Experienced? (1967; MCA, 1997)
★★★★★	Axis: Bold as Love (1967; MCA, 1997)
★★★★★	Electric Ladyland (1968; MCA, 1997)
★★★★★	Smash Hits (1969; MCA, 2002)
★★★★	Band of Gypsys (1970; MCA, 1998)
★★★★½	The Ultimate Experience (MCA, 1993)
★★★½	Woodstock (MCA, 1994)
★★★½	Blues (MCA, 1994)
★★★★	First Rays of the New Rising Sun (1997; MCA, 2003)
★★★½	South Saturn Delta (1997; MCA, 2003)
★★★★½	Experience Hendrix: The Best of Jimi Hendrix (MCA, 1998)
★★★★	BBC Sessions (MCA, 1998)
★★★½	Live at the Fillmore East (MCA, 1999)
★★★½	Live at Woodstock (MCA, 1999)
★★★★½	The Jimi Hendrix Experience (MCA, 2000)
★★★★	Voodoo Child: The Jimi Hendrix Collection (MCA, 2001)
★★★½	Blue Wild Angel: Live at the Isle of Wight (MCA, 2002)
★★★	Live at Berkeley (MCA, 2003)
★★★★	Martin Scorsese Presents the Blues: Jimi Hendrix (MCA, 2003)

Jimi Hendrix is the quintessential rock guitarist, as much as Bob Dylan is the quintessential singer/songwriter and the Beatles are the ultimate rock band. As only classical or jazz players had done before him, Hendrix defined his music's instrument: Expanding the possibilities of the amplified six-string, he confirmed beyond question its status as rock's essential vehicle—as Pablo Casals was to the cello and Charlie Parker to the saxophone, so was Jimi Hendrix to the electric guitar. A psychic successor to Elvis Presley, Hendrix also embodied the politics of rock & roll as a black-white fusion—the twin pillars of his music were the earthiness of the blues and the ethereality of jazz, but his primary contemporary audience was white rock fans and the psychedelic subgenre that provided the context for his particular triumph was a white one. Finally, through lyrics heavily influenced by Bob Dylan, he delivered a message of universal emancipation. A personality large enough to thrive on apparently contradictory impulses, he was both the painstaking artist and the unabashed cock-rocker, a showman whose act presaged the melodrama both of glitter and of punk, a player explosive enough to influence equally jazz perfectionists and heavy-metal thunderers, an erotic liberator and a spiritual force. Sly Stone and Prince obviously learned much from Hendrix; so did Pete Townshend, Gil Evans, and Bob Marley.

The Seattle-born ex-paratrooper began his career, with mythic appropriateness, backing up such originators as B.B. King and Little Richard. Significantly, however, he only hit his stride in Britain—where someone who possessed both Hendrix's looks and talent could pass for an exotic god; Animals bassist Chas Chandler hooked him up with bassist Noel Redding (a former lead guitarist whose playing would subsequently, and felicitously, betray its grounding in melody) and jazz-styled drummer Mitch Mitchell. The interracial Jimi Hendrix Experience was born—ready to come on like psychedelic supermen (already Jimi sometimes soloed with his teeth, and the band's freak-out garb was an acidhead's dream). *Are You Experienced?* was the Summer of Love debut, and it sounded like divine madness—"Purple Haze," "I Don't Live Today," "Manic Depression," and "Fire" were all feedback finesse and arrogant virtuosity wrapped around lyrics sprung from primal wondering, lust, and fear.

Axis: Bold as Love plunged deeper. Ballads ("Little Wing") met mind-warp blues—the songs blurred together, metaphorically implying the fact of Hendrix's creative impatience (and prefiguring his later ventures into jazz freedom). Psychedelia's triumph came next: a double-album manifesto featuring contributions from Steve Winwood, Buddy Miles, and Jack Casady, *Electric Ladyland* showed Hendrix serving notice of his unstoppable ambition. The chord progressions of "Burning of the Midnight Lamp" echoed Bach (and featured perhaps the only example of a wah-wah pedal employed elegantly); "Crosstown Traffic" was the Experience at its most rocking; "All Along the Watchtower" became Hendrix's classic Dylan cover; and, with "Voodoo Child (Slight Return)," the songwriter reached back into gris-gris mythology to fashion a mock-cosmic persona. Like the sounding of a gigantic gong, the album reverberated across the airwaves; it also sounded the death knell for the Experience.

Mitchell held on long enough to join Jimi and new bassist Billy Cox for an appearance at Newport, but the legendary Woodstock gig (including the famous, fiery "Star Spangled Banner") was performed by an ad hoc group called the Electric Sky Church, and by the time of the live *Band of Gypsys,* the drummer's post had been taken by the bombastic Buddy Miles. For once playing with a black band, Hendrix tackled funk. "Machine Gun" and "Message of Love" were the fearsome highlights of *Gypsys,* yet while the power trio achieved the essence of force, it lacked melody—and aesthetic fullness suffered as a result.

Hendrix died in 1970, choking on vomit following barbiturate and alcohol intoxication, at a period of seeming creative transition. He'd been moving further away from rock, alternately returning to blues, delving deeper into funk, and studying jazz fusion. *The Cry of Love* (1971, out of print), however, showed the master, playing with Cox and Mitchell, at his most confident: "Ezy Rider" and "Angel" are the tough and tender faces of the genius at his most appealing.

A deluge of posthumous albums then began. Of the live work, *BBC Sessions* and *Live at Winterland* are the most exciting (we're still waiting for a new package of Hendrix's out-of-print classic Monterey performances). The last decade has seen the Hendrix estate reclaim the guitarist's catalogue from the hands of producer Alan Douglas, who had for years been clogging record-store shelves with albums such as *Crash Landing* and *The Cry of Love,* which combined unreleased Hendrix recordings with new overdubs and production. If you want to hear unreleased Hendrix material, go to the estate's *First Rays of the New Rising Sun* and *South Saturn Delta*—both of these '90s compilations were remastered by Hendrix's original engineer, Eddie Kramer, and feature some blazing material. The fine four-CD *Jimi Hendrix Experience* box also collects some worthwhile unreleased music. And the recently reissued *Smash Hits* best-of is still the tightest collection of killer Hendrix. —P.E./N.B.

Don Henley

★½ I Can't Stand Still (Asylum, 1982)
★★½ Building the Perfect Beast (Geffen, 1984)
★★★★ The End of the Innocence (Geffen, 1989)
★★★½ Actual Miles: Henley's Greatest Hits (Geffen, 1995)
★★½ Inside Job (Warner Bros., 2000)

Heartache and outrage aren't the most obvious bookends for a songwriter's work, but those two emotions are clearly important touchstones for Don Henley. That was true when he was in the Eagles—he, after all, was the voice of both "Desperado" and "Life in the Fast Lane"—and it became even more the case with his solo career, where he scored hits with both the sneering rage of "Dirty Laundry" and the itchy longing of "The Boys of Summer." But while heartache can be timeless and eternal, outrage tends to sour if not leavened with wit or humor, and as such, Henley ultimately went from angry young man to surly old crank—and took his solo career with him.

Of course, he was fairly cranky when he started. His first big solo hit was "Dirty Laundry," a nastily infectious diatribe against media exploitation of personal tragedy. (Presumably Henley, who was arrested in 1980 after a 16-year-old girl was found overdosed in his Los Angeles home, knew whereof he sang.) There's more where that came from on *I Can't*

Stand Still, from the schools-are-going-to-hell rant of "Johnny Can't Read" to the anti–Cold War rocker "Them and Us." Trouble is, those issues now seem as dated as the new-wavey keyboard sounds littering the arrangements, and apart from the deliciously melancholy "Talking to the Moon," the ballads don't really work.

Building the Perfect Beast finds a better balance, thanks in no small part to "The Boys of Summer," which expands Henley's romantic longing to near-cinematic grandeur. Both "Sunset Grill" and "Not Enough Love in the World" also manage a certain emotional frisson, but "All She Wants to Do Is Dance" marries a pallid update of the "Dirty Laundry" groove to a muddled Ugly American story, while the title track is undermined by Henley's strained falsetto.

With "The End of the Innocence," Henley's writing achieves something close to perfection, framing his political commentary with a melody that makes the most of his dry, yearning delivery. While the rest of *The End of the Innocence* rarely matches that apotheosis, neither does it fall much short, thanks to the vividly written and artfully sung "New York Minute," "Heart of the Matter," and "I Will Not Go Quietly."

Assembled largely to fulfill his contractual obligations to Geffen Records, *Actual Miles* augments Henley's hit singles with three new songs, one of which is a cover. Had it also included his duets with Stevie Nicks ("Leather and Lace") and Patty Smyth ("Sometimes Love Just Ain't Enough"), it would have been a much better buy. It would be another five years, however, before Henley delivered an entire album of new material, and *Inside Job* was barely worth the wait. Apart from a sprinkling of ballads—among them the genuinely moving "Annabel"—the album is a nonstop gripefest, with Henley railing against corporate greed ("Goodbye to a River"), rampant consumerism ("Workin' It"), boorish Americans ("Nobody Else in the World but You"), and those punks on MTV ("Damn It, Rose"). —J.D.C.

Joe Henry

★★½	Short Man's Room	(Mammoth, 1992)
★★★½	Kindness of the World	(Mammoth, 1993)
★★★★	Trampoline	(Mammoth, 1996)
★★★½	Fuse	(Mammoth, 1999)
★★★½	Scar	(Mammoth, 2001)
★★★★	Tiny Voices	(Anti-, 2003)

While the typical recording career arcs from more inspired early work to more conventional later stuff, Joe Henry is one of the very few artists (like, say, Tom Waits, Scott Walker) whose music has gotten more challenging and dynamic over time. As such, only the most determined completists need troll the used bins for Henry's out-of-print early albums, 1986's *Talk of Heaven,* 1989's *Murder of Crows,* and 1990's *Shuffletown.* They're full of utterly conventional singer/songwriter fare—at best, a thinking man's Adult Contemporary—that crosses mellow piano-man balladry with a slight Southern twang (Billy Joel gone country-rock? Bruce Hornsby does bluegrass?). In places, though, they point to a still-evolving voice and better things to come. One their own, however, these records sound at best workmanlike.

Short Man's Room, which features Minneapolis country-rockers the Jayhawks as backing band, constitutes Henry's first tentative leap toward a style that would warrant notice. While tracks such as "Good Fortune" and "Sault Sainte Marie" are too reminiscent of the Jayhawks to qualify as a distinct new sound for Henry, elsewhere the influence isn't so obvious. Having been recorded live in the studio gives the album a more lively, immediate feel, while bits of fiddle, mandolin, and banjo root the songs in a country tradition that complements Henry's songwriting.

Kindness of the World continues Henry's fling through the still-nascent world of alt-country Americana, and it's here that his development as a stylist begins to pay real dividends. Again utilizing the talents of the Jayhawks and friends such as Victoria Williams, Henry crafts his first consistently compelling collection. In particular, the subtly tragic optimism of "Fireman's Wedding" and the fatalistic storytelling of "She Always Goes" put him in league with the best country songwriters—in fact, a cover of Tom T. Hall's "I Flew Over Our House Last Night" fits right into the mix. Meanwhile, "Third Reel" hints at the even more artsy and refined writing to come.

After a three-year absence, Henry returned with *Trampoline,* on which he not only shifted his sonic palette once again—embracing a funkier, albeit taut, groove—but also seemed to find his truest voice. As such, it's his best album to date. Country touches resurface on the acoustic "Go With God (Topless Shoeshine)" and with the pedal steel in "Parade," but many of the record's most impressive tracks are completely removed from anything Henry's done before. He was certainly never the obvious choice to cover Sly Stone, as he does here with "Let Me Have It All." "Ohio Air Show Plane Crash" is mesmerizing in its subtle guitar churn, and the lyrics read like a modernist (very) short story. So do the words of "Flower Girl," which, accompanied by pump organ and orchestrations, invites comparison to Tom Waits' off-kilter later work. Tying it all together is a moody, atmospheric production that adds sophistication to Henry's ever-sharpening songcraft.

Fuse and *Scar* not only continue Henry's fascination with highly imagistic, one-word titles, they also push his music further into the intellectual/sophisticate/hipster realm *Trampoline* first entered. Where *Fuse*'s "Monkey" and "Like She Was a Hammer" maximize the juice of a subtle hook using tension and repetition, "Fat," "Want Too Much," and the instrumental "Curt Flood" flirt with jazz colors and riffs. Meanwhile, the New Orleans funeral march of "Beautiful Hat" (courtesy of the Dirty Dozen Brass Band) and "We'll Meet Again," with its David Lynch–style sunny/sinister edge, offer other new settings for Henry's writing. *Scar* embraces jazz even more fully with help from Ornette Coleman ("Richard Pryor Addresses a Tearful Nation") and former Waits guitarist Marc Ribot ("Stop"), and with "Struck" and "Lock and Key" also explores a type of hushed, adult-pop art song not far removed from the work of Brazilian composer Caetano Veloso. While *Scar* can get too artsy and esoteric for its own good, both it and *Fuse* show how Henry has developed into a singularly adventurous songwriter who continues to take chances in expanding his vocabulary.

Tiny Voices further refines the lounge-jazz, art-song approach Henry launched with *Fuse* and *Scar*, achieving here his most rewarding returns of the trilogy. Again backed by first-rate jazz musicians, including clarinetist Don Byron, Henry crafts works that, while mild on the surface, brim with grandeur, edge, funk, poetry, and even a fair number of irresistible hooks. This is for anyone who thinks adult pop doesn't have to be easy listening. —R.M.S.

Herbert

★★★½ Around the House (!K7, 1998)
★★★★ Globus Mix Vol. 5: Let's All Make Mistakes (Tresor, 2000)
★★★★½ Bodily Functions (!K7, 2001)
★★★★½ Secondhand Sounds: Herbert Remixes (Peacefrog, 2002)

Radio Boy

★★½ The Mechanics of Destruction (Soundslike, 2002)

Matthew Herbert Big Band

★★★ Goodbye Swingtime (Soundslike, 2003)

Cerebral Londoner Matthew Herbert was a jazz keyboardist who studied electroacoustic theory at university. But he approaches both record making and record spinning like a grad student at Pleasure Principle U., his detail-oriented approach to beats and textures as gorgeous as anything in dance music. *Around the House* (1998) exemplifies his approach: Its various sounds taken from samples of household objects

(which are then treated until they take on an iridescent glow), it's both comfortable and alien, just like the distracted, mesmerizing croon of Dani Siciliano, who sings the bulk of the songs. *Bodily Functions* (2001) is similarly arranged (the bulk of its samples come from, you guessed it, hearts beating, blood pumping, etc.) but has better songs and a sharper overall feel. Herbert's remixes tend to be as smart as his albums. His remix of Moloko's 1999 single "Sing It Back," for instance, lolls around like mercury on a waterbed; it appears on 2002's two-disc *Secondhand Sounds* alongside 20 other examples of Herbert's dance-floor-oriented work. "Sing It Back" also pops up on the masterful *Globus Mix Vol. 5: Let's All Make Mistakes*, alongside several other tracks he's released under pseudonyms like Doctor Rockit, Wishmountain, and Radio Boy. The mix isn't necessarily representative of Herbert's production work, but it is his best release. *The Mechanics of Destruction*, the 2002 album he made as Radio Boy, is probably the worst, an uninvolving piece of agitprop whose sounds were made from the destruction of various megacorporations' products (McDonald's hamburger wrappers, Starbucks lattes, etc.). Somewhere in between falls *Goodbye Swingtime*, a curious step into big-band jazz arrangements carried off with surprising density and flair. —M.M.

Kristin Hersh

★★★★ Hips and Makers (Reprise, 1994)
★★½ Strings (EP) (Sire, 1994)
★★½ Strange Angels (Rykodisc, 1998)
★★★ Sky Motel (4AD, 1999)
★★★ Sunny Border Blue (4AD, 2001)
★★★ The Grotto (4AD, 2003)

With a gift for raw-nerved, impressionistic lyrics and a history of bipolar disorder, Throwing Muses frontwoman Kristin Hersh had been considered indie rock's answer to Sylvia Plath long before her first solo album, 1994's *Hips and Makers*, sealed the deal. Produced by Lenny Kaye (Patti Smith Group) and recorded in two weeks, *Makers*, both razor-sharp and maddeningly obtuse, is still Hersh's finest solo record, a hushed (especially in comparison to the often clamorous Muses), largely acoustic offering populated with the sort of darkly incisive love songs that are Hersh's stock-in-trade. "Your Ghost," a gorgeous and eerie duet with Michael Stipe that qualifies as Hersh's one modest hit, anchors an album's worth of guitar and piano ballads. Though the songs' sparse arrangements served them well, Hersh released *Strings* soon after, an EP of outtakes and retakes that refashioned some of *Makers'* starkest tracks into chamber music pieces, with a jaunty cover of Zeppelin's "When the Levee Breaks" (!) thrown in.

Hersh spent the next few years shuttling between the on-again, off-again Muses and a series of solo records, most of which varied little from *Makers'* bare-bones template of guitar, piano, and cello. *Strange Angels,* like almost all of Hersh's solo work, is alternately dreamy and harrowing, a typically stripped-down and echoey folk record that in its worst moments tends toward Tori Amos–like spaceyness and in its best ("Like You," "Cold Water Coming") recalls *Makers'* strongest tracks.

Hersh plugged in for 1999's *Sky Motel,* using drums, electric guitars, and keyboards to create a buzzing, Museslike rock album that hits ("Fog," "White Trash Moon") more often than it misses. Hersh played almost all the instruments on the characteristically strange *Sunny Border Blue,* a dark, ambient folk album that boasts all the tangled wordplay fans have reasonably come to expect, with trumpets and a cover of Cat Stevens' "Trouble." With its emphasis on acoustic guitars and pianos, 2003's *The Grotto,* released the same day as the Muses' self-titled reunion disc, is more reminiscent of Hersh's Makers-era solo recordings than anything else in her catalogue. It's affecting and lovely, and unlike some of Hersh's other solo albums, it's not just for completists.   —A.S.

John Hiatt

★★★½	Hangin' Around the Observatory (Epic, 1974)
★★★	Overcoats (Epic, 1975)
★★★★	Slug Line (MCA, 1979)
★★★	Two Bit Monsters (MCA, 1980)
★★	All of a Sudden (Geffen, 1982)
★★★★	Riding With the King (Geffen, 1983)
★★★	Warming Up to the Ice Age (Geffen, 1985)
★★★½	Bring the Family (A&M, 1987)
★★★★	Slow Turning (A&M, 1988)
★★½	Stolen Moments (A&M, 1990)
★★★	Perfectly Good Guitar (A&M, 1993)
★★½	Hiatt Comes Alive at Budokan? (A&M, 1994)
★★★	Walk On (Capitol, 1995)
★★★	Living a Little, Laughing a Little (Raven, 1996)
★★★★	The Best of John Hiatt (Capitol, 1998)
★★★½	Greatest Hits: The A&M Years: '87–'94 (A&M, 1998)
★★½	Crossing Muddy Waters (Vanguard, 2000)
★★★	The Tiki Bar Is Open (Vanguard, 2001)
★★★★	Anthology (Hip-O, 2001)

He stood right at the brink of something bigger for so damn long that you can't really blame John Hiatt for finally sitting back and relaxing on his last decade or so of records. This Indiana-born singer/songwriter has a plethora of slightly neurotic gems sprinkled throughout his bumpy career: witty 'n' warm love songs that have provided hits for Three Dog Night ("Sure As I'm Sittin' Here," from *Hangin' Around the Observatory*) and Bonnie Raitt ("Thing Called Love," from *Bring the Family*). Stylistic uncertainty and a wavering vocal attack marred even the best of Hiatt's own albums, though several have much to recommend them and none (save the Tony Visconti–produced synth-pop disaster *All of a Sudden*) are outright duds. The Epic albums (*Observatory* and *Overcoats*) are his most country-oriented, though Hiatt would return to Nashville in the mid-'80s after a new wave–inspired spell. "Slug Line" failed to establish Hiatt as the American Elvis Costello, but the rangier, nervously rockin' accompaniment accentuates the slightly twisted hooks of "You're My Love Interest," "Radio Girl," and the title track. Despite his flair for sardonic rockers, Hiatt also evinces a talent for disarmingly pretty ballads with "Washable Ink" (exquisitely covered by the Neville Brothers a few years later). "Two Bit Monsters" is a somewhat pallid followup in the same mode; "Pink Bedroom" (later claimed by Rosanne Cash) is the only true keeper in the pile. Hiatt's wicked sense of humor comes to the fore on the confident "Riding With the King," bolstered by the producing and bass-thumping presence of Nick Lowe. The double-edged title track and "She Loves the Jerk" cut far beyond the surface yuks.

Typically, Hiatt follows up this artistic turning point with another shaky holding-pattern album: On *Warming Up to the Ice Age,* a heavy-handed AOR mix sabotages sterling heartbreak sagas like "The Usual" and "She Said the Same Things to Me." Recorded with a band consisting of Lowe, Ry Cooder, and drummer Jim Keltner, *Bring the Family* greatly benefits from their loose, spacious tone and bluesy input. Not quite the breakthrough impatient fans and critics hyped it as, *Bring the Family* is still one of Hiatt's most consistent efforts. Hiatt reaches a mature peak on *Slow Turning,* recorded with his tight regular road band; the heartfelt hearth-and-home scenarios ("Georgia Rae," "Is Anybody There?") lend contrast and depth to the gleefully perverse stompers ("Drive South," "Trudy & Dave," "Tennessee Plates"). But when Hiatt kicks off the too-satisfied "Stolen Moments" by declaring himself "unworthy" of his woman's "real fine love," his self-deprecating gift starts to resemble a glib automatic reaction.

By the time the '90s rolled around, there was no sense in complaining about Hiatt's gargly voice—either you accepted it or you'd already moved on. But his '90s output didn't add too much to his canon—*Perfectly Good Guitar* sounded like the work of a crank who happened to glance at the TV over the bar between sets and catch Nirvana on *SNL*. Among the compilations, Hip-O's *Anthology* is the most comprehensive, Capitol's *Best of* the most consistent. But even here Hiatt's a victim of his own success—he'd have less money in the bank if Bonnie Raitt and Roseanne Cash hadn't seen fit to cover him, but because they did, his own versions of songs like "Thing Called Love" and "The Way We Make a Broken Heart" seem unnecessary.   —M.C./K.H.

Faith Hill

- ★★ Take Me as I Am (Warner Bros., 1994)
- ★½ It Matters to Me (Warner Bros., 1995)
- ★★ Faith (Warner Bros., 1998)
- ★★ Breathe (Warner Bros., 1999)
- ★★½ There You'll Be: The Best of Faith Hill (Warner Bros., 2001)
- ★ Cry (Warner Bros., 2002)

The C&W industry regularly throws a bunch of ingenues at the charts to see what sticks. In 1993, Faith Hill stuck. "Wild One" was #1 for four weeks—an all-but-unheard-of feat for a country gal at the time—and she consolidated her star power with a big-voiced rehash of "Piece of My Heart." However, she didn't have career security until after she conveniently traded in producer-boyfriend Scott Hendricks for hunky Tim McGraw. Nor did McGraw—their connubial synergy has buoyed both their careers, and the pair have reigned as Homecoming King and Queen of Nashville High ever since. They could be a great testament to the joys of married sex if only their duets weren't so DOA. You'd think the two had never fucked with the lights on.

There's no such thing as "real country"—the stuff's been incorporating pop styles since back when they called it hillbilly music—but inauthenticity can be as much a drag as musty traditionalism. The singles Hill's crossed over on—the giddy "This Kiss," the swooning "Breathe," the ditzy "Way You Love Me"—have been such transcendent trifles you might be tempted to dig a little deeper. Bad idea. Given space to stretch out, Hill is oppressive, bombastic, and conniving, in many ways more Mariah than Shania. *Cry* marks Hill's final descent into schlock. On the cover, she looks like she's been greased down for a *Maxim* shoot, and the Instamatic grooves make her no more R&B than David Gray or Phil Collins. She's coated in Teflon. Any time someone whispers she's gotten a little slutty, she flashes her wedding band. Every time someone intimates that she's sold out, she just smiles a little wider and sweeter. Say what you will about Nashville's bland hat acts—at least they're gone in a flash. Faith Hill ain't going nowhere.   —K.H.

Lauryn Hill

- ★★★★½ The Miseducation of Lauryn Hill (Columbia, 1998)
- ★★½ MTV Unplugged 2.0 (Columbia, 2002)

Though the press made much of her balancing the demands of being in one of the most popular hip-hop groups of the mid-'90s and still trying to complete her undergraduate studies at Columbia University, to anyone with eyes and ears, it was clear that Lauryn Hill wasn't long for the Fugees or, for that matter, for school. Instead, she poured her energies into her solo debut, *The Miseducation of Lauryn Hill,* as earnest, unpretentious, and pleasantly sloppy an album as any woman of the hip-hop generation has ever made. Hill was always an outstanding rapper, but *Miseducation* showed her to be a more-than-competent singer as well on songs like "Doo Wop (That Thing)" and "Everything Is Everything." By turns socially engaged, personally revelatory, and, in the hip-hop tradition, a bit arrogant, *Miseducation* managed to filter hip-hop through a womanist lens, resulting in an album that appealed to an improbably wide spectrum of listeners.

Miseducation made Hill a superstar of epic proportions: She earned five Grammys and found herself at the focal point of hip-hop's crossover into the mainstream. But by all accounts, the pressure on her was overwhelming, and she quickly slipped out of the public eye. In her downtime, Hill renounced her old image, radically altering her wardrobe and her hairstyle; rediscovered a profound spirituality; and grappled with problems with both her manager, whom she fired, and her husband, Rohan Marley, one of Bob and Rita's sons. When Hill finally reemerged on *MTV Unplugged,* she was a woman transformed. The two-disc recorded version of the concert captures the performance in all its eccentricity. In between songs, Hill meanders through a set of spoken interludes, in which she discusses spirituality, personal responsibility, and her own struggles with fame. The songs themselves, though they hew to the same subject matter, aren't any more focused. "Adam Lives in Theory" and "Mystery of Iniquity" are just plain confusing, a bizarre set of statements from an artist whose shtick was once self-assuredness. The sentiment of the set, both explicit and implied, can be summed up in one song title: "I Gotta Find Peace of Mind." True enough.   —J.C.

Robyn Hitchcock

- ★★★½ Black Snake Dîamond Rôle (1981; Relativity, 1986)
- ★★½ Groovy Decoy (1982; Relativity, 1986)
- ★★★ Eaten by Her Own Dinner (EP) (1982; Midnight Music, 1986)

★★½ I Often Dream of Trains (1984; Rhino, 1995)
★★½ Invisible Hitchcock (Relativity, 1986)
★★★½ Eye (Twin/Tone, 1990)
★★★ Gravy Deco (The Complete Groovy Decay/Decoy Sessions) (Rhino, 1995)
★★★★ Moss Elixir (Warner Bros., 1996)
★★★½ Uncorrected Personality Traits (Rhino, 1997)
★★★ Storefront Hitchcock (Warner Bros., 1998)
★★★★½ Jewels for Sophia (Warner Bros., 2000)
★★★ A Star for Bram (PAF, 2000)
★★★★ Robyn Sings (PAF, 2002)
★★★½ Luxor (PAF, 2003)

Robyn Hitchcock & the Egyptians

★★★★ Fegmania! (Slash, 1985)
★★★★½ Gotta Let This Hen Out (Relativity, 1985)
★★★ Exploding in Silence (EP) (Relativity, 1986)
★★★★½ Element of Light (Relativity, 1986)
★★★ Globe of Frogs (A&M, 1988)
★★★★ Queen Elvis (A&M, 1989)
★★★★½ Perspex Island (A&M, 1991)
★★★★ Respect (A&M, 1993)
★★★★★ Greatest Hits (A&M, 1996)

One of rock & roll's most gifted eccentrics, Soft Boy frontman Robyn Hitchcock at his best evokes much of the same benign insanity that marked John Lennon's whimsicality—at times, his songs even evoke a similar sense of melody. His first solo album, *Black Snake Dîamond Rôle*, picks up pretty much where his work with the Soft Boys left off, even to the point of employing most of his former bandmates. Still, this suits the material, particularly the manic "Brenda's Iron Sledge" and the lovely, semipsyche-delic "Acid Bird."

Working with a pickup band, Hitchcock then recorded *Groovy Decay*, using ex-Gong guitarist Steve Hillage as producer. Dissatisfied with the result, Hitchcock eventually substituted a revamped version entitled *Groovy Decoy;* although some of the songs are agreeably melodic (especially "America" and "The Cars She Used to Drive"), neither the Hillage record-ings nor the Matthew Seligman–produced remakes are in any way essential. But if you're curious, the whole mess was compiled into *Gravy Deco (The Com-plete Groovy Decay/Decoy Sessions)*. After a two-year hiatus, Hitchcock returned with the drolly titled *I Often Dream of Trains*. Recorded without a band, its lean, guitar-and/or-piano arrangements leave it sounding less like a finished album than a collection of song demos. Thus, although the songs are wonder-ful—particularly "Sounds Great When You're Dead" and the barbershop harmony number "Uncorrected Personality Traits"—the performances rarely do them justice.

Eventually, Hitchcock got tired of being solo and recruited the Soft Boys' original rhythm team of Morris Windsor and Andy Metcalfe (plus keyboardist Roger Jackson) for a new band, the Egyptians. That this was the right thing to do becomes obvious with the first notes of *Fegmania!*, which showcases Hitchcock's cheerful insanity through authoritatively played, tunefully surreal numbers such as "Egyptian Cream" (a perverse fertility song) and "The Man With the Lightbulb Head" (a loopy monster-movie send-up). Even better, Hitchcock and band followed *Feg-mania!* with the spirited concert album *Gotta Get This Hen Out*, which not only righted some of the wrongs done by *I Often Dream of Trains* and *Groovy Decay* by remaking "Sometimes I Wish I Was a Pretty Girl" and "America," but also reclaims the Soft Boys' "Leppo and the Jooves." But Hitchcock and the Egyptians don't really begin to show their true potential until *El-ement of Light*, which augments the usual lyrical whimsy with well-crafted, insinuating melodies such as those to "Winchester," "Lady Waters & the Hooded One," and the homoerotic "Ted, Woody and Junior." (The best of his work to this point is compiled as *Uncorrected Personality Traits*.)

Obviously, others sensed the group's potential, for with *Globe of Frogs*, Hitchcock and the Egyptians made the leap to the majors. Unfortunately, the album doesn't quite live up to the inspired standards of *Element of Light*, for despite the appealing lunacy of "Balloon Man" and the raucous "Sleeping With Your Devil Mask," the album fizzles where it should sizzle. Hitchcock bounces back, though, with *Queen Elvis*, which includes the expected flashes of insanity (for in-stance, the wicked wit of "The Devil's Coachman") but puts the bulk of its energy into tuneful tidbits such as "Wax Doll" or the chiming, Byrdslike "Madonna of the Wasps." Hitchcock hadn't gone completely com-mercial, however, and had by this point assembled enough musical oddities to fill an album; hence, *Eye*, which takes the same stripped-down approach as *I Often Dream of Trains*, although without its predeces-sor's lo-fi sound. It's not a great album, but Hitchcock does seem to need an outlet for his apparently relent-less creativity. After all, up to this point he had been regularly releasing occasional collections such as *Eaten by Her Own Dinner* and *Exploding in Silence;* indeed, *Invisible Hitchcock* compiles more than a dozen songs from such projects.

Hitchcock compensates for those underproduced efforts with the surprisingly slick and accessible *Per-spex Island*. What makes this such a delight isn't that its conventional love songs—"So You Think You're in Love," for instance—are so infectious, but that Hitch-cock's melodic standards are the same regardless of lyrical content. *Respect,* which turned out to be his final album with the Egyptians, is a somewhat more low-key affair, but it doesn't lack for verve—the wacky "Yip Song" sounds as if it was inspired by a four-year-old after too many cookies. From "The Wreck of the Arthur Lee" to "Then You're Dead," it's classic Hitchcock. It's worth owning pretty much all of the A&M albums, but for those on a budget the sterling *Greatest Hits* includes most of the highlights.

Hitchcock went back to playing solo, with a revolving cast of accompanists, with *Moss Elixir,* a mildly folkie effort long on whimsy but packed with melodic punch, especially on "Sinister But She Was Happy" and "The Devil's Radio." *Jewels for Sophia* reflects an unexpected L.A. influence and features such big marquee names as Peter Buck, Jon Brion, and Grant Lee Phillips. Its sound is more traditionally rock & roll than any of Hitchcock's non-Egyptian projects, and tracks such as "Sally Was a Legend" and "You Got a Sweet Mouth on You, Baby" are sassy, nonsensical, and nearly irresistible. Even the outtakes from those sessions, collected on *A Star for Bram,* are pretty fab. But just as Jonathan Demme's concert film *Storefront Hitchcock* failed to generate any buzz outside the music world—or, to be honest, much buzz within it—*Jewels* didn't set the world on fire, and Hitchcock slid back into indie semiobscurity. At least he has his freedom, and makes the most of it on *Robyn Sings,* a serious sort of gag album in which he covers a number of Dylan songs, including the infamous "Royal Albert Hall" bootleg. The mostly acoustic *Luxor* returns to the stripped-down sound of *I Often Dream of Trains* and maintains the usual standards of inspired whimsy through the likes of "Penelope's Angles" and "Solpadeine." —J.D.C.

The Hives

   ★★★   Barely Legal (Gearhead, 1997)
★★★★½ Veni Vidi Vicious (2000; Reprise, 2002)
  ★★★★ Your New Favourite Band (Poptones, 2002)
  ★★★½ Tyrannosaurus Hives (Interscope, 2004)

Coming straight out of Fagersta, Sweden, the Hives formed in 1993 but will be forever known as members of the Class of 2002, when rock was officially declared Back. (See also White Stripes, Strokes, Vines.) On their 1997 debut full-length, *Barely Legal,* it's clear that high-energy '60s garage rock is the foundation idea, but they're tighter and heavier than most of their brethren, like they've absorbed as much Big Black as the Seeds. Singer Howlin' Pelle Almqvist has a knack for good put-downs and pithy social commentary sans self-righteousness. Their rock aliases (Chris Danger-

ous, Dr. Matt Destruction, etc.) and policy of dressing only in black-and-white slacks and button-down shirts made them memorable, but their 2002 return to the studio, *Veni Vidi Vicious,* further made clear they were thinking a lot about this whole allegedly party-hearty, nonthinking genre. "Die, All Right!" is anticorporate garage punk worthy of the Peanuts dance, and the singles are killers—"Main Offender" and the MTV hit "Hate to Say I Told You So." The band's signal strength is the ferocity they bring to every single tune, as if they couldn't possibly be more psyched to be the Hives. *Your New Favourite Band* is on Alan McGee's Poptones label and collects four songs from both full-lengths plus various tracks from EPs and a generous selection of videos. —S.F.J.

Hole

    ★★   Pretty on the Inside (Caroline, 1991)
★★★★★ Live Through This (Geffen, 1994)
   ★★★   Ask for It (EP) (Geffen, 1995)
    ★★   Celebrity Skin (Geffen, 1998)

Courtney Love

    ★★   America's Sweetheart (Virgin, 2004)

Well, you wouldn't want to share a bathroom with her, but let the record show that Courtney Love did, in fact, make a great album once, and even her many enemies must concede, lest they look like total tools, the achievement of *Live Through This,* the album she released only days before the dead body of her husband, Kurt Cobain, was found. Five years earlier or later, her music would have been unthinkable on a major label, let alone the radio. But in 1994 she defined mainstream rock.

Love rips herself apart on *Live Through This,* while backed by a tunefully anonymous grunge band. She howls about needing to be the girl with the most cake, veering from rage-queen guitar explosions such as "Violet" and "Miss World" to the folk-rock beauty of "Softer, Softest" and "Doll Parts." "I've got a blister from/Touching everything I see," Love snarls, and she left her share of blisters on us as well, voicing her female audience's most forbidden fantasies of power and freedom. After Cobain's death, the songs seemed sadder than ever—in terms of emotional intensity, *Live Through This* is a landmark, if not a land mine.

Nothing else in Hole's recorded work has any of the same fire. *Pretty on the Inside* was just routine indie trashola, unnoticed before Love's 1992 marriage to Cobain. *Ask for It* is a stopgap EP of rarities released in the wake of *Live Through This.* Love has repeatedly denied the rumors that Cobain helped her write *Live Through This,* but she hasn't done herself any favors by failing to write new songs. *Celebrity Skin* took four years, with writing help from Smashing Pumpkins' Billy Corgan. But although the title song was great ("when I wake up in my makeup"—nice one), even die-hard fans had trouble finding any songs buried in all the slick verbiage and production goop. It was the sort of made-in-L.A. meatball that could only have come from a professional rock contractor, in the tradition of Rod Stewart's *Body Wishes*, Mick Jagger's *Primitive Cool*, or Stevie Nicks' *Rock a Little*.

By now, Love was concentrating on her movie career, and what can you say about an artist who could have chased Bob Dylan but decided to chase Juliette Lewis instead? Love spent the next few years suing the surviving members of Nirvana, successfully preventing fans from hearing any of the band's unreleased material. She returned to music with the heavily hyped solo debut *America's Sweetheart*, but it was ignored by fans and apparently unnoticed by the artist herself. Love seems to crave the spotlight, and she's welcome to it, but *Live Through This* reminds you she once had something to say there. —R.S.

Billie Holiday

★★★½   The Billie Holiday Songbook (1952; PolyGram, 1990)

★★★½   Lady Sings the Blues (1954; Verve, 1991)

★★★½   All or Nothing at All (1955; PolyGram, 1995)

★★★½   Songs for Distingué Lovers (1956; PolyGram, 1997)

★★★½   Body and Soul (1957; Verve, 2002)

★★★★   Lady in Satin (1958; Columbia/Legacy, 2002)

★★★★   Last Recordings (Verve, 1959)

★★★   The Silver Collection (Uni/Verve, 1984)

★★★   Compact Jazz: Billie Holiday (Uni/Verve, 1987)

★★★★★   The Quintessential Billie Holiday, Vol. 1 (1933–1935) (Columbia, 1987)

★★★★★   The Quintessential Billie Holiday, Vol. 2 (1936) (Columbia, 1987)

★★★★½   Billie's Blues (MCA, 1988)

★★★★★   The Quintessential Billie Holiday, Vol. 3 (1936–1937) (Columbia, 1988)

★★★★★   The Quintessential Billie Holiday, Vol. 4 (1937) (Columbia, 1988)

★★★★★   The Quintessential Billie Holiday, Vol. 5 (1937–1938) (Columbia, 1988)

★★★★★   The Quintessential Billie Holiday, Vol. 6 (1938) (Columbia, 1990)

★★★★★   The Quintessential Billie Holiday, Vol. 7 (1938–1939) (Columbia, 1990)

★★★★   Billie Holiday Live (Verve, 1990)

★★★★★   The Quintessential Billie Holiday, Vol. 8 (1939–1940) (Columbia, 1991)

★★★★★   The Quintessential Billie Holiday, Vol. 9 (1940–1942) (Columbia, 1991)

★★★★½   Lady in Autumn: The Best of the Verve Years (Verve, 1991)

★★★★★   The Legacy (1933–1958) (Columbia, 1991)

★★★★★   The Complete Decca Recordings (GRP, 1991)

★★★★   Billie's Blues (Blue Note, 1991)

★★★   Billie Holiday Live (Uni/Verve, 1991)

★★★   I Like Jazz: The Essence of Billie Holiday (Columbia, 1991)

★★★   Billie's Best (Verve, 1992)

★★★½   The Essential Billie Holiday: Songs of Lost Love (Uni/Mercury/PolyGram, 1992)

★★★   Control Booth Series, Vol. 1 (1940–1941) (Storyville, 1993)

★★★   Solitude: The Billie Holiday Story, Vol. 2 (PolyGram, 1993)

★★★   16 Most Requested Songs (Sony, 1993)

★★★½   Verve Jazz Masters 12: Billie Holiday (Verve, 1994)

★★★½   First Issue: Great American Songbook (PolyGram, 1994)

★★★½   Recital By: The Billie Holiday Story, Vol. 3 (PolyGram, 1994)

★★★   Jazz 'Round Midnight: Billie Holiday (PolyGram, 1994)

★★★½   Jazz at the Philharmonic (PolyGram, 1994)

★★   God Bless the Child (Universal Special Products, 1994)

★★★★★   The Complete Billie Holiday on Verve (1945–1949) (PolyGram, 1995)

★★★½   Lady Sings the Blues: The Billie Holiday Story, Vol. 4 (PolyGram, 1995)

★★★★   Verve Jazz Masters 47: Billie Holiday Sings Standards (Verve, 1995)

★★★½   Music for Torching: The Billie Holiday Story, Vol. 5 (PolyGram, 1995)

★★★½   At Carnegie Hall: The Billie Holiday Story, Vol. 6 (PolyGram, 1995)

★★★   Billie Holiday's Greatest Hits (GRP, 1995)

★★★   Control Booth Series, Vol. 2 (Storyville, 1995)

★★★   Swing! Brother, Swing! (Sony Special Products, 1995)

★★★   Love Songs (Sony, 1996)

★★★½   This Is Jazz, Vol. 15 (Sony, 1996)

★★★   The Ultimate Billie Holiday (PolyGram, 1997)

★★★½   Priceless Jazz Collection (GRP, 1997)

★★★★   The Complete Commodore Recordings (GRP, 1997)

★★★½   This Is Jazz, Vol. 32: Standards (Sony, 1998)

★★★★★   Billie Holiday's Greatest Hits (Columbia/Legacy, 1998)

★★★★★   The Quintessential Billie Holiday: Vols. 1, 2, 3, (Sony, 1998)

★★★★ The Commodore Master Takes (PolyGram, 2000)

★★★★★ Ken Burns Jazz Collection: Billie Holiday (Verve, 2000)

★★★★★ Lady Day: The Complete Billie Holiday on Columbia (1933–1944) (Sony, 2001)

★★★★★ Lady Day: The Best of Billie Holiday (Columbia/Legacy, 2001)

★★ The Best of Billie Holiday (EMI-Capitol, 2001)

★★ Singin' the Blues (MCA Special Products, 2002)

★★★½ A Musical Romance (Columbia/Legacy, 2002)

★★★½ Blue Billie (Columbia/Legacy, 2002)

★★★½ Lady Day Swings (Columbia/Legacy, 2002)

★★★½ The Golden Years, Vols. 1–2 (Columbia, 2002)

★★★½ Billie Holiday for Lovers (Universal, 2002)

★★★ Singin' the Blues (Universal, 2002)

★★★ Love for Sale (Prestige Elite, 2002)

★★★★ The Billie Holiday Collection, Vol. 1 (Sony, 2003)

★★★★ The Billie Holiday Collection, Vol. 2 (Sony, 2003)

★★★★ The Billie Holiday Collection, Vol. 3 (Sony, 2003)

★★★★ The Billie Holiday Collection, Vol. 4 (Sony, 2003)

★★★★ The Golden Years, Vols. 1–2 (Columbia, 2003)

Epitomizing as absolutely as does Charlie Parker the saga of the jazz genius as tragic soul, Billie Holiday's biography reads like a Dostoyevsky novel: Raped at 10 years old by a neighbor (some accounts say "cousin"), she was sent to a home for wayward girls; in her teens she spent four months in jail for prostitution. Starting as a singer in New York's rough-and-tumble speakeasies of the early '30s, she was famous by mid-decade. Heroin and a hard-luck love life began wearing her down in the '40s; with her success, too, came the pressures of song pluggers and aesthetic compromise—all of Tin Pan Alley's hack songwriters dogged Holiday to sing their tunes. Her personality a tense mix of the rebel and the victim, Holiday's life was wholly struggle; self-destructive, incandescent, she died at 44. And she left music that, at its finest, continues to work like a depth charge—few singers of any genre can approach its emotional intensity; few singers, either, command her skill.

Remarkably, Holiday's voice wasn't the natural force that some stars (Sarah Vaughan, Aretha Franklin, even Dionne Warwick) have been given. Instead, her greatness lies in how she deployed it; by 1937, she was in full control of her style. Hitting notes against the beat the way all jazz horn players do (an early influence was Louis Armstrong's trumpet), she shaped rhythmic lines ingeniously—and interpreted lyrics with intuitive savvy. Humor, sass, toughness, and yearning all formed part of her staggering emotive repertoire; Holiday was expert both at laying bare the essence of a great lyric and at tossing off a mediocre one with such happy virtuosity that the words were elevated into pure swinging sound.

A number of massive, worthwhile compilations cover Holiday. Columbia's *Quintessential* series chronicles her work in the 1933–42 heyday; her sessions are grounded on the elegant piano work of Teddy Wilson, and her range of sidemen extends to such legends as clarinetist Artie Shaw and saxophonist Lester Young. (She cut a few sides, too, with the orchestras of both Benny Goodman and Count Basie.) *Volumes 3, 4,* and *5* are the crème de la crème: Billie at the peak of her powers. *Legacy* does a good job of condensing the nine sets of the *Quintessential* series, including such standouts as "I Must Have That Man," "Having Myself a Time," "God Bless the Child," "Summertime," and "Long Gone Blues." Not only does Columbia repackage the first three of the series in a handsome set, all of her Columbia recordings are available on the gargantuan *Lady Day: The Complete Billie Holiday on Columbia.* In 2002, the label subdivided its offerings further, focusing alternately on bluesy, romantic, and swinging Holiday. A year later, it reconfigured the catalogue yet again, this time chronologically. The Commodore period covers the years 1939–44, with Billie swinging staunchly. Her work for Decca was string-laden and lush; with its selections recorded between 1944 and 1950, GRP's *The Complete Decca Recordings* gives us Holiday in her middle period—not quite so swaggering as during her late-'30s reign nor so powerfully desperate as she became later on.

Holiday's later work continues to divide listeners—some jazz purists scorn her experiments with richer string arrangements, others consider her interpretive approach occasionally melodramatic or strained, and some fans of Billie's early, clearer tone find disturbing the roughness that comes into her voice in the mid-'40s. Listen to *The Complete Billie Holiday on Verve,* a 10-record collection that documents her 1946–59 period, however, and discover remarkable music that, for all its hit-and-miss technique (sometimes poorly chosen material, sometimes overwhelming instrumentation), is an astonishing spiritual autobiography—at times, Holiday's singing is the very voice of pain, loss, and hard experience. *Lady in Autumn* encapsulates the Verve years, and it's a bittersweet triumph; in fact, it's often against the lush backdrop of a full orchestra that she achieves her most eerie effect—her singing is acid splashed against velvet. Those who appreciate the fearsome, agonized Holiday might also check out *Lady in Satin* and *The Last Recordings;* Ray Ellis' somewhat soupy arrangements serve (who knows how intentionally?) to set off Lady Day's singing in ways that can provoke feelings of real terror.

At Carnegie Hall is memorable live Holiday. Of the superabundance of Holiday repackagings, perhaps the best place to start is the *Ken Burns Jazz* disc. The songs are very intelligently selected and the chronological range is generous. —P.E.

The Hollies

★★★ The Hollies (EMI, 1965)
★★ Evolution (1967; Sundazed, 1999)
★★½ Dear Eloise/King Midas in Reverse (1967; Sundazed, 1997)
★★ Moving Finger (1970; Sundazed, 1997)
★★★ The Hollies' Greatest Hits (Epic, 1973)
★★ Live Hits (Polydor, 1977)
★★★ The Best of the Hollies, Vol. 2 (EMI America, 1983)
★★★ Epic Anthology (Epic, 1990)
★★ Magic Touch (Hollywood, 1992)
★★ The Midas Touch (Sony Special Products, 1995)
★★★ Archive Alive! (Archive Alive, 1997)
★★ Take Two (Sony Special Products, 2001)
★★ Super Hits (Legacy, 2001)
★★★ Classic Masters (Capitol, 2002)
★★★ The Hollies' Greatest Hits (Sony, 2002)
★★½ What Goes Around (Wounded Bird, 2002)

The Hollies' mid-'60s hits were British Invasion pop of the cute school—sweet-voiced, upbeat, and ultra-crafted. Vocalists Allan Clarke and Graham Nash crooned about teenagers in love on hit singles including "Stop Stop Stop" and "Dear Eloise," in addition to songs by non-Hollies such as Graham Gouldman (later a founding member of 10cc), who provided such valentines as "Here I Go Again," "Look Through Any Window," and "Bus Stop." The band made massive singles but couldn't stretch enough for albums, and bombed when trying anything difficult (their 1969 album of Dylan covers, *Hollies Sing Dylan,* for example). Their better albums have been reissued by Sundazed, and they range from the semipsychedelia of *Evolution* and *Dear Eloise/King Midas in Reverse* to the slick pop of *Moving Finger.* Nash departed for Crosby, Stills & Nash in 1968, but the Hollies, with ex–Swinging Blue Jean Terry Sylvester added on second lead vocal, persevered. The '70s found them scor-

ing big with "Long Cool Woman," "He Ain't Heavy, He's My Brother," and "The Air That I Breathe." Of the abundant compilations, *Epic Anthology* and *Classic Masters* are the strongest. *Archive Alive!* features a fine 1983 concert: It's amazing that they could pull off those complex harmonies live. *What Goes Around* is a nice reunion album of almost all the original members on the 20th anniversary of the Hollies' founding. —P.E.

Buddy Holly

★★★★½ The Chirping Crickets (1957; MCA, 2004)
★★★★★ The Buddy Holly Collection (MCA, 1993)
★★★★½ Greatest Hits (MCA, 1996)
★★★ The Best of Buddy Holly: The Millennium Collection (MCA, 1999)

Buddy Holly was one of rock's first great singer/songwriters, a double threat who inspired the Beatles and countless other recording artists to take control of their own repertoires; he was also a product of country music who made that music's influence on rock & roll clear. But those achievements pale next to Holly's towering achievement: a collection of songs that have become a part of rock's DNA and still sound fresh today, including "That'll Be the Day," "Peggy Sue," "Maybe Baby," "Everyday," "Not Fade Away," "Oh Boy," "Rave On," and more. That run started in 1956, when, having been dropped by Decca Records after the commercial failure of his work with Nashville producer Owen Bradley, Holly took the song "That'll Be the Day" to producer Norman Petty's studio in Clovis, New Mexico. Holly—who had grown up in a musical family and who was performing, writing, and making home recordings in his mid-teens—and drummer Jerry Allison had written the song after being inspired by a line of dialogue spoken by John Wayne's character in director John Ford's classic 1956 film *The Searchers.* With Allison, bassist Jerry Welborn, and new rhythm guitarist Niki Sullivan joining him in the studio, Holly fired off the opening licks and came roaring in with a no-compromises vocal that underscores the narrator's determination to steer a rocky relationship's tenuous course. Holly works the verses masterfully for dramatic effect, and behind him the band charges hard, especially Allison on drums, and Holly adds some razor-edged guitar solos to boot. In May 1957, following some tricky contractual maneuvering, Brunswick, a Decca subsidiary, released "That'll Be the Day" b/w "I'm Looking for Someone to Love" (another Holly original, this one featuring a tough guitar solo rooted in the licks from "Holly Hop"), and by August it was sitting at #1 on the singles chart.

Over the next year, Crickets singles made the Top 20 three times, hit the Top 30 once, and hit #10 in December 1957 with one of Holly's most ferocious performances, "Oh Boy." However, a month ahead of "Oh Boy" came Holly's first solo hit, "Peggy Sue," which topped out at #3 in November. In their brief chart history, Crickets recordings were far more successful than Holly's solo efforts—he was in the Top 20 only once more, in March 1959, a month after his death, with a lilting ballad Paul Anka had written for him, "It Doesn't Matter Anymore." But whereas the Crickets' recordings emphasized the big beat and the basic band, Holly's solo work is where the visionary in him surfaced most dramatically. Disc two of *The Buddy Holly Collection* is virtually a showcase for the artist Holly was on his way to becoming when his life ended in a 1959 plane crash that also claimed the lives of Ritchie Valens and the Big Bopper. The addition of ace guitarist Tommy Allsup to the Crickets lineup (replacing a road-weary Niki Sullivan) freed Holly to focus on other aspects of his performance and sound, so great was his confidence in Allsup's ability to fashion commanding instrumental statements. Sometimes a simple new touch made all the difference, such as pianist C. W. Kendall pounding out ebullient boogie-woogie riffs on his own "Little Baby," a cut from Holly's debut solo album in 1958; piano, in fact, figures prominently in the sound Holly was constructing in those days, as a softening touch, for lack of a better term, even in the midst of an uptempo workout such as "Fool's Paradise," a 1958 cut featuring Vi Petty (Norman's wife) on the 88s. The "Fool's Paradise" session also yielded "Take Your Time," a Holly-Petty collaboration marked by infectious cross-rhythms accented by Allison's thumping on a cardboard box, Holly's softly strummed acoustic guitar, and Petty's robust fills on Hammond organ. It wasn't a single, but in 1958 no rock & roll record really sounded like "Take Your Time," and it would be another four years, in 1962, before Booker T. & the MG's brought an organ-rich sound into the mainstream. The first appearance of a stuttering sax solo on a Holly record came via the acknowledged copyright owner of the style, King Curtis, on the lively, R&B-flavored take on Curtis' own "Reminiscing," from 1958. Recording at the Pythian Temple in New York City in June 1958, Holly took "Early in the Morning," cowritten by Bobby Darin, into gospel territory, with a hearty, free-flowing vocal as the Helen Way Singers provide exultant responsive background vocals and jazz stalwarts Sam "the Man" Taylor (saxophone) and Panama Francis (drums) set a propulsive pace. "True Love Ways," another New York cut from 1958, is as lush and dreamy as any mainstream pop song of the day,

with romantic allure courtesy of Taylor's seductive tenor sax fills, a beautifully arranged string section from Dick Jacobs' orchestra, and a gentle vocal from Holly in which he dispenses with all his eccentricities and sings his vows of enduring love straight and with powerful conviction. Its timelessness is rooted in its simplicity: Despite its grandiose aspirations, the production doesn't call attention to itself, but rather serves to heighten the message the lyrics impart, to the point where a listener could almost regard it as an acoustic ballad. The same approach worked to equal emotional impact in Holly's final studio session, in January 1959, on an incandescent heartbreaker written by Felice and Boudleaux Bryant, "Raining in My Heart."

The amazing journey that is *Collection*'s disc two concludes with four home recordings Holly made in January 1959. The original acoustic recordings have since been overdubbed by Norman Petty, with the Fireballs adding additional instrumentation and backing vocals. All four of these songs are Holly originals, and rank as some of his finest lyric writing: "Peggy Sue Got Married" is no lightweight sequel, but a deeply felt lament over a lost love done to a driving arrangement that subtly evokes the sound of "Peggy Sue"; "Crying Waiting Hoping," which gained some measure of fame when Marshall Crenshaw performed it in portraying Holly in the film bio of Ritchie Valens, *La Bamba,* is about as good a statement as anyone has come up with to describe the hope-against-hope a jilted lover experiences in the aftermath of a breakup; the stolid rhythm and stop-time measures of "Learning the Game" point up the emotional toll love can exact on a vulnerable heart; "What to Do" is a midtempo evocation, gently sung with complete understanding, of postbreakup identity loss.

Over the years, the amount of Buddy Holly in print has expanded and contracted, depending on the vagaries of the record labels. Apart from *The Buddy Holly Collection*, the disc to own is *Greatest Hits*. This 18-song entry is all choice cuts, from "That'll Be the Day" to "Raining in My Heart" and all stops in between, solo and band, flat-out rockers to breathtaking ballads, plus inspired album cuts such as "Fool's Paradise" and "Heartbeat" that offer an intelligent overview of the artist's oeuvre.

Also, don't overlook *The Chirping Crickets*, the only album Holly made with his band before he was given headline billing. Unlike many long players of its day, *The Chirping Crickets* is not a couple of hit singles and throwaway filler. Each cut is a marvel of inspired playing and intelligent singing. The familiar tracks are rather amazing: "Oh Boy," "Not Fade Away," "That'll Be the Day," "Maybe Baby" (which sounds like the basic text for the next decade's British Invasion). There's also a cover of Chuck Willis' R&B gem "It's Too Late" that Holly makes his own; a nice turn on "Send Me Some Lovin'," originally recorded by Little Richard; and an impassioned take on "An Empty Cup (and a Broken Heart)," one of Roy Orbison's early entries in the tear-stained ballad category.

Lesser inspired but no less inspiring, *The Best of Buddy Holly* is in keeping with MCA's 20th Century Masters series in offering only a taste of an artist's most delectable fare. Though its 10 cuts are above reproach—"That'll Be the Day," "Peggy Sue," "Words of Love," "Rave On," "Raining in My Heart," "True Love Ways," etc.—10 cuts is 10 cuts only. There's so much more to say. But then that sentiment's been true since about, oh, February 3, 1959. —D.M.

Holy Modal Rounders

★★★★½ 1 & 2 (1964; Fantasy, 1999)
★★★½ Live in 1965 (1965; DBK, 2002)
★★★ Indian War Whoop (ESP/Calibre, 1967)
★★★½ The Moray Eels Eat the Holy Modal Rounders (1969; Water, 2002)
★★★½ Bird Song: Live 1971 (1971; Water, 2004)
★★★★★ Have Moicy! (1976; Rounder, 1991)
★★★½ Last Round (1978; Adelphi, 2000)
★★★★ Too Much Fun (Rounder, 1999)
★★★★½ I Make a Wish for a Potato (Rounder Heritage, 2001)

Peter Stampfel is that rarest of all creatures, a modest genius. He has one of the most distinctive voices in American music, a twangy screech that somehow he can actually sing in. What makes him so modest is his conviction that all of the really great American music was done a long time ago, and mostly collected on Harry Smith's *Anthology of American Folk Music*. What makes him a genius is that instead of putting his beloved old-timey music up on some pedestal, he makes it an organic part of his own life experience—which is mostly that of a radical '60s speed freak who appreciates nothing better than a cosmic joke.

When Stampfel hooks up with guitarist Steve Weber, as he has infrequently for a third of a century, they knock off a Holy Modal Rounders album. These are filed as Folk, because their first two albums, now known as *1 & 2*, with Stampfel on fiddle and banjo, are full of public domain songs like "Flop Eared Mule" and "Fishing Blues." But it also has a novelty called "Mr. Spaceman," and prophetic songs by future Rounder Robin Remaily and fellow traveler Michael Hurley. It may have sounded weird way back when, but it sounds fresher than ever today. The recently re-leased *Live in 1965* sounds harsh but kicks the energy up a level, and Stampfel's between-song patter is a plus.

The other '60s Rounders albums are curiosities, conceived as psychedelia and sloppily executed, but there is a rousing "I.W.W. Song" on *Indian War Whoop*, and *The Moral Eels Eat* generates dim-witted glee on pieces like "My Mind Capsized" and "The STP Song." The '70s albums are folkier, but most of the songs are originals and the band has devolved into posthippie counterculture. They seem to be crawling back into print, along with old tapes like *Live in 1965* and *Bird Song: Live 1971*. *Good Taste Is Timeless* is blessed with new liner notes by Stampfel, but both it and *Last Round* are very inconsistent: Some of the best songs ("If You Want to Be a Bird") are remakes, and the inspired titles ("Boobs a Lot," "Snappin' Pussy") aren't as good as you'd hope. Meanwhile, the live tapes add period color, like Stampfel's wit in 1965 and the indiscriminate banging and tooting of their loud 1971 band (seven pieces, including sax).

But *Have Moicy!*, attributed to "Michael Hurley/ The Unholy Modal Rounders/Jeffrey Frederick & the Clamtones," is an improbable masterpiece. The extra songwriters broaden the worldview: Hurley is comfy, Frederick has a bitter streak, and Antonia has her mind on sex and drugs. And every song is quotable, from "oh I see the dishes over there/they fill me with despair" to "I got a jug of wine, Griselda/why should you waste your time in sorrow/hold out your hand and have no fear/if we're caught I'll marry you tomorrow."

Stampfel's albums under his own name are out of print, including *You Must Remember This* (Gert Town, 1995), where he reworks pop chestnuts. But Weber surfaced again for 1999's *Too Much Fun*, where the Rounders returned strongly to traditional material, including some of their own. The Rounder compilation *I Make a Wish for a Potato* tries to synthesize another *Have Moicy!* by slipping tracks from Hurley and Frederick solo albums into a passel of Rounders songs, including one that goes, "Superman's/on the can/contemplating synergy." —T.H.

Hoobastank

★★ Hoobastank (Universal, 2001)
★★ The Reason (Island, 2003)

This well-scrubbed California four-piece combine aggressive new-metal riffs, swooning melodies, pained lyrics of masculine anger and self-pity, and big, happy grooves. It all holds together, in the same way that grunge bands have mixed exuberant music and whiny vocals for years. "Running Away" and "Crawling in the Dark," high-octane and tuneful, with achingly earnest lyrics ("Is there something more than what I've been handed?/I've been crawling in the dark looking for the answer") set the tone for the first album. The followup mostly stays the course, with an increase in the ballad quotient ("The Reason," which became a huge smash) and an unwelcome addition that most of their L.A. rock peers wouldn't touch with a ten-foot pole: Hollywood strings.   —B.S.

John Lee Hooker

- ★★★★ House of the Blues (1959; Chess, 1989)
- ★★★½ I'm John Lee Hooker (1959; Collectables, 2000)
- ★★★½ That's My Story: John Lee Hooker Sings the Blues (1960; Riverside, 1991)
- ★★★★½ The Country Blues of John Lee Hooker (1960; Original Blues Classics, 1991)
- ★★★½ Travelin' (1960; Collectables, 2000)
- ★★★★★ John Lee Hooker Plays & Sings the Blues (1961; Chess, 1989)
- ★★★★ The Folk Lore of John Lee Hooker (1961; Collectables, 2000)
- ★★★½ Burnin' (1962; Collectables, 2000)
- ★★★½ The Big Soul of John Lee Hooker (1964; Collectables, 2000)
- ★★★★ Burning Hell (1964; Original Blues Classics, 1992)
- ★★★½ On Campus (1964; Collectables, 2000)
- ★★★★ Concert at Newport (1964; Collectables, 2000)
- ★★★½ Is He the World's Greatest Blues Singer? (1965; Collectables, 2000)
- ★★★½ It Serves You Right to Suffer (1965; MCA, 1999)
- ★★★★ Live at the Café au Go-Go/Live at Soledad Prison (1966, 1972; MCA, 1996)
- ★★★★ The Real Folk Blues (1968; Chess, 1987)
- ★★★★ That's Where It's At! (1969; Stax, 1990)
- ★★½ Endless Boogie (MCA, 1971)
- ★★★★ Boogie Chillun (1972; Fantasy, 1989)
- ★★★½ In Person (1976; Collectables, 2001)
- ★★★★ Alone (1976; Rhino, 1991)
- ★★★★ Gotham Golden Classics (1977; Collectables, 1991)
- ★★★ The Cream (1978; Fuel, 2001)
- ★★★★ Sad and Lonesome (Muse, 1979)
- ★★★★ Detroit Blues 1950–1951: John Lee Hooker/Eddie Burns (1986; Collectables, 1991)
- ★★ Jealous (1987; Pointblank/Virgin, 1996)
- ★★★★★ The Best of John Lee Hooker (GNP Crescendo, 1987)
- ★★★★ The Healer (Chameleon, 1989)

- ★★★ John Lee Hooker and Canned Heat Recorded Live at the Fox Venice Theatre (Rhino, 1990)
- ★★★ More Real Folk Blues: The Missing Album (Chess, 1991)
- ★★★★ Mr. Lucky (Charisma/Pointblank, 1991)
- ★★★★ The Best of John Lee Hooker 1965 to 1974 (MCA, 1991)
- ★★★★★ The Ultimate Collection (Rhino, 1991)
- ★★★★ Boom Boom (Pointblank, 1992)
- ★★★★ Graveyard Blues (Specialty, 1992)
- ★★★½ Get Back Home (Evidence, 1992)
- ★★★★ Everybody's Blues (Specialty, 1993)
- ★★★★★ The Legendary Modern Recordings, 1948–1954 (Flair/Virgin, 1993)
- ★★★★★ The Early Years (Tomato/Rhino, 1994)
- ★★★½ King of the Boogie (Drive Archive, 1994)
- ★★★★★ Alternative Boogie: Early Studio Recordings, 1948–1952 (Capitol Blues Collection, 1995)
- ★★★★ Chill Out (Pointblank, 1995)
- ★★★★ The Very Best of John Lee Hooker (Rhino, 1995)
- ★★★½ The Best of Hooker 'n' Heat (EMI, 1996)
- ★★½ His Best Chess Sides (Chess, 1997)
- ★★★★ Don't Look Back (Pointblank, 1997)
- ★★★★½ The Complete '50s Chess Recordings (MCA, 1998)
- ★★★ The Best of Friends (Virgin, 1998)
- ★★★ The Best of John Lee Hooker: The Millennium Collection (MCA, 1999)
- ★★★★★ Detroit 1948–1949 (Atlantic/Savoy, 2000)
- ★★★★ Live at Sugar Hill, Vol. 2 (Fantasy, 2002)
- ★★★½ Blue on Blues (Varèse Sarabande, 2002)
- ★ Blues Kingpins (Virgin, 2003)
- ★★★ The Early Years, Vol. 1 (Tomato Music, 2003)
- ★★★ The Early Years, Vol. 2 (Tomato Music, 2003)
- ★★★★ Boom Boom and Other Hits (Rhino, 2003)
- ★★★½ Low Down Midnite Boogie (Savoy Jazz, 2003)
- ★★★ I'm the Boogie Man (Collectables, 2004)

John Lee Hooker was born near Clarksdale, MS (the year is in question, as Hooker variously gave 1915, 1917, and 1920 as birthdates), but his music was born farther south, thanks to his stepfather Will Moore, who was raised in Louisiana and played a style of blues built on a one-chord droning tone, relentless vamping, and stinging, lower-strings punctuations. Blind Lemon Jefferson, Blind Blake, and Charley Patton often visited Moore at his house, but their effect on Hooker was virtually nil—Moore's music possessed him and is the most direct influence on a style that became one of the touchstones of blues-based rock & roll. In fact, in the last few years before his death in 2001, Hooker found his "children" coming home to pay homage to the master. In his excellent latter-day releases, *The Healer, Mr. Lucky, Boom Boom,* and *Chill Out,* Hooker is joined by Bonnie Raitt, Albert Collins, Robert Cray, Keith Richards, Carlos Santana, Los Lobos, George Thorogood, Booker T. Jones, Johnnie Johnson, John Hammond, Charlie Musselwhite, a new incarnation of Canned Heat, Ry Cooder, Johnny Winter, and others in what amounts to Hooker's whistle-stop tour through 25-plus years of rock music bearing his signature in the voices of other players. In his twilight resurgence, he was well served by producer Roy Rogers, who didn't let the marquee names overwhelm the proceedings. Indeed, *Chill Out*'s best moments feature not the all-stars but Hooker alone with his guitar, carving out some savage blues all on his own.

Hooker's signature sound isn't easily copied, since its only pattern is no pattern at all. Vamping and droning are its constants, but Hooker regularly breaks down the 12-bar structure in order to extend his story to a conclusion only he envisions; moreover, his fingering and chording follow no discernible logic, and time is without question a moving thing almost from bar to bar. Then Hooker brings everything home with his brooding, low-down vocals, which hint at some impending danger even in the brightest moments. Like Muddy Waters', Hooker's is the deepest of deep blues, and his point of view is that of someone who regards life as a tragedy and humankind as basically no damn good. This is, after all, a bluesman who sang the murder ballad "I'm Bad Like Jesse James" with utter conviction, and whose repertoire included scalding entries such as "When My First Wife Left Me," "I'll Never Get Out of These Blues Alive," "Serve Me Right to Suffer," and, if only to show the universe in perfect alignment, "Serve You Right to Suffer."

After working odd jobs and playing music as a sideline in Memphis and Cincinnati in the late '30s and early '40s, Hooker moved to Detroit. There he made some recordings for a local distributor, Bernard Besman, who had his own small label, Sensation, but leased the first masters to the folks at Modern and proceeded to work extensively in the studio with the artist over the next five years. From that first session, "Boogie Chillen" broke out in 1948 and reportedly sold over a million copies; its success loosed on the world an insistent, brooding, pulsating rhythm—built on a simple ostinato figure played slightly behind the beat—that both heralded the coming of a distinctive new artist and brought traditional blues into step with the accelerating pace of America's postwar society. Thereafter Hooker's masters were leased to a variety of labels and issued with the artist identified by a variety of names: Delta John, Texas Slim, the Booker Man, even John Lee Booker. Regardless of the name

on the labels, most of the songs (and certainly the most effective) featured only Hooker accompanied by his electric guitar and his own foot stomping, in large part because his unusual approach to a song's structure and rhythm made it difficult for other musicians to stay in step with him.

Apart from the late '80s and '90s albums, Hooker's most noted band sessions are those he cut in 1970 with blues revivalists Canned Heat, which started life as a single album, were reissued in a two-CD set, and are now available in a boiled-down single CD from EMI, *The Best of Hooker 'n' Heat.* Rhino's catalogue features a live album as well, *John Lee Hooker and Canned Heat Recorded Live at the Fox Venice,* featuring Hooker, Canned Heat, and, on backup vocals, the Chambers Brothers. In its original incarnation with 300-pound lead singer Bob Hite and ace guitarist/vocalist Al Wilson (both are now deceased), Canned Heat was the foremost exponent of Hooker-style boogie in a blues-rock setting.

Nothing, however, supplants Hooker solo or with minimal backing. His finest records through the years have benefited from a stark approach that elevates the mood of his most personal stories. Rhino's *The Ultimate Collection: 1948–1990* supports this theory even as it shows Hooker sometimes effective in a broader setting. Guitarist Eddie Kirkland, who provided exemplary support on several Hooker sessions, is heard here in good form on "Think Twice Before You Go," and again on a 1968 track, "Back Biters and Syndicators," which also features Louis Myers on harmonica, Eddie Taylor on bass, and Al Duncan on drums. Similarly, a track from Hooker's marvelous *The Real Folk Blues,* "You Know I Know," finds him backed by one of his early accompanists, guitarist Eddie Burns, as well as Lafayette Leake on piano, Willie Dixon on bass, and the incomparable Fred Below on drums.

You don't have to be a purist to appreciate the power of Hooker's earliest sides cut in Detroit. These represent the darkest, rawest tales in the artist's literature as well as his most acerbic slants on life as black Americans knew it in the immediate postwar years. Some of these have the feel of having been carefully prepared and worked out, others are ragged and improvisational. All are powerful statements. Numerous first-rate overviews of this period are now in print, and it's difficult to recommend one over another. However, as a complete package the Capitol Blues Collection's three-CD survey of the Besman-produced sessions, *Alternative Boogie: Early Studio Recordings, 1948–1952,* is hard to beat. In addition to 56 recordings, including some alternate and previously unreleased takes, the set comes with an informed liner essay by Pete Welding and a short piece by Bernard Besman himself, who lays out his argument that Hooker's music is so distinctive it cannot be called blues at all, but rather should be designated "early Americana." Less ambitious but no less essential is Flair/Virgin's 24-track single-CD survey, *The Legendary Modern Recordings 1948–1954*. Other key titles that round out Hooker's early years on various labels include *Detroit Blues 1950–1951,* with solo recordings by Hooker and by Eddie Burns (Hooker's tracks are also available separately in Collectables' *Gotham Golden Classics*); and two fine Specialty titles, *Graveyard Blues* (from 1949–50, its 20 Besman-produced cuts were released on the producer's own Sensation label) and *Everybody's Blues* (a handful of solo Hooker tracks from 1950–51 and others from 1954 recorded for Specialty but seeing the light of day for the first time here). A more recent and equally vital entry, in that it goes far toward completing the picture of Hooker's early years, is the Atlantic/Savoy disc *Detroit 1948–1949,* which finally brings to light 20 sides Hooker cut pseudonymously for Savoy during those years. Most of these tracks are Hooker and solo guitar, but four feature him in a duo with acoustic guitarist Elmer Barbee, and four feature Hooker with Barbee, James Watkin on piano, and Curtis Foster on drums. Check out a searing adaptation of Louis Jordan's "Ain't That Just Like a Woman," here titled "Just Like a Woman," with Hooker flailing his guitar furiously at the outset, then settling into a fierce vamp as he sings/declaims his explanation for dumping a two-timing woman, whom he regards as simply reverting to type. There's also a raw Christmas blues here, "Christmas Time Blues," with the band in tow, and its melody and piano part sometimes bear a striking resemblance to Charles Brown's Yuletide classic, "Merry Christmas, Baby." Deeper into the '50s, another exemplary package comes by way of the 31-track, double-CD Tomato/Rhino set, *The Early Years,* also graced by a Pete Welding essay and covering Hooker's band recordings for the Vee Jay label from 1955 to 1964. On this set the stellar Vee Jay artist Jimmy Reed is heard blowing a mean harmonica and playing guitar on two cuts, Hooker is backed by horns on a 1961 session, and the Vandellas sing backup vocals on two cuts from 1963. An overview that takes Hooker from his solo days into his first band sides is available by way of GNP Crescendo's well-considered *The Best of John Lee Hooker.* For a brief period Hooker also was in the Chess stable in Chicago, and those recordings have been returned to print in MCA's double-CD *The Complete '50s Chess Recordings,* which comprise not only Hooker's recordings while under contract to Chess but also some sides the Chess

brothers leased from other labels (Fortune, HiQ, and Gone). Some of these sides feature Eddie Kirkland on guitar, but in terms of Hooker's development on record the most interesting are three tracks teaming Hooker with a horn section, a precursor to the mainstream R&B bent his music would take later in the decade and into the '60s during his tenure with the Vee Jay label.

The development of Hooker's style within a band context is demonstrated on the sides dating from the late '50s forward, for Vee Jay and several other labels that had the benefit of Hooker's services through the '60s. Not that the style developed all that much—Hooker was resolutely Hooker, no matter the setting; what was interesting was how other musicians respond to the challenge posed by his unorthodox sense of song structure. Thanks to an ambitious reissue program by Collectables, 10 of Hooker's Vee Jay albums have been returned to print (available individually or in a boxed set, *The Man, The Legend*). The place to start in the Vee Jay recordings is the monumental *The Folk Lore of John Lee Hooker.* In the early '60s Hooker had started referring to himself as a folk singer, and emphasized the point by appearing regularly at folk festivals around the country, including Newport (memorialized in the Vee Jay album *Concert at Newport*). The first track on *Folk Lore* is "Tupelo," a deep, dark blues told in a foreboding voice, about the devastation visited upon the Mississippi town when the river overflowed. That live cut (recorded at Newport in 1960) marks the start of an amazing journey that features some of the finest writing, singing, and musical accompaniment Hooker ever delivered on a long player. It's followed on disc by a tale of revenge and murder, "I'm Mad Again," in which Hooker recounts how he took in a down-on-his-luck friend who betrayed his benefactor by sleeping with his wife. "I'm made like Al Capone," Hooker announces in a threatening tone, and then proceeds to describe drowning the lout and watching him sink. Generally there's no going wrong with the Vee Jay albums from the standpoint of arresting music and performances; the only negative is the lack of session info and dates, all too typical of Collectables' reissues.

Apart from Vee Jay, some of the strongest work from this period was done for the Riverside label, starting in 1959 with the potent, stark solo renderings on *The Country Blues of John Lee Hooker,* wherein the Hooker boogie is displaced by a blues style redolent of the Delta. From those same sessions comes *Burning Hell,* issued first in England (and even there not until 1964) and unavailable Stateside until its release on CD in 1992. In 1960 producer Orrin Keepnews cut Hooker with bassist Sam Jones and drummer Louis

Hayes, rhythm masters recruited from Cannonball Adderley's band, for *That's My Story: John Lee Hooker Sings the Blues*. Of interest here is Hooker's "I Need Some Money," which showed up in slightly different form as "Money (That's What I Want)," a Top 30 pop single that year for Barrett Strong and later covered by the Beatles. A brief liaison with jazz producer Bob Thiele, first for Thiele's Impulse label in 1965 and a year later at the Thiele-led ABC–Bluesway, yielded two memorable efforts. For Impulse, Hooker served up fire, brimstone, and a sinister ambience on *It Serves You Right to Suffer* (his blood-curdling scream on the album-opening boogie, "Shake It Baby," is worth the price of admission) accompanied not by die-hard bluesmen but rather by some top names in the jazz–big band world, including Milt Hinton on bass, Panama Francis on drums, Barry Galbraith on guitar, and, on another version of "Money" (now titled as such), trombonist Dicky Wells, a veteran of the Count Basie Band. Purists are adamant in arguing the superiority of undiluted Hooker, but the great players Thiele assembled for this session seem to understand every nuance of the Hooker approach, and respond with support that's as intelligently crafted as it is subtle. When Impulse folded its tent a year later, Thiele founded ABC's Bluesway imprint and cut one more noteworthy session with Hooker, a live album recorded at New York's Café au Go-Go on August 30, 1966. There's not a thing wrong with Hooker's dramatic performances on *Live at the Café au Go-Go,* but what must have been seen by Thiele as a summit meeting of giants doesn't quite pan out. Muddy Waters had preceded Hooker with a set and stayed onstage with his band to accompany his fellow Mississippian, but it turns out to be Waters' piano player, the redoubtable Otis Spann, who gets in the good licks throughout. Nevertheless what's here is choice, from the first cut ("I'm Bad Like Jesse James," which is "I'm Mad Again" retitled) to the eighth and final cut, the wrenching heartbreaker "Seven Days." *Live at the Café au Go-Go* is now paired with another live recording, a searing performance memorialized as *Live at Soledad Prison,* on a must-have MCA twofer. One of the best live Hooker performances ever captured on tape was released in 1972 (reissued in 1989) on Fantasy's double-album *Boogie Chillun.* Recorded at San Francisco's Sugar Hill nightclub—a regular stop for prominent blues artists in its day—these acoustic performances are vivid demonstrations of the mesmerizing power Hooker wrought with only his voice, his guitar, his foot beating time, and a stockpile of lived-in blues sagas. Now 19 more performances from that night have surfaced on *Live at Sugar Hill Vol. 2.* Suffice it to

say, Hooker, in 1962, was at the top of his game, a judgment borne out by every purposeful note played and sung on the second Sugar Hill volume.

Recorded in 1966 (reissued in 1991) as the followup to the outstanding *Real Folk Blues* album for Chess, the engaging *More Real Folk Blues* finds Hooker plugged in and working with a band on some of the most overt efforts he made at chart success. This is a mixed bag, but Hooker does an interesting take on "Mustang Sally & GTO," basing his version on the original "Mustang Sally" cut by Mack Rice in 1965, two years before Wilson Pickett hit paydirt with it. One of Hooker's final '60s recording sessions took place in Paris in late November 1969. Some of these sides were issued on a Black and Blue import, and these plus six other previously unreleased songs comprise Evidence's *Get Back Home.* Among the interesting oddities here: John Lee having a boisterous go at "Hi Heel Sneakers" and a reconsideration of Jimmie Rodgers' "T.B. Blues" in which Hooker's vocal takes on a penetrating Bukka White–style vibrato. Sessions from 1967 and 1969 comprise *Urban Blues,* which finds Hooker dipping ever so slightly into social commentary on the dark, turgid "Motor City Is Burning" (from 1967) and, less successfully, on "I Gotta Go to Vietnam" (a previously unreleased track from 1969); the latter, which borrows generously from "Rollin' and Tumblin'," percolates along steadily, but delivers less in its ho-hum narrative than in its powerhouse riffing (with Earl Hooker's snarling wah-wahed guitar lines most prominent).

Payback time begins in the '70s with the Canned Heat sessions and continues with the above-mentioned guest artists populating his latest recordings. Additionally, *Never Get Out of These Blues Alive* teams Hooker with a band whose numbers are bolstered on several cuts by Elvin Bishop on slide guitar, the Butterfield Blues Band's Mark Naftalin on piano, and, on the title track, Naftalin, Bishop, and Van Morrison, the latter sharing lead vocals with Hooker. *Endless Boogie* (1971) brings Steve Miller on board to add some pungent electric guitar lines to the proceedings, although it is harmonica wizard Dave Berger who steals the show with his Little Walter–style wails and moans. *The Cream* is four sides of live, prime Hooker, recorded in 1977 with a band featuring Charlie Musselwhite on harmonica. Note also that two Hooker albums are titled *Alone.* One of these is available on vinyl from Specialty and contains sides cut between 1948 and 1951 with Bernard Besman in Detroit; the other is a two-CD live album on Tomato featuring Hooker solo at New York City's Hunter College. As for single-CD overviews, both MCA and Rhino have top-notch samplers of Hooker's work, with MCA's covering the years 1965 to 1974, while Rhino's *The Very Best of John Lee Hooker* ranges from the original Modern recording of "Boogie Chillen" through representative tracks from the '50s and '60s cut for Modern, Vee Jay, Riverside, Impulse, Chess, and Bluesway, plus a side from the 1971 *Hooker 'n' Heat* album and an interesting take on Robert Johnson's "Terraplane Blues" recorded for Roy Rogers' 1987 album, *Sidewinder.* It can be argued that Hooker rarely varied his tried-and-true formula; but more than 50 years after that formula was first heard on record, the man's "early Americana" sounds as vital and stirring as ever. Elemental, fundamental, monumental, John Lee Hooker's blues is the stuff of life. —D.M.

Hootie & the Blowfish

★★★ Cracked Rear View (Atlantic, 1994)
★★½ Fairweather Johnson (Atlantic, 1996)
★★★ Musical Chairs (Atlantic, 1998)
★★½ Scattered, Smothered and Covered (Atlantic, 2000)
★★½ Hootie & the Blowfish (Atlantic, 2003)

At press time, 16 million Americans had purchased a copy of Hootie & the Blowfish's *Cracked Rear View.* However much music snobs may shake their heads in disbelief, the major-label debut by these four South Carolinians touched a lot of people, many of whom probably didn't listen to much pop music or hadn't in a long time. The reason? Hootie's brand of classic-flavor Middle American guitar rock was unoriginal and kind of dull, but you could also call it pleasantly familiar. "Hold My Hand," "Let Her Cry," "Only Wanna Be With You," and "Time" became megahits because their melodies are catchy and likable, and because Darius Rucker's mellow voice worked on listeners like a fuzzy security blanket.

Unfortunately, even the best bar bands have trouble with artistic growth, and Hootie proved no exception. *Fairweather Johnson* is more of the same, just not as good. Actually, the tunes hold up well; the central problem is Rucker, who apparently decided between albums that he'd sound more soulful if he sang more gruffly. He only sounds more constipated. *Musical Chairs* is a significant improvement, with less mannered vocals enhancing punchy rockers like "Wishing" and down-home country-style outings like "Michelle Post." Song for song, it's their best so far.

Hootie's next album, an all-covers affair, takes songs by such notables as Tom Waits, R.E.M., and the Smiths and makes them sound like Hootie & the Blowfish originals. Which proves a point: This band, unlike a lot of other pop acts, has an instantly recognizable style. If only it were a little more exciting.

Recorded after a four-year hiatus, *Hootie & the Blowfish* is another helping of meat and potatoes, with slight detours into smoky soul ("Little Brother") and sassy Southern rock ("Go and Tell Him"). As usual, it's pleasant but nothing special. —M.R.

Lightnin' Hopkins

★★★★★ Lightnin' Hopkins (1959; Smithsonian Folkways, 1990)
★★★★★ Last Night Blues (with Sonny Terry) (1960; Original Blues Classics, 1992)
★★★★ Autobiography in Blues (1960; Tradition, 1996)
★★★½ Lightnin' (1960; Original Blues Classics, 1991)
★★★★ The Best of Lightnin' Hopkins (Prestige, 1960)
★★★★ Blues in My Bottle (1961; Original Blues Classics, 1991)
★★★★ How Many More Years I Got (1962; Fantasy, 1989)
★★★★ Lightnin' Strikes (1962; Collectables, 2000)
★★★★ Smokes Like Lightning (1962; Original Blues Classics, 1995)
★★★ Goin' Away (1963; Original Blues Classics, 1990)
★★★★ Soul Blues (1964; Original Blues Classics, 1991)
★★★★ Double Blues (1964; Fantasy, 1989)
★★★½ The Hopkins Brothers: Lightnin', Joel, & John Henry (1964; Arhoolie, 1993)
★★★½ Sometimes I Believe She Loves Me (with Barbara Dane) (1964; Arhoolie, 1996)
★★★ Hootin' the Blues (1964; Original Blues Classics, 1995)
★★★½ Coffee House Blues (with Brownie McGhee & Sonny Terry) (1965; Collectables, 2000)
★★★★ Live at 1966 Berkeley Blues Festival (1966; Arhoolie, 2000)
★★★ Free Form Patterns (1968; Collectables, 1993)
★★★ The Legacy of Blues, Vol. 12: Lightnin' Hopkins (1976; GNP Crescendo, 1992)
★★★★ Mojo Hand/Golden Classics (1987; Collectables, 1990)
★★★ From the Vaults of Everest Records, Part 1: Drinkin' In the Blues (Collectables, 1989)
★★★ From the Vaults of Everest Records, Part 2: Prison Blues (Collectables, 1989)
★★★ From the Vaults of Everest Records, Part 3: Mama and Papa Hopkins (Collectables, 1989)
★★★ From the Vaults of Everest Records, Part 4: Nothing but the Blues (Collectables, 1989)
★★★★ The Herald Recordings—1954 (Collectables, 1989)
★★★★ Texas Blues (1989; Arhoolie, 1993)

Sam Hopkins, who died in 1982, left behind a staggering collection of country and urban blues as personal and topical as any artist of his time. He recorded solo acoustic; he recorded with small backing groups of anywhere from one to four players, some playing acoustic instruments, some playing electric. He talked some of his blues; he sang most of them. In narrative and ambience, his acoustic sides reflect the country life and attitudes he stayed close to from the cradle to the grave; his band sides burn with the fierce energy of rock & roll, as if the artist were acknowledging the quickening pace of society around him. From his songs you sense the man: witty, acerbic, truculent, deep feeling, confident, loyal, giving, somewhat sentimental, sensitive, engaged in the world, and if not misogynistic, certainly quick with his put-downs of the distaff side.

In 1946 Sam was discovered by a talent scout for the Aladdin label and sent to Los Angeles to record with pianist Wilson "Thunder" Smith. Thunder and Lightnin''s single, "Katie Mae Blues," did well in the Houston area, and Hopkins returned to the Aladdin studio, where he was to cut 41 more sides between 1946 and 1948, now collected on the double-CD set *The Complete Aladdin Recordings,* one of the critical early documents in Hopkins' recording history.

Arhoolie's *Early Recordings* and *The Gold Star Sessions* document the beginnings of his career (1947–50), when he was recording a broad variety of material. For example, in the midst of the fairly traditional folk blues on volume 1 of *The Gold Star Sessions,* Hopkins launches into "Zolo Go," accompanying himself on organ. The title is a phonetic misspelling of zydeco, and the song is one of the early recorded examples of that genre, cut several years before Clifton Chenier first appeared on record.

From the 1950s, Hopkins is represented by a set of recordings made for the Herald label, now issued on Collectables as *The Herald Recordings—1954* and *The Herald Recordings Vol. 2;* on BMG/Buddah as *Lightnin' and the Blues: The Herald Sessions;* and by Smithsonian/Folkways' *Lightnin' Hopkins,* recorded in 1959 when he was rediscovered in Houston by blues scholar Samuel Charters. Setting up a tape recorder in Hopkins' drab living quarters, Charters held the microphone in his hand while the artist produced one remarkable performance after another. The chitchat is kept to a minimum here, save for one brief but vivid reminiscence about Lightnin' 's personal encounters with Blind Lemon Jefferson. Otherwise, "Penitentiary Blues," "Bad Luck and Trouble," "See That My Grave Is Kept Clean," "Trouble Stay Away From My Door," and the salacious "Fan It" represent a blues titan at the top of his game.

One of Hopkins' most productive periods occurred between 1960 and 1964, when he recorded for the Prestige label. The seven-CD box set *The Complete Prestige/Bluesville Recordings* is a must-have title. As for individual Prestige/Bluesville titles, *Smokes Like Lightnin'* is highly recommended, both for the quality of the songs—"Prison Farm Blues" is a grim portrait of the bleakest of places a bluesman could and often did land—and for folklorist/producer Mack McCormick's liner notes.

Last Night Blues, with Sonny Terry sitting in on harmonica and singing one song, is quintessential Lightnin'. His vocals are crisp and clear, full of feeling, and he's right there on guitar, strong and cutting and propulsive, as Terry's harmonica snakes it way through the melody line, energizing Hopkins' every lick. *Hootin' the Blues* is a live album from 1962, recorded at the Second Fret in Philadelphia, featuring among its cuts an etiology of the blues ("The Blues Is a Feeling") and an original instrumental dialogue imagining a musical interchange between Lightnin' and Ray Charles ("Me and Ray Charles"). *Straight Blues* (1999) collects a dozen tracks culled from three Prestige/Bluesville albums and also contained on the seven-CD box set. These range from four solo efforts cut in Houston in 1961 to two with bass and drum accompaniment recorded in May 1964 and six solo acoustic live tracks from December 1964. It includes "Get It Straight," one of the artist's few forays into traditional country music.

In 1964, Lightnin' recorded with his brothers John Henry and Joel at John Henry's home in Waxahachie, Texas. This was something of a family reunion, since John Henry had not been in touch with his siblings or mother in years. As evidenced on *The Hopkins Brothers,* this was a reunion full of laughter, love, and some melancholy over time passed—Lightnin''s disc-opening "See About My Brother John Henry" is about as sad as blues gets. Other Arhoolie titles are worthy examples of the variety of blues Lightnin' was proffering in his later years. *Po' Lightnin',* in particular, is recommended.

Sometimes I Believe She Loves Me (1964) finds him accompanying the blues/folk singer Barbara Dane on guitar and vocals on an interesting collection of numbers. Some were written by Dane (whose earthy voice has an appealing rough edge, not unlike, say, Bonnie Raitt's or Maria Muldaur's), some by Lightnin', and covers of two Woody Guthrie songs ("Don't You Push Me Down" and a stirring version of "Deportees") and Malvina Reynolds' "Bury Me in My Overalls."

Arhoolie also has reissued on CD a live album from 1968 featuring Hopkins, Mance Lipscomb, and zydeco king Clifton Chenier (who was Hopkins' cousin by marriage by this time), recorded at the Berkeley Music Festival. Hopkins, playing electric guitar and backed by drummer Francis Clay, is medium-cool throughout, offering up some of his signature songs—"Short Haired Woman," "Lightnin's Boogie," "Black Cadillac"—as well as a strutting take on Big Bill Broonzy's "I Feel So Good." The real star of the show was Chenier, accompanied only by his accordion and Clay on drums. Of special note are his cover versions of Slim Harpo's "Scratch My Back" and a rocking version of Ray Charles' "What'd I Say."

From Hopkins' brief tenure on Chicago's Vee Jay label, two must-have albums remain in print, both from the Collectables catalogue. *Lightnin' Strikes,* from 1962, features Hopkins solo acoustic and electrified with a backing band, and though it's a mere 10 cuts total, it's full of fury, anger, heartbreak, and outrage. "War Is Starting Again" is a surging, outraged blues decrying the waste of human lives in Vietnam, from the moment the news media was starting to document the ever-escalating nature of the war. Equally startling, from a personal standpoint, is the spoken/sung acoustic blues "Walkin' Round in Circles," with Hopkins firing off angry licks to punctuate his litany of life's woes.

Collectables' four-volume *Anthology of the Blues* series is culled from the Everest label's vaults and takes Hopkins from the late '50s into the early '60s. The four albums in the series are available either individually or as a box set titled *From the Vaults of Everest Records,* which is handsomely packaged but poorly annotated, a persistent flaw with Collectables reissues. Another Collectables title, *Mojo Hand,* features some of Hopkins' most searing guitar work, close-miked and violent in its intensity, produced by Bobby Robinson, whose Fire and Fury labels were home to some of the great blues and R&B artists of the '50s.

From later years comes the GNP Crescendo *Legacy of the Blues* entry, which in 1976 reunited Hopkins with Samuel Charters for what proved to be one of the artist's final recording sessions. Collectables also chips in with an intriguing five-volume series titled *The Lost Texas Tapes,* which may be (there's no annotation) recordings Hopkins made in Houston in the '70s for the Home Cooking label. (Collectables has two other Home Cooking releases in its Hopkins catalogue, *Lonesome Life* and *Lightnin' Hopkins Strikes Again.*) Volumes 1 through 3 are Hopkins solo; 4 and 5 bring on guest artists. Volume 4 is a live recording, a true down-home effort done in a club or restaurant; patrons are heard conversing in the background, and on one track a cash register rings as Hopkins plays. He's accompanied by Curley Lee, who blows mean and low harmonica fills throughout and engages Hopkins in some humorous but cutting between-songs banter.

Among several Hopkins overviews, three stand out. Arhoolie's *The Best of Lightning Hopkins* has 17 tracks of choice performances: seven recorded for Gold Star between 1947 and 1950, the other 10 cut in Houston and Berkeley for Arhoolie. The songs run the gamut from classic blues ("Whiskey Blues") to gospel ("Jesus Will You Come by Here," again with Hopkins on piano) to social commentary ("Mr. Crow & Bill Quinn," "Tim Moore's Farm," "Please Settle in Vietnam"). You can't go wrong with this one. Ditto for Rhino's Blues Masters entry, *The Very Best of Lightnin' Hopkins*, with 16 tracks recorded for 10 different labels, beginning with Aladdin in 1947 and concluding with tracks cut for Folkways in 1961.

Finally, for those who really want some sense of the path of Hopkins' career, get *Mojo Hand: The Lightnin' Hopkins Anthology*. This well-annotated double-CD set contains 41 cuts, ranging from the original "Katie Mae Blues" cut for Aladdin with Thunder Smith in 1947 to a 1974 track previously released on a Swedish blues album. Among other things, this set shows that no matter the passing of time and trends, Hopkins remained true to his style and never ran out of things to say. —D.M.

Bruce Hornsby and the Range

★★★	The Way It Is (RCA, 1986)	
★★½	Scenes From the Southside (RCA, 1988)	
★★★	A Night on the Town (RCA, 1990)	
★★★	Harbor Lights (RCA, 1993)	
★★★	Hot House (RCA, 1995)	
★★★	Spirit Trail (RCA, 1998)	
★★★	Here Come the Noise Makers (RCA, 2000)	

Bruce Hornsby's mid-'80s singles were almost aggressively tasteful: ultraprofessional piano pastiches, Americana, and MOR-ready hooks. But "The Way It Is" and "Mandolin Rain" suffered from an air of wistfulness that passed, on first listen, for melancholy but left a "Well-then-who-gives-a-damn?" aftertaste. *Scenes From the Southside* continued in the same vein, producing "The Valley Road," another stainless hit. Hornsby enlisted such diverse talents as Jerry Garcia and Wayne Shorter to help make *A Night on the Town* his most direct, almost bluesy record. Not that great a departure from the Range's earlier sound, it garnered critical encouragement but no big hits. *Harbor Lights* and *Hot House* found Hornsby dropping the Range and moving further jazzward. The double-album *Spirit Trail* was his most ambitious yet, stretching out his playing without resorting to aimless jamming. By this time, he was almost as well known for his part-time membership in the Grateful Dead as he was for his own music. The two-disc live album *Noise Makers* is culled from concerts in 1998 through 2000 and includes hits from "The Way It Is" to "Mandolin Rain." —P.E.

Hot Boys

★★	Get It How U Live! (Cash Money, 1997)	
★★★	Guerrilla Warfare (Cash Money/Universal, 1999)	

Juvenile

★★	Being Myself (Warlock, 1995)	
★★★★	400 Degreez (Cash Money/Universal, 1998)	
★★½	Solja Rags (Cash Money, 1999)	
★★★	Tha G Code (Cash Money/Universal, 1999)	
★★★	Project English (Cash Money/Universal, 2001)	
★★★	Juve the Great (Cash Money/Universal, 2003)	

Lil' Wayne

★★★★	Tha Block Is Hot (Cash Money/Universal, 1999)	
★★★	Lights Out (Cash Money/Universal, 2000)	
★★★½	500 Degreez (Cash Money/Universal, 2002)	
★★★	Tha Carter (Cash Money/Universal, 2004)	

Big Tymers

★★	How You Luv That? (Cash Money/Universal, 1998)	
★★½	I Got That Work (Cash Money/Universal, 2000)	
★★★½	Hood Rich (Cash Money/Universal, 2002)	
★★½	Big Money Heavyweight (Cash Money/Universal, 2003)	

Baby

★★	Birdman (Cash Money/Universal, 2002)	

As soon as New Orleans' Master P and his No Limit Records crew started to cool off in the late '90s, Cash Money Records was there to pick up the bling-bling and run with it. Assembled by producer Manny Fresh under the auspices of label heads Ronald "Suga Slim" Williams and Bryan "Baby" Williams (who later made an ill-advised album under his name), Cash Money's music shared some common traits with their hometown rivals in No Limit: a mix of over-the-top materialism and Run-D.M.C.–era production values; an assembly-line approach to releases and merchandising (new CDs often pictured the next few album covers well before the actual recordings were even finished); and lyrics that introduced thick Big Easy slang into the mainstream vernacular. But if Master P's No Limit Records created the template for successful New Orleans hip-hop, Hot Boys operated on a higher artistic plane, with the nimble playfulness of their raps and the extraordinary futuristic productions of Manny Fresh. Fresh, in codifying the Southern bounce sound, effectively became the most significant rhythmic innovator out of New Orleans since the Meters' legendary Porter/Modeliste rhythm section. The fly-by-night nature of the albums didn't matter to fans: After years of being ignored by the hip-hop scene at large, New Orleans had a huge reserve of enthusiasm and style to be tapped.

Juvenile (born Terius Gray) was the highest-profile member of the crew, which also included Lil' Wayne, B.G., and Turk. Growing up in and around N'awlins' lethal 17th Ward neighborhood, the Hot Boys were immersed in a hard-core existence of drugs and guns from a young age, which makes the fact that they were rhyming on record about this reality before they reached puberty (B.G. waxed his 1993 debut *True Story* at age 11) shocking and sadly credible. These tricky, regional rhythms manifested themselves in a Big Easy version of booty bass, which the Hot Boys gleefully adorned with anthem-making catchphrases. "Back That Azz Up" and "Ha," the hit singles from Juvenile's *400 Degreez,* sounded wildly original when spun on narrowly programmed radio stations in both New York and Los Angeles, and a regional niche sound blew up nationwide. While the Hot Boys' image as baggy-jeaned, heavy-lidded, medallion-wearing adolescents—not to mention their lyrics about platinum-crusted teeth and diamond-toenailed hoes— suggested little depth, tracks like "F*** Tha World" (from *Tha Block Is Hot,* where Lil' Wayne details the murder of his father) carried significant emotional heft. Apparently, Lil' Wayne's drug troubles led to his ouster from the group (Wayne countered with *500 Degreez,* a record that purported to be 100 degrees hotter than Juvenile's hottest release), and producer Manny Fresh took his turn on the mike with his group Big Tymers. Curious listeners should start with *400 Degreez* and B.G.'s *Chopper City in the Ghetto,* and move to *Tha Block Is Hot.* And if all this music fails to entice, mainstream America can nevertheless thank the Hot Boys for popularizing the phrase "bling-bling." —P.R./N.B.

Son House

★★★★½   Father of the Delta Blues: The Complete 1965 Sessions (1965; Columbia/Legacy, 1992)

★★★★   Delta Blues: The Original Library of Congress Sessions From Field Recordings 1941–1942 (Biograph, 1991)

★★★★   Delta Blues and Spirituals (Capitol Blues Collection, 1995)

★★★★★   The Original Delta Blues (Columbia/Legacy, 1998)

Son House's blues universe is like no other Delta artist's, and to some his music is without parallel in its spiritual force. Born in Lyon, MS, and raised in Tallulah, LA, the forever-restless Eddie James "Son" House (1902–88) returned to his native state periodically in his teens in what now seems a search for peace of mind that would consume him throughout his life. A devout churchgoer from childhood, by age 15 he was a dedicated Baptist preacher who loved and sang gospel music but scorned the blues for its evocations of immorality and slovenly behavior.

In his mid-twenties, though, House heard the music with new ears, perhaps because he was on his way to living out the very tales he so despised as he rambled aimlessly from town to town throughout the South, preaching, riding the rails, working a variety of manual-labor jobs, designing his next getaway. From a wandering Mississippi guitarist named Willie Wilson he learned the fundamentals of the bottleneck style that would lend his music its eerie, edgy quality. In another bluesman, Rubin Lacey, he heard the guitar being used almost as a second, inner voice, its hard-flailed chords crying out heartache as Lacey sang dark tales relating the ongoing battles in his soul between the sacred and the profane. In Lyon, he stumbled on James McCoy, whose songs "My Black Mama" and "Preachin' the Blues" House mastered, then rewrote into what are now regarded as Delta blues classics (the former in turn served as the foundation for Robert Johnson's "Walkin' Blues"). With these songs as a springboard, House soon found himself with steady work playing Delta juke joints.

In 1928, at the moment his career was gaining some momentum, House shot a man to death after the fellow had opened fire in a Lyon juke joint where House was performing. Rejecting the defendant's claim of self-defense, a judge sentenced House to serve two years at the notorious Parchman prison farm; he was pardoned before his sentence was up by a judge in Clarksdale, MS, who warned him never to set foot in town again. House agreed, telling the judge he could "cover as much ground as a red fox" if he were set free. From the Parchman experience came another House monument, "Mississippi County Farm Blues," whose tune was adapted from the great Blind Lemon Jefferson's "See That My Grave Is Kept Clean."

More important to House's high standing in the blues pantheon was a 1941 trip through the Delta by a team of field recordists (Alan Lomax among them) working on a documentary project cosponsored by Fisk University and the Library of Congress. These recordings, capturing House at his artistic peak (even though he was recorded playing solo rather than in the blues combo he and Brown had formed), were followed a year later by another session with the same team. House had by then moved to Rochester, NY, where he stayed until 1978. Biograph's *Delta Blues: The Original Library of Congress Sessions From Field Recordings 1941–1942* is the document arising from those sessions, and monumental it is. While he had his share of songs about faithless lovers and general feelings of doom and degradation, House, more so even than Robert Johnson, found his soul in a constant tug-of-war between God and the Devil (a reason, perhaps, for his frequent returns to the pulpit), and this battle lent the music a moral depth rarely encountered in any genre, let alone Delta blues. "Preachin' Blues" may be the most explicit delineation of the artist's inner conflict, but spiritual turmoil shadows him in almost every circumstance. As powerful as the lyrics are in detail and imagery, it is House's deep, gravelly voice, haunted and haunting, that brings the message home with chilling authority. Supporting all this are some rather simple guitar stylings, by Delta standards—no showy polyrhythms, no startling key changes, no sweeping single- or double-string solo runs; rather, House wielded his slide as if it were on the left hand of God: It slashed, it wailed, it howled, it moaned, it wept. In the end, these fundamental parts created a mesmerizing whole.

When Willie Brown died in the mid-'50s, House lost interest in music completely. After moving to Rochester, he left his instrument in its case, preferring various day jobs (railroad porter, cook, etc.) to playing without Brown. By 1964, when blues scholars tracked him down, he didn't even own a guitar. Coaxed out of retirement, House began playing to enthusiastic audiences all over the country, leading to a 1965 contract with Columbia Records. The resulting sessions, produced by John Hammond and Frank Driggs and first issued on vinyl as *Father of Folk Blues*, are now collected on the two-CD set *Father of the Delta Blues: The Complete 1965 Sessions*, the second disc of which is composed entirely of previously unreleased alternate takes ("Death Letter" and "John the Revelator" among them) and seven cuts that didn't make the original vinyl issue. Here he reprises many of the Delta blues landmarks that established his legend—"Death Letter," "Preachin' Blues," "Pony Blues," "Louise McGhee"—along with newer material, including the touching, loving elegy "President Kennedy" (a retooling of a song House had written years before as a tribute to General Douglas MacArthur and then discarded after the general was relieved of his command by President Harry Truman). House is a bit rusty in spots—a blown lyric here, a fumbled guitar lick there—but the imperfections are endearing glitches in otherwise remarkable performances. These sessions are available in a whittled-down version—11 cuts, including two of the previously unissued tracks on the double-CD set—on Columbia/Legacy's *The Original Delta Blues*.

The House canon is rounded out beautifully by Capitol's *Delta Blues and Spirituals*, which wraps four blues songs and four spirituals around a pair of insightful House monologues explaining in folk poetry—which was general conversation for Son House—the link between the two musical styles.

Although House struggled on performing as his health permitted, by 1975 he had played his last show.

After moving in with relatives in Detroit, he was later taken to a rest home, where he died on October 19, 1988. His legacy is a body of work rarely equaled, never surpassed. His guitar is in the Delta Blues Museum in Clarksdale; his voice is in the wind.   —D.M.

House of Pain

   ★★★   House of Pain (Tommy Boy, 1992)
  ★★★★ Same As It Ever Was (Tommy Boy, 1994)
   ★★½ Truth Crushed to Earth Shall Rise Again (Tommy Boy, 1996)

DJ Muggs was one of the most talented hip-hop producers to emerge in the '90s, a real missing link between the wailing artillery barrage of Public Enemy and the claustrophobic minimalism of Wu-Tang. But Cypress Hill's albums hardly tell the full story. Muggs' commercial success with his home crew led him to endlessly imitate himself, and the group's smoked-out fans neither noticed nor cared. Fortunately, he hooked up with a couple of rowdy white guys who fit his groove. The result, House of Pain's *Same As It Ever Was*, is a lost classic—relentless, clever, and free of the sentimental bullshit with which tough guys try to explain away their nastiness.

It had to be all that, if only on account of "Jump Around," probably the only House of Pain track you've ever heard, a party anthem that launched itself recklessly in the air without the slightest care where it might land. It was as inescapable in the summer of 1992 as that other "Jump," by Kris Kross, and it earned House of Pain just as much street cred. But *Same* was a statement of purpose—Everlast represents the first generation of white kids raised on hip-hop who speak its rhythms and lyrical codes as a first language—though he's capable of dropping some punky comparisons ("Like G.G. Allin I'm crazy ill" or "I'm not Phil Collins/More like Henry Rollins"), he has none of the Beasties' indie roots.

Though capable of telling stories (check out the criminal vignettes of *Same*'s "It Ain't a Crime," neither celebratory nor judgmental, just factual) Everlast preferred sticking to ingenious boasts, which only takes you so far. The third album showed that the concept had outlived its usefulness. And Everlast apparently understood that—he went on, of course, to a solo career that ably mixed hip-hop and protest folk, overflowing with genuine empathy.   —K.H.

Whitney Houston

   ★★★   Whitney Houston (Arista, 1985)
   ★★½ Whitney (Arista, 1987)
    ★½ I'm Your Baby Tonight (Arista, 1990)
  ★★★★ My Love Is Your Love (Arista, 1998)

★★★ Whitney: The Greatest Hits (Arista, 2000)
★★★½ Love Whitney (Arista, 2002)
★½ One Wish: The Holiday Album (Arista, 2003)

Soundtrack Appearances
★★ The Bodyguard (Arista, 1992)
★ Waiting to Exhale (Arista, 1995)
★★ The Preacher's Wife (Arista, 1996)

Whitney Houston has one of the most powerful and polished voices in popular music, an instrument exquisitely capable of balladic intimacy, gospel exuberance, and soulful expression, and she has misused that gift in more ways than most singers could imagine. She began her career slinging blandly romantic pap; from there, she became a singing actress and overblown torch song specialist. Eventually, she decided to show she did indeed have soul, but her career had been so battered by erratic behavior and rumored drug use that the achievement almost went unnoticed.

Although utterly calculating, *Whitney Houston* does have its moments, particularly when Houston leans toward R&B, as on "You Give Good Love." *Whitney,* on the other hand, was a shameless attempt to downplay the singer's blackness and thus capitalize on her Top 40 pop following. It made sense as a marketing move—the album generated four #1s, including the insanely chipper "I Wanna Dance With Somebody"—but as music it's not much.

I'm Your Baby Tonight found the singer trying to recapture the increasingly alienated R&B listeners who had been her initial audience, although the music was less soul than vaguely soulful. Houston would pick up this thread at the end of the decade with *My Love Is Your Love,* but in the meantime, Hollywood beckoned. She appeared in three movies and on their soundtracks. *The Bodyguard* contained her biggest hit, the rafter-rattling ballad "I Will Always Love You," but undermined her soul roots with an overwrought remake of Chaka Khan's epochal "I'm Every Woman." *Waiting to Exhale* had only three Houston efforts, including the hit "Exhale (Shoop Shoop)"; the rest was given over to tepid R&B by other artists. *The Preacher's Wife* is a good idea in theory, as it promises to return Houston to her gospel roots, but ends up bland and unconvincing, as if Houston were afraid to cut loose.

My Love Is Your Love boasts cameos by Mariah Carey, Faith Evans, and Missy Elliott, and comes closer to proving Houston's mettle as an R&B star than any album in her catalogue. Unfortunately, personal problems kept her from fully capitalizing on the achievement, and her label resorted to gimmicks—the bloated *Greatest Hits,* the ballad-focused *Love Whit-*

ney, and the lamentable Christmas collection *One Wish*—to keep new product in the stores. —J.D.C.

Howlin' Wolf

★★★★★ Howlin' Wolf/Moanin' in the Moonlight (1958, 1964; Chess/MCA, 1986)
★★★★★ His Greatest Sides, Vol. 1 (1967; MCA/Chess, 1986)
★★ The Super Super Blues Band (Chess, 1968)
★★★★ The London Sessions (1971; Chess/MCA, 1989)
★★★★ The Back Door Wolf (Chess, 1973)
★★★★ Cadillac Daddy: Memphis Recordings, 1952 (Rounder, 1987)
★★★★★ The Memphis Days: Definitive Edition, Vol. 1 (Bear Family, 1989)
★★★★★ The Memphis Days: Definitive Edition, Vol. 2 (Bear Family, 1990)
★★★★★ The Chess Box (MCA/Chess, 1991)
★★★★ Howlin' Wolf Rides Again (Flair, 1993)
★★ Highway 49 and Other Classics (Intercontinental, 1996)
★★ Bluesmaster (Universal, 1996)
★★★★ His Best (The Chess 50th Anniversary Collection) (MCA/Chess, 1997)
★★★ Goin' Down Slow (Classic World, 2000)
★★★ Legendary Blues Recordings: Howlin' Wolf (Direct Source, 2001)
★★ Killing Floor (Magnum, 2001)
★★ Electric Blues (Delta, 2001)
★★ Wolf at Your Door (Arpeggio Blues, 2001)
★★★★ The Real Folk Blues/More Real Folk Blues (MCA, 2002)
★★ In Concert (Prestige Elite, 2002)
★★★ Live at Joe's 1973 (Wolf, 2002)

Along with his lifetime rival, Muddy Waters, Howlin' Wolf was the archetypal Chicago bluesman—raw, electric, deep, and continually astonishing. Born Chester Burnett in 1910, the singer/guitarist was raised in Mississippi, there absorbing the country blues tradition of Robert Johnson and Charley Patton. Picking up on the harmonica style of Sonny Boy Williamson, he formed his first band in Memphis with James Cotton and Junior Parker in the 1930s; he'd go on to play with Ike Turner, Willie Dixon, and other genre greats. While seldom recording as a guitarist, he gripped listeners with his voice in the early '50s: Moving to Chicago, he recorded a series of seminal electrified singles whose appeal—particularly to Brit rock legends such as the Stones, Yardbirds, and Led Zeppelin—was their sheer visceral power.

The Chess Box is the best collection. Extending from 1951 to 1973, its three CDs feature 75 songs, including rarities and all Wolf's hits. "How Many More Years," "Smokestack Lightning," "I Ain't Superstitious," "Killing Floor," and "Back Door Man" are by turns sly, terrifying, spooky, profane, and wise. The Bear Family sets are absolutely scorching early-'50s blues, rawer even than his Chess classics. *His Best* is the finest single-CD compilation; *Rides Again* is also phenomenal—Wolf young and very hungry. The paired *Howlin' Wolf* and *Moanin' in the Moonlight* CD brings together his two most consistent albums. *The London Sessions* is a good late collaboration with Eric Clapton, Stevie Winwood, Charlie Watts, and Bill Wyman; *Cadillac Daddy* is another great review of the earliest work. All of the Chess records are worth seeking out. *The Box,* however, is so thorough (and nicely annotated) that it serves as more than a mere introduction. —P.E.

The Human League

★½	Reproduction (1979; Caroline, 2003)
★★	Travelogue (1980; Caroline, 2003)
★★★	Dare (1981; Caroline, 1997)
★★½	Love and Dancing (1982; Virgin, 1998)
★★	Fascination! (EP) (A&M, 1983)
★½	Hysteria (1984; EMI, 1998)
★★½	Crash (1986; EMI, 2004)
★★★½	Greatest Hits (A&M, 1988)
★½	Romantic? (A&M, 1990)
★	Octopus (East/West, 1995)
★★★	The Very Best of the Human League (Ark 21, 1998)
★½	Secrets (Ark 21, 2001)

The most impressive thing about the Human League's output isn't that the band went from avant pop to Top 40 in three albums, but that its best singles hold up despite all the hokey electronics.

Needless to say, the League's early recordings sound pretty primitive at this point. With its buzzing, clanking synths and dour "postindustrial" perspective, *Reproduction* sounds less like a rock album than an art school project gone awry; even its nod to the mainstream—a cover of the Righteous Brothers' "You've Lost That Loving Feeling"—seems studied and theory-driven. The League loosens up some with *Travelogue,* with songs that are more melodic and accessible. But the rudimentary synth programming renders the arrangements clunky and mechanical.

Between *Travelogue* and *Dare* two unexpected developments dramatically changed the Human League's sound. One was the departure of Martyn Ware and Ian Marsh, the band's original synth wizards; the other was the introduction of the Linn drum, a computerized drum machine that used digitally

sampled drum sounds instead of synthesized equivalents. Original singer Phil Oakey recruited a new lineup, including ex-Rezillo Jo Callis plus singers Joanne Catherall and Susanne Sulley (whom Oakey claimed to have met at a disco), and delivered the first true synth-pop album. In truth, the most radical thing about *Dare* was its instrumentation, since the songs—particularly "Love Action (I Believe in Love)" and the marvelously melodramatic "Don't You Want Me"—were fairly conventional pop numbers. But in 1981, drum machines and sequencers were novelty enough, and helped make *Dare* an international smash.

The League immediately cashed in on its newfound success, releasing an amusing album of dance-oriented remixes entitled *Love and Dancing,* which is credited, in a nod to Barry White, to the League Unlimited Orchestra. An amusing trifle, it's a prelude of sorts to *Fascination!,* a somewhat thinner slice of dance pop whose principal point of interest is the flirtatious "(Keep Feeling) Fascination." Apparently afraid of falling into a rut, the Human League tried to turn serious again with *Hysteria.* Unfortunately, pompous message-heavy numbers such as "The Lebanon" are as ridiculous as dance fluff like "Rock Me Again and Again and Again and Again and Again and Again."

Luckily, the League then decamped for Minneapolis and the studios of Jimmy Jam and Terry Lewis. *Crash* is a fairly schizo affair, with some songs ("Money," for instance) sounding like the Human League of yore, albeit with a better rhythm section, and others ("Swang") coming across like contemporary R&B sung by the generally soulless Oakey, Sulley, and Catherall. Fortunately, "Human," a classic Jam & Lewis ballad, finds the perfect middle ground, thus rescuing the album as well as the group.

"Human," along with the rest of the group's singles, can also be found on *Greatest Hits,* which is understandably the most consistent album in the group's catalogue. (*The Very Best* offers a similar, though slightly inferior, selection.) The League returns to its old tricks with *Romantic?* and seems to have recorded *Octopus* and *Secrets* simply to have a "new album" to flog while working the nostalgia circuit. —J.D.C.

Humble Pie

★★½	Rock On (1971; MCA, 2000)
★★	Performance: Rockin' the Fillmore (1971; A&M, 1990)
★	Smokin' (1972; A&M, 1990)
★	On to Victory (Atco, 1980)
★	Go for the Throat (1980; Atco, 1991)
★★½	Humble Pie Classics (A&M, 1987)

★★ Hot 'n' Nasty: The Anthology (A&M, 1994)
★★ King Biscuit Flower Hour (King Biscuit, 1996)
★★ Natural Born Boogie (Recall, 1999)
★ Natural Born Boogie: BBC Sessions (Varèse, 2000)
★½ Live at the Whisky A-Go-Go '69 (Sanctuary, 2002)

At the peak of the Pie's inscrutably monstrous success—*Performance: Rockin' the Fillmore*—amiable maniac Steve Marriott brandished one of the most annoying voices in rock: a hectoring, sandpaper parody of black authenticity. With the group's platform boots and troglodyte riffing crushing the subtlety out of blues standards, *Fillmore* featured a 16-minute slaughter of Muddy Waters' "Rollin' Stone" that typified the band's "appeal." Now unlistenable, this stuff then was considered soulful, perhaps as a populist headbanging antidote to the smarmy "good taste" of the singer/songwriters who dominated radio.

For Marriott, at least artistically, such tripe was a bringdown. Having begun as a snappy popster with Small Faces, he formed Humble Pie in 1968 as a progressive outfit whose first two albums weren't bad, no matter how fawning their homage to the Band. *Rock On* hit harder, but still nodded toward taste. Peter Frampton helped keep things tuneful. Formerly of the Herd and later to find megastardom as a heartthrob, Frampton on guitar balanced Marriott like sweet does sour. Soon enough, though, Humble Pie headed for the boogie wastelands, never to return.

With more than 30 cuts, *Hot 'n' Nasty* is enough Humble Pie for anyone; the *King Biscuit* CD features characteristic live work from 1973—powerful in a neanderthal kind of way. —P.E.

Hüsker Dü

★★ Land Speed Record (SST, 1981)
★★★ Everything Falls Apart (Reflex, 1982)
★★★★ Metal Circus (EP) (SST, 1983)
★★★★★ Zen Arcade (SST, 1984)
★★★★★ New Day Rising (SST, 1985)
★★★★½ Flip Your Wig (SST, 1985)
★★★★ Candy Apple Grey (Warner Bros., 1986)
★★★ Warehouse: Songs and Stories (Warner Bros., 1987)
★★★ The Living End (Warner Bros., 1994)

You can see Hüsker Dü on the cover of *Zen Arcade:* three Midwestern boys wandering through the junkyard of their souls, seeing their lives piled up like abandoned scrap metal, steeling themselves to build toweringly inspirational cathedrals of industrial-strength punk rock guitar noise. The Minneapolis trio emerged from the hardcore scene, but the Hüskers' savage sound set them apart, as did the stark emotional exorcisms in their songs. The band had two singer/songwriters on the job: Guitarist Bob Mould looked a lot like Charlie Brown, drummer Grant Hart looked a lot like Snoopy, and as they traded vocals back and forth in their happy-sad songs of adolescent turmoil, it was easy for fans to imagine them cheering each other up, even if they hated each other in real life. Bassist Greg Norton didn't write or sing—he was the band's token straight guy, even though he had the gayest mustache in indie rock. The Hüskers had a this-could-be-you realness about them; for one thing, they were easily the ugliest, worst-dressed rock band of all time, which is intended as a compliment. Their records were cheaply recorded, and for that matter badly recorded; but for a few years, everything they touched felt noisy, aggressive, compassionate, human.

Good as the early hardcore records were, the story really begins with the 1983 EP *Metal Circus.* Acerbic but not ironic, including not one but two explicit anti-rape songs, *Metal Circus* burns with moral zeal and guitar bile. The band followed it with a noise-soaked single covering the Byrds' "Eight Miles High" (so far unissued on CD), which set the table for the monster double album *Zen Arcade.* There's a loose plot here about a teenage boy leaving home and running away to the city, but the real surprise is the expansive musical and emotional approach, as the Hüskers stretch from the two-minute acoustic kiss-off "Never Talking to You Again" to the 14-minute psychedelic feedback finale "Reoccuring Dreams," with an unforgettable plug-pulling ending. The songs slam home, especially "Something I Learned Today," "Newest Industry," "Pink Turns to Blue," and "Whatever." Side three is louder than the last 20 minutes of *The Wild Bunch,* and just as moving. Buried in all the noise, an inspirational message: "Don't get up, don't give in, don't let go, don't let on."

Acclaimed as geniuses overnight, despite the fact that they were barely breaking even, the Hüskers released *New Day Rising* just a few months later. The intensity of the guitar kicks harder than ever before, especially on "Powerline," but it's their song album, with a cheerfully carefree kamikaze approach to pop melody and structure. "Books About UFOs" and "I Apologize" sound like garbage trucks trying to sing Beach Boys tunes, while Mould breaks out his acoustic guitar for the devastating "Celebrated Summer" and "Perfect Example." Tune for tune, it's their best album, and a huge influence on Nirvana and all that followed. Later that year, it was time for *Flip Your Wig,* a little straighter but still packed with great tunes, especially Mould's protest song against literally everything, "Makes No Sense At All," and Hart's ode to childhood sledding memories, "Flexible Flyer."

At this point, nobody was making rock records anywhere near as intense as the Hüskers, who were churning them out every six months. They kept their historic roll going with *Candy Apple Grey,* their most downbeat album (and their major-label debut), with the purgative climax of "Eiffel Tower High," "No Promise Have I Made," and "All This I've Done for You." But *Warehouse,* another double album, aimed for professional rock craft, which was beyond the band's skill set—what sounded like mushy pop music to hardcore fans still sounded like sloppy guitar noise to everyone else. There are good songs if you dig them out—"Could You Be the One" even cracked MTV—but the Hüskers were spreading themselves too thin. They broke up acrimoniously, leading to a live epilogue, *The Living End,* which has a swell version of the Ramones' "Sheena Is a Punk Rocker," and solo projects. As they once sang, everything falls apart; Hüsker Dü fell apart more loudly than anybody else. —R.S.

i

Ice Cube

★★★★★	AmeriKKKa's Most Wanted (Priority, 1990)
★★★★	Death Certificate (Priority, 1991)
★★★½	The Predator (Priority, 1992)
★★★	Lethal Injection (Priority, 1994)
★★★	Bootlegs & B-Sides (Priority, 1995)
★★★	Featuring . . . Ice Cube (Priority, 1997)
★★★	War & Peace, Vol. 1 (The War Disc) (Priority, 1998)
★★★	War & Peace, Vol. 2 (The Peace Disc) (Priority, 2000)
★★★★	Greatest Hits (Priority, 2001)

"It's the nigga ya love to hate!" Roaring out of the blocks, holding his mike like a Glock, Ice Cube opened his 1990 solo debut with those words, and for the first half of the '90s, the man born O'Shea Jackson lived up to his pledge with a vengeance. One of the most ferocious and effective rappers ever to pick up a mike, Ice Cube was the first member to defect from notorious gangsta rap pioneers N.W.A, and no matter where you rank him on the shortlist of the Greatest MCs of All Time, it's clear that Cube changed the hip-hop game. While a student at Taft High School in Woodland Hills, CA (where he was bused from his home in South Central L.A.), Cube, who had learned how to combine profanity with hilarity from Richard Pryor records, wrote the seminal story-rap "Boyz N Tha Hood." At the time, Cube had a group called CIA with his buddies Sir Jinx and Kid Disaster. Then Eazy-E recorded "Boyz" and released it in 1987 as the first record on his Ruthless label; the single's success led directly to the creation of N.W.A, a group that consisted of Cube, Dr. Dre, Eazy-E, MC Ren, and Yella. Cube had gone to Phoenix, AZ, to get a one-year degree in architectural drafting, but returned in time to rap and write many of the rhymes on N.W.A's 1988 debut, *Straight Outta Compton*. A genuine street-level phenomenon, *Straight Outta Compton* aroused the ire of the FBI and sold more than 3 million copies with nearly zero radio airplay.

A beef with N.W.A's management prompted Cube to go solo, and Cube teamed up with the Bomb Squad, Public Enemy's production team and the preeminent beatmakers of the time. Together they made *AmeriKKKa's Most Wanted*, an album of menacing, unflinchingly fierce rhymes that took millions of listeners deep into the terrors of South Central L.A.

A year later, *Death Certificate* continued the brutal sonic and lyrical assault, but the multiplatinum album found Cube growing more articulate even as he grew more vulgar. The man who once wrote "F— Tha Police" now took lyrical aim at LAPD Chief Darryl Gates: "Turn him over with a spatula/Now you got Kentucky Fried cracker." Factor in the sensational violence of "Black Korea" (a song that apparently condoned the burning of Korean-owned convenience stores) and *Death Certificate* was roundly condemned by a rattled news media, including *Billboard* magazine. But hey, if you didn't like it, well, like Cube said, you could new jack swing from his nuts.

Followup *The Predator* debuted at #1 on both the pop and R&B charts, the first album ever to do so. With the Bomb Squad out of the mix, production duties were handled primarily by Cube, Sir Jinx, and DJ Pooh, and their collective fondness for P-Funk and Isley Brothers–derived loops was amply evident. By this time Cube had shaved off his Jheri curl and felt comfy enough to release his first laidback classic, "It Was a Good Day." (The fantastic remix of "It Was a Good Day" on *Bootlegs & B-Sides* uses a loop of the Staple Singers' "Let's Do It Again" that ups the blissful sentiments of the original.) *The Predator* also included "Check Yo Self," Cube's hit collaboration with duo Das Efx. On 1994's *Lethal Injection*, Cube's original power seemed to have waned, but typically ill tracks like the musically sweet lowrider classic "You Know How We Do It" shone.

Cube and his estranged running partner Dre eventually buried the hatchet and recorded the duet "Natural Born Killaz" (which appears on 1997's so-so compilation *Featuring . . . Ice Cube*), and in 2000 Dre took Cube out on his Up In Smoke tour (immortalized on a DVD of the same name). Fanatics should also ferret out Cube-related releases by Westside Connection (Cube's group with W.C. and Mack 10), protégés Yo-Yo (1991's *Make Way for the Motherlode*), Kam (1994's *Neva Again*), and Da Lench Mob (1994's *Guerillas in tha Mist*), as well as the soundtracks to films Cube has starred in, including *Higher Learning, Dangerous Ground, Friday,* and *Barbershop.* The out-of-print *Kill at Will* EP, released in 1990, is also worth finding for the awesome "Dead Homiez." While latter-day Cube releases have been maligned as soft (just about anything would seem lightweight when compared to his early work), both *War & Peace* discs have at least a couple great party jams. Now a proven Hollywood actor and screenwriter, Cube commands attention and respect with anything he does; no matter the venue, Ice Cube s presence simply cannot be discounted.   —P.R.

Ice-T

★★★	Rhyme Pays (Sire, 1987)
★★★★	Power (Sire, 1988)
★★★★	The Iceberg/Freedom of Speech . . . Just Watch What You Say (Sire, 1989)
★★★★	O.G.: Original Gangster (Sire, 1991)
★★	Body Count (Sire, 1992)
★★	Home Invasion (Priority, 1993)
★★★	The Classic Collection (Rhino, 1993)
★★½	VI: Return of the Real (Priority, 1996)
★★	7th Deadly Sin (Atomic Pop, 1999)
★★★★	Greatest Hits: The Evidence (Atomic Pop, 2000)

Ice-T's lyrical preoccupations (pimping, police brutality, thug life) are now the most clichéd motifs in hip-hop, but he was the first West Coast rap star to get those themes over to the massive record-buying public of Middle America. While he often wore the de rigueur gangsta uniform of ski cap and wifebeater T-shirt, Ice-T's lightish skin and flowing ponytail gave him a different look, and his unadulterated, intelligent rhymes were often critical of criminality on both sides of the law. Born Tracy Morrow in Newark, NJ, in 1959, Ice-T was raised in the gang-infested streets of South Central Los Angeles, and took his MC handle from the infamous pimp-turned-novelist Iceberg Slim. His first single was 1983's "The Coldest Rap" (much of his early work reappeared on 1993's *The Classic Collection*). He quickly found his opinionated foot-

ing. *Power* (1988) featured "I'm Your Pusher," based around Curtis Mayfield's "Pusherman," a strong antidrug song ("For this bass you don't need a pipe/Just a tempo to keep you hype") where a deadpan Ice-T hooked up a jonesing customer with "dope" 12-inch records. No matter how important such songs were at the time (and their message remains relevant), the tinny drum programming has not dated well. Yet the rolling groove of "Colors" (his theme song to the 1988 film of the same name), where Ice-T tells the first-person tale of a gangster ("I'm a nightmare walking/Psychopath talking"), retains a rugged musical appeal. From the screaming sirens of "Home of the Bodybag" that open 1991's *O.G.: Original Gangster,* Ice-T presented an adrenalized, near-classic: gangsta rap with a minimum of bullshit. In 1992, he fronted his heavy metal group Body Count, and while they were no better than the countless rap/metal acts they spawned, the ensuing media firestorm over their track "Cop Killer" spurred Ice-T to take to the lecture circuit, speaking at Harvard about First Amendment rights and civil liberties. Film and TV work has been a big part of Ice-T's career: a rapping cameo in the 1984 movie *Breakin',* more substantial roles in films *New Jack City* and *Trespass,* and a current starring role (as, of all things, a police detective) in NBC's *Law & Order: Special Victims Unit.*   —P.R.

Idlewild

★★★½	Hope Is Important (Odeon, 1999)
★★★★	100 Broken Windows (EMI, 2000)
★★½	The Remote Part (EMI, 2002)

Coming of age in the last days of Brit Pop's glory years (Oasis, Blur, Suede), Idlewild searched outside of the Brit Rock music tradition of Beatles, Kinks, Bowie, glam rock, and vaudeville to the western shores of America, finding themselves intoxicated by American indie and classic alt-rock. Early R.E.M., Pixies, Nirvana, and Slint records in tow, *Hope Is Important* is very much a love letter to their favorite bands, as spiky anthems such as "Captain," and "When I Argue I See Shapes" betray them as members of the *Nevermind* generation. Idlewild grows up and gets smart ("Roseability" references Gertrude Stein!) on their second album, a gorgeous mixture of jangle pop and heavy rock: *100 Broken Windows* is a step up in songwriting quality, as melody takes precedence over noise, for great results. Sadly, they may have grown up too fast. *The Remote Part* (2002) sees the band coming of age a little too fast. Where earlier records showed vocalist Roddy Woomble as an engaging, idiosyncratic, and above all bravely intelligent lyricist, *The Remote Part* finds him settling for sweeping generalizations. The band follows suit, playing for big crowds with U2-style arena rock. —C.R.

Billy Idol

★★★ Billy Idol (1982; Capitol, 2001)
★★★★½ Rebel Yell (1983; Capitol, 1999)
★★★ Whiplash Smile (Chrysalis, 1986)
★★★★ Vital Idol (1987; Capitol, 2002)
★★★ Charmed Life (Chrysalis, 1990)
★ Cyberpunk (Chrysalis, 1993)
★★★★½ Greatest Hits (Capitol, 2001)
★★★ VH1 Storytellers (Capitol, 2002)

One of the reasons Billy Idol is so dearly beloved is because he obviously didn't know any better. Of all the mindless new-wave haircut rockers of the '80s, he was the most mindless, the most rocking, and the most '80s, shaking his fist, greasing his hair, and boozing and brawling through a rock-star trip that was so unironic, it *had* to be ironic. He began as a punk, singing lead for Generation X. But as soon as that band folded, he launched his solo career with the 1982 single "White Wedding," and it turned out his name wasn't the joke everybody had assumed. "White Wedding" became a monster hit, with Billy cramming himself into skintight black leather pants and singing like Richard Nixon doing an Elvis imitation, and things only got better from there. He remade Generation X's best song, "Dancing With Myself," as a 1983 video in which Billy stands alone at the top of a postnuclear wasteland, a Prometheus in chains, showing off his impressive upper-lip musculature and acting out all his tawdriest fantasies of adolescent idolatry. As the sweat pours out of his body, and the zombies dance all around him, Billy knows the loneliness that only the gods know.

Rebel Yell was a brilliant combination of punk, disco, synth pop, glam rock, metal, and mud wrestling, with producer Keith Forsey cranking the rhythm tracks and guitar sidekick Steve Stevens going *wonka-wonk* at the appropriately dramatic moments. Billy's finest hits are all here: "Blue Highway," "Catch My Fall," and the ludicrously pretentious "Eyes Without a Face" ("Hanging out by the state line/Turning holy water into wine/Drinking it down," and so on). But the killer is the title track, which by federal law was played at every prom for the rest of the decade. "Rebel Yell" preaches a gospel of sex as liberation, with the example of a dancing queen who becomes insatiable in the midnight hour, tormenting Billy with screams for "mo, mo, mo!" of his funky stuff. It was the sort of song you could be proud to get your first speeding ticket to, and the video was one of the cinematic landmarks of the '80s, capturing unbelievable levels of egomania, hostility, sexual hysteria, and narcissistic preening.

Whiplash Smile was a letdown, but "To Be a Lover" is as good as anything on *Rebel Yell* (better than the William Bell original, truth be told), and "Sweet Sixteen" was a smoldery acoustic interlude. The remix album *Vital Idol* had a hit cover of Tommy James' "Mony Mony," inspiring obscene sing-alongs at high school dances across the land. *Charmed Life* was smarmily entertaining enough to make *Rebel Yell* sound subtle, with the manic "Cradle of Love," an idiotic cover of the Doors' "L.A. Woman," the rockabilly standard "Endless Sleep," and the confessional "Trouble With the Sweet Stuff," which attested to Billy's dangerous Clairol Styling Gel habit. Despite his dull *Cyberpunk*, a near-fatal 1990 motorcycle crash, and at least one high-profile drug overdose, Billy remains inexplicably alive, unrepentant, still revered as the New Romantic era's version of Busta Rhymes. He stole the show at MTV's 2001 20th-anniversary special, rocking the house with a torrid "Rebel Yell." He also appeared in *The Wedding Singer,* making the climax one of the funniest 15-minute comic sequences ever filmed. It is an atrocity that Robin Williams has an Oscar for Best Supporting Actor and Billy doesn't. —R.S.

Natalie Imbruglia

★★ Left of the Middle (RCA, 1998)
★★½ White Lilies Island (RCA, 2001)

When Natalie Imbruglia arrived in 1998, the former Australian teen soap star managed to conquer the American pop charts without much battle, thanks to an undeniable hit, "Torn." Resurrected from the catalogue of alt-rock also-rans Ednaswap, the addictively catchy song deserved every bit of radio overplay it got. However, *Left of the Middle,* Imbruglia's debut, never matches its standout track. Instead, the album tries a little of everything—some Alanis Morissette rock ("One More Addiction"), some Portishead trip-hop noir ("Leave Me Alone"), even some old Madonna house ("Impressed")—without much distinction. Imbruglia's voice, with a guileless sweetness that worked so well on "Torn," seems unremarkable elsewhere.

Its followup, *White Lilies Island,* improves upon the debut by offering a more consistent medium-rock sound—less stylized, and seeming less market-researched to capture the latest hot sounds. Here, the reference points are more random: the rushing vocals and swirling music of "That Day" sound like Pink singing Morrissey; "Satellite" is Crosby, Stills, & Nash–style pop-folk. "Wrong Impression," meanwhile, makes a valiant attempt at rewriting "Torn" but doesn't quite match its predecessor's heart-on-the-sleeve tunefulness (or, it turned out, its chart success). Like its predecessor, there's little essential listening on *White Lilies Island,* but the album works perfectly well as somewhat generic, slightly left-of-center mainstream pop. —R.M.S.

Imperial Teen

- ★★★½ Seasick (PolyGram, 1996)
- ★★★½ What Is Not to Love (Slash, 1999)
- ★★★½ On (Merge, 2002)
- ★★★ Live at Maxwell's (DCN, 2002)

The members of Imperial Teen have some loud, crashing noises in their backgound—keyboardist Roddy Bottum was in Faith No More, and drummer Lynn Perko played with the Dicks—but now they specialize in old-school pop-rock and relatively mature themes, making them a happy indie rock oddity. Like bands such as Yo La Tengo or the Go-Betweens, Imperial Teen promise that love among consenting adults is the key to happiness, and that the modest glamour of life in a cult rock band beats having a day job. To communicate this, they employ bright hooks and riffs, delicate harmonies, catchy choruses, and guitar-and-keyboard raveups. Imperial Teen's vibe is both gay and straight, male and female, sweet and a touch sadistic, as Bottum can proclaim, "Why you gotta be so proud?/I'm the one with lipstick on" just as fervently as the whole band can holler "I like you/I like you" until the crowd believes it. Although widely separated in years and recorded for different record labels, their three studio albums are remarkably consistent. *Live at Maxwell's* is full of premium material, but the rougher, flatter sound renders it best for those already in the Imperial court. —M.M.

The Impressions

- ★★★★★ Curtis Mayfield and the Impressions: The Anthology, 1961–1977 (MCA, 1992)
- ★★★★ The Very Best of the Impressions (Rhino, 1997)
- ★★★★★ Ultimate Collection (Hip-O, 2001)

Beginning with "Gypsy Woman," from 1961, the Impressions' *Ultimate Collection* defines the sweet inspiration of soul music. This Chicago-based harmony group amplifies its gospel conviction ("Amen," "Meeting Over Yonder") through a lush, orchestral pop approach ("It's All Right," "You Must Believe Me"). Working with arranger Johnny Pate, group leader Curtis Mayfield constructs a supple wall of sound: His dynamic string arrangements underline rather than undercut the urgency of his messages. "People

Get Ready" and "Keep On Pushing" reflect and reinforce the hard-earned optimism of the civil rights movement. These two spiritual pleas sound more relevant—and necessary—than ever. Original lead singer Jerry Butler left after an initial hit, "For Your Precious Love," in 1958, and was replaced by Fred Cash. (It's no accident that Butler later achieved solo success with producers Gamble and Huff; the precise richness of Curtis Mayfield's songwriting and production strongly foreshadows the Sound of Philadelphia.) Mayfield, Cash, and Sam Gooden carried on together until 1970, when Mayfield departed to pursue a solo career; on its two discs, *The Anthology, 1961–1977* couples most of the essential Impressions sides with Mayfield's socially conscious '70s work. While Motown hits of the mid-'60s go for your gut, the Impressions aim a little higher—and never miss. —M.C./G.F.

Incubus

- ★ Fungus Amongus (Epic/Immortal, 1995)
- ★★ S.C.I.E.N.C.E. (Epic/Immortal, 1997)
- ★★★★ Make Yourself (Epic/Immortal, 1999)
- ★★★ Morning View (Epic/Immortal, 2001)
- ★★★ A Crow Left of the Murder (Epic/Immortal, 2003)

Although it may be only vaguely recalled, the great funk-metal scare occurred at the dawn of the '90s, between the waning of hair metal and the waxing of grunge. Incubus was a latecomer to a boomlet of shirtless suburban funkateers who were greatly influenced by the Red Hot Chili Peppers, Faith No More, and Primus. *Fungus Amongus,* a compendium of slapped bass, atonal guitar noise, and forced wackiness, seemed hopelessly dated in 1995.

S.C.I.E.N.C.E., from 1997, links funk metal to the rap metal (replete with turntable scratches and downtuned guitars), a fusion that had become the dominant rock idiom by the decade's end. But the record is far more emotionally and texturally nuanced than those by peers like Korn, and its Santana-esque "Summer Romance" supports the fact that Brandon Boyd, unlike Anthony Kiedis or Les Claypool, is a fine singer. Hence, *Make Yourself*'s shift toward genuine songwriting was quite welcome. Incubus had found a betamale approach to new-metal: roaring, assymetrical riffs and herky-jerky dynamics coexisting with Boyd's yearning tenor and burgeoning melodic gift. The record yielded two of the finest Modern Rock singles of the era, "Stellar" and "Drive," easily the band's best song.

Morning View purged Incubus' remaining traces of hip-hop (barring the odd scratch) but boasted only one standout cut, the exultant "Wish You Were Here." *A Crow Left of the Murder* commences with the turbulent "Megalomaniac," a barely veiled condemnation of George W. Bush, and dives headlong into art rock reminiscent of the Police and King Crimson. If the album offers few immediate pleasures, at least Incubus demonstrates a glimmer of ambition. During the past decade, it has been much bemoaned that major labels no longer give artists time to develop; Incubus' steadily improving arc is evidence, however scant, to the contrary.   —R.K.

India.Arie

★★★½   Acoustic Soul (Motown, 2001)
★★★   Voyage to India (Motown, 2002)

Combining African head wraps with a folkie sensibility, India.Arie looked like Erykah Badu but sounded more like an upbeat Tracy Chapman when she first arrived on the scene. On her debut album, matter-of-factly called *Acoustic Soul,* neo-soul is the flavor, but with a strong singer/songwriter bent—and a focus on organic over orgasmic. The lyrics spell out the vibes: She's not built like a supermodel, as she sings in the reggaeish single "Video," and she loves brown skin kissed by the sun ("Brown Skin"). She sings of promises, courage, and wisdom, and strives to achieve holistic balance in her life. She also makes sure to pay tribute to her forebears, naming everyone from Billie Holiday to Stevie Wonder in song. And while the moods of *Acoustic Soul* rarely deviate from smooth, laid-back, and occasionally sultry, the album's sameness is more than made up for by the strength of the songs.

The followup, *Voyage to India,* offers few surprises, and because Arie's earth-mother/unplugged-diva thing is now familiar, there's less novelty appeal. Still, "Little Things," her first song not built around acoustic guitar, shows growth, while other tracks ("Talk to Her," "Slow Down," "Good Man") relay a soul classicism that should make her label proud. While her occasional impulse to preach syrupy New Age platitudes and commit other lyrical offenses mar the record (as does a slightly slicker production sheen), on the whole, *Voyage* compares favorably with the debut—and keeps you wanting more.   —R.M.S.

Indigo Girls

★★   Strange Fire (Indigo, 1987)
★★★★   Indigo Girls (Sony, 1989)
★★★½   Nomads Indians Saints (Sony, 1990)
★★★   Rites of Passage (Sony, 1992)
★★★½   Swamp Ophelia (Sony, 1994)
★★   1200 Curfews [live] (Epic, 1995)
★★   Shaming of the Sun (Epic, 1997)
★★★½   Come On Now Social (Epic, 1999)
★★★★   Retrospective (Epic, 2000)
★★★   Become You (Sony, 2002)
★★★   All That We Let In (Sony, 2004)

The Indigo Girls personify what happens when two distinct sensibilities, voices, and worldviews come together to create something transcendently its own. Amy Ray's a lapsed goth girl with an astringent cynicism; Emily Saliers is the pop optimist with the taste for jangle. Together their passion outstripped their polish, but only for the space of one album. Their earnest and folky debut, *Strange Fire,* didn't stoke much interest, but it did beget Emily Saliers and Amy Ray's signature sound—acoustic, passionate, and witty. Some interesting bonus tracks on the 2000 rerelease make informative listening for fans of the outfit's more complex and satisfying later work. But it wasn't until 1989's self-titled album that the Girls came into their own. They had a hand from indie darlings such as Irish singer/songwriter Luka Bloom and R.E.M.'s Michael Stipe, and a hefty label push, but there was much else on the Girls' side—the mainstream visibility of queer activism cleared the way for a young, modern breed of the guitar-toting lesbian, and Ray's and Saliers' rumored lesbianism gave them an edge. It helps that this was some of the most difficult, dangerous, beautifully assembled folk-pop ever made. *Nomads Indians Saints* takes a more generous, poetic, global view of love, faith, and loss: The title song refers to beatific states of being, and the searing "You and Me of the 10,000 Wars" is a mature and unflinching look at the bedroom battlefield. Still struggling not to give in to a sliding scale of morality, Indigo Girls burrow deeper into the own psyches on *Rites of Passage,* exploring the joys of art and the pitfalls of aesthetic solipsism, all the time remaining on the political side of the angels (in the "issue" songs about the plight of the Native American and other left-wing sure things) without alienating the kind of listener who just can't help singing along. *Swamp Ophelia* is brushed across a bigger canvas; it's prog-rock without the pomp. The emotional scope is enormous on the lush and thoughtful love songs, the rich instrumentation (cello, mandolin, violin, viola, bouzouki, dobro, percussion including bongos, vibrachime, and much more) adds depth to the Girls' increasingly sophisticated palette of concerns.

With *Shaming of the Sun,* the formula is firmly in place, but the duo seems to be out of tunes—there isn't much to catch the ear after the kickoff, "Shame on You." But as one century gives way to the next, the Girls seem to perk up, in part because they haul in every indie/folkfest name in their Rolodexes—Joan Osborne, Meshell Ndegéocello, Sheryl Crow, Sinéad O'Connor's backing band, and Kate Shellenbach from girl-funk outfit Luscious Jackson—and in part because Ray and Saliers stretch out of the folk-pop realm and into rockier ones, idling in the roadhouse here and taking a turn at slick country there. Then they throw it all away on *Become You,* sneaking back to their roots and concentrating mightily on the most pained bare-bones folk yet. *All That We Let In,* on the other hand, has a few surprises—the ska-influenced "Heartache for Everyone" and the almost B-52's-like "Perfect World." —A.B.

The Ink Spots

★★★★★ Anthology (MCA, 1998)
   ★★★ We Four: The Best of the Ink Spots (Jasmine Music, 1998)
    ★★ Favorites (MCA, 1999)
   ★★★ Millennium Collection: The Best of the Ink Spots (MCA, 1999)
   ★★★ Rare Air 1937–1944 (Flyright, 2001)

Founded in 1934, the Ink Spots developed a pop-oriented group-harmony style that kept them on the charts from 1939 through 1951 and influenced many of the most important vocal groups of the '50s. The group's trademark was the contrasting voices of lead tenor Bill Kenny and bass singers Orville Jones and Herb Kenny (the latter joining in 1944 after Jones' death). Kenny, in particular, with his impeccable control and diction in the highest register of his tenor, became the singer's singer, a master of technique with a peerless sense of drama. Of the prerock-era vocal groups, perhaps only the Ravens exerted an influence comparable to that of the Ink Spots.

Because there have been several lesser incarnations of the group over the decades, the buyer is advised to beware of any package not featuring the original members. MCA's two-disc *Anthology* is the most complete. It touches all the bases: hits like "When the Swallows Come Back to Capistrano," "Don't Get Around Much Anymore," and "To Each His Own"; the group's classic versions of "We'll Meet Again," "Until the Real Thing Comes Along," and "I Cover The Waterfront"; and collaborations with Ella Fitzgerald on "I'm Making Believe" and "I'm Beginning to See the Light." Also included are the original versions of songs that were hits in the '50s and '60s for the Platters—"My Prayer," "To Each His Own," "If I Didn't Care," and "I'll Never Smile Again"—and one that has become a staple of the Manhattan Transfer's repertoire, "Java Jive." Of the single-disc collections, *We Four* gets the nod because it contains 24 tracks; by comparison,

Millennium Collection offers twelve and *Favorites* only 10. The assembled radio transcriptions and other live tapes that make up *Rare Air 1937–1944* will not replace the familiar studio renditions, but are a welcome addition to a library of music that spawned untold thousands of doo-wop groups. —D.M./B.E.

Insane Clown Posse

     ★ Carnival of Carnage (1992; Island; 1998)
     ★ The Ringmaster (1994; Island, 1998)
   ★½ The Riddle Box (Jive, 1995)
   ★★ The Great Milenko (Island, 1997)
   ★½ Forgotten Freshness, Vols. 1 & 2 (Island, 1998)
   ★★ The Amazing Jeckel Brothers (Island, 1999)
  ★★★ Bizaar (Island, 2000)
  ★★★ Bizzar (Island, 2000)
   ★★ Forgotten Freshness, Vol. 3 (Psychopathic, 2001)
   ★★ Pendulum (Psychopathic, 2002)
   ★★ The Wraith: Shangri-La (Riviera, 2002)

The missing link between Kiss and Eminem, these greasepainted buffoons from Detroit built a small empire around personae of ultraviolent (as well as misogynist, homophobic, and racist) rapping clowns. Coming in the wake of gangsta rap and the explosion of porn, wrestling, and public profanity that characterized the '90s least-common-denominator revolution, ICP's Violent J (Joe Bruce) and Shaggy 2 Dope (Joey Utsler) rode several albums of raunchy rap-metal to far more than their allotted 15 minutes of fame. In time the Clowns revealed a conceptual complexity and self-referential pathos that was a cut above the rest, justifying their fame somewhat, though with the arrival of Eminem and Kid Rock the jig was certainly up.

After several ridiculous early albums of gangsta-inspired wigga posturing, the group came into its own with *The Great Milenko.* But it was dumb luck that brought success: Hours after its release, the album was recalled by Disney-owned Hollywood Records, fearing a conservative Christian boycott. ICP became famous overnight, which never would have happened on the scant merits of "Murder Go Round" and "Bugz on My Nutz" alone.

Island immediately rereleased *The Great Milenko* and launched the group's merchandising gravy train with multiple collectible versions of *The Amazing Jeckel Brothers*—whose "B*itches" and "Another Love Song" ("I could love you and treat you with class/... But thinking about that/I feel I'd rather kill you") established, for any who missed it before, ICP's pathological hatred of women.

Like Kiss before them, ICP are less musicians than hucksters in facepaint, selling special "Joker's Cards" (albums) to their beloved "Juggalos" (fans, a name suspiciously similar to *jigaboos*). On Halloween 2000 the group released two companion concept albums called *Bizaar* and *Bizzar*, which qualify as ICP's masterworks of both merchandising and music. With surprising clarity, J articulates the appeal of fantasy and engages in a hyperbolic, Eminem-like self-analysis, over consistently catchy tracks by the group's longtime studio hand Mike E. Clark. *Bizaar*'s "Take Me Away" questions rap as reality and instead insists on the need for fiction: "You wanna keep it real, walk out your door." Elsewhere J describes strictly bourgeois visions of terror ("I'll walk through Compton alone, sportin' Wranglers and a cowboy hat/. . . I'll hunt Michael Jackson's plastic surgeon, tell him, 'Hey, do me up' ") and wonders what it means to play the clown and turn out a success ("Look beneath the paint, bitch/It's the scrubs who won").

ICP never followed their double albums with anything worthwhile. *Pendulum* is a metal-heavy compilation of tracks included with their comic book series, and *The Wraith*, the storied sixth Joker's Card, drops the ball entirely by revealing that all along the whole thing was some bland divine plan: "Truth is we follow God, we've always been behind him/The Dark Carnival is God and may all Juggalos find Him!" Is this man's final dis of God, or His of us? —B.S.

INXS

★★½	INXS (Atco, 1980)
★★½	Underneath the Colours (1981; Atco, 1984)
★★★	Shabooh Shoobah (Atco, 1982)
★★★	The Swing (Atco, 1984)
★★★½	Listen Like Thieves (Atlantic, 1985)
★★★½	Kick (Atlantic, 1987)
★★★½	X (Atlantic, 1990)
★★★½	Live Baby Live (Atlantic, 1991)
★★★	Welcome to Wherever You Are (Atlantic, 1992)
★★★	Full Moon, Dirty Hearts (Atlantic, 1993)
★★★★	The Greatest Hits (Atlantic, 1994)
★★	Elegantly Wasted (Atlantic, 1997)
★★★½	Shine Like It Does: The Anthology (1979–1997) (Rhino, 2001)
★★★★	The Best Of (Rhino, 2002)

At their best, INXS were almost like an Australian Tom Petty and the Heartbreakers: an honorable pop-rock band, underappreciated by critics at the time, that achieved their relatively modest pop-rock goals, and whose music will survive on the radio long after some of their more pretentious competitors' work fades into obscurity. With singer Michael Hutchence exuding classic rock star bravado and the three Farriss brothers providing the essential instrumental muscle for this sextet, INXS had become an irresistible rock force by the end of the '80s. Finding a cohesive style, though, took them a while. On *INXS*, Hutchence's Jaggeresque vocals are already very developed, but the fusion of Kirk Pengilly's saxophone and the rhythm section's big beats doesn't quite come off. For *Shabooh Shoobah*, the band found their way to the big production sound that suited them, with the help of producer Mark Opitz. The songs are pared down to thick riffs and crunchy rhythms, and Hutchence introduces the deep Jim Morrison–like delivery that would come to define his style. *The Swing*, produced by Nile Rodgers, yielded the elegant funk hit "Original Sin" and hinted that the power of this band lay less in melody or even in hooks than in the dense, glossy beauty of their more atmospheric tracks. *Listen Like Thieves* includes the sax-driven workout "What You Need," and the airy and majestic "Shine Like It Does" and "This Time," which borrowed from U2 a trance-rock momentum. On *Kick*, the band's most successful album, Hutchence applied his telegraphic lyrical style to "New Sensation" and "Devil Inside." With "Never Tear Us Apart" and its gorgeous synth-cello undergirding, INXS proved themselves capable of delivering a truly lovely ballad. *X* was a sort of Son of *Kick*: Rather than breaking ground, INXS continued to write songs that were crafty, spacious, and inviting, but whose meaning remained a teasing mystery. The band finally called it quits when Hutchence hanged himself in November of 1997; his long-anticpated solo debut was released in 1999. —P.E.

Iron Maiden

★★★½	Iron Maiden (1980; Sanctuary/Metal Is, 2002)
★★½	Killers (1981; Sanctuary/Metal Is, 2002)
★★★½	The Number of the Beast (1982; Sanctuary/Metal Is, 2002)
★★	Piece of Mind (1983; Sanctuary/Metal Is, 2002)
★★½	Powerslave (1984; Sanctuary/Metal Is, 2002)
★★	Live After Death (1985; Sanctuary/Metal Is, 2002)
★★½	Somewhere in Time (1986; Sanctuary/Metal Is, 2002)
★★★½	Seventh Son of a Seventh Son (1988; Sanctuary/Metal Is, 2002)
★★★½	No Prayer for the Dying (1990; Sanctuary/Metal Is, 2002)
★★★	Fear of the Dark (1992; Sanctuary/Metal Is, 2002)

★★ A Real Live Dead One (1993; Sanctuary/Metal Is, 2002)
★★★½ Live at Donnington (1993; Sanctuary/Metal Is, 2002)
★★ The X Factor (1995; Sanctuary/Metal Is, 2002)
★★★★ Best of the Beast (1996; Sanctuary/Metal Is, 2002)
★ Virtual XI (1998; Sanctuary/Metal Is, 2002)
★★ Brave New World (Columbia, 2000)
★★½ Rock in Rio (Columbia, 2002)

Iron Maiden may have surfed in on the "new wave of British heavy metal"—the early-'80s movement that inspired Metallica and laid the foundations for death metal and thrash—but the band never made any claims to rock & roll revisionism. Indeed, rather than spurn the excesses of '70s metal, Maiden's early output embraces them, and though *Iron Maiden* and *Killers* are full of hyperdriven blues riffs and wank-arama guitar solos, they're offered with such unabashed passion that even the band's most obvious moves somehow avoid sounding clichéd. No wonder Maiden were the most influential English hard rockers of their generation.

After recording *Killers,* singer Paul Di'anno (whose work was hobbled by too much drinking) was replaced by former Samson vocalist Bruce Dickinson. Even though bassist and founder Steve Harris continued to write most of the band's material, Dickinson's powerful, dramatic voice opened the door to a more song-oriented approach. Although *The Number of the Beast* would never be mistaken for Def Leppard, it moved the band closer to the mainstream through cunningly tuneful numbers like "The Prisoner" and, especially, "Run to the Hills." (The album's references to the Antichrist also earned the band an undeserved reputation as Satanists.) Both *Piece of Mind* and *Powerslave* proceed in kind, albeit with diminished melodic interest, and *Live After Death* is a lengthy but predictable concert document.

With *Somewhere in Time,* the band begins to vary its sonic palette, augmenting its galloping bass lines and wide-vibrato vocals with occasional quiet bits, apparently in an attempt to make the songs more dramatic (note the slow, *Bolero*-like buildup given "Alexander the Great"). *Seventh Son of a Seventh Son* goes even further, adding synth sequences, acoustic guitars, even—gasp!—a ballad of sorts ("Infinite Dreams"), while fleshing out the vocal line with unexpectedly pop-friendly harmonies on "Can I Play With Madness." More of the same can be found on the intricately arranged *No Prayer for the Dying,* which includes the unnervingly catchy "Bring Your Daughter . . . to the Slaughter."

Fear of the Dark wastes much of its energy trying to maintain Maiden's aura of spook-house menace, although "From Here to Eternity" does at least deliver a solid chorus.

Iron Maiden's popularity crested at this point, and the band (understandably) tried to make the most of it by releasing a passel of live albums. The spotty, lackluster *A Real Live Dead One* was originally released as two separate discs; thanks to repackaging, there's now only one title to avoid. *Live at Donnington* is marginally better, with a more hit-intensive set list and genuinely fiery playing (even though Dickinson could no longer hit the high notes in "Run for the Hills").

Dickinson split for a solo career after that tour, and was replaced by Blaze Bayley for the sci-fi blather of *The X Factor.* Bayley's brief tenure is given unmerited emphasis in the otherwise solid retrospective *Best of the Beast,* but after *Virtual XI*—an album that would have been forgettable were it not for the rightwing anthem "The Clansman"—he was given the boot, and Dickinson was brought back into the fold for *Brave New World.* It seems unlikely that this "classic" Maiden will ever regain its late-'80s glory—although the band did reissue its catalogue following his return—but the solidly entertaining *Rock in Rio* indicates the band has quite a future on the nostalgia circuit. —J.D.C.

The Isley Brothers

★★★½ 3+3 (T-Neck/Legacy/Epic, 1973)
★★★ The Heat Is On/Featuring "Fight the Power" (T-Neck/Legacy/Epic, 1975)
★★★ Go for Your Guns (T-Neck/Legacy/Epic, 1977)
★★★ Winner Takes All (T-Neck/Legacy/Epic, 1979)
★★★ Between the Sheets (T-Neck/Legacy/Epic, 1983)
★★★★ Greatest Hits, Volume 1 (T-Neck/Legacy/Epic, 1984)
★★★★ Beautiful Ballads (T-Neck/Legacy/Epic, 1994)
★★★ Shout: The RCA Sessions (RCA, 1996)
★★★★★ It's Your Thing: The Story of the Isley Brothers (T-Neck/Legacy/Epic, 1999)
★★★★ Shake It Up, Baby: Shout, Twist, and Shout (Varèse Sarabande, 2000)
★★★ The Ultimate Isley Brothers (T-Neck/Legacy/Epic, 2000)
★★★½ Love Songs (T-Neck/Legacy/Epic, 2001)
★★★★ 20th Century Masters—The Millennium Collection: The Best of the Isley Brothers (Universal, 2001)

The Isley Brothers Featuring Ronald Isley

★★½ Spend the Night (Warner Bros., 1988)
★★★ Mission to Please (Island, 1996)
★★★ Eternal (DreamWorks, 2001)

Ronald, Rudolph, and O'Kelly Isley came roaring out of Cincinnati with "Shout Parts 1 & 2"; this 1959 rock & roll hit climaxes with a gospel-powered explosion that still gives goose bumps. The Isley Brothers jumped from label to label in the '60s, recording a handful of soul nuggets and a lot of filler (see *Shout: The RCA Sessions* for ample evidence). Lead singer Ronald—a raw, rangy tenor—and his harmonizing brothers connected only twice during their Tamla residency, but "This Old Heart of Mine (Is Weak for You)" and "I Guess I'll Always Love You" number among the great lost Motown songs, and are available on *20th Century Masters*. *Shake It Up Baby: Shout, Twist, and Shout* summarizes this period fairly well, leaving in some ragged edges along with galvanizing soul workouts like "Twist & Shout," "Respectable," and "Nobody but Me."

In retrospect, the turning point for the Isley Brothers was a young sideman they employed in the mid-'60s: Jimi Hendrix. Although he's barely noticeable on the tracks he recorded with the Isleys, Hendrix and his probing psychedelic spirit inspired younger brother Ernie Isley. When guitarist Ernie and bass-plucking Marvin joined the clan in the late '60s, the Isley Brothers constructed a bold, funky new sound to match—a grandly appointed soul castle built on solid rock.

"It's Your Thing" established the Isleys' T-Neck label by crossing over to the pop charts. This horny blast of Stax/Volt-style swagger doesn't hint at the new direction, but subsequent R&B hits like "Lay Away," "Work to Do," and "Pop That Thang" (all from 1972) introduce fresh rhythms and stinging lead-guitar lines to the elder Isleys' rough-hewn harmony attack. And talk about cover versions! At least Stephen Stills' "Love the One You're With" and Dylan's "Lay Lady Lay" are in the Isleys' thematic ballpark; resuscitating Seals and Crofts' "Summer Breeze" qualifies as a miracle. *3+3* and the sweet summer single "That Lady" (a funkadelicized rereading of an earlier track) brought the Isley Brothers mainstream success in 1973. Here the group settles into a comfortable—if increasingly predictable—game plan, splitting its albums between extended party-jam throwdowns and surprisingly tight, satisfying sex ballads. *It's Your Thing: The Story of the Isley Brothers* is the most comprehensive overview of the Isleys' career, emphasizing the cream of the '70s crop. Disc two of the three-disc set mines the deep funk vein of "That Lady," peaking with the politicized throb of "Fight the Power." The third reflects the lusty glow of the group's later years, after beginning with the plaintive "Harvest for the World." Alongside Funkadelic and Earth, Wind & Fire, the Isley Brothers led a crucial musical movement that we've only recently begun to appreciate. Steeped in R&B tradition, the T-Neck years also recall today's metal-funk cutting edge at times, but never when the Isley Brothers are singing. Both *Mission to Please* and *Eternal* demonstrate the Isleys' continuing relevance as well as their influence on today's neosoul crop, and both feature Ronald Isley's hip-hop Mack-(grand)daddy alter ego, Mr. Biggs, concocted with R. Kelly. —M.C./G.F.

Alan Jackson

★★	Here in the Real World (Arista, 1990)
★★½	Don't Rock the Jukebox (Arista, 1991)
★★★	A Lot About Livin' (And a Little 'Bout Love) (Arista, 1992)
★★	Honky Tonk Christmas (Arista, 1993)
★★	Who I Am (Arista, 1994)
★★★½	The Greatest Hits Collection (Arista, 1995)
★★½	Everything I Love (Arista, 1996)
★★	High Mileage (Arista, 1998)
★★	Under the Influence (Arista, 1999)
★★	Super Hits (Arista, 1999)
★★	When Somebody Loves You (Arista, 2000)
★★★★	Drive (Arista, 2002)

Throughout the '90s, mainstream country singer/ songwriter Alan Jackson managed a delicate balancing act. If he grew too boring, he'd degenerate into merely another hat act and soon drop off the charts. But if he grew too interesting, he'd lead his audience into expecting him to develop a real personality, and he didn't have the goods to follow up on that promise. So he balanced mild honky-tonk like "Don't Rock the Jukebox" with restrained heart songs like "Someday," and managed to stay atop the charts without growing into a real persona.

It was a profitable niche. When Jackson first hit, country was in another big crossover period—everybody had, as one Jackson song put it, "Gone Country." That tune, sort of a "Sheena Is a Punk Rocker" for yuppies in Stetsons, defined Jackson's response to the music's new fans—he didn't reach out a hearty handshake like Garth Brooks or glare at 'em from beneath the brim of his hat like Travis Tritt. His voice was personable but hardly distinctive, so he's only as good as the song that's put in front of him—and, as *Greatest Hits* shows, he was no bloodhound when it came to sniffing out great tunes. If, as "Chattahoochee" put it, he had learned "a lot about livin' and

a little 'bout love," very little of that wisdom translated into his mushier material.

Then two planes hit the World Trade Center and, depending on your perspective, Jackson responded with the best song of his career or the worst of all time, "Where Were You (When the World Stopped Turning)." *Drive* is the warmest and most consistent album of his career. The title track is Nashville sentimentality at its most irresistible—first Jackson's dad teaches him to drive, then he teaches his own daughters. As with the best popular culture attuned to the heartland, Jackson creates an everyday world so rich with sentiment that you don't ever want it to stop turning. —K.H.

The Jackson 5

★★★	The Jackson 5 Christmas Album (1970; Universal, 2000)
★★★	Diana Ross Presents the Jackson 5 & ABC (1970; Motown, 2001)
★★½	Third Album & Maybe Tomorrow (1970, 1971; Motown, 2001)
★★	Goin' Back to Indiana & Lookin' Through the Windows (1971, 1972; Motown, 2001)
★★	Skywriter & Get It Together (1973; Motown, 2001)
★★★	Dancing Machine & Moving Violation (1974, 1975; Motown, 2001)
★	Motown Legends: Never Can Say Goodbye (Motown, 1993)
★★★★★	The Ultimate Collection (Motown, 1995)
★½	Pre-History: The Lost Steeltown Recordings (Brunswick, 1996)
★★★	The Millennium Collection—Best of the Jackson 5 (Motown, 1999)
★★★★½	Anthology (Motown, 2000)

The Jacksons

★★★½	The Jacksons (Epic, 1976)
★★★½	Goin' Places (Epic, 1977)

★★★ Destiny (Epic, 1978)
★★★★½ Triumph (Epic, 1980)
★★★½ The Jacksons Live (Epic, 1981)
★★★ Victory (Epic, 1984)

The Jackson 5 were already a huge black music draw when Motown scooped them up in 1968; the mighty mite at the front of the Gary, IN–based family act had left an indelible impression on people right from the start. Eleven-year-old Michael and his brothers (Jackie, Tito, Jermaine, and Marlon) had already been touring around the country when Gladys Knight and then Bobby Taylor recommended them to Berry Gordy. *Pre-History* preserves their earliest hometown recording experiences. There's a certain charm in hearing pint-sized Michael attack "Let Me Carry Your Schoolbooks" or lament "I Never Had a Girl," but this is really just an embryonic audition tape by a group that is obviously going places; their versions of "My Girl" and "Tracks of My Tears" tell you where.

Depending on your perspective, the Jackson 5 were either Motown's last classic gasp or the standard-bearers of a second generation that never quite took over. The group was groomed on the traditional company conveyor belt, but with some major adjustments. The writer/production team called the Corporation (Deke Richards, Freddie Perren, Fonce Mizell, and Gordy himself) was based in Los Angeles, where the J5 records were cut using local session pros instead of Hitsville's fabled Funk Brothers. No matter; the confident kiddie-soul of their first three singles ("I Want You Back," "ABC," and "The Love You Save") is as enduring as anything in the label's hallowed history. These are perfect records, and when the ballad "I'll Be There" (this one produced by Hal Davis) became their fourth consecutive #1 in less than a year, the Jackson 5 became a phenomenon.

Like all Motown performers before them, the Jackson 5 were positioned as a singles act. Nightclub-bound schlock and obvious cover versions pad their hits-plus-filler albums. The flurry of Jackson 5 releases in the first years of the '70s shows the brothers bumping up against the limits of Motown formula. "Never Can Say Goodbye" (from *Maybe Tomorrow*) goes the earlier ballad one better, as the disarming warmth and increased authority of Michael's singing lift this beyond the MOR of the cooing backing vocals and flute trills. But "Sugar Daddy" (from *Maybe Tomorrow*) feels like "ABC" revisited—already. These early albums are all rushed and uneven; Motown's 2001 reissue strategy of putting two on each CD cuts the sting somewhat. Their 1970 Christmas album, however, is a small gem. It wasn't until the Jackson 5 confronted the emergent disco animal in 1974 that

they created their finest overall Motown effort, *Dancing Machine.* Its percolating title track is where the Michael Jackson we know today first emerges. It was their final Motown peak, and a signpost to their CBS future. Their Motown past is captured in *The Ultimate Collection,* which lives up to its name. It contains all the hits and essential tracks, plus four of Michael's solo outings (including "Got to Be There" and "Rockin' Robin") and Jermaine's hit remake of "Daddy's Home." *The Millennium Collection* is a budget compilation of hits, while *Never Can Say Goodbye* is a random and pointless assortment. The double *Anthology* replaces, and improves upon, a previous package of the same name. It has room for top-shelf album material, including their killer versions of Smokey Robinson's "Who's Loving You" and George Clinton's "I'll Bet You," plus a smattering of B-side rarities.

When the group split for CBS subsidiary Epic in 1975, Jermaine stayed behind (he'd married Berry Gordy's daughter Hazel) and was replaced by younger sibling Randy. *The Jacksons* and *Goin' Places* brought the renamed quintet to Philadelphia, though the expansive Gamble and Huff groove has a leveling effect on their newfound dance sound. Moving from one hit factory to another didn't exactly provide the artistic freedom that the Jacksons—especially Michael—craved. Despite somewhat rote songwriting, you can spot Michael developing by leaps and bounds. The 1977 R&B hit "Show You the Way to Go" from *The Jacksons* wraps his deepening vocal twists and turns in a creamy-rich double-tracked chorus; singing rings around himself, Michael sounds like nobody else on earth. His brothers' contributions are now out of print, but shouldn't be completely discounted. Finally producing themselves, the Jacksons and a coterie of sessionmen (led by keyboardist Greg Phillinganes) fashioned a glossy yet progressive pop-soul sound on *Destiny;* they plowed right through the late '70s rock-disco barricade without thinking about it. Michael's skittering, intense vocal workouts on "Blame It on the Boogie" and "Shake Your Body (Down to the Ground)" made dancing seem like very serious business indeed.

Triumph is where the Jacksons reach an audible peak; "Can You Feel It" and "This Place Hotel" are so all-encompassing they teeter on the brink of sonic overkill—without caving in. That air of melodrama adds something, but it's a bit ominous, too. The supernova phase of Michael's solo career soon overshadowed the Jacksons. *Victory* suffered unjustly from the fallout surrounding the group's last tour in 1984. It's not up to the level of the last two, but Jermaine's return signals a consistent, communal effort—and

Michael's somewhat restrained presence never hurts. His absence, however, clearly does: The post-Michael *2300 Jackson Street* (1989) was a major letdown, and has been banished from the catalogue.   —M.C./B.E.

Janet Jackson

★★	Janet Jackson (A&M, 1982)
★★½	Dream Street (A&M, 1984)
★★★★	Control (A&M, 1986)
★★★	Janet Jackson's Rhythm Nation 1814 (A&M, 1989)
★★★	Janet (Virgin, 1993)
★★★★	The Velvet Rope (Virgin, 1997)
★★	All for You (Virgin, 2001)
★★★	Damita Jo (Virgin, 2004)

Even Janet Jackson must have been surprised when her third solo album shot to the top of the pops in 1986. *Janet Jackson* and *Dream Street* sound like bland dance-music ready-mades; perhaps she'd give brother Jermaine a run for his money someday, but Michael's hallowed level of success seemed well beyond Janet's grasp. Then she took a trip to Minneapolis and hooked up with Jimmy Jam and Terry Lewis.

With a scintillating shrug of her shoulders, Jackson asserted her newfound *Control*—quite convincingly, too. She wasn't completely autonomous, of course; *Control* is also where Jam and Lewis perfected their melodic, full-blown funk attack. Not a commanding vocal presence by any means, Jackson filled each track with a breathy believability, yearning romantically on the bittersweet "When I Think of You" or seductively relishing the slinky hook on "Nasty." Cynics accused her of filling in the gap for her brother Michael and rifling through Madonna's closet of castoffs, but *Control* developed a blockbuster momentum all its own. Two years later, a new crop of female singers (such as Paula Abdul and Karyn White) were charged with imitating Janet.

Rather than follow up with an obvious sequel, Jackson continued to stretch. Predictably, *Janet Jackson's Rhythm Nation 1814* is more than a little strained and self-conscious. Heartfelt pleas for racial unity and cloudy musings on the "State of the World" don't obscure the pulsating beat of "Miss You Much," "Rhythm Nation," or "Black Cat." Jackson, Jam, and Lewis worked wonders—when they weren't trying too damn hard to be meaningful, anyway. Although you've got to admire Jackson for pursuing her ambitions, the pseudo-intellectual clutter and windy arrangements compromise *Rhythm Nation*'s underlying groove thang. No matter: A series of exquisitely choreographed video clips helped to cement the disc's multiplatinum sales.

In the years between *Rhythm Nation* and *Janet,* somebody slipped Janet Jackson either some Spanish fly or a copy of *Fear of Flying* or both. She shed that military "Black Cat" suit and started sharing her sexual self, finally meeting Jam and Lewis' teasingly sado-masochistic beats head on. Debuting her newfound confidence, Janet appeared with just two male hands covering her breasts on a ROLLING STONE cover (foreshadowing the much-discussed breast-baring during her duet with Justin Timberlake at the 2004 Super Bowl). Her lyrics on *Janet* took more risks than before. The disc's best single, "That's the Way Love Goes," sounded girlish, but the catalogue of sexual favors—"If," the Princely "Throb," and the disco coo "Anytime, Anyplace"—introduced grown-up desires. Ultimately, however, the record was not as strong as 1997's meditation on stardom and sexual access, *Velvet Rope.* Organized as a kind of inner-sanctum tour (in every way), *Rope*'s tunes are separated by raunchy skits and studio banter meant to show an unfettered, self-possessed Janet. These devices, sounding canned and robotic, sometimes backfire, but her combination of Xanadu and Xanax is never less than intriguing. There's no denying the het-up boldness of the title track's come-on or the pulsing erotic groover "Go Deep." Never simply a Madonna-style romp, *Velvet Rope* gets plenty dark. The scathing "You" takes aim at a sequestered star, perhaps her brother or even herself. Jam and Lewis pull a coup with the video hit "Got 'Til It's Gone," a subtle weave of Janet's panted laments and Q-Tip's nasal rap rejoinders over a wistful loop from Joni Mitchell's "Big Yellow Taxi." While nothing on the record is as transgressive as it pretends to be, you-go moments occur when Janet okays girl-on-girl kicks in "Free Xone," offers her strange take on Rod Stewart's "Tonight's the Night," and revels in rough stuff in "Rope Burn." Amid so much blue, the radio single "Together Again," about her hopes of seeing gone pals in the sunny afterlife, provides a freaky oasis.

As Janet became (or at least valued becoming) more lifelike, the work she was doing on her body made her look more like a manufactured product than ever before. On the cover of 2001's *All for You,* she luxuriates in a towel, proudly jutting out a hip, gym-whittled to the bone. Preserving *Velvet Rope*'s skit structure, *All for You* has a lighter vibe but fewer arresting songs. The title track conjures sexy girl-talk fun under a disco ball, with its "All the girls at the party/Look at that body!" meowing over some boy's "package." But several slow jams bog down the album's flow. A duet with Carly Simon that retools "You're So Vain" as music-biz screed, "Son of a Gun (I Betcha Think This Song Is . . .)" comes off too harsh, with Simon's crunchy rapping sounding silly. The pure-sugar, Latin-tinged "Doesn't Really Matter" claims to privilege the "inner being" over physical atraction. But we feel the wink. She's not swearing off carnality just yet.

Referencing both her own middle name and that of the scorching *Soul Train* dancer who allegedly taught brother Mikey the moon walk, Janet dubbed her 2004 album *Damita Jo*. With beats by current hit gurus like Kanye West, the record sounds like retro soul on a robo planet. Make that a robot planet full of specially-engineered, appletini-swilling sex cyborgs with enhanced proportions and dirty mouths. Single "All Nite" is a frenetic lapgrind in a *Blade Runner* strip club. "Strawberry Bounce" is a short-short Roller Derby sucker-lick about losing control, or at least about losing "Control." Ms. Jackson's own "Escapade" has certainly been a "sexcapade" since *Janet,* and the Timberlake-shake "Sexhibition" makes this redundantly overt. The record's creepy erotics aren't for everyone (sales suggested they weren't for anyone), but history may out their metallic shag appeal. Maybe we'll even get a remix of "Moist," with its euphemistic lyrics, "You know how to make my rain come down," and goofy rhythmic intoning of the icky title. If that track, with its piano plinks and metronomic maraca, or any of the others make you long for old-school, human, Anita Baker moans, Janet's not gonna go there. But you imagine she'd certainly never oppose your getting creative and emitting some yourself. Just don't forget to tip the table-dancing holograms. —L.S.

Joe Jackson

★★★★½   Look Sharp! (1979; A&M, 2001)
★★★½   I'm the Man (1979; A&M, 2001)
★★★½   Jumpin' Jive (1981; A&M, 1999)
★★★★   Night and Day (1982; A&M, 2003)
★★★   Body and Soul (A&M, 1984)
★★½   Big World (A&M, 1986)
★★½   Night Music (Virgin, 1994)
★   Heaven & Hell (Sony Classical, 1997)
★★★   Symphony No. 1 (Sony Classical, 1999)
★★★½   Summer in the City: Live in New York (Sony Classical, 2000)
★★★   Night and Day II (Sony Classical, 2000)
★★★★   The Millennium Collection: The Best of Joe Jackson (Universal, 2001)
★★★★½   Steppin' Out: The Very Best of Joe Jackson (A&M, 2001)
★★★½   Volume 4 (Rykodisc, 2003)
★★★½   Two Rainy Nights: Live in Seattle and Portland (Koch, 2004)
★★★★   Afterlife (Rykodisc, 2004)

Joe Jackson cut a striking figure on his debut album: *Look Sharp!* portrays an angry young tunesmith, a messenger of the new wave who sends stinging telegrams to former lovers ("Is She Really Going Out With Him?") and the world at large ("Sunday Papers"). Jackson displayed a light-fingered pop touch that's entirely his own. *I'm the Man* feels rushed in comparison, but its best moments—"It's Different for Girls," "Don't Wanna Be Like That," "Friday"—are on a par with its predecessor's peaks.

Ironically, the borderline-nasty wit and unchecked exuberance of these albums quickly gave way to self-seriousness and a middlebrow disdain of rock itself. Jackson turned into a bigger crank than his two old rivals Parker and Costello put together—and that's saying a lot! The remainder of his in-print catalogue is marked by restless wandering from one musical genre to another. Sometimes the experiments work brilliantly; more often, they simply bewilder.

Twenty years before Brian Setzer made a mint covering Louis Prima, Jackson was mining the same territory on *Jumpin' Jive,* one of his best stylistic jaunts. He doesn't really have the pipes for '40s R&B, but he does a fair job of conjuring up the horny "Saturday Night Fish Fry" spirit of Louis Jordan and His Tympany Five. *Night and Day* takes a dance-floor spin through Spanish Harlem, and oddly enough, the collision of salsafied disco with Jackson's sour-milk worldview catches fire. (It also garnered him his only Top 10 single, "Steppin' Out.") *Body and Soul's* "Happy Ending" and "Be My Number Two" hark back to the incisive cynicism of Jackson's breakthrough albums; the rest of the record, which incorporates elements of jazz and even musical theater, could do with a little less politeness. *Big World* was clearly meant to be a big deal—three sides of all-new material, recorded live in front of a New York audience, with a solid-rocking quartet sound—but few of Jackson's awkward topical missives find their target, despite the crisp musical accompaniment.

Following two more rock-oriented albums, 1989's *Blaze of Glory* and 1991's *Laughter and Lust,* neither currently in print nor especially memorable, Jackson began to indulge his Serious Composer side, with mixed results: the intermittently diverting *Night Music,* the respectable *Symphony No. 1,* and the god-awful "song cycle" *Heaven & Hell.* Next move? Revisiting past glories. The string-suffused *Night and Day II* is fine overall, but Jackson's self-cannibalism (epitomized by the musical quotes from "Steppin' Out" in "Stay") is disheartening. *Volume 4,* on the other hand, is an unqualified treat. Reuniting with his original band—the guys who recorded *Look Sharp!* and *I'm the Man*—Jackson sounds revitalized on the tartly tuneful "Take It Like a Man" and "Awkward Age." The live *Afterlife* is even better, combining the best *Volume 4* tracks with '70s and '80s nuggets.

The two other recent live albums, *Summer in the City* and *Two Rainy Nights,* each recorded with a different band, are enchanting trips down the Jackson back roads. Either of the existing best-of compilations would serve as a good introduction to his catalogue; the single-disc *20th Century Masters* is cheaper, the double-disc *Steppin' Out* more comprehensive. —M.C./M.R.

Mahalia Jackson

   ★★   The Power and the Glory (Columbia, 1963)
   ★★★   Bless This House (Columbia, 1963)
   ★★★   Mahalia Jackson's Greatest Hits (Columbia, 1963)
   ★★   Sings the Best-Loved Hymns of Dr. Martin Luther King Jr. (Columbia, 1968)
   ★★   Christmas With Mahalia (1968; Columbia, 1990)
   ★★   Sings America's Favorite Hymns (Columbia, 1971)
   ★★   The Great Mahalia Jackson (1972; Columbia, 1991)
  ★★★★   How I Got Over (Columbia, 1976)
   ★★★   Gospels, Spirituals, & Hymns (Legacy/Columbia, 1991)
★★★★★ Live at Newport (Legacy/Columbia, 1994)
  ★★★★   The Best of Mahalia Jackson (Legacy/Columbia, 1995)
   ★★   Mahalia Sings Songs of Christmas (Legacy/Columbia, 1995)
  ★★★★   16 Most Requested Songs (Legacy/Columbia, 1996)
   ★★★   Gospels, Spirituals, & Hymns, Vol. 2 (Legacy/Columbia, 1998)
   ★★★   Sunday Morning Prayer Meeting (Legacy/Columbia, 2001)
★★★★★ The Essential Mahalia Jackson (Legacy/Columbia, 2004)

Inspired by Bessie Smith, Mahalia Jackson is regarded as the singer who brought blues into the gospel field and then brought gospel to a secular audience with greater success than any other artist in the field. Stubborn, contentious, and not altogether a model of propriety, Jackson seemed to use her singing performances to transport herself to more sanctified ground. Her majestic contralto voice could handle a wide range of material, and her gift as an interpreter allowed her to work a lyric with such conviction, you sensed someone unburdening her soul in powerful terms.

Born in New Orleans in 1911, she moved to Chicago in 1927, and in 1936 married a man who wanted her to sing jazz and classics. The marriage ended, and Jackson went back on the gospel circuit and began to build a following. In 1937, she recorded a few sides for Decca, all of them wonderful, but another nine years elapsed before she recorded again. Signed to the Apollo label, she made her most important records in the late '40s and early '50s. These are out of print now, but should any show up in cutout bins, the titles to latch on to are *The Best of Mahalia Jackson* and *1911–1972.*

In the years between her move to Columbia, in 1954, and her death, in 1972, Jackson was by most estimations the most popular gospel artist in America. But at the same time that she was experiencing all this fame, her music was suffering. Columbia saw an opportunity to reach a mass audience by saddling Jackson's arrangements with strings or even a full orchestra (the most egregious example being the out-of-print *Power and the Glory,* with arrangements by Percy Faith, the very model of the corporate studio hack). It is a testament to her consummate artistry that Jackson surmounts most every obstacle placed in her path; every Columbia album contains profound moments, even if no LP is totally successful or representative of the breadth and depth of the woman's power.

Bless This House features her with a small rhythm section, but the inspired accompaniment of her longtime pianist Mildred Falls comes through loud and clear. A male quartet—sounding for all the world like something cooked up by Mitch Miller—disrupts a few otherwise ebullient performances, but these miscalculations are more than offset by powerhouse vocals on "God Knows the Reason Why," "Trouble of the World," and "Precious Lord." The 1976 release *How I Got Over* is the best of the Columbia titles precisely because the tracks are culled from 1954 radio performances and a 1963 television appearance, capturing Jackson close to the form she displayed on her best Apollo sides. A loyal friend and supporter of Dr. Martin Luther King Jr., her album devoted to his memory includes a powerful reading of "We Shall Overcome," as well as "Precious Lord," King's last request of Jackson. Beware of *Greatest Hits,* as it contains rerecordings of some of the Apollo sides as well as newer material. *The Great Mahalia Jackson* is a worst-case example of Columbia's mishandling of this great artist; the disc is rife with pop fluff such as "Danny Boy," "Sunrise, Sunset," and "What the World Needs Now Is Love." The set *Gospels, Spirituals, & Hymns* is a good summary of Jackson's Columbia catalogue, but a summary is all it amounts to: Its 36 tracks represent only a small portion of her output in nearly two decades with the label. In 2004, a definitive Mahalia Jackson collection that demonstrates proper appreciation of her artistry was finally released—the two-disc *Essential Mahalia Jackson*. The *Live in Newport* album is also indispensable, as it captures Jackson's astounding vocal gifts mercifully unadorned by overproduction.   —D.M./G.F.

Michael Jackson

★★★★½   Off the Wall (1979; Epic, 2001)
★★★★★   Thriller (1982; Epic, 2001)
★★   Anthology (Motown, 1986)
★★★½   Bad (1987; Epic, 2001)
★★   Dangerous (1991; Epic, 2001)
★★★   HIStory Past Present and Future—Book 1 (Epic, 1995)
★★★   Blood on the Dance Floor: HIStory in the Mix (Epic, 1997)
★   Invincible (Epic, 2001)
★★★★   Number Ones (Epic, 2003)

First he was a prodigy, then he was a genius, then he was a freak. Actually, Michael Jackson was always a little bit of all three, and his strangeness, along with his overwhelming musical gifts, is the edge that has kept pop-watchers fascinated as Jackson's career ascended to a world-beating peak and collapsed into paranoia and self-pity. Though images of Jackson's dancing feet and constantly resculpted face have been inescapable for the last 30 years, all his dualities—androgyny, adulthood and childhood, shyness and megalomania, vulnerability and fury—were captured in his music alone. In the sound of his voice, desperation and vulnerability came through just as clearly as mastery.

Jackson was five years old when he joined his brothers in the Jackson Family vocal group, and he quickly emerged as the main draw and lead singer when the group became the Jackson 5. He was a boy-man from the beginning; though he sang in a child's piping voice, he danced like a grown-up hoofer and sang with the R&B/gospel inflections of Sam Cooke, James Brown, Ray Charles, and Stevie Wonder.

The best material of Jackson's Motown years, unquestionably, was his hits with the Jackson 5: songs like "I Want You Back," "ABC," and "The Love You Save," which Motown aimed precisely at teens and preteens, complete with references to grade school. The two-CD *Anthology* is all anyone needs, and more, of the four solo albums Jackson made in his teens.

While his voice descended ever so slightly from boy soprano to his current androgynous high tenor between 1971 and 1975, Jackson gamely sang whatever Motown's team brought him: exuberant covers, like

"Rockin' Robin" and a distraught "Ain't No Sunshine," and second-tier Motown originals, which were mostly lonely-love plaints or inspirational hooey—the kinds of songs that would persist as filler on later Jackson albums. Of course, the oddities had begun: Jackson's big solo hit was "Ben," a love song to a pet rat.

But Jackson had learned plenty at Motown, and with his first solo album for Epic, *Off the Wall*, he was unstoppable. Though it was released in 1979, when the disco fad was already abating, *Off the Wall* managed to capture the glitter-ball moment without getting stuck in it. That's because Jackson and producer Quincy Jones went after full-out '70s funk rather than the simplified disco thump. Then they swirled in disco strings and Jackson's airy voice like frothy milk in a latte.

Jackson's own songs, built on his vocal beat-boxing, were the album's funkiest tracks; they also had the nuttiest lyrics, a taste of things to come. And Tim Bahler's "She's Out of My Life" became the prototype for Jackson's better ballads: smooth, sustained, tuneful, and just on the verge of overwrought while staying poised. By the time the album petered out in its final songs, Jackson had already proved himself.

Then he doubled his ambitions and multiplied his audience with *Thriller*. Picking up ideas (and reusing a few riffs) from *Off the Wall*, Jackson went after every pop constituency he could imagine: dancers, rockers, lovers, kids, parents. Paul McCartney shared one song, Eddie Van Halen shredded another. And Jackson was now ready to look beyond the dance floor, to sing about ambition ("Wanna Be Startin' Somethin' "), gang fights ("Beat It"), paternity suits ("Billie Jean"), compulsive cruising ("Human Nature"), and primal fears ("Thriller"), while dispensing irresistible synthesized bass lines.

Thriller had extramusical help in becoming the best-selling noncompilation album of all time: Jackson's dancing feet and dazzling stage presence, amplified by the newfound promotional reach of music video and the Reagan era's embrace of glossy celebrity. But especially in the album's seven hit singles (out of nine songs), the music stands on its own. As the biggest pop star in the world, Jackson followed through by cowriting (with Lionel Richie) the well-intentioned, unctuous, profoundly self-absorbed all-star benefit single "We Are the World," the template for Jackson's pop-gospel anthems to come.

Bad wasn't so bad. But it was an inevitable anticlimax after *Thriller*, offering more variations than advances. The album was full of forced poses that started with the title song; people who are "really really bad" don't say so backed by a chipmunk chorus. But the music had lots of small pleasures: the suddenly accelerating synthesizer in "Speed Demon," the lighthearted affection in "The Way You Make Me Feel," the transparently manipulative but effective anthem "Man in the Mirror."

But Jackson's unruly id also erupts on *Bad:* with rough, choked, hiccupy vocals, nasty scenarios, and music that quashes his sweet side. "Dirty Diana" and "Leave Me Alone" present predatory women—the feared sisters of "Billie Jean"—while "Smooth Criminal" shoots a woman down. Jackson the celebrity continued to present himself as a guy singing love bromides and uplifting thoughts, but Jackson the songwriter was letting loose some demons.

With *Dangerous,* Jackson plunged off the deep end. To update himself, Jackson traded Quincy Jones for new jack swing producer Teddy Riley and allowed some guest rappers on a few songs. Jackson's musical categories were hardening: crisp dance tracks ("Jam"), ultrasmooth ballads ("Gone Too Soon"), anthems ("Heal the World"). And while his ballads clung to convention, a beat could set off anything from a tirade against the media to new complaints about women to a free-association about faith and inner peace. For most of the album, brittle rhythm tracks back a singer who sounds almost unhinged with fury and suspicion, only calming himself to sing about death in "Gone Too Soon."

HIStory started out as a hits collection and turned into a double album that's an inadvertent before-and-after story: the gifted, confident Jackson who made the hits and the isolated, self-pitying, maniacal Jackson who's living through their aftermath. Harsh, near-industrial beats collide with brief pop choruses, as if Jackson's at war with himself. Whether he's ranting about tabloids and money-grubbers or piteously crooning, "Have you seen my childhood?", he sounds like he's running on bile. (Epic would later release the greatest-hits half by itself as *Greatest Hits HIStory Volume 1,* then add a few songs for *Number Ones.*)

The tantrum continued in the five new songs on *Blood on the Dance Floor,* which also included eight beat-added remixes of tracks from *HIStory.* Jackson vowed, "If you want to see eccentric oddities, I'll be grotesque before your eyes." The songs were as raw as Jackson would ever be, even if his complaints were getting redundant.

Jackson regained his composure for *Invincible.* Only allowing himself one anti-tabloid song, he tried to play the gentle, adoring lover and concentrated on ballads. But three decades after he had first charmed the world, his old suavity was gone, and all that was left was grim calculation.   —J.P.

Wanda Jackson

★★★½   Wanda Jackson (1958; Capitol, 2002)
★★★½   Rockin' With Wanda (1960; Capitol, 2002)
★★★★★   Vintage Collections Series (Capitol, 1996)
★★★   Heart Trouble (CMH, 2003)
★★★½   Live and Still Kickin' (DCN, 2003)

One of the coolest women in rock history, Wanda Jackson came roaring out of Oklahoma City in the mid-'50s singing rockabilly, rock & roll, and hard country with a constricted, razor-sharp voice and a monster attitude. Capitol's *Vintage Collections* CD is the best single-disc overview of Jackson's most essential rockabilly and country recordings for Capitol from 1956 through 1961, surveying Jackson in a variety of modes, from full-throttle rock ("Let's Have a Party," originally recorded by Elvis Presley and featured in the film *Loving You*) to rockabilly to traditional country (the weeper "Why I'm Walkin' " gets over via a vocal imbued with the profound sadness so characteristic of Patsy Cline's great tearjerkers). Recently Capitol has reissued Jackson's first two albums, 1958's *Wanda Jackson* and 1960's *Rockin' With Wanda,* both with bonus tracks not on the original vinyl release. The import bins carry a wealth of Wanda Jackson's Capitol recordings for those who want to go deeper into a fairly remarkable body of work; in 2003, Jackson mounted a well-received comeback with the spirited *Heart Trouble.*   —D.M.

Jadakiss
see THE LOX

Mick Jagger

★★★   She's the Boss (Atlantic, 1985)
★★   Primitive Cool (Atlantic, 1987)
★★★★   Wandering Spirit (Atlantic, 1993)
★★★★   Goddess in the Doorway (Virgin, 2001)

Away from the Stones, Mick Jagger has an eye for fashion, which can be good and bad. On *She's the Boss,* he puts himself in the hands of ultraproducer Bill Laswell, and comes up with glossy rock, heavy with all kinds of percolating percussion and studio texturalism. "Just Another Night" is a fine single, enlivened by a catchy acoustic guitar motif. The rest of the record is crunchy funk, intriguing chiefly for the title track and "Hard Woman." Defenses of strong women, both songs are perhaps intended as late-in-the-day correctives to the Stones' exaggerated reputation as misogynists. Big names and studio aces—Jeff Beck, Pete Townshend, Nile Rodgers, Robbie Shakespeare, and Sly Dunbar—help craft the record, and the sound Jagger gets is nothing if not accomplished.

With *Primitive Cool,* this time with Eurythmic Dave Stewart as collaborator, Jagger takes more risks in style and lyrics. It's a commendable effort, but the results are haphazard. The title song finds Jagger in the role of "daddy" and doing nostalgia—a sentiment that does not suit him. "Let's Work" is a paean to the Protestant ethic, but its championing of honest toil comes off as yuppie gospel. The rocker "Shoot Off Your Mouth" is fine, vintage bad boy–ism; "Say You Will" is a lovely ballad; "Peace for the Wicked" is neat, Prince-ish R&B; and "War Baby," for all its clunkiness, is a heartfelt political meditation.

It's with *Wandering Spirit* that he finally comes into his own. Producer Rick Rubin lends him a clean, pared-down sound, nice guest vocals from Lenny Kravitz and the dependable playing of keyboardist Billy Preston and drummer Jim Keltner help as well. The real surprise is Jagger himself. The voice sounds simply terrific, and as he ranges from R&B (a great cover of Bill Withers' "Use Me") to country and even to Celtic ("Handsome Molly") he's actually emoting, not just role-playing. *Goddess in the Doorway* is almost as good. Pete Townshend and Joe Perry turn in strong guitar work and Jagger is once again commanding. There's a little too much gloss on the record (how much empathy can you really have with an artist who announces that "god gave me everything"?) but it's commendable stuff, kind of like one of those "What If?" comic books, if the Stones took a different path. —P.E.

The Jam

★★★★	In the City (1977; Polydor, 1997)
★★½	This Is the Modern World (1977; Polydor, 1997)
★★★★½	All Mod Cons (1978; Polydor, 1997)
★★★	Setting Sons (1979; Collector's Choice, 2001)
★★★★★	Sound Affects (1980; Polydor, 1997)
★★	The Gift (1982; Polydor, 1997)
★★★★	Dig the New Breed (Polydor, 1982)
★★★★½	Snap! (Polydor, 1983)
★★★★★	Greatest Hits (Polydor, 1991)
★★★	Extras: A Collection of Rarities (PolyGram, 1992)
★★	Live Jam (Polydor, 1993)
★★★	The Jam Collection (Polydor, 1996)
★★★★	Direction Reaction Creation (Polydor, 1997)
★★★	The Sound of the Jam (Polydor, 2003)

The Jam, one of the great British bands, was a thick-as-thieves punk trio who bashed out mod anthems, led by the eternally boyish Paul Weller. On albums such as 1978's *All Mod Cons,* 1980's *Sound Affects,* and the 1982 live summary, *Dig the New Breed,* Weller sang his tales of ordinary English life, envisioning a nation of sad-eyed boys dressing up to go race their Vespa scooters through the streets while a hundred lonely housewives clutched empty milk bottles to their hearts. The fantasy struck a chord in the U.K., where Weller came to be revered with fanatical devotion. Although the Jam never had an American hit and broke up 20 years ago, these sharp-dressed mods have influenced practically every decent British rock band since.

Weller, the self-proclaimed "Cappuccino Kid," was only 18 when the Jam debuted in 1977 with *In the City.* He yelled his clumsy youth-explosion lyrics over frantic guitar riffs, but even when the band slowed it down for the naively touching "Away From the Numbers," his Woking accent was too thick for any American to comprehend, one of the reasons the Jam never came close to cracking the U.S. *This Is the Modern World* had weaker songs, as sophomore albums do, except for "Life Through a Window." But *All Mod Cons* made Weller a boy wonder over in Britannia, with a cover of the Kinks' "David Watts" as a touchstone for Weller's catchy little vignettes, especially the funny "A-Bomb in Wardour Street" and the politically charged "Down in the Tube Station at Midnight." (Despite the somewhat bizarre claim in Jon Savage's *England's Dreaming* that the Jam were Tories, they were the U.K.'s most energetically left-wing pop stars.)

From their Who/Kinks/Creation riffs to their mohair suits, the Jam touched off a glorious mod revival, inspiring followers like the Merton Parkas, the Jolt, and Secret Affair, whose 1979 hit "Time for Action" perfectly summed up the mod lifestyle: "Looking good's the answer/And living by night." But *Setting Sons* was a pompous concept album, taking the whole influenced-by-the-Who business a little far, despite "Thick as Thieves," "When You're Young," and "Saturday's Kids," a boyish answer to Blondie's "Sunday Girl." The Jam had its first #1 U.K. hit with "Going Underground" and followed with the magnificent *Sound Affects.* The album offers the poignant teen-boy ache of "Start!," "Monday," and "Boy About Town"; the sha-la-la harmonies of "Man in the Corner Shop"; a Shelley poem on the back cover; and the Jam's best song ever, the acoustic lament "That's Entertainment," which can break your heart even if you have no idea what Weller's saying.

The Jam faltered with the R&B moves of *The Gift*—why these three decidedly unfunky gentlemen decided it was their destiny to get on the good foot, the world will never know. "Town Called Malice" was a gem with an elastic bass line and a howling organ, while "Ghosts" was an elegiac ballad. But the lads were rich adults now and could no longer pretend to be the skinny-tied, bowling-shoe-wearing, Union

Jack–waving, tube-station-frequenting adolescents of "Boy About Town" or "Saturday's Kids." So they bade farewell with the superb single "Beat Surrender," though Weller kept pursuing his R&B and classic-rock influences, first as the Style Council and then solo, aging from the Cappuccino Kid to the Duke of Decaf but still sounding touched by the hand of mod.

Of all the Jam's many overlapping repackages, the original 1983 double-vinyl *Snap!* is still the best, blasting off with the essential early hits "In the City" and "All Around the World." But it's truncated on CD and includes only the inferior demo version of "That's Entertainment," so the 1991 *Greatest Hits* is preferable. *Snap!* has the version of "The Modern World" on which Weller yells, "I don't give a damn about your review!"; on *Greatest Hits*, it's "I don't give two fucks." The poorly selected 2003 *Sound of the Jam* omits necessities like "All Around the World" and "The Bitterest Pill." *Extras* has ace covers of the Who's "So Sad About Us" and the Beatles' "And Your Bird Can Sing"; *Direction Reaction Creation* is an impersonal but functional box set. *Dig the New Breed*, the Jam's superb live album, has dramatic renditions of "Ghosts," "Going Underground," and "In the Crowd," plus a version of "That's Entertainment" even more moving and incomprehensible than the original. A final thought, from "Boy About Town": "There's more than you can hope for in this world." —R.S.

Elmore James

★★★★½   Street Talkin' (with Eddie Taylor, Jimmy Reed) (1975; Muse, 1992)

★★★★   Let's Cut It: The Very Best of Elmore James (Flair Virgin, 1987)

★★★★   The Complete Fire and Enjoy Sessions, Part 1 (Collectables, 1989)

★★★★   The Complete Fire and Enjoy Sessions, Part 2 (Collectables, 1989)

★★★★   The Complete Fire and Enjoy Sessions, Part 3 (Collectables, 1990)

★★★★   The Complete Fire and Enjoy Sessions, Part 4 (Collectables, 1991)

★★★★   Dust My Broom (Rhino/Tomato, 1991)

★★★★★   The Complete Elmore James Story (Capricorn, 1992)

★★★★★   The Sky Is Crying: The History of Elmore James (Rhino, 1993)

★★★★   Golden Classics: Guitars in Orbit (Collectables, 1994)

★★★★   For Collectors Only: The Complete Fire & Enjoy Recordings (Collectables, 1995)

★★★★   The Very Best of Elmore James (Rhino, 2000)

★★★★   Shake Your Money Maker: The Best of the Fire Sessions (Buddah/BMG, 2001)

Elmore James' wailing slide guitar shadows the playing of virtually every important British blues guitarist from the 1960s onward and informs the styles of great American blues guitarists such as Duane Allman, Stevie Ray Vaughan, and Michael Bloomfield. Moreover, in the tracks James cut between 1951 and 1956, he provided the link between Robert Johnson's acoustic howl and Chuck Berry's electrified translation of same—a bridge from the Mississippi Delta to St. Louis, from the dark heart of the blues to the ebullient spirit of early rock & roll. James' first hit, recorded surreptitiously in 1951 for the Trumpet label, was a version of Johnson's "Dust My Broom." A prolific songwriter as well, his lyrics were incisive, eloquent blues poetry about bad love affairs, with vivid descriptions of torment, desire, and mean mistreaters.

Among the single-CD issues of James' work, Rhino's Blues Masters entry, *The Very Best of Elmore James,* is a no-brainer must-have covering 16 tracks from the artist's peak years of 1951 to 1963. "Dust My Broom" kicks off the disc, and other choice cuts include "Standing at the Crossroads," "The Sky Is Crying" (and its companion piece, "The Sun Is Shining"), "It Hurts Me Too," "Shake Your Moneymaker," and James' powerful instrumental showcase "Hawaiian Boogie." The disc also includes an homage to one of James' principal influences, T-Bone Walker, by way of a scorching interpretation of "Stormy Monday." The most succinct overview is provided by *The Sky Is Crying: The Best of Elmore James,* which includes liner notes by Robert Palmer. Apart from the sheer emotional impact of the songs themselves, this set's great virtue is in showcasing both the breadth and depth of James' music. "Something Inside Me," from 1960, is a beautiful slow blues. In "Sunny Land," from 1954, he one-ups Muddy Waters with a tricky stop-time arrangement and abandons the slide in favor of dark, robust single- and double-string solo lines.

More exhilarating in quantity and quality are the two box sets; taken together, these form virtually all of James' recording history for the various labels whose studios he graced. The three-CD box set *The Classic Early Recordings 1951–1956* includes the original "Dust My Broom" as well as the sides he cut in 1952 with Ike Turner playing piano. The casual fan may not be interested in six takes of "Strange Kinda Feeling," or four takes of "Make My Dreams Come True," but devoted James fans will find much to chew on.

Between 1960 and 1962 James recorded prolifically for the New York City–based Fire, Fury, and Enjoy labels headed by Bobby Robinson. Tomato/Rhino's *Dust My Broom* is a fine single-disc survey of these years—15 key tracks recorded between 1959 and 1963, including the essentials: "The Sky Is

Crying," "Anna Lee," "Dust My Broom," "Shake Your Moneymaker," "One Way Out," "Rollin' and Tumblin'." Buddah/BMG has its own James single-disc retrospective from the latter years as well, *Shake Your Money Maker: The Best of the Fire Sessions*. Though it duplicates some of the great cuts available on *Dust My Broom* (and other collections), it also includes stuff that doesn't show up elsewhere, such as "My Bleeding Heart" and "Look on Yonder Wall." Less satisfying is Collectables' *Golden Classics: Guitars in Orbit*, which has some fine (and classic) performances from the Fire/Fury/Enjoy years, but is a bit skimpy at only 12 cuts. The better buy is the thoroughly annotated two-CD box set *The Complete Elmore James* (a truncated version of Capricorn's first James box, the now-deleted *King of the Slide Guitar*), featuring 50 tracks from the various Robinson labels in what stands as the artist's last will and testament. —D.M.

Etta James

★★★★	At Last! (1961; MCA/Chess, 1987)
★★★	Etta James Rocks the House (1963; MCA/Chess, 1992)
★★	Come a Little Closer (1974; MCA/Chess, 1996)
★★★	Deep in the Night (1978; Bullseye Blues, 1996)
★★★	Blues in the Night, Vol. 1: The Early Show (1986; Fantasy, 1990)
★★★★	Blues in the Night, Vol. 2: The Late Show (1986; Fantasy, 1990)
★★★★	R&B Dynamite (1987; Flair/Virgin, 1991)
★★★	Her Greatest Sides (MCA/Chess, 1987)
★★★★★	The Sweetest Peaches: The Chess Years, Vol. Two (1967–1975) (MCA/Chess, 1988)
★★★	Seven Year Itch (Island, 1989)
★★★	Stickin' to My Guns (Island, 1990)
★★★	The Right Time (Elektra, 1992)
★★★½	How Strong Is a Woman: The Island Sessions (4th & Bway, 1993)
★★★★★	The Essential Etta James (MCA/Chess, 1993)
★★★★★	Mystery Lady: Songs of Billie Holiday (Private Music, 1994)
★★★★	Live From San Francisco (Private Music, 1994)
★★★★½	Time After Time (Private Music, 1995)
★★★★	These Foolish Things: The Classic Balladry of Etta James (MCA, 1995)
★★★★	Her Best (MCA/Chess, 1997)
★★★	Love's Been Rough on Me (Private Music, 1997)
★★★½	12 Songs of Christmas (Private Music, 1998)
★★★½	Life, Love & the Blues (Private Music, 1998)
★★★★	The Heart of a Woman (Private Music, 1999)
★★★½	Matriarch of the Blues (Private Music, 2000)
★★★★★	The Chess Box (MCA, 2000)
★★★★	Burnin' Down the House: Live at the House of Blues (Private Music, 2000)
★★★	Love Songs (MCA, 2001)
★★★½	Blue Gardenia (Private Music, 2001)
★★★★½	Tell Mama: The Complete Muscle Shoals Sessions (MCA, 2001)
★★★	Greatest Gospel Hits, Vol. 1 (Curb, 2002)
★★★	Greatest Gospel Hits, Vol. 2 (Curb, 2002)
★★★	Live and Ready (Classic World, 2002)
★★★★	Let's Roll (Private Music, 2003)
★★★	Blues to the Bone (RCA, 2004)

She sings classy ballads, pop, jazz, soul, and rock, too, but at its best, Etta James' work is everything you want from the blues: impassioned, intelligent, deeply felt, and just plain painful. James was born in 1938, and she remains a vital touring and recording artist to this day, but it was during the '60s, recording for Chess Records, that she became one of the crucial R&B singers of our time. *At Last!*, her first for Chess, is the quintessential James album, deeply felt but varied, and featuring classics such as "All I Could Do Was Cry" and the title track. Completists are advised to check out the superb three-CD, 72-song *Chess Box* for the broadest overview of the enduring work she did for the Argo, Chess, and Cadet labels from 1960 through 1975. Here James worked with some of the best producers and arrangers of her time, as well as first-rate songwriters (the subtlety and personality she brings to her performances of several Randy Newman songs cut in the early '70s indicate she might well be that fabled songwriter's preeminent interpreter); whatever the style, whoever the composer, the hurt is always near the surface. An abridged retrospective of these years is provided on a two-CD, 44-song set issued in 1993 as *The Essential Etta James*. *These Foolish Things: The Classic Balladry of Etta James* charts James' torrid treatment of various pop standards. The success of her self-penned "Stop the Wedding," a Top 40 pop hit in 1962, enabled James to dive headfirst into the good life. She wound up a drug addict, and her music assumed a harsh, bitter tone as her life fell into disarray.

The original *Tell Mama* album, released 1968, was one of the decade's exceptional albums; it yielded two Top 30 hits in the title song and the breathtaking, Otis Redding–penned "Security," and included several other breathtaking performances. *Tell Mama: The Complete Muscle Shoals Sessions* supplements the original with some revelatory, previously unissued tracks from those sessions: Everything from Sonny Bono's "I Got You Babe" to soul man Don Covay's "I'm Gonna Take What He's Got," David Houston's country classic "Almost Persuaded," the classic pop evergreen "Misty," and the Chips Moman/Dan Penn soul monument "Do Right Woman, Do Right Man."

In the early '70s James was teamed with rock-oriented producer Gabriel Mekler, whose credits included Janis Joplin, Three Dog Night, and Steppenwolf. *Come a Little Closer* (as well as some cuts on *The Essential Etta James*) was the upshot, but only the abovementioned Randy Newman–penned songs stand out. Following another near-disastrous bout with drugs and another round of rehab, James left Chess. In 1978 she signed to Warner Bros. and delivered the Jerry Wexler–produced *Deep in the Night* (now reissued by Bullseye Blues), which pointed her in the right direction again professionally. James came all the way back with a live album, *Blues in the Night,* recorded at Marla's Memory Lane Supper Club in Los Angeles in 1986 with a band that included alto saxophonist Eddie "Cleanhead" Vinson, and on two solid albums for Island, *Stickin' to My Guns* and *Seven Year Itch* (both are sampled on the 11-track *How Strong Is a Woman*).

As it turned out, the Island years were but prelude to greater glories for Etta James. In 1993 she was inducted into the Rock and Roll Hall of Fame; a year later, after signing with Private Music, she delivered the fantastic *Mystery Lady: Songs of Billie Holiday.* Though her style isn't as winsome and delicate as Holiday's, the sultry, longing quality of James' delivery adds rich subtext to some of Holiday's signature songs. *Time After Time* is a smart move that finds James going back to one of her strengths, pop standards done in a blues-jazz vein. *Love's Been Rough on Me* (1997) is described by James in her liner notes as "a country record" (it was recorded in Nashville, with, for the most part, Nashville-based musicians, and produced in Music City by Barry Beckett), but this being James, the blues is in its veins. From 1998 through 2000, James hit a big trifecta with *Life, Love & the Blues* (1998), *The Heart of a Woman* (1999), and *Matriarch of the Blues* (2000), and threw in a tour de force of interpretive rethinking on *12 Songs of Christmas,* which puts some scintillating, bluesy spins on Yuletide evergreens. There's no going wrong with any of the titles mentioned here, but special attention should be paid to *Heart of a Woman,* as it finds James toning down her fiery style and exploring a pop-jazz bag, complete with Spanish acoustic guitar fills and cool, sensuous arrangements. On 2003's *Let's Roll* she rides roughshod over some vintage roadhouse rock and blues of vintage flavor; more evidence of her ongoing blues prowess is provided on *Burnin' Down the House: Live at the House of Blues,* recorded in West Hollywood, CA, in December 2001. —D.M.

Rick James

★★★	Come Get It!	(Gordy, 1978)
★★½	Bustin' Out of L Seven	(Gordy, 1979)
★★½	Fire It Up	(Gordy, 1979)
★★	In 'n' Out	(Gordy, 1980)
★★	Garden of Love	(Gordy, 1980)
★★★★	Street Songs	(1981; Motown, 2001)
★★★½	Throwin' Down	(Gordy, 1982)
★★½	Cold Blooded	(Gordy, 1983)
★★★★	Reflections: All the Great Hits	(Gordy, 1984)
★★	Glow	(Gordy, 1985)
★½	The Flag	(Gordy, 1986)
★★★★	Greatest Hits	(Motown, 1986)
★★½	Wonderful	(Reprise, 1988)
★★½	Come Get It	(Motown, 1991)
★½	Urban Rhapsody	(Private I/Mercury, 1997)
★★★★½	The Ultimate Collection	(Motown, 1997)
★★★★	The Millennium Collection	(Motown, 2000)
★★★★	Street Songs Deluxe Edition	(Motown, 2001)
★★★★½	Anthology	(Motown, 2002)

Anyone who grew up post-1980s might be excused for thinking that if Rick James didn't exist, the producers of *Behind the Music* would have had to invent him. James' personal saga, which includes liaisons with shapely starlets, long-term drug abuse, a conviction for assault, and an onstage stroke during a "comeback" tour, is outlandish enough to make his musical career seem secondary—and to some extent, it was.

James dressed like a rocker, sang like a soulman, and strutted like a mack daddy. Although there was nothing particularly "street" about his sound, he knew the buzzwords and inserted enough nudge-wink innuendo—particularly drug references like "Mary Jane," from *Come Get It!;* "Cop N Blow," from *Bustin' Out of L Seven;* and "South American Sneeze," from *In 'n' Out*—to convince most of the kids back in the burbs.

James' best albums, *Street Songs* and *Throwin' Down,* owe more to production value than to any sort of originality, though in fairness, *Street Songs'* "Super Freak" (later co-opted by MC Hammer for the pop-rap smash "U Can't Touch This") and "Give It to Me Baby" had terrific hooks. Elsewhere, he relies on everything from secondhand Bootsy Collins (*Fire It Up*) to third-rate Larry Graham (*In 'n' Out*), with varying degrees of success.

James essentially ran out of ideas by 1982, and though *Cold Blooded* is a passable attempt at synthesizing the funk & roll chemistry of *Street Songs,* his subsequent albums for Gordy are a waste. *Wonderful,* his 1988 attempt at regaining cred, is no better, though

Roxanne Shanté's cameo on "Loosey's Rap" is worth hearing. *Urban Rhapsody,* which followed his release from prison, is a cannily conservative attempt to recapture the R&B portion of his audience, but it lacks the fire of his early hits. Of the various anthologies, most boast copious hits, but only *Anthology* gives a real sense of the sweep and breadth of his career. James died in 2004, at the age of 56. —J.D.C.

James Gang

★★★½	Yer' Album (MCA, 1969)	
★★★★	Rides Again (MCA, 1970)	
★★★½	Thirds (MCA, 1971)	
★★★	Live in Concert (Beat Goes On, 1971)	
★½	Straight Shooter (One Way, 1972)	
★★★★½	Bang (Atco, 1973)	
★★★	Miami (Atco, 1974)	
★★★★	Greatest Hits (MCA, 2000)	

As Cleveland, OH's premier classic-rock act, James Gang was a versatile, funky band best known for the two star guitarists who passed through the ever-revolving door on their way up, Joe Walsh and Tommy Bolin, and two rock radio staples, "Funk #49" and "Walk Away." Kent State University buddies Jim Fox (drums), Tom Kriss (bass), and Glenn Schwartz (guitar) formed the band in 1966, before Schwartz headed to San Francisco for the Summer of Love and joined Pacific Gas & Electric (whose 1970 album *Are You Ready* is tremendous). Schwartz was replaced by Joe Walsh in time for James Gang's 1969 debut, *Yer' Album,* on which Walsh's yearning vocals nicely complement the band's power-trio setup. Sophomore album *Rides Again* is even better: Recorded at L.A.'s legendary Record Plant (then brand-new), it includes top-down rocker "Funk #49," seven-minute crunchy-rock head trip "The Bomber," and a Cat Stevens–style acoustic send-off "Ashes, the Rain and I" (the cover photo of the band riding motorcycles in the snow is pretty cool, too). *Thirds,* more easygoing and at times even jazzy, was not accurately represented by its classic-rock radio staple "Walk Away." The extended jamming (particularly from a wah-wah-riding Walsh) gave *Live in Concert* a prog-rock feel. Walsh left to go solo (before raking in millions with the Eagles), and 1972's *Straight Shooter* sounds like tired Grand Funk Railroad (notable only for the comedic country number "Hairy Hypochondriac").

When replacement guitarist Dominic Troiano left to join the Guess Who, Tommy Bolin stepped into the fold, and the band was reborn. *Bang* and *Miami* are generally underrated by those who assume Walsh was the heart of the band. Bolin then went solo himself (he

died from a drug overdose in 1976), and although the James Gang limped through another incarnation, it wasn't until Walsh began gigging sporadically with the band, around MCA's millennium release of remastered versions of its classic albums, that the James Gang rode one more time. Any '70s rock fan should have at least the pared-down *Greatest Hits.* Worth seeing are original guitarist Glenn Schwartz's obsessed sets of suffering electric blues at his long-running Thursday-night residency at Hoopple's, a bar in Cleveland. —P.R.

Jamiroquai

★★	Emergency on Planet Earth (Columbia, 1993)	
★★	The Return of the Space Cowboy (Work, 1995)	
★★½	Travelling Without Moving (Work, 1996)	
★★	Synkronized (Work, 1999)	
★★	A Funk Odyssey (Epic, 2001)	

The new hippies: plugged in, high on touchy-feely ecstasy instead of acid, and proudly multicultural yet as shallow and sanctimonious as always. These British funktopians took their name from *jam* and a Native American tribe *(Iroquois),* and if that weren't silly enough, their Muzak-ready Stevie Wonder rips and people-let's-all-get-together platitudes should be enough to guarantee them a permanent place on the dance floor of hell. Led by a diminutive disco cheerleader named Jay Kay, whose baggy-trousered, wacky-headgeared silhouette graces every release like a chilled-out Mickey Mouse, the group capitalized on two trends that swept Britain in the late '80s and early '90s: rave culture and retro, gourmet R&B. Kay and his keyboardist and chief collaborator, Toby Smith, studied *Innervisions*-era Wonder carefully, and just about everything the group has recorded sounds like it could in fact have been played by the master himself. But the blissed-out rave mind-set reduces every track to an aimless, endless trip with no apparent memory of where the band's been or care for where it's going. And Kay's lyrics—which all fall into either the "I must believe/I can do anything" category or the "Baby, come fly with me/Eternally" category (actual quotes)—emulate the sentimentality of "My Cherie Amour" but miss the harsh and urgent social criticism of, say, "Living for the City" or "Black Man." *Travelling Without Moving* stands out slightly because of "Virtual Insanity" and "Cosmic Girl," two big hits that, vapid as they may be, lightened radio playlists somewhat circa 1996. (But the disc is docked half a point for all that damn didgeridoo.) Everything else is identical. —B.S.

Jan and Dean

- ★★★ Surf City/Folk 'n Roll (1963, 1965; One Way, 1996)
- ★★★½ Jan & Dean Take Linda Surfin'/Ride the Wild Surf (1963, 1964; One Way, 1996)
- ★★★★ Dead Man's Curve/New Girl in School/Popsicle (1964, 1964, 1966; One Way, 1996)
- ★★★½ Drag City/Jan & Dean's Pop Symphony No. 1 (1964, 1965; One Way, 1996)
- ★★★ The Little Old Lady From Pasadena/Filet of Soul (1964, 1966; One Way, 1996)
- ★★★ Save for a Rainy Day (1967; Sundazed, 1996)
- ★★★★★ Jan & Dean Anthology Album (1990; One Way, 1996)
- ★ All-Time Greatest Hits (Curb, 1991)
- ★★★½ Greatest Hits (CEMA Special Products, 1992)
- ★★★ Teen Suite 1958–1962 (Varèse Sarabande, 1995)
- ★★★ The Very Best of the Early Years (Collectables, 2001)
- ★★★ Surf City: The Best of Jan and Dean (K-Tel, 2002)

High-school buddies in Los Angeles, Jan Berry and Dean Torrance had experienced only minor success with a handful of mainstream, ineffectual rock singles in the early '60s before fate intervened and teamed them on a show with the Beach Boys in 1963. Brian Wilson began collaborating on songs with Berry and the duo immediately produced a #1 single in May of '63, "Surf City." Jan and Dean had lithe bodies and surfer-boy good looks, but until Wilson came on the scene they were hurting for material that mapped into their culture and their image. Turnabout being fair play, Jan and Dean often popped into Beach Boys recording sessions. Dean, for instance, sang the uncredited lead vocal on the Boys' hit cover version of "Barbara Ann." The Wilson/Berry team (often with Wilson collaborator Roger Christian in on the action) produced a steady stream of hits for Jan and Dean through the mid-'60s, most all of them trading on a holy trinity of themes—surfing, drag racing, and girl chasing. Along the way Berry became a strong producer, fashioning a sound that packed layer after layer of detail beneath crisply recorded vocals.

In '64 Jan and Dean's finest hour on record occurred in the form of "Dead Man's Curve." Detailing a horrible car wreck, the song makes its terrifying point both in the lyrics and in all-stops-out production flourishes such as screeching tires, breaking glass, a deadpan spoken-word bridge ("Well, the last thing I remember, Doc, I started to swerve . . ."), and a fullbore instrumental blast as J&D's multitracked voices shout, "Won't come back from Dead Man's Curve!" A similar approach was used on "Ride the Wild Surf." Of the 22 tracks on Surf City, 18 are Berry productions, most of them models of inspired choices behind the board. In addition to the hit singles, the album also contains some rather obscure but nonetheless commendable Jan and Dean efforts, most notably "She's My Summer Girl" and "Meet Batman."

Where Jan and Dean were headed artistically became a moot point in April of 1966 when Berry's Corvette crashed into a parked truck near the real Dead Man's Curve in Los Angeles. After being in a coma for a month, Berry regained consciousness; but he had suffered severe aphasia as a result of his head injuries, and it would be another seven years before he performed again. Even then, he had difficulty speaking—and for all intents and purposes could not sing with any degree of professional polish or even amateur enthusiasm—and remained partially paralyzed on his right side.

For the heart of the matter, the best place to start is with One Way's Jan & Dean Anthology Album, which is a repackaging of EMI's essential 1990 reissue Surf City: The Best of Jan and Dean—The Legendary Masters Series, a 26-song double-vinyl collection now contained on a single CD with the original artwork and informative liner notes. On a lesser note, Surf City: The Best of Jan & Dean contains six chart hits, including "Dead Man's Curve," among its 10 selections, but four cuts are covers of Beach Boys songs. More difficult to find is the budget item from CEMA Special Products titled Greatest Hits, another 10-cut album, but all of the tracks here were Top 40 hits, and all the obvious selections are present and accounted for. The must to avoid is Curb's All-Time Greatest Hits. Yes, the songs were hits, but these are inferior rerecordings of those monuments.

One Way has reissued a raft of Jan & Dean albums as twofers, and for completists and historians these offer an abundance of scintillating period teen-pop, as well as some genuinely odd moments, such as the 1965 album Folk 'n Roll—on which J&D tackled items such as Dylan's "It Ain't Me Babe" and Pete Seeger's "Turn, Turn, Turn"—now combined on a twofer with 1963's Surf City. For the early years, two thorough overviews are available, Varèse Sarabande's Teen Suite 1958–1962 and Collectables' The Very Best of the Early Years, each containing all the essential home recordings that brought Jan & Dean from the garage to the mainstream. —D.M.

Jane's Addiction

- ★★★ Jane's Addiction (Triple X, 1987)
- ★★★★½ Nothing's Shocking (Warner Bros., 1988)

★★★★ Ritual de lo Habitual (Warner Bros., 1990)
★★ Kettle Whistle (Warner Bros., 1997)
★★★ Strays (2003, Capitol)

If Kurt Cobain was the Messiah of the '90s rock revival, Perry Farrell was its John the Baptist. Brash, colorful, decadent, and unwilling to be ignored, he and his band Jane's Addiction came among the hair-metal dandies of the late-'80s and announced to any that would hear that a new world was dawning. The Los Angeles–based JA sounded the trumpet with a fury of hard-rock riffage, punk swagger, and glam rock star charisma, attracting a sizable following before Farrell erected a temple in the form of the groundbreaking Lollapalooza road show. And through a history plagued by drugs, tempestuous personality clashes, breakups, and late-'90s reunions, the music always transcended its time.

That heady future was not entirely apparent from the work of Psi Com, the goth-glam band from which New York refugee Farrell (born Perry Bernstein) emerged to team with guitar prodigy Dave Navarro, bassist Eric Avery, and drummer Stephen Perkins. Early Jane's shows were marked by Farrell's tortured-cat wails and the band's Led Zeppelin–leaning dub drones. But by the time of 1987's indie live debut, recorded at the famed Roxy Theatre, the music had started to coalesce around Farrell's lyrical observations of seedy Hollywood bohemia, notably on the acoustic real-life portrait "Jane Says," with Perkins' steel drums giving the song a distinctive signature sound. Farrell soon gained a reputation for outrageous statements in interviews, and the band became the object of a significant major-label bidding war, eventually signing a deal with Warner Bros. that gave the band total artistic control.

The band's debut full-length *Nothing's Shocking* is often stunning. Hardcore fans will argue correctly that the studio version of "Jane Says" is flat compared to the previous live take, but "Ocean Size," "Mountain Song," "Had a Dad," and "Standing in the Shower . . . Thinking" are towering clashes of slinky Zeppelin thunder with personal/poetic imagery recalling Lou Reed. The 1990 followup, *Ritual de lo Habitual*, produced the sly glam-rocker "Been Caught Stealing," which remains a rock radio staple to this day. And the sprawling sex-liberation odes "Three Days" and "Then She Did . . ." with Navarro's snaking guitar lines matched by guest Charles Bisharat's violin (on "Three Days") stand as peaks not just for Jane's, but for new rock of the era.

But as the new age came into being, the pressures and distractions mounted, starting with Farrell's role in creating Lollapalooza, and the band's slot headlin-

ing the inaugural 1991 edition proved to be a farewell tour. The group split in two, Farrell and Perkins founding Porno for Pyros in 1992 (two solid albums further broadening the Jane's sound), and Navarro and Avery taking the moniker Deconstruction (with one belated 1994 album after Navarro abandoned the project to join the Red Hot Chili Peppers).

The inevitable reunion came in 1997, though without Avery, who vowed never to work with Farrell again, leaving the Chili Peppers' Flea to step in as interim bassist. Marking the occasion was *Kettle Whistle*, a hodgepodge of unreleased live and demo tracks with four inessential new songs that sounded like, well, a hodgepodge. On stage, though, the band justified its return to action. (A 1999 Perry Farrell compilation, *Rev*, features both Jane's and Porno hits plus some choice rarities including a "Been Caught Stealing" remix and the lilting Jane's version of the Grateful Dead's "Ripple.") For the next few years it was on-again, off-again for JA, as both Farrell and Navarro worked on solo projects. In Farrell's case, his reconnection with his Jewish upbringing took the fore, with an ecstatically mystical glow that he married to his love for deejay culture (he took to spinning in clubs and at festivals as DJ Peretz, his Hebrew name). His 2001 solo album *Song Yet to Be Sung* was a joyful explosion. Navarro's solo *Trust No One* was a bit more scattered. Neither made much impact, though, and the two teamed again with Perkins (with former Porno bassist Martyne LeNoble taking over for Flea full time) to tour as Jane's and record a new album, their first since 1990. *Strays* didn't have the L.A. cool or Zeppelinesque adventure and majesty of *Shocking* and *Habitual*, but it was still better than half of the rock records in 2003, and proved that the thundering live shows were no illusion. —S.H.

Ja Rule

★★★ Venni Vetti Vecci (Murder Inc./Def Jam, 1999)
★★½ Rule 3:36 (Murder Inc./Def Jam, 2000)
★★★½ Pain Is Love (Murder Inc./Def Jam, 2001)
★★½ The Last Temptation (Murder Inc./Def Jam, 2002)
★★ Blood in My Eye (Murder Inc./Def Jam, 2002)

Murderers

★½ Irv Gotti Presents the Murderers (Murder Inc./Def Jam, 2000)

When he debuted with his solo LP, *Venni Vetti Vecci*, Ja Rule cast himself as an analogue of Tupac and DMX: Not only was Rule a bald, bandanna-sporting, tattooed thug with an affinity for going topless, but he also wrestled with his mortality in long, melodic swipes of rhyme on poignant numbers like "Race

Against Time" and takes a swan dive into hedonism on the R. Kelly–sampled "Suicide Freestyle." The album's highlights are undoubtedly the pogo-bouncing "Holla Holla" and the DMX- and Jay-Z–assisted "It's Murda," a fine example of ego and competition resulting in great synergy.

On *Irv Gotti Presents the Murderers,* Ja, like any successful hip-hop artist with friends, fronts his crew, the Murderers, in a misguided attempt to solidify his street credibility. The Murderers, a group of bottom-tier MCs, plod through this ill-fated project with a barrage of uninspired threats and brain-numbing skits. Songs include "We Don't Give a F**k," "Somebody's Gotta Die Tonight," and "We Getting High Tonight." The album's only saving grace is a remix of "Holla Holla" featuring star turns by Jay-Z and Busta Rhymes.

On *Rule 3:36,* Ja emerged as a hip-hop lothario and radio monster on danceable grooves "Between Me and You" and "Put It on Me." A kinder, more sensitive Ja is heard on "I Cry," while "One of Us" interpolates Joan Osborne's tune with a ghetto perspective. Guest slots by Lil' Mo and Christina Milian apply Ja's formula of teaming with female vocalists; he downs ecstasy on the Barry White–fueled "Extasy" (White refused to clear the sample); and the hyper "6 Feet Underground" and heavy-rock underpinnings of "Die" drip with nihilism.

Originally envisioned as a double-CD package, *Pain Is Love* is Ja's most accomplished record. Ghetto-primed numbers like "Dial M for Murder" and "The Inc." ride with a mix of West Coast G-funk and East Coast bump. Ja indulges in ecstasy once again, this time with the help of Missy Elliott and Tweet on "X," and he performs a posthumous duet with Tupac on "So Much Pain." The record's strength is that Ja has accepted his mainstream acceptance: He mastered radio-friendliness on the Stevie Wonder–sampled, Case-assisted "Livin' It Up"; the gospel-inspired "Always on Time," performed with Ashanti; and the guitar-tinged Bonnie and Clyde ode, "Down Ass B**ch," featuring Chuck (Charli Baltimore). For extra measure, Ja includes his remix of "I'm Real" with Jennifer Lopez—a song that cements his pop-star position while extending the lease on J.Lo's music career.

By the time *The Last Temptation* rolled around, Ja's mix of peck-flexing bangers and pop-friendly duets had become formulaic, so much so that he was able to write and record the entire album in just 12 days. The Neptunes-produced "Pop Niggas"—a speedy, syncopated track on which Ja spits rapid-fire threats and disses—is the best of the bangers, and the Bobby Brown–assisted "Thug Lovin' " is a nice piece of sleazy bling-bling romancing, but Ja's none-too-

menacing boasts and hyperserious rhymes about the trials and tribulations of the multiplatinum thug get tiresome fast. Speaking of tiresome, *Blood in My Eye* was another threat-laden cash-grab straight off the Murder Inc. assembly line, only this time, Ja wrangled some B-list guest MCs (Hussein Fatal, Sizzla, Black Child) to back him up. The cheaply hooky beats sound tossed together as Ja tries his best to regain the street cred he'd lost in a highly publicized fued with 50 Cent, but the disses he hurls at 50, Eminem, and Dr. Dre sound more forced than ever.   —K.X./C.H.

The Jayhawks

★★★　Blue Earth (Twin/Tone, 1989)
★★★★★　Hollywood Town Hall (American, 1992)
★★★★½　Tomorrow the Green Grass (American, 1995)
★★★　Sound of Lies (American, 1997)
★★★½　Smile (American, 2000)
★★★★　Rainy Day Music (American/Lost Highway, 2003)

After a now out-of-print 1986 debut, the Minneapolis country rockers the Jayhawks first gained notice with 1989's *Blue Earth.* The album's production values are shoddy, but the band's core appeal is clear. In songs like "Dead End Angel" and "The Baltimore Sun," you can hear the soulful twang and singer Mark Olson's mournful tenor—as well as his perfect harmonies with guitarist Gary Louris—that first earned the comparisons with cult hero Gram Parsons.

Landing on a major label to work with big-league producer George Drakoulias (Black Crowes, Tom Petty) gave the Jayhawks the added push they needed to make a truly remarkable album. *Hollywood Town Hall* furthers the Parsons influence but tempers it with a strong Neil Young–styled roots-rock edge that, with the record's crisp and bright production, nearly jumps off the disc. *Hollywood* stands out because of its timeless, impeccably crafted songs. From the righteous rock of "Waiting for the Sun" and "Settled Down Like Rain" to the swooning ballad "Take Me With You (When You Go)," there's not a weak track among the lot.

By comparison, the poppier *Tomorrow the Green Grass* seems more lightweight, with the group indulging in the kind of bubblegum roots-rock hybrid that made Grand Funk Railroad stars (even covering GFR's "Bad Time"). However, it stands up extremely well with time, particularly tracks like the soaring "Blue," string-adorned "Nothing Left to Borrow," and prophetic "Miss Williams' Guitar" (a tribute to Olson's future wife Victoria Williams). *Green Grass'* ability to embrace a more immediately accessible sound without forsaking its country-rock approach sounds like real progress for a band that seemed still on the rise.

Olson's departure from the Jayhawks dashed any hopes of further refining the band's greatest strength—the songwriting and harmonic collaboration between him and Louris. For better or worse, Louris decided to forge ahead as lead singer and primary songwriter, and *Sound of Lies,* the band's first release without Olson, marks a substantial shift in the Jayhawks' sound. While the opener, "The Man Who Loved Life," doesn't stray far from the group's established sound—and ironically, neither does "Bottomless Cup," written by new member Tim O'Reagan—elsewhere the group embraces more of a straight rock sound, whether with the driving, sludgy riffs of "Think About It," the Beatlesy arpeggios of "Trouble," or the full-on power pop of "Big Star." While *Sound of Lies'* best tracks suggest the viability of a post-Olson Jayhawks, the album sounds too much like the work of a band in search of itself to fully succeed.

By *Smile,* audaciously named after the Beach Boys' abandoned epic, the Jayhawks once again secure their footing, arriving at a more consistent, unabashedly pop sound that echoes the classic album-oriented radio sound of the '70s. While "What Led Me to This Town" provides a fading glimpse of the Jayhawks' earlier sound, tracks like "Smile," "I'm Gonna Make You Love Me," and "(In My) Wildest Dreams" sound much more like Big Star, Tom Petty, and E.L.O. than Parsons or Young. And it's nearly impossible to recognize "Somewhere in Ohio" and "Queen of the World" as the band that brought us *Hollywood Town Hall.* No matter, *Smile* shows the Jayhawks having once again evolved to a comfortable place where they can continue to create strong, consistent records.

And just when it seemed the Jayhawks' evolution was linear, the group circled around and offered *Rainy Day Music,* a surprising banjo-and-slide-guitar-accented return to its country-rocking roots. More than any disavowal of the group's more recent pop direction, the record represents an assimilation of earlier and later styles into a consistently tuneful, expertly harmonized set of songs steeped in classic-rock idioms. Eleven years after its career record and seven years after the departure of its frontman, the Jayhawks—stripped down to an intimate trio—confound expectations in creating a record that ranks among its best and suggests an endurance well beyond expectations. —R.M.S.

Jay-Z

★★★★★ Reasonable Doubt (Roc-A-Fella, 1996)
★★★½ In My Lifetime, Vol. 1 (Roc-A-Fella/Def Jam, 1997)
★★★½ Vol. 2: Hard Knock Life (Roc-A-Fella/Def Jam, 1998)
★★★★ Vol. 3: Life & Times of S. Carter (Roc-A-Fella/Def Jam, 1999)
★★★½ The Dynasty: Roc La Familia 2000 (Roc-A-Fella/Def Jam, 2000)
★★★★★ The Blueprint (Roc-A-Fella/Def Jam, 2001)
★★★★ MTV Unplugged (Roc-A-Fella/Def Jam, 2001)
★★★ The Blueprint 2: The Gift & the Curse (Roc-A-Fella/Def Jam, 2002)
★★½ The Blueprint 2.1 (Roc-A-Fella/Def Jam, 2002)
★★★★½ The Black Album (Roc-A-Fella/Def Jam, 2003)

Although the late Biggie Smalls used to joke about going from "ashy to classy," his Brooklyn partner in rhyme, Jay-Z, would best embody that shift in style and station. Jay's recording debut, however, was anything but auspicious, spitting a well-constructed yet unremarkable verse on 1993's "Can I Get Open?" by Original Flavor, a group that featured Big Jaz, Jay's mentor in rhyme. At the time, Jay was a small-time hustler trying to make ends meet; "Open" gave him the boost he needed to begin working on his debut album, *Reasonable Doubt.* After shopping it to every major record company with no success, Jay and his business partner, Damon Dash, decided to form their own label, Roc-A-Fella Records, a move that would eventually make them very rich men.

To this day, *Reasonable* stands as one of rap music's essential albums, not to mention one of its greatest debuts. Like Biggie's *Ready to Die,* released two years earlier, *Reasonable* profoundly captures the inner life of the above-average corner boy, especially on songs like "Dead Presidents 2" and "Regrets." Hints of the good life to come were revealed on "Ain't No Nigga" (featuring a then-underage Foxy Brown), and Jay's lyrical dexterity was showcased on "22 Twos." The album also featured "Brooklyn's Finest," Jay's only recorded duet with Biggie, which shows two hungry talents seemingly aware that they had no one to outduel but each other.

By the time Jay's second album, *In My Lifetime, Vol. 1,* dropped, he no longer had any competition: Biggie had been gunned down eight months before its release. Nevertheless, *Vol. 1* seemed like a corrective measure in the opposite direction of *Reasonable Doubt,* bearing all the marks of an artist with his eye on a larger pop prize, to the detriment of his art. The dark ethos of his debut was missing almost entirely. Songs like "Imaginary Player" and "Rap Game Crack Game" had heart, but they were drowned by blatant attempts at radio crossover. "I Know What Girls Like" and "(Always Be My) Sunshine" not only found Jay thinning out his dense rhymes but also employing of-the-moment R&B-inflected production that may have earned him club play at the expense of credibility.

His next move seemed like a certain coffin-nailer: He sampled the theme song from the musical *Annie* and turned it into an inescapable summer pop-rap crossover hit. The result, the quirkily brilliant "Hard Knock Life (Ghetto Anthem)," took him from the ears of the cognoscenti to the disc-changers of casual rap fans and sent *Vol. 2: Hard Knock Life* to the upper reaches of the charts. But where many artists—rappers, especially—would have used this as a jumping-off point to an even more preposterous success, Jay aimed lower, and wisely so. Not particularly cut out for being a true pop artist, Jay used the remainder of *Vol. 2* to showcase the skills that had earned him his reputation. If the production (thanks to Swizz Beatz and Timbaland) was glossier than on albums past, it didn't stop Jay from working his tongue in nimble fashion, and the tracks—such as "Nigga What, Nigga Who," "Money, Cash, Hoes," and "Can I Get A . . ."—were more sonically experimental and less formulaic than his prior attempts at shine.

Life & Times of S. Carter took this combination of style and substance to its apotheosis. In addition to maintaining a strong lyrical presence, Jay also showcased his talents as a master of flow, changing cadences and rhyme patters with impressive regularity and flexibility. "So Ghetto," "Do It Again (Put Ya Hands Up)," "Big Pimpin'," "Dope Man": Nearly every track on this album was sonically unique, and Jay rode each one with aplomb and skill.

By contrast, his next great album (following the merely strong *Dynasty Roc La Familia*) could have been construed as a one-trick pony. *The Blueprint* is one of hip-hop's true coherent masterpieces among the few albums since the advent of radio-friendly pop rap in the early '90s that consciously aimed for an all-encompassing feel. Thanks to the soul-drenched production work of then-rookies Just Blaze and Kanye West, Jay-Z was suddenly grappling with a worldview that surpassed his previous limits. Whether he was taking on rivals ("Takeover") or lamenting lost relationships ("Song Cry"), he sounded like he was coming from the same grounded, mature place, a talent few artists of any genre can access.

In 2001, Jay's celebrity status was confirmed with the filming of an *Unplugged* session, making him one of only a handful of rappers to ever be featured on the MTV show. Backed for the gig by the Roots, he used the forum to continue his squabble with Nas and Mobb Deep, but he also dug into his catalogue, revisiting "Can't Knock the Hustle," from his debut album,

and mid-career classics like "Izzo (H.O.V.A.)" and "I Just Wanna Luv U (Give It 2 Me)."

The *Unplugged* album was modest in execution but long in achievement. Surprising, then, that Jay's next effort was the bloated *Blueprint 2*, the first true misstep of his career. The double album had barely enough strong songs ("Meet the Parents," "Excuse Me Miss," "A Dream") for an EP. And his quickly issued revision, *Blueprint 2.1*, slimmed to one disc and with bonus tracks, was no better.

In 2003, Jay announced his "retirement," though few close to him thought this would hold. *The Black Album*, he said, would be his final bow as a recording artist, and so he recruited a virtual who's who of great hip-hop producers to see him off. Kanye West ("Lucifer"), the Neptunes ("Change Clothes"), and Timbaland ("Dirt Off Your Shoulder") contributed songs, as did Eminem and, in a thrilling move, Rick Rubin (Dr. Dre and DJ Premier missed the cut due to schedule conflicts). Rubin's contribution, the bruising "99 Problems," would prove to be the album's most potent cut, and the most fitting one for Jay to ride into the sunset with. Old-school and utterly modern, it showed Jay at the top of his game, able to reinvent himself as a rap classicist at the right time, as if to cement his place in hip-hop's legacy for generations to come. —J.C.

Wyclef Jean

★★★★	Presents the Carnival Featuring Refugee Allstars (Columbia, 1997)
★★★★½	The Ecleftic: Two Sides II a Book (Columbia, 2000)
★★	Masquerade (Columbia, 2002)
★★	The Preacher's Son (J Records, 2003)

As a member of the Fugees, Haitian-born Brooklyn-raised guitarist Wyclef Jean helped bring a bit of traditional musicality, social awareness, and boho-Caribbean style to hip-hop in the mid-'90s. His solo efforts extend that work far beyond hip-hop: They're showcases for his agile guitar playing and a rhythmic repertoire that includes reggae, calypso, Haitian compass, and other Caribbean styles.

The success of the Fugees' 1996 multiplatinum *The Score* enabled Jean to launch his solo career in a lavish way: *The Carnival*, which features cameos from Fugee cohorts Lauryn Hill and Pras, contrasts doleful ballads ("Gone Till November") with uptempo dance rhythms (the title track), and shows that though Jean isn't the most authoritative MC, he understands how to wedge idealistic sermons on equality and justice into tense, propulsive polyrhythmic schemes. Only Jean could transform the Bee Gees' disco hit "Stayin'

Alive" into an earnest missive on the challenges of survival.

The Ecleftic, which features cameos from Kenny Rogers (reprising "The Gambler") and WWF icon the Rock, continues along the same path. There are pieces expressing outrage (the most persuasive is the mournful "Diallo," in which Jean presents himself as a modern-day Bob Marley, advocating understanding) and pieces that are mindless party jams (the deceptively melodic "Red Light District")—all of them notable for taut production, smart guitar textures, and their Fugee-like mix of singing and rapping.

Jean's penchant for lecturing takes over on *Masquerade,* easily his least satisfying work. Though he continues to recontextualize classic tunes—two key tracks offer new treatments of Frankie Valli's "Oh, What a Night" and Bob Dylan's "Knockin' on Heaven's Door"—Jean is so obsessed with the materialistic, hedonistic bent of current hip-hop that he comes across more as a schoolmarm than a voice of reason. The music surrounding his screeds is equally disappointing, as it deemphasizes the global-village sensibility of Jean's previous works in favor of stock, incredibly ordinary hip-hop beats. Jean's work as a producer ensures that he'll never have a shortage of stars around to do cameos. Just one problem: He still needs decent material. *The Preacher's Son* has a few notable commentaries on the state of hip-hop, and features guest energy from Missy Elliott, Patti LaBelle, and Carlos Santana (among others); in almost every case, their talents are wasted on wandering, too-obvious, begging-for-a-hit refrains. —T.M.

Jefferson Airplane

- ★★★ Takes Off (1966; RCA, 2003)
- ★★★★ Surrealistic Pillow (1967; RCA, 2003)
- ★★★★ After Bathing at Baxter's (1967; RCA, 2003)
- ★★★½ Crown of Creation (1968; RCA, 2003)
- ★★★★ Bless Its Pointed Little Head (1969; RCA, 2003)
- ★★★★ Volunteers (1969; RCA, 2003)
- ★★★ The Worst of Jefferson Airplane (RCA, 1970)
- ★★★ Bark (Grunt, 1971)
- ★★★ Thirty Seconds Over Winterland (Grunt, 1973)
- ★★★ The Best of Jefferson Airplane (RCA, 1980)
- ★★★★★ 2400 Fulton Street (RCA, 1987)
- ★★½ Jefferson Airplane (Epic, 1989)
- ★★★★ White Rabbit and Other Hits (RCA, 1990)
- ★★★ Live at the Monterey Festival (Magnum, 1995)
- ★★★½ Live at the Fillmore East (RCA, 1998)
- ★★★★ Jefferson Airplane Loves You (RCA, 1992)
- ★★ Hits (RCA, 1998)
- ★★ Jefferson Airplane (Sony Special Products, 2000)
- ★★ Through the Looking Glass (Get Back, 2000)
- ★★★ Love Songs (RCA, 2000)
- ★★★ VH1 Behind the Music: Jefferson Airplane (RCA, 2000)
- ★★ Live in Monterey (Town Sound, 2001)
- ★★★ The Roar of Jefferson Airplane (RCA, 2001)
- ★★★★ Ignition (RCA, 2001)

Jefferson Airplane was very much part of the tribal ethic that sparked the Summer of Love in the Bay Area in 1967, but there was something special about them. For one thing, in purely technical terms the band boasted a lineup none of its peers, from the Grateful Dead to Quicksilver Messenger Service, could match: Both Marty Balin and Grace Slick were remarkable singers, Jorma Kaukonen a ferocious guitarist, and Jack Casady the most dexterous American rock bassist. For another, all of them wrote: While rhythm guitarist Paul Kantner's contributions came to dominate, it was the fertile exchange of diverse styles and ideas among the members that produced a vison darker and deeper than any other in acid rock.

Jokingly dubbing themselves after the mythic bluesman "Blind Thomas Jefferson Airplane," the group was formed by Balin in 1965. The first album, *Jefferson Airplane Takes Off,* was sturdy folk rock that highlighted Balin's rich, sensuous singing and ballad writing, but the band's distinctiveness came from featuring a strong second vocalist, Signe Anderson. It wasn't until her departure, however, and the release of *Surrealistic Pillow,* that the group hit its stride. New member Grace Slick's "Somebody to Love" and "White Rabbit" became Airplane anthems, their soaring melodies coaxing inventive arrangements and a new instrumental assertiveness from the rest of the band. And Slick's singing made her the counterpart of San Francisco's other reigning diva, Janis Joplin. Where Janis was raw blues urgency, her persona combining the toughness of a biker mama with the pathos of a strayed waif, Slick was queenly, stentorian, her voice an instrument of almost operatic authority and her beauty dark, mysterious, and remote. *Surrealistic Pillow* was a record commanding enough that the band couldn't be ignored—and by dint of its sheer melodicism it cracked open AM radio. Acid rock insinuated itself into the mainstream.

By contrast, *After Bathing at Baxter's* flipped out into experimentalism of a kind baffling to all but the trippiest of the Airplane's fans. Melody still held on in Kantner's "The Ballad of You and Me and Pooneil" and "Won't You Try/Saturday Afternoon," but such inside jokes as "A Small Package of Value Will Come to You, Shortly" and an overall air of maniacal weirdness made for strange, adventurous music more admirable than likable—and more than a little forbidding. Relative accessibility, at least in terms of the Airplane's music, returned with *Crown of Creation*. By now the group's playing had evolved into a compelling mastery, but the band's thematic concerns were becoming more abstruse—Kantner had become obsessed with sci-fi; drummer Spencer Dryden turned woozily mystical with an odd ditty entitled "Chushingura"; and Grace was working her own sex-as-liberation trip with a version of David Crosby's ménage à trois ode, "Triad." A blistering live set, *Bless Its Pointed Little Head*, removed the band from the hothouse environment the studio had become; when the group returned to record, it emerged with a masterpiece, *Volunteers*. A summing-up of psychedelia, the record featured a host of hippie royalty—Jerry Garcia, David Crosby, Stephen Stills—and the Airplane's most cohesive set of songs. Crosby/Kantner/Stills' "Wooden Ships" blended sci-fi and a bittersweet utopianism; the title track, "We Can Be Together," and the rest of the record rocked with more assurance than the Airplane had ever summoned. With Balin departed, neither *Bark* nor the now-deleted *Long John Silver* flourished the tradmark Airplane sound, and while the addition of violinist Papa John Creach affirmed that the band's experimental edge had not been blunted entirely, neither record was much more than pleasant. *Thirty Seconds Over Winterland*, a live album, hardly packed as much punch as *Pointed Head*—and it served as a fairly uninteresting swan song. The band's live work is better featured on *Fillmore East*. The Airplane came together in 1989 for a reunion album—but the synergy could not be recovered. Because the Airplane was a conceptual band, none of the greatest hits albums really works, but on the grounds of intelligent notes and song-selection, *2400 Fulton Street* is the best, trumping both the *Jefferson Airplane Loves You* box set and the almost exhaustive *The Roar of. Love Songs* focuses essentially on Marty Balin's crooning; the VH1 package folds an Airplane best-of in with hits from their lesser, later incarnations, Jefferson Starship and Starship. *Ignition* repackages the band's first four albums—the Airplane at its zenith.   —P.E.

Jefferson Starship

★★★   Dragon Fly (1974; RCA, 1988)
★★★   Red Octopus (Grunt, 1975)
★★★   Earth (Grunt, 1978)
★★   Freedom at Point Zero (Grunt, 1979)
★★   Winds of Change (Grunt, 1982)
★★   At Their Best (RCA, 1993)
★   Live: Miracles (CEMA Special Markets, 1997)
★★   Live at the Fillmore (CMC, 1998)
★★★½   Windows of Heaven (CMC, 1999)

★★   Extended Versions: The Encore Collection (BMG Special Products, 2000)
★★★½   Across the Sea of Suns (Zebra, 2001)
★★★½   Deeper Space/Extra Virgin Sky (Beyond, 2002)

Starship

★★   Knee Deep in the Hoopla (RCA, 1985)
★★★½   Greatest Hits (Ten Years and Change, 1979–1991) (RCA, 1991)
★★   The Best of Starship (RCA, 1993)

Divisive, extreme, and visionary, the Jefferson Airplane was a band of artists; Jefferson Starship, at its best, became nothing but a band of hitmakers. The transformation of Paul Kantner and Grace Slick into crafty corporate rockers took a while, of course, but by the mid-'70s the changeover had become concrete. Occasionally (and infuriatingly), their music echoed their former adventurousness, but in general they made glossy pop-rock that sounded hideously dated almost the day it came out.

A Kantner project starring Slick and members of the Grateful Dead, "Jefferson Starship" was originally a one-off assemblage responsible for *Blows Against the Empire* (1970), a sci-fi song suite that now suffers from concept-album creakiness but at its time boasted an experimental edge. In 1974 Kantner and Slick put together Jefferson Starship, the actual working group. Their proven songwriting skills and Slick's vocal expertise made the new band appear promising—but the seeds of mediocrity had already been sown.

"Caroline" and "Ride the Tiger," from *Dragon Fly*, and "Play on Love" and "Fast Buck Freddie," from *Red Octopus*, defined the early Starship sound—smooth instrumental work, strong singing, and occasionally interesting lyrics. But with Marty Balin's "Miracles," *Octopus'* massive hit, the band began shifting toward schmaltz. Balin now sounded like a lounge singer, and on the mid-'70s stuff, smarmy expertise ruled, resulting in a passel of hits ("With Your Love," "Count on Me," "Love Too Good," and "Runaway") that quiver with the ersatz "sexiness" typical of '70s AOR fare. Balin departed on the advent of *Freedom at Point Zero*, his place taken by ex–Elvin Bishop Group singer Mickey Thomas. A vocalist with all of the arena-rock aspirations to become another Steve Perry, Thomas perfectly suited Jefferson Starship in its relentless descent into mediocrity.

The hits kept on a-comin'—"Jane" *(Freedom)*, "Sara," "We Built This City" (both from *Knee Deep in the Hoopla*), "Nothing's Gonna Stop Us Now" *(No Protection)*. By 1985, the band had dropped "Jefferson" from its name—thus ditching painful memories of a glorious past. *Gold* is Jefferson Starship's greatest hits, and it's entertaining. *Ten Years and Change* is the strongest Starship best-of, and it's embarrassing. *Windows of Change* featured a reunited version of JS alongside the Tubes' Prairie Prince and the Dixie Dregs' T Lavitz. —P.E.

Waylon Jennings

★★½	Folk Country (1966; Razor & Tie, 1998)
★★½	Love of the Common People (1967; Buddah, 1999)
★★★★	The Taker/Tulsa (RCA, 1970)
★★★★★	Honky Tonk Heroes (1973; Buddah, 1999)
★★★½	This Time (1974; Buddah, 1999)
★★★½	The Ramblin' Man (1974; Buddah, 2000)
★★★★	Dreamin' My Dreams (1975; Buddah, 2000)
★★★★	Waylon Live (1976; Buddah, 1999)
★★★	Ol' Waylon (RCA, 1977)
★★★★	Greatest Hits (RCA, 1979)
★★	Hangin' Tough (MCA, 1987)
★★★	Waymore's Blues (Part 2) (RCA, 1994)
★★½	Super Hits (RCA, 1996)
★★★★	Right for the Time (1996; Buddah, 2000)
★★★	The Essential Waylon Jennings (RCA, 1996)
★★½	Cowboys, Sisters, Rascals & Dirt (RCA, 1998)
★★★	Closing in on the Fire (Ark 21, 1998)
★★	Never Say Die: Live (Columbia, 2000)
★★½	The Millennium Collection (MCA, 2000)
★★★★	RCA Country Legends (Buddah, 2001)
★★★	Phase One: The Early Years 1958–1964 (Hip-O, 2002)

with Willie Nelson, Jessi Colter, and Tompall Glaser

★★★	Wanted! The Outlaws (RCA, 1976; 1996)

Waylon Jennings, who died in early 2002, was the archetypal outlaw's outlaw right up to the very end. In 2001, when the Nashville establishment finally got around to inducting him into the Country Music Hall of Fame, Jennings refused to attend the ceremony; it was one last show of defiance against a straitlaced system he'd spent more than half his life rebelling against. This plainspoken Texas troubadour began his career as Buddy Holly's bass player, and it was Holly who produced Jennings' 1958 debut single, "Jole Blon." Together with a generous sampling of Jennings' folksy, Herb Alpert–produced sides for A&M, that song is preserved on *Phase One: The Early Years 1958–1964*. While there's nothing here that quite heralds the revolution to come, his cover of Bob Dylan's "Don't Think Twice, It's Alright," with its thumping bass line and Johnny Cash–derived rhythm, is vintage Waylon. The Chet Atkins–produced *Folk Country* and *Love of the Common People* are similarly tentative but promising steps in the right direction, with the latter

featuring an earnest crack at the Beatles' "You've Got to Hide Your Love Away." Straining against Nashville slickness, Jennings begins to really assert his rough-hewn sensibility on 1968's taut, rollicking "Only Daddy That'll Walk the Line" (RCA Country Legends) and 1970's *The Taker/Tulsa* (out of print at press time, but surely not for long). That album was distinguished by a handful of smart, literate songs ("The Taker," "Sunday Morning Coming Down") by kindred rebel spirit Kris Kristofferson. By 1973's *Lonesome, On'ry and Mean* (deleted), Jennings had successfully wrestled control of his music away from his label—unprecedented in Nashville at the time, that freedom allowed him to produce his own records, record with his own band, and pick his own songs—even if that meant releasing an album like *Honky Tonk Heroes*, written almost entirely by then unknown fellow Texas renegade Billy Joe Shaver. The title track, "Old Five and Dimers Like Me," and "Black Rose" define the Outlaw stance at its best, before self-awareness turned to self-consciousness.

For a while, however, Waylon Jennings jumped from strength to strength. *This Time* accentuates his quiet side and introduces the first of many genial collaborations with Willie Nelson. *Dreamin' My Dreams* captures the full range of Jennings' talent, from the reflective title cut to the full-tilt rebellion of "Are You Sure Hank Done It This Way" and "Bob Wills Is Still the King." *Waylon Live* sounds damn near punk or, at the very least, as hard-charging as anything on the rock charts in 1976. And yet, by the time the same year's *Wanted: The Outlaws* hit the racks, Jennings was already growing weary of the tag—a sentiment sharply expressed on *Ol' Waylon*'s "Don't You Think This Outlaw Bit's Done Got Out of Hand." *Wanted!*—which pulled together songs by Jennings, Willie Nelson, Tompall Glaser, and Jennings' wife, Jessi Colter—was a monster hit but is now mostly an artifact of historical interest; the best songs are featured on other, superior albums and anthologies. In fact, Jennings' 1979 *Greatest Hits* offers a superb introduction to Jennings and the Outlaws as a whole, moving from "Lonesome, On'ry and Mean" on through to the Waylon and Willie trilogy: "Mamas Don't Let Your Babies Grow Up to Be Cowboys," "Good Hearted Woman," and the heart-shattering "Luckenbach, Texas."

By the late '70s, Jennings' eclectic approach had become inconsistent. His Neil Young cover (from 1976's *Are You Ready for the Country*, deleted) and Buddy Holly medley (from 1978's *I've Always Been Crazy*, also deleted) are well worth searching out, but the fact that the lion's share of his records for MCA and Epic have fallen out of print is probably for the best. MCA's *The Millennium Collection* salvages a few notable keepers, such as mid-'80s country hits "My Rough and Rowdy Days," a rockin' cover of Los Lobos' "Will the Wolf Survive," and his last country chart-topper, "Rose in Paradise." The '90s, though hitless, were a little more fruitful in terms of quality. *Waymore's Blues (Part 2),* which teamed Jennings with rock producer Don Was, suggested that he still had a card trick or two up his sleeve, and the proof came with *Right for the Time.* While lacking the fire of his past glories, the laid-back album nonetheless found Jennings in fine, weather-beaten voice, and the ruminative songs—mostly self-penned—were uniformly excellent.

Closing in on the Fire was livelier but not quite as consistent, though it was a far cry better than *Never Say Die: Live,* which caught Jennings in good humor and robust voice but questionable taste, subjecting his songs to an overblown horn section and guest appearances by latter-day outlaw wanna-be's like Montgomery Gentry. Fortunately, that rather feeble swan song will forever be overshadowed by the formidable legacy of groundbreaking, status quo–shaking music Jennings left behind. —M.C./R.SK.

The Jesus and Mary Chain

★★★★★ Psychocandy (Reprise, 1985)
★★★★ Darklands (Warner Bros., 1987)
★★½ Barbed Wire Kisses (Warner Bros., 1988)
★★★ Automatic (Warner Bros., 1989)
★★★ Honey's Dead (Def American, 1992)
★★★½ Stoned & Dethroned (American, 1994)
★★½ Hate Rock 'n' Roll (American, 1995)
★★ Munki (Sub Pop, 1998)
★★★½ Complete Peel Sessions (Strange Fruit, 2000)
★★★★ 21 Singles (Rhino, 2002)

Coming straight outta East Kilbride, Scotland, with three chords, some distortion, and a whole lot of slouch, the Jesus and Mary Chain caused one of the biggest ruckuses in the British music scene since the Sex Pistols. Deriving their aesthetic directly from the Velvet Underground, brothers William and Jim Reid wrote beautifully simple yet miserable songs using nothing but the rudiments of classic pop and an excess of white noise, and delivered the combination with cynicism and insouciance. *Psychocandy,* one of the most powerfully jarring albums of the '80s, opens with a stark "Be My Baby" drumbeat and a wash of feedback, and the feeling of being lost in a cold, echoey dungeon does not let up until the end. But beneath the pummeling is a tasteful economy of style and a gift for pure melody that harks back to the Beach Boys and '60s girl groups. "Just Like Honey," "The

Living End," "Taste of Cindy," and "Some Candy Talking" are perfectly proportioned pop starlets disfigured by noise.

The Reids made a quick stylistic shift with the barren *Darklands,* cleaning up the sonic picture but leaving the elegance and gloom of their songs intact. Compared to the debut's assault, the silence and relative psychic peace of many of the tracks here—just (clean) guitar and tambourine—are shockingly intimate. "I'm going to the darklands/To talk in rhyme/With my chaotic soul," Jim Reid sings on the title track. The album also introduced the sleek, muted guitar groove that became the group's rhythmic signature. *Psychocandy* was a bold entrance, but the sharp lines, symmetry, and steady pulse of *Darklands* became the model the group followed for the rest of its career.

Barbed Wire Kisses, a collection of B sides and other non-LP material, contains the group's cacophonous pre-*Psychocandy* singles and mystifyingly warped covers of the Beach Boys' "Surfin' USA" and Bo Diddley's "Who Do You Love?," but on the following two albums, the Reids continued to move away from their noise-mongering beginnings. *Automatic* and *Honey's Dead* further streamlined their approach with a cool, mechanical groove dominated by a chug-chugging electric guitar, bare beats, and a never-changing vocal sneer; if not for the occasional flash of brilliance, like *Automatic*'s timeless "Head On" and "Half Way to Crazy," the albums would be ruined by sheer redundancy.

But they weren't out of tricks just yet. *Stoned & Dethroned* returned to the sparse, bleak soundscape of *Darklands,* an act of cleansing (or penitence) that once again resulted in some of their strongest work. With guest vocals from Hope Sandoval and Shane MacGowan, the songs have a delicacy and an emotional depth that hadn't been heard from the band before; MacGowan, sounding vulnerable as ever, sings a plain, earnest prayer, "God Help Me."

Hate Rock 'n' Roll comes out strutting, and although it's not the Reids' strongest material ("I love the BBC/I love it when they're pissin' on me/And I love MTV/I love it when they're shittin' on me," goes the ham-fisted title track), the blast of passion is welcome, at least until they lose the plot halfway through. *Munki,* idiotically bookended by "I Love Rock 'n' Roll" and "I Hate Rock 'n' Roll," is an unfortunate final statement from the band, which broke up the year after its release. Dull and overlong, peppered with no-longer-shocking-or-even-meaningful references to Jesus and television, it could be the work of a Jesus and Mary Chain parody band if not for the sad and humble look back in the many autobiographical songs

("I'm a mean motherfucker now but I once was cool"; "I was just a teenage Jesus freak/Got drunk on punk and then I found my feet").

The contrasting visions of the first two albums say most of what needs to be said about the Jesus and Mary Chain, but the posthumous singles and radio-session collections are handy summaries. For a group that struck a lot of revolutionary (or at least anticommercial) poses, it produced a lot of great three-minute pop tunes. —B.S.

The Jesus Lizard

★★	Pure EP (Touch and Go, 1989)
★★½	Head (Touch and Go, 1990)
★★½	Goat (Touch and Go, 1991)
★★★★	Liar (Touch and Go, 1992)
★★★	Lash EP (Touch and Go, 1993)
★★★	Show (Collision Arts/Giant, 1994)
★★★½	Down (Touch and Go, 1994)
★★★½	Shot (Capitol, 1996)
★★½	Jesus Lizard EP (Jetset, 1998)
★★★½	Blue (Capitol, 1998)
★★★	Bang (Touch and Go, 2000)

While no substitute for its drunk-and-disorderly live performances, the studio albums by the Jesus Lizard are the musical equivalent of Everclear in the hard-rock liquor cabinet. Though utterly terrifying to commercial radio programmers—in large measure because of singer David Yow's coarse subject matter and maniacal vocal spew—the Jesus Lizard forged an original sound that merges the Birthday Party mania with Led Zeppelin stomp. Few bands made such consistently abrasive smash-mouth rock, particularly during the period when the group was a foursome with drummer Mac McNeilly (1990–96), indie-rock's answer to Zep's John Bonham in the way he kept even the band's most belligerent tunes swinging. Guitarist Duane Denison and bassist David Wm. Sims (who with Yow was in the legendary Texas art-punk combo Scratch Acid in the '80s) were masters of punk-metal sonic architecture, and it is their riffs, more than any sense of sustained melody, that make the band's best songs memorable. Yow's voice is the wild card: Clowning one minute, frothing the next, he uses words as rhythmic devices to batter the walls of taste.

Pure is a tentative start recorded with a drum machine, but the band gained confidence in the studio working with veteran noise-rock auteur Steve Albini (another former Sims bandmate in Rapeman). The height of the Albini-engineered albums is *Liar*, which finds Yow actually attempting to sing for the first time, and the band's corrosive power is captured on "Gladi-

ator" and "Puss," later issued as a limited-edition split single with Lizard admirers Nirvana.

The departure of McNeilly after recording *Shot* was a blow the band never quite recovered from, and it broke up in 1999 after releasing its most accessible album, *Blue*, with drummer Jim Kimball. *Bang* is a posthumous collection of outtakes and rarities, and *Show* documents the quartet in its natural element: on stage, where it alternately baits, assaults, and entertains its audience. —G.K.

Jethro Tull

★★	This Was (Chrysalis, 1969)
★★★	Stand Up (Chrysalis, 1969)
★★★	Benefit (Chrysalis, 1970)
★★★½	Aqualung (Chrysalis, 1971)
★★★½	Thick as a Brick (Chrysalis, 1972)
★★★	Living in the Past (Chrysalis, 1972)
★★★	A Passion Play (Chrysalis, 1973)
★★★	Minstrel in the Gallery (Chrysalis, 1975)
★★★	M.U./The Best of Jethro Tull (Chrysalis, 1976)
★★	Too Old to Rock 'n' Roll, Too Young to Die! (Chrysalis, 1976)
★★★★	Songs From the Wood (Chrysalis, 1977)
★★★	Heavy Horses (Chrysalis, 1978)
★★★	Bursting Out/Jethro Tull Live (Chrysalis, 1978)
★★½	Stormwatch (Chrysalis, 1979)
★★★	A (Chrysalis, 1980)
★★★	Broadsword and the Beast (Chrysalis, 1982)
★	Walk Into Light (Chrysalis, 1983)
★	Under Wraps (Chrysalis, 1984)
★★★	Crest of a Knave (Chrysalis, 1987)
★★★½	20 Years of Jethro Tull (Chrysalis, 1988)
★★	Rock Island (Chrysalis, 1989)
★★	Catfish Rising (Chrysalis, 1991)
★★½	A Little Light Music (Chrysalis, 1992)
★★	Roots to Branches (Chrysalis, 1995)
★★	J-Tull.Com (Varèse, 1999)
★★★	The Jethro Tull Christmas Album (Varèse, 2003)

Jethro Tull isn't his name, of course, but it might as well be. At the mere mention of this venerable British art-rock outfit, most people flash on the image of flute-wielding Tull frontman Ian Anderson. *This Was* and *Stand Up*, both from 1969, present the group as jazz- and folk-influenced progressives; Anderson's rasping, meldodramatic style of play takes off from Rahsaan Roland Kirk's multireed explorations. Guitarist Martin Barre contributes heavy, hooky riffs to accompany Anderson's burgeoning songwriting voice on *Stand Up*. And then, Tull clicked with young American audiences.

Aqualung combines heaving melodies and moralistic liberal diatribes against church and state: You know the rest. Thanks to 20 years of radio rotation, heavy-handed manifestos like "Aqualung" and "Wind Up" rank right up there with "Stairway to Heaven" on the overfamiliarity meter. *Living in the Past,* which ably documents Tull to this point, is recommended over the later compilations.

The immediate success of *Aqualung* spurred Anderson to indulge his artistic whims, resulting in two challenging, wildly experimental, and occasionally obtuse theatrical concept albums: *Thick as a Brick* and *Passion Play.* After that strategy backfired, Jethro Tull returned to traditional song structure on *War Child* and the acoustic-flavored *Minstrel in the Gallery.* Things were never quite the same again, though. After the excessively snide 1976 hit "Too Old to Rock 'n' Roll, Too Young to Die!," Tull retreated into a sylvan glade of arty Elizabethan folk-rock. This latter-day approach is best captured on the lovely, smoke-flavored *Songs From the Wood* and *A,* on which former members of Fairport Convention and Roxy Music add crucial support. After releasing a pair of electronic stinkers (*Walk Into Light* and *Under Wraps*) in the '80s, Anderson retired the Tull moniker for several years. The 1988 box-set retrospective *(20 Years of Jethro Tull)* is representative, but mighty tough for the average listener to wade through. Jethro Tull released the folkish *Crest of a Knave* in 1987; from then on, Anderson retreated into a prosaic formula that obliterated most of the pastoral passages and tricky time signatures in favor of shorter songs that rocked in surprisingly conventional ways. Anderson's darkly sarcastic sense of humor and the band's tight instrumental combustion has made Tull an exhilarating live experience to this day—long after its records ceased to hold much interest for anyone but hard-core fans. —M.C./E.L.

Joan Jett

★★★½　Bad Reputation (1981; Blackheart, 1998)
★★★½　I Love Rock 'n' Roll (1981; Blackheart, 1998)
★★★　Album (1983; Blackheart, 1998)
★★★　Glorious Results of a Misspent Youth (1984; Blackheart, 1998)
★★★　Good Music (Blackheart/CBS, 1986)
★★★　Up Your Alley (Blackheart/CBS, 1988)
★★★　The Hit List (Blackheart/CBS, 1990)
★★★　Notorious (Blackheart/CBS, 1991)
★★★½　Flashback (Blackheart, 1993, 1998)
★★★　Pure and Simple (Warner Bros., 1994)
★★★½　Fit to Be Tied (Blackheart, 1997, 2001)
★★½　Fetish (Blackheart, 1999)

Liberated from the Runaways—the '70s all-girl teen rock group masterminded by impresario Kim Fow-

ley—lead guitarist Joan Jett brought her own punk attitude to the Gary Glitter school of glam-pop-metal. What you see is what you get with her first two albums: No, Jett doesn't give a damn 'bout her bad reputation and yes, she loves rock & roll. Both discs are lean rock machines, thanks to a mix of inspired covers ("Crimson and Clover") and po-faced, jackhammer-simple originals (the title tracks). *Album* finds Jett stretching her self-imposed boundaries a bit (see her cover of Sly & the Family Stone's "Everyday People"). She retrenches on *Good Music;* the title track is a backward-gazing Beach Boys tribute. A cover of "Fun, Fun, Fun" fares better, though the best tracks are originals this time: "This Means War," "Just Lust." *Up Your Alley* brings the chartwise song doctor Desmond Child into the picture, and Jett connects with several of the renowned Bon Jovi collaborator's meaty hooks—she turns a by-the-numbers heartbreak anthem ("I Hate Myself for Loving You") into a rocking therapy session. *The Hit List* is entirely composed of covers: newly recorded, if not exactly fresh. There are no surprises, and no letdowns; typical Joan Jett, in other words. *Notorious*—a competent but dull set—could use a few *Hit List* leftovers.

The '90s saw several Jett reinventions. Even during waning popularity, Jett's Blackheart Records label made small pressings for hard-core devotees, and this dedication to her tougher-than-leather music and fanbase would later pay off. Grungy guitars replaced the usual power chords on *Pure and Simple,* which witnessed the original riot-chick and Activity Grrrl teaming up with Bikini Kill's Kathleen Hanna and L7's Donita Sparks and Jennifer Finch. The grrrl-power movement undoubtedly led to a new generation of fans, with the release of retrospectives like *Flashback,* a collection of rarities, and *Fit to Be Tied,* a greatest-hits compilation. Radical feminism informed the badass babe's next incarnation: *Fetish* found a buff-and-butch Jett demanding latex and rough sex on the title track. But the inclusion of bawdier bubblegum covers like "Wooly Bully" and "Hanky Panky" demonstrated that when it comes to raunchy rock-writing, veiled sexuality trumps overt sleaze any day. —C.S.

Jewel

★★★　Pieces of You (East West/Atlantic, 1994)
★★　Spirit (Atlantic, 1998)
★★★½　This Way (Atlantic, 2001)
★★★½　0304 (Atlantic, 2003)

If folk music's fatal weakness is naiveté, Alaska's Jewel Kilcher is the genre's living martyr. At her debut, the fresh-faced 19-year-old was the folk heroine ready for pop fame. *Pieces of You* proved that Jewel could write a beautiful melody and sing with a conviction and accomplishment beyond her years, and also that she was as hopelessly pained and wide-eyed about social and cultural issues as Natalie Merchant is about political ones. Scornfully equating poor nutritional choices with lack of spiritual fulfillment ("Little Sister"); railing gently against looksism in the embarrassing title song ("Ugly girl, ugly girl, do you hate her/'cause she's pieces of you?"); sympathizing with the elderly ("Painters"): Jewel is firmly on the side of the angels. But her "issue" songs can't match the beautiful simplicity of her love songs, notably "Morning Song" and the sweet, lilting hits "Who Will Save Your Soul," "Foolish Games," and "You Were Meant for Me." There are plenty of sparklers that didn't crack the charts—the lovely, rambling "Near You Always" and the slow lament "Don't."

Insofar as there was anything wrong with *Pieces of You*, it wasn't the scatty production, whose rough edges gave Jewel's pretty melodies an admirable folk grit. On her followup recording, released in tandem with her first book of poetry, *Nights Without Armor*, she enlists slick pop producer Patrick Leonard to upsize her sound, fill out the band, and turn the intimate pieces into smooth contemporary hits. Jewel's weakness—her stubbornly girlish point of view toward grand subjects—was merely allowed to flourish. So now she's comparing a broken heart to "grape gum on the ground," seeing the fragile flame inside a "Fat Boy," speculating on the psychosexual component of Hitler's behavior, and telling the world that "we're all okay." While one thanks her for this endorsement, the sensitive-but-clear-eyed-child act wears thin. Then again, the woman writing the songs just becomes more proficient; she can't not write a melody, even when she tries (on the wafting "Kiss the Flame" and the repetitive wordplay of "Jupiter"). The drift away from folk allows Jewel to showcase the strength in her delicate voice, particularly on the popping "Down So Long" and the half-talked "Hey You."

At age 27, Jewel was still writing lyrics with the uninformed compassion of a teen scribbling in homeroom ("the light lends itself to soft repose"—ugh), but with *This Way* she discovered the merits of electric guitar, and her songwriting has blossomed from flower-child-folk through soporific pop into sturdy folk-rock. There's a big old beat in the background and a new sinew in the vocals, and a high percentage of the songs are solid winners—"Standing Still," "Cleveland," the sassy "Everybody Needs Somebody Sometime," the gorgeous love song "Break Me." Jewel deepens her voice and lays off the crystalline falsetto in "Serve the Ego" and the melancholy "I Won't Walk Away."

Jewel was ready for more change, though: With *0304* she reinvents herself with sleek studio effects, plastic dance-rock hooks, and pop-art irony. Helmed by cowriter and producer Lester Mendez (whose credits include Shakira and Enrique Iglesias), *0304* is essentially a wanna-be version of late-career Madonna albums such as *American Life*. It even has its own State of the Union song, "America," with lyrics such as "We shed blood in the name of liberty." Jewel seemed a bit stiff and silly waxing lyrical about hot pants and bumpin' boots, but she was surrounded by pop of such undeniable catchiness that her fakeness somehow fit: She found herself an artificial flavor that tasted good.   —A.B./B.W.

Jimmy Eat World

★★ Static Prevails (Capitol, 1996)
★★★★ Clarity (Capitol, 1999)
★★★ Bleed American (DreamWorks, 2001)

Jimmy Eat World emerged from Arizona in the late '90s, fresh out of high school with a major-label deal. Despite being nominally part of a posthardcore-emo scene (with bands like the Promise Ring and Sunny Day Real Estate) that valued aggression and noise as much as hooks and melody, Jimmy Eat World showed a striking pop sensibility. Its debut, *Static Prevails*, is very much of its time, sporting anxiety-ridden vocals, lyrics of suburban melodrama, and screaming punk guitars. Even then, the band knew a hook when it heard one, as evidenced on the exhilarating "Call It in the Air."

The band found the perfect balance of noise and bliss on *Clarity*. Lead singer Jim Adkins' vocals are lushly layered and harmonize with the chiming guitars, while the group's powerful rhythm section propels the band through full-throttle power-pop (emphasis on the *power*) songs like the title track and "Crush." By the time the band moved to a new label two years later, it had cultivated a devoted following. *Bleed American* made Jimmy Eat World minor celebrities; for the album, the band had thrown themselves into pop-rock craftsmanship, practically abandoning all hints of rebellious noise. Songs like "The Middle" and "Sweetness" became minor hits, and the album contained a half dozen other saccharine treasures.   —C.R.

Antonio Carlos Jobim
Selected Discography

★★★★½ The Composer of Desafinado, Plays (Verve, 1963)
★★★ The Wonderful World of Antonio Carlos Jobim (Discovery, 1965)
★★★★★ Wave (Warner Bros., 1967)

★★★★½ Stone Flower (Epic, 1970)

★★★★★ Elis & Tom (Verve, 1974)

★★★★ Urubu (Warner Bros., 1976)

★★★★ Passarim (Verve, 1987)

★★½ Antonio Brasileiro (Sony, 1995)

★★★ The Man From Ipanema (Verve, 1995)

★★★★½ Antonio Carlos Jobim's Finest Hour (Verve, 2000)

★★★ Tom Canta Vinicius: Ao Vivo (Universal Latino, 2001)

★★★★ The Very Best of Antonio Carlos Jobim (Universal, 2003)

with Frank Sinatra:

★★★★ Francis Albert Sinatra & Antonio Carlos Jobim (Warner Bros., 1967)

Blame "The Girl From Ipanema"—that staple of elevators and supermarkets worldwide—for the notion that the bossa nova is superficial Muzak for lounge aficionados. In reality, the bossa is one of Latin America's most poignant and exquisite genres, light and sophisticated, but at the same time able to distill the full meaning of the word *saudade*—Portuguese for nostalgia, or the inherent bittersweetness of life. And there would be no bossa without Antonio Carlos Jobim and his equally important but criminally ignored songwriting partner, poet Vinicius de Moraes.

What makes Jobim's compositions so deceptively simple is his classically trained harmonic sense, which draws inspiration from mood masters such as Claude Debussy, Maurice Ravel, and Brazil's own Heitor Villa-Lobos, while remaining rooted in popular music. Together with Vinicius, singer/guitarist João Gilberto, and a few other collaborators, Jobim spearheaded the bossa wave in the late '50s. The movement's internationalization would arrive via the movie *Orfeu Negro* (for which Jobim cowrote the soundtrack) and the infamous 1963 Stan Getz and João Gilberto sessions that saw Gilberto's wife Astrud walk into the studio and, presumably at Getz's insistence, make her impromptu recording debut with her timeless, endearingly flat-toned version of "Garota de Ipanema."

Jobim's adequate piano playing and monotone vocals were no match for his extraordinary gift as a composer, which explains why he always surrounded himself with remarkable singers such as Miucha and the late Elis Regina. For a good taste of the velvety bossa free of most of the overexposed hits, try *Elis & Tom.* You'll recognize the opening track, since the impressionistic "Aguas de Marco" (Waters of March) is an obligatory standard for all Brazilian singers (and David Byrne, too). But the 13 other, lesser-known gems showcase Jobim at his peak: sad and playful at the same time, clearly inspired by the presence of the mercurial Regina.

The maestro's jazzy, instrumental side is represented with 1967's *Wave,* which many consider to be the best single work he ever released. The same could be said of *Stone Flower,* a languid, nocturnal masterpiece that was largely ignored upon its release. *Urubu* was even more radical, a violent departure from bossa territory, but well worth exploring. *Antonio Brasileiro,* Jobim's last album before his death in 1994, found him returning to familiar ground, having lost none of his ability to compose new bossa gems. Still, the album's highlight is a smoky duet with Sting on the scorching oldie "Insensatez" (How Insensitive).

Studious Jobim listeners will be tempted by Verve's three-CD set *The Man From Ipanema.* The first two discs offer a fine overview of Jobim's songs and instrumentals. Unfortunately, disc three becomes a trying experience by juxtaposing various versions of the same classics side by side. There are plenty of single-disc compilations out there that do a better job at showcasing the man's ever-influential genius.   —E.L.

Jodeci

★★ Forever My Lady (MCA, 1991)

★★★ Diary of a Mad Band (MCA, 1993)

★ The Show, the After Party, the Hotel (MCA, 1995)

Four vocalists, two sets of brothers, one new image for the hip-hop/doo-wop of New Jack Swing. The melding of smooth street-corner harmonizing with the rhythms and black consciousness of rap worked well for clean-cut outfits like Boyz II Men, New Edition, and Bell Biv Devoe. But it was Jodeci—songwriter DeVante Swing and his brother Dalvin DeGrate, and brothers Joel and Cedric Hailey—who brought some sweat to the satin-sheet contemporary stylings. *Forever My Lady*'s romance-rap broke no musical ground otherwise, but it did showcase the quartet's pleasingly varied vocal strengths and spun off some hits with the title song, cowritten by Al B. Sure!, and the mellow "Come Talk to Me."

With *Diary of a Mad Band,* Jodeci came on strong, with rich, layered production providing a velvet cushion for Swing's gemlike songwriting. Despite the title and the tough posturing of the foursome on the album's cover, *Mad Band* is packed with slowhand grooves, the vocalists sounding more earnest and powerful than in their relatively playful debut. Designed not as a single-machine but as a seduction soundtrack, the record varies little in rhythm and intensity. From the love songs ("My Heart Belongs to U" and "Alone") to the Jamaican-inflected funky business of "You Got It," all the way to the suitably steamy "Sweaty" and the afterglow of "Jodecidal Hotlines," the album rides a single dance-soul arc in 13 movements.

Young, rich, and suddenly the objects of attraction to hundreds of fans, a group can get lost in the celebrity maze. *The Show, the After Party, the Hotel* is a misguided concept album referring specifically to the quartet's own fame, and a long, dull limo ride it is. The grooves are harder and the voices are strong and nimble, but the pompous idea—an album divided into three conceptual parts, each song alternating with an interlude—weighs down the elaborate production. It doesn't take long for the songs to sound repetitive, and the concept is only of interest to someone intimately acquainted with the goings-on at the show, the after party, and the hotel. —A.B.

Billy Joel

★★	Cold Spring Harbor (1971; Columbia, 1988)
★★½	Piano Man (1973; Sony/Columbia, 1998)
★★★	Streetlife Serenade (1974; Sony/Columbia, 1998)
★★★½	Turnstiles (1976; Sony/Columbia, 1998)
★★★★	The Stranger (1977; Sony/Columbia, 1998)
★★★	52nd Street (1978; Sony/Columbia, 1998)
★★★	Glass Houses (1980; Sony/Columbia, 1998)
★★½	Songs in the Attic (1981; Sony/Columbia, 1998)
★★★½	The Nylon Curtain (1982; Sony/Columbia, 1998)
★★★½	An Innocent Man (1983; Sony/Columbia, 1998)
★★★★	Greatest Hits, Volumes 1 & 2 (Columbia, 1985)
★★★½	The Bridge (1986; Columbia, 1998)
★★★	Kohuept (In Concert) (Columbia, 1987)
★★★★	Storm Front (Columbia, 1989)
★★★	River of Dreams (Columbia, 1993)
★★★	Greatest Hits, Vol. 3 (Columbia, 1997)
★★★	Complete Hits Collection, 1974–1997 (Sony, 1997)
★★★	The Bridge/Storm Front/The Nylon Curtain (Sony, 1998)
★★½	2000 Years: The Millennium Concert (Columbia, 2000)
★★★	Fantasies and Delusions (Columbia, 2001)
★★★½	The Essential Billy Joel (Sony, 2001)
★★★	Piano Man/52nd Street/Kohuept (Sony, 2002)

A gift for song in the tradition of Tin Pan Alley, the Brill Building, Burt Bacharach, and Paul McCartney is Billy Joel's most apparent gift; the closer he keeps to it,

the surer his approach. When he tries anything harder, he comes off sounding forced. "She's Got a Way" from *Cold Spring Harbor* set the pattern for the ballads Joel would soon turn out effortlessly on almost every album. "Everyone Loves You Now" is tougher, its note of sarcasm one he'd continue through the years. Already on his first album Joel showed himself a graceful pianist; his singing was harder to assess—an error in the record's mix (corrected in the 1984 rerelease) sped up the vocal track, and he sounds trebly. The title track of *Piano Man* gave Joel his first hit; it also introduced a trademark theme that he's since treated with alternate grace and bitterness—the pathos of the performer. Filled with ambitious story-songs ("Captain Jack," "The Ballad of Billy the Kid"), the record provoked comparisons to Elton John and Harry Chapin.

The narrative vignettes off *Streetlife Serenade* ("Los Angelenos," "The Mexican Connection") strain to be clever, but the ballad "Roberta" and the rollicking "The Last of the Big Time Spenders" are the album's high points. *Turnstiles* shows Joel writing with assurance and loveliness about family and memory ("I've Loved These Days," "Summer, Highland Falls"). "Say Goodbye to Hollywood" is a neat Phil Spector tribute, and "New York State of Mind" is Joel's earliest acme. On *The Stranger,* Joel's commercial breakthrough, "Just the Way You Are" and "She's Always a Woman to Me" boast strong melodies and Joel's elegant singing.

52nd Street, however, is overbearing. The sweet music of "Honesty" is sabotaged by trite lyrics; "Big Shot" is bombastic, though the swagger of "My Life" is a good epitaph for the "Me" Decade. *Glass Houses* displayed Billy in a black leather jacket on its cover, but the album's best tracks are the modest "Don't Ask Me Why" and the brassy "All for Leyna." On *The Nylon Curtain,* "Allentown" deals with unemployment and "Goodnight Saigon" with Vietnam. Examinations of domestic strife and modern-day pressures complete the record.

An Innocent Man—a spiritual tribute to doo-wop, the Four Seasons, the Drifters, and the sound of early rock & roll ("Uptown Girl," "The Longest Time," "Leave a Tender Moment Alone")—is Joel's most pleasing album. *The Bridge* echoes *Innocent*'s lightness, if not in quite so breezy a fashion; its standout remains Billy's fond duet with Ray Charles on "Baby Grand." *Storm Front* finds Joel in the unlikely guise of a stadium rocker. "We Didn't Start the Fire" kicks heartily, as does "I Go to Extremes." With a streamlined production helping out, Joel found a way to sound tough without seeming overwrought.

River of Dreams, billed as Billy's final pop record, is still the work of an ultrapro, especially the fetching gospelish title track. After a long hiatus, Joel returned to recording with a surprisingly good venture into classical music, *Fantasies and Delusions*. It offers mainly sonatas, played by virtuoso pianist Richard Joos. Of Joel's live work, *Kohuept*, a record of his 1987 Leningrad concert, is sharper and more comprehensive than *Songs in the Attic* or the bloated *2000 Years*. Of the greatest-hits sets, *The Essential* is the most efficient.   —P.E.

Elton John

- ★★ Empty Sky (1969; Island, 1996)
- ★★ Elton John (1970; Island, 1996)
- ★★★ Tumbleweed Connection (1971; Island, 1996)
- ★★ 11-17-70 (1971; Island, 1996)
- ★★★ Madman Across the Water (1971; Island, 1996)
- ★★★★★ Honky Chateau (1972; Island, 1996)
- ★★ Don't Shoot Me I'm Only the Piano Player (1973; Island, 1996)
- ★★★★★ Goodbye Yellow Brick Road (1973; Island, 1996)
- ★★★★ Caribou (1974; Island, 1996)
- ★★★★★ Greatest Hits (Rocket/Island, 1974)
- ★★ Captain Fantastic and the Brown Dirt Cowboy (1975; Island, 1996)
- ★★★★ Rock of the Westies (1975; Island, 1996)
- ★ Here and There (1976; Island, 1996)
- ★ Blue Moves (1976; MCA, 1997)
- ★★★★★ Greatest Hits, Vol. #2 (MCA, 1977)
- ★ A Single Man (1978; Island, 2001)
- ★ Victim of Love (1979; Universal, 2003)
- ★★ The Complete Thom Bell Sessions (MCA, 1979)
- ★ 21 at 33 (1980; Universal, 2003)
- ★ The Fox (1981; Universal, 2003)
- ★★½ Jump Up! (1982; Universal, 2003)
- ★★½ Too Low for Zero (1983; Island, 2001)
- ★★ Breaking Hearts (1984; Universal, 2003)
- ★★ Ice on Fire (1985; Island, 2001)
- ★ Leather Jackets (MCA, 1986)
- ★★ Live in Australia (MCA, 1987)
- ★★★ Greatest Hits, Vol. 3 (Geffen, 1988)
- ★ Reg Strikes Back (1988; MCA, 2001)
- ★ Sleeping With the Past (1989; Universal, 2001)
- ★★★½ To Be Continued (MCA, 1990)
- ★★ The One (1992; Universal, 2001)
- ★★½ Duets (MCA, 1993)
- ★★ Made in England (Rocket/Island, 1995)
- ★★½ Love Songs (Mercury, 1996)
- ★★ The Big Picture (Mercury, 1997)
- ★★ Aida (Mercury, 1999)
- ★★ One Night Only (Universal, 2000)
- ★★★★ Songs From the West Coast (Universal, 2001)

The Elton Run is a great road-trip game: Using the radio's scan and seek buttons, see how long you can keep a continuous streak of Elton hits rolling. It's been proven possible to follow the Elton Run up I-95 from Virginia all the way to Boston. The hazard: One sixth of your listening time will be devoted to "Your Song," Elton's most overplayed standard even though everybody hates it. ("If I was a sculptor/But then again, no": Jesus H. Christ on ice and Mary in the penalty box.) But Elton has a staggering number of hits—at least one in the Top 40 every year from 1970 through 1995. With his electric boots and mohair suits, he's the prima of all donnas, sitting like a princess perched in his electric chair. He entertains by picking brains. He sells his soul by dropping names. And for all his camp flamboyance, he's aged into the most beloved entertainer on earth.

Elton's best album is *Greatest Hits, Vol. #2*, the cream of his grand early-to-mid-'70s run: "Philadelphia Freedom" (written for tennis great Billie Jean King), "The Bitch Is Back," "Island Girl," "Levon," and "Someone Saved My Life Tonight." To ward off that annoying great-artist smell, there are also horrific versions of "Pinball Wizard" and "Lucy in the Sky With Diamonds." *Greatest Hits* has too much goop but seven historic classics including "Rocket Man," a Bowie rip that's one of the best songs about husband-hood ever written; the gangsta-gangsta "Saturday Night's Alright for Fighting," where Elton grabs his switchblade and motorbike to hit the leather bars; and the terrifying "Bennie and the Jets," an occult invocation to the pagan goddesses of glam rock, complete with blood, honor, electric music, riots in the streets, and a sacrifice of the fatted calf.

Elton always made erratic albums, but if the hits are all you know, you'd be surprised how many great songs he scattered along the way. Songwriting partner Bernie Taupin provided great stupid lyrics ("Bennie and the Jets") and stupid serious lyrics ("Candle in the Wind"); he also wrote some great serious lyrics ("Rocket Man"), which happened just often enough to keep everyone confused. The Wild West concept job *Tumbleweed Connection* has "Country Comfort" and "Amoreena," the song that plays over the opening credits of *Dog Day Afternoon*. *Madman Across the Water* has "Levon," an excellent imitation of Cher's consonants-only vocal style. *Honky Chateau*, Elton's first actual rock & roll album, has some of his greatest nonhits, such as "Mellow," "Hercules," "Slave," and "Mona Lisas and Mad Hatters." The Truffaut answer record, *Don't Shoot Me I'm Only the Piano Player,* comes down to the hits: "Crocodile Rock," which Elton revived with an all-croc band on *The Muppet Show,* and the extremely annoying "Daniel."

The double-vinyl *Goodbye Yellow Brick Road* is Elton's biggest, best, catchiest, silliest, most pretentious, and most rocking set, a fun house of pansexual perversion. It's packed with mythic hits and oddities, with special praise for side three's femme-fatale triptych of "Sweet Painted Lady," "Dirty Little Girl," and "All the Young Girls Love Alice." ("Getting paid for being laid/I guess that's the name of the game"—oh, that Bernie.) *Caribou* has glitzy bitch-rockers plus the cozy love ballad "Pinky." *Rock of the Westies* has "Island Girl," a much more honest song about prostitution than "Lady Marmalade," and the fantastic self-loathing ballad "I Feel Like a Bullet (in the Gun of Robert Ford)," one of his best songs ever, and buried on the flip side of the awful "Grow Some Funk of Your Own." The autobiographical *Captain Fantastic and the Brown Dirt Cowboy* didn't have many good songs, but it inspired a pinball machine, back when that really meant something.

Elton's popularity took a dive around the time he came out, in the late '70s, and so did his music. He fought his way back with "Mama Can't Buy You Love" (sweet Philly soul), "Little Jeannie" (remembered for the idiotic chorus "I want you to be my acrobat"), and the triumphant "I Guess That's Why They Call It the Blues." He even cracked MTV with the gayest video ever, "I'm Still Standing." On the radio, Elton was rolling like thunder under the covers, but he faded as a songwriter. His '80s hits had occasional glimmers, such as "Kiss the Bride" and "Wrap Her Up." *Duets* had a funny remake of "Don't Go Breaking My Heart," with RuPaul as Kiki Dee.

Songs From the West Coast was such a great idea, you wonder why it took 25 years: Why doesn't Elton just sit down at the piano and make an Elton John album? The result was easily the Captain's most fantastic platter since *Rock of the Westies;* no hits, but Elton had plenty of those already. In fact, some he's had twice, such as "Don't Let the Sun Go Down on Me," which became a 1991 duet with George Michael ("Ladies and gentlemen . . . Mr. Elton John!"), and "Candle in the Wind," rewritten in 1997 for Princess Diana's funeral. He also has many live albums and muddled compilations—the one called *Love Songs* includes "Daniel," even though it's apparently about driving your brother to the airport. The pricey, filler-stuffed box *To Be Continued* is a case of great music in a clunky package. The 1991 tribute album *Two Rooms* features a strange array of celebrities pretending they understand what the songs are about: Kate Bush comes close, but Roger Daltrey and Jon Bon Jovi don't stand a chance. —R.S.

Linton Kwesi Johnson

★★★½ Dread Beat an' Blood (1977; Caroline, 2001)
★★★★½ Forces of Victory (1979; Mango, 1990)
★★★★ Bass Culture (1980; Mango, 1991)
★★★★ LKJ in Dub (1980; Mango, 1992)
★★★½ Making History (1984; Mango, 1990)
★★★★ Reggae Greats (1984; Mango, 1991)
★★½ In Concert With the Dub Band (1985; Shanachie, 1985)
★★★★½ Independent Intavenshen (PolyGram, 1998)
★★★★ Tings an' Times (Shanchie, 1991)
★★★ LKJ in Dub, Vol. 2 (LKJ Records, 1994)
★★½ LKJ A Cappella Live by Linton Kwesi Johnson (LKJ, 1996)
★★★ More Time (LKJ, 1998)
★★★ LKJ in Dub, Vol. 3 (LKJ, 2002)
★★★★½ Straight to Inglan's Head: An Introduction to Linton Kwesi Johnson (Universal International, 2003)

Jamaican-born Linton Kwesi Johnson (LKJ) moved to London when he was 11 and settled with his mother in the largely black West Indian neighborhood of Brixton, an area that would inspire him to become every bit the eye-opening ghetto chronicler for blacks in '70s London as Public Enemy and N.W.A were for their respective 'hoods in New York City and Los Angeles several years later.

Already politically active as a youth (he was a member of the Black Panther Youth League), Johnson was also an established poet—giving public readings and making TV/radio appearances—before setting his work to music. While his words remain some of the most conscious and powerful lyrics ever put on record (his work is now taught at universities and his influence ranges from Mutabaruka to Michael Franti), the reggae rhythms that formed their soundtrack were just as important—and just as appealing. Johnson's formidable partner in this endeavor was producer/bandleader Dennis "Blackbeard" Bovell who, something of a legend in his own right, is considered the grandfather of British reggae music because of his numerous band and production credits. Bovell laid down grooves that were not only tighter and "tuffer" than his dread contemporaries but certainly more so than the easier-going "lovers rock" style prevailing in the U.K. at the time. His deft use of open space and jarring shifts within the music served to underline the rhythmic lilt in Johnson's spoken-word flow. One only need check out the superb *Dub* albums to realize just how well Bovell's music holds up on its own.

Against this backdrop, Johnson released his three most influential albums. The debut *Dread Beat an' Blood* (initially released under the moniker Poet and the Roots) is sparser, its tone choked with outrage at racial mistreatment. *Forces of Victory* doesn't back off from that anger so much as bolster it with hooky choruses and heated instrumental dialogues with Bovell's Dub Band. *Bass Culture* branches out even further, examining the power of music on "Reggae Sounds" and even bringing a love song ("Lorraine"). *LKJ in Dub*, by nature of the form, drops quite a bit of the vocals and plays around with the instrumental tracks, but it's not to be overlooked. While each of these early albums stands strong, the two-disc overview *Independent Intavenshun* is a fantastic primer that scans this era and throws in some interesting 12-inch versions as well. For those who want to start with a smaller taste, the 13 songs on the *Straight to Inglan's Head* collection are top-notch.

After a four-year break, Johnson confidently returned with *Making History*, followed by the generic single-CD retrospective *Reggae Greats* and a somewhat pedestrian live album, *In Concert With the Dub Band*. Johnson's output then slowed further as he turned his focus to other activities, including his own label and book-publishing company. But his eventual return, *Tings an' Times*, is graceful and assured; even while venturing to expand the music beyond its Jamaican roots with touches like accordion and violin solos, the songs remain every bit as lyrically sharp. *More Time* continues his partnership with Bovell and features "Reggae Fi Bernard," a poem about the death of his nephew. But much of the album harbors, along with some nice strings, a more upbeat air, suggesting that Johnson, while no less concerned with black injustices today than he was 20 years ago, is at least entertaining a more positive outlook on life in general. These later releases are available directly from his LKJ Records Web site. —D.S.

Freedy Johnston

★	The Trouble Tree	(Bar/None, 1990)
★★★★	Can You Fly	(Bar/None, 1992)
★★★	Unlucky (EP)	(Bar/None, 1993)
★★★★	This Perfect World	(Elektra, 1994)
★★★★	Never Home	(Elektra, 1997)
★★★	Blue Days Black Nights	(Elektra, 1999)
★★★	Right Between the Promises	(Elektra, 2001)

More than anything else, Freedy Johnston is a storyteller. His stories are as evocative as they are economical, filled with memorable characters and sparkling details while leaving out nearly as much as they in-

clude. They're often quite grim, too. Prisons are a recurring theme in Johnston's songs, not just literal prisons of concrete and steel but the prisons people create within themselves through the choices they make. Yet once his lyrics are endowed with the plain, good-natured melodic backing that Johnston's made his trademark, even his most downhearted tales sound more sweet than bitter.

An inauspicious opening entry, *The Trouble Tree*, is lackluster roots rock rendered almost unlistenable by Johnston's strangled whine. *Can You Fly* is something else entirely: 13 gripping pieces of guitar-driven power folk that present an array of losers, drifters, gamblers, and a mortician's daughter (plus, on "Trying to Tell You I Don't Know," Johnston's own experience of selling his family's Kansas farm to finance his music career) in a harsh yet always sympathetic light. The singing has calmed down, blossoming at times into a high lonesome croon, and the accompanists, who include such major names as Marshall Crenshaw and Syd Straw, are top-notch. One of the album's finest songs, "The Lucky One," also appears on the *Unlucky* EP along with four other worthwhile tracks, the niftiest a cover of Jimmy Webb's "Wichita Lineman."

From this point on, Johnston's done little wrong. His next two releases were moving, eloquent pop records for grown-ups, highlighted by slice-of-life minimasterpieces such as *This Perfect World*'s title cut and *Never Home*'s "Western Sky." *Blue Days Black Nights* and *Right Between the Promises* are slightly less inspired, but both contain songs—"Moving on a Holiday" on the former, "Radio for Heartache" on the latter—that are vintage Freedy, capturing poignant moments with such cheerful precision you're not sure whether to laugh or cry. —M.R.

Joi

★★★★	The Pendulum Vibe	(EMI, 1994)
★★★★	Star Kitty's Revenge	(Universal, 2002)

The daughter of Pittsburgh Steeler great Joe Gilliam, Joi entered the R&B world as a sort of avant-bohemian, doing so-called neosoul music years before Philadelphians like Jill Scott, James Poyser, and Musiq forged a scene to merit the moniker. Produced by the eclectic and savvy Dallas Austin, her first proper album teems with womanist pride and proud race talk. Her (un)love songs, such as "If We Weren't Who We Were," are just as potent. Between her two albums, Joi recorded the sensational, bizarre, never-released *Amoeba Cleansing Syndrome,* sang backup with Curtis Mayfield, and married Goodie Mob's Big Gipp. Accordingly, her return to recording, 2002's *Star Kitty's*

Revenge, reeked of the unique stank of Atlanta's Dungeon Family collective. "Techno Pimp," "Crave," and "Lick" are almost slimy in their lasciviousness, and the sentiment is driven home by crisp, punishing beats. The jungle-meets-gospel "Get On" may well be the cruelest breakup song ever recorded: "I want a vision of me making love inside of your head/But not to you, to someone else/With my legs behind my head." But for all *Kitty's* raunch, Joi still takes the opportunity to flex her impressive, Betty Davis–style vocals on more traditional material. On *Pendulum,* it was the Latin motet "Adoramus Te, Christe"; this time, it's the church standard "Agnus Dei." Joi's rendition is delicate and sure, a reminder that the sacred and secular can coexist comfortably in one soul.　—J.C.

George Jones

★★★½	All-Time Greatest Hits (Epic, 1977)
★★★½	My Very Special Guests (Epic, 1979)
★★★★½	Anniversary: Ten Years of Hits (Epic, 1982)
★★★	First Time Live (Epic, 1987)
★★★½	Sings the Great Songs of Leon Payne (Hollywood, 1987)
★★★★	Super Hits (Epic, 1987)
★★★½	One Woman Man (Epic, 1989)
★★★★½	The Best of George Jones (Rhino, 1991)
★★★★	Walls Can Fall (MCA, 1992)
★★★	High-Tech Redneck (MCA, 1993)
★★★½	Super Hits Vol. 2 (Epic, 1993)
★★★★★	Cup of Loneliness: The Classic Mercury Years (Mercury, 1994)
★★★★★	The Spirit of Country: The Essential George Jones (Epic/Legacy, 1994)
★★★½	It Don't Get Any Better Than This (MCA, 1998)
★★★★	A Picture of Me/Nothing Ever Hurt Me (Koch, 1998)
★★★★	16 Biggest Hits (Epic/Legacy, 1999)
★★★★	Cold Hard Truth (Asylum, 1999)
★★½	Live With the Possum (Asylum, 1999)
★★★½	Memories of Us/The Battle (Koch, 1999)
★★★★½	The Best of George Jones (The Millennium Collection) (Mercury, 2000)
★★★★	I Am What I Am (Epic/Legacy, 2000)
★★★½	The Rock: Stone Cold Country 2001 (BNA/Bandit, 2001)
★★★½	The Best of George Jones Vol. 2: The '90s (The Millennium Collection) (Mercury Nashville, 2002)
★★★½	Hank, Bob and Me (Fuel 2000, 2003)
★★★½	Love Songs (Epic/Legacy, 2003)
★★★	The Gospel Collection (BNA/Bandit, 2003)

with Melba Montgomery

★★★★	Vintage Collections (Capitol, 1995)

with Tammy Wynette

★★★½	Greatest Hits (Epic, 1989)
★★★★	Greatest Hits Vol. 2 (Epic, 1992)
★★★★	George and Tammy Super Hits (Sony, 1995)
★★★½	One (MCA, 1995)
★★★★	16 Biggest Hits (Epic/Legacy, 1999)

George Jones is the greatest pure singer in country music—while his East Texas drawl identifies him both regionally and culturally, it doesn't cloud his remarkably clear and pliant voice, nor does it limit his astonishing vocal technique. But just as important is how profoundly Jones has bound himself to country music tradition, which for him is the religion that saved his life.

Jones' life is by now an open book, but virtually none of it appears in his music. As a child, Jones sang to pacify his alcoholic father. As a teenager, Jones sang on street corners and in honky-tonks to escape his home. Jones sang country music because country was what he grew up with and all that he knew. He tried odd jobs, did a hitch in the Marines, had a couple of messed-up marriages, but the only thing he was ever any good at was singing, and singing was the only thing that kept him going. He channeled Roy Acuff and Hank Williams and countless others, but judging from the numerous covers in his early Mercury recordings, the only singer he had any trouble subsuming was Lefty Frizzell. And within a few years his own voice became such an integral part of that tradition that nothing—not even 18 years of Billy Sherrill—could diminish Jones.

For the first 35 years of his career, Jones' records were produced by two men: Pappy Daily (1955–71) and Sherrill (1972–89). Daily was co-owner of Starday Records, but took over managing as well as producing Jones, and stayed with him through a series of record companies: Mercury, United Artists, Musicor. Jones' first hit, "Why Baby Why," was pure honky-tonk. His first #1 hit was J. P. Richardson's moonshiner novelty "White Lightning," with a panoply of vocal effects. But he also cut songs that became classics, like "The Window Up Above," "Tender Years," and "She Thinks I Still Care." Four good compilations cover this period with a lot of overlap on the hits: By far the most extensive is the 51-cut *Cup of Loneliness,* which gives by far the fullest picture of Jones the hardcore honky-tonker. Rhino's *The Best of George Jones (1955–1967)* adds a few later tracks to the Mercury hits, most of which are duplicated on the first disc in Epic/Legacy's two-disc *The Spirit of Country.*

Aside from the biggest hits, very little of the massive amount of material that Jones and Daily recorded for United Artists (1962–66) and Musicor (1965–71) is in print. *Hank, Bob and Me* restores parts of albums of Hank Williams and Bob Wills songs from 1962. The *Vintage Collections* duets with Melba Montgomery are long on bluegrass and notable for the freak hit "Let's Invite Them Over," about spouse-swapping, and the magnificent "We Must Have Been Out of Our Minds." Jones and Daily recorded something in excess of 300 cuts for Musicor, including 23 chart singles, so it's surprising that the only one seen recently is the fine set of Leon Payne songs.

Jones married Tammy Wynette in 1968. She had just released "Stand By Your Man," making her one of the biggest new stars in Nashville, and he was already a legend, so their marriage kicked off the King and Queen of Nashville hype. More concretely, marriage steered Jones to Wynette's label (Epic) and producer (Billy Sherrill), but it was late 1971 before the first George and Tammy duet came out. They cut another dozen singles after that, hitting #1 three times—twice after the inevitable d-i-v-o-r-c-e. The songs, which have been collected in short, overlapping compilations, are a strange mix of pop artifacts—hopeful, cynical, devout, dejected, and/or funny ("God's Gonna Get'cha"). But one thing that can't be doubted is their utter professionalism, and both can switch on absolute devotion to even the most irrelevant of material. (This continues without a hitch in their 1995 reunion, *One*.)

But the duets were just a sideshow: Jones recorded at least an album a year from 1972 to '89, a vast amount of material, most now out of print (most regrettably 1976's *Alone Again*). Billy Sherrill had a reputation as a guy who never heard a song without thinking that it could use some strings, and anyone with a taste for Jones' honky-tonk roots is likely to view most of the music that Sherrill produced as glop. But for Jones the music was just the launch pad for his singing. While most voices thicken with age, Jones' voice was becoming, if anything, lighter and more pliable, and the ballads that Sherrill preferred often worked best to flatter Jones' singing. Sometimes the pair joined spectacularly, as on "He Stopped Loving Her Today," where the swelling of the strings lifts Jones into the stratosphere. The ballads dominate the compilations from the period, especially *16 Biggest Hits* and *Love Songs*, both full of treasures. *The Spirit of Country* is the broadest selection currently available, the 15 early hits followed by 29 Epic cuts, including five Wynette duets and a couple of curveballs (like inviting Ray Charles to join in on "We Didn't See a Thing"). *All-Time Greatest Hits* were interesting 1977 remakes of early hits, which also surface in the short *Super Hits* volumes. Of Jones' surviving albums, the early twofers on Koch are consistently good; 1980's *I*

Am What I Am is perhaps his peak, with exceptionally strong material throughout; and *One Woman Man* closed out the series on a high note.

During the late '80s Jones finally started to get his oft-wrecked life together. He married again, to Nancy Sepulveda, and this time it stuck. In 1991 he moved to MCA, and his new producers pointed him back toward his old country roots. They also helped him pick better songs—Jones had long since stopped writing his own, but Nashville was full of songwriters who dreamt of servicing him. *Walls Can Fall* was perhaps the best of the '90s albums, with ballads like the title cut and "She Drives Me to Drink," the fast-paced "I Don't Need Your Rockin' Chair," and the definitive "Wrong's What I Do Best."

Others such as *It Don't Get Any Better Than This* and *Cold Hard Truth* are nearly as good, and *The Rock* isn't far behind, but Jones' reunion with Billy Sherrill on *The Gospel Collection* is uninspired profiteering. Perhaps the most surprising thing of all is how consistent Jones has been over a recording career that now approaches 50 years.   —T.H.

Norah Jones

★★★★   Come Away With Me (Blue Note, 2002)
★★★★   Feels Like Home (Blue Note, 2004)

Come Away With Me began 2002 as a quiet little secret, passed among friends as a hot pick among the coffeehouse jazz set. A year later, 22-year-old Norah Jones was a household name and this modest debut won her five Grammy Awards, including Album of the Year.

In any year *Come Away With Me* would be a remarkable album if only because of Jones' extraordinary voice: It is smoky like Diana Krall's, but there's enough warmth to remind you of the vivacious Rickie Lee Jones. Brilliantly produced by Arif Mardin, the spare arrangements serve to frame Jones' breathy vocals and never overpower her atmospheric piano playing. The title track and "Don't Know Why" are the standouts because Jones' laconic phrasing serves to further emphasize the melancholy of these two songs. The rest of the album seems more slight, but when Jones covers Hank Williams' "Cold Cold Heart" and J. D. Loudermilk's "Turn Me On," she proves herself more talented than even the above average piano chanteuse. As debut albums go, few are as promising—and as steadfastly ethereal—as *Come Away With Me*.

Feels Like Home, Jones' second album, is another triumph of the low-key, but it's a bit more varied. There are moments of lithe, coolheaded boho blues ("In the Morning," featuring a coy Jones solo on Wurlitzer electric piano) and downcast salvation-seeking waltzes (the transfixing "Humble Me"). There's a credible excursion into country two-step (the duet with Dolly Parton, "Creepin' In") and a haunted Brechtian tone poem called "Carnival Town." Jones talks about her whirlwind success just a little, with her usual understatement: On the idyllic "Toes," she sings of an idealized, unharried life not in the strident complaining voice of a newly minted star but like any other overwhelmed soul yearning for a moment's peace. *Feels Like Home* extends the *Come Away With Me* template—not by echoing the earlier songs, but by chasing the same ruminative moods and hushed-whisper atmospheres.   —C.R.C./T.M.

Rickie Lee Jones

★★★½   Rickie Lee Jones (Warner Bros., 1979)
★★½   Pirates (Warner Bros., 1981)
★★★   Girl at Her Volcano (EP) (Warner Bros., 1983)
★★   The Magazine (Warners Bros., 1984)
★★★   Flying Cowboys (Geffen, 1989)
★★★½   Pop Pop (Geffen, 1991)
★★   Traffic From Paradise (Geffen, 1993)
★★★   Naked Songs (Warner Bros., 1995)
★★   Ghostyhead (Geffen, 1997)
★★★   It's Like This (Artemis, 2000)
★★★   Live at Red Rocks (Artemis, 2001)
★★   The Evening of My Best Day (V2, 2003)

On *Rickie Lee Jones*, the beret-wearing, boho-pop singer looks and sounds like she just walked out of a Jack Kerouac novel. Her between-the-cracks singing style—a mixture of childlike wonderment, jazzy affectation, and almost sobbing intensity—has its moments, and her songs strive for poetic intimacy. The debut sculpts her quirks into slurred, bebop-light pop tunes such as "Chuck E.'s in Love" and "Danny's All-Star Joint." But for the next decade, glossy production would sanitize her unwashed visions, and the studio-pro fussiness of the more open-ended *Pirates* and the overly self-conscious *The Magazine* now sounds dated. The looser approach adopted on *Girl at Her Volcano*, a stopgap collection of covers including an audacious remake of the Left Banke's wimp-pop classic "Walk Away Renee," suggests what might have been. *Flying Cowboys*, overseen by Steely Dan's Walter Becker, is less grandiose, and Jones' more mature songwriting and singing filter out the affections that marred the earlier albums. *Pop Pop* offers intimate lounge-jazz interpretations of a dozen standards, though Jones lacks the technical expertise to completely pull it off. But there's also a sense that she's breaking off a piece of her heart with each line, as she personalizes everything from the Tin Pan Alley

standard "Bye Bye Blackbird" to Jefferson Airplane's "Comin' Back to Me."

With Jones taking over the production, *Traffic From Paradise* continues in a more intimate, jazz-inspired vein, centered on acoustic instruments and fleshed out with subtle orchestrations. But discipline is lacking: The alluring fragments rarely coalesce into memorable songs. *Ghostyhead* is even more shapeless, a misguided detour into a trip-hop world dominated by spooky atmospherics and decorative programming, but no actual songs. *It's Like This* retools more pop standards to less startling effect than on *Pop Pop*. Some of the vocal tics are toned down on *The Evening of My Best Day*, which presents Jones in elegantly orchestrated settings. This rather transparent attempt at sophistication errs on the side of caution, as the arrangements' all-consuming loveliness never once pushes Jones or the songs outside the comfort zone. Even the anger underlying "Tell Somebody (Repeal the Patriot Act)" is undermined by toothless instrumentation. Two live albums present solid career overviews: *Naked Songs*, including a disturbing new original, "Altar Boy," offers an unplugged perspective, and *Live at Red Rocks* presents full-band versions, including a duet with Lyle Lovett.   —G.K.

Janis Joplin

★★★   Janis Joplin With Big Brother and the Holding Company: Live at Winterland '68 (1968; Columbia/Legacy, 1998)
★★★½   I Got Dem Ol' Kozmic Blues Again Mama! (1969; Columbia/Legacy, 1999)
★★★★   Pearl (1971; Columbia/Legacy, 1999)
★★★   In Concert (Columbia, 1972)
★★★★   Greatest Hits (1973; Columbia/Legacy, 1999)
★★   Farewell Song (Columbia, 1982)
★★★★½   Janis (Columbia/Legacy, 1993)
★★★½   18 Essential Songs (Columbia/Legacy, 1995)
★★★★   Box of Pearls: The Janis Joplin Collection (Columbia/Legacy, 1999)
★★½   Super Hits (Legacy, 2000)
★★   Love, Janis (Columbia/Legacy, 2001)
★★★★   Essential Janis Joplin (Columbia, 2003)

with Big Brother and the Holding Company

★★★   Big Brother & the Holding Company Featuring Janis Joplin (1967; Columbia/Legacy, 1999)
★★½   Cheap Thrills (1968; Columbia/Legacy, 1999)

Equal parts Southern Comfort, honey, and gall, Janis Joplin's voice made her the greatest white female blues singer. And with a hard history of unhappy loves, angst, and a talent so huge that it weighed too heavy, she died at 27 of a heroin OD, ready-made for myth. She survives not only as a singer, but as a sympathetic, if harrowing, archetype. Too rushed to develop the casual confidence of Billie Holiday or Bessie Smith, she remains the all-time singer of the desperate blues.

Her legend began at the 1967 Monterey Pop Festival—redefining grace, sex appeal, and popular singing, the Texas vagabond shrieked and staggered over fevered but formless blues riffing by Big Brother and the Holding Company, whom she'd soon outgrow. Nonetheless, there's a genuine innocence about the group's self-titled, almost folksy debut (featuring "Bye, Bye Baby" and "Down On Me") that makes it easier to swallow today than the histrionic screeching and numbing acid rock of the major label bow (and commercial breakthrough) *Cheap Thrills*. Joplin rises above the din—just—on the volcanic "Piece of My Heart," and the band exercises a certain welcome restraint on the slow burn cover of "Summertime," but you'll mercifully find both of those highlights on *Greatest Hits*. Curiously, *Live at Winterland '68*—which captures a concert recorded right before *Cheap Thrills*—while ostensibly of interest only to hard-core fans, is the easiest to swallow document of Joplin's Big Brother period; you get the best of both albums: Joplin in powerhouse form, and the band, if not exactly tight, at least freshly inspired from its first trip to the East Coast, making for an enjoyable psychedelic trip without the headache. That said, Joplin's raw delivery shocked even more effectively when backed by crack R&B players, as evidenced by her first "solo" album, the horns-and-soul-drenched *I Got Dem Ol' Kozmic Blues Again Mama!* Adding quivering heart to the sturdy pop skeleton of the Bee Gees' "To Love Somebody" and thunder to Jerry Ragovoy's "Try," Joplin was now balancing a Big Mama Thornton fervor with an Aretha Franklin sense of timing. *Pearl*, the album that bore her nickname, found her moving easily and naturally into country, with the definitive take on Kris Kristofferson's "Me and Bobby McGee"; she also does right by Bobby Womack with "Trust Me," drips blood on Ragovoy's "Cry Baby," and flashes her sense of humor in "Mercedes Benz," introduced with tongue in cheek as "a song of great social and political import." From start to finish, *Pearl* was her finest hour, and her last. Joplin died shortly before its completion; ironically, the album's "Buried Alive in the Blues" is the only song she didn't record a vocal for in time.

Of the numerous anthologies and compilations that have been issued posthumously, the lean-and-mean *Greatest Hits* remains the one to beat—a filler-free distillation of a promising career cut short before its time. The latter-day *18 Essential Songs* and the

two-disc *Essential Janis Joplin* offer a bigger picture without necessarily saying more, while the soundtrack to the play *Love, Janis*, which intersperses songs with an actress reading some of Joplin's letters to her mother back home, is a novelty at best. The three-disc *Janis* box set, however, is a treasure trove, collecting not only all of her essential recordings but 18 previously unissued tracks ranging from curio to historic (such as the Big Brother performance of "Ball and Chain" at the Monterey Pop Festival that first ignited Joplin's buzz like wildfire). Additionally, the two original Big Brother albums, *Kozmic Blues, Pearl,* and *Greatest Hits* have all been reissued with bonus tracks. *Box of Pearls* collects the first four albums and adds a fifth, EP-length disc of rarities. —P.E./R.SK.

Louis Jordan

★★★★	One Guy Named Louis (1954; EMI/Blue Note, 1992)
★★★★	One Guy Named Louis: The Complete Aladdin Sessions (1954; Capitol Jazz, 1992)
★★★★★	The Best of Louis Jordan (1975; MCA, 1989)
★★	I Believe in Music (1980; Evidence, 1992)
★★★½	No Moe! Louis Jordan's Greatest Hits (Verve, 1992)
★★★★★	Five Guys Named Moe: The Decca Recordings (MCA, 1992)
★★★★	Rock'n Roll Call: Louis Jordan and His Tympany Five (RCA Bluebird, 1993)
★★★★★	Let the Good Times Roll: Anthology 1938–1953 (MCA, 1999)
★★★	20th Century Masters—The Millennium Collection: The Best of Louis Jordan (MCA, 1999)
★★★★	Swingstation (GRP, 1999)
★★★★½	At the Swing Cat's Ball (MCA, 1999)
★★★	Essential Recordings (Purple Pyramid, 2001)

Born in Brinkley, AR, Louis Jordan got his start playing alto saxophone with Chick Webb's band in 1936; in 1939 he formed his own jump-blues group, the Tympany Five, and set out laying the foundation for R&B and rock & roll. Between 1944 and 1949, Jordan was omnipresent on both the black and pop charts with a succession of swinging, blues-oriented singles. Jordan's big voice and driving arrangements fueled some of the decade's best novelty and dance songs—this is music that is guaranteed to put a smile on your face. Several excellent overviews now document the first, brilliant period of Jordan's career. *Let the Good Times Roll: Anthology 1938–1953* is an essential album: two discs of prime Jordan spanning 1938's Elks Rendez-Vous Band debut, "Barnacle Bill the Sailor," to 1953's Jon Hendricks–penned "I Want You to Be My Baby," with all the Jordan landmarks in between, including "Ain't Nobody Here but Us Chickens" and "Caldonia." The 20-track *At the Swing Cat's Ball* spans the 1938 to 1954 era, with a heavier emphasis on 1938 tracks than can be found on *Let the Good Times Roll: Anthology,* and with little duplication of tracks. *Swingstation* offers the heartiest of party-hearty Jordan performances in its 16 tracks, leading off with the riot-on-wax "House Party." Although *Anthology* is hard to beat, *The Best of Louis Jordan* and *Five Guys Named Moe: The Decca Recordings* still stand out with the best albums in a deep catalogue. In addition to the classic Jordan entries ("G.I. Jive," "Is You Is or Is You Ain't My Baby"), many of the lower-profile tunes here are scintillating. Check out the nodding vocal and the sassy spoken dialogue on "What's the Use of Getting Sober (When You're Gonna Get Drunk Again)"; "I Want You to Be My Baby" requires more complex, jazz-rooted phrasing, and Jordan pulls it off with considerable aplomb and winning humor.

Jordan died from a heart attack on February 4, 1975. His glory days had long since passed, but his music was always out there for the finding, and in the '90s it was revived in spectacular fashion in a hit Broadway revue, *Five Guys Named Moe;* that, plus his induction into the Rock and Roll Hall of Fame, brought Jordan the acclaim he deserved all along for breaking new ground in American popular music. —D.M.

Journey

★	Journey (Columbia, 1975)	
★	Look Into the Future (Columbia, 1976)	
★	Next (Columbia, 1977)	
★★	Infinity (Columbia, 1978)	
★★	Evolution (Columbia, 1979)	
★	In the Beginning (Columbia, 1979)	
★½	Departure (Columbia, 1980)	
★	Captured (Columbia, 1981)	
★★½	Escape (Columbia, 1981)	
★★½	Frontiers (Columbia, 1983)	
★★	Raised on Radio (Columbia, 1986)	
★★★½	Greatest Hits (Columbia, 1988)	
★★★½	Time 3 (Columbia, 1992)	
★	Trial by Fire (Columbia, 1996)	
★	Arrival (Columbia, 2001)	

Somewhere in your town, maybe even right down your street, there is a karaoke bar that stays open long past midnight. That, friend, is the place to experience the music of Journey.

We can pass over Journey's early incarnation as a Frisco hippie band ("Wheel in the Sky") and go straight to the moment when the band figured out that its meal ticket was Steve Perry, who clobbered power ballads like an old Italian lady with an umbrella catching a pickpocket on bingo night. Man, the guy could shred: "Who's Crying Now," "Faithfully," "Only the Young," "Lovin', Touchin', Squeezin'," "Lights," and the love theme to the popular film *The Last American Virgin,* "Open Arms."

Best of all, or maybe just most of all (the distinction is meaningless with Journey), there was "Don't Stop Believin'," a perfect cheese-metal hymn to streetlight people everywhere, the strangers searching up and down the boulevard, paying anything to roll the dice just one more time. (Fun fact: There is no such place as "South Detroit.") It was over much too soon, with the 1986 hit "I'll Be Alright Without You" a poignant farewell. The band fell apart, reunited, and recorded with both Perry and his sound-alike replacement, Steve Augeri. *Greatest Hits* captures Journey in all its mullet-tastic splendor. But it's still no substitute for the karaoke bar: To really comprehend the music of Journey, to understand what Steve and the guys were trying to say, you have to go there and join the streetlight people, as the lights go down in the city. Especially when somebody gets drunk enough to tackle "Don't Stop Believin'." —R.S.

Joy Division

★★★★★	Unknown Pleasures (1979; Qwest, 1989)	
★★★★★	Closer (1980; Qwest, 1989)	
★★★½	Still (1981; Qwest, 1991)	
★★★★	Substance (Qwest, 1988)	
★★★	Preston Warehouse 28 February 1980 (Factory, 1999)	
★★★	Les Bains Douches 18 December 1979 (Get Back, 2001)	
★★½	Permanent (Qwest/Warner, 1995)	
★★★★★	Heart and Soul (Rhino, 1998)	
★★★½	The Complete BBC Recordings (Varèse, 2000)	

"Here are the young men/The weight on their shoulders." Could one line sum up a band's self-image as perfectly as that line (from "Decades") sums up Joy Division? From Manchester, U.K., they slouched: four raincoat-clad youths and one legitimately revolutionary producer. Armed only with a stack of William S. Burroughs and J. G. Ballard novels, a few Iggy albums, and a master-class depressive for a lyricist, Joy Division took punk apart piece by piece and rethought every bit as best they could, creating the most influential sound of their scene and era, as dramatic and severe a rethink of rock's aesthetic parameters as has ever been envisioned.

On the two albums and handful of singles they released as an active band, Joy Division's rolling tom-toms, echoing guitar, and melodic bass created icy, distant rhythms as Ian Curtis' basso *muy* profundo subverted, smashed, and proved generally smarter than the goth clichés they've been cursed with ever since. The quartet created a great, free-floating sense of doom, chaos, and uncertainty, yet you could dance to it; a miracle, that.

On May 18, 1980, days before what would likely have been a wildly successful first American tour, 23-year-old Curtis hanged himself in his home, ending the band and cementing its growing legend for (largely) the wrong reasons. The three remaining members conquered the world as New Order.

Joy Division evolved in leaps and bounds after scrapping an album's worth of tracks the band deemed nonrepresentative (a handful became their first EP). Good call, because *Unknown Pleasures* remains one of rock's most startling debuts. Producer Martin Hannett created moments simultaneously claustrophobic and energetic, displaced and focused, but always jarringly intense and melodramatic. Songs like "Disorder," "Interzone," and "I Remember Nothing" staked out a sonic territory utterly the band's own. Curtis' crystalline voice is anchor and signifier, struggling against chaos, displacement, and that wicked drum sound. *Unknown Pleasures* is a world-historic struggle against darkness.

You can feel the band slip into that darkness on *Closer.* Released after Curtis' death and again produced by the extraordinary Hannett, it's an almost impossibly heavy listen, full of unsettling melodies, sepulchral riffs, and funereal tempos. Even the ripping "Isolation" sounds like a dying-light fight. Curtis vents like he just remembered part of Nietzsche's great epigram, "When you gaze long into an abyss, the abyss also gazes into you"; it's the lament of a doomed singer's long, slow, sad blink.

The band's singles are also remarkable: the "dance, dance, dance to the radio" wail of "Transmission," the tear-jerking melodrama of "Atmosphere," and "Love Will Tear Us Apart," the band's most exquisite pop moment. A great, rolling juggernaut with Curtis doing his best Sinatra and a brilliant quote from the Crystals' "And Then He Kissed Me," tacked onto the coda, "Love Will Tear Us Apart" is the band's most accessible moment and its finest hour.

Still is a "beat the boots" double album collecting stray studio tracks and live material from the band's final show. The production is awfully rough, but you get a good sense of the band's muscular live power (see also "Ceremony," which sounds far more desperate and panicked than New Order's icy studio version). The '90s live albums are better recorded and

present a more well-rounded look at the band's strengths, while the BBC sessions are tight and tough.

The 1988 release of the fabulous anthology *Substance* brought Joy Division a whole new generation of fanatical, deep-feeling, black-clad followers; it was the first time many suburban American kids had ever heard the band, a moment captured note-perfectly in the 2001 film *Donnie Darko.*

Substance is the opposite of *Permanent,* which is a shoddy collection of context-free album tracks better understood in their original settings, while *Heart and Soul* is everything all but the most severe fan would ever need: both albums, the crucial singles. It's a brilliant representation of a moment when four young men wandered into the most profound alienation, just to see what was there.

And hey, they're more fun than the Doors. —J.G.

Judas Priest

★★	Rocka Rolla (RCA, 1975)
★★	Sad Wings of Destiny (RCA, 1976)
★★½	Sin After Sin (1977; Columbia, 2001)
★★½	Best of Judas Priest (1978; RCA, 2001)
★★½	Stained Class (1978; Columbia, 2001)
★★★	Hell Bent for Leather (1979; Columbia, 2001)
★★	Live—Unleashed in the East (1979; Columbia, 2001)
★★★★	British Steel (1980; Columbia, 2001)
★★	Point of Entry (1981; Columbia, 2001)
★★	Screaming for Vengeance (1982; Columbia, 2001)
★★★	Defenders of the Faith (1984; Columbia, 2001)
★★½	Turbo (1986; Columbia, 2001)
★★½	Priest . . . Live (1987; Columbia, 2001)
★★½	Ram It Down (1989; Columbia, 2001)
★★★	Painkiller (1990; Columbia, 2001)
★★	Jugulator (CMC, 1997)
★★	98 Live Meltdown (CMC, 1998)
★★★	Demolition (Atlantic, 2001)
★★★★	Metalogy (Sony/Legacy, 2004)

Judas Priest is the surviving elder prophet of the metal tribes. This English quintet didn't invent a single move, mind you, but its mid-'70s sound codified the previous five years or so of metallic developments, minus any significant blues content. The rigid, intense music was a key influence on the accelerating speed-metal hordes of the 1980s. Since then, Judas Priest has refined its attack with a near-religious zeal. Lead singer Rob Halford can match the range and sharp impact of Robert Plant, but his shrieks and moans aren't nearly as deep. No matter: Glenn Tipton and K. K. Downing trade solos in a dueling-guitar approach, and their best tandem riffs give the Priest a hooky, driving momentum that's usually absent in metal's doomy end. And make no mistake, these guys are doom-oriented; Judas Priest pumped out apocalyptic epics like "Island of Domination" (from the RCA best-of collection) and "Dissident Aggressor" (from *Sin After Sin*) when Metallica and its followers were still in junior high, and both albums contain the group's mincing desecration of Joan Baez's "Diamonds and Rust" (in case anybody thought this music genre lacks a sense of humor).

With its exaggerated leather-'n'-studs theatrical bent and polished musical consistency, Judas Priest encapsulates the metal experience for true believers. There were bigger, better bands pushing hard rock in more interesting directions (AC/DC, Zeppelin, Van Halen, etc.) but by the time *Hell Bent for Leather* was released, Judas Priest could be counted on to fully represent the standard metal sound of the moment. No surprises ever. Every Columbia album sports at least one tuneful, surefire drive-time rocker, though. *British Steel* kicked off the '80s with the fierce "Breaking the Law" and the rollicking, Kiss-like pop of "Living After Midnight," while the coming wave of hair metal found a blueprint in "United," a ready-made anthem for Bon Jovi. *Screaming for Vengeance* maxes out with "Freewheel Burning" (catchy, whatever the hell it means) and the campy send-ups that raised Tipper Gore's foolish ire: "Eat Me Alive" and "Love Bites."

By 1985, the Birmingham rockers had fully implemented the speed-metal tempo they inspired. Priest backed off just a touch on *Turbo*, adding guitar synthesizers, but the high-speed *Painkiller* defied the power-ballad imperative that ultimately killed off the '80s pop-metal scene. And who better than Judas Priest? In the early '90s, Halford quit the band for a more experimental solo career that touched on grunge and industrial rock. Judas Priest was in limbo until Tipton and Downing took the bizarre step, in 1996, of recruiting Halford's replacement from a Priest tribute band in Akron (a story crazy enough to inspire the 2001 Mark Wahlberg movie *Rock Star*). Tim "Ripper" Owens had all the right moves and a voice that could pierce eardrums, but on *Jugulator,* he still sounded like a man who sang for a cover band. *Demolition* was much stronger. Priest stretched out with electronic effects at the margins; on the stormy "Hell Is Home," Owens sounded increasingly like Metallica's James Hetfield. But if Owens had any lyrics in him, songwriters Tipton and Downing don't leave him much room. And the dream was soon over anyway because Halford was back as frontman in 2003. The entire Columbia catalogue was reissued in 2001, with bonus studio and live tracks, and the box set *Metalogy* gathered 65

songs and a live DVD, making a powerful case for Priest's influence and longevity for new generations of needy heshers, but the small number of previously unreleased songs included here are unessential and beside the point. As long as there's heavy metal, Judas Priest will continue to administer the rites of passage to an eager audience.   —M.C./S.A.

Jungle Brothers

- ★★★★ Straight Out the Jungle (Warlock, 1988)
- ★★★★ Done by the Forces of Nature (Warner Bros., 1989)
- ★★★½ J. Beez Wit the Remedy (Warner Bros., 1993)
- ★★½ Raw Deluxe (Gee Street, 1997)
- ★★ V.I.P. (V2, 2000)
- ★★½ Jungllenium Remixes (Gee Street, 2000)
- ★★★½ Best and Rare (Warner Bros., 2000)
- ★★ All That We Do (Jungle, 2002)

A crucial group in hip-hop's evolution, New York's Jungle Brothers embodied the link between the self-respecting street knowledge of Afrika Bambaataa's Zulu Nation and the positive Native Tongues movement that De La Soul brought to prominence at the end of the 1980s. With conscious lyrics over swinging jazz and upbeat funk, *Straight Out the Jungle* was a debut by a group (Afrika Baby Bam, Mike Gee, and DJ Sammy D) fully formed upon arrival. *Done by the Forces of Nature* was another great album, by turns serious and fun: The Afrocentric, Christopher Columbus–dissing "Acknowledge Your Own History" was followed immediately by the chick-specific booty rap of "Belly Dancin' Dina." The "Tribe Vibes" line "Don't eat meat cuz I'm not that mean/ Drink a lot of juice so my insides is clean" told socially conscious homeboys everywhere what they should be putting in their bellies. Jungle Brothers were ahead of their time; the concept and Ashford & Simpson loop of "Black Woman" were copied for Method Man's hit "All I Need" five years later. The album's high point may be "Doin' Our Own Dang"—featuring De La Soul, Queen Latifah, Monie Love, and A Tribe Called Quest—which remains the definitive Native Tongues posse cut. While Jungle Brothers were primed for success, their record label dropped the ball; it wasn't until 1993 that the even more adventurous *J. Beez Wit the Remedy* appeared, and despite the boot-stomping single "40 Below Trooper," the album sold squat. As the group aged, they found success in Europe, and this apparently affected their music. Back in 1988, *Straight Out the Jungle*'s most intriguing cut was "I'll House You," a collaboration with house producer Todd Terry. While the track was great, it spawned the lamentably cheesy subgenre of hip-house, and come 2000's *V.I.P.*, the J.B.s were rapping over beats that sounded more like wine-bar Eurodisco than real hip-hop. For anyone who was a fan of the group's pioneering early work, their latter-day party guise is a bit hard to accept. A number of compilations and remix collections are available, none of which are a better buy than Jungle Brothers' first two albums. —P.R.

Jurassic 5

★★★★ Jurassic 5 EP (Rumble, 1997)
★★★½ Quality Control (Interscope, 2000)
★★★½ Power in Numbers (Interscope, 2002)

Jurassic 5 are old-school hip-hop revivalists—their name harks back to hip-hop's prehistoric age à la Furious Five. But when these these four rappers and two turntablists emerged from the underground of the gangsta-rap-ridden Los Angeles in the mid-'90s, J5's positive vibe and laid-back melodicism sounded downright revolutionary. After years honing its live chops with only a single in circulation, J5 burst onto the burgeoning indie hip-hop scene with a nine-track debut EP that condensed an album's worth of hooks, intricate flows, and virtuosic beat-juggling into just over 26 minutes. Trading between singsong mike-passing ("In the Flesh," "Concrete Schoolyard") and scratch workouts courtesy of Cut Chemist and DJ Nu-Mark ("Lesson 6: The Lecture"), there's not a weak moment on this terrific introduction.

Having earned enough attention to make the jump to a major label, J5's full-length debut, *Quality Control,* mostly offered more of the same. By then, though, the novelty of the group's catchy songs and group dynamics had somewhat worn off, and the sound proved more difficult to pull off over the course of an entire album—one that aimed for commercial success, no less. Still, tracks like "World of Entertainment (W.O.E. Is Me)" proved J5 was no mere gimmick, but rather had the power to suggest that a grassroots playground-rhyming revival was just what hip-hop needed in the new millennium.

Two years later, *Power in Numbers* confirmed J5's enduring dedication to roots hip-hop. Stylistically identical to its predecessor, the record builds on obscure soul and jazz samples, then adds expert scratches, virtuosic rhyming, and a couple stabs at pop crossover—most notably, the catchy "Thin Line," featuring singer Nelly Furtado. If you're not quite convinced of the group's worth, *Power* won't change your mind. If you're already sold, it's just more proof. —R.M.S.

Juvenile
see HOT BOYS

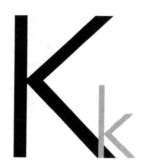

Kansas

- ★ Kansas (1974; Epic/Legacy, 2004)
- ★ Masque (1975; Epic/Legacy, 2001)
- ★ Song for America (1975; Epic/Legacy, 2004)
- ★★ Leftoverture (1976; Epic/Legacy, 2001)
- ★★ Point of Know Return (1977; Epic/Legacy, 2002)
- ★ Two for the Show (Kirshner/CBS, 1978)
- ★ Monolith (Kirshner/CBS, 1979)
- ★ Audio-Visions (1980; Epic/Legacy, 1996)
- ★½ Vinyl Confessions (1982; Epic/Legacy, 1996)
- ★ Drastic Measures (1983; Epic/Legacy, 1996)
- ★★½ The Best of Kansas (1984; Epic/Legacy, 1999)
- ★ Power (MCA, 1986)
- ★ In the Spirit of Things (MCA, 1988)
- ★★ The Kansas Boxed Set (Legacy, 1994)
- ★ Freaks of Nature (Intersound, 1995)
- ★ Always Never the Same (River North, 1998)
- ★ Somewhere to Elsewhere (Magna Carta, 2000)

These corn-fed prog-rock philosophers hit it right exactly once: the 1977 acoustic doomshow "Dust in the Wind," which seems guaranteed to stick around long after the earth and sky are both gone. It's the first riff any guitarist learns to play (very similar to Janis Ian's "At Seventeen," in fact), as well as a sermon on the transience of material things, complete with air-violin solo, dry-ice video, and Steve Walsh's terrifying crumble-to-the-ground screams. ("All your money! Won't another! Minute buy-*hiiiiiiiiy!*") Radiohead tried to rewrite it as "Street Spirit (Fade Out)," but the original's much scarier; it also inspired the best scene in *Bill and Ted's Excellent Adventure.* Compared to "Dust in the Wind," the rest of Kansas' oeuvre just sounds like ordinary prog. Guitarist/songwriter Kerry Livgren was a seeker after the truth, leading to brow-furrowing anthems like "Carry On Wayward Son" and "Point of Know Return." Fond of suites and such, the band at least had a sense of humor, as evinced by titles such as *Leftoverture* and for that matter "Magnum Opus" and "Icarus—Borne on the Wings of Steel." Livgren moved on to become one of the leading lights of '80s born-again Christian rock with his new band, A.D. The usual cycle of breakups and reunions ensued, proving that everything *is* dust in the wind. Tragically, Kansas never got around to making a duet album with Toto. —R.S.

Robert Earl Keen

- ★★★½ No Kinda Dancer (Sugar Hill, 1984)
- ★★★ The Live Album (Sugar Hill, 1988)
- ★★★½ West Textures (Sugar Hill, 1989)
- ★★★★½ A Bigger Piece of Sky (Sugar Hill, 1993)
- ★★★½ Gringo Honeymoon (Sugar Hill, 1994)
- ★★★½ No. 2 Live Dinner (Sugar Hill, 1996)
- ★★★ Picnic (Arista Austin, 1997)
- ★★★★ Walking Distance (Arista, 1998)
- ★★★½ Gravitational Forces (Lost Highway, 2001)
- ★★★ Farm Fresh Onions (Audium/Rosetta/Koch, 2003)
- ★★★ The Party Never Ends: Songs You Know From the Times You Can't Remember (Sugar Hill, 2003)

Singer/songwriter Robert Earl Keen never found quite the level of fame achieved by his Texas A&M buddy Lyle Lovett, but his own considerable grassroots following both within and beyond the borders of the Lone Star State is no fluke. Though he is best known for his beer-friendly live shows (as vividly captured on *No. 2 Live Dinner*) and sing-along anthems (most notably "The Road Goes On Forever," covered by both Joe Ely and the Highwaymen, and the fractured, white-trash Yuletide classic "Merry Christmas From the Family"), closer attention reveals a writer with a novelist's eye for character and narrative detail comparable to forerunners like John Prine, Guy Clark, and Kris Kristofferson. He's got an equally sharp ear for catchy melodies and first-class backing musicians, strengths that more than offset his limited vocal range.

The gently loping *No Kinda Dancer* is a fine, unassuming debut, its laid-back, acoustic charms characterized by the Keen/Lovett cowrite "The Front Porch Song" and the cinematic bluegrass instrumental "Death of Tail Fitzsimmons." But it's the next three studio albums that truly lay the foundation for Keen's career. *West Textures* premieres both the haunting "Mariano" and "The Road Goes On Forever," though the latter's "Born to Run"-with-blazing-guns punch is better captured on *No. 2 Live Dinner* and with the unabashedly rock & roll remake on 2001's *Gravitational Forces. A Bigger Piece of Sky* is, song for song, Keen's best album; "Blow You Away," "Whenever Kindness Fails," and a full-throttle rip through Terry Allen's "Amarillo Highway" are the highlights, though there's really not a weak track here. *Gringo Honeymoon* isn't quite as airtight, though the title track remains Keen's best love song and "Lynnville Train" his most heartbreaking.

Picnic, the first of Keen's three major-label albums, aims a little too earnestly for straight-ahead roots rock and ultimately misses its mark; the songs just aren't as strong, and Keen's voice is outmatched by the muscular arrangements, though two covers (James McMurtry's "Levelland" and Dave Alvin's "Fourth of July") pick up considerable slack, as does "Then Came Lo Mein," a fetching duet with the Cowboy Junkies' Margo Timmins in which an all-you-can-eat Chinese buffet sets the scene for an emotional breakdown. Keen bounded back with *Walking Distance*, his strongest set since *Bigger Piece of Sky,* and *Gravitational Forces,* the latter heavy on covers but distinguished by the terrific "Wild Wind," a portrait of a small Texas town as memorable as a Mayberry populated by eccentric Flannery O'Connor characters. *Farm Fresh Onions* is a freewheelin', anything-goes (including psychedelic garage rock on the title track) mess of an album. But barring a couple of duds (such as "Floppy Shoes"), it's a blast. There's a hell of a great anthology to be culled from all this; unfortunately, *The Party Never Ends*—which samples only three of the Sugar Hill albums (and not even *Bigger Piece of Sky*)—isn't it. —R.SK.

Salif Keita

★★★ Seydou Bathilli (Sonodisc, 1982)
★★½ Soro (Mango, 1987)
★★★½ Ko-Yan (1989; Palm Pictures, 2003)
★★★ Amen (Mango, 1991)
★★★½ Les Ambassadeurs Internationales Featuring Salif Keita (Rounder, 1992)
★★★★ The Mansa of Mali . . . A Retrospective (Mango, 1994)
★★★ Folon . . . The Past (Mango, 1995)
★★★★ Papa (Metro Blue, 1999)
★★★½ Best of the Early Years (Wrasse, 2002)
★★★½ Golden Voice: The Best Of (Wrasse, 2002)
★★★★ Moffou (Universal, 2002)

Mory Kante and Salif Keita
★★★★ Rail Band (Sonodisc, 2000)

Along with Senegal's Youssou N'Dour and Baaba Maal, Mali's Salif Keita is one of the grand trio of African pop voices who have found a big audience among Western listeners by infusing traditional African songs with all kinds of modern sounds. Although he may lack N'Dour's sheer power and the poetic touch of Maal, Keita seems more determined to become a star. He began with strikes against him. Born an albino in a culture that considered such people bad luck, he also belonged to a royal lineage that frowned on playing music as a profession. But he strengthened his voice scaring baboons out of the farm fields, and by the mid-'70s was a member of the legendary Rail Band, the first electrified dance outfit in Mali. (The band also included another celebrated singer, Mory Kante, as documented on the captivating *Rail Band* collection.)

Keita next joined Les Ambassadeurs Internationales, where he began writing songs with his characteristic combination of sweet melody, bits of fable and folklore, and hardheaded advice about work, pride, and respect for the past. Many of these were epic slow burners built around circular guitar figures; they can be sampled on either the Rounder *Les Ambassadeurs Internationales* (slightly more focus on the band) or the Wrasse *Early Years* (slightly more focus on the singer).

Going solo, he was uncertain how to make music that could catch on anywhere in the world. His early Western releases tended to be overly fancy or uneven and indistinct, but *The Mansa of Mali* anthology cuts away the weeds from this era. The huge, throbbing voice, which can express hints of rage or dread prophecies, remains a gripping constant.

"Neotraditional" was an Afropop buzzword in the early 1990s, but only Keita made it mean something vibrant, starting with *Papa*. There seemed to be more folklore and acoustic African instruments than ever before, but under the ministrations of coproducer Vernon Reid, the album shuffled from plaintive street-songs to funk fusions to dreams of the elders designed for modern Bamako. *Moffou* is equally confident, diverse, and even prettier, with a choice guest vocal from Cesaria Evora and some of his most seductive choral arrangements. State-of-the-pop-world art.   —M.MI.

Kelis

★★★½   Kaleidoscope (Virgin, 1999)
★½   Wanderland (Virgin, 2001)
★★★★   Tasty (Star Trak/Arista, 2003)

It wasn't Kelis' fault her strong and soulful debut missed the neosoul train by a year—the single "Caught Out There" was tagged for easy reference to the conventional rock-chick yowlings of Alanis Morissette. But Kelis, a genetic jackpot, with a father who was both a minister and a musician, demonstrated a silky, insinuating voice and a precocious ease in a variety of genres on *Kaleidoscope*.

A curiosity upon its release, this intelligently upside-down R&B album seems almost revelatory. Hip-hop breaks intensify the confidence Kelis exudes on "Good Stuff," as the tune ambles smokily over a slow-thumping bass. She does her own rapping on the sinuous "Mafia," with its serpentine Middle Eastern vocal melody grounded in hard-edged funk. "Caught Out There" subverted traditional song form, burying its title in a lilting throwaway phrase at the end of the verses, and got Kelis attention with her screaming chorus: "I hate . . . you so . . . much right now!" Even her less interesting songs glow thanks to the Neptunes' funky syncopations.

Kelis loses her way on the aptly titled *Wanderland*. The beats that brought *Kaleidoscope* to life are gone, and only Kelis' hippieish and overly self-aware songwriting remains. Still, there's a nice ambiguity on "Popular Thug" (with rapping by Pusha T of Clipse), which includes a bizarre calliope-like synth part and lyrics about the singer's self-delusion over the source of her boyfriend's money. She dabbles in rock, with miserable results in "Perfect Day" and much better ones in "Easy Come, Easy Go," which boasts Korn's Fieldy on bass but could slip unnoticed onto a J.Lo album. Still, the songwriting can be juvenile, and she tries in vain to recapture the magic of "Caught Out There" with the spacy, sassy "Get Even." *Tasty,* her third album, is her best work—lighter and more cohesive than *Wanderland,* more focused and mature than *Kaleidoscope.* Take away the Dallas Austin–produced tracks ("Trick Me" and "Keep It Down"), two Neptunes rock attempts, and the superfreaky, undeniable "Milkshake," and you have a solid R&B album, one that's thickly speckled with hip-hop influences and nods to early Prince and '80s Latin freestyle music.   —E.H./A.B.

R. Kelly

★★★½   12-Play (Jive, 1993)
★★★★   R. Kelly (Jive, 1995)
★★★½   R. (Jive, 1998)
★★★½   TP-2.Com (Jive, 2000)
★★★★   Chocolate Factory (Jive, 2003)
★★★   Happy People/U Saved Me (Jive, 2004)

with Public Announcement
★★   Born Into the 90s (Jive, 1992)

with Jay-Z
★★   The Best of Both Worlds (Universal, 2002)

Probably the most important R&B producer of the hip-hop era, R. Kelly's music has become the default mode of mainstream soul: a mix of syrup and sex, of church-trained vocals and simple keyboards employed in the service of a night out at the booty bar. Kelly isn't as intent on rooting through R&B history as neosoul archaeologists D'Angelo and Musiq, but he has a healthy respect for the past—essentially, he updates the Isley Brothers' slick groove for hip-hop-trained ears. And his persona—the tormented Lothario—is indebted to the darker side of Motown. Like Marvin Gaye and Michael Jackson before him, Kelly plumbs the depths of his sexual neuroses. At his best, he expresses fears and worries that most loverman R&B is too booty-fixated to bother itself with. At his worst, he sounds like he's feigning a divided soul to seem deeper than he is and wheedle some sympathy out of the ladies.

Kelly came up in the last wave of New Jack, and some of that style seeped into his debut. Though he always was a hell of a singer, nothing in the dozen songs of *12-Play* (three times as good as foreplay, get it?) suggested he was in it for the long haul—"Bump & Grind" was so direct that you can't really call it a come-on. Window-fogging was still his MO on the followup, but Kelly managed to keep it in his pants for stretches at a time. "You Remind Me" turned a string of dumb woman-as-car metaphors into a classic single. *R.* has its moments—particularly the astounding cheater's plaint, "When a Woman's Fed Up"—but Kelly can't keep it up for two full discs.

TP-2 is Kelly at his most wacked-out; at one point he assumes the voice of God to lecture himself. In 2002 a videotape surfaced of Kelly allegedly pissing on a teenage girl (he denies it's him), and *Chocolate Factory* was released as Kelly was ducking for cover. But he'd apparently learned from Michael Jackson's publicity mistakes, because the new Kelly was less haunted, if no less horny. The hit "Ignition (Remix)" was his warmest pick-up joint to date, and set the tone for the new record—and maybe a new stage in his career.   —K.H.

Alicia Keys

★★★ Songs in A Minor (J Records, 2001)
★★★ The Diary of Alicia Keys (J Records, 2003)

Pianist and singer Alicia Keys was discovered by legendary record executive Clive Davis, and became one of the first artists Davis introduced after starting his J Records label. As a result, Keys had the kind of debut aspiring artists dream about: A hot single, "Fallin'," created curiosity, and an appearance on *Oprah* just before her album's release helped *Songs in A Minor* enter at the top of the *Billboard* 200, selling 50,000 copies on the day of its release.

Graced with Hanon Studies–style arpeggios and references to the classical piano repertoire, *Songs in A Minor* is basic neosoul, situating Keys' resolute, reed-thin voice within taut production environments. Keys wrote nearly half the songs herself, and while some are enchanting, more—including "Fallin'," which reprises James Brown's "It's a Man's World"—are relatively transparent rewrites of established hits. As a pianist, Keys is totally convincing; vocally, however, she has some growing to do, as her mechanical performance of Prince's "How Come You Don't Call Me Anymore" made clear. Despite a uniformly sexy vibe and whip-smart production on several standout tracks—the Jackson 5–ish "Heartburn," the torchy "You Don't Know My Name"—Keys' followup, *The Diary of Alicia Keys*, didn't quite captivate mainstream listeners the way her debut did. —T.M.

Nusrat Fateh Ali Khan

★★★★ Devotional and Love Songs (Real World, 1993)
★★★½ Mustt Mustt (Real World, 1993)
★★★★ Intoxicated Spirit (Shanachie, 1996)
★★ Night Song (Real World, 1996)
★★★★★ Rapture: An Essential Collection (Music Club, 1997)
★★★★ Supreme Collection, Vol. 1 (Caroline, 1997)
★★★★ Greatest Hits of Nusrat Fateh Ali Khan (Shanachie, 1997)
★★★½ Greatest Hits, Vol. 2 (Shanachie, 1998)
★★★★ Imprint: In Concert (Hi Horse, 1999)
★★★ Magic Touch (Music Club, 2000)
★★★½ Live in London, Vol. 3 (Navras, 2000)
★★★½ Ecstacy: Live (Music Club, 2001)

When Pakistani singer Nusrat Fateh Ali Khan (1948–1997) flashed into the American world music scene in the early '90s, "Pakistan" and "Islam" were not the charged words they have become. But the appeal of the huge man with the huge voice has persisted through the changes of history and his death. Khan sang *qawwali* ("utterance"), a religious mode from the antifundamentalist Sufi culture. The basic lineup of a Party, as qawwali groups are called, is no more than a pair of harmoniums (hand-pumped organs), double-headed *dholak* drums perhaps supplemented by tabla drums, several backup singers who also provide hand claps, and two or three lead singers. Most numbers are devotional meditations that swirl to ecstatic climaxes, though a few *ghazals* (love songs from India) are welcomed for light relief. While Khan sang in typical Indo-Arabic tones that can sound raw to Western ears, he projected atypical warmth, and was an amazingly swift and deft improviser on the repeated phrases that form the heart of qawwali performance. Khan's ability to build passion transcended not only the bounds of language but also, it seems, of the conscious mind, until everyone in range took flight with him. His recorded output was as vast as his girth and his sales, so the above is only a selection. *Rapture, Supreme Collection,* and the two *Greatest Hits* titles are anthologies, with the first offering an irresistible program of varied, compact and vibrant tracks. *Greatest Hits, Vol. 2* is highlighted for those looking for early material recorded for cassette in Pakistan. *Intoxicated Spirit* is the most headlong rush of his straightforward studio recordings. *Devotional and Love Songs, Mustt Musst,* and *Night Song* are meetings with Western instruments and the ministrations of producer Michael Brook. The title tune of *Mustt Mustt* was a hit dance remix by Massive Attack. *Night Song* is for those who don't want to jiggle around too much. *Magic Touch* is the standout techno-remix collection, and those who object should remember Kahn was no purist—he wanted to inspire people through whatever sound it took. The finest vehicle for him, however, was live performance. *Imprint, Ecstacy,* and *Live in London,* particularly the beautifully recorded *Imprint,* are the best available chances to get intoxicated with Khan in concert. —M.R.

Kid Koala

★★★★ Carpal Tunnel Syndrome (Ninja Tune, 2000)
★★★ Nufonia Must Fall (Ninja Tune/ECW Press, 2003)
★★★ Some of My Best Friends Are DJs (Ninja Tune, 2003)

Bullfrog Featuring Kid Koala

★★★ Bullfrog (Ropeadope/Atlantic, 2001)

At some point the DJ replaced the guitarist as the supreme pop virtuoso, whose quick-fingered skills served both musical and theatrical functions. Eventually there arose a school of superspinners—Invisibl Skratch Piklz, DJ Shadow, and the X-Ecutioners chief among them—with such extraordinary powers of pastiche that no band or rapper could ever keep up with them. But this diminutive Chinese-Canadian (né Eric San) made a splash with a lighthearted approach and a genius for comic samples that obscured tremendous chops on the decks.

Carpal Tunnel Syndrome, released after well-received singles and guest spots with Coldcut and on Handsome Boy Modeling School (and an opening gig with the Beastie Boys), is a tour de force of the turntable art, though performed with a rare focus and flair that makes it one of the few DJ-only discs that can be listened to and enjoyed by nonspecialists. Kid churns through libraries of bebop and funk samples, though you barely notice the sleight of hand because of the constant streams of hilarious vocal appropriations, from the stuttering *Revenge of the Nerds* dialogue scratched on "Nerdball" to the *Mad* magazine–esque bad date scenario that emerges from a quilt of samples in "Barhopper" Parts 1 and 2. After more big guest spots—Deltron 3030, Gorillaz, opening for Radiohead—Kid released an album of gorgeous P-Funk–style grooves with his long-running group, Bullfrog. It's a fun and seamless blend of band and DJ—a little too seamless, actually, as Kid Koala's contributions are invisible on all but a few tracks. In early 2003 Kid released the first of several planned book/CD projects, *Nufonia Must Fall*, a 300-page cartoon novel about a robot who falls in love with a human girl (he makes her a killer mix, what else?), with a brief accompanying keyboard/turntable soundtrack. *Some of My Best Friends* continues with the Kid Koala formula of lighthearted comedy and jazz samples. Nothing special there, but the accompanying comic book and short video are adorable vignettes about the DJ lifestyle—scratching, sampling, digging in the crates like kids playing in sandboxes—and offer something that is absent from music made entirely of samples and splices: a fun narrative.   —B.S.

Kid Rock

- ★★½   Grits Sandwiches for Breakfast (Jive, 1990)
- ★★   Fire It Up (Continuum, 1994)
- ★★★★   Devil Without a Cause (Top Dog/Lava/Atlantic, 1998)
- ★★★   The History of Rock (Lava/Atlantic, 2000)
- ★★½   Cocky (Lava/Atlantic, 2001)
- ★★★   Kid Rock (Atlantic, 2003)

Who put the *baw* in the *bawitdaba da-bang-ga-dang diggy-diggy*? His name is Kid Rock, baby, and he hit the big time on *Devil Without a Cause*, a trailer trash triumph of metal guitars, hip-hop beats, and I'm-an-American-band egomania. In scuzzbag anthems such as "Bawitdaba," "Cowboy," and "I Am the Bullgod," the Kid comes on looser and funnier than the rap-metal competition, probably because he doesn't nurse any psychosexual grudges against the world: All he wants to do is rock like Amadeus for his Detroit playas. For all its boozy wallop, the music is full of clever details—"Cowboy" swipes its piano solo from the Doors' "L.A. Woman," while "Bawitdaba" mixes up the Sugarhill Gang's "Rapper's Delight" and the Marcels' "Blue Moon" like it ain't no thing. Giving love to minimum-wage lawn mowers and Heidi Fleiss and topless dancers and midnight glancers, crooning his own ersatz Skynyrd ballad "Only God Knows Why," Kid Rock is a one-man grand funk railroad. And when he urges his peeps, "Get in the pit and try to love someone!" he ain't joking.

Kid Rock had actually been around for years already, even if nobody outside the Detroit methadone clinics had ever heard of him. His early albums are clever ("I like bean burritos from Taco Bell/I like trippin' on acid with Dick Vitale"), but not as much fun as *Devil*. The Bullgod celebrated his breakthrough with *The History of Rock,* a collection of odds and sods from his past, most either remixed or rerecorded entirely. The material wasn't quite dope enough to sell his new fans on the theory that he was a neglected master back when he was taking up fanzine ad space alongside early-'90s hip-hop not-quites like Downtown Science, Dream Warriors, Poor Righteous Teachers, and the Afros. The highlight was the brand-new "American Badass," which shouts out to Johnny Cash and Grandmaster Flash, David Allan Coe, and No Show Jones. *Cocky* was a weak followup, playing down the hip-hop and taking the Southern-rock ballads way too seriously. *Kid Rock* went even further into country-style guitar rock, but with better songs, including the Hank Williams Jr. duet "Cadillac Pussy" and a cover of Bad Company's "Feel Like Makin' Love." But Kid Rock will clearly remain a star on sheer momentum, a Murder City madman with Pabst Blue Ribbon in his veins.   —R.S.

Kid 606

- ★★★★½   Don't Sweat the Technics (Vinyl Communications, 1998)
- ★★★½   Unamerican Activity (Vinyl Communications, 1998)
- ★★★★   Down With the Scene (Ipecac, 2000)
- ★★½   The Soccergirl EP (Carpark, 2000)
- ★★★★   Kid 606 and Friends, Vol. 1 (Tigerbeat6, 2001)
- ★★★★½   P.S. I Love You (Mille Plateaux, 2001)
- ★★★   P.S. You Love Me (Mille Plateaux, 2001)
- ★★★★   The Action Packed Mentallist Brings You the Fucking Jams (Violent Turd, 2002)

★★★½ Why I Love Life (Tigerbeat6, 2002)
★★★½ Kill Sound Before Sound Kills You (Ipecac, 2003)

California sound anarchist Kid 606 saturated the electronic music marketplace in the late '90s and early '00s with a rapid-fire series of releases that took jungle, hip-hop, techno, and ambient music as templates to be utterly disassembled and rebuilt with hyper speed and the attention to detail of an O.C.D.-addled child. The results were some of the most invigorating music ever to emanate from a laptop computer. Screaming vocal samples, Japanese noise music, bleak heavy metal, digital glitches, advertising snippets, insider electronic music jokes, and a healthy fascination for hip-hop offshoots like dancehall and Miami bass: Add these things up and you get maybe half of 606's gift. The other half is making all these aggressively disparate influences sound utterly normal up against one another, copyright and expectations be damned. *Down With the Scene* is as ironic an electronic album as there is. On *The Action Packed Mentallist*, 606 mashes up Black Sabbath, Kylie Minogue, Bubba Sparxxx, and A-Ha, among countless others, adding his trademark snarl on top of theirs. (606's experiments with subtler sounds, as on *Soccergirl* and *P.S. I Love You*, have been less consistent.)

Tigerbeat6, 606's label, also became a home to several like-minded sonic thrashers, who built irregular dance-floor compositions on the shards of musical samples, as heard on the excellent *Attitude* and *Freakbitchlickfly* compilations, as well as the "$" series of seven-inch singles. And in 606's hands, the remix became both a collaborative art form as well as a de facto requirement for all electronic auteurs to follow. Some of his finest work is to be found on the *Kid 606 & Friends Vol. 1* compilation, a set of soundclashes with the likes of Matmos, Cex, and the Rapture. And like any young punk, he wore his sentiments proudly for all to see. As one song title puts it: "Fuck Up Everything You Can Before You Plan on Slowing Down." —J.C.

B.B. King

★★★★★ Live at the Regal (1965; MCA, 1997)
★★★★ Lucille (1968; MCA, 1992)
★★★★ The Electric B.B. King: His Best (1968; MCA, 1988)
★★★★ Live & Well (1969; MCA, 1990)
★★★★ Completely Well (1969; MCA, 1998)
★★★★ His Best: The Electric B.B. King (1969; MCA, 1998)
★★★★ Indianola Mississippi Seeds (1970; MCA, 1989)
★★★ Live in Cook County Jail (1971; MCA, 1998)
★★★ B.B. King in London (1971; MCA Special Products, 2001)
★★★★ The Best of B.B. King (1973; MCA, 1990)
★★★★ B.B. King & Bobby Bland: Together for the First Time Live (1974; MCA, 1987)
★★★★ Lucille Talks Back (1975; MCA Special Products, 1995)
★★½ Bobby Bland & B.B. King: Together Again . . . Live (1976; MCA, 1990)
★★★ Midnight Believer (1978; MCA Special Products, 1999)
★★★ Take It Home (1979; MCA, 1998)
★★★★ Live "Now Appearing" at Ole Miss (1980; MCA, 1991)
★★★★ Great Moments With B.B. King (1981; MCA, 1990)
★★★★ There Must Be a Better World Somewhere (1981; MCA Special Markets, 1998)
★★★★ Love Me Tender (1982; MCA, 1991)
★★★★ Blues 'n' Jazz (1983; MCA, 1988)
★★★★½ The Best of B.B. King, Vol. 1 (1986; Flair/Virgin, 1991)
★★★★½ Do the Boogie! B.B. King's Early 50s Classics (1988; Flair/Virgin, 1994)
★★★ King of the Blues 1989 (MCA, 1989)
★★★★ Live at San Quentin (MCA, 1990)
★★★★ There Is Always One More Time (MCA, 1991)
★★★½ Spotlight on Lucille (Flair/Virgin, 1991)
★★★½ Live at the Apollo (GRP, 1991)
★★★★ Singin' the Blues/The Blues (Flair/Virgin, 1991)
★★★★ The Fabulous B.B. King (Flair/Virgin, 1991)
★★★★ Heart and Soul: A Collection of Blues Ballads (Pointblank/Virgin, 1992)
★★★★ My Sweet Little Angel (Flair/Virgin, 1992)
★★★★ King of the Blues (MCA, 1992)
★★ Heart to Heart: Diane Schuur & B.B. King (GRP, 1994)
★★★½ Blues Summit (MCA, 1993)
★★★★½ How Blue Can You Get? Classic Live Performances 1964 to 1994 (MCA, 1996)
★★★ Deuces Wild (MCA, 1997)
★★★★ Blues on the Bayou (MCA, 1998)
★★★★★ Greatest Hits (MCA, 1998)
★★★★ Blues on the Bayou (MCA, 1998)
★★★★ Let the Good Times Roll: The Music of Louis Jordan (MCA, 1999)
★★★ Best of B.B. King: 20th Century Masters (MCA, 1999)
★★★½ Live in Japan (MCA, 1999)
★★★ Makin' Love Is Good for You (MCA, 2000)

★★★★½   Anthology (MCA, 2000)
★★★★   A Christmas Celebration of Hope (MCA, 2001)
★★★   Here and There: The Uncollected B.B. King (Hip-O, 2001)
★★★★   Martin Scorsese Presents the Blues: B.B. King (MCA, 2003)

B.B. King has done everything a bluesman can do, and he's done it extraordinarily well: He's a great singer, a great guitarist, and he has written dozens of classic songs, including "Paying the Cost to Be the Boss," "Why I Sing the Blues,"and "Sweet Little Angel." King has proved both highly influential and prolific: He's mentored dozens of talented singers and guitarists, and he's toured and recorded at an astonishing rate. King's presence thus looms large in the world of the blues—perhaps larger than that of any other performer.

In his early years, King stayed true to the blues while incorporating elements of other music he enjoyed. Born Riley B. King in 1925 in Itta Bena, MS, he sang in gospel quartets and on street corners in his youth; in the '50s, he often worked with a group of musicians that included singer Bobby Bland and pianist Johnny Ace. At that time King began to develop his deceptively simple single-string guitar technique, taking cues from both Blind Lemon Jefferson and T-Bone Walker. As a disc jockey for Memphis' WDIA radio, which in the late '40s became the first U.S. radio station to feature an all-black format, King gained a reputation for playing the hippest records in town; as an added bonus for listeners, he would often perform along with the records he played.

WDIA's bosses helped land King with Bullet Records, who released two of his singles. In 1950 he was signed to the nascent RPM label, and for the next year King recorded his RPM sides at Sam Phillips' new Memphis Recording Service studio. King's commercial breakthrough came in 1952, when a cover version of Lowell Fulson's 1948 hit "Three O'Clock Blues" reached #1 on the R&B chart. King carved out a place for himself on the blues circuit by touring constantly—as he continues to do—and cutting some potent tracks for RPM, which later became Kent (and sometimes issued on the budget Crown label). Each step of the way King was refining his art: With his supple young voice he could affect the deep, husky timbre that made "Three O'Clock Blues" so poignant, or a bright, almost reedy tenor sound that was especially effective on love ballads such as 1952's "You Know I Love You" and lighthearted, upbeat jump blues tunes on the order of 1954's "You Upset Me Baby." At the same time, his guitar playing became more individual;

he dubbed his axe "Lucille," and increased both the technical facility and emotional depth of his playing.

Working with arranger Johnny Pate at ABC, King fashioned the sound he adheres to today: orchestral, with a prominent brass section, a powerhouse rhythm section, strings used sparingly for maximum emotional impact, and King's guitar and voice hot and out front, where each belongs. Over the years a few variations have been worked on this setup, but only a few: His 1978 album with the Crusaders, Midnight Believer, is all soft edges and mellow moods, a bit more in the jazz mold than blues, and lacking the grit of the straight-ahead blues efforts; four years later he went foursquare into boudoir soul with the gentle stylings collected on Love Me Tender, a well-sustained effort at romantic balladeering on which a tougher mind-set would have been inappropriate. A 1999 tribute to one of his idols, Louis Jordan, Let the Good Times Roll: The Music of Louis Jordan, is a high-spirited affair (appropriately enough) featuring King's guitar playing in an entirely secondary role (guitar not being a prominent feature of Jordan's exciting jump blues workouts) to his personable singing—and King responds with some of his most engaging vocal work on record.

Thanks to an ambitious reissue campaign by the Flair/Virgin label, much of King's early recorded work for Modern/RPM/Kent has been returned to print, along with a good number of sides that had been previously unissued in any form. Start with Singin' the Blues/The Blues, a twofer combining King's first two Crown album releases. Singin' the Blues includes a blazing T-Bone Walker–style assault—all distortion and hard-picked single-string runs—ahead of King's plaintive vocal on "Please Love Me." "Three O'Clock Blues" is here, as well as the earliest versions of two other King classics in his own rich, double-entendre ballad "Sweet Little Angel" and Memphis Slim's "Every Day I Have the Blues." The Blues didn't produce any comparable monuments, but it did spotlight King and his stellar studio band in peak form on uptempo rousers ("Ruby Lee"), slow blues grinders ("Fast Day"), and breakneck boogie-woogie straight from the Kansas City school ("Boogie Woogie Woman," fueled by Willie McDaniels' boisterous solos).

Elsewhere, The Best of B.B. King Volume One and The Fabulous B.B. King are basically greatest hits packages from the early era. Both contain "Three O'Clock Blues," "Please Love Me," "You Upset Me," "Every Day I Have the Blues," and the first "Sweet Little Angel." My Sweet Little Angel features 21 songs recorded with King and his touring band in Chicago, Houston, Little Rock, and Memphis, giving us an idea of what it must have been like to experience King in a small club setting at this seminal stage of his career. *My Sweet Little Angel* has some surprises to offer in the form of alternate takes and rare tracks, while *Do the Boogie: B.B. King's Early 50s Classics* includes a number of sides that have been out of print or available only on bootlegs.

King's tender side is the focus of *Heart and Soul: A Collection of Blues Ballads*. Again, the chart hits are supplemented by previously unissued alternate takes, B sides, and otherwise obscure singles. King fans will appreciate the way he melds blues, R&B, and pop on several tracks. *Heart and Soul* shows that later efforts, such as the aforementioned *Midnight Believer* and *Love Me Tender* albums, are consistent with and rooted in a long-standing, broad stylistic definition of the blues universe. *Spotlight on Lucille* captures a number of early instrumentals, making it a capsule lesson in the development of King's guitar technique.

Of King's many live albums, the best might be 1964's *Live at the Regal,* on which King's superior musicianship is on vivid display as is his exemplary rapport with his audience. Stirring performances of "Every Day I Have the Blues," "Sweet Little Angel," and "Woke Up This Morning" key the show, but the highlight is the hilarious "Help the Poor," which, far from being a socially conscious screed, is B.B.'s own hapless plea for help in rehabilitating his own battered soul in the aftermath of a love war. *Together for the First Time . . . Live,* teaming King with fellow trailblazer Bobby "Blue" Bland, is a spectacular outing, as these two towering figures in American music burn their way through a repertoire that includes "Three O'Clock Blues," "Driftin' Blues," "Goin' Down Slow," and a medley composed in part of "Rock Me Baby," "Driving Wheel," and "Chains of Love." The second King/Bland summit pales in comparison, even though the titular artists manage a few sparks along the way. Those less inclined to wade through all the live albums have a splendid alternative in *How Blue Can You Get? Classic Live Performances 1964 to 1994.* Opening with four powerhouse cuts from *Live at the Regal,* the double-CD makes stops at Cook County Jail, the Village Gate, and the Apollo Theatre in New York City, plus the University of Mississippi, Tokyo, Germany, and England. A first-rate overview of the peak moments of the '60s is available on the invaluable 1998 reissue of *His Best: The Electric B.B. King.*

By 1970 King was a well-established, reliable figure on the concert circuit, and the blues revival of the '60s had brought him a large, multiracial audience. *Completely Well* has its share of bedrock blues, but it is at this point that King's guitar becomes a secondary player—not unheard, but diminished in the overall mix—to the big, booming orchestral arrangements. The players are changing, too, with young rockers stepping in for guest turns backing King: Leon Russell, Carole King, Joe Walsh, and Russ Kunkel all show up on early-'70s albums; on *Live in London,* the backing band includes Gary Wright, Klaus Voorman, Jim Keltner, Ringo Starr, Mac Rebennack, and Jim Gordon.

By 1981 King's music had taken a turn for the philosophical. With *There Must Be a Better World Somewhere,* King set out to chronicle his own worldview in far more personal terms than he had to this point, commenting on social ills while maintaining that the future promises an era of compassion and selflessness.

A year after *There Must Be a Better World Somewhere,* King assembled another group and delivered *Blues 'N' Jazz,* a bit of musical archaeology that hearkened back to the RPM/Kent days in its big t-band approach. After ushering in the '90s with another scorching concert album, *Live at San Quentin,* King dug down deep for *There Is Always One More Time,* another optimistic message arising out of despairing circumstances. Doc Pomus wrote the title song, one of his most optimistic but poignant tracts, as he lay dying of cancer. King, a longtime friend of Pomus', gives it a performance for the ages, honoring its composer with an impassioned reading. King's next album, the Phil Ramone–produced *Heart to Heart,* teaming King with jazz vocalist Diane Schuur, is an odd affair that never quite takes off. The song selection is good—Don Gibson's "I Can't Stop Loving You," Aretha Franklin's "Spirit in the Dark," "Try a Little Tenderness," "It Had to Be You," Irving Berlin's "I'm Putting All My Eggs in One Basket"—but the execution leaves something to be desired, at least when Schuur's reedy voice enters. King got back on track with 1993's *Blues Summit,* a series of scintillating duets with titans on the order of Buddy Guy, Irma Thomas, Lowell Fulson, Koko Taylor, Ruth Brown, Robert Cray, Etta James, John Lee Hooker, and others. Picking out highlights is almost impossible—each cut has something to recommend it. Vocally and instrumentally, King is at the top of his game here, energized by his partners on a boiling rework of Ivory Joe Hunter's "Since I Met You Baby." There's a steadily percolating version of Chris Kenner's "Something You Got" and a dark, haunting treatment given to the Willie Dixon/J. B. Lenoir classic "You Shook Me," which teams King with John Lee Hooker. The duet format was revisited almost as successfully on 1997's *Deuces Wild,* which brings in the likes of Mick Hucknall, Heavy D, David Gilmour, and Paul Carrack, whose performances simply don't measure up to those of artists such as Van Morrison, Joe Cocker, and Willie Nelson (on "Night Life"), who deal their blues from a place nearly as deep as King's.

As he was approaching 73 years of age, and had been recording for nearly 50 years, King decided the time was right for another serious studio album, and he came up with the self-produced *Blues on the Bayou*. King took his road band—which he describes as "my best ever"—to Dockside Studio in Maurice, LA, and delivered the goods over the course of 15 songs, all of them written or cowritten by King himself. The feel is laid-back but spirited, with the impressive synchronicity between the bandleader and the musicians resulting in invigorating instrumental interplay among the soloists. The songs are a mix of old and new King tunes, the most familiar of the lot being "I Got Some Outside Help I Don't Need," a beloved concert tune in King's repertoire, guaranteed to get a crowd going with its wry, sardonic wit and steady rhythmic pulse, on top of which King constructs a series of ruminative solos.

Following the high of *Blues on the Bayou*, the Eric Clapton collaboration on *Riding With the King* is a bit of a letdown. On the plus side, King stands out in any situation, so even on a substandard song such as "Marry You," his gruff vocal carries a certain gravitas, but the wah-wah guitar and hard-rock approach leave him little room to assert his own personality.

The magic King found at Dockside Studio for *Blues on the Bayou* was summoned once more in 2001 for *A Christmas Celebration of Hope*. His road band is characteristically tight and sympathetic to B.B.'s every move, the string arrangements are beautifully nuanced, and King's singing effuses personality and infallible technique. He gets it right on the money, whether he's digging deep to plead his case on "Please Come Home for Christmas," assuming a lonely, despondent demeanor on the winsome "To Someone That I Love," or ratcheting up his saucy side on a delightful reading of Clarence Carter's double-entendre seasonal classic "Back Door Santa."

Recent years have seen the release of several solid career overviews in single- and double-disc packages. For the cream of the early years, Virgin's *Classic Masters* hits the high points of the career-establishing tracks from the 1950s (plus two from the early '60s). Its dozen songs include the original recordings of "Three O'Clock Blues," "Every Day I Have the Blues," "Sweet Little Angel," "Sweet Sixteen," and others. The two-CD *Anthology* encompasses 34 songs, live and studio tracks alike, from the '60s through the '90s, its earliest track being 1962's "Sneakin' Around," its latest the stirring "I'll Survive"

from *Blues on the Bayou*, although the emphasis is on '60s and '70s recordings. This is no mere history lesson; its music is vital and vibrant. Highlights include two cuts from *Live at the Regal* ("Every Day I Have the Blues" and "Sweet Little Angel," which could be taken as the representative '50s tracks, making this collection career-spanning at the time of its release); "The Thrill Is Gone"; the single version of "I Got Some Help I Don't Need"; and the single version of "When Love Comes to Town," recorded with U2. Finally, *Here & There: The Uncollected B. B. King* fills in a few gaps in the catalogue by focusing on soundtrack cuts, songs recorded for other artists' albums, and two tracks previously unreleased in the U.S. These range from a searing rendition of " 'T Ain't Nobody's Business (If I Do)," produced by Robbie Robertson for Martin Scorsese's *The King of Comedy* soundtrack; a sprightly jazz instrumental, "Six Pack," for the like-titled album by vibraphonist virtuoso Gary Burton; a mid-tempo, jazz-inflected version of "Three O'Clock Blues" with organist Jimmy Smith for Smith's *dot.com blues* album; and a potent duet with Willie Nelson on a reinvigorated "The Thrill Is Gone," for Nelson's *Milk Cow Blues* album.

Ultimately, the four-CD box set *King of the Blues* provides the sweeping, exhaustive survey of a remarkable blues odyssey. Its 77 tracks begin with the previously unavailable (on any domestic release) Bullet single "Miss Martha King" that began King's career in 1949, and trace the course of King's high points with RPM, Kent, ABC/Bluesway, and MCA, concluding with a 1992 version of "Since I Met You Baby" cut for Gary Moore's *After Hours* album. This is a smart box in that it hits the high points—"The Thrill Is Gone," "Paying the Cost to Be the Boss," "Three O'Clock Blues," "Every Day I Have the Blues," "Sweet Little Angel," "There Must Be a Better World Somewhere," etc.—but also offers seven previously unreleased recordings and a dozen others that are considerably off the beaten path, such as the 1964 treatment of the Bill Doggett/Louis Jordan gem "Never Trust a Woman," which is making its first appearance here as an album track. In toto, this amounts to nearly five hours of music, all of it fascinating as a short course in the evolution of a great American artist. Better yet, as *Blues on the Bayou* indicates, there's more where this came from.—D.M.

Ben E. King

★★★★ The Ultimate Collection: Ben E. King (Atlantic, 1987)

★½ The Best of Ben E. King (Curb, 1993)

★★★★ The Very Best of Ben E. King (Rhino/Atlantic, 1998)

★★★½   Spanish Harlem/Don't Play That Song (1961, 1962; Collectables, 1998)
★★½   Shades of Blue (Half Note, 1999)

Ben E. King made an indelible mark on his time, both as lead singer of the Drifters and as a solo artist. A North Carolina native who had honed his vocal chops in church and carried the explosive style of the Sensational Nightingales' Julius Cheeks into the secular arena, Benjamin Earl Nelson was an original member of the 5 Crowns, a quintet that made a little bit of noise in 1958 with the Doc Pomus–Mort Shuman song "Kiss and Make Up," recorded for Pomus and Shuman's own R&B label. A year later the remaining original Drifters assembled by Clyde McPhatter fell apart, but the group's enterprising manager, George Treadwell, recognizing the commercial value of the group's name, simply recruited the 5 Crowns to be the new Drifters. Ben E. Nelson then renamed himself Ben E. King, after his favorite uncle, and stepped up to the lead-tenor role, making his 1959 debut with a magnificent song he had written, "There Goes My Baby." It peaked at #2 on the pop charts and inaugurated a bona fide golden era that produced innovative productions largely from the team of Jerry Leiber and Mike Stoller. King's tenure with the Drifters lasted only through 1960, when he went solo with a lovely Jerry Leiber–Phil Spector song "Spanish Harlem," which topped out at #10 on the pop chart. His finest hour as a writer and vocalist came in 1961, with the stark, haunting "Stand by Me" (a cowrite with Leiber-Stoller), a song that is as unsettling in its pronounced sense of dread as it is uplifting in its promise of fidelity, and which has assumed its proper grandeur as a monumental work of popular art. The hits pretty much ceased after "Stand by Me," but he returned to Atlantic in 1975 and produced a substantial #1 R&B and #5 pop single in the two-part "Supernatural Thing." By that time King had adopted a cooler vocal approach, sensual in its muted nuances, and well suited to his maturity.

King's glory years are well documented. The 20-track *Ultimate Collection* and Rhino's 16-track *The Very Best of Ben E. King* hit all the Drifters' high notes in the King era and contain most of the key solo recordings, though neither set includes "Seven Letters," a curious omission. A bracing set of songs comprises the Collectables twofer *Spanish Harlem/Don't Play That Song*, solo albums from 1961 and 1962 respectively. *Spanish Harlem* in particular is fascinating, owing to its focus on exotic, Latin-influenced material such as "Perfidia," "Grenada," "Quiza, Quizas, Quizas," and "Besame Mucho," an obscure Pomus-Shuman gem titled "Souvenir of Mexico," and

of course the title tune. *Don't Play That Song* includes the title song and "Stand by Me," but also a number of seldom-heard album sides penned by Pomus-Shuman ("Here Comes the Night"), Pomus-Spector ("Ecstasy" and "Young Boy Blues"), and Gerry Goffin–Carole King's "Show Me the Way." It's a worthy and essential addition to the King oeuvre. Avoid Curb's *The Best of Ben E. King* as it contains inferior rerecordings of the classic material.

More recently King cut a solo album, *Shades of Blue,* for the Half Note label. This 1999 effort teamed him with some top-notch musicians (tenor sax man David "Fathead" Newman and the great vibraphonist Milt Jackson, for starters) and found him employing his medium-cool crooning voice in service of some classic American pop tunes ("You'd Be So Nice to Come Home To," the Gershwins' "They Can't Take That Away From Me," "Cry," "Learnin' the Blues") as well as Ray Charles' rousing "Hallelujah, I Love Her So." It's not an earth-shaking outing, but it has its moments, and it shows King aging gracefully as a vocalist, which was not always the case in the years leading up to this recording. He's found out that a little goes a long way and that subtlety is a great vocal attribute in an aging singer.   —D.M.

Carole King

★★★   Writer (1970; Epic/Legacy, 1999)
★★★★★   Tapestry (1971; Epic/Legacy, 1999)
★★★   Music (1971; Epic/Legacy, 1999)
★★★   Rhymes and Reasons (1972; Epic/Legacy, 1996)
★★★   Fantasy (1973; Epic/Legacy, 1996)
★★★   Wrap Around Joy (1974; Epic/Legacy, 1996)
★★   Really Rosie (1975; Epic/Legacy, 1999)
★★★   Thoroughbred (1976; Epic/Legacy, 1996)
★★★★   Her Greatest Hits: Songs of Long Ago (1978; Epic/Legacy, 1999)
★★   Speeding Time (Atlantic, 1983)
★★   Colour of Your Dreams (Rhythm Safari, 1993)
★★★★★   A Natural Woman: The Ode Collection (Epic/Legacy, 1994)
★★★★   Carnegie Hall Concert: June 18, 1971 (Epic/Legacy, 1996)
★★★   Now That Everything's Been Said (Epic/Legacy, 1999)
★★★   Love Makes the World Go Round (Koch, 2001)

Carole King is one of the few talents in music to have two full careers: first as a successful Brill Building songwriter, and later as a solo artist. She was a teenager when she began working with Gerry Goffin (eventually her husband), and the duo wrote a string of hits that still light up oldies radio, including "Will You Love Me Tomorrow," "The Loco-Motion," "Take Good Care of My Baby," and "Go Away Little Girl." She divorced Goffin in the late '60s and emerged with *Writer* in 1970, a solid though unassuming start.

Her followup, *Tapestry,* was a career- and decade-defining album. For almost 10 years it ranked as the biggest selling album in history, and rightfully so: It's full of beauty and innocence and blessed with a rare level of songcraft, so emotionally cinematic it almost feels like a great '70s film that Dustin Hoffman and Ali MacGraw might have starred in. "So Far Away," "It's Too Late," and "Home Again" have a resonance that few pop songs approach—which is why they end up in so many movie soundtracks.

Tapestry was a hard act to follow, but King did so with a series of solid '70s records—*Music, Rhymes and Reasons, Fantasy, Wrap Around Joy*—that produced a slew of hits such as "Sweet Seasons," "Been to Canaan," and "Jazzman." *Really Rosie,* her most cohesive effort, was a children's album. King made six less memorable records for Capitol and Atlantic in the late '70s and '80s, but only *Speeding Time* is in print, and it's not at the top of the King checklist. That honor goes to *Tapestry,* and to *A Natural Woman: The Ode Collection,* which contains every song on *Tapestry* plus another two dozen gems.—C.R.C.

King Crimson

★★★½ In the Court of the Crimson King (1969; Caroline, 1999)
★★½ In The Wake of Poseidon (1970; Caroline, 2000)
★★ Lizard (1970; Caroline, 2000)
★½ Islands (1971; Caroline, 2000)
★★ Earthbound (1972; Caroline, 2002)
★★★★★ Larks' Tongues in Aspic (1973; Caroline, 2001)
★★★½ Starless and Bible Black (1974; Caroline, 2001)
★★★★½ Red (1974; Caroline, 2001)
★★★½ USA (1975; Caroline, 2002)
★★★★½ Discipline (1981; Caroline, 2001)
★★★★ Beat (1982; Caroline, 2001)
★★★★ Three of a Perfect Pair (1984; Caroline, 2001)
★★★½ The Compact King Crimson (1986; EG, 1989)
★★★★★ Frame by Frame (Editions EG, 1991)
★★★★ The Abbreviated King Crimson: Heartbeat (Caroline, 1991)
★★★★ The Great Deceiver: Live 1973–74 (Discipline, 1992)
★★★ The Concise King Crimson (Caroline, 1993)
★★★ VROOOM EP (Discipline, 1994)
★★★★ THRAK (1995, Caroline, 2002)
★★½ THRaKaTTaK (Discipline, 1995)

★★★ B'Boom: Official Bootleg, Live in Argentina, 1994 (Discipline, 1995)
★★★½ Epitaph, Vols. 1 & 2 (Discipline, 1997)
★★★ Epitaph, Vols. 3 & 4 (Discipline, 1997)
★★★★ The Night Watch (Discipline, 1998)
★★★★ Absent Lovers: Live in Montreal, 1984 (Discipline, 1998)
★★★½ Cirkus: The Young Person's Guide to King Crimson Live (Caroline, 1999)
★★★ The Deception of the Thrush (Discipline, 1999)
★★½ The ProjeKcts (Discipline, 1999)
★★★ The ConstruKction of Light (Virgin, 2000)
★★★½ Heavy ConstruKction (Discipline, 2000)
★★★ Vrooom Vrooom (Discipline, 2001)
★★★½ Ladies of the Road (Discipline, 2002)
★★★½ Happy With What You Have to Be Happy With (Sanctuary, 2002)
★★★★ The Power to Believe (Sanctuary, 2003)

Despite counting among its alumni members of Bad Company; Emerson, Lake & Palmer; Foreigner; and Asia; King Crimson has never had much truck with the pop end of progressive rock. Instead, the ever-changing ensemble has preferred to haunt the artiest extremes of the prog-rock movement, producing music that can be abstruse, arcane, abrasive, and abstract—but very rarely boring. As such, it casts a long shadow, not just over prog rock but also new wave, alt rock, and metal, echoing audibly in such acts as Gentle Giant, Talking Heads, Dream Theater, Tool, and Opeth.

King Crimson is, by and large, a creature of guitarist Robert Fripp, but that's not quite the same thing as its being Fripp's band. Despite his reputation as a less-than-democratic bandleader, Fripp has long recognized that Crimson's musical identity is more the product of collaboration than direction. The group started out as a collective operation, which should be evident from the chamber-music dynamics found in most of the playing on *In the Court of the Crimson King.* Although best remembered for the sci-fi fury of "21st Century Schizoid Man," the other songs find the band operating in the semiclassical mode favored by early art rockers; apart from occasional mellotron overkill and singer Greg Lake's pompons tendencies, the album remains quite listenable. That's not quite the case with *In the Wake of Poseidon,* on which the band's sound grows more complicated, with jazzy rhythms and knotty, dissonant instrumental lines flavoring "Pictures of a City" and "Cat Food," while lengthy, obtuse improvisation dominates "The Devil's Triangle." *Lizard* pushes those elements even harder but with less success;

apart from the "Bolero" segment of the 24-minute "Lizard," the improvisational sections inevitably degenerate into showy self-indulgence. Live, however, a lot of that fat was burned off in the heat of performance, and the *Epitaph* sets do an admirable job of documenting that intensity. *Vol. 1,* which captures the last performance before this lineup disbanded, is by far the strongest.

Fripp reformed Crimson a year later with a new rhythm section and singer Boz Burrell. This lineup debuts on *Islands,* but apart from "Ladies of the Road," which sets its groupie-adoration lyric to a lean, edgy blues, the songs rank among the group's most pretentious. Nor was this version of Crimson particularly long-lasting, as the other members abandoned ship a year later. (*Earthbound,* a mediocre live album featuring this lineup, was for years the only other document of this version of Crimson; it has since been augmented with the much-superior *Ladies of the Road,* which includes a whole disc of excerpted guitar and sax solos from various versions of "21st Century Schizoid Man").

The next incarnation of King Crimson was on many counts its best. In addition to boasting enormously capable players, this band—violinist David Cross, bassist/vocalist John Wetton, drummer Bill Bruford, and percussionist Jamie Muir—was disciplined enough to keep the improvisational passages sharp and lean and to make the actual songs seem tuneful and direct. As such, the incandescent *Larks' Tongues in Aspic* alternates between crisply played, dramatically paced instrumentals, like the two-part title tune, and quirky vocal numbers, such as "Book of Saturday" and the clankingly catchy "Easy Money." Never before had Crimson's music been so daring and focused. After such heights, *Starless and Bible Black* is a bit of a let down; while "The Great Deceiver" and "Starless and Bible Black" have their moments, the material is generally too fragmented to cohere. *Red,* however, quickly returns to form. With Cross and Muir gone, the chemistry between Fripp, Wetton, and Bruford is intensely dynamic, adding bite to works like "Fallen Angel" and the electrifying "Red." *USA,* a live album recorded with the Cross-Fripp-Wetton-Bruford lineup, was the first of many "official bootleg" recordings by this period Crimson. *The Night Watch* is the best of the lot, though there's also a lot of good stuff squirreled away on the four-CD set *The Great Deceiver.*

King Crimson called it quits again in 1975, but Fripp, never one to say never, brought the band back in 1981 with *Discipline.* Bruford and Fripp were the only carryovers from the previous incarnation; joining them were Peter Gabriel bassist Tony Levin and guitarist Adrian Belew. Even given Crimson's history of never downplaying its chops, this was a player's band in the truest sense of the term, and the quartet's jaw-dropping technique is more than obvious on such knottily rhythmic, harmonically demanding workouts as "Thela Hun Ginjeet," "Elephant Talk," and "Discipline." *Beat,* this crew's sophomore effort, is a little less rigorous, with Belew's melodic instincts adding a pop sheen to the snakily complex instrumental lines beneath "Neal and Jack and Me" and "Waiting Man." *Three of a Perfect Pair* introduces funk elements to the band's rhythmic repertoire and gives a nod to the band's past in "Larks' Tongues in Aspic Part III." Then after a 1984 tour, vividly documented on *Absent Lovers,* King Crimson abdicated yet again.

Not that Fripp would ever fully retire the crown, of course. The next King Crimson emerged in 1994, in what Fripp had dubbed the "double trio" format with two guitarists, two bassists, and two drummers—basically, the entire previous lineup plus bassist Trey Gunn and drummer Pat Mastelotto. *VROOOM* is simply an opening salvo, offering an early take on ideas that would be fleshed out more fully on *THRAK;* the former's principal charm is the fluidity of the intertwining group improvisations. *THRAK,* by contrast, is a more typical Crimson album, offering a couple of solid songs ("Dinosaur," "Sex Sleep Eat Drink Dream") and lots of edgily aggressive playing. Quirky uppercasing aside, *THRaKaTTaK* isn't especially interesting, as its in-depth exploration of synth technology turns the music into something resembling a high-concept sound-effects record. This isn't the most consistent Crimson, but it is extraordinarily well documented, thanks to such goofily titled live albums as *B'Boom* (spotty) and *VROOOM VROOOM* (which is long but boasts a few brilliant bits).

Surprisingly, King Crimson didn't disband after this run; instead, it split into various fractals—or, as Fripp spelled it, "fraKctals." These were four "projeKct" groups featuring various mutations on the last King Crimson, minus Bruford, who presumably got annoyed by the insertion of that stupid capital K. *The ProjeKcts* is a four-CD box documenting these outings, and while the playing is frequently astonishing, the general lack of a melodic anchor more often than not leaves the music adrift. (*The Deception of the Thrush* handily excerpts from the box for those merely interested in a taste.)

ConstruKction of Light marks the post-ProjeKct return of Crimson, now down to a quartet, due to Levin's departure. Again the playing is vigorous, but the writing is too stiff and self-conscious to be completely convincing; there are better versions of "Into the Frying Pan" and "ProzaKc Blues" on the live

Heavy ConstruKction. The four returned to the studio for *Happy With What You Have to Be Happy With,* a *VROOOM*-style prequel to *The Power to Believe.* Each has its charms, with *Happy* showing more grit and raw aggression, while *Believe* showcases the band's subtlety and polish; but the writing is the band's best in years, particularly "Eyes Wide Open" and "Happy With What You Have to Be Happy With," which appear in different versions on both.

There are two King Crimson anthologies out, neither of which captures the entire span of the band's existence. *The Compact King Crimson* is perhaps too compact, as it draws only from *In the Court of the Crimson King, Discipline, Beat,* and *Three of a Perfect Pair.* The boxed anthology *Frame by Frame* is considerably more inclusive, offering one disc's worth of music for each of the band's three periods of development, plus a fourth, live disc; *The Abbreviated King Crimson* reduces its bulk to a single, judiciously edited CD. Since forming his own Discipline label in the mid-'90s, Fripp has also launched a "collector's club" series, which has at this point released more than 20 albums of live recordings and esoterica (available online through www.disciplineglobalmobile.com). —J.D.C.

Kings of Leon

★★★	Holy Roller Novocaine (RCA, 2003)
★★★★	Youth and Young Manhood (RCA, 2003)

Preacher's sons who grew up on the road, laying down the holy-roller boogie in churches across the South, Kings of Leon come by their scuffed, scruffy sound honestly. They rolled out their Strokes-meets-Skynyrd sound on their debut EP, the very solid *Holy Roller Novocaine.* But *Youth and Young Manhood* was where these little red roosters, who range in age from 16 to 23, really kicked down the door, already sounding like old-school greasers who've been around long enough to know how to savor a moment. The Kings are also a Southern rhythm section to the core: They know when to lay back and let things simmer or when to jump up and testify with tambourines banging. Guitar playing in this band is not about Southern-rock virtuosity in the Allmans mold but about staggering-drunk solos that suggest calamity is just around the corner (dig that firecracker dance in "Happy Alone") or that ooze blues slop until it melts into feedback ("Dusty"). Frontman Caleb Followill doesn't sing so much as slouch into his narratives of waywardness. On "Trani," he sounds so busted up he can barely hold a conversation, and it only magnifies the sense of dissolution. Most of the time, every slur and mumble sounds as if he either has just had sex or is dreaming

about it, never more so than on "Molly's Chambers." Mannish boys, they do grow up fast. —G.K.

The Kinks

★★½	Kinks (1964; Rhino, 1988)
★★½	Kinks-Size (1964; Rhino, 1988)
★★★½	Kinda Kinks (1965; Rhino, 1988)
★★★	Kinkdom (Castle, 1965)
★★★½	The Kink Kontroversy (1965; Sanctuary, 2004)
★★★★★	Face to Face (1966; Castle, 1998)
★★★★★	Something Else By the Kinks (1967; Reprise, 1990)
★★★★★	The Kinks Are the Village Green Preservation Society (1968; Reprise, 1990)
★★★★	Arthur (Or the Decline and Fall of the British Empire) (1969; Reprise, 1990)
★★	Lola vs. Powerman and the Money Go Round (1970; Reprise, 1990)
★★	Percy (Castle, 1971)
★★★½	Muswell Hillbillies (1971; Velvel, 1998)
★★★★★	The Kink Kronikles (1972; Reprise, 1990)
★★	Everybody's in Showbiz (1972; Velvel, 1998)
★★★½	The Great Lost Kinks Album (1973; Velvel, 1998)
★★	Preservation: Act I (1973; Velvel, 1998)
★	Preservation: Act 2 (1974; Velvel, 1998)
★	The Kinks Present a Soap Opera (1975; Rhino, 1990)
★½	Schoolboys in Disgrace (1975; Velvel, 1998)
★★	Sleepwalker (1977; Velvel, 1998)
★★	Misfits (1978; Velvel, 1998)
★	Low Budget (1979; Velvel, 1999)
★★	One for the Road (MCA, 1980)
★★	Give the People What They Want (Velvel, 1981)
★★	State of Confusion (Velvel, 1983)
★	Word of Mouth (Velvel, 1984)
★	Think Visual (MCA, 1986)
★★	Come Dancing (Arista, 1986)
★	U.K. Jive (MCA, 1989)
★	Kinks Live: The Road (MCA, 1990)
★	Lost and Found (MCA, 1991)
★★	Phobia (Columbia, 1993)
★★	To the Bone (Grapevine, 1994)
★★★★	BBC Sessions 1964–1977 (Sanctuary, 2001)
★★★★	Singles Collection (Sanctuary, 2004)

In the Kinks' most beautiful song, "The Way Love Used to Be," for some indefensible reason available only on the 1971 *Percy* soundtrack, Ray Davies warbles sadly about two misfits finding each other in the midst of the London crowd, and wandering off to some secret place where they both belong. It's a fantasy he could realize only in music, with the ache of the melody and his gawky, delicate voice underscoring how far out of reach the dream was. Nobody sang about loneliness the way Ray Davies did; a London version of Brian Wilson who'd never seen the beach, he retreated into the beauty he heard in his painfully lavish reveries of the past. The most deeply Brit of all the '60s rockers, he sang about the day-to-day dreams and defeats of ordinary English eccentrics with a tender pathos that barely masked what a creep he could be. The Kinks stuck around so long that they obscured their early achievements a bit, like a great pitcher who doesn't retire until too many years of mop-up relief pushes his career ERA over five. But the Kinks' '60s work, alternately gentle and brutal, still has a strange emotional power.

The Kinks began as the toughest of the British Invasion bands, a North London Mod quartet pitting Davies' whine against his younger, brasher, and better-looking brother Dave's guitar aggression. You could hear how much they hated each other—the Davies brothers would go on to a long history of onstage punch-ups—as they scrapped on top of Mick Avory's amazingly violent drums. Dave practically invented the modern noise-guitar solo in "You Really Got Me," although as with most of the Kinks' innovations, the Who would soon come along behind them and take the lion's share of the credit. *The Kink Kontroversy* has the searing "Till the End of the Day" and "Where Have All the Good Times Gone?"; *Kinda Kinks* has the hopeful ballad "Something Better Beginning" and the more typically downbeat "Nothin' in the World Can Stop Me Worryin' 'Bout That Girl."

The Kinks became more tuneful and reflective with "Set Me Free," "Tired of Waiting for You," "So Long," the seething "I Need You," Dave's plaintive acoustic solo turn "Wait Till the Summer Comes Along," and an early sign of Ray's morbid side, the droning, depressive, and deeply weird 1965 hit "See My Friends." Ray also began to make his name as a social satirist, in hits like "A Well Respected Man" (about the British class system) and "Dedicated Follower of Fashion" (about frilly nylon panties). *BBC Sessions* captures the early Kinks' live power. But the breakthrough came with the 1966 *Face to Face,* one of the great albums of the '60s. Davies refines his obsessions into his own private world, with nostalgic music-hall piano ("Sunny Afternoon"), brooding acoustic ballads ("Fancy," "Rainy Day in June," "Too Much on My Mind"), and swinging London rock ("Most Exclusive Residence for Sale"), as he tells his ruefully witty tales of English losers and outsiders, himself included. "My poor demented mind is slowly going," Davies sings in "Too Much on My Mind," and it's the capper to a relentlessly dark album, even if the finale is the sweet "I'll Remember." The Castle reissue adds a few essential bonus tracks full of urban malaise: "Dead End Street," "I'm Not Like Everybody Else," and "Big Black Smoke."

Something Else went even further, with Davies' gentle compassion for his characters inspiring his loveliest melodies; only Lou Reed has written about city squalor with such an unabashedly romantic eye for beauty. "David Watts" is a peppy curse on childhood, setting up melancholy ballads such as "Afternoon Tea," "End of the Season," and the bossa nova "No Return," as well as Dave's haunting "Death of a Clown" and the harpsichord sibling-rivalry ditty "Two Sisters." (One of the sisters is a swinging socialite, the other a housewife in curlers: Ray, of course, roots for the housewife in curlers.) The climax is "Waterloo Sunset," the ballad of a recluse living near a dreary London train station, watching lovers from his window, making up names and stories for them. "But I don't feel afraid," he sings to himself, with gorgeous guitars and sha-la-la harmonies welling up all around.

The Village Green Preservation Society was Davies' pastoral retreat, with mostly acoustic guitars, high harmonies, and self-consciously quaint small-town sentiments leaving the mad rushing crowds of the city far behind. Song for song, it might be the Kinks' strongest, although Kinks fans will never get sick of arguing over whether that honor goes to *Face to Face* or *Something Else* instead. It has the lonesome regret of "Picture Book" and "People Take Pictures of Each Other," the rustic escapism of "Animal Farm" and "Sitting by the Riverside," the nasty wit of "Starstruck," and the almost mystical resignation of "Big Sky," which transplants "Waterloo Sunset" to an equally unforgiving country locale.

The Kinks then made *Arthur,* an ambitious soundtrack to a British TV drama about a working-class family, a "rock opera" that put the Who's more famous *Tommy* to shame. It doesn't quite hold together, with Davies straining too hard and starting to value his concepts higher than his individual songs, but it does have great moments such as "She Bought a Hat Like Princess Marina," "Young and Innocent Days," and the fantastic rocker "Victoria," his sharpest political song. (It's still the funniest song about Ronald Reagan ever, even if it predated his presidency by over a decade.) The Kinks followed *Arthur* with the 1970 single "Lola," their biggest hit in years and one of their best, a rowdy sing-along about the perverse delights that await runaway farmboys in the dark corners of old Soho. Somehow the BBC censors missed the lines, "I'm not the world's most masculine man / But I know what I am and I'm glad I'm a man / And so is Lola."

The rest of *Lola,* unfortunately, was a tired concept album about the music business. Davies' pomposity and self-pity had begun to strangle his sense of humor, even ruining the pretty ballad "Get Back In Line." The nostalgic *Muswell Hillbillies* was a last gasp. But the Kinks lost their touch in overblown concept jobs such as *Preservation* and *Soap Opera;* now a veteran rock crank, Davies was hard at work thinking thoughts, not an area of expertise for him, as his music went dry and his audience dwindled. Later in the '70s, the Kinks straightened out and had their biggest U.S. success yet as a mainstream arena band, dumbing down for macho hard-rock hits like *Misfits* and *Low Budget.* Davies could still write great songs—"Sleepwalker," "Better Things," "Around the Dial"—but he couldn't even try to hide his contempt for the Americans who were falling for this shit. While the U.K. punk upstarts were taking inspiration from the Kinks' classic period (the Jam had a hit with "David Watts," while the Pretenders did "Stop Your Sobbing") the band itself was lumbering on as an irrelevant dinosaur. The last of their good songs, along with quite a few terrible ones, are on *Give the People What They Want;* "Come Dancing" was a fluke MTV hit in 1983. But by the time the final breakup came, hardly anyone noticed.

Since then, Davies has toured as a solo singer/ songwriter, putting on inspired *Storyteller*-style shows or rocking out with his awful backup band; he and his brother Dave both published books about the rock life. There are many overlapping Kinks anthologies, most focusing on the original '60s hits; *Come Dancing* collects the late U.S. hits, including embarrassing novelties like "A Gallon of Gas" and "Catch Me Now I'm Falling." The briefly available *Great Lost Kinks Album* has essential cult items like "The Way Love Used to Be," "Rosemary Rose," and a shocking satire of British anti-Semitism, "When I Turn Out the Living Room Light." (It is satire, right? But then, one of the things about prime Kinks is that you're never exactly sure enough to feel safe.) *The Village Green Preservation Society* was reissued in 2004 as a three-disc package—one stereo, one mono, and one disc of extras. The best anthology is still the classic *Kink Kronikles,* a 1972 collection of early rockers ("She's Got Everything," "This Is Where I Belong"), hits ("Lola," "Victoria," "Waterloo Sunset"), and weird character studies ("Big Black Smoke," "Mindless Child of Motherhood," "Autumn Almanac"), as well as Dave's greatest song ever, "Susannah's Still Alive." It's a two-disc set that could easily fit on one, if you just prune

away annoyances like "Mr. Pleasant" or "Holiday in Waikiki," but it's still an ideal introduction to the Kinks' world.   —R.S.

Kiss

★★	Kiss (1974; Mercury, 1997)	
★★	Hotter Than Hell (1974; Mercury, 1997)	
★★★	Dressed to Kill (1975; Mercury, 1997)	
★★★★	Alive! (1975; Mercury, 1997)	
★★★½	Destroyer (1976; Mercury, 1997)	
★★★	Rock and Roll Over (1977; Mercury, 1997)	
★★★½	Love Gun (1977; Mercury, 1997)	
★★★½	Alive II (1977; Mercury, 1997)	
★★★★	Double Platinum (1978; Mercury, 1997)	
★	Peter Criss (1978; Mercury, 1997)	
★★½	Gene Simmons (1978; Mercury, 1997)	
★★	Ace Frehley (1978; Mercury, 1997)	
★	Paul Stanley (1978; Mercury, 1997)	
★	Dynasty (1979; Mercury, 1997)	
★	Unmasked (1980; Mercury, 1997)	
★★	Music From "The Elder" (1981; Mercury, 1997)	
★	Creatures of the Night (1982; Mercury, 1997)	
★★	Lick It Up (1983; Mercury, 1998)	
★	Animalize (1984; Mercury, 1998)	
★	Asylum (1985; Mercury, 1998)	
★★	Crazy Nights (1987; Mercury, 1998)	
★★★½	Smashes, Thrashes, and Hits (Mercury, 1988)	
★★	Hot in the Shade (Mercury, 1989)	
★	Revenge (Mercury, 1992)	
★★	Alive III (Mercury, 1993)	
★	MTV Unplugged (Mercury, 1996)	
★★★	You Wanted the Best, You Got the Best (PolyGram, 1996)	
★★★½	Greatest Kiss (Mercury, 1997)	
★	Psycho Circus (Mercury, 1998)	
★★★	The Millennium Collection (Mercury, 2003)	
★★★	The Millennium Collection, Vol. 2 (Mercury, 2004)	

Has there ever been a rock group whose actual studio recordings ever had less to do with anything than Kiss? No way. The Kiss experience was a multimedia spectacle: four costumed characters playing bubble-metal riffs, fireworks, smoke bombs, scary clown makeup, wigs, blood-spitting, fire-breathing, cartoon album covers, a comic book printed in the band's own blood, and the entire Kiss Army chanting the chorus of "Rock 'n' Roll All Nite." Kiss became the hottest band in the world in the '70s by prizing showmanship first—compared to these guys, the Banana Splits were sharecroppers down on the farm, and the Partridges were the Carter Family. Listening to Kiss records has hardly anything to do with the fun of being a Kiss fan, especially since the guys were too tightfisted as businessmen to give away two hooks in the same song, much less put all their catchy songs on one album. But Paul Stanley (the Star Child), Gene Simmons (the Samurai Dragon), Peter Criss (the Cat), and Ace Frehley (the One Who Probably Didn't Save Any of His Money) drove us wild and drove us crazy.

Kiss' early albums are thin, cruddy-sounding hard rock recorded on the cheap, with only occasional lapses into catchiness: You'd be hard pressed to name another band that wrote all its own songs over such a long period of time without ever learning how. But by accident or design, when the men of Kiss hit it right, they really hit it ("Rock 'n' Roll All Nite," "Strutter," "Room Service") and *Alive!* is a nonstop Kiss-krieg of two-note guitar motifs, fake-sounding audience noise, and inspirational chitchat. "I was talking to somebody backstage before," Paul Stanley informs the crowd. "And they were tellin' me there's a lot of you people out there who like to drink vodka and orange juice! Awwww riiiiiight!" *Alive!* is the next best thing to being there, clearly.

Destroyer was the inevitable arty concept album, from the drink-smoke-drive-die saga "Detroit Rock City" to the touching "Do You Love Me" ("You like mah theven-inch . . . high heelth!"). *Rock and Roll Over* offered "Love 'Em and Leave 'Em" and "Calling Dr. Love," while *Love Gun* had Ace's star turn "Shock Me." *Alive II* was the *Bad News Bears in Breaking Training* of '70s metal, a well-made sequel that could not possibly deliver the shock of the original, although it's very impressive how this supposed concert recording of "Beth" features a full orchestra, who must have spent the rest of the show playing cards backstage. Counting down the final minutes until their expiration date, Kiss blew it out in appropriately grandiose style, releasing solo albums by all four members simultaneously. Ace had a hit with the fantastic "New York Groove," but Gene made the best overall album, dribbling blood all over the record-company logo on the label and croaking the Disney ballad "When You Wish Upon a Star."

Strictly speaking, Kiss' classic period was now over. But Gene and Paul continued on a humbler commercial scale, trying disco with *Dynasty,* progging out in the rock opera *Music From "The Elder,"* removing their makeup, periodically reuniting with old buddies, putting the makeup back on for a lucrative and apparently perennial reunion tour in the '90s, doing one of the most pointless *MTV Unplugged* segments imaginable, and in general refusing to get respectable with age. The band's greatest-hits collections have all been

conspicuously incomplete, as if it hates the idea of anyone buying just one Kiss album, but *Double Platinum* is the most solid, though not as much fun as *Alive!* Kiss' '80s hits were utterly undistinctive pop metal that could have been absolutely anyone, despite occasional flourishes like "Reason to Live," "The Street Giveth and the Street Taketh Away," and the long-forgotten 1988 gem "Let's Put the X in Sex," which had a plot Prince would have been proud to call his own. —R.S.

The Klezmatics

★★★½ Rhythm and Jews (Flying Fish, 1993)
★★★★ Jews With Horns (Rounder, 1995)
★★★★ Possessed (Rounder, 1997)

The Klezmatics with Chava Alberstein

★★★ The Well (Rounder, 1998)

Klezmer has always been subject to an almost Talmudic flurry of argument, its form and musical structure beset by an impolite influx of transnational styles. This Yiddish wedding music has also been a paradox, occupying a central space in Jewish communities though performed by traveling musicians, the exiles of an exiled people. And though riotously celebratory in nature, klezmer nonetheless gravitates toward moody minor keys. Brought to the United States at the turn of the century, this "Yiddish jazz" offers a telling counterpoint to the pop integration of Berlin and Gershwin, Jolson and Cantor.

When the klezmer revival hit in the early '80s, the Klezmatics (their name a comic riff off slovenly punk decadents the Plasmatics) were at the forefront. *Rhythm and Jews* is an adequate introduction to the band's high energy dexterity. *Jews With Horns,* however, is a tour de force, alternately giddy and ruminative. David Krakauer's antigravity clarinet flights and Alicia Svigals' passionately sawed violin navigate rhythms that are always quick-pulsed but never hectic. And Lorin Skalberg's tenor is both delicate and surprisingly sturdy, and sometimes soulful.

Possessed delves still deeper into the mix of furious rhythms and traditional themes, especially on "This Undoing World," as mystically secular a hymn to life as you could ask. The lyrics are by playwright Tony Kushner; in fact, the second half of *Possessed* is from the Klezmatics' score to Kushner's *A Dybbuk: Between Two Worlds.* The band's collaboration with Israeli star Alberstein is a similar stylistic stretch, though the results rein in the Klezmatics' liberatory mania for the sake of their more staid guest performer. Still, the band's thirst for collaboration underlines their commitment to klezmer as much more than a novel juxtaposition of old and new sounds. —K.H.

The KLF

★★★½ The History of the JAMS a.k.a. the Timelords
(TVT, 1988)
★★★★ Chill Out (TVT, 1990)
★★★★ The White Room (Arista, 1991)

Between 1987 and 92, music-biz vets Jimmy Caufy and Bill Drummond had enormous critical and commercial success in Britain with their extravagantly catchy and clever technopop, all while snapping at the hand that fed them. First, they released their music under a string of different names—the Justified Ancients of Mu Mu (or the JAMS), then the Timelords, and finally the KLF (or Kopyright Liberation Front)—and then they compounded the confusion with extreme Situationist statements/publicity stunts, including burning a million pounds of their own money, and spraying an unsuspecting awards show audience with blanks from a semiautomatic rifle before announcing their retirement.

Despite that ruckus, the three surviving albums are nothing more or less than succinct and pleasurable exemplars of a bygone era: England in the throes of its acid-house high. *The History of the JAMS a.k.a. the Timelords* compiles cuts from the JAMS' first two English albums, plus a few huge hit singles like the Gary Glitter/*Dr. Who* stomp "Doctorin' the Tardis." Despite the various sources, the tracks are all of a piece, mixing thick Scottish raps, booming club beats, and lengthy samples from famous pop totems (Hendrix, Sly Stone, Whitney Houston). The effect is something like Mike Myers' Fat Bastard imitating the Beastie Boys over a randomly skipping karaoke machine, but it's also redolent of a moment when the possibilities of club music felt boundless. The duo next did an about-face with *Chill Out,* an undulating, ghostly suite of muted synthesizers and dissociated samples—nighttime noises, radio hucksters, Elvis singing "as the snow flies." The JAMS' assault failed to topple the world, but this hermetic move succeeded in helping create a new one, ambient house. *The White Room* marked the duo's return to the dance floor with another remarkably coherent hodgepodge of singles and EP tracks, this time with real rappers and soul singers and a minimum of samples. Finally, the KLF became what they'd mocked with this enduring embrace of Euro-trash club culture. They knew their exit cue.   —F.S.

KMD

★★★½ Black Bastards (SubVerse, 2001)

Until recently, *Black Bastards,* the sophomore album from New York duo KMD, was a lost gem of early-'90s hip-hop. The record was originally slated for release on Elektra in 1994, but rapper Zev Love X's controversial cartoon cover art, which depicted a Sambo character being lynched, got the group dropped from the label. Just completing the album had been a struggle for Zev, since his brother and fellow KMD MC Subroc was killed in a car accident during the making of the record. When it finally emerged on SubVerse in 2001, *Black Bastards* sounded surprisingly upbeat, considering the grim events surrounding its creation. The production is fast and loose; raw drum cracks and jazz samples tumble together with freewheeling ease as Zev and Subroc drop adrenalized rhymes. They touch on everything from the perils of drugs to racist stereotypes, propelling their commentary with sly humor and fearless flows. While the beats move with a swift clip reminiscent of contemporaries like Pete Rock & CL Smooth, they're augmented by spooky metallic clanging ("Gimme"), tinkling keys ("Plumskinzz," "Oh No I Don't Believe It"), and snatches of background chatter ("What a Nigga Know [Remix]"). The group's debut, *Mr. Hood,* is even better, but is still out of print.   —K.M.

The Knack

★★★   Get the Knack (1979; Capitol, 2002)
★★½   . . . But the Little Girls Understand (1980; Capitol, 2002)
★   Round Trip (1981; Capitol, 2002)
★   Serious Fun (1991; Virgin, 2002)
★★★   Proof: The Very Best of the Knack (Rhino, 1998)
★★   Re-Zoom (1998; Zen, 2003)
★★★   Normal as the Next Guy (Smile, 2001)
★★½   Live From the Rock n Roll Fun House (Zen, 2002)

Knack fans will forever contend that their band suffered unduly and irreparably from a critical backlash that followed the group's first album. Less strident lovers of power-pop argue that the group never had much in 'em beyond their mega-hit "My Sharona," and their catalogue bears that out.

Early detractors had a barrel of reasons for hating the Knack: Their lyrics were sexist (though they were mostly just sexual), they copped moves from the Beatles' playbook, they refused to give interviews, and their song was overplayed. But "My Sharona" was a hit for good reason. The beat is urgent, the chorus calls out for drunken shouting along, and the guitar solo is a firecracker flash. Throughout *Get the Knack,* the band winds itself tighter than a hot pair of disco jeans, then does its best to hold on to that energy until it's time to explode.

The title of the second album has less to do with the blues (it comes from Willie Dixon's "The men don't know . . .") than with flipping off critics as out-of-touch geezers. But "Baby Talks Dirty" is cut too much from the same cloth as "Sharona," and the rockabilly licks elsewhere don't do enough to distinguish the disc. The band truly fell flat with the Steely Dan–lite sounds and disco horns of *Round Trip.* For their 1991 resurrection bid, *Serious Fun,* producer Don Was shined up the Knack to sound like a cheesy amalgam of Starship, Boston, and Heart. Sex-obsessed though they are, the band aren't lecherous enough to grow successfully into old-man sleazes à la AC/DC; "Rocket o' Love" is simply embarrassing.

Re-Zoom, a slightly expanded version of the second comeback attempt *Zoom* (1998), features former Missing Persons and Frank Zappa band member Terry Bozzio in the group's oft-vacant drummer slot. While the disc eventually improves, the anti-MTV opener "Pop Is Dead" reveals that 20 years on, the Knack themselves no longer know what the little girls understand. If "Can I Borrow a Kiss" sounds like parody, that's because *The Simpsons* beat the group to the idea by two years with the schlock satire "Can I Borrow a Feeling." With *Normal As the Next Guy,* the Knack get back on the power-pop track with crisp production and smart melodies. *Live From the Rock n Roll Funhouse* is the soundtrack to the DVD of the same name, which depicts the band in 2001 performing their hits on a fictional 1960s-style TV show. *Proof: The Very Best of the Knack* will best serve anyone looking for more than "My Sharona."   —C.N.

Gladys Knight and the Pips

★★★	Letter Full of Tears (Collectables, 1961)
★★★½	Best of: Anthology (Motown, 1974)
★★½	All Our Love (MCA, 1987)
★★★★	Soul Survivors: The Best of Gladys Knight and the Pips, 1973–1988 (Rhino, 1990)
★★★	Neither One of Us (Universal Special Products, 1993)
★★½	Room in Your Heart (Drive Archive, 1995)
★★★	Blue Lights in the Basement (BMG/RCA, 1996)
★★½	Midnight Train to Georgia (BMG Special Products, 1997)
★★★★	The Ultimate Collection (Motown, 1997)
★★½	Live at the Roxy (Sony, 1998)
★★★	Collector's Edition 1 (Platinum Disc, 1999)
★★★	Collector's Edition 2 (Platinum Disc, 1999)
★★★	Collector's Edition 3 (Platinum Disc, 1999)
★★★	Collector's Edition 1–3 (Platinum Disc, 1999)
★★★★	Essential Collection (Hip-O, 1999)

★★½	Every Beat of My Heart (Prestige Elite, 1999)
★★★½	Gladys Knight and the Pips: VH1 Behind the Music Collection (Buddah, 2000)
★★½	Jungle Love (Columbia River, 2000)
★★★★	The Millennium Collection (Motown, 2000)
★★★	Best of Gladys Knight and the Pips (Sony, 2001)

Possessing neither the headstrong genius of Aretha Franklin, the eccentric brilliance of Dionne Warwick, nor the charisma of Diana Ross, Gladys Knight instead has evolved into the most dependable of soul music divas—she's neither a visionary, nor a truly distinctive stylist, nor a megastar, but she delivers consistently. The daughter of two gospel performers, Gladys began singing at age four; while still in her teens she assembled her male backup group, dubbing them the Pips after the nickname of her cousin and manager. Her first single, Johnny Otis' doo-wop "Every Beat of My Heart" (1961), was pleasant enough, but only after Knight signed with Motown in 1966 did the hits begin. And they were tremendous—"Heard It Through the Grapevine," "The Nitty Gritty," "The End of the Road," and "You Need Love Like I Do (Don't You)" carried her into the '70s, establishing her gritty, gospel-derived delivery as one of the strongest in R&B.

In 1973, the Pips signed with the Buddah label and released their strongest album, *Imagination,* featuring the landmark "Midnight Train to Georgia." Soon, however, their style changed; like Diana Ross, Knight embraced AOR. She did so with customary class, but over the next 15 years or so, her truly great albums were infrequent. The Rhino and the Hip-O collections are the most extensive; the Sony set covers only early '80s fare; *The Ultimate Collection* is a strong introduction.   —P.E.

Mark Knopfler

★★½	Local Hero (Warner Bros., 1983)
★★★½	Cal (Mercury, 1984)
★★★	The Princess Bride (Warner Bros., 1987)
★★	Last Exit to Brooklyn (Warner Bros., 1989)
★★★	Screenplaying (Warner Bros., 1993)
★★½	Golden Heart (Warner Bros., 1996)
★★	Wag the Dog (PolyGram, 1998)
★★½	Metroland (Warner Bros., 1999)
★★★	Sailing to Philadelphia (Warner Bros., 2000)
★★½	The Ragpicker's Dream (Warner Bros., 2002)
★★★	A Shot at Glory (Warner Bros., 2002)

Usually, when the main talent from a successful group ditches his old bandmates to go solo, it's because he or she wants to present their musical vision uncorrupted by musical compromise. Mark Knopfler's solo career, by contrast, seems more the work of a man who's made enough money not to have to worry about hits, and so approaches recording the way other people look at gardening. It may be more than a hobby for him, but one has the sense that he wouldn't do it if he didn't enjoy it, and that he's more interested in satisfying himself than any audience.

As such, Dire Straits fans are more likely than not to be disappointed by these albums. There are elements in common, of course. *Local Hero,* for instance, is recorded with Dire Straits alums Alan Clark, John Illsley, and Terry Williams, and at times evokes much the same mood as the quieter bits of *Love Over Gold. Cal* also uses a few Straitsmen in the rhythm section, but pulls more of its color from the Irish folk contributions of Paul Brady and Liam O'Flynn. *The Princess Bride,* assembled with the help of orchestral arranger Guy Fletcher, offers more straight-up movie scoring—lots of suspense-building strings and swashbuckling flourishes, as well as a wonderfully sentimental vocal by Willy DeVille on "Storybook Love." It's fun, and much more satisfying than the empty, mechanical *Last Exit to Brooklyn,* which features some Knopfler guitar but leaves most of the music to Fletcher. (*Screenplaying* draws from the best of these soundtracks.)

Golden Heart, released a year after Knopfler officially disbanded Dire Straits, may open with an Irish traditional flourish, but plays off many of the same tropes as the Straits, from the "Money for Nothing"–ish rhythm guitar that kick-starts "Imelda" to the "Walk of Life"–style shuffle that drives "Don't You Get It." A pleasant album, but hardly as appealing as *Sailing to Philadelphia,* in which Knopfler combines his cinematic flair with his fondness for folk music to create a truly memorable set of story-songs. Nor does it hurt that the album boasts a memorable set of vocal cameos, including James Taylor (on the title tune), Van Morrison ("The Last Laugh"), and Squeeze's Chris Difford and Glenn Tilbrook ("Silvertown Blues").

Knopfler hadn't abandoned movie scoring, of course. *Wag the Dog* is a pleasant mélange of roots rock and country, but clocks in at well under 30 minutes—hardly a bargain. *Metroland* includes a nice sampling of new-wave rockers (Elvis Costello's "Alison," Dire Straits' "The Sultans of Swing") and French pop (tracks by Françoise Hardy and Django Reinhardt), but only a smattering of new Knopfler. But the Scots-inflected *A Shot at Glory* is more like a pop album than a standard soundtrack, and in many ways upstages Knopfler's pleasant but more conventional third album, *Ragpicker's Dream.* —J.D.C.

Kool & the Gang

★★★ Kool & the Gang (1969; Mercury, 1996)
★★★½ Live at the Sex Machine (1971; Mercury, 1999)
★★★ Live at P.J.'s (1971; Mercury, 1999)
★★★ Good Times (1972; Mercury, 1996)
★★★½ Music Is the Message (1972; Mercury, 1996)
★★★½ Wild and Peaceful (1973; Mercury, 1996)
★★★½ Light of Worlds (1974; Mercury, 1996)
★★★½ Spirit of the Boogie (1974; Mercury, 1996)
★★★½ Love & Understanding (1976; Mercury, 1998)
★★ Kool & the Gang Spin Their Top Hits (1978; Mercury, 1990)
★★★ Ladies' Night (1979; Rebound, 1995)
★★★½ Celebrate! (1980; Mercury, 1990)
★★★ Something Special (1981; Mercury, 1990)
★★½ As One (1982; Mercury, 1990)
★★½ In the Heart (1983; Mercury, 1990)
★★½ Emergency (1984; Mercury, 1990)
★★ Forever (Mercury, 1986)
★★★½ Everything's Kool & the Gang (1988; Mercury, 1990)
★★ Sweat (Mercury, 1989)
★★★★ The Best of Kool & the Gang 1969–1976 (Mercury/Chronicles, 1991)
★ Unite (RCA, 1993)
★★★½ Celebration: The Best of Kool & the Gang 1979–1987 (Mercury/Chronicles, 1994)
★★★ State of Affairs (Curb, 1995)
★★★½ Hollywood Swinging (Rebound, 1995)
★★ New York City Kool (Music Deluxe, 1996)
★★★½ Kool Jazz (Mercury, 1997)
★★ Greatest Hits (Mercury, 1998)
★★ All-Time Greatest Hits (Curb, 1998)
★ Greatest Hits Live (Culture Press, 1998; Rhino, 1998)
★ The Great Kool & the Gang Live (Goldies, 1998)
★ Ladies Night: Greatest Hits Live (Cleopatra, 1999)
★★★★ The Very Best of Kool & the Gang (Mercury, 1999)
★★★½ The 12 Inch Collection & More (Mercury, 1999)
★★ The Millennium Collection: The Best of Kool & the Gang (Mercury, 2000)
★ Gangland (Eagle, 2001)
★★ Kool Funk Essentials 1970–1977 (Singular, 2001)
★ Live in Concert (Time, 2002)
★ Live on Stage (Music Deluxe, 2002)
★ Too Hot Live (Brentwood, 2002)

Like the quite similar Earth, Wind & Fire, Kool & the Gang never enjoyed the critical cachet of James Brown or George Clinton but are sampled almost as often by hip-hop DJs and spun just as often by oldies DJs. Maybe Kool & the Gang didn't boast the conceptual innovations or iconoclastic lyrics that impress music writers, but they did have the funky grooves that rappers like and the juicy sing-along hooks that radio fans like.

Jersey City's Bobby Bell was a close friend of Thelonious Monk, so it made sense that his two sons, bassist Robert "Kool" Bell and saxophonist-keyboardist Ronald "Khalis Bayyan" Bell, should become musicians. The brothers recruited neighborhood pals George Brown (drums), Dennis Thomas (alto sax), Robert Mickens (trumpet), Clifford Adams (trombone), Charles Smith (guitar), Ricky West (keyboards), and Woody Sparrow (guitar) to form a soul-jazz band in the style of the Crusaders. They were good enough to back up McCoy Tyner and Pharoah Sanders in local clubs, but audiences preferred the songs where the horn riffs were backed by funky dance grooves. And so the Jazziacs became the Soul Town Band, then the New Dimensions, and finally Kool & the Gang.

They first recorded for the small indie label De-Lite in 1969, featuring their mix of soul-jazz instrumentals and party jams on their studio debut, *Kool & the Gang,* and two subsequent live albums, *Live at the Sex Machine* and *Live at P.J.'s.* They had Top 40 R&B hits right from the start, but it was the 1973 album *Wild and Peaceful* that pushed them into the R&B Top 5 and then the pop Top 10 with three irresistible singles, "Funky Stuff," "Jungle Boogie," and "Hollywood Swinging." This was unabashed party music, full of ensemble chants, bleating whistles, fat bass lines, and sharp horn riffs.

The band continued in that vein on *Light of Worlds, Spirit of the Boogie,* and *Love & Understanding* (the latter is noteworthy for its three impressive live tracks), but 1977–78 was a dry period commercially as the disco era frowned on Kool & the Gang's loose and greasy approach to dance music. Finally the band gave in and hired a true lead singer and an outside producer, as music-biz types had so often advised. Vocalist James "J.T." Taylor (no relation to the pop-folk singer) came aboard in 1977, and producer Eumir Deodato in 1979.

Their first collaboration, "Ladies' Night," topped the R&B charts and hit the pop Top 10. The jazz influence was gone; the funk had been minimized and the disco beat had been accommodated, but the chorus hook was hard to get out of your head. The *Ladies' Night* album included another hit single,

"Too Hot," and the template was set for eight years of hits.

One line in "Ladies' Night" ("Come on, let's all celebrate") inspired Khalis Bayyan to write "Celebration," an anthem so contagious that it not only topped both charts but also became the theme song of the 1980 World Series, the 1981 Super Bowl, the 1981 NBA Championship, and the 1981 return of the Iran hostages. It has been a staple of high school graduations and wedding receptions ever since. The *Celebrate!* album included that single and the like-minded "Take It to the Top."

Deodato also produced *Something Special* and *As One,* which pursued the successful formula with diminishing returns. When Jim Bonnefond became coproducer with the band on *In the Heart* and *Emergency,* the music got softer yet, yielding bland ballad hits such as "Joanna" and "Cherish" and generic dance tracks such as "Fresh" and "Straight Ahead."

Taylor left the group in 1987 to pursue a moderately successful solo career, though he returned to Kool & the Gang for the respectable 1995 comeback album *State of Affairs.* That would be the only listenable Kool & the Gang record recorded after 1987. A live album recorded without Taylor and released under various titles (*Greatest Hits Live, The Great Kool & the Gang Live, Ladies' Night: Greatest Hits Live, Live in Concert, Live on Stage,* and *Too Hot Live*) is mediocre, and *Gangland,* a stab at hip-hop, is embarrassing.

The group's tracks have been divided and sorted into dozens of compilations. The best look at the pre-1979 soul-jazz era is the 16-track *The Best of Kool & the Gang 1969–1976* and the 16-track *Hollywood Swinging. Kool Jazz* focuses on the early tracks that best showcase the band's jazz leanings. The 17-track *Celebration: The Best of Kool & the Gang 1979–1987* best documents the latter period. Both eras are covered on the 21-track, hit-laden *Very Best of Kool & the Gang.* *The 12 Inch Collection & More* and *Everything's Kool & the Gang* both serve up extended club remixes of the dance hits. Budget compilations such as *Kool Funk Essentials, 20th Century Masters—The Millennium Collection, Greatest Hits, All-Time Greatest Hits, Kool & the Gang Spin Their Top Hits,* and *Sweat* offer less than a dozen cuts apiece and should be avoided   —G.H.

Kool G Rap & DJ Polo

★★★½ Road to the Riches (1989; Landspeed, 2001)
★★★★½ Wanted: Dead or Alive (1990; Landspeed, 2001)
★★★★ Live and Let Die (Cold Chillin', 1992)
★★★★ Killer Kuts (Cold Chillin', 1992)
★★★ Rated XXX (Cold Chillin', 1996)

Kool G Rap

★★★ 4, 5, 6 (Cold Chillin'/Epic, 1995)
★★½ Roots of Evil (Illstreet/Downlow, 1998)
★★★ The Giancana Story (Rawkus/Koch, 2002)

Before Kool G Rap, New York didn't really have the street rap that could hold its own against what artists such as L.A.'s Ice-T and N.W.A were churning out. Sure, Run-D.M.C. could get tough, and in the mid-to-late '80s a new generation of rappers, led by Rakim, was beginning to explore this territory. G Rap, though, excelled at the street narrative, a style that would come to define later Queens MCs like Nas (who was hugely influenced by G Rap on his early records) and Mobb Deep. G Rap was also known for his voice: a distinctive, menacing slur that conveyed world-weariness as much as it did impending terror.

Paired with DJ Polo, G Rap's first album, *Road to the Riches,* was a product of its time: compared to G Rap's later work, it's almost a lighthearted affair. The title track brimmed with jook-joint piano, and "Truly Yours" hinged on a spry horn loop later used by Nas. For the most part, G Rap focused on the intricacies of rhyming, and it was only on his second album with Polo, *Wanted: Dead or Alive,* that his storytelling skill truly came to the fore. There was the requisite politically conscious track ("Erase Racism") bumping up against one of hip-hop's erotic classics ("Talk Like Sex"), as well as a cautionary tale to young hustlers in the making ("Rikers Island"). But *Wanted*'s masterpiece is "Streets of New York," a vivid look inside the misery of the hood: "Upstairs, I cover my ears and tears/The man downstairs must've drank too many beers/Because every day of his life, he beats his wife/'Til one night, he decides to pull a butcher knife" (a line chillingly revisited a decade later by New York indie-rap pioneers Company Flow on the domestic-violence tale "Last Good Sleep"). Their third album, *Live and Let Die,* continued G Rap's reign as rap music's premier yarn-spinner, thanks to morose classics like the title track and "Ill Street Blues."

As a solo artist, G Rap never achieved the same heights as he did on these albums, not because of the absence of DJ Polo, but because younger artists such as Notorious B.I.G., Nas, and Ghostface Killah took his street-narrative style to new heights of sophistication. The man himself wasn't able to change with the music, but his template remains. —J.C.

Kool Keith

★★★★ Dr. Octagon/Dr. Octagonecologyst
(DreamWorks, 1997)
★★★½ Sex Style (Funky Ass, 1997)
★★★½ Black Elvis/Lost in Space (Ruffhouse, 1999)

★★★½ First Come, First Served (Funky Ass, 1999)
★★½ Matthew (Funky Ass, 2000)
★★★½ Robbie Analog (Funky Ass, 2000)
★★★½ Analog Brothers Pimp to Eat (Ground
Control, 2000)
★★★½ Spankmaster (TVT, 2001)
★★ Game (Number 6, 2002)
★★ Lost Masters (Dmaft, 2003)
★★★½ Presents Thee Undatakerz (Activate, 2004)

One of indie rap's most prolific and profoundly bugged-out artists, Kool Keith puts out albums with uncommercial, pointedly abstract original music with no samples, almost always creating an entirely new persona for himself from disc to disc. The MC born Keith Thornton came up as part of the Bronx crew Ultramagnetic MC's, the oddball star of their 1988 cult classic *Critical Beatdown.* He appeared on the cover of that album wearing a Budweiser painter's cap sideways while claiming "I swarm around with a thousand bees/Absorb earth and the honey from trees."

After some rocky years during which Keith spent time institutionalized in New York's Bellevue psychiatric hospital and the Ultramagnetic MC's released their excellent, but commercially unsuccessful second album, 1993's *The Four Horsemen,* Keith released his first notable solo single, "Earth People," in 1995, recorded under the name Dr. Octagon. Released by San Francisco–based Bulk Recordings, the record sent shock waves through the hip-hop independent-label underground, setting the stage for the *Dr. Octagonecologyst* album, a slab of mondo bizzaro brilliance. With Dan the Automator making beats and DJ Q-Bert's sick scratching, *Dr. Octagon* was totally unlike anything else and totally right, sending kids, heads, and critics around dazed singing *Twilight Zone*–like tracks "Blue Flowers" and "Halfsharkalligotarhalfman," which drew equally from pulp science fiction and the darker reaches of Keith's noggin. He quickly followed with *Sex Style,* posing lasciviously on the cover in tight pink underwear. Kool Keith's other main mode is dissing other rappers and the record industry. *Robbie Analog* was an entire album swiping at the RZA's Bobby Digital identity; Kool Keith has also taken down OutKast's Andre 3000 for wearing wigs long after Keith went around wearing a rubber Elvis wig for all of 1999. As Keith succinctly put it: "Rappers take it personal/you're wack."

On *First Come, First Served* Keith dished up "hamburgers infested with mice" and delivers the battle track "You Live at Home With Your Mom." In 1998 Keith teamed up with Tim Dogg as Ultra for the My Turn Records 12-inch "The Industry Is Wack." The uncompromising hardcore classic finds Keith claiming he "can't trust Little Richard—Little Bitchard" and utilizes enjambment rhyme on the line "girls today slept with Rock Hudson/the NBA, your favorite ballplayer turned gay." Under the guise of Dr. Doom, Keith even "killed off" the popular Dr. Octagon on record. Notably, Keith teamed up with Ice-T as the Analog Brothers for *Pimp to Eat* with "Bionic Oldsmobile" and "Permsbaldheadsafrosdreads," making the album another must of odd excellence. *Thee Undatakerz* features morgue stories from Keith's new persona Reverand [*sic*] Tom. Also worth hearing is Keith's freestyle insect rap on Jurassic 5's *Power in Numbers*— as usual, Keith is dangerously ill. —P.R.

Kool Moe Dee

★★★½ Kool Moe Dee (Jive, 1987)
★★★★ How Ya Like Me Now (Jive, 1987)
★★★½ Knowledge Is King (Jive, 1989)
★★★ Funke, Funke Wisdom (Jive, 1991)
★★★½ Greatest Hits (Jive, 1993)
★★½ Interlude (Wrap, 1994)
★★★★ The Jive Collection, Vol. 2 (Jive, 1995)

When Kool Moe Dee released his self-titled debut album in early 1987, he benefited from something few popular rappers of the day could claim: experience. The Harlem native had been making crisp, danceable rap records with the now-legendary Treacherous Three since the late '70s, and with *Kool Moe Dee* he caught up with gritty, hard-rocking contemporary hip-hop without smudging his silky white sweats. The breakthrough was "Go See the Doctor," a safe-sex PSA driven home by Moe Dee's wonderfully ribald humor and a young Teddy Riley's irresistible electro-funk production. If Boogie Down Productions' KRS-One was the new school's "Teacher," then "Go See the Doctor" suggested Moe Dee was the school's dapper, charismatic principal, a senior role model who could joke with the boys and flirt with the girls yet still crack the whip.

The rest of *Kool Moe Dee* whips it good, too. With its balance of bawdy braggadocio and pointed parables, the album deserves a place alongside that seminal year's most celebrated hip-hop albums, including Boogie Down Production's *Criminal Minded* and Moe Dee's own amazing followup, *How Ya Like Me Now*. Despite the rushed turnaround, Moe Dee's second album is so confident that it even includes a report card rating the competition. The music is fuller and the raps more urgent than on the debut, too, perhaps inspired by the performer's infamous feud with L.L. Cool J, the target of the slamming title track. If so, Moe Dee also proves he can rise above with his tough, funny look at street beefs, "Wild, Wild West."

Two long years later, however, Moe Dee dropped his heady combination of hardness and humor with *Knowledge Is King,* a disc in which the rapper became just another quality entertainer promising nothing more or less than "I Go to Work." Even so, the album hits hard thanks to the political consciousness that suffused hip-hop in 1989, and thanks to the peak skills of producer Teddy Riley, who by now was a New Jack star in his own right. Moe Dee's work ethic is also evident on his last original album for a major label, *Funke, Funke Wisdom.* But although the disc is musically varied and spiked with clever rhymes, titles like "Here We Go Again" suggest how tired some themes had gotten. *Interlude* is a wishful thought more than a description, as Moe Dee fumbles through various experiments searching for a viable new style in the gangsta-riddled mid-'90s.

In the end, the only "interlude" Moe Dee's last album provided was between his two Jive anthologies. *Greatest Hits* has more cuts, all 15 of them sensibly if predictably selected. *The Jive Collection, Vol. 2* shares nine titles with *Greatest Hits,* but it has chronological sequencing, slightly nicer packaging, and three fine selections not on *Hits,* including "Knowledge Is King," which sums up his message in three sharp words. —F.S.

Korn

★★ Korn (Immortal/Epic, 1994)
★★ Life Is Peachy (Immortal/Epic, 1996)
★★★ Follow the Leader (Immortal/Epic, 1998)
★★½ Issues (Immortal/Epic, 1999)
★★★ Untouchables (Immortal/Epic, 2002)
★★★½ Take a Look in the Mirror (Immortal/Epic, 2003)

In the old DC comic book *The New Gods,* the villain Darkseid was constantly looking for an all-powerful, universe-dominating formula called the Anti-Life Equation. Korn seems to have found it. Mind you, it was impossible to tell back in '94 that these five deeply alienated weirdos from Bakersfield, CA, had stumbled upon one of the most influential hard rock sounds of the next 10 years, but, well, here we are.

Drawing on the will-to-power fury of death-metal and hip-hop dynamics, Korn was one of the very first bands to be termed "new metal," isolating a defiantly ugly brew of chunky, downtuned guitars, clicking bass, and wheezing/screaming vocals. It was as if someone had taken the muffled sound of gangsta rap coming from a moving car and set it to six-string riffs. Add to this the band's status as spokesmodel for the '90s latchkey nation. Busted stuffed animals, distressed cartoon youth heading over a cliff lemming-style or looking zombified, playgrounds with predatory shadows: It was all right there on the album covers.

All of these elements are present in its 1994 debut, and the band hasn't strayed too far from this sonic formula. The music favors shrill riffs that expand into chunks and sickening drones, an incessantly clicking bass, and rudimentary drumming. Jonathan Davis is a new kind of metal hero: He plays the bagpipes, calls himself a "faget," and generally finds pain, horror, and fear pretty much everywhere he looks. Don't mistake the self-loathing for a lack of power: There's a focused, undeniable rage in "Blind," "Clown," and (of course) "Daddy." The martial beats of "Shoots and Ladders" and Davis' nursery rhyme mumble pack a rough wallop. Korn is determined to violate you the way they've been violated.

Life Is Peachy is more of the same, a little darker, a little funnier in spots. "A.D.I.D.A.S." unpacks a hip-hop fetish with aplomb, and there's a cover of Ice Cube's "Wicked." *Peachy* zipped up the charts a little faster. But the thing feels slight and tossed off. Korn had clearly hit a nerve, but wasn't entirely sure how to hit it again. *Follow the Leader* was the first album that lots of critics took seriously. Complete with the smash single "Freak on a Leash," *Follow* sports guest spots by Ice Cube on "Children of the Korn," and Limp Bizkit's Fred Durst on the insult fest "All in the Family." The music still squealed and bumped, screamed and crawled, and Davis' voice began to amplify the preverbal squeaks and clicks that made him sound like an H. R. Giger insect with dreads.

Prior to the release of *Issues,* Korn solicited entries from the public for an album cover; the most well known is the brilliantly aesthetic-defining busted stuffed animal painting. *Issues* continues the boiling over, but oddly, this is both the first album that lets the drums breathe a little, and the first with little or no hip-hop overtones. And like *Life Is Peachy, Issues* has something of a placeholder feel. No new ground broken, or even attempted, just more filth from Davis' spleen.

Produced by Michael Beinhorn, *Untouchables* cost a reported $4 million to create, and all that money went to making a record that pretty much sounds like all their others, just a tad more brutal, a tad more refined and detailed, a tad more more. It's really past time for these guys to evolve just a bit, to move past what were apparently pretty horrible childhoods, to create some art that at least tries to do a little more than force you to feel their pain.

Well, they gave it a shot, anyway. As the new-metal kingdom was being overrun by the likes of Jack White, the Hives, and Beyoncé, Korn reemerged in 2003 with *Take a Look in the Mirror,* the band's least whiny

album to date. The music moved around a bit, from groove monoliths to something a little rougher and a little gnarlier. The video for "Ya'll Want a Single" even gets political, featuring Davis and the boys smashing a record store to pieces and flashing comments such as "only 4 songs are added to the average radio 'playlist' each week" and "hit songs on Top 40 are often repeated over 100 times per week." And who said Korn had issues?   —J.G.

Kraftwerk

★★★½   Autobahn (1974; Astralwerks, 2004)
   ★★   Radio-Activity (1975; Astralwerks, 2004)
★★★★★   Trans-Europe Express (1977; Astralwerks, 2004)
 ★★★★   The Man-Machine (1978; Astralwerks, 2004)
  ★★★   Computer World (1981; Elektra, 1988)
   ★★   Electric Cafe (EMI, 1986)
  ★★★   The Mix (Elektra, 1991)
 ★★½   Expo Remix (Astralwerks, 2001)
  ★★★   Tour de France Soundtracks (Astralwerks, 2003)

When Ralf Hütter and Florian Schneider formed Kraftwerk in 1970 in Düsseldorf, Germany, the concept of an all-electronic pop band was still revolutionary. Since then Kraftwerk's mechanistic minimalism has gone on to shape the course of dance music, rock, modern classical, and hip-hop (most notably, the melodic roots of Afrika Bambaataa's landmark 1982 single "Planet Rock" lie in the title track of *Trans-Europe Express*). Indeed, anyone who uses a drum machine owes Hütter and Schneider big-time.

Autobahn is actually the fourth Kraftwerk album; its three remarkable predecessors, *Kraftwerk 1, Kraftwerk 2,* and *Ralf and Florian,* are currently out of print. But it was the first to capture the attention of American listeners, thanks to its hypnotic title song, on which sighing synth winds rise and fall around a chanted robot refrain, enveloping your senses like an eventless five-hour trip on the expressway. *Radio-Activity* emits a wide range of analog groans and cross-wired giggles that dissolve into the atmosphere without leaving much of an impression. *Trans-Europe Express* and *The Man-Machine* spice the mechanical lull with genuine melodies, sly humor, and a firmer rhythmic pulse.

Subsequent releases saw Kraftwerk fading from the vanguard almost as quickly and silently as it had entered. On *Computer World* and (especially) *Electric Cafe,* the group stops weaving repetitious spells and starts merely to repeat itself. Appropriately enough, *The Mix* juggles and jumbles some of its best-known "numbers" into nearly unrecognizable (though not unlistenable) forms. After more than a decade in retirement, Kraftwerk returned to action with "Expo 2000," written for the event of the same name, followed by a collection of remixes of that song. Its first full album in over 15 years, *Tour de France Soundtracks,* was a sequel of sorts to its 1983 single "Tour de France." While the new tunes are pleasant enough, the overwhelming influence this band has had on nearly everyone becomes a negative here. Simply put, the future that Kraftwerk forecasted in the '70s has arrived, which means that nowadays nobody needs to hear another artist that sounds like Kraftwerk—even if that artist is the real McCoy.   —M.C./M.R.

Alison Krauss

★★★	Too Late to Cry (Rounder, 1987)	
★★★½	Two Highways (Rounder, 1989)	
★★★½	I've Got That Old Feeling (Rounder, 1990)	
★★★½	Every Time You Say Goodbye (Rounder, 1992)	
★★★	I Know Who Holds Tomorrow (Rounder, 1994)	
★★★★	Now That I've Found You: A Collection (Rounder, 1995)	
★★★★	So Long So Wrong (Rounder, 1997)	
★★	Forget About It (Rounder, 1999)	
★★★	New Favorite (Rounder, 2001)	
★★★★	Live (Rounder, 2002)	

The rise of Alison Krauss both presaged and shadowed the most significant country music trend of the '90s: the explosion in the earning power of female talent. Of course, Krauss didn't pull a Shania by morphing country hooks into slick radio pop. Krauss was right at the forefront of the explosion's most adult wing, a violin prodigy from the Midwest who signed with Rounder Records at age 14 and became the best-selling bluegrass musician of all time. And all that was before the million-selling soundtrack to *O Brother, Where Art Thou?,* on which Krauss plays a prominent role, ignited a country/bluegrass/"old-time" music boomlet that proved that the elusive adult audience could be convinced to buy an album in the multimillions.

Krauss has kept a patina of unvarnished authenticity throughout her career; she managed to avoid overslick sounds in favor of bluegrass-indebted purity. *Too Late to Cry* is a solid debut, full of sharp, nuanced fiddling, sprightly tunes, and Krauss' lilting voice; not bad for a 16-year-old. *Two Highways* (1989) was Krauss' first album with Union Station, the backing band that has accompanied Krauss for the balance of her career. It's her purest bluegrass effort, a dynamic collection of traditional tunes ("Wild Bill Jones," "Beaumont Rag") and bassist Joe Pennell's trad-yet-contemporary-sounding tunes ("Here Comes

Goodbye"). *I've Got That Old Feeling* (1990) marked the beginning of Krauss' rise to the top of the neo-trad heap, blending her angelic voice, technical fiddle savvy, and "new grass" structures with soft country, folk, and pop styles, snagging a Grammy in the process. *Every Time You Say Goodbye* is another excellent bluegrass collection, this time incorporating Ron Block's brilliant banjo playing. *I Know Who Holds Tomorrow* is a solid gospel collaboration with the Cox family.

The dam pretty much burst with the release of the million-selling *Now That I've Found You: A Collection,* an excellent retrospective that highlighted both her stellar playing and her exceptionally beautiful voice. Purists had likely lost interest at this point, but Krauss was now a bona fide adult pop star. *So Long So Wrong* feels like a new beginning for the Krauss/Union Station juggernaut (and by now, it *was* a juggernaut). Krauss' voice has never sounded better, guitarist Dan Tyminski's everyguy tenor takes a lead vocal on a couple of numbers, and the band basically sticks to their patented blend of new grass, adult folk, and country.

Krauss slipped a bit on *Forget About It,* turning in a somewhat generic-sounding solo album of adult pop. It's not a terrible album—her voice is still an instrument of deep and lasting beauty—just a slightly dull one, sounding much like any other adult-oriented modern country star, with little of the Union Station fire or skill. Then in 2000, Krauss exploded again as one of the main voices behind the neo-old-timey soundtrack to the Coen brothers' *O Brother, Where Art Thou?* She and Union Station even scored a hit single with a zippy cover of "Man of Constant Sorrow" with Dan Tyminski singing for George Clooney's character in the film.

Krauss again seemed like the head of the authenticity class, even though that year's *New Favorite* was easily the group's slickest effort, relying as much on folky singer/songwriter fare as new grass style. Tyminski's voice is by now as important—and possibly as recognized—as Krauss', and his cuts ("Momma Cried," "The Boy Who Wouldn't Hoe Corn") are just as crucial to the album's vibe. *Live* is an excellent double-CD collection with material spanning her career. Krauss fanatics may blanch at, say, Ron Block's solo tune ("Faraway Land") or the instrumentals, but those just prove this is a band (nothing screams authenticity like a little humility). Some find her a savior, some find her a little dull, mostly she falls right in between; but one thing is certain: Alison Krauss bent a genre to fit her needs, and yanked it back into the public eye in the process. Not many artists in any field can say as much.   —J.G.

Lenny Kravitz

- ★★★½   Let Love Rule (Virgin, 1989)
- ★★★★   Mama Said (Virgin, 1991)
- ★★★   Are You Gonna Go My Way (Virgin, 1993)
- ★★½   Circus (Virgin, 1995)
- ★★   5 (Virgin, 1998)
- ★★★   Greatest Hits (Virgin, 2000)
- ★★½   Lenny (Virgin, 2001)
- ★★★½   Baptism (Virgin, 2004)

Lenny Kravitz is a fanatic, an obsessive student of all things classic rock, soul, funk, and psychedelic. He is the peace-and-love candidate for superstardom, the black hippie Jew with tattoos and dreads and an insatiable jones for Jimi, Sly, and the Beatles. That is how Kravitz first emerged at the end of the '80s, oblivious to hair metal and gangsta, embracing the feel-good soundtrack of his childhood with naïveté and feeling, not merely nostalgia for the Age of Aquarius. And he's faced criticism ever since for appropriating only the finest sounds of the period and for dressing the part in epic rock-star threads, all bell-bottoms and feather boas. He is not groundbreaking. But his early albums at least sound in retrospect like a man tapping genuine emotion, using ancient pop styles as a setting for revealing messages on love and faith that rarely sound secondhand. As later recordings drift into a sound more identifiably his own, the result has mostly been slick, manufactured, and cold. The paradox of Lenny Kravitz is that his most derivative music is also his most personal.

On *Let Love Rule,* he plays virtually everything himself (guitars, bass, organ, drums, etc.). The sound is raw and largely acoustic, just beats, bass lines, and Hammond B-3's, like a collision of Sly Stone and solo Lennon. As a lyricist, he's best served when focused on the personal, and much less so as a rock & roll messiah. He is a flower child in a computer age, singing praises for his wife and daughter ("I Build This Garden for Us") and fighting curbside racism on the anxious "Mr. Cab Driver." *Mama Said* is already a step up in sophistication. "Fields of Joy" opens with light and loving acoustic guitar as Kravitz sings at his most falsetto. He is less of a one-man band, even as he expands his chops as a writer, arranger, and ringmaster. The sticky funk of "Always on the Run" mingles horns with Slash doing Joe Perry on guitar, and Kravitz sheds real tears of commitment and regret on the soulful "Stand by My Woman" and amid breezy Al Green strings of "It Ain't Over 'til It's Over." *Are You Gonna Go My Way* introduces new permanent sideman Craig Ross on lead guitar, unleashing his inner Jimmy Page in time for the Zep textures and Sly Stone preaching ("Being free is a state of mind!") of "Believe." As al-

ways, Kravitz is careful not to sound any slicker than Stevie Wonder circa 1972, even using vintage tape in the studio. The goal isn't lo-fi but high concept, as if the limitation of period technology is as crucial an instrument as his guitar. But the songwriting is slipping on *Circus,* even as he cranks up the guitars and declares that "Rock and Roll Is Dead," making a point that isn't exactly clear ("You can't even sing or play an instrument/So you just scream instead").

With *5,* Kravitz seems to surrender to his critics and resorts to digital technology and computerized sounds, straying deep into other styles, announcing that he's "getting straight in '98, y'all!" But he's no Bowie chameleon. "Black Velveteeen" sounds like a Depeche Mode outtake circa 1988, with cheeseball effects and beats. Kravitz is still a decade behind. He can sometimes hook into a moment of real emotion, but that's less and less often, as if without his core influences, he's lost. The silky soul of "I Belong to You" is as moving and elegant as anything he's done, with a bit of romantic desperation in his voice. A ham-fisted remake of the Guess Who's "American Woman" was a crossover hit, but *5* is his most forgettable album. *Lenny* is a slight improvement, while admitting on "Stillness of Heart" that "the things that were so sweet no longer move my feet/But I keep trying." He goes metal sludge on "Battlefield of Love," as the true funk finally slips away. *Baptism* is where Kravitz finally comes up with a modern sound that reflects his obsession with the rock & roll past without sounding stuck there. Lyrics remain dubious and overblown ("I am a minister of rock & roll/I can heal you, I can save your soul!") whenever he steps away from issues romantic or personal. And yet it is his best album in a decade, riffing easily like a Kiss wanna-be amid pop and handclaps on "California" and the glam funk of "Lady." The agitated "I Don't Want to Be a Star" rocks harder even as he denies his own fabulous lifestyle of limos, furs, and anonymous fashion models: "Just want my Chevy and an old guitar." Right. But this time, the illusion sticks. Kravitz finally sounds like no one but himself.   —S.A.

Kris Kross

- ★★★½   Totally Krossed Out (Ruffhouse/Columbia, 1992)
- ★★★   Da Bomb (Ruffhouse/Columbia, 1993)
- ★★   Young, Rich, and Dangerous (Ruffhouse/Columbia, 1996)

That backward-pants style never bum-rushed the fashion industry, and their expiration date as stars was as inevitable as the descent of their testicles. But Kris Kross did instigate a strange copycat phenomenon, which occurred once before in 1984 and let's hope will at some point in the aughts: A great hit single called "Jump" spontaneously generates another great hit single with *jump* in the title. House of Pain's "Jump Around" isn't quite the Pointer Sisters' "Jump (For My Love)." But if you don't think Jermaine Dupri's high-energy mauling of the Jackson 5's "I Want You Back" belongs on the same jukebox with Van Halen, then you could get the finger. The middle.

The Atlanta duo's actual followup to "Jump" was "Warm It Up," which echoes "Jump" as surely and delightfully as the Jackson 5's "ABC" does "I Want You Back." Far from a hits-plus-filler package, though, *Totally Krossed Out* was so much fun you might not realize how cleverly Dupri streamlined Public Enemy's wail-and-screech for your car radio. This music is accommodating without being compromising, and the Chrisses—Smith and Kelly—are precocious enough to sneak into a club underage on "Party," average enough to lament "I Missed the Bus."

Da Bomb proved that not every kid rap star grows up to be Will Smith, but at least Mack Daddy and the Daddy Mack avoided the oversexualized panting of tykes like Bow Wow and Lil' Romeo. The "dangerous" in the title of their 1996 disc supposedly indicates they know how to use their minds and pose a threat to the powers that be. Unfortunately, the album's tepid G-funk brings to mind the adage "A little knowledge is a dangerous thing." The "Lil Boyz in the Hood" who were haunted by the adult violence they encountered back in 1992 were now toting gats themselves. And that really is whickety-whickety-whickety-wack. —K.H.

KRS-One

see BOOGIE DOWN PRODUCTIONS

Kruder & Dorfmeister

★★★ G-Stoned EP (G-Stone/Island, 1993)
★★ Conversions: A K&D Selection (Shadow, 1996; 1999)
★★★★ DJ Kicks (Stud!o K7, 1996)
★★★ The K&D Sessions (Stud!o K7, 1998)

Despite their minimal output, Austrians Peter Kruder and Richard Dorfmeister cast a long shadow. Indeed, they're accountable for a thousand chill-out compilations that would follow in their wake, and their music (or the countless imitations thereof) would become a staple in clothing boutiques and coffee shops the world over. On their one available release of original material, the EP *G-Stoned*, they successfully crossbreed downbeat, ambient, trip-hop, dub, and mid-tempo electronic music to arrive at their signature sound: cinematic and spliffed-out with gently pulsing breakbeats, minimalist keyboards, and the occasional vocal sample.

Their subsequent studio work would revolve largely around remixing. On the landmark two-disc collection *The K&D Sessions,* the pair rework and effectively bliss-out tunes by everyone from Depeche Mode and Bomb the Bass to Bone Thugs-N-Harmony. *DJ Kicks* shows why their DJ sets frequently draw big crowds. It's a superb mix by the duo that picks up the tempo a bit by mixing smoothed-out versions of house to drum-and-bass tracks alongside the regular chill-out fare. Less interesting is the shorter DJ set *Conversions.* The only original material to be heard from the two since has been via their respective side-projects, Dorfmeister's Tosca and Kruder's Peace Orchestra. —D.S.

Fela Anikulapo Kuti

★★★½ Koola Lobitos/The '69 L.A. Sessions (1964–69; MCA, 2001)
★★★★ Shakara/London Scene (1970–71; MCA, 2000)
★★★½ Fela With Ginger Baker Live: The Africa 70 (1971–78; MCA, 2001)
★★★½ Open & Close/Afrodisiac (1971–73; MCA, 2001)
★★★★ Roforofo Fight/The Fela Singles (1972–73; MCA, 2001)
★★★★ Confusion/Gentlemen (1973–74; MCA, 2000)
★★★½ Expensive Shit/He Miss Road (1975; MCA, 2000)
★★★★ Monkey Banana/Excuse O (1975; MCA, 2001)
★★★½ Everything Scatter/Noise for Vendor Mouth (1975; MCA, 2001)
★★★★ Yellow Fever/Na Poi (1975–76; MCA, 2000)
★★★★ Ikoyi Blindness/Kalakuta Show (1976; MCA, 2001)
★★★★ J.J.D./Unnecessary Begging (1976; MCA, 2001)
★★★★ Zombie (1976–78; MCA, 2001)
★★★½ Upside Down/Music of Many Colours (1976–80; MCA, 2001)
★★★ Stalemate/Fear Not for Man (1977; MCA, 2000)
★★★★ Opposite People/Sorrow Tears and Blood (1977; MCA, 2000)
★★★★ Shuffering and Shmiling/No Agreement (1977–78; MCA, 2000)
★★★ V.I.P./Authority Stealing (1979–80; MCA, 2000)
★★★★ Coffin for Head of State/Unknown Soldier (1979–81; MCA, 2000)
★★★★½ Original Sufferhead/I.T.T. (1980–81; MCA, 2000)

★★★½ Live in Amsterdam (1985; MCA, 2001)
★★★ Army Arrangement (1985; MCA, 2001)
★★★ Teacher Don't Teach Me Nonsense (1986; MCA, 2001)
★★★½ Beasts of No Nation/ODOO (1989–90; MCA, 2001)
★★★½ Underground System (1990–92; MCA, 2001)
★★★★★ The Best Best of Fela Kuti (MCA, 1999)

The man who would become the father of afro-beat was born into the Yoruba tribe in southwest Nigeria, where his father, like his grandfather, was a protestant minister, and his mother was a prominent feminist political activist. Against his father's wishes, Fela sang in highlife bands at age 16. During the '60s he studied music in London, where he formed a highlife band called the Koola Lobitos. In 1969 he spent a year in the U.S., where he linked up with the Black Panthers and others, broadening and radicalizing his political sense, which embraced Kwame Nkrumah's pan-Africanism.

His early work is sampled in *Koola Lobitos/The '69 L.A. Sessions,* where the early cuts sound like an odd mix of Trinidadian calypso with highlife rhythms, but the 1969 sessions unveil the unique musical and political conception that Fela called afro-beat. Rhythmically simple by West African norms, sung in English to broaden the audience, spiced with jazz and funk licks, afro-beat was a musical platform for political activism. In "Viva Nigeria," Fela ends with a message: "Brothers and sisters in Africa/never should we learn to wage war against each other/let Nigeria be a lesson to all."

Nigeria was full of lessons. At the time, it was just coming out of a civil war which had killed over a million people, mostly by starvation. For more than two decades Fela chronicled, heckled, stirred up this turmoil. His band was huge, putting as many as 80 on stage; they lived together, with Fela marrying many of his singers. Fela further challenged the Nigerian establishment by building a fence around his compound and declaring it the independent Kalakuta Republic. The Nigerian authorities, in turn, repeatedly harrassed, arrested, beat, and tortured Fela, at one point sending a thousand soldiers to burn Kalakuta to the ground.

While this oppression eventually took its toll, it worked mostly as fodder for Fela's songs, which early on tended to be sarcastic attacks on neocolonial manners and the incompetence of the officials. Fela's attacks became increasingly strident, as he vehemently decried the military ("Zombie") and corruption. In the end, Fela's last record, *Underground System,* was as unflinching as "Viva Nigeria" was hopeful. He claimed that artists were the true leaders of society, and he lived with the consequences of that conviction.

Fela recorded over 50 albums, which have been heroically remastered and released on 25 CDs, as comprehensive a picture of a major artist as any, and especially unusual for African music. Typically, one CD combines two LPs, where the original LPs typically had one long song per side, or occasionally a song would be split into two parts, one for each LP side. The songs themselves are structured uniformly: A typical song starts out with a drums and bass rhythm, adding funky guitar and keyboard figures that could go on for several minutes, then the horns come in to develop a melody; maybe there's a sax solo, and more horns; then anywhere from 5 to 10 minutes into the piece Fela comes in with short lines often in a patois of English and Yoruba answered by a female chorus. Sometimes the horns cut in sooner, sometimes the keyboard leads off, but it's all pretty much the same.

As popular music goes, Fela's songs are long, but if you've ever sat through evangelical church services, his sermons seem rather concise: He calls the parish together, sets the mood and tone, and delivers his message, smartly orchestrated with his choir. The best of these albums are the ones where the music kicks in hardest, like *Roforofo Fight, Excuse O, Kalakuta Show, Zombie,* and especially *Original Sufferhead/I.T.T.,* with three powerful pieces that never flag over an hour.

The Best Best of Fela Kuti, with 13 signature pieces on two CDs, is a marvelous overview for Fela neophytes. But in order to hold the cuts to an average of 12 minutes, most appear only as "Part 2" or have otherwise been edited. The only problem here is that shorter isn't necessarily better with Fela. While his politics may have been urgent, Fela's Africanism liked to stretch out and enjoy itself. —T.H.

Talib Kweli

★★★★ Reflection Eternal (Rawkus, 2000)
★★★★ Quality (Rawkus, 2002)

Until he released his first solo album, wordy Brooklyn MC Talib Kweli ran the risk of being remembered only as the less naturally charismatic half of Black Star. Paired with the perpetually grinning Mos Def, Talib could seem dour, even though he was responsible for most of the group's wisdom. On his own, though, he shone far brighter than anyone expected. His first album, a full-length collaboration with producer Hi-Tek, was thick with fierce street raps ("Down for the Count" and "Ghetto Afterlife"), maudlin soul ("Love Language"), and the type of insightful versifying Kweli has made his stock-in-trade ("Memories

Live" and "This Means You"). His second album, made without Hi-Tek, continued Kweli's quest to penetrate the mainstream while remaining true to his highbrow lyricism. "Guerilla Monsoon Rap" (which also features Pharoahe Monch and the Roots' Black Thought) is battle-rhyming at its finest, but tracks such as "Get By" and "Where Do We Go" supplant Kweli's tart tongue with heavy doses of vintage soul. It was a combination that made his medicine go down so much more easily. —J.C.

Kyuss

★★½	Wretch (Dali, 1991)
★★★★	Blues for the Red Sun (Dali/Elektra, 1992)
★★★	Kyuss (Chameleon/Elektra, 1994)
★★½	. . . And the Circus Leaves Town (Elektra, 1995)
★★	Muchas Gracias: The Best of Kyuss (Elektra, 2000)

A bunch of metal-worshiping whippersnappers from the California desert, Kyuss (rhymes with "pious") came along just as the hair bands of the '80s were breathing their last and helped inject a much-needed new spirit into hard rock, melding the weighty riffage of classic metal with the high energy of its speedier spawn. And when guitarist and future Queens of the Stone Age leader Josh Homme decided to detune his axe a whole step and beyond, he set a wave in motion that has yet to break. Just think of all the new-metalers—from Korn to Slipknot—who indulge in the crunchy delights of the way, way low end; fact is, they all owe something to Kyuss.

Wretch shows that the band had the requisite pieces in place early on, though not necessarily in the right order. The faster songs are too obviously indebted to Metallica, Danzig, and several others. But when the pace slows, Kyuss finds its zone, summoning up a sound that's relentless, monolithic, and thrilling, particularly on the devastating "Son of a Bitch." *Blues for the Red Sun* musters that sound at every tempo. Greatly improved production conveys a sense of power and menace that *Wretch* strove for but couldn't reach. Highlights include the chugging "Green Machine" and "Thong Song" (no relation to Sisqó), which features lead howler John Garcia intoning these deathless lyrics: "My hair is real long/No brains, all brawn . . . I hate slow songs."

Kyuss' third, self-titled album (also commonly referred to as *Welcome to Sky Valley* after the sign on its cover) is sludgier and less fun; still, the exploratory jam on "N.O." and the pummel-one-chord-and-repeat-until-exhausted ending of "Supa Scoopa and Mighty Scoop" are boss. . . . *And the Circus Leaves Town* offers diverting turns into quasipsychedelia and pseudoreggae, but except for the massive, 11-minute-plus "Spaceship Landing," the big rock songs are nothing special. Despite its best-of billing, *Muchas Gracias* is actually a collection of rarities, most of which should have stayed rare. —M.R.

L

Mark Lanegan
see SCREAMING TREES

k.d. lang

★★	A Truly Western Experience (Bumstead, 1984)
★★★½	Angel With a Lariat (Sire, 1987)
★★★½	Shadowland (Sire, 1988)
★★★★	Absolute Torch and Twang (Sire, 1989)
★★★★	Ingénue (Sire, 1992)
★★★	Even Cowgirls Get the Blues (Warner Bros., 1993)
★★★	All You Can Eat (Warner Bros., 1995)
★★★	Drag (Warner Bros., 1997)
★★★★	Invincible Summer (Warner Bros., 2000)
★★★½	Live by Request (Warner Bros., 2001)
★★★★	Hymns of the 49th Parallel (Nonesuch, 2004)

Like Madonna, k.d. lang has earned more ink for her offstage antics and provocative, chameleonic image than for her music. A pity, because lang not only possesses one of the finest voices in pop music, she's also blessed with the sort of stylistic range most singers can only dream of attaining. She started out performing what could be called postmodern country, but over the course of her career she's proved her mettle in traditional country, flirted successfully with mainstream pop and dance rock, and has even laid convincing claim to various standards.

Born in a Canadian prairie town, lang initially made her name both through her stunning voice and her playful subversion of country & western swing conventions. *A Truly Western Experience*—the title is a joke on her home province of Alberta's status as Canada's Wild West—is a good effort for a bar band, but barely hints at her potential. By the time of *Angel With a Lariat,* lang had become a fully-formed musical personality, and she also found a valuable ally in multi-instrumentalist Ben Mink. A veteran of the prog-rock combo FM, Mink had chops to spare—and

a sense of humor every bit as sharp as lang's. Between them, they filled the album with such giddy treats as the Cajun two-step "Got the Bull by the Horns" and the off-balance dance tune "Watch Your Step Polka." Great stuff, but a bit edgy for American country audiences, which may be why lang felt inclined to prove her bona fides with *Shadowland,* a painstakingly pure tribute to Patsy Cline. Not content with merely singing her heroine's songs, lang recruited Cline's producer, Owen Bradley, and his presence lends an authority to the project no mere re-creation could match. Yet for all her enthusiasm, lang's performance is more impressive as devotion than interpretation, for she often loses her identity in an attempt to seem authentic.

Absolute Torch and Twang brings the focus back to lang herself. She has wondrous fun with the uptempo tunes, whether homegrown (the cool-rocking "Didn't I") or borrowed (her sly, swinging remake of "Full Moon Full of Love"). But the slow songs are where she really proves her mettle, for between the bluesy inflection of "Three Days" and the melancholy yodel tugging at "Trail of Broken Hearts," lang is revealed as one of the most gifted song stylists in country music. And with *Ingenue,* genre distinctions become irrelevant as lang fuses her influences into a unique and distinctive sound encompassing everything from the sophistication of "Miss Chatelaine" to the Patsy Cline–meets–Joni Mitchell angst of "Save Me."

Having thus established her pop credentials, lang and Mink take a bit of a detour with the semi-experimental cowboy songs of *Even Cowgirls Get the Blues,* a soundtrack that's far more likable than the movie to which it's attached. *All You Can Eat* pushes her pop evolution even further. Considering how heavily hunger and longing color the songs here, lang earns points for the deliciously ironic album title. But it's the funk-tinged grooves of "Maybe" and "Acquiesce" that help lang move beyond the torch song expectations of her previous work.

Drag is a bit more self-indulgent, a tobacco-stained collection of covers that ranges from the sublime (an incandescent reading of Albert Hammond's "The Air That I Breathe") to the ridiculous ("Theme From the Valley of the Dolls"). *Invincible Summer* puts her back on track, however, celebrating the wonder of love and glory of happenstance with undisguised delight—"The Consequences of Falling" and "Summerfling" are especially gorgeous. Sadly, these originals would be her last for a while. *Live by Request* is a de facto greatest-hits collection, and it justifies the concert setting with some of lang's most lustrous singing. She also cut an album of standards with Tony Bennett, *Wonderful World.* Finally, she put her own imprint on the notion of standards with *Hymns of the 49th Parallel,* which answers the "American songbook" concept by including only songs by Canadian tunesmiths, Leonard Cohen, Joni Mitchell, Neil Young, and Jane Siberry among them. Typical is "A Case of You," in which lang takes a famously personal and specific pop song and makes it both universal and utterly her own.   —J.D.C.

Jon Langford

- ★★★½   Skull Orchard (Sugar Free, 1998)
- ★★★½   Mayors of the Moon (Bloodshot, 2003)
- ★★★½   All the Fame of Lofty Deeds (Bloodshot, 2004)

The Pine Valley Cosmonauts

- ★★★½   Misery Loves Company: The Songs of Johnny Cash (Bloodshot, 1995)
- ★★★★   Salute the Majesty of Bob Wills (Bloodshot, 1998)
- ★★★   Beneath the Country Underdog (Bloodshot, 2000)
- ★★★★   The Executioner's Last Songs, Vol. 1 (Bloodshot, 2002)
- ★★★½   The Executioner's Last Songs, Vol. 2 & 3 (Bloodshot, 2003)

It's not that unusual for a jazz musician such as Charlie Haden or David Murray to juggle several distinct groups over extended periods of time, but no one in rock has done it more dexterously than Mekons' founder Jon Langford. While Langford has continued to record with the Mekons since 1979, he recorded a dozen albums with the Three Johns in the '80s, and since then has spun out groups such as the Killer Shrews, the Waco Brothers, and the Pine Valley Cosmonauts. His solo album *Skull Orchard* provides a sort of baseline to what Langford brings to his groups: rock & roll that takes simplicity as a virtue, and sharp wordplay that cuts no slack for cliché.

Mayors of the Moon puts Langford in front of a Canadian alt-country group called the Sadies, shaping up a tight set of songs that plays like a slightly lighter version of the Waco Brothers.

All the Fame of Lofty Deeds finds Langford playing a populist ramblin' man, turning out wiseass ditties that sound upbeat and plenty tuneful even when he's going on about lyin' in a cold, dark grave and how there's nothing more perfect than a perfect crime.

The Pine Valley Cosmonauts are another Jon Langford project, where various sets of Waco Brothers and Waco Cousins get together to form left-wing country's foremost backing band. The two tribute albums differ in that the Cash set is sung by Langford only with a teeth-grinding grimness, while the Wills set is pure celebration, rotating standards through guest vocalists (most notably Jimmie Dale Gilmore).

In *Beneath the Country Underdog,* the Cosmonauts play backing band for Kelly Hogan, while *The Executioner's Last Songs* is a benefit for the Illinois Death Penalty Moratorium Project, with guest vocalists taking turns at songs of death, murder, and executions, not that it makes all that much difference. *Vol. 1* sets the course; *Vol. 2 & 3* piles on more of the same, recycling a few songs for alternate singers.   —T.H.

Daniel Lanois

- ★★★   Acadie (Opal/Warner Bros., 1989)
- ★★★   For the Beauty of Wynona (Warner Bros., 1993)
- ★★★   Shine (Anti, 2003)

Whether working on his infrequent but jewellike solo recordings or turning the knobs for high-profile clients such as U2 and Bob Dylan, Daniel Lanois brings a cinematographer's sensibility to production; he creates soundtracks for the mind in the recording studio. Lanois is best known for bringing an avant-garde edge to masterpieces by U2 *(Achtung Baby)* and Dylan *(Time Out of Mind),* as well as albums by Emmylou Harris, Robbie Robertson, and the Neville Brothers, among others. He favors steam-bath atmospherics and heavily treated guitars, but his soundscapes are rooted in ethnic traditions that bridge string-band folk, New Orleans R&B, and delta blues.

Lanois' distinctive brand of roots impressionism informs his solo albums as well. *Acadie* is an eerie, inward-looking debut; it's bittersweet mood music with French-Canadian folk and Cajun accents. It's not far removed in tone from the ambient records Lanois was making earlier in the '80s with Brian Eno. *For the Beauty of Wynona* finds Lanois gaining confidence as a vocalist, and picking up the energy—if only slightly—with a New Orleans–based rhythm section and a more aggressive guitar tone, especially on "Brother L.A."

Shine is even more expansive, flirting with reggae on "Power of One" and Curtis Mayfield–like soul on the pleading "Slow Giving." Though it includes vocal cameos by Harris and U2's Bono, the album retains its moody cohesiveness, thanks in part to three evocative pedal-steel instrumentals that serve as connective tissue between the vocal tracks.   —G.K.

The La's

★★★★   The La's (Go! Discs, 1990)

With just one album in its discography, and one genuine hit—the enduringly charming "There She Goes"—the La's look to be a lock for the one-hit-wonder hall of fame. Which is a shame, because the Liverpool group, which drew its sound from the spiderwebbed guitars of the Byrds and the Hollies, was for a moment or two among the most promising in all British pop.

First established in 1986, the La's recorded their debut with producer Steve Lillywhite. While the fragile, slightly anguished voice of Lee Mavers brings melancholic dimension to "There She Goes," the rest of the album, which later influenced Oasis and others, stretches from fantasy themes to gnarly garage rock to the near-frantic "Way Out." What connects these styles is Mavers' keen melodic sense: Even when he's projecting anger or hostility, there's an ethereal, floating-in-the-clouds effortlessness to the songs, a quality Mavers apparently tried, unsuccessfully, to replicate on a followup that was never released. After the success of "There She Goes," which turned up on the soundtrack to 1998's *The Parent Trap,* Mavers worked for years on a second record, and despite a tour in the mid-'90s, it has never been released; bassist John Power enjoyed some success in the U.K. with his middling, hippieish Brit-pop band Cast.   —T.M.

Latin Playboys

★★★★   Latin Playboys (Warner Bros., 1994)
★★★★   Dose (Atlantic, 1999)

The Latin Playboys is a willfully offbeat but artistically rewarding detour for Los Lobos' primary songwriters David Hidalgo and Louie Perez. Their journey into the hazier end of the sound spectrum is greased by studio alchemists Mitchell Froom and Tchad Blake, the team behind Los Lobos' sonically adventurous 1992 album, *Kiko. Latin Playboys* takes leftover *Kiko* demos and transforms them into weird little pieces of border-music exotica, lo-fi blues-rock and acid-folk. Allusive, dreamlike, and disturbing, *Latin Playboys* is a side project that's anything but frivolous; indeed, it's the equal of any Los Lobos album. *Dose* goes even further

out, employing steel-drum grooves, Javanese gamelan, West African guitar lines, and Eastern violins in the service of Perez's lyrical vignettes about childhood, family, and barrio memories.   —G.K.

Cyndi Lauper

★★★★   She's So Unusual (Portrait, 1983)
★★   True Colors (Portrait, 1986)
★★   A Night to Remember (Epic, 1989)
★★★   Hat Full of Stars (Epic, 1993)
★★★   12 Deadly Cyns and Then Some (Epic, 1995)
★★½   Sisters of Avalon (Sony, 1997)
★★   Merry Christmas . . . Have a Nice Life! (Epic, 1998)
★★★   Shine (Edel America, 2002)

A brilliant debut, Cyndi Lauper's *She's So Unusual* kicked off with a quartet of songs ("Money Changes Everything," "Girls Just Want to Have Fun," "When You Were Mine," "Time After Time") that revealed her as a genre-bending sharpie—mistress of styles varying from post-punk rock to neo-'50s pop to sex-funk to balladry. With a voice that combined the cartoon soul of Little Eva and the wink-wink naughtiness of Betty Boop, Lauper may have backed away from the depth or urgency of the writers whose work she mainstreamed (among them, Prince, Jules Shear, and Tom Gray of Atlanta's underrated Brains), but her transformation of their power into sheer pop was ultimately subversive—giggling all the way, she incited legions of mall rats into orange-hair rebellion and a measure of self-assertion. A homely-pretty, good-bad girl, Cyndi proved that the woman singer need not be "sensitive" nor agonized nor "artful" nor conventionally sexy nor a male imitator. What a drag, then, that her subsequent career was largely a bust commercially. Turning far too soon toward self-parody, she became a figure about as radical and liberating as a Muppet.

In 1993, she won critical, if not commercial, kudos with *Hat Full of Stars,* an uncharacteristically "serious" work that contended with racism and incest, and featured nice guest vocals from Mary Chapin Carpenter. After the fine greatest-hits package *12 Deadly Cyns and Then Some,* with a nifty remix of "Girls Just Want to Have Fun," she came back with *Sisters of Avalon.* As its title suggests, it's heavy on Enya-esque melodies and vaguely New Age philosophies: When it rocks, it's also credible dance music. Her vocals, as always, are terrific, and they show no diminishing of luster on *Shine,* a strong effort, boasting among its distinctions a nice songwriting collaboration between Cyndi and Japanese avant-gardist Ryuichi Sakamoto.   —P.E.

Avril Lavigne

★★½ Let Go (Arista, 2002)
★★★ Under My Skin (Arista, 2004)

Before Avril Lavigne, teenage pop stars were expected to get tarted up and shake their pubescent booties to electro-dance tunes crafted by Swedish hitmakers such as Max Martin. Then along came this pint-size 16-year-old hellion from the tiny Canadian town of Napanee, Ontario, with her kohl-rimmed eyes, baggy skateboarder's pants, and a permanent scowl. Although she probably couldn't tell her Sex Pistols from her Ramones, Avril had the whiff of punk to distinguish her from the Britneys and Christinas. According to lore, she writes her own songs—though the extent of her contribution is debatable. What is certain, however, is that the first three singles from *Let Go*—all "cowritten" by Los Angeles–based production trio the Matrix—were such perfect pieces of sour-apple bubblegum music that they made this teen pop star seem somehow less manufactured than the others. On top of how ridiculously catchy they were, the Matrix songs stood out thanks to the sassy wordplay in "Complicated" and the schoolyard narrative of star-crossed lovers in "Sk8er Boi." But within months of its release, the sound of the album was already dated. The Matrix had their hands on so many artists during late 2002 that their ultrasheen production became more immediately recognizable than the artists themselves.

Lavigne was smart to try new partners for *Under My Skin,* which lacks the immediacy of *Let Go* but makes up for that loss with mood and attitude. Whereas *Let Go*'s aggro number "Losing My Grip" felt affected, the harder-edged songs on *Under My Skin* ("Take Me Away," "Together," and "Forgotten") have more genuine angst. "He Wasn't" is the punkest-sounding punk-pop song she's tackled yet, complete with Ramonesy "hey, hey, hey, hey"-ing. Avril cops some moves from Evanescence singer Amy Lee on a couple of tracks, but she seems to be growing into her own persona: the girl who flips the bird rather than curtsying, or lashes out at boys who didn't love her enough, rather than weeping about it. It's only a hair more authentic than before, but sometimes, a hair is all it takes. —J.E.

Lead Belly

★★★★★ Lead Belly's Last Sessions (1953; Smithsonian Folkways, 1994)
★★★ Leadbelly Sings Folk Songs (1968; Smithsonian Folkways, 1989)
★★★ Bourgeois Blues: Golden Classics (1989; Collectables, 1994)

★★★★ Defense Blues: Golden Classics, Part Two (1990; Collectables, 1994)
★★★★★ Lead Belly, Vol. 1: Midnight Special (Rounder, 1991)
★★★★★ Lead Belly, Vol. 2: Gwine Dig a Hole to Put the Devil In (Rounder, 1991)
★★★★★ Lead Belly, Vol. 3: Let It Shine on Me (Rounder, 1991)
★★★★★ Lead Belly, Vol. 4: The Titanic (Rounder, 1994)
★★★★★ Lead Belly, Vol. 5: Nobody Knows the Trouble I've Seen (Rounder, 1994)
★★★★★ Lead Belly, Vol. 6: Go Down Old Hannah (Rounder, 1994)
★★★★ Storyteller Blues (Drive Archive, 1994)
★★★★ Lead Belly Memorial Album, Vols. 1 and 2: The Stinson Collector's Series (Collectables, 1995)
★★★★ Lead Belly Memorial Album, Vols. 3 and 4: The Stinson Collector's Series (Collectables, 1995)
★★★ Lead Belly Party Songs & Sings and Plays: The Stinson Collector's Series (Collectables, 1995)
★★★★★ Where Did You Sleep Last Night: Lead Belly Legacy, Vol. 1 (Smithsonian Folkways, 1996)
★★★★★ Bourgeois Blues: Lead Belly Legacy, Vol. 2 (Smithsonian Folkways, 1997)
★★★★★ Shout On: Lead Belly Legacy, Vol. 3 (Smithsonian Folkways, 1998)
★★★★ Bridging Lead Belly (Rounder Select, 1999)
★★★ The Best of Lead Belly (Purple Pyramid, 2000)
★★★★ Sings for Children (Smithsonian Folkways, 1999)

Huddie Ledbetter, better known as Lead Belly, rose from penitentiary prisoner to beloved folk troubadour in the '30s, when his influence spread far and wide, most notably to Woody Guthrie, Pete Seeger, Sonny Terry, and Cisco Houston. It was remarkable enough that a black man achieved such widespread popular acclaim at a time when crossover was a near-nonexistent phenomenon. His songs are even more remarkable and enduring. Americans who would otherwise draw a blank at the mention of Lead Belly's name will recognize "Goodnight Irene" and "Rock Island Line," to name but two of his best-known songs.

Lead Belly was discovered in 1933 by folklorist John Lomax and his son Alan, who were touring the South, recording blues, work and folk songs for the Library of Congress. In the course of their travels the Lomaxes often set up their recording gear in prisons, which were a limitless source of the music they were seeking. In 1933, at Louisiana State Penitentiary, they found Lead Belly, who had been convicted of attempted homicide. The Lomaxes recorded him, then brought him to New York in 1935 after his release from prison (he was pardoned after writing a song for the governor of Louisiana). Lead Belly was an instant hit playing in New York clubs and throughout the Northeast, but by the decade's end he was back in prison on an assault charge.

Upon his release in the spring of 1940 he took an apartment in lower Manhattan and soon joined the Headline singers, whose members included Guthrie, Sonny Terry, and Brownie McGhee. At that time he began to record his songs for various labels and in 1945 even made one short film, *Three Songs by Leadbelly.* His touring intensified after World War II, but he fell ill in 1949, was diagnosed with Lou Gehrig's disease, and died late in the year.

The wealth of recordings Lead Belly left behind offer abundant opportunities to examine the full breadth and depth of the man's music. At the top of the list are the 1994 four-CD set *Lead Belly's Last Sessions* and Rounder's six-volume collection of Lomax-recorded work. Recorded over the course of three nights in 1949 in the apartment of a noted folk music enthusiast-scholar, *Last Sessions* is presented with virtually no editing and all the songs sequenced on disc in the order of their performance, with between-songs patter included as well. This is Lead Belly at work, to be sure, but also relaxed and voluble—the man was a born storyteller, and he relates the folklore behind nearly every one of the 100 songs and offers some telling anecdotes from his own life. At times he is accompanied by his wife, but the largest part of this set is the pure, unadulterated, solo folk artist in full flower. Encouraged to go where the muse took him, Lead Belly essays everything from work songs to folk songs to sacred songs to bawdy songs to topical material with sociological bite to the baldly commercial fare that is equal parts folk- and pop-influenced.

Midnight Special documents Lead Belly's earliest Library of Congress sessions, including those recorded while he was still in prison. Like *Last Sessions,* the entire scope of Lead Belly's repertoire is represented on these Rhino collections: Volume 1's and Volume 2's (*Gwine Dig a Hole to Put the Devil In*) blues and work ballads lead to Vol. 3's (*Let It Shine on Me*) focus on sacred songs and spiritually oriented material. *The Titanic* centers largely on topical songs, such as the title number, and musings about specific people and places ("Blind Lemon Blues," "Mr. Tom Hughes," "Henry Ford Blues"), as does *Nobody Knows the Trouble I've Seen,* which includes "Rock Island Line" and the two-part chronicle of a headline-making event, "The Hindenburg Disaster." The set closes on an introspective note with *Go Down Old Hannah,* a collection of spiritual songs ("Amazing Grace," "Old Time Religion") and folk monuments such as "John Henry."

Recorded between 1941 and 1948, the selections on *Where Did You Sleep Last Night . . . , Bourgeois Blues,* and *Shout On* range from a 1943 recording of "Irene" with Sonny Terry sitting in on harmonica; autobiographical songs such as "Cotton Fields," "Bring a Little Water Sylvie," and "4, 5 and 9"; sukey-jump tunes; children's play songs; spirituals (a powerful "Let It Shine on Me," "Meeting at the Building"); and blues. One of the most powerful recordings in the entire Lead Belly legacy is on *Shout On.* It's a version of "John Henry" with Lead Belly on vocals and guitar, Brownie McGhee on guitar, and Sonny Terry wailing away on harmonica in a spitfire musical dialogue that moves at a furious, breathtaking pace.

The *Memorial* albums feature the artist's bold voice and 12-string guitar in a variety of contexts encompassing virtually every type of song Lead Belly played. Vol. 1 is a program of work songs, blues, and spirituals; Vol. 2, more of the same, with Lead Belly playing piano-concertina as well as 12-string; Vol. 3 is a collection of previously unreleased masters and once-rare tracks; Vol. 4 finds Lead Belly telling his life story in song, traveling from the cotton fields to prison to the urban jungle (some of this material is duplicated on Collectables' *Bourgeois Blues*).

Bridging Lead Belly consists of a dozen tracks recorded in 1938 for the BBC but never released in the States, and five others recorded before a live audience in 1946. The idea is to show the artist at two distinctive stages of his career: the first showcases him performing songs almost exclusively related to his experiences in the South, good and bad, including "Governor O.K. Allen," one of the two "pardon" songs he composed in what proved to be a successful effort to win a pardon from prison; the second shows a more mature Lead Belly, more assured on his 12-string guitar and more thoughtful in his singing style. *Sings for Children* includes some fanciful numbers that would captivate a young audience (the "Pig Latin Song," for instance, and "Skip to My Lou"), but the albums is also rich in blues, story-songs, work songs, and spirituals, 28 tracks in all of Lead Belly vocalizing at peak form and bringing his winning personality to bear on his spoken introductions. *Lead Belly Party Songs & Sings and Plays* and *Leadbelly Sings Folk Songs* both find the artist whooping it up with other artists, including Woody Guthrie, Cisco Houston, Sonny Terry, and, on *Sings and Plays,* Josh White. The 16-track *Storyteller Blues* and *Defense Blues* both include material available on better-annotated sets, but are solid if perfunctory overviews of specific aspects of the artist's sensibility, particularly with regard to highly personal songs and other, more socially conscious fare such as that found on *Defense Blues.*   —D.M.

Led Zeppelin

★★★★★   Led Zeppelin (1969; Atlantic, 1994)
★★★★★   Led Zeppelin II (1969; Atlantic, 1994)
★★★★   Led Zeppelin III (1970; Atlantic, 1994)
★★★★★   Untitled (1971; Atlantic, 1994)
★★★★½   Houses of the Holy (1973; Atlantic, 1994)
★★★★   Physical Graffiti (1975; Atlantic, 1994)
★★★   Presence (1976; Atlantic, 1994)
★★   The Song Remains the Same (1976; Atlantic, 1994)
★★★   In Through the Out Door (1979; Atlantic, 1994)
★★   Coda (1982; Atlantic, 1994)
★★★★   Led Zeppelin (Atlantic, 1990)
★★★   Remasters (Atlantic, 1992)
★★   Box Set, Vol. 2 (Atlantic, 1993)
★★★★   The Complete Studio Recordings (Atlantic, 1993)
★★★½   BBC Sessions (Atlantic, 1997)
★★★   Early Days: The Best of Led Zeppelin Vol. 1 (Atlantic, 1999)
★★★   Latter Days: The Best of Led Zeppelin Vol. 2 (Atlantic, 2000)
★★★   Early Days and Latter Days, Vol. 1 & 2 (Atlantic, 2002)
★★★★   How the West Was Won (Atlantic, 2003)

Led Zeppelin is sometimes credited with inventing heavy metal. That's an understandable misconception, given that few songs bring the godless thunder quite like "Whole Lotta Love," from the British quartet's second album. But Zep's scope was far wider. Though the band wrote some indelible songs, its primary innovations were in pure sound: the orchestration of bass, drums, guitar, and voice into music that embraced mayhem and subtlety, light and shade, Eastern drones and city blues, proto-punk ("Communication Breakdown") and centuries-old folk ("Gallows Pole").

Talk about telegraphing your punch: The cover of *Led Zeppelin* shows the Hindenburg airship, in all its phallic glory, going down in flames. The image did a pretty good job of encapsulating the music inside: sex, catastrophe, and things blowing up. The swagger is there from the get-go, on "Good Times Bad Times": Jimmy Page's guitar pounces from the speakers, fat with menace; John Bonham's kick drum swings with anvil force around John Paul Jones' dexterous bass line; Robert Plant rambles on about the perils of manhood. Hard rock would never be the same. Zep dances with Chicago blues, British folk, and Eastern ragas, though subtlety would play a larger

role on later works; on *Led Zeppelin,* the mission is to create music of extremes, a concept that appeals to hard-core album buyers rather than the Top 40 marketplace.

Led Zeppelin II contains the epochal "Whole Lotta Love," which became a starting point for Aerosmith, Guns N' Roses, and Van Halen, among others. It's an amazing song not just for its seismic riff and bingeing-on-lust vocal performance, but for its mind-bending midsection, in which Page orchestrates the aural equivalent of an orgasm (theremin included). Elsewhere on *Led Zeppelin II,* excess abounds: more heavy blues ("Bring It on Home"), more pastoral splendor ("Thank You"), more sex ("The Lemon Song").

Though there are hints of bucolic folk on the first two albums, *Led Zeppelin III* embraces it, the album split evenly between metallic boogie and acoustic reverie. Plant's voice in particular achieves a conversational grace that had eluded him earlier; by dialing down the volume, he begins to approximate the gravity and maturity of the blues singers he admires.

The untitled fourth album weaves together the disparate musical threads of the preceding releases, most auspiciously on "Stairway to Heaven." Though its pleasures have been muted by radio overexposure, "Stairway" is in many ways the quintessential Zep song and arrangement: an electro-acoustic hybrid that builds over seven minutes to a crescendo in support of a fancifully cryptic lyric that sounds like it contains a thousand mysteries, or none at all. Zep's hard-rock blues was never more momentous than on "When the Levee Breaks," and their folk-hippie aspirations peak on "Going to California" and "The Battle of Evermore."

Houses of the Holy is a bit of a letdown, overextending the band's reach to funk ("The Crunge") and reggae ("D'Yer Maker"), while making more extensive use of overdubbed orchestration than ever before. The arrangements and performances are more intricate and less propulsive, yet the classics keep coming: "Thank You," "The Ocean," "Over the Hills and Far Away."

Filler bloats the double-album-length *Physical Graffiti,* but it remains a Zep touchstone, thanks to the epic Eastern swirl of "Kashmir," and the closest thing to a dance tune in the band's discography: "Trampled Underfoot." In contrast, *Presence* is more focused, one-dimensional, and rushed. The ragged force of "Nobody's Fault but Mine" and "Achilles' Last Stand" nearly compensates for the album's lack of diversity.

In Through the Out Door finds the band responding to punk's challenge by making its most experimental, keyboard-heavy album. Maligned upon its release as a retreat from heaviness, it now stands as an art-rock oddity with some alluring tangents. It suggests that Zep, at the very least, never stood still.

Bonham's death a few months after the album's completion left the band to anthologize itself endlessly over the next two decades. *Coda* collects unexceptional studio leftovers; the well-chosen, brilliantly sequenced four-CD box set *Led Zeppelin* includes four rarities (notably the B side "Hey Hey What Can I Do"); while the largely unnecessary *Box Set 2* unearths a first-session outtake, "Baby Come On Home." The desultory *The Song Remains the Same* stood as the band's lone concert document until the arrival 27 years later of *How the West Was Won,* which documents two swaggering 1972 California performances. —G.K.

Ben Lee

★★★	Grandpaw Would (Grand Royal, 1995)
★★½	Something to Remember Me By (Grand Royal, 1997)
★★½	Breathing Tornados (Capitol, 1999)
★★★½	Hey You Yes You (Red Ink, 2003)

Ben Lee was the 16-year-old frontman of Australian teen indie-pop sensations Noise Addict when he released his full-length solo debut, *Grandpaw Would,* in 1995. A strum-heavy lo-fi gem, *Grandpaw* prompted comparisons to Loudon Wainwright III, though Lee's goofy sense of humor and eye for detail also mirrors Jonathan Richman's. Produced by Brad Wood and featuring a guest turn from Liz Phair, the roughly hewn *Grandpaw* was winsome and charming (especially the Pixies' ode "Away With the Pixies"), impossible to dislike, and almost equally impossible to re-create, as the followup, *Something to Remember Me By,* would make clear.

Also produced by Wood, *Something* flirted vaguely with country ("New Song"), but was otherwise *Grandpaw* redux, packed with the sort of moony and clever love songs that had become Lee's stock-in-trade. While Lee's past efforts felt as if they could have been cobbled together in his bedroom, *Breathing Tornados* takes the opposite tack. Leaning heavily on loops, samples, and drum machines, Lee, who seems to be channeling Beck, comes dangerously close to losing the air of easy intimacy that is his greatest strength. Still, "Cigarettes Will Kill You," the opening track and the closest Lee has ever come to an actual hit single, is a keeper.

Hey You Yes You continued in the same vein, with acclaimed producer Dan the Automator fleshing out Lee's mature, brightly melodic tunes with fuzzed-out trip-hoppy ambience. —A.S.

Brenda Lee

★★★½	The Brenda Lee Story—Her Greatest Hits (1973; MCA, 1991)
★★★★★	Anthology, Vols. 1 & 2 (1956–1980) (MCA, 1991)
★★★	In the Mood for Love: Classic Ballads (Hip-O, 1998)
★★★	The Millennium Collection (MCA, 1999)
★★★	Rockin' Around the Christmas Tree (MCA, 1999)
★★★★	The Christmas Collection (MCA, 2003)

Checking in at four feet, eleven inches tall, Brenda Lee was dubbed "Little Miss Dynamite" early on in her career. The reference, though, was as much about her singing style as it was about her height. When she was ruling the pop charts in the '60s, she could be convincing with an almost straight-pop approach to a heartbreaking ballad, then swing into an uptempo number that would reveal a deep streak of blues and honkytonk in her style. A protégé of Patsy Cline's producer, Owen Bradley, Lee recorded her first pop hit in 1960—"Sweet Nothin's," which peaked at #4—and then set about becoming one of the dominant female vocalists of the decade. Pop hit after pop hit ensued, all charting the rocky course of love and its accompanying angst. Bradley, who has been criticized for his extravagant use of strings on Cline's recordings, found a more appropriate vehicle for his lush arrangements in Lee; in fact, it can be said that he made all the right moves in the studio in terms of his decisions to lay on the strings or to let Lee wail with only a basic rock band pushing the beat. The two-volume *Anthology* series collects Lee's most essential sides in their original form (Bradley had a habit of having his artists rerecord their hits for album releases). In particular, "All Alone Am I," "As Usual," "Thanks a Lot," "Break It to Me Gently," "Sweet Nothin's," and "Johnny One Time" are superb examples of the different styles Lee employed in getting a lyric across. Among female pop artists in the '60s, Lee, Lesley Gore, and Dionne Warwick are pretty much alone in terms of their ability to affix an individual stamp to first-rate material.

Anthology's annotation is also superior to that of the other sweeping greatest-hits collection, *The Brenda Lee Story: Her Greatest Hits,* which is otherwise an exemplary gathering of Lee's choice cuts, dating from 1956's "Jambalaya" to 1966's "Coming On Strong." *The Millennium Collection* is a solid but truncated tour of Lee's hit singles. Ten songs and 10 songs only cannot do justice to such an overpowering history, but an album containing "I'm Sorry," "Sweet Nothin's," "Emotions," "Break It to Me Gently," "Fool #1," and especially "All Alone Am I" must be reckoned with, however fleeting its pleasures. Choice cuts these, to be sure, but more like half an entrée than a full platter.

If Lee's album tracks had been less compelling, there would be no advocating Hip-O's *In the Mood for Love: Classic Ballads*. But these 18 cuts spanning the years 1961–71 add an important dimension to Lee's in-print catalogue in collecting some powerful nonsingle sides on one disc. She ranges far and wide here, tackling Bacharach-David's "(There's) Always Something to Remind Me," Clarence "Frogman" Henry's 1961 hit "You Always Hurt the One You Love," "I Left My Heart in San Francisco," the Dusty Springfield evergreens "Wishin' and Hopin' " and "You Don't Have to Say You Love Me," and Willie Nelson's "Funny How Time Slips Away," among others.

And what would a Brenda Lee catalogue be without *Rockin' Around the Christmas Tree*? This remastered, 18-track version of the original 12-track vinyl album *Merry Christmas From Brenda Lee* could be seen as a companion volume to *In the Mood for Love* in that most of its tracks are known only to hard-core Lee fans, and it shows off Lee's assured way with different styles of song. All in all, this is a winner among Christmas albums, its warm atmosphere and fanciful arrangements sounding ever fresh as the years go by. —D.M.

Lemonheads

★★	Hate Your Friends (Taang!, 1987)
★★½	Lick (Taang!, 1989)
★★★	Lovey (TAG/Atlantic, 1990)
★★½	Favorite Spanish Dishes (TAG/Atlantic, 1991)
★★★★	It's a Shame About Ray (TAG/Atlantic, 1992)
★★★	Come On, Feel the Lemonheads (TAG/Atlantic, 1993)
★★½	Car Button Cloth (TAG/Atlantic, 1996)
★★★★	The Best of the Lemonheads: The Atlantic Years (TAG/Atlantic, 1998)

From little punk bands big pop acts grow—or so it seemed when the Lemonheads hit their early-'90s stride. Fronted by alterna-hunk (and occasional Blake Baby) Evan Dando, the group briefly fused low-fi aesthetics with Top 40 ambition, but ultimately lacked the discipline to turn its talent for hooks into an actual career.

Named for a sour candy, the group started out with a sound that touched on hard rock while paying homage to punk icons such as Hüsker Dü. They recorded several cheaply produced albums and EPs for Boston's Taang! label, of which *Lick* showed the sharpest pop instincts, thanks in part to its earnest, balls-out rendition of Suzanne Vega's "Luka."

By *Lovey*, only Evan Dando remained from the original lineup (although guitarist Corey Loog Brennan turns up for two tracks); perhaps as a consequence, the rockers there are augmented by occasionally introspective ballads, the best of which are disarmingly tuneful, and surprisingly moving. *Spanish Dishes* brought out even more of the band's pop smarts, but it wasn't until *It's a Shame About Ray* that the band truly clicked, thanks to the power-poppy title tune and a sly cover of the Simon & Garfunkel oldie "Mrs. Robinson."

But Dando's growing celebrity, combined with an ongoing drug problem, began to take its toll. *Come On, Feel the Lemonheads* felt more like a lemon than a hit, while *Car Button Cloth* was as pointless as its title. Still, there's enough fizz to *The Best of* to leave most listeners wishing that Dando and the Lemonheads had realized more of their potential. —J.D.C.

John Lennon

★★★★★	John Lennon/Plastic Ono Band (1970; Capitol, 2000)
★★★★	Imagine (1971; Capitol, 2000)
★★★½	Mind Games (1973; Capitol, 2002)
★★★	Walls and Bridges (Apple/Capitol, 1974)
★★★½	Rock 'n' Roll (Apple/Capitol, 1975)
★★★	Shaved Fish (Apple/Capitol, 1975)
★★★	Menlove Avenue (Capitol, 1986)
★★★	John Lennon Live in New York City (Capitol, 1986)
★★★★	Lennon (Capitol, 1990)
★★★★½	Lennon Legend: The Very Best of John Lennon (Capitol, 1997)
★★★	John Lennon Anthology (Capitol, 1998)
★★★★	Wonsaponatime (Capitol, 1998)

with Yoko Ono

★★½	Some Time in New York City (Apple, 1972)
★★★★	Double Fantasy (1980; Capitol, 2000)
★★★½	Milk and Honey (Geffen, 1984)
★½	Wedding Album (Rykodisc, 1997)
★½	Unfinished Music Vol. 1: Two Virgins (Rykodisc, 1997)
★	Unfinished Music Vol. 2: Life With the Lions (Rykodisc, 1997)

The shorthand assessment of Lennon as the tough rock genius and McCartney as the sweet pop craftsman has always seemed facile (and unfair to Paul). But with *John Lennon/Plastic Ono Band*, Lennon brutally, brilliantly, and definitively underlined the differences between himself and his ex-Beatle brother. "Love" is one of John's prettiest songs, and "Look at Me" is all fragile yearning, but the rest isn't just antipop; rather, it's rock & roll as Lennon always understood it: anger, catharsis, deliverance. One of the most demanding albums ever made, *Plastic Ono Band* is also one of the finest—singing with more verve than he'd mustered since the Beatles' "Money," his urgency encouraged by primal scream therapy with Arthur Janov, Lennon bares his soul. The trio lineup—John on guitar and piano, Ringo on drums, and longtime Beatle ally Klaus Voorman on bass—keeps the playing fierce, spare, and commanding; the force is helped greatly by Phil Spector's vast, echoing production. "God," "Remember," and "Isolation" find John unburdening himself of an exhausting, mythic past and seeking—through harsh, nihilistic exhilaration—release. "Well, Well, Well" and "I Found Out" are tougher rock than nearly anything released before the Sex Pistols; "Mother" is painful, lovely, and spine-chilling. And with "Working Class Hero" Lennon shucks off his gigantic stardom and reclaims the black-leather spirit of his Liverpool youth.

After the focused intensity of *Plastic Ono Band* came the much steadier *Imagine.* The title track is perhaps Lennon's most popular song, but there are plenty of other highlights, including "I Don't Wanna Be a Soldier Mama I Don't Wanna Die" and "Gimme Some Truth." The famous savaging of Paul, "How Do You Sleep?," however, is John at his nastiest.

Some Time in New York City is a not-bad rocking collaboration with the capable band Elephant's Memory; the ponderous lyrics, about the Attica prison riots, feminism, and Angela Davis, are far below Lennon's standard. On *Mind Games*—distinguished primarily by its sweeping, Spector-ish title track— John rocked tough in places, but it's mainly a holding pattern. From *Walls and Bridges,* "Whatever Gets You Through the Night," a duet with Elton John, gained Lennon his only #1 hit; even better is "#9 Dream," a heavily atmospheric number boasting cool cellos and fine singing.

Critically derided as a step backward, *Rock 'n' Roll* in fact offers delights for those true believers who share Lennon's lifelong insistence that early rock is the only music that really matters. Another Spector production, its standouts include takes on "Ain't That a Shame," "Just Because," and "Stand by Me." Its lack of forced fever ultimately only makes the record stronger—John lends dignity to these classics; his singing is tender, convincing, and fond.

Lennon had always insisted that he and Yoko were artistic equals. While Yoko had achieved distinction on her own as an avant-gardist, *Double Fantasy* comes close to redeeming Lennon's claim on the pop front. John's "Starting Over," with its easy, Fats Domino–like roll, as well as "Watching the Wheels"

and "Woman" are the highlights, and Yoko sounds better than she ever did. But this development took time, as the three formerly rare LPs reissued by Rykodisc show in abundance. Rather than the inert "avant-garde" conceptual sound pieces, the real subjects of these albums are the private art games of John and Yoko. If you are obsessed with the couple, enjoy. Most will settle for a glance at the once-scandalous cover of *Two Virgins.*

Much of Lennon's '80s posthumous releases—the six Lennon songs on *Milk and Honey,* the raucous 1972 concert that makes up *Live*—are good but unspectacular. A bracing exception is the second half of *Menlove Avenue,* containing live and *Walls and Bridges* cuts starkly stripped of Spector's overkill production. It's Lennon as punky minimalist, although the first half is one of his soggiest. Those who come across unfamiliar Lennon albums should be careful to avoid the many all-interview releases out there.

The four-CD *Lennon Anthology* is a beat-the-bootlegs miscellany of studio and home rehearsals, live performances, alternate versions, jokes, and bits of dialogue with Yoko and Sean. The devoted need it, but few others will play it often. The overlooked *Wonsaponatime,* however, is the most magical Lennon release in many years, as it culls 21 potent or fascinating tracks from *Anthology.* Highlights include "I'm Losing You" with backup by Cheap Trick, "Real Love" (the demo that became the final "new" Beatles track after the other members of the band worked on it), and "Serve Yourself," a slap at born-again Bob Dylan in which Lennon is both caustic and witty. *Shaved Fish* is a good, though brief, best-of, but *Lennon Legend,* at least the third try at a single-disc overview, is flawless if a single album is all you need. The 74 songs that make up the *Lennon* box set constitute a comprehensive summary. —P.E./M.MI.

Julian Lennon

- ★★ Valotte (Atlantic, 1984)
- ★★ The Secret Value of Daydreaming (Atlantic, 1986)
- ★★ Mr. Jordan (Atlantic, 1989)
- ★★★ Help Yourself (Atlantic, 1991)
- ★★ Photograph Smile (Fuel, 1999)
- ★★★ VH1 Behind the Music: The Julian Lennon Collection (Rhino, 2001)

To be commended for daring even to whisper after the echo of his formidable father, Julian settles for clean but modest stuff—high-end MOR. More a record maker than a songwriter, he assembles crack studio vets (Michael Brecker, Barry Beckett, Ralph MacDonald) and, through the almost clinical packaging of their playing, turns out compositions that vaguely resemble backing tracks to Steely Dan songs. Genes make sounding like John inevitable, and Julian does so, eerily, on his first album's not-bad title ballad, and, from his second outing, the haunting "Want Your Body." *Valotte* gave Lennon his only two Top 10 hits, the title track and "Too Late for Goodbyes." *Mr. Jordan* found him, for some odd reason, uncannily re-creating David Bowie's vocals. Lennon's records are pervaded with a sort of listlessness, a free-floating pathos. The one thing he hasn't done, even on his comeback "Indie" album, *Photograph Smile*, is rock, and, given the standard he's inevitably compared to, that's one wise move.   —P.E.

Sean Lennon

★★★½   Into the Sun (Grand Royal, 1998)

Sean Ono Lennon made his debut as a force in the family business leading a trio called IMA, a band of grinding minimalist punks recruited by Yoko Ono for 1995's *Rising,* still one of her finest, hardest-rocking albums. Playing guitar behind his mother's apocalyptic-scientist howl, Lennon jammed together hard punk, funk, and urban attitude in a way that suggested a future career as Lou Reed. When Lennon reemerged with *Into the Sun* in 1998, he was ready to rock up and chill out, scanning pop, fuzz guitars, jazzy interludes, sugar and light. His reedy Lennon vocals (as strangely familiar as those of half-brother Julian) are dropped into an indie-rock context, this time relaxed and adrift, singing of spaceships and tainted love in NYC. The title song is a playful bossa-nova duet with girlfriend Yuka Honda of Cibo Matto. And "Home" matches punk riffing with Beatles-style pop at its most sweet and surreal, as Lennon sings, "Watching the shadows on the wall, having seen it all" (already echoing John's tranquil "Watching the Wheels Go Round"). *Into the Sun* is smart and self-indulgent in a gentle, genuine way, introducing Lennon not as a brand name, but as an artist.   —S.A.

Annie Lennox

★★★½   Diva (Arista, 1992)
★★   Medusa (Arista, 1995)
★★★   Bare (J, 2003)

After the 1990 breakup of British synth-pop sensation Eurythmics, both of the duo's members—singer Annie Lennox and guitarist/keyboardist Dave Stewart—launched solo careers. While Stewart perpetrated a couple of atrocious rock records, Lennox let loose with the engrossing *Diva*. Bubbly on the sur-

face but apprehensive underneath, "Walking on Broken Glass" and "Little Bird" do a splendid job of updating the classic Eurythmics sound. Still, it's the moody ballads such as "Why," "Cold," and "The Gift" that truly stand out. Lennox's supple vocals prove once again that she's among the finest white soul singers of our time; given the quality of the goods on offer here, the album's antiseptic sheen is only a minor irritant.

If there had been any question which Eurythmic was the most significant talent, *Diva* seemed to have answered it. Then along came *Medusa,* an ill-advised collection of cover songs that takes the bloodlessness of *Diva*'s production several steps too far. Interesting as it can be to hear Lennox apply other singers' traits—the hesitance of Neil Young ("Don't Let It Bring You Down"), the offhand ease of Bob Marley ("Waiting in Vain"), the romantic yearning of the Blue Nile's Paul Buchanan ("The Downtown Lights")—to her own vocal persona, she turns the Clash's "Train in Vain" and Al Green's "Take Me to the River" into smooth background music appropriate for upscale hair salons.

Eight years passed before Lennox's next solo release; one wishes she'd spent the time coming up with a few more memorable tunes. All the same, *Bare* features some of the most intense singing of her career, and when she does get a decent song to work with— "Wonderful," for example, or "The Saddest Song I've Got"—she's stunning.   —M.R.

Le Tigre
see BIKINI KILL

Huey Lewis and the News

★★   Huey Lewis and the News (Chrysalis, 1980).
★★   Picture This (Chrysalis, 1982)
★★★   Sports (Chrysalis, 1983)
★★   Fore! (Chrysalis, 1986)
★★   Small World (Chrysalis, 1988)
★½   Hard at Play (EMI, 1991)
★★   Four Chords and Several Years Ago (Elektra, 1994)
★★½   Greatest (EMI, 2000)

Huey Lewis found gargantuan mid-'80s success by masquerading as a rock & roller. Due to the News' bar-band competence, the hits were letter-perfect versions of fundamental rock, but Lewis' remarkably unnuanced vocals and jockish sensibility were such that the songs missed the spirit by miles. After a desultory debut, the Bay Area sextet—originally named American Express—scored with "Workin' for a Livin'" and "Hope You Love Me Like You Say You Do" from *Pic-*

ture This. Sports was the band's biggest hit, with radio-friendly tunes such as "I Want a New Drug" and "The Heart of Rock & Roll." Yet the entire record could have passed for the soundtrack to a TV commercial. *Fore!* yielded the bland hit "It's Hip to Be Square." *Small World* and *Hard at Play* offer more of the same. *Four Chords and Several Years Ago,* the group's last studio album, was actually one of their more endearing. Covering chestnuts like "Some Kind of Wonderful," "Blue Monday," and "Stagger Lee," they sound exactly like the competent bar band that, essentially, they were. —P.E.

Jerry Lee Lewis

★★ The Golden Rock Hits of Jerry Lee Lewis (1967; Smash, 1987)
★★★★ Killer Country (1980; Elektra, 1995)
★★★★★ 18 Original Sun Greatest Hits (Rhino, 1984)
★★★★ 20 Classic Hits (1986; Original Sound, 1990)
★★★½ The Mercury/Smash Years Recordings (Collectables, 1996)
★★★★ The Very Best of Jerry Lee Lewis, Vol. 1: Whole Lot of Shakin' Going On (Collectables, 1999)
★★★★ The Very Best of Jerry Lee Lewis, Vol. 2: Invitation to Your Party (Collectables, 1999)
★★★½ A Taste of Country/Ole Tyme Country Music (Collectables, 1999)
★★★½ Monsters/Roots (Collectables, 1999)
★★★★★ Original Golden Hits, Volumes 1 & 2 (Collectables, 1999)
★★★½ Rockin' Rhythm & Blues/The Golden Cream of the Country (Collectables, 1999)
★★★½ The Millennium Collection (Hip-O, 1999)
★★★★ The Very Best of Jerry Lee Lewis (Collectables, 2000)
★★★★ 25 All-Time Greatest Sun Recordings (Varèse Sarabande, 2000)
★★★★ Rockin' the Blues: 25 Great Sun Recordings (Varèse Sarabande, 2002)
★★★½ 16 Thrillers from the Killer (Varèse Sarabande, 2003)
★★★★ Great Balls of Fire and Other Hits (Rhino, 2003)
★★★★ Platinum & Gold Collection (BMG Heritage, 2004)

While Jerry Lee Lewis' behavior throughout his career has created the impression that what was sprung from Memphis by way of Ferriday, LA, in 1956, was something unholy and vile, time has been Lewis' ally. Time hasn't tamed his image, of course, but it has allowed the record to be rolled back via the issuing of all his nearly 300 Sun tracks, which reveal an artist of enormous stylistic range. His bedrock Sun recordings make the progression of his career seem logical; even if he hadn't been forced into it after becoming the scourge of mainstream America by marrying his 13-year-old cousin, torpedoing his rock & roll career in the process, Lewis' natural evolution would have been into country music. If there's anything surprising about Jerry Lee the country artist, it's that the basic rugged concept of his personality hasn't been altered by the trouble he's seen: The furor over his cradle-robbing; the puzzling tendency of his wives to die under mysterious circumstances; a battle with the bottle; unstable health; a hair-trigger temper that's landed him in one jam after another; and the ghost of Elvis hovering to remind the Killer that the one true King of Rock & Roll lived on Elvis Presley Boulevard in Memphis, TN. He remains, as he said in a TV interview, "an old country boy, mean as hell."

The Sun recordings are available in various configurations encompassing greatest hits collections, original albums, and rare tracks. For completists, the import Bear Family box, *Classic Jerry Lee Lewis,* is the ne plus ultra of Lewis retrospectives. Encompassing 287 songs on eight discs, it includes virtually everything Lewis cut in the Sun studio. As a measure of Lewis' artistic reach, this set is staggering in showing the ease with which the artist handled any type of music that came his way. Traditional country ("Deep Elem Blues"), R&B ("Sixty Minute Man"), Dixieland ("When the Saints Go Marchin' In"), pop ("That Lucky Old Sun"), traditional Southern gospel (collected on the 1970 Sun album *Sunday Down South*), folk ("Goodnight Irene"), even minstrels ("Carry Me Back to Old Virginia"). Nearly everything is played with authority, and sung with utter conviction.

Fortunately, the single-disc domestic Sun retrospectives at least offer a taste of this broad range of music, although the focus is, naturally, on the classic and rocking sides. Collectables has done a most estimable job of keeping Jerry Lee's Sun catalogue in print, by way of a series of twofers that not only encompass greatest-hits-type collections but also offer a hard focus on the country and R&B sides. The must-have entries are the two volumes titled *The Very Best of Jerry Lee Lewis,* each containing 24 tracks, with Vol. 1, *Whole Lot of Shakin' Going On,* concentrating on blistering rock & roll, including all the chart monsters, whereas Vol. 2, *Invitation to Your Party,* is a collection of down-home country songs such as the title track, several Hank Williams covers, a bopping treatment of Jimmie Rodgers' "Waiting for a Train," Charlie Rich's beautiful "I'll Make It All Up to You," and others. *Monsters/Roots* blends country and rock & roll tracks, and the content of *Rockin' Rhythm & Blues/The Golden Cream of Country* as well as *A Taste of Country/Ole Tyme Country Music* is explained in the album titles. The annotation for these releases is the same from one disc to the next—a simple biographical sketch—but the music is something else again. Although Jerry Lee didn't have enough Sun hits to warrant more than one Golden Hits album, there are, in fact, two volumes so named, and both are available on another Collectables disc, *Original Golden Hits, Volume 1/Original Golden Hits, Volume 2*. Varèse Sarabande's *25 Great Sun Recordings* is perhaps misleadingly titled, as its only bona fide Killer hit is "Whole Lotta Shakin' Going On," but in an alternate version; otherwise it features some solid R&B/blues-style takes on "C.C. Rider," "My Girl Josephine," "Hound Dog," "Deep Elem Blues," and some good rock & roll on a cover of Gene Vincent's "Be-Bop-A-Lula" and Carl Perkins' "Matchbox" (Jerry Lee had played piano on the classic Perkins track, and was always credited by Perkins with "popping that song alive"). Rhino's *18 Original Sun Greatest Hits* and Original Sound's *20 Classic Hits* are both excellent single-disc surveys of the hits, B sides, and selected other studio recordings, a little bit country, a little bit R&B, a lotta rock & roll. Hip-O's *The Millennium Collection* amounts to some of the best of the post-Sun years—even its versions of "Whole Lotta Shakin' Going On," "Breathless," "High School Confidential," and "You Win Again" (the B side of "Breathless") are rerecordings Lewis cut for the Smash label—and on that count it's pretty darn good: "What Made Milwaukee Famous," "Middle Age Crazy," "She Even Woke Me Up to Say Goodbye," and "Another Place, Another Time," country classics all, are included.

In an attempt to get back on the rock charts in 1963, Lewis rerecorded some of his classic Sun sides for a package titled *The Golden Rock Hits of Jerry Lee Lewis*. Jerry Lee invested each performance with the expected energy, but nothing was going to supplant the magic that took place on Union Avenue in Memphis in the late '50s. A more successful approach was to roll tape when the Killer was doing his thing in front of a live audience, and when that happened, in Birmingham, AL, on July 1, 1964, the resulting album, *The Greatest Live Show on Earth*, was not only a *succés d'estime*, it had a four-month chart run and to fans signaled a return to form by one of rock & roll's authentic giants. A Bear Family import, *The Greatest Live Show on Earth*, contains two live shows, including the Alabama show in its entirety; domestically all that's left in print is the Collectables disc *The Mercury/Smash Years Recordings*, which bolsters nine cuts from *The Greatest Live Show on Earth* with five other studio efforts, including his last Top 40 hit, a 1972 cover version of Kris Kristofferson's "Me and Bobby McGee." It's a real shame that no domestic releases are in print covering the Smash/Mercury years more thoroughly, because Lewis, with Kennedy cut some of the best country music of the late '60s–early '70s in the honky-tonk lament "What Made Milwaukee Famous (Has Made a Loser Out of Me)," "Another Place, Another Time," "Middle Age Crazy," "Boogie Woogie Country Man," "There Must Be More to Love Than This," and others. The only source for this material now is via import, specifically the Bear Family releases, starting with the seven-CD *The Locust Years*, which pretty much documents all of the work for Smash in its 167 cuts (one being a 38-minute-plus interview with the Killer), and concluding with the multidisc *Mercury Smashes . . . And Rockin' Sessions*, its 233 cuts not only documenting the music made during the late '60s–early '70s but also containing several interview sessions with Lewis. Similarly, an intermittently productive tenure with Elektra in the '80s is now reduced to one in-print domestic album, 1980's *Killer Country*, which reunites Lewis with Jerry Kennedy for another strong effort that featured a powerful country tune in "Thirty-nine and Holding" and a whimsical treatment of "Over the Rainbow." —D.M.

Liars

★★★ They Threw Us All in a Trench and Stuck a Monument on Top (2001; Mute, 2002)
★★½ They Were Wrong, So We Drowned (Mute, 2004)

Skeletal punk-funk rhythms, mercilessly repetitive guitar parts, and zombie vocals straight out of Joy Division come together nicely on *They Threw Us All in a Trench*, the debut by this group at the center of New York's post-millennial No Wave revival. The Liars juxtapose bare, erotic dance rhythms with ghostly echo and treble effects, yielding a seductive but implacably chilling overall picture. A death rattle sounds in "Nothing Is Ever Lost or Can Be Found My Science Friend" and the final track, "Why Midnight Walked but Didn't Ring Her Bell," drones on hypnotically for 30 minutes.

The group quickly earned a reputation as one of the strangest and most unpredictable in the New York scene, its concerts often bumbling into chaos. *They Were Wrong*, their second full-length following a series of singles and EPs, is an aggressive and claustrophobic blast that earned comparisons on its release to Lou Reed's famously unlistenable *Metal Machine Music*. But that's not quite fair: Look close and find grinding noise arranged into precise, danceable grooves, and lyrical themes of witch hunts and mass sacrifice that resonate eerily in the George W. era. —B.S.

The Libertines

★★★★ Up the Bracket (Rough Trade, 2002)
★★★★ The Libertines (Rough Trade, 2004)

The history of rock & roll is strewn with libertines, but few bands have lived up to the title to the degree of the Libertines themselves. Drug-addled, smoky-voiced, and boozy, playing rock that threatened to jump the rails and go careening into the countryside, these barmy London urchins served as Britain's answer to 2002's garage-rock revival. On their debut, produced by Mick Jones of the Clash, the Libs unleashed a textbook lesson on shambolic punk rock that would do Jones' band proud. Singer/guitarists Carl Barat and Pete Doherty don't aim for precision. The harmonies are loose, the guitars chaotic, but the result is brilliant. Songs about drugs, dreamers, and hangers-on flirt with collapse. On "The Boy Looked at Johnny," breathless vocals veer into wailing, and on "The Boys in the Band," the Libs create their own mythology. But it's "What a Waster," a rebuke to the junkie lifestyle and the band's first big hit back home, that warns of things to come.

As Doherty's smack and crack addiction spiraled out of control in 2003, the band nearly fell apart, the low point coming when a desperate Doherty burgled Barat's flat to help feed his jones. Thankfully, they held together long enough to record their followup, if anything an even looser collection than the band's debut. By stripping away some of the reckless abandon, the band's tunes shine through. In place of Clashlike punk, we get songs that Beatle and Kink. There's something both tragic and exhilarating about the album: the band proves just how great it could be, but there's a pervading sense that it might not last. This is never more poignant than on the album's closer. "What became of the likely lads," sings Doherty. "What became of the dreams we had/What became of forever?" If the singer indeed follows the well-worn path to rock self-immolation, at least he left us a fitting coda. —D.SW.

Lil' Kim

★★★★½ Hard Core (Undeas/Big Beat, 1996)
★★½ Notorious K.I.M. (Queen Bee/Undeas/Atlantic, 2000)
★★★ La Bella Mafia (Atlantic, 2003)

Hip-hop had never seen anything like Brooklynite Kimberly Jones at the time of her solo debut: She sin-gle-handedly raised the bar for raunchy lyrics in hip-hop, making male rappers quiver with fear with lines like "You ain't lickin' this, you ain't stickin' this . . . I don't want dick tonight/Eat my pussy right" ("Not Tonight").

Riding the wing of Notorious B.I.G.'s *Ready to Die* and Jay-Z's *Reasonable Doubt*, Kim's *Hard Core* helped put East Coast hip-hop back on top in the late '90s. The album's overreliance on old '70s funk samples doesn't detract a bit from the Queen Bee's fearless rhymes: In "Dreams," she demands service from R. Kelly, Babyface, and nearly every "R&B dick" in the field. A landmark of bold, hilarious filth.

The production on *Notorious K.I.M.* is more stylistically varied than that of its predecessor (check the sumptuous sample of José Feliciano's "Esto Es el Guaguanco" on "No Matter What They Say"). But there's far too much standard "mo' money, mo' problems" complaining and not enough humor (the exception is "How Many Licks," another cunnilingus classic). Unlike her main rival, Foxy Brown, Kim didn't know how to be more than a raunchy clotheshorse on album. The same goes for *La Bella Mafia:* The likes of Timbaland and Missy Elliott contribute trademark stuttering tracks, while 50 Cent and Twista accompany Kim's often tedious, defensive rhymes. One rare highlight is "This Is a Warning," an adjustment of R. Kelly's "A Woman's Threat" and Kim's debut as a real singer—her rich, husky vocalizing points toward a potentially tantalizing future. —R.K.

Lil' Romeo

★★½ Lil' Romeo (Priority, 2001)
★★½ Game Time (No Limit, 2002)

His dad, No Limit mogul Master P, packaged prepubescent Lil' Romeo shortly after Lil' Bow Wow began barking up the charts. Romeo followed suit with the smash "My Baby," in which the 11-year-old boasts about his Bugs Bunny bling, girls and "grown women" wanting him, and his planned NBA career—all in all, much more charming stuff than his thuggish father ever delivered. P's sunny productions, built on can't-miss pop interpolations ("My Baby" borrows from the Jackson 5's "I Want You Back"), give Romeo a plush bed to jump around on. But unsurprisingly, the unlimited bounce eventually wears thin. *Game Time* is no better edited, though Romeo charms as never before, rapping to Beyoncé Knowles' younger sister Solange on (ahem) "True Love." —N.C.

Lil' Wayne

see HOT BOYS

Limp Bizkit

★★	Three Dollar Bill Y'all (Interscope, 1998)
★★★½	Significant Other (Interscope, 1999)
★★★	Chocolate Starfish and the Hot Dog Flavored Water (Interscope, 2000)
★★	New Old Songs (Interscope, 2001)
★★★	Results May Vary (Interscope, 2003)

There are a million reasons to despise Fred Durst. But believe it or not, his music isn't one of them. Though Durst's skills are more in the tradition of white rappers like Rodney Dangerfield or even Vincent Price than the Beasties or even Anthony Kiedis, he owns wimp rage's authentic mewl. Sure, Durst is a putz beset by petty indignities of life and he whines indignantly back. But deny ever feeling that way yourself and you're an even putzier putz. True, nobody ever mistook DJ Lethal for a Grandmaster, and the rhythm section takes the phrase "give up the funk" far too literally. But Wes Borland is a guitar hero for the age of sample-and-hold, trading in virtuoso expression for a rudimentary crunch.

The band's moment of glory is *Significant Other*, keynoted by the defensive breakup rant "Nookie" and the offensive break-stuff rant "Break Stuff." The latter, in particular, shows how the standard media line on Bizkit, which links the appeal of its aggression to overdriven Y chromosomes and beer-addled fraternity memberships, falters. Bizkit has never been a band for unapologetic muscleheads. "Break Stuff" is an anthem for closet wusses who ineffectually hurl their phone against the wall when their girlfriends hang up on them.

Chocolate Starfish found the band counterpunching, Durst singing "My Generation" to a fan base a decade younger than himself. Shortly afterward, Borland jumped ship to pursue dreams of art rock and the band released a stopgap remix project called *New Old Songs*—a trifle, really. Time will tell whether they can reclaim the balance of powers integral to any big rock band—the yin of introspective tech geek vs. the yang of spotlight-crazed mouthy geek.

On *Results May Vary*, Limp Bizkit's fourth studio album, Durst is the latest in a series of megasuccessful pop stars to beat you over the head with their pain; he even covers the Who's tears-of-a-clown classic "Behind Blue Eyes." Admittedly, Durst lost his longtime guitarist and broke up with Britney Spears within the span of a year, but you gotta wonder if his hardships warrant rote attempts at pathos such as "[high school] was like a prison with bullies always putting me down/just a little skater boy they could pick on/I learned to forgive 'em, now I got the balls they can lick on." But Durst and his mates—including new guitarist Mike Smith—use mook melancholy as the inspiration for a dark, streamlined attack. With their usual guitar-heavy thrash still in place, songs such as "Creamer" and "Lonely World" get by on Linkin Park–style electronic textures, stutter-step rhythms, and catchy, cathartic choruses. Durst still raps like a linebacker, but he hasn't lost his knack for big, heavy hooks—witness the hard-driving first single, "Eat You Alive." —K.H.

Linkin Park

★★★½	Hybrid Theory (Sony, 2000)
★★½	Reanimation (Sony, 2002)
★★★	Meteora (Sony, 2003)
★★	Live in Texas (Sony, 2003)

Linkin Park must have been designed in a laboratory as the consummate rap-metal band: the angry vocals, the headbanging guitar, the renegades-of-funk rhythm section, the DJ scratching between verses, the baggy pants, the gratuitous use of the letter *K*. Although they got lumped in with bands like Korn and Limp Bizkit, Linkin Park sang sensitive songs about the secret life of boys, hitting a nerve in the audience with their brotherly compassion: *Hybrid Theory* was the biggest seller of 2001. Brad Delson's flash guitar, Mike Shinoda's low-key rapping, and Chester Bennington's Freddie Mercury–has-risen-from-the-grave vocals fused into intensely emotional teen angst. "In the End," their biggest and best hit, was really the flip side of Limp Bizkit's "Nookie," the cry of an embattled young dude who finds out the hard way that nice guys have girl troubles, too, just like the Fred Dursts of the world.

Meteora sucked a few last drops from the rap-metal formula. The quickie *Live in Texas* followed the strategy, "Give the people as much as they can stand of what they want." The remix album *Reanimation* featured underground hip-hop producers such as Kutmasta Kurt, X-ecutioners, Dilated Peoples' Evidence, and the excellently named Jewbacca. Guest vocalists include rockers such as Korn's Jonathan Davis and Staind's Aaron Lewis, as well as indie rappers such as Aceyalone, Rasco, Planet Asia, and Jurassic 5's Chali 2na. —R.S.

Little Feat

★★★½	Little Feat (Warner Bros., 1971)
★★★★	Sailin' Shoes (Warner Bros., 1972)
★★★★	Dixie Chicken (Warner Bros., 1973)
★★★½	Feats Don't Fail Me Now (Warner Bros., 1974)
★★★	The Last Record Album (Warner Bros., 1975)
★★★	Time Loves a Hero (Warner Bros., 1977)
★★★	Waiting for Columbus (Warner Bros., 1979)

★★½　Down on the Farm (Warner Bros., 1979)
★★★½　Hoy Hoy (Warner Bros., 1981)
★★★　Let It Roll (Warner Bros., 1988)
★★　Representing the Mambo (Warner Bros., 1989)
★★　Shake Me Up (Morgan Creek, 1991)
★★★　Ain't Had Enough Fun (Zoo, 1995)
★★½　Live From Neon Park (Zoo, 1996)
★★　Under the Radar (CMC, 1998)
★★　Chinese Work Songs (CMC, 2000)
★★　Down Upon the Suwannee River (Hot Tomato, 2003)
★★　Kickin' It at the Barn (Hot Tomato, 2003)

Little Feat hailed from Los Angeles, but by its mid-'70s prime this funky, bluesy band was embraced by fans below and beyond the Mason-Dixon Line as one of the finest purveyors of the era's popular Southern-fried boogie. Led by ex–Mothers of Invention guitarist Lowell George, Little Feat's overlooked first album introduced a weirder, wilder, West Coast version of the Band, blending and blurring American musical styles like Captain Beefheart leading a garage-rock combo along with Hank Williams, Howlin' Wolf, Duane Allman, and Jack Kerouac. George's warped, travel-weary storytelling on songs like "Truck Stop Girl," "Willin'," "Crack in Your Door," and "Crazy Captain Gunboat Willie" immediately distinguished this outfit from your average California jam band.

Although Little Feat's album art would get even more surreal on subsequent releases, beginning with *Sailin' Shoes* the group began honing its raw, avant-country-rock tendencies into a tight, eclectic blend of lean country, blues, rock, and New Orleans–style funk. In 1972, Lowell George was the missing link between Gram Parsons, Frank Zappa, and Allen Toussaint, and this stylistic recipe would pay off for the band, both critically and commercially. From the raw "A Apolitical Blues" to the shuffling "Tripe Face Boogie" to the full-on rock & roll of "Teenage Nervous Breakdown," Little Feat had found its voice.

With *Dixie Chicken,* the band found its audience. Following a lineup change that replaced bass player Roy Estrada and guitarist Ron Elliott with the more funk-friendly Kenny Gradney and Paul Barrere, as well as conga player Sam Clayton, George and company expanded their rhythmic vocabulary, delivering laid-back, groove-heavy tunes that would be hallmarks of Little Feat's live performances: "Fat Man in the Bathtub," "Two Trains," and the rubbery strut of the title track. It was here that Little Feat—as a razor-sharp unit and not just a vehicle for George's crazy songcraft and slide guitar—reached its apex. By the time of the aptly named *Feats Don't Fail Me Now,* the band had locked into a serious groove. If George's

songwriting had begun showing slight signs of fatigue, the band's powerhouse funk was as strong as ever, due in no small part to Little Feat's constant live performing. For better and for worse, percussionist/keyboardist Bill Payne's rocking "Oh, Atlanta," Barrere's funky "Skin It Back," and George's moaning "Spanish Moon" provided the formula for the band's subsequent albums.

For all intents and purposes, *Feats Don't Fail Me* had been Little Feat's final moment as a boundary-pushing rock band, and when *The Last Record Album* appeared it confirmed that George and company were running out of new ideas. Here the group comes off as little more than a laid-back, middle-of-the-road fusion band, although tracks like "All That You Dream" placed them a notch above similarly inclined contemporaries such as the Atlanta Rhythm Section. Little Feat had lost much of its inspiration by *Time Loves a Hero.* With leader George fighting his addictions and turning his attention toward a solo career, Barrere took the reins and steered Little Feat further into a synthesizer/fusion direction. The title track and "Old Folks Boogie" were the highlights of *Time,* but even those songs sounded more inspired on the band's live album, *Waiting for Columbus.* Fueled by Tower of Power's barrelhouse horn section, *Columbus* was a good document of Little Feat's jam-heavy performances, but by the time of its release the band that Lowell George had built was on its last leg.

George was on tour in support of his exhilarating solo debut *Thanks I'll Eat It Here* when he suffered a fatal heart attack on stage in Virginia. Little Feat had been recording *Down on the Farm* at the time of his death, and the album sounds as patched together as it was. It's clear that George had reserved his best vocal performances for his solo album: *Down on the Farm*'s "Kokomo" was one of the finest songs that Gregg Allman didn't write, but for the most part the album was (understandably) a spotty, uninspired affair, typical of the slick, mellow country rock sounds coming out of California by the late 1970s. For nearly a decade, Little Feat remained dormant.

In 1988, Barrere, Payne, and the others reunited Little Feat, with former Pure Prairie League founder Craig Fuller replacing George on lead vocals. Though it lacks the songwriting edge of the George-era Little Feat, *Let It Roll* is a funky musical feast that finds the band returning to the pre-fusion sound of *Feats Don't Fail Me Now.* Not only that, but the album gets a serious vocal punch from guest spots by Bonnie Raitt and Linda Ronstadt. The reunited Little Feat could not sustain its renewed passion, though, and subsequent releases by this lineup were at best uneven. The band got a brief third wind in the mid-'90s when they recruited the Bonnie Raitt–sound-alike Shaun Murphy for *Ain't Had Enough Fun,* but again, subsequent releases suffered from too much filler and not enough killer. Little Feat continue to tour as one of many jamband replacements for the Grateful Dead, and on a good night they can crank out competent if pedestrian performances of their old chestnuts.

Most of Little Feat's compilation CDs are strong. *Hoy Hoy* collects some of the band's best overlooked songs with rarities and live tracks, but it's hardly an adequate career retrospective; for that, look to *As Time Goes By.* Avoid the slick, live Extended Versions—it's a set of mostly classic songs performed by the reunited Little Feat. The four-CD Rhino collection *Hotcakes and Outtakes* presents a Lowell George–heavy portrait of the band in all its funky, envelope-pushing glory. A top-notch boxed retrospective. —M.K.

Little Richard

    ★★★★   Here's Little Richard (1957; Specialty, 1991)
    ★★★   The Fabulous Little Richard (1959; Specialty, 1991)
    ★★★★★   His Biggest Hits (1959; Specialty, 1991)
    ★★★   Greatest Hits Recorded Live (1967; Epic, 1994)
    ★★★★   The Essential Little Richard (1985; Specialty, 1989)
    ★★★★★   The Specialty Sessions (Specialty, 1990)
    ★★★★★   The Georgia Peach (Specialty, 1991)
    ★★½   Greatest Songs (Curb, 1995)
    ★★★½   Shag On Down by the Union Hall (Specialty, 1996)
    ★★★   God Is Real (MCA, 1999)
    ★★★   Good Golly! (RSP, 1999)
    ★★★   Very Best of the Vee Jay Years, Volume 1 (Collectables, 2000)
    ★★★   Very Best of the Vee Jay Years, Volume 2 (Collectables, 2000)

By this time the basic facts and claims about Little Richard Penniman are well known and, on record, now well documented, thanks to an ambitious reissue program on Specialty's part. All of Little Richard's Specialty albums are now available in their original packaging—vinyl even—and original song selection. So are numerous collections of the songs that form one of the foundations of rock & roll—"Rip It Up," "Long Tall Sally," "Keep A-Knockin'," "Lucille," "Jenny Jenny," "Tutti Frutti," "Good Golly, Miss Molly," and "Ready Teddy." Pause and consider that the Quasar of Rock recorded these Olympian moments, which have influenced each succeeding generation of rock artists and will continue to do so until the

planet destroys itself, in a two-year period dating from September 1955 to October 1957, when Penniman had a religious conversion and retired from rock & roll to study for the ministry. Ranking these collections is something of a problem, because in any setting the hits retain their emotional pull and historical resonance. Those so inclined will find in these tracks more fuel for the argument that New Orleans was the birthplace of rock & roll, as many of Penniman's sessions were cut in the Crescent City with then-unknown musicians who were inventing something new virtually every time they picked up their instruments. So indeed, consumers will get their money's worth from *His Biggest Hits, The Essential Little Richard,* and *The Georgia Peach,* with the latter having an edge over the other titles because of its splendid annotation by Billy Vera. Still, the music carries the day, and all are legitimate classics.

If that is the case, there should be an extra star for *The Specialty Sessions,* because it is the rare box set that can be enjoyed by completists, historians, and casual fans alike. This is, as the title suggests, everything Penniman put on tape for the Specialty label, from previously unreleased demo sessions in February 1955 before he was signed to sessions cut in 1964 when Penniman was making the first of his many comebacks. In between are all the famous songs, alternate takes, demos, false starts, the movie version of "The Girl Can't Help It," even a Royal Crown Hairdressing commercial Penniman cut for radio DJ Gene Noble. In addition, each disc in this three-CD collection comes with a well-researched booklet explaining the who, what, why, when, where, and how of the sessions, as well as keeping track of Penniman's career as limned by the disc in question. To say this is the most important work Penniman has done in his long career is to state the obvious; to say that it ranks with the most important work by any of rock's pioneers may also be stating the obvious, but it needs to be said anyway simply to emphasize the long shadow cast by these songs.

As a corollary to the box set, check out *Shag On Down by the Union Hall,* another Specialty gem that includes some of the Little Richard essentials among its 24 tracks, but also his engaging, swinging interpretations of standards such as "Baby Face" and "By the Light of the Silvery Moon," as well as four key cuts from his 1964 comeback including "Bama Lama Bama Loo." In its own way this disc is a sort of *Specialty Sessions* summary—but hardly a substitute for the real deal. For those looking for the cream of the crop, the hits and best-known songs only, several attractive options are out there. *Here's Little Richard,* originally released in 1957, could well have been titled

Greatest Hits—its dozen cuts are strictly in-his-prime Little Richard, including "Tutti Frutti," "Jenny Jenny," "Ready Teddy," "Long Tall Sally," "Miss Ann," "Rip It Up," and "She's Got It." *His Biggest Hits,* originally released in 1959, is explained by its title. *The Essential Little Richard,* which preceded *The Specialty Sessions* to the market by five years, in its original incarnation as a double-vinyl set foretold the coming of the box set in including the 1955 Macon demos that earned Penniman his Specialty tryout, and 18 other cuts spanning the critical 1955–57 period; its notes also feature the personnel listings that are absent from the box set's liner notes (making their omission there all the more puzzling). Released in 1959 by Specialty, after the artist had retired to the ministry, *The Fabulous Little Richard* features some good, bluesy performances by Penniman ("Shake a Hand," "Lonesome and Blue," "Early One Morning") as well as a credible take on "Whole Lotta Shakin' " and the boisterous version of "Kansas City/Hey-Hey-Hey-Hey" that would become more familiar in a cover version on *Beatles VI.* For those who want to get to the heart of the matter, with no side trips, RSP's 10-cut *Good Golly* collection zeroes in on the evergreens. *The Georgia Peach* is a recommended latter-day anthology of the great songs, with the added bonus of astute liner notes by the always-reliable Billy Vera.

Little Richard's gospel years are almost unrepresented on disc now. He recorded for a number of labels after becoming a man of the cloth, but the only sides still in print are a few recorded for Coral in 1959, on *God Is Real.* Suffice it to say the man is fully in the spirit here: Performances of "Every Time I Feel the Spirit" and "Just a Closer Walk With Thee" indicate how persuasive a servant of God the man would have been, had he stayed in the pulpit.

One of his first stops post-ministry, and following his aborted return to Specialty in 1964, was Chicago's Vee-Jay label. Way too much of his output here was in the form of updated versions of his Specialty catalogue, and though the music is still "poundin'," and Penniman's vocals are as expressive as ever, there's not much reason to recommend these discs, except to completists (and perhaps to fans of Jimi Hendrix, who is reported to have played on these sessions). Unfortunately, the two volumes of Vee-Jay recordings issued by Collectables as *The Very Best of the Vee-Jay Years* contain absolutely no session information. A better stab at rerecordings comes by way of *Greatest Hits Recorded Live,* originally a 1967 release on the Okeh label, now reissued by Epic. As the title indicates, this is a live recording, with Little Richard at his most effusive and fronting a hot band led by none other than his former Specialty labelmate and friend Larry ("Bad

Boy") Williams. Apart from the titles indicated here, all that's left is to hope some label takes a chance on a still-vital Little Richard and puts him back in the studio soon, and that Warner Bros. will one day see fit to reissue the recordings he made for that label in 1969–70, one of which, "Freedom Blues," finds the Quasar in vintage form on a song that had a bit of extra resonance when it was issued at the height of the Vietnam War. Back in the day, "Freedom Blues" was a bold reminder of the special gifts this man Richard Penniman brings to his art. And he's still doing it. —D.M.

Live

★★	Mental Jewelry (Radioactive/MCA, 1991)
★★★★	Throwing Copper (Radioactive/MCA, 1994)
★★½	Secret Samadhi (Radioactive/MCA, 1997)
★★	The Distance to Here (Radioactive/MCA, 1999)
★★½	They Stood Up for Love (Radioactive/MCA, 2000)
★★★½	V (Radioactive/MCA, 2001)
★★½	Birds of Pray (Radioactive/MCA, 2003)

Most bands gradually acquire a sense of self-importance. Not Live. By its second album, the commerical breakthrough *Throwing Copper,* the York, PA, quartet appeared convinced of the righteousness of its mission—postgrunge anthem rock informed by philosophical, vaguely Eastern lyric themes—and as a result was hailed by some as the next coming of U2 and derided by others as self-important blowhards with a messiah complex.

The Live rhythm section—guitarist Chad Taylor, bassist Patrick Dahlheimer, drummer Chad Gracey—began playing music together in middle school as First Aid and by high school had teamed up with singer and songwriter Ed Kowalczyk, who in the years since Live's emergence has carefully followed the Bono/ Michael Stipe playbook, embracing the role of lead singer/spiritual seeker/cryptic interview subject with aplomb.

After kicking around the Northeast original-rock circuit in the late '80s, Live eventually landed a deal with Radioactive Records, and had Talking Head Jerry Harrison produce its uneven 1991 debut *Mental Jewelry.* Three years later came *Throwing Copper,* again produced by Harrison. Much more disciplined than its predecessor in terms of songwriting, the album's stately processionals ("Lightning Crashes") and ferocious rock declarations ("I Alone") became staples of Modern Rock radio; the album stayed on the charts for months, and in the course of several dogged tours the band went from playing clubs to headlining arenas.

The Live story post–*Throwing Copper* has been one of disappointment and a slow crawl back to artistic redemption. The heavy-handed *Secret Samadhi* found the band using turgid, foreboding prog-rock accompaniments to prattle on about modern moral quandries. *The Distance to Here* got the band back on the radio—"The Dolphin's Cry" was a minor hit—but was even more erratic. Sacrificing its metaphysical meditations in favor of pedestrian discussions of romance, Live begged for reconsideration with *They Stood Up for Love,* but it was only with the comparatively breezy *V* that the band hit its stride: Here, the rhythm section roared with a lean efficency that was missing from its previous outings, and Kowalczyk managed to slip wry (and sometimes bitter) observations on life into his songs without turning them into hectoring screeds. And, amazingly, there were genuine vocal melodies—the fervent "Deep Enough" walloped as hard as anything on *Throwing Copper,* and "Overcome," which was used in an oft-seen video surveying the devastation of the Sept. 11 terrorist attacks, was as beautiful as anything the band has recorded. Still, the album failed to galvanize the faithful, much less expand Live's audience.

Birds of Pray, issued in 2003, met the same fate: Though the lyrics offer more personal insights from Kowalcyzk—he mentions his young daughter on "What Are We Fighting For" and others—the high-pomp anthems end up seeming like a pale U2 rehash. —T.M.

Living Colour

★★★★	Vivid (Epic, 1988)
★★★★	Time's Up (Epic, 1990)
★★★½	Biscuits EP (Epic, 1991)
★★★	Stain (Epic, 1993)
★★★★	Pride (Epic, 1995)
★★★★	Superhits (Epic/Legacy, 1998)
★★½	Collideoscope (Sanctuary, 2003)

A lot of hard-rock acts imitate Led Zeppelin, but Living Colour is one of the few that managed to *emulate* the group. Instead of slavishly copping licks from the Zep catalogue, Living Colour appropriated the band's eclecticism and eagerness to experiment, a combination that keeps it from falling victim to the clichés that make most metal so predictable.

After all, how many other hard-rock acts would open an album with a sound bite from Malcolm X? But that's exactly how *Vivid* begins, and not only does the quote fit neatly into the sound and sensibility of "Cult of Personality," it nicely balances the song-ending samples of JFK and FDR. More interesting than the song's message, however, is its method, for

"Cult of Personality" happily augments its bluesy power riffing with modal asides that add to the melody without diminishing the aural impact. It helps that the band's founder, Vernon Reid, built his reputation as a jazz guitarist, and that the rhythm section is as at home with funk beats as metal stomps. But *Vivid* is full of unexpected left turns, from the Beach Boys bridge in "I Want to Know" to the James Brown–isms of "What's Your Favorite Color?" to the furious, fusion-style intro to "Desperate People." Best of all, the band backs its musical vision with insight, offering pointed, perceptive social commentary through songs such as "Funny Vibe" and "Open Letter (to a Landlord)."

With *Time's Up,* Living Colour doesn't just maintain its initial momentum, but actually picks up speed. Musically, the band casts an even wider net, opening the album with a nod to the Bad Brains ("Time's Up") and bringing in such guests as Little Richard, Maceo Parker, and Queen Latifah. Accordingly, its best moments are absolutely stunning: "Elvis Is Dead" is a meditation on the Lord of Graceland; "Type" is a thought-provoking attack on the power of image over substance; while "Love Rears Its Ugly Head" is a modern blues, a song about sex and fear and desire that's as real as life itself. *Biscuits,* released while the band was on hiatus, offers nothing new—a live "Desperate People," a leftover from the *Time's Up* sessions, and three covers—but is worth hearing if only for the band's crunchy remake of Al Green's "Love and Happiness" and Reid's incendiary take on Hendrix's "Burning of the Midnight Lamp."

With *Stain,* bassist Muzz Skillings was replaced by Tackhead (and Sugar Hill Records house band) vet Doug Wimbish. Stylistically, it was a step forward for the band, with samples and slick backing vocals fleshing out the sound. But apart from "Ignorance Is Bliss" and the pointedly political "Auslander," the material was largely unexceptional. Within a year of the album's release, Living Colour called it quits, only to reunite for *Collideoscope,* a messy, slightly overbearing album weighed down by too much experimentation and sociopolitical theorizing.

Pride is an aptly titled best-of that, unlike most of its ilk, saves some of its best stuff for last. *Superhits* is a much more meager offering (10 tunes to *Pride*'s 17), but does at least include "Elvis Is Dead," which *Pride* inexplicably omits. —J.D.C.

L.L. Cool J

★★★★	Radio (Def Jam, 1985)
★★½	Bigger and Deffer (Def Jam, 1987)
★★★	Walking With a Panther (Def Jam, 1989)
★★★★	Mama Said Knock You Out (Def Jam, 1990)
★★½	14 Shots to the Dome (Def Jam, 1993)

★★★   Mr. Smith (Def Jam, 1995)
★★★★½   All World: Greatest Hits (Def Jam, 1996)
★★½   Phenomenon (Def Jam, 1997)
★★   G.O.A.T. Featuring James T. Smith: The
            Greatest of All Time (Def Jam, 2000)
★★   10 (Def Jam, 2002)

Following fast on Run-D.M.C.'s trail, James Todd Smith roared out of Queens, NY, with a Kangol brim and his radio cranked to 10. "I Can't Live Without My Radio" establishes his winning persona: L.L. Cool J is cocksure and quick-witted, but he also comes equipped with disarming frankness and a winning sense of humor. He freely admits the boom box drives pedestrians nuts—even if he wouldn't dream of turning it down. His debut pumps nonstop; "Reduced by Rick Rubin" reads the cover, and that's about right. Boiling funk and heavy-metal riffs down to a potent essence, tracks such as the withering "That's a Lie" display a verbal flair and inventiveness that's rarely been matched.

Bigger and Deffer collapses under the sophomore strain—busier and dumber might be closer to the truth—though the crossover hit "I Need Love" represents the first satisfying example of "ballad rap." ("L.L. Cool J," after all, is short for "Ladies Love Cool James.") *Walking With a Panther* pares down the cartoon samples and toughens the funk. L.L. reasserts himself with some feisty assaults, though his incessant boasting grates after a while. It's hard to tell if "Big Ole Butt" celebrates or lampoons macho sexuality; L.L.'s expertly paced narrative flow and the seductive rhythm track don't give you much chance to think. Two steps forward, one step back: Overall, *Panther* is a little frustrating.

Mama Said Knock You Out lands a whopping blow. Once again, L.L. extends his range and even displays a certain amount of maturity. He exhibits a hard-earned self-awareness on cuts such as the devastating "Cheesy Rat Blues" and the hilarious "Boomin' System," though there are no lectures or sermons here—not even on "The Power of God." Producer Marley Marl constructs firm musical support as L.L. revisits the scene of rap's past triumphs, acknowledges its present state of affairs, and points to possible futures. Few pop albums of the early '90s hold a candle to this one. Unfortunately, that's also true of L.L.'s followup discs. Because he's never lost that inimitable kick-boxer delivery, nothing he's recorded is without interest. But from *14 Shots to the Dome* on, serious deficiencies take hold; the more hardcore cuts can sound forced, while the transparent pandering of the lover-man raps stretches tolerance to the breaking point. Worse, L.L. repeatedly falls victim to a common disease of modern hip-hop: the pointless duet (e.g., *Mr. Smith*'s "Hey Lover" with Boyz II Men, *G.O.A.T.*'s "Back Where I Belong" with Ja Rule, or *10*'s "All I Have" with Jennifer Lopez). Yes, most of these tunes were hits, but time was when L.L. had no problem carrying an entire album on his own. Considering how much he's got going on these days—including a successful career as a film and TV actor—it's doubtful he'll muster the focus for that again.   —M.C./M.R.

Local H

★★   Ham Fisted (Island, 1995)
★★   As Good as Dead (Island, 1996)
★★★★   Pack Up the Cats (Island, 1998)
★★★   Here Comes the Zoo (Palm Pictures,
            2002)
★★★½   Whatever Happened to P.J. Soles? (Studio E,
            2004)

Coming in at the tail end of the alternative-rock era, Local H injected enthusiasm into the genre, if not originality; they seized their moment as if playing hooky from school. A duo from Zion, IL (guitarist Scott Lucas and drummer Joe Daniels, later replaced by Brian St. Clair), Local H were the latest in a long line of post-Nirvana grunge bands, but with a twist. On *Ham Fisted* and *As Good as Dead* they play sternum-smashing melodies that verge on satire, bratty rock & roll Davids poking fun at corporate-rock Goliaths ("Chicago Fanphair '93," "Eddie Vedder") and clueless bullies ("High-Fiving MF"). At its worst, their humor comes off a touch smug and the music derivative.

Pack Up the Cats is a huge leap forward in ambition. The band flushes some of the Nirvana comparisons with '70s-style hard-rock songcraft, crossing Cheap Trick's power pop with AC/DC's Godzilla riffs, and a more deeply textured sound (courtesy of Queen and Cars producer Roy Thomas Baker). It's all put in service of one of the savviest and funniest critiques of the rock biz this side of *This Is Spinal Tap!* This time the humor spares no one, even the band itself, as Lucas dissects the relationship between a band and its fans, and the forces (jadedness, money, the media) that drive a wedge between them. "All the Kids Are Right" isn't just inspired by the Who's "The Kids are Alright" and Cheap Trick's "Surrender," it's an anthem that can stand with the wit, power, and poignance of those earlier classics.

With no overarching concept, *Here Comes the Zoo* returns to the my-fist, your-face approach of the earlier albums, only this time with a more developed sense of song and sonics. Guitars hacksaw their way through a wall of kick-drum dementia, even as Lucas delivers the kind of smart-aleck lyrics that don't call attention to just how smart they really are. Two stoned-immaculate epics—"Baby Wants to Tame Me" and "What Would You Have Me Do?"—provide a respite from the hammering, forging a connection between "Stranglehold"-era Ted Nugent and Queens of the Stone Age, whose Josh Homme makes a cameo. *Here Comes the Zoo* confirms that even though Lucas and St. Clair aren't the future of rock, they are among the best at embodying what rock once meant.

Whatever Happened to P.J. Soles? dispenses with some of the more elaborate production ideas explored on the previous two albums for a more brutally direct approach. Lucas joins gleeful put-downs of the self-deluded, himself included, with an encroaching sense of time passing him by. Introspection never gets in the way of a good rock thrashing, however, and at the tail end of "Buffalo Trace," Lucas and St. Clair sound like the heaviest two-man band ever. —G.K.

Lisa Loeb

★★	Tails (Geffen, 1995)
★★★	Firecracker (Geffen, 1997)
★★★	Cake and Pie (A&M, 2002)

With her thick-rimmed teardrop specs and songs that wordily explored the subtleties of romantic relationships, Lisa Loeb entered the public eye in the mid-'90s, looking and sounding like the epitome of the white collegiate folk chick. Her song "Stay," featured in the soundtrack to 1994's *Reality Bites,* made her a star before she even had a recording contract. Fetching in its modesty but just a tad precious, "Stay" reappeared as the closing track of Loeb's debut album. Few of the other songs match it, although the polite jangle-pop of "Waiting for Wednesday" is nice enough. Undeniably pretty, *Tails* is handicapped by the stuffy creative-writing-class aura that hangs over it.

Firecracker is more musically diverse and more mature, a few overreaching lyrics aside. "I Do" and "Truthfully" affirm that Loeb can pen a catchy tune; the smooth jazz stylings of "Dance With the Angels" are intriguing, if not entirely successful. Five years later, Loeb teamed up with Dweezil Zappa to produce *Cake and Pie.* Easily as good as its predecessor, the album once again demonstrates Loeb's crafty pop touch on songs like "The Way It Really Is" and "Everyday." Several tracks also pile on distorted guitars in an attempt to toughen up her sound—not a bad idea, but unfortunately it falls flat. Try as she might, Loeb just doesn't make a convincing rocker. —M.R.

Lo Fidelity Allstars

★★	How to Operate With a Blown Mind (Skint/Columbia, 1999)
★★★★	On the Floor at the Boutique (Skint/Columbia, 2000)
★★★	Don't Be Afraid of Love (Skint/Columbia, 2002)
★★★	Abstract Funk Theory (Obsessive [U.K.], 2003)

Originally a six-piece band centered around DJ Phil Ward ("the Albino Priest"), with a lead vocalist (Dave Randall) who called himself the Wrekked Train, Leeds' Lo Fidelity Allstars were one of the flagship bands on Brighton's Skint Records—the home of Fatboy Slim and spiritual center of the happy, accessible "big beat" dance movement—during its late-'90s heyday. Unfortunately, their first album, *How to Operate With a Blown Mind,* offered sluggish, prog-rockish grooves that did less body-rocking than just standing around. The disc's only really memorable track, "Battleflag," featured the vocals of Brad Smith of Seattle duo Pigeonhed. So when Randall left the group shortly before a 1999 tour, it's hardly surprising that the group used a revolving door of vocalists for the followup. *Don't Be Afraid of Love* features appearances from Bootsy Collins, Greg Dulli (Afghan Whigs), and Jamie Lidell (Super Collider), and is far tighter, both song- and groove-wise. The poppy instant classic "Feel What I Feel" resembles a collision between Meat Loaf and Basement Jaxx, while "On the Pier" features Collins abetting a twisted soul groove. Between those albums, Ward put together a superb volume of Skint's *On the Floor at the Boutique* DJ-mix series, juggling classics from Boogie Down Productions, Blackstreet, and Armand Van Helden, as well as Feelgood Factor's (a.k.a. Fatboy Slim) aptly titled "The Whole Church Should Get Drunk." The Lo Fi's compilation *Abstract Funk Theory* connected the dots between Mercury Rev, the Jimmy Castor Bunch, and Rhythim is Rhythim. —M.M.

London Suede

★★★★	Suede (Columbia, 1993)
★★★★	Stay Together (Columbia, 1994)
★★★½	Dog Man Star (Columbia, 1994)
★★★½	Coming Up (Columbia, 1996)
★★★½	Sci-Fi Lullabies (Columbia, 1997)
★★★	Head Music (Columbia, 1999)

Suede was one of the first bands to emerge in the great Britpop wave of the '90s, a bunch of Bowie boys led by the hair-flipping, gender-twisting, and falsetto-abusing Brett Anderson. (Unfortunately, they were forced to change their name to the London Suede in

America for legal reasons, although their American cult has always continued to call the band Suede anyway.) Anderson preens all the way through the band's excellent 1993 debut album *Suede,* yelping "This skinny boy is one of the girls!" over the opening riffs of "Animal Lover." Bernard Butler builds a wall of glam guitars as Anderson moans about nightmarish sex-and-drug misadventures in "The Drowners," "Animal Nitrate," and the morbid eight-minute ballad "Breakdown," where he dismisses a rival as "the canine in the A-line." Proclaiming himself "a bisexual man who's never had a homosexual experience," Anderson became a huge U.K. pop star overnight.

The closest the band came to a U.S. hit was probably "Stay Together," from the near-album-length EP of the same name. "Stay Together" and "My Dark Star" are Suede's most passionate love songs, while "The Living Dead" has one quintessential moment where Brett suddenly interrupts a lulling acoustic-guitar interlude with the ear-splitting shriek, "I was the wife of an acrobat!" It's one of the many Suede moments that feels like heaven for cultists, hell for everybody else.

Suede never did crack America, partly because of the mix-up over the band's name, and partly because *Dog Man Star* was one of the most pretentious albums ever released by a major label. It's all dark, druggy guitar textures, topped by purple poesy about wild pigs and running dogs and other fruits of Anderson's overheated brain. (The album's opening lines: "Dog man star took a suck on a pill/And stabbed a cerebellum with a curious quill.") But the best song was "The Wild Ones," a ballad about listening to the radio with someone hot, and there can never be enough songs about that. Although *Dog Man Star* was great in its way, Butler quit before it was even released. Fans figured that the band was finished, and yet with teenaged replacement guitarist Richard Oakes on hand, *Coming Up* was a surprisingly solid and simplified return, featuring the anthem "Trash": "We're trash, you and me/We're the litter on the breeze/We're the lovers on the streets." Suede never really threatened the charts again, but while the surprise may be gone, their albums have delivered consistent quality entertainment for glam fans and connoisseurs of thirdhand decadence everywhere. *Sci-Fi Lullabies* is a two-disc rarities collection; the Butler-era first disc has "To the Birds," "My Insatiable One," and "My Dark Star," while the Oakes-era second disc has lesser, later material. —R.S.

Jennifer Lopez

★★ On the 6 (Sony, 1999)
★★ J.Lo (Epic, 2000)
★★ J. to tha L-O! The Remixes (Epic, 2002)
★★½ This is Me . . . Then (Epic, 2002)

The fact that listening to her records has markedly diminishing returns does no damage to Jennifer Lopez's celebrity. She keeps her fame moments popping like popcorn—film appearance, hit single, sultry video, gossip-page headline, scandal—another kernel exploding just when a previous one has been consumed. A self-crafted multimedia star couldn't put out a more fitting debut than *On the 6:* mildly friendly, mildly sexy hip-hop, and Latin-tinged R&B whose best moments showcase not her thin voice but her great instincts. Sean Combs produces the party-down R&B of "If You Had My Love" and "Feelin' So Good," and Emilio Estefan Jr.'s uncluttered production reveals the strong bones of "Let's Get Loud," a supertight salsa-inflected party song. The remaining dozen numbers exist to fill space between the hits and drift facelessly throughout beauty salons everywhere.

Proving that Lopez needs only a decent song to touch her vocals with in order to have a megahit, *J.Lo* provides four terrific tunes on five tracks. The album is front-loaded with the good stuff—"Love Don't Cost a Thing," "I'm Real," "Play," and "Ain't It Funny," half of which casts Lopez as a humble girlfriend who just happens to have her own Mercedes and won't trouble you for yours. Her voice is stronger here, and she sounds loose and comfortable on the infectious disco-salsa ("Ain't It Funny," "Dame," "Carino"), but the wallpaper ballads and lame R&B are such a drag that even Ja Rule can't save a gangsta reprise of "I'm Real" no matter how many profanities he bellows in the song's corners. *This Is Me . . . Then* includes the deathless "Jenny From the Block," which is sure to be a regular on any future *Best of the '00s* singles collection, along with the painfully dated "Dear Ben"—hey Affleck, you saw the album title, right? —A.B./N.B.

Mary Lou Lord

★★★★ Got No Shadow (Work, 1998)
★★★ Live City Sounds (Rubric, 2001)

As anyone who's spent much time in a major city can attest, street musicians are pretty annoying. For the early part of her career, Mary Lou Lord, who cut her teeth busking in Boston, recorded nothing that made her an exception. Her first batch of singles and EPs, on Kill Rock Stars, presented her as little more than an enthusiastic indie-rock fan (she had a particular weakness for the Bevis Frond and Daniel Johnston) with a nice if wispy voice. During a period when female songwriters were commanding so much attention, the singer—so girlie-voiced she made Juliana

Hatfield sound like Courtney Love—seemed out of step with the spirit of the age.

By the time Lord recorded her first real album, *Got No Shadow,* alt-rock was out of commercial favor. Lord sang like a real adult now, recording solid versions of her own songs and material by Freedy Johnston, along with the folk oldie "Shake Sugaree." "She Had You" is a tale of lingering jealousy, worthy of Elvis Costello, and "Some Jingle Jangle Morning"—a snapshot of an aging post-indie rock scene where "No one sees much of anyone these days"—sounds more timely now than when she'd originally cut it years earlier. Even the album's production sound, a carefully burnished folk rock, seems fitting, as if Lord was making the sort of accommodations to the mainstream that most aging indie types were making in their everyday life.

If anyone had heard it, *Got No Shadow* could have been as much a landmark in its way as Jackson Browne's *Running on Empty* was for post-hippies in the '70s. But the disc did nothing commercially and didn't generate much interest among her fans, and Lord largely stayed out of the studio after that. Her only other full-length disc is a live collection, recorded back where she started, in the subway. The disc offers nice readings of Richard Thompson and Bruce Springsteen ("Thunder Road," believe it or not); it would be a shame if Lord didn't take another crack at a real record. —K.H.

Los Lobos

★★★   Del Este de Los Angeles (1977; Hollywood, 2000)
★★★½   . . . And a Time to Dance (Slash, 1983)
★★★★   How Will the Wolf Survive? (Slash/Warner Bros., 1984)
★★½   By the Light of the Moon (Slash/Warner Bros., 1987)
★★★½   La Bamba (Slash/Warner Bros., 1987)
★★★½   La Pistola y el Corazón (Slash/Warner Bros., 1988)
★★★★   The Neighborhood (Slash/Warner Bros., 1990)
★★★★★ Kiko (Slash/Warner Bros., 1992)
★★★★   Just Another Band From East L.A.—A Collection (Slash/Warner Bros., 1993)
★★★½   Colossal Head (Slash/Warner Bros., 1996)
★★★★   This Time (Hollywood, 1999)
★★★★½ El Cancionero—Mas y Mas: A History of the Band From East L.A. (Rhino, 2000)
★★★★   Good Morning Aztlán (Mammoth, 2002)
★★★★   The Ride (Mammoth, 2004)

One of the great roots-rock bands of the last few decades, Los Lobos have become ever greater as they've gotten more and more creative with their roots. The band has always counted *musica norteño* and other Mexican–folk styles among its sources, but Los Lobos have treated such music as just part of the mix, on par with R&B or country or the blues.

Although Los Lobos cut an album for local consumption in East L.A. in the late '70s *(De Este de Los Angeles)* it was . . . *And a Time to Dance* that introduced the band to America at large. Packed with seven sweatily endearing dance tunes, it ranges from the classic rock & roll of Richie Valens' "Come On, Let's Go" to the spirited Tex-Mex two-step of "Anselma." Still, the accordion-spiked blues of "Let's Say Goodnight" most clearly defines the band, and such rangy eclecticism is also typical of Los Lobos' first full album, *How Will the Wolf Survive?* With stunning ease, the band leaps from the blues-rock snarl of "Don't Worry Baby" to the giddy norteño groove of "Corrida #1" to the delicate string-band interplay of "Lil' King of Everything."

With *By the Light of the Moon,* the group broadens its lyrical perspective, moving from the realm of everyday romance to more explicitly ethical and political ground. But the big-picture efforts often seems forced, and apart from "One Time One Night," which strongly recalls Dave Alvin's later writing for the Blasters, and the lovely "River of Fools," the album is generally disappointing.

Yet with *La Bamba,* a soundtrack album for the Ritchie Valens bio-pic, Los Lobos wound up with a chart-topping single (the title tune) and a second Top 40 hit ("Come On, Let's Go"). On the whole, *La Bamba* manages to convey all of Los Lobos' appeal without any of its essence; perhaps that's why *La Pistola y el Corazón* focused exclusively on Mexican traditional tunes, avoiding rock & roll entirely.

Apparently reinvigorated, the band sounds stronger than ever on *The Neighborhood.* Some of that may have to do with the use of studio drummers to shore up Louis Pérez's sometimes shaky time keeping, but mostly it's the material, which finds the band showing all its strengths, whether in the muscular stomp of "Georgia Slop," the gentle strains of "Little John of God," or the giddy, multiethnic waltz of "The Giving Tree." *Kiko,* produced by the team of Mitchell Froom and Tchad Blake (who, with Los Lobos guitarists David Hildago and Cesar Rojas, would record two albums as the Latin Playboys), broadened the band's palette considerably, transforming its blues impulses and bringing a dreamy sonic gauze to the wistful beauty of "Kiko and the Lavender Moon." *Colossal Head* and *This Time* continued the collaboration with frequently stunning results ("Mas y Mas," from *Colossal Head,* is as good as anything the band ever cut), while *Good Morning Aztlán* found the wolves drawing from an even wider range of South American influences (as on "Luz de Mi Vida" and "Malaqué") without relinquishing its country and blues chops. If that seemed to suggest the group was pulling away from its Americano roots, *The Ride* clarified matters, using a string of celebrity cameos—by Bobby Womack, Elvis Costello, Mavis Staples, Richard Thompson, and Rubén Blades, among others—to add sparkle to the material. Womack's soulful singing on "Across 110th Street" is especially sweet. If anything, the band seems to get stronger with each passing year.

Of the anthologies, *Just Another Band From East L.A.* makes a reasonable hits package, but presents a fairly shallow view of the band. By contrast, the four-CD *El Cancionero—Mas y Mas* includes all the essentials as well as some well-chosen rarities and samples from the band's various spin-off projects. —J.D.C.

Los Lonely Boys

★★★ Los Lonely Boys (Epic/Or/Pedernales, 2003)

Few artists in any genre have inspired as many uninspired imitators as Stevie Ray Vaughan. But among the innumerable knockoffs to come along in the Texas blues icon's wake, Los Lonely Boys distinguish themselves by merit of tight blood-brother harmonies, a pinch of Latin spice, and an infectious enthusiasm for the form. The pride of sleepy San Angelo, TX, Garza brothers Henry (guitar), JoJo (bass), and Ringo (drums, natch) didn't have anything new to say (sample lyric: "Our love is deeper than any ocean/My heart is pounding with real emotions") on their self-titled, bilingual debut, but the passion at play is as undeniable as their vocal and instrumental chops. Predictably, the most reverent Vaughan facsimiles ("Crazy Dream") are the least interesting—a little more Mex in their Tex-Mex would help—but "Real Emotions" makes up for the aforementioned duff lyrics with a snarling, hooky riff, while the sprawling, nine-minute "Onda" channels Santana at his organic best. The ballads "Hollywood," "More Than Love," and "La Contestacion" (the last sung in Spanish, with outspoken fan Willie Nelson pitching in on guitar), meanwhile, showcase the kind of sweetly melodic pop smarts that with further refinement should distance Los Lonely Boys even more from the rest of the blues-brothers crowd. —R.SK.

Love

★★★½ Love (Elektra, 1966)
★★★★ Da Capo (Elektra, 1967)

★★★★½ Forever Changes (Elektra, 1968)
★★★ False Start (One Way, 1970)
★★★½ Love Revisited (Elektra, 1970)
★★★ Out There (Big Beat, 1988)
★★★★ Love Story 1966–1972 (Rhino/Elektra, 1995)
★★★ Comes in Colours (Raven, 1997)
★★★★★ Forever Changes (Deluxe Edition) (Rhino, 2001)

With lead singer/guitarist Arthur Lee as the group's weirdo mastermind, this L.A. quintet made three psychedelicized folk-rock classics in the mid-'60s. *Love* plays like strange, sloppy Byrds: Chiming guitars and dark vocals transmute Burt Bacharach's "My Little Red Book" from fluff into a sly threat; "Hey Joe" is all frenzied jangling; "Signed D.C." is a remarkably candid drug song; and, with titles like "A Message to Pretty" and "My Flash on You," Lee flourishes whimsically hip kiddie lyrics that find parallels only in Donovan or Prince. A critical success, the record engendered a cult that included Robert Plant and the Move; it also introduced, in Lee, a trippy visionary whose singular soul and private humor would preclude any mass acceptance. *Da Capo* is bolder: "7 and 7 Is" outright pounds; "Orange Skies" and "She Comes in Colors" are strange and lovely. Considered Love's *Sgt. Pepper's, Forever Changes* lives up to its hype: Horns and strings enliven Lee's best group of songs wherein melody reigns, without at all softening the band's surreal power. These three albums are the essential Love: After making them, Lee worked with different players and never quite recaptured the fire. *Love Story 1966–1972* is the best best-of. Lee's out-of-print solo album, *Vindicator* (1972), is pretty wild, as such titles as "Ol' Morgue Mouth" and "Love Jumped Through My Window" suggest. —P.E.

Darlene Love

★★★½ Best of Darlene Love (Abkco, 1992)
★★ Unconditional Love (Harmony, 1998)

Darlene Wright was the lead voice of the Blossoms, the Los Angeles vocal group who backed everyone from Sam Cooke to Elvis Presley, and were background regulars on the TV music show *Shindig!* When her booming voice finally got its big break, however, she found herself still in the background. Phil Spector had fallen so under her vocal spell as he was putting together "He's A Rebel" for the Crystals that he made Darlene the lead singer, but still credited it to the group. She was also out front on its "Crystals" followup, "He's Sure the Boy I Love," and as the featured (but uncredited) member on the Bob B. Soxx and the Blue Jeans' hits "Zip-A-Dee Doo-Dah" and "Why Do Lovers

Break Each Other's Hearts." Spector then changed her name to Darlene Love and released a string of singles which, truth be told, showed that he was saving the A-list material for others. "(Today I Met) The Boy I'm Gonna Marry" is impossible to resist, but her obviously mature pipes are miscast on girlie fodder like "Wait Till My Bobby Gets Home" and "Fine Fine Boy." *The Best of Darlene Love* offers an assortment of Spector-produced recordings under all these aliases, lacking only what is arguably her best performance for the master: "Christmas (Baby Please Come Home)" from his *A Christmas Gift for You* album. The singer published her autobiography, *My Name Is Love,* in 1998. That same year she released *Unconditional Love,* a gospel album that showed her voice to be able and willing, but the problem of finding material up to it still unresolved. —B.E.

Lyle Lovett

★★★½   Lyle Lovett (MCA/Curb, 1986)
★★★★   Pontiac (MCA/Curb, 1987)
★★★   Lyle Lovett & His Large Band (MCA/Curb, 1989)
★★★★½   Joshua Judges Ruth (MCA/Curb, 1992)
★★★★   I Love Everybody (MCA/Curb, 1994)
★★★½   The Road to Ensenada (MCA/Curb, 1996)
★★★½   Step Inside This House (MCA, 1998)
★★★   Live in Texas (MCA, 1999)
★★   Dr. T & the Women (MCA, 2000)
★★★   Anthology Vol. One: Cowboy Man (MCA, 2001)
★★   Smile: Songs From the Movies (MCA, 2003)
★★★½   My Baby Don't Tolerate (Curb/Lost Highway, 2003)

As much as it probably made sense for Lyle Lovett's label to introduce him as a country artist, it was soon apparent he wasn't built for mainstream country—not even for the '80s' "new traditionalist" flavor, despite his firmly planted roots. Still, the Texas songwriter's self-titled debut did quite well with mainstream country fans, who embraced the swinging honky-tonk of "Cowboy Man" as well as the pedal-steel waltz of "God Will," an early taste of Lovett's wry humor. And overall, the mix of country, blues, jazz, and folk makes for an impressive introduction. But on slickly produced tracks such as "You Can't Resist It"—the sort of cheesy lite-rock that would become the country music standard in years to come—it sounds like Lovett's swimming around in a suit that just doesn't fit.

Pontiac asserts something closer to Lovett's true personality, with more consistent folk-based material that's too weird ("If I Had a Boat"), too sophisti-

cated ("Give Me Back My Heart"), too edgy ("L.A. County"), or too smart in general for a long stay on the country charts (though it also fared surprisingly well). Dark even beyond Lovett's usual sardonic pall, *Pontiac* can be mildly misogynistic and disarmingly violent ("Black and Blue")—and pretty funny as well. By the time the disc ends with its tense, unresolved title track and the goofy, more-swing-than-Western "She's Hot to Go," Lovett's tenuous connections to mainstream country are, though not discarded entirely, forever thrown into doubt.

Just what its title says, *Lyle Lovett & His Large Band* features over a dozen musicians—horns and strings included. It's not quite a big band, but it swings nevertheless. In fact, the album's first half is straight swing-light jazz arrangements mixed with mannered blues, including a Clifford Brown cover ("The Blues Walk") and show-stealing vocal contributions from backup blues belter Francine Reed. Then suddenly, the pedal steel breaks in and the record reverts to more familiar fare, including an unironic cover of country standard "Stand by Your Man" and some forgettable folksy material. If it sounds schizophrenic, it is. But Lovett's strong songwriting persona—the straight-faced weirdo looking for love—comes through whether it's jazz ("Here I Am") or country ("I Married Her Just Because She Looks Like You").

By finally integrating his various musical impulses and moods, Lovett triumphs with *Joshua Judges Ruth,* his most confident and memorable recording. From the rollicking blues stride of "I've Been to Memphis" to the epic gospel hand-clapper "Church," and from the noir jazz of "All My Love Is Gone" and mournful folk of "Baltimore" to the country croon of "She's Leaving Me Because She Really Wants To," *Joshua* comes packed with joy and sadness, humor and heartbreak—the tales of life and death that make it something of an Americana masterpiece.

While *I Love Everybody* stretches to a sprawling 18 songs, it's an altogether more modest affair. For one, the sound is more consistent and understated—acoustic guitar, bass, drums, and strings (plus the occasional vocal quartet) etch out a sophisticated adult folk. And the material, much of it dating back to the '80s (though all previously unreleased and newly recorded) lacks the weight of its predecessor. But that's not to suggest quirky miniatures like "Skinny Legs" and "Fat Babies," or the uncharacteristically funky "Penguins," or winsome ditties like "Hello Grandma" and "Record Lady," are anything less than delightful—or that a song like "The Fat Girl" can't be disarmingly heartbreaking, even edgy. And with the sappy title-track finale, complete with then-wife Julia

Roberts' backing vocals, Lovett confounds his own misanthropic image once again.

By the time *The Road to Ensenada* kicked off Lovett's second decade as a recording artist, his style (and audience) had morphed so entirely that *Ensenada*'s return to country arrangements probably sounded quite foreign to his fans. "Fiona" would fit right in among *Pontiac*'s dark twang, and "That's Right (You're Not From Texas)" is the kind of high-energy Western swing that would've made *His Large Band* feel more cohesive. With one notable exception—"Her First Mistake," a clever story-song that's more Brazilian pop than country—*Ensenada* brings Lovett's career full circle.

Since Lovett has yet to follow *Ensenada* with an album of new, original material, the rest of the story, unfortunately, seems something like regression. On the two-CD *Step Inside This House*, Lovett pays tribute to the Texas (and Texas-associated) songwriters that shaped his own sensibility. While songs by Guy Clark, Townes Van Zandt, Willis Alan Ramsey, and Robert Earl Keen could be expected, others—most notably, Steven Fromholz's 1969 "Texas Trilogy"—are truly revelatory. The material, whether by friends and mentors or from traditional sources ("Texas River Song"), is uniformly first-rate—in fact, the songs are uniform enough to sound like they could be Lovett's own. Except that Lovett's best writing surpasses that of his heroes—and that's what ultimately limits *Step Inside* as little more than an interesting diversion.

Live in Texas features concert recordings from the summer of 1995—making them four years old at the time of release. The Large Band sounds sharp and supremely polished, drawing from all the original albums—even redeeming "You Can't Resist It" with a rootsier arrangement. Unfortunately, it doesn't include any of Lovett's deadpan stage banter and stories—things that make his concerts particularly entertaining. *Dr. T & the Women* is the soundtrack to a film set in Texas, by director Robert Altman (who has used Lovett as an actor in previous films). Here, Lovett and bandmates Viktor Krause (bass) and Matt Rolling (piano) compose and perform mostly instrumental music in a country and Western-swing vein. Aside from some scary incidental music, it sounds a lot like Lyle Lovett songs without words. Also included: two songs from *Joshua Judges Ruth* and a new, livelier version of "Ain't It Somethin' " (from *I Love Everybody*).

Anthology Vol. One: Cowboy Man compiles 15 songs from Lovett's first two albums, and adds two new songs (one of which, the swinging "San Antonio Girl," received a Grammy nomination). And *Smile:*

Songs From the Movies collects 12 songs, none originals, that Lovett recorded for various film soundtracks. While Lovett's duet with Randy Newman on the Newman-penned "You've Got a Friend in Me" (from *Toy Story*) is plenty charming, his performances on the collection's many standards ("Straighten Up and Fly Right," "Mack the Knife," "Summer Wind") prove that, while he's a very capable singer—particularly of his own material—he's got no special gift as a song stylist.

When it began to appear as if Lovett's well of original material had indeed run dry, *My Baby Don't Tolerate* finally appeared to reaffirm the songwriter as the master of elegant country gospel blues. For fans, it's nothing they haven't heard plenty of before: the sophisticated country ("Truck Song"), the winking blues ("My Baby Don't Tolerate"), the oddball vignettes ("Election Day"), the gospel echoes ("I'm Going to the Place"). But it's nice to hear that Lovett hasn't lost much of his stride so far into his run. —R.M.S.

The Lovin' Spoonful

★★★★ Do You Believe in Magic (1965; Buddha/BMG, 2002)
★★★ Hums of the Lovin' Spoonful (1966; Buddha/BMG, 2003)
★★★ Everything Playing (1968; Buddha/BMG, 2003)
★★★★ Anthology (Rhino, 1990)
★★ Greatest Hits (Hollywood, 1998)
★★ Summer in the City (BMG Special Products, 1997)
★★★ The Very Best of the Lovin' Spoonful (Camden, 1998)
★★ Live at the Hotel Seville (Varèse, 1999)
★★★★ Greatest Hits (Buddha/BMG, 2000)

Taking their band name from a Mississippi John Hurt blues verse, John Sebastian and Zal Yanovsky had been early-'60s New York folkies before founding the Spoonful and heading toward radio triumph with effervescent pop. Notorious merrymakers onstage, the band settled down in the studio to combine folk and jug-band elements with accessible melodies and pop hooks. "Did You Ever Have to Make Up Your Mind" and "You Didn't Have to Be So Nice" were sweet love songs; "Do You Believe in Magic?" remains one of the sunniest and best rock & roll anthems. A very casual, somewhat flat-voiced crooner, Sebastian sang with an aw-shucks sincerity. Finger-picking his guitar, Yanovsky kept the tunes airy and stirring. The fine "Summer in the City," with its effective drill-hammer and car-honk sound effects, is as heavy as the band ever got, its key signature remaining a sense of wonder and deliberate naiveté. The Buddha *Greatest Hits* is the perfect intro; with John Sebastian MIA, *Live at the Hotel Seville* doesn't really work.　—P.E.

Nick Lowe

★★★　The Wilderness Years (1974–77; Demon, 1991)
★★★★　Basher: The Best of Nick Lowe (Columbia, 1989)
★★★★　Party of One (1990; Upstart, 1995)
★★½　Impossible Bird (Upstart, 1994)
★★½　Dig My Mood (Upstart, 1998)
★★★　The Convincer (Yep Roc, 2001)

Brinsley Schwarz

★★　Brinsley Schwarz (1970; One Way, 1995)
★★★★½　Surrender to the Rhythm (1970–74; EMI, 1991)
★★★★½　Nervous on the Road/The New Favourites of Brinsley Schwarz (1972–74; Beat Goes On, 1995)

When the great wave of punk broke on American shores in the late '70s, it swept with it more conventional, pop-oriented songsters who had been pining for a second shot at the British Invasion. Nick Lowe, who had played bass and wrote and sung most of the songs in the pub rock band Brinsley Schwarz, was ready to break big. But by the time Columbia released Lowe's first solo album in the U.S., its title had changed from *Jesus of Cool* to *Pure Pop for Now People,* and the cover, a mosaic of six portraits of Nick the Pop Chameleon, had been altered to give him a tie sporting the stars and stripes.

All that's left of Lowe's seven Columbia albums is the retrospective *Basher,* which favors (14 of 25 cuts) the first two albums. The first album was a smorgasbord of neoclassic rockers like "Heart of the City," darkly wry tales like "Marie Provost" and "36 Inches High," fan letters to David Bowie ("[I Love the Sound of] Breaking Glass") and the Bay City Rollers, and the cynical "Music for Money."

The second album was the risqué *Labour of Lust,* where he takes delight in making Americans squirm, and sings "When I see you I get an extension/And I don't mean Alexander Graham Bell's invention." Those two were tours de force, but in Lowe's later albums the irrepressible humor often turned trite and even sappy ("Time Wounds All Heels" is one of the better ones).

Lowe's 1990 album *Party of One* was a return to form, the music sharpened up by the return of producer Dave Edmunds, and songs like "All Men Are Liars" flashed his old bite. But Lowe's '90s albums

have turned to a soft rock with little to distinguish itself.

Still, Lowe's early work is worth revisiting. *The Wilderness Years* collects solo demos and singles predating *Jesus of Cool;* it's a mixed bag, but has some interesting pieces, including a startling cover of "Born a Woman." Even better are two Brinsley Schwarz reissues, the career-spanning *Surrender to the Rhythm* and the twofer of their last (and best) albums, *Nervous on the Road* and *New Favourites.* The Brinsleys started out as an English analog to L.A.'s country-rock, but they soon settled into the pubs and expanded their repertoire to include R&B such as "I Like It Like That" and "Trying to Live My Life Without You," while their originals fit and often exceeded their inspirations. Lowe became the main songwriter, and two of his greatest songs appeared on *New Favourites:* the beautiful soul ballad "Ever Since You're Gone" and the self-explanatory "What's So Funny About Peace, Love and Understanding?"　—T.H.

The Lox

★★★　Money, Power & Respect (Bad Boy, 1998)
★★★　We Are the Streets (Ruff Ryders/Interscope, 2000)

Jadakiss

★★★½　Kiss tha Game Goodbye (Ruff Ryders/Interscope, 2001)
★★★　Kiss of Death (Universal, 2004)

Styles

★★★★　A Gangster and a Gentleman (Ruff Ryders/Interscope, 2002)

The Yonkers, NY, rap trio the Lox signed with Puff Daddy's Bad Boy Records in the mid-'90s, when Biggie Smalls was still a small-time hustler making good and bling hadn't yet been invented. On their debut, they dutifully tried their best to keep it real with songs such as the title track. But thug bravado aside, the group became best known for "If You Think I'm Jiggy" (word to Rod Stewart) and for rocking improbably shiny suits in the video for Puff's "It's All About the Benjamins." The streets rebelled, culminating in a "Let the Lox Go" T-shirt campaign that swept New York in 1999. By 2000, the Lox had signed with their fellow Yonkers residents the Ruff Ryders, who allowed the group the freedom to revisit where they came from, resulting in fiery street anthems such as "Wild Out" and the title track, and also punishingly ignorant skits such as "Rape'N U Records," on *We Are the Streets.* The street, it appeared, was two-way.

By 2001, the three MCs were beginning to spread their solo wings and, to their credit, find their own distinct voices, something that wasn't always possible in the Lox groupthink. Jadakiss was first out of the gate with *Kiss tha Game Goodbye,* an eclectic affair (guests included Snoop Dogg, Nas, Eightball, and Fiend) that showed he had previously untapped dimensionality. "None of Y'All Betta" is one of the great Lox group efforts, as Jadakiss, Styles, and Sheek breathe true fire, but just as compelling is "Knock Yourself Out," a shimmery Neptunes production that marks Jadakiss' first attempt at wooing the ladies. On *Kiss of Death,* Jadakiss again asserted himself as a master of fine lyrical detail, bringing the same clinical precision to crime sagas ("Air It Out") and pickup lines ("Hot Sauce to Go" featuring Pharrell) alike.

Of the Lox three, Styles was always the grimiest, the most unreconstructed among thugs. His solo debut, *A Gangster and a Gentleman,* certainly didn't disappoint the hardcore. Indeed, it's one of the great rap albums of the post-Biggie era, laserlike in focus and unrelenting in dark mood. Even his jokes are dark: "Don't you ask me what I'm robbing you for/'Cause you was talking big money, and I'm a little broke/And I'm a firm believer in equality, dog." Most of the time, though, smiling's not an option, as on "My Brother," which bemoans the loss of his young sibling, and on the nihilistic "My Niggas" and "Black Magic." Out of a morass of mean mugging, Styles became one of the great poets of the downtrodden, though one senses there's no joy in the task for him.   —J.C.

L7

★★½	L7 (Epitaph, 1987)
★★★★	Smell the Magic (Sub Pop, 1990)
★★★★	Bricks Are Heavy (Slash, 1992)
★★★½	Hungry for Stink (Slash/Reprise, 1994)
★★★½	The Beauty Process: Triple Platinum (Slash/Reprise, 1997)
★★★	Slap-Happy (Wax Tadpole/Bong Load, 1999)

They didn't get the grunge millions, but these wickedly witty witches perfected the metal-punk alloy that generally eluded their many flailing male contemporaries. With Donita Sparks' and Suzi Gardner's twin lockstep guitars racing down the highway to hell, *Smell the Magic* was one of Sub Pop's finest hours (okay, one of its finest 30 minutes). Fleeing L.A.'s late-'80s glam sleaze, L7 glimpsed its innermost self reflected in the Runaways' truant-chick anthem "Cherry Bomb." *Magic* gleefully smashed that mirror with the ass end of the band's guitars, casting a fractured image of every good-girl-gone-bad they could imagine and embody.

With Butch Vig polishing L7's chrome, *Bricks Are Heavy* was as sleek as it was scathing. "Wargasm" calls out armchair generals who confuse SCUDs with their dicks, "Pretend We're Dead" calls out slackers who confuse apathy with cool, "Mr. Integrity" calls out petty punk ideologues. And just to be safe, "Shitlist" calls out every other asshole they might have overlooked elsewhere. *Hungry for Stink* was L7's idea of a groove album. The women trudge diligently through sludge that captures their dissipated jag, while the rape paranoia of "Can I Run" captures the underside of a feminism the founders of Rock for Choice never shied away from.

Beauty Process further distilled the essence of L7 into joyously self-obsessed nastiness, but by *Slap-Happy,* L7 was merely cruising on the fumes of its attitude. But what an attitude. As ever, Sparks spits her spite less with contempt than with utter dismissal—you aren't even worth the effort, but a girl's gotta sing about something. After all, this was a woman who once hurled her used tampon at a crowd of male hecklers.   —K.H.

Ludacris

★★½	Back for the First Time (Def Jam, 2000)
★★★½	Word of Mouf (Def Jam, 2001)
★★★½	Chicken 'N' Beer (Def Jam, 2003)

Blessed with a knack for comic rhymes, a big voice, and a graphic artist's widescreen sensibility, Ludacris is one of the great singles artists of the new decade in hip-hop, and he's made some decent albums along the way, too. Originally released independently as *Incognegro,* Ludacris' debut got picked up by Def Jam South, who rejiggered and reissued the record as *Back for the First Time.* Massive success followed immediately after, thanks to the rolling "Southern Hospitality" and the sexy call-and-response with his buddy Shawna, "What's Your Fantasy?" Still, Luda wasn't yet consistent enough to carry an entire album, and he didn't vary his aggressive, Marv Albert–style of rapping enough.

Quick on the debut's heels, *Word of Mouf* brings more of the same crunked-up barrage, though brighter production and a far more varied sonic palette provide relief from Luda's onslaught. Singles like "Area Codes" and "Saturday" show marked improvement and make for great radio fare; "My Business" is all vibrant bounce, and "Move Bitch" is so much fun you can forgive its nasty sentiment. Still, ever wonder how many times an hour you can hear the word *ho* before you go nuts? Ludacris has your answer.   —R.M.S.

Luna

★★★½	Lunapark (Elektra, 1992)
★★★	Slide (EP) (Elektra, 1993)

★★★★ Bewitched (Elektra, 1994)
★★★★★ Penthouse (Elektra, 1995)
★★★½ Bonnie and Clyde (Beggars Banquet, 1995)
★★★ Luna (EP) (No. 6, 1996)
★★★★ Pup Tent (Elektra, 1997)
★★ The Days of Our Nights (Jericho, 1999)
★★★½ Luna Live! (Arena Rock, 2000)
★★★★ Romantica (Jetset, 2002)
★★★½ Close Cover Before Striking (Jetset, 2002)
★★★★ Rendezvous (Jetset, 2004)

Dean Wareham and his band of New York guitar aesthetes have perfected one of indie rock's slinkiest, sexiest sounds. For sheer sonic pleasure, few bands can match Luna's languid, decadently ethereal pulse, and Wareham's limpid voice adds the right touch of wit. Everyone expected him to fall on his face after the demise of Galaxie 500, but *Lunapark* was an energy jolt—tight, funny songs detailing breakups ("Slash Your Tires"), crushes ("I Want Everything"), innocence ("I Can't Wait"), and experience ("Slide"), kissing off his professional adolescent-depressive past with the album's memorable opening line, "You can never give the finger to the blind." *Bewitched* was even better, thanks to new guitarist Sean Eden, who joined Wareham for the sun-dazed twin-guitar flurries of "Tiger Lily" and "Great Jones Street."

But Luna really got it together in the scandalously beautiful guitar ballads of *Penthouse,* one of those rare albums that can stand up to literally hundreds of listens over the years. Wareham spends the album plumbing his foolish heart in the back of a New York cab, going home alone after yet another night of fancy drinks and lucky toasts. "Chinatown," "Moon Palace," and "23 Minutes in Brussels" have the vinegary guitar burn of classic downtown bands like the Velvets and Television, but with a light touch that just makes the riffs more seductive. Wareham purrs sly one-liners about urban romance ("It's no fun reading fortune cookies to yourself") but the music celebrates the pleasures of being too young, too rich, too pretty, and too single, shopping for true love while getting lost in Chinatown.

Pup Tent was more of a mood piece, meandering sweetly in "Pup Tent," "Beggar's Bliss," and "Tracy I Love You." Wareham continues his eccentric pop-culture fascinations—*Penthouse* was surely the first rock album ever to begin and end with songs named after Faye Dunaway movies—but whether he's pretending to be Ernest Borgnine in a great movie ("Whispers") or Willem Dafoe in a bad one ("Bobby Peru"), he still sounds like the pathetic romantic obsessive he is. Unfortunately, Luna still couldn't sell any records, and *The Days of Our Nights* sounded listless,

with one ace Joy Division rip ("Math Whiz") and a lame Guns n' Roses cover ("Sweet Child o' Mine") that failed to earn a reprieve from the major-label ax. *Romantica* was a welcome return: "Lovedust," "Black Postcards," and "Renee Is Crying" are among Luna's loveliest songs, nicking lyrics from Nabokov and Berryman, with "1995" an appropriately snide farewell to the first golden era. Always a great live band, Luna finally released the chakra-clearing concert album it had in it, *Luna Live!,* which had plenty of guitar jams and the Galaxie 500 classic "4th of July." Luna keeps releasing fans-only EPs of covers and outtakes; the best is 1995's *Bonnie and Clyde,* which has two versions of the Serge Gainsbourg title track with Stereolab's Laetitia Sadier (originally on *Penthouse*), a "Chinatown" remix, and a Talking Heads cover ("Thank You for Sending Me an Angel"). The soundtrack of the terrible 1996 movie *I Shot Andy Warhol* has Luna's hilarious version of Donovan's "Season of the Witch." Dean Wareham and bassist/paramour Britta Phillips teamed up for the duo side project *L'Avventurra,* which featured sincere versions of the Silver Jews' "Random Rules" and Madonna's "I Deserve It," as well as an ace new song, "Ginger Snaps." —R.S.

Luscious Jackson

★★★★ In Search of Manny (EP) (Grand Royal, 1992)
★★★ Natural Ingredients (Grand Royal, 1994)
★★ Fever In Fever Out (Grand Royal, 1996)
★★★ Electric Honey (Grand Royal, 1999)

A vision of hip lower-Manhattan ladies of the '90s, Luscious Jackson kept it short and very sweet on its delightful (though now out-of-print) seven-song debut EP, *In Search of Manny.* Making pale-skinned, live-instrument hip-hop on a label run by friends the Beastie Boys, LJ justifiably earned its reputation as "Beastie girls"—particularly with sassy/silly feminist rhymes like "No family jewels between my legs/My wealth is my brain, my jewels my eggs." But *Manny* also owes a serious debt to the mostly female minimalist funk of early-'80s New Yorkers ESG—a group obscure enough to allow this record to sound like something completely fresh and new circa 1992. Warm, lo-fi production and irresistible melodies make even the clunky, unconvincing raps of Jill Cunniff and Gabby Glaser sound brilliantly audacious. By the EP's final two cuts, the duo is bolstered with a live drummer (onetime Beastie Boy Kate Schellenbach) and keyboardist Vivian Trimble, pointing to the full-band sound of later releases.

With its first full-length, *Natural Ingredients,* LJ begins to develop into something more powerful and sophisticated. The opener, "City Song," adds bleating sax to the group's urban groove, while "Strongman" features a funky flute line. "Here" embraces the club funk/disco of Deee-Lite, while the exotic "Pele Merengue" and "Surprise" make an ambitious move toward a more edgy, almost post-punk/dub grind. The urban-slacker humor has fallen off, but the attitude-heavy feminism—men that drag them down, men who can handle strong women—remains at the forefront. Without attempting to recapture the vibe that made *Manny* so unique, *Natural Ingredients* offers ample evidence of the group's growth potential.

Unfortunately, *Fever In Fever Out* doesn't build on the group's promise, but sounds tired and attitude-free. The single "Naked Eye" kicks the record off with a familiar slice of catchy and cool, and other tracks early on are similarly engaging—the woozy, noirish "Mood Swing," the sexy funk of "Under Your Skin." But mostly—particularly through its second half—*Fever In* relies too heavily on slower tempos, spacey production, and seemingly half-written, largely forgettable melodies.

Following Trimble's departure, a pared-down threesome released *Electric Honey,* which finds LJ's vitality restored. "Nervous Breakthrough," with its handclaps and thumping bass, kicks off with an unmistakable party vibe, while "Ladyfingers" follows with the group's most sophisticated pop sound yet. While dark and dirty production makes "Gypsy" sound like a *Manny* outtake, that debut's sass and fun returns with the guitar-and-strings funk of "Space Diva." What's more, songs like "Devotion," with its Veruca Salt–style heavy-rock riffing and female harmonies, and "Country's A Callin'," with its bluesy guitar line and harmonica (and guest vocals from Emmylou Harris), suggest LJ is back on track and continuing to grow. Unfortunately, with the group disbanding after *Electric Honey,* the record became only a valiant swan song.   —R.M.S.

Frankie Lymon and the Teenagers

★★★★½ Frankie Lymon at the London Palladium
(1958; Collectables, 1991)
★★★★★ Frankie Lymon and the Teenagers: For
Collectors Only (1986; Collectables, 1994)
★★★★★ The Very Best of Frankie Lymon and the
Teenagers (Rhino, 1998)

If all you knew of Frankie Lymon was the wonderful performances on the 20-cut Rhino *Very Best of* set you'd come away with a mental picture of a teenage boy whose every sung note celebrated life. Even his more introspective, pained numbers—"Share," "Out

in the Cold Again"—communicate a bright optimism. Indeed, when Lymon entered the public arena in 1956 at age 13, rock & roll had never seen anything quite like him. His face was a cherub's, but his eyes radiated an intelligence far beyond his years; his voice was a plaintive, malleable tenor that retained its clarity even when Lymon soared into the upper register; onstage he displayed the suave and charm of a wizened pro. He also developed some dazzling dance moves that had a measurable impact on the styles later developed for Motown artists; and he had a touch of the poet about him, too, possibly having written both sides of his group's first single. One of those songs is among the most famous and most performed in American popular music, "Why Do Fools Fall in Love." Its release in 1956 began an 18-month run of international stardom for Lymon and his friends from Manhattan's Washington Heights neighborhood, who had changed their name from the Premiers to the Teenagers before their first record's release.

"Why Do Fools Fall in Love," aided by Lymon's galvanizing stage presence, peaked at #6 on the pop chart and catapulted the group into the upper echelons of the entertainment elite. They appeared on national TV shows, in two Alan Freed movies, and performed for royalty in England; more important, Lymon and the Teenagers brought the doo-wop-harmony sound to mainstream America, adding to it a rock & roll beat and irrepressible energy. In addition to "Fools," the group's next three singles—"I Want You to Be My Girl," "I Promise to Remember," and "The ABC's of Love"—hit the Top 50 on the R&B chart. Although the group continued to cut exemplary singles, it never duplicated the chart success of the first four hits. By late '57, Gee executives had decided to take Lymon solo, and that spelled the beginning of the end for the singer and his backing group. The Teenagers without Lymon went hitless (and made Billy Lobrano, Lymon's replacement, one of the great trivia answers in rock & roll history). "Portable on My Shoulder" and "Thumb Thumb," available on the Rhino and Collectables entries, show that Lymon was in a good-rockin' groove in 1958, even though his voice had begun to change. His last charted single, a remake of Thurston Harris' 1957 hit "Little Bitty Pretty One," came in 1960, though Lymon's vocal had been cut two years earlier and released on his *Rock 'n' Roll* album (now out of print). By 1959, his voice had lost its elasticity; some performances on the Collectables box set *For Collectors Only* (which was originally released as a five-LP vinyl collection on the Murray Hill label in 1986) sound like anyone *but* Frankie Lymon. By the early '60s Lymon was battling heroin addiction, and his personal life was spiraling out of control, culminating in a mid-'60s arrest for stealing drums from a recording studio to finance his habit. A stint in the U.S. Army helped him get his life together again, and his old label, Roulette, responded by scheduling a recording session for him in February 1968. The day prior to the session, Lymon overdosed and died in his grandmother's apartment in New York. He was 25 years old.

The excellent liner notes and prime cuts on Rhino's best-of tell a good chunk of Lymon's story on and off the stage. Collectables' *For Collectors Only* comprises 64 tracks that are at once exciting, revealing, and depressing: exciting because they reveal the solid artistry the youngsters brought to some terrific B sides and nonsingle album tracks, depressing as an aural documentation of Lymon's artistic disintegration. In addition to the Lymon/Teenagers work, a number of tracks are included that feature Lymon solo and the Teenagers post-Lymon. Unfortunately for fans, the new Collectables box omits the complete and invaluable sessionography and recording history that was part of the Murray Hill vinyl edition, an omission for which even Marv Goldberg's solid biographical liner notes cannot compensate. Nevertheless, *For Collectors Only* is essential for anyone interested both in the course of this group's groundbreaking career and in the evolution of doo-wop into a commercially viable music.

For a good single-disc anthology of Lymon's solo work, there's nothing better than Collectables' *Frankie Lymon at the London Palladium*. The title makes it sound like a live album, but it's actually a studio effort released in 1958 to cash in on Lymon's April 1957 appearance at the fabled London venue. Backed by a terrific big band and orchestra assembled by session leader Rudy Traylor, Lymon does a bang-up job with a dozen songs, showing off some dazzling vocal craftsmanship. A brassy, swinging take on Harold Arlen's 1934 gem "Let's Fall in Love" kicks off the album, followed by Lymon easing into a heartfelt, string-laden ballad, "So Goes My Love," that features his keening tenor in full, heartbreaking flight. The pop standard "Fools Rush In" gets a slow, deliberate treatment, with gorgeous, ascending string lines surfacing as Lymon works his way from a muted reading to a soaring, plaintive cry in the chorus—a performance masterful in its use of nuance and timbre to reveal a soul divided. The young man revealed on disc seems to have all the answers, whereas the young man in the real world seemed to have none. —D.M.

Loretta Lynn

★★★	Hymns (1965; King, 1998)
★★★½	You Ain't Woman Enough (MCA, 1966)
★★★	Who Says God Is Dead! (1968; King, 1998)
★★★	Coal Miner's Daughter (MCA, 1971)
★★	Making Love From Memory (MCA, 1982)
★★★★★	The Country Music Hall of Fame: Loretta Lynn (MCA, 1991)
★★★★★	Honky Tonk Girl: The Loretta Lynn Collection (MCA, 1994)
★★★½	All Time Gospel Greats (Time Life, 1998)
★★★½	Millennium Collection: The Best of Loretta Lynn (MCA, 1999)
★★★	Best of the Best: Her Gospel Side (Federal, 1999)
★★★★	Still Country (Audium, 2000)
★★★	Millennium Collection: The Best of Loretta Lynn, Vol. 2 (MCA, 2001)
★★★★	All Time Greatest Hits (MCA, 2002)
★★★★	Van Lear Rose (Interscope, 2004)

with Conway Twitty

★★★½	Very Best of Loretta and Conway (MCA, 1979)
★★½	Two's a Party (MCA, 1981)
★★★	Conway Twitty & Loretta Lynn: 20 Greatest Hits (MCA, 1987)
★★½	Hey Good Lookin' (MCA, 1993)
★★★	Conway & Loretta Sing the Hits (MCA, 1997)
★★★	Millennium Collection: The Best of Conway Twitty & Loretta Lynn (MCA, 2000)

Loretta Lynn (née Webb) of Butcher Hollow, KY, was a 25-year-old housewife and mother when she cut her first record, in 1960. Released on a tiny Canadian label, "Honky Tonk Girl" got the fledgling singer noticed in Nashville. By the mid-'60s, Lynn had offically arrived on Music Row: performing on the Grand Ole Opry, duetting with Ernest Tubb ("Mr. & Mrs. Used to Be"), and, most important, scoring chart singles with weepers like "Success," on which the husband's fast-track career leads to domestic disaster. Something about Lynn's voice—perhaps her unfettered drawl and crystalline high notes—suits this sort of material. She may be waiting at home while her man indulges in "Wine, Women, and Song," but Lynn hardly plays the role of understanding wife on her subsequent hits. "Don't Come Home a Drinkin' (With Lovin' on Your Mind)" (1967) and "You Ain't Woman Enough" (1966) are propelled by her gutsy mixture of humor and indignation. Buttressed by pedal-steel guitar and a clanking railroad-trestle beat, she doesn't suffer fools—whether male ("Drinkin' ") or female ("Woman").

Adhering to the country standard of the time, Lynn recorded prolifically throughout her hit-making years in the '60s and '70s. Most of these records never made it to CD (while several that did have subsequently fallen out of print all over again). What currently survives is a scattershot catalogue of better-than-average gospel albums, 1971's *Coal Miner's Daughter*, and a couple of nonessential '80s efforts. Fortunately, Lynn's career and indelible standing as one of country music's finest voices (as a singer and a songwriter) are served well by a handful of hits collections and anthologies. If you're just after the hits, the 16-track *Country Music Hall of Fame* collection and the 22-track *All Time Greatest Hits* will do the trick (with an edge going to the shorter, former disc for including some of the important early songs curiously skipped over on the latter). Budget permitting, err on the safe side and skip both in favor of *Honky Tonk Girl: The Loretta Lynn Collection,* a three-disc, 70-song box set that covers all her hits as well as a generous sampling of album tracks, charting her rise from the title track and all of the other tunes already mentioned, as well as "Blue Kentucky Girl" and on through the '70s, when she kept the audacious singles coming fast and furious. "Fist City," "Wings Upon Your Horns," and "Your Squaw Is on the Warpath" make good on their comeuppance-threatening metaphors, while "Coal Miner's Daughter" and "You're Looking at Country" offer pungent, revealing slices of autobiography. "One's on the Way" pillories American class distinctions with cutting accuracy, though Lynn takes the inevitable turn toward countrypolitan corn with "Love Is the Foundation." But all these years later, her amazing 1975 birth-control manifesto, "The Pill," has lost none of its knockout feminist punch; even in the modern age of feisty and confident women artists such as the Dixie Chicks and Shania Twain, you *still* don't hear too many songs quite so bold on country radio. The box set also features a trio of Lynn's '60s duets with Ernest Tubb and six of her later Conway Twitty collaborations. Lynn and Twitty recorded a long string of duets throughout the '70s, and their earliest efforts are searing, guilt-drenched honky-tonk cheating scenarios. "It's Only Make Believe" and "Lead Me On" (both on *The Very Best of Loretta and Conway*) can still inspire heated are-they-or-aren't-they debates: The (usually) thwarted desire is downright audible in those teasing, frisky voices. The duo's later hits sank into formula schmaltz as the decade wore on, though the goony 1978 novelty "You're the Reason Our Kids Are Ugly" provided some much-needed comic relief.

Following a lengthy hiatus to tend to her ailing husband (who died in 1996), Lynn returned to the studio for a pair of strong—but radically dissimilar—comeback albums, 2000's Randy Scruggs–produced *Still Country* and 2004's Jack White (of the White Stripes)–produced *Van Lear Rose*. While the latter received far more attention, especially from the rock press, *Still Country* is actually the better Lynn album. Although she had a hand in writing only two of the

tracks ("God's Country" and "I Can't Hear the Music," a suitably tear-jerking tribute to her late husband), the respectful production and pure-country accompaniment recall a much younger Lynn in her prime, while her voice has lost none of its shine. This is Lynn in her element, sounding as at home as she was when she sang "You're Looking at Country" way back in 1970. On *Van Lear Rose,* by contrast, you can tell she's not quite sure *what* she's looking at, though she follows White's garage-rock direction with admirable aplomb. The songs, all from Lynn's own pen, are generally excellent (particularly the title track and "Family Tree," both of which, dressed a little differently, could have been classics had she cut them 35 years earlier). —M.C./R.SK.

Shelby Lynne

★★★★ I Am Shelby Lynne (Island, 2000)
★★½ Epic Recordings (Lucky Dog, 2000)
★★½ Love, Shelby (Island, 2001)
★★★ Identity Crisis (EMI, 2003)

Shelby Lynne impressed critics, country fans, and pop listeners alike with her breakthrough album, 2000's *I Am Shelby Lynne*. Just formerly, she'd been a pissed-off 32-year-old Virginia-born/Alabama-raised ex–country singer of modest commercial success, and Nashville regulars who heard the album routinely wondered why it hadn't more explicitly shown off Lynne's big voice. In fact, Lynne's unusually tedious demonstrations of her instrument, an involving low soprano of pure silk and unfazed regionalism, had represented her cardinal problem. She and L.A. producer Bill Bottrell had conceptualized *I Am Shelby Lynne* with textbook perfection.

From 1989 through 1991 in Nashville, when she recorded with producers as professional as Bob Montgomery and James Stroud, not to mention as all-out legendary and musical as George Jones' and Tammy Wynette's Billy Sherrill, Lynne recorded song after song that always seemed to be about nothing except her voice. It was as though, unhappy with Nashville methodology, she'd decided to bore everyone to tears. For proof, consult *Epic Recordings*, probably her best work from the sulky Music Row years when Lynne was a favorite of singers such as George Jones, Randy Travis, and Willie Nelson.

During this time, Lynne's work recalls a less glossy k.d. lang bereft of concepts. Before *I Am Shelby Lynne,* on albums for Morgan's Creek and Magnatone (1993's *Temptation* and 1995's *Restless,* both out of print), she'd tried on some period nightclub and pop-jazz and wildass-folk stuff; nothing proved the proper fit. But on *I Am Shelby Lynne* it was as though she'd never experienced a creative difficulty in her life; suddenly she sang like a specific person with wildly expressive capabilities instead of a country mannequin hypnotized by technique.

On songs such as "Your Lies" and "Leavin'," Bottrell put Lynne in frankly fucked-up, symphonically inelegant settings that suggested the noisy truth instead of the fluffy memory of Dusty Springfield records; Lynne sounded like no one except herself, a young woman with a tragic past (she grew up orphaned, the victim of parental murder-suicide, looking after her younger sister, the singer Allison Moorer), Alabama roots, a voice that exposed real beauty and woundedness and strength. "Life Is Bad," Lynne sang on a country rocker too skanky to be called Sheryl Crow music; "Gotta Get Back," she declared on a soaring salute to Muscle Shoals greasy pop that seemed like a natural new retro-soul hit.

But commercial success eluded Lynne. Perhaps as a result, she followed up with *Love, Shelby,* made with the superproducer Glenn Ballard. There's really nothing wrong with Lynne's singing here, or with songs such as "Trust" or the sexy "Bend," but Ballard leads her into crassly arranged radio-ready music that, while canny, does nothing to mesh with the conceptual advances of *I Am Shelby Lynne;* it's like he never heard the earlier album. *Love, Shelby* has just one essential track, "Killin' Time," a spray of heartache memorable from the film *Bridget Jones's Diary,* as well as a couple of decent others.

With *Identity Crisis,* Lynne got back on track by stripping her sound down to its roots—acoustic guitars, touches of old gospel and blues, and a gorgeously bummed, torchlit ambience. "Lonesome" is a soulful echo of Patsy Cline, but most of the album is more like "I'm Alive," where Lynne speed-drawls a difficult lyric over roiling gusts from a vintage keyboard. The elegantly disconsolate "If I Were Smart" could be a grainy black-and-white noir about a woman who has finally quit smoking but still gets in fistfights with bad men. —J.H./P.B.

Lynyrd Skynyrd

★★★★ (pronounced leh-nerd skin-nerd) (1973; MCA, 2001)
★★★★ Second Helping (MCA, 1974)
★★★½ Nuthin' Fancy (1975; MCA, 2004)
★★★ Gimme Back My Bullets (MCA, 1976)
★★★★ One More From the Road (1976; MCA, 2001)
★★★★★ Street Survivors (1977; MCA, 2001)
★★★ Skynyrd's First . . . And Last. (MCA, 1978)
★★★★★ Gold & Platinum (MCA, 1979)
★★★ Best of the Rest (MCA, 1982)
★★★ Legend (MCA, 1987)

★★★½ Southern by the Grace of God (MCA, 1988)
★★★ Skynyrd's Innyrds (MCA, 1989)
★★★ Lynyrd Skynyrd 1991 (Atlantic, 1991)
★★★★★ Lynyrd Skynyrd (MCA, 1991)
★★ The Last Rebel (Atlantic, 1993)
★★★½ Endangered Species (Capricorn, 1994)
★★★ Freebird: The Movie (MCA, 1996)
★★ Twenty (CMC, 1997)
★★★★ The Essential Lynyrd Skynyrd (MCA, 1998)
★★ Extended Versions: Encore Collections (BMG Special, 1998)
★★★½ Skynyrd's First: Complete Muscle Shoals (MCA, 1998)
★★ Lyve (CMC, 1998)
★★ Edge of Forever (CMC, 1999)
★★★½ The Millennium Collection (MCA, 1999)
★★½ Solo Flytes (MCA, 1999)
★★★½ All Time Greatest Hits (MCA, 2000)
★★★½ Skynyrd Collectybles (MCA, 2000)
★★½ Then and Now (CMC, 2000)
★ Christmas Time Again (CMC, 2000)
★★★½ The Collection (PolyGram, 2001)
★★ Vicious Cycle (Sanctuary, 2003)

If the Allman Brothers invented Southern rock at the dawn of the '70s, then Lynyrd Skynyrd perfected it as the decade wore on. These shaggy guitar troopers from Jacksonville, FL, really weren't the unequivocal rednecks or wasted all-night jammers of popular description. Their renewed appeal in the latter part of the '90s—surprising after nearly a decade of being the butt of late-'70s arena-rock jokes ("Freeee Bird!")—led to a surge of reissues, repackaged hits, and rarities collections.

Lynyrd Skynyrd boiled down its potent regional influences—blues, country, soul—into a heady, potentially crippling homebrew. They liked to play; those three lead guitars weren't just for show. But a taut command of rhythm drives even Skynyrd's lengthiest excursions. Overexposed as it is, the studio version of "Free Bird" (from *[pronounced leh-nerd skin-nerd]*) climbs to a dizzying height.

Guitarists Allen Collins and Gary Rossington formed the nucleus of Skynyrd's frontline. Bassist Leon Wilkeson and guitarist Ed King (formerly of the pop-psychedelic band Strawberry Alarm Clock!) rounded out the sound. Lead singer Ronnie Van Zant was the band's anchor; the gruff authority of his voice was matched by his forthright and forceful way with words. On *pronounced,* his take on Washington politics ("Things Goin' On") is as startlingly fresh as his perspective of local customs ("Mississippi Kid," "Poison Whiskey"). Producer Al Kooper adds keyboard sweetening to the slow-building "Tuesday's Gone" that sounds unnecessary; Skynyrd's tuneful guitar interplay provides just the right touch of sugar—and salt.

Second Helping served up the band's feisty hard-rock twang to a broad national audience. "Sweet Home Alabama" is the consummate Skynyrd platter; the guitars sigh and sting like a stiff breeze as Ronnie Van Zant draws a line in the dirt: "Well, I heard Mr. Young sing about her/I heard old Neil put her down/Well, I hope Neil Young will remember/Southern man don't need him around anyhow." But if Neil Young's anti-Southern anthems wounded Van Zant's pride, the singer hardly sounds like a card-carrying segregationist on "The Ballad of Curtis Loew." Skynyrd's tribute to a black grocery store owner who played the blues underlines the crucial role music plays in kicking down racial barriers. Though songs about the business of rock and life on the road became clichéd in the '70s, Van Zant wrote some of the best, beginning with *Second Helping*'s searing "Workin' for MCA," the reflective "Was I Right or Wrong," and the cautionary "The Needle and the Spoon."

Nuthin' Fancy kicks off with further proof of Van Zant's independent thinking; "Saturday Night Special," Skynyrd's hardest rocker, is a full-bore assault against handguns. The rest of the album never exactly slacks off, but aside from that opener, Skynyrd seems to be repeating itself on tracks like "On the Hunt" and "Am I Losin'." That goes double for *Gimme Back My Bullets,* especially on the band's cover of J.J. Cale's too-telling "I Got the Same Old Blues." While Skynyrd's musical strength hasn't diminished on these albums, the pressures of constant touring had a clear effect on the group's creativity. That said, live albums don't get much more exciting than *One More From the Road.* With new guitarist Steve Gaines stepping in for the departed Ed King, Skynyrd roars through a set of mostly earlier material and two wholly appropriate covers: Robert Johnson's "Crossroads" (with a nod to Cream) and Jimmie Rodgers' "T for Texas."

Street Survivors is much better than might have been expected. Gaines stimulated Van Zant's songwriting as well as axemen Rossington and Collins' playing. "What's Your Name," "That Smell," "You Got That Right," and "I Never Dreamed" mine familiar Skynyrd territory with a sharpened melodic focus and wide-ranging instrumental reach. What should have been the band's second coming turned out to be its swan song; Ronnie Van Zant, Steve Gaines, and his sister, backup singer Cassie, were killed when the band's private plane crashed in late 1977—just days after *Street Survivors'* release.

After recovering from their loss, Gary Rossington, Allen Collins, Leon Wilkeson, and keyboard pounder Billy Powell hooked up with an assertive female vocalist named Dale Krantz a few years later. The Rossington-Collins Band's two albums—*Anytime, Anyplace, Anywhere* (MCA, 1980) and *This Is the Way* (MCA, 1982)—flash the expected guitar heat, but the songs fall short of Skynyrd's imposingly high standards.

Surprisingly, the revamped-for-the-'90s Lynyrd Skynyrd comes much closer to realizing Rossington-Collins' goal. A decade after the crash, Rossington rounded up Ed King, a then-wheelchair-bound Collins, and lead singer Johnny Van Zant (Ronnie's brother)—along with a few extra Southern rock luminaries—for a wonderfully potent live reunion. On *Southern by the Grace of God,* the younger Van Zant sings his brother's songs with spit and vinegar, but the performance lacks the youthful passion of *One More From the Road.* Though Collins died in 1990, Rossington's reunited Skynyrd hit the studio for a satisfyingly brash boogie session. Ultimately, however, *Lynyrd Skynyrd 1991* fails to deliver the songwriting bite that Ronnie Van Zant gave the original band.

The new Skynyrd continued to tour and release albums throughout the '90s, winning younger Southern rock converts, but the Ronnie Van Zant–less group could never match the grit and drive of the original lineup. Still, when Skynyrd took a cue from MTV's *Unplugged* for *Endangered Species,* performing a handful of its classic songs in the studio on acoustic instruments, the result was remarkably fresh; Van Zant's songs never sounded so appropriately rustic.

The various posthumous releases of the original Skynyrd's music are completely eclipsed by the 1991 box set. *Lynyrd Skynyrd* mixes early demos, unreleased tracks, acoustic outtakes, live cuts, and acknowledged classics in a swaggering, impressive, three-disc package. Most of the other repackaged hits and live collections suffer, to varying degrees, from weak song selections and sluggish performances. The early *Gold & Platinum* and later *Essential Lynyrd Skynyrd* are the best two-disc retrospectives, while the budget-minded would do fine with the single-disc *The Millennium Collection.* Essential for die-hard fans are *Skynyrd's First,* the band's complete earliest Muscle Shoals recordings, and the rarities set *Collectybles.* Of moderate interest is *Solo Flytes,* an uneven compilation of mostly generic bar-band boogie by the various members' post-Skynyrd projects including the Rossington-Collins Band, the Allen Collins Band, and the Artimus Pyle Band. —M.C./M.K.

M m

Baaba Maal

★★★	Wango (1985; Stern's, 1994)
★★★	Baayo (1991; Palm Pictures, 2003)
★★★	Lam Toro (1993; Palm Pictures, 2003)
★★★½	Firin' in Fouta (Mango, 1994)
★★★	Nomad Soul (Palm Pictures, 1998)
★★★	Jombaajo (Sonodisc, 1999)
★★★½	Live at Royal Festival Hall (Palm Pictures, 1999)
★★★★	Missing You . . . Mi Yeewnii (Palm Pictures, 2001)
★★★★	Best of the Early Years (Wrasse, 2003)

Baaba Maal/Mansour Seck

| ★★★★★ | Djam Leelii (1989; Palm Pictures, 1998) |

Mansour Seck

| ★★★ | N'der Fouta Tooro, Vol. 1 (Stern's, 1994) |

Possessing one of the most extraordinary voices in popular music, Baaba Maal became a star in his native Senegal and a favorite of globally attuned listeners everywhere. But the road to international acclaim was a long one. Born in the north of Senegal among the Fula people, Maal did not belong to a clan of griots, (traditional singers of folk history). But after studying music in Paris, he paid his dues and sharpened his skills by traveling with his griot friend, the gentle, blind, charismatic guitarist Mansour Seck. In 1984, they recorded *Djam Leelii,* a song sequence set to guitars, *kora,* and percussion. The tracks are floating, gorgeous, and seemingly tranquil, though with close listening (and a translation of lyrics), passages of intense sadness, tragedy, and want reveal themselves.

Maal then set out to further modernize and electrify his music. The first efforts were uneven, sometimes clumsy or indistinct, but always highlighted by his piercing, unmistakable voice. *Firin' in Fouta* is a romping, all-out fustian album featuring electronic percussion, horns, synths, and guest spots for the finest West African rap team, Positive Black Soul.

(This small landmark also inspired the members of Afro-Celt Sound System to get together.) *Best of the Early Years* cherry-picks *Wango, Baayo,* and *Lam Toto,* with only minimal overlap with *Firin' in Fouta.* In 1999, Maal released *Missing You,* a beautiful, understated acoustic album, and *Live at Royal Festival Hall,* a brief but bubbling set sparked by dramatic contributions from master reggae guitarist Ernest Ranglin, who also costars on the relentlessly eclectic *Nomad Soul.* The artfully selected and sequenced *Best of the Early Years* is a fine choice for those who want only one album besides the essential *Djam Leelii.* —M.MI.

Kirsty MacColl

★★★½	Galore (1995; EMI, 2001)
★★★	What Do Pretty Girls Do? (Hux, 1998)
★★★½	Tropical Brainstorm (Instinct, 2001)
★★★	The One and Only (Metro, 2001)

Before her untimely death, occasional Pogues vocalist Kirsty MacColl had established herself as one of the wittier presences in British pop. Daughter of famed folksinger/songwriter Ewan MacColl, she was a music-biz wunderkind, signed to Stiff records at age 16. "They Don't Know," which became a massive hit for Tracey Ullman, revealed MacColl's exceptional songwriting promise as early as 1979. Later a backup singer for outfits as diverse as the Rolling Stones, the Smiths, and Billy Bragg, she continued to pen brilliant pop—"There's a Guy Works Down the Chip Shop (Swears He's Elvis)"—that scored big in the U.K. The best songs from her earlier albums *(Kite, Electric Landlady)* are collected on *Galore.* After a 10-year hiatus, she returned with *Tropical Brainstorm,* an exuberant take on mambo and samba rhythms, and perhaps her sunniest music. Tragically, she died in a boating accident in Mexico months before its release. *Pretty Girls* is Kirsty on BBC Radio:

live and intimate. *The One and Only* is a decent best-of; *Galore* is stronger.   —P.E.

Madness

★★★½	One Step Beyond . . . (1979; EMI, 1999)
★★★	Absolutely (1980; EMI, 2004)
★★★	7 (1981; EMI, 2004)
★★★½	Complete Madness (1982; Virgin, 2003)
★★★½	Madness Presents the Rise and Fall (Stiff U.K., 1982)
★★★★	Madness (Geffen, 1983)
★★★	Keep Moving (1984; Geffen, 1997)
★★½	Mad Not Mad (Geffen, 1985)
★★★½	Utter Madness (1986; Virgin, 1999)
★★	The Peel Sessions (Strange Fruit U.K., 1986)
★★★½	Total Madness: The Very Best of Madness (Geffen, 1997)
★★★★	Ultimate Collection (Hip-O, 2000)

In its early-'80s prime, Madness was one of England's most beloved pop acts, and no wonder—its blend of irrepressible rhythm, insinuating choruses, and brash music-hall humor all but guaranteed the group a place on the U.K. charts. Here in the U.S., however, Madnessmania was limited, in large part because the band's ska-revival roots and Cockney sensibility didn't quite appeal to general American tastes.

From the R&B revelry of *One Step Beyond . . .* to the Kinksian wit of *7,* the group's early work used ska not as a defining aesthetic but merely as a rhythmic starting point, as made plain on such singles as "My Girl" (from *One Step Beyond . . .*) or "Baggy Trousers" (from *Absolutely*). *Madness* is cobbled together from material originally on *7* and *The Rise and Fall* as well as such English singles as "It Must Be Love" and "House of Fun." The album also includes "Our House," an endearing Kinks-Motown fusion and the band's biggest U.S. hit. Sadly, the ambitious *Keep Moving* failed to match its predecessor's charm or melodic integrity (though the Caribbean-flavored "Wings of a Dove" has its moments), while *Mad Not Mad* finds the lads sinking into unseemly self-reflection.

Even though Madness called it quits in 1986, the group eventually reunited for several annual Madstock concerts before finally going all the way in 1998 with a full tour and new album, the U.K.-only *Wonderful.* Meanwhile, on this side of the Atlantic, fans were given the choice between *Total Madness,* which showcases the band's pop sensibility while almost entirely ignoring its ska roots, and the far more representative *Ultimate Collection* (probably the best Madness disc out there). As for *The Peel Sessions,* it's hard to justify spending good money on 11 minutes of so-so live ska.   —J.D.C.

Madonna

★★★½	Madonna (Sire/Warner Bros., 1983)
★★★	Like a Virgin (Sire/Warner Bros., 1984)
★★★★	True Blue (Sire/Warner Bros., 1986)
★★★	You Can Dance (Sire/Warner Bros., 1987)
★★	Who's That Girl: Original Motion Picture Soundtrack (Sire/Warner Bros., 1987)
★★★★½	Like a Prayer (Sire/Warner Bros., 1989)
★★½	I'm Breathless (Sire/Warner Bros., 1990)
★★★★★	The Immaculate Collection (Sire/Warner Bros., 1990)
★★★★	Erotica (Maverick/Sire, 1992)
★★★½	Bedtime Stories (Maverick/Sire, 1994)
★★★★	Something to Remember (Maverick/Sire, 1995)
★★	Evita: The Complete Motion Picture Soundtrack (Warner Bros., 1996)
★★★★½	Ray of Light (Maverick/Warner Bros., 1998)
★★★★	Music (Maverick/Warner Bros., 2000)
★★★	GHV2 (Maverick/Warner Bros., 2001)
★★★	American Life (Maverick/Warner Bros., 2003)
★★	Remixed & Revisited (Maverick/Warner Bros., 2003)

Madonna's many career sidelights often obscure the fact that she remains one of the greatest pop acts of all time. Yes, she's made some awful movies, but so did Elvis and the Beatles. Simply put, Madonna makes exemplary pop records. They've embraced the trends of the day while showcasing a feisty personality that lesser pop idols and their keepers can't fake. Like David Bowie during his glory days, Madonna has moved from stylistic strength to strength: She's succeeded so fantastically partly thanks to her skill at picking crafty collaborators, but also because behind all the videos, costumes, quotes, and celebrity trappings, she is an exemplary songwriter with a gift for hooks and indelible lyrics, and a better studio singer than her live spectacles attest. Her many albums aren't always perfect, and the early ones include regrettable filler. But when it comes to singles, Madonna has few peers, a deserving candidate for the title of greatest singles artist since the 1960s heyday of the single.

That gift was there on her 1983 debut, which combined proven postdisco club tracks like "Everybody" and "Burning Up" with breakthrough pop hits "Borderline" and "Lucky Star." The knockout remains "Holiday," the first production by DJ, remixer, and then boyfriend John "Jellybean" Benitez. Her debut has aged better than its smash successor of the next year, *Like a Virgin,* which combines two career-making monsters, "Material Girl" and the equally tongue-in-cheek title track, with catchy but less substantial follow-ups, producer/songwriter/rhythm guitarist extraordinaire Nile Rodgers' clattering arrangements, and her weakest album tracks ever.

True Blue magnified her button-pushing ability with a controversial 1986 smash about pregnancy, "Papa Don't Preach," and proved her range, from the dark ballad "Live to Tell" to the Latin kitsch of "La Isla Bonita." *You Can Dance* lengthens previously released singles and album cuts while adding the clubby exclusive "Spotlight," but none of the remixes match the originals' simple urgency. The *Who's That Girl* soundtrack is a mixed bag of four Madonna cuts not found on other albums combined with five forgettable flops from Club Nouveau and other bygone '80s rhythm-pop acts.

After these 1987 trifles, 1989's *Like a Prayer* effectively upped Madonna's ante as a serious artist with the one-two punch of the righteous gospel-inflected title track and the quintessential Madonna manifesto "Express Yourself," as well as a supporting cast of substantial songs that covered topics like spousal abuse ("Till Death Do Us Part") and familial neglect ("Oh Father") with the breezy buzz of self-discovery. Created to coincide with Madonna's credible acting job in *Dick Tracy*, 1990's *I'm Breathless* fails to turn the pop singer into a convincing Broadway belter: She tries too hard and sounds literally out of breath on tracks cowritten with longtime collaborator Patrick Leonard or penned for her by theater songwriting legend Stephen Sondheim. Released later that year, *The Immaculate Collection* leaves off several hits, yet sums up the first stage of Madonna's career flawlessly while including stray essential singles like "Into the Groove" and "Crazy for You," and worthy sensual newies "Justify My Love" and "Rescue Me."

Created with remix kingpin Shep Pettibone to coincide with her button-pushing book, *Sex*, 1992's *Erotica* represents Madonna's fullest immersion in gay culture and sounds, and is also her darkest, least tune-driven album. Not coincidentally, a media backlash intensified. The ever-resilient star responded with 1994's bruised but far more mainstream *Bedtime Stories*, a low-key, R&B-derived confessional defined by its Dallas Austin– and Babyface-assisted smashes, "Secret" and "Take a Bow," respectively. The atypical title track (a flop when released as a single) pointed the way to her next musical incarnation, the sleek electronica of 1998's *Ray of Light*, although the star wasn't yet ready for another commercial risk. First she emphasized her crooning powers with 1995's ballad retrospective *Something to Remember* (key track: the haunted *A League of Their Own* soundtrack hit "This Used to Be My Playground"), then reaped the benefits

of voice lessons with her '96 *Evita* soundtrack. Although she'd dramatically improved her vocal technique since attempting Sondheim, what she tries with Andrew Lloyd Webber's operatic score is far more ambitious, serious—and consequently just as strained.

The elocution lessons learned during *Evita* give her a *My Fair Lady*-esque English accent, but *Ray of Light* achieves another breakthrough akin to *Like a Prayer* in the way it documents the singer's journey to the center of her soul. Pop song doctor Rick Nowles balances producer William Orbit's sonic explorations as the set flips from club anthems like the title track's rock-trance synthesis to the chilled-out heartbreak of "Frozen." With 2000's *Music*, Madonna lightens up, harking back to the early-'80s street disco of her debut with the help her most offbeat collaborator, obscure French synth-popper Mirwais Ahmadzai. The album lacks its predecessor's introspective intensity but offers wise feminist observation ("What It Feels Like for a Girl") and inspired froth (giddy Bond soundtrack hit "Beautiful Stranger"). Unlike her previous hits collections, *GHV2* doesn't include lost singles or new cuts, and the albums it culls from (*Evita* aside) offer stronger, more consistent pleasures. After Madonna's back-to-back successes, 2003's *American Life* disappoints, a rare instance of lesser more-of-the-same from this extraordinarily disciplined trend forerunner. Many missed the joke of the title track's goofy rap about lattés and feeling "super-dooper" in her Mini Cooper, but the scent of stale indulgence is hard to ignore, despite the popsmith's ever-present hooks and Ahmadzai's sportive studio noise. *Remixed & Revisited* improves upon *American Life*'s standout single, "Love Profusion," but the rest botches an opportunity to revive interest in its parent album. Even the casually curious would be advised to investigate the hundreds of remixes found on her many maxi-singles, most of which remain in print and attest to her nearly unerring dance-floor smarts. —B.W.

The Magnetic Fields

The 6ths

Future Bible Heroes

★★★ Memories of Love (Slow River, 1997)
★★★ I'm Lonely (and I Love It) (EP) (Merge, 2000)

The Gothic Archies

★★ The New Despair (EP) (Merge, 1997)

Stephin Merritt

★★ Eban & Charley (Merge, 2002)

If you appreciate someone who revels in rhyming *libertarian* with *Herbert von Karajan*, look no further than Stephin Merritt. Merritt has recorded under several aliases—but in the end, these "groups" come down to one deep-throated, black-humored singer/songwriter/multi-instrumentalist.

The first two Magnetic Fields albums, now on one CD, showcase sexually ambiguous lyrics, loopy arrangements, and the disaffected voice of Susan Anway. But they suffer from an air of inconsequentiality. Merritt took over vocals on *The House of Tomorrow,* and his Eeyore-like baritone added just the right gravitas to his quietly outrageous wordplay. The next three Fields discs mine the same cheesy-Casiodrone-meets-suicidal-comic vein. *Holiday* scores with the infectious "Strange Powers"; *Charm of the Highway Strip* riffs on American folk and country, occasionally revealing more smugness than becomes Merritt; *Get Lost* has moments of genius, but the Merritt method was turning formulaic.

Enter the alter egos. The 6ths are Merritt's very own tribute band, with each song on their two albums handled by a different guest vocalist, ranging from Sebadoh's Lou Barlow (on *Wasps' Nests*) to folk legend Odetta (on *Hyacinths and Thistles*). The results are surprisingly consistent; it's like listening to the original cast album of a particularly warped Broadway show. Merritt and drummer/manager Claudia Gonson trade off crooning duties for Future Bible Heroes, whose album and EP boast a cool, grimly sardonic charm. The Gothic Archies' name is, sadly, the most amusing thing about them.

These side projects must have stoked Merritt's muse, for when the Magnetic Fields reappeared, it was with *69 Love Songs,* which is exactly as advertised: 69 songs covering every aspect of love, from the hilarious to the heartrending, spread over three CDs (available in a box or as separate discs). The inclusion of a handful of throwaways keeps the set from absolute classic status, but it's an awesome achievement all the same, and Merritt's best work. By comparison, the soundtrack to *Eban & Charley*—Merritt's first release under his own name—is only okay, though a couple of smart numbers elevate it above the average disc. *69 Love Songs'* real followup,

i, is centered on a similar attention-getting gimmick; each one of its 14 song titles begins with the letter *i.* Does this kind of thing really set a healthy precedent for Merritt's career? Regardless, the pleasures here are still great, though (obviously) not as many as on the previous Magnetic Fields blockbuster—it's got one of the best opening lines of a song on an album full of them: "So you quote love unquote me" ("I Don't Believe You"). —M.R.

Main Source

★★★★ Breaking Atoms (Wild Pitch, 1991)
★★½ F*ck What You Think (Wild Pitch, 1994)

Large Professor

★★ 1st Class (Matador, 2002)

Main Source's sizable legacy rests almost entirely on its one true album, *Breaking Atoms.* From the candy-colored cover depicting the three members crowded around a fantasy science project to the up-tempo beats and matching fast raps, it's a period piece whose meticulous presentation (particularly the production and rhymes of Large Professor) make it an enduring pleasure from a bygone era. Slightly unconventional in its lineup, Main Source featured two DJs, K-Cut and Sir Scratch (Toronto-bred brothers Kevin and Shawn McKenzie), who roped in native New Yorker William Paul Mitchell (a.k.a. Large Professor) as rapper and producer. *Atoms* is chock-full of great material, including "Looking at the Front Door" (where Large Professor declares that no matter how good his girl might look, if the arguments don't stop he's going to bounce) and "Live at the Barbeque" (notable as the recording debut of Nas, then recording under the name Nasty Nas, who states his intent to "kidnap the president's wife without a plan"). On the tremendous "Peace Is Not the Words to Play," Large Professor rhymes "I've seen people on the streets/shoot the next man and turn around and say peace/but that's leaving people in pieces/it's not what the meaning of peace is" as K-Cut and Sir Scratch demonstrate telepathy on the ones-and-twos. Large Professor left the group after *Breaking Atoms* over money squabbles (the McKenzies' mother had been the group's manager) and made beats for A Tribe Called Quest, Eric B and Rakim, Busta Rhymes, and others, finally releasing an underwhelming solo album in 2002. In his absence, Main Source recruited MC Mikey D and made a second, less impressive album (though recorded in 1994, it apparently did not receive widespread release until 1999). Whatever beef existed was eventually squashed as Main Source, including Large Professor, reunited for a performance in Toronto in December 2002. —P.R.

Stephen Malkmus

★★★★ Stephen Malkmus (Matador, 2001)
★★★★ Pig Lib (Matador, 2003)

When Pavement broke up, no one knew what to expect from Stephen Malkmus, the Natalie Wood of enigmatic American guitar boys. But it's safe to say that no one expected a solo debut as great as *Stephen Malkmus.* Having relocated to Portland, Oregon, he put together a new band of local buddies, the Jicks, and cut a bunch of off-the-cuff songs about love, sex, Greek gods, pirates, and the later work of Yul Brynner ("Perhaps you saw me in *Westworld*/I acted like a robotic cowboy"). In the tradition of Lou Reed and Tom Verlaine, Stephen Malkmus is a songwriter throwing off the constraints of a band that really didn't constrain him much. But he loosens up for the direct emotion of "Church on White," an elegy for a dead friend, and the finale of "Jo Jo's Jacket," mumbling the words "it's alright Ma, I'm only bleeding" before launching into a 30-second frenzy of debris-slide guitar babble.

Pig Lib was more ambitious, defying indie-rock fashion with a move into '70s-style folk–prog rock. Apparently, Malkmus wasn't kidding about all the time he spent listening to old Wishbone Ash and Incredible String Band albums. Not all of it works—the opener "Water and a Seat" is like bad Tull, and don't even start with the godawful album title. But now that he had a real rhythm section to play around with, he could write songs with the subtle punch of "Animal Midnight," "Us," and "The Ramp of Death." His guitar is brazenly beautiful, and, as usual, so is his voice in whispery ballads such as "Craw Song" and "Vanessa From Queens." The album came with a bonus CD of five songs, three of them good, including the best of the Jicks' long guitar jams, "Old Jerry." Still learning new songwriting tricks at a time when most of his indie contemporaries have either flamed out on major labels or shuffled off to grad school, Malkmus will be worth listening to whatever he chooses to do next. —R.S.

The Mamas and the Papas

★★★★½ If You Can Believe Your Eyes and Ears (1966; MCA, 1998)
★★½ The Mamas & the Papas (1966; MCA, 1987)
★★ People Like Us (1971; MCA, 1989)
★★★ Greatest Hits (MCA, 1998)
★★★ The Millennium Collection (MCA, 1999)
★★ California Dreamin' (MCA Special Products, 1994)
★★★★½ All the Leaves Are Brown: The Golden Era Collection (MCA, 2001)

On the cover of their debut album, the Mamas and the Papas are shown lounging happily in one big bathtub. Four personable hippies, they came on in 1966 like lifestyle radicals promising hedonistic freedom. Their true gift, though, was compromise: fusing folk-rock urgency with the gloss of highly commercial studio pop. *If You Can Believe Your Eyes and Ears* was a fresh wonder. By far their best record, it boasts the yearning "California Dreamin' "; the free-spirit manifesto, "Go Where You Wanna Go"; a vaudeville take on Lennon-McCartney's "I Call Your Name"; and a nice, breathy cover of Leiber-Stoller's "Spanish Harlem." John Phillips, Denny Doherty, Michelle Phillips, and especially Mama Cass were clear-voiced singers with solid folk backgrounds, but the group's strength was John's songwriting. Coupling a sure melodic sense with a flair for zeitgeist sloganeering, he made music that was hip yet unthreatening. The band's marketability was also boosted by a clearly delineated visual lineup: John the six-foot-four "genius," Doherty the winsome one, Mama Cass the earth mother, and Michelle the mistily gorgeous hippie chick.

Although the group continued in the folk-rock vein with a handful of singles, it began moving toward a more generic pop sound with the fine "Dedicated to the One I Love." By 1968, the hippie anthems verged on genial parody ("Meditation Mama," "Gemini Childe"), and "Dream a Little Dream of Me" was coy, even by pop standards.

As cultural symbols, the band members remained significant for a few years—John and Michelle organized the Monterey Pop Festival—but they seemed just as comfortable delivering tuneful, innocuous songs. Of their abundant greatest-hits packages, *All the Leaves Are Brown* is the strongest. —P.E.

Aimee Mann

★★★★ Whatever (Imago, 1993; DGC, 1995)
★★★ I'm With Stupid (DGC, 1995)
★★★½ Magnolia: Original Soundtrack (Reprise, 1999)
★★★★ Bachelor No. 2, or the last remains of the dodo (SuperEgo, 2000)
★★★ Ultimate Collection (Hip-O, 2000)
★★★ Lost in Space (SuperEgo, 2002)

Intelligent, tuneful, and loaded with attitude, many of Aimee Mann's songs should be instant pop classics. The only problem is that most of them haven't been very popular. Mann's understandable frustration at this and other hardships has come out increasingly in her music over the years, to the point where it's often tough to tell whether the guys she's venomously kissing off in song are ex-lovers or record company executives. And yet, tart as her lyrics may be, her melodies—expertly crafted pieces of retro-chic that pay homage to all the usual '60s and '70s touchstones—never lose their sugar.

Whatever, Mann's first album following the dissolution of her '80s band 'Til Tuesday, is a veritable encyclopedia of regret, bitterness, and defeat set to glorious Beatles-worthy music. Highlights include the rousing rocker "I Should've Known" and the woman-meets-much-*much*-older-man vignette "Mr. Harris," which manages to be both funny and touching. *I'm with Stupid* is rougher and less compelling, with a few ear-catching exceptions: "Amateur," "You Could Make a Killing," and "All Over Now."

After shuttling from one bad major-label experience to another, Mann finally caught a commercial break with the soundtrack to Paul Thomas Anderson's film *Magnolia.* Although the album isn't completely hers (four of the 13 tracks are by other artists, including two by, ahem, Supertramp), the stuff she's responsible for is some of her finest work, especially the cheeky stroll through Harry Nilsson's "One" and the beautifully somber "Build That Wall." Three *Magnolia* songs reappear on *Bachelor No. 2,* another outstanding disc that would be worth the list price for the poignant "Ghost World" alone. From the vintage Chamberlin tones of "This is How It Goes" to the finely wrought metaphors of "The Moth," nothing on *Lost in Space* will surprise fans of Mann's earlier albums, but nothing on it will turn them off either. Clearly, she's found a good sound and she's sticking with it.

Ultimate Collection, compiled by Mann's former record company to cash in on her *Magnolia* success, cobbles together a few nifty B sides and three 'Til Tuesday cuts (including the band's biggest hit, 1985's "Voices Carry") to bulk up the obvious choices from *Whatever* and *I'm With Stupid.* It's an okay intro to Mann's catalogue, but the original albums are better.   —M.R.

Mantronix

★★★★   Mantronix: The Album (1985; Warlock, 1999)
★★★★   Music Madness (Sleeping Bag, 1986)
★★★½   In Full Effect (Capitol, 1988)
★★★   This Should Move Ya (Capitol, 1990)
★★   The Incredible Sound Machine (Capitol, 1991)
★★★★   I Sing the Body Electro (Oxygen Music Works, 1999)
★★★★½ The Best of Mantronix 1985–1999 (Virgin/EMI, 1999)
★★★★½ That's My Beat (Soul Jazz, 2002)

Born in Jamaica and raised in Canada and the U.S., Kurtis Mantronik (né Curtis Khaleel) is one of hip-hop's sonic innovators, often cited as a founder of "electro," which isn't exactly true, although Mantronik's sound is shiny and voracious enough to accommodate the urge. Working with tape-edits and the limited capabilities of early sampling drum machines, Mantronik helped establish "stabbing," or using a short piece of sound repeatedly, as a dramatic highlight or rhythmic element. His drum patterns are full of sharp edges and counterpoint. Along with MC Tee, he did business as Mantronix. After meeting Sleeping Bag owner Will Socolov at Downtown Records in Manhattan, where Mantronik worked, the duo was signed in 1985 and released their debut single "Fresh Is the Word," revelatory for the force and syncopation of Mantronik's drums. MC Tee was never much of an MC, but he didn't get in the way. (While at Sleeping Bag, Mantronik also signed EPMD, earning him a gold star in any hip-hop lover's book.) Mantronik's work with other artists is just as important as his work with Mantronix (some would say more so): Just-Ice ("Cold Gettin' Dumb," later sampled by Redman), T-La Rock ("Breakin' Bells" and "Back to Burn"), and R&B singer Joyce Sims ("All in All"). The debut Mantronix album is brief and to the point, full of party rhymes and punchy bits and pieces flying by at a rapid tempo that hip-hop abandoned in the '90s until the Dirty South brought it back. (Cash Money producer Mannie Fresh has acknowledged Mantronik's influence repeatedly in interviews.) On "Needle to the Groove," Mantronik replaces much of MC Tee's voice processed through a vocoder. Robotlicious!

Why the second album, *Music Madness,* has never been issued on CD is one of life's great mysteries. Though some of the tracks are available on the great U.K. *Best of, Music Madness* needs to be heard in its entirety. Ratcheting up the number of samples and the sonic width, Mantronik creates a relentless, pulsing sound that still smokes most so-called electronica artists. "Listen to the Bass of Get Stupid Fresh" is a landmark for both hip-hop stabs and harmonica (courtesy of a sample of rock band Area Code 615), while "Who Is It?" is just plain nervous. *In Full Effect* saw the duo move to Capitol and maintain their sound for an effort that stands up nicely with the first two.

Everything changed on their second Capitol LP, and fourth overall, *This Should Move Ya.* MC Tee left the fold for the Air Force, so Mantronik recruited LL Cool J's cousin, Bryce Luvah, to rap, and his own cousin, DJ Dee, to do something, possibly DJ—it's hard to tell. MC Tee's absence was hardly a problem, as Bryce Luvah is a nimble rapper. More relevant was that Mantronik abandoned most of his style and went instead for a very status quo take on current hip-hop a la Big Daddy Kane and dance music somewhere between Chicago house and Britain's Soul II Soul. Neither distinct nor a failure, it's pretty fun (and is notable for the extremely odd cover choice: Ian Dury's "Sex & Drugs & Rock 'n' Roll"). The group scored a big hit in the U.K. with "Got to Have Your Love," a great pop club tune featuring singer Wondress. The final Mantronix album, *The Incredible Sound Machine*, dispenses with the hip-hop elements almost entirely and pushes the club tracks with new singer Jade Trini. The dominant sound is a sort of budget Soul II Soul, though the cover art suggests a budget Deee-Lite. It's perfectly passable, with a couple of great songs.

Mantronik resurfaced in the late '90s as a remixer and producer and issued one solo album as Kurtis Mantronik, *I Sing the Body Electro*. A small, underrated gem and already out of print, *Body Electro* revives his old style and even redoes a few Mantronix songs ("King of the Beats v. 3.0" and "Bass Machine Returned"). Interspersing fast-edit beat tracks with raps by female MC Traylude and a bit of drum and bass, Mantronik sounds absolutely undiminished and the album kicks respectably hard. For his Soul Jazz DJ mix CD, *That's My Beat*, Mantronix curates a fabulous selection of early-'80s N.Y. club music. —S.F.J.

Marah

★★★	Let's Cut the Crap and Hook Up Later On Tonight (Black Dog, 1998)
★★★½	Kids in Philly (Artemis, 2000)
★★	Float Away With the Friday Night Gods (Artemis, 2002)
★★★	20,000 Streets Under the Sky (Yep Roc, 2004)

Think Springsteen in Philadelphia, 20 years later. That said, singer David Bielanko and his crew have the good taste to pick from the best of the book of Bruce: the wrenching detail of working-class strivers, the fleeting earthly pleasures, the poetic clarity of the hard life. *Let's Cut the Crap* is a little heavy on the folksy side of things, but its followup is a fully articulated panorama of life with the lovelorn tramps in a crumbling town. Bielanko's banjo blends gorgeously with the band, adding a dimension of vulnerability, as the lyrics trace a gutter-bound pathos in lines that could have come straight from *Born to Run* (if not the Replacements' *Pleased to Meet Me*): "I'm trying on a beery drunk/You're leavin' me, the fire in your eyes/To be a ship already sunk."

How doubly unfortunate, then, that the band abandoned its hometown roots and the cleansing grit of roots rock entirely and relocated to Wales for their big-money bid, *Float Away*. Produced by Brit-pop czar Owen Morris (Oasis, the Verve), it uncomfortably soups up Marah's sound with sneering vocals and obnoxious electronic dance beats; the only remnant of Philly is "Crying on an Airplane," a disappointingly shallow reflection ("Fly away from the ones that we love/Fly away from one fine day, yeah yeah yeah"). They finally got Springsteen to do a cameo, singing *and* playing guitar on "Float Away," although, inexplicably, it's buried in the mix. But the group wised up fast: *20,000 Streets* sees their return to Philly and to the gritty, passionate ditties of their beginnings. The girl-group cheers on "Freedom Park" are instant fun, though the band's credulous runs through roots-rock tropes—doo-wop makes an appearance here, besides the usual Bruceisms—seem like penance. —B.S.

Marcy Playground

★★½	Marcy Playground (EMI, 1997)
★★	Shapeshifter (Capitol, 1999)
★★	MP3 (Reality, 2004)

Marcy Playground, a trio of arty alterna-rockers, scored its one and only hit in 1997 with the druggy "Sex and Candy." On the band's debut, frontman John Wozniak's lyrics are thoughtful and literate, and his band generates an ably supple, tunefully semi-acoustic backing. But you can listen to this disc three times and still not be able to tell songs such as "Cloak of Elvenkind" and "The Shadow of Seattle" apart. "Sex and Candy," on the other hand, is a shlub's soft-core fantasy that's only slightly better plotted than your average beer commercial. Ah, but that hook: One acoustic guitar figure tripping its light descent down a hesitant scale secured a place for these guys in pop history. Stay tuned for some canny hip-hop producer to recycle it soon, or just wait until the song returns on *Remember the Nineties?, Vol. 3*, sandwiched between "Tubthumping" and "Semi-Charmed Life." —K.H.

Marilyn Manson

★★	Portrait of an American Family (Nothing/Interscope, 1994)
★★	Smells Like Children (Nothing/Interscope, 1995)
★★★	Antichrist Superstar (Nothing/Interscope, 1996)
★★★½	Mechanical Animals (Nothing/Interscope, 1998)
★★	The Last Tour on Earth (Nothing/Interscope, 1999)
★★½	Holy Wood (In the Shadow of the Valley of Death) (Nothing/Interscope, 2000)
★★	The Golden Age of Grotesque (Interscope, 2003)

With much of rock's transgressive allure and star power usurped by hip-hop in the '90s, Marilyn Manson strapped on the bondage gear and went to work at winning it back. The erstwhile Brian Warner's act is mild stuff by the standard set by most death-metal bands, but because he was among the best ever at packaging and marketing the genre, he became the raunch-peddling, storm-trooping inheritor of the shock-rock legacy pioneered by Alice Cooper and Kiss.

Portrait of an American Family, overseen by Nine Inch Nails guru Trent Reznor, encases sick thrills in industrial-metal armor. *Smells Like Children* is a collection of remixes, outtakes, and covers that includes a stomping remake of Eurythmics' "Sweet Dreams (Are Made of This)," which improbably won Manson some mainstream-radio airplay. Ambition creeps into *Antichrist Superstar,* a concept album of sorts that positions Manson as a nihilistic cartoon version of Public Enemy No. 1. As a publicity gambit, it succeeded completely by putting Manson on the radar screens of offended religious leaders, government officials, and parents.

Mechanical Animals strips back the production just enough to let Manson's band establish a personality, and the result is an album that even well-adjusted adults might appreciate. Manson traded his Alice Cooper–goes-industrial sound for strutting glam rock, and his lyrics seem motivated by satire rather than spite. *Holy Wood* is a goth-rock end-of-innocence saga. More melodramatic and bloated than its predecessor, it finds Manson actually trying to sing melodies while teeing off on his usual subjects: mass media, organized religion, and killing your parents. Exhaustion overtakes *The Golden Age of Grotesque,* in which Manson admits "everything's been said before" and so resorts to campy gibberish on the order of "Doll-Dagga Buzz-Buzz Ziggety-Zag" and "Ka-Boom Ka-Boom." When the guilty pleasures run out, Manson, in desperate need of yet another makeover, is left to flirt with new-metal clichés. —G.K.

Marky Mark and the Funky Bunch

★★ Music for the People (Interscope, 1991)
★½ You Gotta Believe (Interscope, 1992)

As the younger brother of New Kids on the Block roughneck Donnie "Donnie D" Wahlberg (who produced and cowrote most of the former's music), "Marky Mark" Wahlberg was a zero-cred rapper who scored with 1991's "Good Vibrations." With a high-energy, hip-house sound similar to that of "The Power" by Snap! and a memorable video featuring Marky Mark curling bricks in the rain, "Good Vibra-

tions" (no relation to the Beach Boys classic) helped *Music for the People* go platinum. Surrounded by an all-black crew (the Funky Bunch) and flexing in Calvin Klein underwear ads, Marky Mark continued to mix pop aspirations with a tough-guy attitude on his second album, *You Gotta Believe,* but he couldn't repeat the commercial success of his debut. Having put himself on ice with couplets like "Freezer might as well be frostin'/Cuz I'm the baddest white boy in Boston" (from "Super Cool Mack Daddy"), Marky Mark appeared to be no more than an extended footnote in the New Kids on the Block story. But soon Marky Marky reverted to his given name and made his acting breakthrough as a studly porn star in Paul Thomas Anderson's acclaimed film *Boogie Nights.* This kicked off a string of major films roles for Wahlberg—including costarring alongside Ice Cube in *Three Kings* and the title role in *Rock Star,* a film based on the Judas Priest story—that remains a going concern. —P.R.

Bob Marley and the Wailers

★★★★½ Catch a Fire (1973; Tuff Gong, 1990; Tuff Gong/Island, 2001)
★★★★★ Burnin' (1973; Tuff Gong, 1990; Tuff Gong/Island, 2001)
★★★★★ Natty Dread (1975; Tuff Gong, 1990; Tuff Gong/Island, 2001)
★★★★ Live! (1975; Tuff Gong, 1990; Tuff Gong/Island, 2001)
★★★★ Rastaman Vibration (1976; Tuff Gong, 1990; Tough Gong/Island, 2001)
★★★★ Exodus (1977; Tuff Gong, 1990; Tuff Gong/Island, 2001)
★★★½ Kaya (1978; Tuff Gong, 1990; Tuff Gong/Island, 2001)
★★★ Babylon by Bus (1978; Tuff Gong/Island, 2001)
★★★★ Survival (1979; Tuff Gong, 1990; Tuff Gong/Island, 2001)
★★★★½ Uprising (1980; Tuff Gong, 1990; Tuff Gong/Island, 2001)
★★★ Confrontation (1983; Tuff Gong, 1990; Tuff Gong/Island, 2001)
★★★★★ Legend: The Best of Bob Marley and the Wailers (1984; Tuff Gong, 1990; Tuff Gong/Island, 2002)
★★★½ Rebel Music (1986; Tuff Gong, 1990; Tough Gong/Island 2001)
★★★½ Talkin' Blues (Tuff Gong, 1991; Tuff Gong/Island 2001)
★★★★ One Love: Bob Marley and the Wailers at Studio One (Heartbeat, 1991)
★★★★★ Songs of Freedom (Tuff Gong/Island, 1992; Tuff Gong/Island, 1999)

If he had done nothing but record *Catch a Fire*, Bob Marley would still be known as the person who introduced reggae music to millions of Americans. But more than just a cultural ambassador, Robert Nesta Marley was a fabulously talented songwriter who could mix protest music and undeniable pop as skillfully as Bob Dylan; even before Marley's death at age 36, he was becoming a true culture hero—the first major rock artist to come out of a Third World country. More than 20 years on, his records sound as fresh as ever, something proved every week by the astonishing continued sales of his greatest-hits package *Legend*.

Although Marley is best known for the string of memorable albums he recorded during the '70s, the original Wailers—Marley, Peter Tosh, and Neville "Bunny Wailer" Livingston—were a leading Jamaican vocal trio in the '60s, cutting R&B-flavored sides with distinctive island rhythms. The development of the Wailers into a self-contained band mirrors the evolution of reggae itself; gradually, the group shook off the singles-minded approach of the early Jamaican studios and forged an expansive new groove from established local styles like ska, *mento*, and bluebeat. Emerging as a fiery topical songwriter and spiritually compelling frontman, Marley led the Wailers to international acclaim with the release of two startling albums in 1973. With stalwart bassist Aston "Family Man" Barrett and drummer Carlton Barrett pumping out incendiary "riddims" behind the Wailers' smoky harmonies, *Catch a Fire* is a blazing debut. "Concrete Jungle" and "Slave Driver" crackle with streetwise immediacy, while "Kinky Reggae" and "Stir It Up" (a pop hit for Johnny Nash in '73) revel in the music's vast capacity for good-time skanking. "Stop That Train" and "400 Years," both written by Peter Tosh, indicate the original Wailers weren't strictly a one-man show. *Burnin'* glows even hotter; "Get Up, Stand Up" backs its activist message with an itchy, motivating beat. "I Shot the Sheriff" (covered by Eric Clapton in 1974) and

"Small Axe" show Marley's verbal and melodic skills growing by leaps and bounds; he expertly blends personal testimony with political philosophy to make enduring points about institutionalized racism.

Tosh and Livingston left for solo careers after that album and were effectively replaced by the "I-Threes" trio: Marcia Griffiths, Rita Marley (Mrs. Bob), and Judy Mowatt. *Natty Dread* captures the refurbished Wailers at an ambitious peak. "No Woman, No Cry" features Marley's most soulful vocal performance; while avoiding crippling despair, "Them Belly Full (But We Hungry)" and "Rebel Music (Three o'Clock Roadblock)" articulate the anger of the oppressed and downtrodden; the title track and "So Jah Seh" posit the tangled web of Rastafarian belief without slipping totally into the cosmos. *Live!* documents a thrilling, tight-as-a-drum 1975 London performance of highlights from the first three albums. On *Rastaman Vibration*, Marley starts to fall back on pat formulas and ganja-stoked rhetoric. But the grimly prophetic "War" and the deceptively feel-good "Positive Vibration" stand out on an album that holds up to repeated listening (and dancing).

Marley opted for a lighter touch on *Exodus* and *Kaya*, adding lead guitars to the bass-defined reggae pocket. These two albums don't command the same attention as the earlier ones, but either effort will grow on a committed fan. Recent converts should begin at the top. *Babylon by Bus* is probably Marley's flattest and least-inspiring effort; this live set isn't bad, but the loose readings of Wailers classics can't compare to the marvelously succinct *Live!* Marley ups the political ante on the impassioned *Survival:* "Wake Up and Live" and "Ride Natty Ride" recast familiar messages in fresh musical surroundings, while "Zimbabwe" and "Africa Unite" confidently extend the Wailers' sphere of influence.

If Marley hadn't been fatally stricken with cancer in 1980, *Uprising* would most likely have ushered in a productive new decade for the world reggae ruler. The final Wailers album deftly summarizes Marley's revolutionary career: "Coming in From the Cold" strikes a measured note of hope; "Real Situation" acknowledges reasons for hopelessness; "Could You Be Loved" incorporates a winning taste of commercial funk; and "Redemption Song" closes the album with a heart-stopping acoustic plea.

Posthumous Marley releases have maintained a fairly high standard of quality. The Heartbeat issues cover Marley and the Wailers' early days at Studio One, when ska, which had emerged as Jamaica's homegrown interpretation of stateside rock & roll, ruled the West Indian nation's airwaves. *Greatest Hits at Studio One* skanks dancehall gems like "Simmer

Down"; *V.1* and *V.2* survey the group's formative years; and *Wailers and Friends* easy-rocks with the legendary Skatalites. *Confrontation* includes rare tracks and outtakes, most notably the minor hit "Buffalo Soldier." *Rebel Music* and *Natural Mystic* collect some of the Wailers' most overtly radical statements in listenable agit-pop broadsides. *Talkin' Blues* mixes live versions and outtakes from their prime mid-'70s period with telling interview snippets. *One Love* needlessly updates *Legend,* an indomitable greatest-hits set; as deep as this sterling single-disc album sounds, it barely scratches the surface. *Songs of Freedom* remedies this. From rock-steady crooner to dreadlocked Rasta, this four-disc box set is a fitting testament to Marley's transformative career.   —M.C./C.S.

Martha & the Vandellas

★★★	Come and Get These Memories (1963; Motown, 1999)
★★★½	Heat Wave (Gordy, 1963)
★★★½	Greatest Hits (1966; Motown, 1990)
★★★	Motown Legends (1993)
★★★	Greatest Hits (Prime Cuts, 1995)
★★	Milestones (Motown, 1995)
★★★★	The Ultimate Collection (Motown, 1998)
★★★★	The Millennium Collection (Motown, 1999)

Because of mid-'60s classics "Nowhere to Run," "Dancing in the Street," and "Heat Wave," Martha Reeves and the Vandellas achieved immortality as one of Motown's edgiest outfits. Recipient of some of Holland-Dozier-Holland's most hard-hitting production work, the group's best songs are all bass, brass, and thunder—the singers have to fight hard just to keep up. The Vandellas hung around longer than their 1963–65 heyday, and Reeves kept recording on her own throughout the '70s, but none of the later efforts could rekindle the early spark.   —P.E.

Ricky Martin

★★	Ricky Martin (Sony, 1999)
★★	Sound Loaded (Sony, 2000)
★★	La Historia (Sony, 2001)

When this former Menudo singer started wooing the pop mainstream in 1999, everybody tipped him as a major star. Yet the Puerto Rican stud was out the door faster than the mocha seductress he sang about in "Livin' La Vida Loca." His English-language debut, *Ricky Martin,* had electric-salsa disco sleaze such as "The Cup of Life" and "Shake Your Bon Bon," but the crap ballads drove all his new fans away. The followup, *Sound Loaded,* flopped despite "She Bangs," a me-want-woman song so unbelievably idiotic it verged on

genius. Adam Ant could have written the chorus, and that's a compliment. He opted to play the Bush inauguration, shaking his bonbon at the Lincoln Memorial and asking, "Mr. President, may I have this dance, please?" Surprisingly, the White House never invited Martin back to sing "Happy Birthday, Mr. President." Not so surprisingly, Martin split with his agent and went crawling back to the Spanish-language market with *La Historia,* a collection of early hits.   —R.S.

The Marvelettes

★★★	The Marvelettes' Greatest Hits (1966; Motown, 1991)
★	The Very Best of the Motorcity Collections (Hot, 1996)
★★★½	The Ultimate Collection (Motown, 1998)
★★★	The Millennium Collection (Motown, 2000)

While still in her teens, Michigan's Georgeanna Dobbins wrote "Please Mr. Postman," and the song so impressed Motown Records head Berry Gordy that he signed Dobbins and four of her girlfriends as the Marvelettes. Illness forced Dobbins' departure soon after, but the upbeat, supercatchy "Postman"—which gave Motown its first #1 pop hit—remains the group's signature tune. "Beechwood 4-5789" is nearly its equal in perkiness (and remains perhaps the best of rock & roll's many "phone number" songs); "Too Many Fish in the Sea" is also prime early Marvelettes; lead singer Gladys Horton exudes good-humored sass.

By 1967, the group went in for a more mature sound—the commanding "The Hunter Gets Captured by the Game" is a classic example—but its pop appeal never wavered. "My Baby Must Be a Magician" and "Here I Am Baby," the latter released in 1968, marked the waning of their heyday; dizzying personnel changes (as reflected on the Hot compilation) ultimately made the Marvelettes seem like an echo of their former glory.   —P.E.

Mase

★★★	Harlem World (Bad Boy/Arista, 1997)
★★	Double Up (Bad Boy/Arista, 1999)

Mase Presents Harlem World

★½	The Movement (All Out/So So Def/Columbia, 1999)

Mason "Mase" Betha was already being groomed for stardom by Sean "Puffy" Combs when the murder of Bad Boy Records star Notorious B.I.G. in 1997 pushed him into the center of the label's universe. On *Harlem World,* Mase played his position with cool, understated flair: "I'm the newest member of the Bad Boy team/And I'ma bring this nigga Puff mad more cream." But Mase's remarkably simple rhymes are filled with weak, unimaginative lines, and his monotone style is more lethargic than laid-back. Still, he epitomized the jiggy late '90s and glorified the luxe life like no rapper before him: "No problem gettin' cars/ Whole entourage in the Mount Airy Lodge/When you very large, never spend cheddar, you charge/Get my daily ménage, Halle Berry massage."

Unlike the average hip-hop album, *Harlem World* features a bevy of singers—112, Monifah, Total, Billy Lawrence—and superslick, highly danceable grooves that owe more to R&B than to hip-hop. Samples of Kool & the Gang, Teena Marie, Curtis Mayfield, and Michael Jackson inform "Feel So Good," "Love U So," "What You Want," and "Cheat on You." Mase frequently plays the tough-guy role ("Niggaz Wanna Act," "Take What's Yours," "Will They Die 4 You?"), claiming, "I was Murder/P. Diddy named me pretty," though there's really no bite in the dimpled playboy's bark.

Capitalizing on the massive success of *Harlem World* (more than 4 million copies sold in the U.S.), Mase formed his own record label and fronts the Harlem World collective on the utterly forgettable *Mase Presents Harlem World: The Movement.* A little more than a month after *The Movement*'s release, Mase shocked the world when he announced his immediate retirement from hip-hop, eventually revealing that he'd decided to become a minister. *Double Up*, recorded before his announcement but released months later, copied *Harlem World*'s formula with few variations. But Mase's rhymes, lazy at their best, seem wholly uninspired as his debut's nouveau riche bliss turns into angry disillusionment on tracks like "Make Me Cry," "Same Niggas," and "Fuck Me? Fuck You." In the summer of 2004, Mase returned with the single "Welcome Back," which sampled the theme from *Welcome Back, Kotter.* Now how did we know this was coming? —K.X.

Dave Mason

★★★   Alone Together (MCA, 1970)
★★½   Let It Flow (Columbia, 1977)
★★½   The Best of Dave Mason (Columbia, 1981)
★★★   Long Lost Friend: The Best of Dave Mason (Columbia, 1995)
★★   Will You Still Love Me? (Sony Special Products, 1998)
★★★½   Ultimate Collection (Hip-O, 1999)
★★★   Super Hits (Sony, 2000)
★★½   Live at Perkins Palace (Pioneer Artists, 2002)

with Jim Capaldi

★★   The 40,000 Headmen Tour (Receiver, 1999)

Dave Mason's pop songwriting contributions— "Feelin' Alright," "Hole in My Shoe," "We Can All Join In"—brought some crucial leavening to his old band's (Traffic) classical-jazz-blues mix. But when he went solo, Mason turned soft and then got softer. The guitarist's way with a hook is apparent throughout his work, but more telling are his limited vocal range, an overall sense of caution, and lyrics that too often descend to pop-psych clichés. His big hit from 1977, "We Just Disagree," was pabulum. Backed by Delaney and Bonnie and their excellent group of players, *Alone Together* was crisp and highly successful. With *It's Like You Never Left* (now deleted), Mason hit a peak, of sorts—Graham Nash's singing is pleasant, as always, but the album's dense instrumentation shows Mason heading toward the glossiness from which he'd seldom depart thereafter. Mason won his biggest audience with his most boring material on *Let It Flow.* Released in 1977, the year punk fully erupted, it was sad, dinosaur music from a former innovator and provided a cautionary tale in the perils of growing comfortable, expert, and redundant. *Ultimate Collection* is the most balanced compilation, from the early Traffic work to the later solo fare. —P.E.

Massive Attack

★★★★★   Blue Lines (Virgin, 1991)
★★★½   Protection (Virgin, 1994)
★★★★   Mezzanine (Virgin, 1998)
★★★   Singles 90/98 (EMI Int'l, 1998)
★★★   100th Window (Virgin, 2003)

Massive Attack created a new template for dance music by merging hip-hop's gritty urban beat, spaced-out dub-reggae texture, chill-out melodies, and soul instrumentation. *Blue Lines* distills this distinctly urban mix into sultry mood music pulse, the core trio of Daddy G, 3-D, and Mushroom creating lush soundscapes for serenely commanding vocalists such as Shara Nelson and reggae master Horace Andy. With *Blue Lines* as the blueprint and the group's hometown of Bristol, England, as its epicenter, this cultish brand of underground club music—later dubbed trip-hop—would eventually infiltrate the mainstream, thanks to proponents such as Portishead, Beth Orton, Sneaker Pimps, and former Massive Attack member Tricky.

On *Protection*, the Massive Attack brain trust does little to alter the *Blue Lines* approach, simply sliding in a new set of vocalists, including Everything but the Girl's Tracey Thorn; the results are less innovative, but no less intoxicating.

A four-year layoff resulted in a much-needed rethink on *Mezzanine* and a complete break with trip-hop, which by this time had become easy-listening music for hipsters. The album slips off the dance floor and into the shadows. It seethes with low-key paranoia and dread, punctuated by bursts of newfound aggression. The emphasis on showcasing the individual vocalist fades in favor of a more cohesive musical statement. If not as melodic or groovy as its predecessors, *Mezzanine* packs a dark allure.

The shadow play continues on *100th Window,* which softens some of the edges that had crept into *Mezzanine* and adds touches of glitch techno alongside Arabic string orchestration and submerged bass lines. The guest vocalists, foregrounded in the mix on previous albums, become just another instrument in the slow-moving, sci-fi gloom; even Sinéad O'Connor sounds strangely muted. It's Massive Attack at its grimmest and most abstract, with music befitting a cold-sweat nightmare rather than disco transcendence. —G.K.

Master P

★★	Get Away Clean (1991; No Limit, 1998)	
★★	Mama's Bad Boy (1992; No Limit, 1998)	
★★½	The Ghetto's Tryin' to Kill Me! (No Limit, 1994)	
★★½	99 Ways to Die (No Limit, 1995)	
★★½	Ice Cream Man (No Limit/Priority, 1996)	
★★★	Ghetto D (No Limit, 1997)	
★★	MP Da Last Don (No Limit, 1998)	
★★	Only God Can Judge Me (No Limit/Priority, 1999)	
★★★	Ghetto Postage (No Limit, 2000)	
★★	Game Face (No Limit/Universal, 2001)	
★★	Good Side, Bad Side (Koch, 2004)	

TRU

★★	Who's Da Killer? (No Limit, 1993)
★★½	Understanding the Criminal Mind (No Limit, 1994)
★★½	True (No Limit/Priority, 1995)
★★	Tru 2 Da Game (No Limit/Priority, 1997)
★★	Da Crime Family (No Limit/Priority, 1999)

504 Boyz

★★	Goodfellas (No Limit/Priority, 2000)
★★	Ballers (No Limit/Universal, 2002)

New Orleans rap kingpin Master P represents the best and worst of hip-hop's transformation into big business in the '90s. As Percy Miller, who rose from the projects to own and operate one of the country's most successful independent record companies, No Limit, he is a model of rugged individualism and old-fashioned American entrepreneurship. Featured on the cover of *Fortune* in 1999, he was for years a mainstay in that magazine's annual list of the richest Americans under 40, his worth hovering at around $300 million (just a little above Puff Daddy and a little below Michael Jordan).

But his rise is tainted by his taste. After studying business at a junior college in Oakland, CA, Miller returned to New Orleans inspired by the rawness (and surely the popularity) of West Coast gangsta rap and began a prodigious output of unapologetic thuggery set to basic, street-rocking beats. The endless product issued by No Limit—besides Master P, there are his younger brothers C-Murder and Silkk the Shocker, and dozens of others—is often indistinguishable even for die-hard fans. With on-the-cheap production and a formulaic script of West Coast G-funk, Southern bounce, and N'awlins slang, No Limit's releases have less to do with quality and expressiveness than quick, assembly-line mass entertainment. Master P likes to call himself the ghetto Bill Gates, but he's also hip-hop's Roger Corman.

His early albums are fairly rote gangsta rap, distinguished in hindsight by the fact that their outlandish boasts of taking over the world and making shit-loads of money actually turned out to be true. Occasional pleas about being forced into a life of crime by society's neglect—exploited heavily on the albums by TRU (The Real Untouchables), his group with C-Murder, Silkk, and others—offer some humanity, but it's nothing that hadn't been said better by N.W.A and Tupac Shakur.

Some lucky occurrences and smart business moves led to No Limit's commercial explosion in the late '90s. The deaths of Tupac and Notorious B.I.G., and the collapse of Death Row Records, left a void in the gangsta marketplace, and aggressive marketing and expansion left No Limit poised to fill it. *99 Ways to Die* and *Ice Cream Man* ("In case y'all wondering what ice cream is/It's anything that you can make profit off of") attempt to do that, but not until the next release did Master P's formula fully come together.

Opening with a step-by-step recipe for making crack, *Ghetto D* (as in dope) has a strong main plotline of drugs and big money ("Let's Get 'Em," "After Dollars No Cents") supported by moments of maudlin sentimentality ("I Miss My Homies") and raunchy comic relief ("Make 'Em Say Ugh," celebrating P's favorite syllable). All the while, a cast of regulars—Silkk, Kane and Abel, Fiend, Mia X, it never ends—hover around the mike like a ghetto Rat Pack. It's a full and self-contained entertainment package, with P at the center and a huge group of marketable sidemen getting exposure for their own thangs: a perfect example of product placement and branding.

MP Da Last Don is a morbid double album that feels like a triple, and *Only God Can Judge Me* (an outright Tupac rip) is no lighter, opening with a stark, pseudomystical invocation and warning ("To my enemies and the media/To the feds and the IRS/Fuck all y'all"). But both further develop P's music-as-marketing strategy, with CD booklets almost entirely devoted to other No Limit products, from upcoming albums and Master P's clothing and shoe lines to No Limit cell phone service and even the Talking Master P doll. With all this to buy, who cares if you're hearing a lazy Boyz II Men copy called "Goodbye to My Homies" or the fourth rap in a row by Fiend?

Ghetto Postage is a comic delight, with head-nodding Southern grooves and irresistible shout-along hooks delivered in a slang language that is barely understandable. *Game Face,* made with a new team of producers, is not as manic as previous releases. By 2001 solo albums seem to be just a pie-slice of activity for Master P, and it shows; by 2004, No Limit fortunes apparently reached their limit, as Master P went to an outside label to release *Good Side, Bad Side,* a bland double album chronicling the rapper's two not-very-different sides.

Of the many No Limit group projects, Master P's role is most significant in TRU and the 504 Boyz. TRU's early albums are mainly notable as the place where P developed his character of the "ice cream man" who likes to bounce, but they also have an angry social conscience absent from his solo releases ("I'm sell 'caine to get my grits because I can't get a job, so/Fuck that shit"). 504 Boyz, founded long after P reached the peak of fame, seems like just another marketing scheme, with a Tupac sound-alike named Krazy and cover artwork that's shoddy even by No Limit standards.   —B.S.

Matchbox Twenty

★★★★ Yourself or Someone Like You (Atlantic, 1996)
★★★ Mad Season (Atlantic, 2000)
★★½ More Than You Think You Are (Atlantic, 2002)

Every generation has its Bryan Adams—a syrupy balladeer cloaked in root-rock affectation. By 1997, the chart-topping Holy Grail that Rob Thomas sought was a gut-wrencher that would sound equally at home on *Now, That's What I Call Eddie Vedder, Vol. 8* and the soundtrack of *Titanic 2.* On the radio, "Push" seemed like standard-issue frat-boy resentment. But "Push" sounds different in the context of an album dedicated to the ruminations of a schlub who's fascinated and repulsed by sexual, psychological, and financial power relations. Not sure if he's "ever been good enough," outclassed by the movers

and shakers of the real world, Thomas settles, in bad conscience, for manipulating his girlfriend and sulking at parties.

For round two, however, the author of Santana's biggest single ("Smooth") could no longer play the underdog. Thomas' empathy had swelled with his bank account, and, unfortunately, so did the string section that began to accompany his ballads. "Bent" distills new-metal dysfunction into everyday desperation even as its riffs forge grunge into a platinum alloy suitable for nine-to-five office radio. On "Rest Stop," Rob takes a nap in the passenger seat during a road trip, and when he wakes up, his girl gives him the boot. Her rationale: "I was listening to the radio/And wondering what you're dreaming/When it came to mind that I didn't care." Wow. Rod Stewart is *never* gonna cover that.   —K.H.

Dave Matthews Band

★★★ Remember Two Things (1993; RCA, 1997)
★★½ Recently (1994; RCA, 1997)
★★★½ Under the Table and Dreaming (RCA, 1994)
★★★★ Crash (RCA, 1996)
★★★½ Live at Red Rocks 8.15.95 (Bama Rags/RCA, 1997)
★★★★½ Before These Crowded Streets (RCA, 1998)
★★★ Listener Supported (RCA, 1999)
★★★ Everyday (RCA, 2001)
★★★½ Live in Chicago 12.19.98 at the United Center (RCA, 2001)
★★★★ Busted Stuff (RCA 2002)
★★★½ Live at Folsom Field, Boulder, Colorado (RCA, 2002)
★★★★ The Central Park Concert (RCA, 2003)

Dave Matthews

★★★ Live at Luther College (RCA, 1999)
★★★ Some Devil (RCA, 2003)

The Dave Matthews Band ignited a quiet revolution in the mid-'90s with a jazzy world-beat stew that appealed to both button-down collegians and peasant-attired neo-hippies looking for a new group to follow. They were the most multicultural and unconventional of all the H.O.R.D.E. ("Horizons of Rock Developing Everywhere") tour acts, helping to launch a jam-band craze that thrives to this day. Their unusual lineup featured violin and saxophone (no lead guitar!), and the exotic configuration allowed them to weave various stylistic strands (jazz, pop, Middle Eastern, African) into an oddly hypnotic sonic tapestry.

When they signed to RCA in 1994, the DMB had already released two discs—*Remember Two Things* and *Recently,* a five-song EP—on their own Bama Rags label and were well established regionally.

Formed in 1991 near the University of Virginia campus in Charlottesville, the Dave Matthews Band—South African–born singer/acoustic guitarist Matthews, sax player Leroi Moore, violinist Boyd Tinsley, bassist Stefan Lessard, and drummer Carter Beauford—built a loyal following at frat houses and clubs around the Southeast. Their grassroots touring strategy became a template for a rising generation of jam bands who saw little for themselves in the conventional record business.

All but two songs from *Remember Two Things* were cut live, and the longish, meandering tracks included the fan favorites "Ants Marching" and "Tripping Billies." More to the point, the album served to introduce the DMB's unique musical syntax. *Under the Table and Dreaming,* their first studio album and major label debut, moved them forward. Producer Steve Lillywhite helped focus and streamline their sound, providing an airtight framework over which the soloists added limber coloration. Matthews' sometimes static songs weren't always as remarkable as the band's grooves and textures, but *Under the Table and Dreaming* succeeded in bringing the DMB to a larger audience, and "Warehouse," "Dancing Nancies," and "Jimi Thing" became cornerstones of their repertoire. Moreover, this unlikely quintet scored an actual pop hit with "What Would You Say," which featured Blues Traveler's John Popper on harmonica.

The group demonstrated further growth and finesse on *Crash,* fine-tuning its studio persona and bucking the notion that jam bands can't make good records. *Crash* included the DMB classics "Two Step" and "#41," and netted them their biggest hit, "Crash Into Me."

Before These Crowded Streets marked the point at which the DMB became a good song band as well as a great jam band. Fans, critics, and Matthews himself consider it their quintessential album. It mixed dark, foreboding songs about what Matthews called the "symphony of death"—i.e., the global bloodletting loosed by religious and political differences—and playful tunes about lust and desire. The DMB's instrumental blend was particularly entrancing on "Rapunzel," where violinist Tinsley's swirling lines and Moore's snake-charmer sax animated Matthews' peppery, seductive vocal.

The group next recorded and abandoned an album, known to fans and bootleggers as *The Lillywhite Sessions* (for producer Steve Lillywhite). In its stead, Matthews split to Los Angeles, where he wrote and recorded a new album, *Everyday,* with producer Glen Ballard (Alanis Morissette, No Doubt), involving the band only in the later stages. On *Everyday,* the emphases shifted dramatically. Matthews assumed an upfront role on electric guitar, while Tinsley and Moore were relegated more to the background. Producer Ballard cowrote every song and played piano throughout, raising eyebrows in DMB land. *Everyday* was a jagged little pill for many fans, but it served its purpose of getting the band out of a rut.

On *Busted Stuff,* the Dave Matthews Band took the unusual step of rerecording their lost album. With a fresh perspective on the material, combined with a tighter approach to arrangements gleaned from their one-off with Ballard, they emerged with a bold, moving musical statement. Matthews' fluid voice ruminated about lost love, emptiness, escape, and "busted stuff" as the band cooked up a quiet storm behind him. "Where Are You Going," featuring 12-string guitar, was as pretty a song as Matthews ever wrote.

The group, looking to outfox bootleggers and satisfy fans, took to releasing live albums early in its career. Including its debut album, half of all band and solo releases have been concert recordings. Among this bevy, *Live at Red Rocks 8.15.95* captured them early at every big-time jam band's favorite venue, while *Live in Chicago 12.19.98 at the United Center* documented a solid show from a much-praised tour in support of *Before These Crowded Streets. Listener Supported* came from an end-of-tour gig in New Jersey in 1999, while *Live at Folsom Field,* recorded in July 2001, found them revamping their set with fresh material from *Everyday* and *Busted Stuff.* The three-hour, three-CD *Central Park Concert* is preferable on DVD, as the spectacle—more than 100,000 fans at a high-profile benefit concert for New York City schools and parks—is well worth seeing as well as hearing.

Live at Luther College came from one of the solo acoustic tours Matthews occasionally undertakes with guitarist Tim Reynolds. In 2003, Matthews released his first solo studio disc, *Some Devil.* The material was highly personal, finding its emotional center in a run of songs that worked its way from misery ("Some Devil Some Angel," "Trouble") to salvation ("Grey Blue Eyes," "Save Me"). "Gravedigger," an extraordinary meditation on life and death, won Matthews a Grammy for Best Male Rock Vocal. —P.P.

The Mavericks

★★	The Mavericks (1990; Hip-O, 1998)
★★★★	From Hell to Paradise (MCA, 1992)
★★★★	What a Crying Shame (MCA, 1994)
★★★	Music for All Occasions (MCA, 1995)
★★★	Trampoline (MCA, 1998)
★★★½	Super Colossal Smash Hits of the '90s: The Best of the Mavericks (Mercury, 1999)
★★★	The Mavericks (Sanctuary, 2003)

The content of this intelligent, eclectic, new-country band's first album is less important than the fact of it: After confusing audiences around Miami by playing original country music in various rock clubs, the Mavericks were signed by a minor label and released an album. *The Mavericks* got them in the door. Once its name was established, the foursome fine-tuned their sound in preparation for a second, more polished release.

And so *From Hell to Paradise* was born. Mavericks frontman and songwriter Raul Malo, a Cuban émigré, taps into the isolation at the heart of great country music—which for Malo means "this country" as much as country & western—and the pains and simple pleasures of a hardscrabble existence come alive in his big earnest tenor and evocative lyrics. *From Hell to Paradise* is amiable and danceable; in addition to the title song (about Malo's family's journey to America) and a zippy cover of Hank Williams' "Hey Good Lookin' " with Trisha Yearwood, four songs are resurrected from *The Mavericks*: the ambling ballad "This Broken Heart," the sly breakup number "A Better Way," the poignant "Mr. Jones," and "The End of the Line," perhaps the only song mocking hypocritical religious zealots that deserves its own line dance.

On *What a Crying Shame,* the Mavericks fold some smooth pop into their honky-tonk mix for their most sophisticated recording yet. The title track, a radio-ready pop weeper with an irresistible chorus, garnered the group Top 40 play. Between the numbers that sound unearthed from the vintage bin ("There Goes My Heart" and "Ain't Found Nobody") are unusual country-based songs performed with little consideration for genre. "The Things You Said to Me" seems loosely wrapped around the bones of "Tonight the Bottle Let Me Down" but sparked with a sneaky bass riff; "I Should Have Been True" and the gorgeous "Oh, What a Thrill" are '50's-prom slow dances; the pretty dance tune "All That Heaven Will Allow" casts a salsa shadow.

On *Music for All Occasions,* the Mavericks stray from their honky-tonk beginnings into the realm of retro easy-listening country. Malo's songs are all about love here, and his rhymes take an attendant plunge in complexity: "say/day," "forever/together," "soul/hold"—it's not pretty. The Cuban-inflected ballads that swayed between the high-steppers of their previous albums constitute the entire recording of *Music for All Occasions,* and even when the melodies are solid and effective, as on "Missing You" and "I'm Not Gonna Cry for You," the pace drags. Fortunately, smack at the center of this 11-song effort, two guests crash the party with a fresh bag of ice and some great new jokes: Flaco Jimenez's accordion playing enlivens

the bright, busy "All You Ever Do Is Bring Me Down"; Rafe Vanhoy's "My Secret Flame," though in the same idiom as Malo's songwriting, is so different in style that the vocals sound entirely new.

Trampoline, like all of the better Mav work, is a good but not great album. A roadhouse band with sterling taste and an interestingly diverse repertoire of styles, the hardworking group is not in the business of transcending its chosen forms, even if it can occasionally transcend itself. When it unleashes the string section for the chorus of "I've Got This Feeling," the group sounds as if meaning every note is the enlightened path to cutting loose. On *The Mavericks* (2003), they get a bit cheesy at times ("I'm Wondering" could have lit up your parents' prom), but they're still as catchy as Toby Keith, and without any backwoods nonsense to boot.   —A.B.

Maxwell

★★★	Maxwell's Urban Hang Suite (Columbia, 1996)
★★	Embrya (Columbia, 1998)
★★★	Now (Columbia, 2001)

With his 1996 debut, good-looking soul man Maxwell sought to create a style of seductive, bedroom-ready R&B that could incorporate pop, funk, jazz, and hip-hop, as though he were some kind of postmodern Marvin Gaye. Maxwell's laid-back romanticism has heat at its core and a powerful groove that grounds the music: By varying the push of the beat but retaining the central mellow vibe, Maxwell creates a sound as felicitous on headphones as it is in the bedroom. Song after song explores the long-dormant possibilities of gentlemanly sexuality, from the kindly "Welcome" to the generous hit "Ascencion (Don't Ever Wonder)" to the come-ons of ". . . Til the Cops Come Knockin'."

Unfocused and pretentious, *Embrya* did not match the success of Maxwell's impressive debut. The album is full of overwrought, underwritten songs with obscure, fancy titles revolving around a sort of sexual gnosticism. He still has his songcraft and beautiful, subtle voice, but the burbling Latin vibe of "I'm You: You Are Me and We Are You (Pt Me & You)," doesn't change the fact that the song is called "I'm You: You are Me and We Are You (Pt. Me & You)," or that the lyrics, half in Spanish, are correspondingly obfuscatory. Despite Maxwell's plunge into the mysteries of desire and the complicated, arcane images he finds to describe them, the songs are disappointingly alike, a single unchanging rhythm arranged around a slow-whipping soul groove marked with traditional touches—pauses for hand claps and spare piano vamping, sexy strings, muted horns, and a low-popping bass.

Now moved whatever was brewing in *Embrya* into the realm of the present and listenable, but not back to *Urban Hang Suite*'s winning formula of bedroom music for the intelligent lover. An expert in crafting smooth, '70s-style love songs—to a point where he seems to be doing it in his sleep—Maxwell has always prized groove over tune. But here he's writing real songs, slow-dance numbers and candlelight sing-alongs, like the mid-tempo "Changed" and the great single "W/As My Girl," a mellow yearner that kicks off each verse with the singer rushing the line, "Turn the lights down low." *Now* even incorporates the dance floor on the snappy, horn-spiked "Get to Know Ya"; the rueful, bass-heavy "No One," with Maxwell's satiny tenor in full effect; and the hot-to-trot "Temporary Nite." His avant-garde leanings are ably served with a cover of Kate Bush's "This Woman's Work," in which his tender falsetto sparkles.   —A.B.

John Mayall

★★★★½ Bluesbreakers—John Mayall With Eric Clapton (1966; Universal, 2001)
★★★ Crusade (Deram, 1967)
★★ Raw Blues (Deram, 1967)
★★ The Blues Alone (1967; PolyGram, 1996)
★★★ A Hard Road (1967; Polydor, 2003)
★★★½ Bare Wires (1968; Rebound, 1995)
★★★ Blues From Laurel Canyon (Deram, 1969)
★★★★ Looking Back (Deram, 1969)
★★★ Empty Rooms (Polydor, 1970)
★★★½ The Turning Point (1970; Polydor, 2001)
★★★ USA Union (Polydor, 1970)
★★½ Thru the Years (London, 1971)
★★★ Jazz-Blues Fusion (Polydor, 1972)
★★ Notice to Appear (1975; Beat Goes On, 2000)
★★ A Banquet in Blues (London, 1976)
★★ Lots of People (ABC, 1977)
★★ A Hard Core Package (1977; One Way Records, 1993)
★★ Primal Solos (Deram, 1977)
★★ Road Show Blues (DJM, 1982)
★★ Behind the Iron Curtain (GNP Crescendo, 1985)
★★ A Sense of Place (Island, 1990)
★★★★ London Blues (1964–1969) (Deram, 1992)
★★★★ Room to Move (1969–1974) (Polydor, 1992)
★★ Wake Up Call (Silvertone, 1993)
★ Return of the Bluesbreakers (Aim, 1994)
★★ Spinning Coin (Silvertone, 1995)
★★ Blues for the Lost Days (Jive, 1997)
★★★★ As It All Began: The Best of John Mayall and the Bluesbreakers, 1964–1969 (Polydor, 1998)
★★ Silver Tones: The Best of John Mayall and the Bluesbreakers (Silvertone, 1998)
★ Rock the Blues Tonight (Indigo, 1999)
★★ Padlock on the Blues (Cleopatra, 1999)
★ Blues Power (Recall, 1999)
★ The Masters (Spitfire, 2000)
★★ Blue for You (Dressed to Kill, 2000)
★★ New Year, New Band, New Company/Lots of People (BGO, 2000)
★ Live at the Marquee, 1969 (Spitfire, 2000)
★ Reaching for the Blues (Purple Pyramid, 2001)
★ Along for the Ride (Red Ink, 2001)
★ Lost and Gone (Movie Play, 2001)
★★★ Stories (Red Ink, 2002)
★★★½ 70th Birthday Concert (Eagle, 2003)

A bit of an eccentric—in his early days he favored a curious nine-string guitar, and later he sported a kind of caveman loincloth (on *Blues From Laurel Canyon*)—John Mayall is the great pedagogue of British blues. The bands he has led function as schools of the form, tutoring young hopefuls in the now-arcane arts of Sonny Boy Williamson and J. B. Lenoir; graduates include such luminaries as Eric Clapton, Mick Taylor, Peter Green, Jack Bruce, and Aynsley Dunbar, among many others. From Mayall, in fact, have sprung the instrumental stars of some of the best bands in rock. Shifting his personnel constantly—he went through more than nine groups between 1963 and 1967 alone—Mayall is a guiding light, but the best playing on his albums comes from his sidemen.

From the start, Mayall's strength as a harmonica player was obvious, as was his very reverent treatment of the blues—even while he wrote many of his songs, they seldom varied from the classic 12-bar pattern—but it would take Clapton's arrival to make Mayall's music catch fire. On *Bluesbreakers—John Mayall With Eric Clapton* it did; the guitarist plays Chicago blues with precocious authority here, and it remains one of Mayall's toughest sets. *Crusade* highlights the teenage Mick Taylor—his stinging lead work an embryonic version of the mastery he would develop with the Rolling Stones—and Mayall begins experimenting with a horn section. For all but blues purists, *Bare Wires* remains one of the more interesting records, with Mayall trying out an early form of jazz-rock fusion; the horns, by Dick Heckstall-Smith and Chris Mercer, add elegance, and Mayall himself—never a very strong singer—finds, in a breathy, whispering style, a haunting delivery that works. Peter Green, who would go on to form Fleetwood Mac with Mayall veterans John McVie and Mick Fleetwood, enlivens *A Hard Road*: his playing is spare, fierce, and supple. On *Blues From Laurel Canyon*, a conceptual album featuring Mayall's musings about L.A., the sound is soft and fluid, jazz-inflected and moody. An entirely acoustic effort, *Turning Point* gave Mayall an FM radio hit in the harp extravaganza "Room to Move." *Jazz Blues Fusion* shows off the trumpet skills of Blue Mitchell.

While many of his records are now mainly of historical interest, they provide fascinating glimpses of talents not yet fully developed, and they certainly testify to Mayall's industry and influence. All the work released after *Jazz-Blues,* however, is primarily for the man's fanatics.

Mayall's early albums remain the most enjoyable; *London Blues* and *Room to Move,* along with the comprehensive *As It All Began,* are good overviews. Of interest is *Stories:* Now over 70, Mayall is in fine, earnest form—still an impassioned devotee of the music to which he's given his life. —P.E.

John Mayer

★★½	Inside Wants Out (1999; Columbia, 2002)
★★★½	Room for Squares (Aware/Columbia, 2001)
★★	Any Given Thursday (Aware/Columbia, 2003)
★★★	Heavier Things (Aware/Columbia, 2003)

Like Huey Lewis before him, this Atlanta-based singer/songwriter proves that there's always room in pop music for a well-groomed young man with an ear for melody and an unpretentious demeanor. Mayer's mix of adult-alternative and light rock combines the pouty swoon of Jeff Buckley, the literate class of Sting, and the nice-guy approachability of Dave Matthews. *Room for Squares* is a deceptively charming record and a perfectly honest reflection of its author: The album soaks in its just-out-of-college white-guyness and all the existential baggage that comes with it—the discovery of adult love ("Your Body Is a Wonderland"), the first lament of lost youth ("No Such Thing," "83"), and the difficulty of settling into one's own skin ("My Stupid Mouth," "Not Myself"). Although its unrepentant mellowness starts to wear by the end, the record's finely sketched lyrical snapshots and subtle melodies seem to be grooming Mayer for soccer-mom heartthrobdom. And to his credit, he sounds like he couldn't think of anything finer.

To capitalize on *Squares'* success without prematurely introducing another new studio album into the marketplace, in late 2002 Columbia reissued Mayer's then three-year-old self-released debut EP, *Inside Wants Out.* While four of the eight tracks appear on *Squares* in a more richly produced form, the remaining, otherwise unavailable songs are hardly throwaways; "Love Soon" and "Comfortable," in particular, stand up to *Squares'* best material. Mayer's label clearly pushes its luck, however, with the two-disc live album, *Any Given Thursday,* the third release in three years to rely on essentially the same material. Like

most concert recordings, it's padded with cover songs ("Message in a Bottle") and previously unreleased material ("Something's Missing"); hearing the proficient Mayer and his band re-create the songs live doesn't prove particularly enlightening.

By the end of 2003, Mayer (finally!) delivered a set of new material in the form of a 10-track studio album, *Heavier Things.* Playing it safe, Mayer made no radical departures from the success of *Squares,* aside from the occasional horn flourish and some off-kilter guitar textures. He's still the young preppy trying to figure out this love thing, and trying to get a handle on this wide new world. It's charming and immaculately delivered, although the record's lack of an undeniable hook—no matter how Mayer might cast it as a sign of newfound "heaviness"—makes the effort decidedly less memorable. —R.M.S.

Curtis Mayfield

★★★½	Curtis (1970; Rhino, 2000)
★★★★½	Curtis/Live! (1971; Rhino, 2000)
★★★★	Roots (1971; Rhino, 1999)
★★★★★	Superfly (1972; Rhino, 1999)
★★★★½	Superfly Deluxe 25th Anniversary Edition (1972; Rhino, 1997)
★★★★	Back to the World (1973; Charly, 1997)
★★★	Curtis in Chicago (1973; Sequel, 1999)
★★★	Sweet Exorcist (1974; Sequel, 1998)
★★★	Got to Find a Way (1974; Sequel, 1999)
★★	There's No Place Like America Today (1975; Curtom/Ichiban, 1989)
★★★	Give, Get, Take and Have (1976; Curtom/Ichiban, 1992)
★★	Never Say You Can't Survive (1977; 1992; Sequel, 2000)
★★★★	Short Eyes (1977; Sequel, 1998)
★★½	Do It All Night (1978; Charly, 1995)
★★½	Heartbeat (1979; Sequel, 2000)
★★½	Something to Believe In (1980; Curtom/Ichiban, 1992)
★★½	The Right Combination (1980; Sequel, 2000)
★★	Love Is the Place (1981; Boardwalk, 2000)
★★	Honesty (1983; Boardwalk, 2000)
★★½	We Come in Peace with a Message of Love (1985; Sequel, 1999)
★★★½	Live in Europe (1988; Sequel, 2000)
★★★½	Live at Ronnie Scott's (1988; Sanctuary/Castle, 2002)
★★★	Take It to the Street (1990; Sequel, 1999)
★★★★★	The Anthology 1961–1977 (MCA, 1992)
★★★½	People Get Ready: A Tribute to Curtis Mayfield (Shanachie, 1993)
★★★½	BBC Radio 1 in Concert (BBC Windsong, 1994)

★★½   A Tribute to Curtis Mayfield (Warner Bros., 1994)

★★★★   Curtis Mayfield's Chicago Soul (Epic/Okeh/Legacy, 1995)

★★½   New World Order (Warner Bros., 1996)

★★★★★   People Get Ready: The Curtis Mayfield Story (Rhino, 1996)

★★★½   I'm So Proud: A Jamaican Tribute to Curtis Mayfield (Trojan, 1997)

★★★★   The Very Best of Curtis Mayfield (Rhino, 1997)

★★★½   Masters (Cleopatra, 1998)

★★★★   Give It Up: The Best of the Curtom Years 1970–1977 (Music Club, 1998)

★★★★   The Ultimate Curtis Mayfield (Recall, 1998)

★★★★   Gospel (Rhino, 1999)

★★★½   Beautiful Brother: The Essential Curtis Mayfield (Metro, 2000)

★★   The Millennium Collection: The Best of Curtis Mayfield (MCA, 2000)

★★★   Singles Anthology (Sequel, 2000)

★★★   Love Songs (Rhino, 2001)

★★★★   Move On Up (Armoury, 2001)

★★   Nobody but You (Brentwood, 2002)

★★   Essentials (Rhino, 2002)

★★★★   Freddie's Dead & Other Hits (Rhino Flashback, 2003)

Curtis Mayfield's only equal as a soul-era triple threat—he was a lyricist, composer, and producer—was Smokey Robinson, but Mayfield was willing to address social issues in a way that Robinson wasn't. It was Mayfield, in fact, who joined Marvin Gaye, Stevie Wonder, Sly Stone, and George Clinton in leading the progressive-soul movement that gave African-American pop a musical sophistication and a lyrical ambition it had never seen before.

Mayfield had been prepared for this role while he was the lead singer, chief songwriter, and producer of the Impressions, a male-harmony trio that scored such pop hits as "It's All Right," "I'm So Proud," "Keep on Pushing," "Amen," "People Get Ready," and "Choice of Colors." Most of these songs combined Mayfield's musical roots in Chicago's black churches with the bright, brisk Northern soul of the '60s to create allegorical rallying cries for the civil rights movement of that decade.

And as a songwriter and producer who worked with such artists as Major Lance, Gene Chandler, Walter Jackson, the Opals, and Billy Butler, Mayfield helped to shape the Chicago-soul scene into a worthy rival to nearby Motown. That non-Impressions production work is nicely anthologized on the 18-track compilation *Curtis Mayfield's Chicago Soul.*

In 1970, however, Mayfield left the Impressions and their clean-cut-soul formula and broke with Brunswick/ABC Records to launch a solo career on his own label, Curtom Records. He used this new freedom to pursue more pointedly political lyrics and funkier arrangements, qualities that reflected the mood on the street at the time. On his greatest solo recordings, clustered early in the decade, he translated that mood into indelible character studies of everyday folks, which were backed up by riveting guitar riffs. Later on, he lost his focus and his lyrics became untethered philosophical rants while his guitar licks became mere noodling.

On his first solo album, 1970's *Curtis,* Mayfield balanced warnings of doom ("If There's a Hell Below We're All Gonna Go") and laments for the state of black America ("We the People Who Are Darker than Blue") with inspiring anthems of hope ("Move On Up," a rewrite of the Impressions' "Keep On Pushing"), and tributes to his people's potential ("Makings of You"). Sometimes the statements are overly sweeping and the production (lush string and horn arrangements, doo-wop harmonies, gimmicky studio effects, rattling conga drums) are too ornate, but the melodies are irresistible and the rhythm section is funky.

The following year, he released *Curtis/Live,* recorded onstage at the Bitter End nightclub in New York, recycling three songs from *Curtis,* recasting some old Impressions tunes in his latest style, and introducing a handful of new songs. The horns, strings, and studio effects are gone, revealing a superb funk band. Riding the groove, Mayfield powerfully evokes the tension of a troubled society yet holds out hope for redemption. Less impressive is 1973's *Curtis in Chicago,* which reunites Mayfield with Jerry Butler, Gene Chandler, and the Impressions in more conventional arrangements.

Roots is in the same mode as *Curtis,* but Mayfield displays better control of the production. With expansive orchestration and political-gospel evangelism, it sounds like the sequel to *What's Going On* that Marvin Gaye never made.

Mayfield made his creative breakthrough when he was commissioned to write and record the soundtrack for the Gordon Parks Jr. blaxploitation film *Superfly.* Mayfield ignored the movie's glorification of drug-dealing and hustling and instead painted an unflinching portrait of the real people who get caught up in street life. Somehow the assignment of writing for specific characters gave his lyrics a new focus, as he zeroed in on specific situations and settings to create his own minimovies. His music acquired a new focus, too; the guitar-driven hooks for "Freddie's Dead" and the title track buoyed the songs into the Top 10, though the portraits "Pusherman" and "Little Child

Runnin' Wild" were just as sharp. The soundtrack is now available in two versions—the original nine songs plus two bonus remixes; or a deluxe version with an additional disc of demos, alternate mixes, a radio spot, and an interview. The latter is a must for Mayfield fanatics but superfluous for everyone else.

Superfly kicked off a cycle of six soundtrack albums written and produced by Mayfield, which represent the best work of his career. Only two of them, however, were released under his name. *Claudine* was credited to Gladys Knight & the Pips in 1974; *Let's Do It Again* to the Staple Singers in 1975; *Sparkle* to Aretha Franklin in 1976; *A Piece of the Action* to Mavis Staples in 1977; and *Short Eyes* to Mayfield himself in 1977. All of these are great albums—Mayfield had a knack for crafting catchy songs that not only fit the narrative of the film but also fit Knight, Franklin, and Staples, whose strong, agile voices were much better vehicles than Mayfield's own thin, immobile tenor. *Short Eyes* is often the forgotten title of the cycle, but Mayfield's songs conjure the film's prison setting even more ruthlessly than the songs on *Superfly* evoke the drug trade.

Back to the World, his followup to *Superfly,* was an impressive album, and though not a soundtrack, it married portraits of a returning Vietnam vet and an innocent child to catchy hooks and funky horn-and-percussion arrangements. But Mayfield soon lost his way when he didn't have a film on which to focus his vision. With each succeeding title—*Sweet Exorcist, Got to Find a Way, There's No Place Like America Today*—the arrangements grew more meandering, the riffs less memorable, and the lyrics more abstract. Not surprisingly, the record-buying public lost interest.

Mayfield reacted by jumping on the disco and Quiet Storm bandwagons. The resulting albums were competent examples of the genres without being special, though Mayfield hadn't lost his rhythmic expertise as a producer or his romantic touch as a songwriter: *Give, Get, Take and Have; Never Say You Can't Survive; Do It All Night; Heartbeat, Something to Believe In; The Right Combination* (with Linda Clifford); and *Love Is the Place.* He tried to reclaim the roles of social critic and musical adventurer on albums such as *We Come in Peace with a Message of Love, Take It to the Street,* and *New World Order,* but they just weren't the same. He also returned to soundtrack work by contributing tracks to *Return of Superfly* and *I'm Gonna Git You Sucka.*

It didn't help matters that Mayfield was never much of a businessman, and as Curtom Records bounced around from distributor to distributor, the titles were poorly promoted and it became difficult to find even Mayfield's best work. He continued to put

on strong live shows, however, and the best outings from the '80s and '90s are on live albums such as *Live in Europe, Live at Ronnie Scott's* (which includes an interview with Paul Weller), and *BBC Radio 1 in Concert.*

There were always at least one or two inventive tracks on Mayfield's solo albums, and the best place to find them is on *People Get Ready: The Curtis Mayfield Story,* the three-CD, 51-track box set. It includes 12 tracks by the Impressions and 17 cuts from the 1970–73 peak years, leaving room for 22 tracks from the 1974–90 solo years—and they all stand up quite well. Over a syncopated funk groove, "Mother's Son" offers a matriarch's advice to her teenage boy, telling him to be proud on the street but not foolish. The serrated dirge "Billy Jack" is the tale of a man who disregarded such advice and ended up "shot with a handgun, body sprawled out." "Only You" and "Show Me Love" are intoxicating love songs.

If you're more interested in the Impressions material than the solo work, the two-CD *Anthology: 1961–1977* offers 30 songs from the 1961–70 trio years and just 10 songs from the 1970–77 solo years. The two-disc *Ultimate Curtis Mayfield* reverses the ratio, offering six Impressions songs and 23 solo tracks. The best single-disc compilations of the solo work are the 16-track *Very Best of Curtis Mayfield,* the 17-track *Masters,* and the 17-track *Move On Up. The Singles Anthology* squeezes 39 tracks onto one disc by using edited 45-rpm versions for nearly half the songs, with predictable sonic sacrifice.

Gospel isolates 13 of Mayfield's spiritual numbers—five of them with the Impressions—on a single disc. *Love Songs* does something similar with his romantic material, offering 16 tracks, all solo. Avoid such budget compilations as *The Millennium Collection, Nobody but You,* and *Essentials,* each of which offers 12 or fewer tracks and skimpy notes.

On August 14, 1990, Mayfield was playing a concert in Brooklyn when an improperly secured lighting scaffold fell on him, broke three of his vertebrae, and left him paralyzed from the neck down. He spent the last six years of his life in a wheelchair, giving upbeat interviews, recording his solo album *New World Order,* and contributing a track to *A Tribute to Curtis Mayfield.*

There are three Mayfield tribute albums. *A Tribute to Curtis Mayfield,* which boasts the biggest names (Bruce Springsteen, Rod Stewart, Eric Clapton, Stevie Wonder, Elton John, Aretha Franklin, etc.), is maddeningly uneven, with many artists trying too hard or not hard enough. More consistent and satisfying is *People Get Ready: A Tribute to Curtis Mayfield,* recorded with one house band, giving the disc a unity that few tribute albums enjoy. Singers such as Jerry Butler, Don Covay, Delbert McClinton, Kim Wilson, and Bunny Wailer find the soul in Mayfield's songs.

But the most revealing project is *I'm So Proud: A Jamaican Tribute to Curtis Mayfield,* a 20-track compilation featuring Bob Marley, Marcia Griffiths, the Heptones, the Uniques, and others. When Jamaicans tuned in to American radio in the '60s, the springy rhythms and sweet harmonies of the Impressions caught the ears of fledgling reggae artists and supplied the biggest impact. —G.H.

Percy Mayfield

★★★★★ Poet of the Blues (Specialty, 1990)
★★★★½ Percy Mayfield, Vol. 2: Memory Pain (Specialty, 1992)
★★★ Percy Mayfield Live (Winner, 1992)

As a songwriter, Percy Mayfield evinced a command of language and a deep, tragic understanding of love's mercurial, often contradictory emotions; as a vocalist, his personable, soulful delivery had all the comfort of a blazing fire on a cold night. As a solo artist, Mayfield was a fixture on the R&B singles chart in the early '50s, but even after the hits ended, his songs found favor with some of America's finest singers, notably Ray Charles, for whose Tangerine label Mayfield became an artist and staff writer in the early '60s. Charles' Tangerine period includes several Mayfield compositions, the best known of which is the rollicking "Hit the Road Jack."

Mayfield's most important work can be found on Specialty's two 25-song retrospectives, *Poet of the Blues* and *Memory Pain.* The highlight of the former collection is "Please Send Me Someone to Love," a #1 R&B single from 1950 that daringly complains of racial prejudice, a topic sensibly ignored at that time by black artists aiming to break into the pop charts. *Poet*'s other tracks cover Mayfield's fertile 1950–54 period, when he had seven Top 10 R&B hits.

Opening with an alternate take of "Please Send Me Someone to Love," *Memory Pain* covers Mayfield's output from 1950 to 1957. Like *Poet, Memory Pain* includes some previously unissued sides as well as a demo for "Hit the Road, Jack" which alone is worth the price of admission.

Mayfield's current catalogue is rounded out by *Percy Mayfield Live,* an album assembled from performances recorded in a California nightclub between 1981 and 1983. "Please Send Me Someone to Love" is beautifully rendered here, and "Strange Things Happening" and "P.M. Blues" have their moments as well. Mayfield was in his early sixties during this time, and although his voice shows the effects of

age and hard living, his phrasing remains sly and sharp. He died a year after the last of these tracks was recorded, on August 12, 1984, at age 64. Mayfield also recorded for Chess, Cash, Imperial, Tangerine, RCA, Brunswick, and, for one Johnny "Guitar" Watson–produced single in 1974, Atlantic. Unfortunately, nothing remains in print from those affiliations. —D.M.

Mazzy Star

★★ She Hangs Brightly (Capitol, 1990)
★★★ So Tonight That I Might See (Capitol, 1993)
★★ Among My Swan (Capitol, 1996)

Pretentious, precious, and pouty-lipped, Hope Sandoval was the perfect vehicle for Mazzy Star's neo-psychedelic downer music. She sings like she could barely bother, an attitude that is a perfect fit for "Fade Into You," the band's 1994 minimalist near hit. Sounding a bit like a sad German ingenue—a sweeter-voiced Marlene Dietrich—she creates an almost perfect piece of pop melancholy with this cut, sighing rather than singing through the song. Guitarist David Roback's subtle slide work adds a spooky undercurrent that gives the track a rare atmosphere. This is Nico meets Bela Lugosi, or music to suck blood by.

"Fade Into You" is the clear highlight of *So Tonight That I Might See,* though "Five String Serenade" was another worthy pared-down amphetamine lullaby. The earlier *She Hangs Brightly* lacked a breakthrough song and seemed too slow, off by maybe 20 BPM. By the time *Among My Swan* rolled around, even Sandoval's dreamy voice couldn't make up for songwriting ideas that seemed like window dressing to her pale but beautiful mannequin of a voice. —C.R.C.

MC Lyte

★★★½ Lyte as a Rock (First Priority, 1988)
★★★ Eyes on This (First Priority, 1989)
★★★½ Act Like You Know (Atlantic, 1991)
★★★ Ain't No Other (Atlantic, 1993)
★★★ Bad As I Wanna B (Elektra/Asylum, 1996)
★★★ Seven & Seven (Elektra/Asylum, 1998)
★★★★ The Very Best of MC Lyte (Rhino, 2001)

When MC Lyte emerged in the late '80s, one could rarely find a woman's perspective in hip-hop—particularly a woman's point of view that was voiced in razor-sharp rhymes and didn't pander to the lovey-dovey R&B world. By the time Lyte dropped her finest full length, *Act Like You Know,* she had a few sisters on the radio with her, notably Queen Latifah, even if, by 1991, gangsta-rap bullshitters were monopolizing the airplay. In this context, "Ruffneck" came off as hip-hop's very own "He's a Rebel"; it was an ode to a tough-talking street thug who had Lyte's back.

In the '90s, hip-hop blew up commercially; by the end of the decade, potty-mouthed sexpots like Foxy Brown and Lil' Kim defined what it meant to be a woman in hip-hop. The genre had also made its peace with R&B, so Lyte went along for the ride: The danceable *Seven & Seven* enlisted help from Missy Elliott and L.L. Cool J, with fine results. Unfortunately, Lyte's lyrics had lost their edge—which is a shame, because hip-hop could use women who trade on skill rather than sex appeal. —K.H.

Paul McCartney

★★½	McCartney (Apple/Capitol, 1970)
★★★	Ram (Apple/Capitol 1971)
★★	McCartney II (Columbia, 1980)
★★★½	Tug of War (Columbia, 1982)
★★	Pipes of Peace (Columbia, 1983)
★★	Give My Regards to Broad Street (Columbia, 1984)
★★	Press to Play (Capitol, 1986)
★★★½	All the Best! (Capitol, 1987)
★★★½	Choba b CCCP (1988; Capitol, 1991)
★★★	Flowers in the Dirt (Capitol, 1989)
★★★	Tripping the Live Fantastic (Capitol, 1990)
★★★★	Unplugged (Capitol, 1991)
★★	Liverpool Oratorio (EMI Classics, 1991)
★★★	Off the Ground (Capitol, 1993)
★★★	Paul Is Live (Capitol, 1993)
★★★	Flaming Pie (Capitol, 1997)
★★	Standing Stone (EMI Classics, 1997)
★★★★	Run Devil Run (Capitol, 1999)
★★★	Driving Rain (Capitol, 2001)
★★★½	Back in the U.S.: Live 2002 (Capitol, 2002)

Wings

★★	Wild Life (1971; Capitol, 1989)
★★	Red Rose Speedway (1973; Capitol, 1988)
★★★★	Band on the Run (1973; Capitol, 1998)
★★★½	Venus and Mars (Capitol, 1975)
★★★	Wings at the Speed of Sound (1976; Capitol, 1996)
★★★½	Wings Over America (Capitol, 1977)
★★	London Town (Capitol, 1978)
★★★★	Greatest (Capitol, 1978)
★★	Back to the Egg (1978; Capitol, 1989)
★★★★	Wingspan (Hits and History) (Capitol, 2002)

Paul McCartney was a lot more than the easy-listening half of the greatest songwriting duo in rock history, but many of his post-Beatles studio albums are larded with sentimental trifles, half-finished songs, and effer-

vescent dreck. He's partially redeemed by his live albums, which portray a charming entertainer who hasn't forgotten how to rock, and by his hits collections, which affirm his engaging melodicism.

In contrast to the emancipatory fury of *Plastic Ono Band*, the first major solo statement by his former partner John Lennon, *McCartney* is so modest it barely registers. Only the white soul of "Maybe I'm Amazed" distinguishes otherwise unbearably slight confections such as "Lovely Linda." *Ram* puts the emphasis on frills, finesse, and songs that, superficially at least, sound more substantial than those on the debut. Although *Ram* boasts the dazzling arrangement "Uncle Albert/Admiral Halsey," the song is little more than an elaborate, inscrutable goof.

McCartney then formed Wings with his wife, Linda, and former Moody Blues guitarist Denny Laine, and went on to record some of his finest post-Beatles albums—as well as some of his worst. Although McCartney managed to craft an indelible single or two on just about every Wings album, he too frequently wasted his time on silly trifles. His Wings' career is best summed up in the hit "Silly Love Songs," from *Wings at the Speed of Sound*, in which McCartney defends his right to be as trivial as he wants to be over a bass line so inescapably perfect that it almost justifies the song's existence.

After the so-so albums *Wild Life* and *Red Rose Speedway* (which includes his soggiest hit, the over-orchestrated "My Love"), McCartney redeemed himself with *Band on the Run*, a near-perfect blend of pop smoothness and rock grit. *Venus and Mars* is nearly as accomplished, though *Wings at the Speed of Sound* took the idea of band democracy too far when McCartney decided to share lead-vocal duties. *London Town* and *Back to the Egg* are pillow soft, and Wings called it a career in 1981. *Wings Over America*, a document of the band's 1975 arena tour, toughens up the sound—a major improvement over most of their studio albums—while *Greatest* and *Wingspan* affirm that Wings were among the most reliable singles bands of the '70s.

McCartney II launches the singer's post-Wings career by consciously evoking the do-it-yourself tone of his first solo album, more a shrug of the shoulders than an emphatic statement of belief renewed. *Tug of War* is more ambitious; despite a mawkish duet with Stevie Wonder on "Ebony and Ivory," it contains enough high points ("Take It Away," "What's That You're Doing?") to qualify as one of McCartney's most accomplished efforts. *Pipes of Peace* sinks into blandness on the back of another ill-advised duet, "Say Say Say," with Michael Jackson.

Give My Regards to Broad Street, a movie soundtrack, and *Press to Play* are expertly crafted fluff. A songwriting collaboration with Elvis Costello jump-starts *Flowers in the Dirt,* but the off-the-cuff rock & roll of the covers-heavy *Choba b CCCP* and *Unplugged* suit McCartney best. On the latter, he brings fresh insight to the familiar: the Brazilian shadings in "And I Love Her," the countryish undertones of "That Would Be Something."

Off the Ground has the usual quota of slight songs and clumsy lyrics, but the animal-rights anthem "Looking for Changes" has McCartney sounding like something more is at stake than mere fun and whimsy, and "Winedark Open Sea" is a hypnotic tone poem. *Flaming Pie* is yet another back-to-basics gambit, with McCartney playing most of the instruments himself. Amid a bunch of songs that sound half finished, he delivers a lovely pair of lullabies ("Little Willow," "Great Day"), a soul-deep ballad ("Souvenir"), and a chamber-pop jewel orchestrated by Beatles producer George Martin ("Somedays").

Backed by Pink Floyd's David Gilmour and Deep Purple drummer Ian Paice, McCartney leaps through a dozen rock & roll oldies and three like-minded originals on *Run Devil Run.* Similar in tone and spirit to *Unplugged,* it's positively bruising compared to much of McCartney's too-precious studio recordings. Great moment: McCartney forgets the words to "Honey Hush," makes up some new ones on the spot, and just keeps tearing it up.

The small-combo approach also energizes *Driving Rain,* with McCartney's voluptuous bass-playing doing the steering. Once again, the songs are mostly forgettable, with a handful of exceptions: "Lonely Road" builds to a growl, while "There Must Have Been Magic" and "From a Lover to a Friend" flirt with introspection. *Liverpool Oratorio* and *Standing Stone* are pleasant if facile excursions into classical music.

McCartney's arena tours are documented on three live albums, all of which rely heavily on Beatles songs; *Back in the U.S.* hits the hardest, thanks to the kicking drumming of Abe Laboriel Jr. —G.K.

MC5

★★★	Kick Out the Jams (Elektra, 1969)
★★★★	Back in the USA (1970; Rhino, 1992)
★★★★	High Time (1971; Rhino, 1992)
★★★	Babes in Arms (1983; ROIR, 1997)
★★	Power Trip (Alive, 1994)
★★	American Ruse (Total Energy, 1994)
★★	Looking at You (Total Energy, 1995)
★★½	Teenage Lust (Total Energy, 1996)
★★★½	Starship: Live at the Armory, June 1968 (Total Energy, 1998)
★★	'66 Breakout (Total Energy, 1999)
★★★★	The Big Bang: The Best of the MC5 (Rhino, 2000)
★★½	Motor City Is Burning (Sanctuary/Trojan, 2000)
★★★	Human Being Lawnmower: The Baddest and Maddest of the MC5 (Total Energy, 2002)
★½	Extended Versions (BMG Special Products, 2002)

About as ballsy as they get, the MC5 were Motor City madmen making punk before its time. House band for the radical lefty White Panther Party, led by John Sinclair (whom John Lennon championed), the MC5 used the '68 Democratic convention as a riotous backdrop for an early gig; the band's first album presaged 2 Live Crew in its First Amendment testing, screaming "Kick out the jams, motherfuckers!"— gravel-voiced Rob Tyner offended delicate sensibilities as well as eardrums. "Rocket Reducer No. 62 (Rama Lama Fa Fa Fa)" revealed the acidhead mind-set of counterculturalists in extremis; the guitar-as-God attack of Wayne Kramer and Fred "Sonic" Smith, however, hinted that, at heart, MC5 was nothing but a party. *Back in the USA* is the essential MC5; combining Little Richard and Chuck Berry with such prophetically slasher-film fare as "The Human Being Lawnmower" and "High School" (the kind of stoked pop the Ramones would later perfect), the band's second album was unrivaled rock & roll. *High Time* was the desperadoes' most ambitious set; the monster features horns, Bob Seger, a full choir, and players from the Salvation Army—and gives up nothing in its rock righteousness. A neat epitaph, *Babes in Arms* is Kramer's collection of rarities—hits and misses from the MC5 vaults. During the '90s, as the seminal Detroit band was getting plenty of retrospective R-E-S-P-E-C-T via a number of reverent if largely lo-fi anthologies (exception: Rhino's typically impeccable single-CD best-of, *The Big Bang*), the hearts of Tyner and Smith both gave out, the latter leaving Patti Smith as his widow. Kramer, who began a solo career in the mid-'90s, joined the two surviving members, drummer Dennis "Machine Gun" Thompson and bassist Michael Davis, for a 2004 reunion tour, using various stand-in frontmen. —P.E./B.SC.

Kate and Anna McGarrigle

★★★★	Kate & Anna McGarrigle (1976; Hannibal/Ryko, 1994)
★★★★	Dancer With Bruised Knees (1977; Hannibal/Ryko, 1994)
★★★	Pronto Monto (Warner Bros., 1978)
★★★★	French Record (1981; Tribu, 2003)
★★★½	Love Over and Over (1982; Hannibal, 1997)

★★★½ Heartbeats Accelerating (Private Music, 1990)
★★★½ Matapedia (Hannibal, 1996)
★★★★ The McGarrigle Hour (Hannibal, 1998)
★★★½ La Vache qui Pleure (Tribu, 2004)

Specializing in tart, tuneful songs that marry the resonance of folk to the emotional immediacy of everyday life, the McGarrigle sisters are probably the finest singer/songwriter team ever to go ignored by the American public. Well, not entirely ignored; Anna's "Heart Like a Wheel" is certainly well known to Linda Ronstadt fans, as is Kate's "(Talk to Me of) Mendocino." But *Kate & Anna McGarrigle,* the album that contains their versions of these songs, has, like much of their catalogue, spent more time out of print than in.

Given the marquee value of the guests on *The McGarrigle Hour*—guests include Emmylou Harris and Linda Ronstadt as well as Anna's ex, Loudon Wainwright III, and son, Rufus—its relative lack of commercial success seems profoundly unfair. No matter. The McGarrigles' music has less to do with the ephemeral quality of fame than with the enduring values of family and tradition, a point deftly driven home by the homey, folk song–laden *The McGarrigle Hour.*

But being traditional doesn't mean emphasizing old songs, nor should the McGarrigles be mistaken for old-timey stylists such as the Watersons. Indeed, *Heartbeats Accelerating* sounds strikingly modern, both in its embrace of synths (as on the title track) and its ability to sketch the mundane truths of modern life ("I Eat Dinner"). Likewise, "Jacques et Gilles" and "Going Back to Harlan," from *Matapedia,* evoke a reality so vivid that even those with no personal connection to the landscapes (physical or psychological) will find themselves filled with longing as they hear each sad, sweet melody.

Being Quebecers, the McGarrigles are as attached to French as to English, and regularly slip francophone tunes into their albums, as on *Love Over and Over,* where they do a delightful translation of Bob Seger's "You'll Accompany Me." They've also released two albums with no English songs whatsoever. *French Record* mixes new recordings such as the bittersweet "Entre la jeunesse et la sagesse" with francophone selections from their first three albums. *La Vache qui pleure*—the title is a joke on the "Laughing Cow" cheese brand—is, by contrast, a fully realized album and brings a strong taste of Acadian folk tradition into what are otherwise contemporary songs about love, longing, and domestic life. *C'est merveilleux.* —J.D.C.

Tim McGraw

★★★ Tim McGraw (Curb, 1993)
★★½ Not a Moment Too Soon (Curb, 1994)
★★½ All I Want (Curb, 1995)
★★★ Everywhere (Curb, 1997)
★★★ A Place in the Sun (Curb, 1999)
★★★ Greatest Hits (Curb, 2000)
★★★ Set This Circus Down (Curb, 2001)
★★★ Tim McGraw and the Dancehall Doctors (Curb, 2002)
★★★ Live Like You Were Dying (Curb, 2004)

Before he became Mr. Faith Hill—and, in his own right, arguably the most successful male country singer since Garth Brooks—Tim McGraw was just another young hat act seemingly cut from the same new traditionalist mold as Alan Jackson. *Tim McGraw,* his modest 1993 debut, is a pleasing if unremarkable set of light honky-tonk ("Two Steppin' Mind") and smoothly sung ballads ("Only Thing That I Have Left") that doesn't quite hint at the highly polished country pop that would soon become his trademark. *Not a Moment Too Soon* gave him his first notable hit in the utterly loathsome "Indian Outlaw," a ridiculous salute to "Cherokee pride" comprised entirely of stereotypes so brazen ("You can find me in my wigwam/I'll be beating on my tom-tom/pull out the pipe and smoke you some"), one suspects even Custer would have been embarrassed singing them. Not McGraw, although at least he didn't write it (or any of his songs, for that matter). The ballad "Don't Take the Girl" was markedly better, and proved McGraw to be a master at delivering admittedly sappy fare in an achingly sincere voice that almost *dares* you to be unmoved. By *All I Want* and its successor *Everywhere,* he was a well-oiled hit machine, effortlessly making the most out of slick, by-the-numbers mid-tempo Nashville pop like "She Never Lets It Go to Her Heart" *(All I Want),* faking it through catchy up-tempo clunkers like "I Like It, I Love It," and knocking the occasional honest-to-goodness contemporary country gold nugget like "Just to See You Smile" *(Everywhere)* clean out of the park. Precious little honky-tonk remains to be found on either *A Place in the Sun* or *Set This Circus Down,* but even with straight-up-the-middle Nashville power balladry, there's something to be said for consistency, and by this point it's clear McGraw and his producers were getting first dibs on the cream of the crop from Music Row's resident tunesmiths. Surprises are few but all the more welcome when they do pop up, as in *Set This Circus Down*'s Bruce Robinson–penned "Angry All the Time," an unflinching portrait of a marriage stretched to the breaking point, sung with Oscar-worthy conviction by McGraw and happy wife Hill. *Tim McGraw and the Dancehall Doctors* doesn't quite deliver on the back-to-basics kick implied by the title (the album was recorded with McGraw's road band rather than Nashville session musicians), but at least he seems to be trying. Covering Elton John's "Tiny Dancer" in the exact same style as the original (or, for that matter, *any* style) isn't the bold rock & roll statement McGraw might have intended it to be, but the teenage abortion drama "Red Ragtop" is an emotional corker, nearly as rife with sugar-free hard truth and regret as Bruce Springsteen's similarly themed "The River." Pity both that song and "Angry All the Time" came *after* the premature *Greatest Hits* set, which gets docked half a star for featuring not only the inevitable "Indian Outlaw" but also the gooey horror of the (much) lesser Faith duet "Let's Make Love," which would be only marginally more icky if Donny and Marie were singing it to each other.   —R.SK.

Roger McGuinn

★★★	Roger McGuinn (1973; Sundazed, 2004)	
★★★	Cardiff Rose (Columbia, 1976)	
★★★	Thunderbyrd (Columbia, 1977)	
★★★★	Back From Rio (Arista, 1991)	
★★★	Live From Mars (Hollywood, 1996)	
★★	Treasures From the Folk Den (Appleseed, 2001)	

Only sometimes does Roger McGuinn strive to echo the astonishing harmonies and buoyant strength of the Byrds, the pioneering '60s folk rockers he once led. Powered by fine playing from L.A. studio stalwarts, his debut concentrated on songwriting collaborations with psychologist Jacques Levy, which was McGuinn's modus operandi for his next three albums as well. *Cardiff Rose,* produced by Mick Ronson, and *Thunderbyrd* are strong sets; maddeningly, they go in and out of print.

Back From Rio, his sixth solo outing, is a powerhouse. Elvis Costello, Tom Petty and his Heartbreakers, Michael Penn, and ex-Eagle Timothy B. Schmit join McGuinn in his stunning return to form. Even though a pinched, adenoidal quality can sometimes mar his vocals, here McGuinn sings with absolute command. The most Byrd-like of his solo work, the record suggests that McGuinn had come to terms with his legacy—a style so ahead of its time that every song on *Rio* sounds sharp and up to the minute. *Live From Mars* presents McGuinn at his most congenial, serving up the classics with accompanying commentary. *Treasures From the Folk Den,* a collection of folk chestnuts McGuinn originally released on the Internet, is mild-

mannered fun with nice guest appearances by the likes of Joan Baez, Pete Seeger, and Judy Collins.   —P.E.

Brian McKnight

★★★	Brian McKnight (Mercury, 1992)	
★★½	I Remember You (Mercury, 1995)	
★★½	Anytime (Mercury, 1997)	
★★★	Bethlehem (Motown, 1998)	
★★★	Back at One (Motown, 1999)	
★★★	Superhero (Motown, 2001)	
★★★½	From There to Here: 1989–2002 (Motown, 2002)	
★★★	U-Turn (Motown, 2003)	

R&B singer Brian McKnight has managed to carve out a successful, if not exactly adventurous, career while avoiding most of the satin-sheets-and-bearskin-rug clichés that have dogged his Quiet Storm contemporaries. A veteran of church choirs, McKnight released his self-titled debut in 1992, when he was still better known as the younger brother of Take 6 member Claude McKnight. Other than an ill-advised, beat-happy cover of Hall & Oates' "I Can't Go For That," *Brian McKnight* was a well-crafted combination of smooth, jazz-influenced jams and mid-tempo soul tracks that helped set the standard for '90s R&B. Less slick than Luther Vandross, manlier than Boyz II Men, McKnight demonstrated a remarkable tenor and boundless tolerance for MOR balladry—most notably on his first hit single, "The Way Love Goes."

McKnight wrote, produced, and played virtually every instrument on his sophomore effort, *I Remember You.* With similarly interchangeable ballads and the same sensitive-yet-rugged romanticism, his followup was a lot like his debut, only less so.

Not only did the Artist Then Known as Puff Daddy take over some of the production duties on 1997's *Anytime,* he also enlisted protégé Mase to rap on the hip-hop–meets–Quiet Storm "You Should Be Mine (Don't Waste Your Time)," one of McKnight's most appealing hit singles. *Anytime,* which would eventually sell 3 million copies, signaled the start of a new phase in McKnight's career; successive albums have found him enlisting guest stars like Nelly, Justin Timberlake, and Nate Dogg to lend him a patina of urban cool.

A year after the release of his holiday album, *Bethlehem,* McKnight issued *Back at One,* on which he again wrote, produced, sang, and played virtually everything. Excepting the occasional boilerplate slow jam, *One* is McKnight's finest effort and worth the price for the Grammy-nominated "Stay or Let It Go" alone. On the more daring but less successful *Superhero,* McKnight—whose previous idea of uptempo funk had involved peppy synthesizer riffs—included almost danceable hip-hop tracks and guitars aplenty.

When *U-Turn* was released, in 2003, McKnight was already an R&B icon, so the cameo appearances by younger crooners Joe, Carl Thomas, and Tyrese seemed homagelike. *U-Turn* successfully mixed mild, *Superhero*-style hip-hop with McKnight's usual smooth jams, most notably on the lead-off duet with Nelly, "All Night Long."

Since McKnight is mainly a singles artist, newcomers might want to try *From There to Here*, a comprehensive hits collection that offers hard-to-find soundtrack cuts and two new tracks. —A.S.

Sarah McLachlan

★★★	Touch (1988; Arista, 1989)
★★★½	Solace (Arista, 1991)
★★★★	Fumbling Towards Ecstasy (Arista, 1993)
★★½	The Freedom Sessions (Arista, 1994)
★★★	Rarities, B-Sides and Other Stuff (Nettwerk, 1996)
★★★½	Surfacing (Arista, 1997)
★★★½	Mirrorball (Arista, 1999)
★★½	Remixed (Nettwerk, 2001)
★★★	Afterglow (Arista, 2003)

Sarah McLachlan was one of the most influential artists of the mid- to late '90s, when she instituted the successful multiartist Lilith Fair tour and ushered a parade of female singer/songwriters into the upper regions of the pop charts. Even with the benefit of hindsight, there's precious little about Sarah McLachlan's 1988 debut, *Touch*, that foreshadows her eventual rise to fame. On *Touch*, she's just a 20-year-old girl from Nova Scotia who sounds like an overly earnest cross between Kate Bush and Enya. Still, there's at least a hint of real drama in the lilting "Vox" and "Sad Clown," and her wordless aria on the title track is, in a word, gorgeous.

Solace represented a considerable leap in maturity and focus. The production is less muddled, and this time most of the songs (notably "Into the Fire," "Back Door Man," and the hypnotic "Black") come with sharper hooks and distinctive melodies, allowing McLachlan's quavering soprano opportunity to do more than just flutter about like an aimless butterfly.

Fumbling Towards Ecstasy is where McLachlan truly came into her own as an artist. While still couched in lush, moody folk pop, the arrangements are notably less airy-fairy, with subtle but effective hip-hop beats pulsing just beneath the surface. McLachlan's lyrics are also sharper, her trademark earnestness now carrying a formidable edge. "This is gonna hurt like hell," she warns a lover in the haunting "Hold On," while

"Possession"—reportedly inspired by an overenamored fan—balances romantic obsession with creepy stalker undertones as craftily as the Police's "Every Breath You Take." *Surfacing*, released the same year McLachlan unleashed Lilith, could use a little more of that lyrical bite, though the album boasts several of her most assured songs. "Adia," "Angel," and "Building a Mystery" were all worthy chart hits, but the aptly titled "Sweet Surrender" is the real prize here. Thanks to a steady drum-machine track and staccato electric guitar, it's one of her most driving songs and also one of her most seductive, as vulnerable in its romantic yearning as "Possession" was determined. If she doesn't have you at the opening "Doesn't mean much," give McLachlan and her music a wide berth, because she's got nothing left to give.

Unfortunately, that seems to be all too true on *Afterglow*, the studio followup to *Surfacing*, released six years later. While not without its moments (the lead single, "Fallen," and the longingly plaintive and genuinely moving "Answer"), far too much of this belated comeback sounds like a fallback. Apart from the post-9/11 references in "World on Fire," there's little to distinguish the songs on *Afterglow* from the filler on *Solace* or *Surfacing*—though the later two albums have more hooks.

Mirrorball, a pristine live album released at the height of McLachlan's popularity, focuses primarily on *Fumbling* and *Surfacing* material, and it's a remarkably effective roundup of McLachlan's career, as even the quietest songs benefit from the (slightly) more energetic performances. The rest of the catalogue is best left to collectors and die-hard fans. *Rarities, B-Sides and Other Stuff* is the most interesting of the lot, gathering 13 of McLachlan's nonalbum tracks, including "I Will Remember You" from *The Brothers McMullen* soundtrack and a fine cover of Joni Mitchell's "Blue." *The Freedom Sessions* is a rather skimpy collection of acoustic *Fumbling* demos and interactive CD-ROM material, self-indulgent and unnecessary but not without some merit, notably McLachlan's smoky pass at Tom Waits' "Ol' 55." On the import-only *Remixed*, DJs including William Orbit and BT do their best to reinvent McLachlan as a dance-floor diva by transforming her languid, potpourri-scented lullabies into trance anthems. —R.SK.

Clyde McPhatter

★★★	Love Ballads/Clyde (1958, 1959; Collectables, 1998)
★★★★	Deep Sea Ball: The Best of Clyde McPhatter (Atlantic, 1991)
★★★	The Mercury Sessions (Collectables, 1996)

★★★½   The Forgotten Angel (32 Jazz, 1998)
★★★   A Shot of Rhythm & Blues (Sundazed, 2000)

For those who loved his lead vocals with Billy Ward and the Dominoes and especially with the original Drifters group that he founded, Clyde McPhatter's solo career is a case of an extraordinary artist forever shy of consistently first-rate material. With the Dominoes, McPhatter sang on some of the decade's best R&B singles ("Have Mercy Baby," "Sixty-Minute Man," "These Foolish Things Remind Me of You"), and then helped lay the foundation for soul music by forming the Drifters and delivering commanding, emotion-rich lead vocals on some beautifully crafted productions ranging from pop fare such as "Bells of St. Mary's" to raunchy R&B ("Money Honey" and "Honey Love") to Christmas standards (a version of "White Christmas" that has been often imitated by succeeding generations of R&B singers). His tenure with the Drifters was cut short when he was drafted by the army in 1954; he began recording some solo sides while on furlough in 1955, and picked up from there upon his discharge in 1956.

Beloved by black audiences, McPhatter was a regular fixture in the R&B Top 10, but he didn't register the same high marks on the crossover front, although having eight Top 40 singles between 1956's beautiful "Treasure of Love" and 1962's cover of "Little Bitty Pretty One" is nothing to sneeze at. Still, as much of his remaining in-print work reveals, McPhatter had plenty of mesmerizing performances left in him after he came home from the army. The depth of his artistry can be measured in the way he made much of some lightweight material, and made everything of the top-drawer songs that came his way. His high, quavering tenor was a most expressive instrument, and his control of vocal dynamics revealed a singer with a deep sensitivity to lyrical nuance, which may explain why he was able to range wide and remain credible in any style. And like Sam Cooke, he knew how to keep the customers satisfied, whether it was an R&B audience who preferred a grittier approach or the pop audience who swooned for his upbeat, happy-go-lucky tunes and plaintive love ballads.

It's no revelation to point to McPhatter's Atlantic sides as his most important work. As is abundantly evident on three releases—the Collectables twofer combining a pair of Atlantic albums, Love Ballads/Clyde; Deep Sea Ball: The Best of Clyde McPhatter; and the two-disc retrospective The Forgotten Angel—it was here, from 1956 to 1959, that McPhatter knew without question who he was as an artist, and brought tremendous authority to everything he touched, whether it was a Latinized treatment of "Heartaches" (later covered by Patsy Cline), some raw, boisterous, early Drifters-style R&B such as "Bip Bam" or the finger-poppin', updated doo-wop pop and pleading vocal of his irresistible #6 pop hit of 1958, "A Lover's Question" (cowritten by Brook Benton). In these selections and others, history resonates in the vocal performances—a straight line can be drawn from these linking Sam Cooke, Jackie Wilson, and Smokey Robinson to the style and sound of Clyde McPhatter.

It's after McPhatter leaves Atlantic in 1959 that the problems begin. His first stop was MGM, where a one-year stint yielded four minor R&B hits. His next move was the right one, going to Mercury, where the gifted A&R director Clyde Otis took charge of McPhatter's recordings, updating his sound with the lush string arrangements Otis had employed so effectively with Brook Benton. The big-band oomph and swinging vocal that drove McPhatter's first ebullient, self-penned single, "Ta Ta," pushed it to #23 pop in 1960. After a dry spell, he returned to the pop Top 10 in early 1962 with an infectious plea to a wandering lover, "Lover Please" (written by then-13-year-old Billy Swann), and later that year his bouncy cover of Thurston Harris' 1957 hit, "Little Bitty Pretty One," ascended to #25 pop. When Otis left the label, McPhatter's recordings were turned over to Nashville veteran Shelby Singleton, and at that point, though the hits ceased, some minor masterpieces ensued, such as the albums Rhythm and Soul and Golden Blues Hits, both recorded in Music City with a lineup of the town's finest session players. In 1964 came a concept album, Songs of the Big City, replete with social content—as reflected in the minor hit "Deep in the Heart of Harlem," a Latin-flavored rendering of hard times and dreary days among the lower class in uptown New York City ("I push and kick and get my feelings hurt downtown/I'm just a little spoke that helps the wheel go 'round," McPhatter laments evenly in one stirring passage), and beautifully realized, full-bodied arrangements by Alan Lorber. Unfortunately, this period is ill-documented on record now: Only Collectables' The Mercury Sessions and a smidgen of The Forgotten Angel offer any Mercury sides; moreover, The Mercury Sessions is mostly a live album from a date at the Apollo Theatre with three studio cuts supplementing its 11 concert tracks. The live cuts were originally issued as Live at The Apollo, which is now out of print. That said, though limited as a review of these years, The Mercury Sessions does feature a powerful live version of "Deep in the Heart of Harlem," a bopping take on "A Lover's Question," and a simply stunning treatment of one of McPhatter's greatest Atlantic sides, "Without Love (There Is Nothing)," a breathtaking demonstration of interpretive brilliance and soulful expressiveness.

From there McPhatter's story takes one final turn that was as aesthetically fruitful as it was commercially unproductive. After being dropped by Mercury, the artist was signed to the small Amy label, where Alan Lorber was now employed and assigned to produce McPhatter. Their first sessions together yielded a romantic, string-laden ballad, "I'll Belong to You," and, best of all, a deep soul approach to Connie Francis' 1960 chart-topper, "Everybody's Somebody's Fool," that ditched the original's upbeat, pop arrangement and took Clyde back to the church. Speaking and singing the verses—combining the testifying of Joe Tex with the soulful belting of Solomon Burke, backed by a fervent female gospel chorus and a basic band plus brass and strings—McPhatter delivered a tour de force, drawing on the fundamentals he learned singing in the Baptist church as a youth in Durham, NC, performing like a minister preaching fire and brimstone to the faithless masses. It was a most unlikely song for such an approach, and McPhatter transformed it into something entirely different and considerably darker in meaning than was suggested in the original version. As documented completely on Sundazed's *A Shot of Rhythm & Blues,* McPhatter's army years found him working at a consistently high level, no matter the circumstances. When the first sessions with Lorber met commercial indifference, McPhatter ventured south, to Muscle Shoals, AL, and Rick Hall's Fame Studios, where he teamed up with the redoubtable swamper session players and came away with some in-the-pocket Southern soul stew, with pumping horns, chirping female choruses, and that insinuating backbeat that never quits. He cut a greasy version of this album's title track; a stomping, party-hearty, Calypso-influenced take on Joe Tex's celebration of a determined day off, "I'm Not Going to Work Today"; an easy-rolling pop confection with "sha-la-sha-la" female choruses and Memphis-style horns, penned by Hall and Billy Sherrill, titled "Sweet and Innocent"; and a Latin-tinged arrangement (right out of the latter-day Drifters textbook) of Roy Orbison's tender-hearted outsider's lament, "Lavender Lace." All for nought—but the failure of these recordings is not in the music nor in McPhatter's approach; rather, it's that enduring music business mystery centered on zeitgeist, catching the cultural wave and locking in for a good ride. To torture the metaphor, McPhatter clearly wiped out. From there it was a slow, excruciating downhill slide, propelled by alcohol, culminating in death on June 13, 1972, five months before he would have celebrated his fortieth birthday. His indeed was a voice sent by angels, and it sings still.   —D.M.

Meat Loaf

★★½ Bat Out of Hell (1977; Sony, 2001)
★ Bat Out of Hell II: Back Into Hell (MCA, 1993)
★½ Welcome to the Neighborhood (1995; MCA, 2002)
★★ The Very Best of Meat Loaf (Sony, 1998)
★★ Couldn't Have Said It Better (Sanctuary, 2003)

Veteran of both *The Rocky Horror Picture Show* and one of Ted Nugent's marauding mid-'70s road bands, the hefty metal belter known as Meat Loaf came roaring out of left field with the inexplicably popular shlock-rock magnum opus *Bat Out of Hell.* Produced by Todd Rundgren, *Bat* positions Meat as an unholy cross between Bruce Springsteen and Freddie Mercury. If that sounds at all appealing, or even listenable, you are probably amused by the sex spiel of "Paradise by the Dashboard Light" and deeply touched by the tuneless shopping-mall balladry of "Two Out of Three Ain't Bad." *Bat* is also recommended to punk and disco scholars—originally, there really was something to rebel against.

Meat Loaf disappeared from the charts soon after, but finally interrupted 16 years of anonymity with an unexpected sequel, openly admitting that *Bat out of Hell II: Back Into Hell* was less a true followup than the title of an excellent marketing plan. It did mark the return of songwriter/arranger Jim Steinman to repeat the original's formula of hysterical angst, melodrama, and dumb jokes. "I'd Do Anything for Love (But I Won't Do That)" at least captures the same mushy flavor and Meat's heavy breathing. Too much of the rest embraces the sound of late-'80s hair metal, arriving like bad show tunes for bored headbangers. Naturally, it went to #1. *The Very Best of Meat Loaf* is drawn mostly from his '70s hits and '80s misses, and includes new helium-filled tunes cowritten by Steinman and pop stage composer Andrew Lloyd Webber. *Couldn't Have Said It Better* and *Welcome to the Neighborhood* are better produced and marginally improved, but the oversized formula is unchanged, with or without Steinman's mouthful of rock kitsch.   —M.C./S.A.

Medeski, Martin & Wood

★★★ Notes From the Underground (Accurate Jazz, 1992)
★★★ It's a Jungle in Here (Gramavision, 1993)
★★ Friday Afternoon in the Universe (Gramavision, 1995)
★★★ Shack Man (Rykodisc, 1996)
★★★½ Combustication (Blue Note, 1998)
★★★ Tonic (Blue Note, 2000)
★★★½ Last Chance to Dance Trance (Perhaps): Best of (1991–1996) (Gramavision, 1999)

★★½ The Dropper (Blue Note, 2000)
★★★★ Uninvisible (Blue Note, 2002)

Comprised of denizens of New York's downtown jazz scene, the keys-bass-drums trio Medeski, Martin & Wood built a reputation as one of the most inventive jam bands of the '90s, the rare act that could entertain Phishheads one night and a fringe-jazz crowd the next.

The group's self-released debut, *Notes From the Underground,* shows why these three were in demand from the beginning: It's loaded with knotty jazz exchanges atop unusual rhythmic beds far from jazz orthodoxy. Keyboardist John Medeski serves as the primary soloist, and after this initial album he switched to organ (and, to a lesser degree, electric piano) to make touring easier. That sassy soul-jazz B3 sound defines *It's a Jungle in Here,* which moved an inch or two closer to the mainstream—though the pairing of Thelonious Monk's "Bemsha Swing" with the Bob Marley standby "Lively Up Yourself" probably left reggae fans scratching their heads.

The group's commercial breakthrough comes with *Friday Afternoon in the Universe,* which remains a groove benchmark: Where MMW's followers were busy yammering over simple chord structures, these guys dig into pieces that are harmonically challenging, and like the best jazz groups, the crosstalk actually lifts tracks like the title tune higher. By the mid-'90s, the trio found itself collaborating with Phish and others far from jazz, and earned a certain amount of attention for recording the 1996 release *Shack Man* entirely in a jungle retreat in Maui.

Those collaborations—particularly with DJ Logic, a regular presence at live shows—became part of MMW's next project, the inspired *Combustication,* for Blue Note. Although many groups utilize DJs to provide hip-hop backgrounds, MMW treat Logic not just as a texture provider but as another solo voice, and some of the juiciest playing happens when the DJ has the floor.

This album sold well, and subsequently, MMW had no problem touring constantly. The trio's challenge was to come up with enough compelling material to put onto record. *Tonic* is a live acoustic date designed to show the group's abiding love for jazz improvisation. *The Dropper* finds the trio veering away from its cherished organ funk in different ways: There's some Latin jazz, bits of odd hip-hop-loop mangling, and several genre-blind, almost rawk solos from guitarist Marc Ribot. The experimental bent continues with *Uninvisible,* which moves from greasy, stock MMW Booker T send-ups to jarring instrumental hip-hop atmospherics to brassy world-beat horns to an ill-advised spoken word foray enunciated, in full gravely glory, by eccentric Southern rocker Col. Bruce Hampton. —T.M.

Megadeth

★★★ Killing Is My Business . . . and Business Is Good (Combat, 1985)
★★★ Peace Sells . . . But Who's Buying? (1986; Capitol, 2004)
★★★ So Far, So Good . . . So What! (1988; Capitol, 2004)
★★★½ Rust in Peace (1990; Capitol, 2004)
★★★½ Countdown to Extinction (1992; Capitol, 2004)
★★★ Youthanasia (1994; Capitol, 2004)
★★ Hidden Treasures (Capitol, 1995)
★★★★ Cryptic Writings (1997; Capitol, 2004)
★★★ Risk (1999; Capitol, 2004)
★★★★ Capitol Punishment: The Megedeth Years (Capitol, 2000)
★★ The World Needs a Hero (Sanctuary, 2001)
★★★ Rude Awakening (Sanctuary, 2002)
★ Still Alive . . . And Well? (Sanctuary, 2002)

Formed by guitarist Dave Mustaine after he was forced out of Metallica, Megadeth long represented the dark and nasty side of American thrash. Between the manic precision of Mustaine's riffage, which unlike most thrash bands locked perfectly with the machine-gun pulse of the kick drum, and the inspired cynicism of his songwriting, Megadeth perfectly captured the mood of those metal fans who thought the world was going to hell, and frankly didn't give a shit. From *Killing Is My Business* to *So Far, So Good,* the albums are largely interchangeable, right down to the ellipses in the titles. *Rust in Peace* upped the ante with "Hangar 18," an impressively expansive conspiracy number, and *Countdown to Extinction* showed unexpected pop savvy with "Symphony of Destruction" and "Sweating Bullets." By *Youthanasia,* the band even managed to deliver credible ballads—well, slow and mostly sensitive songs, anyway—but it's *Cryptic Writings* that marks the band's zenith. Not only has the band broadened its palette to include synths and electronic treatments, but the powerful, confessional "Use the Man" gives the band a single as strong as any in the Metallica songbook. (In between *Youthanasia* and *Cryptic Writings,* Mustaine also released an album under the name MD.45, with punk legend Lee Ving of Fear.) *Risk,* unfortunately, doesn't quite maintain that momentum (although it has its moments), while the sluggish, retrograde *The World Needs a Hero* actually seems a step back for the band.

As it turned out, the album was nearly Megadeth's

last hurrah. Mustaine injured his arm a year after *Hero*'s release, and killed Megadeth. Sanctuary did its best to keep the name alive in lieu of new material, releasing *Rude Awakening,* a live recap of that album and the bulk of the Megadeth catalogue that shows off most of the band's strengths, and *Still Alive,* a shameless attempt to cash in on fans' desire for leftovers. Fortunately, Mustaine eventually recovered from his injury, re-formed Megadeth, and remastered the band's Capitol albums.

Those seeking an overview will find *Capitol Punishment* to be a perfunctory best-of with two previously-unreleased tracks serving as an alleged bonus; *Hidden Treasures* is a compendium of nonalbum tracks that's worth hearing only for "99 Ways to Die." —J.D.C.

The Mekons

- ★★½ The Quality of Mercy Is Not Strnen (1979; Blue Plate/Caroline, 1990)
- ★★ Mekons (1980; Quarterstick, 1997)
- ★★ It Falleth Like Gentle Rain From Heaven: The Mekons Story (1982; CNT, 1993)
- ★★★★½ Fear and Whiskey (1985; Quarterstick, 2002)
- ★★½ Crime and Punishment (EP) (Sin UK; 1986)
- ★★★½ The Edge of the World (1986; Quarterstick, 1996)
- ★★★ Slightly South of the Border (EP) (Sin UK, 1986)
- ★★★ Honky Tonkin' (1987; Quarterstick 2004)
- ★★★½ New York (1987; ROIR, 1990)
- ★★★ So Good It Hurts (Twin/Tone, 1988)
- ★★★★ The Mekons Rock 'n' Roll (1989; Collectors Choice, 2001)
- ★★★½ F.U.N. '90 (EP) (A&M, 1990)
- ★★★★ The Curse of the Mekons (1991; Collectors Choice, 2001)
- ★★★ I ❤ Mekons (Quarterstick, 1993)
- ★★★ Retreat From Memphis (Quarterstick, 1994)
- ★★½ United (Quarterstick, 1995)
- ★★ Untitled (Quarterstick, 1995)
- ★ Pussy, King of the Pirates (Quarterstick, 1996)
- ★★★½ Me (Quarterstick, 1998)
- ★★★½ I Have Been to Heaven and Back: Hen's Teeth . . . Vol. 1 (Quarterstick, 1999)
- ★★ Where Were You? Hen's Teeth . . . Vol. 2 (Quarterstick, 1999)
- ★★★★½ Journey to the End of the Night (Quarterstick, 2000)
- ★★½ New York: On the Road 86–87 (ROIR, 2000)
- ★★★★ OOOH! (Out of Our Heads) (Quarterstick, 2002)
- ★★★★ Punk Rock (Quarterstick, 2004)

No one expected all that much from the Mekons when they emerged in the late '70s from the same Leeds University scene that spawned Gang of Four. A bunch of sloppy, anticapitalist punks who loved country music and liquor, the Mekons expressed their collectivist ideology by making music that sounded like the work of a free-flowing, sometimes anarchic collective, complete with screeching fiddles, shouted coed singing (most often courtesy of main man Jon Langford and elastic-voiced Sally Timms), suffering ballads, arty experiments, wickedly catchy pub-rock, and a boatload of excellently shambling melodies. Their sizable catalogue includes its share of duds, but as punk bands go, the Mekons are as bighearted as the Clash, and unlike their No Future peers, they not only survived but also got better as they got older.

The Quality of Mercy Is Not Strnen is typical of their spotty early stuff. For all the wit of the title and cover (which features a monkey at a typewriter, almost typing . . . Shakespeare?), the music is noisy and brittle, an unsuccessful attempt at fusing the sparse eloquence of Wire with the rhythmic agility of Gang of Four. *The Mekons* (a.k.a. *Devils, Rats and Piggies: A Special Message From Godzilla*) is an unsuccessful stab at pop, so muddled it's hard to tell whether the band is being facetious. Nor is it easy to decode the intentions behind *It Falleth Like Gentle Rain From Heaven,* a collection of outtakes, leftovers, and the like that marks both the band's surrender (the Mekons had more or less disbanded at this point) and its refusal to remain silent; on the whole, though, it's a better gesture than an album.

Three years later, the Mekons became a septet and reinvented themselves by inventing alt country. *Fear and Whiskey* brought the band's roots-music jones to the forefront without surrendering an ounce of their punk-schooled sloppiness. Rousing cuts such as "Hard to Be Human Again," "Lost Dance," and the Hank Williams cover "Lost Highway" bridge the gap between duskily melodic and drunkenly shambolic, as the band gets soused and drives down dirt roads, fights wartime fear with joyful noise, and gives Thatcher hers. If any modern-day cowpunk troubadour gets your blood flowing, you owe it to yourself to check out *Fear and Whiskey.*

The *Crime and Punishment* EP further refines the Mekons' strategies, and includes a credible Merle Haggard cover ("Deep End"), but it's *The Edge of the World* that brings the band's sound into focus (and, not coincidentally, introduces Timms as an additional vocalist). *Slightly South of the Border* trades in *Fear and Whiskey*'s energetic sprawl for a more traditional country sound, and *Honky Tonkin'* cleans things up even further, offering well-schooled playing, vigorous politicking, and boozy roots-rock. (*New York* offers a glimpse of this version of the band on tour, but the album's sub-bootleg sound quality makes it an unreliable document; it was later expanded into *New York: On the Road, 86–87*).

Broadening its stylistic base, the band adds reggae and Cajun elements for *So Good It Hurts,* which compromises its relatively folk-rock tunefulness with some overly bookish lyrics. But *The Mekons Rock 'n' Roll* puts the band back on track with a series of antic, noisy sing-alongs, including Langford's rollicking "Only Darkness Has the Power" and Timms' twangy "I Am Crazy." The four-song EP *F.U.N. '90* is a covers record only the Mekons could conceive, with sprightly, danceable renditions of the Brit-centric traditional song and the Band's "Makes No Difference."

With a greatly expanded lineup (fourteen players, not counting the occasional horn section) and a gutsy, wide-ranging sound, *The Curse of the Mekons* presents an even more eclectic sound. Yet it isn't the album's stylistic sprawl that astonishes (though the mandolin obbligatos on "Wild and Blue" are impressively genuine) so much as the band's vastly increased instrumental competence, which manifests itself in everything from the raging country-rock of "The Curse" to the dub-inflected funk groove beneath "Sorcerer." Not that the performances would fool country or reggae fans, of course, but at least they get the basics right. *I ❤ Mekons* applies this broadened approach to romantic matters, although with a typically political bent; as such, "Millionaire" is a bit stilted, but "Honeymoon in Hell" and especially "All I Want" are delightful.

The Mekons' fearless forays into uncharted musical territory continue with *Retreat From Memphis,* which on "Our Bad Dream" offers what may be presumed to be an attempt at rap (well, there are chanted vocals and a fake funk groove, anyway). Far more pleasant and typical, however, are "Soldier" and the melancholy "Ice Rink in Berlin." Both *United,* a sort of self-tribute disc, and half of the *Untitled* EP dabble in cut-and-paste electronica, and there's even a bit of club groove snuck onto *Pussy, King of the Pirates,* an unlistenable performance-art piece in the shape of a very nasty children's story, performed in collaboration with author Kathy Acker.

After a few years' sabbatical in which various side and solo projects were pursued, the Mekons reconvened for the boozy *Me,* with the likes of "Gin & It" and "Whiskey Sex Shop." *Journey to the End of the Night* finds the band unexpectedly besotted by reggae grooves, which of course are not played straight but instead flavored with everything from Cajun accordion ("Neglect") to electric sitar ("Cast No Shadows"). Still, the singing is lovely, and the writing mostly lives up to its ambitions.

Then, out of nowhere, *OOOH! (Out of Our Heads)* proved to be their best album in forever. Taking an everything-and-the-kitchen-sink tack that seemed to fit not only post-9/11 reality but also their weathered intelligence, the album evokes everything from British folk ("Stinehead") to Arabic music and dub ("Dancing in the Head"), and featured a trio of rousing, near-perfect sing-alongs in "Thee Olde Trip to Jerusalem," "This Way Through the Fire," and "Take His Name in Vain." *Punk Rock* literally takes the band back to roots, rerecording material from its earliest singles and albums. Some are done straight; others are radically remade, with "Building" offered a cappella and "What" transformed into a folkie reverie. Of the handful of rarities compilations, both *I Have Been to Heaven and Back: Hen's Teeth . . . Vol. 1* and *Where Were You? Hen's Teeth . . . Vol. 2* are coherent, very solid collections featuring live versions of their greatest misses. —J.D.C./C.H.

John "Cougar" Mellencamp

★★	Chestnut Street Incident (1976; Original Masters/Snapper Music, 1998)
★★½	The Kid Inside (1977; Original Masters/Snapper Music, 1998)
★★½	Early Years (1976–77, Rhino, 1986)
★★½	A Biography (Riva UK, 1978)
★★½	John Cougar (Mercury, 1979)
★★	Nothin' Matters and What If It Did (Mercury, 1980)
★★★½	American Fool (Mercury, 1982)
★★★½	Uh-huh (Mercury, 1983)
★★★★	Scarecrow (Mercury, 1985)
★★★½	The Lonesome Jubilee (Mercury, 1987)
★★★	Big Daddy (Mercury, 1989)
★★★	Whenever We Wanted (Mercury, 1991)
★★★	Human Wheels (Mercury, 1993)
★★★½	Dance Naked (Mercury, 1994)
★★★★	Mr. Happy Go Lucky (Mercury, 1996)
★★★★	The Best That I Could Do (1978–1988) (Mercury, 1997)
★★★	John Mellencamp (Columbia, 1998)
★★★	Rough Harvest (Mercury, 1999)
★★★½	Cuttin' Heads (Columbia 2001)
★★★½	Trouble No More (Sony, 2003)

If rock & roll is often just a matter of attitude, it's no wonder John Mellencamp is a star. While his music is just pleasantly pedestrian, his understanding of pop mythology and ability to play off of those myths is phenomenal. Whether or not that makes him a great rocker depends in part on how much stock you put into such cultural touchstones as classic rock, small-town life, and the American dream: Mellencamp's albums generally expect his listeners to believe in such things at least as fervently as he does.

It takes more than a leap of faith to be excited by his first five or six albums, however. Mellencamp launched his career as "Johnny Cougar," a sobriquet thrust upon him by then-manager Tony DeFries, and *Chestnut Street Incident* and *The Kid Inside* present an artist whose instincts run to recycled Stones riffs and Springsteen-derived braggadocio—an embarrassing combination. *The Early Years* contains highlights (loosely speaking) of both. Switching labels and management but still stuck with the name, he produced the import-only *A Biography,* which swaps Stonesisms for a sound closer to that of the Faces and is noteworthy only for having produced his first hit (in Australia, anyway), the casually sexist "I Need a Lover." *John Cougar,* which did see domestic release, also includes the song. Mellencamp plows ever deeper into the Great American Rock cliché with *Nothin' Matters and What If It Did,* which pushes his I'm-a-rebel posturing to ever more preposterous extremes.

What changed things was "Jack & Diane," a heart-land slice-of-life number from *American Fool.* Although its lyrics rarely get more than ankle deep, the music strikes an impressive balance between anthemic power and down-home intimacy, a combination Mellencamp returned to for much of *Uh-Huh.* Again, it isn't what he has to say that matters so much as how he says it, as "Pink Houses" couches its small-town odes in cleverly distilled Stones licks (note how the introduction recalls "Tumbling Dice") while "Authority Song" offers an agreeable update on Eddie Cochran's wild-youth raveups. *Scarecrow* is where he makes the most of this approach, with music so astonishingly eloquent that it easily outweighs the ideological over-reach of songs like "Small Town" and the ludicrous "Justice and Independence '85."

Rather than refine that sound, Mellencamp took a sharp left turn with *The Lonesome Jubilee,* moving from heartland rock to an Appalachian-influenced sound that owed more to *Desire*-era Dylan than any Stones album. That's not to say the album abandons rock; just listen to "Rooty Toot Toot" or "Cherry Bomb." *Big Daddy* expands on that fiddle-driven sound, but its folkie flourishes and grand gestures seem to be largely rhetorical, while its songs, apart from the self-serving "Pop Singer," are unmemorable. *Whenever We Wanted* finds the singer returning to the straight-up, Stones-style guitar rock of *Scarecrow* and *Uh-Huh,* and though there's more than enough melodic appeal to the likes of "Love and Happiness"

and "Get a Leg Up," the album's attempts at social commentary are overwrought.

With *Human Wheels,* Mellencamp turns unexpectedly depressive, offering dark, dreary songs that ask the listener to work harder than the music merits. Things perk up, however, with *Dance Naked,* in which Mellencamp again embraces the gutsy, physical aspects of rock & roll. It includes a sterling cover of Van Morrison's "Wild Night"). That feel-good approach takes an unexpected turn with *Mr. Happy Go Lucky,* which finds Mellencamp collaborating with remix star Junior Vasquez, a guy more likely to work with Madonna than a rootsy rocker like Mellencamp. Nonetheless, the combination clicks, and there's a sizzle and spirit to the music that goes well beyond Mellencamp's usual.

After that happy experiment, Mellencamp left his old label, Mercury, for a new one, Columbia. Trouble was, he still owed Mercury two albums—hence the more-or-less greatest-hits collection *The Best That I Could Do* and the semilive odds-and-sods disc *Rough Harvest.* Meanwhile, *John Mellencamp* consolidates the country and urban influences of his last few Mercury studio albums into a vivid, diverse, and unexpectedly coloristic sound. And if the depth of such tracks as "Eden Is Burning" or the beat-driven "Break Me Off Some" comes as a surprise, at least it prepares you for *Cuttin' Heads,* which not only backs Mellencamp with a raucous, soulful sound, but actually includes a cameo by Public Enemy's Chuck D. Admittedly, the music on the album's "political" songs is more fully realized than the words are, but personal songs such as the mildly self-deprecating "Women Seem" are among his best. A pity, then, that *Trouble No More* follows up with mostly covers—well-chosen and beautifully sung, but covers nonetheless. He does provide some new, Dubya-bashing lyrics for the traditional "To Washington," but the album's greatest strengths are his readings of such blues classics as Memphis Minnie's "Joliet Bound" and Robert Johnson's "Stones in My Passway." —J.D.C.

Natalie Merchant

★★★½ Tigerlily (Elektra, 1995)
★★★ Ophelia (Elektra, 1998)
★★★ Live in Concert (Elektra, 1999)
★★½ Motherland (Elektra, 2001)

First as lead singer and songwriter of 10,000 Maniacs and then as a solo artist, Natalie Merchant tapped into a hunger for literate, sometimes mystical singer/songwriter music. Her songs exuded enough pop gloss to land on the radio, but they were also reflective and full of emotional nuance, a combination that established Merchant as one of the guiding lights of the sensitive-gal Lilith Fair explosion of the mid-'90s.

Even before the Maniacs dissolved, Merchant was writing ambitious, unconventional material like "Noah's Dove" (from the band's 1992 swan song *Our Time in Eden*), which made good use of her porcelain voice and exotic lyrical imagery. She didn't tinker much with that approach on her solo debut, *Tigerlily:* While the hit "Carnival" suggests a goosed, more produced Maniacs, the album's elegies and lamentations, notably the eight-minute "I May Know the Word," catch the wistful, inward-looking mood to which her audience had become accustomed.

On *Ophelia*, though, Merchant made conscious changes. Electric guitar, previously used sparingly, is the disc's defining instrument, and the rhythms have a more rocklike assertiveness. A conceptual gallery of strong female archetypes, the album is less consistently engrossing than Merchant's previous work but nonetheless offers several artistic departures, including the ersatz spiritual "When They Ring the Golden Bells." *Motherland*, which follows the relatively predictable live set, is more repetitive, pointing Merchant to places she'd visited—more persuasively—before. —T.M.

Mercury Rev

★★★½ Yerself Is Steam (1991; Columbia, 1992)
★★★ Boces (Columbia, 1993)
★★★ See You on the Other Side (Work/Columbia, 1995)
★★★★ Deserter's Songs (V2, 1998)
★★★½ All Is Dream (V2, 2001)

Blending alumni of the Flaming Lips and disciples of Velvet Underground crony Tony Conrad, Mercury Rev revved up art-punk engines on *Yerself Is Steam*. It's one of the freshest—and weirdest—debut albums of the '90s: A vocalist murmurs non sequiturs, flutes flutter, jarring sound effects intrude and fade, and three heavily distorted guitars whirl and plink. On "Chasing a Bee," white-noise avalanches alternate with the sound of coos and mooing, while "Car Wash Hair" achieves a blurred folk-rock majesty.

Boces and *See You on the Other Side* are as much documents of the band's breakdown as they are coherent musical statements, the aural diary of six musicians simultaneously heading in different directions. *Deserter's Songs* chronicles the repair process; along the way, however, the reconfigured band apparently lost its distortion pedals. In their place is a symphonic tapestry of bowed saws, woodwinds, flutes, and vintage synthesizers, evoking a desolate but still wondrous world. Reference points include old church hymns, scratchy 78 r.p.m. records, Delta blues, and Eastern European folk, and the mood is one of slow healing. *All Is Dream* is nearly as thrilling, with even denser orchestrations heightening the drama of fragile impermanence. —G.K.

The Meters

★★★★ The Meters (1969; Sundazed, 1999)
★★★★ Look-ka Py Py (1970; Sundazed, 1999)
★★★½ Struttin' (1970; Sundazed, 1999)
★★★★ Cabbage Alley (1972; Sundazed, 2000)
★★★★½ Rejuvenation (1974; Sundazed, 2000)
★★★½ Fire on the Bayou (1975; Sundazed, 2000)
★★ Trick Bag (1976; Sundazed, 2000)
★★ New Directions (1977; Sundazed, 2000)
★★★★★ Funky Miracle (Charly U.K., 1991)
★★★½ The Meters Live on the Queen Mary (Rhino, 1992)
★★★ The Meters Jam (Rounder Select, 1992)
★★★★★ Funkify Your Life: The Meters Anthology (Rhino, 1995)
★★★★★ The Very Best of the Meters (Rhino, 1997)
★★★ Zony Mash (Sundazed, 2003)

The Funky Meters

★★★½ Fiyo at the Fillmore (Varèse, 2003)

Joseph "Zigaboo" Modeliste

★★★½ Zigaboo.com (JZM, 2000)

Long the premiere R&B rhythm section in New Orleans, the Meters—guitarist Leo Nocentelli, keyboardist Art Neville, bassist George Porter Jr., drummer Joseph "Zigaboo" Modeliste, and, eventually, percussionist Cyril Neville—worked with producer Allen Toussaint on dozens of sessions, backing Dr. John, LaBelle, Robert Palmer, and others. They also made quite a few records in their own right, recording three albums for Josie between 1968 and 1971 before signing with Reprise in 1972. These early sides are now finally available again, and detail how the Meters went from operating as a funkier version of the MG's to formulating their own synthesis of James Brown funk and New Orleans second-line syncopations. *Zony Mash* gathers stray B sides and singles not on regular early-period LPs. Forever in the groove.

Trying to get established outside the Crescent City, the Meters went looking for a hit on Reprise, initially with salutary changes. Unlike the all-instrumental Josie sides, the Reprise sessions add vocals, which, although they work well enough on titles like *Rejuvenation* (1974), which included the classic "Hey Pocky a-Way" and the relentless rhythm workout "It Ain't No Use," also led to such embarrassments as the foolishly topical "Disco Is the Thing

Today" on *Trick Bag*. The Meters performed *Live on the Queen Mary* at a Paul McCartney–hosted 1975 cruise party; judging from the band's set, it's obvious that fun was had by all. The retrospective single- and double-disc sets are equally ideal, depending on one's collector ambition. And, although the Meters disbanded after failing to find a way onto the charts, the group recently returned as the Funky Meters, combining drummer Russell Batiste and guitarist Brian Stoltz with Art Neville and George Porter. As *Fiyo at the Fillmore* confirms, this is a vibrant outfit that puts so-called jam bands to shame, but lacks the original group's particular sly, inventive quality, which appears in flashes on original drummer Modeliste's solo shot, *Zigaboo.com*. (The *Funky Miracle: Live at the Moonwalker* set, although graced by the JB Horns, is an unauthorized European release that does not pay the band royalties.) —J.D.C./M.MI.

Method Man

★★★½   Tical (Def Jam, 1994)
★★½   Tical 2000: Judgement Day (Def Jam, 1998)
★★½   Tical 0: The Prequel (Def Jam, 2004)

with Redman

★★★★   Blackout! (Def Jam, 1999)
★★★   How High (Def Jam, 2001)

A sandpaper-voiced, elastic rhymer whom both the ladies and thugs could love, Method Man was the first breakout star from the nine-man Wu-Tang Clan. Produced entirely by the RZA, Meth's debut, *Tical*, is equal parts blunt smoke, darkness, and sex appeal. It's packed with masterful moments: the dub-influenced "Bring the Pain," the jubilant horns of "Release Yo' Delf," the nursery-rhyme-inspired "Mr. Sandman." On "Meth vs. Chef," our star battles fellow Wu member Raekwon for the rights to RZA's slow-burning groove. Method rides RZA's music with singsong raps, spit-filled slang, and lots of references to *tical*, his branded term for marijuana.

Tical 2000: Judgement Day is the hip-hop equivalent of *The Road Warrior*: a millennium-weary venture that opens with the end of the world. It's every bit as menacing as its predecessor but channeled through a postapocalyptic view with stripped-down futuristic beats. Even though RZA is on hand for only a handful of tracks, *Judgement Day* is full of powerful musical non sequiturs, like the deep moaning "Sweet Love" and the paranoid, effects-laden title cut. Musically, *Judgement Day* doesn't extend many frontiers—there's an obligatory R&B moment in the D'Angelo-assisted "Break Ups 2 Make Ups," and "Retro Godfather" is all about blaxploitation funk. Skits—like Ed Lover's "Where's Method Man?";

"Donald Trump," featuring the real-estate magnate himself; and Def Jam head Lyor Cohen's "Check Writer"—poke fun at Meth's notoriously slow recording process, adding an air of humor to this otherwise pretty bleak record.

Things lightened up quick when Meth teamed with labelmate and fellow pothead Redman. The hedonistic *Blackout!* finds the self-described Blunt Brothers getting high and bouncing off the walls. As the duo runs through party-rocking grooves like the pneumatic, kinetic "Da Rockwilder," the sparsely soulistic "Cereal Killer," and the raucous "Fire Ina Hole," Redman's unhinged playfulness makes *Blackout!* as fun as Meth's first two records were spooky.

For the serviceable soundtrack to their Hollywood vehicle, *How High*, Meth and Red combine new numbers and old classics. The gem here is RZA's remix of Meth's "All I Need," featuring Mary J. Blige. Method Man completed his journey into mainstream pop culture with the very average "N2Gether Now," a collaboration with Limp Bizkit's Fred Durst. Perhaps inspired by his part-time acting career, Meth titled his next solo album *Tical 0: The Prequel*. But there was no going back to his heyday on this effort, despite a bumping duet with Missy Elliott ("Say What"). —K.X.

George Michael

★★★★   Faith (CBS, 1987)
★★½   Listen Without Prejudice (Columbia, 1990)
★★★   Ladies and Gentlemen: The Best of George Michael (Epic, 1998)
★★★   Song From the Last Century (Virgin, 1999)
★★★   Patience (Sony, 2004)

Because dance music had been George Michael's métier and the nightclub's sexual energy his muse, the former Wham! singer's first solo recording, *Faith*, distilled all of his themes and ambivalences into addictive neodisco. Hit after worthy hit spun off this trim, clean, thoughtful album, usually deeper than other hits of the time but never as deep as Michael thought.

Listen Without Prejudice, a lot less fun than *Faith*, finds Michael running from the form he had helped reshape and discovering he has nowhere to go. His chops are nothing without his beats, and except for the groovy, airy salsa of "Freedom 90," *Listen Without Prejudice* lives up to its sanctimonious title.

Ladies and Gentlemen is a cleverly sequenced collection with a ballad CD and a dance CD, meant to appeal to "heart" and "feet," respectively. The package proves breezily entertaining, covering the hits and some pleasant obscurities, like an as-good-as-all-the-others version of "Desafinado" with Astrud Gilberto.

Songs From the Last Century is an intimate and

often moving group of well-chosen favorites that create a snapshot of the "American century" in music. Using a wide range of instrumentation, Michael burnishes into the mainstream such piffle as "First Time Ever I Saw Your Face," pays his respects to the hardships that produced "Brother, Can You Spare a Dime," and does neither David Bowie nor Gogie Grant any disservice with "Wild Is the Wind." —A.B.

Bette Midler

★★★★	The Divine Miss M (Atlantic, 1972)
★★★½	Bette Midler (Atlantic, 1973)
★★½	Songs for the New Depression (Atlantic, 1976)
★★★	Live at Last (Atlantic, 1977)
★★	Broken Blossom (Atlantic, 1978)
★★	Thighs and Whispers (Atlantic, 1979)
★★★	The Rose (Atlantic, 1979)
★★	Divine Madness (Atlantic, 1979)
★★	No Frills (Atlantic, 1983)
★★	Mud Will Be Flung Tonight (Atlantic, 1985)
★★	Some People's Lives (Atlantic, 1990)
★★★½	Experience the Divine (Atlantic, 1993)
★★★	Bette of Roses (Atlantic, 1995)
★★½	Bathhouse Betty (Warner Bros., 1998)
★★½	Bette (Warner Bros., 2000)
★★★	Bette Midler Sings the Rosemary Clooney Songbook (Sony, 2003)

Bette Midler touched off a nostalgia boom in the '70s with *The Divine Miss M* and "Boogie Woogie Bugle Boy," but warm-'n'-fuzzy tunnel vision really wasn't her style—at first. Her audaciously theatrical delivery and campy, taste-zapping zest for life can still strike a listener like a cold slap in the face. She could play the bawdy mama act to the hilt, yet Midler also found the emotional center in a dumbfounding variety of songs. Of course, her voice—surpisingly supple and delicate at times—helps quite a bit. A true child of the '60s underneath her tacky period glitz, Midler exults in girl-group melodrama ("Chapel of Love") and singer/songwriter homilies (John Prine's "Hello in There") alike on her debut album. If you can bear the chattering show-biz patter on the first version of "Friends" (this acid-etched soundtrack chestnut appears twice), the shameless delights offered on *The Divine Miss M* will melt even the sternest objections to cabaret music. The early Bette Midler falls somewhere between a traditional belter and a modern-day performance artist.

Naturally, this made Bette a dynamite live performer—and also an underdeveloped recording artist. *Bette Midler* repeats the scattershot format of the debut, with respectable-enough results. "Twisted"

prefigures Joni Mitchell's hit version of this bitter '50s cocktail, and signals Midler's widespread influence. The soul cover versions are another matter; despite her élan, Midler can't do justice to the raw lust of Ann Peebles' "Breaking Up Somebody's Home" or the spiritual uplift of Jackie Wilson's "Higher and Higher." You can't do *everything;* Midler shines on "Da Doo Ron Ron" and "Lullabye of Broadway."

From the strained opener ("Strangers in the Night") onward, *Songs for the New Depression* is where Bette Midler's musically adventurous act lapses into shtick. *The Rose* established Midler as an actress; she credibly portrays a Janis Joplinesque doomed rock star in this hit melodrama. *The Rose* album is the first of several very successful Midler soundtracks. "Wind Beneath Your Wings," from the 1988 screen weeper *Beaches,* kick-started Midler's languishing musical career when it charted that year. Up until then, she'd been sadly adrift on record during the '90s. *Live at Last* and the Broadway stage soundtrack *Divine Madness* will more than satisfy fans, however. Ironically, Midler, who started her career singing deceptively witty little ditties, wound up the '80s pumping straight sentimental hokum on *Some People's Lives* and the 1990 smash "From a Distance." Midler's acting career continued to thrive throughout the '90s, and her albums started to feel more and more like sidelights—albeit sidelights that were often pleasurable in a dilettanteish way. Curious newcomers should start with *Divine Miss M* and proceed to *Bette Midler.* Those with an appetite for Midler's megahits as well as her campy beginnings should search out the career overview *Experience the Divine.* —M.C./N.B.

Midnight Oil

★★★	Midnight Oil (Columbia, 1978)
★★★	Head Injuries (Columbia, 1979)
★★★	Bird Noises (EP) (Columbia, 1980)
★★★½	Place Without a Postcard (Columbia, 1981)
★★★★	10, 9, 8, 7, 6, 5, 4, 3, 2, 1 (Columbia, 1983)
★★★½	Red Sails in the Sunset (Columbia, 1984)
★★★	Species Deceases (EP) (Columbia, 1985)
★★★★½	Diesel and Dust (Columbia, 1987)
★★★½	Blue Sky Mining (Columbia, 1990)
★★★	Scream in Blue Live (Columbia, 1992)
★★★½	Earth and Sun and Moon (Columbia, 1993)
★★★	Breathe (Work Group, 1996)
★★★★	20,000 Watt R.S.L. (Columbia, 1997)
★★★½	Redneck Wonderland (Columbia, 1998)
★★★	The Real Thing (Columbia, 2000)
★★★	Capricornia (Liquid 8, 2002)

For more than 25 years, Midnight Oil raged and rolled as the antinuclear, pro-environmental conscience of

Australian rock. At the height of the band's international fame, in the 1980s, Midnight Oil was favorably compared to the Clash, with good reason: The Oils' U.S. debut, *10, 9, 8* is a stunning, sunbaked answer to *London Calling*. Midnight Oil's ferocious jeremiad against corporate greed and American military imperialism is powered by the apocalyptic delivery of bald singing colossus Peter Garrett and the twin-guitar assault of Jim Moginie and Martin Rotsey. But the Oils were never punks; they were heavy-melody activists, pressing their politics with the seductive writing and vocal harmonies of mid-'60s Beatles and the classic Aussie ferocity of AC/DC and Radio Birdman.

Formed in Sydney in 1976, the Oils quickly became favorites of the hard-drinking, pub-brawling surfer communities on the city's North Beaches. *Midnight Oil* and *Head Injuries* crudely bottle the force and fire of early Oils shows. The band's earliest records also reveal a poetic nationalism that bloomed on the outback-tour diary, *Diesel and Dust*. At a time when many Aussie bands sought world approval by slavishly emulating American and British songwriting, the Oils made explicit geocultural references to their pride in Australia and fear for its future in songs like "Lucky Country" and "If Ned Kelly Was King," on *Place Without a Postcard*.

10, 9, 8 was the first Oils record to truly bring out the pop in their pow. Moginie and drummer Rob Hirst wrote much of the Oils' music, and their tuneful instincts made the argumentative drama of *10, 9, 8* torpedoes—"Only the Strong," "Read About It," "The Power and the Passion"—both compelling and convincing.

The Oils' explosive growth on *10, 9, 8* and the nuclear-nightmare followup, *Red Sails in the Sunset*, climaxed with their worldwide commercial triumph, *Diesel and Dust*. Recorded after a pioneering series of shows in remote aboriginal settlements in the Australian desert, *Diesel and Dust* is a vivid examination of Western sociocultural failure and indigenous suffering and spirituality, set against a punishing landscape and including the Oils' finest, tightest writing: the folk-rock strum and foreboding locomotion of "The Dead Heart" and the muscular R&B surge and soaring chorus of the Top 20 hit "Beds Are Burning."

After fighting their way to the top from the bottom of the globe, Midnight Oil hit alternative rock's brick wall in the 1990s. Although sales and airplay fell, their later albums deserve, and reward, rediscovery. The title song of *Blue Sky Mining* is a righteous, garage-band stomp in the local spirit of the Easybeats. "My Country," on *Earth and Sun and Moon*, and *Breathe*'s "Surf's Up Tonight" capture Garrett in dark, magnetic ballad form. *Redneck Wonderland* shakes and snarls

with Black Sabbath–like distortion and outlaw rage. In December 2002, Garrett—a former law student who ran for a seat in the Australian senate on the Nuclear Disarmament Party ticket in 1984—announced that he was leaving Midnight Oil to pursue full-time activism, leaving the group's future in doubt. The best-of set, *20,000 Watt R.S.L.*, is a compact dossier on the power and passion Garrett and the Oils brought to rock, then spread around the world.   —D.F.

The Mighty Mighty Bosstones

   ★★   Devils Night Out (Taang!, 1990)
   ★★   Where'd You Go (EP) (Taang!, 1991)
  ★★★ More Noise & Other Disturbances (Taang!, 1992)
   ★★   Ska-Core, the Devil and More (EP) (Mercury, 1993)
   ★★   Don't Know How to Party (Mercury, 1993)
  ★★★ Question the Answers (Mercury, 1994)
  ★★★ Let's Face It (Big Rig/Mercury, 1997)
  ★★★ Live From the Middle East (Big Rig/Mercury, 1998)
  ★★★ Pay Attention (Big Rig/Island, 2000)
  ★★★ A Jackknife to a Swan (SideOneDummy, 2002)

Back in the mid-'80s, a bunch of Boston high school kids discovered that Jamaican ska and American hardcore punk could be combined to form one exceedingly loud and fast musical tribute, complete with horn section, to testosterone. Since then, many other bands have capitalized on that discovery, and some (No Doubt and Sublime, for instance) have taken it to greater commercial heights. Yet the Mighty Mighty Bosstones' pioneer status remains secure, just as their ongoing dedication to the music is unquestionable.

The Bosstones' debut album doesn't blend ska and hardcore so much as it bashes them together. Like a traffic accident, *Devils Night Out* is horribly fascinating; unlike a traffic accident, you can dance to it. The EP that followed is named for the Bosstones' first truly catchy tune. *More Noise* leans toward pop metal, an interesting development undermined by inconsistent songwriting. Lead vocalist Dicky Barrett sings with all the grace of an angry frog on a weeklong bender, amusing enough on the party tracks but discouraging on the ones striving for personal or social relevance.

The Bosstones' first two major-label releases accentuate the harder side of their music, proving definitively that the band is better at skanking than head banging. *Question the Answers* gets the balance closer to right: more horns, memorable tunes, and less gargling from Barrett. The situation continues to improve on *Let's Face It*, the band's best batch yet, including its long-hoped-for breakthrough hit, "The Impression That I Get." Recorded on home turf in Cambridge, MA, the live album is a well-selected slam dance through the Bosstones' back catalogue.

The Bosstones of *Pay Attention* often sound less like a ska or punk band than a power-pop outfit with two saxophones and a trombone. And it's good power pop, despite the presence of a few too many "Impression That I Get" rewrites. *A Jackknife to a Swan* is the band's first album without founding guitarist Nate Albert, but the personnel change doesn't affect the music much. At this point, it seems very little could. The Mighty Mighty Bosstones have reached a level of dependable professionalism; expect them to be hardworking and fun, but don't expect many surprises. —M.R.

Rhett Miller
see OLD 97'S

Steve Miller Band

★★★½	Children of the Future (1968; Capitol, 1994)
★★★½	Sailor (1968; Alliance, 1996)
★★★½	Brave New World (1969; Capitol, 1994)
★★★	Your Saving Grace (1969; Capitol, 1991)
★★★	Number Five (1970; Capitol, 1991)
★★★★	Anthology (1972; Alliance, 1996)
★★	Living in the U.S.A. (1973; CEMA, 2003)
★★★	The Joker (1973; JVC, 1998)
★★★½	Fly Like an Eagle (1976; Capitol, 1999)
★★★½	Book of Dreams (1977; Alliance, 1996)
★★★★½	Greatest Hits 1974–1978 (1978; DCC, 1997)
★★½	Abracadabra (1982; Alliance, 1996)
★★½	Living in the 20th Century (1987; CEMA, 1995)
★★★	Born 2 B Blue (1988; Alliance, 1996)
★★★★	The Best of 1968–1973 (Capitol, 1991)
★★★★	Steve Miller Band (Capitol, 1994)
★★	Extended Versions (BMG Special Projects, 2003)
★★★★½	Young Hearts: Complete Greatest Hits (Capitol, 2003)

"Take the Money and Run," the winking title of one of Steve Miller's '70s megahits, seems to sum up the blithely commercial drive of this genial radio artiste, but his early work was trailblazing—and even his trifles sound great in the car. Forming his first professional outfit in San Francisco in 1966, the Wisconsin-born guitarist/singer deftly sidestepped the flashier excesses of shopworn psychedelia and concentrated on clean rockers and supple blues. Helped out greatly by Boz Scaggs on vocals and guitar, "Living in the

U.S.A.," "Quicksilver Girl," "Dime-a-Dance Romance" and the bulk of *Children of the Future* and *Sailor* are steady, effortless rock & roll. (*Living in the U.S.A.* packages the two records together.) *Anthology* is also pretty terrific: "Space Cowboy," "Seasons," "I Love You," and "My Dark Hour," an interesting, heavy thumper featuring Paul McCartney, are melodically astute and very catchy. The collection also renders *Number Five, Rock Love,* and *Recall the Beginning . . . A Journey From Eden* (the last two out of print) unnecessary.

With its ultraclean production and the absolute efficiency of its songs, *The Joker* was a record made for radio success—and it reaped it in spades. The title track has become Miller's signature tune, and it shows his complete mastery of the single: punchy bass, a nifty guitar motif, and witty lyrics delivered with laconic assurance. His next two records, *Fly Like an Eagle* and *Book of Dreams,* form, with *The Joker,* the essential big-time Miller trilogy. As Stephen King does with horror stories, so Miller does with Top 40 rock; that is, he delivers, in such hits as "Rock'n Me," "Jet Airliner," and "Jungle Love," surefire pleasures, triumphs not of originality but of craft.

With infinitesimal shifts in tone and style, Miller continued in the vein set by those three albums. "Abracadabra" was a tasty smash, even if the album that bore its title was fairly perfunctory. Only on the deleted *Italian X-Rays* did the formula show signs of real exhaustion; a ditty like "Bongo Bongo" sounds like Miller parodying himself. Miller's gift—and it's a subtle one—is making the familiar sound fresh. Miller's most recent album of new material, 1993's inconsequential *Wide River,* is no longer available. But his oeuvre has been satisfyingly gathered on the 1994 box set *Steve Miller Band,* compiled by the artist himself, and 2003's *Young Hearts: Complete Greatest Hits,* a solid single-disc sampler. —P.E./B.SC.

Milli Vanilli

★★	Girl You Know It's True (Arista, 1989)
★	The Remix Album (Arista, 1990)

Perhaps the only duo in pop music history that's best known for what it didn't sing, Rob Pilatus and Fabrice Morvan of Milli Vanilli made headlines in 1990 when it was revealed that the two never sang a note. According to producer Frank Farian, Pilatus and Morvan were hired only for their looks, which he felt would add street-level credibility to the music. After their disgrace, the group was briefly thrust back into the public eye in the late '90s after they were the subject of one of the first VH1's *Behind the Music.* Rob Pilatus died of a drug overdose in 1998. —J.D.C.

Charles Mingus
Selected Discography
★★★	Pithecanthropus Erectus (Atlantic, 1956)
★★★	The Clown (Atlantic, 1957)
★★★½	New Tijuana Moods (Bluebird, 1957)
★★★★	Blues and Roots (Atlantic, 1959)
★★★★★	Mingus Ah Um (Columbia, 1959)
★★★★	Mingus at Antibes (1960; Sony, 1999)
★★★★	The Black Saint and the Sinner Lady (Impulse, 1963)
★★★★	Let My Children Hear Music (Columbia, 1971)
★★★★	The Very Best of Charles Mingus (Rhino, 2001)

Charles Mingus, the jazz bassist, composer, and arranger, was an intelligent, iconoclastic crank: an incredibly gifted composer who understood how to bring the energy of the blues and gospel into an improvisatory setting; a sideman feared for his angry outbursts; a leader who treated his band like a free-form workshop; and the owner of a label (Debut) that documented some key jazz sessions of the '50s. But that's not all—a victim of racism, Mingus became one of the most outspoken jazz musicians, whose titles offered trenchant commentary on current events (one song, "Fables of Faubus," took aim at the Arkansas governer who sought to continue segregation). He also contributed a classic memoir of jazz, *Beneath the Underdog,* and several ambitious large-ensemble pieces, including the haunting *Epitaph,* which was pieced together from his notation after his death.

After working in several famous bands (including the Jazz at Massey Hall ensemble featuring Charlie Parker), Mingus began his composing career in the conventional manner—as an Ellington disciple, writing out parts for each of his musicians. Sensing this approach denied his musicians the chance to shape the music, he switched tactics, singing the parts to each player and outlining structures in ways that allowed for spontaneous revision. This gave the music a hocketing, sometimes frenetic call-and-response quality, and a sense of rippling invention first heard on 1956's *Pithecanthropus Erectus,* Mingus' first great statement as a leader. The recordings that followed are marvels of extrapolation and motific embellishment that, by the way, yield some of the most visionary writing in jazz: *The Clown* contains the catcalling "Haitian Fight Song," *Blues and Roots* has the revival blues "Better Git It in Yo' Soul." These dates feature some of the sidemen who became crucial collaborators for Mingus—saxophonists Eric Dolphy, Jackie McLean, and Booker Ervin, multi-instrumentalist Rahsaan Roland Kirk, and trombonist Jimmy Knepper all helped Mingus find an inspiring midpoint between uproarious free improv and gutbucket blues, a balance he achieved best on his 1959 Columbia debut, *Mingus Ah Um.* Dolphy, a fixture with Mingus in the early '60s, lights up the consistently energized *At Antibes.* And 1963's *The Black Saint and the Sinner Lady,* written for big band and featuring Dolphy, remains one of the most adventurous long-form pieces in jazz history—a fate that would have been shared by *Epitaph* had Mingus himself been able to finish it.

Active into the 1970s, Mingus continued to record even after Lou Gehrig's disease made it impossible for him to play the bass anymore. Among his last projects was a collaboration with singer/songwriter Joni Mitchell, *Mingus,* which contains her approximations of several of his classics. Because his recordings were issued by many labels, there's no comprehensive career anthology, but there are several era-specific sets; of these, Rhino's *The Very Best* actually is the best. A posthumous recording of *Epitaph* featuring some Mingus sidemen was issued in 1989.   —T.M.

Kylie Minogue
★★★★	Fever (Capitol, 2002)
★★★★	Greatest Hits 87–97 (Jive/BMG, 2003)
★★★	Body Language (Capitol, 2004)

In America, Kylie Minogue is known for 1988's giddy dance-pop remake of Little Eva's "The Loco Motion" and 2002's neo-disco tour de force "Can't Get You Out of My Head." But in every other corner of the English-speaking world (and not a few non-English-speaking ones), the pint-sized Australian is an icon to rival Madonna. Her backside, while far smaller than that of Jennifer Lopez, is the recipient of as much scrutiny overseas. She became wildly famous in the mid-'80s via her role as Charlene in the Australian soap *Neighbors,* and quickly became the preferred vehicle of the English Stock-Aitken-Waterman production juggernaut. Her percolating hits "I Should Be So Lucky," "Got to Be Certain," "Hand on Your Heart," as well as "The Loco Motion" are delightful trifles, each as cheesily and identically redolent of the late '80s as a pair of stone-washed jean shorts. These and 24 other cuts (as well as eight remixes) are collected on *Greatest Hits 87–97,* which samples a decade's worth of dance pop that moved every disco in every nation other than the U.S. to distraction.

In 2001 Minogue resolved to do what had eluded scores of international superstars—break into the U.S. If *Fever* didn't exactly send Britney Spears and Christina Aguilera scurrying away in terror, the calling-card single "Can't Get You out of My Head" was easily the best and most omnipresent dance track of the new century. Like Madonna, Minogue was not a virtuosic singer but a canny trend spotter—hence "Love at First Sight" is a not only wholesale tribute to Daft Punk's metadisco opus *Discovery,* but a damn great one. Completed by the cleverly phrased "Come Into My World" ("Come, come" she trills, as if coaxing a climax out of her partner) and 10 equally effective tunes, *Fever* is a dance-pop masterpiece. 2003's *Body Language,* on the other hand, mined dance-pop styles that were a bit more obscure—electro, the modern house stylings of Basement Jaxx—and thus fell a little short. But Minogue finally took over the entire world with *Fever,* and thus fulfilled her destiny.   —R.K.

Ministry

★★	Twelve Inch Singles 1981–1984 (Wax Trax!, 1985)
★★½	Twitch (Sire, 1986)
★★★½	The Land of Rape and Honey (Sire, 1988)
★★★½	The Mind Is a Terrible Thing to Taste (Sire, 1989)
★★★★	In Case You Didn't Feel Like Showing Up (Live) (Sire, 1990)
★★★★	Psalm 69: The Way to Succeed and the Way to Suck Eggs (Sire, 1992)
★★★	Filth Pig (Sire, 1995)
★½	The Dark Side of the Spoon (Warner Bros., 1999)
★★★	Greatest Fits (Warner Bros., 2000)
★½	Sphinctour (Sanctuary, 2002)
★★	Animositisomina (Sanctuary, 2003)
★★	Houses of the Molé (Sanctuary, 2004)

At its peak, Ministry made the loudest, ugliest, most uncompromising music out there—or at least the loudest, ugliest, most uncompromising music out there worth listening to. Like fellow pop industrialist Trent Reznor, Ministry frontman Alain Jourgensen learned his doofy goth clichés from the inside when he led a drippy synth band. But unlike Reznor, Jourgensen learned to play gloom and doom for laughs later on. By the time production began on *The Mind Is a Terrible Thing to Taste,* he'd figured out that keyboards could sound at least as hard as guitars. Ministry's sound—heavy, fast, anonymous—is showcased in its purest form on *In Case You Didn't Feel Like Showing Up,* six unrelenting slabs of rhythmic oppression with Jourgensen's drill-sergeant bark emanating from somewhere below. On *Psalm 69,* his conceptual gifts caught up with his sonic smarts. The ideas are simple but effective: a loop of George H. W. Bush whinily intoning "A New World Order"; ghastly choirs wailing over a creepy Christian testimonial; and, best of all, the Butthole Surfers' Gibby Haynes ranting dementedly about "Jesus Built My Hotrod."

Jourgensen instantly became a victim of his own success. He found his niche market and he decided to work it. "Lay Lady Lay" is kinda fun, but the rest of *Filth Pig* is sludge. He's been pumping sewage into the marketplace ever since—arty sewage, which is just that much more pathetic. His career trajectory would be less sad if his success hadn't been so limited, his niche so tiny. The joke's on him.   —K.M.

Minor Threat

★★★★	Minor Threat (Dischord EP, 1981)
★★★	In My Eyes (Dischord EP, 1981)
★★★★	Out of Step (Dischord, 1984)
★★★	Salad Days (Dischord EP, 1985)
★★★★★	Complete Discography (Dischord, 1988)
★★★	First Demo Tape (Dischord EP, 2003)

Minor Threat, from Washington, D.C., was not just the quintessential American hardcore punk band of the 1980s; it also was the best that hardcore ever produced. Germs and Black Flag, from Los Angeles, set the tone of the music; D.C.'s Bad Brains expanded its boundaries; and Southern California politicos Minutemen brought in the funk. But their recorded output was spotty. In Minor Threat's brief career, the band never released a bad song. What's more, one of its earliest tracks, "Straight Edge," unintentionally spawned a movement of clean-living young punk fans, and members of Minor Threat would ultimately form the hugely influential Fugazi. But the lesser-known Minor Threat was actually more significant to the development of modern rock.

The members were teenagers when they put out the first EP, which fairly brims with restless passion and creative energy. "I Don't Want to Hear It," "Small Man, Big Mouth," "Screaming at a Wall" and "Bottled Violence" all summed up the feelings of anxious, rebellious, politically progressive young people in the Reagan years. Subsequent EPs are just as passionate and powerful, and the band's first album, *Out of Step,* delivered an extended set of loud, fast, whiplash punk with a sense of humor and alienation. The album and EPs are all too brief, though, which makes the self-explanatory *Complete Discography,* released posthumously, the only essential Minor Threat CD. Any fan of postpunk and hard rock—from Nirvana to Limp Bizkit—should own this collection. The *First Demo Tape* EP is an interesting but inessential set of embryonic material from earlier albums.   —M.K.

The Minutemen

★★★½	Paranoid Time (SST, 1981)
★★	The Punch Line (SST, 1981)
★★★★★	What Makes a Man Start Fires? (SST, 1983)

★★★★ Buzz or Howl Under the Influence of Heat (SST, 1983)
★★★★★ Double Nickels on the Dime (SST, 1984)
★★★ The Politics of Time (SST, 1984)
★★ Project: Mersh (SST, 1985)
★★★½ 3-Way Tie (for Last) (SST, 1985)
★★★★ Ballot Result (SST, 1987)
★★★★ Post-Mersh, Vol. 1 (SST, 1987)
★★★½ Post-Mersh, Vol. 2 (SST, 1987)
★★★½ Post-Mersh, Vol. 3 (SST, 1989)
★★★½ Introducing the Minutemen (SST, 1998)

The Minutemen sang the famous line "Our band could be your life" in "History Lesson—Part II," and listening to their homemade yet intricate punk rock is still an inspiration. Blue-collar nerds from the port town of San Pedro, CA, guitarist D. Boon and bassist Mike Watt grew up together, eventually falling in with drummer George Hurley for a band that expanded the possibilities of what could be said politically and musically in a punk-rock song. They began as a hardcore band, but from the beginning they were more than just thrash, splicing folk, jazz, and funk snippets into a flurry of brief songs with no verses or choruses. A 60-second blast like the 1981 "Joe McCarthy's Ghost" (on *Paranoid Time*) explodes with rage, but it also feels friendly and high-spirited, as the Minutemen rant in the populist style of their heroes, Creedence Clearwater Revival.

Their first great record was *What Makes a Man Start Fires?*, one of the very best American punk albums. Its 18 songs speed by in 27 minutes: the breathtaking stop-start dynamics of "Sell or Be Sold," the slash guitar of "Colors," the dissonant funk of "Life as a Rehearsal," the boyish melancholy of "Fake Contest." You could accuse the political songs of being propapaganda, and you'd be right, because these guys loved propaganda and made it rock. *Buzz or Howl* has D. Boon cutting loose on guitar in "The Product," which has an out-of-nowhere junk-trumpet solo. Their landmark *Double Nickels on the Dime* piles 46 songs onto two vinyl LPs (43 on the CD). There are funny tributes to Steely Dan ("Doctor Wu"), Blue Öyster Cult ("The Red and the Black"), and Van Halen ("Ain't Talkin' 'Bout Love," which lasts 38 seconds). It's an album that's even better when you can program your favorites over and over; if you're overwhelmed at first by the sheer bulk of it, start with the protest anthem "This Ain't No Picnic," the sad "Storm in My House," the matter-of-fact "There Ain't Shit on TV Tonight," or the story of their lives, "History Lesson—Part II."

The band softened its touch a bit, not wholly successfully, on *Project: Mersh* (short for "commercial"),

featuring a bad Steppenwolf cover and the great "Tour Spiel," and *3-Way Tie (For Last)*. On December 22, 1985, a few days after *3-Way Tie* was released, D. Boon was killed in a van crash in Arizona, ending the Minutemen.

Watt began playing with Black Flag's Kira Roessler in the two-bass combo Dos, which was much better than one could hope; devoted Minutemen fan Ed Crawford joined Watt and Hurley in fIREHOSE, which was nowhere near as good as one would hope.

SST has repackaged the Minutemen canon into three volumes: *Post-Mersh, Vol. 1* has *Punch Line* and *Start Fires*; *Vol. 2* pairs *Buzz or Howl* and *Project: Mersh*; *Vol. 3* comprises EPs, *Politics of Time* outtakes, and covers that had been cut from the CD version of *Double Nickels*. *Ballot Result* is a live retrospective of songs chosen by fans who voted on a ballot that was included in original copies of *3-Way Tie*. *Introducing* is a clumsy attempt at a greatest-hits album, with muddled chronology and strange omissions ("The Product," "Sell or Be Sold," "Plight," and more are left out). D. Boon, one of the genuinely humane and imaginative rock heroes of all time, is still missed.   —R.S.

Mission of Burma

★★★★ Signals, Calls, and Marches (EP) (1981; Ace of Hearts/Rykodisc, 1997)
★★★★ Vs. (1982; Ace of Hearts/Rykodisc, 1997)
★★★ The Horrible Truth About Burma (1985; Ace of Hearts/Rykodisc, 1997)
★★ Forget (1987; Taang!, 1994)
★★★ Peking Spring (Taang!, 1993)
★★★½ ONoffON (Matador, 2004)
★★★★ Accomplished: The Best of (Rykodisc, 2004)

Too herky-jerky and too enamored with the joys of noise to ever find mass acceptance during its active years, Mission of Burma has nevertheless garnered a posthumous reputation as a crucial force in U.S. punk history. It wouldn't be inaccurate to call this Boston quartet the missing link between the artier side of late-'70s British postpunk (Wire, Gang of Four, Joy Division) and the American indie rock that flourished in the '80s (R.E.M., the Minutemen, Hüsker Dü). *Signals, Calls, and Marches* introduces the band's central features: Roger Miller's vicious guitar work, Clint Conley's octave-jumping bass lines, Peter Prescott's off-kilter drumming, and Martin Swope's surprising tape-loop textures. The music turns crazy corners with aggro aplenty; the lyrics are as intelligent as they are angry; and Miller, Conley, and Prescott deliver them with appropriate levels of spit and snarl. "That's When I Reach for My Revolver" (later covered by Moby), "Fame and Fortune," and the entrancing in-

strumental "All World Cowboy Romance" are standouts. The Ryko CD reissue also includes the valuable
early single "Academy Fight Song."

If *Signals* was a nasty scuffle, then *Vs.* is a full-
armored onslaught. Although melody is sometimes at
a premium, the band's intensity is astonishing, making
the album's quieter moments—"Trem Two," "Weath-
erbox"—all the more effective. *The Horrible Truth,*
recorded during Burma's last tour in 1983, is less necessary, though "Tremelo," "New Disco," and an extended cover of Pere Ubu's "Heart of Darkness"
testify to the group's live power.

In 2002, nearly two decades after their dissolution
(due to the hearing damage Miller had suffered from
years of playing at top volume), Burma reunited for a
series of shows in England and the U.S. The adoring
response made a new album almost inevitable. Miraculously, *ONoffON* equals its predecessors; judging by
the brittle, manic energy of "Fake Blood" or "Absent
Mind," you'd hardly guess any time had passed.

Burma novices shouldn't start their investigations
with the two haphazard discs of unreleased studio
recordings on Taang! (originally issued in the mid-
'80s; in its initial release, *Peking Spring* was titled simply *Mission of Burma*). But both albums contain good
material: *Peking Spring*'s title track and *Forget*'s "Eyes
of Men," for example. The best Mission of Burma
primer remains Ryko's 1988 single-CD compilation,
also titled *Mission of Burma* and now out of print, but
Accomplished will do in a pinch.   —M.R.

Joni Mitchell

★★★	Joni Mitchell (1968; Reprise, 1990)
★★★½	Clouds (1969; Reprise, 1990)
★★★★	Ladies of the Canyon (1970; Reprise, 1990)
★★★★★	Blue (1971; Reprise, 1990)
★★★★	For the Roses (1972; Asylum, 1990)
★★★★★	Court and Spark (1974; Asylum, 1990)
★★★	Miles of Aisles (1974; Asylum, 1990)
★★★½	The Hissing of Summer Lawns (1975; Asylum, 1990)
★★★½	Hejira (1976; Asylum, 1990)
★★★	Don Juan's Reckless Daughter (1977; Asylum, 1990)
★★★	Mingus (1979; Asylum, 1990)
★★★	Shadows and Light (1980; Asylum, 1990)
★★★	Wild Things Run Fast (1982; Geffen, 1991)
★★½	Chalk Mark in a Rain Storm (1988; Geffen, 1990)
★★★★	Night Ride Home (Geffen, 1991)
★★★	Turbulent Indigo (Geffen, 1994)
★★★★½	Hits (Reprise, 1996)
★★★½	Misses (Reprise, 1996)
★★★	Taming the Tiger (Geffen, 1998)
★★★	Both Sides Now (Reprise, 2000)
★★★	Travelogue (Reprise, 2002)
★★★★	The Complete Geffen Recordings (Geffen, 2003)
★★★½	The Beginning of Survival (Geffen/UME, 2004)

Joni Mitchell strummed her way out of Canada and
into the L.A. music scene in the late '60s. Produced by
David Crosby, her sparse debut album reveals a striking, if somewhat fragile, folksinger in the accepted
acoustic mode. However, Mitchell's heart-piercing
cold-water vocals and restless, self-questioning persona separate her from the competition. Judy Collins
scored a Top 10 hit with Mitchell's "Both Sides Now"
in 1968; Joni's more contemplative version sets the
older-and-wiser tone of *Clouds,* her much-improved
second album. *Ladies of the Canyon* solidifies those
songwriting advances. "Woodstock," too self-
conscious to be an all-out anthem, is still Mitchell's
most outgoing, least analytical moment. "The Circle
Game," the album's closer, asserts Mitchell's ability to
express complex emotional states in plain language. A
supple chorus puts her personalized message across.

Blue raises the autobiographical stakes and intensifies the melodies; arguably, it's Mitchell's masterpiece.
She picks memorable vignettes out of the flood of
memories and reflections that accompany an extended
journey, spinning off songs like "Carey," "California,"
and "This Flight Tonight." Though the musical backing (by Stephen Stills, James Taylor, and others) is
kept to a minimum, Joni's vocals grow in nuance and
complexity. *Blue* stays under your skin for quite a
while.

Starting with *For the Roses,* Mitchell pushes her
musical accompaniment to keep pace with her rapidly
evolving singing and writing skills. She's not always
successful, but few other singer/songwriters extended
their quest to include music as well as lyrics. Certainly,
the cozy L.A. cowboy-rock studio scene must have
beckoned Joni Mitchell with the lure of easygoing hit
singles. True to form, she did it her own way with *For
the Roses.* Saxophone player and bandleader Tom
Scott can be a vapid fusion-Muzak meister on his
own, but his light jazz coloring underscores the subtle
depths of *Roses.* On *Court and Spark,* Mitchell and
Scott concoct a resonant pop-jazz sound that accommodates both swooning melodies ("Help Me") and
blue reflection ("Same Situation") with ease. The
buoyant humor of "Raised on Robbery" and the
Lambert-Hendricks-Ross novelty "Twisted" makes
this Joni's most appealing album (if not her most profound). Recorded on the tour following that album,
Miles of Aisles features revamped version of Mitchell's

better-known early songs. It's a convenient sampler, but the progression from album to album—a big part of the picture—gets lost on both this concert album and the 1980 live set *Shadows and Light*.

Naturally, Mitchell pursued her muse into more adventurous territory on the next two albums. Some of the impressionistic snippets on *The Hissing of Summer Lawns* ("The Jungle Line," "The Boho Dance") never quite register, though the effervescent melancholy of "In France They Kiss on Main Street" and "Don't Interrupt the Sorrow" sinks in deeply over time, as does the hauntingly slow "Shadows and Light." *Hejira* is even more atmospheric—or formless, depending on your attention level. Bassist Jaco Pastorius keeps up with Mitchell's wandering freeform meditations, while the rest of the music—wintry, detached—lulls in the background. No single track leaps out the way *Summer Lawns'* best ones do, but overall *Hejira* leaves the more lasting—if mysteriously vague—impression.

Don Juan's Reckless Daughter seems inevitable now—the double album in search of an editor. This time, a real lack of focus allows the session musicians to hotdog their way through Mitchell's stilted setpieces. *Mingus* represents a brave attempted collaboration with the noted jazz bassist and composer; unfortunately, the results are sketchy at best.

Mitchell didn't retire in the '80s, though her intermittent releases indicate that she'd retreated from the artistic vanguard. *Wild Things Run Fast* is exactly the sort of competent holding-pattern album—complete with cover versions—that Mitchell went out of her way to avoid in the '70s. *Dog Eat Dog*, which came out of left field in 1985, comes closer to being the individualistic challenge fans might expect. Joni confronts producer Thomas Dolby's synthesized sound with feisty vocals and her most pointed set of songs. Rife with withering political opinions and topical insights, this unsettling album is her best of the period—and her only '80s album to be deleted, though it's available on 2003's *The Complete Geffen Recordings.* Avoid *Chalk Mark in a Rain Storm;* a torrent of borderline New Age–easy-listening blandness washes over even the most thoughtful lyrics.

Night Ride Home isn't a comeback so much as a chance to catch up with a long-lost confidante. There's a slight return to the jazz-tinged sound of the mid-'70s; succinct orchestrations and smoky sax lines curl around Mitchell's most tuneful material since *Court and Spark.*

The albums Mitchell has recorded since returning to Reprise in 1994 reveal the extremes of a deeply reflective artist preoccupied with the passage of time and life's ups and downs: *Turbulent Indigo* sets dark themes drawn from an ever more troubling world in understated acoustic settings, while the jazz-inflected *Taming the Tiger* finds her counting her blessings after beginning a relationship with her long-lost daughter, whom she'd given up for adoption in 1965, and grandson. Mitchell's mature voice, darkened to an elegiac timbre through decades of smoking, brings added poignancy to the standards she personalizes on *Both Sides Now* and the original material she revisits with the support of a 70-piece orchestra on the two-CD *Travelogue.* Strangely, Mitchell has yet to receive the career-spanning box-set treatment—the single-disc collections *Hits and Misses* don't begin to cover her expansive oeuvre—but it's only a matter of time before justice is served. She is, after all, the preeminent female singer/songwriter; no one else comes close. —M.C./B.SC.

Mobb Deep

★★	Juvenile Hell (4th & Broadway, 1993)
★★★★★	The Infamous (Loud, 1995)
★★★★	Hell On Earth (Loud, 1996)
★★★	Murda Muzik (Loud, 1999)
★★	Infamy (Sony, 2001)
★★★	Murda Mixtape (Landspeed, 2003)

Prodigy

★★★★	H.N.I.C. (Loud, 2000)

Born out of the infamous Queensbridge projects in New York, Mobb Deep made their debut as something of a novelty act. On *Juvenile Hell* the duo of Prodigy and Havoc come off as Kris Kross' twisted evil twins; postpubescent teenagers talking gunplay. Their debut is memorable only for the DJ Premier–produced, "Cop Hell." With this inauspicious entry into the rap world, it seemed like the Mobb might fade into obscurity.

Instead, they made one of the great rap albums of the '90s. *The Infamous* sounds like a rainy project courtyard at night; tense, morbid, and wary. Havoc's production (noisy drum samples with eerie piano and string loops) set a dark scene, and Prodigy's threats and tales of betrayal, fear, susbtance abuse, and violence colored it all in. The album has practically no filler, but highlights include the anthem "Shook Ones, Pt. 2," "Survival of the Fittest," and "Eye for an Eye," which features the Mobb's Queensbridge neighbor Nas in one of his greatest post-*Illmatic* verses.

Hell on Earth had the unenviable task of following a classic, but it was almost up to the task. If *Infamous* was a chilling documentary, *Hell on Earth* is a crime saga of mythical proportions. The stickup kids of the last album become hitmen and corner drug pushers become crime kingpins. "Drop a Gem on 'Em" and

"Nighttime Vultures," among other tracks, feature Prodigy's increasingly blunt delivery and Havoc's sparse, gothic production at levels they would never again reach. With its deluded dreams of Mafia invincibility, *Murda Muzik* is only decent. It was the source of the East Coast rap radio hit "Quiet Storm," but all in all, it's a case of going back to the well one too many times.

Prodigy experienced something of a rebirth on his solo album, *H.N.I.C.* While he doesn't stray from his kitchen, content-wise, he sounds reinvigorated by carrying an album on his own, with the single "Keep It Thoro" standing as one of his great vocal performances.

By the time the group reunited on *Infamy,* Prodigy had lost his lust for the trife life. He sounds exhausted with the gunplay, and Havoc seems stuck in a production rut. The only memorable track is the single "Burn." Stuck in label limbo, the group released a semiofficial mix tape–style CD called *Free Agents,* which harkened back to their more passionate youth but sounded sketchy and unfinished.   —C.R.

Moby

★★★	Moby (Instinct, 1992)
★★★½	Ambient (Instinct, 1993)
★★★	Early Underground (Instinct, 1993)
★★★★	Everything Is Wrong (Mute, 1995)
★★★	Rare: The Collected B-Sides (Instinct, 1996)
★★	Animal Rights (Elektra, 1997)
★★½	I Like to Score (Elektra, 1997)
★★★★	Play (V2, 1999)
★★★★	18 (V2, 2002)
★★★	18 B Sides (V2, 2003)

It's difficult to assess Moby's influential and wide-ranging musical career solely in terms of his full-length albums. Even before the release of *Moby* in 1992, the activist/vegan/environmentalist (and devout Christian) recorded rave-ready dance singles on his label, Instinct, and became a maverick dance-world superstar in the process. *Moby* compiles his club hits "Go," "Drop a Beat," and "Next Is the E" with a versatile array of tracks that ripened so-called electronica into a complex, emotional pop form. Moby cast his net wider than most programmers, even at this early stage harnessing vocal descants from soul and blues (on "Everything") and looking to the exotic soundscapes of vintage spy films for waves of sound that run like cold water over hot, hiccupping beats (on "Electricity"). A four-note orchestral base fuels heavy action on "Help Me to Believe," and "Have You Seen My Baby?" is as menacing as anything recorded by techno bad boy Aphex Twin. The surprise pop hit

"Go" is an interesting—if not entirely convincing—marriage of Angelo Badalamenti's *Twin Peaks* theme with a brushy, fast break beat and desultory piano.

Ambient's opener, "My Beautiful Blue Sky," sounds like everything good and kind in ambient music—the bubbling African beat; the insistent piano's, clean, intimate tinkle; the serene strings. Too intelligent for sonic wallpaper, Moby's ambient work suffers when heard en masse; each piece has a singular mood whose delicate balance is destroyed when jammed onto a disc with 11 other songs. But Moby proves himself a master of atmospheric effect, whether it's a blissful shimmer on "Heaven," the mournful dialogue between piano and strings on "J Breas," or the isolated wanderings of the keyboard drifting over come-and-play drumbeats on "House of Blue Leaves." The stalking "Bad Days" is like hearing the sounds of a dark carnival from far away—unpleasantly friendly, subconsciously discomfiting—while "Dog" refuses to bloom into a full-fledged dance party.

Rare: The Collected B-Sides includes energetic remixes of singles released on 1993's *Early Underground* on one disc and the collected mixes of "Go" on another. "Voodoo Child (Poor in NY Mix)," "Drug Fits the Face (Drug Free Mix)," and "Drop a Beat (Deep Mix)" are amped up, sped up, and given a more forceful rhythmic line. "Next Is the E" from *Moby* is cartoonishly filled out in the "Club Mix," and for curiosity seekers, there's a nonimport recording of the notorious "Thousand." Reportedly the fastest song ever recorded, "Thousand" revs from the standard disco 128 BPM to an astounding 1,000 BPM then drops the beat out entirely while the confused and exhausted dancers (presumably) regroup. The "Go" remixes aren't markedly better than the overrated original.

Everything Is Wrong—Moby's first album targeted at mass audiences—goes from the heart-stoppingly beautiful "Hymn" and the shivery endless energy of "Feeling So Real" to the punk-rock exclamation of "All That I Need Is to Be Loved" and the sweaty chain-gang thwock of the 37-second-long "Let's Go Free." *Everything Is Wrong* is impossibly busy, its beats ticking at unearthly rates, but the arrangements are coolheaded. Early signs of *Play* appear in the forceful blues-sung intro to "What Love," which dissolves into early signs of Moby's subsequent thrash-rock experiments on *Animal Rights.* But elsewhere, the human touches put flesh on the industrial bones of the chill tracks—vocalist Mimi Goese (of the Los Angeles band Hugo Largo) lends her ethereal tone to "Into the Blue" and "When It's Cold I'd Like to Die."

Moby's ability to write an affecting hook, demonstrated on *Everything Is Wrong,* led him to the delusion that he could be as accomplished a rocker as he is a programmer. Audiences put off by Moby's preachy liner notes were not reassured by *Animal Rights:* Once again, he writes rabble-rousing yet fundamentally sensible essays in praise of Christian goodness and basic human rights, but the album's glowering, amateurish thrash will not help make the world a lovelier place. Moby's voice has no elasticity or timbre. His arrangements are weak—the drums, bass, and guitars tick along with all the repetitiveness of the kind of techno he spent his life trying to overhaul. The good stuff, not surprisingly, is on the swooningly emotional instrumentals "Now I Let It Go" and the gently pushing "Soft." But Moby scored a hit with a cover of Mission of Burma's "That's When I Reach for My Revolver."

I Like to Score compiles his soundtrack contributions. It cheats only a little with the inclusion of British Top 10 hit "Go," which is based on a soundtrack recording but wasn't used as one; the wah-wah-heavy title song, ready for any neoblaxploitation film; and an "inspired by" but uninteresting rev-up of the James Bond theme.

Play is a richly conceived and executed full-length recording that could almost be called a concept album. It's about the construction of rock and the flexible quality of great music; *Play* pulls the thread of musical development back to its source and closes the circle—blues to rock, to pop, to techno, then back to blues; voice to acoustic instruments, to electric instruments, to electronic ones, to voice again. "Honey" layers a dance beat over Bessie Smith's rotund blues. A sizable sample from "Trouble So Hard" is prominently featured on "Natural Blues" (it's more of a remix). "Why Does My Heart Feel So Bad?" uses the Shining Light Gospel Choir as a parable of revelation: Over sweet strings and a yearning piano grounded with bass chords, human voices strive to reach God. Halfway through, Moby begins to shroud the vocals in a sheer curtain of sound, burying them in the mix, then pulls back the curtain to reveal the song's crystalline components. Moby also returns to the mike: On "Porcelain," his weak voice sounds intimate and vulnerable, an extension of the strings that almost mask his lines. The hit single "South Side" breaks from half-spoken verses into a gorgeous, indelible chorus, and "Run On" gives him a hands-shaking gospel loop to mumble along with.

18 synthesizes the Moby repertoire into virtual pop songs with no loss of programming intelligence. As he allowed for more ambiguity in his beliefs (a process delineated in the liner notes), so does his music make room for verse-chorus-verse structures and lyrics that function as story as well as sound. The mood

is warm and mellow, the elegiac piano chords are front and center (particularly on the soulful "One of These Mornings," which also features a gospel-organ cameo), and the vocalists are moving in the extreme. Moby sings "We Are All Made of Stars" and "Extreme Ways," but it's the burnished tones of great female vocalist—Dianne McCaulley, Jennifer Price, an uncredited voice on "Another Woman"—that form the heart of this recording. He still digs the rhythmic joys of hip-hop, which get playful treatment on the funky "Jam for the Ladies." The beautiful "Sunday (The Day Before My Birthday)" is full of fleeting hope, the vocals cheery but wistful, with a piano descant signaling the end of something. Moby's birthday is September 11. —A.B.

Moby Grape

★★★★½   Moby Grape (Columbia, 1967; San Francisco Sound, 1994)

★★½   Wow/Grape Jam (Columbia, 1968; San Francisco Sound, 1992)

★★   Moby Grape (San Francisco Sound, 1984)

★★★   Legendary Grape (Dig Music, 2003)

Moby Grape was a beautiful mess: five seemingly mismatched talents that collided in San Francisco a year before the Summer of Love, managing during their brief existence to embody the antithesis of the prevailing peace-and-love vibe with flash-and-burn brilliance. The Grape's debut album presented a band with breathtaking firepower, as former Jefferson Airplane drummer Skip Spence, Peter Lewis (the son of actress Loretta Young), and Jerry Miller interlocked their individualistic guitar styles to form a jaw-dropping fireworks show, while bassist Bob Mosley and drummer Don Stevenson joined their three bandmates in intricate five-part harmonies. *Moby Grape* was a runaway freight train, with the band blazing through 14 tracks in 32 minutes, shifting from scorching rockers like "Omaha" and "Fall on You" to drop-dead gorgeous ballads like "Sitting by the Window" and "8:05."

After this tour de force, the Grape had nowhere to go but down, and that's exactly where they headed. The followup studio album *Wow* was sabotaged by mediocre material and out-of-sync performances; worse yet, it is now packaged with *Grape Jam*, comprising four of the most aimless extended noodling sessions imaginable. The out-of-print *Moby Grape '69* was a near return to form (although hardly anybody noticed), paced by "It's a Beautiful Day Today," perhaps the Grape's prettiest song. By then, the Grape was collapsing under its own weight; the year before, Spence had wound up in Bellevue suffering from acid-induced psychosis (but still managing to record the solo psycho–cult classic *Oar,* despite—or because of—his condition), while Mosley joined the Marine Corps after completing work on *'69.* The less said about *Truly Fine Citizen*—quickly recorded by the three remaining members later in '69—the better. The '71 reunion album *20 Granite Creek* seemed to promise that the band was ready to get back to business, until a disastrous set at the Fillmore East during which Mosley snapped his fingers rather than playing bass and Spence stared into space, arms akimbo, causing the others to leave the stage, one by one, mortified and disgusted.

But that wasn't the end of Moby Grape, as the original members reconvened from time to time, sometimes even with Spence (whose condition continued to deteriorate; he died in 1999). It's hard to recommend the 1984 album that's also titled *Moby Grape;* yes, it's the original band, but some of the cuts are downright embarrassing—especially "Better Day," which would fit perfectly on the soundtrack to *A Mighty Wind,* and "Hard Road to Follow," which sounds like civic light opera. Spence was too far gone to participate on *Legendary Grape* (although his name is listed on the cover), but the band sounds far more energized on this 1990 studio set, which is worth a pop for hard-core Grape-o-philes.

Columbia/Legacy's definitive two-CD anthology, *Vintage Grape* (1993), was pulled from release as the band members and ex-manager Matthew Katz, who owns the masters and band name, engaged in an ongoing legal battle (the set is available as a Sony import). The first two albums are only available on Katz's San Francisco Sound label (on which he credits himself, and not David Rubinson, as producer), putting Grape fans in something of an ethical bind. One way around it is to spring for the *Vintage* import, which has the entire first album in order, plus the best cuts from *Wow* and *Moby Grape '69.* —B.SC.

Modest Mouse

- ★★★½ This Is a Long Drive for Someone With Nothing to Think About (Up, 1996)
- ★★★★ The Lonesome, Crowded West (Up, 1997)
- ★★★½ Building Nothing out of Something (Up, 2000)
- ★★★½ The Moon & Antarctica (Sony, 2000)
- ★★★ Sad Sappy Sucker (K, 2001)
- ★★★★ Good News for People Who Like Bad News (Epic, 2004)

Isaac Brock's impertinent squawk is the cry of an outsider who, as the title of this Issaquah, Washington, indie-rock band's best album suggests, is at his loneli-

est in a crowd. From the first meandering arpeggio of the band's debut album, Modest Mouse sounds unmistakable—Brock's double-tracked guitars and Eric Judy's loose-lined bass forge seemingly accidental harmonies from their independent chatter until Jeremiah Green's drums insistently pound these goings-on into a constancy that resembles riffs. The only thing that could improve *The Lonesome, Crowded West* would be if the wired, dejected "Doin' the Cockroach" really was their emo-dance-craze answer to the Macarena. On *The Moon & Antarctica* (cold and desolate, get it?), Brock drops cosmic burnout science, such as "The universe is shaped exactly like the earth/If you go straight long enough you'll end up where you were," like that's enough reason to postpone the voyage and fire up the bong, while the band gestures occasionally toward prog-leaning atmospherics. A pack rat till the end, Modest Mouse has accumulated two collections of rarities and B sides: The snippets on *Sucker* are abbreviated and petulant; the ruminations on *Building Nothing* are sprawling and uncertain; and both are of a piece—as if the most perverse act these devout pessimists could envision in the face of the void was to make even their trash consistent in quality.

Good News for People Who Like Bad News was an improbable chart success that showed Modest Mouse could polish their delivery without changing their outlook one bit. The textures are brighter and the instrumentation more diverse on an impressive series of outcast anthems, from the unironically bouncy single "Float On," to the Tom Waits-y rural-blues squall of "This Devil's Work Day," to typically verbose and cutting rants like "Black Cadillacs" and "Bury Me With It." It's not the Modest Mouse older fans had come to love, but it proved that Brock was still a talented sad sack set against a current of booze, laughing at the world with a butter knife always to his throat. —K.H.

Mogwai

- ★★★½ Ten Rapid (Jetset, 1997)
- ★★★½ Young Team (Jetset, 1997)
- ★★½ Kicking a Dead Pig (Jetset, 1998)
- ★★½ Come On Die Young (Matador, 1999)
- ★★★★ EP+2 (Matador, 1999)
- ★★★★ Rock Action (Matador, 2001)
- ★★★★ Happy Music for Happy People (Matador, 2003)

The fire-breathing Scottish space-rockers in Mogwai build spectral mood music out of noise guitar, doing structurally basic quiet/loud/quiet instrumentals that are nonetheless charged with feeling and beauty even at earsplitting volume. They level their audiences in concert, but they make it work on record, too, scattering their work across EPs and singles and, in the case of *Kicking a Dead Pig,* even a remix album. The tracks collected on *EP+2* are positively beautiful, taking off from *Sister*-era Sonic Youth to build long wordless passages of probing guitar fuzz, ebbing and flowing with flourishes of piano, voice-over static, occasional buried voices, room tone, and even a brass band in "Burn Girl Prom Queen." "Rage: Man," "Rollerball," and "Small Children in the Background" build to amazingly dense and lyrical climaxes. *Rock Action* is even better, stretching out with keyboards and even occasional vocal melodies for their most diverse and expansive record, even if the sound was a bit too bright to please some fans. "2 Rights Make 1 Wrong" is Mogwai's finest moment, building a hypnotic groove as banjos, horns, and synthesizers flow together in and out of the guitars for nine unbelievably gorgeous minutes. Mogwai released a single later in 2001, featuring the studio version of a longtime live staple—a killer noise-drenched 20-minute version of the old Jewish devotional song "My Father My King." —R.S.

The Moldy Peaches

★★★★ The Moldy Peaches (Rough Trade, 2001)
★★★ Unreleased Cutz and Live Jamz 1994–2002 (Rough Trade, 2003)

Kimya Dawson

★★★½ I'm Sorry That Sometimes I'm Mean (Rough Trade, 2002)
★★★½ My Cute Fiend Sweet Princess (Important, 2004)
★★★ Knock-Knock Who? (Important, 2004)

Adam Green

★★½ Garfield (Sanctuary, 2002)
★★★ Friends of Mine (Sanctuary, 2003)

The Moldy Peaches were two cracked, charming suburban outcasts who wrote wickedly catchy folk-punk songs that bridged the gap between dadaism and pornography. Their debut caused a minor stir in indie circles, and occasioned the rather amazing sight of a room full of young devotees gleefully yelling out "Who's got the crack?!" The Peaches came together when Kimya Dawson dropped out of college and ran into fellow New Yorker Adam Green; they began writing songs in which they alternated lines that seemed designed mostly to crack each other up. On *Moldy Peaches* winners such as "Who's Got the Crack?" and "Steak for Chicken" they alternate lines like "I like it when my hair is poofy/I like it when you slip me a roofie" and "Who mistook this steak for chicken?/Who'm I gonna stick my dick in?" (with

Dawson taking the latter line at one point). But the album also showed that Dawson and Green—who usually performed in bunny rabbit and Peter Pan costumes—were auteurs full of childlike innocence (dig the sweet, tender "Jorge Regula") and a gift for making oddball juvenalia and superb melodies stick.

After a final show on Halloween of 2002, the pair released the odds-and-ends collection *Unreleased Cutz and Live Jamz 1994–2002* as well as some solo records, several of which had been recorded while the Peaches were still together. Dawson's three albums sound like the work of a bizarro Bob Dylan, offering funny, heartfelt lyrics about pirates, an evil social worker, and how Kenny G wanted to hump one of her friends. *I'm Sorry That Sometimes I'm Mean* features the strongest songs (including "Talking Ernest" and "Trump Style"), but because all three albums feature a similar mix of folkie strumming, toy keyboards, funny sound effects, and Dawson's cute, naked rasp, any one'll do nicely.

Green was always the more smut-minded half of the Peaches, and a heavy reliance on shocking lyrics hurt his relatively polished solo debut, which didn't have enough charm or good tunes to compensate for throwaways like "Baby's Gonna Die Tonight" and "Mozzarella Swastikas." The stronger *Friends of Mine* shows off his promise as a songwriter: The tuneful, well-kempt songs bubble over with swooning string arrangements, pretty melodies, and Green's surprisingly polished crooning. But the real coup is "Jessica," a sweetly comic ode to Jessica Simpson in which Green proves he can be an irreverent weirdo and a sentimental sap at the same time. —C.H.

Momus

★★★★ 20 Vodka Jellies (Cherry Red, 1996)
★★★½ Ping Pong (Le Grand Magistery, 1997)
★★½ The Little Red Songbook (Le Grand Magistery, 1998)
★★ Stars Forever (Le Grand Magistery, 1999)
★½ Folktronic (Le Grand Magistery, 2000)
★★½ Oskar Tennis Champion (American Patchwork, 2003)

Nick Currie, the itinerant Scotsman who calls himself Momus, had already been making odd, wildly smart, dirty-minded records for more than 10 years when his first American album appeared. Originally a Jacques Brel–inspired singer/songwriter (seek out the remarkable *Tender Pervert,* from 1988), he scored hits in Japan with the hyperactive, hyperintellectual songs he wrote for pop idol Kahimi Karie; besides his own work, he's subsequently written for artists including Laila France (the hilariously sex-obsessed album *Orgonon*) and Milky (a.k.a. his ex-wife, Shazna Nessa).

20 Vodka Jellies is a hodgepodge of outtakes, demos (including his own version of Karie's Japanese megahit "Good Morning World"), and stylistic experiments. For all that, it flows deliciously. Momus' jaunt through personae, musical modes, and egghead name-dropping (this may be the first pop album to mention Polish novelist Witold Gombrowicz) just reinforces his pose as a wise, funny old exile, and his melodies have never been as splendid as they are here.

The jokes on *Ping Pong* are somewhat broader—song titles include "Tamagotchi Press Officer" and "Space Jews." Still, "I Want You, but I Don't Need You" is the ultimate statement of mock-chanson cocksmanship, "Lolitapop Dollhouse" (written for Karie) lives up to its title, and Momus isn't yet *quite* too full of himself to be charming.

The Little Red Songbook, an exploration of "analog baroque" (read: lots of fake harpsichord), belabors its wit severely—the disc's most-quoted line is "What is the cultural meaning/Of coming in a girl's mouth?"—and its music is almost entirely incidental. A harmless tune about Walter/Wendy Carlos on the original printing of *Songbook* sparked legal trouble from its subject; to raise money for legal fees, 30 people and organizations each paid $1,000 to be the subject of an original Momus song on the two-CD set *Stars Forever*. It's a cute idea, but the songs are mostly forgettable.

By *Folktronic*, Currie had moved on to another, even weaker conceit: the intersection of cheap technology and folk tradition, which results in dopey jingles about "Finnegan, the folk hero of HTML" and an "electronic mountain girl." Debunking the myths of authenticity is a nice idea, but he doesn't have much with which to replace them.

Oskar Tennis Champion's songs also lean too hard on jokey concepts—the titles of "Is It Because I'm a Pirate?" and "My Sperm Is Not Your Enemy" tell the whole story—but Momus' tunes are back on the upswing, and the ring-tone medley that closes the disc is a nice touch. And the title track is his strongest in years, an elegant little piece of postmodern whimsy. —D.W.

Money Mark

    ★★   Mark's Keyboard Repair (MoWax/FFRR, 1995)
   ★★★   Push the Button (MoWax/London, 1998)
   ★★★   Change Is Coming (Emperor Norton, 2001)

As the story goes, keyboardist Mark Ramos-Nishita (a.k.a. Money Mark) was discovered by the Beastie Boys when he came by their L.A. house/studio to do some carpentry work. Whatever the case, his influence on the Beastie Boys' music during their *Check Your Head* period is undeniable.

Listening to his playful lo-fi debut, *Mark's Keyboard Repair,* is like stumbling on a demo cassette; it's full of rough song ideas and seemingly unfinished tunes (of which there are 30 here). But on *Push the Button,* Mark really finds his groove. Not only does he sing on much of the album, but the songs teem with fun, poppy charm, great melodies, and the Latin-rock vibe of early War and Santana. Legendary session drummer Jim Keltner holds it down on a couple of tracks, including the lovely "I Don't Play Piano." Fans of the Beastie Boys collection *The In Sound From Way Out* (on which Ramos-Nishita shares writing credit on all 13 tracks) will certainly dig *Change Is Coming,* a cool 38 minutes of keyboard-driven instrumentals flavored with funk and bossa nova. Nishita cleary enjoys any opportunity to play around with his collection of vintage keyboards and other curious gear—an activity that's manifest on his three albums —D.S.

Monica

   ★★½   Miss Thang (Rowdy, 1995)
   ★★★   The Boy Is Mine (Arista, 1998)
   ★★½   After the Storm (J Records, 2003)

Monica Arnold was 14 years old and a protégée of producer Dallas Austin when she released her debut in 1995. An assured, streetwise amalgam of soul, pop, hip-hop, and blues, *Miss Thang* established Monica, with her gospel-choir voice and attitude to spare, as the antidote to emerging good-girl teen stars like Brandy. The hit single "Don't Take It Personal" and "Let's Straighten It Out," a duet with Usher, demonstrate Monica's considerable gift for vinegary, uptempo R&B, though the record's many soppy MOR ballads ("Before You Walk out of My Life") don't play to her strengths.

Monica's debut was a modest success, but it wasn't until the release of "The Boy Is Mine"—her musical cage match with Brandy—that she became a star in her own right. Coproduced by Clive Davis, *The Boy Is Mine* contains, among other things, dance pop, groove-happy R&B ("Cross the Room"), orchestral flourishes, a convincing collaboration with OutKast ("Gone Be Fine"), and a cover of Richard Marx's "Right Here Waiting," a song beyond even Monica's redemptive powers.

Although wildly uneven, *Boy* was good enough to suggest that Monica was on her way to the sort of success enjoyed by Aaliyah or Toni Braxton, but the long gap between records didn't bode well. Coproduced by Missy Elliott, Monica's eventual followup, 2003's *After the Storm*, was originally released in a much-altered form as the 2002 import *All Eyez on Me*. Although the disc made reference to Monica's almost Dickensian troubles—one boyfriend in prison, another a suicide, and that's not the half of it— *After the Storm* was a disappointingly tepid mix of slushy ballads and preachy, believe-in-yourself R&B tracks that didn't live up to the promise of its predecessors. —A.S.

The Monkees

★★	The Monkees (1966; Rhino, 1994)
★★	More of the Monkees (1967; Rhino, 1994)
★½	Headquarters (1967; Rhino, 1995)
★½	Pisces, Aquarius, Capricorn & Jones Ltd. (1967; Rhino, 1995)
★½	The Birds, the Bees and the Monkees (1968; Rhino, 1994)
★½	Head (1968; Rhino, 1994)
★½	The Monkees Present (1969; Rhino, 1994)
★½	Instant Replay (1969; Rhino, 1995)
★½	Changes (1970; Rhino, 1994)
★★★½	Greatest Hits (Arista, 1969)
★★★	More Greatest Hits (Arista, 1982; Rhino, 2000)
★★★½	Forty Timeless Hits (EMI, 1980)
★★★½	Missing Links (Rhino, 1987)
★★★	Live, 1967 (Rhino, 1987)
★	Pool It! (Rhino, 1987)
★★½	Missing Links, Vol. 2 (Rhino, 1990)
★★★	Anthology (Rhino, 1998)
★★	Missing Links, Vol. 3 (Rhino, 2000)
★★★	Music Box (Rhino, 2001)

With any number of punkish bar bands semi-ironically recycling "Steppin' Stone" in the late '70s, and a partially reunited Monkees touring and recording in the '80s, there's been a revisionist twist upward in appraisals of this band's slight canon. Cynically manufactured by Don Kirshner and a crew of TV producers looking to dilute *A Hard Day's Night* for the boob tube, Davy Jones, Michael Nesmith, Mickey Dolenz, and Peter Tork were the fill-in fab four who lip synched their way through a few seasons of sitcoms and most of their albums (on later product, they did play on some songs). Tommy Boyce and Bobby Hart, Neil Diamond, and Nesmith wrote the Monkees' 1966–68 hits: "Last Train to Clarksville," "Daydream Believer," "I'm a Believer," and "Pleasant Valley Sunday." Clever and tuneful, along the lines of knockoff Turtles, this was teenybop fare that provoked shudders from anyone who took the Beatles at all seriously. Those teenyboppers grew up and, in a frenzy of nostalgia,

reclaimed their idols. The first greatest-hits package is pleasant—and more than enough Monkees for everyone except cultists. *Pool It!* (1987), the reunion album, is glossy, tired, and redundant. The two-CD *Anthology* and certainly the elaborate box set *Music Box* take the bunch far too seriously. —P.E.

The Monks

★★★½	Black Monk Time (1966; Infinite Zero/American, 1997)
★★★	Five Upstart Americans (Omplatten, 1999)

The Five Torquays were just another garage band of American G.I.s in Germany in 1964. Then they shaved their heads and dressed in black; started calling themselves the Monks; and wrote a bunch of single-minded, bilious one-and-a-half-chord rockers like "I Hate You" and "Shut Up," built around electric banjo and organ. (They claim to have invented feedback by accident, though that's, er, open to debate.) Their sole album, *Black Monk Time*, became a cult favorite, and was finally reissued in the mid-'90s. *Five Upstart Americans* collects even cruder demos and an early single. —D.W.

Bill Monroe

★★★★	Bill Monroe & Doc Watson: Live Duet Recordings, 1963–1980 (1963; Smithsonian Folkways, 1993)
★★★	16 All-Time Greatest Hits (1970; Columbia, 2002)
★★★★	Bean Blossom (MCA, 1973)
★★★	Columbia Historic Edition (Columbia, 1987)
★★★	Bluegrass '87 (MCA, 1987)
★★★★	Live at the Opry—Celebrating 50 Years on the Grand Ole Opry (MCA, 1989)
★★★	Cryin' Holy Unto the Lord (MCA, 1991)
★★★½	The Essential Bill Monroe (1945–1949) (Columbia/Legacy, 1992)
★★★★	Live Recordings 1956–1959 (Smithsonian/Folkways, 1993)
★★★★★	The Music of Bill Monroe (MCA, 1994)
★★★½	Blue Moon of Kentucky (1993; Sony Special Products, 1995)
★★★★	16 Gems (Columbia/Legacy, 1996)
★★★½	The Essential Bill Monroe & the Monroe Brothers (RCA, 1997)
★★★½	The Early Years (Vanguard, 1998)
★★★	The Millennium Collection (MCA, 1999)
★★★★½	The Father of Bluegrass: Early Years 1940–1947 (ASV Living Era, 1999)
★★★★½	Monroe Brothers, Vol. 1: What Would You Give in Exchange for Your Soul? (Rounder Select, 2000)

★★★★½ The Monroe Brothers, Vol. 2: Just a Song of
Old Kentucky (Rounder Select, 2001)
★★★★ RCA Country Legends: Bill Monroe (RCA,
2002)
★★★½ The Very Best of Bill Monroe and His
Bluegrass Boys (MCA, 2002)
★★★★ Anthology (MCA, 2003)

As the first generation of rock & roll artists are revered, so do they, almost without exception, revere Bill Monroe, who in their eyes is one of the most important figures influencing the big beat music that emerged in the '50s. True enough. As Elvis Presley halted a slow version of Monroe's "Blue Moon of Kentucky" in mid-lyric with the words, "That don't move me. Now let's get real gone!," Bill Monroe had much the same thought when he stepped up to the microphone in 1940 to record a bright cover version of Jimmie Rodgers' "Mule Skinner Blues."

Growing up in Kentucky, Monroe had become conversant with blues, traditional country, folk songs, and church hymns. His instrument was the mandolin, primarily because his brothers Birch and Charlie were already the family's fiddler and guitarist, respectively. The brothers began playing together on radio shows, building a loyal following and generating offers from other sponsors. After Birch left the band in 1934, Bill and Charlie continued on as a duo, expanding their repertoire and forging a distinctive style from the disparate musics they favored. In 1936 the Monroe Brothers made their first recordings for the Bluebird label and were soon the most popular brother team in the South. Personal differences over matters relating both to business and music split the brothers in 1938, with each forming separate bands. Bill's Bluegrass Boys won an audition for the Grand Ole Opry in 1939, which led to national exposure via WSM radio and ensuing recording contracts with RCA Victor and Columbia.

Working from a traditional foundation, Bill gradually shaped a unique music keyed by his breakneck mandolin runs and a high, lonesome, pinched voice that packed an emotional wallop. A devotee of discipline and style, Monroe made certain that his bands were well rehearsed and well dressed. He prides himself on having the first band to wear white shirts and ties at the Grand Ole Opry almost as much as he does their being the group to break out of the C, D, and G keys that were most common to Opry groups, thus encouraging spontaneity among the instrumentalists and freeing them for a greater range of expressiveness. Central to all of this was Monroe's own sense of where to take his new music. Rather than adhere to accepted notions of tempo and tuning, he blasted away the barriers, bringing what he called "driving time" and the unusual ambience of open tunings to the songs in his repertoire. And yet his music was traditional in feel and in its concern with family, love, hard times, impending doom, and fear of God. Through the years Monroe has hewed steadily to what worked so successfully for him in the '40s; the most dramatic change was probably the addition of a banjo player to the fiddle-mandolin-guitar-bass lineup. On the personnel side, apart from Monroe himself, the players most responsible for bringing a sharp focus to the bluegrass style were guitarist Lester Flatt and banjo player Earl Scruggs, who joined the Bluegrass Boys in 1945. Flatt and Scruggs were both forward-thinking instrumentalists, and their ideas freed Monroe to add more new touches to his sound.

For an introduction to Monroe, the best place to start is with the Legacy overview, *16 Gems*, which includes the original versions of classics such as "Kentucky Waltz," "Summertime Is Past and Gone," and "Travelin' That Lonesome Road." Although the double-CD, 40-track box *The Essential Bill Monroe 1945–49* would seem to be the set to own—cuts include the original version of "Blue Moon of Kentucky" (which would inspire a young Elvis Presley's barnburning interpretation on his first Sun single, in 1954), "Kentucky Waltz," "Footprints in the Snow," "Rocky Road Blues," and several other monuments; however, 16 of the 40 tracks are not original versions but rather alternate takes. The 16 original versions compose the aforementioned *16 Gems. Columbia Historic Edition* pares the Monroe years down to 10 cuts from the early '40s, which means no "Blue Moon of Kentucky" here, but rather "Kentucky Waltz," Jimmie Rodgers' "California Blues (Blue Yodel #4)," "Bluegrass Special" and other scintillating tracks on a too-skimpy package. A solid overview is to be found on Vanguard's *The Early Years*, comprising 14 tracks spanning 1945 to 1949.

One of the most exhilarating documents from the '50s is Smithsonian/Folkways' *Live Recordings 1956–1959*, which offers 27 tracks of vintage performances recorded not only onstage, but also at workshops and jam sessions—hence the loose, downhome feeling to the whole affair. Another amiable live set, *Live Duet Recordings 1963–1980*, finds Monroe sitting in with gentleman picker Doc Watson; the two men range wide stylistically, but complement each other's artistry and generally have a fine time playing music near and dear to their hearts.

Monroe recorded steadily from 1950 to 1981 for Decca/MCA, and the peaks far overshadowed the valleys. As an overview of these years, *The Very Best of Bill Monroe and His Bluegrass Boys* is a good single-disc compilation containing vivid reworkings of Monroe monuments such as "Uncle Pen," "Footprints in the Snow," and "Blue Moon of Kentucky"; a fervent take on Hank Williams' "I Saw the Light"; and a rousing interpretation of the gospel standard "Working on a Building." A deeper consideration of the same period is available via *Anthology,* a 50-track, four-star meal of solid Monroe artistry ranging from 1950's "New Mule Skinner Blues" to 1981's touching "My Last Days on Earth," all more than worth the price of admission as a perspective on the Decca/MCA years. Finally, the whole enchilada is available in the four-CD, 98-track *The Music of Bill Monroe.* No more thorough overview of Monroe's career is available; the set contains seven decades of recordings made for RCA, Columbia, and Decca/MCA. Pretty simple: This is the master at work, over time. The result of listening to these discs chronologically is to be amazed by the consistency of his music and by his unflagging commitment to bridging technique and heart, regardless of his lineup.   —D.M.

Monster Magnet

★★★	Spine of God (Caroline, 1992)
★★	25 . . . Tab (Caroline, 1993)
★★★	Superjudge (A&M, 1993)
★★★	Dopes to Infinity (A&M, 1995)
★★★½	Powertrip (A&M, 1998)
★★★★	God Says No (A&M, 2001)
★★★½	Monolithic Baby! (SPY, 2004)

Not since Blue Öyster Cult's heyday has heavy rock seen a combination of brains, brawn, and humor quite like that orchestrated by Monster Magnet's Dave Wyndorf. In a style of music that indulges sex- and drug-fueled power fantasies, Wyndorf brings an ability to laugh at himself while still whipping the music into a rabid-dog froth. He creates the soundtrack for a world in which comic-book antiheroes, Hell's Angels, and dominatrixes party in shag-carpeted boogie vans that stink of stale bong water.

Each of Monster Magnet's albums wallows in excess; after a couple of cassette-only releases, *Spine of God* betrays a heavy debt to Hawkwind's sludge-encrusted psychedelia, while *25 . . . Tab* goes off the deep end of acid-drone. *Superjudge* finds the band trying to rein in its indulgences and softening slightly as a result, but *Dopes to Infinity* injects garage rock and welcome doses of self-deprecating humor ("Ego, the Living Planet").

Powertrip is the most concise and physical Monster Magnet album yet; the dawn-of-metal riffs and stadium-worthy choruses are balanced by wicked satire and flashbacks to the sound of Detroit circa early Alice Cooper and MC5. *God Says No* has the

bombast and testosterone of a codpiece-and-leather-pants ensemble. But Wyndorf's leer always comes with a wink; when he promises, "You'll swim in the sweat of a million orgies," he trumps Kid Rock at his game. *God Says No* is about overkill; the false ending of "Melt" lingers for five interminable seconds before revving back into a torrid guitar solo. In contrast to the relatively concise muscle car that Wyndorf fashioned on *Powertrip, God Says No* luxuriates in a decadent psych-rock whirlpool, improbably bridging the chasm between the Music Machine and Nine Inch Nails (NIN coproducer Alan Moulder was enlisted to mix). *Monolithic Baby!* finds them off a major label, but up to the usual high jinks   —G.K.

The Moody Blues

★★★½	The Magnificent Moodies (1966; London, 1988)
★★★	Days of Future Passed (Deram, 1967)
★½	In Search of the Lost Chord (Deram, 1968)
★½	On the Threshold of a Dream (Deram, 1969)
★½	To Our Children's Children's Children (Threshold/PolyGram, 1969)
★½	A Question of Balance (Threshold/PolyGram, 1970)
★	Every Good Boy Deserves Favour (Threshold/PolyGram, 1971)
★½	Seventh Sojourn (Threshold/PolyGram, 1972)
★★½	This Is the Moody Blues (1974; Threshold/PolyGram, 1989)
★★	In the Beginning (Deram, 1975)
★★	Caught Live +5 (London, 1977)
★★	Octave (London, 1978)
★★	Long Distance Voyager (Threshold/PolyGram, 1981)
★★	The Present (Threshold/PolyGram, 1983)
★★★	Voices in the Sky: The Best of the Moody Blues (Threshold/PolyGram, 1985)
★★	The Other Side of Life (Threshold/PolyGram, 1986)
★★½	Prelude (Threshold/PolyGram, 1987)
★★½	Sur la mer (Threshold/PolyGram, 1988)
★★★	Legend of a Band: Greatest Hits, 1967–1988 (PolyGram, 1989)
★★	Keys of the Kingdom (Polydor, 1991)
★★★	A Night at Red Rocks With the Colorado Symphony Orchestra (Polydor, 1993)
★★★	Time Traveller (Polydor/Threshold, 1994)
★★★	The Very Best of the Moody Blues (PolyGram Chronicles, 1997)
★★	Strange Times (Universal, 1999)

No major band has so relentlessly purveyed nonsense as have the Moodies; were it not for their titanic success, in fact, they might easily be dismissed as an odd and overlong joke. Since coming up with a name that offered sly tribute to the British beer M&B (in the hopes of a corporate sponsorship eons before that hideous practice became popular), the Moody Blues have been nothing if not commercial—but it's the artiness of their symphonic rock that's truly crass, their self-importance offensive. Gods of '70s FM radio, they invented a sort of easy-listening psychedelia that resolutely combined the worst of both worlds. Long past their heyday, they've continued to produce mild echoes of the stuff.

Ironically, the Moodies started out great. With Denny Laine on vocals, their first smash was the bold and lovely "Go Now," a ballad version of the British Invasion pop they were masters of, when not performing credible Sonny Boy Williamson numbers and R&B fare along the lines of a sweeter Spencer Davis Group. The reissue of *Magnificent Moodies* captures this fine early period well. Laine soon left, however, and pomposity entered. Justin Hayward and Ray Thomas joined founder Mike Pinder to form the Moodies' new core and to pursue a new direction—the fusing of rock and classical music. Recorded with the London Festival Orchestra, *Days of Future Passed* accomplished exactly that; with its theme of the passage of day into night echoing Vivaldi's *The Four Seasons,* the album produced the haunting "Nights in White Satin" and established the band as pioneers in a subgenre that Procol Harum and, later, ELO would develop much more winningly.

But the record also previewed a pretentiousness that soon became the Moodies' raison d'être. Appalling, often hilarious, poetic introductions to the songs were an innovation. Hippie profundities delivered in a voice-of-God manner, these musings introduced *In Search of the Lost Chord,* a bombastic meditation on Timothy Leary, astral planes and mantras; *Children's Children's Children* and *Threshold* were more of the same, their air of high seriousness underscored by the mellotron, a keyboard capable of producing orchestral sounds. By now, the Moodies had found a pattern they would seldom depart from— a long, portentous intro followed by a smooth, stirring ersatz rocker, and then roughly equal numbers of fast and slow songs trading in wide-eyed philosophizing.

"Question," "Story in Your Eyes" and "I'm Just a Singer" were huge hits, tricked out with furiously strummed acoustic guitars (ripped off from the Who) and played with absolute, unsmiling professionalism. With *Octave,* synthesizers became dominant, but the song remained basically the same. The '80s albums showed a slight but very welcome relaxing of the heavy lyrical content, allowing the band's one sure

strength, melody, to come through clearly. But what the Moody Blues gained in accessibility, they'd lost in distinction; they now just sounded trite.

In the next decade, the band capitalized on its longevity not only by releasing a clutch of greatest-hits packages (*Time Traveller* is the most extensive), but by becoming a fairly massive live act. The bombast is best captured with the Colorado Symphony Orchestra. Outdoors, in the cavernous Red Rocks amphitheater, the band's best songs sound like pop Wagner—which might have been their intention all along. —P.E.

The Moonglows

★★★★   Their Greatest Hits (Chess/MCA, 1997)
★★★½   The Millennium Collection (Chess/MCA, 2002)

One of the earliest and most influential group harmony ensembles, the Moonglows were formed in Louisville in 1951 by Harvey Fuqua, a talented songwriter and arranger who went on to play a key behind-the-scenes role as a producer, arranger, and writer in Motown's early history. Alan Freed discovered the Moonglows in Cleveland and helped them land a recording contract with Chess. One of Fuqua's songs, "Sincerely," cracked the Top 30 in 1955 and established the quintet. Personnel changes became a way of life with the Moonglows, with Fuqua remaining as the constant, and by 1958 the group was being billed as Harvey and the Moonglows. The year 1958 also saw the release of the song that immortalized the Moonglows, "Ten Commandments of Love," the group's last Top 30 hit. The '59 edition of the Moonglows featured the then-unknown Marvin Gaye. *Their Greatest Hits* documents the style that defined the mellow side of doo-wop; *The Millennium Collection* is a slightly abridged counterpart. —D.M.

M.O.P.

★★½   To The Death (Select, 1994)
★★★   Firing Squad (Relativity, 1996)
★★★   First Family 4 Life (Relativity, 1998)
★★★★   Warriorz (Relativity, 2000)
★★★★   10 Years and Gunnin' (Sony, 2003)

How about some hardcore? It's all you get from this punishing Brooklyn duo. Made up of Billy Danze and Lil' Fame, M.O.P. spent the better part of a decade refining their raw, punishing brand of hip-hop. Mainstream rap's pendulum has swung between thugged-out street drama and fantastical materialism, but M.O.P. has always remained the same. Harkening from the same generation as Nas and Notorious B.I.G., the group has stuck to their tried-and-true formula—menacing beats from the likes of Gang Starr's DJ Premier, plus their hyperactive delivery—to make some of rap's most arresting albums.

Powered by their seminal single, "How About Some Hardcore," *To the Death* is a striking if somewhat unrealized debut. Larceny anthems like "Downtown Swinger" and "New Jack City," and a step up in beats (some from Premier), make *Firing Squad* the best place to start. The fireworks really start with 1998's *First Family 4 Life,* which was overseen by DJ Premier. Jay-Z guests on the "Eye of the Tiger"–sampling "Four Alarm Blaze," while Premier remixes the street anthem "Handle Ur Buzness." When it was first released, *First Family* was an antidote to Puffy Combs' bling age; it still sounds fine today.

The group finally found some of the critical acclaim (and commercial payback) they had long deserved on 2000's *Warriorz.* The nuclear single "Ante Up" is a live-wire hip-hop classic. Premier and fellow beatsmith Dr. Period fashion dense boom-bap as Danze and Fame's interplay reaches a stunning new level of sophistication. *10 Years and Gunnin'* collects "Ante Up," "Eye of the Tiger," and eight other stellar examples of how harrowing New York street rap can get.   —C.R.

Morcheeba

★★½	Who Can You Trust? (China, 1996)
★★★	Big Calm (China/Sire, 1998)
★★	Fragments of Freedom (London/Sire, 2000)
★★½	Charango (Reprise, 2002)
★★★½	Parts of the Process (Reprise, 2002)

Female-fronted electronica in the mid-'90s could often be cold and minimal, however appealingly so. But as envisaged by London's Morcheeba, the medium gained warmth and a decided groove. The key was singer Skye Edwards, whose heated purr breathed life into the mix of ambient and trip-hop cooked up by her bandmates, brothers Ross and Paul Godfrey. She coos her way through the trio's debut, upping the sex quotient on already slinky tracks such as "Tape Loop." But it soon becomes apparent that her emotional spectrum begins at sexy and ends no further than sultry. Singing of heartbreak on "Col," she only approximates sadness, and her near-lifeless approach to the mournful "Howling" comes off like a wasted opportunity.

For *Big Calm,* her lack of emotional range proves a perfect fit. Here, the band reveals a flirtatious side on tracks such as "Shoulder Holster" and the opening "The Sea." It also starts to expand its musical repertoire, copping a reggae beat and a midsong toast for "Friction," and adding scratches and vocal samples to the instrumental "Bullet Proof."

On *Fragments of Freedom,* Morcheeba gets overzealous. The trio incorporates a new style into practically every song: dashes of funk on "Love Is Rare," soul on "Rome Wasn't Built in a Day," beat-boxing courtesy of Biz Markie on "In the Hands of the Gods"—even calypso on "A Well-Deserved Break." The followup, *Charango,* is only somewhat less disjointed, and once again Edwards' voice proves ill suited to experimental forays. Pursuing a seemingly obvious connection to hip-hop, Morcheeba invites two rappers to guest on the album: Pace Won, on "Get Along" and the title track, and Slick Rick, on "Women Lose Weight," a cautionary tale about murdering one's wife because she's fat. It's all wrong, and Edwards' vocal turn on "Women Lose Weight" only makes matters worse—her earnest and airy delivery is completely at odds with Rick's wry tone. Her duet with Lambchop's Kurt Wagner, however, on "What New York Couples Fight About," proves more successful: Wagner's ragged near-whisper balances out the bright vocals Edwards can't help but deliver. Ultimately, the 18-track career overview *Parts of the Process* may be the best way to experience Morcheeba.   —N.P.

Alanis Morissette

★★★★½	Jagged Little Pill (Maverick, 1995)
★★★	Supposed Former Infatuation Junkie (Maverick, 1998)
★★	MTV Unplugged (Maverick, 1999)
★★★	Under Rug Swept (Maverick, 2002)
★★	Feast on Scraps (Maverick, 2002)
★★	So-Called Chaos (Maverick, 2004)

A former child television and pop star with two out-of-print releases in her native Canada, 19-year-old Alanis Morissette established herself as a very different sort of star with "You Oughta Know," *Jagged Little Pill*'s first single. Backed by Flea and Dave Navarro, Morissette's wail of a woman scorned blends obsession, rage, blunt sexuality, and raw pain into a mob hit of a pop song. It may be the best kiss-off song since "Positively 4th Street." Elsewhere on *Pill,* Morissette's confessional lyrics are as gawky, awkward, and self-important as their subject, adolescence. "You Oughta Know" is *Jagged Little Pill*'s arresting standout, but the entire album—from "Ironic," "You Learn," to "Hand in My Pocket" has aged extremely well.

Three years later, Morissette and Ballard teamed up again to create *Supposed Former Infatuation Junkie.* Although just as lyrically dense as its predecessor, *Supposed Former Infatuation Junkie* suffers from relative indirectness. In songs like "Front Row,"

Morissette offers paragraphs of lyrics filled with nonsense such as "I'd like you to be schooled and in awe as though you were kissed by God full on the lips." The single "Thank U" and hard rocker "Baba" allow rare moments of Morissette's emotional punch to shine though her lyrical spew.

Besides marking her first tiny step away from Ballard, *MTV Unplugged* is a premature live disc with little to recommend it. In addition to songs from her first two releases, Morissette pads the set with three new songs and a pointless cover of the Police's "King of Pain." *Under Rug Swept* represents Morissette finally taking full control of her muse by writing and producing the entire disc. Less dense than the sonic tapestries she created with Ballard, *Under Rug Swept* nonetheless finds Morissette with more than enough musical intelligence—from thick guitars and hip-hop beats to Middle Eastern flourishes—to go it alone, though her lyrics still read like binge entries in a therapy diary. On "Hands Clean," even her posse turns out to contain an "inner posse." But no matter how ridiculous her lyrics may seem, Morissette's increasingly expressive singing is strengthened by her genuine belief in each and every word. As prolific as she is verbose, she also released *Feast on Scraps,* containing a DVD of a performance from the *Under Rug Swept* tour and an outtakes audio disc.

Narcissism has always been the major drawback of Morissette's music, and it is one that she has, at her best, struggled against. On the dreadful *So-Called Chaos,* she seems to have given up. On "This Grudge" she goes back to the relationship that has haunted all her adult work, although this time even she realizes that it's "this grudge that's grown old." Still, she dutifully adds the detritus up to "14 years 30 minutes 15 seconds I've held this grudge/11 songs 4 full journals, thoughts of punishment I've expended." Yet, at the end of the song Morissette is still no closer to moving on. And so, stuck in a rut, *So-Called Chaos* becomes the sound of Morissette spinning her wheels by revisiting her old themes of verbose insecurity, self-discovery, and empowerment while allowing her music to stagnate under a pop sheen that—like a nervous tick—recycles the techno touches and Middle Eastern flourishes of earlier efforts but this time weds them to the weakest songwriting of her career.   —R.A.

Morphine

★★★	Good (1992; Rykodisc, 1993)
★★★½	Cure for Pain (Rykodisc, 1993)
★★★½	Yes (Rykodisc, 1995)
★★	B-Sides and Otherwise (Rykodisc, 1997)
★★½	Like Swimming (DreamWorks/Rykodisc, 1997)
★★★★	The Night (DreamWorks/Rykodisc, 2000)
★★★	Bootleg Detroit (Rykodisc, 2000)
★★★★	The Best of Morphine (Rykodisc, 2003)

The Boston trio Morphine's unusual lineup—two-string slide bass guitar, baritone sax, and drums—practically guaranteed that some observers would see it as nothing more than a musical freak show. But over the course of five studio albums, the group proved that it wasn't just a purveyor of shtick. Mixing blues, jazz, and goth rock without owing much to any of those genres, Morphine created a sound of unique and timeless cool, which the band's leader, singer/bassist Mark Sandman, aptly dubbed "low rock."

"Rock noir" would also be appropriate. The world presented on *Good, Cure for Pain,* and *Yes* is one of dimly lit bars and pool halls, suffused with cigarette smoke and furtive desire, inhabited by addicts, adulterers, and various other not-so-beautiful losers. All three albums are excellent, but the latter two get the nod for their heavier grooves. *Cure for Pain* is the best place for the curious to start, featuring such gems as "Buena," "Thursday" and "A Head With Wings."

Like Swimming, by contrast, sounds tired. The band's repeating itself, and the shtick has begun to overwhelm the spirit. Sadly, this would be the last Morphine album that Sandman saw released; he died in July 1999 after suffering a heart attack onstage in Italy. Sadder still, the band's posthumously issued final studio recording, *The Night,* is nearly *Cure for Pain*'s equal, and it shows Morphine successfully moving beyond "low rock," incorporating keyboards, cello, and oud on haunting tracks like "Rope on Fire" and "Take Me With You." Where it all would have gone from here we'll never know.

The *Best of* is a good intro; both the B-sides collection and the dodgy-sounding live album are fun but nonessential.   —M.R.

Van Morrison

★★★★	Blowin' Your Mind (Bang, 1967)
★★★★★	Astral Weeks (Warner Bros., 1968)
★★★★½	Moondance (Warner Bros., 1970)
★★★½	His Band and the Street Choir (Warner Bros., 1970)
★★★★★	Tupelo Honey (Warner Bros., 1971)
★★★★★	Saint Dominic's Preview (Warner Bros., 1972)
★★	Hard Nose the Highway (Warner Bros., 1973)
★★★★★	It's Too Late to Stop Now (Warner Bros., 1974)
★★★★★	Veedon Fleece (Warner Bros., 1974)
★★	A Period of Transition (Warner Bros., 1977)
★★½	Wavelength (Warner Bros., 1978)
★★★	Into the Music (Warner Bros., 1979)

★★ Common One (Warner Bros., 1980)
★★ Beautiful Vision (Warner Bros., 1982)
★★ Inarticulate Speech of the Heart (Warner Bros., 1983)
★★ A Sense of Wonder (Mercury, 1985)
★★★½ Live at the Grand Opera House Belfast (Mercury, 1985)
★★ No Guru, No Method, No Teacher (Mercury, 1986)
★★ Poetic Champions Compose (Mercury, 1987)
★★★½ Irish Heartbeat (Mercury, 1988)
★★★½ Avalon Sunset (Mercury, 1989)
★★★★★ The Best of Van Morrison (Mercury, 1990)
★★★ Enlightenment (Mercury, 1990)
★★★★½ Bang Masters (Epic, 1991)
★★★ Hymns to the Silence (Mercury, 1991)
★★★½ Too Long in Exile (Polydor, 1993)
★★★★ The Best of Van Morrison, Vol. 2 (Polydor, 1993)
★★★½ A Night in San Francisco (Polydor, 1994)
★★½ Days Like This (Polydor, 1995)
★★ How Long Has This Been Going On (Verve, 1996)
★★ The Healing Game (Polydor, 1997)
★★★½ The Philosopher's Stone (Polydor, 1998)
★★ Back on Top (Polydor, 1999)
★★½ The Skiffle Sessions (Polydor, 2000)
★★½ You Win Again (Polydor, 2000)
★★★½ Down the Road (Polydor, 2002)
★★★½ What's Wrong With This Picture? (Polydor, 2003)

Them

★★★★ Them (1965; PolyGram, 1990)
★★★★ Them Again (1966; Universal, 1998)
★★★★ The Story of Them Featuring Van Morrison (PolyGram, 1998)

The Irish have no kings, and no Irish knee has ever bowed before one, so it will never do to call Van Morrison the king of the Celtic blues singers. But it's tempting. For the past 40 years, Van the Man has worked his unique style, mixing a soulful Irish growl with poetic rambles inspired by Lead Belly, Ray Charles, Dylan, and Yeats. An eccentric recluse with a mean stare, Morrison started as the singer for Them, the Belfast garage-rock band who did the huge hit "Gloria" as well as lesser-knowns like "One Two Brown Eyes," "Bring 'Em On In," and "My Lonely Sad Eyes." There have been countless Them repackages over the years; *The Story of Them* is almost the complete works on two CDs. Just don't bother with any Them compilation that leaves out Van's first great song, "Friday's Child."

He made his solo debut with *Blowin' Your Mind*,

later repackaged as *T.B. Sheets* and *Bang Masters*. He scat-sings his dark, brooding poetry in "He Ain't Give You None," slurring "you can leave now if you don't like what's happening," either to his girlfriend or his band. "Brown Eyed Girl" became a hit, sung off-key by generations of drunk Tri-Sigmas in Myrtle Beach ever since. But most striking was the ten-minute guitar/organ blues groove "T.B. Sheets," in which Morrison sang of watching a lover die of tuberculosis, sometimes singing as the dying woman, sometimes as the lover left behind, snarling "gotta go" over and over. A strange, sick, obsessive song, announcing a major artist.

After a down-and-out stint in Boston, Morrison made his most beautiful and intense album, *Astral Weeks*. The sound is almost all acoustic, with guitars, stand-up bass, brushed drums, and occasional strings or horns, as Van rants and raves about death ("Astral Weeks"), sex ("Sweet Thing"), lost love ("Beside You"), and childhood memories of Belfast ("Madame George"). His lyrics are full of pain, but he keeps taking off to chant incantations like "you breathe in, you breathe out" or, again, "gotta go." It's impossible to categorize, and it was hard to sell, but despite initial commercial failure *Astral Weeks* is an album that still floors musicians and converts new fans, and it's the basis of Morrison's legend.

For *Moondance*, Morrison came up with the smooth style that made him most famous, a mellow, piano-based hybrid of pop, jazz, and Irish folk. He sings gentle reveries ("And It Stoned Me," "Caravan"), seductive piano ballads ("Crazy Love") and a romantic ode to a polluted and foul Boston-area river ("Into the Mystic"). His voice is intimate, warm, making *Moondance* one of the most rampantly made-out-to of all rock classics. It's also one of the most famously front-loaded—the first five songs are perfect, but until the CD era, nobody ever played Side Two. "Brand New Day" is pretty good, however.

His Band and the Street Choir was a lighter version of *Moondance*, short on songs but ending with the great "Street Choir." *Tupelo Honey* is loose and wild fun, Van's only really cheery-sounding album. He celebrates domestic bliss in rural California with the country charm of "When That Evening Sun Goes Down," the huge title ballad, and "Wild Night," a rocker that celebrates the girls who walk by dressed up for each other, while the inside jukebox roars out just like thunder.

When the marriage broke up, Van responded with *St. Dominic's Preview*, a concept album about feeling homesick in America, looking back on Ireland from California but finding only miles and miles of loneliness in between. The songs combine the bleak melancholy of *Astral Weeks* with the light touch of *Moondance;* he misses with the closing dirge "Almost Independence Day," but he rollicks away in the uptempo R&B stomp of "Jackie Wilson Said (I'm in Heaven When You Smile)," "Redwood Tree," "I Will Be There," and the powerhouse title track. But the only good song on *Hard Nose the Highway* was his bizarre version of Kermit the Frog's Sesame Street classic, "Bein' Green." As a Protestant kid from Belfast, Van's technically Orange, not Green, but it's still a landmark of Muppet soul.

It's Too Late to Stop Now is a warm live album, with an orchestra, vintage blues covers, and vivid band-crowd interaction. It peaks with "Saint Dominic's Preview" and "Listen to the Lion," where the music ebbs away slowly, instrument by instrument, until one fan breaks a roomful of silence by crying out, "All right!" *Veedon Fleece* was another commercial flop, but it was the culmination of everything Van was doing up to that point, all Celtic mystic tumult in the vocals and pastoral beauty in the music. He sums up his vocal reach in the bearlike blues growl of "Linden Arlen Stole the Highlights" and the soft falsetto of "Who Was That Masked Man?" The lyrics are even more eccentric than usual ("Tell me, oh Poe/Oscar Wilde and Thoreau") but *Veedon Fleece* ranks with *Astral Weeks* and *St. Dominic's Preview* as his most majestic music.

Van spent three years in seclusion, returning with the shrill, clumsy *Period of Transition. Wavelength* was a failed mainstream pop move, but the title track was a worthy hit, which like many of his best songs expresses the profound spiritual yearning to listen to the radio. *Into the Music* was hailed by many as a creative come-back, but it sounds stuffy and ornate, with too many violin solos; the one killer is a cover of the '50s oldie "It's All in the Game." Morrison hit a painful slump in the '80s, starting with the jazzy religious blather of *Common One* and *Beautiful Vision. Inarticulate Speech, A Sense of Wonder, No Guru,* and *Poetic Champions* are cranky self-imitation. *Best of Van Morrison, Volume 2* preserves some great songs from this period—the live "Rave On, John Donne," "Tore Down a la Rimbaud"—but Morrison seemed to suck the life out of his past glories. On *No Guru,* he complains about how you don't understand him because you live in an "Ivory Tower," though he obviously hadn't listened to any music in years except his own.

But on *Irish Heartbeat,* a collection of standards with the Chieftains, Morrison kicked up his heels—you would have expected him to do an appropriately soulful "Carrickfergus" or "She Moved Through the Fair," but who would have expected him to have so much fun with "Marie's Wedding"? *Avalon Sunset* was a modest breakthrough that has been paying off

for him ever since. The music wasn't radically different from his recent work—the same scat-singing poetics about love and God over easy-rolling folk rock—but the voice, the songwriting, and the spirit all had a renewed sense of uplift, especially "Coney Island." After years of letting his audience down, Morrison found himself back in touch with a thriving cult, and *The Best of Van Morrison* was a well-timed summary.

Since then, Van has remade the same album every year, usually with at least a couple of worthy songs. *Hymns to the Silence* and *Enlightenment* are the most complex and self-involved; *Too Long in Exile* is the breeziest, including three duets with John Lee Hooker; *Back on Top* has "When the Leaves Come Falling Down"; *Days Like This* has "Songwriter" ("I'm a songwriter and I'm hot on your trail/I'm a songwriter and my check's in the mail"). *The Philosopher's Stone* collects outtakes, and after so many prolific spleen-venting years, who knew Van had outtakes? *A Night in San Francisco* is a good 1994 live album, up there with *It's Too Late to Stop Now* and 1986's *Live at the Grand Opera House Belfast,* and a document of what a marvelous live performer the old man remains. *The Skiffle Sessions* is a strange live collaboration with '50s old-timers Lonnie Donegan and Chris Barber, while *You Win Again* is an even stranger set of mostly Jerry Lee Lewis covers sung with the Killer's daughter, Linda Gail Lewis. For non-cultists, there's little point trying to tell the recent albums apart—you don't need any of them unless you need all of them. But *Down the Road* and *What's Wrong With This Picture?* offer treats like the telling "Hey Mr. DJ" ("Play me something/That I know"), a moving rendition of "Georgia on My Mind," and the original "What Makes the Irish Heart Beat," which deserves to become a pub standard.   —R.S.

Morrissey

★★★★	Viva Hate (Sire, 1988)
★★★★	Bona Drag (Sire, 1990)
★	Kill Uncle (Sire, 1991)
★★★★★	Your Arsenal (Sire, 1992)
★★★	Beethoven Was Deaf (EMI, 1993)
★★★★	Vauxhall and I (Sire, 1994)
★★★★★	World of Morrissey (Sire, 1995)
★★	Southpaw Grammar (Reprise, 1995)
★	Maladjusted (Mercury, 1997)
★★★★	The Best of Morrissey (Rhino, 2002)
★★★★	You Are the Quarry (Sanctuary, 2004)

How fans wept when the Smiths split up in 1987. Without the tender loving care of his musical enabler, guitarist Johnny Marr, Morrissey seemed destined to go back on the dole. But things turned out differently. Johnny Marr floundered around in a failed search for context, from groups such as Electronic to the Healers, proving that you can't just go out and hire yourself a new Morrissey. But Morrissey proved that if you have the dubious luck to be Morrissey, at least you can always go out and find another Johnny Marr. Indeed, he found that England's cheerless marshes were simply crawling with aspiring Johnny Marr imitators, and he kept hiring them to make new Smiths-style solo records with barely a pause. *Bona Drag* collects the best of his early solo hits, picking the highlights from his nasty debut *Viva Hate*—"Suedehead," "Hairdresser on Fire"—with great nonalbum singles like "Interesting Drug," "Disappointed," and "The Last of the Famous International Playboys."

Morrissey's solo peak is 1992's *Your Arsenal,* which bounces back from the tired *Kill Uncle* with a brace of loud, grandiose glam-rock riffs. "We'll Let You Know," "We Hate It When Our Friends Become Successful," and the timely fascist-bashing "The National Front Disco" address the outside world like the Mozzer never had before. "You're the One for Me, Fatty" was true romance, while "Certain People I Know" made fans fantasize about how cool it would be to get flogged with Morrissey's pool cue. *Vauxhall and I* had a softer, subtler approach in hits such as "Now My Heart Is Full" and "The More You Ignore Me, the Closer I Get."

Morrissey dropped off the map with the sketchy *Southpaw Grammar* and the pathetic *Maladjusted,* going into seclusion in his adopted home of L.A. But amid concrete and clay and general decay, nature must still find a way, so Morrissey clawed his way back with the triumphant return, *You Are the Quarry.* "First of the Gang to Die" was a gloriously romantic blast of hooligan lust, even if it was the exactly same song as Suede's "Trash," setting up the surprisingly adult anguish of "I Have Forgiven Jesus" and "I'm Not Sorry." ("The woman of my dreams, well, there never was one"—awesome!) "Irish Blood, English Heart" was one of punk rock's all-time coolest attacks on Oliver Cromwell, up there with Elvis Costello's "Oliver's Army," the Pogues' "Young Ned of the Hill," and the Mekons' "Hard to Be Human Again."

The Best of Morrissey is more fun than a pocket full of gladiolas. *Beethoven Was Deaf* is a live gig with the *Your Arsenal* band. But *World of Morrissey* is definitely the one to buy if you're only buying one, a collection of magnificent singles such as "Boxers," "My Love Life," "The Loop," and "Jack the Ripper." Best tune: Moz's nine-minute, guitar-drenched, bitterly ironic, perversely moving version of "Moon River." —R.S.

Mos Def

★★★★ Mos Def & Talib Kweli Are Black Star (Rawkus, 1998)
★★★★ Black on Both Sides (Rawkus, 1999)

A Brooklyn-based, dimple-faced rapper radiating intelligence and wit, Mos Def represented the next step in the evolution of the hip-hop MC, sporting all the skills and credibility of the underground plus an undeniable charisma that pushed his music seamlessly into the mainstream. Born Dante Terrell Smith in Brooklyn in 1973, Mos Def acted on the short-lived 1994 TV series *The Cosby Mysteries* and formed the short-lived group Urban Thermodynamics with his brother (DCQ, of the group Medina Green) and sister. Mos then appeared on De La Soul's album *Stakes Is High* (Tommy Boy, 1996) and two cuts on da Bush Babees album *Gravity* (Warner Bro., 1996) where he picked up some of da Babees' West Indian flavor. An excellent freestyler and writer with a deep knowledge of hip-hop's old school, Mos's topical range widened as he sought to transcend the "keepin' it real" clichés that had subsumed much of hip-hop's revolutionary potential and stunted its artistic growth. At the same time, Mos was there to rock the party, starting with his languid, funky solo single "The Universal Magnetic," which positioned him as a direct successor to Q-Tip, of A Tribe Called Quest. Mos then teamed up with fellow Brooklyn MC Talib Kweli to form the duo Black Star, named after Marcus Garvey's Black Star Line, the first black-owned ship line to go from the U.S. to Africa ("Black Star Line" was also a track on Brand Nubian's 1993 album, *In God We Trust,* which Mos and Kweli undoubtedly knew). *Black Star* was brilliant lyrically (conscious and clever) as well as musically (fat drums and jazzy loops), catching the attention of hibernating heads who had last checked hip-hop during Native Tongues' late-'80s/early-'90s heyday. Mos ably followed this up with *Black on Both Sides,* an album that runs the gamut from the furiously catchy "Rock N Roll," on which Mos details pioneering African-American musical developments subsequently capitalized on by whites, to "Ms. Fat Booty," a wicked tale of seduction (check the surprise ending) built around an Aretha Franklin sample. Although Mos' album-length oeuvre is brief, he has dropped quite a few nonalbum singles and guest spots. He appears on three tracks on the excellent compilation *Soundbombing II* (Rawkus, 1999), including the tremendous "B-Boy Document 99" with High & Mighty and Mad Skillz; he drops a verse on Floetry's smooth 2003 single "Wanna B Where U R (Thisizzaluvsong)"; his cut "3-Card" opens *Music From the Original Broadway Production Topdog Underdog*

(MCA, 2002), a Suzan-Lori Parks play that costarred Mos and Jeffrey Wright (Mos has also been featured in Hollywood movies including *Bamboozled* and *The Italian Job*); also worth seeking is "Beef," a 2003 single that begins with the memorable couplet "Beef is not what Jay said to Nas/Beef is when working folks can't find jobs." Mos' millennial musical power move was Black Jack Johnson, a black rock supergroup featuring P-Funk keyboardist Bernie Worrell, Bad Brains guitarist Dr. Know, Sugarhill bassist Doug Wimbish, and Living Colour drummer Will Calhoun. But what sounded great on paper didn't translate well to the stage (perhaps it would have helped if Mos could sing better); for once, mighty Mos might've gotten caught up in believing he was bigger than hip-hop.   —P.R.

Mötley Crüe

   ★★½   Too Fast for Love (1981; Mötley/Hip-O, 2003)
   ★★   Shout at the Devil (1983; Mötley/Hip-O, 2003)
   ★★½   Theatre of Pain (1985; Mötley/Hip-O, 2003)
   ★★★   Girls, Girls, Girls (1987; Mötley/Hip-O, 2003)
   ★★★★   Dr. Feelgood (1989; Mötley/Hip-O, 2003)
   ★★★½   Mötley Crüe (1994; Mötley/Hip-O, 2003)
   ★★½   Generation Swine (1997; Mötley/Hip-O, 2003)
   ★★★★   Greatest Hits (1998; Mötley/Hip-O, 2003)
   ★★½   Supersonic and Demonic Relics (1999; Mötley/Hip-O, 2003)
   ★★½   Live: Entertainment or Death (1999; Mötley/Hip-O, 2003)
   ★★   New Tattoo (2000; Mötley/Hip-O, 2003)
   ★★★★   The Millennium Collection (Mötley/Hip-O, 2003)
   ★★   Music to Crash Your Car To, Vol. 1 (Mötley/Hip-O, 2003)

The ultimate hair metal band, Mötley Crüe is in some ways the perfect embodiment of the rock & roll dream. Despite being only modestly talented and not especially attractive, the band nonetheless became rich and famous, not only surviving a life of excess and decadence but actually acquiring a certain celebrity through their relentless partying and porn-star dalliances. Most incredible of all, the Crüe actually made some decent music before descending into well-paid self parody.

For a moment, the band even managed to seem radical and vaguely dangerous. In 1981, when the quartet released its debut album, the glam-referencing Sunset Strip scene that would produce Guns N' Roses, Ratt, and Poison didn't quite exist, and the Crüe's fascination with makeup, attitude, and umlauts seemed genuinely edgy. Pity the music was crap. *Too*

Fast for Love was originally released as an indie, and is nowhere near as ferocious-sounding as the leather-clad crotch shot on the cover would suggest. Indeed, its sound borders on the anemic—but there is a surprising melodic resilience to songs like "Come On and Dance," "Piece of Your Action," and "Merry-Go-Round." (Within a year *Too Fast* was licensed and re-mastered by Elektra; like the rest of the Crüe's albums, it has been reissued with bonus tracks on the band's own UMG-distributed label),

Shout at the Devil aims for a heavier sound but doesn't quite achieve it; as much as the Crüe tries to cultivate its bad-boy image through titles like "Bastard" and "God Bless the Children of the Beast," the music is a distressingly mild-mannered distillation of Kiss and Aerosmith clichés. It's much the same story with *Theatre of Pain*, which, despite its beefier mix, doesn't get any tougher than a tepid remake of Brownsville Station's hoary teen-attitude classic, "Smokin' in the Boys' Room."

But if you do anything long enough you're likely to get better at it, and with time the band's sound begins to catch up to its image. *Girls, Girls, Girls*, whose title tune became famous for its titty-bar-celebrating video, actually put some punch behind the leering lyrics, with such rockers as "Wild Side" and "Bad Boy Boogie" providing plenty of muscular guitar and relentlessly driving rhythm to support the posturing. Still, that was just an hors d'oeuvre compared to *Dr. Feelgood*. With producer Bob Rock behind the boards, the sound is snarling and ferocious, while the songs—from the brutally swinging, guitar-driven title tune, through the breathless surge of "Kickstart My Heart," to the insistent swagger of "Same Ol' Situation (S.O.S.)"—never lets up. Even the ballads seem plausible.

Typically, such success was not to last. After several years of coasting and self-indulgence, the band splintered, with singer Vince Neil being pushed out and replaced by former Scream vocalist John Corabi. (Neil filed a wrongful dismissal suit, then cut a forgettable solo album.) Surprisingly, *Mötley Crüe* sounds tougher and more focused for the change, throwing real sparks with "Hooligan's Holiday" and unleashing a fearsome groove in "Welcome to the Numb." Corabi didn't click with the fans, however, and when the Crüe returned to the studio three years later, Neil was back out front. But apart from a hyped and slightly hysterical remake of "Shout at the Devil," *Generation Swine* is as limp as overcooked spaghetti.

More turmoil ensued, and the band marked time by releasing *Live: Entertainment of Death*, a painfully accurate concert recording. Drummer Tommy Lee—who by this point had become more famous for canoodling with Pamela Anderson than for playing percussion—had left, and was replaced by Randy Castillo, previously of Ozzy Osbourne's Blizzard of Oz. *New Tattoo,* the studio debut by this lineup, is largely pointless, but shows occasional signs of life through the likes of "She Needs Rock N Roll."

Mostly, Mötley Crüe has opted to spend its later years mining the back catalogue for reissues—a wise choice, given the sound of the newer songs. The best value for money is the fun-but-predictable *Greatest Hits* (which supplanted *Decade of Decadence,* a now-deleted best-of that had been released after *Dr. Feelgood*). Those on a budget will find fewer hits but no embarrassments on the *20th Century Masters* anthology, while the leftovers/rarities compilation *Supersonic and Demonic Relics* is strictly for hard-core fans. *Music to Crash Your Car To* (the title is a tasteless allusion to Vince Neil's having killed Hanoi Rocks drummer Nicholas "Razzle" Dingley in a 1984 car accident) is a boxed set that repackages the band's first four albums with a handful of minor rarities. It's docked one star for the title. —J.D.C.

Motörhead

★★★½	Motörhead (1977; Roadracer/Revisited, 1990)
★★★½	Overkill (1979; Roadracer/Revisited, 1992)
★★★½	Bomber (1979; Roadracer/Revisited, 1992)
★★★★½	Ace of Spades (1980; Roadracer/Revisited, 1992)
★★★★½	No Sleep 'til Hammersmith (1981; Sanctuary, 2004)
★★★½	Iron Fist (1982; Bronze/Roadracer, 1990)
★★★★½	No Remorse (1984; Bronze/Roadracer, 1990)
★★★	Orgasmatron (Profile, 1986)
★★★	Rock 'n' Roll (Profile, 1987)
★★★	No Sleep at All (Enigma, 1988)
★★★	The Birthday Party (GWR, 1990)
★★★½	1916 (WTG/Epic, 1991)
★★★½	March or Die (WTG/Epic, 1992)
★★★	Bastards (1993; Steamhammer/SP, 2001)
★★★	Sacrifice (CMC, 1995)
★★★	Overnight Sensation (CMC, 1996)
★★★	Snake Bite Love (CMC, 1998)
★★★	Everything Louder Than Everyone Else (CMC, 1999)
★★★	We Are Motörhead (CMC, 2000)
★★½	Hammered (Sanctuary, 2002)
★★★★	The Very Best of Motörhead (Sanctuary, 2002)
★★★★	Stone Deaf Forever (Sanctuary, 2003)
★★★	Inferno (Metal-Is, 2004)

The black-leather soul of Motörhead emanates from a lanky Brit biker type named Ian Kilmister, better known as Lemmy. A former roadie for Jimi Hendrix,

self-declared speed freak, maniacally propulsive bass guitarist, carnival barker of the sharpest lyrics heavy metal has to offer, and—thanks to the passage of time—a bona fide metal god.

Motörhead are the fathers of speed metal, the band that punks and head bangers could agree on in the '80s (Metallica, for one, would not exist without them). They were punk rock because they play blazingly fast and because they avoid metal's romantic flourish. Also, Lemmy can't really sing: About halfway through most songs, he gives up any semblance of tunefulness and starts to wail; it's the vocal equivalent of guitar feedback, deafeningly crude but effective. Available after a long absence, Motörhead's debut features the hard-charging psychedelic guitar style of Larry Wallis. He was replaced by "Fast" Eddie Clarke not long after the 1975 session, but Wallis helped develop Motörhead's speedy power-trio approach. *No Remorse* culls an hour or so of sustained hysteria from *Overkill* (1979), *Bomber* (1979), the gargantuan *Ace of Spades* (1980), the live in-your-face *No Sleep 'til Hammersmith* (1981), and the reissued *Iron Fist* (1982). Topping it all off is Motörhead's dread masterpiece "Killed by Death," which fully lives up to its title. *The Birthday Party* summarizes Motörhead's comparatively sleeker, "high-tech" phase, drawing on the Bill Laswell–produced *Orgasmatron* (1986), *Rock 'n' Roll* (1987) and *No Sleep at All* (1988), another live set. None of these discs is as urgent as Motörhead's earlier head banging. *1916* reapplies the sonic grit with a trowel, however; only Lemmy could pull off a breathless tribute called "Ramones" that actually outguns the bros themselves.

The sound remains the same, dependably raw and uncompromising across the decades. Motörhead's rotating lineup hardly matters now, since Lemmy never stops or even slows down, cranking out near-identical albums faster than any but the most obsessive fans could possibly consume. *March or Die* easily confiscates Ted Nugent's "Cat Scratch Fever" as another Lemmy anthem, and not even the lo-fi sludge of *Bastards* can fully blunt the hard edge of self-explanatory rockers like "Born to Raise Hell." The big riffs and swagger rarely fail Motörhead, grinding like dragsters on "Dogs of War" *(Snake Bite Love)* or rewiring punk history for "God Save the Queen" *(We Are Motörhead),* with no new concepts and never a disappointment—until 2002's *Hammered,* which cleans up the Motörhead sound. For the first time momentum and attitude are not enough, as the songs are merely loud and forgettable. *Inferno* is back to brutal basics, riffing like a rocket-fueled Chuck Berry: no mercy, no quarter, no prisoners. *Stone Deaf Forever* is the long-overdue box set, a staggering collection of tracks that gathers enough Lemmy for any serious rock fan. Not much on variety, but enough real, timeless metal to rock yet another generation of proudly disaffected head bangers. —M.C./S.A.

Mott the Hoople

- ★★★ Mott the Hoople (Atlantic, 1969)
- ★★ Wildlife (Atlantic, 1971)
- ★★★ Brain Capers (Atlantic, 1972)
- ★★★½ All the Young Dudes (1972; Sony, 1998)
- ★★★★ Mott (Columbia, 1973)
- ★★★★ The Hoople (1974; Columbia, 1990)
- ★★★½ Mott the Hoople Live (1974; Columbia, 1989)
- ★★★½ Greatest Hits (Columbia, 1975)
- ★★★ London to Memphis (Sony, 1992)
- ★★★★ The Ballad of Mott: A Retrospective (Columbia/Legacy, 1993)
- ★★★½ Backsliding Fearlessly: The Early Years (Rhino, 1994)
- ★★ Super Hits (Sony, 1997)
- ★★★ Greatest Hits Live (Cleopatra, 2000)

Combining the swagger of a heavier Rolling Stones and the poetic fervor of a 1966 Bob Dylan sounds like an audacious idea. The amazing thing is that Mott the Hoople pulled it off with remarkable consistency. Kicking in with a debut that featured M.C. Escher cover art and tougher takes on the Kinks' "You Really Got Me" and Doug Sahm's "At the Crossroads," Mott served notice that metallic guitar and introspective lyrics weren't antithetical. With its third album, *Brain Capers,* the roles of its star players gelled. Mick Ralphs—who would later harvest big bucks and grunge simplicity with Bad Company—would keep the riffs and solos hard and tasty; wordsmith Ian Hunter would provide mid-tempo rockers like "Sweet Angeline" that, delivered in an anglicized Dylan drone, mixed tenderness and toughness, irony and compassion.

In the early '70s, David Bowie went slumming with Mott, finding in its rock & roll faith an outlet for the raw impulses his cannier approach too often squelched. When he penned the crunching ballad "All the Young Dudes" for Mott, he wrote an anthem not only for the band, but also a movement—glitter rock, or as its proponents (Mott, T. Rex, Slade, and others) preferred, glam rock. The group hit full, romping stride with *Mott.* Hunter served up road-life sagas ("All the Way From Memphis"), back-alley psychoanalysis ("I Wish I Was Your Mother"), and an outlaw's desperate religiosity ("Hymn for the Dudes"). *The Hoople* was nearly as fine; Gus Dudgeon's Phil Spector–ish, wide-screen production lent

grandeur to bombastic material like "The Golden Age of Rock 'n' Roll" and suited the theatrical bent of the first rock band to play Broadway. *Mott the Hoople Live* captures the band's propensity for baroque gesturing and crowd-inciting heat that, early on, provoked a riot at London's Albert Hall and a subsequent ban on rock shows at that venue.

The early material is best represented by *Backsliding Fearlessly* and the glory days by the generous *Ballad of Mott* (the box set, *All the Young Dudes,* is mainly for fanatics). Mott remains a primer for smart, hard rock & roll. —P.E.

Mouse on Mars

- ★★½ Vulvaland (1994; Beggars, 1998)
- ★★½ Iaora Tahiti (1995; Beggars, 1998)
- ★★★½ Autoditacker (Too Pure/Thrill Jockey, 1997)
- ★★★ Instrumentals (Thrill Jockey, 1997)
- ★★★ Glam (1998; Thrill Jockey, 2003)
- ★★★½ Niun Niggung (1999; Thrill Jockey, 2000)
- ★★★½ Idiology (Thrill Jockey, 2001)
- ★★★ Rost Pocks: The EP Collection (Beggars/Too Pure, 2003)
- ★★★ 7 Radical Connector (Thrill Jockey, 2004)

There's very little precedent in music—pop or otherwise—for the bizarre and amazing electronic spasms created by this German duo at the forefront of the so-called blip-hop movement. In their superfast gushes of micro-musical sounds, they recall Carl Stalling's hyperactive soundtracks for the classic Warner Bros. cartoons, or, more recently, John Zorn's postmodern jazz-metal bands like Naked City. But in their actual sound—the slippery, squiggly, stuttering, spitting jumble of a zillion robotic pulses beating at once—mankind simply had to wait for the invention of the PowerBook to hear stuff like this.

Andi Toma and Jan St. Werner began working together in 1993 with a basic palette of IDM (Intelligent Dance Music) and Eno-meets-krautrock ambitions, and their first two albums show a budding genius for tricky electronic soundscapes that seem vaguely sentient. Curious, humanlike noises and questioning melodies break out of a murky wash of tones, evoking sci-fi films not yet made.

With *Autoditacker,* they sped things up and made a great leap forward into a crazily multifaceted consciousness that can only be described as cartoonish. Suddenly acquiring a sense of humor, Toma and St. Werner strip away the comforting, oceanic background of sounds, and instead give us a never-ending vaudeville show of tiny sounds that can sound divine and otherworldly, nobly jazzy, or familiar as a fart. The song titles are revealing, although they seem as arbitrary as titles for Jackson Pollock paintings: "Tux & Damask," "Schnick Schnack Melimade," "Juju."

Niun Niggung and *Idiology* brilliantly continue the mad blipping and hopping; by this point the group stood at the head of an international movement of similar-minded laptop auteurs. With every album, Toma and St. Werner have sharpened and expanded their approach, which on *Idiology* reaches mind-boggling levels of frantic complexity. What's more amazing is that this is dance music, not just guys making up weird sound effects, and the songs never lose sight of their fundamental rhythmic pulse. Reversing the usual trend, Toma and St. Werner's beats actually get dancier the more they cram them with wild intergalactic funk.

The MoM discography is crowded with singles, vinyl-only albums, and disparities between American and European releases. *Rost Pocks* is a useful collection of miscellany spanning their career; curiously, the tracks with vocals by Laetitia Sadier of Stereolab are the least interesting (this stuff is too hyper to be background music for any vocalist). *Glam* and *Instrumentals,* originally limited-edition, overseas releases, are not groundbreaking but are worth seeking out just for glimpses of their menageries of sounds.   —B.S.

Mudhoney

★★★★	Superfuzz Bigmuff (EP) (Sub Pop, 1988)
★★½	Mudhoney (Sub Pop, 1989)
★★★★	Superfuzz Bigmuff Plus Early Singles (Sub Pop, 1990)
★★★	Every Good Boy Deserves Fudge (Sub Pop, 1991)
★★★	Piece of Cake (Reprise, 1993)
★★	Five Dollar Bob's Mock Cooter Stew (EP) (Reprise, 1993)
★★★	My Brother the Cow (Reprise, 1995)
★★★½	Tomorrow Hit Today (Reprise, 1998)
★★★½	March to Fuzz (Sub Pop, 2000)
★★★	Since We've Become Translucent (Sub Pop, 2002)

When Mudhoney issued its debut EP, *Superfuzz Bigmuff* (named after the vintage distortion pedals used by guitarists Mark Arm and Steve Turner), and a bilious Stooges-worthy single, "Touch Me I'm Sick," it birthed Seattle grunge. Arm and Turner are Green River alums, just like Jeff Ament and Stone Gossard, who went on to form Pearl Jam. Whereas Pearl Jam updated the anthemic possibilities of early '70s arena

rock, Mudhoney played as if it had emerged from the same '60s garage in which Pacific Northwest heroes the Sonics honed their no-frills assault.

Equal parts alienation and inebriation, the quartet's music never caught on commercially like that of their peers Pearl Jam, Nirvana, and Soundgarden. That's because Mudhoney's records boast a caustic, dirty-fingernails sound that falls just short of slipshod. The band's best early work is collected on *Superfuzz Bigmuff Plus Early Singles,* with Arm's cat-scratch wail piercing through a wall of overdriven guitars on the salacious "Sweet Young Thing (Ain't Sweet No More)." Afterward, Mudhoney continued to crank out variations of the same record, distinguished by pithy commentaries on selling out ("Suck You Dry," from *Piece of Cake*) and runaway rock-star ego ("Generation Spokesmodel" and "Into Yer Shtik," from *My Brother the Cow*). *Tomorrow Hit Today* bares a more Southern-fried edge, thanks to production by Memphis legend Jim Dickinson, but it also holds together as the tightest collection of psyche-garage mania since Mudhoney's first handful of singles.

March to Fuzz offers a fine overview of the band's first decade, while *Since We've Become Translucent* repays its debt to side B of the Stooges' 1970 classic *Funhouse,* in which free-jazz saxophone rides the rails of protopunk rhythm. Where *Funhouse* masterfully integrates the worlds of John Coltrane, James Brown, and garage rock, however, *Since We've Become Translucent* is hit or miss. The horns fall flat on "Where the Flavor Is," and the epic "Baby, Can You Dig the Light?" can't sustain the song's initial intensity for eight minutes. But when Mudhoney simply does what it has always done best—namely crank up the fuzz pedals, most notably on "Dyin' for It" and "Sonic Infusion"—they do Iggy proud.   —G.K.

Mya

★★★½	Mya (Interscope, 1998)
★★	Fear of Flying (Interscope, 1999)
★★★	Moodring (Interscope, 2003)

Mya's suburban sexiness, alternately squeaky-clean and ready to get her freak on, made for a fresh, accessible R&B stardom. She seemed like the diva next door, the gal from your chem class who happened to sing and dance her way right onto the radio. Which might be why her divahood seems fleeting despite the fact that she's three albums into her career.

Mya slinks outta the speakers like a virgin touched for the very first time. The beats are the sort of post-Timbaland blip-bumps that dominated pop radio in the late '90s, but Mya's thin voice propels flirtations like "Movin' On," "Keep on Lovin' Me," and the brilliantly titled "If You Died I Wouldn't Cry Cause You Never Loved Me Anyway." The highlight was the amazingly dirty-sounding "It's All About Me." Sisqó, even at his drag-on moanin'-est, can barely keep up; by the end of this five minutes of throbbing foreplay, he sounds as on the edge of exhaustion as we feel. A perfect example of cold-shower R&B, and a smashing opening move.

Mya buried a couple of excellent songs on soundtracks to fairly worthless films. "Ghetto Supastar," from *Bulworth,* her hook-singin' collaboration with former Fugee Pras and Wu-Tang surrealist ODB, was the only thing about the movie that the mass market dug. "Take Me There" was snap-crackle-pop from *The RugRats Movie,* of all things.

But *Fear of Flying* didn't capitalize on her charms. That inner-sleeve photo of Mya looking mighty Mariahesque was not a good sign; the music sounds blandly generic. Perhaps sensing something was amiss, *Fear of Flying* was withdrawn in 2000, and two dishwater-dull ballads, "For the First Time" and "No Tears on My Pillow," were replaced with "Again and Again" and the terrific "Free," a spitfire ode to being "single, sexy, and free," written by Jimmy Jam and Terry Lewis. (The two really should get an award for not having lost a step since they were doing this sort of thing for Janet Jackson in the mid-'80s.)

Mya recovered from the appallingly popular 2001 single "Lady Marmalade"—a misguided ménage between Mya, Pink, Christina Aguilera, Lil' Kim, and Missy Elliott—with the fine *Moodring,* her most even album yet, which hit the charts with the excellently titled Elliott production "My Love Is Like . . . Wo." —J.G.

My Bloody Valentine

  ★★   This Is Your Bloody Valentine (Tycoon, 1985)
★★★½ Isn't Anything (Sire/Warner Bros., 1988)
  ★★★   Ecstasy and Wine (Lazy, 1989)
★★★★★ Loveless (Creation/Sire/Warner Bros., 1991)

It's one of the great losses to music in the '90s that My Bloody Valentine never followed up *Loveless,* its peerless neo-psychedelic masterpiece of 1991. A beguiling mix of breathy, effeminate melodies and storm clouds of guitar noise, warped and bent and twisted into a transcendently beautiful mess, the album stands in the alt-rock pantheon as a genuinely new vision of rock on par with the innovations of Sonic Youth, the Jesus and Mary Chain, and the Velvet Underground. But Kevin Shields, the band's guitarist and mastermind, largely disappeared from the scene after releasing the album, doing remixes and occasional guest

spots but never releasing another record, leaving in his wake one of rock's great what-ifs.

Born in Queens, New York, and reared in Dublin, Shields formed My Bloody Valentine with drummer Colm O'Ciosoig in 1984 and released a deservedly obscure (and out-of-print) goth-punk mini LP called *This Is Your Bloody Valentine* the next year. A flurry of singles and EPs followed (two of which are collected on *Ecstasy and Wine*) before *Isn't Anything,* which defined MBV's basic approach—powerful, sensual washes of feedback surrounding Cocteau Twins–like vocals—and mobilized Britain's nascent "shoegazer" scene. For a lesser band it would have been a high point, but Shields was just getting started. On *Loveless,* he took the elements that made *Isn't Anything* interesting and headed straight through the looking glass, adding layer upon layer of feedback and breaking down the song structures to a plotless, erotic dream state. Pretty is ugly, ugly is pretty, and disorientation is a destination in itself. Shields finally popped up his head with several new songs on the 2003 soundtrack to the film *Lost in Translation;* the clattering "City Girl" recalled some of his old beguiling form, which can only be taken as a good sign for things to come.   —B.S.

Mystikal

   ★★   Mind of Mystikal (Big Boy/Jive, 1996)
★★★½ Unpredictable (Jive, 1997)
★★★½ Ghetto Fabulous (Jive, 1998)
★★★½ Let's Get Ready (Jive, 2000)
★★★½ Tarantula (Jive, 2001)
   ★★★   Prince of the South (Jive, 2004)

Master P turned out a lot of filler during the late-'90s prime of his label, No Limit, but Mystikal stands a cut above his labelmates. Although the croaky-voiced former military man was a local hero in New Orleans before hooking up with P, he didn't find his voice until he joined No Limit. *Unpredictable* lives up to its title— it's more than an hour of manic fury from the Incredible Hulk of hip-hop. Mystikal is genuinely scary when he threatens to off the thugs who murdered his sister, while explosives detonate ominously in the song's background. Maybe he even intimidated No Limit's production hacks, Beats by the Pound, because they had never crafted such a wide range of beats for any other MC. But though he's a force of nature, Mystikal's also a weirdo. "I'm on Fire" (from *Ghetto Fabulous*) finds the rapper running frantically and uncontrollably through his neighborhood, on flames. "I'm blind," he exclaims at one point, before realizing, "Oh, I had my eyes closed."

When Mystikal leaped out of the No Limit tank, he

left behind most of the tired gangstaisms he'd nursed on P's label. It was a new era, and there was no longer any shame in a street MC making a crowd dance—especially with a hip production crew like the Neptunes. His growl, which could have been custom de-signed for their grimy retro-funk, was exploited for its soulful side. "Shake Your Ass" sounded like a great, lost James Brown track. Mystikal still sounds feral, a reminder that, back in the day, R&B most certainly did not mean watered-down.   —K.H.

Leona Naess

   ★★★   Comatised (MCA, 2000)

   ★★   I Tried to Rock You but You Only Roll (MCA, 2001)

 ★★★★   Leona Naess (MCA, 2003)

Bohemian pop singer/songwriter Leona Naess—the daughter of Norwegian shipping billionaire Arne Naess (who died in a 2004 climbing accident) and stepdaughter of soul diva Diana Ross—has won fans with her winningly melodic, openhearted love songs, sung in an enticingly airy voice by a young woman whose favorite fabric appears to be worn denim. Raised in England, Naess moved to the United States at 18 and briefly studied anthropology at NYU. Persistent gigging at Village dives led to a recording contract and the promising *Comatised,* which was recorded with R.E.M. producer Scott Litt and invited easy but accurate comparisons to Edie Brickell and Beth Orton. While Naess has the sultry visual appeal and breathy vocalisms of Mazzy Star's Hope Sandoval, her songs are much more emotionally engaged. A year later, *I Tried to Rock You but You Only Roll* showed a progression in Naess's songwriting, but producer Martin Terefe's radio sheen did the material a disservice. Rigidly programmed drums effectively robbed the songs of any potential organic appeal, as the New Order–ish dance rock stylings of "All the Stars" and "Boys Like You" showed. After *I Tried to Rock You*'s release, Naess gigged extensively in and around her New York City home, reclaiming "I Tried to Rock You" and the lovely soft-rocker "Mexico" from lo-cal Sheryl Crow AOR hell. Engaged briefly to prolific rock jerk Ryan Adams, Naess got the better of the deal by escaping without Adams but with the services of Adams' longtime producer Ethan Johns. Johns (son of longtime Who producer Glyn Johns) and Naess were an entirely simpatico recording combination who set to work in a computer-free North Hollywood pad.

The warm, earthy *Leona Naess* ideally suited the singer's full-blooded studies of love in all its facets. "Don't Use My Broken Heart" is an especially fine song (with the memorable Jim Webb–style image "nothing is as sad as a man with bells on his shoes") that one could imagine being sung by Roberta Flack. Or even Naess' soul diva stepmom.   —P.R.

Nappy Roots

 ★★★★   Watermelon, Chicken & Grits (Atlantic, 2002)

   ★★★   Wooden Leather (Atlantic, 2003)

Nappy Roots' debut was one of the most pleasant surprises of 2002. The six Kentucky boys managed to put together a swirling good-time concoction of country, soul, and funk, making a hip-hop hoedown in the process. The single "Awnaw," with producer Jazze Pha's organ stabs and its wailing chorus, was one of the best things on the radio that year, a feel-good song you could actually feel good about liking. Other tracks on the album, such as "Po' Folks," made it one of the more striking debuts to come along in some time.

Wooden Leather is much the same. Despite enlisting the help of top-notch producers like Kanye West and Lil' Jon, the album doesn't have anything on it as magnetic as "Awnaw," and often the unremarkable voices and lyrics of the six different members blend together in undifferentiated songs.   —C.R.

Nas

 ★★★★★   Illmatic (Columbia, 1994)

  ★★★★   It Was Written (Columbia, 1996)

   ★★½   I Am (Columbia, 1999)

   ★★½   Nastradamus (Columbia, 1999)

   ★★★   Stillmatic (Columbia, 2001)

  ★★★½   The Lost Tapes (Columbia, 2002)

  ★★★½   God's Son (Columbia, 2002)

Emerging out of the hip-hop wellspring of New York's Queensbridge projects, Nasir Jones burst onto the early-'90s rap scene as something like a phenomenon. With his razor-sharp eye for detail, his entrancing delivery, and his penchant for braggadocio bordering on self-mythology, the kid formerly called Nasty Nas raised the bar for MCs both in New York and worldwide. After a breathtaking debut appearance on Main Source's classic 1991 single "Live at the BBQ," upon which this son of jazz trumpeter Olu Dara introduces himself by saying, "When I was 12/I went to hell for snuffing Jesus," he set out to work on what would become one of the greatest debut albums in hip-hop history. *Illmatic* saw the finest producers in rap, all at the top of their creative skills, working with an MC operating at a fevered creative pitch. With beats by DJ Premier, Pete Rock, Large Professor, and A Tribe Called Quest's Q-Tip, Nas set out to write the first part of his musical autobiography. A portrait of an artist as a hood, loner, tortured soul, juvenile delinquent, and fledgling social critic, it still stands as one of rap's crowning achievements.

Unfairly maligned upon its release, *It Was Written* faced the unenviable challenge of following a masterpiece. Nas had his whole life to write *Illmatic* and only two crazed years to write the followup, years that would see him declared rap's savior and New York's rhyme king by adoring fans and critics alike. *It Was Written*'s strengths lie in Nas' blossoming skills as a storyteller. While it succeeded commercially and spawned the radio hit "If I Ruled the World," critics and die-hard fans accused Nas of succumbing to the materialism sweeping the rap world. True, his infatuation with jewelry had become more pronounced, and the beats were not up to par with the classic material of his debut, but tracks like "Shoot-outs," "I Gave You Power," and "The Message" are narrative-driven classics that stand up against any of *Illmatic*'s hits.

Taking three years off between solo albums, Nas saw his commercial stock dip with the chart failure of his "supergroup" the Firm (which featured Foxy Brown, AZ, and Nature). When he returned in 1999 he seemed to have lost the plot. *I Am* and *Nastradamus* both have their share of solid material, but ultimately fail in the face of Nas' inability to navigate the divide between the street reporting that made him a legend and the commercial hits that made him a star. Then, in 2001, a rhyme war with Jay-Z reignited his creative flame and led to *Stillmatic*, a return to form. Powered by the diss track "Ether," *Stillmatic* finds Nas sticking with what works, creative story-raps and trenchant social commentary. He still errs when he makes attempts at club tracks, but the album is largely a success.

Stillmatic marked the beginning of a second phase in Nas' career. He continued with *The Lost Tapes*, a collection of shelved tracks deemed not commercial enough for the *I Am/Nastradamus* period. While somewhat inconsistent, and certainly too scattered to be considered an album per se, it contains some classics, such as the nostalgic "Doo Rags," that are not to be missed.

Nas continued to strike while the iron was hot in 2002, releasing *God's Son*, coming on the heels of the old-school-flavored single "Made You Look." Nas operates with a palpable sense of confidence spinning tales ("Get Down"), teaching the children ("I Can"), and flirting with the girls ("Hey Nas"), striking out to extend his legend rather than rest on his legacy. —C.R.

Milton Nascimento

★★★	Travessia (1967; Dulas Musica, 2002)
★★★	Courage (1969; A&M, 1989)
★★★★	Milton (EMI Brz., 1970)
★★★½	Clube da Esquina (EMI Brz., 1971)
★★★★	Minas (1972; EMI, 1995)
★★★½	Milagre dos Peixes (1973; Capitol/Intuition, 1988)
★★★	Milagre dos Peixes (Gravado Ao Vivo) (EMI Brz., 1974)
★★★★	Geraes (1976; EMI, 1998)
★★★★★	Milton (A&M, 1976)
★★★½	Clube da Esquina 2 (1978, World Pacific, 1995)
★★★	Journey to Dawn (A&M, 1979)
★★★	Sentinela (1980; Verve, 1990)
★★★½	Missa dos Quilombos (1982; EMI, 2002)
★★★½	Ănĭmă (Verve, 1982)
★★½	Ao Vivo (1983; Philips, 1990)
★★½	Paixão a Fé (EMI Brz., 1985)
★★★	Encontros e Despedidas (Polydor, 1985)
★★★	A Barca dos Amantes (Verve, 1986)
★★★½	Yauaretê (1987; Columbia, 1988)
★★★	A Arte de Milton Nascimento (Verve, 1988)
★★★	Milton's (1988; Columbia, 1989)
★★★½	Personalidade (Philips, 1990)
★★★½	Txai (Columbia, 1991)
★★★★	Angelus (Warner Bros., 1994)
★★★	Amigo (Warner Bros., 1994)
★★★½	Nascimento (Warner Bros., 1997)
★★★½	Musica do Mundo (EMI Brz., 1998)
★★★	Crooner (Warner Bros., 1999)

One of Brazil's most talented singer/songwriters, Milton Nascimento is blessed with one of pop music's most perfect voices—rich and soulful in its lower register, angelically pure in falsetto—as well as the sort of melodic instincts that can exploit such a voice to its fullest. Understandably, that combination has made him a superstar in his homeland, where his recordings are treated with the fervor and respect Americans once lavished on Stevie Wonder. Yet even though numerous attempts have been made to translate Nascimento's appeal into American terms, he remains a cult artist at best in this country, a situation that is less an indictment of U.S. pop fans than a reflection of how quintessentially Brazilian Nascimento's music is.

That's not to say he's strictly a samba singer or bossa nova act. Like many Brazilian musicians who came up under the sway of *tropicalismo,* Nascimento was as in awe of the Beatles as any American rock fan; indeed, the first selection on *Milton* is a version of the Lõ Borges tune "Para Lennon e McCartney" ("For Lennon and McCartney"). But Nascimento's first American album, *Courage,* shows no hint of this, as his songs are given the same lush Creed Taylor production that had been lavished on similar efforts by samba stars like Antonio Carlos Jobim (who also worked with Taylor). Consequently, the album, though listenable enough, fails to offer any real sense of Nascimento's talents.

It would take seven years before he assembled another album for U.S. consumption, but Nascimento's Brazilian output improved steadily, offering a masterful synthesis of Brazilian pop styles, from the childlike cadences of "Ponta De Areia" (from *Minas*) to the hypnotic primitivism of "Promessas Do Sol" (from *Geraes*) and the dramatic splendor of "Milagre dos Peixes" (from *Milagre dos Peixes*). *Musica do Mundo* nicely summarizes this period.

In 1975, Nascimento was featured on the Wayne Shorter album *Native Dancer,* and Shorter returned the favor a year later by appearing—along with Herbie Hancock—on *Milton,* his second U.S. release. A wonderfully alluring album, it neither diluted Nascimento's sound nor made it seem in any way foreign, and the remakes of "Raca" and "The Call (A Chamada)" rival the Brazilian originals. But *Journey to Dawn,* which backs away from Milton's jazzy insouciance, isn't quite as exciting, and Nascimento's option with A&M was not renewed.

Meanwhile, back in Brazil, Nascimento was going strong, and made a major step forward with the politically charged mass, *Missa dos Quilombos* in 1982. That same year, the remarkably assured *Ănĭmă* was released in the U.S., which found the singer holding his own even against such a luminary as Caetano Veloso on "As Várias Pontas de Uma Estrela." Although his music was no more jazzy than before, Nascimento continued to record with American jazz-men. Shorter gets guest-star billing on the live *A Barco dos Amantes,*

while Pat Metheny adds some delightfully colorful guitar to "Vidro e Corte" on *Encontros e Despedidas* (although that album's highlight is undoubtedly the Winnie Mandela tribute "Lágrima do Sul").

Yauaretê strikes an inspired balance between American and Brazilian music, thanks in part to the Paul Simon cameo on "O Vendedor de Sonhos." (Nascimento appears on Simon's *Rhythm of the Saints*). The album is something of a turning point for Nascimento, as subsequent albums made much freer use of guest stars (such as James Taylor, who appears in a bilingual version of "Only a Dream in Rio" on *Angelus*) and cover songs (a dreamy "Old Man River" on *Nascimento,* a hushed remake of the Beatles' "Hello Goodbye" on *Angelus*). That's not to say Nascimento entirely left Brazil behind, as the winningly exotic *Txai* offers a breathtaking evocation of his homeland's indigenous culture. But the all-covers, multilingual *Crooner* seems to suggest that Nascimento would like a worldwide following, something he may yet achieve. —J.D.C.

Naughty by Nature

★★★	Naughty by Nature (Tommy Boy, 1991)
★★★	19 Naughty III (Tommy Boy, 1992)
★★★★	Poverty's Paradise (Tommy Boy, 1995)
★★★★	Nature's Finest (Tommy Boy, 1999)
★★½	Nineteen Naughty Nine: Nature's Fury (Arista, 1999)
★★★	IIcons (TVT, 2002)

During the early '90s, the talented, pop-friendly rap trio Naughty by Nature helped to connect rap's old and new(er) schools by turning out irresistible, sample-laden hits ("O.P.P.") and verbose, streetwise rhymes. *Poverty's Paradise* is an invite to the actual block party, the perfect straddle between pop smarts and street cred, as MCs Treach and Vinnie (a.k.a. Vin Rock) power-rhyme their way through bright hooks and booming beats. NBN's later hits were less satisfying—when other acts caught on to their party-jam recipe, Treach and crew began to sound less essential. "Jamboree" (from *Nineteen Naughty Nine*) was an obvious update of the Treacherous Three's update of "Yes We Can Can." *IIcons,* recorded after KayGee left and Tommy Boy dropped the group, relies too heavily on guest spots. Although the crew had fewer greatest hits than the 17-track compilation suggests, *Nature's Finest* is their truest legacy. Today, the declaration that rap/hip-hop music is here to stay may generate nostalgia for a time when the assertion seemed defiant rather than redundant. But that doesn't undercut its power or joy of "Hip Hop Hooray." It's an anthem, so get your damn hands up! —K.H.

Meshell Ndegeocello

★★★★ Plantation Lullabies (Maverick, 1993)
★★★½ Peace Beyond Passion (Maverick, 1996)
★★★★ Bitter (Maverick, 1999)
★★★ Cookie: The Anthropological Mixtape (Maverick, 2002)

Like Curtis Mayfield, Sly Stone, George Clinton, and Prince before her, Meshell Ndegeocello grabbed influences wherever she found them, combining James Brown funk, Beatlesque rock, and iconoclastic lyrics into songs that put the listener in motion at both ends of the spinal column. Because she was born in 1969 and debuted in 1993, she added hip-hop and go-go to the mix; because she was a bisexual woman, she added a fearless form of feminism; all this anticipated the later arrival of Erykah Badu, India.Arie, Lauryn Hill, and Jill Scott.

Born Michelle Johnson, the young bohemian adopted the Swahili name for "free like a bird" (she originally spelled it Me'Shell NdegéOcello but later dropped the strange punctuation and capitalization; she pronounces it mih-SHEL en-DAY-gay-oh-CHEL-lo). She was first and foremost a monster bass player, and that emphasis on a fat, percolating bottom made all her music—even her gloomiest ruminations on race, sex, and power—funky. Her instrumental skills also led her to melodic and harmonic adventures that distinguished her tunes from most hip-hop.

An army brat who was raised in Europe and D.C., she wound up in New York after college, joined the Black Rock Coalition, and signed with Madonna's label. Her debut, *Plantation Lullabies,* garnered three Grammy nominations and wound up on lots of year-end 10-best lists. Virtually a Prince-like one-person production, it bristled with irresistible hooks—rhythmic, melodic, and verbal ("I'm digging you like an old soul record"). She celebrated African-American culture, but she also criticized its self-betrayals in the form of addiction and misogyny.

She enjoyed a modest hit single with "If That's Your Boyfriend (He Wasn't Last Night)" from her debut and a bigger hit single with Van Morrison's "Wild Night," a duet with John Mellencamp from his album. But rather than build on this initial success by refining her formula, Ndegeocello took a left turn on her much-delayed second album, *Peace Beyond Passion.* Her music was thickened with vocal and keyboard harmonies; her lyrics adopted biblical imagery to discuss racial and sexual politics in pointed detail. The hooks weren't as sharp as before, but her big ambitions clicked more often than they misfired.

Bitter replaced dance tracks with chamber pop in a shift as radical as Prince's move from *1999* to *Around the World in a Day* or the Beach Boys' move from *The Beach Boys Today* to *Pet Sounds.* Ndegeocello and producer Craig Street used a string quartet, Prince alumni Wendy and Lisa, and a tasteful rhythm section to create the hushed intimacy and bruised intensity that goes with fresh heartbreak. Not just the lyrics but also the melodies and arrangements capture that period right after a breakup when every pore in your skin becomes a deep-dish antenna for hurt and hope.

As the title implies, *Cookie: The Anthropological Mixtape* pulls together all of Ndegeocello's far-flung interests, scrambling hip-hop, leftist politics, synth strings, street-corner observations, deep funk, romantic confessions, D.C. go-go music, sexual boundary-crossing, pretty pop keyboards, and sampled black orators. The sprawling, 19-track, 71-minute CD has its peaks ("Pocketbook," "Barry Farms"), but it also has plenty of valleys where the melody, groove, and imagery remain underdeveloped. —G.H.

Youssou N'Dour

★★★½ Immigrés (1984; Earthworks/Virgin, 1989)
★★★½ Inédits '84–'85 (1985; Earthworks/Virgin, 1999)
★★★ Nelson Mandela (Verve, 1986)
★★★ The Lion (Virgin, 1989)
★★★½ Set (Virgin, 1990)
★★★★ Eyes Open (Columbia, 1992)
★★ The Guide (Wommat) (Chaos/Columbia, 1994)
★★★★ Best of the '80s (Celluloid, 1998)
★★★½ Best of Youssou N'Dour (EMI, 1999)
★★★ Lii! (Jololi, 2000)
★★★★ Joko (The Link) (Nonesuch, 2000)
★★★★ Nothing's in Vain (Coono du réér) (Nonesuch, 2002)
★★★★½ The Rough Guide to Youssou N'Dour & Étoile de Dakar (World Music Network, 2002)
★★★ 7 Seconds: The Best Of (Sony, 2004)

Before "7 Seconds," his hit duet with Neneh Cherry on the otherwise mediocre *The Guide (Wommat),* Americans knew Youssou N'Dour, if at all, as Peter Gabriel's duet partner on "In Your Eyes." But in Senegal—indeed, in much of Africa—N'Dour is perhaps the most famous singer alive. Blessed with a voice as expressive as it is spectacular, N'Dour combines the soaring lyricism of the West African singing-historian griots with the fluttering virtuosity of the great Islamic vocalists. As a singer, he has no peer. But there seemed to be no satisfactory way to explain him to the Western marketplace. Not only does N'Dour sing almost exclusively in Wolof, his native language, but the m'balax—literally, "rhythmic accompaniment"—sound he has developed seems nowhere near as pop-friendly as Fela's Afrobeat, or the South African mbaqanga Paul Simon co-opted.

Consequently, even though there's much to recommend the recordings N'Dour intended for his African audience—*Inédits* and the wonderfully moving *Immigrés*—the potential for crossover seemed maddeningly elusive. *The Lion* augmented the singer's own Étoile de Dakar with members of Peter Gabriel's band, but this tended to dilute the music. *Set,* by contrast, fleshed out N'Dour's band with synth sequences and funk licks without crowding its own sound, thereby enlivening the group's indigenous groove while creating a middle ground for his singular vocals. N'Dour took further strides toward graceful fusion with *Eyes Open,* in which he was able to deliver a track as instantly accessible as "Africa Remembers" while holding on to the rhythmic exoticisms of material such as "Yo Lé Le (Fulani Groove)."

After "7 Seconds" was all over American radio, N'Dour could have declared his conquest of world pop over. Instead, he went home to Dakar and built the Xippi studio, which has quietly turned into an artist-owned enterprise to rival Lee Perry's famous Black Ark. Most of the Xippi recordings that reach the U.S. market are N'Dour's own, but they are masterpieces of modern Afropop production and arrangements. N'Dour is now more precisely in tune with folk bases and visionary about urbane energy than anyone except possibly Salif Keita. *Joko (The Link)* and especially *Nothing's in Vain (Coono du réér)* are where to begin the new, heady N'Dour trip. They have rich sound, varieties of passion, and complexity of tone on a par with classic rock or R&B albums. *Best of the '80s* is a waste-free display of the toil and thrills that led up to N'Dour's current high plane. *7 Seconds: The Best Of* offers the smartest possible case for N'Dour's more Westernized works. He's too clever a performer and too transcendent a vocalist for it to be less than sturdy fun—but it's not the material that will make him last. Finally, *The Rough Guide to Youssou N'Dour & Étoile de Dakar* is the logical listen after the three previous albums, and may outlast them all as a favorite. Mbalax takes form and takes flight here, and with guidance from N'Dour's current work, you can hear his primal tunes mesh with his primo band. He creates a country's modern pop sound, with pattering tama drums, scampering electric guitars, and his arcing voice all filled with the rush of discovery and the flash of stardom.   —J.D.C./M.M.

Fred Neil

★★★★   Bleecker & MacDougal (1965; Elektra, 2001)
★★★½   The Many Sides of Fred Neil (Collector's Choice, 1998)

Reclusive, mysterious, and extravagantly gifted, Fred Neil was a pivotal figure in the transition from folksinger to singer/songwriter. Little is known for certain about his early years, though myth places him in Memphis with the Sun gang and in Clovis, New Mexico, with Buddy Holly (who recorded one of his songs). Neil was known to have haunted the halls of the Brill Building in the '50s, where he sold songs to Roy Orbison ("Candy Man"), Jack Scott ("Grizzly Bear"), and others, while recording a succession of obscure pop and rockabilly singles. He discovered Greenwich Village and the burgeoning folk scene, in which he could give full vent to the bluesier side of his personality. His calling card was his extraordinary voice, an impossibly deep and rich baritone Odetta once described as "a healing instrument."

After a 1964 album as part of a folk duo with Vince Martin, Neil bowed on his own the following year with the epochal *Bleecker & MacDougal.* "The Water Is Wide" demonstrates his mastery of tradition; "Blues on the Ceiling" shows the master bluesman's ability to make something fresh from familiar materials. He transcends genre with the tender ballad "Little Bit of Rain," while "Other Side to This Life" would become a favorite of folk rockers from the Youngbloods to the Jefferson Airplane. With a supporting cast of guitarist Peter Childs, future Lovin' Spoonful founder John Sebastian on harp, and Mountain architect Felix Pappalardi on bass, this is folk that often rocks. (They even throw in "Candy Man," just to make it obvious.) *Bleecker & MacDougal* is one of the albums that best captures its era, but its greatness is also in the future it predicts.

The Many Sides of Fred Neil presents his three subsequent albums for Capitol and an album's worth of unreleased material, all on two CDs. The 1967 album, called simply *Fred Neil,* is five-star stuff, surpassing *Bleecker & MacDougal.* "I've Got a Secret," "That's the Bag I'm In," and "Sweet Cocaine" (the latter two featuring Canned Heat's Alan Wilson on harp) are among his best blues adaptations, but two exquisite songs of longing mark this as a classic: "The Dolphins" ("I've been searching for the dolphins in the sea/and sometimes I wonder, do you ever think of me?") and "Everybody's Talkin'." When the latter was covered by Harry Nilsson and used as the theme for the film *Midnight Cowboy,* it became a hit and then a standard. Neil actively resisted the fame this brought him; his performing antipathy was such that he had to be begged, cajoled, and even tricked into making records. *Sessions* documents this antipathy, as well as the drug problem that had always hounded him; the fog lifts only for "Felicity" and a bravura reading of Percy Mayfield's "Please Send Me Someone to Love." *Other Side of This Life* is a 1971 contract-satisfier, half live and half disappointing duets with the likes of Les McCann and Gram Parsons. Fred Neil never released another record, disappearing into the Florida Keys, where he lived anonymously off songwriting royalties until his death in 2001, an enigma to the end.   —B.E.

Nelly

★★★	Country Grammar (Universal, 2000)
★★★½	Nellyville (Universal, 2002)
★★★★	Da Derrty Versions: The Reinvention (Universal, 2003)
★★★½	Sweat (Universal, 2004)
★★★	Suit (Universal, 2004)

Under the name Nelly, St. Louis rapper Cornell Haynes Jr. became one of the decade's hottest stars by honing two hip-hop fundamentals, both of which are often forgotten when the bling starts to sing. First, he kept it real by keeping it local, proving yet again that hip-hop is the world's biggest pop style because it's the most proudly parochial. Equally important, he matched his "back there" with a "back then," taking the playas to the playground, where flossing and rhyming are reborn with every new generation.

The result was Nelly's huge breakthrough hit of 2000, "Country Grammar (Hot . . .)" the lead single off his major label debut of the same name. The song's "down, down baby" chorus was lifted from a double-dutch rhyme that, in one version or another, can be heard at school recesses across the country. Nelly's St. Louis version, however, was located in the country's center, a position that allowed it to mix up Dirty South bounce, West Coast flash, and even the junior thug harmonies that once emanated from Cleveland. And if it borrowed from everywhere, it gave back to everyone. The music mostly concerned itself with riding in cars and women (in that order), and his honeyed flow— perched halfway between rapping and singing—and Jason "Jay E" Epperson's airy production invited all comers along.

Country Grammar's catchiest, most convivial tracks became hits (the Spanglish-flavored "E.I.," the definitive "Ride Wit Me"), but the rest was mostly competent filler, stretching out the St. Louis tour to fill the requisite hour-plus of a mainstream rap CD. Two years later, though, Nelly proved the depth of his talent with an album that nearly doubled his hit quotient by transforming St. Louis into "Nellyville," a utopian fantasyland where everyone gets "40 acres and a pool." Produced by the Neptunes, the single is flashier than anything on *Country Grammar,* and the rest of the album follows suit, especially on the numbers where Nelly and a guest artist dives into mainstream pop and R&B waters, like "Dilemma" with Kelly Rowland or "Work It" with Justin Timberlake. At the album's best, it's thrilling to see this former ballplayer swing so confidently (even if he sometimes still whiffs).

Da Derrty Versions remixes all the hits, but Epperson's "reinventions" are so offhand that this quick cash-in could be Nelly's most winning product yet. David Banner turns "Air Force One" into a demonic grunge assault, Ron Isley ("Mr. Biggs himself") reimagines a blaxploitation "Pimp Juice," and "Ride Wit Me" starts as stripped-down cipher and morphs into a chunky pop hit that would sit comfortably in a mix between No Doubt and John Mayer—and slyly outshine them both. Everyone can ride along, but only one man will drive.   —F.S.

Rick Nelson

★★★½	Ricky/Ricky Nelson (1957, 1958; Capitol, 2001)
★★★½	Ricky Sings Again/Songs by Ricky (1959, 1959; Capitol, 2001)
★★★½	More Songs by Ricky/Rick Is 21 (1960, 1961; Capitol, 2001)
★★★½	Rick Sings Spirituals/Album Seven by Rick (1960, 1962; Capitol, 2001)
★★★½	Garden Party (MCA, 1972)
★★★	Playing to Win (1981; Capitol, 2001)
★★★½	The Best of Rick Nelson (EMI, 1987)
★★★	Live 1983–1985 (1986; Rhino, 1989)
★★★	The Best of Rick Nelson 1963–1975 (MCA, 1990)
★★★★	Ricky Nelson (Volume One): The Legendary Masters Series (EMI, 1990)
★★★★½	The Best of Rick Nelson, Vol. 2 (EMI, 1991)
★★★	The Best of Rick Nelson (Curb, 1991)
★★★½	Stay Young: The Epic Recordings (Sony, 1993)
★★★½	A Night to Remember (Varèse Sarabande, 1999)
★★★½	A&E Biography (Capitol, 1999)
★★★½	Absolutely the Best . . . Live! (Varèse Sarabande, 2000)
★★★★	Legacy (Capitol, 2000)
★★★½	The Greatest Hits: Revisited (Varèse Sarabande, 2001)
★★★★	Greatest Hits (Capitol, 2002)

If he had to die young and under tragic circumstances, then at least Rick Nelson went to his grave knowing he had won the respect he had been seeking from the outset of his career. At the time of his death, Nelson was widely acknowledged as an important artist whose recordings from the late '50s through the early '60s not only constituted some of the most important contributions by any artist of that time, but also performed the valuable service of keeping the rootsy rock & roll flame alive after the army had taken Elvis. Although he wasn't blessed with the great pipes of his idol, Elvis, Nelson, along with producer Jimmie Haskell and his father/mentor, former big-band leader (and TV's most genial dad) Ozzie Nelson, chose terrific material by good writers and employed consummate studio musicians. Rick brought it home by employing his smooth, almost monotone tenor with feeling and subtlety, conveying a broad spectrum of emotions in songs that mostly relate to teen angst in all its forms, from lovesickness and alienation to wanderlust and living it up with the gal of your dreams.

Marketed as a teen idol and given a springboard to national recognition on his family's weekly sitcom, *The Adventures of Ozzie and Harriet,* Nelson could have coasted all the way to the bank. Even though his initial inspiration for recording was to impress a girl-friend who was deep in the throes of Elvismania, once he got started—via a straight-out-of-the-box hit in 1957 with a cover of Fats Domino's "I'm Walkin' " (which he introduced on the TV show) and its flip side, "A Teenager's Romance," an atmospheric dirge lamenting the emotional turmoil of young love—Nelson took nothing for granted. With each new record, it seemed as if he had grown, singing more effectively (especially on his warm love ballads) and getting great support from some of the finest musicians in Los Angeles. In addition, incomparable studio guidance was provided by his father and certainly by Haskell, whose arrangements were practically flawless. Through the early years, Nelson championed the emerging young rock & roll songwriters of the day as well as the pop giants of an earlier era: One of his favorite writers, Baker Knight, penned "Lonesome Town" and "Never Be Anyone Else but You" and numerous album tracks; Dorsey and Johnny Burnette, together and singly, contributed a wealth of songs to the Nelson canon, including "It's Late," "Believe What You Say," "Waitin' in School," and "One of These Mornings"; Gene Pitney was the source for "Hello Mary Lou." From 1957 through 1964, Nelson placed 33 singles in the Top 40, 17 of those in the Top 10, two of them—1958's "Poor Little Fool" and 1961's "Travelin' Man"—topping the chart.

Nelson had his demons, though. As the '60s wore on, drugs did a number on him, and his storybook marriage to Kristin Harmon (daughter of college football legend Tom Harmon) broke up when the two of them were battling substance abuse and Ricky was struggling to reestablish himself as a viable music artist after his hits had ceased. His recovery, personally and artistically, is one of the most heartening stories in rock & roll lore. In the late '60s, he went foursquare into one of his lifelong passions, country music, and formed a new band, the Stone Canyon Band, to help him get back on track. Inspired by Bob Dylan's *Nashville Skyline* album, Nelson sculpted a fusion of rock, folk, and country that was slightly ahead of its time and helped serve as the foundation for the country-rock explosion of the '70s. In 1970, he returned to the Top 40 for the first time in six years with a lilting, seductive cover of Dylan's "She Belongs to Me." A year later, he played an oldies show at Madison Square Garden and was booed by fans who resented his new look and sound. His response was to dig in deeper with what he had going, and to those fans who wanted to see Ricky instead of Rick, he warbled, "If memories were all I sang/I'd rather drive a truck," in his song "Garden Party," his final Top 10 hit, which peaked at #6, in 1972. That he had no further chart hits before his death in a plane crash on New Year's Eve 1985 is no reflection on the quality of his music in the years between 1972 and 1985. With both Epic and Capitol he made some solid albums, one of the best of his career being 1981's Capitol LP, *Playing to Win,* which features a sizzling cover of John Fogerty's "Almost Saturday Night," and a potent interpretation of John Hiatt's "It Hasn't Happened Yet," as well as two strong originals, "The Loser Babe Is You" and "Call It What You Want." The Epic overview, *Stay Young: The Epic Recordings,* is a succinct roll call of some unjustly ignored work.

Early Ricky Nelson is amply and well documented in several collections, from single-disc hits volumes to twofer album reissues. For annotation and song selection, high marks go to EMI's two-volume *The Best of Rick Nelson,* which covers his first #1, 1958's "Poor Little Fool," to 1962's "It's Up to You," with interesting stops in between. For one solid disc of chart monsters, Capitol's *Greatest Hits* is just this side of awesome. Its 20-track tune stack kicks off with "I'm Walkin' " and concludes with "She Belongs to Me" and "Garden Party," and also features juiced-up single versions of "Be Bop Baby" and "Believe What You Say."

Capitol has done a great service to Nelson fans by reissuing all seven albums and the one EP that Nelson cut for Imperial between 1957 and 1962 on four discs of twofers. These are remarkable recordings, particularly if you're a Nelson fan interested in hearing his progression from nervous moonlighter to assured professional.

For a fairly full and complete story of a productive 30-year recording career, the four-CD box set, *Legacy*, is the winning ticket. In addition to all the hits, the fare includes a number of the bonus tracks from the Capitol/Imperial discs (including the above-mentioned alternate take of "Lonesome Town"); two fine, previously unissued Christmas songs (Mel Torme's "The Christmas Song" and "Jingle Bells"); previously unissued recordings (from the 1974–1985 period) of Buddy Holly's "Rave On" and John Hiatt's "Doll Hospital"; and, among several previously unissued live tracks, a rousing duet with Don Everly on the Everly Brothers' hit "Bye Bye Love." An accompanying booklet lays out Nelson's history, and the liner notes to each disc contain complete session info as well. This one's as good as box sets come, and serves as a worthy tribute to a man who conducted his career and lived his too-short life with great personal dignity and compelling artistic integrity.   —D.M.

Willie Nelson

- ★★★½ Country Favorites Willie Nelson Style (1966; BMG, 2002)
- ★★★ Shotgun Willie (Atlantic, 1973)
- ★★★★ Phases and Stages (Atlantic, 1974)
- ★★★★ Red Headed Stranger (Columbia, 1975)
- ★★½ The Sound in Your Mind (Columbia, 1976)
- ★★★ To Lefty From Willie (1977; Columbia/Legacy, 2003)
- ★★★★½ Stardust (1978; Columbia/Legacy, 1999)
- ★★★½ Willie and Family Live (1978; Columbia/Legacy, 2003)
- ★★★ Sings Kristofferson (Columbia, 1979)
- ★★★ Honeysuckle Rose (1980; Columbia/Legacy, 2003)
- ★★★½ Somewhere Over the Rainbow (Columbia, 1981)
- ★★★½ Greatest Hits (And Some That Will Be) (1981; Columbia/Legacy, 2003)
- ★★★★ Old Friends/Funny How Time Slips Away (1982, 1985; Koch, 2002)
- ★★★★½ In the Jailhouse Now/Brand on My Heart (1982, 1985; DCC, 2000)
- ★★ Always on My Mind (1982; Columbia/Legacy, 2003)
- ★★★★ Me and Paul (DCC, 1985)
- ★★½ Half Nelson (Columbia, 1985)
- ★★★ What a Wonderful World (Columbia, 1988)
- ★★★★★ Nite Life: Greatest Hits and Rare Tracks (Rhino, 1990)
- ★★★½ Across the Borderline (Columbia, 1993)
- ★★★½ The Early Years (Scotti Bros., 1994)
- ★★★½ Six Hours at Pedernales (Step One, 1995)
- ★★★★ The Essential Willie Nelson (RCA, 1995)
- ★★★½ Revolutions of Time: Journey (Columbia, 1995)
- ★★★★ Spirit (Island, 1996)
- ★★★★ I Let My Mind Wander (Kingfisher, 1997)
- ★★★★ 16 Biggest Hits (Columbia/Legacy, 1998)
- ★★★½ Teatro (Island, 1998)
- ★★★★ Night & Day (Pedernales, 1999)
- ★★★★½ Country Willie—His Own Songs (Buddha, 1999)
- ★★★½ The Very Best of Willie Nelson (Columbia/Legacy, 1999)
- ★ Love Songs (Columbia/Legacy, 2000)
- ★★★★ Me & the Drummer (Luck, 2000)
- ★★★ Milk Cow Blues (Island, 2000)
- ★★★½ Oh Boy Records Classics Presents: Willie Nelson (Oh Boy, 2000)
- ★★★½ Rainbow Connection (Island, 2001)
- ★★★½ Face of a Fighter (Delta Blue, 2001)
- ★½ Great Divide (Lost Highway, 2002)
- ★★ Stars & Guitars (Lost Highway, 2002)
- ★★★ RCA Country Legends (RCA, 2002)
- ★★★½ Crazy: The Demo Sessions (Sugar Hill, 2003)
- ★★★★ Broken Promises (Proper, 2003)
- ★★★★½ The Essential Willie Nelson (Columbia/Legacy, 2003)

Waylon Jennings/Willie Nelson

- ★★★½ Wanted: The Outlaws (RCA, 1976)
- ★★★ Waylon & Willie (1978; Buddha, 2000)
- ★★★ WWII (1982; Buddha, 2000)

Willie Nelson/Leon Russell

- ★★½ One for the Road (Columbia, 1979)

Willie Nelson/Ray Price

- ★★★½ San Antonio Rose (1980; Columbia/Legacy, 2003)
- ★★★★ Run That by Me One More Time (Lost Highway, 2003)

The Highwaymen

- ★★★½ The Road Goes on Forever (Liberty, 1995)
- ★★★ Super Hits (Columbia, 1999)

To make any sense at all out of Willie Nelson's discography, you first have to realize that he has reinvented himself at least four times. In the '60s, he was Country Willie, the Nashville songwriter, who wrote hit songs for the likes of Ray Price, Faron Young, and Patsy Cline but couldn't buy a hit for himself. Then, in the '70s, he became Outlaw Willie, the Austin alternative to Nashville pablum, and that gave him his first big set of hits. But as he eased up on the songwriting, Nelson emerged as an astonishing Interpretive Singer, his voice instantly recognizable and his songbook ranging far beyond country turf. Finally, there is Willie the Superstar, the good-natured chum of celebrities everywhere. Each of these Willies dominates a decade, but they also overlap and mix, and ultimately, there's just one man who binds them all together.

Nelson grew up in Texas, raised by his grandparents along with his sister/pianist Bobbie. He wrote a few songs and, in 1960, moved to Nashville. His house burned down in 1970, and he took that as a sign to leave Nashville, so he headed back to Austin, a booming confluence of longhairs and/or rednecks, not to mention old-fashioned Texas liberals. While in Nashville, Nelson recorded two albums for Liberty and a dozen for RCA—few of which are still in print, though RCA has started to make amends: *Essential* is a good overview, while *RCA Country Legends* focuses on obscure 1972 material that was shelved when Nelson left the label. But the prize is the reissue of *Country Willie*, on which Nelson recut 12 of his own songs so simply and eloquently that, for once, countrypolitan producer Chet Atkins didn't even try to mess things up.

But Nelson was a songwriting legend, and most of what's in print from the early '60s are the simply arranged song demos that he cut for Pamper Music. The "Pamper Demos" have been so loosely licensed that we now have lots of competing, overlapping, poorly documented sets: Kingfisher's *I Let My Mind Wander* is the most consistent; Delta Blue's *Face of a Fighter* is more complete; Sugar Hill's *Crazy* has some rare cuts; the *Oh Boy* set has better-known songs; and Proper's 40-cut *Broken Promises* is the best overall deal—but none of these are definitive. Rhino's *Nite Life* pulls Nelson's '60s together; it's an outstanding package on which the greatest hits are, if anything, eclipsed by rare tracks, like the unreleased "You'll Always Have Someone" and the B side "Me and Paul."

Nelson's outlaw mystique emerged gradually but was certified in 1976, when hype and opportunism converged in RCA's release of a passel of leftovers titled *Wanted! The Outlaws.* With solos and duets by Waylon Jennings and Willie Nelson, extras by Jennings' wife, Jessi Colter, and sureshot covers by Tompall Glaser, *Outlaws* sounded old and tough and crossed over enough to become the first country album to go platinum. Jennings got top billing, but Nelson was the real talent and had the legend to back it up: His exodus from Nashville to the promised land of Austin and the series of ambitious albums he cut after freeing himself from the countrypolitan yoke— *Shotgun Willie*, recorded in Muscle Shoals with the Memphis Horns, and two concept albums built around repeated themes, *Phases and Stages* and *Red Headed Stranger*, the latter a huge hit. *Red Headed Stranger* went a step further in sketching out a story line: A jealous preacher kills his wife and her lover, wanders dazed and lovesick, kills again, and finally finds redemption in the love of another woman. What you think of that story may depend on how you estimate the life span of the second woman, but the album was unique, its ambiguity befitted an outlaw, and it sold miraculously well. It made Nelson a star. It was also the last ambitious artistic statement he ever made—but not the last brilliant one.

Nelson's followup, *The Sound in Your Mind*, had little new and lots of filler. Then he knocked off *To Lefty From Willie*, a set of covers that even at best just remind you how incomparable Frizzell was. Then Nelson thought he'd try even older songs, pop standards such as "Moonlight in Vermont" and "Georgia on My Mind," which he sang with such delicate conviction as to suggest that he owed more to Hoagy Carmichael than to Hank Williams. And that album, *Stardust*, sold some 3 million copies: It was his biggest hit ever, and all the legendary songwriter had to do was sing. That lesson, of course, wasn't lost on Nelson: He wrote less than ever and covered damn near everything—often brilliantly. But his later pop-standards albums, *Somewhere Over the Rainbow* and *What a Wonderful World*, fell short and shorter. And there are atrocities among the covers, including most of *Always on My Mind* and all of *Love Songs*.

Nelson's long stay at Columbia produced a lot of everything, which is the main reason the compilations are such mixed affairs. Although the three-CD box *Revolutions of Time* has a nice booklet, it sags in the middle (too much *Half Nelson*); the two-CD *Very Best of Willie Nelson* starts strong but gets sandbagged in uninspired collaborations and overpowered covers; and while *16 Biggest Hits* is short, it is the most consistently listenable, perhaps because it's the most consistently country. So the compilations really don't have much advantage over the better albums, which include: *Willie and Family Live,* a feel-good concert album; *Honeysuckle Rose,* the mostly live soundtrack to a movie in which Nelson expertly played himself; *Me and Paul,* with three good Billy Joe Shaver songs and a bunch of vintage Nelson classics; and a delightful series of duet albums with Nelson's old Nashville mentors: Ray Price, Webb Pierce, Hank Snow, Faron Young, and Roger Miller. The common denominator on his best albums is that they are loose, intimate, and personal, such as the lovely reunion with Price, 23 years later, *Run That by Me One More Time.*

But Nelson's last Columbia album was anything but loose: He brought in Don Was to produce *Across the Borderline* and called in celebrity connections to decorate the album with bits of Paul Simon, Bonnie Raitt, Sinéad O'Connor, Bob Dylan, and plenty more. The album has some impressive-sounding pieces but also seems arty and contrived. Nelson's later albums flip between fancy superstar confabs and the sort of minor projects that he really excels at. Among the latter form are *Spirit,* a spare set of originals done with just guitar, piano, and fiddle; *Night and Day,* a set of jazz-tinged instrumentals that show his delight in his band; and *Me & the Drummer,* on which he revisits his own vintage songbook.

On the other hand, when Nelson hooks up with fellow celebrities, he tends to get lost. *Milk Cow Blues*— with wannabes like Francine Reed crowding the spotlight and veterans such as B.B. King stealing the show—reminds you that Nelson never was much of a bluesman. But if *Great Divide* is any indication, Nelson's future in heavy-metal power ballads and New Jack R&B promises even less. And the live *Stars & Guitars,* even more laden with guest stars, fares better only because it hangs on to more old songs.

Over the years, Nelson has collaborated prolifically. The success of *Wanted! The Outlaws* led to *Waylon & Willie* and *WWII,* both of which have good cuts, including the latter's sarcastic "Write Your Own Songs." Waylon and Willie were joined by Johnny Cash and Kris Kristofferson to form the Highwaymen. Much of the thrill of their first two albums (cut down to *Super Hits*) is in hearing the unmistakable voices of Nelson and Cash trade turns, but their third album, *The Road Goes On Forever,* features better songs, starting off with Steve Earle's "The Devil's Right Hand." But Nelson's collaborations have more often than not been just a way to knock out some easy product. That turns out fine when he is working with his country-music peers—*Brand on My Heart,* with Hank Snow, is as much pure pleasure as anything he's ever done.

Columbia/Legacy's new two-CD *The Essential Willie Nelson* is the first serious attempt at a career-spanning sampler, starting with Nelson's 1961 "Night Life" single and working its way through to a riotous superstar encounter with Aerosmith 42 years later. Given Nelson's cornucopia, the set necessarily omits a lot and includes things one would rather forget, but in its big picture, it reminds us what a wonder Willie is.   —T.H.

N.E.R.D.

★★★½   In Search Of . . . (Virgin, 2002)
★★★½   Fly or Die (Virgin, 2004)

As the Neptunes, Pharrell Williams and Chad Hugo have quickly become one of the world's top pop and hip-hop production teams, crafting hits for everyone from Britney Spears to Snoop Dogg. But Williams and Hugo apparently desire something more from their career than the accolades and cash that come

from making other people's music. And so in 2001, with help from colleague Shae, they formed their own band, N.E.R.D. Their debut, *In Search Of . . . ,* is a preposterous blend of influences—'60s psychedelia, '70s AM pop, classic R&B, '90s rap metal—held together by unshakable hooks and Williams' charmingly wayward falsetto. It's hard to know whether these guys actually believe in the Neanderthal lyrics of "Lapdance" or "Rock Star," but damn, those tunes are catchy.

With *Fly or Die,* N.E.R.D. continues to score high on the guilty-pleasure chart, offering loose-limbed paeans to "Backseat Love" and putting Steely Dan chords to flamenco rhythms on "She Wants to Move." Hugo and Williams are clearly the funkiest producers-turned-performers going. Alan Parsons, eat their dust.   —M.R.

Aaron Neville

★★★   Orchid in the Storm (EP) (1985; Rhino, 1990)
★★½   Greatest Hits (Curb, 1990)
★★★½   My Greatest Gift (Rounder, 1990)
★★½   Tell It Like It Is (Curb, 1991)
★★★½   Warm Your Heart (A&M, 1991)
★★★   The Grand Tour (A&M, 1993)
★★★   The Tattooed Heart (A&M, 1995)
★★★   To Make Me Who I Am (A&M, 1997)
★★½   Devotion (Chardant, 2000)
★★★½   The Very Best of Aaron Neville (A&M, 2000)
★★★★   Ultimate Collection (Hip-O, 2001)
★★★   The Millennium Collection (A&M, 2001)
★★½   Humdinger (EMI, 2002)
★★½   Love Songs (A&M, 2003)
★★★   Nature Boy: The Standards Album (Verve, 2003)

"Tell It Like It Is," Aaron Neville's 1966 hit single, is arguably the greatest New Orleans R&B ballad ever, and Neville has every right to reprise the song at any and every opportunity. Unfortunately, a lot of what he recorded up to that point is fairly forgettable, which is why *Tell It Like It Is* seems to have less meat than filler. Still, the New Orleans flavor of its material at least seems a bit more genuine than the secondhand Memphis soul and imitation–Bacharach/David material included among the late-'60s singles on the obviously mistitled *Greatest Hits* (although that album, like *Tell It Like It Is,* takes care to include "Tell It Like It Is" and "Over You").

There's a different version of "Tell It Like It Is" on *My Greatest Gift,* but the bulk of these '70s-vintage tracks find Neville working with producer Allen Toussaint, a combination that produces memorably funky results on the likes of "Hercules" and "Mojo Hannah." Astonishingly, there isn't a version of "Tell It Like It Is" on *Orchid in the Storm,* but this 1985 ballad session (produced by Joel Dorn) does offer sterling renditions of oldies like the Johnny Ace hit "Pledging My Love" and Jerry Butler's "For Your Precious Love."

Yet it wasn't until *Warm Your Heart*—produced by Linda Ronstadt, with whom he'd recorded a set of Grammy-winning duets in 1990—that Neville had his first Top 40 success since "Tell It Like It Is." Again, there are a fair number of oldies here, with "Everybody Plays the Fool" being the standout, but as the more contemporary sound of "Angola Bound" makes plain, Neville is not just an oldie, but a goodie. Casual fans should go straight to Hip-O's fine *Ultimate Collection.* —J.D.C.

Neville Brothers

★★½	The Neville Brothers (Capitol, 1978)
★★★★	Fiyo on the Bayou (A&M, 1981)
★★★★	Neville-ization (Black Top, 1984)
★★★	Live at Tipitina's (Spindletop, 1985)
★½	Uptown (EMI America, 1987)
★★★★	Treacherous: A History of the Neville Brothers (Rhino, 1988)
★★★½	Yellow Moon (A&M, 1989)
★★★½	Treacherous Too! (Rhino, 1991)
★★★★	Legacy: A History of the Nevilles (Charly, 1990)
★★★	Brother's Keeper (A&M, 1990)
★★★½	The Millennium Collection (A&M, 2004)
★★½	Family Groove (A&M, 1992)
★★★	Live on Planet Earth (A&M, 1994)
★★	Mitakuye Oyasin Oyasin: All My Relations (A&M 1996)
★★★★	The Very Best of the Neville Brothers (Rhino, 1997)
★★★★	Live at Tipitina's 1982 (Rhino, 1998)
★★★	Valence Street (Columbia, 1999)
★★★★	Uptown Rulin' The Best of . . . (A&M, 1999)

Despite having a fearsomely soulful lead singer, flawless harmony vocals, and the finest rhythm section in New Orleans, the Neville Brothers have never achieved a level of success commensurate with their talent. Although the four Nevilles, Aaron, Art, Charles, and Cyril, had been kicking around the New Orleans music scene since the mid-'50s, when Aaron and Art were members of the Hawketts, the Neville Brothers as such didn't come together as a band until after the quartet had united behind the Wild Tchoupitoulas. What made the Tchoupitoulas album so exciting was the ease with which the group meshed contemporary funk licks with traditional Mardi Gras parade rhythms. But there's almost no sign of that sound on *The Neville Brothers,* where the group wastes its time on such calculated attempts at R&B currency as "Dancin' Jones" (an insipid paean to the Rolling Stones) and "Vieux Carré Rouge" (a pleasant-but-pedestrian soul ballad). Only "All Nights, All Right" and a version of John Hiatt's "Washable Ink" save the album from irrelevancy. *Fiyo on the Bayou* puts the band back on track. Some of the added punch can be attributed to the addition of guitarist Leo Nocentelli (who'd played in the Meters with Art and Cyril) to the rhythm section, but the real secret to this album's success is the shift in focus away from the R&B charts and toward the Crescent City. Apart from "Mona Lisa" and "The Ten Commandments of Love," a pair of oldies included to frame Aaron's otherworldly tenor, the songs are mostly traditional, lending the album a rootsy richness. Yet despite rave reviews, *Fiyo on the Bayou* made barely a blip on the pop charts; likewise, the stunning *Neville-ization,* which documents the group's legendary live act, failed to reach beyond the faithful. (*Live at Tipitina's* offers additional material from the same concert). Perhaps that explains the desperation of *Uptown,* an ill-advised attempt at mainstream respectability that not only downplays the New Orleans elements, but actually stiffens the groove with sequencers and electronic percussion.

By this point, the Nevilles' past appeared far more promising than their future—hence the intoxicating nostalgia of *Treacherous,* which mixes early solo singles by Art, Aaron, and Cyril with selections from *The Wild Tchoupitoulas, The Neville Brothers,* and *Fiyo on the Bayou. Treacherous Too!* continues in that vein, with more solo stuff and excerpts from *Neville-ization,* while Charly's *Legacy* takes a pre–Neville Brothers approach, augmenting its Art and Aaron tracks with tunes by the Meters. But just when it seemed the Nevilles would never find a way to reconcile their sound with the modern pop market, the group went into the studio with producer Daniel Lanois, emerging with the triumphant *Yellow Moon,* an album that manages to find room for such contemporary touches as rap ("Sister Rosa," a tribute to civil rights figure Rosa Parks) without compromising or corrupting the Nevilles' identity. Having found their formula, the Nevilles went back for more on *Brother's Keeper,* which may lack the eerie atmospherics of *Yellow Moon* but otherwise maintains its musical balance, thanks to touches like the low-key funk of "Witness" or the thick, dark harmonies of "Brother Blood." With the exception of the rootsy *Valence Street,* none of the band's recent work has come close. —J.D.C.

Neu!

★★★★ Neu! (1972; Astralwerks, 2001)
★★★ Neu! 2 (1973; Astralwerks, 2001)
★★★½ Neu! 75 (1975; Astralwerks, 2001)

Harmonia

★★★ Musik von Harmonia (1974; Universal/PolyGram, 1996)
★★★½ Deluxe (1975; Universal/PolyGram, 1996)
★★ Tracks & Traces (Rykodisc, 1997)

Michael Rother

★★★ Chronicles, Vol. 1 (Cleopatra, |1998)

Throughout the '80s and '90s, the mysterious German band Neu! (meaning "new," as in "New! Improved!") was a strong presence in avant-garde rock circles, partly because, at the time, only bootleg versions of their albums were available. Neu! gathered praise from Brian Eno, Sonic Youth, and Radiohead, while Stereolab owed a good deal of its sound directly to an outfit that started playing nearly 30 years earlier—and still sounds futuristic.

Rother and Dinger met during their brief stay in an early version of Kraftwerk, but they wanted to crank up their own music machine. Although both were urban technophiles, the dreamy Rother and the sullen Dinger were not a stable partnership. They were, however, among the first to grasp the implications of the Velvet Underground's stark, stiff beat applied to rock music. Dinger lubricated the VU momentum and called the Neu! beat "motorik." The long, triumphant tracks of the first album, "Hallogallo" and "Negativland," combine Dinger's head-down drive with the stretchy, curling guitar figures of Rother and engineer Conny Plank's farsighted, ever-present distortion effects. Neu! is not a joyride; it's an anxious flight into an unknown tomorrow. Neu 2 builds on the debut for the first side, then collapses into trite tape-speed manipulations, used when the band had depleted its studio-time funds.

By Neu! 75, the band had separated into its components. Rother's tunes were pacific, Dinger's more pissed-off (a valuable old wad of protopunk). Neu! 75 still feels rambunctious, though. Rother, who went on to explore the limits of peaceful machinery on the first two Harmonia albums and eight solo releases (well selected for Chronicles, Vol. 1), dwindled into a figure of fascination for cultists and guitarists. Dinger's group La Dusseldorf does not have anything in print. But time will never catch up with Neu!: It remains the once and future band of tomorrow. —M.MI.

Neutral Milk Hotel

★★★½ On Avery Island (Merge, 1996)
★★★★ In the Aeroplane Over the Sea (Merge, 1998)
★★½ Everything Is (Orange Twin, 2001)

Jeff Mangum

★★½ Live at Jitter Joe's (Orange Twin, 2001)

Although psychedelic retro-pop and neohippie experimentalism defined the cadre of affiliated bands known as Elephant 6 (including Apples in Stereo and Olivia Tremor Control), Jeff Mangum's Neutral Milk Hotel stands out as the unique, even visionary, one of the collective—and the most enigmatic. With Mangum (the group's only constant member) aided primarily by Apples chief Robert Schneider, Neutral Milk Hotel made an impressive debut with On Avery Island. Somewhere between the gloomy Smog and the classic-rocking Guided by Voices on the spectrum of notable mid-'90s lo-fi indie sounds, the record succeeds in blending surrealist lyrics and Sgt. Pepper–like instrumental coloring with punk-rock urgency and nearly gothic atmospheres. Its production limitations and a still-developing songwriting voice were the only slight weaknesses of this terrific effort.

By the followup, In the Aeroplane Over the Sea, Mangum had put together something resembling an actual band, resulting in a far richer and more organic sound. What's more, the songwriting had blossomed far beyond the bounds of Elephant 6 (or indie rock as a whole), with Mangum etching out timeless transcendentalist pop steeped in a century of American music (from funeral marches to driving punk). All sorts of triumphant brass and quavery organs dress up Mangum's passionate acoustic-guitar strums, irresistible melodies, and lyrics that rarely feel obtuse even when they're nonsensical. Although Aeroplane lacks a single weak track, an opening stretch—from the brisk introductory chords of "The King of Carrot Flowers Pt. One" to the fuzzed-out raveup of "Holland, 1945," halfway through—breezes by particularly flawlessly, shifting without notice among fragile, creaky, dignified, and even ballsy to create the core of a truly great record.

Aeroplane's accomplishment would be hard to top, and in fact Mangum thus far has found it impossible to follow up. While he spent three years in the apparent throes of writer's block and off making field recordings in Bulgaria, the Elephant 6–affiliated label Orange Twin finally interrupted his absence with a pair of archival recordings. Everything Is, which reissued Neutral Milk Hotel's 1995 European-only EP plus a previously unreleased track from the same period, features material that wouldn't have sounded out of place on On Avery Island. The second is a live solo recording by Mangum from a 1997 performance in an Athens, Georgia, coffeehouse. The set combines material from both albums, plus a cover of Phil Spector's "I Love How You Love Me" and previously unreleased Mangum songs. —R.M.S.

New Edition

★★★	Candy Girl (1983; Warlock, 1991)
★★★½	New Edition (MCA, 1984)
★★½	All for Love (MCA, 1985)
★★	Christmas All Over the World (MCA, 1985)
★★	Under the Blue Moon (MCA, 1986)
★★½	Heart Break (MCA, 1988)
★★★★	Greatest Hits (MCA, 1991)
★★½	Home Again (MCA, 1996)
★★	Lost In Love: The Best of the Slow Jams (MCA, 1998)
★★★★	All the Number Ones (Hip-O Universal, 2000)
★★★★	Hits (Geffen, 2004)

Originally assembled by songwriter/producer Maurice Starr in the hope of creating a latter-day Jackson 5, New Edition went from teen idols to hip-hop godfathers in less than a decade. The New Edition of *Candy Girl* is endearing but ragged, a bit unsure in the high register and none-too-close in its harmonies. That's not to say the album doesn't work: "Candy Girl" is a near-perfect gloss on the Jackson 5's "ABC," while "Is This the End" does an admirable job of rewriting "I'll Be There."

By *New Edition*, the group had moved into the mainstream, dumping Starr (he later concocted New Kids on the Block as a form of revenge) and working with top-flight L.A. studio talent. It paid off, thanks to insinuatingly tuneful material like "Cool It Now," which worked rap-style exchanges around Ralph Tresvant's boyish tenor, and the calculatedly innocent "Mr. Telephone Man." *All for Love* takes the same tack, though less successfully; "Count Me Out" comes across as a "Cool It Now" retread, and ballads like "Whispers in Bed" find the group in over its head. Even so, "A Little Bit of Love (Is All It Takes)" boasts one of the Edition's most memorable choruses, while "School" shows how much the quintet has learned about rap.

New Edition suffered its first defection at this point, when Bobby Brown left for a solo career that would eventually turn his flair for hip-hop into massive crossover success. Meanwhile, the group's remaining members went in the opposite direction, delivering an album of doo-wop oldies, *Under the Blue Moon*. It was a cute idea but a big mistake. Hoping to regain lost ground, the group brought in gruff young soulman Johnny Gill and recruited producers Jimmy

Jam and Terry Lewis to make *Heart Break*. Although the disc updates the group's rhythmic base and incorporates many of the ideas Brown exploited, not even songs as strong as "If It Isn't Love" or "Boys to Men" are enough to overcome the clunky conceptualism of the album's let's-pretend-this-is-a-concert presentation.

Heart Break may not have salvaged New Edition's fortunes as a group, but its respective members found themselves well-positioned for personal glory. Bell Biv DeVoe (that is, Ricky Bell, Michael "Biv" Bivins, and Ronnie DeVoe) generated hits as performers and producers, while Tresvant and Gill parlayed their New Edition visibility to solo success. But the public's appetite for New Edition hadn't diminished, so in 1996, the group—including Brown and Gill—reunited for *Home Again*. Although the material was somewhat predictable, the performances (honed by such top-drawer producers as Jam and Lewis, Jermaine Dupri, and Sean "Puffy" Combs) were strong enough to ensure the album's success. The comeback came and went, however, and when Brown walked out on the group, New Edition's final chapter appeared to have been written. *All the Number Ones* and the lamentable slow-jam collection *Lost in Love* are essentially contract-obligation albums, but *Number Ones* and *Hits* are extremely listenable overview of the New Edition saga. —J.D.C.

New Kids on the Block

★½	New Kids on the Block (Columbia, 1986)
★★	Hangin' Tough (Columbia, 1988)
★★	Step by Step (Columbia, 1990)
★★½	Greatest Hits (Columbia, 1999)
★★	Super Hits (Sony, 2001)

As the biggest teen-pop group of the late '80s and early '90s, New Kids on the Block are an integral link in the chain connecting the Osmonds to the Backstreet Boys and 'N Sync—Max Martin certainly learned a thing or two from listening to the music that impresario Maurice Starr penned for the New Kids. Starr, who had founded New Edition several years earlier, wrote a fresh chapter in the twisty, turny saga of rock 'n' miscegenation, finding five white kids to make famous (for a little while, at least). *Step by Step* signaled that the bloom was already off the rose, and teenypop would go into deep freeze for a half dozen years.

Alas, NKOTB's music hasn't aged well, mostly because Starr played it so safe. The albums are dominated by harmless, light pop funk that has neither the spritz of schlock nor the exuberance of true pop. While "I'll Be Loving You Forever" is a serviceable ballad and "You Got It (The Right Stuff)" a peppy dance tune, no one born after Reagan left office will care. (If you care, seek out Jordan Knight's self-titled 1999 solo disc, featuring "Give It to You" and a surprisingly credible version of "I Could Never Take the Place of Your Man" rendered in ballad form). Evolution—you never know where it's going to take you.   —K.H.

Randy Newman

- ★★★★ Randy Newman (1968; Warner Bros., 1995)
- ★★★★★ 12 Songs (1970; Warner Bros., 1990)
- ★★★½ Live (1971; Warner Bros., 1995)
- ★★★★★ Sail Away (1972; Rhino 1992)
- ★★★★ Good Old Boys (Warner Bros., 1974)
- ★★ Little Criminals (Warner Bros., 1977)
- ★★★½ Born Again (Warner Bros., 1979)
- ★★½ Trouble in Paradise (Warner Bros., 1983)
- ★★★½ Land of Dreams (Warner Bros., 1988)
- ★★ Randy Newman's Faust (Warner Bros., 1995)
- ★★★½ Guilty: Thirty Years of Randy Newman (Rhino, 1998)
- ★★★★ Bad Love (DreamWorks, 1999)
- ★★★★ The Best of Randy Newman (Rhino, 2001)

Randy Newman emerged in the late '60s as the slyest, meanest, and funniest of the post-Dylan singer/ songwriters. His music was steeped in old-time Tin Pan Alley piano; his sardonic lyrics inhabited sleazy characters from the B side of Nixon's America, hustlers and racists and glad-handers and backslappers. Newman sang in the ragged croak of a crazed old piano man, the Jewish Fred Sanford whose drawl was half "wanna kiss you" and half "get off my lawn." He started out in L.A. as a hack songwriter-for-hire with Hollywood connections, Hoagy Carmichael with a hard-boiled dark side. But he also had a feel for New Orleans R&B and the blues, making the two-bit Sun Belt con man he played on record sound like an American archetype as vivid as Duke Ellington or Fats Domino.

His debut album stunned musicians, who rushed out to cover its songs, and confused consumers, who rushed out to not buy it—a commercial slump that has lasted his whole career. Despite some Allen Sherman moments, *Randy Newman* had brilliant songwriting and orchestrations, especially the lonely piano ballad "I Think It's Going to Rain Today," recorded by everyone from Dusty Springfield and Neil Diamond to UB40 and Nina Simone. But *12 Songs* is where Newman got loose as a rock & roller, ditching the complex orchestrations for a bluesy, easy-swinging satire of America as a land of lonely gas-station attendants ("If You Need Oil"), desperate cuckolds ("Have You Seen My Baby?"), psychopaths ("Suzanne"), cranks

("Uncle Bob's Midnight Blues"), and bigots (a twisted cover of the '30s chestnut "Underneath the Harlem Moon"). The only folks on the album who escape the alienation long enough to have fun are in "Let's Burn Down the Cornfield," the tale of two sexy young pyromaniacs in love.

Sail Away hit even harder in the painfully beautiful title hymn, a slave-ship captain's invitation to the New World, where "you'll just sing about Jesus and drink wine all day." Very much a product of the New Hollywood of the *Easy Riders, Raging Bulls* era, *Sail Away* is Newman's broadest American portrait, especially the cold-blooded "Old Man," the nostalgic "Dayton, Ohio—1903," the blasphemous "God's Song," and the romantic "You Can Leave Your Hat On." *Good Old Boys* went all out for a concept album about the South, the home of "College men from LSU/Went in dumb, come out dumb too/Hustlin' 'round Atlanta in the alligator shoe/Getting drunk every weekend at the barbecue." Miraculously, Newman failed to get beaten within an inch of his life by angry Lynyrd Skynyrd roadies, but his musical and vocal warmth add a crucial touch of compassion to the album, particularly when he cuts back on the irony for ballads like "Rollin' " and "Louisiana 1927." (And the joke was ultimately on Newman: In the '90s, ex-Klansman politician David Duke used "Louisiana 1927" in campaign ads.) The 2002 Rhino reissue of *Good Old Boys* adds a bonus disc, *Johnny Cutler's Birthday*, a rough-draft demo version with just Newman at the piano, that includes the great previously unreleased song "My Daddy Knew Dixie Howell."

Newman got to feel up the radio for a few weeks in early 1978, when the catchy New Orleans piano shuffle "Short People" briefly became a novelty hit. *Little Criminals* was a bore, though the lyric to "You Can't Fool the Fat Man" sums up his worldview if anything does. *Born Again* went for nasty laughs, peaking with the hysterical "It's Money That I Love" and the achingly sad "Ghosts." But by now, Newman was getting serious about movie soundtracks and paying less mind to the record business. His work got spottier, stranding occasionally great songs in appallingly overproduced cheese. *Trouble in Paradise* and *Land of Dreams* perk up whenever Newman busts out his favorite comic persona, the egomaniac Hollywood sleaze pimp who slobbers his way through "My Life Is Good," "I Want You to Hurt Like I Do," and his signature hit, "I Love L.A." ("Look at these women! Ain't nothin' like 'em, *nowhere!*"). *Land of Dreams* opens with two killer autobiographical songs about his New Orleans childhood, "Dixie Flyer" and "New Orleans Wins the War." It would have been great to hear him follow this theme further—although the blatantly fake

"Falling in Love" was charming as well. His musical version of *Faust*, featuring guest vocals from Bonnie Raitt, James Taylor, Don Henley, and Linda Ronstadt, would have been a fine idea if he'd written a half-decent song or two.

As his movie-soundtrack career took off, Newman became a weird Hollywood star: nominated for countless Oscars, famous enough to play the ceremony every year, but not famous enough to win. Newman obviously got a perverse kick out of composing for stomach-turning treacle—pick a Top 10 of the schlockiest movies you've ever seen, and the odds are that Randy worked on at least three of them. Sometimes he knocked off a nice one: "You've Got a Friend in Me" from *Toy Story*, or "That'll Do" from *Babe: Pig in the City*. But it took Bill Clinton—a Newman character if ever there was one—to put the bite back in Newman's music. On *Bad Love*, his most inspired album since *Good Old Boys*, Newman sang "My Country" and "The World Isn't Fair" with a nasty rock & roll twitch that had seemed lost to him years ago. "Shame" was the most hilarious vocal performance on an album full of them; muttering "You know, I have a Lexus now" in a haze of heavy-breathing lust and piano boogie, the Randy Newman of *Bad Love* was the *real* pig in the city.

Guilty is a clumsily selected box set with ugly packaging and dumb liner notes, useful mainly for rounding up stray gems like "Gone Dead Train" (from *Performance*). "Change Your Way" (from *Ragtime*), and "Vine Street" (definitively recorded by Harry Nilsson on his 1970 *Nilsson Sings Newman*). *Live* was a concert quickie featuring a boffo version of "Lonely at the Top," originally written for Frank Sinatra, who wouldn't touch it. There's another box set out there waiting to be compiled: the greatest hits of Newman's early mercenary/songwriter years, including buried treasures like Dusty Springfield's "I Don't Want to Hear It Anymore," Jackie DeShannon's "Take Me Away," Claudine Longet's "Snow," and Irma Thomas' "While the City Sleeps." Fans may also wish to investigate Tony Randall's 1967 LP *Warm and Wavery*, which has a most distinctive version of "The Debutante's Ball." In 2002, after a record-tying 15 losing nominations, Randy Newman finally won his first Oscar, for a *Monsters, Inc.* throwaway that was forgotten before Randy even finished his acceptance speech. You can't fool the fat man. —R.S.

New Order

★★★ Movement (1981; Qwest, 1992)
★★★★½ Power, Corruption & Lies (1983; Qwest, 1992)
★★★½ Low-Life (Qwest, 1985)
★★★★ Brotherhood (Qwest, 1986)
★★★★★ Substance (Qwest, 1987)
★★★★½ Technique (Qwest, 1989)
★★★ Peel Sessions (Strange Fruit, 1990)
★★★ Republic (Qwest, 1993)
★★★½ The Best of New Order (London, 1995)
★★★½ BBC Radio 1 Live in Concert (Varèse, 2000)
★★★½ Get Ready (Reprise, 2001)

In short order, New Order combined dance music's physicality with postpunk guitar rock and pop songwriting. This innovation made New Order one of the most important rock bands of its era, and one of the most ripped-off. Indie rock copped the band's melodic, high-end bass sound, just-folks fashion sense, and disco revisionism. New Romantics admired its emotional inscrutability. Techno and hip-hop traded beat sciences with the band. Everyone stole from New Order, and everyone's music improved as a result.

When Joy Division's singer, Ian Curtis, took his life on the eve of the band's first American tour, the three surviving members—guitarist Bernard Sumner, bassist Peter Hook, and drummer Stephen Morris—joined with keyboardist Gillian Gilbert, renamed themselves New Order, and tried to carry on. *Movement* is no fun; it's the sound of shattered pals working through survivor's guilt via emotionally sludgy synths and leftover Joy Division ideas. Everyone sounds exhausted, and new singer Sumner sounds terrified as well—it's a well-meant bummer. The BBC Sessions are better: still very Joy Division, but livelier.

Which makes the followup EP, *1981–1982*, that much more miraculous. The keeper is "Temptation"—New Order finds a formula and congeals it into joy. Graced with an infinite hook, rhythmic rapture, a killer bass line, and Sumner's mediocre singing, "Temptation" is majestic, ravishing, and hypnotic in equal measure, qualities that became N.O. trademarks.

As did the band's 1983 single "Blue Monday." Like most seismic shifts in pop, "Blue Monday" still sounds totally shocking, the ultimate in flawlessly programmed, LSD-driven, push-button dance-pop, complete with Sumner's funny, who-cares vocal and an astonishing drum break—a totemic accomplishment and a well-deserved hit.

Fully into its rebirth, the band set the bar insanely high; *Power, Corruption and Lies* is the first fully conscious N.O. album. There is no real revelation, and Sumner's vocals still refuse to grow a personality, but *PCL* fits the band's world-historical sound into the gorgeous ("Your Silent Face") and the cheeky ("Age of Consent"). (The CD version includes both sides of the "Blue Monday" single.)

The American debut, *Low-Life*, is prized as the

band's apex by many connoisseurs, but it has aged oddly. The opener, "Love Vigilantes," is almost a non sequitur, a folk-ballad short story with a black punch line; narrative ain't Sumner's strong suit. "The Perfect Kiss" and "Sub-Culture" are perfect subcultural kisses, and the rest of the disc moves and shakes like a band truly hitting its stride. But in a career context, *Low-Life* has an off-putting feel—the songs' sense of vigorous elation replaced with stately pretension.

Brotherhood is an underrated rocker, full of grand hooks ("Bizarre Love Triangle," "Weirdo") and hooky grandeur ("All Day Long," "Every Little Counts"). Sumner begins to hint at a personality, but he freely ignores content. It's New Order's most recognizable collection; when bands sound like New Order, they usually sound like *Brotherhood*.

Focusing on dance mixes of key singles, including "Temptation," "Blue Monday," and the spectacular near-hit "True Faith," the double-CD *Substance* is pure pleasure, moving from strength to exhilarating strength. A guidebook to 1980s pop, along with Madonna's *Immaculate Collection* and Prince's *Purple Rain*.

Soaked in proto-acid house ("Fine Time," "Run") and perfectly formed pop hooks ("All the Way," "Love Less"), *Technique* flows like a bacchanalian ode to getting royally blitzed on Ibizan Ecstasy. The pop is stellar, but the dance tracks seem absentminded, as if the band was, well, really, really high. Astonishing in spots, vapid throughout, *Technique* is New Order's masterwork of weightlessness.

Totally sick of each other, the members of New Order spent the next few years on side projects: Sumner with Pet Shop Boy Neil Tennant and Smith Johnny Marr in the fop-pop supergroup Electronic; Hook in the appallingly rockist Revenge; Gilbert and Morris on the appropriately faceless the Other Two. New Order knocked out a World Cup anthem in 1990 ("World in Motion") and returned to active duty in 1993, with *Republic*. The catchy "Regret" was the band's first true American hit, but most of *Republic* is a serious phone-in: slick, dull dance-pop landscape dominated by indie-rock dreams. So New Order vanished again. *The Best of,* which includes key album tracks and '90s material, is fine, but it should be considered a companion to *Substance,* not a replacement.

The BBC Radio 1 Concert, a solid 1987 show by a spotty live band at the peak of its power, is notable for the live debut of "True Faith" and an amazing cover of the Velvet Undergound's "Sister Ray."

Fans hoped for a miracle comeback, but it's a dark day when New Order thinks it needs Billy Corgan and Primal Scream's help, which is where *Get Ready* left us in 2001. Finally realizing they had invented much of '90s indie rock by guiding '80s pop, New Order released *Get Ready,* the most straight-ahead rock album (the single "Crystal" is almost *heavy*) it had produced since *Brotherhood.*　—J.G.

The New Pornographers

★★★★½　Mass Romantic (Mint, 2000)
★★★★　Electric Version (Matador, 2003)

Conceived as a one-off studio project, Vancouver indie group the New Pornographers became a full-on band when their debut turned out better than anyone could have imagined. Singer/songwriters Carl Newman (of Zumpano) and Dan Bejar (a.k.a. Destroyer) devised a smart, winningly eccentric variation on Cheap Trick and Utopia's exuberant power pop, crammed every available aural space with blockbuster hooks, and produced it with full-throttle AM-radio gusto—hand claps! organs! four-part harmonies! The secret ingredient, alt-country torch singer Neko Case, tears into unstoppable rockers like "Letter From an Occupant" with relish. A delight.

Case is less of a presence on *Electric Version* (she only sings lead on two songs, one of them the stunningly catchy crypto-political anthem "The Laws Have Changed"), and Bejar pops in to contribute three peculiar little songs—one of which quotes Wittgenstein—then disappears again. (He didn't tour with the band, either.) But Newman, now clearly in charge, is on overdrive, pinning the tunefulness meter in the red, pushing the group's energy over the top, and layering the album's production like baklava—sweet, nutty hooks never stop emerging from its depths.　—D.W.

The New Radicals

★★　Maybe You've Been Brainwashed Too (MCA, 1998)

With the New Radicals, Michigan singer/songwriter Gregg Alexander gave up the ponderous experimentalism of his solo work for a band, a bucket hat, and a pleasant, professional rock sound. In the process, he scored a summer hit with the power-poppy "You Get What You Give." Soul-inflected rock is the going currency, and Alexander explores the Big Themes against oversize arrangements that recall Hall & Oates. But his confidence in the realm of the sociopolitical is as glib as his former faith in his sexual prowess was precocious, and there's something suspect about a singer who professes the benefits of freethinking while making the most eager-to-please corporate soft-rock imaginable. The title song is better than the hit, which was such a blatant made-for-MTV move that a century from now historians will be able to date it to within a month of its release.   —A.B.

New York Dolls

★★★★★   New York Dolls (Mercury, 1973)
★★★★½   In Too Much Too Soon (Mercury, 1974)
   ★★½   Lipstick Killers (1981; ROIR, 1990)
    ★★   Red Patent Leather (Fan Club, 1984)
   ★★★   Hard Night's Day (Norton, 2000)
   ★★★   Actress: Birth of the New York Dolls (Get Back, 2000)
    ★★   Great Big Kiss (Sanctuary, 2002)
   ★★★   From Paris With Love (L-U-V) (Sympathy for the Record Industry, 2002)
     ★   The Millennium Collection (Mercury, 2003)

The smeared-on clothes, the screwed-down eyes and screwed-up hairdos, the gnarlier-than-thou-bitch sound: Rock & roll still hasn't gotten over the Dolls. They cooked up the Crystals and the Velvets' fuck-you swagger by mugging the Stones and turning their London blooze into Bowery lust. They boiled down glam from Kabuki lite to the picked-up trash at its core. They were tougher than the Ramones and dressed like trannie hookers who would kill you as soon as look at you cuz they knew the right chicks would dig it. The Dolls' junk- (and junkie-) rock vibe has been aped by every scene from punk, hair metal, and neoglam to whatever generation the Strokes belong to. Many regard the Dolls as the single greatest thing to ever happen to Manhattan, and when you hear David Johansen's unholy sneer (yes, his sneer is audible) or Johnny Thunders' and Syl Sylvain's skanky guitars wrestling over lipstick like the bad girls they wanna fuck or be, it's mighty hard to argue.

Produced by a sympathetic Todd Rundgren, their 1973 debut is epic sleaze, the sound of five young men shaping the big city in their own scuzzy image. From Johansen's shouting over the burlesque piano clamor on "Personality Crisis" and the subtle power ballad of "Lonely Planet Boy" to the surrealism of "Frankenstein" and the roar of "Jet Boy," *The New York Dolls* is in love (L-U-V) with its smarts, a sloppy, fearless sense of self, and its own crass brashness. This is rock that's giving you all you ever wanted fast, cheap, and out of control, and it is entirely possible that no one has ever had as much fun recording a rock & roll record as these twisted doofs seemed to be having. *The New York Dolls* is absolutely essential.

But few bought the thing, so the band turned to girl-group producer Shadow Morton for *Too Much Too Soon,* in an attempt at radio airplay. It didn't work, probably because with a slicker sound, background choruses, and cleaner riffs, the Dolls just

sounded skankier, wallowing in earnest-yet-bizarre covers of the Cadets' "Stranded in the Jungle," Archie Bell's "(There's Gonna Be a) Showdown," Leiber and Stoller's "Bad Detective," and Sonny Boy Williamson's "Don't Start Me Talkin'." "Babylon" is an ode to the place, "Puss 'n' Boots" positions them as the ultimate underworld dandies, and "Human Being" is a statement of purpose ("If I'm acting like a king/ Well, that's cuz I'm a human being"). Commercially, that didn't really work, either, and after a wildly ill-advised turn with Malcom McLaren (red leather outfits! Communism!), the Dolls fell to pieces, with Johansen starting a campy-as-hell solo career and Thunders beginning his occasionally brilliant career as a tragic genius, first with the Heartbreakers, then solo, before dying, way after anyone expected him to, in 1991. Thirteen years later, in 2004, bassist Arthur "Killer" Kane died suddenly of leukemia.

A series of live albums, anthologies, and demos of varying quality, dubious legality, and variable print status have been the Dolls' recorded legacy ever since they went tits up. The anthologies are maybe the worst buy of all. *Rock 'n Roll* (Mercury, 1994) is all originals, which eliminates much of the band's crucial context. *The Millennium Collection* is an 11-song rip-off.

From Paris . . . is the latest version of a hot French-radio tape, but *Red Patent Leather* is still one of the worst-recorded live albums in history, though it documents one of the band's final shows before Thunders and drummer Jerry Nolan quit and the New York Dolls dissolved in a pool of drunken vomit. *Great Big Kiss* is a two-CD set that pairs *Leather* with *Seven Day Weekend,* a collection of rough-and-tumble '73 demos also available in expanded form as *Hard Night's Day.* *Lipstick Killers* collects raw demos from '72, but the most interesting demo collection might be *Actress,* a pre-Johansen rehearsal tape dating from 1971, with Thunders on lead vocals. But these are for the hard core: Any serious rock collection needs the first two Dolls albums, and crappy leftovers can't dim their flashy luster. True trash lives forever, baby.   —J.G.

Nickelback

   ★½   Curb (1996; Roadrunner, 2002)
   ★★   The State (Roadrunner, 2000)
   ★★½   Silver Side Up (Roadrunner, 2001)
   ★★   The Long Road (Roadrunner, 2003)

Without the hit "How You Remind Me," which dominated the rock airwaves in 2002, Canadian hard rockers Nickelback might have been just another forgotten late-'90s hard-rock act of half warmed-over grunge riffs and half new-metal charm. Instead, it was a half warmed-over grunge band that got a little famous. It didn't hurt matters that singer Chad Kroeger is about as hot as a bootstrapping Canadian crooner can get.

Nickelback got the name from bassist Mike Kroger, who worked at a coffee shop. A cup of joe was $1.45, and he found himself frequently saying, "Here's your nickel back." What's amazing is that they actually admitted this exceptionally '90s tale in interviews: It's like running into a band named Gas Crisis that was active during the Ford administration. *The Curb* was released in 1996 (and rereleased after fame hit in 2002), and its generic heft got the band nowhere. But Nickelback toured like the little bubble-grunge band that could.

The State fared better, adhering to the band's self-improvement regime: The songs were more focused (read: tailor-made to the rock/metal radio format), and "Old Enough" showed up on the soundtrack to *Blair Witch 2.* But over the long haul, *The State* rocks a late-'90s sound so by-the-numbers, it's weirdly inspirational.

Since some girls like guys who write annoying self-deprecatory lyrics and will hold their hair as they barf, said girls became integral to the success of Nickelback's next album, the pretty-much-a-breakthrough *Silver Side Up,* propelled up the charts by "How You Remind Me." "Never Again" sticks up for abused spouses, but who didn't in 2002?

The band scored another huge hit with "Hero," from the *Spider-Man* soundtrack. *The Long Road* capitalizes on this success, becoming more dour. Only in a mainstream rock landscape this dull could these bootstrappers thrive. Throughout many interchangeable albums to come, Nickelback's essential facelessness will remain intact, and like so many hard-rock bands of their era, the group generates but one thought: Eddie Vedder, you have so much to answer for. —J.G.

Stevie Nicks

★★★½   Bella Donna (Modern, 1981)
★★★   The Wild Heart (Modern, 1983)
★★   Rock a Little (Modern, 1985)
★★   The Other Side of the Mirror (Modern, 1989)
★★★★   Timespace: The Best of Stevie Nicks (Modern, 1991)
★★   Street Angel (Modern, 1994)
★★★½   Enchanted (Atlantic, 1998)
★★   Trouble in Shangri-La (Reprise, 2001)

Stevie Nicks is the high priestess of her own religion, ruling a world of prancing Gypsies, gold-dust princesses, and white-winged doves, all without going anywhere near a sensible shoe. Like David Bowie or Bryan Ferry, she has spent a career turning her private fantasies into an elaborate pop mythology. As she confesses in 1983's "Nightbird," "I wear boots all summer long." The Nicks mystique has inspired everything from Sandra Bernhard's performance piece "The Women of Rock & Roll" to the annual New York drag-queen festival Night of a Thousand Stevies. And even when Stevie gets carried away, she still has that husky ache in her voice.

The Fleetwood Mac siren made her solo debut with *Bella Donna,* which included her Don Henley duet "Leather and Lace," her Tom Petty duet "Stop Draggin' My Heart Around," and "Edge of Seventeen (Just Like a White-Winged Dove)." After *The Wild Heart,* which has the great "Stand Back," the solo albums bog down in bloated production and vague songwriting. *Enchanted* is a definitive three-CD retrospective; the emotional highlight is "Ooh My Love" (originally buried on the otherwise forgettable *The Other Side of the Mirror*), a fabulous song about a princess who feels like a prisoner in her own castle even though she's terrified of the world outside. It's Nicks' love letter to her fans, and it makes you admire her compassion for the lost girls in her flock. She's lasted so long because she remembers how it feels to teeter in high heels on the edge of 17. —R.S.

Nico

★★★   Chelsea Girl (1967; PolyGram, 1990)
★★★½   The Marble Index (1969; Elektra, 1990)
★★★½   Desertshore (1971; Reprise, 1993)
★★★½   The End . . . (1974; Island, 1996)
★★½   Drama of Exile (1981; Cleopatra, 2004)
★★★   Do or Die Diary 1982—Nico in Europe (ROIR, 1982)
★★   Live Heroes (Performance, 1986)
★★½   Icon (Cleopatra, 1996)
★★★★   The Classic Years (PolyGram, 1998)
★★½   Nico's Last Concert: Fata Morgana (Steamhammer/SPV, 2000)

She's more than just another dour (if shockingly beautiful) face and a terrifying, Germanic drone-voice, but even haters admit that goth rock—everything good and bad about it—begins with the late Christa Päffgen (1938–1988), known to the world as Nico. Starting out as a European model and all-around rock scenester before dropping like a bomb(shell) into Andy Warhol's Factory, Nico ended up in the Velvet Underground, sticking around long enough to write herself into history as the scary blond chanteuse on *The Velvet Underground & Nico* before embarking on a solo career. She gained a rep as the ice queen to end them all (allegedly breaking up with Lou

Reed by telling him, "I can no longer sleep with Jews."). She had a son by Alain Delon, lived for years with a monster heroin habit, and made a couple of the creepiest rock albums ever recorded. She died falling off a bike, in 1988. All in all, an epic life, at least for a while.

The woman, as unpleasant as her rep might be, made some pretty sui generis music, and everything between 1967 and 1974 is worth a spin if you like your (non)rock remote, arty, and colder than a Valkyrie's armored tit. Unfortunately, the shelves now sag with exploitative death-tripping compilations of live shows, remixes, limited-edition outtakes, and other bullshit that all but the most devout of fans should avoid on principle alone.

Chelsea Girl, her solo debut, is sort of the first great lost Velvets album. Lou Reed, John Cale, and Sterling Morrison play on various songs and between them wrote five, including the oddly sweet "Little Sister," "It Was a Pleasure Then," and the haunting title track. (Think of it as an early version of "Walk on the Wild Side.") The music is folk rock as only the Velvets could have imagined it: strings, a wandering flute, minimalist guitar thrum, and little else. Other highlights are by Tim Hardin and Jackson Browne, including the old-before-his-time genius of Browne's "These Days" and "The Fairest of the Seasons." A lovely debut, and not too scary. (The Reed tunes have been added to the deluxe reissue of *VU and Nico.*)

The Marble Index, on the other hand, is where the difficult listening starts, and it's pretty amazing for it. The songs, Nico compositions all, are spare melodic frames that Cale, perhaps feeding on post-Velvets rage and feeling a bit anti-American, gives a stark, high-church-of-art feel to, adding droning harmonium, flashes of percussion, and generally creating one seriously dislocating vibe. "Ari's Song," dedicated to her son, might be the least-comforting lullaby ever recorded. Totally uncompromised, deeply European art music that stands in total contrast to the American roots music that was obsessing folks like, say, Dylan and the Band.

Desertshore is essentially *Marble Index II: Teutonic Boogaloo,* somehow even starker than *Index.* Cale again relies on the harmonium for musical weight, layering it into towering, droning waves. Nico still sounds pretty much like death chilled over, but that's kind of her thing, and it's still quite beautiful if you're the type who drinks his Céline straight.

The End is as strange and removed an album as the '70s could have spawned. Produced again by Cale (complete with some vocals and about a billion instruments by him) and featuring Roxy Music's Brian Eno and Phil Manzanera. Guitar and piano textures flicker

in and out, muffled instrumental screams flicker in and out, and over it all is Nico's stately manner. The only thing preventing this obelisk from unreservedly rolling into the avant-rock canon is her wretched yet brilliantly revealing taste in covers. Nico closes the album with a reading of the Doors' "The End" so straight-faced and melodramatic as to render Jim Morrison's already overwrought Freudian bullshit *totally* comic. Far less cute (though somehow not as annoying) is a monolithic, droning take on "Das Lied der Deutschen" (or "Deutschland Uber Alles"). Perhaps *The End* is Nico's most totally idiosyncratic album: creepy, morally suspect, and occasionally inadvertently funny as hell; it fit her like a velvet glove cast in onyx. (*The Classic Years* draws on all of these albums for a very handy sampler.)

Fascinating, then, that when she returned to rock in 1981, she dismissed her earlier work as "really boring" (a sentiment many might totally agree with). It was the perfect time for the ice queen to thaw, as bands like Bauhaus, Echo and the Bunnymen, and Sisters of Mercy were stealing her moves. So, no surprise that *Drama of Exile* pairs her with a thin new-wave band that wouldn't have sounded out of place on, say, Rough Trade. The tighter material is strange after so much ambience, but her lyrics are still intriguing reflections on the doom of it, all and her taste in covers has gotten much better: She tries to slay the father (or ex-boyfriend) on VU's "Waiting for the Man," and Bowie's "Heroes" gets a charged, jumpy makeover, and, yes, her accent sells it brilliantly. (Maybe the Wallflowers should have tried doing the German version . . . uh, never mind.) *Camera Obscura,* from 1985, is her final studio album and only available as an import.

Before the CD era, *Do or Die* was the closest thing to a hits package Nico's cult ever got, a set of live tunes from various shows, many with the live band from her 1982 European tour. But thanks to that same CD era, there are a bunch of somewhat exploitative and totally inessential live albums that fall in and out of print, most of them available on import. Each has some nice moments, but there's a lot of studio product to get through before anyone needs to dig this deep. *Live Heroes* drones through six songs, including the Bowie tune and "My Funny Valentine." *Chelsea Girls/Live* is a brutally misleading title for an set of live '80s synth stuff. *Icon* appends the interesting "Vegas/Saeta" 7-inch with some *Drama of Exile* outtakes and some live material. Solid. *Fata Morgana* is, as you might expect, from 1988, as she moved back to drones. Nico died of a cerebral hemorrhage on July 18, 1988. The goth nation has yet to declare this cruel day some sort of holiday, but it's only a matter or time. —J.G.

Harry Nilsson

- ★★★ The Pandemonium Shadow Show (RCA, 1967; out of print)
- ★★★½ Aerial Ballet (1968; RCA/Camden, 1980; out of print)
- ★★★ Harry (1969; DCC Compact Classics, 1997)
- ★★★★ Nilsson Sings Newman (1970; Buddha/BMG, 2000)
- ★★★ The Point! (1970; RCA, 2002)
- ★★★½ Aerial Pandemonium Ballet (1971; Buddha/BMG, 2000)
- ★★★★ Nilsson Schmilsson (RCA, 1971)
- ★★★ Son of Schmilsson (RCA, 1972)
- ★★ A Little Touch of Schmilsson in the Night (RCA, 1973)
- ★★★★ Pussy Cats (1974; Buddha/BMG, 1999)
- ★★ That's the Way It Is (RCA, 1976; out of print)
- ★★★½ All-Time Greatest Hits (RCA, 1989)
- ★★★★ Personal Best: The Harry Nilsson Anthology (RCA, 1995)
- ★★★½ Greatest Hits (RCA, 2002)

Nilsson added his voice—slight, yet very distinctive—to the outer fringes of the singer/songwriter movement. His early writing and singing hinted of a close familiarity with the work of Burt Bacharach and Hal David as well as Bob Dylan. "Everbody's Talkin' " (used in the film *Midnight Cowboy*) and "One" (a hit for Three Dog Night) are the catchiest examples of his orchestrated folk rock; both are included on *Aerial Ballet*. Along with the now-deleted late-'60s records *The Pandemonium Shadow Show* and *Harry*, this album earned Nilsson a cult following and a variety of well-placed fans. (In 1971, Nilsson selected and remixed tracks from his first two albums to create the whimsically titled *Aerial Pandemonium Ballet*, which might have legitimate claim to be the first-ever remix album.) *The Point!*, the soundtrack for an animated television special, positions seven sweetly melodic little song snatches between installments of a hippie-era children's fable.

Somewhere in between the underrated *Nilsson Sings Newman* and his 1971 breakthrough, Harry Nilsson discovered rock & roll. Perhaps exposure to Newman's acute cynicism and corrosive insights toughened Nilsson's artistic stance. Many Newman fanciers insist that Nilsson gently waters down the impact of these songs, but his polished vocal style puts Newman's point across with unaccustomed subtlety. *Nilsson Sings Newman* offers a fine introduction to either artist.

The juiced-up charge that illuminates *Nilsson Schmilsson* quickly turns into a hangover on subsequent followups. But what a party! A guest list of stu-dio-session heavies brings in the rock element, while producer Richard Perry harnesses Nilsson's diffuse genius to a variety of musical settings. "Without You" could be a Perry Como outake, and "Jump Into the Fire" throbs like a funkier Humble Pie or James Gang. In between those extremes, cuts like "Down" and "Gotta Get Up" temper the melodic ache of Nilsson's older work with exuberance and humor. *Son of Schmilsson* lays on the sloppy charm with a trowel. Though several cuts—most notably "Spacemen"—could hold their own on *Nilsson Schmilsson*, the album's title isn't as ironic as Nilsson obviously intends. *A Little Touch of Schmilsson in the Night* finds Nilsson reaching for prerock elegance; despite the presence of Sinatra arranger Gordon Jenkins, it winds up sounding like self-conscious Muzak. The out-of-print *Pussy Cats* is a dark companion piece to John Lennon's *Rock 'n' Roll;* produced and accompanied by the former Beatle, Nilsson barrels through soul-baring cover versions of sacred cows like Dylan's "Subterranean Homesick Blues." Unsettling stuff, but fans of Neil Young's *Tonight's the Night* or Bryan Ferry's *These Foolish Things* should be intrigued by *Pussy Cats*—if they can find it.

Harry Nilsson continued releasing albums until his death in 1994 to little notice or effect. Save for a couple of tracks on the now-deleted *That's the Way It Is* (including a revelatory cover of America's "I Need You"!) from 1976, his lost years are mostly worth rediscovering insofar as they've been anthologized. (There are three best-ofs on the market, the best and most thoroughgoing being the two-CD *Personal Best*.) And as Nilsson's best work proves, even the friendliest clown routines often possess a fascinating yet tragic dimension. —M.C./M.M.

98°

- ★★ 98° (Motown, 1997)
- ★★ 98° and Rising (Motown, 1998)
- ★★ This Christmas (Motown, 1999)
- ★★ Revelation (Motown, 2000)
- ★★½ The Collection (Motown, 2002)

Check out 98°'s ever so slightly sullen album covers: These are the cranky half smiles of men who wish to be thought of as Four Aspiring Tops or at least White Boyz II White Men, not Color Me Badder. Because 98°—L.A.-based, Ohio-raised soulboys Justin Jeffre, Jeff Timmons, and brothers Nick and Drew Lachey—couldn't even hack the teen scene, they mostly acted like they were too good for it: Their pale bubble-crooning, even with Montell Jordan producing, made 'em sound like old-school dullards next to the Backstreet Boys' teen-pop juggernaut. The group soon drifted into the background of the late-'90s louder-than-love pop epoch, becoming known even to fluff-pop connoisseurs as merely "the muscled ones" or "those guys in the really tight T-shirts."

In '97, 98° dropped a modest set of pop R&B harmonies, New Jack swing production, and generally civilized pop songwriting. The gold single "Invisible Man" pines for a girl who won't look at him, while "Was It Something I Didn't Say?" is typically amorphous Diane Warren balladry—it's compulsively competent, perfectly well sung, and completely forgettable.

Released in '98, which should have been their year, 98° and Rising covered a country hit, "I Do (Cherish You)," a smash for Mark Wills; got Trackmasters to juice "Heat It Up"; and featured Stevie Wonder on "True to Your Heart." But the group's attempts to have it both ways—as R&B singers and teen heartbreakers—produce neither pure soul nor pure cheese, obviously failing on both fronts.

A Christmas collection reminded the market that the group hadn't discarded the shtick while plotting a comeback. Revelation, released a good two years after their name stopped making any sense, took that inevitable last step in boy bandhood: the "serious music" album. At this point, 98° must have know they would never be a Backstreet, they'd never be an 'N Sync, they'd never even be a New Kids. So they enlisted Anders Bagge and Arnthor Bigisson for the potential big single, the vaguely Latin "Give Me Just One Night (Una Noche)." Okay so far. Then our heroes go on to cowrite 11 of the album's 13 tracks. Not a good idea.   —J.G.

Nirvana

★★★★	Bleach (Sub Pop, 1988)
★★★★★	Nevermind (Geffen, 1991)
★★★	Incesticide (Geffen, 1992)
★★★★	In Utero (Geffen, 1993)
★★★★★	Unplugged in New York (Geffen, 1994)
★★★★	From the Muddy Banks of the Wishkah (Geffen, 1996)
★★★	Nirvana (Geffen, 2002)

Only a handful of musicians have been able to catch their zeitgeist and watch their music resonate far beyond their fan base into the culture at large. Despite the best efforts of demographers and businesspeople to manufacture such phenomena, they always come as a surprise to everyone, especially the artist. Kurt Cobain's legacy and mystery have continued to reverberate, long after his moment overwhelmed his capacity to cope.

A native of Aberdeen, WA, whose parents divorced when he was eight, Cobain found solace from familial and cultural dysfunction in music—first the Beatles, then metal, then the hardcore-punk subculture. His first bands, Fecal Matter and the (redundantly) Stiff Woodies, reflected the punk gross-out ethos of rejecting yourself before anyone else can and becoming so offensive that selling out seems impossible. When Nirvana coalesced (Cobain on guitar and vocals, Chris Novaselic on bass, Chad Channing on drums) and released its first album, Bleach, in 1988, the band had already progressed to something beyond punk. Recorded for a mere $600, the album sounded as good as anything could for that amount of money. Indeed, it sounded better than most albums recorded for vastly greater sums, separating Nirvana from the lo-fi punk pack right out of the chute. Bleach became a moderate hit on college radio and the underground/DIY circuit.

The lyrics make no attempt at narrative. They create moods with images, and those moods are mostly tortured, ranging from angst to defiance and back again. The vocals create an unfathomable depth and are clearly the work of someone who has not erected the normal neurotic defenses against the nasty world. "Floyd the Barber" turns the old Andy Griffith Show into a den of child molesters, with the child ending up "smothered in Andy's butt." Punk humor, yeah, but also a critique of idyllic small-town America. Cobain illustrated a long list of other horrors: his own body; his inability to communicate; everyone's bad motives (including his own); and a malicious, utterly confusing adult world that offered relief only in alcohol, cigarettes, and other drugs. These were the themes of his life. The only thing missing was a killer hook.

Picking up drummer Dave Grohl and jumping from Sub Pop to Geffen, where the band notched up the sonics to A-level with producer Butch Vig, Nirvana delivered the killer hook on "Smells Like Teen Spirit." Nevermind's first single proved to be the song of the decade. Overnight, the hair bands of the '80s knew what it felt like to be Frankie Avalon when the Beatles landed at Idlewild. Everything underground came upstairs and became "grunge" (with flannel shirts as the new uniform of corporate rock), and everything previously upstairs went out the door.

The killer hook is a stuttering chord progression similar to the stuttering chord progression in Boston's "More Than a Feeling," a hit 15 years earlier, utterly transformed through Nirvana's trademark loud/soft dynamic and dark, surreal mood. Following Ezra Pound's call to arms, Cobain made it new. Following the Talking Heads' dictum, he stopped making sense. And he stopped making it in a way that made total sense to those who shared his alienation. It was like the

James Dean of *Rebel Without a Cause,* the Bob Dylan of "Subterranean Homesick Blues," the Eddie Cochran of "Summertime Blues," and the Johnny Rotten of "Pretty Vacant" had been rolled into one shy kid with beautiful eyes and unwashed blond hair. And if there was any doubt about the meaning of the mulatto/albino/mosquito/libido nonsense, there was the video, the most riveting three minutes in the history of MTV. At last, high school portrayed as the pep rally in hell that it is. Millions of post–education-stress-disorder survivors immediately identified. The rest of the album is a relentless run of monster riffs and monstrous imagery, all punched along by arguably the greatest rock rhythm section since Led Zeppelin.

Genuinely ambivalent about success and his own musicality, Cobain avoided the issue and got married to Courtney Love, Hole's front woman, who modeled herself after Sid Vicious' notorious girlfriend, Nancy Spungen. Rather than wait for the followup to the massive success of *Nevermind,* Geffen collected outtakes and demos and released them as *Incesticide,* in 1992. Cobain's singing generally lacks the depth he achieved on *Bleach* and *Nevermind,* and the killer hooks were simply more standard punk fare. Not bad, not transcendent. His rant in the liner notes is a must-have for any fan in search of clues.

In Utero, produced by Steve Albini, shows Cobain careening wildly between screaming dissonance, with all the needles in the red ("Scentless Apprentice"), and the irresistible hooks that made *Nevermind* a masterpiece ("Heart-Shaped Box," "All Apologies"). If you time the album, the dissonance would probably outweigh the melody by a factor of three to one—but the dissonance is compelling. The imagery again reveals someone who can't be anything but nakedly vulnerable and is wondering what he's doing in this world ("Throw down your umbilical noose so I can climb right back").

Amid reports of Cobain's heroin problem and suicide attempts, Nirvana recorded its second masterpiece, *Unplugged in New York,* in December 1993. Perhaps it's a cliché that the true test of songwriting is to play a song without a loud band bashing away behind you and if it still sounds good with just an acoustic guitar, you know you've got a great song, but Cobain proved this cliché and displayed the scope of his talent with the stark drama of his ravaged yet strangely innocent voice. He also demonstrated an uncanny ability to pick cover songs, giving the Meat Puppets a moment of deserved aboveground fame ("Lake of Fire" is hilarious and haunting) and Lead Belly his only MTV airtime (the stunning "Where Did You Sleep Last Night").

Could Cobain have revolutionized folk music the

same way he had rock? Yeah, but we won't see it. He shot himself on April 5, 1994, leaving millions of fans bereft, desperate to understand, and wanting more of the talent that had flamed out so quickly. Cobain's estate has been a mess ever since, with band members Grohl and Novaselic feuding with Love about what should be released. The 1996 live album *From the Muddy Banks of the Wishkah* captures the Dionysian essence of the band, adding dimension of energy where none seemed possible. The 2002 greatest-hits compilation is a sad reminder of the definitive box set that may never come. The songs feel starkly ripped from context without the surrounding dissonance, while the one new cut, "You Know You're Right," is a powerhouse—it's not quite "Teen Spirit," but what is? Pray for the survivors to settle their issues. —C.Y.

No Doubt

★★ No Doubt (Interscope, 1992)
★★★½ Tragic Kingdom (Trauma/Interscope, 1995)
★★★ Collector's Orange Crate (Interscope, 1997)
★★★½ Return of Saturn (Interscope, 2000)
★★★★ Rock Steady (Interscope, 2002)
★★★★ The Singles 1992–2003 (Interscope, 2003)

No Doubt started out in Southern California's fertile ska-punk scene of the early 1990s and eventually blossomed into something more exotic and hydra-headed; a hit-making machine whose interests range from tender ballads to tense electronica and taunting hard rock, fronted by quintessential SoCal siren Gwen Stefani.

First gathering around Stefani and her brother, Eric, in 1987 as an Orange County answer to Madness, No Doubt spent three years developing a local following, eventually attracting interest from several majors. The eponymous first album is mostly forgettable, a cloying attempt to lighten up everyday rock attitude with a scholarly reduction of ska, and though No Doubt toured, record sales didn't soar. After a contract dispute, the band returned with its basic musical strategy for *Tragic Kingdom,* but this time the songs hit a sweet spot: "Don't Speak," "Just a Girl," and "Spiderwebs," all singles, were inescapable in 1996. *Collector's Orange Crate* assembles early demos, material the band issued on its own during the Interscope contract tussle, and other rarities in a box designed to exploit the group's newfound success.

With *Return of Saturn,* ska and island rhythms are subordinated, and the band sounds emboldened, even experimental. The singles don't reach out and grab you quite as aggressively—though some would say "Simple Kind of Life" is a quintessential Gwen Stefani petulant whine—but the production and the songwriting show a nuanced sophistication missing from previous work.

The band returned in 2002 with the blazing single "Hey Baby" (sample lyric: "I'm just sipping on chamomile, watching boys and girls with their sex appeal") and the dub-heavy, overtly poppy *Rock Steady*. It's a culmination of sorts—partially recorded in Jamaica, the island flavor is strong, spiced with outbreaks of crunchy guitar dissonance and electronic loops, and though the songs are simple, they do indeed rock steady. The *Singles* anthology catches all the No Doubt radio songs, and adds only a few rarities—a live acoustic version of "Underneath It All," and the collaboration with Bounty Killer "Girls Get the Bass in the Back." —T.M.

NOFX

★★	S&M Airlines (Epitaph, 1989)
★★	Ribbed (Epitaph, 1990)
★★	Liberal Animation (Epitaph, 1991)
★★★½	White Trash, Two Heebs and a Bean (Epitaph, 1992)
★★★★	Punk in Drublic (Epitaph, 1994)
★★★	I Heard They Suck Live (Fat Wreck Chords, 1995)
★★★	Heavy Petting Zoo (Epitaph, 1996)
★★★	So Long and Thanks for All the Shoes (Epitaph, 1997)
★★★	Pump Up the Valuum (Epitaph, 2000)
★★★	45 or 46 Songs That Weren't Good Enough to Go on Our Other Records (Fat Wreck Chords, 2002)
★★★	Regaining Unconsciousness (EP) (Fat Wreck Chords, 2003)
★★★½	The War on Errorism (Fat Wreck Chords, 2003)

NOFX/Rancid

★★★★	BYO Split Series/Volume III (BYO, 2002)

NOFX are smart-assed political punks, originally from Berkeley but transplanted to Los Angeles in the early '80s and, beginning with 1989's *S&M Airlines*, one of the signal bands of Epitaph Records' roster for over a decade. The band's speedy, hooky style has rarely changed, but their songwriting eventually became strong enough to mark them from the pack. *S&M Airlines*, *Ribbed*, and *Liberal Animation* are uncertain and messy, but *White Trash, Two Heebs and a Bean* is the group's breakthrough, the always-humorous lyrics acute rather than silly, the hooks stronger (and tempos speedier) than ever. ("Bob" even showed the group to have a tighter grip on Jamaican skank than many of their punk peers.) *Punk in Drublic* was even better, from the snarky "Punk Guy (Because He Does Punk

Things)" to the rousing "Don't Call Me White." After an excellent split album with Rancid, on which each band covered six of each other's songs—Rancid remaking "Bob" into a flashy rockabilly number and performing a hostile takeover of "Don't Call Me White," with gravel-voiced bassist Matt Freeman on vocals, and NOFX turning "Radio" from speed rock to organ-driven ska and making the "Let California fall into the fucking ocean" wishes of "Antennas" sound even more sincere—NOFX jumped from Epitaph to Fat Wreck Chords, issuing the excellent *War on Errorism*, whose title and cover art are a direct slap at George W. Bush, and whose heartfelt spleen on songs such as "Franco Un-American" make it an up during a lousy, disheartening political time. —M.M.

Northern State

★★★½	Dying in Stereo (Northern State, 2002)
★★★	All City (Columbia, 2004)

They may hail from the suburbs of New York City, but the members of Long Island white-girl rap trio Northern State are no clueless Prada-wearing princesses: Julie Potash (a.k.a Hesta Prynn), Correne Spero (Guinea Love), and Robyn Goodmark (DJ Sprout) think very deeply about bombing Baghdad, police brutality, and a woman's right to choose. Like a certain white-male rap trio before them, they also like a smart, silly reference and sports.

Hip Hop You Haven't Heard, the critically acclaimed 2001 EP, veered from strip-mall tease to flaunting college degrees, with educated rapper Hesta Prynn rhyming "Chekhov wrote *The Seagull*" with "Snoopy is a beagle" on "A Thousand Words." Three of the four tracks were rereleased on 2001's *Dying in Stereo*, which found the posse theorizing in full effect. "Vicious Cycle" perhaps exemplifies their liberal linguistics best, with Prynn rapping, "Open your minds and rewrite your texts, cuz there's a lot you can learn from the opposite sex."

All City, their major-label debut, features a much pricier sound, courtesy of Cypress Hill's DJ Muggs and the Roots' ?uestlove, among others. Their flows still evoke the Beastie Boys circa 1988, but tracks such as "Girl for All Seasons," "Last Night," and "Think Twice" are packed with hooky funk, group-chant choruses, and New Yawk toughness, and the group's playfulness and unpretentious intelligence evoke hip-hop's golden age without a hint of retro self-consciousness. —C.S.

North Mississippi Allstars

★★★½	Shake Hands With Shorty (Tone-Cool, 2000)
★★★½	51 Phantom (Tone-Cool, 2001)
★★½	Polaris (Tone-Cool/ATO, 2003)

Luther and Cody Dickinson, sons of the legendary Memphis producer Jim Dickinson (Rolling Stones, Big Star, Replacements), love the blues enough to make it their own. *Shake Hands With Shorty* is a raucous, juiced-up run through classics by Fred McDowell, Furry Lewis, and Junior Kimbrough, with occasional blasts from samplers and drum machines. Decades after most of this stuff was written, and decades still after much of it was first interpreted by white rock bands, it's amazing how effortlessly the Dickinson brothers are able to return to the core of the blues and reveal its essential lust, joy, and honesty. Following the '90s blues experiments by Jon Spencer and G. Love, the NMA's musical surgery is no shock or surprise; what's impressive is that they never get carried away with it.

51 Phantom is a big step forward, a lean toward the full-band sound of the Allman Brothers and latter-day jammers like Widespread Panic. Less jarring than the debut, it has a bigger, cozier sound and an unhurried, self-assured pace. A cover of the Staple Singers' "Freedom Highway" is, like the original, groovy without being preachy, despite its hippy-dippy message ("Yes we want peace if it can be found/We're gonna stay on Freedom Highway, we're not gonna turn around"). Given the good taste and quick development shown on the first two albums, *Polaris*, with cheesy, overwrought jams that recall the worst of Lynyrd Skynyrd and the Allmans, doesn't make much sense. Bad Skynyrd is perhaps still better than most mediocre blues bands, but these boys are capable of much more. —B.S.

The Notorious B.I.G.

★★★★★ Ready to Die (1994; Bad Boy, 2004)
★★★★★ Life After Death (Bad Boy, 1997)
★★ Born Again (Bad Boy, 1999)

As the Roots' Ahmir Thompson memorably put it, when it comes to MCs, "Rakim is the Father, Biggie's the Son, and Jay-Z's the Holy Ghost." Biggie Smalls spread love the Brooklyn way, doing more than anyone else to revitalize New York hip-hop after years of West Coast dominance. His classic debut, *Ready to Die*, mapped out the sound of '90s cool: He came on as the baddest chronic-smoking, Oreo-cookie-eating, pickle-juice-drinking stud on the block, and he was the *man*, girlfriend. The street visions are bleak, from "Suicidal Thoughts" to the love song that hinges on the line "I swear to God I hope we fuckin' die together." (They don't—at the end of the song, while he's out dealing, his enemies come by and shoot her.) But Biggie's voice was also full of high-spirited fun, bringing the pleasure principle back to hip-hop. In "Big Poppa," his idea of a romantic evening includes a T-bone steak, cheese, eggs, and Welch's grape juice, and that's just while the Jacuzzi heats up. Best line: "Honeys play me close like butter play toast."

His voice and lyrics were deeper on *Life After Death,* which brought the different sides of his soul together for a filler-free two-disc rush of musical bravado. The brutal gangsta scenarios "Niggas Bleed," "Somebody's Gotta Die," and "You're Nobody (Til Somebody Kills You)" were genuinely scary, while radio hits like "Hypnotize" and "Mo Money Mo Problems" were hilarious, virtuosic pop outreach. Never one to get high on his own supply, Big enlisted Puff Daddy as his comic foil, the Joe Pesci to his De Niro, as well as supporting playas like Lil' Kim, Lil' Cease, and Mase—the team effort of a true pop community. But three weeks before the album was released, Biggie was murdered by an unknown assailant with a handgun in L.A. He was 24. He was also one of the few young male songwriters in any pop style writing credible love songs; even gritty tales like "Me & My Bitch" and funny boasts like "#!*@ You Tonight" engaged the pleasures and struggles of romantic commitment. The posthumous *Born Again* proved Biggie was still dead, but his place in the MCs Hall of Fame remains untouchable. —R.S.

NRBQ

★★★★½ Scraps (1972; Rounder, 2000)
★★★ All Hopped Up (1977; Rounder, 1989)
★★★★ At Yankee Stadium (1978; Mercury, 1988)
★★★½ Kick Me Hard (1979; Rounder, 1989)
★★★½ Tiddlywinks (1980; Rounder, 1990)
★★½ Grooves in Orbit (1983; Bearsville/Rhino, 1990)
★★★ Tapdancin' Bats (1983; Rounder, 1998)
★★★½ Uncommon Denominators (Rounder, 1986)
★★★ RC Cola and a Moon Pie (Rounder, 1986)
★★★½ God Bless Us All (Rounder, 1987)
★★★★ Diggin' Uncle Q (Rounder, 1988)
★★½ Wild Weekend (Virgin, 1989)
★★★★½ Peek-a-Boo: The Best of NRBQ 1969–1989 (Rhino, 1990)
★★★½ Honest Dollar (Rykodisc, 1992)
★★★★ Stay With We/The Best of NRBQ (Columbia/Legacy, 1993)
★★★½ Message for the Mess Age (Rhino, 1994)
★★★ Tokyo (Rounder, 1997)
★★★ You're Nice People You Are (Rounder, 1997)
★★★½ You Gotta Be Loose (Rounder, 1998)
★★★½ NRBQ (Rounder, 1999)
★★★ Ridin' in My Car (Rounder, 1999)
★★★★ Scraps Companion (Edisun, 2000)
★★ Music's Been Good to You (Edisun, 2002)

★★★   Live From Mountain Stage (Blue Plate, 2002)
★★★   Atsa My Band (Edisun, 2002)

During the '70s NRBQ—New Rhythm and Blues Quartet (Quintet, in the early five-member days)—became one of America's most beloved cult bands by turning out a good-timey, jam-heavy mix of jazz, blues, funk, and pop. Although keyboardist Terry Adams, whose influences run from Jerry Lee Lewis to Thelonious Monk, has always been the de facto leader, this is an all-for-one, all-American band. The classic lineup comprised Adams, bassist Joey Spampinato, drummer Tom Ardolino, and guitarist Al Anderson. They cheerfully toss jazz and country strains into their chunky rock & roll, spicing it up with a dose of unadulterated, even juvenile fun.

Rootsy yet eclectic, NRBQ started recording in 1969, releasing a weird, wonderful debut, *NRBQ*, that introduced Eddie Cochran to Sun Ra at a cosmic roadhouse where beer and laughter were plentiful. The band collaborated with Carl Perkins on 1970's *Boppin' the Blues*, introducing the '50s legend of "Blue Suede Shoes" fame to the late-'60s rock crowd. While these early albums have long been out of print, tracks from each were culled for *Stay With Me/ The Best of NRBQ*, a CD survey of their brief stint at Columbia.

NRBQ moved to Kama-Sutra for its third album, 1972's *Scraps*, which is almost perfect. The first two tracks illustrate the group's considerable strengths. Anderson and Adams are unusually subtle instrumental wizards not given to flashy solo intrusions. Anderson effortlessly grafts a chicken-scratching funk riff onto the joke-rock opener, "Howard Johnson's Got His Ho-Jo Workin'," and then Adams weaves a cool blue bebop piano through "Magnet," a mid-tempo shuffle. *Scraps* never lets up on ingenuity or high spirits. (Lovers of *Scraps* may be interested to know that in 2000, the band briefly made available *Scraps Companion:* a live radio broadcast from 1972 and a half dozen outtakes.) *Scraps* was followed by *Workshop* (1974), which came and went quickly. The original LP was distressingly hard to find even when it was in print, but a mid-1980s CD on Rounder, *RC Cola and a Moon Pie*, collects most of it. Mention should also be made of *She Sings, They Play*, on which the group backs country singer Skeeter Davis, whom Joey Spampinato married in 1983; *Christmas Wish* (1985), a kid-themed EP of silly seasonal tunes; and *Lou and the Q* (1986), cut with pro-wrestling manager Captain Lou Albano, who became the band's manager, too.

Many hard-core fans cite 1978's *At Yankee Stadium* as the 'Q's most solid studio work, and it is a rocking, seamless, start-to-finish pleasure. The CD nonsensically leaves off the LP's best song: Al Anderson's sweetly nostalgic "Ridin' in My Car." By contrast, the CD release of 1979's *Kick Me Hard*—which found NRBQ moving to the independent Rounder label, a safe haven where the band remained for many years—appends eight additional tracks. Next came *Tiddlywinks*, a winningly eclectic set that includes the classic car song "Me and the Boys." Subsequently recorded by Dave Edmunds and Bonnie Raitt, it has become something of a rock & roll standard.

NRBQ flinched on the few occasions their momentum led to major-label signings. *Grooves in Orbit*, released on Warner Bros.' Bearsville subsidiary, and *Wild Weekend*, issued on Virgin, were tame and timid by NRBQ standards, as if it didn't really want to be there and was holding back on principle.

More recent albums tend to be live souvenirs, the idea being that NRBQ is best caught in concert. Among the worthier releases are 1988's *Diggin' Uncle Q* and 1998's *You Gotta Be Loose*. The deluge of predictable, overdone live recordings didn't do much to broaden NRBQ's appeal beyond its hard-core fan base, but that probably didn't concern the band in the least.

NRBQ novitiates may want to start with *Peek-a-Boo: The Best of NRBQ 1969–1989*. This double-disc Rhino compilation sifts golden nuggets from two decades of recorded work. Rounder released another nifty compilation, *Uncommon Denominators*, a few years earlier. The group keenly felt the loss of Al Anderson in 1996, who went on to become a successful Nashville-based songwriter, slinging less interesting songs at country singers than he wrote while with NRBQ. Yet the indomitable quartet rebounded, enlisting Joey Spampinato's guitar-playing brother Johnny (formerly of the Incredible Casuals) as a replacement. Keeping it all in the family has made the bonds even tighter. Johnny debuted on *Tokyo*, recorded live in Japan on a 1996 tour. In 1999, the group celebrated its 30th anniversary with *NRBQ*, whose 15 tracks played up the musicians' innovative, offbeat side and jazzy chops. *Atsa My Band*, which mixed covers and originals, is more loopy fun from these never-say-diehards. —P.P.

'N Sync

★   'N Sync (RCA, 1998)
★★   Home for Christmas (RCA, 1998)
★★★   No Strings Attached (Jive, 2000)
★★★   Celebrity (Jive, 2001)

Even if the sugar-spun balladeering of wildly successful late-'90s guy group the Backstreet Boys wasn't your thing, by the time you saw the first video for 'N

Sync, you knew their crooning, Armani-suited elders were set for some *Tiger Beat* whup-ass. For one thing, the Syncs proved they could laugh at themselves (which, granted, didn't take much). The upstarts had also heard and liked hip-hop, which ultimately counted for plenty. Former *New Mickey Mouse Club* kids Justin Timberlake and J.C. Chasez brought their Space Mountain child-slave work ethic and above-average pipes to the service of Max Martin–penned machine music, infusing it with spiking-hormonal clean-teen sex appeal. Early songs and videos from their eponymous debut, product-tested by their label in Germany, remained safely Europop, but once stateside success was a lock, the tracks funked up with first ersatz and finally legit shimmy. Our five feisty, muscle-shirted lads threw themselves into athletic, just-this-side-of–MC Hammer–style pop-'n'-lock choreography. And with their image dialed to street-level sporty, they eventually succeeded in making the champagne- and rose-bearing Backstreets look like pedophile math teachers.

Their 1998 eponymous U.S. debut utilized some of the production whizzes from the Backstreet camp. "Tearin' Up My Heart" and "I Want You Back" bear the smooth Swedish melodies that powered early hits by Britney Spears. But the rest of the record is filled with schmaltz such as the adult contemporary "I Drive Myself Crazy" and the acoustic guitar plucks and water-drip beats of the New South love song "God Must Have Spent a Little More Time on You." That year's *Home for Christmas* is a reliable set for fans—if you caught their a capella Bee Gees tribute at the 2003 Grammy Awards, you have some idea of the adequately tight harmonic skills employed.

If they were nipping at Backstreet heels in 1998, things had changed by 2000, when the band dropped *No Strings Attached,* their "Look, Ma, no manager!" declaration of independence. The video for "It's Gonna Be Me" ushered in a newly self-conscious phase, with our tykes insisting they were no longer just puppets, they were self-conscious, rebellious puppets! The songs on *No Strings* are consistently stronger than the drivel on the debut. On the jet-revving "Bye Bye Bye," Timberlake revealed a snotty persona that suited Wayne Isham's train-top-hopping action video. By the time Eminem blasted one chatty Sync-er for off-the-cuff moralizing, "Chris Kirkpatrick you can get your ass kicked" (Kirkpatrick was reportedly psyched about the name check), fame had become onerous for the fab five, or at least that was their chosen coming-of-age narrative. *Celebrity* takes a dark view of said condition, but that pique serves the songs well. Timberlake got songwriting credit for the best ones, claiming the Jackson mantle with the BT-produced "Pop." His lyrics challenged

radio listeners to strike the guilt from guilty pleasure, though the song is more confrontational than pleasurable. "Girlfriend" (produced by the Neptunes) is another confident R&B track, as is the Rodney Jerkins–helmed "Celebrity." —L.S.

Ted Nugent

★★★	Ted Nugent (Epic, 1975)
★★★	Free-for-All (Epic, 1976)
★★★★	Cat Scratch Fever (Epic, 1977)
★★★½	Double Live Gonzo! (Epic, 1978)
★★½	Weekend Warriors (Epic, 1978)
★★½	State of Shock (Epic, 1979)
★★½	Scream Dream (Epic, 1980)
★★★½	Intensities in Ten Cities (Epic, 1981)
★★★★	Great Gonzos: The Best of Ted Nugent (Epic, 1981)
★	Nugent (Atlantic, 1982)
★	Penetrator (Atlantic, 1984)
★	Little Miss Dangerous (Atlantic, 1986)
★	If You Can't Lick 'Em . . . Lick 'Em (Atlantic, 1988)
★★★	Spirit of the Wild (Atlantic, 1995)
★★★½	Live at Hammersmith '79 (Sony, 1997)
★★★½	Full Bluntal Nugity (Spitfire, 2001)
★★★	Craveman (Spitfire, 2002)

Ted Nugent and the Amboy Dukes

★★★½	Ted Nugent and the Amboy Dukes (1968; DCC Classics, 1987)
★★★½	The Best of the Original Amboy Dukes (Mainstream, 1969)
★★★	Survival of the Fittest (Polydor, 1971)
★★½	Call of the Wild (1975; Enigma Retro, 1988)
★★★	Tooth, Fang and Claw (1975; Enigma Retro, 1988)

Ted Nugent asserted his maniac presence from the 1965 beginning of the Amboy Dukes. "Journey to the Center of the Mind" (1968) would be just another pleasant psychedelic excursion without that lead guitar: Nugent makes the instrument snarl and stutter like a Harley-Davidson in low gear, shifting into a high-pressure whoosh on the solo breaks. Along with Motor City peers such as the MC5, Nugent and the Amboy Dukes built a bridge between the scruffy garage rock of the late '60s and the gargantuan structures of '70s heavy metal. The Mainstream *Best of* captures this transition, splitting the difference between acid-laced pop songs and Nugent's full-bore instrumental frenzy. The Amboy Dukes recorded several disappointing albums for Polydor (all now deleted), with varying lineups. The muddled opus *Marriage on the Rocks/Rock Bottom* (1971) offers vivid and frightening evidence of Nugent's secret art-rock bent—his Bartók interpretation doesn't come off any better than Emerson, Lake and Palmer's Mussorgsky.

Nugent's solo career really begins with the two Amboy Dukes albums on Discreet. *Survival* never quite catches fire, but the taut, rangy guitar workouts on *Tooth, Fang and Claw*—"Hibernation," "Great White Buffalo"—can floor an unsuspecting listener. Nugent worked the arena circuit hard in the mid-'70s, cultivating a flamboyant stage persona to accompany his bag of riffs. Sporting a loincloth, shaking his torrents of dirty blond hair, wielding a massive hollow-body Gibson like it was a shotgun: he was an act you couldn't ignore. Producer Tom Werman effectively reins in the Neanderthal on his early Epic albums, placing his stream of banshee peals and power chords in an ever-shifting group format. (An up-and-comer named Meat Loaf provides lead vocals on *Free-for-All.*)

Cat Scratch Fever is the catchiest and most fevered entry in the Nugent catalogue. Hot-dog guitar licks and slobbering choruses push the sexist swill of "Wang Dang Sweet Poontang" and "Cat Scratch Fever" into the comedy zone. "Live It Up" draws up a blueprint for the Bon Jovi school of pop metal, "Fist Fightin' Son of a Gun" declares Ted's allegiance with Skynyrd-style Southern boogie, and "Death by Misadventure" skids into a wall of granite guitars about halfway through.

Despite the fact that *Great Gonzos!* succinctly demonstrates the considerable influence his '70s singles had on the '80s hair-metal boom, Terrible Ted's slicked-up forays in the following decade were completely unsuitable, which goes as well for his misbegotten stint with Damn Yankees, a creation of Night Ranger's Jack Blades and Styx's Tommy Shaw. But in the '90s, the rock & roll caveman began to trumpet his far right (some might say Paleolithic) sociopolitical views regarding hunters' rights, the criminal justice system, and the environment, and his public profile was reborn. *Spirit of the Wild* and *Craveman* restore Nuge to his wild and woolly modus operandi: unrestrained feral soloing, recklessly hilarious self-aggrandizement and political incorrectness, and, in the case of the latter's "Pussywhipped," the first recorded instance of Nugent deferring to someone—namely, his wife. But the truest manifestation of Tedness can be found on his live albums—on the excavated *Live at Hammersmith '79*, 1981's *Double Live Gonzo* and 2001's *Full Bluntal Nugity;* his trademark stage raps show that even a loudmouthed right-winger can lay claim to the status of rock & roll original.   —M.C./R.K.

N.W.A

★★ N.W.A and the Posse (1987; Ruthless/Priority, 1989)

★★★★★ Straight Outta Compton (1988; Ruthless/Priority, 2002)

★★½ Niggaz4life (1991; Ruthless/Priority, 2002)

Various Artists

★★½ The N.W.A Legacy, Vol. 1: 1988–1998 (Priority, 1999)

★★½ The N.W.A Legacy, Vol. 2 (Priority, 2002)

Whether you believe this seminal Los Angeles rap supergroup (including future solo superstars Ice Cube, Dr. Dre, and Eazy-E) was the first act bold enough to express the horrible truths of inner-city life, or did irreparable harm to hip-hop and race relations by marketing black criminality to the masses, there's no doubt N.W.A ranks among the most influential rap groups of all time. The group's arrival shifted the genre's locus to the West Coast and forever changed hip-hop's vocabulary and associations.

The group was still a loose collective of rappers and DJs in search of a sound when it released *N.W.A and the Posse,* an 11-song compilation crediting four tracks to N.W.A (mostly featuring Ice Cube)—including "8 Ball" and "Dope Man," which reappear as remixes on *Straight Outta Compton*—three to Eazy-E (solo or with Ron-De-Vu), and four to the Fila Fresh Crew featuring the D.O.C. Aside from N.W.A's gritty tracks and Eazy-E's seminal "Boyz-n-the-Hood," many songs—Eazy's "Fat Girl," the Fila Fresh Crew's "3 the Hard Way," and "Drink It Up" (a sloppy, minimalist rewrite of "Twist and Shout")—are played for laughs. The record's most musically compelling track, "Panic Zone," harks back to hip-hop's long-gone electrofunk era. Because most of the best material is available elsewhere, *The Posse* would be mostly of interest as a snapshot of a group in the process of finding its powerful voice.

The real action begins with *Straight Outta Compton,* on which N.W.A fully embraces its image as "gangstas" (thus naming the subgenre) and combines Public Enemy–style sonic barrages with lyrics full of violence and rage, particularly on the opening title track and the incendiary second song, "Fuck tha Police." While it's impossible to condone the "bloodbaths" promised by Ice Cube and MC Ren, it's also difficult—given revelations of LAPD abuses following 1991's Rodney King beating—to write off these threats and revenge fantasies as pure unprovoked bluster. And while N.W.A's slash-and-burn rants seemed a perversion of P.E.'s more politically sophisticated style, the group's hard-core fusillade sprayed a more righteous fury than the hundreds of copycats it spawned. The album's reissue adds four nonessential tracks: two remixes, a *Posse* retread, and some spare beats.

If there was any thought that N.W.A might refine its powerful rage into something more constructive, *Niggaz4life* dispeled those hopes. Dre's production (and rapping) skills continued to sharpen and move in the direction that would earn him massive solo success. And the group actually sounds like it has something to say on openers "Real Niggaz Don't Die" and the title track (both tracks include samples from revolutionary '60s proto-rappers the Last Poets). But the record soon devolves into exercises in puerility and pointlessness. The group expends an awful lot of time in its dishonorable attempt to degrade departed member Ice Cube, when in fact the record clearly suffers from his absence. And with its second half focused particularly on misogynistic displays—"One Less Bitch," "She Swallowed It," even the country-music parody "Automobile"—the group sounds less like "niggas with attitude" than "niggas with intimacy issues." *Niggaz4life*'s reissue tacks on the group's 1990 EP, *100 Miles and Runnin'*.

N.W.A's label released two posthumous compilations that mix a smattering of N.W.A hits with solo tracks and songs by the many N.W.A-affiliated spin-offs. While both volumes of *The N.W.A Legacy* attest to the group's massive ongoing influence, for every notable protégé (Dre's Snoop Doggy Dogg; Eazy-E's Bone Thugs-N-Harmony) there's a forgotten third-generation also-ran (Tha Dogg Pound, Daz Dillinger). The two-CD *Vol. 1* covers many of the high points up through 1998, including Ice Cube's and Dre's solo singles, Dre's collaboration with Tupac and Roger Troutman ("California Love"), and Snoop Dogg's breakthrough ("Murder Was the Case"). *Vol. 2* picks up with more recent Snoop material and some N.W.A reunion tracks (including 1999's "Chin Check," with Snoop filling in for Eazy-E, who died in 1995), plus older Eazy-E cuts and other tracks omitted from *Vol. 1*. Both volumes offer decent surveys of the group members' output, yet just a taste of the enduringly popular mayhem that their gangsta style hath wrought. —R.M.S.

Laura Nyro

- ★★★½   The First Songs (1966; Columbia/Legacy, 1988)
- ★★★★   Eli and the Thirteenth Confession (1968; Columbia/Legacy, 2002)
- ★★★½   New York Tendaberry (1969; Columbia/Legacy, 2002)
- ★★½   Christmas and the Beads of Sweat (Columbia, 1970)
- ★★★½   Gonna Take a Miracle (1971; Columbia/Legacy, 2002)
- ★★★   Smile (Columbia, 1976)
- ★★★   Walk the Dog & Light the Light (Columbia, 1993)
- ★★★★   Stoned Soul Picnic: The Best of Laura Nyro (Columbia/Legacy, 1997)
- ★★½   Live from Mountain Stage (Blue Plate, 2000)
- ★★★★½   Time and Love: The Essential Masters (Columbia/Legacy, 2000)
- ★★★   Angel in the Dark (Rounder, 2001)
- ★★★½   Live/The Loom's Desire (Rounder, 2002)

Laura Nyro was just a couple of years ahead of her time. Her late-'60s heyday as composer-of-the-moment helped pave the way for the female singer/songwriters of the '70s. Strong R&B influences and a dash of Tin Pan Alley reveal Nyro's New York roots; she was definitely a departure from the Joan Baez–Judy Collins school in terms of both songs and singing. Nyro's whoops and sighs sometimes cross the line into screechiness; her ruminative and intensely personal lyrics can easily slip into obscurity. As the hit cover versions of her very best songs suggest, however, Nyro can also bait a melodic hook with the confidence of a Brill Building pro. Three Dog Night ("Eli's Coming"), Blood Sweat & Tears ("And When I Die"), and Barbra Streisand ("Stoney End") reaped the benefits, while the Fifth Dimension served as her personal messengers: The pop-soul harmony group scored hit singles with "Wedding Bell Blues," "Sweet Blindness," and "Stoned Soul Picnic." Nyro's original versions—contained on *The First Songs* and *Eli and the Thirteenth Confession*—bristle with an electrifying confessional charge. *Eli* was Nyro's second album and breakthrough; it's a more accurate portrayal of her soulful sound than the slightly popified debut *More Than a New Discovery* (later reissued as *The First Songs*), confidently negotiating a stunning compromise between personal statement and melodic outreach. The challenging *New York Tendaberry* is even more stark, often just the singer and her piano. It contains the reassurance of "Save the Country" and "Time and Love," but much of the rest ducks down darker New York City side streets where the Fifth Dimension were not likely to follow. By *Christmas and the Beads of Sweat* her song sense is taking a backseat to alternating currents of free-floating anxiety and preciousness, though a loving cover of "Up on the Roof" hints at an antidote.

Gonna Take a Miracle comes close to pulling a miracle off. Produced by Gamble & Huff and backed vocally by a cobilled LaBelle, Nyro tackles an assortment of R&B and girl group material that allows her to both kick up her heels ("The Monkey Time") and bare her soul (Nolan Strong's doo-wop masterwork "Wind"). She then returned to her own songs with a somewhat lighter touch on *Smile*. That 1976 work appeared after a five-year break, and it would be decades until her next album of new material. *Walk the Dog & Light the Light* (1993) was the last released before her death in 1997, and it brings her personal politics—feminism in "The Descent of Luna Rose" ("dedicated to my period") and "A Woman of the World," animal rights in "Lite a Flame"—to the fore. The majority of her catalogue has been reissued, most with bonus cuts, and is anthologized in the flawless single disc *Time and Love* (flawless because it contains nothing cut after 1975) and the double but consequently not quite as essential *Stoned Soul Picnic*. There have been two posthumous collections,

both distinguished by some of her best singing ever. She was finally in control of her upper register (or maybe, with the wisdom of age, she was simply less inclined to push it where it wouldn't go). *Angel in the Dark* contains her final studio recordings, led by the beguiling title track and moving versions of "Let It Be Me" and "Will You Love Me Tomorrow." The two-disc *Live/The Loom's Desire* documents her 1993 and '94 Christmas Eve concerts at New York's Bottom Line club. With only piano and backing singers for support, she offers the faithful sets that lean on the later songs, using her signature pieces and golden-oldie interpretations as spice. In such a setting the hits aren't terribly missed; whether she's singing about a plum wine reverie in "Japanese Restaurant" or sending the crowd on its way with a tender reading of Smokey Robinson's "Ooh Baby Baby," Laura Nyro was one of a kind.   —M.C./B.E.

Paul Oakenfold

★★★ Journeys by Stadium DJ (Moonshine, 1994)
★★ Perfection: Perfecto (Warner Bros., 1996)
★★ Sessions V.2 (Ministry of Sound, 1996)
★★½ Global Underground: Live in Oslo (Global Underground, 1997)
★★★★ Tranceport (Kinetic, 1998)
★★★ Perfecto Presents Another World (Sire/Ada, 2000)
★★½ Voyage Into Trance (Cleopatra, 2001)
★★★½ Ibiza (Perfecto/K7!, 2001)
★★½ Perfecto Presents Travelling (Perfecto/K7, 2001)
★★ Swordfish: The Album (London/Sire, 2001)
★★½ Global Underground: NY (Global Underground, reissue, 2002)
★ Bust a Groove (Cleopatra, 2002)
★★ Bunkka (Maverick, 2002)
★★½ Perfecto Presents: Great Wall (Reprise, 2003)
★★★ Greatest Remixes (Topaz/Phase One, 2004)

Paul Oakenfold has been called the king of club DJs, the king of trance, and even the king of cheese. He's listed in *The Guinness Book of World Records* as the world's most popular DJ, though ravers the world over debate the artistry of his music, which augments house music's 4/4 thump with sweeping major-chord melodics, orchestral synthesizers, and big, dramatic crescendos for the masses. Oakenfold's shamelessly populist jams have led dance music's transpotter purists to tug their beards in consternation.

The London-born Oakenfold started out in the '80s as a hip-hop head, rocking the funky beats of the day and gaining fame by signing the likes of Will Smith and Salt-n-Pepa to their first U.K. deals. Then, captured by the hippieish Balearic grooves coming out of Spain's nightclubbing paradise Ibiza, he became an advocate of England's acid-house revolution. In the early '90s, he was tapped as producer to pump up the dance-floor funk for bands like Happy Mondays, served as U2's tour DJ, and took to the decks at club and rave gigs.

Oakenfold enhanced his reputation with a series of mix CDs. *Journeys by Stadium DJ* features classic tracks by acid-house legends the Shamen and Oakenfold's own "Perfecto" mix of U2's "Lemon." However, *Sessions V.2* and *Perfecto: Perfection*—which primarily collects releases on Oakey's Perfecto label—now sound hopelessly dated.

Bust a Groove, a.k.a. *Sampladelica: The Roots of Paul Oakenfold,* is a collection of dusty old-school DJ tools (discreet break beats and sounds, not songs per se). *Voyage Into Trance* reveals Oakenfold's early-'90s obsession with Goa (or "psy-trance"), a trippy-hippie, utopian rave sound, while *Global Underground: NY* combines darker grooves with more New Agey epics over two discs with, er, mixed results.

Oakenfold truly hit his stride during the late '90s. On *Global Underground: Live in Oslo* collection, Oakenfold stretched out, tossing some drum-and-bass grooves and chill-out ambience among the anthems. Its followup, *Tranceport,* is considered a classic trance record. One of the best-selling mix CDs ever, *Tranceport* features revised Ibiza favorites like Energy 52's "Cafe del Mar" and tracks courtesy of Oakey's superstar-DJ peers Sasha and Paul Van Dyk. *Another World* finds him pushing the stylistic boundaries, which lead to effective jams (his dance-floor twist on Led Zeppelin's "Babe I'm Gonna Leave You" brought many nonbelievers into the fold) and pretentious excesses (the snatches of film dialogue and tracks from New Age icon Vangelis are a bit much).

On *Ibiza,* Oakenfold returned to his Balearic roots, mixing together surging break beats and darkly tribal New York house via John Creamer and Danny Tenaglia alongside the usual euphoric epics. Oakenfold even drops in Radiohead's "Idioteque" and a re-vamp of U2's "Beautiful Day" for extra diversity points.

Swordfish: The Album is a reimagined soundtrack to the awful John Travolta action movie of the same name. The album includes some anonymous inciden-tal music used in the film, but other songs display an increased interest in hip-hop, which isn't always a good thing: His neo-electro twist on N.E.R.D.'s "Lapdance" saps the original's aggro tension, while a remix of Afrika Bambaataa's early '80s hip-hop masterpiece "Planet Rock" doesn't veer far from the original.

On *Bunkka*, his first album of all-original material, Oakenfold tried to break out of the "epic trance." *Bunkka* even scored a Top 40 hit, "Starry Eyed Sur-prise," a perkily saccharine ode to all-night raving with an insidiously catchy refrain supplied by Crazy Town singer Shifty Shellshock. Other than token trancer "Hypnotised," most of *Bunkka*'s tracks fea-ture Crystal Method–lite break beats (check the opener, "Ready Steady Go") with bold-faced guest vocalists Perry Farrell, Tricky, Nelly Furtado, and even Hunter S. Thompson. *Bunkka* epitomizes the trade-mark inconsistency of Oakenfold's career—dance music for the masses mixed with stylistic leapfrogging, producing frequently listenable, often danceable, but rarely exciting results. —M.D.

Oasis

★★★★★   Definitely Maybe (Creation/Epic, 1994)
★★★★★   (What's the Story) Morning Glory
           (Creation/Epic, 1995)
  ★★½   Be Here Now (Creation/Epic, 1997)
★★★★   The Masterplan (Creation/Epic, 1998)
   ★★   Standing on the Shoulders of Giants
           (Creation/Epic, 2000)
   ★★   Familiar to Millions (Creation/Epic, 2000)
 ★★½   Heathen Chemistry (Epic, 2002)

"Tonight I'm a rock and roll star!" Liam Gallagher brayed in the first minute of Oasis's debut album, and although it was all the poor boy has ever had to say for himself, it was enough. The lager-swilling Manchester louts in Oasis probably couldn't have counted to 20 without eating their shoes, but damn, they knew how to shake up a song. Former Inspiral Carpets roadie Noel Gallagher played guitar and wrote spine-rattlingly great tunes, while his little brother Liam sneered through the lyrical platitudes with all the con-tempt they deserved. The boozing, brawling Gallagher brothers were true sons of the peat, prone to punching each other out, quitting the band midtour, marrying movie stars, moving into stately homes with names

like "Supernova Heights," and other feats of rock-star debauchery. But amid all the chaos, Oasis also pro-duced some of the '90s' finest rock & roll in the cos-mic guitar climaxes of "Live Forever," "Wonderwall," and "Slide Away."

Definitely Maybe, which brought Oasis fame and fortune, is a celebration of "Cigarettes & Alcohol" swaggering with hooks nicked from the Beatles, Bowie, T. Rex, the Sex Pistols, and practically every-one ever. Brilliantly crafted, appropriately grandiose, emotionally rousing, *Definitely Maybe* gets sentimen-tal and slovenly in all the right places. The lads bash out thirdhand glam riffs as if they've spent a lifetime worshiping Bowie without ever giving a moment's thought to his sex life, while the lyrics achieve some kind of cretin haiku: "I know a girl called Elsa/She's into Alka-Seltzer/She sniffs through her cane/On a supersonic train." Genius!

(What's the Story) Morning Glory?, by all the laws of U.K. rock stardom, should have been the flop fol-lowup. Instead, it's a triumph, full of bluster and bravado but also moments of surprising tenderness, such as the offhand love ballad "Wonderwall," the ma-jestic "Some Might Say," and the climactic "Cham-pagne Supernova." *Morning Glory* capped a true golden age for Britpop, the heady days of Blur and Elastica and Suede and Pulp and, er, Menswear. At this point, Oasis was recording more top-drawer tunes than it could cram onto its albums; the fantastic B sides and outtakes collected on *The Masterplan* in-clude "Listen Up," "Talk Tonight," and "Fade Away." Fans should chase down the definitive acoustic "Fade-away" on the 1995 compilation *Help,* maybe Oasis' most moving moment ever.

And then what happened? "I know where we lost it," Noel once observed with customary tact. "Down the drug dealer's fuckin' front room is where we lost it." *Be Here Now* was Oasis's version of Elton John's *Captain Fantastic and the Brown Dirt Cowboy,* a con-cept album about how long all the songs were. It was also the sound of a great songwriter turning his brain to cocaine crispies, with only two kickers: the title tune and the ridiculous "It's Getting Better (Man!!)." Noel quit drugs, shuffled the band lineup, and promised the sequel would be better. It wasn't. *Standing on the Shoulder of Giants* was the nostalgic mush Oasis-bashers had always accused the band of peddling, complete with sitar, mellotron, and lyrics like "Life is precocious/In a most peculiar way." *Familiar to Millions* is a live album about as exciting as its title; *Heathen Chemistry* is a studio album nowhere near as exciting as its title, though "Stop Crying Your Heart Out" is a great one and Liam's tambourine playing has definitely improved. —R.S.

Phil Ochs

- ★★★½   All the News That's Fit to Sing (1964; Hannibal, 1995)
- ★★★½   I Ain't Marching Anymore (1965; Carthage, 1986)
- ★★★½   Phil Ochs in Concert (Elektra/Rhino, 1997)
- ★★★   Pleasures of the Harbor (A&M, 1967)
- ★★★½   Tape from California (A&M, 1968)
- ★★★   Rehearsals for Retirement (A&M, 1969)
- ★★★★   Greatest Hits (A&M, 1970)
- ★★   Gunfight at Carnegie Hall (A&M, 1971)
- ★★★★   Chords of Fame (A&M, 1976)
- ★★★½   The War Is Over: The Best of Phil Ochs (A&M, 1988)
- ★★★★   There but for Fortune (Elektra, 1989)
- ★★★   A Toast to Those Who Are Gone (Archives Alive, 1986)
- ★★★   The Broadside Tapes: 1 (Folkways, 1989)
- ★★½   There and Now: Live in Vancouver, 1968 (Rhino, 1991)
- ★★★   Live at Newport (Vanguard, 1996)
- ★★★½   Fantasies & Farewells (Rhino, 1997).

Of all the major figures of the early-'60s folk boom, Phil Ochs adhered longest to Woody Guthrie's tradition of songs fired by social activism. Dylan moved toward more idiosyncratic poetry; Eric Andersen and others shifted their emphasis toward love songs and the softer singer/songwriter material; Joan Baez kept pace with Ochs in terms of political engagement, but the material she chose to cover lacked the edge of topicality that sharpened the typical Ochs protest song. Like Guthrie himself, a patriot of the most optimistic kind, his righteousness fueled by a populist faith, Ochs in time became a tragic hero—a seer ignored, his idealism shaken by the long agony of Vietnam and America's internal dissension. Not long before his 1976 suicide at age 35, Ochs was attacked mysteriously while traveling in Africa, and with bizarre, metaphoric appropriateness, his vocals cords were damaged. He sang again, but his spirit was shot.

All the News That's Fit to Sing, I Ain't Marching Anymore, and *In Concert* present Ochs' definitive protest songs. Lean, graceful acoustic guitar carries the simple melodies; Ochs's voice is strong; and his delivery is sharp, witty, and precise. "Talking Cuban Crisis," "The Ballad of Oxford (Jimmy Meredith)," "A.M.A. Song," and "Draft Dodger Rag" are aimed at specific targets, which he assails with zest and sardonic wit. *Pleasures of the Harbor* is introspective Ochs. No longer relying upon the three-chord melodies of classic folk, the orchestrated song arrangements on *Pleasures* recall 19th-century Impressionism. "Cross My Heart," "I've Had Her," and

the title track are brooding elegies; "Crucifixion" is a remarkable treatise on martyrdom; "The Party" and "Outside of a Small Circle of Friends" feature Ochs' typical satiric sneer.

With Van Dyke Parks turning in an atypically straightforward production, *Tape From California* stands as Ochs's most solid set, even if, at the time, it continued his descent into relative obscurity. "When in Rome" masterfully delineates American history as an epic of conquest; "The War Is Over" is strange, bitter, and moving; the title track is almost pop. While the songcraft reaches new levels of skill, the record's tone of melancholy and defeat came to overpower its followup, *Rehearsals for Retirement. Greatest Hits* has always been derided by fans of the singer's activist music, but it sounds riveting today. Van Dyke Parks provides strange, almost saccharine string arrangements, but nostalgic songs like "Jim Dean of Indiana," "Chords of Fame," "No More Song," and "One-Way Ticket Home" show profound soul racked with anguish. With its cover picturing the singer tricked out in gold lamé in some inscrutable Elvis homage/parody, *Gunfight at Carnegie Hall* ends the story on a painful note of confusion: Covering "Okie from Muskogee," oldies, and his own "best hits," Ochs reveals nothing but desperation.

There but for Fortune and *Chords of Fame* generously cover Ochs' entire career; *The War Is Over* concentrates on the more difficult later period. The *Fantasies & Farewells* box set gives you the whole picture in four CDs. *A Toast to Those Who Are Gone* presents strong material recorded before 1964; the cuts are demos, but they're excellent. *Live at Newport* is early, protest-folk Phil in concert, passionate and committed.   —P.E.

Sinéad O'Connor

- ★★★★   The Lion and the Cobra (Chrysalis, 1987)
- ★★★½   I Do Not Want What I Haven't Got (Chrysalis, 1990)
- ★★★   Am I Not Your Girl (Chrysalis, 1992)
- ★★½   Universal Mother (Chrysalis, 1994)
- ★★½   Gospel Oak (EP) (EMI, 1997)
- ★★★★   So Far . . . The Best of Sinéad O'Connor (EMI, 1997)
- ★★★½   Faith and Courage (Atlantic, 2000)
- ★★   Sean-Nos Nua (Vanguard, 2002)

For some, Sinéad O'Connor will forever be the tortured, sensitive soul whose doe eyes and tear-stained cheeks dominated the video for "Nothing Compares 2 U." For others, she's the wild-eyed radical who kept her head shaved and tore up a picture of the pope on *Saturday Night Live.* Lovelorn waif or crazy chick—

no matter which side of that coin comes up, O'Connor ends up the loser. A more sympathetic reading would be simply to take O'Connor during the '80s and much of the '90s as a perpetual adolescent—gifted but headstrong, given to impulsive acts and overpowering waves of emotion, and a sucker for heartbreak and unpopular causes. Of course, there are times when you wish she'd just grow up, but even at her most maddening, there's no denying the powerful musicality of her work.

From the first, it was clear that O'Connor was an artist of unusual precocity. Not only was her achingly personal debut, *The Lion and the Cobra,* entirely self-produced, but it moves through its mix of arty ballads, postpunk ravers, and slick, synth-smart dance tunes with an ease and assurance that would elude many established stars. Yet as striking as the songs often are—the ululating mystery of "Mandinka," for instance, or the insinuating heat of "I Want Your (Hands on Me)"—it's O'Connor's voice that ultimately carries the album. When the protagonist of "Jackie" rages against the sea that took her lover, you can hear the rage in O'Connor's voice, just as there's genuine tenderness in "Jerusalem." And when she assumes the role of the betrayed lover in "Troy," her fearsome, flamboyant performance would be the envy of any Medea.

O'Connor's ability to convey emotion through her singing paid huge dividends on *I Do Not Want What I Haven't Got.* The chart-topping "Nothing Compares 2 U," a Prince song, perfectly captures the sorrow and desperation of someone on the losing end of an infatuation. O'Connor touches on similarly strong emotions elsewhere on the album, but rarely with the same intensity; the emphasis instead seems more on the music than the words. That's fine, especially when her ideas are as interesting as on "I Am Stretched on Your Grave," which juxtaposes Celtic fiddle with a James Brown drum loop.

Most pop stars would see having a #1 single as good reason to repeat the formula. O'Connor, by contrast, seems to have seen it as an excuse for doing something completely different. And so *Am I Not Your Girl* finds her abandoning rock for a selection of torch songs associated with Billie Holiday and Ella Fitzgerald. Her performances, though idiosyncratic, were quite winning, but the album was a disaster commercially. After a two-year break and several controversies (including the pope-picture incident), she returned with *Universal Mother,* a powerful but perplexing album in which she seemed to recast all the world's problems in terms of parent/child relationships. (Take *that,* Dr. Freud!) While the politics are often wearying, the singing can be spectacular, as on her version of Nirvana's "All Apologies."

O'Connor then took a turn at acting, which explains the brevity of her not-gospel EP *Gospel Oak.* *Faith and Courage,* which brilliantly expanded upon the Afro-Celtic fusion first explored with "I Am Stretched on Your Grave," should have revitalized her career, but by this point the peculiarity of her personal life had, for the mainstream media, completely overshadowed interest in her artistic merit, and the album was largely ignored. Undaunted, she returned to roots with *Sean-Nos Nua,* a maddeningly uneven fling at Irish traditional music that is by turns wonderfully insightful and hopelessly clichéd.   —J.D.C

The Offspring

★★ Offspring (Epitaph, 1989)
★★½ Ignition (Epitaph, 1993)
★★★★ Smash (Epitaph, 1994)
★★★ Ixnay on the Hombre (Columbia, 1997)
★★★½ Americana (Columbia, 1998)
★★★ Conspiracy of One (Columbia, 2000)
★★★ Splinter (Columbia, 2003)

The Offspring was one of the biggest bands to emerge from the pop-punk explosion of the mid-'90s, boasting hooked-filled, frat-friendly anthems and a metallic gleam that referred back to the old-school sludge that L.A. punks fell for when they burned out on adrenaline. Singer Dexter Holland didn't try to evoke the pain and suffering of adolescence—instead, his voice was just plain authoritative, the commanding bark that skinny kids in malls across America wish they wielded.

The Offspring's early albums could have been made by any number of Orange County punks. But *Smash* is a powerful document. "Come Out and Play" imagines gang warfare as a game between street kids, without reducing it to a cheap joke; the song describes how self-mythologizing MCs can be when addressing the subject. And the female sex predator of "Self Esteem" teaches our hero some hard-won nerd wisdom: Under the wrong circumstances, sex can be demeaning, even if you're a guy.

Success didn't spoil the Offspring, but it sure made the band's immediate authority less attractive. By *Americana,* it sounded like the king of the hill picking on the little people. And yet the wigger-bashing "Pretty Fly (for a White Guy)," the welfare-to-work anthem "Why Don't You Get a Job?" and the beleaguered-boyfriend plaint "She's Got Issues" are irresistible.

Neither original nor particularly pranky, "Original Prankster," from *Conspiracy of One,* was pretty spry for a white lie, but "I Want You Bad" is fun. "Your one vice/Is you're too nice," Holland sings to a pretty, prim thing he wants to deck in whips and leather.

Having struck the perfect balance between the punk novelty single that sells albums and the serious thrash that appeases diehards, the Offspring learned to milk that formula with style.

Three years later, *Splinter* served up a familiar collection of party-hearty and slamming sounds: catchy pogo punk ("Long Way Home"), sludgy pseudogrunge ("Race Against Myself"), reggae-lite jams ("The Worst Hangover Ever"), and lighthearted ditties about romantic dysfunction ("Spare Me the Details"). Ironically, *Splinter* drags when the Offspring is most faithful to its roots—trad-punk numbers such as "Lightning Rod" are a bit too reverential. But like jokey pioneers the Ramones, the Offspring could keep riding its dumb humor and smart riffs well into middle age.   —K.H.

Ohio Players

   ★★½   Pain (Westbound, 1971)
   ★★½   Pleasure (Westbound, 1972)
   ★★½   Ecstasy (Westbound, 1973)
   ★★½   Climax (Westbound, 1974)
   ★★½   Skin Tight (Mercury, 1974)
   ★★★   Fire (Mercury, 1975)
   ★★★   Honey (Mercury, 1975)
   ★★½   Contradiction (Westbound, 1976)
★★★★★   Gold (Mercury, 1976)
   ★★   Angel (Mercury, 1977)
   ★★   Mr. Mean (Mercury, 1977)
   ★★★½   Funk on Fire: The Mercury Anthology (Mercury/Funk Essentials, 1995)
   ★   Jam (Mercury, 1996)
   ★★   Ol' School (Intersound, 1997)
   ★★★½   Orgasm: The Very Best of the Westbound Years (Southbound, 1998)
   ★★★★   The Millennium Collection (Mercury, 2000)

After stirring a lumpy Funkadelic-derived stew during their early years, Dayton's Ohio Players signed to Mercury Records in 1974 and cut their recipe back to the basics; soon, gleaming proto-disco concoctions like "Fire" and "Love Rollercoaster" would leave entire dance floors slavering for more. Notorious for their silly S&M-themed album covers, Ohio Players backed up the salacious cartoon flash of vocalist Leroy "Sugar" Bonner with a spare, supple groove. *Gold,* released in 1976, remains definitive; even "Sweet Sticky Thing" leaves a peppery aftertaste of bass-heavy, finger-poppin' funk. *Orgasm* covers the early years nicely; the two-disc *Funk on Fire* is a good, though overlong, overview. Surprisingly, the group's *The Millennium Collection* edition is nearly as good as *Gold. Jam* and *Ol' School,* latter-day live sets, are best avoided.   —M.C./M.M.

The O'Jays

   ★★   Back on Top (1968; Collectables, 1996)
★★★★½   Back Stabbers (1972; Epic/Legacy, 1996)
★★★★½   Ship Ahoy (1973; Sony, 2001)
   ★★★   Survival (1975; Epic/Legacy, 2000)
   ★★★½   Family Reunion (1975; Columbia, 1991)
   ★★★   Message in Our Music (1976; The Right Stuff, 1993)
   ★★★★   Collector's Items (1977; Columbia, 1991)
   ★★★   So Full of Love (1978; The Right Stuff, 1993)
   ★★★★   Greatest Hits (1984; Sony, 1995)
   ★★½   From the Beginning (1984; Universal, 1994)
   ★★★½   Emotionally Yours (1991; Alliance, 1996)
   ★½   Home for Christmas (1991; Alliance, 1996)
   ★★★   Love Train: The Best of the O'Jays (Epic/Legacy, 1994)
   ★★★   Let Me Make Love to You (Epic/Legacy, 1995)
   ★★★   Give the People What They Want (Epic/Legacy, 1995)
   ★★   Love You to Tears (Volcano, 1997)
   ★★   Super Hits (Epic/Legacy, 1998)
   ★★½   Live in London (Epic/Legacy, 1998)
   ★★★★   The Best of the O'Jays 1976–1991 (The Right Stuff, 1999)
   ★★★½   Smooth Love (AMW, 1999)
   ★★★   The Best of the Old School (AMW, 1999)
   ★★★   For the Love . . . (MCA, 2001)
   ★★★   The Best of the O'Jays (EMI-Capitol, 2001)
   ★★★★   The Ultimate O'Jays (Columbia/Legacy, 2001)
   ★★   I'll Be Sweeter Tomorrow: The Bell Sessions 1967–1969 (Sundazed, 2002)
   ★★   Love Songs (Epic/Legacy, 2003)

In 1972, a danceable message of societal paranoia called "Back Stabbers" struck like a thunderbolt, giving the O'Jays their first pop hit and propelling the sleek Sound of Philadelphia into the Top 10, where it ruled for the next several years, eventually spawning disco. There was little prior indication that such things were in store for the Cleveland vocal group. The late-'60s material that fills the collections *Back on Top* and *I'll Be Sweeter Tomorrow* gave the O'Jays a taste of success on the R&B charts but failed to provide an identity to build upon. Producers Kenny Gamble and Leon Huff, however, found a perfect vehicle in this vocal power trio. Buoyed by the smooth harmonies of Walter Williams and William Powell, lead singer Eddie Levert's growling authority pushes the O'Jays through the trickiest Gamble and Huff soundscapes. *Back Stabbers* may be the pinnacle of Philly Soul. Although the edgy title track and the musically related "992 Arguments" are vague evocations of personal travail, the feel-good anthems "Love Train" and "Time to Get

Down" are danceable winners. "Put Your Hands Together," the lead single from the followup album, *Ship
Ahoy,* sounds like another upbeat love march, but it's
calling for something "Love Train" took for granted. If
"Don't Call Me Brother" edges toward hostility, the
epic title cut depicts the slave passage with impassioned clarity all the more devastating because so few
artists have tried to tell this shameful story.

After those two magnificent albums, social commentary took a backseat. "Let Me Make Love to You,"
from *Survival,* and "I Love Music" and "Livin' for the
Weekend," from *Family Reunion,* sum up the O'Jays'
later Philly period: simple sentiment elevated by towering voices and majestic production. "Stairway to
Heaven" (no, not Zep's) captures the group at its
most gospel-flavored, but the Philly formula was
beginning to stagnate. The O'Jays didn't notice, and
continued to supply pleasing singles—from "Use ta
Be My Girl" in 1978 to "Lovin' You" in 1987—long
after the albums became routine. In the late '80s, the
group moved to EMI, where it attempted various
forms of cross-generational fusion, often with the assistance of Eddie's sons Sean and Gerald and their
group Levert. *Emotionally Yours* (1991) comes closest
to accomplishing that fusion with the smoking, politically charged "Something for Nothing." And the two
versions of the title track—an obscure late-Dylan
number taken out dancing and then escorted to
church—indicate that those blazing voices could still
strike like lightning. *Love You to Tears* is a low-key
effort that concentrates on ballads, but the O'Jays
greeted the new century with the equally smooth *For
the Love . . . ,* which contains the surprisingly frisky
single "Let's Ride," proving the old love train has
plenty of room for new passengers.

Given the group's long and illustrious lifespan, it
hasn't been adequately anthologized. *The Ultimate
O'Jays* succeeds because it includes the group's best-
known work, but the disc covers less than the first half
of the O'Jays' tenure with Philadelphia International
Records. *Best of the O'Jays 1976–1991* picks up
where *Ultimate* leaves off; taken together, the two
packages provide a bare-bones outline of the group's
story. The mistitled *Collector's Items* is a random
1972–76 grab bag of hits and album cuts that contains
nothing rare or unreleased (though nothing that isn't
great, either). By contrast, *Smooth Love* purposefully
cherry-picks ballads from the albums to show that the
group was much more than the the the sum of its hits. *Let
Me Make Love to You* and *Give the People What They
Want* are companion pieces—romantic and political
songs, respectively—and make the same point about
the depth of their catalogue. With such an impressive
arsenal of album tracks to buttress their four decades

of hitmaking, surely the O'Jays have earned the honor
of a box set.   —M.C./B.E.

Ol' Dirty Bastard

★★★★	Return to the 36 Chambers: The Dirty Version (Elektra, 1995)	
★★	N***a Please (Elektra, 1999)	
★★	The Dirty Story: The Best of ODB (Elektra, 2001)	
★	The Trials and Tribulations of Russell Jones (D3, 2002)	

Ol' Dirty Bastard, a.k.a. Russell Jones, was the most distinctive personality on the first few Wu-Tang Clan
records, but then again, he'd also be the most distinctive
personality in a Fellini movie: pure id run wild, an MC
with a mangled voice that constantly erupts into rage
and grotesquerie. Blessed with *delirium tremens*–style
production by fellow Wu-Tang soldier RZA, ODB's solo
debut, *Return to the 36 Chambers,* is a miracle of
messed-up-ness, like someone feigning drunkenness
while walking a tightrope. "Shimmy Shimmy Ya" is the
hit (dig the backward verse), but the extended gurgle
that opens "Goin' Down" is the peak of insanity.

During the next four years, ODB made more headlines than music—getting arrested repeatedly, announcing he was changing his name to Big Baby Jesus,
and so on. On *N***a Please,* he no longer sounds like
he's pretending to be out of control—he sounds like
he's being eaten alive by his own shtick. Aside from the
Neptunes' lithe (and Kelis-augmented) track for "Got
Your Money," the production is a major comedown
from *Return.* And ODB's cover of "Good Morning
Heartache" belongs to precisely the same creepy category as Sid Vicious' "My Way."

The Dirty Story is a feeble and badly sequenced
piece of catalogue exploitation: five tracks apiece from
the first two albums, plus the infamous remix of
Mariah Carey's "Fantasy," on which ODB groans,
"Me an' Mariaaaah go back like a baby and a pacifi-
aaaah." It's still better than the disastrous *Trials and
Tribulations*—ODB was already imprisoned when
record execs decided to milk another album out of his
name, and the result is a cold, sticky mash of snippets
of his voice, recycled verses from other records,
cheap-ass synth production, and gratuitous "guest
verses" to mark time.   —D.W.

Old 97's

★★½	Hitchhike to Rhome (Big Iron, 1994)	
★★★½	Wreck Your Life (Bloodshot, 1995)	
★★★★	Too Far to Care (Elektra, 1997)	
★★★★	Fight Songs (Elektra, 1999)	
★★★	Early Tracks (Bloodshot, 2000)	

★★★★½   Satellite Rides (Elektra, 2001)
★★★½   Drag It Up (New West, 2004)

Rhett Miller

★★★½   The Instigator (Elektra, 2002)

When they convened in Dallas in the early '90s, the Old 97's were looking for an excuse for hotshot guitarist Ken Bethea to sift some nifty guitar licks out of the history books and for wide-eyed Rhett Miller to perform a marathon autopsy on his broken heart. They discovered something more: rootsy, heartfelt, and oh-so-tuneful songs demonstrating that wheedling a willing lovely off the bar stool and into bed may get you through the night but rarely results in love-true-love.

After a few warm-ups, the 97's hit their stride with *Too Far to Care.* "My name's Stuart Ransom Miller/ I'm a serial lady-killer," our hero declares to a soon-to-be one-night stand on the standout track "Barrier Reef," his achy purr undercutting the gawky bravado even as Bethea's brawny twang undercuts his romantic fatalism. On *Fight Songs,* the band learned to insinuate rather than muscle the hooks across. Miller sets out to charm you the way prepunk romantics used to—with elegantly upbeat tunes, earnest come-ons, and a boatload of great melodies. There isn't a single dud on the record, but Miller really gets his star-crossed mojo working on "Lonely Holiday," "Indefinitely," "Oppenheimer" (named for the road where Miller says he fell in love, but also, not coincidentally, for one of the creators of the atomic bomb), and the acoustic tearjerker "Valentine."

Satellite Rides is as punchy and direct as premium power-pop, but it's grounded in easygoing rootsyness. A more upbeat Miller is in full flirt, admitting, "I'd be lyin' if I said I didn't have designs on you," and even offers to take you bowling on the irresistible "Rollerskate Skinny." That song ends with Miller declaring, "I believe in love, but it don't believe in me," which sums up Miller's impressive oeuvre as well as any one line ever could. Following Miller's very good solo foray, fussily groomed by producer Jon Brion, the Old 97's edged back toward country rock on *Drag It Up.* Despite a glut of slow tunes, the album includes its share of winners, including "The New Kid," "Won't Be Home," and "Friends Forever," where Miller starts reminiscing about his teenage years and ends up writing a cowpunk-flavored graduation anthem.   —K.H.

Olivia Tremor Control

★★★   Music From the Unrealized Film Script—
         "Dusk at Cubist Castle" (Flydaddy, 1996)
★★½   Black Foliage: Animation Music, Vol. One
         (Flydaddy, 1999)
★★½   Singles and Beyond (Emperor Norton, 2000)

Part of the loose coalition of neo-psychedelic bands known as the Elephant 6 Collective, Olivia Tremor Control made its full-length debut with *Music From the Unrealized Film Script—"Dusk at Cubist Castle,"* a sprawling 27-track disc that reveals some great pop instincts—and a serious need for editing. The main references throughout are *Revolver*-era Beatles, *Smile*-era Beach Boys, and various other classic-rock signposts roughened up by lo-fi production and a loose, informal playing style. The record's centerpiece, the 10-track suite "Green Typewriters," displays OTC's strengths and weaknesses: Promising musical ideas emerge—a pretty harmony here, an explosive riff there—but soon get replaced by some noisy "experiment." Still, *Cubist Castle* is the group's most cohesive recording, revealing a band clearly capable of creating solid retro-pop songs.

Its followup, *Black Foliage: Animation Music, Vol. One,* is another 27-track opus with heavy conceptual strains. This time, higher fidelity and production values turn the Beatles/Beach Boys references into more overt imitation. German tape-collagers Faust also loom large in the recurring *musique concrète* of five "animation" tracks, which feature instrumental themes and bits cobbled together from the title track and other sources. Here again, though, an admirable sense of playful experimentation gets clouded by the group's lack of focus or restraint.

A posthumous compilation, *Singles and Beyond,* collects a pair of early EPs as well as singles and compilation tracks. While the sound and vision of later inclusions are mostly familiar from the group's two studio albums, recordings from 1992–93 (released originally on the *California Demise* EP and as a single from the same era) reveal an unpolished, lo-fi fuzz-rock approach that manages to be retro and catchy without drawing too obviously on the band's influences. Here, sounding more like the Tall Dwarfs or fellow Elelphant Six act Neutral Milk Hotel, OTC still brims with the promise it never quite attained.   —R.M.S.

Yoko Ono

★★★   Yoko Ono/Plastic Ono Band (Rykodisc, 1970)
★★   Fly (Rykodisc, 1971)
★★   Approximately Infinite Universe (Rykodisc,
         1973)
★★★½   Feeling the Space (Rykodisc, 1973)
★★★   Season of Glass (Rykodisc, 1981)
★★★   It's Alright (I See Rainbows) (Rykodisc, 1982)
★★★   Starpeace (Rykodisc, 1985)
★★½   A Story (Rykodisc, 1992)
★★★★   Walking on Thin Ice (Rykodisc, 1992)
★★★★   Onobox (Rykodisc, 1992)

★★★ Rising (Capitol, 1995)
★★½ Rising Mixes (Capitol, 1996)
★★★ Blueprint for a Sunrise (Capitol, 2001)

Gathered together on the six-CD *Onobox,* the early work of Yoko Ono—an influence on punk and alternative bands from the late '70s onward—attains a charged, hypnotic power. Her later, slightly more pop-oriented material is less distinctive, though more listenable in conventional terms. While John Lennon's instrumental work can be heard on *Onobox,* the collection focuses mainly on Ono's solo oeuvre—including *A Story,* a previously unreleased album from when she and Lennon were separated in the mid-'70s. *Walking on Thin Ice* is the one-CD sampler of tracks drawn from *Onobox;* it's fine on its own terms, but lacks the substantiality of the longer collection. Regarding the individual albums, *Plastic Ono Band* is the companion piece to Lennon's astonishing solo debut; *Feeling the Space* is full of righteous feminist anthems (representative cut: "Angry Young Woman") that anticipate riot grrrl indignation; *Approximately* finds Yoko rocking convincingly; *It's Alright* is more pop oriented; and *Starpeace* pairs her with ultrahip producer Bill Laswell as Ono tries her hand at reggae and funk. *Season of Glass,* recorded right after John's murder, is harrowing and profound. *Blueprint for a Sunrise* proves that she's still vital and revolutionary. *Rising* marks the high point of her '90s comeback; a new generation of bands such as Sonic Youth was acknowledging her influence on them, and she was recording crunching hard rock with her son Sean's band, IMA. —P.E.

The Orb

★★★½ The Orb's Adventures Beyond the Ultraworld (Big Life/Mercury, 1991, 1994)
★★★ Peel Sessions (Strange Fruit/Dutch East India, 1991)
★★½ Aubrey Mixes: The Ultraworld Excursions (Caroline, 1991)
★★★★ U.F. Orb (Big Life/Mercury, 1992)
★★½ Live 93 (Island Red Label, 1993)
★★½ Pomme Fritz (Island Red Label, 1994)
★★★ Orbus Terrarum (Island, 1995)
★★½ Peel Sessions 92–95 (Strange Fruit (U.K.), 1996)
★★ Orblivion (Island, 1997)
★★★ U.F. Off: The Best of the Orb (Island, 1998)
★★ Cydonia (Island, 2001)

The Orb consists of "Dr." Alex Paterson and a rotating crew of sidekicks, notably Kris "Thrash" Weston, Thomas Fehlmann, and Andy Hughes; over the years, their prog-electronic innovation has gradually tapered off to insignificance. The group's breakthrough single, "Little Fluffy Clouds," was one of the most excitingly original records of the summer of '91. A bumping dance track built on samples of Steve Reich's "Electric Counterpoint" and a Rickie Lee Jones interview record, "Fluffy Little Clouds" has the sweetly elegiac undertone of a celebration that has ended. The rest of *The Orb's Adventures Beyond the Ultraworld* (abridged to a single disc for its first American release) is elegant chill-out music: long, blurry, near-ambient tracks that occasionally burble up into low-end grooves. The first *Peel Sessions* contains alternate mixes of three long tracks from *Aubrey Mixes: Ultraworld* and is more of the same, but less effective.

If *Ultraworld* was the warning shot, *U.F. Orb* was the ambient-dub bomb. Its centerpiece is the mighty "Blue Room," which circles a throbbing bass line for more than 17 minutes (the single version made that almost 40 minutes); "Towers of Dub," an abstracted take on dancehall reggae, is another extended powerhouse. For a few years, the Orb became the hot remixers for anyone who wanted to sound dark, mysterious, and vaguely spaced-out. (Two volumes of Orb remixes have appeared as *Auntie Aubrey's Excursions Beyond the Call of Duty,* which is worth investigating.) *Live 93* is pleasant enough, but it's clearly a stopgap product and the fifth time the same damn material had been reworked.

The Orb finally ditched the old repertoire and outer-space references for *Pomme Fritz,* billed as "the Orb's little album." The title track, constructed around a contrapuntal chime, is charming and willowy; after that, the musicians basically run out of material and doodle amiably for another half hour. Whooooooosh. Things improve a bit with the grainy, foggy *Orbus Terrarum,* whose beats are mostly either absent or muted to a point that summons not much more body motion than head-nodding. There are few if any hooks to speak of, though the 17-minute "Slug Dub" has exactly the sort of stoned pulse suggested by its title. The second *Peel Sessions* disc is of interest because Paterson and friends strap on guitars for a faithful and decidedly uncharacteristic reading of the Stooges' "No Fun."

After that, it's all downhill. *Orblivion* recalls *Ultraworld* without the hooks or centered grace, and clichéd ranting-preacher samples don't help. *Cydonia* attempts to bring the franchise up to date with drum-and-bass-influenced beats and even vocals (by Aki Omori and Nina Walsh) on a couple of tracks, but it's still pretty dull. The greatest-hits set *U.F. Off* is a weird one—it marks virtually all of the Orb's career high points, but most appear in condensed three- or four-minute versions. It's never dull, but it rarely achieves the spaced-out buzz along the way to dullness, which is really the Orb's sweet spot. —D.W.

Roy Orbison

★★★★★   The All-Time Greatest Hits of Roy Orbison (1972; Sony, 1990)

★★★★   For the Lonely: A Roy Orbison Anthology (1956–1964) (Rhino, 1988)

★★★½   Black & White Night Live (1988; Orbison, 1998)

★★½   Laminar Flow (Elektra/Asylum, 1989)

★★★   The Sun Years (Rhino, 1989)

★★★   Mystery Girl (Virgin, 1989)

★★★★★   The Legendary Roy Orbison (CBS Special Products, 1990)

★★★½   Our Love Song (Sony, 1990)

★★★   The Best of His Rare Solo Classics (Curb, 1991)

★★★½   Sings Lonely and Blue (Sony, 1994)

★★★½   Super Hits (Sony, 1995)

★★★   The Very Best of Roy Orbison (Virgin, 1997)

★★★½   Greatest Hits (Orbison, 1997)

★★★   Combo Concert: 1965 Holland (Orbison, 1998)

★★★★   Ooby Dooby: The Very Best of Roy Orbison (Collectables, 1999)

★★★★   16 Biggest Hits (Sony, 1999)

★★★   Anthology (Orbison, 1999)

★★★½   Roy Orbison: Authorized Bootleg Collection (Orbison, 1999)

★★★★★   The Complete Sun Sessions (Varèse Sarabande, 2001)

★★★½   Lost and Found: The Unreleased 1956 Recordings (Varèse Sarabande, 2001)

★★★   Shades of Roy Orbison (Collectables, 2002)

Death is always untimely, but rarely more so in the case of Roy Orbison, who succumbed to a heart attack in 1988 as his career was moving into high gear for the first time since his glory days in the '60s. In 1985, film director David Lynch, entranced by the dark beauty of Orbison's 1963 hit "In Dreams," featured the song in his oddball mystery *Blue Velvet,* sparking renewed interest in Orbison's early sides. In the aftermath of *Blue Velvet,* Orbison signed with the Virgin label and rushed out a set of newly recorded versions of his '60s hits, *In Dreams: The Greatest Hits,* now reissued as *The Very Best of Roy Orbison.* Then he hooked up with top contemporary artists—Bruce Springsteen, Tom Waits, Bonnie Raitt, k.d. lang, and Jackson Browne, among others—for a concert filmed by HBO and titled *A Black & White Night Live,* which also produced an album. Both were unqualified successes, and Orbi-

son demonstrated that his voice had lost little over the years. Moreover, he introduced two new songs he had already recorded for a studio album, one a strong interpretation of Elvis Costello's "The Comedians" and the other a tepid rocker titled "(All I Can Do Is) Dream You." He had been touring all along and had cut one splendid album in a group with Tom Petty, Bob Dylan, Jeff Lynne (whaaa?), and George Harrison, a loose configuration called the Traveling Wilburys. Everything was in place for a full-fledged and most welcome comeback when he died.

Released in early 1989, *Mystery Girl* yielded an atmospheric hit single in the Jeff Lynne–produced "You Got It." Written by Orbison, Lynne, and Petty, the song was a perfect showcase for Orbison's vocal brilliance. Lynne's other productions are ham-handed and ill-considered, but tracks produced by T Bone Burnett ("The Comedians" and "[All I Can Do Is] Dream You"), Orbison and Heartbreaker Mike Campbell (notably "The Only One"), and especially U2's Bono bring out the best in Orbison's awesome interpretive skills. The one to build on would have been the Bono-produced track, "She's a Mystery to Me," written by Bono and his mate the Edge. Rather than a big production number, Bono opted for a stark approach, discarding an orchestral arrangement in favor of stripped-down support provided by guitars, drums, and piano, and he lets Orbison breathe life into a song about obsessive, blind love and its attendant pain. Bono had it right: Keep the voice out there, give it a good song, and let it play.

This is hardly a revelation. Bono took his cue from Fred Foster, who established the classic template when producing the '60s sides that earned Orbison his legendary stature (he scored 15 consecutive Top 40 hits between 1960 and 1965); it can be heard on *The All-Time Greatest Hits of Roy Orbison,* Rhino's *For the Lonely: A Roy Orbison Anthology (1956–1964)* collection, *16 Biggest Hits,* the skimpy 10-track *Super Hits,* and the essential four-CD box set, *The Legendary Roy Orbison.* Foster believed in big productions—nothing about Orbison's Monument recordings can be considered "stripped down," and those sessions were among the first in Nashville to use large string sections—but the voice was always hot in the mix. The voice established the mood, and the arrangements were sculpted to heighten the tension and to mirror the stories' fevered, anxiety-riddled atmosphere. Teamed primarily with Joe Melson in the early '60s and with Bill Dees in the late '60s, Orbison delivered songs that broke with standard songwriting formulas and came on instead like mini-operas, minus the bloodlust. Paranoia, dread, and fatalistic anticipation were the dominant states of mind of those early '60s gems—"Running

Scared," "Only the Lonely (Know How I Feel)," "Crying," "In Dreams," "It's Over," "Leah" (perhaps his most stunning moment on record, with a song that builds tension incrementally from verse to verse, without a chorus ever rearing its head)—but there were also moments of heartfelt tenderness in "Blue Angel," "Blue Bayou," and "Dream Baby." And, of course, Orbison could kick it into a higher gear and rock out—he had, after all, started his career in a wild-ass rock & roll band in Vernon, TX, called, first, the Wink Westerners and then the Teen Kings—and in that mode he produced, in 1964, "Oh, Pretty Woman," his last #1 single but, more significant, an acknowledged rock & roll classic that still ignites a dance floor whenever it's played on the P.A. or covered by a band. Orbison's voice was one of the most remarkable instruments in rock, and he used it to full capacity, most effectively on "In Dreams" when that full-bodied tenor rose from a strong, straightforward delivery to a plaintive wail, followed by a piercing falsetto shriek—always in tune, mind you—in a performance of breathtaking majesty and passion. Rarely have a producer, an artist, and the material been so ideally matched as when Fred Foster was behind the board rolling tape on Roy Orbison.

In 1965, following two mediocre followups to the mammoth "Oh, Pretty Woman," Orbison signed with MGM. *The Classic Roy Orbison 1965–1968* documents the ill-fated association that saw Orbison disappear from the charts altogether. He continued to cut some good records, but they disappeared quickly. Only hard-core Orbison fans will be interested in the '70s albums. *Regeneration* (now out of print) brought the artist back to Monument and Fred Foster in 1977, but the old spark was gone. The voice was there, but the songs were bland, the performances listless, save for a take on Tony Joe White's "(I'm a) Southern Man." A brief tenure with the Elektra label is represented by 1979's *Laminar Flow* (now back in print), which featured three Orbison collaborations among its songs, but these and other tracks were dead in the water. The one indisputably great Orbison track from the '70s, "That Loving You Feelin' Again," was recorded for the soundtrack of one of the most forgettable movies in history, *Roadie* (Meat Loaf was in it—need more be said?). Although the movie soundtrack has long been out of print, the track in question is available on the 2001 Rhino/Warner Archives box set *Emmylou Harris Anthology: The Warner/Reprise Years*. It's a warm, touching duet between two voices well matched in texture, cast in a spare, discreet arrangement and unobtrusive production, and singing tender lyrics expressing everlasting love.

Before Orbison arrived at Monument, in 1960, he had put in time at two other labels, Sun and RCA, without notable success. He cut some wonderful records at Sun, garnering only one near-hit, 1956's dance song, "Ooby Dooby." Two Varèse Sarabande releases—*The Complete Sun Sessions* and *Lost and Found: The Unreleased 1956 Recordings*—and Collectables' *Ooby Dooby: The Very Best of Roy Orbison* show Orbison and the Teen Kings laying down some hot rockers and a few lovely ballads, even if Orbison is sometimes affecting the hiccuping vocal style of either his fellow West Texas rocker Buddy Holly or his former Sun labelmate Elvis Presley. One of the treats on *The Complete Sun Sessions* is a section of acoustic run-throughs of five songs, including a devastating treatment of an Orbison original, "The Clown." This is Orbison unplugged, worth the price of admission. Both *The Complete Sun Sessions* and *Ooby Dooby: The Very Best of Roy Orbison* feature Orbison's version of a song he cowrote with Harold Jenkins (before he changed his professional name to Conway Twitty), "Rock House," and Orbison's rocking paean to his first wife, Claudette, which was later covered by the Everly Brothers.

After Sun, Orbison signed with RCA; his 1958–'59 stay there has been documented on the Bear Family import *RCA Sessions*. Producer Chet Atkins clearly knew what he had: He sweetened up the arrangements with jazzy guitars, saxophones, and close-harmonizing background singers (which, to be fair, had also shown up on some of the later Sun recordings). But of these recordings, only the Boudleaux Bryant love song "Seems to Me" approaches the style Orbison would thrive on during the following decade, with Fred Foster producing.

Posthumously, Orbison's widow, Barbara, has formed the Orbison label and released several live albums, including *Black & White Night Live;* a limited-edition box set; *Anthology,* a collection assembled from *Black & White Night Live* and *Mystery Girl;* a 1965 live set recorded largely in Holland (some tracks are from a show in Paris), *Combo Concert: 1965 Holland,* which is marred by thin sound and uneven mixes; and a four-CD box titled *Roy Orbison Authorized Bootleg Collection.* The latter comprises live concert recordings, four from English tour dates and one from Birmingham, AL. Given that Orbison's sets varied little through the years, this collection is for completists only.

Ultimately, *The Legendary Roy Orbison* box set overshadows all other releases. For a concise overview of the most critical recordings of an important career, it's hard to beat. A couple more decades of work were yet to come when Orbison left Monument, but here, on four CDs, is the stuff of legend.   —D.M.

Orbital

★★★ Orbital (FFRR, 1992)
★★★★ Orbital 2 (FFRR, 1993)
★★ Diversions (FFRR, 1993)
★★★★ Snivilisation (FFRR, 1994)
★★★ In Sides (FFRR, 1996)
★★ The Middle of Nowhere (FFRR, 1999)
★★★ The Altogether (FFRR, 2001)
★★★★ Work 1989–2002 (Warner Strategic Marketing/Rhino, 2002)

As Orbital, brothers Paul and Phil Hartnoll gave the faceless electronic-dance-music scene of early-'90s Britain an indelible image: two wildly bobbing miner's helmets topped by twin flashlights (their standard stage headgear). The Hartnolls also differentiated themselves from most techno artists by crafting their albums as coherent statements and by showing an interest in melody and harmony as well as in the groove.

That Orbital's music is designed as much for listening as for dancing becomes clear on the very first track of its debut, *Belfast,* which slows down drastically from one section to another. Cool but never clinical, *Orbital* is electronica with a very human spirit. But it's just a warm-up for *Orbital 2,* a triumph of minimalist composition. The album blends subtle textures—a tamboura drone, a darting flute line, a synth patch that sounds like dripping water—to mesmerizing effect. Nominally an EP, the album-length *Diversions* compiles interesting but nonessential remixes and live recordings.

On *Snivilisation,* the Hartnolls add Alison Goldfrapp's winsome vocals to the mix; the clattering frame-drum beat of "Are We Here?" is one of many high points. *In Sides* lacks some of the duo's drama, but its final track, the burbling epic "Out There Somewhere?," compensates for the tedious moments. *The Middle of Nowhere* and *The Altogether* (which includes a nice cameo by David Gray on "Illuminate") up the rhythmic-aggression quotient while lowering the general complexity level. The discs are the closest Orbital has come to making standard-issue club fare and, as such, aren't bad, but considering the near-symphonic character of the previous four albums, it's hard not to feel that the brothers are slacking. *Work 1989–2002* is a solid best-of, though newcomers are advised to start with *Orbital 2.* —M.R.

Orchestral Manoeuvres in the Dark

★★★ Orchestral Manoeuvres in the Dark (1980; Virgin, 1987)
★★★ Organisation (1980; Virgin, 1987)
★★★ Architecture and Morality (Virgin/Epic, 1981)
★★½ Dazzle Ships (Virgin, 1983)

★★★½ Crush (Virgin/A&M, 1985)
★★★ Sugar Tax (Virgin, 1991)
★★★ Liberator (Virgin, 1993)
★★★½ The Singles (Virgin, 1998)
★★½ In the Dark (Virgin, 2003)

A Brit synth duo with brains under their sleek haircuts and hooks aplenty programmed into their keyboards, OMD were the best of their genre—while seldom forgoing the dance-floor punch of electronic pop, the band revved beyond the form's limits by stressing experiment over formula, melody over beat. From the beginning, OMD, featuring Liverpool's Paul Humphreys and Andy McCluskey—and, subsequently, an ever-shifting cast of players—feverishly joined inventive sound textures and odd themes ("Electricity," "Enola Gay") to undeniable riffs. With *Architecture and Morality,* they strained for seriousness—and found it in a tribute to "Joan of Arc," the tough thud of "The New Stone Age," and the languor of "She's Leaving." Spacey instrumental passages mar the record, but a live drummer compensates. *Dazzle Ships* is about as recherché as mainstream music gets; a postmodern critique-celebration of technology, the concept album percolates with sound effects, treated vocals, and the occasional slice of strange loveliness. With *Crush,* pure, luscious melody rules. Disowned (of course) by the band's cult, *Crush* is OMD at its most purely pop—"So in Love" and "Secret" are flawless singles. *The Singles* is radio music made in heaven.

By 1991, Humphreys had split. And on *Sugar Tax,* McCluskey plays it pretty safe—but "Pandora's Box," "Walk Tall," and nearly all of the album's 12 mechano-ditties make for dance-floor wonder. *Liberator* is even more dance-happy, though even less adventurous. —P.E.

Organized Konfusion

★★★★½ Organized Konfusion (Hollywood, 1991)
★★★½ Stress: The Extinction Agenda (Hollywood, 1994)
★★½ The Equinox (Priority, 1997)

Representing the creatively fertile hip-hop class of 1991, the underground hip-hop duo Organized Konfusion released their self-titled debut to little commercial success, but platinum records weren't the point. This proto-"undie" hip-hop group consisted of Prince Poetry and Pharoahe Monch, the latter of whom would dominate street-wise mix tapes throughout the 1990s. As Organized Konfusion, the two bounced rhymes off each other like an Olympic table-tennis team, turning them into thesaurus rap champions revered by an army of head-nodding backpackers. One of their weaknesses was keeping too much of the production in-house. At best this results in strange, ear-bending quilts of sound, but too often they settle on rather indistinguishable instrumental tracks—the Buckwild-produced "Why" from *Stress: The Extinction Agenda* is a notable exception. Unfortunately, their own tracks on 1997's *The Equinox* substitute dullness for what they were really going for: darkness (something that was far too common on late-'90s underground hip-hop albums). Even so, both MCs could transcend even the most uninspired beats, which is why Organized Konfusion will be remembered. —K.M.

Beth Orton

★★★★½ Trailer Park (Heavenly, 1996)
★★★ Best Bit (EP) (Heavenly, 1997)
★★★★ Central Reservation (Deconstruction/Arista, 1999)
★★★½ Daybreaker (Arista, 2002)
★★★ The Other Side of Daybreak (Astralwerks, 2003)

Beth Orton has one of rock & roll's strangest job descriptions: a boho folkie who strums her acoustic guitar for everyone from punk rockers to club kids. She got her start hanging around dance producers William Orbit and the Chemical Brothers, lending her voice to give their break beats a human touch; she sings the hangover rhapsodies "Alive: Alone" and "Where Do I Begin" on the early Chemical Brothers albums. On the chemical sister's stunning 1996 debut, *Trailer Park,* her bleak voice and guitar weave in and out of moody dance beats in "Someone's Daughter," "She Cries Your Name," a heartbroken cover of Ronnie Spector's "I Wish I Never Saw the Sunshine," and the fantastic 10-minute sex-and-death finale "Galaxy of Emptiness." All over *Trailer Park,* she wails like a bummed-out angel in the badlands of love.

On *Central Reservation,* Orton sounds none too chemical, ditching the techno beats of the debut for a woozy folk-rock record that recalls Big Star's *Sister Lovers* and Nick Drake's *Five Leaves Left:* piano, strings, vibes, congas, and an acoustic guitar with a bad case of the shakes. Orton moans bleary love songs like "Stolen Car," "Sweetest Decline," and "Feel to Believe," and even when they end in tears, she makes you feel how much fun it is to drink ale at dawn with the boy with the cinnamon eyes. "Pass in Time" is a seven-minute duet with British folk legend Terry Callier; the two collaborated on Orton's 1997 *Best Bit* EP, which is strictly for fans of British folk legends. *Daybreaker* blends the organic style of *Central Reservation*

and the debut's techno experiments, offering mixed but still impressive results. She reunites with both Orbit and the Chemicals while teaming up with country mavericks Emmylou Harris ("God Song") and Ryan Adams ("Concrete Sky"). But the sound is the one she's long since established as her own, particularly the melancholy splendor of "Mount Washington." Whenever Orton opens her mouth, she's bitching and bewitching, a space cowgirl with a stolen-car heart. —R.S.

Joan Osborne

★★★ Relish (Blue Gorilla/Mercury, 1995)
★★ Early Recordings (Womanly Hips/Blue Gorilla/Mercury, 1996)
★★½ Righteous Love (Interscope, 2000)
★★★½ How Sweet It Is (Compendia, 2002)

Joan Osborne is best known for asking the poignant question "What if God was one of us?" over a glistening guitar riff. But truth be told, the pop sensibility Osborne displayed on "One of Us" was out of character. For most of her career, she's striven to be a Janis Joplin–style blues-rock mama, with ho-hum results.

In the early '90s, Osborne put out a couple of records on her own, now largely available on *Early Recordings.* Eight of the 11 songs are live cuts; they're basically decent bar-band fare with overwrought singing. The studio tracks are okay but baffling; the best is a spaced-out version of Captain Beefheart's "His Eyes Are a Blue Million Miles."

Thanks in part to producer Rick Chertoff and songwriter/multi-instrumentalists Eric Bazilian and Rob Hyman—the same guys who contributed to Cyndi Lauper's triumph *She's So Unusual*—Osborne scored big with *Relish.* Besides "One of Us," highlights include the jaunty "Spider Web" (which imagines Ray Charles regaining his sight), the pensive "Lumina," and the roadhouse rocker "Right Hand Man." But the album is uneven, to put it kindly; the cover of Sonny Boy Williamson's "Help Me" is downright atrocious, and Osborne's yodeling renders "Pensacola" almost unlistenable.

Five years in the making, *Righteous Love* was considered a disappointment by many, which is unfair. Yes, Mitchell Froom's production is a trifle overbearing, but Osborne compensates with the horn-stoked "Baby Love" and a twangy take on Bob Dylan's "Make You Feel My Love." In fact, *Righteous Love* mirrors its predecessor: pleasant, workmanlike, and essentially anonymous.

Quality of material certainly isn't an issue on the covers record *How Sweet It Is,* a collection of mostly

'60s and '70s soul classics. Though it's sometimes hard to see the point in modern retreads of Aretha Franklin's "Think" or Otis Redding's "These Arms of Mine," the comfy vibe and judiciously restrained performances make this Osborne's most enjoyable work. —M.R.

Ozzy Osbourne

★★★★½	Blizzard of Ozz (Jet/Epic, 1981)
★★★	Diary of a Madman (Jet/Epic, 1981)
★★	Speak of the Devil (Jet/Epic, 1982)
★★	Bark at the Moon (CBS Associated, 1983)
★★	The Ultimate Sin (CBS Associated, 1986)
★★★★½	Tribute (CBS Associated, 1987)
★★	No Rest for the Wicked (CBS Associated, 1988)
★★	Just Say Ozzy (CBS Associated, 1990)
★★★★	No More Tears (Epic, 1991)
★★	Live and Loud (Epic, 1993)
★★★	Ozzmosis (Epic, 1995)
★★★	Down to Earth (Epic, 2001)
★★½	Live at Budokan (Epic, 2002)

Emissary of the devil or lovable, befuddled TV dad? The march of time (as well as MTV) has witnessed the perception of the onetime Black Sabbath frontman evolve from the former to the latter. Despite dabblings in diabolism and well-known misadventures with drug and drink, Ozzy Osbourne's solo career has supplied a sort of avuncular presence to 25 years of heavy-metal music.

First heard on the spotty but revelatory *Blizzard of Ozz,* Ozzy's first backing band was one of the most influential in all of metal, primarily due to late guitar virtuoso Randy Rhoads, perhaps Eddie Van Halen's only peer. Rhoads' disciplined attack—flashy but fleet—is best sampled on the posthumous *Tribute,* from 1987. On that recording of a 1982 concert, Rhoads buoys Ozzy's apocalyptic shtick with his arsenal of distorted chords and machine-gun solo outbursts. There's a strong note of empathy running through Osbourne's horrific metal melodrama: "Suicide Solution," "Crazy Train," and "Flying High Again" are nowhere near as exploitative as their titles might suggest. The naked, open-wound vulnerability of his voice, far more than his proclivity for rock & roll nuttiness and cartoon, is the key to his appeal. After Rhoads died in a plane accident while on tour in 1982, Osbourne soldiered on through the decade, gamely trying to compete with the hair bands he partly sired. Finally, with harmonics-happy guitarist Zakk Wylde, Ozzy pulled ahead of the pack with *No More Tears.* Several taut tracks, cowritten by Lemmy Kilmister of Motörhead, bring a gravitas that balances the L.A.-metal sheen; the

pathos-ridden, psychedelic title track is one of Osbourne's greatest achievements.

Although separated by six years, *Ozzmosis* and *Down to Earth* are essentially interchangeable—both contrast molasses-thick riff epics with charmingly mawkish ballads. Around the time that he and his family became reality-TV icons via *The Osbournes,* his entire back catalogue was re-released—with an intriguing wrinkle: Due to a contentious legal dispute, the bassist and drummer's contributions on Ozzy's first two solo records were replaced by their '90s equivalents. If this succeeded in spiting the original instrumentalists, only the most gifted audio engineer could possibly discern a difference. With the exception of *Tribute,* Ozzy's live albums are notable for their homogeneity; each one includes songs from its studio-album contemporary. The constant is Ozzy's hoarse exhortations to the audience: "I love you all!!" "Let me see your hands!" For it's not Mephistopheles that Ozzy worships, but his fans. —M.C./R.K.

Os Mutantes

★★★★	Everything Is Possible!: The Best of Os Mutantes (Luaka Bop, 1999)

Led by Brazilian songwriters Caetano Veloso and Gilberto Gil, tropicalia fused traditional Brazilian folklore with the anarchic spirit of late-'60s rock and protest folk. But there was a side to tropicalia that Veloso and Gil were a tad too tender and poetic to convey: a certain dissonance, a loopy sense of humor, and overt psychedelic tendencies that the trio known as Os Mutantes (Arnaldo Baptista, Rita Lee Jones, Sérgio Dias) gleefully explored during a short-lived but impressive career.

Thanks to David Byrne, that enthusiastic trader in exotic musical goods, mainstream America got a taste of the Mutantes. *Everything Is Possible!* is the only domestic release available, though the band's entire output can be easily found as import reissues. Still, Byrne's anthology does a wonderful job of capturing Os Mutantes' mystique, which centers around nonsensical spoofs of established genres ("Cantor de Mambo," "Adeus Maria Fulo") and mini–pop symphonies that sound like *Magical Mystery Tour* outtakes (the undeniably lovely "Fuga No. 2"). It's no coincidence that the majority of the 14 tracks are culled from Os Mutantes' self-titled debut, the best psychedelic album you've never heard.

Os Mutantes disbanded in 1978, and during its last few years, the group shuffled its lineup and released some forgettable prog-rock-flavored albums. Fortunately, Os Mutantes will probably be remembered for their earlier, quirkier aesthetic, which has influenced artists as diverse as Beck, Nirvana, and Stereolab. —E.L.

OutKast

★★★★	Southernplayalisticadillacmuzik (LaFace/Arista, 1994)
★★★	ATLiens (LaFace/Arista, 1996)
★★★★★	Aquemini (LaFace/Arista, 1998)
★★★★½	Stankonia (LaFace/Arista, 2000)
★★★½	Big Boi and Dre Present . . . OutKast (LaFace/Arista, 2001)
★★★★½	Speakerboxxx/The Love Below (Arista, 2003)

Dungeon Family

★★★½	Even in Darkness (Arista, 2001)

There had been plenty of albums by Southern hip-hop groups before OutKast's 1994 debut, *Southernplaya-listicadillacmuzik,* but nothing as good—and nothing with its Southern sense so proudly on display. As such, the record marked a coming out for a region that would dominate hip-hop by the decade's end. Full of local color and Southern slang ("ain't no thang but a chicken wang"), old-school rap's attention to mundane topics (talk of high school graduation in "Call of da Wild"), and an even older-school embrace of the African-American oral tradition ("Player's Ball"), the record is surprisingly deep for a then-teenage duo's first try. With clear debts to East Coast bohos like the Native Tongues and a West Coast level of attention to live instruments and smooth, irresistible melodies, Andre 3000 and Big Boi helped define a new stream of hip-hop that would rejuvenate the music in the late '90s and early 2000s.

Although *ATLiens* promised expanded vistas with its interstellar motif, the record delivered something of a sophomore slump. Except for a few standout tracks, including the single "Elevators (Me & You)" and the plaintive, piano-driven "13th Floor/Growing Old," much of the album feels flat. While the rapping remains strong, the music suffers as the duo make their first attempt at self-producing. Lost in the process are the rich, soulful melodies of their main producers and Dungeon Family cohorts, Organized Noize. At best, *ATLiens* is the sound of an ambitious group searching for its voice.

By *Aquemini,* though, OutKast has regained its stride and then some, delivering a career record that staked the group's claim as one of hip-hop's most important acts. Beginning with a statement of purpose—"Let's talk about time traveling, rhyme javelin, something mind unraveling, get down!"—*Aquemini* ebbs and flows with hardly any filler, mixing pop hits soaked in Southern tradition ("Rosa Parks," with its acoustic guitar strum and harmonica breakdown);

P-Funk tributes (complete with a George Clinton cameo); dub-influenced spoken-word bits ("SpottieOttieDopalicious"); blistering rock-guitar romps ("Chonkyfire"); and a soul-stirring epic starring Erykah Badu ("Liberation") that's more gospel blues than hip-hop. In the process, OutKast created the first masterpiece of Dirty South hip-hop.

If *Stankonia* is not as consistently brilliant as *Aquemini,* it's even more musically adventurous. The album sees OutKast growing simultaneously in opposite directions. With tracks including the Prince-like "I'll Call Before I Come," the silky smooth "So Fresh, So Clean," and the indisputable pop smash "Ms. Jackson," the duo engages conventional pop while exploring more mature themes than had been seen in mainstream hip-hop. Elsewhere, OutKast pushes toward something far more avant-garde—something *post*-hip-hop, perhaps—via songs that lift the genre's basic elements out of their comfort zone, injected with angry rock ("Gasoline Dreams") and sensuous psychedelia ("Slum Beautiful," "Stankonia"). Most striking is "B.O.B.," offering a frantic beat, ambient atmosphere, rapid-fire cadences, rock-guitar solos, and gospel choruses. It's all over the map yet amazingly cohesive, making it one of the most unusual, and energizing, rap singles of all time.

Big Boi and Dre Present . . . OutKast is a solid best-of that sprinkles three new tracks among early material and later hits like "Rosa Parks" and "Ms. Jackson." None of the new tunes are worthy of the best that OutKast has to offer, but they're at least unconventional. And one, "The Whole World," leaves you with unshakable nursery-rhyme melody.

The Dungeon Family's *Even in Darkness,* released only a few weeks before OutKast's compilation, makes good on a long-discussed project starring the group's larger Atlanta-based collective, which includes production team Organized Noize, groups Goodie Mob and Society of Soul, and solo rappers Cool Breeze, Witchdoctor, and Backbone. Although the album is surprisingly cohesive given the number of voices and producers, performances by the crew's top stars stand out—especially OutKast with Goodie Mob's Cee-Lo and Gipp on the single "Trans DF Express"—but don't overshadow the work of the others. With rousing horns and gospel swells, "Excalibur" is the climactic track—the key to a record that imagines the Dungeon crew as a Dirty South version of the Knights of the Round Table. Maybe not, but the always tuneful and inventive tracks are inspiring nevertheless.

Speakerboxxx/The Love Below continues where *Stankonia* left off, with OutKast's trajectory veering ever further off the course of conventional hip-hop and further into the annals of pop history. The album's structure—two solo records packaged together as a double CD—offers a fractured view of the duo's aesthetic: Big Boi's *Speakerboxxx* drops cutting-edge hip-hop that's at turns freaky and socially aware; Andre 3000's *The Love Below* eschews hip-hop almost entirely with a set of jazzy pop funk steeped in the eclectic influence of Prince. Both discs score big singles (Big Boi's "The Way You Move," Andre's "Hey Ya!") and loads of great album cuts— plus enough filler to make the duo vulnerable to charges it might have been better off with a tight single album. But for sheer breadth, ambition, and musical vision, there's little doubt *Speakerboxxx/The Love Below* is a classic. —R.M.S.

Buck Owens

★★★★   Buck Owens (1961; Sundazed, 1995)
★★★   Sings Harlan Howard (1961; Sundazed, 1997)
★★★½   You're for Me (1962; Sundazed, 1995)
★★½   On the Bandstand (1963; Sundazed, 1995)
★★★½   Sings Tommy Collins (1963; Sundazed, 1997)
★★★   Together Again/My Heart Skips a Beat (1964; Sundazed, 1995)
★★★   I Don't Care (1964; Sundazed, 1995)
★★★★   I've Got a Tiger by the Tail (1965; Sundazed, 1995)
★★★½   Before You Go/No One but You (1965; Sundazed, 1995)
★★   The Instrumental Hits of Buck Owens and His Buckaroos (1965; Sundazed, 1995)
★★   Christmas With Buck Owens (1965; Sundazed, 1999)
★★★   Roll Out the Red Carpet (1966; Sundazed, 1995)
★★★★   Carnegie Hall Concert (1966; Sundazed, 2000)
★★★½   Open Up Your Heart (1966; Sundazed, 1995)
★★½   Buck Owens and his Buckaroos in Japan! (1967; Sundazed, 1997)
★★★   Your Tender Loving Care (1967; Sundazed, 1997)
★★½   It Takes People Like You to Make People Like Me (1968; Sundazed, 1997)
★★   Christmas Shopping (1968; Sundazed, 1999)
★★★   Hot Dog (1988)
★★½   Act Naturally (1988)
★★★   All-Time Greatest Hits, Vol. 1 (Curb, 1990)
★★½   All-Time Greatest Hits, Vol. 2 (Curb, 1992)
★★★★   The Hits of Buck Owens (Rhino, 1992)
★★★★½   The Buck Owens Collection (1959–1990) (Rhino, 1992)
★★½   All-Time Greatest Hits, Vol. 3 (Curb, 1993)
★★★   Young Buck: The Complete Pre-Capitol Recordings (Audium, 2001)

Thanks to his hammy run on TV's *Hee Haw* coupled with a lengthy retirement from recording, it's easy to forget that throughout the '60s, Buck Owens ruled the country charts. Although he continued to score hits into the early '70s, the lion's share of his 42 Top 10 country hits came in the '60s—including 20 that went to #1. Most remarkably, he did it all by bucking the system, forgoing the traditional, string-laden Nashville sound in favor of the Telecaster-and-pedal-steel-fueled honky-tonk characteristic of California's Bakersfield sound. And what his songs might have lacked in emotional depth (compared to those of say, fellow Bakersfield pioneer Merle Haggard), they made up for in sheer, almost Beatlesque catchiness. The Fab Four, in fact, were such avowed Owens fans that they covered his 1963 hit "Act Naturally" almost note-for-note on *"Yesterday" . . . and Today*. Owens, who openly expressed his admiration for the Beatles despite grumblings from country traditionalists, repaid the honor by covering "Twist and Shout"—at Carnegie Hall, no less, with his whole band wearing mop-top wigs.

Although Owens' best-known '60s hits ("Act Naturally," "Together Again," "I've Got a Tiger by the Tail," etc.) are well represented on various anthologies (the best of which are Rhino's three-disc *Buck Owens Collection* and its single-disc counterpart, *The Hits of Buck Owens*), Sundazed's exhaustive reissue series of his Capitol albums better illustrates the extent of Owens' popularity; at last count, 18 titles originally released between 1961 and '68 were available on CD. A pair of perfunctory Christmas albums and an instrumental collection are included, but it's a testament to Owens' consistency that there's not a dud in the bunch. Like the Ramones, he was essentially a one-trick pony: His records sounded essentially the same—genial, upbeat, well played, and chock-full of catchy tunes—and he never dropped a turkey on his fans by straying off the tried-and-true track. So unless you're searching for a particular song, pick up any title—even the crystal-clear *In Japan*—and you'll get the picture: at least one, two, or three #1 hits sung (and usually written) by Owens, a half-dozen non-hits that sound less like filler than equally worthy singles candidates, an instrumental or two, and a couple of songs featuring Buckaroos guitarist/fiddler Don Rich or bassist Doyle Holly on lead vocal.

That said, three titles do stand out by merit of historical significance: the shuffle-heavy *Buck Owens*, which predates his Bakersfield sound bonanza; *I've Got a Tiger by the Tail*, representing said bonanza at its most bountiful; and *Carnegie Hall Concert,* in which Buck and the Buckaroos take Manhattan in high aw-shucks cornball style.

Owens recorded several more albums for Capitol during the first half of the '70s, and a few for Warner Bros. later in the decade, though none have yet been reissued. After the motorcycle-accident death of Don Rich in 1974, Owens showed little interest in recording or performing, until Dwight Yoakam—for whom Owens had written several songs—coaxed him out of retirement in 1988. That year's *Hot Dog!* and 1989's *Act Naturally* featured likable but lesser remakes of his earlier recordings. *Hot Dog!* boasts some borderline rock & roll, while *Act Naturally* presents Owens chumming it up with Ringo Starr on the title tune and harmonizing beautifully with Emmylou Harris on "Crying Time." Both albums have since fallen out of print, but as long as his vintage recordings remain (newly) readily available, neither is likely to be missed. —P.E./R.SK.

Jimmy Page & Robert Plant

★★★½ No Quarter (Atlantic, 1994)
★★★½ Walking Into Clarksdale (Atlantic, 1998)

Contrary to the insistence of Pagey and Percy, this is Led Zeppelin, version 2.0, despite missing drummer John Bonham (dead) and bassist John Paul Jones (not invited). *No Quarter* is a live *MTV Unplugged* spectacle, featuring Robert Plant and the not-strictly-unplugged Jimmy Page supplemented by the London Metropolitan Orchestra, a percussion-and-strings Egyptian ensemble, a quartet of Marrakech musicians, and veterans from Plant's band dressing up a handful of Zeppelin's more folksy or world-music-inspired material in full-on "Kashmir" regalia. Predictably, it's portentous as hell but not without moments of genuine beauty and power: "Nobody's Fault but Mine" and "Gallow's Pole" manage to transcend the original versions, while the new song "Wonderful One" sounds of a piece with the more delicate selections from *Led Zeppelin III*.

Released four years later, *Walking Into Clarksdale* was a back-to-basics (i.e., minimal strings) studio set featuring a dozen new tunes penned by Page and Plant with bassist Charlie Jones and drummer Michael Lee. But even more than on *No Quarter*, the songs remained the same, like two long-lost sides of *Physical Graffiti*. While the absence of John Paul Jones remains puzzling, the new Jones and Lee hold their own on the thunderous back end while Page and Plant go through the motions with conviction, if not quite over-enthusiasm. Plant's wails inject real majesty into "Most High," the album's most overtly Middle Eastern–themed track, while Page, seemingly lacking for much new to say with his Les Paul, still gets his message across with authority. Bottom line: Led Zep fans will love it. It's a lot better than *Coda* and Page's heavy-handed album with David Coverdale, though truth be told, Plant's solo albums are a lot more inspired. —R.SK.

Robert Palmer

★★★½ Sneakin' Sally Through the Alley (1974; MCA, 1990)
★★★ Pressure Drop (1975; MCA, 1990)
★★½ Some People Can Do What They Like (Island, 1976)
★★½ Double Fun (Island, 1978)
★★★ Secrets (Island, 1979)
★★½ Clues (Island, 1980)
★★ Maybe It's Live (1982; MCA, 2000)
★★ Pride (Island, 1983)
★★★ Riptide (Island, 1985)
★★ Heavy Nova (EMI Manhattan, 1988)
★★★½ "Addictions," Vol. One (Island, 1989)
★★ Don't Explain (EMI, 1990)
★★ "Addictions," Vol. Two (Island, 1992)
★★ Ridin' High (EMI, 1992)
★★½ Honey (EMI, 1994)
★★ Rhythm & Blues (Pyramid, 1999)
★★★ Live at the Apollo (Eagle, 2001)
★★★½ Best of Both Worlds: The Robert Palmer Anthology (1974–2001) (Hip-O, 2002)
★★½ Drive (Compendia, 2003)

An impressive range of influences, impeccable good taste, and an immediately identifiable voice don't necessarily equal soul, and Robert Palmer's career has always oscillated between style and substance. A cool blue sense of detachment pervades his New Orleans stopover (*Sneakin' Sally Through the Alley*), his various reggae trips (*Pressure Drop, Some People Can Do What They Like*), his macho-rock fling (*Secrets*), his half-serious new-wave jaunt (*Clues*), his dance-pop excursion (*Pride*), and his soft-core model-rock adventures (*Riptide* and *Heavy Nova*). Which pretty much leaves *"Addictions," Vol. One*. It's heavy on Palmer's massive synthed-up '80s hits and light on his pan-global '70s cult favorites. "Addicted to Love" (originally from *Riptide*) never fails to get under your skin, while Palmer ably handles some astute R&B covers like the System's "You Are in My System" *(Pride)* and Cherrelle's "I Didn't Mean to Turn You On" *(Riptide)*. On the other hand, "Simply Irresistible" *(Heavy Nova)* is a brazen, callow rewrite of "Addicted to Love," which naturally proved to be just as popular. Jumping around from Marvin Gaye to Mose Allison, and from Bob Dylan to Rodgers and Hammerstein and beyond on *Don't Explain,* Palmer sounds like an accomplished show-off.

A volatile concert performance culled from a 1988 tour, *Live at the Apollo* delivers thunderous versions of his '80s hits. Palmer engineered a comeback of sorts with the sparsely arranged meta-blues collection *Drive,* but he suffered a heart attack and passed away while vacationing in Paris on September 26, 2003. He was fifty-four years old. His early death was made even more tragic by the fact that, more often than not, his studio recordings left you with the feeling of unfulfilled promise. A pity, considering that Palmer's uniquely textured voice and significant songwriting skills could have secured him a more substantial place in the pantheon of elegant pop-rock megasellers. —E.L.

Eddie Palmieri

★★★★	Echando Pa'lante (Tico, 1964)	
★★★★	Mozambique (Tico, 1965)	
★★★★★	Azúcar pa' Ti (Tico, 1965)	
★★★½	Champagne (Tico, 1968)	
★★★★	Live at Sing Sing Vol. 1 (Tico, 1972)	
★★★★	Live at Sing Sing Vol. 2 (Tico, 1972)	
★★★★★	The Sun of Latin Music (Coco, 1974)	
★★★★★	Unfinished Masterpiece (Coco, 1976)	
★★★★	Lucumí, Macumba, Voodoo (Epic, 1978)	
★★★★	Eddie Palmieri (Barbaro, 1981)	
★★★★	Palo pa' Rumba (Fania, 1984)	
★★★★	El Rey de las Blancas y las Negras (Sony, 1991)	
★★★½	Palmas (Elektra, 1994)	
★★★½	Arete (RMM, 1995)	
★★★½	Vortex (RMM, 1996)	
★★★★	El Rumbero del Piano (RMM, 1998)	
★★★½	Live! (RMM, 1999)	
★★★½	La Perfecta II (Concord, 2002)	
★★★★	Absolutely: The Best of Eddie Palmieri (Varèse, 2003)	

with Cal Tjader

★★★★★	El Sonido Nuevo: The New Soul Sound (Verve, 1966)	
★★★★	Bamboléate (Tico, 1967)	

with La India

★★★½	Llegó La India vía Eddie Palmieri (RMM, 1992)	

with Tito Puente

★★★½	Masterpiece/Obra Maestra (RMM, 2000)	

Wildly original, moody, and dissonant, keyboardist Eddie Palmieri is, sonically speaking, the closest to a visionary rock star the Afro-Caribbean field has ever known. Although he draws mainly from the salsa and Latin jazz worlds, Palmieri has consistently transcended genres. But he never forgot the dancers, delivering some of the most devastatingly funky jams in the history of tropical music. Understandably, during his 40-plus-years career, he managed to attract some of the key players and vocalists in the Latin biz, from percussionist Manny Oquendo and trombonist Barry Rogers to illustrious singers such as Cheo Feliciano and Lalo Rodríguez.

Palmieri began his career as a *timbalero,* which explains his highly percussive piano playing—those crackling, crunchy chords are instantly recognizable. In 1961, he founded La Perfecta, a flavorful *charanga* orchestra that today sounds a bit tame compared to subsequent efforts. Think of Azúcar pa' Ti as the first real display of Palmieri's orgiastic take on tropical motifs. It was no coincidence that the album's "Azúcar" became a huge hit with New York's African-American dancers. With its sticky chorus, sinuous piano lines, and rock-solid percussion, it still stands as one of the ultimate salsa anthems.

It was during the '70s that Palmieri would produce the most fascinating and unique recordings of his career. Inspired, perhaps, by the atmospheric experimentations that were going on at the same time in the rock field, he began toying with electronics and off-the-wall fusions. *The Sun of Latin Music* is salsa's very own *Dark Side of the Moon.* It begins, innocently enough, with the conventional party tune "Nada de Ti"—after which Palmieri proceeds to demolish our expectations of what a tropical album is supposed to sound like. The 14-minute epic "Un Día Bonito" begins with a bizarro, abstract six-minute-long piano solo. "Una Rosa Española" translates the Beatles' "You Never Give Me Your Money" into Spanish—then wraps it up in a gleeful, sing-along Afro-Cuban chorus. Most important, the record's overall vibe was trippy and psychedelic, taking Latin music into brilliant, uncharted territory.

Having no intention of slowing down, Palmieri began the recording of a project that would eventually be truncated by the Coco label and released without his approval as *Unfinished Masterpiece*—an apt title indeed. *Lucumí, Macumba, Voodoo* (1978), a dark, raucous concept album based on the influence of African religions in the Americas, added funk and R&B to the mix. It was ignored by a public that was clearly having difficulty connecting with Palmieri's vision.

Subsequently, the maestro tamed somewhat his iconoclastic tendencies, but continued releasing highly danceable material. He won a bunch of Grammy Awards, discovered future Nuyorican diva India, and then, disgusted with the state of commercial salsa, retreated into Latin jazz for a trilogy of albums *(Palmas, Arete, Vortex)* that make other artists in the genre sound like tired old farts in comparison.

A triumphant return to salsa was engineered through 1998's *El Rumbero del Piano,* complemented by high-voltage live appearances and the introduction of the excellent Hermán Olivera as the band's new vocalist. Never one to shy away from commerce as long as his eccentric tendencies are not compromised, Palmieri resurrected La Perfecta in 2002 for a flawless collection that brought the old hits up to speed with the digital era while introducing a handful of new tunes, as jazzy and percolating as ever.   —E.L.

Pantera

★★★½	Cowboys From Hell (Atco, 1990)
★★★★	Vulgar Display of Power (Atco, 1992)
★★★	Far Beyond Driven (EastWest, 1994)
★★★	The Great Southern Trendkill (EastWest, 1996)
★★★	Official Live: 101 Proof (EastWest, 1997)
★★★	Reinventing the Steel (EastWest, 2000)
★★★★	Best of Pantera (Elektra, 2003)

You'd never know it from looking at, or listening to, 'em now, but Pantera, one the '90s' very heaviest metal bands, started life as a hair-metal act. After four albums of fluffy metal that these Texans naturally have let fall out of print and out of mind, the lineup of singer Phil Anselmo, guitarist Diamond Darrell, hellacious drummer Vinnie Paul, and bassist Rex Brown self-consciously reinvented themselves as dramatically as any one of David Bowie's reboots. On *Cowboys From Hell,* they became one of the few truly *heavy* metal bands to remember the groove, which is a nice way of saying some of their rhythmic brutality probably gave rise to new metal, for which they can (more or less) be forgiven. Songs like the title track, "Cemetery Gates," and "The Art of Shredding" found a heavy (sweet) spot between death metal's cultish separatism, speed metal's velocity, and doom metal's sludge.

Vulgar Display of Power is the first-tier breakthrough, a thick, nasty, rolling tank of an album. Anselmo sounds like a rabid dog, Darrell buzzes and howls under the influence of heat, and the rhythm section is simply massive. Picks to click: "Fucking Hostile," "Mouth for War," and slower yet no less scary tracks like "Hollow." Like the man said, Totally. Fucking. Hostile. *Far Beyond Driven* went all number one,

and platinum 'n' shit, but it's no *Vulgar* or *Cowboys.* Heavy as hell, sure, but also unfocused and meandering. "I'm Broken" and "Slaughtered" show signs of the old rage; "Good Friends and a Bottle of Pills" finds Anselmo taking inventory, while a cover of Black Sabbath's "Planet Caravan" tries to chill out. It was an exhausting album that spoke to an exhaustion just around corner.

After taking some time off, Pantera returned in '96 with *The Great Southern Trendkill,* a morose bit of work that found the band changing up tempos while Anselmo ranted about pain and self-destruction. He was falling deeper into a well of drugs and chaos, culminating in a near-fatal heroin overdose two months after the album was released. Good riffs, of course, but the vibe is so fucked, it's hard to enjoy.

After they toured for years and released a solid if uninteresting live album, *Reinventing the Steel* doesn't quite, but who can be expected to do that twice in one career? Instead, it finds them moving back toward the old *Cowboy* power. Although it leans too heavily on newer albums, *Best of Pantera* charts their evolution nicely. Besides, any self-respecting metal fan should know these Texans' hostility inside and out. By 2004, the band's hiatus seems indefinite, with compulsive side-project starter Anselmo in Down and Superjoint Ritual, and Paul and Darrell in Damageplan.   —J.G.

Papa Roach

★★★★	Infest (Dreamworks, 2000)
★★★½	Lovehatetragedy (Dreamworks, 2002)
★★★½	Getting Away With Murder (Universal, 2004)

With so many hang-ups on its plate—disgust at oneself, one's parents, women—you can understand why so many rap-rock bands forgot to, you know, rock. But no new-metal band so conscientiously kept its obligation to rock out as Papa Roach did on *Infest.* Lots of metalheads seek grandeur through an inflated sound, but these guys have a simpler M.O. Jerry Horton plays really big riffs, like those Ozzy came up with in the '80s; drummer Dave Buckner pounds the songs past any hint of self-pity; and frontman Coby Dick exclaims dour observations like, "It's in our nature to kill ourselves/It's in our nature to kill each other/It's in our nature to kill kill kill." But rather than use the "Broken Home" of his youth to justify his actions, Dick struggles for sanity to "break the cycle." "Last Resort" is a suicide note that seems especially creepy because the chorus emits a potent whiff of teen spirit; the band thrashes with such determination, though, that actual self-destruction is not an option.

For the followup, Dick—perhaps realizing that his nom de guerre was just as wussy as his given one—

became Jacoby Shaddix again. (Keep it real, brother.) Having exorcised its familial demons, the band turns an eye to intimate relationships on *Lovehatetragedy.* Yet rather than lash out at women whose only crime is digging a dude with major issues, Shaddix excoriates himself for not being able to love correctly. When Shaddix closes "She Loves Me Not" by screeching "Life's not fair" over and over, he renders a whole century of lost-love pop poetry redundant. —K.H.

Charlie Parker

Selected Discography

★★★★★ Yardbird Suite: The Ultimate Collection (1945; Rhino, 1997)
★★★★★ The Complete Savoy Sessions (1946; Savoy, 1989)
★★★★★ The Complete Dial Sessions (1946; Stash, 1995)
★★★½ Bird at the Roost, Vol. 1 (1946; Savoy, 1948)
★★★½ Now's the Time (1949; PolyGram, 1990)
★★★★ Bird With Strings (1950; PolyGram, 1994)
★★★½ South of the Border (1953; PolyGram, 1995)
★★★ Jazz at Massey Hall (1953; Debut, 2004)
★★★ One Night in Washington (Blue Note, 1953)

No jazz musician carries more mythology than Charlie "Yardbird" Parker, the Kansas City alto saxophonist whose lightning-fast runs and equally reckless lifestyle became the torrid intertwined legacies of bebop. Bird, as he was known, was a speed-demon technician and a famously voracious learner interested in Bartók and Stravinsky. Both an imp and a genius revered for his warm sense of humor and glib irreverence, he was the prototypical heroin addict, who pawned his horn repeatedly and made many a session playing a plastic saxophone.

Right from the beginning, his life has the stuff of legend: Parker got the name "Yardbird" as a teen because he'd hang out in the back yards and alleys of Kansas City's nightclubs, soaking up the sounds. An early formative experience came on one of his first attempts at playing in public: Parker got lost in a tune, and according to legend, drummer Jo Jones hurled a cymbal at him. From then on, Parker became a determined student who learned by copying the recorded solos of such established masters as tenor saxophonist Lester Young. Parker's recording career began in 1940, after he landed a gig with Jay McShann's band; the early sides, collected on *Early Bird,* are of erratic quality but show that the altoman's basic approach—playing on the upper ends of chords, stringing short motifs into extended lines—was in place.

Parker met trumpeter Dizzy Gillespie in 1940, and with him joined several seminal big bands, including

Earl Hines' 1943 band, unrecorded due to the wartime ban, and Billy Eckstine's legendary 1944 ensemble. Bird and Diz became partners late in 1944, and the following year began to record the glib blues and pirouetting themes of bebop. The early sessions, best sampled on *The Complete Savoy,* are legendary, and by 1946, Bird was recording for several different labels. Some ornithologists prefer the material he made for Dial Records, which is collected on *The Complete Dial Sessions.* A two-disc overview, *Yardbird Suite: The Ultimate Collection,* culls the best of both.

Parker's recording career diminished after the Dial dates. Although signed to a bigger label, Verve, his work was less frenetic and less consistently surprising: *Swedish Schnapps,* recorded between 1949 and '51, shows the altoman's virtuosity, as does Parker's collaboration with Machito's Afro-Cuban Orchestra, the torrid *South of the Border.* Parker's Cole Porter songbook offers only scattered thrills, and a new version of the classic *Bird With Strings* captures the leader reeling off solos that are far more sophisticated than their surrounding arrangements.

A score of Parker's live recordings are available, but most deserve a "buyer beware" label: The sound quality of *Jazz at Massey Hall* is fuzzy even though the music blazes, while *One Night in Washington* suffers from the exact opposite problem. Those just beginning their Bird collections are advised to start with Rhino's *Yardbird Suite: The Ultimate Collection,* an excellent primer that more than explains the phrase "Bird Lives!" —T.M.

Graham Parker

★★★★ Howlin' Wind (Mercury, 1976)
★★★★ Heat Treatment (Mercury, 1976)
★★★ Stick to Me (Mercury, 1977)
★★★★ Squeezing Out Sparks/Live Sparks (1979; Arista, 1996)
★★★ The Up Escalator (1980; Diablo, 2001)
★★★ Another Grey Area (Arista, 1982)
★★★ The Real Macaw (Arista, 1983)
★★½ Steady Nerves and the Shot (Elektra, 1985)
★★★½ The Mona Lisa's Sister (RCA, 1988)
★★★ Human Soul (RCA, 1989)
★★½ Live! Alone in America (RCA, 1989)
★★★ Struck by Lightning (RCA, 1991)
★★★½ Burning Questions (Diablo, 1992)
★★ Live Alone (Gadfly, 1993)
★★★ 12 Haunted Episodes (Razor & Tie, 1995)
★★★ Acid Bubblegum (Razor & Tie, 1996)
★★ Loose Monkeys: Spare Tracks and Lost Demos (Razor & Tie, 1999)
★★★ Deepcut to Nowhere (Razor & Tie, 2001)
★★★★ Ultimate Collection (Hip-O, 2001)

★★ King Biscuit Flower Hour Presents Graham
     Parker (King Biscuit, 2003)
★★★½ Your Country (Bloodshot, 2004)

Although he's widely perceived as a progenitor of
punk and new wave, Graham Parker came on like
a younger, more angst-ridden version of Van Morrison right from the start. *Howlin' Wind,* his volcanic
Nick Lowe–produced debut album, anchors personal
exploration worthy of the best singer/songwriters in
rock-solid, updated white R&B. Assured enough to
wrestle with reggae rhythms (the title track), rockabilly ("Back to Schooldays"), his pessimistic nature
("Don't Ask Me Questions"), and horn-peppered
blue-eyed soul, Parker possesses the talent—and the
backing band—necessary to pull it all off. Led by guitarist Brinsley Schwarz, the assembled pub-rock vets
known as the Rumour provide bristling support for
Parker's pointed eruptions. *Heat Treatment* is a
slightly weak followup; the energy level registers high,
but only "Turned Up Too Late" and "Fools' Gold" deliver the unaffected, haunting resonance of *Howlin'
Wind.* Muddy production and lackluster songwriting
make *Stick to Me* sound like a rush job.

Aggressively clearheaded and laden with pissed-off
hooks, *Squeezing Out Sparks* is a triumphant turnaround for Parker. His spleen-venting ("Local Girls")
is balanced by romantic conviction ("Passion Is No
Ordinary Word"), and feelings of dislocation ("Discovering Japan") are offset by a moral center ("You
Can't Be Too Strong"). You don't have to agree with
the antiabortion message of that last song to be affected by its strength.

Puzzlingly, after attaining that confident peak,
Parker lapsed into mercurial inconsistency and outright grouchiness. Hesitant, frustrated and frustrating, full of coulda-been-a-contender bitterness, his
next few albums exhaust the patience of all but
his most committed fans. There are moments when
his muse peeks out, of course, usually when he's not
trying too hard to be deep. *The Up Escalator* and (especially) *Another Grey Area* suffer from acute symptoms of Springsteenitis: gusty, overwrought vocals;
clunky, ham-fisted arrangements. *The Real Macaw*
is an admirable but half-convincing attempt at a
mellowed-out celebration of monogamy; "You Can't
Take Love for Granted" hits its target.

After bottoming out with the blandly gruff *Steady
Nerves,* Parker reemerged for round three in 1988
with *Mona Lisa's Sister,* his best release since *Squeezing Out Sparks.* Coproducer Brinsley Schwarz sparks
the gratifyingly spare accompaniment with spiky guitar lines, and Parker is fired-up throughout. Followup
Human Soul is almost as good; Parker grafts some of

the old R&B pizzazz onto his family-man profile, with
hummable results ("Big Man on Paper," "Call Me
Your Doctor").

Although Parker sounds a little too relaxed or
pleased with his circumstances at the acoustic outset of
Struck by Lightning, the bolt of inspiration eventually
finds him. "A Brand New Book" and "Ten Girls Ago"
update and embellish the pub-rock strut and stutter
rather than merely echo it. "Children and Dogs" is so
warm and funny, you may believe Parker's assertions
of hard-won maturity. Even better is *Burning Questions,* for which Parker manages to fire himself up
again for tracks like "Release Me" and "Love Is a
Burning Question."

Parker's studio work has become increasingly laid-
back and self-satisfied. Parker's most recent discs
(*Acid Bubblegum, 12 Haunted Episodes,* and *Deepcut
to Nowhere*) have moments of maturity and inspiration, and Parker's performances are never less than reliable. When it comes to rock & roll, even the "adult"
variety, a little pent-up fury never hurt.

After a few years' hiatus from the studio, Parker re-
turned in 2004 with a disc on the alt-country label
Bloodshot. Lacking the reverence with which Elvis
Costello approached his country phase, the songs on
Your Country are firmly rooted in that particularly
British version of country rock that owes more to
"Dead Flowers" than any "Blue Yodel." But as a result
Your Country winds up feeling more like a slightly too
mellow Graham Parker disc than a genre exercise.
That said, Parker has come up with a fine batch of
songs, including "Cruel Lips," which features contri-
butions from Lucinda Williams, and an enjoyable remake of "Crawling From the Wreckage." Almost three
decades into his career, Parker's voice has become too
distinctive to be much disguised by a little twang.

Parker has also been the subject of archive releases
that include concerts, rarities, and greatest-hits collections. *Loose Monkeys* is an outtakes collection—
from an artist who has always packed his releases with
filler—that will appeal only to completists. *The King
Biscuit* disc captures an indifferent Parker onstage in
1983, the valley between the peaks of *Sparks* and
Mona Lisa's Sister. The Ultimate Collection provides a
perfect single-disc introduction to this prolific but uneven artist.   —R.A.

Junior Parker

★★★½ Mystery Train (1990; Rounder Select, 1992)
★★★★ Junior's Blues: The Duke Recordings, Vol. 1
       (MCA, 1992)
★★½   The Mercury Recordings (Collectables, 1996)
★★★½ I'm So Satisfied: The Complete Mercury and
       Blue Rock Recordings (PolyGram, 1998)

The circuitous route that brought West Memphis, AR, native Herman "Junior" Parker to prominence in the R&B field originated in an impulse. During a 1948 concert, Sonny Boy Williamson (Rice Miller) asked his audience if there was a harmonica player in the house. Parker jumped onstage, and a career was under way. He toured the rest of the year with Williamson, joined Howlin' Wolf's band (featuring Ike Turner on piano) in 1949, and two years later was fronting it after Wolf began a short-lived retirement. By 1952 he had his own group, the Blue Flames, and a recording contract with Modern, for which he cut one single, with Turner (who had signed him) on piano. But it was a move to Memphis' Sun label in 1953 that got things going full throttle, when Parker's self-penned "Feelin' Good," a driving boogie assault in the style of a John Lee Hooker number, became a substantial R&B hit.

But though Parker could sell a raucous workout, his smooth, light voice and his crooner's sense of phrasing were most effective in service of a sorrowful blues lyric, such as on the jazzy, urban flip of "Feelin' Good," "Fussin' and Fightin' (Blues)." In fact, Parker's Sun tenure, brief as it was, showed him to have considerable potential as a balladeer. No matter what else he did at Sun, though, Parker's place in history was secured by way of an eerie, recondite slow blues he wrote and recorded in 1953, "Mystery Train." It's not quite a shuffle, it's not quite a boogie, but it's a little of both; Parker's vocal is all dark tones and conflicting emotions, as if he were describing an event he feared but had accepted as inevitable; an unidentified baritone sax player approximates the train's steady drone of a warning whistle; and the lyrics extend the inscrutability of it all by leaving open the question of whether the lover Parker sings of is dead, leaving him, or coming back to him. Hence the mystery of the train in question. Two years later, Elvis Presley stood in the same studio where Parker had recorded and, with Scotty Moore on guitar and Bill Black on bass, reconsidered "Mystery Train" in terms so emotionally and instrumentally searing that his and his band's performance became something akin to a gold standard by which all other rock & roll recordings would be measured. Rounder's *Mystery Train* encompasses the title song and eight other Parker Sun recordings (four of them making their first appearance on a domestic release), as well as three Sun cuts by James Cotton, including the epochal, defiant 1954 recording of "Cotton Crop Blues," featuring guitarist Pat Hare's blistering solo; and two previously unissued Hare solo recordings, "Bonus Pay" and the prescient "I'm Gonna Murder My Baby," which he did (murder his girlfriend, that is) six years later, for which he was sentenced to 99 years in prison. (One of

the most gifted of the many exceptional musicians who walked into the Memphis Recording Service studio on Union Avenue, Hare died behind bars in 1980.)

In 1954 Parker jumped to the Duke label, where he had a productive decadelong stay that saw him landing consistently in the upper reaches of the chart during those years as he lit the transitional path from R&B to rock & roll, both in his swaggering, bluesy vocal style and in the work of his newly acquired guitarist Hare, whose forceful style and use of distortion as a complementary voice marked his forward-looking sound. Working with producer/trumpeter Joe Scott at Duke, Parker, like his labelmate, touring partner (in a package dubbed Blues Consolidated), and friend Bobby Blue Bland, augmented his blues band with a horn section for extra ballast and blast. His nine-year association with Duke produced a steady stream of R&B hits, including three that rose into the Top 10: "Next Time You See Me" (1957), "Annie Get Your Yo-Yo" (1962), and the towering "Driving Wheel" (1962), which along with "Mystery Train" constitute the lasting monuments of Parker's career. Parker's Duke years are chronicled domestically on MCA's *Junior's Blues: The Duke Recordings, Vol. 1*. Note here the presence of the song "Stand by Me," which in feel and sentiment would seem to have been the inspiration for the like-titled Ben E. King classic from 1961.

From 1966 to 1968 Parker recorded for the Chicago-based Mercury label (and its Blue Rock subsidiary), hoping to cash in on the burgeoning blues revival of the time. Still working with a basic band and horn section, but updating his sound to embrace the style of soul coming out of Memphis' Stax Records, Parker cut some tough, swinging sides for Mercury, but his most substantial hits, the funky workout "I Can't Put My Finger on It," and 1969's "Ain't Goin' Be No Cuttin' Loose," both peaked at #48 on the R&B chart. But there's a lot of meat on these bones, as Parker's studio band included some top-rank players, including arranger Doug Sahm (who also penned a few tunes for Parker), Reggie Young on guitar, Bobby Emmons on organ, Willie Mitchell on trumpet, and Tommy Cogbill on guitar. PolyGram's *I'm So Satisfied: The Complete Mercury and Blue Rock Recordings*, with 31 tracks, is the most thorough overview of the these years and is further recommended for its sessionography and Billy Vera's always intelligent liner notes; at 14 tracks, the Collectables release, *The Mercury Recordings*, is a bit incomplete, but still a good bang for the buck for those who only want a taste.

After leaving Mercury, Parker bounced around from label to label for a few years, creeping back into the Top 50 on a couple of occasions but otherwise floundering commercially. During these years he recorded for Minit, United Artists, Bluesway, Groove Merchant, and Capitol (where he covered a couple of Beatles songs along the way, "Taxman" and "Lady Madonna"), but none of this work remains in print domestically. On November 18, 1971, following surgery for a brain tumor, Junior Parker passed away. —D.M.

Parliament

★★★½	Up for the Down Stroke (1974; Universal, 2003)
★★★½	Chocolate City (1975; Universal, 2003)
★★★★★	Mothership Connection (1976; Universal, 2003)
★★★★★	The Clones of Dr. Funkenstein (Casablanca, 1976)
★★★½	Parliament Live—P. Funk Earth Tour (Casablanca, 1977)
★★★★½	Funkentelechy vs. the Placebo Syndrome (Casablanca, 1977)
★★★½	Motor-Booty Affair (Casablanca, 1978)
★★★	Gloryhallastoopid (Casablanca, 1979)
★★★	Trombipulation (Casablanca, 1980)
★★★★	Tear the Roof Off: 1974–1980 (Casablanca/Universal, 1993)
★★★½	First Thangs (Fantasy, 1995)
★★★★	The 12" Collection and More (Universal, 1999)
★★★★★	Funked Up: The Very Best of Parliament (Universal, 2002)

The Parliaments began as a doo-wop quintet in Plainfield, NJ. Former barber George Clinton and crew— Fuzzy Haskins, Calvin Simon, Grady Thomas, Ray Davis—moved to Detroit in the mid-'60s. They landed a Motown contract, only to wind up on the bench. The group finally got a single out on Revilot Records; "(I Wanna) Testify" hit on the R&B and pop charts in 1967, but lousy distribution and an ensuing contractual dispute prevented a followup. In the meantime, Clinton was busy immersing himself in Sly Stone and Jimi Hendrix, studying the Beatles and Bob Dylan. Once he discovered the power in those big amplifiers, soul—and rock—would change forever.

Unable to use the Parliaments name, Clinton renamed the band Funkadelic and signed it to Westbound records. At the same time, the *exact* same band was rechristened Parliament and recorded *Osmium* for Holland-Dozier-Holland's Invictus label in 1970. (*First Thangs* collects all the Parliament recordings done for Invictus between 1970 and 1972.) Many of the Parliament songs recorded during these sessions showed up later, confusingly, on Funkadelic records ("Red Hot Mama," "Loose Booty," "I Call My Baby

Pussycat"), proving the two bands weren't exactly two bands, not yet. The furious funk rock is in place, as is Clinton's self-conscious humor ("Little Old Country Boy") and skill with vocal arrangements ("Come In Out of the Rain"). It's not a footnote, and works better as an album than several Funkadelic records.

Up for the Down Stroke was the moment when Clinton decided what made this band distinct from Funkadelic: punchline vocals and intricate harmony arrangements; Bernie Worrell's keyboard as bass line, melody, and Harpo-like vocal respondent; an easygoing sense of humor; horns, keyboards, and interlocking percussion rather than rock aesthetics and guitar solos. Veteran James Brown sidemen like bassist Bootsy Collins and the newly named Horny Horns (Maceo Parker, Fred Wesley) pump up the beat, with an ever-shifting cast of singers. The title track is one for the time capsule, as Clinton plays ringmaster with end to end hooks and beats that won't stop. The group's first single, "Testify," gets a decent reworking, and "All Your Goodies Are Gone" is a funky left turn that became a hip-hop sample. From there, the forays into ballads ("Whatever Makes Baby Feel Good") and drum machines ("The Goose") range from atmospheric to negligible but don't stop the flow. (The 2003 remastered reissue adds two alternate mixes and one very strong unreleased track, "Singing Another Song.")

The title track of *Chocolate City* is one of Clinton's most successful political concepts; an AM radio DJ trying to paint the White House black with the best band in town. The funk stays strong for five songs and then Clinton leads the band into some pleasant, if thin, male vocal harmony tracks that sound more like the old doo-wop style than Clinton's new approach, which used female voices to better effect. The Isaac Hayes–style funeral funk of the underrated "I Misjudged You" sounds like trip-hop now, and "Big Footin' " brings back the bottom with a crazed Fuzzy Haskins vocal (and a quote from Funkadelic's "A Joyful Process"!). The reissue adds 2 alternate mixes and one unreleased comedy track, "Common Law Wife."

That was it for fine-tuning. Parliament began a serious run. *Mothership Connection* featured Clinton as MC, rapping, teasing, and herding his band through a new pop music with links to Africa, deep space, and urban politics. The balance here is perfect—the endless manifesto "P. Funk," the knee-buckling sweetness of the horns and vocals calling back and forth across the aisle on the title track, and their best-known sing-along, "Give Up the Funk," which probably started as many bands as the Ramones' first album. The groove undergirds everything, so that comedy tracks ("Unfunky UFO" and "Handcuffs") flow into the whole without a drop in bumpa-tivity.

On *The Clones of Dr. Funkenstein,* the band is in its prime and knows it. The Funky Trinity of George Clinton, Bootsy Collins, and Bernie Worrell are almost the Beatles of funk on this one, stringing sex, funk, and mad science into a seamless thing that doesn't know how to not please. The horns echo '40s swing without threatening the funk, and the vocal interplay is playful and deeply embedded. Choose any track—the low-slung title track, which is pure hip-hop attitude before the fact, or the lovely "Everything Is on the One," a slower, sweeter blend—and you'll be rewarded.

Funkentelechy vs. the Placebo Syndrome goes heavier on space travel than sex and introduces a new Clinton character, Sir Nose D'Voidoffunk, enemy of all things danceable (and a stand-in for the rock and pop audiences not understanding Clinton's too-black, too-strong circus crew). Again, the flow from track to track is impeccable, with Bootsy's watery, enveloped bass running like a live wire through everything. They're having such a good time in their atomized cloud of riffs and funny voices, you can't help but get carried along. "Wizard of Finance" is one of Clinton's best nonfunk tunes, a Broadway-ready slow tune about finance and romance. The album ends with one of the 20th century's greatest songs about absolutely nothing, "Flash Light," which is criminally short at 5:46. (Go to the *12" Collection* for the full 10:42 version.) Bernie Worrell will one day be elected Emperor of the World for his work on this song. So it has been written, so shall it be done!

Motor-Booty Affair is a slight step backward, with Clinton concentrating on the cartoon characters and offering the first weak opening track in Parliament history: "Mr. Wiggles." "Aqua Boogie" is a masterpiece, but again, go for the longer version. The band is good enough to dress everything up nicely, but there are too many longueurs and too few hooks to make this a good ride. (There is some fascinating comedy and musical madness buried in the last track, "Deep," possibly their oddest track ever.) You'd be better off at this stage in P-Funk history with spinoffs like Parlet (responsible for one of P-Funks' most monstrous moments, "Huff 'n' Puff") or Bootsy's excellent solo LPs.

Gloryhallastoopid and *Trombipulation* boast general product quality but few killer tracks, especially on *Trombipulation.* (*Gloryhallastoopid* does have the obscene but pretty great "Theme From the Black Hole," and "The Big Bang Theory," featuring the synth bass line that showed up the next year in Stevie Wonder's "Master Blaster.") *Tear the Roof Off* is a two-disc best-of, while *Funked Up* is one, long, re-mastered best-of. Both are excellent, as is *The 12" Collection,* which presents the long versions of some of their masterpieces, plus lesser-known tracks like Parlet's "Ridin' High" and the original version of "Testify," which reveals a very strong Sly Stone influence. —S.F.J.

Gram Parsons

★★★½ GP (Reprise, 1973)
★★★★★ Grievous Angel (Reprise, 1974)
★★★½ Sleepless Nights (A&M, 1976)
★★★ Gram Parsons: The Early Years 1963–65 (Sierra, 1979)
★★★ Gram Parsons and the Fallen Angels Live, 1973 (1982; Rhino, 1995)
★★★★★ GP/Grievous Angel (Reprise, 1990)
★★★½ Another Side of This Life (Sundazed, 2000)
★★★ Warm Evenings, Pale Mornings, and Bottled Blues (Raven, 1991)
★★★★½ Sacred Hearts and Fallen Angels: the Gram Parsons Anthology (Rhino, 2001)

International Submarine Band

★★★½ Safe at Home (1968; Shiloh, 1996)

Various Artists

★★★ Conmemorativo: A Tribute to Gram Parsons (Rhino, 1993)
★★★★ Return of the Grievous Angel: Tribute to Gram Parsons (Almo Sounds, 1999)

Gram Parsons didn't completely master country music in his brief life, but he had a much firmer grasp on the genre than his rock contemporaries. Although Parsons virtually invented country rock during his stints with the International Submarine Band, the Byrds, and the Flying Burrito Brothers, his sound barely resembles the sleek, glamorized radio fare churned out by bands like the Eagles just a few years later. Parsons concocted his notion of country soul, or "Cosmic American" music, after pursuing folk as a teenager, with the Shilohs (rereleased on *The Early Years*). During a quick stint in college in 1965, he dug in to the relatively bitter literary side of the urban-folk revival, documented on *Another Side of This Life,* which edges closer to the *GP* of legend. Parsons then formed possibly the first country-rock (*rock* as in R&B) aggregation, the International Submarine Band, and recorded an album that was promptly ignored (a remastered version is now available on Shiloh). Parsons's next stop was the Byrds, but by the time fans began to accept the band's country turn on *Sweetheart of the Rodeo,* he had already ended his brief, influential tenure. Soon joined by Byrds bassist Chris Hillman, Parsons went further down the country road with his new band, the Flying Burrito Brothers, staying long enough to contribute to two albums. Material from this period, along with later solo recordings, makes up *Sleepless Nights*. Parsons continued in a pure country direction for his abbreviated solo career. (He died in 1973, just after the completion of his second solo album.)

Parsons didn't cast off the rock influence so much as outgrow it. On *GP*, Parsons finds a soul mate in backup singer Emmylou Harris. The album's melancholy edge cuts deep on songs like "Streets of Baltimore" and "New Soft Shoe," though *GP* could stand a touch of *Gilded Palace of Sin*'s warped humor. That dolorous charge is what cultists have come to idolize about Parsons, of course. *Grievous Angel* displays the full range of his talents. Emmylou Harris is front and center, singing pristine harmony to Parsons' quavery lead—a far cry from the salty "he said, she said" duets of early-'70s mainstream country. This space-cowboy/earth-mother duo works wonders with familiar material ("Love Hurts") and its own neotraditionals ("In My Hour of Darkness"). On "Brass Buttons" and "$1000 Wedding," Parsons pinpoints the telling details of heartbreak with surgical precision. And a cover of Tom T. Hall's raucous "I Can't Dance" adds a welcome what-the-hell dash of spirit to an otherwise somber—but never depressing—album. Paired on a single-CD reissue, *GP/Grievous Angel* form a monumental document.

Parsons' influence just kept spreading deeper and wider. For groups like the Jawhawks and Wilco and performers like Gillian Welch, Parsons assumed the role that Hank Williams had held for Parsons' generation: a primal country muse, gloriously doomed and nearly inviolable. A bit too romanticized, this version of Parsons drags down *Conmemorativo*. But the surge of interest encouraged Emmylou Harris, among others, to put forth a more rounded portrait that's brilliantly represented on *Return of the Grievous Angel*, which is an ideal supplement to the splendid *Sacred Hearts and Fallen Angels* retrospective. It's a shade slow-moving for a legend with rock & roll bones, but it swiftly makes the case for Parsons as a songwriter and interpreter based deep in the American grain. In memory, Parsons now suggests a younger, forever-unfinished brother of Johnny Cash, with one foot in sacred water and the other on blood-soaked ground, nursing love dreams and a wound that cannot heal. —M.C./M.MI.

Dolly Parton

★★★★   Just Because I'm a Woman (1968; BMG Heritage, 2003)
★★★   Joshua (RCA, 1971)
★★★★   Coat of Many Colors (1971; Buddha, 1999)
★★★   The World of Dolly Parton Volume One (1972; CBS Special Products, 1988)
★★★   The World of Dolly Parton Volume Two (1972; CBS Special Products, 1988)
★★★★   My Tennessee Mountain Home (1973; Buddha, 1999)
★★★★   Jolene (1974; Buddha, 1999)
★★★★★   The Best of Dolly Parton (RCA, 1975)
★★   Here You Come Again (RCA, 1977)
★★   Heartbreaker (1978; Buddha, 1999)
★★★½   9 to 5 and Odd Jobs (1980; Buddha, 1999)
★★   Greatest Hits (RCA, 1982)
★★★   Dolly Parton Collector's Series (RCA, 1985)
★★   The Best There Is (RCA, 1987)
★★   Rainbow (Columbia, 1987)
★★½   White Limozeen (Columbia, 1989)
★★½   Eagle When She Flies (Columbia, 1991)
★★   Straight Talk (soundtrack) (Hollywood, 1992)
★★   Slow Dancing with the Moon (Columbia, 1993)
★★★★   The RCA Years: 1967–1986 (RCA, 1993)
★★★   Heartsongs: Live From Home (Columbia, 1994)
★★   Something Special (Columbia, 1995)
★★★★★   I Will Always Love You: The Essential Dolly Parton, Volume One (RCA, 1995)
★★★   Treasures (RCA, 1996)
★★★½   The Essential Porter Wagoner and Dolly Parton (RCA, 1996)
★★★★★   The Essential Dolly Parton, Volume Two (RCA, 1997)
★★★★   Hungry Again (Decca, 1998)
★★★★   The Grass Is Blue (Sugar Hill/Blue Eye, 1999)
★★★★   Mission Chapel Memories: 1971–1975 (Raven, 2001)
★★★★½   Little Sparrow (Sugar Hill/Blue Eye, 2001)
★★★½   Halos & Horns (Sugar Hill/Blue Eye, 2002)
★★★½   RCA Country Legends (RCA, 2002)
★★½   For God and Country (BMG/Blue Eye, 2003)
★★★★   Ultimate Dolly Parton (RCA, 2003)
★★★   Platinum & Gold Collection (RCA, 2004)

Born in the Blue Ridge Mountains of Tennessee, Dolly Parton made her radio singing debut at age 10. Her first Nashville sides, cut a decade later for the Monument label in the mid-'60s, are compiled on the two *World of Dolly Parton* albums. Signs of an indomitable singing and writing talent leap out right away, especially on *Volume One;* "Dumb Blonde" is exactly what she ain't. Teaming up with veteran singer Porter Wagoner after that, the bubbly Parton quickly stole the spotlight from her poker-faced benefactor. Between their hit duets (sampled on the 1996 collection *The*

Essential Porter Wagoner and Dolly Parton) and syndicated television variety show, Parton and Wagoner ruled the country roost at the turn of the '70s. It was around the same time that Parton began to shine with a singular, disarming brilliance as a solo artist—although, predictably for an artist this prolific, many of her earliest albums have fallen out of print, including 1970's terrific *The Best of Dolly Parton*. Fortunately, the double-disc anthology *The RCA Years: 1976–1986* (2003) picks up some of the slack, as does *The Essential Dolly Parton, Volume Two* (1997). Her version of Jimmie Rodgers' "Mule Skinner Blues (Blue Yodel #8)" skips and soars with effortless grace. But Parton distinguished herself early on as a formidable writer as well as singer. Deep-running bluegrass and folk roots inform her lyrics as well as her singing. She addresses traditional subject matter—often dark or morbid reflections on life's cruel inconsistencies—in a convincing modern context. "My Blue Ridge Mountain Boy" and "In the Good Old Days (When Times Were Bad)" (both on *The RCA Years*) examine the consequences of leaving the simple life behind, administering an unexpected dose of realism. She wouldn't go back if they paid her, Dolly rightly concludes on "Good Old Days." Her gift for empathetic narrative comes to the fore on "Down From Dover" (a pregnant teen's sad awakening) and "Daddy Come and Get Me" (from a padded cell!), while the title track of 1968's *Just Because I'm a Woman* (finally reissued on CD in 2003) lays down a sharply worded protofeminist manifesto.

Parton took advantage of her superstar clout at first, cutting two loosely conceptual albums in the early '70s. Autobiographical but not overly sentimental, *Coat of Many Colors* (childhood inspiration) and *My Tennessee Mountain Home* (music-biz aspirations) contain some of Parton's strongest work. The title tracks of both albums provide unforgettable hits, as does the haunting title tracks of *Jolene* (1974) and the deleted *Bargain Store* (1975). Both *Coat* and *Jolene* have been domestically reissued by Buddha, while BMG International has issued twofer discs pairing 1971's *Joshua* with *Coat*, and *Jolene* with *My Tennessee Mountain Home*. While various anthologies—including 1975's *The Best of Dolly Parton*, Raven's *Mission Chapel Memories* (2001) and the aforementioned *RCA Years* and *The Essential Volume Two*—offer good overviews of Parton's dizzying peak, and catch several key tracks from still out-of-print albums like the unbearably sexy "Touch Your Woman," the original albums that have made it to CD are all worth exploring on their own. *Coat* features the wonderfully randy "Travelin' Man," while *Jolene* offers up Wagoner's guilt-racked "Lonely Comin' Down" and

Parton's own indelible "I Will Always Love You," a country #1 years before Whitney Houston got ahold of it.

Of course Parton herself had aspirations beyond the country charts; if the dream of a pop crossover was hinted at with "I Will Always Love You," it became explicit on 1974's icky, string-laden "Love is Like a Butterfly" *(The Essential Volume Two)*. By the time Parton achieved that goal a couple of years later, she'd left her distinctive, rootsy musical approach behind almost entirely. Her 1977 pop hit "Here You Come Again" could just as easily have been recorded by Helen Reddy. Despite its peppy title hit, however, *9 to 5 and Odd Jobs* (1980) marks a refreshing (and underrated) return to country. After years of ever-blander releases, it's a pleasure to hear Parton's pure mountain warble latch on to Woody Guthrie's "Deportee," among others. But while the rest of her crossover period is not without winning moments (like the catchy "Two Doors Down" and even the Kenny Rogers duet "Islands in the Stream," an inexhaustible source of guilty pleasure), 1982's slim *Greatest Hits* and 1995's more generous *I Will Always Love You: The Essential Dolly Parton Volume One* both offer grim, glitzy testament to the soul-sapping power of media celeb4yhood.

Apparently sparked by the success of the *Trio* album with Linda Ronstadt and Emmylou Harris (1987), Parton returned to making records in Nashville, though it would take a while for her to find her muse again. Ricky Skaggs produced *White Limozeen* (1989), though it's a shame he couldn't bring more of a calming bluegrass influence to bear on the post-Hollywood Parton. She sounds nervous and breathy on "Why'd You Come in Here Lookin' Like That," a fidgety uptempo strut. *Eagle When She Flies* is a good deal more confident and assured, though Parton still doesn't quite connect with these polished countrypolitan love songs—even the ones she cowrote. The crowd of guests (including Billy Ray Cyrus) clutters up *Slow Dancing with the Moon*, and *Something Special* really isn't, unless you really need the Vince Gill duet remake of "I Will Always Love You." *Treasures,* a collection of covers ranging from Merle Haggard's "Today, I Started Loving You Again" to Katrina & the Waves' "Walking on Sunshine," is more pleasant diversion than timeless keepsake.

But just when it seemed Parton had lost the plot, she came back with a vengeance. The stripped-down *Hungry Again* delivers on the promise of its name with ravenous conviction. Parton's rootsiest record (and best collection of original songs) in ages, it proves you *can* go home again. From there, she got even rootsier, releasing a trio of honest-to-goodness bluegrass records: *The Grass Is Blue, Little Sparrow,* and *Halos & Horns.* Teamed with ace musicians like Sam Bush, Stuart Duncan, and Jerry Douglas and singing at the top of her game, Parton shines on songs new (the title track to *The Grass Is Blue; Little Sparrow*'s tremendous "Mountain Angel"), old (the Louvin Brothers' "I Don't Believe You've Met My Baby"), and unexpected (turning the rock band Collective Soul's anthem "Shine" into glorious gospel on *Little Sparrow* and even having a go at "Stairway to Heaven" on *Halos & Horns*). *Little Sparrow* is the best of the bunch, and the formula starts to wear a little thin by *Halos,* but the three albums still represent one of the most inspiring creative runs of her career—no small achievement. Rather less inspiring—at least musically—is the patriotic *For God and Country.* It's better than you might expect, given its limited scope, though the best thing about it is the priceless cover shot of Parton as a cheesecake USO pinup.   —M.C./R.S.

Charley Patton

★★★★★   Founder of the Delta Blues 1929–34 (1988; Yazoo, 1991)
★★★★★   King of the Delta Blues: The Music of Charley Patton (Yazoo, 1991)
★★★★★   Masters of the Delta Blues: The Friends of Charley Patton (Yazoo, 1991)
★★★★★   Charley Patton: The Complete Recorded Works (Peavine, 1992)
★★★★★   Screamin' and Hollerin' the Blues: The Worlds of Charley Patton (Revenant, 2001)

Robert Johnson gets all the headlines, but it was Charley (also spelled "Charlie") Patton who established so many of the stylistic standards of Delta blues as to rightfully deserve the title of "founder" and "king." Among the prominent Delta bluesmen of his time, Patton was the ultimate individualist; his home was wherever the four winds blew him, and changed when the first strong wind—or jealous husband or boyfriend—came along.

He left behind choice sides that continue to startle in their rhythmic complexity and structural innovation. Singing in a gruff voice that became harsher after his throat was slashed at a dance, Patton employed his voice as a percussive instrument, making his lyrics difficult to understand. Yet the emotion came through undampened and even enhanced when Patton used his slide to echo his vocal. The rhythmic devices he used have been traced back to West African drumming; Patton further complicated his sound by adhering to no set pattern of rhythmic structure. Also, he often disdained the standard eight- and 16-bar blues formula, working instead in 13-and-a-half-bar verses,

harkening back to a 19th-century folk drumming style.

Though no less bedeviled than Johnson, Patton nonetheless crafted some of the most harrowing accounts of Delta life—"Pony Blues," "Tom Rushen Blues," the two-part "High Water Everywhere," "Moon Going Down," and "Bird Nest Bound" are Delta classics, songs that inspired succeeding generations of bluesmen. The tracks on *Founder of the Delta Blues* represent many of Patton's classic blues recordings—some have been lost—but, almost without exception, these are the most important. In addition to his gut-wrenching blues, another side of Patton the performer of gospel and preblues songs and country tunes is presented on *King of the Delta Blues. Masters of the Delta Blues* is an anthology of recordings by Patton's friends and pupils (Son House, Tommy Johnson, and Bertha Lee, among others), all under the sway of Patton's style and themes. The three Yazoo albums together represent "the finest introduction to pre–Robert Johnson Delta blues imaginable," according to Robert Palmer, author of *Deep Blues.*

Palmer might have revised that opinion had he lived to experience the exhaustive seven-CD box set from the late John Fahey's Revenant label, *Screamin' and Hollerin' the Blues: The Worlds of Charley Patton.* It contains all of Patton's 54 known recordings and four alternate takes, along with tracks recorded by other artists at Patton's sessions, including House, Willie Brown, Henry Sims, Louise Johnson, Lee, the Delta Big Four gospel quartet, and others, with Patton appearing on some tracks in a supporting role. Another disc is a blues overview spanning the years 1924 to 1957, spotlighting songs that were inspired by or in some way related to Patton's style, by everyone from Muddy Waters to Ma Rainey. There's also an all-interview disc with people like Howlin' Wolf, and 120 pages of liner notes. If you're looking for just straight-up Patton at a cheaper price, the three-CD Peavine import *The Complete Recorded Works* is a fine way to go.   —D.M.

Sean Paul

★★½   Stage One (VP, 2000)
★★★   Dutty Rock (Atlantic, 2002)

Dancehall-reggae crossover hits tend to be deliciously simple, and former Jamaica water-polo star Sean Paul (born Sean Paul Henriques) knows how to make them. *Dutty Rock* contained both "Gimme the Light," a sticky ode to toking, with a twinkling beat and an undeniable hook, and "Get Busy," which rides the undeniable *diwwali* rhythm to great effect. Whether the average American listener can comprehend what's going on lyrically is moot, which is good news for Paul, because he's at best a middling MC. But even the most dowdy numbers on *Dutty Rock* sparkle on the chorus, which is sometimes just enough. Like most dancehall stars who have U.S. hits, Paul has been making records for some time in Jamaica; 2000's *Stage One* is a collection of those '90s hits; most of it is only for dancehall fans. The highlights are the ominous, sizzling "Infiltrate" and the stark "Hot Gal Today." —J.C./N.B.

Pavement

★★★★★ Slanted and Enchanted (Matador, 1992)
★★★★ Watery, Domestic (EP) (Matador, 1992)
★★★★ Westing (By Musket and Sextant) (Drag City, 1993)
★★★★★ Crooked Rain, Crooked Rain (Matador, 1994)
★★★★ Wowee Zowee (Matador, 1995)
★★★★ Pacific Trim (Matador, 1996)
★★★★★ Brighten the Corners (Matador, 1997)
★★★½ Terror Twilight (Matador, 1999)
★★★★★ Slanted and Enchanted: Luxe and Reduxe (Matador, 2002)

Oh, the summer of '92. Nirvana was on the radio. Corporate rock was dead. The end of the Reagan-Bush era was so close we could taste it. We were young and in love and the world was changing. All summer long, we sang along with the songs of Pavement, and we knew every word we sang was true, even the song that went "Lies and betrayals/Fruit-covered nails/Electricity and lust." *Slanted and Enchanted* was so damn good, no one even cared if Pavement would ever make another album, let alone go on to a decadelong run as the great American rock band of the '90s. But it did.

Two guitar boys from Stockton, CA, Stephen Malkmus and Spiral Stairs, headed into the garage studio of their hippie drummer, Gary Young, and knocked off a few songs for a laugh. As Pavement, they revamped the avant-noise experiments of Sonic Youth and Big Black, but goosed them with playful energy, wiseass humor, stolen guitar hooks, and unironically beautiful sha-la-la melodies. For all the art-punk excesses and lyrical goofs, the album flowed like a Buddy Holly song. The guys never thought anyone would hear it, but *Slanted and Enchanted* shook up the rock underground and became one of the '90s most influential albums, inspiring countless imitations (not mentioning any names, weezer blur).

Pavement was already making noise before *Slanted* on three limited-edition indie vinyl EPs, later collected on the excellent *Westing (By Musket and Sextant)* CD. First came *Slay Tracks 1933–1969,* featuring the jangly breakup tune "Box Elder," followed by the heavier *Demolition Plot J-7,* which had the hard-sludging "Forklift" and the odd love ballad "Perfect Depth." Over a wave of lo-fi guitar fuzz, Malkmus warbled plaintively, "I wasted all your precious time . . . I wasted it all on you." Singing about girls? On an indie-rock 7-inch? It was true. The 10-inch *Perfect Sound Forever* was just unbelievable, with "Debris Slide" celebrating and parodying 10 years of hardcore pretension in under two minutes. Pavement was a breath of fresh air, bringing miles of style to an indie-rock scene starved for a little excitement and, to the band's surprise, stumbling across a real audience.

Slanted and Enchanted was even better than anybody had hoped. Malkmus and Spiral Stairs had the songs to turn their homemade tape of guitar clatter into a full-blown California fantasy of girls and boys dreaming big on the ridge where summer ends. It was the sound of sweet suburban boys who loved the Velvet Underground's "The Black Angel's Death Song" without ever wondering what the words meant. "Zurich Is Stained," "In the Mouth a Desert," "Trigger Cut," "Here"—these songs still hold up as some of the freshest, funniest indie-rock gold sounds ever recorded.

Slanted sold something like 100,000 copies, an astronomical number for a small-town band on an indie label. Pavement started touring with bassist Mark Ibold and second drummer, backup singer, and onstage booty shaker Bob Nastanovich, an old friend from Malkmus' college days in Charlottesville, VA. The *Watery, Domestic* EP followed, featuring four cleanly recorded tunes as great as anything on *Slanted,* especially "Texas Never Whispers." The 10th-anniversary *Slanted and Enchanted* reissue documents Pavement on a roll in 1991 and 1992, when even its lackadaisacal throwaways were touched with greatness. The collection has B sides, BBC sessions, *Watery, Domestic,* and a December 1992 gig in London. The rarities include three of Pavement's best songs: "Circa 1762," "Greenlander," and the woozy space-guitar ballad "The Secret Knowledge of Backroads."

Crooked Rain, Crooked Rain was a daring move—instead of consolidating its noise-rock cred, Pavement got together in a real studio as a real band. Malkmus wrote an album's worth of juicy melodies, with the guitars ringing and chiming in emotional stray-slack surges. It's the band's most immediately lovable music, and "Cut Your Hair" even became a modest MTV hit. "Range Life" dabbles in a country-rock tinge that comes from living near too many college-town parrot-head bars, and like most of the other songs it waves goodbye to youth with ironic wit. Between "Gold Soundz," "Silence Kid," and "Fillmore

Jive," *Crooked Rain* is practically a concept album about turning 28.

Wowee Zowie is Pavement's most divisive moment: It turned off the fans who'd come on board with *Crooked Rain,* but many diehards call it their favorite. Pavement breathed in the mellow California air and went all soft and woogly, ditching any last trace of noise for 18 eccentric tracks that range from twee folk ditties to lazy instrumental doodles. When it's bad it's embarrassing, but in true White Album style, the overall what-the-fuck? effect adds to the fun of "Black Out," "Kennel District," "Father to a Sister of Thought," and other highlights. "Brinx Job" really blows, however. The best is "AT&T," which has nothing to do with the phone company—it's a breathy love song to a groovy, groovy kitty.

Brighten the Corners was a song album, high on the guitar power and group interaction that *Wowee Zowee* lacked. For some, it was too smooth, but by now Pavement was an avowed ballad band that only played rockers as filler; the ballads never got any more beautiful than "Old to Begin" or "Starlings in the Slipstream." Malkmus proves himself the great guitar romantic of an era replete with them, his voice barely afloat on a sea of girl worship, scared shitless by sexual attraction but sensible enough to let himself feel awestruck by it anyway. His words are funny in their sentimental way, or sentimental in their funny way, and as always, they accrue emotional meaning by flowing through his voice and guitar. The solo at the end of "Fin" is a real corker.

Terror Twilight was the same album with fewer songs and some really bad harmonica solos. Pavement soon fell apart, as haphazardly as it had come together. Spiral Stairs, using his real name, Scott Kannberg, started a new project, the Preston School of Industry. Malkmus made solo records with his new Portland band, the Jicks, and kept playing in David Berman's band, Silver Jews. The 2002 DVD *The Slow Century* features a documentary, live slop, and the immortal video for "Gold Soundz." Pavement still has another album's worth of great songs out there, scattered on singles and compilations. All the singles are essential for their nonalbum B sides; fans should hunt down "Strings of Nashville," "Harness Your Hopes," "Easily Fooled," "Raft," "No Tan Lines," and Kannberg's "Coolin' by Sound." The two best *Terror Twilight* songs, "Major Leagues" and "Spit on a Stranger," came out on singles with B sides that add up to a stronger unit than the actual album. Have fun looking for "Nail Clinic" (on the 1994 *Hey Drag City* comp) and "Sensitive Euro Man" (on the 1996 *I Shot Andy Warhol* soundtrack). The band covered R.E.M.'s "Camera" on the "Cut Your Hair" single; the 1993

benefit *No Alternative* has "Unseen Power of the Picket Fence," a very strange ode to R.E.M. (" 'Time After Time' was my least favorite song!/'Time After Time' was my least favorite song!"). *Pacific Trim* has three stellar tunes, including "Give It a Day," the best song ever written about the sex drive of Cotton Mather's daughter.   —R.S.

Pearl Jam

★★★★	Ten (Epic, 1991)
★★★★	Vs. (Epic, 1993)
★★★★½	Vitalogy (Epic, 1994)
★★★★	Merkin Ball (Epic, 1995)
★★★	No Code (Epic, 1996)
★★★	Yield (Epic, 1998)
★★★	Live on Two Legs (Epic, 1998)
★★★½	Binaural (Epic, 2000)
★★★½	Riot Act (Epic, 2002)

Selected Live Discography

★★★★	Live: 16/6/00 Katowice, Poland (Sony, 2000)
★★★★½	Live: 9/4/00 Washington, D.C. (E2K, 2001)
★★★★★	Live: 11/6/00 Seattle, Washington (Sony, 2001)

Of the four juggernauts that came to represent the Seattle scene of the '90s, Pearl Jam started off with the sound that was the most overtly commercial. Where Nirvana had punk influences, Soundgarden were metalheads, and Alice in Chains began as a glam band, Pearl Jam never gave the impression that they wanted anything other than to headline arenas, which they did within a year of San Diego surfer Eddie Vedder hooking up with the remains of Seattle's Mother Love Bone. Their debut album, *Ten,* was a runaway success, they were MTV favorites, and ticket sales set off the kind of hysteria not seen in rock since the Beatles. Success happened so quickly the band faced an immediate backlash: Nirvana's Kurt Cobain labeled them "careerists" (true, but it's not as though he wasn't himself), and critics described them as the '90s' Aerosmith, when they really wanted to be the '90s' Who.

Their early albums are better than those first reviews suggest, perhaps because only a band gunning to be the best in the world can play with the kind of narcissism and conceit that is needed to fuel such arena anthems as *Ten*'s "Jeremy," "Even Flow," and "Alive." Released a month before Nirvana's *Nevermind, Ten* is the more derivative album, but it does showcase Vedder's unique, driving vocal style and the delicate interplay between guitarists Stone Gossard and Mike McCready.

Vs. was a far better example of what Pearl Jam could do live, and by this second album the group was already consciously unplugging from the trappings of fame by refusing to make videos and starting to battle with Ticketmaster. As a result, riff-heavy songs like "Animal," "Daughter," and "Dissident" sound large without being bombastic, perhaps because they were never in regular MTV rotation. Still, the band's songwriting skills left something to be desired: Tracks like "Rats" and "Leash" come off as arrogant experiments by a band with a fan base that can't be disappointed.

By *Vitalogy* PJ hit their apex, combining their driving brash sound with the level of songwriting that keeps tunes on classic radio for decades to come. Stripped a bit from icon status, Vedder turns in vocal performances on "Better Man," "Spin the Black Circle," and "Not for You" that seem possessed. *Vitalogy* was the band's creative zenith, finding them doing a *Led Zeppelin III* on acoustic tracks like "Corduroy" and turning in a Tom Waits–like weird attack on "Bugs."

Both *No Code* in 1996 and *Yield* in 1998 were minor disappointments. *No Code* did contain the classic single "Who You Are" and the ferocious "Lukin," but the band seemed adrift, remembered more for off-album political battles with Ticketmaster and for testifying before Congress. On *Yield* the band shared songwriting duties, but when Vedder sang some of the other players' tunes, he seemed to be dialing in his performance. Additionally, Vedder's voice is mixed too low on most of *Yield*'s songs, almost as if he appeared on the album grudgingly, perhaps at gunpoint.

The best Pearl Jam album of the mid-'90s wasn't a Pearl Jam album: In 1995 they teamed with Neil Young and did service as his backing band on *Mirror Ball*. Although songwriting takes a backseat to spontaneous riffing, the results here are inspired and searing rock. An EP titled *Merkin Ball* is credited to Pearl Jam, and the two songs it includes, "I Got ID" and "Long Road," were the band's best work of the year.

In 1998, PJ released *Live on Two Legs,* their first live album. Although Pearl Jam has always been better in concert than on record, this tour highlighted tunes from the *Yield* album, which made it less powerful than some of the fan-produced bootlegs from earlier tours. By 2000's *Binaural,* the band had upgraded drummers, wisely grabbing Matt Cameron from the ashes of Soundgarden. Vedder also began playing guitar with more intent, and songs like "Breakerfall" and "Insignificance" suggested the kind of enthusiasm found on the band's first records. Pearl Jam took a break but came back together for 2002's *Riot Act,* a solid effort that contained the hit "I Am Mine," their first FM smash in years.

Pearl Jam has always allowed fans to tape their shows, and Vedder has openly admitted he's a fan of bootleg recordings himself. But in 2000 Pearl Jam took that enthusiasm farther than any band had before

by releasing 72 different shows—every concert from their world tour of that year. The sound quality on these shows was first-rate, and the tour found the band playing at their best. For casual fans, the three best live sets are shows in Poland; Washington, D.C.; and the one that ended the tour, in hometown Seattle. Pearl Jam mix up their set every night, but the Seattle show in particular found the band experimenting during the course of their 30-song set. Mixing rarely performed classics like "Alive" with energetic covers of the Who's "The Kids Are Alright" and "Baba O'Riley," Pearl Jam for a moment sounded like the most important band in the world again.   —C.R.C.

Pere Ubu

★★★★	The Modern Dance (1977; Geffen, 1998)
★★★★½	Dub Housing (1978; Thirsty Ear, 1999)
★★★½	New Picnic Time (1979; Thirsty Ear, 1999)
★★★	The Art of Walking (1980; Thirsty Ear, 1999)
★★★	Song of the Bailing Man (1982; Thirsty Ear, 1999)
★★★★	Terminal Tower: An Archival Collection (1985; Thirsty Ear, 1999)
★★★½	The Tenement Year (Enigma, 1988)
★★★½	Cloudland (Fontana, 1989)
★★★½	Worlds in Collision (Fontana, 1991)
★★★½	Story of My Life (Imago, 1993)
★★★½	Ray Gun Suitcase (Tim/Kerr, 1995)
★★★★	Datapanik in the Year Zero (Geffen, 1996)
★★★½	Pennsylvania (Tim/Kerr, 1998)
★★★★	Apocalypse Now (Thirsty Ear, 1999)
★★★½	St. Arkansas (spinART, 2002)

Pere Ubu prefigured the punk revolution. The maverick band was spawned by Cleveland's infamous Velvets-obsessed rock underground during the bone-dry mid-'70s. Founded by guitarist/critic Peter Laughner and singer David Thomas (a.k.a. Crocus Behemoth), the original Ubu mixed posthippie psychedelia and bargain-basement surrealism into a dense, scarifying hard-rock sound. As the group's early propaganda proudly announced, Pere Ubu's music could only have been produced in an "avant garage." The "30 Seconds Over Tokyo"/"Heart of Darkness" single, released in 1975 on the Hearthan label, helped usher in the heyday of independent recording. Those cuts and the 1976 followup "Final Solution" make the *Terminal Tower* retrospective essential listening for any student of punk or new wave.

By the time of Pere Ubu's debut album, Laughner's fluid Hendrixisms had been replaced by Allen Ravenstine's shocking electronic vocabulary of synthesizer rattles, hums, and screeches. *The Modern Dance* introduces rock to the concept of "industrial music." But unlike today's brutal clang-banging dance brigades, Pere Ubu's horrible noise and urbanized teen angst are tempered by the infusion of humanity: Tom Herman's curtly strummed rhythm guitar, Tony Maimone's probing bass, and David Thomas's quirky, passionate vocal eruptions.

Pere Ubu cuts loose from its rock grounding on *Dub Housing,* and the music takes off into uncharted territory that's alternately beautiful and grim. The group's discipline and implicit sense of structure separate it from raving new wavers and noodling art rockers alike; even the abstract electronic splashes and chattering tape splices on "Codex" congeal into fascinating patterns. There's always a purpose behind Pere Ubu's perverse humor and perplexing logic, and an eerie sense of reality pervades even the wildest sonic forays on *Dub Housing.*

New Picnic Time feels much looser; the band reaches for a semi-improvised experimental groove, nailing it more often than not. Guitarist Mayo Thompson replaces Tom Herman on the next two albums, and the overall sound slips into arid, arty repose. Most of the familiar elements are present on *The Art of Walking* and *Song of the Bailing Man,* but David Thomas no longer exudes the warped, wonderful essence that so enlivens Pere Ubu's groundbreaking earlier work. Pere Ubu broke up after a sour 1982 tour; 1987 saw the band's reunion with the satisfying album *The Tenement Year,* an unnostalgic blast of the old alchemy. "We've got the technology!" Thomas croaks and sputters with reactivated glee over the outmoded din of Allen Ravenstine's EML synthesizers.

Characteristically, Pere Ubu didn't remain long at the juncture. *Cloudland* and *Worlds in Motion* confront traditional song structures and melodies head on. The middle-aged Pere Ubu managed to sound more confident than compromised, though the closest it came to pulling off a commercial coup came when Geffen issued *Datapanik in the Year Zero,* a five-CD box set containing all of the band's pre–*Tenement Year* work as well as a disc of related prepunk Cleveland bands. The band has continued to put out good record after good record of noirish rock, keeping its heart of darkness intact well into its third decade. —M.C./M.M.

Carl Perkins

★★★★ Original Sun Greatest Hits (1986; Rhino, 1990)
★★★½ Honky Tonk Gal (1989; Rounder, 1992)
★★★ Silver Eagle Cross Country Presents Live: Carl Perkins (Silver Eagle, 1997)
★★★ Blue Suede Shoes: The Very Best Of Carl Perkins (Collectables, 1999)
★★★ Live At Gilley's (Q/Atlantic, 1999)
★★★ Blue Suede Shoes/Original Golden Hits (Collectables, 1999)
★★★½ The Complete Sun Singles (Varèse Sarabande, 2000)

Carl Perkins will forever be linked to his 1956 classic, "Blue Suede Shoes," and well he should be. In one fell swoop, this Tennessee sharecropper's son gave voice to emerging language, symbols, and attitudes, capturing the spirit of rock & roll's first generation and of the '50s as well. The first song to become a hit on the pop, country, and R&B charts simultaneously, it seemed to herald the start of an important career. But at the moment of his greatest triumph, Perkins found the rug pulled out from under him when he was seriously injured in a car wreck while traveling to New York to appear on *The Perry Como Show.* At the time of the accident "Blue Suede Shoes" was jockeying at the top of the chart with "Heartbreak Hotel," the first RCA single by Perkins' friend and former Sun labelmate Elvis Presley. A month later Presley released his own cover of "Blue Suede Shoes" and, although Perkins' original outsold Presley's, the song became identified with the King.

"Blue Suede Shoes" casts such an immense shadow that it nearly obscures the wealth of music Perkins recorded both during and since the Sun years. Moreover, Perkins overshadowed all the Sun artists as a picker; combining blues, country, and boogie, his forceful, economical lead style, unusual progressions and impeccable timing made a profound impression on succeeding generations of guitarists. Both Eric Clapton and George Harrison have pointed to Perkins as one of the players who influenced their styles.

As well, Perkins has carved out a solid history as a songwriter. The Beatles covered three of his songs— "Matchbox," "Everybody's Trying to Be My Baby," and "Honey Don't"; Patsy Cline had a hit with "So Wrong"; Johnny Cash had one of the biggest country singles of the '60s with "Daddy Sang Bass"; and in '91 Mark O'Connor's New Nashville Cats charted with an updated version of "Restless," and Dolly Parton scored with her tender "Silver and Gold," written by Perkins and his sons. When he gets down to looking at his life Perkins becomes a great writer: "Blue Suede Shoes" was inspired by an incident he witnessed at a dance, when a boy upbraided his date for stepping on his blue suede shoes. Even more dramatic are songs reflecting the habits and privations of the rural environment in which Perkins grew up. His first single, "Movie Magg" (issued on Sam Phillips' Flip label), is an account of dating mores in backwoods Tennessee; "That's Right" expresses a jealous man's feelings toward a woman whose infidelities are only imagined; "Dixie Fried," his greatest Sun side, is a dark recounting of the violent, whiskey-soaked nights Perkins observed in the honky-tonks where he plied his trade. In his post-Sun years Perkins has turned inward for material, producing sides notable for self-revelation and eloquence: "Just for You," "A Love I'll Never Win," "Someday, Somewhere, Someone Waits for Me."

Perkins and his brothers Jay and Clayton, along with drummer W. S. Holland, had been playing in the honky-tonks around Jackson, TN, when they signed to Sun in 1954. The Perkins brothers had grown up in Lake County, TN, where theirs was the only white family on a sharecropper's farm. From the black farmhands Carl learned to play blues guitar; from the radio on Saturday night, he learned of traditional country and bluegrass by way of the Grand Ole Opry. When the Perkins Brothers Band began playing dances around Lake County, Carl was already working out a more rhythmically driving style of music that was neither country nor blues, but had elements of both. Hearing Presley's "That's All Right (Mama)" on the radio in 1954 convinced Carl that Sun was the place to be. Indeed, Sam Phillips understood what Perkins was doing, but he already had Elvis doing the same thing, so after signing the Perkins brothers he directed them to country music. Heavily indebted to Hank Williams, Perkins delivered with songs such as "Honky Tonk Gal," "Turn Around," and "Let the Jukebox Keep on Playing." After Presley left Sun for RCA, Perkins was given the go-ahead to cut uptempo material. "Blue Suede Shoes" was the upshot.

After his wreck, Perkins made some of the best music of his life, but failed to approach the success of "Blue Suede Shoes." Along with Cash, he signed with Columbia in 1958. By this time Perkins was deep in the throes of alcoholism. Most of his Columbia efforts were tepid country affairs that met with little enthusiasm, although a couple showed some of the old spark. Signed to Decca in 1963, Perkins got it together long enough to make some startling, pure country records. A 10-year stint with Johnny Cash's revue was part of a regrouping process that saw Perkins kick his alcohol habit and regain his confidence. Signed to Mercury in 1973, he cut a brilliant country album, *My Kind of Country,* notable both for the honesty of its songs and the palpable feeling in Perkins' performances. When yet another generation of British rockers rediscovered rockability, Perkins responded with a first-rate return to his roots in *Ol' Blue Suede's Back* (1978).

Again, sustained success on record proved elusive, but Perkins, backed by a band that included his sons Stan and Greg, worked steadily through the '80s. Signed to the new Universal label in 1989, Perkins re-

leased *Born to Rock,* an album that comes down strong on his rockability heritage ("Born to Rock," "Charlene," "Don't Let Go") even as it attempts to establish a contemporary country foundation. It's hardly Perkins' strongest effort, and his vocals, particularly on the slower songs, sound forced at times.

Of the in-print recordings, Bear Family's five-CD *Classic Carl Perkins* offers all the Sun sides as well as Perkins' early Columbia and Decca recordings. It's pricey, but it sheds light on some years undocumented on other available releases. *Jive After Five* offers a broad sweep of post-Sun recordings; among its more important tracks are the solo guitar entry "Just Coastin'," from an album Perkins recorded with NRBQ, *Boppin' the Blues* (1970); "I'm in Love Again," from *Ol' Blue Suede's Back;* and three tracks from *My Kind of Country.* Both *Up Through the Years* and *Original Sun Greatest Hits* summarize the best of the Sun sides, with the former offering 24 tracks to the latter's 16. Being comprised of rare and previously unissued Sun masters otherwise available only on the Perkins box, Rounder's *Honky Tonk Gal* serves as a complementary disc to the Sun hits collections.

The Sun years are the only ones in Perkins' long career still well documented on CD. After leaving Sun, he made good records for a number of labels, including Columbia, Dollie, and Mercury, but those are available only in import collections. Rhino's *Original Sun Greatest Hits,* Collectables' two Perkins titles, and Varèse Sarabande's *The Complete Sun Singles* are all worthwhile buys for the essential, best-known recordings. Collectables' *Blue Suede Shoes: The Very Best of Carl Perkins* gets extra credit for including the non-single, but highly inflammatory "Right String, Baby, Wrong Yo-Yo," a 1951 R&B hit for Willie Perryman that the Perkins band absolutely scorched in a performance that must be heard to be believed. For the best of the off-sides, for lack of a better term, Rounder's *Honky Tonk Gal* is a must-have. Not only does this album contain "Right String, Baby, Wrong Yo-Yo," it also includes a red-hot Perkins original, "You Can't Make Love to Somebody," another powerhouse showcase for the entire band.

Those who want to check out the import sections for Perkins releases are advised to start with Bear Family's *The Classic Carl Perkins,* a five-CD box set covering nearly everything Carl recorded for Sun and Columbia, supplemented by alternate takes (and some home recordings Carl made during the Sun years, the rarest of all Perkins recordings). Diehards are also advised to check cut-out bins for *My Kind of Country,* a 1973 masterpiece of intimate, autobiographical songwriting released by Mercury. A morbid, haunting masterpiece, produced by the estimable Jerry Kennedy, it's an unapologetic account of the demons that were stalking Carl as he battled alcoholism and struggled to keep his career and his family in one piece.   —D.M.

Pernice Brothers

★★★★   Overcome by Happiness (Sub Pop, 1998)
★★★★   The World Won't End (Ashmont, 2001)
★★★½   Yours, Mine & Ours (Ashmont, 2003)

Joe Pernice

★★★½   Big Tobacco (Ashmont, 2000)

The Pernice Brothers are the longest-running musical project of Boston singer/songwriter Joe Pernice. Pernice's other musical ventures were less explicitly pop in influence: The Scud Mountain Boys and Chappaquiddick Skyline both mine territory closer to the world of country rock, desolate in arrangement and folksy in tone. In the Pernice Brothers, though, he takes those lyrical influences and pairs them with impossibly lush arrangements that date back two or three decades. As a songwriter, Pernice sounds like a world-weary combination of Woody Guthrie and Stephin Merritt, making songs like the transcendent "Working Girls (Sunlight Shines)" and "Crestfallen" sound something like art nuggets burnished for popular consumption. *Overcome by Happiness,* the PB debut, is lush and spacious, and the followup, 2001's *The World Won't End,* is even more so—the songs on both brim with promise musically, even if Pernice's lyrics are always wry and winking. *Yours, Mine & Ours* is Pernice's most moping project; on songs like "Number Two" and "Waiting for the Universe," he shows himself to be a true master of rendering dark thoughts in optimistic tones. Pernice was a writer outside of the studio context as well. In 2002, following an earlier book of poetry, *Two Blind Pigeons,* he penned a book based around the themes of the Smiths' *Meat Is Murder* album.   —J.C.

Lee "Scratch" Perry

★★★   Return of Django (1969; Trojan, 2003)
★★★   Rhythm Shower (Trojan, 1972)
★★★★   Africa's Blood (1972; Trojan, 2001)
★★★★   Cloak & Dagger (1973; Black Art, 1979)
★★★★★   Roast Fish Collie Weed and Cornbread (1976; VP, 1992)
★★★★   Super Ape (1976; Island, 1991)
★★★★   Scratch Attack (Clocktower/RAS, 1979)
★★★   The Return of Pipecock Jackxon (Black Star Liner, 1980)
★★★★   Mystic Miracle Star (Heartbeat, 1982)
★★   History, Mystery, Prophecy (Mango/Island, 1984)
★★★★½   The Upsetter Box (Trojan, 1985)

★★★   Satan Kicked the Bucket (Wackies/Rohit, 1988)
★★   Battle of Armagideon (Trojan, 1986)
★★★   Time Boom X De Devil Dead: Lee Perry & The Dub Syndicate (On U Sound, 1987)
★★★   Give Me Power (1988; Trojan, 2001)
★★★   On the Wire (Trojan, produced by Perry in 1988; released in 1999)
★★★   Open the Gate (Trojan, 1989)
★★★   Chicken Scratch (Heartbeat, 1989)
★★★   Satan's Dub—Lee "Scratch" Perry Meets Bullwackie (ROIR, 1990)
★★★   Spiritual Healing (Black Cat/Sound Service, 1990)
★★★   Mystic Warrior—Lee Perry & Mad Professor (Ariwa/RAS, 1990)
★★★   Mystic Warrior Dub—Lee Perry & Mad Professor (cassette only: ROIR, 1990)
★★★   Message From Yard (Rohit, 1990)
★★★   Lord God Muzik (Heartbeat, 1991)
★★★★   From the Secret Laboratory (Mango/Island, 1990)
★★   The Dub Messenger (Tassa, 1990)
★★   The Upsetter and the Beat (Heartbeat, 1992)
★★★★   Soundz From the Hot Line (Heartbeat Records, 1992)
★★   Smokin' (VP Records, 1994)
★★★★   Experryments at the Grassroots of Dub (Ariwa/RAS, 1995)
★★★   Black Ark Experryments—Lee Perry & Mad Professor (Ariwa/RAS, 1995)
★★   Who Put the Voodoo 'pon Reggae (Ariwa/RAS, 1996)
★★★★½   Arkology (Island, 1996)
★★   Dub Take the Voodoo out of Reggae (Ariwa/RAS, 1996)
★★★   Technomajikal (ROIR, 1997)
★★★   Live at Maritime Hall (2B1, 1997)
★★★★   Upsetter in Dub: Upsetter Shop Vol. One (Heartbeat, 1997)
★★★★   Dub Fire (Ariwa/RAS, 1998)
★★★★   Fire in Dub (Ariwa/RAS, 1998)
★★★★   Lee "Scratch" Perry and the Upsetters: The Upsetter Shop, Vol. 2 (Heartbeat, 1999)
★★★   Jamaican E.T. (Trojan, 2002)
★★★   Baffling Smoke Signal: The Upsetter Shop Vol. 3 (Heartbeat, 2002)
★★★   Cutting Razor: Rare Cuts from the Black Ark (Rounder, 2003)

Crazy like a fox, or just crazy? High jinks like introducing his willy on MTV Europe as "God" don't cancel out Lee "Scratch" Perry's unfettered brilliance as producer, songwriter, recording artist, mixologist, and even, perhaps, self-described shaman. Perry began his career in the late '50s as a gofer for legendary Studio One boss Coxsone Dodd, graduated to spinning discs for Dodd's Downbeat sound system, and then engineered, recorded, and produced for the nearly-as-legendary producer Joe Gibbs. Like other DJs, Perry patterned his between-disc chatter after stateside race-radio jocks to fill in blank air while he was changing records on the set's sole turntable. After engineer King Tubby figured out how to pull out the vocals from a two-track mix, "toasting" over the instrumentals became the featured attraction at dances. It wasn't long before "DJs" like Perry moved their acts indoors, to the many jerry-built "roots" studios springing up like weeds all over Kingston, Jamaica.

By 1968, as ska was giving way to rock steady, Perry broke with Gibbs and recorded a musical bomb on his own Upsetter label. Kicking off with a baby's wails, "People Funny Boy" was merely the first of countless jaw-dropping testaments to Perry's plastic musical imagination. He went on to incorporate all manner of previously unimagined sound effects, even scratching on the vinyl long before Grand Master Flash had the idea. By 1969, Scratch was a leading Kingston producer and had formed his Upsetters band, which later morphed into the future Wailers' rhythm section. The sound was raw, chugging, and juiced with baroque flourishes of spaghetti Western drama.

Bob Marley came to Scratch during a lull in the Wailers' career following their initial Studio One success. Though the Wailers soon persuaded the Upsetters to abandon Scratch and join them, Perry wasn't furious enough to refuse an offer to produce the trio of Bob, Bunny, and Peter. Those recordings—among them "Small Axe," "Duppy Conqueror," and "Fussing and Fighting"—are viewed as the Wailers' finest by reggae purists (and are also the most bootlegged), not least for the satisfyingly squishy drum beats that are a trademark Scratch touch. After Scratch sold the rights to his Wailers recordings to Trojan, without permission (they were eventually released as Soul Rebels and as singles tracks), the Wailers signed with Island in 1973. Scratch kept the Upsetters name for the floating group of musicians who recorded and played with him, and despite their feud, Marley returned to record with the original Upsetter in the early '70s, when Scratch was at his most boldly experimental. Scratch wreaked permanent delirious havoc on the worldwide musical order, introducing the sounds of breaking glass, animals, and whatever other aural signs of life took his fancy. After completing his Black Ark studio in 1974, he continued to create magic through inven-

tive uses of rudimentary technology and by working with a litany of reggae's finest, including the Heptones, Max Romeo, Dr. Alimantado, Junior Marvin, Marley, and, of course, himself. Paul McCartney, the Clash, Robert Palmer, and others were beating a path to Black Ark's door, but the pressure of freeloaders, local gangstas, and loiterers turned Scratch's eccentricity into something more serious. By 1979, things fell apart. A Dutch impresario tried to resuscitate the vandalized studio and Scratch's shattered psyche. With his financing, Scratch recorded the bizarre *Return of Pipecock Jackxon,* titled after his new, albeit temporary, name. In 1983, Scratch reportedly torched Black Ark, was briefly jailed, and then took off for England. *History, Mystery, Prophecy,* recorded with Adrian Sherwood in 1983, testifies to Scratch's unbridled madness at the time. In 1984, though, Scratch launched a longtime collaboration with Mad Professor, who despite his name possesses enough well-grounded calm to release a new set almost yearly that features Scratch's free-form ramblings over the Professor's sinewy dubs. The results have been mixed, but every few years, the two set off to tour the world so Scratchheads can witness live his riddimic rants on angels, vampires, excrement, world banks, his dick, and his genius. And Scratch continues to record with Sherwood and just about anyone with enough patience and greenbacks to coax Scratch off the Swiss mountaintop where he now lives with his Swiss wife and two children. —E.O.

Pet Shop Boys

★★★★	Please (EMI America, 1986)
★★★	Disco (EMI America, 1986)
★★★★	Actually (EMI America, 1987)
★★★★	Introspective (EMI America, 1988)
★★★★½	Behavior (EMI America, 1990)
★★★★★	Discography: The Complete Singles Collection (EMI America, 1991)
★★★★½	Very (Capitol, 1993)
★★½	Disco 2 (EMI America, 1994)
★★★½	Alternative (EMI America, 1995)
★★★★	Bilingual (Atlantic, 1996)
★★★½	Night Life (Parlophone/Sire, 1999)
★★★★	Please/Further Listening 1984–1986 (Parlophone, 2001)
★★★★	Actually/Further Listening 1987–1988 (Parlophone, 2001)
★★★★	Introspective/Further Listening 1988–1989 (Parlophone, 2001)
★★★★	Behavior/Further Listening 1990–1991 (Parlophone, 2001)
★★★★	Very/Further Listening 1992–1994 (Parlophone, 2001)

★★★½   Release (Sanctuary, 2002)
★★★★   Disco 3 (Sanctuary, 2003)

Neil Tennant sang, "I was faced with a choice at a difficult age/would I write a book? or should I take to the stage?/but in the back of my head I heard distant feet/Che Guevara and Debussy to a disco beat." Which is roughly what the Pet Shop Boys have done. Tennant was a journalist with a history degree when he met Chris Lowe, an architect, and they found common interests in synthesizers and disco. They started their collaboration in 1981 but didn't produce a hit until "West End Girls" went #1 on both sides of the Atlantic in 1985. Over the next six years they followed up with 11 more Top 10 singles (in the U.K., that is—the only one that charted in the U.S. was the one that went "Let's make lots of money").

The first album, *Please,* is the only one that sounds like hits plus filler, where the latter mostly lack finishing touches such as the dogs that haunt "Suburbia" or the innuendos of "Love Comes Quickly" and especially "Opportunities (Let's Make Lots of Money)"— the latter pointedly anti-Thatcher yet reducible to a pro-Reagan sound bite. *Actually* is a more completely realized album, with singles—four more, including the Dusty Springfield vehicle "What Have I Done to Deserve This?" and "It's a Sin" with its thunderclaps and triumphal horns—but also fully formed songs, ranging from the dance kick of "One More Chance" to the undanceable elegy "It Couldn't Happen Here." On the other hand, *Introspective* aimed straight at the disco audience, with six cuts averaging eight minutes, including the Latin-tinged "Domino Dancing" and the Elvis deconstruction "Always on My Mind."

Behavior was a change of pace: Its subdued midtempo rhythms didn't burn up the dance floor, nor did its singles scale the charts as before, but its songs were elegant and complex and often downright beautiful. "Being Boring" opens up a letter from the '20s about never feeling bored, then draws a line to unimagined loss in the present. "(It Hurts So Much) to Face the Truth" is a poignant breakup song. "My October Symphony" ponders what will happen to the music celebrating Russia's October Revolution, closing with a bit of Shostakovich. "Nervously" wraps its shy young boy in shimmering sound. And "Jealousy" closes with a towering burst of orchestra. *Discography* capped the period, gathering 18 singles, including three not on any album: their version of U2's "Where the Streets Have No Name" which morphs into Frankie Valli's "I Can't Take My Eyes off You," the anti–Gulf War "DJ Culture," and the affirmative "Was It Worth It?" ("I reserve/the right to live/my life this way/and I don't give/a damn when I/hear people

say/I'll pay the price/that others pay"—Tennant's most direct lyric yet on AIDS and being gay).

Some critics couldn't get past the word "boring" with *Behavior,* but few were unconvinced by *Very.* For one thing, songs like "Can You Forgive Her?," "Yesterday, When I Was Mad," "One in a Million," and especially the cover of the Village People's "Go West" jump out of the grooves. For another, the love songs were unusually direct, with most making more sense gay than not. "Dreaming of the Queen" was also their most direct AIDS song ("and [Lady] Di replied that/'There are no more lovers left alive . . . and that's why love has died' ").

Bilingual is more out ("Metamorphosis"), more Latin ("Discoteca," "Se a vida é"), and not above a rare bit of stupid fun ("Single"). *Nightlife* had a U.S. hit in "New York City Boy," with its Village People reprise, but mostly entailed a return to simpler dance beats ("I Don't Know What You Want But I Can't Give It Any More") and more elaborate productions, such as the choral effects on "Footsteps." *Release* seems to break apart more cleanly into separate songs, including the single "Home and Dry" and "The Night I Fell in Love," a one-night stand haunted by Eminem's Stan ("next morning we woke/he couldn't have been a nicer bloke/over breakfast made jokes/about Dre and his homies and folks").

Beyond the main studio albums, the Pet Shop Boys have released a bewildering array of remixes, alternate versions, experiments, and trivia. From outside this looks like product padding, not to mention profiteering, but the other view is that dance music is a very promiscuous culture, where everything is subject to remix. So sure, these collections are mostly of interest to fans and pros, and they are inevitably mixed bags, because most of the currency is in singles. *Disco* and *Disco 2* were mostly third-party remixes—Arthur Baker, Shep Pettibone, Jam & Spoon, Farley & Heller—they rarely add much. *Alternative* was more interesting—two CDs of things that didn't make the albums, such as their souped-up version of Weill/Brecht's "What Keeps Mankind Alive." *Disco 3* has a couple of remixes from *Release,* but it has some good new songs as well—"Positive Role Model" and the recontextualized cover of "Try It (I'm in Love With a Married Man)"—and the relatively stripped-down beats redeem some of what seemed excessive in *Release.* The studio albums from *Very* on have initially appeared with bonus discs, and now the albums from *Please* through *Very* have been rereleased in sets with a second *Further Listening* disc. The extras tend to be well programmed, spiked with further variations on their hits, and the sets come with exemplary booklets.   —T.H.

Tom Petty

★★★½	Tom Petty & the Heartbreakers (Warner Bros., 1976)
★★½	You're Gonna Get It! (Warner Bros., 1978)
★★★½	Damn the Torpedoes (MCA, 1979)
★★★	Hard Promises (MCA, 1981)
★★★	Long After Dark (MCA, 1982)
★★★★	Southern Accents (MCA, 1985)
★★★	Pack Up the Plantation: Live! (MCA, 1986)
★★★	Let Me Up (I've Had Enough) (1987; MCA, 2002)
★★★½	Full Moon Fever (MCA, 1989)
★★★	Into the Great Wide Open (MCA, 1991)
★★★★	Greatest Hits (MCA, 1993)
★★★½	Wildflowers (Warner Bros., 1994)
★★★½	Playback (MCA, 1995)
★★★	Songs and Music From "She's the One" (Warner Bros., 1996)
★★★	Echo (Warner Bros., 1999)
★★★½	Anthology: Through the Years (MCA, 2000)
★★★	The Last DJ (Warner Bros., 2002)

One thing you can say about Tom Petty is he's consistent. Except for the predictable sophomore slump, all of his albums are, at the very least, good. Some are real good, some are merely good, none are bad. The problem is, Petty's never made a great album, and his very reliability renders most of his merchandise redundant.

In the mid-'70s, when Petty left his native Florida for Los Angeles, the environment was ripe for his Southern counterclaim to the chiming guitars of the Byrds and the cocky strut of the Rolling Stones. Between 1976 and 1978, when *Tom Petty & the Heartbreakers* and *You're Gonna Get It* came out, the Southern rock of Lynyrd Skynyrd was dying and punk was on the rise. This was the backdrop for the controlled anger of such early Heartbreakers songs as "Breakdown," "Rockin' Around (With You)," "The Wild One, Forever," "Too Much Ain't Enough," and "Restless." But Petty was always more of a simple, Southern-bred fan of classic '60s and '70s album rock. On songs such as "Mystery Man" and "Luna," from the first album, the Heartbreakers dip their toes into *Exile*-era Stones and "Warm Love"–period Van Morrison. In the anthemic "American Girl," Petty and the boys beat the Byrds at their own game. The Heartbreakers got derailed on *You're Gonna Get It!* Some of the songs sounded like the group had traded Byrds and Stones fixations for Foreigner and Foghat, though "I Need to Know" stood up to the best of the new-wave era's revamped power pop.

If none of the songs on the Heartbreakers' first two albums hit the ball out of the park, "Refugee," from *Damn the Torpedoes,* did. The fuck-you snarl of

Petty's nasal, Dylan-via-Jagger delivery and the bright, crunchy drive of Mike Campbell's Telecaster rendered "Refugee" 1980's most powerful radio anthem. *Torpedoes* stormed the charts and established a formula for the Heartbreakers that they would milk on nearly every subsequent release: two or three hook-filled singles ("Here Comes My Girl," "Even the Losers," "Don't Do Me Like That"), a pseudoserious ballad ("Louisiana Rain"), and too much boring filler. The band employed that formula to massive commercial success on the folk-rocking *Hard Promises* and synth-embellished *Long After Dark,* which together spawned hits in "The Waiting," "A Woman in Love (It's Not Me)," "You Got Lucky," and "Change of Heart." Those tracks are the highlights, though; the rest is just competent frat-house party fodder.

Midway into the '80s, Petty and the Heartbreakers threw a serious curveball. Their sixth album, *Southern Accents,* is a top-notch collection of songs written and performed from the disparate perspectives of characters from Petty's Gainesville, Florida, childhood. With an expanded musical palette—courtesy of producer Dave Stewart, who brought in horns, sitar, background vocalists, and a beautifully restrained electronics foundation—the music was unlike anything the Heartbreakers had ever done. In spirit, *Southern Accents* recalls Randy Newman's *Good Old Boys,* but the music embraces everything from country and funk to straight-ahead rock and even psychedelia. "Don't Come Around Here No More," the album's big hit, is a powerful song whose hypnotically sung title is a central theme in the Deep South. The album's centerpiece is the gorgeous title song, with an opening line that resonates for folks born and raised below the Mason-Dixon line: "There's a Southern accent, where I come from/The young 'uns call it country/The Yankees call it dumb." *Southern Accents* is a critical but loving look at the South from the frustrated point of view of a displaced Southerner. Unfortunately, Petty would never again attempt such depth or scope.

On *Let Me Up,* the Heartbreakers return to the winning formula of their early-'80s hits. Kicking off with the AC/DC crunch of "Jammin' Me" (cowritten with Bob Dylan), the band is clearly back to punching the rock & roll time clock. Aside from the rueful, mandolin-fueled "It'll All Work Out" and the surprisingly soulful "All Mixed Up," the album serves up more of the same old, same old. In 1988, Petty took a break from his Heartbreakers and joined the Traveling Wilburys, a side project featuring Bob Dylan, Roy Orbison, George Harrison, and former Electric Light Orchestra frontman Jeff Lynne. The influence of those rock & roll giants is evident on his next album, *Full Moon Fever.* Produced by Lynne, the songs get their charge from his big, ELO-style vocal sound and sparkling, electronics-treated guitars. The hits ("Free Fallin'," "I Won't Back Down") are infectious, and even the filler ("Love Is a Long Road," "Face in the Crowd") sounds as sweet as hard candy. What's more, with Lynne sharing songwriting credits on most of the tracks, the melodies are more ambitious and the music more eclectic than Petty's usual fare.

Into the Great Wide Open picks up the old formula, but with Lynne's bright pop sound, the music seems fresher. To be sure, Petty's songs have more of a George Harrison–Jeff Lynne feel to them here, and on "Learning to Fly" he even mimics Harrison's vocal style. Petty seems to be trying to age gracefully on *Wide Open,* and to a certain extent he succeeds, offering more acoustic guitars and less attitude. But as with most of his work, he still lacks the creative juice to deliver a fully developed album. All the dressing in the world can't make mediocre material like "Two Gunslingers," "Out in the Cold," or "Makin' Some Noise" sound interesting.

Petty's move from MCA to Warner Bros. found him working with producer Rick Rubin, who had successfully revitalized the career of the legendary country star Johnny Cash with a set of stripped-down folk music. He does the same for Petty, whose new folk and country-style songs on *Wildflowers* are well served by Rubin's simple production. Tracks like the title song and "You Don't Know How It Feels" recall the grace and dignity of Neil Young, while "Cabin Down Below" cribs from another of Petty's influences, Creedence Clearwater Revival's John Fogerty. The album's biggest weakness is its length. Petty has a difficult enough time realizing a normal 40-minute album; at more than an hour, *Wildflowers* becomes tedious. The Heartbreakers' spotty soundtrack album *She's the One* continues in the vein of *Wildflowers* but with more of a Lindsey Buckingham pop feel. It's most notable for an interesting cover version of Beck's self-deprecating "Asshole." *Echo,* Petty's darkest, most desperate album, was recorded after the singer's divorce from his wife of more than two decades. With Rubin at the controls again and Petty's voice becoming more raggedly Dylanesque than ever, these songs of sorrow and regret appear in an appropriately spare context. The *Last DJ* is just as dark, but this time his anger is pointed outward, at the corrupt modern record industry. For all his crotchetiness and redundancy, Petty has managed to cross over into middle age with dignity.

The live *Pack Up the Plantation* offers competent performances of Petty's best-loved songs, but it's unnecessary, since the band brings absolutely nothing new to the material. Petty's best collection is *Greatest Hits:* in fact, aside from *Southern Accents,* it's his best album. For those who prefer to dig a bit deeper than just the singles, *Anthology* is a fine compilation, too. The six-disc *Playback* is overkill. —M.K.

P. Funk All-Stars

   ★★★★   Urban Dancefloor Guerillas (1983; Columbia, 1989)
     ★★★   Live at the Beverly Theatre in Hollywood (Westbound, 1990)
   ★★★★   Hydraulic Funk (Westbound, 1995)

Few artists have danced their way out of their constrictions like funkmeister George Clinton. When his Parliament-Funkadelic empire started coming apart in the early 1980s, the bandleader exploded into a solo career with one good foot and renegotiated the contracts of some of his best players with the other. In time, the new P. Funk All-Stars became the solo artist's backing band, but on one very fine album and legendary tour, they also served as a great coda to his phenomenal collective creations of the 1970s. *Urban Dancefloor Guerillas* features a different lineup on every cut (including Sly Stone and Bobby Womack as occasional guests), and it ranges from surprisingly straightforward pop songs like "One of Those Summers" to typically surreal electrofunk jams like "Hydraulic Pump." Oddly enough, none of those tracks are included in the undated show captured on *Live at the Beverly Theater in Hollywood.* Instead, the loose and lively double-disc set focuses on high-quality hits from "Cosmic Slop" to "Atomic Dog," all of it somewhat undercut by the less-than-high-quality recording. *Hydraulic Funk* includes longer versions of the tracks on the original studio album. —F.S.

Liz Phair

   ★★★★   Exile in Guyville (Matador, 1993)
     ★★★   Whip-Smart (Atlantic/Matador, 1994)
     ★★★   Whitechocolatespaceegg (Capitol, 1998)
    ★★½   Liz Phair (Capitol, 2003)

Liz Phair, a struggling visual artist from a wealthy suburban Chicago family, caused a mild sensation in the indie-rock underground when her Girlysound bedroom recordings began circulating. These combined her idiosyncratic, self-taught guitar playing with salty (if sometimes sophomoric) lyrics about boyfriends, breakups, and the toxic consequences of intimacy; the songs formed the basis of her debut album. Phair claims that *Exile in Guyville* was her song-by-song response to the Holy Grail of rock albums, the Rolling Stones' *Exile on Main Street,* but the connection is nearly impossible to discern. What matters is that the album packs a giddy wallop, despite its lo-fi budget, with sturdy if rudimentary guitar riffs riding spare grooves in a variety of settings: folkish mood pieces, spooky piano nocturnes, Patti Smith–style dialogues, and, yes, Stonesy rockers. Phair drew leers with her explicit sexual lyrics, but the frankness was in keeping with the album's agenda of unfettered self-expression, the sound of a long-repressed voice (not just Phair's, but that of a generation of women) finally airing its innermost thoughts and desires. Phair's deadpan delivery makes her most outrageous confessions sound matter-of-fact, even as she subtly acknowledges her vulnerability and revels in tart humor. At one point, she breaks into an Ethel Merman voice to sing, "I get away, almost every day, with what the girls call murder."

That audacity is missing on the more refined but inconsistent *Whip-Smart,* which reunites her with producer/drummer Brad Wood. The songs are in some ways even more ambitious, with men and women swapping roles in a fairy-tale world. On the album's title track, a male Rapunzel is locked in an ivory tower while his mother offers a prescription for escaping it. But with more conventionally constructed songs, the music lacks the debut's offhand authority.

Whitechocolatespaceegg is sprawling: four producers (including Wood) and 16 tracks encompassing everything from churning club beats to a solo-guitar piece. The Wood collaborations work best, particularly on the sly, sexy "Johnny Feelgood," the infectious chorus of "Polyester Bride," and the minisymphony "Uncle Alvarez." But much of the rest sounds labored and fussy.

Whereas *Exile in Guyville* presented a self-taught original who had no idea how the music industry operated, *Liz Phair* is the work of a pro-fessional who is as interested in pandering as she is in provoking. Cringe-inducing come-ons lard songs that belie Phair's strengths as a lyricist. Only "Little Digger," which explores the emotional challenges of single parenthood, is on a par with her best work. The unimaginative production—including lacquered contributions from Avril Lavigne's studio gurus, the Matrix—embraces the pop-rock formulas Phair once gleefully subverted. But go figure: *Phair* went on to become the singer's best-selling album to date. —G.K.

Pharcyde

  ★★★★   Bizarre Ride II the Pharcyde (1992; Rhino, 2000)
  ★★★★   Labcabincalifornia (1995; Rhino, 2000)
  ★★½   Plain Rap (Edel America, 2000)
  ★★★★   Cydeways: The Best of Pharcyde (Rhino, 2001)

Released at a time when hip-hop was getting "realer" by the second, *Bizarre Ride II* is a goofy, zigzagging party full of gleeful energy and batty rhymes. Like a pack of class clowns set loose in a studio, these four Los Angeles MCs—Imani, Bootie Brown, Fat Lip, and Slim Kid Tre—had a field day, rhyming about prank calls ("4 Better or 4 Worse"), jack-off sessions ("On the DL"), and schoolboy crushes ("Passing Me By"). Paired with producer J-Swift's jitter-quick drums and jazzy bass lines, the crew's manic, high-pitched quips and group-chanted hooks are hard to resist. The album's most memorable cut, "Ya Mama," is a marathon game of the dozens set to a beat ("Ya mama's got a peg leg with a kickstand"; "Ya mama's got an Afro with a chin strap.")

By 1995, when it released its sophomore album, *Labcabincalifornia,* the Pharcyde had outgrown the antic energy. "Every time I step to the microphone/ I put my soul on two-inch reels that I don't even own," the group testifies on "Devil Music." This introspective approach pays off. The nostalgic, pulsing "Runnin'," a melodic rumination on shouldering adult responsibility, taps emotions while evoking head nods, and the lovely slow-dance number "She Said" rocks with syrupy, hip-swiveling heft.

After a five-year hiatus, the Pharcyde returned, minus Fat Lip, for 2000's *Plain Rap,* a disappointingly generic effort that sounds woefully deflated compared to the group's previous albums. —K.M.

Sam Phillips

  ★★★   The Indescribable Wow (Virgin, 1988)
  ★★★   Cruel Inventions (Virgin, 1991)
  ★★★★   Martinis & Bikinis (Virgin, 1994)
  ★★½   Omnipop (It's Only a Flesh Wound Lambchop) (Virgin, 1996)
  ★★★   Zero Zero Zero (Virgin, 1998)
  ★★★½   Fan Dance (Nonesuch, 2001)
  ★★★★   A Boot and a Shoe (Nonesuch, 2004)

Interested in a deeper spiritual perspective than her brief career as a contemporary Christian artist would allow, Leslie Phillips transformed herself into Sam Phillips in the late '80s and instantly began mulling moral and spiritual puzzles over melodies that evoked the baroque neo-psychedelia of the Beatles' *Revolver.*

Paired with future husband T Bone Burnett on *The Indescribable Wow,* she sounds tentative, though "What You Don't Want to Hear" and especially "Holding On to the Earth" show a distinct vision taking shape.

On *Cruel Inventions,* Burnett's subtle instrumental colorations illuminate Phillips' longing, her quest to "find the dreams under cynical wreckage." Phillips' wordplay can be frustratingly convoluted, but her voice conveys longing tinged with hope and humor ("Now I Can't Find the Door," about an unexpected marriage proposal).

Martinis & Bikinis ranks as her finest album. Every sonic element has a purpose, with a sophistication that cannot be mistaken for fussiness. The melodies are abundant, the lyrics assertive even as they examine the world of the morally ambivalent. A cover of John Lennon's "Gimme Some Truth" neatly summarizes the singer's quest. Although unfulfilled, her outrage is bracing, her wonderment intoxicating.

Omnipop sheds melody in favor of soundscapes, and its exotic edges obscure Phillips' strengths. *Zero Zero Zero*, a career summation, continues the experimentation with several remixes and a creepy reinvention of "Holding On to the Earth."

Fan Dance pulls back from the ornamentation of the earlier albums to offer a more bare-bones perspective, both sonically and lyrically. Every vestige of excess is excised, and the songs—appointed with subtle chamber-pop orchestration—acquire a new sharpness.

A Boot and a Shoe is equally sparse, with Phillips distilling her twin themes of romantic dissolution and new beginnings to their essence. Even with drums in the foreground, the singer delivers her melodies with a measured, gimmick-free assurance that is haunting.   —G.K.

Phish

★★½	Junta (1988; Elektra, 1992)
★★	Lawn Boy (1990; Elektra, 1992)
★★★	A Picture of Nectar (Elektra, 1992)
★★	Rift (Elektra, 1993)
★★½	Hoist (Elektra, 1994)
★★★★	A Live One (Elektra, 1995)
★★★★	Billy Breathes (Elektra, 1996)
★★★★	Slip, Stitch & Pass (Elektra, 1997)
★★★½	The Story of the Ghost (Elektra, 1998)
★★★★	Hampton Comes Alive (Elektra, 1999)
★★★★	Farmhouse (Elektra, 2000)
★★½	The Siket Disc (Elektra, 2000)
★★★½	Live Phish 01: 12.14.95, Broome County Arena, Binghamton, NY (Elektra, 2001)
★★★	Live Phish 02: 7.16.94, Sugarbush Summerstage, North Fayston, VT (Elektra, 2001)
★★★	Live Phish 03: 9.14.00, Darien Lake Performing Arts Center, Darien Lake, NY (Elektra, 2001)
★★½	Live Phish 04: 6.14.00, Drum Logos, Fukuoka, Japan (Elektra, 2001)
★★	Live Phish 05: 7.8.00, Alpine Valley Music Theater, East Troy, WI (Elektra, 2001)

★★★	Live Phish 06: 11.27.98, The Centrum, Worcester, MA (Elektra, 2001)
★★★★	Live Phish 07: 8.14.93, World Music Theatre, Tinley Park, IL (Elektra, 2002)
★★½	Live Phish 08: 7.10.99, E Centre, Camden, NJ (Elektra, 2002)
★★★	Live Phish 09: 8.26.89, Townshend Family Park, Townshend, VT (Elektra, 2002)
★★★	Live Phish 10: 6.22.94, Veterans Memorial Auditorium, Columbus, OH (Elektra, 2002)
★★★½	Live Phish 11: 11.17.97, McNichols Sports Arena, Denver, CO (Elektra, 2002)
★★	Live Phish 12: 8.13.96, Deer Creek Music Center, Noblesville, IN (Elektra, 2002)
★★★½	Live Phish 13: 10.31.94, Glens Falls Civic Center, Glens Falls, NY (Elektra, 2002)
★★★	Live Phish 14: 10.31.95, Rosemont Horizon, Rosemont, IL (Elektra, 2002)
★★★★	Live Phish 15: 10.31.96, The Omni, Atlanta, GA (Elektra, 2002)
★★	Live Phish 16: 10.31.98, Thomas & Mack Center, Las Vegas, NV (Elektra, 2002)
★★½	Round Room (Elektra, 2002)
★★½	Live Phish 17: 7.15.98, Portland Meadows, Portland, OR (Elektra, 2003)
★★★½	Live Phish 18: 5.7.94, The Bomb Factory, Dallas, TX (Elektra, 2003)
★★★	Live Phish 19: 7.12.91, Colonial Theatre, Keene, NH (Elektra, 2003)
★★★★	Live Phish 20: 12.29.94, Providence Civic Center, Providence, RI (Elektra, 2003)
★★★★	Undermind (Elektra, 2004)

Want to know what a jam band is? You came to the right place: Phish was the living, breathing, noodling definition of the term. From its humble start in the mid-'80s touring around the New England college circuit, this Vermont quartet—Trey Anastasio (guitar), Page McConnell (keyboards), Mike Gordon (bass), and Jon Fishman (drums)—grew to become a cultural phenomenon, followed across the country from summer shed to summer shed by thousands of new-generation hippies and hacky-sack enthusiasts, and spawning a new wave of bands oriented around group improvisation and superextended grooves.

Comparisons to the mother of all jam bands, the Grateful Dead, are unavoidable, and in some cases warranted. Like the Dead, Phish had a pronounced fondness for the rustic and drew from a seemingly bottomless well of cover tunes. Like the Dead, Phish was helmed by a guitarist with a casual, conversational lead style who enjoys playing lots of notes. And like the Dead, Phish lacked a singer who's any more than competent. But in its frequent bursts of prog-style musical complexity as well as its taste for goofy humor (this is a band, after all, that incorporated trampolines, vacuum cleaners, and a giant hot dog into its concerts), Phish shows that it was very much its own entity.

It took a while for Phish to get its sound convincingly onto disc. The first five albums listed above all have great moments (the stunning replication of early-'70s Genesis on *Lawn Boy*'s "The Squirming Coil," the Thelonious Monkish twists on *A Picture of Nectar*'s "Magilla"), but inconsistency plagues them. *Billy Breathes*, *The Story of the Ghost*, and *Farmhouse* are much more like it, presenting an appealing rock/jazz/folk hybrid with a tasteful mix of looseness and precision. Cut quickly following a two-year hiatus, *Round Room* sounds undercooked, while *The Siket Disc* collects a few in-studio jams that are less than revelatory.

That brings us to the teensy-weensy matter of Phish's live albums, of which there are, at this writing, a mere 23. Though purists will argue, rightly, that you could only get the full Phish experience in person, many of these discs make a pretty decent substitute. The best is *Hampton Comes Alive*, which documents two November 1998 concerts in full. Only problem: It's six CDs. Those desiring something less pricey to start out with should spring for either *A Live One*, *Slip, Stitch & Pass*, or *Live Phish 15*; on the latter, Phish covers Talking Heads' *Remain in Light* in its entirety, to surprisingly powerful effect.

Shortly before the release of *Undermind*, Phish announced that it was breaking up for good. Luckily, the album's far from a white flag; in fact, it's one of the band's most cohesive collections, produced with warmth and flair by Tchad Blake, combining outlandish psychedelia ("A Song I Heard the Ocean Sing") with winning folk rock ("The Connection"). Whether or not it was intended to be Phish's final statement, *Undermind* is a fitting sendoff. —M.R.

Photek

★★★   Modus Operandi (Astralwerks, 1997)
★★★   Solaris (Astralwerks, 2000)

Hailed by drum-and-bass knob-twiddlers as a producer's producer, Photek—a.k.a. Rupert Parkes—gained great admiration from his peers for immense attention to detail; he was able to split a million beats in a single bound. Unlike many producers who were DJs before they got in the recording game, Parkes was a producer who'd never DJed, and the results were plain in his work. His complex version of drum-and-bass was not made for the dance floor. Flitting somewhere between the heady atmospherics of LTJ Bukem and techno's minimalism, the jazzy riffs on "The Hidden Camera" on his debut were at odds with

what most jungle fans were listening to—namely, big booming bass and a sense of foreboding thick enough for a slasher flick.

More experimental in nature than other drum-and-bass producers (most of whom stuck to a tried and true dance-floor-friendly formula), Parkes became bored and disenchanted with the increasingly menacing, macho drum-and-bass scene and tried his hand at a tech-house record. His penchant for perfectionism carried over into his new form of choice on *Solaris*—and the response to his tracks with house DJs was overwhelming. On "Mine to Give," he brought old-school house music singer Robert Owens out of slumber and scored big; "Glamorama" is a sexy ice capade, with a female French vocal topping a sparse, spooky backdrop. There is just one drum-and-bass track on the record, "Infinity"—a searing testament to his technical prowess and his ability to innovate within a stale genre. —T.R.

Wilson Pickett

★★★★★   Greatest Hits (Atlantic, 1973)
★★★★★   A Man and a Half: The Best of Wilson Pickett (Rhino, 1992)
★★★★   The Very Best of Wilson Pickett (Rhino, 1993)
★★★   If You Need Me (Prime Cuts, 1996)
★★★½   It's Harder Now (Bullseye Blues, 1999)
★★★   The Magic of Wilson Pickett (Dressed to Kill, 2000)
★★★   I'm in Love (Collectables, 2002)
★★★   The Essentials (Rhino, 2002)

Wilson Pickett's R&B was not the blowtorch burst of almost surreal funk that James Brown invented, nor did it boast Otis Redding's gorgeous melodicism, but it was the most insistently earthy of all soul music. Flourishing an ultrastud persona, "the Wicked Pickett" coaxed fierce energy out of the great Muscle Shoals players, and "In the Midnight Hour," "Land of 1,000 Dances," "Mustang Sally," "Funky Broadway," and "I'm a Midnight Mover" remain some of the most urgent singles ever released. Staccato horn parts and surging bass lines were key to the sound, but it was Pickett's growling vocal style that made the records hot—every note he sang was propulsive. "Hey Jude" proved that Pickett could tackle ballads, too. For a while in the mid-'70s he sounded confused, but at the end of the decade, he reemerged with at least some of his trademark fury. *It's Harder Now* is excellent latter-day Pickett; he still sounds ferocious. *The Magic of* features very early work, and it's groundbreaking funk. All the greatest-hits packages are decent; *A Man and a Half*, with its nifty chest-pounding title, is the most extensive. —P.E.

Pink

★★	Can't Take Me Home (LaFace/Arista, 2000)
★★★½	Missundaztood (Arista, 2001)
★★★	Try This (Arista, 2003)

With a hot-pink crew cut and her place as the lone white girl on urban label LaFace, Philly native Pink stood out just fine on arrival. But there was little about the mostly slick, by-the-numbers R&B of her debut, *Can't Take Me Home*, that suggested the singer, then just out of her teens, would warrant a second look come her 21st birthday. No doubt, her label crafted the best R&B/pop money could buy: Production and songwriting was supplied by the best in the biz (She'kspere, Babyface). Pink sounds plenty sassy and suitably cool on hits like "There You Go" and "Most Girls," but she never truly takes control of the material.

Not so with Pink's surprising followup, *Missundaztood*. Forsaking the faceless R&B of her debut, she enlisted the help of both TLC producer Dallas Austin, whose R&B embraces mainstream pop, and former 4 Non Blondes frontwoman Linda Perry, whose rock leans toward funky. The collaborations provided just the transition Pink needed to remake herself into the pop diva most likely to stick around. While it's not above the occasional corn, *Missundaztood* delivers the stuff of great, even eclectic, contemporary pop—the electro-boogie anthem "Get the Party Started," the Alanis-lite rock of "Don't Let Me Get Me," the slow and straight blues of "Misery" (featuring Aerosmith's Steven Tyler). Moreover, Pink's lyrics let loose, expressing the angst and aspirations of teen-girldom in a way that puts her pop peers (and her own lightweight debut) to shame. *Missundaztood* defines Pink as a voice worth noting.

Try This takes Pink's new direction even further. While Linda Perry reappears to cowrite songs including the Heart-like "Waiting For Love," Pink's main collaborator is Rancid's Tim Armstrong, who lends a full-on rock approach to tracks like "Trouble" and "Humble Neighborhoods." With Pink's transformation nearly complete, the lone R&B slow jam "Catch Me While I'm Sleeping," which would have fit just fine on her debut, sounds downright out of place here. Regardless of style, though, pop hooks remain central to any Pink song, and *Try This* delivers the goods with only slightly less flair than its predecessor. —R.M.S.

Pink Floyd

★★★★★	The Piper at the Gates of Dawn (Capitol, 1967)
★★★	A Saucerful of Secrets (Capitol, 1968)
★★½	Ummagumma (Capitol, 1969)
★★	More (Capitol, 1969)
★	Atom Heart Mother (Capitol, 1970)
★★★½	Relics (Capitol, 1971)
★★★½	Meddle (Capitol, 1971)
★★	Obscured by Clouds (Capitol, 1972)
★★★★★	Dark Side of the Moon (Capitol, 1973)
★★★★★	Wish You Were Here (Capitol, 1975)
★★	Animals (Capitol, 1977)
★★★	The Wall (Capitol, 1979)
★★★	A Collection of Great Dance Songs (Capitol, 1981)
★★★	Works (Capitol, 1983)
★★	The Final Cut (Columbia, 1983)
★★	A Momentary Lapse of Reason (Columbia, 1987)
★	Delicate Sound of Thunder (Columbia, 1988)
★★★½	Shine On (Columbia, 1992)
★	The Division Bell (Columbia, 1994)
★	Pulse (Columbia, 1995)
★	Is There Anybody Out There? The Wall: Live 1980–1981 (Columbia, 2000)
★★★★★	Echoes (Columbia, 2001)

One of the most popular and successful rock bands of all time, Pink Floyd is actually a brand name linking three different eras. The '60s Floyd, led by singer/songwriter Syd Barrett, was a pioneering psychedelic band from Cambridge, England, recording a handful of hits before Barrett succumbed to massive acid damage. The '70s Floyd, led by bassist Roger Waters and guitarist David Gilmour, recorded the high-tech art-rock classics *Dark Side of the Moon, Wish You Were Here,* and *The Wall,* memorized in their entirety by generations of stoners, who used the original LP covers as spliff-rolling tray tables. Since Waters split bitterly in the early '80s, Pink Floyd has carried on as an oldies act, occasionally releasing new albums that nobody listens to.

Much to Pink Floyd's chagrin, and occasionally its indignation, the group has never escaped the shadow of Syd Barrett, the original "lunatic on the grass." He founded the band as a conspicuously blues-free U.K. echo of San Francisco psychedelia, as in the guitar/organ jams "Astronomy Domine" and "Interstellar Overdrive"; his Floyd recorded a couple of hits ("See Emily Play," "Arnold Layne") and one classic album, *The Piper at the Gates of Dawn.* Syd had a taste for whimsy, leaning to lyrics about cats and gnomes, but his daft wit and eerie melodies made the album a rock version of the Mad Hatter's tea party. In "Flaming," "Matilda Mother," "Lucifer Sam," and "Bike," his voice and guitar teeter between euphoria and mental collapse. "Astronomy Domine" is a thunderstorm of stargazing guitars and scary keyboards, full of druggy optimism but exploring the "icy waters underground" of the psyche.

But Barrett was already cracking in the summer of 1967, one of rock's first drug burnouts and a doomed figure who barely lasted six months as a functional songwriter. "I'm full of dust and guitars," Barrett once said. By *A Saucerful of Secrets,* he was down to the disturbing "Jugband Blues," with Waters providing the other standout track, "Set the Controls for the Heart of the Sun." Syd's childhood friend David Gilmour came on board; with Waters, he also went on to produce and play on Barrett's two excellent solo albums. Without Syd, Pink Floyd struggled through a couple of miserable prog albums, *Ummagumma* and *Atom Heart Mother,* the former at least padded with good 1969 live performances, including a ten-minute "Astronomy Domine." *Relics* was a 1971 retrospective; *More* and *Obscured by Clouds* were dull film soundtracks. But *Meddle* introduced the Floyd's mature style in the 23-minute instrumental "Echoes," coloring the slow guitar ripples with deep-in-the-studio sonic details that only the truly baked would notice, much less appreciate.

Pink Floyd finally achieved peak "like wow man" heaviosity with *Dark Side of the Moon,* a meditation on death and madness that stayed on the bestseller charts for nearly 15 years. This most hip-hop of rock classics is all about flow, shifting through the headphones from stereo sine waves to spoken word fragments ("there is no dark side of the moon, really—matter of fact it's *all* dark"), gospel piano, sax, the early VCS3 synth, ticking clocks, heartbeats, and soulful surges from guest singers Doris Troy and Clare Torry. The stoned keyboard dribbles get boring, and so does the whining annoyance "Money," but the tone is stately and somehow brotherly as well, especially the morose grandeur of "Time," "The Great Gig in the Sky," and "Brain Damage/Eclipse." It's the sonic equivalent of one of those 3-D placemats where you can see Jesus' eyes move.

If Barrett's mental breakdown was the subtext of *Dark Side, Wish You Were Here* was an explicit tribute to their lost friend. "Shine On You Crazy Diamond" was a sad space-rock elegy for Barrett, built in several long segments based around a four-note slide guitar phrase from Gilmour. The futuristic instrumental textures have real bite and drive, especially "Welcome to the Machine" and "Wish You Were Here." It's not as famous as *Dark Side* or *The Wall,* but *Wish* tops them both because the special effects have so much emotional resonance, mourning lost innocence in the spirit of male camaraderie that was always the band's most underrated strength.

But *Animals* was just a laser show looking for a soundtrack. If there's one ironclad rule of rock & roll, it's that songs about pigs are *always* lame. *The Wall* was Waters' big autobiographical rock opera, the tale of a sensitive musician oppressed by the cold cruel world, including but not restricted to his wife, his mother, his teachers, their wives, the government, the bleeding hearts and artists, and chicks in general. If you went to high school in the '80s, you probably recall *The Wall* fondly. But if you go back and try listening to "Waiting for the Worms," "Run Like Hell" or "Young Lust," you may be aghast at how *The Wall* sucks much worse than you remember—the music is just tossed-off atmospherics, and Rog never shuts up. Still, it's a piece of history, and there are a few good songs: "Comfortably Numb," a hymn for adolescents already nostalgic over their lost youth; "Hey You," a rewrite of Funkadelic's "Maggot Brain"; and "Nobody Home," which never gets played on the radio but holds up as the album's most touching moment. (Even when Waters complains about "the obligatory Hendrix perm"—didn't anyone tell him Jimi's hair could do that naturally?)

The Wall was the last croak of vintage Floyd. *A Collection of Great Dance Songs* and *Works* were pointless "hits" collections from a band that disdained hits, and *The Final Cut* was basically a mediocre Waters solo album of antiwar rants. He can't sing, by the way. Floyd's subsequent studio reunions, *A Momentary Lapse of Reason* and *The Division Bell,* are fluffy tour merch cut without Waters; the only echo of past success is the 1987 hit "Learning to Fly." *Shine On* is a redundant eight-CD box with no previously unreleased material. The Floyd have released various live albums *(Pulse, Delicate Sound of Thunder, Is There Anybody Out There?),* pointlessly re-creating their meticulous studio effects onstage. But the two-CD *Echoes* is an ideal career summary, with "Shine On You Crazy Diamond" segued together into a 17:32 whole, a generous helping of five ace Barrett songs, highlights from *Dark Side* and *Wish You Were Here,* all 16:31 of "Echoes," and one unbelievably bad song from *The Final Cut.* —R.S.

Gene Pitney

★★ It Hurts to Be in Love (Musicor, 1964)
★★ I'm Gonna Be Strong (1965; Goldies, 2002)
★★★ Town Without Pity (Hallmark, 1975)
★★★ Greatest Hits (1981; Prime Cuts, 1995)
★★★★ Anthology (1961–1968) (Rhino, 1986)
★★ Golden Classics (Collectables, 1991)
★★★½ Hits and Misses (Bear Family, 1994)
★★ Greatest Hits (Curb, 1995)

★★★   Blue Gene/Gene Meets the Fair Young Ladies of Folkland (Sequel, 1997)

★★★   I'm Gonna Be Strong/Looking Through the Eyes of Love (Sequel, 1997)

★★★   Sings the Great Songs of Our Time/Nobody Needs Your Love (Sequel, 1997)

★★★   The Many Sides of Gene Pitney/Only Love Can Break a Heart (Sequel, 1997)

★★★   Gene Pitney Sings Bacharach and Others/Pitney Today (Sequel, 1997)

★★★   Young and Warm and Wonderful/Just One Smile (Sequel, 1997)

★★★   Gene Pitney Sings Just for You/World Wide Winners (Sequel, 1998)

★★★   Golden Greats/This Is Gene Pitney (Sequel, 1998)

★★★   Ten Years Later/New Sounds of Gene Pitney (Sequel, 1998)

★★★★   25 All-Time Greatest Hits (Varèse, 1999)

★★★   Looking Through: The Ultimate Collection (Sequel, 2000)

Along with Johnnie Ray and Roy Orbison, Gene Pitney was one of pop's great sufferers: Almost his entire, vast canon consists of weeping and wailing. But if Orbison's melodramatic hurt was grand and earned, and Ray's pathological and forced, the cute Pitney's lush pain seemed almost winsome, a theatrical sobbing for strange, sheerly musical effect. Emotionalism laid on with a trowel, it's pretty intriguing and eccentrically pretty.

Debuting during the early '60s rock & roll hiatus that came after early Elvis and before the Beatles, Pitney careered wildly between pathos and bathos. He never hit the smarmy lows of the period's worst exemplar, Bobby Vinton; yet he was miles away, too, from the swagger of its minor monarch, Bobby Darin. Collaborating in turn with Phil Spector and Burt Bacharach, Pitney staked out his own wounded ground—sweeping, orchestral singles that forefronted the baroque quiver of his trebly, sometimes falsetto, pleading.

For his 1961 debut single, "(I Wanna) Love My Life Away," the then–college student wrote the song himself, multitracked his voice 12 times, and played all the instruments in the arrangement. A trademark style soon evolved, and whether tricked out in the ersatz Western trappings of "(The Man Who Shot) Liberty Valance" and "Town Without Pity" or the mariachi theater of "24 Hours From Tulsa," the effect was of B-grade, queasily moving, cinematic excess. In 1964 the Rolling Stones gave "That Girl Belongs to Yesterday" to Pitney when they discovered that some of the Beatles' big money came from writing originals: the

first Jagger-Richard song ever to hit the U.S. charts, it's a not bad Spectorish tidbit. Later that same year, Pitney unleashed Mann-Weill's "I'm Gonna Be Strong"—it's definitive, heartbreakingly Pitney.

More curiosities soon followed. Driven by apt instinct toward the hammy glory of operatic bel canto, Pitney began recording in Italian; these albums are out of print. Searching around for an actual C&W collaborator, he unerringly teamed up with moody extremist George Jones on *Famous Country Duets* and *It's Country Time;* both albums are worth searching for. The masterful Rhino *Anthology* includes all the singles listed above; it's a heady, if somewhat guilty, pleasure. Nicely, the man is well-represented on other best-ofs and reissues: Sequel has released a generous clutch of his '60s finest, all with original cover art. They've also turned out the massive *Looking Through,* a wondrous compilation with all his best (even some gems in Italian). For a great, briefer intro, try Varèse's *25 All-Time Greatest Hits* or Bear Family's *Hits and Misses.* —P.E.

The Pixies

★★★½   Come On Pilgrim (1987; 4AD, 2003)

★★★★★   Surfer Rosa (1988; 4AD, 2003)

★★★★½   Doolittle (1989; 4AD/Elektra, 2003)

★★★   Bossanova (1990; 4AD/Elektra, 2003)

★★★★   Trompe le Monde (1991; 4AD/Elektra, 2003)

★★½   Death to the Pixies (4AD/Elektra, 1997)

★★★   Pixies (spinART, 2002)

★★★   Wave of Mutilation (4AD, 2004)

★★★½   Live in Minneapolis, MN (Disk Live, 2004)

When most bands send out demos, they include three or, at most, four songs. The Pixies crammed 17 onto their legendary "Purple Tape," and eight of those tracks became their debut, *Come On Pilgrim.* The Boston quartet, still figuring itself out, was definitely onto something: Black Francis jitters and yelps in English and a little Spanish, bassist Kim Deal (Mrs. John Murphy) chimes in sourly, guitarist Joey Santiago plays like a punk raised on Ennio Morricone and flamenco, and drummer David Lovering puts the pedal to the floor. The tape's other nine tracks (including a cover of "In Heaven," from the movie *Eraserhead*) finally surfaced 15 years later as *Pixies,* serving as evidence that the band had written its biggest hits, *Doolittle's* "Here Comes Your Man" and *Trompe le Monde's* "Subbacultcha," before anyone had heard of the band.

Steve Albini, not yet an alt-rock household name, recorded the unstoppable *Surfer Rosa,* honing the Pixies' sound to scalpel sharpness. The songs are harder and, in places, more fragmented than *Pilgrim's,* but incredible tunes poke out from behind the wall of smashed bottles and rusty needles. Black Francis sounds genuinely insane as he giggles at the top of "Broken Face," and Deal comes into her own with "Gigantic," a joyful, twisted anthem about childhood voyeurism that became a college-radio standard.

The first half of *Doolittle* is an alternative-rock landmark, years ahead of its time and a model for later bands, so it's a shame that the second half falls off. But for 20 minutes, the Pixies can do no wrong. Francis screams his lungs out on the opening, the Luis Buñuel tribute "Debaser," then scarily shrieks the chorus of "Tame." The band radically contracts song structure wherever possible and employs the quiet-verse/explosive-chorus formula three years before everyone else figured out how to copy it. "Here Comes Your Man" and "Monkey Gone to Heaven" strip away the Pixies' bristles to bare their bizarre, masterful songwriting.

Bossanova is a serious stumble, with inappropriately bombastic production and songwriting that suggests the Pixies had finally started listening to their college-rock contemporaries (not a good thing). "Is She Weird" and "Velouria" have held up surprisingly well, but that's about it. The band's farewell, *Trompe le Monde,* on the other hand, rocks—it's not the kamikaze punk-rock attack of *Surfer Rosa* (aside from the Roman candle that is "Distance Equals Rate Times Time"), but Francis and Santiago pull out one massive guitar riff after another. (The riff that powers "U-Mass" is as stupid as any ever written, and as effective.) Black Francis' outer-space obsession doesn't explain the Jesus & Mary Chain cover, "Head On." Don't try to figure it out; just bang your head.

Death to the Pixies collects a disc's worth of singles and album tracks, which lose something out of context, and appends a fairly dull live set from 1990, *Wave of Mutilation.* Released to cash in on the band's 2004 reunion, it improves on the earlier best-of a bit—the almost-chronological approach serves it better, and the B side "Into the White" is an inspired inclusion. That year the Pixies mounted a comeback tour and played the Coachella Festival; *Live in Minneapolis* showed they hadn't lost a step.   —D.W.

Robert Plant

★★★	Pictures at 11	(Swan Song, 1982)
★★★½	The Principle of Moments	(Es Paranza, 1983)
★★★½	Shaken 'n' Stirred	(Es Paranza, 1985)
★★★½	Now and Zen	(Es Paranza, 1988)
★★★½	Manic Nirvana	(Es Paranza, 1990)
★★★	Fate of Nations	(Atlantic, 1993)
★★★½	Dreamland	(Universal, 2002)
★★★½	Sixty Six to Timbuktu	(Atlantic, 2003)

with the Honeydrippers
★★★   Volume One (EP) (Es Paranza, 1984)

It is a credit to Robert Plant's solo career that the *worst* thing he's ever done post–Led Zeppelin was hooking back up with guitarist Jimmy Page for a nostalgia tour of duty in the mid-'90s. While the Page and Plant albums came closer to capturing the spirit of their old band than anyone had a right to expect, the whole endeavor was a giant step backward for Plant after more than a decade of forward motion. Sure, *Now and Zen* nodded to the past with its Zeppelin quotes and crisp Page solo on "Tall Cool One"—but it was a nod and a wink, rather than a full-on embrace. Ditto *Manic Nirvana*'s cheeky "Big Love," in which Plant hits on a stewardess with the pickup line, "I slept in the same room with Jimmy Page!" After years in which Plant seemingly went out of his way to explore everything *but* classic hard rock, his return to the form with those two albums was heralded as a return to his Zeppelin roots; the problem with that theory is, exactly when in the Zep days did Plant ever sound like he was having this much fun?

All of which is not to say that Zeppelin fans need steer clear, as they'll find much to feast on even on the early-'80s albums. *Pictures at 11* boasts two cavernous crushers; on "Burning Down One Side" and "Worse Than Detroit," guitarist Robbie Blunt pierces Plant's molten lava cries with peals of thunder. *The Principle of Moments* spawned two hits in 1983; the floating art rock of "Big Log" and the warm R&B nostalgia of "In the Mood" neatly represent Plant's diverse interests. *Shaken 'n' Stirred* was even more eclectic, with Plant mixing strong doses of hip-hop beats and world rhythms into tracks like "Hip to Hoo" and "Too Loud"; even the familiar-sounding rockers ("Little by Little," "Easily Lead") benefit from the judicious addition of synthesizers to the guitar-led strut. The Honeydrippers' *Volume One* is a one-off EP of vintage soul and R&B covers; excessive orchestrations distract from Plant's restrained interpretations, while the guest hotshots (Jimmy Page, Jeff Beck, Nile Rodgers) are underutilized.

Distinguished by sharp material and an equally focused band, both *Now and Zen* and *Manic Nirvana* hold up much better than most hard rock albums released in their era. Indeed, after hair metal, grunge, rap metal, and every other trend since *Now and Zen*, the taut snap and swagger of "Tall Cool One"—once vaunted/criticized as a throwback—make it sound fresher today than it did way back in 1988. *Manic Nirvana* (released a year before *Nevermind*) delivers on the heady promise of its title with a vengeance, confidently skipping from jumpin' boogie ("Hurting Kind

[I've Got My Eyes on You]") to brutal funk metal ("Nirvana") to sardonic psychedelia ("Tie Die on the Highway") to gale-force blooze wailing ("Your Ma Said You Cried in Your Sleep Last Night"). The much mellower *Fate of Nations* suffers from a muddled second half (and one of the worst album covers in rock history), but its strengths are considerable—notably the gorgeous "29 Palms" and "I Believe," Plant's moving memorial to his deceased son. His fine cover of folkie Tim Hardin's "If I Were a Carpenter," meanwhile, hinted at the direction he would take years later on *Dreamland*. Comprised of four originals and six covers, *Dreamland*, like the Honeydrippers, finds Plant paying respect to his early influences—this time focusing on psychedelia and folk with strikingly fresh passes at Bob Dylan ("One More Cup of Coffee"), Tim Buckley ("Song to the Siren"), Skip Spence ("Skip's Song"), and the obscure Tim Rose, via "Morning Dew" and a menacing, seven-minute "Hey Joe" that also points to Arthur Lee and Love. In sharp contrast to those Page and Plant efforts, this look backward seems to stem from true inspiration, not the lack of it.

The same goes for the excellent double-disc anthology, *Sixty Six to Timbuktu*. The first disc covers high points from the solo albums (although "In the Mood" is conspicuously missing); the second is a treasure trove of hit-and-miss rarities, ranging from his pre-Zep days (including two Band of Joy tracks with drummer John Bonham) to soundtrack and tribute album contributions and the "Kashmir"-colored "Win My Train Fare Home," recorded live at the 2003 Festival in the Desert in Timbuktu. —M.C./R.SK.

Plastikman
see RICHIE HAWTIN

The Platters

★★★★★ The Magic Touch: Platters Anthology (Polygram, 1991)
★★★ The Platters (King, 1994)
★★★ The Musicor Years (Collectables, 1995)
★★★ The Very Best of the Platters 1966–1969 (Varèse Sarabande, 1997)
★★★½ Enchanted: The Best of the Platters (Rhino, 1998)
★★★ The Millennium Collection: The Best of the Platters (MCA, 1999)

In the end the story of the first and best incarnation of the Platters comes down to two dominant personalities, those of lead tenor Tony Williams and the group's manager/producer/songwriter, Buck Ram. Linda Hays, Williams' sister (a singer who was managed by Ram's Los Angeles–based Personality Promotions) introduced her brother to the budding music business mogul at a time when the Platters lineup included future Coaster Cornel Gunter, brothers Alex and Gaynell Hodge, Joe Jefferson, and Zola Taylor. The Hodge brothers, Gunter, and Jefferson moved on to other endeavors, and were replaced by Herb Reed, David Lynch, and Paul Robi, who joined with Taylor and Williams in the quintet Ram brought to Syd Nathan at King Records; he signed them in 1954 to King's Federal subsidiary. The Platters' earliest sides failed to catch on in the pop marketplace, although a couple of singles, "Love All Night" and "Tell the World," made some noise on the R&B charts. At this stage the group evinced a greater gospel influence in its vocal stylings, and also showed an assured touch on jump blues tunes. The King budget reissue, *The Platters*, contains 12 of the reported 23 tracks the group cut for Federal, including the aforementioned singles, and an early, stripped-down version of a plaintive, Ram-penned ballad, "Only You (and You Alone)."

Another group under Ram's aegis, the Penguins ("Earth Angel"), was being courted by Mercury; as part of the deal, Ram leveraged a contract for the Platters as well. Reviving "Only You (and You Alone)," Ram beefed up the arrangement (which now included a series of rapid piano arpeggios by Ram himself, and a solid backing band led by Ernie Freeman), and otherwise turned Williams loose to let his soaring, plaintive tenor work its magic. It did, to the tune of a Top 10 hit in 1955 that launched the Platters on a career that remained commercially viable into the late '60s, long after Williams had departed and been replaced by a new lead singer, Sonny Turner. But it's Williams' voice that shaped the Platters' legend and was out front on 20 Top 40 singles and four #1s between 1955 and 1961. In the early days of rock & roll, romantic, even melodramatic, ballads still occupied an honored place in the canon, and the Platters, despite formidable competition from the likes of the Moonglows and the Flamingos, were in a league of their own. They appeared in films and on TV, played to wildly enthusiastic receptions all over America, Europe, and Australia, and developed a following very nearly as rabid as Elvis'.

Stylistically Williams had learned some artful lessons from the Ink Spots' Bill Kenny and the Ravens' two outstanding tenors, Maithe Marshall and Joe Van Loan, taking from Kenny an unerring sense of the dramatic and infallible control of his keening upper register; from Marshall and Van Loan he developed an impeccable instinct for the art of control and release as a means of adding dramatic tension to his readings.

The greater good that came out of the Platters' success was the group's appeal across racial boundaries, which helped kick open pop charts that had been racially segregated and provided yet another signal, at the dawn of the modern civil rights movement, that a change was gonna come.

Like that of many other '50s vocal groups, the Platters' repertoire was a blend of original material (mostly written by Ram) and revered pop songs of earlier eras. Back-to-back #1 singles in 1958 were "Twilight Time," a Top 20 hit for the Three Suns in 1944, and "Smoke Gets in Your Eyes," a Jerome Kern tune that had been a #1 single in 1933 for Paul Whiteman and His Orchestra. "Harbor Lights," a Top 10 single for the Platters in 1960, dates to 1937, when it was a Top 10 single for Frances Langford. It's a measure of the depth of Ram's artistry that his own songs compare favorably to those classic American pop entries (and thanks to the great feeling Williams brought to everything he sang, even Ram's rare substandard lyric came out like poetry). The first three Ram songs the group cut display an impressive sophistication in both lyric and melody and advance a view of love that didn't condescend to teens but spoke to them in articulate, heartfelt terms. One of those Ram efforts, "The Great Pretender," was a #1 single in 1955, whereas the other two, "Only You" and "The Magic Touch," peaked at #5 and #4 (1957), respectively.

In 1959 the male members of the group and their white girlfriends were arrested on morals charges (which were later dropped), but the resulting publicity undermined a once-spotless image. Then Williams decided to bow out and pursue a solo career. Ram quickly replaced his peerless lead tenor with a young Cleveland nightclub performer, Sonny Turner. Turner had to bide his time, however, because for two more years Mercury continued to release, and have hits with, recordings featuring Williams in the lead role, culminating in 1962's #91-charting single, "It's Magic," and the end of the group's Mercury contract.

When Ram secured a new recording deal for the Platters in 1965 with the Musicor label, the lineup consisted of Turner, original members Lynch and Reed, Nate Nelson (whose eerie, beautiful tenor voice had graced some of the Flamingos' classic recordings) and Sandra Dawn, replacing Zola Taylor. At Musicor they were teamed with Luther Dixon, who had already fashioned a breathtaking résumé as a producer-arranger-writer for the Shirelles and Chuck Jackson, among others. Dixon updated the Platters' sound with Motown-style arrangements, diminishing the orchestra, bringing a steady-grooving instrumental ensemble up in the mix, with the harmony vocals doing the job of the strings, as the story was carried forward by Turner's emotive tenor—not nearly as striking in its theatrics as Williams' but more telling of the singer's gospel roots in the way he phrased in his fragile upper register before returning to a forceful middle range. As well, Dixon recognized what he had in Nate Nelson and put him out front on several sides, which allowed him to show off not only his glorious, high-pitched approach—the pleading, romantic single "I'll Be Home" sounds like the Flamingos single that never was—but a gritty, R&B shouter's voice in items such as his self-penned, streetwise directive "Don't Hear, Speak, See No Evil." They would never reach the height of popularity they had enjoyed in the previous decade, but the Platters, with Dixon at the helm (and butting heads with Ram over the group's direction), made their Musicor debut in 1966 with their new producer's self-penned "I Love You 1,000 Times." It went to #6 on the R&B chart and peaked at #31 pop, bringing the Platters back into the game. In 1967 they did even better on the pop chart with an infectious, uptempo love song, "With This Ring" (a Dixon co-write), which peaked at #12 R&B but rose to #14 on the pop chart. From that high it was all downhill, as succeeding singles charted only in the lower regions of the Top 100 and the group members became disenchanted with their fate. In 1967 David Lynch left the group, followed two years later by the only other remaining original group member, Herb Reed. At that time the group was a popular attraction on the Carolinas' beach music scene, but virtually nowhere else. In 1971 Turner called it quits too. Buck Ram, undeterred, continued to put groups of Platters out on the road to sing the old songs and bask in the applause that belonged to Tony Williams (who died in 1992) and his mates.

For definitive Platters recordings, *The Magic Touch: Platters Anthology* can't be beat. This two-CD set offers a comprehensive overview of the group's history (with thorough annotation) from the beginning to the end of the Tony Williams era and even includes a Williams solo track. Rhino's *Enchanted: The Best of the Platters* hits the high points of the Williams era and also includes three Musicor tracks. Both Varèse Sarabande and Collectables have worthwhile overviews of the Musicor years, with Collectables' 18-track *The Musicor Years* bettering by four Varèse's *The Very Best of the Platters: 1966–1969.* —D.M.

P.O.D.

★★ Brown (Butterfly, 1996)
★★★ The Fundamental Elements of Southtown (Atlantic, 1999)

★★★★ Satellite (Atlantic, 2001)
★★ Payable on Death (Atlantic, 2003)

After a decade woodshedding on the Southern California hardcore circuit, this multicultural San Ysidro quartet burst onto a new-metal scene drowning in recrimination and self-pity in 2001. What set P.O.D. (short for "payable on death") apart was a rhythmic agility born of Latin music, reggae, and the metallic fusion of late-'80s Bad Brains, as well as a righteous, generous Christian viewpoint that offered something other than the endless grievances of their peers. P.O.D.'s debut, *Brown,* is an unfocused series of grooves and rants that sets the scene for the much better realized *Southtown,* heralded by "Rock the Party," an echo-soaked exhortation to Jah and their fans.

Satellite, from 2001, is the easily the band's best, containing twin rap-metal classics: "Alive" is a pile-driving, syncopated salute to the Almighty, and the solemn "Youth of a Nation" updates Pink Floyd's "Another Brick in the Wall" for a generation rocked by the Columbine murders. Alas, 2003's *Payable on Death,* recorded after the departure of the band's guitarist Marcos Curiel, lacked the sheer exuberance and purpose of *Satellite,* though P.O.D.'s positivity still seems striking in light of the relentless negativity of their fellow rap rockers. —R.K.

The Pogues

★★★ Red Roses for Me (1984; Enigma, 1986)
★★★★ Rum, Sodomy & the Lash (MCA, 1985)
★★ Poguetry in Motion (EP) (MCA, 1986)
★★★★ If I Should Fall From Grace With God (Island, 1988)
★★½ Peace & Love (Island, 1989)
★½ Yeah Yeah Yeah Yeah Yeah (EP) (Island, 1990)
★★★ Hell's Ditch (Island, 1990)
★★ Essential Pogues (Island, 1991)
★½ Waiting for Herb (Chameleon, 1993)
★½ Pogue Mahone (WEA, 1995)
★ Streams of Whiskey (Castle, 2002)

Sounding at times like a cross between the Clancy Brothers and the Clash, the Pogues are a rollicking, rowdy, drunken brawl of a band. At its best, the group is a marvel, matching the tuneful spirit of traditional Irish folk with near-poetic lyrics and a straight-to-hell punk attitude. More often, though, the group comes across as loutish buffoons, a sort of musical Pat and Mike routine portraying Irish culture as little more than drunken dissolution.

There's more than a hint of that on *Red Roses for Me,* particularly on Shane MacGowan's self-satisfied "Streams of Whiskey" and "Boys From the County

Hell." But the traditional tunes—raucous ravers like "Waxie's Dargle"—tip the balance in the band's favor, showing off the fervor that gave the band its name (shortened from the Gaelic *pogue mahone,* or "kiss my ass") and reputation. But it's the Elvis Costello–produced *Rum, Sodomy & the Lash* that proves there's more to the Pogues than a bad reputation. Granted, the album's best songs are covers (Ewan MacColl's lovely "Dirty Old Town" and Eric Bogle's chilling antiwar anthem "And the Band Played Waltzing Mathilda"), and MacGowan still at times comes across as a second-rate Tom Waits. But when he hits his mark, as on the swirling "The Sick Bed of Cuchulainn," it's worth indulging his excesses.

After *Poguetry in Motion,* an EP more noteworthy for its title than its music, the Pogues began self-mythologizing in earnest with *If I Should Fall From Grace With God.* The cover photo uses trick editing to slip James Joyce into their ranks, which says something of the Pogues' ambition; it's doubtful, though, that Joyce would have resorted to such doggerel as "You scumbag/You maggot/You cheap lousy faggot."

"Turkish Song of the Damned" makes an interesting connection between Turkish tunes and Irish reels, but even that bit of experimentalism comes a-cropper on *Peace & Love,* where the band attempts to augment its Irish groove with unconvincing stabs at jazz, Caribbean, and other non-Irish styles. *Yeah Yeah Yeah Yeah Yeah* is a lurch toward straight rock that's every bit as silly as the psychedelic title tune suggests, but thanks to MacGowan's "The Ghost of a Smile" and "The Sunny Side of the Street," *Hell's Ditch* is, if not a return to form, a reminder at least of the strengths that made the Pogues worth hearing in the first place. *Essential* is hardly that, ignoring as it does anything before *Fall From Grace.*

Sadly, MacGowan's drinking became a proper stinking, and he was asked to leave the Pogues the following year. Clash singer (and *Hell's Ditch* producer) Joe Strummer stepped in for a year, but didn't record with the band; he was succeeded in 1992 by Spider Stacy, who fronted the band through its final, forgettable studio albums, *Waiting for Herb* and *Pogue Mahone. Streams of Whiskey* is a live recording from 1991 that the band has disavowed. —J.D.C.

Poison

★★★★ Look What the Cat Dragged In (Capitol, 1986)
★★★½ Open Up and Say . . . Ahh! (Capitol, 1988)
★★ Flesh and Blood (Capitol, 1990)
★★ Swallow This Live (Capitol, 1990)
★ Native Tongue (Capitol, 1993)
★★★★ Poison's Greatest Hits: 1986–1996 (Capitol, 1996)

In the credits on Poison's debut album *Look What the Cat Dragged In*, we find Bret Michaels ("Vocalizin' & Socializin' "), Rikki Rockett ("Sticks, Tricks & Lipstick Fix"), Bobby Dall ("Bass Rapin' & Heartbreakin' "), and C.C. DeVille ("Guitar Screechin' & Hair Bleachin' "). These guys were the quintessential '80s hair-metal band, dolled up in spandex, leg warmers, feather boas, top hats, leopard-skin vests, and more makeup than any glam band before or since; they looked like four slices of wedding cake that just escaped out the bakery window. And Rockett was a former hairdresser, just like the guy in A Flock of Seagulls, confirming their glam credentials. Their first hit, "Talk Dirty to Me," is a timeless rush of hormonal overload, with a riff stolen from the New York Dolls, lyrics stolen from "My Jolly Playmate," maybe the best ending of any song ever, and a demented guitar solo introduced with the shriek, "C.C., pick up that guitar and uh, *talk* to me!"

Look What the Cat Dragged In is actually a terrific album, everything fast and flashy and sensationalistic about glam with none of the ponderous macho bits, just catchy tunes like "Cry Tough" (you have to believe in your dreams), "Let Me Go to the Show" (you have to sneak out the window and steal your parents' car to go rock, because that's part of believing in your dreams), and "I Want Action" (why yes, it *does* rhyme with "satisfaction"—how did you guess?). *Open Up* is more serious about the metal cred, though that doesn't spoil "Nothin' But a Good Time," the absurd '70s schlock cover "Your Mama Don't Dance," the tearjerker "Every Rose Has Its Thorn," and the perfect win big, lose big Sunset Strip melodrama "Fallen Angel." By *Flesh and Blood,* the band was running low on energy, although "Ride the Wind" was ten times better than a song with that title has any right to be. The hits and the hair spray both dried up, but Poison continues to enjoy success on tour, playing their '80s hits for grateful audiences of former high school hellraisers, still rolling the dice of their lives. —R.S.

The Police

Unlike most punk rockers—who spent albums honing their chops—the Police entered from the other end of the spectrum. Founder Stewart Copeland cut his teeth with the art-rock combo Curved Air, while guitarist Andy Summers was an alumnus of the jazzy progressive band Soft Machine; even bassist/vocalist Sting, a relative unknown, had made a name in fusion bands. But because punk favored passion over technical prowess, musical skill was useless to the band. So the Police traded overt flash for a sort of covert virtuosity, burying its talent in intricate rhythm arrangements and quietly complex reggae grooves.

It wasn't punk, of course, but it wasn't like anything else in rock, either. *Outlandos d'Amour* mixes jazzy reggae workouts like "Masoko Tanga" with predictable punk fare along the lines of "Born in the 50's." The band's commercial potential didn't seem manifest at the time, but "Roxanne" (a U.S. Top 40 single), "So Lonely," and "Can't Stand Losing You" have become '80s pop classics. *Reggatta de Blanc*'s "The Bed's Too Big Without You" and "Message in a Bottle" are powered by the instrumentation, not melody. Instead of the typical power-trio approach, in which the guitar carries the tune while drums and bass offer rhythmic support, the Police invert the formula: Copeland's swirling polyrhythms lead the way while Sting's bass grounds the pulse and Summers' phased-and-flanged guitar adds color.

This sly twist on tradition placed most of the band's energy in the groove, which paid off big-time with *Zenyatta Mondatta.* The emphasis on rhythmic intensity made the band's songs catchier (as "Voices Inside My Head" shows, the band certainly knew how to work a vamp), and the rhythmic dynamics add a singular punch to the material. So despite the flirty-student melodrama of its lyrics, the groove's ebb and flow underscores the dramatic tension in "Don't Stand So Close to Me." The band augments its instrumentation with keyboards and even a little saxophone in *Ghost in the Machine* but otherwise maintains *Zenyatta*'s approach via well-modulated singles like "Every Little Thing She Does Is Magic" and "Spirits in the Material World" (though the most interesting and entrancing rhythmic ideas are lavished on nonpop numbers like the funky "Too Much Information" and the relentless "Demolition Man").

Synchronicity is the band's swan song. The playing is clearly collaborative, and the band is at its most supple and inspiring, from the percolating exoticism of "Walking in Your Footsteps" and the full-throttle fury of "Synchronicity I" to the slow boil of "Every Breath You Take." The fact that Sting's writing so conspicuously dominated the band's songbook clearly began to grate on the other members, whose input amounted to one song each on this album (Copeland's wry "Miss Gradenko" and Summers' irritatingly Freudian "Mother"). Consequently, the band fell apart soon after *Synchronicity*, reuniting only long enough to cut an unimpressive update of "Don't Stand So Close to Me" for the best-of package *Every Breath You Take: The Singles* (which was slightly enlarged and reissued nine years later as *Every Breath You Take: The Classics. Message in a Box: The Complete Recordings* compiles all of the band's studio recordings, including B sides and rarities, making it perfect for completists who somehow neglected to buy the original albums. *Live!* pairs a sprightly, raw 1979 club show with a staid 1983 arena performance, but it delivers nothing revelatory. *The Very Best of Sting & the Police* exists largely to cash in on the tiny amount of nostalgia generated when Sean "Puffy" Combs copped "Every Breath You Take" for his Biggie Smalls tribute, "I'll Be Missing You." It includes a Combs remix of "Roxanne," which is drolly described as a "bonus." —J.D.C.

Polyphonic Spree

★★★	The Beginning Stages (2001; Hollywood, 2003)
★★★★	Together We're Heavy (Hollywood, 2004)

While in Tripping Daisy, a '90s alt-rock also-ran, singer Tim DeLaughter dreamed of creating lush, melodic middle-age symphonies to the sun. Two years after guitarist Wes Berggren died of an overdose, DeLaughter reconvened Daisy bassist Mark Pirro and drummer Bryan Wakeland and added a few other musicians . . . then a few more . . . and a few more . . . as he augmented his basic rock trio with horns, brass, a choir, percussion, a harp, a theremin, and 25 white robes—and the Polyphonic Spree was born. DeLaughter's rubbery whelp, his penchant for singing about the sun and the sky, and the group's robust sound suggest a strange intersection of the Flaming Lips, ELO, and the Fifth Dimension.

The Beginning Stages was recorded in a whirlwind 48-hour session, as a demo to land the unorthodox group some gigs. It boasts booming choruses and instrumentation on songs like "It's the Sun" and "Hanging Around the Day." "Light and Day" was its breakthrough single, landing a prominent slot on movie soundtracks and a Volkswagen commercial. *Stages* contained a jolting dose of sunshine pop in an age of emo, teen pop, and new metal and went on to cult success, though the record suffered from spartan production and a lack of focus.

There's no such problem with 2004's *Together We're Heavy*. The Spree's shtick takes a backseat to a dramatic production with tighter arrangements that don't necessarily lean on the Spree's thunderous sound. The bombast does surface on "We Sound Amazed" and "Hold Me Now," but quieter songs like "Suitcase Calling" and "One Man Show" are more intricately crafted and find the Polyphonic Spree playing a more subdued and sophisticated brand of chamber pop. *Heavy* suggests a musically restless troupe with a highly stylized form that nevertheless follows its function. —A.D.

Iggy Pop

★★★★	The Idiot (1977; RCA/Virgin, 1990)
★★★★	Lust for Life (1977; RCA/Virgin, 1990)
★★	TV Eye Live (RCA, 1978)
★★★½	New Values (Arista, 1979)
★★½	Soldier (Arista, 1980)
★★	Party (Arista, 1981)
★★	Zombie Birdhouse (Animal, 1982)
★★★★½	Choice Cuts (RCA, 1984)
★★½	Blah Blah Blah (A&M, 1986)
★★	Instinct (A&M, 1988)
★★★½	Brick by Brick (Virgin, 1990)
★★	American Caesar (Virgin, 1993)
★★½	Naughty Little Doggy (Virgin, 1996)
★★★	Avenue B (Virgin, 1999)
★★½	Beat 'Em Up (Virgin, 2001)
★★★	Skull Ring (Virgin, 2003)

"I'm just a modern guy/Of course I've had it in the ear before." That quote from "Lust for Life" (which became a quasi-hit in 1996 via its use in the opening sequence of *Trainspotting*) sums up the former Stooge's solo attitude: A cutting, ironic distance replaces the self-lacerating edge of his legendary early-'70s performances. Producer David Bowie modernizes the dense psychedelic blare of the Stooges, substituting synth moans for guitar wails and keeping the jackhammer beat largely intact. This stark, electronic sheen alienated more than a few old Pop fans, but the Bowie association and the advent of new wave brought Iggy to a much larger audience. A unique sensibility inhabits the crunching rockers and burnt-out torch songs on these two albums: brooding, sardonic, restless, outraged, perceptive, funny as hell, slightly bitter. *The Idiot* knowingly pokes through the residue of hedonism-run-amok on "Funtime" and "Nightclubbing," while *Lust for Life* highlights like the title cut and "The Passenger" portray Iggy Pop as a punk survivor. He's battle-scarred, but still searching. Reuniting with latter-day Stooges guitarist James Williamson, Iggy cooks up a lean, keyboard-enhanced hard-rock sound on *New Values*. If he doesn't quite consummate the title track's ambitious quest, Iggy does find strength in the old verities. "Endless Sea" perfects his post-Doors romantic doomsayer stance, and sets the stage for hundreds of mopey underground sensations to come. This initial stage of Iggy's career wielded a tremendous influence over the '80s; he translated the glittery innovations of Bowie and Roxy Music into a streetwise argot any art-school dropout could understand. After that, however, the dreaded roadshow syndrome set in. Through the '80s, each successive Iggy album sounds more dispiriting and uninspired than the next.

It's hard to decide which A&M album is worse: The slick Bowie reunion *(Blah Blah Blah)* mysteriously fails to spark either participant's batteries, while the numbing dinosaur-rock return *(Instinct)* stumbles into the tar pits. Ever the phoenix, Iggy stumbles halfway back from artistic oblivion with the surprisingly consistent *Brick by Brick*. This self-consciously "mature" effort offends the faithful, but Iggy curls his lip and lets his delightfully twisted mind roam the contemporary media landscape.

By 1993, our hero had been lionized by Seattle bands such as Mudhoney. But his response to grunge was *American Caesar*, wherein producer Malcolm Burn applies the same swampy, reverb-drenched glop that his colleague Daniel Lanois had dumped all over records for U2 and the Neville Brothers—an approach that suits Iggy not one whit. Conversely, *Naughty Little Doggy* sounds as if it had been recorded in the same time it takes to listen to it and for about 25 bucks, besides. This was a step too far in the other direction, but the strutting, leering "Pussy Walk" may be his funniest tune ever. And then came *Avenue B,* a baffling if often amusing excursion into crooning and spoken word, accompanied largely by organ trio Medeski, Martin & Wood. If that record seemed ill-advised, at least it wasn't the same old scum rock retread that *Beat 'Em Up* was. Finally, Iggy gave his fans the Stooges reunion they had salivated after for three decades—*Skull Ring* includes four tunes recorded with his old comrades, as well as cuts with Green Day, Sum 41, and Canadian porno-rap diva Peaches. Sadly, each of the latter is far more energetic than the reconstituted Stooges' tracks. —M.C./R.K.

Porno for Pyros

- ★★ Porno for Pyros (Warner Bros., 1993)
- ★★★ Good God's Urge (Warner Bros., 1996)

Between Jane's Addiction and Jane's reunions, singer Perry Farrell indulged himself with Pornos for Pyros. Whereas Jane's best work was a smart nexus for punk, funk, and metal, Porno's debut simply spins in alt-rock circles. Farrell's worldview—women are virtuous and put-upon, men are stupid, and he can save us because he is free to masturbate and has a black girlfriend—revels in self-aggrandizement. But *Good God's Urge* shows genuine progress: The band sloughs off the imperative to prove itself to be freakier than thou as it follows a muse toward world-flavored music and less ham-fisted, occasionally tender lyrics. —C.N.

Portishead

- ★★★★ Dummy (Go!, 1994)
- ★★★★ Portishead (Go!, 1997)
- ★★★ Roseland, NYC Live (Island, 1998)

The retiring British quartet Portishead brought together various cultish musical strands—spy-movie jazz, lounge, acid house, atmospheric ambience, chilly techno—and somehow created a blend more widely popular than the sum of its influences. Portishead's brand of trip-hop, more urbane than the gritty sound Massive Attack had pioneered a few years prior, was a kind of languorous neocabaret whose cool vocals, courtesy of Beth Gibbons, were fired up by the tricky, layered production her bandmates laid down as the songs' base. Taken as a whole, *Dummy* is a seamless, gorgeous piece of atmospherics, and its singles—notably "Sour Times" and the fittingly titled "Numb"—stand on their own as hypnotic, deeply tuneful pop. The formula proved just as lovely and absorbing on the group's self-titled followup. By then, however, Portishead had numerous competitors and imitators on both sides of the Atlantic, and its reluctance to play the press game gave the band the unfortunate status of admired innovators rather than the stunning, intelligent hitmakers they were well on their way to becoming. —A.B.

The Presidents of the United States of America

- ★★★ The Presidents of the United States of America (Columbia, 1995)
- ★★ II (Columbia, 1995)
- ★★★ Pure Frosting (Columbia, 1998)
- ★★★ Freaked Out and Small (Music Blitz, 2000)

The Presidents of the United States of America were Seattle's antidote to Kurt Cobain's angst, arriving on the scene virtually moments after his death in 1994. They owed as much to Saturday-morning cartoons as they did to sludgy feedback, so it was an upbeat wake. Presidents Chris Ballew, Dave Dederer, and Jason Finn were conducting a deconstructionist experiment, to see how much noise they could make playing songs about *The Brady Bunch* on two-stringed guitars.

The experiment foamed over into their self-titled debut, a record that combined the Three Stooges with Iggy and the Stooges. Frat boys and postpunkers went crazy over the songs about canned peaches, mobile homes, and crop pests and the childishly simple three chords of "Lump," which dominated airwaves during the summer of 1995.

Although it was fun, and often funny, the band was quickly tagged a "novelty act" by critics. "Toob Amplifier," from *II*, proves that slight wrong; the song is reminiscent of latter-day Replacements, though it does share album space with "Puffy Little Shoes," a song in search of an overstuffed cartoon character. The Presidents broke up in 1998; *Pure Frosting* served as a posthumous B-sides album. By 2000's *Freaked Out and Small*, the band was back together, still writing ditties that were clever and always weird. In no small bit of irony for a band truly rooted in Seattle, their cover of "Cleveland Rocks" became the theme to *The Drew Carey Show.* —C.R.C.

Elvis Presley

★★★★★ Elvis Presley (1956; RCA, 1999)
★★★★★ Elvis (1956; RCA, 1999)
★★★★★ Elvis' Christmas Album (1957; RCA, 1990)
★★★★★ Elvis' Golden Records, Vol. 1 (1958; RCA, 1999)
★★★★★ His Hand in Mine (1960; RCA, 1999)
★★★★★ 50,000,000 Elvis Fans Can't Be Wrong: Elvis' Golden Records, Vol. 2 (1960; RCA, 1999)
★★★ Blue Hawaii (1961; RCA, 1997) (expanded, with 14 bonus tracks)
★★★★ Elvis' Golden Records, Vol. 3 (1963; RCA, 1997)
★★★★★ How Great Thou Art (1967; RCA, 1999)
★★★★★ Elvis (TV Special) (1968; RCA, 1999)
★★★★ Elvis' Golden Records, Vol. 4 (1968; RCA, 2001)
★★★★★ From Elvis in Memphis (1969; RCA, 1999)
★★★★ On Stage—February, 1970 (1970; RCA, 1999)
★★★★ Elvis in Person at the International Hotel, Las Vegas, Nevada (1970; RCA, 2001)
★★★★ Elvis Sings the Wonderful World of Christmas (1971; RCA, 1990)
★★★★★ He Touched Me (1972; RCA, 1999)

★★ As Recorded at Madison Square Garden (1972; RCA, 2001)
★★★ Aloha from Hawaii (Via Satellite) (1973; RCA, 1999)
★★ From Elvis Presley Boulevard, Memphis, Tennessee (1976; RCA, 1999)
★★★ Moody Blue (1977; RCA, 2000)
★★★★ Memories of Christmas (1982; RCA, 1990)
★★★★ Elvis' Gold Records, Vol. 5 (1984; RCA, 1997)
★★★★★ Known Only to Him: Elvis Gospel, 1957–1971 (RCA, 1989)
★★★★ The Million Dollar Quartet (1990; RCA, 2002)
★★★★★ The King of Rock 'n' Roll: The Complete '50s Masters (RCA, 1992)
★★★★★ The Top Ten Hits (RCA, 1987)
★★★ Christmas Classics (RCA, 1992)
★★★½ Blue Christmas (RCA, 1992)
★★★★★ From Nashville to Memphis: The Essential '60s Masters (RCA, 1993)
★★★★★ Amazing Grace: His Greatest Sacred Songs (RCA, 1994)
★★★★★ If Every Day Was Like Christmas (RCA, 1994)
★★★★ Heart and Soul (1995; RCA, 2003)
★★★★ Command Performances: The Essential '60s Masters II (RCA, 1995)
★★★★★ Walk a Mile in My Shoes: The Essential '70s Masters (RCA, 1995)
★★★★ Elvis 56 (1996; RCA, 2003)
★★★ Great Country Songs (1996; RCA, 2003)
★★★½ An Afternoon in the Garden (RCA, 1997)
★★★½ Platinum: A Life In Music (RCA, 1997)
★★★ Greatest Jukebox Hits (RCA, 1997)
★★½ A Touch of Platinum, Vol. 2 (RCA, 1998)
★★★½ Rhythm and Country (RCA, 1998)
★★★★ Tiger Man (RCA, 1998)
★★★★ Memories: The '68 Comeback Special (RCA, 1998)
★★★★★ Sunrise (RCA, 1999)
★★★ The Home Recordings (RCA, 1999)
★★★★ Suspicious Minds (RCA, 1999)
★★★★ Tomorrow Is a Long Time (RCA, 1999)
★★★½ Artist of the Century (RCA, 1999)
★★★½ Burning Love (RCA, 1999)
★★★ The Collection (RCA, 1999)
★★★★ Can't Help Falling in Love: The Hollywood Hits (1999; RCA, 2003)
★★★ It's Christmas Time (RCA, 1999)
★★★★ That's the Way It Is: Special Edition (RCA, 2000)
★★★★½ Peace in the Valley: The Complete Gospel Recordings (RCA, 2000)
★★★ White Christmas (RCA, 2000)
★★★★ Elvis Ballads, Vol. 2 (RCA, 2001)
★★★ Live in Las Vegas (RCA, 2001)

★★★★ The 50 Greatest Love Songs (RCA, 2001)
★★★★ The Country Side of Elvis (RCA, 2001)
★★★★ He Is My Everything: The Gospel Series (RCA, 2001)
★★★★ Today, Tomorrow & Forever (RCA, 2002)
★★★★ Elvis: 30 #1 Hits (RCA, 2002)
★★½ Roots Revolution: The Louisiana Hayride (Tomato, 2002)
★★★★★ 30 #1 Hits (BMG, 2003)

There was no model for Elvis Presley's success; what Sun Records head Sam Phillips sensed was something in the wind, an inevitable outgrowth of all the country and blues he was recording at his Union Avenue studio. Enter Presley in 1954, bringing with him a musical vocabulary rich in country, country blues, gospel, inspirational music, bluegrass, traditional country, and popular music—as well as a host of emotional needs that found their most eloquent expression in song. His timing was impeccable, not only as a vocalist, but with regard to the cultural zeitgeist: emerging in the first blush of America's postwar ebullience, Presley captured the spirit of a country flexing its industrial muscle, of a generation unburdened by the concerns of war, younger, more mobile, more affluent, and better educated than any that had come before.

The Sun recordings tower over Presley's later work, which, exemplary as most of it was, could not possibly have the overweening and broad import of his explosive first sessions. These were the first salvos in an undeclared war on segregated radio stations nationwide. (His initial Sun single, "Blue Moon of Kentucky" b/w "That's All Right, Mama," was released in 1954, the same year the Supreme Court outlawed segregation in public schools and Dr. Martin Luther King arrived in Montgomery to take the pulpit at Dexter Avenue Baptist Church. Overnight, it seemed, "race music," as the music industry had labeled the work of black artists, became a thing of the past, as did the pejorative "hillbilly" music. Suddenly Elvis Presley could be heard fusing musical styles on stations that would also play Ray Charles or Al Hibbler, who in turn might follow Ernest Tubb, who might follow Jo Stafford or Tony Bennett.

The Sun years, once represented by *The Complete Sun Sessions,* have been given a makeover on disc by way of the double-CD *Sunrise* collection. Unlike the previous Sun collection's random track order, *Sunrise* features one disc devoted entirely to 19 original takes; the second disc features the alternate takes, live cuts from 1955, and four tantalizing private demos recorded in 1953 and 1954. The other essential document from the Sun era is the legendary *Million Dollar Quartet* session, a December 4, 1956, summit meeting of Presley, Carl Perkins, Jerry Lee Lewis, and Johnny Cash that took place during one of Perkins' hottest Sun sessions. We hear Elvis telling the others of an exciting new R&B singer whose act he had caught in Las Vegas. "He was out there cuttin' it, man," Elvis exclaims, "and I was goin' way up in the air! I went back four nights straight, man." The singer was Jackie Wilson, then a member of Billy Ward's Dominoes, and the song Elvis was so excited about having heard this young singer perform was his own "Don't Be Cruel."

The must to avoid from this era is Tomato's woeful *Roots Revolution: The Louisiana Hayride.* Elvis's appearances on this popular Louisiana barn dance–style radio show are documented on various small labels and imports, but this release offers the unbelievably insensitive (or simply plain stupid) idea of overdubbing new musical tracks to supplement the music being made live by Elvis, his guitarist Scotty Moore, and his bassist, Bill Black. There's simply no excuse for doctoring the original tapes in this manner, even if Scotty and Bill were so far off mike as to be completely inaudible, which they aren't.

In late 1955 Sam Phillips sold Elvis' recording contract to RCA in order to keep his own business running. The artist spent the rest of his career on RCA, and since his death in 1977 the label has fed the Elvis industry with numerous reissues and box sets; has reconfigured studio albums with bonus tracks to the point where the original configurations no longer exist in the form remembered by millions of fans whose connection with Elvis predates the CD era; has deleted almost all of the '60s soundtrack albums (placing the key tracks on box sets and themed single-disc albums); and has issued so many themed albums (e.g., *Great Country Songs, Heart and Soul*) that it's hard to keep track of them all. Wading through all this is a daunting task, but the bottom line on Elvis' in-print recordings is that the quality remains high, whether it's a roiling Sun track from the early '50s or one of his final recordings, such as 1977's "Moody Blue." The discography here represents the albums RCA shows as being in print, but a visit to a record store or an online retailer will reveal numerous other, supposedly deleted titles in stock as well, including almost all of the movie soundtracks, which RCA reissued in the '90s as twofer CDs (the best of the bunch being *Viva Las Vegas/Roustabout,* which contain some of Elvis's finest studio performances of the '60s). Being an out-of-print Elvis album seems to be a temporary condition at best. Also, the shops at Graceland will from time to time offer special, limited edition CD titles unavailable anywhere else on the planet. With that in mind, the lay of the land looks something like this:

Studio and Live Albums:

Elvis' first two RCA albums remain two of the finest rock & roll albums ever released. The reissues from 1999 replete with bonus tracks don't alter that fact, but will frustrate anyone who grew up remembering *Elvis Presley* kicking off with a rousing cover of Carl Perkins' "Blue Suede Shoes" or the first sound on the monumental *Elvis* being D.J. Fontana's swinging cymbal intro to "Rip It Up." The bonus tracks represent songs that were hit singles but nonalbum tracks at the time of the original albums' releases. The big question is why the sequencing of the albums couldn't have been retained and the bonus tracks added to the end of the CD. It's an insult to an album that was great in 1956 and has lost none of its luster in the ensuing 48 years.

That said, both *Elvis Presley* and *Elvis* belong in any serious rock & roll collection, even though each album's tracks are also available on the essential box set, *The King of Rock 'n' Roll: The Complete '50s Masters*. *Elvis Presley* is a statement nonetheless of Elvis' deep roots in Americana, and of the remarkable chemistry among Elvis and his trusted musical trio, guitarist Scotty Moore, bassist Bill Black, and drummer D.J. Fontana (with RCA house producer Chet Atkins sitting in on rhythm guitar). The fare roams from country into pop ("Blue Moon"), R&B (Ray Charles' "I Got a Woman," the Drifters' "Money Honey"), blues, and the jet-fueled rockabilly Elvis had sculpted into rock & roll ("Blue Suede Shoes"). *Elvis* is even more impressive. This was Elvis' first total RCA album effort, and it couldn't have come out any better. The cover photo of a backlit, crooning Elvis in profile in a cool, light purple shirt, hair slicked back, strumming a guitar, is eye-catching in its warm tones and simple presentation. The uncredited liner notes, by an RCA staff member named Chick Crumpacker, are among the smartest ever written in the '50s. Rather than crack wise and jivey about the new teen idol, Crumpacker made a sober, sensible case for Elvis as a folksinger extending into the contemporary R&B field, a tradition established by Jimmie Rodgers, and noted the influence of important Southern gospel quartets of the day on Elvis' style. The song selections include three Little Richard covers ("Rip It Up," "Long Tall Sally," "Ready Teddy"), Leiber and Stoller's dramatic ballad "Love Me," jazzman Joe Thomas' laconic, swinging "Anyplace Is Paradise," Red Foley's heart-tugging tale of a boy and his dog, "Old Shep"—which Elvis had first performed in 1945 at the Mississippi-Alabama Fair and Dairy Show—and Aaron Schroeder and Ben Wiseman's poignant love song, "First in Line," which produced one of Elvis' most deeply felt balladeering performances (despite doing 27 takes of the song before he was satisfied). With each cut Elvis' mastery as an interpreter becomes more breathtaking, his command of nuance and subtlety (the vulnerability in his voice in "First in Line," the strength he exudes in "Ready Teddy") more astonishing in so young an artist. He was deep inside every song on *Elvis,* maybe more so than he ever would be again until his 1969 masterpiece, *From Elvis in Memphis.*

Years later, at the moment he was in danger of becoming a rock relic, Presley bid adieu to Hollywood and returned to live performing. The public found out about this in a dramatic way, when, on December 3, 1968, Elvis' face filled TV screens everywhere, his eyes set in a commanding glare, and he snarled, "If you're lookin' for trouble/you came to the right place." Tough and unequivocal, "Trouble" set the tone for an evening in which Presley reasserted his primacy as a rock & roll artist. His ammo was blues, gospel, and powerhouse rock & roll; in the special's most memorable sequence, he played live in the round with his former band members Scotty Moore and D.J. Fontana (and other friends, including his army buddy guitarist Charlie Hodge, who in the '70s would be noted mostly for handing Elvis his scarves onstage), all of them rocking out on some of the songs Elvis made famous back in the day. He showed even greater command of ballad stylings in goosebump-raising versions of "Memories" and "Love Me Tender," added an appropriate seasonal touch in his signature Christmas song, "Blue Christmas," and revealed a hitherto-unexpressed social conscience in closing the show without comment, but instead offering a dramatic reading of "If I Can Dream." It was a performance of emotional grandeur and historical resonance, Presley refusing to be discarded by the music he helped create and seizing his moment with a fury that remains astonishing still.

While the triumph of the TV special was still fresh in the public consciousness, Presley returned with one of the finest studio albums of his career in 1969's *From Elvis in Memphis.* Recording in January 1969 at Memphis' famed American Sound Studio, Presley produced 21 usable tracks in less than a week, with another 14 tracks cut in six nights a month later. Recording in Memphis for the first time since 1955, Elvis enlisted as his producer the flamboyant Chips Moman, whose own history in the Bluff City dated back to the formation of Stax Records. With a house band that included some of the city's best players (including a large horn section and a female background chorus that became a defining feature of Elvis' '70s concerts), Moman fashioned an album that was conceptually and aesthetically whole, integrating strings and other interesting instrumental flourishes seamlessly with the rock-solid core provided by a basic Southern soul band. *From Elvis in Memphis* finds the artist moving with grace and ease from Jerry Butler's forthright, gospel-tinged advisory "Only the Strong Survive" to John Hartford's languorous "Gentle on My Mind," and he goes on to assay in compelling fashion Hank Snow's "I'm Movin' On," Johnny Tillotson's "It Keeps Right On a-Hurtin'," and Chuck Jackson's "Any Day Now," closing it out with another barbed bit of social commentary in the form of Mac Davis' "In the Ghetto." The definitive take on the Memphis sessions is provided by *Suspicious Minds,* supplanting the out-of-print *Memphis Record* as the most complete document of those critical recordings. Nine alternate takes of classics such as "Suspicious Minds" and "In the Ghetto" illuminate the critical choices that resulted in some of the most memorable recordings of Elvis' entire career. In 1973 Elvis was back in the studio in Memphis, but this time at the Mecca of Southern soul, the Stax studio, where over the course of 12 days he fashioned not hit records but some interesting excursions into his singular style of contemporary country fused with R&B, gospel, blues, and rock & roll. Eighteen of those cuts form the Stax sessions overview *Rhythm and Country,* ranging from the beautiful pop ballad popularized by Al Martino, "Spanish Eyes," to Jerry Reed's rambunctious "Talk About the Good Times" to Dottie Rambo's soaring song of faith and inspiration "If That Isn't Love."

As his comeback mirrored his arrival nearly two decades earlier, so did the live albums of the '70s approximate the movie years of the '60s—that is, wildly uneven, sporadically uninspired, but nonetheless replete with startling, penetrating performances on occasion. On the road Presley expanded the sound Moman had crafted during the Memphis sessions, adding a full orchestra behind a crack band that included the estimable James Burton on guitar, Glen D. Hardin on piano, Ronnie Tutt on drums, and Jerry Scheff on bass; in addition, he employed male and female gospel groups. *On Stage—February 1970* (now featuring six bonus tracks) and *Elvis in Person at the International Hotel, Las Vegas, Nevada* are indicative of the hard edge common to those early-'70s shows—coming off his celebrated TV special, Elvis is lean and hungry, intensely engaged at every moment in his concerts. By 1972, though, the concerts had become ritual anointings and the music spotty. Still, Elvis cut some great singles in the '70s, and the live versions of "Suspicious Minds" and "Burning Love" invariably were highlights, even when much of the rest of the fare was mostly rote. The 1973 *Aloha from Hawaii* tele-

vised spectacular brought out the best in Elvis, as he delivers, before an international audience connected by satellite, his finest self-defining treatment of Mickey Newbury's "American Trilogy"—a rich weaving of "All My Trials," "The Battle Hymn of the Republic," and "Dixie" that spoke to Presley's Southern pride and sense of mortality—and concludes with a bombastic, Baroque finale that becomes a jaw-dropping showcase of vocal muscle on Presley's part. Elvis' celebrated Madison Square Garden show from 1972 was finally issued as *An Afternoon in the Garden,* 25 years following the show in question, and spotlights a commanding if not transcendent performance. The 1968 comeback special is the focus of two recent overviews, *Tiger Man* and *Memories: The '68 Comeback Special.* The former captures the second of the two in-the-round sets filmed for the special, whereas the latter is a double-CD expanded version of the original soundtrack album, fleshed out with 22 previously unissued recordings. It's a valuable document, but more for fanatics, historians, and completists than the casual Elvis fan, for whom the original will suffice.

Gospel Albums:

Arguably the greatest white gospel singer of his time, throughout his career Elvis put the Word into the culture, and he's really the last rock & roll artist to make gospel as vital a component of his musical personality as his secular songs. Gospel pervaded Elvis' character and was a defining and enduring influence all of his days. Even in his sad last years, when he was ballooning to unrecognizability and shuffling around in a druggy haze, he always delivered the goods in concert when it came time to perform "How Great Thou Art." The individual albums Elvis cut in his lifetime are all magnificent, moving testimonies of a man's deep and abiding faith in God and God's word. *His Hand in Mine* is closest to the country church Elvis knew as a lad in its spare arrangements and scintillating blend of quartet voices, with "Working on a Building" and the potent "In My Father's House" ranking with the finest gospel performances he ever committed to tape. *How Great Thou Art* (Elvis' only Grammy winner ever, for Best Engineered Album) features a bigger band than its predecessor and even more of a pop feel, certainly by way of its hit single, a cover of the Orioles' "Crying in the Chapel." On each cut here Elvis is given splendid vocal support by the Imperials Quartet, who are especially effective on the dramatic "Somebody Bigger Than You and I" and "Where Could I Go But to the Lord," a song that surfaced again in a production number on the 1968 comeback special. From its first cut to its twelfth and last cut, 1971's *He Touched Me* is a wonder, featuring great songs and powerful performances by Elvis and the Imperials Quartet. Even with well-worn testimonials such as "Amazing Grace" and "Bosom of Abraham," *He Touched Me* has a buoyant, light spirit about it, and you can sense the depth of all the singers' commitment to the material. Elvis' version of "An Evening Prayer" rivals that of Mahalia Jackson, and the Jerry Reed–penned country-pop treatise, "A Thing Called Love," gets a nice, bouncy treatment worthy of repeat listenings. Beyond the individual studio albums, it's almost pick-'em with the excellent anthologies of Elvis' gospel music. The big enchilada of the bunch is *Peace in the Valley: The Complete Gospel Recordings,* a three-CD collection that encompasses all the recordings from the three studio albums, a host of previously unreleased alternate takes, and an entire disc compiled from various sources, such as the *Million Dollar Quartet* session, the *Ed Sullivan Show* (featuring the national debut of "Peace in the Valley"), and the gospel medley from the 1968 comeback special. If that's too much ephemera, check out the double-CD *Amazing Grace: His Greatest Sacred Songs,* which is tightly focused on the official studio releases, starting with the four cuts that fleshed out the B side of Elvis' first Christmas album (including "Peace in the Valley"), winding through 54 other cuts from the three gospel LPs, before concluding with a septet of songs comprised of two live recordings (including a powerful reading of "How Great Thou Art") and five previously unreleased songs—not least of all the full version of "Lead Me, Guide Me," the song featured in a scene from the documentary, *Elvis: That's the Way It Is,* in which Elvis and J.D. Sumner and the Stamps do a verse and chorus at the piano between shows. A truncated overview of the gospel highlights is provided by *He Is My Everything: The Gospel Series,* with 14 tracks from Elvis' gospel catalogue, the highlight being an informal performance of "The Lord's Prayer."

Compilations:

The various compilations in the Presley catalogue offer both greatest-hits surveys and single-genre spotlights. The standard-bearer of this category is the wonderful five-volume series of *Elvis' Golden Records* (Vol. 5 is titled "Gold" records, but it's part of the same series as the first four volumes), all of which have been remastered and expanded with bonus cuts. Even in their original 12-song editions, these volumes were a great way for the Elvis fan to follow the arc of the King's career, from "Heartbreak Hotel" to "Moody Blue," even though there is little in the way of liner copy to offer any critical perspective on the work. The music speaks volumes, though, and with each disc having additional tracks, the portrait of the artist

through the years is more complete and complex. As an alternative to the multiple Golden Records discs, the 38-track, double-CD *Top Ten Hits* spotlights every Top 10 hit of Presley's career. That's a lot of good music, but it also omits anything from the Sun years, all of his gospel recordings, and a few other significant but non–Top 10 singles. Much the same problem attends *30 #1 Hits*—what's here is choice, but only part of a much larger and exceedingly important story. Besides, it happens to have 31 #1 hits, with JXL's 2002 dance remix of "A Little Less Conversation" bringing up the rear of the album. For the tender, romantic side of Elvis, nothing beats the superb ballad performances to be found on *Heart and Soul, Elvis Ballads, Vol. 2,* and, most highly recommended, *The 50 Greatest Love Songs. Great Country Songs* and the 51-track overview, *The Country Side of Elvis,* show him at ease with almost every style of country music and, on a more interesting note, incorporating pop influences in a way that only enhances the country elements in his arrangements—something contemporary mainstream Nashville has yet to learn. Released originally in 1996 and remixed (with the same tracks; no bonus cuts here) in 2003, *Elvis 56* is heavily weighted toward material that appeared on Presley's first two studio albums, supplemented by nonalbum singles, including such key entries as "Hound Dog," "Don't Be Cruel," "Too Much," "Any Way You Want Me," and "I Want You, I Need You, I Love You." The material favors Elvis' R&B/blues bent, ranging from covers of a couple of Little Richard hits, Lloyd Price's R&B boiler "Lawdy Miss Clawdy," Ray Charles' "I Got a Woman," two Arthur "Big Boy" Crudup tunes, and the first of many Leiber and Stoller songs in the Presley canon, including "Love Me" as well as "Hound Dog."

Movie Albums:

If any aspect of Presley's career is more readily dismissed than his movies, it would be the music in those 33 films (including two documentaries). But even the least among the films often featured a couple of interesting songs that Elvis made the most of, and a good number of bona fide hits sprang from the soundtracks—sometimes well after the fact: witness 2002's surprise hit remix of "A Little Less Conversation" from the soundtrack of *Live a Little, Love a Little.* Twenty-two soundtrack songs comprise *Can't Help Falling in Love,* a remixed, remastered reissue of a 1999 anthology. Elvis' favorite writers are well represented: Leiber and Stoller are on board with five classics (including three title songs: "Jailhouse Rock," "Loving You," and "King Creole"); Doc Pomus and Mort Shuman are here with the exquisite, exciting, and right-on "Viva

Las Vegas"; Otis Blackwell is cowriter of three terrific songs, including "Return to Sender" and "One Broken Heart for Sale"; and three songs from the pens of Fred Wise and Ben Weisman are featured, most notably the self-affirming "Follow That Dream." Nothing here will ignite an aesthetic reassessment of the movies in question, but these tracks prove that the "movie years," far from being a waste, found Elvis producing a lot of good music, not all of which has ever been properly acknowledged for the excellent work it is. A compilation that might well have been titled "essential" is the 18-track *Tomorrow Is a Long Time,* which gathers 18 tough tracks from Elvis' '60s precomeback years. Anyone who has studied Elvis' soundtrack recordings from that time knows that in between "(There's) No Room to Rhumba in a Sports Car" and "He's Your Uncle, Not Your Dad," Elvis was filling out the LPs with some spirited, committed vocal performances. This disc represents a healthy portion of those cuts, although the best release in this vein is no longer in print—*The Lost Album.* But *Tomorrow Is a Long Time* is a winner, whether it's in tender ballad performances of "Love Letters" or Eddy Arnold's country classic "You Don't Know Me"; hard-charging rock & roll on the order of a gritty take on Chuck Berry's "Too Much Monkey Business" (which might be heard as a metaphor for Elvis' career at that point); Jerry Reed's "Guitar Man," Willie Dixon's "Big Boss Man," or certainly the sensitive treatment he gives Dylan's "Tomorrow Is a Long Time."

Box Sets:

RCA has done right by Elvis in the box set department. Apart from the $400-plus, 30-CD *The Collection* and the 30-disc, velvet-covered *Blue Suede Shoes Collection,* the various Elvis boxes are solid, reasonably priced journeys through an amazing career, and there are enough options to satisfy the hard-core fan who collects everything as well as those on a limited budget who still want a sense of a towering 20th-Century artist's career arc. The three key boxes are 1992's *The King of Rock 'n' Roll: The Complete '50s Masters,* 1993's *From Nashville to Memphis: The Essential '60s Masters,* and 1995's *Walk a Mile in My Shoes: The Essential '70s Masters.* Note that only one of the three is billed as *Complete;* the '60s box omits soundtrack and gospel recordings (which are available in other collections—in fact, the double-disc *Command Performances: The Essential '60s Masters II* is nothing but soundtrack highlights, as a supplement to the first '60s box), whereas the five-CD '70s box breaks down into two discs of singles, two of studio essentials, and a live show comprised of highlights from several concert dates. Still, in three multiple-CD boxes, these collections offer a breathtaking journey through the Elvis era, even without the soundtrack music (although the '50s box does include the three songs Elvis performed in *Love Me Tender*) and the gospel. Well annotated and profusely illustrated, these boxes are model presentations of a monumental body of work. The four-CD *Platinum: A Life in Music* is consistently interesting, but it's a completist's package, as most of its 100 tracks are alternate takes of material ranging from the Sun years to "Way Down" from the *Moody Blue* sessions. *Platinum*'s big selling point upon release was the inclusion of a 1954 demo of "I'll Never Stand In Your Way," with a tentative but bristling Elvis accompanying himself on acoustic guitar. You can hear the pent-up energy in his voice, the sense of wanting to break free of the song and soar, and it's exhilarating, knowing what was indeed to come only a short while later. Five months following the release of *Platinum: A Life in Music* came a sequel, *A Touch of Platinum, Vol. 2,* a two-disc set featuring 44 of the 50 tracks on discs two and three of its predecessor, with 18 of the tracks being alternate takes. Mark this one for completists only. A juggernaut of hits defines the three-CD *Artist of the Century* box, released in 1999. A self-contained alternative to the various *Golden Records* volumes, the set begins with "That's All Right" from 1954 and winds up three discs and 74 cuts later in 1976, with "For the Heart." Curiously "Kentucky Rain" (not merely one of his best '70s singles, but one of his best ever) and "Moody Blue" are absent.

One of the weirder boxes in the catalogue is 2002's *Today, Tomorrow & Forever.* Over the course of 100 tracks on four discs, this collection focuses on alternate takes, soundtrack recordings, and live recordings. A show taped in Arkansas on May 6, 1956, is the big news: as it shows Elvis, newly ensconced at RCA and with his star still ascending, fiery but in command, already a polished pro in his presentation but very much the Hillbilly Cat in his attitude and energy. The title song is one of the *Lost Album* cuts that features some exceedingly sensitive singing on Elvis' part.

As for *The Collection,* its 30 CDs and $400-plus price tag come without any Sun recordings or late-'60s to early-'70s Memphis sessions. The CDs seem haphazardly assembled—some are the original versions of earlier CD releases, others have supplemented the original releases with bonus tracks. On the other hand, it does contain the entire *Elvis Country* album, a 1971 gem that ranks among the finest albums of his career. Its song selection leans heavily toward country, and within that framework toward songs of loss and longing: "Tomorrow Never Comes," written by Johnny Bond and Ernest Tubb; the Bill Monroe–Lester Flatt bluegrass standard "Little Cabin on the

Hill"; Willie Nelson's "Funny How Time Slips Away"; Bob Wills' "Faded Love"; and Hank Cochran's "Make the World Go Away." It's by far the strangest and most beautiful album Presley ever recorded, and you don't have to be a fan to find its melancholy mood a bit unsettling. Clearly the songs are ones to which Elvis felt a profound emotional connection; something in their lyrics touched him down deep, as his gripping performances attest, but the narratives seem an eerie precursor to his own sad, final days when his world was collapsing around him. The 30 discs of the equally pricey *Blue Suede Shoes Collection* feature 21 complete Elvis albums, with 653 tracks in all of generally top-drawer gospel, rock & roll, country, pop, Christmas songs, and blues—but no Sun recordings. Better to opt for the '50s, '60s, and '70s box sets for a more complete story at a more reasonable price. —D.M.

The Pretenders

★★★★★	Pretenders (Sire, 1980)
★★★½	Extended Play (EP) (Sire, 1981)
★★★	Pretenders II (Sire, 1981)
★★★★★	Learning to Crawl (Sire, 1984)
★★★★	Get Close (Sire, 1986)
★★★★½	The Singles (Sire, 1987)
★★★½	packed! (Sire, 1990)
★★★½	Last of the Independents (Sire, 1994)
★★★½	The Isle of View (Warner, 1995)
★★★★	¡Viva el Amor! (Warner, 1999)
★★★	Loose Screw (Artemis, 2002)

Today the Pretenders are little more than an outlet for singer Chrissie Hynde, but in the beginning they were a band, and a great one at that. Much of the *Pretenders'* appeal is that it is *such* a band album—this was a group that was relentlessly in the pocket, and combined the energy of punk with a healthy respect for their '60s rock elders. They also combined America (Hynde) and England (feral guitarist James Honeyman-Scott and the rest of the band) as well as, in their makeup, guys and gals. Here was a band for everyone! The only track on the album that seems wholly Hynde's is "Stop Your Sobbing"—which happens to be a Kinks song and the album's only cover. Elsewhere, the music is a group effort, from the way Hynde's wry delivery plays off the churning, odd-metered guitar riffs of "Tattooed Love Boys" to the perfectly locked rhythm work propelling "The Wait" from chorus to chorus. *Extended Play* and *Pretenders II* were relative disappointments. Sure, the players acquit themselves admirably on "Message of Love" and "Talk of the Town," but instead of adding the necessary edge to "The Adultress" or putting some bite into "Jealous Dogs," the group merely goes through the motions, playing with minimal energy and conviction.

This version of the Pretenders fell apart when bassist Pete Farndon left in early 1982, and guitarist James Honeyman-Scott died of a drug overdose soon after. Surviving Pretenders Hynde and Martin Chambers then recorded "Back on the Chain Gang" and "My City Was Gone" with ex-Rockpile guitarist Billy Bremner and bassist Tony Butler before completing *Learning to Crawl* with guitarist Robbie McIntosh and bassist Malcolm Foster. Even though this game of musical chairs affects the album's sound, it doesn't undermine the group's identity. If anything, songs like "Time the Avenger," "Watching the Clothes," and "I Hurt You" sound more like the original Pretenders.

On *Get Close*, the Pretenders are down to two members, Hynde and McIntosh. But the mood of the music is radically different, trading the aggressive rhythms of "Middle of the Road" and "Thumbelina" for the airy arabesque of "Tradition of Love" and the gentle bop of "Don't Get Me Wrong." With *packed!*, the arrangements on "Sense of Purpose" and "Hold a Candle to This" take on a low-key confidence that's halfway between the gentleness of *Get Close* and the cool maturity of *Learning to Crawl*. The album seems to be yet another "band" effort, but it's worth noting that the only Pretender pictured anywhere on the cover is Hynde. Then again, given the generally lax quality of the *packed!* performances, it's possible that the backing musicians didn't want to own up to their involvement.

Original drummer Martin Chambers (who'd left after *Get Close*) was back on board for *Last of the Independents*, which also found Hynde returning to snarling form in lyrics and attitude. New blood Adam Seymour (guitar) and Andy Hobson (bass) rose to the challenge, rocking out with such abandon you almost don't notice that the songs aren't as strong as Hynde's better moments on *packed!*; "Night in My Veins" was a tough, terrific single, as was the surging "I'm a Mother," but the hit power ballad "I'll Stand by You" has Hynde peddling the kind of Hollywood-soundtrack mush best left to pop-schlock writers like Dianne Warren. That said, Hynde sings it like she means it.

After getting her rocks off with *Independents*, Hynde slipped them quietly back in pocket for *The Isle of View*, an "unplugged" live album that featured the band supplemented by a string quartet and Blur's Damon Albarn on piano. For the most part, the experiment works on the revamped classics, like "Back on the Chain Gang" and "2000 Miles," as well as lesser-known album tracks like *packed!*'s "Criminal." With *¡Viva el Amor!*, the Pretenders were back in full-on rock mode, this time with considerably more satisfying results than on *Independents*. Hynde is at her best when she conveys both strength and vulnerability, and she does just that on standout tracks like "Nails in the Road" and the superb "Human," singing "I can be a little cold/But you can be so cruel."

From start to finish, ¡Viva el Amor! was the Pretenders' finest hour in more than a decade, and the comparatively underwhelming Loose Screw, while not without its moments (notably, the disarmingly sweet and self-analytical reggae-flavored "Complex Person"), does little to steal the crown.   —J.D.C./R.SK.

Primal Scream

★★	Sonic Flower Groove (Elevation, 1987)
★★	Primal Scream (Mercenary, 1989)
★★★	Screamadelica (Sire, 1991)
★★★	Give Out but Don't Give Up (Sire, 1994)
★★★★½	Vanishing Point (Sire, 1997)
★★★★	XTRMNTR (Astralwerks, 2000)

The members of Primal Scream encapsulate the past 20 years of British rock: They've been twee popsters, baggy-pants ravers, retro rockers, reggae mystics, and noise-rock anarchists, convincing in nearly every role. Bobby Gillespie began as the Jesus and Mary Chain's drummer, which had to be one of the easiest jobs in '80s rock; Primal Scream's early records, such as the ace 1986 single "Velocity Girl," were standard indie pop. The Scream really got its own myth going with the drug-addled, dance-crazed, techno-frazzled Screamadelica, which sucked up acid house and recast it in prog-rock terms. Screamadelica wasn't all that great—did the world need a funkier Moody Blues, really?—but since the Brits didn't have any Prince or hip-hop of their own, tracks like "Loaded" seemed quite innovative and made the band U.K. stars.

Give Out but Don't Give Up was another stylistic makeover; this time, the Primals baffled their fans by pretending to be shit-kicking blues-rockers, even sticking a Confederate flag on the cover. Silly, to be sure, but good fun—"Rocks" has a slippery sex groove the Black Crowes would sell their Lava lamps for. Next time out, though, Primal Scream actually made the psychedelic dance-trance masterpiece of its dreams, the still-astonishing Vanishing Point. The tunes were steeped in head-spinning dub textures, sweetly spliffed melody, and '70s pulp cinema, from the harrowing techno dystopia of "Kowalski" and "If They Move, Kill 'Em" to the ethereal soul hymn "Star." It's an album to disappear into for days at a time. XTRMNTR was a ridiculous move into big ugly Stooges-style guitar noise, with a couple of casting coups: The band now included not only Stone Roses bassist Mani but long-lost My Bloody Valentine gui-

tarist Kevin Shields. The tempos were good and fast and stupid; the lyrics were bomb-tossing political broadsides. All around, a hilarious listen, and the Scream really shook its bones in feedback freakouts like "Accelerator." It's gratifying to hear a bunch of haggard old pros willing to experiment—and to keep getting better with age.   —R.S.

Primus

★★½	Suck on This (1989; Prawn Song, 2002)
★★★	Frizzle Fry (1990; Prawn Song, 2002)
★★★½	Sailing the Seas of Cheese (Interscope/EastWest, 1991)
★★★	Pork Soda (Interscope/Atlantic, 1993)
★★½	Tales from the Punchbowl (Interscope/Atlantic, 1995)
★★	Brown Album (Interscope, 1997)
★★	Rhinoplasty (Interscope, 1998)
★★	Antipop (Interscope, 1999)

Blending serpentine arrangements and tarantula-fingered bass patterns that Rush might admire, and vocals that suggest alternative-rock's answer to Mel Blanc, Primus became one of the '90s' more improbable success stories. Singer-bassist Les Claypool brings a demented gleam to his tall tales on the live recordings that make up Suck on This, and an offbeat but engaging sense of song ("To Defy the Laws of Tradition," the antiwar "Too Many Puppies") to Frizzle Fry. Claypool's 10-finger dances up and down the fretboard are fanned into blue-flame conflagrations by Tim Alexander's agile drumming and Larry LaLonde's strafing guitar. Sailing the Seas of Cheese again pours on the virtuosity, this time with a greater sense of menace. The satire takes on darker overtones, with help from guest vocalist Tom Waits on "Tommy the Cat." Pork Soda is a mind-boggling exercise in technique, particularly during the giddy Welcome to this World, and Bob is an eerie evocation of suicide. But by "Tales from the Punchbowl," the humor curdles into sophomoric songs such as "Wynona's Big Brown Beaver," a novelty hit. Brown Album suffers from a reconfigured lineup, with Alexander's departure hindering the interplay. Rhinoplasty bides time with radical reinterpretations of songs by XTC, Stanley Clarke, and Metallica, among others. On Antipop, Claypool insists, "I'll run against the grain till the day I drop," but he and the band are reduced to repeating themselves, save for the atmospheric Pink Floyd homage "Eclectic Electric."   —G.K.

Prince

★★½	For You (Warner Bros., 1978)
★★★★	Prince (Warner Bros., 1979)

★★★★★ Dirty Mind (Warner Bros., 1980)
★★★½ Controversy (Warner Bros., 1981)
★★★★½ 1999 (Warner Bros., 1982)
★★★★★ Purple Rain (Warner Bros., 1984)
★★½ Around the World in a Day (Paisley Park, 1985)
★★★★½ Parade (Paisley Park, 1986)
★★★★★ Sign O' the Times (Paisley Park, 1987)
★★★½ The Black Album (Warner Bros., recorded 1987, released 1994)
★★★½ Lovesexy (Paisley Park, 1988)
★★ Batman (Warner Bros., 1989)
★★★ Graffiti Bridge (Paisley Park, 1990)
★★½ Diamonds and Pearls (Paisley Park, 1991)
★★★★ The Love Symbol Album (Paisley Park, 1992)
★★★★ The Hits 1 (Paisley Park, 1993)
★★★★ The Hits 2 (Paisley Park, 1993)
★★★★ The Hits/The B-Sides (Paisley Park, 1993)
★★½ Come (Warner Bros., 1994)
★★★★ The Gold Experience (Warner Bros., 1995)
★★★½ Chaos & Disorder (Warner Bros., 1996)
★★★★ Emancipation (NPG/EMI, 1996)
★★★ Crystal Ball (NPG, 1998)
★★ The Vault . . . Old Friends 4 Sale (Warner Bros., 1999)
★½ Rave Un2 the Joy Fantastic (NPG/Arista, 1999)
★★★★ The Very Best of Prince (Rhino, 2001)
★ The Rainbow Children (NPG, 2001)
★★½ One Nite Alone . . . Live! (NPG, 2002)
★★★½ Musicology (NPG/Columbia, 2004)

James Brown may have been the hardest-working man in show business, but no one in the history of rock & roll has covered more ground than Prince. As a songwriter—for himself and for others ranging from the Time, Sheila E., and Vanity 6 to the Bangles and Chaka Khan—he ranks with Lennon and McCartney, Bob Dylan, and Smokey Robinson; as a guitarist, with Hendrix and Steve Cropper. He was the most influential record producer and arranger of the '80s and the most influential creative speller in all of pop (though Slade came close). No artist has swung as fluently from style to style (hard rock, stripped-down funk, jazzy show tunes, intoxicated balladry, kid-pop, dance raunch), and only JB has put on more incendiary live shows. And if Prince had done nothing but stand stock still onstage and sung other people's material, he'd have locked up his place in the Rock and Roll Hall of Fame; in the last three decades, popular music has produced few finer singers.

He started as a wunderkind, a black teenager from a north Minneapolis broken home (his father played jazz piano and led a trio; his mother sang) who'd taught himself every basic instrument while playing in cover bands during high school. Minneapolis is an isolated city, eight car-hours away from Chicago, the nearest large city, and with a small African-American population. Prince cut his teeth playing and listening to rock as well as R&B, and on *For You,* the debut cut when Prince was 20 (his bio trimmed two years off his age to make him appear even more of a prodigy), he leaned on light funk (the black-radio hit "Soft and Wet"), balladry ("Baby"), and R&B but also ended it with a hard rock song, "I'm Yours." 1979's *Prince* was even rockier and a lot more assured, with one hit ("I Wanna Be Your Lover," #11 pop and # 1 R&B), one future classic ("I Feel for You," a hit for Chaka Khan in 1984), and plenty else to chew on, most notably "Bambi" (a heavy-metal tale of a frustrated crush on a lesbian) and the molasses-tempo "When We're Dancing Close and Slow."

Dirty Mind remains one of the most radical 180-degree turns in pop history. Here, Prince flavored his rock with funk rather than the other way around, and the tinny keyboard hooks of the title cut, "Do It All Night," and the outrageously great "When You Were Mine" owed plenty to new wave. He also honored the title concept to the letter: cuts like the droll "Head" and the frantic "Sister" can still raise eyebrows. Throughout, Prince sounds furious, either at war ("Partyup") or with desire (take your pick), and his forthrightness marked him as a rock hero in the vein of Johnny Rotten or John Lennon as well as an heir to the soul-music throne. *Controversy* pushed this direction further ("Sexuality," "Jack U Off"), but also expanded his sonic palette with an increasing emphasis on synthesizers, although the best song is the most conventional: "Do Me Baby," a gorgeous, piano-led love song that features what may still be his best vocal performance.

1999 may be Prince's most influential album: its synth-and-drum machine–heavy arrangements codified the "Minneapolis sound" that loomed over mid-'80s R&B and pop, not to mention the next two decades' worth of electro, house, and techno. The first half is all anthems: "1999," "Little Red Corvette" (the rock-radio breakthrough he'd been after since the beginning; it reached #6 on the pop chart), "Delirious," the nervous grind of "Let's Pretend We're Married," and the sardonic "DMSR" ("All the white people clap your hands on the four now . . . one, two, three [clap]"). The rest is more experimental (the sound effects on the bridge of "Lady Cab Driver," the ominous textures of "Something in the Water"), although the rock ballad "Free" hinted at what was to come.

Which, as it turned out, was world domination. The movie was cartoonishly melodramatic, but the music of *Purple Rain,* made with his band the Revolution, remains the most accessible of Prince's career. Guitar heroics? Check ("Let's Go Crazy," "Computer Blue," "Purple Rain"). Plush candy pop? Double-check ("Take Me With U"). Edge-of-frenzy slow jams? You got it ("The Beautiful One"). And oh yeah—an abstract lyric about a deteriorating relationship set to a weird drum-machine pulse and no bass line. That must be the hit, right? It was: "When Doves Cry" topped the charts for a month and was the biggest single of 1984, not exactly a bad year for pop singles.

Around the World in a Day, released a scant ten months after *Purple Rain,* proved that, just in case you missed *Dirty Mind,* Prince would do things his way or not at all. And miss it you might, because most of *Around the World* feels like an exercise in pop-psychedelia instead of a full-fledged immersion in it. Luckily, *Parade,* the soundtrack to the dreadful *Under the Cherry Moon,* Prince's second film, fitted a leaner, more finely polished psychedelia with a healthy shot of funk; cuts like the steel drum–happy "New Position" and the bushy-tailed "Mountains" were coy without cutesiness, and "Kiss" remains Prince's best single.

Sign O' the Times, made after the Revolution's breakup, remains his best album, the most complete example of his artistry's breadth, and arguably the finest album of the 1980s. The electroblues title hit was frequently identified as the source of the disc's tone, but mostly it served as a somber keynote to a wild party: "U Got the Look" is what funk metal might have sounded like if it weren't for slap-bass; the live-in-Paris "It's Gonna Be a Beautiful Night" is more live than you'll ever be; and "Housequake" is the quirkiest and funniest James Brown homage ever. But it's his lyrics that take the real leap: "If I Was Your Girlfriend" and "I Could Never Take the Place of Your Man" are among the most honest relationship songs he or anyone else has ever written, and "The Cross" works as much for the black-and-white sketch of its lyric as for its equally monochromatic music, which unexpectedly calls up the Velvet Underground.

His next disc would not be so devout. The funky, ribald *Black Album* is an excellent throwaway, and would have remained so had Prince not had a religious epiphany (brought on, according to biographers, by having been dosed with the drug ecstasy in a Minneapolis nightclub) and decided to shelve it. (It would be released in 1994 as part of his get-out-of-contract card.) In its place came *Lovesexy,* infuriatingly programmed as a single audio track on the CD version, which meant you had to take the bad ("Positivity," the *Black Album* leftover "When 2 R in Love") with the good ("Alphabet St.," "I Wish U Heaven"). This set the tone for pretty much every Prince album of the

'90s, though the good on them is a lot better than it's usually given credit for.

Following the sleepwalking *Batman,* Prince issued another bad movie with a good soundtrack, *Graffiti Bridge,* which is interesting primarily for its guest stars (Mavis Staples, the Time, a teenage Tevin Campbell) and for the fact that it now sounds as dated as the new-jack swing it apes. *Diamonds and Pearls,* on the other hand, aims at hip-hop with the addition of Tony M, a rapper who cannot rap. Its thick, cushy sound is also a blatant aim for commercial appeal that only occasionally hits its target, although when it does— "Cream," "Gett Off," the surprisingly biting "Money Don't Matter 2 Nite"—it's pretty great.

The Love Symbol Album sounds like Prince on autopilot, but that's one reason it's a rebound from the overthought and lifeless *Diamonds and Pearls.* (It's also the last Tony M album, thank God.) It's the true beginning of Prince's second phase, in which his genre multitasking feels less like a state-of-the-pop-union address and more like variations on the theme that is Prince himself, who wasn't Prince anymore—in 1993, he changed his name to the title of his most recent album, whatever that was. By now, the vast majority of his nonfervent followers were off the bus, and Prince decided he didn't like his Warner Bros. contract anymore. Bad timing, guy. His next album, *Come,* was blatant contract-fulfiller, credited to "Prince 1958–1993," but when he put out a single, "The Most Beautiful Girl in the World," on indie label Bellmark the same year, it went to #1 (thanks in no small part to some heavy spending on independent promotion by Prince himself), and the fight was on. Prince was a slave, and his public would suffer.

How much it suffered tends to be exaggerated; while *Chaos & Disorder,* another contract-fulfiller, was obviously tossed off, its offhandedness has a frisky appeal, and it was sandwiched by a pair of more major works. *The Gold Experience* occasionally tries too hard, but "P Control" is his funniest and therefore best rap excursion (hint: the *P* doesn't stand for "princess"), while "319" and "Billy Jack Bitch" successfully resurrect his *Controversy*-vintage synth sound. *Emancipation,* conceived long before Prince got out of his Warners contract and issued five months after *Chaos,* is surprisingly short on filler and features some of his most underrated songs: "In This Bed I Scream" harks back to the Revolution days, while the house beats of "Slave" and "The Human Body" hint at what he could have done with the form he'd so heavily influenced. And the covers—the first he'd ever commercially recorded—kill, particularly a fiery take on Joan Osborne's "One of Us" and an astonishingly supple version of the Delfonics' "La, La, La Means

I Love U." At three discs, *Emancipation* is too long, but it's rich nevertheless, and considering how many used or remaindered copies are out there, it's a bargain besides.

From there, Prince just seemed to keep sliding. *Crystal Ball* is three discs of interesting, sometimes great ("Crucial," the prototype for *Sign O' the Times'* "Adore") outtakes and rarities, plus an okay bonus acoustic album, *The Truth. The Vault . . . Old Friends 4 Sale* is exactly what it sounds like: contractual obligation outtakes. *Rave Un2 the Joy Fantastic* is loaded with guest stars (Chuck D, Gwen Stefani, Ani DiFranco) and not one single interesting song. Which doesn't mean it's worse than 2001's *The Rainbow Children,* which was sold with a sticker advertising it as "controversial," probably because no one had ever combined lite-jazz treacle with Jehovah's Witness dogma to such an unprecedented degree. That's not quite what we meant when we asked for another groundbreaking album, Prince.

After *Rainbow,* even diehards thought Prince was finished, but when you hit bottom, there's nowhere to go but up. *One Nite Alone . . . Live!* isn't perfect, but some of the rearranged older material shines, and when Prince strolled back into public consciousness in early 2004, thanks to appearances at the Grammys and his Rock and Roll Hall of Fame induction, his new good-guy stance was still trumped by his blazing showmanship. *Musicology* isn't quite the great comeback it's claimed to be, but after nearly a decade in the wilderness, its solid groove and modest feel will certainly do. As for that wilderness era, maybe someday he'll let some corporate entity make a compilation. Speaking of which, 1993's three-disc *The Hits/ The B-Sides* box is full of great music, but the sequencing could be sharper and the strict division between two discs of hits (also available separately) and one of B sides feels too neat to do his frequent tangents justice, while the single-disc Rhino collection is—for the most protean, prolific, and brilliant artist of his generation—completely useless. —M.M.

Prince Paul

★★★½   Psychoanalysis: What Is It? (WordSound, 1996)
★★★★½   Prince Paul Presents a Prince Among Thieves (Tommy Boy, 1999)

Handsome Boy Modeling School

★★★★   So . . . How's Your Girl? (Tommy Boy, 1999)

It seems like every time rapper, DJ, producer, and hip-hop conceptualist Prince Paul (Paul Houston) undertakes a major project, something new happens. He innovated as a young teen DJ'ing for Stetsasonic,

where he added jazz licks to James Brown samples. But his big wave hit after he produced De La Soul's 3 *Feet High and Rising.* As Jimi Hendrix was to guitar in rock, this album was to the sonic possibilities of hip-hop: Prince Paul showed how to incorporate sound effects, comedy and drama sketches, and types of music limited only by the imagination of how to use them. He was an in-demand producer for 3rd Bass and Big Daddy Kane, but he put his fascination with pulp culture on full display in 1994 with the "horrorcore" rap group the Gravediggaz (see separate entry). Although Prince Paul barely integrated the sketches and gags with the music on 3 *Feet High and Rising,* he had advanced well beyond that by his solo debut, *Psychoanalysis: What Is It?.* He understood that his hip-hop collages should not simply be like movie soundtracks with dialogue left in, but more like vintage radio plays—theater in the mind. Paul applies cathartic therapy to his own distressed brain in *Psychoanalysis* by satirizing or just putting his stamp on a manic sequence of hip-hop styles: happy, murderous, and plain loony. Dancing in your head, indeed.

His next two releases would put Prince Paul on top as all-time hip-hop dramatist. *Prince Paul Presents a Prince Among Thieves* is one of the sharpest and most penetrating blaxploitation movies ever made, and it happens to be a CD. The album works as pure soundtrack, but never flags as it tells the story of aspiring rapper Tariq (played by Sha), his friend the slick and savvy True (Breeze), and the strange tangle of their destinies in an underworld scam led by crime boss Mr. Large (Chubb Rock) and his goons such as gun master Crazy Lou (Kool Keith). Like they say—hardboiled.

The Handsome Boy Modeling School, though telling a daft and witty tale, is almost as biting. A team production from Paul and Dan the Automator, *So . . . How's Your Girl?* includes protest and sex interludes, but the running themes are self-image and self-love, succeeding in this celebrity-soaked universe, and humanity's addiction to bullshit talk and stupid swindles. The sounds flow with variety and surprise equaled only by the best of DJ Shadow, who produces a standout track. The many other players include Money Mark, DJ Kid Koala, and . . . Father Guido Sarducci? Everyone contributes a lively texture or turn of phrase, however, instead of the usual guest-star slop-through. Prince Paul has a wide-open future. —M.MI.

John Prine

★★★★★   John Prine (Atlantic, 1971)
★★★½   Diamonds in the Rough (Atlantic, 1972)
★★★½   Sweet Revenge (Atlantic, 1973)
★★★½   Common Sense (Atlantic, 1975)

★★★ Prime Prine (Atlantic, 1976)
★★★ Bruised Orange (Asylum, 1978)
★★★ Pink Cadillac (Asylum, 1979)
★★★½ Storm Windows (Oh Boy, 1980)
★★★ Aimless Love (Oh Boy, 1984)
★★★ German Afternoons (Oh Boy, 1985)
★★★★½ The Missing Years (Oh Boy, 1991)
★★★ A John Prine Christmas (EP) (Oh Boy, 1994)
★★★★★ Great Days: The John Prine Anthology (Rhino, 1993)
★★★ Lost Dogs and Mixed Blessings (Oh Boy, 1995)
★★★ Live on Tour (Oh Boy, 1997)
★★★★★ In Spite of Ourselves (Oh Boy, 1999)
★★ Souvenirs (Oh Boy, 2000)

Wielding a wicked tongue and a sharp eye, John Prine introduced an unforgettable cast of characters on his eponymous 1971 debut. There's an OD-bound Vietnam vet ("Sam Stone"), a pair of loveless lovers ("Donald and Lydia"), and several neglected elderly people who can still speak their minds ("Angel From Montgomery," "Hello in There"). And who's John Prine? That guy with the "Illegal Smile" over there, the one "digesting the *Reader's Digest* in the back of the dirty bookstore." Prine's deep, reedy voice takes some getting used to, but he manages to turn his croak into an affecting country twang. The generous amount of pedal steel guitar helps quite a bit, coaxing melody out of Prine's tightly constructed sketches and reveries. That twang comes to the fore on the raucous "Yes I Guess They Oughtta Name a Drink After You" (from *Diamonds in the Rough*). But the rest of this followup reworks the debut's themes—Vietnam, Jesus—in a less striking fashion. Prine's career continued under the "difficult but rewarding" banner for the remainder of the '70s and '80s. He loves throwing curveballs and boomerangs.

Laden with more tart country influences, *Sweet Revenge* is, like its name, somewhat bitter; the tersely observed "Christmas in Prison" and "Grandpa Was a Carpenter" capture Prine's high standard. *Common Sense* administers a moody rock thrashing to what are probably sensible-enough songs; the words get swallowed up in the melancholy blur. The best-of format *(Prime Prine)* hardly suits this mercurial artist because even Prine's fans can't agree on what his best tracks are. *Bruised Orange*, which features a collaboration with Phil Spector ("If You Don't Want My Love"), is a subdued, quietly sung outing. *Pink Cadillac* is the polar opposite; muddy-sounding, insanely raucous rockabilly recorded at the source, Sun Studios in Memphis. Prine's vocal control (never faultless) seemed to waver a bit on his self-produced, lo-fi

'80s albums *Great Days*, a superb two-CD anthology, skims the cream from his first two decades and, along with *John Prine*, is the best introduction to his work.

Prine came back as strong as ever with 1991's *The Missing Years*. Subtle assists from various friends and the most graspable set of Prine originals since the '70s—songs like "It's a Big Old Goofy World" and "Jesus, the Missing Years"—reintroduced him as a skewed folk-rock elder. *Lost Dogs and Mixed Blessings* continued in the same vein with less memorable results, though "Lake Marie," a spoken meditation on the bitterness of divorce (a subject the much-married singer knows well), may be Prine's greatest moment on record. *In Spite of Ourselves*—a disc of country covers on which Prine duets with several female singers, most memorably Iris DeMent—may be his greatest record, period. The performances equal or better the originals, and the songs earn that highest of accolades: They could have been written by Prine himself. *Souvenirs* is a disc of self-covers: great songs, frayed voice. Like his Christmas-themed EP and live disc, it's a for-fans-only stopgap. —M.C./M.M.

Procol Harum

★★★★ A Salty Dog—Plus (West Side, 1969)
★★ The Prodigal Stranger (Zoo, 1991)
★★½ The Long Goodbye (RCA Victor, 1995)
★★★★ Greatest Hits (A&M, 1996)
★★★★ 30th Anniversary Anthology (West Side, 1997)
★★★★ Procol Harum—Plus! (West Side, 1998)
★★★½ Home Plus (West Side, 1999)
★★ Pandora's Box (West Side, 1999)
★★★ Greatest Hits (Metro, 2000)
★★★ A Whiter Shade of Pale (Disky, 2001)
★★★ Classic Tracks and Rarities: An Anthology (Metro, 2002)

Ever since Paul McCartney underscored the melody of "Eleanor Rigby" with a string quartet, many pop players have attempted a fusion of rock and classical music. The Moody Blues and Emerson, Lake and Palmer contrived grandiose hybrids; ELO nursed a much more pleasant mix; but the band that absolutely mastered the concept was Procol Harum. United by tremendous ambition, each musician was an adept soloist; Pianist Gary Brooker's voice was not only a first-rate blues vehicle, but it was graced with the command to handle Procol's ofttimes thunderous lyrics; Matthew Fisher played organ with rare subtlety; B.J. Wilson was a drummer as unique in his way as Keith Moon or John Bonham; Robin Trower brandished technique as well as sheer rock power. And in Keith Reid, a literary figure who wrote the words to their songs, Procol found a lyricist whose odd, vaguely surreal poetry matched the musicians' distinctive vision.

Even if Trower and Wilson were brought on board after its release, the staggering "Whiter Shade of Pale" provided the blueprint for Procol's early glory. Based on Bach's Suite no. 3 in D Major, this music had a haunting resonance; the single remains the centerpiece of the group's impressive debut. The two-keyboard approach, heard first on Dylan's *Highway 61 Revisited* and *Blonde on Blonde,* was employed with a fresh majesty, and Brooker's singing summoned the urgency of a prime R&B vocalist's. *Shine on Brightly* (1968) developed the group's sound; "Shine on Brightly" nearly matched the power of "Pale." Procol purveyed spacious, crafty epics with 1969's *A Salty Dog,* featuring such standout cuts as the title track, "Wreck of the Hesperus," and "Boredom." Brooker favored classical progressions; he virtually never limited himself to the standard three rock & roll chords, and while the playing was always first-rate, the group seldom came off as self-indulgent.

Matthew Fisher, however, then departed—the first of Procol's significant personnel losses. *Broken Barricades,* from 1971 (now out of print), showed the group going for a heavier, less leisurely style, especially on the full-out attack of "Simple Sister"; Procol proved it could rock with undeniable credibility in "Whiskey Train," from 1970's *Home.* Trower, the group's only true rocker, left next, and the band developed signs that it had lost its initial creative tension. *The Prodigal Stranger,* Procol Harum's 1991 comeback, was deeply uninspired. Somewhat better was the symphonic followup, *The Long Goodbye.* With its *Plus* series, West Side has done an excellent job of reissuing the band's classic albums, all with bonus tracks. Of the compilations, *30th Anniversary Anthology* is the best and the fullest. *Greatest Hits* and the now-deleted *The Best of* are interchangeable and excellent; also of note is the outstanding 1972 live album that produced a great symphonic reworking of "Conquistador," a classic from the debut.   —P.E.

The Prodigy

- ★★ Experience (Elektra, 1993; 2001)
- ★★ Music for the Jilted Generation (Muse, 1995)
- ★★★★ The Fat of the Land (Maverick/Warner Bros., 1997)
- ★★★ Prodigy Present the Dirtchamber Sessions Volume One (XL Recordings/Beggars Banquet, 1999)
- ★★★★ Always Outnumbered, Never Outgunned (Maverick/XL, 2004)

The Prodigy erupted from the British working-class county of Essex to lead a '90s techno revolution that never was, delivering electronic fire and relentless beats deep into the mainstream. They did it by colliding the astonishing mix skills of beat maestro Liam Howlett with sneering punk-rock attitude, crafting a techno blend sometimes as explosive and terrifyingly beautiful as Jimi Hendrix or the Sex Pistols. The ferocious "Firestarter" (on *The Fat of the Land*) finally took the rave to rock radio, but aside from Moby and a small crowd of one-hit beat scientists, the revolution did not take hold. Not yet.

Experience and *Music for the Jilted Generation* predate the band's embracing of punk and instead offer hypnotic, unremarkable patterns, not songs (though a 2001 reissue of *Experience* was expanded with a second disc of antic remixes and B sides). Vocals are mostly irrelevant sound effects deep in the background. Only Howlett's vivid textures hint at the muscle to come. *The Fat of the Land* was an unexpected blast of testosterone and dense beats anchored by the vocals of rapper Maxim and shouter Liam Flint, a punk cipher in cartoonish Johnny Rotten drag. Dance-floor lifers sneered at the Prodigy's sudden commercial fortunes, but reaching the masses was a real breakthrough for rave culture. Lyrics were empty of any content worth remembering, just dumb rantings on sex and violence (see "Smack My Bitch Up"). No matter. Grooves that rock as hard as metal sell the concept, closing with L7's lustful "Fuel My Fire." *Prodigy Present the Dirtchamber Sessions Volume One* suggests the full flowering of Howlett's mixing skills, spanning hip-hop to industrial-strength rock. Recastings of obscure and well-known recordings by the likes of Meat Beat Manifesto and Jane's Addiction were hardly necessary, but are a dazzling display just the same.

With 2004's *Always Outnumbered, Never Outgunned,* Howlett abandons technopunk and locks Maxim and Flint out of the studio, recruiting instead a disparate crowd of vocalists (Oasis' Liam Gallagher, Kool Keith, and Princess Superstar among them) to be mixed deep into his new postmillennial storm, erupting with the harsh Arabic mediations of "Spitfire." Beats, samples, guitars, more beats. The twitchy "Action Radar" could be early Devo or Gary Numan, redefined via lap-top. The result is less immediate than *Fat of the Land,* but just as inventive, this time more about driving grooves than songs and hooks destined for mass airplay. Rock radio is so passé.   —S.A.

Professor Longhair

- ★★★★ New Orleans Piano (Blues Originals, Vol. 2) (1953; Atlantic, 1989)

★★★★ House Party New Orleans Style (1971; Rounder, 1987)
★★★ Rock 'n' Roll Gumbo (1974; Dancing Cat, 1985)
★★★ Live on the Queen Mary (Harvest, 1978; One Way, 1993)
★★★ Crawfish Fiesta (Alligator, 1980)
★★★★★ Mardi Gras in New Orleans (Nighthawk, 1981)
★★★★ The Last Mardi Gras (Atlantic, 1982)
★★★★ Mardi Gras in Baton Rouge (Rhino, 1991)
★★★★★ 'Fess: The Professor Longhair Anthology (Rhino, 1993)
★★★★ Rum and Coke (Rhino, 1993)
★★★★ Big Chief (Rhino, 1993)
★★★★ Big Easy Stomp (Varèse Sarabande, 2002)

The New Orleans school of rock & roll is inconceivable without the depth and baroque grandeur of Professor Longhair's piano style. Longhair, born Henry Roeland Byrd, perfected the synthesis of mambo, rumba, and boogie-woogie rhythms that became the trademark of New Orleans music. With his indefatigable left hand, he maintained the rhythmic base of his work, having absorbed and broadened the styles of pioneers Jimmy Yancey, Pete Johnson, and a host of New Orleans barrelhouse giants. With his dexterous right hand, he swooped, trilled, and soared through the melody lines, bringing into play the Caribbean music of his heritage and adding complexity in the form of the traditional country and blues quotations he worked into this blend. What's more, in a city full of idiosyncratic vocalists, he may have been the most idiosyncratic of them all. Yelps, yodels, and whistles were part of his trick bag, but that's not to dismiss the warmth or personality evident in his stylish approach. His rocking interpretation of Hank Williams' "Jambalaya (On the Bayou)" finds him singing one verse in a deep, Fats Domino voice; likewise, on Muddy Waters' "Got My Mojo Working," he slurs some lyrics in a lascivious style that echoes Elvis Presley's.

Rhino's two-CD set, 'Fess: The Professor Longhair Anthology, is the must-have comprehensive overview of Longhair's career, beginning with his first and only R&B hit, "Bald Head," which rose to #5, and concluding with the previously unreleased "Boogie Woogie," the last recording Longhair made before his death in 1980. Nighthawk's Mardi Gras in New Orleans and Atlantic's New Orleans Piano collect Longhair's most important late-'40s and early-'50s recordings, including "She Ain't Got No Hair," "Mardi Gras in New Orleans," "Professor Longhair's Boogie," and "Tipitina."

From 1964 to 1971, Longhair dropped out of music and worked as a manual laborer in New Orleans until a talent scout for the New Orleans Jazz and Heritage Festival persuaded him to perform again, which he did until he passed away. Crawfish Fiesta, his final studio album, and The Last Mardi Gras, his final live album (recorded in 1978 at Tipitina's, named after the Longhair song), show no diminution in the master's touch or his feisty approach to the material. Live on the Queen Mary, the first live recording of Longhair's career, was made at a 1975 party hosted by Paul McCartney. Houseparty New Orleans Style was Longhair's first postretirement recording, and it's notable for including more than the usual evergreens dotting most of the artist's releases: "Tipitina" is here, but so is "She Walks Right In" and "Cherry Pie." Mardi Gras in Baton Rouge collects 18 tracks recorded in 1971 in Baton Rouge and in 1972 at Ardent Studios in Memphis; remarkably, neither disc is rendered superfluous by the essential Rhino title. Baton Rouge boasts a wonderful, rollin'-and-tumblin' Fats Domino medley made all the more impressive for comprising lesser-known titles from the Domino canon. "Sick and Tired," a Top 30 pop single for Domino in 1958, is featured as well (it's also on 'Fess), with guitarist Snooks Eaglin constructing a blazing, staccato-rich solo run around and through Longhair's riotous disjointed boogie.

Rock 'n' Roll Gumbo, originally issued in France in 1974 and released stateside in 1985, teams the Professor with Louisiana blues guitarist Clarence "Gatemouth" Brown, who also adds some friendly fiddling to buttress Longhair on "Jambalaya." The closest thing to a greatest-hits title in 'Fess's catalogue is Big Easy Stomp, containing 14 signature Longhair performances. A fitting final tribute to Longhair's genius came with the 1993 releases of Big Chief and Rum and Coke, live albums recorded on two nights in the early '70s at Tipitina's. In these sets, Longhair pulls out all the stops by displaying the huge vocabulary at his command: the jubilant calypso of "Rum & Coca-Cola"; the powerhouse R&B propelling the medley of "She Walks Right In/Shake, Rattle & Roll/Roberta" (both on Rum and Coke); the scalding mix of ragtime and jump blues on the instrumental "Mess Around" (from Big Chief); and the languorous, moody, slow blues of "Little Blues" (Big Chief). In a nice touch on Rum and Coke, Longhair pays tribute to James Booker with a buoyant take on the latter's "Junco Partner"—yet another example of the great heart evident in Henry Roeland Byrd's art over the course of three decades. —D.M.

The Psychedelic Furs

★★★★½ The Psychedelic Furs (1980; Columbia, 2002)
★★★★½ Talk Talk Talk (1981; Columbia, 2002)
★★★★ Forever Now (1982; Columbia, 2002)
★★★ Mirror Moves (1984; Columbia, 2002)

★★ Midnight to Midnight (Columbia, 1987)
★★★★½ All of This and Nothing (Columbia, 1988)
★ Book of Days (Columbia, 1989)
★ World Outside (Columbia, 1991)
★★½ B-Sides and Lost Grooves (Columbia, 1994)
★★★★ Should God Forget: A Retrospective (Columbia, 1997)
★★★★ Greatest Hits (Columbia, 2001)
★★ Beautiful Chaos: Greatest Hits Live (Columbia, 2001)

Richard Butler obviously slept late the morning God was handing out singing voices, so he only got the Bowie voices that Bowie didn't want. But Butler's grating voice was the key element in the Psychedelic Furs, and for a few years there the Furs were the kitten's knickers, blasting out London postpunk art trash with a name that combined hippie and glam clichés just because it was such a punk rock thing to do. The Furs raised a racket of droning guitars and sax, with a great pound-pound-pound rhythm section in drummer Vince Ely and bassist Tim Butler, Richard's brother and apparently a man who had real trouble finding three of the four strings on his instrument. Richard Butler was a sarcastic romantic who loved to sing his favorite word, "stupid," often making four syllables out of it. He specialized in songs about weird girls whom nobody understands, especially not their bonehead boyfriends, and not Richard himself either, although he'll gladly offer them meaningless sex anyway because it would be in bad taste not to. "I've been waiting all night for someone like you/But you'll have to do," went one of his typical pickup lines (from the 1983 hit "Run and Run"), and he was a seductive poseur because he never pretended to be anything else.

The Furs' classic debut is a hectic rush of punk guitars and scathing wit, highlighted by the ballad "Susan's Strange" and the rocker "Imitation of Christ." In the theme song "We Love You," Butler snarls about how much he loves Frank Sinatra, the Supremes, Brigitte Bardot, and the Twist, pushing his sarcasm way past self-parody into a parody of self-parody, if that makes sense. *Talk Talk Talk* is even louder and catchier, beginning with "Pretty in Pink," the story of a sad girl named Caroline who gets betrayed by all her lovers. The song went on to inspire the John Hughes movie of the same name. Butler elaborates his ideal of hypocrisy-free no-strings lust in "I Wanna Sleep With You" ("He wants to be your guard/I just want to sleep with you"), "She Is Mine," and "Into You Like a Train," playing a prematurely world-weary roue who wouldn't dream of insulting your intelligence by pretending he'll call you later. It

was the only scam he had, but it was a great one, and judging from his photos he needed it.

Things were smoother on *Forever Now,* produced by a typically heavy-handed Todd Rundgren as the band started to fragment. It has "Run and Run," "President Gas," and the Furs' biggest hit, "Love My Way," featuring Ed Buller's marimba hook. In the excellent title track, Butler sings, "He isn't very honest, but he's obvious at least," which is such an accurate self-description it can't be improved. *Mirror Moves* was softer synth pop, leaving the trashy punk sound behind except in Butler's still-harsh vocals. By now, Butler's sentimentality was a lot more interesting musically and emotionally than his cynicism, and the two great songs are his most sentimental ever: "The Ghost in You," about another misunderstood girl with a heart of gold, and "Heaven," about the home of our hearts.

The movie *Pretty in Pink,* which starred Molly Ringwald as the girl in the song, gave the Furs a big mainstream break, but they had already run out of tunes. They recorded a lame new version of "Pretty in Pink" for the soundtrack, and faded away with *Midnight to Midnight, Book of Days,* and *World Outside,* as Butler sounded increasingly seduced by his own mirror moves. The 1988 best-of *All of This and Nothing* leaves out too many early hits ("Run and Run," "Into You Like a Train"), but 11 of the 14 songs are great ones, the omission of the terrible 1984 hit "Heartbeat" is a major plus, and it's still the best album to include "The Ghost in You" or "Heaven." Other posthumous P-Furs reissues include *B-Sides and Lost Grooves,* the 2001 *Greatest Hits* (which goes 9 for 17), and the 1997 double-disc *Should God Forget* (which goes 16 for 33, getting the nod for quantity if not efficiency). After the Furs split in 1991, Richard Butler went on to found the drab '90s alternative act Love Spit Love; the Furs did a reunion tour in 2001, documented on *Beautiful Chaos.* Old poseurs never die, and that's not such a bad thing. —R.S.

Public Enemy

★★★★½ Yo! Bum Rush the Show (Def Jam, 1987)
★★★★★ It Takes a Nation of Millions to Hold Us Back (Def Jam, 1988)
★★★★★ Fear of a Black Planet (Def Jam, 1990)
★★★★½ Apocalypse 91 . . . The Enemy Strikes Back (Def Jam, 1991)
★★★ Greatest Misses (Def Jam, 1992)
★★★ Muse Sick-n-Hour Mess Age (Def Jam, 1994)
★★★ He Got Game (Def Jam, 1998)
★★½ There's a Poison Goin' On (Play It Again Sam, 1999)
★★★★ The Best of Public Enemy (Def Jam, 2001)
★★★½ Revolverlution (Koch, 2002)

Believe the hype: Public Enemy created as potent a musical and lyrical brew as any era or genre has ever witnessed, unleashing a coruscating sequence of revolutionary hip-hop albums that induce a physical and mental disorientation that can profoundly effect one's outlook on social living and the power of music. Carlton Ridenhour (aka Chuck D) was a student at Long Island's Adelphi University when he rhymed over fellow radio DJ Hank Shocklee's beat; that track became "Public Enemy No. 1." Shocklee became the head of the Bomb Squad, PE's sound designers, while PE grew to include formidable DJ Terminator X, "media assassin" Harry Allen, Nation of Islam mouthpiece Professor Griff, a plastic-machine-gun-toting foot-soldier step team called the Security of the First World, and, most importantly, Chuck's manic foil, the clued-in jester and superb rapper Flavor Flav, who wore a giant clock around his neck (get it? Flav always knew what time it is). Their 1987 debut, *Yo! Bum Rush the Show,* heralded hip-hop's great leap forward, placing listeners squarely in the crosshairs (as embodied by the PE logo) of bristling, defiant jams like "You're Gonna Get Yours."

Nation of Millions is the band's stone-cold masterpiece, and perhaps the first truly great hip-hop album. Basing their tracks on the noisiest James Brown samples they could find, Shocklee and his crew created beats that both screamed and rocked the boulevard. Tracks like "Prophets of Rage," "Bring the Noise," "Night of the Living Baseheads," and "Rebel Without a Pause" were uptempo, banshee-like tracks that dropped names from Louis Farrakhan to black nationalist JoAnne Chesimard. The album had an inspiring effect on a generation of hip-hop and electronic producers, not to mention artists from Björk to Dead Prez. More than one critic has claimed Chuck D's booming baritone to be as stirring an instrument as John Coltrane's saxophone—heck, Chuck weighed in on the topic on "Noise": "Writers treat me like Coltrane, insane/Yes to them, but to me I'm a different kind/We're brothers of the same mind, unblind."

Fear of a Black Planet was more varied stylistically and more downtempo ("Pollywannacracka," "Brothers Gonna Work It Out"), but its greatest tracks contain just as much lightning. "Can't Do Nuttin' for Ya Man" is a funky Flavor Flav showcase. "Fight the Power" found PE in a fit of poetic, political pique, with Chuck's intelligent opinions indivisible from the sonics (particularly the saxophone squeals of Maceo Parker, a Bomb Squad staple). The track begins in overdrive and never lets up. After dissing Elvis (while Flavor Flav takes out John Wayne), Chuck D lays it out: "I'm black and I'm proud/I'm ready and hyped plus I'm amped/Most of my heroes don't appear on no stamps." Taking its tagline ("We gotta fight the powers that be!") from the Isley Brothers' 1975 #4 chart hit of the same name, "Fight the Power" was the ultimate antiestablishment rallying cry by a group whose plentiful protests included "By the Time I Get to Arizona" (about that state's refusal to recognize Martin Luther King Jr. Day).

Rocked by controversy in '91 (Griff's anti-Semitic remarks led to his expulsion), PE was losing ground artistically and commercially by 1994's *Muse Sick-n-Hour Mess Age,* but every PE release has something to recommend it. In 1999, Terminator X went on sabbatical to concentrate on his North Carolina ostrich farm and was replaced by DJ Lord Aswod. PE, a pioneering Internet presence, remains an active unit to this day, while Chuck D lectures on the college circuit and does talk radio. Jocked by David Byrne, bitten by Madonna, and quoted by Weezer, Public Enemy had a massive effect on popular music and youth consciousness. If rampant jigginess has subsequently squandered much of hip-hop's revolutionary potential, anyone who ignores the recorded legacy of Public Enemy might as well, in the words of Flavor Flav, "pick your teeth with tombstone chips." —P.R.

Public Image Ltd.

★★★	Public Image/First Issue (Virgin, 1978)
★★★★	Second Edition/Metal Box (Island, 1980)
★★	The Flowers of Romance (Warner Bros., 1981)
★★½	This Is What You Want . . . This Is What You Get (Elektra, 1984)
★★½	Album (Elektra, 1986)
★★	Live in Tokyo (Elektra, 1986)
★★½	Happy? (Virgin, 1987)
★★½	9 (Virgin, 1989)
★★★½	The Greatest Hits, So Far (Virgin, 1990)
★★½	That What Is Not (Virgin, 1992)
★★★	Plastic Box (Virgin, 1999)

The Sex Pistols didn't leave much room for an encore. *Public Image/First Issue* reflects the confusion of John Lydon (né Johnny Rotten) as he gropes for a new attack mode. The title rant is both the most convincing and most traditional track on the album. *Second Edition* is anything but tentative or traditional. Originally released as three EPs in a canister *(Metal Box), Second Edition* is one of rock's most powerful records, with Lydon's bitter diatribes and cautionary mantras propelled by the wildly imaginative guitar playing of Keith Levene, who spews forth near-psychedelic outbursts and oddly lyrical Middle Eastern asides, and by bassist Jah Wobble, who plies slippery, reggae-flavored space dub from the punishing beat. Postpunk's—and postrock's—visionary high point.

On *The Flowers of Romance*, however, Lydon already seems to have run out of ideas. Pseudoethnic percussion and free-ranging spleen don't add up to much of a statement—let alone an antidote to boredom. Bored is exactly how Lydon sounds on *This Is What You Want . . . This Is What You Get*. From this point on, his albums are sleekly produced walk-throughs: The former Rotten one does his scattershot thing to state-of-the-art "alternative rock" accompaniment, even getting off a zinger now and then: "This Is Not a Love Song" from *What You Want*, "Rise" from *Album*, "Seattle" from *Happy?* "Anger is an energy," Lydon dutifully snarls on "Rise" over a churning Siouxsie and the Banshees imitation. But it comes across as an easy one-liner, not a defiant statement of purpose. Lydon reaches his cynical nadir on the best-of collection, though. "Don't Ask Me" is pure stand-up shtick. "Don't blame me, I told you so," he declares at the end of a snide ecological rap. It's a long way from "No future" to the optimistically titled *Greatest Hits, So Far*, whose faith proved unfounded; PiL broke up in 1993. The four-disc *Plastic Box* is an appropriate epitaph, with Peel Sessions and 12-inch versions of classic early material bulking up the first two discs, and the depressing decline of the later years providing the majority of the rest. —M.C./M.M.

Puddle of Mudd

★★★ Come Clean (Flawless, 2001)
★ Life on Display (Flawless, 2003)

A man so amused by toddlers urinating that he put a picture of one on his first album, St. Louis native Wes Scantlin hit it big in late 2001. After dumping his long-time band, he befriended Fred Durst, who hooked him up with three journeyman rockers. The group's album *Come Clean* signified, along with best-selling albums from Nickelback and Three Doors Down, that Nirvana's sense of discontentment and alienation was no longer an outsider's creed—it had been the default setting of mainstream rock for a decade.

But even as he clung to the Nirvana and Alice in Chains template, Scantlin, seeming almost like a grunge-lite John Fogerty, demonstrated a gift for catchy, plainspoken songcraft that his peers couldn't approach. With the punishing "Control" and the playful "She Hates Me," Scantlin made misogyny oddly palatable, while "Blurry," a power lullaby to his son, remains genuinely touching. *Come Clean* is one of the hard-rock success stories of 2001–02, but a year later, *Life on Display* indicated that Scantlin's big bag of tunes was empty. —R.K.

Tito Puente

★★★★ Mamborama (1956; Charly, 1993)
★★★★★ Puente in Percussion (1956; Fania, 2003)
★★★★ Cuban Carnival (1956; RCA, 2003)
★★★★½ Top Percussion (1958; RCA, 1992)
★★★★★ Dance Mania (1958; RCA, 1991)
★★★★ Mucho Cha-Cha (1959; RCA, 1992)
★★★★★ Tambo (1960; RCA, 2003)
★★★★ Pachanga con Puente (1961; Tico, 1995)
★★★½ El Rey Bravo (1962; Fania, 2000)
★★★½ Bossa Nova by Puente (1962; Palladium, 1995)
★★★★½ More Dance Mania (RCA Victor, 1963)
★★★ My Fair Lady Goes Latin (Roulette, 1965)
★★★★ The Mambo King: 100th LP (Sony, 1991)
★★★★★ The Best of Dance Mania Plus Unreleased Outtakes (BMG, 1994)
★★ Tito's Idea (RMM, 1995)
★★★★★ 50 Years of Swing (RMM, 1997)
★★★½ Live at Birdland/Dancemania '99 (RMM, 1998)
★★★½ Mambo Birdland (RMM, 1999)
★★★ The Best of the Concord Years (Concord, 2000)
★★★★★ The Complete RCA Recordings, Vol. One (BMG, 2001)
★★★★★ The Complete RCA Recordings, Vol. Two (BMG, 2001)
★★★ Live at the Playboy Jazz Festival (Playboy Jazz, 2002)

with La Lupe
★★★★½ Tito Puente Swings, the Exciting La Lupe Sings (1965; Tico, 1992)
★★★★ Tú y Yo (1965; Tico, 1993)
★★★★ Homenaje à Rafael Hernandez (1966; Tico, 1993)
★★★★ The King and I/El Rey y Yo (Tico, 1967)
★★★★ La Pareja (1978; Tico, 1992)

with Celia Cruz
★★★★½ Cuba y Puerto Rico Son . . . (1966; Tico, 1992)
★★★★ Quimbo Quimbumbia (1969; Fania, 2003)
★★★★ Etc. Etc. Etc. (1970; Tico, 1993)
★★★★ Alma con Alma (Tico, 1971)
★★★½ En España (1971; Tico, 1995)
★★★★ Algo Especial Para Recordar (1972; Tico, 1995)

with India
★★★ Jazzin' (RMM, 1996)

with Eddie Palmieri
★★★★ Masterpiece (RMM, 2000)

Eddie Palmieri might be a much better composer and Machito a more charismatic bandleader, but of the three Afro-Cuban giants to emerge from NYC in the '50s, Tito Puente was the only one who managed to become an indelible part of the American mainstream. And how could he not? Taking the rambunctious timbales (until then, an underrated percussion instrument) to the forefront of the stage, he delighted audiences with his pyrotechnical solos and flamboyant attitude.

Exploring the Puente discography can prove to be an intimidating task; the man expressed his voracious appetite for music through 100-plus albums, which, taken together, trace the development of Latin music from the '40s to the late '90s. (Puente passed away in the year 2000 at age 77.) Indeed, Puente did it all: bigband jazz, Cuban cha-cha and bolero, rumba rituals and mambo marathons, bossa nova and *pachanga,* instrumentals, and songs with some of Latin music's finest vocalists. He wrote new music, rearranged old standards, conducted mystically tinged percussion ensembles, and occasionally left his beloved timbales aside in favor of the vibes, performing slow tunes with a delicate, assured touch.

Beginners should concentrate on the Nuyorican's recordings for the RCA label from the late '50s and early '60s. *Dance Mania* is the inevitable starting point, a bubbly collection of irresistible, three-minute hit singles, from the instantly hummable "El Cayuco" to the explosive "Mambo Gozon" and the retro charm of "Hong Kong Mambo." *Tambo* showcases Puente at his atmospheric best, extracting deep layers of texture from his big band of jazz virtuosos on the silky "Call of the Jungle Birds." True to its title, *Cuban Carnival* is unabashedly sunny and optimistic, with a feistier-than-usual Puente showing off his youthful brio. (The interplay between congas and timbales on the classic "Pa' Los Rumberos" is definitely not for the faint of heart.)

Much of the '60s found Puente recording with two Cuban vocalists who could not have been further apart from one another in looks and style. La Lupe was fleshy and risqué, infamous for her tendency to disrobe onstage, moaning loudly whenever the orchestra reached the climax of the hotter boleros—a dangerous performer, reckless and soulful. Celia Cruz, on the other hand, kept a prudent emotional distance from the material at hand. She wasn't into selling sex; her potent, chocolate voice celebrated life with an almost endearing naïveté and unfailing sense of decency. Puente, whose discography reveals a veritable fetish for championing glamorous divas, enjoyed performing with both. The La Lupe and Cruz collaborations are especially noteworthy because they showcase Puente's wisdom as a bandleader—namely, his ability to retreat into the background and let the divas' talent speak for itself.

During the '80s, Puente recorded a number of albums for the Concord jazz label. Elegant and reliable as these recordings are, they lack the fire of the '50s classics. Fortunately, the *timbalero* recovered some of the vigor of his youth during his last few years. He released a couple of solid live albums as well as a collaboration with keyboard maestro Eddie Palmieri—a much-hyped affair that, miraculously, did not disappoint.

Casual fans looking for a single Puente fix will be satisfied with the flawless *50 Years of Swing,* which offers a perfect encapsulation of his work in only three discs. Completists should apply for a loan, then obtain the two separate six-CD box sets collecting Puente's complete output for RCA. The information on the booklets is skimpy, but the music—remastered to enhance the originals' inviting warmth—speaks for itself, emphasizing Puente's eclectic musicality over his undeniable showmanship.   —E.L.

Puff Daddy

★★★   No Way Out (Bad Boy/Arista, 1997)
★★   Forever (Bad Boy/Arista, 1999)
★★★½   The Saga Continues . . . (Bad Boy/Arista, 2001)

All these years later, it's still hard to believe that *No Way Out* was the album that launched an empire. A record executive named Sean Combs renamed himself Puff Daddy, gathered all the rappers and singers he signed, and led them through an album that was both a celebration of Combs' hip-hop-meets-R&B style and a tribute to his protégé, the late Notorious B.I.G., who had been murdered a few months earlier. In short, *No Way Out* sounds like a funeral set in a nightclub, and that's the best thing about it: the disc captures the grimly gleeful attitude that would continue to dominate hip-hop for the next few years.

The album's biggest hits tug in different directions. There's "It's All About the Benjamins (Remix)," the era-defining posse cut backed by producer Derrick "D-Dot" Angelettie's brilliant sample of a one-note guitar line from an old Love Unlimited Orchestra record. And near the end comes "I'll Be Missing You," an ode to B.I.G. based on the Police's "Every Breath You Take": At the time many critics called it over-the-top, but in hindsight what's impressive is the song's restraint, especially Combs' plainspoken eulogy, which was ghostwritten by Sauce Money. The rest of the album floats by in a haze of disco-inspired beats and rapping guest stars: B.I.G. appears on four songs, and Mase adds mushmouthed boasts to "Can't No-body Hold Me Down," a brash reworking of "The Message" by Grandmaster Flash and the Furious Five.

The followup, *Forever,* has a handful of irresistible

beats, but overall the album seems a bit aimless: two years removed from the tragedy that helped inspire his first album, Combs spends 74 minutes trying to live down his shiny-suit image without forfeiting his right to brag. The result is lots of wheel-spinning: "They ain't true like us/If they only knew like us/It's less than a small few like us." The exceptions usually involve special guests, like R. Kelly's electropop love song "Satisfy You" and a menacing remix of B.I.G.'s "Real Niggas."

Combs came back as P. Diddy for *The Saga Continues . . .* , a return to form driven by a series of addictive singles: the Neptunes-produced spelling lesson "Diddy," the hip-hop ballad "I Need a Girl," the back-to-basics bragfest "Let's Get It," the lopsided club track "Bad Boy for Life." Combs is smart enough to put the microphone down sometimes—he doesn't even appear on some tracks: "Can't Believe," for example, is a sinuous duet between Faith Evans and Carl Thomas. By the time the album came out, Diddy was well established as a fashion designer, philanthropist, and all-purpose celebrity; he had survived a weapons charge, a weak sophomore album, and a relationship with Jennifer Lopez. Perhaps it's no surprise, then, that this, his best album, is also the one that sounds the most like a compilation: as he himself would be the first to tell you, his main musical talent is making hits, by any means necessary. —K.S.

Pulp

	It (Velvel, 1983)
★	Freaks (Velvel, 1986)
★★	Separations (Razor & Tie, 1992)
★★½	His 'n' Hers (Island, 1994)
★★★★½	Different Class (Island, 1995)
★★★	This Is Hardcore (Island, 1998)
★★★★	We Love Life (Rough Trade/Sanctuary, 2002)

In the '90s, England's class war was transported to our shores via Blur and Oasis, though only ardent Anglophiles bothered to suss the subtext beneath the singles and the interviews. But Pulp dropped the bomb with "Common People," in which a posh art-school bird propositions broke bloke Jarvis Cocker for the sake of a little life experience, and your man tells her what for while lifting a synth bit from Men Without Hats' unjustly forgotten "Pop Goes the World."

While Pulp's early albums (particularly *His 'n' Hers*) offer ripe moments, nothing prepared listeners for Cocker's emergence on *Different Class* as a startling new Britpop hybrid—an amalgam of Morrissey's wit (and acerbic resentment) and Bryan Ferry's dandyish charm (and grand libido), plus a dash of his own footloose abandon. 'Twas all very Brit, but Pulp's

danceable trash, not above copping a lick from Laura Branigan's "Gloria" here or masterfully faking pop techno there, was a universal language. Alas, the sourness of followup *This Is Hardcore* was a real turnoff, with Cocker hopping joylessly from one musty bedroom to another. Only "Help the Aged," on which he wryly propositions some sweet young thing for a sympathy fuck, is a keeper.

Both lush and understated, *We Love Life* was a mild triumph. "The Trees," with its lovely New Order–style melody, is typical of Cocker's new melancholy but unbowed perspective. Sure, those titular organisms create oxygen, but did they tell him his sweetie was gonna skip out on him? Realizing that his flashiest stuff was behind him and reverting to fop mode would seem really callow, Cocker gambled in the shade of gorgeous electropastoral arrangements and told himself that everything would be fine as long as he didn't forget to breathe. —K.H.

Pussy Galore

★★	Right Now! (1987; Matador, 1998)
★★½	Sugarshit Sharp (EP) (1988; Matador, 1998)
★★	Dial 'M' for Motherfucker (1989; Matador, 1998)
★★½	Live: In the Red (In the Red, 1998)

It sounds quaint today (a decade after the Butthole Surfers found themselves to be MTV sweethearts) that a band like Pussy Galore could have once forged an existence with repugnance as its golden rule. Unlike shock-rockers chasing cash, Pussy Galore strove to offend on a purely aesthetic level, though the band often missed its mark. From the band's moniker and trash-heap sound to songs like "You Look Like a Jew" (out of print) and the audacity of rerecording the Stones' sacrosanct *Exile on Main Street* (also out of print), Pussy Galore was the band for hipsters with a taste for distaste. It was also the farm team for the Jon Spencer Blues Explosion (featuring Pussy guitarist Spencer, natch), Royal Trux (guitarist Neil Hagerty), Boss Hog (guitarist Cristina Martinez and Spencer), and Free Kitten (guitarist Julia Cafritz).

The ruckus that saturates *Right Now!* would make a fine noise for a single, but its not nearly enough to carry 19 songs of pseudo-sickness. For every burst of focused adrenaline ("NYC 1999!") there are four other tunes that sound like they were forgotten as soon as Steve Albini stopped the tape machine. *Sugarshit Sharp* adds color to the sketches, but it's nothing to make you stare. Still, a cover of Einstürzende Neubauten's "Yü Gang" smartly slips dance samples and Public Enemy snippets into snatches of Link Wray chicken-scratch geetar, a portent of the disco strings and remixes that Spencer would later dabble in with the Blues Explosion.

Cafritz split during the recording of *Dial 'M' for Motherfucker,* and Pussy Galore picked up guitarist Kurt Wolff. Although the noise is further refined (drummer Bob Bert, ex–Sonic Youth, masters his rattletrap kit), the band continues to talk loud and say nothing. The perfect example is "DWDA," which starts off in a meditative state but drops into mind-numbing gibberish. *Live: In the Red* captures the band's final gig, a 1989 show at New York's CBGB. It's the band's most accessible set, perhaps because the Pussies are forced to entertain a crowd instead of amuse themselves. Nonetheless, while solos pop up above the dense hedges of feedback, distortion, and noise, nothing especially threatens. The band that shot for obnoxious comes up innocuous, and that spelled the end. —C.N.

Q-Tip

★★★ Amplified (Arista, 1999)

When A Tribe Called Quest's Q-Tip dropped his solo debut, fans of Tribe's rootsy aesthetic were caught off guard. From the album's cover, which pictures the rapper bare-chested and draped in fur, to boneheaded track titles like "Go Hard" and "Do It," *Amplified* makes plain Tip's desire to curb the intellect, buy out the bar, and party naked. Followers balked at his transformation from abstract poet to libidinous, brand-conscious baller, but those who loitered felt the motor-booty beats and raspy rhymes work their magic. *Amplified* bounces from the bubbly head rush of "Let's Ride" to the jangly, buoyant "Do It" without losing its champagne buzz. Tip and Jay Dee handle most of the production, crafting cuts that snap and crackle with bowel-loosening bass and caffeinated claps. Although it may not have the staying power of Tribe's classics, *Amplified* is the ideal soundtrack for a carefree night at the club. —K.M.

Quasi

★★½   Early Recordings (Key-Op, 1996)
★★★   R&B Transmogrification (Up, 1997)
★★★★ Featuring "Birds" (Up, 1998)
★★★½ Field Studies (Up, 1999)
★★½   The Sword of God (Touch & Go, 2001)
★★★   Hot Shit (Touch & Go, 2003)

In the early '90s, keyboardist/guitarist Sam Coomes (formerly of the Donner Party) and drummer Janet Weiss got married and started a band called Motorgoat. The rest of the group fell away; the material on *Early Recordings*, made in 1993 and 1994, finds Coomes and Weiss taking a dry run at the ideas on their later, more fully developed records and testing their chemistry as a duo.

The musical chemistry is what kept Quasi going as a band, even when Coomes and Weiss divorced in the mid-'90s. On *R&B Transmogrification*, Coomes writes from the perspective of someone who might not actually want to die but needs to be convinced. He's also hit on his instrument of choice, the Roxichord—a vintage analog synth that approximates the sound of an electric harpsichord, which he pounds at like Jerry Lee Lewis, while Weiss (by now also the drummer in Sleater-Kinney) batters and rolls with flair.

Featuring "Birds," though, is where the gloves come off. The lyrics are corrosively, spastically bitter, from the vicious little science-fiction vignette "Our Happiness Is Guaranteed" to withering couplets like "You fucked yourself and now you don't know where to go/Split wide open like a sturgeon for the roe." Even a nominal love song, "It's Hard to Turn Me On," sprays venom everywhere. But the music is stunningly catchy and energetic, and the two sing like they can't believe how cathartic it is. It's the *Rumours* of indie rock, a perfect album for a horrible breakup. "Birds," incidentally, is a short nature recording.

Before *Field Studies*, Quasi toured as backing band for Coomes' old Heatmiser bandmate Elliott Smith, and Smith returned the favor by playing elegant bass lines on a few of the album's songs. Coomes has hardened his heart considerably—"I feel much better when I'm under a cloud," he deadpans—although Weiss' "Two by Two" sounds genuinely wounded. The ex-couple has eased off the attack long enough to allow a string section in, too, and this time, "Birds" is an actual song.

Recorded slowly and painfully in their own studio (with a synthesized approximation of the defunct Roxichord), *The Sword of God* sounds utterly exhausted by the process—Coomes starts to repeat himself, which doesn't do Quasi's still-vibrant give-and-take any favors. Only the New Orleans–R&B–inspired "It's Raining" is up to the band's standards.

Fortunately, Coomes and Weiss pull themselves together for *Hot Shit*. Heavy on the rock heroics (wailing solos! slide blues! Weiss channeling her inner Bill Bruford!) and light on the keyboards, it shifts the band's tension from romance to politics: "Master & Dog" is a shudder of revolt at the two-party system, and both "Good Times" and "Good Time Rock 'n' Roll" are titled with ichor-dripping irony. —D.W.

Queen

★★	Queen (1973; Hollywood, 1991)
★★½	Queen II (1974; Hollywood, 1991)
★★★	Sheer Heart Attack (1974; Hollywood, 1991)
★★★½	A Night at the Opera (1975; Hollywood, 1991)
★★	A Day at the Races (1977; Hollywood, 1991)
★★½	News of the World (1977; Hollywood, 1991)
★★	Jazz (1978; Hollywood, 1991)
★★	Live Killers (1979; Hollywood, 1991)
★★★	The Game (1980; Hollywood, 1991)
★★	Flash Gordon (1980; Hollywood, 1991)
★★	Hot Space (1982; Hollywood, 1991)
★★	The Works (1984; Hollywood, 1991)
★★	A Kind of Magic (1986; Hollywood, 1991)
★★½	Live Magic (Hollywood, 1986)
★★	The Miracle (1989; Hollywood, 1991)
★★★	Innuendo (Hollywood, 1991)
★★	Classic Queen (Hollywood, 1992)
★★★	Greatest Hits (Hollywood, 1992)
★★★	Live at Wembley '86 (Hollywood, 1992)
★★★	Queen at the BBC (Hollywood, 1995)
★★★★	Greatest Hits, Vols. 1 and 2 (Hollywood, 1995)
★★½	Made in Heaven (Hollywood, 1995)
★★½	Rocks (Hollywood, 1997)
★	Greatest Hits III (Hollywood, 1999)
★★	Greatest Hits I, II, and III (Hollywood, 2002)

Excessive, decadent, theatrical, androgynous, tasteless, mocking, ironic, self-conscious: Queen lived up to its moniker with gleeful abandon. It could only have happened in the '70s. In fact, the British quartet's popularity in the States plummeted immediately after the career peak of 1980's *The Game*. With good reason, too; the font of crafty hooks suddenly dried up. But in the group's prime, guitarist Brian May and irrepressible lead singer Freddie Mercury provided a steady flow of bombastically catchy schlock-rock hits. Although the albums drag with mediocre filler that sinks the group far below the level of, say, Led Zeppelin in terms of overall achievement, the triumphant pomp of Queen's biggest hits—"Another One Bites the Dust," "We Are the Champions," "Bohemian Rhapsody"—eclipses the copious weak material. Mercury stands apart as a sexual sphinx in

the decade of not-entirely-liberated excess: A gay man who lived out the classic straight-male fantasy of leading a rock band, he paraded his sexuality before millions—it remained unspoken, an open secret—and though stricken with AIDS, he did not publicly admit to having the disease until the day before his death, in late 1991.

The group began as a somewhat crude glam-metal outfit with arty underpinnings. Gradually, the members' college degrees and musical chops emerged. On *Sheer Heart Attack*, "Killer Queen" and "Stone Cold Crazy" weld Mercury's creamy falsetto strut to propulsive, tightly wound arrangements. You can get winded just listening to all those multitracked Freddies singing rings around each other. That's nothing compared to "Bohemian Rhapsody," of course: The notorious six-minute centerpiece of *A Night at the Opera* is either a prog-rock benchmark or the most convoluted novelty song ever recorded. The over-the-top approach is precisely what makes Mercury and company so endearing, but it's also responsible for Queen's downfall. A little too predictable, *A Day at the Races* is a quickie sequel to *A Night at the Opera*. *News of the World* sports two songs that have become so popular, they've transcended mere chart success to reign eternally as ubiquitous anthems: the jackboot jock-rock pomp stomp of "We Will Rock You" (written by May) and the ultimate gloat, "We Are the Champions" (by Mercury), heard around the world at sports stadiums and wherever else thousands of people gather for some form of gladiatorial combat.

The decline starts with *Jazz*, which has the quickie operetta "Bicycle Races" but is otherwise utter jive. *The Game* offers two more megahits, of dubious achievement for the band: "Another One Bites the Dust" (credited to bassist Roger Deacon), a shameless rip-off of Chic's "Good Times" and "Crazy Little Thing Called Love," a bit of pseudo-rockabilly hokum that introduces an ominous new element to the Queen mix: nostalgia.

From this point forward, Queen's output seems neutered and obsessed with gloss, whether with outright nostalgic projects (the tuneless *Flash Gordon* soundtrack) or albums that exhibit the hollow glamour of the times *(Hot Space, The Works);* the only track from this period that has any life at all is "Under Pressure," an impromptu collaboration with David Bowie. Mercury began to suffer from AIDS during this period, and everything from *A Kind of Magic* on was driven by an unspecified philosophy promoting all races, creeds, etc. ("One Vision," "The Miracle"). He was on this trip until his death, as evidenced by the posthumous *Made in Heaven*—for which he recorded vocal tracks to be finished later by the band—and we can only hope the project brought him peace. Though not the band's best work, the earnest, joyful later albums remain poignant as an epitaph for Mercury.

After the film *Wayne's World* made "Bohemian Rhapsody" a #2 hit in 1992, the band's new label, Hollywood, rushed a hits collection into the stores: *Classic Queen* omits "We Will Rock You," "Another One Bites the Dust," "Killer Queen," and a half-dozen other essentials; *Greatest Hits* offers these tracks but does not include "Bohemian Rhapsody," "Under Pressure," and others that were on *Classic Queen.* The double *Greatest Hits, Vols. 1 and 2* corrects the oversight, though many of the inclusions weren't U.S. hits ("Breakthru," "Headlong," "I Want to Break Free"). *Greatest Hits III* is a junkyard of rarities, remixes, and solo tracks, valuable mostly for Mercury's ingenious cover of "The Great Pretender." *Greatest Hits I, II, and III* is a rather expensive doorstop, and *Rocks,* a decent collection of '70s classics, gets docked half a star for sloppy editing. The BBC set, eight tracks recorded in two sessions in 1973, is an intriguing glimpse of the band just before the release of its first album; clearly excited yet delicately precise about every move, Queen appears almost fully formed as rock's most dramatic perfectionists. —M.C./B.S.

Queen Latifah

★★★★ All Hail the Queen (Tommy Boy, 1989)
★★ Nature of a Sista' (Tommy Boy, 1991)
★★★ Black Reign (Motown, 1993)
★★½ Order in the Court (Motown, 1998)
★★★★ She's a Queen: A Collection of Hits (Universal, 2002)

Formerly Dana Owens of East Orange, NJ, distaff rapper Queen Latifah earned that Afrocentric crown with her debut album. *All Hail the Queen* is a masterful sampler package, a dance-floor tour of hip-hop at the dawn of its second decade. Working with sympathetic producers (Daddy-O from Stetsasonic, the members of De La Soul, KRS-One of Boogie Down Productions, DJ Mark, the 45 King), Latifah displays an uncommon versatility, especially for an up-and-comer. She moves comfortably from soul-music roots to house-music echoes, from spacious dub-reggae to cosmic funk, and from feminist insistence to convincing romance: Even without a surefire hit single, this is one of the most consistently listenable—and inspired—rap albums ever assembled. Latifah even introduces British rapper Monie Love on an insistently sharp duet called "Ladies First." Latifah is somewhat overwhelmed by *Nature of a Sista*'s various producers and their tradition-bound musical outlook. The disco elegance of "Give Me Your Love" and

"How Do I Love Thee" is a turnaround from the no-nonsense groove on earlier tracks like "Ladies First" or "Mama Gave Birth to the Soul Children."

Black Reign offered a toughened-up Latifah, while *Order in the Court* attempted a mishmash of styles to little notable effect. By this time, though, Latifah was making more headway as an actress (the sitcom *Living Single,* the movies *Set It Off* and *Chicago,* the latter of which garnered her an Oscar nomination as Best Supporting Actress in 2002) than as an MC, and the strain showed. *She's a Queen,* a best-of, seemed to put a cap on a career that had begun on the mike but flourished in front of the camera. —M.C./M.M.

Queens of the Stone Age

★★★★ Queens of the Stone Age (Loosegroove, 1998)
★★★½ Rated R (Interscope, 2000)
★★★★ Songs for the Deaf (Interscope, 2002)

Guitarist Josh Homme—who, with his golf shirts and altar-boy haircut, couldn't look less like a metal-guitar hero—had a great idea: Strip down the menacing, Cali-desert-fried rumble made mildly famous by his former band Kyuss ("stoner rock") and blend it with krautrock's circular rhythmic chug. Viola: minimalist hard rock as hypnotic as it is meaty.

After a few formative (now out-of-print) EPs, the desert storm *Queens of the Stone Age* appeared in '98. Guitars and bass churn in near loops, like a tank engine turning over. Vocals are kept to a minimum, embracing traditional metal sentiments such as "I wish we'd get away/Drink wine and screw." *QOTSA* is that rare bird, an aesthetically innovative hard-rock debut.

Rated R is slicker and more diverse, if not as exciting. Arrangements are more precise, vocals are more prominent, and on "Feel Good Hit of the Summer," Judas Priest's Rob Halford helps sing: "Nicotine, Valium, Vicodin, marijuana, ecstasy and alcohol/C-c-c-c-c-cocaine!!!" "In the Fade" is a ballad, and polyrhythms abound. The followup isn't quite as promising as the debut, but it's still miles apart from anything else on the mainstream-metal landscape.

They've had fine drummers in the past, but Queens can't help but benefit from Dave Grohl's guest pounding on *Songs for the Deaf.* "Millionaire," "Song for the Dead," and the seasick title track are tough, high-desert scorchers, while "Mosquito Song" is an acoustic-horns-strings ode to the little bloodsuckers. Although *Deaf* is largely a return to bulldozer grooves, the band baffled Ozzfest fans—but for the rest of us, the band acts as a weirdly adult respite from new metal's adolescent tantrums. —J.G.

Quicksilver Messenger Service

★★★	Quicksilver Messenger Service (Capitol, 1968)
★★★½	Happy Trails (Capitol, 1969)
★★	Shady Grove (Capitol, 1970)
★★★	Just for Love (Capitol, 1970; Beat Goes On, 2000)
★	Comin' Thru (Capitol 1972; Beat Goes On, 2001)
★★★½	Anthology (Capitol, 1973; Beat Goes On, 1996)
★★★	Best of Quicksilver Messenger Service (Capitol, 1990)
★★★★	Sons of Mercury: The Best of Quicksilver Messenger Service 1968–1975 (Rhino, 1991)
★★★½	Unreleased Quicksilver: Lost Gold and Silver (Collector's Choice, 2000)
★★★	Classic Masters (Capitol, 2002)

With its blend of folkie song sense, bluesy improvisation, and a nod to rock's Bo Diddley roots, Quicksilver Messenger Service was one of the more personable bands to come out of the first wave of San Francisco psychedelia. QMS became a ballroom favorite despite some real shortcomings: colorless vocals courtesy of bassist David Freiberg and guitarist Gary Duncan, and a loosey-goosey rhythm section. Quicksilver was distinguished by the guitar playing of Duncan and John Cipollina, the latter's slashing runs and whammy-bar punctuation making for one of the era's most recognizable styles. The duo spun off endless solos of the sort encouraged by the Butterfield Blues Band's epic jams. Surprisingly, on ASM's debut album, only the shorter songs—principally versions of Hamilton Camp's "Pride of Man" and Dino Valenti's "Dino's Song"—register. The lysergic-acid reworking of Brubeck's "Take Five," called "Gold and Silver," has its moments, but the live energy needed to sustain extended pieces like "The Fool" is a no-show in the studio. The band remedied this by recording most of Happy Trails at the Fillmore; the album's centerpiece is a sidelong "suite" of improvisations on "Who Do You Love," which, despite being the sentimental fan favorite and a telling artifact, has not aged terribly well. (The majority of the early live material and studio outtakes on Lost Gold and Silver have been floating around on bootleg, but the double-disc collection offers considerably improved sound quality.)

Shady Grove found Gary Duncan departed and English pianist Nicky Hopkins on board, but nary a song in sight. Duncan returned for Just for Love with singer/songwriter Dino Valenti in tow. Despite Valenti's annoying penchant for vocal overkill, the focus he brought to the writing resulted in Quicksilver's only (semi-)hit single "Fresh Air." That song features a Duncan solo that is a marvel of guitar architecture, as sharp as anything played by his more publicized partner, Cipollina. From there it was all downhill, as Quicksilver's final four albums took the band further away from the heady '60s atmosphere that made its magic possible. Rhino's double-disc Sons of Mercury remains the most comprehensive overview, though hippie diehards who insist on the full 25:22 minutes of "Who Do You Love" will still reach for Happy Trails. —B.E.

Radiohead

According to the script, Radiohead was supposed to disappear after its flukey 1993 smash, "Creep," leaving only fond memories of Thom Yorke's Martin-Short-after-electroshock yodel and that wukka-wukka guitar hook. Certainly nothing else on *Pablo Honey* hinted at things to come. But then Radiohead shocked the world with the wide-screen psychedelic glory of *The Bends,* the album that raised these pasty British boys to a very '70s kind of U.K. art-rock godhead. The depressive ballad "Fake Plastic Trees" turned up in *Clueless,* in which Alicia Silverstone memorably tagged the band "complaint rock." In big-bang dystopian epics like "High and Dry," "Planet Telex," and "Street Spirit (Fade Out)," Yorke's choir-boy whimper runs laps around Jonny Greenwood's machine-head guitar heroics. U2 would have sold crack to nuns to make this record.

Radiohead officially became king of rock with its next album, *OK Computer,* which zooms even further into futuristic mind games and headphone textures than *The Bends,* even if it's not quite as lyrical. *OK Computer* kicks off with "Airbag," the catchiest song ever written about a car crash, disintegrating into electronic chaos at the end as guitarists Jonny Greenwood and Ed O'Brien warp their instruments into a DJ Shadow–inspired glitch-core coda. Things only get bleaker from there, in darkly emotional ballads such as "Let Down," "No Surprises," and "Exit Music for a Film." The seven-minute nervous breakdown "Para-noid Android" became a surprise U.K. pop hit. If Pink Floyd ever made an album this good, they kept it to themselves. Radiohead was claiming the high ground abandoned by Nirvana, Pearl Jam, U2, R.E.M., everybody; and fans around the world loved them for trying too hard at a time when nobody else was even bothering. Naturally, the band celebrated success with *Meeting People Is Easy,* a rockumentary about how depressed they were.

Radiohead's response to all the acclaim was to get even weirder, laboring over the sessions that spawned *Kid A* and *Amnesiac. Kid A* is a detour into electronics riddled with anxiety and paranoia, but once again, Radiohead defied all expectations by reinventing themselves and only getting more popular. "Morning Bell," "How to Disappear Completely," and "Idioteque" were brutally beautiful ballads of emotional disintegration, caught between the lines "this isn't happening" and "this is really happening." Some fans hailed *Kid A* as a masterwork; others feared the band was turning into Jefferson Laptop. But Radiohead saved even better songs for the second half, *Amnesiac.* "You and Whose Army?" beams in from the fifth side of the White Album; "I Might Be Wrong" rewires the Allman Brothers even as "Knives Out" rewires the Smiths' *The Queen Is Dead;* and it all reaches an unlikely emotional peak in the two-minute guitar solo "Hunting Bears." *I Might Be Wrong* is an ace live album featuring a new song, "True Love Waits." Topping the charts with zero airplay, refusing to kiss a square inch of ass, too busy rewriting the rules to follow anyone else's, Radiohead remains king, and the worst you can say is that the band is willing to fall on its face. If you can forgive them for taking themselves so seriously—try, you'll grow as a person—they can take your ears somewhere new. *I Might Be Wrong* is an ace live album featuring a new song, "True Love Waits." *Hail to the Thief* offers their hardest rock since *The Bends,* going for punk aggression and disoriented electronic angst at the same time. "Sit Down. Stand Up," "There There," "Sail to the Moon," "2 + 2 = 5": The new tunes were pretty brief, rarely venturing longer than five minutes but raging from top to bottom with adult confidence, no messing around, and once more leaving bewildered fans in their wake.   —R.S.

Raekwon

★★★★★   Only Built 4 Cuban Linx (Loud, 1995)
  ★½   Immobilarity (Loud, 1999)
  ★★★   The Lex Diamond Story (Universal, 2003)

Corey Woods is Raekwon of the Wu-Tang Clan, a "black stallion wildin' on the island of Shaolin"—that is, a Staten Island MC with a bad overbite and what sounds like two plugs of wool stuffed between cheeks and gums. In the opening round of Wu solo albums, Raekwon teamed with Ghostface Killa to make Raekwon's *Only Built 4 Cuban Linx* and Ghostface's *Ironman,* appearing together on both album covers, sharing marquee billing and complementing each other on nearly every track with extraordinary synergy. Both albums feature the RZA's sinuous, insidious hip-hop beats, anchoring them at the molten core of the Wu canon. *Cuban Linx* introduced Raekwon's story-based "ghetto mafiosi" mythology, codifying the Cosa Nostra mob/rap corollaries first elucidated by Kool G Rap. Any Wu novitiate needs *Cuban Linx:* "Ice Cream" finds Method Man hanging off the truck with Rae, the latter checking out Ms. Black America: "car'mel complexion/breath smelling like cinnamon/excuse me hon, the don mean no harm/turn around again/goddam backyard's banging like a Benzi/if I were jiggy/you'd be spotted like Spuds McKenzie." "Verbal Intercourse" was an incredible Rae and Nas team-up (the pair would reconnoiter over a nyabinghi RZA beat on "Met My Niggas Live" from Wu-Tang Clan's 2000 album *The W,* Rae laying down the law: "Handle your bid and kill no kids.")

The followup, *Immobilarity,* without RZA behind the boards or Ghostface riding shotgun, was not good. The exception is the Pete Rock–produced "Sneakers," where Raekwon confesses to a "thousand pair a week freak" footwear fetish. After another four-year hiatus, Raekwon returned with *The Lex Diamond Story,* playing to his stately strengths and revisiting *Cuban Linx*'s hard-carved gangster mythology (although the RZA was again conspicuously absent behind the boards). *Lex Diamond* sported "All Over Again," with the Chef delivering a *Beyond the Glory*–style redux of his career from Wu year one until now, the charmingly titled drug tale "Pa-Blow Escablow," and the memorable ensemble effort "Musketeers of Pig Alley," with Masta Killa and Inspectah Deck.   —P.R.

Rage Against the Machine

★★★★   Rage Against the Machine (Epic, 1992)
  ★★★   Evil Empire (Epic, 1996)
★★★★★   The Battle of Los Angeles (Epic, 1999)
  ★★★   Renegades (Epic, 2000)

It's hard to say whether it was Rage Against the Machine's good fortune or misfortune to have flourished during the Clinton years rather than the Constitution-shredding age of John Ashcroft, when a revolution-rallying rock band led by a black man and a Chicano would surely have confronted the specter of Guantanamo Bay. During the band's late-'90s heyday, the dot-com bubble made Rage's agit-prop rap rock seem quaint, even retro. But whether you were a follower or a nonbeliever, there was no denying the never-say-die conviction with which singer Zack de la Rocha carried himself onstage, or that guitarist Tom Morello, emulating turntablists with his toggle switch and whammy pedal, whipped out the first new set of tricks by an axeman since the birth of Eddie Van Halen. Less indelible were the nicked Hendrix riffs the band considered songwriting and a rhythm section that could barely keep up. These elements, combined with the screaming monotony of De la Rocha's delivery, ensured that if you heard one Rage song, you heard them all.

And yet like most bands who quickly run a shallow formula into the ground, Rage crafted songs that jumped out of the bushes and grabbed you, including "Bullet to the Head," a standout on their very strong, very aggro debut album. De la Rocha found his singing voice by way of Chuck D (which may be why Zack turns out to be a damn smart lyricist when you care enough to decipher the words). The group sticks to its formula on *Evil Empire,* to wearying effect. Still, "Bulls on Parade" and "Year of the Boomerang" wrings a couple of minor punk-funk miracles out of Rage's self-imposed clichédom. The sinister and provocative boy-superhero cover art is priceless because the band's rowdy Wonderbread fan base included many look-alikes.

The Battle of Los Angeles was the last stand for the street fightin' quartet. But wouldn't you know, this is also when they decided to cut the bs and drop a bona fide killer worthy of the hard-rock canon. Unlike most rock & roll closeout parties, Rage's demise was publicly precipitated by a beef between the singer and *the bass player,* the former accusing the latter of not taking the group's image seriously when the latter engaged in a drunken MTV Awards prank. (It might only be rock & roll to you, homeboy, but *I'm* a revolutionary.) There's evidence of real musical growth here, particularly in vilified party-boy Tim Bob's thick and more Bootsylicious Mutron-filtered bass sound. Morello raises his game riffwise and magic-wand-wise, too. The machine-shop tricks are deployed more pungently, lyrically, and orchestrally than before. As Bomb Squad–inspired as ever but also more surreal, psychedelic, and Morricone-like than Public Enemy ever was; more Frusciante-like and Aphex Twin-like, even. De la Rocha almost considers crooning to be an option in a couple of places. The quiet, whispery voice he would sneak into *Renegades'* "Beautiful World" makes several even scarier, sardonic appearances on the disc. Above and beyond all critical ranking, this sucker swings, funks, rocks, moshes, and rolls from track to track. After which another good band on the way to greatness bit the dust. Truly a loss for the ages, especially in this age of right-wing terror. A goddamn pity too.

Released postbreakup, *Renegades* is a covers record. Some of the choices seem almost laughably obvious—"Street Fighting Man" and "Kick Out the Jams" in particular. Springsteen's "The Ghost of Tom Joad" and Dylan's "Maggie's Farm" weren't great ideas, but there is a magic moment when de la Rocha makes like a sexy beast delivering the line. "It's a shame how she makes me scrub the floor" as Morello uncharacteristically drops a diminished chordal riposte into the mix. Although Rage's hip-hop covers—Rakim's "Microphone Fiend," Cypress Hill's "How I Could Just Kill a Man," and EPMD's "I'm Housin' "—are shot full of love, balls, and admiration, the leaden funk-metal workout reminds us that a good beat is akin to God in the flesh and that history isn't kind to rapping rockers who commit the cardinal sin of having no flow. Still, De la Rocha's exuberant reading of the Rakim joint is charmingly, bitterly punk, and the hushed, haunting cover of "Beautiful World" is oddly affecting. Also not to be slept through is the bonus live version of "Kill a Man," with Cypress Hill helping out.   —G.T.

Raincoats

- ★★★★   The Raincoats (1980; Geffen, 1997)
- ★★★   Odyshape (1981; Geffen, 1997)
- ★★★   The Kitchen Tapes (1983; ROIR, 1998)
- ★★   Moving (1984; Geffen, 1997)
- ★★   The Raincoats (EP) (Smells Like Records, 1995)
- ★★★★   Looking in the Shadows (Geffen, 1996)

The Raincoats, a British all-female quartet formed in the do-it-yourself crucible of punk, released three albums before breaking up in 1984. Commercially they were a bust, but to a generation of young rockers their albums were an inspiration, a model of how amateur musicians could make extraordinary music out of their everyday lives.

The Raincoats opens with "Fairytale in the Supermarket," which declares, "No one teaches you how to live." The quartet proceeds to make up the rules as it goes along; the band's angular drone-and-strum punk is not for those who prefer compact, in-tune arrangements. But get your head around the odd song shapes, woozy violin solos, and yelping vocals and a strange beauty, born of sincerity and daring, begins to emerge. A cover of the Kinks' "Lola" puts a feminist spin on the song's gender-bending lyrics. Even during an era when everything seemed up for grabs, *The Raincoats* sounds like nothing else.

Odyshape finds the band in deconstruction mode, gleefully ripping apart pop convention. Without a full-time drummer, however, they stray further from punk's directness. The aptly titled *Moving*, posthumously released, is all about refusing to stand still, and the band ventures into pancultural grooves with enthusiasm, if not coherence.

Popular demand (at least from high-profile fans such as Kurt Cobain and Sonic Youth) prompted a 1994 reunion by founding members Gina Birch and Ana Da Silva. They recorded *The Raincoats*, a tentative EP with Sonic Youth's Steve Shelley on drums. But *Looking in the Shadows* picks up where *Moving* left off, integrating dub rhythms and feedback with off-kilter pop melodies. Thankfully, Da Silva and Birch still can't seem to write a normal pop song, their efforts typified by the antianthem "57 Ways to End It All," which withholds its strangely celebratory chorus, "Dying again, dying again," until the tune is nearly done.   —G.K.

Bonnie Raitt

- ★★★   Bonnie Raitt (1971; Rhino, 2001)
- ★★★★   Give It Up (1972; Rhino, 2002)
- ★★★★   Takin' my Time (1973; Rhino, 2002)
- ★★★   Streetlights (1974; Rhino, 2001)
- ★★   Home Plate (1975; Rhino, 2001)
- ★★   Sweet Forgiveness (1977; Rhino, 2001)
- ★★★   The Glow (1979; Rhino, 2001)
- ★★★   Green Light (1982; Rhino, 2001)
- ★★★   Nine Lives (1986; Rhino, 2001)
- ★★★★   Nick of Time (Capitol, 1989)
- ★★★★   The Bonnie Raitt Collection (WB, 1990)
- ★★★   Luck of the Draw (Capitol, 1991)
- ★★★   Longing in Their Hearts (Capitol, 1994)
- ★★★½   Road Tested (Capitol, 1995)
- ★★★★   Fundamental (Capitol, 1998)
- ★★★½   Silver Lining (Capitol, 2002)

When Bonnie Raitt picked up three Grammys for her 1989 album *Nick of Time*, she wasn't earning long-overdue credit. Rather, the Grammys were testimony to eighteen years' worth of evolution and growth. Time and tide finally brought her to producer Don Was for *Nick of Time*. Which is not to suggest that Raitt's previous producers were hacks: Of the many with whom she has worked, only Paul Rothchild (whose credits include the Doors, Paul Butterfield Blues Band, and Janis Joplin) misfired wildly, attempting to convert Raitt into a country-rock chanteuse on *Home Plate* and *Sweet Forgiveness*. Peter Asher, who produced *The Glow*, moved Raitt closer to the grit of her early albums even as he put a pop sheen on the proceedings. Looking back over Raitt's career, it's clear that the problem lay not with the producers but with the star. Simply put, it took a long time for Bonnie Raitt to grow up.

As an artist, she's always had the right idea—sliding the blues she loves into a smattering of tough-rocking originals and smart outside material written by many of the best and brightest of her generation—but she hasn't always had undeniable presence. That quality sporadically *is* there on all of her Warners albums, and it produces some exhilarating moments. *Give It Up* is first-rate, with electrifying performances of Jackson Browne's "Under the Falling Sky" and Eric Kaz's tormented "Love Has No Pride" as well as her own forthright "Give It Up or Let Me Go." Thoughtful interpretations of songs by Kaz ("Cry Like a Rainstorm"), Browne ("I Thought I Was a Child"), and Randy Newman ("Guilty") enliven *Takin' My Time*, with Mississippi Fred McDowell's "Write Me a Few of Your Lines/Kokomo Blues" adding a raw-nerve edge to the disc. On the otherwise muddled *Sweet Forgiveness*, she delivers a delicate take on Paul Siebel's enigmatic "Louise" that approaches Siebel's own definitive version. Still, even her best work seemed too eclectic for its own good. She appeared too polished to be completely convincing as a blues singer, too gritty to be a pop singer, and too restrained to be an out-and-out rocker.

By the time Raitt reached Don Was, she was ready to make a statement. Was provided the rock-steady focus: crisp, stripped-down, bottom-heavy arrangements, with Raitt's voice riding strong over everything and her slide-guitar lines mixed hot and played tastily and soulfully. Raitt responded with one well-modulated performance after another. Where once her singing had been an example of studied casualness, here she emerges with a voice that is easy, confident, free, robust, and alive. The uptempo material—notably "Thing Called Love," written by John Hiatt—cooks righteously, and Raitt sounds utterly absorbed in its emotion. On meditative numbers such as the title song and Michael Ruff's "Cry on My Shoulder," she works from knowledge learned the hard way.

She builds on these strengths on *Luck of the Draw*, which sounds of a piece with *Nick of Time*. Co-produced by Was and Raitt, the album serves up Raitt's forthright originals—"I ain't lookin' for the kind of man/Can't stand a little shaky ground/He'll give me fire and tenderness/And got the guts to stick around," she sings on "Come to Me"—and material that speaks most directly to her newfound self-assurance. When she gets down with Delbert McClinton on "Good Man, Good Woman," their ebullience is infectious; and her yearning on "I Can't Make You Love Me" is profound and real, a serious turn inward to unburden the heart of sadness born of love gone wrong. A variety of moods, a variety of settings; regardless of the context, Raitt's choices are impeccable.

By *Longing in Their Hearts*, however, the Raitt and Was formula seemed a little long in the tooth. The songs were mostly terrific, particularly the title track, cowritten by Raitt and her husband, Michael O'Keefe, and a lovely cover of Richard Thompson's "Dimming of the Day," but a distinct sense of déjà vu smothered the high-gloss, adult-contemporary blues-pop production. After the safe but satisfying career-spanning double-disc live set *Road Tested*, Raitt shifted gears by teaming with the more experimental duo of Mitchell Froom and Tchad Blake (Los Lobos, Suzanne Vega) for the refreshingly challenging *Fundamental*. The album's organic, woodsy grooves were dark and sexy, more back-alley voodoo than prime-time VH1, though with the uptempo "Blue for No Reason" Raitt threw a curveball straight into Sheryl Crow territory, and a heartfelt reading of John Hiatt's "Lover's Will" proved she could still nail a ballad with devastating conviction. The livelier *Silver Lining*, again produced by Raitt, Froom, and Blake, is markedly more polished but equally satisfying, showcasing Raitt at her most refined (the stately, atmospheric David Gray–penned title track) and her most down and dirty. Raitt's own "Gnawin' on It" is exceptionally ferocious, with her slide-guitar standoff with guest Roy Rogers matched nudge for raunchy nudge with lines like, " 'Cause what I got in mind'll put a grin on your face." Proof, just in the nick of time, that while Raitt the artist has indeed grown up, she's still got plenty of youthful playfulness. —D.M./R.SK.

Rakim

★★★   The 18th Letter (Universal, 1997)
★★★   The Master (Universal, 1999)

The greatest MC of all time sat out some serious competition in the early '90s—Biggie, Snoop, and Tupac, to name just three—and came back somewhat diminished after a five-year hiatus. But who wouldn't? That's three lifetimes in hip-hop, and if he sounds only great now instead of unbelievable, chalk that up to history and the disappearance of most conscious rap. No, chalk it up to other things, like production. *The 18th Letter* features some great beats from DJ Premier ("It's Been a Long Time" and "New York (Ya Out There)" and Clark Kent ("Guess Who's Back"), but without a good dose of the signature Eric B. & Rakim sound—uptempo sampled drums and fierce, weird ostinatos—Rakim sounds a bit lost. He's neither easy listening nor callous, and over the wrong beats, his calm style implies something he's not. (Eric B. & Rakim was more of a fusion than we realized, eh?) *The Master* finds the R sounding solid but also stiff, occasionally aping the thugisms of the day. Aside from Premier's "When I B on tha Mic" and the 45 King's fabulous "How I Get Down," the producers don't inspire Rakim to his previous lexical heights.   —S.F.J.

Joey Ramone

★★★   Don't Worry About Me (Sanctuary, 2002)

Don't Worry About Me was the last gasp of Joey Ramone—he was working on this solo album at the time of his death, in 2001, from lymphoma. Thus, what was supposed to be a new beginning for Ramone (born Jeffrey Hyman) now serves as an epitaph of sorts. As the title of this set suggests, Ramone died courageously and with a certain grace: His cover of Louis Armstrong's "What a Wonderful World" might seem strange coming from a punk godfather who was dying from cancer, but it reflects Joey's eternal optimism.

Although early Ramones albums like *Road to Ruin* demonstrate the band's undying adolescent-boy stance, *Don't Worry About Me* is a more adult Joey, albeit with snippets of his childish sweetness. "Searching for Something" is a simple love song, even by Ramones standards, but also an eloquent one. The title track is unpretentious and winning with its buoyancy, a quality effused by every great Ramones song. Even the Armstrong cover, while punked up, comes across like a fight song, which is exactly how one would have expected Joey Ramone to go out—an iconoclast to the last.   —C.R.C.

The Ramones

★★★★★   Ramones (1976; Rhino, 2001)
★★★★½   Leave Home (1977; Rhino, 2001)
★★★★★   Rocket to Russia (1977; Rhino, 2001)
★★★½   Road to Ruin (1978; Rhino, 2001)
★★★★   It's Alive (1979; Warner Bros., 1995)
★★★   End of the Century (1980; Rhino, 2002)

★★   Pleasant Dreams (1981; Rhino, 2002)
★★   Subterranean Jungle (1983; Rhino, 2002)
★½   Too Tough to Die (1984; Rhino, 2002)
★★★★   Ramones Mania (Sire, 1988)
★★★   Loco Live (Sire, 1992)
★★½   Acid Eaters (Radioactive, 1994)
★★   Greatest Hits Live (Radioactive, 1996)
★★★½   Hey Ho Let's Go! (Rhino, 1999)
★★★   Loud Fast Ramones: Their Toughest Hits (Rhino, 2002)
★★★½   NYC 1978 (King Biscuit Flower Hour, 2003)

The Ramones invented punk rock—its sound, its style, its speed—and kept at it for 20 years of steadily diminishing returns. Singer Joey Ramone was their candy-pop heart, with his adenoidal fake British accent and love for '60s radio hits; tormented bassist Dee Dee (the one who started every song by yelling *onetwothreefour!*) provided the darkness beneath the surface; Johnny created a new style of playing guitar by discarding everything but distorted bar chords. A thrilling live band that played well over 2,000 concerts, they never got the Top 40 hit they knew they deserved, but the "brothers" from Forest Hills, Queens, emerged from the gutter and reached for the stars.

Ramones is one of the happiest albums ever made: fourteen songs recorded for $6200, all about the joys of cartoon stupidity ("Now I Wanna Sniff Some Glue"), cartoon violence ("Beat on the Brat"), cartoon male prostitution ("53rd & 3rd"), and gigantic cartoon riffs. "Second verse, same as the first," Joey chirps like he's just discovered the secret of pop; the whole thing sounds a lot simpler than it is. (The reissue adds some demos made before they figured out that they'd be better off keeping the recording as simple as humanly possible.) If it'd been their only record, their place in rock history would have been assured.

But they kept going. *Leave Home* is pretty much the same album, just with different songs: Instead of "Judy Is a Punk," we get "Suzy Is a Headbanger" and so on. They're mostly great songs, though. "Gimme Gimme Shock Treatment" and "Pinhead" became Ramones standards, and "I Remember You" and "Swallow My Pride" are actually wistful. The 2001 reissue adds a 16-song live set from a '76 show that single-handedly kicked off the L.A. punk scene—they're not quite the unstoppable live machine they later became, but you can hear the crowd being won over.

By *Rocket to Russia*, the Ramones had decided it was time for the big time: They wanted a hit single. Their not-yet-embittered attempts are a delight, and their fabulous summertime anthem "Rockaway

Beach" and the love song to their audience, "Sheena Is a Punk Rocker," have had a considerably longer shelf life than most of the songs that *did* make the Top 10 in 1977. The album is tough, catchy, and frequently hilarious. "Teenage Lobotomy" ("Now I guess I'll have to tell 'em/That I got no cerebellum") would seem self-mocking, but so was virtually everything else they did.

On New Year's Eve, 1977, the Ramones played in London, each song separated only by Dee Dee's *onetwothreefour,* and the result was released as *It's Alive,* the best of their live albums. One week later, they did almost exactly the same set, in the same order, in New York City; it eventually appeared as *NYC 1978* though not quite as well recorded as *Alive.* The hits keep coming—27 of them in less than 54 minutes.

Tommy Ramone left in 1977 and was replaced on drums by his previously unknown brother Marky Ramone, who toughens up the band's sound a bit on *Road to Ruin* (still coproduced by Tommy, under his real name, T. Erdelyi). It's got two stone Ramones classics, "I Wanna Be Sedated" (another failed attempt at a hit) and a heart-tugging cover of the Searchers' "Needles & Pins." (The 2001 reissue adds their contributions to the *Rock 'n' Roll High School* soundtrack, including the daffy theme song.) *Road to Ruin* still recognizably follows the template of their first three albums, though. You can't say as much for the bizarre misfire *End of the Century,* for which they hooked up with legendary producer Phil Spector, who scarcely understood them. Only "Do You Remember Rock 'n' Roll Radio?" benefits from the hyperproduced wall-of-sound treatment, though Dee Dee's heroin memoir "Chinese Rock," and Joey's wistful tour diary "Danny Says" assert themselves from beneath the murk.

By *Pleasant Dreams,* the Ramones were barely on speaking terms, so Joey steered them toward their fluffiest pop album, a vision, perhaps, of what Spector might have done for them 20 years earlier. The Ronettes-on-a-bad-trip anthem "The KKK Took My Baby Away" became a live standard; Dee Dee's songs, though, are almost embarrassing. *Subterranean Jungle,* another attempt at radio-friendly production, almost recasts the group as an oldies act, with three covers, including the Chambers Brothers' "Time Has Come Today," and self-recycling originals like "Psycho Therapy." Marky got the boot before *Too Tough to Die* and was replaced by Richie Ramone; Joey only wrote or cowrote three songs because of health problems. The result is a nasty, grisly punk-metal album, with Dee Dee as its dominant songwriting voice (he even sings a couple cuts, tunelessly). Tough, yes, but also no fun.

Animal Boy, released in 1986, includes the Ra-

mones' last great original song—"My Brain Is Hanging Upside Down (Bonzo Goes to Bitburg)," Joey's protest of Ronald Reagan's visit to the graves of Nazi storm troopers—but little else of note. *Halfway to Sanity,* from 1987, and 1989's *Brain Drain* (for which Marky took over the drum seat again) are eminently forgettable; all three discs are now out of print. Dee Dee left the Ramones in 1989, ostensibly to pursue a hip-hop career, though he continued to write songs for the band until the end. (If you ever see a copy of *Standing in the Spotlight,* which he recorded as Dee Dee King, run the other way.) The subsequent not-bad double-live contract fulfiller, *Loco Live,* debuted his (much younger) replacement, C.J. Ramone. 1992's *Mondo Bizarro* is a flaccid disaster, mercifully out of print.

The much-maligned *Acid Eaters,* a collection of '60s covers, is better than its rep; for one thing, it solved the Ramones' songwriting problem. Pete Townshend helps out with backing vocals on the Who's "Substitute," but the band does better with a thundering race through Love's "7 and 7 Is" and a poignant Ramonesification of the Rolling Stones' "Out of Time." Still, they were clearly spinning their wheels, and the subsequent (now out-of-print) studio farewell, *Adios Amigos,* finds them creatively exhausted, aside from Joey's Ronnie Spector tribute, "She Talks to Rainbows" (which Ronnie later recorded), and a cover of Tom Waits' "I Don't Want to Grow Up."

Not exactly what the title promises, *Greatest Hits Live* is a live set from early 1996. Joey has given up on getting the lyrics across and is just sort of hiccuping bits of them (C.J. even fills in for him a few times), and the band plays so fast that the songs melt into a single long polka. The sole highlight is a cover of Motörhead's "R.A.M.O.N.E.S.," which is a little sad. *We're Outta Here!* is yet another unnecessary (and deleted) goodbye, this time a document of their final show.

Of the three Ramones best-of collections, *Ramones Mania* is the most entertaining; it's sequenced for listenability rather than chronology, and came out too early to include anything from the dire final albums. The two-disc *Hey Ho Let's Go!* has all the hits but flows awkwardly, especially the second disc. *Loud Fast Ramones,* compiled by Johnny, omits anything that smacks of Joey's romanticism, which leaves out a crucial part of the Ramones story. Joey died from lymphoma in April 2001, and his solo album, *Don't Worry About Me,* was released almost a year later. In March 2002, the Ramones were inducted into the Rock and Roll Hall of Fame; three months later, Dee Dee died from a heroin overdose. In September 2004, Johnny succumbed to prostate cancer. —D.W.

Rancid

★★★ Rancid (Epitaph, 1993)
★★★½ Let's Go (Epitaph, 1994)
★★★★ . . . And Out Come the Wolves (Epitaph, 1995)
★★★ Life Won't Wait (Epitaph, 1998)
★★★★ Rancid (2000) (Epitaph, 2000)
★★★ BYO Split Series, Vol. 3 (BYO, 2002)
★★★½ Indestructible (Hellcat, 2003)

Rancid never got the memo—distributed, by 1991, as far away as D.C., L.A., New York, and Seattle—that there was nothing less cool than ripping off the Clash. Stealing from Sabbath? Hello, Soundgarden. Aping X-Ray Spex? Just ask the riot-grrrl nation. Even Green Day knows to lift from the Buzzcocks and Stiff Little Fingers. But the Clash? Sweet Jesus, no. Phony Beatlemania may have bitten the dust, but Strummer and Jones were Rancid's Lennon and Mc-Cartney and the only inspiration these four Berkeley City Rockers ever needed. (Well, the Clash and the Specials.)

But Rancid, formed in '91 out of the ashes of ska-core pioneers and East Bay scenesters Operation Ivy, never gave a shit about hipster chic; they were too busy transcribing *Give 'Em Enough Rope,* looking like crusty homeless punks, and writing some of the catchiest, most hilariously derivative pop-core of the '90s. Ivy bassist Matt Freeman and guitarist/singer Tim Armstrong, along with drummer Brett Reed (and, from *Let's Go* forward, guitarist Lars Frederiksen), just wanted their hair to stand up, London to burn, and the music to go bang. The whole thing was pretty touching, really.

Oddly enough, Rancid's self-titled debut is the band's least flagrantly Clash-inflected album, and the least interesting. The generic East Bay punk ramalama certainly bangs away, never quite reaching hardcore velocity but getting there, never manifesting the flawless hooks Rancid later leaned on for emotional sustenance. This is a punk record about getting drunk and breaking stuff, and there's nothing on *Rancid* that indicates the group would be anything other than a Gilman St. stalwart for the rest of its career.

Then came *Let's Go,* on which Rancid smashes the Clash's windows and steals whatever openhearted chords and anthemic earnestness it can grab. Frederiksen's guitar thickens the sound, and the Armstrong/Freeman songs just got sharper and catchier. "Nihilism" couldn't sound less so, "Radio" was co-written with Green Day's Billie Joe Armstrong, and the band scored a real-live hit single with the infectious sing-along "Salvation." MTV picked it up, born-too-late alt-kids latched on to Rancid's warmed-over

'77 enthusiasm, and suddenly one of the least probable bidding wars in indie history was on.

Call Rancid derivative, but praise the band's smarts (and, uh, integrity) in ignoring the major labels, making itself and its indie label mountains of cash when the followup album became one of the defining rock records of 1995. Sporting a sleeve that screamed "Minor Threat," 1995's *. . . And Out Come the Wolves* is Rancid's finest hour. Hipsters get a shout-out on "Olympia Wa." (and Rancid got its own hip-card punched by appearing on a Kill Rock Stars compilation the same year); and the band scored an even bigger hit with "Rubie Soho." The ska influences are still all over the place—"Time Bomb" and "Roots Radicals" are 2-Toned love letters—but Rancid's unbridled eagerness sells these reenactments as true feelings. After playing the '96 Lollapalooza, the band took a break.

This might not have been such a hot idea career-wise, as mass-market punk revivalism was as dead as Sid Vicious in '98. Parts of *Life Won't Wait* don't fall too far from *Wolves'* pile-driving pop, but the disc is pure *Sandinista!* sprawl, hopping genres and hanging out with guest stars like Buju Banton, Stephen Perkins from Jane's Addiction, and the Bosstones' Dicky Barrett. Armstrong and Freeman's politics are still up-with-people simple—"Cash, Culture and Violence," for example—and the Clash-isms have never been more apparent ("Crane Fist" is about two notes away from "The Guns of Brixton"), but the music is sheer ambition, moving from punkabilly to arena rock to reggae in the space of a slightly exhausting but musically fearless hour.

Rancid is all velocity-blurts and hard-core swagger, a return to scenester purity. It is a brutal set, 22 blurts in less than 40 minutes, covering Rwanda, game shows, Radio Havana, and more. The songwriting is still sharp, and Freeman is still a deft, melodic bassist, but *Rancid* 2000 steps back from world-music leanings and into the comforts of a safe East Bay home. Two years later, Rancid participated in a fun EP, split with NOFX, and then headed into the studio to record *Indestructible,* on which the band softened up *Rancid*'s blitzing oi! anthems by returning to their raggedly tuneful stuff of old. On the punk-soul "Fall Back Down" and the piano-driven, almost lounge-y "Arrested in Shanghai," Rancid finds just the right amount of hard-charging beats, snaggle-tooth melodies, and deep convictions about punk and the President. Only a curmudgeon would want them to stop here. —J.G.

Shabba Ranks

★★★ Rappin' With the Ladies (1988; PowWow, 1991)

★★★★ As Raw as Ever (Sony, 1991)
★★★ Rough & Ready, Vol. 1 (Epic, 1992)
★★★ X-tra Naked (Epic, 1992)
★★ Rough & Ready, Vol. 2 (Epic, 1993)
★★★ A Mi Shabba (Epic, 1995)
★★★ Shabba Ranks and Friends (Sony, 1999)
★★★★ Greatest Hits (Sony, 2001)

With his gruff, pulsating toasts and tireless boasts of sexual prowess, Shabba Ranks became the first worldwide crossover dancehall star with hits such as "Mr. Loverman," "House Call (Your Body Can't Lie to Me)," and "Slow and Sexy." His international stardom peaked at the turn of the '90s, as he reputedly released more than 50 singles between 1989 and 1991. His significant crossover success in the U.S. was due in major part to his pioneering hybridization of dancehall with hip-hop, scoring a 1992 hit duet with KRS-One, "The Jam," and soliciting production from Naughty by Nature and Puff Daddy on his 1995 album, A Mi Shabba.

Ranks, born Rexton Rawlston Fernando Gordon in 1966, grew up in Trenchtown, Kingston, (famous as the ghetto home of Bob Marley), releasing his debut single "Heat Under Sufferer's Feet" under the name Co-Pilot in 1985. He was soon being mentored by his hero, the toaster Josey Wales, and brought in to record at Jamaica's premier digital studio, King Jammy's. With producer Bobby Digital (not to be confused with the alias of the RZA), Ranks perfected his nonmelodic chanting style over chugging electronic rhythms. As Raw as Ever was awarded the 1991 Grammy for Best Reggae Album, making Ranks the first dancehall artist ever to notch a win. The album had a pop sensibility, and tracks such as "Trailer Load a Girls," with its chant "girls, girls every day/from London, Canada, and USA," typified the nursery-rhyme simplicity of his vocal hooks. Sporting the same scrawny musculature and asymmetrical hairdo as new-jack star Bobby Brown (a decided favorite of Ranks), Shabba crystallized the image of the flashy, sex-mad Jamaican dancehall star, setting the stage for Shaggy and Sean Paul to follow. —P.R.

The Rapture

★★★ Mirror (Gravity, 1999)
★★★ Out of the Races and Onto the Tracks (EP) (Sub Pop, 2001)
★★★ Echoes (DFA, 2003)

New York City's postmillennial music scene was divided between punk, indie, and electro. With "House of Jealous Lovers," the Rapture combined all three, earning the group spots in seemingly every local DJ's

rotation and on every critic's year-end lists, as well as spreads in hipster lifestyle magazines.

Three years before, the Rapture had released the postpunk-reprising romp Mirror on Gravity, San Diego's venerable noise-rock label. Singer/guitarist Luke Jenner and drummer Vito Roccoforte, originally from that city, moved to Brooklyn, where bassist/singer Matt Safer joined the band. The bracingly raw Out of the Races and Onto the Tracks introduced the basic format, lifted from dance punks like Blondie and James Chance, for "House of Jealous Lovers." On the title track, Roccoforte rides his hi-hat like he'd heard that disco doesn't suck but stomp, Safer drops rudimentary funk, and Jenner complements his stinging guitar with a keening yowl and a raspy admonishment to "shake, shake, shake!"

The Rapture put out the revelatory "House of Jealous Lovers" 12-inch, which drops an absolutely frantic chorus into a rubbery, cowbell-accented groove, along with another single, "Olio," a sleek electronic ode to the Cure. Both cuts ended up on the full-length Echoes, and good thing: So did a Beatlesque ballad called "Open Up Your Heart," where Jenner croons like a tone-deaf Paul McCartney instead of a junior Robert Smith, and the wandering dirge "Infatuation," on which Jenner echoes Thom Yorke. The dance-punk and plain dance numbers, though long on style and short on hooks, do provide some dirty fun: The spastic "Heaven" features a tightly wound a cappella chorus, "Killing" pounds with a heart-attack pulse, and "I Need Your Love" recalls C + C Music Factory—but not, impressively enough, punk, indie, or '80s electro. —N.C.

The Rascals

★★★ The Young Rascals (1966; Warner Bros., 1990)
★★★★ Collections (1967; Warner Bros., 1990)
★★★ Groovin' (1967; Warner Bros., 1990)
★★ Peaceful World (1971; Sundazed, 1999)
★★ The Island of Real (1972; Sundazed, 1999)
★★★ The Ultimate Rascals (Warner Bros., 1986)
★★★★ The Rascals Anthology (1965–1972) (Rhino, 1992)
★★★½ The Very Best of the Rascals (Rhino, 1994)

No matter how silly they looked in their Brit-aping stage gear of knickers and Fauntleroy collars, the Young Rascals (the Young was dropped after three LPs) were one soulful unit, desperate to copy their Stax and Motown idols. Singer/organist Felix Cavaliere handled the rawer fare and Eddie Brigati crooned the pop—such radio cookers as "I Ain't Gonna Eat out my Heart Anymore" and "Good Lovin'" (from the 1966 debut) and "Groovin'" (from

Groovin', 1967). Making keg-party "blue-eyed soul" before the term was coined, Cavaliere-Brigati enjoyed the sort of tough-tender exchange that furthered the Lennon-McCartney partnership, a freer vocal delivery than that of later white R&B singers, plus the secret weapon of Dino Danelli's stop-on-a-dime drum style. From definitive covers of R&B bar-band classics ("In the Midnight Hour," "Mustang Sally") to love songs and feel-good pop ("How Can I Be Sure," "A Beautiful Morning"), they brought class and punch to all their hits. Not content with Top 40 brilliance, the boys tried their hand at pseudo-jazz on *Peaceful World,* and long after their mid-'60s heyday, Cavaliere returned with a decent comeback. But it was their brief summertime moment that made the Rascals great: a funky-sweet alternative to the British Invasion. The highlights of the band's entire career can be found on the excellent *Anthology* (1992). —P.E.

Ratt

★★★★	Out of the Cellar (Atlantic, 1984)
★★★	Invasion of Your Privacy (Atlantic, 1985)
★★½	Dancin' Undercover (Atlantic, 1986)
★★★	Reach for the Sky (Atlantic, 1988)
★★	Detonator (Atlantic, 1990)
★★★★	Ratt & Roll 81–91 (Atlantic, 1991)
★★	Ratt (Portrait, 1999)

Ratt may be the platonic ideal of '80s pop metal/hard rock. Well, okay, there's Poison, but Ratt could play way better, dude. Totally killer riffs? Check. Half-naked chicks crawling around the album covers? Check. One totally classic hit? Check. Giant hair? Cool logo? Sleaze to spare? Check, check, check, baby. This is pure Jaeger-shot music.

Singer/vocalist Stephen Pearcy's limited but effective voice had that high tough thing down cold, guitarist Warren DeMartini had tough ditzy solos to spare, and guitarist Robbin Crosby (R.I.P.), bassist Juan Croucier, and drummer Bobby Blotzer could make all this banality swing pretty hard.

After they did time in the L.A. scene, their major-label, full-length debut, *Out of the Cellar* is about as all-killer-no-filler as this stuff got. "Round and Round" is one of metal's great anthems, built on an absurdly catchy chorus. "She Wants Money" states the obvious, "Lack of Communication" laments the same, and "Back for More" brings us back for more (really, this stuff is almost critic-proof.) Awesomely dumb, dumbly awesome, *Out of the Cellar* holds up damn nicely.

As for the rest of their albums, well, if you can tell them apart, you're probably already a fan.

Ratt & Roll 81–91 anthologizes the band just brilliantly. The hard core may quibble here and there (five tracks from *Detonator* at the expense of "She Wants Money"? Absurd . . .) but all the hits are here, along with less-well-known demiclassics such as "I Want a Woman," "Lay It Down," and "Nobody Rides for Free," from the soundtrack to (yes) *Point Break.* The perfect soundtrack to your Sunset Strip revival party. (*The Essentials* isn't. Avoid.)

Ratt wisely split up in '92, returning in '97 for the out-of-print *Collage,* which sported a cover so blinding ugly even serious fans skipped it. *Ratt* is just kinda sad; guys rehashing the riffs that brought them old glories. After *Ratt,* Pearcy split again, the band continued without him, and in 2002, guitarist Robbin Crosby, who had struggled with heroin over the years, died of AIDS. But wherever Aquanet is used and pointy guitars are plugged in, "Round and Round" will forever go around and come around. —J.G.

Raveonettes

| ★★★★ | Whip It On (2002; Columbia, 2003) |
| ★★★★ | Chain Gang of Love (Columbia, 2003) |

From the first 10 seconds of *Whip It On,* it's clear that this Danish boy-girl duo means business: a painful squeak of feedback, then right into a dark, hollow groove that sounds like the best riff the Jesus and Mary Chain never played. Though stripped and streamlined to a cold, accelerated minimalism, the influence of the JAMC's Reid brothers is all over the eight songs on the Raveonettes' debut mini-LP. But Sune Rose Wagner and Sharin Foo—the former a short, plain man who seems more like a photographer's assistant than a rock star, the latter a tall suicide blonde who seems more like an icy supermodel than a rock star—never lose sight of the sexy violence of their distorted pop vision, nor for a minute grow maudlin or self-obsessed, neither of which can be said of the Reids.

Whip It On—"Recorded in Glorious B-flat Minor"—blazes through its 21½ minutes without a care in the world, not even for the fuzz on their backs in "Cops on Our Tail." (Their response: "Fuck you.") The full-length *Chain Gang of Love* shifts the key to B-flat major and lets in a little light. From "Remember" and "The Great Love Sound," two blasts that could have been on *Whip It On,* the album moves to girl-group, rockabilly, and, in the title track, novelty pop (complete with chain gang grunts a la Sam Cooke and the Pretenders). It's a pastiche of whole swaths of prehippy Americana (leather gangs, Buddy Holly and Everly Brothers melodies, black-and-white B movies), with a curiosity that could only come from foreigners in love and awe. —B.S.

Lou Rawls

★★★	Stormy Monday (1962; Blue Note, 1990)
★★★★	Soulin' (1966; Capitol, 2001)
★★★	Live! (1966; Capitol, 1990)
★★★½	All Things in Time (1976; Capitol, 1993)
★★★½	When You Hear Lou, You've Heard It All (1977; Capitol, 1993)
★★★	Lou Rawls Live (1978; Capitol, 1994)
★★★½	At Last (Blue Note, 1989)
★★★½	Greatest Hits (1990; Capitol, 1995)
★★★★	Anthology (Capitol, 2000)
★★★	Rawls Sings Sinatra (Savoy Jazz, 2003)

Gifted with a remarkable voice—deep, rich and slightly wearied—Lou Rawls has for years purveyed a sophisticated soul style that owes as much to Nat "King" Cole and jazz-lite vocalists as it does to those of classic R&B. He hit biggest in the mid-'70s with Gamble and Huff's "You'll Never Find Another Love Like Mine," a song whose Philly Soul smoothness encapsulated his appeal. Hardly a visionary, the singer instead is a dependable craftsman: Rarely does he catch real fire, yet even less often does he turn in a weak performance. Capitol's two-disc *Anthology,* with "Dead End Street" and "Tobacco Road," remains his strongest collection. *Rawls Sings Sinatra,* from 2003, is just that: a set of swinging songs associated with Ol' Blue Eyes.   —P.E./G.F.

Otis Redding

Selected Discography

★★★★	Pain in My Heart (1964; Atlantic, 1991)
★★★★★	Otis Blue/Otis Redding Sings Soul (1966; Atlantic, 1991)
★★★★	The Otis Redding Dictionary of Soul (1966; Atlantic, 1991)
★★★★★	The Soul Album (1966; Atlantic, 1991)
★★★★	Live in Europe (1967; Atlantic, 1991)
★★★★½	The Dock of the Bay (1968; Atlantic, 1991)
★★★★★	History of Otis Redding (Atco, 1968)
★★★★★	The Immortal Otis Redding (1968; Atlantic, 1991)
★★★★★	In Person at the Whisky-a-Go-Go (1968; Rhino, 1992)
★★★★	Love Man (1969; Atlantic, 1992)
★★★★	Tell the Truth (1970; Atlantic, 1992)
★★★★	Monterey International Pop Festival: Otis Redding/Jimi Hendrix Experience (Reprise, 1970)
★★★★	The Best of Otis Redding (1972; Atlantic, 1985)
★★★★	Recorded Live (1982; Atlantic, 1992)
★★★★	The Legend of Otis Redding (Pair/Atlantic, 1986)

★★★★★	Otis! The Definitive Otis Redding (Rhino, 1993)
★★★	Love Songs (Rhino, 1998)
★★★★½	Very Best of Otis Redding (ATCO, 2002)

with Carla Thomas

★★★★	King & Queen (1967; Atlantic, 1991)

Otis Redding was the premier Southern soul singer. Providing counterpoint to Motown, the Memphis-based sound Redding defined made the '60s R&B renaissance a glorious tension of complementary styles. While Motown, as Peter Guralnick explains in *Sweet Soul Music,* was string-laden, melodic, and tended toward pop, Stax/Volt/Atlantic, adhering more closely to gospel and blues roots, was horn-driven and primarily rhythmic, its fierceness the product of stellar solo vocalists and a lean rhythm section. Otis Redding remains its quintessence. In league with the Muscle Shoals studio players—Booker T. Jones (organ), Steve Cropper (guitar), Donald "Duck" Dunn (bass), and Al Jackson (drums)—Redding tested the limits of his quick musical intelligence. His horn parts alone were radically innovative: By employing trumpets as exclamation points, for example, he altered forever the syntax of the brass section in popular music, and his use of difficult, unexpected key signatures added density to the simple melodic lines his horn parts accompanied. Cowriting many of his hits with Cropper, Otis spared R&B down to its lean core—in Stax/Volt, no note was redundant. All of Redding's technique, however, served emotion, and that emotion, celebratory or anguished, was conveyed by the absolute urgency of his remarkable voice.

The title track on *Pain in My Heart* (1965) set the pattern for all his ballads to come—Otis triumphed at rendering agony. Signs of the singer's virtuosity are already apparent in the almost teasing way he lingers over some lyrics and spits out others; virtually never would he sing a line the same way twice. *The Great Otis Redding Sings Soul Ballads* continues his rapid development as a style setter: "Mr. Pitiful" sums up his tortured-romantic persona. "That's How Strong My Love Is" demonstrates his skill at transforming gospel witnessing into erotic testifying.

With *Otis Blue,* he achieves his first masterwork. "Respect" becomes not only a soul standard but also a black pride anthem; "I've Been Loving You Too Long (to Stop Now)" may be Otis' strongest ballad; the assertiveness of B.B. King's "Rock Me Baby" and Sam Cooke's "Shake" finds him equally at home with blues and rockers as well as ballads. His furious cover of the Stones' "(I Can't Get No) Satisfaction" is prescient, suggesting the spirit of later R&B-rock fusions by Hendrix, Sly Stone, and Prince. "Chain Gang" and the moody swing of "Cigarettes and Coffee" highlight *The Soul Album; In Person at the Whisky-a-Go-Go* is dependably intense; and by the time of *Dictionary of Soul,* Otis had arrived at another plateau. "Try a Little Tenderness," first recorded by Bing Crosby, is Stax/Volt at its most sophisticated; in an elegant, almost jazzy setting, Redding, for all his customary fervor, delivers one of his most mature performances, smoky and at times almost langorous.

"Fa-Fa-Fa-Fa-Fa (Sad Song)" is more typical Southern soul: hard and precise but swinging. From *King & Queen,* his duet with Carla Thomas, "Tramp," offers a rare display of Otis' sassy humor; their cover of Steve Cropper and Eddie Floyd's "Knock on Wood" is almost assaultive in its drive. By 1967, the singer had reached a point of such assurance that he seemed ripe for even more ranging explorations of style and new shifts in tone. But even his record company didn't quite know what to do with the latest product of his impatient creativity—the soft, acoustic-guitar ballad "(Sittin' on) The Dock of the Bay." As the first soul singer to absorb the influence of Bob Dylan, Redding turns out a folk melody of indelible, simple force; his lyrics have all the immediacy of conversation, but he sings the line with an undertone of yearning that makes the record unmistakable soul music, and the final triumph of his deep, swift career.

By the end of the year, the singer had died in a plane crash; given the potential suggested by *The Dock of the Bay* as well as the consistent, challenging beauty of all the music he'd made up until the recording of that album, the loss incurred by Redding's death remains immeasurable. Rhino's superb *Otis! The Definitive Otis Redding* is required listening for anyone remotely interested in classic R&B. A lovingly annotated four-CD box set, it compiles all of the singles and essential album tracks, culminating with an entire disc of various live performances assembled to create the definitive Redding concert experience. Other single and double-disc compilations are simply underwhelming by comparison. Of the many live sets, the best are *Live in Europe* and *In Person at the Whisky-a-Go-Go.* —P.E.

Red Hot Chili Peppers

★ The Red Hot Chili Peppers (1984; EMI, 2003)
★★ Freaky Styley (1985; EMI, 2003)
★★ The Uplift Mofo Party Plan (1987; EMI, 2003)
★★★ Mother's Milk (1989; EMI, 2003)
★★★½ Blood Sugar Sex Magik (Warner Bros., 1991)
★★★ What Hits!? (EMI, 1992)
★ Out in L.A. (EMI, 1994)
★★½ One Hot Minute (Warner Bros., 1995)
★★★ Californication (Warner Bros., 1999)
★★★ By the Way (Warner Bros., 2002)
★★★★ Greatest Hits (Warner Bros., 2003)

Long before the idea of making a puree out of funk, punk, hip-hop, and metal became fashionable, the Red Hot Chili Peppers were terrorizing audiences in Los Angeles and beyond with a musical approach no more disciplined than a band of runaway orangutans. Their emergence as a headlining arena act in their second decade coincided with a dialing down of the high jinks (and the experimental flair) in favor of a more song-oriented approach.

For years, the Chili Peppers' me-Tarzan-you-Jane booga-booga shtick camouflaged serious musical deficiencies—namely, the first two albums contain not a single memorable song despite the production assistance of Gang of Four's Andy Gill *(The Red Hot Chili Peppers)* and George Clinton *(Freaky Styley).* The California quartet brings a modicum of structure to *The Uplift Mofo Party Plan,* but their humor—as their famous "party on your pussy" chorus demonstrates—wouldn't merit an audience in a high-school locker room.

The death of guitarist Hillel Slovak, due to a drug overdose, prompted a retooling on *Mother's Milk,* which yielded their first hit—a cover of Stevie Wonder's "Higher Ground" that jumps on the back of Flea's mind-melting bass and never lets go. The era is summed up on *What Hits!?* and *Out in L.A.,* which gather early-'80s demos that are essentially an homage to Flea's bass playing and little else.

Things get better when the band recruits fanboy-guitar-wunderkind John Frusciante as Slovak's replacement. With *Blood Sugar Sex Magik,* producer Rick Rubin focuses on the quartet's songwriting and sets the elastic bass lines, syncopated drumming, and Frusciante's scratchy, punk-Hendrix guitars in uncluttered arrangements that bring the melodies closer to the surface. Singer Anthony Kiedis even became something of a crooner on the breakthrough ballad "Under the Bridge," an unlikely development that turned the band into Lollapalooza-era stars.

One Hot Minute, made with guitarist Dave Navarro, marks the mainstreaming of the Peppers, with the ratio of throwaways to keepers leveling off. An unexpected lightness surfaces on "Aeroplane," and a social consciousness permeates "Shallow Be Thy Game" and "Pea." (The band has since disavowed the album.) An outright pop sensibility, unimaginable a decade before, pervades *Californication.* The return of prodigal guitarist John Frusciante gives the band a second strong instrumental voice to complement Flea's, while Kiedis focuses on increasingly vibrant vocal melodies. Almost all vestiges of the band's funk-monkey persona have been expunged in favor of textured sing-alongs. It adds up to the quartet's most consistent recording.

Something is missing, though, which becomes apparent on *By the Way*. Even though the disc boasts a bevy of multihued pop tunes, it forgets to rock. Flea's hyper bass lines take a holiday, but Frusciante's myriad guitar voicings nearly compensate: choppy funk accents ("By the Way"), trickle-to-a-monsoon dynamics ("Don't Forget Me"), flamenco flourishes ("Cabron"). Kiedis digs deeper emotionally, but ballads have never been his forte—and *By the Way* is full of them. —G.K.

Red House Painters

★★★	Down Colorful Hill (4AD, 1992)
★★★	Red House Painters 1 (4AD, 1993)
★★★★	Red House Painters 2 (4AD, 1993)
★★★★	Ocean Beach (4AD, 1995)
★★½	Songs for a Blue Guitar (Supreme/Island, 1996)
★★★	Old Ramon (Sub Pop, 2001)

San Francisco's Red House Painters burst onto the scene in the early '90s like an extra-slow rocket covered in molasses. Their lugubrious, lyrical, and literate singer/songwriter alt rock was a natural fit for 4AD Records, Great Britain's number-one exporter of tears, fears, gloom, and atmosphere, and the four albums that the RHPs recorded for that label proved they could hold their own with fellow Yank signees Throwing Muses and Lisa Germano in a game of More Miserable Than Thou.

Down Colorful Hill (1992) is made up of unaltered demo recordings that the band sent to the label. It's a spare and echoey album filled with lead Painter Mark Kozelek's dulcet moans and inward melodramas of pain and regret set to acoustic guitars and a wash of gentle drums and droning feedback. *Hill* is possibly one of the finest albums ever for shut-ins who consider a move from the bed to the couch one of the few goals in life worth achieving.

In 1993 the Painters released two separate self-titled albums. The first is notable for the lovely "Grace Cathedral Park" and the slowly evolving metallic dirge "Funhouse." More cohesive and powerful is the second self-titled album, which features "Evil," a note-perfect summation of childhood discontent that's possibly the band's finest hour, as well as the first of many inspired (and at times misguided) cover songs, including Simon & Garfunkle's loner anthem "I Am a Rock" and "The Star-Spangled Banner" (!).

Ocean Beach lightens the mood considerably. It's more mannered, layered, and complex than earlier al-

bums, but somehow more accessible and satisfying, too. *Songs for a Blue Guitar* has Cowboy Junkie–ish loner-folkie acoustic songs, a cover of Yes's "Long Distance Runaround" reconfigured as a Neil Young guitar jam, and a genius cover of the Cars' "All Mixed Up." *Old Ramon,* which was recorded in 1998 but released in 2001, hints at an older and wiser Kozelek settling down to a life of boring domesticity, as evidenced on "Wop-a-din-din," a love song for his cat. Happily, there are enough C&W-tinged ballads, weeping drums, and proud last stands for loneliness on *Old Ramon* to keep even the most destitute of travelers satisfied year after godforsaken year. —S.S.

Redman

★★½	Whut? Thee Album (Def Jam, 1992)
★★★	Dare Iz a Darkside (Def Jam, 1994)
★★★	Muddy Waters (Def Jam, 1996)
★★★★	Doc's da Name 2000 (Def Jam, 1998)
★★½	Malpractice (Def Jam, 2001)

Redman and Method Man

| ★★★★ | Blackout! (Def Jam, 1999) |

Newark, New Jersey, ain't the Bronx or the Bridge— or Compton, either, while we're at it. There's nothing glamorous about its poverty and grime, and the city's poet laureate knows better than to pretend otherwise. Although Redman blurs the line between talking tough and bullshitting with a trickster's glee, he's more of a realist than most of hip-hop's supposed truth-talkers. At his sharpest, he sketches a Newark that's recognizable as an actual city, populated by recognizable characters struggling to survive. And he tells their stories with a brilliantly foul mouth and a gift for comic exaggeration that makes him the most eloquent nut job in hip-hop this side of Ol' Dirty Bastard.

Of course, when you're driven by a need to prove your insanity, your shtick can grow tiresome. Early in his career, Red could come off like a one-man Onyx (not a compliment), and the tracks Erick Sermon had given him to rhyme over were recycled George Clinton so stale they'd make Dr. Dre blush. But Da Funk Doctor Spot (as Red called himself) improved incrementally until he found his voice on *Doc's da Name 2000,* which has more laughs than most comedy records, with the MC unleashing absurd gags like "My middle name must be He Ain't Shit/Cause every time bitches see me, they be like 'He ain't shit.'"

Then in 1999, a wonderful thing happened— Redman hooked up with Method Man. They dubbed themselves "the rap Cheech & Chong," and they made plenty of cheeba gags (while gagging from cheeba), but they're funnier than the original pothead jokesters ever were. They're one of the great pairings in hip-hop, on record and on film, genuinely bringing out the best in each other. Unfortunately, Red seems to be putting no more effort into his solo career than necessary; he sounds no more invested in *Malpractice* than he does when he drops nonsense on big-money R&B tracks like Christina Aguilera's "Dirrty." —K.H.

Jimmy Reed

★★★	I'm Jimmy Reed (1958; Collectables, 2000)	
★★	Rockin' With Reed (1959; Collectables, 2000)	
★★★	Found Love (1959; Collectables, 2000)	
★★★	Now Appearing (1960; Collectables, 1996)	
★★★½	Jimmy Reed at Carnegie Hall (1961; Collectables, 2000)	
★★★★	Just Jimmy Reed (1962; Collectables, 2000)	
★★★½	12 String Guitar Blues (1963; Collectables, 2000)	
★★★	The Best of the Blues (1963; Collectables, 2000)	
★★★★	T'ain't No Big Thing but He Is Jimmy Reed (1963; Collectables, 2000)	
★★★	Jimmy Reed at Soul City (1964; Collectables, 2000)	
★★★★	The Legend-the Man (1965; Collectables, 2000)	
★★★★★	The Best of Jimmy Reed (1974; GNP Crescendo, 1992)	
★★★½	Blues Is My Business (1976; Collectables, 2000)	
★★	Jimmy Reed Is Back (Collectables, 1994)	
★★★	Big Legged Woman (Collectables, 1996)	
★★★★	Lost in the Shuffle (32 Jazz, 1997)	
★½	Cry Before I Go (Drive Archive, 1995)	
★★★★	Blues Masters: The Very Best of Jimmy Reed (Rhino, 2000)	
★★★★★	Big Boss Man (Collectables, 2001)	

Raised in the Mississippi Delta on Delta blues, Jimmy Reed made the exodus to Chicago in 1953, and two years later he had a national hit with "You Don't Have to Go." For the next six years, Reed was rarely off the charts, and on occasion he crossed over from R&B to the national pop chart. During that time, he built the monuments at which many young British rockers genuflected in the '60s: "Ain't That Lovin' You Baby," "Baby What You Want Me to Do," the Willie Dixon–penned "Big Boss Man" and, in 1961, the instant classic "Bright Lights Big City." Like Bo Diddley, Reed found a groove and stuck with it. His was a lazy but relentless shuffle, spiced with elemental blues progressions, crying harmonica, and a vocal style that was personable and mellow. He was the definition of medium cool.

Reed's catalogue is in great shape nowadays,

thanks to Collectables' ambitious reissue program on the artist's behalf. Check out the instrumental album *12 String Guitar Blues,* which features Reed on acoustic 12-string guitar, fashioning some steadily percolating renditions of a dozen familiar songs, including "Bright Lights Big City," "Hush-Hush," and "Baby What You Want Me to Do." *Just Jimmy Reed,* from 1962, is slight at only ten cuts, but it finds Reed going straight into an R&B bag on the first track, "I'll Change That Too"; expanding his instrumental lineup to include a horn section and a Hammond B3 organ; and thriving in the big, dramatic sound the band sculpts behind one of his most powerful vocal performances. This essential album is highlighted by five cuts taken directly from the studio sessions, complete with chatter between Reed and the musicians, false starts, and Reed appearing to make up a song on the spot, "Kansas City Baby."

Sifting through the Vee-Jay titles in the Collectables reissue series, certain albums stand out. *T'ain't No Big Thing but He Is Jimmy Reed* and *Rockin' With Reed* (he's accompanied by Albert King on guitar on the latter) are notable for the ferocity of the rocking tracks. Also ranking with the essential Reed albums is *The Legend the Man.* Originally released in 1965, this 12-song long player serves as a career overview, its tune stack kicking off with Reed's first Vee-Jay single, 1953's "High and Lonesome," and includes "You Don't Have to Go" and other Reed evergreens.

At the other end of the scale is Collectables' *Big Legged Woman,* comprising 10 of what turned out to be Reed's final recordings made for the Canyon label. Fans who treasure the spirit and liveliness of Reed's Vee-Jay cuts will find this collection difficult to negotiate, owing to the ravaged, morose quality of Reed's singing. It's a sad document, but some may find it essential because it's the final installment of the life's work of an important artist. Reed's first album, *I'm Jimmy Reed* (released in 1958) contains the original recording of "Honest I Do," a Top 5 R&B hit. On this track, Reed was joined by Chicago jazz guitarist Remo Biondi, who added a new wrinkle to Reed's sound with a series of delicate, descending lines that serve as an instrumental counterpoint to Reed's vocal. This track alone elevates the album into the top tier of Reed's studio efforts.

For those who want only the prime cuts, several first-rate Reed retrospectives are available. Rhino's *Blues Masters: The Very Best of Jimmy Reed* has the best-known Reed numbers and other vital tracks such as "Take Out Some Insurance," "Going to New York," the eerie "Odds and Ends" (complete with violin parts!), and its boogying opposite, "Ends and Odds." GNP Crescendo's *The Best of Jimmy Reed* is a wonderful package tracing the arc of Reed's Vee-Jay years, from the early sides to "I'm Goin' Upside Your Head," with the added benefit of liner notes by veteran jazz writer Leonard Feather. Another solid overview of the Vee-Jay years comes by way of *Lost in the Shuffle* on the 32 Records label.

As a companion to *Big Legged Woman,* Collectables' *Jimmy Reed Is Back* fills in more of the artist's final, unsuccessful years as a recording artist, when he was signed to ABC Bluesway and Exodus. Its 12 tracks, recorded between 1966 and 1971, show Reed getting solid support from Eddie Taylor, Lefty Bates, and Phil Upchurch, among others. Among the highlights: a semiautobiographical blues, "Just a Poor Country Boy," built on "Big Boss Man"; a raucous harmonica raveup on "Tribute to a Friend," an homage to Sonny Boy Williamson; and a deep, slow blues, "I'm Leavin'," which takes off behind Reed's soulful vocal. Drive Archive's entry, *Cry Before I Go,* a collection of recordings made for the Roker label in 1970, is an unfortunate experiment, updating Reed's sound with funk rhythm and wah-wah pedals galore. —D.M.

Lou Reed

★★★★	Lou Reed (RCA, 1972)
★★★★	Transformer (1972; RCA, 2002)
★★★★	Berlin (RCA, 1973)
★★★★	Rock 'n' Roll Animal (1974; RCA, 2000)
★★★	Sally Can't Dance (1974; RCA, 2001)
★★★	Lou Reed Live (RCA, 1975)
★	Metal Machine Music (1975; Buddha/BMG, 2000)
★★★½	Walk on the Wild Side: The Best of Lou Reed (1972–76; RCA, 1977)
★★★★	Different Times: Lou Reed in the '70s (1972–76; RCA, 1996)
★★★	Street Hassle (Arista, 1978)
★★★	The Bells (1979; Buddha/BMG, 2000)
★★★	Growing Up in Public (1980; Buddha/BMG, 2000)
★★★	Rock and Roll Diary: 1967–1980 (Arista, 1980)
★★★★½	The Blue Mask (RCA, 1982)
★★★★½	Legendary Hearts (RCA, 1983)
★★★★	New Sensations (RCA, 1984)
★★★	Between Thought and Expression (1972–86; RCA, 1992)
★★★★	New York (Sire, 1989)
★★★	Magic and Loss (Sire, 1992)
★★★½	Set the Twilight Reeling (Warner Bros., 1996)
★★★	Perfect Night: Live in London (Warner Bros., 1998)
★★★★	Ecstasy (Warner Bros., 2000)
★★★½	The Raven (Sire/Reprise, 2003)
★★★★½	NYC Man: The Collection (RCA/BMG Heritage, 2003)
★★★★	Animal Serenade (Sire/Reprise, 2004)

Lou Reed/John Cale

★★★½	Songs for Drella (Sire, 1990)

Lou Reed was a young poet who had studied under Delmore Schwartz. John Cale was a young composer who had studied under Cornelius Cardew and worked with La Monte Young. (While none of those mentors were famous names, each had genuine underground cachet.) They joined in a band called the Warlocks; they were arty and intellectual and subversive, all of which appealed to Andy Warhol, who incorporated them into his Exploding Plastic Inevitable and renamed them the Velvet Underground. Their early songs dealt with the major issues of New York intellectual life in the late '60s: transvestites, sadomasochism, scoring heroin. Warhol and superstar chanteuse Nico left after one album. Cale packed up his electric viola after the second. Their later songs dealt with love and having your life saved by rock & roll. Reed quit the band after four albums. When Lou Reed embarked on his solo career he was known to a small but intense cult as the singer/songwriter of the Velvet Underground.

Lou Reed entered the '70s hankering for success, but when he found some—a Top 20 single, "Walk on the Wild Side," and a Top 10 album, *Sally Can't Dance.* He didn't seem to care for it much. In fact, his next move was a double album of amplifier feedback called *Metal Machine Music,* which he followed with albums of indifferent songs and live abuses, until even his most devoted fans cried uncle.

Reed's first solo album, *Lou Reed,* might have been a fifth Velvets album—indeed, many of the songs eventually surfaced on outtake albums such as *VU*— but the studio pros sounded hollow compared to the band. It went nowhere and is still out of print. But for *Transformer* Reed wrote a bunch of clever new songs and tried to cash in on producer David Bowie's trendily androgynous glam rock, which worked well enough to break "Walk on the Wild Side." There's actually much to enjoy on the album: the intro riff on "Vicious," the maturing "Hangin' 'Round," the tricked-up "Satellite of Love," the trivial "New York Telephone Conversation." But with a hit single Reed started looking to move into the arenas, so he recruited Alice Cooper producer Bob Ezrin and cut his ambitious, gloomy, brutal song cycle *Berlin*—his most controversial album: strong songs, weak stories, bloated arrangements. Then came *Rock 'n' Roll Animal,* with its four Velvets standards scaled up to arena size, which they do remarkably well.

This set the stage for the flash success of *Sally*

Can't Dance—the album was effectively presold on Reed's recent successes and his ever-growing Velvet Underground fame, so it shot straight up the charts—and then flopped like a duck. It is at best a confusing album, laden with blaring horns, but the title track was funky, and there are two nice ballads ("Ennui," "Billy"). The next few years were nasty, but the first whiffs of Reed comeback hype surfaced with *Street Hassle*—some old Velvets-era songs and a long suite built around a violin riff, ambitious but cold and inconsistent. *The Bells* was another twist: cut with jazz trumpeter Don Cherry, it offered exceptionally dense but not really jazzy music. *Growing Up in Public* returned to simpler songs and much more straightforward writing, such as his mother's admonition not to smile, and his petrified marriage proposal.

Reed's 1980 marriage to Sylvia Morales was a turning point for him, but what really jump-started his music was renewed interest in playing guitar in a real band, especially one with another ace guitarist, Robert Quine. Reed wrote better songs for *The Blue Mask* (see "Average Guy" and "Day John Kennedy Died"), but the most impressive cuts were guitar raveups such as "Heavenly Arms," "Waves of Fear," and especially the title track. *Legendary Hearts* and *New Sensations* had less guitar flash but, if anything, even better songs—for example, "Don't Talk to Me About Work," "Bottoming Out," "Doin' the Things That We Want To," and "My Friend George."

If Reed's early-'80s album streak did anything it was to get him out from under the ever-growing VU legend and establish a new standard for him to fail to meet (but a more benign one). Reed's albums ever since have been marvelously diverse. *New York* is his acidic hometown tourist flyer, *Songs for Drella*, an elegy for the late Mr. Warhol. *Magic and Loss* has more funeral notices. *Set the Twilight Reeling* is a loud digression, and renewal of sorts. *Ecstasy*, perhaps the best of the run, is the revenge of the guitars.

The Raven, Reed's reworking of Edgar Allan Poe, is further proof that reading is fun (although rock & rollers are advised to stick to the single-CD version, story line be damned).

Reed's three-CD box set, *Between Thought and Expression*, is the sort of mess you'd expect from such an inconsistent, idiosyncratic artist. RCA's two 1972–76 comps are decent samplers, with only five cuts in common—*Different Times* gets the nod for being longer and more adventurous. The RCA and Arista records, now owned by BMG, are in a chaotic state of disrepair—the recent remastered editions of *Transformer* and *Sally Can't Dance* may be the start of a revival, although as of this writing several of the best are available only as German imports.

Reed's most recent releases show he's been thinking about his legacy. *NYC Man* is the artist's own idea of an epitaph: an unobvious but smartly sequenced two-CD retrospective that tightly binds together his every twist and turn from the Velvet Underground to his latest album. Compared to it, *Between Thought and Expression* is just a grab bag, and RCA's 1972–76 comps are narrow slices. *Animal Serenade* also plumbs his songbook, in the guise of a live album. Like *Rock 'n' Roll Animal*, it recasts old songs on a new soundscape—this one staged to draw out the drama of the words, framed starkly with guitar, synths, and cello. Then he rocks out with his old standard "Heroin." —T.H.

R.E.M.

★★★★★ Murmur (I.R.S., 1983)
★★★★½ Reckoning (1984; A&M, 1990)
★★★★½ Fables of the Reconstruction (1985; Capitol, 1998)
★★★★★ Lifes Rich Pageant (1986; Capitol, 1998)
★★★★½ Document (1987; Capitol, 1998)
★★★★½ Dead Letter Office (1987; A&M, 1990)
★★★★½ Eponymous (1988; Capitol, 1998)
★★★★ Green (1988; Warner Bros., 1990)
★★★½ Out of Time (Warner Bros., 1991)
★★★★½ Automatic for the People (Warner Bros., 1992)
★★★½ Monster (Warner Bros., 1994)
★★★½ New Adventures in Hi-fi (Warner Bros., 1996)
★★★ Up (Warner Bros., 1998)
★★★ Reveal (Warner Bros., 2001)
★★★★ In Time: The Best of R.E.M., 1988–2003 (Warner Bros., 2003)

R.E.M. came roaring out of Athens, GA, in 1981, spearheading the college-rock movement of the '80s and introducing the word *jangle* to the world of music. Bursting with melody, R.E.M. had the good fortune to sound like a band assembled with new, raw parts, so that Peter Buck's percussive guitar playing sounded fresh against Mike Mills' fluid bass lines, Michael Stipe's vocals were cryptic and languid when not downright inaudible, and Bill Berry's drums skittered underneath everything, driving it all forward with a danceable momentum. That sound has been intact from the band's first 1981 single, "Radio Free Europe," and the 1982 EP *Chronic Town*. "Radio Free Europe" also kicked off their first proper album, *Murmur*, a murky, alarmingly original collection that wasn't punk, hard rock, country, new wave, or anything else on the radio in 1983. It was the first true shot of what came to be called college rock. *Murmur* showcased Buck's wandering semileads on gorgeous but inscrutable tracks like "Moral Kiosk" and "Catapult." *Murmur* would have almost been folk rock if not for Stipe's self-consciously opaque vocals: "Standing assumed shoulders high in the room," he seems to say on the chorus of "Perfect Circle."

Reckoning lightened things a bit, with the effervescent pop of "(Don't Go Back to) Rockville" and the classically constructed, moody "so. Central Rain (I'm Sorry)" nearly becoming hits. The songwriting was as strong as *Murmur's* though the atmospherics were more conventional. *Fables of the Reconstruction* was significantly darker; even the single "Driver 8" tells a story of death and destruction. The instrumentation broadened slightly, with punchy horns on "Can't Get There From Here" and the banjo arpeggios of the heartbreakingly beautiful "Wendell Gee" exploring the shadowy corners of Americana, even though the record was made in England. Existing almost entirely in minor keys, *Fables* was somewhat overlooked, but it stands up nearly as well as the first two albums.

After getting off to such a strong beginning, R.E.M. continued to step forward on 1986's *Lifes Rich Pageant,* which may be the band's best album. Equal parts gorgeous and whimsical, *Pageant* is highlighted by the stunning, swooning "Fall on Me," and the almost-as-perfect Civil War reverie "Swan Swan H." Openhearted and accessible, *Pageant* starts off with the rollicking "Begin the Begin" and doesn't let up until Mills takes his first solo vocal on the Clique's "Superman."

Document kept the momentum going; it was a commercial breakthrough as well as another landmark record. "The One I Love" became the band's first Top 10 hit, though the anthemic single "It's the End of the World As We Know It (and I Feel Fine)" had more lasting power. If the songwriting wasn't as consistently extraordinary as on the previous albums, Stipe was showing more political sensibility, not to mention enunciation, on "Exhuming McCarthy" and "Welcome to the Occupation."

Green, released on Election day, 1988, ended the first phase of R.E.M.'s career with the bubblegum classic "Stand," complete with wah-wah-guitar solo and double key changes at the end; it found a deserved second life as the theme to Chris Elliott's deeply weird Fox sitcom *Get a Life.* Buck took the album's lead, from the churning near-metal guitar of "Turn You Inside-Out" to the chiming mandolin on "Hairshirt" and the harmonics ringing through "Orange Crush." It was followed by the B-side collection *Dead Letter Office,* which demonstrated that even in its throwaway efforts, R.E.M. had more ideas than most bands could put into an entire album. They covered Aerosmith,

Roger Miller, and Pylon; reworked their own songs for no reason other than amusement; and tucked meaty hooks into jokey toss-offs, like their attempted theme for Walter's Barbecue. While far from great, *Dead Letter Office* is an enjoyable trip through a terrific band's most lighthearted moments; the CD version, with *Chronic Town* tacked onto the end, is a don't-miss.

R.E.M. returned in 1991 with *Out of Time* and the intricately constructed single "Losing My Religion." But aside from that gorgeously fragile piece, the band sounded bored, switching instruments for no apparent purpose and tarting up unfinished song ideas with string arrangements and Kate Pierson (e.g., "Shiny Happy People"). The experiments work the best, including "Country Feedback," with Stipe spewing vitriol over a lone Western guitar, and the half-spoken fable "Belong." (*Out of Time* is also the third R.E.M. album, after *Murmur* and *Green,* to begin with a song about the radio, in this case, "Radio Song.")

The pensive *Automatic for the People* found Stipe not just clear and direct but almost didactic on paeans to the kids on Top 30 hits like "Drive" and "Everybody Hurts." The Andy Kaufman tribute "Man on the Moon" was an unlikely smash, but more of the album was given over to dark, death-haunted ballads like "Sweetness Follows," "Try Not to Breathe," and the rippling "Nightswimming." Although the songs were straightforward in their construction, the lyrics' open emotions combined with some of R.E.M.'s sweetest compositions resulted in what many consider the band's finest hour.

Monster, the followup, couldn't have been more different: The guitars were amped up, but the songwriting was far less consistent and the emotions had returned to opacity. Buck storms through the excellent single "What's the Frequency, Kenneth?," complete with backward guitar solo, and his flamethrower chords power through "Circus Envy." Again, the experiments—the River Phoenix tribute "Let Me In," with its scrabbling distorted guitar and lack of drums; the audacious, falsetto "Tongue"—work better than the conventional songs: "Crush With Eyeliner" and "Band and Blame" were simply interminable exercises in subpar songwriting. *New Adventures in Hi-fi,* from 1996, feels like a retreat—it was largely recorded live on tour and lacked anything resembling a hit single. The songs were drawn out; Many of them clocked in at five minutes; the siren-fueled "Leave" tops seven. While "New Test Leper" and "E-Bow the Letter," with guest vocals from Patti Smith, sound like classic R.E.M., the album as a whole was too unfocused for many listeners.

In 1997, Bill Berry, who had suffered a brain

aneurysm during a show in Switzerland in 1995, retired from R.E.M. to operate his farm in his hometown of Macon, GA. When R.E.M. regrouped without Berry for 1998's *Up,* it seemed as if the band wanted to forgo drums altogether. While the songwriting was still strong, particularly on the single "Daysleeper" and the *Pet Sounds* tribute "At My Most Beautiful," the arrangements were sluggish, almost mushy, without much to differentiate one track from the next. The experiments, such as the Brian Eno–ish "Airportman," weren't exactly unsuccessful, but they weren't memorable either. *Reveal,* from 2001, was more of the same: The rhythmic drive of R.E.M.'s best work was missing, despite the sweetness of tracks like "Imitation of Life" and "All the Way to Reno." Layered arrangements and strings couldn't compensate for the lack of sharp edges the band's best work had displayed. R.E.M. had always been the most democratic of bands; every song was credited to all four members, and each musician brought a distinctive tone and set of strengths to the band. Without Berry, however, the brilliant, groundbreaking R.E.M. may be a thing of the past.

The first R.E.M. best-of, 1988's *Eponymous,* is worth owning, as it compiles every hit through *Document,* but those early albums are must-haves for fans anyway. *In Time* picks up most of the best of the latter half of R.E.M.'s career and may make more sense to own than *Eponymous,* since the later albums are less essential.   —T.N.

REO Speedwagon

★★★	REO Speedwagon (Epic, 1971)
★★★	R.E.O./T.W.O. (Epic, 1972)
★★★	Ridin' the Storm Out (Epic, 1973)
★★	Lost in a Dream (Epic, 1974)
★★	This Time We Mean It (Epic, 1975)
★★	R.E.O. (Epic, 1976)
★★½	Live: You Get What You Play For (Epic, 1977)
★★★	You Can Tune a Piano, but You Can't Tuna Fish (Epic, 1978)
★★	Nine Lives (Epic, 1979)
★★★	A Decade of Rock & Roll: 1970 to 1980 (Epic, 1980)
★★★	Hi Infidelity (Epic, 1980)
★★	Good Trouble (Epic, 1982)
★★	Wheels Are Turnin' (Epic, 1984)
★★	Life as We Know It (Epic, 1987)
★★★½	The Hits (Epic, 1988)
★	The Earth, a Small Man, His Dog and a Chicken (Epic, 1990)
★★	The Second Decade of Rock & Roll: 1981 to 1991 (Epic, 1991)
★½	Building the Bridge (Castle, 1996)
★★★	The Ballads (Epic/Legacy, 1999)
★★	Styx and REO Speedwagon—Arch Allies: Live at Riverport (Sanctuary, 2000)
★★	Plus (Sanctuary, 2001)

Perseverance paid off in buckets for this Illinois-based outfit. REO Speedwagon barreled out of the college region of Champaign-Urbana in the early '70s, carrying a hefty load of generic bar-band boogie. The first three albums register at a slightly higher octane than you might expect, though they contain nothing that the house combo down at the local gin mill couldn't kick out on a Saturday night. *Ridin' the Storm Out* features lead singer Mike Murphy, a temporary (and indistinguishable) replacement for squeaky-clean longtime frontman Kevin Cronin. When Cronin rejoined the group on *R.E.O.* (1976), the band slid into a stretch of mediocre records relieved only by ceaseless touring. *Live: You Get What You Play For* managed to trade on some of that collected goodwill, but *REO Comes Alive!* it ain't. Finally, *Hi Infidelity* put this journeyman quintet on the chart map in 1980; the album sat at #1 for 15 excruciating weeks. Soft-rocking hits like "Keep on Loving You" emphasized Cronin's numbingly earnest "regular dude" stance over guitarist Gary Richrath's tattered sack of Berry-derived riffs. The LP is docked a notch or two for begetting the power ballad in all its mock-sensitive glory.

After *Hi Infidelity,* the followups to REO's out-of-nowhere blockbuster become increasingly less tuneful (and successful), until cofounder Richrath split the band in 1989. As for the continuing saga, running on empty (*The Earth, a Small Man, His Dog and a Chicken* and *Building the Bridge*) didn't stop REO Speedwagon from releasing albums through the '90s and into the 21st century. That said, *The Hits* is a guilty-pleasure feast, albeit one best played at home alone or with the car windows safely rolled up. The first *Decade of Rock & Roll* set, which mixes live and studio tracks, also has its moments, but the second volume, spanning the '80s, pushes it. *Plus* and *Arch Allies* are wheezy nostalgia-tour souvenirs; *Allies,* a two-disc set with fellow Midwest survivors Styx, captures the package-deal spirit of such shows with something akin to charm. "We were joined at the hip, or should I say the unhip," quips a refreshingly self-deprecating Cronin in the liner notes. Then he blows it with the unnecessary *The Ballads* collection, for which he writes, "So, you may ask, how is it that the loudest, fastest, rowdiest rock band in Champaign, Illinois, has come to release a CD called *The Ballads*? I mean in concert, these guys rock!" Ah, yes. And in my dreams, you love me.   —M.C./R.S.

The Replacements

★★★½   Sorry, Ma, Forgot to Take Out the Trash (1981; Restless, 2002)

★★★★½   Stink (1982; Restless, 2002)

★★★★   Hootenanny (Twin/Tone, 1983)

★★★★★   Let It Be (Twin/Tone, 1984)

★★★   The Shit Hits the Fans (Twin/Tone, 1985)

★★★★½   Tim (Sire, 1985)

★★★★   Boink! (Glass U.K., 1986)

★★★½   Pleased to Meet Me (Sire, 1987)

★★   Don't Tell a Soul (Sire, 1989)

★★   All Shook Down (Sire, 1990)

★★★   All for Nothing/Nothing for All (Reprise, 1997)

The Replacements were one of the all-time great American garage bands, a freewheeling mess of four Minnesota punk rockers who knew how to turn dead-end adolescent malaise into a grand joke. They burst out of the '80s hardcore underground with music that told you something about where they came from and what they wanted: Here were songs about dads, songs about jobs, songs about drinking buddies you couldn't get away from and long boring drives through the Midwestern winter and quitting school and going to work and never going fishing. In their legendary live shows, the 'Mats would shamble through drunken destructions of '70s pop trash before blasting off into one of Paul Westerberg's amazing original tunes, while Westerberg choked on his own raggedy voice and guitarist Bob Stinson urged the crowd, "You gotta boo!" From hilarity to heartbreak, the Replacements' emotional realness made other hardcore bands sound like sitcoms.

The early records hold up smashingly well, especially the cleanly recorded and brilliantly played *Stink,* which offers the ballad "Go" between manic sure shots like "Gimme Noise," "Fuck School," and "God Damn Job" ("God damn it/God damn it/God damn/I need a god damn job"). But *Let It Be* is where the 'Mats went overboard and claimed a national audience. Westerberg rasps with the nyuk-nyuk-nyuk snicker of the wiseass kid who learned early how to joke his way out of getting his ass kicked. The band charges through breathlessly funny brat-punk tantrums and a cover of Kiss' "Black Diamond." But behind all the noise, Westerberg bares his tender heart in "Favorite Thing," "I Will Dare," and the surprise acoustic ballad "Unsatisfied." An American adolescence in all its agony and ecstasy.

Tim sealed the triumph with growing-up tales like "Bastards of Young," "Left of the Dial," and "Swingin Party." Westerberg channels the voice of a young, scared John Lennon in the album-closing "Here Comes a Regular," the devastating acoustic confessional of a party commando who ages into a bitter old man right before your ears. You can hear a typically rowdy Replacements show on the live cassette *The Shit Hits the Fans,* confiscated from a fan's tape recorder during an Oklahoma City gig. Paul serenades the crowd with the Jackson 5's "I'll Be There," singing the first verse over and over because he can't remember the others, until the band locks into the guitar blowout "Can't Hardly Wait," Bob Stinson's finest moment. Around this time, the band also put on *Saturday Night Live*'s best musical performance ever, playing "Kiss Me on the Bus" and "Bastards of Young" on the show of January 18, 1986.

Like so many other youthful rock hellions, the 'Mats flailed when it came time to grow up or blow up. They fired Bob Stinson under cloudy circumstances, in late 1986, and never got close to their old guitar fire again. *Pleased to Meet Me* is well sung, poorly played, terribly recorded, and often spoiled by a two-bit horn section (who must have offered the band a ride to the studio) despite the excellence of songs like "Alex Chilton," "Skyway," and especially "I.O.U." *Don't Tell a Soul* was a nod to Modern Rock radio, which did not nod back. *All Shook Down* had an ace ballad about crashing an old flame's wedding, "Nobody," which pointed to the rugged, mature solo style that Westerberg never followed through on. The 'Mats even priced themselves out of the indie-rock live scene, opening for Tom Petty instead—believe it or not, that sort of thing was considered a shrewd business move in the '80s. The band's final years are summed up in a moment on the live bootleg *Shit, Shave, and Shower,* where you can hear the Petty fans jeer and boo. Bassist Tommy Stinson mutters, "Fine, we'll play 'Achin' to Be' for the little nimrods." And then the band plays "Achin' to Be." Sad.

Of course there were solo albums, and lousy ones they were, too, though Tommy's live shows have always been a gas. We all expected too much from Paul, didn't we? Westerberg rocked on his 1993 solo debut *14 Songs,* but after it tanked, his music became so forced and grudging that it was depressing to hear—the man really seemed to hate his job. Tommy Stinson recorded solo, after leading the bands Bash & Pop and Perfect, and joining Guns n' Roses. Even weirder, he appeared in Puff Daddy's "It's All About the Benjamins" video—hell, on a good night for the Replacements, it was barely even about the Abrahams. Bob Stinson died from drugs in 1995. *Boink!* is the nearest thing to a Replacements best-of, with rarities like the lost classic "Nowhere Is My Home," an '85 outtake that would have been the best song on *Tim. All for Nothing/Nothing for All* is a poorly selected two-

CD summary of the Sire years, emphasizing crap like "The Ledge" and "Talent Show." But at least it gathers "I'll Be You," "Nobody," and a studio mix of "Can't Hardly Wait" cut during the *Tim* sessions: at long last, a properly big-sounding version of this big-hearted song. —R.S.

Paul Revere and the Raiders

★★½	Here They Come! (Columbia, 1965)
★★½	Midnight Ride (Columbia, 1966)
★★½	The Spirit of '67 (Columbia, 1966; Sundazed, 1996)
★★	Just Like Us! (Columbia, 1966)
★★	Revolution! (1967; Sundazed, 1998)
★★	Goin' to Memphis (1968; Sundazed, 2000)
★★	Something Happening (Columbia, 1968; Sundazed, 1996)
★★	Hard 'n' Heavy (With Marshmallow) (Columbia, 1969)
★★★	Greatest Hits (Columbia, 1969)
★★	Alias Pink Puzz (Columbia, 1969; Sundazed, 2000)
★★★½	All-time Greatest Hits (Columbia, 1972)
★★½	The Legend of Paul Revere (Columbia/Legacy 1990)
★★★	The Essential Ride, '63–'67 (Sony Legacy, 1995)
★★★	The Best of Paul Revere and the Raiders (Sony Special Products, 1997)
★★	Mojo Workout (Sundazed, 2000)
★★★	Super Hits (Sony, 2000)

Tricked out in silly Revolutionary War frock coats and gaiters, keyboardist and ultraham Paul Revere, together with darling ponytailed frontman Mark Lindsay, reigned supreme on Dick Clark's mid-'60s afternoon TV show *Where the Action Is.* Given this nifty platform from which to deliver their product, the Raiders capitalized on the exposure, scoring massively with "Hungry," "Just Like Me," "Him or Me—What's It Gonna Be?" and Barry Mann and Cynthia Weill's antidrug number "Kicks." All these hits were slick popcraft; Lindsay's breathy, well-trained voice was made for radio; and the frenzy displayed on the studio dance floor made the songs seem like rock & roll. But the band's "we're just entertainers" spirit was even then apparent, and it became more so as the shtick got tired. Revere, however, is still at it, touring maniacally with a new crew whose synchronized dance steps and general foolery are kitsch beyond parody. Either *All-time Greatest Hits* or *The Essential Ride* is probably enough Raiders for anyone. *The Legend of Paul Revere* is bafflingly comprehensive: 55 songs presented with enough brouhaha to convince the unsuspecting that this was a significant band. Don't be fooled. —P.E.

Reverend Horton Heat

★★½	Smoke 'Em if You Got 'Em (Sub Pop, 1991)
★★	The Full Custom Gospel Sounds of the Reverend Horton Heat (Sub Pop, 1993)
★★	Liquor in the Front (Sub Pop, 1994)
★½	It's Martini Time (Interscope, 1996)
★	Space Heater (Interscope, 1998)
★★	Holy Roller (Sub Pop, 1999)
★★	Spend a Night in the Box (Time Bomb, 2000)
★½	Lucky 7 (Artemis, 2002)

"It's a psychobilly *freak-out!*" declares Texas' own Reverend Horton Heat, a.k.a. James C. Heath, in the middle of his first album, and that's his raison d'être— retro rockabilly played at meltdown speed. Unsurprisingly, he's better known for his live shows than for his records. *Smoke 'Em if You Got 'Em* is entirely derivative, right down to the guitar reverb and slapback echo, but it's also got plenty of verve and a touch of wit. "Eat Steak" would make a fine Beef Council ad, if not for the verse about the slaughterhouse.

Things start going downhill on *The Full Custom Gospel Sounds,* produced by the Butthole Surfers' Gibby Haynes. Heat cranks up the distortion and vehemence, but the shtick's starting to wear thin; tracks like "Bales of Cocaine" and "400 Bucks" are little more than shaggy-dog stories with rockabilly riffs appended. *Liquor in the Front* (hidden half of title: "Poker in the Rear") was produced by Al Jourgensen of Ministry, and its single, "Yeah, Right," is full-on industrial-billy, electronic beats and all.

Arriving a couple of years too late for the lounge revival (and replacing drummer "Taz" Bentley with Scott Churilla), *It's Martini Time* is a total mess, alternating unctuous swingin' retro tracks ("Big Red Rocket of Love"—talk about subtle!) with overblown stompers that seem left over from *Liquor.* The songwriting finally gives out altogether on *Space Heater,* and the bombastic production just exposes how little is holding the record up. *Holy Roller* compiles songs from the first five albums (plus a few rarities), and somehow manages to miss a lot of what good stuff there is.

Spend a Night in the Box (again produced by a wayward Butthole, this time Paul Leary) is a tentative step up. Heat has evidently decided he wants to be Jerry Lee Lewis with a guitar, and the title track and a couple of stabs at jump blues show off his trio's groove to fine effect. More energetic than anything the Rev's done in a while, *Lucky 7* suffers from disastrously rote songwriting. "Sermon on the Jimbo" and

"You've Got a Friend in Jimbo," both concerning Heat's longtime bass player Jim "Jimbo" Wallace, are the kind of traveling-preacher parodies you'd expect from a man in Heat's robes—if only the routines were funny.   —D.W.

Keith Richards

★★★½   Talk Is Cheap (Virgin, 1988)
★★★★   Live at the Hollywood Palladium, December 12, 1988 (Virgin, 1991)
★★★½   Main Offender (Virgin, 1992)

Reportedly, Keith Richards has years of solo jams stored in vaults; no doubt by the year 2010, they'll all come out in box sets. For now, apart from a late-'70s single that reworked Jimmy Cliffs "The Harder They Come" and Chuck Berry's "Run, Run Rudolph," his 1988 *Talk Is Cheap* will have to do. And it does fine. This collaboration with funksters (Bernie Worrell) and L.A. rock pros (Waddy Wachtel) is one strong set. "How I Wish" has swagger, but most of the other tunes are torrid one-riff jobs. An Al Green–ish tune featuring Sarah Dash is a nice beauty-and-the-beast duet, and "Locked Away" is a good Richards ballad. Keith proudly mixes his relatively on-key vocals a bit high, and it's arguable that "better" singing makes him more expressive. The Richards guitar, however, is in top form—unflanged, unwah-wahed, and irresistible. *Live at the Hollywood Palladium* is even better. *Main Offender* lacks a bit of the abandon of in-concert Keith, but it's still dependable.   —P.E.

Jonathan Richman

★★★★★   The Modern Lovers (1976; Beserkley/Rhino, 1986)
★★★★½   Jonathan Richman & the Modern Lovers (1977; Beserkley/Rhino, 1986)
★★★   Rock & Roll With the Modern Lovers (1977; Beserkley/Rhino, 1986)
★★   Live (1977; Beserkley, 1995)
★★½   Back in Your Life (1979; Beserkley/Rhino, 1986)
★★½   Jonathan Sings! (Sire, 1983)
★★★   Rockin' and Romance (Twin/Tone, 1985)
★★   It's Time for Jonathan Richman and the Modern Lovers (Upside, 1986)
★★★   The Beserkley Years: The Best of Modern Lovers (Beserkley/Rhino, 1987)
★★½   Modern Lovers 88 (Rounder, 1988)
★★½   Jonathan Richman (Rounder, 1989)
★★   Jonathan Goes Country (Rounder, 1990)
★★★   Having a Party With Jonathan Richman (Rounder, 1991)
★★★★   I, Jonathan (Rounder, 1992)
★★½   Jonathan, Te Vas a Emocionar! (Rounder, 1994)
★★★   You Must Ask the Heart (Rounder, 1995)
★★½   Surrender to Jonathan (Vapor, 1996)
★★★   I'm So Confused (Vapor, 1998)
★★★   Her Mystery Not of High Heels and Eye Shadow (Vapor, 2001)
★★★   Action Packed: The Best of Jonathan Richman (Rounder, 2002)

Punk avatar, folkie imp, bilingual crooner, movie star: Richman's been them all and more in the course of more than three decades since he founded the Modern Lovers in Boston. Yet in each context, he's exactly the same person, a gawky Peter Pan preaching the love of rock & roll at its simplest and most direct, and the rock & roll of love at its most open and passionate, all in his nasally Boston burr. The idiosyncrasies that would be present throughout his career can be found on "Roadrunner," one of his very first songs, a two-chord burst of unbridled joy about driving down the road "with the radio on." Like the Velvet Underground's "Rock & Roll," which inspired Richman's song, it extols music as a life-giving force, but with a sense of wide-eyed wonder rather than Lou Reed's cynical bite and seedy bent. Like its predecessor, "Roadrunner" seemed to exist outside the context of anything else that was happening in its day.

"Roadrunner" is the center of the Modern Lovers' repertoire, which is heard at its best on their official debut album, produced by former Velvet John Cale. Originally recorded in 1973 as a Warner Bros. demo, the material was rejected and released in 1976 by Bay Area upstart Beserkley Records. Other highlights include the bitterly dry "Pablo Picasso" and "I'm Straight." The band's 1971 demos for gadfly Kim Fowley were eventually released in 1981 as *The Original Modern Lovers* (which includes two versions of "Roadrunner"), and while the LP shows promise, it doesn't present the band in a great sonic light. *Precise Modern Lovers Order*, released in 1994, captures spiritedly rough live performances from 1971 and 1973. The Lovers, which included future Talking Heads keyboardist Jerry Harrison and future Cars drummer David Robinson, split up in 1973. *The Beserkley Years* is a good overview of this period.

After a three-year break, Richman formed a new Modern Lovers (with Robinson as the only holdover), sporting a scruffy, largely acoustic sound, putting his inner child up front—not that it had ever been hidden before—on 1977's *Jonathan Richman & the Modern Lovers*. "Abominable Snowman in the Market," "Hey There Little Insect," and "Here Come the Martian Martians" could have been big on the preschool hit parade. But then there's "Important in Your Life," a yearning pledge of troth worthy of a Jerome Kern or Richman's beloved doo-wop idols. If you can reconcile the two sides of the coin, you'll find this album among the most charming ever made. If not, you'll have little patience for this or much anything else Richman has done. *Rock & Roll With the Modern Lovers,* released later that year, continues much the same, but adds whimsical yet sincere forays into world music, with tunes from Japan and South America in the mix, as well as the jaunty faux-world instrumental "*Egyptian Reggae.*" *Back in Your Life* (with Richman dropping the Modern Lovers and going solo) fits somewhere between its two predecessors, led by the gorgeous title track. *Live* pushes the kiddie appeal a bit too far and, though earnest, gets annoying.

After another layoff, Richman rebounded refreshed for 1983's *Jonathan Sings!,* rhapsodizing about his kind of music ("This Kind of Music") waxing nostalgic ("That Summer Feeling," "Give Paris One More Chance") and casting himself as a pure romantic. And that's more or less the pattern from there on out, with an album every year or two. He is not always emotionally upbeat—as a romantic, he's just as prone to sorrow as to joy. But the differences from one album to the next are subtle, often simply a matter of setting, even on such diversions as *Jonathan Goes Country* (very funny cover photo of Richman considering Western footwear) and *Jonathan, Te Vas a Emocionar!* (translation: "Jonathan, you are going to touch yourself!"), featuring occasionally tortured Spanish translations of his songs. At this point, the biggest news for Richman was being tapped by the Farrelly brothers to serve as the strolling, strumming, singing Greek chorus in *There's Something About Mary.* Collecting tracks from the late '80s through mid-'90s, *Action Packed: The Best of Jonathan Richman* is a fine starting point for the post–Modern Lovers years.   —S.H.

Amy Rigby

★★★★	Diary of a Mod Housewife (Koch, 1996)
★★★½	Middlescence (Koch, 1998)
★★★½	The Sugar Tree (Koch, 2000)
★★★★	18 Again: An Anthology (Koch, 2002)
★★★½	Til the Wheels Fall Off (Signature Sounds, 2003)

Amy Rigby is a mess. She's a single mom who wants to rock, have a good time, and find true love—roughly in that order. When will she grow up and start packing lunch boxes? But the singer/songwriter's sense of humor lets you in on the cruel joke that is her perpetual dissatisfaction, because in the end, Rigby is an East Village mom with a punk-era past (the Last Roundup,

the Shams) and a failed marriage (to Will Rigby of the dB's), and what aging hipster can't relate to that?

At its best, *Diary of a Mod Housewife* transforms the anonymous experiences of city living into the highly personal accounts of country music; in "Knapsack," Rigby sees potential where others find only shrugged-off ambivalence—the security bag-check ("He took my knapsack and his fingers brushed my wrist/Gave me a number but it wasn't even his"). It's also naively hopeful: "Beer and Kisses" is poignant not only for its everydayness but because the doomed husband and wife—drinking but no longer kissing—decide to give it one more go.

A vulnerable Rigby lowers such expectations on *Middlescence:* All she wants on "All I Want" is human recognition; she pines for "The Summer of My Wasted Youth," and it's sublime because it's not far from her wasted adulthood. Since she's got nothing to lose, she sets her sights on Nashville for *The Sugar Tree,* which finds her "Rode Hard" until she's "Cynically Yours." Could be that her label's giving her heartache: After Koch let all her work fall out of print, she released a greatest-hits anthology to fulfill her contract. She added the grown-up opus *Til the Wheels Fall Off* to her alternative-adult oeuvre the following year.   —C.S.

The Righteous Brothers

★★★	Greatest Hits (Verve, 1967)
★★★★	Anthology (1962–1974) (Rhino, 1989)
★★★½	Best of the Righteous Brothers (Curb, 1990)
★★★★	Unchained Melody: The Very Best of the Righteous Brothers (Polygram, 1990)
★★★★	The Moonglow Years (Polygram, 1991)
★	Reunion (Curb, 1991)
★	Rock 'n' Roll Heaven (CEMA Special Products, 1992)
★	The Best of the Righteous Brothers, Vol. 2 (Curb, 1993)
★★★	Universal Masters Collection (Universal, 2003)

With Bill Medley moaning low and Bobby Hatfield wailing high over the grandest Wall of Sound production Phil Spector ever achieved, "You've Lost That Lovin' Feelin'," from 1964, may be the most dramatic ballad single ever released. All echoes, kettledrums, and surging strings, the instrumental track is wonderful, ersatz Wagner, but it's the vocal duel, mounting from resignation to longing to hysteria, that provokes the chills and the erotic/divine madness. It's odd then, that this California duo's 1963 debut, "Little Latin Lupe Lu," had been such a dud. Medley actually wrote the sassy rocker, but it was left to Mitch Ryder to fire it up; the Brothers, in fact, with the exception of the nifty

Little Richard–like "Justine" (1965), never could rock convincingly at any speed past mid-tempo—their art-form was rhapsodic ballads. Dark and Lincolnesque, Medley was the baritone and brains behind the operation, and his stellar moments were many: He tends to dominate such glories as "(You're My) Soul and Inspiration" and "Hung on You." A small, blond ex-jock, Hatfield was the more tender deliverer—it's his warm elegance that carries "Unchained Melody," the 1965 hit that, recycled, got Demi Moore and Patrick Swayze all hot and bothered in *Ghost.* No fools, the pair spent much of their career attempting reruns of "You've Lost That Lovin' Feelin'," either by working with Spector or covering Mann-Weill songs. Only "See That Girl" bordered on self-parody, however, and while "Ebb Tide" and "The White Cliffs of Dover" were sappy clunkers, most of the Brothers' hits carried a rare dignity, especially considering the ultra-romantic songs they covered.

Rhino's brilliant two-CD *Anthology* collects all the best Righteous Brothers performances—and these epics remain riveting. *Unchained Melody,* not quite as comprehensive or well-packaged, runs a close second. *The Moonglow Years* is a good representation of the duo's early days. Each time out, the boys go for broke, overpowering the listener with feeling. The *Reunion* album, sadly, doesn't work; especially embarrassing, too, is *The Best of the Righteous Brothers, Vol. 2,* an album of lame rerecordings of their classics. —P.E.

LeAnn Rimes

★★★★   Blue (Curb, 1996)
★   You Light Up My Life: Inspirational Songs (Curb, 1997)
★   Unchained Melody: The Early Years (Curb, 1997)
★   Sittin' on Top of the World (Curb, 1998)
★   LeAnn Rimes (Curb, 1999)
★   I Need You (Curb, 2001)
★   God Bless America (Curb, 2001)
★   Twisted Angel (Curb, 2002)
★★★   Greatest Hits (Curb, 2003)

Just when all country music seemed to be arriving via overnight express from Nashville's canny song factories—in tidy laminated packages indistinguishable from one another—along came one of music's favorite finds: a little girl with a great big voice. Fifteen-year-old Rimes mixes up ambling oldtime country with the kind of springy, youthful back-talk numbers that the peppier female C&W singers make careers out of. The surprise hit "Blue" made the diminutive blonde with the puppyish features a household name; with her sweet, unbridled yodel and precocious huski-

ness, Rimes sounded as if she were channeling Patsy Cline. But "Blue" the song was no novelty, and *Blue* the album was no fluke—the 11 beautifully chosen and sequenced songs have a charming, old-fashioned lope that seems to refute the lacquered craft of countrypolitan that was then numbing the airwaves.

After the fluky success of *Blue,* the only way the teenage country singer could squander her considerable talent would be to take herself too seriously, or, more likely, to listen to rapacious promoters who wanted to hit the jackpot again by pushing her forward as America's Wholesome Sweetheart. Which she promptly proceeded to do, releasing the goopy, patriotic Christianity of *You Light Up My Life: Inspirational Songs.*

"Ka-ching" is the only sound that lingers after *Unchained Melody* spins into silence. Along with *You Light Up My Life,* this collection of studio floor–sweepings is an incoherent mess of Western fluff ("Cowboy's Sweetheart") and overblown ballads (a cover of Dolly Parton's "I Will Always Love You" even more attenuated, though not as bombastic, as Whitney Houston's version). Many of the songs are quite fine (the ballad "Broken Wing" and the perky "Sure Thing"), but the arrangements are poisoned with bad decisions: The racing honky-tonk classic "Blue Moon of Kentucky" begins with a "dramatic" a cappella intro featuring Rimes' econosize vocals slowly filling every molecule of space, and to hear a teenager sing Lennon-McCartney's autumnal "Yesterday" is absurd.

"God Bless America" is a great song—neat, evocative, and heartfelt—and the last thing it needs is rock-like production and me-me-me vocals, which is exactly the treatment it gets on *God Bless America,* a trashy collection of God-and-country uplift. Rimes mutates into Tennessee Ernie Ford on this shameless recording, with such sentimental CCM (contemporary Christian music) as "The Sands of Time" and "Middle Man" sharing space with "The Lord's Prayer" (set to music), the national anthem, "I Believe," and "Amazing Grace." Rimes' big, round voice sounds threadbare at the edges as she holds notes into eternity and forgoes the charming yodel of her carefree secular sass. The only song worth hearing is David E. Nowlen's "A Broken Wing," resurrected from 1997's *Unchained Melody: The Early Years.*

I Need You was released to the indifference of both country and pop audiences and to the dismay of critics, all of whom retained enough goodwill toward Rimes to expect that she had another *Blue* in her. But soon after *I Need You* hit the charts, Rimes renounced this collection of bland pop ballads as studio experiments she had deemed unfit for release. She was right, proving that, as her fans had hoped, she still had taste.

Rimes continued her losing streak into the new millennium. *Twisted Angel* was touted as the diminutive country starlet's Britney move, a recording of "modern" pop songs with slick, dancey production meant to appeal to a widespread audience approximately her own age. It does and it doesn't—the extreme care with which Rimes' handlers negotiate her career curve precludes any kind of Britney-style self-knowledge. *Twisted Angel* is glossy countrypolitan with a click track—pint-size ballads ("The Safest Place") that could just as well have been sold to Shania Twain, tough-girl club numbers ("Trouble With Goodbye") that don't showcase her voice any better than they would have that of a Jennifer Lopez, dorky rock ("Suddenly"), and a heap of would-be prom ballads. —A.B.

Robbie Robertson

   ★★★   Robbie Robertson (1987; Capitol, 2002)
  ★★★½   Storyville (Geffen, 1991)
   ★★★   Contact from the Underground of Redboy (Capitol, 1998)

Robbie Robertson and the Red Road Ensemble

  ★★½   Music for "The Native Americans" (Capitol, 1994)

A decade after retiring as the Band's guitarist and primary songwriter, Robbie Robertson launched a solo career that had very little in common with his previous band's rustic-soul sound. Although his former Bandmates Rick Danko and Garth Hudson play on *Robbie Robertson,* the album is more indebted to the singer's movie-soundtrack experience (composing scores for Martin Scorsese's *Raging Bull* and *The Color of Money,* among others). Guest stars (U2, Peter Gabriel, the Gil Evans horn section) lurk behind every chord change, and the arrangements move with a ponderous self-importance through Daniel Lanois' trademark production mist.

Storyville is essentially a Frankie-and-Johnny love story set in New Orleans and told through the voices and rhythms of some of the city's most distinctive talents: the Nevilles, the Meters, the Zion Harmonizers. Robertson arrays the backing voices like characters in a play, and the expansive arrangements percolate with an understated yet sensual pulse.

The soundtrack to a television special, *Music for "The Native Americans"* reconnects Robertson to his Native American heritage. He melds *Storyville*-style production haziness with traditional tribal chants and instruments, but his overly earnest lyrics occasionally disrupt the vibe.

Just as *Music for "The Native Americans"* brokered a sometimes inspired middle ground between technology and tradition, *Contact from the Underworld of Redboy* weaves the voices and rhythms of Robertson's boyhood past into futuristic electronic textures created by DJ-mixers Howie B and Marius de Vries. At its best, the album is hypnotic; Robertson punctuates the grooves with barbed guitar incisions and the voice of imprisoned activist Leonard Peltier. Robertson's own sense of quiet devastation emerges on "Unbound." But the singer still hasn't figured out how to record his voice; his overly processed vocals frequently come off as mannered, and his lyrics verge on preachiness. —G.K.

Smokey Robinson and the Miracles

  ★★½   Cookin' With the Miracles (Tamla, 1961)
  ★★★★ Doin' Mickey's Monkey (1963; Motown, 1986)
 ★★★½ Miracles Going to a Go-Go (1964; Motown, 1989)
  ★★★★ The Miracles Greatest Hits, Vol. 2 (Tamla, 1966)
 ★★★½ The Tears of a Clown (1970; Motown, 1991)
 ★★★½ Great Songs and Performances (1989; Motown, 1991)
 ★★★½ Whatever Makes You Happy: More of the Best (Rhino, 1993)
   ★★★ Motown Legends: I Second That Emotion (Motown, 1993)
   ★★★ The 35th Anniversary Collection (Motown, 1994)
 ★★★½ The Ballad Album (Motown, 1995)
★★★★½ Best of: The Ultimate Collection (Motown, 1998)
   ★★★ 20th Century Masters: The Millennium Collection (Motown, 1999)
   ★★★ Motown Lost and Found: Along Came Love 1958–1964 (Motown, 1999)

Smokey Robinson

   ★★★ A Quiet Storm (Motown, 1975)
 ★★★½ Blame It on Love and All the Greatest Hits (1983; Motown, 1991)
  ★★★★ One Heartbeat (Motown, 1987)
 ★★★½ Love, Smokey (Motown, 1990)
   ★★★ Motown Legends: Cruisin' (Motown, 1995)
  ★★★★ The Ultimate Collection (Motown, 1997)
   ★★★ Intimate (Uptown/Universal, 1999)
  ★★★★ 20th Century Masters: The Millennium Collection (Motown, 2000)
 ★★★½ Solo Anthology (Motown, 2001)

Not only is "Tears of a Clown" (1970) the definitive song for Smokey Robinson and the Miracles, but it's also one of pop's few perfect singles. Kicked off by a sprightly flute and oboe interchange, soon followed by sassy trombone, and featuring an ingenious Jew's harp twanging exactly as the chorus's key line arrives, the arrangement is audacious—it's pure pop frosting piled atop Motown's customarily delicious bass and drums. Smokey sings in his unerring falsetto, and his lyrics justify Bob Dylan's only half-outrageous claim that Robinson qualifies as America's greatest living poet. Master of supple half rhymes (*public* and *subject*) and virtuosic language games (Robinson works in the name of the classic Italian clown Pagliacci without sounding at all arch), the songwriter delivers his tour de force.

And "Tears" remains only one of a barrage of Miracles classics. Along with the Temptations, the Four Tops, and the Supremes, the Detroit quartet defined Motown—and cinched its ingenious wedding of R&B's depth and physicality to pop's airy melodicism. Robinson, however, as composer and producer, was arguably Motown's most significant creative force besides owner Berry Gordy: Nearly all of the label's acts were lucky recipients of his songs. While Smokey's "Got a Job" (1958)—an answer to the Silhouettes' "Get a Job"—was little more than (very capable) doo-wop, the band's followup, "Bad Girl," hinted at the Miracles' later greatness; for one thing, it properly forefronted Smokey's lead vocals; for another, it featured in embryo the glossy instrumentation that would stamp the group's ballads.

Throughout the '60s, the Miracles alternated between great rave-ups and elegant love songs. Particulary fetching were the crowd-noise intros to "Mickey's Monkey" and "Going to a Go-Go"—while Motown 45s became known as ultratight productions, Smokey's dance fare often began with the tape rolling as the musicians casually led off, only to kick in with absolute assurance. "Ooo Baby Baby" (1965) was the first great slow song, notable primarily for Robinson's tender singing; that year also saw the release of the staggering "The Tracks of My Tears," a triumph of the songwriter's gift for metaphor. With Marvin Tarplin on guitar, the group continued to produce epic radio fare until the early '70s, climaxing in "Tears of a Clown." Although Robinson departed in 1972, the Miracles continued successfully for another six years; "Do It Baby" (1974) and "Love Machine (Part 1)" (1975) remain their finest moments, even if none of their singles managed to reproduce Smokey's panache. *The Ultimate Collection* is the definitive Smokey and the Miracles compendium.

On his own, Robinson managed to do what few Motown artists (with the notable exceptions of Marvin Gaye and Stevie Wonder) were able to accomplish: continue to make vital music after the label's '60s hey-day. His solo work lacks some of the obvious freshness of his early Miracles efforts; instead, it's an exercise in seamless expertise. The obvious shift has been in his records' arrangements; he has concentrated on developing albums as well as singles, and where the best Miracles songs often featured melodic motifs and instrumentation that borrowed from classical music ideas, Smokey's later style is jazzier, the rhythms often langorous, and the ambience sometimes recalling that of such classic pop writers as Cole Porter and the Gershwins. While never conceding totally to the predominant R&B genres of the late '70s and early '80s (disco and funk), he still engaged them, while concentrating primarily on the romantic ballad. He remains a master of the art of the love song—he does "mellow" better than just about any other pop composer.

With such standouts as "Sweet Harmony" and "Just My Soul Responding," *Smokey* (now out of print) ushered in the mature Robinson, as well as a series of fine, subtle albums that met with a bewildering lack of commercial success. The singer's older audience kept the faith—the elegant sexiness of Smokey's material found favor, too, with critics—but younger R&B fans seemed to prefer the blatant flash of Rick James or the cartoon sensuality of Barry White. Six years after his solo debut, Smokey's style coalesced with a great single ("Cruisin' ") and some of the singer's most assertive vocals in years. By then, he'd also released *A Quiet Storm*, enough of a landmark recording that the album's title has come to characterize a certain kind of lush, warm contemporary R&B. *The Ultimate Collection* does justice to his solo work, concentrating on great cuts from *Warm Thoughts*, a fluid masterwork and one of his strongest collections of love songs; *Being With You*; and *One Heartbeat*—all of which confirmed that Smokey had finally lived up to the promise of his early legacy. *Intimate*, his first non-Motown release, shows him at his smoothest. —P.E.

The Roches

★★★★★	The Roches (Warner Bros., 1979)
★★★	Nurds (Warner Bros., 1980)
★★★½	Keep On Doing (Warner Bros., 1982)
★★½	Another World (Warner Bros., 1985)
★★	No Trespassing (EP) (Rhino, 1986)
★★★½	Speak (MCA, 1989)
★★★	We Three Kings (1990; MCA, 1995)
★★★★	A Dove (MCA, 1992)
★★½	Will You Be My Friend? (Baby Boom, 1994)
★★★	Can We Go Home Now? (Rykodisc, 1995)
★★★	The Collected Works of the Roches (Rhino, 2003)

If they thought about it at all, most pop fans would probably be tempted to sum up all contemporary folk acts with the title of the Roches' second album—*Nurds*. In assuming the label, the three Roche sisters felt free to indulge many of the faults that are often expressed by the brightest, most talented nerds: artiness, overexertion, insularity, even a touch of primness. The disc was just barely saved by the closing number by eldest sister Maggie, the group's lowest-pitched singer and highest-caliber songwriter (at least at first). Even so, *Nurds* was still a major step down from the unprecedented thrill of the trio's spare, loose, pointed 1979 debut. Heard at the time, its folksiness seemed less important than its New York–ness. From the gorgeous harmonies of "Hammond Song" to the tidy slyness of "Pretty and High," it was a Greenwich Village compatriot of the miraculous punk sounds that had so recently emanated from the Bowery, or a musical version of the naturally sexy, proto-feminist exuberance of the three comediennes who graced the first lineup of *Saturday Night Live,* where the Roches enjoyed their first national exposure.

The trio's well-named third album, *Keep On Doing,* returned some of the debut's poise, thanks partly to the return of their original über-formalist taskmaster, producer Robert Fripp. Among its treasures is "Losing True," a ballad as harmonically enrapturing as anything by the Byrds or My Bloody Valentine. But the folkie taint proved impossible to completely shake. *Another World* and *No Trespassing* only underscored it, with their middle-of-the-road rock arrangements and happy, shiny sentimentality. Though often overlooked, *Speak* again returned focus by toning down the arrangements and moderating the tempos. But the next non-Christmas, nonkids album, *A Dove,* suggested something more was at work—the group had grown into their MOR light rock, had learned to make their nerdiness inextricable from their grace (and Suzzy and Terre had learned to take the weight off Maggie). Of course, this was a testament to their maturity, to having survived being almost famous and come through some of the biggest relationships of their lives while still having miles to go before they sleep. Given its pointed title, it's no surprise the Roches' last album was just a decent collection of gentle afterthoughts. Their 2003 collection highlighted the women at both their best and their worst, which might be how they wanted it.   —F.S.

Pete Rock & C.L. Smooth

★★★★ All Souled Out (EP) (Elektra, 1991)
★★★★★ Mecca and the Soul Brother (Elektra/Asylum, 1992)
★★★★ The Main Ingredient (Elektra, 1994)

Pete Rock

★★★ Soul Survivor (RCA, 1998)
★★★ PeteStrumentals (BBE, 2001)
★★★½ Soul Survivor 2 (BBE, 2004)

One of hip-hop's great duos, Mount Vernon, NY's Pete Rock (the DJ/producer with an omniscient command of vintage jazz, funk, and soul), and Queens native C.L. Smooth (the clean-cut, dulcet-voiced storyteller) created a virtually flawless body of work that exemplifies the craftsmanship and dedication of hip-hop's extended golden age. But while they never made a bad (or even mediocre) record, their landmark achievement remains "They Reminisce over You (T.R.O.Y.)." The lead single off their debut full-length has been known to move the hardest B-boy to tears, with its dreamy Tom Scott saxophone sample wound around C.L.'s extended eulogy for longtime friend Trouble T-Roy (a member of Heavy D & the Boyz). Throughout their career, the pair demonstrated an extraordinary symbiotic energy, each of Rock's signature rolling productions complementing C.L.'s centered, highly aware rhymes with often transcendent results. *Mecca and the Soul Brother,* at nearly 80 minutes, is remarkably free of filler (the same can seldom be said of hip-hop albums half as long), while the tighter followup *The Main Ingredient* dealt the hypnotic, soul-stirring single "Take You There." In the mid-'90s, based on his undeniable musical acumen, Elektra gave Pete Rock the run of his own imprint label, Soul Brother Records; but when Elektra began shelving Pete's production projects, both he and C.L. left, stowing their group in the deep freeze. Rock then produced for the likes of Common and Rakim, while C.L. went on extended sabbatical. However, the appearance of two tracks featuring C.L. Smooth on Pete Rock's *Soul Survivor 2* album set the stage for an enticing full-length reunion mooted for 2005.   —P.R.

The Rolling Stones

★★★★ The Rolling Stones: England's Newest Hitmakers (ABKCO, 1964)
★★★★ 12 x 5 (ABKCO, 1964)
★★★★★ The Rolling Stones, Now! (ABKCO, 1965)
★★★★½ Out of Our Heads (ABKCO, 1965)
★★★★½ December's Children (and Everybody's) (ABKCO, 1965)
★★★★★ Big Hits (High Tide and Green Grass) (ABKCO, 1966)
★★★★★ Aftermath (ABKCO, 1966)
★★★ Got Live if You Want It! (ABKCO, 1966)
★★★★★ Between the Buttons (ABKCO, 1967)
★★★★★ Flowers (ABKCO, 1967)

★★★★	Their Satanic Majesties Request (ABKCO, 1967)
★★★★★	Beggars Banquet (ABKCO, 1968)
★★★★★	Through the Past, Darkly (Big Hits, Vol. 2) (ABKCO, 1969)
★★★★★	Let It Bleed (ABKCO, 1969)
★★★★	Get Yer Ya-Ya's Out! (ABKCO, 1970)
★★★★★	Sticky Fingers (1971; Virgin, 1994)
★★★★★	Hot Rocks 1964–1971 (ABKCO, 1971)
★★★★★	Exile on Main St. (1972; Virgin, 1994)
★★★★★	More Hot Rocks (Big Hits and Fazed Cookies) (ABKCO, 1972)
★★★	Goats Head Soup (1973; Sony, 1990)
★★½	It's Only Rock & Roll (1974, Virgin)
★★	Metamorphosis (ABKCO, 1975)
★★★½	Made in the Shade (Rolling Stones, 1975)
★★★	Black and Blue (1976; Virgin, 1994)
★★	Love You Live (1977; Virgin, 1998)
★★★★★	Some Girls (1978; Virgin, 1999)
★★★★	Emotional Rescue (1980; Virgin, 1994)
★★★½	Sucking in the Seventies (Rolling Stones, 1981)
★★★★½	Tattoo You (1981; Virgin, 1994)
★★	Still Life (1982; Virgin, 1998)
★★★	Undercover (Virgin, 1983)
★★★★½	Rewind: 1971–1984 (Virgin, 1984)
★★★★	Dirty Work (Virgin, 1986)
★★★★★	The Singles Collection: The London Years (ABKCO, 1989)
★★★	Steel Wheels (Virgin, 1989)
★★★	Flashpoint (Virgin, 1991)
★★★½	Jump Back (Virgin, 1993)
★★★	Voodoo Lounge (Virgin, 1994)
★★★	Stripped (Virgin, 1995)
★★★	Bridges to Babylon (Virgin, 1997)
★★	No Security (Virgin, 1998)
★★★★★	Forty Licks (Virgin, 2002)

In the '60s, they shouted and screamed and killed the king and railed at all his servants; in the '70s, they gave it away on Seventh Avenue; in the '80s, they did their dirty work; and they're still around today, celebrating 40 years as the World's Greatest Rock & Roll Band. Mick Jagger was the decadent, slither-hipped rogue singer; Keith Richards was the sinister guitar despot outglowering all the demons that hovered around him. They were the Glimmer Twins, the beggars at the banquet, the vandals who took the handles. They had Charlie Watts as the greatest drummer in rock & roll history, Bill Wyman's jazz-bred bass, and a sweet blond angel named Brian Jones. Put on "Jumpin' Jack Flash" and feel the acoustic guitars suck you into a cross-fire hurricane. Thrill to the Keith-vs.-Brian guitar battle in the final minute of "It's All Over Now."

Savor the self-parodic machismo of "Under My Thumb," where Mick flounces like a Siamese-cat-whipped gigolo over Bill's swishiest bass and Brian's cocktail-lounge marimba. Those torn and frayed harmonies. That Charlie Watts kick drum. It's all better than sex. Well, better than sex with Bill or Brian, that's for sure, and probably better than sex with Mick. Not sure about sex with Keith—anybody know?

The Stones started out as a British blues band, but what they played was unmistakably rock & roll, revving up everything fast and loud and mean about the blues—not just chasing good times, but insisting on them. As a slippery character, Mick Jagger wasn't too interested in faking soulful sincerity; he pranced and wiggled through his sexual guises, relishing his role as a white guy singing black, an English guy singing American, a young guy singing old, a jaded guy singing sincere, and most of all, a male guy singing female. You couldn't pin him down, and that's the way he liked it, pouting "Don't hang around/ 'Cause two's a crowd" with a sullen charisma you still can't take your ears off. As Chuck Berry once put it (in a song the Stones covered), "You Can't Catch Me." And the relentless forward motion of the Stones' music kept Mick one step ahead of anyone trying to hang a name on him.

Jagger and Richards had to learn songwriting on the job—it took them a few years to notice that there was such a thing as melody. But even from the beginning, they could slap together brooding originals like "Tell Me," "Grown Up Wrong," and "Empty Heart." The early Stones records are hodgepodges full of R&B covers going horribly wrong ("Under the Boardwalk," "Come On") or shockingly right ("It's All Over Now," "Around and Around"). *The Rolling Stones, Now!* is their first consistently great LP, with the mean "Heart of Stone," the funky "Off the Hook," and the Leiber-Stoller oldie "Down Home Girl," where Mick has a blast playing the wide-eyed city boy rendered helpless by his sweetie's Southern-gal sex drive. There's also a fantastic version of the '40s jump blues "Down the Road Apiece," where the old line "Come on before they lose their lease" becomes "You can lose your lead," and you realize that Mick, a spoiled rock & roll prince, has never had to sign a lease and has no idea what one is.

Out of Our Heads adds "Satisfaction," the 1965 breakthrough single that continues to inspire garage-rock imitators today. Poor Mick: flying around the world with no girlie action, only his cars and clothes and cigarettes and TVs to keep him company. He sounds bored enough to blow up the world; Keith sounds like he just lit the fuse. There's also "The Spider and the Fly," a groupie blues with Mick's positively filthy languor as he breathes the vowels of the line, "She said she liked the way I held the microphone." *December's Children,* a compendium of tracks from the completely different U.K. version of *Out of Our Heads,* leaps out with the 90-second blast of "She Said Yeah," plus live rips through "I'm Moving On" and "Route 66." It also has "The Singer Not the Song," a chiming Beatle-style ballad that's all narcissistic mod glamour, especially the way Mick and Keith harmonize on the killer couplet, "It's not the way you give in willingly/Others do it without thrilling me."

Aftermath was the first album of Jagger-Richards originals and the first album the Stones recorded as a coherent whole. It showcases the sauciest Mick, the broodiest Keith, the prettiest Brian, the funkiest Bill, and Charlie—now and forever, Charlie. It's blues-rock flower power, but all the flowers are painted black, with Brian's marimba and dulcimer adding color to these tough, lean, desperately lonely songs. If the Velvet Underground had ever made an album with the Stax house band, it might have sounded like this: the outrageously funny country honk "High and Dry," the gentle acoustic longing of "I Am Waiting," the 11-minute "Going Home." The U.S. version improves on the original by losing "Mother's Little Helper," always a song worth losing, and adding the sitar-crazed death chant "Paint It Black." Mick trips through the Swinging London scene with tirelessly bitchy ditties like "Under My Thumb," "Think," and "Doncha Bother Me," coming up with sharp lines even when he's just shaking the maracas of his mind to the beat to give his lips something to do.

Between the Buttons is lighter and thinner, heavy on piano and a Kinks-like touch of ye olde Englandisms; having belatedly discovered pop melody, Jagger and Richards were suddenly overdosing on the stuff. The songs that stand out are the ones that bite: "Connection," "My Obsession," "Yesterday's Papers," and the *Blonde on Blonde* rip "Who's Been Sleeping Here?" "Something Happened to Me Yesterday" is a remarkably moving and confused finale, chronicling either a first acid trip or a first experience with gay sex, depending on whether you think Mick is singing "trippy" or "drippy." David Bowie obviously guessed the latter, since he based most of his early career on this song, turning it into his debut hit "Space Oddity."

Flowers collects stray singles from this period, but it holds together as one of the Stones' best records, a concept album about the social scene that gathers around five rich young men with an appetite for sex, drugs, and gossip. There's the acoustic "Sittin' on a Fence," the sad accordion waltz "Backstreet Girl,"

and best of all, the dizzy harpsichord watusi "Ride On Baby," one of the great unknown Stones classics. *Their Satanic Majesties Request* was the Stones' big psychedelic statement, with the band looking silly in medieval wizard costumes on the cover. Despite its bad rep, though, it's an inspired mess, layering all the airy, effete melody of a Donovan or Kaleidoscope song on top of the powerhouse Stones rhythm section. There's a heap of sci-fi twaddle, but you still get a buzz from spooky space drones like "Citadel," "The Lantern," and "2,000 Light Years From Home." The band's brief but tasty psych period, well summed up by the 1969 singles collection *Through the Past, Darkly,* includes high-water marks of British pop such as "Child of the Moon" and "Dandelion." This Stones era ended much too soon—except that even better sounds were on the way.

Brian, never a day at the beach in the human-being department, was increasingly lost as a musical presence, but he has his final great moments on *Beggars Banquet,* the album on which the Stones stripped down for some kind of mutant acoustic blues. When Brian plays a ghostly slide guitar on "No Expectations," he sounds like he's playing at his own funeral. (He died in his swimming pool in 1969, soon after the Stones finally kicked him out.) *Beggars Banquet* has ironic roots moves like "Parachute Woman," "Jigsaw Puzzle," and a cover of Reverend Robert Wilkins' country-gospel "Prodigal Son," where Keith utters a friendly "Hey!" at the end, as though he fully expected the fatted calf all along. In "Stray Cat Blues," Mick lures the kittens to his scratching post with a lazy post-coital mumble, as if forming consonants is too much work to expect from a guy with such a demanding sexual schedule. And "Sympathy for the Devil" is one of their best singles, with a conga beat, one of Keith's rare straight-razor solos, a chorus of presumably restless natives from central casting chanting "hoo hoo," and Mick chewing right through the scenery in his guise as the Prince of Darkness.

On *Let It Bleed,* the Stones face up to the end of the '60s, starting with the dread guitar rumble of "Gimme Shelter." It's all over now: the fast times of Swinging London have degenerated into death and despair, the banality of Mister Jimmy waiting in line for his fix at the drugstore. The Stones rock through the darkness with the bluesy punch of "Monkey Man," a great cover of Robert Johnson's "Love in Vain" (with Ry Cooder on mandolin), and "You Got the Silver," with Keith singing a ragged lead vocal as the ultimate romantic supplicant. "Let It Bleed" might be the Stones' sexiest song. Mick slips in a very unconvincing "she said" before the first verse, but he's the one offering us his body, shaking his hips to turn us on and drinking our health in scented jasmine tea, as blood and sweat and other bodily fluids spill all over the honky-tonk guitars. By the end of the song, Mick is dancing on the tables while Charlie tries to calm him down, and for a few minutes, the sex drive wins over the death drive.

Sticky Fingers, coming after the disastrously violent concert at Altamont, was a chance for the Stones to clean up their act. Needless to say, they declined. The songs are full of drugs, often as a metaphor for sexual loss ("Moonlight Mile"), but sometimes just as drugs ("Sister Morphine"). New guitarist Mick Taylor adds rich instrumental textures, despite the dull lite-jazz coda for "Can't You Hear Me Knocking." The incomprehensibly terrifying "Sway" destroys your notion of circular time, "Bitch" riffs on the nature of lust with unbelievably rabid guitars, and "Dead Flowers" is a country goof on decadence. "Brown Sugar" is the album's most famous song, a Chuck Berry rip connecting the 19th-Century slave trade to the birth of 20th-Century rock & roll, raising disturbing questions about American culture while refusing to answer any of them, just dissolving into a chant of "yeah yeah yeah, wooo!"

The Stones fled to France to cut the double album *Exile on Main St.* Recorded in the basement of Keith's French villa with electricity allegedly stolen from the French railway system, it's their most physically jolting album and, ultimately, their most emotionally inspiring. Mick's vocals are just another instrument in a glorious rush of high-velocity electric noise, his lyrics barely perceptible in all the guitar, sax, and harmonica; whatever he's saying, he just wants to plug in and flush out and fight and fuck and feed. Keith channels all his nasty habits and internal chaos into the guitars, from the convulsive opener, "Rocks Off," to the weary acoustic stomp of "Sweet Virginia." Charlie Watts' understated performance in "Shake Your Hips" demands some sort of Nobel Prize.

Exile was the Stones' biggest musical triumph, but all the decadence was catching up with them. The band lost focus, with Keith's attention diverted by the pressing concern of stuffing as many toxic chemicals into his veins as possible. *Goats Head Soup* is overbaked melodrama, enlivened only by "Angie" and the groupie anthem "Star Star," in which Mick finds himself traded in for Steve McQueen. *It's Only Rock & Roll* is formula, and the nearly song-free *Black and Blue* comes down to a pair of sincere ballads ("Fool to Cry," "Memory Motel") and the silly but shitkicking cowboy tale "Hand of Fate." *Some Girls* brought the band back to life, taking on punk and disco as the Stones rediscovered their sense of musical aggression with new guitarist Ron Wood, who made up in spirit what he lacked in guitar chops. "Miss You" combines funk beats, sax, guitars, urban loneliness, Sugar Blue's harmonica, and some Puerto Rican girls just dying to meet you. While Mick bites the Big Apple and spits out the New York sleaze of "Shattered" and "When the Whip Comes Down," Keith sings himself a heart-tugging theme song, "Before They Make Me Run."

Their comeback in the can: the Stones kept it up for the next few years. *Emotional Rescue* was a high-spirited lark, racing through the hooks of "Let Me Go," "Where the Boys Go," and the fabulous "She's So Cold." *Tattoo You* had the necrophiliac hit "Start Me Up," the doo-doo-doo ditty "Hang Fire," and Keith's sincere pro-bitch statement, "Little T&A," with Sonny Rollins blowing sax on the big ballad "Waiting on a Friend." *Undercover* was a serious but failed attempt to adjust their political lyrics to hip-hop production. Mick started to act on his long-threatened solo career, and the Stones began to fall apart, this time apparently for good. *Dirty Work* sounded like the band's nasty kiss-off to one another, even though all the nastiness made the album feel alive, not to mention Stonesy. Too hard and bitter for mainstream acclaim, *Dirty Work* has a thriving cult, especially the title song, in which Jagger rails against Reagan with what sounds like authentic rage.

But the Stones didn't really break up, of course; they were just sitting on a fence. After three years, they reunited for *Steel Wheels* and assumed their present roles as elder statesmen, road warriors, voodoo loungers, and men of wealth and taste. Their post-reunion albums have been muffled by the soft retro production of Don Was—it takes a real studio whiz to make Charlie Watts sound like a click track. But *Bridges to Babylon* has its moments, especially Mick's "Might as Well Get Juiced" and Keith's "Thief in the Night." The double-disc anthology *Forty Licks* has four new songs, including Mick's "Don't Stop," a plea for emotional rescue, and Keith's piano ballad "Losing My Touch" (which he isn't).

For more than 20 years, the 1971 double-album anthology *Hot Rocks* was the standard introduction to the Stones' music, the first one most of us ever heard, with a great doomy cover. Along with its predecessor, *Big Hits,* and its superb companion volume, *More Hot Rocks,* it's been superseded by *The Singles Collection: The London Years. Hot Rocks* does, however, have the ten-minute "Midnight Rambler," the highlight of the live *Get Your Ya-Ya's Out!,* from 1970, and a truly frightening listen. Forget Altamont—this is the real death of the '60s, as Mick preaches about bad news on the way, bad news of death and destruction, bad news that everybody's got to know because everybody's got to go. But the crowd just cheers wildly, because they don't understand that the bad news is for them. The moment when a happy fan screams "Goddamn!" and Jagger answers, "Honey, it's not one of those," is much scarier than "Sympathy for the Devil" ever was.

Forty Licks is the closest thing to a comprehensive career-spanning intro, featuring daring picks ("Have You Seen Your Mother, Baby, Standing in the Shadow?"), but it's not as strong song-for-song as *Hot Rocks* or *The Singles Collection*. So far, there hasn't been a completely satisfying collection of the post–*Hot Rocks* hits, despite some worthy-at-the-time artifacts now out of print, such as the 1975 *Made in the Shade*, the 1984 *Rewind*, and let us now remember the brilliantly titled 1981 *Sucking in the Seventies*. Of the many Stones live albums, *Ya-Ya's* is the only keeper; *Love You Live* and *Still Life* are the real dogs. *Jamming With Edward* is an aimless jam session never intended for release; the outtakes collection *Metamorphosis* includes the irresistible "I'd Much Rather Be With the Boys." As for *The Singles Collection*—of course, three-disc sets are kind of a dubious idea by definition, especially from a band whose original albums are classics. But we're talking the Stones here, and as an introduction, it's only one disc longer than *Hot Rocks* or *Forty Licks*, and not only brings together all the '60s hits, but also digs much deeper into the weird corners of the Stones work. (If you've never heard "Child of the Moon" or "Who's Driving Your Plane," you'll love them.) A desert-island-worthy relic of the 20th Century for sure, the collection takes a journey from the demand for "Satisfaction" to the realization that "You Can't Always Get What You Want," and then back again. Honey, it's not one of those. —R.S.

Sonny Rollins
Selected Discography
★★★★	Saxophone Colossus (Prestige, 1956)
★★★★★	Tenor Madness (Prestige, 1956)
★★★½	Way Out West (Prestige, 1957)
★★★★	Newk's Time (Prestige, 1957)
★★★★★	A Night at the Village Vanguard (Blue Note, 1957)
★★★★	The Bridge (RCA, 1962)
★★★½	Next Album (Milestone/OJC, 1972)
★★★	Don't Stop the Carnival (Riverside, 1978)

Sonny Rollins has been called the greatest living improviser and the last great master of the tenor saxophone. But he's also a vital living link to the ideals and macho discipline of jazz's hard-bop heyday. His long, heroic solos, laced with daunting technical passages and quotes from prerock pop tunes, are brilliant, motif-building displays of theme-and-variation solo-

ing that showcase his robust tone and a film director's knack for exploring ideas step-by-step.

Rollins made his first big impression working in the Clifford Brown–Max Roach band in the mid-'50s. Although he recorded under his own name as early as 1951, his most consequential recordings start in 1956, with *Tenor Madness* (which includes a blues duel with John Coltrane), and run through a series of remarkable recordings he made with just bass and drums at the Village Vanguard in 1957. Rollins retired for the first time in 1960—according to legend, he spent his nights practicing on New York's Williamsburg Bridge—before resurfacing in 1962 with another gem, *The Bridge*. He soldiered on through the late '60s and '70s with his usual mix of blues, bop, and calypso (Rollins authored several now-ubiquitous island themes, including "St. Thomas" and "Don't Stop the Carnival"), best appreciated on *Next Album*, and was featured on the Rolling Stones' hit "Waiting on a Friend." Since returning from a second retirement, the enigmatic Rollins has recorded several polite albums; some, like 2000's *This Is What I Do*, contain flashes of brilliance, others (such as 1988's *Dancing in the Dark*) fail to display the fire he still summons in live performance. —T.M.

The Romantics
★★★	The Romantics (1980; Nemperor/Epic, 1992)
★★★½	What I Like About You (and Other Romantic Hits) (1990; Nemperor/Epic, 1993)
★★★	Super Hits (Sony, 1998)
★★	Live (EMI-Capitol Special Markets, 2000)
★★★	Extended Versions (BMG Special Projects, 2002)
★★★½	61/49 (Web Entertainment, 2003)

Along with dozens of other new wave bands, the Romantics displayed a winning knack for Beatlesque power pop. What set this Detroit quartet apart from the turn-of-the-decade competition was a strong command of roots. Yes, the Romantics *did* wear skinny ties and shiny suits on their album covers, but they also tipped their caps to the blues and R&B greats behind Merseybeat. Having a stalwart drummer helped that cause mightily; Jimmy Marinos makes that immobile 4/4 really jump, and he sings most of the Romantics' best songs with a raggedy-assed vulnerability that can be quite affecting. Once power pop started to fizzle, the Romantics inched closer and closer to arena rock (the out-of-print *Strictly Personal* is a botched Loverboy album). Two years later, the re-formed group hit the rebound when "Talking in Your Sleep" became an early MTV staple. The rest of *In Heat* pales in comparison to that love-it-or-loathe-it single, which may account for its disappearance—but what the hey, the Romantics were always a singles band anyway.

Collecting half of *In Heat* and a handful of earlier gems like the title track, *What I Like About You* contains a perfect dose of the Romantics: almost 40 minutes' worth of rock & roll songs played short, sweet, and straight to the point; later budget collections from EMI-Capitol and BMG duplicate that still-available original collection. Their 2003 reunion album, *61/49,* showed that the Romantics hadn't lost a step, nearly a quarter century later. —M.C./B.SC.

The Ronettes

★★ The Ronettes: The Early Years (1965; Rhino, 1992)
★★★★★ Best of the Ronettes (Abkco, 1992)
Ronnie Spector
★★★ She Talks to Rainbows (EP) (Kill Rock Stars, 1999)

With their short skirts, mile-high hairdos and tough come-hither-at-your-own-risk pose, the Ronettes might have qualified as the quintessential '60s girl group on looks alone. But the New York trio of Veronica "Ronnie" Bennett, her sister Estelle, and their cousin Nedra Talley had something that would forever separate them from the mascara pack. They had the voice of Ronnie, an aching, quavery throb of an instrument, the sound of which can still make grown men weak in the knees. Oddly enough, in the beginning, her voice was not considered an asset; it was thought of as a somewhat freakish thing, as if she were Frankie Lymon in drag. *The Early Years,* a collection of prefame sides cut for Colpix, is average go-go fare that shows how clueless their first producers were; only the Jackie DeShannon–Sharon Sheely song, "He Did It" and "I'm Gonna Quit While I'm Ahead," tap into Ronnie's potential.

Phil Spector had no such difficulty discerning what made the Ronettes special: The producer found the perfect complement to his fabled Wall of Sound in Ronnie Bennett's voice. From its opening drum figure, the 1964 Ronettes single "Be My Baby" was the record Spector's career had been leading up to, a pop valentine so sublime that Brian Wilson has obsessed over it for nearly 40 years. That none of the followups—including "Baby, I Love You," "(The Best Part of) Breakin' Up," "Do I Love You?" and the magnificent "Walking in the Rain"—cracked the Top 20 probably had to do with the roller-coaster nature of Spector's independent Philles label; every one of these records is eternal. *Best of the Ronettes* contains all of them, as well as lesser hits like "Born to Be Together"

and nonhit but no less heartwarming material like "You Baby," "I Wish I Never Saw the Sunshine," and the Veronica solo "You Came, You Saw, You Conquered." (The only chart entry missing is their last, "I Can Hear Music," later to become a bigger hit for the Beach Boys. Was the cut excluded because it was the only one not produced by Phil Spector?)

Sadly, the escalation of Phil and Veronica's personal relationship was marked by a corresponding decline in the producer's professional attention; in making her Ronnie Spector, he allowed the Ronettes to wither on the vine. Ronnie eventually escaped the marriage, but she never got out from under her ex-husband's creative shadow. Most of her subsequent producers attempted to recapture Phil's glory. Joey Ramone was no exception—he even recut "I Wish I Never Saw the Sunshine"—but his downtown small-band reverence is so good-natured that the 1999 EP *She Talks to Rainbows* succeeds largely on goofball charm. Joey does his best Sonny to Ronnie's Cher on "Bye Bye Baby"; elsewhere, he has her tackle Johnny Thunders' "You Can't Put Your Arms Around a Memory" and Brian Wilson's own bit of eternity, "Don't Worry Baby," which was written with the voice of Ronnie Spector very much in mind. —B.E.

Roni Size/Reprazent

★★★½ New Forms (Talkin' Loud/PolyGram, 1997)
★★ In the Mode (Talkin' Loud/PolyGram, 2000)
★★ Touching Down (Full Cycle, 2002)

One of the only drum-and-bass artists to score a major-label deal, Roni Size and his Reprazent collective—a contingent of producers, DJs, and vocalists including DJ Die, Krust, Suv, MC Dynamite, and singer Onallee—received critical accolades for their sprawling two-disc debut, *New Forms,* which won the coveted Mercury Prize.

In the mid-'90s, the music industry had high hopes for drum and bass. Usually fueled by quickened beats and apocalyptic bass, Size offered a less threatening but undiluted version of jungle that could be enjoyed at home as well as on a booming dance floor.

Size hails from Bristol, England, a southwestern port steeped in Jamaican music; the city was also home to trip-hop pioneers Portishead, Massive Attack, and Smith & Mighty. Like the trip-hop musicians, Size and his crew attended early-'90s Wild Bunch parties, where they gleaned dub's thundering bass and later paired it with quicksand rhythms. Big hip-hop and American R&B fans, the Reprazent crew injected personality into *New Forms* with Onallee's soul-diva croonings, featured on singles like "Share the Fall" and "Watching Windows," while MC Dynamite's smooth patter crowned crowd favorite "Brown Paper Bag."

Drum and bass developed a strong cult following by the end of the '90s—Size and Reprazent were among the underground's favorite artists—but the style failed to capture the attention of mainstream America. The collective's second release was an outright attempt to sway the masses by using big-name collaborators like Rahzel, Method Man, and Redman (whom Size had always dreamed of working with). Even Rage Against the Machine's Zach de la Rocha lent his rage-fueled voice to an ill-conceived track titled "Center of the Storm." But *In the Mode* was inharmonious and failed to attract either the general public or the critics who had gushed so heavily over *New Forms.* Hip-hop fans didn't understand or care for drum and bass' fast pace, and fans of the genre didn't necessarily want to hear hip-hop rappers over drum and bass—seemingly, the talented MCs couldn't handle the accelerated pace. The best track on the album, "Snapshot," isn't a crossover attempt; it's a straightforward dance-floor tune with a killer hook (which had been released on Size's own label, Full Cycle, to great success), proving that sometimes artists should stick to what they do best. Size seemed to have realized that the crossover thing was wearing a bit thin by the time he recorded 2002's *Touching Down.* Without a single producer, MC, or musician helping out, Size turns out spare, high-velocity drum-and-bass that sacrifices hook-filled accessibility for frenetic nondanceability. —T.R.

Linda Ronstadt

★★★½   Linda Ronstadt (1971; Capitol, 1995)
★★½   Don't Cry Now (1973; Asylum, 1990)
★★★★★   Heart Like a Wheel (1974; Capitol, 1990)
★★★   Prisoner in Disguise (1975; Asylum, 1990)
★★★   Hasten Down the Wind (1976; Asylum, 1990)
★★★★   Greatest Hits (1976; Asylum, 1990)
★★★★   Simple Dreams (1977; Asylum, 1990)
★★★   Living in the U.S.A. (1978; Asylum, 1990)
★★½   Mad Love (1980; Asylum, 1990)
★★★   Greatest Hits, Volume II (1982; Asylum, 1990)
★★   Get Closer (1982; Asylum, 1990)
★★★   What's New (1983; Asylum, 1990)
★★★   Lush Life (1984; Asylum, 1990)
★★★   Sentimental Reasons (1986; Asylum, 1990)
★★★   'Round Midnight With Nelson Riddle and His Orchestra (1986; Asylum, 1990)
★★★   Canciones de Mi Padre (1987; Elektra, 1990)
★★★½   Cry Like a Rainstorm, Howl Like the Wind (Elektra, 1989)
★★★   Mas Canciones (Elektra, 1991)
★★   Frenesi (Elektra, 1992)
★★★½   Winter Light (Elektra, 1994)
★★★   Feels Like Home (Elektra, 1995)
★★   Dedicated to the One I Love (Elektra, 1996)
★★½   We Ran (Elektra, 1998)
★★★★   Western Wall: The Tucson Sessions (Elektra, 1999)
★★★★½   The Linda Ronstadt Box Set (Elektra, 1999)
★★★   A Merry Little Christmas (Elektra/Asylum, 2000)
★★★★   The Very Best of Linda Ronstadt (Rhino, 2002)
★★★½   Mi Jardin Azul: Las Canciones Favorites (Elektra/Rhino, 2004)

The dulcet purity—and sheer power—of her voice stands out right from the start, though it took Linda Ronstadt several years to corral her talents. "Different Drum," her 1967 folk-rock hit with the Stone Poneys, hinges on that sweet lonesome wail. In the '70s, Ronstadt rose to prominence as a keen, often definitive interpreter of young singer/songwriters. While her first two, deleted Capitol albums are somewhat tentative, exploratory efforts, the self-titled third LP benefits from strong material and the backing of the soon-to-be Eagles. On *Heart Like a Wheel,* producer Peter Asher and the cream of L.A.'s session-playing crop provide impeccable backing; more important, Ronstadt finds the material her voice had been crying out for. She leaps out of the Southern rock–flavored guitar mesh on "You're No Good" and "When Will I Be Loved"; tackles contemporary material both well-known (James Taylor's "You Can Close Your Eyes") and undiscovered (Anna McGarrigle's title track); and asserts a natural command of country roots (with an assist from backup singer Emmylou Harris) on Hank Williams's "I Can't Help It (If I'm Still in Love With You)." Deservedly, *Heart Like a Wheel* made Ronstadt a superstar. Her subsequent pop success with lightweight cover versions of rock & roll classics soon came to overshadow her vital connection to country and folk—too bad. The further Ronstadt ventures from *Heart Like a Wheel*'s comfortable mix, the more inconsistent her albums become. Some of her biggest hits completely miss the mark.

Two Motown nuggets carry *Prisoner in Disguise:* her peppy readings of "Heatwave" and "Tracks of My Tears" neither subtract nor add much to the originals. *Hasten Down the Wind* centers on a trilogy of lovelorn, somewhat lugubrious songs by Karla Bonoff: "If He's Ever Near," "Lose Again," and "Someone to Lay Down Beside Me." However, *Simple Dreams* pulls off this eclectic old-new-borrowed-blue approach. Ronstadt's strident treatment of Roy Orbison's "Blue Bayou" and the Stones' "Tumbling Dice" will sound like sacrilege to some listeners. But Ronstadt's acoustically spare, heart-piercing takes on "I Never Will Marry" (a Dolly Parton oldie) and the traditional "Old Paint" seem just right. Then-fledgling songwriter Warren Zevon benefits from Ronstadt's patronage here, and vice versa: she concocts a nearly convincing "wild side" for "Carmelita" and "Poor Poor Pitiful Me."

Living in the U.S.A.—a.k.a. "Rollerskates"—is where Linda coasts into trouble. Retooled classics by Chuck Berry and Smokey Robinson fall flat, while more adventurous covers of Zevon ("Mohammed's Radio") and Elvis Costello ("Alison") never quite connect.

Her chart momentum unabated, Ronstadt drops her first bomb at the dawn of a new decade. *Mad Love* is her new-wave fashion travesty—every artist of this period should be allowed one, anyway. Amid the herky-jerky tempos and three uncertain Costello covers, Ronstadt sounds downright relieved when she gets to Neil Young's pretty "Look Out for My Love." Penned by future "Like a Virgin" cowriter Billy Steinberg, "How Do I Make You" proves that Ronstadt can still bait a hook quite alluringly. The bulk of *Mad Love*, however, suggests that the foremost female singer of the '70s is rapidly losing touch with the pop marketplace. On *Get Closer* she no longer wields the attention-grabbing power of old; for the first time in ten years, Ronstadt appears totally out of the loop.

Starring in Gilbert & Sullivan's *Pirates of Penzance* on Broadway during the early '80s, Ronstadt apparently got bitten by the prerock-pop bug. She released three albums of orchestrated standards with former Frank Sinatra arranger and conductor Nelson Riddle: every perfect note in place, *What's New, Lush Life,* and *Sentimental Reasons* (issued together in the set *'Round Midnight*) are tasteful to the point of seeming dispassionate. Those torch songs are meant to smolder, spark, and glow. Ronstadt's two albums of Spanish-language traditionals are far warmer—and more involving. Growing up in Arizona, Ronstadt obviously developed an ear for Mexican folk melodies and Spanish phrasing. *Canciones de Mi Padre* and *Mas Canciones* are enjoyable side-trips, though hardly transcendent. Ronstadt returned to the pop field in 1989; *Cry Like a Rainstorm, Howl Like the Wind* hinges on the elegant hit single "Don't Know Much," a duet with the shivery-voiced New Orleans giant Aaron Neville. Believe it or not, the onetime Queen of Bombast gives her guest room to soar this time. The rest of *Cry* is pleasant, if slightly pedestrian adult-contemporary fare.

During the '90s, Ronstadt dabbled in her various modes: *Frenesi* revisits Latin music, *Winter Light* and *Dedicated to the One I Love* focuses on oldies (the latter reinterpreting them as children's songs), *Feels Like*

Home is a return to country rock and *We Ran*—on which she's teamed with producer Glyn Johns and stalwart session men—features material by A-listers like Dylan, Springsteen, and John Hiatt. All are solid, professional records that demonstrate the enduring strength of her pipes and phrasing, and will appeal to fans of her '70s work. But Ronstadt's most striking recent record by far is *Western Wall,* a Johns-produced collaboration with Emmylou Harris that benefits from the latter's career-long knack for choosing exceptional material. The two *Greatest Hits* albums get to the heart of the matter but could do with expanded reissues, while the 1999 box set impeccably covers the stylistic expanse of the singer's first three decades. Nonetheless, Ronstadt's individual albums—for all their highs and lows—offer a more accurate, telling portrait. —M.C./B.SC.

The Roots

★★★ Organix (Remedy Records, 1993)
★★★½ Do You Want More?!!!??! (DGC, 1995)
★★★★ Illadelph Halflife (DGC, 1996)
★★★★ Things Fall Apart (MCA, 1999)
★★★★ The Roots Come Alive (MCA, 1999)
★★★★½ Phrenology (MCA, 2002)
★★★★ The Tipping Point (MCA, 2004)

First dismissed as a novelty—hip-hop MCs backed by a live band—then as a curiosity, the Roots have quietly become one of the most influential ensembles in hip-hop history. Through near-constant touring and a series of lyrically enlightened, musically genre-blind recordings, the collective has helped spark alternative hip-hop (lending a hand on recordings by Common and others) and defined the basic sound of neosoul via collaborations with such vocalists as Eyrkah Badu, Jill Scott, and D'Angelo.

The Roots started spreading in the late 1980s at Philadelphia's High School for Creative Performing Arts, where drummer Ahmir "?uestlove" Thompson, whose father is a singer, shared classes with future jazz lions (bassist Christian McBride) and singing heartthrobs (Wanya Morris of Boyz II Men) and began collaborating with rapper Tariq Trotter (Black Thought). Setting up in the city's South Street District, the group played for passersby and earned a rep for replicating the hip-hop hits of the day with spot-on accuracy. The self-produced *Organix*, from 1993, catches the group at its jazziest, with sparkling electric piano punctuating tongue-twisting proclamations of prowess from rapper Black Thought.

National buzz about *Organix* led to a bidding war; the Roots became the first hip-hop act signed to Geffen Records' DGC imprint. The band's first major-label effort, *Do You Want More?!!!??!*, set the basic Roots approach: some freestyle, some elaborate production pieces, and several tracks accessible enough to attract radio play, most notably "Proceed." The band's loose, vamping grooves—accomplished with minimal sampling and human beat-box scratching—weren't exactly radical, but they were hailed as an important development (even though from a narrative standpoint, the album is repetitive).

The messages grow more focused on 1996's *Illadelph Halflife,* which includes several strident anti-gangsta tirades and taunts. Black Thought replaced the bellicose, confrontational bravado of so many rappers with discussions of fidelity and responsibility. The Roots hit their stride with *Things Fall Apart,* which brought the group its first hit ("You Got Me," written by Scott and sung by Badu) as well as mountains of critical acclaim for its sharply observed accounts of urban life. The song won a rap Grammy and set the stage for a series of tours, documented on the intense, highly caffeinated live disc *The Roots Come Alive.*

After a personnel change and a hiatus for various projects (Black Thought acted in the movie *Brooklyn Babylon;* ?uestlove provided the foundation for D'Angelo's second record, *Voodoo*), the Roots regrouped for *Phrenology.* The band had been moving in a rock direction in live performance, and that directional shift is obvious here: There are blasts of snarling uptempo punk and a slithering rocker, "The Seed 2.0," featuring guitarist/singer Cody Chesnutt, and a piece called "Water" that begins with the age-old Bo Diddley beat and ends as an extended *musique concrète*–style instrumental fantasia.

The Roots followed *Phrenology*'s resolute weirdness with the lean and mean *Tipping Point,* which finds Black Thought dispensing more overtly political insights over grooves that are stun-gun direct. Several pieces were born in jam sessions and sound that way, including the brisk shuffle "I Don't Care" and the reggae-tinged "Guns Are Drawn." —T.M.

Roots Manuva

★★★★ Brand New Second Hand (Big Dada/Ninja Tune, 1999)
★★★★ Run Come Save Me (Big Dada/Ninja Tune, 2001)
★★★½ Dub Come Save Me (Big Dada/Ninja Tune, 2002)

Ever since the earliest hip-hop singles were exported across the Atlantic, U.K. rappers had tried, and largely failed, to articulate a uniquely British hip-hop vision. Some rappers rapped with American accents; some just couldn't rap at all. Roots Manuva made neither of those mistakes. A South London resident of Jamaican descent, Rodney Smith had been rapping for almost a decade before his debut album, *Brand New Second Hand,* was released, and with songs like "Juggle Tings Proper," Roots Manuva was the first British rapper to succeed on the U.K. pop charts. More important, he was the first to nail what would become a distinctive U.K.-rap swagger: accented, melodic, and decidedly local. No longer was the British accent a source of shame, and when paired with a dancehall aesthetic (England's significant Jamaican community had made dancehall reggae the sound of choice in black London for more than three decades), it became a mature tool. *Run Come Save Me,* Roots Manuva's second album, was a little more esoteric, a little more bugged, a little more buzzed than its predecessor (a dub-remix album was even more so), with jagged, irregularly thumping beats underlying free-associative lyrical jaunts that are not for the faint of mind. —J.C.

Diana Ross

★★★ Diana Ross (1970; Universal, 2002)
★★★½ Lady Sings the Blues (1972; Motown PGD, 1992)
★★★ Touch Me in the Morning (1973; Universal Spectrum, 2003)
★★★½ Diana & Marvin (1973; PolyGram, 2001)
★★½ Mahogany (1975; PolyGram, 2000)
★★★½ Diana Ross (1976; Motown PGD, 1992)
★★★½ An Evening With Diana Ross (1977; Motown PGD, 1992)
★★★ Baby It's Me (1977; Motown PGD, 1992)
★★★ The Boss (1979; Motown PGD, 1999)
★★★½ Diana (1980; Motown PGD, 2003)
★★★ To Love Again (1981; Universal, 2003)
★★★½ All the Great Hits (1981; Universal, 2000)
★★★ Why Do Fools Fall in Love? (1981; BMG Special Products, 1997)
★★½ Silk Electric (RCA, 1982)
★★★ Diana Ross Anthology (Motown, 1983)
★★★ Red Hot Rhythm and Blues (1987; RCA 1990)
★★½ Workin' Overtime (Motown, 1989)
★★★ Diana Ross's Greatest Hits (Motown, 1991)
★★ Stolen Moments: The Lady Sings Jazz & Blues (1993; Universal, 2002)
★½ Forever Diana: Musical Memoirs (Motown, 1994)
★★★★ The Ultimate Collection (Motown, 1994)
★★½ Take Me Higher (Motown, 1995)
★★★ Greatest Hits: The RCA Years (RCA, 1997)
★★★ Every Day Is a New Day (Motown, 1999)
★★★ The Millennium Collection (PolyGram, 2000)
★★★½ The Motown Anthology (Motown, 2001)

Leaving the Supremes in 1970—and with them, Motown's expert songwriting team, Holland-Dozier-Holland—Diana Ross embarked pellmell on a pursuit of superstardom. With Motown investing $100,000 in her stage act, and with her own show-biz instincts honed to a razor's edge during her years as the Supremes' only high-profile singer, she soon achieved that goal—but at considerable aesthetic cost. Holding on only fitfully to her R&B credibility, she came across alternately as an ingratiating Vegas showstopper and an ebony Streisand. Sheer professionalism remains her signal "virtue"—by the end of the '80s, she had become an out-of-touch diva, her success gained only by her dogged following of obvious trends.

With the exception of her movie soundtracks—*Lady Sings the Blues,* and its flashy renditions of Billie Holiday standards, and the much less interesting *Mahogany*—Ross' early-'70s albums mixed predictably strong hits and an overabundance of filler. Ashford and Simpson's "Reach Out and Touch (Somebody's Hand)" and "Ain't No Mountain High Enough" made *Diana Ross* a credible glossy-soul debut; soon, however, she began working with weaker writers and such slick pablum as "Touch Me in the Morning and "Last Time I Saw Him" were the sad result. Her duets with Marvin Gaye, *Diana and Marvin,* displayed her comfortable expertise, but by mid-decade Ross was lost in disco-land. Her endless dance epic "Love Hangover" was a smash, but the fact that it sounded like Donna Summer suggested that Diana was in need of new direction.

She chose, however, to coast. The inflated double-album *An Evening with Diana Ross* epitomized her Vegas period. Chic's Nile Rodgers and Bernard Edwards came to the rescue with *Diana,* the ace producers providing streamlined designer-funk; the sessions produced such disco classics as "I'm Coming Out" (since made immortal by Puff Daddy and Co. as the basis of Biggie Smalls' "Mo' Money, Mo' Problems") and "Upside Down." A deluxe reissue of *Diana* contains the version of the album that the Chic guys originally recorded, which will interest hardcore fans but few others. *Why Do Fools Fall in Love?* was a diluted version of the same sort of dance-pop, with "Work That Body" generating frenzy in aerobics classes. Capitalizing on that single's success, Ross then released Michael Jackson's shameless "Muscles," off *Silk Electric. Silk*'s Warhol cover-art summed up Ross's fully realized upward mobility—she'd reached a safe pinnacle from which she'd rarely descend. *Red Hot Rhythm and Blues* didn't live up to its title, but it at least showed the singer moving onto the right track.

The '90s Diana was mainly a tale of her ascension into a kind of diva emeritus. Concerts, magazine covers, and acting forays all kept her busy, even if she rarely released stellar new material. *Stolen Moments* was Diana doing Billie Holiday, and only pointed up that Billie she's not. *Take Me Higher* was decent contemporary R&B, with a nifty version of the disco chestnut "I Will Survive." *Every Day Is a New Day,* a comeback bid, scored with "Not Over You Yet," Diana's venture into electronica.

Of the bewildering array of best-ofs, the RCA *Greatest Hits* and Motown's *The Ultimate Collection* (with a few Supremes classics thrown in) cover all you need. *The Motown Collection* is more extensive; *Forever Diana,* the box set, is for fanatics only.   —P.E.

David Lee Roth

  ★★★½ Crazy from the Heat (EP) (Warner Bros., 1985)
    ★★ Eat 'Em and Smile (Warner Bros., 1986)
    ★★ Skyscraper (Warner Bros., 1988)
  ★★½ A Little Ain't Enough (Warner Bros., 1991)
    ★★ Your Filthy Little Mouth (Warner Bros., 1994)
   ★★★ The Best (Rhino, 1997)
     ★ DLR Band (Wawazat Records, 1998)

When David Lee Roth was Van Halen's vocalist, his ribald wit and unabashed showmanship were the perfect counterpoint to the inventive anarchy of Eddie and Alex Van Halen. On his own, though, Roth more often than not comes across as a self-impressed boor, the kind of not-funny clown most of us try to avoid at parties. *Crazy from the Heat,* recorded just before Roth's split with Van Halen, is the best of his solo efforts; he may not have the voice for "California Girls," and "Just a Gigolo" may go a little heavy on the borscht-belt shtick, but overall the EP is entertaining and energetic.

With *Eat 'Em and Smile* and *Skyscraper,* Roth forgoes such indulgences, relying instead on an ersatz Van Halen built around Steve Vai, a guitarist whose earliest claim to fame was a transcription of Eddie Van Halen's "Eruption" solo, and Billy Sheehan, who had previously been known as the "Eddie Van Halen of bass." Instrumental firepower is no substitute for songs, though, and apart from "Just Like Paradise" (from *Skyscraper*), Roth had little in the way of memorable melodies. *A Little Ain't Enough,* recorded after Vai and Sheehan had departed, recaptured a little of Roth's early vitality, but not enough to make the album matter. Perhaps tired of banging his head against the wall, Roth changed direction with *Your Filthy Little Mouth,* moving away from heavy rock and toward more Adult Contemporary fare. What little audience he had promptly evaporated.

Roth's solo career to this point is anthologized in the generously indulgent *The Best.* In 1996 he reunited with Van Halen, but that only lasted two songs, and he was back on his own again. The band he assembled for *DRL Band* eschews virtuosity in favor of meat-and-potatoes hard rock; sadly, the CD sounds more like a demo than a finished album. —J.D.C.

Roxy Music

★★★★	Roxy Music (EG/Reprise, 1972)
★★★★★	For Your Pleasure (EG/Reprise, 1973)
★★★★	Stranded (EG/Reprise, 1973)
★★★★★	Country Life (EG/Reprise, 1974)
★★★★★	Siren (EG/Reprise, 1975)
★★	Viva! (EG/Reprise, 1976)
★★★★★	Greatest Hits (EG/Reprise, 1977)
★★★½	Manifesto (EG/Reprise, 1979)
★★½	Flesh + Blood (EG/Reprise, 1980)
★★★★½	Avalon (Warner Brothers, 1982)
★★★	The High Road (EG/Reprise, 1983)
★★★★	The Atlantic Years; 1973–1980 (Atco, 1983)
★★★★½	Street Life: 20 Greatest Hits (EG/Reprise, 1986)
★★★	Heart Still Beating (EG/Reprise, 1990)
★★★★	More Than This (Virgin, 1999)
★★★½	Slave to Love: Best of the Ballads (Virgin, 2000)

The key to understanding Bryan Ferry's career is watching the opening credits of *Fantasy Island*. Ricardo Montalban's Mr. Rourke, a character blatantly based on Bryan Ferry, spends his life fulfilling everybody else's wildest fantasies while keeping his own private heartache discreetly tucked away inside his white dinner jacket. He makes tragic faces and murmurs words of regret in an all-purpose pan-European accent. Note that during the opening credits of the television show, Mr. Rourke looks out his window and sees the plane landing before Tattoo rings the bell and yells, "The plane, boss! The plane!" Of course, Mr. Rourke already knows the plane is landing: He can hear it. So why make Tattoo go through this? Because he loves the ritual, the elaborate performance of his *Fantasy Island* melodramas, just as Bryan Ferry loves the pop song and its inherent ritualistic romantic repetition. Also like Mr. Rourke, Bryan Ferry makes sure he never gets upstaged by always surrounding himself with much uglier men in public.

With Ferry on hand as the prime singer and songwriter, Roxy Music made the most seductive glam rock of the '70s. Bryan Ferry explored his obsessions— the allure of romantic delusion, the narcissism of "looking for love in a looking-glass world," the compulsion to dash his heart on the rocks of beauty over and over again—amid Phil Manzanera's guitar, Andy MacKay's sax, and Brian Eno's synthesizer. Stranded

in his own world, where music and passion are always the fashion, Ferry indulged his most pathetic romantic fantasies. His blatantly artificial lounge-lizard trill and ironic Eurotrash glam moves sent up every tawdry emotion that has ever been buried in a pop song, without washing his hands clean of any of them. The debut, *Roxy Music,* is an explosion of wit and imagination, even if the songwriting and sound still seem a little thin, with the Humphrey Bogart tribute "2 H.B." and the proggy epic "If There Was Something." There was a vaguely sinister fashion model preening on the cover, which became a Roxy tradition.

For Your Pleasure was a bigger, richer, fuller-sounding album, giving Eno more room to experiment in the dense instrumental rush of "The Bogus Man" and "For Your Pleasure" (which didn't keep him from leaving the band for a solo career immediately afterward). Ferry soars in the glitter-gasmic convulsions of "Do the Strand," "In Every Dream Home a Heartache," and, best of all, "Beauty Queen," a tortured torch song pledging eternal devotion to an invisible sex wraith. The vocals drip with wit and remorse, while the music ventures into outer space. Eno was gone by *Stranded*, but that just gave Ferry a bigger stage to dance on, and Eno himself called it his favorite Roxy album. "Just Like You" refines the piano-based cocktail-ballad style that became a Roxy trademark; "Mother of Pearl" veers from abrasive art-rock clamor to moody introspection; and "Street Life" settles for fast sex.

Country Life and *Siren* hold up alongside *For Your Pleasure* as Roxy Music's best; somehow, the music got glossier and bolder at the same time. *Country Life* opens with the ultimate Roxy tune, "The Thrill of It All," a roaring, bombastic, self-lacerating, but unabashedly passionate love song named after a terrible old Doris Day movie. "Prairie Rose," "All I Want Is You," and "Casanova" are sleek guitar rockers; "A Really Good Time" is all piano and strings, as rock's most Wildean dandy finds himself out on a quiet spree, vainly fighting the old ennui. *Siren* is smoother; it's the first Roxy Music album without any failed moments, as the debonair funk grooves of "Love Is the Drug" and "Both Ends Burning" set up the world-weary balladry of "Sentimental Fool," "Could It Happen to Me?," and the climactic "Just Another High," on which the Divine Bryan finally breaks down and confesses that he's just another crazy guy. When Ferry's on fire, smoke gets in your eyes.

After a layoff and the weak live album *Viva!*, Roxy returned in 1979 as a very different band: The surface was all gloss and the guitar freakery was kept to a minimum. Roxy became, for all purposes, an arty disco band. This phase of its career was hugely influential on the New Romantic synth pop and Euro-disco of the '80s, inspiring tribute bands like Duran Duran, ABC, and the Blow Monkeys. On *Manifesto* and *Flesh + Blood,* superb U.K. pop hits—"Dance Away," "Over You," "Oh Yeah"—are surrounded with filler, including the worst version ever of "In the Midnight Hour" *Avalon* was the culmination of Ferry's pop obsessions; in steamy synth-pop ballads like "More Than This," "True to Life," and "Avalon," he became the sincere romantic smoothie he'd always halfway wanted to be, and a great one at that. The world has been swapping spit to this album ever since.

Avalon was an appropriate way for Roxy to blow a kiss and wave good night, though the band's last official release, the live quickie EP *The High Road,* had a cover of John Lennon's "Jealous Guy" that became a huge U.K. hit, no doubt because of Ferry's impeccably elegiac whistling solo. *Heart Still Beating* is a live rehash. *Street Life* contains the best of the band's various best-ofs, collecting the early art rock (1977's *Greatest Hits*), the pop success (1983's *The Atlantic Years*), and the best of Ferry's solo work. *More Than This* is a lesser *Street Life,* with too much solo Ferry. Beginners who start with *Street Life* are guaranteed not to stop there. Roxy's best line, from 1979's "Dance Away," is: "I hope and pray, but not too much/Out of reach is out of touch/All the way is far enough." For better or for worse, all the way was *never* far enough for Roxy Music. —R.S.

Ruff Ryders

★★	Ryde or Die Compilation, Vol. 1 (Interscope, 1999)
★★½	Ryde or Die, Vol. 2 (Interscope, 2000)
★½	Ryde or Die, Vol. 3: In the "R" We Trust . . . (Interscope, 2001)

More a business association than a hip-hop crew, the group synergistically fuses together the production talents of Swizz Beatz, DJ Clue, P.K., and DJ Shok, along with the rhyming skills of DMX, Eve, the Lox, and others to make a partnership that is, unfortunately, less than the sum of its parts. The excitement that was generated by the first volume of *Ryde or Die* was quickly quelled upon a first listen, when it revealed itself to be an odds-and-sods collection of tracks that sound like they were discarded from each individual artist's solo albums. You'd do better to buy DMX's *The Great Depression* or Eve's *Scorpion.* —K.M.

The Runaways

★★	The Runaways (Mercury, 1976)
★★	Queens of Noise (Mercury, 1977)
★★	Waitin' for the Night (Mercury, 1977)
★★	Little Lost Girls (Rhino, 1981)
★★½	Best of the Runaways (1982; Mercury, 1987)

Hype dies hard. The Runaways helped pave the way for female punkers, perhaps, but that sure doesn't render this shrieky L.A. fivesome's inept metal albums any more listenable. "Cherry Bomb," from the debut, detonates its trashy hook with youthful glee—and that's it. Shlockmeister-producer Kim Fowley wields a tuneless, overweening hand at the controls, so guitarist Joan Jett's emerging lead vocals and presence get lost in the bright plastic din. No wonder she titled her first solo album *Bad Reputation.* (Lead guitarist Lita Ford's subsequent career as a metal vixen is a different story altogether.) Either way, you'd never figure the Runaways for a launching pad on the basis of these records; even *Best of the Runaways* fails to deliver the expected quota of escapist fun. —M.C.

Todd Rundgren

★★★½	Runt (1970; Bearsville/Rhino, 1987)
★★★★	Runt: The Ballad of Todd Rundgren (1971; Bearsville/Rhino, 1987)
★★★★★	Something/Anything? (1972; Rhino, 1987)
★★★	A Wizard a True Star (1973; Rhino, 1987)
★★½	Todd (1974; Bearsville/Rhino, 1987)
★★	Initiation (1975; Bearsville/Rhino, 1987)
★★★½	Faithful (1976; Bearsville/Rhino, 1987)
★★★½	Hermit of Mink Hollow (1978; Bearsville/Rhino, 1987)
★★★	Back to the Bars (1978; Rhino, 1987)
★★	Healing (1981; Rhino, 1987)
★★	The Ever Popular Tortured Artist Effect (1983; Bearsville/Rhino, 1987)
★★	A Cappella (1985; Rhino, 1988)
★★★★	Anthology (1968–1985) (Rhino, 1989)
★★★½	Nearly Human (Warner Bros., 1989)
★★	2nd Wind (Warner Bros., 1991)
★★★½	An Elpee's Worth of Productions (Rhino, 1992)
★★	No World Order (Forward/Rhino, 1993)
★★½	The Individualist (Ion, 1995)
★★★	With a Twist . . . (Guardian, 1997)
★★★	The Very Best of Todd Rundgren (Rhino, 1997)
★★★	One Long Year (Artemis, 2000)
★	Reconstructed (Cleopatra, 2000)
★★★	Live (King Biscuit Flower Hour, 2000)
★★★	The Essentials (Rhino, 2002)
★★	Todd Rundgren & His Friends (Cleopatra, 2002)
★★½	Bootleg Series, Vol. 1: Live at the Forum, London '94 (Sanctuary, 2002)

★★½ Bootleg Series, Vol. 2: KSAN 95 FM Live '79
(Sanctuary, 2002)

★★½ Bootleg Series, Vol. 3: Nearly Human Tour,
Japan '90 (Sanctuary, 2003)

★★★ Liars (Sanctuary, 2004)

Utopia

★★½ Todd Rundgren's Utopia (1974;
Bearsville/Rhino, 1987)

★★½ Another Live (1975; Bearsville/Rhino, 1987)

★★½ RA (1977; Bearsville/Rhino, 1987)

★★★ Oops! Wrong Planet (1978; Bearsville/Rhino,
1987)

★★★ Adventures in Utopia (1980; Bearsville/Rhino,
1987)

★★½ Deface the Music (1980; Bearsville/Rhino,
1987)

★★ Swing to the Right (1982; Bearsville/Rhino,
1987)

★★½ Utopia (1983; Bearsville/Rhino, 1987)

★★★ Anthology (1974–1985) (Rhino, 1989)

Buoyed by an uncanny skill in the studio and a well-developed ego, Todd Rundgren floated between two extremes during the '70s: sainted pure-pop balladeer (his solo albums) and bedeviled hippie technocrat (Utopia). That's when he wasn't working as a producer for Meat Loaf, Grand Funk Railroad, Badfinger, the New York Dolls, or Patti Smith. Perhaps as a reaction against spending so much of his time crafting hits for profitability's sake, his own music grew increasingly complex and unapproachable, not quite as "experimental" as he might like us to believe but opposed to easy consumption nonetheless. After *Something/Anything?*, the delectable 1972 magnum opus on which he played (nearly) every instrument and recorded every sound, Rundgren engaged in a continuing game of cat-and-mouse with an audience that seemed less interested in him with each passing decade. By the '90s, he was working on a unique Internet-based music subscription system, a genuine experiment that purported to allow fans closer access to his creative process—while the notoriously reclusive musician was far away in his Hawaii home.

Rundgren learned his way around a recording studio while leading Nazz in the late '60s. That Philadelphia quartet's debt to the Beatles is obvious from the first three notes of "Open My Eyes" (1968), but Todd also had an ear cocked toward his hometown's R&B scene. Rundgren's taste for scorchingly ironic hard rock rises to the top of *Runt*, though the vulnerable hook of "We Gotta Get You a Woman"—poor "Leroy boy"—is what attracted mainstream interest. Except for one crazed raveup ("Parole"), *The Ballad of Todd Rundgren* is exclusively devoted to melodic heartbreak

scenarios: beautiful three-minute songs that hark back to various '60s styles without directly quoting or mimicking. Rundgren "does it all" on *Something/ Anything?* (actually, he gets some help on the last fourth), and damn near everything works: the irresistibly sweet hit singles ("I Saw the Light" and "Hello It's Me"), the ominous metal hunk ("Black Mariah"), the taut, psychedelically enhanced rocker ("Couldn't I Just Tell You"). Even the jokey nostalgia ("Wolfman Jack") holds up, and the tracks on which Todd and pals run amok in the studio have their unforgettable moments, too.

Enter the "unpredictable" phase of Rundgren's career, which is going on 35 years now. *A Wizard a True Star* is an endurance test of stylistic diversity, with just three fully realized songs ("Sometimes I Don't Know What to Feel," "International Feel," and "Just One Victory") stranded in the midst of so much half-baked sonic decoration. Too loose and largely tuneless, the rambling double album *Todd* finds Rundgren playing the self-indulgent cult-hero role to the hilt. It's the polar opposite of *Something/Anything?* and a blatantly anticommercial act that seems less like an artistic statement than a dare to his fans to remain interested. Those that did heard puzzling exercises in studio verisimilitude (*Faithful* eerily re-creates songs by the Yardbirds, Beatles, Beach Boys, Dylan, and Hendrix, along with sonically correct homages by Todd) and virtuosic self-indulgence (*Healing*).

Yet another twist in the Todd legend emerged with Utopia, his celestial multikeyboard art-rock band, which began far, far away indeed (there are just four superlong fusion odysseys on the debut), but within a few years coalesced into a pop-rock vehicle for Rundgren in the highly stylized manner of Styx or Electric Light Orchestra. *Oops! Wrong Planet, Adventures in Utopia,* etc., all turn out the kind of easy-on-the-ears radio pop that Rundgren avoided in his solo albums from this period—an inversion of the usual relationship of solo artist to group.

When he wanted to, Rundgren could still write gorgeously sentimental tunes in the noblest Brill Building/Philly Soul tradition, such as *Hermit of Mink Hollow*'s "Can We Still Be Friends" and Utopia's "Love Is the Answer." He also developed a profitable knack for writing novelty tunes: he may have stuck "Bang the Drum All Day"—the '80s version of "Take This Job and Shove It"—on an album called *The Ever Popular Tortured Artist Effect,* but you can be sure that royalties from that song paid his rent long after his latest album of studio tricks (*A Cappella,* for example) was forgotten.

After a quiet spell in the mid-'80s, Rundgren rebounded on a new label with *Nearly Human,* his tightest and most tuneful outing in years, from the subtly haunting "Parallel Lines" to several synthed-up Philly Soul salutes. *2nd Wind* fails in the usual Todd way, a melodramatic, overreaching attempt at fusing elements of Broadway theater and rock. Geniuses never learn.

In the '90s, Rundgren threw himself headlong into the intoxicating new technologies of computers and the Internet. In some ways computer-aided music making is perfect for him: solitary, logical, and infinitely complex, computers offer a level of control never before possible in the studio. And indeed Rundgren seems newly energized on *No World Order* and *The Individualist,* which are credited to his digital alter ego TR-i. He expounds lucidly on broad cultural issues such as religion ("Fascist Christ"), the working life ("Day Job"), and pseudo-populist right-wing propaganda ("Family Values"). But the isolating effects of computing are also apparent in these projects, from the utter staleness of the sound to his out-of-date hangups (sampling Dan Quayle in 1995, three years into the Clinton-Gore administration).

By the end of the decade Rundgren was wholly devoted to his PatroNet project, a truly innovative Internet-based service in which he made music for a group of paying subscribers. *One Long Year* collects 10 highlights from this venture, with lots of industrial grooves (the latest addition to his stylistic utility belt) and his second big novelty score, "I Hate My Frickin I.S.P." It's spunky and vivacious, unlike the ridiculous *Reconstructed,* for which TR-i handed over old vocal tracks to various electronic remixers, with predictable results. Rundgren's continuing efforts are so far only available to his Web patrons, an appropriate exit from the marketplace at the dawn of the 21st Century. A surprise came in early 2004 with *Liars,* an angry and impassioned song cycle that is Rundgren's return to the album as a high-concept, self-contained art form. An elegant rant from beginning to end about a mendacious and callous culture that has degraded religion ("Mammon"), relationships ("Happy Anniversary"), and—most important for Rundgren—honesty, it is his most powerful and heartfelt work in years. But it's also a puzzle worthy of a veteran contrarian like Rundgren: is a '70s-style concept album a return to the marketplace of pop or a retreat into nostalgia?

For an artist who has compulsively made records since the late '60s, Rundgren's discography of collections and anthologies is remarkably simple. His solo *Anthology* is a worthwhile sampler, though it sacrifices some quality to even representation of his career; including a few Utopia tracks would eliminate the need for that collection. *The Very Best* has all the hits ("I Saw the Light," "We Gotta Get You a Woman,"

"Hello It's Me," "Bang the Drum") but is heavy on the '70s soft ballads; *The Essentials* evens the mix a little but adds some nonessentials ("Compassion," "Time Heals"). *An Elpee's Worth of Productions* showcases his career as a producer of others, from Fanny to XTC to the New York Dolls, with all the eclecticism and professional finesse one would expect.

Rundgren flooded the late-'90s market with live albums and reworkings of hits, which test redundancy (how many versions of "Love Is the Answer" and "Bang the Drum" can you stand?) but can occasionally be charmingly clever (the all–bossa nova *With a Twist . . .*). If that's not Todd Rundgren, then what is? —B.S.

Run-D.M.C.

★★★★½ Run-D.M.C. (Profile, 1984)
★★½ King of Rock (Profile, 1985)
★★★★★ Raising Hell (Profile, 1986)
★★★½ Tougher than Leather (Profile, 1986)
★★★ Back From Hell (Profile, 1990)
★★ Down With the King (Profile, 1993)
★★ Crown Royal (Arista, 1999)
★★★★★ Greatest Hits (Arista, 2002)

When Run-D.M.C. got into the game in the early '80s, hip-hop was seen as a novelty by some, and as an upstart ghetto artform by others—something that was good for the occasional pop hit. Grandmaster Flash and the Furious Five had proven it didn't have to all be party records with "The Message," "White Lines," and "New York New York," but their tight leather cutup outfits bordered on funk kitsch. Run-D.M.C. was the first major hip-hop band to transform basic B-boy style—sneakers, track suits, and jeans—into an influential style.

We can trace the origins of hip-hop—the culture and the artform—beyond the Bronx to ancient Africa, but if we want to talk about hip-hop the modern industry it all begins with *Run-D.M.C.* Under the guidance of Rick Rubin and older brother Russell Simmons, Joseph "Run" Simmons, Daryl "D.M.C." McDaniels and Jason "Jam Master Jay" Mizell would go on from this debut album—basically a collection of stellar singles—to initiate a number of hip-hop firsts: first hip-hop act to break MTV's forgiven but never forgotten color barrier; first hardcore hip-hop act to make canonical heavy metal; first and last hip-hop act to collaborate with Aerosmith; first hip-hop act to pull down a major corporate endorsement and be on the cover of ROLLING STONE.

The energy and exuberance of their initial work can still give you chills. You can practically feel the concrete rumbling beneath your feet in the wake of their debut—they are the true beginning of hip-hop as a shouting and testifying force to be reckoned with in the world beyond black radio. The two-man MC concept has never been better synchronized or more dynamic than as practiced by these cats in their prime. Their debut is already a greatest hits collection, stocked with an embarrassment of rich, stark, big beat classics. Stone monster jams like "Rock Box," "30 Days," "Hard Times," "It's Like That," and "Sucker MCs" are still definitive examples of what real hip-hop can be: streetwise, socially conscious, boisterously and boastfully witty, and irresistible when getting on the good foot. In the multinational tagged, branded, and labeled world of hip-hop today, "Rock Box' "s deathless "Calvin Klein is no friend of mine/don't want nobody's name on my behind" comes from a more innocent time as the entrepreneurial battle cry that would eventually give us the Phat Farm, Sean John, Wu-Wear, and Roc-A-Wear labels.

King of Rock was the followup; unfortunately, the title track, a dope metalled-out successor to "Rock Box," is the only classic track. The rest of the album seems somewhat mashed together from outtakes and less scintillating attempts to pepper their rap with rock flava. By their third disc, Run-D.M.C. had more than figured out how to concoct a meaty, long-playing sucker. *Raising Hell*'s "My Adidas" made sneakers a definitive a hip-hop topic, just as "Rocket 88" had made cars a prime subject for rock & roll. "Walk This Way," their crossover hit with Aerosmith, made rock-rap more than a notion. Unquestionably Rick Rubin's high water moment as their producer, *Raising Hell* made it clear that neither hip-hop nor Run-D.M.C. was going to be denied an all-access pass to MTV's suburban subscribers. And if anyone needed proof that they could still bring the hardcore sound, they provide it on "Is It Live" and "Hit It Run." The group was also unashamed to take a page or two from the Beastie Boys, as is clear from the gung-ho goofiness of "Its Tricky," "You Be Illin' " and "Dumb Girl."

On *Tougher Than Leather*'s most memorable tracks—"Run's House" and "Beats To The Rhyme"—you can feel the pressure to keep with the scratch-mad sampledelic frenzy of Public Enemy. The lyric writing geniuses emerging from hip-hop's third wave (PE, EPMD, De La Soul, Eric B. and Rakim, A Tribe Called Quest) were making Run-D.M.C. sound thematically and linguistically limited by comparison, but Run-D.M.C. could still command our attention with rhythm and tone alone. The metal grind redux of the title track proves you can only punish rock-rap so much before the beast asks to be shot and put out of its misery.

Greatest Hits has not an ounce of fat nor filler;

"Christmas in Hollis" (originally on the soundtrack to the Robert Downey flick *Less than Zero*) will probably always be the only hip-hop holiday song worth mentioning. *Back From Hell* is another Run-D.M.C. impression of a Public Enemy album, and not such an awful one at that. Our two heroes probably made Chuck D. blush with such naked flattery. Still, all good pop vehicles run eventually out of gas. By the time 1993's *Down With the King* rolled around, their gig was more than about to be up; the group turned over production chores to Pete Rock, The Bomb Squad, and EPMD for tracks that run from hot (the title tune) to barely blazing. It doesn't sound like fun anymore.

Comeback albums are hard on everybody. Old schoolers have to deny the wear of time and fashion, New Jacks have to play the role of the humble re-animators. That said, there's still no excuse for how low they went on *Crown Royal*. Even in their twilight, Run (who, by the way, now prefers to be known as the ordained Reverend Run, if you please) and D.M.C. should have never had to dignify sharing album space with such worthies as Fred Durst, Kid Rock, Stephen Jenkins, Jermain Dupri, or Sugar Ray. Okay, we like Everlast too, but not so much here. Nas and Prodigy are the redemptive factors on the 'hood-rallying "Queens Day," and the lush hip-hop soul that the Run-D.M.C. and Jagged Edge drop on "Let's Stay Together (Together Forever)" ain't so bad, really. Method Man collects another easy cameo check on the not-so-def closer "Simmons Incorporated," and you gotta hope, as with Michael Jordan's third retirement—and out of respect to the late Jam Master Jay, who was murdered in 2002—this will be all she wrote. —G.T.

Rush

★★	Rush (1974; Mercury, 1997)
★★	Fly by Night (1975; Mercury, 1997)
★★	Caress of Steel (1975; Mercury, 1997)
★★½	2112 (1976; Mercury, 1997)
★★½	All the World's a Stage (1976; Mercury, 1997)
★★½	A Farewell to Kings (1977; Mercury, 1997)
★★★	Hemispheres (1978; Mercury, 1997)
★★★½	Permanent Waves (1980; Mercury, 1997)
★★★½	Moving Pictures (1981; Mercury, 1997)
★★★	Exit . . . Stage Left (1981; Mercury, 1997)
★★★	Signals (1982; Mercury, 1997)
★★½	Grace Under Pressure (1984; Mercury, 1997)
★★½	Power Windows (1985; Mercury, 1997)
★★	Hold Your Fire (1987; Mercury, 1997)
★★	A Show of Hands (1989; Mercury, 1997)
★★	Presto (Atlantic, 1989)
★★½	Roll the Bones (Atlantic, 1991)
★★★	Counterparts (Atlantic, 1993)
★★★	Test for Echo (Atlantic, 1996)

★★★ Retrospective, Vol. 1 1974–1980 (Mercury, 1997)

★★★ Retrospective, Vol. 2 1980–1987 (Mercury, 1997)

★★★½ Different Stages (Atlantic, 1998)

★★★ Vapor Trails (Atlantic, 2002)

★★★ The Spirit of Radio: Greatest Hits 1974–1987 (Universal, 2003)

★★★½ Rush in Rio (Atlantic, 2003)

Geddy Lee

★★½ My Favorite Headache (Atlantic, 2000)

Rush pumps out a more approachable brand of sci-fi fusionoid pomposity than, say, sophisticated prog-rock practitioners such as Pink Floyd or King Crimson. The vaguely populist bent suits this musicianly Canadian power trio, while hinting at its preconceptual roots as dull, perennially second-billed metal plotzers. Drummer Neil Peart, guitarist Alex Lifeson, and bassist Geddy Lee have developed fearsome chops over the years; their love of tricky time signatures and busy solos is what hypnotizes fans and bores everybody else. Lyricist Peart's mystifying cosmic bent and lead singer Lee's Donald Duck–on-acid howl inspire similar love-it-or-loathe-it debates.

2112 and *All the World's a Stage* mark the end of Rush's muddy space-plowboy phase; with *Permanent Waves* ("Spirit of the Radio," "Jacob's Ladder") and *Moving Pictures* ("Limelight," "Tom Sawyer"), the group sculpts a more tuneful, AOR-friendly approach without forsaking its trademarks—middlebrow philosophizing and flashy instrumental trappings. After *Signals* and "New World Man," popular tastes shifted from the '70s-identified progressive-rock sound—of course, Rush has continued to follow its quest, regardless of trends. The '90s found the trio returning to the more organic, instrumentally complex aesthetic of its youth, albeit with the benefits of digital technology and a heavier sound (those power chords on *Counterparts'* "Stick It Out" are pure postgrunge menace.) But the tragic death of Peart's wife and daughter within a 10-month span brought to the group to a halt. Fortunately, the lifelong friends stuck together and, after a forgettable Geddy Lee solo outing, returned in 2002 with a new, geeky-as-ever album and subsequent world tour. A double DVD documenting a triumphant Rio de Janeiro gig was released the following year.

Of the handful of compilations available, the two-volume *Retrospective* captures the band's classic output at its muscular best. An elephantine DVD/CD package recorded live in Rio, *Rush in Rio* is, by far, the most satisfying of the band's many live collections. —M.C./E.L.

Mitch Ryder and the Detroit Wheels

★★½ Take a Ride (1966; Sundazed, 1993)

★★½ Breakout . . . !!! (1966; Sundazed, 1993)

★★ Sock It to Me! (1967; Sundazed, 1993)

★★★★ All Mitch Ryder Hits! (1967; Sundazed, 1994)

★★★★½ Rev Up: The Best of Mitch Ryder and the Detroit Wheels (Rhino, 1989)

If the term *blue-eyed soul* wasn't coined to describe Mitch Ryder, it could've been. Born William Levise, he came up on Detroit's demanding early-'60s R&B circuit as Billy Lee, the only white member of vocal groups like the Peps. Inspired by the guitar-wielding British Invasioneers, he assembled Billy Lee & the Rivieras to marry this new energy with his organic grasp of his city's black music heritage, something the Brits could only ape from afar. The band was built around lead guitarist Jim McCarty, who found a dynamic middle ground between the economy of Steve Cropper and the more solocentric style favored by the emerging guitar gods, and drummer John Badanjek's monster drive and explosive fills.

Billy Lee & the Rivieras were excitement personified, soon attracting local crowds by the thousands. They were signed by Four Seasons producer Bob Crewe, who rechristened them Mitch Ryder and the Detroit Wheels and devised a unique strategy for capturing the group's live energy. They didn't write, so Crewe and his charges fashioned medleys of familiar material that, in the hands of this impassioned singer and his shit-hot band, sounded fresh and invigorating. The first was "Jenny Take a Ride!" in December 1965, which combined "Jenny Jenny" by Little Richard with Chuck Willis' venerable "C.C. Rider"; the strategy reached a sweaty apogee the following year with "Devil With a Blue Dress On/Good Golly Miss Molly"—as electrifying a blast of basic rock & roll energy as has ever scorched the charts. Despite this and other hits, like the lascivious "Sock It to Me—Baby!," the formula would be reduced to "Too Many Fish in the Sea & Three Little Fishes" within a year. The Wheels were ditched, and Ryder soon fronted a 40-piece orchestra in a misguided attempt to be an "all-around" entertainer.

The band's ride had been short and intense. They ground out three albums in barely more than a year. As a result, none can be recommended. Each is a quickie, with a couple of singles padded by hastily tossed-off covers of Motown, James Brown, and other jukebox items from their club sets. (*What Now My Love*, Ryder's 1967 album of solo syrup, is an unlamented deletion.) Mitch Ryder and the Detroit Wheels were a singles band, so *All Mitch Ryder Hits* was the only album issued during their lifetime that mattered. Even better is the *Rev Up* anthology, because it includes tracks from Ryder's 1969 solo album, *The Detroit-Memphis Experiment,* on which he was backed by Booker T. and the MGs, and from his 1971 band, Detroit, which reunited him with drummer Johnny Bee and introduced guitarist Steve Hunter. Ryder's Detroit also introduced the Velvet Underground to the singles chart via Ryder's heavied-up version of Lou Reed's "Rock & Roll" (a sound Reed would, with the assistance of Hunter, replicate to great success during his *Rock 'n' Roll Animal* period). Since the mid-'70s, Mitch Ryder has maintained a separate recording career in Europe, one that is not based on his Detroit Wheels style or history. Many of these albums are readily available as imports. —B.E.

RZA

★★★★	RZA as Bobby Digital in Stereo (Gee Street, 1998)
★★★★	The RZA Hits (Epic, 1999)
★★★	Digital Bullet (Koch, 2001)

Without RZA, there would be no Wu-Tang Clan as we know it. As the group's original in-house producer and elder statesman, RZA, it can conclusively be said, is the only Wu member who is in no way expendable. RZA himself takes this truth to be self-evident—his 1999 release, *The RZA Hits,* is a masterful collection of RZA-produced cuts drawn from all corners of the Wu catalogue. (Never mind that *The RZA Hits* is padded with dull between-song commentary by the man himself.) Hailing from Staten Island, New York, RZA came up in the group All in Together Now (which

also included a young GZA and Ol' Dirty Bastard) before, as Prince Rakeem, releasing the solo EP *Ooh We Love You Rakeem* on Tommy Boy in 1991. Soon after the success of Wu-Tang's 1993 debut, members of the collective started spinning off solo albums, many produced in part or whole by RZA. It wasn't until 1998, however, that he released his own solo album, under the alias Bobby Digital. RZA and Kool Keith had a heated land-grab-style beef over the futuristic hip-hop superhero concept, and after *RZA as Bobby Digital in Stereo* came out, Keith responded with releases under his alias, Robbie Analog. RZA had said that his Bobby Digital alter ego was created under the effect of angel dust, and one can almost hear the zooted spittle flying from the corners of his mouth as he delivers rhymes like "Classic like Marley Marl/Tie you ass down and run you over with a trolley car." The music is murky and layered; its purposefully plodding beats and dive-bombing synthesizers induce disorientation. Bobby Digital's lyrical tone is emotionally charged, borderline hysterical, and reaches its crux on the brutal "Domestic Violence." Even the loved-up sonic bubble bath "Love Jones" has an undercurrent of foreboding. Fantastic artwork by longtime Marvel Comics artist Bill Sienkiewicz completed the package. *Digital Bullet,* a comparable installment in Bobby Digital's fearsome, libidinous saga, followed three years later. Fans of Ol' Dirty Bastard will feast on ODB's rabid rhyming on tracks "Kiss of a Black Widow" and "Black Widow Pt. 2," on the first and second Bobby Digital albums, respectively. In 2000, RZA created the moodily effective soundtrack to the Jim Jarmusch movie *Ghost Dog: The Way of the Samurai.* Although an album inspired by the movie was released domestically, the actual soundtrack was issued in Japan only. —P.R.

Sade

★★★★   Diamond Life (1984; Epic, 2000)
★★★½   Promise (1985; Epic, 2000)
  ★★★   Stronger Than Pride (Epic, 1988)
  ★★★   Love Deluxe (Epic, 1992)
★★★½   The Best of Sade (Epic, 1994)
  ★★★   Diamond Life/Promise/Love Deluxe (Epic, 2000)
★★★★   Lovers Rock (Epic, 2000)
  ★★★   Lovers Live (Epic, 2002)

Sweetback

  ★★½   Sweetback (Epic, 1996)
★★★½   Stage 2 (Epic, 2004)

With a string of hit singles and platinum albums, Nigerian-born British vocalist Sade and her trio of collaborators—also known collectively as Sade—have ranked among pop's most enduring acts, largely without the glare of celebrity or much fooling with their proven formula. At its center is Sade's warm, fragile voice, which more than makes up in style and distinction what it may lack in range and power. Her band's jazz lite dresses up very pleasant, Burt Bacharach–style adult pop with saxophones, icy keys, and rolling funk bass; as such, Sade provides a link between the mid-'80s British jazz/soul revival (Style Council, Everything But the Girl) and the '90s neosoul movement in the U.S. (most notably Maxwell, who collaborated with Sade multi-instrumentalist Stuart Matthewman).

Sade's largely interchangeable first two albums, *Diamond Life* and *Promise,* appeared in rapid succession. Both offer catchy sets of love songs—sometimes breezy, sometimes yearning, always cool—and the occasional social message. The former album, though, packs more consistent songwriting and more of Sade's signature tunes ("Smooth Operator," "Your Love Is King," "Hang on to Your Love"). The latter includes the group's best song, "The Sweetest

Taboo," with its insistent rim-shot syncopation, as well as "Never as Good as the First Time," which has a more transparent '80s-pop foundation than most of the group's material.

Stronger Than Pride tweaks the sound only slightly while scoring another hit with the memorable, though lightweight, "Paradise." Backing vocals now bolster Sade's attractive yet somewhat thin croon, while "Turn My Back on You" gives disco funk a whirl without embarrassing the group too much. Four years later, *Love Deluxe* revisits Sade's standard sound (as if the group had ever veered), adding subtle divergences. "Kiss of Life" stands out, combining Motown groove with smooth jazz, while "Pearls" builds drama through orchestration, crafting a tale of third-world misery that strongly evokes Sting. Most significant, "No Ordinary Love"—the group's only major single of the '90s—hints at what would be Sade's one major stylistic shift: toward the sleeker, more digital sound of modern British pop.

Two years into the eight-year absence that followed *Love Deluxe,* the group collected its hits and favorites on *The Best of Sade.* While Sade's fairly homogenous body of work seems ideal for a cream-of-the-crop retrospective, *Best of* would have been more useful and truer to its name by including fewer than the five tracks from *Love Deluxe* (which was only two years old at the time) and more of *Diamond Life*'s early cuts. Still, it hits the mark more often than not. A second retrospective—this one a three-CD box set including the entirety of *Diamond Life, Promise,* and *Love Deluxe* (why not *Stronger Than Pride?*)—appeared in early 2000, perhaps to reacquaint fans with the group after the long hiatus.

Lovers Rock arrived later that year and, amazingly, revealed no rusty parts whatsoever. In fact, it ranks among the group's best work. Fully embracing the hip-hop/trip-hop beats and technology that had blossomed since the group's earlier days, the record eschews Sade's prototypical sax-and-synth schmaltz for a contemporary blend of programmed beats, instrumental loops, and organic elements: nylon-stringed guitars, churchy organs, strings, and classic-soul songwriting ("By Your Side," "It's Only Love That Gets You Through"). The effect is quite similar in places to Massive Attack (particularly the dub reggae of "Slave Song"), Beth Orton, and Everything but the Girl's more recent material.

Lover's Live documents Sade's 2001 comeback tour, specifically two Los Angeles–area shows; the smooth set is heavy on recent material, and it also joyfully revisits older hits. Halfway into the group's extended vacation, Sade's three instrumentalists—Matthewman, keyboardist Andrew Hale, and bassist Paul Denman—convened as Sweetback for a one-off record. Closer to the digital groove of *Lovers Rock* than the threesome's earlier lounge-jazz sound, *Sweetback* uses vocalists Amel Larrieux and Maxwell to fill Sade's shoes. A lead vocal from rapper Bahamadia and many moody instrumental tracks, however, attest that Sweetback is up to more than just passing time. Eight years later, inspiration hit again and Sweetback returned with *Stage 2*, this time featuring vocals from Chocolate Genius (Mark Anthony Thompson), Aya, and rapper Ladybug from Digable Planets. The high quality of the material—just about all of it stylistically compatible with Sade—suggests her backing band is not looking for new directions, but simply creating more material than its singer can keep up with. —R.M.S.

Doug Sahm (The Sir Douglas Quintet)

★★★	Hell of a Spell (Takoma, 1979)
★★★★	Border Wave (Takoma, 1981)
★★½	Quintessence (1983; Varrick, 1995)
★★★½	Juke Box Music (1988; Musicraft, 1997)
★★★★	The Best of Doug Sahm (1968–1975) (Rhino, 1991)
★★★★	The Best of Doug Sahm and Friends: Atlantic Sessions (Rhino, 1992)
★★★★	The Best of Doug Sahm (1968–1975) (Sequel, 1993)
★★½	Day Dreaming at Midnight (Elektra, 1994)
★★★	The Last Real Texas Blues Band (1995; Musicraft, 1997)
★★½	Texas Fever (AIM, 1998)
★★★	She's About a Mover (The Crazy Cajun Recordings) (Edsel, 1999)
★★½	The Return of Wayne Douglas (Tornado, 2000)
★★½	San Antonio Rock: The Harlem Recordings (Norton, 2000)
★★½	In the Beginning (Aim, 2000)
★★½	Son of San Antonio: The Roots of Sir Douglas (Music Club, 2001)
★★★★	He's About a Groover: The Essential Collection (Fuel 2000, 2004)

With a jukebox mind under his 10-gallon hat, Doug Sahm has explored everything from psychedelia, country, and horn-heavy blues to a unique mix of garage funkiness and Merseybeat. The Sir Douglas Quintet's "She's About a Mover" started the trip. The 1965 hit laid a mop-top catchiness atop Augie Meyers' Farfisa organ syncopations, revealing a gift for eccentric fusion that would stamp the band's subsequent efforts. *Honkey Blues* featured James Brownish horns overlaid with San Francisco guitar noodling; *Together* was Latino swagger meeting the blues meeting C&W. *Mendocino* produced another hit in the flower-power title track; "At the Crossroads" was Doug doing Dylan.

Doug faltered on forgettable albums such as *Doug Sahm and Band,* and *Hell of a Spell*. His guitar sounds better when reined in, and earnestness is his voice's greatest virtue—but his musical imagination paid off consistently in happy, novel ways. It's a bit confusing that the Rhino and Sequel compendiums have the same title, but they're both terrific—and they concentrate on the Tex-Mex sound that Sahm trademarked. *Juke Box Music* contains more straightforward roots rock; *San Antonio Rock* collects early, pre-Quintet gems. The Rhino Atlantic set give us the psychedelic and the countrified Sahm. —P.E.

Saint Etienne

★★★	Foxbase Alpha (Warner Bros., 1991)
★★★★	So Tough (Warner Bros., 1993)
★★★	Tiger Bay (Waner Bros., 1994)
★★	Good Humour (Creation, 1996)
★★★★	Sound of Water (Sub Pop, 2000)
★★★	Finisterre (Beggars Banquet, 2002)

The Saint Etienne that club audiences fell in love with was not quite the Saint Etienne that released *Foxbase Alpha*. The 1990 indie single "Only Love Can Break Your Heart," an ice-cream-cool cover of Neil Young's song, featured vocals by Faith Over Reason singer Moira Lambert, whose chocolaty tones added a plangency to the otherwise distanced Europop arrangement. The second single under the Saint Etienne flag was the dreamy girl-group pop of "Kiss and Make Up," sung by New Zealand vocalist Donna Savage of Dead Famous People.

It wasn't a huge leap from these women's voices to the blankly sweet, opaque stylings of Sarah Cracknell, whose recruitment settled St. E's lineup. Perhaps arranger/composers Bob Stanley (a former music journalist) and Pete Wiggs were looking for the sound of utter detachment that Stephen Merritt cherishes. Whatever the case, Cracknell's girlish unflappability suited the St. E ethos of marrying pastel '60s sophisto pop to the laid-back textures of ambient dance. Even though *Foxbase Alpha* did little more than realize this goal, its ironic invocation of trance wallpaper is not always ironic enough. But as an introduction to an inevitable—and deeply pleasurable—genre invention, it gets the job done with the inclusion of both singles ("Kiss and Make Up" sung by Cracknell, "Only Love" in the original) and coy, funny, lyrical moves like "Willie would you like some sweets" where "sweets" morphs imperceptibly into "LSD."

Stanley and Wiggs expanded their palette for *So Tough*, adding flute, tiny splashes of hip-hop syncopation, and digitally processed percussion, building up the layers with care and structuring the tracks to sound less like punch lines about pop ephemera than the actual thing. What's handy about ephemera is that it has nothing to prove, so St. E got a chance, if for only an album or two, to become that impossibility: a relaxed concept band. *Tiger Bay*, with its pretensions to being a soundtrack to a nonexistent film, rocked a little harder, invoked full orchestration a little more unnecessarily, and generally made the right choice in leaving pure sonic experimentation behind. The record features the monumentally lovely singles "I Was Born on Christmas Day" and "Like a Motorway," so it's not unthinkable that Saint Etienne was a pop band all along. Or, you know, not. Because the band took a breather in the mid-'90s, releasing the singles compilation *Too Young to Die* and a remix album rather hopefully called *Casino Classics* before returning with the ultracool, all-wallpaper, inaccessibly boneless *Good Humour*. The group righted itself for 2000's *Sound of Water*, in which Stanley and Wiggs stopped worrying about how many more sounds they could get out of their keyboards and started writing songs solidly within their previous formula, possibly inspired by the way artists like Beth Orton and Air could wring emotional verities from landscapes, memories, and ellipses. —A.B.

Salt-n-Pepa

- ★★★★ Hot, Cool & Vicious (Next Plateau, 1986)
- ★★★½ A Salt With a Deadly Pepa (Next Plateau, 1988)
- ★★★ Blacks' Magic (Next Plateau, 1990)
- ★★★½ Blitz of Salt-n-Pepa Hits (Next Plateau, 1992)
- ★★★★ Very Necessary (Next Plateau/London, 1993)
- ★★★ Brand New (Red Ant/London, 1997)
- ★★★½ The Best Of (London, 1999 U.K.)

Like many early female rappers, Salt-n-Pepa (Cheryl "Salt" James, Sandy "Pepa" Denton, and DJ Dee Dee "Spinderella" Roper) began their career with a back-at-ya answer record to a macho rapper's hit. "The Showstopper," the group's first single, was a response to "The Show" by Slick Rick and Doug E. Fresh. Changing their name from Supernature to Salt-n-Pepa when they hooked up with producer Hurby "Luv Bug" Azor, the group forged a sassy, distinct musical identity on *Hot, Cool & Vicious*. "Tramp" skillfully plays off the Otis Redding–Carla Thomas duet, arriving at the (half-serious) conclusion that all men are bums. The irresistibly sexy jams "Push It" and "My Mic Sounds Nice" suggest that these independent women, while hardly pushovers, are willing to make the best of the best possible situation. Salt-n-Pepa continue to rap rings around each other on *A Salt With a Deadly Pepa*, alternating and then combining their rich, throaty voices. They try to sing a bit this time as well, and if the cover of the Isley Brothers' "Twist and Shout" doesn't get over, the sputtering chorus of "I Gotcha" by Joe Tex perfectly lends itself to hip-hop interpretation. Backed by the powerhouse go-go band E.U. (of "Da Butt" fame) as well as by Spinderella, Salt-n-Pepa put a feminist spin on another Isley stomper ("It's Your Thing"). While the rappers turn the tables ("It's my thing!"), Spinderella splices the male voices from the original version between Salt-n-Pepa's declaration of sexual independence: "Do what you wanna do," the Isleys encourage, and the women do, until everyone's satisfied. The samples and verbal sallies on *Blacks' Magic* aren't quite as inspired, though "Let's Talk About Sex" provided an articulate and funny dose of frankness on the pop charts in 1991.

The trio's peak came with the hit-heavy *Very Necessary*. Sex-positive and socially aware, the album is a vivid streetwise statement of self and a bridge between those '80s block parties back in the Bronx and the new decade's generation of sophisticated hip-hop divas (Missy Elliott, Beyoncé Knowles). A cover of Linda Lyndell's 1968 song "What a Man" is the sound of women utterly conscious and in control, funky-smooth with elegant background wailing from En Vogue. "None of Your Business" is all righteous attitude and self-determination, while "Shoop" is soulful body rock and nasty tales of affection. Some rap purists called it a crossover sellout, but *Very Necessary* dominated its hip-hop moment, as universal as Motown.

With *Brand New*, Salt-n-Pepa finally broke from Azor, producing themselves in Salt's basement studio and finding a new comfort zone in jazzy, organic sounds featuring muted horns, a light touch on the funk guitar, and slow jams for miles. All that's missing is Barry White's growl. But the rappers lose none of their edge or sexual power. Sheryl Crow steps in for a funky good-time statement against prejudice on "Imagine," and the hip-hop gospel of "Hold On," with Kirk Franklin, is a genuinely moving declaration of faith ("I praise the Lord every day/That's how I get high"). A 1999 U.K.-only *Best Of* gathered the hits and remixes, but the group soon disbanded for side projects, acting, marriage, and children. Salt shelved a planned solo album *(Salt of the Earth)* and retired, apparently for good.   —M.C./S.A.

Sam & Dave

★★★	Sam & Dave (Roulette, 1966)
★★★★	Best of Sam & Dave (1969; Atlantic, 1985)
★★★★	The Very Best of Sam & Dave (Rhino, 1995)
★★★★	Sweat 'n' Soul: Anthology, 1965–1971 (Rhino/Atlantic, 1993)
★★★★	Soul Man & Other Favorites (Collectables, 2004)

In terms of emotional depth and stylistic innovation, Sam and Dave fall far short of Otis Redding, the giant with whom they helped create '60s Southern soul. But the propulsiveness of Sam & Dave's hits makes them irresistible. Precision of attack was this duo's trademark: Very few bands kick into their material with the immediacy and confidence Sam & Dave managed, and the pair never let the energy flag. Between 1966 and 1968, they released a catalogue of bass-and-horn-driven soul smashes—"You Don't Know Like I Know," "Hold On! I'm Comin'," "Soul Man," and "I Thank You," among others—that have lost none of their immediacy over the years. As craftsmen, then, if not visionaries, they remain significant; their sound informs virtually every R&B bar band that has followed in their wake. *Sweat 'n' Soul,* the Rhino collection, is both massive and definitive—and relentless.   —P.E.

Pharoah Sanders

Selected Discography

★★★	Tauhid (1967; GRP, 1993)
★★★★	Karma (Impulse!, 1969)
★★★½	Jewels of Thought (1970; GRP, 1998)
★★★	Deaf Dumb Blind/Summun Bukmun Umyun (Impulse!, 1970)
★★★½	Thembi (1971; Impulse!, 1987)
★★★½	Black Unity (1971; GRP, 1997)
★★½	Priceless Jazz Collection (GRP, 1997)

Renamed by Sun Ra, the former Farrell Sanders became the howling, screeching saxophone foil to John Coltrane in Trane's final years, and continued to col-laborate with Alice Coltrane after his death. On his own, though, he made a series of expansive, soul-inspired albums, gradually coming around to a heavily Coltrane-inspired lyricism. (Sanders has made plenty of records besides the ones listed here—a few before, many after—but his Impulse! Records period is far and away his most important.)

Tauhid, recorded (while Coltrane was still alive) with a group that included guitarist Sonny Sharrock, is an extension of what Sanders was doing a few months earlier on Coltrane's *Live in Japan:* The material is more about extravagant extended techniques (humming through a piccolo, speaking through a tenor sax) than melody, and there's a thematic focus on astrology. Sanders even half yodels a little on "Japan."

Two years later, he hooked up with a real yodeler, singer Leon Thomas, and recorded his greatest hit. "The Creator Has a Master Plan" occupies almost all of *Karma* and became a soul-jazz standard. Built around an eight-note cycle that recalls the first part of *A Love Supreme* and hooked by Thomas' extraordinary ululations, it's gentle in a way Sanders had rarely been before and really lovely if you've got the patience for it. Thomas returns for *Jewels of Thought,* two more long tracks cowritten by pianist Lonnie Liston Smith: "Sun in Aquarius" meanders pleasantly for almost half an hour, but "Hum-Allah-Hum-Allah-Hum Allah" is a delicious 15-minute soul jam, with everyone pitching in on bells and African percussion.

For *Summun Bukmun Unyun,* Sanders switches to soprano sax (as well as "cow horn, tritone whistle, cowbells, wood flute, thumb piano, and percussion"), Thomas departs, and bylophone player Nathaniel Bettis contributes a touch of yodeling, but it's not the same. The title track is another casual two-chord groove; its companion is a loose, lyrical free-tempo hymn. With pronounced roles for Smith and bassist Cecil McBee, *Thembi* fits neatly into the electric jazz/fusion scene of its time. The only sign of Sanders' old fury is the multitracked sax freak-out "Red, Black & Green," but he's finally learning to edit himself—six whole tracks on an album!

Black Unity goes all the way in the other direction: a single 37-minute piece with two bassists, three drummers, and all the cosmic funk juice you could hope for. The sprawl is pretty much the point, and Sanders and trumpeter Hannibal Peterson tear off some wild solos. Other discs from the same era have yet to be reissued, notably *Izipho Zam* and *Elevation.* The *Priceless Jazz Collection* best-of (two tracks apiece from *Tauhid* and *Thembi,* three from a 1987 Coltrane tribute, and an abridged "The Creator Has a Master Plan") misses the boat on Sanders—you really have to hear his best work at its full duration to appreciate it.   —D.W.

Mongo Santamaria

★★★★ Yambu (1958; Original Jazz Classics, 1987)
★★★★ Mongo's Greatest Hits (1958; Fantasy, 1995)
★★★★½ Our Man in Havana (1960; Fantasy, 1993)
★★★★ At the Black Hawk (1962; Fantasy, 1994)
★★★★ Mongo at the Village Gate (1963; Original Jazz Classics, 1990)
★★★½ Mongo Introduces La Lupe (1963; Milestone, 1993)
★★★★ Sabroso (1963; Original Jazz Classics, 1991)
★★★ Mongo '70/Mongo at Montreux (1970, 1971; Collectables, 1999)
★★½ Feelin' Alright (1970; Collectables, 2001)
★★★½ Mongo's Way/Up From the Roots (1971, 1972; Collectables, 1999)
★★★½ Afro Roots (1972; Prestige, 1989)
★★★½ Skins (1976; Milestone, 1991)
★★★½ Summertime (1981; Original Jazz Classics, 1991)
★★★ Mongo y Su Charanga (Fantasy, 1987)
★★★ Soy Yo (Concord Picante, 1987)
★★★ Mucho Mongo: Soca Me Nice/Olé Ola (1988, 1989; Concord Jazz, 2001)
★★★★ Live at Jazz Alley (Concord Picante, 1990)
★★★½ Afro Blue: The Picante Collection (Concord Jazz, 1997)
★★★★½ Skin on Skin: The Mongo Santamaria Anthology (1958–1995) (Rhino, 1999)
★★★★½ Afro American Latin (Columbia/Legacy, 2000)
★★★ Montreux Heat (Pablo, 2003)

When Dizzy Gillespie and the Cuban conga player Chano Pozo collaborated on the song "Manteca," they suggested a new direction for jazz that another Cuban native, percussionist/bandleader Mongo Santamaria seized upon and broadened. Inspired by the fusion of Cuban dance rhythms and harmonic ideas rooted in jazz composition (played with the improvisational feel of jazz solos) on "Manteca," Santamaria delivered his own Afro-Cuban masterpiece in the form of 1960's "Afro Blue," in which a 6/8 tempo common to African folk music met a minor-key blues melody. Pressing the point, Santamaria made a greater impact on popular music three years later, when his recording of Herbie Hancock's "Watermelon Man"—itself an irresistible amalgam of blues, jazz, and Afro-Cuban rhythms—became a Top 10 pop hit.

Culled from the 10 albums he recorded for Columbia, *Mongo Santamaria's Greatest Hits* collects his most overt stabs at pop crossover success. It's inter-

esting to hear him put his own funky spin on the likes of the Temptations' psychedelic hit "Cloud Nine" and Booker T. and the MG's' steadily percolating "Green Onions." By far the best work to surface from the Columbia vaults is the previously unreleased *Afro American Latin* album, recorded in 1969. Spurred by his producer David Rubinson and music director/arranger/composer (and confidant) Marty Sheller, Santamaria cut a deep, moving, sometimes dark, often celebratory rhythmic exploration of Santería, the Afro-Cuban religion. From "Obtala," the almost 10-minute opening African-blues tribute to the Santería god, to the five closing tracks recorded live at Pep's Lounge in Philadelphia in 1968 (which include a near eight-minute version of "Obtala"), *Afro American Latin* is a mesmerizing philosophical and musical discourse.

Collectables has reissued four of Santamaria's Atlantic Records albums on two twofer discs. Of these, the must-have is *Mongo's Way/Up From the Roots*, albums released in 1971 and 1972, respectively. The former happens to be a fiery showcase for the dueling congas of Santamaria and the irrepressible Armando Peraza; they strike up dialogues on unlikely choices such as the Box Tops' pop hit, "The Letter." *Up From the Roots* joins the select group of Santamaria albums on which the artist returned, metaphysically speaking, to his native Cuban soil for inspiration and came up with a song selection comprised of some obscure, traditional Afro-Cuban material and some new songs (penned by Santamaria, Marty Sheller, and Eddie Martinez, among others) in the bright, Latin-jazz style he had made popular. Another Atlantic album (his first for the label, in fact) reissued by Collectables, 1970's *Feelin' Alright*, is a strange bird indeed, in that its eleven songs are covers of contemporary R&B, pop, soul, and rock songs, such as the Dave Mason–penned title track, Booker T. and the MG's' "Hip-Hug-Her," the Drifters' "On Broadway," Smokey Robinson's "The Tracks of My Tears," even Jim Webb's "By the Time I Get to Phoenix."

From Santamaria's late-'80s/early-'90s association with Concord Jazz comes a recent anthology of highlights, *Afro Blue: The Picante Collection*, featuring 10 choice tracks culled from *Soy Yo, Soca Me Nice/Olé Ola,* and *Live at Jazz Alley.* It's not a substitute for the complete albums, but it suffices as a taste of the main courses offered on those four interesting long players. And not least, Rhino delivers a big winner in the career overview on two discs titled *Skin on Skin: The Mongo Santamaria Anthology (1958–1995).* Its 34 tracks range from "Afro Blue" and "Watermelon Man" to a workout on James Brown's "Cold Sweat" and a previously unreleased track, "Panamanian Aire," as well as a conga-drum solo titled "My Sound."

Our Man in Havana found Santamaria back in his native Cuba in 1960, accompanied only by the ever-reliable Willie Bobo and a team of Fantasy engineers; when he arrived, he assembled a group of esteemed Cuban musicians, including Yeyito, Cuba's foremost bongo player; a top-flight flute player known simply as Julio; and most important of all, Nino Rivera, a master of the *tres* (a native six-string instrument that is something of a cross between a mandolin and a guitar) and a peerless, daring arranger. The result is an exhilarating blend of masterful ensemble and individual playing and deeply felt material that is by turns ruminative and jubilant, always speaking to the soul—*Our Man in Havana* is an important recording whose fresh, vital aura, still undiminished, sets a formidable standard for contemporary musicians who would call themselves pioneers. Following a stroke, Santamaria died in Miami in February 1, 2003.   —D.M.

Santana

- ★★★★ Santana (1969; Columbia/Legacy, 1998)
- ★★★★★ Santana: Abraxas (1970; Columbia/Legacy, 1998)
- ★★★★ Santana 3 (1971; Sony, 1998)
- ★★★★ Caravanserai (1972; Columbia, 1986)
- ★★★½ Welcome (Columbia, 1973)
- ★★★★★ Santana's Greatest Hits (1974; Columbia, 1984)
- ★★★½ Borboletta (1974; Columbia, 1990)
- ★★★★★ Lotus (1974; Columbia, 1991)
- ★★★★ Amigos (1976; Columbia, 1986)
- ★★★ Festival (1977; Columbia, 1990)
- ★★★ Moonflower (1977; Columbia, 1990)
- ★★ Inner Secrets (1979; Columbia, 1985)
- ★★ Marathon (1979; Columbia, 1986)
- ★★ Zebop! (1981; Columbia, 1984)
- ★★ Shango (Columbia, 1983)
- ★★ Beyond Appearances (Columbia, 1985)
- ★★½ Freedom (Columbia, 1987)
- ★★★★ Viva Santana! (Columbia, 1988)
- ★★★ Spirits Dancing in the Flesh (Columbia, 1990)
- ★★★★ Dance of the Rainbow Serpent (Columbia/Legacy, 1995)
- ★★★ Live at the Fillmore '68 (1997)
- ★★★★ Best of Santana (Columbia, 1998)
- ★★★ The Essential Santana (Legacy, 2002)

Carlos Santana

- ★½ Carlos Santana & Buddy Miles Live! (Columbia, 1972)
- ★★★ Love, Devotion, Surrender (Columbia, 1973)
- ★★½ Illuminations (Columbia, 1974)
- ★★½ Oneness (Columbia, 1979)

- ★★★ Silver Dreams–Golden Reality (Columbia, 1979)
- ★★½ The Swing of Delight (Columbia, 1980)
- ★★★ Havana Moon (Columbia, 1988)
- ★★★★ Blues for Salvador (Columbia, 1988)
- ★★★ Santana Brothers (Island, 1994)
- ★★★★ Supernatural (Arista, 1999)
- ★★ Shaman (Arista, 2002)
- ★★½ Ceremony—Remixes & Rarities (BMG, 2003)

In one of the most remarkable comebacks in pop history, Carlos Santana scored nine Grammys for *Supernatural*, a 1999 outing that boasted big-time radio hits ("Smooth," with Matchbox Twenty's Rob Thomas on vocals), an all-star cast (Eric Clapton, Lauryn Hill), and impressive critical credibility. As Santana's successful bid for youth-market favor, the album reached out demographically but did not compromise aesthetically—at its center was Santana's riveting guitar. *Supernatural*, his 36th album, followed nearly 20 years during which Santana still had his adherents, though he had long left the limelight. The album rekindled the excitement of the guitarist's early days and showed how enduring the power of his Afro-Cuban sound remained.

The box set, *Dance of the Rainbow Serpent*, as well as *Lotus*, a compelling 22-song live offering, best captures Santana's considerable appeal. Formed in San Francisco in 1967, the band fed the scene's appetite for long open-air jams with an athletic mixture of blazing guitar and frenetic percussion. Santana's novelty lay in employing the jam format for Latin music. Leader/guitarist Carlos Santana, drummer Michael Shrieve, and percussionist Jose "Chepito" Areas were the band's anchors; fusing Hispanic danceforms and bluesy rock, they achieved a synthesis of the familiar and the exotic. *Lotus* finds Santana at its peak; throughout its history, the band was marked by frequent personnel changes, and this lineup is its strongest. With Leon Patillo, they'd enlisted a singer markedly more soulful than either original vocalist Gregg Rolie or later mainstay Alex Ligterwood, and the entire eight-member unit achieves a remarkable, instinctive symbiosis. Charging through early hits (Fleetwood Mac's "Black Magic Woman," Tito Puente's "Oye Como Va"), this outfit is both fiery and fluid, and with Airto Moreira's "Xibaba (She-Ba-Ba)" and Richard Kermode's "Yours Is the Light," the group suggests its coming direction—jazz-rock fusion and flights into the mystic.

Because its rhythmic basis was so strong and the music itself a solid mix of genres, Santana's would-be jazz fusion was of a less irritating variety than most (the band drew heavily on Miles Davis' *Bitches Brew*—

period aggressiveness and rarely stooped to jazz lite). But at its late-'70s height of experimenting with complex chord structures and aimless "atmosphere" *(Moonflower, Inner Secrets)* Santana had become something unimaginable for such a passionate ensemble: boring. After the jazz foray came the pop—starting with *Zebop!* and continuing to the present—when Santana began to border on the trite.

Santana's first albums were brilliant, and they hold up very well. World beat ahead of its time, Santana riveted Woodstock audiences with one of the festival's most exciting stage acts. Carlos' playing continued to delight, even when squandered on inferior material, throughout the band's career.

On his own, Carlos Santana flexed his guitar in a number of settings. An instantly recognizable musician—with an intense B.B. King–style clarity of tone, he achieves long, fluid lead lines that resemble those of a violinist—Carlos sounds best when he's juxtaposed against heavy percussion. He became a devotee of Indian guru Sri Chinmoy in the early '70s (and took the name Devadip, or "Light of the lamp of the Supreme") and recorded the drifty *Love, Devotion, Surrender* with fellow disciple and guitar wizard, John McLaughlin, in 1974. The even driftier *Illuminations* came that same year, boasting another Chinmoy adherent, jazz composer Alice Coltrane. Despite the presence of such big-name (if unlikely) collaborators as Willie Nelson, the Fabulous Thunderbirds, and Booker T. Jones, *Havana Moon* was fairly bland; *Blues for Salvador* remains one of his strongest efforts. *Supernatural* sold more than 10 million copies within a year of its release, garnering Santana the kind of superstar status that had long been denied him. His years in eclipse were over.   —P.E.

Sasha & Digweed

★★★★   Northern Exposure, Vol. 1 (Ultra, 1997)
★★★★   Northern Exposure, Vol. 2: East Coast Edition (Ultra, 1998)
★★★★   Northern Exposure, Vol. 2: West Coast Edition (Ultra, 1998)
★★★   Northern Exposure, Vol. 3: Expeditions (Incredible, 1999)
★★½   Communicate (Kinetic, 2000)

Of all the disparate electronic music to bubble up from the underground during the '90s, perhaps none moved more bodies than the ecstatic synth sounds of trance. Unlike the black and gay street beats of house music, trance attracted large numbers of glowstick-wielding suburban youths, loved up on E. And no one did trance and its close cousin, progressive house, better than tag-teaming Sasha and John Digweed, the British DJ duo whose long, sweeping soundscapes defined the genres. The pasty pair began their partnership in 1993 at the Manchester club Renaissance, releasing a debut mix of that name the following year.

The wildly successful epic mixes of the *Northern Exposure* series, however, rocketed them to superstar status and later landed them a monthly residency at the New York megaclub Twilo. *Vol. 1* features wave upon wave of lysergic transcendence—sometimes terrifying, always awe-inspiring—and tracks from a roster of rave-arena acts like Rabbit in the Moon and Underworld. *Vol. 2: East Coast Edition*'s pretty, deep breaks stretch and yawn to a melting sunrise, disturbed now and then by a gust of wind like rustling moth wings; the trancey house of *Vol. 2: West Coast Edition* resembles an electronic storm that slackens to a drizzle before the next downpour. Both approaches appear on *Expeditions*, which finds the duo picking records that change up the formula, with the occasional funky hand clap, techno thud, or voluptuous female vocal. Sasha & Digweed continue to move in a progressive-house direction on *Communicate*, with a thumping bass line that steadily supplants the usual trancey keybs. But with the shuttering of Twilo, the new millennium has found the duo working increasingly apart: Digweed focuses on Bedrock—his Brit-based party, label, and production alter ego—while Sasha has released production CDs, most notably his 2002 *Airdrawndagger*.   —C.S.

Savage Garden

★★½   Savage Garden (Columbia, 1997)
★★   Affirmation (Columbia, 1999)

The mind-blowing success of the first Savage Garden album cannot be separated from the rise of the WB network as a wildly popular font of teen-junk culture. You'll get into serious chicken-egg territory when you try to figure out if *Felicity*'s, *Jack and Jill*'s (we'll never forget you), and, above all, *Dawson's Creek*'s navel-gazing emotions created a market for Savage Garden's marshmallow-soft dance pop, or vice versa. But make no mistake: Songs like "Truly Madly Deeply" and "I Want You" have a serious white-on-rice relationship with breathlessly earnest teen melodrama, and James Van Der Beek and the gents in Savage Garden—Darren Hayes and Daniel Jones—owe each other Christmas cards until the end of time.

The Australian duo began writing together in the mid-'90s, and in late 1996 released "I Want You" in Australia, where it was a hit, before migrating to the States in '97. *Savage Garden* contains their three biggest hits, right in a row, right at the beginning: "To the Moon and Back" does its damnedest to send you there, but the massive "I Want You" completes the trip. Darren Hayes mumbles breathlessly about closing his eyes, seeing you, standing close, getting to you, holding tight, and something called a "chic-a-cherry cola." A total pop wipeout and one of 1997's more ubiquitous pieces of fluff. Afterward, the middle-school makeout epic "Truly Madly Deeply" drifts you gently back to earth. It's unlikely that anyone has ever listened to anything else on the album, or would ever need to, but the rest is appropriately faceless. It sold more than 11 million copies worldwide.

Reportedly recorded long distance, with Hayes now in the U.S. and Jones still in Oz, *Affirmation* shows very little growth whatsoever. "I Knew I Loved You" was a hit, the sort of adult-oriented radio ballad that very few adults would ever actually listen to. Indeed, in the blink of a TV season, Savage Garden's moment had passed. But it made its mark, and no one in human history will ever be able to unpack the mysteries of chic-a-cherry cola, no matter how many recipes for Diet Coke and red cordial show up on the Internet.   —J.G.

Boz Scaggs

★★★★½ Boz Scaggs (Atlantic, 1969)
★★★★ Moments (1971; Columbia, 1990)
★★★ Boz Scaggs and Band (1971; Columbia, 1990)
★★★ My Time (1972; Columbia, 1990)
★★★ Slow Dancer (1974; Columbia, 1990)
★★★★★ Silk Degrees (1976; Columbia, 1990)
★★★ Down Two Then Left (1977; Columbia, 1990)
★★★½ Middle Man (1980; Columbia, 1998)
★★★½ Hits! (Columbia, 1980)
★★ Other Roads (Columbia, 1988)
★★★½ Some Change (Virgin, 1994)
★★★ Fade Into Light (MVP Japan, 1996)
★★★ Come On Home (Virgin, 1997)
★★★★ My Time: A Boz Scaggs Anthology (1969–1997) (Columbia/Legacy, 1997)
★★★½ Dig (Virgin, 2001)
★★★ But Beautiful: Standards, Vol. 1 (Gray Cat, 2003)

Urbane blues crooner William Royce "Boz" Scaggs first gained notice as a rhythm guitarist and occasional singer with the Steve Miller Band. Scaggs and Miller played together as teenagers in Texas (the Marksmen) and on the fringes of the college scene in Madison, Wisconsin (the Ardells). After bumming around the world for several years, Scaggs was encouraged by Miller to join him in San Francisco. Miller's band was something of a square peg: a tight, rootsy R&B outfit in a generally loose, psychedelic scene. You can hear Scaggs emerging from within the Steve Miller Band

on the mellow "Baby's Calling Me Home" (from *Children of the Future*) and the sizzling "Overdrive" (from *Sailor*), both released in 1968.

Scaggs' self-titled solo debut marked a confident departure from the sound of San Francisco (his adopted home). Recorded at the legendary Muscle Shoals studio in Alabama—and coproduced by ROLLING STONE editor/publisher Jann S. Wenner—*Boz Scaggs* contained a number of striking, soulful originals ("I'll Be Long Gone") and covers (Jimmie Rodgers' "Waiting for a Train"). The album's centerpiece is the 13-minute "Loan Me a Dime," on which guitarist Duane Allman engages in a deliciously down-and-out, voice-and-guitar duet with Scaggs, a highlight of both men's careers.

Back on the West Coast, Scaggs signed to Columbia Records for what would be a long run. 1971's *Moments* is a gorgeous album of sweet hippie pop soul that has much in common with the work that Van Morrison—who also lived in the Bay Area—was doing at the time. Consider *Moments* to be Scaggs' *Moondance,* and by all means seek out this forgotten gem. Scaggs' plainly titled third album, *Boz Scaggs and Band,* found him paying tribute to the horn-stoked R&B big bands (like Ray Charles') that had turned his head as a youth. The inconsistent *My Time,* which included the uptempo favorite "Dinah Flo," mixed Muscle Shoals and San Francisco sessions. Scaggs worked with longtime Motown producer Johnny Bristol on *Slow Dancer,* his most overt "soul" outing, with a special nod to the sound of Philadelphia.

Scaggs' brand of sleek romantic soul struck pay dirt when he moved into the disco era with *Silk Degrees.* The album rocked harder than its reputation might otherwise suggest (check out the slide-drenched "Jump Street"), but the grooves had never been so exquisitely manicured, thanks to such sidemen as keyboardist David Paich, bassist David Hungate, and drummer Jeff Porcaro (all members of Toto), plus guitarists Fred Tackett and Louie Shelton. The Top 5 hit "Lowdown" mixed bluesy grit, string-section elegance, and cross-talking percussion with an unaffected grace. The album went to #2, sold 5 million copies, and gave Scaggs his first Top 40 hits. Moreover, it established him as a classy, poised soulman who made a disco album that rock and R&B fans could enjoy without blanching.

Silk Degrees' followup, the bloodlessly slick *Down Two Then Left,* displayed a refinement bordering on sterility and didn't fare as well as its predecessor. Fine-tuned studio precision was also the approach on *Middle Man* (1980), but there was more of a red-hot soul core here, as Scaggs explored the glamorous but reckless life of a city-dwelling romantic in a very urbane time.

And then Scaggs dropped out, remaining hidden for most of the '80s. He finally reemerged in 1988 with *Other Roads,* but it was a surprisingly cold, synthetic, and directionless comeback attempt, and it remains his worst record.

The '90s were much kinder, as a small-scale renaissance found Scaggs slipping back into a musical groove that felt as comfortable as the years and albums before *Silk Degrees* catapulted him to fame. *Some Change* (1994) was an affecting, down-home return to form that focused on his pet theme of romantic loss. *Come On Home* (1997) took him back further in time, as he fondly revisited his blues influences. The cool, meticulous grooves of *Dig* (2001) were the closest Scaggs has ever come to making *Silk Degrees* redux; appearing exactly a quarter-century after that milestone, the notion of lightning striking twice was no doubt on his mind.

Scaggs launched his own label, Gray Cat, in 2003 with *But Beautiful,* an album of standards ("Sophisticated Lady," "Bewitched, Bothered and Bewildered") that matched his silken voice with a classic jazz quartet.—P.P.

Scarface
see GETO BOYS

Jill Scott

★★★½	Who Is Jill Scott? Words and Sounds, Vol. 1 (Hidden Beach, 2000)
★★★	Experience: Jill Scott 826+ (Hidden Beach, 2001)
★★★	Beautifully Human (Sony, 2004)

In much the same way as Erykah Badu, around-the-way girl, poet, R&B crooner, and sympathetic hip-hop soldier Jill Scott found a way to realize the promise of a neosoul movement that's long on heart and cool hairdos but often short on good songs. *Who Is Jill Scott?* bubbles over with hummable songs and Scott's honeyed tones, which are soothing but never soporific. The jazz-inflected instrumentation, complemented by the rap-derived beats that are now de rigueur for most modern R&B, is never Quiet Storm–boring, but rather gently stoned and spaced-out, like dub. The result is a thoroughly modern production, with tracks such as the swinging and swaying "Gettin' in the Way" and the beat-driven "Show Me" gently convincing the listener that presence, atmosphere, and charisma go a long way when you're trying to cram big ideas about self-empowerment and sexual freedom into a four-minute pop song.

The hurry-up-and-feed-the-hype disc *Experience,* released as soon as humanly possible after the success of her debut, has some new songs in the same vein and live tracks that showcase Jill's ample talents as a performer. Live, songs like "A Long Walk" and "It's Love" reveal a crowd-pleasing actor who could just as easily be on Broadway or in the movies. The other small miracle is that her spoken-word moments, such as "Thickness," are way less cringe-inducing and cloying than those found at most poetry slams.   —S.S.

Gil Scott-Heron

★★	Small Talk at 125th and Lenox (1970; BMG International, 2001)
★★★	Pieces of a Man (1971; BMG International, 2001)
★★★	Free Will (1972; BMG International, 2001)
★★½	Winter in America (1973; Get Back, 2001)
★★★½	The Revolution Will Not Be Televised (Bluebird/RCA, 1974)
★★★	The First Minute of a New Day (1975; TVT, 1998)
★★★½	From South Africa to South Carolina (1975; TVT, 1998)
★★★	It's Your World (Arista, 1976)
★★★	The Mind of Gil Scott-Heron (1978; TVT, 2001)
★★★★	The Best of Gil Scott-Heron (1984; Arista, 1991)
★★★	Spirits (TVT, 1994)
★★★	Minister of Information (Castle, 1994)
★★★½	Evolution and Flashback: The Very Best of Gil Scott-Heron (RCA, 1999)
★★★½	Ultimate Gil Scott-Heron (RCA, 2003)

Gil Scott-Heron's '70s albums were jazzy funk of an intelligence notably lacking in the Age of Disco, and his political wordplay anticipated rap. As a novelist *(The Vulture, The Nigger Factory),* poet, and pianist, Scott-Heron achieved an arresting synthesis of laid-back soul music—with jazz-fusion embellishment borrowed from *Bitches Brew*–period Miles Davis—and class-struggle sermonizing. As evidenced by the title track and "Whitey on the Moon" from *The Revolution Will Not Be Televised* (1974), the singer often leavened his heavy messages with crafty wit, but at his most direct ("Home Is Where the Hatred Is"), he could come on with all of the significant fury—if little of the furious noise—of Public Enemy or the Clash.

Even though "Johannesburg," off *From South Africa to South Carolina* (1975), gave him FM-radio airplay, Scott-Heron has generally remained a critical success only. Playing with expert musicians (Bernard Purdie, Ron Carter, David Spinozza), he's made extremely competent records, but his vocals have lacked distinction, and an overreliance on the glossy flute work of Hubert Laws and collaborator Brian Jackson has sometimes blunted the rhythmic edge of his songs. "Re-Ron," a biting anti-Reagan diatribe from *The Best of,* shows him working with a tougher sound, courtesy of Material's Bill Laswell; his '80s work, as a whole, gained in force.

But Scott-Heron proves most noteworthy as an early influence on urban-message music. Ahead of his time in a decade when most funk was escapism, Scott-Heron prophesied while others partied. His 1994 comeback, *Spirits,* underscores his commitment and breadth: "Message to the Messengers" is straight-talk advice to upcoming rappers, while the title track puts words to prime John Coltrane.   —P.E.

Screaming Trees

★★★	Uncle Anesthesia (Epic, 1991)
★★★	Sweet Oblivion (Epic, 1992)
★★★★	Dust (Epic, 1996)

Mark Lanegan

★★★	The Winding Sheet (Sub Pop, 1990)
★★★★	Whiskey for the Holy Ghost (Sub Pop, 1994)
★★★	Scraps at Midnight (Sub Pop, 1998)
★★★	I'll Take Care of You (Sub Pop, 1999)
★★★	Field Songs (Sub Pop, 2001)
★★★	Here Comes that Weird Chill (Beggars Banquet, 2003)

Because they came from Seattle, had long greasy hair, and wore big lumberjack shirts, Screaming Trees were called a grunge band. Yet even a cursory listen to their music reveals how little they had in common with, say, Soundgarden or Alice in Chains. Instead of welding '70s punk to '70s metal, the Trees built their imposing roar by going back to the original punk: the crude garage psychedelia of the mid- to late '60s. Brothers Gary Lee Conner (guitar) and Van Conner (bass) were the musical core of this sadly undervalued collective, but it was the ominous gravity of Mark Lanegan's voice that really made the Trees special.

The early Screaming Trees catalogue—including three fine '80s albums on SST—is now out of print, but fortunately, the Trees were one of those bands that only improved with age. On fierce yet tuneful songs like "Bed of Roses" and "Something About Today," *Uncle Anesthesia* suggests how a collaboration between the Byrds and the 13th Floor Elevators might have sounded. *Sweet Oblivion* is a grander, heavier take on classic American folk rock, highlighted by "Nearly Lost You," the closest the Trees came to a hit. *Dust* is their final, crowning achievement, book-ended by two majestic, Indian-flavored tracks, "Halo of Ashes" and "Gospel Plow."

Mark Lanegan's solo career began well before the Trees' breakup at the end of the '90s. His albums differ significantly from the band's; steeped in country, folk, and blues and dominated by acoustic guitar, their mood ranges from somber to creepy to downright morbid. *The Winding Sheet* is notable for featuring Nirvana's Kurt Cobain and Chris Novoselic on Lead Belly's "Where Did You Sleep Last Night?" (a song that Nirvana would later do in a remarkably similar manner). *Whiskey for the Holy Ghost* is Lanegan's best—his charged performances on "Borracho" and "Riding the Nightingale" are angsty masterworks. *I'll Take Care of You* is a quirky collection of covers by the likes of Fred Neil and Tim Hardin. Early in the new millennium, Lanegan joined forces with hard-rock supergroup Queens of the Stone Age, whose leaders Josh Homme and Nick Oliveri return the favor by guest-starring on *Here Comes that Weird Chill.* Touted as a precursor to a full album to come late in 2004, the EP cranks the amps higher than Lanegan's usual solo levels while maintaining the expected air of claustrophobia on tracks like "Methamphetamine Blues" and a cover of Captain Beefheart's "Clear Spot."   —M.R.

Screamin' Jay Hawkins

★★★	I Put a Spell on You (1957; Collectables, 1994)
★★★	Voodoo Jive: The Best of Screamin' Jay Hawkins (Rhino, 1990)
★★★	Cow Fingers and Mosquito Pie (Epic/Legacy, 1991)

Although he had only one major hit, Screamin' Jay Hawkins has left his mark on rock & roll by way of a wild-man persona quite unlike anything anyone had ever seen in the '50s. Little Richard was weird, Chuck Berry had his duckwalk, the Big Bopper favored loud suits, but Screamin' Jay was in his own league. Carried onstage in a coffin, he would emerge decked out in a suit of the unlikeliest color and pattern, with a silk cape around his shoulders and a human skull in his hand.

His only major hit, "I Put a Spell on You," retains its luster today, and Hawkins has done a good job of riding that one hit from 1956 into legend. Apart from this, the cuts on *Best of* and Epic/Legacy's newer *Cow Fingers and Mosquito Pie* show him to be a marginal R&B singer who was at his best when he didn't really have to sing: "I Put a Spell on You," recorded when Hawkins and his backing band were drunk, is mostly ominous growl and ghostly laugh. The *Best of* includes two of Hawkins' rare pre-"Spell" tracks "(She Put the)

Wamee (on Me)" and "This Is All," which show him playing it straight. He might have made a name for himself as an R&B vocalist had he stayed on this early path; after "Spell," he seemed in relentless pursuit of the bizarre, which resulted in one other minor hit, Leiber and Stoller's "Alligator Wine," a 1958 single that is fairly unremarkable. Among *Cow Fingers'* oddities are a version of Cole Porter's "I Love Paris" and of "There's Something Wrong With You," which may be much funnier that Hawkins intended. —D.M.

Scritti Politti

★★   4 A-Sides (Rough Trade, 1979)
★★   Works in Progress (Rough Trade, 1979)
★★★★ Songs to Remember (1982; Rough Trade, 2001)
★★★★ Cupid & Psyche 85 (Warner Bros., 1985)
★★★   Provision (Warner Bros., 1988)
★★   Anomie & Bonhomie (Virgin, 1999)

Scritti Politti's Green Gartside was one of the most pretentious rock stars in history. He began in 1978 as an art-school anarchist squatting in London's Camden Town, diddling around with dour, abstract indie-rock rants attached to titles such as "Skank Bloc Bologna." Then, after a few Rough Trade 12-inch singles, he made a sudden and drastic conversion to pop, although on his own hyperintellectual terms. "Pop music is of the Other, of the ironic," Green proclaimed to the *New Musical Express* in 1981. "It's about criminality, sexuality, madness. Antithesis of sameness. Though of course we have to bring out that Other, by listening, by recognizing the unspoken, not by gauche attempts to construct more of the mythical 'alternative,' or metaspeech." And all this to explain why he called his new single "The Sweetest Girl."

Green sighed the low-key pop melodies of *Songs to Remember*, reflecting his newfound passion for soft soul and funk, even if his idea of a catchy chorus was still "I'm in love with Jacques Derrida." He began spending lots of somebody's money on designer suits and mousse, no doubt performing a self-conscious parody of pop stardom, but writing songs catchy enough to turn him into the real thing. *Cupid & Psyche 85* remains one of the great New Romantic albums, all a-glimmer with sparkly synth melodies and sleek beats and ironically overproduced pop flash, as Green contemplates romantic love as "a margin of error for two." His crushed-out-schoolgirl voice is a love-or-hate deal, but he spins off dazzling puns in great tunes such as "Perfect Way" (the only U.S. hit), "The Word Girl," and "A Little Knowledge," brooding over faith and doubt ("Now I know to love you/Is not to know you") over the breathless bounce of the music. It's a maddeningly perfect album that continues to bewitch and bedevil '80s-pop obsessives long after it should have been forgotten.

Unfortunately, Scritti fizzled. Fans continue to swear by side one of *Provision*, where Green rhymes "I got Gaultier pants" with "I got a reason, girl, like Immanuel Kant's." The fantastic lead-off single "Boom! There She Was" features Zapp singer and future hip-hop icon Roger Troutman; Miles Davis, a huge Scritti fan (he covered "Perfect Way" on his 1986 album *Tutu*), plays the trumpet solo on "Oh Patti (Don't Feel Sorry for Loverboy)." But he who lives by the ironically overproduced pop trifle dies by the ironically overproduced pop trifle, and nobody was listening closely enough to bother with the mind games of *Provision*. Green dropped one more single, a 1990 dancehall cover of the Beatles' "She's a Woman" featuring Shabba Ranks, before heading home to lie low in his South Wales cottage. His much-ballyhooed 1999 return, *Anomie & Bonhomie*, had rock guitars, MeShell Ndegeocello's bass, and guest rappers like Mos Def. It wasn't any good, but it could not quite squash the hopes of die-hard Scritti fans, who were waiting for Green to woo back his pop muse in time for the next album: *Cupid & Psyche 2005?* —R.S.

The Sea and Cake

★★★★ The Sea and Cake (Thrill Jockey, 1994)
★★★   Nassau (Thrill Jockey, 1995)
★★★   The Biz (Thrill Jockey, 1995)
★★★   The Fawn (Thrill Jockey, 1997)
★★   Two Gentlemen (EP) (Thrill Jockey, 1997)
★★★   Oui (Thrill Jockey, 2000)
★★★★ One Bedroom (Thrill Jockey, 2003)

On its first three albums, released within 13 months in 1994–95, the Sea and Cake shaped a guitar-based vocabulary that had nothing to do with grunge, punk, or other alternative trends of that era. Sam Prekop and Archer Prewitt played intricate, interlocking guitar patterns that suggest the influences of bebop, African juju music, and bossa nova without mimicking any of those styles; Eric Claridge brought a bright, melodic dimension to his bass playing, stamping him as indie pop's answer to Paul McCartney; and drummer John McEntire treated percussion not as an opportunity to take out his aggression on stationary objects but as a tool for sculpting sound and heightening texture.

Prekop's conversational voice floats airy melodies through a delicate latticework of instruments on *The Sea and Cake*. Layered keyboards play a more prominent role on *Nassau*, while *The Biz* flirts with standard rock riffs, albeit with disarming charm (the churning "Leeora").

The Fawn refreshed the Chicago quartet's approach, blending the sounds of typewriters, keyboards, and other electronic enhancements with the guitar/bass/drums vocabulary. It's more trancelike, layered, and groove-oriented, with loops taking over for live drums and Claridge's bass bubbling over the guitars.

Oui is the band's most delicately engrossing album; its charms are illustrated in tiny moments of bliss such as the ghostly, Jobim-like fade of "The Colony Room" or the lush yet fragile orchestrations of "Seemingly."

After a three-year break, *One Bedroom* found the band newly invigorated. The album closes with a relatively faithful cover of David Bowie's Berlin-era classic "Sound and Vision," its sighing voices and swooning synthesizers a perfect fit for the band's sound. The guitars are once again sublimated to the synthesizers and keyboards, and McEntire's beats motor along, free of kick-drum bombast. Claridge is particularly crucial; the tunes retain their buoyancy, and "Hotel Tell" and "Shoulder Length" boast a dance-floor kick as well. —G.K.

Seal

★★½	Seal (Sire/Warner Bros., 1991)	
★★★★	Seal (ZZT/Sire/Warner Bros., 1994)	
★★★★	Human Being (Warner Bros., 1998)	
★★★½	Seal IV (Warner Bros., 2003)	

Sealhenry Samuel burst onto U.S. radio in the early '90s with "Crazy," which climbed to #7 on the pop charts. Full of strobey dissolves and crowded rhythmic percolation, the song's lyrics maintained ardently that, in a world packed with various people and their often conflicting agendas, "We're never going to survive/ Unless we get a little crazy." Seal was offering undeniable pop that knew its way around the dance floors of the U.K. and Europe.

In fact, this Englishman, born to Nigerian and Brazilian parents, had come from the U.K. house scene; the year before, Seal had provided vocals on "Killer," an Adamski single that had enjoyed #1 status at home. On his debut, Seal left no one in doubt that he had a top-drawer soul voice; on a turn such as "Whirlpool," producer Trevor Horn slowed down the tempo and refrained from overdubs while Seal, singing in an acoustic setting, testified with the slightly rough tone and streaming flow of a modern soul champ.

With limber, harmonically alive jams such as "Whirlpool," Seal's debut is a nice record, undated, unlike most clumsy attempts to mate rave and pop. But the great Seal music begins with his followup (also

titled *Seal*). There, he and Horn unveil a rare kind of ultraslick and scrupulously arranged studio craft that combines the London sonic-luxury tradition of late Roxy Music with the superpro sessions of '80s Los Angeles. The result suggests Roxy with an open heart, or Toto with Knightsbridge cool.

When *Seal* was released, it was already going strong on the basis of "Prayer for the Dying," a surging ballad on which Seal, who holds a degree in architecture, and Horn, whose past productions—even with the far less adept Buggles and Frankie Goes to Hollywood—seriously pursued dimension and elegance and solidified their approach. The pianos sail; the acoustic guitars fly around vibrantly; Seal testifies with the grace and fire of a great contemporary soulman; and Ann Dudley, the finest string arranger at work in pop music today, provides gorgeous symphonic drifts and lifts. "Kiss From a Rose," a rock song done in this highly arranged sweet-soul manner (it appeared on the *Batman* soundtrack), marked another hit for the album.

Seal, which moved more than 4 million copies in the U.S., offers this approach, plus major hits; the far less commercially successful *Human Being,* which was in some ways musically superior to its predecessor, does not. If *Seal,* with its gigantic tunes, accesses the Toto side of Seal/Horn music, then *Human Being* clings—in a thoroughly late-'90s dance-music way—to late Roxy. The arrangements remain lucidly dense as their components mull over ambient trance passages. The melodies on pieces such as "State of Grace" and the title track pursue a relative amelodicism until Seal zooms off toward career-best ballads such as "No Easy Way" and the magnificent "When a Man Is Wrong." Still, the effect is stunning, a virtual case study of how musical daring, technological know-how, bottomless soul, and time and money can yield music far too elevated to be called mere adult contemporary.

Seal IV is a more accessible soul-pop album. Seal retains his unwavering, if bruised, faith in the powers of love and forgiveness, but he sounds as though he's been immersed in Stax, Bobby Womack, and Sam Cooke. And his gorgeously granulated voice is never less than sublime. —J.H.

Sebadoh

★★	The Freed Man (Homestead, 1989)	
★★	Weed Forestin (Homestead, 1990)	
★★	The Freed Weed (Homestead, 1990)	
★★★★½	III (Homestead, 1991)	
★★★½	Rockin' the Forest (Domino, 1992)	
★★★½	Sebadoh vs. Helmet (Domino, 1992)	
★★★★	Smash Your Head on the Punk Rock (Sub Pop, 1992)	

★★★½ Bubble and Scrape (Sub Pop, 1993)
★★★★ Bakesale (Sub Pop, 1994)
★★★ Harmacy (Sub Pop, 1996)
★★ The Sebadoh (Sire, 1999)

In Dinosaur Jr, bassist Lou Barlow was the sullen dork who never said anything, except to scream in anguish, usually after the song was already over. But just a few years later, he was an acoustic troubadour warbling emotional ballads like "It's So Hard to Fall In Love" into his 4-track. His new incarnation was Sebadoh, the always erratic but oft-splendid band that epitomized indie-rock introspection. Never before have so few felt so much on behalf of so many who heard so many of their own feelings so fully expressed by so few on such a low budget. As the band announced in the 1991 breakthrough single "Gimme Indie Rock," it was "a whole new generation of electric white-boy blues."

Barlow teamed up with Eric Gaffney for the early albums, just pot-smoking tape-hiss demos long forgotten even by those of us who took them seriously at the time. But when Jason Loewenstein joined, the trio opened up for the exuberant mess that was *Sebadoh III*, a dog's breakfast of ironic art punk, lo-fi acoustic pop, tape-twiddling jokes, and sensitive girlfriend songs. Gaffney and Loewenstein made funny noises at best and blood-pressure-baiting filler at worst, but Barlow bloomed into an unlikely love man, writing gems like "Kath," "Spoiled," and "The Freed Pig," though the album also made room for reverent tributes to the Minutemen and Johnny Mathis. Writing more good tunes than he could fit onto Sebadoh albums, Barlow released a steady stream of side projects, most notably the Folk Implosion (a separate story in itself) and the solo 4-track Sentridoh. *Smash Your Head on the Punk Rock* plucked highlights from two import EPs, including a swell cover of David Crosby's "Everybody's Been Burned." It also had the magnificent "Brand New Love," tied for first place in the Sebadoh canon with *Bubble and Scrape*'s "Soul and Fire." These anthemic losercore ballads are Barlow's specialty: music that feels intimate and homemade even when—no, especially when—the band is bashing away.

Gaffney finally left before *Bakesale*, which came as a relief: There is such a thing as too much democracy. It's the most accessible Sebadoh record, peaking high with "Magnet's Coil." *Harmacy* had great slow stuff—"Perfect Way" ranks up there with Scritti Politti's, while "Willing to Wait" used an actual string section. But the still-sketchy hit-to-miss ratio had begun sounding like a contrivance, and *The Sebadoh* sounded tired; while the king was moping around, Elliott Smith stole his thorny crown. It was time to move

on anyway, and there will surely be more music to come from both Barlow and Loewenstein. —R.S.

Pete Seeger
Selected Discography

★★★ Pete Seeger Sampler (Smithsonian Folkways, 1954)
★★★★ Talking Union and Other Union Songs (Smithsonian Folkways, 1955)
★★★★ With Voices Together We Sing (Smithsonian Folkways, 1956)
★★★★ Love Songs for Friends and Foes (Smithsonian Folkways, 1956)
★★★★ American Ballads, Vol. 1 (Smithsonian Folkways, 1957)
★★★★ American Favorite Ballads, Vol. 1 (Smithsonian Folkways, 1957)
★★★★ American Favorite Ballads, Vol. 2 (Smithsonian Folkways, 1958)
★★★★ Pete Seeger and Sonny Terry (Smithsonian Folkways, 1958)
★★★★ American Favorite Ballads, Vol. 3 (Smithsonian Folkways, 1959)
★★★★½ Songs of Struggle and Protest, 1930–50 (Smithsonian Folkways, 1959)
★★★★ Pete Seeger at the Village Gate with Memphis Slim and Willie Dixon (Smithsonian Folkways, 1960)
★★★★ American Favorite Ballads, Vol. 4 (Smithsonian Folkways, 1961)
★★★★ Sing Out with Pete! (Smithsonian Folkways, 1961)
★★★ Six Songs for Democracy (Smithsonian Folkways, 1961)
★★★½ Pete Seeger at the Village Gate, Vol. 2 (Smithsonian Folkways, 1962)
★★★★ American Favorite Ballads, Vol. 5: Tunes and Songs as Sung by Pete Seeger (Smithsonian Folkways, 1962)
★★★★½ Waist Deep in the Big Muddy and Other Love Songs (1962; Sony, 1994)
★★★ Broadside Ballads, Vol. 2 (Smithsonian Folkways, 1963)
★★★ Broadsides (Smithsonian Folkways, 1964)
★★★ Dangerous Songs?! (1966; Sony, 1998)
★★★ Sings Traditional Christmas Carols (1967; Smithsonian Folkways, 1989)
★★★ God Bless the Grass (1967; Smithsonian Folkways, 1982)
★★★★ Wimoweh and Other Songs of Freedom and Protest (Smithsonian Folkways, 1968)
★★★½ Pete Seeger Sings Lead Belly (Smithsonian Folkways, 1968)

Pete Seeger deserves the same deep respect we give Elvis Presley and Louis Armstrong—other artists who created something new and lasting out of the music that preceded them. Seeger's achievement, however, rests not on innovation but on conscience and commitment. Born in New York City in 1919 to parents who were faculty members at the Juilliard School of Music, Seeger found his calling at age 16 when he attended a folk festival in Asheville, NC. After dropping out of Harvard in 1938, Seeger began wandering the country, banjo in hand, and eventually befriended Woody Guthrie, a fellow traveler (using the phrase in its literal rather than political sense) who had the gift of song. Along the way he absorbed hundreds of songs—folk songs, topical songs, blues, pop, and songs from foreign lands—and began writing his own original tunes based on his experiences on the road and the lives he saw Americans, especially those on the lower rungs of the social order, living. He studied and developed an abiding faith in humanitarian socialism as a cure for society's ills; as his personal political views crystallized, Seeger became more vocal in his support of workers and labor unions and was quick to advance their point of view in his music.

Through it all Seeger remained fixed on the idea of the song as a source of information, as a link between the past and the present, as a window into other worlds. In addition to workers' songs, he plumbed the folk songs of other countries and other cultures, becoming a master storyteller and a master synthesist, weaving contemporary ideas and perspectives into ballads centuries old. He became a repository of traditional American songs of all types. Being a bit of a musicologist (his father's profession), Seeger tracked down the stories behind the old songs he was digging

up and used this background to bring a compelling historical sweep to his concerts. Though he could be contentious with anyone he perceived as not being suitably libertarian and sanctimonious in the certainty of his opinions, he also was endearingly childlike in the sense of awe and wonder with which he conveyed to his audiences the stories behind his songs.

The folk revival of the '50s and '60s officially began in 1948, when Seeger, Hays, Ronnie Gilbert, and Fred Hellerman joined together as the Weavers and continued the work the Almanac Singers had begun earlier in the decade. Accused of being Communists during the '50s Red Scare, the Weavers—one of the most popular groups in the country at that time—were forced to disband, and Seeger took his place among the blacklisted artists whom radio and television shows would not book. He did continue to record for the Columbia label, though, remaining as active on that front as he had been before joining the Weavers. A Weavers reunion in 1955 marked the beginning a new phase in Seeger's career, one that would find him on the front lines supporting the civil rights movement and, in the '60s, raising his voice in protest against the Vietnam War.

Seeger's bully pulpit for advancing his message was the concert stage—he toured constantly and globally. How many people first heard Bob Dylan's songs at a Pete Seeger concert is impossible to calculate, as is the number whom Seeger introduced to the music of Jimmie Rodgers, Lead Belly, Woody Guthrie, and other great American artists. Johnny Cash has been celebrated, justifiably, for the breadth and depth of his recording career; the unacknowledged template for Cash's explorations beyond the country realm is Pete Seeger's career on record. Recording continuously since 1940, he has constructed a catalogue that is some kind of repository of the entire history of song. A surge of interest in African music in the late '80s and early '90s must have amused him, since his recording of *Bantu Choral Folk Songs* (now out of print) dates from 1955. And when Ken Burns' powerful *Civil War* series made the War Between the States fashionable again in 1990, Seeger could look back to 1943, when he recorded his first album of Civil War songs. There's no end to this: Pick a Pete Seeger album and on it will be something of interest that is virtually unavailable anywhere else. The catalogue is replete with whimsical but enlightening children's albums, instructional albums (*How to Play the 5-String Banjo*, from 1954; another how-to on Lead Belly's 12-string guitar technique, *The 12-String Guitar as Played by Lead Belly*, which is now back in print; and for good measure there's 1955's *Folksinger's Guitar Guide, Vol. 1: An Instruction Record*), blues-folk summit meetings (1958's *Pete Seeger and Sonny Terry*), work songs, protest songs, Christmas songs from all lands, nature songs, numerous tributes to other artists, even a self-interview album, *Pete Seeger Sings and Answers Questions.* Seeger also has cut two fine live albums with Arlo Guthrie (with whom he still appears in concert every Thanksgiving week at Carnegie Hall), now available on the two-CD set *Precious Friend,* both shows offering a capsule history of 20th-century American popular music. In 1996 Seeger returned to the recording studio for his first album in 17 years, and the result, *Pete,* produced by Paul Winter and Tom Bates, is typically galvanizing, even though Seeger's voice is a bit thin. Still, the Seeger intellect and spirit remain formidable. These attributes show up in songs such as his memoir of the young Lead Belly, "Huddie Ledbetter Was a Helluva Man," his incandescent psalm to the spiritual renewal the earth brings in "Sailing Down My Golden River," and a stirring reprise of the Reverend R. Lowry–Anne Warner's mission statement, "How Can I Keep from Singing," which is not only the title of Seeger's autobiography, but also a political broadside that leaves no doubt as to which side Pete is on in a world of tyrants. If there are no more new Pete Seeger albums, *Pete* is a fine and compelling closing statement, and one of the best LPs in his awesome catalogue. Remarkable and of unassailable integrity, Seeger's music renews the spirit as it feeds the mind. Dip freely into this well, as it provides nourishment aplenty. —D.M.

Bob Seger

- ★★★ Ramblin' Gamblin' Man (Capitol, 1969)
- ★★★ Noah (Capitol, 1969)
- ★★★ Mongrel (Capitol, 1970)
- ★★★ Smokin' O.P.'s (1972; Capitol, 1977)
- ★★★ Back in '72 (Reprise, 1973)
- ★★★½ Seven (Capitol, 1974)
- ★★★½ Beautiful Loser (1975; Capitol, 1988)
- ★★★★ Live Bullet (Capitol, 1976)
- ★★★★ Night Moves (Capitol, 1976)
- ★★★★ Stranger in Town (Capitol, 1978)
- ★★★½ Against the Wind (Capitol, 1980)
- ★★★ Nine Tonight (Capitol, 1981)
- ★★★★ The Distance (Capitol, 1982)
- ★★★½ Like a Rock (Capitol, 1986)
- ★★★ The Fire Inside (Capitol, 1991)
- ★★★★ Greatest Hits (Capitol, 1994)
- ★★★ It's a Mystery (Capitol, 1995)

Whether gigging in long, tireless obscurity in the journeyman bars and clubs of his native Michigan or gliding through his late-'70s success, Bob Seger remained in spirit a working-class hero. Gruff-voiced and dramatic, he's a premier rock & roll singer, and his best songs render with dignity and empathy the hard victories and close defeats of ordinary lives. A sort of John Fogerty with more of a naturalist approach than that expressed by Creedence's ruralist myths, or a Springsteen without the vast sweep of the Boss' vision, Seger balances romance and realism—for all its inspirational verve, his work mainly is honest, solid, and strong.

Heavy rock along the lines of Free or Cream, *Ramblin' Gamblin' Man* boasts a great, Mitch Ryder-ish title track and very tough, bluesy stompers driven home with raw assurance. *Mongrel* hasn't quite the same crude, lean power—a remake of Ike and Tina Turner's "River Deep, Mountain High" betrays Seger's occasional tendency toward bombast—but with "Big River," the record sees the singer debuting the kind of confident midtempo ballad writing he'd later perfect with such hits as "You'll Accomp'ny Me" and "Against the Wind." A grab bag of covers as oddly diverse as Stephen Stills' "Love the One You're With" and Chuck Berry's "Let It Rock," *Smokin' O.P.'s* features "Heavy Music," its swagger recalling Spencer Davis' "Gimme Some Lovin'" and a reading of Tim Hardin's "If I Were a Carpenter" that shows Seger capable as ever of fierce conviction, if not yet of much restraint. "Get Out of Denver," from *Seven,* is Seger at his fast-rocking finest; "U.M.C. (Upper Middle Class)" shows him flourishing a political conscience—and the album introduces the Silver Bullet Band, whose no-frills dependability makes possible a growing confidence in the singer that soon pays off in a new refinement that sacrifices little of his earlier energy.

Beautiful Loser's stately title track and its punchy cover of Tina Turner's "Nutbush City Limits" begin Seger's mature period. The trilogy that follows (*Live Bullet, Night Moves,* and *Stranger in Town*) is remarkable stuff—"Night Moves" is not only Seger's best song, but one of rock's most moving exercises in elegy, and the vigor of the fast songs testifies not only to the pleasures of craft, but the rewards of keeping faith with fundamental rock & roll. Seger's glory moment, these three records sum up his strengths: clarity, endurance, and heart.

While "The Horizontal Bop" and "Betty Lou's Gettin' Out Tonight" rock with the offhand assurance Seger had unassailably gained by then, *Against the Wind*'s ballads betray strain and a certain softness. *Nine Tonight* is expert but unnecessary. *The Distance* marks a return to form in its moody remake of Rodney Crowell's "Shame on the Moon" and in Seger's Detroit valediction, "Makin' Thunderbirds"—but the note of nostalgia he'd first sounded in *Stranger in*

Town with "Old Time Rock 'n' Roll" is beginning to seem perfunctory. *Like A Rock,* however, testifies to Seger's survivalist courage. While the breakthrough intensity of his best work is missing, this is wise and confident music. A cover of Fogerty's "Fortunate Son" truly kicks, and in "The Ring" and its lament for an exhausted love, the veteran is doing what he—and few others—can do with frankness and focus: make rock & roll for full-grown men and women. *The Fire Inside* carries on the good fight, as does *It's A Mystery,* which ranges from his trademark nostalgia ("Rite of Passage") to a terrific cover of Tom Waits' "16 Shells from a Thirty-Ought-Six." —P.E.

Semisonic

★★★   Pleasure (EP) (CherryDisc/MCA, 1995)
★★★★   Great Divide (MCA, 1996)
★★★½   Feeling Strangely Fine (MCA, 1998)
★★★½   All About Chemistry (MCA, 2001)
★★★★   The Millennium Collection (MCA, 2003)

Minneapolis-based trio Semisonic were still basking in the afterglow of their breakthrough 1998 smash "Closing Time" when MTV crashed the party by featuring them in a "One-Hit-Wonders" special. Granted, they've yet to prove the epitaph wrong commercially, but the insistent charm of "Closing Time," from *Feeling Strangely Fine,* was no anomaly. While the seven-song *Pleasure* EP was little more than a tease, their full-length debut *Great Divide* is a dizzying head rush of immediately engaging power-pop hooks, clever melodies and studio smarts, not unlike a more literate, indie-rock answer to Boston's first album. While hardly groundbreaking, *Great Divide* stands up better than most modern rock of the era, a testament to the band's sly balance of sheer tunefulness and prog-pop inventiveness. (Singer/guitarist/songwriter Dan Wilson and bassist John Munson both played in the arty college rock band Trip Shakespeare, while drummer Jacob Slichter also handles keyboards—live, he plays both at once.) The result is a nearly flawless batch of top tunes like "Down in Flames" and "Across the Great Divide" that connect at once both head on and left of center. *Feeling Strangely Fine* introduces filler to the equation, but only a pinch. "Closing Time," a few years down the line from over-playedville, remains a great sing-along pop song, as do the prophetic loser's anthem "This Will Be My Year" and "Singing in My Sleep," which captures the giddy thrill of a mix tape from a new lover. The decidedly lower-key *All About Chemistry* didn't deliver the goods quite as generously (and its lackluster sales put a sobering stop to the band's all-too-short chart reign), but the opening "Chemistry"

ranks as one of Wilson's catchiest compositions. It fits right in with the rest of the winners on *The Millennium Collection,* a seemingly premature best-of that nonetheless gives Semisonic the last laugh; casual fans picking up the disc for "Closing Time" will think they've discovered one of the best unheard singles bands of the '90s. —R.S.

Brian Setzer Orchestra

★★½   The Brian Setzer Orchestra (Hollywood, 1994)
★★★   Guitar Slinger (Interscope, 1996)
★★★½   The Dirty Boogie (Interscope, 1998)
★★   Vavoom (Interscope, 2000)

At first former Stray Cat Brian Setzer's big-band jump-blues revue looked like a rock star's indulgence: When he issued *The Brian Setzer Orchestra,* in 1994, grunge was king, and though the album was a competent re-creation of the dance music of the 1940s and '50s complete with a rip-roaring cover of "Route 66," it seemed like a curious throwback, a one-and-done anachronism.

But Setzer persisted, and a funny thing happened with the Orchestra's third work, *The Dirty Boogie:* Its flip, highly caffeinated swing caught on, igniting a full-scale cultural phenomenon. *The Dirty Boogie,* easily the best recording to come from the swing revival that birthed bands such as Big Bad Voodoo Daddy, showcases Setzer's period-perfect guitar leads and features a campy duet between Setzer and No Doubt's Gwen Stefani on "You're the Boss," the Elvis Presley–Ann Margret showstopper from *Viva Las Vegas,* as well as several irreverent Setzer originals, including "This Cat's on a Hot Tin Roof." Though it contains covers of swing classics (Glenn Miller's "Pennsylvania 6-5000," Ellington's "Caravan") the followup, *Vavoom,* is far more formulaic, and less rewarding. —T.M.

Sex Pistols

★★★★★   Never Mind the Bollocks, Here's the Sex Pistols (Warner Bros., 1977)
★★★   The Great Rock 'n' Roll Swindle (Virgin, 1979)
★★   Filthy Lucre Live (Virgin, 1996)

The Sex Pistols fired a shot heard 'round the world; it's just that at the time, it seemed to be a blank. For a strange couple of weeks in 1978, anyway, the avatars of British punk made a significant dent in the American media landscape. Then the group promptly broke up—at the end of an abbreviated U.S. tour, before its music and general attitude had a chance to infect the mainstream here. And truth be told, *Never Mind the Bollocks* is just too raw and corrosive to qualify as any kind of pop. Thousands of lousy imitations have dulled punk's jagged edge over the years, but the Pistols' recorded legacy still cuts deep into the heart of rock & roll—and still draws blood.

Here are the nihilistic singles that brought an empire to its knees during 1976–77 ("Anarchy in the U.K.," "God Save the Queen"), alongside the scornful anthems that shocked a previous generation of rebels ("Pretty Vacant," "No Feelings"). Steve Jones rips blaring anti-riffs out of his guitar, while Johnny Rotten taunts us with alternating flashes of wild insight and utter rudeness. The astounding cuts "Bodies" and "Holidays in the Sun" suggest that the once (and future) John Lydon sensed something basic about the sanctity of human life, as well as the rotten way human beings have come to live it.

The Great Rock 'n' Roll Swindle is a soundtrack compilation, documenting the Sex Pistols' dissolution in more detail than necessary. Rotten is long gone by this point, and the concepts of manager Malcolm McLaren loom large over the proceedings: choral foreign-language versions of the hits, Steve Jones and drummer Paul Cook's tasteless matchup with Great Train Robber Ronald Biggs, and so on. *Swindle*'s only essential moment is a poignant mauling of "My Way" by the late Sid Vicious. *Filthy Lucre Live* documents the band's dispiriting 1996 reunion tour (with original bassist Glen Matlock); eminently avoidable.   —M.C.

Ron Sexsmith

★★★½	Ron Sexsmith	(Interscope, 1995)
★★★	Other Songs	(Interscope, 1997)
★★★	Whereabouts	(Interscope, 1999)
★★★½	Blue Boy	(Cooking Vinyl/spinART 2001)
★★★★	Cobblestone Runway	(Nettwerk, 2002)

Toronto singer/songwriter Ron Sexsmith has a smooth, unornamented tenor, which he deploys to spread dark moods over sunny arrangements. The effect is languorous, and his melodies are incredibly detailed. Sometimes Sexsmith's work seems close to prerock titans such as Irving Berlin and Johnny Mercer; like those artists, Sexsmith's ego often seems to evaporate, swallowed completely by his craft and performances.

His first three albums add another element: The ideas of L.A. producer Mitchell Froom, a fusion-minded musician with a classical sense of balance and proportion. Froom demonstrates an aversion to genre; his songs seem to float outside any style, trend, or approach. From masterly ballads such as "Secret Heart" (from *Ron Sexsmith*) or "April After All" (from *Whereabouts*), to finely wrought mood pieces and dramatically acute narratives, Sexsmith's songs are couched in musical soundscapes that are always smart and

often a little baffling—the production's cool tone can be a little alienating. These collections represent the unusual instance where a little confusion, bad taste, inaccuracy, or strived-for chic actually might have improved things.

Sexsmith's major-label debut years past *Blue Boy* finds him in Nashville working with producers Steve Earle and Ray Kennedy, who give Sexsmith a Lucinda Williams–style beer-joint looseness; this makes sense, because country's lyric clarity as well as Americana awareness and humility have always partly informed Sexsmith's sensibility. Finally, Sexsmith has something Froom always studiously avoided: a sound. This makes Sexsmith gems such as "This Song" and "Cheap Hotel" even better, relaxing into their own articulate expressiveness, rubbing up against warm organs, down-home horns, and relatively noisy rhythms.

Cobblestone Runway, Sexsmith's best album to date, continues this direction, although it takes a more English path. With terrific work from the Swedish producer Martin Terefe, Sexsmith immerses this blue-ribbon batch of songs in fine everyday things like groove, background choruses, guitar hooks, easy atmospheres—all avenues that Froom's severity closed. On trademark ballads such as "Former Glory" and "The Less I Know"—not to mention "Dragonfly on Bay Street," a fun rhythmic setting—Sexsmith seems reborn. The Froom years might have made some theoretical musical sense, but *Cobblestone Road* finds the chief melodic talent of his generation feeling—and sounding—good. And feeling good makes a difference.   —J.H.

Shakira

★★½	Pies Descalzos	(Sony, 1996)
★★★★	Dónde Están los Ladrones?	(Sony, 1998)
★★★½	MTV Unplugged	(Sony, 2000)
★★½	Laundry Service	(Sony, 2001)
★★★½	Grandes Exitos	(Sony, 2002)
★★★	Live & Off the Record	(Sony, 2004)

Before she dyed her hair blond and got all tarted up for crossover success in the English-speaking world, Shakira Isabel Mebarak Ripoll was already a huge and well-respected young rock star throughout Latin America and Spain, and among Spanish-speaking fans elsewhere. The Colombian-born singer recorded two successful albums in her early teens before releasing her international breakthrough, *Pies Descalzos* ("Bare Feet"). But Shakira was still developing her voice, and while *Pies* has its bright spots (the sweet, acoustic folk rock of "Te Necesito" and light power pop of "Vuelve"), its mix of rock, dance pop, ballads, and a stab at Brazilian-flavored pop jazz never quite meshes.

It was clear Shakira was willing to push musical boundaries, though, and her sense of adventure pays off handsomely on *Dónde Están los Ladrones?* ("Where Are the Thieves?"), which mines familiar territory but holds together with stronger songs, a beefier sound, and more confident vocals. On *Ladrones,* Shakira (whose mother is Colombian and father Lebanese) pays tribute to her Latin roots in the Spanish guitars and trumpets of "Ciega, Sordomuda," and to her Middle Eastern heritage in the snaky melody and rhythms of "Ojos Así," sung partly in Spanish and partly in Arabic. The music on *Ladrones* spans from ancient traditional styles to contemporary dance pop to the experimental leanings of British and American artists such as the Beatles, Led Zeppelin, Depeche Mode, Nirvana, and even the twang of Texas and West Coast Americana. It's hard to imagine a singer barely into her 20s having written and recorded such an inventive set of songs. Even the production of the powerful Miami music mogul Emilio Estefan Jr. is surprisingly tasteful and evenhanded.

Laundry Service is a case of American music industry arrogance gone awry. Purportedly produced by Shakira, her English-language crossover is a checklist of transparent marketing hooks—from the album's J.Lo–esque cover image to the emphases on Shakira's Alanis Morissette–like vocal quirk and capacity to belt ballads like Céline Dion. Indeed, Morissette svengali Glen Ballard cowrote one of the more overblown songs ("The One"), and the fingerprints of the Estefan crew are all over the record. In spite of its cynical pandering to mainstream U.S. audiences, *Laundry Service* is not an awful CD. Shakira offers some of the eclecticism of her previous album with the Astor Piazzola–like accordion in the cool, gritty "Te Aviso, Te Anuncio (Tango)" and moody twang of "Que Me Quedes Tú." But the English translations are clunky, and the production is way overcooked. Not that pop fans minded: Shakira's videos for "Whenever, Wherever" and "Under Your Clothes" catapulted the album to #3 on the Billboard 200. Within a year *Laundry Service* had sold triple platinum, and Shakira wound up with a Grammy and a Pepsi endorsement.

In between studio albums, Shakira has released remix collections and live albums. *MTV Unplugged* is a strong, intimate set of songs mostly from *Dónde Están los Ladrones?* The hit-and-miss *Live & Off the Record* includes a DVD that's more interesting than the CD. *Grandes Exitos* is a good collection of some of Shakira's better songs, substituting Spanish versions of her English-language hits. —M.K.

Tupac Shakur
see 2PAC

Shangri-Las

★★ Remember . . . The Shangri-Las at Their Best (Collectables, 1994)
★★★½ Myrmidons of Melodrama (RPM, 1994)

This girl-group foursome had all the earmarks of a novelty act: two of them were twins, they once released a record under the name of the Beatle-lettes, and their heavy Queens accents sounded wonderfully kitschy. Breathless sincerity, however, remains the strongest of their considerable charms: Only in high school when they began recording, the girls tried so damn hard to be the Ronettes that they're quite endearing. "Leader of the Pack," that great 1964 anthem for juvenile delinquents, is still their most winning moment, but "Remember (Walking in the Sand)" is excellent fake Phil Spector, too. "Out in the Streets" and "I Can Never Go Home Anymore" (with its fine, drippy spoken confessional) round out an impressive quartet of hits. A real-life version of *Grease*, these gal wonders are lots of fun. The fabulously entitled import *Myrmidons of Melodrama* gives us oodles of Shangri-Las (33 cuts) and it's all great, weepy stuff. —P.E.

Del Shannon

★★★★ Runaway/One Thousand Six Hundred Sixty-One Seconds (1961, 1965; Taragon, 1997)
★★★ Drop Down and Get Me (1981; Varèse Sarabande, 1998)
★★★★★ Greatest Hits (Bug/Rhino, 1990)
★★★½ Greatest Hits (Curb, 1995)
★★★★★ 25 All-Time Greatest Hits (Varèse Sarabande, 2001)
★★★ Absolutely the Best: Del Shannon & Eddie Cochran (Fuel 2000/Varèse Sarabande, 2001)
★★★★★ Runaway: The Very Best of Del Shannon (Collectables, 2002)
★★★½ Classic Masters (Capitol, 2003)

Conventional wisdom holds that the late '50s and pre-Beatles '60s were a fallow period for rock & roll. This can be disputed on several fronts, one of the strongest being the music erupting from the angst-ridden psyche of Battle Creek, MI's Del Shannon. His classics—"Runaway," "Little Town Flirt," "Hats Off to Larry," "Keep Searchin' "—are tough, aggressive tunes full of fears of abandonment, sadistic glee in revenge, and all sorts of other extreme emotions raging within the teenage soul. Shannon put them across with brio, digging in with a tenor voice that had more than a little country in it, and a sandpapery edge that established the overwrought atmosphere of his stories before he delivered the coup de grace with a howling, eerie falsetto, singing nonsense syllables, rhetorical questions ("Why, why, why?"), or simply the end of a lyric line in a way that usually celebrated a triumphant moment over an unfaithful girlfriend. On the instrumental side, he was an accomplished and fiery guitarist, although guitar solos did not occupy the most prominent place on his enduring recordings; that honor went more to his buddy Max Crook, who had developed an organlike instrument called the Musitron (sort of an early synthesizer, actually) that produced one of the weirdest sounds in rock & roll history—its piercing tone, in fact, served as the instrumental complement to Shannon's forays into the falsetto stratosphere, never with greater or more enduring impact than on the 1961 debut single, the immortal "Runaway," a #1 right out of the box. A "Runaway" sequel, "Hats Off to Larry," which celebrated, with hyper-delirious enthusiasm, the "Runaway" girl's being dumped, ascended into the Top Five, followed by "So Long Baby," a Homeric kiss-off in which Shannon not only sends his deceiving girl packing but, to a furiously bleating horn section's taunts, cheerfully admits to his own illicit affair and a corresponding and complete absence of shame over his actions. However, in the finale of 1961's four-part morality play, "Hey Little Girl," Shannon, now contrite, tries to mend fences with his broken-hearted flame on the theory that he knows what it's like to be left high and dry too, in an arrangement that employs a steady, driving beat with Latin overtones, another evocative Max Crook Musitron solo, and a section of violins supplying a lush, supportive backdrop. Shannon came back strong in 1962 with a merciless dissection of the "Little Town Flirt," which returned him to the upper reaches of the chart. Shannon's next substantial hit didn't come until 1964, with a propulsive, double-tracked treatment of the 1960 Jimmy Jones hit "Handy Man," which rose to #22; later that year he found himself back in the Top 10 with one of the best of all his monumental singles, "Keep Searchin'," a desperate tale of a man bent on taking a woman away from an abusive situation, even if it means "we gotta keep on the run." The band backing Shannon on all these Amy label singles was formidable, numbering among its members guitarist Dennis Coffey, who would move on to join the Funk Brothers at Motown, as did the nonpareil bassist Bob Babbitt. In the midst of a British Invasion that was taking over the charts, Shannon closed out 1964 with this #9 single, his final appearance in the Top 10. 1965's paranoid-drenched "Stranger In Town," the sequel to "Keep Searchin'," wherein the fugitive narrator and his gal discover a sinister figure in relentless pursuit of them, peaked at Number 30.

Shannon's career for the rest of the '60s and the '70s was more or less constant label hopping and promising but unsuccessful recordings. A comeback of sorts seemed at hand in 1981, when Tom Petty stepped in as producer and brought in his band the Heartbreakers to back Shannon on *Drop Down and Get Me*. A single, an easy rolling treatment of Phil Phillips' 1959 classic "Sea of Love," seemed to portend good things when it rose to #33; nothing else happened commercially, but *Drop Down and Get Me* has aged well. Almost 10 years later he was working on another comeback album, *Rock On,* with Jeff Lynne producing, when he killed himself on February 8, 1990. As right as Petty was as a producer for Shannon, so was Lynne—with his booming ELO orchestral arrangements—a horrible mismatch. Three tracks from the posthumously released *Rock On* are included at the end of Varèse Sarabande's *25 All-Time Greatest Hits,* which makes them conveniently skippable.

The essential Shannon recordings are available on three excellent collections: one being the above-mentioned *25 All-Time Greatest Hits,* which includes everything from "Runaway" to the final, Lynne-produced cuts; Collectables' awesome 30-track *Runaway: The Very Best of Del Shannon* hits all the hit highlights and fills in some gaps in the Varèse Sarabande collection with priceless rarities such as an alternate take of "Runaway." Rhino's *Greatest Hits* is a 20-track summary of the '60s, with no Petty- or Lynne-produced cuts; Capitol's skimpy 12-track *Classic Masters* entry does contain the great '60s work and concludes with the Petty-produced "Sea of Love," whereas Curb's *Greatest Hits,* while hitting the chart high notes, checks in at an even sparser 10 tracks. For a good look at the artist in his commercial prime, the Taragon twofer, *Runaway/One Thousand Six Hundred Sixty-One Seconds,* can't be beat. —D.M.

Roxanne Shanté

★★★½   The Best of Cold Chillin' (1995, Landspeed)
★★★½   Greatest Hits (1995, Cold Chillin')

Fifteen-year-old Lolita Gooden of Queens, NY, cut a scorching, definitive answer record to "Roxanne, Roxanne," the 1985 rap hit by U.T.F.O. "Roxanne's Revenge" (included on *Bad Sister*) rolls out a funky tongue-lashing with verbal relish and saucy beats. No one-hit wonder, Roxanne Shanté ups the ante with two saltier-still singles: "Have a Nice Day" and "Go on Girl" are further pumped by ripping lyrics (from Big Daddy Kane) and raw, scratched-up jams (from producer Marly Marl). After a delay that stretched several years, Shanté delivered a debut album that matched the impact of those classic in-your-face performances. Even the sole "message" track on *Bad Sister,* "Independent Woman," is gripped with the same indomitable do-it-yourself spirit that guides randy raps like "Fatal Attraction," "Feelin' Kinda Horny" and "Knockin' Hiney." The subsequent *The Bitch Is Back* (1992) revealed a more mature and consistent artist whose tongue remained as sharp as before. Both albums are out of print, but *Greatest Hits* and *Best of Cold Chillin'* pretty much cover it between them. Shanté began her second act at 25 when she gave up rap to become a full-time student, eventually receiving her Ph.D. in psychology and starting her own practice. —M.C./B.SC.

Shellac

★★★★	At Action Park (Touch and Go, 1994)	
★★★	Terraform (Touch and Go, 1998)	
★★★½	1000 Hurts (Touch and Go, 2000)	

In between engineering sessions for such luminaries as Nirvana, PJ Harvey, and Robert Plant and Jimmy Page (as well as countless obscure punk bands), Steve Albini has fashioned three art-damaged postpunk albums with two veterans of the '80s indie-rock scene, bassist Bob Weston and drummer Todd Trainer. These discs draw on the noise aesthetic Albini pioneered with Big Black and later Rapeman: corrosive guitars that often sound more like trash compactors, machinelike rhythms, and lurid lyrics.

Trainer's drums are mixed way out front, and take on the roll of lead instrument, while Weston's bass parades like Godzilla down Main Street. Albini's guitar converses in terse anecdotes and accents rather than in run-on sentences; there are no "solos," per say. Vocals are treated with disdain, occasionally erupting in strangled, staccato bursts. It's neither pretty nor comforting, but for those who like their rock rough and rude, *At Action Park* pays huge dividends. "A Minute" squeezes more sparks out of a single chord and one relentless groove than most bands muster in a lifetime.

Terraform is more forbidding, kicking off with an extended experiment in hypnotic trance-beats that suggests Kraftwerk running low on batteries. *1000 Hurts*, in contrast, is as satisfying as a well-made slasher movie. "Prayer to God" sounds like ritual beating, a revenge fantasy so tactile that even Eminem might be licking his chops in envy, and "Squirrel Song" will make any nature lover squirm. "Watch Song" takes a perfectly nice rock riff, the kind of stuff that has fueled countless arena anthems, and mutilates it beyond recognition, proof that Albini and company still make rock dangerous enough to both love and loathe. —G.K.

Johnny Shines

★★★	Johnny Shines with Big Walter Horton (1969; Testament, 1995)	
★★★★	Too Wet to Plow (1977; Blue Labor, 2001)	
★★★★	Hey Ba-Ba-Re-Bop (Rounder, 1978)	
★★★	Johnny Shines (HighTone, 1991)	
★★	Traditional Delta Blues (Biograph, 1991)	
★★	Mr. Cover Shaker (Biograph, 1992)	
★★	Johnny Shines/Snooky Pryor: Back to the Country (Blind Pig, 1992)	
★★★	Standing at the Crossroads (Testament, 1995)	
★★	1915–1992 (Wolf, 1998)	
★★★½	Evening Shuffle (Westside, 2002)	
★★★	Johnny Shines/Robert Jr. Lockwood: Sweet Home Chicago–Job Sessions (P-Vine import, 2003)	
★★★½	Skull & Crossbones Blues (HighTone, 2003)	

Born outside of Memphis in 1915 and taught guitar by Howlin' Wolf, the exemplary Delta bluesman Johnny Shines traveled extensively with Robert Johnson and developed a solid, stirring repertoire of traditional Delta blues before electrifying his music to rousing effect. In his youthful prime, he recorded relatively few sides, notably for the JOB label, and then dropped out of music from the middle '50s to the middle '60s. The proper way to hear these stomping sides is on the *Evening Shuffle* collection, which omits middling contemporary material done by Robert Jr. Lockwood. Shines rebounded with his contribution to the third volume of the celebrated *Chicago/the Blues/Today!* series and went on to make several vibrant albums for Pete Welding's Testament label, now reissued on HighTone; the savviest mix of acoustic and electric sides is compiled by ex-Blasters Dave Alvin on *Skull & Crossbones Blues*. A live album recorded in 1974, *Hey Ba-Ba-Re-Bop*, catches a powerful Shines solo performance, his propulsive slide guitar lines providing stirring counterpoint to troubled tales of bad luck, bad women, and the search for spiritual redemption. As usual, Shines throws in a few Johnson songs—"Kind Hearted Woman," "Terraplane Blues"—and delivers moving versions of each. *Too Wet to Plow* is an unusually potent, spare acoustic set with a heavy, overcast feel, underscored by Sugar Blue's ghostly harmonica and some of Shines' most anguished vocals. Right up to his death in 1992, Shines exemplified a forward-thinking approach to blues that helped shape the eclectic but blues-rooted style of Robert Cray and others. —D.M./M.MI.

The Shins

★★★½	Oh, Inverted World (Sub Pop, 2001)	
★★★★½	Chutes Too Narrow (Sub Pop, 2003)	

Anybody can swipe inspiration and riffs from the Beatles or the Stones (or at least try), but it takes a very special little band to evoke the arch, pillowy-soft prog pop of the Zombies and the dreamy falsetto melodies of the Association. Especially one from Albuquerque, NM, the proverbial middle of nowhere from which the Shins hatched their bewitching 2001 debut, *Oh, Inverted World.* "Far above our heads are the icy heights that contain all reason," muses frontman James Mercer on the swirling, jangly opener, "Caring Is Creepy," which lays out the plot in no uncertain terms: lots of words too self-important to mean much to anyone but Mercer himself, all beautifully sung and wrapped up in some of the most exquisitely bittersweet melodies this side of "Time of the Season." The record peaks with the catchy but melancholic stunner "New Slang," which only hints at the sweeping but understated grandeur to come on *Chutes Too Narrow.* From the strum-softly-and-carry-a-*big*-chorus cloudburst of "Kissing the Lipless" to the sublime chamber-pop tapestry of "Saint Simon," *Chutes* unfolds like nothing less than a 21st-century indie-pop band's version of Love's 1967 masterpiece *Forever Changes.* It's a bummer in the summer, all right, and an unfailingly lovely one at that. —R.SK.

Matthew Shipp

★★★½   Circular Temple (Infinite Zero/American, 1990)
★★★   Critical Mass (213 CD, 1994)
★★½   2-Z (Thirsty Ear, 1996)
★★★★   Zo (Thirsty Ear, 1997)
★★★   Thesis (Hatology, 1997)
★★★½   The Flow of X (Thirsty Ear, 1997)
★★★   Strata (Hatology, 1997)
★★★★   The Multiplication Table (Hatology, 1998)
★★★   Gravitational Systems (Hatology, 1998)
★★★½   DNA (Thirsty Ear, 1999)
★★★★   Pastoral Composure (Thirsty Ear, 2000)
★★★½   Matthew Shipp's New Orbit (Thirsty Ear, 2001)
★★★★   Expansion, Power, Release (Hatology, 2001)
★★★★½   Nu Bop (Thirsty Ear, 2002)
★★★½   Songs (Splasch, 2002)
★★★★½   Equilibrium (Thirsty Ear, 2003)
★★★½   Antipop Consortium vs. Matthew Shipp (Thirsty Ear, 2003)

with DJ Spooky

★★★★   Optometry (Thirsty Ear, 2002)
★★★★   Dubtometry (Thirsty Ear, 2003)

In jazz circles, Matthew Shipp is perhaps best known as the pianist in the David S. Ware Quartet. Although Ware plays raw, bracing tenor sax rooted in Sonny Rollins and Albert Ayler, he more closely resembles something we might conjure from the painful searching of John Coltrane's last works. But with Shipp and bass titan William Parker, the Ware Quartet is more than the sum of its parts, and albums like *Earthquation* (DIW, 1994), *Godspellized* (DIW, 1996), and *Go See the World* (Columbia, 1998) stand as '90s landmarks of free jazz.

Shipp also recorded frequently as the leader of small groups, where his distinctive piano (think of a more muscular Monk and a more deliberate Powell exploring in depth the terrain that Cecil Taylor first flew over) engaged in intimate dialogue with other stalwart avant-gardists. The early series of albums is mostly of interest to specialists, though *Zo* is a sparkling duo with Parker; *The Multiplication Table* is a fine showcase for Shipp, perhaps because it was recorded by a conventional piano trio; and the albums with violinist Mat Maneri (*The Flow of X,* a quartet, and *Expansion, Power, Release,* a trio with William Parker on bass) suggest, then transcend, some form of quasiclassical chamber jazz.

But Shipp's career took a sharp turn in 1999, when he became creative director of Thirsty Ear's jazz line, the Blue Series, which not only gave him carte blanche to explore the future of free jazz, but also put him on the hook to sell some records. *Pastoral Composure* featured a quartet with Roy Campbell on trumpet, a more conventional lineup that picked up the rhythm and let Shipp play more percussively, bringing to the fore the heavy block chords and clusters that have long been his signature. On *New Orbit,* Campbell was replaced by another trumpet player, Wadada Leo Smith, for a slower and more lyrical outing.

But Shipp was also producing other Thirsty Ear artists, and his work with Spring Heel Jack assembled elements of free jazz, DJ culture, and hip-hop in fruitful ways. On *Nu Bop,* Shipp's acoustic free-jazz group was joined by Chris Flam on synths and programming, setting up fast regular beats and brooding soundscapes. *Equilibrium* consolidates this progress, adding further rhythmic finesse with Khan Jamal's vibes.

What made this something other than just another twist in the tangled web of fusion was attitude: Shipp's view of jazz was formed by growing up on punk and finding both genres to be what he calls "fuck you music." Under Shipp's direction, the Blue Series has exploded with similar experiments, including notable albums by jazz cohorts William Parker, Guillermo E. Brown, and Mat Maneri. Shipp's group also forms the sonic tapestry for collaborations with DJ Spooky (*Optometry*) and Antipop Consortium, both of which add raps to what is fast becoming a trademark sound. And *Dubtometry* turns that sound into sonic hash, relying even more on the rhythm in the *Optometry* remix.

Meanwhile, Shipp has also brought the muse back to Ware, playing synths instead of piano on *Corridors & Parallels* (Aum Fidelity, 2001), one of the Ware Quartet's most invigorating albums. Turns out that the age-old problem with fusion wasn't selling out—it was losing the will to say "fuck you" when it did.   —T.H.

The Shirelles

★★★	Baby, It's You (1962; Sundazed, 1993)
★★★	The Shirelles Sing to Trumpets and Strings (1963; Sundazed, 1994)
★★★	Foolish Little Girl (1963; Sundazed, 1994)
★★★★★	The Shirelles Anthology (Rhino, 1986)
★★★	Golden Classics (Collectables, 1991)
★★★	The Very Best of the Shirelles (Rhino, 1994)
★★★★	For Collectors Only: The Shirelles (Collectables, 1995)
★★★	25 All-Time Greatest Hits (Varèse Sarabande, 1999)

The Shirelles' longevity can be traced to a couple of factors: a steady procession of captivating songs penned by top-drawer writers and a guiding visionary in producer/songwriter Luther Dixon, whose studio savvy translated into memorable, sophisticated productions unlike the typical teen fare of the day. Moreover, Dixon brought his own considerable songwriting skills to bear on the Shirelles' repertoire, and he proved himself capable of being as fanciful ("Boys," later covered by the Beatles) or as dramatic ("Tonight's the Night") as any of the more heralded tunesmiths in the Shirelles' camp.

The group came together in 1958, in Passaic, New Jersey, when Beverly Lee and three of her schoolmates—Shirley Alston (née Owens), Doris Kenner, and Addie "Micki" Harris—got together in her basement to harmonize on their favorite songs of the day. The story goes that one evening while they were baby-sitting for a family friend, the girls came up with an original song that both celebrated and lamented a quickie (as in weeklong) romance. Titled "I Met Him on a Sunday" and featuring an irresistible "do-ronde-ronde" chorus, the song met an enthusiastic reception when the girls performed it at a school talent show. A classmate told her mother about the quartet, and the classmate's mother, who happened to be Florence Greenburg, recorded the girls and released the single on her own Tiara label. Searching for a name that reminded them of the Chantels, the girls came up with the Shirelles.

After generating some regional heat, "I Want You to Be My Boyfriend" was picked up by Decca for national distribution, and the song made a respectable showing on the national chart. Two more Decca releases followed, both unsuccessful, and the Shirelles then moved over to Greenburg's new label, Scepter Records. Their first release was a cover version of the 5 Royales' "Dedicated to the One I Love," with Doris Kenner singing a plaintive, heartfelt lead vocal. "Tonight's the Night," cowritten by Dixon, followed. A marvelous evocation of sexual anticipation on Alston's part, Dixon fleshed it out with a herky-jerky rhythm pattern derived from West Indian sources and an ebullient, go-for-it reading by Alston, who battles her instinct to hold off on the big moment and finally declares, as the song fades out, "Let's take a chance/It's gonna be a great romance."

The Shirelles were on a roll, and although Dixon kept the group in its familiar bag sonically, he was not averse to varying the stylistic pattern from time to time. "Mama Said," the #4-peaking followup to "Dedicated to the One I Love," found the other three Shirelles chanting exuberantly behind Alston's husky-voiced dissertation. "Abra Ka Dabra" features an eerie, almost detached vocal from Alston, which laments a boyfriend who's flown the coop. The whole affair is somber and haunting but not lacking for suspense in its Spector-ish arrangement, which serves to heighten the morose feeling Alston evokes in her reading. "Abra Ka Dabra" is found on Rhino's *Anthology* and on Sundazed's *Foolish Little Girl*.

"Foolish Little Girl," from 1963, culminated the Shirelles' hit years, and if they had to go, they went in style: The single uses two lead vocalists, with Alston playing the role of a woman gleefully putting down another who let a good man get away. One more Top 30 single followed in 1963—"Don't Say Goodnight and Mean Goodbye"—but the die was cast when Luther Dixon left Scepter for Capitol Records. There would be no more hits, only five years' worth of low- or non-charting singles, some of them appalling attempts to cash in on earlier triumphs. Alston left the group in 1969, formed Shirley and the Shirelles, cut some singles for Bell, reunited with the original Shirelles, and recorded some sides for United Artists and RCA, but everything stiffed. Alston then recorded two solo albums for Strawberry Records, including one with the backing of Billy Vera's band. Original members reunited in 1983 (with Louise Bethune replacing the late Micki Harris) to back their former Scepter labelmate Dionne Warwick (once a substitute Shirelle) on Warwick's version of "Dedicated to the One I Love."

The Shirelles' history on Scepter is well represented on CD now. Rhino's *Anthology* is a double-disc collection of the hits and interesting album cuts, and it will probably suffice for all but completists. Collectables' impressive three-CD *For Collectors Only* set also covers the post-Scepter years, which is a way of saying Disc 3 is a bit tough to get through, what with "I Met Him on a Sunday '66" and "Hippie Walk, Parts 1 & 2" among the song selections, as well as "Que Sera Sera." Still, this is the whole story, complete and mostly unabridged, for those who care to chart the entire Shirelles arc. Rhino's 16-song collection, *The Very Best of the Shirelles*, tells the story of the group's commercial success in fine fashion—everything of note is here, including all the Top 50 hits and lesser-charting items that were good performances but simply didn't click with the record-buying public. Sundazed's album reissues are not strictly for collectors only. There's a lot of good music on these albums, some wonderful Luther Dixon productions, and more than a few surprises. *Foolish Little Girl* features a sprightly interpretation of Jessie Hill's New Orleans–flavored "Ooh Poo Pa Doo"; a stylish pop take on the Sam Cooke–penned "Only Time Will Tell"; and a tender rendition of the Bob Crewe/Bob Guadio gem, "Talk Is Cheap." *The Shirelles Sing to Trumpets and Strings* features not only several first-rate Luther Dixon songs, but a rousing, string-rich production of Goffin/King's "What a Sweet Thing That Was" that's just as charming and memorable as many Shirelles hits. Van McCoy contributes a blues ballad in uptempo form, "The First One," that blends some R&B sax lines with country-styled chicken-pickin' guitar ostinatos. Dixon's beautiful blues lament, "Blue Holiday," is given ballast by a string arrangement worthy of Nelson Riddle in its ornate beauty; a muted, distant trumpet solo clearly meant to evoke the specter of Miles Davis; and an earthy, moaning vocal by Alston that brooks comparison with Etta James. Hardly filler, these album tracks make a rich story richer still.   —D.M.

Shyne

★★★ Shyne (Bad Boy/Arista 2000)
★★★ Godfather Buried Alive (Def Jam, 2004)

Perhaps the most buzzed-about rapper of the late '90s, Jamal "Shyne" Barrow sparked a bidding war of absurd proportions, thanks to his voice—a full-throated, gravelly instrument that bore striking similarity to the tones of the late Notorious B.I.G. It was only natural that Shyne would sign to Biggie's old label, Bad Boy, which is part of label don Sean "Puffy" Combs' grave-milking strategy. Shyne's solo debut, though, showed him to be something more than a vocal carbon copy, as Shyne spun compelling 'hood yarns. The Belize-born MC also imported fantastic flavor from south of the continental 48, most notably reggae don Barring-

ton Levy on "Bonnie & Shyne" and the outstanding single "Bad Boyz." Just as hip-hop was in materialistic overload, Shyne kept it grimy, thereby shortening his shelf life. His gangster tales proved prophetic when he was sentenced to 10 years in prison for his role in a 2000 New York nightclub shooting that saw Puffy tried, and acquitted, of attempted murder.   —J.C.

Sigur Rós

★★ Von (Bad Taste, 1997)
★★★★ Agætís Byrjun (PIAS America, 1999)
★★★ ( ) (Fat Cat, 2002)

Move over Godspeed You Black Emperor, make way for Godspeed You Blue Icelanders. If you grew up on the volcanic island, maybe you'd invent your own language, too. If it wasn't the Sugarcuban yelps and bleats of Björk, it might sound like the singing of whales. The beautiful boyhood pals in Sigur Rós took the latter route when in the mid-'90s they began their wistfully moody saga through love's bare tundras and frozen straits, pulling down a local record deal on the strength of a 1994 EP. Already buzzworthy in Britain, idiosyncratic vocalist-guitarist Jon Thor Birgisson and his mates were on their third album when their second found favor among Europhiles and art rockers in the States.

Suggesting a modern-classical take on the sweeping ethereal pop of '80s groups such as Cocteau Twins and Dead Can Dance, the group's songs use hushed tones, submerged acoustic melodrama, and vocal obfuscation as a subversion of the multinational pop forces they austerely dismiss in interviews. But if they prefer murmurs to the language of hegemony, their best music strives for the same epic glories of the classic rock it abjures. "Svefn-G-Englar," which opens 1999's breakthrough *Agætís Byrjun* with the ice-prince siren beckoning *"its youuuuuo,"* eventually plods along like Led Zeppelin looking for Moby Dick in the fog. "Vidrar Vel til Loftárasa" has a lush funereal elegance that suggests a vigil at a northern lights laser show. The rest is one long mournful last call from the land that pop forgot. Of course, now the pop world was watching (one of the most poignant bootleg mashups featured Ny Batteri's "Bíum Bíum Bambaló" woven into Céline Dion's mawkish *Titanic* sinker "My Heart Will Go On"), and music snobs soon uncovered a small army of bashfully blipping Icelandic newbies such as Múm. Expertly playing both sides of the high-low equation, Sigur Rós joined forces with fellow pensive lamenters Radiohead, scoring a dance piece and playing to the velvet-seat crowd as well as fans on the club and fest circuit. But their 2002 followup *( )* went too far out of its way to court high-art bona fides, even eschewing song names to assure its sonic purity. Unfortunately, the music itself is little more than a less-powerful rehash of what's come before, only minus the thrill of initial discovery.   —L.S.

Silver Jews

★★	A Dime Map of the Reef (Atlantic, 1992)
★★	The Arizona Record (Atlantic, 1993)
★★★½	Starlite Walker (Atlantic, 1994)
★★★★	The Natural Bridge (Drag City, 1996)
★★★★★	American Water (Drag City, 1998)
★★★½	Bright Flight (Drag City, 2001)

The Silver Jews' David Berman, a Texan holed up in Nashville by way of Virginia, stands tall among our nation's singer/songwriters: He's a veritable Timbaland of the spoken word, a wandering honky-tonk bard murmuring feverish, fractured one-liners in his handsome country-rock growl. He's had more success in the U.K., where artists such as Badly Drawn Boy have built whole careers around imitating him, but he taps into all-American small-town nightmares, dropping his bourbon-soaked ruminations ("It is autumn and my camouflage is dying," say, or "Most wars end in the fall") with poetic flair. Indeed, Berman published an excellent book of poetry in 1999, *Actual Air.*

He debuted with the 7-inch EP *A Dime Map of the Reef,* featuring frequent collaborators (and Charlottesville, Virginia, friends) Stephen Malkmus and Bob Nastanovich of Pavement. *The Arizona Record* had a couple of real songs buried in lo-fi static ("The War in Apartment 1812," "The Secret Knowledge of Backroads"). But *Starlite Walker* and *The Natural Bridge* had nothing to do with the suffix *-fi* at all— just cleanly produced guitar twang with an easy, shambling feel, topped by Berman's deadpan verbals. *Starlite Walker* boasts the hysterically funny "Living Waters" and the boozy instrumental shindig "The Silver Pageant." The dark, brooding *Natural Bridge* is even better, with simpatico backup from New Radiant Storm King. In the showstopper "Black and Brown Blues," Berman finds himself stuck in a mysterious border town where it rains triple sec and the radio always plays "Crazy Train." Tom Waits, eat your heart out.

For *American Water,* Berman finally put a great band of Jews together, bringing back Malkmus on guitar and prominent harmonies; the resulting album is loose as a goose and twice as much fun when wet. The archly titled "Like Like the the the Death" is some kind of mongrel masterpiece; "Random Rules," "Blue Arrangements," and "The Wild Kindness" are just a notch below. Too many great lines to quote, so a quatrain from "Random Rules" will have to suffice: "I asked the painter/Why the roads are colored black/He said, 'Steve, it's because people leave/And no highway will bring them back.' " It's the Jews' best by a crooked mile. *Bright Flight* is a much more somber affair, featuring members of Lambchop. The peak is "Death of an Heir of Sorrows," a country ballad mourning and cursing an old friend who died alone.   —R.S.

Carly Simon

★★	Carly Simon (Elektra, 1970)
★★½	Anticipation (Elektra, 1971)
★★★½	No Secrets (Elektra, 1972)
★★	Hotcakes (Elektra, 1974)
★★	Playing Possum (Elektra, 1975)
★★★½	The Best of Carly Simon (Elektra, 1975)
★★★	Another Passenger (Elektra, 1976)
★★★	Boys in the Trees (Elektra, 1978)
★★★	Spy (Warner Bros., 1979)
★★½	Come Upstairs (Warner Bros., 1980)
★★½	Torch (Warner Bros., 1981)
★★	Spoiled Girl (Epic, 1985)
★★★	Coming Around Again (Arista, 1987)
★★★	Greatest Hits Live (Arista, 1989)
★★½	My Romance (Arista, 1990)
★★★	Have You Seen Me Lately (Arista, 1990)
★★	This Is My Life: Music From the Motion Picture (Qwest, 1992)
★★★	Letters Never Sent (Arista, 1994)
★★★½	Clouds in My Coffee 1965–1995 (Arista, 1995)
★★★	Film Noir (Arista, 1997)
★★★★	Anthology (Rhino, 2002)
★★½	Christmas Is Almost Here (Rhino, 2002)
★★★★	Reflections: Carly Simon's Greatest Hits (BMG, 2004)

Long on atmosphere and short on vocal precision, Carly Simon's first few hits left a deep impression nevertheless. "That's the Way I've Always Heard It Should Be" (from *Carly Simon*) hangs in the air like an unfinished argument; Simon's postadolescent discovery— that many marriages are empty facades—echoes amid a hushed, somewhat melodramatic setting. This confessional approach can sound unbearably self-conscious when Simon doesn't have a catchy chorus at her disposal, which is most of the time on the debut. *Anticipation*'s title track and "Legend in Your Own Time" match the lush, musing tone of "That's the Way I've Always Heard It Should Be" sigh for sigh, positioning Carly as a natural singles artist and a (mild) feminist presence on the pop charts.

Hooking up with producer Richard Perry seemed to bolster Simon's confidence as a singer and writer.

On the 1972 #1 "You're So Vain," Simon (with backup singer and lookalike Mick Jagger) lacerates a self-satisfied playboy with a double-edged hook: "You probably think this song is about you, don't you?" The rest of *No Secrets* integrates Simon's tell-all assertiveness with Perry's post-folkie pop craft, while Carly's marriage to James Taylor is celebrated on "The Right Thing to Do." These sources of inspiration soon ran dry, however. *Hotcakes* (home of the squawky duet "Mockingbird") is James and Carly's attempt to open a mom-and-pop record franchise; in this case, the couple that played together didn't stay together. On *Playing Possum,* Perry and Simon's collaboration starts to go sour; the est-disco groove of "Attitude Dancing" comes off as glib and irritating. *Another Passenger* resembles the typical L.A. supersession of the period, but Simon's strengthened voice is more than up to the task of covering the Doobie Brothers ("It Keeps You Runnin' ") and Little Feat ("One Love Stand"). *Boys in the Trees* reemphasizes Simon's own relationship songs and moody set pieces, though "You Belong to Me" (cowritten by Doobie Michael McDonald) projects a pop-soul warmth that's quite unlike her previous work. *Spy* contains a couple of her most incisive lyrics since "You're So Vain" ("Vengeance," "We're So Close"), while "Jesse" (from the otherwise lackluster *Come Upstairs*) reached #11 in 1980. *Torch* (1981) and *My Romance* (1990) find Simon negotiating prerock balladry with surprisingly stiff results. She's better at interpreting her own words.

Simon reached a nadir on *Spoiled Girl,* as too many meddling producers spoiled her always distinctive soup. *Coming Around Again* follows the same multiproducer format, but the songs are better and the production more attuned to the source; it was a platinum comeback, though too polished and commercially calculating to be the major album it wants to be. *Have You Seen Me Lately* was not as "big" a record, but it is deeper. The music moves along at a stately, almost New Age–influenced pace, which suits these meditations on the encroachment of middle age. On "Happy Birthday," Carly Simon commits a grown-up-and-sober anthem that sounds as clear and unsentimental as her warbly, weathered voice. She turns the emotional heat back up with *Letters Never Sent;* then, with the assistance of Jimmy Webb on *Film Noir,* Simon finally finds appropriately relaxed settings for her third stab at an album of standards.

Surprisingly, there is no adequate single-disc collection of her work. *The Best of Carly Simon* came too early in her career, and *Greatest Hits Live,* while an unexpectedly strong concert from one so notoriously stage-shy, is not a substitute for the originals. *Reflections* is the best single-disc overview of her career, the

only one to collect the high points from every stage of her career. The double *Anthology* gets it right, but at an expanded price. The 1995 *Clouds in My Coffee* box set is almost a curio. Its three CDs were organized (by the subject herself) into "The Hits," "Miscellaneous & Unreleased," and "Cry Yourself to Sleep," the last consisting of her favorite album cuts. The second disc is unsurprisingly erratic, and the third reveals some questionable choices by the singer—particularly the excessive number of standards—at the expense of fan favorites like "Waterfall" and "Come Upstairs," making for a set that is personalized but less than definitive. —M.C./B.E.

Paul Simon

★★★★★ Paul Simon (Warner Bros., 1972)
★★★★ There Goes Rhymin' Simon (Warner Bros., 1973)
★★★★★ Still Crazy After All These Years (Warner Bros., 1975)
★★★★★ Greatest Hits, Etc. (Warner Bros., 1977)
★★ One Trick Pony (Warner Bros., 1980)
★★★★ Hearts and Bones (Warner Bros., 1983)
★★★★★ Graceland (Warner Bros., 1986)
★★ The Rhythm of the Saints (Warner Bros., 1990)
★★★ Paul Simon's Concert In The Park (Warner Bros., 1991)
★ Songs From the Capeman (Warner Bros., 1997)
★★ You're the One (Warner Bros., 2000)
★★★★ The Paul Simon Collection: On My Way, Don't Know Where I'm Goin' (Warner Bros., 2002)
★★★★ The Studio Recordings (Warner Bros., 2004)

When Simon and Garfunkel broke up in 1970, the custody battle was simple. Art Garfunkel got the voice, the hair, and the honor of starring in Sherilyn Fenn's finest film, *Boxing Helena.* Paul Simon got the songs. He is America's favorite poet of New York alienation, dabbling stylistically in a variety of Third World and Tin Pan Alley genres. He can write brilliant songs in his snide mode ("Me and Julio Down by the Schoolyard") or his sad mode ("Slip Slidin' Away") and enjoy massive success either way. When Simon's off his game, his fussy approach can sound belabored and self-defeating—he's never developed a signature beat of his own. But when he's on—*Paul Simon, Still Crazy After All These Years, Graceland*—he's an inspired wit, doing for Manhattan what Steely Dan did for L.A.

His '70s masterworks still stand out in his career like Phil Rizzuto's 1950 MVP season. The first remains the best: *Paul Simon* is a blast of city-kid humor and Latin-inflected acoustic grooving, with classics like "Run That Body Down," "Papa Hobo," and "Armistice Day." Simon cuts back on the flowery poesy of his early work, stripping the songs down to make room for his nimble doo-wop voice and guitar. "Mother and Child Reunion" mourns the death of the '60s with a reggae rhythm section recorded in Kingston, Jamaica. "Me and Julio Down by the Schoolyard" has to be the funniest Catholic-guilt song ever written by a Jewish guy—Simon stumbles into a sordid sexual awakening, boogies to Airto Moreira's percussion, and knocks off a world-class whistling solo. Simon would go on to have bigger hits, even get splashier reviews, but he's never made another album with the punch of *Paul Simon*.

Simon had more success with the sequel *There Goes Rhymin' Simon*, featuring the bouncy pop hits "Kodachrome" and "Loves Me Like a Rock." On *Still Crazy After All These Years*, his second-best album, he's a gloomy poet with a weakness for fluffy keyboards, but he atones for all the electric-piano schlock with his funniest, nastiest urban romances, especially "You're Kind," "Have a Good Time," and "50 Ways To Leave Your Lover." Best line: "You're so good/You introduced me to your neighborhood." Around this time he also appeared in *Annie Hall*, reportedly because Woody Allen wanted to lose the girl to a shorter guy.

Simon floundered for a few years, releasing only the clock-watching soundtrack to his film *One Trick Pony*. But he found his feet on *Hearts and Bones*, inspired by his brief show-biz marriage to Carrie Fisher. Ignored at the time, forgotten now, it's a hidden gem. It also introduced the tart songwriting style that paid off on *Graceland*, his big 1986 comeback. Simon traveled to Johannesburg to collaborate with South African mbaqanga musicans, resulting in one of the '80s most acclaimed hits, not to mention the first Paul Simon album where anybody noticed the basslines. As a songwriter, he got back in touch with his sarcastic side in "I Know What I Know." He also displayed his sappy side in "Homeless" and "Under African Skies," a horrendous duet with Linda Ronstadt. Simon failed to address apartheid in any significant way, but he did sing about making the scene at Hollywood parties. This guy gets invited to parties?

The Rhythm of the Saints tried to redo *Graceland*, except with Brazilian drummers and weak songs. Since then, he's only revisited the studio for minor efforts like *Songs from the Capeman* (a failed rehab job on his flop Broadway musical *The Capeman*) and *You're the One*. His 1979 collection *Greatest Hits, Etc.* is long out of print, sad to say, and *The Paul Simon Collection* is an inferior substitute that emphasizes his softer side. *Live Rhymin'* was a stiff 1974 concert LP; *Concert in the Park* remakes his most famous songs

with busy new arrangements, though Garfunkel doesn't show up. *The Paul Simon Songbook* was a U.K.-only 1965 folk one-off, and doesn't really count except as a Simon and Garfunkel footnote. *The Studio Recordings* is a box that augments each of Simon's individual studio albums with bonus tracks, mostly demos and work tapes—Simon has never been prolific enough to leave finished songs off his albums. But the rarities are prime, especially the 1971 demo of "Me and Julio," featuring an alternate third verse, and the gorgeous "Let Me Live in Your City."   —R.S.

Simon and Garfunkel

★★	Wednesday Morning, 3 A.M. (1964; Columbia, 2001)
★★★	Sounds of Silence (1966; Columbia, 2001)
★★★★	Parsley, Sage, Rosemary and Thyme (1966; Columbia, 2001)
★★★½	The Graduate (Columbia, 1968)
★★★½	Bookends (1968; Columbia, 2001)
★★★★★	Bridge Over Troubled Water (Columbia, 1970)
★★★★★	Greatest Hits (Columbia, 1972)
★★★★½	Collected Works (Columbia, 1981)
★★★	The Concert in Central Park (Warner Bros., 1982)
★★★★	Old Friends (Legacy, 1997)
★★★★½	The Best of Simon and Garfunkel (Legacy, 1999)
★★★½	The Columbia Studio Recordings 1964–1970 (Legacy, 2001)
★★★½	Live from New York City 1967 (Legacy, 2002)
★★★★★	The Essential Simon and Garfunkel (Legacy, 2003)

Although Simon and Garfunkel made their name as America's most accessible folk act, in truth the duo's success represented something altogether different— acoustic pop's transition from the sing-along simplicity of folk music to the commercially savvy craft of the singer/songwriters. Ironically, it was a role the duo fell into almost by accident, having split up after releasing a fairly conventional folk album entitled *Wednesday Morning, 3 A.M.* But "The Sounds of Silence" became a massive hit after producer Tom Wilson dubbed electric guitar and drums onto that album's acoustic arrangement, and they reunited to record an album of similarly flavored folk rock. In addition to the revamped version of its title tune, *Sounds of Silence* also includes "Richard Cory" and "I Am a Rock," but for the most part, the album downplays its pop ambitions, sticking close to understated guitar-and-voice arrangements.

With *Parsley, Sage, Rosemary and Thyme*, the

duo's break with folkie convention becomes more pronounced. Although the album-opening "Scarborough Fair/Canticle" maintains Simon and Garfunkel's attachment to tradition, the music's point of reference shifts from the coffeehouse to the drawing room, as Simon's songwriting moves toward the increasingly personal perspective of songs such as "The Dangling Conversation" and "For Emily, Whenever I May Find Her." Of course, as the Dylan-savaging "A Simple Desultory Philippic" makes plain, there's a world of difference between the personal and the solipsistic, and Simon's buoyant sense of melody ensures that these songs are pop-friendly; indeed, "Homeward Bound" was a Top 5 single. *Bookends* continues that progression, with a wider range of songs and even more ambitious arrangements than its predecessor. Yet its strength has less to do with the uncluttered appeal of songs such as "Mrs. Robinson" or "A Hazy Shade of Winter" than the way the duo managed to make the rambling melodies of "Fakin' It" and "America" seem just as straightforward.

From there, it's an easy leap past the soundtrack album from *The Graduate* (which merely reiterated tracks from *Sounds of Silence, Bookends,* and *Parsley, Sage, Rosemary and Thyme*) to *Bridge Over Troubled Water,* the pair's final and most successful studio album. A stunning piece of pop craft, it finds hooks in the most unlikely places—the Peruvian folk tune that was the basis for "El Condor Pasa," say, or the way Garfunkel's angelic tenor contrasts with the gospel piano of "Bridge Over Troubled Water," or the bass-harmonica groove that fires up the last verse of "The Boxer"—and remains one of the most irresistibly tuneful albums of its day. It, along with all of *Bookends, Parsley, Sage, Rosemary and Thyme, Sounds of Silence,* and *Wednesday Morning, 3 A.M.,* is included in the set *Collected Works.*

Simon and Garfunkel never cut another album's worth of new material, but they did record together after *Bridge Over Troubled Water.* Unfortunately, their first postbreakup hit, "My Little Town," is not included on Simon and Garfunkel's *Greatest Hits,* but can be found on Simon's *Still Crazy After All These Years* and Garfunkel's *Breakaway.* "Wake Up Little Susie" is one of the few nonnostalgic moments on *The Concert in Central Park,* which documents Simon and Garfunkel's 1981 reunion show. —J.D.C.

Nina Simone

★★★ Little Girl Blue (1957; Bethlehem, 1993)
★★★½ The Best of the Colpix Years (1959; Blue Note, 1993)
★★★½ Nina at the Village Gate (1961; Blue Note, 1991)

★★★½ Nina Simone at the Village Gate (1962; Collectables, 1993)
★★★½ The Best of Nina Simone (PolyGram, 1962)
★★ Nina's Choice (1963; Collectables, 1999)
★★★ Pastel Blues/Let It All Hang Out (Mercury, 1964)
★★★ Wild Is the Wind/High Priestess of Soul (1964; Mercury, 1990)
★★★★ Verve Jazz Masters 58: Nina Sings Nina (PolyGram, 1964)
★★★ The Ultimate Nina Simone (Verve, 1964)
★★★★ Verve Jazz Masters 17 (Verve, 1964)
★★★★ The Blues (1966; Novus, 1991)
★★★ The Essential Nina Simone (RCA, 1967)
★★★ The Essential Nina Simone, Vol. 2 (RCA, 1967)
★★★ Nina Simone and Piano! (1970; RCA, 2001)
★★★ The Best of Nina Simone (Jive/Novus, 1970)
★★½ Baltimore (1978; CTI, 1995)
★★ Nina Simone 1980 (Just a Memory, 1980)
★★★ Live at Ronnie Scott's (DRG, 1984)
★★★½ Let It Be Me (Verve, 1987)
★★★½ Don't Let Me Be Misunderstood (Verve, 1989)
★★★ In Concert/I Put a Spell on You (Mercury, 1991)
★★★ Compact Jazz: Nina Simone (Verve, 1991)
★★★½ A Single Woman (Elektra/Asylum, 1993)
★★★ Tomato Collection (Tomato, 1994)
★★ Something to Live For (Drive, 1995)
★★★ After Hours (Verve, 1995)
★★★ In Concert (Remember, 1996)
★★★★ Anthology: The Colpix Years (Rhino, 1996)
★★ Private Collection (Music Deluxe, 1997)
★★★ Saga of the Good Life and Hard Times (RCA, 1997)
★★ The Great Nina Simone (Music Club, 1998)
★★★ The Very Best of Nina Simone (RCA, 1998)
★★★ Forbidden Fruit/Nina Simone at Newport (Collectables, 1998)
★★★ Folksy Nina/Nina with Strings (Collectables, 1998)
★★★½ At Newport, the Village Gate and Elsewhere (WestSide, 1999)
★★★ The Amazing Nina Simone/Nina Simone at Town Hall (Collectables, 1999)
★★ Quiet Now: Night Song (PolyGram, 2000)
★★★ Forbidden Fruit/Nina Simone Sings (WestSide, 2000)
★★★ The Legend at Her Best (Collectables, 2000)
★★ Nina: The Essential Nina Simone (Metro Music, 2000)
★★★ Sings Duke Ellington/At Carnegie Hall (Collectables, 2000)
★★ Nina Simone's Finest Hour (PolyGram, 2000)
★★ Platinum Series (D-3, 2000)

★★ Bittersweet: The Very Best of Nina Simone (7-N, 2000)
★★★ Misunderstood (Recall, 2000)
★★ Nina Simone (DJ Specialist, 2001)
★★★ Live and Kickin': In New York and London (Meteor, 2001)
★★★ Touching and Caring (Prestige Elite, 2002)
★★ My Baby Just Cares for Me (303 Recordings, 2002)

Dubbed "the High Priestess of Soul," Nina Simone isn't so much an R&B singer as a highly artful interpreter of all kinds of music—jazz, traditional ballads, African songs, folk, and pop. A skillful, understated pianist, she's also an inventive arranger; virtually all of her covers transform the original songs into music more elegant, leaner, more haunting. Her mid-'60s hits ("I Put a Spell on You," "Don't Let Me Be Misunderstood") established her as a vocalist of unmistakable, idiosyncratic power; she also developed a powerhouse, somewhat thorny persona, highly political and militantly self-confident. Both on keyboard and at the mike, she swings with a nearly austere finesse—her trademark is authority.

Rhino's anthology of her work on Colpix collects the best of her early work; she primarily concentrated on jazz standards. Virtually always a riveting live performer, she's represented well by Roulette's *At the Village Gate* and Verve's *Let It Be Me*, a strong later set. Both *Verve Jazz Masters 58* and *17* are excellent, generous, career-spanning collections; the Tomato set, too, is fairly comprehensive. The best intro to her work, though, is probably Novus's *The Blues*: with such ace musicians as drummer Bernard Purdie and guitarist Eric Gale, she takes on Dylan's "I Shall Be Released" and Hoyt Axton's "The Pusher," sets Langston Hughes' "Backlash Blues" to music, and, accompanied only by herself on piano, delivers one of the strongest of her own compositions, "Nobody's Fault but Mine." Nothing Simone ever did lacked class, however, so all her albums are worth checking out. Especially noteworthy are the twofer sets, reissued by Collectables, which repackage her classic '60s albums. *A Single Woman* is Nina in her mature prime, a comeback of sorts; *After Hours* is the best of Simone's jazz ballads. —P.E.

Jessica Simpson

★½ Sweet Kisses (Sony, 1999)
★ Irresistible (Sony, 2001)
★★ In This Skin (Sony, 2004)

A terrifying creature of marketing, Simpson was originally presented as a demure, secular-Christian variation on Sony Music's successful pop-diva model: a virgin Mariah Carey. But as a singer, Simpson is no Carey: Her voice is pretty but nondescript (every groan sounds like it was focus-grouped), and the bombastic production of *Sweet Kisses* doesn't mask the anonymous blandness of the songs. Only "I Think I'm in Love With You" has any juice at all, thanks to a riff borrowed from John Mellencamp's "Jack and Diane."

Improbably, *Irresistible* (its packaging includes an ad for hair-care products) is even worse. The dominant mode this time is post–Spears/Aguilera teeny-pop, with touches of Destiny's Child–style R&B; the songs appear to have been written (and performed) by entering those parameters into a computer, then filtering out every hook. The result is wholly generic, adding nothing to the genres. —D.W.

Frank Sinatra

Selected Discography

★★★★ In the Wee Small Hours (Capitol, 1954)
★★★★½ Songs for Swingin' Lovers (Capitol, 1955)
★★★★½ A Swingin' Affair (Capitol, 1957)
★★★★ Only the Lonely (Capitol, 1958)
★★★½ Nice 'N Easy (Capitol, 1960)
★★★★ Sinatra-Basie (Reprise, 1962)
★★★★ September of My Years (Reprise, 1965)
★★★★ Sinatra at the Sands With Count Basie (Reprise, 1966)
★★★ Strangers in the Night (Reprise, 1966)
★★★★★ Francis Albert Sinatra & Antonio Carlos Jobim (Reprise, 1967)
★★½ Ol' Blue Eyes Is Back (Reprise, 1973)
★★½ Trilogy (Reprise, 1980)
★★ L.A. Is My Lady (Reprise, 1984)
★★★★★ The Capitol Years (Capitol, 1990)
★★★★★ The Reprise Collection (Reprise, 1990)
★★ Duets (Capitol, 1993)
★★★ The Voice: The Columbia Years 1943–1952 (Columbia, 1999)

Frank Sinatra was the singer's singer and the swinger's swinger—a titanic figure who brought the suave phrasing of the big-band era into modern popular music and taught generations of singers the value of poise and cool. And although his womanizing, hard-partying, Rat Pack–leading ways contributed to what is now a towering legend, his influence on contemporary pop is far greater than many might realize: One of the first artists to helm his own label (Reprise), Sinatra is the father of the modern-day "concept" album and was the first star to create a synergized career between recording, live performance, and film.

The best way to appreciate Sinatra is to view his evolution in four parts: the early Columbia years, which include the surprisingly durable sides he cut with Tommy Dorsey; the Capitol heyday; the thematic (and schmaltzy) recordings on Reprise; and the resting-on-laurels later years, typified by the dismal *Duets*.

Columbia did a good job with Sinatra's work there—almost everything of consequence, including several Dorsey gems, turns up on the *Columbia Years* set, which has been carefully remastered.

At Capitol, Sinatra blossomed from band singer into full-fledged star; here, he figured out how to use his mellow baritone in velvet brass or string surroundings and put his own spin on standard songs by Cole Porter, George and Ira Gershwin, and others. *In the Wee Small Hours* is the first fully great album, and it's followed by a string of classics that should be required listening for anyone who cares about singing. Working with several great arrangers including Nelson Riddle and Billy May, Sinatra suggested both general atmosphere and specific counterlines in the studio, and he delivered his lines in ways that made the arrangements of "Night and Day" (from *A Swingin' Affair*) and "What's New?" (from the tremendous ballad collection *Only the Lonely*) sparkle. Coy and casual, his singing of this era is romantic longing cut with a splash of glib cool, and whether the backing was a studio orchestra or the Count Basie Band (as on the fiery *Sinatra at the Sands With Count Basie*), Sinatra made each song sound like another clue to the mysteries of his heart.

After setting up Reprise in 1961 (he sold it in '63), Sinatra entered his most ambitious recording period, characterized by unusual collaborations (one, with Duke Ellington, *Francis A. and Edward K.*, was a great idea that didn't quite click), overt schmaltz (1966's *Strangers in the Night* sets off a wave of parodic shooby-doo scat singing), and everything in between. Among the most impressive titles is his 1967 summit meeting with Brazilian composer Antonio Carlos Jobim; by this time, many U.S. singers had interpreted bossa nova, but none had captured the wistfulness and precarious vulnerability that Sinatra attained here.

After a brief retirement in the early '70s, Sinatra returned with a triumphant 1973 TV special *Ol' Blue Eyes Is Back,* a corresponding album, and several concert tours. He had less success in the studio, though 1980's *Trilogy* contains his biggest chart hit in years, "New York, New York." The Quincy Jones–produced *L.A. Is My Lady* attempted to bring coastal parity to Sinatra's city-song catalogue, and although the track was a dud, the album includes a surprisingly swinging version of "Mack the Knife."

Sinatra was in full artistic twilight when he enlisted contemporary pop stars Bono, Gloria Estefan, and others to join him for *Duets;* most recorded their contributions seperately from the reclusive Sinatra, and as a result, even the pleasant moments feel forced.   —P.E.

Siouxsie and the Banshees

★★★★ The Scream (1978; Geffen, 1990)
★★½ Join Hands (1979; Universal, 2003)
★★★ Kaleidoscope (1980; Geffen, 1992)
★★★ Juju (1981; Geffen, 1992)
★★★★ Once Upon a Time/The Singles (1981; Geffen, 1990)
★★★ Nocturne (Geffen, 1983)
★★★ Hyaena (Geffen, 1984)
★★★½ Tinderbox (Geffen, 1986)
★★½ Through the Looking Glass (Geffen, 1987)
★★½ Peepshow (Geffen, 1988)
★★★ Superstition (Geffen, 1991)
★★★½ The Best of Siouxsie and the Banshees (Interscope, 2002)
★★★★ The Seven Year Itch (Sanctuary, 2003)

Along with Billy Idol and Sid Vicious, Siouxsie Sioux (formerly Susan Dallion) first gained notoriety as a highly visible and vociferous early Sex Pistols fan. She started her own band in short order; Siouxsie and the Banshees' debut performance in late '76 consisted of one number, an epic desecration of the Lord's Prayer. Cohering around bassist Steve Severin, guitarist John McKay, and drummer Kenny Morris, the Banshees later forged a unique, introspective strain of punk rock. Even if you can't figure out exactly what makes Siouxsie wail the way she does, *The Scream* creates a rich, claustrophobic maelstrom of crude sound and half-submerged feelings. Though Siouxsie & Co. never quote the '60s directly, their debut draws a vital connection between punk and psychedelia. The Cure and the Psychedelic Furs—just for starters—were directly inspired by *The Scream*. Bless her or blame her, Siouxsie is the Godmother of Mope.

The atypical single "Hong Kong Garden," a British hit in 1978, evinces the Banshees' flair for melody and hooky exotica. *Join Hands,* however, indicates just how easily the brooding trance music can slip into dankness. Substituting guitarist John McGeoch and drummer Budgie for the departed McKay and Morris, *Kaleidoscope* and *Juju* refine the Banshees' attack, diversifying the sound without losing its swirling impact. *Once Upon a Time* neatly documents the group's development; at its catchiest and most direct, Siouxsie's stylized Gothic weirdness is surprisingly inviting.

Robert Smith of the Cure had jumped on board

for a spell during the tour documented on *Nocturne*. His surprisingly disciplined influence can be felt on *Hyaena's* best cuts: the liquid-mercury "Dazzle," the sparse "Swimming Horses," and a lushly appointed cover of the Beatles' "Dear Prudence." But *Tinderbox*, recorded with a virtual Smith clone named John Valentine Carruthers on guitar, is just as good. "Cities in Dust" sports a knockout chorus and Siouxsie's most confident vocals to date. If she's not exactly warm, well, she certainly sounds inflamed about something.

Through the Looking Glass presents overpolished covers of the group's obvious influences: Roxy Music, Bowie-era Iggy Pop, Television. *Peepshow* integrates synthesizers and a lighter pop touch with the Banshees' trademark howl, but it lacks spark. The similarly inclined *Superstition* has the advantage of a great single; "Kiss Them for Me" weaves a bewitching electronic stitch through Siouxsie's familiar cloth.

In the '90s, Siouxsie and Budgie's growing preoccupation with their side project, the Creatures, spelled doom for the Banshees. Their 1995 album, *Rapture*, is a lackluster affair now mercifully out of print. *The Best of* is decent but far from complete; you'd be better off tracking down *Once Upon a Time* and its out-of-print 1992 sequel, *Twice Upon a Time*. Recorded during the Banshees' 2002 reunion tour, seven years after their breakup (thus the title), *The Seven Year Itch* focuses on material from the band's first three albums. It's a vibrant reminder of the power of goth. —M.C./M.R.

Sir Mix-a-Lot

★★½ Swass (Nastymix, 1988)
★★★ Seminar (Nastymix, 1989)
★★★½ Mack Daddy (Def American, 1992)

Sir Mix-a-Lot may hail from Seattle, but *Swass* is pure Miami—it has the same singsong raps and thumping 808 grooves as Miami Bass acts such as 2 Live Crew and Gucci Crew. That was the sound that gave him his first hit, "Posse on Broadway," but it was the metal-rap fusion of "Iron Man" (recorded with Seattle thrash legends Metal Church) that set him apart from the pack. Even so, Mix-a-Lot's music doesn't really mature until *Seminar*, which not only upgrades his musical approach—check the Prince "Batdance" sample that flavors "Beepers"—but also adds an angry political edge to his material, as "National Anthem" makes plain. Mix-a-Lot continues to grow with *Mack Daddy*, grounding his aggressive delivery with deeply funky rhythm beds such as the clavinet-driven loop beneath "One Time's Got No Cause." Yet as hard as these rhymes are, Mix-a-Lot avoids most gangsta-rap clichés and relies more on humor (as in "Swap

Meet Louie" and the big-butt tribute "Baby Got Back") than on violence. —J.D.C.

Skatalites

★★★ Scattered Lights (Alligator, 1984)
★★★★ Stretching Out (ROIR, 1986)
★★★½ Hi Bop Ska (Shanachie, 1994)
★★★ Greetings From Skamania (Shanachie, 1996)
★★★ Ska Voovee (Shanachie, 1993)
★★★ Ball of Fire (Island, 1998)
★★★★ Foundation Ska (Heartbeat, 1996)
★★★ Musical Communion (Culture Press, 1999)
★★★ Ska Boo-Da-Ba: Top Sounds From Top-Deck, Vol. 3 (Westside, 1998)
★★★ Nucleus of Ska (Music Club, 2001)

Before reggae came ska—relentlessly upbeat syncopated Jamaican dance fare. In the early '60s, the Skatalites were the music's masters, incredibly assured instrumentalists who, over an endless, pumping beat, wailed wildly melodic jazz riffs. Two tenor saxophonists, Tommy McCook and Roland Alphonso, were the band's twin powers, engaged in happy, honking wars. Thirty-five cuts of the band's choicest '60s material—the Skatalites at their sharpest, rawest height—*Foundation Ska* is by far the best collection. *Scattered Lights* is a strong 1984 studio set, and *Stretching Out* is a tuneful marvel: 90 minutes of a live reunion, it captures the fire of the band's nine players (and three guest horns) as they blaze through "Confucius," "Lee Harvey Oswald," "Fidel Castro," and 14 other ska delights. *Greetings From Skamania* features tasty instrumentals, and *Hi Bop Ska* is intriguing: a '90s version of the group playing off the sax work of avant-garde maestro Lester Bowie. *Ball of Fire* finds latter-day Skatalites reworking and jamming on the outfit's early work. —P.E.

Slayer

★★★ Show No Mercy (Metal Blade, 1983)
★★★ Haunting the Chapel (Metal Blade, 1984)
★★ Live Undead (Metal Blade, 1985)
★★★★ Hell Awaits (Metal Blade, 1985)
★★★★½ Reign in Blood (Def Jam, 1986)
★★★★ South of Heaven (Def Jam, 1988)
★★★½ Seasons in the Abyss (Def American, 1990)
★★★ Live: Decade of Aggression (Def American, 1991)
★★½ Divine Intervention (American, 1994)
★★ Undisputed Attitude (American, 1996)
★★ Diabolus in Musica (American/Columbia, 1998)
★★★ God Hates Us All (American, 2001)
★★★★ Soundtrack to the Apocalypse (American, 2003)

Though they remain growling idols to the metallic millions who knew Kiss was more into money and makeup than Satan and suffering, Slayer's relentless, cryptic slaughter hasn't really changed all that much in the 20 years since they established themselves as one of the most important metal bands of all time. But having accidentally set the bar impossibly high after irrevocably changing the direction of metal and hard rock, Slayer has spent nearly 15 years trying to figure out exactly what to do next.

Blending crass, apocalyptic lyrical images (Satan, the Holocaust, Lucifer, human decomposition, Satan, insanity, man's inhumanity to Satan, you get the idea) with hardcore tempos, singer/bassist Tom Araya's bleat, and faster, tougher versions of the twin lead-guitar flameouts Iron Maiden and Judas Priest made famous, Slayer's blood-boiling sound became the brutal touchstone for, let's see, death metal, speed metal, grindcore, black metal . . . pretty much any metal subgenre that came along after punk rock.

Show No Mercy and *Haunting the Chapel* are early exercises in figuring out how to piss off as many parents as possible. *Mercy* is mostly power metal played fast and loose, complete with leather armor and makeup, while the latter contains a few choice moments (the neck-snapping "Chemical Warfare" is a classic) while they get up to full speed. *Live Undead* gives you an idea of what those early shows were like.

Hell Awaits is the first sign that with warp-speed velocity came a fundamentally different (read: more violent, more chaotic, more MORE) kind of metal. "Kill Again" and "In Praise of Death" are pure rock fury, while the title track is almost prog in its complexity. A wonderfully nasty piece of work.

While *Hell Awaits* has aged quite well with the rise of such chaotic, no-fi subgenres as black metal and grindcore, it's *Reign in Blood* that was the breakthrough and remains the classic. Produced and reduced by Rick Rubin, he honed their sound to a diamond-tipped, impossibly heavy bullet, the soundtrack to a million skater wipeouts. Killers such as "Criminally Insane" and "Angel of Death" (hello, Josef Mengele!) whip by, but not before turning your stomach. Old fans were thrilled, and punks who avoided metal couldn't deny this thing's sheer rage and velocity. Articulate, rude, and, once again, really, really fucking fast, *Reign in Blood* was a watershed moment for speed metal, its fans, and the parents who were scared of both.

Having refined themselves to a laserlike focus, *South of Heaven* introduced tempo shifts that didn't dim the band's considerable power, while *Seasons in the Abyss* continued the band's relentless will to power by displaying everything in the skill set, from blinding speed to complex riffs to mid-tempo heft. Moving away from fantasy and into the hells here on earth ("War Ensemble," "Hallowed Point"), this is music to conquer nations by (or at least play while you mow the lawn). Hey, we're now up to four straight albums that cast as long a shadow as Satan would allow over the metal underground, in spite of steadily becoming a gold-selling act.

The live, exhausting *Decade of Aggression* double album was released one month after Nirvana's *Nevermind,* and suddenly punk angst began to outsell metal's cruelty. Rage suddenly had a more melodic sound, and Slayer, still a big seller, was neither the cultural force of grunge nor the stadium-filling rock of their one-time peers Metallica. *Divine Intervention* stays the course, which is worthy of admiration, but it still sounds like the sound of no new ideas. *Undisputed Attitude* is a here's-our-hardcore-influences covers album, ranging from Minor Threat ("Filler/I Don't Wanna Hear It" good; "Guilty of Being White" moronic) to D.R.I. and more. Interesting to fans, historians of punk/metal interface, and pretty much nobody else. *Diabolus in Musica* moves further toward, if not orthodox hardcore, then a simpler metal that tries to find new music in old riffs. It feels like more of the same, as does *God Hates Us All,* which feels like simply being savage for its own sake. Fans who think they're as good now as they've ever been, as well as old-school devotees, will love *Soundtrack to the Apocalypse,* four CDs of album cuts, demos, rarities, and live insanity. Taken in toto, it's clear that Slayer prides itself on not budging an inch, nor caving to popular, new-metal taste, nor really giving much of a fuck about anyone but themselves, and this is to be admired—which is different from giving them your money.   —J.G.

Sleater-Kinney

★★★	Sleater-Kinney (Chainsaw, 1995)
★★★★★	Call the Doctor (Chainsaw, 1996)
★★★★	Dig Me Out (Kill Rock Stars, 1997)
★★★	The Hot Rock (Kill Rock Stars, 1999)
★★★	All Hands on the Bad One (Kill Rock Stars, 2000)
★★★★	One Beat (Kill Rock Stars, 2002)

Almost from the moment Sleater-Kinney struck its first chord, in 1994, the punk trio has delivered one of the most arresting sounds in rock: a hailstorm of chiming, percussive guitars and keening harmonies that deliver polemics both personal and political. The trios' best music is fired by righteous outrage—at a desiccated rock scene, at sexism, at suffocating social conformity. But unlike many of its indie-rock peers of the '90s, Sleater-Kinney has grown with time and its vocabulary of outrage has grown with the band.

Inspired by the burgeoning riot-grrrl movement, fronted by bands like Bikini Kill, singer/guitarists Corin Tucker and Carrie Brownstein formed Sleater-Kinney in Olympia, WA, in 1994. With Australian-born Lora McFarlane on drums, they released their bass-free, self-titled debut album a year later on Team Dresch honcho Donna Dresch's Chainsaw label. *Sleater-Kinney*—like the band, named for an Olympia street—earned critical plaudits for what would soon become the band's stylistic signature of symbiotic guitar chords grounded by punk-simple drums and Tucker's operatic vibrato.

Dropped into the middle of grunge's downward spiral, *Call the Doctor* offered a new manifesto for alterna-kids foundering in the post-Nirvana backwash. Mixing fury and chants as anthemic as football slogans, the album's 12 tracks crackled with some of the most heart-wrenching female-fronted punk rock since Poly Styrene of X-Ray Spex. "I'm Not Waiting" eloquently voiced teen longing by alternately blowing loud as a tantrum and as soft as a sob; the title track opened the CD with a primal guitar bellow. The effect was compelling and irresistible. By the time Tucker wailed, "I'm the queen of rock & roll" on the album's finest track, "I Wanna Be Your Joey Ramone," few were inclined to argue.

Sleater-Kinney quickly became the band of choice for latent riot grrrls and precious hipsters jonesing for punk mythos. Rap rock ruled the charts in 1997, but Sleater-Kinney topped critics' polls. *Dig Me Out* marked the band's switch to Olympia's Kill Rock Stars label and the debut of drummer Janet Weiss, while also signaling a shift from purist punk to melodic complexity. Catchy without sacrificing an inch of fury, songs such as "Not What You Want," "One More Hour," and "Dance Song 97" redefined Sleater-Kinney as a power trio whose chops transcended gender and genre issues.

Although the euphoric rock of *Dig Me Out* won praise, it also drew criticism from hard-core fans who deplored its pop overtures. Perhaps in response, Sleater-Kinney delved into more oblique sounds on 1999's *The Hot Rock*. Brownstein's guitar abandoned power chords to slither in abstract patterns, backed by Weiss' increasingly subtle and complex drumming. Tucker expanded her vocal range, steering from bellow to fragile ululations in songs like "Don't Talk Like That." "The End of You" played with disjunctive vocal duets, and "Get Up" marked a foray into spoken word reminiscent of early Sonic Youth.

In 2000, *All Hands on the Bad One* both embraced more accessible rock and created pastiches of it, blowing a raspberry at pundits who dismissed *The Hot Rock* as too cacophonous. As the most playful album of the band's career, it still inserted a few barbs into the cotton candy: "I could be demure like girls who are soft for boys who are fearful of getting an earful," declared Tucker on the soaring "Ballad of a Ladyman," "But I gotta rock!" After a two-year hiatus, in which Tucker had a baby and Sleater-Kinney was declared America's Best Rock Band by *Time* magazine, the trio returned with its sixth and most ambitious album, *One Beat*. Its riotous manifesto remained, but the musical dialect had expanded to include blues, soul, and even traces of vintage metal. Instruments such as theremin and organ fleshed out the trio's two-guitar-and-drums minimalism. A tinge of Jimmy Page ran through Brownstein's wailing guitar lines, and Tucker continued to stretch her formidable voice beyond her signature punk wails, incorporating '60s soul with a power-to-the-people delivery. Whether whupping their axes or singing the blues, Sleater-Kinney have consistently proved that punk spirit is more than banging out three chords—it means pushing rock to the boiling point. —N.CH.

Percy Sledge

★★★	The Best of Percy Sledge (Atlantic, 1969)
★★	I'll Be Your Everything (Capricorn, 1974)
★★	Percy! (Monument, 1983)
★★★★	The Ultimate Collection, Percy Sledge: When a Man Loves a Woman (Atlantic, 1987)
★★★½	It Tears Me Up: The Best of Percy Sledge (Rhino/Atlantic, 1992)
★★★	Star Power: Percy Sledge (Direct Source, 2001)
★★★	The Soulful Sound of Percy Sledge (Prism, 2001)
★★	A Collection of 20 Hits (Double Play, 2002)
★★	Warm and Tender (Brentwood, 2002)
★★	The Essentials (Warner Bros., 2002)

Spooner Oldham's haunting Farfisa organ sets the mood, the Muscle Shoals rhythm section kicks in, Percy wails, and the song climaxes with a great horn-section ostinato—released in 1966, "When a Man Loves a Woman" is one of the great soul ballads, its message of sacrifice and surrender remaining timelessly romantic. Coarse-voiced and absolutely passionate, Sledge hadn't the endurance or distinctiveness to be one of R&B's premier figures, but he's one of the most heartfelt—his delivery is rich in its equal capacity for transcendence and sheer physical force. "When a Man Loves a Woman" is clearly the standout, but any number of Sledge's songs hit with devastating force. Working with great Southern songwriters like Dan Penn and Eddie Hinton, Sledge is best when he wails about suffering, as on "Dark End of the Street." The 1992 anthology *It Tears Me Up* is a wonderful summation of Sledge's career highlights, including material recorded from 1966 to 1971. *Warm and Tender* covers the '70s fare.   —P.E.

Grace Slick

★★½	Grace Slick & the Great Society Collector's Item (1971; Columbia, 1990)
★★★	The Best of Grace Slick (RCA, 1999)
★★	The Best of Grace Slick (BMG Special Products, 2000)

Along with the recorded output of Hot Tuna, Jorma Kaukonen, Marty Balin, and Jefferson Starship, Grace Slick's four solo albums (now out of print) prove that the greatness of Jefferson Airplane was a matter of synergy—together, its members sparked great collisions of creativity; on their own, they touch off merely a slight bang.

Sadly, solo Slick isn't well represented in compilations. The RCA set is marginally better, but it mainly concentrates on her Airplane/Starship years. While chiefly of documentary interest, *Collector's Item* is kind of intriguing, gathering two albums (*Conspicuous Only in Its Absence, How It Was*) of pre-Airplane work with a nondescript crew called the Great Society. The CD features the original versions of "Somebody to Love" (very lame drumming drags it down) and "White Rabbit" (the Society jams for four and a half minutes with an inscrutable woodwind wailing along before Slick finally joins in). More fun is the strange meditation from Rex Reed, reprinted from a 1970 *Stereo Review*. While chuckling your way through Rex's arch, baffled prose, you'll learn that the singer's real name is Grace Wing, and that she's nuts about *Peer Gynt*, Irving Berlin, and Miles Davis' *Sketches of Spain*.   —P.E.

Slick Rick

★★★★	The Great Adventures of Slick Rick (Def Jam/CBS, 1988)
★★★½	The Ruler's Back (Def Jam/Sony, 1991)
★★	Behind Bars (Def Jam, 1994)
★★★★	The Art of Storytelling (Def Jam, 1999)

Having made his name as the English-accented rapper on Doug E. Fresh & the Get Fresh Crew's 1985 12-inch, "The Show"/"La-Di-Da-Di," London-born Slick Rick (a.k.a. Ricky Walters) produced one of the most anticipated debut albums of hip-hop's golden age with *The Great Adventures of Slick Rick*. The album has aged surprisingly well, thanks mostly to

Rick's liquid rhymes, though the wiggy trumpet hook of "The Ruler" helps, too. However, songs like "Treat Her Like a Prostitute" helped propagate hip-hop's ugly, know-nothing tradition of misogyny. Soon thereafter, Rick was jailed for six years for attempted murder, and recorded *The Ruler's Back* in three weeks while out on bail. It sounds just about as hurried as you'd expect, but between the jazzy groove and the offhand spin of the raps, it's strangely compelling. "I Shouldn't Have Done It" teases with the promise of autobiographical detail; the song turns out to be a reluctant father's grudging acceptance of responsibility—too little, too late. The tired *Behind Bars*, recorded while on work release three years later, fares far less well. In 1999, however, Rick came back with the excellent *The Art of Storytelling*. Guest appearances from OutKast and Snoop Dogg (who'd covered "La-Di-Da-Di" on his debut *Doggystyle* as "Lodi Dodi") didn't help the album sell any, but *Storytelling*, like De La Soul's later works, showed that you can age in hip-hop without sounding irrelevant.   —M.C./M.M.

Slint

★★½	Tweez (1989; Touch & Go, 1994)
★★½	Spiderland (Touch & Go, 1991)
★★★	Slint EP (Touch & Go, 1994)

During its brief existence, this boldly experimental Louisville, Kentucky, quartet attracted little attention. Its posthumous career, on the other hand, has been an unqualified success. In fact, Slint has arguably become one of the most influential bands of the past decade. Rockcrit types now view the group as an early example of that arty, abstract subgenre "postrock." Too bad the term neither does justice to the unhinged vigor of Slint's music nor explains its inability to make one consistently good record.

Vocalist Brian McMahan's half-mumbled, half-shouted non sequiturs are a mere afterthought on *Tweez;* the main focus is Slint's ensemble playing, which veers wildly from brittle punk riffing (not surprising, since McMahan and drummer Britt Walford were both vets of the hardcore outfit Squirrel Bait) to brooding ambient passages to almost jazzlike improvisation. Jarring dynamic shifts abound, with little heed paid to time signature, tempo, or harmonic conventions. Undeniably original, at times thrilling, *Tweez* also tends to be tough on the ears.

Spiderland is an easier listen, with longer, more developed songs but less energy. The absence of anything resembling a tune continues to nag, and the mood improves when McMahan keeps his mouth shut. Still, "Nosferatu Man" and "Good Morning,

Captain" achieve a twisted grandeur that almost justifies their pretensions.

At this point, Slint broke up. Its members have since gone on to form or join several celebrated '90s acts, including the Breeders, Tortoise, the For Carnation, and Will Oldham's Palace posse. The two untitled instrumental leftovers on the 1994 EP are, oddly enough, the band's best work, astutely balancing invention, aggression, and discipline. Yet from the recorded evidence, it's hard not to conclude that Slint's innovations have been better applied by those who followed them. —M.R.

Slipknot

★★½   Slipknot (Roadrunner, 1999)
★★½   Iowa (Roadrunner, 2001)
★★★★   Vol. 3: The Subliminal Verses (Roadrunner, 2004)

Kiss got the joke. So did Gwar. Slipknot doesn't think it's funny at all. These angry boys from Des Moines, Iowa, wear their Halloween masks with pride and conviction. They are nine mystery men, disguised as clowns, monsters, and supercreeps. Slipknot may be all about cartoon horror, crafting a dark but ultimately safe nightmare metal fantasy, but they're crazy serious about it. Feel their pain on "Surfacing," from the band's self-titled major-label debut, as Corey Taylor screams the Slipknot manifesto: "Fuck it all! Fuck this world! Fuck everything that you stand for!" The uninitiated will find all this deeply disturbing, but it's nothing Slayer and a thousand other speed/death metal bands haven't done since the '80s. Except that there is something undeniably powerful and subversively melodic beneath the noise of Slipknot's gears grinding into your skull.

Slipknot establishes a pattern of cataclysmic riffs and overlapping machine-gun beats, as if your fave metal act collided with a hyperactive high school drum corps. Taylor's guttural shriek is not just a dull roar, but somehow musical, even slipping into an occasional smooth tenor (on "Liberate"), and sounding far more 311 than Cannibal Corpse. Much of the album evokes little more than anger and noise, which has its place on the metal landscape, but it's also easy to come by. High energy and a dizzying, fully realized horror persona are all that make the band worth exploring. *Iowa* may be more cinematic, but it strays little from the formula: livid beats, snarky riff patterns that too often fail to pay off, plus the usual explicit lyrics. There is a fine frenetic twist of electronic and turntable sounds to "Disasterpiece." And the band swings hard on "Left Behind" before Taylor whines about whiners on "I Am Hated" (inspirational message: "Shut up/

Nobody gives a fuck!"). Other than the by-now unavoidable presence of turntables, Slipknot shares little with others in the exhausted new-metal scene. But a little variety in their attack modes wouldn't hurt.

Which only makes the depth of rock horror on *Vol. 3: The Subliminal Verses* an unexpected, impossible feat. Producer Rick Rubin finds the truth in the fantasy, turning a sometime joke band into the second coming of Beelzebub, delivering what Slipknot could only hint at before. The Midwestern cartoon thugs actually sound inspired, daring to slow down on the understated industrial melody of "Prelude 3.0" before erupting with the snarling guitars of "The Blister Exits." Taylor sings not just of hate, but loss, contemplation. It's enough to invite comparisons to the maximum metal of Metallica (although James Hetfield's anger jams are still scarier even without a costume). Which is a kind of miracle. Some heshers are bound to hate it. And Taylor also hinted that the album might be Slipknot's last. *Vol. 3* makes retirement seem a little premature. Send in the clowns. —S.A.

The Slits

★★★★   Cut (Antilles, 1979)
★★★½   In the Beginning (Cleopatra, 1997)

It is one of the great discographical catastrophes of modern times that almost nothing by the Slits is currently in print in America. Fronted by Ariane Forster, a reggae-loving German newspaper heiress who called herself Ari Up (imagine it in a Cockney accent), the initially all-female quartet toured with the Clash and the Sex Pistols in 1977; their early punk screamers and some practice-room doodles are preserved on an alternately great and dreadful (and long-out-of-print) "official bootleg" from 1980, informally known as *Once Upon a Time in a Living Room,* which sounds about 15 years ahead of its time.

Inexplicably, the Slits didn't manage to get a record out until 1979. By that point, drummer Paloma "Palmolive" Romero had defected to the Raincoats, and their verve and ineptitude had given way to the subdued and subtly bizarre dub pulse of *Cut.* It's the handsome, stateless child of punk and reggae, propelled by Forster's chants and trills and by the twitchy inventiveness of Viv Albertine's guitar playing; no other record sounds like it. Still, they saved their best ideas for nonalbum singles—search out, especially, their brilliant cover/mutations of "I Heard It Through the Grapevine" and John Holt's "Man Next Door." Their second and final studio album, *Return of the Giant Slits,* is slicker and much duller.

The uneven live retrospective *In the Beginning* starts with some haphazard tracks from 1977 and ends with a long jam from the Slits' final show, in 1981 (after a young Neneh Cherry had joined the band). It's a fascinating document if you already know the better studio versions of these songs, but it shouldn't be anyone's first Slits record. —D.W.

Sly and Robbie

★★★	Language Barrier (1985; Palm Pictures, 2003)
★★★	Taxi Fare (1986; Heartbeat, 1990)
★★½	The Summit (1988; Ras/Sanctuary, 1990)
★★★	The Many Moods of Sly, Robbie & the Taxi Gang (Sonic Sounds, 1991)
★★★★	Sly & Robbie Hits 1978–1990 (Sonic Sounds, 1991)
★★★	Overdrive in Overdub (Sonic Sounds, 1993)
★★★	Sound of Sound (Pow Wow, 1993)
★★½	Meet King Tubby (House of Reggae, 1997)
★★★	Friends (Elektra, 1998)
★★★½	Drum & Bass Strip to the Bone by Howie B (Palm Pictures, 1999)
★★★½	Hail Up the Taxi, Vol. 2 (Tabou, 1999)
★★★	Massive (NYC Music, 1999)
★★★	Dance Hall Killers (Tabou, 2000)
★★★	Dub Fire (NYC Music, 2000)
★★★	Gold Dubs: Ultimate Reggae Collection (Fine Tune, 2000)
★★★	Reggae Stylee (Recall, 2000)
★★★★	In Good Company: Ultimate Collection (Hip-O, 2001)
★★★	Dub Transmission Specialists: At Prince Jammy's (Varèse, 2002)
★★	Romantic Reggae (Rhythm Club, 2003)
★★★★	Riddim: The Best of Sly and Robbie in Dub 1978–1985 (Sanctuary/Trojan, 2004)
★★★½	Dub Revolutionaries: Sly and Robbie Meet the Mad Professor (Earmark, 2004)
★★★	Unmetered Taxi (Pressure, 2004)

Drummer Sly Dunbar and bassist Robbie Shakespeare were premier Kingston sessionmen who struck up a creative partnership at the tail end of the '70s. At first, they produced and accompanied a broad variety of Jamaican artists, from the politically charged trio Black Uhuru to "lovers' rock" crooners like Gregory Isaacs and Dennis Brown. Laying bare the bedrock bass lines, trimming away the keyboard and guitar excesses, allowing room for cosmic dub effects and ricocheting syndrums: Sly and Robbie brought roots reggae skanking into the '80s. The partners branched off into pop with immediately satisfying results: rehabilitating Grace Jones' credibility with three strong albums, and supplying several tracks for Bob Dylan, among other projects.

Under their own names, Sly and Robbie began releasing singles compilations culled from their Taxi label at home, featuring a host of guest vocalists from Jamaica and beyond. While none of these early albums (including seminal LPs like *Sly and Robbie Present Taxi, Sixties Seventies + Eighties*—both from 1981— and 1984's *A Dub Extravaganza*) are currently available, numerous retrospectives have been released in recent years, of wildly varying quality and packaging. The most definitive and most expertly remastered of these are the single-disc *In Good Company: Ultimate Collection*, which gathers the best of their work as producers, and *Riddim*, two discs' worth of dub. Only die-hard dubbies need to dig deeper into the confusing array of anthologies, and it's prudent to avoid the cheapos on labels you've never heard of.

Sly and Robbie moved toward a more conceptual, ensemble-oriented approach in the '80s, working with avant-garde producer Bill Laswell on *Language Barrier* (1985) and KRS-One from Boogie Down Productions on *Silent Assassin* (1989), but most of these cross-genre experiments failed to gel, and they've slipped out of print without generating any discernible hue and cry. More lamentable is the disappearance of 1987's *Rhythm Killers,* the duo's second hookup with Laswell, which is so coherent and smooth that you could mistake it for a suite if it wasn't also so thoroughly down and dirty. Progressive hip-hopper Shinehead and P-Funkateer Bootsy Collins, among others, all do their respective thangs while riding that impeccable bottom-heavy groove.

Sly and Robbie have continued to crank out records of new material since that time as if their lives and livelihoods depended on it, right up to 2004's *Dub Revolutionaries*, on which they're teamed with second-generation dub master, the Mad Professor. —M.C./B.SC.

Sly and the Family Stone

★★★	A Whole New Thing (Epic, 1967)
★★★½	Dance to the Music (Epic, 1968)
★★★	Life (Epic, 1968)
★★★★★	Stand! (Epic, 1969)
★★★★★	Greatest Hits (Epic, 1970)
★★★★★	There's a Riot Goin' On (Epic, 1971)
★★★★	Fresh (Epic, 1973)
★★★★	Anthology (Epic, 1981)
★★★★★	The Essential Sly & the Family Stone (Epic/Legacy 2002)

"Different strokes for different folks." The tagline of "Everyday People," from *Stand!* sums up both Sly and the Family Stone's musical philosophy and the group's magnetic appeal. Sylvester Stewart, a former San Francisco DJ, forged an ecumenical rock & soul sound on the Family Stone's three earlier, now out-of-print Epic albums: *A Whole New Thing, Life,* and *Dance to the Music.* The latter album's title track, "I Want to Take You Higher" and "Everyday People" (both of which can be found on *Greatest Hits*) got over as hippie anthems and hit singles; an uplifting vibe carried Sly's message to the masses, although he never sugarcoated the counterculture's dark side—quite the opposite. *Stand!* is balanced by "Don't Call Me Nigger, Whitey" and the instrumental throb of the 15-minute "Sex Machine." *Greatest Hits* adds the sweat-dripping "Thank You (Falletinme Be Mice Elf Agin" and the breezy "Hot Fun in the Summertime" to Sly's string of jewels.

There's a Riot Goin' On drops the hopeful dance-party rhetoric and turns the band's musical reach inward. Sly concocts a brooding, lethal-funk setting for his dark and dissolute musings on the state of the nation—from Woodstock to Watts. "Family Affair" and "Runnin' Away" couch bleak scenarios in hauntingly light tunes; even at rock bottom, Sly can nail a catchy hook when it suits his mood. Canceled shows and erratic performances plagued Sly and the Family Stone at this point, adding to the air of dread surrounding *Riot.* However, Sly rebounded with the playful, sharp *Fresh* in 1973. "If You Want Me to Stay" became the Family Stone's last Top 20 single; if that sounds a bit coy coming from Sly, "Thankful 'n' Thoughtful" and the acid-drenched "Que Sera, Sera" carry the expected sting, along with a newfound mellow glow. That grace period turned out to be cruelly short-lived, though. Sly's subsequent Warner Bros. releases probably deserve to remain out of print: The sound of such a brilliant inventor turning imitative of his followers is just too much to bear. Surfacing on Funkadelic's *The Electric Spanking of War Babies* and the *P-Funk All-Stars* album in the early '80s, Sly convincingly kicked out a few jams and then promptly faded from view. He's popped up a couple times since then, most recently to program the excellent *Essential Sly* 2-CD set. —M.C.

The Small Faces

★★★½ There Are but Four Small Faces (1967; Immediate, 1991)
★★★★ Ogden's Nut Gone Flake (Abko, 1968)
★ Playmates (Atlantic, 1977)
★ 78 in the Shade (Atlantic, 1978)
★★★ Big Hits (Dressed to Kill, 1999)
★★★½ The Definitive Collection (Recall, 1999)
★★ Nice (Pilot, 2001)
★★★½ Absolutely the Best (Fuel 2000, 2001)
★★★½ Odds and Mods (Varèse, 2002)
★★★½ Hits, Misses, Thrashers & Crashers (Fuel 2000, 2004)

Cute and tiny and flashing a giddy, soaring arrogance, the Small Faces, circa 1966, had the mod pose down better even than fellow-Londoners the Who. And they were tunesmiths, too. Frontman (former kiddie actor) Steve Marriott, organist Ian McLagan, drummer Kenney Jones, and bassist Ronnie Lane made jaunty R&B-ish rock & roll that highlighted Marriott's on-stage dramatics, bluesy guitar, and patented scratchy vocal stylings he'd later parody gratingly with Humble Pie. "Itchycoo Park" (1967) was a great flower-power single whose outsized influence reaches down to the Raspberries and Prince. *Ogden's Nut Gone Flake* may be the best contemporary *Sgt. Pepper's* clone: Everything about it was nicely quirky—a round record sleeve, a sweet mix of psychedelia and R&B, and the charm of "Afterglow." When Marriott left in 1969 for Humble Pie, Ron Wood and Rod Stewart joined up, and the band became the Faces. Later, Jones replaced Keith Moon in the Who for a time; McLagan moved to the States and has released a bunch of albums under his own name; Marriott was poised for a comeback with Peter Frampton when he perished in a fire at his home in 1991; and Lane accumulated an impressive body of solo work before succumbing to MS in 1997. While the Small Faces legacy is beloved in the U.K., where Sanctuary's *Ultimate Collection* lives up to its title, the band has yet to get the proper archival treatment in the U.S. —P.E./B.SC.

Smashing Pumpkins

★★★★ Gish (Virgin, 1991)
★★★★ Siamese Dream (Virgin, 1993)
★★ Pisces Iscariot (Virgin, 1994)
★★★★ Melon Collie and the Infinite Sadness (Virgin, 1995)
★★ Adore (Virgin, 1998)
★ Machina/The Machines of God (Virgin, 2000)

Zwan

★★★★ Mary Star of the Sea (Reprise, 2003)

One of the most ambitious alt-rock bands of the 1990s was also one of the most old-fashioned. For 10 years, Billy Corgan led his band, the Smashing Pumpkins, on a sublime—and often ridiculous—quest for 1970s-style rock & roll glory at a time when lots of bands seemed more skeptical than ever about the rewards of fame. Corgan's dream came true, at least for a while, and like most rock stars worth talking about, he earned enemies who were, if anything, even more passionate than his fans.

The first Smashing Pumpkins album was *Gish,* a grand, furious album full of expansive guitar solos and other indulgences that underground rockers were supposed to disavow. Corgan's airy, supple voice spilled out in wisps and bursts, often matching the shifting sounds of the guitar; one of his most effective tricks was to match a guitar line exactly, so that voice and instrument blended into one semihuman sound.

Gish includes the band's extraordinary break-through single, "Siva," which crams eight minutes' worth of twists and turns into a song half that long. The lyrics, by turns whiny ("Don't wanna live in your misery") and whimsical, seem to refract hard-rock themes from across the decades without committing to any of them, and the refrain captured the mixture of urgency and apathy that would define the band for years: "Tell me, tell me what you're after/I just wanna get there faster."

Siamese Dream was even grander, prettier, and more atmospheric than *Gish:* Drummer Jimmy Chamberlin toned down his funk backbeats, letting the bumblebee swarms of guitar notes drive the fuzzy songs forward. And Corgan wrote a batch of songs that captured something more disquieting than sadness: the dismal suspicion that you might not feel anything at all. One of the album's biggest hits, "Today," has a deceptively blissful opening that soon gets subtly and bitterly modified: "Today is the greatest day I've ever known" becomes "Today is the greatest day I've never known."

After the success of *Siamese Dream,* the band threw hard-core fans (and, perhaps, impatient record executives) a bone with *Pisces Iscariot,* a compilation of B sides and demos. It's uneven by design, but there's plenty to amuse the faithful, including "Blew Away," a Beatles-damaged ballad sung by guitarist James Iha; a quiet, Bowie-fied cover of Fleetwood Mac's "Landslide"; and, best of all, Corgan's petulant liner notes, which end, "and fuck you to those who will never understand."

Of course, nothing says "fuck you" like a sprawling double album, so Corgan got to work, and in 1995 the band released *Melon Collie & the Infinite Sadness,* two CDs that gave Corgan plenty of space to embrace, renounce, and mock his new reputation as rock's most self-pitying swaggerer. (The album includes some of his most famous and most ridiculous lines, such as, "Despite all my rage, I am still just a rat in a cage.") It's not flawless, but there are plenty of hits (the gorgeous ballad "Tonight, Tonight," the gently tangled "1979"), and lots of surprises, too, including a thick electrometal experiment called "Love."

And then something went wrong. The band split with Chamberlin and recorded *Adore,* a single-disc album that felt twice as long as *Melon Collie,* full of overlong atmospheric songs that never got going. Chamberlin returned for *Machina/The Machines of God,* a return to form that wasn't: The arrogance and

dreaminess of the best Smashing Pumpkins albums were gone, replaced by lukewarm tunes and oddly straightforward songwriting.

Corgan didn't produce a proper followup to *Melon Collie* until years later, when he recruited a group of alt-rock veterans (including Chamberlin) and formed the short-lived Zwan, which produced a surprisingly strong album called *Mary Star of the Sea* before disbanding. The first track, "Lyric," skips forward on Paz Lenchantin's bass line; one of the last, "Jesus, I/Mary Star of the Sea," is a glorious blast of Pumpkinish excess. —K.S.

Smash Mouth

★★★★ Fush Yu Mang (Interscope, 1997)
★★★½ Astro Lounge (Interscope, 1999)
★★½ Smash Mouth (Interscope, 2001)
★★★ Get the Picture? (Interscope, 2001)

Intent on probing the psychology of a party animal who "ain't the sharpest tool in the shed," songwriter Paul Delisle deposits Smash Mouth singer Steve Harwell into various comic situations on *Fush Yu Mang.* His girl calls out her lesbian ex's name in bed, he deliberately blinds himself with "Beer Goggles," and, on "Let's Rock," he even ruminates upon the meaning of life atop a gentle skank. Then the music abruptly cranks into hardcore rant, and Harwell desperately and repeatedly shouts the title. Another bout of deep thinking narrowly averted!

Delisle built off the success of SM's cover of "Can't Get Enough of You Baby" (from the *Can't Hardly Wait* soundtrack) and constructed glossy garage pop for *Astro Lounge.* Purists say that garage rock is all about the kind of tube amp you use. But listen to Rhino's *Nuggets* box and you'll hear kids who wanted stardom battering the boundaries of three-chord troglodyte stomps with fuzz guitar, weirdo organ, and hectic instrumentation. With its exuberant pop outreach, "All Star" hews closer to this garage spirit than preservationists like the Barons.

Musically, *Smash Mouth* continues this omnivorous influx of musical styles. "Pacific Coast Party" seamlessly blends disco strings and guitar stomp. A dip in sales indicates that this synthesis might have been a bit over the head of many party animals. But it's the lyrics that point to a bleak future when Harwell muses, "We ain't so dumb just now." *Get the Picture?* returns to the hook-filled, beach-ready mold—there's the reggae-filled first single ("You Are My Number One"), the usual Farfisa-driven surf rockers ("Hot," "Fun") and Harwell's mushy musings on the world and its discontents ("Hang On"). Harwell may be the only rocker to sing worse than Ja Rule, but he and his mates are still plenty adept at turning out good-timey throwaways. —K.H.

Bessie Smith

★★★★★ Bessie Smith: The Collection (Columbia, 1989)
★★★★ The Complete Recordings, Vol. 1 (Columbia/Legacy, 1991)
★★★★ The Complete Recordings, Vol. 2 (Columbia/Legacy, 1991)
★★★★ The Complete Recordings, Vol. 3 (Columbia/Legacy, 1992)
★★★★ The Complete Recordings, Vol. 4 (Columbia/Legacy, 1993)
★★★★ The Complete Recordings, Vol. 5: The Final Chapter (Columbia/Legacy, 1996)
★★★★★ The Essential Bessie Smith (Columbia, 1997)

Few artists—particularly pioneers whose work predates the advent of the long-playing record—have been as well served by the CD reissue as Bessie Smith, the aptly nicknamed Empress of the Blues. In 1970, Smith's label, Columbia, and the man who signed her, the late John Hammond, restored order to Smith's catalogue by way of a two-year reissue of her work in a series of well-annotated, handsomely packaged double-album collections. In 1989, as the demise of vinyl neared, the label launched yet another Smith reissue series with *Bessie Smith: The Collection,* a solid, if incomplete, overview of the artist's decade-long recording history. A more ambitious project was launched in 1991 with the release of the first two of five multi-CD box sets, under the rubric *The Complete Recordings,* which is exactly what it claims to be—166 Columbia and Okeh sides—and more. In 1997 Columbia offered noncompletists a viable alternative in *The Essential Bessie Smith,* a two-CD set featuring 36 prime cuts that get the job done in terms of spotlighting what it was that made Smith special and her art enduring.

Born in Chattanooga, TN, Smith began performing on the street, and by her late teens was a local star on the strength of her ratings in amateur shows. In 1912 her brother Clarence came through town as a member of the Moses Stokes minstrel show. Stokes' featured vocalist was Ma Rainey, whose widespread popularity had pretty much dashed the notion that women couldn't, or shouldn't, sing the sort of hard blues that the circuit's male performers trafficked in. Smith joined up with Stokes, but Rainey's influence on her approach was minimal. Musicians who were around at that time asserted that Smith already had developed a distinctive style that needed no further grooming; if Rainey made an important contribution to Smith's career, it doubtless came in enlightening the impressionable young lady to the ofttimes nefarious ways of showbiz types. That said, it's difficult to dismiss the notion that Rainey's way of taking hold of a song and infusing it with her own personality didn't rub off on Smith, no matter how developed Smith's own approach.

In 1923 Smith recorded her first sessions for Columbia (published reports exist of her having recorded for the Chicago-based Emerson label in 1921, but none of this work has ever surfaced), with Frank Walker, head of the label's race records division, overseeing the sessions. Her cover of Alberta Hunter's "Downhearted Blues" sold 780,000 copies in its first six months of release and catapulted Smith to headliner status; at the same time, her touring schedule expanded to include dates in Chicago, Detroit, and Cleveland, a rarity at a time when the black revues' rigorous road trips were confined to the Southern states.

Smith's singing was fueled by rage and defiance. Being both black and female—something of a double whammy in those prefeminist, Jim Crow days—she was conscious of artificial barriers preventing her from living the good life her success had earned. Add this simmering resentment to a hair-trigger temper, and the result is an emotional cauldron that boiled over, on record and off. Numerous tall tales abound of her attacks on others (being physically prepossessing, she feared no one, male or female), perhaps the most memorable occurring when she learned of her husband's infidelity and proceeded to trash their hotel room and him all at once. Deep blues is defined in her expressive singing, in all its dark, brooding moodiness and chilling, nuanced moans and wails. The text of her songs, and the kinetic performances of them, suggest someone who is nursing wounds so severe they might never be healed.

Throughout the '20s, Smith recorded with the best musicians of her era, but it was a fleeting session with Louis Armstrong that has justifiably entered into legend. In 1925, with pianist Fred Longshaw the only other player on the date, they recorded five songs—including a monumental summit of voice and instrument on "St. Louis Blues"—and challenged each other in the way geniuses must be challenged in order to produce art of this caliber. Theirs is one of the most compelling conversations in blues history, preserved on *The Collection, The Essential,* and Vol. 2 of *The Complete Recordings.*

Vol. 3 of *The Complete Recordings* covers the years 1925–28, when Smith was at the peak of her interpretive powers, her writing was at its sharpest, and her recordings were instant classics ("I'd Rather Be Dead and Buried in My Grave," "Send Me to the 'Lectric Chair," "Muddy Water [A Mississippi Moan]," and "Backwater Blues" among the many standouts here). On Vol. 4 the arc is still ascending in the years 1928–31, when the material takes a revealing but disturbing personal turn in its bluest moments, offering a glimpse into the artist's tormented offstage life. "Me and My Gin," "Shipwreck Blues" (parts one and two), "Nobody Knows You When You're Down and Out," and "I've Got What It Takes (But It Breaks My Heart to Give It Away)" tell a story as intimate and revealing as any artist offered in the 20th century.

The Depression upended Smith's career, although she continued to record into 1933, with her final sides cut for the Columbia subsidiary Okeh, a label that had rejected her 10 years earlier for being "too rough." These, along with her last Columbia sessions, define Vol. 5 and illustrate an artist in transition. Still a magnet for top-drawer musicians, Smith was backed on the Okeh sides by the remarkable Buck Washington band, whose members included Washington on piano, Frankie Newton on trumpet, Jack Teagarden on trombone, Chu Berry on tenor sax, Bobby Johnson on guitar, Billy Taylor on bass, and, on the romping "Gimme a Pigfoot," a barely audible Benny Goodman on clarinet. At this stage of her career Smith isn't abandoning the blues, but she is moving away from the relentlessly downbeat, moaning style that was her stock-in-trade in earlier years. Still direct and commanding, she adopts a lighter tone and a more jocular approach to her tales of romantic skullduggery, as if shrugging off her bad luck instead of railing against it. Behind her the band settles into a brisk pace that sets up some exciting solos, such as Newton's trilling trumpet turn and Washington's loping, lazy interjection on "Do Your Duty," a lighthearted, double-entendre scolding of a feckless lover. In fact, much of the Okeh material is of the wink-and-a-nudge variety, with Smith laughing and growling her way through risqué scenes such as those described in "Gimme a Pigfoot" and in a steamy, comic masterpiece of lust and longing, "Need a Little Sugar in My Bowl," one of her final Columbia recordings and a memorable one, with pianist Clarence Williams providing the sole, spare bit of instrumental support. For a little added oomph, Vol. 5 also includes a disc containing a 70-minute interview with Smith's niece, Ruby Smith, who recounts memories of Aunt Bessie's life, some of them loving, some amusing, some profane, some harrowing, all riveting as eyewitness reports of an incredible life journey.

Smith's legend endured, darkly, after she was fatally injured in a car wreck in Mississippi in 1937 and Hammond published an article in *Down Beat* in which he claimed, without any documentation to support his theory, that a white hospital's refusal to treat Smith led to her demise. So powerful was the cultural pull of this myth that Pulitzer Prize–winning playwright Edward Albee reimagined it for the stage in his 1959 play *The Death of Bessie Smith*. The booklet accompanying Vol. 5 settles the questions surrounding Smith's death by reprinting recollections from a 1971 interview with the doctor who found Smith's broken body on the side of the road and a letter from the doctor who treated Smith at the Clarksdale, MS, black hospital where, he writes, "we gave her every medical attention, but we were never able to rally her from the shock." Bessie Smith's death was a tragedy that didn't need Hammond's outrageous fabrication to make it more heartbreaking. Focus instead on what remains unsullied—the music. Resonant, stirring, troubling, electrifying, the art of Bessie Smith is a national treasure. —D.M.

Elliott Smith

★★★★ Roman Candle (Cavity Search, 1994)
★★★★★ Elliott Smith (Kill Rock Stars, 1995)
★★★½ Either/Or (Kill Rock Stars, 1997)
★★★ XO (DreamWorks, 1998)
★★★★★ Figure 8 (DreamWorks, 2000)
★★★½ From a Basement on the Hill (Anti-, 2004)

Lo-fi, folk punk, and other mid-'90s buzzwords didn't help the ferociously talented Smith when he debuted *Roman Candle* to a public already softened up for the charms of post-grunge acoustics by the likes of Lou Barlow. Perhaps the album fell through the cracks because of the limited resources of its tiny label, or maybe because so much of *Roman Candle* sounds like Simon and Garfunkel after an idealism bypass. The album set the Smith template: unflinching portraits of bad love in a low-down town, recorded with sparkling clarity, his guitar squeaking, his voice unemphatic to say the least, the rolling prom rhythms hypnotic and terribly, unrelentingly sad.

If total lack of effect is going to be your thing, you'd better know something about songcraft. Fortunately for Elliott Smith, he's not just depressed, angry, and sarcastic, he's also observant, literate, and musically accomplished. Never has "folk punk" been as classically defined as in Smith's second album, his premiere effort for the indie anticorporate rock label Kill Rock Stars. He spins a disorienting acoustic web of strums and plucks on guitar; his voice has all the substantiality of wet tissue paper. But the music burrows, digging up gems of structure, melody, and lyrical vividness that belie his naive delivery. He tries to distance himself from the tales of misery, shifting from second to first person as his characters—"I," "you"—get thrown out of bars, hunt down a fix buzz-brained, and fumble their love lives. On the page, it's literary punk rock, all fury at the Man (in "Christian Brothers") and weary poems of self-examination in a substance-altered state (in almost everything else). But the sound is hummable pop, slowed and drugged, with tricky but unshowy guitar work driving the melodies forward, and sung in a numb near-whisper. "The Biggest Lie," "St. Ides Heaven," and especially the stunning look into the head of a middle-class addict, "Needle in the Hay" (heard on the soundtrack to the 2001 film *The Royal Tenenbaums*), are some of the loveliest songs about the dissolution of the soul ever written.

Smith is so coruscatingly self-aware that he's the first person to fret that a move to Hollywood might corrupt his defiant outsider stance. So it's no surprise, only a bit of a disappointment, that when he not only contributed a song to a big-budget movie but got a Grammy nomination for it ("Miss Misery," written for *Good Will Hunting*) and then moved to the West Coast, he would make the kind of album that complained about how fake Tinseltown is. Nor is it coincidental that he uses variations of the phrase "Pleased to meet you" to evoke the false bonhomie of SoCal business, since the last great postpunk album about the soul-draining pleasures of big-time coopting was the Replacements' *Pleased to Meet Me*. Smith didn't mislay his talent for *Either/Or*, just his perspective. His use of a full band sounds rich and real—"Alameda" is a beautiful Beatlesque march, "Ballad of a Big Nothing" such pitch-perfect folk pop it's a shock the Mamas and the Papas didn't think of it first, and "Say Yes" indicates he might be ready to crawl out of his navel and look at the real world more with rose-colored glasses and less of a jaundiced eye. But moaning about the absurdity of seeing "Pictures of Me" all over town or shaking his head over the big, messy (meaningless, yes, but fabulous) "Rose Parade" is just juvenile. It's most frustrating when his best and worst impulses collide, as on the gorgeous finger-picked "Angeles," another slap at sunlit phoniness painted with exhilarating delicacy: "Someone's always coming around here trailing some new kill/Says I seen your picture on a hundred-dollar bill/And what's a game of chance to you, to him is one of real skill." Smith could hang on like Tom Waits if he'd learn to appreciate the glitz as much as he revels in the grime.

Was Smith's fear of an industrial buyout a self-fulfilling prophecy? *XO* finds him in the same seedy hotel room surrounded by bottles, metaphorically speaking, but his melody-making powers seem to be running on fumes. With the possible exception of "Independence Day," there's nothing as beautiful here as the least impressive number on any previous record, but what *XO* lacks in riveting songwriting it makes up for in weirdly widescreen instrumentation. Horns,

brass, and strings wax orchestral while Smith retreads some of his favorite melodic tropes. "Amity" benefits from a crashing, textural wall of cymbals, but otherwise the arrangements don't add much besides bulk to the songs.

Recording musicians make their mistakes in public, and if *XO* was an experiment, *Figure 8* is the smoothly working invention it resulted in. There's something exhilarating about the joy inherent in a gorgeous melody, and Smith capitalizes on the frisson that results from anger, addiction, and madness being expressed in such transcendent means. So he incorporates some of the elaborate instrumentation of *XO*—strings—in small doses, using the guitars, drums, bass, piano, and backup vocals to give his songs a shimmering chime, Beatlesque march, or intimate folk strum. Gem-packed and less irredeemably tragic than his four previous releases, *Figure 8* shows the artist at the peak of his powers, as reconciled to his professionalism as he is to his outsider status—or at least it seemed that way. Smith committed suicide in 2003 while working on a followup album, the uneven but often lovely *From a Basement on the Hill*.   —A.B.

Patti Smith

★★★★★   Horses (1975; Arista, 1996)
★★★½   Radio Ethiopia (1976; Arista, 1996)
★★★★½   Easter (1978; Arista, 1996)
★★★   Wave (1979; Arista, 1996)
★★★   Dream of Life (1988; Arista, 1996)
★★★★   Gone Again (Arista, 1996)
★★   Peace and Noise (Arista, 1997)
★★★   Gung Ho (Arista, 2000)
★★★½   Land (Arista, 2002)
★★★★   Trampin' (Columbia, 2004)

With the very first utterance of her debut album, Patti Smith declares war on the musical complacency of the mid-'70s: "Jesus died for somebody's sins but not mine." *Horses* defies the reigning rock conventions of its time, and deflates a few current notions, too. Smith's idiosyncratic mix of Beat poetry and the big beat still has the power to either entice or offend. Teeming with ambition, primitivism, anybody-can-do-this chutzpah, and casual androgyny, *Horses* demands a reaction. On the basis of attitude alone, Smith inspired every punk and riot grrrl artist who followed in her wake. A published poet and rock critic, she began reciting her Beat-tribute "Babelogues" over fellow writer Lenny Kaye's guitar accompaniment in the early '70s. It was a perfect match: mixing Kaye's protopunk Nuggets riffs with Smith's poesy. On *Horses*, her visionary metaphors collide with the inviting din of late-'60s-style garage-band rock. The title track refers both to stallions as a psychosexual image and to "doin' the pony." Smith expands the words of oldies like "Gloria" and "Land of 1,000 Dances," although the band's furious pounding never obscures the power of those three mighty chords. Quieter, reflective tracks like "Kimberly" and "Elegie" underline the passionate romanticism in her voice.

Radio Ethiopia boasts the Patti Smith Group's growing power as a band, broadcasting a gritty, hard-rocking rhythm guitar sound. "Pumping (My Heart)" and "Ask the Angels" ring out like anthems, but the grueling title cut reveals the Achilles' heel among Patti's pretensions: Her squalling guitar-feedback orgies never reach beyond the annoyance level.

On *Easter,* producer Jimmy Iovine makes good on Smith's professed rebel stance by moving her sound even closer to solid, meat-and-potatoes mainstream rock. You can hear the newfound confidence in her singing, and the more traditionally structured approach doesn't dull the jagged conviction of "25th Floor," "Space Monkey," and "Till Victory." Maybe Bruce Springsteen did Smith a big favor by giving her a song (which she lightly edited) for this album, finally rendering her skittery energy accessible. But another way of hearing "Because the Night" suggests that this so-called punk priestess breathes a much-needed air of subtlety into the Boss's lofty anthemic construct.

Wave continues that melodic roll with "Dancing Barefoot" and "Frederick," though for the rest of the album Smith sounds uncharacteristically fuzzy, even disengaged. Once the Patti Smith Group had completed a successful tour in 1979, Patti Smith abruptly retired from the music scene. Perhaps her mission felt complete.

After eight subsequent years of marriage (to Detroit rocker Fred "Sonic" Smith) and two children, Smith quietly resurfaced; perhaps the only low-profile comeback of the late '80s. Overproduced by Jimmy Iovine (with Fred "Sonic" Smith), *Dream of Life*'s net effect underwhelms most expectations. Oddly, it sounds a bit out of time: more 1983 than 1977, of all things. Not that Smith needs to monitor current trends: When her rekindled vision clicks into overdrive beside Fred Smith's zinging guitar lines on "Up There Down There," "Where Duty Calls," or "People Have the Power," *Dream of Life* sounds timeless. But mostly *Dream of Life* sounds tentative, and after its release Smith once again fell silent for years. The death of her husband at the end of 1994 brought Smith slowly back to music with a series of concerts. Then with *Gone Again* in 1996, Smith launched her most sustained productive period since the '70s.

Gone Again is dedicated to Fred "Sonic" Smith, and not surprisingly, the songs on *Gone Again* focus on death and loss. Though not nearly as aggressive as her classic '70s work, the hard-rocking title track and "Summer Cannibals" (both cowritten by her late husband) both prove that Smith has no plans to go gentle. Another highlight is the building, emotional "Beneath the Southern Cross," where Smith once again benefits from her powerful partnership with Lenny Kaye. A sharp cover of Dylan's "Wicked Messenger" gives Smith plenty of opportunity to growl and grunt, as well as providing a certain dark gravitas to balance against Smith's more uplifting spirituality. In all, *Gone Again* is a true return to form for the original punk priestess.

Peace and Noise, on the other hand, is a disappointment. Some of the songs, like "Dead City" and "Spell," are weakened by the busy out-of-place metal guitar of Oliver Ray, and others, like the far stronger "1959," feel like leftovers from *Gone Again.* Far better is *Gung Ho,* where on songs like "New Party" and "Strange Messengers" Smith returns to bringing political and social commentary into her vatic pronouncements. "Lo and Beholden" is another fantastic collaboration with Lenny Kaye. Only on the nearly 12-minute title track does Smith seem to get bogged down by the pretentious overreaching for grandeur that has been her trademark throughout her career.

After a four-year hiatus, Smith moved to Columbia, the first label change of her career, and responded to the post–September 11 world with the fully reinvigorated *Trampin'*, an affirming mix of her vatic poetry, leftist politics, and driving rock. At the core of *Trampin'* are the lengthy tracks "Gandhi" and "Radio Baghdad," which hark back to "Piss Factory" with a loose musical structure building in intensity as the lyrics move from hallucinatory vision to inspiring incantation. A remarkable disc in every way, against the odds, *Trampin'* is arguably the most successful Patti Smith album since *Horses* and shows that Smith's visionary gifts, at age 57, are undiminished, an extraordinary rarity in rock.

Hardly a traditional greatest hits collection, *Land*'s first disc is mostly a career-spanning retrospective that many will find a bit too focused on Smith's '90s work. The second disc of *Land*—a rarities, live recordings, and outtakes collection—is even more heavily weighted to the '90s. But no matter how perverse Smith's choices on *Land* seem, what is most important to fans is that this legendary artist is once again looking to the future.   —R.A.

Will Smith

★★½ Big Willie Style (Columbia, 1997)
★★ Willennium (Sony, 1999)
★★ Born to Reign (Columbia, 2002)
★★★ Greatest Hits (Columbia, 2002)

Will Smith was never going to fade into old-school history as a footnote for his mid-'80s boy-next-door rap. Cute, smart, determined, and possessed of that ineffable thing called charisma, Smith parlayed his early fame as half of DJ Jazzy Jeff and the Fresh Prince into a television career, reclaimed his name when he took to the big screen, garnered an Academy Award nomination, and, not incidentally, started making hit records again, this time for a bigger audience. *Big Willie Style* toys with Smith's past, with an intro that fakes a public appearance by "the artist formerly known as Fresh Prince" and forces Smith to defend his music as something more than novelty. The album is a genial collection of pleasant-enough background hip-hop, casting Smith as an unmenacing love man ("I'ma call you," he promises on "Candy"), sensitive balladeer, and goofy braggart, with multiple "uhn"s thrown in for street cred. Pop radio made a beeline for the three terrific, sample-heavy singles: the party anthem "Gettin' Jiggy wit It," busy, bouncy, and undeniably dancey; Smith's tribute to his son, "Just the Two of Us," and the synergistic plug "Men in Black"—just in case you're not sure if it's *that* Will Smith.

A hardcore Will Smith is a relative notion, and the planned obsolescence implied by the title of his second all-grown-up solo album is but a gnat on his gigantic shoulder—Smith isn't going anywhere, however precisely he dates the landmarks of his maturation. He gathers another roll call of pals and costars for this eclectic, high-energy party-in-a-jewel-box, quick lipped on the revved-up salsa of "La Fiesta," helping himself to some of Bob Dorough's idiosyncratic jazz on "Afro Angel," and once again shouts out the title of his latest film—here, the box-office bomb *Wild Wild West.* "Will 2K" didn't do the business of "Gettin' Jiggy wit It," but it gets the party started with just as much energy and some help from the piano riff from "Rock the Casbah." Smith gets a little freakier (and a lot boastier) than he's been, talking big about his cash flow on "Freakin' It" and trying to keep up with the effortlessly dirty-minded Li'l Kim on "Da Butta." Smith is a fan's celebrity, and *Willennium* mints nothing but his determination to let no one down. *Born to Reign* is another nice try from a nice guy, but that's about all you can say to recommend it.   —A.B.

The Smithereens

★★★	Beauty and Sadness (EP) (1983; Enigma, 1988)
★★★½	Especially for You (Enigma, 1987)
★★★	The Smithereens (EP) (Restless/Enigma, 1987)
★★★½	Green Thoughts (Enigma/Capitol, 1988)
★★★½	The Smithereens 11 (Capitol, 1989)
★★★½	Blow Up (Capitol, 1991)
★★★	Date With the Smithereens (RCA, 1994)
★★★½	God Save the Smithereens (Koch, 1995)
★★★½	Blown to Smithereens: The Best of the Smithereens (Capitol, 1995)

Expert at mining some jukebox version of the collective unconscious, frontman/guitarist Pat DiNizio writes great pop songs that recall Brit mod glory but don't sound at all cute or slavishly recycled. *Especially for You* is clean, tough, and snappy—the four-piece group doesn't mess with DiNizio's hooks, which, fortunately, overpower the so-so quality of his singing. With *Green Thoughts,* the players get subtler, their style verging in places on the mid-tempo numbers of Elvis Costello. *Smithereens 11* is heavier; while "William Wilson" (its title taken from Poe's short story) recalls the Kinks, the record's thick guitar tones sound more '70s than '60s. "Maria Elena" (a song for Buddy Holly's widow) is smart and tender, proving that DiNizio's skill at ballads rivals his flair for ravers. *Blow Up* and *Date* still found the Smithereens honest and tough, even if their style of hooky rock & roll had begun to fall out of favor. Never ones to follow trends, they persevered with *God Save,* their strongest work in years.   —P.E.

The Smiths

★★★★	The Smiths (Sire, 1984)
★★★	Hatful of Hollow (Sire, 1984)
★★	Meat Is Murder (Sire, 1985)
★★★★★	The Queen Is Dead (Sire, 1986)
★★★★★	Louder Than Bombs (Sire, 1987)
★★★★	Strangeways, Here We Come (Sire, 1987)
★★★	Rank (Sire, 1988)
★★	Best Of, Vol. 1 (Sire, 1992)
★★	Best Of, Vol. 2 (Sire, 1992)
★★★★	Singles (Sire, 1995)

Oh, Manchester—so much to answer for. The Smiths managed to make a career's worth of timeless rock & roll out of completely unpromising elements. Morrissey was an utterly batshit choirboy obsessed with Oscar Wilde, James Dean, and the New York Dolls, moaning and droning about sexual confusion and youthful malaise with a voice that only got weirder when he started hitting actual notes. Johnny Marr was a shy Manchester guitar geek fixated on the Beatles and the Stones who knocked on the door of the local literary recluse and asked him to start a band. The result: local indie-rock cult status, huge international pop success, countless terrible imitators, 30 or 40 classic songs, and an enduring legend as the greatest British band of the past 20 summers.

The Smiths' debut was an instant sensation, thanks

to gems like "Reel Around the Fountain" and "This Charming Man." Tonally and emotionally, it's a little skimpy, with Morrissey chasing tropes such as "dig a shallow grave and I'll lay me down" over Marr's thin guitar jangle. But Morrissey had unprecedentedly dippy star power, often appearing in public wearing love beads, government-issue glasses, and a hearing aid. The Smiths added a few excellent singles to the import collection *Hatful of Hollow* ("William, It Was Really Nothing," "How Soon Is Now"), with a first few glimmers of wit. Morrissey sings, "You've been in the house too long, she said/And I naturally fled," probably the first time he'd ever done anything naturally in his life. But all the good songs here are also on the much stronger *Louder Than Bombs,* and the filler is so appallingly bad ("Accept Yourself," "Back to the Old House," the live BBC remakes) that Caligula would have blushed. *Meat Is Murder* was tuneless cow-humping self-parody, hammering away at the lyrical messages: meat is murder, love is larceny, girls are gruesome, etc. Fans sadly figured that the Smiths had moped their last mope.

So it may be hard for latter-day Smiths fans to appreciate how shocking *The Queen Is Dead* was in the summer of 1986. Johnny Marr suddenly discovered that he was born to rock, while Morrissey turned into rock's dishiest wit, playing around with rough boys in cemeteries and "writing" poetry during knee tremblers behind the Salford Lads' Club. Morrissey decided he'd rather be famous than righteous or holy, so he just chased his loud loutish lovers all over "Bigmouth Strikes Again," "Cemetry Gates," and "I Know It's Over." "There Is a Light That Never Goes Out" is a sacred song by now, one that makes fans across the globe join hands and mope together. Someday he'll have to explain "Some Girls Are Bigger Than Others," won't he?

The Smiths were on a truly historic roll by now, dropping unbelievably great singles and B sides faster than fans could absorb them. "Half a Person" may be their most moving song, as Morrissey leaves his humdrum town and runs away to London, where he volunteers to be a backscrubber at the YWCA. In "Panic," he heads back to his humdrum town in defeat, vowing revenge against the world, especially the DJ playing the pop music that filled his head with big dreams in the first place. "Ask," "Is It Really So Strange?," and "Stretch Out and Wait" reach out to unlovable teen misfits everywhere with a tuneful compassion that still makes converts today. *Louder Than Bombs,* a vastly improved U.S. version of the U.K. collection *The World Won't Listen,* collects all these great songs, and picks everything worth picking off *Hatful of Hollow.* Good times, for a change.

Morrissey and Marr severed their alliance during the making of *Strangeways,* and the band broke up just as it was released. It drags quite a bit, though there are still some great songs, especially the one that begins "Last night I dreamt that somebody loved me" and the one that begins "I've come to wish you an unhappy birthday/Because you're evil." The *Best of* collections are annoyingly programmed, and while *Singles* is an improvement, it's hard to imagine how anyone could consciously contemplate picking it over *The Queen Is Dead* or *Louder Than Bombs. Rank* is a live album memorable for a strange rendition of Elvis Presley's "Marie's The Name (His Latest Flame)." From the Leeds side streets that you slip down to the provincial towns that you jog around, the Smiths remain hugely influential and beloved fifteen years after breaking up. Morrissey went on to a memorable solo career; the rest of the Smiths didn't.   —R.S.

Smog

★★	Sewn to the Sky	(Drag City, 1990)
★★	Forgotten Foundation	(Drag City, 1992)
★★★★	Julius Caesar	(Drag City, 1993)
★★★½	Burning Kingdom	(Drag City, 1994)
★★★½	Wild Love	(Drag City, 1995)
★★★	Kicking a Couple Around	(Drag City, 1996)
★★★½	The Doctor Came at Dawn	(Drag City, 1996)
★★★★½	Red Apple Falls	(Drag City, 1997)
★★★★½	Knock Knock	(Drag City, 1999)
★★★½	Dongs of Sevotion	(Drag City, 2000)
★★★	'Neath the Puke Tree	(Drag City, 2000)
★★★	Rain on Lens	(Drag City, 2001)
★★★	Accumulation: None	(Drag City, 2002)
★★	Supper	(Drag City, 2003)

Bill Callahan, the underground singer/songwriter known as Smog, made his name as indie rock's most pathetic misery goat, the kind of guy who writes a mean tune but really shouldn't be allowed to cross the street by himself. He sings beautifully tragic ballads about how love has let him down, although his romantic life might be a little less bleak if he didn't think "Spread Your Bloody Wings" was a nice title for a love song. He started releasing his lo-fi home recordings in the late '80s, attracting fanzine attention with *Sewn to the Sky* and *Forgotten Foundation.* But *Julius Caesar* is where he became a big-deal songwriter, pouring out his heart in the frail ballad "Chosen One" ("I wanted to ride that wild horse into the sun/But I no longer think that I'm your chosen one"). "37 Push-Ups" (he's cranking *Highway to Hell* and he's in a bad mood) and "Your Wedding" (he's gonna get real, real drunk) keep up the pace, while "I Am Star Wars!" is a ridiculous blast of avant-noise hooked around what sure sounds like a homemade tape loop of the guitar lick from the Stones' "Honky Tonk Women." Brilliant stuff.

With each release, Smog kept establishing himself as the passivest aggressing man in show business, often employing the vocals of his paramour Cynthia Dall and bringing a little joy into the lives of his dangerously undermedicated fan base. *Burning Kingdom* includes the devastating "Renee Died"; *Wild Love* has the theme song "Bathysphere," later covered by Cat Power; *Kicking a Couple Around* has the wacko cowboy ballad "I Break Horses." He summed himself up neatly with the 1994 single "A Hit" (on the rarities collection *Accumulation: None*): "I'll never be a Bowie/I'll never be an Eno/I'll only ever be a Gary Numan." His plaintive tunes and self-parodic misogyny both hit new levels on *The Doctor Came at Dawn*—according to legend, the seven-minute "All Your Woman Things" is the one that inspired a female audience member to hop onstage at one L.A. show and punch him out. (Maybe it was the line about the "spread-eagle dolly"?)

But the wolfboy started to mature on 1997's *Red Apple Falls*. The music opened up into sumptuous folk-rock splendor, with steel guitar, French horn, and even synths to bring out nuance earlier records had just implied. The epic "Inspirational" lived up to its title: "If you're living the unlivable/By loving the unlovable/It's time to start changing the unchangeable." *Knock Knock* hit even harder—the songs involve actual emotional contact with another person, quite a breakthrough in indie-rock terms. It's a funny song cycle about rural love gone bad, from the hopeful anticipation of "Let's Move to the Country" to "Hit the Ground Running," the catchiest tune about fleeing the country since the Velvets' "Train Round the Bend." Acoustic droopers like "Teenage Spaceship" and "River Guard" illustrate with piano, cello, even a children's choir. The moral of the story is "If someone offers you some sugar/You should eat it," and if it can happen to this guy, *Knock Knock* truly offers hope for everyone. Subsequent albums don't hit the same heights, though *Dongs of Sevotion* has a fine summary of the Smog philosophy: "Dress Sexy at My Funeral." —R.S.

Snoop Dogg

★★★★★ Doggystyle (Death Row, 1993)
★★½ Tha Doggfather (Death Row, 1996)
★★★ Da Game Is to Be Sold Not to Be Told (No Limit, 1998)
★★½ No Limit Top Dogg (No Limit, 1999)
★★ Dead Man Walkin' (D3, 2000)
★★★★ Tha Last Meal (No Limit, 2000)

★★★★ Death Row's Snoop Doggy Dogg Greatest Hits (Death Row, 2001)
★★★★ Paid tha Cost to Be da Bo$$ (Priority, 2002)

Every dog has his day, but not many have them on the multiple supersize order of the double-G born Calvin Broadus: He's evolved from hip-hop phenom and nearly washed-up MC to a TV personality, while bringing a sense of humor to the hardest gangsta rap and choice West Coast slang into the national lexicon. Along the way, he's made a few classic rap records. Snoop Doggy Dogg (the cute appellation by which he was then known) debuted on the Dr. Dre–produced theme song to the 1992 film *Deep Cover,* rapping about killing undercover cops in his already signature languid Long Beach, CA drawl. It was a quick leap to *The Chronic,* Dre's weeded-out gangsta masterpiece on which Snoop starred on "Nuthin' but a 'G' Thang," and the album's companion, Snoop's debut, *Doggystyle.* If you're not one of the 5 million people who bought *Doggystyle,* please do so now: Tracks like "Gin and Juice" and "Murder Was the Case" sound as fresh today as when they came out in 1994, helping to define West Coast hip-hop.

But Dre didn't contribute to followup *Tha Doggfather,* which resulted in rote funk tracks that brought out nothing new in Snoop; the album's best moment is its cover of Biz Markie's classic "The Vapors," with Snoop sabbing the names of homies Warren G and Nate Dogg into the story rap. With Death Row boss Suge Knight running a label whose name was becoming all too apt, Snoop jumped ship to Master P's lowball lifeboat, No Limit Records. Although generally considered to be the nadir of his career, *Da Game Is to Be Sold* has its redeeming qualities, starting with the incredible Pen & Pixel–designed CD case (a mass-produced ghetto objet d'art if ever there was) and extending to the organic funk duet with No Limit's first lady Mia X, "Picture This." Nine months later, *No Limit Top Dogg* was another slab from the No Limit production line; by now, Snoop's gangsta clichés made him seem hopelessly passé. Then something interesting happened: Suge Knight cobbled together a doggie bag of leftovers, hatefully titled *Dead Man Walkin',* making it seem like a new Snoop album by rush-releasing it mere weeks before Snoop dropped his next proper album, *Tha Last Meal.* But *Tha Last Meal* effected Snoop's first genuine reinvention by replacing his worn-out gangsta mask with a Ronnie Isley–meets–Iceberg Slim playa-pimp persona that was an easy-to-love natural fit. It also reunited Snoop with Dre, on the G-funk essential "Lay Low," and with Timbaland, on the bounce cut "Set It Off." *Jeah!*

Suge Knight cashed in again with *Death Row's*

Snoop Doggy Dogg Greatest Hits, a cobble job padded with intriguing but inessential rarities and remixes. But Snoop had regained control of his own damn self, thank you, releasing the artist-showcase album *Snoop Dogg Presents Doggy Style Allstars: Welcome to tha House, Vol. 1* (Doggystyle, 2002), worth buying for Lady of Rage's DJ Premier–produced "Unfucwitable." (Rage would appear again on *Paid tha Cost to Be tha Bo$$*'s "Batman & Robin," another Premier-produced track; props to Snoop for keeping her in the game). *Paid tha Cost* is the peak of a long, strange comeback trip, an omrapotent chef d'oeuvre whose single bobowack moment, "Wasn't Your Fault" (a remake of Robert Palmer's "Didn't Mean to Turn You On") can be laughed over as one gorges on highlights like the Neptunes-produced "Beautiful" and the filthy McNasty "Lollipop," with Jay-Z and Nate Dogg. It's proof that this singular Dogg is able to teach (and turn) new tricks. —P.R.

Phoebe Snow

★★★★	Phoebe Snow (1974; DGC, 1988)
★★★½	Second Childhood (Columbia, 1976)
★★★½	It Looks Like Snow (Columbia, 1976)
★★★	Never Letting Go (Columbia, 1977)
★★★	Against the Grain (Columbia, 1978)
★★★	Something Real (Elektra, 1989)
★★★★	The Very Best of Phoebe Snow (Columbia/Legacy, 2001)
★★★	Natural Wonder (Eagle, 2003)

A bluesy and assured alto voice sets Phoebe Snow apart from her kindred pale singer/songwriters, right from the start of her debut album, *Phoebe Snow.* The indelible intro of the hit "Poetry Man"—when she soars over a spare acoustic guitar—gives you some idea of her astounding range and emotional control. Actually, that isn't the strongest performance on the album: "Harpo's Blues" epitomizes her high-flying (and high-strung) approach to singing and writing. Snow opts for a fuller, jazz-flavored sound on *Second Childhood,* accompanying a set of psychologically subtle lyrics. The overall effect is a little underwhelming after the quiet rush of the debut, though she breathes immediacy into the lines about "dying on the vine in suburbia" (from "Two-Fisted Love"), among other telling moments. *It Looks Like Snow* casts her in an appealing, uptown-R&B light with covers of "Shakey Ground" (late Temptations), "Don't Let Me Down" (late Beatles), and "Teach Me Tonight" (Dinah Washington). *Never Letting Go* and *Against the Grain* are slicker and less satisfying, but *The Very Best of Phoebe Snow* (an expanded update of the deleted *The Best of Phoebe Snow*) offers a highly listenable recap of

her career, including a previously unreleased 1977 live pass at Sam Cooke's "Good Times" and a 1991 cover of the Etta James standard "At Last" lifted from Donald Fagen's *New York Rock & Soul Revue: Live at the Beacon* album. It's a strictly Columbia affair, though, meaning her long-deleted 1981 set for Mirage/Atlantic *(Rock Away),* her 1989 Elektra comeback *Something Real* (featuring the modest hit "If I Can Just Get Through the Night"), and 1998's already out-of-print venture for House of Blues *(I Can't Complain)* are unrepresented. —M.C./R.SK.

Social Distortion

★★★	Mommy's Little Monster (1983; Time Bomb, 1995)
★★★	Prison Bound (1988; Time Bomb, 1995)
★★★½	Social Distortion (Epic, 1990)
★★★★	Somewhere Between Heaven and Hell (Epic, 1992)
★★	Mainliner: Wreckage From the Past (Time Bomb, 1995)
★★★★★	White Light White Heat White Trash (550/Epic, 1996)
★★★	Live at the Roxy (Time Bomb, 1998)

Rock classicists despite their L.A. punk origins, Social Distortion took a tough-but-tuneful approach to their music, a tack that produces fairly predictable results on the punkish *Mommy's Little Monster* (and even more so on the ultra-early tracks comprising *Mainliner*), but pays dividends with *Prison Bound.* There the group develops an interest in country music—not the sweet, Gram Parsons–ish country rock you'd expect of Stones fans like this crew, but a sound more akin to the brusque, edgy tone of Johnny Cash's Sun recordings. This change shifts the band's focus slightly, moving its emphasis away from the guitars and toward Mike Ness' rough-hewn vocals, a shift that adds emphasis to "Like an Outlaw (for You)" and "No Pain No Gain."

Social Distortion plays down the hillbilly influence (though it does include a cover of "Ring of Fire") and generally toughens the group's attack, but maintains many of the same musical values, as "Ball and Chain" and "It Coulda Been Me" make plain. As such, the only change offered by *Somewhere Between Heaven and Hell* is a slight increase in guitar noise and a marked strengthening of the songwriting. But *White Light White Heat White Trash,* recorded after a four-year hiatus, brings all of the band's strengths and influences to bear for an album of twangy, tuneful, and intense rockers—including the band's first real hit, the snarlingly catchy "I Was Wrong."

Sadly, the band called it quits not long after, but

Ness continued as a solo artist, releasing the rootsy, ambitious *Cheating at Solitaire* as well as an album of country covers called *Under the Influences.* —J.D.C.

Soft Boys

★★★ Live at the Portland Arms (1978; Glass Fish UK, 1987)
★★★½ A Can of Bees (1979; Rykodisc, 1992)
★★★★½ Underwater Moonlight (1980; Matador, 2001)
★★★ Two Halves for the Price of One (1981; Glass Fish UK, 1990)
★★★ Invisible Hits (1983; Rykodisc, 1992)
★★★ 1976–81 (Rykodisc, 1993)

Seriously strange and terrifically tuneful, the Soft Boys were perhaps the most engagingly deranged act to have washed up with the English new wave. Between the deadpan insanity of singer/guitarist Robyn Hitchcock and the pure-pop virtuosity of lead guitarist Kimberley Rew, the Soft Boys had a rock-solid front line, while the rhythm section—drummer Morris Windsor and bassists Andy Metcalfe or Matthew Seligman—was as supple as it was expert. But what really made the Soft Boys sizzle were the songs—delightfully droll numbers like "Sandra's Having Her Brain Out" or "Do the Chisel." Both appear on *A Can of Bees,* along with such should-have-been hits as "Leppo & the Jooves" and "The Pigworker." The only thing that keeps these entertainingly played and exceedingly melodic songs from being career highlights is that the stuff on *Underwater Moonlight* is even better. Of course, it's hard to argue with any album that can slip from something called "I Wanna Destroy You" into "Kingdom of Love," but the Boys not only manage that transition with aplomb, but outdo it later on as they move from the triumphant Beatle-isms of "Tonight" into the spacey, Pink Floyd-ian "You'll Have to Go Sideways." (The Matador reissue of *Underwater Moonlight* augments the original album with bonus tracks and a second disc of rehearsal rarities.)

Invisible Hits is a bit of a disappointment, being merely terrific when its predecessors are absolutely marvelous, but the presence of "Let Me Put It Next to You," "Have a Heart, Betty (I'm Not Fireproof)," and "Rock 'n' Roll Toilet" is more than enough to recommend it. The all-acoustic *Live at the Portland Arms* is quite fun but given to such unexpected selections as "I Like Bananas (Because They Have No Bones)" and an all-vocal rendition of Glenn Miller's "In the Mood." Had the band landed any actual hits, *1976–1981* would include the greatest thereof. By contrast, *Two Halves for the Price of One* is mostly given over to outtakes and oddities—which, given how strange the official releases were, is saying something. —J.D.C.

Soft Cell

★★★ Non-Stop Erotic Cabaret (1981; Mercury, 2002)
★★½ Non-Stop Ecstatic Dancing (1982; Mercury, 1999)
★★ The Art of Falling Apart (Sire, 1983)
★½ Soul Inside (EP) (Sire, 1984)
★ This Last Night in Sodom (Sire, 1984)
★★★ Memorabilia: The Singles (Mercury, 1991)
★★★½ The Singles (Mercury, 1998)
★★★ The 12-inch Singles (Mercury, 2001)
★★★★ The Very Best of Soft Cell (Mercury, 2002)
★★★ Cruelty Without Beauty (Cookin', 2002)

Few groups took as much pleasure in perversity as Soft Cell. It wasn't just the kinky sex described in *Non-Stop Erotic Cabaret* or the glee with which the duo dubbed its farewell album *This Last Night in Sodom;* Soft Cell also got off as much on assaulting rock & roll notions of decency—that is, respect for such classics as Gloria Jones' "Tainted Love" or Jimi Hendrix's "Purple Haze," both of which get royally buggered by the band (on *Erotic Cabaret* and *Falling Apart,* respectively).

Of course, after two decades of ecstasy-fueled, rave-driven dance depravity, Soft Cell's kinks seem a bit tame now. As far as full albums go, *Erotic Cabaret* is the only one that still stands up. A conceptual salute to the sex industry, it makes the most of both Marc Almond's mannered tenor and David Ball's electronic soundscapes, and in this context, the exaggerated sense of shame lent "Tainted Love" seems almost like comic relief. *Non-Stop Ecstatic Dancing* is a jokingly cynical attempt by the group to cash in its pop currency, but only "Memorabilia" actually repays the effort.

The Art of Falling Apart is an impressively earnest effort, but that doesn't always work to the group's benefit—the charming domesticity of "Kitchen Sink Drama," for instance, is undercut by Almond's resolute refusal to stay on pitch, while the warts-and-all portrayal of prostitution in "Baby Doll" ends up sounding more vicious than realistic. Even so, it's worth enduring such excesses if only to hear the deliriously goofy "Hendrix Medley" offered as a bonus track. It's hard, however, to have the same enthusiasm for *Soul Inside* or *This Last Night in Sodom.* Somehow, though, *Cruelty Without Beauty* (the obligatory reunion effort) manages to reignite the duo's spark, both in the disco abandon of "Monoculture" and the cartoonish depravity of "Caligula Syndrome."

On the whole, though, Soft Cell was a singles band, and the best-ofs are the most consistent items in their catalogue. *Memorabilia* mixes original singles with dance mixes, but not as successfully as *The Very Best of; The Singles* is recommended for those who prefer their pop mixes unextended. —J.D.C.

Sonic Youth

★★ Sonic Youth (1982; SST, 1987)
★★★ Confusion Is Sex (1983; SST, 1987)
★★ Kill Yr Idols (Zensor, 1984)
★★★ Bad Moon Rising (Homestead, 1985)
★★ Death Valley 69 EP (Homestead, 1985)
★★★★ Evol (SST, 1986)
★★★★★ Sister (SST, 1987)
★★ Master-Dik (SST, 1988)
★★★★★ Daydream Nation (Enigma/Blast First, 1988)
★★★ Goo (DGC, 1990)
★★★ Dirty (DGC, 1992)
★★★ Experimental Jet Set, Trash and No Star (DGC, 1994)
★★★★ Screaming Fields of Sonic Love (DGC, 1995)
★★★½ Washing Machine (DGC, 1995)
★★★ SYR 1 (SYR, 1997)
★★½ SYR 2 (SYR, 1997)
★★½ SYR 3 (SYR, 1997)
★★★★ A Thousand Leaves (DGC, 1998)
★ Silver Session for Jason Knuth (SYR, 1998)
★★ Goodbye 20th Century (SYR, 1997)
★ NYC Ghosts and Flowers (DGC, 2000)
★★★★ Murray Street (DGC, 2002)
★★★½ Sonic Nurse (DGC, 2004)

Sonic Youth's best song is "Kotton Krown," from their 1987 breakthrough album *Sister*. It starts as an ungodly eruption of New York feedback noise, until the noise starts humming a melody through the amp fuzz, and guitarists Thurston Moore and Lee Ranaldo play along with the melody, over and over. Moore and bassist Kim Gordon sing their mumbled vocals, repeating the line "Angels are dreaming of you" as if it's a lullaby, and the repetitions build until the guitars start to sound like antennas, picking up otherworldly signals and channeling them through the scuzziest urban noise. It's a hypnotic, unforgettable song, wreaking eerie beauty out of the clang. It typifies what Sonic Youth has always been up to, making art rock in the visionary New York tradition, standing tall on the third rail in between Television's "Marquee Moon" and Eric B. & Rakim's "Follow the Leader."

It took them a while to get their sound down. Moore and Ranaldo began as apprentices to noise composer Glenn Branca, and got pigeonholed as Branca clones, causing them much irritation, although maybe it was just a polite way of saying that whatever they were, it wasn't rock. Very Euro, very punk, heavily influenced by the late-'70s no wave

bands, Sonic Youth tried out their own distinctive guitar tunings, often with drumsticks or screwdrivers jammed into the strings. Many of their guitar tones sounded "wrong" to rock ears on *Sonic Youth, Confusion Is Sex*, and *Kill Yr Idols*, but they were definitely on to something new, and by *Bad Moon Rising* the Youth had learned to emit some serious sonic shock waves. The excellent 1985 single "Flower"/"Halloween" was a turning point, a 12-inch single pairing the two most intense tracks they had recorded up to that point. But *Evol*, their first album with new drummer Steve Shelley, took the band's unique guitar textures and shaped them into compelling music. The macabre tones of the guitars really ring out in "Shadow of a Doubt," "Secret Girls," and "Star Power"; the violent guitar explosions of "Expressway to Yr Skull" build to a locked-groove finale. The CD version adds the '70s trash-rock cover "Bubblegum," from the "Star Power" single, a must for Kim Gordon fans.

The next step turned out to be *Sister*, an album so good that the band's previous glories sounded a little dim by comparison. "Schizophrenia" and "Tuff Gnarl" are corrosively lyrical guitar-noise reveries, while Steve Shelley brings forward motion to the rockers "Stereo Sanctity," "White Cross," and the amazing "Catholic Block." The lyrics veer from Philip K. Dick–style science fiction ("Pipeline/Kill Time") to real-world feminist anger ("Beauty Lies in the Eye"), and the beauty of *Sister* holds up from the first minute to the last. The best line, even if it's stolen from Philip K. Dick: "I can't get laid 'cause everyone is dead."

Daydream Nation was *Sister*'s double-album companion piece, and it was also the Youth's triumph. Instead of continuing the succinct punch of *Sister*, the band tries something new every track, stretching out for long multidimensional instrumental passages of headphone-friendly guitar exploration that burst into noise ("Silver Rocket") or slow down for mood music ("Total Trash"). *Daydream Nation* doesn't exactly go down easy—lots of curious people who bought it found that they couldn't take it—but the cleaned-up production only makes the guitars sound weirder and more complex, combining prog-rock structures with punk propulsion (there's even an offbeat somewhere on side two, in the second third of " 'Cross the Breeze"). The highlights: Moore's wistful rock elegy "Teen Age Riot," Ranaldo's fond psychedelic anthems "Eric's Trip" and "Rain King," Gordon's rock-goddess fantasies " 'Cross the Breeze," "Kissability," and "The Sprawl." Hearing Gordon scream "I wanna know!/I wanna *know!*" over the necromantic groove is a powerful experience.

Having blown the collective mind of the rock underground, the Youth sought new worlds to conquer, and signed with a major label in search of a wider audience. They also decided to devote themselves to something they'd never shown much interest in before—concise, catchy rock songs. Unfortunately, the effort required more expertise and a snappier sense of rhythm than the band could muster. The initial Geffen albums had their moments: "Kool Thing" and "Dirty Boots" on *Goo*, "Purr" on *Dirty*, "Bull in the Heather" on *Experimental Jet Set*. But for better or worse, Sonic Youth is a groove band, not a song band, so it was a relief when they began stretching out again on 1995's *Washing Machine*. Alongside some truly sad attempts at tunecraft ("No Queen Blues," "Junkie's Promise") there were amazing jams on the title track and the 20-minute finale, "Diamond Sea." *A Thousand Leaves* took this approach further—it was utterly ignored on its release, but it was their spaciest and best after *Daydream Nation*. Program it 2-4-5-7-8-10 for a six-song, 46-minute groove album as intense as *Sister*, topped by the Ranaldo ballads "Hoarfrost" and "Karen Koltrane." *NYC Ghosts and Flowers* was a mainly instrumental throwaway, bringing in Jim O'Rourke as a full-fledged fifth member. *Murray Street* and *Sonic Nurse* were up there with *A Thousand Leaves*. Long, engrossing drones like "Rain on Tin," "Sympathy for the Strawberry," "Stones," and "Dripping Dream" summed up the music Sonic Youth could keep making for the next 20 years.

Sonic Youth has always strewn odds and ends about for their fans: places to experiment (*Goodbye 20th Century*), places to jam (*Silver Session*), places to cover "Beat on the Brat" (*Master-Dik*). *Goodbye* covers avant-garde compositions by the likes of John Cage and Christian Wolff. The three self-released instrumental SYR EPs of 1997 mess around with improvised atmospherics. All four have done various solo projects; the prize goes to Moore's fine *Psychic Hearts*. As Ciccone Youth, they did a novelty album *(The Whitey Album)* with Kim Gordon's brilliant karaoke version of "Addicted to Love." *Screaming Fields of Sonic Love* is an '80s best-of that does a remarkable patch-up job on the early, sketchier records, and is the closest thing to a best-of, although newbies should definitely start with *Daydream Nation*.   —R.S.

Son Volt

★★★★	Trace (Warner Brothers, 1995)
★★★	Straightaways (Warner Brothers, 1997)
★★★	Wide Swing Tremolo (Warner Brothers, 1998)

After breaking up the revered Midwestern roots-rock band Uncle Tupelo that he founded in the late '80s

with fellow singer/songwriter Jeff Tweedy, Jay Farrar formed a similarly styled combo in Son Volt to showcase his songs exclusively. *Trace* makes good on Tupelo's twang-and-thrash promise. A surprising optimism surfaces, with the chorus of "Windfall" the equivalent of a blessing. On "Tear Stained Eye," Farrar finds an almost Zen-like commitment in life's relentless passage. It's the sound of Farrar's sonorous voice, with its melancholy, wise-beyond-its-years tone, rather than the sensibility of his often cryptic lyrics, that makes the biggest impact. And, at its finest, the guitars whine and crash like Belleville, Illinois', answer to Crazy Horse.

Straightaways pares back the volume to reveal Son Volt unplugged. The opening "Caryatid Easy" evokes the roar of the debut, but the group gradually narrows its focus until the album winds down with just the sound of Farrar's voice, acoustic guitar, and harmonica on "Way Down Watson."

Wide Swing Tremolo finds the band breaking no new ground and presages its eventual breakup a year later, with Farrar setting off on a solo career.   —G.K.

Soul Asylum

★★	Say What You Will Clarence. Karl Sold the Truck (Twin/Tone, 1984)
★★	Made to Be Broken (Twin/Tone, 1986)
★★★	Time's Incinerator (Twin/Tone, 1986)
★★★½	Clam Dip & Other Delights (Twin/Tone, 1988)
★★★½	Grave Dancer's Union (Columbia, 1992)
★★★½	Let Your Dim Light Shine (Columbia, 1995)
★★½	Candy From a Stranger (Columbia, 1998)
★★★½	Black Gold: The Best of Soul Asylum (Columbia, 2000)

Dave Pirner deserves more respect than he gets, though not a lot more. No matter how many records his band sells, they'll always be overshadowed by their legendary Minneapolitan neighbors, Hüsker Dü and the Replacements. No matter how long Pirner keeps making hits, he'll never be as archetypal an alt figure as Kurt Cobain. At least he can take comfort in the fact that he made it with Winona Ryder back when Beck was still sleeping on couches.

The sloppy, hardcorish records the band made in the early '80s sound fierce and pretty damn OK, just like a lot of sloppy, hardcorish records made at the time. The majors suspected there was something to these grungy underground bands, and Soul Asylum was snatched up and slicked down. The resulting albums are now out of print, but you could argue that there would have been no alternative rock without blind alleys like *And the Horse They Rode In On*, which proved that you really could make a hard-rock record that didn't sound like Warrant or G n' R (though shades of Aerosmith's *Pump* do pop out).

But the band stuck around until their sound made more sense commercially. On *Grave Dancer's Union* Pirner commits Sammy Hagar–level crimes against the vernacular—"Standing in the sun with a Popsicle/Everything is possible" is a better line than "Only time will tell if we stand the test of time," only if you prefer faux cleverness to faux profundity. He also rhymes "Runaway Train" with pain, rain, brain, and insane. (What, no "membrane"? Cypress Hill please advise). And yet the songs are great—the choruses swell in all the right places, and Pirner's choked sob, while not always palatable, is always convincing. The stuff is as meat-and-potatoes in its way as John Cougar Mellencamp in its way—Pirner and Co. made heartland rock for a postpunk era, and for that, respect is due.   —K.H.

Soul Coughing

- ★★★★   Ruby Vroom (Slash/Warner, 1994)
- ★★★½   Irresistible Bliss (Slash/Warner, 1996)
- ★★★½   El Oso (Warner, 1998)
- ★★★½   Lust in Phaze: The Best of Soul Coughing (Rhino, 2002)

Mike Doughty

- ★★½   Skittish (Superspecialquestions.com, 2000)
- ★★★½   Smofe + Smang Live in Mpls. (Superspecialquestions.com, 2002)

New York quartet Soul Coughing arrived fully formed with 1994's remarkably inventive *Ruby Vroom.* Each of the group's individual parts stood out as distinct and formidable: snap-sharp drumming, springy elastic bass, *musique concrète* sampling (incorporating everything from seagull chirps to Raymond Scott cartoon music), and hip-hop Beat poetry (from the pop and subcultural appropriations of "Casiotone Nation" and "Blue Eyed Devil" to the storytelling of "Screenwriter's Blues"). Like Talking Heads, Soul Coughing offered downtown art-pop experimentalism with a funky rhythm section, and like Beck or Cake, it was peopled by geeky postmodern white guys who embraced hip-hop as part of a much wider aesthetic continuum—from the avant-garde composer to the singer/songwriter. All this is abundantly clear on *Ruby Vroom,* and that, combined with the novelty of this group's ultimately unique sound, makes it the group's definitive statement.

Irresistible Bliss is a terrific record marred only by the fact that it offers more of the same, with the novelty wearing off. More hip-hop faux-bravado ("Super

Bon Bon") and mock–race politicking ("White Girl"); more poetic cant from the world of commerce ("4 out of 5"); more complex blending of nourishment for the mind (lyrics and samples) and body (bass and drum groove). If there's anything new here, it's what sounds like Soul Coughing's first real stab at a radio single with the appropriately catchy "Soundtrack to Mary." The group's final studio recording, *El Oso,* goes one step further, scoring an actual (if minor) hit with "Circles." Otherwise, the third album takes only small steps away from the signature sound: a little more explicit with its social messages here ("Blame"), a little moodier there ("St. Louise Is Listening"), a little more varied throughout. Overall, though, *El Oso* is perfectly consistent with Soul Coughing's first-rate recorded output. *Lust in Phaze,* a posthumous compilation from 2002, collects 16 tracks from the three albums, plus one outtake, one nonalbum cut, one remix, and one live recording. It's totally legit as an overview—but since the group was so consistent, it's no better than any of the individual records. Fans, though, will likely find the enlightening liner notes by vocalist Mike Doughty worth the cost alone.

Doughty's debut, *Skittish,* is mostly acoustic singer/songwriter fare—albeit rich in his skewed sensibility—that sometimes reveals new sides to the vocalist but just as often feels like demos in need of Soul Coughing. The concert recording *Smofe + Smang Live in Mpls.* is better, partly because it mixes solo and Soul Coughing material as performed alone on electric guitar, but mostly because Doughty's easy humor and audience rapport shine like they never could sharing time with a full band.   —R.M.S.

Souls of Mischief

- ★★★★   93 'Til Infinity (Jive, 1993)
- ★★½   No Man's Land (Jive, 1995)
- ★★★½   Focus (Hieroglyphics Imperium, 1999)
- ★★★   Trilogy: Conflict, Climax, Resolution (Hieroglyphics Imperium, 2000)

During the early '90s, Souls of Mischief—along with their Hieroglyphics crewmates Del the Funky Homosapien and Casual—were the architects of the sound and sensibility of the independent West Coast hip-hop scene with its minimal loops, verses that stick mostly to playground battle themes, and choruses that largely eschew sung melodies. Their debut, *93 'Til Infinity,* established them as both old-school and forward-thinking. But there's also a bohemian-flavored jazz element to the record, and the rapid-fire rhymes sing with poetry, varied cadences, and dynamic voicings. While not self-consciously "alternative"—there's gun talk and plenty of n-words flying—*Infinity* introduced a level of intelligence and vocabulary that was more middle-class and college-bound than the typical Cali gangsta fare.

No Man's Land attempted to build on the debut's promise and establish Souls commercially, but instead it sealed the deal on sending the group packing to indie-land. A darker, more aggressive tone informs tracks like "Secret Service," but mostly the record stays stylistically close to its predecessor. While "Times Ain't Fair" ends *No Man's Land* on a high note, too much of what comes before it is forgettable.

While Souls of Mischief stayed relatively busy releasing music as part of the larger Hieroglyphics crew, it was four years before they reappeared as a distinct unit, on the independently released cassette *Focus*. Here, the foursome's typically jazzy backing gives way to the funkier grooves of "Way 2 Cold" and even a stab at R&B/pop on the bouncy "Step Off." Sung melodies are still virtually absent, but the rapped hooks sound fresh enough to make *Focus* a welcome return to form. The Souls' MCs still concern themselves mostly with battle themes—how good they are, how bad you are—but on tracks like "Pay Due" and "Shooting Stars," a newfound self-consciousness takes root. The group seems to settle into its role as independent elder statesmen who stayed true to hip-hop and paid the price.

Souls returned quickly with a proper CD release, *Trilogy: Conflict, Climax, Resolution*. Its high-concept title suggests an attempt to weave unity through the album's tracks—and that, in turn, suggests a desire to stretch beyond the fairly narrow parameters in which the group has thrived. A stab at spoken word on "Save the Babies (Conflict)," delivered by guest J. Crow, furthers the implication of newfound sophistication. But while tracks like the love song "Mama Knows Best" show how the Souls' MCs have clearly grown up in the group, not much about *Trilogy* offers evidence that it has evolved into something more than the sum of its parts. They remain four great freestyle battlers without the musical gifts to craft great songs. —R.M.S.

The Soul Stirrers

- ★★★ Going Back to the Lord Again (1972; Specialty, 1990)
- ★★★ Tribute to Sam Cooke (Chess/MCA, 1986)
- ★★★ Resting Easy (Chess/MCA, 1986)
- ★★★★★ Sam Cooke With the Soul Stirrers (Specialty, 1992)
- ★★★★★ Shine on Me (Specialty, 1992)
- ★★★★★ Jesus Gave Me Water (Specialty, 1992)
- ★★★★★ Heaven Is My Home (Specialty, 1993)
- ★★★★★ The Last Mile of the Way (Specialty, 1994)

The greatest of all gospel groups, the Soul Stirrers created the modern gospel sound, pioneered the use of co-lead singers, and brought a level of showmanship to their staid world that remains the standard by which all other groups have been judged. This latter achievement was due almost solely to the group's legendary lead singer from 1951 to 1955, Sam Cooke, who was 20 years old when he replaced a gospel giant, R.H. Harris, as the group's frontman. Cooke's unbridled energy and youthful charisma were singular forces in the gospel world, a combination made doubly potent by his angelic voice and uncanny interpretive instincts, both of which were far advanced beyond his tender years.

Cooke's shadow looms large in Soul Stirrers history, but it has been enhanced by his later success in the secular world, where he laid the foundation for modern soul while achieving significant crossover success. In fact, though, the Soul Stirrers have always been about great lead singers: The man who preceded Cooke, R.H. Harris, did not possess Cooke's showmanship, but then Cooke, for all his magnificence, was no match for Harris' superb vocal craftsmanship, as exemplified by the latter's unparalleled flair for expressive phrasing and dramatic emotional control. After Cooke departed for the secular world in 1956, in stepped Johnnie Taylor, called up from the Highway Q.C.'s (a fine group, but something of a farm team for the Soul Stirrers), a dynamic lead in his own right, with improvisational skills almost on a par with Cooke's. (Taylor, too, would follow Cooke into the secular realm, first as an artist on Cooke's own SAR label, and later with Stax and Epic.) But there were also Paul Foster, James Medlock, and Willie Rogers, each of whom brought powerful conviction and presence to their testimonials. And briefly, very briefly, one of the undisputed gospel giants, the Sensational Nightingales' Julius Cheeks (the direct link to hard soul shouters such as Wilson Pickett), was a Soul Stirrer.

In 1950 the group signed with Specialty Records and made its debut with one of Harris' most powerful performances, "By and By," which was surpassed by another song he cut at the initial February 24 session, the towering "In That Awful Hour," a haunting verbal depiction of imminent death that will give a body chills. For reasons that remain unexplained, Harris abruptly retired and returned to Chicago, where he performed with other groups, well out of the spotlight. For years much of Harris' work with the Soul Stirrers was out of print, but now the entirety of his two 1950 sessions, one on February 24, the other on July 28, is available on the single-disc *Shine on Me*.

Enter Sam Cooke. His years with the Soul Stirrers

were always the best documented in the group's long history, and nothing has changed in that regard during the CD era. *Sam Cooke With the Soul Stirrers, Jesus Gave Me Water,* and *The Last Mile of the Way* all chart Cooke's course from 1951 through 1955, and all come highly recommended. Cooke's voice is already fully developed, and all the nuances that would prove so affecting on his secular recordings are abundantly evident here: The Harris-taught emphasis on precise diction and the modulated timbre and the delicate "whoa-whoa-oa-o" that became a signature Cooke flourish are employed to stirring effect on "Wonderful," in a vibrant double lead with Foster on "He'll Welcome Me," and especially on the monumental "Touch the Hem of His Garment," on which the twists and turns of his phrasing hit with shattering impact. Both *Jesus Gave Me Water* and *The Last Mile of the Way* are essential surveys of the development of Sam Cooke's art.

Although its star power cannot compare to the other albums here, *Heaven Is My Home* should not be overlooked. The focus is on the post–Sam Cooke Soul Stirrers, when first Paul Foster and then Johnnie Taylor stepped into the spotlight. Other than three cuts featuring Foster's lead voice in 1953, the other 21 tracks here encompass recordings made between 1956 and 1958, several of them featuring Taylor and Foster in double lead roles. Those who know Taylor only from his Stax recordings in the '60s will be surprised to hear how much he sounds like Cooke here, not only in the timbre of his voice, but in the vocal tics he employs, and especially in that fluttering, upper-register "whoa-whoa-oa-o," which is a dead ringer for the master's voice. The recordings from 1959 find the instrumental lineup expanding from solely guitar to guitar-piano-organ-drums, and including fresh texts, such as James Cleveland's "The Lord Laid His Hands on Me," but without diminishing a whit the effectiveness of the classic Soul Stirrers double-lead strategy, one of the most distinctive in any genre.

Going Back to the Lord Again, Resting Easy, and *Tribute to Sam Cooke* feature latter-day configurations of the Soul Stirrers. Lead singers Richard Miles and Martin Jacox are powerful in their own right, but the material isn't as consistently moving as it was back in the day. Still, the Soul Stirrers were early adopters, if you will, of modern instrumental backing, and these later albums are full-blown productions, their arrangements betraying the influence of Memphis soul music. *Resting Easy* might have been better titled *Tribute to Sam Cooke, Vol. 2,* so close is it in style to Cooke's music, in addition to being graced by lead singers Willie Rogers and Martin Jacox, whose voices and techniques recall Cooke's. With that caveat considered, all of these albums have their virtues, making them worthy additions to the Soul Stirrers' magnificent body of work.   —D.M.

Soul II Soul

★★★★	Keep On Movin' (Virgin, 1989)	
★★★½	Vol. II 1990—A New Decade (Virgin, 1990)	
★★★	Vol. III Just Right (Virgin, 1992)	
★★½	Vol. V Believe (Virgin, 1995)	
★★★★	Club Classics, Vol. 1: 10th Anniversary (Virgin, 1999)	

Soul II Soul started out as a sound system—a sort of roving disco setup—and even though it never completely coalesced into a band, it somehow managed to invent a new and wholly British approach to R&B. By folding rumbling, hypnotic reggae bass lines into snappy, swaggering hip-hop drum patterns, bandleader/DJ Jazzie B and programmer/producer Nellie Hooper generated a groove that was at once languorous and urgent. The duo augmented that irresistible pulse with a stunning set of fresh, new voices: Caron Wheeler on "Keep On Movin' " and "Back to Life" (from *Keep On Movin'*), Victoria Wilson-James on "A Dream's a Dream" (from *A New Decade*), and Kym Mazelle on "Missing You" (also from *A New Decade*). Sadly, that was about as good as it was going to get. Hooper moved on to high-profile production gigs with the likes of Björk and No Doubt, and *Just Right* wasn't quite, despite a sultry performance from Wheeler on "Take Me Higher." Volume four in the Soul II Soul saga, *The Classic Singles,* wasn't even strong enough to see U.S. release, while *Believe* found Jazzie B and company resorting to such sentimental tripe as "Be a Man." Unsurprisingly, the group's next album, *A Time for Change,* went unreleased in the U.S. *Club Classics* merely reiterates the band's debut with a handful of remixes tacked onto the end.   —J.D.C.

Soundgarden

★★½	Screaming Life/Fopp (1987, 1988; Sub Pop, 1990)	
★★★	Ultramega OK (SST, 1988)	
★★★★	Louder Than Love (A&M, 1989)	
★★★★½	Badmotorfinger (A&M, 1991)	
★★★★★	Superunknown (A&M, 1994)	
★★★	Down on the Upside (A&M, 1996)	
★★★★	A-Sides (A&M, 1997)	

Nirvana and Pearl Jam emphasized grunge rock's punk attitude, but the genre owed at least as much to the sound and fury of heavy metal, and no band in Seattle made that connection more obvious than

Soundgarden. However much Chris Cornell's sinewy tenor recalled Led Zeppelin's Robert Plant, and Kim Thayil's grinding, slo-mo riffage inspired comparisons to Black Sabbath, Soundgarden avoided the stylistic excesses typical of mainstream metal. Solos were few and far between, and there was more to each song than a sturdy, head-banging riff. Indeed, the group's biggest hit, "Black Hole Sun" (from *Superunknown*), was almost Beatlesque in its approach to melody and texture.

Soundgarden didn't start off so ambitiously, of course. *Screaming Life/Fopp* (which compiles two late-'80s EPs) is far less interesting when the group performs its own tunes than when it covers the Ohio Players ("Fopp"), while *Ultramega OK,* despite its texturally adventurous use of feedback and multitracking, squanders the band's fevered intensity on forgettable, post-Sabbath riff rockers.

But *Louder Than Love* upgrades the melodic content and better exploits the contrast between Cornell's keening vocals and Thayil's slab-o-metal guitar grind, lending a sense of majesty to "Hands All Over," and a dizzying, hypnotic power to "Loud Love." *Badmotorfinger* continues in that vein, from the relentless momentum of "Rusty Cage" and "Outshined" to the savage psychedelia of "Searching With My Good Eye Closed." But it's with *Superunknown* that the band truly makes its mark. Although suffused with melancholy, it turned grunge on its head, painting downcast self-obsession in hues of grandeur, giving an epic sweep to "Fell on Black Days" and "The Day I Tried to Live." Meanwhile, the semipsychedelic "Black Hole Sun" and vaudeville-ish "Spoonman" significantly broadened the band's palette.

Sadly, Soundgarden lost its edge soon after. *Down on the Upside* offers a reasonable simulacrum of the band's sound and attitude but lacks anything in the way of a first-rate melody (though "Blow Up the Outside World" comes close). The group disbanded not long after; the ironically titled *A-Sides* compiles what would have been the band's singles, had it ever released any.   —J.D.C.

Spacemen 3

★★★	Sound of Confusion (Glass, 1986)
★★★★½	The Perfect Prescription (Glass, 1987)
★★	Performance (Glass, 1988)
★★★★½	Playing With Fire (Glass, 1989)
★★★½	Taking Drugs to Make Music to Take Drugs To (Father Yod, 1990)
★★★	Dreamweapon (Fierce, 1991)
★★	Recurring (Dedicated/RCA, 1991)
★★★★½	The Singles (Taang; 1995)
★★★	Live in Europe 1989 (Bomp, 1995)

★★	For All the Fucked Up Children of the World We Give You Spacemen 3 (Sympathy for the Record Industry, 1995)

Spacemen 3 titled one of its records *Taking Drugs to Make Music to Take Drugs To,* winning the all-time psychedelic truth-in-advertising award. But whatever the Spacemen's personal health habits, its indie trance-rock assuredly holds up with no chemical assistance at all. Their signature sound: distorted guitar drones, heavy repetitions, gospel flourishes, a bit of organ, very slight percussion, just skinny Brit boys tuning out the world behind their shades and listening to the reverberations of their inner space. They took off from touchstones like the Velvets, Can, the 13th Floor Elevators, and the early Dream Syndicate, to make music nobody else at the time was trying. *Taking Drugs* has their definitive moment, the 1986 nine-minute demo version of "That's Just Fine." Sonic Boom and Jason Pierce pluck away at their guitars, Bassman noodles over his bass, and Sonic mumbles the mantra "That's just fine/Outta my mind." He wheezes, huffs, puffs, coughs into the mike, occasionally humming a bit of Brian Wilson melody, as the guitars ebb and flow through his head, back and forth, dissolving into a gorgeous space-rock haze that seems to last for hours.

The Perfect Prescription stretches this formula to album length with zone-out grooves like "Take Me to the Other Side," "Come Down Easy," and "Ode to Street Hassle," full of incantations to Jesus and music that captures the sound of zero gravity. *Playing With Fire* is a more mellow and acoustic version, with a great exception in the insane "Revolution," a screaming rant about fighting authority by staying inside and taking drugs all day, just because the Man can't tell you not to, man. Both albums were excellent and influential. But the Spacemen always flew too close to the sun, and they were getting a bit crispy by the 40-minute drone *Dreamweapon*, subtitled "An Evening of Contemporary Sitar Music." *Recurring* was just bad imitation acid house: In the "Big City" video, Sonic even tried to dance, a shameful surrender of principle. *Performance* and *Live in Europe* are live sets that try to rock out (not a Spacemen specialty). *For All the Fucked Up Children* is early demo work; *Sound of Confusion* is the premature debut, too much punk and not enough trance. The comically titled *Singles* combines the *Walkin' With Jesus, Transparent Radiation*, and *Take Me to the Other Side* EPs into an 80-minute stroll through the ozone, lifted by the dreamy acoustic "Feel So Good" and the weightless version of Red Krayola's "Transparent Radiation." Pierce went on to extend the Spacemen sound with his new band, Spiritualized. Sonic Boom continued under the names Spectrum and Experimental Audio Research.   —R.S.

Spain

★★★   The Blue Moods of Spain (Restless, 1995)
★★★   She Haunts My Dreams (Restless, 1999)
★★★   I Believe (Restless, 2001)

While not exactly a landmark in the annals of depressive alt-rock, the debut from L.A.–based collective Spain, *The Blue Moods of Spain*, was a languid and moody offering that made up in style what it lacked in musical variation. Formed under the aegis of bassist/singer Josh Haden, the son of famed jazz bassist Charlie Haden and the brother of that dog's Petra Haden, Spain's output can best be described as jazzy slowcore, with more heart than copacetic outfits like the Red House Painters or Low, and less of a sense of musical adventure. Their sophomore release, *She Haunts My Dreams*, maintained the same level of artfully arranged mopiness, but 2001's *I Believe* opens things up somewhat, emphasizing a more layered and organ-intensive sound and featuring two tracks, "You Were Meant for Me" and "If We Kissed," that stand as the group's finest.   —A.S.

Spandau Ballet

★½   Journeys to Glory (Chrysalis, 1981)
★   Diamond (1982; Chrysalis, 1986)
★★★   True (Chrysalis, 1983)
★★   Parade (Chrysalis, 1984)
★★½   The Singles Collection (Chrysalis, 1985)
★½   Through the Barricades (Epic, 1986)
★★½   The Collection (EMI, 1999)
★★★   Gold: The Best of Spandau Ballet (Chrysalis, 2001)

Eyebrows arched and strutting gamely, London's Spandau Ballet joined Duran Duran in initiating the New Romantic fad—a bombastic fusion of frilly shirts and neodisco. Spandau's debut sounded an awful lot like Duran Duran and contained only one decent cut, the single "To Cut a Long Story Short." The rest, featuring songs with such portentous titles as "Musclebound" and "Reformation," sounded thin and monotonous; the band's appeal wasn't helped by its air of vaguely fascist snobbery. *Diamond* was more of the same; its offhand attempts at experimentalism didn't help.

With *True*, however, Spandau found a style. Tony Hadley developed a way of vocalizing that joined the heavy dramatics of Bryan Ferry to the lounge-act "feeling" of a Gary Puckett or a bad Bobby Darin.

And guitarist Gary Kemp, with "Gold" and "True," provided Hadley perfect songs for hamming it up: lush MOR that would've been clever if it had been intended ironically. Guitarist/percussionist Steve Norman switched over to sax, and added fittingly smarmy fills. *Parade* was a lesser *True*, but with *Through the Barricades*, Spandau took a bizarre turn toward arena rock and power ballads. *The Singles Collection* is an all right greatest hits package, while *Gold* contains a few later hits; *True*, however, remains creepily fascinating. Incidentally, Kemp and his bassist brother, Martin, starred in the gangster movie *The Krays* and were brilliant. Perhaps, after all, their years of posing paid off.   —P.E.

Sparklehorse

★★½   Vivadixiesubmarinetransmissionplot (Capitol, 1995)
★★★   Good Morning Spider (Capitol, 1998)
★★★   It's a Wonderful Life (Capitol, 2001)

On its surface, *Vivadixiesubmarinetransmissionplot* is a fairly normal set of Southern-sun-baked alt-rock, mostly on the slow side. Listen more carefully, though, and there are premonitions of something creepy in almost all of singer/multi-instrumentalist Mark Linkous' songs, like the "Rainmaker" who wakes up "with spiders on his eyelids." Linkous sings like he's passing on an uncomfortable secret, and likes to frost the edges of his recordings with blurts of noise or voice-garbling filters. It's a promisingly ambitious record, if dull.

Following the *Vivadixie . . .* tour, Linkous nearly died in a medical disaster. Unsurprisingly, pain and fear are the major themes of *Good Morning Spider*'s lyrics, although he tries to conceal them behind veils of electronic interference, voice-torturing tricks, and explosions of white noise. Even so, it's remarkably varied, with its simple tunes dressed up in a costume store's worth of freaky arrangements. The high point is a juicy cover of Cracker's cracking-up anthem "Sick of Goodbyes."

It's a Wonderful Life doesn't bury its melodies quite so deeply, and they're some of Linkous' prettiest, especially the title track and the Vic Chesnutt homage "Little Fat Baby." The arrangements are as ingenious as ever, with peculiar vintage keyboards and digital static popping up all over. But Linkous' gifts as a stylistic chameleon too often let him avoid sounding like himself: "Dog Door," guest-starring Tom Waits, is so Waitsian it doesn't even hint that it's a Sparklehorse record. And too many of these songs are slowed down to a funereal plod to disguise their scantiness.   —D.W.

Britney Spears

★★★ Baby One More Time (Jive, 1999)
★★ Oops! . . . I Did It Again (Jive, 2000)
★ Britney (Jive, 2001)
★★★ In the Zone (Jive, 2003)

More a cultural phenomenon than a musical artist, Britney Spears was the center of a teen-pop movement in the late '90s that pedophiles everywhere surely remember as a droolly heyday. In a bizarre but wildly successful PR campaign, Britney's persona was designed to be that of a chaste floozy. Every photo, video, outfit, and lyric had erotic zoom, while every interview underscored her upstanding Christian values. But whether or not you spent time trying to look up her skirt on the cover photo of her debut album or panted over her Catholic schoolgirl lusciousness in the video for "Baby One More Time," you have to admit that the singles like that record's title track and "(You Drive Me) Crazy," produced by Swedish maestro Max Martin, are something special.

By infinity-tracking her thin vocals, Martin makes her sound like the nubile robot of every boy's dreams, and the instrumentation has the metallic crash and wind-tunnel woosh of a sci-fi nightmare. All this happening over vaguely hip-hop dance beats makes sexy, danceable trifles out of the fearsome noise of modernity.

The title track of her next record, "Oops . . . I Did It Again," almost reaches the melodic heights of "Baby One More Time," but the whole affair sounds much more menacing. The robot is gloating, amoral, out of control. Perhaps it was to soften the backhanded apology of the song's lyrics that Britney's handlers decided she should perform it as a faux striptease in a glittering, skin-colored bodysuit at the MTV Video Awards. The performance remains a landmark of family-television pornography, and did have the effect of reestablishing her as a hard-working sex object. The rest of the songs here are rather lackluster in comparison, with "Stronger," an attempt at inspirational crooning, ending up only garnering unfavorable comparisons to first-rate singers like rival and fellow former Mouseketeer Christina Aguilera.

Her third effort, Britney, was the inevitable attempt to allow her to grow up and overtly claim some of her sexuality. But in the same manner as before, handlers deemed it necessary to ensure she was still a subservient male fantasy figure. The video for the tuneless, hyperventilating "I'm a Slave 4 U" found her writhing in that Flashdance combo of pleasure and pain while making close friends with a large snake. The spell-it-out ballad "I'm Not a Girl, Not Yet a Woman," sounded saccharine, and her tabloid-

reading fans didn't buy it. Attempts to seize the spotlight on In the Zone included a video for the title track with Madonna, followed by the famous MTV smooch between the famously shrewd elder sexpot and her prefab heir. "Me Against the Music" is another overly busy, not very danceable dance track. Max Martin's hooky handiwork is missed here, but the record, made with a grab bag of star producers from Moby to the Neptunes, has definite club cred. Bloodshy and Avant get it very right with the sexily infectious "Toxic." Moby provides a chic track for "Early Mornin," and "Breathe on Me" makes great use of Britney's intuitive breathiness. Planned stunts around this album also included being snapped pantless for Esquire, while unplanned ones included a shotgun annulment after a drunken hitch in Vegas, followed by an engagement with one of her dancers. And much to Christian chagrin, tabloid readers know that former girl Britney is yet a woman several times over. —L.S.

Specials

★★★★★ The Specials (1979; EMI, 2002)
★★★★½ More Specials (1980; EMI, 2002)
★★★★★ Ghost Town (EP) (Two Tone/Chrysalis, 1981)
★★★★★ The Singles Collection (Chrysalis, 1991)

Special Aka

★★★½ In the Studio (Two Tone/Chrysalis, 1984; EMI, 2002)

The British ska revival of the early '80s was more than just a big sales boost for skinny ties and porkpie hats. Dubbed the Two Tone movement after a record label and the racially integrated bands on its roster (Specials, Madness, the Beat, Selecter), this loose conglomeration of bands used the shuffling rhythm of pre-reggae Jamaican pop as a foundation but not an outside limit. Music hall tunes, '60s pop, roots reggae—a whole primer of English pop is buried in the Two Tone catalogue, much of which was incredibly strong for the first few years.

Madness became the long-running UK singles act, the Beat got the U.S. hits, but the Specials were the bravest of the bunch. Their debut single, "Gangsters," announced Terry Hall, one of the great voices of the 1980s, and a band that thought old Kingston ska was punk. Produced by Elvis Costello of all people, The Specials is the kind of debut a band spends its life living up to. Forget love songs—the Specials were all about average British citizens and their problems. Ska might have been their inspiration, but mastermind Jerry Dammers always had Margaret Thatcher in the back of his mind. "Concrete Jungle" and "Nite Klub" are as much George Orwell as they are Prince Buster.

For *More Specials,* Dammers cast away the fast tempos of ska (and most of ska, period) and brought in calypso and lounge music way before the hipsters got to it in the '90s. "Man at C&A" deals with nuclear war, "Stereotypes" is newspapers being torn up and rewritten, literally, and "Do Nothing" is one of the best unemployment songs ever written. But the best unemployment song ever was their last single ever; the "Ghost Town" 12-inch, one of the most beautiful songs ever recorded. Starting with a haunted-house organ and a synth sound that mimicked the wind whipping through an empty factory, "Ghost Town" is the lament Thatcher couldn't hear. Rico Rodriguez's trombone solo is heartbreaking and perfect, and the whole thing feels like a dance in a graveyard, unprecedented even in reggae's vast catalogue of dread and suffering. (This track is available on *The Singles Collection.*) "Ghost Town" and *More Specials* created a sound that later acts like Tricky (who worked with Terry Hall on the *Nearly God* album) would develop further.

Terry Hall, Lynval Golding, and Neville Staples left to form Fun Boy 3 (whose debut is deeply underrated), and Dammers kept the remaining crew together, adding Rhoda Dakar, and made records that suffered in the shadow of the first two Specials albums. Their first single, "The Boiler," was a groundbreaking rape narrative, still terrifying. (Not on the album, it is included on *The Singles Collection.*) *In the Studio* doesn't have the magical fuzz of *The Specials,* but Dammers' social critique is fierce, and songs like "Lonely Crowd" and "House Bound" prove how important Dammers was in the development of the later Bristol sound. The exuberant "Free Nelson Mandela" is the album's signature tune, yet more evidence that Dammers could see into the future. An album worthy of revival. (All three reissues have videos added.) —S.F.J.

Phil Spector

★★★★★ Back to Mono (1958–1969) (Abkco, 1991)

Phil Spector's life story is full of enough discomforting twists and turns—accusations of spousal abuse, substance abuse, a fondness for firearms, and first-degree murder charges—to keep biographers busy for years, but his gifts to pop music are undeniable. Spector's artistic legacy is in full view on *Back to Mono,* four CDs packed with grand, glorious, visionary pop productions aimed squarely at the heart of anyone who ever felt the explosions—hormonal, emotional, whatever—that made adolescence the best and worst of times. During the crucial years that *Back to Mono* chronicles, Spector refined and rede-

fined the concept of record producer as auteur, which he had learned as a protégé of Jerry Leiber and Mike Stoller in sessions with the Coasters and the Drifters. But Spector took rock production far beyond anything Leiber and Stoller—or anyone else at that time—ever envisioned. Layer upon layer of guitars, drums, pianos, and strings, and a couple of warehouses' worth of percussion mesh into a solid roar behind some of the best pop, rock, and soul singers of the era documented here, creating an aural extravaganza that had no parallel in popular music. More than 30 years after the last cuts in this set were recorded, it's easy to draw a line from the Spector style to the grand visions of Spector acolyte Brian Wilson (the dense layers of sound on the single "I Can Hear Music" are pure Spector, breathtaking and beautiful all at once) to the Beatles' *Sgt. Pepper's Lonely Hearts Club Band* to Bob Ezrin's rich, theatrical productions for Lou Reed *(Berlin),* Kiss *(Destroyer),* and Pink Floyd *(The Wall),* and to such contemporary masters of mise-en-scène as Trent Reznor, the RZA, and Dr. Dre. Spector, though, linked his sound signature to opera: he spoke of his "Wagnerian approach to rock & roll," and somewhere along the way it became "the Wall of Sound."

Back to Mono really delivers the Spector goods, encompassing the essential recordings from '58 through '69, a healthy sampling of rare Ronettes tracks and several breathtaking Darlene Love solo sides. One of the rarest tracks is the Crystals' 1962 recording of Goffin-King's "He Hit Me (It Felt Like a Kiss)," which Spector withdrew shortly after release, fearing the lyrics were too controversial for pop radio. A special treat is the inclusion of the great *A Christmas Gift to You,* Spector's vibrant 1963 Yuletide album featuring all of his Philles stars in vivid, atmospheric renditions of seasonal favorites such as "Frosty the Snowman" and "White Christmas." In a wonderful bit of sequencing symmetry, the album kicks off with Darlene Love's white-hot wailing on the now-classic "Christmas (Baby Please Come Home)" and closes with a sincere spoken message from Spector himself. With "Silent Night" playing in the background, and sounding duly humble, he thanks his artists and bids the listener a merry Christmas, then lets the music and chorus fade out gently—a nice, quiet touch to close out a celebration marked by high spirits and energetic productions. Only Elvis Presley's first Christmas album is even in the same league with this one in its seamless balance of rock fervor and Christmas sentiment.

Some of the earliest Spector productions—those by the abovementioned Kell Osborne and Spector's Three—are not included on *Back to Mono* but can be found on an out-of-print Rhino Records vinyl album, *The Early Productions 1958–1961,* which is well worth tracking down on eBay or elsewhere. Ditto for the sine qua non of the producer's oeuvre, the six-volume *Phil Spector Wall of Sound* series issued in the mid-'70s by the Phil Spector International label. The set includes two volumes of *Rare Masters,* including tracks by April Stevens, Betty Willis, and Bonnie and the Treasures. Other volumes include a hits album *(Yesterday's Hits Today)* and individual albums devoted to the Crystals, the Ronettes, and Bob B. Soxx and the Blue Jeans.

Back to Mono is indeed in glorious monophonic sound, and is packaged with a "Back to Mono" button for the diehards, and a book with song lyrics, sessionography, personnel listings, a 1965 profile of Spector penned by Tom Wolfe, and a solid appreciation of Spector's legend and legacy by writer David Hinkley. —D.M.

Jon Spencer Blues Explosion

★★	Jon Spencer Blues Explosion (Caroline, 1992)
★★★	Extra Width (Matador, 1993)
★★★½	Orange (Matador, 1994)
★★½	Now I Got Worry (Matador/Capitol, 1996)
★★★★	Acme (Matador/Capitol, 1998)
★★★½	Plastic Fang (Matador, 2002)

This is blues from the lunatic fringe, an indie-rock obliteration of everything Son House and Robert Johnson might have intended. It is ancient Delta hoodoo refitted as postpunk irony, qualifying as both insult and celebration, just like when British blues purist John Mayall called Zeppelin a "parody" of the blues for the band's high-octane overkill and outright thievery. Jon Spencer staggers beyond parody and into dementia, drawing on his days cranking out urban white noise as part of Pussy Galore. The singer/shouter/guitarist is not the first white punk to tussle with the old masters, not with the Cramps still ripping '50s rock to horror-movie extremes. But Spencer and his Blues Explosion partners wallow in that madness. Later records drift toward modern hip-hop and rock textures, but their core inspiration in madman blues rarely wavers. Whether you hear Spencer as a master deconstructionist or as a New York clown in Mississippi blackface may depend on your mood.

The band's debut is all theory and fuzzy guitar noise, a gathering of 20 barely contained tracks of real and imagined ecstasy and worry. Songs offer neither salvation nor clarity, though "Eye to Eye" at least hints at song structure, while "Eliza Jane" is anxious, furious, and raw. Spencer is already the feral blues front-man, a new barbarian for a new decade, neither B.B. nor ZZ. He shouts and weeps amid overlapping fuzzy guitars and drummer Russell Simins' relentless thump! thump! thumping! But the Blues Explosion was merely a promising notion until *Extra Width,* which suggested a sound and songwriting skills of their own. "History of Lies" is wild and mean, with frayed guitars and theremin mingling at the edges, and Spencer swaggers like a possessed Elvis on "Back Slider." *Orange* is just as charged, only this time more playful than desperate and loose enough to slip into the rock groove of "Ditch" and the sunny, funky soul of "Very Rare." By now, Spencer's songwriting had caught up with his flair for the conceptual, yet the songcraft too often fails on *Now I Got Worry.* A growing sophistication permeates the grooves, but aside from the bristling "Wail," little sticks to the ribs or eardrums. Not even the hallowed presence of Stax-Volt legend Rufus Thomas and Mississippi bluesman R.L. Burnside can make up the difference. Underwritten and overcooked.

During the same decade, Spencer explored multiple musical side projects, including Boss Hog (with wife Cristina Martinez) and a 1996 album of amusing if ultimately unsatisfying jam sessions with Burnside, called *A Ass Pocket of Whiskey.* The Blues Explosion remained the most fertile setting for his inner hound dog, closing the '90s with its best album yet, *Acme.* It begins with the ironic announcement, "This is blues power!" The joke is that Spencer and the band here fully embrace a sticky soul vibe of warmth and torrid grace, more Stax-Volt smooth than Delta gutbucket, while using hip-hop as a fresh tour guide. There is a wider range of sounds and influences, from the Spencer falsetto on "Magical Colors" to mad-scientist ranting and turntable scratches of "Talk About the Blues." Polish does not mean compromise. On *Plastic Fang,* the Blues Explosion erupts with straight-up '50s rock & roll on "Sweet N Sour" and country-fried rock on "Down in the Beast," of the *Exile on Main Street* variety. Not many ancient blues echoes here, just tight, tough indie-rock songs, and all the better for Spencer's new ideas. —S.A.

Spice Girls

★★★	Spice (Virgin, 1996)
★★★	Spiceworld (Virgin, 1998)
★★	Forever (Virgin, 2000)

Future generations will wonder why all the fuss. In fact, they probably already do. But with pop feminist expectations raised by indie rock's early-'90s brush with the mainstream, the debate did rage. Q: "Girl Power"—mass-marketing as subversive tool for preteen empowerment, or sisterhood commodified into this season's hippest fashion accessory? A: Both. Discuss.

Of course Girl Power wasn't riot grrrl—the femininity these five unkempt spazzes celebrated had less in common with assembling your 'zine at Kinko's than with enrolling your daughter in soccer camp. But no matter what shadowy fellow may have originally organized the audition, each gal was her own woman by the time they hit the tabloids—not a single Spice was a fashion-plate knockout, none was a Kewpie-voiced singer. They stood shoulder to shoulder in solidarity, fiercely demanding of the entrenched patriarchy, "You're going to wear *those* shoes with *that* outfit?"

Spice remains a buoyant capsule of their moment, a series of tunefully reasonable demands of potential suitors (be nice to my girlfriends, unlock your hips when you hit the dance floor). Sure, "Wannabe" sounded like EMF's "Unbelievable" run through the Stock/Aiken/Waterman Defunkerator, but "Tell me what you want, what you really really want" neatly boiled 40 years of rock & roll yearning into a demand for an immediate answer. As for the Girls' own response, well, "I wanna zig-a-zig-ahh" was suitably and polyamorously open-ended. It might mean an infinity of gently expanding orgasms. It might mean a lifetime's supply of push-up bras. It might mean awopbopalubopabopbamboom.

Spiceworld worked similar, if less magical, variations on the vanilla Motown the suburban Brits had been patting their feet to for years. But *Forever* is a 12-track hangover, a punishment for three years of irrational exuberance, foolishly enlisting "real" producer/ writers (Rodney Jerkins, Jimmy Jam and Terry Lewis) to combat those critics who accused the Spices of fluff. Which is kinda like Stephen King composing a sonnet cycle to prove he's a real writer. Solo albums exist for several of the Girls. Don't say nobody warned you. —K.H.

Spin Doctors

★★★	Pocket Full of Kryptonite (Epic, 1991)	
★★	Homebelly Groove (Epic, 1992)	
★★	Turn It Upside Down (Epic, 1994)	
★	You've Got to Believe in Something (Epic, 1996)	
★	Here Comes the Bride (Uptown/Universal, 1999)	
★★½	Just Go Ahead Now: A Retrospective (Epic, 2000)	

Mommy, make the scary clown stop singing! Make him *stop!* Oh, and while you're at it, remind him that hairy white guys who call women "mama" stopped

getting laid around the time the Steve Miller Band went disco, okay? The Spin Doctors were basically a pop version of a hippie jam band, playing those rubber-band Deadhead rhythms for four catchy minutes at a time, but the really surprising thing about them was how fast they came and went. Lead singer Chris Barron was one of the most visually arresting MTV stars of his day—for those of you too young to remember, he kind of looked like Boris Karloff risen from the grave, after smearing his head with Krazy Glue and then getting lowered head-first into a vat of boiling human earwax.

The Doctors' first hit was "Little Miss Can't Be Wrong," where Barron called his ex-girlfriend a *bitch*—not as a big statement, but casually, the way someone might say the word in a real-life conversation. It made the word *bitch* shocking again, quite an achievement in the gangsta era. (Naturally, he called her "mama" in the same song.) *Pocket Full of Kryptonite* spun off plenty of other hits; the one you still hear on the radio today is "Two Princes," a spunky little marriage proposal. After the live stopgap *Homebelly Groove*, the followup, *Turn It Upside Down*, was obviously supposed to be a smash—upon its release, *Newsweek* proclaimed it the album of the year, displaying its usual rock acumen. But consumers had apparently had all they could stand of those wacky Spin Doctors, leaving unbelievably awful songs like "You Let Your Heart Go Too Fast" dead on the vine. Of the band's comeback attempts, perhaps the most garish is *You've Got to Believe in Something*, which features Biz Markie on a cover of K.C. and the Sunshine Band's "That's the Way (I Like It)." Friendly recommendation: Why not try covering "The Bitch Is Back"? —R.S.

The Spinners

★★★★½	Spinners (1972; Rhino, 1995)	
★★★★	Mighty Love (1974; Rhino, 1995)	
★★★	New and Improved (1974; Rhino, 1995)	
★★★★½	Pick of the Litter (1975; Rhino, 1995)	
★★½	Happiness Is Being With the Spinners/8 (1976/1977; Collectables, 1998)	
★★½	Yesterday, Today & Tomorrow/Labor of Love (1977/1981, Collectables, 1998)	
★★★★½	Best of the Spinners (1978; Motown, 1990)	
★★½	From Here to Eternally/Love Trippin' (1979/1980; Collectables, 1998)	
★★½	Down to Business (Volt, 1989)	
★★★★★	A One of a Kind Love Affair: The Anthology (Rhino/Atlantic, 1991)	
★★★★½	The Very Best of Spinners (Atlantic/Rhino, 1993)	
★★★½	The Chrome Collection (Rhino/Atlantic, 2003)	

The liner notes for *Mighty Love* say it best: "Whenever Thom wants a hit he simply has to keep still long enough to hear it coming." For a stretch in the early '70s, it really did seem as though this Philadelphia producer had the magic touch. Using the same studios and many of the same musicians as crosstown rivals Kenny Gamble and Leon Huff, Thom Bell carved out a distinct niche in the emerging Philly Soul spectrum. He worked well with falsetto-drenched harmony groups such as the Delfonics and the Stylistics, but his subtle dynamics clicked into place with the Spinners: second-string Motown vets with an unproven new lead singer, Philippé Wynne.

Under Bell's direction, Wynne quickly asserted himself as a different kind of soul man: sensitive (but never hesitant), thoughtful (not impulsive), ever ready to throw down when the rhythm section kicks in. His warm tenor embraces listeners in a conversational tone; Wynne never lets emotion or his ample technique overwhelm the melody. *Spinners* is also a shining example of Thom Bell's soul pop. The simple, stunning arrangements isolate each voice—human and instrumental—and then gently weave the diverse strands into an indelible melody. "I'll Be Around" leads the charge, but followups such as "One of a Kind Love Affair," "Could It Be I'm Falling in Love," and "Ghetto Child" aren't too far behind. "How Could I Let You Get Away" establishes Wynne's devastating ballad prowess and elevates a sterling collection of singles to classic album status.

The 1991 two-CD Atlantic anthology *A One of a Kind Love Affair* superbly summarizes the Spinners' brilliant career, from 1961 (the minor doo-wop hit "That's What Girls Are Made For") to 1982 (the Spinners covering Al Green covering Willie Nelson's "Funny How Time Slips Away"). Also included are all the aforementioned songs plus "Mighty Love," the Dionne Warwick duet "Then Came You," and "Sadie" from *New and Improved,* the (full-length) boogiedown epic "The Rubberband Man" from *Happiness Is Being with the Spinners,* and, of course, *Pick of the Litter*'s "Games People Play." That song may be Thom Bell's masterpiece: immediately catchy yet structurally complex, it draws you into dozens of listens until the lyrical non sequiturs—a Thom Bell hallmark—somehow develop a deeply touching emotional logic.

There's not a wasted note or expendable breath on *Pick of the Litter,* but Thom Bell's increasingly grand orchestral designs inevitably begin to overshadow the natural tension between Wynne's passion and his partners' plush restraint. Wynne left after the disappointing *Yesterday, Today & Tomorrow,* and the Spinners achieved only one more undeniable hit with replacement John Edwards: the offhand Frankie

Valli remake "Workin' My Way Back to You/Forgive Me Girl" (from the out-of-print 1979 album *Dancin' and Lovin'*), also included on the Atlantic '91 anthology. Wynne toured and recorded intermittently with the P-Funk clan until his death in 1984, while Thom Bell's singular productions became less and less frequent during the group's last 10 years. Despite its insistent claim to the contrary, *The Chrome Collection* goes too far in committing one of its three CDs to that final decade.   —M.C./F.S.

Spiritualized

★★★½	Lazer Guided Melodies (RCA/Dedicated, 1992)
★★★	Pure Phase (Dedicated, 1995)
★★★★½	Ladies and Gentlemen We Are Floating in Space (Arista, 1997)
★★★	Royal Albert Hall October 10 1997 (Arista, 1998)
★★★★	Let It Come Down (Arista, 2001)
★★★	Complete Works, Vol. 1 (Arista, 2003)
★★½	Amazing Grace (Sanctuary, 2003)
★★★	Complete Works, Vol. 2 (Arista, 2004)

A member of the infamous hallucinogenic British outfit Spacemen 3, singer/guitarist/auteur J. Spaceman (Jason Pierce) went on to form Spiritualized after the former band's early-'90s implosion. Tormented by addiction and intra-band controversy, Spiritualized nevertheless set the gold standard for brainy, expertly realized space rock. The band's full-length debut (after a series of EPs), *Lazer Guided Melodies,* observed all the usual prog/fuzz-rock conventions: drony guitars and vocals, a slavish adherence to the Velvet Underground, but seasoned with unexpected touches such as harmonicas and horns.

More aggressively tasteful than *Lazer, Pure Phase* boasts string quartets, dulcimers, Farsifa organs, trumpets, and banjos but still manages to sound like a triumph of minimalism. Pierce's reputation for crafting trippy and spacious orchestral pop records was growing as rapidly as his offstage reputation for Brian Wilson–size nuttiness. Both would reach full flower with *Ladies and Gentlemen,* Spiritualized's unrivaled headphone masterpiece. A kitchen-sink record that added gospel choirs and blues and R&B influences to the group's already crowded sonic palette, *Ladies and Gentlemen* may be the least likely record ever to feature a cameo by Dr. John (who plays piano on the record-ending "Cop Shoot Cop"). Early the next year, Spiritualized returned with a two-disc live album that drew heavily from *Ladies and Gentlemen*—while neglecting that album's blissful title track—and managed to sound just as lush and evocative as its source material. (There's an excellent version of the Spacemen 3 chestnut "Walking with Jesus" as well).

As is his wont, Pierce fired just about all the members of Spiritualized and recast the group with session musicians on the unjustly neglected *Let It Come Down*, which continued his fascination with religious imagery ("Won't Get to Heaven [the State I'm In]," "Lord Can You Hear Me?") and American roots music. Though *Come Down* features the usual assortment of gospel choirs, string sections, and a veritable cast of thousands, the album's most restrained tracks, in particular the gorgeous hymn "Lord Can You Hear Me?," are its finest.

Reportedly influenced by Pierce's newfound love of the White Stripes, *Amazing Grace* attempts to combine the group's usual outsized theatrics with a rawer, garage-inspired sound, with mostly unhappy results. *Grace* is the first Spiritualized offering to ever feel messy: Its orchestral numbers and gospel choirs bump up uncomfortably against pared-down rock tracks such as "Never Goin' Back" and "She Kissed Me (It Felt Like a Hit)," a would-be subversion of the girl-group classic "He Hit Me (It Felt Like a Kiss)." *Grace* doesn't live up to the promise of its title.

Released in early 2003, the double-disc *Complete Works, Vol. 1* is a rarities collection that includes tracks from early EPs and 7-inches as well as the impossible-to-find Mercury Rev split single, "Good Dope/Good Fun." The two-disc *Vol. 2*, which focused mostly on the group's 1995–2001 output, followed in early 2004.   —A.S.

Spoon

★★★	A Series of Sneaks (1998; Merge, 2002)
★★★★	Girls Can Tell (Merge, 2001)
★★★★	Kill the Moonlight (Merge, 2002)

Spoon probably named themselves after the verb. The Austin, TX, foursome's songs are insinuating morsels, savored one riff, turn of phrase, or sentiment at a time. After releasing two albums on Matador during the mid-'90s (both of which are now out of print), they solidified their formula by the time they recorded *Series of Sneaks*. Drummer Jim Eno and bassist Andy Maguire lock down grooves tight enough to bounce Britt Daniel's surgical-strike guitar riffs off of; the hoarseness in Daniel's controlled keen gives the grooves a menacing tint you might not otherwise hear. The handclaps and whistling embedded in "The Guestlist/The Execution" flow with the song's subtle exuberance, but so does the wall of fuzz and reverb that eventually overwhelms "30 Gallon Tank."

Although *Girls Can Tell* shared the spirit of its minimalist predecessor, the album was a leap forward.

Daniel's lyrics are as opaque as ever (or plain frivolous, as on "Fitted Shirt," an ode to Dad's button-down), but he steps forward in the mix, betraying the punky passion of his inspiration, Wire, and varying his tone to ruffle the band's smooth dynamics. It helps that many of his melodies stick like burrs, and songs like "Take the Fifth" turn Motown bubble up to a running boil.

After six years at it—and with one particularly unpleasant experience with a major-label stiff, bitterly documented on the "Agony of Lafitte" single, under his belt—Daniel finally found a muse appropriate to his aesthetic: minimum wages. *Kill the Moonlight* isn't about making a few bucks an hour but about making do. "The Way We Get By" celebrates small pleasures, minor epiphanies, and life outside the big city. The buoyant piano and astringent bass kick would light up a jukebox anywhere. But Daniel fears settling, too. Jittery and dogged, "Small Stakes" cocks a cold eye at the sometimes sad business of self-preservation; it ends with the clamor of willfully drubbed drums and Daniel stutter-scatting. Hey—you've got to allow the guy at least one grand gesture.   —N.C.

Dusty Springfield

★★★½	Stay Awhile—I Only Want to Be With You (1964; Mercury, 1999)
★★★★	Dusty Springfield's Golden Hits (1966; Polydor, 1985)
★★★½	The Look of Love (1967; Mercury, 1999)
★★★★★	Dusty in Memphis (1969; Rhino, 1992)
★★	A Very Fine Love (Columbia, 1995)
★★★★	Anthology (Mercury, 1997)
★★★½	Stay Awhile—I Only Want to Be With You/Dusty (Tarragon, 1997)
★★★★	The Very Best of Dusty Springfield (Mercury, 1998)
★★★	The Millennium Collection (Mercury, 1999)
★★★½	Love Songs (Rhino, 2001)
★★★	Beautiful Soul: The ABC/Dunhill Collection (Hip-O, 2001)
★★★	Ultimate Collection (Hip-O, 2001)
★★½	Heart and Soul (Varèse, 2002)

After flirting with Peter, Paul and Mary–style folk and scoring big with "Silver Threads and Golden Needles" (1962), Dusty Springfield left a band she'd formed with her brother (and titled, obviously enough, the Springfields) to triumph with "I Only Want to Be With You," in 1963. Heavily influenced by Motown, the single's rhythmic drive and sure melody freed the singer to flourish one of the best (and huskiest) voices English pop ever delivered. "Wishin' and Hopin'" and "I Just Don't Know What to Do With Myself," both by Bacharach and David, came next, establishing her as a star. Finally, "You Don't Have to Say You Love Me" (1966) made her Britain's queen of the dramatic ballad.

In 1969 she released her finest effort, *Dusty in Memphis.* Produced by Jerry Wexler and featuring Atlantic's crack soul players, it was commanding R&B, including a phenomenal version of "Son of a Preacher Man." (The Rhino 1992 deluxe-edition reissue boasts great bonus tracks.) Floundering throughout the '70s (during which she was reduced for a while to singing backup for Anne Murray), she unsuccessfully attempted a comeback at the end of the decade; as a late-in-the-game disco diva, Dusty came off sounding strained. In 1987, she turned in a great guest performance on the Pet Shop Boys' "What Have I Done to Deserve This," but her earlier work remains her most memorable. *Stay Awhile—I Only Want to Be With You/Dusty* repackages her excellent debut along with *Dusty,* another great '60s disc; *Love Songs* ranges from Gamble and Huff to Antonio Carlos Jobim; *Heart and Soul* features good mature Springfield (especially live performances culled mainly from TV specials). And the three-disc *Anthology* isn't only for Dusty devotees but also for anyone intrigued by this still underrated giant.   —P.E.

Bruce Springsteen

★★★	Greetings From Asbury Park, N.J. (Columbia, 1973)
★★★★	The Wild, the Innocent, and the E Street Shuffle (Columbia, 1973)
★★★★★	Born to Run (Columbia, 1975)
★★★★★	Darkness on the Edge of Town (Columbia, 1978)
★★★★	The River (Columbia, 1980)
★★★★★	Nebraska (Columbia, 1982)
★★★★★	Born in the U.S.A. (Columbia, 1984)
★★★★	Live 1975–85 (Columbia, 1986)
★★★★★	Tunnel of Love (Columbia, 1987)
★★	Human Touch (Columbia, 1992)
★★	Lucky Town (Columbia, 1992)
★★	The Ghost of Tom Joad (Columbia, 1995)
★★★★	Greatest Hits (Columbia, 1995)
★★	MTV Plugged (Columbia, 1997)
★★★★	Tracks (Columbia, 1998)
★★★	18 Tracks (Columbia, 1999)
★★★½	Live in New York City (Columbia, 2001)
★★★★	The Rising (Columbia, 2002)
★★★★	The Essential Bruce Springsteen (Columbia, 2003)

One question: Are they waiting until Springsteen dies before they name a New Jersey Turnpike rest stop after

him? Is that the rule? Or can they go right ahead? And can they save another one for Clarence? Really—what has Vince Lombardi or Woodrow Wilson done for Jersey lately, anyhow? Well, the powers that be can stall if they want, but Bruce Springsteen has already earned his legend as the Garden State's poet laureate, and despite the fact that his mythic stature rubs a lot of people the wrong way, and for perfectly good reasons, the Boss di tutti Bosses remains a one-of-a-kind rock star. He's one of the few male rockers of any generation who sings about women without turning into a pushy little creep. He has never passed out into a toilet, or worn a mullet, or bought a castle, or announced his tantric sex prowess. His live shows are still the stuff of legend. He was smart enough to hire Max Weinberg as his drummer. Bon Jovi wasn't really his fault. Oh, and he rocks.

The young Springsteen made his entrance as a scruffy acoustic Dylan clone on *Greetings From Asbury Park.* It's rhythmically sludgy and vocally overwrought, but there's still a spark in songs like "For You." True, at the end of the song he sings, "Who am I to ask you to lick my sores"—but hey, he was learning. Still young, still eager to please, still reluctant to shave, Bruce scored his first triumph with *The Wild, the Innocent, and the E Street Shuffle,* with ridiculous car/girl mythos and jazzy rhythms and horns and guitars all over the place. The highlight: "Rosalita," a pile-driving eight-minute anthem roaring up from deep in the swamps of Jersey, celebrating the ultimate us-against-the-world teen romance.

For *Born to Run,* Springsteen got the E Street Band together to stomp all over some jaw-droppingly great songs, ascending into a Zen realm of pure carness and girlness. He also obviously watched De Niro in *Mean Streets* about a hundred times. The result was his breakthrough hit. "Born to Run" was all drama and lust and sax and drums and glockenspiels and one of the great "1-2-3-4!" screams in rock history. "Tenth Avenue Freezeout" sat back right easy and laughed, while "Jungleland" was a fabulously overblown epic about a rumble under an Exxon sign, starring the Magic Rat, his sleek machine, and a supporting cast of Jersey boys and their automotive enchantresses. Some of us are *still* trying to figure out the plot to this one. (Does the Rat crash in the tunnels uptown? Or does the girl turn him in to the cops? Suggestions, please.)

Darkness on the Edge of Town was grim, bitter, adult. Springsteen added more bite to the music, and more everyday detail to the lyrics, even noting the right kind of engine heads to put in a '69 Chevy. He also obviously watched Al Pacino in *Dog Day Afternoon* about a hundred times. His working-class heroes hang tough in "Prove It All Night," "Candy's

Room," and "The Promised Land," where the dogs on Main Street howl for the soul of a small-town kid in the Utah desert. And "Racing in the Streets" is still the best Springsteen song ever. *The River* was a more erratic double-vinyl set, divided between long slow ones with plots and short catchy throwaways. The throwaways are the ones you remember, especially the joyous "Out in the Street" and the morbid "Cadillac Ranch." But the real stunner is the long slow title song. If you love "The River," you should rent the concert flick *No Nukes* and fast-forward to the scene where Springsteen sings it for a crowd who have never heard it before, but who are singing along by the second chorus. Good question: "Is a dream a lie if it don't come true? Or is it something worse?"

Nebraska, which he recorded at home on a four-track tape machine, and carried around as a cassette in his pocket for two weeks before realizing he wanted to release it, is a bleak, unforgiving acoustic portrait of the dark side of Reagan's America. Releasing these stark demos should have meant commercial disaster, but *Nebraska* struck a nerve with the audience and became a surprise hit. Despite the slow pace, the sheer sonic punch of the thing is still shocking, especially "State Trooper," one of the scariest songs ever recorded. No happy endings, just the terrifying menace of "Nebraska," "Highway Patrolman," and "Atlantic City," the tale of a husband driven to the edge by debts that no honest man could pay. The Notorious B.I.G. would have understood.

With *Born in the U.S.A.,* Springsteen took the stripped-down songcraft of *Nebraska* back to his band. He also obviously stopped going to the movies so much, and started spending more time in the gym. The result: *Born in the U.S.A.* blew up like the Chicken Man, pushing Bruce to the level of fame reserved for Jesus, Elvis, and Cher. Even at the time, the synthesizers sounded dated and cheesy, but that didn't keep anyone from hearing how great the songs were, especially given Springsteen's most passionate singing. "I'm Goin' Down," "I'm on Fire," and "Bobby Jean" are desolate yet catchy; "Downbound Train" steals a melody from Jethro freakin' Tull and turns it into country blues. "Born in the U.S.A." is a long nightmare of American betrayals from Vietnam to Reagan, driven by punk-rock screams and Max Weinberg's even angrier drums. The song gets more intense the longer it builds, with Springsteen's howl giving way to a furious instrumental outro, kicking back in for one last chorus just so Max and the band can beat up on the riff a little more.

But fame was clearly taking its toll on a rock star who tried so hard to cultivate his regular-guy cred. His response was *Tunnel of Love,* a low-key, mostly acoustic meditation on his marriage, exploring good love ("All That Heaven Will Allow"), bad love ("Two Faces"), and the detours in between ("Cautious Man"). Even if the marriage didn't last, the music does; ballads like "One Step Up" and "Walk Like a Man" are alive with hurt and wit and Catholic angst. Unfortunately, it was the last shot of Springsteen's amazing '80s run. He basically dropped out, dissolved the band, and retired to L.A., of all places.

After a five-year layoff, he tried to get a solo career going, but without his rhythm section, he was just another klutzy singer/songwriter, his audience split down the middle by Garth Brooks on the right and Eddie Vedder on the left. (Indeed, two of his E Street comrades, Max Weinberg and Steve Van Zandt, became TV stars and enjoyed better solo success in the '90s than the Boss did.) He simultaneously released two heavily hyped comeback albums, *Human Touch* and *Lucky Town,* but the songs were lugubrious and out of focus, overplayed by the hack L.A. studio band, and his fans didn't bite. *The Ghost of Tom Joad* was a self-conscious attempt to remake *Nebraska,* this time with a real studio, a big budget, and preachier lyrics—but the songs just weren't there. *The Rising* was rightly hailed as Springsteen's best since *Tunnel of Love,* an E Street reunion inspired by the September 11 terrorist attacks. It was still heavy-handed in the lyrics department ("Land of Hope and Dreams," hoo-hah), but the music was punchy and vivid, especially the clincher "Counting on a Miracle."

Springsteen's first archival retrospective came in 1986 with the five-record *Live* box, which had massive production numbers, "This Land Is Your Land," Edwin Starr's "War," and too many *Born in the U.S.A.* remakes. But the *Nebraska* tunes were revelatory—especially "Reason to Believe," which became a blasphemous country-gospel hoedown that blew the studio version away. *Chimes of Freedom* was a weak 1988 live EP; *MTV Plugged* was a little-watched MTV gig that failed to shore up the sagging sales of *Human Touch* and *Lucky Town.* *Tracks* was a generous if belated four-CD box of rare and unreleased tunes, most notably "Shut Out the Light," originally the B side of the "Born in the U.S.A." single; it's the same Vietnam vet singing, but the guitars are acoustic and the pain is brand-new. *18 Tracks* was a rip forcing fans to pay twenty bucks for three songs foolishly left off *Tracks.* *Live in New York City* documented the E Street Band's 2000 reunion tour.

As for *Greatest Hits,* it's an argument-starter for sure. There are brave choices ("Atlantic City," "The River"), but the final third is all filler; none of the new songs was ever called a hit again, and just because his theme for the movie *Philadelphia* won an Oscar doesn't make it suck any less. And where oh where is

"Rosalita"? "Prove It All Night"? "I'm Goin' Down"? But this is a good place to hear why Bruce remains a legend, particularly when you get to that moment in "Thunder Road" when he sings "from your front porch to my front seat." Consider how easy it would have been for him to sing "my back seat." Easier, in fact—catchier, more crowd-pleasing, more poetic in a way, more pandering definitely. He just had something else to say. If you're one of those people who has trouble understanding why Springsteen still inspires such fervor in his fans, it's all there in that moment. —R.S.

Squarepusher

★★★	Feed Me Weird Things (Rephlex, 1996)
★★★½	Hard Normal Daddy (Warp, 1997)
★★★★	Big Loada (Warp, 1997)
★★★	Burning 'n' Tree (Warp, 1997)
★½	Music Is Rotted One Note (Warp, 1998)
★	Budakhan Mindphone (Warp, 1999)
★★	Selection Sixteen (Warp, 1999)
★★★	Go Plastic (Warp, 2001)
★★	Do You Know Squarepusher (Warp, 2002)
★★½	Ultravisitor (Warp, 2003)

Techno breeds weirdos, but they don't come much more willfully weird than Tom Jenkinson, a.k.a. Squarepusher, a master of high-speed breakbeat flip-outs who's dedicated most of his career to not doing what's expected of him. The first sound on *Feed Me Weird Things* is a crisply strummed acoustic guitar; "Squarepusher Theme" rapidly develops into a pleasant bit of fusion jazz, notable for its freaky drum-program rolls and wanky fretless bass parts—the two constants of Jenkinson's subsequent career. The beats on the rest of the album are fearfully strong, fast, and varied, though they're sometimes shoehorned into fluffy jazz arrangements. When they're not, as with the almost-all-percussion "North Circular," they herald a major new electronic stylist.

Hard Normal Daddy finds Jenkinson mostly leaving his bass untouched and even more divided about what to do with his rhythms. He's a natural grandstander, and loves nothing more than to double, quadruple, and octuple the velocity of his beats, then send them off into a rattling skid. Here, though, he either sublimates them to tunes like "Cooper's World" that approximate an early-'70s sort of funk-jazz hybrid, or makes them carry delirious tracks like "Chin Hippy" with almost no help. (*Burningn'n Tree* collects several early singles in much the same vein.)

Big Loada is a massive whirling video-game spasm of drum and bass—mostly drum. "Come on My Selector" and "A Journey to Reedham" are almost im-

possibly fast and detail-crammed, flitting and exploding like skipping stones that turn into fireworks. The keyboard and bass parts aren't too developed, but who cares? Jenkinson's beats are effectively one long, magnificent jazz percussion solo, as fast as a deck of cards being riffled. (The American version appends the *Port Rhombus* E.P.)

Big Loada was also kind of a stylistic terminus—there's no way the beats could've gotten any faster—but *Music Is Rotted One Note* still came as a shock: Jenkinson put drum and bass aside altogether, in favor of a tepid, tuneless approximation of early electric Miles Davis, "collectively improvised" by a collective that consisted of himself. With the exception of "My Sound," it's a thoroughly failed experiment. *Budakhan Mindphone* is more of the same, but even worse; a subsequent EP, *Maximum Priest*, found him playing around with snail's-pace dub.

By the time *Selection Sixteen* came out, Mu-Ziq and others had pretty much taken over Squarepusher's spatterbeat niche. The album alternates some leftover jazz doodles with some beat workouts that rev the tempo way up again. But it's nowhere near as much fun as the early stuff; only the monomaniacal thump of "Snake Pass" delivers the goods. *Go Plastic*, on the other hand, really is a return to form: not as spastic, but much more developed and controlled. It leads off with the delirious single "My Red Hot Car," on which Jenkinson actually sings. The thoroughly scattered *Do You Know Squarepusher* encompasses the *Big Loada*–style title track, a couple of Autechre parodies (with titles like "Conc 2 Symmetriac"), a 10-minute showdown between skidding rhythms and synth ambience, and a Joy Division cover. The album also includes a live-in-Japan disc that's basically the *Go Plastic* repertoire with some digital feedback and crowd noise added. *Ultravisitor* is pretty much a straight recapitulation of everything Jenkinson has done to date—the superspeed beat workouts, the jazz doodles, the ambient timbres—none of which seems to have evolved from earlier appearances. It's listenable if a bit overlong, but when an artist who recorded a track called "Iambic 5 Poetry" names a new piece "Iambic 9 Poetry" four years later, you know he's running out of ideas. —D.W.

Squeeze

★★½	U.K. Squeeze (A&M, 1978)
★★★½	Cool for Cats (A&M, 1979)
★★★★	Argybargy (A&M, 1981)
★★★★	East Side Story (A&M, 1981)
★★★½	Sweets From a Stranger (A&M, 1982)
★★★★½	Singles: 45's and Under (A&M, 1982)
★★★	Cosi Fan Tutti Frutti (A&M, 1985)
★★★	Babylon and On (A&M, 1987)

★★★½ Frank (A&M, 1989)
★★½ A Round and A Bout (I.R.S., 1990)
★★ Play (Warner Bros., 1991)
★★ Some Fantastic Place (A&M, 1993)
★½ Ridiculous (ARK 21, 1996)
★★★ Piccadilly Collection (A&M, 1996)
★½ Domino (Valley, 1999)
★★★★ Big Squeeze: The Very Best of Squeeze (Universal, 2002)

A writers' band in the most literal sense, Squeeze is essentially the creature of its principal songwriters, Chris Difford and Glenn Tilbrook. Squeeze bubbled up at about the same time as Elvis Costello and Joe Jackson, but the band's allegiance to the new wave was more a matter of instrumental color than musical attitude. Its John Cale–produced debut, *U.K. Squeeze*, does include such game efforts as "Sex Master," but *Cool for Cats* is much closer to what the band is about. Despite such period touches as the sequenced synths on "Slap & Tickle," these songs make their point through a deft combination of melody and characterization, and with the wicked wit of keyboardist Jools Holland acting in counterpoint to Difford and Tilbrook's songcraft, the group serves up several gems, including the breathless "Goodbye Girl" and the gorgeous "Up the Junction."

With *Argybargy* and *East Side Story*, Squeeze truly hits its stride. *Argybargy* starts off strong with the endearing "Pulling Mussels (From the Shell)" and builds from there, with songs that range from the personal ("Another Nail in My Heart") to the picaresque ("Misadventure"). *East Side Story* fleshes out the band's approach further, adding a country feel for "Labelled with Love" and—with the aid of new keyboardist Paul Carrack—bringing a bit of blue-eyed soul to "Tempted," perhaps the group's most memorable single.

From there it's a slow slide into cliché. *Sweets From a Stranger*, recorded with yet another new keyboardist, has its moments (particularly "Black Coffee in Bed") but lacks the sparkle of its predecessors. No wonder; the band was falling apart, and in fact disbanded right before releasing *Singles: 45's and Under*, a best-of with one new song, "Annie Get Your Gun."

The group's main men cut an album as Difford and Tilbrook, but it lacked group chemistry, and eventually Squeeze reorganized, with Holland back in the fold. Yet *Cosi Fan Tutti Frutti* didn't have that Squeeze chemistry either, and it wasn't until *Babylon and On* that the group regained its footing. "Hourglass," a tuneful trifle, is the album's standout track, but "Trust Me to Open My Mouth" and "853-5937" are equally charming. Charm, though, is about as much as the band has to offer by this point. Although

Frank is well-crafted, it's only occasionally involving, while the live *A Round and A Bout* will be of interest only to completists. Even hard-core fans would be forgiven for losing interest at this point, as *Play*, *Some Fantastic Place*, *Ridiculous*, and *Domino* reduce the Squeeze recipe to thinner and thinner gruel.

Of the various hits collections, *Big Squeeze* is the most comprehensive, but all include the group's few actual hits. —J.D.C.

Billy Squier

★★★ The Tale of the Tape (1980; J-Bird, 2000)
★★★½ Don't Say No (Capitol, 1981)
★★ Emotions in Motion (Capitol, 1982)
★★ Signs of Life (1984; J-Bird, 2000)
★ Enough Is Enough (1986; J-Bird, 2000)
★ Hear & Now (Capitol, 1989)
★ Creatures of Habit (Capitol, 1991)
★ Tell the Truth (Capitol, 1993)
★★★½ 16 Strokes: The Best of Billy Squier (Capitol, 1995)
★★★ Reach for the Sky: The Anthology (Capitol, 1996)
★ Happy Blue (J-Bird, 1998)

Billy Squier was the first pop-metal yelper to slip into the void left by Led Zeppelin, with his smash *Don't Say No* in 1981. "Lonely Is the Night" was a Zep imitation so obvious, it made bands around the country slap their foreheads and declare, "But of course!" Squier had been scuffling around the Boston area for years before his big break ("Who's Your Boyfriend," from 1980's *The Tale of the Tape*, was a great power-pop nugget, and Jam Master Jay cited "The Big Beat" as an unlikely hip-hop inspiration), and he was beloved in New England for the unreconstructed townie accent he flaunted in hits such as "In the Dark" ("in the dock") and "My Kinda Lover" ("my kind-ah lov-ah"). *Don't Say No* invented the pretty-boy hard-rock style that would soon make Jon Bon Jovi a rich man, and delivered a bona fide classic with "The Stroke," which made going to third sound like some depraved medieval torture ritual, complete with a choir of disembodied succubi chanting, "Stroke! Stroke!"

Squier squeezed out a few more hits with *Emotions in Motion*, which had "Everybody Wants You," and *Signs of Life*, which had "Rock Me Tonight." Unfortunately, the "Rock Me Tonight" video also displayed Squier's unique terpsichorean skills. The man was the silliest dancer in MTV history—yes, even worse than the chick from Scandal. Squier had his own unique repertoire of moves: the deep-knee duck wobble, the elbow-swinging double-finger snap, the pointy-toe backward kick, and so on. As ROLLING STONE memorably put it at the time, he flapped his wrists like a French pastry chef whose soufflés had just fallen. *16 Strokes* is the most efficient of his hits packages, although it includes far too many of his later comeback efforts.   —R.S.

Staind

★★½	Dysfunction (Flip/Elektra, 1999)
★★★	Break the Cycle (Flip/Elektra, 2001)
★★★	14 Shades of Grey (Elektra, 2002)

New metal is born free but is everywhere Alice in Chains. Aaron Lewis is a key figure in metal's shift in vocal fixation from the constipated sincerity of Eddie Vedder to the chilly modalities of Layne Staley. But if Staley's voice was numbed with a narcotic chill, Lewis was restless, as if jonesing for a far more insidious opiate—the quest for the ideal childhood that troubled rockers as dissimilar as John Lennon and Axl Rose. In the process, he's come to typify what critics find most unstomachable about mope rock: an utter humorlessness undercut with a somewhat cynical hint that if you mock these sentiments, you have no respect for the screwed-up kids who share them.

Musically, however, Staind is not merely a missing link between grunge and new metal; they are more like chromosomal evidence that they're the same damn species. On *Dysfunction,* guitarist Mike Mushok's riffs shift around, their attack as potent, yet unfocused, as early Alice or Soundgarden. But while those bands were still finding their feet, Staind seemed to argue that riffs *should* have a mind of their own, as if sharing Korn's unstated credo that catharsis is for pussies.

Unlike Korn, however—who seem like the kind of creepy shop teachers who forget that while adults should identify with kids, they should be capable of an adult perspective, too—Staind came up with a heartfelt approach to the problems of its times on *Break the Cycle.* Unfortunately, Lewis ignores the fact that families are fucked up in subtle ways, berating straw parental figures with accusations like "Your daughters are porno stars/And your sons sell death to kids." As its title suggests, *Break the Cycle* was a way out, supposedly—power ballads as family therapy, or some such therapeutic dodge. Tolstoy be damned, Staind insists—all unhappy families are unhappy in exactly the same fucking way.   —K.H.

The Standells

★★★	The Best of the Standells (1966–1968) (Rhino, 1987)
★★	Ban This! Live From Cavestomp! (Varèse, 1999)
★★	The Live Ones! (Sundazed, 2001)

The Standells' "Sometimes Good Guys Don't Wear White" was a good, snarling defense of teenage misfits, and "Try It" was banned for suggestive lyrics by right-wing radio stations—but nothing this L.A. outfit did ever measured up to the sludge-rock power of their 1966 smash, "Dirty Water." Written by producer Ed Cobb and sung by drummer Dick Dodd, the song remains a trashy monolith. Rhino gives us the best in toto; *The Live Ones!* is prime 1966 screaming, and *Ban This!* finds Dodd still in fine outta-control form live in 1999.   —P.E.

The Staple Singers

★★★½	Uncloudy Day (1959; Koch, 2002)
★★★½	Swing Low Sweet Chariot (1961; Collectables, 2000)
★★★	Swing Low (1962; Collectables, 2001)
★★★★	Freedom Highway (1965; Sony Legacy, 1991)
★★★	Soul Folk in Action (1968; Stax, 1991)
★★	We'll Get Over (1970; Stax, 1994)
★★★	The Staple Swingers (1971; Stax, 1996)
★★★½	Be Altitude: Respect Yourself (1972; Stax, 1989)
★★★	Be What You Are (1973; Stax, 1991)
★★	City in the Sky (1974; Stax, 1996)
★★★★★	The Best of the Staple Singers (1975; Fantasy, 1991)
★★★	Let's Do It Again (1975; Spy, 2002)
★★★½	Great Day (1975; Milestone, 1991)
★★★★½	Chronicle (Stax, 1979)
★★★	Let's Do It Again: Greatest Hits Live in Concert (Aim, 1998)
★★★	The Very Best of the Staple Singers, Vol. 1 (Collectables, 1998)
★★★	The Very Best of the Staple Singers, Vol. 2 (Collectables, 1998)
★★★½	The Staple Singers Greatest Hits (Fantasy, 1999)
★★½	Too Close (MCA, 1999)
★★★½	The Gospel According to the Staple Singers (Dressed To Kill, 2000)
★★★½	Pray On, My Child (Liquid 8, 2002)
★★★★★	Glory! It's the Staple Singers (Recall, 2002)

Mavis Staples

★★½	Mavis Staples (1984; HDH, 1995)
★★★	Only for the Lonely (Stax, 1993)
★★★	Spirituals to Gospel: Dedicated to Mahalia Jackson (Verve, 1996)

Pops Staples

| ★★★½ | Peace to the Neighborhood (Virgin, 1992) |

Of all the great gospel groups, the Staple Singers were the most adept at moving between the spiritual and the secular, and the only group to do inspired work on both sides of the fence. Roebuck "Pops" Staples was already a highly regarded gospel guitarist when he formed a singing group with his children—son Pervis and daughters Cleotha, Yvonne (who would replace Pervis in 1970), and the mighty Mavis—in Chicago in 1951. Throughout that decade they recorded a series of albums for Vee Jay that featured their passionate vocal assault on traditional songs ("Will the Circle Be Unbroken") and the new traditionals Pops was showing a talent for composing ("This May Be the Last Time," which a certain English rock band may have stumbled upon), often requiring little more than the patriarch's shimmering guitar lines for accompaniment. The available early albums are all worthwhile, especially *Uncloudy Day* and *Swing Low Sweet Chariot*. Because they never met a gospel song they couldn't command, there is no filler on these albums, unlike later when they relied on pop sources. There are several serviceable compilations of Vee Jay material (*The Gospel According to the Staple Singers; The Very Best of the Staple Singers, Vol. 2; Pray On, My Child*), but the double-disc *Glory!* is the most comprehensive. These performances stand as joyously tall as anything they ever recorded and made the Staple Singers gospel stars, but Pops had a wider vision of what his group could be. He spent much of the '60s perfecting the Staples as the connection point between gospel music and contemporary concerns. *Great Day* is drawn from the 1960–63 sessions for Riverside, which sought to align them with the social conscience of the exploding folk scene, and includes a very prescient 1963 cover of Dylan's "Masters of War." *Freedom Highway* dates from their brief mid-'60s tenure with Epic, where they lifted their voices in support of the civil-rights movement, and made their first significant pop-chart appearance with their funky take on Buffalo Springfield's "For What It's Worth." It was a sign of things to come.

Those things didn't come right away. The Staple Singers signed with Stax in 1968. *Soul Folk in Action* was a promising beginning, as producer Steve Cropper and the MGs (minus Booker T.) make the Staples feel right at home in Memphis, but *We'll Get Over* works a bit too hard to make the crossover point with songs like "Everyday People" and "Games People Play." Al Bell replaced Cropper and moved recording to Muscle Shoals for *The Staple Swingers*. It produced their first big hit, the simplistic "Heavy Makes You Happy," but this was just a warm-up. 1972's *Be Altitude: Respect Yourself* was the watershed. Like all the records the Staples made for Stax, it downplays Pops' writing and overtly churchy trappings, but here the company's song factory gives the group material that

accomplishes what good gospel does. "Respect Yourself" and "I'll Take You There" are inspirational songs, set to equally uplifting grooves that deliver the messages to the heart of the pop and soul mainstream. On them Mavis is revealed as the soul diva her gospel fans always knew her to be, and seldom has salvation sounded so sensual. *Be What You Are* and *City in the Sky* aren't quite up to that standard, but they do offer treats like "Touch a Hand (Make a Friend)" and the ever-relevant "Washington We're Watching You." The group's feel-good agenda is sometimes too heavily handled on the individual albums, but the three main compilations from this golden era are all recommended. You can base the decision on your budget: *Greatest Hits* (eight songs), *Chronicle* (12), or *Best Of* (16). *Greatest Hits Live in Concert* is worthwhile, though mistitled; apart from the title track, this fairly recent set eschews their biggest numbers in favor of their pre-'70s repertoire. The group's fervor and Pops' guitar make *Too Close* noteworthy, though the poor recording quality of these live tracks from the '60s will keep all but the most devoted followers at bay.

They moved to Curtis Mayfield's Curtom label in 1975 for *Let's Do It Again*. The title track was a chart-topping single, but the overall results were more slick than soulful, disappointing in light of Mayfield's own gospel leanings. The Staple Singers continued recording into the '90s, though none of the later albums are presently in print. Mavis began making solo albums in 1969. *Only for the Lonely* combines the first two on one disc, and contains her definitive reading of Bacharach/David's "A House Is Not a Home." *Mavis Staples* was an unfortunate mid-'80s attempt by Edward and Brian Holland to contemporize her, but *Spirituals to Gospel: Dedicated to Mahalia Jackson* gets it right by taking her back—the pairing of her voice with the solo accompaniment of Lucky Peterson's Hammond B-3 organ recalls her relationship with Pops' guitar, and many of the songs associated with Mahalia had been in the Staples' book for decades. Pops didn't test the solo waters until 1992, when he was 78, but *Peace to the Neighborhood* was surprisingly cohesive considering its multiple artist/producer collaborations (including Bonnie Raitt, Jackson Browne, Willie Mitchell, and Ry Cooder), and more satisfying than its now-deleted followup for which Pops was awarded a Grammy. —B.E.

Edwin Starr

★★★ Hell Up in Harlem (1974; Motown, 2001)
★★★ Motown Legends: War (Motown, 1995)
★★★ The Very Best of Edwin Starr (Hot, 1996)
★★★ The Millennium Collection (Uptown/Universal, 2001)

★ Agent OO Soul: The Ultimate Live
Performance (Cargo Music, 2002)
★★★ Essential Collection (PolyGram International,
2002)

In the mid-'60s, gruff-voiced Edwin Starr scored a few hits for Detroit's tiny Ric-Tic label, and then moved on to the mother ship, Motown. There, he's chiefly remembered as an early proponent of message music—"War" (1970) became a #1 pop hit and was later covered by Bruce Springsteen; its followup, "Stop the War Now," reached #26 on the pop charts. His albums are sturdy soul music, not the work of a true trailblazer, but certainly the commendable product of an ace craftsman. *Hell up in Harlem* is the tough soundtrack to one of the representative blaxploitation films of the era; *Legends* gives up the most solid stuff; *The Millennium Collection* is an okay Starr primer. —P.E.

Ringo Starr

★★½ Sentimental Journey (Capitol, 1970)
★★ Beaucoups of Blues (Capitol, 1970)
★★★ Ringo (Capitol, 1973)
★★ Goodnight Vienna (Capitol, 1974)
★★★ Blast From Your Past (Capitol, 1975)
★★ Ringo's Rotogravure (Atco, 1976)
★★ Ringo the 4th (Atco, 1977)
★★ Bad Boy (Epic, 1977)
★★ Stop and Smell the Roses (Boardwalk,
1981)
★★ Old Wave (RCA Canada, 1983)
★★★ Starr Struck: Best of Ringo Starr, Vol. 2 (Rhino,
1989)
★★★ Ringo Starr and His All-Starr Band (Rykodisc,
1990)
★★★ VH1 Storytellers (PolyGram, 1998)
★★ I Wanna Be Santa Claus (PolyGram, 1999)
★★ Ringo Starr and His All-Starr Band: The
Anthology (Koch, 2001)
★★★ Ringorama (Koch, 2003)
★★ Tour 2003 (Koch, 2004)

Blast From Your Past and *Starr Struck* contain all the necessary Ringo. *Blast* mines mainly his early records: his best single, the punchy "It Don't Come Easy"; the tolerably silly "You're Sixteen"; the plodding "Photograph"; Hoyt Axton's novelty number "No No Song"; and his reminiscence of the Beatles' demise, "Early 1970" (it's cute, not maudlin). Aside from reprising numbers from *Beaucoups of Blues,* the affable country album Ringo made with Nashville session legend Pete Drake, *Starr Struck* covers the later stuff, emphasizing McCartney's tuneful tidbits from *Stop and Smell the Roses,* and oldies off a Canadian LP, *Old Wave* (peppy

takes on Doug Sahm's "She's About a Mover" and Leiber and Stoller's "I Keep Forgettin' "). Trading on the clownish sweetness he'd developed in his Beatle role, Ringo's solo output is cheerful fluff, aided greatly by crack sidemen (Gary Brooker, Dr. John, Joe Walsh, not to mention John, Paul, and George). His drumming remains unspectacular but unerring (none of his own records demand the flashes of brilliance he'd displayed with the Beatles), and his vocalizing makes feckless hit-or-miss passes at singing. A collection of Tin Pan Alley standards dripping with strings, *Sentimental Journey* is Ringo's oddest album (and maybe his most interesting). Ringo made a comeback of sorts in 1990 with his All-Starr Band roadshow, recorded for posterity on the Rykodisc CD (*Anthology* and *Tour 2003* feature updated, lesser incarnations of the band), and he was also in fine, upbeat form on *VH1 Storytellers. Ringorama* is a return to original material, as Ringo crafts lush, nostalgic pop songs that pay homage to George ("Never Without You"), John ("Imagine Me There"), and Paul ("English Garden"). —P.E.

Starsailor

★★½ Love Is Here (Capitol, 2002)
★★½ Silence Is Easy (Capitol, 2004)

Is that the Goo Goo Dolls? No, they're British. Is it Coldplay? No, too depressing. Is it Travis? Nope, these guys are more electric. (But good guess.) Is it Radiohead? No, but the singer (James Walsh) sure wails like Thom Yorke. Well, who is it? It's Starsailor. Who? Starsailor. You know, swoony nouveau-shoegazer stuff; luxurious Neil Young–meets–U2 acoustic-electric arrangements, vague sense of heartache and agony ("You've got your daddy's eyes/ Daddy was an alcoholic"). Their first album is somewhat small in scale, almost cabaret; the second one is bigger, with two songs ("Silence Is Easy," "White Dove") produced with appropriate grandiosity by Phil Spector just before his arrest on murder charges in early 2003. You know, Starsailor. —B.S.

Static-X

★★★★ Wisconsin Death Trip (Warner Bros., 1999)
★★★ Machine (Warner Bros., 2001)
★★ Shadow Zone (Warner Bros., 2003)
★★ Beneath . . . Between . . . Beyond (Warner
Bros., 2004)

This quartet emerged as the smartest industrial crossover since Ministry because it understood the finer points of aural torture. Its pounding lockstep could be called "unrelenting," but it actually relents quite often, letting up momentarily with breaks for guitar squall and keyboard squeal before bearing down again. *Wisconsin Death Trip,* named for a creepy art house documentary about one small Midwestern town's murderous past, is full-throttle nightmarish death metal. Frontman Wayne Static and Koichi Fukuda, who share guitar and programming duties, definitively mimic the appalling scrape of metal against bone, and Static barks instructions such as "Tune it in/Chill out/Drop dead/I need a fix" like a drill sergeant. Such precision will only carry you so far, however. *Machine* is too well-oiled, leaving the listener to wish Static and Fukuda would jam a few gears. *Shadow Zone* is vacuous new-metal sludge that could almost pass for a Korn record, and *Beneath . . . Between . . . Beyond* is a negligible collection of rarities, remixes, and B sides dating back to 1996.   —K.H.

Steel Pulse

★★★★	Handsworth Revolution (Mango, 1978)
★★★½	Tribute to the Martyrs (Mango, 1979)
★★★	Caught You (Mango, 1980)
★★★	True Democracy (Elektra, 1982)
★★★½	Earth Crisis (Elektra, 1983)
★★★★	Reggae Greats (Mango, 1984)
★★½	Babylon the Bandit (Elektra, 1986)
★★½	State of . . . Emergency (MCA, 1988)
★★	Victims (MCA, 1991)
★★	Rastafari Centennial: Live in Paris (MCA, 1992)
★★	Vex (MCA, 1994)
★★½	Rage and Fury (Atlantic, 1997)
★★½	Sound System: The Island Anthology (Island, 1997)
★★★★	The Ultimate Collection (Hip-O, 2000)
★★★	The Millennium Collection (Hip-O/Island, 2004)

Britain's premier reggae unit of the '70s and early '80s, Steel Pulse inspired a slew of younger bands in its hometown of Birmingham, including UB40 and the English Beat. Led by singer and guitarist David Hinds, Steel Pulse picked up on the crossover-era (mid-'70s) sound of Bob Marley and the Wailers. Keyboardist Selwyn Brown lends a sweetening touch with both voice and hands, while Hinds blends aggressive rock lead guitar lines into politicized musings. Loose-limbed and accessible, the Steel Pulse groove is further strengthened by saucy horn lines and dub echoes on *Handsworth Revolution.* The title track, "Soldiers," and "Ku Klux Klan" all contrast pointed messages with giving rhythms; the lighthearted melodies underline, rather than obscure, the all-too-realistic lyrics. *Tribute to the Martyrs* is a worthy followup; the title track haunts, while "Sound System" pumps up an irresistible party-time buzz. Originally released as *Reggae*

Fever in the United States, *Caught You* (the English title) leans a little too heavily on Steel Pulse's poppier side. "Reggae Fever" itself simply sounds like a rote self-celebration, and the romantic motif of "Caught You Dancing" doesn't subtly elbow you the way the slice-of-life tale in "Drug Squad" does.

Perhaps *True Democracy* dips too far in the opposite direction; for the first time, Hinds sinks in a sea of incomprehensible Rasta ideology, and even the band's light-fingered touch can't save him. However, *Earth Crisis* goes a long way toward striking a balance between commercial aspirations and Armageddon. After a slow start, Steel Pulse kicks into comfortable high gear on the album's second half: the title track, "Bodyguard," "Grab Education," and "Wild Goose Chase" mix harmonies with a fresh array of tuneful synths and crisp beats.

Reggae Greats draws heavily on *Handsworth* and glances at the subsequent Mango albums, including the early single "Prodigal Son." Like the later *Ultimate Collection* and *Sound System* compilations, this is a choice introduction to Steel Pulse. On later albums, the group strives for an American black-pop crossover with surprisingly stiff results. Even the presence of guest producers like the Family Stand ("Soul of My Soul") and former Madonna henchman Steven Bray ("Can't Get You [Out of My System]") doesn't enliven the sodden mush. Adjusting to the lightweight dance grooves on those tracks seems to take a toll on Steel Pulse, because the more familiar reggae protest numbers (like the title track and "Gang Warfare") don't catch fire, either.   —M.C./M.M.

Steely Dan

★★★★	Can't Buy a Thrill (1972; MCA, 1998)
★★★★★	Countdown to Ecstasy (1973; MCA, 1998)
★★★★★	Pretzel Logic (1974; MCA, 1999)
★★★★½	Katy Lied (1975; MCA, 1999)
★★★	The Royal Scam (1976; MCA, 1999)
★★★½	Aja (1977; MCA, 1999)
★★★½	Greatest Hits (MCA, 1978)
★★	Gaucho (1980; MCA, 2000)
★★★★	Gold (MCA, 1982)
★★★★	A Decade of Steely Dan (MCA, 1989)
★★★★	Citizen Steely Dan (MCA, 1993)
★★	Alive in America (Giant, 1995)
★★★	Two Against Nature (Giant, 2000)
★★★★	Showbiz Kids: The Steely Dan Story 1972–1980 (MCA, 2000)
★★★	Everything Must Go (Giant, 2003)

In the mellow California soft-rock scene of the '70s, Steely Dan's Donald Fagen and Walter Becker came on as cynical robber barons. They were New York hepcats stuck on the West Coast, hung up on bebop and Beat poetry, refusing to play live so they could hole up in the studio to polish their twisted jazz-rock songs. Fagen and Becker became notorious for their obsessive studio perfectionism, as well as some of the nastiest lyrics ever sung on the radio. Steely Dan sums up the L.A. of the coked-out 1970s—no other band's music has been so identified with one particular drug. Indeed, it's a fact of life that in any rock scene, Steely Dan becomes trendy about two weeks after cocaine does.

Steely Dan's music always sounds slick on the surface, thanks to producer Gary Katz, but underneath there's real despair, growing out of the band's doomed love affair with L.A. The '70s trilogy of *Countdown to Ecstasy, Pretzel Logic,* and *Katy Lied* is a rock version of *Chinatown,* a film noir tour of L.A.'s decadent losers, showbiz kids, and razor boys. It's hard to understand Fagen and Becker's taste for the cheesiest sidemen money could buy—how could anyone write a song as vicious as "Black Friday" and then hire the guys from Toto and the Doobie Brothers to play it? But somehow, all that jazzy schlock just adds to the music's mystery. Forget it, Jake—it's pretzel logic.

Steely Dan debuted with the mellow folk rock of *Can't Buy a Thrill,* bringing a little urban alienation to smooth-sounding ballads such as "Brooklyn (Owes the Charmer Under Me)" and "Only a Fool Would Say That." It's softened by vocalist David Palmer, who sounds like he's nervous about where his wallet is. But keyboardist Fagen sang lead on both hits, "Do It Again" and "Reeling in the Years," while Becker played bass and sidemen handled the rest. The album became a huge hit, making Steely Dan a favorite among FM disc jockeys in fuzzy sweaters, high school music teachers, and other folks frazzled by too much '60s chaos. Fagen took over all the vocals on *Countdown to Ecstasy,* the album in which he and Becker fleshed out their vision of America as one big Las Vegas, with gangsters and gurus hustling for souls to steal. It's cold-blooded L.A. studio rock tricked out with jazz piano and tough guitar, from the ironic boogie of "Bodhisattva" to the stately dread of "The Boston Rag." It ends with "King of the World," a catchy little ode to nuclear apocalypse. A thoroughly amazing, hugely influential album.

Pretzel Logic is warmer, with more acoustic guitar and slightly more humane songs ("Charlie Freak," "Any Major Dude Will Tell You"), although the hit was the sinister "Rikki Don't Lose That Number." Steely Dan's songwriting and Fagen's singing were at their peak of fluid power: The whole album is flawless, but highlights include "Barrytown" (which Lou Reed could have written), "Monkey in Your Soul,"

and Duke Ellington's "East St. Louis Toodle-Oo." *Katy Lied* is much fluffier musically, but darker lyrically, starting off with "Black Friday," which sounds like the nastiest Bill Clinton song ever, even if it came out in 1975. "Dr. Wu" is Steely Dan's sharpest tune, with Fagen croaking the cryptic tale of a drugged-out Vietnam veteran over an ominously rumbling piano. Steely Dan's studio precision meant that while the music sometimes sounded slick and sterile, it could also gleam as brightly as "Your Gold Teeth II" or "Daddy Don't Live in That New York City No More."

The Royal Scam is a luxuriantly zonked-out concept album about drug dealers: very gangsta, especially the killer title song. *Aja* is one of the band's most popular records, although fans of rock & roll (as opposed to wussy jazz fuzak) may find their attention wandering. It peaks with "Peg" and "Deacon Blue," two affectionate send-ups of the band's roots in the early-'60s college-hipster scene. The other tracks have less to offer in the songwriting department and more in the "long boring solos by the sidemen" department. Much, much more. But *Gaucho* was so slick it slid right off the turntable into the wastebasket, except for the hit single "Hey Nineteen," a celebration of March–July romance with Cuervo Gold, fine Colombian, and a rollergirl tenderoni who's never heard of Aretha Franklin.

Steely Dan didn't cut another album for two decades, sidelined by drug and other problems, but oddly enough, they just kept getting bigger, remaining in heavy rock rotation while getting sampled by hip-hoppers. (Fagen and Becker stick it to people who try to sample them, even though they never had to pay for the riffs they borrowed from Horace Silver and Charlie Parker, but there's no point letting lawyers ruin music for you.) Steely Dan anthologies kept appearing, as did the box *Citizen Steely Dan.* The original '70s albums got reissued in the late '90s with brilliantly funny liner notes from Fagen and Becker; they complain that the engineering on *Countdown to Ecstasy* is too sloppy, and they're not even kidding. *Alive in America* is a weak 1995 reunion concert. The comeback albums *Two Against Nature* and *Everything Must Go* found Steely Dan unchanged, reeling in the years with slick, malicious satire. Deep down inside, Fagen and Becker must be disappointed that California still hasn't tumbled into the sea, but they still know how to make decadence and desperation move to their own beat, not quite rocking and not exactly swinging, just the sound of the monkey in their soul.   —R.S.

Stereolab

★★★ Switched On (Too Pure, 1992)
★★½ Peng! (Too Pure, 1992)

★★★ The Groop Played "Space Age Bachelor Pad Music" (Too Pure, 1993)
★★★★ Transient Random-Noise Bursts With Announcements (Elektra, 1993)
★★★★ Mars Audiac Quintet (Elektra, 1994)
★★★½ Refried Ectoplasm (Switched On, Vol. 2) (Duophonic/Drag City, 1995)
★★★★½ Emperor Tomato Ketchup (Elektra, 1996)
★★½ Dots and Loops (Elektra, 1997)
★★★ Aluminum Tunes: Switched On, Vol. 3 (Drag City, 1998)
★★★ Cobra & Phases Group Play Voltage in the Milky Night (Elektra, 1999)
★★½ The First of the Microbe Hunters (Elektra, 2000)
★★★ Sound-Dust (Elektra, 2001)
★★★½ Margerine Eclipse (Elektra, 2004)

It seems only appropriate that a group as prolific as London's Stereolab would make its 1992 full-length debut with not one but two records—*Switched On*, a collection of early singles, released almost simultaneously with *Peng!*, the proper first album. From the start, Stereolab had much of the distinct sound it fine-tuned on a dozen or so releases over the following decade.

Switched On's opener, "Super-Electric"—and any number of other tracks on both of these releases—kicks in with the steady motorik beat associated with '70s kraut-rockers such as Neu!, the repetitive grind of organs and guitars, and the ghostly yet facile melodies of French-born lead singer Laetitia Sadier (whose vocals, which alternate between French and English, often come accompanied by a second female voice). While elements of Stereolab's sound have their antecedents in a number of obscure sources, the group's sonic combination was among the most novel to emerge in the '90s. But Stereolab's early releases seem more focused in exploring this unique approach than in distinguishing individual songs from one another. As such, the records are more refreshing than they are memorable.

The same pretty much goes for the group's second studio album, *The Groop Played "Space Age Bachelor Pad Music"*, though a newly expanded lineup begins to open Stereolab's sound to new textures and colors (such as marimbas). While its title would associate Stereolab with the budding lounge-music revival, the album has only tangential connections to the easy-listening music of the '50s and '60s—and when it does draw from that well, it's only in combination with far more adventurous elements, including postpunk and Teutonic rock. In fact, *Bachelor Pad*'s individual song titles are more indicative of Stereolab's aims:

Songs like "Avant Garde M.O.R." and "Ronco Symphony" highlight the band's interest in juxtaposing disparate elements from an extremely wide sonic vocabulary.

With *Transient Random-Noise Bursts With Announcements*, things got even more interesting. Although it was Stereolab's major-label debut, the record took the group a few steps back in terms of audio fidelity. In doing so, Stereolab became prime examples of the so-called "low-fi" movement brewing at the time, and arrived at its meatiest, most satisfying sound to date. The group unequivocally embraced classic pop melody ("Pack Yr Romantic Mind") and even some funky grooves ("Lock-Groove Lullaby"), creating more conventional songs that are both catchy and, with the emergence of Mary Hansen as a co–lead singer, increasingly complex (such as on "Our Trinitone Blast").

Mars Audiac Quintet went a step further in turning Stereolab into the discerning record collector's favorite contemporary pop band. With its futurist takes on classic rock riffs ("Transona 5"), fully conventional verse/chorus structures ("International Colouring Contest"), and plenty of familiar pop touches, it's the group's most accessible album. And with vocals appearing clearer and more prominent in the mix—spewing the familiar Marxist philosophy, plus tributes to eccentric cult singers—it's also the group's most topical and least oblique collection.

By *Emperor Tomato Ketchup*, Stereolab was on a roll, delivering its most well-rounded, confident, and accomplished statement yet. While staying song-oriented, the album neatly balances the sonic adventures of interlocking rhythms and a wonderfully wide sonic palette (strings, skronky sax, punky guitars, percolating synths) with a groove that, on tracks like "Metronomic Underground," can be downright funky. Having moved away from its earlier lo-fi productions with *Mars Audiac*, Stereolab forsakes it entirely with an impeccably produced, creatively mixed collection that's a joy to behold in its full high-fidelity glory.

Dots and Loops marked yet another major shift for the group, and this time the results were not so welcome. Working with Chicago "postrock" producer John McEntire, the album marks Stereolab's jump from the analog sound world, where the group had made its reputation on wheezing keyboards and chugging guitars, to a digital universe of cut-and-paste elements and immaculately clean production. Blame, perhaps, a lack of experience with the new computer tools on which these songs are constructed, but *Dots and Loops* suffers from an overwhelming sense of superficiality. The music—full of horns, vibraphones, even an acoustic guitar—sounds extremely pretty, but enduring songs don't emerge from the mix. While some tentative dabblings with electronic beats show the promise of potential new directions (such as on the drum-and-bass–inflected "Parsec"), more often the album displays the pitfalls of electronica (lack of melody and song structures) rather than the benefits.

On subsequent albums—*Cobra & Phases Group Play Voltage in the Milky Night* and *Sound-Dust*—Stereolab continued its work with McEntire, as well as with his fellow Chicago new-music star Jim O'Rourke. To some extent, these albums smooth out the digital gloss that hurt *Dots and Loops,* and occasionally hit on some really soulful songs (*Cobra*'s "Come and Play in the Milky Night"). But comparing these songs to those of Stereolab's mid-'90s heyday suggests that the group has permanently shifted from being the great-pop-band-of-the-future-here-today to more of a fringe, lite jazz–inflected prog-rock thing. *Sound-Dust*—as well as the seven-song mini album *The First of the Microbe Hunters*—seems particularly interested in exploring compositions with radical internal shifts.

After enduring the death of longtime member Mary Hansen and taking its longest-ever break, Stereolab returned in 2004 with *Margerine Eclipse.* Here, the group seems to be reintegrating the analogue burps and churns that were so mesmerizing on earlier records. Tracks such as "Margerine Rock" and "Bop Scotch" have some real rock teeth to them, while many of the other songs revisit the organ-spooked Euro funk that goes so well with Sadier's dreamy swoon. Of course, there's a downside of this return to form: It's all too familiar and fans might be better off just sticking with their earlier favorites. If *Margerine* displays a band getting reacquainted with what it does best, it also finds Stereolab seemingly at a loss for new direction.

Two followups to *Switched On,* Stereolab's initial compilation of nonalbum tracks, have appeared over the years. *Refried Ectoplasm (Switched On, Vol. 2)* and *Aluminum Tunes: Switched On, Vol. 3,* like many odds-and-ends collections, are essential listening only for obsessives and completists. But they offer some of Stereolab's most experimental material, and occasionally—as with *Refried*'s early singles ("Lo Boob Oscillator")—some of the group's more accessible tracks as well.   —R.M.S.

Stereo MC's

★★★½   Supernatural (Gee Street/4th & Broadway, 1990)
★★★½   Supernatural America Mix (Gee Street/4th & Broadway, 1992)
★★★½   Connected (Gee Street/4th & Broadway, 1992)

★★★   DJ Kicks (Studio K7!, 2000)
★★★   Deep Down & Dirty (Island/Def Jam, 2001)

Other than Slick Rick—who doesn't really count because he was raised in the Bronx—Stereo MC's are the only British hip-hoppers to reach America's pop charts. Then again, the reason for that is most likely that they're not trying to be pure hip-hop, they're just being their oddball selves; from Soul II Soul and Massive Attack on down to Roots Manuva, the English artists that have succeeded stylistically with hip-hop have turned it inside out with their own British cultural idiosyncrasies, and Stereo MC's are no different.

London based, Stereo MC's formed in 1985 as a joint venture between rapper/frontman Rob Birch (a.k.a. Rob B.) and the group's producer/DJ Nick Hallam (a.k.a. Nick Head). They released an independent album in the U.K. in 1989, but it was their 1990 second release *Supernatural* that put them on the international map. From the groovy time good vibes (and title) of *Supernatural*'s hit single "Elevate My Mind" to the album's psychedelic cover art, it was clear that Stereo MC's were rocking funky hip-hop beats with a sensibility clearly influenced by England's late-'80s Summer of Love driven by the acid house movement. That meant big sing-along choruses dedicated to positivity driven by a multi-culti collective of singers, dancers, and instrumentalists that gave off a rave-meets-block-party aesthetic; while the rest of *Supernatural*'s tracks too closely followed the path of the singles, they were at least equally good as dance-floor dynamite (*Supernatural America Mix* features four songs left off the initial release).

Stereo MC's next album, *Connected,* didn't vary much from *Supernatural*'s template, but it was again consistent in quality and contained great sing-along singles like "Connected" and "Step It Up." Despite the album's popularity, Stereo MC's wouldn't release a full studio album for nine years, their only release being *DJ Kicks,* an amiably shambling party collection that blended golden-age hip-hop a la Kool G. Rap and Ultramagnetic MCs alongside contemporary Brit neo-funktionaries like Herbaliser and Red Snapper. Then, seemingly out of nowhere, Stereo MC's released a new studio album in 2001, *Deep Down & Dirty.* Despite the extensive time gap between releases, this recording sounded almost exactly like the previous two albums—not exactly groundbreaking, but still satisfying and, in its own smiley-faced retrofunky way, refreshing.   —M.D.

Cat Stevens

★★★   Matthew and Son/New Masters (1967, 1968; London, 1971)

★★★   Mona Bone Jakon (A&M, 1970)
★★★   Tea for the Tillerman (A&M, 1971)
★★★   Teaser and the Firecat (A&M, 1971)
★★½   Catch Bull at Four (A&M, 1972)
★★   Foreigner (A&M, 1973)
★   Buddah and the Chocolate Box (A&M, 1974)
★★★   Greatest Hits (A&M, 1975)
★   Izitso (A&M, 1977)
★★   Cat's Cradle (London, 1977)
★   Back to Earth (A&M, 1979)
★★★   Footsteps in the Dark: Greatest Hits Volume Two (A&M, 1984)
★★★   Classics Volume 24 (A&M, 1988)
★★★   The Very Best of Cat Stevens (A&M, 2000)
★★★★   Cat Stevens: Box Set (A&M, 2001)

Cat Stevens was a British folkie who scored a Top 10 pop hit at home with "Matthew and Son" in 1967. Sidelined by tuberculosis for several years, he emerged on the American scene several years later. *Mona Bone Jakon* fit right in to the emerging singer/songwriter movement: Stevens delivers his romantic sentiments, simplistic homilies, and hokey hippie mysticism with an affecting, gentle acoustic touch. *Tea for the Tillerman* and the likably underwrought hit "Wild World" established Stevens as a more reserved British version of James Taylor. *Teaser and the Firecat* continues working this vein, yielding two more U.S. hits: the chug-chug-chugging "Peace Train" and the pretty-verging-on-precious "Morning Has Broken." With *Catch Bull at Four*, Stevens began to lard his approach with strings, horns, guitar-led rock arrangements—anything and everything that came to mind, it seems. His delicate melodies and mewling voice all but collapse under the weight, though. Either *Greatest Hits* or the slightly longer *Classics Volume 24* redeem what few catchy choruses poke through the growing fog ("Sitting" from *Catch Bull*, "Oh Very Young" from *Buddah and the Chocolate Box*). Stevens converted to Islam and changed his name to Yusuf Islam in the late '70s, leaving his pop career behind. He made brief return to the spotlight in 1989, when it was widely reported that Stevens supported Iran's fatwa against *Satanic Verses* author Salman Rushdie.

During the '90s, Stevens' music was repacked in a handful of best-of's and odds-and-ends collections, most of which are now out of print. *Box Set* offers just about all the Cat Stevens anyone should ever need, including a handful of rarities. If you love "Peace Train," "Wild World," "(Remember the Days of the) Old Schoolyard," and "Moon Shadow" but can't take too large a dose of earnest, emotive, acoustic guitar–based music, stay away from the enormity of such a collection and stick to one of the best-of's. —M.C./W.Z.

Rod Stewart

★★★★½   The Rod Stewart Album (1969; Mercury, 1998)
★★★★½   Gasoline Alley (1970; Mercury, 1998)
★★★★★   Every Picture Tells a Story (1971 Mercury, 1998)
★★★★   Never a Dull Moment (1972; Mercury, 1998)
★★★   Atlantic Crossing (1975; Warner Bros., 2000)
★★★½   A Night on the Town (1976; Warner Bros., 2000)
★★★   The Best of Rod Stewart (Mercury, 1976)
★★★   The Best of Rod Stewart, Vol. 2 (Mercury, 1977)
★★★   Foot Loose and Fancy Free (1977; Warner Bros., 2000)
★★½   Blondes Have More Fun (1978; Warner Bros., 2000)
★★★★   Rod Stewart Greatest Hits, Vol. I (Warner Bros., 1979)
★★½   Tonight I'm Yours (1981; Warner Bros., 2000)
★★★   Absolutely Live (Warner Bros., 1982)
★★★   Camouflage (Warner Bros., 1984)
★★★   Out of Order (Warner Bros., 1988)
★★★★★   Storyteller: The Complete Anthology: 1964–1990 (Warner Bros., 1990)
★★★   Downtown Train (Selections From Storyteller) (Warner Bros., 1990)
★★★★   Vagabond Heart (Warner Bros., 1991)
★★★   Unplugged . . . and Seated (Warner Bros., 1993)
★★★   Vintage (PolyGram 3145, 1993)
★★★   Spanner in the Works (Warner Bros., 1995)
★★★   If We Fall in Love Tonight (Warner Bros., 1996)
★★★   When We Were the New Boys (Warner Bros., 1998)
★★   The Rock Album (Rebound, 1998)
★★   Human (Atlantic, 2000)
★★★   Millennium Edition (Universal, 2000)
★★★   1964–1969 (Pilot, 2000)
★★   It Had to Be You . . . : The Great American Songbook (J-Records, 2002)

An object lesson in the perils of pandering, Stewart's career proves that "selling out" wasn't just some thought-crime dreamed up by '60s idealists. For a golden hour, Rod the Mod was one of rock's finest singers, with a lock on, of all things, sincerity, taste, and self-mocking humor. In the much longer period since then, exactly those values have been sacrificed, as, rushing headlong after megabucks and artistic bankruptcy, the working-class Scot became the Hollywood tart, the definitive parody, the saddest poseur. He continues to get it up for brilliant bits, and even his worst echoes a truly remarkable voice—it's only that, given his promise, the bulk of his product radiates pathos and a certain shame.

In the late '60s, no one rocked harder. Paired with ex-Yardbird Jeff Beck in the Jeff Beck Group, Stewart debuted the protometal Led Zep would later perfect; heavy blooze, "You Shook Me" and scorchers like "Let Me Love You" made *Truth* and *Beck-Ola* exercises in brilliant bombast. Two talents this huge, however, weren't easy roommates, and Stewart moved on to replace Steve Marriott as frontman of the (Small) Faces and thrive on the giggly fraternity of that band. In the interim, he'd put out an astonishing solo debut. Keith Emerson on Mike D'Abo's "Handbags and Gladrags," guitarist Ronnie Wood at his most ambitious, and the sloppy thunder of drummer Mick Waller, provided much of *The Rod Stewart Album*'s pleasure—but the star was Stewart, revealed as a highly original interpreter whose skill at selecting material encompassed the Stones' "Street Fighting Man" and Ewan MacColl's lovely "Dirty Old Town." Even better, Rod's songs, "Cindy's Lament," "Man of Constant Sorrow," and "An Old Raincoat Won't Ever Let You Down" ushered in a writer capable of startlingly bare emotion and compassion for the hard-hit strivers, misfits, and survivors who peopled his songs.

The songs on *Gasoline Alley* were equally strong. With Stewart's folk heart thumping, the dignified empathy of "Only a Hobo" saw him beginning a minicareer of covering Dylan consistently better than anyone else; "Gasoline Alley" marked the cementing of the Stewart-Wood alliance—the blending of slide guitar and hoarse-voiced yearning is a thing of rare beauty, and when the duo elsewhere kick it up on homages to the Stones and Eddie Cochran, rock seldom sounds freer or more fun. "Maggie May" and the title track of *Every Picture Tells a Story* made for Rod and Ron's finest hour—happy lads wearing their hearts on their sleeves. *Never a Dull Moment* was still strong, raw and honest, Stewart refreshing his narrative skills with the lusty travelogue, "Italian Girls," and paying his debt to Sam Cooke on "Twistin' the Night Away."

With the now-deleted *Smiler,* danger signals began to flash. Dylan's "Girl From the North Country" was fine, but Chuck Berry's "Sweet Little Rock 'n' Roller" was far too obvious, and trans-sexing Aretha, on "(You Make Me Feel Like) A Natural Man," was shockingly misguided. Also, a fatal tendency toward hokum reared its head. *A Night on the Town,* with an excellent take on Cat Stevens' "The First Cut Is the Deepest" and a gallant nod toward Stewart's gay following ("The Killing of Georgie [Part I and II]"), was Rod's last cohesive and respectable set for quite some time—subsequent album titles, *Foolish Behaviour* and *Blondes Have More Fun* (Stewart reaches his nadir on

"Da Ya Think I'm Sexy")—spell out his disastrous turn toward stadium-mediocrity and soft-porn eroticism.

Throughout the '80s, Stewart's singles—for example, "Lost in You" and "Forever Young," from *Out of Order*—were competent hitcraft. And (shockingly, felicitously) he began to revive at the end of the decade—*Vagabond Heart* (1991) was Stewart's best in years. While hardly a full return to his early form, a Tina Turner duet, material by Robbie Robertson, and help from the Stylistics show a singer beginning at last to think again. *Unplugged* revived memories of the early years; *Spanner in the Works* continued the progress, with a fine Tom Petty cover. And on *When We Were the New Boys,* he even rocked convincingly again—turning in, of all things, a nice version of an Oasis number. *Human* marked another downturn, with Rod trying for slick, up-to-the minute contemporary R&B; *It Had to Be You* was a bit of a puzzler—Stewart sings prerock standards—not exactly with knowing grace, but with the Voice in fine sandpaper form. *Storyteller* collects a ton of the better Rod, and it's terrific. Even better, get the first four records of his shining moment—and honor an incredible singer by forgoing his tripe. —P.E.

St Germain

★★★ Boulevard (1996; Pias America, 2002)
★★★½ Tourist (Blue Note, 2000)

St Germain is the working name of Ludovic Navarre, a Frenchman who sets jazz improvisations over laidback dance beats to produce what he, on one track, calls "easy-listening underground house music." The original release of *Boulevard* found a popular niche for such light fare, and sold more than 200,000 copies. This has, in turn, emboldened Navarre to make his later work jazzier and more upbeat. The *Boulevard* reissue adds two tracks: one a Latin feast with congas, piano, and flute; the other a disco throwback.

Tourist is denser and richer. Kicked off by a fast beat and a sample that goes "I want you to get together" and interwoven with trumpet and sax solos, it sets up tension, but the rest of the album delivers only a series of syncopated soundscapes as the jazz musicians play one-on-one against the rhythm. —T.H.

Sting

★★★½ The Dream of the Blue Turtles (A&M, 1985)
★★★½ Bring On the Night (A&M, 1986)
★★★★ . . . Nothing Like the Sun (A&M, 1987)
★★★ Nada Como el Sol (A&M, 1988)
★★★½ The Soul Cages (A&M, 1991)
★★★ Ten Summoner's Tales (A&M, 1993)

★★ Demolition Man (A&M, 1993)
★★★★ Fields of Gold: The Best of Sting (A&M, 1994)
★★★ Mercury Falling (A&M, 1996)
★★★★½ The Very Best of Sting and the Police (A&M, 1997)
★★½ Brand New Day (Interscope, 1999)

Sting had been playing in a fusion jazz band when he was spotted by drummer Stewart Copeland and recruited into the Police, so it's hardly surprising that his first post-Police project would be built around jazz musicians. He had quite an ear for talent, recruiting future *Tonight Show* bandleader Branford Marsalis and eventual Rolling Stones bassist Daryl Jones, among others. But his writing style remained anchored in pop, and it's the balance between the melodic appeal of his songs and the improvisational fire of his band that gives *The Dream of the Blue Turtles* its distinctive character. How that works varies somewhat from song to song, but for the most part it's a matter of mood in which the arrangements set the emotional context for each song, like the chilly anxiety of "Russians" or the jazzy melancholy of "Moon Over Bourbon Street." The approach is not without its risks—his remake of the Police tune "Consider Me Gone" says more about the band than the song—but when the playing manages to bring the song into focus, as with the soulful "If You Love Somebody Set Them Free," its success is stunning.

With . . . *Nothing Like the Sun,* Sting shifts gears slightly. For one thing, his band is no longer a jazz outfit, for despite the continued input of saxophonist Marsalis and keyboardist Kenny Kirkland, the addition of drummer Manu Katché (who powered Peter Gabriel's *So*) pulls the groove in an entirely new direction; for another, the songs on this album are more word-centered than their predecessors. Fortunately, that never seems to get in the way of the melody, allowing Sting the luxury of his elaborate imagery without compromising the music's allure. Some of that, admittedly, is simply a matter of his vocal phrasing, as in "Be Still My Beating Heart," where Sting's polysyllabic melody dances around the metronomic pulse of Katché's drumming. But the most accessible songs—the jovial "Englishman in New York," or the danceable "We'll Be Together"—simply repeat the strengths of Sting's previous efforts. (His Gil Evans–arranged cover of "Little Wing," though, is sumptuously solemn.)

The Soul Cages marks a turning point in Sting's solo career. Although he was never shy about revealing his musical or literary erudition, that element of his creativity previously took a backseat to his pop in-

stincts. Beginning with *The Soul Cages,* Sting actively celebrates his smarts, both in the heavy metaphors of the lyrics and the underlying complexity of the music. So even though "All This Time" manages to be as tuneful and accessible as anything in his songbook, the bulk of the album takes some effort to fully appreciate. *Ten Summoner's Tales* is even more abstruse, as Sting indulges himself with sly musical jokes (e.g., the oddly metered country song "Love Is Stronger Than Justice") and high-flown allusions (e.g., "St. Augustine in Hell"), but even that is mitigated by the direct melodic appeal of "Fields of Gold" and the tart melancholy of "It's Probably Me." *Mercury Falling* repeats that formula without the compensating pop appeal, although the single-dad blues "I'm So Happy I Could Cry" has its moments. *Brand New Day* is almost masturbatory in its self-satisfied cleverness (there's a guest rapper, but of course the rapping itself is in French). Fortunately for Sting, there was enough exotic appeal in the Rai-flavored "Desert Rose" (thanks in no small part to Algerian guest vocalist Cheb Mami) to turn the album into a chart success, but the rest is just extremely sophisticated background music.

Nearly half of Sting's catalogue is devoted to repackages of one sort or another. The first is a concert album, *Bring on the Night,* which pushes the *Blue Turtles* band and dynamic a level beyond what was achieved in the studio, though the Police covers seem oddly perfunctory. . . . *Nada Como el Sol* sprang out of "They Dance Alone (Cueca Solo)," a song about the "disappeared" victims of political violence in Chile (from . . . *Nothing Like the Sun*), and offers a version of that song and others in Spanish, plus a Portuguese translation of "Fragile." How cosmopolitan. *Demolition Man* is a soundtrack that manages to be even more forgettable than the B-movie it accompanied, while *Fields of Gold* is a solid, conventional best-of drawn from Sting's first four solo albums. Song for song, *The Very Best of Sting and the Police* is probably the best buy in his catalogue; it's docked half a star for the irritating and unnecessary Puffy Combs remix of "Roxanne." —J.D.C.

Angie Stone

★★★★ Black Diamond (Arista, 1999)
★★★★ Mahogany Soul (J, 2001)
★★★½ Stone Love (J, 2004)

Blessed with a rich, smoky voice and an attitude of confident restraint, Angie Stone is one of the most outstanding members of the neosoul crew that livened up the pop scene of the late '90s. A devoted student of '60s and '70s soul, Stone often incorporates elements of classic records into her own songs, but she's no retro freak; even at her most traditional, she manages to sound fresh and contemporary.

Between her first taste of the spotlight—as the lead singer of early-'90s R&B group Vertical Hold—and her 1999 solo debut, Stone collaborated with such artists as Lenny Kravitz and D'Angelo (who's also her ex-boyfriend and father of one of her kids). Both appear on *Black Diamond,* but it's Stone's contributions that take center stage on sinuous numbers like "No More Rain (in This Cloud)," "Everyday," and "Love Junkie." Her spot-on cover of Marvin Gaye's "Trouble Man" is an appropriate choice, since Stone's dense vocal arrangements share the same mix of warmth and eeriness that characterized Gaye's best work.

Mahogany Soul offers further delights: the heartfelt racial-pride anthem "Brotha," the quietly dramatic "Wish I Didn't Miss You," and "The Ingredients of Love," which converts the slinky chord pattern of jazz trumpeter Freddie Hubbard's "Red Clay" into the base for an imposing wall of bob-and-weave voices. The album drags a bit toward the end, but its overall excellence confirms that Stone's one to watch.   —M.R.

The Stone Roses

★★★★   The Stone Roses (Silvertone/RCA, 1989)
★★★   Turns Into Stone (Silvertone/RCA, 1992)
★★   Second Coming (Geffen, 1994)

In Manchester in 1989, the Stone Roses were *it:* dreamy, druggy, dancey, the populist evolutionary climax of the guitar-pop genre the British called "indie." They had a skinny, pretty lead singer, Ian Brown, who sang "I Wanna Be Adored" and clearly meant it; a guitarist, John Squire, who could pull off wah-wah freakouts and nimble fingerpicking with equal aplomb; and a rhythm section that understood why people in clubs would want to wave their hands in the air. And, by the time they released *The Stone Roses,* they had at least half a dozen fantastic songs, especially "Elephant Stone" (hedonistic dance-psychedelia) and "Fools Gold" (10 minutes of a mutated James Brown beat and a stripped-down groove that comes off like "Theme From *Shaft"* on some really killer E). Then the silence came.

When it became clear that a followup wasn't coming any time soon, the Roses' label slapped together *Turns Into Stone,* a collection of nonalbum singles and B sides (plus "Elephant Stone" and "Fools Gold" again). It's mostly throwaways, but surprisingly fun, especially the imitation-Byrds "Mersey Paradise." Between lawsuits, label troubles, and legendary laziness, the Stone Roses took five years to get their second and

final real album recorded. *Second Coming* is anything but; it somehow manages to ape the sound of the debut (and its leisurely pace—the opening "Breaking Into Heaven" runs 12 minutes) while abandoning most of its energy and wit. Squire had taken over most of the songwriting by himself, and he got off one solid tune in the familiar style ("Love Spreads"), but the album's otherwise forgettable.   —D.W.

Stone Temple Pilots

★★★   Core (Atlantic, 1992)
★★★½   Purple (12 Gracious Melodies) (Atlantic, 1994)
★★★   Tiny Music . . . Songs from the Vatican Gift Shop (Atlantic, 1996)
★★½   No. 4 (Atlantic, 1999)
★★½   Shangri-La Dee Da (Atlantic, 2001)
★★★½   Thank You (Atlantic, 2003)

Scott Weiland

★★½   12 Bar Blues (Atlantic, 1998)

Stone Temple Pilots managed to benefit as much as anyone from the '90s grunge movement without ever leading it. Nirvana and Pearl Jam had more juice and headlines, but STP enjoyed as many radio-ready hits, if not staying power. The West Coast quintet first invaded radio and MTV rotation with grunge minus the punk, as led by charismatic (and troubled) frontman Scott Weiland, who finally became recognized less for his rugged wail than for time wasted with drugs, arrest, and rehab. Bad habits took him from brooding grunge wannabe to gaunt glam peacock, though he still managed to finish the decade alive.

Core would have been a marginal, forgettable debut if not for a small cache of career-defining singles. It begins badly with the chest-beating sludge of "Dead and Bloated," but soon shifts into the churning, psycho riffing of "Sex Type Thing," as Weiland drops the metal pose to sing his rape fantasy a la Jim Morrison, while the acoustic "Creep" has him as sensitive stooge. *Purple (12 Gracious Melodies)* delivered another string of edgy hits, and this time even the non-singles show some grace and ease of delivery. The playing is better, more confident, and looser as a result. "Meat Plow" shows a touch of the Spiders from Mars (plus the inevitable aping of Soundgarden), while "Lounge Fly" and "Still Remains" are pure Zeppelin.

During Weiland's rehab sentence in '95, his long-suffering band mates found time to stretch out musically while awaiting his return. The result was *Tiny Music . . . Songs from the Vatican Gift Shop,* a sudden and welcome shift into pure pop. Cobain was gone now, and the grunge wave was crashing under the weight of endless exploitation. So "Pop's Love Suicide" offered Beatles-style hard rock, with Weiland doing a Lennon rasp and some "yeah yeah yeahs." "Trippin' on a Hole in a Paper Heart" was frantic, churning pop and the only hit. Two instrumentals fill the spaces left vacant by Weiland's uncertain presence, but the band stuck beside him long enough to make a meaningful album. Weiland repaid that gesture with a solo career. *12 Bar Blues* teamed him with producer Daniel Lanois, where he discovered renewed energy if not focus. The tunes are less assured, but the album peaks early with the rock carnival of "Lady, Your Roof Brings Me Down," with gypsy strings and an accordion squeezed by Sheryl Crow.

STP reunited for *No. 4,* erupting with a return to balls-out rock on "Down," a hard-charging strut that had some melody in its grooves. Other songs offered the same dark rumble, but never quite came together. The band reaches for the same aimless diversity, from grunge to pop, on *Shangri-La Dee Da,* without much success or notice. *Thank You* gathered the hits with one new song ("All in the Suit That You Wear"), leaving a scattered, unsatisfying legacy, as Weiland quit to join Velvet Revolver with Guns n' Roses survivors Slash, Duff, and Matt Sorum, interrupted only by more busts and rehab. Just like old times.   —S.A.

The Stooges

★★★★	The Stooges (Elektra, 1969)
★★★★★	Fun House (Elektra, 1970)
★★★★	Raw Power (Columbia, 1973)
★★½	Metallic K.O. (Freud, 1976)
★★½	Open Up and Bleed! (Bomp, 1995)
★★★	Double Danger: Live 1973 (Bomp, 2000)

Lies, legends, half-truths, tales of drug-fueled lunacy, and wax-museum amounts of after-the-fact nostalgia will never be able to mute the stunning, violent, visceral recorded legacy of a band that made jaws drop in both horror and awe. The difference is striking from the get-go between *The Stooges* and almost everybody else recording at the time. "1969," the opening track, isn't a call to arms or a vision of an idyllic psychedelic future. It's about being bored. "I Wanna Be Your Dog" invents punk and then destroys it in three minutes by being both dumber and smarter than any punk could ever hope to be. Of the million-plus bands inspired by *The Stooges* later, the ones who were most successful realized that simplicity, volume, repetition, and primitivism could be a shortcut to transcendence, but that it takes brains to get it just right. "No Fun" is so perfect it's breathtaking: Scott Asheton's metronomic drumbeat, brother Ron's inspired fuzz guitar solo—there isn't a note out of place. Credit producer John Cale with helping to create what in effect are Stooges

miniatures, contained and tight (unlike their already chaotic, anarchic live shows), yet oozing with menace underneath it all. To the Stooges, and unlike other bands of the era like the Doors, decadence was just another word for Friday night. No need for baroque flourishes or bad poetry to describe their hearts of darkness.

To say that their second album, *Fun House,* is one of the greatest rock & roll records of all time risks hyperbole, but the evidence is inescapable. As great as they were, the Stones never went so deep, the Beatles never sounded so alive, and anyone would have a hard time matching Iggy Pop's ferocity as a vocalist. The dirt-simple riffs of "Loose" and "T.V. Eye" mask the quantum-physics-level complexities at play in songs that can elicit from the listener emotions of pure joy and the simultaneous impulse to tear shit up and bust skulls. Heightened emotion is an element in all great music, but few pieces or albums can summon the strength to keep reaching higher and higher until by the end everything comes crashing down under the weight of its own power and ambition. Optimally, after a spin of *Fun House,* the listener should be a little weary and a little bloody.

If Stooges albums don't sound dated, it's because the whimsy, wooziness, or strident agitprop of the day is absent from their music, being replaced instead with the timeless constancy of lust, fear, and hate. They were white bluesmen making Detroit tribal music, and their last studio album, *Raw Power,* is no exception. Producer David Bowie still catches heat for the sound of the album. Described as "muddy," the in-and-out-of-clarity mix is actually the perfect approach for the last incarnation of the group. The Stooges sound like they are trapped at the bottom of a dark pit, and every minute or so Iggy or guitarist James Williamson reaches up and tries to drag you in with them. There aren't enough synonyms for the word "slashing" to describe Williamson's guitar tone on the album. And you know a group is communing with gods and monsters when even the acoustic guitars sound malevolent. "Raw Power," "Search and Destroy," "Gimme Danger," and "I Need Somebody" are required listening for students of epochal milestones, failed coup attempts, and the restorative powers of nihilism.

The innumerable amount of shitty-sounding live and demo recordings of the Stooges can be overwhelming and less than illuminating for anyone but the most rabid fan. *Open Up and Bleed,* part of Bomp Records' archival Iguana Chronicles series, is notable for featuring only songs that would have presumably made it onto a fourth Stooges album had there been one. The live and rehearsal recordings of "Cock in My Pocket" and "Cry for Me" are worth hearing. The live *Metallic K.O.* was the first posthumous album to document the end of the road for the band, and it's worth getting just to hear Iggy's desperate attempts to be put out of his misery. The great thing about a Stooges show in 1974 was that everyone in the crowd was joined together in a mutual desire for oblivion. Half the audience wanted to get high and have fun, and the other half couldn't wait to go home, put on their boogie shoes, and forget the whole thing. —S.S.

The Stray Cats

★★★	The Best of the Stray Cats (1990; EMI/Capitol, 1998)
★★★	Greatest Hits (Curb, 1992)
★★★	Choo Choo Hot Fish (Rhino/Pyramid, 1994)
★★★★★	Runaway Boys: A Retrospective '81–'92 (Capitol, 1997)
★★★★	Live (Cleopatra, 1999)
★★★★½	Greatest Hits (Capitol, 2000)
★★★	Feline Frisky (Recall, 2001)

Right from the get-go the Stray Cats had it right: At the beginning of the Long Island trio's hit single, "(She's) Sexy + 17," frontman Brian Setzer lets go with an attitudinous statement that brooks no argument: "Hey man! I don't feel like goin' to school noooo more!" The Cats were long past their school days when "(She's) Sexy + 17" became a Top 10 hit in 1983, but with their baby faces, pompadours, retro garb, multiple tattoos, and sneering postures, they sure fit the bill of real gone rockers who might have stepped into the modern era through a seam in time.

Formed in Massapequa, NY, in 1979, the Cats included Brian Setzer on guitar, and his school buddies Lee Rocker (né Leon Drucker) and Slim Jim Phantom (né James McDonnell) on bass and drums, respectively. Finding no audience for their classic rockabilly and roots rock sound, the trio emigrated to London and its burgeoning rockabilly revival movement. Befriended by producer Dave Edmunds, an old and respected hand at roots rock styles, the Cats cut their debut album and scored three hit singles; a followup album fared poorly, however, and drove the band back to the States, where a contract with EMI ensued, and a U.S. debut in 1981 with *Built for Speed*, which in fact was built from the best tracks on the two British albums. Hitting the States just when MTV was shaking up popular culture, the photogenic Cats chewed up the scenery in music videos and scored two Top 10 hits in the nuclear-powered rockabilly of "Rock This Town" and the swaggering, bluesy "Stray Cat Strut." 1983's now out of print *Rant N' Rave With the Stray Cats* took off on the strength of "(She's) Sexy + 17,"

and yielded a minor hit in the ballad, "I Won't Stand in Your Way." Setzer pulled the plug in 1984. Two years later the band reunited for *Rock Therapy*, a skimpy 10-track album that blended some originals with covers of Buddy Holly's "I'm Looking for Someone to Love," Chuck Berry's "Beautiful Delilah," and Gene Vincent's "Race With the Devil." It bombed. Following another break for solo projects, the trio reassembled in 1989 for *Blast Off*, toured with Stevie Ray Vaughan, and in 1990 worked with producer Nile Rodgers on another long player, *Let's Go Faster*. All of these are now out of print, but only completists need be upset.

Reunited with original producer Dave Edmunds in 1992, they almost got back on track with the evocatively titled *Choo Choo Hot Fish*. The rockabilly is solid on the waitin'-and-waitin'-on-my-date song, "Cry Baby," and Setzer cuts loose with an astonishing, speed-picked top-strings solo midway through; a cover of Santo and Johnny's timeless instrumental "Sleepwalk" offers Setzer another showcase for the dreamy side of his playing. The end, on record at least, came in 1996, following the tepid response to an album of covers, *Original Cool*, which deserved a better fate, then and now (it's out of print, too).

Phantom and Rocker have continued on with their solo projects, and Setzer had a high-profile flirtation with big-band music in the late '90s via his powerhouse Brian Setzer Orchestra. —D.M.

The Streets

★★★★	Original Pirate Material (Vice/Atlantic, 2002)
★★★½	A Grand Don't Come For Free (Vice/Atlantic, 2004)

When Mike Skinner, a.k.a. the Streets, released his debut record, *Original Pirate Material*, he was hailed as a lot of things: the British Eminem, the gutter poet of a loutish generation, the long-awaited pudding proof that limeys can rap. In fact, he was more of a historical inevitability: a wiseass kid schooled in the kind of au courant electronica that had dominated British music during the '90s but in love enough with hip-hop to get on the mike and claim suburban English life as a source of prime rhyming material. *Original Pirate Material* had almost nothing to do with hip-hop's black urban roots, and Skinner's cockney accent was as English as Big Ben, but the album had the over-the-top verbosity, vibrancy, and goofy-charm personality of lots of great old-school rap records. Over a series of spare but engaging beats—bouncy distillations of 2-step and garage augmented by synths and orchestral samples—Skinner chronicled the daily dramas of a cash-strapped twentysomething in love with E,

PlayStation, and the one that got away. "Has It Come to This?" was a 2-step club hit on which Skinner noted that "We walk the tightrope of street cred/Keep my dogs fed, all jungle all garage heads;" on "The Irony of It All," Skinner played both Tim, a pot-smoking engineering student, and Terry, a drunken workaday bloke whom Tim infuriates with clever defenses of his lazy-student lifestyle. And on the excellently groovy single "Let's Push Things Forward," Skinner dropped a calling card as good as any other on the album: "Around 'ere we say 'birds,' not 'bitches.' "

A Grand Don't Come for Free was simpler in sound and scope than *Pirate,* but also much more ambitious. Think *Quadrophenia* with E: *A Grand* tracks a week or two in the life of a drugging, drunken, and nearly lovable heel; in the course of it, several affairs begin and end, a load of money goes missing, and the narrator's mum gets her feelings hurt. "Blinded by the Light," which documents a night out, itches with a cherubic female vocal and an insistent rave-synthesizer sample, which dissolves into aquatic sound just as the song's narrator starts to come on to his drugs. "Dry Your Eyes" is the most impressive moment: With a simple acoustic-guitar strum, a high, delicate vocal from singer Matt Sladen, and a very precise, descriptive rhyme, Skinner beautifully captures a tiny instant that devastates the narrator, as his girl tells him it's all over, babe. Skinner's skills at tickling and tearing vowels, adverbs, and lexicons is impressive enough, but his real gift is literary. *Grand* is cool because it's thoroughly mundane—the narrator spends a lot of time complaining about his cell phone—yet Skinner's ear for language and detail keeps it vivid, and hilarious. Surprisingly enough, at the end of the album, after lots of spare, excellent beats, there's even a cosmic lesson at the bottom of the pint glass: Be your own hero, and what will be will be. Call it Zen hooliganism. —P.B./C.H.

The Strokes

> ★★★★   The Modern Age EP (Rough Trade, 2001)
> ★★★★★   Is This It? (RCA, 2001)
> ★★★★   Room on Fire (RCA, 2003)

The continuing story of the black leather jacket, starring five New York dolls. As 2001 dawned, the Strokes were still playing local dive bars, with puffy-lipped leather-boy Julian Casablancas saying things like "Awww, don't fuckin' yawn!" before tumbling drunk off the stage. But the Strokes seduced the world with their all-mod-cons flash and New York punk guitar attack. The band's first release was the three-song *Modern Age* EP, featuring raw, never-topped versions of

"Last Nite" and "Barely Legal." *Is This It?* was a flawless debut album, making you jump up and down at the rhythm-guitar action of manic lust-for-lust anthems like "Soma," "Someday," and "Hard to Explain," in which drummer Fab Moretti (everyone's favorite!) steals the show. It's a much better album than the Vibrators, the Merton Parkas, Secret Affair, Bram Tchaikovsky, or even the Only Ones ever made. Julian had the philosophical query of the year, too: "Life seems unreal/Can we go back to your place?" The Strokes foolishly censored their original leather-glove-on-bare-ass cover, so you'll have to download your own; also, "New York City Cops" was replaced by "When It Started," although you want both. ("New York City Cops" is on the U.K. CD single of "Hard to Explain.")

From the sounds of *Room on Fire,* the Strokes have encountered a girl or two in their recent adventures, so it's a wonder they found time to come up with another album, let alone one this great. It's their answer to the Stones' *Flowers,* with Julian running the romantic gauntlet from "Meet Me in the Bathroom" to "You Talk Way Too Much." Guitarists Nick Valensi and Albert Hammond Jr. devise perfect new-wave handclap hooks in "12:51" and "The End Has No End," the rhythm section raves in "Reptilia," and Julian proves he can do Marvin Gaye ("Automatic Stop"), although Smokey Robinson is beyond his grasp ("Under Control"). It will end in tears, no doubt, but right now the Strokes are the most fun band around: so fast, so slatternly, so generous with the amphe-fe-fe-fetamine hooks. —R.S.

Joe Strummer

> ★★½   Walker (Virgin, 1987)
> ★★   Earthquake Weather (Epic, 1989)
> ★★★   Rock Art and the X-Ray Style (Epitaph/Hellcat, 1999)
> ★★★½   Global a Go-Go (Epitaph/Hellcat, 2001)
> ★★★★   Streetcore (Epitaph/Hellcat, 2003)

In front of the Clash, Joe Strummer seemed the ideal rock & roller—intelligent, impassioned, and ebullient, full of good humor and great ideas. Unfortunately, those qualities didn't manifest themselves in his solo career. It wasn't for lack of trying; his 1986 single "Love Kills," from the soundtrack to *Sid and Nancy,* managed to recall both the raucous charm of "Train in Vain" and the punchy guitars of "Clash City Rockers." But Strummer's next venture into film music, the score to *Walker,* is a disappointment, whether taken as a rock album (which it isn't) or as an exercise in approximating Central American folk idioms (which it tries in vain to do).

Apparently starstruck, Strummer returned to Hollywood yet again, to bestow the *Permanent Record* soundtrack (Epic, 1988) with four forgettable performances by his band, the Latino Rockabilly War. *Earthquake Weather,* his first noncinematic solo album, arrived a year later; empty and enervated, it's an embarrassment.

Chastened, Strummer took the next decade off, returning refreshed and reinvigorated. Recorded with his spitfire backing band the Mescaleros, *Rock Art and the X-Ray Style,* is an endearing trifle that neither furthers his reputation nor undercuts his legacy. The world-beat crazed *Global a Go-Go* followed, and despite sessions so loose it's easy to wonder if they even rehearsed, the album has a loose-limbed charm that with the likes of "Mondo Bongo" and "Bhindi Bhagee" overcomes the occasional sagginess of the playing.

Streetcore, recorded just before Strummer died of a stroke, is a good record that could have been great. There's impressive power in "Get Down Moses" and "Arms Aloft," and the cover of Bob Marley's "Redemption Song" is one of Strummer's best vocal performances, period. But there's a ragged casualness to other performances that makes the album, like his solo career itself, seem sadly unfinished. —J.D.C.

The Style Council

★★½ My Ever Changing Moods (Geffen, 1984)
★★★½ Internationalists (Geffen, 1985)
★★ Home & Abroad (Geffen, 1986)
★★ The Cost of Loving (Polydor, 1987)
★½ Confessions of a Pop Group (Polydor, 1988)
★★★ The Singular Adventures of the Style Council (Polydor, 1989)

After the Jam dissolved in 1982, Paul Weller dabbled with cocktail-lounge eclecticism on the Style Council's initial releases. The title track of *My Ever Changing Moods*—the U.S. debut that absorbs some U.K. singles and a previous EP—is the only really coherent thing to be found amid the demi-jazz tinkling and half-baked orchestrations. Reactivating his politicized bent, Weller turned in a much more convincing followup, *Internationalists.* With a soulful assist from backup singer (and future wife) Dee C. Lee, he wraps those somewhat rusty pipes around fervent neo-'70s funk anthems such as "Shout to the Top!" and "Walls Come Tumbling Down!" It might not be the British *Superfly,* but it's not bad. And "Come to Milton Keynes" is Weller's most closely observed bit of Kinks-style sociology since the Jam's late heyday. *Home & Abroad* is a sterile live album taken from post-*Internationalists* tours. Awkward lyrics and klutzy

rhythms sink *The Cost of Loving,* while *Confessions of a Pop Group* marks a bitter, frustrated return to the rambling experimentation of the debut. The Style Council's abrupt skid into muddy indulgence is reflected in the spotty quality of *The Singular Adventures of the Style Council.*   —M.C.

Styles

see THE LOX

Styx

★ Styx (Wooden Nickel, 1972)
★ Styx II (Wooden Nickel, 1973)
★ The Serpent Is Rising (Wooden Nickel, 1973)
★ Man of Miracles (Wooden Nickel, 1974)
★ Equinox (A&M, 1975)
★ Crystal Ball (A&M, 1976)
★ The Best of Styx (Wooden Nickel, 1977)
★★½ The Grand Illusion (A&M, 1977)
★★½ Pieces of Eight (A&M, 1978)
★½ Cornerstone (A&M, 1979)
★★½ Paradise Theater (A&M, 1981)
★★★ Kilroy Was Here (A&M, 1983)
★★ Caught in the Act: Live (A&M, 1984)
★★★ Classics Volume 15 (A&M, 1987)
★ Edge of the Century (A&M, 1990)
★★½ Greatest Hits (A&M, 1995)
★ Greatest Hits Part 2 (A&M, 1996)
★ Return to Paradise (CMC, 1997)
★ Brave New World (CMC, 1999)
★ Arch Allies: Live at Riverport (With REO Speedwagon) (Sanctuary, 2000)
★ Styx World: Live 2001 (CMC, 2001)

This Chicago band hit the bloat-rock jackpot at the tail end of the '70s, milking a basic strategy: goopy ballads for girls, hard-rock anthems for boys. The ballads ran the gamut from "Lady" to "Babe," all marked by the earsplitting keen of lead singer Dennis De Young, who never met a high note he didn't strangle to death with his bare hands. Meanwhile, male fans were placated by heavy guitars, Easter Island–style cover art, and vaguely metallic rockers like "I'm O.K." (teen self-discovery), "Too Much Time on My Hands" (teen frustration), and "Renegade" (oh mama, he's in fear for his life from the long arm of the law). The band's early work, the proggy nadirs of which are not to be braved by timid spirits, culminated in the ultimate psycho-alpha-mystic Stygian epic, the 1977 hit "Come Sail Away," where De Young navigates the ocean of his soul in the boat of truth, or something, as the wussy piano trills give way to guitar bombast. But he'll try, oh Lord, he'll try, to carry on.

And carry on Styx did, straight to the *Paradise The-*

ater, where it briefly reigned as the most popular rock group in America. The relatively catchy sci-fi concept joint *Kilroy Was Here* foretold a futuristic society where music is banned (okay, a total rip of Rush's *2112*) until the arrival of a heroic savior named Robert Orin Charles Kilroy, whose initials . . . hey! . . . have something to do with a computerized spirit named "Mr. Roboto," to whom all we who rock must be grateful. The 1984 single "Music Time" wasn't on the album, but it was Styx's best song ever, as well as the only video in MTV history to contain the disclaimer, "We Now Interrupt This Video for the Guitar Solo." Styx burned out, but after a discrete interval of a few years, the guys swallowed their pride, strapped those guitars back on, and tried to remember the chords to "Mr. Roboto." By all accounts, they're still working on it. De Young ended up on Broadway, singing the role of Pontius Pilate in the 1995 revival of *Jesus Christ Superstar.* The two-volume *Greatest Hits* shamefully omits "I'm O.K.," "Heavy Metal Poisoning," and "Music Time," all to make room for "Lady '95." Styx's comeback work has been nothing to domo arigato about, but they'll try. Oh Lord, they'll try. To carry on. —R.S.

Sublime

★★	40 Oz. to Freedom (Skunk, 1992)
★★½	Robbin' the Hood (MCA, 1994)
★★★★½	Sublime (MCA, 1996)
★★	Second Hand Smoke (Gasoline Alley, 1997)
★★½	Stand By Your Van (MCA, 1998)
★★★	Acoustic: Bradley Nowell and Friends (MCA, 1998)
★★★	Greatest Hits (MCA, 1999)
★★½	20th Century Masters (MCA, 2002)

Forget what Keith Richards says—there sure are some heavy drug albums out there, and plenty of them dropped in the '90s. But—although frontman Brad Nowell's life had been cut short by a heroin overdose by the time the smartly laid-back "What I Got" made the band's third album a smash—*Sublime* is not one of those albums. Nowell neither writes nor sings with the detached lethary of a nodding junkie or the cranky anxiety of a jonesing addict, but with the thoughtful ease of a guy who's in it for the long haul. Even when he toys with violent impulses, on the hit "Santeria" or the revisionist history of "April 29, 1992 (Miami)," he seems like a reasonable dude.

Sublime had been bouncing around the Long Beach, CA, punk scene since the late '80s, so they come by their secondhand ska influences honestly. On their early albums, Sublime is the rare punk band that can play ska and dub fluently without muscling those styles into submission. But the band's songwriting really didn't blossom until its eponymous breakthrough, and so *Greatest Hits* is fine, if redundant. On the other hand, *20th Century Masters,* like most of Universal's consumer-bilking series, is a ripoff quickie. It's a shame, because Nowell did seem to be developing a lyrical vision to match his band's versatility, but for all intents and purposes, *Sublime* is sublime. —K.H.

Sugar

★★★★	Copper Blue (Rykodisc, 1992)
★★★★	Beaster EP (Rykodisc, 1993)
★★★½	File Under: Easy Listening (Rykodisc, 1994)
★★★½	Besides (Rykodisc, 1995)

After the collapse of his magnificent postpunk trio Hüsker Dü, Bob Mould uncorked a couple of cathartic solo albums (see separate entry) and then formed Sugar with indie-rock veterans David Barbe on bass and Malcolm Travis on drums. Though comparisons to his earlier trio were inevitable, there were more differences than similarities. Sugar's songs had a tighter, ultramelodic pop-rock focus, and Travis' piston-precision drumming was tauter than that of Hüsker Dü's loose-limbed Grant Hart. Melody ruled, while some of the Dü's more open-ended delirium was sacrificed. But what Sugar did, it did very well.

Copper Blue blasts out of the gates with an intensity that raised the notion of power pop to new speaker-shattering heights. Mould's voice and guitar are mixed at ungodly levels, but Barbe and Travis do not shrink from the challenge, and the music at times suggests a three-man sprint, slowing to a chug only for the harrowing "The Slim." The sturdy melodies don't break under the assault; played at more tolerable volume levels, one could almost imagine the likes of "If I Can Change Your Mind" as a Top 40 hit.

Beaster is the equal of *Copper Blue,* but with less emphasis on melody and an even greater sense of goggle-eyed passion that picks up where "The Slim" left off. The music drones and thrashes as if locked in a straitjacket, building to a shattering and shattered peak with "JC Auto," which rivals Mould's Hüsker Dü–era classics.

File Under: Easy Listening is more about pop and less about power, and there's a brooding disquiet in the lyrics that presages Sugar's imminent breakup. The posthumous *Besides* mines a treasure trove of B sides, including a galvanizing romp through the Who's "Armenia City in the Sky" and Barbe's poignant but bruising "Where Diamonds Are Halos." Some editions include an extra disc that documents a typically ferocious concert. —G.K.

The Sugarcubes

★★★★ Life's Too Good (Elektra, 1988)
★★★ Here Today, Tomorrow Next Week! (Elektra, 1989)
★★★½ Stick Around for Joy (Elektra, 1992)
★★★½ It's-It (Elektra, 1992)
★★★★ The Great Crossover Potential (Elektra, 1998)

Even though it's meant ironically, *The Great Crossover Potential*—the title of the Sugarcubes' best-of retrospective—really does sum up this Icelandic sextet's strengths. Because despite its nonconformist arrangements and willfully eccentric vocals, the Sugarcubes possessed an enduring, endearing pop sensibility, which made even the band's strangest singles seem hummable.

Make no mistake—these six boldly went where few bands had gone before. "Motorcrash," from *Life's Too Good,* is a case in point. Initially, it seems straightforward enough, with Björk Gudmundsdottir emotionally recounting the aftermath of a car accident. Then second vocalist Einar Orn Benediktsson chimes in, snarkily suggesting Björk is faking her breathless compassion—at which point the listener begins to notice that the music behind the two singers is a tad cheery for the soundtrack to a tragedy.

Like "Birthday," the single that made the band's reputation in Britain, "Motorcrash" offers all the elements of the Sugarcubes' aesthetic: deadpan wit, supple grooves, jazzy instrumental flourishes, and deceptively catchy melodies. *Life's Too Good* is packed with such strengths, but *Here Today* falters. Its playing may be as good as *Life's Too Good,* but the writing isn't, apart from such admirable efforts as "Regina" and "Hot Meat." *Stick Around for Joy* is more consistent, downplaying Einar's irritating interjections while emphasizing the band's instrumental strengths. Thus, as much as Björk's vocals might add to "Hit," "Chihuahua," or "Gold," it's the churning interplay of guitarist Thor Eldon Jonsson and the rhythm section that ultimately carries the album.

Unfortunately, the Sugarcubes didn't stick around, disbanding not long after the release of their third album. Björk embarked on a solo career, and *It's-It* was released as a career summation, a job it does well, but not as convincingly as the less gimmicky *The Great Crossover Potential.* —J.D.C.

Sugar Ray

★★ Lemonade & Brownies (Atlantic, 1995)
★★½ Floored (Atlantic, 1997)
★★★½ 14:59 (Atlantic, 1999)
★★★ Sugar Ray (Atlantic, 2001)
★★½ In the Pursuit of Leisure (Atlantic, 2001)

Give Mark McGrath credit. He didn't have to go through all this trouble—joining a band, touring the world, talking to dimwitted morning jocks—just to get laid. Good-looking guy like him, he could have done just as well as a bartender or a ski instructor. So at least he was big-minded enough to do the world a service—after all, someone was going to be shoveling innocuously melodic, vaguely rhythmic pop on the radio, and it may as well have been a guy who knows a good tune when he hears it. Quibble all you want, but for a few minutes there, Sugar Ray was the world's most adequate rock & roll band.

Early on, Sugar Ray had a bunch of musical ideas—funk-metal, ska-pop, like that. Unfortunately, better bands had had the same ideas years before. (Though SR did have a pointless DJ back before it was *de rigueur.*) They broke through with "Fly" (from *Floored*), which was indeed about wanting to fly. Dumb, for sure, but countless rockers have made clumsier use of the cliché (Lenny Kravitz comes to mind). For their next trick, they made an album you could listen to all the way through, *14:59.* The title was a cute, understated Warhol joke (their fifteen minutes are almost up, get it?) and the single, "Every Morning," was a cute, oblique tune about McGrath's bed-hopping.

By this time, Sugar Ray had hit upon a formula. And like most formulas, it sucked. *Sugar Ray* was catchy, but it boasted about as much originality as its album title. "When It's Over" was the single. I bet you'd remember it if you heard it. And I bet you wouldn't remember it if you didn't hear it. By the time of *In the Pursuit of Leisure,* it was clear that the band had traded in identity for airplay, and if they're not careful they might innocuous themselves right out of a career. Don't worry about McGrath—he'll always get by—but wouldn't it be sad if DJ Homicide wound up playing weddings? —K.H.

Sum 41

★★★ Half Hour of Power (Big Rig, 2000)
★★★★ All Killer No Filler (Aquarius, 2001)
★★★ Does This Look Infected? (Island/Def Jam, 2002)

When Heatmiser-haired young Deryk Whibley first crammed his yowl down our halfpipe in 1999, he and his Canadian band of Offspring offspring seemed as though they started a band for the sheer joy of jumping in the air and landing on the same power chord. Of course their high-voltage mosh pop also got them paid and laid on the summer tour circuit. 2001's *All Killer No Filler* was a skatepark smash. The brat rap of "Fat Lip" made Pennywise look almost pound foolish, and

"In Too Deep" was a pleasure-punk ode to the shallows. 2002 saw the drop of a new album whose title riffed on the many magazine cover stories calling Sum 41's music infectious. *Does This Look Infected?* gave us the antic "Hell Song" whose video featured the bathead-biting demon Oz paterfamilias himself. —L.S.

Donna Summer

★★★	Love to Love You Baby (Casablanca, 1975)
★★★	Love Trilogy (Casablanca, 1976)
★★★½	Four Seasons of Love (Casablanca, 1976)
★★★½	Once Upon a Time . . . (Casablanca, 1977)
★★★½	Live and More (Casablanca, 1978)
★★★★	Bad Girls (Casablanca, 1979)
★★★★	On the Radio (Greatest Hits) (Casablanca, 1979)
★★★★	She Works Hard for the Money (Mercury, 1983)
★★★½	The Dance Collection (Casablanca, 1987)
★★★	Another Place and Time (Atlantic, 1989)
★★★★	The Donna Summer Anthology (Casablanca, 1993)
★★★★	Endless Summer (Casablanca, 1995)
★★½	VH1 Presents: Live & More Encore! (Epic, 1999)
★★★★	The Best of Donna Summer: The Millennium Collection (Mercury, 2003)
★★★★★	Bad Girls (Deluxe Edition) Mercury/Chronicles, 2003)
★★★★	The Journey: The Very Best of Donna Summer (UTV/Mercury, 2003)

When Donna Summer broke her first hit, little more than whispers and moans over a tepid eurodisco beat, her career didn't seem to promise more than another Andrea True. That the best song on her second album was written by Barry Manilow wasn't very promising, either. But two things changed all that: Producer Giorgio Moroder figured out how to deploy the string synth, and Summer took charge of her material.

Turns out that she could sing, belt even. Turns out that she liked rock & roll as much as disco. Turns out that she discovered that niche at the crosshairs of rock, soul, dance, and showbiz pop that Madonna exploited so successfully a decade later.

Summer was born in Boston but went to Europe to sing onstage in productions of *Hair* and *Godspell*. There she hooked up with Giorgio Moroder and Pete Bellotte, who were cranking out disco fluff as the Munich Machine, and they had a hit with "Love to Love You Baby." Summer became an instant disco icon, and her early records exploited that: The first two albums were more Moroder/Bellotte than Summer, with side-long disco suites on the first side, and filler on the second. Indeed, one of the things that we notice now is that all of Summer's albums were conceived as LP sides, usually laid out in a continuous mix, which makes for some inconsistencies as the sides were piled up on CDs. *Four Seasons of Love,* a cycle of disco songs for each season, is one of the few albums that benefit from being heard whole; the transitional *I Remember Yesterday,* with its strong first side and filler plus hit on the second, is less consistent. But two songs there portended where Summer was going: "Love's Unkind" was updated girl-group rock, while "I Feel Love," her second big hit, was so propulsive that Brian Eno called it "the future of music."

Summer's next album, *Once Upon a Time,* was an ambitious double-LP retelling of the Cinderella story, a suite of songs connected by a relentless disco beat. It was a lot to swallow at the time, but it contains some of her strongest work, especially Act One with "Fairy Tale High" and "Say Something Nice." This was an intensive period for Summer, with four double-LPs in a two-year stretch from 1977 to 1979. *Bad Girls* was the next new studio set, another big advance in songcraft and a broadening of her music: more rock, more soul, one side of ballads, and hits as compelling as "Hot Stuff," "Bad Girls," and "Sunset People." The other two doubles were the improbable *Live and More* and the inevitable *On the Radio.* The much-panned live album actually sounds remarkably fresh now, the sound clear, the energy palpable. Perhaps the reason for the pans was the side-long "MacArthur Park Suite," moved from the *Live and More* CD to *The Dance Collection,* but even though it's built around one of rock's all-time worst songs, the extended music is some of Moroder's most elegant disco, and there's nothing wrong with two interpolated Summer songs. As for *On the Radio,* it not only sums up Summer's oeuvre to date, half of it was new to LP, coming from singles and soundtracks.

Summer's discography falls apart after 1980: She divorced, changed labels and producers several times, remarried, proclaimed herself born again, moved to Nashville. Not much of her post-1980 work is in print. (Hard to say why; maybe God is punishing her for blaspheming her gay fans.) Still, the Michael Omartian–produced *She Works Hard for the Money* is one of the best things she's ever done. *Another Place and Time,* produced by Bananarama braintrust Stock Aitken Waterman, is more rigid rhythmically, but she's more than ever a skilled, powerful singer. This period is chronicled, for better or worse, on the second disc of *The Donna Summer Anthology.* Since then, we have only the second coming of *Live and More*—if tragedy returns as farce, perhaps ambition returns as conceit. Then there are the comps: The first disc of *Anthology* ends with "Bad Girls," a fine selection from the rising slope of her career. *Endless Summer* compresses *Anthology*'s two discs down to one, including two new cuts not likely to stand the test of time.

The Millennium Collection shows only that less is less: 11 cuts, 51 minutes, a bare canonical minimum. *The Journey* is almost a carbon copy, with two (not bad) new songs added, but both comps thin out after the 1980s output. *The Millennium Collection* is more canonical, using longer mixes to stretch its not quite a dozen songs to nearly an hour. But the most effective use of her long dance mixes is on the extra disc of *Bad Girls (Deluxe Edition).* —T.H.

Sun Kil Moon

★★★½   Ghosts of the Great Highway (EMI, 2003)

It's easy to compare Mark Kozelek to Neil Young, but the horse that Kozelek rides is much more sad and wild than it is crazy. As leader of the San Francisco gloom-rock combo Red House Painters, Kozelek made six albums of elegant English-major despair that you might expect to hear at Sylvia Plath's favorite coffee shop. With Sun Kil Moon, Kozelek remains as inscrutable as ever, but he avoids the archness that sometimes infected his earlier work. Six of the album's 10 tracks run longer than five minutes; "Duk Koo Kim," which elegizes a Korean boxer who died from injuries sustained in the ring in 1982, stretches to nearly 15. Kozelek's squalling dirges turn despair into a kind of elemental beauty. The autumnal, haunted tone reaches its peak in the album's best song, "Carry Me Ohio," a lament to lost love in which he searches for "the stars that I just don't see anymore." Kozelek seems in no danger of finding them, which is good news as long as it means he keeps making music this strong. —W.D.

Sunny Day Real Estate

★★★   Diary (Sub Pop, 1994)
★★½   Sunny Day Real Estate (Sub Pop, 1995)
★★★★   How It Feels to Be Something On (Sub Pop, 1998)
★★★   Live (Sub Pop, 1999)
★★★★   The Rising Tide (Time Bomb, 2000)

The Fire Theft

★★★½   The Fire Theft (Rykodisc, 2003)

When Sunny Day Real Estate first emerged from the Seattle scene of the early '90s, it immediately stuck out from its grungy contemporaries. SDRE liked hardcore punk as much as any bunch of urban white kids, but its principal goal was to harness the emotionalism and heroic earnestness of bands such as U2 and the Clash. Critics called it "emocore," and a new movement was launched. But in truth, few of the many other bands so tagged can match Sunny Day's balance of power and grace.

Diary is a promising although occasionally monotonous debut. Jeremy Enigk's thin, reedy voice is an acquired taste, but when he howls over Dan Hoerner's intense guitar rhythms on "Song About an Angel," it's pretty overwhelming. After *Diary,* Enigk underwent a born-again experience, and the band responded by breaking up; bassist Nate Mendel and drummer William Goldsmith joined Dave Grohl's Foo Fighters. Sunny Day's self-titled second album, released after the split, is surprisingly dull despite a couple of great songs, "Red Elephant" and "J'nuh."

Three years later, Sunny Day Real Estate was once again a going concern, with Goldsmith (but not Mendel) back in the fold. *How It Feels to Be Something On* is the band's best work to date. Enigk's melodies are subtler than before, with a pronounced raga influence, and his guitar interplay with Hoerner is spiky and intricate. A live album followed, its principal interest being that it improves on several songs from the first two records.

In 2000, SDRE made the jump to a major label (or, more accurately, a label distributed by a major conglomerate). And you sure can tell; *The Rising Tide* is punchier and more rock-radio-friendly than *How It Feels.* Fist-waving anthems such as "One" are delivered with total commitment. There still isn't much humor in Sunny Day Real Estate's songs, but when great music is played this passionately, it's hard to complain.

Staying true to their tumultuous nature, SDRE broke up once again after *The Rising Tide.* Enigk, Mendel, and Goldsmith regrouped as the Fire Theft; their self-titled debut ups Sunny Day's drama level, adding prog-rock touches such as chamber orchestra, children's choir, chiming glockenspiel, and raging guitar solos. Strangely, it works.

Fans of Sunny Day's more recent work should also check out Jeremy Enigk's 1996 solo album, *Return of the Frog Queen* (Sub Pop). No emocore here—file this one under dazzling, if enigmatic, orchestral pop. —M.R.

Sun Ra

★★★★   Angels and Demons at Play/The Nubians of Plutonia (1956; Evidence, 1993)
★★★★   Visits Planet Earth/Interstellar Low Ways (1956; Evidence, 1992)
★★★½   We Travel the Spaceways/Bad and Beautiful (1956; Evidence, 1992)
★★★   Sun Song (1956; Delmark, 1993)

★★★ Super-Sonic Jazz (1956; Evidence, 1992)
★★★½ Sound of Joy (1957; Delmark, 1994)
★★★★ Jazz in Silhouette (1958; Evidence, 1992)
★★½ Fate in a Pleasant Mood/When Sun Comes Out (1960; Evidence, 1993)
★★★½ Holiday for Soul Dance (1960; Evidence, 1992)
★★★ Cosmic Tones for Mental Therapy/Art Forms of Dimensions Tomorrow (1961; Evidence, 1992)
★★ Futuristic Sounds of Sun Ra (1961; Savoy, 1994)
★★ Other Planes of There (1964; Evidence, 1992)
★★★★ The Heliocentric Worlds of Sun Ra, Vol. 1 (1965; Get Back, 1999)
★★★★ The Heliocentric Worlds of Sun Ra, Vol. 2 (1965; Get Back, 1999)
★★★ The Magic City (1965; Evidence, 1993)
★★★ Nothing Is (1965; Get Back, 1999)
★★ Monorails and Satellites (1966; Evidence, 1992)
★★★★ Atlantis (1967; Evidence, 1993)
★★★ My Brother the Wind, Vol. 2 (1969; Evidence, 1992)
★★ It's After the End of the World (1970; Universe, 2003)
★★★ The Solar Myth Approach, Vols. 1–2 (1970; Varèse, 2001)
★★★★ Sound Sun Pleasure (1970; Evidence, 1992)
★★★ Space Is the Place (1972; GRP, 1998)
★★★★ Space Is the Place (1972; Evidence, 1993)
★★★ Concert for the Comet Kohoutek (1973; Get Back, 2000)
★★★ A Quiet Place in the Universe (1976; Leo, 2000)
★★★½ Languidity (1976; Evidence, 2000)
★★ Strange Celestial Road (1980; Rounder, 1990)
★★ Nuclear War (Unheard Music, 1982)
★★ Love in Outer Space: Live in Utrecht (1983; Leo, 1999)
★★★ Live at Praxis '84 (1984; Golden Years of New, 2000)
★★ Sun Ra Arkestra Meets Salah Ragab in Egypt (1984; Golden Years of New, 2000))
★★ Cosmo Sun Connection (1985; ReR, 1997)
★★★ A Night in East Berlin/My Brothers the Wind and the Sun (Leo, 1986)
★★ Live at Pitt-In, Tokyo (1988; DIW, 1999)
★★★ Somewhere Else (1988; Rounder, 1993)
★★★½ Second Star to the Right: Salute to Walt Disney (Leo, 1989)
★★★ Live From Soundscape (DIS, 1994)
★★★★ The Singles (Evidence, 1996)
★★★ Janus (1201 Music, 1999)

★★½ Outer Space Employment Agency (Total Energy, 1999)
★★★ At the Village Vanguard (Rounder, 1999)
★★★ Life Is Splendid (Total Energy, 1999)
★★ Live at the Hackney Empire (Leo, 2000)
★★★ Stardust From Tomorrow (Leo, 2000)
★★★ When Angels Speak of Love (Evidence, 2000)
★★★½ Great Lost Sun Ra Albums: Cymbals and Crystal Spears (Evidence, 2000)
★★★½ Standards (1201 Music, 2000)
★★★★ Greatest Hits: Easy Listening for Intergalactic Travel (Evidence, 2000)
★★ It Is Forbidden (Total Energy, 2001)
★★★ The Solar Myth Approach, Vols. 1–2 (Varèse, 2001)

The fact that legendary composer/pianist Sun Ra listed the planet Saturn as his birthplace was only one of the obvious indicators of his lifelong commitment to eccentricity—his mad, joyous jazz is the more profound index of his 70-year pursuit of idiosyncratic, aesthetic freedom. While Ra's head was adamantly in the clouds, his insistence on the work ethic was hardly extraterrestrial—whether he dubbed his outfits the Solar Arkestra, the Myth-Science Arkestra, the Band from Outer Space, or the Astro-Intergalactic-Infinity Arkestra, Ra pulled off the incredible feat of keeping a working big band together for decades. His sax players, especially, were titans—John Gilmore on tenor, Marshall Allen on alto, Pat Patrick on baritone—but virtually all his sidemen were aces.

An innovator, back in the '50s, on electric keyboards, Ra managed to work his own subtle twists on Ellington-derived big-band jazz, incorporate the rhythmic whimsy of Thelonious Monk, and collaborate with McCoy Tyner, Quincy Jones, Mongo Santamaria, and Art Blakey, all the while furthering the product of his own weird muse. A deft and often subtle pianist, his work builds on the stride tradition—and, in ways unheard of in serious jazz, he always insisted that live performance incorporate theater (outlandish African-Martian costumery, percussion marathons, huge, ritual gestures). Think of P-Funk playing jazz on Mars.

A way to begin grappling with Ra might be to pick up *Second Star to the Right*, his salute to Walt Disney, which morphs those kiddie-happy movie tunes into something very strange. *Greatest Hits*, a sampler from the late '50s to the early '70s, is also very approachable. His late-'50s fare remains, in some ways, his most trailblazing; Evidence has put out a fine crop of twofers—try out *Angels and Demons at Play/The Nubians of Plutonia* or *Visits Planet Earth/Interstellar*

Low Ways. Standards is nice: Sun Ra and Gilmore shining on recognizable versions of jazz staples. His magnum opus and seminal set remains the two volumes of *The Heliocentric Worlds of Sun Ra,* a pathfinding work of atmospheric free jazz. For those willing to dare Sun Ra getting really out there, *Cosmic Tones for Mental Therapy/Art Forms of Dimensions Tomorrow* and *Pathways to Unknown Worlds/Friendly Love* ought to do the trick. So assured, however, is the rhythmic sense of any Arkestra that Ra has fashioned, that his music is rarely wholly inaccessible—the term "joyful noise" suits Sun Ra perfectly. Live, of course, was the way to truly enjoy the Sun Ra experience: *At the Village Vanguard* and *Live at Praxis '84* (with a great "Mack the Knife") are fairly representative of the in-concert buzz—long before Beefheart, Zappa, John Zorn, or any of a number of exponents of musical surreality, Ra had the act down. —P.E.

Superchunk

★★½ Superchunk (Matador, 1990)
★★★ No Pocky for Kitty (Matador, 1991)
★★★½ Tossing Seeds (Singles 89–91) (Merge, 1992)
★★★★ On the Mouth (Matador, 1993)
★★★ Foolish (Merge, 1994)
★★★½ Incidental Music 1991–95 (Merge, 1995)
★★★ Here's Where the Strings Come In (Merge, 1995)
★★★½ Indoor Living (Merge, 1997)
★★★★ Come Pick Me Up (Merge, 1999)
★★★ Here's to Shutting Up (Merge, 2001)
★★★½ The Clambakes Series, Vol. 1: Acoustic In-Stores East and West (Merge, 2002)
★½ The Clambakes Series, Vol. 2: Music for Kinugasa's "A Page of Madness" (Merge, 2003)
★★★ Cup of Sand (Merge, 2003)

Pogoing onstage like jumping beans, cranking out records on its own Merge label in Chapel Hill, NC, and burying frontman Mac McCaughan's yowl in a cloud of distorted guitars, Superchunk was the archetypal indie-rock band of the '90s. It's surprising, then, that it's evolved into something rather different and more delicate—and arguably better—over the last decade or so, as it's changed from a singles band into an album band. Its publishing company is called All the Songs Sound the Same Music, and on its self-titled debut, there's some truth to that: The band hasn't quite figured out how to project its personality through its murky, metal-derived rock stance. It does have the group's best-known song, though: the anti-laziness anthem "Slack Motherfucker."

No Pocky for Kitty, with new guitarist Jim Wilbur, is a little better defined, and even more enthusiastic, starting with the energy-through-the-roof opener "Skip Steps 1 & 3." The roaring never lets up, but you can hear McCaughan's ingenious power-pop ideas starting to assert themselves through the barrage, and the dueling guitars articulate hooks as often as they simply hurtle and squeal. Two hits apiece from each of the first two albums recur on the singles compilation *Tossing Seeds,* along with some clever covers and a few more cryptic full-speed-ahead rockers.

On the Mouth is everything the early Superchunk was aiming for: marvelously inventive rock & roll songwriting (check out the mileage "Precision Auto" gets from its two-note hook) delivered with unflagging rocket force. There are still squalls of feedback everywhere, and McCaughan is shouting (more or less on key!) most of the time, but the volume works in the service of the songs. The band's not opposed to a little subtlety, either—it even lets "The Question Is How Fast" build for a minute or so before it slams it into overdrive. Snare-battering new drummer Jon Wurster completes the lineup the band's maintained for the past decade.

Foolish is mostly much slower, and audibly bummed-out: McCaughan and bassist Laura Ballance had split up, and there's obvious emotional strain in his songwriting and singing. There are a couple of fine songs, especially "The First Part" and the elegiac "Driveway to Driveway" (reprised in acoustic form on a single), but none of *On the Mouth*'s sense of fun. *Incidental Music,* another singles comp, conversely, is inconsistent but wildly entertaining, with tossed-off covers of the Verlaines' "Lying in State" (perfect for them) and the Magnetic Fields' "100,000 Fireflies" (totally wrong for them, and they don't care), as well as the fantastic originals "Ribbon" ("When will our fuckin' hearts cease to riot?" goes the chorus) and "Cadmium." The secret bonus track is Mark Robinson's deranged remix of "Precision Auto."

"Hyper Enough" opens *Here's Where the Strings Come In* in vintage 'Chunk style, but the rest of the album is generally moving in a new direction. What the band's lost in speed (which honestly isn't much—Wurster keeps things moving at a nice clip), it's gained in complexity and density, with organ sneaking into the mix and lots of long-sustained tension. (Robinson remixed "Eastern Terminal" a few years later and made it sound exactly like Joy Division.) It even tries for a sustained, hypnotic groove on "Certain Stars," although it doesn't quite work out. (The *Laughter Guns* EP, now out of print, features a hilarious, extended deconstruction of "Hyper Enough" from a Chapel Hill radio station.)

The keyboards are fully integrated into *Indoor Living*, especially on its gorgeous single "Watery Hands." Superchunk revs up the tempo a couple of times, to show that it still can; but mostly, the mood is close to McCaughan's mellower solo project Portastatic, and the band's wall of guitars no longer acts like armor against the world outside punk rock. When "Song for Marion Brown" climaxes with a riff borrowed from "Baba O'Riley," it feels like a reconciliation.

By the splendid *Come Pick Me Up*, two things are evident about McCaughan's voice: First, that years of screaming have irreparably changed it, and second, that he's figured what to do about its change more effectively than anyone since Stevie Nicks, relying on his tender falsetto and treating it to some of his smartest, twistiest songs. With the aid of producer Jim O'Rourke and crack Chicagoan string and horn sections, the band rethinks and micromanages its sound. It's still recognizably Superchunk, but every note sounds like a conscious decision rather than an automatic reflex.

With its gentle strumming and brushed drums, *Here's to Shutting Up* is a little less recognizable as the band that made *No Pocky for Kitty*, a little too self-consciously mature. It's pretty and lively, but the languid shuffle "Late-Century Dream" is its only real 'Chunk classic. *The Clambakes Series, Vol. 1* is a quickie live album drawn from acoustic in-store performances on the subsequent tour, and surprisingly excellent—the material spans the band's entire career, and it's rearranged it all with care, especially "Art Class," a *Shutting Up* tribute to polka-dot-and-phallus-obsessed artist Yayoi Kusama. The second *Clambakes* disc, though, is negligible: a live recording (with Wurster's drums prerecorded) of their instrumental accompaniment to a 1927 silent film by Teinosake Kinugasa. The two-disc *Cup of Sand* is a third odds-and-ends collection, including the actual songs from *The Laughter Guns*, turbo-boosted 1992 covers of Adam Ant's "Beat My Guest" and Government Issue's "Blending In," and some wistful outtakes from the *Come Pick Me Up* period.   —D.W.

Super Furry Animals

★★★ Fuzzy Logic (Creation, 1996)
★★★ Radiator (Flydaddy, 1997)
★★½ Guerrilla (Flydaddy, 1999)
★★★★ Mwng (Flydaddy, 2000)
★★★★★ Rings Around the World (Epic, 2002)
★★★★ Phantom Power (Epic, 2003)

Think fast. How many bands can you name from Wales? Even harder, how many of those bands have released full-length albums sung entirely in Welsh?

Only a perverse bunch of weirdos would pack their catchiest pop album with lyrics that only 0.005 percent of the world's population can understand, which is what they did with *Mwng*, their followup to the more oblique *Guerrilla*. Formed in Cardiff during the mid-1990s, Super Furry Animals quickly carved out a presence on the British charts with their debut, *Fuzzy Logic*, which became a surprise radio hit across the pond. Meanwhile, in America, SFA slowly but surely earned the "critics' darlings" label with each new album, culminating in their epic mind fuck, *Rings Around the World*. With this release, SFA took the dirty digital production aesthetic of the Wu-Tang's RZA and applied it to their version of psychedelic Brit pop, producing an infectious album of beautiful noise that's akin to riding a Tilt-a-Whirl while drugged out of your mind, although you wouldn't necessarily know that by hearing the stringed-out cheese of their Beatlesque single "It's Not the End of the World?" Here, they skid all over the proverbial map, hopping and hot-wiring genres on a sonic field trip (with the emphasis on trip) that mixes scuzzed-out electronica ("No Sympathy"), Philly soul ("Juxtaposed With U"), ELO pap gone wrong ("Receptacle for the Respectable"), and straight-up balladry ("Presidential Suite"). In sum, SFA comes off as a demented Pink Floyd for a fractured, postmodern world. The Pink Floyd connection was made all the more obvious when the group released DVD companions to *Rings Around the World* and *Phantom Power*, in which SFA one-ups Floyd's dream of a quadraphonic audio world by remixing each album in full Dolby 5.1 Surround Sound.   —K.M.

Supergrass

★★★ I Should Coco (Capitol, 1995)
★★★★ In It for the Money (Capitol, 1997)
★★★ Supergrass (Island, 2000)
★★★★ Life on Other Planets (Island, 2002)

With their mod hairdos, bushy sideburns, and diminutive stature, these three young (as in barely out of their teens) lads from Oxford hit the British charts in the mid-'90s looking like the second coming of the Small Faces. Even better, they sounded great, mixing '60s pop smarts with postpunk verve and a distinctively youthful exuberance. *I Should Coco* is a giddy romp that peaks with "Caught by the Fuzz," a slashing early Who-style number, and "Alright," a perfect teen summer anthem if ever there was one. A few songs are undercooked, and Gaz Coombes' voice is limited, but overall, the album's a joy.

On *In It for the Money*, Supergrass takes a major leap forward. This is one big-sounding record, balancing mighty rock ("Sun Hits the Sky," "You Can See Me") with majestic ballads ("Late in the Day," "It's Not Me"). Coombes' singing remains a weak link, but he makes the best out of his strained croak, and the stellar songs do the rest.

In comparison, the band's self-titled third album is a letdown. For every positive moment—such as the delicate "Shotover Hill," the supercharged nouveau-glam of "Pumping on Your Stereo," and the soaring acoustic guitar–powered verses of "Moving"—there's a dull or sophomoric track to match it. *Life on Other Planets* proves that the slump was temporary, as Gaz and his pals cleanly hit every one of their targets with nod-and-wink zest. One song, "Seen the Light," is the catchiest single T. Rex never made; the disc's other 11 are almost as good. —M.R.

Supertramp

- ★ Supertramp (A&M, 1970)
- ★ Indelibly Stamped (A&M, 1971)
- ★★★ Crime of the Century (A&M, 1974)
- ★★ Crisis? What Crisis? (A&M, 1975)
- ★★★ Even in the Quietest Moments . . . (A&M, 1977)
- ★★★ Breakfast in America (A&M, 1979)
- ★★½ Paris (A&M, 1980)
- ★★ Famous Last Words (A&M, 1982)
- ★ Brother Where You Bound (A&M, 1985)
- ★ Free as a Bird (A&M, 1987)
- ★★★ Classics, Volume 9 (A&M, 1987)
- ★★★ The Very Best of Supertramp (A&M, 1992)
- ★ Some Things Never Change (Chrysalis, 1997)
- ★ Slow Motion (EMI, 2002)

Here's one of those eternal rock & roll questions: Did the saxophone player from Supertramp ever get any action? Like, could he swagger into a rock club and say, "Hey babe, dig my embouchure on 'The Logical Song,' " and expect to get laid? Did groupies primp for Supertramp shows and tell one another things like, "I'm gonna see if that ligature-licker can *really* take the long way home, if you know what I mean"? For the answers to these and other questions, we can only turn to the collected works of Supertramp. These English art rockers had their own sound, with a strange electric-keyboard device apparently unique to their band. They also had two singer/songwriters, squeaky-voiced Roger Hodgson and mumbly-voiced Rick Davies, pondering the weighty moral issues of their time. And they also had a saxophone player.

Supertramp's early prog work is slight: rhythmi-cally underfed, lyrically facile, all the way treble. Like every other band in the '70s, they were required to do a song called "Lady" (on *Crisis? What Crisis?,* one of

the decade's worst album covers). Like everyone else who writes a song about "School," they complained about being forced to learn "the golden rule" (it rhymes, see), seeking solace in astrology ("Aries") and keyboard solos. But there are nice moments on *Crime of the Century,* which has "Dreamer" and "Bloody Well Right," and *Even in the Quietest Moments . . . ,* which has "Give a Little Bit." The breakthrough hit *Breakfast in America* was all nice moments: the jolly "Take the Long Way Home," the adjectivally crazed "Logical Song," the bitchy fuck-and-run ditty "Good-bye Stranger." Unfortunately, Hodgson's voice got even higher and hit genuinely painful treble levels on *Famous Last Words,* until he went straight through the roof to a solo career. The band tried to regain its prog cred with the unbearable *Brother Where You Bound,* and has intermittently progged it out ever since. Daft Punk paid homage to the Supertramp keyboard sound in the 2001 tribute single "Digital Love." That same year, "Give a Little Bit" became a Gap commercial, with Robbie Robertson, Liz Phair, Dwight Yoakam, and lots of other worried mortgage-payers each taking a line of the song and singing their hearts out. —R.S.

The Supremes

- ★★ The Supremes Sing Country, Western and Pop (1965; Motown, 1991)
- ★★★ I Hear a Symphony (1966; Motown, 1991)
- ★★½ Supremes a Go Go (1966; Motown, 1989)
- ★★★★ Diana Ross and the Supremes Greatest Hits, Vol. 1 (1967; Motown, 1989)
- ★★★ Reflections (1968; Motown, 1991)
- ★★★ Diana Ross and the Supremes Join the Temptations (Motown, 1968)
- ★★½ T.C.B. (With the Temptations) (Motown, 1968)
- ★★ Live at London's Talk of the Town (Motown, 1968)
- ★★★★ The Ultimate Collection (Motown, 1997)
- ★★★★ The Millennium Collection (Motown, 1999)

Although it was Florence Ballard who first led the girl group who went on to rival the Temptations as Motown's most successful act, Diana Ross very soon took over. With Ross at the helm—a figure with a commanding stage presence and a singular voice (a tense balance of the cool and the flirtatious)—the Supremes ruled soul radio in the mid-'60s by turn-ing out a prodigious series of hits. Holland-Dozier-Holland assembled overpowering finger-snapping, bass-thumping backing tracks for the singers—and the group delivered an awesome five-in-a-row clutch of #1 smashes: "Where Did Our Love Go?" "Baby Love," "Come See About Me," "Stop! In the Name of

Love," and "Back in My Arms Again." As certainly pop records as they were R&B ones, these 45s made soul music safe for white audiences—without costing Motown any of its massive black following. And had the Supremes retired in, say, 1967, their achievement would've been mythic—sweet, short, and perfect.

As it was, they moved on—to the Copa, internal dissension, glitz, and confusion. With Ross departing in 1970 (Jean Terrell took over on lead), they put out exactly one magnificent single, "Stoned Love" (1970), and descended, as did most of their Motown labelmates, into mere professionalism. The length of their discography shouldn't trick anyone into thinking that all (or even most) of their albums were significant—even more of a singles band than most Motown acts, they're best represented on compilations: *The Ultimate Collection* should do the trick. —P.E.

Sweet

★★★	Funny How Sweet Co-Co Can Be (RCA, 1972)
★★★	Sweet (Bell, 1973)
★★½	Sweet Fanny Adams (RCA, 1974)
★★★½	Desolation Boulevard (Capitol, 1974)
★★	Give Us a Wink (Capitol, 1976)
★★	Level Headed (Capitol, 1978)
★	A Cut Above the Rest (Capitol, 1979)
★	Water's Edge (Capitol, 1980)
★★★★★	The Best of Sweet (Capitol, 1992)
★★★★	The Best of Sweet (Camden U.K., 1997)

If there's a more depraved song of sexual awakening than Sweet's "Wig Wam Bam," the world isn't ready for it yet—three minutes, idiot poetry about Hiawatha and Minnehaha, sucrose-splattering glam guitars, cowbells, handclaps, and the utterly demented way Brian Connolly shrieks the chorus, "Wig wam bam, gonna make you my man/Wham bam bam, gonna get you if I can." A perfect song, from a perfect band. Sweet rang up an incredible string of glam bubblegum U.K. hits in the early '70s, most written by the Chapman/Chinn production team, and it ranks up there with T. Rex in the pantheon. The most famous hit was "Ballroom Blitz," but there's more: "Little Willy" (the kid came to dance, and nobody can make him stop), "Blockbuster" (psycho killer on the loose), "Teenage Rampage" (smells like teen spirit), "Action" (everybody wants some), "Hell Raiser" (groupies), "Co-Co" (steel drums), "Funny Funny" (dumb), "Chop Chop" (dumber), "Tom Tom Turnaround" (irreversible brain damage). It's all electric, so frantically hectic.

Sweet didn't waste its time on album tracks, although it accidentally made a good album anyway with 1974's *Desolation Boulevard,* source of the classics "Fox on the Run," "The 6-Teens," and "AC/DC." It tried to grow up and get serious, resulting in its last radio shot, the great 1978 bubble-prog hit "Love Is Like Oxygen" ("Get too much, you get too high/Not enough and you're gonna die," far out). Beware of the many greatest-hits collections: Band members kept deceitfully rerecording bad new versions of their old hits under the Sweet name (for shame!), so if you see a cheap compilation, assume it's a rip-off until you hear otherwise with your own ears. Start with the 1992 Capitol best-of, which collects eight or nine absolute classics of teenage rampage. Try a little touch, try a little too much—just try a little wig wam bam. —R.S.

Matthew Sweet

★★★½	Inside (Columbia, 1986)
★★★	Earth (A&M, 1988)
★★★½	Girlfriend (Zoo/BMG, 1991)
★★★	Altered Beast (Zoo, 1993)
★★	Son of Altered Beast (EP) (Zoo, 1994)
★★½	100% Fun (Zoo, 1995)
★★½	Blue Sky on Mars (Volcano/Zoo, 1997)
★★★	In Reverse (Volcano, 1999)
★★★	Time Capsule: The Best of Matthew Sweet (Volcano, 2000)

During the early '90s, Matthew Sweet was at the forefront of a power-pop revival that found would-be alt rockers indulging in the simple pleasures of crunchy guitar hooks, double-tracked harmonies, and winsome romantic longing. Sweet didn't have much to say about love—it was exhilirating, it sucked, it was alternately reminiscent of childhood happiness and death's icy grip, that sort of thing—but he was a talented songwriter with an artiste's touch in the studio and had two ace guitarists backing him up: Television's Richard Lloyd and well-traveled gun-for-hire Robert Quine, both of whom gave his records an edginess not found in Sweet's smooth, mild-mannered voice.

Sweet's first two albums are slightly muddled affairs that flopped commercially. On *Inside* he's joined by members of the Bangles, Tom Petty's Heartbreakers, and the dB's, as well as such interestingly paired playmates as Valerie Simpson and Anton Fier. The tunes, however, don't sound at all like guest-star jams—they come across like the snappy work of a brainy Tommy James or a looser Dwight Twilley. Sweet's songwriting remains impressive on *Earth,* but aside from great guest-guitar work by Quine and Lloyd, the album suffers from synthitis.

Girlfriend proved to be Sweet's breakthrough. Again Lloyd and Quine help out, along with Lloyd Cole, as Sweet meditates on love supreme ("Divine Intervention," "Holy War") and love fleshly

("Winona" is a fine mash note to the actress). The driving, hooky guitar-o-rama title track became a Top 5 hit, and Sweet turned out near-perfect pop-rock in "I've Been Waiting" and "Evangeline," a riff-laden winner about a crush-worthy comic book character who "only thinks about the Lord above."

Not one for playing it safe, he moved beyond simple catchiness as his music progressed. *Altered Beast* is tough, smart pop, with a curious all-star cast, from Mick Fleetwood to ex–Rolling Stones pianist Nicky Hopkins. Some of the songs—"Someone to Pull the Trigger," "Dinosaur Act," "Knowing People"—are equal to anything on *Girlfriend,* but Sweet's studio perfectionism is beginning to run amok, as he goes a little nuts with overdubs and tries to pack in too many ideas and too many guitar solos. (The *Son of* sequel, a hodgepodge of live work, outtakes, and covers, stands nicely on its own.)

Sweet simplified his approach for *100% Fun,* which proved a brief return to form. Either Sweet had dusted off some Big Star records or else he learned to ease up in studio, but whatever the case, "Sick of Myself," "We're the Same," and "Lost My Mind" were crunchy, super-tuneful nuggets that could have fit nicely onto *Girlfriend. Blue Sky on Mars* is more of the same, only with weaker songwriting. *In Reverse* is an ambitious and moderately successful attempt to update Phil Spector's Wall of Sound for the '90s. Sweet piles on flugelhorns and harpsichords and theremin (sometimes there are 15 musicians playing at once), which at least hold your attention when the songs fail to deliver. —P.E./C.H.

Swell Maps

★★★★	A Trip to Marineville (Rather/Rough Trade, 1979)	
★★★★½	. . . in "Jane From Occupied Europe" (Rather/Rough Trade, 1980)	
★★★½	Whatever Happens Next . . . (Rather/Rough Trade, 1981)	
★★½	Collision Time (Rough Trade, 1982)	
★★★★	Train Out of It (Antar, 1987)	
★★★	Collision Time Revisited (Mute/Restless, 1989)	
★★★	International Rescue (Alive, 1999)	
★★★½	Sweep the Desert (Alive, 2000)	

Swell Maps never quite fit onto the punk bandwagon, never had a hit, never reunited, and never had much of an influence on anyone else, including their own members' subsequent musical careers—they were too strange to be imitated. But their arty, wildly creative records have also never been out of print for long, and they've aged better than almost all of their peers.

The brothers who called themselves Nikki Sudden (sneers and guitar) and Epic Soundtracks (drums and piano) had been recording together as early as 1974. By the time punk broke, they hooked up with singer/bassist Jowe Head, guitarist Richard Earl, and a couple of auxiliary members, and released a string of twisted, messy singles, some under pseudonyms. *A Trip to Marineville* impersonates a straightforward punk-pop album for just over a minute, then collides with a free-form solo on an out-of-tune piano. Thereafter, it races off in a daze, incorporating toy instruments, improvised noise, a jam called "BLAM!!" that ended up in a Honda commercial 23 years later, the whole band screaming about midget submarines, and (best of all) "Vertical Slum," 72 seconds of flawlessly snotty riff heaven.

Their followup, *Swell Maps . . . in "Jane From Occupied Europe,"* is one of the crowning glories of the postpunk era: disciplined, rich with detail, deeply mysterious, and practically bursting into flames with energy. The lyrics Sudden whines are obliquely poetic bulletins from the rear guard of some kind of war, submerged beneath torrents of resonant guitar and rawly inventive noise. Half the album is gorgeous collaborative instrumentals like "Big Maz in the Desert"; Head also contributes a goofy but dignified love song, "Cake Shop." *Jane* isn't what you'd call pop (Sudden couldn't carry a tune with a hydraulic lift), but its chaos is punctuated everywhere by unforgettable moments, most of which probably count as hooks.

The band collapsed shortly thereafter, but left behind a mountain of uncompiled material that's been filtering out ever since. *Whatever Happens Next . . .* collects demos, experiments, and a couple of BBC radio sessions (including one that features X-Ray Spex's saxophonist Lora Logic gloriously honking away). *Collision Time* is a chronological singles-and-LP-cuts survey that somehow misses the point; it was later replaced by the double album *Collision Time Revisited,* which throws in a few unreleased scraps but doesn't flow right, either. The much better *Train Out of It* compiles most of their nonalbum singles along with a bunch of winningly bizarre instrumentals, even more of which appeared on the CD editions of *Marineville* and *Jane.*

Released a couple of years after Soundtracks' 1997 death, *International Rescue* is practically revisionist history, presenting the Swell Maps as a feisty but sort of inept punk band unambiguously fronted by Nikki Sudden—all of which was only true some of the time. Its whine-and-bash rockers and oddities (like a mock-oldies single originally credited to the Phones Sportsman Band) hang together surprisingly well, although the remixes of Maps classics are suspect. The mostly instrumental *Sweep the Desert* is more like it, with the weirdest passages of both studio albums carefully sequenced among compatible curiosities from the rest of their catalogue.   —D.W.

System of a Down

★★★★   System of a Down (American, 1997)
★★★★   Toxicity (Columbia, 2001)
★★★   Steal This Album (Sony, 2002)

Admirers tend to talk up System of a Down's committed left politics as a remarkable occurrence, as if a certain strain of heavy metal hasn't always encouraged a contemplatively antiauthoritarian streak. And sure, while the L.A. quartet backs up its ideology with reams of facts, agitprop railing against the U.S. government for "Utilizing drugs to pay for foreign wars around the globe" isn't the real hook, no matter how much it may echo your beliefs. Instead, System gets over with its flair for the exotic (credited to its Armenian heritage), which juices its riffs into a thrashy whorl primed to belly dance blithely into the mosh pit.

The most surprising thing about listening to the band's self-titled debut now, after *Toxicity* has been all-but-unanimously declared the new millennium's first masterpiece for the thinking metalhead, is how well that first shot stands up. All the explosive charges are in place, ready to be detonated. The band's mix of sludge and thrust is powered by a flexible sense of dynamics—just when you suspect System's detours into apparent culs-de-sac of prog-rock complexity into which arty depressives like Tool waywardly stray, the band busts free. This balance of tone is managed by frontman Serj Tankian, who is just as willing to explore the humor in his manic tirades as he is to bellow with drill-sergeant ferocity.

Toxicity was a reminder that rock summons up dangerous thoughts we'd all rather sublimate. Hardly a new proposition, but if Fred Durst presiding over the Woodstock wilding was a challenge to banality, System placed its violence in a deliberate context with lyrics like "Why won't you trust in my self-righteous suicide?" The analysis was there in the music as well—a fascination with the empowering energy that violence unleashes. And yet, goofball sideswipes like the pogo-friendly "Bounce" insisted that the band has no intention of winding up self-righteous suicides themselves. *Steal This Album* is a better-than-average odds-and-sods collection.   —K.H.

Tt

Taj Mahal

Rising Sons

By the late '60s the blues had evolved from a humble, outlaw Southern folk style and grown into one of the most influential musical forms of the 20th century. Any aspiring bluesmen faced a choice: they could either revisit the music's past glories or accept the difficult challenge of reinventing it once again.

Taj Mahal did both. Born Henry St. Clair Fredericks in 1942, he enjoyed a middle-class life and a college education in Springfield, MA, far away from the Delta. But from the beginning he showed a keen musical intellect and curiosity about the potential of the blues, and over the years he has boldly taken it to new places: to reggae, to sunny Calypso, to India, and even to its deep roots in West Africa.

His first group, Rising Sons, was formed in Los Angeles with a fellow blues traveler, Ry Cooder. Though signed to Columbia, the group's music remained in the vaults for more than 25 years; probably for the best, since its Paul Butterfield–like electric boogies were nothing new, and its versions of several Taj Mahal standbys ("Statesboro Blues," "Corinna," "Dust My Broom") were better served on later solo albums.

As a solo artist, Taj emerged as a stylish and lovable devil with a wide-brimmed hat and a dandyish bandana around his neck: a John Lee Hooker for the Woodstock generation. "Leaving Trunk," "Statesboro Blues," and "EZ Rider" balance tight, rock-tinged grooves with the narrative looseness of a born raconteur. *The Natch'l Blues* is even better, with the gorgeous keyboard-based ballad "Corinna" and even more confident discursiveness on "She Caught the Katy and Left Me a Mule to Ride" and "Going Up to the Country, Paint My Mailbox Blue."

Giant Step and *De Ole Folks at Home,* separate albums long packaged as a double, are the pinnacle of Taj's early career. Covering Buffy Sainte-Marie, the Band, and the Monkees, he shows that he can make anything his own, using the blues not for self-pity or mere sexual braggadocio, but as a sensitive tool for revealing a song's life force. Stripped down in the extreme, *De Ole Folks* links him with Lead Belly, his closest blues ancestor. On "A Little Soulful Tune," he conjures the childlike pleasures of song with a true minimum of sounds: just his voice and handclaps.

Mo' Roots has the first of his many excursions into Caribbean music, including a cover of Bob Marley's "Slave Ship" that burns with all the passion and authority of the original. After further testing the island waters on some now-deleted Columbia discs, Taj signed to Warner Bros. in 1976 and released three heavily calypso- and reggae-influenced albums. Collected on *Sing a Happy Song*, they show a bluesman who has found sweetness and peace in steel drums and a lyrical steel guitar.

After some dormant years, Taj returned in 1986 for the difficult third phase of his career, which was marked by a mix of first-class musical ambassadorship and dull bluesploitation. *Taj* belatedly brought him into the *Miami Vice* age with cold synths and mechanical beats, though the distant chime of steel drums and Taj's Howlin' Wolf–like growls put a ghost in the machine. Still, it's an embarrassment, as are the shamelessly commercial albums he made for Private through the mid-'90s. From *Dancing the Blues* to *Phantom Blues* to *Señor Blues,* he's painting by numbers for an audience that is certainly easy to please: *Dancing* was nominated for the contemporary blues Grammy and *Señor* won it.

At the same time, Taj was doing some of his most ambitious and intelligent work. *Mumtaz Mahal,* a collaboration with two Indian musicians, N. Ravkiran and V. M. Bhatt, is pretty far out there, though there are moments where Taj's blues heartily shakes hands with the bending, wailing Indian quartertones. Better still are *Sacred Island,* his greatest and most heartwarmingly sweet blues/calypso experiment, and *Kulanjan,* recorded with the master Malian musician Toumani Diabate. Like Cooder on his *Talking Timbuktu* album with Ali Farka Toure five years before, Taj digs deep into the blues' African roots with wide eyes and plenty of licks to trade. *Hanapepe Dream* brings the blues to Hawaii, Taj's island home since the mid-'80s.

Along the way Taj has made some great oddball albums, including several excellent children's discs. In *Shake Sugaree*'s cheerful sing-alongs and rambling autobiographical asides, he seems like the very reincarnation of Lead Belly. *Mule Bone* collects his songs for a play written by Langston Hughes and Zora Neale Hurston that was lost for decades. And on his soundtrack for the 1972 film *Sounder* (long out of print), he expertly evokes the hard life of sharecropping-era southern blacks.

Of the many collections, none captures the full breadth of Taj Mahal's talent and ambition. Most rely on the market-proven blues standards and avoid or ghettoize his experiments; only *In Progress and in Motion,* an excellent three-CD box, combines them, and even then his first five years gets two discs and everything else is crammed onto the third. Avoid *The Best of the Private Years:* It picks from everything except *Sacred Island,* which is the only Private disc worth listening to. —B.S.

Talking Heads

★★★½ Talking Heads: 77 (Sire, 1977)
★★★★½ More Songs About Buildings and Food (Sire, 1978)
★★★★½ Fear of Music (Sire, 1979)
★★★★★ Remain in Light (Sire, 1980)
★★★★ The Name of This Band Is Talking Heads (Sire, 1982)
★★★★ Speaking in Tongues (Sire, 1983)
★★½ Stop Making Sense (Sire, 1984)
★★ Little Creatures (Sire, 1985)
★★ True Stories (Sire, 1986)
★★ Naked (Sire, 1988)
★★★★ Sand in the Vaseline: Popular Favorites 1976–1992 (Sire, 1992)
★★★ Stop Making Sense: Special Edition (Sire, 1999)
★★ Once in a Lifetime (Sire, 2003)
★★★★ The Best of Talking Heads (Rhino, 2004)

The Heads

★ No Talking, Just Head (Radioactive, 1996)

Talking Heads plowed through art rock, CBGB punk, funk, bubblegum, even African polyrhythms, making beautiful sounds out of frontman David Byrne's malaise about life during Reagantime and the late '70s. The Heads' paradox was that the harder they tried to imitate music from around the world, the more they sounded exactly like four clean-cut American college kids: eager to please, embarrassed about their privilege, working hard at their chosen career.

Talking Heads: 77 is quirky singer/songwriter pop; while the band plays stiff, clean nerd rock, Byrne squawks one-liners about how it takes a tough man to be a tender chicken. But for *More Songs About Buildings and Food,* producer Brian Eno opens up the music so that Byrne now has the sonic spritz he needs to hone his comic persona: the company man who learned everything he knows from reading in-flight magazines and the warnings on the back of sugar packets. For the killer finale, "The Big Country," Byrne warbles over pastoral guitars about looking down from an airplane at ordinary American life ("Look at that kitchen!/All of that food!") and concludes, "I wouldn't live there if you paid me to."

Eno stuck around to produce the band's two finest records, *Fear of Music* and *Remain in Light*. *Fear of Music* is science-fiction comedy arranged for electric guitar, fleshing out Byrne's paranoid vision of an urban world where air can hurt you, animals are setting a bad example, and heaven is a place where nothing ever happens. "Mind" and "Heaven" are beautiful ballads, while the climactic "Drugs" can scare the bejeezus out of you if you're properly sleep-deprived. *Remain in Light* is an expertly paced, intricately layered album of future-shock Afro-disco polyrhythms, revved up and spliced together with hypnotic melodies, dense electronics, Adrian Belew's crazed guitar shrieks, and echoes of Nigerian highlife. In "Cross-eyed and Painless," "Houses in Motion," and "The Great Curve," the Heads found their groove; for all the awe and mystery in the music, *Remain in Light* rocks like a monster.

The Heads pursued solo projects for the next few years, releasing the excellent live retrospective *The Name of This Band Is Talking Heads,* which improbably turned "Drugs" into an arena anthem. After collaborating with Eno on a diffuse ethno-fusion album, *My Life in the Bush of Ghosts,* Byrne composed a Twyla Tharp ballet score, *The Catherine Wheel.* Guitarist Jerry Harrison's solo album *The Red and the Black* rehashed *Remain in Light.* Husband/wife team drummer Chris Frantz and bassist Tina Weymouth's Tom Tom Club seemed the slightest of the Heads-related projects, but proved the most complex. As the Tom Tom Club's twitchy synth-pop hit "Genius of Love" crossed over to rap radio and got mixed into early Sugar Hill singles, the Heads' fascination with pop became a two-way dialogue for the first time. *Speaking in Tongues* sounds inspired by "Genius of Love" and by the prospect of a real live audience joining in the fun. The result is the Heads' most festive album, full of big flippy-floppy drums, although Eno's gone and the songwriting's thinned out. The P-Funk-inspired party chant "Burning Down the House" made a great radio hit, while "This Must Be the Place (Naïve Melody)" was Byrne's surprisingly pretty attempt at a sincere love song.

The Heads followed their hit concert film *Stop Making Sense* with a redundant soundtrack that left out the movie's highlight, an acoustic "Heaven" (restored on the 1999 edition). Byrne's next solo project, *Music for "The Knee Plays,"* mixed New Orleans brass

bands with clever stand-up. For *Little Creatures,* Byrne reconvened the Heads to play some foursquare folk-rock ditties he'd written solo, no polyrhythms or funny business; unfortunately, Byrne needs polyrhythms and funny business, because he doesn't have much knack for hooky rock tunes. *Little Creatures* has some lively moments ("And She Was," "Perfect World"), but the beat is flat and the vocals are too cutesy for words. *True Stories* collects leftovers from the same session into a dubious soundtrack to Byrne's dubious debut film.

Naked rallied the Heads for one last attempt at African music, this time soukous, with the usual glut of gee-whiz humor and pedigreed guest musicians. *Naked* was obviously inspired by the success of Paul Simon's *Graceland,* but times had changed, and the world-music industry had come into its own. *Remain in Light* fans had little access to Nigerian highlife in 1980, but by 1988, if you wanted to check out soukous, you could just buy a Kanda Bongo Man or Rochereau CD instead of a well-meaning imitation. Rap, freestyle, and house had bum-rushed the airwaves, making the Heads' theoretical approach to polyrhythms sound smug and fussy.

Tasteful as always, the Heads had the good form to quit. Harrison became a prolific producer, while Frantz and Weymouth succumbed to the temptation to keep milking the Tom Tom cash cow. Byrne made pallid solo albums in the *Naked* mode (1989's *Rei Momo,* 1992's *Uh-Oh*). For 1994's *David Byrne,* he made himself over as a long-haired sensitive folksinger, with oppressively wordy guitar ballads; 1997's *Feelings* and 2001's *Look into the Eyeball* reverted to stale '80s art funk. His label Luaka Bop has given U.S. fans access to Os Mutantes, Tom Zé, and other important global artists. Bonnie Raitt covered "Burning Down the House" on a live album once, and the world will never know why. Sans Byrne, the band regrouped in 1996 as "The Heads" to make *No Talking, Just Head* with a lineup of guest vocalists that resembled a halfway house for '80s refugees (Michael Hutchence! Maria McKee! Gordon Gano!). You couldn't blame them for trying, and they couldn't blame you for not buying. *Once in a Lifetime* is a box set flawed by banal liner notes, poor song selection, and unbelievably ugly design: all told, a package that sums up the band's cute side rather than the abrasive intelligence and acerbic wit that made them special. *Sand in the Vaseline* collects the band's hits into a bulky two-CD package. For such a concept-album band, this obviously isn't the way to get to know them. But there's no denying that radio shots such as "Once in a Lifetime," "Psycho Killer," and "Wild Wild Life" still burn down the house. —R.S.

T.A.T.U.

★★½ 200 KM/H in the Wrong Lane (Interscope, 2003)

As the quip put it, this pair of teenage girls arrived "from Russia with love"—complete with casual curses, shrieking climaxes, a chilly Russian rap, and a marketing gimmick that implied they were lesbians. None of these audience-baiting elements was quite enough to make up for the mousy vocals and predictable disco beats; and there's also just not quite enough on this disc to make an entire album: Of the 11 cuts, three are alternate versions, one a cover of the Smiths' "How Soon Is Now?" ("I am human and I need to be luft!"). —F.S.

James Taylor

★★★½ James Taylor (Apple, 1969)
★★★★★ Sweet Baby James (Warner Bros., 1970)
★★★½ Mud Slide Slim and the Blue Horizon (Warner Bros., 1971)
★★ One Man Dog (Warner Bros., 1972)
★★ Walking Man (Warner Bros., 1973)
★★★½ Gorilla (Warner Bros., 1975)
★★ In the Pocket (Warner Bros., 1976)
★★★★½ Greatest Hits (Warner Bros., 1976)
★★★½ JT (Columbia, 1977)
★★ Flag (Columbia, 1979)
★★★ Dad Loves His Work (Columbia, 1981)
★★ That's Why I'm Here (Columbia, 1985)
★★ Never Die Young (Columbia, 1988)
★★★½ New Moon Shine (Columbia, 1991)
★★★ James Taylor (Live) (Sony, 1992)
★★★ JT/Flag/Dad Loves His Work (Sony, 1995)
★ James Taylor & the Original Flying Machine (Gadfly, 1996)
★★★ Hourglass (Sony, 1997)
★★★★ Greatest Hits Vol. 2 (Sony, 2000)
★★★ New Moon Shine/Never Die Young/That's Why I'm Here (Sony, 2000)
★★★ October Road (Sony, 2002)
★★★★ The Best of James Taylor (Warner Bros., 2003)

James Taylor's 1969 debut was one of the first releases on the Beatles' Apple label. Though nearly capsized by heavy-handed orchestration, it was an eye-opening collection of songs whose highlights—"Knocking 'Round the Zoo," "Something in the Way She Moves" and "Carolina in My Mind" (the latter two rerecorded for the 1976 Greatest Hits)—point toward the path he'd pursue in the next decade. Sweet Baby James, Taylor's landmark second release, heralds the arrival of pop music's sensitive phase. "Fire and Rain" epitomizes the singer/songwriter stance: acoustic-based

autobiography, where the arresting musical sparseness casts Taylor's gentle melodies and warm, unassuming vocals in full relief. On "Steamroller Blues," he effectively mocks the straining pomposity of then-current white bluesmen—though Taylor became entrapped by his own laid-back image soon enough. (Following this breakthrough, early demo tapes surfaced of the Flying Machine, Taylor's Greenwich Village band with Danny Korchmar. These green versions of some of the Apple album songs are not worth your investment.)

It's easy to hear Taylor's reflective bent as self-satisfaction; he's never really pushed himself musically (in the way, for example, Joni Mitchell has). The fact that Taylor actually improved in the role of MOR crooner is the saving grace of his recording career. Mud Slide Slim cemented Taylor's superstar status. But the hit reading of Carole King's "You've Got a Friend" drops some strong hints about the inherent flaccidity of this mellow troubadour approach that the rest of the album doesn't heed (save for "Long Ago and Far Away," with Joni Mitchell's backing vocals). Taylor spent the next few years casting around for a broader-based sound; One Man Dog is so wispy it nearly evaporates, while Walking Man sums up the confusion of this period with its near-stationary title track. (The less said about James and Carly Simon's hit version of "Mockingbird," the better.) Gorilla is where Taylor regains his balance. "Mexico" introduces a welcome strain of humor, the title track is a natural children's song, and "You Make It Easy" positions Sweet Baby James as a posthippie torch singer. And despite the generic clunk of its track, Taylor handles the hit remake of "How Sweet It Is (to Be Loved By You)" with such breezy vocal ease that even Marvin Gaye expressed admiration. Apart from the sturdy "Shower the People," In the Pocket misses the mark. Greatest Hits marked a record-label move, but at a fortuitous juncture when such a summing-up would include nothing but gems.

As so often happens with first efforts for new labels, JT ranks right up there with his best. Taylor reaches back for another upbeat pop classic to tenderize, and nails down "Handyman" with his most insinuating vocal performance ever. A slight rock influence sparks the rest of JT, though the goofy blues-rap "Traffic Jam" and the relaxed pace of "Your Smiling Face" feel as familiar as faded denim. Flag turned out to be a verb rather than a noun, but Dad Loves His Work finds JT back on the beam. It was led by the gently incisive divorce song "Her Town Too," among his finest pieces of writing and his last hit single. Late-'80s albums That's Why I'm Here and Never Die Young offer little beyond pleasantry. Instead of fading into the sunset, though, Taylor reemerged in 1991 with *New Moon Shine,* his most focused and tuneful release in more than 10 years; the reflective "Copperline" and the frisky "(I've Got to) Stop Thinkin' 'Bout That" would stand out on *any* of his albums. In "Slap Leather" and "Native Son" he provides affecting and still-relevant takes on the human cost of the first Persian Gulf war.

Taylor has settled comfortably into his 1990s role as an elder statesman of song. *(Live)* ably commemorates the warmth of his relationship with his audiences, though ultimately it can't escape souvenir status. Both *Hourglass* and *October Road* are brimming with the acceptance and grace that Taylor's younger self—frequently referenced here lyrically and melodically—often had trouble locating. "I had to have my way/Which was bleak and gray," he admits in "Mean Old Man," a song about how much life can lie on the other side of these feelings. *Greatest Hits Vol. 2* may lack the chart firepower of its predecessor, but strongly rebuts the notion that there are no second acts in American creative life. The 20-song *Best of James Taylor* is the first career-spanning domestic collection, but in his quiet, easygoing way, James Taylor has amassed too great a legacy to be adequately represented by a single disc. —M.C./B.E.

Teenage Fanclub

★★★	A Catholic Education (Matador, 1990)
★★★★	Bandwagonesque (DGC, 1991)
★★½	Thirteen (DGC, 1993)
★★★★	Grand Prix (DGC, 1995)
★★★	Songs From Northern Britain (Columbia, 1997)
★★★½	Howdy! (2000; Thirsty Ear, 2002)
★★★★	Four Thousand Seven Hundred and Sixty Seconds: A Short Cut to Teenage Fanclub (Sony, 2003)

Ragged grunge and delicate pop songcraft met on these Glaswegians' breakthrough 1991 album, *Bandwagonesque,* making them seem, at the time, a sort of mild Scottish analogue to Nirvana. But the similarity turned out to be only riff-deep: Soon Teenage Fanclub dropped the noisy haze and concentrated on the simple clarity of Byrds-y, Big Star-y guitar pop. The group's three songwriters, Norman Blake, Gerard Love, and Raymond McGinley—three George Harrisons, not an agitator or egotist among them—never had much rage anyway and so, as it turns out, neither burned out nor faded away.

Filled with languid, fuzzy head-nodders with titles such as "Everything Flows" and "Eternal Light," *A Catholic Education* melded the sounds of Alex Chilton, Neil Young, and Thurston Moore. Much gen-

tler than anything happening in Seattle, the sound was also totally removed from the head-rush dance music infecting most of the rest of Britain at the time.

Bandwagonesque, produced by then-ubiquitous Don Fleming, sharpened the band's approach, replacing the sleepy aimlessness of *A Catholic Education* with crystalline sound and vastly improved songwriting skills. The result was some of the tastiest guitar pop of the decade, self-effacing enough to be called indie but still bursting with melody. "What You Do to Me" is the guitar-mad radio song that '80s British rock never produced; the same could be said for "December," "I Don't Know," and most of the rest of the album, each track a joyous, worthy tribute to the band's heroes, Chilton and Gene Clark.

Thirteen is a fairly dense experiment in prog pop that, despite some interesting spots, mostly sounds like a false start. But the band hit its stride again with *Grand Prix,* which is possibly even more gorgeous and exuberant than *Bandwagonesque.* Fuzz boxes gone, the guitars ring bright and clear, with ace harmonies by Blake, McGinley, and Love sailing effortlessly through the entire disc. The songwriting, too, has matured beyond the adolescent narcissism of previous albums, aiming for "something simple, unaffected," as Blake sings in "I'll Make It Clear," a love song that doubles as a statement of renewed musical purpose.

The band made another smart stylistic shift on the following two albums, taking the excitement of *Grand Prix* down a couple of notches to the level of intimate, domestic folk song. Following the Fannies' pattern of dud-then-gem, *Songs From Northern Britain* is sonically lovely if occasionally tedious; it's improved upon immensely by *Howdy!,* the band's prettiest and most emotionally direct statement. The guitars still chime, but organ, vibes, and other chamber-pop elements give it a warmer, more nuanced sound as the songs trace a calm quest for musical and emotional peace. *Four Thousand . . .* is an outstanding retrospective, with well-chosen tracks from every album and, sensibly, one new song each from Love, Blake, and McGinley. —B.S.

Television

★★★★★	Marquee Moon (1977; Elektra/Rhino, 2003)
★★★★	Adventure (1978; Elektra/Rhino, 2003)
★★★★	The Blow Up (ROIR, 1982)
★★★	Television (Elektra, 1991)
★★★★★	Live at the Old Waldorf (Rhino Handmade, 2003)

Television was one of the greatest rock & roll bands New York City ever coughed up, mystical guitar boys dressing up like punks and singing like poets while exploring the mind-expanding properties of the Fender Jazzmaster solo. Onstage at CBGB, Tom Verlaine and Richard Lloyd would sail away on ten-minute twin-guitar jams such as "Kingdom Come" and "Little Johnny Jewel." Their 1977 debut, *Marquee Moon*, remains one of the all-time classic guitar albums. But unfortunately, they broke up just as they were hitting their musical peak because the band members were reportedly high-strung freakazoids who hated one another.

Tom Verlaine's strangled voice takes some getting used to, but *Marquee Moon* shimmers with urban grime and psychedelic imagination. In the trebly twang of "See No Evil," "Guiding Light," and "Venus," you can hear how Television inspired bands from U2 and R.E.M. to Joy Division and Sonic Youth. In the epic title song, Verlaine probes the outer contours of six-string consciousness like a mix of William Blake, Sam Fuller, and the Shadows. *Adventure* is slighter, but it still has great songs such as the spastic rocker "Glory," the brooding "Carried Away," and the gorgeously sad "Days." "Marquee Moon" was a Top 30 single in the U.K., and *Adventure* cracked the Top 10, but that didn't help keep the band together. Television reunited briefly for a lightweight 1991 album, and have also gigged periodically in recent years, mostly at European festivals. The 2003 Rhino reissues of *Marquee Moon* and *Adventure* feature rare goodies, including the inferior studio "Little Johnny Jewel" and a great alternate version of "See No Evil" with additional guitars.

The weird part: Most of Television's best stuff has never been released. The band's live jams make the studio albums sound tame, but for the most part they're only available on rare bootlegs. *The Blow Up* is a collection picked by Verlaine from live 1978 New York shows, featuring attacks on Dylan's "Knockin' on Heaven's Door" and the 13th Floor Elevators' "Fire Engine." Even better (in terms of sound quality as well as playing), *Live at the Old Waldorf* finally got officially released in 2003, via Rhino's Handmade imprint. It's a legendary San Francisco show from the summer of 1978, when Television was topping itself every night. The 11-minute version of "Little Johnny Jewel" is an absolute peak of human/guitar telepathic interaction. As Television's legend keeps growing, more of their live work will get officially released—hopefully starting with the Portland show from July 3, 1978, featuring a definitive 17-minute "Marquee Moon" that gets religion. —R.S.

The Temptations

★★★★ Gettin' Ready (1966; Motown, 1991)
★★★★½ The Temptations Greatest Hits (1966; Motown, 1988)
★★½ Temptations Live! (Motown, 1967)
★★★★ Temptations Greatest Hits, Vol. 2 (1970; Motown, 1988)
★★★ Sky's the Limit (1971; Motown, 1990)
★★★★ All Directions (1972; Motown, 1989)
★★★ Masterpiece (1974; Motown, 1991)
★★★★★ Anthology 64–73 (1973; Motown, 1986)
★★ A Song for You (1974; Motown, 1986)
★ Give Love at Christmas (Gordy, 1980)
★★★½ Reunion (Gordy, 1982)
★★½ To Be Continued (Gordy, 1986)
★★★ Together Again (Gordy, 1987)
★★ Special (Motown, 1989)
★★★★ Hum Along and Dance: More of the Best (1963–1974) (Rhino, 1993)
★★★★ Emperors of Soul (Motown, 1994)
★★ For Lovers Only (Motown, 1995)
★★ Phoenix Rising (Motown, 1997)
★★★★ The Ultimate Collection (Motown, 1997)
★★★★ The Millennium Collection Vol. 1: '60s (Motown, 1999)
★★★ Ear-Resistible (Interscope, 2000)
★★★★ The Millennium Collection Vol. 2: '70s, '80s, '90s (Motown, 2000)
★★½ Awesome (Universal, 2001)
★★★★½ Get Ready (EMI, 2002)

In their early-'60s prime, the Temptations boasted a lineup of singers whose individual talents and skillful ensemble work has rarely been equalled in pop music. With three leads (gritty tenor David Ruffin, supple, high tenor Eddie Kendricks, assured baritone Paul Williams) and two backup vocalists (baritone Otis Williams, bass Melvin Franklin), the group became the Motown flagship, finding, primarily in the songs of Smokey Robinson, the blend of R&B assertiveness and pop melodies a formula for radio greatness. Smokey's "The Way You Do the Things You Do" and "My Girl" began a remarkable series of tight, perfectly arranged singles that only slowed down as the '60s waned. Produced by Norman Whitfield, "Ain't Too Proud to Beg," "(I Know) I'm Losing You," and "I Wish It Would Rain" were also among the standouts of a style whose fluid grace provided counterpoint to the tortured soul of Otis Redding and Stax-Atlantic soul, making Motown the essential vehicle for R&B crossover. The Temptations' impact was enormous, not only influencing native soulsters but also priming the emulation of the Stones, Beatles, and other British rhythm & blues fanatics; highly choreographed and ultra-precise, the Temps' stage show embodied the music's pristine efficiency—and yet, under the tuxedos, the singers worked up a righteous sweat.

At the end of the decade, the Temps (with new lead

singer Dennis Edwards) turned funkward. Influenced by both Sly Stone's rock-inflected jams and Marvin Gaye's explorations of concept material, their songs got longer, roomier, edgier. When the newer material worked—"I Can't Get Next to You," "Psychedelic Shack," "Papa Was a Rollin' Stone," "Ball of Confusion (That's What the World Is Today)"—the band achieved a new gritty realism that nearly compensated for their abandonment of their trademark violins-and-love-lyrics grace (and the departure, as well, of Eddie Kendricks). Often, however, they seemed to be overreaching; long gone was their early, remarkable concision.

As a whole, the Temptations' '70s and '80s work was haphazard. Sly, P-Funk, and, later, Prince had captured R&B's harder, more experimental edge—and the Temps, however occasionally impressive, seemed retrograde. Years of performing meant that the band could be counted on for extremely professional product, but their best moments came when they worked hardest at recapturing the sound of their earliest glory.

Of the many greatest hits sets, *Anthology* is the strongest, with nearly 50 cuts. *Emperors of Soul* is also terrific, but five CDs' worth of the group make it for fanatics only. —P.E.

10,000 Maniacs

★★★	Human Conflict Number Five (EP) (Christian Burial, 1982)
★★★	Secrets of the I Ching (Christian Burial, 1983)
★★★	The Wishing Chair (Elektra, 1985)
★★★★	In My Tribe (Elektra, 1987)
★★★	Blind Man's Zoo (Elektra, 1989)
★★★	Hope Chest (Elektra, 1990)
★★★	Our Time in Eden (Elektra, 1992)
★★★½	MTV Unplugged (Elektra, 1993)
★★½	Love Among the Ruins (Geffen, 1997)
★½	The Earth Pressed Flat (Bar/None, 1999)
★★★★	Campfire Songs (Elektra, 2004)

Sounding anything but maniacal, 10,000 Maniacs emerged from tiny Jamestown, NY, with an approach that was complex and distinctive—and, at first, not entirely focused. *Human Conflict Number Five*, the sextet's debut EP, offers an awkward mix of folk-tinged new wave ("Orange") and odd, reggae-flavored rock ("Planned Obsolescence") that emphasizes guitarist Robert Buck at the expense of singer Natalie Merchant. Fortunately, things improve considerably with *Secrets of the I Ching*, as the Maniacs rein in their excesses while honing their material. (Both *Human Conflict Number Five* and *Secrets of the I Ching* are combined on *Hope Chest*).

With *The Wishing Chair*, the group makes its move to the majors. Although the album repeats three songs from *Secrets of the I Ching*, the band's sound exudes a confident eclecticism that at its best recalls the Band. Still, that wasn't enough to give the group the mass audience it deserved, and so the Maniacs moved from folkie auteur Joe Boyd, who produced *The Wishing Chair*, to James Taylor/Linda Ronstadt producer Peter Asher, who handled *In My Tribe*. Although decried at the time as an obvious move for mass acceptance, the album's success didn't quite come as expected, as an ill-advised cover of Cat Stevens' "Peace Train" flopped, while idiosyncratic originals such as "What's the Matter Here" and "Like the Weather" found an audience. And no wonder, as the band's arrangements were leaner (as was its lineup, after the departure of guitarist John Lombardo) and its sound more melody-intense. But best of all was the writing, which made the most of Merchant's luscious melodies and subtle narrative cadences.

Blind Man's Zoo isn't quite as cheerful, but despite its issue-oriented focus, Merchant and her bandmates never turn the songs into a social-commentary bully pulpit. *Our Time in Eden* broadened the band's sound with horns and the like, but kept enough of the original flavor to ensure the success of "These Are Days." Much the same held true for the string-laden *MTV Unplugged*, which recapped various oldies while adding Patti Smith and Bruce Springsteen's "Because the Night" to their hit parade.

Merchant then left the band, and was replaced by Mary Ramsey, at which point no one cared. *Campfire Songs* compiles the best of the Merchant era, plus enough rarities to keep late-arriving fans from feeling bad about not being able to buy vinyl. —J.D.C.

Ten Years After

★★½	Undead (Deram 1968)
★★	Stonedhenge (Deram, 1969)
★★½	Ssssh (1969; BGO, 1997)
★★★	Cricklewood Green (1970; EMI-Capitol Special Markets, 2001)
★★½	Watt (Deram, 1970)
★★½	A Space in Time (1971; Chrysalis, 1987)
★★★	Essential Ten Years After (Chrysalis, 1991)
★★★	Live at the Fillmore East 1970 (EMI, 2001)

Charisma and blinding speed made guitarist-singer Alvin Lee a standout at Woodstock—especially in that tie-dyed context, the boogie fever and early rock & roll swagger of all 13 minutes of "I'm Going Home" were mightily refreshing. But while Lee and keyboardist Chick Churchill were better players than, say, Savoy

Brown, TYA now sounds like one more middling English blues band, lacking even the crude distinctiveness of Humble Pie.

Not a strong vocalist, Lee never developed an interesting style of nonsinging, either—and while the faster, grittier TYA is punchy, few of the ballads work, and the blues the band made is wearisome. "I'd Love to Change the World," TYA's big hit off *A Space in Time,* is melodic, but its lyrics creak with an odd mixture of grumpy conservatism and hippie defeat. *Cricklewood Green* stands as the band's most cohesive album—again, though, it's really only Lee's guitar that smokes. *Essential* is a decent greatest hits, and includes the entire epic of "I'm Going Home." *Live at the Fillmore East* is probably their most representative set, stage rather than studio work being their raison d'être. —P.E.

Tenacious D.

★★★½   Tenacious D. (Epic, 2001)

Jack Black and Kyle Gass were the twin visionaries behind Tenacious D.: two sloppy dudes strumming and wailing the hysterically funny '70s faux-metal ballads that had made them legendary for their L.A. club gigs. (Black went on to a big-time screen career in movies such as *School of Rock* and, um, *Shallow Hal.*) The D's long-awaited debut album is an angel-dustrial bong-water brew of Styx, Rush, and Triumph, with a dollop of Journey, a soupçon of Kansas, loads of Zep and Sabbath, a pinch of Black Oak Arkansas, maybe a dash of the Ozark Mountain Daredevils. Not since Bob and Doug McKenzie have two jokers nailed the clod-metal aesthetic so accurately: Nearly every lyric here comes straight from your high school's bathroom wall.

Tenacious D sounds like it was bashed out in one dazed and confused all-nighter, with musical help from famous pals such as Foo Fighters' Dave Grohl, Phish's Page McConnell, and producers the Dust Brothers. But what makes the D such noble warriors is their mastery of every '70s-rock cliché, from the Skynyrdesque groupie-chasing boogie "The Road" to the perfect Steve Howe–style guitar filigree in the middle of "Rock Your Socks." You also get the best song ever written about Ronnie James Dio ("Dio"), the best song ever written about kielbasa ("Kielbasa"), tormented battle-of-evermore prog narratives such as "Wonderboy" and "Tribute," and the for-lovers-only acoustic ballad "Fuck Her Gently," where Black adopts his most sensitive Steve Perry voice to charm the ladies with sweet nothings such as "I'm gonna hump you sweetly/I'm gonna ball you discreetly." —R.S.

They Might Be Giants

★★★½   They Might Be Giants (1986; Restless, 1997)
★★★★   Lincoln (1988; Restless, 1997)
★★★★   Flood (Elektra, 1990)
★★★   Miscellaneous T (1991; Restless, 1997)
★★½   Apollo 18 (Elektra, 1992)
★★★   John Henry (Elektra, 1995)
★★½   Factory Showroom (Elektra, 1996)
★★★   Then: The Earlier Years (Restless, 1997)
★★   Severe Tire Damage (Restless, 1998)
★★★★   Best of the Early Years (BMG Special Products, 1999)
★★★   Live (BMG Special Products, 1999)
★★★   Mink Car (Restless, 2001)
★★★   No! (Idlewild/Rounder, 2002)
★★★★★   Dial-a-Song: 20 Years of They Might Be Giants (Rhino, 2002)
★★★   The Spine (Idlewild/Rounder, 2004)

New-wave smart alecs who at times sound like jingle writers run amok, John Flansburgh and John Linnell—the guys who Might Be Giants—specialize in songs that are relentlessly catchy and hopelessly cheesy, full of giddy non sequiturs, cartoonish combinations of instruments, and hooks that leave listeners feeling like a freshly landed trout. Working with cheap drum machines and overdubs instead of a band, the tracks they deliver for *They Might Be Giants* are mostly novelty tunes and marginalia, but the best songs—"Don't Let's Start," "Put Your Hand Inside the Puppet Head," "(She Was a) Hotel Detective"—are insanely tuneful, avoiding any pretense to deeper meaning (or even surface content) in their headlong pursuit of melody. *Lincoln* maintains that standard even as it unleashes puns of cosmic awfulness.

Flood, however, finds the Giants taking a few tentative steps toward pop convention, with arrangements that flirt with commercial competence, and even a couple of songs that dare to have a message. As always, though, what drives the album is the duo's melodic impetuosity, whether manifested in pop-rock moves such as "Birdhouse in Your Soul" or genre spoofs such as "Istanbul (Not Constantinople)." There's even more ambition evident in the sound of *Apollo 18,* which finds the Giants fleshing out their sound with guest musicians. There's even a cantata of sorts on "Fingertips," which is impressive but not much fun—a fatal flaw for a band so dependent on whimsy. *John Henry* steps back toward the short and silly, and shines brightest on the concept joke "Subliminal" and the giddy "Dirtbike," but *Factory Showroom* is undone by an unfortunate fondness for overly clever fare such as "XTC Vs. Adam Ant."

By this point in their career, the Giants had put together a mighty impressive band for concert performances, which gets shown off on *Severe Tire Damage.* Slightly self-indulgent but often wickedly entertaining, it boasts the least tedious drum solo—actually, more like a round of "stump the drummer"—ever. A cutdown version may be found on *Live.* TMBG had also been doing a fair amount of TV theme work, most notably contributing the theme to *Malcolm in the Middle,* which turns up on the *Malcolm* soundtrack; the group also performed the theme (written by Bob Mould) for Comedy Central's *The Daily Show.* They also dabble in kiddie pop on the relentlessly winsome *No,* a children's album secretly intended for grown-ups.

With *Mink Car* the group takes chances stylistically, flirting with electro beats on "Man, It's So Loud In Here" and working with Soul Coughing rapper Mike Doughty on "Mr. Xcitement," but otherwise it's the same old, same old. That sense of predictable unpredictability also permeates *The Spine,* though there's enough zip to "Prevenge" to make the rest forgivable.

They Might Be Giants have, over the years, been heavily anthologized. *Then* compiles the first two albums along with a fistful of bonus tracks and B sides, a number of which also appear on the aptly titled *Miscellaneous T.* At just 10 tunes, *Best of the Early Years* is certainly short, but quite sweet, thanks to the nonstop hooks. Still, you're better off spending a little more and getting the heaping pile of melodies that is *Dial-a-Song,* a far more inclusive document of the duo's quirky charm and inexhaustible melodic gifts. —J.D.C.

Thin Lizzy

★★ Thin Lizzy (1971; PolyGram, 1990)
★★½ Night Life (1974; PolyGram, 1990)
★★½ Fighting (1975; PolyGram, 1990)
★★★½ Johnny the Fox (1976; PolyGram, 1990)
★★★★ Jailbreak (1976, Mercury; PolyGram, 1990)
★★½ Bad Reputation (1977; PolyGram, 1990)
★★★½ Live and Dangerous (1978; Warner Bros., 1990)
★★★½ Black Rose: A Rock Legend (1979; Wounded Bird, 2001)
★★★ Chinatown (1980; Wounded Bird, 2001)
★ Renegade (1981; Wounded Bird, 2002)
★★½ Thunder and Lightning (1983; Wounded Bird, 2002)
★★★★½ Dedication: The Very Best of Thin Lizzy (PolyGram, 1991)
★★ Life Live (1993; Wounded Bird 2001)
★★★ Remembering, Part 1 (1998; Rebound, 2003)
★½ One Night Only (CMC, 2000)
★ Extended Versions (BMG Special Projects, 2002)

The melancholy tear in Phil Lynott's rich voice sets Thin Lizzy far apart from the braying mid-'70s metal pack. Projecting a dissolute sensitivity above dueling lead guitars, this black-Irish bass player chiseled out a distinct, lyrical hard-rock niche for his band. Thin Lizzy's only hit album, *Jailbreak,* is also its only consistent one. "The Boys Are Back in Town," a lingering hit single in 1976, set the tone: celebratory riffs cut by bittersweet reflection. Though Lynott gets caught up in macho adventures like *Jailbreak*'s definitive "Cowboy Song," the band's spacious arrangements and propulsive rhythms usually carry him forward. Thin Lizzy's discipline and drive are in evidence on *Live and Dangerous,* though filler sinks most of the Mercury albums (as well as the other, out-of-print Warner Bros. albums). Perhaps Thin Lizzy was overtaxed by clockwork recording schedules; the seamless best-of compilation *Dedication* successfully taps each stage of the band's bumpy decade-plus career, serving Thin Lizzy's memory well. Those seeking full immersion have no choice but to shell out for the import box set *Vagabonds Kings Warriors Angels.* Lynott succumbed to a drug overdose in 1986; by all means avoid *One Night Only* and *Extended Versions,* which feature entirely new lineups of the band. —M.C./B.SC.

3rd Bass

★★★★½ The Cactus Album (Def Jam, 1989)
★★★ Cactus Revisited (Def Jam, 1990)
★★★★ Derelicts of Dialect (Def Jam, 1991)

The two white MCs of 3rd Bass made much of the fact that they deserved the respect that they had won from the hip-hop community. MC Serch (Queens native Michael Berring) was a chubby four-eyes with a bottomless supply of lyrical put-downs; rockabilly-coiffed partner Pete Nice (Brooklyn-born Pete Nash, an English major at Columbia University) maintained a slightly slicker microphone mien. Backed by DJ Richie Rich (the Jamaican-born Richard Lawson), Serch and Pete Nice were meticulous, dues-paying hip-hop scholars whose debut *The Cactus Album* became an instant classic. On "Gas Face," they effectively used witty disses to stake out their territory; "Triple Stage Darkness" was just one of the album's amped-up anthems. *Cactus Revisited,* an early example of hip-hop's now-ubiquitous remix album (note to P. Diddy: you didn't invent it) was inessential then, and still is.

Proper second album *Derelicts of Dialect* was just as solid and even more expansive, as the group, like Serch said, got "cool to the cut/shaking butts off of ledges/came a longer way than Benson & Hedges." Serch plainly relished detailing his hip-hop credentials on "Portrait of the Artist as a Hood," just one *Derelicts* track that benefited from production by Sam Sever, whose funky, buoyant beats had the propulsion of Public Enemy's Bomb Squad but with warmer corners. (Side note: Sever and Bosco Money's duo Downtown Science put out a fantastic, nearly forgotten self-titled album in '91, also on Def Jam.) *Derelicts'* hit single "Pop Goes the Weasel" looped Peter Gabriel's smash "Sledgehammer" and had a memorable video in which 3rd Bass pummeled the crap out of a Vanilla Ice stand-in (a trick that the similarly skin-tone-sensitive Eminem used in concert against Everlast a decade later). But while 3rd Bass got busy dissing Vanilla Ice, the footloose Serch was leveled on wax by Beastie Boy MCA with the infamous couplet "you're wack, son/dancing around like you think you're Janet Jackson."

3rd Bass disbanded in 1992, but postsplit releases such as MC Serch's *Return of the Product* (with its smoking single "Back to the Grill Again") and Prime Minister Pete Nice & DJ Daddy Rich's 1993 *Dust to Dust* suggested separation did not mean death. All parties soon faded from the frontlines, however. Serch became an A&R man at Wild Pitch (his most famous discovery was Nas) while Pete Nice opened up a baseball memorabilia store in Cooperstown, New York. —P.R.

Third Eye Blind

★★★	Third Eye Blind (Elektra, 1997)
★★½	Blue (Elektra, 1999)
★★½	Out of the Vein (Elektra, 2004)

San Francisco–based Third Eye Blind is responsible for one of the few truly undeniable rock singles of the late '90s, the sardonic "Semi-Charmed Life." Released in the summer of 1997, the song balances blaring power chords against a mindlessly catchy wordless vocal refrain, and hit the top of the Modern Rock radio charts as well as #11 on the Billboard 100 singles chart. The band parlayed its "Semi-Charmed" success into several other singles—the punkish "Graduate" and the more sedate, melodic "How It's Gonna Be." Third Eye Blind returned in 1999 with the competent, less-inspired *Blue,* an album that is notable for its attempts at re-creating the giddy earlier magic. "An Ode to Maybe" appropriates the "Semi-Charmed" vocal hook, while other tracks reveal Stephan Jenkins' affinity for borrowing melodies and chord sequences from new-wave hits. Only one song from the second album, "I'll Never Let You Go," had a (brief) life on the charts. Guitarist/songwriter Kevin Cadogan departs before *Out of the Vein,* leaving Jenkins as the driving musical force. He guides Third Eye Blind into utterly ordinary modern-rock-anthem territory, and though several songs have the fervent air of earlier works

("My Hit and Run," "Blinded"), they lack the undeniably alluring, incandescent hooks of the band's previous work. —T.M.

Carla Thomas

★★★	Gee Whiz (Atlantic, 1966)
★★★	Memphis Queen (Stax, 1969)
★★★	Hidden Gems (Stax, 1992)
★★★	Gee Whiz: The Best of Carla Thomas (Rhino, 1994)
★★½	Sugar (Stax, 1994)
★★★½	Love Means Carla Thomas/Memphis Queen (Stax, 1997)
★★★	Gee Whiz and Other Hits (Rhino, 1997)

with Rufus Thomas

★★★½	Chronicle: Their Greatest Stax Hits (Stax, 1979)

Daughter and labelmate of Stax novelty hitmaker Rufus Thomas, Carla Thomas delivered the first hit for the legendary Memphis record company in "Gee Whiz" (1960), a song she'd written when she was 16. A sweet, doo-wop love song, the ballad was distinguished only by Carla's precociously adept singing— a warm delivery that would strengthen to power as Thomas and Stax Records matured. Thomas enjoys a deserved cult following among R&B insiders, but despite a star turn with Otis Redding on "Tramp" (1967) she never achieved a lasting success. The Rhino collection is terrific—from her 1966 trademark hit "B-A-B-Y" to even funkier funk. *Hidden Gems* proves that even her Stax outtakes could rival a lesser singer's chart-toppers. *Love Means Carla Thomas/Memphis Queen* presents two of her classic mid-career albums: vintage soul. —P.E.

Irma Thomas

★★★	Soul Queen of New Orleans (Maison de Soul, 1978)
★★★½	The Best of Irma Thomas: Breakaway (EMI America, 1986)
★★★★	The New Rules (Rounder, 1986)
★★★★	The Way I Feel (Rounder, 1988)
★★★	Something Good: The Muscle Shoals Sessions (Chess, 1990)
★★★★½	"Live: Simply the Best" (Rounder, 1991)
★★★	True Believer (Rounder, 1992)
★★★★	Time Is on My Side: The Best of Irma Thomas (EMI-America, 1992)
★★★	Walk Around Heaven: New Orleans Gospel Soul (Rounder, 1993)
★★★½	Sweet Soul Queen of New Orleans: The Irma Thomas Collection (Razor & Tie, 1996)
★★★	The Story of My Life (Rounder, 1997)

★★★ My Heart's in Memphis: The Songs of Dan Penn (Rounder, 2000)

★★★ If You Want It, Come and Get It (Rounder, 2001)

Summing up 30 years in soul music, Irma Thomas' *Simply the Best* is one of the great live R&B recordings. A scorching "Time Is on My Side" makes even prime Jagger sound feeble; an Otis medley honors the master; Crescent City classics such as "Iko Iko" never were zestier; and Allen Toussaint's "It's Raining" is balladry of a heart-stopping order.

Debuting in 1958 with the swaggering "You Can Have My Husband (but Please Don't Mess With My Man)," this powerhouse from Ponchatoula, Louisiana, went nationwide Top 20 in 1964 with "Wish Someone Would Care." The consistent big time eluded her, however, and Thomas retreated to the congenial intimacies of New Orleans night clubs. There, she reigns. *The Way I Feel* and *The New Rules* are prime Thomas, as is *My Heart's in Memphis* (classic and new songs by Dan Penn, perhaps the preeminent Southern soul songwriter). She's also an epic gospel singer: Witness *Walk Around Heaven*. *Simply the Best* and *Time Is On My Side* are the essential recordings, nearly in a class with vintage Aretha. —P.E.

Rufus Thomas

★★★ Walking the Dog (Stax, 1964; Sundazed, 2003)

★★★ That Woman Is Poison! (Alligator, 1988)

★★ Can't Get Away from This Dog (Stax, 1992)

★★★ Rufus Thomas Live! (Stax, 1995)

★★★ Did You Heard Me?/Crown Prince of Dance (Stax, 1995)

★★★½ The Best of Rufus Thomas: Do the Funky Something (Rhino, 1996)

★★ Funky Chicken (Stax, 1997)

★★ Swing Out With Rufus (High Stacks, 1999)

★★★ Funkiest Man Alive: The Stax Funk Sessions 1967–1975 (Stax, 2003)

Clown prince of rhythm & blues, Rufus Thomas was already a legend in Memphis when the fledgling Stax label recorded him in 1960; he'd had a 1953 Sun Records hit with "Bear Cat" (a song spun off Big Mama Thornton's "Hound Dog") and, as a sly, jive-talking DJ, he'd gained a massive local following. For Stax, he put the humor to music: "Walking the Dog" (1963) became his signature tune; the single is party music with a slightly ribald twist. In the early '70s, the gruff-voiced Thomas scored with "Do the Funky Chicken" and the mildly naughty "(Do the) Push and

Pull, Part 1," two prime examples of his novelty funk. The Rhino collection presents all the essential Thomas, and it's still a truly funky giggle. *That Woman Is Poison!* features the elder, but certainly no more mature, Rufus, and the 1995 live release kicks. —P.E.

Richard Thompson

★★★ Starring as Henry the Human Fly! (1972; Hannibal/Rykodisc, 1991)

★★★ (Guitar, Vocal) (1976; Hannibal/Rykodisc, 1991)

★★★½ Strict Tempo! (Hannibal, 1981)

★★★★ Hand of Kindness (1983; Hannibal/Rykodisc, 1991)

★★★½ Small Town Romance (Hannibal, 1984)

★★★½ Across a Crowded Room (Polydor, 1985)

★★★★ Daring Adventures (1986; Beat Goes On, 2001)

★★★½ Amnesia (Capitol, 1988)

★★★★ Rumor and Sigh (Capitol, 1991)

★★★★½ Watching the Dark: The History of Richard Thompson (Hannibal, 1993)

★★★½ Mirror Blue (Capitol, 1994)

★★★ You? Me? Us? (Capitol, 1996)

★★★½ Mock Tudor (Capitol, 1999)

★★★★ Action Packed: Best of the Capitol Years, (Capitol, 2001)

★★★★ The Old Kit Bag (Spin Art, 2003)

★★★½ 1000 Years of Popular Music (Beeswing, 2003)

with Danny Thompson

★★★½ Industry (Hannibal, 1997)

Although Richard Thompson released his first solo album in 1972, his solo career really doesn't properly begin until 1983 with *Hand of Kindness*. In large part that's because after recording *Henry the Human Fly!*, Thompson married singer Linda Peters (who sings backup on that first album), and the two began touring and recording as Richard and Linda Thompson; as such, Thompson had no real need for a solo career until the marriage failed and the duo fell apart.

Besides, *Henry the Human Fly* sounds less like a genuine solo effort than an ersatz Fairport Convention album. Granted, it comes by the resemblance honestly, since Thompson (himself a Fairport alum) is backed by several ex-Conventioneers, including singers Sandy Denny and Ashley Hutchings. Moreover, the material is in the same vein as Fairport's fusion of rock and Celtic folk, from the mournful drone of "Wheely Down" to the self-explanatory "Roll Over Vaughn Williams." *Strict Tempo!*, although recorded without Linda or anyone else except drummer Dave Mattacks (and even then only on a few tracks), is also not typical of his subsequent albums, consisting entirely of instrumental treatments of traditional-style tunes. And despite the fact that *(Guitar, Vocal)* is listed under his name, its contents actually consist of Fairport Convention B sides augmented by Richard and Linda outtakes, making it interesting, but hardly essential.

Then, in 1983, *Hand of Kindness* picks up where Richard and Linda's *Shoot Out the Lights* left off. Although it's probably a mistake to read these broken-love songs as commentary on the demise of the Thompsons' marriage, it's hard not to notice the vitriol in tunes like "Tear Stained Letter" or "A Poisoned Heart and a Twisted Memory." But nastiness becomes Thompson, and the angrier his lyrics get, the stronger the performances seem to be, adding a gleeful edge to the Celtic-style melodies. *Small Town Romance* has a completely different feel, but then, it was recorded under dissimilar circumstances. Unlike the full-band *Hand of Kindness*, this album features Thompson in an acoustic setting (it was recorded live in New York) and alternates between witty folk-style songs like "Woman or a Man?" and solo versions of Richard and Linda tunes.

Thompson is back with his band for *Across a Crowded Room*, which finds him returning to the subject of romantic recrimination ("She Twists the Knife Again," "When the Spell Is Broken"), but this time with a greater sense of wit (the biting "You Don't Say") and poetry ("Love in a Faithless Country"). He hits his stride with *Daring Adventures*, thanks to songs as tuneful and assured as "How Will I Ever Be Simple Again" or the wickedly biting "A Bone Through Her Nose." His work up to this point is handily summarized in the superb three-CD set, *Watching the Dark*.

Thompson, now signed to Capitol Records, widens his scope with *Amnesia*, but as ambitious as the lyrics often are, the music is maddeningly uneven. *Rumor and Sigh* more than compensates, however, as Thompson excels both in character songs, like the wickedly funny "Read About Love" and the frighteningly intense "I Feel So Good," and wonderfully evocative sketches like "1952 Vincent Black Lightning" and "Mystery Wind." *Mirror Blue* continues in that vein, adding a bit of new-wave edge to Thompson's sound and continuing pursuit of vehicular nostalgia with "MGB-GT." But the album's best moments are more understated, as with the lovely "Beeswing." By this point, Thompson had emerged sufficiently from cult status that even MTV paid mild attention, and the subsequent double album, *You? Me? Us?*, even picked up a Grammy nomination. A pity the album wasn't more deserving. Despite some lovely acoustic work on the second disc, the songs (apart from the spirited "Razor Dance") don't really stand up to repeated listening. *Mock Tudor* takes him back to roots—quite literally, as the album is an evocation of the English suburbia of his youth, while the arrangements offer folk-rock directness in place of the studio gloss found on his three previous albums. Hard-core Thompsonites loved it, especially "The Sights and Sounds of London Town" and the spirited "Cooksferry Queen." (The album also featured performances by Thompson's son, Teddy, on guitar and voice.) But sales, which had been sliding, slipped below expectations, and Capitol cut him loose, marking his departure with *Action Packed*—a best-of that makes his Capitol stint seem better than it was.

Thompson had no doubt been feeling the itch for some time, however; two years before *Mock Tudor,* he cut *Industry* with bassist Danny Thompson (no relation), a pleasant if inconsequential foray into light jazz. Perhaps chastened by his tenure with the majors, he started his own label, Beeswing (available online at www.richardthompson-music.com), and released a number of titles, ranging from the live *Semi-Detached Mock Tudor* and *ducknapped* to the well-researched and surprisingly accessible *1,000 Years of Popular Music,* which ably covered the whole millennium, from madrigals to Britney Spears (and concluded by combining them, rendering "Oops! I Did It Again!" as "Marry, Ageyn Hic Hev Donne Yt"). *The Old Kit Bag,* a raw and rocking quartet session, was picked up for U.S. distribution by Spin Art; with Thompson relying mostly on his acerbic guitar and bassist Danny Thompson's swinging counterpoint, selections such as "Gethsemane," "Pearly Jim," and "A Love You Can't Survive" rank with his best work to date. —J.D.C.

Richard and Linda Thompson

★★★★½   I Want to See the Bright Lights Tonight (1974; Hannibal/Rykodisc, 1991)
★★★★   Hokey Pokey (1974; Hannibal/Rykodisc, 1991)
★★★★   Pour Down Like Silver (1975; Hannibal/Rykodisc, 1991)
★★★½   First Light (Chrysalis, 1978)
★★★   Sunnyvista (Chrysalis, 1979)
★★★★★   Shoot Out the Lights (1982; Hannibal/Rykodisc, 1991)
★★★½   The Best of Richard & Linda Thompson (Uni/Island, 2000)

Fairport Convention may have originally popularized the idea of marrying rock & roll to Celtic folk styles, but it was Richard and Linda Thompson who perfected the approach. Richard's is the first voice heard on *I Want to See the Bright Lights Tonight*—which was originally released in the U.S. as half of the now-deleted *Live (More or Less*)—but Linda's is by far the most resonant, and that's not simply because she delivers the album's best songs. His singing tends to build off the mood of the music itself (as in "The Calvary Cross"), while hers sets the tone on its own, filling the plain melodic lines of "The Great Valerio" with revealing layers of nuance or fleshing out the wry wit of "The Little Beggar Girl." Add in some slashing guitar fills like those Richard adds to the title tune, and the Thompsons are already beating Fairport at its own game.

With *Hokey Pokey,* they refine their sound further, thanks to knowingly revisionist trad-style tunes such as "Smiffy's Glass Eye" and the ice-cream-mania number, "Hokey Pokey." But *Pour Down Like Silver,* recorded after their conversion to Sufism, replaces its predecessors' whimsy with a somber solemnity that shines brilliantly through songs such as "For Shame of Doing Wrong" and the wonderfully elegiac "Night Comes In" (which also boasts some of Richard's most memorable guitar playing). *First Light* doesn't change the duo's mood much, but it does increase the music's energy, particularly on the rollicking "Layla" (not the Eric Clapton tune). Mood, though, doesn't really seem to be the answer. After all, *Sunnyvista* is almost oppressively cheerful, but that doesn't make its music any better. Indeed, the duo's approach on that album seems at times almost a parody of pop ambition, as songs such as "Why Do You Turn Your Back?" and "Lonely Hearts" are given arrangements that leave them seeming absurdly overdressed.

Shoot Out the Lights, on the other hand, is absolutely perfect. Between the vividly emotional writing and the stirringly impassioned playing, the album would be a winner even if neither Thompson sang a note. But sing they do, from the gentle resignation of "Walking on a Wire" to the gleeful snarl of "Back Street Slide," to the electric energy of "Shoot Out the Lights." Unfortunately, part of the album's emotional power came from the fact it was the duo's swan song; after a final, tumultuous tour, the Thompsons divorced, personally and professionally.

Sadly, *The Best of Richard & Linda Thompson* isn't. Because it draws only from material released through Island Records in the '70s, it includes nothing from *First Light, Sunnyvista,* or *Shoot Out the Lights* while adding three selections from Richard's solo albums, two of which don't involve Linda at all. —J.D.C.

3 Doors Down

   ★★★   The Better Life (Uptown-Universal, 2000).
   ★★★   Away from the Sun (Best Buy Co., 2002)

Able to leap tall radio charts with a single song, these coastal Mississippians unleashed crunch-stomper "Kryptonite" to much success, making good on the same heavy-lite formula that made Bush and Stone Temple Pilots the head-bangingest girlfriend-rock on the radio. The band kept fans happy with energetic live shows until the 2002 followup *Away From the Sun* birthed the lesser hit "When I'm Gone" —L.S.

311

   ★½   Music (Capricorn, 1993)
   ★★   Grassroots (Capricorn, 1994)
   ★★½   311 (Capricorn, 1995)
   ★★   Transistor (Capricorn, 1997)
   ★½   Live! (Capricorn, 1998)
   ★½   Soundsystem (Capricorn, 1999)
   ★★   From Chaos (Volcano, 2001)
   ★★   Evolver (Volcano, 2003)
   ★★★   Greatest Hits '93–'03 (Volcano, 2004)

You never can tell. Perhaps if posterity deems Limp Bizkit the Led Zep of the '90s, these wooly Nebraskans will be recognized as pioneers of a rap-rock fusion others would later cash in on more dramatically. Most likely, 311 will be remembered for the cheeseball skank of "Down," the one-hit testament of these well-intentioned Chili Peppers fans, who sound like they never got around to checking out Parliament-Funkadelic.

311 are indefatigably professional purveyors of perhaps rock's most undying genre—music you can dance to without spilling your beer. S.A. Martinez's lyrics are so to the point they verge on unnecessary. When 311 cooks up a rock-out number they title it "In Your Face," and their messages of "positivity" would get less-buff persons smacked upside the head in study hall. Meanwhile, Tim Mahoney makes a variety of fun noises with his guitar, the aural equivalent of a way-cool laser light show.

Distinguishing among 311's strikingly similar releases is more work than such a laid-back band deserves. Always obliging, the band put the hits ("Down," "All Mixed Up") on the disc with the easiest title to remember—*311. Live!* is what it says, though that exclamation point is overstating the case. *From Chaos* keeps on keeping on, ending with a track entitled "I'll Be Here Awhile"—no empty boast from a band that, despite the fact that it's commercial peak is more than half a decade gone, seems no more likely to fade from existence than spring break itself. —K.H.

Three 6 Mafia

   ★★★½   Mystic Stylez (SOH, 1995)
   ★½   Da End (Prophet, 1996)
   ★★½   Chapter 2: World Domination (Relativity, 1997)

   ★★★   When the Smoke Clears (Relativity, 2000)
   ★½   Choices (Relativity, 2001)
   ★★   Da Unbreakables (Columbia, 2003)

Not all Southern rappers crave booty-bass beats like a crackhead needs a hit. Although the cheesy Photoshop-generated cover art might fool you, Three 6 Mafia—a Memphis, TN–based collective of six sick rappers—is not another generic crew of Southern rappers signed in the post–Master P prospecting bonanza. MCs Lord Infamous, Koopsta Knicca, Crunchy Black, and Gangsta Boo (who are joined by producers Juicy J and DJ Paul) lay down their blood-drenched rhymes atop slow, sinister soundscapes that are about as far removed as you can get from the New Orleans bounce of Juvenile and his Cash Money cohorts. The first album suffers from poor, muddy production, which turns out to be an advantage rather than a liability. The lo-fi sound only intensifies the creepiness of their murder rhymes, giving the Southern synthetic production aesthetic a deeply surreal quality that defies easy categorization. You might call it Southern hip-hop folk art (though don't call it that to the Mafia's face or you might be on the receiving end of a serious beatdown). Once they could afford a good studio, unfortunately, the quality of their music went down, though they did recover with the glossy and flossy (but still dark and disturbing) *When the Smoke Clears*. —K.M.

Throbbing Gristle

   ★★   2nd Annual Report (Mute, 1977)
   ★★★   D.o.A.: The Third and Final Report of Throbbing Gristle (Mute, 1978)
   ★★★   20 Jazz Funk Hits (Mute, 1979)
   ★★★   Heathen Earth (Mute, 1980)
   ★★★½   Greatest Hits: Entertainment Through Pain (Mute, 1990)

In 2003, after a rock critic announced he would listen to live Throbbing Gristle CDs for a continuous 24-hour period, band member Chris Carter warned, "I hope your ears don't bleed." He wasn't kidding. Twenty-seven years after a member of British Parliament referred to them as "wreckers of civilization," this English quartet remains best known as inventors of industrial music. For half a decade they churned out made-to-shock music and married it with abrasive skull-crushing noise. Today, their records play like Monty Python skits without the jokes.

Starting in 1976, Carter, Peter "Sleazy" Christopherson, Genesis P-Orridge, and Cosey Fanni Tutti challenged listeners with Burroughs-esque "cut-ups," and twisted lyrics on subjects like mutilation, murder,

sex, and Nazism. Their first full-length, *2nd Annual Report,* is a chaotic debut that snidely embraces redundancy by including three versions of "Slug Bait," four cuts of "Maggot Brain," and a disturbing tune called "Zyclon B Zombie" about an insecticide used for murder at Auschwitz. There is a lot of noise here, and it doesn't always seem choreographed. TG's second record, *D.o.A.: The Third and Final Report,* is a modicum more accessible. The most intense track, "Hamburger Lady," is also one of the band's most intriguing. "There's no end in site," murmurs P-Orridge under a Doppler synth-and-sample collage that drones as he tells the story of a suffering burn victim. None of this is dinner-party music, but this CD is worth spinning once or twice for friends, not least for the one legitimate electro-dance track, "AB/7A." The reissue also includes two tracks from an early EP: "Five Knuckle Shuffle" (a treatise on masturbation) and "We Hate You (Little Girls)." *20 Jazz Funk Hits* is neither jazz nor funk, but there are complete tunes here that are less chaotic than on the band's previous albums. For the uninitiated listener who hates compilations, this is a decent place to start. "Still Waiting" plays like a blueprint for '90s techno-texture outfits like Autechre. "Exotica" is a lovely ambient piece, and "Hot on the Heels of Love" could easily have Xed-up ravers humping on the dance floor. TG's final album, *Heathen Earth,* continues the band's momentum, and would be worth the purchase if the album's best track, "Adrenalin," wasn't already included on *Greatest Hits: Entertainment Through Pain*. In fact, for listeners who are only mildly interested, TG's *Greatest Hits* is probably the best deal of all since it really does include (surprise!) the best stuff from TG's albums. Although the foursome split in 1981, they dipped into the archives and went on to release dozens of live records. After a reunion in 2004, they announced that their last ever show would go down in April, 2005. —D.MA.

Johnny Thunders

   ★★★★   So Alone (1978; Warner Bros., 1992)
   ★★★   New Too Much Junkie Business (1983; ROIR, 1999)
   ★★★   Stations of the Cross (ROIR, 1987)
   ★★   Belfast Nights (Triple X, 2000)
   ★★★   In the Flesh (Triple X, 2000)
   ★★   Endless Party (Amsterdamned, 2000)
   ★★★★   You Can't Put Your Arms Around a Memory (Sanctuary/Castle, 2002)
   ★½   Anthology (Anarchy, 2004)

The Heartbreakers

   ★★★   Live at Max's Kansas City '79 (1979; ROIR, 1996)
   ★★★   What Goes Around (1991; Bomp, 1997)

In a perversely brilliant casting maneuver, filmmaker Lech Kowalski picked Johnny Thunders to play Jesus in a 1982 documentary on New York junkie life. In actuality, Thunders was a Jesus noir, a trashy Jean Genet saint, his hard-fated life a furious, unfocused rebellion. Never more than a cult figure, he died in 1991, ready made for myth—the last of the hell-bent rock & roll true believers. Even when Thunders started out in the '70s, that faith was anachronistic— in the New York Dolls, playing Keith Richards to David Johansen's Jagger, the guitarist was trapped between two forms of parody: glitter (which inflated basic rock & roll) and punk (which deflated it). Thunders was instrumental in making the waters semisafe for the Sex Pistols, the Dead Boys, and the like, but his own playing, however sloppy, contained no irony: He rocked straight out of Chuck Berry. The zeitgeist, though, demanded caricature—and Thunders soon became a pathetic one, a kamikaze sadder than Sid Vicious, because Thunders had real talent.

When the Dolls predictably imploded, he just as predictably continued—and his records have all the power of an apocalyptic party, a stumbling dance toward annihilation. *So Alone,* with help from ex-Pistols Paul Cook and Steve Jones, the underrated Only Ones, Steve Marriott, and Phil Lynott, remains his most cohesive set, and it's terrific, dangerous music. With the Heartbreakers (guitarist Walter Lure, ex-Doll Jerry Nolan on drums, ex-Television bassist Richard Hell) his work was shakier, but *D.T.K.* (with Billy Rath, who replaced Hell) features savage live versions of the band's anthems "Chinese Rocks" and "Born To(o) Lo(o)se," while *L.A.M.F.,* the Heartbreakers' ragged debut (which has seen several expanded reissues over the years) remains the definitive Thunders statement; like *D.T.K.,* it kicks with a desperate power. While these 1977 recordings are out of print domestically, the three-disc career retrospective *You Can't Put Your Arms Around a Memory* contains both *L.A.M.F.* and *D.T.K.,* along with most of two other unavailable LPs, *Live at the Speakeasy* and *Live and Wasted: Unplugged, 1990. Que Sera, Sera* (currently available only as an import) is surprisingly tidy Stones-ish rock, lacking only an imaginative drummer. *New Too Much Junkie Business,* despite the presence of veteran Stones producer Jimmy Miller, suffers from wretched sound; it's worth checking out, however, for Thunders elegy for Sid Vicious, "Sad Vacation." *Stations of the Cross,* music originally intended for the Kowalski documentary, isn't a bad intro to Thunders—the live release collects almost all his "greatest hits." Thunders met his inevitably sad end in 1991, setting off the equally inevitable flurry of archival releases on obscure indies (primarily in the U.K., where he enjoys a greater cache than stateside), the bulk of which will take some effort to track down, if you must. —P.E./B.SC.

'Til Tuesday

★★ Voices Carry (Epic, 1985)
★★½ Welcome Home (Epic, 1986)
★★★½ Everything's Different Now (Epic, 1988)
★★★ Coming Up Close: A Retrospective (Legacy, 1996)
★★★ All About Love (Columbia Special Products, 1998)

Before she became known as a solo artist, Aimee Mann was the bassist and singer for this punk-schooled Boston band, which produced her only Top 10 hit, the deliciously melancholy "Voices Carry." That Cars-like single is by far the strongest song on *Voices Carry,* but Mann and company more than make up for that inconsistency with *Welcome Home,* on which the achingly lovely "What About Love" (another Top 40 hit) is matched by such richly melodic material as "Lovers' Day" and the Simon and Garfunkel–ish "On Sunday."

So why is it that the group's best album, *Everything Is Different Now,* had the least commercial success? Maybe it's because the subject matter—the end of Mann's affair with songwriter Jules Shear—seemed too emotionally loaded for some listeners. Or perhaps the fact that these two mourn their lost love by writing songs for each other struck listeners as a trifle weird. But regardless of inspiration or circumstance, songs such as "Everything's Different Now," " 'J' for Jules," and "Crash and Burn" are too emotionally vibrant and melodically memorable to be denied, offering listeners a taste of Mann's musical future.

Coming Up Close is a by-the-numbers best-of, which offers most of the band's singles but underplays *Everything's Different Now;* as such, the more thematic (and less hit-packed) *All About Love* will likely prove more satisfying to Mann fans. —J.D.C.

Justin Timberlake

★★★★ Justified (Jive, 2002)

By the time ex–'N Sync heartthrob Timberlake went solo in 2002, the teen-pop movement had been heading toward the cliff of adulthood, with each adorable entertainer either falling or making it to the other side. Britney Spears completed the jump by a hair; LeAnn, we're glad you wore that parachute. But with *Justified,* Timberlake and producers the Neptunes (with Timbaland in a sidecar) straight-up vaulted over the canyon and Timberlake became the biggest male pop star in the world. The Neptunes' brilliant, impertinent, full-body funk is, for the most part, what stays with you from *Justified;* their songs, spacious and shot through with ecstatic ahhhs, outshine their neighbors on the album. In "Like I Love You," a nasty funk rhythm on loud, live drums shares the space with a tiny guitar strum and Timberlake's breathy, studied tenor; it's minimalism influenced by Michael Jackson. The album's lyrics, similarly, invoke scenes of the tenderest understanding here, of full-on booty calls there. By most other measures, Timbaland's contributions (especially "Cry Me a River") are on a high level; in this context, they're a bit dull and claustrophobic. —B.R.

Cal Tjader

★★★	Extremes (1951/1977; Fantasy, 2001)
★★★★	Tjader Plays Mambo (Fantasy, 1954)
★★★★	Los Ritmos Calientes (1954/1957; Fantasy, 1992)
★★★★	Monterey Concerts (Fantasy, 1959)
★★★★	Latino! (Fantasy, 1960)
★★★½	Several Shades of Jade (Verve, 1963)
★★★	Breeze from the East (Verve, 1963)
★★★★★	Soul Sauce (Verve, 1964)
★★★★★	Primo (Fantasy, 1970)
★★★★	Amazonas (Fantasy, 1975)
★★★	Grace Cathedral Concert (Fantasy, 1976)
★★★	La Onda Va Bien (Concord, 1979)
★★★★	Heat Wave (Concord, 1982)
★★★★½	Greatest Hits (Fantasy, 1995)
★★★	The Concord Jazz Heritage Series (Concord, 1998)
★★★	Cuban Fantasy (Fantasy, 2003)
★★★★	Best of the Concord Years (Concord, 2004)

with Eddie Palmieri

★★★★★	El Sonido Nuevo: The New Soul Sound (Verve, 1966)
★★★★	Bamboléate (Tico, 1967)

Latin music's most influential non-Latin bandleader, Cal Tjader had an uncanny ability to concoct genuine Afro-Cuban dance fever. Although he was not necessarily a virtuoso, Tjader played the vibes (and, occasionally, the *timbales*) with impeccable feeling and precision, and his bands created a sophisticated combination of cool jazz and simmering Afro beats. Tjader's output is distinguished by a certain emotional distance that sets it apart from more visceral efforts by, say, Machito or Tito Puente, but ultimately evokes an effortlessly elegant, strangely nostalgic feeling.

If you're into crisp arrangements and short, *sabroso* sessions, then Tjader's '50s stint with the Fantasy label is the place to start. Like many of the company's CD reissues, *Los Ritmos Calientes* compiles two separate LPs into an extended Latin jazz workout. Tjader was a generous leader, and on tracks such as "Mongorama" and "Cubano Chant" he steps aside and lets his percussionists shine. The same happens in *Monterey Concerts,* a particularly inspired live outing that includes a memorable rendition of Santamaría's sinuous "Afro-Blue."

During the '60s, Tjader switched to the Verve label and began to experiment. The unexpected commercial success of the *Soul Sauce* LP and the "Guachi Guaro" single must have cheered him up, as evidenced by his subsequent collaborations with pianist Eddie Palmieri on *El Sonido Nuevo* and *Bamboléate*—both of them required listening for Latin jazz aficionados.

Returning to Fantasy, Tjader continued stretching the boundaries of his own signature sound. *Primo* was the Hispanic community's ultimate declaration of love: Tito Puente himself contributed *timbales* on Mario Bauza's standard "Tanga" (slang for marijuana), Charlie Palmieri (Eddie's older brother) provided arrangements and exuberant keyboard playing, and *salsero* Ismael Quintana took care of the vocal choruses. Like every jazz player of his time, Tjader was also touched by the Brazilian wave of the '60s. *Amazonas* forsakes the bossa craze in favor of a more psychedelic sound, with collaborations by Brazil's enfants terribles Airto Moreira and Egberto Gismonti.

Tjader ended his career on a quiet note, recording a string of albums for the Concord label that saw him returning to the traditionalist approach of his youth. *La Onda Va Bien* is textbook Tjader, alternately crunchy and velvety, whereas *Heat Wave* ups the ante through Carmen McRae's vocal bravado. A staple of Tjader's latter-day band was young *conguero* Poncho Sánchez, who was by his side when the bandleader died while on tour in the Philippines, and since then has founded his own Latin jazz band, paying constant tribute to that enigmatic, reserved white man who played the mambo with the swing of a real *Cubano.* —E.L.

TLC

★★	Ooooooohhh . . . On the TLC Tip (LaFace, 1992)
★★★½	CrazySexyCool (LaFace, 1994)
★★★	Fan Mail (LaFace, 1999)
★★★	3D (LaFace, 2002)

Tionne "T-Boz" Watkins seduced, the late Lisa "Left-Eye" Lopes rapped, Rozonda "Chilli" Watkins sang, and they were all hip-hop tomboys whose up-front heterosexuality and sisterly camaraderie were as aggressive as their baggy layers and quirky accessories were schoolyard bright. Under the guiding hands of Atlanta superproducers L.A. Reid and Babyface, with song contributions by Marley Marl, Dallas Austin, and other leading lights of AM-radio dance-'n'-soul, TLC mixed girl-pride rap with sensuous R&B a la Salt-'n'-Pepa. But the trio's jumping-bean energy and childish look made for an intriguing disconnect with their bid for sexual responsibility as represented by the condoms pinned to their shorts. Which is all to say: It was a boffo marketing concept wagging the dog of tinny, unimpressive, up-with-peeps cheerleading. The trio's debut is stuffed with filler, a wearying 15 tracks that keep a frantically "positive" vibe humming like a mosquito. Only the ballad "Baby-Baby-Baby" finds a groove and nestles in.

A calmed-down, Chanel-wearing TLC grew up virtually overnight with *CrazySexyCool,* which vaulted the group's exceptional video of "Waterfall" into heavy rotation and showed off a newly mature sound, as well as the girls' newly impressive abs. The love songs are dull but acceptable, and the novelty moments—the silly "Case of the Fake People" and an ill-advised cover of Prince's "If I Was Your Girlfriend"—grasp the wrong end of the stick. But the group gets vulnerable on the deep-dish R&B of "Creep," and on "Waterfall" it takes the safe-sex warnings of its earlier incarnation to an operatic extreme. "Red Light Special" is as low-down carnal as anyone can get on pop radio, satin sheets and all.

After impressively dramatic intra-band troubles—notably the troubled Lisa Lopes' attempt to burn down her boyfriend's house, and threats to leave the group—the Atlanta trio find their instincts, for better or worse, intact. It can't keep away from the New Jack trope of structuring its albums around whispered "interludes" and faux phone calls, and its vulnerability, like its cheerful vigor, can be cloying. Once again, nothing on *Fan Mail* rises above autopilot hip-hop–R&B except the singles. The preachy "Unpretty" is fueled more by its stunning video than anything found in the music, but "No Scrubs" elegantly reconciles TLC's sisterly solidarity with its blunt sass, and the song started a sexual skirmish that kept 1999's radio airwaves hopping before Destiny's Child picked up the banner. Then in 2001, Lisa Lopes died in a car crash in Honduras. The other two members of TLC did honor to her memory with *3D,* which was only partially finished when Lopes passed away. "Damaged" is written from the perspective of a woman asking her new boyfriend for the patience to forgive insecurities bred by previous bad relationships, and draws on the hidden folk-rock element of "Waterfalls." It's the kind of heartfelt, vulnerable song that's rare in today's tough-as-platinum

girl-group world. TLC doesn't appear to be finished: at press time, the group was looking for a replacement for Lopes.   —A.B./B.W.

Tom Tom Club

★★★½   Tom Tom Club (1981; Warner Bros., 1990)
★★½   The Good, the Bad and the Funky (Rykodisc, 2000)

Tom Tom Club was originally a side project for the husband-and-wife team of Chris Frantz and Tina Weymouth, the Talking Heads' drummer and bass player, who made three albums while waiting around for David Byrne to reconvene the band and a fourth after he pulled the plug. The self-titled debut (and the only one of the early albums still available) sounds like a delightful accident: funky beats collide with dub reggae keyboards; rap ("Wordy Rappinghood") bumps into new wave ("Genius of Love") on the dance floor. Like a vacation trip on which everything clicks into place, this insouciant groove seems impossible to duplicate. "Pleasure of Love" is about as close as the followup comes. By the time of the forced, hollow-sounding *Boom Boom Chi Boom Boom* from 1989, Tom Tom Club couldn't help but reflect some of Frantz and Weymouth's frustration with the uncertain status of their old band. Ironically, Tom Tom Club's sense of wonder (and of humor) is exactly what's missing from much of Byrne's solo work. After an eight-year break, Franz and Weymouth cut an uneven fifth album immediately following a Talking Heads reunion minus Byrne (now there's a genius idea). Tom Tom Club's intermittent career winds up proving an old rock & roll adage: Breaking up is hard to do.   —M.C./B.SC.

Tone-Lōc

★★½   Lōc'd After Dark (Delicious Vinyl, 1988)
★★½   Cool Hand Lōc (Delicious Vinyl, 1991)

A two-hit wonder from a glorious era for hip-hop radio, L.A. rapper Tone-Lōc arrived in late 1988 with "Wild Thing," which reigned for a while as the best-selling single of all time. It was a low-down but friendly sex growl ("I tipped the chauffeur when it was over") with Dust Brothers production, a sample from Van Halen's "Jamie's Crying," lyrics written by Delicious Vinyl labelmate Young M.C., and Lōc's funny rasp. Arnold Schwarzenegger eventually saved his own career when he quoted Lōc's signature line, "Hasta la vista, baby," in *Terminator 2,* but Lōc did it better, yo. "Funky Cold Medina" was even funnier, driven by beats from Kiss's "Christine Sixteen" and Foreigner's "Hot Blooded," with the immortal plot twist "Sheena was a man!" But fans who bought the album *Lōc'd After Dark* felt ripped off when they found out that it included "Medina" only in an inferior alternate version, although "Cheeba Cheeba" was pretty good. *Cool Hand Lōc* was a better all-around album, but there were no hits. Tone-Lōc moved on to a surprisingly successful acting career; you can see him get roughed up by Al Pacino in *Heat,* which does strain the credibility a bit. —R.S.

Tony! Toni! Toné!

★★½ Who? (PolyGram, 1988)
★★★ The Revival (PolyGram, 1990)
★★★★½ Sons of Soul (PolyGram, 1993)
★★★★★ House of Music (Mercury, 1996)
★★★★ Hits (Mercury, 1997)
★★★½ The Millennium Collection
(Motown, 2001)

Though this R&B trio eventually succumbed to a fraternal feud, the career of brothers Dwayne and Raphael Wiggins and cousin Timothy Christian Riley also exemplified a much rarer pop phenomenon— sustained artistic growth that led to a truly original sound.

At the beginning, Tony! Toni! Toné!'s most distinguishing characteristic was the wry black comedy that spiked their standard-issue New Jack Swing.

Their wit was in full display on *Who?,* the trio's 1988 debut. "Little Walter" is the fatal tale of a smug player and "Born Not to Know" a jab at his inverse, a dogged do-gooder who loses out on the good times bursting around him. These moments are so pointed they leave the disc's love ballads sounding flat. Almost lost between the two are also a few references to R&B classics that Tony! Toni! Toné! would later expand on.

Apart from "Oakland Stroke," which drops Sly Stone's name into its combo of New Jack Swing and hip-hop, *The Revival* mostly avoids history and humor for improved songwriting and production on dance tracks such as "Feels Good" and love ballads such as "Whatever You Want." Although the disc falters on its mushy second half, it still proves the group's lyrical cleverness is matched by its musical talent.

There's no such slippage on *Sons of Soul,* which kicks off with a five-song tour de force that bounces from Motown to New Jack Swing and back before breaking for a series of ballads as sexy as they are sweet, a first for Tony! Toni! Toné!. Suddenly Raphael Wiggins' high tenor glides as smoothly and confidently as his songwriting: He drops Sly Stone's name before channeling his druggy style with equal parts love and humor on "Tonyies! in the Wrong Key."

House of Music consolidates the triumph of *Sons of Soul* for a masterpiece of 1990s R&B, an album that is as steeped in soul tradition as anything by Maxwell or D'Angelo, but that mixes the homage with humor and deft contemporary touches, thereby creating a new space all its own. The opener, "Thinking of You," is pure Al Green, complete with nonsensical asides. Raphael Wiggins, renamed Raphael Saadiq, then drops a ballad as sultry as Smokey himself, only to get up again on "Let's Get Down," a paean to clubbing whose lyrics offer another bewildering mix of love and mockery. And so it goes. Though the 70-minute disc doesn't deliver hooks from start to finish, the mood and groove never falter, standing with the best product ever put together by Gamble and Huff. On "Party Don't Cry," the Tonyies even nab the kind of existential profundity that so often escaped the Philadelphia producers' grasp.

And that was it. Of the obligatory greatest hits packages, *Hits* is preferable for its length and elegant design, even if the error-ridden lyric sheet seems to have been transcribed by someone's bored, fifth-grade nephew. —F.S.

Tool

★★★ Opiate (EP) (Zoo, 1992)
★★★½ Undertow (Zoo, 1993)
★★½ Aenima (Zoo, 1996)
★★★ Salival (Volcano/Zomba, 2000)
★★★★ Lateralus (Volcano/Zomba, 2001)

Tool bridged the gap between the heavier end of grunge and the art-metal fringe, staking out territory where fans of Smashing Pumpkins, King Crimson, and Metallica might all find something worth savoring. Their blend of brooding theatricality, eye-popping visuals, and progressive-rock chops cultivated an aura of genuine mystique and unlikely mainstream staying power. On *Opiate,* the quartet doesn't do much to differentiate themselves from the pack of hard-edged alternative bands stirring up mosh pits in the Lollapalooza era; the violence and concision of the performances are thrilling, but there are only hints of the discomfiting darkness to come.

Undertow spirals out from the hammering riffs of "Prison Sex" and "Sober" into progressively more complex terrain. Adam Jones' guitar playing discards traditional solos in favor of texture, the stranger the better, while drummer Danny Carey steers the band through a maze of tempo shifts with dazzling agility.

With *Aenima,* the band's ambitions nearly get the best of them. The increasing density of their relentlessly downcast music, augmented by occasional electronic noises, begins to feel ponderous. "I've been wallowing in my own chaotic insecure delusions," Maynard James Keenan mutters, and the music indulges him. The claustrophobic production doesn't help. *Salival* packages a handful of live performances and two new songs with some of Tool's deeply disturbing cutting-edge videos, which serve as a nightmarish backdrop for its concerts.

Brains and brawn meld on *Lateralus*, one of the more accomplished hard-rock albums of its time. "Reflection" is an unfortunate holdover from the droning *Aenima* era, but otherwise Carey and bassist Justin Chancellor explore the rhythmic possibilities from every angle, while Jones makes dramatic entrances in "The Patient" and "Schism." In "Parabol" and "Parabola," the hymnlike chants are disquieting, the cries of "This body, this body holding me" disconcertingly ecstatic. —G.K.

Toots & The Maytals

★★★★★	Monkey Man (1971; Sanctuary/Trojan, 2003)
★★★★★	Funky Kingston (Island, 1973)
★★★½	Reggae Got Soul (Island, 1976)
★★★½	Pass the Pipe (Mango, 1979)
★★★	Just Like That (Mango, 1980)
★★★	Toots Live (Mango, 1980)
★★★★★	Reggae Greats: Toots and the Maytals (Mango, 1984)
★★★★	Toots in Memphis (Mango, 1988)
★★	True Love (V2, 2004)

The title of Toots and the Maytals' American debut says it all: *Funky Kingston* forges a rock-solid connection between the spiritual lilt of reggae and the gut-bucket roar of Memphis soul. Toots Hibbert is clearly an admirer of Otis Redding, though he brings his own light touch to the proceedings. The Maytals pump up a sparse yet bottom-heavy groove that drops hints about New Orleans, too. *Funky Kingston* collects the singles that made Toots a Jamaican superstar: "Pressure Drop" (which also appears on the soundtrack to *The Harder They Come*) and "Time Tough" ring out with humble streetwise urgency, while the radical versions of "Louie Louie" and John Denver's "Country Road" just couldn't sound any more natural or unforced. *Reggae Got Soul* and *Pass the Pipe* push this proposed merger a little harder than the somewhat hackneyed material can bear, though each album contains three or four rock-solid vocal workouts. *Just Like That* is a bit skimpy in comparison, while some excessive audience-pleasing maneuvers mar the otherwise fine *Toots Live*. Along with the expected hits, *Reggae Greats* includes the definitive "54-46"—an ex-con's stunning anthem that was left off *Funky Kingston*. Another revealing title brings Toots Hibbert's career full circle: *Toots in Memphis* is an exultant set of Stax-Volt covers, featuring many songs Toots had performed live

for years but never recorded. His affectionate mastery of soul music is obvious, while the shifting riddims (supplied by Sly and Robbie) are anything but.

In 2003, the Maytals scorching 1971 debut LP *Monkey Man* (including the original version of "Pressure Drop") was reissued, buffed out to 25 tracks with the inclusion of early rare singles, making it as important a pick-up and pick-me-up as *Funky Kingston*. While 2004's *True Love* found Toots in fine voice, the album's duet concept paired Hibbert with everyone from Ryan Adams and No Doubt to Willie Nelson and Jeff Beck with inherently embarrassing results, although the version of "Funky Kingston" with Bootsy Collins and The Roots was legit —M.C./P.R.

Tortoise

★★★	Tortoise (Thrill Jockey, 1994)
★★★★	Millions Now Living Will Never Die (Thrill Jockey, 1996)
★★★½	Remixed (Thrill Jockey, 1998)
★★	TNT (Thrill Jockey, 1998)
★★★½	Standards (Thrill Jockey, 2001)
★★★	It's All Around You (Thrill Jockey, 2004)

The instrumental Chicago band Tortoise didn't set out to create a genre, or a scene; it just happened to the band after the fact. Its debut is an experiment in low-end theory—emphasis on the theory. Almost all basses, drums, marimbas, and mixology (this last courtesy of drummer John McEntire), it doesn't have much in the way of tunes, but it's got some splendidly throbbing textures and tricks, like the two-bass pas de deux "Tin Cans & Twine." A canny journalist decided that they (and a few other bands with whom they'd never worked) were "postrock," and a genre was born—and it didn't hurt that the members of Tortoise were also involved in half a dozen other sort-of-likeminded bands.

With *Millions Now Living Will Never Die*, the band proved itself worthy of the hype. McEntire, in particular, took advantage of the studio's capability for making live instruments do impossible things. "Djed" is the first masterpiece of modern digital editing, a 20-minute epic in which a little melodic figure and a drone-based background perpetually shift their forms. "Dear Grandma and Grandpa" hints at European techno; "Along the Banks of Rivers" brings new guitarist David Pajo (formerly of Slint) out front, with a beefy melody that twangs like Duane Eddy. *Remixed* collects a series of transformations of *Millions* pieces by the likes of Jim O'Rourke and Oval's Markus Popp; the best is probably U.N.K.L.E.'s remix of "Djed," which nods to Steve Reich's minimalist classic "Come Out."

TNT is something of a wet firecracker: The pitty-pat beats, sparse textures, mellow-electric-jazz inflections, failed techno experiments, and general retreading of ideas the first two albums did better mostly add up to second-rate fusion. Fortunately, *Standards* is a return to form. The jazz gestures are largely absent, replaced by a throw-it-all-into-the-pot attitude they share with Stereolab, a few of whose albums McEntire has coproduced. There's even a slab of space funk, "Monica." McEntire's drum tones are like no others in the world—they sound like they're made of liquid and alien bones rather than metal and plastic—and he's started to open up his ultraprecise tone-doctoring to messier sounds. *It's All Around You* is even more studio-intensive and micromanaged—the model seems to be Miles Davis' early-'70s tape-and-funk experiments. It's definitely not the sound of six musicians in a room: Instruments flutter around the stereo field, change their timbre mid-note, materialize and evaporate with no notice. Artifice is the point, and if even the album's "spontaneous" bursts of noise seem artificial, that's the price they pay. Still, there are some nicely constructed themes beneath all the trickery. —D.W.

Peter Tosh

★★★★ Legalize It (1976; Sony, 1999)
★★★★ Equal Rights (1977; Sony, 1999)
★★★ Bush Doctor (1978; Capitol, 2002)
★★★ Mystic Man (1979; Capitol, 2002)
★★★ Wanted Dread & Alive (1981; Capitol, 2002)
★★★ Mama Africa (1983; Capitol, 2002)
★★ Captured Live (EMI America, 1984)
★★ No Nuclear War (1987; Capitol, 2002)
★★★★ The Toughest (Heartbeat/Capitol, 1988)
★★★★ Collection Gold (Tristar, 1994)
★★★★ The Best of Peter Tosh: Dread Don't Die (EMI, 1996)
★★ The Gold Collection (EMI, 1996)
★★★★ Scrolls of the Prophet: The Best of Peter Tosh (Columbia, 1997)
★★★★ Honorary Citizen (Sony, 1997)
★★ The Best of Peter Tosh (Disky, 1998)
★★★½ Live at the One Love Peace Concert (JAD/Koch, 2000)
★★★½ Arise Black Man (Earmark, 2000)
★★★½ Live & Dangerous Boston 1976 (Sony, 2001)
★★★★ Arise! The Best of Peter Tosh (Trojan/Music Club, 2001)
★★★ Stand Up! (Sony Special, 2001)
★★★ Super Hits (Sony, 2001)
★★ I Am That I Am (Jad, 2001)
★★★ Peter Tosh Live at the Jamaica Music Festival (Jad, 2002)
★★★★ Complete Capture Live (Capitol, 2002)
★★★★ The Essential Peter Tosh: The Columbia Years (Sony, 2003)

For each of the Rastamen who made up reggae's holy trinity—Bob Marley, Bunny Livingston Wailer, and Peter Tosh—music was The Message. All three sang for "equal rights and justice," as defined by the Jamaican-bred blend of Marcus Garvey's worldview and Old Testament fire and brimstone known as Rastafari. But Tosh, a.k.a. reggae's Stepping Razor, came the hardest and, less fortunately, proved to be the most didactic. Once the world heard "The Tosh," Jamaica transformed from a vacation paradise for the wealthy into a mecca for the disenfranchised. His urgent baritone bore a threat of danger, sharpening Bunny's and Bob's sufferahs' dreams and Rastafarian plaints into lessons for heathens and militant demands aimed at "downpressors."

Born in the rural western part of Jamaica, this life-long foe of the "shitstem" made his way at age fifteen to the Trench Town tenement yard in Kingston where he met musical youths Bob Marley and Bunny Livingston and formed the Wailers. After the Wailers broke up, each asserted himself as an individual crossover reggae force. Tosh won his own worldwide following with *Legalize It*, his first Stateside major-label release, and its followup, *Equal Rights*. Tosh and his crack band, featuring Santa Davis on bass, concoct a euphoric, bottom-heavy stew, with reggae's one-drop riddim leavened by an occasional guitar lead. *Legalize It* zeros in on Tosh's paramount cause—free the herb!—while *Equal Rights* levels his scathing attack against a range of societal offenses in "Equal Rights," "Downpressor Man," "Stepping Razor," "African," and the remade "Get Up Stand Up." All tracks exude the trademark Jamaican musical buzz, yet the take-no-prisoners messages and aggressive stance could easily suit today's politicized rap.

The Toughest collects the best tracks from Tosh's out-of-print albums for the Rolling Stones label and EMI; tellingly, it sticks to the earlier albums for soulful grooves such as "Don't Look Back" (a hit duet with Mick Jagger from *Bush Doctor*). Even though Tosh's voice sounds strained around the edges on *No Nuclear War*, his deliriously schizoid wordplay and unflagging indignation power the title cut, and there are signs of life throughout. Sadly, this inconclusive but encouraging album stands as his last testament; Tosh was murdered in 1987. Far more worthy of Tosh's biting humor and righteous rage are his posthumous box sets and compilations, including *Scrolls of the Prophet, Honorary Citizen, Live at the One Love Peace Concert, Arise!*, and *Live and Dangerous*. —E.O.

Traffic

- ★★★½ Mr. Fantasy (1968; Island, 1989)
- ★★★½ Traffic (1968; Island, 1989)
- ★★★ Last Exit (1969; Island, 1988)
- ★★★ Heaven Is in Your Mind (1969; Island, 2000)
- ★★★★ The Best of Traffic (United Artists, 1970)
- ★★★★ John Barleycorn Must Die (1970; Island, 1989)
- ★★★ Welcome to the Canteen (1971; Island, 1988)
- ★★★ The Low Spark of High Heeled Boys (1971; Island, 1989)
- ★★★ Shoot Out at the Fantasy Factory (1973; Island, 2003)
- ★★ On the Road (1974; Island, 2003)
- ★★½ When the Eagle Flies (1974; Asylum, 2003)
- ★★★★ Smiling Phases (Island, 1991)
- ★★★ Far From Home (Virgin, 1994)
- ★★★½ Feelin' Alright: The Very Best of Traffic (Island, 2000)
- ★★★ The Millennium Collection (PolyGram, 2002)

Traffic boasted the reedy, soulful vocals, cerebral keyboards, and guitar of Steve Winwood, the sharp grace of lyricist Jim Capaldi's drumming, the elegance of Chris Wood's flute and sax, and Dave Mason's way with melody. Copping ideas from a range of genres—jazz, classical, and Eastern—for a kind of embryonic world music, the band epitomized the ambitious impulse of the best British late-'60s art rock. *Mr. Fantasy* is psychedelia for brain people: Dave Mason's sitar lifts "Paper Sun" toward sonic majesty; "Hole in My Shoe" is clever; "Dear Mr. Fantasy" is that rarity, an epic pop song that (almost) justifies its length. *Traffic*, with Mason's insistent "Feelin' Alright" and Winwood sounding otherworldly on "Forty Thousand Headmen" and "Who Knows What Tomorrow May Bring," is the band's strongest—an album of dense, swirling musicality. After Mason left to pursue a mediocre solo career of caution and craft, Traffic turned jazzish with *John Barleycorn Must Die.* The band would later push jamming to the point of exhaustion on *The Low Spark of High Heeled Boys,* but on *Barleycorn,* the extended flourishes of instrumental virtuosity are exhilarating—leavened with the folk poetry of the lyrics and Winwood's freest singing, the title song and "Freedom Rider" reveal dazzling playing that never obscures sheer melody.

Mason rejoined briefly on *Welcome to the Canteen,* on which the African percussion of Reebop Kwaku Baah adds zest to the Traffic style. Endless personnel shifts and exhaustion led to the band's mid-'70s demise; *Far From Home,* a reunion of sorts (only Winwood and Capaldi participate), was good, but a bit more Winwood than actual Traffic. *Smiling Phases,* a two-CD set, is the best compilation. —P.E.

Transplants

- ★★★★½ Transplants (Epitaph, 2002)

Although they were the greatest punk band of the '90s, Rancid never escaped the shadow of their musical and spiritual forebears, the Clash. It took this side project, featuring Blink-182 drummer Travis Barker and newbie Rob Aston, for Rancid leader Tim Armstrong to finally catch up with the hip-hop generation. Mixing together soulful organ, big-beat loops, fist-pumping choruses, barrelhouse piano, Aston's hoarse gangsta raps, and Barker's snappy beats, *Transplants* reinvents gutter punk for turn-of-the-millennium California, where steamy streets teem with thugs of all ethnicities, and everyone carries a blaring boombox. On the album's best cut, "Tall Cans in the Air" (chorus: "Lemme see 'em/Fuck you!"), Aston vividly describes lives spent dealing dope, pulling guns, drinking Budweiser tallboys, and cruising around on low-rider bikes. Armstrong infuses the glorious mess with strains of melancholy, slurring tributes to dead buddies, and tempering Aston's shout with a croon that recalls Shane MacGowan of the Pogues. And the hip-hop generation contributes directly: Funkdoobiest's Son Doobie rhymes on "Diamonds and Guns," and a cover of the Wu-Tang Clan classic "C.R.E.A.M." recasts the original's money-grubbing assurance as down-and-out desperation. Never before has there been combat rock like this. —N.C.

Traveling Wilburys

- ★★★½ Traveling Wilburys, Vol. One (Wilbury/Warner Bros., 1988)
- ★★★ Vol. 3 (Wilbury/Warner Bros., 1990)

The Rutles-ish humor and determined casualness of the Traveling Wilburys counter understandable fears for this "band" of '60s gods (Bob Dylan, George Harrison), the '50s idol they dug (Roy Orbison), and the aging pups who worshipped them, Tom Petty and ELO's Jeff Lynne. Giddy with the freedom of their winking "anonymity," these significant figures doff their crowns and get down to effortless, and remarkably fresh, rocking. Dylan sings better on the first Wilburys than he has in years; Harrison again proves that he's best when surrounded by real talents, not sidemen; Orbison's "Not Alone Any More" is a weeper (almost) up there with his classics. With Roy departed, the second try isn't quite so fine. But Lynne again turns in expensive garage production, Petty matches his mentors, and Dylan's ease is infectious. —P.E.

Travis

★★★ Good Feeling (Epic/Independiente, 1997)
★★★½ The Man Who (Independiente, 1999)
★★ The Invisible Band (Epic, 2000)
★★★ 12 Memories (Epic, 2003)

During the late '90s, after Blur decided it had no interest in challenging Radiohead as the U.K.'s Biggest Band and Oasis mounted a sad, Larry Holmes-esque bid to reclaim the crown, Brit-pop fans turned to Travis, who was actually more like the Little Scottish Band That Could. Judging from its unassumingly pretty folk pop, Travis had no interest in being world beaters, but when he didn't have his head the clouds, frontman Fran Healy could write a painfully sincere love song really pushed your pleasure buttons.

On *Good Feeling* Travis is your average mid-'90s Brit-pop band, mixing in reverb-drenched melancholia and big-ass anthems such as "All I Want to Do Is Rock," which is much less dumb than its title suggests. But Travis didn't really find itself until *The Man Who,* the cuddliest Brit-pop record in forever. A huge hit in Britain, *The Man Who* got by on a string of lovestruck ballads that ignored sci-fi trendiness in favor of modestly beautiful melodies and Healy's little-lost-boy croon. The moony, gorgeous "Why Does It Always Rain on Me" gave sustenance to pop fans waiting for Radiohead to remake *The Bends,* and Travis fleshed out its lightweight folk-strum with understated atmospherics on great songs such as "Slide Show" and the Oasis-referencing "Writing to Reach You," where Healy asks, "What's a Wonderwall, anyway?"

After the massive success of *The Man Who,* Travis felt no need tinker with its formula, and *The Invisible Band* turned out to be just so much useless beauty. "Indefinitely," "Sing," and "The Humpty Dumpty Love Song" are packed with well-wrought melodies, but the songs are so lightweight and down-in-the-mouth that you want to grab Healy by the collar just to see if he fights back. On *12 Memories* Travis put a bit of swagger in its sound by turning to darker, vaguely spectral sounds and tackling weighty post-9/11 issues on "The Beautiful Occupation" and "Peace the Fuck Out." But aside from on the embarrasingly ponderous "Mid-Life Krysis," Healy proves that winsome tunefulness is still his only stock-in-trade. —C.H.

T. Rex

★★★ My People Were Fair and Had Sky in Their Hair, but Now They're Content to Wear Stars on Their Brows (A&M, 1968)
★★★ Prophets, Seers, and Sages, the Angels of the Ages (A&M, 1968)
★★★ Unicorn (Fly, 1969)
★★★★ A Beard of Stars (A&M, 1970)
★★½ T. Rex (Reprise, 1970)
★★★★★ Electric Warrior (Reprise, 1971)
★★★★ The Slider (Mercury, 1972)
★★★ Tanx (Mercury, 1973)
★ Zinc Alloy and the Hidden Riders of Tomorrow (Mercury, 1974)
★ Bolan's Zip Gun (Mercury, 1975)
★ Futuristic Dragon (Mercury, 1976)
★ Dandy in the Underworld (Mercury, 1977)
★★★★ T. Rexstasy: The Best of T. Rex 1970–1973 (Warner Bros., 1985)
★★★½ Great Hits 1972–1977, Vol. One: The A Sides (Mercury, 1994)
★★★ Great Hits 1972–1977, Vol. Two: The B Sides (Mercury, 1994)
★★★ A Wizard, a True Star (Edsel, 1996)

Marc Bolan was glitter rock's prettiest boy child, a cosmic dancer strumming his Les Paul under the mambo sun, living out all his silver-studded saber-toothed dreams, attended by a flock of gong-banging handmaidens. Bolan's band T. Rex ruled the U.K. charts in the early '70s—his fey vocals, wild humor, and indefensibly sexy egomania really did conjure up their own musical world. The early, difficult-to-find albums (as Tyrannosaurus Rex) are acoustic hippie folk in the Donovan style, with *A Beard of Stars* the best. But Bolan truly became the elemental child when he plugged in his guitar and started writing manic chant-along glam-rock hits such as "Metal Guru," "20th Century Boy," "Solid Gold Easy Action," and "Children of the Revolution." The lone U.S. hit was the addictive sex drivel of "Bang a Gong (Get It On)."

T. Rex's most famous album is deservedly *Electric Warrior,* with a heavy-lidded, dreamy guitar buzz in classics such as "Planet Queen," "Jeepster," and "Cosmic Dancer." *The Slider,* just a notch below, adds the acoustic slow-motion gem "Spaceball Ricochet" (the universe as pinball machine, with Bolan and his lover as the flippers) and "Metal Guru" (so great the Smiths borrowed it and retitled it "Panic"). When the end came, it came fast. Bolan kept recording prolifically, but he never wrote another decent song after the erratic *Tanx.* A definitive one-disc best-of would be welcome, but because different corporations own different tracks, there isn't one—*Great Hits* doesn't even have "Bang a Gong." So the place to start is definitely *Electric Warrior.* Bolan died in a car crash in 1977. But as far as T. Rex fans are concerned, he just danced himself into the tomb. —R.S.

A Tribe Called Quest

★★★★ People's Instinctive Travels and the Paths of Rhythm (Jive, 1990)
★★★★★ The Low End Theory (Jive, 1991)
★★★★½ Midnight Marauders (Jive, 1993)
★★★ Revised Quest for the Seasoned Traveller (Jive, 1994)
★★★ Beats, Rhymes, and Life (Jive, 1996)
★★★ The Love Movement (Jive, 1998)
★★★★½ Anthology (Jive, 1999)
★★★★ Hits, Rarities, & Remixes (Jive, 2003)

At the turn of the '90s, as hip-hop entered its second decade and gangsta rap hardened into hip-hop's default mode, a counterstrain emerged, shunting aside macho boasting and grim urban reportage in favor of whimsical storytelling, intelligent but still verbally dexterous takes on social issues, and laid-back samples from old jazz, or at least jazzy, records. Among the leading proponents of this more reflective style (including De La Soul and the Jungle Brothers), A Tribe Called Quest was arguably the most accomplished.

People's Instinctive Travels shows the Tribe's sound already firmly in place. The delivery of MCs Q-Tip and Phife Dawg is low-key and relaxed, and their rhymes —covering a variety of topics, including venereal disease ("Pubic Enemy") and high-cholesterol food ("Ham 'n' Eggs")—flow in loose, rolling cadences. Meanwhile, DJ Ali Shaheed Muhammad mixes jazz piano with sitar on "Bonita Applebum" and nabs from Lou Reed's "Walk on the Wild Side" on "Can I Kick It?" Laid-back but far from lacking in intensity, *People's Instinctive Travels* is a powerful debut, but A Tribe Called Quest was only getting started.

On *The Low End Theory,* Muhammad's jazz samples have become even more seamless, matching Q-Tip and Phife's deceptively casual flow. At times, the tracks sound as if they're barely there; acoustic bass (some courtesy of Ron Carter) and slyly insistent drum patterns are often a song's sole nonvocal components, and yet the sparseness only adds to the music's impact. *The Low End Theory* is a hip-hop masterpiece.

Though perhaps a tad more mainstream than its predecessor, *Midnight Marauders* certainly doesn't skimp on the funk. Among its many highlights are the infectious hit "Award Tour" and "Sucka Nigga," a much-needed commentary on rappers' use of the N-word. *Revised Quest* is a neat but hardly necessary collection of remixes.

With *Beats, Rhymes and Life,* A Tribe Called Quest hits the wall. The music's not terrible by any means; the bottom-heavy "Phony Rappers" is only one of several excellent cuts. Still, no new ground is broken, and the MCs' sense of growing inertia is palpable.

The Love Movement is more consistent, but energy levels are dipping. Not surprisingly, the group called it quits shortly thereafter. Both *Anthology* and *Hits, Rarities & Remixes* are well-selected compilations, but you really can't go wrong with any of the first three albums. —J.D.C./M.R.

Tricky

★★★★½ Maxinquaye (Island, 1995)
★★★½ Pre-Millennium Tension (Island, 1996)
★★★½ Angels with Dirty Faces (Island, 1998)
★★★★ BlowBack (Hollywood, 2001)

Nearly God

★★★ Nearly God (Island, 1996)

Tricky with DJ Muggs and Grease

★★★½ Juxtapose (Island, 1999)

After squinting into the glare of nightlife notoriety for more than half a decade as an adjunct member of Bristol, England, beatmongers Massive Attack, Tricky took a deep huff and released his brilliant debut *Maxinquaye,* a long, distorted shadow of utopian '90s club culture that draws from the techno, hip-hop, and rock underground.

The soundtrack to a morning after in which the sun never rises, *Maxinquaye* coughs up disjointed sonic details like so much technicolor phlegm—an echoed dockside clang, a hyper piano tinkle, sluggish funk guitar scrapes. Sometimes Tricky rasp-raps, often he cedes the mike to ladies, particularly the imperturbably deviant Martina Topley-Bird, who claims Public Enemy's "Black Steel in the Hour of Chaos" as her own and declares "I'll drink till I'm drunk/And I'll smoke till I'm senseless." Descending into this garish, ominous, and self-aware soundscape is like watching a Disney cartoon on bad acid, itching with fear even as you retain the sense that it's all an illusion.

Critics bestowed the term *trip-hop* on Tricky's pallid imitators, who often unimaginatively propped a blank thrush atop a moody beat—a trick he promptly one-upped by cannily producing a series of women (Björk, Alison Moyet, Neneh Cherry) on the chilly *Nearly God.* After that, the wizened imp became a virtuoso of self-imitation: Each time he repeated himself, his tracks constricted further, reveling in their claustrophobia. Though the work retained its power, many listeners lost interest—what kind of pop masochist deliberately seeks out a hangover? That was a shame, because Tricky was compiling the catchiest, most discrete songs of his career. Featuring cameos from guests as prominent and varied as Alanis Morissette and the Red Hot Chili Peppers, *BlowBack* is an eerie facsimile of a pop record, a collection of smash hits for an alternate reality. *Vulnerable* is business-as-usual

Tricky, spotlighting guest-diva vocals and tweaked covers (XTC's "Dear God," The Cure's "Love Cats") that don't seem so special anymore. —K.H.

The Troggs

★★★	Live at Max's Kansas City (MKC, 1981)
★★★½	The Best of the Troggs (Rhino, 1984)
★★★	Archeology (1967–1977) (Mercury, 1992)
★★	Athens Andover (Rhino, 1992)
★★★	Wild Thing (See for Miles, 1994)
★★★	Best of the Troggs (Fontana, 1994)

With its leering vocal, its goose-stepping rhythm stomping the life out of even the merest suggestion of swing, and—oddest of all—its naively graceful ocarina solo, "Wild Thing," from 1966, was a trash-rock classic of a decidedly wacky stripe. The Troggs' only other Top 10 hit, "Love Is All Around" (1968) was pale Brit Invasion stuff (later featured in the film *Four Weddings and a Funeral*) but the rest of this foursome's catalogue nearly outdistanced "Wild Thing"—not in crude rock power, but in sheer strangeness. "I Can't Control Myself" and "Give It to Me," both banned by the BBC, were lecherous little numbers played poorly enough to achieve a primitive fascination. "Cousin Jane," a brief, breathy ballad, was downright creepy—sort of like the perverse "Uncle Ernie" bit off the Who's *Tommy*. Ozzy Osbourne and other metal minds claim to be influenced by the Troggs, and you can believe it: Reg Presley was one bent nonsinger and his "vision" remains a warped one. *Archeology,* at 52 tracks, is almost too much of a good thing. An intriguing curio, *Athens Andover* teams the Troggs with members of R.E.M.

Live at Max's Kansas City is pure rock & roll power—raw, romping versions of chestnuts such as "Walking the Dog," "Memphis," and "Satisfaction." —P.E.

Trouble Funk

★★★	Saturday Night (Live From Washington, D.C.) (1985; Island, 1990)
★★★★	Live and Early Singles (2.13.61 Records, 2004)

Despite massive hype, the funky go-go sound of Washington, D.C., failed to take the nation by storm in the mid-'80s. Above all else, go go is a live event: Drums and assorted percussion cook up itchy polyrhythmic jams, spiced by floating JB-style horn riffs, spare keyboard washes, call-and-response vocals, and the occasional rap. Audience participation is key, and, unlike the early hip-hop scene, so is traditional musicianship. Go go bands like Trouble Funk, E.U., or Chuck Brown and the Soul Searchers could

indeed play their instruments, and loved to prove it all night.

Released on the pioneering rap label Sugar Hill, *Drop the Bomb,* Trouble Funk's debut (currently out of print) is probably the most accurate and exciting transcription of the go-go experience. The anti-nuke title track and the aerobics workout "Pump It Up" qualify as bona fide songs, although it's the breathless, refreshing rhythms that establish *Bomb* as a classic groove album—a perfect party-peak explosion. Trouble Funk's major label debut, *Live From D.C.,* actually splits the difference, backing a representative live set with stiff, overproduced studio tracks. The 1987 followup, *Trouble Over Here, Trouble Over There* (also out of print), gets mired in clichéd R&B moves. Having failed as both revolutionaries and crossover ambassadors, Trouble Funk returned to the Washington, D.C., scene which nurtured it, where the group continued to drop the bomb on its longstanding audience well into the '90s. In 2004, material from the band's peak period was collected on the two-CD collection *Live and Early Singles,* which boasts four extended untitled jams on the first disc and eight studio recordings on the second—and all of it on CD for the first time. —M.C./B.SC.

Ike & Tina Turner

★★★½	The Soul of Ike & Tina Turner (1960; Collectables, 1994)
★★★★★	Dance with Ike & Tina Turner & Their Kings of Rhythm (1961; Collectables, 1996)
★★★	River Deep—Mountain High (A&M, 1966)
★★★½	Dynamite! (1968; Collectables, 1994)
★★★	Ike & Tina Turner's Greatest Hits—Volume Two (SAJA, 1988)
★★★	Ike & Tina Turner's Greatest Hits—Volume Three (SAJA, 1988)
★★★★	Proud Mary: The Best of Ike and Tina Turner (EMI, 1991)
★★★★	Back in the Day (32 R&B, 1997)

Many years have passed since Tina Turner suffered at the hands of her violent, coked-up former husband, and it's high time to acknowledge that Clarksdale, MS's, Isaac Lustre Turner, for all his inexcusable and shameful behavior behind closed doors, is as much a monster on the stage and in the studio as he is off. Turner has an exemplary track record as a bandleader (his Kings of Rhythm were as formidable a combo as any in the South during the mid-'50s), talent scout, producer (for both Elmore James and Howlin' Wolf, and musician (his boogie-woogie piano style was distinctive and incendiary, and when he took up the guitar, he explored some uncharted territory marked by ferocious hurricane blasts of distortion and dirty, chunky blues riffs). On the recommendation of B.B. King, Sun Records owner Sam Phillips cut a session with Ike and the Kings on March 3, 1951, featuring Ike's cousin (and Kings saxophonist) Jackie Brenston singing lead on a propulsive ode to one of the day's most powerful motor vehicles, "Rocket 88," a song modeled after Jimmy Liggins' "Cadillac Boogie." His recordings with the Kings can be heard in all their majesty on Rhino's 1994 anthology *I Like Ike,* truly a thing of wonder. More recently, Ike proved that age and all his trials haven't robbed him of his muse, as his 2001 solo album, *Here and Now,* on the Ikon label, was nominated for a Grammy.

Then there's Tina. Born Annie Mae Bullock in Brownsville, TN, she was only 18 when she joined Ike and the Kings of Rhythm just as the band was ruling the roost of a lively club scene in East St. Louis, IL. She stepped up as lead vocalist in late 1959 and was christened Tina Turner by Ike. The former Ms. Bullock made her incendiary debut on the Sue Records single "A Fool in Love," with a full repertoire of blistering, hoarse R&B shouts framed by a singsong girl chorus and the Kings' steady rocking pulse pushing the whole affair forward. A Top 30 pop and #2 R&B hit, "A Fool in Love" set the template for a succession of rousing singles in the early '60s: Tina's gravel-throated blues shouts and cries answered by a pop-ish female chorus, all set against a churning, muddy soundscape with occasional spoken double-entendre-laden byplay between Ike and Tina.

Onstage, Tina's shapely, athletic figure and sexually charged performances became the stuff of legend, while Ike directed the proceedings behind her. Of course that energy could never quite be captured on disc, but producer Ike knew how to use the studio as a creative tool. Ike & Tina Turner singles from the Sue era (and the non-single album tracks as well) were some of the most ferocious performances ever set down on wax; there was very little in the way of calm introspection going on in those days. Tina sings with abandon and overwhelming emotion; most of her shouts wind up in the red, slightly distorted. The Collectables reissues of *Dynamite!* and *The Soul of Ike & Tina Turner* are essential documents of the Sue era. There is some duplication of tracks, as both contain "A Fool in Love," "Sleepless," the scalding mission statement called "Letter from Tina," "I Idolize You," and the string-laden R&B ballad "I'm Jealous," but only *Dynamite!* contains the priceless ditty "Tra La La La La," with its ingenious muted trumpet solo rising out of the mix like Miles on a bender. Another interesting document from this period is the all-instrumental outing *Dance.* Ike and Tina are on the cover, but this

one's all Ike and the Kings of Rhythm, and it's a beautiful thing. Not only is it a showcase for the individual Kings, who were strictly powerhouse (especially the sax player), but it makes a prima facie case for Ike being considered with the all-time guitar greats.

In 1966, a now-legendary pairing took place when Ike yielded the producer's chair to Phil Spector for the album that was titled, after its key single, *River Deep—Mountain High.* By most accounts, Spector had expected this to be the jewel in his crown. But despite its grandeur—both in production and in Tina's vocal attack—the single bombed in the U.S. after being a Top 10 hit in Britain, driving Spector into seclusion for three years. The ensuing album, produced in part by Spector, in part by Ike, reveals that Spector's Wall of Sound was a most inappropriate vehicle for Tina's coarse, bluesy shouting, which thrived in the tight R&B combo setting of Ike's old-school productions.

A 1969 tour with the Rolling Stones proved to be the beginning of the end for Ike and Tina. On the plus side, it brought them more attention than they had ever received—and justifiably so—and reinvigorated their recording career. But after their Top 10 cover version of "Proud Mary" for Liberty Records in 1971 (a rendition famously captured on film in the *Gimme Shelter* tour documentary, featuring Tina suggestively stroking and admiring the head of her microphone), the group faltered commercially and didn't get back to the Top 30 until 1973 with an autobiographical song written by Tina, "Nutbush City Limits." Their failure to achieve any consistency in the studio mirrored the decline in the quality of their live performances and Ike's descent into drugged-out oblivion. In 1975 the group cut a cover version of Pete Townshend's "Acid Queen" that took Tina out of her R&B base and pointed her in the pop-soul direction she would explore so fruitfully as a solo artist in the ensuing decades.

The best document of the early-'70s pre-breakup period comes by way of 32 R&B's *Back in the Day* collection. Most of the 15 songs here had never been issued before, and a few others are cast in radically different versions from the original recordings. Ike was experimenting with new approaches at this point, and it shows in the first cut, a medley of "Don't Fight It/Knock on Wood," which fuses Memphis-style horns of the '70s to the tight Memphis groove Ike fashioned in the '50s. Typical of the experiments going on at this time is a down-and-dirty version of the Archies' "Sugar Sugar," complete with a pumping horn section, a pulsating groove, funky wah-wah guitar, Ike's roadhouse piano, and a moaning, grunting, screaming vocal from Tina, who interprets the lyrics so salaciously you might believe someone was going down on her while she was standing at the microphone.

For a single-disc retrospective, EMI's *Proud Mary: The Best of* is a well-rounded collection, beginning with "A Fool in Love" and systematically rolling through the years before concluding with "Acid Queen." Its liner notes provide a good thumbnail sketch of the duo's recording history as well.   —D.M.

Joe Turner

★★★★★   Big Joe Turner's Greatest Hits (1951; Atlantic Jazz, 1989)
★★★★   The Boss of the Blues (1956; Atlantic, 1988)
★★★½   The Trumpet Kings Meet Joe Turner (1974; Original Jazz Classics, 1991)
★★★   Nobody in Mind (1976; Original Jazz Classics, 1993)
★★★½   In the Evening (1976; Original Jazz Classics, 1995)
★★★   Things That I Used to Do (1977; Original Jazz Classics, 1995)
★★★½   Everyday I Have the Blues (1978; Original Jazz Classics, 1991)
★★★   The Midnight Special (1980; Pablo, 2002)
★★★★   Tell Me Pretty Baby (1980; Arhoolie, 1992)
★★★½   The Best of Joe Turner (1980; Pablo, 1990)
★★★   Life Ain't Easy (1983; Original Jazz Classics, 1994)
★★★½   Blues Train (1983; Muse, 1989)
★★★★   Kansas City Here I Come (1984; Original Jazz Classics, 1996)
★★★   Patcha, Patcha All Night Long: Joe Turner Meets Jimmy Witherspoon (1985; Original Jazz Classics, 1996)
★★★★★   Memorial Album: Rhythm & Blues Years (Atlantic, 1986)
★★★   Flip, Flop & Fly (1989; Pablo, 1991)
★★   Joe Turner and T-Bone Walker: Bosses of the Blues—Vol. 1 (RCA Bluebird, 1989)
★★★★★   I've Been to Kansas City, Vol. 1 (MCA, 1990)
★★★★   Stormy Monday (Fantasy, 1991)
★★★   Texas Style (Evidence, 1992)
★★★½   Shouting the Blues (Specialty, 1992)
★★★★★   Jumpin' with Joe: The Complete Aladdin and Imperial Recordings (EMI, 1993)
★★★★★   Every Day in the Week (MCA, 1993)
★★½   Shake, Rattle & Roll (Tomato, 1994)
★★★★★   Big, Bad & Blue: The Big Joe Turner Anthology (Rhino, 1994)
★★★½   Have No Fear, Big Joe Turner Is Here (Savoy Jazz, 1995)
★★★★   The Very Best of Big Joe Turner (Rhino, 1998)
★★★★★   Joe Turner/Rockin' The Blues (Collectables, 2000)

★★★   Atomic Boogie: The National Recordings 1945–1947 (Savoy Jazz, 2001)

"Boss of the Blues" Joe Turner owns the distinction of laying legitimate claim to being one of the founding fathers of both rhythm & blues *and* rock & roll; this in addition to being regarded as one of the most powerful bluesmen in history, a physically imposing man with a huge voice and a singing style unadorned by gimmickry. The very straightforwardness of his approach was its own recommendation: Whether shouting it out or getting into what passed for a gentle mode, Turner's voice remained a stately instrument: dynamic without being ostentatious, long on legato, short on melisma, always moving.

Turner's career dates to the mid-'20s, when he landed a job tending bar in his native Kansas City; as an extracurricular activity he took up shouting the blues with pianist Pete Johnson. Turner, Johnson, Sam Price, and Jay McShann became the key figures in a vital Kansas City music scene that merged blues and jazz into the boogie-woogie which swept the country after Turner's appearance at New York's Carnegie Hall in 1938. Turner remained in New York, ensconced at Café Society, and recorded under his own name and with other prominent jazz and blues artists. A 1956 Atlantic release, *Boss of the Blues*, re-creates the fertile Kansas City period of Turner's career, reuniting him with the estimable Johnson and other first-rate players on the tunes that secured Turner's early acclaim: "Cherry Red;" and "Wee Baby Blues" and "Low Down Dog," both Turner originals. In their original recordings, these and other sides that Turner cut in the late '40s constituted a new sound that would evolve into rhythm & blues—spurred in no small measure by Turner's own voluminous 1950s recordings for Atlantic. It wasn't a long leap from Turner's style of R&B to rock & roll, as evidenced by the success of Turner's "Shake, Rattle, and Roll" in a sanitized cover version by Bill Haley and His Comets. Other of Turner's sides remain important genre-busting entries that are considered rock & roll by some, R&B by others: Of these, the most prominent are "Flip, Flop and Fly," "Honey Hush," "Corrina, Corrina" and "Sweet Sixteen." This fruitful era is well documented on *Big, Bad & Blue, Big Joe Turner's Greatest Hits, Memorial Album—Rhythm & Blues Years,* and Rhino's succinct 16-song overview, *The Very Best of Big Joe Turner.*

Turner continued to record sporadically through the '60s, then found his career in high gear again come the '70s, thanks to producer Norman Granz, who teamed Turner with jazz giants Count Basie, Milt Jackson, Roy Eldridge, and others on several recordings for the Pablo label. Age hardly diminished the authority of Turner's singing; moreover, his stellar accompanists inspired him to fine performances. Of note here are *Flip, Flop & Fly*, with the Count Basie Orchestra (recorded in 1972), *Nobody in Mind*, with Milt Jackson, Roy Eldridge, and Pee Wee Clayton among the supporting cast; and *In the Evening*, a moody set featuring Turner's swaggering, laconic take on George Gershwin's "Summertime." A remarkable summit meeting defines the whole of *The Trumpet Kings Meet Joe Turner*, a 1974 project that found the sine qua non of blues shouters holding forth with a quartet of equally imposing trumpet masters in Dizzy Gillespie, Roy Eldridge, Harry "Sweets" Edison, and Clark Terry.

In 1983 Turner got together with the great songwriter Doc Pomus to cowrite a new tune, "Blues Train," that became the centerpiece of Turner's final album. Coproduced by Pomus (who had been inspired to become a singer and songwriter after hearing Turner's recording of "Piney Brown Blues" in 1941) and Bob Porter, *Blues Train* rumbles and roars mightily, with Turner backed by Roomful of Blues and Dr. John on nine cuts that take him all the way back to Kansas City and bring him forward into the present. Two years later he proved conclusively that age and experience were virtues for a blues singer, when he teamed with another master, Jimmy Witherspoon, for some low-down carousing on *Patcha, Patcha, All Night Long*. It was the last great testament of a great singer. Turner died in 1985, but oh, how those melodies linger on   —D.M.

Tina Turner

  ★★★★   Private Dancer (1984; Capitol, 2000)
    ★★★   Break Every Rule (1986; Capitol, 1998)
    ★★★   Tina Live in Europe (Capitol, 1988)
  ★★★½   Foreign Affair (Capitol, 1989)
  ★★★½   Simply the Best (Capitol, 1991)
    ★★★   What's Love Got to Do With It (Virgin, 1993)
  ★★★★   The Collected Recordings—Sixties to Nineties (Capitol, 1994)
  ★★★½   Wildest Dreams (Virgin, 1996)
    ★★★   Twenty Four Seven (Virgin, 2000)

Following an unproductive stint with United Artists in the late '70s, following an escape from an abusive Ike Turner, a wiser and harder Tina Turner emerged in 1984, having forsaken R&B entirely in favor of a high-gloss, high-tech, hard-rock sound heavy on electronic drum programs and synthesizer flourishes. In one fell swoop, *Private Dancer* (now out of print) captured the zeitgeist of the Me Decade with its cynicism and its solipsism. It made Turner an international star on her

own considerable merits. The song that got her over was "What's Love Got to Do with It," which logged three weeks at #1, and in its title alone, much less its scabrous lyrics, said it all about a decade in which romance took a major hit. "Private Dancer" was even more insidious: Its bluesy patina, irresistible hook, and gritty, R&B-drenched vocal sucked in listeners who then heard the song being rendered from the disengaged viewpoint of an erotic dancer whose only pleasure is in the money men give her.

But Turner was indeed speaking only for herself, not for America, no matter what dimensions her song took on. It was left for her autobiography, *I, Tina*, written with Kurt Loder, to cut away the scar tissue left by her impoverished childhood and the wrenching years with Ike, and allow her to come out whole and to enjoy flexing her muscle as a solo act.

Through the '80s she built up an enormous reservoir of goodwill with fans and critics who saw in her struggle a genuine triumph over forces that would overwhelm less hardy souls. She toured incessantly after *Private Dancer* broke big, so it was unsurprising that the similarly-styled followup, *Break Every Rule*, failed to generate the heat or sales of its predecessor. *Foreign Affair* was closer to the bone. Featuring a number of songs by the redoubtable swamp rocker Tony Joe White (who also contributed some suitably grungy guitar licks), the album had more of a blues edge than anything Turner had done since leaving Ike, even though its sound is grounded in contemporary rock. The old ebullience has returned to her voice here, especially in her alluring moans. On "The Best" she brought virtue to the big, booming, and justifiably maligned power ballad simply on the strength of her ferocious approach to the lyrics. Even better, "Undercover Agent for the Blues" took her back to her roots in its blues shadings and right into the present with its pop sheen. *Simply the Best* kicked off a new decade by summarizing Turner's '80s work, but also takes a broader overview by including the towering Ike and Tina single, "River Deep, Mountain High," remastered by original producer Phil Spector, as well as the " '90s Version" of Ike and Tina's 1973 hit, "Nutbush City Limits."

But the '90s proved to be the time when Tina stopped and smelled the roses. She didn't release a new studio album until 1996's *Wildest Dreams*, a feisty set of tunes and performances highlighted by a suggestive duet with Barry White on the title cut. But it's not as if she had disappeared: Virgin's *What's Love Got to Do With It* and Capitol's multidisc *The Collected Recordings—Sixties to Nineties* remind anyone who hears these CDs of the serious work she had done in her long career. *What's Love Got to Do With It* is the soundtrack to her similarly-titled biopic, whereas *The Collected Recordings* is an essential set, three discs, 48 tracks, covering the years with Ike, the finest of the solo recordings, and a third disc of rarities from different periods. By 2000, she was billing herself solely as "Tina" and promoting a new studio album, *Twenty Four Seven.* Changing producers, she teamed up with Brian Rawling and Mark Taylor (who had masterminded Cher's comeback hit, "Believe") for a result that was more rock than soul, and way overproduced; however, Turner seems incapable of giving it less than all she has, and the sheer energy emanating from her keeps things interesting here. She speaks now of cutting back even more on her road schedule and seems to be enjoying every little nuance of her success. To that one can only say she deserves all the success she's experienced, because she is, after all, Tina.   —D.M.

The Turtles

★★½	It Ain't Me Babe (1965; Sundazed, 1994)
★★½	You Baby (1966; Sundazed, 1994)
★★★	Happy Together (1967; Rhino, 1983)
★★★	The Turtles Present the Battle of the Bands (1968; Sundazed, 1994)
★★★	20 Greatest Hits (Rhino, 1982)
★★★½	The Best of the Turtles (Rhino, 1987)
★★½	Turtle Wax: The Best of the Turtles, Vol. 2 (Rhino, 1988)
★★½	Captured Live (Rhino, 1992)

While hitting the Top 10 in 1965 with Bob Dylan's "It Ain't Me Babe" and releasing a number of P.F. "Eve of Destruction" Sloan songs, this L.A. band proved too gigglesome an outfit for the philosophical strainings of folk rock; they moved on to infectious, and exuberantly slight, radio fluff. With Howard Kaylan and Mark Volman, the Turtles possessed two strong lead singers—of a visual mold riotously at odds with rockstar stereotypes—and their combination of careful song selection and self-mocking humor made them successful and endearing. "Happy Together" (1967) remains their most memorable track; released the same year, "You Know What I Mean" and "She'd Rather Be With Me" were also crafty rock candy. With the same eccentricity that later found Volman and Kaylan recording with Frank Zappa, and, as "Flo and Eddie," singing backup for T. Rex, the Turtles expressed a laudable, if occasional, discontent with their limited role as hitmakers. They flexed this urge not only on the concept album *The Turtles Present the Battle of the Bands* (the album has the group doing sendups of a vast range of styles) but also in an artful choice of songwriters, Harry Nilsson and Warren Zevon among them. Rhino's *20 Greatest Hits* exhaus-

tively covers the straighter Turtles; *Turtle Wax* does the same for the bent.   —P.E.

Shania Twain

★	Shania Twain (Mercury, 1993)
★★★★	The Woman In Me (Mercury, 1995)
★★★★½	Come On Over (Mercury, 1997)
★★★	Up! (Mercury, 2002)

In the mid '90s, a one-time lounge singer from Timmons, ON, who had suffered childhood poverty and the deaths of both parents in a car crash turned the country music establishment on its ear. Despite Nashville's need for a rags-to-riches backstory, Shania Twain was resisted at first by many in the Music City, not only because she was Canadian (and thus an outsider), but also because she often wore midriff-baring outfits which didn't fit the traditional image of a chaste country chanteuse.

At first, Twain was presented as a harmless novelty—the cover of her first album portrays her in a fur-lined parka, next to a wolf, and the music is conveyor-belt Nashville fare, sung with a Southern trill. But then Robert John "Mutt" Lange, the architect of such multiplatinum hard-rock opuses as Def Leppard's *Hysteria* and AC/DC's *Back in Black* proposed a collaboration (Twain and Lange would eventually marry), and the result was *The Woman In Me.* Twain and Lange wrenched conventional pop-country from its genteel moorings by outfitting *The Woman In Me* with sexy come-ons, boom-boom-bap beats, and massed vocal choruses straight out of Leppard's "Pour Some Sugar On Me." Singles like "Any Man of Mine" and "If You're Not In It For Love" not only rocked every line-dance club in the U.S., but the foundations of Music Row itself.

But *Woman*'s achievements were chicken feed compared to those of *Come On Over*, the sixth biggest selling record of all time. Fiddles and steel guitar provide nominal country window dressing, but this album is pristine pop that boasts a Sistine Chapel–level of craftsmanship. Whether squeaking a la Cyndi Lauper or purring as if she were caught in coital bliss, Twain articulates various states of romantic satisfaction and dissatisfaction: She tells her man to quit micromanaging her ("Don't Be Stupid") or celebrates a relationship's endurance (the monumental wedding band staple "You're Still the One"). Unlike Garth Brooks, her only peer in the country crossover sweepstakes, Twain's music burns ahead without a touch of egotism or vague gravitas, and women around the world identified with her while humming the tunes.

Up! released after a five-year pause, contains two discs: one mixed for the country market, one for the pop market (an eastern mix is available overseas). Here, *Come On Over*'s reach was expanded to ABBA tributes ("C'est la Vie") and Latin-pop ("Juanita"), but the album is also larded with filler. Still, Twain and Lange had managed a truly rare feat: making borderless, omnivorous pop from one of the most closed-off American idioms. —R.K.

The Twilight Singers

- ★★ Twilight as Played by the Twilight Singers (Sony, 2000)
- ★★★ Blackberry Belle (One Little Indian, 2003)

Greg Dulli, leader of heavy-breathing rockers the Afghan Whigs, started the Twilight Singers in 1997 as a folk/trip-hop collaboration with two other singers, Harold Chichester (Howlin' Maggie) and Shawn Smith (Brad). Due to various band and record-company obligations, *Twilight* wasn't released until 2000; in the meantime, Dulli had significantly revised the album, with help from the British remixing duo Fila Brazillia. The result is a hodgepodge. Folkier songs such as "That's Just How That Bird Sings" fail to convince, while the bleak electronic vistas of "Annie Mae" and "Last Temptation" are only intermittently engaging.

Blackberry Belle features Dulli as lead vocalist on all but one track (the closing "Number Nine," graced by Mark Lanegan's funereal croak) and hangs together much better. From the very first couplet of opener "Martin Eden"—"Black out the windows/It's party time"—the Twilight Singers set a dark and desperate mood that suits the harder, denser sound. Dulli's obsession with misery can be hard to take, but at least his tunes have more body this time out. —M.R.

Twisted Sister

- ★★ Under The Blade (Secret, 1982)
- ★★ You Can't Stop Rock And Roll (Atlantic, 1983)
- ★★★ Stay Hungry (Atlantic, 1984)
- ★★ Come Out And Play (Atlantic, 1986)
- ★★ Love Is For Suckers (Atlantic, 1987)
- ★★★ We're Not Gonna Take It (Rhino, 2003)

Twisted Sister had the metal anthem of summer 1984, "We're Not Gonna Take It." Dee Snider, a Long Island biker dude in Kinko-the-Clown makeup and a blonde mane, used SAT words like "trite," "jaded," and "confiscated" as he bellowed against the oppressive forces holding him down. Sister was kind of like the hair-metal version of their Strong Island homey in Public Enemy—Snider even vows, "We'll fight the powers that be!" Sister never had another big hit, but came close with "I Wanna Rock" (answering the ques-

tion, "What do you want to do with your life?") and the Alice Cooper duet "Be Cruel To Your School." Snider walked it like he talked it, testifying in the U.S. Senate against the PMRC censors. Always a talk show fixture, he bizarrely became MSNBC's official voiceover man in 2002. But his most memorable moment may be in the liner notes to *Come Out And Play.* After the standard equipment endorsement blurbs, there's a blurb explaining that Snider neither uses nor endorses the latest Vidal Sassoon hairstyling gel: "You blew it, Vidal!" —R.S.

2 Live Crew

- ★★★ The 2 Live Crew Is What We Are (Luke, 1986)
- ★★★ Move Somethin' (Luke, 1987)
- ★★★★ As Nasty as They Wanna Be (Luke, 1989)
- ★★★ Banned in the U.S.A. (Little Joe, 1990)
- ★½ Sports Weekend: As Nasty as They Wanna Be, Pt. 2 (Luke, 1991)
- ★★★★ 2 Live Crew's Greatest Hits (Luke, 1992)
- ★½ The Real One (Little Joe, 1998)
- ★★★ Greatest Hits, Vol. 2 (Little Joe, 1999)

On the one hand, Miami's 2 Live Crew were true hip-hop pioneers, crossing over to the mainstream with pornographic raps and booty bass beats, setting legal precedents while lowering the bar (and making sure the bar stayed open) for a flood of foul-mouthed and/or party-centric music to follow (everyone from Lil' Kim and Lil Jon to 95 South and Insane Clown Posse owe them big time). On the other hand, if filling-rattling uptempo 808 beats and wildly puerile rhymes are not to your taste, 2 Live Crew can be dismissed. Despite 2 Live Crew's being a ubiquitous presence on Florida's musical map, they actually started out in California, releasing the single "Revelation" on the Macola label in 1985. When they moved to Miami, local record pimp Luther Campbell (a.k.a. Luke Skyywalker) both signed and joined the group, and 2 Live Crew thus assumed their classic incarnation. With their green satin jackets, gold-toothed leers, and the paunchy presence of "The Chinaman" (a.k.a. MC Fresh Kid Ice) in their ranks, 2 Live Crew looked considerably different from your average East Coast crew. Raunchy and proud, the group's 1986 release "We Want Some Pussy" (which had echoes of both Richard Pryor's blue humor and blueswoman Lucille Bogan's 1930s hit "Shave 'Em Dry") kicked their notoriety into high gear. By 1989's multiplatinum *As Nasty as They Wanna Be*, the group was something like a filthy rap version of Weird Al Yankovic, flipping songs by Jimi Hendrix and Roy Orbison into potty-mouthed sing-alongs. Song titles such as "Me So Horny" and "If You Believe in Having Sex" tell the tale. In short order, 2 Live Crew and massive litigation became frequent bedfellows. George Lucas sued Skyywalker/Campbell for trademark infringement, and Luther shortened his alias to Luke. Numerous serpentine suits alleged that *As Nasty as They Wanna Be* was legally obscene and therefore illegal to sell. And in 1994, the Orbison estate alleged that a parody of "Oh, Pretty Woman" was in fact plagiarism—a suit that went all the way to the Supreme Court (2 Live Crew won). In 1995 Luke left the group, who continued flaccidly without him.   —P.R.

2Pac/Tupac Shakur

★★★	2pacalypse Now (Interscope, 1991)	
★★★★★	Strictly 4 My N.I.G.G.A.Z. (Jive, 1993)	
★★★	Me Against the World (Interscope, 1995)	
★★★★★	All Eyez on Me (Death Row, 1996)	
★★★	Don Killuminati: The 7 Day Theory (Death Row, 1996)	
★★	R U Still Down? (Remember Me) (Jive, 1997)	
★★★★★	Greatest Hits (Death Row, 1998)	
★	Still I Rise (Interscope, 1999)	
★★	The Rose That Grew From Concrete (Interscope, 2000)	
★	Until the End of Time (Interscope, 2001)	
★	Better Dayz (Interscope, 2002)	
★★	Tupac: Resurrection (Interscope, 2003)	

In roughly five short years of recording, Tupac Shakur became the epitome of everything that was right, wrong, and way over the line about hip-hop. He was born to his Black Panther mom while she was in jail, convicted for a case that became known as the New York 21. He was raised mostly in poverty by his mom in New York, Baltimore, and Oakland, where he would meet the members of Digital Underground, who gave him a start as a dancer and a roadie. His debut album, *2Pacalypse Now,* was released to almost immediate acclaim in 1991. Because we think of Tupac Amaru Shakur as one who lived fast and died young in the name of thug life, we can forget that he emerged on *2Pacalypse Now* as a very militant, conscious, anti-po-po rapper, not to mention one who came on riding Ice Cube's lyrical jock. Before Tupac became the epitome of black genocide and misogyny in gangsta form, Pac, true to his Panther genealogy, was only out to get the cops and the government. On the flip side of his mau-mau wrath was his remarkable capacity to see the world through the eyes of the 'hood's female survivors; "Brenda's Got a Baby" is one of his storytelling masterpieces—perhaps the only hip-hop song to identify and empathize with a tragic ghetto girl driven to dump her baby in the trash.

Strictly 4 My N.I.G.G.A.Z. picks up where *2pacalypse* left off. In search of his own voice, he continues to impersonate Cube when not biting Pete Rock. At the end of the day, Pac was arguably a better actor than an MC, as his appearances in *Fresh,* John Singleton's *Poetic Justice* (with Janet Jackson), and *Gridlocked* prove. What Pac lacked in lyrical invention and wit he made up for in passion, urgency, and charisma. The difference between him and a lyric lover's MC like Ice Cube, Snoop, Chuck D, or Biggie is that the truly great MCs have so much music in their voice, they can make a hook out of how they pronounce one word into. Hell, Biggie could do your phone number and make it sound like butter. Pac has a big stage voice, but it's not so jazzy. He has to be saying something of deep meaning, to himself at least, to move those of us who aren't cult members. Thankfully, *Strictly* finds him with a lot on his mind. He comes with a sense of drive and eruptive, dissident, dissonant fervor worthy of *Fear of a Black Planet* and *AmeriKKKa's Most Wanted.* In many ways, it's his best constructed and most coherent album, and it's also his most militantly political. As with *2Pacalypse,* when *Strictly* breaks for sensitivity, it's all about the sistas in the struggle: "Keep Ya Head Up" may be the most universally embraced song he ever wrote; it manages to pay tribute to black women without pandering, patronizing, or getting all soporific. By the same token, "I Get Around" is his catchiest and bounciest sex song. The presence of Pac's former employer Shock G, from Digital Underground, certainly doesn't hurt the cause in that regard.

By the time 1995's *Me Against the World* came out, Pac had spent the previous year caught up in a world of trouble. He was shot during a robbery attempt in the lobby of a studio while on the way to a Notorious B.I.G. session. By suggesting that Biggie had participated in a setup, he began the war with the East Coast that would culminate in his and Biggie's shooting deaths in 1996 and 1997, respectively. In 1995 Pac was cleared of attempted murder charges against two off-duty cops but was sentenced for four years imprisonment on a rape charge. No wonder, then, that every song on *Me Against the World* seems obsessed with death, betrayal, and a world of pain. At every turn, the morbidity is undercut by warm, laid-back R&B production moves that would soothe a Brian McKnight fan. The album reminds us once again that Pac's powerful life force and equally powerful death urges were locked inside the most tortured soul hip-hop has ever seen. (Eminem notwithstanding—not even hardly.) Of course, there's also "Dear Mama," yet another song for his mother and for all the indefatigable ghetto matriarchs everywhere. Play it to a roomful of the rock-hardest negroes you can find, and we guarantee there won't be a dry eye in the house. (P.S. This was also the first hit album by an artist in lockdown.)

During the 10 months or so Pac spent in California's Clinton Correctional Facility, he came fully under the sway of the estimable Suge Knight, the gang-affiliated label owner of his label. This may be the reason *All Eyez on Me* contains not only the most ruggish-thuggish sentiments he'd ever commit to tape but also the horniest. Hypersexed groupie girls are given ample attention, as are the Dodge City codes of West Coast gang culture. By this time, the thug-life thing had taken hold of Pac's mind, body, and soul; it was his bailiwick, and he was sticking with it. Still, this may be the only gangsta-rap album you need to own, and perhaps the only one that ever needed to have been made. It's music for riding for sure, and every connotation of riding that one can imagine. Besides the preponderance of sex romps, easily explained by our antihero's many moons in the slammer, three of his best songs are here: the top-down cruising anthem "California Love," the foreplay-enabling "How Do You Want It?" (both proof that no one fused smoove and hardcore with more aplomb than this man, and "I Ain't Mad at Ya," a gospel-tinged love song to a cherished homie who came out of prison a straight-arrow Muslim and thought it wise to give Pac a wide berth.

Tupac's death came in September, 1996, just days after he was shot while sitting in Knight's car in a Las Vegas parking lot. This might have been the end of his life on earth, but it was hardly the end of his terrestrial recording career. With his mother overseeing his estate, it was guaranteed that every visit Pac had made to the studio would eventually see the light of day—mostly to diminishing effect. *Don Killuminati: The 7 Day Theory,* came from a marathon production period held just weeks before his death. Right down to its bloody-Jesus cover art, this ranks as Pac's creepiest—and in places most violent—album. On the opening track, "Bomb First (My Second Reply)," he marks the entire East Coast hip-hop pantheon for death. "Hail Mary" lays out the dread, paranoia, and morbidity of hip-hop's most deserved martyr complex, complete with tolling bells, chiming glockenspiels, and liturgical instruction befitting DMX. "Revenge is the sweetest joy next to getting pussy" is the bon mot here. The Teddy Riley knockoff "Toss It Up" tricks you, coming on first as a bumping bedroom breather, then attacking Dr. Dre for leaving Death Row, among other "dumb" moves.

Thankfully, the inevitable *Greatest Hits* collection turns out to be the hands-down winner among all hip-hop best-ofs. Like Madonna, Pac knew a few things some of his more lyrically skillful peers did not, like what a hook was and how a melody could help you find your way onto the radio. For these reasons, *Greatest Hits* easily earns its two-disc amplitude—not bad for a guy who only made records under his own name for five years. In hip-hop, we generally stop expecting hits from any artist after two albums or so because nearly every MC has used up his 25 years of being black and angry by his sophomore effort—and 15 minutes passes quicker than we often realize. Pac, on the other hand, the product of a dramatic upbringing, increased his bounty of experiences exponentially between each release. His propensity for stirring up stuff also had the effect of keeping his public's ear cocked to hear what he might say about his latest arrest, fight, shooting, court case, conviction, lockdown, hospital stay, gang association, or revenge cuckolding. Few MCs, hell, few artists in any genre have so obliterated the distinction between autobiography and imagination. That said, if you wonder what all the hoopla about Tupac is, this ample compilation will provide substance to the rumors that this guy had talent and songs and probably spent as much time perfecting his art as he did getting in and out of trouble.

By the time Mama Shakur got around to approving the release of *R U Still Down? (Remember Me),* she was already on shaky ground. The two disc album was full of more songs about thugs, blunts, bitches, and gats for sure, but they aren't even his second-best songs. Should you wonder if you're possibly missing out on leftovers, trust us, the wellspring of posthumous Tupac has officially run dry. As for *Until the End of Time,* a double album composed mainly of filler, well, there's a reason they're called outtakes, Ma. Tupac will surely be with us as long as there are cash registers and bar-code scanners, but some of these afterlife joints only serve to remind us that the most gangsta sound in the world is "ch-ching!" Ditto for *Still I Rise,* in which Tupac and some young friends try their hand at gangsta rap. "Letter to the President" is a song Dead Prez would've been proud to cut, but otherwise, this one is a long yawn. What do you call it when even the abyss stops winking back? What do you call it when history is doomed to repeat itself as neither tragedy nor farce? *Ch-ching!*

All you can say about *Better Dayz* is wow, there's not a speckle of irony in sight. Its saving grace: the acoustic-guitar-bedded duet with Nas on "Thugz Mansion." *The Rose That Grew From Concrete* is spoken-word tribute album featuring readings of Pac's poetry by Mos Def, Q-Tip, Dead Prez, Outlaws, Russell Simmons, Danny Glover, the late Babatunde Olatunji, and black poet/goddesses Sonia Sanchez and Nikki Giovanni. As a recognition of Tupac's iconic status by the tribe elders, it's nonpareil, sui generis, and all that. But the musical tracks are soft-core MOR funk, and it's tough to argue that every line from Pac's journals scans as poetic profundity. More ch-ching, yes, but in the name of love, struggle, and tribal closure, which might make it kind of okay.

Tupac: Resurrection is the soundtrack to a not-bad documentary from 2003. Eminem, 50 Cent, and Notorious B.I.G. completists will be interested for the rigged, Natalie Cole–esque cameos, and if you simply must have Tupac's first recorded appearance with Digital Underground, come on down. Otherwise, ch-ching! —G.T.

U2

"I told the people who came to our club gig last week that we were applying for the job," Bono told ROLLING STONE in 2001. "There were shouts of, 'What job?' And I said, 'Whaddya mean what job? The job of the best band in the world!'" That sentiment sums up a large part of U2's appeal: During an era when many great rock bands have been embarrassed by grand gestures, powerful anthems, and stadium tours, U2 has fulfilled millions of fans' desires for a larger-than-life band that speaks directly to their emotions. This was true from the band's beginnings in postpunk Ireland. Because albums such as *Boy, October,* and *War* had a grandiose sound long before the band's lyrics had anything especially grand to say, some listeners assumed that the quartet was self-impressed and shallow. But despite the occasional eloquence of issue songs like "Sunday Bloody Sunday," most U2 songs emphasize the sound of the band over the sense of the lyrics—an approach that, at its best, lends a majesty to the band's albums.

The ten tunes of the band's debut, *Boy,* are sturdily constructed and winningly melodic, from the rousing refrain of "I Will Follow" to the elegiac quiet of "The Ocean." But by far the most arresting thing about the band is its sound. U2's instrumental approach is fairly minimal, but the band parts company with its contemporaries by making sure that every part in its stripped-down arrangements is played for maximum impact. The ringing ostinatos and colorful chording provided by the Edge's echo-laden guitar play a large part in this, but he hardly carries all the melodic weight. Adam Clayton's bass line in "Twilight," for instance, doesn't just shore up the beat, but supplies a secondary melodic line; likewise, Larry Mullen's drums in "Stories for Boys" don't merely keep time, but also provide musical cues to underscore the song's inner drama. Between them, the band's instrumental voices manage an almost greater eloquence than Bono's amiably heroic vocals.

The same principle holds for *October,* although not for the same reasons. The band as a whole suffers from sophomore slump here, and Bono seems particularly at a loss, making an impressive noise but precious little sense in "Gloria," "With a Shout," and "I Threw a Brick Through a Window." But *War* more than makes up. Not only is the writing more tightly focused, but the band leaps nimbly between the personal ("New Year's Day," "Two Hearts Beat as One") and the political ("Sunday Bloody Sunday") without a single misstep. Even better, the instrumental palette is richer and more varied, finding room for everything from the martial funk of "Sunday Bloody Sunday" to the shimmering acoustic touches of "Drowning Man."

The EP *Under a Blood Red Sky* offers a hint of how this translated in concert, but the vivid, bristling presence that producer Jimmy Iovine gets for it is worlds away from the rich, atmospheric aura producers Brian Eno and Daniel Lanois give the music on *The Unforgettable Fire.* On that album, the instrumental sound is blurred, giving the band a warmer, more intimate sound, one that brings out the emotional immediacy in

"Bad," and adds soul to the insistent thrust of "Pride." But that isn't the only change introduced by *The Unforgettable Fire:* With this album, Bono begins to explore his obsession with America. The intensely personal *Joshua Tree* album doesn't entirely avoid the political—how could it, with songs like "Mothers of the Disappeared"?—but such concerns seem secondary to the quest for love and identity described in songs like "With or Without You" and "I Still Haven't Found What I'm Looking For." Yet vivid as the album's wordplay may be, it's still the music that carries these songs, from the itchy throb of "Bullet the Blue Sky" to the racing pulse of "Where the Streets Have No Name."

At this point, the next logical move for U2 would have been a live album, but the bloated semi-live soundtrack album *Rattle and Hum* isn't quite what fans expected. Sure, it includes concert versions of hit singles like "Pride" and "I Still Haven't Found What I'm Looking For," but those are accompanied by cover material like "Helter Skelter" and "All Along the Watchtower." Moreover, not all of the album is live; indeed, some of the strongest performances, like the Bo Diddley–style "Desire" or the bluesy "When Love Comes to Town," are studio recordings. Granted, those inclined to nitpick will find plenty to niggle over, but as usual, it's wiser to pay less attention to the words than the notes.

And that goes double for *Achtung Baby.* Thanks to the sound-shaping technology applied to the Edge's guitar and Larry Mullen's drums, the band's sound is more intricate and articulate than ever, affording the album a stylistic range that runs from the techno grunge of "Zoo Station" to the hip-hop-inflected groove of "Mysterious Ways." That's not to say the lyrics don't deserve attention, for some—such as "So Cruel"—are as vividly evocative as the music they adorn. But just as his conspiratorial whisper inflames the desperate clangor of "The Fly," Bono's delivery often says more than the words themselves.

The quickly recorded *Zooropa* attempts to expand the band's new horizons even further, but gets mired in a quicksand of unwise groove and texture experiments—the result is an album with overlong, mostly unmemorable songs. *Pop* puts more emphasis on the songwriting; the best song is the one that sounds the most like classic, pre-*Achtung* U2: the sweeping "Staring At the Sun."

U2 emerged triumphantly with *All That You Can't Leave Behind,* having learned from the '90s to control their most excessive urges, but having lost none of their dramatic heft. "Walk On," "Beautiful Day," and "Stuck in a Moment You Can't Get Out Of" reveal a band that learned to draw inspiration from small personal victories, and to keep evolving. Make way for the biggest band in the world.   —J.D.C./N.B.

UB40

★★½	Signing Off	(Graduate UK, 1980)
★★½	The Singles Album	(Graduate UK, 1980)
★★★	Present Arms	(DEP UK, 1981)
★★½	Present Arms in Dub	(DEP UK, 1981)
★★★★	UB44	(DEP UK, 1982)
★★★	Live	(DEP UK, 1983)
★★★	1980–83	(A&M, 1983)
★★★½	Labour of Love	(A&M, 1983)
★★★	Geffery Morgan	(A&M, 1984)
★★½	The UB40 File	(Graduate UK, 1985)
★★★	Baggariddim	(DEP UK, 1985)
★★★	Little Baggariddim	(A&M EP, 1985)
★★★	Rat in the Kitchen	(A&M, 1986)
★★½	CCCP—Live in Moscow	(A&M, 1987)
★★★	UB40	(A&M, 1988)
★★½	Labour of Love II	(A&M, 1989)
★★★	Promises and Lies	(Virgin, 1993)
★★★	The Best of UB40, Vol. 1	(Virgin, 1995)
★★★	The Best of UB40, Vol. 2	(Virgin, 1995)
★★½	Guns in the Ghetto	(Virgin, 1997)
★★½	Labour of Love III	(Virgin, 1999)
★★★★	The Very Best of UB40 1980–2000	(Virgin, 2000)
★★½	Present the Fathers of Reggae	(Virgin, 2002)

UB40 earned its status as Britain's most popular reggae act not because the group is racially mixed or homegrown but because it has consistently taken a pop-friendly approach to the music. That's not to denigrate UB40's way with riddim, for the group has done a remarkable job in keeping up with the changes in reggae over the decades. But however supple or insinuating the beat, it's Ali Campbell's warm tenor and the group's melody-centered songwriting that make UB40 consistently worth hearing.

Although its earliest material (that is, the Graduate recordings, which include *Signing Off* and the compilations *The Singles Album* and *The UB40 File*) is fairly traditional reggae fare, the group's sound becomes progressively funky and dubwise through *Present Arms* (which features the throbbing "One in Ten") and *UB44* (which boasts the soulful, rhythmically vibrant "So Here I Am"). The compilation album *1980–83* introduced the band to American audiences, with no noticeable reaction, but U.S. interest picked up with *Labour of Love,* a collection of cover tunes that reprises many of the band's favorite early reggae hits. Campbell's vocals are particularly expressive, and the album eventually became a hit on the strength of the chart-topping single "Red Red Wine." Trouble is, it took four years, during which time UB40 had long since moved on. Indeed, *Geffery Morgan* picks up where *UB44* left off, adding more dub effects and continuing to play off the resilience of the rhythm section. There's also a growing eloquence to the songs' social content, for even though UB40—whose name derives from the standard U.K. unemployment compensation card—always had a political edge, songs such as "Riddle Me" and "As Always You Were Wrong Again" expertly articulate anti-Thatcherite class resentment.

UB40's next album, *Baggariddim,* wasn't released in its entirety in this country. In the U.K., the album combines an EP featuring a charming "I Got You Babe" (cut with Chrissie Hynde) with an album of dub remakes of tracks from *Labour of Love* and *Geffery Morgan;* in the U.S., *Little Baggariddim* delivers the EP plus a couple of dubs for a less-satisfying package. Nor does *Rat in the Kitchen* entirely return the band to strength, for despite the urgently percolating pulse of "All I Want to Do" and the engaging groove behind the title tune, songs such as "Don't Blame Me" and "The Elevator" seem forced.

With *UB40,* the band's pop instincts return to full working order. Hynde makes another guest appearance, this time covering the Sheila Hylton hit "Breakfast in Bed," but the band hardly needs the help, as the songs are wonderfully strong, from the relentless "Dance with the Devil" to the insinuating "I Would Do It for You." *Labour of Love II* isn't quite as appealing as its predecessor, despite the soul-cum-reggae groove of the Al Green tune "Here I Am (Come and Take Me)," but *Promises and Lies* is as strong as any album in their catalogue, thanks to "Bring Me Your Cup" and the irresistible "Reggae Music."

Unfortunately, that was the band's last truly great album of original material. *Guns in the Ghetto* has good instincts and solid playing but generally weak material, while both *Labour of Love III* and *Fathers of Reggae* depend on oldies, although in the latter case, the oldies were written by UB40 and are sung by such reggae greats as Toots Hibbert, John Holt, Ken Boothe, Gregory Isaacs, and Alton Ellis. (Think of it as *Labour of Love* in reverse.)

As for the various best-of collections, *The Very Best of,* is, in fact, the very best, distilling the cream of the band's work into 18 solid-gold tracks. The other two sets offer more depth, but frankly would be a better buy as a double-disc set than as two individual albums. —J.D.C.

James Blood Ulmer

★★★★ Tales of Captain Black (1979; DIW, 1999)
★★★½ Are You Glad to Be in America (1981; DIW, 1995)
★★★ Free Lancing (Columbia, 1981)
★★★½ Black Rock (Columbia, 1982)
★★★★ Odyssey (1983; Columbia, 1996)
★★★½ Part Time (Rough Trade, 1984)
★★★½ Live at the Caravan of Dreams (Caravan of Dreams, 1986)
★★★ America: Do You Remember the Love? (Blue Note, 1987)
★★★ Blues All Night (In + Out, 1990)
★★ Black and Blues (DIW, 1991)
★★★ Blues Preacher (1992; DIW/Columbia, 2002)
★★★ Live at the Bayerischer Hof (In + Out, 1995)
★★★ Music Speaks Louder Than Words (Koch Jazz, 1997)
★★★½ Blue Blood (Innerhythmic, 2001)
★★★★ Memphis Blood: The Sun Sessions (2001; Sin-Drome, 2003)
★★★★ No Escape From the Blues: The Electric Lady Sessions (Sin-Drome, 2003)

Guitarist James "Blood" Ulmer got his start with saxophonist Ornette Coleman, a jazzman most noted for his pioneering efforts with free jazz, and later for harmolodics, an arcane (if influential) theory of collective improvisation. All of which makes Coleman—and, by extension, Ulmer—seem pointy-headed and off-putting.

But Ulmer, like Coleman, has his roots in the blues, and it's that gut-level urtext that ultimately shapes the guitarist's sound and sensibility. No matter how "outside" his improvisations may get, they're generally blessed with an emotional grounding that makes them approachable, if not embraceable.

Sounding like an especially trippy acid-rock outing, *Tales of Captain Black* (which credits Ulmer as "James Blood" and features Coleman) is thrilling and intimidating, pushing the envelope in terms of harmony, melody, and rhythm. Avant-jazz fans should be pleased.

But with *Are You Glad to Be in America?,* Ulmer moves to a more blues-oriented sound, working off obviously backbeat-grounded grooves as well as singing on a few numbers. The disparity between selections such as the R&B-oriented title tune and the free-blowing "Revelation March," however, may be a bit much for listeners whose blues experience doesn't extend beyond B.B. King and Eric Clapton.

Moving up to the majors, Ulmer consolidates his focus and tones down the experimental elements of his sound. *Free Lancing* even brings in backup singers for one track. *Black Rock* (a pun that refers both to the sound he evokes and the building that was then Columbia Records' New York headquarters) attempts to broaden Ulmer's appeal by taking a more varied approach instrumentally, but it was the stripped-down and rootsy sound of *Odyssey,* featuring a bassless trio with violinist Charles Burnham, that most successfully bridged the gap between his blues roots and jazz ambition. A pity the band did not find the audience it deserved.

Part Time and *Live at the Caravan of Dreams,* recorded live and emphasizing the more experimental end of his music, are fine companions to Coleman's electric albums from that era. But Ulmer, ever eager to broaden his audience, moved back toward mainstream fare with *America: Do You Remember the Love?,* a halfhearted attempt at crossover acceptability recorded under the aegis of fusion auteur Bill Laswell. This was followed by several albums in which Ulmer approached the blues through the intellectual filter of Coleman's theories, which was a reasonable strategy aesthetically, but not especially satisfying as music. By this point, Ulmer's desire to be accessible and intellectually impressive begins to verge on the schizophrenic, to such a degree that *Music Speaks Louder Than Words* finds him vacillating between emotionally charged covers of Ornette Coleman tunes and half-assed attempts at pop such as "Rap Man" (which, yes, boasts some very lame rapping).

Laswell reenters the picture with *Blue Blood,* which ups the pop ante by backing Ulmer with actual R&B musicians, among them P-Funk alum Bernie Worrell and Jerome "Bigfoot" Bailey. But it's *Memphis Blood* that finally gets the formula right. Produced by ex–Living Colour guitarist Vernon Reid and built around blues standards from the '50s ("Spoonful," "Little Red Rooster," "Back Door Man"), it's sufficiently grounded in conventionality that even Ulmer's most outside riffing connects with the listener. *No Escape From the Blues,* made with the same band, is even better. Had Howlin' Wolf followed Dave Brubeck's lead and made *Blues Goes to College,* it probably would have sounded like this. —J.D.C.

Ultramagnetic MC's

★★★★½   Critical Beatdown (Next Plateau, 1988)
★★★★   The Four Horsemen (Wild Pitch, 1993)
★★½   B-Side Companion (Next Plateau, 1997)

The Bronx-based Ultramagnetic MC's—MC Kool Keith, MC/producer Ced Gee, and DJs Moe Love and T. R. Love—debuted with 1988's *Critical Beatdown,* which blasts off with frenetic scratching on "Watch Me Now" and inflamed tea-kettle whistles on "Ease Back," and keeps the energy level off the meters. Funky James Brown samples and raw boom-bap beats fly at a fast and furious pace, while Ced Gee's commanding bellow and Kool Keith's urgent blurts take

turns snapping necks. Keith steals the show, maintaining a razor-sharp delivery even when spitting odd insults such as "Your head is triangle/Like a mango/Something I snack on" or rhyming over a "Louie Louie"–esque party riff on "Traveling at the Speed of Thought." The result was a bona fide classic of hip-hop's "golden age" of the late '80s and early '90s, an album that was mostly ignored at the time but whose reputation has grown exponentially in the years since.

Five years later, Ultramagnetic released the almost-as compelling *The Four Horsemen.* "This ain't no Flintstone or no Bedrock type shit," Kool Keith assures on "Checkin' My Style," and he follows through with seeds of the unhinged lyricism that would later mark his solo efforts. The beats pack the same unstoppable energy that *Critical Beatdown* delivered, but producers Ced Gee and Godfather Don also add chaotic layers and abstract tangents into the mix. The jazzy vibe of "See the Man on the Street" bristles into an abrasive underlying buzz, and "Raise It Up" is fueled by a rowdy group chant. The album's highlight, though, is "Saga of Dandy, the Devil & Day," an earnest, slow-rolling tribute to the unsung talents of baseball's Negro Leagues.

B-Side Companion, a collection of remixes, live cuts, and radio promo versions, is essential only for Ultramagnetic fanatics; many of the remixes aren't substantially different from their originals, and the collection never really gels. —K.M.

Uncle Tupelo

★★★½   No Depression (1990; Columbia/Legacy, 2003)
★★★   Still Feel Gone (1991; Columbia/Legacy, 2003)
★★★½   March 16–20, 1992 (1992; Columbia/Legacy, 2003)
★★★★   Anodyne (Sire, 1993)
★★★   89/93: An Anthology (Columbia/Legacy, 2002)

Uncle Tupelo started out as a punk band that didn't discriminate against acoustic instruments. The Belleville, IL, band was founded by boyhood friends Jay Farrar and Jeff Tweedy (who would later go on to greater fame in Son Volt and Wilco, respectively). From the start, they blended rock dynamics with string-band textures, scorching electric guitars with whining pedal steels, and Appalachian-style ballads with blasts of feedback. These guys would've been booted out of any self-respecting bluegrass festival for their lack of chops, but the songs were unusually mature. "No Depression," the title track of the debut album, is an old Carter Family tune, also adopted by the group's following as an umbrella term for an emerging neo-country movement. But the four Uncle Tupelo albums are broader in scope than that narrow definition might suggest. *No Depression* at times sounds more like the Minutemen than it does a neo-country band, with its herky-jerky arrangements and harsh guitar spasms. Farrar sings of the "same town blues" in the opening "Graveyard Shift," and the album details Rust Belt life with first-person authenticity: dead-end jobs, the solace found at the bottom of a whiskey bottle, "the sound of people chasin' money and money gettin' away."

Still Feel Gone is more of the same; in one song the trio of twentysomething Midwesterners tries to sound like 70-year-olds pickin' and grinnin' 'round the still, in the next it's paying homage to the Minutemen's D. Boon. *March 16–20, 1992* is an all-acoustic detour, produced by R.E.M.'s Peter Buck. Nearly half the album is traditional country and folk ballads, including the Louvin Brothers' "Atomic Power." Many in the band's hard-core following consider this Tupelo's crowning achievement, but the earnestness of the first-person coal-miner and moonshiner narratives is overbearing at times.

By the time of *Anodyne*, Tweedy and Farrar were collaborators only for publishing purposes, taking their songs down separate roads as a prelude to their breakup the following year. Farrar delivers plaintive ballads, Tweedy the twangy pop. But the unsung star is a new addition to the band, multi-instrumentalist Max Johnston, whose battery of stringed instruments gives the potentially schizophrenic album a cohesion and consistency that make it Tupelo's finest effort. —G.K.

Underworld

★★★★	Dubnobasswithmyheadman (Wax Trax!, 1993)
★★★★	Second Toughest in the Infants (Wax Trax!, 1996)
★★	Beaucoup Fish (Junior Boy's, 1999)
★★★½	Everything, Everything (JBO, 2000)
★★★	A Hundred Days Off (JBO, 2002)
★★★★	Underworld 1992–2002 (V2, 2003)

Karl Hyde (vocals) and Rick Smith (guitar) were just another couple of new-wave wankers until DJ Darren Emerson joined them in 1990, helping reenvision Hyde's moody sonnets for a techno-conscious world. The crew eventually became so successful at programming subversiveness into the commercial realm they've even formed a cutting-edge graphic-design company, Tomato, boasting Pepsi and Nike as clients.

Their *Dubnobasswithmyheadman* debut was released stateside in 1995. Its soulful techno careened

from the thoughtful new wave of Depeche Mode to the industrial dance grooves of Nine Inch Nails, with Hyde's existential crisis verging on nihilism. "Mmm Skyscraper I Love You" discovers God in Elvis while "Dirty Epic" imagines "Christ on crutches." Rick Smith's guitar lends avant atmospherics to the album's more somber moments. The trio sounds more cyborg on its followup, *Second Toughest in the Infants*, with the gritty mutating breakbeats steamrolling into jungle before easing up on tracks such as "Blueski," which finds Hyde "wearing stone-washed jeans again, carrying something wrapped in plastic" and Smith's guitar invoking a 23rd-century John Fahey. That album was propelled by the hit single "Born Slippy"—a frantic, pounding rush that ebbed into junkie-fix clarity—featured on the *Trainspotting* soundtrack. Too bad the trio come off as plain pretentious on *Beaucoup Fish* with Hyde's spoken word and faux blooze the ultimate test of listener patience, but they manage to salvage some of the better tracks on the live *Everything, Everything*, exciting if only for the cheering arena of ravers. Emerson left the band in 2000 to explore his own music, with some of his mixes featured in the excellent Global Underground series. Hyde and Smith released *A Hundred Days Off* without him, and the results are surprising: a highly danceable progressive house album that sounds only occasionally derivative. —C.S.

UNKLE

★★★★	Psyence Fiction (Mo' Wax, 1998)
★★	Never Never Land (Island/Mo' Wax, 2003)

UNKLE was founded in the early '90s by Mo' Wax label chief James Lavelle and engineer/producer Tim Goldsworthy (who would later go on to form the influential DFA production team and label). Like the late-era Beastie Boys who took in disparate sounds and styles to form one unique, utterly hip front, UNKLE's sound and vision was an amalgamation of British rave culture, American hip-hop, skateboarding, graffiti, and science fiction: the B-boy-centric version of the trip-hop subgenre that included Massive Attack, Portishead, and Tricky.

The group, its core members of Lavelle and Goldsworthy with a shifting cast of collaborators, rose to prominence with the Mo' Wax label in the mid-'90s, executing a number of remixes for then "it" bands such as Tortoise and the Jon Spencer Blues Explosion. Lavelle was always an idea man, a Warholian figure who was good at finding himself in the right place at the right time, with the right people. When it came time to make UNKLE's first proper album, he aligned himself with Mo' Wax's flagship artist, DJ Shadow. *Psyence Fiction* seemed to take an eternity to make, finally arriving in 1998 under a mountain of hype, with its rumored label-breaking budget and all-star cameos. Because it wasn't Shadow's *Endtroducing* or the electronica answer to Radiohead's *OK Computer* as some had hoped, and because of that, it was seen as a critical and commercial disappointment. But time has been kind to the debut. On "Guns Blazing (Drums of Death Pt.1)," New York rhyme legend Kool G Rap rages over Shadow's rampaging drum programming, while elsewhere Radiohead's Thom Yorke and the Verve's Richard Ashcroft guest on two stellar, longing ballads ("Rabbit in Your Headlights" and "Lonely Soul," respectively). If *Psyence Fiction* was awaited with baited breath, the followup, *Never Never Land*, barely raised an eyebrow. With Shadow long gone to work on his own projects, Lavelle enlisted the help of singer/songwriter Richard File and released an album of scatterbrained, unfinished-sounding ideas. With Mo' Wax folded, and UNKLE no longer a group of note, Lavelle has since taken to DJing, releasing several solid mix CDs. —C.R.

The Upper Crust

★★★½ Let Them Eat Rock (Upstart, 1995)
★★★ The Decline and Fall of the Upper Crust (Emperor Norton, 1997)
★★★ Entitled (Reptilian, 2000)
★★★ Once More Into the Breeches (Emperor Norton, 2001)

Dismiss Boston's Upper Crust as a joke rock band if you must, but give them this much: They're actually funny, *and* there's as much rock as mock to their singular brand of "roque." Moreover, you can see and hear elements of their shtick rock in a slew of bands that have come since, from the Darkness to Les Savy Fav. The gimmick—a hedonistic band of foppish, powdered-wigged 18th-century aristocrats—might suggest limited returns if not for the method-actor conviction delivered by frontman Lord Bendover, guitarists Duc D'istortion and Lord Rockingham (a.k.a. Ted Widmer, who left to write speeches for President Bill Clinton), drummer Jackie Kickassis, and bassist Count Bassie (successor to the Marquis de Roque). They don't just put on airs for cover shoots and stage wear; they stay gleefully in highfalutin character for every single song—from the opening title track of their 1995 debut, *Let Them Eat Rock*, to the gentry's lament, "You Can't Get Good Help," which closes 2001's *Once More Into the Breeches*. Granted, the musical attack suggests a range of influences that begins and ends with AC/DC (right down to Bendover's dead-on Bon Scott sneer), and the debut claims the

lion's share of the best material—most notably the saucy "Little Lord Fauntleroy" and the hilarious "Friend of a Friend of the Working Class." But there's plenty of worthy riffs and double-entendre wit to go around on *The Decline and Fall*, the swaggering double-live *Entitled*, and especially *Into the Breeches*, which earns an extra half star for the salacious kick Bendover brings to "Badminton." —R.SK.

Urge Overkill

★★ Jesus Urge Superstar (Touch and Go, 1989)
★★ Americruiser (Touch and Go, 1990)
★★½ The Supersonic Storybook (Touch and Go, 1991)
★★★ Stull (EP) (Touch and Go, 1992)
★★★★ Saturation (Geffen, 1993)
★★★ Exit the Dragon (Geffen, 1995)

Urge Overkill initially trafficked in smirks and sarcasm, with matching suits, shades, and swinging U.O. medallions that made the Chicago trio the flannel decade's answer to the Rat Pack. *Jesus Urge Superstar* and *Americruiser*, produced by indie-rock icons Steve Albini and Butch Vig, respectively, are pretty impenetrable, if not downright unlistenable mélanges of kitsch-culture posturing and unjustified swagger. *The Supersonic Storybook* is slightly more focused, with new drummer Blackie Onassis ratcheting up the energy; the rough-hewn vocals and ultradry humor coalesce around some actual songs (notably the chugging "Candidate" and a creepy cover of the melodramatic "Emmaline").

Stull holds some of Urge's darkest originals, and its breakthrough song, a cover of Neil Diamond's "Girl, You'll Be a Woman Soon," was immortalized in Quentin Tarantino's movie *Pulp Fiction*.

Saturation is to grunge what Cheap Trick's *In Color* was to punk; it filters the era's earnest aggression into its arena-ready guitars, delirious drumming, and tongue-in-cheek chic. But Urge also injects eroticism and dark, droll humor, especially on "Bottle of Fur." The precision production by the Butcher Brothers, Joe and Phil Nicolo, makes the case that it's not just the style that sets Urge apart, but the songs.

In contrast, *Exit the Dragon* has the feel of a gritty demo tape, with stripped-down guitars and scruffy voices playing over spare drumbeats, topped off by bleak lyrics: "Hey, hey, I'm dead on arrival." Things bottom out on "The Mistake," presaging the trio's demise. The last thing one expected from a band that once mocked self-serious punks and grunge-rock grumps is an album preoccupied with breakups, burnout, and death, but that's exactly what *Exit the Dragon* is. —G.H.

Usher

★★½   Usher (LaFace/Arista, 1994)
★★★½   My Way (LaFace/Arista, 1997)
★½   Live (LaFace/Arista, 1999)
★★★   8701 (LaFace/Arista, 2001)
★★★½   Confessions (LaFace/Arista, 2004)

"Teen pop" is a term so broad it's practically useless—as if 13-year-olds and 19-year-olds have identical fantasy needs from their idols. Like a driver's license, the heavy breathing Usher Raymond is best reserved for the older girls. And like a driver's license, Usher spirits those girls far away from the security of parental supervision. Sure he's got a song called "Nice and Slow," but lines such as "I got plans/To put my hands/In places I ain't never seen" suggest that he has quite an elastic definition for both "nice" and "slow."

Since producer Puff Daddy didn't know what to make of him, *Usher* falls flat—Bad Boy on autopilot. But *My Way* is a persona coming into his own, ushered, if you will, by Jermaine Dupri. "U Make Me Wanna," with its yearning for "a new relationship," would be an unusually considered cheating song even by Nashville standards. Dupri's combo of hi-hat titters and Isley-styled acoustic guitar arpeggios can wear a little thin over 10 tracks, especially with guest raps from Lil' Kim and JD himself bogging down the proceedings, but this was the work of a major up-and-comer.

But when it came to following up *My Way*, Usher did take it nice and slow—except for a live album (which, since you can't hear a pelvic thrust, is less redundant than useless), he was mostly silent for four years. And then a Napster leak led Arista to delay the album *All About U*, which was released, with new tracks, as *8701* on, well, 8-7-01. The lead single, "U Remind Me," nails a particular romantic problem—trying not to fall for someone who reminds you of your ex—but it does so in a self-serving way disguised as sensitivity. Let's hope the little girls set him straight on that. While they're at it, they could let him know he has the worst case of cutesy pronounitis since Prince at his heights—eight U's in 15 songs, if you count "U-Turn." It all came together on *Confessions*—by now Usher had grown a personality and a famous ex-girlfriend (Chilli of TLC) whom he could allude to on record. The jumpy, Lil Jon–produced "Yeah" became a Godzilla-sized hit, and Usher was now the biggest male R&B singer on the scene.   —K.H./N.B.

Utah Saints

★★★★   Utah Saints (London, 1992)
★★★   Two (Nettwerk America, 2001)

Even if their celebratory sensibilities hadn't been at odds with the prevailing early-'90s mood of spooky techno and dour grunge, Utah Saints would have been an aberration. The giddy propulsion Tim Garbutt and Jez Willis generated seemed sparked not by MDMA brain frenzy but by old-time pop innovation. The club smash "Something Good," which looped Kate Bush over a staccato synth piano, sounded inevitable (Bush's voice had always seemed to have been electronically treated already). Elsewhere, the duo's self-titled debut set minimalist electronic patterns against a sledgehammer wallop—as if Philip Glass had written a marimba concerto for the NCAA Final Four.

Almost a decade after label squabbles sidelined them, Garbutt and Willis returned with *Two*, a more lively reunion than you might expect. In the intervening decade, the Big Beat wallop of Fatboy Slim and the Chemical Brothers had upped the stakes of instant gratification, and Utah Saints rose to the challenge with self-explanatory slabs of fun such as "Funky Music" and "Punk Club." But Big Beat's jock appeal had also burned itself out in the clubs. The Saints had returned to a world where the featureless pulse and ebb of trance music had flooded the dance floors. Back in '92, could even the most dire prophet have guessed that the end of the world would be this dull?   —K.H.

Ritchie Valens

★ La Bamba '87 and Other Great Rock n' Roll Classics (Original Sound, 1987)
★★★½ The Ritchie Valens Story (Del-Fi, 1993)
★★★½ Rockin' All Night: The Best of Ritchie Valens (Del-Fi, 1995)
★★★★ The Lost Tapes (Del-Fi, 1995)
★★★★★ Come On, Let's Go (Del-Fi, 1998)

Unlike Buddy Holly, with whom Ritchie Valens is forever linked by virtue of the 1959 plane crash that claimed their lives and that of the Big Bopper, Valens didn't leave behind a treasure trove of unreleased recordings; like Holly, though, what Valens did leave gives only a tantalizing hint of where he might have taken his music. While Holly may well have become the quintessential American pop artist and a producer of note, Valens seemed headed for more exotic turf, where he would have made explicit the connection between Afro-Cuban and Mexican song forms and rhythms and those of the then-nascent style called rock & roll. Valens remains a touchstone for Mexican-American artists who have followed him—you can't get to Los Lobos without going through Ritchie Valens. To get an idea of his indelible contribution to rock & roll, consider the critic Lester Bangs' citation of Valens as the prototypical punk guitarist whose signature "La Bamba" riff links Valens to a hard-edged, no-frills style of rock & roll later advanced by the Kingsmen, the Kinks, the Stooges, and the Ramones.

Born of Mexican Indian–American parents, Valens (né Richard Stephen Valenzuela) cherished the tradition of the Mexican song and honored it. By the time he entered Pacoima Junior High he was a competent instrumentalist and, like many of his peers, was fired up by the first blasts of rock & roll radio. At age 16 he joined a local band, the Silhouettes, as a guitarist, and in short order was also handling lead vocals. Eventually Valens met producer-manager Bob Keane, who began the painstaking process of shaping promising-but-primitive ideas into professional sounding, radio-friendly songs that captured the energy and hormone-driven passions of the archetypal '50s teen all at once. (This process is documented on disc two of the Come On, Let's Go box set and The Lost Tapes, both of which provide a cavalcade of previously missing material).

The slow-hushed "Donna" became Valens' biggest hit, peaking at #2 in December 1958. Valens' best-known song, "La Bamba," is based on a Mexican wedding huapango said to have as many as 500 verses in its original, ancient form (it dates back at least to the 14th century), and although it rose no higher than #22 in January 1959, its impact musically and culturally far outstrips any considerations of chart performance. (The song title also served as the title of a 1987 film bio of Valens, starring Lou Diamond Phillips as Ritchie, that reignited interest in his life and music. Los Lobos' recreations of Valens' music were nothing short of stunning.) Those who would rather bypass the history and go straight to the music without any alternate-take offroads will find the 22-track Rockin' All Night the best bang for the buck. Of the 23 total cuts on Valens' two officially released studio albums, only two are missing from this disc: "My Darling Is Gone" and a beautiful heartbreaker, "Now You're Gone" (the title sentiment is taken from a discarded lyric to "Donna"). For those who want maybe a dollop of history, The Ritchie Valens Story fits the bill nicely. Opening with a 21-minute narration by Valens' producer-manager, Bob Keane, who offers a fine thumbnail sketch of Ritchie's life and career and insights on the recording process, the album offers both the incomplete demo recording of "Come On, Let's Go" and the official release, as well as a demo and official version of "Donna," a demo of "Malaguena," the live cover of Eddie Cochran's "Summertime Blues" recorded at the Pacoima Jr. High concert, and the official release of "La Bamba," plus an eerie commercial Valens made promoting the Winter Dance Party tour followed by a radio air check from Des Moines, IA, announcing the deaths of Holly, Valens, and Richardson in a plane crash. Disc one of the *Come On, Let's Go* box contains all the tracks on Valens' two studio albums, titled *Ritchie* and *Ritchie Valens*, along with an alternate take of "Cry Cry Cry" and stereo recordings of "That's My Little Suzie" and "La Bamba."

Responding in 1960 to fans' requests for more Valens material, Keane released *In Concert at Pacoima Jr. High*, a live recording made in December 1958 and included now in the *Come On, Let's Go* box set. Given that the show seems to have been recorded by someone sitting in the audience, the sound on the original vinyl release was thin and cheesy; recent developments in audio restoration technology have allowed Keane to bring up Valens' performance in the mix, although he's mixed down the fierce audience reaction as well. Accompanied only by drummer Don Phillips ("a real swingin' cat," as Valens says in introducing him), Valens turns in an engaging performance, kicking off with a version of "Come On, Let's Go" with almost completely different lyrics than those on the official single, segueing into a lovely take on "Donna" and then rocking the house with a ferocious reading of his new buddy Eddie Cochran's "Summertime Blues." The live portion of the album encompasses only six cuts; the original side two of the vinyl edition featured some of the demos that have now shown up on *The Lost Tapes* and the *Come On, Let's Go* box (such material appearing on a 1960 release is almost unheard of, given that the labels had no interest in the historical merit of alternate takes and demos). In addition to "Malaguena," these tracks include a fragment titled "Rhythm Song," which is a Valens homage to Bo Diddley, with whom he had shared the bill (along with Eddie Cochran—imagine) at an Alan Freed Christmas show in New York. The CD version of the live album includes seven tracks unavailable on the vinyl version, two of them Keane's home-studio recordings, four of them Gold Star outtakes (including the band track of "La Bamba" and the "Ooh My Soul" fragment), plus the Winter Dance Party commercial.

With so much legit Valens material available, the Original Sound disc, *La Bamba '87 and Other Great Rock n' Roll Classics*, is rendered even more useless than it was in 1987. It purports to be a sampling of how Valens might have tailored his music for another era. Four versions of "La Bamba" are thus transfigured with an eye toward the contemporary dance market, including a Latino Power Mix and a Hi-tone Rock Box Mix, all of which add up to a rather arrogant dissing of an artist unable to defend himself. You can put

all manner of maracas, horns, and sampled vocals on a disc, and tell us "this is how 'La Bamba' would have sounded had Ritchie Valens lived to record it today," and the question remains, "Sez who?"   —D.M.

Paul Van Dyk

- ★★½   45 RPM (1994; Mute, 1998)
- ★★★   Seven Ways (1996; Mute, 1998)
- ★½   Paul Van Dyk's Nervous Tracks (Nervous, 1999)
- ★★½   Out There and Back (Mute, 2000)
- ★★½   The Politics of Dancing (Ministry of Sound, 2001)
- ★★★½   Global (Mute, 2003)

Nobody will ever accuse Berlin DJ and producer Paul Van Dyk of changing the face of anything but the people occupying his dance floors. Still, there's something to be said for sticking to your guns, and Van Dyk certainly has. Over a decade, he's become one of the most popular dance artists in the world, pushing a progressive-trance style that differs from its more punishing cousin thanks to sweeping synths, lush melodic refrains, and airy diva vocals. That style is best heard on the recent *Global*, a best-of featuring a bonus DVD. If you want to go further, 1994's *45 RPM* and 1996's *Seven Ways* are useful historically: Their mirror-smooth feel and pleasurably uncomplicated textures sent a ripple through the dance community, showing prog-trance's potentially wide appeal; when the latter was reissued in America a few years later, the spangly, evanescent 1998 single "For an Angel" was included on a bonus disc. *Out There and Back*, from 2000, offered more of the same, including vocal appearances by Saint Etienne singer Sarah Cracknell. *The Politics of Dancing* is a rather humdrum DJ mix, while *Paul Van Dyk's Nervous Tracks* is a cheap cash-in featuring four versions of a Joe T. Vanelli song and a couple of Van Dyk remixes.   —M.M.

Van Halen

- ★★★★   Van Halen (Warner Bros., 1978)
- ★★★★½   Van Halen II (Warner Bros., 1979)
- ★★½   Women and Children First (Warner Bros., 1980)
- ★★½   Fair Warning (Warner Bros., 1981)
- ★★★★   Diver Down (Warner Bros., 1982)
- ★★★★½   1984 (Warner Bros., 1984)
- ★★★   5150 (Warner Bros., 1986)
- ★★★   OU812 (Warner Bros., 1988)
- ★★   For Unlawful Carnal Knowledge (Warner Bros., 1991)
- ★★   Van Halen Live: Right Here, Right Now (Warner Bros., 1993)

During the '70s heyday of AC/DC, Aerosmith, and Led Zeppelin, girls could dance to hard rock but they couldn't really *strip*. Van Halen eagerly remedied that with a gloriously sleazy act that combined the power and finesse of fine heavy metal, the poofery of glam, and the outlandish showmanship of James Brown. David Lee Roth became a new archetype for the oversexed hard-rock frontman, displacing Robert Plant and Steven Tyler with vaudevillian panache. And Eddie Van Halen's fretboard prestidigitation created a radically new rock-guitar technique; only Page and Hendrix match up in terms of pure originality. With drummer Alex Van Halen and bassist Michael Anthony, they transformed hard rock into a rollicking burlesque show and paved the way for a whole generation of pop-metal followers.

Van Halen contains all of the band's hallmarks: the bad-boy boogie of "Runnin' with the Devil," the otherworldly guitar wizardry of "Eruption," a swaggering ode to a slut ("Jamie's Cryin' "), and a hyperenergized, this-is-the-way-we-do-it-in-Hollywood cover song (the Kinks' "You Really Got Me"). The group's major weaknesses are evident too, such as its lack of lyrical depth, side two duds, and penchant for oldtimey numbers hammed up for minstrelsy effect ("Ice Cream Man," a lecherous ditty originally by bluesman John Brim). The blistering *Van Halen II* takes the approach further, with an even more over-the-top cover ("You're No Good") and yet more inspired guitar pyrotechnics. Roth also steps more confidently into his character, developing his trademark bawdy squeal into a leitmotif and stepping back now and then to laugh at it all with canny self-awareness.

The band tried a tougher, more heavy-metal sound on *Women and Children First* and *Fair Warning,* but it flops due to the poor material and, significantly, a fairly humorless approach overall. Eddie Van Halen shows off a few new guitar tricks, but the most significant musical development is the synthesizer introduced at the end of *Fair Warning,* which would be exploited to greater effect on later albums.

Diver Down finds the band back in top form, entertaining with a smile and lots of squeals. The album contains a ridiculous five covers, but they're some of the band's best: "(Oh) Pretty Woman," "Dancing in the Street," and another Kinks cover, "Where Have All the Good Times Gone?," which jettisons the melancholy tone of the original in favor of a sexed-up

strut, something that has never done them wrong. The band's masterpiece and greatest commercial success, *1984,* is loaded equally with pop hits and rockers as hot as anything Van Halen had done before. But it was the pop numbers that broke: "Jump" is a trifle constructed wholly around the synth; guitars enter only as backup, and the solo is split between guitar and keyboard. Along with "Hot for Teacher" and "Panama," it was a megahit on MTV and established the band as one of the giants of the video age.

In 1985 Roth was kicked out and replaced by Sammy Hagar. Roth went solo and took with him the band's longtime producer, Ted Templeman. Both were key losses, and the bulk of the post-Roth material is insufferably dull and humorless. A majority of *5150,* like "Love Walks In" and the monster hit "Why Can't This Be Love," grew out of the synth work on *1984,* but at best it sounds like an imitation of the old band, and at worst sluggish and adrift. *OU812* is marginally better, mainly because of "Finish What Ya Started," a hilarious faux-country toe-tapper that is the best (i.e., funniest) song they recorded without Roth. The other hits, "When It's Love" and "Feels So Good," are astonishingly sedate for a band that tore so lustfully through "Hot for Teacher" just four years before.

Templeman returned to coproduce *For Unlawful Carnal Knowledge,* and some of the old fire returned with him. "Poundcake," the first track, is a tough, libidinous stomp that could have been a Roth cut back in the day. But from there the band sounds lost: "Judgement Day" (spelling courtesy of the band) is built on a Judas Priest–circa-'81 riff, something they should have been avoiding since '81; "Spanked" is a flaccid white-funk ode to a TV commercial for a phone sex line with painfully bad lyrics ("Both feet up, watchin' TV/Some place to feast my eyes/I always drift on commercials/But this one blew my mind"). Exit Templeman again; *Balance,* the last with Hagar before *his* ouster, is a disgrace, from the pseudo-religious "The Seventh Seal" (featuring, for real, the Monks of Gyuto Tantric University in Tibet) to Hagar's ode to smoking "Panama red" in "Amsterdam."

In 1996 Hagar was replaced by . . . Roth. But the reunited lineup lasted only long enough to record two songs for the greatest-hits album. The songs, "Can't Get This Stuff No More" and "Me Wise Magic," sound like Hagar cuts, and though it's nice to hear Diamond Dave again, it only tarnishes the memory. *Best of Vol. 1* is itself not a very useful retrospective; it omits "(Oh) Pretty Woman," "Hot for Teacher," "Dancing in the Street," and "You're No Good" and is dominated by mediocre post-Roth tracks. Two years after the aborted reunion with Roth, the band recruited its third singer, Gary Cherone of Extreme, who has even less personality than Hagar, though he can't really be blamed for the lifelessness of the music on *Van Halen III;* he's just hired pipes. In 2004 the band released the mishmash *Best of Both Worlds,* which featured alternating tracks from Roth and Haggar; the band hit the road with Haggar that same year. —B.S.

Armand Van Helden

★★★   Live from Your Mutha's House (Lightyear, 1997)

★★½   Enter the Meatmarket: Armand Van Helden's Sampleslaya (Columbia/Ruffhouse, 1997)

★★★   Greatest Hits (Strictly Rhythm, 1997)

★★★½   2 Future 4 U (Armed Records, 1999)

★★   Armand Van Helden's Nervous Tracks, Nervous Innovators Series, Vol 1. (Nervous, 1999)

★   Killing Puritans (Armed Records, 2000)

★★   Gandhi Khan (Armed Records, 2001)

★★★   Repro (Armed Records, 2001)

★★   Funk Phenomena, The Album (ZYX, 2003)

★★½   New York: A Mix Odyssey (Tommy Boy, Southern Fried, 2004)

Dance producer/superstar DJ Armand Van Helden's obsession with hip-hop has always informed his look, his attitude, and his music, in subtle and not-so-subtle ways. His paean to old-school hip-hop, *Sampleslaya,* is corny, but infectious, ripping huge riffs from notable sources like A Tribe Called Quest and Nas. While the early tribal tracks on the *Greatest Hits* compilation from Strictly Rhythm are top notch, he made his true mark on dance music with his late-'90s remixes of Tori Amos' "Professional Widow," CJ Bolland's "Sugar Is Sweeter," Nuyorican Soul's "Runaway," and the Sneaker Pimps' "Spin Spin Sugar"—the latter three of which can be found on his mix disc compilation *Repro.* With this run of singles, Van Helden essentially created a subgenre of dance music whole hog. By slurring the vocals, adding hiccupy effects, and shifting the basslines into double gear, he gave birth to speed garage, igniting a sensation that burned out as quickly as it burned up the dance floors. While others tried to follow his lead, they never succeeded like Van Helden. (Those seeking prespeed garage hits can hear them on *Nervous Tracks,* which follow in the tradition of New York garage, or the more exciting and better-produced *Live from Your Mutha's House.*)

The turn-of-the-century records were brave forays that more often faltered than succeeded in bridging the gaps between dance music and rock and rap. Van Helden tried to break from the constraining confines of four-on-the-floor house music. While he'd had

some success in mutating it, he decided to throw out the blueprint altogether with *Killing Puritans* and *Gandhi Khan,* two aggressive and uneven records. He sampled the Scorpions on *Puritans'* "Little Black Spiders" and Gary Numan on "Koochy," and the near-pornographic *Gandhi Khan* features the unintentionally hilarious throbbing deep house single "I Can Smell You." Van Helden's most coherent record, while also preaching eclecticism, is *2 Future 4 U,* which jumps gracefully from classic deep vocals ("Flowerz") to the salsa inflections of "Entra Mi Casa." "Alienz" proves that Van Helden could still bring the dark side to house music, with him rediscovering the distorted bass line. But this time, Van Helden slows it down and stretches it across the song's skeleton for an effect that resembles tech-step drum and bass. His latest releases find the producer resting on his once-ambitious laurels—by either rehashing his past (*Funk Phenomena,* which boasts the bubbly, unbeatable title track, and "Witch Doktor," his breakout 12-inch)—or other eras altogether. On *New York: A Mix Odyssey,* Van Helden mixes songs from '80s artists (Soft Cell, Blondie)—after the '80s revival had come and gone—with other producers who played their '80s card well (Felix Da Housecat). —T.R.

Vanilla Ice

★★★   To the Extreme (SBK, 1990)

★   Mind Blowin' (SBK, 1994)

★★★   Hard to Swallow (Universal, 1998)

★   Bipolar (Liquid, 2001)

For a million-selling pop star, Robert Van Winkle, a.k.a. Vanilla Ice, has had a pretty rough ride. His debut *To the Extreme* hit #1 in early 1991, and immediately, due to his numerous dubious claims to street cred, he became the willing punch line to any number of jokes regarding white rappers.

He has never recovered from that one blistering year in the sun. And yet his chart-topping Queen- and David Bowie–interpolating single from that year, "Ice Ice Baby," is a landmark that has never truly faded from view. The remainder of *To the Extreme* is a regrettable yet oddly charming curio of late '80s hip-hop production tropes, a rewrite of L.L. Cool J's "I Need Love" called, ahem, "I Love You," and some truly dumbfounding rhymes. To wit, this boast from "Play That Funky Music": "You're amazed by the V.I.P. posse/Steppin' so hard like German Nazi." The album, in addition to his thunderous lack of self-consciousness, doomed his public profile so completely that by the time his feature film *Cold as Ice* appeared a year later, he was drummed out of show business.

In 1994 he reappeared with dreadlocks and an astonishingly inept and hilarious "gangsta" record, *Mind Blowin.* Even the contemporaneous release of MC Hammer's *The Funky Headhunter* couldn't make Ice's paeans to marijuana ("Roll 'Em Up") or numerous attacks on persistent critics and fellow white rappers 3rd Bass seem less desperate by comparison. Again banished, he reappeared in 1998 with *Hard to Swallow,* in which he hitched his cart to the burgeoning rap-metal idiom. Produced by genre kingpin Ross Robinson, the record sounds as thick and vicious as Korn, and (surprise) the Iceman dumps eight years of resentment and recrimination into the mix, emerging with furious responses to his critics, as well as "Too Cold," an aggro retooling of "Ice Ice Baby." His most convincing music came when he appropriated the metallic white-MC style that he presaged. But it was all for naught; *Hard to Swallow* failed and was followed by 2001's utterly listless *Bipolar.* —R.K.

Little Steven Van Zandt

★★★½   Men Without Women (EMI, 1982)
★★★   Born Again Savage (Pachyderm, 1999)

Steve Van Zandt contributed much to the drama of Springsteen's early albums before departing from the E Street Band in 1984, and his writing and production for Southside Johnny and the Asbury Jukes helped elevate them to something more than merely the best bar band in the country. Absolutely committed to classic rock & roll in the Rolling Stones tradition, Little Steven, with his gypsy head-rag and flamboyant stage presence, then came on convincingly as a frontman—*Men Without Women* was a scorching debut, and it seemed, for a short while, that the Disciples of Soul might stand as a Great Last Hope for rock undiluted either by postpunk irony or revivalist over-reverence. But neither *Men* nor its two capable, now-deleted '80s successors, *Voice of America* and *Freedom—No Compromise,* found much of an audience. America lost its chance to embrace a kind of homegrown Clash, but Steven continued his admirable apostolic work in the late '80s as one of the guiding lights behind Artists United Against Apartheid. In 1999 Little Steven came roaring back with *Born Again Savage*—a guitar showcase that featured him turning in pyrotechnics in the style of Hendrix and prime Yardbirds. —P.E.

Townes Van Zandt

★★★   First Album (1968; Rhino, 1993)
★★★   For the Sake of the Song (1968; Tomato, 2003)
★★★½   Our Mother, the Mountain (1969; Tomato, 1989)
★★★   Townes Van Zandt (1969; Tomato, 1989)

★★½   Delta Momma Blues (1971; Tomato, 1989)
★★★   High, Low and In Between (1972; Rhino, 1994)
★★★   The Late Great Townes Van Zandt (Tomato, 1972)
★★★   Flyin' Shoes (1978; Tomato, 1989)
★★★   At My Window (Sugar Hill, 1987)
★★★½   The Great Tomato Blues Package (Tomato, 1989)
★★★   Live and Obscure (Sugar Hill, 1989)
★★★   Roadsongs (Sugar Hill, 1994)
★★★   No Deeper Blue (Sugar Hill, 1995)
★★★   The Highway Kind (Sugar Hill, 1997)
★★★   Abnormal (Normal, 1998)
★★★½   A Far Cry From Dead (Arista/Austin, 1999)
★★★★   The Best of Townes Van Zandt (Tomato Music, 2002)

Texas singer/songwriter Townes Van Zandt never gained much more than a long-lasting cult following for his well-crafted, mildly countryish folk pop, but his best record, *Our Mother, the Mountain,* remains powerful—and he deserves a revival. He hasn't the fine voice that Eric Andersen had circa Andersen's classic *Blue River* (1972), but he shares some of the same sensibility—he writes well about loss and yearning, and conveys subtle emotions through telling images. Willie Nelson and Merle Haggard scored a country hit with his "Poncho and Lefty," a song with pervasive, dark nostalgia that encapsulates Van Zandt's approach. A deft finger-picking guitarist and a careful lyricist, he delivered work that stands the test of time.

The lyric "a beautiful and scary song" from "St. John the Gambler," off *Our Mother, the Mountain,* describes Van Zandt's songwriting—it's always lovely, and often haunting. An extremely consistent artist, he never released a bad album—a good place to start might be with *A Far Cry From Dead.* Released posthumously, the album features ace Nashville players fleshing out stark tapes of the singer's vocals and guitar (the tapes were discovered after Van Zandt's death in 1997). The voice is sepulchral, but astonishingly effective: "Cowboy Junkies Lament" could serve as the singer's epitaph, and "The Hole" is a harrowing tour of the underworld. Also remarkable is *Roadsongs*—eclectic covers (The Rolling Stones, Springsteen, Johnny Cash) made absolutely personal. *The Best of Townes Van Zandt* does him justice, but every individual album is worth a listen. —P.E.

Stevie Ray Vaughan

★★★★   Texas Flood (Epic, 1983)
★★★½   Couldn't Stand the Weather (Epic, 1984)

★★★ Soul to Soul (Epic, 1985)
★★★ Live Alive (Epic, 1986)
★★★ In Step (Epic, 1989)
★★★★ The Sky Is Crying (Epic, 1991)
★★★ In the Beginning (Epic, 1992)
★★★★ Greatest Hits (Epic, 1995)
★★★ Live at Carnegie Hall (Epic, 1997)
★★★★ The Real Deal: Greatest Hits, Vol. 2 (Epic/Legacy, 1999)
★★★ Blues at Sunrise (Epic/Legacy, 2000)
★★★★ SRV (Epic/Legacy, 2000)
★★★★ Live at Montreux 1982 and 1985 (Epic/Legacy, 2001)
★★★★ The Essential Stevie Ray Vaughan & Double Trouble (Epic/Legacy, 2002)
★★★★ Martin Scorsese Presents the Blues: Stevie Ray Vaughan (Epic/Legacy, 2003)

Among the generation of blues guitarists who came of age in the early '80s, only Robert Cray approaches the late Stevie Ray Vaughan's skill and influence, with Vaughan's brother Jimmie probably sneaking in there as well on the strength of his powerful work with the Fabulous Thunderbirds. To be sure, though, Vaughan kicked the latest blues revival into high gear with his first two albums, *Texas Flood* and *Couldn't Stand the Weather*, which came out of nowhere to become best-sellers in the midst of a rock world being consumed by techno pop.

Texas Flood pays its debts to traditional Texas blues and R&B, sounding a tad muddy, the better to experience the slice-and-dice solos Vaughan delivers. Stylistically, Vaughan was a true eclectic whose hard-driving, steely sound achieved individuality while incorporating quotes from Hubert Sumlin, Buddy Guy, T-Bone Walker, Lonnie Mack, Albert Collins, B.B. King, and Jimi Hendrix. That's a broad palette, but it also shows how Vaughan built on the best influences to express the emotional extremes of his songs.

Couldn't Stand the Weather finds Vaughan broadening out a bit beyond R&B to include a stirring rendition of Hendrix's "Voodoo Child" and a Charlie Christian–Kenny Burrell flavor on the jazz-tinged "Stang's Swang." *Soul to Soul* represents Vaughan and his band Double Trouble's great leap forward. First the addition of keyboardist Reese Wynans expands the sound, adding textural possibilities. Wynans makes his presence felt most dramatically on a version of Hank Ballard's "Look at Little Sister." Vaughan shows more facility with melody in his songwriting, producing his first outstanding ballad in "Life Without Love." Vaughan had a tender side that he could express effectively with either a delicate vocal or pained

guitar solo. *Live Alive* sums up the first part of Vaughan's career in a rousing live set recorded at the Montreux Jazz Festival, and in Austin and Dallas. Of note is Jimmie Vaughan's special guest appearance on four tracks cut in Austin. *In Step*, Vaughan's last studio album, collects more well-turned Vaughan originals, along with a tasty selection of covers of songs by Howlin' Wolf, Buddy Guy, and Willie Dixon. Vaughan's "Crossfire" is one of his peak solo turns in a pure, gut-wrenching style.

A Texas flood of live recordings and greatest hits collections has followed: Most are inessential—buy the albums—except for *Live at Montreux*, which features some searing performances, and the four-CD box *SRV*, which covers Vaughan's entire career and features some revelatory, previously unreleased tracks. The other exception is the lovingly assembled posthumous album, *The Sky Is Crying*, which contains 10 studio performances recorded between 1984 and 1989, with only one track—"Empty Arms"—having appeared on a previous Vaughan album (*Soul to Soul*), but in a different version. Whether by design or by accident, the tunes offer a good overview of Vaughan's stylistic range. Most pronounced are the nods to Albert King, but there are also touches of Kenny Burrell (whose "Chitlins con Carne" is covered), Hubert Sumlin, Lonnie Mack ("Wham," a Mack classic), and of course Hendrix ("Little Wing"). A somber note closes the album, "Life by the Drop," Vaughan's first recorded acoustic solo. It's a moment you don't want to end. But it does. —D.M.

Suzanne Vega

★★★ Suzanne Vega (A&M, 1985)
★★★½ Solitude Standing (A&M, 1987)
★★★★ Days of Open Hand (A&M, 1990)
★★½ 99.9 Degrees F (A&M, 1992)
★★ Nine Objects of Desire (A&M, 1996)
★★★ Songs in Red and Gray (A&M, 2001)

New Yorker Suzanne Vega's third album, *Days of Open Hand* (1990) isn't her bestselling disc, but it is her finest—its cryptic lyrics sophisticated melodies, and complex, crack-jazz playing reveal a formidable progression from her impressive debut five years before. Starting off as a folkie, Vega hit big with "Luka," a haunting, cinema verité portrait of domestic violence. Taken from her second album, *Solitude Standing*, the single was surrounded by equally strong material—the jaunty, a capella "Tom's Diner" showed that a writer capable of songs akin to Leonard Cohen's high-flown poetics could also encompass the street smarts of Lou Reed. Vega is her own woman, though. Compassion, hope, and mystery are themes not very subtly handled in pop music: Vega delves into them with an almost philosophical acuity.

The lank-haired folk waif stiffens her spine for *99.9 Degrees F,* widely and erroneously reported to be Vega's "techno effort." It's folk-rock to its barefoot soul, a kind of exploration of dark and difficult emotional byways just as intense but less intellectually distanced than her previous albums. While synthesizers and the like drive the melodies, Vega's hushed, precise vocals whisper urgently in the listener's ear, and the result is pretty, strange, and unsettling. It could have been predicted that her next step would move into ponderous artiness, and with *Nine Objects of Desire,* Vega and new husband Mitchell Froom show no restraint. What the singer has to say becomes less important than the fancy keyboard arrangements, faux-junky percussion, and oversize production, and despite the touching poetics of her lyrics, the songs are overwhelmed. Divorce informs *Songs in Red and Gray,* which isn't half as pretentious as its title. Confusion battles with incisive observation as Vega works her way through the emotional fallout, and while she speak-sings the lyrics, a piercing sense of pain and sadness cut through the elliptical imagery. —P.E./A.B.

Caetano Veloso
Selected Discography

★★★★	Caetano Veloso (Philips, 1968)
★★★★½	White Album (Philips, 1969)
★★★	Transa (Philips, 1972)
★★★★	Qualquer Coisa (Philips, 1975)
★★★★	Caetano Veloso (Nonesuch, 1986)
★★★	Estrangeiro (Nonesuch, 1989)
★★★★	Circulado Vivo (Philips, 1993)
★★★★½	Caetano e Gil: Tropicalia 2 (Nonesuch, 1994)
★★★	Fina Estampa (PolyGram, 1994)
★★★★½	Livro (Nonesuch, 1998)
★★★★	Live in Bahía (Nonesuch, 2002)
★★★	Eu Não Peço Desculpa (with Jorge Mautner) (Universal, 2002)
★★★★	A Foreign Sound (Nonesuch, 2004)

Throughout a career spanning 40 years and countless experiments, Brazilian singer and songwriter Caetano Veloso has been tagged with every conceivable comparison to English-language pop and rock royalty. One year he's the "Brazilian John Lennon," a rebel who shakes up the staid bossa nova. The next he's the "Brazilian Bob Dylan" for his poetic, sharply observed lyrics. He's been mentioned alongside Miles Davis (for his restlessness) and Paul McCartney (for his earnestness) and David Byrne (for his determined artiness).

While most of these comparisons are apt, none fully captures the range of Veloso's talent—he's a sublime and seductive melodist, a curious musician capable of sharp left turns, a historian whose compositions tie past and present together in a way no other pop-music figure has managed, at once upholding tradition and transcending it. And the Bahia native makes everything he does, from a rudimentary Carnaval samba to his more pensive recent pastels, sound as effortless as wind whistling through the trees.

Veloso gets his start in the late '60s, at the moment the Musica Popular Brazil, or MPB, begins to open up to Western rock influences. He and Gilberto Gil start with regional rhythms, then add electric guitars and thick studio production—elements alien to Brazilian pop at the time. The music, called "tropicália" after Veloso's anthemic song, became a political lightning rod, and Veloso and Gil were forced into exile in 1971, after issuing only several albums—his 1968 breakthrough, recorded with Brazilian rockers Os Mutantes, and the following year's gorgeously orchestrated "white" album, are among the most rewarding.

Veloso continues to experiment with rock and jazz-fusion touches—one record he made in exile, 1972's *Transa,* transforms typically Brazilian chanted choruses via glossy and occasionally psychedelic production. Veloso doesn't stay in that zone for long, however: His 1975 gem, *Qualquer Coisa,* is built around meditative acoustic guitar in the style of the legendary João Gilberto, an album-length spell marred only by three Beatles covers sung in halting English. Veloso continues to record and tour through the late '70s, and becomes an important cultural figure in Brazil—he writes poetry, paints, and collaborates with Gil and other figures associated with bossa nova and MPB.

His recordings begin to get worldwide attention in the mid-'80s: His eponymous first effort for Nonesuch is another acoustic marvel, and this time the covers ("Eleanor Rigby," Michael Jackson's "Billie Jean") are handled with Veloso's customary elegance. Next comes the Arto Lindsay–produced *Estrangeiro,* which expands his U.S. profile even though, in hindsight, it sounds cluttered and unnecessarily conceptual. Veloso and Gil reunite to mark the 25th anniversary of tropicalia with *Tropicalia 2,* an incredibly spirited, gloriously rhythmic document that argues the duo's movement was more than a fad. From there, Veloso pays tribute to Latin American composers including Ernesto Lecuona and Astor Piazzolla with the erratic *Fina Estampa,* and then begins developing a more orchestral approach to pop that blossoms on 1998's *Livro,* a brilliantly moody song cycle flecked with Gil Evans orchestrations and hip-hop rhythms. This is, arguably, his masterpiece.

Veloso has a habit of following studio works with live recordings from the subsequent tours. Among the best of these are *Circulado Vivo,* from his 1993 trip, and *Live in Bahia,* an emotional homecoming show from 2002. Among his many collaborations with other artists, the 2002 set with Jorge Mautner, *Eu Não Peço Desculpa,* is notable for its lighthearted, whimsical embrace of electronica—further proof that though he could easily retire on his catalogue, Veloso is one of those rare souls for whom music is not a job, but a kind of quest. Veloso's valentine to classic English–language pop songcraft, *A Foreign Sound,* is a work of sly daring: In between conjuring spare, deliciously moody treatments of torch songs like "Smoke Gets in Your Eyes," Veloso offers illuminated updates of Nirvana's "Come As You Are" and Stevie Wonder's "If It's Magic" and even rehabilitates that '70's treacle pit, "Feelings." —T.M.

Velvet Revolver

★★★★ Contraband (RCA, 2004)

The debut album by these refugees from hard-rock superstars Guns n' Roses and '90s alt-rock combo Stone Temple Pilots is a rare, fine thing: the sound of the perfect A&R sales pitch turning into a real band. In fact, *Contraband* is tighter and hotter in construction and attack than you have any right to expect from a group that started out auditioning vocalists at the end of 2002 while being filmed for a VH1 reality show. The ex-G n' R trio of guitarist Slash, bassist Duff McKagan and drummer Matt Sorum, plus former STP singer Scott Weiland (who joined in June 2003) are not shy about flashing their pedigree on this snarling update of '80s Sunset Strip classicism. "Sucker Train Blues" opens the album like G n' R's *Appetite for Destruction* in miniature—zooming underwater bass, pneumatic gallop, flying chunks of superfuzz guitar—while Weiland pulls out his police bullhorn–style bark from STP's "Sex Type Thing." But Velvet Revolver (with Dave Kushner, ex–Wasted Youth, on second guitar) energize their combined histories with original snort, like the skewed skittering riff in "Set Me Free," and punchy vocal choruses that sound like dirty Def Leppard. Weiland, in particular, shows that he is far more than the sum of his well-publicized drug problems and rehab stints during his STP years. Lyrically, he nails the sweet selfish oblivion and dumb-ass self-destruction of addiction with explosive clarity and no excuses. And Weiland's grainy yowl—which, at STP's height, earned him a lot of lazy, cruel comparisons to Pearl Jam's Eddie Vedder—is actually a precision instrument that cuts through the double guitar crossfire with a steely

melodic purpose that, when Weiland piles up the harmonies, sounds like sour, seething Queen. —D.F.

The Velvet Underground

★★★★★ The Velvet Underground and Nico (MGM/Verve, 1967)
★★★★★ White Light/White Heat (MGM/Verve, 1968)
★★★★★ The Velvet Underground (MGM, 1969)
★★★★★ Loaded (Cotillion, 1970)
★★★½ Live at Max's Kansas City (Cotillion, 1972)
★ Squeeze (Polydor U.K., 1973)
★★★★ 1969 Live (Mercury, 1974)
★★★★ VU (Verve, 1985)
★★★½ Another View (Verve, 1986)
★★★½ The Best of the Velvet Underground (Verve/PolyGram, 1989)
★★★ Live MCMLXXXXIII (Sire, 1993)
★★★★★ Peel Slowly and See (Polydor, 1995)
★★★★ Bootleg Series, Vol. 1: The Quine Tapes (Universal, 2001)

The Velvet Underground invented the New York noise that became punk rock, sinister and slinky at the same time. Even in its darkest, most demonic moments, you can hear a unique band—John Cale's viola, Sterling Morrison's jittery guitar, Maureen Tucker's drums, Lou Reed's sneer of sneers—having a real good time together. The Velvets had a beat, ripping all the country out of James Brown and Bo Diddley breaks for pure urban momentum. The Velvets had guitars, fashioning hooks and harmonies out of speed-freak feedback. The Velvets had songs—oh baby, did they have songs. Painful songs, often desolate songs, that were nonetheless full of rock & roll fun. "Sister Ray," "Femme Fatale," "I'm Waiting for the Man," and other walks on the wild side present a romantic vision of big-city nightlife over music that's tough enough to pass for gritty realism. Black leather and shades would never sound the same.

All four of the band's original studio albums are musts, but *The Velvet Underground and Nico* is the must-est. A sexy New York sociopath in a motorcycle jacket, schooled in surf music and doo-wop but inspired by the decadent Warhol Factory demimonde, Lou Reed led his band of art punks as they turned the big bad city into the sublimely beautiful rock & roll noise of "Sunday Morning," "Venus in Furs," and "The Black Angel's Death Song." Born-to-be-dead German chanteuse Nico adds her creepy old-world charisma to the ballads "Femme Fatale," "All Tomorrow's Parties," and "I'll Be Your Mirror." The street narratives "Heroin" and "I'm Waiting for the Man" ride on ruthless guitar clatter, stopping and restarting time at will, all glamour and danger. Every song here inspired countless other bands; more important, every song here inspires you to hear the rest. Well, maybe not "Run Run Run" or "There She Goes Again." That Andy Warhol—what a producer!

White Light/White Heat turns up the guitar fuzz to obsessive levels, climaxing with "Sister Ray," 17 blissful minutes of amps screaming in ecstasy. "Here She Comes Now" is the flip side, a two-minute acoustic incantation falling softly on your ears, almost all rhythm. "Lady Godiva's Operation" has perfect comic singing from Cale and Reed, while "I Heard Her Call My Name" and "White Light/White Heat" detail psychic horrors under the dumb fun of the guitars. That leaves "The Gift," an eight-minute spoken narrative that proves the world didn't lose a great novelist when Lou chose music. *White Light* makes vibrant music out of all the urban bleakness until it ends up sounding transcendently sweet, captured in the perfect moment when Reed struggles to force the word "am-fe-fe-fe-fetamine" out of his wracked throat.

The Velvet Underground, on the other hand, is all sweetness. After John Cale's exit, the Velvets became acoustic folkie balladeers, with a surprisingly warm Lou Reed warbling the sad doo-wop melodies of "Pale Blue Eyes," "I'm Set Free," and "Jesus," as well as the urgent rave-ups "Beginning to See the Light" and "What Goes On." Every song is a classic, with Maureen Tucker's "After Hours" an unforgettable last word. *Loaded* is even mellower, with new bassist Doug Yule taking over too many of the lead vocals. It's the Velvets' most conventional album, but when you're in the mood for the glistening guitar shimmer of "I Found a Reason" or "Sweet Jane," nothing else will do. This record was designed to translate fast, to go places, to give instant pleasure, and that's a key part of the Velvets' story. Lou was too much of a rocker at heart to turn up his nose at the redemptive power of pop trash, and so "Rock and Roll" is his version of the radio's version of the rock & roll that saved his life. "Train Round the Bend" has some of his best lyrics, and that back-cover photo is a gem: lonely guitars on a rainy day, hoping someone will pick them up and make them sing.

Reed quit the band during the *Loaded* sessions. Yule went on to make *Squeeze* under the Velvet Underground name; it's the sort of pricey collector's item you really shouldn't ever pay money for, lest you get laughed at by whomever you're trying to impress. On the other hand, so many people have been willing to shell out for Velvets' bootlegs *(Sweet Sister Ray! Live '68!)* that the band has been repackaged archivally ever since. *VU* and *Another View* collect great outtakes such as "Foggy Notion," "Stephanie Says," "Hey Mr. Rain," and "Temptation Inside Your Heart."

The *Peel Slowly and See* box collects this arcana (inexplicably leaving out *VU*'s "She's My Best Friend"), adds more ("Guess I'm Falling in Love"! "Satellite of Love"!), throws in the four original albums, and restores the full-length version of "Sweet Jane" to *Loaded.* Essential—although there's even more where that came from (the 10/2/68 live version of "Pale Blue Eyes" is a *killer*). *Best of* is a well-selected sampler that's still beside the point. *Live MCMXCIII* documents the Velvets' brief 1993 European reunion tour, and you had to be there, though John Cale sounds great bellowing "All Tomorrow's Parties." *The Quine Tapes* collects dim-sounding but fierce live performances, with some *looong* versions of "Sister Ray." Despite rotten sound quality, *Live at Max's Kansas City* rocks, with Reed in a hilariously Santa-like mood ("Wow, it's really fun to be able to play all these for you!") as the barflies chat about Tuinols between songs.

The album *1969 Live* shows off the Reed-Morrison-Tucker-Yule lineup on one frantic rave-up after another, catching your breath with quiet interludes such as "Over You" and "Sweet Jane." Listen to "Sweet Bonnie Brown/It's Just Too Much"—the lyrics are hardly there at all, the vocal is a callow Otis Redding rip, the melody is a shambles, but the guitars coast and zoom and rocket their red glare for five, six, seven minutes of beautiful blur. You can hear the Velvets pummeling away at this trifle, mixing up the heavy with the frivolous, the most obscure rock emotions with the most obvious ones. Plenty of Velvets' imitators have gotten louder, but nobody's ever managed to duplicate the Velvets' sense of adventure and romance. No one has ever duplicated the sound of Mo Tucker's drums, either; for all Reed's singer/songwriter tendencies, the Velvets were an irreplicable tribute to the spirit of teamwork and collective creation. Those were different times. —R.S.

Tom Verlaine

★★★★ Tom Verlaine (1979; Collector's Choice, 2003)
★★★ Dreamtime (1981; Warner Bros., 1995)
★★ Words from the Front (Warner Bros., 1982)
★★★½ Cover (Warner Bros., 1984)
★★★½ Flash Light (1987; Collector's Choice, 2003)
★★ The Wonder (Fontana, 1990)
★★ Warm and Cool (Rykodisc, 1992)
★★★½ The Miller's Tale: A Tom Verlaine Anthology (Virgin, 1996)

Tom Verlaine made his lifelong reputation in a few years of '70s punk glory with Television; since then, he's taken a leisurely approach to his role as a New York guitar god. His trademark sound is exploring the intricate modulations of his Fender Jazzmaster's upper register, giving his guitar that distinctive lunar quiver, and along with his strangled Richard Widmark voice, it goes with the enigmatically pretty songs Verlaine writes whenever he's in the mood. His first solo album is still his best, dusting off the old Television live staple "Breakin' in My Heart," which features a killer rhythm guitar line from the B-52s' Ricky Wilson. It's an example of how high Verlaine could soar with a little instrumental kick from a real band, although since he was a natural-born control freak, it's a side of his music that he never explored very far.

Dreamtime was a more conventional singer/songwriter album: Verlaine wrote and sang some poetic mid-tempo sketches with a backup rhythm section. Unfortunately, the sound is shrill and thin—there's no producer credit, and who would want one?—so even when the songs are pretty great, they sound like badly recorded demos. *Words from the Front* was mostly filler, despite one magnificent tune that should have been a hit, the sweetly foppish loverboy ballad "Postcard from Waterloo." *Cover* was so subtle that it disappeared instantly on release, and has stayed disappeared ever since, but in fact, side two is a kick-ass synth-pop suite, with four powerful songs in a row. With touches of Byrne/Eno in the vocals and a light hand at the keyboards, Verlaine blends his distinctive guitar twang into the liquid synth grooves of "Dissolve/Reveal," "Rotation," and "Swim" for his most impressive solo music. The man was born to shimmer, and this music shimmers.

Flash Light returned to guitar-with-backup rockingness, with punchier songs and production than usual. It was a comeback of sorts, earning Verlaine his biggest acclaim in years. But he hasn't made a proper solo album since, even though recent gigs (solo and with the reunited Television) reveal that he hasn't lost a stroke as a lead guitarist. *The Wonder* and *Warm and Cool* are dull diddling, while *The Miller's Tale* is a bungled anthology—the first disc is a good 1982 live gig, the second a mishmash of solo and Television tracks, apparently selected at random and leaving out almost all of his studio work. Tom Verlaine remains a legendary rock crackpot who, despite his hermetic habits and sketchy work ethic, has managed to record some gorgeously inspired moments.   —R.S.

Veruca Salt

   ★★★★   American Thighs (Minty Fresh/DGC, 1994)
   ★★★½   Eight Arms to Hold You (Outpost, 1997)
   ★★★½   Resolver (Beyond, 2000)

Nina Gordon

   ★★½   Tonight and the Rest of My Life (Warner Bros., 2000)

One of the worst parts about the alt-rock onslaught of the early '90s was that every half-serious rock fan started sounding like the most sniveling sort of fanzine editor. Fun wasn't enough anymore—the "petty little ayatollahs," denounced by Cracker's David Lowrey, were demanding authenticity as well—many fine pop bands were written off as conniving carpetbaggers. The most insidious analogy of the era? How about this: Veruca Salt are to the Breeders as Stone Temple Pilots are to Pearl Jam. Sure, Nina Gordon and Louise Post copped their nice-girl voices from Kim Deal—but like the generation (or two) of indie boys who uncovered limitless possibility in Lou Reed's monotone, Gordon and Post were expanding that vocal blueprint, not cashing in on it.

If you must compare, *American Thighs* thumps seductively (and nastily) where the Breeder's *Last Splash* lolls about goofily (and distractedly). At first, "Seether" outpaces the other songs so handily, you'd mistake the rest for filler, but where the hit explodes, the remaining songs here actually do, well, seethe, with insinuating melodies that slowly sink their tendrils into your earholes. The playing loosens up and the volume pumps up on *Eight Arms*, produced by heavy-metal veteran Bob Rock—the band finally earns the AC/DC quote of its first album title. But they're just as interested in indulging the not particularly original but loopy and endearing Beatlemania indicated by the album's title: "Volcano Girls" echoes the White Album's "Here's another hint if you please/The Seether's Louise" and features a truly ferocious count off.

When they failed to take over the world, Gordon jumped ship to make the sort of conventional singer/songwriter move that'll probably ensure a continuing career. A Beatles fan to the last, Post made like her idols and wrote nasty, barely coded swipes at her former band mate. She also kept the band's name, and the debut of VS 2.0, *Resolver*, was snotty and punchy yet vulnerable. Gordon's *Tonight* earned a home on the new adult-rock stations aimed at aging Gen Xers, but Post's effort disappeared on impact.   —K.H.

The Verve

   ★★★½   A Storm in Heaven (Vernon Yard, 1993)
   ★★★★   A Northern Soul (Vernon Yard, 1995)
   ★★★★   Urban Hymns (Virgin, 1997)

The Verve fit the classic British rock model: Richard Ashcroft was the lippy sex poet on the mike, a long, tall swirl of cheekbones and pretension, while Nick McCabe was the shy, perfectionist guitar wizard. For a while, they struck brilliant musical sparks by driving each other up the wall, regularly throwing crockery in the studio and breaking up after each album. *A Storm in Heaven* was a top-notch debut, full of long, druggy jams, shoegazing guitar excursions, and Mad Richard's shambolic, shamanic vocals. *A Northern Soul* kicked home with the gorgeous breakup ballad "On Your Own" and the epic "History," which opened with a reading from William Blake before exploding into the massive chorus, "You and me/We're history." It was their breakthrough, and the Verve celebrated by splitting up almost immediately.

The lads kissed and made up for the triumphant international smash *Urban Hymns*, which included "The Drugs Don't Work," "Weeping Willow," and "Come On." They even cracked America with "Bittersweet Symphony," a brooding doom-show ballad coasting on a heavenly string sample nicked from an orchestral version of the Stones' "The Last Time." The sample cost the Verve all the publishing rights to their biggest hit. (Of course, the Stones nicked "The Last Time" from James Brown, who nicked it from the Staple Singers, who nicked it from an ancient African-American spiritual, but that's showbiz.) When Ashcroft and McCabe suddenly remembered how much they loathed each other, the Verve split again. Ashcroft lost cred with his 2000 solo debut *Alone With Everybody*, typified by the perfectly titled, absolutely moronic "C'mon People (We're Making It Now)." But he still possesses superhuman levels of sullen rock-god charisma and contributed excellent lead vocals to the Chemical Brothers' *Come with Us*. Ashcroft turned 30 on September 11, 2001. The odds are still excellent that he will write a terrible song about it. —R.S.

Luke Vibert

   ★★★   Big Soup (Mo' Wax, 1997)
  ★★★½ Stop the Panic (Astralwerks, 2000)

Plug

 ★★★★ Drum 'N' Bass for Papa/Plug EP's 1, 2 & 3
         (Nothing/Interscope, 1997)

Wagon Christ

    ★★   Phat Lab Nightmare (Rising High, 1993)
 ★★★★ Throbbing Pouch (Moonshine, 1995)
 ★★★½ Tally Ho! (Astralwerks, 1998)
 ★★★½ Musipal (Ninja Tune, 2001)

Releasing a headache-inducing array of CDs, LPs, EPs, singles, and compilation tracks—under various aliases, no less—Luke Vibert became one of the most well-known names of the 1990s electronic dance music scene. Vibert makes dance music for the head, music that challenges the intellect more than it taxes the feet. Under the guise of Plug, he speeds up hip-hop break beats, sometimes close to 200 b.p.m.s, cre-

ating his own very original take on drum-and-bass electronica that is so mathematical and abstract that it threatens to rip open a hole in the space-time continuum. *Drum 'N' Bass for Papa/Plug EP's 1, 2 & 3* collects the majority of his work as Plug; it stands as one of the best full-length albums within the genre of jungle/drum and bass. As Wagon Christ, he slows things down to a trip-hop crawl, crafting a psychedelic musical bed that might best be described as a kind of vocal-less postapocalyptic rhythm & blues. Perhaps because *Throbbing Pouch* was instantly hailed as a classic of the trip-hop canon, you can feel him resisting the trip-hop label on *Tally Ho!*, which is far more eclectic than his previous effort. *Tally Ho!* zips all over the map, embracing spaced-out ambience, hyperfrenetic drum and bass, and the hazy murk of slo-mo hip-hop beats. Taken together, his entire catalogue suggests a kind of musical attention deficit disorder, particularly the music he released under his own name, Luke Vibert. *Stop the Panic* is a great example of this, a collaboration between Vibert and pedal steel guitar player B.J. Cole. The album integrates abstracted hip-hop beats with an instrument that is traditionally associated with country music, but which becomes totally detached from its earthly origins, revealing it to be capable of producing the most spacey, ethereal sounds this side of the Theremin. —K.M.

Village People

   ★★★   Village People (Casablanca, 1977)
   ★★★   Macho Men (1978; Casablanca, 1996)
  ★★★½ Cruisin' (1979; Casablanca, 1996)
   ★★★   Go West (1979; Casablanca, 1996)
    ★★   Can't Stop the Music (Casablanca, 1980)
   ★★★   Live and Sleazy (Casablanca, 1980)
    ★★   Renaissance (RCA, 1981)
 ★★★★ The Best of the Village People (Casablanca, 1994)

Let us now praise famous men: the Cowboy, the Construction Worker, the Sailor, the Indian, the Traffic Cop, and the Leather Biker. Strange as it would have seemed in 1977, the Village People have become one of the disco decade's most enduring phenomena. There is not a sporting event, wedding reception, or monster-truck rally in the country where anyone would be surprised to hear "Y.M.C.A.," even though it's a disco anthem about gay sex at the gym, sung by six men who looked like they were just getting home from their Halloween party in mid-November. The Village People were originally recruited by disco producer Jacques Morali to chant and grunt over explicitly gay-themed club hits such as "Macho Man" and "San Francisco (You've Got Me)." But his rhythm tracks were so undeniable—that pumping bass, those splashy horns—and the costumes so lovable that the group turned into a surprise crossover hit. Middle America got a massive crush on the Village People, even after straight people started to figure out exactly why it's so much fun to stay at the Y.M.C.A.

Even more than most disco artists, the VP are best enjoyed one song at a time, although their original albums were all pretty good. *Cruisin'* has "Y.M.C.A.," the touching "My Roommate," and "The Women," which didn't fool anybody. *Go West* has "In the Navy," with patriotic cries of "come and join your fellow man!" above the hot-and-heavy panting of the chorus, "They . . . want . . . you!" It also has the title song's irresistible call to a California utopia. As disco started to fizzle, the VP began their film career with *Can't Stop the Music* and ended it about two hours later. Then they dropped the inevitable *Live and Sleazy,* featuring "Ready for the 80s." *Renaissance,* their 1981 attempt at a new-wave comeback, is a prized collectors' item in some extremely specialized circles, though the Europe-only *Fox on the Box* and *Sex on the Phone* remain obscure. The Village People eventually hit the oldies circuit, where they have remained immensely popular ever since, as they became gay-pride icons—Morrissey wrote the "Y.M.C.A." answer song "Half a Person," while the Pet Shop Boys elegiacally covered "Go West" on *Very.* Glenn Hughes, the Biker, died in 2001. At his request, he was buried in his black leather suit. —R.S.

Gene Vincent

   ★★★★   Capitol Collectors Series (Capitol, 1990)
     ★★   Ain't That Too Much! The Complete Challenge Sessions (Sundazed, 1995)
  ★★★★★   The Screaming End: The Best of Gene Vincent & His Blue Caps (Razor & Tie, 1997)
  ★★★★½   Bluejean Bop!/Gene Vincent and the Blue Caps (Collectables, 1998)
  ★★★★½   Gene Vincent Rocks! And the Blue Caps Roll/A Gene Vincent Record Date (Collectables, 1998)
   ★★★½   Sounds Like Gene Vincent/Crazy Times (Collectables, 1998)
    ★★★   The Lost Dallas Sessions 1957–1958 (Dragon Street, 1998)
   ★★★★   The Legend at His Best (Collectables, 2000)

Gene Vincent's recording history, once almost completely out of print domestically—especially the critical years with the Capitol label from 1956 through 1960—is now well documented. His fleeting stateside stardom aside, Vincent recorded prolifically from the time of his first hit in 1956 (the immortal "Be-Bop-a-

Lula") up to his death in 1971 at the age of 36 (injured in the car crash that killed Eddie Cochran, Vincent's health suffered further as he became increasingly dependent on alcohol). While only a smidgen of his prolific output is as inspired as his early work, at least Vincent stayed on the rock & roll course to the end: He always favored black leather and the big beat. He wasn't as primitive as Link Wray, but he shared with Wray an unswerving commitment to keep on rocking when other stars of their generation were attempting to transform themselves into country or MOR singers.

Vincent never again equaled the chart success of "Be-Bop-a-Lula" (his only other Top 40 singles were "Lotta Lovin' " in late 1957, which peaked at #13, and "Dance to the Bop," a #23 pop single in early '58). But Vincent did cut some absolutely riveting, ferocious rock & roll, full of sneers, attitude, breathless passion, and blazing-hot instrumental work. The music is uniformly inspired, even when the band's lineup is fluid, and virtually the entire recorded output for Capitol can be heard now. A concise survey of the 1956–57 barn burners is available on the Razor & Tie compilation, aptly titled *The Screaming End: The Best of Gene Vincent & His Blue Caps,* and on Capitol's 21-track *Collectors Series* entry.

An interesting entry in the catalogue is Dragon Street's *The Lost Dallas Sessions 1957–1958,* which documents Vincent's first studio work with a new lineup of Blue Caps. For a deeper probing into Vincent's Capitol years and various Blue Caps incarnations, Collectables has reissued all six albums the artist released on Capitol from 1956 through 1960. These are all on twofer single-CD packages: from 1957, *Bluejean Bop!* and *Gene Vincent and the Blue Caps* showcase Vincent and Gallup at the outset of their journey, although neither album includes "Be-Bop-a-Lula" or "Woman Love." The twofer composed of Vincent's 1958 albums—*Gene Vincent Rocks! And the Blue Caps Roll* and *A Record Date with Gene Vincent*—does include "Be-Bop-a-Lula" as a bonus track, plus its followup, "Race With the Devil." In addition to the original material here, these albums also find Vincent and company dipping into their country bag for exemplary renditions of Hank Williams' "Your Cheatin' Heart," "Hey Good Lookin'," and "I Can't Help It If I'm Still in Love with You"; some classic pop by way of the Gershwins' "Summertime" and Rodgers and Hammerstein's inspirational "You'll Never Walk Alone" (yes, in a Gene Vincent rendition); and a little taste of honky-tonk in Mel Tillis' "Five Feet of Lovin'." The third Collectables twofer features 1959's *Sounds Like Gene Vincent* and 1960's *Crazy Times* and includes three nonalbum singles, "Lotta Lovin' " (his 1957 hit single), "Wear My Ring," and "Dance to the Bop," with Vincent and the Blue Caps rocking furiously. —D.M.

The Vines

- ★★★ Highly Evolved (Capitol, 2002)
- ★★ Winning Days (Capitol, 2004)

Arriving on the hipster radar around the same time as the similarly named but better-dressed Swedish retro-rockers the Hives, these Aussie grunge babies were adopted by 2002's "rock-is-back," who found enough protopunk swagger and '60s-style songcraft to anoint their processed Nirvana dirges as part of the garage revolution.

Pretty and petulant frontman Craig Nicholls seems to have come out of the womb with just the right sort of marketable disdain for the paparazzi who would surely plague his future. After the band wowed the Brits with its pop-slanted single "Factory," alt-rock über-producer Rob Schnapf stepped in and offered to guide their debut, *Highly Evolved.* His precision lushness makes the band's rawness sound a bit canned, though the single "Get Free" survives with its vroom and fractured bash intact. The grunge millstone hangs heavy on the rest, including the redeemingly energized "Highly Evolved" single, the middling tantrum "Outtathaway!," and the dreary reheated growler "In the Jungle." As things progress, though, Nicholls reveals himself to be also a partisan of *Abbey Road*–era Paul McCartney, with songs like the dolorous folkie pastoral "Autumn Shade," and the piano-flecked Cali dream "Sunshinin'." Unfortunately, in these moments, Schnapf can't resist slathering on the treacle. Followup *Winning Days* heads even further in that dazed direction. The heavier stuff is boilerplate SUV rock, with none of the uptempo cuts approaching the abandon of "Get Free." Curiously, though still overly filigreed, the folk-pop tunes on *Days,* especially the countryfied "Rainfall," evidence Nicholls' melodic sense emerging more inspired and nuanced than his Silverchair-hurling hissy fits. —L.S.

Violent Femmes

- ★★★★ Violent Femmes (1983; Rhino, 2003)
- ★★★ Hallowed Ground (1985; Rhino 2000)
- ★★★½ The Blind Leading the Naked (1986; Warner Bros., 1990)
- ★★½ 3 (1989; Warner Bros., 1990)
- ★★ Why Do Birds Sing? (Reprise, 1991)
- ★★ New Times (Elektra, 1994)
- ★★ Rock!!!!! (Cold Front, 2000)
- ★★★ Add It Up (1981–1993) (Slash/Reprise, 1993)

This Milwaukee trio took punk's revenge-of-the-nerds aspect to heart; clean-cut choirboy Gordon Gano gleefully wheeled out his tales of sexual frustration and impending psychosis, while bassist Brian Ritchie and stand-up drummer Victor DeLorenzo both slammed away on acoustic instruments. Violent Femmes really stood out on the fledgling alternative circuit, and the group capitalized on its barebones mobility by playing impromptu street-corner gigs—talk about punk pragmatism! The debut album gets over mostly on that loose ensemble feel; strumming and haranguing, Gano works up a compelling neurotic fury on three-chord classics such as "Blister in the Sun" and "Add It Up."

Gano did tend to sound unpleasantly nasal on the band's inevitable, talky mid-tempo melodramas. That tendency peaks on *Hallowed Ground*'s pointlessly overwrought "Country Death Song"; between its shallow roots excavations and sarcastic fits, Violent Femmes' second album is nearly unlistenable. Producer Jerry Harrison (of Talking Heads) turns things around on *The Blind Leading the Naked,* focusing some of the group's manic energy and filling in some of the gaps in their technique. Gano responds with a far more considered set of songs, even looking out beyond his own cracked world: "Mother Reagan" stands as one of the best politico-rockers of the '80s, and the cover version of Marc Bolan's "Children of the Revolution" is actually less ironic than the glittery T. Rex original. Violent Femmes began to draw a younger, much-enthused audience around this time, and the prospect of MTV-fueled teen idolatry must've frightened the group off its feed. The album *3* is a jumbled stylistic grab bag, reflecting the members' various solo projects. (Gano formed a gospel band called Mercy Seat, and Brian Ritchie has recorded for the independent SST label.) The acoustic return of *Why Do Birds Sing?* makes a sad, brazen play for the early-'80s nostalgia market—too bad the Violent Femmes' tuneless take on Culture Club's "Do You Really Want to Hurt Me?" actually makes you pine for Boy George. DeLorenzo went solo just after 1993 retrospective *Add It Up* was released (he was replaced by BoDeans drummer Guy Hoffman), and the Femmes have continued to slog along since then, intermittently releasing albums to little fanfare, the most recent being 2001's download-only rarities collection *Something's Wrong.* —M.C./B.S.

Waco Brothers

★★★½ To the Last Dead Cowboy (Bloodshot, 1995)
★★★ Cowboy in Flames (Bloodshot, 1997)
★★★ Do You Think About Me? (Bloodshot, 1997)
★★★ Wacoworld (Bloodshot, 1999)
★★★½ Electric Waco Chair (Bloodshot, 2000)
★★★½ New Deal (Bloodshot, 2002)

The Waco Brothers is Jon Langford's local bar band, a side project for the founder and mainstay of the Mekons. But while the Mekons are still as artistically viable and commercially marginal as ever, they work together only occasionally, having scattered to the far corners of the globe. Langford, originally from Wales, wound up in Chicago, where he found a few congenial fellows to gig with. But while Langford is the first name one associates with the Wacos, it makes just as much sense to view them as the second coming of Wreck, Dean Schlabowske's alt-country band. Langford produced Wreck's last album, and found in Dean a kindred spirit with an aesthetic firmly rooted in honky-tonk and a clear, cynical gaze on the capitalist rot all around.

Still, it's hard for an outsider to tell who does what here. The Wacos are a six-man band who over six albums have had only one personnel change (Allen Doughty replacing Tom Ray on bass starting with the second album), with three vocalists and all compositions credited to the group. This distinguishes them from the singer/songwriters who dominate alt country, although volume (loud) and tempo (fast) are also distinctive. As are the often-biting lyrics, which are pure class consciousness from "Plenty Tuff, Union Made" (on *To the Last Dead Cowboy*) to "Dragging My Own Tombstone" (on *Electric Waco Chair*).

The six albums are remarkably consistent, the main difference being that the first one is both artier and more country, like a Mekons album. But by the second album they had simplified the songs and punched up the volume, spiced with the occasional country cover such as "Wreck on the Highway" or "Johnson to Jones." And if the latter albums have a slight edge, that just means that their songcraft is getting sharper.   —T.H.

Loudon Wainwright III

★★★★ Album III (1972; Sony, 1990)
★★★★ Attempted Moustache (1973; Columbia/Legacy, 1998)
★★★★½ Unrequited (1975; Columbia/Legacy, 1998)
★★★ A Live One (Rounder, 1979)
★★★ Fame and Wealth (Rounder, 1983)
★★★½ I'm Alright (Rounder, 1984)
★★★½ More Love Songs (Rounder, 1986)
★★★ Therapy (Silvertone, 1989)
★★★½ History (Charisma, 1992)
★★★★½ Career Moves (Virgin, 1993)
★★★½ The BBC Sessions (1971–93; Fuel 2000, 1998)
★★★★ Grown Man (Virgin, 1995)
★★★ Little Ship (Charisma, 1998)
★★½ Social Studies (Hannibal, 1999)
★★★★ Last Man on Earth (Red House, 2001)
★★★½ So Damn Happy (Sanctuary, 2003)

Loudon Wainwright III grew up rich and whiny in Beverly Hills and the New York suburbs of Westchester County. He went to prep school, studied acting (and has done a little), wrote some songs. He was touted as a new Dylan, signed by Atlantic, and cut two out-of-print albums there. His next record, *Album III*, spawned a Top 20 hit single, "Dead Skunk"—he claimed to have written that one in 15 minutes, but it took him years to convince the major labels that he'd never write another one. But when he wasn't boorish ("Clockwork Chartreuse") or pathetic ("Red Guitar," "The Man Who Couldn't Cry"), he could be quite funny: "B Side" deals with the sex life of bees; "Swimming Song" extols the virtues of going informal; "I

Am the Way" catches Jesus kissing Magdalen (done with a laugh track for anyone who needed the hints); "Guru" mocks sham holiness ("they're proselytizing and it's mesmerizing and they're making moolah every day"). "Rufus Is a Tit Man" admires his infant son's culinary tastes; and "The Untitled" (introduced as "The Hardy Boys at the Y") revels in good clean sex. But the real theme of *Unrequited* was the turmoil and breakup of his marriage to Kate McGarrigle, from "Whatever Happened to Us" ("You told me that I came too soon/But it was you who came too late") to "On the Rocks" ("On Park Avenue South/I punched my baby on the mouth") to the postseparation but ultimately fruitless "Absence Makes the Heart Grow Fonder."

Wainwright's Rounder albums figured to be folky, but he moved to England and fell in with some real musicians—Richard Thompson and unrelated bassist Danny Thompson are constants, and Tony Coe turns in some nice clarinet. *A Live One* looks backward, sometimes derisively. But *Fame and Wealth* has fond memories of country club swimming pools in "Westchester County"; *I'm Alright* declares that he's survived divorce; *More Love Songs* threatens to make a career out of it, in songs such as "Unhappy Anniversary" and "Your Mother and I" ("are living apart/I know that sounds stupid/But we weren't very smart"). *Therapy* concerned itself more with parenthood, as in "Me and All the Other Mothers"; and in *History* he seems to come to some hard-learned realizations: that "Hitting You" just made things worse, that "my songs about you were all about me" ("So Many Songs"), and finally that "I'd Rather Be Lonely." As he grew older, Wainwright's skill shifted from comedy (although he could still sling out "Talking New Bob Dylan") to trenchant observation, not that it ever extends far beyond himself.

Career Moves is career-capping: a live album that works both as a best-of and as a showcase for his showtime comedy. The songs on *The BBC Sessions* are mostly familiar, recorded simply over two decades—although "It's Love and I Hate It" is scabrous and shameless and ever so typical. *Grown Man* consolidates his gains—for instance, his "Five Years Old" daughter has grown up into "Father/Daughter Dialogue": "Dearest Daddy with your songs/Do you hope to right your wrongs?" For his part, dearest Dad denies that the guy in his songs is him. If the songs on *Little Ship* seem less detailed, perhaps he's working on his deniability. The songs on *Social Studies* were mostly written as news commentaries for NPR and, I gather, mostly rejected: There's something to offend everyone, so caveat emptor. *Last Man on Earth* is an improvement, the death of his mother focusing his

thoughts on his own mortality. But when he concludes that "I feel like I'm homeless," he's testifying that even the rich and whiny have to struggle to be all right. —T.H.

Rufus Wainwright

★★★½ Rufus Wainwright (DreamWorks, 1998)
★★★★ Poses (DreamWorks, 2002)
★★★★ Want One (DreamWorks, 2003)

American-born, Canadian-bred Rufus Wainwright comes from first-class singer/songwriter stock—his dad's Loudon Wainwright III, his mom's Kate McGarrigle—but his music has little in common with his parents' homespun folk. As his debut album demonstrates, Wainwright's talent is for making urbane pop of such sweeping drama that a Broadway stage could barely contain it. The long, convoluted melodies, fervently lovelorn lyrics, and ornate arrangements of tracks such as "Baby" and "Foolish Love" recall generations of American songwriters, from Stephen Foster to Cole Porter to Randy Newman, even as they maintain their own distinct personality.

Poses is even better. The lyrics express Wainwright's homosexuality both forthrightly and poetically ("Grey Gardens," for example, refers repeatedly to Tadzio, the young male object of desire in Thomas Mann's *Death in Venice*), while the music is practically drunk on its own beauty (listen to the twists and turns of the vocal harmonies on "Shadows," or the swelling chorus of the title track). And Wainwright's grainy, sorrowful voice—think Radiohead's Thom Yorke without the existential despair—is a marvel.

With *Want One*, Wainwright's claim to major artist status is cemented for good. Whether incorporating orchestral quotes from Ravel's *Bolero* into a bemused statement of world-weariness ("Oh What a World") or reading the line "My phone's on vibrate for you" as the most elegant expression of devotion imaginable ("Vibrate"), Wainwright blends whimsy and deep feeling in a way that few contemporary artists can match. —M.R.

Tom Waits

★★★★½ Closing Time (1973; Asylum, 1990)
★★★★ The Heart of Saturday Night (1974; Asylum, 1990)
★★★★ Nighthawks at the Diner (1975; Asylum, 1990)
★★★★ Small Change (1976; Asylum, 1990)
★★★½ Foreign Affairs (1977; Asylum, 1990)
★★★ Blue Valentine (1978; Asylum, 1990)
★★★ Heartattack and Vine (1980; Asylum, 1990)
★★★★ One from the Heart (1982; Columbia/Legacy, 2004)

★★★★½ Swordfishtrombones (1983; Island, 1990)
★★★★★ Rain Dogs (1985; Island, 1990)
★★★½ Anthology of Tom Waits (1985; Asylum, 1990)
★★★ Franks Wild Years (1987; Island, 1990)
★★★ Big Time (1988; Island, 1990)
★★★★ The Early Years, Vol. 1 (1991; Manifesto, 1995)
★★★½ Bone Machine (1992, Island)
★★★★ The Early Years, Vol. 2 (1993; Bizarre/Straight; 1998, Manifesto)
★★ The Black Rider (Island, 1993)
★★★★ Beautiful Maladies: The Island Years (1998, Island)
★★★★½ Mule Variations (Island, 1999)
★★★★½ Used Songs (1973–1980) (Rhino, 2001)
★★★★ Alice (Anti-Epitaph, 2002)
★★★★ Blood Money (Anti-Epitaph, 2002)

Rasping his way through comic-nostalgic cocktail jazz and garrulous streams of Beat-derived wordplay, Tom Waits rose from the seamy side of Los Angeles in the '70s. Some of his first recordings from 1971 are on the 1991 release *The Early Years*. Lingering like a bad hangover, he eventually developed a musical approach to match both his devil-may-care wit and his bluesy sense of despair. Waits' early albums are dreadfully uneven, thanks mostly to his parched voice and well-lubricated point of view: He sounds like he's had a bottle in front of him and a frontal lobotomy for quite some time. The less he tends to marinate his tales of floozies and losers in alcoholic sentiment, the better his albums get. *Small Change* is where his half-mad maundering style gels into something more than a hip novelty act. The slippery-sly evasions of "The Piano Has Been Drinking (Not Me)" and the amphetamine pitchman spiel of "Step Right Up" hold up to close and repeated inspections—more than you can say for many spoken comedy albums. Singing might not be an accurate description of what he does on *Foreign Affairs*, but Waits does expand his somewhat rigidly defined boundaries, duetting with Bette Midler on "I Never Talk to Strangers" and offering the disquieting "Burma Shave" amid the expected bleary reveries. After releasing two comparatively rote thumb-twiddlers (*Blue Valentine* and *Heartattack and Vine*), Waits jumped labels and opted for a challenging, clear-headed approach on *Swordfishtrombones* and *Rain Dogs*. The down-and-out subject matter remains the same, but Waits seems to be in full control of his voice—writing and croaking—now. Stellar session crews on both albums flesh out the compositions with abrasive rock and schizzy jazz motifs. More substantial than his early albums could ever have suggested, it's still not what you'd call easy to digest. Naturally attracted to the theater, Waits followed his triumphant re-emergence with the sketchy *Franks Wild Years* (excerpts from a musical play) and the even-vaguer soundtrack *Big Time* (drawn mostly from its predecessor and *Rain Dogs*) before getting it right with *Alice* and *Blood Money*, a pair of collaborations with Waits' wife, Kathleen Brennan, which were staged in Europe by dramatist Robert Wilson (who'd also been involved in the earlier, less satisfying *Black Rider*) prior to the simultaneous release of these LPs. They followed 1999's *Mule Variations*, annointed by the critics as a return to peak form for the defiantly idiosyncratic artist. —M.C./B.SC.

Junior Walker and the All Stars

★★★★ Shotgun (Motown, 1965)
★★★★ Greatest Hits (Soul, 1969)
★★★ Motown Superstar Series, Vol. 5 (Motown, 1992)
★★★★ The Ultimate Collection (Motown, 1997)

Whether it's Bobby Keys, David Sanborn, or Clarence Clemons, every time a pop sax player starts to blow, it's hard not to hear echoes of Junior Walker. With his specialty being a passionate, sweet growl, he made great, hard soul music in the mid-'60s; such fun cuts as "(I'm a) Road Runner," "Pucker Up Buttercup," "Hip City—Pts. 1 & 2," and his trademark, "Shotgun," are now classics. He sang tough, too, with a scratchy, swinging delivery. The later work got swamped in glossy arrangements, but any of his best-of records still sound tough. By now "Junior Walker" is a style in itself, one that Foreigner deployed excellently on "Urgent" by getting the man himself to sit in. *The Ultimate Collection* is the more comprehensive, an undying testimony to the "cool" of sax. —P.E.

Jerry Jeff Walker

★★★½ Mr. Bojangles (1968; Rhino, 1993)
★★★½ Driftin' Way of Life (Vanguard, 1969)
★★ Five Years Gone (1969; Koch, 2000)
★★★ Bein' Free (1970; Wounded Bird, 2000)
★★★★ Viva Terlingua (MCA, 1973)
★★★½ Ridin' High (MCA, 1975)
★★★½ The Best of Jerry Jeff Walker (MCA, 1980)
★★★★ Gypsy Songman: A Life in Song (Tried & True, 1988)
★★½ Live at Gruene Hall (Tried & True, 1989)
★★★½ Great Gonzos (MCA, 1991)
★★½ Viva Luckenbach! (Rykodisc, 1994)
★★½ Christmas Gonzo Style (Rykodisc, 1994)
★★★ Night After Night (Tried & True, 1995)
★★★ Scamp (Tried & True, 1996)
★★★½ A Man Must Carry On, Vol. 1 (MCA, 1997)
★★★ A Man Must Carry On, Vol. 2 (MCA, 1997)

★★★ Lone Wolf: The Best of Jerry Jeff Walker (Warner, 1998)

★★ Cowboy Boots & Bathin' Suits (Tried & True, 1998)

★★½ Best of the Vanguard Years (Vanguard, 1999)

★★★ Gonzo Stew (Tried & True, 2001)

★★★★½ Ultimate Collection (Hip-O, 2001)

★★★ The Millennium Collection (MCA, 2002)

★★★½ Jerry Jeff Jazz (Tried & True, 2003)

With Circus Maximus

★★ Circus Maximus With Jerry Jeff Walker (1967; Vanguard, 1991)

In the world of Texas singer/songwriters—a clan including such idiosyncratic mavericks as Townes Van Zandt, Billy Joe Shaver, and Joe Ely—few names loom as large as Jerry Jeff Walker. Along with Willie Nelson, Walker was one of the key players on the progressive country scene that sprang up in Austin in the early '70s, and he remains one of the state's most popular musical ambassadors with both old-timers and college kids alike, as well as a major influence on scores of latter-day Texas songwriters and performers. The fact that Walker—born Ronald Clyde Crosby—is a native New Yorker who borrowed many of his best-loved songs ("L.A. Freeway," "Up Against the Wall, Redneck Mother") from other writers has hampered his Lone Star cred not a whit.

Walker's earliest recordings with the New York–based (but Texas-formed) psychedelic folk band Circus Maximus—1967's *Circus Maximus* and 1968's *Never Land Revisited* (out of print)—offer little hint of what was to come, but by 1968's *Mr. Bojangles,* the template for his career was set, four years before he even settled in Austin. Comprised entirely of Walker originals reminiscent of Bob Dylan by way of Ramblin' Jack Elliot, *Mr. Bojangles* features his definitive version of the title track, later covered by both the Nitty Gritty Dirt Band and Sammy Davis Jr. *Driftin' Way of Life* was just as strong, as was his self-titled debut for MCA in 1972. *Jerry Jeff Walker* (out of print) marked his first invigorating dip into Texan Guy Clark's songwriting well, surfacing with fine versions of "That Old Time Feeling" and "L.A. Freeway." While technically not much more of a singer than Clark—both performers sing-speak in the kind of dry rasp generally deemed unfit for country radio—Walker turns Clark's understated song about getting the hell out of Los Angeles (featured on *The Best Of* and *The Ultimate Collection*) into a rousing battle cry. The stage was set for *Viva Terlingua,* a hybrid studio/live album recorded in the sleepy town of Luckenbach (later immortalized in song by Waylon and Willie) that captured both Walker in peak form and the freewillin' spirit of the progres-

sive country movement at its apex. Featuring Clark's "Desperados Waiting for the Train," Walker's own "Sangria Wine," Gary P. Nunn's "London Homesick Blues," and Ray Wylie Hubbard's "Up Against the Wall" (the slyest ironic "tribute" to the American redneck this side of Merle Haggard's "Okie From Muskogee"), *Terlingua* remains Walker's most enduring album—and his last bona fide classic. The followup, *Ridin' High,* found him still doing just that, and 1977's sprawling *A Man Must Carry On* (another live/studio set, frustratingly split into two volumes in '97) holds myriad charms, but subsequent mid-'70s albums for MCA and Elektra (all out of print) added little to Walker's already fully formed persona as a self-styled gonzo troubadour: part tireless champion of Americana's finest underappreciated songwriters (himself included), part rabble-rousing, honky-tonk Jimmy Buffett.

Although his concerts remained rowdy crowd pleasers, Walker's independently released records from the '80s to the present find him mellowing out some. *Gypsy Songman* is the pick of the litter, featuring solo acoustic versions of his favorite originals, while *Scamp* and *Gonzo Stew* mark his return to songwriting after years of coasting on covers. *Jerry Jeff Jazz,* on the other hand, is all covers—a remarkably pleasing and effective collection of stripped-down standards ("My Funny Valentine," "In the Wee Small Hours") that begs the question: What took Texas' most beloved carpetbagger so long in getting around to pinching inspiration from Willie's *Stardust?* —R.SK.

Scott Walker

★★½ It's Raining Today: The Scott Walker Story (1967–70) (Razor & Tie, 1996)

★★ Tilt (Drag City, 1997)

American-born Noel Scott Engel moved to England in the early '60s and became a teen idol as a third of the Walker Brothers (their big hit was "The Sun Ain't Gonna Shine Anymore"). By the time they split up in 1967, though, Scott was less David Cassidy than Ingmar Bergman: On the five early solo albums excerpted on *It's Raining Today,* he'd become devoted to the emotion-wracked, hyperserious songs of Jacques Brel (Walker's originals were along the same lines) and surrounded his lugubrious baritone with bombastic orchestral arrangements that haven't aged well. Remarkably, the kids stuck with him: His version of Brel's "Jackie" is probably the only '60s chart hit whose chorus includes the word "stupid-ass," and his British fan club was bigger than the Beatles'.

Walker's only other American release is the impenetrable *Tilt,* written in the early '90s and originally released in the U.K. in 1995. It's overwhelmingly dark and ambitious, musically and lyrically, but it's hard to get past Walker's vibrato-soaked baritone, which comes off like Berlin-era David Bowie in an 8-foot-deep vat of margarine. And the album is top-heavy with pretentious abstraction, self-consciously difficult and often actively unpleasant. —D.W.

T-Bone Walker

★★★★   T-Bone Blues (1960; Atlantic, 1989)
★★★   I Want a Little Girl (1967; Delmark, 1993)
★★★★   Stormy Monday (1973; LRC Limited, 2001)
★★★★   Well-Done (1973; Collectables, 1994)
★★★★★   The Complete Imperial Recordings, 1950–1954 (EMI, 1991)
★★★★★   The Complete Capitol/Black & White Recordings (Capitol Blues Collection, 1995)
★★★★   Blues Masters: The Very Best of T-Bone Walker (Rhino, 2000)
★★★½   The Very Best of T-Bone Walker (Koch International, 2000)
★★½   Blue on Blues (Fuel 2000/Varèse Sarabande, 2002)

Trace the arc of blues history from the country blues to big-band swing to postwar electrified urban blues to R&B to the dawn of soul music, and one name is everywhere: Aaron Thibeaux Walker, popularly known as T-Bone Walker. Through most of these eras, Walker was more than a mere participant—he was doing much of the reshaping of the landscape around him before moving on to discover new worlds.

The Texas-born Walker was a protégé of Blind Lemon Jefferson, whose uncommonly individual guitar stylings and lyrical folk poetry left an indelible imprint on the budding artist. Jefferson's raw, emotional approach informed Walker's first recordings, "Trinity River Blues" b/w "Wichita Falls Blues," made in 1929 for Columbia. When that record didn't sell, Columbia elected to dispense with a followup. By that time Walker had a full schedule playing with a group of school friends in the Lawson-Brooks big band, an affiliation that continued until 1936, when he headed west to Los Angeles' thriving R&B scene; his place in Lawson-Brooks was assumed by a promising young guitarist named Charlie Christian.

Walker signed to the nascent Capitol label in 1942 and made a statement with his early release "I Got a Break, Baby." Nearly a minute passes at the outset with nothing but soloing from Walker, everything from frisky single-line runs to sustained bent notes, ostinato riffs morphing into screaming three-note chords, rich, legato phrases, and speed-picked single notes cartwheeling one over the other. Then Walker

the vocalist enters, casual but confident, swinging his phrases with Joe Turner–like assurance. The whole package was there, and from that foundation he would move on to write his name large on virtually every succeeding trend in black music up to his death in 1975.

Walker jumped to another new label, Black & White, in 1946, after the lifting of wartime restrictions on materials used for recording. The 50-plus songs he recorded in a variety of contexts over the next five years are now considered among the most important body of blues work ever committed to tape. In it are contained signposts to B.B. King's warm, single-string lyricism, Albert Collins' blazing, hard-picked attacks, Albert King's hearty but unusually tender voicings—the list goes on and on, encompassing about every important guitarist who came after him in the '50s, '60s, and '70s. Moreover, he had the vocal chops to work persuasively in a number of styles. A mid-1949 session produced "Don't Give Me the Runaround," a languorous jazz-pop fusion in the style of the King Cole Trio, singing in a silky, seductive voice that could easily be mistaken for the smoky gray crooning of Cole himself; a swinging bit of Louis Jordan–style small-band novelty, "I Know Your Wig Is Gone"; and Walker's self-penned Mount Rushmore of a blues song, "Call It Stormy Monday (but Tuesday's Just as Bad)." Walker was also a galvanic live performer; his club dates across the country invariably drew packed houses, and many of his '40s and '50s singles routinely peaked in the upper reaches of the R&B chart.

The Capitol Blues Collection's fine three-CD package, *The Complete Capitol/Black & White Recordings*, is, as its title suggests, the complete picture of Walker's early artistic breakthroughs, including "I Got a Break, Baby"; the first version of "Mean Old World" (which became a staple of his live shows and something of a signature song); two versions of "T-Bone Shuffle"; and the original and alternate versions of "Call It Stormy Monday (but Tuesday's Just as Bad)." An absence of personnel or other detailed sessionography information is puzzling given the scope of this project, but the music alone makes it an essential buy. This information is in abundance on *The Complete Imperial Recordings, 1950–1954,* along with all 52 songs Walker recorded for the label (minus six alternate versions excluded owing to space limitations), including four tracks cut in New Orleans with Dave Bartholomew and some of the same musicians who played on Bartholomew-produced Fats Domino recordings.

In 1955, with the rock & roll era dawning, Walker signed with Atlantic, and over the next four years cut 15 sides with producers Jerry Wexler, Ahmet Ertegun, and Nesuhi Ertegun. By the end of his Atlantic tenure, R&B, child of gospel and blues, was mutating into soul, child of gospel, blues, R&B, and pop, and bringing with it a broad-based young audience that regarded Walker's generation as yesterday's news, as these artists' declining sales figures indicated. Yet the Atlantic recordings, issued in 1960 as *T-Bone Blues,* were swept up in the folk and blues revival of that time, and jump-started Walker's career, albeit on a smaller scale than he had experienced in the previous two decades. Walker did some solid work for Atlantic, recording in 1955 in Chicago with Junior Wells and Jimmy Rogers and, toward the end of his tenure with the label, in Los Angeles with the likes of Barney Kessel, and, as the cuts on this disc attest, always rising to the occasion. Working small clubs, colleges, and festivals, he won a new following and gained recognition as an important jazz instrumentalist.

Although 1967's *I Want a Little Girl,* for the Delmark label, is interesting in showcasing Walker in a swinging mode that finds him putting some air into his sound in opting for a terse soloing approach remarkable for its understated eloquence, 1973's effort for the Home Cookin' label (now available on Collectables), *Well-Done,* is the gem of the later years. Walker energizes the place with his smoky, gritty vocals, and gets off some startling solos along the way. Both albums boast an intimate, after-hours club feel and offer periodic displays of vocal and instrumental prowess. As final testaments of a great artist, these are worthy additions to the catalogue.

Of the various single-disc compilations of Walker's music, Koch International's *The Very Best of T-Bone Walker* offers an excellent sampling of the Black & White and Imperial recordings from 1949 through 1954, including "T-Bone Shuffle," "They Call It Stormy Monday," "Midnight Blues," and 13 other choice cuts. A slightly broader overview—16 tracks—is available on Rhino's well-considered *Blues Masters: The Very Best of T-Bone Walker.* All the obvious commercial highlights are here, including some not available on the Koch title (because the Rhino disc covers more territory, its tracks ranging from 1945 through 1957), such as "West Side Baby," a Top 10 R&B hit from 1948. Fuel 2000/Varèse Sarabande's *Blue on Blues* series release devotes six cuts to T-Bone and six to another distinctive blues guitarist, Lowell Fulson, but neither artist is represented by his best work. —D.M.

The Wallflowers

★★ The Wallflowers (Virgin, 1992)
★★★★ Bringing Down the Horse (Interscope, 1996)

★★★ Breach (Interscope, 2000)
★★½ Red Letter Days (Interscope, 2002)

It's not surprising that Bob Dylan's son Jakob would try his hand at making music; what is surprising is the level of success he and his Wallflowers have achieved, well beyond most of the other '60s' rock-star progeny who flooded the market in the '90s. Cynics may say it's all due to Jakob's family connections and striking cheekbones, but the fact is that the guy has developed some songwriting chops. And the rest of the Wallflowers are no slouches either; they're a talented band that knows how to play good old-fashioned no-nonsense American-heartland rock & roll.

As their first album shows, they needed time to find direction. Influenced less by Dylan the elder than by Robbie Robertson, Bruce Springsteen, and Tom Petty, *The Wallflowers'* best songs are its most modest ones: the country-tinged "Shy of the Moon," the solo acoustic "Asleep at the Wheel." Long, sprawling numbers such as "Somebody Else's Money" and "Honeybee" shoot for high drama, but Dylan's stiff vocal delivery sinks them. (His voice is mixed low, too, suggesting a lack of confidence.)

Four years and one record label later, only Dylan and keyboardist Rami Jaffee remained from the original lineup. The change did them good; *Bringing Down the Horse* is light-years better than its predecessor. Dylan's singing has vastly improved—imagine a gruffer Don Henley with a hint of Dad's rasp—and his songs ("One Headlight," "6th Avenue Heartache," "The Difference") are punchy and instantly appealing. *Breach* continues the positive trend. Coproducer Michael Penn's retro-pop leanings blend well with witty tracks such as "Hand Me Down" (which seems to address those critics who still compare Jakob, unfavorably, to his father) and "Murder 101" (featuring Elvis Costello on backing vocals, a smart call since it sounds just like a Costello song). Though better than the Wallflowers' debut, *Red Letter Days* lacks the personality of *Bringing Down the Horse* or *Breach.* The tender piano ballad "Closer to You" stands out, along with the mild salsa inflections of "Too Late to Quit," but much of the remainder fails to engage.

A final note: Is it mere coincidence that since the emergence of his son as a pop music force, Bob Dylan has been doing his best work in at least two decades? Perhaps we should be doubly grateful for the Wallflowers. —M.R.

War

★★½ War (1971; Rhino, 1992)
★★★½ All Day Music (1971; Rhino, 1992)

★★★½ The World Is a Ghetto (1972; A Street, 1995)
★★★½ Deliver the Word (1973; A Street, 1995)
★★½ War Live (1974; Rhino, 1992)
★★★ Why Can't We Be Friends? (1975; A Street, 1995)
★★ Youngblood (1978; Rhino, 1996)
★★ Life (Is So Strange (1983; Rhino, 1996)
★★★½ The Best of War and More (1990; Rhino, 1991)
★★ Peace Sign (Rhino, 1994)
★★★★½ Anthology (1970–1994) (Rhino, 1994)
★★½ Platinum Jazz (1977, MCA; A Street, 1995)
★★★½ The Best of War and More, Vol. 2 (Rhino, 1996)
★★ Coleccion Latina (Rhino, 1997)
★★★½ Grooves & Messages: Greatest Hits of War (Rhino, 1999)
★★★★½ The Very Best of War (Rhino, 2003)
★★★ Cisco Kid and Other Hits (Rhino Flashback, 2003)

As soon as this Los Angeles–bred funk band shook free of Eric Burdon, it was in business. You can hear traces of War's jazzy dance groove on "Spill the Wine," its 1971 hit with the croaking ex-Animal. The two acts parted ways after the unfortunately titled *The Black Man's Burdon,* and the band recorded *War* sans Burdon. With the release of *All Day Music,* War became an impeccable source of earth-moving singles. Lee Oskar's wide-ranging harmonica dances around chanted vocals, snazzy horn charts, and a Latin-tinged bottom; War cuts its ominous rhythmic power with beguiling melodies. "All Day Music" displays the group's lush seductive side, while the equally atmospheric "Slippin' Into Darkness" administers an unflinching shot of social realism.

War's exploratory impulses often lead from fusion into Muzak, making for inconsistent-at-best albums. The vocal high points outweigh the instrumental valleys on *The World Is a Ghetto* (title track, "Cisco Kid"), *Deliver the Word* ("Gypsy Man," "Me and Baby Brother"), and the slightly sweeter *Why Can't We Be Friends?* (title track, "Low Rider"). But a plethora of career retrospectives, the most satisfying of which is the two-CD *The Very Best of War,* keeps the good stuff coming and the filler at bay. One to avoid is *Grooves & Messages,* a two-disc set with the second CD containing nothing but lame remixes. Another iffy collection is *Platinum Jazz,* which surveys War's jazz-fusion excursions—the group's Achilles heel revealed. Like many preeminent funk bands, War seemed to be shaken by the rise of disco, unsure of how to proceed; the group drifted off into a sea of rudderless, MOR-friendly albums. However, hip-hop samplers and rap-

pers have dug deep into War's catchy and complex early-'70s classics. Don't miss the originals, though; Rhino and A Street have reissued all six of these hugely influential albums. —M.C./B.SC.

Warren G

★★★ Regulate . . . G Funk Era (Def Jam/PolyGram, 1994)
★★ Take a Look Over Your Shoulder (Def Jam, 1997)
★★★ I Want It All (Restless, 1999)
★★ Return of the Regulator (Universal, 2001)

Warren G (born Warren Griffin III) is a crucial player in the story of g-funk, the most musical and enduring strain of gangsta rap. As a teenager, Warren formed the group 213 with his Long Beach, CA, running mates Snoop Doggy Dogg and Nate Dogg, and the group cut a demo in the back room of Long Beach's famous V.I.P. record store. Warren, convinced of its worth, pestered his half brother Dr. Dre to give it a listen. When Dre remained uninterested, Warren surreptitiously slipped the tape into the mix at a party. Dre was hooked by Snoop's voice, and the g-funk era was born. This dogged persistence on Warren's part is an early instance of what is perhaps the key quality that has sustained his career. Warren is a talented producer, but not on the level of Dre, and a competent rapper, but without a classic voice à la Snoop. Warren knows his limits, however, and has never overextended himself or strayed far from the breezy, rolling g-funk sound.

From the beginning, Warren collaborated with the cream of the g-funk scene. His debut album went triple platinum and peaked at #2 on the *Billboard* charts on the strength of its massive hit single "Regulate," a duet with Nate Dogg that also appeared on the *Above the Rim* soundtrack.

Take a Look Over Your Shoulder fell prey to the sophomore slump both artistically and saleswise, but even as Warren's national profile took a nosedive, his Southern California stronghold remained. "Smokin' Me Out," his soulful collaboration with Ronnie Isley, was a ubiquitous presence on Los Angeles–area radio stations in 1997.

His 2001 album, *Return of the Regulator,* was in part an attempt to revisit past glories, a fact made plain by the album cover, on which Warren is shown standing on the same street corner as on his debut. The album includes "Yo' Sassy Ways," a 213 reunion of Warren with Snoop and Nate Dogg, and "Ghetto Village," a tasty track that, much like Coolio's "Gangsta's Paradise," is wholly derived from a Stevie Wonder song. The album's most interesting track is "Young

Locs Slow Down," a cautionary tale about the gangsta lifestyle in which Warren laments seeing a ghetto youth "trying to be bold/A hog and a pimp/18 years old/With HIV and a limp." The role of reliable elder statesman suits Warren to a T or, more accurately, to a G. —P.R.

Dionne Warwick

★★★	Dionne (Warner Bros., 1972)
★★½	Track of the Cat (Warner Bros., 1975)
★★★	Friends (1985; Arista, 1990)
★★★★	The Dionne Warwick Collection/Her All-Time Greatest Hits (Rhino, 1989)
★★½	Friends Can Be Lovers (Arista, 1993)
★★★	Aquarela Do Brazil (Arista, 1995)
★★½	Dionne Sings Dionne (River North, 1998)
★★★	Greatest Hits (1979–1990) (Arista, 1989)
★★	Dionne Warwick Sings the Bacharach and David Songbook (MCA, 1995)
★★	Walk On By (Audiophile, 1997)
★★★	Her Classic Songs (Curb, 1997)
★★★	Her Classic Songs, Vol. 2 (Curb, 1998)
★★★	Definitive Collection (Arista, 1999)
★★★	I Say a Little Prayer for You (BCI, 2000)
★★★	The Very Best of Dionne Warwick (Rhino, 2000)
★★★	Love Songs (Rhino, 2001)

Starting out in the very early '60s with the Gospelaires—a quintet whose superabundance of talent included her aunt Cissy Houston, sister Dee Dee, and their friend Doris Troy—Dionne Warwick caught the attention of composer Burt Bacharach. With Warwick, the ace songwriting team of Bacharach and Hal David found their perfect vehicle, and the trio went on to make pop hits whose crafty complexity and disarming effervescence has rarely been equalled. Not only was Warwick's range astonishing, but her delivery—cool, swinging, and unerring—was one of effortless grace, particularly fetching in rendering David's busy, staccato lyrics, her voice projected a sassy elegance. From the early '60s through the end of the decade the singer thrived; while contemporary R&B and rock audiences were chary of her music's classiness, its sleek arrangements, and absolute lack of funk, she hit big on MOR radio, and the songs hold up extremely well. Almost all her '60s albums contain gems, and each of the 24 cuts on Rhino's *Her All-Time Greatest Hits*— from "Walk On By," "Message to Michael," and "I Say a Little Prayer" to "Do You Know the Way to San Jose?" and "Promises, Promises"—is a marvel of craft. After Bacharach-David's bitter split, Warwick floundered. She recovered slightly with "Then Came You," a 1975 duet with the Spinners that hit #1, but

her post-'60s output didn't live up to her glory days. Basically, Warwick never found material as strong as Bacharach-David's and, especially in the disco '70s, her particular finesse was out of style. Her Arista records have been slightly duet-crazed—she's been paired with Luther Vandross, Johnny Mathis, Barry Manilow, and Stevie Wonder—and her distinctiveness has suffered. *Aquarela Do Brazil* turns her loose on an excellent, and apt, set of bossa nova tunes. Still, in her mature years, Warwick remains a staggering talent in search of direction. —P.E.

Muddy Waters

★★★★★	Muddy Waters at Newport, 1960 (1960; Chess, 1986)
★★★★	Muddy Waters Sings Big Bill Broonzy/Folk Singer (1960/1964; Chess, 1987)
★★★★	Folk Singer (1964; Chess, 1999)
★★★	The Real Folk Blues (1966; Chess, 1990)
★	Muddy, Brass and the Blues (1966; Chess, 1987)
★★★	More Real Folk Blues (1967; Chess, 1988)
★★★	Super Blues: Muddy Waters, Little Walter, Bo Diddley (1968; Chess, 1992)
★	Electric Mud (1968; MCA, 1996)
★★★½	Fathers and Sons (1969; MCA, 2001)
★★★★	They Call Me Muddy Waters (1971; Chess, 1990)
★★★★	Live at Mr. Kelly's (1971; Chess, 1992)
★★★	The London Muddy Waters Sessions (1972; Legacy, 2003)
★★★	Can't Get No Grindin' (1973; Chess, 1990)
★★	The Muddy Waters Woodstock Album (1975; MCA, 1995)
★★★★	Hard Again (1977; Legacy, 2004)
★★★½	I'm Ready (1978; Legacy, 2004)
★★★★	Muddy "Mississippi" Waters Live (1979; Sony, 1990)
★★★★	King Bee (1981; Legacy, 2004)
★★★½	Muddy & the Wolf (1982; Chess, 1986)
★★★★	Rare and Unissued (1982; Chess, 1991)
★★★★★	Trouble No More (Singles, 1955–1959) (Chess, 1989)
★★★	Muddy Waters Live (Sony, 1989)
★★★★★	The Chess Box (Chess, 1989)
★★★½	Blues Sky (Epic/Legacy, 1992)
★★★★★	The Complete Plantation Recordings: The Historical 1941–42 Library of Congress Field Recordings (Chess/MCA, 1993)
★★★★★	One More Mile: Chess Collectables, Vol. 1 (Chess, 1994)
★★★	Chicago Blues Masters, Vol. 1: Muddy Waters and Memphis Slim (Capitol, 1995)
★★★	Collaboration (with Otis Spann) (Rhino, 1995)

★★★ Muddy Waters Blues Band featuring Dizzy
      Gillespie (Delta, 1996)
★★★ Hoochie Coochie Man (Delta, 1996)
★★★★ His Best: 1947 to 1955 (MCA, 1997)
★★★★ His Best: 1956 to 1964 (MCA, 1997)
★★★ King of the Electric Blues (Sony, 1997)
★★★ Paris, 1972 (Pablo, 1997)
★★★ Best of Muddy Waters: 20th Century Masters
      (MCA, 1999)
★★★★½ Rollin' Stone: The Golden Anniversary
      Collection (MCA, 2000)
★★★★ The Anthology: 1947–1972 (Chess, 2001)

Muddy Waters stands in a select group of artists whose work altered the landscape of American music, reaching across the years to mark everything that has come in its wake. His 1950s recordings for the Chess label transformed his native Delta blues into a music with widespread popular appeal, both here and abroad, thereby laying a huge chunk of rock & roll's foundation. This he accomplished by giving the blues a new shape crafted by electric instruments and amplification; along the way he introduced a stop-time riff that has since become one of the most familiar sounds in blues and rock, and penned eloquent, culturally revealing lyrics rooted in the folklore and traditions of African-Americans. Moreover, musicians who accompanied Waters always profited from his rigorous discipline, many of them going on to form their own bands and make important records. And while the blues is acknowledged as a limited musical form, Waters, sometimes solely through the sheer force of his own personality, demanded attention be paid to his work, even to noble but failed experiments such as 1966's *Muddy, Brass and the Blues.*

Waters, who died in 1983, left behind a substantial body of recordings, many of which remain in print. Most indispensable, naturally, are the Chess albums, which document the most fertile period of his artistry, but it would be a mistake to ignore his later work, because the man was still going strong in the late '70s, buoyed by an association with the Blue Sky label that paired him with Johnny Winter, whose energizing presence as producer reinvigorated Waters both personally and artistically.

Had Waters never made it out of the Delta, *Down on Stovall's Plantation* (a vinyl release on the Testament label) and its unabridged version on Chess/ MCA, *The Complete Plantation Recordings,* would show only the raw beginnings of an artist much admired in his own region, albeit one whose style was imitative of other Delta giants who had preceded him or were his contemporaries; in fact, at the time of these recordings made by Alan Lomax for the Library

of Congress, Waters' reputation for brewing the best moonshine in Mississippi's Coahoma County was on a par with his standing as a musician.

Born McKinley Morganfield in 1915 in Rolling Fork, MS, Waters grew up in Clarksdale on the Stovall Plantation, where he was raised by his grandmother, who bestowed upon him the nickname Muddy, to which his friends appended Waters. In 1932, when he was 17, he took up the guitar. Taught by a friend, Waters' most direct influences were Charley Patton, Son House, and Robert Johnson.

Folklorist Alan Lomax, heading a field recording team for the Library of Congress, came to Clarksdale in 1941 looking for Robert Johnson, unaware that he had been dead for nearly three years. Told that the man on Stovall's played a lot like Johnson, Lomax tracked down Waters at home and recorded him performing two songs; a year later he came back and recorded more sides, some with Waters playing solo acoustic; some with Waters and a primitive string band, the Son Sims Four; some with Waters and guitarist Charles Berry. Encompassing 18 sides in all, these recordings, cut in Waters' cabin, are raw, moving, and suggestive of things to come. One of the 1941 tracks, "Country Blues Number One," is descended musically and lyrically from House's "My Black Mama" and Johnson's "Walkin' Blues." Thus a pattern emerged: Over the course of his career Waters would make frequent figurative forays back to the Delta for material, building new songs out of folktales and fragments of choruses he had absorbed in his youth, adding new and sometimes bolder lyrics to material otherwise decades old. As for thematic focus, Waters' songs were in the Delta tradition of brooding ruminations on death and faithless love, aptly summarized in titles such as "You're Gonna Miss Me When I'm Dead and Gone," "You Got to Take Sick and Die Some of These Days," and "Why Don't You Love So God Can Use You?" Vocally he displays mastery of the nuances of Delta blues singing, but while the stark authority of his voice is commanding, he's not yet the overpowering presence he would become a few years later after relocating to Chicago.

In 1943, Waters packed his belongings in a suitcase and boarded the Illinois Central Railroad, joining the mass exodus of black people out of Mississippi to greater opportunity in the North, Chicago in this case. In the mid-'40s he got his first electric guitar and began working with various combinations of musicians headed by an older Delta-born bluesman, Sunnyland Slim. With Slim and bassist Big Crawford he recorded some unsuccessful sides for the Columbia and Aristocrat labels, the latter a Chicago-based operation run by brothers Leonard and Phil Chess.

In 1948, Waters cut two Aristocrat sides in the Delta bottleneck style, "I Can't Be Satisfied" b/w "(I Feel Like) Going Home," which sold rapidly in Chicago and in the South. By this time Waters was working clubs with a band that included Claude Smith on guitar, Jimmy Rogers doubling on guitar and harmonica, Baby Face Leroy on guitar and drums, and Little Walter Jacobs doubling on guitar and harmonica. This configuration, which later included Elgin Evans on drums, began recording in 1950 and developed the hard-driving sound of modern urban blues on "Louisiana Blues," "She Moves Me," "Honey Bee," "Still a Fool," and "Long Distance Call," all heard (along with the early Aristocrat sides) on disc one of the three-CD *Chess Box.* "Louisiana Blues" was a significant track in that it was Waters' first recording to feature Little Walter's amplified harmonica and it was his first national R&B hit; also, it was the single that established the Chess label, which had been formed in early 1950 after the brothers Chess bought out their Aristocrat partner.

Leonard Chess was producing Waters in these days, and his lack of musical training worked in his and the artist's favor. Like Waters, Chess went on instinct and feel. In 1954, bassist Willie Dixon penned three songs for Waters that became major R&B hits and, as subsequent years have shown, blues masterpieces—"Hoochie Coochie Man," "Just Make Love to Me," and "I'm Ready." That same year saw pianist Otis Spann and drummer Fred Below (replacing Elgin Evans) join Waters, and the band develop such rhythmic innovations as stop-time patterns and a driving backbeat that quickly found their way into other artists' songs. Disc one and the first half of disc two in *The Chess Box* document the groundbreaking period from 1947 through 1956 and demonstrate most dramatically Waters' growing confidence in his artistry. He was surrounded by great musicians, and in Dixon and Chess he had the support and advice of two mentors, one an artist himself, the other a technician, both of whom understood where this music was headed and knew how to get it there.

Come 1956 (and the second half of *The Chess Box*'s second disc), Waters' band was undergoing change. Late in the year Little Walter left to form his own band and was replaced by James Cotton; in early '57 Rogers left and was replaced by one of the early masters of distortion, Pat Hare. This combination proved even more combustible than Waters' first band.

In 1958, Waters and Spann toured England with great success, which led to a booking at the 1960 Newport Jazz Festival. The live album from that date, *Muddy Waters at Newport, 1960,* was a substantial hit in England, where it had enormous impact on the then-emerging generation of young white blues musicians. It remains available and is one of the most important in the entire catalogue, marked as it is by outstanding vocal performances from Waters and revelatory guitar support from Pat Hare.

The early '60s brought new personnel into the band, including guitarists Buddy Guy, Sammy Lawhorn, and Pee Wee Madison and drummers Willie "Big Eyes" Smith and S.P. Leary. This was a time of experiments, with Waters cutting an album on which horns were later overdubbed (a mistake), *Brass and the Blues. The London Muddy Waters Sessions* united Waters with some of his British acolytes (Georgie Fame, pre–Blind Faith Rick Grech, pre-Hendrix Mitch Mitchell) for fair-to-middling results (some of these tracks, along with those cut in London by Howlin' Wolf, found their way onto the 1982 compilation *Muddy & the Wolf*). A disastrous attempt to psychedelicize Waters' blues resulted in the horrendous *Electric Mud,* about which the less said the better; only completists need invest in it. In 1969 a group of young American blues artists got together with Waters and Otis Spann for their own salute to the master on the *Fathers and Sons* album. The lineup's heavy hitters included Paul Butterfield on guitar and two alumni of his Butterfield Blues Band, Michael Bloomfield on guitar and Sam Lay on drums. Sitting in with them are Booker T. and the MG's bassist Donald "Duck" Dunn, and, making an appearance on the rousing live version of "Got My Mojo Workin'," drummer Buddy Miles. The album is composed of studio sessions recorded over three days, and a short live set taped at the Super Cosmic Joy-Scout Jamboree in Chicago. Studio or live, the whole affair cooks with a vengeance, as the young acolytes of Chicago blues and Waters in particular mesh perfectly with the elder statesmen. The remastered CD version of the album offers four previously unissued studio cuts, making *Fathers and Sons* more than a passing curiosity. Two alternate takes from those sessions are featured on *The Chess Box*'s third disc, with Waters and Spann accompanied by Paul Butterfield, Michael Bloomfield, Donald "Duck" Dunn, and Phil Upchurch, among others.

Other titles showcase the breadth and depth of Waters' blues over the years. The remastered, expanded *Folk Singer* (originally issued in 1964) is a return to the Delta blues in a stirring all-acoustic session teaming Waters and Buddy Guy on guitars and Willie Dixon on bass. It's also now available in a recommended twofer CD with Waters' heartfelt homage to the towering figure who preceded him as the major domo of Chicago blues, Big Bill Broonzy, *Muddy Waters Sings Big Bill Broonzy.* Taking a page out of RCA's

Elvis repackaging strategy, MCA has made a continuing project of reissuing Waters' work in configurations to suit any budget. The least of these is the *20th Century Masters* entry, *Best of Muddy Waters,* not because its material is weak—in fact, some of the gems are here, including "Mannish Boy," "Rock Me," "Got My Mojo Workin'," and "Hoochie Coochie Man"—but because there's so little of it: 11 cuts only. Still, it's a good low-priced buy, however incomplete. Otherwise, MCA offers three first-rate, in-depth overviews of the body of work in question. *His Best: 1947 to 1955* and its companion volume, *His Best: 1956 to 1964,* are single-disc, 20-cut compilations of choice Muddy, no filler allowed. About the only complaint possible is the 1947–55 disc's inclusion of a curious alternate take of "Hoochie Coochie Man," instead of the issued track, featuring a searing vocal from Muddy that diminishes the familiar version but is undermined by faltering harp support from a clearly confused Little Walter, who at one point stops playing rather than continue wandering around the track in search of his niche. The disc of material covering 1956–64 spotlights eight cuts from 1956, then moves on to 1958, when Waters' formidable band members included James Cotton, Pat Hare, Luther Tucker, and Francis Clay (except on "You Shook Me" and "You Need Love"—the latter being the blueprint for Led Zeppelin's "Whole Lotta Love"—which feature an entirely different lineup). *The Anthology: 1947–1972* is pretty much *The Chess Box* boiled down to 50 cuts on two CDs. In addition to the obvious tracks from this quarter-century of work, the song selection includes powerful but lesser-known entries such as the moving reminiscence, "I Feel Like Going Home." Easily falling into the "Essential" category is the double-CD, 50-track retrospective, *Rollin' Stone: The Golden Anniversary Collection.* Here in one package are all the known recordings of Waters' 1947–52 tenure at Aristocrat and Chess. An accompanying 16-page booklet puts it all in proper historical perspective. Most of the first disc features Waters accompanied only by bassist Earnest "Big" Crawford; Little Walter joins later in the proceedings to make it a trio, but the effect of listening to the tracks in chronological order is to hear the modern Chicago blues scene taking shape as each note is played. This is where Waters was at when he moved to the Windy City from the Mississippi Delta, and the fury of his slide work on the early cuts suggests the bigger, more propulsive sound to come as he fleshed out his lineup with gifted instrumentalists.

Ample documentation exists of Waters' sizzling live shows, which remained powerful right up to the end of his life as a performer. The above-mentioned *Newport, 1960* is first among unequals, but a performance from two years earlier, in 1958, finishes a close second to, if not in a dead heat with, the more celebrated Newport show. *Collaboration* was recorded at the Free Trade Hall in Manchester, England, on October 26, 1958, with Waters accompanied only by Otis Spann on piano and an unidentified British drummer believed to be Graham Burbridge. The audio quality could be better—the sound is hollow, as would be the case if someone were recording from the audience rather than directly from the sound board—but the dialogue between Waters and Spann is scintillating, the latter filling the spaces with dexterous riffs, and Waters offering his own stinging commentary on electric guitar. The low-down version of "Hoochie Coochie Man" is foreboding and seductive in one fell swoop. Another fine live album (though there's nary a hint of an audience on it) from 1971, *Live at Mr. Kelly's,* features the Waters band with Pinetop Perkins on piano (Otis Spann died in 1969) and the redoubtable Willie "Big Eyes" Smith on drums, with James Cotton blowing some harsh, protesting harmonica solos on three cuts. Waters is at his fine, weary-voiced best on this outing, and the band is about note-perfect behind him with the Smith and Calvin Jones (bass) rhythm section especially coming up with a powerhouse performance. Another smart choice among the live discs is Pablo's *Paris, 1972.* On this outing Waters is joined by a full band, members of which include Pinetop Perkins on piano, Calvin Jones on bass, Willie "Big Eyes" Smith on drums, with George "Mojo" Buford wailing and crying on harmonica like the second coming of Little Walter, and Louis Meyers rounding out the roster on guitar. Everyone gets into a deep, surging groove on the set-opening "Clouds in My Heart," with Perkins and Buford engaging in an impressively stormy instrumental set-to about midway through the seven-minute-plus number. A stripped-down interpretation of Robert Johnson's "Walking Blues" evokes the spirit of Waters' earliest inspiration even as it rethinks the song's dramatic structure. Instead of attacking the guitar a la Johnson, Waters heightens the song's sinister ambience with a few choice, robust upper-strings licks as his supporting musicians stay resolutely in the background, filling out the sound just so but giving Waters a wide berth for his stark testifying. Despite the presence of the Band's Levon Helm and Garth Hudson, plus Paul Butterfield, Waters' final Chess LP, *The Muddy Waters Woodstock Album,* released in 1975, is an uninspired effort, with the musicians trudging through their paces and Waters straining to get something out of half-baked material.

Following the disappointment of the Woodstock album, Waters came roaring back two years later on the Blue Sky label, with the appropriately titled *Hard*

Again, on which Johnny Winter provided the sensitive production touch otherwise lacking on some of the early '70s recordings. Old hands James Cotton and Bob Margolin, among others, are back on board; Jimmy Rogers shows up on the followup to *Hard Again, I'm Ready,* as does Walter Horton. The live album *Muddy "Mississippi" Waters Live* demonstrates what everyone who saw Waters in the late '70s learned: On any given night the man could cut any other artist who stepped on a stage, a point he made explicit on this set with an explosive version of "Mannish Boy" performed as if it were freshly written. All three of these titles are now packaged in a single, slip-cased set—a threefer, that is—as well as remaining available as separate entities. *King Bee* is a fitting final testament, with Waters mixing in some stirring originals ("Too Young to Know," "Sad Sad Day") with covers of Slim Harpo's "I'm a King Bee" and Arthur Crudup's "Mean Old Frisco Blues." 1992's *Blues Sky* was the first issued overview of the Blue Sky years, but the 1997 *King of the Electric Blues* is a solid followup in 15 tracks, although the end result of listening to these tracks will likely drive fans back to the complete albums from which each was culled (probably the point of the sets, anyway). The cover photo of *King Bee* shows Waters smiling beatifically and relaxing in an ornate chair. Atop the chair is a king's crown, which rests directly above Waters' head. It looks like a good fit. —D.M.

Roger Waters

★★	The Pros and Cons of Hitchhiking (Columbia, 1984)
★★★	Radios KAOS (Columbia, 1987)
★★	The Wall—Live in Berlin (Mercury, 1990)
★★★	Amused to Death (Columbia, 1992)
★★★	In the Flesh Live (Sony, 2000)
★★★	Flickering Flame: The Solo Years, Vol. 1 (Columbia, 2002)

Ron Geesin/Roger Waters

★★½	Music from The Body (1970; EMI, 2000)

Bassist Roger Waters left Pink Floyd in 1983, taking his concepts and lead vocals along with him. Assembling a weighty studio crew for his debut solo venture, Waters ponders *The Pros and Cons of Hitchhiking.* Eric Clapton drips rivulets of blues guitar in between the floating story segments, somewhat incongruously, but Waters' wandering tale doesn't amount to much without a tune or three to hang it on. And even the full-blown chorus on the climactic title track can't quite pull that out of thin air. *Radio KAOS* is a more successful attempt at constructing an art-rock-enhanced narrative. Resolutely unswinging rhythms and mellow

voiceovers from archetypal FM DJ Jim Ladd enhance Waters' depiction of a wheelchair-bound computer genius: a saintly hacker and phone freak who zaps the nuclear "Powers That Be." Despite the stiffened beat and occasional horn lines, *Radio K.A.O.S.* sounds exactly like a transmission from another time. That's a large part of its appeal, too.

Waters commemorated the fall of communism by re-creating Pink Floyd's 1979 concept rock opus at the Berlins Wall with an all-star cast: Bryan Adams, Joni Mitchell, Cyndi Lauper, Sinéad O'Connor, and the Scorpions all joined in the fun. The souvenir live album's more a pleasant reminder of an exciting moment in history than a statement of lasting artistic worth. Waters' most piercing indictment of modern society to date, *Amused to Death* reaches a positively corrosive level of irony on "What God Wants" and "Perfect Sense." The choice of Jeff Beck as stunt guitarist is inspired, but the melody quotient remains low, and Waters' voice sounds ravaged.

More than a decade later, fans are still waiting for *Amused to Death*'s successor. *In the Flesh Live* documents two late-'90s tours, cogently blending old Floyd and solo material, while the import-only *Flickering Flame* compiles random album cuts and a few movie soundtrack numbers. Speaking of which, Waters' 1970 collaboration with avant-gardiste Ron Geesin, *Music from The Body,* was originally meant to provide the aural backdrop for a subunderground film. Boasting titles like "More than Seven Dwarfs in Penis-Land," this collection of bizarre sound effects and jaunty acoustic ditties is little more than an amusing footnote to Waters' discography. —M.C./M.R.

Ween

★★★½	GodWeenSatan: The Oneness (1990; Restless, 2001)
★★½	The Pod (1991; Elektra, 1995)
★★★½	Pure Guava (Elektra, 1992)
★★★★	Chocolate & Cheese (Elektra, 1994)
★★★	12 Golden Country Greats (Elektra, 1996)
★★★★	The Mollusk (Elektra, 1997)
★★★	Paintin' the Town Brown: Ween Live 1990–1998 (Elektra, 1999)
★★★½	White Pepper (Elektra, 2000)
★★★	Quebec (Sanctuary, 2003)
★★★	Live in Chicago (Sanctuary, 2004)

Following a number of self-released cassettes, Ween's official debut, *GodWeenSatan: The Oneness* documents the awesome possibilities that result from two bong-addled suburban Pennsylvania kids with a four-track recorder, a sick 'n' twisted aesthetic sense, and a love for popular music at its most bloated and dramatic. Across 26 tracks (bolstered to 29 in the anniversary edition reissue), Gene and Dean Ween romp through Beefheart/Zappa-style dadaist blues with an anything-goes '80s punk sensibility that also encompasses quirky minimalism, bubblegum pop, boogie rock, folk rock, art rock, Satanic metal (and Satanic gospel!), reggae, folk, mariachi, Prince, the Boss, and more, all chainsawed and mutilated into small, pulpy chunks that only sometimes reveals its brilliance. Just as often, it's tough to stomach.

Its followup, *The Pod,* is just as low-fi and almost as sprawling (23 tracks), but not nearly as joyfully eclectic. Instead, the duo wallows mostly in a demonic acid rock that can be ponderous and overly murky. At its best, though, the album reveals glimpses of Ween's later genius at mocking rock conventions while simultaneously relishing them. Tracks such as the psychedelic art-rock indulgence "Right to the Ways and the Rules of the World," the glam-rock "Captain Fantasy," or "Sketches of Winkle"—equal parts galloping proto-metal and Who-style Brit rock—could serve as models for retro rockers Guided by Voices or metal parodists Tenacious D.

The duo's major-label debut, *Pure Guava,* pares the song list down to a more manageable 19 tracks, but only slightly smoothes the rough edges and the compositional excesses. The catchy 'n' cutesy novelty "Push th' Little Daisies" was presentable enough to earn significant airplay, and—along with other catchy, totally twisted nuggets such as "Big Jilm" and "Pumpin' 4 the Man"—shows Ween developing its own oddly accessible, relatively consistent sound.

Then *Chocolate & Cheese* pushed Ween into a whole other realm. Here, the low-fi noodlings get discarded almost entirely, replaced by a full band of players proficient in rock and pop vernaculars. "Freedom of '76" works as a nicely crafted, more subtlely humorous Philly-soul parody (or low-rent tribute?), while "Voodoo Lady" offers a spastic Latin-rock send-up (think Santana fronted by Cheech and Chong) that's not too far over the top to enjoy on its own musical merits. With *Chocolate & Cheese,* Ween graduates from the fringe to take its place alongside truly accessible eccentrics such as They Might Be Giants.

Taking a detour from its increasingly dynamic trampings of familiar pop styles, Ween headed to Nashville to record *12 Golden Country Greats* with a cast of famed country sessionmen. The album's pedal steel, fiddles, and banjos scream "stunt," and white-trash parodies offer predictable mockings of Southern culture. But tracks such as "I'm Holding You" at least attempt earnest graftings of classic country music over Ween's warped images. As an exercise in testing the group's ability to stretch its sensibility across genre lines, it's pretty convincing.

The Mollusk picks up where *Chocolate & Cheese* left off, continuing Ween's renaissance as stylistically nimbly, musically rich idiot savants. Among the album's many water-themed songs, the title track—a wonderfully goofy bit of folk psychedelia inspired by Donovan's "Atlantis"—is most notable. "Ocean Man" is nearly as infectious, though, and the sea chanty "She Wanted to Leave" breaks new ground for the group by daring to trade formalistic in-jokes for some truly heartbreaking balladry.

The two-disc live retrospective, *Paintin' the Town Brown: Ween Live 1990–1998,* offers 19 songs from all stages of Ween's development: early on, as a duo with a drum machine, later as a full band, plus some selections featuring backup from Nashville sessionmen. All this, plus the inclusion of some rare songs not found on other albums, makes *Paintin' the Town Brown* a draw mainly for hard-core devotees.

Returning to studio releases after three years away, the group offered *White Pepper,* its most straightforward, pop-oriented album yet. While suitably populated with clever *Chocolate & Cheese*–style parody/tributes—the Jimmy Buffet–style "Bananas and Blow"; Steely Dan–like "Pandy Fackler"—the record also features a surprising number of catchy, mainstream rock songs ("Even If You Don't," "Stay Forever") utterly devoid of sonic and lyrical mutations.

Since parting ways with Elektra, Ween has released two more live albums through its own Chocodog label: 2001's *Live in Toronto, Canada* and the following year's three-disc *Live at Stubb's,* neither of which are officially in print. And yet another live release, the two-disc CD/DVD combo *Live in Chicago,* followed once the group landed on new label Sanctuary. But not before Ween returned with a new studio record, *Quebec.* The record finds Ween moving even further toward a straightforward approach in the vein of *White Pepper*—where the music was once truly twisted, it's now merely psychedelic, and often quite mildly at that. Aside from a Motörhead-inspired power-metal opening track ("It's Gonna Be a Long Night"), the old-timey "Here There Fancypants," and some Residents-style synth weirdness ("So Many People in the Neighborhood"), the majority of *Quebec* consists of breezy midtempo or folksy progressive rock. Vocal distortions and bits of weirdness still abound, but relative to the group's most creative work, *Quebec* is strictly easy listening Ween.   —R.M.S.

Weezer

★★★★ Weezer (DGC, 1994)
★★★★★ Pinkerton (DGC, 1996)

★★★★ Weezer (Interscope, 2001)
★★★★ Maladroit (Interscope, 2002)

Weezer is one of the strangest rock stories of our time: Rivers Cuomo and his L.A. geek-punk band hit the MTV grunge jackpot in 1994, fizzled out after the flop 1996 concept album *Pinkerton,* and then began a second career as a shockingly successful cult phenomenon. Weezer's self-titled debut (later known to fans as the "Blue Album") has a couple of guitar-heavy radio hits in "Buddy Holly" and "Undone (The Sweater Song)," suffused by Cuomo's presence as the ultimate suburban nerd, writing madly catchy pop gems inspired by Kiss, comic books, and 12-sided dice. Nobody took it very seriously. *Pinkerton* was a textbook case of the difficult second album: a confessional song cycle, based on the opera *Madame Butterfly,* about a lonely young rock star nursing furtive crushes on lesbians ("Pink Triangle") and teenage Japanese fans ("Across the Sea"). People took it even less seriously. Excellent though it was, *Pinkerton* was too raw and weird for the radio, and it looked like the "Buddy Holly" boys had gotten their asses abandoned to the buzz bin of history.

Except that unbeknownst to normal people, Weezer not only kept hanging in there, it continued to hold a Rasputin-like grip on its fanatical, ever-increasing cult of emo kids and suburban punks, until its triumphant 2000 comeback tour shocked the music biz. As the die-hard Weezer kids rose out of the woodwork to pump their fists and sing along with "My Name Is Jonas," the only other sound you could hear was multiple jaw-floor collisions—and maybe also the sound of Sponge, Nada Surf, and Better Than Ezra frantically paging their agents. *Weezer* (a.k.a. the "Green Album") and *Maladroit* are totally crunk half-hour albums buzzing through crunch-guitar nuggets such as "Dope Nose," "Hashpipe," and the should've-been-a-hit "Simple Pages." Cuomo has gotten more oblique about his girl troubles—there's no "El Scorcho" or "Pink Triangle" on these albums, which is a shame. But no matter how hard he tries, he can't quite keep from exposing his wracked personality, and with ballads such as "O Girlfriend" taking that crucial millimeter of a step toward maturity, Weezer deserves a huge hand for making the world safe again for frayed cardigans and corduroys.

Of Weezer's four albums, *Pinkerton* is the best by far, with a big raw guitar sound to flesh out Cuomo's psychosexual contortions. Despite "The Good Life," "Tired of Sex," and "El Scorcho," the highlight is "Pink Triangle," especially its chorus hook, "We were good as married in my mind/But married in my mind's no good." Much derided upon its release, and disavowed by an understandably embarrassed Cuomo, *Pinkerton* has taken its rightful place as a classic anyway. —R.S.

Bob Weir

★★★ Ace (Warner Bros., 1972)
★★½ Heaven Help the Fool (1978; Arista, 1988)
★★½ Bobby and the Midnights (1981; Arista, 1988)
★★★ Weir/Wasserman Live (Arista, 1998)

Bob Weir and Ratdog

★★★ Evening Moods (Arista, 2000)
★★★½ Weir Here: The Best of Bob Weir (Hybrid, 2004)

Rhythm guitarist and singer for the Grateful Dead, Weir doesn't stray far from that band's sound and spirit on his debut, *Ace* (1972)—his band mates provide backup, and the record is smooth, clean, and unsurprising. Undercut by Keith Olsen's overglossy production and the busy drumming of Nigel Olsen and Mike Baird, *Heaven Help the Fool* is more distinctive, but it's a weaker album. In very clear voice, and deftly assisted by session vet Waddy Wachtel on guitar, Weir delivers accomplished midtempo numbers—some so slick and burdened with a backup choir as to verge in passages on high-end MOR. Much tougher, *Bobby and the Midnights* joins Weir with Dead keyboardist Brent Mydland and jazz drummer Billy Cobham. The highlights from Weir's best set include the reggae-ish "Book of Rules," the graceful "Carry Me," and a neat, bluesy shuffle, "Josephine." In the mid-'90s Weir teamed up with bassist Rob Wasserman, and began turning out his best work outside the Dead. The pair became the nucleus for his post-Dead band, Ratdog. And on *Evening Moods,* with guest drummer Mickey Hart (also formerly of the Grateful Dead), the ensemble dazzles, Wasserman's bass a perfect counterpoint for Weir's idiosyncratic guitar. —P.E.

Gillian Welch

★★★½ Revival (Almo Sounds, 1996)
★★★ Hell Among the Yearlings (Almo Sounds, 1998)
★★★★ Time (The Revelator) (Acony, 2001)
★★★ Soul Journey (Acony, 2003)

On a debut album that came out of nowhere and raised lots of questions about what bluegrass could be, this Los Angeles–born singer/songwriter does more than impersonate the hard-times praise music of Bill Monroe: She inhabits it. With partner, David Rawlings, Welch sings strong, sad ballads that invoke and do not redirect classic bluegrass and folk idioms—

faith in God, fast old cars, ties to the land, moonshining, sharecropping. The mournful "Orphan Girl" finds strength in its incantatory, repetitive structure as the lyrics spiral heavenward; "Annabelle" is a delicately plucked ballad that harbors a tragedy like a scrub-covered landmine; "By the Mark" recalls the Carter Family's harmonizing as it invokes a raw vision of Christianity very like the blunt, bloody imagery of traditional Appalachian music. Her melodies are thoroughly beautiful, and T Bone Burnett's clean, balanced production allows every aspect of the performances to shine.

Welch's tunes remain as strong as ever on her anticipated followup to *Revival*, but even as she strips down the production—paring the use of drums and electric guitar—her imagery grows more lurid and hopeless, the songs slower, and the strings skewed toward the minor. While the bluegrass-country-folk axis she mines for inspiration provides a direct route to a certain set of values and emotions, her insistence on expressing those values in antiquated terms is troubling.

Songs such as "Good Til Now," "Miner's Refrain," and "My Morphine" are sung from a male point of view, and her tales of hardship seem to take place on a shabby back porch of the long-ago past. Only when Welch speeds up the pace—on the roadhouse blues "Honey Now"—or crafts one of the circularly constructed ballads of Christian faith at which she excels (in this case the death-directed "Rock of Ages") does *Hell Among the Yearlings* rise above the melancholy but archaic litany of sin, rape, lost girls, bad boys, cut throats, and gunshot wounds.

Exactly the record that Welch needed to make, *Time (The Revelator)* is also the record her fans wanted to hear, proving that her songwriting could transcend the dated idioms in which she previously trafficked. Cowritten with David Rawlings, the songs are neither trendy nor dated but fresh, thoughtful, and full-blooded modern folk with gritty rock edges and meltingly lovely melodies. Welch's simple voice does complicated things on the tough "My First Lover," and muses gently on the anti-Napster "Everything Is Free." On "I Want to Sing That Rock and Roll," Welch and Rawlings cast rock & roll as anything that makes a joyful noise unto the Lord—in this case, a peppy midtempo ballad. "Dear Someone" is as gentle and pure as a Stephen Foster tune, the earthy "Red Clay Halo" is rousing in her older style, and "Elvis Presley Blues" is a gimlet-sharp and heartfelt examination of Elvis' instinctive genius.

On *Soul Journey*, Welch's slow, earnest songs don't have the texture of those from her three previous albums. Tracks such as "Lowlands" and "One Monkey" are meant to sound stately and austere, but they just seem stagnant. Welch does rise to the occasion on the album's few uptempo numbers: On the bluegrass session "No One Knows My Name," which owes debts to Ralph Stanley and Charley Patton, she laments, "My mother was just a girl, seventeen/It's a wonder that I'm in this world at all." And on "One Little Song," she pines for "One little word that ain't been abused a thousand times/In a thousand rhymes." Sometimes, she even finds it. —A.B./J.C.

Mary Wells

★★★ You Beat Me to the Punch (Motown, 1995)
★ The Very Best of the Motorcity Recordings (Hot, 1996)
★★★½ The Ultimate Collection (Motown, 1998)
★★★ The Millennium Collection (Motown, 1999)
★★½ My Guy: The Best of Mary Wells (Prestige Elite, 2002)

Motown's reigning diva until the arrival of Diana Ross, Mary Wells began making hits at 16 with "Bye Bye Baby," which she wrote herself, and went on to release a stirring round of singles, generally cowritten with the label's in-house genius, Smokey Robinson. Her light, airy approach stamped her as more of a '50s-style doo-wopper than a soul singer, and her trademark songs—"My Guy," "You Beat Me to the Punch," "The One Who Really Loves You"—were more snappy than fervent. With Marvin Gaye, however ("What's the Matter With You Baby," "Once Upon a Time"), she swung with more confidence. Holland-Dozier-Holland produced her one exceptional go-for-broke number, "You Lost the Sweetest Boy", and it remains a fine treatise on agonized romance. *The Ultimate Collection* is the most thorough compilation; *You Beat Me to the Punch* is a strong set of all-Smokey productions. Wells lost her battle with throat cancer in 1992. —P.E.

Kanye West

★★★★ College Dropout (Roc-A-Fella, 2004)

Kanye West first made his name by letting his production—not his voice—do the talking for him. As the man behind Jay-Z's "Izzo (H.O.V.A.)" and Scarface's "Guess Who's Back," he perfected a warm, almost sentimental brand of hip-hop, using bright, soulful beats and melodic choruses to humanize otherwise chilly gangsters. His multiplatinum debut, *College Dropout,* has made him a singular hip-hop star, one whose aesthetic spans both hard-nosed mainstream rap and hip-hop's more introspective underground scene. "Wasn't talking 'bout coke and birds," he fesses on his plaintive, "Through the Wire." "It's more like spoken word." West revels in odd juxtapositions— "Get Em High," for instance, references both Beck and Pastor Troy. The half-serious twelve-minute monologue "Last Call" details the hard knocks he suffered to make the album a reality, and there are several skits—part comedy, part pure bitterness—about the uselessness of higher learning.

West isn't quite MC enough to hold down the entire disc; carefully sprinkled A-list guests such as Jay-Z and Mos Def help. His ace in the hole is his signature cozy sound—dusty soul samples, gospel hymns, drums that pop as if hit for the very first time. He has also succeeded in showing some vulnerability behind a glossy, MTV-ready hip-hop sheen. On "All Falls Down," he says, "We all self-conscious/I'm just the first to admit it." Let's hope he's not the last.   —J.C.

Paul Westerberg

> ★★★★ 14 Songs (Sire, 1993)
> ★★ Eventually (Reprise, 1996)
> ★★ Suicaine Gratification (Capitol, 1999)
> ★★★★ Mono/Stereo (Vagrant, 2002)
> ★★★ Come Feel Me Tremble (Vagrant, 2003)

Paul Westerberg could have made *Pet Sounds* after the Replacements broke up and it still probably wouldn't have been good enough. So beloved was his old band that his solo output never got out of the shadow of the Replacements' legacy and catalogue. But that doesn't mean he hasn't released some solid records. The album *14 Songs* came shortly after the breakup of the band and picks up where their swan song, *All Shook Down,* left off. The musicianship had a sense of professionalism, and songs seemed finely crafted, especially cuts such as "World Class Fad" and "Someone I Once Knew." But the album didn't garner the kind of fanaticism that greeted Replacements records. Westerberg followed up *14 Songs* with a string of mediocre singer/songwriter records. *Eventually* and *Suicaine Gratification* sounded like Westerberg was lost at sea, unable to capture the loose glory that marked his best work. It seemed as if old age was being unkind to the man who once personified youthful exuberance.

It wasn't until 2002's *Mono/Stereo* that Westerberg found his footing again. Released on the emo/punk label Vagrant, the double album—one CD of loose rock and roll, the other of hushed folk—saw Westerberg at his most tuneful and charming, with songs such as "Silent Film Star" and "Only Lie Worth Telling." Westerberg continued his relationship with Vagrant, and his renaissance with 2003's *Come Feel Me Tremble.*   —R.S.

Wham!

> ★★ Fantastic (Columbia, 1983)
> ★★★★ Make It Big (Columbia, 1984)
> ★ Music From the Edge of Heaven (Columbia, 1986)

Did Andrew Ridgley and George Michael's dopey little record have to be put together so cheesily, its disco so uninformed, the synths so gawky? Apparently, yes. That way, the pretty-good songs ("Bad Boys," "Club Tropicana," the great disco novelty "Young Guns") had the cheap snap of sweatshop plastic novelties, while the bad ideas (the robotic dance tune "Come On," and "Wham! Rap"—don't ask) just fall over and stay down. A misguided cover of the Miracles' "Love Machine" showcased the creamy, dark soul voice that Michael would develop in his subsequent solo career.

With the help of a blow-dryer and a little self-knowledge, Wham! pledges—and proceeds—to *Make It Big.* Now two slick young romancers with a little political consciousness and a lot of rhythm, Michael and Ridgley know exactly how to get over with English and U.S. audiences, and they do it in eight slender songs. The pop absurdity of "Wake Me Up Before You Go-Go" made them superstars, its soul-lite handclaps and Michael's mature voice turning a dopey party song into an anthem of good times. Wham! also had hits with the dance ballad "Everything She Wants" and the mournful cheating song "Careless Whisper." In between, it's all cheerful, infectious pop, such as the smart rhymes of the big, rolling "Heartbeat," the poolside cool of "Like a Baby," the horn-driven British soul of "Freedom," and the silly bubblegum of "Credit Card Baby." There's not a dud on this record; just great melodies, terrific singing, and utter conviction that it's everything it sets out to be, even if that means both a seminal classic and a fizzy little time capsule.

Once Ridgley and Michael realized their music was worth taking seriously, they began to take themselves seriously, and on the third and last Wham! recording, *Music From the Edge of Heaven,* they jettison decent melodies in favor of "mature" songwriting. Tuneless electro-flotsam like "Battlestations" is the result, a song about squabbling lovers that features an outro in pointless French. The ballads droop and the lyrics try too hard, although two hits pull themselves from the muck: "The Edge of Heaven" is muscular disco poised between the fluff of Wham!'s previous work and the thoughtful strength of Michael's solo songwriting, and "I'm Your Man," despite its lack of syncopation, is infectious dance-soul with an indelible chorus.   —A.B.

Whiskeytown

★★★★ Faithless Street (Outpost, 1996)
★★★ Stranger's Almanac (Outpost, 1997)
★★ Pneumonia (Lost Highway, 2001)

These whiskey-swilling North Carolina boys brought together the rash fury of punk with the outsider braininess of indie rock and fused them both with the sensibility of classic country—loping, alienated, spare. In keeping with the punk ethos, *Faithless Street* is a beautiful mess; it has an immediacy of purpose that blows a fresh wind through with increasingly polished notions of country music. The plangent violin on "Drunk Like a River" and the hard-luck stories of, well, "Hard Luck Story" and "Mining Town" couldn't be more roadhouse rock, but the improvisatory feel and startlingly direct voice of singer/songwriter Ryan Adams made the album sound like nothing else. The band expanded on *Stranger's Almanac*, and Adams' tendencies to pretentious meandering came to the fore. It's still an impressive effort, but the unnecessarily eclectic instrumentation and chunky horn section weigh down the slow, rambling songs. The itchy feet that would eventually send Adams to embark on a successful solo career in which he could be in love with his own voice full-time are apparent in *Pneumonia*, a cluttered, soporific, and altogether disappointing album from a band bursting with early promise. The rerelease of *Faithless Street* includes nine "previously unavailable" tracks. —A.B.

Barry White

★★★★½ Greatest Hits, Volume 1 (PolyGram, 1975)
★★★½ Greatest Hits, Volume 2 (PolyGram, 1981)
★★½ The Man Is Back (A&M, 1988)
★★½ The Right Night & Barry White (A&M, 1989)
★★★½ Put Me in Your Mix (A&M, 1991)
★★★★ Just For You (PolyGram, 1992)
★★½ The Icon Is Love (A&M, 1994)
★★★½ Staying Power (Private Music, 1999)

The image of Barry White at his peak remains indelible: The Man himself, looming over his gold grand piano, decked out in tux, tails, and cape, flanked by the full Love Unlimited Orchestra—who could forget those female backup singers, statuesque doesn't even begin to . . . too much, whew, you givin' your love to me babe is just too much. White revels in excess, no question about that. But he also made some of the sharpest, most satisfying music of the disco era. Behind his velvet bedroom raps and penchant for lush orchestration, White wields the sure, steady hand of a naturally gifted musician. His arrangements are lean and rhythmically compelling, while his melodies are simply put and consistent. White picked up on the innovations of the Philly Sound producers, applying his own outrageous pleasure principle to their meticulous studio-soul blueprints. Of course, the fact that most Barry White songs revolve around sex—offering "hands on" experience and play-by-play commentary at times—may have something to do with the platinum success of *Greatest Hits, Volume 1*. He's not Al Green, but his crushed-velvet baritone rumbles through seduction preambles ("You're the First, the Last, My Everything") and straight ballads ("I've Got So Much to Give") with equal aplomb. Overkill isn't his style; not even on "Love Serenade," all seven heavy-breathing minutes of it. This prolonged slow-motion stab of audio erotica makes Prince's *Dirty Mind* sound like bathroom graffiti. *Greatest Hits, Volume 2* doesn't document a decline so much as a leveling off; the late-'70s disco boom that *Volume 1* helped inspire soon rendered White's approach hopelessly square. As the almighty Beat came to dominate dance music, White kept right on doin' it, impeccably: "It's Ecstasy When You Lay Down Next to Me," because "Your Sweetness Is My Weakness," so turn out the lights and "Let the Music Play." After an extended break, White reemerged just as a new strain of dance music—rap—began to reach mainstream audiences. On *Put Me in Your Mix*, Barry White laces the title track with his signature strings and soulful moans. "I'll make your toenails curl," he declares and then proceeds to do so. In general, though, the A&M albums occupy an uncertain position between old and new, as though White couldn't decide whether to preserve or update his signature sound.

The hits had slowed to almost nothing by the end of the '80s, but the man kept right on wanting, craving, and working, forever locked in a formula that edged dangerously close to camp, until he pulled you into one of his "hypnotic, neurotic, sexy little games." Too often during those years, White traded the timeless for the temporary, dumping the lush strings of the old Love Unlimited Orchestra for something slick, polished, and cold. *The Icon Is Love* was a promising return to form. The stormiest passions were behind him, but White's bedroom growl was as intimate as ever, begging his woman, "Don't say anything, don't say one word, just lay there and let me unwind a little." Promising ballads ("I Only Want to Be With You") dissolve into corn. He smolders on "Baby's Home," but too often the fire is out. The final album before his death in 2003 came in the aftermath of his rediscovery via appearances on *The Simpsons* and *Ally McBeal* as a figure either of camp or of ultimate romance (depending on your point of view). With *Staying Power*, he returned to spread the White gospel to a new generation, a love god ready with a steamy, heavy-breathing soundtrack to your most lustful moments. It's a step up, but still no return to the '70s, only a taste of the smooth operator he once was. A modern take on Sly Stone's "Thank You" (remixed by Sean "Puffy" Combs) updates the sound but goes nowhere. The original songs are better, including two duets on the torrid "The Longer We Make Love" with Chaka Khan and Lisa Stansfield.

For an artist with such a massive catalogue, a little still goes a long way. The inevitable box set, *Just for You*, gathers all the hits and near-misses, the mistakes, the quiet, quivering narration, and the euphoric Love Unlimited Orchestra. The original hits packages are still all anyone needs. Your desire for more will depend on your dependence on mood enhancement. —M.C./S.A.

The White Stripes

★★★½ The White Stripes (1999; V2, 2002)
★★★★ De Stijl (2000; V2, 2002)
★★★★½ White Blood Cells (2001; V2, 2002)
★★★★½ Elephant (V2, 2003)

The White Stripes were part of a wave of retro-minded young bands who gave rock music a much-needed jolt in the first few years of the 21st century, but they're less nostalgic bashers than a brilliant conceptual creation: a divorced Detroit couple who masqueraded as brother and sister, named themselves after their band (or vice versa), wore alternating white-and-red outfits, and rewired the blues for the new generation. Jack White proved himself one of the best rhythm guitarists of all time while wrenching all kinds of deliciously brooding melodies out of his ragged coffee-and-cigarettes croon, and button-cute Meg White assaulted her simple trap set and said a lot by not saying much at all.

The White Stripes combines big, jagged blues riffs, Meg's dirt-simple pounding, and Jack's tortured howl into a gloriously shambolic mess. The songs don't push your pleasure buttons as well as the later, more well-wrought stuff, and the slightly clumsy attack of "Screwdriver" and "Astro" veer too close to forgettable punk bashing. But "Jimmy the Exploder" and "The Big Three Killed My Baby" channel the White Stripes' roots-music obsession into fuzzed-out barn-burners that foreshadow their later triumphs, and two well-chosen covers—Dylan's "One More Cup of Coffee" and Blind Willie Johnson's "John the Revelator"—manage to sound nothing like the originals and are all the better for it.

On *De Stijl*, named for an early-20th-century minimalist art movement, the Stripes upped the songwrit-ing ante, turning out another wildly noisy affair but filling in the blanks with newfound tunefulness. The album kicks off with an excellent one-two punch: "You're Pretty Good Looking" is sunny '60s pop refracted through the Stripes' dark prism, and "Hello Operator" is the finest of White's deceptively simple riff-based numbers. Elsewhere, Jack and Meg delve into acoustic surrealism ("I'm Bound to Pack It Up"), Kinksesque vaudeville pop ("Apple Blossom"), and a jokey country cover (Blind Willie McTell's "Your Southern Can Is Mine").

White Blood Cells is even more meticulously crafted, as Jack and Meg deliver a series of highly memorable, high-impact rock & roll songs that stay true to the Stripes' deliciously original aura. "Dead Leaves and the Dirty Ground," "I'm Finding it Harder to Be a Gentleman," and "The Same Boy You've Always Known" turn down the intensity level in favor of slightly dark, scorched-earth tunefulness and some of Jack's best cracked-throat crooning, and "Hotel Yorba" is a gleeful acoustic sing-along about a hotel where "all they got inside is vacancy." Elsewhere, "The Union Forever" is a creepy, slow-burning meditation on marriage with a bizarro midsection that quotes *Citizen Kane,* and "Fell in Love With a Girl" is a high-velocity number that squeezes all the promise of neo–garage rock into a verbose diatribe about a bewildering affair.

White Blood Cells put the White Stripes on the verge of stardom, and *Elephant* made them household names. Recorded over a two-week stretch in London on an eight-track machine that dated from the early '60s, *Elephant* finds the Stripes coming up with an ever more full-bodied attack. The opener, "Seven Nation Army," uses a six-note bass riff like a call to arms, and from there Jack and Meg channel their sound into a series of dark-not-desolate rockers such as "The Hardest Button to Button," "Black Math," and "Girl, You Have No Faith in Medicine." The stylistic quirks of the previous album are no longer present, but the duo manage to increase their power by focusing their energy, as Jack turns out his most memorably rough melodies and sexiest, most agile singing yet. —C.H.

White Zombie

★★★ La Sexorcisto: Devil Music Volume One (Geffen, 1992)
★★★ Astro-Creep: 2000 (Geffen, 1995)
★★ Supersexy Swingin' Sounds (Geffen, 1996)

Of course White Zombie is a cartoon. Rob Zombie, né Rob Cummings, started as an illustrator and designer, and White Zombie began its undead life as another New York scumrock band with a fondness, not uncommon to their scene, for campy grindhouse sci-fi, horror, and comic book imagery. Except, over time, White Zombie emphasized the grindhouse more than the scum, and turned into one of the most visually entertaining bands of the '90s alt-rock belch.

Their early, gnarly days are out of print, but their 1992 major label debut is where most of the uncool heard about them anyway. *La Sexorcisto* split the difference between old school noise rock and major label metalism, throwing in odes to Russ Meyer ("Thunder Kiss '65") and producing nothing less than fully self-conscious carny-rock, far more than threatening.

Astro-Creep nailed the mad scientist formula perfectly, entered the Top 10, spawned the genius hit "More Human Than Human," which turns a line from *Blade Runner* into a mosh-worthy piece of industrial rock candy corn. Utterly without depth but with charming, rubber-mask glee to spare, *Astro* is a golden moment in junk-rock history.

In spite of *Supersexy*'s misleading cover (trying to exploit the then-dying lounge-music revival), it's just a remix album, calling in folks like the Dust Brothers and P.M. Dawn (!?!!) to wring new life out of *Astro-Creep*'s decaying tunes.

White Zombie rarely seemed more than a reflection of whatever piece of '50s nerd-kitsch Rob was obsessing over at the time anyway, so it was no surprise that Zombie retired the name and launched a solo career that sounded exactly like White Zombie. *Hellbilly Deluxe* is a triumph of pure formula, while *American Made* is another remix album, this one a little more industrial than *Supersexy*. *The Sinister Urge* tries to expand the sound a bit, with acoustic flourishes here and some crooning there ("House of 1000 Corpses," the theme to his attempt at an actual grindhouse movie). *Past, Present and Future* boils Zombie's career into one handy set. Unless you burn for his juvenilia, it's all the Zombie any Fangoria-obsessed head banger will ever need.   —J.G.

The Who

★★★★★ The Who Sings My Generation (MCA, 1965)
★★★ A Quick One (MCA, 1966)
★★★★★ The Who Sell Out (MCA, 1967)
★★ Magic Bus—The Who on Tour (MCA, 1968)
★★★★ Tommy (MCA, 1969)
★★★★★ Live at Leeds (1970; MCA, 1995)
★★★★★ Who's Next (MCA, 1971)
★★★★★ Meaty Beaty Big and Bouncy (MCA, 1971)
★★★★ Quadrophenia (MCA, 1973)
★★★ Odds & Sods (MCA, 1974)
★★★ The Who by Numbers (MCA, 1975)
★★★ Who Are You (MCA, 1978)
★★★★ The Kids Are Alright (MCA, 1979)

★★★ Face Dances (MCA, 1981)
★★½ It's Hard (MCA, 1982)
★★★ Hooligans (MCA, 1982)
★★★ Who's Greatest Hits (MCA, 1983)
★ Who's Last (MCA, 1984)
★★★ Who's Missing (MCA, 1985)
★★★ Who's Better, Who's Best (MCA, 1988)
★ Join Together (MCA, 1990)
★★★ Thirty Years of Maximum Rock & Roll (MCA, 1994)
★★★½ My Generation: The Very Best of the Who (MCA, 1996)
★★½ The Millennium Collection (MCA, 1999)
★★★★ The BBC Sessions (MCA, 2000)
★★★★ Live at Leeds (Deluxe Edition) (MCA, 2001)
★★★★ The Ultimate Collection (Universal, 2002)
★★★ Live at the Royal Albert Hall (Steamhammer, 2003)
★★★★ Then and Now: Maximum Who (Geffen, 2004)

It's been said that the Rolling Stones, the Beatles, and the Who are the Holy Trinity of '60s British Invasion–era rock. If that's true—and if the Beatles represent the Father and the Stones the Son—then the Who fits squarely into the role of Holy Spirit.

From the outset, the Who stormed the Mod scene of West London with a sound and vision that distilled the pure essence of post-'50s rock & roll. Their music was fast, furious, and noisy, and three of the four members—singer Roger Daltrey, guitarist Pete Townshend, and drummer Keith Moon—performed with the obnoxious abandon of juvenile delinquents. Above all, the musicianship was first rate. In their performances, Townshend's muscular feedback and fuzz locked into a groove with the thunderous clatter of Moon's unbridled drumming, and the blistering throb of John Entwistle's complex bass runs like gas in a combustion engine. At the vortex of this din, Daltrey would stalk the stage with a thuggish swagger, hurl his microphone cord about him like a lasso, and howl like a banshee. The Who created a tension that always seemed ready to explode, and indeed most of the band's shows ended with Townshend and Moon destroying their instruments. But there was an air of sophistication behind the brute force, and by their early-'70s prime the Who was performing rock operas.

With its ferocious blend of grungy distortion, rumbling bass and percussion, and brutish vocals, *The Who Sings My Generation* became the blueprint for much of the subsequent garage rock, heavy metal, and punk. In contrast to debut albums from the Stones (whose take on Southern American rock & soul was fairly earnest) and Beatles (who spread the word of rock & roll through sweet harmonies and easily digestible melodies), *My Generation* positively shoved at the boundaries of popular music. Townshend's fiercely original guitar experiments here predate the innovations of his later American rival Jimi Hendrix. Though *My Generation* includes everything from two James Brown covers ("I Don't Mind" and "Please, Please, Please") to a noisy, beefed-up surf tune ("The Ox") to a jangly, Beatlesque pop song ("The Kids Are Alright"), it all sizzles and crackles as though the band was playing through broken amps. The title tune remains a timeless expression of teenage angst.

The Who expanded its musical vocabulary on *A Quick One,* a decent but flawed collection of experimental pop and rock. Except for one R&B cover ("Heat Wave"), the band's earlier nods to American rock & roll were diminishing, replaced by original songs by each band member. Though Townshend is clearly the visionary here, Entwistle reveals his clever songwriting eccentricities on the delightfully morbid "Boris the Spider" and "Whiskey Man." Moon's and Daltrey's contributions are less compelling. The highlight of the album comes in the pure pop of Townshend's "So Sad About Us," but the centerpiece is the nine-minute, multipart mini-opera "A Quick One, While He's Away," the guitarist's first stab at high-concept rock. (The original American version of *A Quick One,* titled *Happy Jack,* included the hit song of the same name. Unfortunately, MCA's 1995 reissue of *A Quick One* is diluted by the addition of a full album's worth of throwaway outtakes, B-sides and EP tracks, including two annoying covers of surf hits by the Beach Boys and Jan & Dean. "Happy Jack" appears here in an emasculated acoustic form.)

The Who Sell Out is Townshend's first (and best) album-length concept piece, paving the way for the full-blown operatic sprawl of *Tommy* and *Quadrophenia.* On *Sell Out,* a satirical yet celebratory look at the folly of Top 40 radio, Townshend successfully does what he would overdo in the two operas. Every song shines—none are mere transitions to the next part of the story—and the mock ads and jingles are hilarious. *Sell Out* works because there's no fixed narrative to take away from the music. And the music is sensational, from the backward-tape-loop psychedelia of "Armenia City in the Sky" to the Latin buzz of "Mary Anne With the Shaky Hand" to the Who's all-time best song, "I Can See for Miles."

Magic Bus, with its misleading subtitle *The Who on Tour* (it's not a live album) and shameless rip-off of the Beatles' *Magical Mystery Tour* vibe, is a baffling step backwards. Composed of random repeats of songs from *A Quick One* and *Sell Out,* a few B-sides and EP tracks, it's a hodgepodge of wrong turns and dead ends. Even before most of this stuff was available on other collections, the strongest songs—the Bo Diddley–inspired title track and "Pictures of Lily"—were not worth the price of admission to this haphazard funhouse.

In retrospect, *Tommy* isn't quite the masterpiece it was hyped to be when it first appeared. There's no doubting its excellence as a narrative-based set of Who songs, but it's not nearly as much fun, or even as enlightening, as *Sell Out. Tommy*'s ultimately spiritual plot—it's a dark, twisted tale of recovery from abuse—is thin. If anything, rock's first opera betrays the inherent contradiction of such a concept: The restrictions and complexities of opera take away from the simple power of rock. Still, in Townshend's hands, this ambitious though flawed effort spawned more than a handful of bone fide classic songs: "Amazing Journey," "Christmas," "Sensation," "I'm Free," "We're Not Gonna Take It," "Tommy, Can You Hear Me?" and "Pinball Wizard." *Tommy*'s biggest crime is that it inspired lesser artists to attempt the same trick, and by the late '70s, bands like Styx had turned operatic concept albums into rock's lamest joke.

The Who hit its peak in the early '70s, releasing a brutal, balls-to-the-wall performance set *(Live at Leeds),* an impeccable new studio album *(Who's Next),* and a perfectly sequenced collection of its finest moments from the '60s *(Meaty Beaty Big and Bouncy).* The Who was at a turning point in 1971, straddling the transition from British Invasion pioneers to arena-rock gods. On *Who's Next,* the band crossed that line with power and grace. The album spawned the concert classics "Baba O'Riley" and "Won't Get Fooled Again"; the great Daltrey vocal vehicles "Bargain" and "Song Is Over"; Entwistle's scorching, anxiety-ridden "My Wife"; and Townshend's most delicate song on record, "Behind Blue Eyes." On *Who's Next,* Townshend unleashed the power of the synthesizer as a rock & roll instrument, to be used like guitar or bass rather than as a special-effects novelty.

Quadrophenia was Townshend's next stab at the rock opera, and though it is a more muscular piece of music than *Tommy,* its narrative—about a teenager afflicted with a four-way multiple personality disorder—is even weaker than that of its predecessor. Still, as an exemplary set of '70s hard rock, *Quadrophenia* cornered the market. No other contemporary rock band—not Led Zeppelin, nor Pink Floyd, nor Deep Purple—could crank out Big Arena Rock like "The Real Me," "The Punk and the Godfather," or "Love, Reign O'er Me."

By the mid-'70s the Who was in a holding pattern, delivering slick, high-quality album-oriented rock and singer/songwriter fare but no longer pushing boundaries. *The Who by Numbers* and the electronics-informed *Who Are You* are both decent albums with varying mixes of great, good, and mediocre material. But Townshend's heart no longer seemed to be in the songwriting, and Daltrey's commanding voice had become a parody of itself. When Moon drank himself to death in late 1978, the Who got a big punch in the stomach. While the band's first post-Moon album, *Face Dances,* turned out to be a passable collection of New Wave–inspired, MTV-era rock, by the time of the aptly named *It's Hard,* the Who had lost all inspiration.

Who's Last and *Join Together* are pointless live albums. The former comes off like a contractually obligated release from a tired, directionless band on its half-hearted farewell tour. The latter is more insidious. Recorded seven years after the aforementioned "farewell" tour—and featuring an all-star cast that includes Phil Collins and Patti LaBelle—it's a musically tolerable but cynical financial ploy, a greatest hits of rock opera that comes off more like the Ringling Brothers, Townshend, and Daltrey Circus. This isn't the Who—it's a Vegas revue.

Of the various Who compilations, only *Meaty Beaty Big and Bouncy* and *Ultimate Collection* truly capture the scope and drama of the band's oeuvre. The others lack essential songs or are poorly sequenced, or—particularly in the case of the box set *Thirty Years of Maximum R&B*—include entirely too much residue. *The Kids Are Alright* is a fine collection of great Who songs, mostly caught live, that captures scorching performances of "My Generation" (from *The Smothers Brothers Comedy Hour*), "Magic Bus" (from the German TV show *Beat Club*), "A Quick One, While He's Away" (from *The Rolling Stones Rock and Roll Circus*), as well as the concert faves "Long Live Rock," "Baba O'Riley," and "Won't Get Fooled Again." *BBC Sessions* is a comprehensive document of the Who's recordings for British radio from 1965 to 1973. It's not a starting point for the uninitiated, unless said uninitiated is a fan of lo-fi punk rock: The sound is tinny and the performances are ragged, but it's absolutely glorious, from start to finish.

Live at Leeds (Deluxe Edition) is an expanded version of the remastered 1995 single-disc restoration of the original six-song classic. That edition had added extra songs from the band's famed Leeds performance of February 14, 1970; this edition tacks on an entirely new disc of music from the same show—a live performance of the entire *Tommy* opera, from beginning to end. The sound has been improved, and diehard Who fans will relish the extra music and onstage patter. That said, the original, stripped-down *Live at Leeds*

cannot be topped. Not only does it remain the most sonically intense document of that evening's performance, but it's also one of rock's all-time best live albums.

John Entwistle died of a heart attack in 2002; *Live at the Royal Albert Hall* captures him and the band in 2000, with guest spots from Paul Weller and Eddie Vedder; the disc also includes four tracks from Entwistle's final gig with the Who.   —M.K.

Wilco

★★★½ A.M. (Reprise, 1995)
★★★★ Being There (Reprise, 1996)
★★★★ Summerteeth (Reprise, 1999)
★★★★★ Yankee Hotel Foxtrot (Nonesuch, 2002)
★★★★½ A Ghost Is Born (Nonesuch, 2004)

Billy Bragg and Wilco

★★★★½ Mermaid Avenue (Elektra, 1998)
★★★½ Mermaid Avenue Vol. II (Elektra, 2000)

After the breakup of alternative-country mainstays Uncle Tupelo, primary songwriters Jay Farrar and Jeff Tweedy split to form distinctly different bands: Farrar's Son Volt pursued a moody brand of rustic guitar rock that wasn't that far removed from the Tupelo template, while Tweedy's Wilco began pursuing musical ambitions that encompassed everything from avant-rock to orchestral pop.

Those aspirations weren't immediately apparent on *A.M.* Tweedy recruited three former Tupelo band mates to craft an engaging, no-frills blend of twang-encrusted guitar rock and ballads. The album opens in deceptively high spirits, punctuated by clanging booze bottles in "Casino Queen," and then winds down with a bunch of breakup songs cast against a backdrop of aimless small-town life.

Being There instantly announces its more grandiose intentions with the confrontational blast of noise that ushers in "Misunderstood." The 19 tracks are spread across two CDs—a sound aesthetic decision. Each disc functions as a self-contained entity digestible in a single 40-minute sitting. Together, both halves aspire to the nervy sprawl of such double-album predecessors as *London Calling* and *Exile on Main Street,* records that forged unified personal statements out of a bewildering variety of styles. The most significant sonic advance since *A.M.* is the greater prominence accorded the keyboards, with Jay Bennett's army of pianos and organs shading the music in ways that reflect the more nuanced perspective in Tweedy's lyrics. His is a tale of faith—in oneself, in a lover, in rock & roll itself—tested by time and distance, but it's the accomplished music that ultimately justifies the album's epic scope.

Summerteeth marks another progression, with Wilco shifting toward more elaborate studio creations that blend guitars, drums, and a thrift-shop array of vintage keyboards. The songs themselves chronicle a relationship that takes some sickening turns; the morbid tone of the lyrics ("She begs me not to hit her") contrast with the layered pop-friendly arrangements.

Yankee Hotel Foxtrot became a cause célèbre when it was rejected by Wilco's Reprise label for its lack of commercial potential, eventually surfacing nearly a year after its completion to become the band's fastest-selling album. To be sure, *Foxtrot* sounds a galaxy removed from the pop-friendly innocence of *A.M.* It creates tension by merging opposites: the ingratiating melodies of pop and the chaos of noise, the reassuring strum of an acoustic guitar and the discomforting hum of radio static, the warmth of Tweedy's voice and the icy swirl of lost-in-space keyboards. Yet it hangs together thanks to the brilliant sequencing, a world unto itself that rewards repeat visits.

A Ghost Is Born backs off from the elaborate studio maneuvers of *Foxtrot* for a live-in-the-studio approach built on stately mid-tempo pop songs and skronky guitar solos. Exploring themes of identity and self-definition, Tweedy often prefers to let his guitar do the talking, peppering the 10-minute trance-rocker "Spiders (Kidsmoke)" with spastic fills and bombastic power chords. Though not quite as cohesive as its predecessor, *Ghost* nonetheless finds Wilco pursuing new avenues of expression. The most radical of these is the droning 12-minute instrumental coda to "Less Than You Think," which suggests Wilco's response to Lou Reed's "Metal Machine Music."

British folk-rocker Billy Bragg recruited Wilco to help him dive into an archive of lyrics left behind by the late folk legend Woody Guthrie. Together, they wrote new music for Guthrie's lyrics, which offered a fresh perspective on the earnest Dust Bowl balladeer; Woody, it turns out, was every bit as lusty, fallible, and funny as the deportees, migrant laborers, and hobos he portrayed in song. The performances brim with in-the-moment playfulness ("Walt Whitman's Niece"), radiant wistfulness ("California Stars"), and staggering poignancy ("One by One"); it's a watershed.

The sequel, *Mermaid Avenue Vol. II,* plays down Guthrie's playful leer in favor of his snarl. *Vol. II* blasts the verbal buckshot; the agit-punk Bragg wails Guthrie's "All You Fascists," taking obvious relish in spitting out what was once the nastiest of the *f* words as Wilco's Jay Bennett plays along with rootin', tootin' harmonica. On "Meanest Man," Bragg stumbles through junkyard percussion worthy of Tom Waits while staving off the hellhounds in his head. But once

again it's the more personally expansive songs that bring us closer to Guthrie's inner world, and Wilco's. "Secret of the Sea" wrestles with the unanswerable over a small army of guitars, their tonal centers shifting from the Far East to George Harrison's *All Things Must Pass* to Nashville in the space of a few bars. Best of all is the six-minute "Remember the Mountain Bed," a tour de force without a chorus that ends more quietly than it began, with Bennett and bassist John Stirratt's whispered harmony briefly, almost subliminally shadowing Tweedy's husky baritone, as though the ghost of Guthrie himself had slipped into the recording session. —G.K.

Hank Williams

★★★★★   40 Greatest Hits (Mercury, 1978)
★★★½   Rare Demos: First to Last (Country Music Foundation, 1990)
★★★★★   The Original Singles Collection . . . Plus (Mercury, 1992)
★★★½   Alone and Forsaken (Mercury, 1995)
★★★½   Low Down Blues (PolyGram, 1996)
★★★★★   The Complete Hank Williams (Mercury, 1998)
★★★★   Alone With His Guitar (Mercury, 2000)
★★★½   Beyond the Sunset (Mercury, 2001)
★★★★★   The Ultimate Collection (Universal, 2002)

Hank Williams lived fast, died young, and left a beautiful memory. He was born in Alabama in 1923, and died less than 30 years later, having recorded 36 Top 10 country & western singles in less than six years. He wrote over two thirds of those songs, leaving one of the major songbooks in American music. But it was Williams' performance that had the most immediate impact, virtually defining the hard, spare style of modern country music that took its name from his early hit "Honky Tonkin'."

Williams had an extraordinary ability to convey naked emotion. He could be exuberant, but more often he played sad, lonesome, dejected, defeated, downright miserable. For every "Hey, Good Lookin' " there's a whole mess of "I'm So Lonesome I Could Cry" and "Moanin' the Blues" and "Alone and Forsaken" and "I'll Never Get Out of This World Alive." Even his love songs portray a man hopelessly out of control, from the lovestruck "Howlin' at the Moon" to the hopeful "Half as Much" to the troubled "I Can't Help It (If I'm Still in Love With You)" to the frazzled "Please Make Up Your Mind" to the hopeless "You Win Again." It's easy to take these as clues to Williams' own doomed life, and it doesn't seem accidental that Williams finalized his second (and last) divorce from Miss Audrey with the vicious "Your

Cheatin' Heart." But not everything Williams did was first person: "Kaw-Liga" chronicled a heartsick piece of knotty pine.

After Williams' death, his recorded legacy was looted and plundered for spurious singles, fake stereo, and even overdubbed duets and trios with his progeny. But in the CD era there started a systematic effort to restore the original recordings and round up as much trivia as possible. The remastering of *40 Greatest Hits* went back to the original mono tapes and 78-r.p.m. discs, including only one overdubbed single. Then came *The Original Singles Collection . . . Plus,* which filled two and a half CDs with original singles then filled out the third CD with the undubbed demo sources for the posthumous singles. While *40 Greatest Hits* is an impeccable selection, the extra material in *Original Singles* gives a much fuller accounting of Williams' work.

Then came *The Complete Hank Williams,* a sprawling 10-CD box with four CDs of studio recordings in chronological order, followed by six CDs of song demos, radio programs, and live recordings. The studio recordings add 22 cuts to *Original Singles:* the spoken lectures released as *Luke the Drifter* (collected separately in *Beyond the Sunset*), gospel songs sung with wife Audrey, and a few alternate takes, but hardly anything that could be called a miss. The other six CDs have their moments, but the early Montgomery demos are very scratchy, the demo songs tend to be lackluster, and the live material is sometimes marred by bad sound and too much patter. The Shreveport radio performances tend to be better performances. So overall, the box is too much.

The other anthologies slice this work up in various ways. *Low Down Blues* and *Alone and Forsaken* take an almost perverse delight in Williams' lowest-down material, and therefore overlap quite a bit. *Rare Demos* originally uncovered many of the song demos, concentrating on the earliest and roughest. *Alone With His Guitar* also selects from the demos, much more expertly. *The Ultimate Collection* is the latest attempt to sum up Williams in two CDs: The main difference between it and *40 Greatest Hits* is that it is selected more broadly from the box, including demos and live cuts instead of sticking to the studio singles. And in that it may have a slight edge, presenting a more complex and rounded portrait of a singer who was much more than "just another guy on the lost highway." —T.H.

Lucinda Williams

★★ Ramblin' on My Mind (1979, Rounder, 1991)
★★★ Happy Woman Blues (1980; Rounder, 1991)
★★★★½ Lucinda Williams (Rough Trade/Koch, 1998)
★★★★ Sweet Old World (Chameleon, 1992)
★★★★★ Car Wheels on a Gravel Road (Polygram, 1998)
★★★★ Essence (Lost Highway, 2001)
★★★ World Without Tears (Lost Highway, 2003)

Born in Louisiana, Lucinda Williams honed her style in Houston, in a fertile local scene where Nanci Griffith and Lyle Lovett were working their own intriguing variations on music rooted in country, western swing, blues, and folk. Williams' college-professor father was a Hank Williams fan, and the family's home often resonated with all manner of country and folk music. Williams financed two albums released on the Smithsonian/Folkways label (which were reissued on Rounder in 1991), then held out for creative control when major labels began bidding for her services. In the late '70s she moved to Los Angeles and signed with Rough Trade. Although that company evaporated just as *Lucinda Williams* was beginning to find an audience, the vibrant record returned to circulation just in time to take advantage of her late-'90s breakout.

Of the two earlier albums, *Ramblin' on My Mind* is the less satisfying. That is, until she gets to "The Great Speckled Bird," the strange quasi-hymn indelibly linked with Roy Acuff. In Williams' hands, the song sounds vital and mesmerizing as her crystalline, keening voice evokes the unsettling mystery of larger forces shaping our lives. As the one honest, deeply felt performance on the album, it points the way to *Happy Woman Blues,* where Williams comes back with a collection of original songs more representative of her own life and better suited to her style. "Lafayette" and "Louisiana Man" are loving reminiscences of places and people in her home state. Otherwise, Williams appears ambiguous and compelling in recounting some dangerous and ill-fated liaisons.

Lucinda Williams is such a startling advance over her first two releases that it seems to have been done by a different artist. The writing is sharp and tough with plenty of tender moments rendered in a heartfelt manner. She's moved foursquare into rock & roll, with conviction and assurance. "I Just Wanna See You So Bad," the album's opener, comes out of the Springsteen school, but the rest of the album hews closer to country-rock and folk-rock arrangements. Williams hasn't resolved her ambiguous feelings regarding commitment and love—expressed with devastating clarity in "Side of the Road," when she implores, "I wanna know you're there, but I wanna be alone"—but the search becomes more interesting as she spills blood on the tracks. There's not a false step, and the depth of feeling is powerful.

Sweet Old World showed Williams was a damned determined artist: She'd already overcome enough delays and setbacks to destroy two ordinary careers. The parameters of her perspective—adult, Southern, female, sensual but neurotic—firmed up here, and all of her subsequent releases have focused on either characters or the landscapes in which they struggle and strive for a drop of redemption. *Sweet Old World* is essentially an album about characters shadowed by death—its tragedies, its allure, how it unites the living. So much so that Williams has to tell audiences when she performs "Little Angel, Little Brother," her affectionate sibling portrait, "He's not dead, you know."

Car Wheels on a Gravel Road is a masterpiece about growing up and getting older in the Louisiana and Texas that Williams knows. Fussed over through three producers and six years, *Car Wheels* pays off with a faultless accumulation of faces, fights, keening swamp guitar and sighing accordion, strong drink and stronger lust in an album about places shadowed by memory. Williams' mix of songs and sound are so enduring and deep here that everything she did before them seems like sketches.

An obsessive detail-stickler will have trouble following a perfectly imperfect work. Adding to the strain, Williams is no longer pop music's most worthy unknown and is instead another backlash target. So the consensus of admiration around *Car Wheels* has not carried on to *Essence* and *World Without Tears.* Yet the best tracks from both albums would make a single collection as potent as that landmark. *Essence* is her slowest, smoothest album, with Williams' voice and fancy touches such as harmony choruses filling in the vivid emotive bits that more concrete lyrics have on other albums. But if you offer even one unguarded moment, she can hook you even with old notions such as the love-addict metaphor of the title track. *World Without Tears* is her hardest-rocking album, recorded quickly in Bob Dylan's bang-it-out mode, which results in some infelicities, especially with vocals (better the talking blues of "American Dream" than the semi-rap of "Sweet Side"). Despite a few wistful interludes, the album is the opposite of its title, filled with currents of sexual violence, drug damage, and "how sorrow finds a home." Messy (not sloppy), gloomy, and grand, *World Without Tears* appeared with ideal, mordant timing when America was at war, sunk in a morass of confusion and doubts. Lucinda Williams remains the muse you need. —D.M./M.MI.

Robbie Williams

★★★½ The Ego Has Landed (Capitol, 1999)
★★½ Sing When You're Winning (Capitol, 2000)
★★★ Escapology (Capitol, 2003)

Über-pop star Robbie Williams enjoyed his first round of mega-success as one-fifth of Take That, Britain's most popular boy band since the Beatles. His solo career began in 1995 when the rest of Take That—a rather straight-arrow bunch—parted ways with the drinking-and-drugging Williams. The playboy's revenge came in the form of two #1 U.K. albums: his debut, 1997's *Life Thru a Lens,* and its followup, 1998's *I've Been Expecting You.*

Those two discs were combined to make *The Ego Has Landed,* a delicious guilty pleasure that served as Williams' official introduction to American ears. Standouts here include the pop trinkets "Lazy Days" and "Millennium" and the swoon-inducing ballad "Angels"—expected fare from a boy-band alumnus. But within the album's fluff lurks plenty of cheek: The sing-songy "Strong" is an exercise in self-deprecation, while "Let Me Entertain You"—quintessential Williams—sees the singer both reinventing and promoting himself as the human embodiment of show business.

If the ego had landed for Williams' first two records, it had invaded and conquered by the time of *Sing When You're Winning:* "Single-handedly raising the economy," he boasts on the Kylie Minogue duet "Kids," "ain't no chance of the record company dropping me." The album has its inspired moments— "Supreme" puts a dark spin on the Gloria Gaynor classic "I Will Survive"—as well as a number of questionable mushy ballads.

In 2002, EMI signed Williams to a megamillion-dollar deal and declared its intention of pushing him hard in the United States. *Escapology* sounds like a more self-conscious effort to craft a pop-rock blockbuster. Williams does a fine job belting out power ballads such as "Monsoon" and "Come Undone," but the best tracks here are the ones least likely to become hits: for instance, "Me and My Monkey," a seven-minute saga with mariachi horns about checking into a Las Vegas hotel with an out-of-control chimp. —N.P./G.E.

Saul Williams

★★★½ Amethyst Rock Star (American, 2001)

A fixture on New York's spoken-word scene long before he entered the recording booth, Saul Williams made a name for himself in the late '90s with a series of incendiary 12-inch singles and as the star of the movie *Slam.* His commanding baritone evoked the stylings of a chastising preacher, and his moral and intellectual certitude made him an impressive, and unusual, musical force. By the time über-producer Rick Rubin got to him, Williams decided he wanted to be a rock star, and his debut album, *Amethyst Rock Star,* is a bizarre long-form concerto on post-rap confusion, featuring turntable wizardry, psych-roch guitar runs, boom-bap percussion, and viola workouts. It's an ambitious, sloppy, dense, and utterly unaffected album, if not an unpretentious one. But when Williams breaks down into pure love-lost squall on "Fearless," or tongue lashes naive young hip-hoppers on "1987," it's hard not to ride with him, even if the car sometimes crashes. —J.C.

Victoria Williams

★★★★	Loose (Mammoth, 1994)
★★★	This Moment: In Toronto with the Loose Band (Mammoth/Atlantic, 1995)
★★★★	Musings of a Creek Dipper (Atlantic, 1998)
★★★	Sings Some Ol' Songs (Dualtone, 2002)

The Original Harmony Ridge Creek Dippers

| ★★½ | The Original Harmony Ridge Creek Dippers (Original, 1997) |
| ★★½ | Pacific Coast Rambler (Koch, 1998) |

The trouble with most hippie eccentrics is that they ain't all that eccentric. Like punks or hip-hoppers or stalwarts of any other subculture, they gravitate toward norms of belief, dress, and cant. But Victoria Williams is her own weird, wonderful woman, with an adventurous warble and a goofball sense of humor that mark her as an original. She's a dear heart whose music feels spontaneous at its most elaborate and orchestrated, and who sounds as though she sings primarily to amuse herself without ever seeming self-absorbed. *Swing the Statue,* now out of print, established Williams' voice, but it was on *Loose* that she came into her own. She covers both the pop standard "What a Wonderful World" and the Rare Earth nugget "Nature's Way" in her loopy way—for Williams, both Tin Pan Alley and studio rock are folk music. "My Ally," a duet with Dave Pirner, may be the loveliest song ever written about a male-female nonsexual friendship; it's definitely the loveliest vocal of Pirner's career. Williams coproduced *Musings* with Trina Shoemaker, and her sound expanded to include more meandering piano, more textural strings and horns as her song structures became more rambling and elastic. Her mood wasn't always as unrelentingly nostalgic as on "Train Song (Demise of the Caboose)," an elegy for locomotive travel, but sentiments such as "I wish I could fly and see everyone I love in the blink of an eye" pervaded.

Given her tendency to glance backward, it's not surprising that Williams has since been content to rely on others' material. *Sings Some Ol' Songs* is her

second disc of covers; the other, *Water to Drink,* is now out of print. Here, as on her collaborations with hubby Mark Olson, the former Jayhawk, as the Original Harmony Ridge Creek Dippers, Williams' homeyness has come to the forefront. This is private music, and listening to it is like paging through a stranger's family photo album—you can sense the love, but you can only experience it from a distance. —K.H.

Bob Wills and His Texas Playboys

★★★★	The Tiffany Transcriptions, Vol. 1 (Rhino, 1982)
★★★★	The Tiffany Transcriptions, Vol. 2 (Rhino, 1986)
★★★★	The Tiffany Transcriptions, Vol. 3 (Rhino, 1986)
★★★★	The Tiffany Transcriptions, Vol. 4 (Rhino, 1986)
★★★★	The Tiffany Transcriptions, Vol. 5 (Rhino, 1986)
★★★	Columbia Historic Edition (1987; Sony, 1992)
★★★★★	The McKinney Sisters (Rhino, 1990)
★★★★★	Anthology 1935–1973 (Rhino, 1991)
★★★★	The Tiffany Transcriptions, Vol. 9 (Rhino, 1991)
★★★★½	The Essential Bob Wills (Sony, 1992)
★★★★	For the Last Time (Capitol, 1994)
★★★	The Millennium Collection (MCA, 2000)
★★★★★	Take Me Back to Tulsa: The Original Columbia Recordings, Vol. 1 (Rounder Select, 2001)
★★★★★	Stay a Little Longer: The Original Columbia Recordings, Vol. 2 (Rounder Select, 2002)

Bob Wills was not the father of Western swing—several prominent bands were championing the style well ahead of Wills' arrival on the scene—but he quickly became its most popular and most adventurous practitioner, its reigning visionary, and its conscience; in the end his music so dwarfed all the Western swing that came before him that Wills was widely regarded not merely as the King of Western Swing, but as the genre's founding father as well. Certainly the template he shaped out of all the varieties of music he heard in his west Texas childhood had a sui generis quality, and the passage of a half century plus since his heyday has only deepened the impression of Wills as a visionary trailblazer. His in-print catalogue is not as deep as it once was, but the titles extant provide a persuasive argument for Wills' preeminence in the Western swing pantheon. That there was ever a band in America as soulful and at the same time as technically accomplished as Bob Wills and His Texas Playboys is one of the wonders of the 20th century.

A fiddler in the traditional style, like his father before him, Wills *fils et père* played west Texas house parties together, with the son moving on to work with medicine shows touring the region. The roots of Wills' style can be traced to several key influences. The fiddle and guitar duets of virtuoso jazz players Eddie Lang and Joe Venuti were popular with musicians throughout the Southwest, not the least being young Bob Wills, who also had an affection for blues, Dixieland jazz, mariachi, Cajun music, and the native dance music of the central European immigrants who had settled in the Lone Star state. One of the first important influences in the shaping of Wills' vocal style was Emmett Miller, an enigmatic blackface singer who starred on the minstrel circuit in the late '20s and early '30s, and recorded some amazing sides for OKeh (including "Lovesick Blues," which became Hank Williams' breakthrough hit, and "Right or Wrong," which became a Bob Wills classic) that had a major impact not only on Wills but on Jimmie Rodgers and Hank Williams as well.

In 1931 a trio of Wills, guitarist Herman Arnspiger, and vocalist Milton Brown landed a steady gig as the Light Crust Doughboys plugging a like-named flour on a Fort Worth, TX, radio station. Brown left the group in 1932 to form his own band, and Wills followed suit a year later with his banjo-playing brother Johnnie Lee in tow, along with the versatile vocalist Tommy Duncan. Christening his group the Texas Playboys, Wills relocated to Tulsa, OK, dispensed with the traditional country band lineup and assembled a large group to play dance halls. Adding a drummer and, later, horns and electric instruments to his lineup was a revolutionary step for a country artist, but it made perfect sense to Wills. Nevertheless, in his "big band" approach to country music Wills maintained the fiddles as the immediately identifiable signature of the music that has variously been called country jazz and Western swing. Always, Wills attracted stellar musicians, many of whom rank with the giants on their instruments: Wills, Duncan, and Arnspiger would be on that list, along with the inventive guitarist Eldon Shamblin; Al Stricklin, who was dealing some honky-tonk piano solos before honky-tonk as a style had even been identified; steel guitarist nonpareil Leon McAuliffe, the gold standard by which all succeeding generations of steel players have been measured; jazz-influenced electric mandolin player Tiny Moore; and such maestros of the fiddle as Jesse Ashlock, Joe Holley, and Johnny Gimble.

From the time of his first sessions in 1935 through his last productive sessions in the early '60s, Wills was about change and movement, his band's membership shrinking and expanding, his music taking on different hues and textures that reflected his drive to keep it fresh, his popularity exploding throughout the South, Southwest, and West Coast as his grueling tour schedule brought Western swing to new audiences. His disdain for the commonly accepted definitions of country music enabled Wills to redefine and broaden conventional boundaries he found too limiting for a vision as

expansive as his. Had he written only "New San Antonio Rose," "Faded Love," and "Take Me Back to Tulsa," he would be considered a significant figure in country music history. That his grasp was equal to his considerable reach ranks him with the likes of Louis Armstrong, Bill Monroe, and Charlie Parker, who dreamed different dreams, and then subsequently pioneered music that changed the course of history.

Wills' catalogue is accessible from a number of vantage points. For the hits and other familiar tracks, look no further than Rhino's two-CD set, *Anthology 1935–1973*, which kicks off with "Maiden's Prayer," an evocative instrumental cut at Wills' first session, and ends with two tracks from the powerful final tribute to the King, *For the Last Time*, a reunion of Wills and several former Playboys, along with contemporary disciples such as Merle Haggard, which has finally been restored to print on CD. *Anthology*'s 32 vital cuts show the band's remarkable range in its execution of varied styles—check out Wills' own bluesy vocal on "Corrina, Corrina"—as well as the evolution of Wills' sound with different configurations of Playboys. Rounder's two volumes of Wills recordings, *Take Me Back to Tulsa* and *Stay a Little Longer*, take a narrower focus, centering on the years 1935 to 1947 when Wills was recording for the American Record Corporation and Columbia and building monuments almost every time he and the Playboys stepped into the studio. The portrait that emerges from these tracks is that of a man aggressively pursuing new ideas. An early cut, "Spanish Two Step" (on *Take Me Back to Tulsa*) is equal parts swing and traditional Western. The band's first-ever recording, "Osage Stomp," is derived from "Bugle Call Rag" and a rowdy jazz workout, "Rukus Juice Shuffle," and sounds not unlike a wildly swinging ensemble jazz number Jelly Roll Morton might have cooked up for his Red Hot Peppers in 1927. To a Bob Nolan classic Western song, the beautiful, poetic "Away Out There," Wills adds an insistent, controlled swell of horns to heighten the effect of a train rumbling across the Texas plains en route to Amarillo, "the land of good-lookin' women," as Duncan croons one of his most affecting vocals in service to a vivid lyric. The first of several Cindy Walker–penned classics that Wills cut, "Blue Bonnet Lane," is a lovely mid-tempo reminiscence that fuses pop and country elements in its arrangement. So it goes: blues; two-steps; pop songs (the romantic classic "I'll See You in My Dreams," also on *Stay a Little Longer*); traditional fiddle tunes and Wills gems such as the incandescent "San Antonio Rose" and the band's first hit, "Steel Guitar Rag," a landscape-altering cut that gave Leon McAuliffe a self-penned signature song and made the steel guitar a required feature in Western swing bands forever after.

For Wills completists and historians alike, *The Tiffany Transcriptions* series is the Holy Grail. Originally nine volumes when released on vinyl by Kaleidoscope Records between 1982 and 1990, the recordings are now on Rhino and pared down to six volumes, Volumes 1–5 and 9, with 6, 7, and 8 missing in action. Otherwise the exemplary packaging and song selections are identical to the original vinyl versions.

The *Tiffany Transcriptions* story begins in 1945 when Wills, Cliff Sundlin (a monied businessman and aspiring songwriter who was hoping to persuade Wills to cut some of his tunes), and disc jockey Clifton "Cactus Jack" Johnson formed the Tiffany Music Company intending to offer for radio syndication live performances of Wills and the Playboys, who were then based in California. The sets were recorded in San Francisco in 1946 and '47, and accompanied by a script for a disc jockey to read between songs. Of the more than 370 selections recorded, only 50 sets had been issued when the Tiffany company went out of business, and the remaining transcriptions sat in Cliff Sundlin's basement in Oakland, CA, for 30 years before the folks at Kaleidoscope obtained the release rights.

It's fair to say that Wills and the Playboys functioned at their highest level during those San Francisco sessions. Duncan's singing is amazing throughout—his mastery of blues, pop, country, ballads, and uptempo numbers alike is almost as astonishing as the powerful feeling and ingratiating personality he projects in even the most casual or lightweight of lyrics. The staggering range of music on these discs is indicated in subtitles such as "Basin Street Blues" and "You're From Texas." Virtually no genre goes unexplored. Those who would be satisfied with the tried and true Wills oeuvre are directed to Vol. 2, with "Faded Love," "San Antonio Rose," "Cotton Eyed Joe," the haunting "Time Changes Everything," and other Wills standards; those who want great music that spans everything from the Nat King Cole–penned "Straighten Up and Fly Right" (on Vol. 1) to Duke Ellington's "Take the 'A' Train" (on Vol. 3) to "Red River Valley" (Vol. 4) to Woody Herman's "At the Woodchopper's Ball" (on Vol. 5) are advised to purchase the entire Tiffany collection and cherish it until death do you part.

As if having Tommy Duncan as a lead singer weren't enough, Wills also employed the services of the sister duo Dean and Evelyn McKinney, who are heard extensively throughout *The Tiffany Transcriptions* albums. Twenty-two of their recordings with Wills and the Playboys, all recorded for Tiffany in 1946–47, have been preserved on a single-disc collection, *The McKinney Sisters.* No question about it, the McKinneys, with their bright, cheery voices, represented the pop end of the band's spectrum, even though their singing was often supported by arrangements that were more indebted to blues, Western swing, and jazz than to pop. *The McKinney Sisters* ranks as essential fare as well.

In the caveat emptor category, MCA's *Millennium Collection* entry, *The Best of Bob Wills,* contains a dozen familiar tracks, but these aren't the original, classic versions of monuments such as "New San Antonio Rose" and "Time Changes Everything." The recordings span 1947 to 1969, when he was recording for MGM, Kapp, and Decca. Only the two 1947 songs, "Keeper of My Heart" and "Bubbles in My Beer," feature Tommy Duncan, who left the band in 1948, after a falling out with Wills. Not that Johnny Preston, who is featured on a couple of tracks (including the Duncan-penned "Time Changes Everything") was a bad singer, but Duncan was an indisputably towering singer who invested his classic vocal style with personality to burn; Preston, and every singer who followed in Duncan's wake, paled in comparison to the master. As a result, *The Best of Bob Wills* is rather a depressing look at an illustrious, groundbreaking career in its endgame, although to Wills' credit the music is expertly executed and still retains a certain vibrancy of feeling and spirit.

On the other hand, Sony's *The Essential Bob Wills* lives up to the promise of its title. Its 20 cuts are prime Wills, spanning the glory years of 1935 to 1946 and featuring the original, enduring versions of Wills' monuments. "Right or Wrong," "Time Changes Everything," "New San Antonio Rose," "Steel Guitar Rag," "Maiden's Prayer," "Sugar Moon," "Deep Water"—everything here is remarkable and more. There's no better single-disc overview of Wills' career than this one.

After suffering a crippling stroke on May 31, 1973, Wills recovered enough to participate in one last, truly remarkable recording session, with many of the surviving members of the Texas Playboys. Never was an album title more appropriate and more poignant all at once than the document fashioned in those late spring days, *For the Last Time.* The group assembled at the Sumet-Burnet Studio in Dallas, TX, on December 3–4 to reprise some of the greatest moments in the King of Western Swing's career on the 40th anniversary of the band's founding. Special guest Merle Haggard, paying tribute to a personal hero, sang on three cuts and joined the fiddle ensemble on others. Wills himself, then wheelchair-bound, his voice affected by the stroke, was energized enough to deliver a homespun recitation of Cindy Walker's "What Makes Bob Holler." The reunion took an unfortunate turn after the first session ended: Wills suffered another, more serious stroke, lapsed into unconsciousness, and died 18 months later. The Playboys recorded as scheduled the next day, closing out the session with a joyous version of "That's What I Like About the South." Here the story of Bob Wills and His Texas Playboys ends, four decades after it began, in the same town where they started the journey that wrought lasting changes in American music in general and country music in particular. This is one powerhouse coda, unlike anything else in American music—and being unlike anything else in American music is what made Bob holler in the first place.   —D.M.

Brian Wilson

- ★★ Brian Wilson (1988; Warner Archives/Rhino, 2000)
- ★★★½ I Just Wasn't Made for These Times (MCA, 1995)
- ★★ Imagination (Giant, 1998)
- ★★★ Live at the Roxy Theatre (Brimel, 2000)
- ★★½ Brian Wilson Presents Pet Sounds Live (Brimel, 2002)
- ★★★ Gettin' In Over My Head (Rhino, 2004)
- ★★★★ Brian Wilson Presents Smile (Nonesuch, 2004)

Brian Wilson and Van Dyke Parks

- ★★★½ Orange Crate Art (Warner Bros., 1995)

Brian Wilson has spent decades living in the towering shadow of his 1960s masterworks with the Beach Boys. During that time, Wilson's mental illness turned him into a virtual recluse, and then a pawn in the manipulations of various would-be caretakers and collaborators. Yet his return to recording and touring without his longtime band, from whom he had become personally estranged, was among rock's most heartwarming stories. Here at last was an opportunity for Wilson to bask in the glow of his past achievements and to create songs that, while hardly the equal of his best works, suggested that he was once again engaged with his audience and the world outside his bedroom.

For his solo debut, Wilson demonstrates that his songwriting muse has not abandoned him completely with the man-out-of-time innocence of "Love and Mercy," "Baby Let Your Hair Grow Long," and "Melt Away" harkening back to his mid-'60s heyday, while the weird mix of paranoia and vampirish anticipation on "Night Time" bespeaks Wilson's troubled life. But dated synth-heavy production makes the album almost unlistenable.

Oddly, it's the Don Was–produced soundtrack to the documentary I Just Wasn't Made for These Times that best represents the post–Beach Boys Wilson. It presents him in a small-combo setting, singing with a frayed openness that is oddly moving. In this setting, "Love and Mercy" and "Melt Away" bloom, while some of his more profound if lesser-known Beach Boys songs ("The Warmth of the Sun," "'Til I Die") are illuminated. There's also a harrowing moment, a 1976 demo of "Still I Dream of It," with a ragged and off-key Wilson pouring out his pain at the piano.

Imagination suffers from many of the same problems as Brian Wilson: personal, sometimes wrenching songs obscured by vapid production and watered down by inappropriate collaborators, including Jimmy Buffett.

Live at the Roxy Theatre is a connoisseur's survey of Wilson's career, focusing not so much on overly familiar Beach Boys hits as relative rarities. Wilson's in high spirits, even though his choirboy voice wobbles in search of notes he once reached effortlessly. But his excellent backing band casts a safety net of harmony and musicianship that does justice to his most ambitious material. The backing ensemble's performances are even more accomplished on Pet Sounds Live; the 1966 masterpiece had never been performed in its entirety until Wilson took it on the road in 2002. But his voice sags beneath the weight of these beautifully demanding ballads.

Orange Crate Art reunites Wilson with Van Dyke Parks, the master arranger and lyricist who was his collaborator on the aborted 1967 Beach Boys album, Smile. Rather than participating in a full-blown union, Wilson is essentially a hired-gun vocalist. But he's in fine voice, his multioctave range stretched by long-lined melodies. Parks' orchestrations evoke California's sun-kissed geography and an era of pop songwriting when melody rather than rhythm was the guiding force. At the core of the album is a longing for a California that doesn't exist, and a sound that couldn't be less fashionable. In its own way, Orange Crate Art is a quirky little song cycle that defies categorization, a hint of what Smile might have been if circumstances had allowed these two mavericks to ever complete it.

Gettin' In Over My Head, Wilson's first studio album in six years, is an agreeable piece of work with cameos from Eric Clapton, Paul McCartney, and Elton John. Wilson is still frighteningly detached from the moment, though; it's best to think of this one as a celebrity children's record.

Thirty-eight years after he abandoned Smile, Brian Wilson was nudged back into the studio to re-create the album he once intended to be his masterpiece. And while rock's most famous lost recording could not possibly live up to its own legend, Smile 2004 is a joy on its own terms—filled with majestic harmonies, lush string and horn arrangements, gorgeous melodies, and Wilson's sly sense of humor. Shaped largely by

Darian Sahanaja, the musical director of Wilson's touring band, the album is arranged into three suites built around key compositions: "Heroes and Villains," "Surf's Up," and "Good Vibrations." And while none of these familiar songs is necessarily better sounding than the original version listeners have heard before (Wilson's voice is nowhere near as expressive as it once was and clearly strains in parts), the arrangements are terrific: *Smile* pieces together bits and pieces of Wilson's humor and genius into a majestic song cycle that's funny, poignant, irreverent, and totally wonderful. —G.K./M.MI.

Cassandra Wilson

★★★	Point of View (1985; Winter & Winter, 2001)
★★★	Days Aweigh (1987, Winter & Winter, 2001)
★★★★	Blue Skies (JMT, 1988)
★★½	Jump World (JMT, 1989)
★★★	She Who Weeps (PolyGram, 1991)
★★★★	Blue Light 'Til Dawn (Blue Note, 1993)
★★★★½	New Moon Daughter (Blue Note, 1995)
★★★½	Rendezvous (Blue Note, 1998)
★★★	Traveling Miles (Blue Note, 1999)
★★★★	Belly of the Sun (Blue Note, 2002)
★★★½	Glamoured (Blue Note, 2003)

Cassandra Wilson began her career as a sullen jazz diva, a purveyor of dramatic, if relatively tradition-minded, takes on standards. Frustrated with the insularity of the jazz world, she abandoned that pedestal to investigate more earthy music, and in the '90s carved out her own genre—dusty, blues-influenced songs of longing and woe backed by acoustic guitars and hand drums.

The "before" period—her straight-ahead jazz and occasional avant experimentation (she was a member of the Brooklyn-based '80s collective M-Base)—is best documented on *Blue Skies*. Taking tempos almost painfully slow, Wilson offers spare, hauntingly fragile treatments of timeworn ballads such as "My One and Only Love," and finds genuinely new drama within the warhorses. Other records were less consistent—though *She Who Weeps*, from 1991, has moments of brilliance.

Wilson signed to Blue Note in 1993 and immediately set out to dismantle the jazz-diva reputation: Her Craig Street–produced label debut includes an eerie rendition of Robert Johnson's "Hellhound on My Trail" and a smart reworking of Joni Mitchell's "Black Crow," followed by two introspective, charcoal-hued originals. The *Blue Light* formula—Wilson's smoldering voice nestled in a webbing of acoustic instruments, reimagining pop favorites and rural blues—has changed little since then. The magnificent *New Moon Daughter* finds

her transforming the Monkees' "Last Train to Clarksville" into an expression of pent-up longing; the album's originals, her strongest yet, include the biblical allegory "Solomon Sang" and a spry samba, "A Little Warm Death." Though *Belly of the Sun* continues in the same general terrain, it is notable for the increased warmth and nuance of Wilson's singing, and the daring of her choices—particularly the Band's "The Weight" and Jimmy Webb's "Wichita Lineman."

Wilson's approach, which has been copied by Dianne Reeves and others, served her well on other projects: the Miles Davis tribute *Traveling Miles* is a typically moody exploration, while a duo recording with pianist Jacky Terrasson proves that though she rarely scats like a jazz diva, her improvisatory gifts are formidable, and her kind of singing transcends genre to be timeless. Wilson's formula grows a bit more predictable as time goes on: Though sumptuous texturally, *Glamoured*'s treatments of Dylan ("Lay Lady Lay") and Willie Nelson ("Crazy") follow now-expected pathways by adding a bit of blues, or a whispered moan, to well-known melodies. The draw, as ever, is Wilson's intimate, easygoing phrasing—here best appreciated on "If Loving You Is Wrong." —T.M.

Jackie Wilson

★★½	Jackie Wilson at the Copa (1962; Brunswick, 2000)
★★★½	Whispers (1966; Brunswick, 2002)
★★★	Higher and Higher (1967; Brunswick, 2000)
★	Christmas Eve with Jackie Wilson (Brunswick, 2000)
★★★	Jackie Wilson and Count Basie (EMI-Capitol, 2002)
★★	Live (EMI-Capitol, 2002)
★★★★	The Greatest Hits of Jackie Wilson (1969; Brunswick, 1988)
★★★★	The Very Best of Jackie Wilson (Rhino, 1994)
★★★½	Uptown and Upnorth (Westside, 1999)
★★★★★	20 Greatest Hits (Brunswick, 2002)
★★★	The Very Best of Jackie Wilson, Vol. 1 (EMI-Capitol, 2002)
★★½	The Very Best of Jackie Wilson, Vol. 2 (EMI-Capitol, 2002)

Influenced heavily by Roy Brown and Clyde McPhatter, Detroit native Jackie Wilson broke into the music business in 1953 as McPhatter's replacement in Billy Ward's Dominoes. Three indifferent years produced only one minor hit, "St. Therese of the Roses," before Wilson went solo and cut a Top 20 R&B hit out of the box, "Reet Petite," written by Berry Gordy, then a struggling songwriter, later the founder of Motown Records. The next year produced the Top 30 pop hit

"To Be Loved," and ended with Wilson in the Top 10 with the enduring "Lonely Teardrops," all courtesy of Gordy. From that point through 1968 Wilson was found regularly in the Top 40. Among his hits are a couple of early soul classics in "Baby Workout" and "Higher and Higher," as well as a raft of powerful performances of both uptempo and ballad material. His appeal was further bolstered by frenetic live performances, with Wilson using his athlete's grace and physical command (he had been a Golden Gloves champion) to whip his audiences into a frenzy. Spins, splits, slides, and a smooth, single-foot skate were all among his arsenal of moves, which have been studied by every great R&B dancer from James Brown to Michael Jackson.

Jackie Wilson also possessed a voice of near-operatic proportions, which he loved to show off on show tunes and hoary old standards such as "Danny Boy." The supper-club conservatism of *Jackie Wilson at the Copa,* tempered only by tame arrangements of "Lonely Teardrops" and "What'd I Say," likely required no strong-arming. Wilson was happy to croon "Love for Sale" or belt out selections from *West Side Story.* As the '60s progressed and Wilson saw what was happening with his onetime song provider Berry Gordy, however, he also had no problem going with the modern flow. An association with Chicago producer Carl Davis resulted in the excellent 1966 album *Whispers.* The hit "Whispers (Gettin' Louder)" put Wilson in the soul mainstream, and was a career break for its writer, singer Barbara Acklin. "Just Be Sincere" and "I Don't Want to Lose You" were also chart successes in the lilting Chi-town style. The following year Davis and Wilson had their greatest success together with "(Your Love Keeps Lifting Me) Higher and Higher," on which backing is provided by moonlighting members of Motown's fabulous Funk Brothers. The *Higher and Higher* album also contains a convincing version of Darrell Banks' "Open the Door to Your Heart," but lacks the consistency of *Whispers.* The 1968 collaboration of Jackie Wilson and Count Basie's orchestra promised much but delivers little. It was not a jazz session, and the stiff big-band arrangements of such songs as "Funky Broadway" and "In the Midnight Hour" get the vocal performances they deserve. If your taste runs to Wilson's later soul sides, the *Uptown and Upnorth* collection is an instant party. Brunswick's 1969 *Greatest Hits* package still holds up, though Rhino's *Very Best* offers a better overview. (The two albums EMI also calls *Very Best* are decent budget items divided into 1957–1965 and 1966–1975 volumes.) The single most useful compilation is *20 Greatest Hits,* but the real heavyweight champ, the triple-CD box *Mr. Excitement,* is regrettably no longer available. —D.M./B.E.

Steve Winwood

★★★   Steve Winwood (Island, 1977)
★★★★½   Arc of a Diver (Island, 1980)
★★★   Talking Back to the Night (Island, 1982)
★★★½   Back in the High Life (Island, 1986)
★★★★   Chronicles (Island, 1987)
★★★   Roll With It (Virgin, 1988)
★★½   Refugees of the Heart (Virgin, 1990)
★★★★   The Finer Things (Island, 1995)
★★½   Junction 7 (Virgin, 1997)
★★★★   The Millennium Collection (Island, 1999)
★★★   About Time (Wincroft/SciFidelity, 2003)

Boy wonder of British blues, Winwood powered through "Gimme Some Lovin' " (1966) and "I'm a Man" (1967) for the Spencer Davis Group, his Hammond organ played with banshee intensity and his soaring vocals sounding like a mod Ray Charles. The brain behind the bluesy elegance of Traffic, Winwood took dazzling guitar solos, and edged rock further into harmonic complexity, without capitulating to the crass synthesis of jazz-rock fusion. After dominating Blind Faith, the brilliant but strife-ridden supergroup he'd formed with Eric Clapton and Ginger Baker, Winwood became for a while a virtual hermit.

His return was impressive. "Vacant Chair" and "Time Is Running Out" display his trademark classiness—even if he sounds a little tentative in places throughout *Steve Winwood,* whose atmosphere is one of restraint and careful polish. With *Arc of a Diver,* however, Winwood takes total control. With poetically suggestive lyrics by, of all people, Viv Stanshall, formerly head of the loopy comedy troupe the Bonzo Dog Band, the album's title track and "While You See a Chance" are pop of a brilliant caliber: Winwood's keyboards concoct gorgeous sound tapestries, through which his keening vocals shimmer coolly—and then take off. Winwood's best, this is the kind of mature pop that proves that "AOR" needn't be read as a mild obscenity: while played with intimidating craft, the songs demonstrate no lack of passion.

A one-man band on *Talking Back to the Night,* Winwood seems slightly exhausted; the record is, of course, accomplished, but the singer's moves are beginning to sound calculated, and the material trades more heavily on skill than heart. *Back in the High Life* is absolute gloss. "Higher Love" sounds amazing at first listen, and, if you forget the beer commercial it eventually became, so does the title track—but this is yuppie soul music, a triumph only of artful design. *Roll With It* is even blander, particularly when, as on the boring title tune, it tries for funk. With *Refugees of the Heart,* Winwood edges tentatively back toward music fired by more than fearsomely intelligent technique: "I

Will Be Here" and "In the Light of Day" are ballads that mark a return to grace, but the fully dimensional art Winwood had achieved in the past remains missing in action. *Junction 7*, a bid for urban-contemporary credibility produced by Narada Michael Walden and featuring guest turns by Lenny Kravitz and Des'ree, is slick, accomplished, and tastefully mild. He mercifully rediscovers his Hammond B-3 organ on *About Time*, which sounds a little more like the Winwood of Traffic, but not enough to give you a reason to listen to *Time* instead of the original albums. Aside from *Arc of a Diver*, the *Chronicles* hit collection contains the only essential solo music (the *Finer Things* box set is terrific, but mainly for the Traffic work; the same goes for *The Millennium Collection*). —P.E.

Wire

★★★★★	Pink Flag (1977; Restless Retro, 1989)
★★★★	Chairs Missing (1978; Restless Retro, 1989)
★★★★½	154 (Automatic/Warner Bros., 1979)
★★	Document and Eyewitness (1981; Mute, 1991)
★★★	Snakedrill (EP) (1986; Mute/Enigma, 1987)
★★★	The Ideal Copy (Mute/Enigma, 1987)
★★½	A Bell Is a Cup Until It Is Struck (Mute/Enigma, 1988)
★★	It's Beginning to and Back Again (Mute/Enigma, 1989)
★★★★	On Returning (1977–1979) (Restless Retro, 1989)
★	Manscape (Mute/Enigma, 1990)
★★	The First Letter (Mute, 1991)
★★	The Drill (Mute, 1991)
★★★★	Wire 1985–1990: The A List (Mute/Elektra, 1993)
★★★	Coatings (WMO, 1997)
★★★★	Read & Burn 01 (EP) (UK pinkflag, 2002)
★★★★	Read & Burn 02 (EP) (UK pinkflag, 2002)
★★★★	Send (UK pinkflag, 2003)

Wire were the sharpest, most inventive guys in the punk class of '77. Singer Colin Newman, guitarist Bruce Gilbert, bassist Graham Lewis, and drummer Robert Gotobed were a little older, a little more adventurous, and a little more visionary than most of their three-chord peers, and the four instantly (and rightly) perceived punk as a music of maximum possibility. For nearly three decades, for good and ill, Wire followed nothing but its muse. When they got bored with an idea, they dropped it; when they got bored with the band, they scrapped it for years on end. Wire achieved total art and total provocation, total rock and (occasionally) total boredom. They did it their way like Sinatra, and no wonder they're worshiped by punks to this day.

Well, at least one album is. *Pink Flag* is one of rock's all-time great reimaginings, 21 tracks whizzing by in 37 minutes, every one blindingly fresh in its expansion of rock's parameters and utterly familiar in its tunefulness. Produced with a deft hand by Mike Thorne, who oversaw the band's first three, groundbreaking albums, Wire reduces every song it touches to a streamlined, minimalist essence, moving from war-torn drama (the utterly harrowing and sadly ever-relevant "Reuters") to triumphant pop ("Ex Lion Tamer") to shots at squaresville ("Mr. Suit," "Mannequin") to surprisingly direct love songs ("Fragile"). *Pink Flag* is the explosive sound of brainiacs tossing off staggering musical insights like so much bread to birds. Many of those birds were a whole generation of American indie rockers—from the Minutemen to R.E.M. to Superchunk to Pavement to Spoon and dozens more—who aped not just the sound but the urge. (Minor Threat turned the perfect shouter "12XU" into a hardcore standard and Elastica built a whole career around "Three Girl Rhumba.") Decades later, *Pink Flag* is still pure lightbulb-over-the-head music, and an essential rock document. (Various CD pressings append various singles; mine comes with the wonderfully new-wavey single "Dot Dash/ Options R.")

But Wire got bored fast and evolved at an inhuman pace. *Chairs Missing* slows things down, as Thorne adds keyboard and moves toward abstraction, drones, and obtuse gestures: more blurry French films, less dotdash. The pink flag waves here and there: "Outdoor Miner" discovers the Kinks and "Heartbeat" perfects their minimalism (and got covered by Big Black). But a self-consciousness has taken to the fore: The dislocating "I Am the Fly" and the raging "Sand in My Joints" are autocritique.

154, the final album of Wire's first career arc, continued to complicate their sound with more elaborate arrangements, a thicker sound, and more complex, studio-enabled melodies. Lewis' "I Should Have Known Better" and "The Other Window" point disturbingly toward something gothic, while "On Returning" is synthy, dance rock fire, and "The 15th" is simply lovely. *On Returning* anthologizes these years, but you need the albums.

By February 1980, their ambitions had finally caught up to their ability to translate them, and after a really annoying show, which can be found on *Document and Eyewitness*, they put the band to sleep for five years, producing a library's worth of side projects in the interim.

Wire returned with a weird beat and body music. The *Snakedrill* EP contains two songs that defined their worldview for the next five years. "A Series of Snakes" is tuneful dance pop with obscure lyrics while "Drill" is about nothing in particular but is built around a gnarly little rhythm called "dugga" (say it "duggaduggadugga"—yeah, it sounds like that). Most of the songs recorded by Wire Mark Two were aspects of these two ideas. *The Ideal Copy* is straight-up minimalist dance rock, filled with stiff rhythms and affected, Britwuss vocals, the kind of throb New Order and, say, Sisters of Mercy had already mastered. The thrill is gone, but there's still something deeply intriguing about them, and with the '00s dance-punk revival, much of *The Ideal Copy* sounds disturbingly contemporary.

A Bell Is a Cup turns up the pop and adds back guitars, as if someone had been listening to R.E.M.'s covers of *Pink Flag* songs. Only "Kidney Bingos," with its melodic glossolalia, resonates. *It's Beginning to* cuts some live tracks to pieces to make new songs, an interesting if failed experiment at best. The cool, both pounding and flighty "Eardrum Buzz" is the highlight. The drum-machine-driven *Manscape* just plain sucks, while *The Drill* remixes the ur-dugga tune to the point of exhaustion. (The dugga era has been extremely well-anthologized on the fan-selected *The A List* and the hardcore can pick up remixes from the same period on *Coatings*.) *The First Letter,* credited to a Gotobedless Wire, is near-generic electronic fuckery, and on that weak note, Wire split once again until 1999.

Then, outta nowhere, Wire found its fury again. In 2000, they played a few shows, and in 2002, released the scorching, self-recorded, -released, and -distributed *Read & Burn 01* EP in which they combined *Pink Flag*'s speed and power with the dugga era's thick, digital sounds. "The Art of Stopping" and nearly hardcore "Comet" are as raging as anything Wire ever waxed. The sequel *Read and Burn 02* EP is even heavier. Pieces of both were combined with four new songs for the aggressive *Send,* and suddenly we find guys approaching 60 giving their 20-something selves a decent run for their money.   —J.G.

Bill Withers

★★★★	Still Bill (1972; Columbia/Legacy, 2003)	
★★★½	Live at Carnegie Hall (1973; Columbia/Legacy, 1997)	
★★½	Menagerie (1977; Columbia/Legacy, 2003)	
★★★	Greatest Hits (Columbia, 1981)	
★★★★½	Lean on Me: The Best of Bill Withers (Columbia/Legacy, 1994)	
★★★	Top Bill (AMW, 1999)	
★★★	Super Hits (Columbia/Legacy, 2002)	
★★★	Lean on Me (Collectables, 2002)	

Bill Withers was already in his 30s when his debut album caught on, and his voice conveys an unfazed assurance. "Ain't No Sunshine" is the single that rocketed Withers into the national spotlight, its insinuating folk-soul cadence accentuated by producer Booker T. Jones' spare arrangement and subtle, funky support. Tracks such as "Grandma's Hands" and "Harlem" from the album *Just As I Am* (presently unavailable) indicated that he would be more than a one-hit wonder. The self-produced followup *Still Bill* made good on that promise, artistically and commercially. The gospel-tinged "Lean on Me" and the scintillating "Use Me" broadened his range even as they took him to the top of the charts; the many covers of each (including the 1987 Club Nouveau version that made "Lean on Me" #1 a second time) attest to Withers' strength as a writer. Having composed and sung three classic singles and two excellent albums in his first year, Bill Withers was soaring when he recorded *Live at Carnegie Hall*. Backed by a crack band, he delivers sharp versions of his best songs, tosses in a few new ones, and closes with a medley of "Harlem/Cold Baloney" that sounds more appetizing than it looks.

After this, Withers seemed to back off from the challenge of maintaining this level a little more with each successive album. After switching to Columbia in the mid-'70s, he discreetly stepped over to the middle of the road. *Menagerie* was the best of his albums there. "Lovely Day" was an engaging single, and Motown vet Paul Riser's orchestrations are, well, lovely, but material such as "Lovely Night for Dancing" and "She Wants to (Get on Down)" is too insubstantial to stick. His quiet-storm collaborations with Grover Washington Jr. (*Just the Two of Us*) and the Crusaders (*Soul Shadows*) wound up overshadowing the last few of his own albums, as his career quietly drifted into well-compensated semiretirement. There are several hits collections available (*Top Bill* and *Lean on Me* offer the exact same songs), but only *Lean on Me: The Best of Bill Withers* (no relation to the other compilation titled after that hit) contains more than 10 tracks.   —M.C./B.E.

Andrew W.K.

★★★★	I Get Wet (Island, 2001)	
★★½	The Wolf (Island, 2003)	

Andrew W.K.'s debut album, *I Get Wet*, was such a crystalline example of dumb fun that it raised an unusual set of questions: Is this guy serious, or is he being ironic? And, if he's being ironic, does that mean it's wrong to like it so much? W.K. (short for Wilkes-Krier) preaches the gospel of good times on songs that combine hair-metal riffs and pop melodies into a straight shot of adrenaline. Much like the Ramones, W.K. is smart enough to know the value of keeping things simple, and his songs rely on little more than a few choice power chords, lunkheaded lyrics, and the constant feeling that he's having way more fun than you are. Like, all the time. Exhibit A: Three of 12 songs on *I Get Wet* have "party" in the title, including "It's Time to Party," "Party Til You Puke," and the pop-metal masterpiece "Party Hard." Even when he gets sentimental, he's still in character. In "She Is Beautiful," he says little more than "She is beautiful!/The girl is beautiful!" repeated ad nauseam.

If *I Get Wet* was W.K.'s *Ziggy Stardust*, *The Wolf* is *Aladdin Sane*: He's still in character, but the songs simply aren't as great. On "Long Live the Party," W.K. hollers, "You cannot kill the party," but the truth is that you can. Without the kind of killer hooks he used on *I Get Wet*, the headbanging licks and goofy motivational lyrics start to wear thin. He assumes a Queen-like grandiosity on the ballad "Never Let Down," which provides a welcome change of pace. But W.K. has so fully inhabited the character he's created that even he doesn't seem to know anymore where the line is between honesty and irony.   —J.E.

Peter Wolf

★★★½ Lights Out (EMI America, 1984)
★★½ Come As You Are (EMI America, 1987)
★★★ Up to No Good (MCA, 1990)
★★★ Long Line (Reprise, 1996)
★★★ Fool's Paradise (Mercury, 1998)
★★★★ Sleepless (Artemis, 2002)

After leaving the seminal white-R&B party group the J. Geils Band, at the very height of their hard-won popularity, vocalist Peter Wolf released his first solo album, *Lights Out*, in 1984. It was a promisingly eclectic and electric outing, with Boston hip-hop maven Michael Jonzun (head of the Jonzun Crew) overseeing a rangy program that showcased the blues-belting rocker in a flattering contemporary light. However, Wolf seemed to lose his manic spark thereafter, recording only one more album (the so-so *Come As You Are*) in the '80s—another veteran rocker stranded by the new wave.

The '90s began promisingly for Wolf with *Up to No Good*, which recaptured some of the manic intensity and irreverence of his R&B-fueled work with J. Geils. But although that and subsequent albums were all solid, fan-pleasing efforts, they emerged sporadically (six years passed between *Up to No Good* and *Long Line*) while Wolf played major-label roulette, making it difficult for him to recover any career traction. Happily, he landed on Artemis in the new millennium, where he released a late-career masterpiece, *Sleepless*. Members of Bob Dylan's band provided sympathetic

backup on this spare, reflective album of old-school R&B, blues, country, and reggae.   —P.P.

Stevie Wonder

★★½ The Jazz Soul of Little Stevie Wonder (Motown, 1963)
★★★ The 12 Year Old Genius (Motown, 1963)
★★ Tribute to Uncle Ray (Motown, 1962)
★★ With a Song in My Heart (Motown, 1963)
★★★ Up-Tight (Motown, 1966)
★★½ Down to Earth (1966; Motown, 1986)
★★★½ I Was Made to Love Her (Motown, 1967)
★★★½ Greatest Hits (Motown, 1968)
★★★ Alfie (Motown, 1968)
★★★½ For Once in My Life (Motown, 1968)
★★★ My Cherie Amour (Motown, 1969)
★★★ Signed Sealed & Delivered (Tamla, 1970)
★★★★ Where I'm Coming From (Motown, 1971)
★★★★ Stevie Wonder's Greatest Hits Vol. 2 (Tamla, 1971)
★★★★½ Looking Back (Motown, 1978)
★★★★ Music of My Mind (Motown, 1972)
★★★★★ Talking Book (Tamla, 1972)
★★★★★ Innervisions (Motown, 1973)
★★★★ Fulfillingness' First Finale (Motown, 1974)
★★★★★ Songs in the Key of Life (Motown, 1976)
★★★★ Journey Through the Secret Life of Plants (Tamla, 1979)
★★★★ Hotter Than July (Tamla, 1980)
★★★★ Stevie Wonder's Original Musiquarium I (Tamla, 1982)
★★★ The Woman in Red (Motown, 1984)
★★★ In Square Circle (Tamla, 1985)
★★½ Characters (Motown, 1987)
★★★½ Jungle Fever (Motown, 1991)
★★ Conversation Peace (Motown, 1995)
★★★ Natural Wonder (Motown, 1995)
★★★★ Song Review—Greatest Hits (Motown, 1996)
★★★★★ At the Close of a Century (Motown, 1999)

Perhaps the most singular talent ever to grace the Motown roster, Stevie Wonder began his recording career at age 11. At his peak, he scored five #1 singles in six years, and was a perennial favorite at such awards shows as the Grammys. Even more amazing is the fact that Wonder did so entirely on his own terms, building a catalogue of songs that managed to retain the harmonic sophistication of prerock pop while remaining completely up to date rhythmically.

It would be an exaggeration, though, to suggest that the scope of Wonder's potential was evident from the first. True, his second album did bill him as *The 12 Year Old Genius*, but "prodigy" would have been a more appropriate term. His debut, *The Jazz Soul of Little Stevie,* is an instrumental album featuring Wonder on piano, organ, harmonica, drums, and bongos, and while it's impressive from a technical standpoint, musically it sounds too much like the work of an adolescent. Fortunately, one track from that album, a bongo number called "Fingertips," is transformed into an absolutely incandescent harmonica showcase on *The 12 Year Old Genius,* a concert recording that became Wonder's first chart-topping single. But it's the only real bright point on Wonder's first four albums; *Tribute to Uncle Ray* finds the young singer reprising some of Ray Charles's better-known hits, while *With a Song in My Heart* is an appallingly earnest attempt at MOR ballad slinging.

Wonder doesn't get a proper Motown sound until *Up-Tight,* which even kicks off with the Motown tribute "Love a Go Go." Still, his commitment to the style is far from absolute, as *Up-Tight* finds room for a version of "Blowin' in the Wind," while *Down to Earth* has him handling such seemingly inappropriate material as "Bang Bang (My Baby Shot Me Down)" and "Sixteen Tons." *I Was Made to Love Her* has much better taste in cover material, tending more toward classic soul tunes such as "My Girl" and "Can I Get a Witness" (although Wonder doesn't quite know what to do with James Brown's "Please Please Please"), but even so, it's the title tune, with its incredible James Jamerson bass line, that makes this album—or the subsequent *Greatest Hits Vol. 1*—worth owning.

And yet he continued to yo-yo stylistically, swinging from the innocuous instrumentals of *Alfie* to the jazz-tinged soul of *For Once in My Life* to the sentimental balladry of *My Cherie Amour* to the straight-up soul of *Signed Sealed & Delivered.* The last was the first album Wonder produced on his own, but he doesn't truly begin to take control of his music until *Where I'm Coming From,* an album in which he uses his multi-instrumental virtuosity to provide nearly all the parts himself. It sounds dated today, but that's more a function of technology (primitive synths and the like) than the music itself, which is often striking. Wonder's *Greatest Hits Vol. 2* covers most of his big singles since the last hits, but a far better overview (if you can find it) is the now-deleted *Looking Back,* which not only highlights his albums to this point but also includes a number of non-LP singles.

With *Music of My Mind,* Wonder's albums turn a corner. His work from this point finds him acting as a self-sufficient, completely independent recording entity, handling the writing, production, and most of the instrumental chores himself—an unprecedented move for a Motown artist at that time. Unlike *Where I'm Coming From, Music of My Mind* arrives fully realized, with a resonant sound and songwriting that pushes his melodic instincts in unexpected directions. Yet as "Superwoman (Where Were You When I Needed You)" makes plain, this change of approach hasn't hurt his pop appeal. *Talking Book,* for instance, is a pop tour de force, with Wonder's work running the gamut from the blissful romanticism of "You Are the Sunshine of My Life" to the melodic exuberance of "I Believe (When I Fall in Love It Will Be Forever)" to the snaky funk of "Superstition," and *Innervisions* continues in kind, thanks to songs as accessible and inspired as the jazzy "Don't You Worry 'Bout a Thing" or the deliciously melancholy "All in Love Is Fair." *Innervisions* also finds Wonder addressing deeper issues, as "Living for the City" dramatizes the injustice of black urban life while "Higher Ground" and "Jesus Children of America" evoke a sense of spiritual struggle. Those topics crop up again on *Fulfillingness' First Finale,* and, indeed, spark one of its highlights, the bitingly anti-Nixon "You Haven't Done Nothin'." Still, Wonder's playful side dominates, and it's a pleasure to hear his almost bashful profession of lust in "Boogie on Reggae Woman."

By *Songs in the Key of Life,* Wonder is clearly at his peak, effortlessly sustaining the focus required of a double album while demonstrating an almost frightening capacity for hit singles. Even better, he's able to deal with an astonishing range of material, writing memorably about anything from childhood ("I Wish") to childbirth ("Isn't She Lovely"), and from ardent love ("Knocks Me Off My Feet") to fervent fandom ("Sir Duke"). But rather than try to top that album, Wonder went off in an entirely different direction, spending three years on *The Secret Life of Plants.* Although ridiculed at the time for its lack of commercialism, the album doesn't entirely deserve its reputation as a pop-star boondoggle, for not only does this atmospheric soundtrack succeed on its own terms, but it manages to do everything expected of a New Age album without succumbing to the usual directionless noodling. And it does have its share of pop elements, including "Send One Your Love" and the insinuatingly rhythmic "Race Babbling."

Even so, Wonder wasn't forgiven until he delivered the buoyantly tuneful *Hotter Than July,* an album most fans considered a return to form. To the extent that it produced two Top 20 singles ("I Ain't Gonna Stand for It" and "Master Blaster [Jammin']") as well as the shoulda-been-a-hit "Happy Birthday" (a Martin Luther King tribute), that's a fair assessment. Wonder's methods are different this time around, though, as many tracks are recorded with either an all-star backing choir, a full rhythm section, or both, while "Do I Do," one of the four new numbers on the greatest-hits package *Stevie Wonder's Original Musiquarium I,* actually finds him jamming with a live band (and guest soloist Dizzy Gillespie).

From there, Wonder's output becomes maddeningly unpredictable. His soundtrack album from *The Woman in Red* has some astonishingly lovely melodies, including "Love Light in Flight" and a charming collaboration with Dionne Warwick entitled "Moments Aren't Moments," but it also presents Wonder at his schlockiest in "I Just Called to Say I Love You."

In Square Circle is even more uneven, as Wonder backs lusciously melodic songs such as "Part-Time Lover" and "Stranger on the Shore of Love" with gratingly mechanical rhythm programs, while *Characters* undercuts its obvious ambition with a near-complete lack of musical edge. The dearth of great material guaranteed the lightweight-but-likeable soundtrack to *Jungle Fever* a lukewarm reception, and left the earnest-but-unsuccessful attempts at relevance on *Conversation Peace* almost completely ignored. The live-in-Japan *Natural Wonder* showed that his chops, at least, hadn't suffered, but Wonder's uncertain place in the pop world was made painfully obvious by the distinctly middle-of-the-road pitch of *Song Review,* which seems to suggest he was the black Paul McCartney. Fortunately, the richer, funkier, hit-packed *At the Close of a Century* offers a more realistic model, placing Wonder in a continuum with Louis Armstrong and Ray Charles as one of American popular music's most gifted and innovative performers. —J.D.C.

Wu-Tang Clan

★★★★★ Enter the Wu-Tang (36 Chambers) (Loud, 1993)
★★★ Wu-Tang Forever (Loud, 1997)
★★★★½ The W (Loud, 2000)
★★★★ Iron Flag (Loud, 2001)

A nine-man hip-hop group in the decade of the solo star, black to the back but too weird for any iteration of urban radio, the Wu-Tang Clan earns that most threadbare cultural assessment: real, if that means "internal contradictions not disguised." Everybody in the pop culture universe namechecks the Wu, yet no Wu album has sold more than 2 million records. Wu members have worked with Björk, Mariah Carey, and Shaquille O'Neal, but most of the group stays permanently below the celebrity waterline. If folks buying records at chain stores have moved on, it is likely because the Wu are not really pop. The Wu don't give immediate thrills, don't cut to the chase (if they even know what road they're on), don't know when to stop, don't know how to make their strengths read to a larger audience, don't engage the world beyond the inside of their minds. But then, keeping your own counsel could be an operational definition of "artist," and the Wu are, above all, listening only to themselves, and to their thousands and thousands of insular, hilarious, gnomic, crackling words. On the Wu's full-length debut, the RZA's beats are in a cloud of Cypress Hill smoke, fuzzy thumps indebted to DJ Muggs' style. The RZA's melodic moves are more unexpected, though, and soon enough they'll be his private property forever: minor-key piano clumps, quavering strings, random clicks and cracks, samples from the Stax and Hi records catalog and dialogue from Hong Kong kung fu movies. *Enter* still sounds like the product of one long night in front of the mike, 20-odd years of dreams and sketches tumbling out. Jump-up tracks such as "Method Man" and "Wu Tang Clan Ain't Nothing to Fuck Wit" gave U.K. junglists a lifetime of sound bites and made the album, atypically, a mover, but the heart of the RZA's project is in laments such as "Can It All Be So Simple" and "C.R.E.A.M." The RZA was building a new house for hip-hop, a place to mourn and think and wander. If anyone happens to dance or have fun along the way, bully for them.

Pace Spice Girls and Puffy, beware followup albums called *Forever* that answer an imagined question with wishful thinking. The RZA and his B-team producers go straight for the bin with off-the-rack keyboards and drum machines on this endless two-CD affair. The tracks are slow as ever, but drag-assing instead of dread-filled. Shame, because the MCs are in strong form. Method Man delivers one of my favorite lines ever here: "We at odds until we even." On "The Projects," Raekwon continues to expand his food-based thesaurus ("light up the broccoli, put the relish in my back pocket") and "A Better Tomorrow" finds GZA worrying about his family convincingly, but listeners without a programmable CD player should proceed with caution. Putatively addressing somebody else, Genius delivers a perfect capsule review on "As High as Wu Tang Get": "Too many songs, weak rhymes that's mad long/Make it brief, son—half short and twice strong." The era of RZA-produced albums is officially over. From here on in, the brunt of Wu-Tang production work falls to associates and disciples. (Perversely, this is the biggest selling album in the Wuevre.)

If you want proof that the Wu are a living contradiction, *The W* is it. After being absent as producer from some of the Wu's best work, and about to record one of the weakest Wu records yet *(Digital Bullet)* under his own name, the RZA comes through here with possibly his most consistent productions yet, handling every single song on the album. *The W* is a ferocious return to form for everybody involved. "Careful" and "Click Click" are mudfests in the tradition of Method Man's *Tical,* and "Protect Ya Neck (The Jump Off)" is good enough to earn its title. The standout tracks are some of the highest points in Wu history: "Hollow Bones" is simply staggering. Over nothing more than a loop from Syl Johnson's "Is It Because I'm Black?," Ghostface and Raekwon percolate and striate a crime narrative with enough swing to fuel an entire album. "I Can't Go to Sleep" features fake crying, Isaac Hayes, and plausible apocalypse scenarios while the icy "Jah World" is the RZA's lament come full circle: a funeral march. The combination of Memphis soul shout and Kingston soul cry first heard on RZA's *Ghost Dog* soundtrack comes to full bloom here.

Iron Flag was a disappointment at the checkout counter, but there isn't much reason to lament. "In the Hood" and "Uzi (Pinky Ring)" are two of the most charging Wu anthems yet, and "Babies" is Ghostface at his journalistic best. It's as solid as Wu gets, and blows *Wu-Tang Forever* away. But it's become clear—hip-hop is a fashion system with ruthless turnover. The Wu just do what they do, long may they buzz. —S.F.J.

Wyclef

see WYCLEF JEAN

Tammy Wynette

★★★	Your Good Girl's Gonna Go Bad (Epic/Legacy, 1967)
★★½	Stand by Your Man (Epic/Legacy, 1968)
★★	Til' I Get It Right (Platinum Disc, 1999)
★★★★	Tammy's Greatest Hits (Epic, 1969)
★★★	Biggest Hits (Epic, 1983)
★★★★	Anniversary: 20 Years of Hits (Epic, 1987)
★★★	Tears of Fire: The 25th Anniversary Collection (Epic, 1992)
★★	Always Gets It Right (Sony Special Products, 1995)
★★	Winners (Sony Special Products, 1995)
★★	Super Hits (Epic, 1994)
★★★	Inspirational Favorites (Ranwood, 1996)
★★	Super Hits, Vol. 2 (Sony, 1998)
★★	Collector's Edition (Sony, 1998)
★★	16 Biggest Hits (Epic/Legacy, 1999)

While Tammy Wynette continued to pile up sales in the decades following the late '60s, her groundbreaking work was accomplished during that Nashville heyday—the most passionate of all women country singers, she established herself as a riveting musical force, and patented her problematic persona as the antifeminist.

In hindsight, the perception of her as the C&W equivalent of Phyllis Schlafly, however, seems condescending and facile—while it's true that she parlayed more than her share of long-suffering-wife apologias, not only do such songs as "Your Good Girl's Gonna Go Bad," "The Only Time I'm Really Me," and "I Stayed Long Enough" counter her perceived submissiveness, but the dismissal of Wynette specifically reads like the more general loathing of white Southern life that afflicted many critics of the time. Basically, Wynette, a former beautician, embodied the sensibility of a certain culture; Bobbie Ann Mason and Andre Dubus would later write stories about the kind of character she represented—Wynette, however, sang directly from inside the scene, and she gave it authentic, soulful expression.

While her first Epic single, "Apartment #9," didn't fare well (Keith Richards later covered it with the New Barbarians), the title track of *Stand by Your Man* made Tammy a star—and provoked the early trashing of her as slavish wifey. In actuality the song was both tougher and more compassionate than its opponents averred; it also set the pattern for the very affecting approach Wynette would deploy on many of her ballads—she begins singing with a dramatic hesitancy and then builds to a startling intensity. Produced by Billy Sherrill (and cowritten by Wynette and Sherrill in about 20 minutes), the single has a melodramatic force, and while the album's uptempo numbers were capable, it's the songs of agony that remain riveting. Understandably, Wynette concentrated on heartache for the rest of her career, with either formulaic results or impressive ones. In the '80s, Wynette's sound, courtesy of producer Chips Moman, had progressed past the gooey arrangements Sherrill provided, but the results were iffy—she no longer came across as quaint, but her records occasionally suffered from glossiness. Her first greatest-hits album remains her strongest, by far; *Anniversary* is a fair career overview; and *Tears of Fire* gives us the most of the best. —P.E.

X

The most literary and musically adventurous light on the early Los Angeles punk scene, X absorbed all the fury of its contemporaries but outshone them in communicative power and subtlety of craft. Founded in 1977 by singer Exene Cervenka and bassist John Doe after they met in a poetry class, X explored topics uncommon to punk rock: marital fidelity, mourning, making a home in the squalor of bohemia. The group's hallmarks—crying male-female harmonies, buoyant rockabilly-punk guitars—were completely unique at the time.

Los Angeles is a spitfire punk classic, capturing the dissolute, strung-out population of the modern Babylon with nightmarish vignettes and mercilessly slashing guitars. "Johny Hit and Run Paulene" is a deadpan account of a drug-fueled abduction and rape; the despairing "Nausea" tells of "poverty and spit" with throbbing, dissonant chords by guitarist Billy Zoom and a headache beat by the aptly named D.J. Bonebrake; in the title track, unrelenting hostility forces a young woman out of the city of dreams. Not since the Doors had Los Angeles been painted in such a hellish light. No coincidence, then, that the album was produced by Ray Manzarek, and the band paid tribute with a blistering cover of the Doors' "Soul Kitchen."

A slow but steady evolution toward a distinctly Californian blend of punk, rockabilly, and country occurs on the next three albums, with Manzarek still at the helm. *Wild Gift,* the band's second, and even greater, classic album, is another glimpse of the dark side of the SoCal soul, though the scope narrows to the personal and domestic. "The Once Over Twice," "Adult Books," and "White Girl" find Cervenka and Doe (a married couple by this point) struggling with the demands of monogamy in a world bent on seduction, while "We're Desperate" and "When Our Love Passed Out on the Couch" dryly describe the unglamorous hipster life. *Under the Big Black Sun,* another triumph, has panicked dispatches from the road ("Motel Room in My Bed") and more about marital strains ("What kind of fool am I?/I am the married kind," the couple howl on "Because I Do"). "Riding With Mary," with a propulsive bass-guitar counterpoint by Doe and Zoom, digs deeper with a story about Exene's sister, who died in a car crash while cheating on her husband (and had a Virgin Mary figurine on her dashboard).

The first signs of identity crisis came on *More Fun.* It starts off great, with "The New World" and "I Must Not Think Bad Thoughts" lampooning Reagan-era propaganda and apathy ("Honest to goodness, the bars weren't open this morning/They must've been voting for a new president or something") with tense unison vocals and a nervous groove that in the able hands of Zoom and Bonebrake—one of the few drummers of the era with the chops to make a punk beat swing—rises to a maddening boil. But the album's second half wanders, ending up unhappily in the white funk domain of "True Love Pt. #2." Blondie and Talking Heads did it better years earlier.

The real disappointment came with *Ain't Love Grand,* an abrupt shift toward the hollow, radio-friendly "heavy rock" sound of the mid-'80s that sounds like an abandonment of all that X had worked for. The Knitters, the band's country project with Dave Alvin of the Blasters, followed a more sensible path to snappy acoustic honky-tonk tunes, but it was lost in the shuffle. The band tried to make amends with *See How We Are* (with Zoom now replaced by Tony Gilkyson), though there's not much fire. By this point Cervenka and Doe had divorced, and the best song, the bleak "4th of July," is by Alvin.

X disbanded in 1988 after a series of concerts in L.A., documented on *Live at the Whisky a-Go-Go,* and Cervenka and Doe concentrated on their solo careers (which included, for Doe, a good bit of acting). But five years later the group (with Gilkyson) was back with *Hey Zeus!,* which picks up where *See How We Are* left off but lacks real chemistry. The most promising element is a calming acoustic guitar, and two years later the band released an unplugged set, *Unclogged,* which is strong even if the loungey takes on their songs grow tire-some. The only X anthology is *Beyond & Back,* a two-disc set larded with uninteresting demo takes and live recordings.   —B.S.

X-Ray Spex

★★★★★   Germfree Adolescents (1978; Caroline, 1992)
★★★★   The Anthology (Sanctuary/Castle, 2002)

Marion Elliot was a typical confused London teen-ager with a mouthful of braces until she renamed herself Poly Styrene, formed X-Ray Spex, and hollered about her philosophical conundrums at the top of her lungs. The result was one of the greatest records of the original punk moment, 1978's *Germfree Adolescents.* Her lyrics are eloquently hilarious, aphoristic, and self-lacerating ("I wanna be instamatic/I wanna be a frozen pea"), she sings them like her house is on fire, and guitarist Jak Airport and saxophonist Rudi Thompson somehow manage to match her hurri-cane force. Shortly after the record's release, Styrene dropped out to become a Hare Krishna (later joined by original saxophonist Lora Logic). When *Germfree Adolescents* finally appeared in America, 14 years late, it appended their unforgettable debut single, "Oh Bondage Up Yours!," and a few other singles and B sides. *The Anthology* inexplicably (and badly) re-sequences the original album, and pads it out to two discs with some uninteresting demos of the same songs, a recording of the squawky young X-Ray Spex's second-ever gig (same songs again), and three tracks from their dreadful, preachy 1995 reunion

album *Conscious Consumer.* Any way *Germfree* can be heard is better than no way at all, though.   —D.W.

XTC

★★★½   White Music (1978; Caroline, 2002)
★★★   Go 2 (1978; Caroline, 2002)
★★★★   Drums and Wires (1979; Caroline, 2002)
★★★★   Black Sea (1980; Caroline, 2002)
★★   English Settlement (1982; Virgin, 2002)
★★   Mummer (1983; Virgin, 2002)
★★★   Beeswax: Some B-Sides 1977–1982 (Virgin, 1982)
★★★★   Waxworks: Some Singles 1977–1982 (Geffen, 1984)
★★★½   The Big Express (1984; Caroline, 2002)
★★★★★   Skylarking (1986; Caroline, 2002)
★★★   Oranges & Lemons (1989; Caroline, 2002)
★★★   Explode Together: The Dub Experiments . . . 1978–1980 (Virgin, 1990)
★★   Rag & Bone Buffet (Geffen, 1991)
★★   Nonsuch (1992; Caroline, 2002)
★★★★   Fossil Fuel: The XTC Singles 1977–1992 (Virgin, 1996)
★★★   Upsy Daisy Assortment (Geffen, 1997)
★★★★   Transistor Blast: Best of the BBC Sessions (TVT, 1998)
★★★★   Apple Venus, Pt. 1 (TVT, 1999)
★★   Homespun (TVT, 1999)
★★★   Wasp Star (Apple Venus, Pt. 2) (TVT, 2000)
★★★   Homegrown (TVT, 2001)
★★★★   Coat of Many Cupboards (Virgin, 2002)

Dukes of Stratosphear

★★★   25 O'Clock (Virgin, 1985)
★★★   Psonic Psunspot (Geffen, 1987)
★★★★   Chips From the Chocolate Fireball (1987; Caroline, 2002)

If you were 23 and English in 1977, you were a punk. Such is history. Raised on Beatles and Kinks then perverted by nutso blues rockers Patto and Cap-tain Beefheart's honeycomb patterns, Swindon's Andy Partridge used punk as an excuse to torque up and ab-breviate pop music. (Think of the band name, itself an abbreviation of joy.) Very much the work of Smart Young Men, for better or worse, XTC's debut, *White Music,* clanks more than it rocks: "Radios in Motion" and "This Is Pop" are signature tunes and manifestos. Known today for their nerdy tendencies and generous hooks, XTC were a strong live band. (Go to the *Coat of Many Cupboards* box set for a fierce live version of "Spinning Top," or try the entire 1979 BBC concert on *Transistor Blast.*) Drummer Terry Chambers was appropriately thuggish, Partridge had secret guitar mojo, and Barry Andrews is one of the few punk-era keyboardists who *fit in,* all Halloween swirls and over-driven chords. (Check out his work on the breakbeat classic waiting to happen, "All Along the Watchtower.") Bassist Colin Moulding would eventually challenge Partridge's dominance with his pastoral viewpoint and McCartney bass lines, but at first he simply aped Partridge's spastic side (see "Do What You Do" and "Instant Tunes").

Slagged at the time, *Go 2* draws on secondary sources—dub, some telegraphed idea of funk, and all kinds of social alienation—and makes something new out of it all, though it's not always listenable. "Are You Receiving Me?" was the hit, but "Meccanik Dancing" was better, capturing the tumescent fear and energy of young men on the make. (*Explode Together* gathers the dub EP version of *Go 2, Go +,* and Partridge's solo dub album from the time, *The Lure of Salvage.* It's active, freaky stuff.)

On *Drums and Wires,* guitarist Dave Gregory replaced the recently demobbed Andrews. With the organ mayhem gone, the sound hardened into a twangy brick, and Moulding's new songs turned the band into contenders. Moulding's "Making Plans for Nigel" was the band's first big transatlantic hit, an impossibly sad song about parents with diminished expectations, driven by a guitar that sounds like wind whistling through an abandoned mining town. "Ten Feet Tall" was another Moulding triumph, a lost Kinks song for a first date that never ends. Partridge's "Life Begins at the Hop" is "Meccanik Dancing" set 10 years earlier, without the fear, and it was the first XTC song most Americans heard.

Black Sea toughened up their good nature, opened the social eyeball, and brought a stressed-out intensity to the playing. On "Respectable Street," the band traded jerky for heavy (hello, Terry) and Partridge replaced peevish with angry (hello, autobiography). The hooks got deeper—"Towers of London" was *Abbey Road* come back to haunt punk—and even though "Generals and Majors" wasn't breaking new ground in the Opinions of War Dept., Moulding and Partridge weren't settling for science fiction anymore. "No Language in Our Lungs," especially the live version on *Cupboards,* was cathartic, even.

English Settlement was a search for something that never came. "Senses Working Overtime" was Partridge's first great song of his second stage, acoustic guitars and good vibes replacing the grinding teeth and right angles. But social protest is one of XTC's weaknesses—they keep doing it, even though they have no knack for it. "It's Nearly Africa" was inept and Moulding's "Runaway" unctuous. The faux world music didn't help—leave that to Peter Gabriel, guys.

After the *English Settlement* tour, the band retired in 1982 from live performance because of Partridge's somewhat surprising stage fear. Halfway through recording *Mummer,* Chambers left the band and was replaced by Pete Phipps of the Glitter Band. The upheavals were audible. Except for the luminous "Love on a Farmboy's Wages," *Mummer* was a spasm of uncertainty, Partridge caught between imitating former glories ("Deliver Us From the Elements") and sketching out the new style ("Ladybird"). Partridge had proven he could be as effortlessly melodic as Paul McCartney or Elvis Costello, but his wacky preciousness and tendency to cram songs with details tended to marginalize his work.

The Big Express gave a nod to *Black Sea* with the opening track "Wake Up," a sort of sequel to "Respectable Street." Gregory's guitar is articulate throughout, and Partridge is in the pure pop zone—"You're the Wish You Are I Had" is the song every long-suffering Wife of a Genius is hoping to wake up to. The band had shaken the hex.

For *Skylarking,* the band was aided (and interfered with, say fans) by producer Todd Rundgren. The rustic romanticism that sounded hokey on *Mummer* and *English Settlement* became felt, confident, light. Moulding, unexpectedly, wrote the band's best sex 'n' drugs song, "Grass" ("things we did on grass"), and Partridge expanded his set of workingman odes with the heartbreaking "Earn Enough for Us." The songs roll into one another with remarkable fluidity, and the band's quirks are submerged beneath the beauty. It was a quick single appended to the U.S. release that brought the band its biggest American hit, "Dear God." Partridge's politics were stuck on gee whiz, but the song showed his knack for concepts and conversational melodies.

Oranges & Lemons is a fun, if baggy, album. "Garden of Earthly Delights" is Partridge's jiggling leg turned into an engine, a polyrhythmic broadside in support of general enthusiasm. "The Mayor of Simpleton" rides a great corkscrew bass line from Moulding and one of Partridge's best lyrics, a clever proclamation about lacking cleverness that Cole Porter might have liked. (If the '60s hangover is your thing, check out the "secret" side band Dukes of Stratosphear, Partridge's homage to '60s psych bands. Purposely derivative and awash in echo, these records are often better than they needed to be, as on "Vanishing Girl." *Chips From the Chocolate Fireball* collects their two releases, *25 O'Clock* and *Psonic Psunspot.*)

After an extended hiatus, the band returned as a duo, sans Gregory, in 1999 for *Apple Venus, Pt. 1,* following with *Wasp Star (Apple Venus, Pt. 2)* in 2000.

Occasionally magnificent ("Harvest Festival" and "River of Orchids" from *Venus* and "Stupidity Happy" from *Wasp*), Partridge had lost none of his power, focusing on near–a cappella harmonies for *Venus* and strapping guitars for *Wasp*. (Moulding's role is somewhat vestigial at this point.) Economically aware that their fan base is the fanatics now, the band released companion albums of home demos for both *Venus* and *Wasp*.

The collections are what the consumer expects. *Rag & Bone Buffet* is great for fans, baffling for anyone else. *Waxworks* and *Fossil Fuel* serve the tourist, concentrating on the band's impressive run of '70s and '80s singles.   —S.F.J.

Yy

Weird Al Yankovic

★★★	Weird Al Yankovic (Scotti Bros., 1983)
★★★	In 3-D (Scotti Bros., 1984)
★★★	Dare to Be Stupid (Scotti Bros., 1985)
★★★½	Polka Party (Scotti Bros., 1986)
★★	Even Worse (Scotti Bros., 1987)
★★★	UHF (Rock 'n Roll, 1989)
★★★½	Greatest Hits (Scotti Bros., 1989)
★★★½	Off the Deep End (Scotti Bros., 1992)
★★½	Alapalooza (Scotti Bros., 1993)
★★★	The Food Album (Rock 'n Roll, 1993)
★★★½	Permanent Record (Scotti Bros., 1994)
★★★½	Greatest Hits, Vol. 2 (Scotti Bros., 1994)
★★	The TV Album (Scotti Bros., 1995)
★★	Bad Hair Day (Scotti Bros., 1996)
★★★½	Running with Scissors (Volcano, 1999)
★★	Poodle Hat (Volcano, 2003)

It's been said that the worst reception an artist can get is complete indifference. This hasn't been a problem for Weird Al Yankovic, the accordion-wielding, ultra-prolific, long-reigning pop parody champ. No, they've always loved or hated Weird Al—"they" being the artists whose songs Al has subjected to his incorrigible lyrical rewrites. In fact, "My Bologna"—Al's take on the Knack's "My Sharona"—so tickled the Knack that they successfully petitioned Capitol Records to release the single. Similarly, Michael Jackson let Al use the "Bad" video set for his "Fat" clip. On the flip side, Ray Davies for many years blocked the release of "Yoda" (Al's masterful rewrite of the Kinks' "Lola") and Coolio groused about "Amish Paradise," Al's gut-busting send-up of "Gangsta's Paradise." From his teenage days as the darling of the nationally syndicated *Doctor Demento Radio Show* to his later alliance with Steven Spielberg, Weird Al's witty script-flipping and under-acknowledged musical talents have irreverently skewered the pop music of any given year. Still, after all these years, Al is hitting career high points—his nasal whine has never been put to more appropriate use than on his 1999 Yiddish-sprinkled Offspring goof "Pretty Fly for a Rabbi." —P.R.

Yardbirds

★★★½	Clapton's Cradle: The Early Yardbirds Recordings (Evidence, 1995)
★★★	Five Live Yardbirds (1964; Rhino, 1990)
★★★	Sonnyboy Williamson and the Yardbirds (2002)
★★★★★	Roger the Engineer (1966; Warner Archives, 1996)
★★★	The Little Games Sessions & More (1967; Capitol, 1992)
★★★★	Greatest Hits, Vol. 1 (1964–66) (Rhino, 1986)
★★★★	Live at the BBC (Warner Archive, 1997)
★★★★★	Ultimate (Rhino, 2001)

Although other English blues bands tried to play R&B the American way, with the emphasis on the singing or the groove, the Yardbirds saw it as a means of showcasing guitar playing. That this should be the case hardly seems surprising, given the quality of guitarist the band favored; this, after all, was where Eric Clapton and Jeff Beck made their names, and where Jimmy Page laid the foundations for what would become Led Zeppelin. But at the time, the Yardbirds' approach to blues and R&B transformed rock & roll, making the music harder and more exciting than before, while in the process inspiring successive generations of bands, from blues rockers to heavy metalists to punks.

What made the Yardbirds distinctive is almost immediately apparent in the raucous interplay of *Five Live Yardbirds*. Despite Keith Relf's lackluster vocals and a set list entirely given over to cover material, the Yardbirds nonetheless set themselves apart from their peers, through both the quality of the guitar playing and the feral energy of the ensemble. Just listen to the way these five rip through the Isley Brothers' "Respectable"; not only do the Yardbirds make the original sound tame, but their rhythm work converts the Isleys' breathless backbeat into something far more insistent than swinging. This music doesn't roll—it just rocks.

Other material from that era remains, unfortunately, harder to pin down. *Clapton's Cradle* is an impressive document of that guitarist in his nascent stage, and says much about the Yardbirds' early development. But it's hardly exhaustive, and such periodically deleted titles as now import-only *Sonny Boy Williamson and The Yardbirds* provide valuable clues to understanding how these young Britons absorbed and processed the blues.

A key turning point was the hit "For Your Love." Although the single finally put the Yardbirds on the charts, the recording was too pop for Clapton, who left the group in disgust. But his replacement, Jeff Beck, was more than happy to try other colors, and the singles he played on—"Heart Full of Soul," "Shapes of Things," "The Train Kept a Rollin' "—find the Yardbirds breaking significant new ground. As such, *Roger the Engineer* stands as the Yardbirds' crowning achievement, an album that, through the likes of "Over, Under, Sideways, Down" and "Jeff's Boogie," pushes the band well into the psychedelic era without betraying its sound or roots. (Live, the band took these tunes even further, as the Beck-era material from *Live at the BBC* attests.)

Bassist Paul Samwell-Smith left the group shortly after *Roger*, and was replaced by Page, who later moved over to colead (and, eventually, sole lead) guitar. Both Page and Beck are heard on the dramatic "Happenings 10 Years Time Ago" (originally a single, but now included on *Roger the Engineer*), as well as "Stroll On," a none-too-subtle rewrite of "The Train Kept a Rollin' " the group cut for the Michelangelo Antonioni film *Blow Up* (and is included on *Ultimate Yardbirds!*). That, though, was the group's last bit of greatness, for it fell apart after cutting *Little Games*, a disastrous attempt at conventional pop that nonetheless led Page to the sound that would become Led Zeppelin.

Although five albums' worth of Yardbirds material was released in the U.S. during the band's prime, at this writing, nothing resembling the original vinyl remains in print. That's not entirely a complaint, as the CD version of *Roger the Engineer* is far superior to its vinyl analog, and *Ultimate* manages to squeeze pretty much every track a nonfanatic could want onto two ultrainstructive CDs. Beyond that, it's up to the collector's instinct in every listener.   —J.D.C.

Yeah Yeah Yeahs

★★★★ Yeah Yeah Yeahs (Shifty, 2001; Touch & Go, 2002)
★★★½ Fever to Tell (Interscope, 2003)

This Brooklyn trio debuted during the 2001 celebration of All Things Rock and instantly made their case for good-old-fashioned attitude. Guitarist Nick Zinner has borrowed licks from the Cramps and 8-Eyed Spy, drummer Nick Chase calls on most of classic-rock timekeeping, and singer Karen O has been compared to so many people she can only be entirely original. (Pat Benatar, Poly Styrene, and Chrissie Hynde have all come up.) Screeching, throwing beer, and reviving torn clothing in one fell swoop, Karen O provided a downtown scene of skinny boys with a bona fide killer queen bee. Their guitar-voice-drums setup is unusually rich, able to produce an unlikely party tune such as "Bang" (containing the immortal line "as a fuck son, you suck") and the Ronettes-gone–Glenn Branca mashup "Our Time," which became an inadvertent 9/11 anthem (both from their debut EP). *Fever to Tell* (unexpectedly on Interscope) doesn't clean up their sound much, and has their loveliest tune, "Maps," an actual love song. "Pin" and "Rich" combine rhythm and noise and attitude in a way that somehow hasn't been done, though you'll swear it has. Over a full LP, their high-end sound suffers but their live show doesn't.   —S.F.J.

Trisha Yearwood

★★★½ Trisha Yearwood (MCA, 1991)
★★★½ Hearts in Armor (MCA, 1992)
★★★ The Song Remembers When (MCA, 1993)
★★★ The Sweetest Gift (MCA, 1994)
★★★ Thinkin' About You (MCA, 1995)
★★★ Everybody Knows (MCA, 1996)
★★★★ Songbook: A Collection of Hits (MCA, 1997)
★★★ Where Your Road Leads (MCA, 1998)
★★½ Real Live Woman (MCA, 2000)
★★★ Inside Out (MCA, 2001)

Sometime in the '90s, while nobody was looking, the Eagles became the granddaddies of contemporary country—or maybe folks just finally realized that their L.A. slicko production and the SoCal cult of individuality weren't much different from Nashville slicko production and the outlaw cult of individuality. Embattled malcontents responded by griping about God and Hank and malls and housewives. But Trisha Yearwood managed to stay above the fray, even as she split the difference between L.A. professionalism and down-home style. Stylistically, Yearwood's no purist—she dueted (and more) with Garth himself—but there is an element of purity in her performances. Like Linda Ronstadt, she's a transparent interpreter who puts the song before her own ego, and so she truly earns the old cliché: She's only as good as her material.

Fortunately, that material has often been very good. Yearwood's first hit, "She's in Love With the Boy," was a lively tale of first love that took the kids' side against the parents. And the joyous "Xxx's and Ooo's (An American Girl)" remains a hallmark of Nashville feminism—or maybe just a happy notice that at least a few basic feminist tenets had sunk so deep into American culture even Nashville couldn't backlash against them. Stack 'em all up and you've got *Songbook*, a snapshot of '90s country at its most tasteful and distinguished. Since then, Yearwood's most significant moment has been her attempt to use her care and discernment to redeem "How Do I Live," a tower of Diane Warren megaschlock. She came within a tonsil's width of doing so, but it was a Pyrrhic victory for a woman who once knew how to pick her battles. —K.H.

Yes

★★	Yes (1969; Rhino, 2003)
★★	Time and a Word (1970; Rhino, 2003)
★★★	The Yes Album (1971; Rhino, 2003)
★★★★	Fragile (1972; Rhino, 2003)
★★★★	Close to the Edge (Atlantic, 1972)
★★	Yessongs (Atlantic, 1973)
★★★★	Tales from Topographic Oceans (Atlantic, 1974)
★★★★	Relayer (Atlantic, 1974)
★	Yesterdays (Atlantic, 1975)
★★★½	Going for the One (Atlantic, 1977)
★½	Tormato (Atlantic, 1978)
★★★★	Drama (Atlantic, 1980)
★★½	Yesshows (Atlantic, 1980)
★★★	90125 (Atco, 1983)
★	90125 Live: The Solos (Atco, 1985)
★★★	Big Generator (Atco, 1987)
★★	Union (Arista, 1990)
★★★★	Yesyears (Atlantic, 1991)
★★½	Talk (Victory, 1994)
★½	Keys to Ascension (CMC, 1996)
★½	Keys to Ascension, Vol. 2 (Purple Pyramid, 1997)
★★	Open Your Eyes (Beyond, 1997)
★★	The Ladder (Beyond, 1999)
★	House of Yes: Live from House of Blues (Beyond, 2000)
★★	Magnification (Beyond, 2001)
★★★★	In a Word (Rhino, 2002)
★★★	The Ultimate Yes (Rhino, 2004)

You can say a lot of nasty things about progressive rock, and many people have—most frequently, that the genre emphasizes musical chops over soulful expression. But in the case of Yes, the British band's often overbearing pretentiousness resulted in moments of rare grace and beauty, a bizarre and fleeting—if totally unrealistic—coupling of classical textures with rock & roll pathos.

Curiously enough, Yes' 1969 debut is a relatively down-to-earth affair—and a not very inspired one at that. The quintet's reworking of the Beatles' "Every Little Thing" illustrates its knack for mysterioso, angelic harmonies, led by singer Jon Anderson. But the band's original compositions are sketchy at best. The psychedelic *Time and a Word* offers little improvement, perhaps because of the dubious decision to attach an entire symphony orchestra to the already cluttered arrangements.

It was the addition of Steve Howe's guitar pyrotechnics that finally allowed Yes to find their true identity. *The Yes Album* is a gigantic leap forward, with extended workouts such as the ethereal "Starship Trooper" emphasizing the band members' individual virtues. In Bill Bruford, Yes had a hip, jazzy drummer; in Chris Squire, a bassist willing to dominate the mix with his elephantine lines; and in Tony Kaye, an organist who used his Hammond sparingly, for funkier effect.

Kaye was unceremoniously dismissed so that virtuoso Rick Wakeman could join in, perfecting the definitive Yes sound. *Fragile* is quintessential classic rock. "Roundabout" is an undeniable prog-pop singalong, but the album's happiest moments are subtle, brief passages such as the bucolic instrumental segment of "South Side of the Sky" and the gleefully baroque line that Wakeman repeats hypnotically during the climax of "Heart of the Sunrise."

At that moment, the band threw caution to the wind and indulged its appetite for excess without a hint of guilt. *Close to the Edge* is not really a rock record, but rather a symphony that happens to be performed by a rock band. The decidedly trippy 20-minute-long title track is occasionally shrill and breathtakingly intense, whereas "Siberian Khatru," with its staccato attack and tribal vocalizing, remains, to this day, strangely hip. A bewildered Bruford quit the group, reasoning that Yes could never reach such heights again. He was replaced by Alan White, a more economical drummer.

Depending on your point of view, *Tales from Topographic Oceans* is either prog rock's absolute nadir or its dreamy masterpiece. Sure enough, this overblown double LP set finds true redemption only when seen as an exercise in mood. *Relayer* is probably Yes' best opus, a manic jam session that places the group's instrumental dexterity at the service of a ferocious combination of free jazz and heavy metal.

After an extended hiatus that yielded the inevitable, sub-par solo excursions, the band returned with *Going for the One*, a flashy record whose shorter, punchier tunes displayed an instinctive reaction to the emerging punk movement. The layers of church organ on "Awaken" were decidedly epic, but Yes had run out of steam. So misguided and pedestrian was 1978's *Tormato* that both Anderson and Wakeman jumped ship after its release.

It seemed as if Yes could simply not carry on without Anderson's celestial vocalizing. But carry on it did, enlisting future superstar producer Trevor Horn and his Buggles cohort Geoff Downes to bring a touch of poppy new wave to the proceedings. With its tongue-in-cheek riffs and hummable melodies, *Drama* is the band's most underrated album. Touring with Horn as lead singer proved to be a disaster, however, and Yes called it quits.

Horn would return as producer for a 1983 lineup that included South African guitarist Trevor Rabin and Anderson back in the fold for a surreal twist of fate: Yes as an American-sounding arena-rock outfit, complete with a smash single ("Owner of a Lonely Heart") and best-selling album *(90125)*. The band spent the next decade trying to duplicate its success— as if winning the lotto twice was a feasible option.

Since 1996, Anderson and a revolving cast of former and new members have attempted a return to the classically influenced Yes sound of yesteryear. Truth be said, there are bits and pieces of the old magic to be found in the underwhelming *The Ladder* and the orchestrally enhanced *Magnification*. For the most part, however, Yes has left its maddening grandeur behind. Of the band's two box sets, *Yesyears* includes most of the essential classics. *In a Word* spends way too many discs on the latter-day fluff. The triple disc *Ultimate Yes* juxtaposes some of the band's finest music with a forgettable disc of unplugged numbers. —E.L.

Yo La Tengo

★★ Ride the Tiger (1986; Matador, 1996)
★★★ New Wave Hot Dogs (Coyote, 1987)
★★★★ President Yo La Tengo (Coyote, 1989)
★★★★ Fakebook (Bar/None, 1990)
★★★★ New Wave Hot Dogs/President Yo La Tengo (Matador, 1990)
★★ May I Sing with Me (Alias, 1992)
★★★★★ Painful (Matador, 1993)
★★★★★ Electr-O-Pura (Matador, 1995)
★★ Genius + Love = Yo La Tengo (Matador, 1996)
★★★★★ I Can Hear the Heart Beating as One (Matador, 1997)
★★★½ Strange but True (Matador, 1992)
★★★½ And Then Nothing Turned Itself Inside Out (Matador, 2000)
★★ The Sounds of the Sounds of Science (Egon, 2002)
★★ Summer Sun (Matador, 2003)
★★★ Today Is the Day (Matador, 2003)

Yo La Tengo is one of the all-time great American garage bands, operating out of Hoboken, NJ, for almost 20 years now without running out of ideas. Guitarist Ira Kaplan and drummer Georgia Hubley are a married couple who seem to like each other, quite the rock-world novelty. Together, they do for monogamy what the Velvet Underground did for heroin—even their screaming feedback drones have the down-home feel of neighbors jamming on the back porch. Ever since bassist James McNew joined in the early '90s, the trio has been one of indie rock's most adventurous and most beloved bands. They experiment constantly, so all their albums have tracks that are too awful to even count as filler; the closest they've come to flawless is *Painful*. But no Yo La Tengo fan would be interested in flawless. They do folkie ballads, they do noise, they try endless guitar jams, they play around with keyboards and drum loops, they cover any song that pops into their heads, and they were great on *The Simpsons*.

The first two jangle-rock records sounded good at the time, but the band really made its early reputation with the 28-minute *President Yo La Tengo*. (The title is an arcane *Get Smart* reference—Yo La Tengo has always had trouble with titles, but this is one of their better tries.) "Barnaby, Hardly Working" and "Drug Test" were space-rock drones with a jagged guitar sound, announcing that everybody's favorite cover band had turned into songwriters. Ira sang like Lou Reed's librarian uncle, but he traded stunning harmonies with Hubley on "Alyda." *Fakebook* was a summer-time set of acoustic tunes, mostly covers, giving Hubley plenty of room to sing like Maureen Tucker's librarian niece. They did oldies by the Kinks, the Flamin' Groovies, NRBQ, and John Cale, although the best song was a new original, "The Summer." The touching cover of Daniel Johnston's "Speeding Motorcycle" became one of Yo La Tengo's most enduring faves.

At first, James McNew seemed like the latest in a long line of temporary bassists, but he was already a formidable talent in his own right, recording solo under the name Dump, and he pushed the band to a new level. You can't really hear him in the dull instrumental murk of *May I Sing with Me,* but he became an essential part of the sound on *Painful,* the 1993 album that kept every promise Yo La Tengo ever made and blew their previous highlights away. The premise was New Zealand–style indie rock muscled up with a sharper song sense and a louder bottom, resulting in riffs such as "Sudden Organ" and "From a Motel 6." Even the vocals came on strong. They did "Big Day Coming" twice, first as a lullaby, then as a surging rave-up; Hubley and Kaplan harmonized on a hushed version of the Only Ones' "The Whole of the Law," and the record climaxed with the fantastic seven-minute guitar instrumental "I Heard You Looking."

Even the band's biggest fans were taken aback by *Painful.* So which one is the best—*Painful, Electr-O-Pura,* or *I Can Hear the Heart Beating as One*? It's a tough call. *Painful* is the one that doesn't let up for a minute. *Electr-O-Pura* has the best songwriting. *I Can Hear the Heart* covers the most stylistic ground. *Electr-O-Pura* is guitar, guitar, guitar, with tons of propulsive organ and drums and rugged little tunes such as "Tom Courtenay" and "False Alarm." "Blue Line Swinger" is definitely their best song ever, a nine-minute groove that you never want to end, and it feels like it never does, until the final moments when Hubley's vocals lift off into a human feedback loop.

I Can Hear tries a much wider variety of sonic inventions and gets away with most of them, covering all the bases like an indie-rock version of Prince's *Sign o' the Times.* Kaplan sails away on perfect guitar drones such as "Deeper into Movies" and "We're an American Band" (not the Grand Funk song of the same name). "Moby Octopad" is a mysterious synthed-up psychedelic loop, "Stockholm Syndrome" is acoustic folk rock, "Green Arrow" is a surf instrumental, "Center of Gravity" is mock bossa nova, and "Little Honda" turns a Brian Wilson oldie into a punk-rock celebration. So it looks like a tie between *Electr-O-Pura* and *I Can Hear.* Newcomers should start with the latter, as it's the one that practically everybody likes, although the really bad song on *I Can Hear* ("Spec Bebop") lasts over 10 minutes, while the two really bad songs on *Electr-O-Pura* are over pretty quick. Your call.

Since then, the band has kept experimenting for its loyal fan base. *And Then Nothing Turned Itself Inside Out* was a drastic step, turning down the volume for a set of low-key and apparently autobiographical musings on married life. It's often beautiful, especially "Our Way to Fall," although the loud guitar of "Cherry Chapstick" makes you hungry for a little more. *Summer Sun* was a throwaway with one not-bad song, "Season of the Shark." Warning: Ira's rap is on side two. *The Sounds of the Sounds of Science* is an instru-mental film soundtrack, the sort of thing Yo La Tengo do well when they're trying, but not here. *Genius + Love = Yo La Tengo,* the most awful album title in a career full of them, collects rarities through 1996, such as their version of the *Fast Times at Ridgemont High* love theme "Somebody's Baby." Inexplicably, it omits their great 1991 cover of the Beach Boys' "Farmer's Daughter," from the "Upside Down" single. More recently, the 2003 "Nuclear War" single is a timely antiwar protest with a kids' choir chanting an old Sun Ra song, while *Today Is the Day* has "Styles of the Times." *Strange but True* is an album of the band backing up Half Japanese singer Jad Fair while he reads *Weekly World News* articles out loud. The strange-but-true aspect of this album is that it's pretty great, especially "Circus Strongman Runs for PTA President." James McNew's solo project Dump has done amazing work for years: try *I Can Hear Music, A Plea for Tenderness,* his album of Prince covers titled *That Skinny Motherfucker with the High Voice* (nice "Pop Life"), or his head-spinning 1995 *International Airport.* —R.S.

Dwight Yoakam

★★★	Guitars, Cadillacs, Etc., Etc. (Warner Bros., 1986)
★★★	Hillbilly Deluxe (Warner Bros., 1987)
★★★★	Buenas Noches From a Lonely Room (Warner Bros., 1988)
★★★½	Just Lookin' for a Hit (Warner Bros., 1989)
★★★½	If There Was a Way (Warner Bros., 1990)
★★★½	This Time (WB, 1993)
★★★	Gone (WB, 1995)
★★★	Dwight Live (WB, 1995)
★★★	Under the Covers (WB, 1997)
★★★½	Long Way Home (WB, 1998)
★★★★	Last Chance for a Thousand Years: Greatest Hits from the '90's (WB, 1999)
★★★★	dwightyoakamacoustic.net (WB, 2000)
★★★	Tomorrow's Sounds Today (WB, 2000)
★★★½	South of Heaven, West of Hell (WB, 2001)
★★★★	Reprise Please Baby: The Warner Bros. Years (WB, 2002)
★★★½	Population: Me (Audium, 2003)
★★★½	In Other Words (Reprise, 2003)

Coming out of Los Angeles by way of Pikeville, KY, Dwight Yoakam made a statement when he kicked off his first major-label release with a cover version of Johnny Horton's "Honky Tonk Man." (Yoakam had cut an EP in 1984 for the Oak label that features songs rerecorded for his Reprise debut.) Everything he's done in the intervening years has been a testament to his diligent pursuit of a roots sound and unsentimental point of view. Nominally a country artist, Yoakam has no truck with Nashville, nor it with him. Yoakam and his producer and guitarist, Pete Anderson, keep things lean and mean with a basic band supplemented by fiddles, mandolins, steel guitars, and dobros, with little regard for mainstream country niceties. Yoakam is pretty much an outcast as a country artist, never honored by the Country Music Association, and hardly a staple on country radio; even his videos are seldom seen on TNN or CMT.

Ultimately the path leads to California, where Yoakam resides, and specifically to Bakersfield, where in the '60s Buck Owens and Merle Haggard came on with a searing blast of rock- and blues-informed country that wilted the sanitized, string-laden efforts being packaged as the Nashville Sound. It was Yoakam, in fact, who lured Owens out of retirement and back into the recording studio for a rocking remake of Owens' paranoiac classic, "Streets of Bakersfield." Yoakam writes often of family, dislocation (both spiritual and physical), and love wars. *Guitars, Cadillacs* and *Hillbilly Deluxe* deal most directly with reminiscences of his early life ("South of Cincinnati," "Readin', Rightin', Rt. 23," "Johnson's Love") and his family ("Miner's Prayer"), but the overriding theme of his music is the difficulty of finding true love. This all comes to a head on *Buenas Noches From a Lonely Room,* which sounds torn from the deepest part of a man who's utterly bereft of friends and lovers. In the title song he tells of a woman who bore him a child, then ran off with the baby, and of how he hunted her down and blew out her brains. Even the cover choices are telling: "Streets of Bakersfield," Johnny Cash's "Home of the Blues," and Hank Locklin's "Send Me the Pillow."

After a respite for the best-of collection, *Just Lookin' for a Hit,* Yoakam returned with another first-rate effort, *If There Was a Way.* Less tortured than *Buenas Noches, If There Was a Way* is nonetheless almost totally about loss and self-recrimination. Yet there's tenderness in "If There Was a Way" and in "Send a Message to My Heart." Ending with a cover of Wilbert Harrison's "Let's Work Together" bespeaks an optimism foreign to Yoakam's bleak sensibility, but he makes it work. For good measure, throw in a touch of Duane Eddy twang at the end of "The Distance Between You and Me" and quotes from Link Wray's "Rumble" in "If There Was a Way," and you get a sense that this album represents a summing up of the past and present that finds light, albeit faint, illuminating a path once enveloped in darkness and pain.

It would be almost three years before Yoakam returned with *This Time,* and the wait was worthwhile, even if the hard edges seemed to have become harder—in his on-record persona, that is. "Pocket of a Clown" finds him bemoaning being made a fool of again by a woman, and the final song, "Lonesome Road," finds him alone again, naturally. But in between are some of the finest recordings of his career: the sizzling "Thousand Miles From Nowhere," the brutal "Ain't That Lonely Yet," the spiteful, hard-rocking "Fast As You," and a heart-tugging missive, "Try Not to Look So Pretty." Anderson became bolder in his arrangements, incorporating pop influences as well as subtle nods to the Nashville mainstream of the '50s and '60s. By comparison, *Gone* and *Long Way Home,* despite amazing moments such as "Sorry You Asked?" (on *Gone*) and a tough-minded bit of country philosphizing in "Things Change" (on *Long Way Home*), are the least accessible of Yoakam's studio efforts. That sense of a holding pattern being in effect continued through *Dwight Live* and an album of interesting cover choices, *Under the Covers;* however, a solo acoustic set aired on Internet radio and released as *dwightyoakam acoustic.net* was a powerful statement by an artist at the peak of his powers. Produced by Anderson again, but featuring him on guitar only on "Little Sister," this one belongs solely to Yoakam, whose voice is in full, unadorned splendor and who reveals himself to be one heck of a guitar picker along the way.

The solo acoustic album set the stage for an artistic resurgence, starting with 2000's *Tomorrow's Sounds Today.* The approach here is at once familiar and fresh, as Yoakam weds his hard, Bakersfield-style country to rockabilly rhythms, rock & roll production touches, and honky-tonk heartache in sculpting captivating mise-en-scènes for his lurid tales of love gone frightfully wrong.

A year later came *South of Heaven, West of Hell,* the companion soundtrack to a movie cowritten and directed by Yoakam. Minus the nine snippets of film dialogue interspersed throughout, it ranks as one of the artist's deepest, most stirring albums. This being a Western movie, Yoakam's hard-country approach undergoes little in the way of alteration. But when Yoakam and Anderson push the envelope a bit, the results are uniformly compelling. The dense atmosphere, twangy guitar, ominous kettledrums, and soaring, Billy Rose–style strings of "Somewhere" come out of Bakersfield by way of Phil Spector—an instant Yoakam classic.

For those who want the Yoakam story in succinct form, the four-CD box set, *Reprise Please Baby: The Warner Bros. Years,* is the place to go. All of the essential studio recordings are here, including the above-mentioned demos cut before Pete Anderson's arrival on the scene, which comprise part of disc four's

21 previously unissued recordings. That disc's early take on "You're the One," done as a slow, tearjerking lament, stands in stark contrast to the ferocious, Anderson-assisted version (heard on disc one) that scalded both the country and pop charts a decade later. In addition, there are enough new recordings (three) and previously unissued live and studio tracks (including two stunning duets with Kelly Willis, on the George Jones–Tammy Wynette classic "Golden Ring" and on Jones' "Take Me") to compose an entire new Dwight Yoakam album in the midst of this breathtaking retrospective. Most recently Yoakam departed the Warner Bros. fold to start his own label venture. —D.M.

Neil Young

★★★	Neil Young (Reprise, 1969)
★★★★★	Everybody Knows This Is Nowhere (Reprise, 1969)
★★★★★	After the Gold Rush (Reprise, 1970)
★★	Journey Through the Past (Reprise, 1972)
★★★★	Harvest (Reprise, 1972)
★★	Time Fades Away (Reprise, 1973)
★★★★	On the Beach (Reprise, 1974)
★★★★★	Tonight's the Night (Reprise, 1975)
★★★★½	Zuma (Reprise, 1975)
★★★	American Stars 'n' Bars (Reprise, 1977)
★★★★½	Decade (Reprise, 1978)
★★★★★	Comes a Time (Reprise, 1978)
★★★★★	Rust Never Sleeps (Reprise, 1979)
★★★★½	Live Rust (Reprise, 1979)
★★★½	Hawks and Doves (Reprise, 1980)
★★★½	Re-Ac-Tor (Reprise, 1981)
★★	Trans (Geffen, 1982)
★	Everybody's Rockin' (Geffen, 1983)
★	Old Ways (Geffen, 1985)
★	Landing on Water (Geffen, 1986)
★★	Life (Geffen, 1987)
★	This Note's for You (Reprise, 1988)
★★★★	Freedom (Reprise, 1989)
★★★★★	Ragged Glory (Reprise, 1990)
★★★½	Weld (Reprise, 1991)
★★	Arc (Reprise, 1991)
★★★★	Harvest Moon (Reprise, 1992)
★★	Lucky Thirteen (Reprise, 1993)
★★★★	Unplugged (Reprise, 1993)
★★★★½	Sleeps With Angels (Reprise, 1994)
★★★½	Mirror Ball (Reprise, 1995)
★★★½	Broken Arrow (Reprise, 1996)
★★★	Year of the Horse (Reprise, 1997)
★★★	Silver and Gold (Reprise, 2000)
★★	Road Rock, Vol. 1 (Reprise, 2000)
★	Are You Passionate? (Reprise, 2002)
★★★	Greendale (Reprise, 2003)

After all these years, Neil Young still plays rock & roll as if the offbeat were just a nasty rumor. His voice still creaks like the back-porch stair you try not to step on when you're sneaking in after three, and his guitar still shatters windows across the street. The most durable and independent of rock's elder visionaries, he's taken unpredictable twists and turns all through his career while gaining a certain eccentric wisdom along the way. But his music has always divided neatly into soft, pretty folk ballads and loud, pretty rock ballads, with the stomp-on-the-floor folkie pulse amplified into the dinosaur rumble that Young has kept reverberating from "Cinnamon Girl" in 1969 to "I'm the Ocean" in 1995. His favorite backing band is the crude, tough Crazy Horse, who embody his commitment to outlaw hippie swagger the way Crosby, Stills, Nash & Young embody his commitment to simple-minded hippie good times, and in both groups he's there to be one of the boys. But no matter who he plays with, he forces them to wing it, which gives even his most serious songs a throwaway feel. For Neil Young, throwaways are a Zen spiritual exercise, a way of keeping his aging hippie bones loose and limber.

He began with Buffalo Springfield in the late '60s, in an uneasy alliance with Stephen Stills, writing some of the band's greatest songs: "Mr. Soul," "Out of My Mind," and "Flying on the Ground Is Wrong." For his first solo move, he explored the style he'd begun toying with in Buffalo Springfield songs such as the great "Expecting to Fly" and the not-so-great "Broken Arrow," with ornate, heavily overdubbed pop productions. But he abandoned that tactic and began jamming with the L.A. garage band Crazy Horse for the sloppy guitar splendor of *Everybody Knows This Is Nowhere,* his first classic and still one of his best. Young sums up his whole musical philosophy in the brain-shredding one-note solo of "Cinnamon Girl"; "The Losing End" and "Everybody Knows This Is Nowhere" are wistful Topanga Canyon folk rock; most important, the key tracks "Down by the River" and "Cowgirl in the Sand" are long, violent guitar jams, rambling over the nine-minute mark with no trace of virtuosity at all, just staccato guitar blasts sounding as though Young is parachuting down into the middle of the Hatfield-McCoy feud.

He joined up with Crosby, Stills, and Nash for 1970's *Déjà Vu,* contributing the ballad "Helpless" and the hastily recorded Kent State protest single "Ohio." *After the Gold Rush* sweetens the raw attack of *Everybody Knows* with CSNY's mellow approach, going back to Young's folkie roots for the gorgeous melancholy of "Tell Me Why," "Till the Morning Comes," and "Only Love Can Break Your Heart." The title song is a piano ballad with a cryptic lyric about

Mother Nature on the run in the 1970s, with Young hitting eerie high notes he'd never reach again. Young took this sound to the bank with the huge country-flavored soft-rock hit *Harvest,* which had the #1 single "Heart of Gold," "Old Man," and "The Needle and the Damage Done." "Out on the Weekend" has some of his prettiest harmonica playing; "A Man Needs a Maid" has some of his most unintentionally hilarious lyrics.

If Young had stuck to the *Harvest* approach, he could have had more hits, but as he famously proclaimed, the middle of the road was a bore, so he headed for the ditch. *Journey Through the Past* was an eccentric soundtrack to Young's unreleased film debut; *Time Fades Away,* a live album of new songs recorded with a terrible backup band called the Stray Gators, has a lot of cult cachet, partly because Young refused for years to issue it on CD, but it's one of his duller albums, despite "Don't Be Denied." *On the Beach,* also disavowed by Young and unreleased on CD until 2003, is weirder but sharper, with harrowing lows and an amazing high in the off-the-cuff, apparently improvised eight-minute folk song "Ambulance Blues."

Tonight's the Night was recorded in 1973, inspired by the heroin deaths of Crazy Horse guitarist Danny Whitten and roadie Bruce Berry, but it remained in the can until 1975. It's Young's rawest, messiest album, 12 grief-stricken songs with the Crazy Horse rhythm section, guitarist/pianist Nils Lofgren, and steel guitarist Ben Keith. They all sound drunk, off-key, and ferociously emotional as they mourn the open-hearted '60s people they see burning out all around them. "Roll Another Number," "Lookout Joe," and "Speakin' Out" have terror behind their lonesome hippie smile; "Come On Baby Let's Go Downtown" is a 1970 live cut with Whitten singing about dope, right before it killed him; "Tired Eyes" is a slow-motion collapse that ranks as one of Young's most beautiful songs, high harmonies straining to the breaking point over an open grave. According to legend, Ronnie Van Zandt of Lynyrd Skynyrd was buried in his *Tonight's the Night* T-shirt.

Zuma is more cowboys-and-Indians mythos with the Horse, showcasing Young's wildest guitar since *Everybody Knows This Is Nowhere* in "Barstool Blues" and the somber "Cortez the Killer." *American Stars 'n' Bars* has the home-recording oddity "Will to Love," Young overdubbing himself while he sings about salmon swimming upstream—it's better than it sounds—while "Like a Hurricane" remains Young's most reliable live warhorse, with roaring guitar and a bittersweet tale of a mystic cowgirl who dances on the light from star to star. *Comes a Time* was an acoustic

triumph, heavy on dobro, banjo, and fiddle, with a rugged country groove and harmony vocals from Nicolette Larson. It's a clear-eyed adult version of *Harvest,* offering his truest love song, "Peace of Mind" ("She knows your weak spot/But she still gets you hot"), "Look Out for My Love," "Human Highway," and a cover of the folkie standard "Four Strong Winds." The catchiest song is also the funniest, "Field of Opportunity."

Just in time for the end of the '70s, Young brought it all back home with *Rust Never Sleeps,* one side of acoustic folk elegy and one side of unbelievably brutal Crazy Horse rampage. His greatest songs are here: "Powderfinger," an exorcism of male violence with shotgun power chords rising to the challenge of punk rock; "Pocahontas," an agonizingly lonely ballad; "Thrasher," a farewell to Crosby, Stills, and Nash; "Hey Hey, My My (Into the Black)," a feedback-heavy tribute to Elvis Presley and Johnny Rotten that lives up to the credo "It's better to burn out than to fade away." Young meditates on youth and age, home and exile, cowboys and Indians, and he's honest enough to admit he learned about Indians from watching *The Brady Bunch* (well, what other TV show had a "Grand Canyon rescue episode"?). With *Live Rust,* he picked an ideal time for a definitive summary that kicks the dump in the rump; the folkie first half is pretty good, with Neil sounding surprisingly feisty in the killer version of "Sugar Mountain," but it's the Crazy Horsed second half that you actually want to listen to, especially "Like a Hurricane."

Sometimes in a bar, you will hear someone try to defend Neil Young's '80s albums. This is technically known as a "desperate cry for help." They actually *are* as bad as they seemed at the time. He started out the decade strong with *Hawks and Doves,* a brief folk set including the scary "Captain Kennedy," and swung to the other extreme for the long, robotic guitar jams of *Re-Ac-Tor.* But he began to rust out with the campy synth-pop parody *Trans:* dismissed on its release, later burdened with retro charm, *Trans* is now his most overrated record. Young spent the next few years floundering in search of a hit, trying a new marketing hook with every album but he failed to sell out no matter how much he dumbed down. *Everybody's Rockin'* was cutesy rockabilly; *Old Ways* a more sincere and therefore more annoying country album, with guest shots from Waylon Jennings and Willie Nelson; *Landing on Water* an eager-to-please Aldo Nova imitation. The Crazy Horse reunion *Life* coincided with the CSNY reunion *American Dream,* both albums reeking of flop sweat. *This Note's for You* was a big-band parody, complete with inept horn section, apparent evidence that Neil was ready to close his tired eyes for good.

But fans started to revive hope with the import-only *El Dorado* EP, which featured Young's first real guitar playing in years, and *Freedom* offered proof with the Bush-bashing hit "Rockin' in the Free World." *Freedom* was at least one-third overproduced '80s dreck, but it was also a sign of life, combining three *El Dorado* tracks with Springsteen-style ballads ("Wrecking Ball"), spruced-up oldies ("Too Far Gone"), and the heartbreaking Linda Ronstadt duet "Hangin' on a Limb," a ballad about a man who abandons a lover because "there was something about freedom he thought he didn't know." With noise-loving Neil Young acolytes such as Sonic Youth, Nirvana, and Dinosaur Jr. on the rise, the old man completed the most well-timed comeback in rock history with *Ragged Glory,* stealing back some of his own thunder in an album of wild Crazy Horse guitar jams: "Country Home," "Fuckin' Up," and best of all, "Over and Over," a joyfully noisy celebration of the kind of long-term love that turns time into a joke.

Ragged Glory established Young as rock's elder statesman, the one '60s veteran who was both learning and teaching new tricks, sounding relaxed and affable with his hipness level at an all-time high. No rocker this old had ever been this relevant, and Young kept his creative roll going all decade long. *Harvest Moon* was his long-threatened country sequel to *Harvest,* with a title track celebrating a marriage that lasted and "From Hank to Hendrix" mourning one that didn't. *Sleeps With Angels,* partly inspired by Kurt Cobain's burnout, has beautifully elegiac rockers such as "Change Your Mind," "Trans Am," and "Piece of Crap." *Weld* was a live revamp of *Live Rust* (with many of the same songs); *Arc* was a static feedback piece a la Lou Reed's *Metal Machine Music. Unplugged* obviously doesn't push very hard, but it's surprisingly potent and listenable, ranking just behind *Comes a Time* for when you're in the mood to hear Neil get mellow. Particularly welcome is the official debut of one of his greatest ballads, the longtime bootleg fave "Stringman," which he recorded in 1974 but never got around to releasing.

Mirror Ball was a one-off collaboration with Pearl Jam, and while there's only one great song on the album, it's the best thing he's done since *Rust Never Sleeps*—"I'm the Ocean," a surging nightmare about love and death that ends with Young stranded in his Cutlass Supreme in the middle of an intersection, trying to turn against the flow, as Kurt Cobain, O. J. Simpson, Bill Clinton, and other rock stars battle it out in his soul. *Broken Arrow* had three lazy gems, "Big Time," "Slip Away," and "Scattered." *Year of the Horse* was live slop with no track listings, which made it even harder than usual to tell the jams apart. At one point, a fan yells, "They all sound the same," and Young cheerfully replies, "It's all one song!" *Road Rock* was definitely one live album too many, with an 18-minute "Cowgirl in the Sand"; the backup all-stars get pitifully lost trying to follow Young until he abandons them around the 13-minute mark to take off on two minutes of shriek guitar. The much-maligned *Silver and Gold* was very lightweight country rock, but with a few ace tunes, especially the poignant "The Great Divide," the oft-bootlegged "Razor Love," and the shameless '60s nostalgia of "Buffalo Springfield Again." He also contributed three (out of four) good songs to the universally ignored CSNY reunion *Looking Forward. Are You Passionate?* was a muddled attempt at R&B; giving this guy a subtle rhythm section is like giving a gorilla a Palm Pilot. But *Passionate* was noteworthy as the first genuinely bad album he'd made since the '80s, a conceptual achievement of sorts. *Greendale* was an improvement, an extended narrative filled with righteous political anger, but he hadn't been writing any good songs lately, and his skills were a little too soft to handle such an ambitious project.

Decade is an excellent three-vinyl-disc, 35-song retrospective that invented a whole new genre, the deluxe box set. The only problem with *Decade* is that most of its good songs are already on albums worth owning, but it still serves as a map for new fans and a sampler for nonfans. *Lucky Thirteen* attempted a one-disc salvage job on the '80s Geffen years, but there's less to the picture than meets the eye. Still in command of his crazy grin and unkempt guitar, too busy working on new music to start unloading the hoards of unreleased treasures he's left behind in the vaults, Neil Young remains the model of the rock star who gets old without turning to rust. He can't possibly keep this up more than another 20 years or so.   —R.S.

Z

Frank Zappa

★★★★ Freak Out! (1966; Video Arts, 2001)
★★★★½ Absolutely Free (1967; Video Arts, 2001)
★★★½ Lumpy Gravy (1967; Video Arts, 2001)
★★★★★ We're Only in It for the Money (1968; Video Arts, 2001)
★★★ Cruising With Ruben & the Jets (1968; Video Arts, 2001)
★★★★★ Uncle Meat (1969; Video Arts, 2001)
★★★★ Hot Rats (1969; Video Arts, 2001)
★★★★ Burnt Weeny Sandwich (1970; Video Arts, 2001)
★★★★ Weasels Ripped My Flesh (1970; Video Arts, 2001)
★★★★ Chunga's Revenge (1970; Video Arts, 2001)
★★ The Mothers: Fillmore East—June 1971 (1971; Video Arts, 2001)
★★ Just Another Band From L.A. (1972; Video Arts, 2001)
★★★★ Waka/Jawaka (1972; Video Arts, 2001)
★★★★ The Grand Wazoo (1972; Video Arts, 2001)
★★★ Over-Nite Sensation (1973; Video Arts, 2001)
★★★ Apostrophe (1974; Video Arts, 2001)
★★★ Roxy & Elsewhere (1974; Video Arts, 2001)
★★★½ One Size Fits All (1975; Video Arts, 2001)
★★★ Bongo Fury (1975; Video Arts, 2001)
★★★ Zoot Allures (1976; Video Arts, 2001)
★★★ In New York (1978; Video Arts, 2001)
★★★ Studio Tan (1978; Video Arts, 2001)
★★★ Sleep Dirt (1979; Video Arts, 2002)
★★½ Sheik Yerbouti (1979; Video Arts, 2002)
★★★ Orchestral Favorites (1979; Video Arts, 2002)
★★★ Joe's Garage: Acts I, II & III (1979; Rykodisc, 1995)
★★★★ Shut Up 'n Play Yer Guitar (1981; Video Arts, 2002)
★★★½ Tinseltown Rebellion (1981; Video Arts, 2002)
★★★½ You Are What You Is (1981; Video Arts, 2002)

★★★ Ship Arriving Too Late to Save a Drowning Witch (1982; Video Arts, 2002)
★★½ Baby Snakes (1983; Video Arts, 2002)
★★ The Man From Utopia (1983; Video Arts, 2002)
★★★ Boulez Conducts Zappa: The Perfect Stranger (1984; Rykodisc, 1995)
★★★ Them or Us (1984; Zappa Family Trust, 2002)
★★★½ Thing-Fish (1984; Vack, 2002)
★★ Francesco Zappa (1984; Vack, 2002)
★★★½ Meets the Mothers of Prevention (1985; Rykodisc, 1995)
★★★★ Jazz From Hell (Barking Pumpkin/Rykodisc, 1986)
★★★ Does Humor Belong in Music? (1986; Rykodisc, 1995)
★★★★ Guitar (Barking Pumpkin/Rykodisc, 1988)
★★★★½ You Can't Do That on Stage Anymore, Vol. 1 (Barking Pumpkin/Rykodisc, 1988)
★★★★½ You Can't Do That on Stage Anymore, Vol. 2 (Barking Pumpkin/Rykodisc, 1988)
★★★ Broadway the Hard Way (Barking Pumpkin/Rykodisc, 1988)
★★★★½ You Can't Do That on Stage Anymore, Vol. 3 (Barking Pumpkin/Rykodisc, 1989)
★★★★½ You Can't Do That on Stage Anymore, Vol. 4 (Barking Pumpkin/Rykodisc, 1991)
★★★½ The Best Band You Never Heard in Your Life (1991; Rykodisc, 1995)
★★★ Make a Jazz Noise Here (1991; Rykodisc, 1995)
★★★★ You Can't Do That on Stage Anymore, Vol. 5 (Rykodisc, 1992)
★★★★ You Can't Do That on Stage Anymore, Vol. 6 (Rykodisc, 1992)
★★ Playground Psychotics (1992; Rykodisc, 1995)
★★★½ Ahead of Their Time (1993; Rykodisc, 1995)
★★★★ The Yellow Shark (1993; Rykodisc, 1995)

Frank Zappa dabbled in virtually all kinds of music—and, whether guised as a satirical rocker, jazz-rock fusionist, guitar virtuoso, electronics wizard, or orchestral innovator, his eccentric genius was undeniable. Cross Dion and the Belmonts with Harry Partch, and you get some idea of Zappa's musical sensibility; as a humorist—and humor is crucial to Zappa—he comes on like a hybrid of Lenny Bruce and the Three Stooges. Elusive, indulgent, at times inscrutable, Zappa's tone and intention are often hard to determine; they seem calculated to provoke equal measures of fury, awe, and giggling. An early crusader against rock censorship, he was always political, if sometimes perplexingly so, but his ultimate significance resides in his music. Brandishing as his motto a quote from French avant-garde icon Edgard Varèse, "The present-day composer refuses to die!," Zappa was indeed as much a modern classical composer as a rock legend, and his erasure of the lines between high and pop art remains one of the most emancipatory gestures of the '60s.

With a riff aping the Stones' "Satisfaction," "Hungry Freaks, Daddy" provided the anthemic intro to Freak Out! Lyrically, the record's antilove songs and daft non sequiturs raised the rebel flag for the misfit clowns and underdogs Zappa and his first band, the Mothers of Invention, would henceforth champion; the music was both a triumph and mockery of psychedelia, folk rock, blooze, and doo-wop. Considerably more demanding, Absolutely Free pushed the envelope even further—comprising fragmentary jazz allusions, vibraphone noodlings, chanting, and operatic vocals, its determined messiness seemed totally mad. On "Plastic People," a "Louie, Louie" guitar motif disintegrates into freeform swinging, all in service of a poke at LBJ and American suburbia. By 1968 and We're Only in It for the Money, with its mock–Sgt. Pepper's cover art, orchestral segments, and general ferocity, the Mothers had already achieved their masterpiece.

The prototype of the technically brilliant aggregations upon which Zappa would come to insist, the late-'60s Mothers were basically a crack rock outfit with woodwind capability. Money was, of course, in large part the musicians' work, but the vision was assuredly Zappa's. "Who Needs the Peace Corps?," "Flower Punk," and "Harry, You're a Beast" were early explorations of his trademark themes: paranoia, political and sexual; hatred for the bourgeoisie; and a utopian insistence on completely free expression. In search of that goal, Zappa detoured from the Mothers in 1967 by putting out Lumpy Gravy, his first solo work. Recorded with a 50-piece orchestra, this difficult but often lovely record of John Cage–ish modern music paved the way for the Mothers' second major set, Uncle Meat. A collage of 31 sound bites—tape edits, nonsense phone conversations, "songs," mind-boggling instrumental passages—Meat was an inspired monstrosity, a kind of musical version of William Burroughs' "cut-up" method of literary construction (the insertion of random passages within an otherwise linear text). This album reinvented pop music; the only problem was that its zonked brilliance could never be "popular," so Meat also marked the coalescence of one of Zappa's characteristic stances: the cryptic prophet howling in the wilderness.

On Hot Rats, Burnt Weeny Sandwich, Weasels Ripped My Flesh, and Chunga's Revenge—all four released within a single 12-month period—Zappa's creative juices flowed with a consistent quality that he never again achieved. While members of the Mothers would resurface throughout his career, the band as such was kaput, and Zappa began working with a bewildering array of talents (Little Feat's Lowell George, violinist Don "Sugarcane" Harris, drummer Aynsley Dunbar, keyboardist George Duke). There were vocals on all these albums, but it was the music that mattered. Propulsive neojazz alternated with gorgeous classically derived pieces evoking phantasmagorical dreams. A collaboration with childhood friend Captain Beefheart resulted in Hot Rats' gritty standout "Willie the Pimp," and on the same album's "Peaches en Regalia," Zappa the composer reached a majestic peak.

In comparison, the next Mothers records, Fillmore East and Just Another Band, sounded either lame or silly. Adding ex-Turtles singers Howard Kaylan and Mark Volman, a.k.a. Flo and Eddie, only increased the yu(c)ks factor. The Miles/Mahavishnu-style fusion of Grand Wazoo, Waka/Jawaka, and One Size Fits All made for an impressive clutch of Mothers-less outings; Over-Nite Sensation and Apostrophe, however, were squawking, predictable, and only desperately "hilarious" (despite good work by ex-Cream bassist Jack Bruce).

Although Zappa's approach resists generalization, it became apparent by the mid-'70s that the albums concentrating on humor would be the least satisfying; the musical experiments would be the ones to watch out for. The records that balanced both approaches varied—*Bongo Fury* was a stronger Beefheart performance than a Zappa one; *Zoot Allures* was comparatively bland—but the "funny" *Sheik Yerbouti,* with its disco parodies and churlishness ("Broken Hearts Are for Assholes"), was much less engaging than *Shut Up,* a three-disc set wherein Zappa simply turned loose his astonishing guitar playing. By the time of *Joe's Garage* and such fare as "Why Does It Hurt When I Pee?," the sophomoric smuttiness of Zappa's humor had gotten very old (sexism remained this freethinker's egregious blind spot), and his turn toward strictly instrumental music was welcome. *You Are What You Is* found the naughty lad reclaiming the stand-up stage, but this time, the musical parodies were varied enough to carry the day. Mock versions of reggae, ska, Journey-style power ballads, and country music, plus a hilarious Doors takeoff, produced the most inventive comedy he'd attempted in years.

Later joke-predominant albums *(Tinseltown, Broadway)* were fairly tasty, especially the rock send-up *Them or Us,* but the real excitement was elsewhere. *London Symphony Orchestra,* originally released as two separate discs in the '80s, finally found Frank in an all-orchestral setting, with impressive results; *Jazz From Hell,* executed mostly solo by Zappa on Synclavier, displayed his longtime mastery of music tech. His most ambitious releases, however, were retrospectives: *Guitar,* a sequel to the *Shut Up* series that featured 32 live solos recorded between 1979 and 1984; and the staggering 12-CD *You Can't Do That* package. Twenty years in the making, the set presents previously unreleased live work from 1968 to 1988. Obviously intended for Zappaddicts, it's hardly the best place for a neophyte to start, but its monumentality is unquestionable.

A far more modest project, *The Yellow Shark,* features the Ensemble Modern's wonderfully simpatico readings of some of Zappa's thornier compositions. His finest "classical" venture, it was also the last album he saw completed before his untimely death in December 1993. The absence of any new Zappa music in the past decade hasn't stemmed the tide of new releases one bit. Most are mixed bags, although *Ahead of Their Time, The Lost Episodes,* and *Mystery Disc* are all noteworthy for presenting rare or never-heard selections from the Mothers' late-'60s/early-

'70s golden era. *Cucamonga,* a collection of Zappa's pre-Mothers (mainly doo-wop) recordings, is intriguing, but only for established fans. Compiling the best of Zappa on a single disc is an impossible task; considering that, *Strictly Commercial* and *Strictly Genteel* are surprisingly effective. But the real prize is Ryko's first *Threesome,* which brings the first three Mothers albums together in a single box. If you're looking for a perfect Zappa entry point, your search is over. —P.E./M.R.

Tom Zé

★★★★★ The Best of Tom Zé—Massive Hits (Luaka Bop, 1990)
★★★★ The Hips of Tradition (Luaka Bop, 1992)
★★★★ Com Defeito de Fabricacao (Fabrication Defect) (Luaka Bop, 1998)

Tom Zé was a legend in Brazil years before he was introduced to North American audiences on David Byrne's eclectic world-music label Luaka Bop. Born Antônio José Santana Martins, Zé was a pioneer of the late-'60s tropicália movement, which blended Brazilian folk and dance traditions including bossa nova and samba with the metaphorical politics of a Bob Dylan or George Clinton, and the experimentation of psychedelic rock, jazz, and funk. Zé's Brazilian contemporaries include the great Caetano Veloso, Gilberto Gil, and Gal Costa.

After nearly two decades away from the music business (the singer was working in a gas station when Byrne caught up with him), Zé came back into the public eye with *Massive Hits,* a collection of his songs from the 1970s. The album is a feast of jarring guitar hooks and gorgeous melodies, all mixed with layered, rhythmic percussion, horns, and experimental found instruments. This music had a notable influence on budding American and European avant-pop acts of the early '90s such as Beck, Stereolab, the High Llamas, Tortoise, and various electronics artists. With Byrne at the production helm, *The Hips of Tradition* finds Zé working alongside a group of New York experimental musicians including the Brazilian-born guitarist Arto Lindsay, formerly of the downtown avant-punk band DNA; Lindsay by then had begun mixing his dissonant guitar textures with jazz, rock, funk, and Latin rhythms, and sweet Brazilian melodies. On *Hips,* Lindsay, Byrne, and the other musicians never overwhelm Zé's vision; the album simply adds updated tape loops and grooves to the bedrock quirkiness of his earlier music.

Following another, shorter hiatus, Zé came back with an ambitious concept album, *Com Defeito de Fabricacao,* wherein his dark emotional-political narrative of an overpopulated Brazil takes a front seat to the music. The odd rhythms and melodies are still very present, but Zé puts a series of powerful stories to the music: Tales of a poverty-stricken third world in which first-world capitalism has forced the poor to become mindlessly toiling androids with "defects"—the abilities to think, create, dream, and dance. People not unlike Zé himself.   —M.K.

Zero 7

★★½   Simple Things (Palm Pictures, 2001)
★★½   When It Falls (Palm Pictures, 2004)

Henry Binns and Sam Hardaker, the two British producers behind this ultrasuave studio project, have the same reverence for jazzy, spacey retro sounds as Air, but seem to share none of that pioneering group's imagination or ambition. *Simple Things* is a strictly-by-the-book tour through a post-trip-hop, post-acid-jazz soundscape of groovy bass lines, analogue synthesizers, and languid, impersonal vocals. The blend is seamless, making it perfect as background chill-out music or wallpaper in an expensive bar, but it's pretty tedious otherwise. *When It Falls* is even a bit more chilled, its pulse rarely raising above a semicomatose level.   —B.S.

Warren Zevon

★★½   Wanted Dead or Alive (1969; Virgin, 2003)
★★★★★   Warren Zevon (Asylum, 1976)
★★★★★   Excitable Boy (Asylum, 1978)
★★★   Bad Luck Streak in Dancing School (Asylum, 1980)
★★★★   Stand in the Fire (Asylum, 1980)
★★★½   The Envoy (Asylum, 1982)
★★★★½   A Quiet Normal Life: The Best of Warren Zevon (Asylum, 1986)
★★★★   Sentimental Hygiene (1987; Virgin, 2003)
★★★★   Transverse City (1989; Virgin, 2003)
★★★   Mr. Bad Example (Giant, 1991)
★★½   Learning to Flinch (Giant, 1993)
★★   Mutineer (Giant, 1995)
★★★★½   I'll Sleep When I'm Dead (Rhino, 1996)
★★★★½   Life'll Kill Ya (Artemis, 2000)
★★★½   My Ride's Here (Artemis, 2002)
★★★★   Genius: The Best of Warren Zevon (Rhino, 2002)
★★★★½   The Wind (Artemis, 2003)

Warren Zevon openly defied the "*muy* sensitive" stereotype of the L.A. singer/songwriter. Literate, satiric, violence-obsessed, funny as hell, piano-pounding, equally capable of deranged rock-outs and beautifully sustained melodies: You'd never guess that

Warren Zevon, his first Asylum album (his true debut was the enjoyable apprentice work *Wanted Dead or Alive*, released six years earlier), was produced by Jackson Browne! "Desperadoes Under the Eaves" brilliantly skewers the self-deluded "Life in the Fast Lane" pose. "Today I'm angry at the sun," sneered Zevon's protagonist—before a fully orchestrated, Randy Newman–esque finale cleared the air. Zevon's terse, dynamic readings of "Carmelita," "Poor Poor Pitiful Me," and "Mohammed's Radio" put Linda Ronstadt's cover versions in their proper perspective.

Excitable Boy established Zevon as a commercial comer; his deadpan, finger-on-the-trigger delivery drove home the sardonic hooks on "Werewolves of London" and the title track. "Roland the Headless Thompson Gunner" and "Lawyers, Guns, and Money" defined his probing geopolitical mode. Although *Excitable Boy* remains Zevon's biggest chart success and best-known work, its middling second half renders *Warren Zevon* his overall best.

Bad Luck Streak in Dancing School landed a flat followup blow, especially after such a stunning one-two punch. The ever-mercurial Zevon sounded overextended. No rest, however: *Stand in the Fire* is a galvanizing live album. Rather than appear with the expected slew of studio pros, Zevon led a band of nobodies through a riveting set of fiery uptempo material that lost none of the original nuance. *The Envoy* is where he stepped back from the edge. At first, the move feels tentative, but the loved-and-learned message of "Looking for the Next Best Thing"—and its melody—really sink in over time. Reassuringly, the title track asserts Zevon's (over)active imagination, while "Ain't That Pretty at All" flaunts his remaining wild hair.

After a quiet spell, Zevon came out sober and swinging on *Sentimental Hygiene*. "Detox Mansion" and "Trouble Waiting to Happen" look at both sides of the rehab process with a pitiless, unsentimental eye. Musically supported by three quarters of R.E.M., Zevon turned his perceptive gaze to the boxing ring ("Boom Boom Mancini") and Springsteen-Mellencamp territory ("The Factory") with tuneful results. Even the most loyal Zevon followers got thrown for a loop by *Transverse City*. It's a sci-fi concept album, of all things. With a head filled with ideas lifted from "cyber-punk" paperbacks and an imposing synthesizer arsenal, Zevon set out to do for art rock what he had done for the singer/songwriter movement—kick it in the ass. By and large, he succeeded by matching his new complex, multilayered sound with observant lyrics that considered the "Turbulence" in Russia as well as the local action ("Down in the Mall"). Overall, *Transverse City* is an unmitigated downer—its mood is summed up by a heart-opening closer called "Nobody's in Love This Year." But given some time, Zevon's bleak projection of the future will definitely grow on you. *Mr. Bad Example* took a giant leap backward. Vitriolic spurts such as "Finishing Touches" sound like answers to a long-unanswered, nagging question: "Hey, Warren, couldn't you do another one like that excitable werewolves number, you know, the one that goes woo-woo-woo, like that?" For the first time, Zevon came across as cynical and nasty; the note of hope lurking behind those cathartic rants of old was now long gone. Only the country-tinged "Heartache Spoken Here" hints at the emotional depth that was once Zevon's signature as a singer and songwriter.

Seemingly short on inspiration, Zevon released the live *Learning to Flinch,* featuring lethargic acoustic performances. Despite the beautiful title track, *Mutineer* is the most forgettable album of Zevon's career. Tracks such as "Seminole Bingo" and "Piano Fighter" are inferior takes on familiar territory for Zevon.

It would be five years and a new century before Zevon returned, but *Life'll Kill Ya* is perhaps his best album since the '70s. Lost causes, despair, and the macabre had always inspired Zevon, and here he'd found the perfect subject: the intractability of mortality. On the title track, "My Shit's Fucked Up," "Fistful of Rain," and "Don't Let Us Get Sick," Zevon gave death a come-hither look with brutal black humor. Dying relationships are also aplenty here; "For My Next Trick I Need a Volunteer" and "I'll Slow You Down" are two of Zevon's strongest weepers. The show stealer, though, is a heartrending cover of Steve Winwood's "Back in the High Life," which offers the song's optimistic lyric of restoration with the desperation and hopelessness of a deathbed fantasy. There is a sophistication in the design of *Life'll Kill Ya,* pulling it all together with almost literary construction.

For *My Ride's Here,* Zevon actually collaborated on songs with a bunch of literary writers such as gonzo journalist Hunter Thompson and poet Paul Muldoon. Maybe that is why, though it is as death-haunted as its predecessor, *My Ride's Here* lacks the relentless focus of *Life'll Kill Ya.*

In 2002, it was announced that Zevon had been diagnosed with terminal lung cancer. After the diagnosis, Zevon went to work on finishing a final studio album. Although the Grammy arrived posthumously, Zevon lived just long enough to appreciate the irony that *The Wind* got more attention (including a documentary of its creation) than perhaps any other disc in his career because of the news of his imminent death. Clearly ailing, Zevon is helped on *The Wind* by numerous cameos from celebrity friends such as Bruce Springsteen, Jackson Browne, Dwight Yoakam,

and Tom Petty. Obvious references to his illness include the cover of "Knockin' on Heaven's Door" and the tear-inducing goodbye prayer "Keep Me in Your Heart." Other tracks focus on familiar Zevon themes like fading outlaws ("Dirty Life and Times") and sabotaged romance ("She's Too Good for Me"). In all, *The Wind* contains typical Zevon songs from a singer who for decades wrote—with a wink—about a world where things were bad and the worst was just about to happen, and so he was ready to face facts when it did. *The Wind* is a fitting coda to a remarkable legacy.

Of the greatest-hits sets available, the two-disc *I'll Sleep When I'm Dead* is the preferable choice. Focusing too much on novelty numbers at the expense of essentials such as "Mohammed's Radio" and "Accidentally Like a Martyr," *Genius: The Best of Warren Zevon* is a—just—adequate single-disc introduction to the many facets of this brilliant, twisted, and moving artist. —R.A.

Rob Zombie

★★★½ Hellbilly Deluxe (Geffen, 1998)
★★ American Made Music to Strip By (Interscope, 1999)
★★★ The Sinister Urge (Universal, 2001)
★★★★ Past, Present & Future (Geffen, 2003)

As industrial music merged with metal and dance in the late '80s and early '90s, two problems kept it from mass popularity: It took itself far too seriously, and it lacked a front man, a figure with the charisma and vision to serve as its scowling, tattooed public face. Enter Rob Zombie, who with his group White Zombie showed that he'd never heard a Ministry riff he couldn't make groovier, never saw a low-budget horror movie he couldn't produce a big-budget video homage to, and could never be accused of taking himself too seriously.

After finding his musical epiphany with White Zombie's "More Human Than Human," an irresistible chunk of metal-industrial bubblegum that became a huge hit in 1995, Zombie disbanded the group and went solo for *Hellbilly Deluxe.* Further developing the stylistic elements of White Zombie at their peak—thunderclap guitars, lyrics like Marvel comics strips on acid, beats that merge the terror of Ministry and KMFDM with the bouncier side of techno—he bends the music's extremes into a carnival sideshow of pure, loud pop. "Dragula" is *The Munsters* meets "Dead Man's Curve"—an ode to a monster roadster that races through every fun monster-movie cliche before pulling over for some good old-fashioned backseat sex: "Dig through the ditches/And burn through the witches/And slam in the back of my Dragula!" Not since Ozzy Osbourne and Alice Cooper had there been a metal god so lovable.

American Music is an insignificant remix disc, and *The Sinister Urge* stays the course but with fewer killers. The keeper is *Past, Present & Future*, whose 19 songs from Zombie's solo and group career prove his pop mastery. Every song is a zinger, and the bonus DVD of music videos—most directed by Zombie—puts his vision into its proper multimedia context. It's a circus, and Zombie is happy to serve as the ringmaster or—in the case of "Living Dead Girl," his lovingly thorough rock homage to the classic 1919 silent film *The Cabinet of Dr. Caligari*—the mad scientist who does it all just to see a twinkle in his audience's eyes. —B.S.

The Zombies

★★★★	Zombie Heaven (Big Beat, 1997)
★★★★	Odessey and Oracle 30th Anniversary Edition (Big Beat, 1998)
★★★	Absolutely the Best (Varèse, 1999)
★★★★	The Singles Collection: A's and B's 1964–1969 (Big Beat, 2000)
★★★	Best of the '60s (Simply the Best, 2000)

Propelled by Rod Argent's jazzy keyboards, the Zombies were the most musically intriguing of the British Invasion bands. Hauntingly catchy, "She's Not There" served as a blueprint for their sharper work—pop that wrestled the genre's limits, yet still triumphed on the radio. Colin Blunstone's sexy choirboy vocals on "Time of the Season" made the group sound like few of its peers; Blunstone insinuated rather than shouted—his elegance suiting a band that swung more than it rocked. *Odessey and Oracle* is the Zombies' best, a sort of concept album including mildly precious musings on World War I and faded love.

Very well represented by their reissues, the Zombies are particularly well served by the excellent *Zombie Heaven* box set, a massive collection that takes them commendably seriously. The Varèse CD is a good intro; *The Singles Collection* proves that Top 40 in the mid-'60s was an incredible place to be. —P.E.

Zwan

see SMASHING PUMPKINS

ZZ Top

★★	ZZ Top's First Album (1970; Warner Bros., 1979)
★★	Rio Grande Mud (1972; Warner Bros., 1979)
★★★	Tres Hombres (1973; Warner Bros., 1979)
★★½	Fandango! (1975; Warner Bros., 1979)
★★½	Tejas (1976; Warner Bros., 1979)

★★★½	The Best of ZZ Top (1977; Warner Bros., 1979)
★★★★	Deguello (Warner Bros., 1979)
★★★½	El Loco (Warner Bros., 1981)
★★★½	Eliminator (Warner Bros., 1983)
★★★	Afterburner (Warner Bros., 1985)
★★★½	Six Pack (Warner Bros., 1987)
★★★	Recycler (Warner Bros., 1990)
★★★★	Greatest Hits (Warner Bros., 1992)
★★★	Antenna (RCA, 1994)
★★★½	Rhythmeen (RCA, 1996)
★½	XXX (RCA, 1999)
★★★½	Mescalero (RCA, 2003)
★★★★	Chrome, Smoke & BBQ: The ZZ Top Box (Warner Bros., 2003)
★★★★½	Rancho Texicano: The Very Best of ZZ Top (Rhino, 2004)

This Texas trio slogged around the arena circuit for years, bashing out metalized boogie 'n' blooze that never quite survived the transition to record. Except for the apocalyptic quiver of "Jesus Just Left Chicago" (from *Tres Hombres*), the early recorded efforts of guitarist Billy Gibbons, bassist Dusty Hill, and drummer Frank Beard form a largely undifferentiated mass—a parched riverbed, if you will. By the mid-'70s, ZZ Top began to sprout a juicy hook here and there: first the incongruous lingo of "Tush" (from the half-live *Fandango!*) and then the sober slide of "Arrested for Driving While Blind" (from *Tejas*). All the roadwork paid off, both financially and artistically. *The Best of ZZ Top* dryly contradicts the band's previous cartoon status, and after a three-year layoff, *Deguello* proves these old boys really are capable of more than barbecuing a few borrowed riffs. From the steely pulse of "I'm Bad, I'm Nationwide" to the kicking version of "Dust My Broom," this is a superior white blues album—with a wickedly catchy single to boot: "Cheap Sunglasses" (propelled by a pounding riff yanked clean off of fellow Texan Edgar Winter's lumbering "Frankenstein"). *El Loco* isn't too far behind that, but ZZ Top takes another sharp left turn with *Eliminator*. Video-friendly and enhanced with digitally processed guitars and new-wave–style drum synths, the Top's retooled cartoon image takes some getting used to. The hit single "Legs" provided the opportunity; while the thematic, ah, thrust is a little primitive, the sight of these sharp-dressed, bearded gents on MTV was extremely gratifying in 1984. As was the sound of Billy Gibbons leaning—head on—into a taut, drawling solo during the Top 40 countdown. But that winning formula already starts to wear thin on *Afterburner* ("Sleeping Bag," "Velcro Fly"). *Recycler* is one of the least propitious titles in recent memory. *Greatest Hits* picks up where *The Best Of* left off, spanning all of the group's big '80s hits and adding an unessential but nifty (and appropriately trashy) ZZ-fied electro-fuzz cover of Elvis Presley's "Viva Las Vegas." The *Six Pack* box set gathers together the first five albums and *El Loco* (but no *Deguello*) onto three CDs, but purists beware: in an apparent effort to bring the old albums up to '80s speed, Beard's drums were digitally "enhanced" during the remastering—a source of considerable frustration to veteran Top fans for years. The later individual CD reissues of all six albums feature the same revisionist mix.

After *Recycler* and a move from Warners to RCA, ZZ Top made a concerted effort to reembrace their grittier, bluesier roots. *Antenna* was an appealing if somewhat tentative first step backward in the right direction; while nowhere near as down and dirty as *Tres Hombres* or even *Deguello,* songs such as "Pincush-ion" and "Fuzzbox Voodoo" found them easing away from synths without sacrificing big, meaty hooks. *Rhythmeen,* on the other hand, was a monster unleashed; while none of the songs jump out as standouts, the growling, swampy sound maintained from start to finish is wholly satisfying; it makes even the '70s albums—particularly the remastered versions—sound positively tame in comparison. The depressingly tuneless *XXX,* however, sounds like ZZ Top smothered under a fire blanket. Even the four live tunes tacked on at the end sound D.O.A. On the upside, that only helps to enhance the 90-proof kick of *Mescalero.* Armed with their catchiest songs since their MTV renaissance (and, in "Punk Ass Boyfriend," the best song title of their career), *Mescalero* is proof that these grizzled road dawgs still have legs, and know how to use them.   —M.C./R.SK.

Anthologies and Soundtracks

★★★ **24 Hour Party People Original Soundtrack** (Warner Strategic Marketing, 2002)

Bookended by portraits of Joy Division's depressive postpunk and Happy Mondays' hedonistic acid house, *24 Hour Party People* chronicled 15 years' worth of hedonism, eccentricity, and postpunk music in Manchester, using the rise and fall of Tony Wilson's Factory Records as the film's framework. Not surprisingly, 13 of the 18 tracks were cut by Mancunian acts between 1978 and 1990, and most of those—New Order's "Blue Monday," Buzzcocks' "Ever Fallen in Love," a handful of Happy Mondays and Joy Division tracks—rank as subculture classics. Even so, they don't cohere on CD like they do on the screen. The divergent styles fit Manchester's postindustrial decay like a wrecking ball, but combined out of context, they make a disjointed souvenir, which is almost exactly what Wilson says a soundtrack should be "at worst." Then again, he always aimed high.   —F.S.

★★★★ **'80s Underground Rap** (Rhino, 1998)

The title notwithstanding, not everything on this three-CD set is "underground"—De La Soul, Public Enemy, and EPMD, among others, might take umbrage at the description. But quibbles aside, this is a worthy snapshot of mostly New York hip-hop just before gangsta rap exploded on the West Coast. Early tracks from the aforementioned artists, plus Boogie Down Productions, the Jungle Brothers, and Chubb Rock, capture a time when hip-hop was happy to pat itself on the back for its verbal acuity and crisp, dynamic beats, then go out for a night of carefree dancing at the club. Even better, enshrined here are the few sharp spitters who time and fate have left behind: Masters of Ceremony (the first group of Brand Nubian's Grand Puba); unheralded rappers Three Times Dope and Super

Lover Cee & Casanova Rud; and Chill Rob G, author of "Let the Words Flow," which was the template for "The Power," a 1990 club-pop crossover smash by Snap!, much to the Chill one's chagrin.   —J.C.

★★★★ **Africa Raps** (Trikont, Germany, 2001)

Actually, that should be *West Africa Raps,* since the 16 performers showcased on this ear-opening hip-hop collection are from Mali, Senegal, and the Gambia. Although most of the beats are mixed down further than the U.S. hip-hop norm and many artists here (Gokh-Bi System and Les Escrocs) hew closer to traditional West African music than stateside rap, the producers have nevertheless learned plenty from their American idols. BMG 44's "Kam" chops up a Youssou N'Dour track a la DJ Premier letting loose on a crate of Stax, while C.B.V.'s "Art. 158" imagines Dr. Dre bumping trunks in Dakar rather than Compton (with a far rougher, choppier flow replacing g-funk's smoothness). The most exciting track is Tata Pound's "Badala," for which the only description is "Malian Dirty South": circular guitar riffs, relentless vocal trade-offs, and a quick-stepping Dirty South 808 beat.   —M.M.

The Anthology of American Folk Music

★★★★½ The Anthology of American Folk Music (1952; Revenant, 2000)
★★★★ Harry Smith's Anthology of American Folk Music, Volume Four (Revenant, 2000)

The *Anthology of American Folk Music* is associated less with the artists who appear on it than with the all-around weirdo genius who compiled it: film-maker, collector, and alchemist Harry Smith. The first three volumes, released in 1952, compile raw, eccentric, individualistic 78s made between 1927 and 1932; Smith classified them respectively as "ballads," "social music," and "songs." They include blues, gospel, American adaptations of traditional songs from the British Isles, and whatever else passed for pop in those days and tapped into something much older, sung and played by the famous (the Carter Family, Blind Lemon Jefferson) and the wildly obscure. The '50s folk scene picked up on these songs in a big way—Bob Dylan in particular has covered plenty of them. Virtually every track is remarkable in some way, but Smith's peculiar, miraculous sequencing and annotation make them work as a set. (All three double-disc volumes were reissued as a box set with extensive liner notes) in 1997.

In his original notes, Smith planned three more volumes of the *Anthology;* he went on to assemble the sequence for *Volume Four* only, which appeared in 2000, nine years after his death. The final collection doesn't have a theme and consists mostly of recordings made between 1933 and 1940 in the styles of the earlier period (no jazz, little or no electric guitar). Like the other set, it's phenomenal stuff, including stunning songs by Bukka White and Sister Clara Hudmon; but as a whole, it's more cryptic than the previous volumes.   —D.W.

★★★★★ Atlantic Rhythm & Blues
1947–1974 (Atlantic, 1991)

Besides a cavalcade of great early R&B, this collection offers nothing less than a capsule history of the evolution of modern black music styles. *Volume 1* focuses on urban blues, group harmony, and New Orleans jump blues; over the course of the succeeding volumes we hear Ray Charles evolving soul out of R&B, Chuck Willis bringing rock & roll and R&B together, Solomon Burke and Aretha Franklin bringing the church into their secular music, the rise of Southern soul in sessions cut in Memphis and Muscle Shoals with Franklin, Otis Redding, Percy Sledge, and others, early New Orleans pop in Barbara Lewis' first recordings, and, in *Volume 7,* the last gasp of traditional soul via the great Tyrone Davis and Clarence Carter and the first stirrings of the soft black pop that dominated the mainstream in the early '70s and led directly to modern-day Love Men such as Luther Vandross and Freddie Jackson. In addition to the obvious hits and classic tracks contained in this set, the first three volumes in particular include songs by some artists who may not be in the pantheon but whose contributions were important: The Cardinals' "Wheel of Fortune," Harry Van Walls' "Tee-Nah-Nah," Joe Morris' "Applejack," the two Ivory Joe Hunter tracks on *Volume 3,* and the Cookies, as well. All in all, an extraordinary history of a once-great label whose artists, even the

minor ones, had a spirit and style that remains invigorating and instructive to this day.   —D.M.

Beats and Rhymes: Hip-Hop of the '90s
　　★★★　Beats & Rhymes: Hip-hop of the '90s, Part 1 (Rhino, 1997)
　　★★★★　Beats & Rhymes: Hip-hop of the '90s, Part 2 (Rhino, 1997)
　　★★★½　Beats & Rhymes: Hip-hop of the '90s, Part 3 (Rhino, 1997)

These three CDs don't try to document the entire decade in which hip-hop took over the world; instead, they chronicle just one strand of the decade's first three years. But not only does the narrow focus cohere better than a broad overview might, it's also more illuminating. As the liner notes point out, between Public Enemy's radical *Fear of a Black Planet* in 1990 and Dr. Dre's ghettocentric *The Chronic* in '92, a quick, trippy style developed that blended militant politics, bohemian attitude, and street grooves, which became the direct antecedent of today's underground hip-hop.

All three discs hone to the center of that post–Daisy Age style, mostly ignoring the era's boldest experiments and biggest party hits for tracks that—as Daisy Age inventors De La Soul once boasted—might blow up but would never go pop. *Part 1* has plenty of undeniable cuts, but it's also the most uneven set, as masters like A Tribe Called Quest, the Jungle Brothers, and Boogie Down Productions show up minor artists like Lord Finesse and Special Ed. *Part 2* kicks off with Leaders of the New School rapping fast and joyous on "Case of the P.T.A.," and most of the acts who follow the Leaders are in top form, from young talents Brand Nubian to Xtra Large journeyman Chubb Rock, who, for some reason, gets three selections. And veterans Run-D.M.C., Eric R. & Rakim, and DJ Jazzy Jeff and the Fresh Prince transcend "school" altogether. *Part 3* grinds away through earthy pleasures like "Hot Sex" (A Tribe Called Quest) before hitting a rarefied zone with the surreal classics "Mistadobalina" (Del tha Funky Homosapien), "Ya Mama" (the Pharcyde), and "La Shmoove" (Fu-Schnickens). On "Paugh-Paugh," Romy-Dee takes the style to Jamaica and out.   —F.S.

Bombay the Hard Way
　　★★★★　Bombay the Hard Way: Guns, Cars & Sitars (Motel, 1999)
　　★★★★　Bombay 2: Electric Vindaloo (Motel, 2001)

Bollywood, India's proudly idiosyncratic film industry, is a strange and wonderful marriage of Western pop styles and Eastern traditions. *Bombay the Hard Way* is a collection of remixed soundtracks from '70s spy flicks and bad-guy action adventures—a B-list genre known as *masala* ("mixed spice"). Using raw material from actual masala films (all composed by brothers Kalyanji and Anandji Shah), underground producer supreme Dan the Automator takes the *Shaft*-like bass grooves, noodling sitars, and corny Moogs and sweetens them all in his '90s hip-hop kitchen. Thus, "Professor Pyarela" gets an asymmetric, upbeat groove and a sinister haze of psychedelia in the flutes and keyboards, and the grandiose strings of "Satchidanandra" meet a stark break beat seemingly straight out of the Ultramagnetic MCs. If this isn't true globalism, then what is?

The second volume passes all sequel tests by focusing on the *Miami Vice*–like films of the '80s, with shadowy drug dealers and high-flying cops replacing the cynical private eyes and casino-lounge girls of the previous decade. This time, a top-notch roster of DJs and producers have worked on the tracks, including Mix Master Mike, Kid Koala, Dynamite D, and Ursula 1000. The results are just as fun and culturally multiplicitous, and the scratch-happy fingers of so many DJs pushes the limits of the music even further. —B.S.

★★★★★ Can You Dig It? The '70s Soul Experience (Rhino, 2002)

Few '70s soul LPs were solid; more often than not, one or two hits would be packaged with a bunch of filler. Because the genre was singles-driven, Rhino's six-CD set *Can You Dig It?* is the ideal way to listen to this essential period of American groove. The set contains 136 songs, and remarkably, almost half were #1 pop or R&B chart hits, including such blockbusters as "I'll Be Around" by the Spinners, "Love Train" by the O'Jays, and the Temptations' "Papa Was a Rollin' Stone." Maybe more significant, though, is the inclusion of minor classics that didn't top the charts but deserved archiving. Songs like Johnny Taylor's "Cheaper to Keep Her" and King Floyd's "Groove Me" prove that soul—perhaps the most American of all music genres—continued to evolve outside the mainstream.

Rhino's earlier collection of '60s soul *(Beg, Scream & Shout!)* is also highly recommended, though it's now out of print. Yet the '70s box may be the more important anthology, if only because it illustrates that in a decade usually remembered for disco and British punk, soul became mainstream pop with the success of Sly Stone, Al Green, and Marvin Gaye. This is a lovingly crafted collection, with excellent liner notes,

exceptional sound, and even a bit of exuberance in the packaging, which resembles an 8-track carrying case. If you're old enough to remember what an 8-track even looks like, this set just might be the soundtrack to your youth. —C.R.C.

★★★★★ Chess Blues (MCA, 1992)

During the post–World War II era, as the blues moved from the Mississippi Delta to the northern industrial cities, the musical genre's gradual development into an urban pop form was most vividly documented by, of all people, a pair of Polish-born nightclub owners in Chicago named Leonard and Phil Chess. Through a combination of luck and old-fashioned hustling, they built the Chess label into the nation's strongest and most recognizable depository of the blues and what is now known as R&B: two rough, small, insular styles that, with a dash of country, spawned rock & roll.

This four-disc compilation, one of many issued by MCA in the years after it acquired the Chess catalogue, is a brisk chronological tour through the Chess story, from its beginnings in 1947 to its last significant singles in 1967. It starts incongruously, with the hokey jump blues then in vogue, but before long, a proper starting-off point presents itself in a raw, desperate moan: Muddy Waters' "I Can't Be Satisfied" and "Feel Like Going Home," released as two sides of a 1948 single. Finger-snapping rhythms keep the songs deceptively in the pop realm, while Waters' slurring come-ons and slithery slide guitar are irresistibly, shamelessly sexual. More than any music that came before it, the blues was capable of expressing erotic pains, viscerally and simply, and Chess caught a generation's greatest moans: Besides Waters, this 101-song set features key tracks by Howlin' Wolf, John Lee Hooker, Robert Nighthawk, Little Walter, Lowell Fulson, Jimmy Witherspoon, Sonny Boy Williamson, Etta James, Albert King, Buddy Guy, Elmore James, and Hound Dog Taylor, to name just a dozen.

Things take a big step toward pop with the arrival of Willie Dixon in 1954. He wrote a good deal of the label's subsequent hits, including Howlin' Wolf's "Evil," Little Walter's "My Babe," and Waters' "Hoochie Coochie Man," bringing a level of showbiz finesse to what was then still largely seen as a peculiar folk style popular among homesick Southern blacks. Dixon's genius was in marrying the lawless urges of the blues to pop's catchy formulas, maintaining and even increasing the erotic tension through slick hooks and a driving backbeat. (Chuck Berry and Bo Diddley, two Chess stars essential to the blues' transition to rock, are excluded, but they have great boxes of their own.) Others made timeless contributions as well:

Howlin' Wolf's gruff and unflinching vocal stare-downs are still chilling; John Lee Hooker's back-porch mutterings are an undiluted voice of blues purity; Little Walter and Sonny Boy Williamson reinvented the harmonica for the age of urban, electric blues. In later years, as the blues spread around the world—a 1962 deal with two British labels brought Chess singles into the stores and ears of a hungry new generation—Buddy Guy, Otis Rush, and Albert King gave the music a new muscularity and focus; their rock-based sound jives with Jimi Hendrix, Eric Clapton, and Keith Richards, and remains dominant in contemporary blues. —B.S.

Didn't It Blow Your Mind!: Soul Hits of the '70s (Rhino, 1991)

★★★½	Volume 1
★★★½	Volume 2
★★★★	Volume 3
★★★½	Volume 4
★★★★	Volume 5
★★★½	Volume 6
★★★½	Volume 7
★★★★	Volume 8
★★★★	Volume 9
★★★★	Volume 10
★★★½	Volume 11
★★★	Volume 12
★★★	Volume 13
★★★★	Volume 14
★★★	Volume 15

Didn't It Blow Your Mind! documents a brilliant moment in pop history, when listening to the radio could be exciting and entertaining, informative and inspiring—for hours at a stretch. Though the early '70s are generally perceived as a hangover from the highs of the late '60s, the set extends soul music's peak through 1972. That year, mind-blowing Top 10 hits like "Back Stabbers," "Freddie's Dead," "I'll Take You There," "Lean On Me"—included on volumes 8 and 9—crossed over without a trace of compromise. Musically bold and frankly topical, most of these golden oldies still pack a mighty wallop. The early volumes establish a comfortable mix: Sweet Southern grit from studios in Memphis and Muscle Shoals, soaring Philly slickness from producers Thom Bell and Gamble and Huff, psychedelic post-Motown from the Holland-Dozier-Holland team, and some truly wonderful one-shots. *Volume 3* collects two Motown gems (The Spinners' "It's a Shame" and "War" by Edwin Starr), along with Charles Wright's funky "Express Yourself." *Volume 5* adds reggae to the blend, while addressing racial paranoia ("Smiling Faces Sometimes" by the

Undisputed Truth) and the rise of feminism (Jean Knight's "Mr. Big Stuff"; "Treat Her Like a Lady" by Cornelius Brothers & Sister Rose).

The Sound of Philadelphia exerts its dominance on the later albums; you can here how those concise orchestrations, gripping arrangements, and life-affirming harmonies overwhelmed—and influenced—the competition. The Staple Singers, Curtis Mayfield, and Bill Withers do more than hold their own on the breathtaking eighth and ninth volumes, though. *Volume 10* captures the emergence of a sexier, rhythm-based groove, making room for Sylvia's "Pillow Talk" amid the pessimism of Mayfield's "Superfly" and War's "The World Is a Ghetto." Taking its name from the idiosyncratic producer Thom Bell's first hit single—"Didn't I (Blow Your Mind This Time)" by the Delfonics—and signing off with his last gasp before disco—"I'm Doin' Fine Now" by New York City—the first ten volumes of *Didn't It Blow Your Mind!* feel reasonably complete. And unlike most various-artists compilations, it's remarkably coherent and clearheaded.

Strains in the fabric of the soul coalition begin to show during the final installment of the series. In the mid-70s, black music split off into diverse subgroups like funk, disco, and "quiet storm" classicism. Volumes 11 through 14 compile one-shots rather than serve as a definitive guide. There are some classic tracks, but that unifying buzz ever-present through *Volume 10* completely slips away by the scattershot *Volume 15*. Barry White ("I'm Gonna Love You Just a Little More, Baby") and his underlings Love Unlimited ("Walkin' in the Rain With the One I Love") kick off *Volume 11* in an elegantly orchestrated style, but the subsequent leaps seem abrupt: from soulful R&B throwbacks (the Dells' "Give Your Baby a Standing Ovation" and Ann Peebles' "I Can't Stand the Rain") to kicking, straight-up groove jams (Eddie Kendricks' "Keep On Truckin' " and Fred Wesley and the JBs' "Doing It to Death") to eclectic pop crossovers (Gladys Knight and the Pips' "Midnight Train to Georgia" and the Pointer Sisters' "Yes We Can Can")—it never quite adds up. *Volume 12* focuses on some solid vocal nuggets that are best enjoyed on the respective groups' greatest-hits albums: Harold Melvin & the Blue Notes' "The Love I Lost, Part 1," the O'Jays' "Love Train," and the Chi-Lites' Philly-by-way-of-Chicago "Stoned out of My Mind"; Al Wilson's winning "Show and Tell" and William DeVaughns' low-riding "Be Thankful for What You Got" are invaluable rarities; Joe Simon's "Theme From Cleopatra Jones" and Bobby Womack's "Lookin' for a Love" prove that even the expansive '70s soul sound had its formulaic moments. "Rock the

Boat" by the Hues Corporation and "Rock Your Baby" by George McCrae open *Volume 13* with another smoothly satisfying predisco salvo, but uneven stylistic shifts mar the rest of the album. Forward-looking funksters like Kool and the Gang ("Hollywood Swinging") and Rufus ("Tell Me Something Good") bump rumps with old-school soul acts like Blue Magic ("Sideshow") and the Impressions ("Finally Got Myself Together [I'm a Changed Man]"). Corny pop trifles from Billy Preston ("Nothing From Nothing") and Carl Carlton ("Everlasting Love") tip the set in the wrong direction.

A fairly consistent pulse is sustained throughout *Volume 14,* from the hot Ohio Players ("Fire") to the sultry LaBelle ("Lady Marmalade"), with a little full-fledged dance mania from Shirley and Company ("Shame, Shame, Shame") and Gloria Gaynor ("Never Can Say Goodbye"). The "dooby dooby dooby" chorus of the Tymes' "You Little Trustmaker" alone justifies the price of admission. Several veterans' disco misfires deflate *Volume 15:* "Supernatural Thing—Part 1" by Ben E. King, Joe Simon's "Get Down, Get Down (Get on the Floor)," and "Let's Do It Again" by the Staple Singers—each one stumbles. And Minnie Riperton's annoying "Lovin' You" belongs on a collection of novelty hits even if it was produced by Stevie Wonder. Gwen McCrae's swaying "Rockin' Chair" can be sampled on Rhino's own *The Best of T.K. Records* collection (along with the aforementioned George McCrae gem and others). For that matter, Tavares' "It Only Takes a Minute" probably belongs on one of Rhino's sterling *Disco Years* compilations. If you can swing with the rhythm, those albums pick up where the earlier versions of *Didn't It Blow Your Mind!* leave off. —M.C.

The Disco Years

★★★	Volume One (Rhino, 1990)
★★★	Volume Two (Rhino, 1990)
★★★½	Volume Three (Rhino, 1992)
★★½	Volume Four (Rhino, 1992)
★★★½	Volume Five (Rhino, 1992)
★½	Volume Six (Rhino, 1995)
★★½	Volume Seven (Rhino, 1995)

During the mid-to-late '70s, the beat was king, and straight-up, four-on-the-floor dance music eclipsed rock as the primary life-force in pop music. The seven volumes of *The Disco Years* gather many of the era's divas and Svengalis, all the strings, the giddy pop, and stupid lyrics into a funky time capsule not exclusively for the nostalgic. Much of it is utterly disposable, yet each disc has at least one or two precious tracks that deserve to live forever. The "disco sucks" backlash of

the day tainted the sound for nearly a generation of the mainstream, but the songs still managed a powerful influence on what came after. The Sugarhill Gang lifted the opening riff from Chic's "Good Times" (on *Volume Four*) to create hip-hop on 1979's "Rapper's Delight"; Missy Elliott and Timbaland deconstructed Eruption's "Can't Stand the Rain" *(Volume Seven)* into a '90s hit; while Foxy's "Get Off" *(Volume Three)* sounds like an early blueprint for OutKast. In short, music from the disco era produced some euphoric R&B as lasting as what had come the previous decade, and even provided a contemporary setting for Diana Ross and other soul vets to thrive. The orgasmic synth salvo of Donna Summer's "I Feel Love" *(Volume Five)* was followed by a tidal wave of lust, one-hit wonders, and forgotten minor hits still worth another listen. This series avoids anything too experimental or far from pop (say, Kraftwerk's "Trans-Europe Express"), focusing instead on the girlish funk of "Shame, Shame, Shame" by Shirley & Company *(Volume One)* or Anita Ward's "Ring My Bell" *(Volume Two)*. Blondie's new-wave disco hit "Heart of Glass" *(Volume Two)* is a rare, and welcome, wild card. Still, this series is nowhere near complete. Missing are such major players as the Bee Gees and crossover disco hits by veteran rockers of the day dabbling desperately in the beat (see the Rolling Stones, Rod Stewart, even the Grateful Dead). By the final volumes of *The Disco Years,* the emphasis is on the early '80s, as the genre was losing steam fast, even if the Weather Girls' "It's Raining Men" *(Volume Seven)* lit up one final blast of jubilation in 1982. And by 1983's lifeless "Give It Up" *(Volume Six),* deposed disco king KC had even dumped the Sunshine Band. The best tracks of this series could easily be distilled into half as many CDs. Some of it does suck, but the best remains music of pure, mindless escape, with little substance beyond the one message that truly matters on the dance floor: shake your booty. —S.A.

The Doo Wop Box

★★★★★	The Doo Wop Box (Rhino, 1993)
★★★★	The Doo Wop Box II (Rhino, 1996)
★★	The Doo Wop Box III (Rhino, 2000)

Before hip-hop, before soul, before even rock & roll, there was doo-wop, the first black vocal music to captivate white teens. And, as Rhino Records' series of three box sets proves, this oft-trivialized genre was much more than kiddie pop. The first *Doo Wop Box* is essential listening for any serious popular music fan, as it anthologizes rock & roll's early foundation. Beginning with the Orioles' (yep, they were from Baltimore) 1948 swooning "It's Too Soon to Know," the set captures all the street-corner giants, be they birds (Ravens, Crows, Flamingos), cars (Cadillacs, El Dorados, Jaguars), or natural wonders (Moonglows, Rainbows, Jewels). The Penguins' garage-made demo-turned-smash "Earth Angel" is as raw and emotive as any music you'll ever hear, and the Flamingos' three-minute vocal symphony "I Only Have Eyes for You" is as beautiful. Other classic popular favorites include the Imperials' "Tears on My Pillow," the Crests' "16 Candles," and the Platters' "The Great Pretender." The four CDs also showcase the best of doo-wop's women (the Chantels' "Maybe"), its mighty white boys (Dion and the Belmonts' "I Wonder Why"), and tragic geniuses (Clyde McPhatter's "Money Honey" and Frankie Lyman's "Why Do Fools Fall in Love"). A definitive genre's definitive statement.

Rhino didn't originally plan for a sequel to *The Doo Wop Box* and thus used almost all of the genre's most influential and popular tracks on the first set; however, what *The Doo Wop Box II* lacks in familiarity it more than makes up for in revelation. A sort of doo-wop *Nuggets,* the second set unearths lost treasures like the Vocaleers' nasally ballad "Is It a Dream," the Cufflinks' love-is-war song "Guided Missiles," and the Collegians' bouncy boy-girl sing-along "Zoom Zoom Zoom." You won't hear this stuff on oldies stations.

Unfortunately, the third time is not a charm for the *Doo Wop Box* series. To supplement the first two solid discs of hits and misses, Rhino compensated for a dearth of material by resorting to gimmicks like a disc of celebrity picks from Paul Simon, Quincy Jones, and Keith Richards (good call by Richards on "Maybe"— too bad it's already on the first box) and a disc of "modern doo-wop" from the likes of the Stray Cats and Boyz II Men. For doo-wop fanatics only. —B.C.

★★★½ **8 Mile: Original Soundtrack**
(Interscope, 2002)

8 Mile is a nice exception to the flood of subpar hip-hop-oriented soundtracks that have washed up in record stores during the last few years. Where most rappers take soundtracks as an opportunity to simply spread the word on their personal brand, Eminem took the musical companion to his semiautobiographical film a bit more seriously. The album is notable for a number of reasons, not the least of which is the impressive caliber of talent featured. It spawned Em's mega-hit "Lose Yourself," a change in speed for the comic instigator, upon which he speaks of his struggle to make it as an MC coming out of an impoverished Detroit neighborhood. Other highlights include the legendary Rakim's return to the spotlight on "R.A.K.I.M." and 50 Cent's first appearance under

Eminem's banner ("Wanksta"). The production, handled in places by Dr. Dre and DJ Premier, is usually excellent, and none of the artists come with anything less than their A-game. —C.R.

Ethiopiques

★★★★ Ethiopiques 1: Golden Years of Modern Ethiopian Music 1969–1975 (Buda Musique/Allegro, 1998)

★★★ Ethiopiques 2: Tetchawet! (Urban Azmaris of the 90s) (Buda Musique/Allegro, 1998)

★★★★ Ethiopiques 3: Golden Years of Modern Ethiopian Music 1969–1975 (Buda Musique/Allegro, 1998)

★★★★ Ethiopiques 4: Ethio-Jazz & Musique Instrumentale 1969–1974 (Buda Musique/Allegro, 1998)

★★★½ Ethiopiques 5: Tigrigna Music 1970–1975 (Buda Musique/Allegro, 1998)

★★★ Ethiopiques 6: Mahmoud Ahmed "Almaz" 1973 (Buda Musique/Allegro, 1998)

★★★ Ethiopiques 7: Mahmoud Ahmed "Erè Mèla Mèla" 1975 (Buda Musique/Allegro, 1998)

★★★★ Ethiopiques 8: Swinging Addis 1969–1974 (Buda Musique/Allegro, 2000)

★★★ Ethiopiques 9: Alèmayèhu Eshèté 1969–1974 (Buda Musique/Allegro, 2001)

★★★½ Ethiopiques 10: Tezeta—Ethiopian Blues & Ballads (Buda Musique/Allegro, 2001)

★★★ Ethiopiques 11: Alemu Aga—The Harp of King David (Buda Musique/Allegro, 2002)

★★★ Ethiopiques 12: Konso Music and Songs— Kirba afaa Xonso (Buda Musique/Allegro, 2003)

★★★ Ethiopiques 13: Ethiopian Groove—The Golden Seventies (Buda Musique/Allegro, 2003)

★★★ Ethiopiques 14: Gétatchew Mekurya—Négus of Ethiopan Sax (Buda Musique/Allegro, 2003)

★★★ Ethiopiques 15: Europe Meets Ethiopia (Buda Musique, 2003)

★★★½ Ethiopiques 16: Asnaqètch Wèrqu—The Lady With the Krar (Buda Musique, 2004)

In the CD booklet for several volumes of the *Ethiopiques* series, a photo captures Ethiopian record producer Amha Eshèté wearing a single-breasted red jacket over a black turtleneck and striking a devil-may-care pose. In the liner notes of *Ethiopiques 8: Swinging Addis,* though, that photo is placed next to a tiny reprint of the cover of 1966's *The Exciting Wilson Pickett,* and what do you know—the Man and a Half is wearing the same outfit. It wasn't just the fashion sense of American soul artists that fed Eshèté's imagination. Between 1969 and 1975, his independently owned Amha Records released some 250 titles documenting a sometimes bizarre, frequently arresting hybrid of Southern soul fervor from the States and traditional North African cadences. These sides make up the bulk of the French label Buda Musique's *Ethiopiques* series, originally planned as a ten-disc set but now stretched to 14 discs that include titles from other labels' catalogues.

The discs are somewhat confusingly ordered. Six are dedicated to single artists (*6* and *7* belong to hypnotic vocalist Mahmoud Ahmed, *9* to singer Alèmayèhu Eshèté; *11* to meditative vocalist/harpist Alemu Aga; *14* to saxophonist Gétatchew Mekurya; and *16* to Asnaqètch Wèrqu, a female vocalist), while the rest are compilations. Volumes *1* through *5* (sans *2*), *8*, and *13* feature the region's heady mixture of funk, soul, and jazz. Recorded in 1996, *2* is mostly acoustic and more traditional-sounding than the funky fire of the '70s music, while *12* is traditional, period. *Ethiopiques 10: Tezeta—Ethiopian Blues & Ballads* is smoky, gorgeous, and contemplative late-night music that's less jittery rhythmically than much of the rest of the series. Volume *15* is again contemporary, a collaboration between a European jazz quartet and several Ethiopian players, most notably vocalists Yezinna Negash and Guennet Masresha.

Funk fans will get the most out of volumes *1*, *3*, and *8*, the series' high points. Volume *1* peaks with a handful of Muluqèn Mèllèssè cuts (whose horns have a Chicago-soul feel) and the jutting organ riff of Mahmoud Ahmed's "Aynotché Tèrabu." Ahmed's snaking funk bomb "Kulun Mankwalèsh" opens *3*, which just goes on from there with Hirut Bèqèlè's "Almokèrkum Nèbèr" a near ringer, language aside, for James Brown's "There Was a Time." Volume *8* features Samuel Bèlay's "Aynotchesh Yerèfu," whose Vox organ solo and boisterous horns could have scored the Ethiopian equivalent of *Superfly*, and Bahta Gèbrè-Heywèt's "Tessassatègn Èko," a Stax-Volt–style mid-tempo beauty.   —M.M.

★★★★½ **Go Go Crankin'** (1985; 4th & Broadway, 1990)

While funk bands across the nation began evaporating in the 1980s, a pool around George Clinton's fabled "Chocolate City" (Washington, D.C.) gained attention with a regional style that just wouldn't dry up: go go. The music's polyrhythms were almost Afro-Cuban in their complexity and good cheer, yet its edgy drive was completely African-American, with vocals that bobbed and popped against a backdrop of congas,

timbals, and cowbells. "Can we drop the bomb on the white boy crew?" asked Trouble Funk in "Drop the Bomb," one of the classics featured on this definitive compilation. In the end, that mission was handled by go go's Bronx-born sibling, hip-hop.   —F.S.

★★★★ **Gimme Indie Rock, Vol. 1**
(K-Tel, 2000)

In the late 1990s and early years of 2000, indie-rock compilations flew fast and plentiful (*Short Music for Short People*, anyone?) but it took K-Tel to do the seemingly impossible: make a compilation that impressed both indie snobs and those who think alternative rock began and ended with Nirvana. Considering that the acts here run the gamut from obscure to slightly less obscure, *Gimme Indie Rock, Vol. 1* definitely leans more toward the former than the latter. Most of the necessary touchstones are accounted for (Mudhoney, Hüsker Dü, Meat Puppets, Scrawl, and Dinosaur Jr, among others), but there's a distressing lack of contributions from mainstays like Fugazi, the Pixies, and the Replacements. Otherwise, *Gimme Indie Rock* is faultless, meandering cheerfully from shoegazers (Galaxie 500, Wedding Present) to nascent alt-country (Eleventh Dream Day) to seminal two-chord punk (the Minutemen, Black Flag). Even at 30 songs (spread over two discs), *Gimme* feels brief, but it may have to do. Three years after the release of the first volume, the second has yet to materialize.   —A.S.

Guitar Paradise of East Africa

    ★★★★   Guitar Paradise of East Africa (Earthworks, 1990)
    ★★★½   The Nairobi Beat: Kenyan Pop Music Today (Rounder, 1992)
    ★★★½   Kenya Dance Mania (Earthworks, 1995)

In the 1970s and '80s, Kenya was a stable retreat for three countries' worth of musicians: the local performers who refined the urban pop, or *benga;* Tanzanian players searching for a more developed music industry; and, particularly, expatriate bands from what is now the Republic of the Congo, who left when President Mobutu made life too difficult in the country he called Zaire. The cross-pollination produced a rich blending of the Zairean variant on Cuban rumba, called *soukous,* with the intricate fingerpicking of Tanzania and the sweet, light vocals of Kenya, which shifted among at least three languages. The best benga numbers work like the double strands of DNA. The airy lyrical melodies wrap around twin guitars that spiral over the undulating patter of drums and bass. The precise balance of elements was hard to maintain, but for the vintage sides on these anthologies, the guitars are electric; the voices, earthy; and the beat, ecstatic. The finest benga showcase ever released, *Guitar Paradise* (which is sadly out of print), built momentum through a flawless program of mid-length dance singles. But while the vocals are not as consistently sweet and the guitar swirls aren't as weightless on *Nairobi Beat* or *Kenya Dance Mania,* they deliver much of the folk-wisdom-in-the-big-city attitude that characterizes the golden age of pop music. Even better, the three collections touch on bandleaders Samba Mapangala and D.O. Misiani, who make wondrous albums that are ripe for exploration. —M.MI.

★★★★★ The Harder They Come (Island, 1972)

Although Bob Marley may be the saint of Jamaican music, Jimmy Cliff deserves at least one book of the reggae gospel for the soundtrack to this seminal movie. Cliff's songs make up half this album, though the title song and "You Can Get It If You Really Want" are repeated. Both are worth hearing again and again because they perfectly encapsulate the pop side of reggae with their underdog themes and understated rhythms. But the diverse collection made this album groundbreaking: It served many as the first reggae sampler.

Desmond Dekker's "Shanty Town" is an anthem of the outlaw lifestyle, and the Slicker's "Johnny Too Bad" shares thematic turf with rappers like Tupac Shakur, while existing on a different rhythmic planet. The Maytals seal this album's place in history, however; "Pressure Drop" and "Sweet and Dandy" bring a hyperkinetic energy to reggae, foreshadowing dancehall hits to come.

This album—and the cult-classic movie—did more than just make Jimmy Cliff a star: Album and movie served as effective cultural ambassadors, bringing an outside world into the blossoming of roots reggae. Few incubators are as sweet. —C.R.C.

★★★★ Hillbilly Music . . . Thank God! Vol. 1 (Capitol, 1989)

Featuring 24 California country hits and rarities from the 1940s to the 1960s, this sparkling collection happily contradicts the contemporary notion that "real" country is all about melancholy and primitivism. The numbers range from smooth Western swing to rough hillbilly boogie, tender male-harmony ballads to crass male-female duets, and avuncular folk to sneering rockabilly, yet they're held together by the musicians' sprightly polish, winking humor, and pop reach. If that means they share as much with compiler Marshall Crenshaw as with the Carter Family, then they also

never polish away the rural twang and sass that's so winning, it's no wonder Dwight Yoakam has spent his career chasing it. —F.S.

★★★★★ The History of Township Music
(Wrasse, U.K.; 2001)

Spanning 40 years, this compilation is an indispensable history lesson. Between 1939, when Solomon Linda's Original Evening Birds recorded "Mbube" (a.k.a. the first incarnation of "The Lion Sleeps Tonight" and Africa's most famous melody) and 1981, when this disc ends, South African pop went from imitating American jazz (really well, too) to a groove all its own, with weird but infectious jumps. From the airy swing of '50s tracks like Royal Players' "Khala Zo'Me" and the Solven Whistlers' "Something New in Africa," to the jazzy girl-group harmonies of Young Stars' "Ulova" and the gutty township jive of Big Four's 1966 "Mr. Music" and Mahotella Queens' "Mama Thula," from 1967, there's rarely a dull moment. And it leaves off right where *The Indestructible Beat of Soweto* begins, just in case you like your history in neat increments. —M.M.

★★★★ The Indestructible Beat of Soweto (Shanachie, 1986)

After Paul Simon's *Graceland,* the gorgeous a cappella choral work of Ladysmith Black Mambazo and the joyfully ferocious concert tours of Mahlathini and the Mahotella Queens, nothing boosted the South African music awakening of the '80s like *The Indestructible Beat of Soweto.* This collection delivers rare unity of sound and force of presentation. It draws from recordings made only from 1981 to 1984 (well after the supposed '60s heyday of the eclectic, hard-stomping, urban-dance-music style *mbaqanga*). With performers backed by the Makgona Tsohle Band's core of musicians, this disc is more *The Indestructible Voices of Soweto*—defiant, persistent, and headed for victory over apartheid. The momentum keeps rising from the mellow greeting of Udokotel Shange Namajaha's "Awungilobolele" (a song about working hard to get money for marriage) to the beneficent farewell of, yes, Ladysmith Black Mambazo's "Nansi Imali" (a praise song to miners). What strikes first are Joseph Makwela's elastic bass lines and the low groans of Mahlathini—his voice so deep it seems to boil up from the bottom of the ocean. But other charms entice, such as the wonderfully sour fiddle of Moses Mchunu's "Ohwahilahe" and the steely pride of the female voices including Nelcy Sedibe's. Everyone who feels the vitality of rebel music, from Elvis to Bob Marley, will respond to these grooves. Conventional wisdom held that mbaqanga was hopelessly out of fashion, a black-power sound drowned by disco. *The Indestructible Beat of Soweto* is one long shout of truth in the teeth of official lies.　—M.MI.

★★★½　**Ken Burns Jazz: The Story of America's Music** (Columbia/ Legacy, 2000)

★★★　**The Best of Ken Burns Jazz** (Columbia/Legacy, 2000)

Ken Burns' 19-hour documentary on the history of jazz spawned a virtual cottage industry: best-of sets by 22 individual artists, plus a five-disc best-of-the-best box and its one-disc best-best-best condensation. *The Story of America's Music*, 94 tracks including a lot of drop-dead classics, isn't a bad introduction for jazz neophytes. Burns was criticized, rightly, for scarcely acknowledging the avant-garde movement of the '60s and most of what came after it: The '70s are represented by three tracks, the '80s by two, the '90s by a hip-hop crossover and covers of two ancient standards. And you could argue that Louis Armstrong is overrepresented with 11 tracks—if any of them were less than great, but they aren't. The set is best understood as a grand tour from a rather fogyish perspective—a collection of suggestions for further exploration.

The Best of compounds the weaknesses of the box, containing exactly one track from the past 45 years and rushing from peak to peak. Those peaks are mighty tough to argue with: Thelonious Monk's "Straight, No Chaser," Duke Ellington's "The Mooche," Miles Davis' "So What." But arranging these wildly disparate masterpieces in a gleaming trophy cabinet such as this stifles their individuality.　—D.W.

The Langley Schools Music Project
★★★★　Innocence and Despair (Bar None, 2001)

Any attempt to explain the *Langley Schools Music Project* sounds lunatic: What would happen if you put 60 Canadian schoolchildren in front of a two-track recorder in the middle of rural British Columbia? That's what Hans Fenger did in the late '70s, teaching his students vocal arrangements of contemporary pop songs by the likes of Fleetwood Mac and the Beach Boys. He had no commercial intent with the project, though LPs were made up for the students' parents.

What sounds like folly ends up as mad-scientist inspiration, and the result is a remarkable album that no less than David Bowie (whose "Space Oddity" is covered) called "astounding." The recordings are full of miscues, naiveté, and the innocence you'd expect to find in a middle-school music class. There is something almost supernaturally odd about pairing these juvenile voices with "Space Oddity," and the result is eerie. Others, like listening to a young girl struggle through the Eagles' "Desperado," provide the same sort of pleasure that comes from watching a child favorite win on *Star Search*. Most of the charm comes from the fact that these kids are in love with music and they embrace it without commercial or celebrity considerations. There is also a voyeuristic appeal to the record, like a thrift-store treasure find. To hear middle schoolers echo Brian Wilson's melancholy on "In My Room" is to remember that all transcendent music springs from innocence and despair.　—C.R.C.

★★★★★　**Motown: The Classic Years** (UTV, 2000)

This plainly packaged collection would seem to be another example of the overexposure that has put a big chill on succeeding generations' interest in the one-time Sound of Young America. But the 40 hits on these two discs are so gracious, confident, and unrelenting that the set miraculously brings Motown's spirit to yearning, burning life again. "The Corporation" machine, formed just before the birth of Camelot, tooled a dream of pop-R&B integration that rode shotgun through the most tumultuous decade of social change any living American had ever seen. The selection and sequencing here never falters as Motown's house bassist, James Jamerson, syncopates the revolution to its bittersweet end.　—F.S.

The Music in My Head
★★★★½　The Music in My Head (Stern's, 1998)
★★★★　The Music in My Head 2 (Stern's, 2002)

The *Music in My Head* albums are accompaniments to compiler Mark Hudson's already hard-to-find novel of the same name, which concerns the harrowing, hilarious ins and outs of the music business in Senegal. But these anthologies, especially the first, are superb, stand-alone works. Famous names contribute—Youssou N'Dour, Salief Keita, Franco—though that's incidental. Not a single flabby track intrudes on *The Music in My Head*, but more important, the album boasts its own sound and complex mood. The guitars can scatter single notes or spray light distortion; the wavelike pattering of the *tama* drums hold the arrangements together; and the tart, nasal voices wail above it all in an evocation of urban bustle, airy but manic. It's the soundtrack for a nation of young people on the move.

Singer N'Dour is 18 years old on one cut, 35 on another, but his message feels the same: Senegalese heritage with bite. *Music in My Head 2* is merely a bit less of the same. The musical gestures seem broader, the songs a shade more conventionally pretty. The music still never stops refilling your head. After you warm up to the styles with N'Dour and Keita's finest albums, Hudson's tour of African R&B is the road trip to take.   —M.MI.

Now That's What I Call Music!

★★★	Vol. 1 (Virgin, 1999)
★★★½	Vol. 2 (Virgin, 1999)
★★★	Vol. 3 (Universal, 1999)
★★★	Vol. 4 (Universal, 2000)
★★★½	Vol. 5 (Sony, 2000)
★★★★	Vol. 6 (Epic, 2001)
★★★★	Vol. 7 (Virgin/EMI, 2001)
★★★½	Vol. 8 (Virgin, 2001)
★★★	Vol. 9 (Universal, 2002)
★★½	Vol. 10 (Sony, 2002)
★★★	Vol. 11 (Universal, 2002)
★★★	Vol. 12 (Capitol, 2003)
★★	Vol. 13 (Universal, 2003)
★★★	Vol. 14 (Sony, 2003)
★★	Vol. 15 (Capitol, 2004)

In their own way, the mega-successful *Now That's What I Call Music!* compilations are as big a teen-baiting, disposable income–gobbling franchise as Six Flags and Abercrombie & Fitch. On one level, these collections have replaced the entire U.S. singles market—unless you buy the actual albums or download these tracks, there's no other way you can get them. You can quibble with song selection and complain about how obvious all the hits are, but most of the volumes boast at least a handful of great pop pleasures, and almost all of them hold up way better than your average Britney album. Even the most annoying stuff—including Cherry Poppin' Daddies' "Zoot Suit Riot" (*Vol. 1*), Blackstreet and Mya's "Take Me There" (*Vol. 2*), Jagged Edge's "Walked Outta Heaven" (*Vol. 14*), as well as two tracks from Creed and three from 98°—is kind of fun in that time-capsule sort of way.

Vol. 1 outlines *Now's* format-crossing, hits-only formula, setting Backstreet Boys' "As Long as You Love Me" and Hanson's "MMMBop" alongside hits by Radiohead, Everclear, and the justly forgotten Marcy Playground. One thing these discs prove is how soul-suckingly godawful most rock radio was in the late '90s and early '00s, and most of the time the beatwise stuff—including 'N Sync and Nelly's "Girlfriend" (*Vol. 5*), N.O.R.E.'s "Nothin' " (*Vol. 11*), and all but one of the four Destiny's Child tracks—kicks the shit

out of hits by Saliva, 3 Doors Down, and Lifehouse. If you still believe in the spirit of radio, you can't go too wrong with any volume, but look out for some of the later ones, which pile on formulaic modern rock and bland dance-pop from fresh-faced up-and-comers. The best disc is probably *Vol. 7*, which surrounds a string of danceable winners—Destiny's Child's "Survivor," Nelly's "Ride wit Me," R. Kelly's "Fiesta," Eve and Gwen Stefani's "Let Me Blow Ya Mind"—with Aerosmith's big-ass ballad "Jaded," American Hi-Fi's pop-punk "Flavor of the Weak," and the scorned-diva melodrama of 3LW's "Playas Gon' Play."   —C.H.

Nuggets

| ★★★★★ | Nuggets: Original Artyfacts From the First Psychedelic Era, 1965–1968 (Rhino, 1998) |
| ★★★★★ | Nuggets II: Original Artyfacts From the British Empire and Beyond (Rhino, 2001) |

For archivists, freaks, musos, geeks, and miner-hat-wearing record prospectors found scouring flea markets and yard sales, the *Nuggets* box sets are an invaluable resource that provide an alternate history of '60s rock, not to mention hours of butt-kicking fuzz, yowls, and manic drum-kit abuse. That many of the one- and no-hit wonders and oddities included on both sets were shamelessly ripping off better-known groundbreakers such as the Yardbirds and the Pretty Things should in no way detract from their youthful efforts to be snottier, louder, and wilder than the next band. Instead, it highlights how amazingly vital and infinitely malleable that overamped sped-up R&B beat-racket was.

The first *Nuggets* box, which is essentially a three-disc addendum to the original and highly influential 1972 Lenny Kaye–compiled double-album, features American garage rock of every conceivable stripe. All the chestnuts and garage standards are here (with the notable absence of ? & The Mysterian's "96 Tears"): "Louie, Louie," "Dirty Water," "Psychotic Reaction," as well as the Syndicate of Sound's perfect pop creation "Little Girl," the very bedrock of mid-'60's teen-boy angst. None of these guys were as cute as Paul or John or even Ringo, and they used the newfound freedom of rock, a couple of chords, and some cheap amps to let all the little girls know exactly how they felt. There is Beatles worship to be found in the Knickerbockers' "Lies," Dylan parody in the Mouse & the Traps ditty "Public Execution," and more astounding overblown out-of-their-minds, feedback-drenched guitar solos than you could shake a Thai-stick at. In fact, one of the more entertaining aspects of the *Nuggets* box is that it allows you to play that game beloved of freak-beat connoisseurs, "Who cut the most demented proto-punk single of all time?" Was it the revered Sonics with either their pro-poison anthem "Strychnine" or their equally unhinged "Psycho"? Was it the Elastik Band with their immortal "Spazz"? Or was it the Bees with their uncategorizable 1966 oddity "Voices Green and Purple"? There is no shortage of nominees to be found and *Ugly Things* magazine editor Mike Stax makes a case for each of them in his incisive and informative track-by-track notes, giving a name and a face to bands of dangerous kids that often made only five or six minutes of inspired noise and then disappeared without a trace.

Perhaps less essential, depending on your appetite for a steady stream of Beatles/Stones/Pretty Things/Animals emulators from around the world (all with the standard Jagger/May screamer and raveup drumbasher, but not always possessing a distinct personality of their own), is the second *Nuggets* box set that centers on the original beat-group explosion and the subsequent psychedelic era that would replace everyone's lager and speed with acid and pot. The U.K., Europe, Asia, and South America are all represented, and the history involved is certainly fascinating to read about courtesy of Stax's track listings and the essays of other erudite fuzzologists. The heavy hitters of the time are represented: the Small Faces, Van Morrison's Them, the Creation (no Yardbirds, though, the band that practically started it all and influenced so many!). But it's the stuff you've either never heard or heard the likes of that will have the jaws dropping: the simply staggering "Save My Soul" by Wimple Winch, the amps-on-11 blitzkrieg of the Syndicats' "Crawdaddy Simone," the infectious and hilarious sounds of Holland's the Zipps and their prodrug "Kicks & Chicks," to name a few. The set also performs the service of turning people on to great overlooked acts like Holland's the Outsiders and the hauntingly beautiful "It's a Sin to Go Away" by Peru's We All Together. Stylistically, a lot more ground is covered on the second box, given the longer time frame. This sometimes results in whiplash upon hearing a '65 Mod stomper next to some '68 fairy-tale psych epic. Maybe a more chronological or thematic approach would have worked better. Quibbling aside, though, both boxes make digging for gold a helluva lot of fun.   —S.S.

O Brother, Where Art Thou?

- ★★★★ O Brother, Where Art Thou? (soundtrack) (Universal, 2000)
- ★★½ Down From the Mountain: Live Concert Performances by the Artists & Musicians of "O Brother, Where Art Thou?" (Universal, 2001)
- ★★★½ Down From the Mountain (The "O Brother, Where Art Thou?" Concert) (DVD) (Artisan Entertainment, 2002)

When moviemakers Joel and Ethan Coen recast Homer's *Odyssey* as a darkly whimsical trip through the Depression-era South, they did not expect to be giving the biggest boost to old-timey music in a generation. But producer T Bone Burnett's recipe of authentic performances and dated tunes was inspired: Bluegrass veterans such as Ralph Stanley played off new stars like Alison Krauss; sweet harmonizing by the Peasall Sisters leavened harsh protocountry shouts like "I Am a Man of Constant Sorrow"; the gospel of the Fairfield Four met the Delta blues of Chris Thomas King. A huge public who hadn't had a chance to hear such music for many years was captivated. After the soundtrack had sold an astonishing 4 million copies, a good number of the featured players banded together for a series of Down From the Mountain tours, which revived the dormant country-folk-bluegrass variety-show format to sparkling effect. The homey atmosphere of the shows—particularly Ralph Stanley's unsurpassed ability to bring church into a concert hall—doesn't transfer well to audio documentation, though the concert CD features several loose, vigorous renditions of the beloved material. The DVD version of *Down From the Mountain* improves the experience with flavorful stage visuals, but it is not the straight documentary of all the songs performed that some fans may want.   —M.MI.

★★★★ OHM: The Early Gurus of Electronic Music: 1948–1980
(Ellipsis Arts, 2000)

From sine waves to musique concrète, treated field recordings to Hollywood soundtracks, audiotape experiments to manipulated vinyl, *OHM* offers a concise, highly listenable overview of the development of electronic music from post-WWII academic labs to postpop soundscapers. (Actually, the set's title is misleading: The earliest track, Olivier Messiaen's "Oraison," is actually from 1937, while Brian Eno's "Unfamiliar Wind (Leeks Hills)," is from 1982.) Shrewdly, compilers Thomas Ziegler and Jason Gross sequenced OHM's three discs nonchronologically, arranging them to flow, a gambit that works especially well on disc three, a "chill-out" disc of sorts that features pieces by David Behrman, Robert Ashley, Alvin Curran, Alvin Lucier, Jon Hassell, and Brian Eno. Not everything goes down easy, particularly an excerpt from a La Monte Young drone piece. But in light of grindcore, turntablism, and the crankiest experimental lap-top music, it's easier to hear the joy that imbues John Cage's "Williams Mix" and Steve Reich's "Pendulum Music" (performed here by Sonic Youth). And plenty else, from Pauline Oliveros' deconstruction of "Bye Bye Butterfly" to Hugh Le Caine's "Dripsody" (Aphex Twin fans, take note), which is a straight-up gas. —M.M.

The Perfect Beats

★★★★ Vol. 1 (Timber!/Tommy Boy, 1998)
★★★★★ Vol. 2 (Timber!/Tommy Boy, 1998)
★★★½ Vol. 3 (Timber!/Tommy Boy, 1998)
★★★★ Vol. 4 (Timber!/Tommy Boy, 1998)

The four volumes of *The Perfect Beats* serve as a definitive primer of the period's club sounds, with a heavy emphasis on electro and hip-hop. The discs aren't intermixed, but on several occasions, the songs are segued tightly enough to create the illusion of a DJ set, an entirely appropriate programming decision—as indeed are most of the selections. *Vol. 1* is keynoted by Afrika Bambaataa & Soul Sonic Force's 1982 "Planet Rock," one of the most influential records in history, before unleashing a fusillade of synth-leaning classics from Yaz, Yello, Rockers Revenge, Peech Boys, and electro-granddaddies Kraftwerk. *Vol. 2,* without question the best disc in the series, expands the focus to include punk-funk acts like ESG and Liquid Liquid, protohouse from Strafe and Dominatrix, and Shannon's "Let the Music Play," a #1 hit and the acknowledged birth of Latin freestyle. *Vol. 3* contains the weakest overall selection but gets points for Hashim's "Al Naafiysh (The Soul)," spooky electro that sounds like Detroit techno's most plangent moment half a decade before the fact. *Vol. 4* honors both the future—via Cybotron's (a.k.a. Juan Atkins) "Clear," widely considered the first techno record—and the past, with ten '70s funk, disco, and R&B jams (James Brown's "Give It Up or Turnit a Loose," Candido's "Jingo," Eddie Kendricks' "Date With the Rain") that influenced everything else in the collection. The last song, appropriately enough: Bambaataa's "Looking for the Perfect Beat." Mission accomplished. —M.M.

★★★★ Pulp Fiction: Music From the Motion Picture (MCA, 1994)

In 1994, *Pulp Fiction* arrived like a hyperstylized tsunami blown in from an alternate universe, proving to be, if not the hands-down best movie of the '90s, then by far the most quotable. The soundtrack, like Quentin Tarantino's dialogue, is an ace mood-setter as well as a series of brilliantly placed affectations, as Tarantino dusted off a bunch of prepunk nuggets that hold up individually but nowadays seem inextricably linked to the film. Rather than just use snippets of the songs, Tarantino often employed long stretches in scenes that play like first-rate music videos. A handful of songs—Al Green's "Let's Stay Together," Kool & the Gang's "Jungle Boogie," and Dusty Springfield's "Son of a Preacher Man"—didn't really need dusting off, but they fit in perfectly, anyway. Even the five tracks' worth of dialogue hold up on multiple listens; the best snippet is Samuel L. Jackson's "Ezekiel" speech, which ensured that Gen Xers could quote at least one Old Testament verse. —C.H.

Rai Rebels

★★★★ Rai Rebels (Earthworks, 1988)
★★★ Pop-Rai and Rachid Style (Earthworks, 1990)

Modern Algerian *rai* ("opinion") music, with its big electronic beats, fiercely shouted vocals, insistent rolling groove, and blunt tales of forbidden booze and teenage desires, is world pop that rock and hip-hop fans can grab onto. But while there are numerous rai samplers out there for the uninitiated, much of it may look forbidding or sound low on personality. Many single-disc introductions, such as *The Rough Guide to Rai,* are eclectic but generic, and the almost-as-numerous boxed anthologies (which all seem to have titles like *Total Rai, Maxi Rai,* and *Absolute Rai*) are both padded and too much for a starter.

Rai Rebels and *Pop-Rai and Rachid Style* were among the earliest anthologies released to the general Western market and remain the first picks. *Rai Rebels* is more relentless, particularly since it begins with Chaba Fadela and Cheb Sabroui's male-female duet "N'Sel Fik (You Are Mine)." This is a primal rai number that corresponds to Chuck Berry's "Roll Over Beethoven" or Grandmaster Flash's "The Message"—if you immediately want to hear more tunes like it, you'll enjoy rai. Both collections are the work of star producer Rachid Baba Ahmed, a visionary who made the links between modern electrodance and roots rai sound graceful and natural. Tragically, he was machine-gunned down by terrorists in 1995, and the music has never been able to find the same perfect balance since. —M.MI.

Red Hot + Blue

★★★★½ Red Hot + Blue (Chrysalis, 1990)
★★ Red Hot + Dance (Sony, 1992)
★★★½ No Alternative (Arista, 1994)
★★½ Red Hot + Country (Mercury Nashville, 1994)
★★★½ Stolen Moments: Red Hot + Cool (GRP, 1994)
★★★½ Red Hot on Impulse! (GRP, 1994)
★★★ Red Hot + Bothered (Warner Bros., 1995)

★★½   Offbeat: A Red Hot Soundtrip (TVT/Wax Trax!, 1996)

★★   America Is Dying Slowly (Elektra/Asylum, 1996)

★★★   Red Hot + Rio (PolyGram, 1996)

★★   Silencio = Muerte: Red Hot + Latin (Hola, 1997)

★★½   Red Hot + Rhapsody (Red Hot–Antilles/Verve, 1998)

★★½   Onda Sonora: Red Hot + Lisbon (Bar/None, 1999)

★★½   Red Hot + Indigo (Red Hot Organization, 2000)

★★½   Red Hot + Riot (MCA, 2002)

When *Red Hot + Blue* was released in 1990, it seemed like a hugely original idea: a tribute album to the classic American songwriter Cole Porter, with its proceeds dedicated to AIDS relief. It's got an all-star cast of performers from all over the genre map, some treating Porter's songs reverentially (k.d. lang's "So in Love"), some fooling around with them considerably (Debbie Harry and Iggy Pop Rat-Packing through "Well, Did You Evah!"), and some all but throwing them out the window (the Jungle Brothers' "I Get a Kick Out of You"). But everybody seems enthusiastic, and Porter's songs hold up beautifully to almost every treatment.

Subsequent AIDS-benefit compilations put together by the Red Hot Organization haven't been quite as consistent. *Red Hot + Dance* is essentially a three-song George Michael EP (including "Too Funky") with a bunch of remixed songs by other big-name dance-pop artists tacked on—only Brian Eno's affectionate hatchet job on EMF's "Unbelievable" is especially good. *No Alternative* is a peculiar snapshot of 1994's alt-rock scene, with negligible tracks by the likes of Smashing Pumpkins and Urge Overkill. It's probably best remembered for Nirvana's otherwise unavailable screamer "Verse Chorus Verse" and a ridiculous Pavement song about R.E.M.'s discography, but it's also worth seeking out for two terrific Verlaines compositions: "Heavy 33," played by the New Zealand band themselves, and "Joed Out," covered by Barbara Manning.

Red Hot + Country's contributors include an impressive cross-section of country stars covering country and folk-rock songs (plus an unfortunate Billy Ray Cyrus original), some guest-starring the people who originally sang them—Crosby, Stills, and Nash back up Suzy Bogguss; Alison Krauss and Kathy Mattea on "Teach Your Children," and Johnny Cash helps out Brooks & Dunn with "Folsom Prison Blues" (and sings Bob Dylan's "Forever Young" himself). But too many of the performances are halfhearted indulgences

in Nashville clichés. The old-and-new collaborations on *Stolen Moments: Red Hot + Cool* are considerably more fruitful—hip-hop artists work with jazz musicians, many of them veterans of the '60s avant-garde. Digable Planets' "Flyin' High in the Brooklyn Sky," guest-starring Lester Bowie, is one of their career high points, and the Roots/Roy Ayers combination sounds great, too. *Red Hot on Impulse!* was its companion release—an introduction to the label's late-'60s and early-'70s favorites, including great stuff by the lesser-known Oliver Nelson and Archie Shepp alongside the expected Coltrane/Sanders/Mingus classics.

Red Hot + Bothered attempts to reach out to the indie-rock and fanzine crowd, with impressive songs by Heavenly (whose "Snail Trail" includes a sharp little dis of Liz Phair) and Future Bible Heroes, and less impressive throwaways by Freedom Cruise (Guided by Voices under a pseudonym), Built to Spill, Caustic Resin, and the Grifters. A mostly dismal survey of the mid-'90s art-electronics scene, *Offbeat* is notable mostly for Laika's slow-grooving "Looking for the Jackalope" and two rare recorded appearances by My Bloody Valentine's Kevin Shields (including a nice collaboration with Mark Eitzel).

America Is Dying Slowly is Red Hot's hip-hop compilation, and probably the weakest in the series—big names including the Wu-Tang Clan, De La Soul, and Coolio pitch in, but everyone seems to be saving their good rhymes and beats for their own records, and a few contributors act like AIDS is the fault of "nasty hos." Ick. *Red Hot + Rio* is a distinct improvement, and a return to theme-based compilations: contemporary artists, Brazilian and otherwise, recording new versions of bossa nova classics. The highlight is Stereolab and Herbie Mann's long, loving jam on "One Note Samba/Surfboard," but there are plenty of other little treats, including Everything but the Girl's "Corcovado" and a duet on "Waters of March" by David Byrne and Marisa Monte.

Perhaps the latter is why Cibo Matto's own version of "Aguas de Março" ended up on the subsequent *Silencio = Muerte*, which takes "rock en español" as its starting point and ends up encompassing hip-hop, reggae, metal, salsa, Latin hard-core and, er, Melissa Etheridge singing in Spanish. It's ambitious for sure, but not much fun to listen to as a whole. *Red Hot + Rhapsody* attempts to directly copy the formula of *Red Hot + Blue*, this time substituting the songs of George Gershwin, which aren't quite as resilient as Porter's—Natalie Merchant and even David Bowie seem out of their league. The more irreverent interpretations are the best here, especially Baaba Maal's "Bess, You Is My Woman Now" and Money Mark's nutty cutup "Peter Sellers Sings George Gershwin."

The low-key *Onda Sonora,* whose theme is music with its roots (one way or another) in Portugal, means still more Brazilian artists (both Caetano and Moreno Veloso appear), as well as tracks by Brazilian expatriates Arto Lindsay and DJ Soul Slinger and Brazilophiles like Smoke City and the Durutti Column. *Red Hot + Indigo* gets its cast to play around the Duke Ellington catalogue, a little too respectfully, aside from the Roots' "Caravan," from which they keep nothing but the hook, and Mary J. Blige's bumping "Do Nothin' Till You Hear From Me." About half the disc is actually by Medeski, Martin & Wood, some with guests such as Don Byron and Art Baron.

Red Hot + Riot is an unlikely success—Afrobeat creator Fela Kuti's 20-minute-long songs don't seem like ideal tribute fodder, but stripping them down to a few minutes and throwing posses of rappers, soul singers (like D'Angelo and Macy Gray), and contemporary African pop stars at them works out just great, actually. It turns out Fela's grooves are ideal for hip-hop ping-pong matches by the likes of Dead Prez and Talib Kweli, and the first two thirds of the album sound like one big party, though it falls off by the end—what's a remix of Sade's "By Your Side" doing here?   —D.W.

Rough Guides to World Music
Selected Discography

- ★★★½ The Rough Guide to the Music of Brazil (World Music Network, 1998)
- ★★½ The Rough Guide to the Music of Cuba (World Music Network, 1998)
- ★★★ The Rough Guide to the Music of Japan (World Music Network, 1999)
- ★★★ The Rough Guide to Bhangra (World Music Network, 2000)
- ★★★ The Rough Guide to the Music of Scandinavia (World Music Network, 2000)
- ★★½ The Rough Guide to the Music of Haiti (World Music Network, 2000)
- ★★★½ The Rough Guide to the Music of Indonesia (World Music Network, 2000)
- ★★★½ The Rough Guide to the Music of Nigeria and Ghana (World Music Network, 2002)
- ★★★ The Rough Guide to Highlife (World Music Network, 2003)
- ★★★½ The Rough Guide to the Music of Morocco (World Music Network, 2004)
- ★★★½ The Rough Guide to Gypsy Swing (World Music Network, 2004)
- ★★★½ The Rough Guide to Bollywood Legends: Lata Mangeshkar (World Music Network, 2004)

Most evaluations of world-music collections ask the wrong question: Does this anthology provide an excellent introduction to this music style? Or country? Or region of the world? The query should be: Is this album pleasurable to hear all the way through? Because if it is, the newly enthusiastic audience will likely go on to fill in any historical or scholarly gaps. Given these criteria, the *Rough Guides* fare better than most world surveys, and they seem to get stronger as time goes on.

Beyond that, it's hard to generalize. Of the four *Rough Guides* devoted to Cuban forms, only the *Music of Cuba* is a lively, consistent presentation. The *Indonesia* and *Japan* guides, which could stumble through sheer variety, succeed because they maintain a consistent temperament throughout: pacific and hooky for Indonesia, bright and zany for Japan.

Nigeria and Ghana, Brazil, Highlife, and the sampler of the India-pop electronica known as *bhangra* click because they connect to already familiar Western grooves. (But the CD devoted to *Asian Underground,* which should be a natural after *Bhangra,* is a too-mild bore.) The intros to *Haiti* and *Scandinavia* are recommended first choices in part because the one-disc competition is weak. The best advice may be to go for countries or styles that you know a little about already. But even going in cold, the *Rough Guides* offer the best odds for pleasure right now.

Some of the finest *Rough Guides* triumph by being selective rather than inclusive: the throbbing, bass-lute *sintir* dominates *Music of Morocco;* lesser-known numbers sustain the Django Reinhardt spirit of *Gypsy Swing,* and an emphasis on melodic and instrumental variety as well as plain, strong tunes enable *Lata Mangeshkar* to demystify the Indian film superstar's peculiar little-girl voice for Western ears.   —M.MI.

★★★★ Rushmore: Original Motion Picture Soundtrack (PolyGram, 1999)

In director Owen Anderson's slightly cracked universe, the devil is most certainly in the details. His movies are stylized portraits of a J. D. Salinger–inspired past that never quite existed, American-gothic fairy tales that focus on lovable losers and the eccentrics and oddballs with whom they surround themselves. For the most part, Anderson's artfully constructed soundtracks are light, breezy, wistful, and full of '60s folk, mod, and rock gems that bring to mind Cat Stevens' *Harold and Maude.* In fact, on the *Rushmore* soundtrack, Stevens has two tracks ("Here Comes My Baby" and "The Wind"), both of which fit in just fine alongside Chad and Jeremy's folky, calypso-ish "A Summer Song," Zoot Sims' swanky

"Blinuet," and Yves Montand's ultrasuave "Rue St. Vincent." The centerpiece is the Who's mod minimasterpiece, "A Quick One While He's Away," but the real hidden gem is the rocker "Making Time," by the Great but almost forgotten British beat group the Creation.

Fleshing out the soundtrack is the orchestral score by former Devo kingpin Mark Mothersbaugh, which (just like Anderson's films) manages to be simultaneously sentimental and weird, mixing subtle strings with the kind of offbeat pop orchestrations you might hear in some long lost '60s caper flick. This is all you could ask for from a soundtrack: Nonobvious pop pleasure that deftly supports the story on-screen. —S.S.

★★★★★ Saturday Night Fever: The Original Movie Sound Track (RSO, 1977)

The Bee Gees' "Stayin' Alive" not only provides the disco pulse of this blockbuster album, it also communicates the spirit of the film: corny, but somehow deeply resonant. And the Bee Gees' falsetto harmony wails still project an arresting, almost painful innocence. *Saturday Night Fever* brought a largely urban movement to the rock-saturated hinterlands, and millions of middle-Americans didn't have to think twice about hustling aboard. Collecting the best of the Gibb brothers' born-again funk phase (like the itchy "Jive Talkin' ") and some authentic dance-floor jams (like the Trammps' blazing "Disco Inferno"), *Saturday Night Fever* deserves its preeminent status. Unlike 90 percent of the rip-offs that followed, you can *still* dance to it. —M.C.

Soundbombing

★★★★	Soundbombing (Rawkus, 1997)
★★★★	Soundbombing Volume II (Rawkus, 1999)
★★★	Soundbombing Volume III (Rawkus, 2002)

The first Soundbombing compilation announced the arrival of indie-rap powerhouse Rawkus Records in 1997. Started in New York in the mid-'90s, Rawkus was home to underground hip-hop's most creative talents. The first volume of the series is an essential piece of rap history as well as a fantastic compilation. Collecting most of the label's best seminal 12-inch-single releases, mixed together by Black Moon's DJ Evil Dee, Soundbombing is a collection of classics, from Reflection Eternal's (Mos Def & Talib Kweli) "Fortified Live" to Indelible MCs' raw "Fire in Which You Burn." *Volume II* is another solid collection, though it lacks its predecessor's genre-making cache. Pharaohe Monch's "Mayor" and Company Flow's "Patriotism"

are politically charged anthems, and Common's "1-9-9-9" features some of the Chicago rapper's smoothest verses. Sadly, Rawkus fell victim to bad major-label partnership deals and general financial mismanagement. By the time *Volume III* of the series appeared, most of the artists on the label were in limbo. The template seems to be to mix Rawkus' underground heroes with mainstream artists, but it only works in one case, the lovely "The Life," with Monch and the Lox's Styles. —C.R.

Source Lab

★★½	Source Lab (Source/Virgin, 1995)
★★★	Source Lab 2 (Source/Virgin, 1996)
★★★½	Source Lab 3 (Source/Virgin, 1997)
★★★½	Source Lab Classiques de 1995 à 2002 (Source/Astralwerks, 2003)

In the mid-'90s, it looked as if the French were going to take over the dance-music world, and the *Source Lab* compilations provided the most interesting view of the battleground. Source was a French label that specialized in thickly layered trip-hop and disco-laden house; the first *Source Lab* leans toward the former genre, but standouts by Air and DJ Cam are suffocated by too many forgettable drum-and-bass cuts. On *Source Lab 2,* house rears its impeccably groomed head, most impressively on Daft Punk's fabulous EQ exercise "Musique," a B side that's arguably its greatest record ever. The third volume is the series' most eclectic, a 150-minute panorama of buoyant house (Fantom), dusted down-tempo (Tele Pop), synth wig-outs (Chateau Flight), and Mozesli's wonderful "Sunshine," which samples Diana Ross' "Love Hangover" and Al Green's "Loving You." *Source Lab Classiques*—like the first volume, two shortish CDs—scoops up the most irresistible moments from all three collections. It's a good way to remember a heady time. —M.M.

★★★★ Star Maps: Original Soundtrack (Geffen, 1997)

In terms of its cinematic virtues, the Latino-themed indie film *Star Maps* didn't quite capture the full artistic potential of Puerto Rican director Miguel Arteta (*The Good Girl*). The movie's soundtrack, however, remains to this day the most representative sampling of rock en español ever released, a veritable manifesto of the genre's youthful freshness and exuberant eclecticism. Compiled by producer Gustavo Santaolalla (Café Tacuba, Molotov) and Chicana singer/songwriter Lysa Flores, *Star Maps* focuses less on parading Latin rock's indispensable heavyweights and more on creating an indelible impression of everything the movement stands for: the creation of a new pop language that borrows freely from the mainstream (rap, punk, folk) while drawing heavily from the musicians' own cultural heritage (mariachi, bossa, vallenato).

Fittingly, established names such as Colombia's tropical rockers Aterciopelados and Mexican rappers Control Machete are joined by lesser-known but equally intriguing artists like La Portuaria and Juana Molina (think of her as Argentina's answer to Suzanne Vega). 1997 was a great year for *rock en español,* marked by a number of transcendental albums and promising new artists. *Star Maps* captures a moment in time when Latin music was poised to take over the world. —E.L.

The Stax-Volt Singles

★★★★★   Complete Stax-Volt Singles; 1959–1968 (Atlantic, 1991)

★★★★½   Complete Stax-Volt Soul Singles, Vol. 2: 1968–1971 (Fantasy, 1993)

★★★★   Complete Stax-Volt Soul Singles, Vol. 3: 1972–1975 (Fantasy, 1994)

★★★★★   The Stax Story (Fantasy, 2000)

The decade and a half of soul music that poured from the Stax label and its imprints starting around 1960 is one of the greatest periods of American music in the 20th Century, and these scholarly, lovingly produced boxes rightly treat the label's legacy as a treasure of civilization. Founded inexplicably by a white fiddler and his sister, Stax recorded some of the best music of the time and defined the Memphis Sound, a deliciously gritty, greasy, warm sound achieved through tight, uncomplicated arrangements and the unique acoustics of the label's in-house studio, built in an old movie theater. That room (and the famed studios in Muscle Shoals, AL, used for later sessions) saw the complete works of Otis Redding and the best of the best by Sam and Dave, Booker T. and the MG's, the Bar-Kays, William Bell, Rufus and Carla Thomas, the Staple Singers, Isaac Hayes, Eddie Floyd, and literally hundreds of others. Like Motown, its competitor to the north, Stax was a paradise of black music that should make every American proud and everybody else jealous.

The first set, covering the label's beginnings through the death of Otis Redding and the its break with early benefactor Atlantic, is unspeakably great. Disc two sees Booker T.'s "Green Onions" and the debut of Redding, whose masterly, fully mature "These Arms of Mine" was recorded at the tail end of a session for one Johnny Jenkins, Redding's then employer. Disc four has the arrival of Sam and Dave, the Astors' great toe-tapping harmony hit "Candy" ("Gee whiz, you oughta see my girl / Gee whiz, she's out of this world"), and Redding's "Mr. Pitiful" and "I've Been Loving You Too Long (To Stop Now)." And so it goes through nine CDs—Sam and Dave's "Soul Man"; Eddie Floyd's "Knock on Wood"; Rufus Thomas' many "Dog" gags ("Walking the Dog," "Somebody Stole My Dog"); classic instrumentals by Booker T. and the MG's and the Bar-Kays; and lovable goofs like "That's My Guy," by the onetime-only duo of Cheryl and Pam Johnson, who are described in the otherwise exhaustive liner notes only as "two white Memphis girls that were recorded for no apparent reason." But the real story of Stax in the '60s is Redding, who came from nowhere to become the hardest-driving and most passionate soul singer of all time. The embodiment of the Stax sound, Redding had a rough and homely voice but poured his heart into it, using exquisite care but no lack of spontaneity. It's one of the cruel ironies of history that he died, in a plane crash in December 1967, just weeks after recording his incredible "(Sittin' on) The Dock of the Bay."

Shortly after Redding's death, Stax ended its contract with Atlantic and thus lost Sam and Dave, leaving the label instantly bereft of distribution and its two biggest acts. Given that, it's remarkable how quickly things rebound on the nine-disc second box. The company still had its powerhouse songwriting team, Isaac Hayes and David Porter, churning out hits ("Tighten Up My Thang," "I'll Understand"), and Hayes immediately began his solo career, eventually hitting #1 with the ridiculous "Theme From *Shaft.*" But the biggest news is the Staple Singers, who had been recording for various labels since the '50s but would do groundbreaking work at Stax. In "Respect Yourself" and other "message" songs, they linked the Stax sound with forceful messages of black empowerment. And thanks to ace guitarist and songwriter Steve Cropper and the rest of the Stax musical family, they did it with up-to-the-minute funk that stands with the best of James Brown and Sly Stone. But unlike the first box, there are drops in quality that can't quite be excused by the hits, like Margie Joseph's pointlessly protracted version of "Stop! In the Name of Love" and Hayes' similar treatments of "Walk on By" and "By the Time I Get to Phoenix." The 10-disc third box accentuates this disparity. There are still brilliant hits, like Frederick Knight's falsetto fantasy "I've Been Lonely (For So Long)," Eddie Floyd's "Soul Street," the Emotions' "Baby I'm Through," and the Staple Singers' "I'll Take You There" ("I know a place / Ain't nobody cryin' /. . . Ain't no smilin' faces / Lyin' to the races"), though the label starts to show its age as it tries to keep up with funk and disco.

Still, the history recorded on the boxes is essential, and the voluminous liner notes and other data make these collections models of the art of the box set itself. For those who aren't scholars, or at least aren't interested in a 28-CD investment for the full series, the four-disc *Stax Story* is an excellent guide to the highlights, with one full disc of outstanding live tracks. —B.S.

Trojan Box Sets

★★★½ Trojan DJ Box Set (Trojan, 1998)
★★★½ Trojan Dub Box Set (Trojan, 1998)
★★★ Trojan Rocksteady Box Set (Trojan, 1998)
★★★½ Trojan Ska Box Set (Trojan, 1998)
★★★½ Trojan Instrumentals Box Set (Trojan, 1999)
★★★ Trojan Jamaican Hits Box Set (Trojan, 1999)
★★★ Trojan Jamaican Superstars Box Set (Trojan, 1999)
★★½ Trojan Lovers Box Set (Trojan, 1999)
★★★½ Trojan Producer Series Box Set (Trojan, 1999)
★★★½ Trojan Rare Groove Box Set (Trojan, 1999)
★★★ Trojan Roots Box Set (Trojan, 1999)
★★ Trojan Singles Box Set (Trojan, 1999)
★★ Trojan Tribute to Bob Marley Box Set (Trojan, 1999)
★★½ Trojan Club Reggae Box Set (Trojan, 2000)
★★★½ Trojan Dancehall Box Set (Trojan, 2000)
★★ Trojan Dub Box Set, Vol. 2 (Trojan, 2000)
★★★ Trojan Jamaican Hits Box Set (Trojan, 2000)
★★★ Trojan Rastafari Box Set (Trojan, 2000)
★★★ Trojan Ska Box Set, Vol. 2 (Trojan, 2000)
★★★ Trojan Soulful Reggae Box Set (Trojan, 2000)
★★★½ Trojan "Tighten Up" Box Set (Trojan, 2000)
★★★ Trojan: A Jamaican Story Box Set (Trojan, 2001)
★★ Trojan Bob Marley & Friends Box Set (Trojan, 2002)
★★ Trojan British Reggae Box Set (Trojan/Sanctuary, 2002)
★★★★ Trojan Calypso Box Set (Trojan, 2002)
★★★ Trojan Jamaican R&B Box Set (Trojan/Sanctuary, 2002)
★★★½ Trojan Mod Reggae Box Set (Trojan/Sanctuary, 2002)
★★★ Trojan Revive Box Set (Trojan, 2002)
★★★ Trojan Rude Boy Box Set (Trojan/Sanctuary, 2002)
★★★ Trojan Skinhead Reggae Box Set (Trojan/Sanctuary, 2002)
★★★★ Trojan U.K. Hits Box Set (Trojan/Sanctuary, 2002)
★★★ Trojan Upsetter Box Set (Trojan/Sanctuary, 2002)

★★★½ Trojan X-rated Box Set (Trojan/Sanctuary, 2002)
★★★ Trojan Reggae Sisters Box Set (Trojan/Sanctuary, 2003)
★★★★ Trojan Originals Box Set (Trojan, 2003)
★★★★ Trojan Nyabinghi Box Set (Trojan, 2003)
★★★½ Trojan 12-Inch Box Set (Trojan, 2003)
★★★ Trojan Reggae Brothers Box Set (Trojan, 2003)
★½ Trojan Ska Revival Box Set (Trojan, 2003)
★★★ Trojan Suedehead Reggae Box Set (Trojan, 2003)
★★ Trojan Christmas Reggae Box Set (Trojan, 2003)
★★★ Trojan 35th Anniversary Box Set (Trojan, 2003)
★★★ Trojan Chill Out Reggae Box Set (Trojan, 2003)
★★★ Trojan Carnival Box Set (Trojan, 2003)
★★★ Trojan Ganja Reggae Box Set (Trojan, 2003)
★★★ Trojan Reggae Duets Box Set (Trojan, 2004)

Packaged in attractive, colorful, puffy cases and featuring three discs and 50 tracks apiece, the Trojan box-set series is the ultimate proof of the influential British reggae label's total lack of shame. For one thing, most of them are "boxes" only by dint of packaging; their tracks would fit comfortably on two discs (the *Dancehall, Roots,* and *Upsetter* sets are exceptions). Also, only a few of the more recent volumes have anything resembling the curatorial ambition, historical interest, or detailed annotation normally associated with box sets: The *Calypso* and *Jamaican R&B* collections, for instance, shed light on two underrecognized aspects of the label's history (its ties to Trinidadian and early-'60s pre-ska "boogie" tunes, respectively). But few other sets in the series attempt such an overview, and only one, *U.K. Hits,* seems definitive—until it's derailed by the schlock-ridden pop reggae the label began specializing in around the turn of the '70s, when artists like Greyhound and Judge Dread made some of the corniest music in existence. Most of the Trojan box sets are grab bags that seem less generous in light of how much filler they're stuffed with—or, in the case of *Singles,* the fact that the majority of the selections sound like they were mastered from battered 45s.

Still, the best volumes contain plenty of enjoyable music. The series' best early sets—*DJ, Dub, Ska, Instrumentals*—are good overviews of their respective styles; *Instrumentals* is the best of these, peaking with Harry J Allstars' roaring organ version of the Beatles' "Don't Let Me Down." *Producer Series* highlights the crevices of six producers' catalogues (Lee Perry,

Niney, Clancy Eccles, Alvin Ranglin, Harry J, and Joe Gibbs) to terrific effect. *Rare Groove* is that rare thing, a vault-clearing exercise that excavates songs worth knowing, particularly Jerry Lewis' "Rhythm Pleasure." And *Dancehall* is a useful survey of the period right after the Marley/roots explosion and before the advent of digital recording. The later sets get more ambitious, and while the quality doesn't necessarily improve, the concepts do, particularly the *Rude Boy, Mod Reggae, Skinhead Reggae,* and thematically inevitable *X-rated* boxes. If you really want to splurge, *A Jamaican Story* rounds up 10 of the sets: *Ska, Dub, Rocksteady, DJ, Lovers, Tribute to Bob Marley, Instrumentals, Roots, Jamaican Superstars,* and *Producer Series.* —M.M.

2 Many DJ's

★★★★ As Heard on Radio Soulwax, Pt. 2 (Pias, Belgium; 2002)
★★★★ As Heard on Radio Soulwax, Pt. 1 (Waxed Soul, U.K.; 2002)
★★★★ As Heard on Radio Soulwax, Pt. 3 (Waxed Soul, U.K.; 2002)

Yes, those discs are listed in the right order. That's the sequence in which the three mix CDs by 2 Many DJ's, a.k.a. Belgian brothers David and Stephen Dawaele, were issued—though truthfully, they only released *Pt. 2,* which was the only "official," fully-licensed album. No matter: All three equally impress.

The Dawaeles began their musical career in a band called Soulwax; when the brothers began creating mash-up bootlegs—welding the vocal of one song to the music of another—they continued using the name. Soon, they began assembling hour-long mixes of their efforts for the radio, exhibiting catholic tastes and an infectious sense of mischief. *As Heard on Radio Soulwax, Pt. 2* demonstrates that sensibility on inspired pairings like Skee-Lo's "I Wish" and the Breeders' "Cannonball," or Emerson, Lake and Palmer's "Peter Gunn Theme (Live)" and Basement Jaxx's "Where's Your Head At." And hearing Dolly Parton's "9 to 5" segue flawlessly into the chill-out techno of Royksopp's "Eple" is like watching the skies open.

Pt. 1 and *Pt. 3* are harder—but wholly worthwhile—to track down. *Pt. 1* offers the audio spectacle of the Beach Boys' "God Only Knows" riding the opening beat of Michael Jackson's "Billie Jean," not to mention David Bowie, Kenny Loggins, and Hairy Diamond speeding up the beat until they hand off the relay to Freelance Hellraiser's infamous Strokes/Christina Aguilera mash-up, "A Stroke of Genius." It's one of the most absurdly thrilling sequences on any DJ mix. *Pt. 3* offers an even more ingenious string

that begins with Garbage's "Androgyny," ends with Modjo's "Lady," and takes in "girl" and "boy" songs by Blur, Prince, the Chemical Brothers, Sabrina, Mötley Crüe, the Waitresses, and the Moments. Residual culture has seldom been so much fun. —M.M.

Ultimate Breaks & Beats

★★★★★ Volumes 1–25 (Street Beat)

Ultimate Breaks & Beats was a series of vinyl compilations of classic soul, R&B, and occasionally rock songs (sometimes snippets of songs, almost always the funky break) that had been made popular in discos and at block parties in the '80s and/or sampled on famous hip-hop records. The series, begun in 1986 by Lenny Roberts on the Street Beat label, was a sequel to earlier bootleg vinyl comps (the most famous being Paul Winley's *Super Disco Breaks* releases), but *UBB* eventually grew to encompass 25 volumes and became a ubiquitous resource for DJs, producers, and fans who didn't have the resources or would not devote the time to tracking down the original records. In that sense, the *UBB* records were like Cliff's Notes, or condensed versions of otherwise painfully assembled record collections. For example, *UBB Vol. 4* contained "Different Strokes" by Syl Johnson, "I Know You Got Soul" by Bobby Byrd, "I Think I'd Do It" by Z.Z. Hill, "Sing Sing" by Gaz, and "Breakthrough" by Isaac Hayes—coveted breaks that might've taken someone like Kool Herc years to assemble. While this galled some—Prince Paul once remarked that using a *UBB* break instead of owning the original was considered cheating—the records helped new fans understand what a finished product should sound like. *UBB* were not scholarly aboveboard compilations, to say the least (no liner notes and sketchy credits), but they did inspire the legitimate work of labels like Stones Throw (with their *Funky 16 Corners* comp from 2001). Never released on CD, some *UBB* volumes have popped up again recently re-pressed as double-vinyl duplicate packages for easier mixing. —P.R.

★★★★ Uneasy Listening (Against the Grain, Vol. 1) (2-Trip, 2001)

In 2001, the mash-up phenomenon hadn't yet found its legs, but DJs Z-Trip and P were already collecting and dissecting their influences for this album-length party set. Like all good DJs, they understood that a successful party mix relied on familiar sounds delivered in an unexpected fashion. From the album-opening gambit—"Rhinestone Cowboy" reborn as "Rhinestone B-Boy"—until the end, when "Yesterday" gets assaulted by bottomless drums, it's clear that all sounds are ripe for reinvention and recontextualization. Along the way, Newcleus mixes it up with Depeche Mode and Bruce Hornsby, the Tubes dance with Herbie Hancock, and Pat Benatar backs up the Pharcyde. Even Kansas' "Dust in the Wind" is made to sound like a dance-floor classic. Within a year or so, the concept had been disseminated, exploited, and diluted, but this original document remains one of the best. —J.C.

When the Sun Goes Down

★★★½   Vol. 1: Walk Right In (Bluebird, 2002)
★★★½   Vol. 2: The First Time I Met the Blues (Bluebird, 2002)
★★★★   Vol. 3: That's Chicago South Side (Bluebird, 2002)
★★★★   Vol. 4: That's All Right (Bluebird, 2002)
★★★★½   Vol. 6: Poor Man's Heaven (Bluebird, 2003)

When the Sun Goes Down reaches for a concept (the alternate title is *The Secret History of Rock & Roll*) while the promotion emphasizes how many of these songs have been covered by big-name rockers. But more often than not, the collection feels like something the cat dragged in, its merit an eclectic smorgasbord from RCA's deep-blues catalogue. As samplers go, it also helps that the four CDs are available separately as well as in a slipcase.

Vol. 1: Walk Right In is the old stuff, judged not by date but by a sense of primitivism. For instance, Trixie Butler's "Just a Good Woman Through With the Blues" was recorded in 1936 but harks back to her vaudeville act in the 1910s. Lead Belly's 1940 "Ham an' Eggs," recorded with the Golden Gate Quartet, re-creates the sound of a chain gang. Tommy Johnson moans one of the most primeval blues lines ever, "I asked for water and she gave me gasoline." Amédé Ardoin crawls out of the Louisiana swamp, while Mil-

ton Brown stomps the "Garbage Man Blues," DeFord Bailey plays his harmonica on the Grand Ole Opry, Frank Crumit eulogizes "Frankie and Johnnie," and Paul Robeson sings proletarian opera. Stark, diverse stuff.

Vol. 2: The First Time I Heard the Blues and *Vol. 3: That's Chicago South Side* are more typical sets of prewar acoustic blues. The former features jazz-backed female blues (Victoria Spivey has a top-notch band that features Red Allen, while Lizzie Miles makes do with Jelly Roll Morton) and the blues across the South, including Blind Willie McTell in Atlanta, Bo Carter in New Orleans, and a whole lotta Memphis in between. The latter, of course, is the first wave of Chicago blues, centered around Big Bill Broonzy and Tampa Red. Perhaps because it is more focused, the Chicago set is the most listenable in the series.

Vol. 4: That's All Right collects later material, from "Pearl Harbor Blues" up to 1951, when RCA lost interest in the blues. But during this period, there was a rich assortment of diverse material not all that far removed from what was to become rock & roll. Some highlights include Lil Green's "Why Don't You Do Right," Arthur Crudup's pre-Elvis "That's All Right," Red Allen's jump blues "Get the Mop," Piano Red's "Right String, but the Wrong Yo-Yo," and the first ditty that Little Richard recorded. A fun set.

In 2003, Bluebird added five more volumes to the initial set, each with similar layout and artwork. Four of these were single-artist compilations (Lead belly, Arthur "Big Boy" Crudup, Sonny Boy Williamson, and Blind Willie McTell). The other, *Poor Man's Heaven*, dug deep into its catalogue for songs linked to the Great Depression: more country than blues, tunes like "Brother Can You Spare a Dime," and rarities including a tearful comedy bit by stock speculator Eddie Cantor. It's a unique, extraordinary document—just in time for another Great Depression. —T.H.

Acknowledgments

Many people helped make this book possible. The editors would like to thank Jann Wenner, the editor and publisher of ROLLING STONE, for making this book a reality, along with Holly George-Warren—who provided invaluable help and advice as we began—and literary agent Sarah Lazin. Many thanks to the ROLLING STONE fact-checkers.

Thanks to everyone at Simon & Schuster: Brett Valley, Dominick Anfuso, the saintlike Tricia Wygal, and Emily Remes. Having copy editors who were knowledgeable music fans made this much easier: thanks to Sean Bell-Thomson, Josh Cohen, Suzanne Fass, Liz Gall, Robert Legault, and John McGhee.

The contributors are the heart of this book; all of them took time off from their more lucrative writing careers to be a part of this, and all have our deepest gratitude. One deserves a special thanks: ROLLING STONE contributing editor Rob Sheffield was the first to sign on to the project and delivered many of the most important entries here—including the Beatles, Bob Dylan, the Rolling Stones, David Bowie, Radiohead, and Neil Young, to name only a few—with his usual brilliance and humor.

Thanks to Bob Love, who made sure this book happened during a time of transition at Rolling Stone Press. Many past and present ROLLING STONE staffers helped the book along: Joe Levy, Jason Fine, David Fricke, Jenny Eliscu, and Ed Needham, along with some hardworking interns, notably Kara Norman.

This book could not have happened without the help of the following record company staffers, independent publicists, and other friends in the music industry: Alex Seitz at Red House, Alexandra Greenberg at MSO, Alison Tarnofsky at Astralwerks, Allyson Polak, Alvin at Rap-A-Lot, Amy Welch at DreamWorks, Anthony Musiala at Minty Fresh, Barbara Deyo at KMS Productions, Beth Jacobson Kiefetz and Pearl Lee at Tommy Boy, Bill Bentley, Arvella Kinkaid and Rick Gershon at Warner Bros., Bob Pickering at Oarfin, Bobbie Gale and Michael Ruthig at EMI, Brendan Gilmartin at spinART, Carise Yatter at Artemis, Charlie Mackey, Jana Fleischman at Def Jam, Chris Jacobs at Sub Pop, Clark Warner at Minus, Curtis Casella at Taang!, Dan Schmeltekop at Luna, Katy Krassner and Jason Wheeler at Sanctuary, David Dorn and Kevin Kennedy at Rhino, Elizabeth Goodman, Gina DeYoung at Red Liquorice, Giovanna Melchiorre at Koch, Hillary Okun and Hector Martinez at Epitaph, Katherine Profeta, Jeff Hunt at Table of the Elements, Jennifer Ballantyne, Jim Flammia at Lost Highway, Jo Foster at Concord Records, John Dow at Bluebird, Adam Shore at Vice, Karen Moss, Dave Cirilli and Ken Weinstein at Big Hassle, David Aaron at Thirsty Ear, Kim Fowler at Sugar Hill, Lee Gutowski and Stolie at Bloodshot, Lisa Markowitz at Epic, Lisbeth Cassaday at Virgin, Mandy Eidgah at BMG Heritage, Mark Loewinger at Universal, Martin Hall at Merge, WTJU Radio in Charlottesville, VA, Michelle Jaeger at Rykodisc, Mika El-Baz and Ian Hofmann at Interscope, Nick Stern at Atlantic, Nils Bernstein and Lisa Gottheil at Matador/Beggars

Group, Ben Goldberg, Pam Nashel Leto and Heidi Anne-Noel at Girlie Action, Papa D at Landspeed, Pat Thomas at Runt, Patti Conte, Paul Caparotta at Runt, Paula Witt at Shorefire, Perry Serpa at Good Cop, Pete Ritche at Up, Tom Cording and Randy Haecker at Epic/Legacy, Regina Joskow Dunton at Verve, Robert Bennett at Bennett Management, Robert Griffin at Scat, Roberta Magrini at Jive, Scott Giampino at Touch & Go, Scott King at Oh Boy, Shelby Meade, Fresh and Clean, Maureen Coakley, Anne Kristoff at Elektra, Sherry Ring, Steven Joerg at Aum Fidelity, Susan Zimmerman at Formula PR, Syd McCain at V2, Tamra Wilson, Terri Hinte at Fantasy, Tice Merriwether at Arista, Sandro Grancaric and Tom Muzquiz at Sony, Tracy Mann at MG Limited, and Vicki Marshall at Collectables Records.

Two of the great record-guide writer/editors, Ira Robbins of the Trouser Press guides and Robert Christgau of *Christgau's Consumer Guides,* provided both advice and inspiration. Finally, the following people helped in various ways: Gavin Edwards, Tracy Westmoreland, David Malley, Andy Gensler, Chiara Barzini, Kate Burton, Minna Brackett, and Leo Brackett.